THE WEEKLY LAW REPORTS
1981

VOLUME 1

London
THE INCORPORATED COUNCIL OF LAW REPORTING
FOR ENGLAND AND WALES
3 STONE BUILDINGS, LINCOLN'S INN, LONDON, WC2A 3XN

*Published by the Incorporated
Council of Law Reporting for
England and Wales · 3 Stone
Buildings, Lincoln's Inn, London,
WC2A 3XN, and printed by The
Eastern Press Ltd., London and
Reading*

THE INCORPORATED COUNCIL OF LAW REPORTING FOR ENGLAND AND WALES

HOUSE OF LORDS

Lord Chancellor: LORD HAILSHAM OF ST. MARYLEBONE

LORDS OF APPEAL IN ORDINARY

LORD WILBERFORCE
LORD DIPLOCK
LORD EDMUND-DAVIES
    (retired September 30, 1981)
LORD FRASER OF TULLYBELTON
LORD RUSSELL OF KILLOWEN

LORD KEITH OF KINKEL
LORD SCARMAN
LORD ROSKILL
LORD BRIDGE OF HARWICH
LORD BRANDON OF OAKBROOK
    (appointed September 24, 1981)

COURT OF APPEAL

Lord Chancellor: LORD HAILSHAM OF ST. MARYLEBONE

Lord Chief Justice of England: LORD LANE

Master of the Rolls: LORD DENNING

President of the Family Division: Sir JOHN LEWIS ARNOLD

Sir DENYS BURTON BUCKLEY
    (retired February 6, 1981)
Sir JOHN FREDERICK EUSTACE STEPHENSON
Sir FREDERICK HORACE LAWTON
Sir ROGER FRAY GREENWOOD ORMROD
Sir SEBAG SHAW
Sir GEORGE STANLEY WALLER
The Hon. Sir JAMES ROUALEYN HOVELL-
    THURLOW-CUMMING-BRUCE
Sir EDWARD WALTER EVELEIGH
Sir HENRY VIVIAN BRANDON, M.C.
Sir SYDNEY WILLIAM TEMPLEMAN

Sir JOHN FRANCIS DONALDSON
Sir JOHN ANSON BRIGHTMAN
Sir DESMOND JAMES CONRAD ACKNER
Sir ROBIN HORACE WALFORD DUNN, M.C.
Sir PETER RAYMOND OLIVER
Sir TASKER WATKINS, V.C.
Sir PATRICK MCCARTHY O'CONNOR
Sir WILLIAM HUGH GRIFFITHS
Sir MICHAEL JOHN FOX
    (appointed February 9, 1981)
Sir MICHAEL ROBERT EMANUEL KERR
    (appointed September 24, 1981)

CHANCERY DIVISION

Lord Chancellor: LORD HAILSHAM OF ST. MARYLEBONE

Vice-Chancellor: Sir ROBERT EDGAR MEGARRY

Sir JOHN PATRICK GRAHAM
    (retired January 26, 1981)
Sir PETER HARRY BATSON WOODROFFE
    FOSTER
Sir JOHN NORMAN KEATES WHITFORD
Sir ERNEST IRVINE GOULDING
Sir RAYMOND HENRY WALTON
Sir MICHAEL JOHN FOX
Sir CHRISTOPHER JOHN SLADE
Sir NICOLAS CHRISTOPHER HENRY
    BROWNE-WILKINSON

Sir JOHN EVELYN VINELOTT
Sir GEORGE BRIAN HUGH DILLON
Sir MARTIN CHARLES NOURSE
Sir DOUGLAS WILLIAM FALCONER
    (appointed January 27, 1981)
Sir JEAN-PIERRE FRANK EUGENE WARNER
    (appointed March 3, 1981)
Sir PETER LESLIE GIBSON
    (appointed April 27, 1981)

QUEEN'S BENCH DIVISION

Lord Chief Justice of England: LORD LANE

Sir ALAN ABRAHAM MOCATTA
(retired May 31, 1981)
Sir JOHN THOMPSON
Sir HELENUS PATRICK JOSEPH MILMO
Sir JOSEPH DONALDSON CANTLEY
Sir HUGH EAMES PARK
Sir STEPHEN CHAPMAN
(retired April 17, 1981)
Sir BERNARD CAULFIELD
Sir HILARY GWYNNE TALBOT
Sir WILLIAM LLOYD MARS-JONES
Sir RALPH KILNER BROWN
Sir PHILLIP WIEN (died June 11, 1981)
Sir PETER HENRY ROWLEY BRISTOW
Sir HUGH HARRY VALENTINE FORBES
Sir ROBERT HUGH MAIS
Sir NEIL LAWSON
Sir DAVID POWELL CROOM-JOHNSON
Sir JOHN RAYMOND PHILLIPS
Sir LESLIE KENNETH EDWARD BOREHAM
Sir JOHN DOUGLAS MAY
Sir MICHAEL ROBERT EMANUEL KERR
Sir ALFRED WILLIAM MICHAEL DAVIES
Sir JOHN DEXTER STOCKER
Sir KENNETH GEORGE ILLTYD JONES
Sir HAYDN TUDOR EVANS
Sir PETER RICHARD PAIN
Sir KENNETH GRAHAM JUPP
Sir STEPHEN BROWN
Sir ROBERT LIONEL ARCHIBALD GOFF
Sir GORDON SLYNN (appointed Advocate-
General, European Court of Justice,
February 26, 1981)
Sir ROGER JOCELYN PARKER

Sir RALPH BRIAN GIBSON
Sir WALTER DEREK THORNLEY HODGSON
Sir JAMES PETER COMYN
Sir ANTHONY JOHN LESLIE LLOYD
Sir FREDERICK MAURICE DRAKE, D.F.C.
Sir BRIAN THOMAS NEILL
Sir RODERICK PHILIP SMITH
(died April 12, 1981)
Sir MICHAEL JOHN MUSTILL
Sir BARRY CROSS SHEEN
Sir DAVID BRUCE MCNEILL
Sir HARRY KENNETH WOOLF
Sir THOMAS PATRICK RUSSELL
Sir PETER EDLIN WEBSTER
Sir THOMAS HENRY BINGHAM
Sir IAIN DEREK LAING GLIDEWELL
Sir HENRY ALBERT SKINNER
Sir PETER MURRAY TAYLOR
Sir MURRAY STUART-SMITH
(appointed April 27, 1981)
Sir CHRISTOPHER STEPHEN THOMAS
JONATHAN THAYER STAUGHTON
(appointed April 27, 1981)
Sir DONALD HENRY FARQUHARSON
(appointed April 27, 1981)
Sir ANTHONY JAMES DENYS MCCOWAN
(appointed June 2, 1981)
Sir IAIN CHARLES ROBERT MCCULLOUGH
(appointed June 9, 1981)
Sir HAMILTON JOHN LEONARD
(appointed September 15, 1981)
Sir ALEXANDER ROY ASPLAN BELDAM
(appointed September 24, 1981)

FAMILY DIVISION

President: Sir JOHN LEWIS ARNOLD

Sir JOHN BRINSMEAD LATEY
Sir ALFRED KENNETH HOLLINGS
Sir CHARLES TREVOR REEVE
Sir FRANCIS BROOKS PURCHAS
Dame ROSE HEILBRON
Sir BRIAN DREX BUSH
Sir ALFRED JOHN BALCOMBE
Sir JOHN KEMBER WOOD
Sir RONALD GOUGH WATERHOUSE

Sir JOHN GERVASSE KENSINGTON SHELDON
Sir THOMAS MICHAEL EASTHAM
Dame MARGARET MYFANWY WOOD BOOTH
Sir CHRISTOPHER JAMES SAUNDERS FRENCH
Sir ANTHONY LESLIE JULIAN LINCOLN
Dame ANN ELIZABETH OLDFIELD
BUTLER-SLOSS
Sir ANTHONY BRUCE EWBANK

Attorney-General

Sir MICHAEL HAVERS Q.C.

Solicitor-General

Sir IAN PERCIVAL Q.C.

CASES REPORTED

(Vol. 1)

PAGE

A

A.C.T. Construction Ltd. v. Customs and Excise Comrs. - 49, 59c, 1542

A.G. Thames Holdings Ltd., Impex Transport Aktieselskabet v. - - - - - 1547

Abergavenny's (Marquess of) Estate Act Trusts, In re - - 843

Abergavenny (Marquess of) v. Ram - - - - - 843

Anderton, McQuaid v. - - 154

Armar Shipping Co. Ltd. v. Caisse Algérienne D'Assurance et de Réassurance - - - 207

A/S Awilco of Oslo v. Fulvia S.p.A. di Navigazione of Cagliari - - - - - 314

Ashcroft v. Cambro Waste Products Ltd. - - - - 1349

Attorney-General v. Ho Pui-yiu - 395

Attorney-General ex rel. Tilley v. Wandsworth London Borough Council - - - - - 854

Attorney-General of Hong Kong, Hang Wah Chong Investment Co. Ltd. v. - - - - 1141

Attorney-General of Trinidad and Tobago, Chokolingo v. - - 106

Attorney-General's Reference (No. 4 of 1979) - - - 667

Attorney-General's Reference (No. 1 of 1980) - - - 34

Attorney-General's Reference (No. 2 of 1980) - - - 148

Attorney-General's Reference (No. 4 of 1980) - - - 705

Attorney-General's Reference (No. 5 of 1980) - - - 88

B

B. (A Minor) (Wardship: Medical Treatment), In re - - 1421

B.P. Exploration Co. (Libya) Ltd. v. Hunt (No. 2) - - - 232

Barnett v. French - - - 848

Barnett v. Hassett - - - 1385

Barrass v. Reeve - - - 408

Barrington, Reg. v. - - - 419

Bates (Thomas) and Son Ltd. v. Wyndham's (Lingerie) Ltd. - 505

PAGE

Beard v. Beard - - - - 369

Beer v. Bowden (Note) - - 522

Bernard, Ex parte - - - 116

Berrill, Inland Revenue Comrs. v. 1449

Berry v. Warnett - - - 1

Bickenhall Engineering Ltd., Selim v. - - - - - 1318

Block (Derek) (Holdings) Ltd., Grappelli v. - - - - 822

Bloxham, Reg. v. - - - 859

Boers (D.) B.V., Davis Freight Forwarding (Hull) Ltd. v. (pet. all.) - - - - 1467

Bolton Supplementary Benefits Appeal Tribunal, Ex parte Fordham, Reg. v. - - - 28

Boorman v. Godfrey - - - 1100

Borag, The - - - - 274

Boulton v. Coral Racing Ltd. - 1176

Bowden, Beer v. (Note) - - 522

Brandrose Investments Ltd., Windsor and Maidenhead Royal Borough Council v. - 1083

Brikom Investments Ltd. v. Seaford - - - - - 863

Brooker, Reg. v. - - - 1048

Brown, Thompson v. - - 744

Buckingham Travel Ltd., Chester v. - - - - - - 96

Bunge Corpn., New York v. Tradax Export S.A., Panama - 711

Burnes v. Trade Credits Ltd. - 805

C

C. B. (A Minor) (Wardship: Local Authority), In re - - - 379

Cadbury-Schweppes Pty. Ltd. v. Pub Squash Co. Pty. Ltd. - 193

Caisse Algérienne d'Assurance et de Réassurance, Armar Shipping Co. Ltd. v. - - - 207

Caltex Oil (Australia) Pty. Ltd. v. Feenan - - - - - 1003

Cambro Waste Products Ltd., Ashcroft v. - - - - 1349

Cam Gears Ltd. v. Cunningham - 1011

Camden London Borough Council, Ex parte Ebiri, Reg. v. - 881

Cargill v. Gotts - - - - 441

vii

PAGE

Carmel Exporters (Sales) Ltd. v.
Sea-Land Services Inc. - - 1068
Castle, Ex parte - - - - 217
Chanel Ltd. v. F. W. Woolworth
& Co. Ltd. - - - - 485
Chaplin, Clowser v. - - - 837
Chester v. Buckingham Travel
Ltd. - - - - - 96
Chief Constable for Hampshire,
Kaur (Dip) v. - - - - 578
Chief Constable of Kent, Taylor
v. - - - - - - 606
Chikuma, The - - - - 314
Chin Choy alias Chin Chong Kim
v. Collector of Stamp Duties - 1201
Chokolingo v. Attorney-General
of Trinidad and Tobago - - 106
Cicutti v. Suffolk County Council 558
City of London Corpn., Ex parte 985
Clark v. Oceanic Contractors Inc. 59
Clarke v. Coventry City Council - 1325
Clear v. Smith - - - - 399
Cleaver, decd., In re - - - 939
Cleaver v. Insley - - - 939
Clipper Maritime Co. Ltd. of
Monrovia v. Mineralimport-
export - - - - - 1262
Clowser v. Chaplin - - - 837
Collector of Stamp Duties, Chin
Choy alias Chin Chong Kim v. 1201
Company, In re A (No. 003324 of
1979) (Practice Note) - - 1059
Comr. of Police of the Metropolis,
Ex parte - - - - 112
Comr. of Police of the Metropolis,
Gold Star Publications Ltd. v. 732
Compania Financiera " Soleada "
S.A. v. Hamoor Tanker Corpn.
Inc. - - - - 274, 992
Coral Racing Ltd., Boulton v. - 1176
Coventry City Council, Clarke v. 1325
Coventry City Council v. Doyle - 1325
Coventry City Council v. Quinn - 1325
Crompton v. General Medical
Council - - - - - 1435
Croydon Crown Court, Ex parte
Bernard, Reg. v. - - - 116
Cunningham, Cam Gears Ltd. v. - 1011
Cummins Engine Co. Ltd. v.
Davis Freight Forwarding
(Hull) Ltd. - - 1363, 1467
Customs and Excise Comrs.,
A.C.T. Construction Ltd. v.
49, 59c, 1542

PAGE

Customs and Excise Comrs.,
G.U.S. Merchandise Corpn.
Ltd. v. - - - 1309, 1318

D

Daly v. General Steam Naviga-
tion Co. Ltd. - - - - 120
Dartford Justices, Ex parte Dhesi,
Reg. v. (pet. all.) - - - 1382
Davey, In re - - - - 164
Davis Freight Forwarding (Hull)
Ltd., Cummins Engine Co. Ltd.
v. - - - - 1363, 1467
Davis Freight Forwarding (Hull)
Ltd. v. D. Boers B.V. (pet. all.) 1467
Davies, Ex parte - - - 1080
Davies (Neil), Ex parte - - 374
Debtor (No. 6864 of 1980), In re
A, Ex parte The Debtor v.
Slater Walker Ltd. - - - 1205
Dennis v. McDonald - - - 810
Denton, Reg. v. - - - - 1446
Department for National Savings,
Howard v. - - - - 542
Derby City Council, Fenclose
Securities Ltd. v. - - - 173
Derby City Council, Provident
Mutual Life Assurance Asso-
ciation v. - - - - 173
Dhesi, Ex parte (pet. all.) - - 1382
Director of Public Prosecutions,
Gold Star Publications Ltd. v. - 732
Dodds v. Walker - - - 1027
Doyle, Coventry City Council v. - 1325
Drayton Commercial Investment
Co. Ltd., Stanton v. - - 1425
Drummond, Mallalieu v. - - 908
Dunbar, Reg. v. - - - - 1536
Dunkley v. Evans - - - 1522

E

E.M.I. Records Ltd. v. Riley - 923
East Midlands Housing Associa-
tion Ltd., North West Leicester-
shire District Council v. - - 1396
Ebbw Vale and Merthyr Tydfil
Supplementary Benefits Appeal
Tribunal, Ex parte Lewis, Reg.
v. - - - - - 131
Ebiri, Ex parte - - - - 881
Edmonton Justices, Ex parte
Hughes, Reg. v. (pet. all.) - 1382
Evans, Dunkley v. - - - 1522
Evans v. London Hospital Medi-
cal College (University of Lon-
don) - - - - - 184

PAGE

Exxon Corpn. *v.* Exxon Insurance Consultants International Ltd. - - - - - 624
Exxon Insurance Consultants International Ltd., Exxon Corpn. *v.* - - - - 624

F

Faith Panton Property Plan Ltd. *v.* Hodgetts - - - - 927
Faulkner *v.* Talbot - - - 1528
Feenan, Caltex Oil (Australia) Pty. Ltd. *v.* - - - - 1003
Feltham, Frost *v.* - - - 452
Fenclose Securities Ltd. *v.* Derby City Council - - - - 173
Ferrymasters Ltd., Thermo Engineers Ltd. *v.* - - - - 1470
Finnigan *v.* Sandiford - - - 837
Firth, Johnson *v.* - - - 475
Firth, Wicks *v.* - - - - 475
Folkestone and Hythe Juvenile Court Justices, *Ex parte* R. (A Juvenile), Reg. *v.* - 1501, 1509H
Fordham, *Ex parte* - - - 28
Forsdyke, Hoye *v.* - - - 1442
Frater *v.* The Queen (Note) - 1468
Freilich, McCarney *v.* - - - 431
French, Barnett *v.* - - - 848
Frost *v.* Feltham - - - 452
Fulvia S.p.A. di Navigazione of Cagliari, A/S Awilco of Oslo *v.* 314

G

G., Veater *v.* - - - - 567
G.U.S. Merchandise Corpn. Ltd. *v.* Customs and Excise Comrs. 1309, 1318
Galbraith, Reg. *v.* - - - 1039
Garvin, Inland Revenue Comrs. *v.* 793
General Medical Council, Crompton *v.* - - - - 1435
General Steam Navigation Co. Ltd., Daly *v.* - - - 120
Godfrey, Boorman *v.* - - - 1100
Gold Star Publications Ltd. *v.* Comr. of Police of the Metropolis - - - - - 732
Gold Star Publications Ltd. *v.* Director of Public Prosecutions 732
Gotts, Cargill *v.* - - - - 441
Governor of Pentonville Prison, *Ex parte* Singh (Harmohan), Reg. *v.* - - - - - 1031
Grappelli *v.* Derek Block (Holdings) Ltd. - - - - 822

PAGE

Great Atlantic Insurance Co. *v.* Home Insurance Co. - - 529
Green *v.* Green - - - - 391
Guilfoyle *v.* Home Office (pet. dis.) - - - - - 1080
Gunton *v.* Richmond-upon-Thames London Borough Council (pet. dis.) . . . 28

H

H. (A Barrister), *In re* - - 1257
H.M. & S. Ltd., New Zealand Government Property Corpn. *v.* - - - - - 870
Habib Bank A.G. Zurich, Habib Bank Ltd. *v.* - - - 1265
Habib Bank Ltd. *v.* Habib Bank A.G. Zurich - - - - 1265
Hackney London Borough Council, Watson *v.* - - - 650
Hadmor Productions Ltd. *v.* Hamilton (pet. all.) - - - 1128
Hall (Peter Michael), Reg. *v.* 1510, 1515F
Hamilton, Hadmor Productions Ltd. *v.* (pet. all.) - - 1128
Hammersmith and Fulham London Borough Council, Harrison *v.* - - - - 650
Hamoor Tanker Corpn. Inc., Compania Financiera "Soleada" S.A. *v.* - 274, 992
Hang Wah Chong Investment Co. Ltd. *v.* Attorney-General of Hong Kong - - - 1141
Haringey London Borough Council *v.* Mosner - - - 650
Harman, Home Office *v.* (pet. all.) - - - - - 529
Harris (Lord) of Greenwich, Payne *v.* - - - - - 754
Harrison *v.* Hammersmith and Fulham London Borough Council - - - - - 650
Hassett, Barnett *v.* - - - 1385
Hatfield Justices, *Ex parte* Castle, Reg. *v.* - - - - - 217
Haymarket Publishing Ltd., Westminster City Council *v.* - 677
Hayward *v.* Thompson (pet. dis.) 1309
Heaton, Nabi (Ghulam) *v.* - 1052
Hereford and Worcester Local Education Authority, *Ex parte* Jones, Reg. *v.* - - - 768
Heron, Reg. *v.* - - 1480, 1485E
Hill, *Ex parte* (pet. all.) - - 1382
Hodgetts, Faith Panton Property Plan Ltd. *v.* - - - 927

PAGE

Holder, Reel v. - - - - 1226
Holmes, Spectrum Investment
  Co. v. - - - - - 221
Holt, Reg. v. - - - - 1000
Home Insurance Co., Great
  Atlantic Insurance Co. v. - 529
Home Office, Guilfoyle v. (pet.
  dis.) - - - - - 1080
Home Office v. Harman (pet. all.) 529
Ho Pui-yiu, Attorney-General
  of Hong Kong v. - - - 395
Horsepower Ltd., McCormick v. 993
Howard v. Department for
  National Savings - - - 542
Howell (Errol), Reg. v. (pet. dis.) 1468
Hoye v. Forsdyke - - - 1442
Hughes, Ex parte (pet. all.) - - 1382
Hulley v. Thompson - - - 159
Hunt, B.P. Exploration Co.
  (Libya) Ltd. v. (No. 2) - - 232
Hussain (Iftikhar), Reg. v. - - 416

I

Immigration Appeal Tribunal,
  Ex parte Shaikh (Munir Ah-
  med), Reg. v. - - - - 1107
Impex Transport Aktieselskabet
  v. A.G. Thames Holdings Ltd. - 1547
Inland Revenue Comrs. v. Berrill 1449
Inland Revenue Comrs. v. Garvin 793
Inland Revenue Comrs. v.
  Metrolands (Property Finance)
  Ltd. - - - - - 637
Inland Revenue Comrs., Pil-
  kington Brothers Ltd. v. - - 781
Insley, Cleaver v. - - - 939

J

Janov v. Morris - - - 1389
Jenkins v. Kingsgate (Clothing
  Productions) Ltd. (Case 96/80) 972
Jogoo, The - - - - 1376
Johnson v. Firth - - - 475
Jones, Ex parte - - - - 768
Jordan, Whitehouse v. - - 246
Joyce v. Yeomans - - - 549

K

Kaur (Dip) v. Chief Constable
  for Hampshire - - - 578
Kaye, Reg. v. - - - - 355
Kent County Council, Rootkin
  v. - - - - - 1186
Kingsgate (Clothing Productions)
  Ltd., Jenkins v. (Case 96/80) 972

PAGE

L

Laceward Ltd., In re - - - 133
Lambert (A.) Flat Management
  Ltd. v. Lomas - - - 898
Lambie, Reg. v. - - - - 78
Lands Tribunal, Ex parte City
  of London Corpn., Reg. v. - 985
Landy, Reg. v. - - - - 355
Law Society, The, Manley v. - 335
Lewis, Ex parte - - - - 131
Lewis (J. P.), Ex parte - - 328
Lewisham London Borough
  Council v. M. - - - 1248
Littell, Reg. v. - - - - 1146
Lloyds Bank Ltd. v. London
  College of Music - - - 493
Lloyds Bank Ltd., Worringham
  v. (Case 69/80) - - - 950
Lomas, Lambert (A.) Flat
  Management Ltd. v. - - 898
London College of Music, Lloyds
  Bank Ltd. v. - - - - 493
London Hospital Medical
  College (University of London),
  Evans v. - - - - 184
Lydall, Wadsworth v. - - 598
Lyon Group Ltd., Property
  Discount Corpn. Ltd. v. - 300,
                                    313

M

M., Lewisham London
  Borough Council v. - - 1248
McCarney v. Freilich - - - 431
McCormick v. Horsepower Ltd. 993
McDonald, Dennis v. - - 810
McQuaid v. Anderton - - 154
Malcherek, Reg. v. - - - 690
Mallalieu v. Drummond - - 908
Manchester Stipendiary Magis-
  trate, Ex parte Hill, Reg. v.
  (pet. all.) - - - - 1382
Manley v. The Law Society - 335
Marcus, Reg. v. - - - - 774
Meaney, Wadham Stringer
  Finance Ltd. v. - - - 39
Mears v. Safecar Security Ltd. - 1214
Mellor, Reg. v. - - - - 1044
Metrolands (Property Finance)
  Ltd., Inland Revenue Comrs. v. 637
Mineralimportexport, Clipper
  Maritime Co. Ltd. of Mon-
  rovia v. - - - - 1262
Monahan, Westminster City
  Council v. - - - - 698
Morris, Janov v. - - - 1389

PAGE

Mosner, Haringey London Borough Council v. - - 650
Munro, In re, Ex parte Singer v. Trustee in Bankruptcy - - 1358

N

Nabi (Ghulam) v. Heaton - - 1052
Nadler Enterprises Ltd., In re - 23
National Bank of Kuwait S.A.K., Power Curber International Ltd. v. - - 1233
National Insurance Comr., Ex parte Secretary of State for Social Services, Reg. v. - - 1017
National Westminster Bank Ltd., Safeguard Industrial Investments Ltd. v. - - - 286
National Westminster Bank Ltd. v. Stockman - - - 67
Nembhard v. The Queen - - 1515
New Zealand Government Property Corpn. v. H.M. & S. Ltd. 870
Nicholson, Pascoe v. - - 1061
North Devon District Council, Ex parte Lewis (J. P.), Reg. v. - - - - - - 328
North West Leicestershire District Council v. East Midlands Housing Association Ltd. - 1396
Norvell, Ex parte - - - 413

O

Occasions Textiles Ltd., Suedeclub Co. Ltd. v. - - 1245
Oceanic Contractors Inc., Clark v. - - - - - 59
Oldfield, Windsors (Sporting Investments) Ltd. v. - - 1176
Olugboja, Reg. v. (pet dis.) - - 1382
Orpwood, Reg. v. - - - 1048

P

Pascoe v. Nicholson - - - 1061
Patel (Bharat), Patel (Mahendra Kumar) v. - - - 1342
Patel (Mahendra Kumar) v. Patel (Bharat) - - - - 1342
Payne v. Lord Harris of Greenwich - - - - - 754
Perdana Properties Bhd. v. United Orient Leasing Co. Sdn. Bhd. - - - 1496
Perrons v. Spackman - - 1411
Pharmaceutical Society of Great Britain, Ex parte - - 886
Phekoo, Reg. v. - - - 1117

PAGE

Pilkington Brothers Ltd. v. Inland Revenue Comrs. - - - 781
Plummer v. P. W. Wilkins & Son Ltd. - - - - - 831
Port Jackson Stevedoring Pty. Ltd. v. Salmond and Spraggon (Australia) Pty. Ltd. - - 138
Power Curber International Ltd. v. National Bank of Kuwait S.A.K. - - - - - 1233
Powis, Ex parte - - - - 584
Practice Direction (Adoption: Jurisdiction Application) - - 1212
Practice Direction (Chancery: Setting Down for Trial) - - 322
Practice Direction (Costs: Acquittal of Defendant) - - 1383
Practice Direction (Crime: Crown Court Business) (No. 7) - - 1324
Practice Direction (Divorce: Welfare Report) - - - - 1162
Practice Direction (Divorce Registry: Failure to Maintain) - 274
Practice Direction (E.A.T.: Procedure) - - - - - 323
Practice Direction (Family Division: Case Stated) - - - 138
Practice Direction (Family Division: Filing Affidavits) - - 106
Practice Direction (House of Lords: Costs: Security) - - 1213
Practice Direction (Juries: Length of Trial) - - - - - 1129
Practice Direction (Justices: Clerk to Court) - - - 1163
Practice Direction (Pre-trial Review: Ancillary Relief) - - 1010
Practice Direction (Probate: Representation Grant) - - 1135
Practice Direction (Tape Recorders) 1526
Practice Direction (Taxation: VAT) (No. 3) - - - - 327
Practice Direction (Trials in London) - - - - - 1296
Practice Note (Bankruptcy: Affidavit of Search) - - - 474
Practice Note (Chancery: Deposition) - - - - - 1560
Practice Note (Domestic Violence: Power of Arrest) - - 27
Property Discount Corpn. Ltd. v. Lyon Group Ltd. - - 300, 313
Provident Mutual Life Assurance Association v. Derby City Council - - - - - 173
Pub Squash Co. Pty. Ltd., Cadbury-Schweppes Pty. Ltd. v. - 193

PAGE

Q

Quinn, Coventry City Council v. 1325

R

R. (A Juvenile) Ex parte - - 1501, 1509H
Ragho Prasad v. The Queen - 469
Ram, Abergavenny (Marquess of) v. - - - - - - 843
Ramsden, Regalian Securities Ltd. v. - - - - - 611
Reel v. Holder - - - 1226
Reeve, Barrass v. - - - 408
Regalian Securities Ltd. v. Ramsden - - - - - 611
Reg. v. Barrington - - - 419
Reg. v. Bolton Supplementary Benefits Commission, Ex parte Fordham - - - - 28
Reg. v. Bloxham - - - 859
Reg. v. Brooker - - - 1048
Reg. v. Camden London Borough Rent Officer, Ex parte Ebiri - - - - - 881
Reg. v. Croydon Crown Court, Ex parte Bernard - - 116
Reg. v. Dartford Justices, Ex parte Dhesi (pet. all.) - - 1382
Reg. v. Denton - - - - 1446
Reg. v. Dunbar - - - 1536
Reg. v. Ebbw Vale and Merthyr Tydfil Supplementary Benefits Appeal Tribunal, Ex parte Lewis - - - - - 131
Reg. v. Edmonton Justices, Ex parte Hughes (pet. all.) - - 1382
Reg. v. Folkestone and Hythe Juvenile Court Justices, Ex parte R. (A Juvenile) 1501, 1509H
Reg., Frater v. (Note) - - - 1468
Reg. v. Galbraith - - - 1039
Reg. v. Governor of Pentonville Prison, Ex parte Harmohan Singh - - - - - 1031
Reg. v. Hall (Peter Michael) 1510, 1515F
Reg. v. Hatfield Justices, Ex parte Castle - - - - 217
Reg. v. Hereford and Worcester Local Education Authority, Ex parte Jones - - - 768
Reg. v. Heron - - 1480, 1485F
Reg. v. Holt - - - - 1000
Reg. v. Howell (Errol) (pet. dis.) 1468
Reg. v. Hussain (Iftikhar) - - 416
Reg. v. Immigration Appeal Tribunal, Ex parte Shaikh (Munir Ahmed) - - - - 1107

PAGE

Reg. v. Kaye - - - - 355
Reg. v. Lambie - - - 78
Reg. v. Lands Tribunal, Ex parte City of London Corpn. - - 985
Reg. v. Landy - - - - 355
Reg. v. Littell - - - - 1146
Reg. v. Malcherek - - - 690
Reg. v. Manchester Stipendiary Magistrate, Ex parte Hill (pet. all.) - - - - - 1382
Reg. v. Marcus - - - 774
Reg. v. Mellor - - - - 1044
Reg. v. National Insurance Comr. Ex parte Secretary of State for Social Services - - 1017
Reg., Nembhard v. - - - 1515
Reg. v. North Devon District Council, Ex parte Lewis (J. P.) 328
Reg. v. Olugboja (pet. dis.) - 1382
Reg. v. Orpwood - - - 1048
Reg. v. Phekoo - - - - 1117
Reg., Ragho Prasad v. - - 469
Reg. v. Secretary of State for the Environment, Ex parte Powis - 584
Reg. v. Secretary of State for the Home Department, Ex parte Santillo (pet. dis.) - - - 529
Reg. v. Southampton Justices, Ex parte Davies (Neil) - - 374
Reg. v. Statutory Committee of the Pharmaceutical Society of Great Britain, Ex parte Pharmaceutical Society of Great Britain - - - - - 886
Reg. v. Steel - - - - 690
Reg., Tsang Ping-nam v. - - 1462
Reg. v. Uxbridge Justices, Ex parte Comr. of Police of the Metropolis - - - - 112
Reg. v. Uxbridge Justices, Ex parte Davies - - - - 1080
Reg. v. White - - - - 355
Reg. v. Worthing Justices, Ex parte Norvell - - - - 413
Richmond-upon-Thames London Borough Council, Gunton v. (pet. dis.) - - - - 28
Riley, E.M.I. Records Ltd. v. - 923
Robinson v. Scott Bader Co. Ltd. 1135
Rootkin v. Kent County Council - 1186

S

Safecar Security Ltd., Mears v. - 1214
Safeguard Industrial Investments Ltd. v. National Westminster Bank Ltd. - - - - 286

PAGE

St. Margaret's, Eartham, *In re* - 1129
St. Mark's, Haydock, *In re* - - 1164
St. Mark's, Haydock, *In re* (No. 2) 1167
St. Martin's, Ashton-upon-Mersey, *In re* - - - 1228
St. Mary's, Fawkham, *In re* - 1171
St. Piran Ltd., *In re* - - 1300
Salmond and Spraggon (Australia) Pty. Ltd., Port Jackson Stevedoring Pty. Ltd. *v.* - - 138
Sandiford, Finnigan *v.* - - 837
Santillo v. Secretary of State for the Home Department (pet. dis.) - - - - - 529
Scott Bader Co. Ltd., Robinson *v.* - - - - - 1135
Secretary of State for Social Services, *Ex parte* - - 1017
Seaford, Brikom Investments Ltd. *v.* - - - - - 863
Sea-Land Services Inc., Carmel Exporters (Sales) Ltd. *v.* - 1068
Searose Ltd. *v.* Seatrain U.K. Ltd. - - - - 894
Seatrain U.K. Ltd., Searose Ltd. *v.* - - - - - 894
Secretary of State for the Environment, *Ex parte* Powis, Reg. *v.* - - - - 584
Secretary of State for the Home Department, *Ex parte* Santillo, Reg. *v.* (pet dis.) - - 529
Secretary of State for the Environment, South Oxfordshire District Council *v.* - - 1092
Selim Ltd. *v.* Bickenhall Engineering Ltd. - - - 1318
Shaikh (Munir Ahmed), *Ex parte* 1107
Singer *v.* Trustee in Bankruptcy, *Ex parte* - - - 1358
Singer *v.* Trustee of the Property of Munro - - - 1358
Singh (Harmohan), *Ex parte* - 1031
Smith, Clear *v.* - - - 399
Sony Corpn. *v.* Time Electronics - 1293
Southampton Justices, *Ex parte* Davies (Neil), Reg. *v.* - 374
South Oxfordshire District Council *v.* Secretary of State for the Environment - - - 1092
Spackman, Perrons *v.* - - 1411
Spectrum Investment Co. *v.* Holmes - - - - 221
Stafford Winfield Cook & Partners Ltd. *v.* Winfield - 458
Stanton *v.* Drayton Commercial Investment Co. Ltd. - - 1425

PAGE

Statutory Committee of the Pharmaceutical Society of Great Britain, *Ex parte* Pharmaceutical Society of Great Britain, Reg. *v.* - - - - 886
Steel, Reg. *v.* - - - - 690
Stockman, National Westminster Bank Ltd. *v.* - - - - 67
Stone Toms & Partners, Townsend *v.* - - - - - 1153
Suedeclub Co. Ltd. *v.* Occasions Textiles Ltd. - - - 1245
Suffolk County Council, Cicutti *v.* 558

T

Talbot, Faulkner *v.* - - - 1528
Taylor *v.* Chief Constable of Kent - - - - - 606
Thermo Engineers Ltd. *v.* Ferrymasters Ltd. - - - 1470
Thompson *v.* Brown - - - 744
Thompson, Hayward *v.* (pet. dis.) 1309
Thompson, Hulley *v.* - - 159
Thompson & Riches Ltd., *In re* - 682
Time Electronics, Sony Corpn. *v.* 1293
Townsend *v.* Stone Toms & Partners - - - - - 1153
Tradax Export S.A., Panama, Bunge Corpn., New York *v.* - 711
Trade Credits Ltd., Burnes *v.* - 805
Trustee of the Property of Munro, Singer *v.* - - - - 1358
Tsang Ping-Nam *v.* The Queen - 1462

U

United Orient Leasing Co. Sdn. Bhd., Perdana Properties Bhd. *v.* - - - - - - 1496
Uxbridge Justices, *Ex parte* Comr. of Police of the Metropolis, Reg. *v.* - - - 112
Uxbridge Justices, *Ex parte* Davies, Reg. *v.* - - 1080

V

Veater *v.* G. - - - - 567

W

Wadham Stringer Finance Ltd. *v.* Meaney - - - - - 39
Wadsworth *v.* Lydall - - - 598
Walker, Dodds *v.* - - - 1027
Wandsworth London Borough Council, Attorney-General *ex rel.* Tilley *v.* - - - 854
Warnett, Berry *v.* - - - 1

PAGE

Watson v. Hackney London
  Borough Council -   -   -   650
Westminster City Council v. Hay-
  market Publishing Ltd. -   -   677
Westminster City Council v.
  Monahan -   -   -   -   698
White, Reg. v. -   -   -   -   355
Whitehouse v. Jordan -   -   -   246
Wicks v. Firth -   -   -   -   475
Wilkins (P. W.) & Son Ltd., Plum-
  mer v. -   -   -   -   -   831
Windsor and Maidenhead Royal
  Borough Council v. Brandrose
  Investments Ltd. -   -   - 1083
Windsors (Sporting Investments)
  Ltd. v. Oldfield -   -   - 1176

Winfield, Stano...
  & Partners Ltd. v.
Woodhams, decd., In re
Woolworth (F. W.) & Co. L...
  Chanel Ltd. v. -   -   -
Worringham v. Lloyds Bank Ltd.
  (Case 69/80) -   -   -   -   950
Worthing Justices, Ex parte Nor-
  vell, Reg. v. -   -   -   -   413
Wyndham's (Lingerie) Ltd., Bates
  (Thomas) and Son Ltd. v. -   505
Wynne v. Wynne -   -   -   69

Y

Yeomans, Joyce v. -   -   -   549

The Weekly Law Reports

Volume 1

Containing those cases of value to practitioners which are not intended to be included in The Law Reports, together with practice notes and directions.

[COURT OF APPEAL]

* BERRY *v.* WARNETT (INSPECTOR OF TAXES)

1980 May 20, 21; July 15   Buckley, Ackner and Oliver L.JJ.

Revenue—Capital gains tax—Tax avoidance—Taxpayer transferring shares to Guernsey company on trust for his benefit—Sale of reversionary interest in trust fund for value—Subsequent sale of life interest to company within exemption from charge to tax—Whether transfer of shares to trustees " gift in settlement " so as to be deemed disposal at market value—Whether tax chargeable on sale of reversionary interest as being part disposal—Finance Act 1965 (c. 25), ss. 22 (2) (4), 25 (2), Sch. 7, paras. 17, 21

For the purpose of reducing liability to capital gains tax on the sale of shares and stock, the taxpayer on April 4, 1972, executed a deed of settlement whereby he transferred shares and loan stock to a Guernsey company who were to hold them as trustees for his benefit during his life and to pay income arising from the fund to him. By the same settlement a Jersey company paid £14,500 to the taxpayer in consideration for the sale to it of the reversionary interest in the trust fund. It was agreed that £14,500 represented the market value of that interest in remainder. On April 6, 1972, the taxpayer executed a deed of assignment whereby he disposed of his life interest in the income arising from the settlement to an investment company in the Bahamas for £130,753. The taxpayer appealed against an assessment to capital gains tax for the year 1971–72 in a sum of £150,483 made on the basis that during that year he had made a total disposal of the shares and loan stock that had been transferred to the trustees. The special commissioners rejected the argument put forward by the taxpayer that the sale of the interests in remainder to the Jersey company constituted a part disposal of an asset within the meaning of section 22 (1) of the Finance Act 1965 and that the chargeable gain amounted to £14,839, and dismissed the appeal. Goulding J. allowed the taxpayer's appeal, holding that the taxpayer had made a part disposal on the sale of the reversionary interest, and reduced the assessment to £14,839.

On appeal by the revenue : —

Held, dismissing the appeal (Buckley L.J. dissenting), that

1

2

Berry v. Warnett (C.A.)   **[1981]**

since in the same instrument as the transfer of the entire   A
property of shares and stock to the trustees, the taxpayer sold
his reversionary interest therein for value, consideration was
given and accordingly the transaction was not a gift in settlement within section 25 (2) of the Act; that on the transfer to
trustees part of the property, namely the taxpayer's equitable
life interest therein, remained undisposed of and hence the
transaction was a part disposal of the assets within section
22 (2); and since by the same instrument there could not be   B
both a total and a partial disposal of the property, it followed
that the taxpayer had made a part disposal only of the
property within section 22 (2) in the tax year 1971–72, and
the assessment of £14,839 was the correct one (post, pp. 6D–F,
7H–8A, 9E, 10A, 11C–G, 15B, D–F).

Per Buckley L.J. Since there was an entire disposal of
the taxpayer's shares and stock to the trustees without consideration, nothing remained undisposed of and there was a   C
gift in settlement within section 25 (2); because the trustees
acquired the property otherwise than by way of a bargain made
at arm's length the trustees were deemed to have paid market
value for them, so the decision of the commissioners should
be restored and their assessment to tax on a capital gain of
£150,483 confirmed (post, pp. 18F–H, 20D, 22B–C).

Decision of Goulding J. [1978] 1 W.L.R. 957; [1978] 3
All E.R. 267 affirmed.   D

The following cases are referred to in the judgments:

Attorney-General v. *Beech* [1899] A.C. 53, H.L.(E.).
Attorney-General v. *Milne* [1914] A.C. 765, H.L.(E.).
Canadian Eagle Oil Co. Ltd. v. *The King* [1946] A.C. 119; [1945] 2 All
     E.R. 499, H.L.(E.).
Cape Brandy Syndicate v. *Inland Revenue Commissioners* [1921] 1 K.B. 64.   E
Earl Fitzwilliam's Agreement, In re [1950] Ch. 448; [1950] 1 All E.R.
     191.
Greenberg v. *Inland Revenue Commissioners* [1972] A.C. 109; [1971]
     3 W.L.R. 386; [1971] 3 All E.R. 136; 47 T.C. 240, H.L.(E.).
Inland Revenue Commissioners v. *Gribble* [1913] 3 K.B. 212, C.A.
Inland Revenue Commissioners v. *Joiner* [1975] 1 W.L.R. 1701; [1975]
     3 All E.R. 1050; 50 T.C. 449, H.L.(E.).   F
Inland Revenue Commissioners v. *Plummer* [1979] 3 W.L.R. 689; [1979]
     3 All E.R. 775, H.L.(E.).
Ransom v. *Higgs* [1974] 1 W.L.R. 1594; [1974] 3 All E.R. 949; 50 T.C.
     1, H.L.(E.).
Rose, In re [1949] Ch. 78; [1948] 2 All E.R. 971.
Tennant v. *Smith* [1892] A.C. 150, H.L.(Sc.).
                                                               G

The following additional cases were cited in argument:

Aberdeen Construction Group Ltd. v. *Inland Revenue Commissioners*
     [1978] A.C. 885; [1978] 2 W.L.R. 648; [1978] 1 All E.R. 962; T.C.
     Leaflet No. 2675, H.L.(Sc.).
Sargaison v. *Roberts* [1969] 1 W.L.R. 951; [1969] 3 All E.R. 1072; 45
     T.C. 612.

                                                               H

APPEAL from Goulding J.

The taxpayer, Norman Charles Berry, and his wife, executed settlements dated April 4, 1972, whereby shares and loan stock in Rothschild
Investment Trust Ltd. having a market value of £219,880 were assigned to
Investors Trustees Ltd, of Guernsey, as trustees, to hold for the benefit of
the taxpayer and his wife. The settlements also recited that in consideration of the sums of £14,500 and £7,550 paid by First Investors and Savers

(C.A.)

...ayer and his wife respectively, the trust funds and ... thereof were to be held by the trustees after the death of the taxpayer or of his wife upon trust for that Jersey company absolutely. On April 6, 1972, the taxpayer and his wife executed deeds of assignment selling their life interests in the income of the trust funds for £130,753 and £57,344 respectively. The taxpayer appealed against an assessment to capital gains tax for the year 1971–72 in the sum of £150,483. The commissioners, rejecting his argument that, by virtue of section 22 (2) of the Finance Act 1965 the assessment should be reduced to £14,839, dismissed the appeal. Goulding J. allowed the taxpayer's appeal, holding that the only transfer within the charge to tax was the sale of the taxpayer's reversionary interest in the Jersey company and accordingly the taxpayer had made a part disposal within section 22 (2) and the judge reduced the assessment to £14,839. The Crown appealed.

The facts are stated in the judgment of Oliver L.J.

Andrew Morritt Q.C. and *C. H. McCall* for the Crown.
D. C. Potter Q.C. and *David Braham Q.C.* for the taxpayer.

Cur. adv. vult.

OLIVER L.J., reading the first judgment. This is an appeal by the Crown from a judgment of Goulding J. delivered on March 22, 1978, in which he reversed the decision of the special commissioners.

The facts fall within a fairly short compass. The appellants from the special commissioners, the taxpayer and his wife, were the beneficial owners of certain shares and units of convertible unsecured loan stock of Rothschild Investment Trust Ltd., which were either registered in their respective names or were held on their behalf by Lloyds Bank (Branches) Nominees Ltd. The question on this appeal arises out of settlements made by the taxpayer and his wife respectively of their holdings. The settlements are identical except for the settlors and the amounts of their respective holdings, and there is no question but that the same legal consequences attend the transactions carried out by the wife as attend those carried out by the taxpayer. Nor is there any question but that, if a liability to tax arises from her dealings, he as her husband is responsible for discharging it. The total market value of the shares and stock at the date of the settlements was £219,880.

Since the question in each case is the same, I can confine myself to the transactions carried out by the taxpayer himself. On March 15, 1972, he transferred, or caused to be transferred, the whole of his holdings of shares and stock (consisting of 10,854 shares and a sum of £49,931 stock) to a Guernsey company, Investors Trustees Ltd. That company was not, as a matter of machinery, actually registered as the holder of the stock transferred until April 28, 1972, and did not become the registered holder of the shares until May 12, 1972, but nothing turns on the date of registration save this, so far as it is material, that at the end of the financial year 1971–72 the taxpayer or his nominee was still the registered holder.

In the meantime two documents were executed. On April 4, 1972 (that is, in the financial year 1971–72), a settlement was executed to which the parties were the taxpayer (described as " the vendor "), First Investors & Savers (Jersey) Ltd. (a Jersey company described as " the purchaser ")

Oliver L.J.

A (Jersey) Ltd. to the income the taxpayer

Berry v. Warnett

1 WLR.

The Weekly Law Reports, January 16, 1981

and Investors T̶... beneficial ownership o̶... being in the vendor, and con̶...

"And whereas the vendor and ... agreed for the consideration hereinaft... shall be settled in manner hereinafter app... witnesseth as follows: 1. 'The Trust Fund' means ... specified in the schedule hereto and the property for the ... representing the same. 2. In pursuance of the said agreement an... consideration of the sum of £14,500 now paid by the purchaser to the vendor (the receipt whereof the vendor hereby acknowledges) the vendor as beneficial owner hereby assigns unto the trustees all that the trust fund and the income thereof to hold the same unto the trustees absolutely and the vendor hereby directs and declares that the trust fund and the income thereof shall henceforth be held after the death of the vendor and subject in the meantime to the life interest of the vendor and the powers and provisions hereinafter reserved and contained upon trust for the purchaser absolutely. 3. Provided always that during the life of the vendor the trustees shall pay the income of the trust fund to the vendor for his own use and benefit absolutely."

There followed a trust for sale or retention at the discretion of the trustees, which I do not think I need read, an unrestricted investment clause, a power in the vendor to appoint new trustees (but excluding the vendor himself) and a charging clause enabling trustees to charge for work done in the execution of the trusts and entitling a trust corporation to remuneration in accordance with its scale of fees in force at the date of appointment. Finally, the shares and stock were described in the schedule.

On April 6, 1972 (that is, in the financial year 1972–73), a further document was executed. That was an assignment, made between the taxpayer of the one part and First Investors International Ltd. (a Bahamas company) of the second part. It recited the settlement and the composition of the trust fund and it continued, in recital (C), as follows:

"The vendor has agreed with the purchaser for the sale to it at the price of £130,753.72 of the said life interest of the vendor in the trust fund," and the operative part was in these terms: "Now this deed witnesseth that in pursuance of the said agreement and in consideration of the sum of £130,753.72 paid by the purchaser to the vendor (who acknowledges the receipt thereof) the vendor as beneficial owner assigns to the purchaser all the dividends interest and income to become payable or accrue henceforth during the remainder of the life of the vendor from or in respect of the trust fund and the investments and property from time to time and for the time being representing the same to hold the same unto the purchaser absolutely."

As I have said, the taxpayer's wife executed identical documents relating to her holdings, so the effect was that between April 3 and April 7, 1972, the taxpayer and his wife had effectively divested themselves of their entire beneficial interests in the shares and stock concerned in favour of companies which, being resident abroad, would not be liable

The Weekly Law Reports, January 16, 1981

5

1 W.L.R.   **Berry v. Warnett (C.A.)**   Oliver L.J.

A for any capital gains tax upon the distribution of the trust funds or on any subsequent disposals. It is accepted, of course, that there was a disposal by the taxpayer and his wife of their reversionary interests in favour of the Jersey company and that capital gains tax is payable on the gain made out of the consideration received from that disposal, calculated on the basis that this was a partial disposal only. It is agreed that on this basis the chargeable gains amount to £14,839.

B It is not in issue that there is no chargeable gain in respect of the subsequent assignment of the life interest reserved to the vendor, having regard to the provisions of paragraph 13 of Schedule 7 to the Finance Act 1965, but the Crown contend that there was, on the execution of the settlement, a complete disposition of the shares which results in a chargeable gain of £150,483. The special commissioners upheld that

C contention. They said:

> ". . . the scheme of the tax appears to be that a taxpayer who declares himself to be a trustee of property, or transfers property to a trustee other than a bare trustee for himself, makes a disposal for a consideration equal to the market value of the property in respect of which trusts are declared or which is transferred to the
>
> D trustees. Assets which previously belonged to the taxpayer cease so to belong: prima facie there is a disposition of the whole of the assets. Does it affect this conclusion that the transaction here in question appears to fall within the description of a part disposal in section 22 (2) (b) of the Finance Act 1965? We think not: what matters is that in relation to the shares and loan stock there was a disposal. Whether that disposal was a gift in settlement within the meaning
>
> E of section 25 (2) is similarly not the decisive question: as between the taxpayer and the trustee there was a disposal of the shares and loan stock. Sale of an asset to the trustee of a settlement would be a disposal of the asset notwithstanding that the seller was interested under the settlement. It seems possible that section 25 (2) is intended to do no more than make clear that a gratuitous transfer to the
>
> F trustee of a settlement is in no different category."

Goulding J. felt unable to accept the reasoning of the commissioners and he allowed the taxpayer's appeal. From that decision the Crown now appeals. The point is ultimately a fairly narrow one and it turns on the provisions of sections 22 and 25 of the Finance Act 1965, which are not altogether easy to follow.

G There is no doubt that, upon the execution of the settlement, the shares and stock settled became settled property as defined in section 45 (1) of the Act. That is not in dispute. That subsection defines " settled property " as follows: " ' settled property ' means, subject to subsection (8) below," which does not matter for present purposes, " any property held in trust other than property to which section 22 (5) of this Act

H applies." Settled property is regulated by section 25 of the Act, subsection (1) of which provides that in relation to such property the trustees of the settlement shall be treated as a single and continuing body of persons (distinct from the persons who may from time to time be the trustees) and that body is to be treated as being resident and ordinarily resident in the United Kingdom except in certain circumstances which do not matter for present purposes.

It is pointed out by the Crown that the section goes on to recognise

6

that the interest arising under the settlement is something quite different   A
from the settled property. Thus when the beneficiary becomes absolutely
entitled to the settled property as against the trustee, section 25 (3)
provides that the assets to which he becomes entitled are deemed to have
been disposed of by the trustee and immediately reacquired by him in
his capacity as trustee for a consideration equal to their market value.
So it is the trustee who makes the notional gain, if any. A similar result   B
ensues on the termination of a life interest in the settled property under
subsection (4). These provisions are prayed in aid in support of what is
the mainspring of the Crown's case, namely the contention that whenever
property becomes settled property, the entire property in settlement is
disposed of, with the result that any increase which has at that point
arisen over the appropriate base value of the settled property becomes a
chargeable gain. That contention is based on the provisions of section   C
25 (2) which is in the following terms:

> "A gift in settlement, whether revocable or irrevocable, is a disposal
> of the entire property thereby becoming settled property notwith-
> standing that the donor has some interest as a beneficiary under the
> settlement and notwithstanding that he is a trustee, or the sole
> trustee, of the settlement."   D

The submission, then, may be summarised thus. (1) The expression
"a gift in settlement" is not referring simply to a voluntary settlement.
It is looking, not at the position as between the settlor and the beneficiaries, but at the position as between the settlor and the trustees and
it means merely the transfer of the settled property to the trustees, for
which the trustees give no consideration and which can therefore properly   E
be described as "a gift."
  In the instant case, therefore, there was a transfer of the entirety of
the settled property, notwithstanding that the taxpayer retained an
interest, and the fact that he received consideration from the purchaser
for making the settlement which created the purchased reversion does
not prevent the transfer to the trustees from being a "gift in settlement."   F
(2) The second stage, it is submitted, is then to find out what is the
consideration deemed to be paid by the trustees on this acquisition by
them, because unless one can do that there is no machinery for ascertaining what is the chargeable gain. That, it is submitted, is found in
section 22 (4), which is in these terms:

> "Subject to the provisions of this Part of this Act, a person's   G
> acquisition of an asset and the disposal of it to him shall for the
> purposes of this Part of this Act be deemed to be for a consideration
> equal to the market value of the asset—(a) where he acquires the
> asset otherwise than by way of a bargain made at arm's length and
> in particular where he acquires it by way of gift or by way of
> distribution from a company in respect of shares in the company,
> or "   H

and paragraphs (b) and (c) are immaterial.
  Hence the Crown's contention that the chargeable gain here is the
sum of £150,483, the difference between the market value of the settled
property and the amount for which it was acquired by the taxpayer and
his wife.
  Goulding J. indicated that he would have felt himself able to accept

A   the first of these submissions, but he did not feel able to accept the second. He said [1978] 1 W.L.R. 957, 963:

"... I have to take the deed of April 4, 1972, as showing the true situation. It recites a preliminary agreement between two parties, the taxpayer and the purchaser, and goes on to effect a single and indivisible transaction between three persons. The taxpayer assigns
B   the fund to the trustees, grants a beneficial remainder to the purchaser, receives £14,500, and retains a beneficial life interest. The purchaser pays £14,500 and receives the beneficial remainder. The trustees accept the fund, undertake the duty of holding it as trustees, and receive a right to remuneration. On the evidence there was one arrangement between all three parties, and the taxpayer was at arm's length vis-à-vis both the purchaser and the trustees. In my judgment
C   section 22 (4) clearly does not catch the present case even if, as Mr. McCall asked me to do, I alter the expression ' a bargain made at arm's length' to read ' a bargain made by him at arm's length.' In relation to section 22 (4), it seems to be that I am invited, not so much to strain the language of the Act as to distort the facts of the case. Therefore, I reject the Crown's main argument."

D   For the taxpayer, it is submitted in the first place that, since there is no equity about a taxing statute, the special commissioners were wrong to seek to find the intendment of the Act. They should, it is submitted, have been looking to see whether there were clear words which resulted in the instant case in tax becoming payable. It is not disputed for one moment that the taxpayer's purpose in making the elaborate arrange-
E   ments which I have described was to make a non-taxable profit on his holding of the stock and shares. That, it is submitted, is his privilege. He is not obliged to arrange his affairs for the benefit of the fisc and equally he is entitled so to arrange them as to benefit himself if the words which the legislative draftsmen have chosen to employ fairly enable him to do so.

        That leads, then, to the attack on the Crown's central proposition.
F   Section 25 (2), upon which the Crown's case rests is, it is submitted, expressed in terms which make it applicable only to a settlement by way of gift, and not one executed for consideration in money or money's worth. The appropriate section to apply to the instant transaction is therefore, it is submitted, section 22 (2), and that is in the following terms:

G   "For the purposes of this Part of this Act—(a) references to a disposal of an asset include, except where the context otherwise requires, references to a part disposal of an asset, and (b) there is a part disposal of an asset where an interest or right in or over the asset is created by the disposal, as well as where it subsists before the disposal, and generally, there is a part disposal of an asset where, on a person making a disposal, any description of property derived
H   from the asset remains undisposed of."

The very wide words " any description of property derived from the asset " are clearly, it is submitted, apt to refer to the equitable life interest retained under the settlement and therefore, it is argued, all that was disposed of here was the reversionary interest sold to the purchaser under the deed and it was on that disposition that the real gain arose in the year in question.

If there is to be superimposed some notional gain, that can only be done by finding clear words in the statute imposing such a charge, and the submission is that section 25 (2) which, it is conceded, overrides section 22 (2) in cases to which it applies, does not contain such clear words. It applies in terms only to a " gift in settlement," which this is not. Attention is drawn to other provisions in the Act in which references to " gifts " appear: see, for instance, section 22 (4) (*a*), section 27 (2), section 31 (1) and (7), section 32 (1) and section 34 (1). Particular attention is directed to section 31 (3) (*a*), where there is a significant reference to the concession which is to be allowed in certain circumstances on a disposal of an object of national, scientific, historical or artistic interest " by way of gift, including a gift in settlement." Mr. Morritt has argued that this express reference supports the construction for which he contends, because it demonstrates that " gift in settlement " means something more than merely a voluntary settlement. I find that difficult to accept. It seems to me that what the draftsman was seeking to do was to ensure that the concession was available whether the disposal was by way of outright gift or of a settled gift, but that in either case what the subsection is referring to is a gift," a gift in settlement " being merely a particular type of gift. I find it difficult here to give any secondary meaning to the expression and there is no readily explicable reason why the same expression should have different meanings in separate sections of the same Act.

The other provision to which Mr. Potter draws attention is in paragraph 19 of Schedule 7. The paragraph is concerned with the recovery of tax from the donee in cases of gifts. Subparagraph (4) is in these terms:

"In this paragraph references to a gift include references to any transaction otherwise than by way of a bargain made at arm's length so far as money or money's worth passes under the transaction without full consideration in money or money's worth, and ' donor ' and ' donee ' shall be construed accordingly; . . ."

The only significance of this is that it can be said to demonstrate that, where the legislature wishes to bring under the umbrella of gifts, transactions which are not in fact gratuitous, it does so in express terms.

I confess that, for my part, I find considerable difficulty in giving to the expression " gift in settlement " the meaning sought to be attached to it by the Crown. It is true that, as mentioned by Goulding J., a citation from *Sheppard's Touchstone* 7th ed., (1820) p. 227, might indicate that " gift " has the rather wide connotation simply of a transfer of property, but I entertain some little doubt whether that work (which originated in 1641 and the last edition of which was in 1820) formed part of the staple reading of our parliamentary draftsmen in 1965 and, furthermore, if it did, they must presumably also have had in mind that the extended meaning there suggested was decisively rejected by Danckwerts J. in *In re Earl Fitzwilliam's Agreement* [1950] Ch. 448, as the touchstone for the construction, in previous fiscal legislation, of the words " immediate gift inter vivos." Not only does the construction urged by the Crown put a strained meaning upon the word " gift," but if, as Mr. Morritt suggests, it is really looking at the position vis-à-vis the settlor and the trustees alone and means simply a transfer to trustees, it is impossible to fit that concept with the case which the section itself envisages, of the settlor being the sole trustee of the settlement. Here there is clearly contemplated

A   the case where there never was a transfer but merely a unilateral declaration of trust, and in that context " gift in settlement " can only be referring to the creation, as against the trustee, of the beneficial interests under the settlement.

To give effect to the scheme and intendment of the Act Mr. Morritt must therefore read the expression simply as meaning " a settlement " or " the making of a settlement." That, I agree, would make much more

B   sense if one has regard to what the legislation was trying to achieve, but it is not what the Act says, and unless the court is entitled to put a gloss on the term in order to bring within the subsection a transaction of a type which the draftsman almost certainly did not contemplate, I do not think either that the reference to a gift can be simply ignored or that the word can be given a meaning which it does not naturally bear. That

C   approach to construction is not, as I understand the authorities, permissible in the case of a taxing statute: see Canadian Eagle Oil Co. Ltd. v. The King [1946] A.C. 119, 140 and Ransom v. Higgs [1974] 1 W.L.R. 1594, 1616.

Thus, to take a simple example, if A, the tenant under a 99-year lease, grants a sub-lease to B for 20 years at a premium equal to the value of

D   the sub-lease, he has clearly made a part disposal of the lease as defined in section 22 (2). If he achieves the same result, in consideration of the same premium and of a covenant by B to observe the covenants in the lease, by declaring himself a trustee of the lease for B for a term of 20 years and thereafter for himself, he has equally clearly converted the lease into settled property within section 45 (1) of the Act, since it is now property held in trust, but property to which section 22 (5) does not

E   apply. But to describe that transaction as a " gift in settlement " seems to me at any rate to strain the meaning of that expression beyond the limits both of possible construction and of common sense. The judicial conscience may sometimes be required to display a certain flexibility in questions of construction where the context is clear, but I do not think that it should be, or can be, stretched beyond the point of credibility

F   simply because of an uneasy suspicion that the legislature, if it had given more thought to the matter, would have done more effectively what it seems to have set out to do.

As Mr. Potter submits, it is a dangerous guide to seek to construe a taxing statute by looking for logic. To read the section as he would read it, that is to say, as meaning no more than it says in terms and as confined to cases of gift does, it is true, lead to the strange result that,

G   unless section 22 (4) (a) applies, there is no ascertainable base value upon which to assess the gain on any subsequent disposition by the trustees of the settled property, a result which might be highly disadvantageous to the taxpayer on any initial change of investment by the trustees. That subsection is in the following terms, so far as material for present purposes:

H   " Subject to the provisions of this Part of this Act, a person's acquisition of an asset and the disposal of it to him shall for the purposes of this Part of this Act be deemed to be for a consideration equal to the market value of the asset—(a) where he acquires the asset otherwise than by way of a bargain made at arm's length "

and so on; I have already read that subsection. But if that result follows, it indicates in my judgment no more than that there is a casus omissus for

Oliver L.J.   **Berry v. Warnett (C.A.)**   **[1981]**

which the legislature has failed to provide. It does not fit comfortably   A
with the logic of the scheme and intendment of the Act, but for my part
I do not feel justified, as a result, in giving to the words " gift in settlement " in section 25 (2) a meaning which they do not naturally bear.
I would therefore reject the Crown's primary contention based on that
subsection.

That, however, is not necessarily the end of the matter. Merely
because a disposal to, and an acquisition by, trustees does not fall within   B
section 25 (2) it does not follow that there is no disposal and acquisition.
The only consequence is, so far as I can see, that such a disposal and
acquisition does not oust the provisions of section 22 (2) where those
provisions apply. Under section 22 (9) the amount of gain accruing on the
disposal of assets is to be computed in accordance with the provisions of
Schedules 6, 7 and 8, and section 22 (4) (a) contains the important   C
"deeming provision" in relation to acquisitions otherwise than by way
of arm's length bargain, to which I have already referred. One has,
therefore, as it seems to me, still got to look to see whether there has
been a disposal and acquisition and to compute by reference to the
statutory formulae whether there has been a chargeable gain.

A transfer to the trustees of a settlement, whether voluntary or not,   D
is clearly a disposal by the settlor of the legal interest in the property
which is transferred to the trustees and an acquisition by the trustees
of that legal interest. Whether and to what extent it gives rise to a
chargeable gain depends upon whether apt words can be found in the Act
to produce that result.

The Crown's contention is that, looked at realistically, the settlement
constituted a transfer to the trustees of the stock and shares and that   E
that transfer, being a disposal which, vis-à-vis the trustees, was not the
result of an arm's length bargain, is deemed by section 22 (4) (a) to be a
transfer for a consideration equal to the value of the stock and shares.
This seems to me unanswerable if, but only if, (i) the disposal can be said
to have been otherwise than by way of a bargain at arm's length; and
(ii) it does not fall to be treated only as a part disposal under section   F
22 (2) (b). Goulding J. felt himself unable to accept the Crown's contention that condition (i) was satisfied, and I shall return to that point
a little later; but the first and anterior question seems to me to be whether
the disposal falls within the statutory definition of a part disposal only,
and thus subject only to the limited charge on a gain calculated in
accordance with the statutory provisions relating to such a disposal.

Mr. Morritt contends that it cannot fairly fall within the definition   G
of a part disposal. The property disposed of consisted of the stock and
shares. What was created in the taxpayer and in the purchaser consisted
of interests in " the trust fund " which simply happened, perhaps even
momentarily, to be represented by the stock and shares but which might
equally well have been a fund of gilt-edged stock if the trustees had sold
under their trust for sale and reinvested. There was thus, he argues, no   H
interest or right created in or over " the asset " within section 22 (2) (b)
because " the asset " was the stock and shares and the right or interest
created was in " the trust fund." Equally there was no species of property
remaining " undisposed of," but the creation of some quite different
property—an equitable interest in a trust fund. This argument has an
attraction, particularly if, as the special commissioners held, one is to
look at the scheme and intendment of the Act. But I do not feel able to

A accept it, having regard to the actual terms of the settlement and the proprietary interests which existed prior to it and were created by it. At the date of the settlement the taxpayer had already set in train the necessary steps to transfer the legal title in the shares and stock to the trustees, although those steps had not been completed. He retained the beneficial interest and this is reflected in the form of the settlement. It
B begins by reciting the taxpayer's beneficial ownership of the property described in the schedule which (in clause 1) is included in the definition of the trust fund; it then recites a bargain between the taxpayer and the purchaser for the settlement for the consideration stated below, and then, in clause 2, the taxpayer, as beneficial owner, assigns " the trust fund and the income thereof " to the trustees absolutely and directs that the trustees hold it after the vendor's death and meanwhile subject to his
C life interest on trust for the purchaser. There follows, in clause 3, the proviso that the trustees shall pay the income of the trust fund to the vendor for his own use and benefit absolutely.

When I look at this in the light of the express provisions of section 22 (2), I am bound to say that I find it very difficult to escape from the conclusion that it amounts to a part disposal. All that could be transferred
D to the trustees by this document was the vendor's beneficial interest in the trust fund. Quite apart from the fact that transfers to the trustees had already been executed, the document itself was inappropriate to transfer the shares and stock which, under the articles and terms of issue, require instruments of transfer in the usual common form or, in the case of the stock, in the form authorised by the Stock Transfer Act 1963. What the settlement did was to create out of the beneficial interest assigned a right
E in the purchaser in reversion and to reserve from the beneficial interest the absolute right to payment of income during the vendor's life. That life interest clearly, in my view, remained undisposed of. Equally clearly it seems to me that it was property derived from the asset which was assigned, namely the beneficial interest in the stock and shares.

Mr. Morritt argues that the proper analysis is that the taxpayer
F disposed of his whole interest in the shares and then got something different back, and that therefore his life interest, albeit derived from the asset, did not " remain undisposed of." This seems to me to be unreal, if I may say so respectfully. There was no moment of time under this document when the vendor did not have the absolute right to receive the income from the trust fund. The effect of the settlement was to cut that right
G down to a life interest only, by creating a reversionary interest in the capital in favour of the purchaser. The income arising during the vendor's life therefore seems to me to be properly and literally described as " undisposed of " by the settlement.

Now if this is right, then the Crown's claim must, as I see it, fail, for there cannot be, by the same instrument, both a total disposition and a partial disposition, nor is it argued that there can be.
H   One cannot, as Mr. Potter submits, overcome the effect of section 22 (2) by praying in aid the provisions of section 22 (4), for that subsection applies only " subject to the provisions of this Part of this Act," which includes section 22 (2) itself and the related section 22 (9) and Schedule 6 which lays down (in paragraph 7) how gains on part disposals are to be computed.

That would be sufficient to dispose of the case, but I turn to consider the ground upon which Goulding J. decided the case in the taxpayer's

favour. He would, as I read his judgment, have felt disposed to read the   A
expression " gift in settlement " in section 25 (2) in the sense for which
the Crown contends, notwithstanding the difficulties which he saw in
reconciling the word " gift " in that section with the context in which,
in other parts of the Act, the word is clearly used. The difficulty, however,
which he found, and which he felt was insurmountable, was in ascertaining, on the assumption that section 25 (2) applied, any provision for
ascertaining the amount of the gain upon which tax could be charged.   B
The deeming provisions of section 22 (4) apply only where the acquirer
of the asset acquires it " otherwise than by way of a bargain made at
arm's length," and this was, as he held, indeed such a bargain as between
the vendor and the purchaser. For my part, I do not feel the same
difficulty as that felt by Goulding J. Granted that this was one document
and that the trustee was party to it, there was not in any real sense any   C
bargain between the trustee and the vendor for the acquisition of the
property. I cannot regard the inclusion in the document of a charging
clause, as seems to be suggested in the judge's judgment, as part of a
bargain made at arm's length for the acquisition of the trust property.
The trustees were parties merely as a piece of necessary machinery and
I find some difficulty in reading " by way of a bargain made at arm's
length " as comprehending an acquisition resulting from a bargain made   D
between two other persons. On that analysis if A transfers property to
trustees for B's children in consideration of B transferring property of
equivalent value to trustees for A's children, the subsection would apply
to neither set of trustees because each would acquire the property by
way of the bargain made between A and B. It does not seem to me to
be necessary, even allowing for the strict construction of taxing statutes,   E
to construe the subsection so as to produce so bizarre a result and I do
not myself feel inhibited from accepting Mr. Morritt's submission that
the section is referring to a bargain for the acquisition of the property
made at arm's length between disponor and acquirer.

It is, on the view which I take, strictly unnecessary to consider the
alternative route which the Crown sought to take by way of paragraphs   F
17 and 21 of Schedule 7, but put shortly the submission is that the
settlement here is a settlement as defined in paragraph 21 (which incor-
porates the definition of " settlement " in section 454 of the Income and
Corporation Taxes Act of 1970). The result of that is, it is submitted,
that the settlor and the trustees then became " connected persons " as
defined in paragraph 21 (3) and accordingly paragraph 17 (1) and (2)
apply.   G

Referring briefly to these, paragraph 21 (3) provides as follows, so
far as is material: " A person, in his capacity as trustee of a settlement,
is connected with any individual who in relation to the settlement is a
settlor, . . ." and paragraph 17 (1) and (2), reads:

" (1) This paragraph shall apply where a person acquires an asset and
the person making the disposal is connected with him. (2) Without   H
prejudice to the generality of section 22 (4) of this Act the person
acquiring the asset and the person making the disposal shall be
treated as parties to a transaction otherwise than by way of a bargain
at arm's length."

The difficulty here is that in *Inland Revenue Commissioners* v. *Plummer*
[1979] 3 W.L.R. 689, the House of Lords has clearly stated the limitations

A   on the definition of " a settlement " in section 454. That definition clearly involves the concept of bounty, which is not present in the instant case, and I feel the same difficulty as that felt by Goulding J. in accepting the submission that the definition, having been expressly incorporated into the Act of 1965, can nevertheless be treated as modified by its application in this different context. It seems to me that if a definition from one

B   statute is incorporated in another, it must be subject to the same limitations in both, in the absence of some clear contrary intention or express modification.

However, for the reasons which I have given, I would not feel the same difficulty about the application of section 22 (4) (a) if I could once accept either that the settlement constitutes a " gift in settlement " within section 25 (2) or if I could accept the Crown's submission that the trans-

C   action was not, apart from that provision, a part disposal under section 22 (2) (b).

For the reasons which I have endeavoured to state, I feel unable to accept that submission and I would, therefore, although for reasons rather different from those given by Goulding J., dismiss the appeal.

D   ACKNER L.J. The dispute in this case, although narrow, is one I have found difficult to resolve. It is accepted that upon the execution of the settlement made on April 4, 1972, the shares and stock referred to in the schedule, and which had previously belonged to the taxpayer, became " settled property " as defined by section 45 (1) of the Finance Act 1965. The contest is whether section 25 (2) or section 22 (2) applies to the

E   circumstances of this case.

Section 25 (2) provides:

" A gift in settlement, whether revocable or irrevocable, is a disposal of the entire property thereby becoming settled property notwithstanding that the donor has some interest as a beneficiary under the settlement and notwithstanding that he is a trustee, or the sole

F   trustee, of the settlement."

Section 22 (2) provides:

" For the purposes of this Part of this Act—(a) references to a disposal of an asset include, except where the context otherwise requires, references to a part disposal of an asset, and (b) there is a part disposal of an asset where an interest or right in or over the

G   asset is created by the disposal, as well as where it subsists before the disposal, and generally, there is a part disposal of an asset where, on a person making a disposal, any description of property derived from the asset remains undisposed of."

It is common ground that if section 25 (2) applies, then it must exclude section 22 (2), because it expressly provides that a settlement to which it

H   applies is " a disposal of the entire property thereby becoming settled property." Again it is common ground that the crucial words in section 25 (2) are " gift in settlement," and in section 22 (2), " there is a part disposal of an asset where, on a person making a disposal, any description of property derived from the asset remains undisposed of."

It is well established that in a taxing Act clear words are necessary in order to tax the subject. This means that in a taxing Act one has to look merely at that which is clearly said. There is no room for any intendment.

There is no equity about a tax. There is no presumption as to a tax. A
Nothing is to be read in, nothing is to be implied. One can only look fairly
at the language used. (*Cape Brandy Syndicate* v. *Inland Revenue Commissioners* [1921] 1 K.B. 64, *per* Rowlatt J., approved in *Canadian Eagle
Oil Company Ltd.* v. *The King* [1946] A.C. 119, 140.) Therefore if the
Crown claims duty under a statute it must show that the duty is imposed
by clear and unambiguous words (see *Tennant* v. *Smith* [1892] A.C. 150,
154; *Attorney-General* v. *Beech* [1899] A.C. 53, 59; *Inland Revenue*   B
Commissioners v. *Gribble* [1913] 3 K.B. 212, 219; and *Attorney-General*
v. *Milne* [1914] A.C. 765, 781, to quote but a few of the cases). Although
it may now be questionable whether this strict rule of construction still
applies where the legislation is specifically designed to prevent varying
forms of tax avoidance devices (see *Greenberg* v. *Inland Revenue
Commissioners* [1972] A.C. 109, 137, *per* Lord Reid, and *Inland Revenue*   C
Commissioners v. *Joiner* [1975] 1 W.L.R. 1701, 1706, *per* Lord Wilberforce), the legislation with which we are here concerned is not of such
a character.

I agree with Buckley L.J., whose judgment I have had the much
appreciated advantage of reading in advance, that the ordinary primary
meaning of " gift " is a voluntary transfer of property made without
consideration. It cannot thus, on the ordinary use of language, be made   D
to cover a transaction for full consideration in money or money's worth.
It is not contended that the sum of £14,500 paid for the reversionary
interest was other than its market value. The taxpayer himself retained
the rest of the beneficial interest, so that there was no act of bounty
involved. Since Parliament has chosen, in section 25 (2), by express words,
to limit the transaction to one in which a gift is made, how then, applying   E
the proper approach to the construction of the words " gift in settlement,"
can section 25 (2) be said to apply here?

The Crown contends that in relation to any disposal of assets the Act
looks primarily at the relations between the disponor and the disponee
of the trust property. It is therefore contended that as in the present case
the trustees gave no consideration for the transfers of the shares and   F
stock, then as between the taxpayer and the trustees the transfers were
voluntary. But, as Oliver L.J. in his judgment, which I have also had the
benefit of studying prior to writing this judgment, points out, the final
words in section 25 (2) " . . . notwithstanding that he is . . . sole trustee,
of the settlement " must contemplate the creation of a settlement by an
owner merely declaring that he holds the property on trust. Since the
creation applies to this method of creating a settlement, it must do so   G
on the footing that the words " gift in settlement " are directed at the
relationship between the disponor and the *beneficiaries* and *not* the
trustees.

Thus when the draftsman speaks of " gift in settlement " he is in fact,
as one would normally expect, looking not at the transfer of the legal
estate to the trustee (which he recognised may not occur at all because the   H
trustee may have it already) but to the creation of beneficial interests.
If this was not the case then " gift in settlement " would have two
different meanings in the same Act.

I accept that if the facts of this case do not come within section 25 (2),
then there is no method provided by the Act for fixing the base value of
the trust securities in the hands of the trustees, since there has not been
a disposition of the shares as such, and therefore there is no value at

A which they can be disposed of. Accordingly, the consequences of adopting the natural and ordinary meaning of the word " gift " may well produce an unforeseen result. However, as Mr. Potter, for the taxpayer, submitted, it is rarely profitable to look for logic in a taxing statute, and in particular one where the legislature takes upon itself the burden of taxing not only real gains, but deemed gains on deemed disposals. That the draftsman has left a lacuna in the Act is to me more acceptable than that, when he used the word " gift " to qualify " settlement," he intended to mean a settlement whether by way of gift or for full consideration or valuable consideration. I therefore take the view that the Crown's contention, based upon the meaning of the words " gift in settlement," fails.

B However, the Crown further contends that, when a settlor disposes of property to trustees so as to become settled property, there is for the purpose of the Act a complete disposal of that property. It is contended that since the trustees had power to vary the investment of the fund, interests created by or arising under the settlement are not to be regarded as interests in the specific assets held for the time being by the trustees on the trusts of the settlement, but only as interests in the trust fund. Thus, the Crown contends, there was no interest or right created in or over " the asset " within section 22 (2) (b) because " the asset " was the stock and shares and the right or interest created was in, and only in, " the trust fund."

C

D I accept that there were two quite distinct disposals in this case: first, the transfer of the shares and the stock to the trustees. By that transfer the taxpayer transferred the legal ownership of those assets to the trustees. However, he retained the beneficial ownership as distinct from the legal ownership. Accordingly, the second transfer was the disposal in favour of the purchaser of the settlor's beneficial interest subject to his retaining a life interest in the same property.

E Section 22 (2) (b) provides that there is a part disposal of an asset where an interest or right in or over the asset is created by the disposal. I can find no justification in confining the interest or right to a legal interest or right. To my mind the life interest comes within the words " any description of property." Further, it was " derived " from the settlor's beneficial interests and it remained under the settlement " undisposed of." Accordingly there was a " part disposal " of the asset, namely the beneficial interest in the stock and shares.

F I too would accordingly dismiss this appeal.

G BUCKLEY L.J. This case raises, in my view, difficult questions upon the construction and effect of certain sections contained in Part 3 of the Finance Act 1965, which created the capital gains tax. With regret, I have reached a different conclusion from that of my brethren upon these questions. Like Oliver L.J. I shall confine my observations to the settlement made by the taxpayer. Precisely the same considerations apply to the settlement made by his wife and exactly the same conclusions must follow.

H It is common ground that by virtue of the settlement executed by the taxpayer on April 4, 1972, the ordinary shares and loan stock of Rothschild Investment Trust Ltd. referred to in the schedule to that settlement (which I shall call " the shares and stock ") became " settled property " as defined by section 45 (1) of the Act. The section of the Act which relates to settled property is section 25. The crucial question in the

present case is, in my view, whether section 25 (2) applies in the circum-   A
stances of the case. It it does, the claim of the Crown in this appeal must
succeed, but if it does not, the Crown's claim must fail.

In the case of an ordinary voluntary settlement, where a settlor
transfers property of his to trustees to be held on the trusts of the settlement, he makes a disposal to the trustees of the settled property which
for the purposes of the Act is a disposal of the entire property, notwithstanding that the settlor may have some beneficial interest under the   B
settlement (section 25 (2)). Since the trustees acquire the settled property
otherwise than by way of a bargain at arm's length, (a) the disposal by
the settlor, and (b) the acquisition by the trustees, are to be deemed to
be for a consideration equal to the market value of the settled property
(section 22 (4) (a)). The price so deemed to have been paid by the trustees
applies for the purposes of (a) calculating what capital gain or allowable   C
loss is to be treated as having accrued to the settlor on the disposal; and
(b) ascertaining the amount or value of the consideration which the
trustees are to be treated as having given for the acquisition of the settled
property for the purposes of calculating any capital gain or allowable
loss which the trustees may later realise upon a subsequent actual or
notional disposal by them of the settled property or any part of it. For   D
this latter purpose the trustees of the settlement are given what can
appropriately be called a quasi-corporate character by section 25 (1), so
that changes in the personal identities of the trustees shall not complicate
the ascertainment of capital gains liabilities in respect of dealings with
the corpus of the trust property. If during the continuance of the trust
the trustees sell a trust asset which was part of the property initially
settled by the settlor, the trustees will realise a chargeable gain or an   E
allowable loss by reference to a notional cost of acquisition (or " base
value ") equal to the market value of that asset at the date of the
settlement, and the base value to the trustees for capital gains tax
purposes of the newly acquired asset will be the price paid for it by the
trustees. When anybody becomes absolutely entitled to the settled
property or any part of it as against the trustees, the trustees are to be   F
deemed to have disposed of that property under section 25 (3). Under
section 22 (4) this deemed disposal is to be deemed to be for a consideration equal to the then market value of the property. So the trustees must
be treated as having made a capital gain or sustained an allowable loss
by reference to whatever may then be historically the notional or actual
base value of that property to the trustees. A similar situation will arise
under section 25 (4) on the termination of a life interest in possession   G
in all or any part of the settled property. In this way, so long as the settled
property remains in settlement and on the occasion of its ceasing to be
settled by reason of some person becoming absolutely entitled to the
property as against the trustees, the trustees are the persons chargeable
to capital gains tax in respect of all disposals, whether actual or notional,
of the settled property or any part of it. They are, of course, entitled   H
under the general law to pay the tax out of the settled property, so that
the burden falls on the beneficiaries in accordance with their several
interests under the settlement.

No chargeable gain arises on the disposal by a beneficiary of any
beneficial interest created by or arising under a settlement, whether it is
made for a consideration or voluntarily, but, if the disposal is for a
consideration in money or money's worth, the acquirer will be liable to

A capital gains tax on any subsequent disposal of that interest by him in just the same way as anyone else who realises an investment which he has made (paragraph 13 (1) of Schedule 7) or on his becoming absolutely entitled to the property as against the trustees (paragraph 13 (2) of Schedule 7).

B I have thus set out the effect of the sections in relation to an ordinary voluntary settlement at some length because it seems to me that it affords a helpful background to the consideration of the contentions in this case.

The Crown contends that when a settlor disposes of property to trustees so as to become settled property, there is for the purposes of the Act a complete disposal of that property; and that, where the trustees have power to vary the investment of the fund, interests created by or arising under the settlement are not to be regarded as interests in the C specific assets held for the time being by the trustees on the trusts of the settlement, but as interests in the trust fund of whatever assets it may consist from time to time. The Crown contends that interests arising under the settlement are not, for the purposes of section 22 (2) (*b*), property " derived from " specific assets.

The Crown further submits that in relation to any disposal of assets D the Act looks primarily at the relations between the disponor and the disponee, any bargain made between them and any consideration moving from one of them to the other. In the present case the trustees gave no consideration for the transfers of the shares and stock. As between the taxpayer and the trustees the transfers were voluntary.

In any event, the Crown says, the expression " a gift in settlement " used in section 25 (2) means no more than a transfer whereby property E becomes settled property. In the further alternative the Crown contends that the taxpayer as settlor and the trustees were, when the settlement was made, " connected persons " within paragraph 21 of Schedule 7, so that under paragraph 17 of that Schedule the settlement must be treated as a transaction otherwise than by way of a bargain at arm's length, with the consequence that under section 22 (4) the disposal of the shares and F stock must be deemed to have been made for a full market value consideration.

Mr. Morritt, for the Crown, submits that the assets comprised in the trust and the interests under the trust should be regarded as distinct items of property. He says that there are two quite distinct disposals in this case, viz., first, the transfers of the shares and stock to the trustees and, secondly, a sale by the taxpayer, as settlor, of a reversionary beneficial G interest in the trust fund to First Investors and Savers (Jersey) Ltd. (whom I shall call " the purchasers "). The first of these is a disposal of the whole property in the shares and stock. The fact that the second does not extend to the whole beneficial interest in the trust fund but only to a reversionary interest does not, Mr. Morritt submits, mean that the disposal of the shares and stock left any property in the shares and H stock undisposed of. Moreover, the price paid for the reversion was not given for the acquisition of the shares and stock by the trustees.

Mr. Potter, for the taxpayer, on the other hand, submits that the taxpayer made an actual capital gain of £14,839 in the year of assessment by reason of the sale of the reversionary interest, but that no disposal of the corpus of the trust fund for a notional consideration equal to its market value should be treated as having taken place. According to this argument there was no " gift in settlement " (section 25 (2)) because the

transaction was not a gratuitous one: there was no more than a " part A
disposal " of the shares and stock, because a life interest in the fund
remained undisposed of (section 22 (2) (b)). The true nature of the transaction, it is said, was the sale of a reversionary interest in the settled
property, not a " gift in settlement " of anything, since that expression
imports an act of bounty and there was no bounty involved here.

The contest is between section 22 (2) and section 25 (2). The latter,
if it applies to the facts of the present case, must exclude the former B
because it expressly provides that a settlement to which it applies is a
disposal of the entire settled property and so excludes the possibility of
its being a part disposal only of that property. The answer must depend,
I think, upon the meaning in section 25 (2) of the expression " gift in
settlement." This is not defined in the statute. The word " gift " is used
in a number of other places in the Act in contexts which do not suggest C
that it is there used in any but its ordinary primary sense. Notwithstanding
the passage to which we were referred in Sheppard's Touchstone (7th ed.),
(1820) p. 227, I think that the ordinary primary meaning of " gift " is now
a voluntary transfer of property made without consideration. There is, so
far as I am aware, only one other place in the Act where the expression
" gift in settlement " is used; that is section 31 (3) (a). That subsection D
provides for a concession to be made, as specified in that section, in
respect of a disposal of a work of art or other object of national, scientific,
historic or artistic interest in circumstances prescribed in the subsection.
I do not gain much help from this. The inclusive words may, it is true,
have been inserted because the draftsman considered that without them
the word " gift " would not have covered a " gift in settlement "; but
they may, as it seems to me, equally well have been inserted ex majori E
cautela to make clear that the word " gift " is apt to cover not only an
immediate out and out voluntary transfer to a single individual or a
group of individuals, but also whatever is meant by a " gift in settlement."
The expression " gift in settlement " sounds somewhat strangely in a
lawyer's ear, at any rate in the ear of a conveyancer. One thing is, I think,
clear, that the expression does not mean a disposition in consequence of F
which the disponor ceases to have any beneficial interest in the subject
matter, for section 25 (2) makes clear that the settlor may retain some
beneficial interest under the settlement. It also makes clear that the
settlor may be the sole trustee of the settlement; so a settlor may by
declaring himself a trustee of property for beneficiaries, who may include
himself, effect a " gift in settlement " without disposing of any part of
the legal ownership in the property.   G

One wonders why the draftsman selected the expression " gift in
settlement." Two possible explanations suggest themselves to me and no
more: first, that he used the expression to describe a purely voluntary
settlement, made without any consideration being given for it, or at any
rate without any consideration in money or money's worth, and secondly,
that he used the expression to distinguish a disposal of an asset to trustees H
of a settlement by a settlor, for which the trustees gave no consideration,
from a disposal of an asset to trustees of a settlement by a vendor upon
a purchase by the trustees out of their trust fund.

Property may become settled property in either of two ways: (a) by
the settlor transferring it to trustees upon trust, or (b) by the trustees
investing their settled fund or some part of it in the purchase of that
property. In either case the property equally becomes settled property

A held upon the trusts of the settlement. In the former case the transaction can, in my view, not inappropriately be described as " a gift in settlement," and I think that it would not be an abuse of language so to describe it even in a case in which the settlor receives some personal advantage from making the settlement or some consideration for doing so, so long as the transaction does not amount in substance to a sale of the subject matter to the trustees.

B   Counsel for the taxpayer have contended that the settlement of the shares and stock contained no element of gift: the party who became entitled to the reversionary interest paid £14,500 for it (which I will assume to have been its market value) and the taxpayer himself retained the rest of the beneficial interest, so that there was no act of bounty involved. There was, according to the taxpayer's argument, merely a part

C disposal of the shares and stock, the life interest therein remaining undisposed of in the taxpayer. This argument looks exclusively at the beneficial interests in the subject matter and ignores the transfer of the legal ownership to the trustees, for, if there was a part disposal, it was not a part disposal of the legal ownership, but a disposal of part of the beneficial interest. This appears to me to fit very awkwardly, if it can be said to fit at all, with the scheme of the Act as a whole. As I hope

D I have demonstrated, normally in the case of settled property, so long as the property remains vested in the trustees of the settlement, they are treated as the owners of the capital assets comprised in the settlement and it is upon actual or notional disposals by them of any of those assets that chargeable gains or allowable losses arise. The liability to the tax follows the legal ownership of the corpus of the trust fund. For the

E purpose of calculating such gains or losses, it is necessary to discover what it notionally or actually cost the trustees to acquire each asset of the trust. This is achieved initially by the trustees being treated as if they had bought the original assets of the trust fund from the settlor at their market value. Dealings by beneficiaries with their beneficial interests may render those beneficiaries liable to tax at some stage, but such dealings

F have no effect upon the liability of the trustees.

      If in the present case there was no " gift in settlement " within section 25 (2), no disposition by the taxpayer of the entire ownership of the shares and stock to the trustees, and no acquisition of that entire ownership by the trustees for a deemed consideration equal to the market value, there would be no way, so far as I can see, of fixing any notional cost of acquisition which the trustees would be entitled to deduct in computing

G what gain or loss, if any, had accrued to them on a subsequent sale by them of any of the settled shares or stock, or upon any notional disposal by them of the corpus of the settled property. The price paid by the purchasers for the reversionary interest would be irrelevant in this respect because it was not paid by the trustees and, moreover, was not a price paid, or to be deemed to have been paid, by anyone for the shares and

H stock, but a price paid for something else, viz. a limited equitable interest in the settled fund, which would not be the asset of which the trustees would be disposing. It would follow that, if the trustees were to sell any part of the settled shares and stock, they would only be entitled to deduct incidental expenses for the purposes of calculating the notional capital gain upon which they would be taxable. They would be taxable on the entire net proceeds of sale, notwithstanding that the sale might in fact be at a loss in relation to the taxpayer's expenditure in acquiring it, or to

its market value at the date of the settlement. This surely could not be A
a consequence which Parliament intended.

On the other hand, if there was in the present case a " gift in settlement " within section 25 (2), the liability to tax would follow the
ownership of the corpus of the settled property in the manner I have
indicated, accompanied by a right for the trustees to deduct appropriate
actual or notional base values whenever liability to tax should arise during
the subsistence of the settlement. This would be a result which would   B
conform to the apparent design and policy of the statute.

Mr. Potter has submitted that we should not concern ourselves with
what the apparent design or policy of the statute is. He has reminded us
of Rowlatt J.'s dictum in *Cape Brandy Syndicate* v. *Inland Revenue
Commissioners* [1921] 1 K.B. 64, 71, that in construing a taxing statute
one has to look merely at what is clearly said without regard to intend-   C
ment. When what is said is clearly said, this is no doubt so; but I do
not think that the expression " a gift in settlement " is a clear one.
One must first construe the Act in order to discover what it says in this
respect, and for that exercise the context of the enactment as a whole
is, in my opinion, clearly not only a legitimate aid but one to which the
court is bound to have regard.   D

These considerations dispose me strongly to construe " gift in settlement " in the second of the two senses which I have indicated earlier;
but let me test the position further by a consideration of section 22 (2).
It cannot, in my view, be disputed that when the taxpayer transferred
the shares and stock to the trustees, he transferred the whole legal ownership in the shares and stock. Indeed I did not understand counsel for the
taxpayer to suggest otherwise. What is said is that for the purposes of   E
the statute he must be treated as having made only a part disposal of the
subject matter.

It must be borne in mind that the tax is a tax on capital gains (section
19 (1)), that is to say, gains accruing on the disposal of assets (ibid.).
The expression " assets " comprises in this context all forms of property
(section 22 (1)). The shares and stock were, immediately before the   F
settlement, undoubtedly assets of the taxpayer. After the settlement the
reversionary interest in the settled fund then represented by the shares
and stock was undoubtedly an asset of the purchasers. The shares and
stock were equally undoubtedly assets held by the trustees upon the trusts
of the settlement. There was no direct disposal of any asset by the
taxpayer to the purchasers. In law the taxpayer disposed of his entire
ownership in the shares and stock to the trustees. He did so upon terms   G
which resulted in the purchasers' becoming entitled to a reversionary
interest in the property so transferred, expectant on his own death, and
in himself becoming entitled to an immediate life interest in the same
property. The taxpayer had, however, no proprietorial rights or interests
specifically in the shares and stock once the settlement took effect. He
could neither require nor forbid the sale of any part of them. He could   H
not control the trustees in the exercise of their powers as holders of the
shares and stock in any way. He became entitled to a life interest in the
income of the settled property, however it might be invested from time
to time.

It is contended that in these circumstances the taxpayer made a part
disposal of the shares and stock within section 22 (2). The words relied
on are " there is a part disposal of an asset where, on a person making

A a disposal, any description of property derived from the asset remains undisposed of." These words might well be held to fit the present case if it had taken the form of a grant by the taxpayer to the purchasers of a reversionary interest expectant on his own death specifically in the shares and stock, the taxpayer reserving to himself a life interest in them, thus constituting himself a trustee of the shares and stock. In such circumstances the only disposal would have been of the reversionary

B interest, and the life interest might be accurately described as having " remained undisposed of." But that was not the form of the transaction. The property disposed of was the shares and stock. The property in which the purchasers acquired a reversionary interest was not specifically the shares and stock, but a fund which, for the time being only, was represented by the shares and stock. Strictly speaking, nothing, in my view,

C remained undisposed of. The taxpayer acquired a new asset consisting of a life interest under the settlement, not specifically in the shares and stock, but in the fund for the time being represented by the shares and stock. Mr. Potter contends that the life interest was " properly derived from " the shares and stock. I see the force of that argument, but I find difficulty in regarding the taxpayer's life interest as being accurately described as " derived from " specific investments which might only

D transiently represent the fund in which the life interest existed.

What principally weighs with me is that the assets of which the taxpayer disposed were, as it seems to me, indisputably the shares and stock. He must either have made an entire disposal of them or a part disposal. The disponees were the trustees. In ordinary terms it cannot be denied that the disposal of them was entire, nothing remaining undisposed of.

E One can only discover possible grounds for the view that there was no more than a part disposal by considering the beneficial ownership distinct from the legal ownership. As I have endeavoured to show, in this Act capital gains tax on property held in trust, except in the case of property held in the name of a nominee or vested in a bare trustee (section 22 (5)), is exacted from the trustees as the legal owners of the corpus of the settled

F property, and disregards beneficial interests except in the case of a beneficiary who has bought his interest. In these circumstances, reading section 22 (2) and section 25 (2) together, I reach the conclusion that on the true construction of the Act there was not merely a part disposal of the shares and stock in the present case, but an entire disposal of them to the trustees.

G Mr. Potter submits that the trustees acquired the shares and stock by way of a bargain made at arm's length for the purposes of section 22 (4), for he says that the shares and stock were transferred to the trustees as the result of the bargain between the taxpayer and the purchasers, which was a bargain made at arm's length. That the purchasers acquired the reversionary interest by way of a bargain at arm's length cannot, I think, be doubted. The reversionary interest did not exist as

H such before the settlement took effect. It seems to me reasonable to regard the settlement as a consequence of that bargain. But can it sensibly and accurately be said that the trustees acquired the shares and stock by way of that bargain? It seems to me that the language of section 22 (4) (a) poses the question whether the acquisition of the asset (in this case the shares and stock) was the subject matter of a bargain between the disponor and the disponee (in this case the taxpayer and the trustees) which was at arm's length. The object of this provision is surely to ensure

that market value is treated as the consideration actually given for the A
disposal of the asset where the circumstances are not such as to demonstrate that a full and fair price was paid for it. The fact that someone
other than the disponee can be taken to have paid a full and fair price for
something other than the subject matter of the disposal under consideration has no bearing on this. Goulding J. regarded the taxpayer's
settlement of April 4, 1972, as a tripartite bargain in respect of which the
settlor was at arm's length with both the purchasers of the reversionary B
interest and the trustees. With deference to Goulding J. I feel unable to
regard the taxpayer as having made a bargain at arm's length with the
trustees, although I accept that he did so with the purchasers. Accordingly, in my judgment, section 22 (4) (a) applies to the present case upon
the footing that the acquisition of the shares and stock by the trustees
was otherwise than by way of a bargain made at arm's length, so that C
the trustees must be deemed to have paid market value for the shares and
stock, unless the words " subject to the provisions of this part of this
Act" produce a contrary result. It is said that they do so because, by
reason of section 22 (2), there was only a part disposal of the shares and
stock. I have already given my reasons for thinking that this was not
the case.
                                                                        D
    For these reasons I have, with diffidence, reached a different con-
clusion from that reached by Goulding J. in his exceptionally clear and
careful judgment.

    This makes it strictly unnecessary for me to consider the " connected
persons" argument, but I should perhaps state my opinion about this.
This argument depends on paragraph 21 (3) of Schedule 7 to the Act.
As Goulding J. pointed out, the word "settlement" does not have the E
same meaning in that subparagraph as it has elsewhere in the Act,
because the definition of " settlement " which is to be found in section 454
of the Income and Corporation Taxes Act 1970 is imported into paragraph
21 (3) of the Schedule, but does not apply elsewhere in the Act. The
House of Lords has held that bounty is an essential element of a settlement within that definition (Inland Revenue Commissioners v. Plummer F
[1979] 3 W.L.R. 689), with the consequence that the taxpayer's settlement
would not, as it seems to me, fall within the terms of the subparagraph.
For this reason I agree with Goulding J. that the subparagraph cannot
apply to the present case.

    I have not so far found it necessary to mention the fact that the
transfers of the shares and stock were not registered until May 12, 1972,
and April 28, 1972, respectively. It is true that until that occurred the G
trustees were not, vis-à-vis Rothschild Investment Trusts Ltd., the holders
of the shares and stock, but at April 4, 1972, the trustees had in their
possession executed transfers of all the shares and stock registered in
the names of the taxpayer and his wife as well as the relative certificates.
As regards the shares and stock owned by the taxpayer but registered
in the name of Lloyds Bank (Branches) Nominee Ltd., the transfers were H
signed on March 21, 1972. They and the relative certificates were received
by the trustees' agents " on or shortly after April 6, 1972." There is no
finding about precisely when they were despatched by the nominee
company to the trustees' agents, nor is there any finding that the taxpayer
was in any way responsible for any delay there may have been between
March 21 and April 6 or that he was even aware of it. I should be very
unwilling to hold that the fiscal consequences of the transaction depended

A upon the degree of diligence with which the nominee company or the trustees carried out the purely ministerial steps of transmitting or registering the transfers or handing over the certificates. On the findings of the commissioners I for my part think that the taxpayer and his wife should be regarded as having done all that lay in their power to transfer the shares and stock to the trustees before the date of the settlements and that the ownership of the shares and stock must be treated as having

B passed to the trustees at the latest when the taxpayer and his wife executed the settlements. From that time, as it seems to me, neither the taxpayer nor his wife could have asserted an equitable interest in any of the shares and stock otherwise than under and by virtue of the settlements. See in this connection the decision of Jenkins J. in *In re Rose* [1949] 1 Ch. 78, 88–90.

C   For these reasons I for my part would allow this appeal. The Crown does not seek to levy tax upon both the £14,500 paid for the reversionary interest and the market value of the shares and stock, but on the latter only. I would restore the decision of the commissioners and the assessment to tax on a capital gain of £150,483. Goulding J. thought that no chargeable gain or allowable loss would have accrued if the purchasers

D had subsequently disposed of the reversionary interest, because that interest was created by the settlement for the benefit of the purchasers. I should not be taken as agreeing with this view, for it seems to me that the purchasers (if otherwise amenable to a charge to tax) would not have been entitled to exemption under paragraph 13 of Schedule 7. The purchasers would, it seems to me, have been a beneficiary who acquired his interest under the settlement for a consideration in money and so

E would have been disentitled to exemption.

Appeal dismissed with costs.
Leave to appeal.

    Solicitors: *Solicitor of Inland Revenue; Norton, Rose, Botterell &*
F *Roche.*

[Reported by Susan Denny, Barrister-at-Law]

[CHANCERY DIVISION]

G
* *In re* NADLER ENTERPRISES LTD.

[No. 003087 of 1976]

1980 Feb. 27   Dillon J.

H *Company—Winding up—Preferential debt—Group treatment for*
    purposes of value added tax—Whether claim to tax preferential
    in winding up of non-representative member of group—Finance
    Act 1972 (c. 41), ss. 21 (1), 41 [1]

        On May 5, 1976, E. Ltd. and its parent company, E.N.L.,
    went into creditors' voluntary liquidation. The companies,

---

[1] Finance Act 1972, s. 21 (1): see post, p. 25C–E.
S. 41: see post, p. 25G–H.

with another subsidiary of E.N.L., had been accorded group **A**
treatment under section 21 of the Finance Act 1972 for the
purposes of value added tax, E.N.L. having been made the
representative for the group. The Customs and Excise
Commissioners claimed £80,038 from E.N.L. of which £53,443
was claimed for the period from May 5, 1975, to May 4, 1976,
as a preferential debt, owed jointly and severally by all the
companies in the group. If that claim was correct, the
unsecured creditors of E. Ltd. were likely to receive little or **B**
nothing.

On the liquidator's application to the court pursuant to
section 307 (1) of the Companies Act 1948, to determine
whether the commissioners were entitled to claim preferentially
in the liquidation of E. Ltd. all or any amounts owing by it
in respect of unpaid value added tax by E.N.L., the representative member of the group: —

Held, that the tax became due as soon as it was payable **C**
and since by virtue of section 21 of the Finance Act 1972 the
liability of members of a group was a joint and several liability
for any tax due from the representative member, the commissioners were entitled to preference in E. Ltd.'s liquidation in
respect of any tax at the relevant date due from E.N.L.

Ex parte Kemp, In re Fastnedge (1874) L.R. 9 Ch.App. 383
applied.

 D

The following cases are referred to in the judgment:

Baker (A Bankrupt), In re, Ex parte Eastbourne Waterworks Co. v. *Official
Receiver* [1954] 1 W.L.R. 1144; [1954] 2 All E.R. 790.
Kemp, Ex parte, In re Fastnedge (1874) L.R. 9 Ch.App. 383.

No additional cases were cited in argument. **E**

SUMMONS

On May 5, 1976, Nadler Enterprises Ltd. (" Enterprises ") and its parent
company, Elizabeth Nadler Ltd. (" E.N.L.") went into creditors' voluntary
liquidation and Leonard Cyril Curtis was appointed as liquidator of both
companies. As from April 1, 1973, E.N.L., Enterprises and another subsidiary of E.N.L., namely, Hillingdon Enterprises (U.K.) Ltd., had been **F**
accorded group treatment for the purposes of value added tax, E.N.L. being
chosen as the representative member of the group. In an affidavit sworn
by the liquidator it was stated, inter alia, that Hillingdon Enterprises (U.K.)
Ltd. was not in liquidation, but had no assets; that the Customs and Excise
Commissioners claimed £80,038 from E.N.L., of which £53,443 was claimed
in respect of the period, May 5, 1975 to May 4, 1976, as a preferential **G**
debt; that the commissioners claimed that such debt was a joint and several
debt of all the companies within the value added tax group; that the assets
of E.N.L., all of which had been realised, were unlikely to provide anything
for distribution amongst any class of creditors; that gross realisations in
the administration of Enterprises were about £80,000, and that subject to
commissioners' claim there were no preferential creditors; that if the commissioners were correct in claiming jointly and severally as a preferential **H**
creditor of Enterprises in respect of the debt due from E.N.L., then the
unsecured creditors of Enterprises were likely to receive little or nothing;
that if, however, the joint and several claim against Enterprises was not
preferential, then there would be something to distribute amongst unsecured
creditors of Enterprises, who had debts amounting to £915,000, of which
about £900,000 was owed to the Wang Hang Bank.

By a summons dated September 4, 1979, the liquidator sought an order,

A pursuant to section 307 (1) of the Companies Act 1948, to determine whether the Customs and Excise Commissioners were entitled to claim preferentially in the liquidation of Enterprises, all or any amounts owing by it in respect of unpaid value added tax by E.N.L., the representative of the group of which Enterprises was a member.

B *Muir Hunter Q.C.* and *Michael Crystal* for the liquidator.
Peter Gibson for the commissioners.

DILLON J. I am concerned on this summons with a company called Nadler Enterprises Ltd. which has been referred to as " Enterprises." Enterprises was a subsidiary of a company called Elizabeth Nadler Ltd. which has been referred to as " E.N.L." Both Enterprises and E.N.L.
C went into creditors voluntary liquidation on May 5, 1976. Before that both Enterprises and E.N.L. and another subsidiary of E.N.L. called Hillingdon Enterprises (U.K.) Ltd. with which I am not otherwise concerned had been the subject of group treatment for value added tax purposes under section 21 of the Finance Act 1972. Section 21 (1) reads:

D   " Where, under the following provisions of this section, any bodies corporate are treated as members of a group any business carried on by a member of the group shall be treated as carried on by the representative member, and—(*a*) any supply of goods or services by a member of the group to another member of the group shall be disregarded; and (*b*) any other supply of goods or services by or to a member of the group shall be treated as a supply by or to the representative member; and (*c*) any tax paid or payable by a member of
E   the group on the importation of any goods shall be treated as paid or payable by the representative member and the goods shall be treated for the purposes of . . ." certain other sections of the Finance Act 1972 ". . . as imported by the representative member; and all members of the group shall be liable jointly and severally for any tax due from the representative member."

F This group treatment was accorded to the group constituted by E.N.L., Enterprises and Hillingdon Enterprises (U.K.) Ltd., and E.N.L. was the representative member. It is accepted that Enterprises is jointly and severally liable for any tax due from E.N.L. What I am concerned with is the extent to which the Customs and Excise Commissioners are entitled to rank as preferential creditors in the winding up of Enterprises in respect
G of the value added tax due from E.N.L. as representative member for which Enterprises was jointly and severally liable with E.N.L. Priority of tax in winding up or bankruptcy is dealt with by section 41 of the Finance Act 1972, which provides:

H   " There shall be included among the debts which . . . —(*d*) under section 319 of the Companies Act 1948 . . . are to be paid in priority to all other debts in the winding up of a company . . . the amount of any tax due at the relevant date from the . . . company and having become due within the 12 months next before that date."

The meaning of the phrase " tax due at the relevant date . . . and having become due within the 12 months next before that date " is the subject of elucidation in section 41 (2) of the Finance Act 1972 and section 22 of the Finance Act 1976, which brings in certain apportionment provisions where the relevant date is not at the end of a prescribed accounting period for

26

value added tax purposes, but I do not need to read those provisions.   A
Under section 319 of the Companies Act 1948, the relevant date in the
case of a company which has gone into voluntary liquidation is the date of
the passing of the winding up resolution, namely, in this case May 5, 1976.
The argument for the liquidator is that the priority given by section 41
does not extend to tax due from E.N.L. at the relevant date, but that the
scheme, it is said, of group treatment of value added tax is that although
all members of the group including Enterprises are jointly and severally   B
liable for the tax, the tax is only due from E.N.L. as the representative
member.

    Mr. Muir Hunter appearing for the liquidator has referred me to
observations of Danckwerts J. in *In re Baker* (*A Bankrupt*), *Ex parte
Eastbourne Waterworks Co.* v. *Official Receiver* [1954] 1 W.L.R. 1144
1148, where in referring to sections conferring special preference on certain   C
debts he said:

    ". . . there must be care not to extend unduly the privilege or prefer-
    ence in question. The words [of the section], therefore, must be
    construed with some strictness."

Bearing that in mind however I am nonetheless wholly unable to draw the
distinction that Mr. Muir Hunter would have me draw between tax due at   D
the relevant date from the company and tax for which at the relevant
date the company was jointly and severally liable to the Customs and Excise
with E.N.L.

    Section 33 of the Finance Act 1972 provides in subsection (1): "Tax
due from any person shall be recoverable as a debt due to the Crown."
I see no reason why that section should not be applied in the context of   E
this group against Enterprises just as much as against E.N.L. The Act
is not wholly consistent in its wording throughout. There are references
to tax due. There are references to tax payable. There are references to
amounts assessed which are to be deemed to be an amount of tax due,
and there are references to amounts recoverable as if they were tax due.
I do not think the words "tax due" are a term of art. I think the tax
becomes due as soon as it is payable and in the group context provided   F
for by section 21 there is a liability on all members of the group which is
a joint and several liability affecting all members including the representative member. Since it is a joint as well as a several liability there
must be a single obligation, and therefore the tax must automatically be
due from the various other members of the group as soon as it is due
from the representative member E.N.L. Moreover some support for the   G
arguments of the Customs and Excise Commissioners is in my judgment
provided by the observations of Mellish L.J. in *Ex parte Kemp, In re Fastnedge* (1874) L.R. 9 Ch.App 383. The actual question the court had to
consider in that case was whether certain contingent liabilities due to a
firm called Messrs. Fastnedge & Co. were debts due to that firm which
were therefore recoverable by the trustee in the liquidation of the firm.
Mellish L.J. said, at p. 387:   H

    "I think that prima facie, and if there be nothing in the context to
    give them a different construction, the words [debts due to him]
    would include all sums certain which any person is legally liable
    to pay, whether such sums had become actually payable or not."

I do not see that there can in principle be much difference between the
phrase "debts due to him" and the converse "debts due from him."

A   Therefore by analogy to what Mellish L.J. said the tax for which Enterprises is liable is due from Enterprises.

In my judgment therefore the commissioners are right in contending that they are entitled to preference in respect of the amount of any tax due at the relevant date from E.N.L. as the representative member of the group. That tax is also due at the same date from Enterprises.

B   [Following discussion on costs his Lordship continued:] The precise form of the declaration then will be that the commissioners are entitled to claim preferentially in the liquidation the sum of £55,443·13 in respect of unpaid V.A.T., and then no order as to costs except the liquidator's costs to be costs and expenses of liquidation.

Declaration accordingly.

C   Solicitors: *Markbys; Solicitor to H.M. Customs and Excise.*

T. C. C. B.

D
[FAMILY DIVISION]

* PRACTICE NOTE
(DOMESTIC VIOLENCE: POWER OF ARREST)

E   *Injunction—Domestic violence—Power of arrest—Injunction with power of arrest attached—Desirability of limiting order to period of not more than three months—Domestic Violence and Matrimonial Proceedings Act* 1976 (c. 50), s. 2

The police are holding some thousands of orders containing a power of arrest made under the Domestic Violence and Matrimonial Proceedings Act 1976. Experience has shown that the police are rarely called
F   upon to take action upon an injunction which is more than three months old, and the requirement that they should retain indefinitely the orders containing a power of arrest imposes an unnecessary burden upon them.

The practice note dated July 21, 1978, *Practice Direction (Injunction: Domestic Violence)* [1978] 1 W.L.R. 1123, recommended that consideration be given to imposing a time limit of three months on injunctions
G   excluding a party from a matrimonial home or a specified area.

To assist in easing the burdens of the police and in enabling them to concentrate on the cases where action may be required, judges should consider, at the time a power of arrest is attached to an injunction, for what period of time this sanction is likely to be required. Unless a judge is satisfied that a longer period is necessary in a particular case, the period should not exceed three months. In those few cases where danger
H   to the applicant is still reasonably apprehended towards the expiry of the three months, application may be made to the court to extend the duration of the injunction.

Issued by the President with the concurrence of the Lord Chancellor.

R. L. BAYNE-POWELL,
Senior Registrar.

December 22, 1980.

A

[HOUSE OF LORDS]

* GUNTON . . . . PETITIONER

AND

RICHMOND-UPON-THAMES LONDON
    BOROUGH COUNCIL . . . . . . RESPONDENTS   B

1980 Dec. 18   Lord Wilberforce, Lord Edmund-Davies
                                         and Lord Keith of Kinkel

Petition by the petitioner for leave to appeal from the decision of the
Court of Appeal in *Gunton* v. *Richmond-upon-Thames London Borough
Council* [1980] 3 W.L.R. 714; [1980] 3 All E.R. 577.   C
The Appeal Committee dismissed the petition.

F. C.

D

[COURT OF APPEAL]

* REGINA *v.* BOLTON SUPPLEMENTARY BENEFITS
    APPEAL TRIBUNAL, *Ex parte* FORDHAM

1980 June 30   Lord Denning M.R.,
                                            Waller and Dunn L.JJ.   E

*Social Security—Supplementary benefit—Resources—Wages paid
in advance—Claimant going on strike and obliged to repay in
future—Whether payment " resources "—Supplementary Benefits Act 1976 (c. 71), Sch. 1, para. 27* [1]

On November 14, 1977, the claimant came out on strike.
The following day, in accordance with normal pay arrange-   F
ments, he received from his employers a sum representing
wages for the period from November 1 to November 30, 1977.
When the claimant sought supplementary benefit on behalf of
his wife and children, the Supplementary Benefits Commission
refused to make any payment of benefit before December 15,
1977, which would have been his next pay day. The claimant
appealed to the Supplementary Benefits Appeal Tribunal, contending that, as part of the payment made on November 15   G
related to the period November 15 to November 30 when he
was not working and would have to be repaid, it was not
income for the purposes of assessing his resources. The
tribunal dismissed his appeal, but in proceedings by the
claimant for a judicial review the judge quashed the tribunal's
decision.
On appeal by the Supplementary Benefits Commission: —
Held, allowing the appeal, that when the payment was made   H
to the claimant on November 15, 1977, it could properly be
regarded as his resources for each of the next four weeks and
it so remained regardless of the claimant's being on strike
and the consequential obligation to repay part of it (post, pp.
31F–G, 33A–B, E).
Decision of Sheen J. reversed.

[1] Supplementary Benefits Act 1976, Sch. 1, para. 27: see post, p. 32F.

1 W.L.R.   **Reg. v. Benefits App. Tribunal, Ex p. Fordham (C.A.)**

A   The following cases are referred to in the judgment of Lord Denning M.R.:

Reg. v. Manchester Supplementary Benefits Appeal Tribunal, Ex parte Riley [1979] 1 W.L.R. 426; [1979] 2 All E.R. 1.
Reg. v. Preston Supplementary Benefits Appeal Tribunal, Ex parte Moore [1975] 1 W.L.R. 624; [1975] 2 All E.R. 807, C.A.

The following additional cases were cited in argument:

B   Reg. v. Barnsley Supplementary Benefits Appeal Tribunal, Ex parte Atkinson [1977] 1 W.L.R. 917; [1977] 3 All E.R. 1031, C.A.
Reg. v. West London Supplementary Benefits Appeal Tribunal, Ex parte Taylor [1975] 1 W.L.R. 1048; [1975] 2 All E.R. 790, D.C.

APPEAL from Sheen J.

C   By notice of motion dated June 14, 1978, the claimant, Michael Roy Fordham, applied, by leave of the Divisional Court of the Queen's Bench Division, for an order of certiorari for the purpose of quashing the decision of the Bolton Supplementary Benefits Appeal Tribunal made on January 10, 1978, by which the tribunal held that the claimant and/or his dependants were not entitled to a payment of supplementary benefit before December 15, 1977. On November 24, 1978, Sheen J. granted
D   an order of certiorari to quash the tribunal's decision.

The Supplementary Benefits Commission appealed by notice dated January 15, 1979, on the grounds that the judge erred in law in (1) concluding that two of the four weeks' wages which the claimant received on November 15, 1977, as wages in advance were not resources for the purposes of the Supplementary Benefits Act 1976 because (a) he
E   was on strike for the two weeks to which those wages related and they were not capital, earnings or other income specified in Part III of Schedule 1 to the Act; (b) he was under an obligation to repay the sums by deductions from his salary after he returned to work; (c) if the wages were earned they should be attributed to those months when they were deducted from his salary after he returned to work; and (2) not holding that wages could be resources if they were available
F   to the recipient as the means of support irrespective of whether they had been earned or had to be repaid.

The facts are stated in the judgment of Lord Denning M.R.

Simon D. Brown for the commission.
John Hoggett for the claimant.

G   LORD DENNING M.R. This case raises one of the burning questions today. When men come out on strike, how much supplementary benefit ought to be paid for their wives and children?

In November 1977 all the firemen in England came out on strike. In particular 1,800 firemen employed by the Greater Manchester Council. They came out on strike on November 14, 1977: and remained out
H   until January 16, 1978. That is two months. Under section 8 of the Supplementary Benefits Act 1976, when a man comes out on strike, his own requirements are to be disregarded: but not the requirements of his wife and children.

In this case the Greater Manchester Council pay their firemen in a strange way. It is their practice to pay them for any one calendar month on the 15th day of that month. So the claimant in this case, Mr. Fordham, received his net salary for the whole month of November

Lord Denning M.R.   Reg. v. Benefits App. Tribunal, Ex p. Fordham (C.A.)   [1981]

1977 on November 15. It came to £261. That was expected to carry A him on to the 15th of the next month—in this case December 15, 1977.

As the firemen came out on strike on November 14, this meant that half of the £261 had been paid to Mr. Fordham for the first fortnight in November when he had been working: and half for the second fortnight when he was out on strike. Mr. Fordham says that the Supplementary Benefits Commission ought not to have regard to the payment for the second fortnight. He says that it was not part of his B resources because he would have to pay it back.

The Supplementary Benefits Commission and the Supplementary Benefits Appeal Tribunal decided against him. But the judge below found for him. Now there is an appeal to us.

Under the Supplementary Benefits Act 1976, when a man applies for supplementary benefit, an account has to be taken as to his " resources " C and as to his " requirements." If his resources are such that they cover his requirements, he does not get supplementary benefit.

In this case it appears true that the £261 (which Mr. Fordham was paid on November 15) meant that he had sufficient resources to carry him on until December 15. That would have been his next pay day if he had not been on strike. The Supplementary Benefits Commission say that that sum should be taken as Mr. Fordham's resources for the D period up to December 15. If that is so, he had sufficient resources to meet the requirements of his wife and children: and he is not entitled to claim supplementary benefit for them.

On the other hand, Mr. Fordham says that that argument is wrong: because he will have to repay £125 of that sum: because he was out on strike during the last fortnight of November. So that £125 ought not E be taken into account in assessing his resources.

Reading through the Supplementary Benefits Act 1976, it seems to me that the answer is found by remembering that the claimant's position has to be assessed on a weekly basis. Under paragraph 1 (2) (a) of Schedule 1 to the Act, his weekly requirements are calculated, taking into account his weekly earnings. Payment of supplementary benefit is made on a weekly basis. The whole system is run on a weekly basis. F When one takes that into account, it goes a long way towards solving the question in this case: because for the four weeks from November 15, 1977, until December 15, 1977, Mr. Fordham's weekly resources were £61 a week. That sum exceeded his weekly requirements. So he did not qualify for supplementary benefit over that period.

It is true that in due course Mr. Fordham would have to repay £125 G of the £261. That was made clear on November 30, 1977, when the council's county treasurer wrote to all the firemen involved in the dispute:

> ". . . members of the service who were paid to November 30, 1977, in advance on November 15 under the calendar monthly pay arrangements, should be advised that any overpayment will be recovered from salary at some future date." H

That date would depend on the length of the strike and internal arrangements.

At the time when the tribunal heard the case there was no evidence of any repayment having been made by Mr. Fordham at all. But we have been told what happened. When the firemen went back to work on January 16, 1978, they were entitled to be paid for the second

The Weekly Law Reports, January 23, 1981

31

1 W.L.R.   Reg. v. Benefits App. Tribunal, Ex p. Fordham (C.A.) Lord Denning M.R.

A fortnight of January. But they received no pay for that fortnight at all. The council said that they had already been paid for the second fortnight in November—when they were on strike. So no pay was due. Nevertheless, although no salary was payable for that fortnight, to avoid any hardship the council lent each man £200 to go on with. Then from March or April onwards £20 a month was deducted from their salary in repayment of the loan.

B The point is whether those repayments should be set against the £125 he received in November 1977. It seems to me that they are not relevant to the weekly position. When the weekly requirements and resources were being assessed in November 1977 no one knew what was going to happen in the future. No one knew how long the strike would last: whether Mr. Fordham would remain in the employment of C the council or not: or on what date or to what extent the refund would be made. It was so uncertain that no one could properly take that into account in considering what the weekly resources and requirements were.

A parallel point was considered by this court in *Reg.* v. *Preston Supplementary Benefits Appeal Tribunal, Ex parte Moore* [1975] 1 W.L.R. 624. I said, at p. 630:

D " Again his earnings are to be calculated at a weekly sum, even though they are paid monthly, or quarterly. Suppose he is paid monthly in advance. He may spend it all in the first day or two in buying a new stove or a suit of clothes. Yet his resources during the whole of that month are to be taken as the weekly equivalent. Suppose he is paid monthly in arrear, he has no actual E resources in the first month: and he is not to be regarded as notionally having them. But thereafter he has resources which are to be calculated at a weekly sum, and when he leaves at the end of the last month, he has a month's pay in hand as his resources for the following month."

That passage—especially the last sentence—was adopted by Sheen J. F in the recent case of *Reg.* v. *Manchester Supplementary Benefits Appeal Tribunal, Ex parte Riley* [1979] 1 W.L.R. 426.

So it seems to me that the payment to Mr. Fordham on November 15, 1977, of £261 was a payment which was to last him for the next four weeks. It could be calculated in his resources for the next four weeks until December 15. Those being his resources, they covered his G requirements. Therefore, he was not entitled to supplementary benefit for his wife and children during that time.

Looking at the case as a whole, it seems to me that the decision of the Supplementary Benefits Commission, which was followed by the tribunal, was correct. I take a different view from the judge. He seemed to think that Mr. Fordham's obligation to repay meant that he had not earned anything during the relevant period—and that he had H not had any payment in advance, and the like. I take a different view because of the indefinite, uncertain and almost unforeseeable obligation to refund the money. It was so far ahead that it would not affect the immediate resources available to Mr. Fordham.

I would be in favour of allowing the appeal and restoring the decision of the tribunal.

WALLER L.J. I agree. Lord Denning M.R. has already set out the

facts in this case. The subsection with which we are primarily con- A
cerned is section 1 (1) of the Supplementary Benefits Act 1976, which
says:

"... every person in Great Britain ... whose resources are insufficient to meet his requirements shall be entitled to benefit"—as
thereinafter follows.

It was submitted on behalf of the claimant that that part of the B
payment which was attributable to work which should have been done
after the strike had started was not income and was not earnings because
it had to be repaid. The factual position, as I see it, was this, that,
when a month's wages were paid on November 15, they related to the
period of two weeks which had already elapsed and were a payment
covering the two weeks immediately following November 15. In the
ordinary way, when the employee continued to work, there would be no C
obligation for repayment because the work would be done—the work
which covered the second half of that payment. But the argument is
that, because the strike started on that very day, November 14, thereafter the second half of the payment had to be repaid and therefore
was no longer to be regarded as a resource.

Lord Denning M.R. has drawn attention to the letter from the D
Greater Manchester Council which said that members of the service
who were paid to November 30 in advance on November 15 under the
calendar monthly pay arrangements " should be advised that any overpayment will be recovered from salary at some future date." So notice
was then given that at some future date there would have to be a
repayment. It is because of that that it is submitted on behalf of the
claimant that the money was no longer a resource. E

The sum was clearly not capital; and therefore, as it seems to me,
it was income of some sort. The division in the various sections of the
Act appears to be division between income and capital, and there is
no other possibility. The calculation is set out in Schedule 1 to the
Act. Part II of the Schedule is the calculation of requirements and
Part III is the calculation of resources. There are several paragraphs in F
Part III which indicate that resources can be of a great variety of kinds.
Paragraph 21 deals with net weekly earnings. Then paragraph 27 says:

"Any resources not specified in the foregoing provisions of this
Schedule may be treated as reduced by such amount (if any) as may
be reasonable in the circumstances of the case."

A very wide provision indeed. Then paragraph 28 deals with resources G
deliberately abandoned and paragraph 29 deals with discretionary trusts.
So it is clear from the whole of that part of Schedule 1 that those things
which can be income in some way or another are of a very great variety.
Furthermore it is clear that the specific parts of that Schedule are not
all-embracing.

The judge, when dealing with the question of whether this was
capital or not, said that it was a misuse of language to describe the H
money as capital. He said:

"It was paid as income. It represented two weeks' salary paid
in advance. It did not change its character with each day the
strike lasted."

In my opinion, the judge was quite right in that statement. Where he
was in error, in my view, was in coming to the conclusion that in some

The Weekly Law Reports, January 23, 1981

33

1 W.L.R.   Reg. v. Benefits App. Tribunal, Ex p. Fordham (C.A.)   Waller L.J.

A way that indicated that this should not be treated as a resource. In my view, it can properly be said that, when the payment was made on November 15, it was a resource for each of the next four weeks—that is, until the next payment was made on December 15. It remained income, albeit that there was an obligation to repay at some future date when the strike was over. It remained as a resource for each of the next four weeks. It started as a resource for each of those four weeks, and

B the fact of a strike with a consequential obligation to repay at some future date did not alter the fact that it was a resource for each of the four weeks.

In those circumstances, I also agree that this appeal should be allowed and the decision of the tribunal restored.

C DUNN L.J. I agree. In refusing the application for supplementary benefit, the supplementary benefits officer said:

" Mr. Fordham receives his earnings from his employer two weeks in arrears and two weeks in advance. Although he did not subsequently work for the money paid for the period November 15 to 30, he nevertheless received it under the terms of his employment.

D Therefore it is regarded as available to him, together with the two weeks earned, for living expenses. Since the total amount received is the equivalent of one month's wages he is not entitled to benefit until December 15, 1977."

That seems to me to be a clear and entirely accurate statement of the position, and I agree that the tribunal were right in holding that those sums paid as wages should be treated as a resource.

E The Supplementary Benefits Commission were dealing with the period December 1 to 15, and only with that period. Mr. Fordham had received wages covering that period. The fact that at some indeterminate future date those wages were to be repaid does not prevent them constituting resources available to Mr. Fordham to meet his requirements during the relevant supplementary benefits period.

F I too would allow the appeal and restore the decision of the tribunal.

Appeal allowed with costs.

Solicitors: *Solicitor, Department of Health and Social Security; Brian Thompson, Manchester.*

G
C. N.

H

A

* ATTORNEY-GENERAL'S REFERENCE (No. 1 of 1980)

1980 Oct. 3; 24   Lord Lane C.J., Stocker and Glidewell JJ.

B
*Crime — Theft — False accounting — False material particulars —
Personal loan proposal form with false statements—Whether
document " required for any accounting purpose "—Theft Act
1968 (c. 60), s. 17 (1) (a)*

The defendant gave to householders personal loan proposal
forms addressed to a finance company to enable them to borrow
money to pay for domestic appliances which he was selling.
He advised some of the householders to enter false particulars   C
on the forms to ensure that the proposals were acceptable to
the finance company. The forms, when considered and
accepted, were used to make up the finance company's accounts
on a computer. The defendant was tried on an indictment
two counts of which charged him with an offence, contrary
to section 17 (1) (a) of the Theft Act 1968,[1] in that he had
dishonestly, and with a view to gain for himself and his
company, falsified the specified proposal form, being a docu-   D
ment required for the accounts of the finance company. The
trial judge ruled that, at the time the proposal form was
falsified it was not a document " made or required for any
accounting purpose " within the meaning of the section and
he directed the jury to acquit the defendant on those two
counts.
On a reference by the Attorney-General on the question
whether a person who dishonestly falsified a personal loan   E
proposal form which he then sent to a finance company, and
which the finance company used in their accounting process,
falsified a document " required for any accounting purpose "
contrary to section 17 (1) (a): —
Held, that the words " made or required " in section
17 (1) (a) indicated that there was a distinction to be drawn
between a document made specifically for the purpose of
accounting and one made for some other purpose but which   F
was required for an accounting purpose; that a document
might fall within the section if it was made for some purpose
other than an accounting purpose but was required for an
accounting purpose as a subsidiary consideration (post, pp.
38B–C); and that, in the present case, the nature and content
of the form was such that the question referred was to be
answered in the affirmative (post, pp. 38H—39A).

G
The following case is referred to in the judgment:

Reg. v. *Mallett* [1978] 1 W.L.R. 820; [1978] 3 All E.R. 10, C.A.

No additional cases were cited in argument.

REFERENCE by the Attorney-General under section 36 of the Criminal
Justice Act 1972.   H
The Attorney-General referred a point of law for the opinion of the
Court of Appeal in the following terms:
" 1. The point of law referred for consideration by the court is:
' Whether a person who dishonestly falsifies a personal loan proposal
form in material particulars which he sends thereafter to a finance

[1] Theft Act 1968, s. 17 (1): see post, p. 37D.

A company, and which they use in their accounting process, falsifies
a document " required for any accounting purpose " contrary to section
17 (1) (a) of the Theft Act 1968 '.
   " 2. The material facts of the case which give rise to this reference
are as follows: —(i) The [defendant] was engaged at the material times
in selling domestic appliances to householders. (ii) For that purpose he
B gave to householders personal loan proposal forms addressed to a finance
company to enable them to borrow money to pay for the appliances. (iii)
With the intention of ensuring that the proposals were acceptable to the
finance company he advised some of the householders to give false
particulars on their proposal forms. Two examples of this conduct were
proved. In the first case the householder at the suggestion of the
C [defendant] understated the number of his dependants and falsely stated
that he had no outstanding instalment commitments. In the second case
the householder was induced by the [defendant] similarly to understate
the number of his dependants and falsely to state that he had a National
Savings Bank account. (iv) The personal loan proposal forms when
received by the finance company were considered and accepted. The
forms were marked by the company and were used to make up its
D accounts on a computer. They were used as 'input' documents for
computer records. The forms set aside blank spaces in which the servants
of the company would make entries showing the amount of the loan,
the net interest and various other particulars relating to the methods of
repayment and the dates of payments made by the proposer.
   " 3. The indictment contained four counts. The first two are not
E material to this reference. Counts 3 and 4 were in similar terms and both
charged the [defendant] with an offence contrary to section 17 (1) (a) of
the Theft Act 1968. The particulars of both counts alleged that he had
dishonestly and with a view to gain for himself and his company falsified
the personal loan proposal form specified, being a document required for
the accounts of the finance company.
F   " 4. At the close of the Crown case after hearing submissions the judge
directed the jury to acquit the [defendant] on these counts. He ruled
that, although the personal loan proposal form was used for an accounting
purpose when accepted by the finance company, at the time that it was
falsified it was not a document 'made or required for any accounting
purpose' within the meaning of the section. (He also ruled on the facts
that there was no sufficient evidence that the false statements were false
G in a material particular.)
   " 5. . . . It is submitted that the personal loan proposal forms were
designed to be submitted to the finance company and to be used by the
finance company inter alia for an accounting purpose. Thus they were
' required for any accounting purpose ' within the meaning of the section.
Section 17 (1) (a) refers to a document 'made or required for any
H accounting purpose.' A document 'made for this purpose' is one which
was created for the purpose. But a document which is 'required' for
the purpose may be one which was created originally for another purpose
but which is needed to complete accounting records. It is an offence
dishonestly to falsify for gain either of these categories of documents.
   " The judge's ruling in this case if correct would mean that it was not
an offence against the section to falsify a document required for an
accounting purpose until it had been used to form part of the accounting

system. Such an interpretation would exclude from the ambit of the
section many situations which at present give rise to charges under it."

   David Tudor Price for the Attorney-General.
   David Jeffreys as amicus curiae.

Cur. adv. vult.

October 24. LORD LANE C.J. read the judgment of the court. This
is a reference by the Attorney-General under the provisions of section
36 of the Criminal Justice Act 1972. The reference is in these terms:

> " Whether a person who dishonestly falsifies a personal loan proposal
> form in material particulars which he sends thereafter to a finance
> company, and which they use in their accounting process, falsifies
> a document ' required for any accounting purpose ' contrary to
> section 17 (1) (a) of the Theft Act 1968."

   The facts of the case are as follows. The defendant was engaged at
the material times in selling domestic appliances to householders. For
that purpose, he gave to householders personal loan proposal forms
addressed to a finance company to enable the householders to borrow
money to pay for the appliances. So that the proposals would be accepted
by the finance company, he advised some of the householders to give
false particulars on their proposal forms. Two examples were proved.
In the first the householder, at the suggestion of the defendant, understated the number of his dependants and falsely stated that he had no
outstanding instalment commitments. In the second, the householder
was induced by the defendant similarly to understate the number of his
dependants and to state falsely that he had a National Savings Bank
account.

   The proposal forms when received by the finance company were
considered and accepted. The information set out on the reverse side
of the forms was used by the company to make up its accounts on the
computer. The relevant forms were exhibited at the trial and were
similar to each other. They are headed with the name of the finance
company and are entitled " Personal Loan Proposal Form." There then
follows a section entitled " Particulars of Proposer," the particulars to be
supplied including the name and address of the proposer, his nationality,
personal details of his marital and family circumstances, including the
number of his dependants, his employer's name and address and other
personal details. Also included in this section on the form is a space
in which the proposer is required to state the details of other hire purchase
commitments then existing. It was this section of the form which
contained the false answers in the present case.

   The next section requires details of the house in which the equipment
is to be installed, including any relevant mortgage details. Finally, the
form on its face contains a section " For office use only " in which the
finance company would enter the details needed to be fed into their
computer. At the bottom is a space designated " signature of witness."
At the head of the reverse side of the forms is a request signed by the
proposer and addressed to the finance company requesting the loan " for
the purpose described below " and certifying the truth of the particulars
given.

A   Beneath this request is a section in which the purpose for which the loan is required is stated. There then follow details of the cash price of the equipment and the amount of the initial payment, the amount of the advance, the interest charged and the total sum due and the number of the monthly instalments by which the loan is to be paid and the amount repayable on each instalment. Finally there are blank forms for direct debit authority and promissory note.

B   The defendant was charged in four counts. Two of these are immaterial to this reference. The remaining two give rise to the question posed in this reference; they were in similar terms and each charged the defendant with an offence under section 17 (1) (a) of the Theft Act 1968. The particulars of each count allege that he had dishonestly with a view to gain for himself or his company falsified the personal loan proposal C form specified being a document required for the accounts of the finance company.

          The judge at trial ruled that the proposal form was used for an accounting purpose when the loan had been accepted by the finance company, but that at the time that it was falsified it was not " made or required for any accounting purpose " within the meaning of the section.

D   The question at issue is therefore whether or not the proposal forms were documents required for an accounting purpose within the meaning of section 17 (1) (a). The relevant parts of the section read:

          " (1) Where a person dishonestly, with a view to gain for himself or another or with intent to cause loss to another,—(a) . . . falsifies any . . . document made or required for any accounting purpose; . . ."

E   The judge ruled that the proposal forms in question were not documents made or required for an accounting purpose and expressed his ruling in the following terms:

          " I find it a great help, as always, to look at the document itself and it is headed ' Personal Loan Proposal Form,' and then there are set out particulars of the proposer and it is those particulars which are F   alleged to be false in this case. It is true that over the page the purpose for which the loan is required is set out and the amount of the loan, the amount of interest and the amount of the monthly instalments are all set out, but the point is made broadly that on the face of it this document is not made or required for an accounting purpose. If the proposal were accepted—and it was in this case— G   there is evidence for the jury that the proposal form is used for an accounting purpose because once the proposal form is accepted, various parts of the form are filled up on the front of the form and it is used for what the witness called ' computer input.' So undoubtedly if the proposal is accepted the form is used for an accounting purpose and material is put on the face of the form. . . . Right until the moment that the proposal is accepted, the borrower H   would be under no duty whatever to account: that would only arise after the proposal were accepted. In my opinion it would be a misuse of words of the statute to refer to it as a document made or required for any accounting purpose. In my view the highest that the evidence goes is that this document was for use in an accounting process, but there was no duty of any sort to account until after the proposal was accepted and ceased to be a proposal. . . . I have come to the conclusion that there is no evidence on which a jury could

find that this was a document made or required for any accounting   A
purpose."

The judge based his conclusion, so it seems, on two grounds: (1) that
the document was not required for an accounting purpose until after
it had been received and considered by the finance company and after
the decision had been reached to grant a loan; and (2) that there was no
duty to account until after this decision had been made. As to the   B
second ground, it does not seem to us that the moment at which any
duty to account arose had any relevance to the question of whether the
document was or was not required for an accounting purpose.

As to the first ground, it is to be observed that section 17 (1) (a) in
using the words " made or required " indicates that there is a distinction
to be drawn between a document made specifically for the purpose of   C
accounting and one made for some other purpose but which is required for
an accounting purpose. Thus it is apparent that a document may fall
within the ambit of the section if it is made for some purpose other than
an accounting purpose but is required for an accounting purpose as a
subsidiary consideration.

In the present circumstances the borrower would be making the   D
document for the purpose of his loan proposal to be considered, whereas,
at the same time, the document might be " required " by the finance
company for an accounting purpose. Can it be said that the document
is so required when the proposal may upon consideration by the finance
company be rejected? We think it can. The purpose, or at any rate
one of the purposes, of the figures on the reverse side of the form was
in due course to provide the necessary information for the computer.   E

The fact that the necessity might not arise in the event does not, it
seems to us, mean that the information was not required in the first
instance for the eventual accounting purpose. One can imagine the
conversation: " What do you need this for?" Answer: " We need it
for our computer accounting system in the event of the proposal being
accepted."   F

For these reasons we think that the judge was wrong in the conclusions
which he reached.

The other point argued before us was this: that the part of the form
which was falsified (that is the obverse side) was not in any way required
for an accounting purpose. It was only the reverse side which was
material for accounting, and consequently no offence was committed.   G
We do not think that the words of the section permit of that interpretation. This was one entire document; it was as to part required for an
accounting purpose; it was as to part falsified. The fact that these two
parts were not the same does not exonerate the man who was responsible
for the falsification. Indeed, the reverse side containing the figures also
carries the borrower's signature and declaration.   H

We were referred to Reg. v. Mallett [1978] 1 W.L.R. 820 but the
question we have to decide was not debated in that case and we do not
think the judgment helps our decision.

It follows from what we have said that much will turn in a case of
this sort upon the precise nature and content of the proposal form in
question. In giving the answer " Yes " to the question posed in the
Attorney-General's reference, we add the proviso that the answer might

A well be different were the form which has been falsified to be materially different from that which we are considering here.

Opinion accordingly.

Solicitors: *Director of Public Prosecutions*; *Treasury Solicitor.*

B   [Reported by Mrs. Maria Fleischmann, Barrister-at-Law]

C   [QUEEN'S BENCH DIVISION]

* WADHAM STRINGER FINANCE LTD. *v.* MEANEY

1980   June 30;
       July 1; 18   Woolf J.

D *Hire-Purchase — Conditional sale agreement — Enforceability —
Accelerated payment clause—Seller entitled to call for balance
of purchase price and property in goods to pass to buyer—
—Default in payment of instalments—Seller claiming moneys
due under accelerated payment clause—Whether clause void
as restriction on buyer's right to terminate agreement—
Whether unenforceable as penalty—Hire-Purchase Act 1965
(c. 66), ss. 27 (1), 29*

E   Section 27 (1) of the Hire-Purchase Act 1965 provides:
       " At any time before the final payment under a . . . con-
       ditional sale agreement falls due, the . . . buyer shall . . .
       be entitled to terminate the agreement by giving notice
       of termination in writing to any person entitled or auth-
       orised to receive the sums payable under the agreement."
       Section 29 provides:

F   " (1) Any provision to which this subsection applies shall
       be void.   (2) The preceding subsection applies to any
       provision in any agreement . . . (b) whereby the right
       conferred by section 27 of this Act to terminate a . . .
       conditional sale agreement is excluded or restricted. . . ."

       The buyer entered into a conditional sale agreement
governed by the Hire-Purchase Act 1965 for the purchase of a
G motor car. The total purchase price of £2,145·63 was to be
paid by a deposit of £307·35, one instalment of £53·98 and 35
consecutive monthly instalments of £50·98. The buyer paid
the deposit but failed to pay any of the instalments. The agreement contained an accelerated payment clause which provided
that in the event of failure on the part of the buyer to make
punctual payment of instalments the seller might serve notice
on the buyer calling for payment within 10 days of the balance
H of the sum financed, any unpaid deposit and such charges as
would have accrued in the three months following the next
instalment after the notice. Upon the expiry of the 10 day
period property in the goods passed to the buyer. The seller
served a notice calling upon the buyer to make the accelerated
payment specified in the clause. When the buyer failed to
make the payment the seller brought an action claiming
£1,386, the amount due under the clause. There was no dispute as to the amount of the moneys alleged to be due under
the agreement.

Wadham Stringer Ltd. v. Meaney (Q.B.D.)   **[1981]**

A On the issues whether the clause was void by reason of the provisions of the Hire-Purchase Act 1965 as being a restriction of the buyer's right to terminate the agreement or, albeit valid, was unenforceable as a penalty at law: —

Held, (1) that where the seller chose to implement the accelerated payment clause, if after 10 days the buyer had not paid the outstanding arrears then the accelerated payment fell due and the buyer lost the right to terminate the agreement,
B but, since the accelerated payment was the final payment due under the agreement, the buyer's right to terminate the agreement came to an end after the time specified in section 27 (1), and, accordingly, was not excluded or restricted by the provision for the accelerated payment (post, pp. 45G—46A).

(2) That since the charges under the accelerated payment clause could be a genuine pre-estimate of the seller's loss by reason of the early termination of the agreement, the clause was not unenforceable as being penal in its effect and, accord-
C ingly, the seller was entitled to judgment for £1,386 (post, p. 48G—H).

The following cases are referred to in the judgment:

Campbell Discount Co. Ltd. v. *Bridge* [1962] A.C. 600; [1962] 2 W.L.R. 439; [1962] 1 All E.R. 385, H.L.(E.).
Dunlop Pneumatic Tyre Co. Ltd. v. *New Garage and Motor Co. Ltd.* D [1915] A.C. 79, H.L.(E.).
Glasgow Navigation Co. v. *Iron Ore Co.* [1910] A.C. 293, H.L.(Sc.).
Protector Endowment Loan and Annuity Co. v. *Grice* (1880) 5 Q.B.D. 121.
Sun Life Assurance Co. of Canada v. *Jervis* [1944] A.C. 111; [1944] 1 All E.R. 469, H.L.(E.).
Wallingford v. *Mutual Society* (1880) 5 App.Cas. 685, H.L.(E.).   E

The following additional cases were cited in argument:

Associated Distributors Ltd. v. *Hall* [1938] 2 K.B. 83; [1938] 1 All E.R. 511, C.A.
Attorney-General v. *British Broadcasting Corporation*, The Times, June 13, 1980, H.L.(E.).
Cooden Engineering Co. Ltd. v. *Stanford* [1953] 1 Q.B. 86; [1952] 2 All F E.R. 915, C.A.
Financings Ltd. v. *Baldock* [1963] 2 Q.B. 104; [1963] 2 W.L.R. 359; [1963] 1 All E.R. 443, C.A.
Lombank Ltd. v. *Excell* [1964] 1 Q.B. 415; [1963] 3 W.L.R. 700; [1963] 3 All E.R. 486, C.A.
McEntire v. *Crossley Brothers Ltd.* [1895] A.C. 457, H.L.(I.).
Powell v. *Kempton Park Racecourse Co. Ltd.* [1899] A.C. 143, H.L.(E.). G
Sterling Industrial Facilities Ltd. v. *Lydiate Textiles Ltd.* (1962) 106 S.J. 669, C.A.
United Dominions Trust (Commercial) Ltd. v. *Ennis* [1968] 1 Q.B. 54; [1967] 3 W.L.R. 1; [1967] 2 All E.R. 345, C.A.
White and Carter (Councils) Ltd. v. *McGregor* [1962] A.C. 413; [1962] 2 W.L.R. 17; [1961] 3 All E.R. 1178, H.L.(Sc.).
White (Marion) Ltd. v. *Francis* [1972] 1 W.L.R. 1423; [1972] 3 All E.R. H 857, C.A.

SPECIAL PAPER

By a writ dated November 27, 1979, the seller, Wadham Stringer Finance Ltd., claimed £1,386 under the accelerated payment clause of a conditional sale agreement entered into between the seller and the buyer, Christine Anne Meaney, on July 12, 1979, in respect of a Triumph

A motor car. The buyer had defaulted on the instalments due under the agreement and had failed to pay the accelerated sum due within 10 days of the seller's written notice dated November 14, 1979, in accordance with the agreement. The buyer contended that the accelerated payment clause was contrary to the provisions of the Hire-Purchase Act 1965, or alternatively that the sum claimed was irrecoverable as being a penalty.

B
The facts are stated in the judgment.

Richard Southwell Q.C. and *Richard Mawrey* for the seller.
Michael Hutchison Q.C. and *Simon Tuckey* for the buyer.

Cur. adv. vult.

C   WOOLF J. This is an action by the seller, a company which is jointly owned by Wadham Stringer Ltd., and the United Dominions Trust Ltd., for a sum of money alleged to be due, under the terms of a conditional sale agreement.

At the outset of the case, Mr. Southwell, who appears on behalf of the seller, explained that the action is a test action to ascertain the effect

D of the Hire-Purchase Act 1965 and the law as to penalties on certain clauses in the seller's standard conditional sale agreement, the points raised being of general application on which, surprisingly, there is no previous authority which is directly applicable.

He placed before me a bundle of correspondence which showed that an agreement had been reached between the parties, the effect of which

E can be summarised by saying that the liability of the buyer would be the same whatever the outcome of the action. She would only have to pay the balance of the cash price, and not the charges, by instalments which were not to exceed the amount of the contractual instalments of £50·98. She was also to have an indemnity as to her costs.

After Mr. Southwell had referred me to the relevant authorities, I

F intimated that my view was that it would be wrong as a matter of principle for me to proceed with an action which was so clearly academic; particularly as the seller regarded the case as involving an important point of law which could well result in an appeal whatever the outcome.

Having made known my views, the parties asked for an adjournment, which I granted. When the hearing resumed I was informed that the agreement had been varied so that if the buyer succeeded in the action

G the seller would waive all further rights against her. This, in my view, made a real difference to the situation. Both the seller and the buyer now had a real interest in succeeding in the action and I no longer regarded the case as being academic and covered by the principles laid down in the authorities to which I have been referred, including *Glasgow Navigation Co.* v. *Iron Ore Co.* [1910] A.C. 293 and the *Sun Life*

H *Assurance Co. of Canada* v. *Jervis* [1944] A.C. 111. Accordingly I continued with the hearing; the facts of the case being as follows.

The buyer entered into the conditional sale agreement on July 12, 1979, in respect of a Triumph motor car. Under the agreement, which was subject to the Hire-Purchase Act 1965, the total purchase price of £2,145·63 was payable by a deposit of £307·35 and one instalment of £53·98 and 35 consecutive monthly instalments of £50·98. The buyer, having paid the deposit, made no further payments and in these proceed-

42

ings the seller claims £1,386 under what has been described as " the A accelerated payment clause " of the agreement.

The first issue in this case is whether that clause is void because it contravenes the provisions of the Hire-Purchase Act 1965. The second issue is whether, assuming the clause is valid, it provides for the recovery of a penalty which is unenforceable in law.

In order to consider these issues it is necessary to set out the relevant terms of the agreement. The agreement begins with a schedule which sets B out the name of the buyer, the make and description of the goods, details of insurance and the relevant figures. This is followed by a statement that:

" The statutory notices set out below are to be deemed to form part of this agreement only if the transaction evidenced by this agree- ment is one to which the provisions of the Hire-Purchase Act 1965, C as from time to time amended, apply."

The notice as to the right of the buyer to terminate agreement, in the standard form required by the Hire-Purchase Act 1965, is duly set out. Below this there is a heading " Terms " which is followed by the various clauses of the agreement, the majority appearing overleaf. It is not necessary to refer to all the terms, but I am afraid I must refer to some. D

" Terms of Payment. 1. On or before the making of this agree- ment the buyer shall pay to the seller the deposit specified in the schedule and shall punctually pay the several instalments of the balance of the total purchase price as set out in the schedule on the dates therein specified. Punctual payment of the said instalments shall be of the essence of this agreement and the buyer agrees to E pay interest at the rate of $1\frac{1}{2}$ per cent. per month on any overdue instalment until payment thereof such interest to accrue on a daily basis as well after as before judgment. The rights of the seller here- under shall not be affected by any time or other indulgence that the seller may see fit to grant to the buyer.

" Early Settlement. 10. The buyer may settle this transaction early F (provided each previous instalment of the balance of the total pur- chase price has been paid when due) by paying to the seller a sum comprising such of the balance financed as remains unpaid any unpaid acceptance fee and such percentage of the charges specified in the schedule as remains unpaid and will accrue down to a date three months after the date of the instalment which would have next followed the date of early settlement (instalments being appropriated G first to charges by the rule of 78 and then to part payment of the balance financed): the resulting total is then rounded off upwards if ending in 50p or more or downwards if less to the nearest whole £1.

" Default in Payment. 11. Should the buyer fail to pay the deposit in full at the time when this agreement is made or make default in the punctual payment of two or more monthly instalments of the balance H of the total purchase price or where instalments fall due at intervals of more than a month in the punctual payment of such an instalment for 32 days or more the seller may if it elects to do so call upon the buyer for an acceleration in payment of moneys payable under this agreement in preference to pursuing its rights under the termination clause hereof. In the event that the seller elects to call for an acceleration in payment hereunder the seller shall: (a) by written

A notice to the buyer (either served personally on the buyer or sent to the buyer by post to the buyer's usual or last-known address) call upon the buyer within a period of 10 days from the date of such notice to pay to the seller a sum comprising such of the balance financed as remains unpaid at the date of notice, any unpaid deposit and/or acceptance fee and such percentage of the charges specified in the schedule as will accrue down to a date three months after the

B date of the instalment which would next have followed the date of notice (instalments being appropriated first to charges by the rule of 78) and also to pay interest on such sum from the expiration of the said period of 10 days until payment thereof at the rate of 1½ per cent. per month and on the expiration of the said period of 10 days title to and property in the goods shall pass to the buyer notwith-

C standing the provisions of the title to the goods clause hereof save that should the buyer have paid the arrears within the period of 10 days from the date of such notice the agreement shall continue in full force and effect unless the transaction evidenced by this agreement is one to which the provisions of the Act apply and the buyer shall have exercised the buyer's right of termination set out in the statutory notice overleaf (b) not to be entitled after service

D of the notice referred to in paragraph (a) above to terminate this agreement under the termination clause hereof unless the buyer shall have paid the arrears under paragraph (a) hereof and sub-sequently makes further default in payment. But should the agree-ment terminate automatically under the provisions of the termination clause hereof during the currency of any acceleration notice served

E under paragraph (a) above the said notice shall cease to have any effect.

" Termination. 12. (a) Should the buyer fail to pay the deposit in full at the time when this agreement is made or make default in the punctual payment of two or more monthly instalments of the balance of the total purchase price or where the instalments fall due at intervals of more than a month in the punctual payment of such an

F instalment for 32 days or more and fail to pay the same within 10 days of the seller having demanded the same or, where the trans-action evidenced by this agreement is one to which the provisions of the Act apply, within 10 days after the service upon the buyer of a notice of default as prescribed by section 25 of the Act or if the buyers does or suffers anything whatsover which in the seller's opinion

G bona fide formed upon reasonable grounds will or may have the effect of jeopardising the seller's right of property in the goods (if any) then in each and every such case the seller may by written notice (either served personally on the buyer or sent to the buyer by post to the buyer's usual or last known address) forthwith and for all purposes terminate this agreement and thereupon the buyer

H shall no longer be in possession of the goods with the seller's consent. Should the buyer or anyone included in the expression ' the buyer ' have a receiving order made or be made bankrupt or if any body corporate included in the expression ' the buyer ' calls a meeting of or makes any arrangement or composition with its creditors is wound up compulsorily goes into liquidation or is otherwise dis-solved or has a receiver of any of its assets appointed or if the goods or any part thereof are seized under any execution or legal process

or under any distress for rent then this agreement shall forthwith and   A
without any notice determine and thereafter the buyer shall no
longer be in possession of the goods with the seller's consent. Should
the agreement be terminated by the seller or determine under this
clause after one-third of the total purchase price has been paid and
the transaction evidenced by this agreement is one to which the
provisions of the Act apply then unless the buyer has put an end to
the agreement the seller may not take back the goods from the buyer   B
without the buyer's consent unless the seller obtains an order of the
court in accordance with the statutory notice overleaf. Should the
agreement be terminated by the seller or determine under this clause
in any circumstances other than those set out in the last preceding
sentence the seller may without notice retake possession of the goods
and for this purpose shall be entitled freely to enter into and upon   C
any premises occupied by or under the control of the buyer.
(b) Where the transaction evidenced by this agreement is one to
which the provisions of the Act apply the buyer shall have a statutory right to terminate this agreement and such right and the buyer's
liability upon exercise of such right are set out in the statutory
notice overleaf.

"Payment on Termination or Determination. 13. Should this   D
agreement be terminated by the seller or determine under the termination clause hereof the buyer shall forthwith pay to the seller the
amount of any deposit and/or acceptance fee due but unpaid
together with any instalments which are in arrear at the time of such
termination or determination and, on demand, shall pay to the
seller any expenses reasonably incurred by the seller in tracing and/   E
or recovering possession of the goods (if title to and property in the
goods remains vested in the seller at the date of such termination
or determination) together with an amount representing the seller's
loss on the transaction. It is hereby agreed that for the purpose of
this clause the seller's loss shall be an amount equal to the amount
by which the total purchase price set out in the schedule exceeds   F
the aggregate of (a) any payments made by the buyer by way of
deposit, acceptance fee and instalments of the balance of the total
purchase price; (b) a sum representing the rebate of charges which
would have been allowed in respect of the accelerated payment of
all or part of the total purchase price had the transaction been
settled under the provisions of the early settlement clause hereof at   G
the date of such termination or determination; and (c) if title to and
property in the goods remains vested in the seller at the date of
termination or determination the ' net ' proceeds of sale of the goods
after allowing for any sums reasonably expended by the seller in
putting the goods into good order and repair for the purpose of sale.
Provided always that where the transaction evidenced by this agree-   H
ment is one to which the provisions of the Act apply the amount payable by the buyer in respect of such loss shall not exceed the amount
by which one half of the total purchase price exceeds the total of
the amount paid and the amount due by way of instalments of the
total purchase price immediately before such termination or determination but without prejudice to paragraph 3 of the statutory
notice overleaf."

A   The first contention made on behalf of the buyer turns on the interpretation of section 27 of the Hire-Purchase Act 1965. The relevant
parts of that section read as follows:

"(1) At any time before the final payment under a hire-purchase
agreement or conditional sale agreement falls due, the hirer or buyer
shall (subject to the next following subsection) be entitled to ter-
B   minate the agreement by giving notice of termination in writing to
any person entitled or authorised to receive the sums payable under
the agreement. (2) In the case of a conditional sale agreement,
where the property in the goods, having become vested in the buyer,
is transferred to a person who does not become the buyer under
the agreement, the buyer shall not thereafter be entitled to terminate
the agreement under this section. (3) Subject to the last preceding
C   subsection, where a buyer under a conditional sale agreement terminates the agreement under this section after the property in the
goods has become vested in him, the property in the goods shall
thereupon vest in the person (in this subsection referred to as "the
previous owner") in whom it was vested immediately before it
became vested in the buyer: Provided that if the previous owner
D   has died, or any other event has occurred whereby that property, if
vested in him immediately before that event, would thereupon have
vested in some other person, the property shall be treated as having
devolved as if it had been vested in the previous owner immediately
before his death or immediately before that event, as the case may
be. (4) Nothing in this section shall prejudice any right of a . . .
buyer to terminate a . . . conditional sale agreement otherwise than
E   by virtue of this section."

What the buyer says is that clause 11 of the agreement interferes
with the right to terminate contained in section 27 (1) and as such, it is
void under section 29 (2) (b) which provides that any provision in a conditional sale agreement is void "whereby the right conferred by section
27 of this Act to terminate . . . a conditional sale agreement is excluded
F   or restricted." Whether the buyer's contention is correct depends on the
meaning of the words "At any time before the final payment under a
hire-purchase agreement or conditional sale agreement falls due."

Mr. Hutchison, on behalf of the buyer, says the effect of those
words is that the right of termination only comes to an end on the date
when the thirty-sixth of the monthly instalments would become payable
G   under the agreement, and that date is not affected by the fact that the
seller chooses to activate his rights to accelerate the time for payment
under clause 11 of the agreement.

On the other hand, the seller contends that if the seller elects to call
for accelerated payment and gives the necessary notice, and the 10 days
thereafter expire without the buyer having paid off the arrears, the
H   accelerated payment, which is the final payment under the conditional
sale agreement, falls due, for the purposes of section 27 (1); so the right
to terminate under section 27 (1) comes to an end. On the seller's interpretation there is no interference with the buyer's right to terminate
under the Act, because up until the sum under clause 11 falls due the
right to terminate is expressly recognised, and whereas the right to
terminate is lost thereafter, the loss occurs after the time specified, on
this interpretation, in section 27 (1).

Although I recognise that the seller's interpretation can substantially restrict the protection given to a hirer or buyer by section 27, I am forced to the conclusion that it is the right interpretation. The result of the rival contention is that because under the agreement there is a provision for instalments continuing for three years, the right to terminate must continue for a like period. This is irrespective of whether the seller has exercised his rights under the clause 11 at an early stage of the agreement which could lead to the right to terminate continuing for a period of many months after the buyer acquired title to the vehicle. Although I accept that because of the terms of section 27 (2) and (3) the date on which title passes cannot be conclusive, it still seems remarkable that there should be a right to terminate under section 27 long after any payment in fact falls due and after title has passed.

The seller being correct on his interpretation, clause 11 does not restrict the seller's rights to terminate. The concluding words of clause 11 (a) make it clear that during the period of 10 days following the service of the notice under clause 11, the hirer can still exercise his statutory right, so there is no restriction during that period. As the right to terminate has thereafter ceased to exist it cannot be cut down.

The remaining points taken by the buyer do not assist her in view of my decision on the interpretation of section 27 (1). However, it is desirable that I should deal with them in case this case goes further as they have been fully argued.

The first is that the sum specified in clause 11 (a) could not be the final payment because of the provisions as to interest on failure to pay the accelerated payment. However I cannot accept that the right to terminate can be extended by failing to make the accelerated payment as section 27 (1) specifies the limit for termination as when the payment "falls due," not when it is paid; and the liability for interest only arises after the accelerated payment has fallen due.

The buyer's next argument turns on the wording of section 28 (1) (b) combined with the second half of section 29 (2) (b). It is argued that clause 11 is void because if a buyer exercises his statutory right to terminate after a buyer has become liable to pay an accelerated payment under clause 11, the buyer will be under a liability in excess of that referred to in section 28. Once again I accept the seller's arguments. The second half of section 29 (2) (b) only applies to a liability imposed on the buyer " by reason of the termination of a . . . conditional sale agreement." The liability under clause 11 does not arise by reason of such termination but because the seller exercises his rights under the clause. Furthermore, the liability under clause 11 would be one which falls within the words " without prejudice to any liability which has accrued before the termination " in section 28 (1) if those words are given their literal meaning. The only argument to support a contrary interpretation depends on the surprising fact that the statutory notice which purports to set out the buyer's liability on termination sets out a liability which does not accord with section 28. In particular it makes no reference to the " without prejudice to any liability which has accrued before the termination " in section 28, and because of this Mr. Hutchison says those words must, when the Act is read as a whole, mean no more than the instalments which are in arrear, because this is what is stated in the statutory notice. Were there no other conflicts between what is said in the statutory notice and section 28, the argument in favour of the buyer would be

A much stronger. However this is not the case. It is to be observed that that statutory notice makes no reference to the provisions of section 28 (4) and the limits on the court's powers not to order the return of the goods to the seller after a buyer's termination. Accordingly I do not consider that the statutory notice can be regarded as the key to the meaning of section 28 and I reject the buyer's argument.

B There is an additional reason why the buyer cannot rely on section 28 to render clause 11 void. The statement that the statutory notice shall " be deemed to form part of this agreement " together with the wording of clause 12 (b) makes the statutory notice one of the terms of the agreement. Accordingly, in addition to the statutory right to terminate, the buyer has a contractual right to terminate on the terms set out in the statutory notice, and if he exercises that right his liability cannot exceed

C that provided for in the agreement. So that upon his exercising that right to terminate, the liability specified in the statutory notice must supercede his liability, if any, under clause 11.

That brings me conveniently to the buyer's last argument on the statutory provisions. This turns on the wording of section 29 (2) (c). Initially Mr. Hutchison described this as an esoteric argument but later rather

D regretted using that adjective in case it should be thought to detract from it. He says that although clause 11 of the agreement is not headed " termination," when the seller exercises his right under clause 11 he, in effect, is terminating the agreement and should be treated as such. Accordingly, as the amount payable under clause 11 is in excess of that provided for in section 29 (2) (c), it is void. I am not sure whether it was because of its esoteric qualities, but initially I was attracted by this argu-

E ment. It did seem to me that to regard the conditional sale agreement as still being in existence after clause 11 had been activated, the property in the goods had passed to the buyer and all the buyer was left to do was to make the accelerated payment, was unreal. However, quite clearly the fact that the goods had become vested in the buyer was not intended to mean that the right to terminate could not be exercised

F because otherwise section 27 (2) and (3) would be unnecessary. It therefore seems that the legislature intended an agreement to continue even though the property had passed from the seller and because of this, with some reservations, I have come to the conclusion that the fact that an accelerated payment has fallen due under clause 11 does not terminate the agreement. The agreement remains in force not only until the seller has played his part but until the buyer has also played his part, even

G though that is confined to making an accelerated payment.

In expressing the view which I have about the statutory provisions, I am conscious that in the majority of cases they must apply to hire-purchase agreements as well as conditional sale agreements, and this could have an adverse effect not only on buyers under conditional sale agreements but also hirers under hire-purchase agreements. By skilful drafting

H of agreements it could well be possible to deprive hirers and purchasers of the protection Parliament intended them to have. While recognising this, it is also necessary to take into account the very drastic effect upon the supplier of the goods were the interpretation to be otherwise than that which I have adopted. If the buyer was right in her contentions, it would be virtually impossible to design an accelerated payment provision which did not contravene the sections of the Act under consideration. As there is a special limitation, inter alia, on accelerated payments, in

the case of the death of a buyer in section 30 (1), Parliament did not   **A**
intend that there should never be an accelerated payment provision
and accordingly I regard the conclusions to which I have come as being
in accord with the literal terms of sections 27 and 28 and the Act of
1965 as a whole.

The buyer's remaining argument does not turn upon the provisions
of the Act. It is a contention that clause 11 is penal in effect. Mr.
Southwell's initial argument was that it was wrong to regard the payment   **B**
under clause 11 as being capable of being a penalty. It did not fall within
the classic statement in *Dunlop Pneumatic Tyre Co. Ltd.* v. *New
Garage and Motor Co. Ltd.* [1915] A.C. 79. He contended the correct
approach was that indicated in *Wallingford* v. *Mutual Society* (1880)
5 App.Cas. 685 and *Protector Endowment Loan and Annuity Co.* v.
Grice (1880) 5 Q.B.D. 121, which cases were not considered by the   **C**
House of Lords in the *Dunlop* case, or in *Campbell Discount Co. Ltd.* v.
Bridge [1962] A.C. 600. If this be the position a buyer under a conditional sale agreement would be in a much worse position than he would
be if he had entered into a hire-purchase agreement. Such an outcome
would be highly undesirable. However, it is clear that the seller's right to
serve a notice under clause 11 arises because of the buyer's breach of
the agreement in failing to pay instalments and as the right to call for   **D**
accelerated payment only arises upon such a breach, I would apply the
principles as to penalties to the seller's right to recover accelerated payments under a conditional sale agreement in the same way as they apply
to hire-purchase agreements. It is accordingly necessary to consider
whether the provisions of clause 11 are penal in effect.

In considering this it is important to bear in mind that under clause 11   **E**
the title in the goods vests in the buyer. Furthermore, there is an allowance because the obligation of the buyer is only to pay a proportion of
the charges calculated at a date three months after the date of the instalment which would next have followed the date of notice, the instalments
being appropriated first to charges by the rule of 78. Until this case I had
not heard of the rule of 78 and I am sure that in this regard I am in   **F**
the same position as many purchasers who enter into credit sale agreements with the sellers. However the rule is well recognised in the trade
and now has considerable repectability because it is adopted, as being
the appropriate formula to apply, in the White Paper on the reform of
the law on consumer credit (Cmmd. 5427 at p. 17). The only difference
between the recommendations and the formula used in clause 11 is that
the proposals in the White Paper take a date three to three and a half   **G**
months, while in clause 11 a date is taken which is four months, after
the date of the notice. Mr. Hutchinson conceded that were it not for
this difference the penalty argument would fail because to have adopted
the proposals in the White Paper could not be said to be unreasonable.
I have no hesitation in saying that while the difference between the two
is not de minimis, it is not sufficient to prevent clause 11 containing a   **H**
genuine pre-estimate of the seller's loss. Clearly the charges were not
confined to interest so far as the seller is concerned and while the four
month period could in some cases bear heavily upon the buyer, this
does not mean that the accelerated payment is penal. It can still be a
genuine pre-estimate of what the seller will lose because of the early
termination of the agreement.

It follows that notwithstanding the arguments advanced so skilfully by

A   Mr. Hutchison, the buyer is liable to the seller for the claim under clause 11 and I will therefore give judgment for the seller in the sum of £1,386 which, as I understand it, is the maximum amount of the buyer's liability.

Judgment for the seller for £1,386.

B   Solicitors: *M. J. Sechiari; Graham & Graham, St. Austell.*

[Reported by SUSAN DENNY, Barrister-at-Law]

C

[COURT OF APPEAL]

*A.C.T. CONSTRUCTION LTD. *v.* CUSTOMS AND EXCISE COMMISSIONERS

D   1980   Oct. 8, 9

Lord Denning M.R.,
Brandon and Ackner L.JJ.

Revenue—Value added tax—Zero-rating—Alteration of building— Foundations underpinned to prevent subsidence—Whether work of " maintenance "—Whether zero-rated—Finance Act 1972 (c. 41), Sch. 4, Group 8, item 2, note (2) (as varied by Value Added Tax (Consolidation) Order 1976 (S.I. 1976 No. 128), Sch. 1, Group 8, item 2, note (2) (a))
Statute—Construction—Meaning of word—Word used in ordinary sense—Primary facts found by tribunal—Whether underpinning work maintenance—Whether question of law

F   A construction company underpinned houses which had too shallow foundations by constructing a further foundation, consisting of a new concrete beam with pillars, beneath the existing foundation in order to prevent subsidence. A value added tax tribunal upheld the Customs and Excise Commissioners' assessment of the company to value added tax on the basis that although the work done was a service in the course of the alteration of a building and so within item 2 of Group 8 of Schedule 4 to the Finance Act 1972 [1] it was not zero-rated because it came within the exception " maintenance " in note (2) (*a*) to Group 8. Drake J. allowed the company's appeal.

G   On appeal by the commissioners: —
Held, dismissing the appeal, (1) that the question whether the work of underpinning which the tribunal had found that the company had done was capable of coming within the expression " maintenance " in note (2) (*a*) to Group 8 of Schedule 4 to the Finance Act 1972 was a question of law (post, pp. 54D–E, 56E, 57E).

H   *British Railways Board* v. *Customs and Excise Commissioners* [1977] 1 W.L.R. 588, C.A. and *Pearlman* v. *Keepers and Governors of Harrow School* [1979] Q.B. 56, C.A. considered.
(2) That the underpinning work, which involved the construction of an additional foundation, was an alteration of the building which did not fall within the ordinary and natural

[1] Finance Act 1972, Sch. 4, Group 8, item 2: see post, p. 57G.
Note (2) to item 2 (as varied): see post, p. 58A.

50

meaning of the word " maintenance " and accordingly should   A
be zero-rated under item 2 of Group 8 of Schedule 4 to the
Act of 1972 (post, pp. 55F–G, 56B–C, 57C–D, 58C).

Per Lord Denning M.R. and Ackner L.J. " Alteration " in
item 2 of Group 8 of Schedule 4 to the Act of 1972 does not
necessarily involve a structural alteration (post, pp. 53H—54A,
57G).

Decision of Drake J. [1979] 1 W.L.R. 870; [1979] 2 All
E.R. 691 affirmed.   B

The following cases are referred to in the judgments:

Brew Brothers Ltd. v. *Snax (Ross) Ltd.* [1970] 1 Q.B. 612; [1969] 3
   W.L.R. 657; [1970] 1 All E.R. 587, C.A.
British Railways Board v. *Customs and Excise Commissioners* [1977] 1
   W.L.R. 588; [1977] 2 All E.R. 873, C.A.
Company, In re A [1980] 3 W.L.R. 181; [1980] 2 All E.R. 634, H.L.(E.).   C
Customs and Excise Commissioners v. *Morrison Dunbar Ltd.* [1979] S.T.C.
   406.
Davies (T. G.) v. *Customs and Excise Commissioners* [1976] V.A.T.T.R.
   205.
Pearlman v. *Keepers and Governors of Harrow School* [1979] Q.B. 56;
   [1978] 3 W.L.R. 736; [1979] 1 All E.R. 365, C.A.

                                                              D

The following additional cases were cited in argument:

Collins v. *Flynn* [1963] 2 All E.R. 1068.
Lister v. *Lane & Nesham* [1893] 2 Q.B. 212, C.A.
Lurcott v. *Wakely & Wheeler* [1911] 1 K.B. 905, C.A.
Ravenseft Properties Ltd. v. *Davstone (Holdings) Ltd.* [1980] Q.B. 12;
   [1979] 2 W.L.R. 897; [1979] 1 All E.R. 929.
Sotheby v. *Grundy* [1947] 2 All E.R. 761.   E

APPEAL from Drake J.

On August 8, 1978, a value added tax tribunal sitting in London
upheld an assessment of £1,072·44 value added tax on services rendered
by the company, A.C.T. Construction Ltd. ("A.C.T.") made by the
Customs and Excise Commissioners on March 22, 1978. The services   F
consisted of underpinning dwelling houses and the method adopted
was to improve the " load bearing capacity by the construction of a
further foundation beneath an existing foundation;" a new concrete
beam was constructed " beneath the existing foundation " and " in
addition beneath the concrete beam were inserted two, or possibly
three concrete piers." The tribunal held that the underpinning operation " amounted to an alteration of the building " and " that under-   G
pinning ... was a work of maintenance " so that value added tax was
payable. On March 16, 1979, Drake J. allowed the company's appeal.
The judge [1979] 1 W.L.R. 870 held that work that substantially
altered the character and nature of a building could not be " maintenance " within the meaning of note (1) to item 2 of Group 8 of
Schedule 4 to the Finance Act 1972.   H

The commissioners appealed on the grounds that the judge was wrong
in law in holding that (1) the appeal by the company to the Queen's
Bench Division of the High Court of Justice raised a point of law; (2)
the underpinning work carried out by the company was not work of
repair or maintenance: and (3) the underpinning work was not subject
to value added tax at the standard rate.

The facts are stated in the judgment of Lord Denning M.R.

A   *Simon D. Brown* for the commissioners.
     Michael Beloff for the company.

LORD DENNING M.R. The question is this: when the foundations
of a house are insufficient, and contractors are employed to remedy
the insufficiency by inserting a concrete beam (underpinning the house),
is the work liable for value added tax or not? Or—in technical
B   language—is it zero-rated or positive-rated? It depends on whether the
work of underpinning comes within the description of " repair or maintenance." If it comes within that description, it is positive-rated. If it
does not come within that description, then it is zero-rated.
     That is the point in this case. But we have discussed other points
which are important to the building industry: such as, is the insertion
C   of a damp-proof course zero-rated or positive-rated? Is the insertion of
double-glazing instead of single-glazing zero-rated or positive-rated?
If you put a tiled roof instead of a thatched roof, is that zero-rated or
positive-rated? In all these cases it depends on the words, " Is it repair
or maintenance?" If it is work of repair or maintenance, then it is
positive-rated. If it is not work of repair or maintenance, then it is
zero-rated.
D
     The Finance Act 1972 imposed value added tax from 1973 onwards.
The tax is under the care and management of the Customs and Excise
Commissioners—not the Inland Revenue. Section 12 says that certain
supplies and services are to be zero-rated. They are set out in Schedule
4. In it there are groups which have been up-dated by the Value
Added Tax (Consolidation) Order 1976 (S.I. 1976 No. 128). So we
E   have to look at that order and the schedules to it to see whether any
supplies or services are zero-rated or not.
     The particular group which applies to this case is Group 8
" Construction of Buildings, etc." One of the items which is to be
zero-rated is item 2:

     " The supply, in the course of the construction, alteration or demo-
F   lition of any building or of any civil engineering work, of any
     services . . ."

I will stop there because there is a note (note 2) to that item, which
says: " Item 2 does not include . . . (*a*) any work of repair or maintenance . . ." So the construction or alteration of building work is zero-
rated: but not any work of repair or maintenance.
G   I now turn to our particular problem. In the 1930s many houses
were built in which the foundations were too shallow. (Such foundations would not be allowed under the modern regulations). Builders
in the 1930s did not realise that they were putting in foundations which
were too shallow. The result was that during the drought of 1976 there
was subsidence—especially in houses built on clay soil. There was
movement in the structure of the houses. Cracks appeared. The
H   houses were unsafe.
     To remedy this, some wise owners had their foundations under-
pinned: not only of houses that had already been affected—but also of
houses which might be affected. They had their houses underpinned,
even though movement had not yet started.
     One of the firms which specialised in underpinning work was A.C.T.
Construction Ltd. (" A.C.T."). Their method was to leave the shallow
foundation in place: but a foot or two underneath it they would put a

52

big concrete beam, with pillars sunk in the earth to hold it, so as to hold up the older foundation. It was not an actual raft—but an underlying structure. It had to be done in short stages. It was a specialist job.

A.C.T. took advice as to whether this work should be zero-rated or not. They were advised that it was zero-rated. On October 18, 1977, they gave this quotation for the underpinning of a house:

" . . . our fixed price quotation for the works are as follows: Provide 1·2 m deep reinforced concrete footing to all elevations of property . . . For the sum of £7,271·00 . . . rated zero."

That was the quotation they gave. It was no doubt accepted by the householder: and the work was done on that footing.

Now the commissioners say that A.C.T. were wrong: and that the work should be positive-rated. Value added tax has been assessed at £1,072·44. A.C.T. had to pay that sum. But they ask that it should be returned to them as the work should have been zero-rated.

The matter was discussed with insurance assessors. They wrote to the commissioners on September 3, 1977, saying:

" We have been advised by certain underpinning contractors that their local value added tax offices have given different rulings in that underpinning is to be treated as alterations or new works and therefore zero-rated."

So it seems that different rulings were given by various value added tax officers.

The Customs and Excise Commissioners said that they had already given a ruling on the matter. They issued a booklet as far back as 1975. It was HM Customs and Excise Notice No. 715. It had a blue cover. So I will call it the blue booklet. It gives examples of work which is zero-rated, and examples of work which is positive-rated. Paragraph 4 (a) says: " The following are examples of work which is **positive-rated** as repair or maintenance . . . Shoring up and underpinning buildings."

In further correspondence the commissioners said in a letter of January 9, 1978:

" The meaning of the word ' maintenance ' which we accept is the one adopted in the value added tax tribunal case of T. G. Davies. . . . The tribunal in the decision defined maintenance as ' the keeping of something in proper order before the thing falls out of condition.' When underpinning of buildings is undertaken to prevent the building falling into disrepair, we regard this as work of maintenance and therefore subject to a positive rate of value added tax."

On April 6, 1978, they said:

" . . . we have already given our ruling that underpinning of buildings following subsidence is chargeable with value added tax, as indeed is clearly stated in Public Notice 715, paragraph 4 (a)."

So there is the head office of the Customs and Excise making it as plain as can be that in their view the work of underpinning is positive-rated and not zero-rated.

This matter being of so much importance to the industry, A.C.T.

The Weekly Law Reports, January 23, 1981

53

1 W.L.R.   A.C.T. Construction v. Customs & Excise (C.A.)   Lord Denning M.R.

A appealed to a value added tax tribunal. The tribunal gave a considered judgment. They expressed sympathy for the contractors because they had consulted their accountants and had been told that it was not work of repair or maintenance: but the tribunal felt driven to the conclusion that it was maintenance and was positive-rated. This is the crucial passage in the decision of the tribunal: " We adopt the defini-
B tion of ' maintenance ' set out in the decision of the London Tribunal in *T. G. Davies* v. *Customs and Excise Commissioners* [1976] V.A.T.T.R. 205, 213," As that is the definition on which they rested, I think I will read it:

C
> " The third question is whether or not the supplies under consider-
> ation amounted to ' work of repair or maintenance ' so as to be
> excluded from items 2 and 3 of Group 8 by paragraph (a) of note
> (2) thereto. We were not greatly assisted during the hearing by
> the quotation of authorities on the meaning to be given to these
> words. In our view ' repair ' means the restoration to a sound
> condition after injury or decay; in its ordinary context it indicates
> the putting back into good condition of something that, having
> been in a good condition, has fallen into a bad condition. The
D
> word ' maintenance ' in the context of ' work of repair or main-
> tenance ' is harder to define. We think it extends to the keeping
> of something in proper order before the thing falls out of condi-
> tion. It does not, in our opinion, exclude improvements. In
> performing works of maintenance on a building, the householder
> may substitute for one article a reasonable improvement thereto.
> For example, in ' maintaining ' a house in relation to its central
E
> heating, a householder may substitute an oil-fired boiler for a coal-
> fired boiler. So, in our view, one may maintain something by
> ensuring that it remains in the same good condition, or by
> improving it. But each case must be considered individually, an
> improvement may or may not be ' maintenance '."

F Applying that definition, the tribunal in this case held that underpinning was not " repair " but that it was " maintenance ": and
therefore positive-rated.

A.C.T. appealed to the judge. Drake J. [1979] 1 W.L.R. 870 reversed the tribunal's decision. He disagreed with the test of " maintenance " as propounded by the tribunal: see p. 874. He considered a number of cases of landlord and tenant on repair or maintenance.
G He said that he could not give an exhaustive definition: but he was inclined to see whether the work had changed the character of the building so that it became something different. Applying that test, he held at p. 876 that this was not " maintenance." He also said that on the ordinary meaning of the word the underpinning of the house was not " maintenance." It should be zero-rated. The Customs and Excise Commissioners appeal to this court. It comes down to the
H construction of the few words in Schedule 4.

First, I would like to mention the word " alteration " in the opening sentence. Neill J., in *Customs and Excise Commissioners* v. *Morrison Dunbar Ltd.* [1979] S.T.C. 406, 413, decided on July 5, 1978, said " . . . that the alteration to which item 2 applies is an alteration *of the building* and therefore one which involves some structural alteration."

I am afraid I cannot share that view. I do not think that the word " structural " should be inserted. It seems to me that " altera-

54

tion" means any alteration of a building whether it is structural or not. But nothing depends on it in this case. Clearly the work of underpinning was an "alteration."

I agree with the judge—and with the tribunal—that underpinning was not "repair." I understand that in one or two of the houses cracks had to be plastered over, or work had to be done on the actual defects that then appeared. That would be "repair": and that would be positive-rated. But the work with which we are concerned was the underpinning—putting the concrete beam underneath the foundations. That is not "repair."

The great contest in the case is whether it is "maintenance" or not. Mr. Brown for the commissioners said that the question whether a particular work is "maintenance" or not is a matter on which two opinions can easily be held without either being unreasonable at all. Quite reasonably one person might say that underpinning is "maintenance." Another person might equally reasonably say that it is not "maintenance." So he said there is a band in which either view is reasonable. He said that in such a case the courts should not interfere with the decision of a tribunal, whichever way it decided. He said that the courts should not interfere with the decision of a tribunal unless it was right outside the band of reasonableness—so unreasonable that no reasonable man could come to that conclusion. He sought to find some support for this argument in some observations of Lord Diplock in the recent case of *In re A Company* [1980] 3 W.L.R. 181, 187–188. But I cannot accept that submission. Once you have the primary facts established—as you have here—about the underpinning, then the question, whether the work comes within the word "maintenance" or not, is a question of law for the judges to decide. Brandon and Ackner L.JJ. pointed out that in hundreds of arbitrations in the City of London the arbitrators state their findings of fact and then ask the court whether on the true construction of the document (the charter-party or whatever it may be) they came to the right conclusion. In everyday practice, once the primary facts are found, the interpretation of a word is a question of law for the judges to decide.

Many a time we have expressly so held. We so held in a value added tax case, *British Railways Board* v. *Customs and Excise Commissioners* [1977] 1 W.L.R. 588; and we so held in an analogous case not involving value added tax but structural alterations: see *Pearlman* v. *Keepers and Governors of Harrow School* [1979] Q.B. 56. With regard to the latter case, I would say that the whole court were unanimous in thinking that the circuit judge below was wrong in his construction of the words "structural alterations": and accordingly he had made a mistake of law. The only ground on which Geoffrey Lane L.J. dissented at pp. 73–76 was that he thought it was an error within their jurisdiction which was not subject to correction. But, on whether it was a point of law, Geoffrey Lane L.J. agreed with the rest of us.

I would add that this is especially important in work which is repetitive—and frequently arising—as in this case of underpinning. Throughout the industry it is essential that contractors and their employers should know whether the work is to be positive-rated or zero-rated. It would be intolerable if one tribunal were to give one view and another tribunal were to give another view: and that no one

The Weekly Law Reports, January 23, 1981

55

1 W.L.R.   A.C.T. Construction v. Customs & Excise (C.A.)   Lord Denning M.R.

A could decide between them. You would have different rulings in relation to similar work in different parts of the country; according to which tribunal happened to be hearing the case. That cannot be right. I would ask, if there are two tribunals giving different decisions, what are the Customs and Excise to do? Are they to be the arbitrators between the differing views? I hope not. Tax-gatherers should not be judges in their own cases. Surely not. When a definite ruling is
B needed for the guidance of builders and customers everywhere, it must be for the courts of law to give a definite and final ruling as to the meaning of a word such as " maintenance."

So I will turn to the meaning of the word " maintenance." Was this underpinning maintenance? " Repair " and " maintenance " are used in conjunction throughout the industry: and in the landlord and
C tenant cases. In the context of repair and maintenance to buildings, they are used every day. They are ordinary English words. Judges have tried from time to time to define them.   They do the best they can. Always in relation to the particular case in hand. To my mind, definitions are not much help. I go by the observations made by Sachs L.J. on this line of cases in *Brew Brothers Ltd.* v. *Snax (Ross)*
D *Ltd.* [1970] 1 Q.B. 612, 640. That was a case about a bulging wall: and the question was about a covenant for repair and maintenance. Sachs L.J. said:

" In the course of their submissions counsel referred to a number of varying phrases which had been used by judges in an endeavour to express the distinction between the end-product of work which constituted repair and that of work which did not. They included
E ' improvement,' ' important improvement,' ' different in kind,' ' different in character,' ' different in substance,' ' different in nature,' ' a new and different thing,' and just ' something different ' . . . For my part I doubt whether there is any definition— certainly not any general definition—which satisfactorily covers the above distinctions: nor will I attempt to provide one." Then
F he went on: " . . . the correct approach is to look at the particular building . . . and then come to a conclusion as to whether, on a fair interpretation of those terms in relation to that state, the requisite work can fairly be termed repair."

I would look at this case in that way. I ask myself what would an ordinary reasonable man say if he was asked, " Look at this work of
G underpinning this house at a cost of £7,000 or more. Is that repairing the house? Is it maintaining the house?" I am sure he would say: " Certainly not. I know what to ' repair ' a house is. If a window is broken, or one of the stairs is broken, that is ' repair.' I also know what ' maintaining it ' is. It has to be painted from time to time. It has to be cleaned. It has to be kept in good condition. That is ' maintenance.' But underpinning a house, that is not ' maintenance '."

H A word about the blue booklet (Notice No. 715). If I were asked, is putting in a damp course to a house which has never had one " repair " or " maintenance," I would agree with the commissioners that it is not maintenance. It should be zero-rated. If I were asked, if you are installing double-glazing for the first time, is that maintenance or is it not, I would say it is clearly not maintenance. It should be zero-rated. So also if you are putting fixed cupboards in the house. It is " alteration," but it is not " maintenance." I would agree with the commissioners on all those items. But, when I turn the page and find the things which are said to be positive-rated, I do not agree with some of these. They say that " shoring up and underpinning buildings " is maintenance. I do not agree. Take this case. It cost over £7,000 to underpin this building. That is not maintenance. Take an old wall which has to be kept up by making buttresses. That is not maintenance. Then again: " Replacing one type of roof by another, e.g., slates by tiles." The commissioners say that that is maintenance. I do not think so. It is an alteration which is far more than " maintenance " requires.

I have given those illustrations to show the problems which do arise in this particular Act. For myself, I think that each case has to be decided as it comes up according to the ordinary meaning which the ordinary man would give to these words. As each case is decided, the courts will build up a body of law so that people will know whether or not the work is zero-rated or positive-rated. In some respects the blue booklet gives good guidance. In other respects it does not. So far as the law is concerned the ultimate decision must rest with the judges and not with the tribunals as to whether these cases—which occur time after time— are zero-rated or positive-rated.

In the result I come to the same conclusion as Drake J. [1979] 1 W.L.R. 870. I think that this was not maintenance. It was an alteration to a building, and under the provisions it should be zero-rated. I would therefore dismiss this appeal.

BRANDON L.J. The question of law which appears to me to arise in this case is this: is the work of underpinning which the value added tax tribunal found was done to the building concerned capable of coming within the expression " maintenance " contained in note (2) to Group 8 in Schedule 1 to the (Value Added Tax Consolidation) Order 1976? I limit the question in that way because it has been conceded on behalf of the Customs and Excise Commissioners that the work is not capable of coming within the other word, " repair," also contained in note (2).

If the work concerned is capable of coming within the expression " maintenance " in note (2), the decision whether it does or not is a decision of fact for the value added tax tribunal. This court, which only has power to hear an appeal on a question of law, cannot interfere even though it would have decided the question of fact differently itself. If the work concerned is not capable of coming within the expression " maintenance " in note (2), the decision of the tribunal that it did so was wrong in law, and this court has both the power and the duty to set it aside.

It is possible to take up two extreme positions on the meaning of the expression " maintenance " in note (2). One extreme position is to say that, if the work done involves an improvement to the building, it can never be maintenance. The other extreme position is to say that, if the work has the purpose of remedying an existing defect in the building or preventing a future defect from developing, it must always be maintenance. In my view, neither of these extreme positions is correct. The expression " maintenance " should be given its ordinary and natural meaning. In regard to the first extreme position, there may well be cases where the work done, although it involves some

57

1 W.L.R.   A.C.T. Construction v. Customs & Excise (C.A.)   Brandon L.J.

A   degree of improvement (for instance, because of the use of modern or better materials or methods) is nevertheless maintenance in the ordinary and natural meaning of that word. For example, if metal gutters, which are liable to decay in time, are replaced with plastic gutters which are not liable to decay however long they remain there, that is an improvement to the building, but I would still regard that

B   work as maintenance. With regard to the second extreme position, there may well be cases where, although the purpose of the work is to remedy existing or to prevent future defects in the building, it is nevertheless not within the expression " maintenance " in the ordinary and natural meaning of that word. For example, if a building has a flat roof which leaks continuously and the owner decides to replace the flat roof with a pitch roof so as to eliminate that defect, then, although

C   that work was designed to eliminate a defect, it would not in my view be maintenance in the ordinary and natural meaning of that word.

In the present case the work done was not done to any existing part of the building; it was entirely new work. It involved a radical and fundamental alteration to the construction of the building as it had been before. It involved an extension of the existing building in a

D   downward direction. Such work in my view is not capable of coming within the expression " maintenance " in the ordinary and natural meaning of that word. It is conceded that, if that is right, then the work was work of alteration within the meaning of that expression in item 2 of Group 8 and is accordingly zero-rated.

For the reasons which I have given, I agree with decision of Drake J. that the value added tax tribunal was wrong in law and their decision

E   should be set aside on that ground. I would dismiss the appeal.

ACKNER L.J. I agree. To my mind this appeal raises a short question of law, viz., whether on the true construction of the relevant section of and Schedule to the Finance Act 1972, as applied to the undisputed facts in this case, there was a zero-rated supply of service.

F   Value added tax was imposed by the Finance Act 1972. Section 12 provides that the supply of certain specified goods and services shall be treated as a taxable supply, and yet no tax shall be charged on those goods and services. The goods and services which are zero-rated are specified in Schedule 4 to the Act, and it is Group 8 of that Schedule, which is headed " Construction of Buildings, etc.," with which we are concerned. Item 2 is the relevant one, and that reads:

G   " The supply, in the course of the construction, alteration or demolition of any building or of any civil engineering work, of any services other than the services of an architect, surveyor or any person acting as consultant or in a supervisory capacity."

I agree with Lord Denning M.R. that the word " alterations " has no limit placed upon it. The particular item to my mind covers the

H   three phases in the life of the building: its birth—namely, its construction; its continued existence; and, finally, its demolition. I therefore respectfully do not agree with Neill J.'s decision in Customs and Excise Commissioners v. Morrison Dunbar Ltd. [1979] S.T.C. 406, 413, but I accept that that part of his judgment is not necessary for the decision in this case. What occurred here was clearly structural alterations.

Section 46 (2) of the Act of 1972 is an odd provision because it

provides that Schedule 4 should be "interpreted in accordance with A
the notes contained" in the Schedule; and the relevant note, which
is note (2), as varied by the Value Added Tax (Consolidation) Order
1976, provides: "Item 2 does not include—(a) any work of repair or
maintenance;. . ."

The issue therefore is, was the alteration, which is the subject
matter of this appeal, properly described as work of maintenance, it
being accepted that that tribunal reached the correct conclusion that it B
was not work of repair.

The agreed facts are very short. I take them from the value added
tax tribunal's decision. The underpinning was properly defined as
being "New and permanent support for an existing structure so as to
increase the load-bearing capacity of a building." It consisted in the
construction of an additional foundation to a structure, which already C
existed. The method adopted by A.C.T. improved its load-bearing
capacity by the construction of a further foundation beneath an existing
foundation. No work was carried out on the existing foundations.

I have no hesitation in concluding, having regard to the nature,
scale and effect of this work, that it was not work of maintenance in
the ordinary accepted sense of that word. On the agreed facts it is D
easy to imagine the substance of the expert advice which A.C.T. would
have given to the building owners. They would have said in effect.
"It is useless to try and carry out any work on the existing foundations of these houses. You would only be throwing good money after
bad. You need to put in an entirely new foundation."

Mr. Brown submits that if you carry out work which is designed
to safeguard the building from future deterioration, that is main- E
tenance. I cannot accept that such a test could be conclusive. I
respectfully agree with the example referred to by Brandon L.J. in relation to the pitch roof which takes the place of a flat roof. Equally,
the first-time provision of a damp proof course, which the commissioners in their own booklet accept is not maintenance. I think there
is force in Mr. Beloff's submissions that, without entering into the F
realms of definition, maintenance generally involves the following
characteristics: first, an element of repetition, because the object is to
keep the building in the condition in which it started; secondly, that
the work is generally speaking foreseeable, whereas this was
dramatically unforeseeable; thirdly, again generally speaking, that the
work is of a minor character and habitual, although naturally there are
exceptions as in the case of roof works; fourthly, that generally G
speaking in maintenance one does not add something substantial which
is new; and, lastly, that you do not in ordinary maintenance make a
substantial improvement to that which you maintain. Significantly
here it is not the omission of any one of those characteristics which is
of particular importance; it is the omission of all those characteristics.

The landlord and tenant authorities seem clearly to establish that H
the provision of an entirely new foundation cannot be considered as
work of maintenance. In none of those cases was there any attempt
to construe the word "maintain" in other than its ordinary sense.
Drake J. [1979] 1 W.L.R. 870, 874–875, correctly placed some reliance
upon those cases, although he properly said that caution is required
because of the fact that landlord and tenant cases are dealing with
positive obligations on the tenants and involve on occasions considera-

The Weekly Law Reports, January 23, 1981

59

1 W.L.R.   A.C.T. Construction v. Customs & Excise (C.A.)   Ackner L.J.

A tion of the condition of the premises in question at the date of the demise.

I too would affirm the decision of Drake J. and accordingly dismiss this appeal.

Appeal dismissed with costs.
Leave to appeal refused.

B

Solicitors: *Solicitor, Customs and Excise ; Herbert Smith & Co.*

A. H. B.

December 18. The Appeal Committee of the House of Lords (Lord Wilberforce, Lord Edmund-Davies and Lord Keith of Kinkel) allowed
C a petition by the commissioners for leave to appeal.

—————

D
[CHANCERY DIVISION]

* CLARK (INSPECTOR OF TAXES) *v.* OCEANIC
CONTRACTORS INC.

1980   July 21, 22; 29   Dillon J.

E *Revenue—Income tax—P.A.Y.E.—Exploration work in designated areas of North Sea—Non-resident employer—Employees work-ing in both United Kingdom and foreign sectors of North Sea—Whether employees' duties carried on in United Kingdom —Whether P.A.Y.E. provisions applicable to employer— Income and Corporation Taxes Act 1970 (c. 10), s. 204 (1)* [1] *—Finance Act 1973 (c. 51), s. 38 (4) (6)* [2]

F   The taxpayer company, a wholly owned subsidiary of an American company, was not resident in the United Kingdom for tax purposes. From an operating base in Antwerp it carried on activities installing platforms and laying pipelines in the United Kingdom and Norwegian sectors of the North Sea. Under the provisions of the Continental Shelf Act 1964 rights in "designated" areas of the United Kingdom sector of the North Sea were vested in the Crown and were exercisable under licences from the Crown. In 1977 the taxpayer company
G employed 400 men, both British and foreign, to work in its exploration activities operating from barges that were at times positioned in the United Kingdom sector and at times in the Norwegian sector of the North Sea. Those employees were paid, under contracts not governed by United Kingdom law, in United States currency by cheque from the taxpayer company's office in Brussels. No P.A.Y.E. deductions in respect of Schedule E income tax were made by the taxpayer
H company when making those payments. A determination was made by the inspector of taxes that £2,033,254 was payable by the taxpayer company to the collector of taxes in respect of income tax that it was required by section 204 of the Income and Corporation Taxes Act 1970 to deduct from the payents it made to its North Sea employees during the fiscal year 1977–78. The special commissioners allowed an appeal

[1] Income and Corporation Taxes Act 1970. s. 204 (1): see post, pp. 63H—64A.
[2] Finance Act 1973, s. 38: see post, pp. 62E—63A.

Clark v. Oceanic Contractors Inc. (Ch.D.)   **[1981]**

A

by the taxpayer company against the determination, holding
that the employment was not within the United Kingdom and
section 204 therefore had no application.

On appeal by the Crown: —

Held, allowing the appeal, that the requirement to deduct
Schedule E tax, under section 204 (1) of the Income and
Corporation Taxes Act 1970, applied whenever the duties of
the employment were carried on within the United Kingdom
and for that purpose it was immaterial where the employer
was resident and whether or not the employees were paid
abroad; that although the " designated areas " in the United
Kingdom sector of the North Sea were not part of the United
Kingdom, the provisions of section 38 (4) and (6) of the
Finance Act 1973 were consistent with treating exploration
activities in such areas as trade carried on in the United
Kingdom and, accordingly, section 204 should be construed
as requiring the taxpayer company to deduct Schedule E
income tax from payments made to their employees working
in the designated areas (post, pp. 66D—67A).

Ex parte Blain (1879) 12 Ch.D. 522, C.A.; *In re Pearson*
[1892] 2 Q.B. 263, C.A. and *Hardwick Game Farm* v. *Suffolk
Agricultural Poultry Producers Association* [1969] 2 A.C. 31,
H.L.(E.) considered.

B

C

The following cases are referred to in the judgment:

E

Beevers v. *Mason* (1979) 37 P. & C.R. 452, C.A.
Blain, Ex parte (1879) 12 Ch.D. 522, C.A.
Colquhoun v. *Heddon* (1890) 25 Q.B.D. 129; 2 T.C. 621, C.A.
Draper (C. E. B.) & Son Ltd. v. *Edward Turner & Son Ltd.* [1965]
    1 Q.B. 424; [1964] 3 W.L.R. 783; [1964] 3 All E.R. 148, C.A.
Hardwick Game Farm v. *Suffolk Agricultural Poultry Producers Associa-
tion* [1969] 2 A.C. 31; [1968] 3 W.L.R. 110; [1968] 2 All E.R. 444,
H.L.(E.).
Pearson, In re [1892] 2 Q.B. 263, C.A.
Rhokana Corporation Ltd. v. *Inland Revenue Commissioners* [1938] A.C.
    380; [1938] 2 All E.R. 51; 21 T.C. 552, H.L.(E.).
Whitney v. *Inland Revenue Commissioners* [1926] A.C. 37; 10 T.C. 88,
    H.L.(E.).

E

F

The following additional cases were cited in argument:

Colquhoun v. *Brooks* (1889) 14 App.Cas. 493; 2 T.C. 490, H.L.(E.).
Kenmare (Countess of) v. *Inland Revenue Commissioners* [1958] A.C.
    267; [1957] 3 W.L.R. 461; [1957] 3 All E.R. 33, H.L.(E.).
Robson v. *Dixon* [1972] 1 W.L.R. 1493; [1972] 3 All E.R. 671; 48 T.C.
    527.
Stokes v. *Bennett* [1953] Ch. 566; [1953] 3 W.L.R. 170; [1953] 2 All
    E.R. 313.
Theophile v. *Solicitor-General* [1950] A.C. 186; [1950] 1 All E.R. 405,
    H.L.(E.).
Westminster Bank Executor and Trustee Co. (Channel Islands) Ltd. v.
    National Bank of Greece S.A. [1971] A.C. 945; [1971] 2 W.L.R. 105;
    [1971] 1 All E.R. 233; 46 T.C. 472, H.L.(E.).

G

H

CASE STATED by the Commissioners for the Special Purposes of the
Income Tax Acts.

The taxpayer company, Oceanic Contractors Incorporated, a wholly
owned subsidiary of an American company, was incorporated under the
laws of Panama and was not resident in the United Kingdom for tax
purposes. Its operations extended throughout the world. In 1977 it had
approximately 400 employees engaged in its North Sea exploration

A activities who were paid from its headquarters in Brussels. The taxpayer did not operate the P.A.Y.E. provisions in relation to those North Sea employees. It appealed against a determination by the inspector of taxes under regulation 29 of the Income Tax (Employments) Regulations 1973 (S.I. 1973 No. 334) that tax amounting to £2,033,254 was payable by it to the collector of taxes under regulation 26 of those Regulations for the year 1977–78. The commissioners allowed the appeal holding that
B section 204 of the Income and Corporation Taxes Act 1970 did not apply to the circumstances of the case. The Crown appealed.

The facts are set out in the judgment.

P. V. Baker Q.C. and *Peter Gibson* for the Crown.
Frank Heyworth Talbot Q.C. and *John Gardiner* for the taxpayer
C company.

Cur. adv. vult.

July 29. DILLON J. read the following judgment. This is an appeal by the Crown against a decision of the special commissioners. The special commissioners held that the taxpayer company, Oceanic Contractors
D Incorporated, which is a foreign company, is not liable to operate the P.A.Y.E. procedures of tax collection in respect of the wages of its employees engaged in exploration or exploitation activities in the United Kingdom sector of the North Sea.

The facts are fully set out in the case stated, but can be shortly summarised as follows. (1) The taxpayer company is a company in-corporated in Panama which is a wholly-owned subsidiary of an American
E company whose principal place of business is in Louisiana and whose common stock is listed on the New York Stock Exchange. (2) The taxpayer company is not resident for tax purposes in the United Kingdom. It does indeed have a design office at Wembley in Middlesex, a platform fabrication yard near Inverness and a branch in Aberdeen, but I am not concerned with its employees in these premises. It operates the P.A.Y.E.
F system in respect of those employees. (3) The taxpayer company's activities, however, which extend throughout the world, include a North Sea division whose headquarters are in Brussels and which is engaged in the installation and maintenance of platforms and the laying of pipelines thereto in both the United Kingdom and the Norwegian sectors of the North Sea. The operating base of the North Sea division is at Antwerp,
G which was selected for its practical suitability as a port. Oceanic has derrick barges, pipe-laying barges and other vessels which work out of Antwerp for a six month operational season in the North Sea in each. year. In the winter these vessels return to Antwerp for maintenance. Maintenance workers, who continue to maintain the vessels throughout the winter, have 12 month contracts, but the construction workers who put together and lay the pipelines are normally engaged for a season of
H 180 days only. (4) Approximately 60 per cent. of those employed by the North Sea division are United Kingdom nationals. The remainder are citizens of other countries, principally the United States of America. There was evidence before the commissioners that since 1973 40 per cent. of the taxpayer company's activity has been in the United Kingdom sector of the North Sea as opposed to other sectors. (5) A form of service contract for employees of the North Sea division was annexed to the case stated. The particular contract annexed is with a United States

national. The only relevant difference in the case of employees of other **A**
nationalities is indicated in the case stated. The wording of the service
contract indicates, in my view, that it is intended to be governed by
United States law, and there is nothing to suggest that it is governed by
English or Scottish law. The contract provides for the employee to be
paid in United States currency by any two of the following methods
selected by the employee: that is to say, (a) deposit of a cheque in a **B**
bank designated by the employee; (b) payment of a cheque to any person
designated by the employee; and (c) payment of a cheque direct to the
employee. In practice, cheques under (a) and (b) are posted by the
taxpayer company from Brussels to the banks or designated persons
concerned, whether in England or elsewhere. Cheques under (c) are,
while the employee is engaged in operations in the North Sea, delivered
to him in his barge or vessel; he can then cash the cheque on board for **C**
dollars and spend them for his day-to-day requirements.

What I have referred to as the United Kingdom sector of the North
Sea is not part of the United Kingdom. By international treaty the
United Kingdom became entitled to exercise rights outside territorial
waters with respect to the seabed and subsoil and their natural resources
and, by section 1 of the Continental Shelf Act 1964, these rights were **D**
vested in the Crown (save in relation to coal, with which I am not
concerned). The scheme of the Act of 1964 provided for areas to be
designated as designated areas within which the rights were to be
exerciseable under licences from the Crown. It follows as a practical
matter that the activities of the taxpayer company's North Sea division,
in so far as they are carried on in the United Kingdom sector, are carried
on in these designated areas. **E**

So far as taxation is concerned, section 38 of the Finance Act, 1973
provides:

"(1) The territorial sea of the United Kingdom shall for all purposes
of income tax, capital gains tax and corporation tax (including the
following provisions of this section) be deemed to be part of the
United Kingdom. (2) . . . (a) ' exploration or exploitation activities ' **F**
means activities carried on in connection with the exploration or
exploitation of so much of the seabed and subsoil and their natural
resources as is situated in the United Kingdom or a designated area;
and . . . (e) ' designated area ' means an area designated by Order in
Council under section 1 (7) of the Continental Shelf Act 1964. (3)
Any profits or gains from exploration or exploitation activities carried **G**
on in a designated area or from exploration or exploitation rights
shall be treated for the purposes of income tax or corporation tax
as profits or gains from activities or property in the United Kingdom;
and any gains accruing on the disposal of such rights shall be treated
for the purposes of Part III of the Finance Act 1965 as gains accruing on the disposal of assets situated in the United Kingdom. (4) Any
profits or gains arising to any person not resident in the United **H**
Kingdom from exploration or exploitation activities carried on in
the United Kingdom or in a designated area . . . shall, for the
purposes of corporation tax or capital gains tax, be treated as profits
or gains of a trade, . . . carried on by that person in the United
Kingdom through a branch or agency. . . . (6) Any emoluments
from an office or employment in respect of duties performed in a
designated area in connection with exploration or exploitation

The Weekly Law Reports, January 23, 1981

63

1 W.L.R.   Clark v. Oceanic Contractors Inc. (Ch.D.)   Dillon J.

A activities shall be treated for the purposes of income tax as emoluments in respect of duties performed in the United Kingdom."

It is not in dispute that as a result of this section the taxpayer company is liable to United Kingdom tax in respect of its profit from the activities of its North Sea division in the designated areas, and the taxpayer company's employees, whether British subjects or not and whether resident
B or ordinarily resident in the United Kingdom or not, are liable to United Kingdom income tax under Schedule E in respect of their pay for their duties performed in a designated area.

Before I turn to the machinery for the collection by the P.A.Y.E. system of tax under Schedule E, I should indicate the scope of Schedule E. This is set out in section 181 of the Income and Corporation Taxes Act 1970. That section provides that tax under Schedule E " shall be
C charged in respect of any office or employment on emoluments therefrom which fall under one, or more than one, of the following " three Cases. Case I, in its present form, as amended by section 31 (3) of the Finance Act 1977, reads:

"Case I: where the person holding the office or employment is resident and ordinarily resident in the United Kingdom, any emolu-
D ments for the chargeable period, subject, however, to the deduction or exception provided for in Schedule 2 to the Finance Act1974 if the emoluments are foreign emoluments and to the deduction provided for in Schedule 7 to the Finance Act 1977 if in the chargeable period he performs the duties of the office or employment wholly or partly outside the United Kingdom; . . .".

E In the original form of section 181, Case I was worded somewhat differently and related to the position where the person holding the office or employment was resident and ordinarily resident in the United Kingdom and did not perform the duties of the office or employment wholly outside the United Kingdom. Case II applies where the person concerned " is not resident or, if resident, then not ordinarily resident in the United
F Kingdom "; and the emoluments then are " any emoluments for the chargeable period in respect of duties performed in the United Kingdom." Case III did not figure in the argument and so it is not necessary for me to read it. It is concerned, however, particularly, with emoluments received in the United Kingdom.

The P.A.Y.E. system is a scheme for the collection of tax under Schedule E. The essence of the scheme is that the burden is thrown on
G to the employer to collect the tax for the Crown by deduction from the employees' wages or salaries. Mr. Talbot stressed that Schedule E tax existed and was collected before the P.A.Y.E. system was introduced, but I do not derive any assistance from this. I do not doubt that the P.A.Y.E. system is administratively convenient for the Crown and leads to the prompt collection of very much more tax under Schedule E than would
H otherwise be collectable. The legislative authority for the operation of the P.A.Y.E. system is section 204 of the Act of 1970. Subsection (1) reads:

"On the making of any payment of, or on account of, any income assessable to income tax under Schedule E, income tax shall, subject to and in accordance with regulations made by the Board under this section, be deducted or repaid by the person making the payment, notwithstanding that when the payment is made no assessment has

been made in respect of the income and notwithstanding that the A
income is in whole or in part income for some year of assessment
other than the year during which the payment is made."

There is then provision for regulations to provide the machinery, and
these regulations are to have effect notwithstanding anything in the Income
Tax Acts.

The primary question in this appeal is as to how far section 204 is B
applicable in a case with a foreign element. Mr. Talbot took his stand on
the principles stated in *Ex parte Blain* (1879) 12 Ch.D. 522, where, at
p. 526, James L.J. speaks of

"the broad, general, universal principle that English legislation,
unless the contrary is expressly enacted or so plainly implied as to
make it the duty of an English court to give effect to an English C
statute, is applicable only to English subjects or to foreigners who by
coming into this country, whether for a long or a short time, have
made themselves during that time subject to English jurisdiction."

In the same case Cotton L.J. said, at p. 531:

"I take it the limitation is this, that all laws of the English Parliament
must be territorial—territorial in this sense, that they apply to and D
bind all subjects of the Crown who come within the fair interpretation
of them, and also all aliens who come to this country, and who,
during the time they are here, do any act which, on a fair interpretation of the statute as regards them, comes within its provisions."

Ex parte Blain was concerned with bankruptcy law, but the principles
which I have cited were stated by Fry L.J. in *In re Pearson* [1892] 2 Q.B. E
263, 268, to be of general application, and they were in fact applied to the
construction of a taxing Act in *Colquhoun* v. *Heddon* (1890) 25 Q.B.D.
129, 135. Therefore, said Mr. Talbot, section 204 does not apply to
these North Sea activities of the taxpayer company.

For the Crown Mr. Baker's primary argument was that the wide,
general words of section 204 are to be given their full natural meaning, F
and the only territorial limitation is that provided by the scope of Schedule
E itself. Thus, under Case II of Schedule E a person who is not resident
and not ordinarily resident in the United Kingdom is only liable to tax
under Schedule E on his emoluments in respect of duties performed in the
United Kingdom. Accordingly, a French employer, for instance, would
not be required to operate the P.A.Y.E. system in respect of wages paid G
to his French employees in France for their service in France because such
wages are not subject to Schedule E tax. Mr. Baker pointed to *Whitney*
v. *Inland Revenue Commissioners* [1926] A.C. 37, where, although *Ex
parte Blain* and *Colquhoun* v. *Heddon* were cited, the House of Lords
held, affirming the Court of Appeal, that the term "any individual" in
the section of the Income Tax Act 1918 which imposed super tax, included
a foreign national domiciled and resident abroad, who was thus liable to H
super tax on his income from property in the United Kingdom although
not (because it was outside Schedule D and so not part of his total income
for tax purposes) on income from property outside the United Kingdom.

The difficulty about this wide construction of section 204 is that it
would mean that a foreign employer who employed abroad a person who
was resident and ordinarily resident in the United Kingdom—for instance,
if a young man, to gain experience, took employment for some months

The Weekly Law Reports, January 30, 1981

65

1 W.L.R.   Clark v. Oceanic Contractors Inc. (Ch.D.)   Dillon J.

A with an American bank in New York, or a British engineer worked for some months on a project in an Arab state—the foreign employer would be under a statutory duty to operate the P.A.Y.E. scheme in respect of the employee's emoluments and to account to the Crown here for United Kingdom tax payable by the employee under Case I of Schedule E. Slightly less stark difficulties would have arisen under Case I in its original

B form, and there could also be problems of applying P.A.Y.E. to a foreign employer in respect of emoluments falling within Case III. I cannot conceive that it was the intention of Parliament to throw such liabilities on to foreign employers in respect of businesses not in any sense carried on within the United Kingdom or connected with the United Kingdom. I cannot believe that it is a correct construction of section 204 that it should

C extend to foreign employers in such circumstances.

By contrast, as one of the ways of putting the taxpayer company's case, Mr. Talbot drew my attention to Lord Denning M.R.'s reference in *C. E. B. Draper & Son Ltd.* v. *Edward Turner & Son Ltd.* [1965] 1 Q.B. 424, 432, to " the general rule that an Act of Parliament only applies to transactions within the United Kingdom and not to transactions outside."

D He submitted that the relevant transaction for the purposes of section 204 was the making of a payment of income and that the payments were made in Brussels where the cheques were posted, and where any deduction from emoluments would be effected.

In *Rhokana Corporation Ltd.* v. *Inland Revenue Commissioners* [1938] A.C. 380, 399, Lord Maugham referred to the well known common

E law rule that where a cheque is sent in payment of a debt the date of payment, if the cheque is duly met, is the date when the cheque was posted. The decision of the Court of Appeal in *Beevers* v. *Mason* (1979) 37 P. & C.R. 452 is to the same effect. If the payment is made at the time when the cheque is posted, it seems to me that it must follow that the payment is made in the country where the cheque is posted and not

F in a country which the cheque did not reach until a later date. I do not see any significant distinction between alternative (a) in the service agreement, the deposit of a cheque in a bank designated by the employee, and alternative (b), the payment of a cheque direct to any person designated by the employee. In either case what was envisaged and done was that the cheque was sent by post from the administrative headquarters of the North Sea division in Brussels to the bank or person concerned. Deposit

G merely indicates that the cheque was to be sent to the bank for the account for the employee, rather than for the bank's own benefit.

I therefore agree with Mr. Talbot that the payments by cheque made by the taxpayer company under alternatives (a) and (b) are to be regarded as made in Brussels and not in the United Kingdom. But that does not, in my judgment, solve the problem. Lord Denning M.R. in *C. E. B.*

H *Draper & Son Ltd.* v. *Edward Turner & Son Ltd.* [1965] 1 Q.B. 424 was not laying down a new rule. He was merely stating, in the wording which he considered appropriate to the case before him, the well-established rule which had been enunciated in such cases as *Ex parte Blain*, 12 Ch.D. 522 and *Colquhoun* v. *Heddon*, 25 Q.B.D. 129. That, however, is merely a rule of construction and not a rule of law. In other words, it is merely a factor to be taken into account to a greater or lesser extent, and in whatever way may in the circumstances be appropriate, when the court A has to construe apparently general wording in a statute of the United Kingdom Parliament. It is the statute which has to be construed, and the rule, such as it is, is merely an aid to reaching the right construction of the statute. In fact, the decision of the Court of Appeal in *Draper's* case was overruled by the House of Lords in *Hardwick Game Farm* v. *Suffolk Agricultural Poultry Producers Association* [1969] 2 A.C. 31, and a different construction of the relevant statute was adopted by a majority B of the House. The test which had been adopted by the Court of Appeal in *Draper's* case was regarded by Lord Pearce in the *Hardwick Game Farm* case at p. 120 as " too whimsical a test." It seems to me that much the same comment is warranted by Mr. Talbot's suggestion that whether section 204 is to be applied depends solely on whether the payment of the relevant emolument is technically made in the United Kingdom or over- C seas by despatch to the United Kingdom. If Mr. Talbot were right, the P.A.Y.E. system would not have to be operated by a foreign employer who ran a factory in England if he paid his employees by posting their cheques to them from abroad, but might have to be operated if he paid them by bank telegraphic transfer or telex from abroad.

It seems to me that section 204 must apply where the duties of the D office or employment are carried out within the United Kingdom, whether the employer is foreign or not and whatever method be adopted for paying the emoluments for those duties. An employer who comes to this country and carries on a business here must comply with domestic tax law require- ments such as section 204. Now the designated areas in the United Kingdom sector of the North Sea are not part of the United Kingdom. E They are, however, not part of the territory of any other state, either. The distinction is drawn in section 38 of the Finance Act 1973. Sub- section (1) provides that the territorial sea of the United Kingdom is to be deemed to be part of the United Kingdom, but this subsection does not refer to the designated areas. Subsection (4) refers to activities carried on " in the United Kingdom or in a designated area." Section 38 (4) and (6) F are consistent in treating exploration or exploitation activities in a designated area as being a trade carried on in the United Kingdom and in treating emoluments in respect of duties performed in a designated area in connection with exploration or exploitation activities as emoluments in respect of duties performed in the United Kingdom. It was in my judgment competent to the United Kingdom Parliament to enact such G provisions. The rights which the Crown has in the seabed and subsoil and their natural resources provide an ample link between these designated areas and the jurisdiction of the Parliament of the United Kingdom, and I can accordingly see no reason, on the basis of *Ex parte Blain* or otherwise, why section 204 should be construed so as not to extend to emoluments H in respect of duties performed in a designated area. This is in no way inconsistent with the court's approach in the *Hardwick Game Farm* case.

On the contrary, the direction in section 38 (6) of the Act of 1973 that these emoluments are to be treated for the purposes of income tax as emoluments in respect of duties performed in the United Kingdom, appears to me to include the purposes of collection, and not merely assess- ment, of income tax, and thus to underline that section 204 does apply

1 W.L.R.   **Clark v. Oceanic Contractors Inc. (Ch.D.)**   **Dillon J.**

A to these emoluments. I accordingly conclude that the special commissioners were wrong in law, and this appeal should be allowed.

> *Appeal allowed with costs.*
> *Case remitted to commissioners for*
> *determination of amount payable.*

B
Solicitors: *Solicitor of Inland Revenue; Slaughter & May.*

[Reported by MRS. HARRIET DUTTON, Barrister-at-Law]

C

[QUEEN'S BENCH DIVISION]

* NATIONAL WESTMINSTER BANK LTD. *v.* STOCKMAN

D
1980   Aug. 18
                                                               Russell J.

*Execution—Charging order on land—Trust for sale—Judgment
debtor and his wife holding property under trust for sale—
Whether judgment creditor entitled to have order imposed on
judgment debtor's beneficial interest—Charging Orders Act
1979 (c. 53), s. 2*

E
Section 2 of the Charging Orders Act 1979 provides:
" (1) . . . a charge may be imposed by a charging order
only on—(*a*) any interest held by the debtor beneficially—
(i) in any asset of a kind mentioned in subsection (2)
below, or (ii) under any trust; . . ."
On August 30, 1978, the plaintiffs obtained judgment against
the defendant for £11,604 together with costs. By June 1980,
the judgment remained unsatisfied and the plaintiffs applied
for a charging order to be made over the defendant's interest
F
in his matrimonial home that he held jointly with his wife
under the terms of a trust for sale. The application for the
order was refused by a Queen's Bench master on the ground
that the provisions of section 2 of the Charging Order Act
1979 did not enable the order to be made.
On appeal by the plaintiffs: —
Held, allowing the appeal, that the effect of section 2 (1)
of the Act was to extend the availability of charging orders to
G
cover cases where the interest sought to be charged was a
beneficial interest in the proceeds of sale of land held under
a trust for sale; and that, accordingly, the plaintiffs were
entitled to have an order imposed on the defendant's interest in
the house.
Irani Finance Ltd. v. *Singh* [1971] Ch. 59, C.A. distinguished.

H
The following case is referred to in the judgment:

Irani Finance Ltd. v. *Singh* [1971] Ch. 59; [1970] 3 W.L.R. 330; [1970]
3 All E.R. 199, C.A.

No additional cases were cited in argument.

APPEAL from Master Ritchie.
On August 30, 1978, the plaintiffs, National Westminster Bank Ltd.,

The Weekly Law Reports, January 30, 1981

68

Nat. West. Bank v. Stockman (Q.B.D.)   [1981]

obtained judgment of £11,604 and costs of £49 against the defendant, **A** Hugh Stockman. The judgment debt remained unsatisfied and by June 16, 1980, together with interest, it amounted to £13,764. The plaintiffs applied to Master Ritchie for a charging order to be imposed on the defendant's beneficial interest in 12, Priory Gardens, Old Basing, Basingstoke. On June 19, 1980, Master Ritchie refused the plaintiffs' ex parte application for a charging order nisi to be imposed on the defendant's beneficial interest in 12, Priory Gardens. **B**

The plaintiffs appealed against the refusal. On July 11, 1980, Mustill J. ordered that the notice of appeal be served on the defendant. The appeal was heard in chambers, Russell J. delivering judgment in open court.

The facts are set out in the judgment.

C

G. A. Mann for the plaintiffs.
D. G. M. Marks for the defendant.

RUSSELL J. This is an appeal against the refusal of Master Ritchie to make a charging order nisi in respect of property at 12, Priory Gardens, Old Basing, Basingstoke. The plaintiffs obtained judgment against the defendant in default of defence in the sum of £11,604·10 together **D** with costs, on August 30, 1978. The ex parte application for the order nisi was dismissed by the master on June 19, 1980. I was told that apparently he was not satisfied that the provisions of the Charging Orders Act 1979 and in particular section 2 of that Act, enabled the order to be made. On July 11, 1980, the matter came on appeal before Mustill J. who ordered that notice of appeal should be served on the defendant. **E** Consequently I have had the advantage of argument from Mr. Marks on behalf of the defendant as well as from Mr. Mann on behalf of the plaintiffs.

The facts can be stated very shortly. The judgment was in respect of moneys owing by the defendant to the plaintiffs in an overdrawn bank account. The defendant's matrimonial home was held by him and his wife, as so often happens, under a trust for sale. The conveyance of **F** the house to the defendant and his wife was a conveyance to them as joint tenants both legally and beneficially.

I have been referred to section 35 of the Administration of Justice Act 1956 and to the judgments of the Court of Appeal in *Irani Finance Ltd.* v. *Singh* [1971] Ch. 59. Section 35 (1) of the Act of 1956 provided:

> " The High Court and any county court may, for the purpose of **G** enforcing a judgment or order of those courts respectively for the payment of money to a person, by order impose on any such land or interest in land of the debtor as may be specified in the order a charge for securing the payment of any moneys due or to become due under the judgment or order . . . ."

The judgment of the court in the *Irani* case, delivered by Cross L.J., **H** traced the history of charges in favour of judgment creditors on the land of judgment debtors. I need not do so. The ratio of the judgment was that the words " interest in land " to be found in section 35 did not include interests under trusts for sale of land. Such interests were not interests in land but interests in the proceeds of the sale of land. Those equitable interests, therefore, were not caught by the provisions of section 35 and no charging order could be made.

The Weekly Law Reports, January 30, 1981

69

1 W.L.R.   Nat. West. Bank v. Stockman (Q.B.D.)   Russell J.

A   Section 35 of the Act of 1956 has now been repealed by section 7 of the Charging Orders Act 1979. The short point for my consideration is whether section 2 of the Act of 1979 has removed the limitations of section 35 of the Act of 1956, as interpreted by the Court of Appeal in the *Irani* case, so as to permit charges on the interests of those, such as the defendant in the instant case, who hold real property under the terms of a trust for sale. Section 2, so far as it is relevant, provides:

B
"(1) . . . a charge may be imposed by a charging order only on— (*a*) any interest held by the debtor beneficially—(i) in any asset of a kind mentioned in subsection (2) below, or (ii) under any trust; . . . (2) The assets referred to in subsection (1) above are—(*a*) land . . ."

Is the defendant caught by these words? In my judgment it was plainly the intention of the legislature that the availability of charging
C   orders should be extended to cover cases in which the interest sought to be charged is a beneficial interest in the proceeds of sale of land held under a trust for sale. I think that that object has been achieved by the plain wording of section 2, despite the interesting arguments to the contrary advanced by Mr. Marks. There are various safeguards available to the debtor when application is made to make the order absolute
D   and to his wife whose position can be protected in the event of any application by the creditor which would have the effect of defeating the purpose for which the trust was established. These, however, are not matters before me. I shall allow the appeal and grant the charging order nisi.

E   *Appeal allowed.*
                                                      Charging order nisi.

Solicitors: *Wilde Sapte*; *Ward Bowie, Basingstoke.*

[Reported by Mrs. HARRIET DUTTON, Barrister-at-Law]

F

[COURT OF APPEAL]

G   * WYNNE *v.* WYNNE AND ANOTHER

1980 May 16   Bridge, Cumming-Bruce and Eveleigh L.JJ.

*Husband and Wife—Divorce—Ancillary relief—Court's jurisdiction
—Wife seeking order for co-respondent to file affidavit of means
—Whether jurisdiction to make order—Matrimonial Causes
Rules 1977 (S.I. 1977 No. 344 (L. 6)), r. 77 (5)*
H
By the wife's petition, the woman with whom the husband was living was made a co-respondent. In proceedings for ancillary relief, the wife issued a summons asking, inter alia, that the co-respondent file an affidavit of her means. No order was then made on that application but subsequently the husband was ordered to pay to the wife maintenance pending suit of £6,000 a year and periodical payments for each of the two children of £3,300 a year. Shortly afterwards when the husband's employment was terminated, he ceased to make

A payments under the order and at a later stage the order was suspended.

The wife was granted a decree dissolving the marriage on the ground of the husband's admitted adultery: no finding was made against the co-respondent. In the proceedings for financial relief, the wife renewed her application that the co-respondent be ordered to file an affidavit of her means. The registrar refused to make the order and, on the wife's appeal, the judge, in dismissing the appeal, held that there was B no power under rule 77 (5) of the Matrimonial Causes Rules 1977 [1] to order the co-respondent to file an affidavit of means as she was not a party to the proceedings.

On appeal by the wife: —

Held, dismissing the appeal, that, although the court had jurisdiction under rule 77 (5) to order the attendance at the hearing of an application for ancillary relief of " any person " for the purpose of giving oral evidence, the power C under the latter part of the paragraph to order discovery, production of documents or require affidavits at any stage of the proceedings was limited to the parties to the lis; that the co-respondent was not a party to the proceedings for financial relief and, accordingly, the court had no jurisdiction to order her to file an affidavit of her means (post, pp. 73G–H, 74F, 76C–D, 77A–C, F).

Decision of Bush J. affirmed.

D

The following cases are referred to in the judgment of Bridge L.J.:

West v. *West*, The Times, December 16, 1972, Brandon J.
W. v. *W.* (unreported), October 11, 1979, Booth J.

No additional cases were cited in argument.

E

APPEAL from Bush J.

By her petition of May 25, 1978, for a decree of judicial separation, the wife alleged that the husband had committed adultery with the co-respondent. She subsequently amended her petition to pray for a decree dissolving the marriage. In the proceedings for maintenance pending suit, she issued a summons dated October 12, 1978, for an order that the F husband make a list of all documents relevant to the application and verify that list by affidavit. She also asked that the co-respondent be ordered to make and file an affidavit of her means. No order was made requiring the co-respondent to file an affidavit and, on March 16, 1979, the husband was ordered to pay the wife maintenance pending suit at the rate of £6,000 a year and to make periodical payments for the G two children.

On May 24, 1979, the wife was granted a decree nisi on the admitted adultery of the husband but no finding was made against the co-respondent. On September 3, the husband was ordered to make interim periodical payments to the wife at the rate of £6,000 a year and the decree was made absolute on September 14.

Shortly after the order for maintenance pending suit had been made H in March 1979, the husband's employment was terminated and by August 1979 he ceased to make any payments under that order. He applied for a variation of that order and the wife issued a judgment summons. On November 8 the orders in respect of periodical payments for the wife of September 3 and for the children of March 3 were

[1] Matrimonial Causes Rules 1977, r. 77 (5): see post, p. 73A–B.

A suspended and on November 14 the judgment summons was adjourned generally.

The wife renewed her application for an order that the co-respondent file an affidavit of her means. Mr. Registrar Kenworthy dismissed the application and, on appeal, Bush J. held on February 22, 1980, that he had no jurisdiction under rule 77 (5) of the Matrimonial Causes Rules 1977 to order a co-respondent, who was not a party to the proceedings, B to file an affidavit.

The wife appealed on the grounds that the judge misdirected himself in holding (1) that the High Court had no power to order the co-respondent to file an affidavit of means where her means were relevant to a wife's application for ancillary relief; (2) that no power was given to the registrar or judge of the Family Division by the Matrimonial C Causes Rules 1977 or otherwise to order the co-respondent to file an affidavit of means; and (3) that the final words of rule 77 (5) of the Rules related solely to further affidavits being filed by parties to the application for ancillary relief and did not refer to affidavits by a co-respondent.

The facts are stated in the judgment of Bridge L.J.

D   *Joseph Jackson Q.C.* and *J. J. Davis* for the wife.
   John Samuels for the husband.
   J. P. Harris Q.C. and *Christopher Sumner* for the co-respondent.

BRIDGE L.J. This is an appeal from an order of Bush J. made on February 22, 1980, dismissing an appeal from Mr. Registrar Kenworthy E on December 27, 1979, whereby he refused an application by the petitioner wife in the course of ancillary proceedings for financial relief against the respondent husband, for an order that the lady co-respondent should file an affidavit of her means.

As the sole point in the appeal is whether the court has jurisdiction to make such an order as that which the petitioner wife was seeking, it will be possible to deal with the matter quite shortly. Both the F registrar and the judge held that there was no such jurisdiction. It is against the judge's decision to that effect that the present appeal is brought.

The parties are American. They were married in June 1960 in the United States. There are two children, sons, born in 1966 and 1968. The parties have lived in England since 1967—since 1972 in Maida G Vale. In February 1978 the husband left the wife and set up house with the co-respondent in Knightsbridge. On May 25, 1978, the wife petitioned initially for judicial separation on the ground of her husband's adultery. In due course the petition was amended to seek dissolution of marriage and on May 24, 1979, a decree nisi was pronounced on the husband's admitted adultery, albeit with no finding of adultery proved against the co-respondent. The decree was made absolute on September H 14, 1979.

At the time when the parties separated, the husband was in lucrative employment and, when that state of affairs still subsisted on March 16, 1979, Mr. Registrar Kenworthy made an order for maintenance pending suit in favour of the wife in the sum of £6,000 a year and in favour of each child in the sum of £3,300 a year. Very shortly after that order was made, the husband's employment was terminated in circumstances which have aroused considerable suspicion on the part of the wife and

her advisers. The husband continued to comply with the order for **A**
maintenance for a time but ceased, I think, in about August 1979. On
November 8, 1979, an order was made suspending payment as from
October 1, 1979. Meanwhile the husband continued to live in Knightsbridge with the co-respondent in an extremely luxurious house or apart-
ment. He says that these premises belong to his former employers and
that he is under threat of eviction from them but so far that threat has **B**
not materialised. The wife's case is that he is being supported to a
substantial extent by the co-respondent who herself has a business which
she carries on.

The basis of the application for an order that the co-respondent
should make an affidavit of her means is that her means would be
relevant to two questions which, in the wife's application for ancillary
relief, the court will have to consider under section 25 (1) (*a*) and (*b*) of **C**
the Matrimonial Causes Act 1973, namely, the income and earning
capacity, property and other financial resources which each of the
parties to the marriage has or is likely to have in the foreseeable future
and the financial needs, obligations and responsibilities which each of
the parties to the marriage has or is likely to have in the foreseeable
future.   **D**

When the wife's application for the order in dispute was originally
made, it was made on the basis that she was entitled to know what the
co-respondent's means were in order to minimise any suggestion that
might be made by the husband that she was a burden to him. Now the
position is reversed and it is now contended that the relevance of the
co-respondent's means is to show the extent to which she is able to
support—and is in fact supporting or contributing to the support of—the **E**
husband.

In the end, the issue of jurisdiction raises a short point on the construction of the Matrimonial Causes Rules 1977. It is to those rules
that I now turn. By rule 73 (2) and (3) it is provided:

" (2) Where a respondent or a petitioner is served with a notice in
Form 11 or 13 in respect of an application for ancillary relief, not **F**
being an application to which rule 74 or 75 applies "—I interpose
that this is not such an application—" then, unless the parties are
agreed upon the terms of the proposed order, he shall, within 14
days after service of the notice, file an affidavit in answer to the
application containing full particulars of his property and income . . .
(3) Within 14 days after service of any affidavit under paragraph (2) **G**
or within such other time as the court may fix, the applicant
shall file an affidavit in reply containing full particulars of his property and income."

So the effect of that rule is that, as soon as proceedings are instituted
for ancillary financial relief, both spouses are under an obligation, within
the stated limits of time, under the rule to file affidavits containing **H**
" full particulars " of their property and income.

I do not think I need refer to anything in rules 74 or 75, which, as
I have said, are not applicable to the present case and I can go straight
on to rule 77 and read paragraphs (4) and (5):

" (4) Any party to an application for ancillary relief may by letter
require any other party to give further information concerning any
matter contained in any affidavit filed by or on behalf of that other

A   party or any other relevant matter, or to furnish a list of relevant documents or to allow inspection of any such document, and may, in default of compliance by such other party, apply to the registrar for directions."

Then we come to what is in the end the crucial paragraph:

B   " (5) At the hearing of an application for ancillary relief the registrar shall, subject to rules 78, 79, 80 and 81, investigate the allegations made in support of and in answer to the application, and may take evidence orally and may order the attendance of any person for the purpose of being examined or cross-examined, and may at any stage of the proceedings order the discovery and production of any document or require further affidavits."

C   Before approaching the construction of paragraph (5) on which in the end this appeal turns, it is right that I should refer to two decided cases which have been drawn to our attention by Mr. Jackson for the wife. *West* v. *West* is reported very shortly in *The Times*, December 16, 1972. It was a case where a dissolution was sought on the ground of five years' separation and was opposed by the wife on the ground of

D grave financial hardship. The report records that the judge in the course of the proceedings made an order that an affidavit should be made by the lady with whom the husband was then living disclosing her income and financial resources. There is nothing to indicate that the court was presented with any argument on the rule which then applied which was in similar terms, so far as material, to the rule with which

E we are concerned, to the effect that under the rule there was no jurisdiction in the judge to make such an order as he did make.

    A much more recent decision was by Booth J. in *W.* v. *W.* (unreported), October 11, 1979, where she was asked to make—and did make—an order at the instance of the first wife that the petitioner husband's second wife, whom he had married since the divorce proceedings, should make an affidavit of her means. In that case the hus-

F band was not represented by counsel. Although the judge pays tribute to the skill with which he had presented his case, it again does not appear from the judgment, of which we have a transcript, that the point of jurisdiction now raised before us was canvassed there. What was canvassed there was the question as to whether the affidavit of means which the first wife was seeking from the second wife was one

G which would properly be relevant. The judge resolved that question affirmatively and therefore made the order requiring it.

    I do not regard either of those cases, which would not in any event, of course, be binding on this court, as having much—if any—significance in throwing light on the point which we are called on to decide since, as I have indicated, it does not appear that in either of them the point was argued. It is, of course, perfectly clear from the language of

H rule 77 (5) of the Matrimonial Causes Rules 1977 that when it comes to the effective hearing of this wife's claim for ancillary financial relief the co-respondent can be ordered to attend and to give evidence, to be examined or cross-examined, but the critical question is whether the concluding words of the rule on their true construction permit an order to be made now that she should make an affidavit of her means. I will read those concluding words again. They follow the comma after the word " cross-examined ": ". . . and may at any stage of the

proceedings order the discovery and production of any document or A
require further affidavits." It is to be observed that rule 77 (5) falls
into two parts because the whole of the paragraph down to the word
" cross-examined " is concerned with the proceedings at the hearing
of the application, whereas the concluding words, which I have just
re-read, are, as they expressly state, concerned with the power of the
court exercisable at any stage of the proceedings.

B

Having been much assisted by the argument of counsel on both
sides, in the end I have reached a clear conclusion in this matter that
the registrar and the judge were right in the view that they reached
that they had no jurisdiction to order an affidavit to be made by the
co-respondent in this case. Mr. Jackson has put his argument boldly
on the footing that rule 77 (5) gives power to the court to order an
affidavit to be made by any third party—any person, that is to say, who C
is not a party to the proceedings. In a subsidiary argument he did rely
on the circumstance that this co-respondent was a party to the suit. In
my judgment that really is quite irrelevant. Apart from the fact that
there was no finding against her in the suit, on any view she cannot
properly be regarded as a party to the lis which is involved in ancillary
proceedings for financial relief. So, in my judgment, Mr. Jackson is D
right to put his argument on the broad proposition that the rule empowers an order to be made against any stranger requiring that stranger
to make an affidavit, because only if it is so widely construed is it
available for the purpose for which it is invoked in this case.

I think the reasons which have brought me to the conclusion that
the registrar and the judge were right in giving the words of the paragraph the restrictive construction they did give them may fairly be put E
under five headings. First, it seems to me that the whole phrase:
". . . may at any stage of the proceedings order the discovery and
production of any document or require further affidavits " must be
read in the same sense. To put it conveniently in the form in which
the question was posed by Mr. Samuels for the husband, the question
is whether one should read that entire phrase as if it concluded with the F
words " from the parties " or with the words " from any person." I
have no doubt whatsoever that the power which the paragraph confers
of ordering discovery of any document must be understood as a power
which is limited to the exercise against one of the parties to the lis.

Secondly, in my judgment, one is entitled to draw a significant conclusion from the contrast between the concluding phrase of the paragraph and the phrase which immediately precedes it, because the phrase G
immediately preceding it includes the words in terms: ". . . may order
the attendance of any person for the purpose of being examined or
cross-examined." If the draftsman of the rule thought it necessary to
include that phrase " of any person " in order to make clear the breadth
and scope of the power which he was conferring, then had he intended
the same breadth and scope to attach to the power to order discovery H
and production of documents or further affidavits, I should have
expected him to say so in terms.

The third, and perhaps most significant, pointer, in my judgment, to
the proper construction of this rule lies in this consideration, that it will
only be in the rarest cases that it will be possible to say that a person
who is a stranger to the lis involved in a party's claim to ancillary
financial relief ought, in the words which are used in rule 73, as the

A spouses are required to do, to make an affidavit containing full particulars of his or her property and income. It will only be in the rarest cases where it will be possible to say that full information about the property and income of the third party, whether the third party is a new spouse, a new mistress, a new lover, a rich uncle or a mother or any other friend or relation from whom one of the spouses has expecta-
B tions, will be relevant to the issue which the court has to consider under section 25 of the Matrimonial Causes Act 1973. Indeed, at the end of the day, I do not think Mr. Jackson in this case was contending that, if the court had jurisdiction, the order which it would be appropriate to make against this co-respondent would be an order that she gave full particulars of her property and income. In his reply he formulated the order which he was suggesting would define the scope of the affidavit
C which she should be required to make, namely, that she should be required to state from February 1978—the date when she and the husband began co-habiting—what contributions she had made, in what form and from what source, to the support of the husband. But once it is recognised that if this power is a power to order strangers to the lis to make affidavits, it will, in 99 cases out of 100, be necessary carefully to define the scope of the affidavit they are required to make, one is
D really driven to recognise that so construed this is an order which empowers the court to interrogate, in advance of the hearing, a witness who is not a party to the lis. That is such an exceptional proceeding that I would need the clearest possible statutory language to drive me to the conclusion that that was what the legislature had intended.

Fourthly, it has been pointed out that, whereas only minimal
E expense, for which a witness can in any event expect to be recompensed, is involved in attending a hearing as a witness, if a witness is a stranger to the lis and is required by such an order as is suggested should be made here to make an affidavit that will almost inevitably involve that witness in incurring a good deal of expense. It is a little difficult to see that such an order can properly be made and how the witness can be
F recompensed for that expense. It may indeed be, if a witness who is required to make a full affidavit of means has complicated financial affairs on which his or her means depend, that he or she will be involved in a very large investigation in order to make full disclosure. Moreover, however carefully the terms of the order requiring the witness to make an affidavit were to be formulated, the witness would
G never under such an order enjoy the same degree of protection as he or she would enjoy giving evidence orally at the hearing against being required to disclose matters which are not really relevant. If a witness is simply ordered to attend a hearing to be examined or cross-examined, each question which is put can be the subject of objection if it is not a proper question and does not seek to elicit relevant information. A blanket order, however carefully formulated, requiring a witness to
H make an affidavit covering defined subject matter will always be in danger of requiring that witness to put in evidence in his or her affidavit more than is strictly relevant and more than is strictly necessary.

Fifthly and finally, it does seem to me that, if one looks simply at the language of these concluding words of rule 77 (5), they bear very much more naturally the restricted construction for which Mr. Harris and Mr. Samuels have contended, and which the registrar and the judge adopted, than the very wide construction urged on us by Mr.

Jackson. I rely particularly on the last two words of the paragraph **A**
" further affidavits." What are the affidavits further to? Mr. Jackson
submits that " further affidavits " simply means affidavits in addition to
those which are already in evidence in the proceedings: affidavits which
may come from anybody. If that were so, I find it very difficult to see
what the purpose was of introducing the word " further." It would
have been perfectly simple to say " may require affidavits." To my **B**
mind, in carefully drafted rules such as these, one expects each word
to have its own particular significance. If I ask myself, what is the
significance of the word " further " in the phrase " require further
affidavits " at the end of rule 77 (5), I find the answer by harking back
to rule 73. Under rule 73 both the spouses have been required to
make affidavits containing full particulars of their property and income.
If those particulars were not as full as they ought to be, then further **C**
particulars of their property and income would be required and, in
order that those further particulars should be forthcoming, it is the
most natural phrase in the world to use to say those parties should be
required to make " further affidavits."

For those reasons I have come to the conclusion that the registrar
and the judge were right in the view they took here that they had no **D**
jurisdiction. I would dismiss this appeal.

CUMMING-BRUCE L.J. I agree with the order proposed by Bridge
L.J. The power that the court exercises in relation to financial provisions is to be collected from section 23 of the Matrimonial Causes
Act 1973, and the matters to which the court is to have regard under
sections 23 and 24 are to be collected from section 25 of that Act. It **E**
is perfectly clear from the words of section 25 that all the circumstances
of the case are to be regarded and matters specifically regarded as
possibly being relevant will include the financial resources which each
of the parties have or are likely to have in the foreseeable future and
their financial needs, present and in the foreseeable future. So where
one of the parties, whether the applicant or the respondent to an **F**
application for financial provision or property adjustment, is in fact
receiving support from a third party which increases his or her resources
or reduces his or her needs or, alternatively, if the party is likely to be
in that position in the foreseeable future, the facts relevant to such
present or foreseeable support or reduction of needs are relevant to the
inquiry that is imposed on the court under sections 23, 24 and 25 of **G**
the Act.

In my view, the machinery for the conduct of the investigation is
to be collected from the Matrimonial Causes Rules 1977, rules 73 and
74 and for this purpose particularly rule 77 of the Matrimonial Causes
Rules. Rule 73, as Bridge L.J. has explained, empowers the court at
the inception of the application to require of the parties the filing of the
affidavits to give full particulars of property and income. When one **H**
comes to rule 77, paragraphs (4) and (5) are the relevant paragraphs. Paragraph (4) provides for the eliciting of information from
another party, and, like Bridge L.J., I take the term " other party "
to mean parties to the lis with which the application for ancillary
relief is concerned. It does not include a third party, even though
such third party may be indirectly interested in the result. By paragraph (5) the wide power given in the last two lines to the court,

A that it: ". . . may at any stage of the proceedings order the discovery and production of any document or require further affidavits " in my view, should not be construed to give the court a power to exercise what I regard as a drastic power against strangers to the suit.

Mr. Jackson made a forceful submission that in many cases it was not practicable to do justice to an applicant or a respondent without the powers now sought. I disagree. I take the view that the first four
B lines of rule 77 (5) award the court all the necessary powers to elicit relevant evidence and to see relevant documents. Where I differ from Mr. Jackson is about the stage at which the court has the power to obtain the information and as to the method by which the information may be obtained. I cannot find in paragraph (5), as I interpret it, any power to require an affidavit from a stranger to the lis. There is
C a power on the hearing of the application to take evidence orally, to order the attendance of any person for the purpose of being examined or cross-examined and, in my view, after the exercise of such powers on the hearing of the application, the court then has the power to take such steps as are necessary with a view to ordering the production of any document.

I fully agree with the reasons given by Bridge L.J. with this qualifi-
D cation. My experience in relation to applications for financial provision is limited, but such experience as I have has led me to the view that it is not an infrequent situation for the court to need, in order to do justice, to have full information about the financial resources of third parties who are either spouses or co-habitees to a party to the suit. Where I depart from the submission of Mr. Jackson is as to the stage
E and the machinery for obtaining such information when it is necessary. In my view there is no jurisdiction either to order an affidavit of means from a stranger to the suit or to order the more limited affidavit that Mr. Jackson submitted might be more appropriate, namely, an affidavit setting out the factual quantum of support. I too would dismiss this appeal.

F   EVELEIGH L.J. I agree that the appeal should be dismissed for the five reasons stated by Bridge L.J.

> *Appeal dismissed with costs to be
> paid out of legal aid fund unless
> objection taken by Law Society.
> Legal aid taxation for wife.*

G

Solicitors: *Bernard Sheridan & Co.; Jaques & Co.; Plant, Gold & Co.*

[Reported by MISS HENRIETTA STEINBERG, Barrister-at-Law]

H

A

[COURT OF APPEAL]

* REGINA v. LAMBIE

1980   June 30;   Cumming-Bruce L.J., Stocker and Smith JJ.
         July 1; 30

B

Crime—Fraud—Obtaining pecuniary advantage by deception—
Credit card used for purchases after credit limit exceeded—
Whether representation of authority to use card—Whether shop
assistant induced by false representation to sell goods on credit
—Theft Act 1968 (c. 60), s. 16 (1)

A bank issued a credit card to the defendant, with a credit
limit of £200. On November 14, 1977, the balance owing on   C
her account was £140·38. By December 13 the balance had
risen to £921·61. On December 15 the defendant selected some
goods in a store and indicated that she wished to pay by credit
card. The shop assistant checked her signature against that on
her card, and that the card number was not on the "stop
list." As the value of the goods was within the "floor limit"
agreed between the shop and the bank the goods were then
handed over to the defendant. She was charged with obtaining   D
a pecuniary advantage by deception contrary to section 16 (1)
of the Theft Act 1968, namely, the evasion of a debt for which
she made herself liable by deception, namely by false representations that she was authorised to use a credit card to obtain
goods. She was convicted.
On the defendant's appeal against conviction: —
Held, allowing the appeal, that in order to secure a
conviction under section 16 (1) of the Theft Act 1968 the   E
prosecution had to establish that the defendant made a false
representation and that the victim acted on the strength of that
representation (post, p. 85D–E); that although use of a credit
card at a time when the credit limit had been exceeded was
evidence upon which a jury could find that there was a false
representation that the user was authorised to use the card
for that transaction, it also had to be shown that the victim
relied on that representation (post, p. 83H); that, since the   F
evidence disclosed that the shop assistant had relied solely on
the contractual relationship between the shop and the bank
issuing the credit card when supplying the defendant with
goods, there was no evidence on which the jury could find
that the defendant had obtained the pecuniary advantage by
deception (post, p. 87A–C).
Reg. v. Charles [1977] A.C. 177, H.L.(E.) distinguished.

G

The following cases are referred to in the judgment:

Reg. v. Charles [1977] A.C. 177; [1976] 3 W.L.R. 431; [1976] 3 All
     E.R. 112, H.L.(E.).
Reg. v. Kovacs [1974] 1 W.L.R. 370; [1974] 1 All E.R. 1236, C.A.

The following additional case was cited in argument: H
Reg. v. Laverty [1970] 3 All E.R. 432, C.A.

APPEAL against conviction.
On August 10, 1979, the defendant, Shiralee Ann Lambie, having
pleaded guilty at Bedford Crown Court (Judge Counsell) to an offence of
being carried in a conveyance without authority, was convicted on a count
of obtaining a pecuniary advantage by deception, in that on December 15,

A 1977, she dishonestly obtained for herself a pecuniary advantage namely the evasion of a debt for which she made herself liable by deception, namely, by false representations that she was authorised to use a Barclaycard number 4929–874–294–347 to obtain goods to the value of £10·35. She was acquitted of a similar count of obtaining the evasion of a debt of £9·70 on December 5, 1977. She was sentenced to community service orders of a total of 180 hours and her driving licence was endorsed.

B The defendant appealed against conviction on the grounds, inter alia, (1) that the judge was wrong in rejecting the submission of no case, as (a) the only representation made was that she was the person to whom the Barclaycard had been issued; (b) the prosecution evidence merely showed that she had used the card which had been issued to her; (c) the evidence did not show that any deception was operative; (2) that the judge mis-

C directed the jury as to (i) the importance of the deception being operative; (ii) the necessity for the Crown to prove (i); any inference that could be drawn that the presenter of a card had authority to enter into the transaction.

The facts are stated in the judgment.

D *John Plumstead* (assigned by the Registrar of Criminal Appeals) for the defendant.

Michael Pert and *Louise Coghlan* for the Crown.

Cur. adv. vult.

E July 30. CUMMING-BRUCE L.J. read the judgment of the court. On August 10, 1979, in the Crown Court at Bedford the defendant was arraigned on an indictment with three counts. She pleaded guilty to an offence of being carried in a conveyance taken without authority (count 3). She pleaded not guilty to two counts laid under section 16 (1) of the Theft Act 1968. In the first count she was charged:

" *Statement of Offence.*

F " Obtaining a pecuniary advantage by deception contrary to section 16 (1) of the Theft Act 1968.

" *Particulars of Offence.*

" Shiralee Ann Lambie on December 5, 1977, dishonestly obtained for herself a pecuniary advantage namely the evasion of a debt for which she made herself liable by deception namely by false representations that she was authorised to use a Barclaycard number

G 4929–874–294–347 to obtain goods to the value of £9·70."

The jury acquitted her on this count.

She was charged in the second count with an exactly similar offence, save that the date alleged was December 15, and the value of the goods was £10·35. The jury convicted on this count. She now appeals to this court.

The perfected grounds of appeal raise the question of the nature of the

H representation made by one who uses a credit card, and the question whether the deception (if any) operated upon the mind of the shop assistant who sold the goods so as to induce her to sell them on credit. These problems have not arisen for consideration in this court in the context of a credit card transaction. In *Reg.* v. *Charles* [1977] A.C. 177, this court and the House of Lords considered a series of dishonest cheque card transactions.

Mr. Plumstead, for the defendant, submits that on the evidence relevant

A

to the second count in the instant case (1) there was no evidence upon which the jury could find, in relation to the second count, that the defendant made any representation that she was authorised by the bank to use her credit card, and (2) there was no evidence upon which the jury could find that the shop assistant was induced to act upon that representation. He submits that the legal relationships between bank, credit card holder and retailer are different from those that exist in a cheque card transaction, and that this case should be distinguished from the situation that existed in *Reg.* v. *Charles.*

B

At the trial, the evidence for the prosecution consisted of unchallenged statements and exhibits put in before the committing justices and depositions taken before them. This evidence was read to the jury. No evidence was called on behalf of the defence.

C

The evidence related to four areas of primary fact: (1) the contractual relations of the bank with the defendant and with the shops concerned with counts 1 and 2; (2) the history of the defendant's transactions upon her account with the bank; (3) the events when the defendant bought the goods on December 5 from a shop called Braggins (count 1) and when she bought goods on December 15 from a shop called Mothercare (count 2); (4) the admissions by the defendant to the police. Though this appeal is only concerned with the conviction on count 2, it is necessary to refer to evidence relevant to count 1, because the summing up of the judge cannot otherwise be properly understood.

D

In April 1977 the defendant applied to the Barclaycard headquarters of Barclays Bank for a credit card. The bank agreed to grant her credit facilities up to a limit of £200. They gave her a Barclaycard, whereby the bank guaranteed to pay on her credit account up to the sum of £50 upon any single transaction by which the defendant bought goods from a retailer with whom the bank had entered into an agreement relating to sales to purchasers who presented a Barclaycard. Such shops were guaranteed payment of Barclaycard vouchers. The course of dealing between the bank and the defendant provided for the posting of a monthly statement to the defendant at the address which she had given. The statement showed the then state of her account with the bank. The credit limit continued unless and until another limit was agreed.

E

Barclays had entered into contracts with retailers, and at all material times had contracts with the two shops named in counts 1 and 2. The terms of those contracts were not strictly or comprehensively proved, but their general effect was described by a Barclays Bank investigator who had access to the records held by the Barclaycard organisation. The bank agreed to pay the shop the sums shown on a voucher signed by the credit card holder, provided that five simple conditions were complied with by the retailer. These conditions were (1) that a voucher was properly completed; (2) that the card presented is current in date; (3) that the card does not appear on the current " stop list "; (4) that the shop check the signature of the customer with the specimen signature on the card; (5) that either the transaction is individually checked and authorised by Barclaycard or the transaction falls within " the floor limit " of the shop. The last condition was explained as follows. The bank agree with retailers that any transaction above a certain figure will be individually reported to the bank, who retain power to authorise or refuse payment. In the case of Mothercare, the shop concerned in the second count, the " floor limit " was agreed at £70. But upon any single Barclaycard transaction less than £70 at Mothercare the bank agreed to pay the sum shown on the voucher without

F

G

H

A   requiring or expecting any inquiry from the shop as to the state of the
customer's account with the bank.

The object and effect of the contracts entered into between Barclays and
the retailers was to relieve the retailer of any concern with the state of the
card-holder's account with the bank, provided that the " floor limit " was
not exceeded. Upon the contract between the bank and the retailer, the
retailer agreed to pay to the bank a commission in order to enjoy the
B   bank's guarantee of payment of vouchers made out by the retailer in
compliance with the five conditions, and the convenience of being able to
trade with Barclaycard holders without any regard to the question whether
the customer is overdrawn upon her Barclays Bank account, provided only
that the " shop limit " is not exceeded. Both the witness from the bank
and the shop assistant concerned in the second count agreed that, if the
C   shop carried out its business in accordance with the five conditions, it
received something as good as cash. Barclaycard made their profits in two
ways: by charging the shops commission for the security which the Barclaycard transactions provide, and by charging customers on the money forwarded by Barclaycard. No cheque is drawn by the customer, who simply
presents a Barclaycard and signs the voucher upon which the shop assistant
has entered particulars of the transaction.

D   The defendant, then 18 years of age, received her Barclaycard in April
1977 and until November used it without exceeding her agreed credit limit
of £200. The bank sent her monthly statements showing the state of her
account. On the statement dated November 14 she was in debit of £140·38.
She then rapidly carried out a series of transactions with the result that
when she used the card in the shop called Braggins (count 1) on December
E   5 she owed the bank £553·20. The " shop limit " agreed between the bank
and Braggins was £30. The defendant used her card to buy goods for
£9·70, so there was no occasion for Braggins to concern themselves with
the customer's credit. The shop assistant concerned was Mrs. Walker.
She said: " At the time of the transaction I considered the purchaser
authorised to use the card. As far as I was concerned, the transaction was
quite straightforward." On this count the jury acquitted, probably because
F   the jury were not sure that it was proved that by December 5 the defendant
was already dishonest.

The defendant continued to use her card, without taking any step to
reduce her debit balance at the bank. She had given up her job. She had
no money save what she procured by use of her Barclaycard. By
December 13 her debit balance as recorded in Barclaycard records had
risen to £921·61. Before December 15 she knew that Barclays were
G   trying to get in touch with her, so she changed her address without
telling the bank where they could find her, and went on using the card,
largely to buy for her lover whatever he wanted, and to provide herself
and him with means of livelihood.

Against this background she carried out the transaction the subject of
the second count with which alone this appeal is concerned. She bought
H   goods in Mothercare for £10·35. She produced her Barclaycard to Miss
Rounding, the shop assistant. The " floor limit " agreed between Barclays
and Mothercare was £70, so there was no reason for Miss Rounding to
concern herself with the defendant's credit standing with the bank. Miss
Rounding checked the " stop list." The defendant's name was not on it.
The defendant signed the voucher. Miss Rounding compared the signature with that on the card and delivered the goods. The voucher was duly
dispatched by Mothercare to Barclays, and Barclays paid up, presumably

82

less the commission that had been agreed. Miss Rounding described her A
state of mind. Her evidence about it is so important that we quote what
she said in cross-examination and re-examination:

" If someone came into the shop and wanted to buy something for cash
I wouldn't go through with the transaction unless they produced the
cash. It is a company rule that management have to deal with
Barclaycard transactions. The procedure already outlined is all part B
of the company policy. The company rules exist because of the
company's agreement with Barclaycard. If I follow the rules because
of the agreement it means that Barclaycard will pay my company anything up to £70. As far as I know it is a private agreement with
Barclaycard and Mothercare. The floor limit of £70 is not something
that Mothercare advertise. It is a confidential thing only known by
management and staff that are authorised to accept Barclaycard at C
Mothercare. Provided I check everything including my stop list a
Barclaycard voucher for under £70 is as good as cash. By looking
at Barclaycard one cannot tell a person's own credit limit. I have no
means of telling whether a person can afford the goods or not. If a
Barclaycard matches up to all checks I don't give a second thought
whether the person can afford the goods. As far as I am concerned D
once the transaction is done whatever dealing the customer has with
Barclaycard is their own business. If someone comes to me and buys
a pram for cash I am not concerned how they are going to pay the
next week's housekeeping. I am only concerned that my store gets
paid. I can only remember this particular transaction because someone came and asked me about it after it had taken place. All Barclaycard means to me is that if I check things properly we will in due E
course get the cash. I would not be popular with my shop if I asked
people buying things if they would really afford them. It is not my
business or the shop's business if someone goes into debt to buy goods
from me. I cannot remember thinking on this occasion anything else
other than it was a normal transaction as good as cash. I did all the
things necessary to get paid by Barclaycard in this case. I would
expect the shop to be paid after such a transaction. From my experi- F
ence I or my shop is not any more worried about accepting a Barclaycard as accepting the same number of pound notes.

" If someone came into the shop and offered pound notes for a
maternity garment there would be no problem with that transaction.
If someone comes in and pays with a Barclaycard I scrutinise that
card. I check to see if the card is date valid and also the two signa- G
tures. If for any reason they were something unusual I would not go
through with the transaction. Provided everything was normal with
the card the transaction would go through normally and I would hand
over the goods. I would not worry what went on between the customer
and Barclaycard."

Later on December 15 the defendant gave her Barclaycard to her H
mother, who returned it to the bank. The Barclaycard organisation had
begun inquiries about her on December 6. They never instituted any
criminal proceedings. At some stage they made some arrangement with the
defendant for repayment of her debt, and at the date of the committal
proceedings she had repaid them by four instalments of £10, in respect of
a debt then amounting to some £1,700. On January 12 she was arrested
when she was a passenger in a car stolen by her lover. She then disclosed

A to the police that she was in trouble because she owed Barclays Bank
£1,000. On that date and the next she told the police how she had been
using the card, and signed two statements in which she admitted that she
went on using the card although she knew that she should not have done
so. She said that she was not using the card honestly, but that she
wanted to pay the money back when she could get a job.

B Upon these facts there was ample evidence that on December 15 she
knew that she was acting dishonestly in using the card. The two questions
raised by this appeal are whether on the facts there was evidence of a false
representation to the shop assistant at Mothercare, and evidence upon
which the jury could find that Miss Rounding was induced to rely upon
the false representation.

In a cheque card transaction the bank authorises its customer to
C identify himself to a seller of goods or services by presenting a card stating
the number of his account with the bank and displaying his signature.
The bank offers to the seller a guarantee to pay a cheque drawn by the
buyer, provided certain simple conditions of identification and comparison
of signatures are fulfilled. It is clear that this court was troubled by the
submission that there was no necessity, in order to give business efficacy to
the transaction, that there should be any collateral representation implied on
D the part of the drawer of the cheque who presents the cheque and the card
as to the state of his account with the bank or as to his authority to draw
on that account. Further, this court was inclined to regard with favour
the submission that there was no basis for an inference that any such
representation operated on the mind of the recipient of the cheque as an
inducement persuading him to accept it, because he relied exclusively upon
E the bank's undertaking embodied in the cheque card. But this court held
that it was bound by the earlier decision of the court in *Reg. v. Kovacs*
[1974] 1 W.L.R. 370. The House of Lords analysed the representations
implied by the action of the purchaser. Their Lordships held that the
purchaser acted as agent of the bank in presenting the cheque card, whereby
the bank gave the guarantee to the seller that the cheques drawn by the
purchaser would be met up to the limit of £30 on each cheque that he drew.
F The House held that on drawing the cheque backed by the card the
drawer impliedly represented that he was authorised by the bank to give
the guarantee on the bank's behalf, as stated on the face of the cheque card,
but that authority was conditional upon the drawer's account with the bank
being in credit or within his agreed borrowing limit. Upon the question
of inducement the House held that the evidence of the representee could
G lead to an inference that he was induced by the deception because he
believed the representation that the drawer of the cheque was then authorised as agent of the bank to use the card. The witness had made it clear
that, although he regarded the state of the drawer's account with the bank
as irrelevant, he would not have accepted the cheques if he had known
that the accused was using his cheque book and cheque card " in a way
in which he was not allowed or entitled to use them."
H In our view, the ratio of the decision in *Reg. v. Charles* [1977] A.C.
177 establishes as a matter of law that on the evidence the jury could find
that the defendant had made a representation that she was authorised by
the bank to use her credit card. The judge correctly explained to the jury
the law upon that implied representation, and the jury by their verdict held
that she made the representation and that it was false. It is the question
of inducement that gives rise to difficulty. Was there evidence upon which
the jury could find that the false representation induced Mothercare to sell

her the goods upon the credit given by the bank to the defendant, and the   A
guarantee given by the bank to Mothercare that the bank would pay the
price of the goods?

There has been much discussion by distinguished academic criminal
lawyers about the effect and implications of the speeches in the House of
Lords in *Reg.* v. *Charles* upon the inducement which has to be proved in
a charge of an offence under section 16 of the Theft Act 1968 in a cheque
card transaction. We have considered the powerful argument propounded   B
by Professor J. C. Smith in his commentary upon *Reg.* v. *Charles* in
[1977] Crim.L.R. 615, and in his textbook *The Law of Theft*, 4th ed
(1979), paragraph 158. In *Reg.* v. *Charles* the representee gave evidence
that he accepted the cheque because he did not know that the accused
had no authority to use the card. Professor Smith points out that
that is by no means the same thing as a belief that he had authority to use   C
it. So the argument runs that *Reg.* v. *Charles* is a special and unusual case
because the ratio does not apply to what Professor Smith describes as " the
typical case " where the representee is indifferent whether the card-holder
had authority or not. In that situation he argues that there is no inducement, because the only reason that the cheque is usually accepted is because
the conditions on the cheque card were satisfied, and for no other reason.
Professor Glanville Williams expresses the same view in *Textbook of*   D
Criminal Law (1978), pp. 846–847 :

> " If the creditor is an ordinary mortal who simply goes by the words
> on the cheque card, then the courts ought to hold that no offence is
> committed. . ."

He adds that no offence is likely to be committed against section 16 of the   E
Act of 1968 in a dishonest credit card transaction, because most sellers
could not honestly say that they regarded the position between the buyer
and the credit company of any importance to them.

We are impressed by the analysis of the relation between the deception
and obtaining made by Professor Griew in his textbook *The Theft Acts*
1968 and 1978, 3rd ed. (1978), paras. 6.20 to 6.28, we quote paragraphs
6.21 and 6.22 :   F

> " 6.21 The effect of representation on P's mind (i) *What state of*
> *mind must the representation induce?* ' To deceive is, I apprehend,
> to induce a man to believe that a thing is true which is false? This
> well-known statement by Buckley J. in *In re London and Globe*
> *Finance Corporation* [1903] 1 Ch. 728, 732 was cited with approval
> in *Director of Public Prosecutions* v. *Ray* [1974] A.C. 370. It   G
> appears at first sight to state the obvious and to require no elabora-
> tion. Yet there is, on reflection, a good deal of uncertainty attaching
> to the notion of ' believing that a thing is true '; and there has been no
> judicial consideration of what amounts to ' believing ' for this purpose.
>
> " It is submitted that, if indeed ' believing ' is an appropriate word
> in this context, it should not be understood only in the sense of firmly
> accepting the truth of the statement in question. The deception   H
> offences can hardly be limited to cases in which P is induced to hold
> a strong positive belief. P may be well aware he does not know D,
> that there are rogues and liars abroad and that D may be one of them.
> He may act ' on the strength ' of D's assertion and in reliance upon
> it, but without in any positive sense either believing or disbelieving it.
> If D is lying, P is surely ' deceived ' for the purposes of section 15. It
> may in fact be better to abandon the word ' believe ' and to say that

A   to deceive is to induce a man to act in reliance upon a false
representation."

"6.22 It is further submitted that this view is consistent with the
decision of the House of Lords in *Reg.* v. *Charles* [1977] A.C. 177,
183, 193. P accepted D's cheques because they were backed by a
cheque card. He would not have done so if he had known that D
had no authority to use the card. D's conviction under section 16
B   of obtaining a pecuniary advantage by deception was upheld. It is
quite clear from the evidence that P was at best agnostic on the
question of D's right to use the cheque card. "Their Lordships,
in asserting that P 'believed' that D was authorised to use it, must,
on the facts, have been using 'belief' to stand for ignorance of the
truth plus reliance on the representation of authority; firm acceptance
C   of the truth of that representation was not in question.

"The situation in a cheque card case is peculiar in that P stands
to lose nothing if D's assertion is untrue; the bank will certainly pay.
But this is merely the particular reason why in such a case P is prepared
to act without a positive belief in the representation. When in any
other situation he acts in reliance on D's representation, he may or
D   may not be aware that he is taking a risk as to its truth. It is submitted
that in either case, if the representation is untrue, he is 'deceived.'"

In our view, this analysis is helpful and correct, and the opposite view
expressed by Professor Smith and Professor Glanville Williams is explained
by their different understanding of the kind of belief which has to be
proved for the purpose of establishing that a false representation induced
E   the action of the representee. The analysis of the problem by Professor
Griew was made in relation to offences against section 15 of the Act of
1968, but it applies equally for the purposes of section 16 of that Act.

So we approach consideration of the evidence of Miss Rounding, and
the way in which the judge presented the question of inducement to the
jury in relation to the second count. In order to understand it, it is necessary to consider also the way in which the judge put the issue of inducement
F   to the jury, by considering his summing up upon the first count as well as
the second count. On December 5 the shop assistant at Braggins' shop had
followed the same procedure as that described by Miss Rounding at
Mothercare. We quote from the summing up:

"Is it dishonest conduct on the part of the defendant on any particular
presentation in relation to the transactions involved? Did it affect the
G   mind of the shop assistant who knew that she was going to get paid
or that the shop would be paid in the end? The assistant said, 'I
would have no reservation in accepting a Barclaycard for payment.'
She would if the signature differed on the documents she has to complete in accordance with the procedure she has to follow, but she does
not say to the customer 'Are you over your limit'? She doesn't even
know what the limit is. A card presented in this way is accepted at its
H   face value; you will have to consider whether that face value is a
representation in itself that all the conditions, including the condition
as to the limit allowance, in this case one of £200, are being complied
with and acted upon by the shop assistant without that knowledge as
to the cash limit imposed or the credit limit imposed who allows the
goods, in good faith, to be taken away with the knowledge that she
will eventually be paid. The shop assistant said, 'Over £30 we ring
up and ask authorisation. The card itself, under £30 is evidence that

that is what it is good for.' You can buy goods up to £30, going   **A**
through the proper procedure which the shop assistant has to go
through. She checks that the signatures are the same. Mrs. Walker
said, ' At the time of this transaction I considered the purchaser
authorised to use the card. As far as I was concerned, the transaction
was quite straightforward. If there had been anything untoward we
would have got the manager, seized the card and telephoned Barclaycard.' She later said, ' Under the limit of £30 Barclaycard will pay   **B**
regardless. The steps taken for transactions under £30 is to satisfy
myself that the card is in date, the voucher is filled in correctly and the
signatures are the same.' She thought that the person was authorised,
that is, that she was the holder of this card. You will have to consider,
members of the jury, was this part of the dishonesty in the defendant's
mind? Was this presentation of the Barclaycard in that manner a   **C**
deception upon the stores assistant where the defendant—and this is a
matter for you to judge—may have had the knowledge that she was
well over her credit limit, nevertheless, was getting the benefit of the
use of the Barclaycard presented, although the store was paid eventually
by Barclaycard, the debt still remains and has, therefore, been evaded
as at that date "?

  D

Having thus dealt with the question of the alleged inducement on the first
count, he came to the evidence of Miss Rounding in relation to the count
now under appeal:

"The transaction on December 15, count two, is in similar vein. I
must remind you directly of the evidence of Miss Rounding. This was
at Mothercare in Luton. She said, ' If someone came into the shop   **E**
and gave me a Barclaycard and I found the number to be on the
' stop list ' I would not go through with the transaction. Provided the
card appears to be valid I would normally proceed with the transaction.'
Is that a reliance by her, Miss Rounding of Mothercare, upon the
presentation of the card as being due authority within the limits as
at that time as with count one "?

  F

It is to be observed that Mrs. Walker had given evidence:

"At the time of the transaction I considered the purchaser authorised
to use the card. As far as I was concerned, the transaction was quite
straightforward."

This evidence may be compared with that of Miss Rounding, that provided
the card appeared to be valid she would normally proceed with the trans-   **G**
action, and that having gone through the prescribed procedure she concluded the transaction. Miss Rounding made it perfectly plain that she
regarded the state of the customer's credit with Barclays as nothing to do
with her. It was not her business to inquire. And it appears from the
evidence of the witness from Barclays that, if Miss Rounding had for some
extraordinary reason rung up Barclays to inquire about the defendant's
credit standing, the bank would have refused to disclose anything about it.   **H**
    Using the test of belief suggested by Professor Griew, was it proved that
Miss Rounding was induced by false representation in the sense that she
acted " on the strength " of its truth?
    We would pay tribute to the lucidity with which the judge presented
to the jury the law which the House of Lords had declared in relation to
deception in a cheque card transaction. If that analysis can be applied to
this credit card deception, the summing up is faultless. But, in our view,

A   there is a relevant distinction between the situation described in *Reg.* v. *Charles* [1977] A.C. 177 and the situation devised by Barclays Bank for transactions involving use of their credit cards. By their contract with the bank, Mothercare had bought from the bank the right to sell goods to Barclaycard holders without regard to the question whether the customer was complying with the terms of the contract between the customer and the bank. By her evidence Miss Rounding made it perfectly plain that she

B   made no assumption about the defendant's credit standing at the bank. As she said, " the company rules exist because of the company's agreement with Barclaycard." The flaw in the logic is, in our view, demonstrated by the way in which the judge put the question of the inducement of Miss Rounding to the jury:

C   " Is that a reliance by her, Miss Rounding of Mothercare, upon the presentation of the card as being due authority *within the limits as at that time* as with count one? "

    In our view, the evidence of Miss Rounding could not found a verdict that necessarily involved a finding of fact that Miss Rounding was induced by a false representation that the defendant's credit standing at the bank gave her authority to use the card.

D   For those reasons we allow the appeal.

    The court has reached this conclusion with some hesitation and with reluctance. Hesitation, lest the court has fallen into the same error into which another division of this court fell in *Reg.* v. *Charles.* Reluctance, because the dishonest deception of the defendant was manifest. If we are right, Barclays Bank has by its contractual arrangements opened a gateway to fraud, which may have for the bank such commercial advantages that

E   the bank has no great incentive to make a change in their contracts. If this is the case, Parliament may decide to frame legislation specifically to deal with the credit card fraud.

                        Appeal allowed.

                        Certificate under section 33 (2) *of the*

F   *Criminal Appeal Act* 1968 *that point*
                      of law of general public importance
                      was involved in decision, namely,
                      " In view of the proved differences
                      between a cheque card transaction
                      and a credit card transaction, were
                      their Lordships right in distinguish-

G   *ing this case from Reg.* v. *Charles*
                      [1977] A.C. 177 *upon the issue of*
                      inducement? "
                      Leave to appeal refused.
                      Legal aid to defendant for counsel to
                      attend prosecutor's petition for leave
                      to appeal.

H

    Solicitors: *David Picton & Co., Luton.*

    November 6. The Appeal Committee of the House of Lords (Lord Diplock, Lord Keith of Kinkel and Lord Scarman) allowed a petition by the prosecutor, the Chief Constable of Bedfordshire, for leave to appeal.

    [Reported by MISS EIRA CARYL-THOMAS, Barrister-at-Law]

A

[COURT OF APPEAL]

* ATTORNEY-GENERAL'S REFERENCE (No. 5 of 1980)

1980 Sept. 1   Lawton L.J., Chapman and Boreham JJ.

B

Crime—Obscene libel—Obscene article—Video cassette—Whether use publication of obscene article—Obscene Publications Act 1959 (7 & 8 Eliz. 2, c. 66), s. 1 (2) (3) (b)

Police officers with search warrants issued under the Obscene Publications Act 1959 entered premises where two audiences were watching screens with images displayed thereon. The audience appeared to be watching a conventional sound film of an obscene nature but the display was by means of video equipment. When that equipment was used, images were seen on the screen by means of electric signals from a tape in a cassette conducted by means of a cable to a television receiver containing a cathode ray tube which emitted light. An indictment was preferred against the respondents alleging that they had published an obscene article, namely, a video cassette. At the end of the prosecution's case, the judge ruled that the words "any film or other record of a picture or pictures" in the definition of "article" in section 1 (2) of the Act [1] were to be construed ejusdem generis and, as a video cassette was not in the same genus as a film, it was not an article within the definition. He directed the jury to acquit the respondents.

On a reference by the Attorney-General for the court to give its opinion on the question whether a person providing an obscene display of images on a screen by means of video tape published an obscene article: —

Held, answering the question in the affirmative, that the definition of "article" in section 1 (2) of the Act was to be construed as a whole and was wide enough to include any article that produced words or pictures or sounds which were obscene within the Act; that those obscene articles were published if, within the definition of subsection (3) (b), they were shown, played or projected and, even if there was no showing of the article when a video cassette was used, there was probably a playing of the cassette and definitely a projection when the electric impulses recorded on the tape were thrown onto the screen by means of an electric current (post, pp. 93A—95B–F).

Derrick v. Customs and Excise Commissioners [1972] 2 Q.B. 28, D.C. applied.

Per curiam. The subsequent amendment to the Act by section 53 of the Criminal Law Act 1977 did not affect the construction of section 1 (2) and (3) of the Act (post, p. 95A–B).

C

D

E

F

G

The following case is referred to in the judgment of the court:

Derrick v. Customs and Excise Commissioners [1972] 2 Q.B. 28; [1972] 2 W.L.R. 359; [1972] 1 All E.R. 993, D.C.

H

The following additional cases were cited in argument:

Barker v. Wilson [1980] 1 W.L.R. 884; [1980] 2 All E.R. 81, D.C.
Cox v. Stinton [1951] 2 K.B. 1021; [1951] 2 All E.R. 637, D.C.
Straker v. Director of Public Prosecutions [1963] 1 Q.B. 926; [1963] 2 W.L.R. 598; [1963] 1 All E.R. 697, D.C.

[1] Obscene Publications Act 1959, s. 1 (2) (3): see post, p. 91E–F.

A   REFERENCE by the Attorney-General under section 36 of the Criminal
Justice Act 1972.

The Attorney-General referred a point of law for the opinion of the
Court of Appeal in the following terms:

" 1. The Court of Appeal is asked to give its opinion on the following
point of law: —Does a person who provides an obscene display of images
B   on a screen to persons who are likely to be depraved or corrupted by that
display publish an obscene article contrary to section 2 of the Obscene
Publications Act 1959 in a case where the images are derived from video
tape?

" 2. The material facts which give rise to this reference are as follows:—(a) Police officers in possession of a warrant to search the premises
issued under the Obscene Publications Act 1959 visited basement premises
C   in London. (b) These premises were set out as two small cinemas to which
persons were admitted on payment of money. There were other immaterial
restrictions on entry. (c) In each of the cinemas obscene displays with
sound, indistinguishable to the watcher from conventional film shows, were
being shown on screens to audiences who were present. (d) Three persons
admitted responsibility for these activities and admissions of responsibility
D   for the shows were made on behalf of the company which received the
profits thereof. (e) The displays were not conventional film shows but were
derived from video cassettes. A video cassette contains video tape. When
a video tape is played electric signals from it are fed by way of cable
to a conventional television receiver containing a cathode ray display tube.
This display tube within the display screen provides the means by which
E   the images derived from the video tape are displayed upon the screen. The
electric signals are fired down the display tube to produce the images.
The system used in this case did not involve the projection of light on to
a screen. The light to provide the images was emitted from the cathode
ray display tube.

" 3. The indictment charged three persons and a company with pub-
F   lishing an obscene article namely a video cassette contrary to section 2 of
the Obscene Publications Act 1959 at a date prior to the coming into force
of the provisions of section 53 of the Criminal Law Act 1977.

" 4. At the end of the case for the Crown the learned judge directed
the jury to return a verdict of not guilty against all the defendants upon
the ground that a video cassette was not an obscene ' article ' as defined
by section 1 (2) of the Obscene Publications Act 1959 and thus there was
G   no publication of an obscene article as alleged.

" 5. Three submissions had been made to the learned judge at the end
of the Crown case as follows: —(i) A video cassette was not an ' article '
as defined by section 1 (2) of the Act. The words ' any film or other
record of a picture or pictures ' should be construed ejusdem generis and
a video tape was not of the same genus as a film. (ii) That because the
H   process by which a video tape was made in the first instance included
the projection of light the showing of a video tape was a ' cinematograph exhibition ' and therefore exempted from the provisions of section
1 (3) (b) of the Act by the relevant words of the proviso of the subsection that were in force at the time of the offence charged; and (iii)
In the alternative because the Crown expert had agreed that the process
of display could be described as ' television ' that the display was one
shown ' in the course of television ' and was therefore exempted by that

part of the proviso to section 1 (3) (*b*) which was then and is now in A force.

" 6. (1) The learned judge ruled in favour of the defence submission on the first point as already described in paragraph 4 above. (2) On the second submission he ruled that, if the evidence at the end of the case showed merely that the video tape was initially recorded by means of the projection of light then its showing would not be a ' cinematograph exhibition.' But the learned judge stated that he would have left as a B question of fact for the jury to determine whether or not the process of showing it did include the projection of light so as to make it a ' cinematograph exhibition.' (3) He ruled that even if the process of showing the video cassette was something done in the course of television ' its showing to an audience in one set of premises did not amount to ' broadcasting' so as to bring the activity within the exemption conferred by C the proviso to section 1 (3) (*b*) of the Act.

" (7) The unfortunate result of the judge's ruling from the point of view of public order is as follows: —(i) If a video cassette is not an ' article ' within the meaning of section 1 (2) of the Obscene Publications Act 1959 then presons can only be proceeded against for showing obscene video tapes at common law. (ii) However, if a jury found on the evidence in a particular case that the showing of a video tape was as a D matter of fact a ' cinematograph exhibition ' then by reason of the terms of section 2 (4A) of the Act of 1959 (now in force) the obscene display could not be proceeded against at common law. Thus it would be exempt from all criminal process.

" 8. It is desired to contend before the Court of Appeal (Criminal Division) in this reference that a video cassette is an " article " within E the meaning of section 1 (2) of the Obscene Publications Act 1959. . . . It is submitted that this subsection was intended to embrace any article whatsoever which could be used to show images. This is demonstrated by the wide terms of section 1 (3) (*b*). It is submitted that any record including video tape which when showed, played or projected produces images is an " article " within the definition of section 1 (2) of the Act. It is further submitted that the proper approach to the construction of F this subsection should be the approach adopted by the Queen's Bench Divisional Court in construing section 42 of the Customs Law Consolidation Act 1876 in *Derrick* v. *Customs and Excise Commissioners* [1972] 2 Q.B. 28 not cited to the (learned) judge."

D. W. Tudor Price for the Attorney-General. G

Stuart Shields Q.C. and *Geoffrey Robertson* for the first and second respondents.

Geoffrey Robertson for the third respondent and respondent company.

LAWTON L.J. delivered the opinion of the court. In this matter the Attorney-General, acting under section 36 of the Criminal Justice Act 1972 has asked this court to give its opinion on the following point of law : H

" Does a person who provides an obscene display of images on a screen to persons who are likely to be depraved or corrupted by that display publish an obscene article contrary to section 2 of the Obscene Publications Act 1959 in a case where the images are derived from video tape? "

[His Lordship stated the facts, the Crown's three submissions and

A Judge Lewisohn's rulings upon them, as set out in paragraphs 2 to 6 of the Attorney-General's reference, ante, pp. 89B—90C, and continued:] We have not been concerned with the second submission made to the judge. Whether the judge was right or wrong on the evidence which was before him is of no interest now because, as a result of the provisions of section 53 (1) of the Criminal Law Act 1977, that which took place, even if it had been a cinematograph exhibition, would now be an

B unlawful publication of an obscene article.

As to the third submission, Mr. Tudor Price on behalf of the Attorney-General has been content that the law should be as the judge ruled it was and he has not asked us to deal with the element of television. Mr. Shields on behalf of the respondents to this reference, has said that whether a particular display via a video cassette was or was not a television broadcast

C would depend on the evidence. He has not asked us to deal with the third of the submissions made to the judge.

It follows therefore that the sole issue before us has been whether a video cassette is an " article " within the definition of an obscene article in section 1 (2) of the Obscene Publications Act 1959.

In so far as that Act provides a definition of an obscene article, it has not been affected by subsequent legislation amending the Act of 1959 but

D nevertheless, because of a point taken by Mr. Shields, it may be necessary to look at some of the amending legislation.

Mr. Tudor Price on behalf of the Attorney-General puts his submissions succinctly. He says that section 1 (2) was intended to embrace any article whatsoever that could be used to show images. This, he submitted, was demonstrated by the words of subsection (2) itself and by the wide terms of

E section 1 (3) (b). The definition of an " article " contained in section 1 (2) is as follows:

" In this Act ' article ' means any description of article containing or embodying matter to be read or looked at or both, any sound record, and any film or other record of a picture or pictures."

Section 1 (3) in its relevant parts, is as follows:

F
" For the purposes of this Act a person publishes an article who . . . (b) in the case of an article containing or embodying matter to be looked at or a record, shows, plays or projects it " :

There then followed two provisos: one relating to a cinematograph exhibition and the other to television or sound broadcasting.

G Mr. Tudor Price submitted that the wide words of subsection (2) indicate that any article which brought about the reproduction of an obscene image was within the contemplation of the Act and that the only kinds of reproduction of obscene images which were outside the Act were the two exemptions set out in the provisos. He went on to point out that in subsection (3) publication embraces a person who, in the case of an article containing or embodying matter to be looked at, or a record, shows, plays

H or projects it. He went on to remind the court that in subsection (2) the word " record " occurs twice. On one occasion it has the adjective " sound " in front of it and in the other case the adjectival phrase " any film or other " comes before the word " record." It followed, so submitted Mr. Tudor Price, that an accused publishes an obscene article if it is in the form of a record and he shows, plays or projects it. The record may be either of sound or of pictures. A video tape does in fact constitute a record of pictures, albeit that it is a record which is made up of electrical impulses

recorded on a video tape. As neither of the exemptions apply, so says Mr. **A**
Tudor Price, it follows that a video cassette, being a record of pictures,
does constitute an " article " within the meaning of section 1 (2). As in
this case there was clearly a publication of the video cassette, it follows that
the judge ought not to have ruled as he did.

To that submission, Mr. Shields, whose argument has been adopted by
Mr. Robertson, on behalf of the other respondents, has made the following **B**
answer. He has reminded the court that in 1959, when the Obscene Publications Act was passed, video tapes had not got much beyond the experi-
mental stage. They were probably used by broadcasting bodies (such as
the British Broadcasting Corporation) but they were not on sale to the
public as they are now. It follows, says Mr. Shields, that it is inconceivable
that Parliament had video tapes in mind when it was deciding what articles
should come within the description " obscene articles " for the purposes of **C**
the Obscene Publications Act 1959. He says that this court should be slow
to apply the words to a piece of electronic equipment which probably had
not been within the contemplation of Parliament. We have kept in mind
that particular admonition made by Mr. Shields, but if the clear words of
the statute are sufficiently wide to cover the kind of electronic device with
which we are concerned in this case, the fact that that particular form of **D**
electronic device was not in the contemplation of Parliament in 1959 is an
immaterial consideration. In any event in 1959 Parliament would almost
certainly have had in mind the fact that electronic equipment for reproducing words and pictures was something likely to come about in the near
future. In those circumstances it is not all that improbable that words were
chosen which were wide enough to embrace any developments in the electronic field. But speculation as to what Parliament had in mind and what **E**
it probably had not got in mind is neither here not there. It is the duty
of this court to consider the wording of the Act and to construe the words
in it (if they are words of ordinary English usage) in the ways in which
they would have been understood by ordinary literate persons at the
material time, namely in 1959.

Mr. Shields has submitted that even when that test is applied, the words **F**
are not apt to embrace what happens when a video cassette is played. He
points out that subsection (2) embraces three different situations. The first is
an " article containing or embodying matter to be read or looked at or
both "; secondly, a " sound record " and, thirdly, " any film or other
record of a picture or pictures." He did not seek to say (as counsel who
appeared on behalf of his client at the trial sought to do) that the ejusdem **G**
generis rule applied. The judge thought it did. He put the matter in this
way in his ruling:

> " Does a video cassette fall within the words ' or other record of a
> picture or pictures '? Let me start this consideration by saying that
> I accept the submission that these words form part of one phrase
> or division, starting with the words ' any film.' Therefore the other **H**
> record of picture has to have some kinship with film."

He was wrong in that approach because what he had to do was to construe
the words " film or any other record " in the context of subsection (2). It
is clear that subsection (2) embraced a number of articles, starting with
those which contained or embodied obscene matter, those which were in
the form of a soundtrack and those which were a film or other record of
pictures. The judge did not have the advantage of having cited to him the

A decision of the Divisional Court in *Derrick* v. *Customs and Excise Commissioners* [1972] 2 Q.B. 28. Had he had the benefit of having that decision referred to him, he would have appreciated that he had to look at the subsection as a whole and not to pick out any particular group of words in the subsection. But the fact that he was mistaken in applying the ejusdem generis rule does not mean that there is no force in what Mr. Shields has submitted to this court, because his submission has proceeded as follows.

B There being three types of article, each of them was dealt with, so he submits, specifically in section 1 (3) (*b*) of the Act. That, he says, is shown by the way in which that paragraph is worded, because under it " a person publishes an article who—in the case of an article containing or embodying matter to be looked at "— that is the first category of obscene article—" or a record "—which could cover both the second and third categories—

C " shows, plays or projects it."

Mr. Shields submitted that a video cassette shows nothing. Anyone looking at it merely sees a piece of magnetised tape. There is nothing on that tape to indicate the presence of electrical impulses and certainly nothing on the tape to show pictures, So, so he submits, the word " shows " is inapplicable. He went on to submit that the word " plays," bearing in mind

D the year in which this statute was passed, namely, 1959, clearly applied to a sound record mentioned in section 1 (2). A video tape is not played in any sort of way that a sound record would have been played in 1959. For myself I am not all that certain of that because in 1959 there were many tape recorders and, in ordinary English, those who use tape recorders, play them. But be that as it may, assuming for the moment that the word " plays " is inappropriate to a video cassette, Mr. Shields went on to sub-

E mit that the word " projects " is inapplicable to a video cassette. He submitted, again bearing in mind that the statute was passed in 1959, that the word " projects " envisaged the kind of projection which there is for films, namely by projecting light behind the film and producing an image on a screen. That, he submitted, was not a concept which could be applicable to a video cassette.

F Mr. Shields went on to point out that if video cassettes were to be distinguished from films (and he was submitting that the words " other record of a picture or pictures " meant something in the nature of a film, if not a film) then anomalies would arise in the administration of the law relating to obscene publications. Those anomalies come about (so Mr. Shields submitted) in this way. After 1959, as is common knowledge, video

G cassettes became freely available to the public and in recent years they have been the vehicle for the publication of obscene pictures. The Act of 1959, as I have already said, exempted cinematograph exhibitions from its application. Mr. Tudor Price has told us (and we accept) that the reason was that in 1959 it was thought that the controls which existed under the Cinematograph Acts 1909–1952 together with the existence of the British Board of Film Censors, provided adequate protection to the public from

H the showing of obscene films in, for want of a better term, I am going to call, the commercial cinema. But for various reasons, with which we are not concerned, that protection turned out to be inadequate. A difficulty arose (some might describe it as a nuisance) as a result of private persons prosecuting the owners of commercial cinemas for publishing obscene films. It was thought that this was undesirable. As a result, by section 53 of the Criminal Law Act 1977 which in its material part came into operation on December 1, 1977, no prosecution of anyone for showing films

in commercial cinemas could be undertaken without the consent of the A
Director of Public Prosecutions.

The way the provision was enacted was this—and I quote from section
53 (2) of the Criminal Law Act 1977:

"In section 2 of that Act " . . . —that is, the Obscene Publications
Act 1959—"at the end of subsection (3) there shall be inserted the
following subsection:— ' (3A) Proceedings for an offence under this B
section shall not be instituted except by or with the consent of the
Director of Public Prosecutions in any case where the article in
question is a moving picture film of a width of not less than 16
millimetres . . .' "

and then there are other provisions. Commercial films are always of not less
than 16 millimetres. It follows, said Mr. Shields, that although the consent C
of the Director is required for a prosecution in respect of the showing of
indecent films of a size of 16 millimetres and over, it would not be required
for the showing in cinemas of video cassettes. The consequence would be
that private prosecutions could be started in respect of such shows, although
had they been on 16 millimetre film in commercial cinemas they could
not have been shown. There is a difference there.

The next difference arises in this way. Under section 4 of the Obscene D
Publications Act 1959 there was a defence of public good. That defence
was in these terms:

" (1) A person shall not be convicted of an offence against section two
of this Act . . . if it is proved that publication of the article in question
is justified as being for the public good on the ground that it is in the
interests of science, literature, art or learning, or of other objects of E
general concern."

In 1968 Parliament decided to free theatres from the control of the
Lord Chamberlain. That was done by the Theatres Act 1968. Section 3
of that Act provided:

" (1) A person shall not be convicted of an offence under section 2
of this Act if it is proved that the giving of the performance in question F
was justified as being for the public good on the ground that it was
in the interests of drama, opera, ballet or any other art, or of literature
or learning."

When Parliament decided to amend the Obscene Publications Act 1959
in relation to (I use a wide term) the interests of the commercial cinema,
it provided in section 53 (6) that there should be no prosecution of such G
a performance in a commercial cinema " if it is proved that publication of
the film or soundtrack is justified as being for the public good on the ground
that it is in the interests of drama, opera, ballet or any other art, or of
literature or learning." In other words, in relation to films, there was to
be the same test of public good as there was in relation to the theatre. But
that test was in different words from the general defence of public good H
provided by section 4 of the Act of 1959.

It followed, submitted Mr. Shields, that if there were a showing in a
commercial cinema of a film which was alleged to be obscene, the test
would be different from that which there would be if there was a showing
by means of a video cassette in a cinema of the type found to exist in this
case. There is something in that argument, but not much. It seems to us
that what the Theatres Act 1968 and the Criminal Law Act 1977 were

A doing was making it clear what the word " art " in section 4 of the Act of 1959 embraced, namely, drama, opera and ballet. That, in our judgment, is shown by the use of the additional words " or any other art." Quite clearly Parliament regarded drama, opera and ballet as being forms of art. It would have been surprising if they had not taken that view.

So although there is a very slight difference between the tests to be applied in the different cases, in our judgment, it is not sufficient to make B any difference to the construction of section 1 (2) and (3) of the Act of 1959.

The basic question is whether there is any substance in Mr. Shields' submission that the words in subsection (2) and subsection (3) are not apt to cover a video cassette. In our judgment they are. As Mr. Tudor Price rightly submitted, the object of subsection (2) was to bring all articles which produced words or pictures or sounds within the embrace of the Act. There C were to be only two exceptions.

In our judgment the words " shows, plays or projects " in section 1 (3) (*b*) are sufficiently wide to cover what happens when pictures are produced by way of a video cassette. It may be that Mr. Shields was right in his submission that the word " show," in the context of subsection (3) (*b*), implies looking at, but the words " play or project " cover, in our judg- D ment, what happens when a video tape is used in such a way as to produce pictures. As I have already indicated in ordinary parlance (this would have been the same in 1959 as it is today) when a tape recorder is used it is talked about as being played. We see no reason why the same sort of language should not apply to a video cassette which produces not sounds but pictures. Even if that is not right (and we think it is right) the word " project " would be apt to cover what happens when a video cassette is E brought into use, because what is happening is that the electrical impulses recorded on the video tape are thrown onto the television screen by means of the use of an electric current. In ordinary parlance, they are projected onto the television screen.

Accordingly, we find that the answer to the question posed to us by the Attorney-General in this reference is to the effect that a video F cassette is an article within the meaning of section 1 (2) of the Obscene Publications Act 1959.

Opinion accordingly.
Leave to appeal refused.

G Solicitors: *Director of Public Prosecutions; Cowan, Lipson, Rumney.*

[Reported by MISS HENRIETTA STEINBERG, Barrister-at-Law]

H

96

A

[CHANCERY DIVISION]

* CHESTER v. BUCKINGHAM TRAVEL LTD.

[1972 C. No. 3985]

1980   July 1, 14, 15, 16, 17, 18; 30

Foster J.

B

*Landlord and Tenant—Agreement for lease—Usual covenants—
Business premises—Tenant allowed into immediate possession
—Covenants to be included as usually to be found in 1971
commercial lease*

On March 25, 1971, the defendants entered into an agreement, whereby they agreed to grant to the plaintiff a lease of
certain garage workshops for 14 years at a rent of £6,000 per
annum exclusive of rates, and, pending completion of the
lease, to allow the plaintiff to take immediate possession of
the premises. The premises were situated in a predominantly
residential area and formed part of a complex of properties
consisting of the plaintiff's own premises, a garage, a yard, and
four residential flats. At the date of the agreement, the
defendants were holding over under a previous head lease and
were not granted a new lease until May 21, 1971, when they
were granted a lease of 14 years as from June 24, 1970, so
that at the date of the agreement the defendants were in fact
unable to grant a 14 year term as from March 25, 1971.
The plaintiff went into possession and in 1972 he sued for
specific performance of the agreement. On April 14, 1975,
Foster J. ordered specific performance, but only of so much
of the term specified in the agreement as the defendants were
enabled to grant under the new head lease of May 21, 1971.
After further litigation as to the area of land to be included
in the lease, the defendants' solicitors submitted a draft lease,
the terms of which proved unacceptable to the plaintiff.
The matter was therefore referred to conveyancing counsel
to the court, who submitted a draft lease. This, while acceptable to the plaintiff, was not considered satisfactory by the
defendants, who wanted certain further covenants added.
Accordingly the matter was referred back to the judge, pursuant to R.S.C., Ord. 31, rr. 5 and 6.

On the question of what covenants should be included in
the lease as usual covenants: —

Held, (1) that in determining what covenants were to be
regarded as to be usually found in a lease, the same test
was to be applied whether what was under consideration was
an open contract for a lease or an agreement to assign a
lease (post, p. 99F–G).

(2) That, in addition to the five well known "usual"
covenants in a lease, namely, covenants by the tenant (i) to
pay rent, (ii) to pay taxes, except such as were expressly
payable by the landlord, (iii) to keep and deliver up the
premises in repair, (iv) to allow the lessor to enter and view
the state of repair, and (v) a covenant by the lessor for
quiet enjoyment, it was a question of fact to be determined
by the court as to what covenants were usually to be found
in a lease in 1971 (post, pp. 100B–C, 101D–E); that in a commercial lease of premises of the type let to the plaintiff,
having regard to the purpose for which they were let and
the length of the term of the letting of those business premises,
the only extra covenants required by the defendants that
should be included on the basis that they were usually to be
found in leases of such lettings in 1971 were that the tenant

C

D

E

F

G

H

A   would not alter the plan, height, elevation or appearance of the building without the landlord's consent; that the tenant would not obstruct windows or lights or knowingly permit any encroachment easements to be acquired against the demised premises; that the tenant would not alter the user of the premises without the landlord's consent, such consent not to be unreasonably withheld; that the tenant would not suffer any part of the premises to be a nuisance or cause B   annoyance, and that the landlord should have a right of re-entry for breach of any covenant (post, pp. 102A–C, G—103A, E–G, H—104B, 105E–G).

    Hampshire v. *Wickens* (1878) 7 Ch.D. 555 and *Flexman* v. *Corbett* [1930] 1 Ch. 672 applied.

    The following cases are referred to in the judgment:

C   *Allen* v. *Smith* [1924] 2 Ch. 308.
Flexman v. *Corbett* [1930] 1 Ch. 672.
Hampshire v. *Wickens* (1878) 7 Ch.D. 555.
Liverpool City Council v. *Irwin* [1977] A.C. 239; [1976] 2 W.L.R. 562; [1976] 2 All E.R. 39, H.L.(E.).
Moorcock, The (1889) 14 P.D. 64, C.A.
Shirlaw v. *Southern Foundries* (1926) *Ltd.* [1939] 2 K.B. 206; [1939] D   2 All E.R. 113, C.A.

    The following additional cases were cited in argument:

Anderton and Milner's Contract, In re (1890) 45 Ch.D. 476.
Bennett v. *Womack* (1828) 7 B. & C. 627.
Bishop v. *Taylor & Co.* (1891) 60 L.J.Q.B. 556, D.C.
Blakesley v. *Whieldon* (1841) 1 Hare 176.
Brookes v. *Drysdale* (1877) 3 C.P.D. 52.
E   *Charalambous* v. *Ktori* [1972] 1 W.L.R. 951; [1972] 3 All E.R. 701.
Church v. *Brown* (1808) 15 Ves.Jun. 258.
Doe d. *Marquis of Bute* v. *Guest* (1846) 15 M. & W. 160.
Henderson v. *Hay* (1792) 3 Bro.C.C. 632.
Hodgkinson v. *Crowe* (1875) L.R. 10 Ch.App. 622.
Hyde v. *Warden* (1877) 3 Ex.D. 72, C.A.
Jones v. *Jones* (1806) 12 Ves.Jun. 186.
F   *Lander and Bagley's Contract, In re* [1892] 3 Ch. 41.
Van v. *Corpe* (1834) 3 My. & K. 269.
Vere v. *Loveden* (1806) 12 Ves.Jun. 179.
Wilbraham v. *Livesey* (1854) 18 Beav. 206.

    FURTHER CONSIDERATION OF ACTION

G   In 1972 the plaintiff, Jack Chester, commenced proceedings against the defendants, Buckingham Travel Ltd., claiming specific performance of an agreement dated March 21, 1971, whereby the defendants agreed to let to the plaintiff certain garage workshop premises at 18/20 Danvers Street, Chelsea, London S.W.3, for a period of 14 years at an annual rent of £6,000, exclusive of rates. On April 14, 1975, Foster J. gave judgment in favour of the plaintiff granting specific performance, but H   only in respect of so much of the term of 14 years contracted for as the defendants were able to grant under their head lease, dated May 21, 1971, under which the defendants held a term of 14 years as from June 24, 1970. The order made provided that if the parties should differ as to its terms the lease was to be settled by one of the conveyancing counsel to the court. The draft lease submitted by the defendants' solicitors proved unacceptable to the plaintiff, and accordingly Mr. John Bradburn was appointed to settle a draft lease. His draft proved unacceptable

to the defendants and the matter was therefore referred back to the   A
judge, pursuant to R.S.C., Ord. 31, rr. 5 and 6.   The matter thus came
again before Foster J. on July 1, 1980.

The facts are stated in the judgment.

Vivian Chapman for the plaintiff.
C. P. F. Rimer for the defendants.
                                                                             B
                                                          Cur. adv. vult.

July 30.   FOSTER J. read the following judgment.   In this case, I
am concerned with what are the so-called " usual covenants " to be
inserted in a lease.   As long ago as March 25, 1971, the defendants
agreed to let to the plaintiff certain premises at 18/20, Danvers Street,   C
Chelsea, S.W.3., for a period of 14 years at an annual rent of £6,000
exclusive of rates.   The actual agreement, which was signed by both
parties, was in these terms: it was between J. Chester Esq. of West
Tower, Little Gaddesden, Berkhamsted and Buckingham Travel Ltd.:

" (1) It is agreed that the garage workshops situated at 18/20 Danvers
Street, London, S.W.3 are let by Buckingham Travel Ltd. to
J. Chester Esq., for a period of 14 years at the annual rental of   D
£6,000 exclusive of rates, the rent to be paid quarterly in advance
on quarter days as from March 25, 1971.   (2) It is further agreed
that pending completion of a lease contract between the two parties,
J. Chester Esq. will take immediate possession of the leased premises.
(3) Both parties will, at the same time, come to a separate agreement as to the stock and equipment contained in the premises leased   E
which Buckingham Travel Ltd. will sell to J. Chester Esq. for cash
at prices to be mutually agreed.   (4) It is further agreed that, provided their agreement is first sought and obtained, such members
of the staff as are at present employed in the leased garage-work-
shops by Buckingham Travel Ltd. will be re-employed by J. Chester
Esq. at rates of pay not lower than those at present obtaining.   F
" Signed in London on March 25, 1971. . . ."

and both the defendants and the plaintiff signed it.

In 1972, the plaintiff sued the defendants for specific performance
of that agreement and the defendants defended that action and in the
alternative counter-claimed for the agreement to be rectified in respect
of four clauses.   I heard the case as long ago as April 1975 and gave
judgment on April 14, 1975.   During the case, the defendants dropped   G
the claim that the plaintiff was only a licensee and not a lessee but
proceeded on their counter-claim that the agreement should be rectified
to include four terms: (a) that there should be a rent review clause at
five and ten years; (b) that there should be a full repairing covenant;
(c) that the plaintiff should pay a proportion of the insurance premiums
and (d) that there should be a covenant restricting the user of the   H
premises to that of garage workshops.

On April 14, 1975, I granted the plaintiff specific performance of the
agreement and dismissed the counter-claim.   At the date of the agreement on March 25, 1971, the defendants were holding over under a
previous lease and they were not granted a new lease until May 21,
1971.   This new lease granted the defendants a lease of 14 years from
June 24, 1970, so that the defendants were unable to grant to the plaintiff

A   a term of 14 years from March 25, 1971. But, the plaintiff was prepared to take the term—a little over 13 years—which the defendants could grant. It is common ground that the plaintiff, on March 25, 1971, had no knowledge of the contents of the lease of May 21, 1971, or of any of the covenants contained in it. In my order of April 14, 1975, it was provided that the agreement of March 25, 1971, should be specifically performed and carried into execution but only in respect of so much of

B   the term of 14 years specified in the agreement, as the defendants under the head-lease dated May 21, 1971, were enabled to grant. The parties were agreed that the term should not be for the whole term but should have a reversion of, say, less one day. The order went on to order " . . . such lease to be settled by one of the conveyancing counsel to the court in case the parties differ. . . ."

C   Further litigation ensued between the parties as to what land was to be included in the agreement and on April 28, 1977, Lord Granchester Q.C., sitting as a deputy High Court judge of the Chancery Division, decided what land was to be incorporated in the lease. The defendants' solicitors accordingly submitted a draft lease to the plaintiff's solicitors which was unacceptable to them as it was said that it contained several covenants which were not usual. Accordingly, instructions were deli-

D   vered to Mr. John Bradburn, then one of the conveyancing counsel to the court, and on April 2, 1979, he settled a draft lease. This draft is acceptable to the plaintiff, but the defendants wish to have some further clauses added to this draft lease and under R.S.C., Ord. 31, rr. 5 and 6, it is possible, if a party is not satisfied with a document produced by counsel, to have the matter referred back to the judge. It is in these

E   circumstances that the matter comes before me.

The questions which face me can, I think, be stated as follows: (1) is there any distinction between cases where there is an assignment of an existing lease and cases where there is an open contract as in this case? (2) What does the expression " usual covenant " mean in 1971 and on what evidence should the court act? (3) What individual

F   covenants which the defendants seek to have inserted should I allow to be inserted?

Assignments and open contracts

Mr. Chapman, for the plaintiff, submitted that the usual covenants were much more limited in open contracts than where there is an agree- ment to assign a lease, which it is said contains the usual covenants. No

G   less than 22 cases were cited to me and I confess I find that nowhere is any distinction made between the two. The test to be applied seems to be the same in each case. It is well settled that in the technical sense, the term " usual covenant " is limited to those which are set out clearly in the judgment of Sir George Jessel M.R. in *Hampshire* v. *Wickens* (1878) 7 Ch.D. 555. He said, at pp. 561–562:

H   " Usual covenants may vary in different generations. The law declares what are usual covenants according to the then knowledge of mankind. Lord Eldon L.C., in *Church* v. *Brown* (1808) 15 Ves.Jur. 258, 264, puts it thus: ' Before the case of *Henderson* v. *Hay* (1792) 3 Bro.C.C. 632, therefore, upon an agreement to grant a lease with nothing more than proper covenants, I should have said they were to be such covenants as were just as well known in such leases as the usual covenants under an agreement to convey

an estate.' Now what is well known at one time may not be well   A
known at another time, so that you cannot say that usual covenants
never change. I have therefore looked at the last edition of
Davidson's Precedents in Conveyancing, to see whether the usage
is said to have changed. He says, [2nd ed.] vol. V, pp. 48, 49: 'The
result of the authorities appears to be that in a case where the
agreement is silent as to the particular covenants to be inserted
in the lease, and provides merely for the lease containing "usual"   B
covenants," or, which is the same thing, in an open agreement
without any reference to the covenants, and there are no special
circumstances justifying the introduction of other covenants, the
following are the only ones which either party can insist upon,
namely, covenants by the lessee   1. to pay rent, 2. to pay taxes,
except such are expressly payable by the landlord, 3. to keep and   C
deliver up the premises in repair, and 4. to allow the lessor to enter
and view the state of repair. And the usual qualified covenant by
the lessor for quiet enjoyment by the lessee.'

    " When he refers to ' special circumstances ' he means peculiar
to a particular trade, as for example, in leases of public houses,
where the brewers have their own forms of leases, the ' usual
covenants ' would mean the covenants always inserted in the leases   D
of certain brewers.

    " There is no mention of any other ' usual covenants,' and as
nothing in this case has been lost for want of industry on the part
of the counsel who have argued it, I am justified in saying that there
is nothing in any text-book or book of precedents to show that a
covenant not to assign is a usual covenant.   E

    " I am therefore of opinion that it is not a usual covenant, and
I dismiss the action with costs."

I reiterate that in this case also there has been nothing which has been
lost for want of industry on the part of the counsel who have argued it.
    In *Flexman* v. *Corbett* [1930] 1 Ch. 672, Maugham J. said, at pp.
680–681:   F

    " I will add only that my view that the question is one of fact is
supported by the authority of *Bennett* v. *Womack* (1828) 7 B.C.
627 and *Hampshire* v. *Wickens* (1878) 7 Ch.D. 555, 561 and...
Allen v. *Smith* [1924] 2 Ch. 308. I might also add the case of
Brookes v. *Drysdale* (1877) 3 C.P.D. 52, in which it was held that
a condition that assignments or under-leases shall be registered by   G
the lessor's solicitor and the fee paid to him, was not a usual
covenant."

Of the four cases there cited, the first and fourth were assignment
cases and the second and third were open contract cases. In my judgment, there is no distinction between the two and the test as to what is
or what is not a usual clause is the same in both.   H

Meaning of usual covenants

    If, in the agreement, these are not defined or not even mentioned,
the court inserts them and the usual covenants in the technical sense
are always included. For the defendants, it was submitted that " usual "
means occurring in ordinary use: see Maugham J. in *Flexman* v. *Corbett*
[1930] 1 Ch. 672, 678. For the plaintiff, it was submitted that for a
covenant to be usual it must pass the test of what the court will imply

A into an agreement. He put his submission in this way: " In an open contract for the grant of a lease there is an implied term that the lease should contain usual and proper covenants—that is the usual covenants in the strict sense, together with such other covenants that on the particular facts of the case the parties must have impliedly intended the lease to contain." He referred me to three cases. (a) *The Moorcock*
B (1889) 14 P.D. 64 (the business efficacy test). (b) *Shirlaw* v. *Southern Foundries (1926) Ltd.* [1939] 2 K.B. 206 (the officious bystander test) and (c) *Liverpool City Council* v. *Irwin* [1977] A.C. 239, 251 (the necessary implication test). In my judgment, these cases deal with quite another subject, namely, what the court will imply into a formal document. But when the court has to decide what is a usual covenant it is not implying anything into a document but merely deciding, in an assign-
C ment case, whether the existing lease includes an unusual covenant which should have been disclosed and in an open contract case, what covenants should be inserted. In my judgment, the cases where the court implies something are irrelevant and I reject the plaintiff's submission. I only have to decide what covenants which are usual should be included in the lease.

D *Usual covenants in 1971*

    In coming to a conclusion on this question, in my judgment, it is a question of fact to be determined by the court, not necessarily on the view of conveyancing counsel but by looking at the nature of the pre-mises, their situation, the purpose for which they are being let, the length of the term, the evidence of conveyancers and the books of
E precedents. In *Flaxman* v. *Corbett* [1930] 1 Ch. 672 Maugham J. said, at p. 678:

    " I think it right to express my opinion, after having heard and con-sidered all the numerous authorities which have been cited to me, that the question whether particular covenants are usual covenants is a question of fact, and that the decision of the court on that
F point must depend upon the admissible evidence given before the court in relation to that question. I think that it is proper to take the evidence of conveyancers and others familiar with the practice in reference to leases and that it is also permissible to examine books of precedents. It is permissible to obtain evidence with regard to the practice in the particular district in which the premises in question
G are situated. I would add that in my view it is a complete mistake to suppose that the usual covenants in regard to a lease, for instance, of a country house are necessarily usual covenants in regard to the lease of a London residence, and I would add that it seems to me that it may very well be that what is usual in Mayfair or Bayswater is not usual at all in some other part of London such, for instance, as Whitechapel. Further, in my opinion, ' usual ' in this sense
H means no more than ' occurring in ordinary use,' and I think that it is an error to suppose that the court is entitled to hold that a particular covenant is not usual because it may be established that there are some few cases in which that covenant is not used. If it is established that (to put a strong case) in nine cases out of ten the covenant would be found in a lease of premises of that nature for that purpose and in that district, I think that the court is bound to hold that the covenant is usual. The court must bear

A in mind here the ultimate question which is being decided, which is
whether the form of the covenant is such as to constitute a defect
in the subject-matter of the contract: and if it were established
that the lease is in the form in which it would be anticipated as
being in the great majority of cases, having regard to the nature
of the property and to the place where it is situated and to the
purposes for which the premises are to be used, it does not seem
B to me reasonable to say that there is a defect in the subject-matter
of the contract."

In this case, the premises are situated in Chelsea, in a predominantly
residential area and the premises are part of a complex of properties
consisting of (1) the plaintiff's premises (2) a garage (3) a yard and
(4) four residential flats. The term is under 14 years but, of course,
C as these are business premises, a new lease may be granted by statute.
I was quoted three precedents and I had before me an affidavit filed on
behalf of the defendants by Mr. M. J. Woodrow, a solicitor since 1959,
who is second senior partner out of nine in the property department of
Norton Rose, Botterell and Roche and who has, during the last 15 or
20 years, had considerable experience of commercial leases in London,
acting for both landlords and tenants.
D

What extra covenants should be inserted in the draft lease, if any?

The defendants asked the court to insert a further seven covenants
and to enlarge the proviso for re-entry. I refer to the covenants as
numbered in the defendants' draft lease.

(i) The first is clause 2 (13), which is in these terms: E

" Not without previous written consent of the landlords in any way
to alter the plan height elevation or appearance of the demised
premises or of any part thereof or to cut or injure any of the party
or other walls or the principal or bearing timbers iron steel or any
supports of the demised premises except for the purpose of making
good any defects thereof or to erect or place any building or erection
F upon the demised premises or any part thereof additional to the
building and existing at the date hereof."

I was referred to clause 2 (7) of a precedent of a lease of premises for
the purpose of garage and petrol filling station, contained in *The Encyclopaedia of Forms and Precedents*, 4th ed., vol. 12 (1966), p. 1006 which
has a similar, though simpler, clause. Mr. Woodrow, in his affidavit,
G says:

" Clause 2 (13) Prohibition of alteration of a building in a qualified
or absolute form is a usual covenant in modern commercial leases
and, in the context of the building we are dealing with, and the full
repairing covenants imposed, I think it is reasonable that some
control should be retained by the defendants."
H

It must be remembered that there are other users and the lease is a short
one. In my judgment, this is a usual covenant in 1971, provided that
the clause contains a provision that the landlords' consent should not be
unreasonably withheld.

(ii) Clause 2 (14) reads:

" Not to stop-up darken or obstruct any window or light belonging
to the demised premises or any adjoining buildings now or hereafter

A   belonging to the landlords nor knowingly permit any encroachment
or easements to be acquired against or upon the premises and in
case any window light opening doorway path passage drain or other
encroachment or easement shall be opened or made or attempted
to be opened made or acquired upon receiving notice to give immediate notice thereof to the landlords and at the request and cost
of the landlords to take and do all such proceedings acts and things
B   and to carry out all such works as may be reasonably required or
deemed proper for preventing any such encroachment or the acquisition of any easement; and if a tenant shall omit or neglect to take
do or carry out all or any such things as aforesaid to permit the
landlords or the superior landlords with or without workmen to enter
upon the demised premises and to take do or carry out the same
C   and on demand pay to the landlords the whole or such part as the
landlords' agents may certify as fairly payable by the tenant of the
costs of any such proceedings acts things or works."

Mr. Woodrow said that it is a normal clause to find in a modern
commercial lease and could be particularly important with common
access and differing users on the site.   At one stage in the negotiation
D   the plaintiff was minded to agree that the clause should be inserted.
In my judgment, this was a usual covenant in 1971 and should be inserted.
(iii) Clause 2 (15) reads:

" Not to use or permit or suffer the demised premises to be used
otherwise than as garage/workshops in connection with the tenant's
business."

E
It was pointed out that in the agreement itself, not only was there a
reference to garage/workshops but there was a clause providing that
the plaintiff should employ such members of the staff as are at present
employed in the leased garage/workshops by the defendants.   Mr.
Woodrow said that it is now entirely usual to find in commercial leases
a clause restricting the user of premises and certainly the covenant is
F   to be found in the precedent book, see The Encyclopaedia, vol. 12, form
10 : 2, clause 2 (15), p. 1007, and form 9 : 1, clause 3, p. 883.   But,
these contain the words " not without the consent of the landlords " to
which, I think, should be added the words " such consent not to be
unreasonably withheld."   If these words were inserted and the last six
words deleted, I think that such covenant would be a usual one and
G   ought to be inserted.
(iv) Clause 2 (17)
Only the last two lines of clause 2 (17) namely: " not to hold or
permit or suffer to be held any sale by auction on the demised premises
or any part thereof " are now sought by the defendants to be inserted.
Mr. Woodrow, in his evidence, says that such a clause is not essential.
I agree with him and, although it is to be found in The Encyclopaedia,
H   vol. 12, form 10: 2, clause 2 (18), p. 1008, I do not think that it is a
usual covenant and it should not be inserted.
(v) Clause 2 (21) is a long clause but the defendants only seek to
have inserted the first seven lines which read:

" Not to do or permit or suffer to be done on any part of the
demised premises any act or thing which may grow to be a nuisance
annoyance disturbance or discomfort to the landlords or the superior

landlords or any tenant of the landlords or to the owner or occupier A
of any premises in the neighbourhood. . . ."

and the rest of the clause they do not now seek to have inserted.   Mr.
Woodrow says in his affidavit: " I would certainly regard such a clause
as usual in a commercial lease these days and relevant to a lease of a
garage."   I would regard it as usual provided the words " or discomfort "
and the words " or the superior landlords " and the words " or to the B
owner or occupier of any premises in the neighbourhood " are deleted
and " or " is inserted between annoyance and disturbance.
    (vi) Clause 2 (24) and (25)
    These seem to me to stand or fall together.   Clause 2 (24) reads:

    " Not to assign under-let part with possession or occupation of the
    demised premises or any part thereof except with the prior written C
    consent of the landlords and the superior landlords such consent
    not (in the case of the landlords) to be unreasonably withheld."

And clause 2 (25):

    " To procure that every permitted underlessee of the demised pre-
    mises shall covenant with the landlords to observe and perform the
    covenants on the part of the tenant herein contained (except the D
    covenant to pay the rents hereby reserved) and a covenant not to
    assign underlet or part with possession or occupation of the property
    comprised in any such underlease except with the prior written
    consent of the landlords and the superior landlords such consent
    (in the case of the landlords), not to be unreasonably withheld."

Mr. Woodrow says that it is entirely common for provisions governing E
alienation to be inserted in commercial leases these days, although
those clauses differ considerably from lease to lease.   Such covenants
are to be found in the precedent books The Encyclopaedia, vol. 12, form
10: 2, clause 2 (12), p. 1007 and form 9: 1, clause 3 (15), p. 885, but
they differ considerably and it cannot, I think, be said that these particular clauses are " usual."   In my judgment, they should not be inserted
and particularly in view of the decision in Hampshire v. Wickens, F
7 Ch.D. 555.
    (vii) Clause 2 (30) reads:

    " To pay all costs, charges and expenses (including legal costs and
    surveyors fees) incurred by the landlords (or the superior landlords)
    for the purpose of or incidental to the preparation or service of
    any notice under sections 146 and 147 of the Law of Property Act G
    1925 (or any statutory modification thereof) notwithstanding that
    the forfeiture may be avoided otherwise than by relief granted by
    the court. . . ."

and the defendants do not seek now to have inserted the last four lines.
    Mr. Woodrow's evidence falls far short of what is required and in
view of the decision of Eve J. in Allen v. Smith [1924] 2 Ch. 308 H
where he held that such a covenant was not usual, I do not think it
should be included.

The proviso for re-entry

    Clause 4 (1) of the defendants' lease reads:

    " (1) If the rent hereby reserved or any part thereof shall remain

A   unpaid for 21 days after becoming payable (whether formally demanded or not), or if any of the covenants on the tenant's part herein contained shall not be performed or observed or if the tenant shall have a receiving order in bankruptcy made against him or if the tenant shall make any assignment or composition for the benefit of his creditors or suffer any distress or process of execution to be B   levied upon his goods or (being a corporation), shall enter into liquidation whether voluntarily or by the court (otherwise than for the purposes of reconstruction or amalgamation) then and in any of the said cases it shall be lawful for the landlords at any time thereafter to re-enter upon the demised premises or upon any part thereof in the name of the whole and thereupon this demise shall absolutely determine but without prejudice to any right of action of the land-C   lords in respect of any antecedent breach or non-observance of the tenant's covenants and conditions herein contained."

The defendants do not now seek to have inserted sub-clauses 4 (2), (3), (4) and (5) of the proviso in clause 4. In Mr. Bradburn's draft the power of re-entry is limited to non-payment of rent and does not include the power of re-entry if there is a breach of covenant. In *Flexman* v. D   *Corbett* [1930] 1 Ch. 672 Maugham J. said, at p. 682:

"I do not think that the evidence in this case is sufficient to enable me to express the opinion that the proviso for re-entry "—and he was dealing with the re-entry for breach of covenant—" is in the usual form, although I think that, even with regard to the proviso for re-entry, the matter is one which might usefully and properly be E   reconsidered in the light of modern evidence at some future time."

In this case, the right of re-entry in the defendants' draft lease includes the right of re-entry on breach of any of the covenants in the lease. I confess, until I read Mr. Bradburn's draft, I myself had never seen a right of re-entry in a lease limited to non-payment of rent only. Every precedent contains a right of re-entry for breach of covenant and I have F   no doubt that it was usual in 1971. On the other hand, this clause seeks a right of re-entry if the tenant has a receiving order in bankruptcy made against him and other matters in regard to insolvency. In my judgment, these provisions are far too wide. I think that the proviso should be inserted with the deletion of the words in line 5 'or if the tenant shall have . . ."—down to and including the words—". . . then and in any of G   the said cases." In view of what I have held, I will discuss with counsel the form of the order which I shall make.

Order accordingly.
No order as to costs.

Solicitors: *Carlson & Co.; A. Banks & Co.*

H

T. C. C. B.

A

[FAMILY DIVISION]

*PRACTICE DIRECTION
(FAMILY DIVISION: FILING AFFIDAVITS)

*Husband and Wife—Practice—Affidavit—Principal Registry—Fixed
date of hearing—Filing affidavits and documents*

B

1. Where, in any cause or matter proceeding in the Principal Registry, a party wishes to file an affidavit or other document in connection with an application for which a hearing date has been fixed, the affidavit or other document must be lodged in the Principal Registry *not less than 14 clear days* before the appointed hearing date.

C

2. Where insufficient time remains before the hearing date to lodge the affidavit or other document as required by (1) above, it should be retained and handed to the clerk to the registrar, or associate in attendance upon the judge, before whom the application is to be heard immediately before the hearing. Service should be effected upon the opposing party in the normal way.

3. The registrar's direction of October 31, 1972, *Practice Direction (Family Division: Affidavit)* [1972] 1 W.L.R. 1519 is amended by substituting " 14 days " for " 8 days " and the registrar's direction of July 24, 1956, is amended by substituting " 14 days " for " 7 days."

D

R. L. BAYNE-POWELL,
Senior Registrar.

E

January 12, 1981.

[PRIVY COUNCIL]

*PATRICK CHOKOLINGO . . . . . . APPELLANT
AND

F

ATTORNEY-GENERAL OF TRINIDAD
AND TOBAGO . . . . RESPONDENT

[APPEAL FROM THE COURT OF APPEAL OF TRINIDAD AND TOBAGO]

G

1980 July 14;
Oct. 13

Lord Diplock, Lord Edmund-Davies,
Lord Keith of Kinkel, Lord Scarman
and Lord Roskill

*Trinidad and Tobago—Constitution—Human rights and funda-
mental freedoms—High Court ordering journalist's imprisonment for contempt—Subsequent application for redress—
Whether contravention of constitutional rights—Trinidad and
Tobago (Constitution) Order in Council 1962 (S.I. 1962 No.
1875), Sch. 2, ss. 1 (a), 6.*

H

Section 1 of the Constitution of Trinidad and Tobago provides:
"It is hereby recognised . . . that . . . there have existed and shall continue to exist . . . the following human rights and fundamental freedoms, namely, (*a*) the right of the

A   individual to life, liberty, security of the person and enjoyment of property, and the right not to be deprived thereof except by due process of law; . . ."

Section 6 of the Constitution provides:

". . . if any person alleges that any of the provisions of the forgoing sections . . . of this Constitution has been . . . contravened in relation to him, then, without prejudice to any other action with respect to the same matter which

B   is lawfully available, that person may apply to the High Court for redress."

The applicant was the editor of a newspaper and the author of a short story attacking the judiciary which he published in the newspaper on May 26, 1972. The Trinidad and Tobago Law Society applied to the High Court for an order committing the applicant to prison for contempt and " scandalising the court." At the hearing the applicant conceded that the story

C   and its publication had been a contempt and on August 17, 1972, the court ordered that he be committed to prison for 21 days. He served 12 days of that term. In January 1975 the applicant applied to the High Court under section 6 of the Constitution for a declaration that the order of August 17 was unconstitutional and that the imprisonment was illegal and a violation of his fundamental rights and freedoms guaranteed by section 1 (a) of the Constitution. On the applica-

D   tion the High Court considered whether the story and its publication had constituted a criminal contempt, decided that it had and dismissed the application. The Court of Appeal dismissed the applicant's appeal.

On the applicant's appeal to the Judicial Committee: —

Held, dismissing the appeal, that the " law " referred to in section 1 of the Constitution was the law as interpreted or declared by the judges in the exercise of the judicial power

E   of the state and since the Constitution enshrined the rule of law, it was fundamental that the decision of the court was final as between the parties to the litigation; that, accordingly, even if there had been an error of substantive law in the decision, the applicant had been deprived of his liberty by due process of law in accordance with the provisions of section 1 of the Constitution (post, p. 111A–D).

Maharaj v. *Attorney-General of Trinidad and Tobago*

F   (*No. 2*) [1979] A.C. 385, P.C. applied.

Decision of the Court of Appeal of Trinidad and Tobago affirmed.

The following cases are referred to in the judgment of their Lordships:

Ambard v. *Attorney-General of Trinidad and Tobago* [1936] A.C. 322; [1936] 1 All E.R. 704, P.C.

G   *Maharaj* v. *Attorney-General of Trinidad and Tobago* (*No. 2*) [1979] A.C. 385; [1978] 2 W.L.R. 902; [1978] 2 All E.R. 670, P.C.

The following additional cases were cited in argument:

Dillet, In re (1887) 12 App.Cas. 459, P.C.

Director of Public Prosecutions v. *Nasralla* [1967] 2 A.C. 238; [1967] 3

H   W.L.R. 13; [1967] 2 All E.R. 161, P.C.

Harrikissoon v. *Attorney-General of Trinidad and Tobago* [1980] A.C. 265; [1979] 3 W.L.R. 62, P.C.

Maharaj v. *Attorney-General of Trinidad and Tobago* [1977] 1 All E.R. 411, P.C.

Mootoo v. *Attorney-General of Trinidad and Tobago* [1979] 1 W.L.R. 1334, P.C.

Scott v. *Scott* [1913] A.C. 417, H.L. (E.).

Thompson v. *City of Louisville* (1960) 362 U.S. 199.

APPEAL (No. 20 of 1979) by Patrick Chokolingo (the applicant) with A leave of the Court of Appeal of Trinidad and Tobago against a judgment (December 28, 1979) of the Court of Appeal (Hyatali C.J., Corbin and Kelsick JJ.A.) dismissing the applicant's appeal from a judgment of Cross J. delivered on April 28, 1975, in the High Court by which he dismissed the applicant's application for relief under section 6 of the Constitution in respect of the applicant's committal for contempt by the High Court in its criminal jurisdiction (Hassanali J.) on August 17, 1972.

The facts are stated in the judgment of their Lordships.

David Turner-Samuels Q.C. and *Stephen Sedley* for the applicant.

Jean Permanand, Solicitor-General, Trinidad and Tobago and *George Newman* for the Attorney-General.

Cur. adv. vult.   C

October 13. The judgment of their Lordships was delivered by LORD DIPLOCK.

On May 26, 1972, there was published in a newspaper *The Bomb*, of which the applicant was the editor, what was described as a " Short story by P. David Lincott " entitled " The Judge's Wife." P. David D Lincott was a nom de plume of the applicant who was the author of the story. It was written in the vernacular current in Trinidad and purported to be an account by a servant recently dismissed from a judge's household of the way in which the judge and his wife and, it was suggested, his fellow judges, habitually conducted themselves. A box heading to the story accurately summarised its contents: " The old domestic was bent on E exposing bribery, corruption and fraud in the household."

The Trinidad and Tobago Law Society took the view that, under a thin disguise of fiction, this was an attack upon the probity of the judiciary of Trinidad and Tobago as a whole. It charged them with corruption and was calculated to undermine the authority of the courts and public confidence in the administration of justice. The Law Society, which is F incorporated by an Act of Parliament, applied to the High Court for an order for committal of the applicant and the publisher of the newspaper for contempt of court. At the hearing of the application by Hassanali J. the applicant was represented by both senior and junior counsel. After certain preliminary objections to the form of the proceedings had been overruled by the judge, the applicant filed an affidavit in which he stated that he had been advised that the short story amounted to a contempt G of court for which he unreservedly apologised. His counsel also conceded that the publication of the so-called short story was a criminal contempt.

On July 17, 1972, Hassanali J. held the applicant and the publisher of *The Bomb* guilty of contempt of court and ordered the applicant to be imprisoned for 21 days, of which he in fact served 12, the remainder having been remitted by the Crown. He and the publisher, who was fined H $500, were also ordered to pay the costs of the Law Society.

In 1972, no appeal lay to the Court of Appeal from committal by the High Court for contempt. An appeal lay directly to Her Majesty in Council by special leave of this Board (*Ambard* v. *Attorney-General of Trinidad and Tobago* [1936] A.C. 322); but no such leave was sought by the applicant, no doubt in view of what in effect had been a plea of guilty on his part. Two and a half years later, on January 31, 1975, the applicant

A   sought to resurrect the matter by applying to the High Court, under
section 6 (1) of the Constitution of Trinidad and Tobago, for declarations
that the order of Hassanali J. for his committal was unconstitutional and
void and that his subsequent imprisonment under that order was in breach
of the human rights and fundamental freedoms guaranteed to him by
section 1 (a), (i) and (k) of the Constitution, viz:

B   " (a) the right of the individual to life, liberty, security of the person
          and enjoyment of property, and the right not to be deprived thereof
          except by due process of law; . . . (i) freedom of thought and
          expression; . . . (k) freedom of the press."

Against the Trinidad and Tobago Law Society who were (mistakenly)
made respondents to the application, he also claimed damages for wrongful
C   imprisonment and repayment of the costs of the contempt proceedings in
1972, which he had been ordered to pay. Notice of this application was
given to the Attorney-General as is required by section 13 of the Supreme
Court of Judicature Act 1962 but he was not made the respondent to
the application, as he should have been.

The application came on for hearing before Cross J. in March and
D   April 1975, some three years before the judgment of this Board in
Maharaj v. Attorney-General of Trinidad and Tobago (No. 2) [1979]
A.C. 385 had been delivered. He took the view that, upon an application
under section 6 of the Constitution, it was incumbent upon him to re-open
the whole question of whether the applicant had been guilty of criminal
contempt of court in 1972, notwithstanding the unappealed judgment to
that effect of Hassanali J. and the concession made at the hearing before
E   that judge by the applicant's own counsel that the applicant had been
guilty of contempt. Cross J. accordingly proceeded to consider the various
grounds on which the applicant's counsel relied for their submission that
Hassanali J. had erred in law in holding the applicant guilty. Of these
the only ground to which their Lordships need refer is a submission that,
whatever may have formerly been the law, " scandalising the court " by
F   a scurrilous attack on the judiciary as a whole, impugning their probity and
accusing them of corruption, was no longer capable of amounting to a
criminal contempt of court in Trinidad and Tobago. Cross J., after a
careful survey of the authorities from English and other Commonwealth
jurisdictions, rejected this and the other submissions that had been made
on behalf of the applicant and dismissed the application.

From this dismissal of his application, the applicant appealed to the
G   Court of Appeal. The effective hearing of the appeal took place in
October 1978, after the judgment of this Board in Maharaj v. Attorney-
General of Trinidad and Tobago (No. 2) [1979] A.C. 385 had been
reported. At the hearing the applicant's counsel expressly abandoned any
claim that his rights under section 1 (i) or (k) had been infringed; reliance
was placed solely upon section 1 (a). All three members of the court
H   (Hyatali C.J., Kelsick and Corbin JJ.A.) held that the only grounds upon
which the applicant's application under section 6 of the Constitution was
based, consisted of allegations of errors of substantive law in the original
judgment of Hassanali J. or mere irregularities in procedure; and that
nothing that was alleged was capable of amounting to a failure to observe
one of the fundamental rules of natural justice. Applying what was said
in the majority judgment in Maharaj v. Attorney-General of Trinidad
and Tobago (No. 2)—the minority judgment was more restrictive of the

scope of section 1 (a)—the Court of Appeal held that such errors, even A
if they were established, were not capable of constituting an infringement
of the applicant's right, under section 1 (a), not to be deprived of his
liberty except by due process of law.

All three appellate judges, however, did go on to consider whether
Hassanali J. had made an error in substantive law in holding that
scandalising the court, in the way that the so-called story complained of
did, amounted to a criminal contempt of court. All three were of opinion B
that his judgment to this effect was correct, though Kelsick J.A. was of
opinion that the proper procedure for dealing with this kind of contempt
was by criminal prosecution rather than by the summary procedure that
had in fact been adopted by the Law Society. Kelsick J.A.'s opinion on
this matter was not shared by the majority of the Court of Appeal; nor
has it been relied upon before this Board. Even if it were right, it would at C
most amount to a mere irregularity of procedure which, as this Board
pointed out in *Maharaj* v. *Attorney-General of Trinidad and Tobago*
(No. 2) [1979] A.C. 385, 399, does not of itself constitute an infringement
of rights protected by section 1 (a) unless it involves a failure to observe one
of the fundamental rules of natural justice. There was no such failure here.
The applicant had been fully informed of the charges against him in the D
contempt proceedings in 1972; he had ample opportunity to prepare his
defence. He was represented at the hearing by both senior and junior
counsel; it was on their advice that, in effect, he pleaded guilty to the
charge. The applicant exercised his right under section 82 (1) (c) of the
Constitution to appeal to the Judicial Committee of the Privy Council
from the decision of the Court of Appeal and by leave of this Board the
Attorney-General was substituted for the Law Society as respondent, so E
that the application under section 6 (1) should be properly constituted.

In dismissing the applicant's application under section 6 (1) the Court
of Appeal had relied upon the statement by this Board in *Maharaj* v.
Attorney-General of Trinidad and Tobago (No. 2) [1979] A.C. 385, 399:

> ". . . no human right or fundamental freedom recognised by Chapter
> 1 of the Constitution is contravened by a judgment or order that is F
> wrong and liable to be set aside on appeal for an error of fact or
> substantive law, even where the error has resulted in a person's
> serving a sentence of imprisonment. The remedy for errors of these
> kinds is to appeal to a higher court. Where there is no higher court
> to appeal to then none can say that there was error."
>   G

It may be that technically this statement was obiter, but as the context
indicates it had been the subject of careful deliberation by the Board in the
light of the judgments of Hyatali C.J. and Corbin J.A. in the Court of
Appeal and the minority judgment in the Judicial Committee itself.

The arguments addressed to their Lordships in the instant appeal,
however, call for some expansion of that statement. Under a constitution H
on the Westminster model, like that of Trinidad and Tobago, which is
based on the separation of powers, while it is an exercise of the legislative
power of the state to make the written law, it is an exercise of the judicial
power of the state, and consequently a function of the judiciary alone, to
interpret the written law when made and to declare the law where it still
remains unwritten, i.e. the English common law and doctrines of equity
as incorporated in the law of Trinidad and Tobago by section 12 of the

A   Supreme Court of Judicature Act 1962. So when in Chapter 1 the Constitution of Trinidad and Tobago speaks of "law" it is speaking of the law of Trinidad and Tobago as interpreted or declared by the judges in the exercise of the judicial power of the state.

The normal way in which this interpretative and declaratory function is exercised is by judges sitting in courts of justice for the purpose of deciding disputes between parties to litigation (whether civil or criminal),
B   which involves the application to the particular facts of the case of the law of Trinidad and Tobago that is relevant to the determination of their rights and obligations. It is fundamental to the administration of justice under a constitution which claims to enshrine the rule of law (preamble to the Constitution, paragraphs (d) and (e)) that if between the parties to the litigation the decision of that court is final (either because there
C   is no right of appeal to a higher court or because neither party has availed himself of an existing right of appeal), the relevant law as interpreted by the judge in reaching the court's decision is the "law" so far as the entitlement of the parties to "due process of law" under section 1 (a) and the "protection of the law" under section 1 (b) are concerned. Their Lordships repeat what was said in *Maharaj* v. *Attorney-General of*
D   *Trinidad and Tobago (No. 2)* [1979] A.C. 385. The fundamental human right guaranteed by section 1 (a) and (b), and section 2, of the Constitution is not to a legal system which is infallible but to one which is fair.

It was argued on behalf of the applicant that, if he could persuade the Board that, because it had become obsolete long before 1962, no such offence as "scandalising the court" was known to the common law in force in Trinidad at the commencement of the Constitution, this would
E   entitle the applicant to redress under section 6 for his having been imprisoned by the state for exercising his constitutional rights of freedom of expression and freedom of the press. But giving a separate label to what Hassanali J. held in the contempt proceedings to be a species of the genus of offences known as "contempt of court" does not, in their Lordships' view, assist the applicant. "Scandalising the court" is a convenient way
F   of describing a publication which, although it does not relate to any specific case either past or pending or any specific judge, is a scurrilous attack on the judiciary as a whole, which is calculated to undermine the authority of the courts and public confidence in the administration of justice. Even if it were possible to persuade their Lordships that publication of written matter which has these characteristics no longer constituted a criminal contempt of court in Trinidad and Tobago in 1972, it would
G   merely show that the judge had made an error of substantive law as to a necessary ingredient of the genus of common law offences which constitute contempt of court. In their Lordships' view there is no difference in principle behind this kind of error and a misinterpretation by a judge, in the course of an ordinary criminal trial, of the words of the Act of Parliament creating the offence with which the accused is charged. If
H   the former is open to collateral attack by application to the High Court under section 6 (1) of the Constitution so must the latter be.

Acceptance of the applicant's argument would have the consequence that in every criminal case, in which a person who had been convicted alleged that the judge had made any error of substantive law as to the necessary characteristics of the offence, there would be parallel remedies available to him: one by appeal to the Court of Appeal, the other by originating application under section 6 (1) of the Constitution to the

High Court with further rights of appeal to the Court of Appeal and to   A
the Judicial Committee. These parallel remedies would be also cumulative
since the right to apply for redress under section 6 (1) is stated to be
"without prejudice to any other action with respect to the same matter
which is lawfully available." The convicted person having exercised
unsuccessfully his right of appeal to a higher court, the Court of Appeal,
he could nevertheless launch a collateral attack (it may be years later)   B
upon a judgment that the Court of Appeal had upheld, by making an
application for redress under section 6 (1) to a court of co-ordinate
jurisdiction, the High Court. To give to Chapter I of the Constitution an
interpretation which would lead to this result would, in their Lordships'
view, be quite irrational and subversive of the rule of law which it is a
declared purpose of the Constitution to enshrine.

For the sake of completeness their Lordships will deal briefly with the   C
other argument addressed to them on behalf of the applicant. It was that
he had been convicted by Hassanali J. without there being any evidence
that he had committed an offence and that accordingly his conviction was
not obtained by "due process of law." But this, on analysis, is only
another way of saying that the judge made an error of substantive law in
holding that to constitute a criminal contempt of court it is not necessary   D
that a publication attacking the judiciary should refer to a specific case or
to a specific judge. The publication of the issue of The Bomb containing
the so-called short story "The Judge's Wife" was proved, the applicant's
authorship was admitted. The only fact of which evidence was missing was
one which on Hassanali J.'s view of the substantive law was unnecessary
viz. that the short story related to a specific case or a specific judge.

The application under section 6 (1) was misconceived. The appeal   E
must be dismissed with costs.

Appeal dismissed with costs.

Solicitors: *Ingledew, Brown, Bennison & Garrett; Charles Russell*
& Co.

T. J. M.   F

[QUEEN'S BENCH DIVISION]
                                                                            G
* REGINA v. UXBRIDGE JUSTICES, *Ex parte* COMMISSIONER
OF POLICE OF THE METROPOLIS

1980 July 2   Donaldson L.J. and Kilner Brown J.

Justices—Costs—Property held by police—Claim for return of   H
property—Whether "application" to be made by way of
complaint—Jurisdiction to make order for costs—Police
(Property) Act 1897 (60 & 61 Vict. c. 30), s. 1 (1)—Magistrates'
Courts Act 1952 (15 & 16 Geo. 5 & 1 Eliz. 2, c. 55), s. 55

Section 1 (1) of the Police (Property) Act 1897 provides:
"Where any property has come into the possession of the
police in connection with any criminal charge . . . a court
of summary jurisdiction may, on application either by an

The Weekly Law Reports, February 6, 1981

113

1 W.L.R.   Reg. v. Uxbridge JJ., Ex. p. Police Comr. (D.C.)

A officer of police or by a claimant of the property, make an order for the delivery of the property to the person appearing to the magistrate or court to be the owner thereof, or, if the owner cannot be ascertained, make such order with respect to the property as to the magistrate or court may seem meet."

Section 55 (1) of the Magistrates' Courts Act 1952 provides:

B " On the hearing of a complaint, a magistrates' court shall have power in its discretion to make such order as to costs —(a) on making the order for which the complaint is made, to be paid by the defendant to the complainant; . . . as it thinks just and reasonable: . . ."

The police held money which had come into their possession during an investigation into currency offences. The respondent applied to the justices by summons, expressed to be by way of

C complaint, under section 1 of the Police (Property) Act 1897 for the return of the money to him. The police did not oppose the matter. The justices made the order and, on an application on behalf of the respondent, they awarded him £350 costs.

On an application by the Commissioner of Police for an order of certiorari to quash the order for costs on the ground that the justices had no power to make the order on an " application " under section 1 of the Act of 1897: —

D *Held,* dismissing the application, that in exercising their jurisdiction under section 1 of the Act the justices were usually determining rights of property between parties and, in so doing, they were exercising a judicial function and not a regulatory function (post, p. 114H); that in the present case the justices were exercising a judicial function and, therefore, the respondent had rightly made his claim by way of complaint

E and, accordingly, the justices had power under section 55 (1) of the Magistrates' Courts Act 1955 to make an order for the police to pay the respondent's costs (post, p. 115E–F).

Per curiam. Where the police hold property but have no means of knowing who is entitled to the property and apply to the justices for an order under section 1 of the Act of 1897, it can be argued that there is no lis between the police and anybody else and the justices perhaps could be said not to be

F acting in a judicial capacity. They are acting in a regulatory capacity authorising the police to take some action (post, p. 115B–C).

No cases are referred to in the judgment or were cited in argument.

G APPLICATION for order of certiorari.

The applicant, the Commissioner of Police of the Metropolis, sought an order of certiorari to quash an order made by the Uxbridge justices on January 11, 1979, that the applicant should pay the costs of the respondent, Sukh Deo Prasad, in the sum of £350. The grounds of the application were that the order was wrong in law; that the order was in excess of the jurisdiction of the court; that there was no power to make

H an order for costs on the hearing of an application under section 1 of the Police (Property) Act 1897; and that it was irregular to make an application under section 1 of the Act of 1897 by way of complaint.

The facts are as stated in the judgment of Donaldson L.J.

Laurence Marshall for the applicant.
Michael Harington for the respondent.

The Weekly Law Reports, February 6, 1981

114
Reg. v. Uxbridge JJ., Ex. p. Police Comr. (D.C.) [1981]

DONALDSON L.J. This is a very curious dispute which has arisen A
between the Commissioner of Police of the Metropolis and Mr. Prasad
concerning some currency which came into the hands of the Commissioner of Police in circumstances to which the Police (Property) Act
1897 applies.

Section 1 of that Act gives justices power to make orders with respect
to property in the possession of the police. That is the sidenote. Subsection B
(1) provides that, where any property has come into the possession of the
police in connection with any criminal charge or under various statutes,
a court of summary jurisdiction may, on application either by an officer
of police or by a claimant of the property, make an order for the delivery
of the property to the person appearing to the magistrate or court to be
the owner thereof, or, if the owner cannot be ascertained make such order
with respect to the property as to the magistrate or court may seem meet. C

Mr. Prasad claimed this property and the justices made an order in
his favour. Then the question arose as to whether there was any power
in the magistrates' court to award costs against the police or indeed against
anybody else in favour of the applicant.

Magistrates' courts have no power at common law to make any order
for costs. If the justices in this case, who did make an order for costs, D
were acting with jurisdiction, that jurisdiction is to be found in section
55 of the Magistrates' Courts Act 1952. That section gives power to a
magistrates' court to make an order for costs "on the hearing of a
complaint."

The problem reduces itself to this. If either an officer of police or a
claimant of property makes application under the Police (Property) Act E
1897, are those proceedings properly brought by way of complaint or
should they be by way of application or notice of motion or some other
form of initiating process? If they are properly brought by complaint,
there is power to award costs under section 55 of the Act of 1952. It it has
to be brought in some other way, there being no other statutory power
to order costs which could be applicable in this case, there is no power to
order costs. F

We are told that the *Justice of the Peace,* admirable journal though
it is, has adverted to this question on three occasions and has twice come
down on one side of the fence and once on the other, so that I am not
sure that takes the matter very much further.

I think we have to approach this on the basis of principle and I am
impressed by Mr. Harrington's argument that justices have two different G
functions—a judicial function and a regulatory function. The most obvious
example of their regulatory function is in relation to the Licensing Acts.
He submits, in relation to their regulatory function, that one has to find
special provisions as to costs, the procedure by complaint being inappropriate, but that the procedure by complaint is appropriate to initiate
proceedings calling upon justices to exercise a judicial function. H

I think that is right. I then turn again to section 1 of the Police
(Property) Act 1897 and it seems to me that under that section the
justices are usually being asked to exercise a judicial function. They are
being asked to determine rights of property, albeit on a nisi basis, because
under section 1 (2) any party who claims to be entitled to possession of
property which has been delivered to somebody else pursuant to an order
made under the Act is entitled within six months to apply to some other

The Weekly Law Reports, February 6, 1981

115

1 W.L.R.   Reg. v. Uxbridge JJ., Ex. p. Police Comr. (D.C.)   Donaldson L.J.

A   court of appropriate jurisdiction, and the justices' order does not act as any bar to whatever order that court sees fit to make. But, subject to that, it is essentially a judicial function.

I said "usually" because there is one case in which it does not appear to be a judicial function. Normally there will be a claimant who says that the property is his. There may be several claimants, all of whom say the property is theirs.

B   Then there will be a lis between the claimants inter se and between the claimants and the police as the holder of the property, and that lis will be determined for the time being by the justices' order. But one could get a case as the statute contemplates in which the police are in possession of property, but have no means of knowing who, if anybody is entitled to the property. They then go to the justices and say

C   "What do we do with this property?" The order which will be made by the justices will be their authority for doing whatever the order requires. But there it can be argued that there is no lis between the police and anybody else, and the justices perhaps could be said not to be acting in a judicial capacity. They are acting in a regulatory capacity authorising the police to take some action.

D   I was at one time a little concerned that we should have the position in which, if the police apply, there being no claimant to the property, they should be unable to get costs because it would be inappropriate to begin such proceedings by complaint (it would clearly be by application), whereas if there was a claimant on the horizon, either he or the police ought to proceed by complaint because, as I say, it would be a judicial proceeding. But although I think it is untidy that the logic of what I have

E   been saying should lead to that result, it has no practical significance because, of course, if there is no other party, no defendant to the complaint, there is nobody against whom the police could get costs anyway.

Subject to that, I think that this is a judicial function. It is therefore appropriate to be brought by way of complaint. It being brought by way of complaint, there is jurisdiction to award costs under section 55 of the

F   Act of 1952, but of course justices will no doubt exercise their discretion as to whether costs are awarded and will take account of the conduct of the police who may or may not contest a claim. They will no doubt take very full account of the fact that the police, as the involuntary bailees of the property, have to get some form of authority to hand it over to anyone. If they are doing no more than acceding to an application or "interpleading," they may well think that it will be wholly inappropriate

G   that they should be asked to pay any costs at all. If they contest the claim and fail, that is a different matter, but if they are interpleading then I think the justices have a discretion and it would be an unusual case in which it was appropriate to make an order for costs.

KILNER BROWN J. I agree. I think the matter can further be tested

H   in this way, as Donaldson L.J. has indicated. Suppose that the application is made by a claimant of the property and the police sensibly think that it is a bogus application. They may be compelled to come to court and put the matter before the justices on the basis that this is a bogus application. In those circumstances I would have thought that the police would be entitled to their costs, though only if the justices in their discretion felt that the police intervention was proper and they were forced to intervene. As Donaldson L.J. has pointed out, in circumstances such as

Kilner Brown J.   Reg. v. Uxbridge JJ., Ex. p. Police Comr. (D.C.)   **[1981]**

A

this one ought to leave it to the good sense of the justices to decide whether or not there should be an order for costs and, if so, what amount.

Application refused.
No order as to costs.
Legal aid taxation.

B

Solicitors: *Solicitor, Metropolitan Police; Edward Mackie & Co., Ealing.*

[Reported by MISS LESLEY HEWLETT, Barrister-at-Law]

[QUEEN'S BENCH DIVISION]

C

* REGINA *v.* CROYDON CROWN COURT, *Ex parte* BERNARD

1980 May 6   Lord Lane C.J. and Woolf J.

Crown Court—Jurisdiction—Appeal against conviction—Committal for sentence—Sentence imposed on applicant—Applicant seeking to appeal against conviction—Whether court functus officio

D

The applicant, who had been convicted by the juvenile court of two offences and committed to the Crown Court, under section 28 of the Magistrates' Courts Act 1952, for a sentence of borstal training, wished to appeal against conviction. As a result of a misunderstanding, counsel, who then appeared for the applicant, was under the impression that his instructing solicitors had advised against an appeal and, when asked by the judge in the Crown Court whether he wished to apply for leave to appeal out of time against conviction, he stated that he was not instructed to make the application. The judge then sentenced the applicant to a period of borstal training. Thereafter the applicant wrote to his solicitors stating that he still wished to appeal against conviction. The solicitors applied to the judge, who granted the applicant leave to appeal out of time. The appeal came before a recorder, who refused to hear and determine the matter on the ground that the court was functus officio.

E

F

On an application for a judicial review: —
Held, granting an order of mandamus, that the Crown Court, in determining the sentence to be imposed on a defendant committed to the Crown Court by justices, was exercising a distinct and separate function from its power to hear and determine an appeal from the justices; that, therefore, the fact that the applicant had been sentenced to a period of borstal training did not prevent the court from entertaining his appeal against conviction and, accordingly, the Crown Court would be ordered to hear and determine that appeal.

G

The following case is referred to in the judgment of Lord Lane C.J.:
Rex v. *Faithful* [1950] 2 All E.R. 1251, C.C.A.

H

The following additional case was cited in argument:
Reg. v. *Tottenham Justices, Ex parte Rubens* [1970] 1 W.L.R. 800; [1970] 1 All E.R. 879, D.C.

JUDICIAL REVIEW
The applicant, Peter Burchill Bernard, applied for a judicial review of a decision of the recorder sitting at Croydon Crown Court on March 12,

A 1980, refusing to entertain his appeal against conviction.   He sought the remedy of either an order of mandamus directing the Crown Court to hear and determine his appeal against conviction of two offences by the juvenile court at Croydon on November 26, 1979, or an order of certiorari to bring up and quash an order of borstal training and a sentence of one day's detention passed on him on December 20, 1979, by the Croydon Crown Court for the two offences.   The grounds of the application were

B that the sentence had been passed on the applicant after counsel, under a misapprehension of the true position, had informed the court that he had instructions not to proceed with an appeal against conviction; and that on March 12, 1980, the Crown Court had refused to entertain the applicant's appeal against conviction notwithstanding that leave to appeal out of time had been granted on January 22.

C   The facts are stated in the judgment of Lord Lane C.J.

David Barnard (who did not appear in the earlier proceedings) for the applicant.
Charles Byers for the respondent prosecutor.

D   Lord Lane C.J.   In this case the applicant applies for judicial review pursuant to leave granted by the vacation judge on April 9, 1980.
There are two alternative remedies which are suggested in this case. The first is an order of mandamus directed to the Crown Court at Croydon to hear the applicant's appeal.   The second remedy suggested in the alternative is an order of certiorari to bring up and quash a sentence passed by a different judge at the Croydon Crown Court in respect of

E the offence.
The facts of the case are unusual, but it is necessary to go into them in a little detail in order to explain how this appeal comes about.   On November 26, 1979, the applicant was convicted by the Croydon Juvenile Court of two offences; assaulting a police officer was the first and attempting to steal a tape recorder was the second.   He was committed

F by the justices to the Crown Court for sentence under section 28 of the Magistrates' Courts Act 1952, which as amended reads:

"(1) Where a person is convicted by a magistrates' court of an offence punishable on summary conviction with imprisonment, then, if on the day of the conviction he is not less than 15 but under 21 years old and is a person who, under section 1 (2) and (4) of the Criminal Justice Act 1961, may be committed for a sentence of

G   borstal training, the court may commit him in custody or on bail to the Crown Court for sentence in accordance with the provisions of section 20 of the Criminal Justice Act 1948."

That is the section, brought up to date by section 56 of the Criminal Justice Act 1967, under which the justices committed him.
Before the justices and throughout the subsequent proceedings he was

H represented by counsel, not counsel who appears for him today, who is Mr. Barnard, but a young man of very recent call to the Bar.   It seems that after his conviction before the justices, the applicant was expressing his wish to appeal against his conviction.   That wish was again apparently conveyed to the solicitors who were acting for him.   An employee of the solicitors' firm gave the impression to the young member of the Bar that a partner in the firm had advised against an appeal, though it seems that impression was due to a misunderstanding.

118

Lord Lane C.J.   Reg. v. Croydon Crown Court, Ex p. Bernard (D.C.)   [1981]

The next step in the proceedings was the appearance of the applicant
before Judge Graham Hall on December 20, 1979, at the Crown Court
at Croydon. All that was before that court was of course the question
of sentence. Nevertheless, in his address to the judge, young counsel
alleged and said that his client was still questioning the correctness of the
conviction. The judge then very properly, if we may respectfully say
so, asked whether the applicant wished to seek leave to appeal against
conviction out of time. If everything had gone right, the young member
of the Bar would have taken further instructions from his client and
asked him what the true situation was. But counsel took instructions
only from the solicitors' clerk who was there. He did not take the
precaution of seeing the client himself, and the clerk who was attending
upon counsel gave the impression that the instructions of the firm's
partner were that no appeal against conviction should be launched.
Thereupon counsel told the judge that he had no instructions to appeal
against conviction, so the hearing with regard to sentence continued.

The applicant was sent to borstal for the attempted theft and one day's
detention in respect of the charge of assault. So the matter seemed to
have ended.

But in January 1980 a letter was sent by the applicant to the solicitors
and in it he maintains his innocence of the offences charged against him
and suggests that he still wants to appeal against the conviction because
he thinks that he is in borstal for something that he never did.

That letter came to the notice of one of the partners in the firm of
solicitors, who made investigations about the history of the matter and
at once applied by letter to the court for leave to appeal out of time
against conviction. By a letter dated January 22, 1980, a reply came
from the Crown Court saying that the judge who had heard the matter
of sentence, Judge Graham Hall, had granted the required extension.

The next scene is Croydon Crown Court again when an appeal against
conviction was sought to be launched. That was on March 12, 1980,
before a recorder. When the matters were explained to the recorder he
formed the view that because the applicant had been sentenced in respect
of these two offences there had been a final adjudication with regard to
conviction and sentence, and accordingly the court was functus officio
and had no basis on which to continue.

The matter rests there. The recorder has declined to hear the appeal
because he thinks the court has no power to hear it. Mr. Barnard, on
behalf of the applicant, submits to us as his first proposition that it was
the duty of the recorder to hear that appeal and he was mistaken when
he came to the conclusion that he had no power.

The case which was cited to the recorder was Rex v. Faithful [1950]
2 All E.R. 1251. The circumstances of that case appear from the head-

"On August 30, 1950, the applicant was committed, under the
Criminal Justice Act 1948, section 29 (1) to the County of London
Quarter Sessions for sentence on his conviction of larceny by a
metropolitan magistrate, and on September 8 he was sentenced to
three years' corrective training. On September 11 he gave notice
of appeal to the quarter sessions against his conviction, and on
October 5 the appeal was dismissed.

"Held: (i) an appeal committee of quarter sessions which meet
frequently, before passing sentence on an offender after a committal
under section 29 (1), should satisfy themselves that the time for

A   appealing against the conviction has expired. If the time for appealing has not expired and the offender informs them that he intends to appeal, the committee should adjourn consideration of the sentence.

"(ii) an appeal committee which do not meet so frequently, before passing sentence in any case in which the time for appealing against conviction has not expired, should ascertain whether the

B   offender intends to appeal. If he informs them he intends to appeal, the committee should offer an adjournment and inform the offender of the possible delay and that he must remain in custody."

The passage which apparently was said to be relevant to the present case is, at p. 1252:

C   "On October 5 that appeal was heard by the appeal committee of quarter sessions and was dismissed. Thus, it is seen that the applicant's appeal against conviction was heard and disposed of after he had been committed for sentence and had been sentenced. That, in the view of this court, is an undesirable state of affairs."

It does not seem to me that that decision is of any assistance in the

D   present case for determining whether the court at Croydon was functus officio in the circumstances which I have related. What it does make clear, however, is this. The judge who passed the sentence at Croydon, Judge Graham Hall, acted with complete propriety in addressing the questions she did address to the applicant's counsel before passing sentence.

The way in which the matter is put on behalf of the applicant here is

E   this. The Crown Court has two separate forms of jurisdiction. It has the task of hearing and determining committals for sentence, the task of deciding (having inquired into all the circumstances) what is the proper sentence which should be passed upon someone who has been sent from the justices to be sentenced by the Crown Court. The second duty and power which it has is the right to hear appeals from the justices.

F   The submission is that a determination made under the first of those powers or duties does not render the court functus officio so far as the second form of power or duty is concerned, that is to say that the passing of a sentence does not mean that the court has finished its functions so far as the right to hear appeals against conviction is concerned. With that contention I would respectfully agree.

G   The suggestion made by Mr. Byers, who appears in what he describes as a state of benevolent neutrality on behalf of the Metropolitan Police, does not seem to me to be attractive, because he suggests that, if the answer is as the applicant would have it, then one might get a situation where the conviction has been quashed whereas the sentence still remains. He says, as in this case, one might get a person in borstal whose conviction has been quashed.

H   The answer to that rather extraordinary proposition seems to be that once a conviction has gone then so has everything which depends upon the conviction, and one of the things which depends upon the conviction is the sentence. When the conviction has gone, then so has the sentence.

Consequently, it seems to me that the proper order in this case is an order of mandamus directed to the Croydon Crown Court to hear this appeal and determine it.

120

Lord Lane C.J.   Reg. v. Croydon Crown Court, Ex p. Bernard (D.C.)   [1981]

In those circumstances the other alternative put forward by Mr.   A
Barnard on behalf of the applicant does not seem to fall for decision. He
suggests that an order of certiorari should be directed to the Croydon Crown
Court in respect of the sentence which was imposed upon this applicant by
Judge Graham Hall, and that once that order of certiorari has gone and
that sentence is quashed, then the applicant would be back in his previous
state and could carry on his appeal thenceforward.

Whether that is a correct submission or not I do not propose to say.   B
It is not necessary for the decision of this court. It obviously raises all
sorts of difficult problems. In my judgment, the true answer to the
present case is an order of mandamus directed in the way I have
explained.

WOOLF J.   I agree.   C

> Order of mandamus.
> Applicants' costs to be paid out of
> central funds.

Solicitors: Robert Blackford & Co., Croydon; Solicitor, Metropolitan
Police.

H. J.   D

[COURT OF APPEAL]   E

* DALY v. GENERAL STEAM NAVIGATION CO. LTD.

1980   May 20   Ormrod, Bridge and Templeman L.JJ.

Damages—Personal injuries—Loss of amenities—Wife's inability
   to perform housekeeping duties—Husband's loss of earnings   F
   incurred as result of assisting wife—Estimated cost of employing domestic help — Whether proper measure of damages
   notwithstanding possibility of award not being used for that
   purpose—Whether husband's loss of earnings recoverable
Interest—Award of damages—Personal injury cases—Interest on
   amount for pain and suffering and loss of amenities
Ships' Names—Dragon
    G
The plaintiff housewife, who was a passenger on the defen-
ants' vessel, was injured in an accident and had to be treated
over a long period both in and out of hospital. She became
partially incapable of undertaking housekeeping duties and
ran her home with the assistance of her husband, who lost
£930 in part-time earnings as a result. She did not employ a
home help. On her claim for damages against the defendants,
she was awarded £21,116 damages, consisting of £1,689 special   H
damages (not including the amount of the husband's loss of
earnings), £2,691 for " partial loss of housekeeping capacity "
before the trial, £8,736 for such loss in the future (the last
two sums being the estimated costs of home help for the
respective periods), and £8,000 for pain and suffering and loss
of amenity; she was awarded interest only under the first two
heads of damage.

On appeal by the defendants against the awards for loss
of housekeeping capacity, and on cross-appeal by the plaintiff

1 W.L.R.   **Daly v. General Steam Navigation Co. (C.A.)**

A
against failure to award interest on the sum for pain and suffering and loss of amenity: —

Held, dismissing the appeal, (1) that the estimated cost of providing the housekeeping services which the plaintiff would need in the future was the proper measure of damages for her future partial loss of housekeeping capacity, even if the award might not be used for that purpose (post pp. 127c–E, 129B–C, G).

B
(2) That in respect of the period before the trial it was not a correct method of evaluating the partial loss of capacity, which was essentially an element in the plaintiff's damages for pain and suffering and loss of amenity, to take the figure which it would have cost to employ someone whom she had not, in fact, employed, but that in assessing special damages it was proper to include the amount of the part-time earnings which the plaintiff's husband had lost because of the necessity

C
of assisting the plaintiff and, in the result, the global figure was not wrong but should, have been arrived at by increasing the special damages by the amount of the husband's loss of earnings (£930) and awarding £9,761, instead of £8,000, for pain and suffering and loss of amenity; and that the figures would be adjusted accordingly (post, pp. 128A–D, G–H, 129C, E–F, G).

Donnelly v. *Joyce* [1974] Q.B. 454, C.A. applied.

Per Ormrod L.J. The words " incapacity " and " capacity "

D
are extraordinarily vague words upon which much can be built on rather insecure foundations. What the court has to do is to look to see, so far as the pre-trial loss is concerned, the actual loss that has been sustained (post, p. 130A).

Held further, allowing the cross-appeal, that interest at the short-term investment rate should be awarded on the sum for pain and suffering and loss of amenity from the date of the writ to the date of trial (post, pp. 129A–B, C, 130E).

E
Pickett v. *British Rail Engineering Ltd.* [1980] A.C. 136, H.L.(E.) applied.

Decision of Brandon J. [1979] 1 Lloyd's Rep. 257 affirmed in part.

The following cases are referred to in the judgments:

Cookson v. *Knowles* [1977] Q.B. 913; [1977] 3 W.L.R. 279; [1977] 2 All

F
E.R. 820, C.A.

Donnelly v. *Joyce* [1974] Q.B. 454; [1973] 3 W.L.R. 514; [1973] 3 All E.R. 475, C.A.

Hay v. *Hughes* [1975] Q.B. 790; [1975] 2 W.L.R. 34; [1975] 1 All E.R. 257, C.A.

Pickett v. *British Rail Engineering Ltd.* [1980] A.C. 136; [1978] 3 W.L.R. 755; [1979] 1 All E.R. 774, H.L.(E.).

G
No additional cases were cited in argument.

APPEAL from Brandon J.

The plaintiff, Veronica Daly, by specially indorsed writ dated June 14, 1974, claimed damages against the defendants, General Steam Navigation

H
Co. Ltd., for personal injuries sustained by her on their sailing vessel as a result of an accident which occurred on July 7, 1971, and which she alleged was caused by the negligence of the defendants or the members of the crew in the course of their employment. The defendants denied negligence. Brandon J., on July 10, 1978, gave judgment for the plaintiff in the sum of £21,116 together with interest on £4,380 of that sum.

By notice of appeal, dated September 18, 1978, the defendants appealed on the ground that the judge erred in law and/or principle in the respects that (1) he awarded general damages which were excessive in all the cir-

122

cumstances; (2) he wrongly awarded damages in respect of future loss to   A
the plaintiff, a woman of 42, on the basis of a multiplier of 15; (3) he
wrongly awarded damages for loss of amenity on the same basis as general
damages for future economic loss; (4) he wrongly awarded damages in
respect of the plaintiff's loss of housekeeping capacity as if that were a
head of damages separate from loss of amenity generally (while nonetheless treating the claims in respect of such lost capacity as being a claim   B
only in respect of loss of amenity; (5) he wrongly awarded the plaintiff
damages for loss of her housekeeping capacity by reference to the economic
cost of the replacement of such housekeeping capacity when it was neither
alleged nor proved that such replacement was essential, the plaintiff's
allegation being only in the event of being awarded damages such replacement would in fact be obtained; (6) he wrongly awarded the plaintiff   C
damages for loss of her housekeeping capacity prior to the trial of the
action by reference to the economic cost of the replacement of such capacity although the plaintiff had not in fact suffered that loss, but had suffered
a lesser loss; (7) he wrongly awarded the plaintiff interest on a part of the
general damages which represented economic loss suffered before the trial.

By a respondent's notice dated October 6, 1978, the plaintiff contended
that the judgment should be varied to allow sums awarded therein for the   D
plaintiff's loss of amenity and/or loss of housekeeping capacity to be added
to the plaintiff's general damages; and by a cross-notice of appeal dated
May 20, 1980, the plaintiff appealed from so much of the judgment and
order as adjudged that the plaintiff should not recover interest on her
general damages of £8,000.

The facts are stated in the judgment of Bridge L.J.
                                                                          E

Patrick Bennett Q.C. and *M. N. Howard* for the defendants.
Adrian Hamilton Q.C. and *Alan Pardoe* for the plaintiff.

BRIDGE L.J. delivered the first judgment. On July 7, 1971, the plaintiff
was a passenger on a vessel belonging to the defendants. She was going to
travel from Rosslare in Ireland to somewhere on the continent of Europe,   F
when she met with a most grievous accident which caused extremely serious
injuries to her right shoulder and arm. In due course, she claimed damages
against the defendants, and the matter came for trial before Brandon J.
who, on July 10, 1978, gave judgment for the plaintiff in a sum of
damages which was made up of a number of different items. He awarded
£1,689 special damages; £2,691 for what he described as the " plaintiff's
partial loss of housekeeping capacity " up to the date of trial, and £8,736   G
in respect of the plaintiff's future partial loss of housekeeping capacity;
finally, for pain and suffering and loss of amenity, he awarded a sum of
£8,000. He aggregated the special damages with the partial loss of housekeeping figure up to the date of trial, making a total of £4,380, and on
that figure he awarded interest from the date of the accident to the date
of judgment at half the short-term investment rate, and on the balance of   H
the judgment he awarded no interest.

The essence of the appeal before the court against the judgment is
directed at the awards which the judge made for partial loss of housekeeping capacity, and at a late stage a cross-appeal has been entered on behalf
of the plaintiff, complaining of the judge's failure to award interest on the
damages in respect of pain and suffering and loss of amenity.

I have said that the plaintiff suffered extremely severe injuries to her

The Weekly Law Reports, February 6, 1981

123

1 W.L.R.   Daly v. General Steam Navigation Co. (C.A.)   Bridge L.J.

A right shoulder and arm. The nature of those injuries, the history of the long series of visits to hospital which the plaintiff had to undergo, and the consequences of the injuries are all accurately and succinctly summarised in the judgment of the judge. I could not equal, let alone improve, upon that summary if I tried. I therefore propose to adopt what the judge said in the following passage of his judgment.

B " *The damages issue.* After the accident the plaintiff was taken by ambulance to Wexford County Hospital and detained there. She was found to have a comminuted fracture of the right shoulder and paralysis of the right arm. An operation was carried out on her during the night, consisting of open reduction and fixation with a four hole plate with four screws. This involved a surgical incision on the anterolateral surface of the right shoulder. On July 9, 1971, the plaintiff was transferred to St. Mary's Orthopaedic Hospital, Cappagh. She was found to have extensive bruising of the right side of the neck, the right shoulder and the right arm, and laceration of the medial side of the arm. There was no muscle reaction at all in the right arm. She was treated with physiotherapy and discharged home on August 6, 1971.

D " On August 22, 1971, a plaster was applied, and on September 8 she was examined again at Cappagh Hospital where fresh X-rays were taken. It was found that the bruising had gone and that a four inch surgical incision on the anterolateral side of her arm and a three inch laceration on the posterolateral side had both healed. The fracture, however, had not united and there was very little movement of the shoulder joint. There was some flexion movement in the fingers and thumb of her right hand, but no dorsiflexion movement in either the fingers or the wrist joint.

E " The conclusion was reached that there had been damage to the nerve supply of her right arm. Arrangements were made to have her return to the hospital for a further bonegraft operation consisting of the removal of bone from the iliac crest and the placing of it round the fracture in the right shoulder.

F " On September 13, 1971, the plaintiff was re-admitted to Cappagh Hospital, and on September 15 the bonegraft operation was carried out. On September 22 a plaster was applied, and on November 4 she was discharged home again. On November 29 she went into Cappagh Hospital again and the plaster was removed. On December 22 she was allowed home again.

G " On the last day of December 1971 and during the first two weeks of January 1972 the plaintiff attended as an out-patient at St. Vincent's Hospital for treatment by physiotherapy. She was in Cappagh Hospital again from January 12 to 21, presumably for observation, and from January 26 to 28, when a pin which had been put in her shoulder was removed. She had further spells in Cappagh Hospital: from January 31 to February 4, and from February 7 to February 11. She then continued to receive physiotherapy as an out-patient at St. Anthony's Rehabilitation Centre until May 19, 1972.

H " The plaintiff's shoulder was still very stiff and it was recommended in May that she should have manipulative treatment in hospital. She went into Cappagh Hospital again from September 26 to 28, 1972, to receive such treatment, and there was a slight increase in the movement of her shoulder as a result.

" In May 1973, a further examination showed that there had been

124

some improvement in the function of the plaintiff's right hand. The A
main problems were stiffness in the shoulder and the absence of any
extension movement of the wrist. The fracture itself had now united.

" In August and September 1973, the doctors decided that the
plaintiff should have a further operation, consisting of tendon transplant, but, due to industrial action, there was a delay of several
months in making the necessary arrangements. On February 4, 1974, B
she went into Cappagh Hospital again for this further operation, in
which flexor muscles were transferred to the back of her wrist.

" On February 14 she returned home again in plaster, which remained on until March 19. From then until the end of April she
received further treatment by physiotherapy at St. Vincent's Rehabilitation Centre.

" On May 2, 1974, she was examined again. Her shoulder was C
painful. She had a quarter of the normal range of movement at the
shoulder joint. The transplanted tendons were working and there was
some extension movement at the wrist.

" On July 15, 1974, there was another examination, the transplant
was working and the grip of her hand was fair, but there was no
extension movement of the wrist against resistance. Exercises at home D
were recommended.

" The last examination of the plaintiff took place on July 28, 1975.
There was abduction movement at the right shoulder of 90°, but this
was only possible when the arm was held forward. She was unable
to lift her arm above shoulder level. All the movement was between
the shoulder blade and the underlying chest wall. There was no active
or passive abduction movement at the shoulder joint. There was only E
a very small amount of rotation at the shoulder. As regards the elbow
joint, there was full extension movement, flexion of 10° from a right
angle position, full pronation movement, and a quarter of normal
supination movement. As regards the fingers, there was full extension
movement except for a slight terminal restriction of the little finger
which was slightly clawed; full flexion at all finger joints and half F
normal flexion at all knuckle joints. The hand grip was fair. As regards
the wrist, there was good power of wrist flexion but dorsiflexion,
though present, was not active against resistance. As regards the
muscles, charting showed that there was good power in the small
muscles of the right shoulder; the deltoid muscle had more than half
normal strength; there was some slight weakness of the elbow flexor
muscles; there was considerable weakness of all the muscles which G
extend the wrist and fingers; the flexor muscles were strong; there was
some weakness in the small muscles of the hand; and there was some
diminution of sensation in the hand and forearm.

" There was no evidence that the plaintiff's condition had improved
significantly since that last examination of July 1975, which can therefore be regarded as showing her final condition after all medical H
treatment to improve it had been given.

" The plaintiff's accident, besides producing the physical injuries
and consequences of them which I have described, also had a serious
psychological effect on her. She suffered from severe depression, and
there was an adverse effect on her relationship with Mr. Daly which
put her marriage under strain. She has also suffered from dizzy spells
from time to time and from insomnia."

1 W.L.R.   **Daly v. General Steam Navigation Co. (C.A.)**   **Bridge L.J.**

A   The consequences of the extremely grave injuries which she sustained the plaintiff summarised in particulars which are also adopted by the judge as part of his judgment and held by him to have been fully substantiated, which I will read:

B
" (i) As a result of the injuries caused to her in the accident the plaintiff, who was before the accident right-handed, has been rendered unable to carry out activities requiring full use of her right arm including—(a) ordinary housework such as ironing and vacuum-cleaning and making of beds; (b) gardening; (c) driving, bicycling (this has entailed giving up singing with a choral society since a car is essential to get to rehearsals); (d) washing her own hair; (e) playing tennis.
C
(ii) In addition because she is more prone to falling because she cannot hold on with her right hand and because the consequences of falling on her right arm would be serious she cannot use easily public transport or go out on ice or snow or stand on chairs or ladders. (iii) She is in continual pain which increases in winter. (iv) The scars have affected her appearance and attractiveness. She and her husband have had consequential problems in their marriage. There has been considerable stress and depression. (v) She is no longer able to enjoy
D
the beach which she did before. (vi) She has found it difficult to exercise a proper supervision of her children and the consequent family difficulties have distressed her. Her son is now at a boarding school. She has been precluded from increasing her family. (vii) The opportunities of paid work have diminished because she used her right hand to write."

E   The plaintiff was a lady of 34 years of age at the time of the accident, so presumably she is now 42 or 43. At the time of the accident she had two children, a boy aged 10 and a daughter aged 11. The judge accepted that the intention of the plaintiff and her husband was to increase their family by up to another two children, but that the consequences of the accident have been such as to render that impracticable, so that one of
F the matters to be weighed in the scale in assessing general damages was her loss of a chance of an enlarged family.

    The special damages of £1,689 included an amount of £633 which had been paid or which was due to be paid to the plaintiff's sister-in-law, who had come into the household and who had undertaken the housekeeping work for the husband and the children during the very considerable
G period when the plaintiff had been in hospital. In addition, as originally pleaded, there had been a claim for loss of earnings suffered by the husband in giving up part-time employment which he would otherwise have been in a position to undertake and would have undertaken, but which he had been unable to do because of the necessity to assist his wife in running the home.

    At the trial, the claim for that loss of part-time earnings by the husband
H was abandoned, and there was substituted a claim on behalf of the plaintiff to recover damages in respect of the impairment of her ability to undertake housekeeping duties, both in respect of the years between the accident and the trial, and in respect of future years, based on the estimated cost of employing the domestic help which would be necessary to make good the plaintiff's own inability to undertake all the work needed to be done in and about the household. It is essentially this claim which forms the subject matter of the dispute in this appeal.

The judge said this about the argument which had been addressed to A
him:

> "I have considered first whether it is right to treat the plaintiff's
> partial loss of housekeeping capacity as a separate head of damage,
> or whether it should be regarded only as one element in the loss of
> the amenities of life for which general damages have to be awarded."

B

That single sentence really summarises the issue which has been canvassed
before us in this court. The judge went on:

> "Having considered the matter, I have reached the conclusion that this
> disability should be treated as a separate head of damage. When a
> person in paid employment suffers a total or partial loss of earnings
> by reason of disability, such loss is invariably treated as a separate
> head of damage, with separate assessments of past and future loss. C
> Where the person concerned is a housewife, who is disabled wholly
> or partly from doing housekeeping in her own home, she does not
> suffer an actual loss of earnings, and unless a substitute is employed,
> she may not suffer any pecuniary loss at all. Nevertheless, she is just
> as much disabled from doing her unpaid job as an employed person
> is disabled from doing his paid one, and I think that she is, in prin- D
> ciple, entitled to be compensated separately for her loss in a similar
> way."

Basically, that is the proposition which Mr. Bennett, for the defendants,
challenges. The judge went on:

> "As to the method of assessing the amount of the loss, I think that one
> way of doing it, though not necessarily the only way, is to take the cost E
> of employing someone else to do the work which the plaintiff has been
> in the past, and will be in the future, incapacitated from doing. It was
> contended for the defendants that this method was only permissible if
> another person had in fact been so employed in the past, and would
> in fact be so employed in the future. I do not, however, accept this
> contention as correct. The Dalys did not have the resources to em- F
> ploy such assistance in the past, but I do not think that the plaintiff's
> loss should be assessed at a lower figure on this account. The loss
> occurred and the cost of employing someone else is no more than a
> way of measuring it."

The judge then proceeded to adopt that measure of quantifying this
head of damage, and he came to the conclusion that, excluding the periods G
of time when Miss Daly, the sister-in-law, had been engaged in housekeeping duties in the absence of the plantiff, the total period when the
plaintiff was coping as best she could, with the aid of her husband and
daughter, amounted to 299 weeks, and that the reasonable figure to take
as an average figure for the cost per hour of employing a daily help during
those weeks would be 90p., and that the assistance which the plaintiff H
had needed but had not had in the shape of paid daily help would have
been 10 hours per week. That is how he arrived at the figure, which I have
mentioned earlier in this judgment, for partial loss of housekeeping capacity
up to the date of trial, of £2,691, which was 299 weeks at £9 a week.

He then went on to deal with future loss, and said:

> ". . . I think that it would be reasonable to regard the average num-
> ber of hours for which assistance will be needed in the future as eight

The Weekly Law Reports, February 6, 1981

127

1 W.L.R.   Daly v. General Steam Navigation Co. (C.A.)   Bridge L.J.

A   per week. As to cost, on the footing that the present rate is £1·40 per hour, the weekly cost comes to £11·20, and the annual cost to £582·40."

He then pointed out that the necessity to continue housekeeping was one which would remain with the plaintiff for the rest of her life and was likely to be 30 years or more, and so the judge took a multiplier of 15, and that is how he arrived at his estimate of the future partial loss of house-

B keeping capacity in the figure of £8,736.

    I approach, first, the judge's assessment of the future loss in this respect. It has been energetically argued by Mr. Bennett, for the defendants, that before future loss of capacity to undertake housekeeping duties can properly be assessed at the estimated cost of employing some third person to come in and do that which the plaintiff is unable to do for herself, the plaintiff

C has to satisfy the court that she has a firm intention in any event that such a person shall be employed. For my part, I am quite unable to see why that should be so. Once the judge had concluded, as this judge did, that, to put the plaintiff, so far as money could do so, in the position in which she would have been if she had never been injured, she was going to need, in the future, domestic assistance for eight hours a week, it seems to me that it was entirely reasonable and entirely in accordance with principle in

D assessing damages, to say that the estimated cost of employing labour for that time, for an appropriate number of years having regard to the plain-tiff's expectation of life, was the proper measure of her damages under this heading. It is really quite immaterial, in my judgment, whether having received those damages, the plaintiff chooses to alleviate her own house-keeping burden, which is an excessively heavy one, having regard to her considerable disability to undertake housekeeping tasks, by employing

E the labour which has been taken as the basis of the estimate on which damages have been awarded, or whether she chooses to continue to struggle with the housekeeping on her own and to spend the damages which have been awarded to her on other luxuries which she would otherwise be unable to afford.

    The essence of the matter is that the eight hours' domestic assistance,

F which is the basis of the estimate on which the damages are awarded, represent the court's view of what she reasonably needs to compensate her for her own disabilities. Accordingly, so far as the appeal challenges the inclusion in the overall estimate of damages of the judge's figure of £8,736 as an estimate of the plaintiff's future partial loss of housekeeping capacity, I think it fails.

G   As a matter of strict logic it might seem to follow from that that the same reasoning ought to apply to the period elapsing before trial, but if that is the strictly logical conclusion, then I think there is a fallacy in the logic somewhere. Looking at the matter as one not so much of logic as of practical reality, the fact is that the plaintiff is unable to say that she has incurred the cost of employing the labour which no doubt she needed in the years which intervened between the accident and the trial,

H ignoring the times when she was in hospital. What she has done and what she has had to do for lack of means to do otherwise, has been to manage as best she could with all the disabilities from which she was suffering and with the assistance of such help as her husband and daughter were able to give her.

    Mr. Hamilton, for the plaintiff, has argued strenuously that the judge's award under this head, the figure of £2,691 based on 299 weeks' domestic help at £9 a week, can be understood as his evaluation of the domestic

help which was rendered to the wife by her husband and daughter; but, **A** although this may have been pleaded and argued, I can find no trace of any such finding in the reasoning of the judge's judgment. With the utmost respect to the judge, I cannot think that, as a matter of principle, it is a correct method of evaluating what is essentially an element in the plaintiff's pain and suffering and loss of amenity, caused by the additional difficulties she had had in doing her housekeeping work, to take the figure which it **B** would have cost her to employ someone, whom she has not in fact employed in the past, to take that burden off her shoulders.

What the judge certainly could have done, and I think should have done if the claim had been maintained, would have been to have added to the special damages the amount of the loss of part-time earnings which the husband had sustained, which was a figure either proved or agreed, as I have mentioned earlier, in the sum of £930, which was necessitated **C** by his obligation to spend his time assisting his wife in the home. But apart from that element of strictly special damages, I think the proper approach to this aspect of the case would have been for the judge to ask himself to what extent the difficulties which the plaintiff had had to contend with in performing her housekeeping duties in the face of the disabilities from which she suffered ought to have increased the sum **D** awarded to her for pain and suffering and loss of amenity.

Having said that, when I come to look at the figures awarded by the judge for damages here, and in particular at what I must say seems to me to be the rather parsimonious figure of £8,000 for pain and suffering and loss of amenity, even accepting that the judge was going to add to that £8,736 for future loss of housekeeping capacity, although I am satisfied that the judge arrived at his global figure by the wrong route, applying **E** strictly accurate principles of assessment of damages, I am by no means satisfied that in the event the global figure at which he arrived was the wrong figure.

I test the matter in this way. If the judge had accepted that he was going to add £8,736 for future loss of housekeeping capacity, which as I have already explained I think he was entitled to do, and if the judge had **F** said: damages for pain and suffering and loss of amenity, £10,000, and an additional £930 special damages for the husband's loss of part-time earnings which had resulted from his necessity to assist his wife in the house, then I do not think he could have been faulted at all. In fact, if I took those figures, that would be increasing the total award, and that is something which, subject to the question of interest, we were not invited **G** to do on the plaintiff's behalf.

So the way in which I would adjust the figures is this: I would add to the £8,000 as the judge's award for pain and suffering and loss of amenity, first £2,691, which is the judge's assessment of partial loss of housekeeping capacity up to the date of trial, making £10,691, but I would deduct from that £930, the husband's partial loss of earning capacity which ought to be treated as special damages. That results in the general damage **H** figure coming to £9,761 and the special damage figure becoming £2,619, that is £1,689 plus £930. Subject to the adjustment of the method by which the global award is arrived at, and subject to the question of interest which is the subject of a cross-appeal, I would dismiss the defendant's appeal.

So far as interest is concerned, it is true that the cross notice of appeal, claiming interest on the award of damages for pain and suffering and loss of amenity in accordance with the decision of the House of Lords in

The Weekly Law Reports, February 6, 1981

129

1 W.L.R.   Daly v. General Steam Navigation Co. (C.A.)   Bridge L.J.

A *Pickett* v. *British Rail Engineering Ltd.* [1980] A.C. 136, was made at a
late stage. The reason why the judge did not award interest on that element
in the damages was because he was guided at the date of the trial by the
observations of the Court of Appeal in *Cookson* v. *Knowles* [1977] Q.B.
913, which has been subsequently disapproved in *Pickett's* case. Once the
cross notice was allowed to be entered, as clearly it should be, Mr. Bennett
B concedes he has no answer to the claim for interest on that part of the
award of general damages which represents pain and suffering and loss
of amenity at the short-term investment rate from the date of the writ to
the date of trial. I would, accordingly, allow the cross-appeal to the extent
that it is necessary to give effect to that adjustment.

C TEMPLEMAN L.J. I agree. The figure for special damages was £1,689,
including the cost of employing Miss Daly as a full-time housekeeper during
the period when the plaintiff was in hospital. That figure of £1,689 is the
actual loss suffered prior to the trial. In addition, there was an actual loss
suffered prior to the trial of £930, being the sum lost by Mr. Daly by having
to give up his part-time employment, and the justification for including
that as a loss by the plaintiff is to be found in *Donnelly* v. *Joyce* [1974]
D Q.B. 454. That gives a total special damage figure of £2,619. That leaves
general damages, and those general damages had to take into account
past and future. There were past damages in so far as the plaintiff's
inability to perform her housekeeping duties exceeded the actual loss for
which account has already been taken, namely, the amount paid the
plaintiff and the sums paid to Mr. Daly. Then of course, there must be
general damages for loss and damage in the future.
E The future loss is estimated at £8,736, that being the cost of providing
housekeeping services which the plaintiff in future will be unable to perform. Then there are the future damages in respect of pain, suffering and
loss of amenities but excluding housekeeping loss for which credit has
already been given. Adding all those three together, namely, damages for
the past and loss and damage for the future, the global figure which the
F judge gave, as Bridge L.J. has said, is well within bounds, and the £1,761
damages for the past has merely to be added to the £8,000 for the future,
producing under the third head the figure of £9,761.
   In the result, it seems to me the special damages amount to £2,619 and
the general damages amount to £18,497; and the addition of general
damages and special damages brings up to figure to the global figure
reached by the judge, namely, £21,116.
G
   ORMROD L.J. I agree with both judgments which have been given. The
basic principle in all these cases is to arrive at a figure of compensation
for the plaintiff which is fair to both parties. So far as the special damage
is concerned, that, as I have always understood, represents actual loss—
" actual " as opposed to " estimated " loss. So far as the general damage is
H concerned, that loss necessarily has to be estimated.
   By reason of the rules relating to interest, it is necessary now to sub-
divide these awards in order to distinguish between that part of the award
which the plaintiff was entitled to have paid to her, in theory at the time
of the issue of the writ, and sums the loss of which she will only experience
in the future.
   So far as the approach to the loss of housekeeping ability is concerned,
I would deprecate talking about " capacities " in this connection. The

Ormrod L.J.   **Daly v. General Steam Navigation Co. (C.A.)**   **[1981]**

words " incapacity " and " capacity " are extraordinarily vague words upon A
which much can be built on rather insecure foundations. What we have
to do is to look to see, so far as the pre-trial loss is concerned, the actual
loss that has been sustained. It is perfectly true that the plaintiff is entitled
to some compensation for the loss of her ability to do her housekeeping
during that period, but I agree that properly the compensation is to be
included in the estimated general damage.

I would venture to repeat what I said in my judgment in *Hay* v. *Hughes* B
[1975] Q.B. 790, 818, namely, that in trying to assess what is a fair
compensation in an internal family situation, it is not necessarily at all
reliable to have regard to market values of housekeepers or other comparable people. It introduces a wildly artificial concept if one resorts to that
and talks about compensating the husband in this case at a rate of a daily
woman at so many hours a week. It simply does not represent reality at all. C
The nearest one can get to reality in a case like this is to see what the
husband has actually lost, and thanks to *Donnelly* v. *Joyce* [1974] Q.B.
454 we are no longer in any difficulty about replacing such loss for members of the family.

So far as the future loss is concerned, I entirely agree with what Bridge
L.J. has said. The judge's method of assessing that part of general damage,
represented by the future cost, at least in theory, of supplementing the D
plaintiff's capacity to do her housework, seems to be to be perfectly reasonable. It has to be quantified in some way, not on a £.s.d. basis, but one has
to be able to get the order of magnitude of the sum to be awarded, and
the way the judge did it, by calculating the number of days a week, and
hours per day and cost per hour of the housekeeping assistance, seems to
me to be a reasonable approach to it—maybe too high a figure, in which E
case it can be scaled down—but it is as good a guide as one could think of.

In the result, I agree with the order proposed by Bridge L.J., unless
counsel has anything to say on the question of interest.

> *Appeal dismissed.*
> *Cross-appeal allowed.*
> *Special damages of £2,619 to carry* F
>   *interest at half short-term invest-*
>   *ment rate from date of accident.*
> *General damages of £9,761 to carry*
>   *interest at short-term investment*
>   *rate from date of writ.*
> *Plaintiff's costs of appeal, cross-appeal* G
>   *and respondent's notice.*

Solicitors: *Ingledew, Brown, Bennison & Garrett; Stocken & Co.*

B. O. A.

H

A

[QUEEN'S BENCH DIVISION]

* REGINA v. EBBW VALE AND MERTHYR TYDFIL
SUPPLEMENTARY BENEFITS APPEAL TRIBUNAL,
Ex parte LEWIS

B

1980   June 25

Donaldson L.J. and Kilner Brown J.

*Social   Security — Family   income   supplement — Entitlement —
Claimant absent from work due to sickness at time of appli-
cation — Whether   engaged   in   full-time   " work " — Family
Income Supplements Act 1970 (c. 55), ss. 1 (1) (a), 6 (2) (a)*

C

The applicant, who was employed by a local authority, was
absent from work by reason of ill health from November 14
until December 12, 1977.   He claimed family income supplement under section 1 of the Family Income Supplements Act
1970 [1] on November 17, 1977.   By section 6 (2) (*a*) of the Act,
the question of his right to the supplement fell to be decided
as at the date of his claim.   The Supplementary Benefits Com-

D

mission ruled that as he was ill and not at work on the date of
his claim, he was not " engaged, and normally engaged, in
remunerative full-time work " within the meaning of section 1
(1) (*a*).   He unsuccessfully appealed against that decision to a
supplementary benefits appeal tribunal.

On his application for judicial review and the relief of an
order of certiorari to quash the tribunal's decision: —

Held, granting   the   order   of   certiorari,   that   in   section

E

1 (1) (*a*) of the Family Income Supplements Act 1970 the term
" work " rather than " employment " was used because the
Act applied both to the employed and the self-employed; that
a claimant for benefit had to satisfy two conditions at the time
of the claim, namely, that he was engaged in remunerative
full-time employment or self-employment and that he was
normally so engaged; and that, since the applicant fulfilled
those two conditions, he qualified for benefit although at the
time of making the application he was not actually working

F

because he was ill.

The following case is referred to in the judgment of Donaldson L.J.:

Fuggle (R. F.) Ltd. v. *Gadsden* [1948] 2 K.B. 236; [1948] 2 All E.R. 160,
C.A.

G

No additional cases were cited in argument.

APPLICATION for judicial review.

The applicant, Stephen John Lewis, applied for a judicial review of the
decision of the Ebbw Vale and Merthyr Tydfil Supplementary Benefits
Appeal Tribunal on June 14, 1978, that he was not entitled to family
income supplement under the Family Income Supplements Act 1970.   The

H

relief sought was an order of certiorari to quash that decision and the
ground of the application, inter alia, was that the tribunal erred in law in
holding that, because the applicant was away from work on account of
sickness on the date of his claim, he could not on that date be " engaged
in remunerative full-time work " within the meaning of section 1 of the

[1] Family Income Supplements Act 1970, s. 1 (1) (*a*): see post, p. 132D.
S. 6 (2) (*a*): see post, p. 132D–E.

Family Income Supplements Act 1970 and in distinguishing the judgments   A
of the Court of Appeal in *R. F. Fuggle Ltd.* v. *Gadsden* [1948] 2 K.B. 236.
The facts are stated in the judgment of Donaldson L.J.

John Howell for the applicant.
Simon D. Brown for the Supplementary Benefits Commission.

                                                                         B
DONALDSON L.J.   This is an application brought on behalf of Stephen
John Lewis for judicial review to quash a decision of the Ebbw Vale and
Merthyr Tydfil Supplementary Benefits Appeal Tribunal dated June 14,
1978, which confirmed a decision of the Supplementary Benefits Commission that the applicant was not entitled to family income supplement
under section 1 of the Family Income Supplements Act 1970.

The grounds upon which his application was rejected can be simply   C
stated.   The applicant was, at the material time, subject to a contract
of employment with a local authority, but he had been sick from
November 14, 1977.   He made his application on November 17 when he
was still off work due to sickness and, indeed, he remained off work until
December 12.

The Act provides, by section 1 (1):   D

"For the purposes of this Act a family shall consist of the following
members of a household—(a) one man or single woman engaged,
and normally engaged, in remunerative full-time work; . . ."

Section 6 (2) provides: "Except where regulations otherwise provide"—
which they do not—"(a) any such question"—that is the entitlement to
family income supplement—"shall be determined as at the date when   E
the claim . . . is made; . . ."   The claim, as I say, was made on November
17 and at that time the applicant was sick and all concerned have held
that it follows that on that day, although he was normally engaged in
remunerative full-time work, he was not so engaged.   Full-time work is
work involving attendance for more than 30 hours a week.

Mr. Brown has submitted that there is a very clear distinction drawn
in section 1 (1) (a) between the concept of employment and the concept   F
of work.   He draws our attention to the decision of the Court of Appeal
in *R. F. Fuggle Ltd.* v. *Gadsden* [1948] 2 K.B. 236, which is in fact a
Rent Act case, but one which was concerned with obtaining possession
of property required for the occupation of a person in the owner's whole-
time employment.   Evershed L.J., at p. 246, said that the employee
concerned was at the relevant time "under an existing obligation by   G
contract to work whole-time for the plaintiffs, though in fact he was
not able to work owing to illness."   Mr. Brown says that single sentence
epitomises the distinction that is made between working and employment
and that the tribunal was correct in drawing the same distinction under
section 1 (1).

The consequences are surprising because it means that had the
applicant applied four days earlier he would have qualified and, subject   H
to figures, have been able to receive his family income supplement for
52 weeks whether he was ill or not, whether he was working or not
and whether he was in employment or not.   Leaving that aside, I have
come to the conclusion that this involves a misconstruction of section 1
(1) (a).   The term "work" rather than employment is used because this
Act applies not only to the employed but to the self-employed who are
not working under a contract of employment.   If it is not used for that

The Weekly Law Reports, February 6, 1981

133

1 W.L.R.   Reg. v. Ebbw Vale Tribunal, Ex p. Lewis (D.C.)   Donaldson L.J.

A reason at any rate it is a much more appropriate term to use than
" employment," in the context of the self-employed.

As it seems to me, the Act requires two conditions to be fulfilled.
The first is that the person concerned should be, at the time of the application, actually engaged in remunerative full-time employment or self-
employment. That would apply, for example, to a student who was
working, as contrasted with studying, during his vacation. The second
B condition is that he should *normally* be engaged in remunerative full-time
employment or self-employment. That is a condition which the student,
in those circumstances, could not fulfil. By contrast, the man who is
normally employed as a sheet metal worker, or whatever, but who is
temporarily unemployed, fulfils the second condition of being normally
engaged in remunerative full-time work but not the first condition of
C being at the time of the application so engaged. This construction gives
full effect to both conditions without embarking on the refinement which
the tribunal has adopted and which Mr. Brown has sought manfully to
uphold, regardless of the practical consequences. In my judgment the
applicant remained engaged in remunerated full-time work notwithstanding
that sickness prevented him from doing anything on the date of his
application.

D   I think that the tribunal erred and that the construction which I give
to this section is not only right but also meets the criterion which Mr.
Brown urged should be met in this sort of statute, that of simplicity. I
would accordingly quash the decision.

KILNER BROWN J.   I agree.

E   *Order of certiorari.*
                         Legal aid taxation of applicant's costs.
                         Liberty to apply on behalf of legal aid
                              fund for order for costs.

Solicitors: *R. J. E. Smith for R. I. Martin, Merthyr Tydfil; Solicitor,*
Department of Health and Social Security.

F
[Reported by FELIKS KWIATKOWSKI, ESQ., Barrister-at-Law]

G
[CHANCERY DIVISION]

* In re LACEWARD LTD.

[No. 002157 of 1980]

1980   Oct. 13, 14   Slade J.

H Solicitor—Costs—Non-contentious business—Recovery of costs—
      Omission to inform client company of its right to require soli-
      citors to obtain certificate from Law Society that bill fair and
      reasonable—Petition to wind up company—Whether solicitors
      creditors — Whether petition abuse of process — Solicitors'
      Remuneration Order 1972 (S.I. 1972 No. 1139 (L. 14)),
      art. 3 (2)

      The petitioners, a firm of solicitors, undertook work for
   a company in respect of non-contentious business between

October 1977 and April 1978. When presenting their bill of   A
costs, they omitted to inform the company of its right, under
article 3 (1) of the Solicitors' Remuneration Order 1972,[1] to
require the solicitors to obtain from The Law Society a certificate that their bill of costs was fair and reasonable. The
bill was not paid and the solicitors presented a petition for
the winding up of the company. The company then learnt
of its right under article 3 (1) and indicated that it wished to
avail itself of that right and to have a taxation of the costs.   B

On the question whether the petition should be struck out
as being premature and constituting an abuse of the process
of the court as infringing article 3 (2) of the Order and
because the solicitors had no locus standi as creditors in that
the alleged debt was disputed on bona fide and substantial
grounds: —

Held, (1) that the phrase " proceedings to recover costs on
a bill for non-contentious business " in article 3 (2) of the   C
Order was to be construed so that it carried out the intention
of the article, namely, that no client or former client of a
solicitor should be subjected to proceedings for the recovery
of such costs without having been informed of his right under
article 3 (1); that, accordingly, the phrase was wide enough
to include any proceedings where costs were sought to be
recovered whether specifically or indirectly and, therefore, the
present petition had been presented in violation of article 3 (2)   D
and should be dismissed.

(2) That, since there could be no certainty, before taxation took place, that all or any specific part of the alleged
debt was due, the debt relied on by the petitioners was
manifestly disputed on bona fide and substantial grounds; that,
accordingly, the petitioners had no locus standi to present
the petition and on that ground also the petition should be
dismissed.   E

In re North Bucks Furniture Depositories Ltd. [1939] Ch.
690 distinguished.

The following cases are referred to in the judgment:

Clement-Davies v. *Inter G.S.A.* (unreported) July 5, 1979; Court of
    Appeal (Civil Division) Transcript No. 434 of 1979, C.A.
North Bucks Furniture Depositories Ltd., In re [1939] Ch. 690; [1939]   F
    2 All E.R. 549.

No additional cases were cited in argument.

PETITION

By a petition dated May 23, 1980, a firm of solicitors, Messrs.
William F. Prior & Co., sought a compulsory winding up order in respect   G
of the company, Laceward Ltd. The petition was based on an alleged
debt in respect of work done by the solicitors for the company between
October 1977 and April 1978 in connection with non-contentious business.

The facts are stated in the judgment.

J. D. Martineau for the petitioning solicitors.
M. A. Todd for the company.   H

SLADE J. This is a petition by which a firm of solicitors, Messrs.
William F. Prior & Co., seek the usual compulsory winding up order
in respect of the company concerned, Laceward Ltd. The petition is
founded on an alleged debt arising in consideration of work done by the

[1] Solicitors' Remuneration Order 1972, art. 3: see post, p. 135B–D.

A petitioners for the company, as solicitors, between October 1977 and April 1978. It is common ground that the work in question was non-contentious business.

Article 2 of the Solicitors' Remuneration Order 1972 provided that a solicitor's remuneration for non-contentious business should be such sum as might be " fair and reasonable having regard to all the circum-
B stances of the case." The article then proceeded to list a number of particular matters which should be taken into account in this context. Article 3 (1) provided:

"Without prejudice to the provisions of sections 69, 70 and 71 of the Solicitors Act 1957 (which relate to taxation of costs) the client may require a solicitor to obtain a certificate from The Law Society stating that in their opinion the sum charged is fair and reasonable
C or, as the case may be, what other sum would be fair and reasonable, and in the absence of taxation the sum stated in the certificate, if less than that charged, shall be the sum payable by the client."

Article 3 (2) provided:

"Before the solicitor brings proceedings to recover costs on a bill
D for non-contentious business he must, unless the costs have been taxed, have informed the client in writing—(i) of his right under paragraph (1) of the article to require the solicitor to obtain a certificate from The Law Society, and (ii) of the provisions of the Solicitors Act 1957 relating to taxation of costs."

Article 5 (1) of the order of 1972 provided:

E "After the expiry of one month from the delivery of any bill for non-contentious business a solicitor may charge interest on the amount of the bill (including any disbursements) at a rate not exceeding the rate for the time being payable on judgment debts, so, however, that before interest may be charged the client must have been given the information required by article 3 (2) of this
F Order."

I have been told that, notwithstanding the passing of the Solicitors Act 1974, the relevant provisions of the Order of 1972 remain in full force and effect.

Though other points have been taken by the company in evidence in answer to this petition, a preliminary point has been taken on its
G behalf in reliance on the provisions of the Order of 1972, with which this judgment is concerned.

It is common ground that before the petition was presented, the relevant costs had not been taxed and the petitioners had never informed the company in writing of its right under article 3 (1) of the Order of 1972 to require the petitioners to obtain a certificate from The Law Society. In these circumstances Mr. Todd, on behalf of the company,
H has put forward substantially two propositions as reasons why this petition should be dismissed in limine. First, he has submitted, the petition constitutes " proceedings to recover costs on a bill for non-contentious business," within the meaning of article 3 (2) of the Order of 1972. In these circumstances, he has submitted, since the requisite information had not been given to the company before the petition was presented, the petition was premature and constituted an abuse of the process of the court, as infringing article 3 (2).

136

A

Further or alternatively, Mr. Todd has submitted that the petitioners have no locus standi to present this petition in their purported capacity as creditors, in that the alleged debt is bona fide disputed on substantial grounds. The company accepts that almost certainly some moneys are due to the petitioners, but asserts that, in advance of the taxation of the relevant costs which it now seeks, it does not know what the true sum is. It submits that the sum should be ascertained on a taxation of the petitioners' bills and that, since it had never been informed of its right to taxation before presentation of the petition, the petition is misconceived and oppressive.

B

The correctness or otherwise of Mr. Todd's first submission depends on the true construction of the phrase " proceedings to recover costs on a bill for non-contentious business," in article 3 (2) of the Order of 1972. Mr. Martineau, on behalf of the petitioners, submitted that this phrase should be construed narrowly, in such manner as to include only those proceedings in which recovery of costs is specifically sought. For this reason, he submitted that a winding up petition, such as the present, would not fall within the ambit of the phrase. Mr. Todd, on the other hand, substantially submitted that the phrase is wide enough to include not only proceedings where costs are specifically claimed but also proceedings such as the present, whose obvious purpose is to recover as much of the relevant costs as may prove possible.

C

D

I think that the narrow construction put forward on behalf of the petitioners is certainly an arguable one. On balance, however, I prefer the construction propounded by the company, which seems to me to be justifiable not only by reference to the wording of article 3 (2), but also by reference to what one must assume was the intention of the makers of the rules. I take it to have been their clear intention that a client, or former client, should not be subjected to proceedings of any kind by a solicitor in respect of costs for non-contentious work, until the solicitor had informed him of his rights under article 3 (1). Furthermore, it would appear from the decision of the Court of Appeal in *Clement-Davies* v. *Inter G. S. A.* (unreported) July 5, 1979; Court of Appeal (Civil Division) Transcript No. 434 of 1979, which I have been shown, that the court will expect the relevant information to have been given to the client in an explicit manner, before it will treat the client as having been given the information required by article 3 (2). That was a case relating to a solicitor's claim for interest, so that it was governed by article 5 (1), read in conjunction with article 3 (2).

E

F

On these grounds alone, therefore, I would be prepared to hold that the presentation of this petition was in violation of article 3 (2) and that the petition should accordingly be dismissed. In case my conclusion on this point is wrong, however, I think I should briefly refer to Mr. Todd's second point.

G

It is the well established practice of this court to refuse to allow petitions for the winding up of companies brought at the suit of alleged creditors, whose debts are disputed bona fide on substantial grounds. It has been said in several reported cases that the procedure of a winding up petition is not an appropriate course by which to attempt to resolve such a dispute. In the present case, following the presentation of the petition, the company, I am told, took advice from new solicitors, who advised it of its rights under the Order of 1972, of which it was previously unaware. The company then indicated to the petitioners its

H

A desire to rely on these rights and to have a taxation of its costs.   Before such taxation takes place there is no certainty whatever as to whether all or any specific part of the debt alleged by the petition will be found truly due to the petitioners.   In these circumstances, it seems to me that, in the events which have happened, the alleged debt on which the petition is founded is manifestly disputed on bona fide and substantial grounds.

B   Mr. Martineau pointed out that the request for taxation had not been made at the time when the petition was presented.   But, at best, this point would in my judgment only avail the petitioners in respect of the costs of the petition arising before the point had been taken on behalf of the company, and I do not think that, in all the circumstances, it even avails the petitioners to this extent.   In my judgment, the case is one where the debt is truly disputed on grounds which cannot be said to be insubstantial.

C   Mr. Martineau referred me to the decision of Crossman J. in *In re North Bucks Furniture Depositories Ltd.* [1939] Ch. 690, in which it was held that a local authority to which unpaid rates were due was a creditor within section 170 of the Companies Act 1929 and was entitled to present a petition, after having issued a distress warrant and having recovered nothing thereby.   This decision, that a creditor-debtor relationship existed, was reached, as Mr. Martineau pointed out, even though

D Crossman J. recognised that an action by a local authority to recover unpaid arrears of rates would not lie, the proper recovery being by way of distress.   In my judgment, however, the decision is of no real assistance to the petitioners in the present case.   On the facts of *In re North Bucks Furniture Depositories Ltd.,* I think it clear that a presently owing debt of an ascertained sum existed in favour of the petitioners,

E even though one particular remedy for enforcing that debt, namely, an action for payment, might not have been available to them.

      In the present case, as I have indicated, there is no clearly ascertained sum in respect of which the petitioners have a claim to be creditors in advance of a taxation.   Correspondingly, in my judgment, they have no locus standi to present a petition on this second, alternative ground.

F For this reason also, I therefore find that the petition must be dismissed and I order accordingly.

Petition dismissed.

Solicitors: *W. F. Prior & Co.; Mendoza Segal.*

G   T. C. C. B.

H

[1981]

[FAMILY DIVISION]   A

* PRACTICE DIRECTION
(FAMILY DIVISION: CASE STATED)

*Practice — Family Division — Appeal — Appeal by case stated —
Hearing by single judge — Application for hearing outside
London—R.S.C., Ord. 56, rr. 4A, 5*   B

The President has issued the following practice direction with the
concurrence of the Lord Chancellor.

With effect from January 12, 1981, R.S.C., Ord. 56, rr. 4A and 5 are
amended so that appeals by case stated in any of the types of proceedings
therein set out are taken by a single judge as a general rule and only by
a Divisional Court of the Family Division if the court so directs.   C

The rules require that all relevant papers be lodged in the Principal
Registry of the Family Division but there is no requirement in the rules
that the single judge must be a single judge sitting in London. Accordingly, any party wishing the appeal to be heard and determined by a
single judge outside London should apply to the President for a direction
to this effect. The application should be made by letter addressed to
the Clerk of the Rules. Where such a direction is given, the Clerk of   D
the Rules will inform the appellant of the relevant divorce town and will
refer the papers to the listing officer of the appropriate circuit office for
a date of hearing to be fixed and notified to the appellant.

R. L. BAYNE-POWELL,
Senior Registrar.   E
January 22, 1981.

———————

[PRIVY COUNCIL]
F
* PORT JACKSON STEVEDORING PTY. LTD. .   .   APPELLANT

AND

SALMOND AND SPRAGGON (AUSTRALIA)
PTY. LTD.   .   .   .   .   RESPONDENT

[APPEAL FROM THE HIGH COURT OF AUSTRALIA]   G

1980 May 12, 13, 14, 15;   Lord Wilberforce, Lord Diplock,
      July 10   Lord Fraser of Tullybelton,
                                       Lord Scarman and Lord Roskill

*Shipping—Bill of lading—Exemption clause—Goods discharged and
placed in stevedore's warehouse—Goods obtained by thieves
without presentation of bill of lading — Whether stevedore
entitled to rely on exemption clause in bill of lading*   H
Ships' Names—New York Star

Consignors delivered goods to a carrier for carriage by sea
from St. John, New Brunswick, to Sydney. The carrier issued
a bill of lading to the consignor. Clause 2 (a Himalaya clause)
extended the benefit of defences and immunities conferred on
the carrier by the bill of lading to independent contractors

A   employed by the carrier. Clauses 5, 8 and 14 regulated the care, delivery and discharge of the goods. The consignee accepted the bill of lading. When the carrier's ship arrived in Sydney a stevedore engaged by the carrier unloaded the goods and placed them on a part of the wharf which was under the stevedore's control. A servant of the stevedore wrongly delivered the goods to thieves without production of the bill of lading so that later, when the consignee presented the bill of

B   lading, the stevedore was unable to deliver the goods. The consignee brought an action against the stevedore alleging negligence in failing to take care of the goods, delivery to an unauthorised person and non-delivery to the consignee. In the Supreme Court of New South Wales the trial judge found that the stevedore had been negligent in caring for the goods and had misdelivered them but that it was protected from liability by clause 2 of the bill of lading and he dismissed the action.

C   The Court of Appeal allowed the consignee's appeal. The stevedore appealed to the High Court of Australia. That court, dismissing the appeal by a majority, decided that the bill of lading had ceased to have any effect at the time of the misdelivery; that, accordingly, the stevedore was a bailee of the goods independent of the terms of the bill of lading and that therefore it was not protected by clause 2 and was liable for the loss of the goods.

D   On the stevedore's appeal to the Judicial Committee: —

Held, allowing the appeal, that clauses 5, 8 and 14 of the bill of lading had to be interpreted in the light of the practice that a consignee seldom took delivery from the ship's rail but usually did so from the wharf and the parties to the bill of lading must have contemplated (and on the facts did contemplate) that the carrier would either himself store the goods on the wharf or would employ another person to do so; that,

E   accordingly, after the goods left the ship's rail and while they lay on the wharf, the bill of lading continued to apply and the carrier continued to be liable for them as bailee under the contract; and that, therefore, since clause 2 was capable of conferring the defences and immunities provided for by the contract on the carrier's independent contractor as if that contractor had himself been a party to the contract and, on the facts, in storing the goods, the stevedore had been acting

F   as the carrier's independent contractor fulfilling the carrier's obligations under the bill of lading, the stevedore was protected by clause 2 and was not liable to the consignee for the loss (post, pp. 143E–F, 147E, H—148A, B–D).

New Zealand Shipping Co. Ltd. v. *A. M. Satterthwaite & Co. Ltd.* [1975] A.C. 154, P.C. applied.

Decision of the High Court of Australia (sub nom. *The New York Star*) [1979] 1 Lloyd's Rep. 298 reversed.

G

The following cases are referred to in the judgment:

Heyman v. *Darwins Ltd.* [1942] A.C. 356; [1942] 1 All E.R. 337, H.L.(E.).

Keane v. *Australian Steamships Pty. Ltd.* (1929) 41 C.L.R. 484.

Midland Silicones Ltd. v. *Scruttons Ltd.* [1962] A.C. 446; [1962] 2 W.L.R. 186; [1962] 1 All E.R. 1, H.L.(E.).

H   *New Zealand Shipping Co. Ltd.* v. *A. M. Satterthwaite & Co. Ltd.* [1975] A.C. 154; [1974] 2 W.L.R. 865; [1974] 1 All E.R. 1015, P.C.

Photo Production Ltd. v. *Securicor Transport Ltd.* [1980] A.C. 827; [1980] 2 W.L.R. 283; [1980] 1 All E.R. 556, H.L.(E.).

Suisse Atlantique Société d'Armement Maritime S.A. v. *N.V. Rotterdamsche Kolen Centrale* [1967] 1 A.C. 361; [1966] 2 W.L.R. 944; [1966] 2 All E.R. 61, H.L.(E.).

Thomas National Transport (Melbourne) Pty. Ltd. v. *May & Baker (Australia) Pty. Ltd.* (1966) 115 C.L.R. 353.

Port Jackson Ltd. v. Salmond & Spraggon Ltd. (P.C.)   [1981]

The following additional cases were cited in argument: A

Adamastos Shipping Co. Ltd. v. *Anglo-Saxon Petroleum Co. Ltd.* [1959]
    A.C. 133; [1958] 2 W.L.R. 688; [1958] 1 All E.R. 725, H.L.(E.).
Australasian United Steam Navigation Co. Ltd. v. *Hiskens* (1914) 18
    C.L.R. 646.
Australian Woollen Mills Pty. Ltd. v. *The Commonwealth* (1954) 92 C.L.R.
    424.
Automatic Tube Co. Pty. Ltd. v. *Adelaide Steamship (Operations) Ltd.*   B
    [1966] W.A.R. 103; [1967] 1 Lloyd's Rep. 531.
Brandt v. *Liverpool, Brazil and River Plate Steam Navigation Co. Ltd.*
    [1924] 1 K.B. 575, C.A.
Carlill v. *Carbolic Smoke Ball Co.* [1893] 1 Q.B. 256, C.A.
Chartered Bank of India, Australia and China v. *British India Steam
    Navigation Co. Ltd.* [1909] A.C. 369, P.C.
Circle Sales & Import Ltd. v. *The Tarantel* [1978] 1 F.C. 269.   C
Eisen und Metall A.G. v. *Ceres Stevedoring Co. Ltd.* [1977] 1 Lloyd's
    Rep. 665.
Federal Schelde, The [1978] 1 Lloyd's Rep. 285.
Firestone Tyre & Rubber Co. Ltd. v. *Vokins & Co. Ltd.* [1951] 1 Lloyd's
    Rep. 32.
Frost v. *Knight* (1872) L.R. 7 Exch. 111.
Great Northern Railway Co. v. *Witham* (1873) L.R. 9 C.P. 16.
Hain Steamship Co. Ltd. v. *Tate and Lyle Ltd.* (1936) 41 Com.Cas. 350,   D
    H.L.(E.).
Herrick v. *Leonard and Dingley Ltd.* [1975] 2 N.Z.L.R. 566.
Hollins v. *J. Davy Ltd.* [1963] 1 Q.B. 844; [1963] 2 W.L.R. 201; [1963]
    1 All E.R. 570.
Lummus Co. Ltd. v. *East African Harbours Corporation* [1978] 1 Lloyd's
    Rep. 317.
Metropolitan Asylums Board, Managers of v. *Kingham and Sons* (1889)   E
    6 T.L.R. 217.
Meyerstein v. *Barber* (1866) L.R. 2 C.P. 38.
Mitsubishi International Corporation v. *S. S. Eurymedon* [1977] A.M.C.
    2370.
North General Wagon & Finance Co. Ltd. v. *Graham* [1950] 2 K.B. 7;
    [1950] 1 All E.R. 780, C.A.
Portuguese Consolidated Copper Mines Ltd., In re (1890) 45 Ch.D. 16,   F
    North J. and C.A.
Prins Willem III, The [1973] 2 Lloyd's Rep. 124.
Rex v. *Clarke* (1927) 40 C.L.R. 227.
Suleyman Stalskiy, The [1976] 2 Lloyd's Rep. 609.
Sydney City Council v. *West* (1965) 114 C.L.R. 481.
Sze Hai Tong Bank Ltd. v. *Rambler Cycle Co. Ltd.* [1959] A.C. 576;
    [1959] 3 W.L.R. 214; [1959] 3 All E.R. 182, P.C.   G
Tozer Kemsley & Millbourn (A/Asia) Pty. Ltd. v. *Collier's Interstate
    Transport Service Ltd.* (1956) 94 C.L.R. 384.
Watson v. *Swann* (1862) 11 C.B.N.S. 756.
Wilson v. *Darling Island Stevedoring and Lighterage Co. Ltd.* (1956) 95
    C.L.R. 43.
York Products Pty. Ltd. v. *Gilchrist, Watt & Sanderson Pty. Ltd.* [1968]
    3 N.S.W.R. 551.   H

APPEAL (No. 5 of 1979) with special leave by Port Jackson Steve-
doring Pty. Ltd. (the stevedore) from a judgment (April 3, 1978) of the
High Court of Australia (Stephen, Mason, Jacobs and Murphy JJ.;
Barwick C.J. dissenting) by which that court dismissed an appeal by the
stevedore from a decision (August 19, 1976) of the Court of Appeal of
New South Wales (Hutley, Glass and Mahoney JJ.A.) allowing the

A appeal of Salmond and Spraggon (Australia) Pty. Ltd. (the consignee) from a judgment (14 July, 1975) of Sheppard J. in the Supreme Court of New South Wales. By his judgment of July 14 Sheppard J. dismissed the consignee's action (begun on June 2, 1971) against the stevedore for negligence in caring for, misdelivery of and failure to deliver a consignment of razor blades shipped by Schick Safety Razor Company Division of Eversharp of Canada Ltd. on the Blue Star Line's *New*
B *York Star* from St. John, New Brunswick, to the consignee in Sydney.

The relevant clause of the bill of lading was clause 2, which provided:

"It is expressly agreed that no servant or agent of the carrier (including every independent contractor from time to time employed by the carrier) shall in any circumstances whatsoever
C be under any liability whatsoever to the shipper, consignee or owner of the goods or to any holder of this bill of lading for any loss, damage or delay of whatsoever kind arising or resulting directly or indirectly from any act, neglect or default on his part while acting in the course of or in connection with his employment and with prejudice to the generality of the foregoing provisions in
D this clause, every exemption limitation condition and liberty herein contained and every right, exemption from liability, defense and immunity of whatsoever nature applicable to the carrier or to which the carrier is entitled hereunder shall also be available and shall extend to protect every such servant or agent of the carrier acting as aforesaid and for the purpose of all the foregoing provisions of this clause the carrier is or shall be deemed to be acting
E as agent or trustee on behalf of and for the benefit of all persons who are or might be his servants or agents from time to time (including independent contractors as aforesaid) and all such persons shall to this extent be or be deemed to be parties to the contract in or evidenced by this bill of lading."

F The facts are stated in the judgment.

A. M. Gleeson Q.C. and *B. W. Rayment* (both of the New South Wales Bar) for the stevedore.

J. S. Hobhouse Q.C., *Brian Davenport Q.C.* and *Jonathan Gaisman* for the consignee.

G   *Cur. adv. vult.*

July 10. The judgment of their Lordships was delivered by LORD WILBERFORCE.

This is an appeal, by special leave, from the judgment of the High Court of Australia dated April 3, 1978, which, by majority, dismissed an appeal from the Court of Appeal of the Supreme Court of New
H South Wales. That court had allowed an appeal from a decision of Sheppard J. sitting in Commercial Causes by which he dismissed the action.

The action was brought by the respondent (the consignee) in respect of a consignment of razor blades in 37 cartons, shipped from Canada to Australia on the *New York Star*, a ship of the Blue Star Line. The relevant bill of lading dated March 27, 1970, was issued in Montreal, Quebec: the port of loading was St. John, New Brunswick; and the port of discharge was Sydney. The shipper, named in the bill of lading A was Schick Safety Razor Company Division of Eversharp of Canada Ltd.; the respondent was named as consignee. The bill of lading was issued to the shipper and was transmitted to and accepted by the consignee. The appellant carried on business as stevedore in the port of Sydney. 49 per cent. of its capital was owned by Blue Star Line Australia Ltd. and it commonly acted as stevedore in Sydney for the B Blue Star Line.

The *New York Star* arrived in Sydney on May 10, 1970. On her arrival—and there was evidence that this was in accordance with the normal practice in the port—the packages of razor blades were discharged from the ship and placed by the stevedore in part of a shed (called " the dead house ") on the wharf which was under its control. Later the goods were stolen from the wharf, having been delivered by C servants of the stevedore to persons who had no right to receive them, so that when the consignee presented the bill of lading they were unavailable. The consignee brought this action against the stevedore and against the ship's agent (Joint Cargo Services Pty. Ltd.) alleging negligence in failing to take proper care of the goods, delivery of the goods to an unauthorised person and non-delivery to the consignee. The action against the ship's agent failed at first instance and D has not been the subject of appeal. The trial judge, however, found that the stevedore had been negligent in the care of the goods and that there had been a misdelivery: these findings have not been disputed.

The bill of lading contained a " Himalaya clause " extending the benefit of defences and immunities conferred by the bill of lading upon E the carrier to independent contractors employed by the carrier, and also a time bar (similar to that contained in the Hague Rules) barring any action if not brought within one year after the delivery of the goods or the date when the goods should have been delivered: this action was not so brought. These provisions were in substance identical with those considered by this Board in *New Zealand Shipping Co. Ltd.* v. *A. M. Satterthwaite & Co. Ltd.* [1975] A.C. 154, an appeal from the Court of F Appeal in New Zealand. The stevedore relied upon these provisions as affording a defence to this action. It is now necessary to state in detail the issues which were contested, and the decisions which were given in the three courts in Australia.

Before Sheppard J. it was contended by the consignee: (i) that there had been a fundamental breach by the stevedore of its obligations as G bailee of the goods (the " fundamental breach " point); (ii) that one of the necessary conditions for applying the " Himalaya clause " had not been satisfied, in that it had not been shown that the carrier had authority to act on the stevedore's behalf in accepting the bill of lading (the " agency " point); (iii) that the bill of lading ceased to have any operation after the goods passed over the ship's rail (the " capacity " point). Sheppard J. rejected all these contentions, though he found that H the necessary agency was established only by ratification. He gave judgment for the stevedore.

In the Court of Appeal the same three contentions were put forward, and were rejected by the court. The court found that the necessary agency was directly established by the evidence, so that reliance on ratification was not necessary. In addition, however, the consignee was given leave to take a fresh point, namely: (iv) that there was no proof

The Weekly Law Reports, February 6, 1981

143

1 W.L.R.   Port Jackson Ltd. v. Salmond & Spraggon Ltd. (P.C.)

A of consideration moving from the stevedore so as to entitle it to the benefit of defences and immunity clauses in the bill of lading (the "consideration" point). The Court of Appeal accepted that contention, allowed the appeal and gave judgment for the consignee for $14,684.98 damages.

   In the High Court of Australia: the "agency" point and the "conB diseration" point were again argued, but rejected by the majority of the court (Barwick C.J., Mason and Jacobs JJ.). There was also argument upon the "fundamental breach" point, but this was not dealt with in the judgments. As to the "capacity" point, senior counsel for the consignee expressly disclaimed reliance upon it (not suprisingly since Glass J.A. had described it as "without substance") and argument upon it was not heard. However, the majority of the court (Barwick
C C.J. dissenting) decided the appeal in favour of the consignee upon this point. Finally, it should be mentioned that the Board's decision in *New Zealand Shipping Co. Ltd. v. A. M. Satterthwaite & Co. Ltd.* [1975] A.C. 154 was followed without question by the trial judge and by the Court of Appeal. Their Lordships understand that there was no argument in the High Court upon the correctness of this decision. However,
D two members of the majority (Stephen and Murphy JJ.) expressed disagreement with it. It was upon this situation that their Lordships decided, exceptionally, to grant special leave to appeal to Her Majesty in Council. It will be seen from the foregoing that the point which calls for decision by their Lordships is the "capacity" point. This was fully argued by both sides to the appeal. Before dealing with it, their Lordships must briefly state their position upon the other points, upon
E which argument was addressed by the consignee.

   First, as to the Board's decision in *New Zealand Shipping Co. Ltd. v. A. M. Satterthwaite & Co. Ltd.* [1975] A.C. 154. This was a decision, in principle, that the "Himalaya clause" is capable of conferring upon a third person falling within the description "servant or agent of the carrier (including every independent contractor from time
F to time employed by the carrier)" defences and immunities conferred by the bill of lading upon the carrier as if such persons were parties to the contract contained in or evidenced by the bill of lading. But the decision was not merely a decision on this principle for it is made clear that in fact stevedores, employed by the carrier, may come within it; and moreover that they normally and typically will do so. It may indeed be said that the significance of *Satterthwaite's* case lay not so
G much in the establishment of any new legal principle, as in the finding that in the normal situation involving the employment of stevedores by carriers, accepted principles enable and require the stevedore to enjoy the benefit of contractual provisions in the bill of lading. In the words of Mason and Jacobs JJ. [1979] 1 Lloyd's Rep. 298, 321:

     "When the circumstances described by Lord Reid [in *Scruttons*
H   *Ltd. v. Midland Silicones Ltd.* [1962] A.C. 446] exist, the stevedore will on the generally accepted principles of the law of contract be entitled to his personal contractual immunity. The importance of [*Satterthwaite's* case] is the manner in which on the bare facts of the case their Lordships were able to discern a contract between the shipper and the stevedore, and, we would add, to do so in a manner which limited the approach to those commercial contexts in which immunity of the stevedore was clearly intended in form and

almost certainly known by both the shipper and the stevedore to be   A
intended."

Although, in each case, there will be room for evidence as to the
precise relationship of carrier and stevedore and as to the practice at
the relevant port, the decision does not support, and their Lordships
would not encourage, a search for fine distinctions which would
diminish the general applicability, in the light of established com-   B
mercial practice, of the principle. As regards its applicability in Australia, their Lordships are content to leave the matter as it was left by
the Australian courts, including the High Court. They are the more
satisfied to do so in view of the reasoned analysis of the legal principles
involved which appears in the judgment of Barwick C.J. Their Lordships find, as his Honour himself declares, this to be in substantial   C
agreement with and indeed to constitute a powerful reinforcement of
one of the two possible bases put forward in the Board's judgment. The
applicability of the decision was accepted in their joint judgment by
Mason and Jacobs JJ. although their Honours reached a decision
adverse to the stevedore on the " capacity " point.

Secondly, as to the factual ingredients needed to confer on the
stevedore the benefit of the contract. From what has already been said   D
it follows that this issue requires no prolonged discussion. Not only is
the factual situation in the present case in all respects typical of that
which the Board, in *New Zealand Shipping Co. Ltd.* v. *A. M. Satterthwaite & Co. Ltd.* [1975] A.C. 154, thought sufficient to confer that
benefit, but each relevant ingredient has, in fact, been found to exist.
Agency has been found, as a fact, by all three courts, with only the
qualification as regards the judgment of Sheppard J. already mentioned.   E
The provision of consideration by the stevedore was held to follow from
this Board's decision in *Satterthwaite's* case and in addition was
independently justified through Barwick C.J.'s analysis.

Thirdly, as to " fundamental breach." The proposition that exemption clauses may be held inapplicable to certain breaches of contract as
a matter of construction of the contract, as held by the House of Lords   F
in *Suisse Atlantique Société d'Armement Maritime S.A.* v. *N.V. Rotterdamsche Kolen Centrale* [1967] 1 A.C. 361 and *Photo Production Ltd.*
v. *Securicor Transport Ltd.* [1980] A.C. 827 and endorsed in Australia
by Windeyer J. in *Thomas National Transport (Melbourne) Pty. Ltd.*
v. *May & Baker (Australia) Pty. Ltd.* (1966) 115 C.L.R. 353, 376 was
not disputed. But Mr. Hobhouse for the consignee put forward a
special, and ingenious, argument that, because of the fundamental   G
nature of the breach, the stevedore had deprived itself of the benefit of
clause 17 of the bill of lading—the time bar clause. A breach of a
repudiatory character, which he contended that the breach in question
was, entitles the innocent party, unless he waives the breach, to claim to
be released from further performance of his obligations under the
contract—so far their Lordships of course agree. One of these obliga-   H
tions, counsel proceeded to argue, was to bring any action upon the
breach within a period of one year, and the innocent party was released
from this obligation. An alternative way of putting it was that the
bringing of suit within one year was a condition with which the innocent
party was obliged to comply: the repudiatory breach discharged this
condition. A further point made was that clause 17 applied at most to
actions for breach of contract: the stevedore's negligence as bailee,

The Weekly Law Reports, February 6, 1981

145

1 W.L.R.   Port Jackson Ltd. v. Salmond & Spraggon Ltd. (P.C.)

A however, gave rise to an action in tort which was not governed by the time bar.

Their Lordships' opinion upon these arguments is clear. However adroitly presented, they are unsound, and indeed unreal. Clause 17 is drafted in general and all-embracing terms:

B " In any event the carrier and the ship shall be discharged from all liability in respect of loss or damage unless suit is brought within one year after the delivery of the goods or the date when the goods should have been delivered. Suit shall not be deemed brought until jurisdiction shall have been obtained over the carrier and/or the ship by service of process or by an agreement to appear."

C The reference to delivery of the goods shows clearly that the clause is directed towards the carrier's obligations as bailee of the goods. It cannot be supposed that it admits of a distinction between obligations in contract and liability in tort—" all liability " means what it says. Moreover it is quite unreal to equate this clause with those provisions in the contract which relate to performance. It is a clause which comes into operation when contractual performance has become impossible, or has been given up: then, it regulates the manner in which liability for breach D of contract is to be established. In this respect their Lordships find it relevantly indistinguishable from an arbitration clause, or a forum clause, which, on clear authority, survive a repudiatory breach: see *Heyman* v. *Darwins* [1942] A.C. 356, *Photo Production Ltd.* v. *Securicor Transport Ltd.* [1980] A.C. 827, 849. Mr. Hobhouse appealed for support to some observations by Lord Diplock in *Photo Production* E *Ltd.* v. *Securicor Transport Ltd.*, at p. 849, where reference is made to putting an end " to all primary obligations . . . remaining unperformed." But these words were never intended to cover such " obligations " to use Lord Diplock's word, as arise when primary obligations have been put an end to. There then arise, on his Lordship's analysis, secondary obligations which include an obligation to pay monetary compensation. Whether these have been modified by agreement is a matter of construc- F tion of the contract. The analysis, indeed, so far from supporting the consignee's argument, is directly opposed to it. Their Lordships are of opinion that, on construction and analysis, clause 17 plainly operates to exclude the consignee's claim.

Their Lordships now deal with the " capacity " argument. This rather inapposite word has been used, for convenience, in order to indi- G cate the general nature of the submission. More fully, this was that at the time when the loss occurred, the goods had been discharged and were no longer in the custody of the carrier. Consequently, the stevedore was acting not as an independent contractor employed by the carrier to perform the carrier's obligations under the bill of lading but as a bailee. Its liability, in that capacity, was independent of and not H governed by any of the clauses of the contract. This point enables a distinction to be made with *New Zealand Shipping Co. Ltd.* v. *A. M. Satterthwaite & Co. Ltd.* [1975] A.C. 154 for there, since the goods were damaged in the course of discharge, the capacity of the stevedore as a person acting on behalf of the carrier was not contested.

Their Lordships can at this point dispose of one question of fact. It appears to have been the view of both Stephen J. and of Mason and Jacobs JJ. that the stevedore was remunerated for its services in stacking

Port Jackson Ltd. v. Salmond & Spraggon Ltd. (P.C.)   [1981]

A

and storing the goods on the wharf by the consignee: this, if correct, might be an argument for finding that it was not, in respect of these matters, acting in the course of employment by the carrier. In fact, however, the evidence, including the actual account, showed that these charges were paid by the ship's agent on behalf of the carrier, thus, if anything, giving rise to an inference the other way. Their Lordships put this matter aside and proceed to deal with the point on the construction of the relevant provisions of the bill of lading.

B

On its face, the document stated that delivery would be effected "by the carrier or his agents" in exchange for the bill of lading, and the preamble provided that the goods were

"... to be transported subject to all the terms of this bill of lading ... to the port of discharge ... and there to be delivered or transhipped on payment of the charges thereon ..."

C

and further

"It is agreed that the custody and carriage of the goods are subject to the following terms on the face and back thereof which shall govern the relations, whatsoever they may be, between the shipper, consignee, and the carrier, master and ship in every contingency, wheresoever and whensoever occurring ..."

D

Clause 5 was as follows:

"The carrier's responsibility in respect of the goods as a carrier shall not attach until the goods are actually loaded for transportation upon the ship and shall terminate without notice as soon as the goods leave the ship's tackle at the port of discharge from ship or other place where the carrier is authorised to make delivery or end its responsibility. Any responsibility of the carrier in respect of the goods attaching prior to such loading or continuing after leaving the ship's tackle as aforesaid, shall not exceed that of an ordinary bailee, and, in particular, the carrier shall not be liable for loss or damage to the goods due to: flood; fire, as provided elsewhere in this bill of lading; falling or collapse of wharf, pier or warehouse; robbery, theft or pilferage; strikes, lockouts or stoppage or restraint of labor from whatever cause, whether partial or general; any of the risks or causes mentioned in paragraphs (a), (e) to (l) inclusive and (k) to (p) inclusive, of subdivision 2 of section 4 of the Carriage of Goods by Sea Act of the United States; or any risks or causes whatsoever, not included in the foregoing, and whether like or unlike those hereinabove mentioned, where the loss or damage is not due to the fault or neglect of the carrier. The carrier shall not be liable in any capacity whatsoever for any non-delivery or misdelivery, or loss of or damage to the goods occurring while the goods are not in the actual custody of the carrier."

E

F

G

Clause 8 was as follows:

H

"Delivery of the goods shall be taken by the consignee or holder of the bill of lading from the vessel's rail immediately the vessel is ready to discharge, berthed or not berthed, and continuously as fast as vessel can deliver notwithstanding any custom of the port to the contrary. The carrier shall be at liberty to discharge continuously day and night, Sundays and holidays included, all extra expenses to be for account of the consignee or receiver of the goods notwith-

The Weekly Law Reports, February 6, 1981

147

1 W.L.R.   Port Jackson Ltd. v. Salmond & Spraggon Ltd. (P.C.)

A   standing any custom of the port to the contrary. If the consignee
or holder of the bill of lading does not for any reason take delivery
as provided herein, they shall be jointly and severally liable to pay
the vessel on demand demurrage at the rate of one shilling and six-
pence sterling per gross register ton per day or portion of a day
during the delay so caused: such demurrage shall be paid in cash
day by day to the carrier, the master or agents. If the consignee or
B   holder of the bill of lading requires delivery before or after usual
hours he shall pay any extra expenses incurred in consequence.
Delivery ex ship's rail shall constitute due delivery of the goods
described herein and the carrier's liability shall cease at that point
notwithstanding consignee receiving delivery at some point removed
from the ship's side and custom of the port being to the contrary.
C   The carrier and his agents shall have the right of nominating the
berth or berths for loading and discharging at all ports and places
whatsoever any custom to the contrary notwithstanding. The
carrier shall not be required to give any notification of disposition
or arrival of the goods."

Clause 14 was as follows:

D   " Neither the carrier nor any corporation owned by, subsidiary
to or associated or affiliated with the carrier shall be liable to answer
for or make good any loss or damage to the goods occurring at any
time and even though before loading on or after discharge from
the ship, by reason or by means of any fire whatsoever, unless such
fire shall be caused by its design or neglect."

E   These provisions must be interpreted in the light of the practice that
consignees rarely take delivery of goods at the ship's rail but will nor-
mally collect them after some period of storage on or near the wharf.
The parties must therefore have contemplated that the carrier, if it did
not store the goods itself, would employ some other person to do so.
Furthermore, a document headed " Port Jackson Stevedoring Pty. Ltd.
F   Basic Terms and Conditions for Stevedoring at Sydney, N.S.W." showed
that it was contemplated that the stevedore would be so employed.
These practical considerations, which are developed in the judgment of
Barwick C.J., explain the somewhat intricate interrelation of clauses
5 and 8.

It is convenient to start with clause 8. This, in the first sentence,
creates an obligation on the consignee to take delivery from the ship's
G   rail the moment that the ship is ready to discharge: if he does not, he
must pay demurrage. This provision, which is in line with the decision
in Keane v. Australian Steamships Pty. Ltd. (1929) 41 C.L.R. 484 is a
valuable protection for the carrier, upon which he may, or may not,
insist. The bill of lading takes account of both possibilities. The first
sentence of clause 5, quite consistently, provides that the carrier's
H   responsibility as a carrier terminates as soon as the goods leave the ship's
tackle. But, since the carrier may not have insisted that the consignee
take delivery at this point, the rest of clause 5 continues by recognising
that the carrier may continue to have some responsibility for the goods
after discharge. He cannot after all dump them on the wharf and leave
them there. So to suppose would be commercially unreal and is not
contemplated by the bill of lading. Clause 5 in terms attributes responsibility to the carrier as bailee and defines the period in express terms as

" continuing after leaving the ship's tackle." There is nothing in the A
latter part of clause 8 that is inconsistent with this. It merely provides
that *delivery* ex ship's rail shall constitute *due delivery* and that the
carrier's liability shall cease at that point. But that leaves open the
option not to insist on delivery ex ship's rail, and leaves, to be governed
by clause 5, his responsibility if he does not.

The question may be asked, what is the carrier's position if he acts
as his own stevedore and himself stacks and stores the goods. In the B
High Court, Stephen J. did not provide an answer to this but, in view
of the provisions referred to above, their Lordships think that the
answer is clear: namely that he would be liable for them, as bailee,
under the contract. If that is so, it seems indisputable that if, instead,
the carrier employs a third party to discharge, stack and store, that
person would be acting in the course of his employment, performing C
duties which otherwise the carrier would perform under the bill of
lading, and so would be entitled to the same immunity as the carrier
would have. Their Lordships would add that both clause 5, in references to theft or pilferage (which may be expected to occur, if it does
occur, on the wharf) and clause 14, referring to fire occurring after discharge, also recognise that the carrier may have responsibilities after
this event. It is made clear by clause 5 that, irrespective of the period D
of carriage defined by the contract, the immunity of the carrier is not
co-extensive with this period but extends both before and after it. The
stevedore's immunity extends, by virtue of clause 2, over the same
period.

On this point (and indeed on the appeal as a whole) their Lordships
are in agreement with the judgment of Barwick C.J. They will humbly E
advise Her Majesty that the appeal be allowed. The costs order of the
High Court of Australia will remain undisturbed and the costs of this
appeal will be borne by the stevedore in accordance with the undertaking which it gave.

Solicitors: *Richards Butler & Co.; Clyde & Co.*

T. J. M.   F

[COURT OF APPEAL]

* ATTORNEY-GENERAL'S REFERENCE (No. 2 of 1980)   G

1980 Oct. 3; 24   Lord Lane C.J., Stocker and
                                                    Glidewell JJ.

*Crime—Forgery—False document—Falsification of witness state-
    ment—Statement tendered as evidence—Whether forgery of
    " document . . . made evidence by law "—Forgery Act* 1913 H
    (3 & 4 Geo. 5, c. 27), s. 3 (3) (g)

During a trial, the defendant, who was a police officer in
charge of a summary prosecution, handed to the clerk of the
court a written witness statement which he was tendering
under the provisions of section 9 of the Criminal Justice Act
1967.[1] He later admitted that he, not the purported witness,

---

[1] Criminal Justice Act 1967, s. 9 (1): see post, p. 151B.

A   had written the statement. The defendant was tried on an indictment containing two counts: first, forgery of a document made evidence by law contrary to section 3 (3) (g) of the Forgery Act 1913 [2]; secondly, uttering a forged document made evidence by law contrary to section 6 (1) of the Act. The trial judge ruled that there was no case to go to the jury since, under section 3 (3) (g), the document only became evidence when tendered to the court and at the time of the
B   forgery had not achieved the status of "a document made evidence by law." As a result of that ruling, there was no evidence under section 6 (1) that a forged document had been uttered and the defendant was acquitted on both counts.

    The Attorney-General referred for the opinion of the court the questions whether a person who forged with intent to deceive a written statement which was later tendered to a court under section 9 of the Criminal Justice Act 1967 committed
C   an offence under section 3 (3) (g) of the Forgery Act 1913 and whether a person who knowingly handed to the court such a document committed an offence under section 6 (1) of the Act of 1913 of uttering a forged document which was made evidence by law: —

    Held, answering the questions in the affirmative, that the phrase "document . . . made evidence by law" was descriptive of a class of documents and was not descriptive of the moment
D   when a document was received in evidence and, therefore, became evidence; that, accordingly, an offence was committed under section 3 (3) (g) of the Forgery Act 1913 when there had been a deliberate making of a false document and that document was tendered in evidence in accordance with the relevant provisions of a statute (post, p. 153E–H).

E   No cases are referred to in the judgment or were cited in argument.

    REFERENCE by the Attorney-General.
    The Attorney-General referred, under section 36 of the Criminal Justice Act 1972, points of law for the opinion of the Court of Appeal in the following terms:
    " 1. (a) Whether a person who forges with intent to deceive a written
F   statement which is later tendered to a masgistrates court under section 9 of the Criminal Justice Act 1967 commits an offence under section 3 (3) (g) of the Forgery Act 1913 of forging a document which is made evidence by law?
    " (b) Whether a person who knowingly hands to the court [such] a written statement which he is tendering under section 9 of the Criminal Justice Act 1967 commits an offence under section 6 (1) of the Forgery
G   Act 1913 of uttering a forged document which is made evidence by law?
    " 2. The material facts of the case which give rise to this reference are as follows: (i) The [defendant] who was a police officer was in charge of a summary prosecution. (ii) At the hearing of this prosecution in open court he handed to the clerk of the court a written statement which he was tendering under the provisions of section 9 of the Criminal Justice
H   Act 1967 with the consent of the defence. (iii) The court received the statement in evidence. (iv) The [defendant] later admitted that the purported witness had neither made the statement nor signed it. (v) The matters contained in the statement were capable of proof by two witnesses but the [defendant] stated that because he had forgotten to approach them by the date of the trial he wrote the purported statement to cover up his omission.

    [2] Forgery Act 1913, s. 3 (3) (g): see post, p. 150H—151A.

A

" 3. Count 1 of the indictment charged the [defendant] with forgery of
the statement contrary to section 3 (3) (g) and averred that the statement
was a document made evidence by law. Count 2 of the indictment
charged him with uttering a document made evidence by law.

" 4. The learned judge ruled that the written statement became a " document made evidence by law " when it was received in evidence but because
it was not such a document at the time it was forged the [defendant] did
not commit an offence against section 3 (3) (g). In respect of the

B

offence of uttering a forged document as alleged he ruled that the
uttering occurred when the statement was handed to the clerk of the
court and before it had been received in evidence by the court and thus
there was no uttering of a document made evidence by law."

David Tudor Price for the Attorney-General.

C

Peter Digney for the defendant.

Cur. adv. vult.

October 24. STOCKER J. read the following judgment of the court.
This is a reference by the Attorney-General under the provisions of
section 36 of the Criminal Justice Act 1972, a proceeding whereby the

D

Attorney-General can institute steps for the testing of a direction on a
principle of law decided in the Crown Court which seems to have been
wrongly decided and which may be in danger of reproduction in later
cases if not corrected.

This case concerns the tendering as evidence at the trial of the
defendant before a magistrates' court of a statement pursuant to section

E

9 of the Criminal Justice Act 1967. The statement had not been made
or signed by the person by whom it purported to have been made and
signed but had been written and signed by the defendant. The judge
at the trial of the defendant for forgery and uttering a forged document
ruled that there was no case to go to the jury under section 3 (3) (g) of
the Forgery Act 1913 since the document only became evidence when
tendered to the court, and at the time of the forgery had not achieved

F

the status of " a document made evidence by law " and ruled that
accordingly there was no evidence under section 6 (1) that a forged
document had been uttered.

The point of law which this court had been asked to decide has been
stated in the reference in the following terms:

G

" (a) Whether a person who forges with intent to deceive a written
statement which is later tendered to a magistrates' court under section 9 of the Criminal Justice Act 1967 commits an offence under
section 3 (3) (g) of the Forgery Act 1913 of forging a document
which is made evidence by law. (b) Whether a person who knowingly hands to the court a forged written statement which he is
tendering under section 9 of the Criminal Justice Act 1967 com-

H

mits an offence under section 6 (1) of the Forgery Act 1913 of
uttering a forged document which is made evidence by law."

[His Lordship stated the facts set out in the reference and continued:]
The defendant was charged upon an indictment containing two counts:
first, forgery contrary to section 3 (3) (g) of the Forgery Act 1913;
secondly, uttering such document contrary to section 6 (1) thereof. The
Forgery Act 1913 by section 3 (3) makes it an offence to forge " the

A following documents . . . with intent to defraud or deceive . . . (g) . . . any document which is made evidence by law."

It was not disputed that the document tendered, if genuine, was properly admitted in evidence in accordance with section 9 of the Criminal Justice Act 1967, which states:

B " (1) In any criminal proceedings . . . a written statement by any person shall, if such of the conditions mentioned in the next following subsection as are applicable are satisfied, be admissible as evidence to the like extent as oral evidence to the like effect by that person."

It is unnecessary for the purpose of this judgment to recite in detail the conditions referred to in subsection (1) save to observe that subsection (2) states the form and necessary contents of the statement and requires
C that before the hearing at which it is tendered a copy shall be served on each of the other parties to the proceedings and that no objection to it being tendered in evidence is received from any party within seven days. Subsection (3) sets out further procedural requirements which must be fulfilled before that statement can be admitted. Subsection (4) confers power on parties to the proceedings or the court of its own
D motion to require the person who made the statement to give oral evidence notwithstanding that the statement is admissible in evidence, all requirements having been fulfilled.

The judge's ruling was in these terms:

" What was the nature of that written statement at the time it was so falsely, on the evidence dishonestly, prepared or forged by the
E accused? At this stage it was no more than a witness statement, or purported to be a witness statement made by the witness. At the time it was forged it was not, on any view, a document made evidence by law."

The judge continued later:

" When was the uttering? In my view it must be, at the latest, the
F tendering of the statement to be used in evidence. It is right that it was subsequently read, but that was the administrative process of dealing with it after it had been accepted in evidence. At the moment of tendering it was not a document made evidence by law and it could not be until it had been accepted in evidence."

Counsel for the defendant in his submissions to this court supported
G this part of the judge's ruling quoted above upon the same grounds that he had advanced to the trial judge when advocating such ruling.

His first submission was that section 9 of the Criminal Justice Act 1967 did not make the document itself evidence but only its contents and that the words in section 9 (1) " shall . . . be admissible as evidence to the like extent as oral evidence to the like effect by that person " properly construed meant that the document was the medium through which the
H evidence of the matter contained in the statement would be put before the court. He supported this construction of the section by the contention that in practice statements under section 9 were not put in evidence but were read either wholly or in part to the court. This court while accepting that the reading of statements rather than their being put in evidence as documents may be common practice in the Crown Court, doubts whether in the magistrates' court this is a universal practice. In any event, such practice does not assist in the construction of

the section of the Act, the wording of which states in terms which seem   A
unequivocal " a written statement by any person shall . . . be admissible as
evidence. . . . " The trial judge rejected counsel's contention and held that
the written statement itself was made evidence by the Act. We agree
with this part of his ruling and do not propose further to consider it.

Counsel's second submission which was accepted as correct by the
judge and is the basis of his ruling, the correctness of which this court   B
has been asked to consider, was that the document itself when made and
forged is not at that stage evidence at all or admissible as such. It
becomes evidence under the Act if, and only if, the requirements of
section 9 (2), (3) and (4) of the Act have been complied with and the
document tendered to the court as evidence. He argued that until these
requirements were fulfilled, the document was simply a document and
not evidence at all, either under the Criminal Justice Act 1967 or in any   C
other sense and thus could not be the subject of forgery under section
3 (3) (g) of the Forgery Act 1913 since it was not at the time at which
the " forgery " took place a " document . . . made evidence by law." In
support of this submission he sought to draw a distinction between
certain classes of documents made evidence under certain other statutes
and statements tendered under the Criminal Justice Act 1967. It is
manifest that in 1913 when the Forgery Act became law statements   D
under section 9 of the Criminal Justice Act 1967 could not have been
in contemplation and he sought to argue that the documents which at
that date might have been tendered which were the subject matter of
section 3 (3) (g) of the Act of 1913 were documents which the relevant
statutes relating to them made " evidence " in the sense that they were
themselves evidence at all stages and did not require any conditions to be   E
fulfilled as a pre-requisite of their admissibility. He submitted that the
proper formula to apply in reaching the decision whether a document was
or was not " evidence " for the purpose of section 9 of the Criminal
Justice Act 1967, and if forged for the purpose of conviction under section
3 (3) (g) of the Forgery Act 1913, was " does anything remain to be done
before the document can be admitted in evidence? "

He submitted that documents made evidence by statute prior to 1913   F
and which were accordingly documents " made evidence by law " had
the characteristic that nothing remained to be done to render them
admissible. He cited a number of Acts and documents made evidence
under them such as section 1 of the Evidence Act 1845, section 7 of the
Evidence Act 1851 and such documents as the Official Gazette, which
were themselves evidence of the proclamation, order or regulations pub-   G
lished therein. His contention was that the definition of documents
" made evidence by law " for the purpose of section 3 (3) (g) of the
Forgery Act 1913 was confined to such documents and excluded documents which were admissible only upon the performance of certain conditions, for the reason already stated—that at the time they were forged
they were no more than statements and had no status as evidence.

In our view the judge's ruling and the arguments advanced in sup-   H
port of it are erroneous and should be rejected. We accept that there
are classes of documents which by statute are themselves " evidence "
proving the facts contained in them upon production without further
formality, such as certificates of birth or marriage (covered by section
3 (2) (a) of the Forgery Act 1913), Queen's printers' copies of statutes or
other official orders, but these, too, in our view become " evidence " only
when tendered as such to the appropriate court or other tribunal. If the

A judge's ruling and counsel's argument in support of it are correct, even this class of document would not be capable of being forged until tendered in evidence (subject to specific statutory enactments regarding this). Nor do we accept as valid counsel's formula that documents within the ambit of section 3 (3) (g) are confined to documents which require nothing further to be done before they can be admitted, since, for example, the Bankers' Books Evidence Act 1879 which renders a

B copy of an entry in a banker's book receivable as evidence, prescribes a number of requirements and formalities to be fulfilled before an entry in a banker's book is so receivable, with the consequence that if the judge's ruling and counsel's argument are correct, no false copy of such entry would support a conviction under section 3 (3) (g) of the Forgery Act 1913 until it was tendered in evidence, nor could it be uttered until

C after it was so received. We cite these examples in support of our view that the judge's ruling renders impossible in every, or almost every, case any conviction under section 3 (3) (g) of the Act of 1913 unless the forgery takes place after the document is received as evidence.

This rather startling consequence is not necessarily conclusive of the point in issue but in our view stems from a misconstruction of the meaning of the word " evidence " in section 3 (3) of the Forgery Act 1913. In

D our view no " evidence " can exist, be it documentary, oral or in the form of an exhibit until it is received as such in proceedings in which it is evidence of the fact then in issue. It seems contrary to the manifest intention of the Forgery Act 1913 to confine offences under section 3 (3) (g) to documents after they have become evidence in that sense.

We think it so improbable that the draftsman of section 3 (3) (g)

E had in mind that the subject matter of that section should be forgery after the document had been tendered in evidence that any conclusion which confines the subject matter of this section to that situation can be regarded as fanciful. On this basis the judge's ruling would for practical purposes deprive this subsection of all subject matter.

In our judgment, on its proper construction, section 3 (3) (g) is concerned with documents which if made and tendered in accordance with

F the provisions and conditions of the relevant Act become documents " made evidence by law " and it is the forgery of such class of documents which is the subject matter of this subsection. Thus the phrase " document . . . made evidence by law " is descriptive of a class of documents and is not descriptive of the moment when its reception in evidence renders it " evidence."

G Consequently any person commits an offence under section 3 (3) (g) of the Forgery Act 1913 if he, with intent to defraud or deceive, forges any document which if made and tendered in evidence in accordance with the terms and conditions of the relevant statute relating thereto will become a document made evidence by law.

For these reasons, in our view, the ruling of the judge upon this point was wrong and we would answer each question posed in the reference

H in the affirmative and will so advise the Attorney-General.

Opinion accordingly.

Solicitors: *Director of Public Prosecutions; Bertram White & Co., Epsom.*

[Reported by MARIA FLEISCHMANN, Barrister-at-Law]

A

[QUEEN'S BENCH DIVISION: MANCHESTER]

* McQUAID v. ANDERTON

1980 Feb. 20   Lord Widgery C.J., Roskill L.J. and Heilbron J.

Road Traffic—Driving or attempting to drive—" Driving "—Motor-   B
ist in driver's seat of towed vehicle with steering wheel and
operative braking system—Whether driving—" Drives "—Road
Traffic Act 1972 (c. 20), s. 99 (b)

The defendant, who was disqualified for holding or obtaining
a licence to drive a motor vehicle, was sitting in the driver's seat
of a motor vehicle being towed on a road by another vehicle
with a rope. The towed vehicle was equipped with a steering   C
wheel and the braking system was operative. The defendant
was convicted by justices of driving while disqualified, contrary
to section 99 (b) of the Road Traffic Act 1972.[1]

On appeal against conviction: —

Held, dismissing the appeal, that a person in the driver's
seat of a motor vehicle being towed on a road was driving
the vehicle for the purposes of section 99 of the Road Traffic
Act 1972 if he steered, controlled and had the ability to brake   D
when necessary; and that, accordingly, the defendant had been
rightly convicted.

Reg. v. *MacDonagh* [1974] Q.B. 448, C.A. applied.
Wallace v. *Major* [1946] K.B. 473, D.C. not followed.

The following cases are referred to in the judgments:

Andersen v. *Transport Department* [1964] N.Z.L.R. 881.
Reg. v. *MacDonagh* [1974] Q.B. 448; [1974] 2 W.L.R. 529; [1974] 2   E
All E.R. 257, C.A.
Reg. v. *Roberts* [1965] 1 Q.B. 85; [1964] 3 W.L.R. 180; [1964] 2 All
E.R. 541, C.C.A.
Wallace v. *Major* [1946] K.B. 473; [1946] 2 All E.R. 87, D.C.

The following additional cases were cited in argument:
                                                                       F
Ames v. *MacLeod,* 1969 J.C. 1.
Davis v. *Johnson* [1979] A.C. 264; [1978] 2 W.L.R. 553; [1978] 1 All
E.R. 1132, H.L.(E.).
Reg. v. *Whitlow* [1965] Crim.L.R. 170.

CASE STATED by Manchester justices.

On August 29, 1977, an information was preferred by the prosecutor,   G
Cyril James Anderton, a police officer, against the defendant, Eugene
Francis McQuaid, that he, on August 29, 1977, being a person dis-
qualified for holding or obtaining a licence to drive, did drive a motor
vehicle on Matthews Lane, contrary to section 99 of the Road Traffic
Act 1972.

The justices heard the information on November 1, 1977, and found
the following facts. On August 29, 1977, the defendant was a dis-   H
qualified driver by order of the court. On August 29, 1977, a motor
vehicle, registered number LBA 57E, was being towed along Matthews
Lane, Manchester, by another vehicle. The defendant was sitting in
the driver's seat of the motor vehicle which was being towed. The
vehicle was equipped with a steering wheel, it was being towed by means

[1] Road Traffic Act 1972, s. 99 (b): post, p. 155H.

A   of a tow rope and the braking system of the vehicle was operative. All the evidence before the court was admitted in accordance with the provisions of section 10 of the Criminal Justice Act 1967.

It was contended on behalf of the defendant (i) that the decision in *Wallace* v. *Major* [1946] K.B. 473 was authority for saying that the person sitting in the driver's seat of a towed vehicle was not a driver

B   for the purposes of the Road Traffic Act 1972; (ii) that *Wallace* v. *Major* was a precedent binding on the magistrates' court; and (iii) that, consequently, on the agreed facts it was not open to the bench to find that the defendant was a driver.

It was contended on behalf of the prosecutor (i) that it was only the ratio decidendi in *Wallace* v. *Major* which was binding, and that that was contained in the approach adopted by Lord Goddard C.J. in that

C   case to the question of who should be regarded as a driver; (ii) that that approach was followed and reaffirmed by the Court of Appeal in *Reg.* v. *MacDonagh* [1974] Q.B. 448 where, however, the court doubted whether the Divisional Court in *Wallace* v. *Major* had correctly applied its own approach to the facts of the case before it; (iii) and that, consequently, it was open to the bench, while following *Wallace* v. *Major*,

D   to find that the defendant was a driver.

The justices were of the opinion that on the admitted facts the defendant was driving the vehicle LBA 57E within the meaning of section 99 of the Road Traffic Act 1972, they imposed on him a fine of £3 and ordered that his driving licence be endorsed.

The defendant appealed.

The question for the opinion of the court was whether the justices'

E   determination was right in law.

F. E. Coles for the defendant.
D. J. Brennan for the prosecutor.

HEILBRON J. delivered the first judgment. This is an appeal by way

F   of case stated by Manchester justices who, on November 1, 1977, convicted the defendant of driving a motor vehicle whilst disqualified within the meaning of section 99 of the Road Traffic Act 1972. He was fined £3 and his driving licence was endorsed.

The justices found the following facts which were not disputed. On August 29, 1977, the defendant was a disqualified driver by order of the

G   court; a motor vehicle was being towed along Matthews Lane, Manchester by another vehicle by means of a tow rope; the defendant was sitting in the driver's seat of the motor vehicle being towed. Mr. Coles for the defendant conceded that he was steering by means of the vehicle's steering wheel and that the braking system of the towed vehicle was operative.

Section 99 of the Road Traffic Act 1972 provides:

H
"If a person disqualified for holding or obtaining a licence . . . (b) while he is so disqualified drives on a road a motor vehicle . . . he shall be guilty of an offence."

There is no definition in the Act of the word "drive" or "drives" and that word clearly encompasses a variety of ways in which a person may be described as driving a motor vehicle.

That activity primarily envisages a person sitting in the driving seat

A

directing and controlling the movement of the vehicle by means of a steering wheel, using the brakes as and when required, the engine being used for propulsion. But, that apart, many of the other ways in which a person may be said and has been held to drive, have been considered in authorities covering such widely diverse types of driving as, for example, a man sitting in the driving seat controlling the vehicle by means of the steering wheel and brakes, whilst another person or persons or another car pushes the relevant vehicle. The vehicle in question may be allowed to coast down hill in neutral with the engine switched off, but still with the person sitting in the car at the steering wheel with his foot at the ready, to apply the brakes. There are instances of a person being held to be a driver though not sitting in the driving seat but exercising sufficient, though not necessarily full control, from the passenger seat to cast himself in the role of a driver.

B

C

The matter is not devoid of authority and reliance has been placed, by Mr. Coles in his most helpful submission, on *Wallace* v. *Major* [1946] K.B. 473 where, in a case concerned with a charge of dangerous driving the respondent, who was at the steering wheel of a broken down car on tow to another car, was acquitted by the justices: Lord Goddard C.J. held, when the matter came before him by way of case stated, that, first of all—and this was the prime matter with which he was concerned— section 121 of the Road Traffic Act 1930 did not apply because the provision in that section contemplated two persons being in charge of the same vehicle and the respondent was not a driver in any event within the meaning of that Act. Mr. Coles has referred us to the judgment of Lord Goddard C.J. in which he stated that in his view the person in the driving seat of a towed vehicle could not be described as a driver. One reason was that although he was controlling it to some extent, he did not have full control and, another, that he could not retain a full view of the road and traffic ahead. Lord Goddard C.J. also referred to the latter difficulty arising under the Motor Vehicles (Construction and Use) Regulations 1941.

D

E

Counsel submitted that in reliance on the decision in *Wallace* v. *Major* the defendant should have been acquitted.

F

The matter was, however, recently and authoritatively considered by the full Court of Appeal, Lord Widgery C.J., Scarman L.J., Thesiger, Bristow and May JJ. in *Reg.* v. *MacDonagh* [1974] Q.B. 448. Lord Widgery C.J. gave the judgment of the court. *Wallace* v. *Major* [1946] K.B. 473 was considered and its authority doubted. Although the facts in *Reg.* v. *MacDonagh* were not the same as the facts in the instant case, save that the appellant was also disqualified from driving, it was there held that " driving " could not extend to the activity of a person who was not in the car, had both feet on the road and was making no use of the controls apart from an occasional adjustment of the steering wheel. The appeal was allowed but the facts of that case were far removed from those in the present case for the appellant in *Reg.* v. *MacDonagh* was not in the car at all.

G

H

Lord Widgery C.J. at p. 451, referred to the infinite number of ways in which a person may control the movement of a motor vehicle apart from the orthodox one of sitting in the driving seat and using the engine for propulsion, including some of the manifold ways to which I have referred in which a car can be driven, and he pointed out that, although the word " drive " must be given a wide meaning, the courts must be

A   alert to see that the net is not thrown so widely that it includes activities which cannot be said to be driving a motor vehicle in any ordinary use of that word in the English language. Unless that is done absurdity may result. Although Mr. Coles did not restrict himself to that particular aspect he would no doubt want to rely on it. What he would say, I assume from the rest of his submission, is that the net cannot be thrown wide enough to encompass the man at the seat of a towed vehicle.

B   Lord Widgery C.J. said, at p. 451:

> "The Act does not define the word 'drive' and in its simplest meaning we think that it refers to a person using the driver's controls for the purpose of directing the movement of the vehicle."

Pausing there, certainly the driver in this case was directing the move-
C ment of the vehicle.

> "It matters not that the vehicle is not moving under its own power, or driven by the force of gravity, or even that it is being pushed by other well wishers. The essence of driving is the use of the driver's controls in order to direct the movement, however that movement is produced."

D   As to the argument put forward by Mr. Coles that propulsion is at the basis of these cases, it was made clear in *Reg.* v. *MacDonagh* that it is not. Lord Widgery C.J. referring to the decision of Lord Goddard C.J. in *Wallace* v. *Major* [1946] K.B. 473, said, at p. 452:

> "While we adopt the approach of Lord Goddard C.J. to penal legislation, we respectfully doubt whether the correct conclusion was
E   reached on the facts of that case. The court seems to have regarded the defendant as merely a steersman, and to have ignored his responsibility for the use of the brakes."

Lord Widgery C.J. with reference to *Reg.* v. *Roberts* [1965] Q.B. 85, added:

> "We would draw attention to the two factors to which Lord Parker
F   C.J. refers: first, that the alleged driver must be in the driving seat "—the defendant was certainly in the driving seat—" or in control of the steering wheel "—the defendant was in control of the steering wheel—" and, secondly, that his activities are nevertheless not to be held to amount to driving unless they come within the ordinary meaning of that word."

G   Mr. Coles submitted that the word "driver" in this case was not used in the ordinary way. The justices in this case, no doubt exercising their common sense as justices usually do, apparently had no hesitation in coming to the conclusion that the defendant was a driver.

    One can, I think, test this matter in a number of different ways by asking oneself certain questions. Suppose, for instance, there was no
H one at the wheel of the towed vehicle: would not an ordinary bystander, in common sense, say, perhaps with some alarm, "There is no driver in that car "? Although the facts were somewhat different in *Andersen* v. *Transport Department* [1964] N.Z.L.R. 881 when a towed vehicle snaked dangerously about the road due to the careless control of the man who was at the wheel of the other car, he was held to be guilty of dangerous driving. What would happen therefore if there was no one to

brake the towed vehicle when an emergency arose ahead of the leading A vehicle? One might also ask oneself the question not answered by the newspaper report of *Reg.* v. *Pearson* (unreported) May 8, 1978, Bodmin Crown Court produced by Mr. Coles: could a drunken man safely purport to steer, and control the brakes of a towed vehicle? One has only to ask that question to see how naturally the word " driver " covers the position of a person steering, controlling and having the ability, as he should have, to brake when necessary. As to the criticism that the B word " driver " is not used in its natural and ordinary meaning when a person is in the driver's seat of a towed vehicle, the only alternative word that could be suggested was that of " towee."

Therefore, without straining its connotation, giving the word its ordinary meaning, and adopting the test proposed in *Reg.* v. *MacDonagh* [1974] Q.B. 448, in my judgment " the extent and degree " to which C the defendant must have been controlling this vehicle, comprises an activity which the justices correctly described as driving, and he was rightly convicted.

ROSKILL L.J. I entirely agree that this appeal fails and should be dismissed. The case stated by the justices of this city is, if I may be allowed to say so, a model of its kind. It occupies no more than 2½ pages D of typescript. The facts are set out with admirable succinctness and we are asked to say whether their decision that the defendant was guilty of the offence charged is right in point of law.

Mr. Coles, in this court—and whoever represented the defendant in the court below made the same submission—rested largely on the decision of the Divisional Court in *Wallace* v. *Major* [1946] K.B. 473. I confess E with the utmost respect for Lord Goddard C.J. that when Mr. Coles read the relevant passages I wondered if that case had been correctly decided, though of course sitting in the Divisional Court we would have been bound by the decision if there had been no subsequent authority. I was not then aware of the decision to which attention has been drawn of a five judge Court of Appeal, Criminal Division, in *Reg.* v. *Mac-* F *Donagh* [1974] Q.B. 448. Heilbron J. has read the relevant passages in the judgment of this court delivered by Lord Widgery C.J. and I will not repeat what was there said. It seems to me plain that what Lord Goddard C.J. and the other members of the court said in *Wallace* v. *Major* [1946] K.B. 473 cannot stand alongside with the judgment of the full court in *Reg.* v. *MacDonagh* [1974] Q.B. 448. This appeal will G have served a useful purpose if the ghost of *Wallace* v. *Major* is now finally exorcised.

It is worth drawing attention to the fact that in *Stone's Justices Manual,* 112th ed. (1980), vol. 2, p. 3607 *Wallace* v. *Major* is referred to but, correctly, is doubted with a reference to *Reg.* v. *MacDonagh.* That passage will, no doubt, be revised in the next edition much to the H relief of justices hereafter concerned with these problems.

I agree the appeal should be dismissed and the question we are asked, whether the determination was right in point of law, we answered, " Yes, it was."

LORD WIDGERY C.J. I agree with both judgments. The law hereafter on these points is that laid down in *Reg.* v. *MacDonagh* [1974] Q.B. 448

A and justices will be well advised to apply that authority and no other. The appeal will be dismissed.

Appeal dismissed.
Prosecutor's costs out of central funds.

B Solicitors: *Pariser & Co., Manchester; D. S. Gandy, Manchester.*

L. N. W.

C [QUEEN'S BENCH DIVISION]

* HULLEY *v.* THOMPSON

1980 May 12   Waller L.J. and Stephen Brown J.

Social Security—Supplementary benefit—Maintenance—Father's
D *liability to maintain children—Consent order in divorce pro-*
ceedings—Father to pay no maintenance for children but to
transfer interest in matrimonial home—Effect of consent order
on father's liability—Supplementary Benefits Act 1976 (c. 71),
ss. 17 (1), 18 (3)

On the divorce of the father and mother of two children,
an order was made by consent in the county court providing,
E inter alia, that the father pay no maintenance for the mother or
the children, but that he transfer to the mother all his interest
in the matrimonial home. The mother received supplementary
benefit for the children. The appellant, an officer of the Supplementary Benefits Commission, made a complaint to the justices
under section 18 of the Supplementary Benefits Act 1976 [1] for
an order that the father, the respondent, being a person liable
to maintain his wife and children under section 17 (1) of the
Act, pay to the Department of Health and Social Security such
F sum as the court considered appropriate. The justices had
regard to the county court order, and made no order on the
complaint.
On appeal by the appellant:—
Held, allowing the appeal, that by virtue of section 17 (1) of
the Act of 1976 the respondent had a continuing obligation to
maintain his children which could not be avoided by a con-
G sent arrangement such as that made in the county court, and
the obligation was not discharged by the transfer of his interest
in the matrimonial home, although that was a matter which
could be taken into account in assessing the level of maintenance; and that, since both parents had a continuing liability to
maintain the children under the subsection, prima facie the
father ought to pay the balance of what the mother was unable
to pay for the children's maintenance and, therefore, the matter
H would be remitted to the justices to consider all the financial
circumstances of the respondent and the mother and make an
order accordingly.

The following case is referred to in the judgments:
Diss Urban Sanitary Authority v. *Aldrich* (1877) 2 Q.B.D. 179, D.C.

[1] Supplementary Benefits Act 1976, s. 17 (1): see post, p. 162A.
S. 18: see post, p. 162B–C.

The following additional case was cited in argument: A

National Assistance Board v. *Parkes* [1955] 2 Q.B. 506; [1955] 3 W.L.R.
347; [1955] 3 All E.R. 1, C.A.

CASE STATED by Derbyshire justices sitting at Buxton.

On February 27, 1978, a complaint was preferred by the appellant,
Michael Donald Hulley, an officer of the Supplementary Benefits Commission, against the respondent, Frank Thompson, that the respondent was   B
the father of two children whom he was liable to maintain pursuant to
section 17 of the Supplementary Benefits Act 1976 and to meet whose
requirements, benefit had been paid and continued to be paid within the
High Peak Petty Sessional Division. The appellant applied for an order
under section 18 of that Act for the respondent to pay to the Secretary of
State for Social Services such sum as the court considered appropriate, by C
weekly instalments, or otherwise.

The justices heard the complaint on June 21, 1978, and found the
following facts. The respondent was the father of two children born on
May 28, 1965. He was a person liable to maintain the children. He was
divorced at Derby County Court from Beryl Thompson, the mother of the
children. On November 29, 1976, the Derby County Court made an order,   D
by consent, containing the following provisions: that the respondent not
pay any maintenance to the mother either for herself or for any children
of the family; that within two months of the date of the order, the respondent transfer to the mother all his interest in the matrimonial home at
150, Green Lane, Buxton, in the county of Derby, without payment of any
consideration by the mother to the respondent; that the proceeds of a
policy of insurance on the life of the respondent be paid to the mother if E
not already done at the date of the order; and that the mother should
not take any steps to enforce the arrears under the existing interim order
dated August 10, 1976. The approximate value in 1976 of the property
transferred, in which the respondent had a half share, was £25,000, free
of mortgages. The value of the insurance policy was approximately £100.
The respondent's net wage was between £55 and £70 weekly. Benefit had   F
been paid by the Department of Health and Social Security for both
children.

It was contended by the appellant that the respondent was the liable
relative under section 17 of the Act of 1976, and that his resources were
such that he could pay a reasonable sum for the maintenance of the
children. It was also contended that the order made by the Derby County
Court was irrelevant.   G

It was contended by the respondent that the order made by the Derby
County Court was relevant, that for a magistrates' court to make an order
for the respondent to pay maintenance would be inconsistent with that
order, and that the respondent had in any event met his liability to maintain by assigning his interest in the matrimonial home, estimated at £12,500,
to the mother.   H

The justices were of the opinion that section 18 (3) of the Act of 1976
required the court to " have regard to all the circumstances and in particular, to the resources of the liable relative, and . . . order him to pay
such sums, weekly or otherwise, as it may consider appropriate." They
felt that if they had not considered the Derby County Court order they
would not have been considering all the circumstances of the case, and
that the wording of the subsection gave them a discretion whether or

A not to make an order. They were further of the opinion that the ruling in *Diss Urban Sanitary Authority* v. *Aldrich* (1877) 2 Q.B.D. 179 was applicable in the case in that where discretion was involved a court was not wrong in law in the manner in which it exercised that discretion. They accordingly declined to make an order, save that the appellant pay costs up to £150.

B The appellant appealed. The questions for the opinion of the High Court were (1) whether the order of the Derby County Court as to financial provision for the children was a relevant consideration for the purposes of a complaint under section 18 of the Supplementary Benefits Act 1976, and (2) whether as a matter of law the justices were entitled to make no order.

C *Simon D. Brown* for the appellant.
Thomas Hegarty for the father.

WALLER L.J. This is an appeal by way of case stated from a decision of Derbyshire justices in respect of an adjudication made on June 21, 1978.

A complaint had been preferred by the appellant against the respondent
D as father of two children whom he was liable to maintain pursuant to section 17 of the Supplementary Benefits Act 1976 that benefit had been paid for those children and continued to be paid. The Supplementary Benefits Commission were applying for an order under section 18 of the Act for the respondent to pay such sums as the court considered appropriate.

E The respondent was the father of two children born on May 28, 1965. He was the person liable to maintain the children. He was divorced at the Derby County Court. When the decree was granted there was an order by consent ordering that the respondent do not pay any maintenance to the petitioner for either herself or for any children of the family, and within two months of the date of the order that the respondent transfer to the petitioner all his interest in the matrimonial home. There was a further
F provision about the proceeds of a policy of insurance and about the enforcement of arrears, and a statement that the approximate value of the property transferred was some £25,000 free of mortgages—that was in 1976, that the respondent's net wage was between £55 and £70 weekly, and that benefit had been paid by the Department of Health and Social Security for both children.

G The justices having found those facts, came to the conclusion that they had a discretion as to whether or not they made an order, and they declined to make an order, ordering the appellant to pay costs.

The first thing I should say is this: they purported to make the order on the basis of *Diss Urban Sanitary Authority* v. *Aldrich* (1877) 2 Q.B.D. 179. But having looked at that case, in my view it gives no authority whatever to the conclusion to which the justices came in this case. So we
H have to approach it on the basis of the facts found.

It is submitted on behalf of the respondent that the discretion given by section 18 is a very wide discretion and that the justices were entitled to take into account the agreement that had been made in the county court, which had provided that the wife would not make a claim for maintenance for the children. It was submitted that the transfer by the husband of the half share in the house was in the nature of a capital sum which this

court should infer was in lieu of maintenance not only for the wife, but A
for the children.

Section 17 of the Supplementary Benefits Act 1976 reads:

" (1) For the purposes of this Act—(*a*) a man shall be liable to maintain his wife and his children; and (*b*) a woman shall be liable to
maintain her husband and her children . . ."

Section 18 provides: B

" (1) Where supplementary benefit is paid or claimed to meet requirements which are, or include, those of a person whom another person
is, for the purposes of this Act, liable to maintain (in this section
referred to respectively as ' the dependant ' and ' the liable relative ')
the commission may make a complaint against the liable relative to
a magistrates' court for an order under this section . . . (3) On the C
hearing of a complaint under subsection (1) above the court shall
have regard to all the circumstances and, in particular, to the resources
of the liable relative, and may order him to pay such sum, weekly or
otherwise, as it may consider appropriate . . ."

It was under section 18(1) that this complaint was made, and it is submitted by Mr. Hegarty on behalf of the respondent that subsection (3) D
gives a discretion to the justices sufficiently wide to justify the decision
which they made in this particular case.

In my judgment the liability of both wife and husband is unambiguously set out in section 17(1) of the Act. That indicates that each of them
is liable for the maintenance of their children and while there may be cases
where, as between husband and wife, other arrangements might be made, E
in the case of children it is difficult to see how a consent arrangement can
avoid the husband's or wife's liability to maintain the children. In this case
the Supplementary Benefits Commission have paid benefit to the wife in
respect of the children. It follows from that that the wife herself must
have been entitled to benefit for the children. In those circumstances the
question must arise as to what the father is doing in respect of his liability, F
because prima facie he would be responsible for all that which the wife
was unable herself to provide. Mr. Hegarty submits that the respondent
has provided for that liability by the capital sum of half his share in the
house which he transferred to the wife.

In my judgment it is quite impossible to take that simplistic view. The
justices should have been considering how much the husband could pay
towards the maintenance of the children. Prima facie he should be paying G
the balance of that which the wife was unable to pay. But it may well be
that on consideration some deduction should be made in the circumstances
of the case, which would take into consideration the whole of the terms of
the consent order at the county court.

In my judgment the justices came to the wrong conclusion in exercising the discretion which they did, and this case must go back to be recon- H
sidered. They should reconsider this case on the basis that the husband
is liable to maintain these two children. Prima facie the amount he is
earning, £55 to £70 per week, does include resources sufficient to enable
him to meet his responsibility to maintain these children. Is there something in the light of the order made at the county court which would
reduce that responsibility in any way? It may be that the justices could
come to either conclusion: either there is nothing to reduce it or there is

A something to reduce it. That would be a matter for them. I would send this case back with that indication.

STEPHEN BROWN J. I agree that this appeal should be allowed. The Supplementary Benefits Act 1976, by section 17(1), makes it clear that it is a continuing liability on the part of a man to maintain his children. The facts found by the justices in this case indicate that the children were
B not in fact being maintained by either the father or the mother—at any rate to the extent necessary for their ordinary welfare—since they found that benefit had been paid by the Department of Health and Social Security for both children to the mother.

It would appear that the present unfortunate situation arises in large measure from the rather extraordinary order which was made at the
C Derby County Court in November 1976 when there was a financial settlement between the father and the mother of these children consequent upon their divorce. It was then ordered that the respondent " do not pay any maintenance to the petitioner for either herself or any children of the family." A transfer to the petitioner, as she was then, of the respondent's share in the matrimonial home was ordered by consent, but this was not
D a provision for the children, although it is true that it resulted in them having a roof over their heads. It is unfortunate that a consent order of that kind is on the record, since it may later mislead a court having to consider an application of this kind. Certainly no provision was made in the terms of that order for the maintenance of the chilldren.

That being so, the liability undoubtedly falls upon the respondent, as it does upon the mother, to maintain these children. It seems to me that
E the justices have really considered the consent order at Derby County Court as being rather in the nature of a bar to their making any order of the kind sought on this occasion. They do not record it as being a bar, but merely say that in their discretion, which they seem to think was absolute, they decided they need not make any order of any kind.

Having regard to the facts which they found, particularly as to the
F income of the respondent, it would appear that the respondent should be able to provide something towards the maintenance of his children. The justices should consider the financial circumstances. I do not consider that the fact that in the past a transfer of property order has been made between the father and the mother should obscure the continuing obligation of the father to maintain his children. Accordingly I agree that this case must be sent back to the justices to consider the matter in the light
G of the circumstances obtaining and, as section 18 (3) stipulates, in the light of the resources of the liable relative—in this case both the father and the mother.

Appeal allowed.
Case remitted to justices.

H   Solicitors: *Solicitor, Department of Health and Social Security; Lomax, Geddes & Co., Manchester.*

[Reported by MICHAEL HAWKINGS, ESQ., Barrister-at-Law]

[1981]

A

[COURT OF PROTECTION]

In re DAVEY

1980   March 12, 13;   Fox J
           April 2

B

> Mental Disorder — Court of Protection — Execution of statutory
> will—Application for order after patient's secret marriage—
> Husband not made party to application—Evidence of patient's
> incapability of making will—Order made on basis of urgency
> and doubt as to validity of marriage—Whether proper exercise
> of discretion to make order—Validity of will—Mental Health
> Act 1959 (7 & 8 Eliz. 2, c. 72), s. 103 (1) (dd) (3) (b) (as
> amended by Administration of Justice Act 1969 (c. 58), s. 17)

C

In June 1979 the patient, then aged 92, entered a private
nursing home. On September 10, she made a will and the
beneficiaries, with one exception, were relatives by blood or
marriage. On October 30, unknown to her relatives, she
married an employee at the nursing home, who was aged 48.
The Court of Protection, having received an application
requesting it to take control of her affairs, with which was
sent a copy of the marriage certificate, on December 18
appointed the Official Solicitor as receiver. On December
20, the Official Receiver applied to the Court of Protection,
under section 103 (1) (dd) of the Mental Health Act 1959,[1]
for an order for the execution of a statutory will for the
patient in similar terms to the will made by her in September,
which had been revoked on her marriage. The deputy master,
after hearing evidence, from which it was apparent that the
patient was incapable of making a will, and being satisfied
that because of the patient's age and poor health the matter
was one of urgency, made an order for the execution of the
will without notice being given to either the husband or
relatives. The will was executed in compliance with section
103A of the Act of 1959. On December 21 the husband was
informed of the order. On December 27 the patient died.
The husband appealed against the order.

D

E

F

On the question whether the order should be discharged
and the will set aside on the ground that the master had
wrongly exercised his discretion in making the order without
giving the husband notice of the application and without
assuming the validity of the marriage: —

Held, dismissing the appeal, (1) that the deputy master,
being satisfied that the patient was incapable of making a will,
had jurisdiction, under section 103 (1) of the Mental Health
Act 1959, to order that a will be executed (post, pp. 168E, 169C,
E–F).

G

(2) On the assumption that the court could entertain an
appeal on the question of discretion, that there were no
grounds for interfering with the exercise of the discretion to
make the order for, in a situation of urgency and where there
were grounds for doubting the validity of the marriage, the
deputy master had properly decided that unreasonable delay
would have been caused by ordering the husband to be
joined as a party and, in the circumstances, and taking into
account that if the patient lived the husband could make an
application for a further statutory will in his favour or if
the patient died he could claim under the Inheritance
(Provision for Family and Dependants) Act 1975, he had

H

[1] Mental Health Act 1959, s. 103 (1) (dd): see post, p. 167G–H.

A   rightly come to the conclusion that the proposed will was a proper will to make as it would offer an opportunity for investigation of the matter and for achieving a just result between the husband and the beneficiaries under the September will (post, pp. 170B, E–H—171C, F–G).

     Per curiam. The court does not have jurisdiction to set aside a statutory will, which complies with the provisions of section 103A of the Act, and it must be treated as the last

B   will of the deceased patient. The order of the deputy master had no dispositive effect and, even if it were discharged, the will of the deceased patient could not be revoked for, on her death, the powers of the Court of Protection over her affairs and property ceased (post, pp. 171G, 172E–G, H—173A).

     The following cases are referred to in the judgment:

C   *Bennett, In re* [1913] 2 Ch. 318.
     D. M. L., In re [1965] Ch. 1133; [1965] 3 W.L.R. 740; [1965] 2 All E.R. 129.
     Roberts, decd., In re [1978] 1 W.L.R. 653; [1978] 3 All E.R. 225, Walton J. and C.A.
     Wheater, In re [1928] 1 Ch. 223, C.A.

D   The following additional cases, supplied by courtesy of counsel, were cited in argument:

     De Reneville v. *De Reneville* [1948] P. 100; [1948] 1 All E.R. 56, C.A.
     Gale, decd., In re [1966] Ch. 236; [1966] 2 W.L.R. 571; [1966] 1 All E.R. 945, C.A.
     H. M. F., In re [1976] Ch. 33; [1975] 3 W.L.R. 395; [1975] 2 All E.R. 795.

E   *Osenton (Charles) and Co.* v. *Johnston* [1942] A.C. 130; [1941] 2 All E.R. 245, H.L.(E.).
     Park, decd., In the Estate of [1954] P. 89; [1953] 3 W.L.R. 307; [1953] 2 All E.R. 408; [1954] P. 112; [1953] 3 W.L.R. 1012; [1953] 2 All E.R. 1411, C.A.

F   APPEAL from an order of the Deputy Master of the Court of Protection.

     The appellant, Wallace Lindsay Davey of 20 Fitzjames Avenue, London W.14, husband of the patient, whose property and affairs were under the Control of the Court of Protection, appealed from an order dated December 20, 1979, of the Deputy Master of the Court of Protection directing the execution by the Assistant Official Solicitor (as

G   receiver) of a statutory will under the Mental Health Act 1959 in the name and on behalf of the patient. He asked that the order should be discharged and the will set aside. The patient had died on December 27, 1979. The appeal was heard in chambers, judgment being given in open court.

H   *Hazel Williamson* for the husband.
     Peter Rawson for the executors.
     D. G. A. Jackson for the Official Solicitor.

                           Cur. adv. vult.

     April 2. Fox J. read the following judgment. This is an appeal from an order of the Deputy Master of the Court of Protection directing the execution of a statutory will.

166

Miss Olive St. Barbe (to whom I will refer as "the patient") A
was born in the year 1886. For many years she lived in her own house
in Highgate. Then, in June 1979, when she was 92 years old, she moved
into a private nursing home in London. She had never married and her
nearest relatives were two nephews, Major George St. Barbe and Mr.
Peter St. Barbe.

On July 3, 1979, the patient granted a power of attorney for the
management of her affairs to two London solicitors, Mr. Riou Benson B
and Mr. Russell. They managed the patient's affairs from then until the
appointment of the Official Solicitor as receiver of the patient in
December 1979. It seems that on August 8, 1979, the patient executed
another power of attorney in favour of other solicitors, though Mr.
Benson in his affidavit sworn in support of the application for a receiver
states that the patient confirmed that she had no recollection of doing so. C

On September 10, 1979, the patient made a will by which, after
appointing Mr. Benson and Lloyds Bank Ltd. as executors and bequeath-
ing two small pecuniary legacies, she gave her residuary estate upon
trust for division in equal shares between such of 17 named persons as
should survive her. Those persons, with the exception of a Mrs Klouda,
were related to the patient by blood or marriage; they were Major St.
Barbe, Mr. Peter St. Barbe, their children and grandchildren, the wife D
and former wife of Major St. Barbe, and the wives of Major St. Barbe's
children. Mrs. Klouda, I am informed by counsel, ran the nursing
home.

On October 15, 1979, the patient was examined at the nursing home by
Dr. De Mowbray, a consultant psychiatrist. He found her disorientated
in place and time and showing marked impairment of memory, particu- E
larly for recent events. For example, she gave her age as 84 and the
date as December 25, which she was unable to identify as the date of
Christmas. She was unable to state the day of the week; she stated that
she was living in St. John's Wood though she was in fact living in
Kensington. Dr. De Mowbray's view was that the patient was suffering
from senile mental deterioration of a degree which rendered her incapable F
of properly managing her affairs, though she was able to express definite
wishes about their broad disposal. Dr. De Mowbray was strongly in
favour of the patient's affairs being placed under the control of the Court
of Protection.

On November 9, 1979, Mr. Benson applied to the Court of Protection
for an order appointing him receiver for the patient. The affidavit of
kindred and fortune sworn in support of the application showed that the G
patient's main assets consisted of (i) a house valued at between £70,000
and £100,000 and (ii) cash amounting to about £30,000.

On November 15, the patient was examined by Dr. Donald Blair, also
a consultant psychiatrist, who advised that so far as he could judge the
patient's mentality was sufficiently impaired to warrant the whole of
her estate being placed under the control of the Court of Protection. H
"There is no doubt," he said, "that her mind is greatly enfeebled
through senility."

Major St. Barbe was not agreeable to the proposal that Mr. Benson
be appointed receiver. Ultimately he agreed to the appointment of the
Official Solicitor as receiver; this was notified to the Court of Protection
in a letter from his solicitors dated December 10, 1979. On December 6,
Dr. Blair examined the patient again. His opinion was that "Her

A mentality is definitely permanently and constantly enfeebled and her memory, reasoning, judgment and other intellectual faculties are greatly impaired." He thought that her mind and intellect had wilted to such an extent that she was not of testamentary capacity.

On December 14, 1979 (which was a Friday), Mr. John Witzenfeld, a solicitor, wrote to the Court of Protection stating that provided the
B Official Solicitor was appointed as receiver, the patient herself had no objection to the Court of Protection taking control of her affairs. The letter enclosed a copy of the patient's marriage certificate. In this manner it emerged that the patient had, on October 30, 1979, at the Fulham Registry Office, married the present appellant (to whom I will refer as Mr. Davey). He was 48 years of age. He was an employee of, and resided at, the nursing home. None of the patient's relatives were
C informed of the marriage until it came to their notice in consequence of the letter of December 14.

It is common ground that Mr. Witzenfeld's letter of December 14 reached the Court of Protection on Monday, December 17. On December 18 the Court of Protection made an order appointing the Official Solicitor as receiver.

D On December 20, the Official Solicitor, at the instance of the Court of Protection, made an application to the Court of Protection for an order for the execution of a statutory will for the patient in the same terms as the will of September 10, 1979. The latter will would, by the operation of section 18 of the Wills Act 1837, have been automatically revoked by a marriage of the patient.

E The jurisdiction of the Court of Protection to make a will for a patient is contained in section 103 (1) (dd) of the Mental Health Act 1959, as added by section 17 (1) of the Administration of Justice Act 1969.

It will be convenient if I first set out the provisions of section 102 (1) of the Mental Health Act 1959 which are as follows:

F "The judge may, with respect to the property and affairs of a patient, do or secure the doing of all such things as appear necessary or expedient—(a) for the maintenance or other benefit of the patient, (b) for the maintenance or other benefit of members of the patient's family, (c) for making provision for other persons or purposes for whom or which the patient might be expected to provide if he were not mentally disordered, or (d) otherwise for
G administering the patient's affairs."

Section 103 (1) provides:

"Without prejudice to the generality of the foregoing section, the judge shall have power to make such orders and give such directions and authorities as he thinks fit for the purposes of that section, and
H in particular may for those purposes make orders or give directions or authorities for—. . . (dd) the execution for the patient of a will making any provision (whether by way of disposing of property or exercising a power or otherwise) which could be made by a will executed by the patient if he were not mentally disordered, so however that in such cases as a nominated judge may direct the powers conferred by this paragraph shall not be exercisable except by the Lord Chancellor or a nominated judge; . . ."

Section 103 (3) (b) provides that the power to order the execution of a   A
will for a patient "shall not be exercised unless the judge has reason to
believe that the patient is incapable of making a valid will . . ."

By *Practice Direction (Court of Protection: Wills)* [1970] 1 W.L.R.
259 of November 28, 1969, Ungoed-Thomas J., a nominated judge,
directed that the powers conferred by section 103 (1) (dd) should not be
exercisable except by the Lord Chancellor or a nominated judge unless
by reason of the amount involved or the general circumstances of the   B
case unreasonable expense or delay would be caused.

By section 100 (4), the functions expressed to be conferred by the
Act on the judge are, in general, exercisable by the Lord Chancellor or
by any nominated judge and are also exercisable by the Master or Deputy
Master of the Court of Protection.

The Official Solicitor's application for the execution of a statutory   C
will was heard by the deputy master on December 20, 1979 (the same day
as the application was issued). That was the penultimate day of the
term and I think that unreasonable delay would have been caused by
referring the matter to the judge. The contrary indeed is not asserted.

Neither Mr. Davey nor any of the beneficiaries under the will of
September 10, 1979, was given notice of the application. Mr. Benson   D
gave oral evidence upon oath to the deputy master. He said that he
visited the patient on Thursday, December 13, 1979. She was sitting
up but very much slouched. Mr. Davey was present but did not mention
the marriage. The patient, according to Mr. Benson, made no communication either in reply to him or to Mr. Davey. Mr. Benson formed
the view that she did not have any testamentary capacity and would not
be capable of appreciating any matter relating to property. On this   E
evidence and that of Dr. Blair's examination on December 6 I think
that the deputy master would certainly have had reason to believe
that the patient was incapable of making a valid will and that accordingly
the prohibition contained in section 103 (3) (b) was not applicable. Mr.
Davey does not assert otherwise on this appeal.

At the hearing on December 20 the deputy master made an order   F
directing Mr. Venables, the Assistant Official Solicitor, in the name and
on behalf of the patient to execute a will in the form of a specified draft
(which for practical purposes was the same as the patient's will of
September 10, 1979).

On December 21, 1979, Mr. Venables duly executed the will on
behalf of the patient. The various formalities which are required in
respect of the execution of such a will by section 103A (as added by   G
section 18 of the Administration of Justice Act 1969) were complied with.
The patient died six days later, on December 27.

The deputy master's reasons for ordering the execution of a will
without notice to Mr. Davey were, in effect, as follows. (i) If Mr.
Davey was joined as a party there would inevitably be delay before the
matter could be determined. The patient was 93 years old and in   H
poor health. The matter was, accordingly, one of considerable urgency.
(ii) If the patient died before the court could give directions for the
execution of a will, it would no longer be possible to challenge the
validity of the marriage and the estate would devolve under an intestacy.
The basis of that view is the decision of the Court of Appeal in *In re
Roberts, decd.* [1978] 1 W.L.R. 653, where it was held that a voidable
marriage, whether subsequently annulled or not, is a marriage for the

169

A   purposes of section 18 of the Wills Act 1837 and therefore automatically revokes an existing will of a party to the marriage. Upon an intestacy Mr. Davey would take, if the estate was sufficient, the statutory legacy of £55,000 plus half the residuary estate. (iii) The marriage was apparently clandestine, embarked on at short notice and without notification to the patient's relatives. (iv) If a statutory will was executed as proposed (that is to say in effect restoring the will of September 1979) Mr. Davey
B   could, if he wished, make application for a further statutory will in his favour. If the patient died before that could be dealt with, Mr. Davey could make an application under the Inheritance (Provisions for Family and Dependants) Act 1975.

Mr. Davey was informed of the order for the execution of the statutory will by letter from the Court of Protection dated December
C   21, 1979.

The present notice of appeal asks that the order for the execution of the statutory will be discharged and that the will be set aside.

In my view it is clear that the deputy master had jurisdiction to direct the execution of the statutory will. The power is expressly conferred by section 103 (1) of the Mental Health Act 1959. It is true that
D   the power conferred by section 103 (1), including the power to direct the execution of a will, are conferred for the purposes of section 102. It is said that the case does not fall within section 102 (1) (b) since the will is not for the benefit of members of the patient's " family "; it is said that " family " does not include collaterals: see In re D.M.L. [1965] Ch. 1133. But it seems to me that the case falls within section 102 (1) (c) on the ground that the will makes provision for persons for whom the
E   patient might be expected to provide if she were not mentally disordered. The persons for whom the statutory will makes provision are the same persons as those for whom the patient herself had made provision only three months previously by the September will.

Accordingly, since it is not in dispute that, on December 20, the deputy master had reason to believe that the patient was incapable of
F   making a will, I see no reason to doubt the existence of the jurisdiction.

Mr. Davey contends, however, that, accepting the existence of jurisdiction, the deputy master exercised his discretion wrongly and that his decision cannot be allowed to stand. It is said that he erred in that (1) he reached his decision without notice to Mr. Davey, and (2) that he should have assumed the validity of the marriage.

G   The circumstances with which the deputy master was faced on December 20 were the following. Only three days previously it had come to the notice of the Court of Protection that, on October 30, the patient had married while she was a patient in the nursing home. She was 93 and Mr. Davey was 48. The marriage certificate together with Mr. Benson's evidence showed that he was an employee of the nursing home and resided there. Since the patient had only entered the nursing
H   home in June, their acquaintance was presumably comparatively short. From the marriage certificate it appeared that the patient had started to sign her name but only wrote the letter " O "; she then added her mark. On October 15 (two weeks before the marriage) Dr. De Mowbray had found the patient disorientated in place and time and showing marked impairment of memory; she was suffering from senile mental deterioration. The marriage itself was by licence, so there was no previous publication. In fact no relative of the patient had been informed of it. As

regards the patient's expectation of life she was a very great age and   A
Mr. Benson's evidence before the deputy master was that, at the visit
on December 13, Mr. Davey told him that " She was getting worse
quite quickly."   Dr. Blair in his report of his visit on November 15 says
that the patient was, " obviously suffering from senile physical enfeeble-
ment."

From these facts, two things emerge.   First, the circumstances of the
marriage were suspicious, and it is quite unreal to say that the Court of   B
Protection should have proceeded on the basis that the marriage was
necessarily valid.   Secondly, the matter was urgent.   In view of the
patient's age and condition, she might die at any time.   In fact she
only lived for a few days.

As to the joinder of parties, by rule 12 (1) of the Court of Protection
Rules 1960 (S.I. 1960 No. 1146 (L. 7)), it is provided: C

" The court may direct that all or any of the relatives of the patient
or any other person who appears to the court to be interested in the
relief sought by a summons shall be made a respondent to or given
notice of the summons."

And by rule 21, as amended, it is provided that, on an application under
section 103 (1) (dd):   D

" (2) . . . the receiver shall, unless he is the applicant or one of the
applicants, be made a respondent to the application, but except as
aforesaid no person shall be made a respondent unless and until the
court so directs."

The court, therefore, has a discretion as to what persons are to be
made respondent to or given notice of the application.   No doubt in the   E
normal case the court would generally insist on the joinder of a person
who was adversely affected by the relief sought, but in circumstances of
urgency the position may be different.   The deputy master quite clearly
directed his mind to the question whether Mr. Davey should be joined as
a respondent and decided against it on the ground of delay.   In the
circumstances I think that that was a reasonable view for the deputy   F
master to take.   If Mr. Davey had been joined as a respondent it is
probable that he would have asked for time to consider putting in
evidence and prepare his case; since the application was being heard on
December 20 that would, very likely, have delayed matters until well after
Christmas.   If the deputy master had refused time, it seems most probable that Mr. Davey would simply have asserted the validity of the
marriage and would have asked that substantial provision be made for   G
him.   But that might have affected the interests of the relatives of the
patient who would themselves have to be brought before the court to
allow them to make representations.   All that was bound to cause delay
in circumstances where time might be crucial.   Looking back, it seems
unlikely that it could all have been achieved by December 27 when the
patient died.   H

If the deputy master had decided to do nothing, then if the patient
died before the matter could be investigated Mr. Davey would, under the
intestacy, take irrevocably a very substantial portion of her estate.   That
might, on an investigation of the whole matter, and particularly the circumstances of the marriage, prove very unfair to the beneficiaries under
the September will.   On the other hand, by adopting the course which
he did, the deputy master preserved, in effect, the opportunity for all

A parties to represent their claims fully to the court. Either the patient would live long enough for that to be done in her lifetime or she would not. If she lived, it could be done in the application of Mr. Davey for a new statutory will. If, as happened, the patient died quickly it seems to me that substantially the same result can be achieved by an application under the Inheritance (Provision for Family and Dependants) Act 1975. Under section 1 of that Act Mr. Davey, as the husband of the patient,

B is entitled to apply to the court for an order under section 2 of the Act on the ground that the patient's will does not make reasonable provision for him. Under section 2, the court could, if it thought proper, make an order, inter alia, for any one or more of the following: (i) periodical payments to Mr. Davey out of the estate; (ii) payment to Mr. Davey of a lump sum out of the estate: (iii) transfer to Mr. Davey of any property

C comprised in the estate. Upon such an application Mr. Davey and the persons interested under the statutory will could put their respective claims before the court. I should add that it does not appear that any of the beneficiaries under the statutory will would themselves qualify as applicants under section 1 of the Act of 1975.

I do not think that, in substance, there is any material difference in the present case between the factors which the Court of Protection would

D have been required to consider if the question of what was a proper testamentary disposition for the patient had been fully argued before it and those which the High Court would have to consider on an application under the Inheritance Act. I can see that there may be some difference of emphasis; in an application under the Inheritance Act, Mr. Davey as applicant has to establish that the will does not make reasonable financial

E provision for him. But in the Court of Protection, the essential question in the end would have been what if anything would be reasonable provision in all the circumstances for the various contestants.

It is said on behalf of Mr. Davey that for the deputy master to allow himself to be influenced by the availability of the Inheritance Act was an abrogation of his responsibilities. I do not agree with that. The deputy

F master, in a situation of urgency, had to balance various factors with a view to reaching a just conclusion. It is clear, in my view, that he considered whether the proposed will was a proper will to be made in the circumstances. He concluded that it was. In my judgment, the deputy master in exceptional and difficult circumstances came to a sensible and fair conclusion. If I have any jurisdiction to entertain this appeal I see no reason to interfere with the deputy master's conclusion. I think he

G was right. It seems to me that the order which he made was one which offered the widest opportunities for a full investigation of the matter and, therefore, the best prospect of a just result in the end.

In fact I do not think that I have any jurisdiction to interfere with the statutory will. It is not necessary for me to decide the matter, but I have heard argument on it and I set out the position broadly as it appears

H to me.

I should refer first to the provisions of section 103A of the Mental Health Act 1959. Section 103A (1) provides:

" Where under section 103 (1) of this Act the judge makes or gives an order, direction or authority requiring or authorising a person . . . to execute a will for a patient, any will executed in pursuance of that order, direction or authority shall be expressed to be signed by the patient acting by the authorised person, and shall be . . ."

172

Then certain formalities as to signing, attestation and sealing are set A
forth. These formalities were complied with in the present case. Section
103A (3) provides:

> " Subject to the following provisions of this section, any such will
> executed in accordance with subsection (1) of this section shall have
> the like effect for all purposes as if the patient were capable of
> making a valid will and the will had been executed by him in the B
> manner required by the Wills Act 1837."

The subsequent provisions of section 103A are not material for present
purposes.

In this case the deputy master had jurisdiction to order the execution
of the will. Further the will was executed in accordance with section
103A (1). The result is that by the operation of section 103A (3) the will C
is to have the like effect, " for all purposes," as if the patient were capable
of making a valid will and the will had been duly executed by her.

The patient is now dead. It seems to me, therefore, that the effect
of section 103A (3) is that the statutory will must be treated as if it were a
will duly made by her and as if she were of testamentary capacity when
she made it. It was her last will. One cannot, I think, in this case get D
rid of the will simply by attacking the order. The order had no dispositive effect at all. If the patient had died after the order but before
Mr. Venables executed the will, the patient would have died intestate
just as a person of full capacity who gave instructions for a will who died
before executing it would die intestate (assuming he left no other will).
But the statutory will having been executed, section 103A (3) makes it
the patient's will for all purposes. Suppose the deputy master was wrong E
and that I took the view that the proper order would have been to
direct a will under which the estate was divided in some way between
Mr. Davey and the beneficiaries, or some of them, under the September
will. It does not seem to me that the Court of Protection now has any
jurisdiction to procure such a distribution. It could not be achieved by
order alone. It could only be achieved by revoking the statutory will F
and making a new will in its place. But that, I think, is impossible.
First, it seems to me that the powers of the Court of Protection under
section 102 of the Mental Health Act came to an end on the patient's
death: see, for example, *In re Wheater* [1928] 1 Ch. 223 and *In re
Bennett* [1913] 2 Ch. 318. Secondly, it is not possible to make a will
for or to revoke the will of a deceased person, and it cannot, I think, be
right to say that in such a case, even though it was not possible G
to achieve the disposition contemplated by the appellate tribunal, nevertheless the order of that tribunal would, in some way, by itself invalidate
the existing will; that seems to me to be wrong in principle and quite
likely, in many cases, to produce an unintended (and unfair) intestacy.

In short, the position seems to me to be as follows. The deputy
master had jurisdiction to make the order directing the execution of H
the statutory will. The order, right or wrong, was not a nullity. Accordingly, the will was a will executed in accordance with section 103A (1),
and, therefore, by the operation of section 103A (1), has effect, for
all purposes, as the patient's will. The patient is dead and the will is
irrevocable.

I should add that this is a case where the deputy master had jurisdiction. If he had no jurisdiction (for example because there was no

A reason to believe that the patient was incapable of making a valid will)
different considerations would apply.

The result in my view is that the appeal fails.

Appeal dismissed.

B Solicitors: *John Witzenfeld*; *Charles Russell & Co.*; *Official Solicitor.*

K. N. B.

C   [HOUSE OF LORDS]

* PROVIDENT MUTUAL LIFE ASSURANCE
ASSOCIATION   .   .   .   .   APPELLANTS

AND

D DERBY CITY COUNCIL   .   .   .   .   .   .   RESPONDENTS

FENCLOSE SECURITIES LTD.   .   .   .   .   .   APPELLANTS

AND

DERBY CITY COUNCIL   .   .   .   .   .   .   RESPONDENTS

E   [CONSOLIDATED APPEALS]

1980 Nov. 24, 25;   Lord Wilberforce, Lord Simon of Glaisdale,
1981 Jan. 29   Lord Keith of Kinkel, Lord Roskill and
                            Lord Bridge of Harwich

F *Rating—Unoccupied hereditament—Completion notice—Notice on
photocopied form with blanks completed by rating authority
assistant—Assistant's opinion of expected date of completion
—Validity of notice—Whether provisions administrative in
character—Treasurer validly appointed for proper administration of rating authority's financial affairs—Whether including
collection of rates — Whether giving of notice making and
levying rate—Whether action and opinion of assistant part
of proper administration — General Rate Act 1967 (c. 9),*
G *s. 17 (1), Sch. 1, paras. 1 (1), 8 (1) (4)* [1]*—Local Government
Act 1972 (c. 70), ss. 111 (1) (3), 151* [2]

On October 24, 1973, the respondent rating authority
resolved that their treasurer be the proper officer for, inter alia,
the administration of their financial affairs pursuant to section
151 of the Local Government Act 1972. On February 12,
1975, they resolved that, pursuant to section 17 of the General
H Rate Act 1967, the provisions of Schedule 1 to that Act regarding the rating of unoccupied property should apply in their
area. On June 2, 1976, in purported compliance with Schedule
1, completion notices were served on the appellants, the owners
of new buildings in the rating authority's area. The notices

[1] General Rate Act 1967, s. 17 (1): see post, p. 176c.
Sch. 1, paras. 1 (1), 8 (1) (4): see post, pp. 176G–H, 177A–C.
[2] Local Government Act 1972, s. 111 (1) (3): see post, pp. 178H—179C.
S. 151: see post, p. 178H.
VOL. 1 ·   10

were completed photocopies of a typed form with blanks, A
the original having been signed by the treasurer's fascimile
signature.   The blanks for, inter alia, the dates on which the
buildings were to be treated as completed for the purposes of
Schedule 1, had been completed by the rating authority's
principal rating assistant.   The treasurer had not seen the
notices before they were sent out.   The appellants appealed
to the county court under paragraph 8 (4) of Schedule 1
against the completion dates specified in the notices.   At the B
hearing, they took the point that the notices were a nullity.
The judge upheld that submission.   He found that the opinion
that the work remaining to be done on each building could
reasonably be expected to be completed in three months had
been the opinion of the principal rating assistant alone and
that neither the rating authority nor any committee of theirs
nor their treasurer had had the opportunity of considering the
matter or of forming any opinion on it.   He held that there C
was no power in the rating authority to delegate their function
of forming an opinion for the purposes of paragraph 8 (1) of
Schedule 1, that if there were such a power that there had
been no such delegation to the treasurer and that if there
were power to delegate and there had been a delegation to
the treasurer he had never formed the requisite opinion.   The
Court of Appeal allowed an appeal by the rating authority. D
    On appeal by the building owners : —
    Held, dismissing the appeals (Lord Bridge of Harwich
dissenting), (1) that the operation of section 17 of and the consequent coming into force of Schedule 1 to the General Rate
Act 1967 and the giving of a notice under paragraph 8 could
not be described as making and levying a rate and, accordingly,
no formal resolution of the rating authority had been required
before a valid opinion could be formed for the purposes of E
paragraph 8 (1) and a valid notice served (post, p. 180E–H).
    (2) That the rating authority's treasurer had been properly
appointed under section 151 of the Act of 1972 for the proper
administration of their financial affairs including the collection
of rates to which they became entitled by law, the powers
accorded by section 151 being additional to those accorded
by section 111; that Parliament had plainly contemplated that F
the actual machinery of enforcement and collection of rates
would be operated not by a senior official of the rating authority but by his staff; that the provisions of the latter part
of Schedule 1 to the Act of 1967 were administrative in
character; and that what the principal rating assistant had done
had been part of the proper administration of the rating
authority's financial affairs, namely the collection of rate
revenue, and his actions and opinions had accordingly com- G
plied with the requirements of paragraph 8 (1) (post, pp.
179A–C, 181G—182A, D).
    Per curiam.   The rating authority's documentation in
relation to the exercise of their powers and functions by their
staff was admittedly in some respects open to criticism.   No
doubt they and other rating authorities will wish to review
their arrangements and ensure that the appropriate powers do
lie where they are required to lie (post p. 182A–C). H
    Decision of the Court of Appeal affirmed.

The following cases are referred to in their Lordships' opinions:

Bar Hill Developments Ltd. v. *South Cambridgeshire District Council*
    [1979] R.A. 379, D.C.
Kettle (B.) Ltd. v. *Newcastle-under-Lyme Borough Council* (1979) 77
    L.G.R. 700; [1979] R.A. 223, C.A.

A   The following additional cases were cited in argument:

Graylaw Investments Ltd. v. *Ipswich Borough Council* (1978) 77 L.G.R. 297, C.A.

Nelms v. *Roe* [1970] 1 W.L.R. 4; [1969] 3 All E.R. 1379, D.C.

Westminster City Council v. *London University King's College* [1958] 1 W.L.R. 920; [1958] 3 All E.R. 25.

B   APPEALS from the Court of Appeal.

These were appeals by Provident Mutual Life Assurance Association and Fenclose Securities Ltd. from orders of the Court of Appeal (Megaw and Shaw L.JJ. and Sir Patrick Browne) on June 13, 1980, allowing appeals by the Derby City Council (formerly the Derby Borough Council) from a judgment of Judge Brooke-Willis at Derby County Court on

C   January 4, 1979.

The appellants appealed to the county court against completion notices served on them by the council under the provisions of section 17 of and Schedule 1 to the General Rate Act 1967. The judge allowed their appeals. The council appealed to the Court of Appeal on the grounds, in each case, that the judge had been wrong in law in holding that there was no power in the council to delegate their function under paragraph 8

D   (1) of Schedule 1; that if there was such a power there had been no such delegation to the council's treasurer; and that if there was such power to delegate and if there had been such a delegation the treasurer had never formed the requisite opinion. The Court of Appeal allowed the appeals and refused the appellants leave to appeal. On July 24, 1980, the Appeal Committee of the House of Lords (Lord Wilberforce, Lord Salmon and

E   Lord Russell of Killowen) granted them leave.

They appealed, the appeals being consolidated.

The facts are set out in the opinion of Lord Roskill.

William Glover Q.C. and *Guy Roots* for the appellants.
Raymond Sears Q.C. and *Christopher Cochrane* for the council.

F

Their Lordships took time for consideration.

January 29, 1981. LORD WILBERFORCE. My Lords, I have had the opportunity of reading in draft the speech about to be delivered by my noble and learned friend, Lord Roskill, with which I agree. For the reasons which he gives I would dismiss these appeals.

G

LORD SIMON OF GLAISDALE. My Lords, I have had the privilege of reading in draft the speech about to be delivered by my noble and learned friend, Lord Roskill, with which I agree. For the reasons which he gives I would therefore dismiss these appeals.

H   LORD KEITH OF KINKEL. My Lords, I have had the benefit of reading in advance the speech to be delivered by my noble and learned friend Lord Roskill. I agree with it, and for the reasons which he gives I too would dismiss these appeals.

LORD ROSKILL. My Lords, the respondents are the rating authority for their area pursuant to section 1 (1) of the General Rate Act 1967. The appellants were at the material time each the owners of certain new

176

buildings in Derby. The details of those buildings and their respective A
ownerships will be found in the judgment of the learned judge in the
county court before whom the present, and other closely connected, proceedings, came in the first instance. Nothing now turns on those details.
From his judgment in favour of the appellants only two appeals were
taken by the respondents to the Court of Appeal. It was common ground
that the decision in those two appeals, one concerning each of the
appellants, governed all the other 24 appeals initially before the learned B
judge.

My Lords, the two appeals, and the others, concerned the rating of
unoccupied property in Derby. Section 17 of the Act of 1967 provides
as follows:

" (1) A rating authority may resolve that the provisions of Schedule 1
to this Act with respect to the rating of unoccupied property—(a) C
shall apply . . . to their area, and in that case those provisions shall
come into operation . . . in that area on such day as may be specified
in the resolution . . ."

My Lords, on January 20, 1975, the general purposes finance sub-
committee of the respondents passed the following resolution under the
rubric " Rating of Unoccupied Property ": D

" Resolved that pursuant to section 17 of the General Rate Act
1967, as amended by section 15 of the Local Government Act 1974,
the provisions of Schedule 1 [to] the General Rate Act 1967, as
amended by section 15 of the Local Government Act 1974, shall
from April 1, 1975, apply throughout the borough of Derby to the
extent that the owners of unoccupied hereditaments within the classes E
specified in column 1 of the schedule to this resolution shall be
liable to pay the proportions specified in column 2 of the schedule
as applicable to such classes of the rates which would be payable if
any such owners were in occupation of any such hereditament."

The schedule to that resolution specified what liability that sub-committee
had resolved should thereupon fall upon the owners of such unoccupied F
property. It was common ground that this resolution was adopted by
the respondents on February 12, 1975.

My Lords, on March 3, 1976, the respondents passed a resolution
under section 2 of the Act of 1967 making the general rate for the rating
year 1976/77, and fixing the rate percentage for that year.

My Lords, the effect of the respondents' resolution of February 12, G
1975, was to put into operation the provisions of Schedule 1 to the Act
of 1967. Paragraph 1 (1) of Schedule 1 reads thus:

" Where, in the case of any rating area in which, by virtue of a
resolution under section 17 of this Act, this Schedule is in operation,
any relevant hereditament in that area is unoccupied for a continuous
period exceeding three months, the owner shall, subject to the H
provisions of this Schedule, be rated in respect of that hereditament
for any relevant period of vacancy; and the provisions of this Act
shall apply accordingly as if the hereditament were occupied during
that relevant period of vacancy by the owner."

It follows, therefore, that subject to the due fulfilment of the remaining
provisions of Schedule 1, the effect of that resolution was that " the

A owner shall . . . be rated." What then are the relevant provisions of Schedule 1? Paragraph 8 (1) reads thus:

"Where a rating authority are of opinion—(a) that the erection of a building within their area has been completed; or (b) that the work remaining to be done on a building within their area is such that the erection of the building can reasonably be expected to be completed within three months, and that the building is, or when
B completed will be, comprised in a relevant hereditament, the authority may serve on the owner of the building a notice (hereafter in this paragraph referred to as ' a completion notice') stating that the erection of the building is to be treated for the purposes of this Schedule as completed on the date of service of the notice or on such later date as may be specified by the notice."

C Paragraph 8 (4) provides:

"A person on whom a completion notice is served may, during the period of 21 days beginning with the date of service of the notice, appeal to the county court against the notice on the ground that the erection of the building to which the notice relates has not been or, as the case may be, cannot reasonably be expected to be completed
D by the date specified by the notice."

My Lords, on June 2, 1976, the respondents, in purported compliance with these statutory requirements, served completion notices on the appellants over a facsimile signature of the respondents' treasurer. Those notices were completed photocopies of a typed form with blanks, the original blank form having been signed by the respondents' treasurer. The
E blanks in those photocopies were completed by a Mr. Wells. Mr. Wells was the respondents' principal rating assistant. Mr. Wells filled in the name of the addressees, the description of the building in respect of which the notice was given, and the date upon which that building was to be treated as completed for the purposes of Schedule 1. Mr. Wells also completed the date of the notice on each form.

The appellants thereupon, as they were entitled to do under paragraph
F 8 (4) of Schedule 1, gave notice of appeal to the county court against the completion dates respectively specified in the various notices. But at the hearing Mr. Glover, for the appellants, for the first time took the point that the notices were a nullity. At first sight at least, it seems curious that the appellants, having given notice of appeal on the basis that the notices were valid for the purpose of asserting to the judge that the wrong
G completion dates had been included in them, should subsequently in those same proceedings be able to turn round and deny the validity of the very notices the existence of which gave rise to their right of appeal. The learned judge considered this matter and held that he had jurisdiction to determine the issue of validity. Indeed, he determined that issue in favour of the appellants. No complaint has been made of his decision on jurisdiction, either in the Court of Appeal or before your Lordships'
H House. I therefore say no more about it save to observe that there is obvious convenience in the course adopted, rather than first to proceed by way of judicial review and then, if that attack upon the notices failed, proceed with the factual appeals to the county court, for which a 21-day limit is specified in paragraph 8 (4).

The learned judge in a long and most careful judgment given on January 4, 1979, upheld the appellants' contention that the notices were a nullity. He said that he did so for three reasons. First, that there was

no power to delegate; second, that if there were such a power there was   A
no delegation to the respondents' treasurer, and third, if there were the
power to delegate and there were a delegation to the respondents' treasurer,
the respondents' treasurer never formed the requisite opinion for the purposes of paragraph 8 (1) of Schedule 1. But most helpfully he also determined the factual issues lest his decision upon the nullity issue were
reversed by an appellate court. He resolved those factual issues substantially in favour of the respondents, though he varied certain dates   B
specified in the disputed notices. From his decision, both parties appealed
to the Court of Appeal. The Court of Appeal (Megaw and Shaw L.JJ. and
Sir Patrick Browne) on June 13, 1980, in a reserved judgment prepared by
Sir Patrick Browne, allowed the respondents' appeal on the nullity issue
but dismissed the appellants' cross-appeal on the factual issues. The Court
of Appeal refused leave to appeal to your Lordships' House but on   C
July 24, 1980, leave to appeal was granted to the appellants by an Appeal
Committee of this House. The appellants did not, however, seek further to
appeal in respect of the factual issues upon which they had failed in both
the lower courts. The only issue argued before your Lordships' House
was therefore whether the notices were valid or were a nullity.

The first submission in support of the contention that the notices were   D
invalid and therefore a nullity was that there was no power in the respondents to delegate the performance of their rights and duties under
section 17 of the Act of 1967. The second submission was that if there
were such a power to delegate there had been no such delegation to the
respondents' treasurer. The third submission was that, if there had been
a power to delegate to the respondents' treasurer, he did not form the
" opinion " required by paragraph 8 (1) of Schedule 1, and that, there   E
being no delegation to Mr. Wells, Mr. Wells's opinion could not be that
of either the respondents or the respondents' treasurer. There was
never, it was said, any relevant paragraph 8 (1) " opinion " of the respondents for which that sub-paragraph called, and therefore no valid
notices existed.

Before considering these submissions in more detail it will be convenient   F
to deal with the position both of the respondents' treasurer and of Mr.
Wells. First as to the position of the respondents' treasurer: on October
1, 1973, the respondents' appointments panel resolved to recommend to
the respondents that the treasurer be the proper officer for the purposes of
section 115 (2) and section 151 of the Local Government Act 1972. That
recommendation was accepted by the respondents' policy committee on
October 16, 1973. It was adopted by the respondents by resolution   G
dated October 24, 1973. Section 115 (2) deals with the accountability of
officers employed by a local authority. Section 151 of the Act of 1972,
which to my mind is of great importance in connection with this appeal,
reads thus:

  " Without prejudice to section 111 below, every local authority shall
  make arrangements for the proper administration of their financial   H
  affairs and shall secure that one of their officers has responsibility
  for the administration of those affairs."

Section 111 reads thus:

  " (1) Without prejudice to any powers exercisable apart from this
  section but subject to the provisions of this Act and any other enactment passed before or after this Act, a local authority shall have

A power to do any thing (whether or not involving the expenditure, borrowing or lending of money or the acquisition or disposal of any property or rights) which is calculated to facilitate, or is conducive or incidental to, the discharge of any of their functions . . . (3) A local authority shall not by virtue of this section raise money, whether by means of rates, precepts or borowing, or lend money except in accordance with the enactments relating to those matters

B respectively."

I would emphasise that the opening words of section 151 are " Without prejudice to section 111 " and not " subject to section 111." It follows that the powers accorded by section 151 are additional to those accorded by section 111. Thus to my mind it is clear that the respondents' treasurer was the officer properly appointed for the proper administration of the

C respondents' financial affairs which clearly include the collection of rates to which the respondents become entitled by law. Equally clearly, the performance of such duties as in consequence fall upon the respondents' treasurer could not possibly all be performed by him personally, and Parliament cannot possibly have intended that this should be so. The respondents' treasurer required staff to carry out the financial affairs which

D he is enjoined to administer. See also section 112 (1) of the Act of 1972.

Next as to Mr. Wells's position. The learned judge's note of his uncontradicted evidence reads thus:

" Principal rating assistant, Derby City Council. March 1976 my job to implement resolution of council about rating of unoccupied buildings. March 11, 1976, to Heritage Gate development. Norman

E [House] and Saxon [House] appeared complete. Celtic [House] and Roman [House] work still going on. March 11 I thought would be completed on June 6. June 1 finished Celtic and Roman. Workmen had gone and landscaped and everybody gone. I was then of opinion that my six months from March was right and so completion notices made out. I spoke to the senior rating officer. I assume the city treasurer is rating officer. City treasurer did not see

F the notices. Notices never get near city treasurer. A.R.V.A. my qualification. Form typed with blanks and signed by city treasurer. Supply of forms photocopied and in this case I filled in the ink writing and served by recorded delivery."

The learned judge in his judgment summarised that evidence accurately thus:

G " Mr. Wells the principal rating assistant to the respondent gave evidence that in March 1976 it was his job to implement the resolution of the council about the rating of unoccupied buildings, that on March 11, 1976, he went to the Heritage Gate development, Norman and Saxon Houses appeared complete, work was still going on in Celtic and Roman Houses and he thought they would be

H completed by June 6. He went again on June 1, 1976, and found all the workmen had gone and Celtic and Roman Houses were finished. He said he was of opinion that six months from March was right so he filled in the blanks in ink on forms of photocopied notices of which he had a supply and served them. He spoke to the senior rating officer before serving the notices but the city treasurer never saw the notices; they never went near the city treasurer."

Having thus accurately summarised Mr. Wells's evidence, the learned A
judge continued:

> " I find on that evidence that the then borough treasurer had
> signed a typed form of completion notice with blanks, that Mr. Wells
> had a supply of photocopies of that form, that the opinion that the
> work remaining to be done on each building, referred to in each
> completion notice, could reasonably be expected to be completed B
> in three months was the opinion of Mr. Wells alone and neither
> the council nor any committee of the council nor the city treasurer
> had had the opportunity of considering the matter or of forming any
> opinion thereon."

Is the learned judge's conclusion upon those findings of fact correct?
It was submitted first, as already stated, that the exercise of the council's C
rights and duties consequent upon the passing of the section 17 resolution
could not be delegated. This argument started from section 1 (3) and
section 3 of the Act of 1967. The former, it was said, empowered the
respondents to make and levy rates. The making and levying of a rate
requires a resolution of the respondents as the rating authority. Section
111 (3) of the Act of 1972 expressly prohibits the use of the powers D
accorded to local authorities by section 111 (1) for the raising of money
by rates. The operation of section 17 by resolution and the consequent
bringing into force of Schedule 1 to the Act of 1967 are steps towards
and conditions precedent to the obtaining of rates by the respondents
from particular owners of particular unoccupied property. The respondents are in this way by service of the relevant notices making and
levying rates upon those owners. Accordingly, a resolution of the res- E
pondents was required before any valid opinion could be formed for the
purpose of paragraph 8 (1) of Schedule 1, that is to say, before any valid
notice could be served.

My Lords, in my opinion this argument is unsound. It breaks down at
the outset for two reasons. First, the operation of section 17 and the
consequent coming into force of the Schedule 1 provisions cannot legiti- F
mately be described, to my mind, as making and levying a rate. The rate in
question will already have been made, or, if not already made, is likely
to be made shortly after any such notice is served. What section 17
and Schedule 1 enable a rating authority to do is to bring within the fold
of ratepayers owners of the unoccupied property specified in the particular
notices. It is true that it is difficult to discern in the Act of 1967 any
consistent use of the words " make " or " levy " but whatever the precise G
significance of those words in other parts of the statute may be I am
quite unable to treat the giving of a paragraph 8 notice as " making or
levying " a rate, and thus to require a formal resolution of the respondents.

The second reason why in my opinion the argument breaks down is
the material difference of language between " A rating authority may H
resolve " in section 17, and " Where a rating authority are of opinion "
in paragraph 8 (1) of Schedule 1. Not only is there that difference of
language but a similar phrase " in their opinion " is used in paragraph
6 (1) of Schedule 1 while paragraph 6 (2) of that Schedule uses the
phrase " if they think fit." Pressed to say if he contended that the rating
authority could only " think fit " if they expressed their thoughts by
resolution, learned counsel for the appellants disclaimed any such sub-

A mission. He was clearly right so to do. But if no resolution is required for the purpose of paragraph 6 (2) I am unable to see why such a resolution should be required for the purposes of paragraph 6 (1), and if it is not required for the purposes of paragraph 6 (1) why should such a resolution be required for the purposes of paragraph 8 (1)?

This submission therefore fails as a matter of construction of the relevant statutory provisions. Such authority as there is also points
B against it. In *B. Kettle Ltd.* v. *Newcastle-under-Lyme Borough Council* (1979) 77 L.G.R. 700, the whole argument proceeded upon the footing that there was power to delegate by resolution the power accorded to a rating authority by paragraph 6 (2) of Schedule 1. The only question was whether the particular resolution sufficiently delegated the power in question to the particular officer concerned. I cannot think that the
C learned Master of the Rolls [Lord Denning M.R.] or the learned Lords Justices (Lawton and Lane L.JJ.) would have expressed themselves as they did in their several judgments if they had contemplated for one moment that there was no power to delegate. The decision of the Divisional Court in *Bar Hill Developments Ltd.* v. *South Cambridgeshire District Council* [1979] R.A. 379 is clearly against the appellants' contention on this issue.
D My Lords, I now turn to consider the other matters. It is clear that the respondents' treasurer never personally applied his mind to any of the matters covered by the notices. The crucial question is therefore whether the action and opinion of Mr. Wells complied with the requirements of paragraph 8 (1) of Schedule 1. It is important to note at the outset that what is required by these provisions is simply the formation of an
E opinion. The opinion so formed is not final or conclusive. There is a right of appeal accorded by paragraph 8 (4) to the county court. It is the learned judge's opinion which is finally decisive. I did not understand learned counsel for the appellants to dispute that (assuming his argument on the first issue fails, as it does) the respondents' treasurer could himself have formed the relevant opinion had he been consulted by Mr. Wells and had he applied his own mind to what Mr. Wells reported to him, and
F thereupon formed an independent view on the basis of the material placed for his consideration. This part of the appellants' argument therefore involves the highly technical submission that the opinon of the qualified relevant official is not good enough but the opinion of his administrative superior who may or may not be similarly qualified based on a report of that qualified relevant official is good enough.

G My Lords, the statutory conditions precedent to the imposition of a fiscal liability must obviously be properly complied with and the ratepayer like the taxpayer is entitled to full protection against the improper exaction of revenue by local as well as by central government. But Parliament has conferred very wide powers on local authorities and Parliament plainly contemplated that the actual machinery of enforcement and collection would not be operated personally by some senior local government official
H but would be so operated by the relevant senior official's staff.

My Lords, I regard the provisions of the latter part of Schedule 1 as administrative in character. Section 151 of the Act of 1972 empowers local authorities to make arrangements for the proper administration of their financial affairs. The respondents' treasurer was, as already stated, the respondents' responsible officer for this purpose. For my part I am quite unable to see why that which Mr. Wells did was not done as part

of the proper administration of the respondents' financial affairs, namely A
the collection of rate revenue. Of course the filling up of blank forms
previously signed with a facsimile signature can in some cases lead to an
abuse and indeed to an illegal exercise of power. It is the clear duty of the
courts to see that this method of administration does not lead to any such
abuse. Mr. Sears for the respondents accepted that the respondents'
documentation in relation to the exercise of their powers and functions by
their staff was in some respects open to criticism. No doubt, since, had B
the view of the learned judge prevailed, the respondents would in consequence have lost some £½ million of rate revenue, they will if they have
not already done so take steps to see that they do not again expose themselves to a possible huge loss of revenue of this kind because of some
administrative failure of the kind suggested against them in this case. No
doubt other rating authorities will be similarly prudent and wish to review C
their arrangements and ensure that the appropriate powers do lie where
they are required to lie.

My Lords, in the result I find myself in complete and respectful agree-
ment with the Court of Appeal for the reasons given by Sir Patrick
Browne, at p. 18 of the transcript. On this part of the case the question
is not whether the respondent's treasurer delegated power to Mr. Wells.
The question is whether what Mr. Wells did was authorised by the D
respondents' treasurer so as to be the relevant opinion of the respondents.
For the reasons I have given, I think that it was and for those reasons
I would dismiss these appeals.

LORD BRIDGE OF HARWICH. My Lords, finding myself unhappily in
disagreement with the Court of Appeal and the rest of your Lordships, E
my opinion will not affect the outcome of these appeals and can, I hope,
be expressed shortly.

The appeals turn upon the validity of notices which the respondents
purported to serve upon the appellants pursuant to Schedule 1, paragraph 8 (1) to the General Rate Act 1967. That sub-paragraph provides:

" Where a rating authority are of opinion—(a) that the erection of a F
building within their area has been completed; or (b) that the work
remaining to be done on a building within their area is such that the
erection of the building can reasonably be expected to be completed
within three months, and that the building is, or when completed will
be, comprised in a relevant hereditament, the authority may serve
on the owner of the building a notice (hereafter in this paragraph
referred to as ' a completion notice ') stating that the erection of the G
building is to be treated for the purposes of this Schedule as completed on the date of service of the notice or on such later date as
may be specified by the notice."

My Lords, I entertain no doubt that the formation of the requisite
opinion which must precede the service of a notice under this provision H
is a function of the rating authority. It is a function of a kind which one
would certainly expect to be delegated to a suitably qualified officer.
But in the absence of such delegation, I fail to understand how any
officer can claim to be empowered to form the requisite opinion on the
authority's behalf.

Delegation of functions by local authorities to committees, sub-
committees or officers is provided for by section 101 of the Local

A Government Act 1972. I agree with your Lordships that the restriction on delegation imposed by section 101 (6) is not applicable to the function here in question.

The respondents rely on the appointment of their treasurer as " the proper officer for the purposes of section . . . 151 of the Local Government Act 1972 " as empowering that officer to form the requisite opinion and to subdelegate that function to the principal rating assistant by whom

B it was in fact performed.

Section 151 of the Act of 1972 provides:

> " Without prejudice to section 111 above, every local authority shall make arrangements for the proper administration of their financial affairs and shall secure that one of their officers has responsibility for the administration of those affairs."

C My Lords, it does not seem to me that relevant light for present purposes is cast on the construction of this section by the reference to section 111. I find it impossible to construe section 151 as concerned in any way with the delegation of functions which the Act of 1972 or any other statute assigns to the authority itself. The responsibility which, in my opinion, is required by section 151 to be imposed on one of the

D local authority's officers is that of supervising all the routine operations, such as the keeping of proper books, the operation of necessary bank accounts and the collection and payment of debts, which are involved in the administration of the financial affairs of any corporate body but which do not involve the exercise of any statutory functions of the authority. If the necessary appointment of a responsible officer under section 151 involves the necessary delegation of an undefined range of

E statutory functions of the authority, there must be room for endless debate and uncertainty as to what that range of functions comprises. I cannot believe that this was what Parliament intended. But if I am wrong in this view and an appointment under section 151 of the Act of 1972 is capable of delegating statutory functions of a local authority which properly belong in the province of " the . . . administration of

F their financial affairs," I do not think this expression is apt to embrace the formation of an opinion under paragraph 8 (1) of Schedule 1 to the Act of 1967 as to when the erection of a new building can reasonably be expected to be completed. The ability to form such an opinion lies within the competence, not of a financial administrator, but of a building surveyor.

I would allow the appeals.

G
                                                    Appeals dismissed with costs.

Solicitors: *Braby & Waller; Sharpe, Pritchard & Co.*

                                                                 M. G.

H

[QUEEN'S BENCH DIVISION]

* EVANS *v.* LONDON HOSPITAL MEDICAL COLLEGE
(UNIVERSITY OF LONDON) AND OTHERS

[1977 E. No. 2287]

1980 July 3;
Sept. 25

Drake J.

B

*Practice—Pleadings—Striking out—Action for negligence—Post
mortem investigation by defendants—Report to police indicating death due to poisoning—Arrest and prosecution of plaintiff
for murder—Prosecution offering no evidence at trial—Plaintiff alleging contamination of organs due to defendants'
negligence in post mortem investigation—Whether disclosing
reasonable cause of action—Whether defendants immune from
suit*

C

The first defendants provided post mortem investigations
and reports and toxological investigations at the request of the
police or the Director of Public Prosecutions. The other defendants were employed by the first defendants. The plaintiff's five-
month old son died on July 7, 1975, and a post mortem investigation was carried out by the second defendant and certain
organs were removed, which on July 8 were found on analysis
by the third and fourth defendants to contain various concentrations of morphine. The results of the analysis were communicated to the police in the form of statements, and the
plaintiff was arrested and charged with the murder of her son.
Following further investigations on behalf of the plaintiff the
prosecution offered no evidence at her trial at the Central
Criminal Court and she was acquitted. The plaintiff claimed
damages as a result of her arrest, detention and trial, alleging
that the defendants had been negligent, inter alia, in allowing
the organs removed at the post mortem to become contaminated with morphine and in failing to withdraw their statements in the light of the findings of the investigations carried
out on behalf of the plaintiff, so that when offering no evidence
at the trial the prosecution reaffirmed that the son's death was
due to morphine poisoning. The proceedings were served only
on the first, third and fourth defendants. On October 17, 1978,
Master Warren dismissed the plaintiff's statement of claim as
disclosing no reasonable cause of action since the defendants
were at all times preparing evidence for a possible prosecution
and were therefore immune from civil proceedings ensuing
from such acts.

D

E

F

On appeal to the judge, and on an application to amend the
statement of claim to include a claim for malicious prosecution:—

G

Held, (1) refusing leave to amend the statement of claim,
that all that was alleged against the defendants was that
they provided reports for the purpose of placing them before
the police or the Director of Public Prosecutions and, accordingly, since it was for the police or the Director of Public
Prosecutions to decide whether or not to prosecute, a claim
for malicious prosecution was misconceived (post, pp. 188H—
189A).

H

(2) Dismissing the appeal, that the immunity from a civil
action given to a witness in judicial proceedings in respect of
evidence given by him during those proceedings covered statements made prior to the issue of a writ or the commencement
of a prosecution provided that such a statement was made for
the purpose of a possible action or prosecution and at a time

A   when a possible action or prosecution was being considered; that the immunity extended to the collection and analysis of material relevant to an offence or possible offence under investigation and was not confined to the preparation of a formal statement or proof of evidence; and that, accordingly, since the defendants' statements could fairly be said to be part of the process of investigating a crime or possible crime with a view to prosecution, at the time when they were alleged to

B   have been negligent they were protected by the immunity and no reasonable cause of action was shown against them (post, pp. 191F–G, 192A–B, D–E).

     Marrinan v. *Vibart* [1963] 1 Q.B. 528, C.A. applied.
     Saif Ali v. *Sydney Mitchell & Co.* [1980] A.C. 198, H.L.(E.) considered.

C   The following cases are referred to in the judgment:

     Marrinan v. *Vibart* [1963] 1 Q.B. 234; [1962] 2 W.L.R. 1224; [1962] 1 All E.R. 869; [1963] 1 Q.B. 528; [1962] 3 W.L.R. 912; [1962] 3 All E.R. 380, C.A.
     Rees v. *Sinclair* [1974] 1 N.Z.L.R. 180.
     Saif Ali v. *Sydney Mitchell & Co.* [1980] A.C. 198; [1978] 3 W.L.R. 849; [1978] 3 All E.R. 1033, H.L.(E.).

D   *Watson* v. *M'Ewan* [1905] A.C. 480, H.L.(Sc.).

     No additional cases were cited in argument.

     APPEAL from Master Warren in chambers.
     By a statement of claim dated December 2, 1977, the plaintiff, Michelle

E   Evans, claimed damages for negligence from the first defendants, the London Hospital Medical College (University of London), and the second, third and fourth defendants, Peter Vanezis, Anne Robinson and Anne Holder. No proceedings were ever served on the second defendant. The plaintiff alleged that as a result of post mortem and analysis results prepared by the defendants in various capacities she had been arrested

F   and charged with the murder of her five-month old son by morphine poisoning. After further investigation by toxicologists on her behalf the prosecution had offered no evidence at her trial and she had been acquitted. She alleged that the second, third and fourth defendants had been negligent, inter alia, in allowing the organs removed from the deceased infant's body to become contaminated with morphine, in failing to appreciate that the concentration of morphine revealed by analysis was

G   so high that it was unlikely that it could have existed in the infant while he was still alive and that it therefore came from contamination, in failing to act upon the information given to them after the toxological examination on her behalf and in failing to retract or amend their report to the police or the Director of Public Prosecutions. She alleged that the hospital had been negligent, inter alia, in failing to act upon the infor-

H   mation given to them as a result of the toxological examination on behalf of the plaintiff or to set up an inquiry, in failing to withdraw or disclaim the statements made by the individual defendants to the police or the Director of Public Prosecutions and in failing to ensure that the individual defendants carried out a proper analysis of the organs removed.

     On October 17, 1978, Master Warren set aside the statement of claim on the ground that it disclosed no reasonable cause of action, and he dismissed the action. The plaintiff appealed against the decision.

Evans v. London Hospital (Q.B.D.)   [1981]

The hearing was in chambers. Drake J. delivered judgment in open   A
court on September 25, 1980.

The facts are stated in the judgment.

Philip Otton Q.C. and *John Hunter* for the plaintiff.
Hugh Carlisle Q.C. and *T. J. Briden* for the defendants.

                                                    Cur. adv. vult.   B

September 25.   DRAKE J. read the following judgment. This is an
appeal by the plaintiff from a decision of Master Warren, given as long
ago as October 17, 1978, in which, on the application of the first, third
and fourth defendants, he ordered that the plaintiff's statement of claim
against them be struck out and the action dismissed on the grounds that   C
it disclosed no reasonable cause of action. I was informed that the second
defendant had not been served with any of the proceedings; therefore,
save where I state otherwise, any references to " the defendants " will
exclude him. I am also concerned with a summons taken out by the
plaintiff on June 5, 1980, whereby she applies for leave to amend the
writ and statement of claim. The amendments proposed at the time that   D
summons was taken out were altered in two respects during the hearing
before me. The defendants did not oppose the proposed amendments as
such but argued that even with such amendments the writ and statement
of claim still show no reasonable cause of action. I was invited by Mr.
Carlisle, appearing for the defendants, to deal with the appeal and
summons on the basis of the writ and statement of claim as proposed to
be amended and to allow the amendments if, but only if, I considered   E
that the pleadings as amended disclose a reasonable cause of action
against the defendants.

The plaintiff's claim endorsed on the writ is for

" damages for injury and loss occasioned by the negligence of the
defendants and each of them in issuing inaccurate post-mortem
and toxicological reports to the police and/or Director of Public   F
Prosecutions whereby the plaintiff was on or about July 13, 1975,
falsely charged with the murder of Jamie Evans."

The proposed amendments added an alternative claim for malicious
prosecution.

Jamie Evans was the five-months-old son of the plaintiff and the facts
alleged in the statement of claim may be summarised as follows. The first   G
defendants (" the hospital ") provided, through its department of forensic
medicine, post-mortem reports for the purpose of placing such reports
before the police and the Director of Public Prosecutions (" the D.P.P.").
The three individual defendants were employed by the hospital as lec-
turers in that department. On July 7, 1975, Jamie Evans died from a
condition known as " sudden infant death syndrome." On the same day   H
at Deptford Public Mortuary the second defendant carried out a post-
mortem on the infant during which he removed from the body a number
of organs and specimens which were sent to the third and fourth defendants for toxicological analysis. On July 8 at the hospital they carried
out tests on these organs and specimens and purported to find in them
concentrations of morphine. They reported their findings to the police
and/or the D.P.P. and to the second defendant, and on August 5, 1975,

A they made statements in accordance with the Criminal Justice Act 1967, sections 2 and 9, setting out the results of their analysis. On the same day the second defendant made a statement under the same statutory provisions in which he alleged that the infant's death had been caused by morphine poisoning. As a result of the reports made by the three individual defendants to the police and/or the D.P.P. the plaintiff was arrested on July 13, 1975, and charged with the murder of her infant son by morphine

B poisoning. On August 18, 1975, the plaintiff's solicitors, through the D.P.P., informed the defendants (a) that further organs had been removed from the body of the infant by a pathologist (Professor Mant) acting for the plaintiff, and toxicological analysis had shown these organs to be free from morphine and (b) that it followed that it was not possible for there to have been any morphine in the organs removed by the second defen-

C dant on July 7 at the time of such removal because the morphine would have contaminated all the organs in the body. It also followed that the organs analysed by the third and fourth defendants must have become contaminated with morphine after they had been removed from the body, and whilst they were in the care of the defendants. On receipt of this information the defendants took no action to retract or amend the state-

D ments they had made on August 5. On February 16, 1976, the plaintiff appeared at the Central Criminal Court on the charge of murder, but the prosecution offered no evidence against her and she was acquitted. However because of the failure of the defendants to retract their statements or in any way indicate that they were unreliable in the light of Professor Mant's findings, the prosecution, whilst offering no evidence against the

E plaintiff, reaffirmed that the infant's death was due to morphine poisoning.

    That is a summary of the facts alleged in the statement of claim. When addressing me counsel for the defendants invited me to consider a transcript of the proceedings at the Central Criminal Court to show what prosecuting counsel had then stated as the reasons why the prosecution still believed that the infant had died from morphine poisoning. He read out to me some of the transcript: but I declined to give any effect to it

F because it is well settled that in deciding whether a statement of claim discloses any reasonable cause of action the court should *not* consider any evidence. My decision is based solely on the allegations contained in the pleadings.

    The statement of claim on the basis of those allegations alleges negligence. In its unamended form the allegations made against the second,

G third and fourth defendants are, summarised: (i) permitting the organs to become contaminated; (ii) failing to appreciate that the concentration of morphine revealed by analysis was so high that it was very unlikely that it could have existed in the infant whilst he was alive, and that it therefore got there by contamination; (iii) failing to act upon the information given to them as a result of Professor Mant's examination; and (iv) failing to

H retract or amend their reports made to the police and/or D.P.P. or the written statements made on August 5.

    The allegations against the hospital are, summarised: (i) failing to act upon the information given to them as a result of Professor Mant's examination; (ii) failing to set up an inquiry into the way in which the removed organs had become contaminated; (iii) failing to disclaim or withdraw the statements or reports made by the individual defendants to the police and/or D.P.P. and failing to ensure that the prosecution of the

plaintiff did not proceed any further; and (iv) failing to ensure that the   A
individual defendants carried out a proper analysis of the removed organs.

A proposed amendment would have the effect of making these allegations not only in respect of acts or omissions of the second, third and
fourth defendants as servants or agents of the first defendants but against
" the defendants their servants or agents " without identifying the servants
or agents referred to: in other words it would cover the possible contamination of the infant's removed organs by anyone employed by or   B
acting on behalf of the hospital. It would, for example, cover the possible
contamination by a cleaner or porter who had no direct connection with
the examination of the organs for the purpose of submitting a report to
the police or the D.P.P. It is right to say that the particulars of negligence
do not contain any suggestion that contamination occurred in this or
indeed in any specified manner: and the proposed amendment was only   C
put forward during the hearing before me. An amendment proposed at
the time the summons for leave to amend was issued would not have
covered any negligence save that of " the defendants."

A further proposed amendment made the alternative allegation of
malicious prosecution by the defendants and each of them in that they
made a false analysis and communicated it to the police and/or the   D
D.P.P. and procured the arrest and prosecution of the plaintiff. By way
of malice the plaintiff relies on the allegations set out as particulars of
negligence.

The defendants' successful application to the master to strike out the
writ and statement of claim was made on the ground that the defendants
were at all times acting in the course of preparing evidence for a possible
prosecution and for that reason were immune from any civil proceedings   E
arising from such acts. This ground was relied on in the present hearing
to give immunity from the additional cause of action in malicious prosecution as well as negligence: but it was further submitted that the statement of claim disclosed no basis for alleging malicious prosecution since
the defendants had not initiated the prosecution but had merely passed on
information to the police and/or the D.P.P. Mr. Otton, for the plaintiff,   F
whilst conceding that the defendants had immunity in respect of negligence after the criminal proceedings had started, argued that the negligent
acts or omissions relied on were prior to the prosecution being
commenced. As to malicious prosecution he submitted that it was because
of the defendants' acts and omissions that the plaintiff had been charged
and that the defendants, judged by their entire conduct had in reality   G
" caused the law to be set in motion."

I will deal first with the proposed amendment to claim damages for
malicious prosecution, because it seems to me that this can be briefly disposed of. As is said in Clerk & Lindsell on Torts, 14th ed. (1975), para.
1887:

"To prosecute is to set the law in motion, and the law is only set in
motion by an appeal to some person clothed with judicial authority in   H
regard to the matter in question . . . If a charge is made to a police
constable and he thereupon makes an arrest, the party making the
charge, if liable at all, will be liable in an action for false imprisonment, on the ground that he has directed the arrest and therefore it
is his own act and not the act of the law."

In my judgment the statement of claim in the present case makes it

A clear that all that is alleged against the defendants is that they provided reports ". . . for the purpose of placing such reports before the police and/ or the Director of Public Prosecutions." It was for the police or the D.P.P. (in reality, clearly for the D.P.P.) to decide whether or not to prosecute and I think the proposed addition of a claim of malicious prosecution against the defendants or any of them is misconceived. That is sufficient to dispose of that proposed cause of action. However, I think
B there are other grounds for doubting whether the defendants can be said to have " set the law in motion." As I have just stated the statement of claim avers that the hospital " purported to provide . . . post-mortem investigation and reports . . . for the purpose of placing such reports before the police and the Director of Public Prosecutions." When the second defendant carried out a post-mortem on the deceased infant he must
C have been requested by some other person—probably a police officer—so to do. In the circumstances it is certainly arguable that it was not the defendants who " set the law in motion."

The cause of action in negligence gives rise to more difficulty. The cases show clearly that a witness in criminal proceedings enjoys absolute immunity from any form of civil action in respect of evidence given by him
D during those proceedings: and, further, that such immunity extends to cover statements made by him in preparing a proof for trial or in a report to the D.P.P.: see *Marrinan* v. *Vibart* [1963] 1 Q.B. 234, applying *Watson* v. *M'Ewan* [1905] A.C. 480. But how far does this absolute immunity extend to cover the acts or omissions of a witness or potential witness during the stage when they are collecting or considering material with a view to its *possible* use in criminal proceedings?
E The decision of the Court of Appeal in *Marrinan* v. *Vibart* [1963] 1 Q.B. 528 does, it seems to me, make the position clear. In the leading judgment given by Sellers L.J. with which the other two members of the court, Willmer and Diplock L.JJ., agreed, he said, at p. 535:

> " Whatever form of action is sought to be derived from what was said or done in the course of judicial proceedings must suffer the
F > same fate of being barred by the rule which protects witnesses in their evidence before the court *and in the preparation of the evidence which is to be so given.*" (My italics.)

Mr. Otton for the plaintiff concedes that these words are apparently wide enough to make it difficult for the plaintiff to bring her claim in this action. But he seeks to overcome the difficulty on two grounds. First
G he says that " the preparation of the evidence " applies only to preparing the statements or proof of evidence containing what the witness is expected to say at the trial. Second he argues that the alleged negligence of the defendants arose before the judicial process had started, and was in the course of the routine administrative inquiries which follow a death such as that of an infant in its cot.

H I do not accept either of these arguments. I think it essential to keep in mind the reason for the immunity. Mr. Otton suggests that the main reason is to prevent disgruntled convicted prisoners from seeking to have their cases retried in a civil suit. I think that that is undoubtedly one of the reasons for the existence of the immunity: but I think that the reason is in fact more broadly based than this. It was stated by Salmon J. in his judgment at first instance in *Marrinan* v. *Vibart* [1963] 1 Q.B. 234, 237:

" This immunity exists for the benefit of the public, since the A
administration of justice would be greatly impeded if witnesses were
to be in fear that any disgruntled and possibly impecunious persons
against whom they gave evidence might subsequently involve them
in costly litigation."

The judgment of Salmon J. was approved by all three members of
the court on the subsequent appeal. It seems to me that this immunity B
would not achieve its object if limited to the giving of evidence in court
and to the preparation only of the statements or proof of evidence given
by the witness. Any disgruntled litigant or convicted person could
circumvent the immunity by saying he was challenging the collection and
preparation of the evidence, to be taken down as a statement or proof of
evidence later, and *not* challenging the statement or proof itself. In other
words he would seek to base his claim on things said or done by the
witness at some time prior to the statement or proof being given by him.

In my opinion this would largely destroy the value of the immunity.
Equally I think that it would open the way to convicted persons seeking
to have their cases re-tried in the civil courts. An action could be brought
alleging negligence against police officers in their investigations and the
collection of evidence which at some later date resulted in criminal D
proceedings being commenced.

I think that the wide language used by the Court of Appeal in
Marrinan v. *Vibart* [1963] 1 Q.B. 582, that the immunity " protects
witnesses in their evidence before the court and in the preparation of the
evidence which is to be so given, was deliberately given in those very wide
terms.
E
It remains, of course, a question to be decided on the facts of each
case (or, in the present instance of an application to strike out, on the
alleged facts) whether or not the negligent act or omission arose during the
course of preparation of the evidence. In the present case I think it did
arise during the course of preparing or collecting evidence.

Although the scope of the decision in *Marrinan* v. *Vibart* may be clear
it remains to consider to what extent if at all it has been narrowed by F
the more recent decision of the House of Lords in *Saif Ali* v. *Sydney
Mitchell & Co.* [1980] A.C. 198. That decision was concerned with the
immunity from being sued enjoyed by a barrister or solicitor when
engaged in the conduct of litigation.

The majority decision which can conveniently be taken from the
headnote to the report reads, so far as is relevant to the present case, G
at p. 199:

" that in principle those who undertook to give skilled advice were
under a duty to take reasonable care and skill, and that a barrister's
immunity from suit for negligence in respect of his conduct of litigation on the ground of public policy was an exception and applied
only in the area to which it extended; that the immunity was not con- H
fined to what was done in court but included some pre-trial work,
but that protection should not be given any wider application than
was absolutely necessary in the interests of the administration of
justice and each piece of pre-trial work had to be tested against the
one rule, namely, that the protection existed only where the particular work was so intimately connected with the conduct of the
cause in court that it could fairly be said to be a preliminary decision

A   affecting the way that cause was to be conducted when it came to a hearing."

It was further held that the same immunity attaches to a solicitor acting as an advocate in court as attaches to a barrister.

So if the limits to the immunity enjoyed by a witness were in all respects similar to those of the advocate's immunity, then the test to be
B   applied would be to consider whether the statement or conduct of the witness was so intimately connected with the conduct of the cause in court that it could fairly be said to be a preliminary decision affecting the way the case was to be conducted at the hearing. On that test the immunity would not cover all of the negligence alleged against these defendants, as at least some of it related to a time before any proceedings were in being.
C   The post mortem examination and toxicological analysis on some of the infant's organs was carried out as part of the investigations necessary to decide *whether* any prosecution should be brought. If it is possible to compare the position of a barrister to that of the defendants in this case I think it clear that the barrister would not be immune from being sued for negligence.

But although the immunity attaching to barristers exists for reasons of
D   public policy, as does that attaching to witnesses, I think it clear that it is not identical. The immunity enjoyed by a witness does in fact protect everyone engaged in proceedings in court—not merely the witnesses, but the judge, counsel, jurors and the parties: see Lord Wilberforce in *Saif Ali* v. *Sydney Mitchell & Co.* [1980] A.C. 198, 214 and *per* Lord Diplock, at p. 222. The barrister's immunity from action in respect of his conduct
E   of the litigation is a separate even if in some ways related branch of immunity. Public policy gives immunity to the barrister so that he may be free, without any fear of civil action, in his conduct of litigation: it is not, however, right that he should be given any wider immunity than is necessary for that purpose. The immunity given to a witness or potential witness is because

F   ". . . the administration of justice would be greatly impeded if witnesses were to be in fear that . . . persons against whom they gave evidence might subsequently involve them in costly litigation ": see *per* Salmon, J. in *Marrinan* v. *Vibart* [1963] 1 Q.B. 234, 237.

If this object is to be achieved I think it essential that the immunity given to a witness should also extend to cover statements he makes prior
G   to the issue of a writ or commencement of a prosecution, provided that the statement is made for the purpose of a possible action or prosecution and at a time when a possible action or prosecution is being considered. In a large number of criminal cases the police have collected statements from witnesses before anyone is charged with an offence; indeed sometimes before it is known whether or not *any* criminal offence has been
H   committed.

If immunity did not extend to such statements it would mean that the immunity attaching to the giving of evidence in court or the formal statements made in preparation for the court hearing could easily be outflanked and rendered of little use. For the same reason I think that the immunity must extend also to the acts of the witness in collecting or considering material on which he may later be called to give evidence. If it does not so extend then a convicted person could, for example, sue the

police officers for the allegedly negligent manner in which they had   A
investigated the crime, by complaining that they had wrongly assessed the
evidential value of certain matters or had failed to interview possible
witnesses whose evidence was thought by the accused to be favourable
to him.

It is for these reasons that I think that the words used by the Court of
Appeal in *Marrinan* v. *Vibart* [1963] 1 Q.B. 528, that immunity protects   B
witnesses in their evidence before the court and in the preparation of the
evidence which is to be given, cover and were intended to cover the
collection and analysis of material relevant to the offence or possible
offence under investigation, and were not intended merely to cover the
preparation of the witness's formal statement or proof of evidence.

Applying, to the immunity to be given to a witness, the test suggested
by McCarthy P., in the New Zealand Court of Appeal in *Rees* v. *Sinclair*   C
[1974] 1 N.Z.L.R. 180, 187, cited and approved by the majority of the
House of Lords in *Saif Ali* v. *Sydney Mitchell & Co.* [1980] A.C. 198,
I would alter it to apply it to the immunity attaching to a witness or
possible witness in a criminal investigation, thus: the protection exists
only where the statement or conduct is such that it can fairly be said to
be part of the process of investigating a crime or a possible crime with a   D
view to a prosecution or possible prosecution in respect of the matter
being investigated. Applying this test to the present case I think it clear
that the defendants and each of them were so engaged at the time when
they were allegedly negligent in the different ways set out in the statement
of claim as proposed to be amended. Accordingly I hold that they are
protected by immunity and that no reasonable cause of action is shown
against them. It follows that in my judgment this appeal against the   E
master's order must be dismissed and I dismiss also the plaintiff's application for leave to amend.

As I have adjourned this summons into open court, at the request of
counsel for the plaintiff and because I think the decision is one of interest
beyond the interests of the parties themselves, I think it right to repeat
that I have been required by the rules to consider this matter entirely on   F
the basis of allegations made by the plaintiff, without hearing or in any
way considering whether these allegations could be supported by evidence.
No negligence or wrongful conduct of any kind whatsoever has been
proved against any of the defendants: and it has been made clear to me
that were the action to go to trial these allegations would be very vigor-
ously defended and strenuously denied.

G

> *Appeal dismissed with costs, taxa-*
> *tion not to be proceeded with*
> *without futher order.*
> *Legal aid taxation of plaintiff's*
> *costs.*
> *Leave to appeal.*   H

Solicitors: *Sheratte Caleb & Co.; L. Watmore & Co.*

R. C. W.

A

[PRIVY COUNCIL]

* CADBURY-SCHWEPPES PTY. LTD. AND OTHERS . APPELLANTS

AND

PUB SQUASH CO. PTY. LTD. . . . . . RESPONDENT

B
[APPEAL FROM THE SUPREME COURT OF NEW SOUTH WALES,
EQUITY DIVISION]

1980 June 23, 24, 26, 30;   Lord Wilberforce, Lord Edmund-Davies,
    July 1;   Lord Fraser of Tullybelton, Lord Scarman
    Oct. 13   and Lord Roskill

Passing Off—Risk of confusion—Imitation of trading style—Use
C   *of name " Pub Squash " for lemon drink—Name, get-up and*
advertising campaign imitative of slogans and visual images
used in competitor's advertising—Whether sufficient to establish
passing off—Relevant date for establishing reputation of
product

     In 1974 the plaintiffs launched on the market a new canned
lemon drink. The launch was supported by an extensive
D   advertising campaign on radio and television. In 1975 the
defendant launched a similar drink and adopted an advertising
campaign and chose and registered as a trade mark a name
based on the theme and slogans of the plaintiffs' advertising.
The sales of the plaintiffs' drink declined and they brought an
action against the defendant for damages and an injunction
in respect of passing off, expungement from the Register of
Trade Marks and a claim in respect of unfair trading. In
E   giving judgment the judge first considered the issue of passing
off and decided that on the facts the defendant had sufficiently
differentiated its product from that of the plaintiffs. He then
considered the issue of unfair trading and found that the
defendant had deliberately set out to exploit the market created
by the plaintiffs but that since the defendant had made no
relevant misrepresentation there had been no unfair trading.
He also decided that the relevant date for determining whether
F   a plaintiff had established the necessary goodwill to support a
claim of passing off was that of the commencement of proceedings. He dismissed the action.
     On the plaintiffs' appeal to the Judicial Committee: —
     Held, dismissing the appeal, (1) that although the tort of
passing off was wide enough to encompass descriptive material
such as slogans and visual images used in an advertising campaign on radio and television provided that they had become
G   part of the goodwill of the product, a deliberate imitation of
another's goods, get-up, method of trading or trading style
did not in itself amount to a deception sufficient to constitute
passing off and that to establish the tort it was necessary for
a plaintiff to show that the defendant had confused or misled
the market into thinking that his product was that of the
plaintiff; and that, accordingly, since the judge's findings that
the defendant had sufficiently differentiated its drink from that
H   of the plaintiffs and that the defendant had made no relevant
misrepresentation were inferences which could properly be
drawn from his primary findings of fact and, taking the
judgment as a whole, the judge had not misled himself by its
structure as to the relevance to the issue of deception of the
defendant's intention to take advantage of the plaintiffs'
advertising campaign, the judge had not erred in finding that
the plaintiffs had not made out their case of passing off and
unfair trading (post, pp. 198F–G, 200D–H, 202H, 203G—204B,
205 G–H).

(2) That the relevant date for determining whether a   A
plaintiff had established the necessary goodwill or reputation
of his product to support an action of passing off was the date
of the commencement of the conduct complained of but that
since it was clear that in coming to his decision the judge
had directed his mind to the facts as they had been at that
date, his error in stating that the relevant date was that of
the commencement of proceedings was immaterial to the result
(post, p. 204C–E).   B

Decision of the Supreme Court of New South Wales, Equity
Division affirmed.

The following cases are referred to in the judgment of their Lordships:

Cheney Brothers v. *Doris Silk Corporation* (1929) 35 F. 2d. 279.
Felton v. *Mulligan* (1971) 124 C.L.R. 367.
Hornsby Building Information Centre Pty. Ltd. v. *Sydney Building*   C
     Information Centre Pty. Ltd. (1978) 52 A.L.J.R. 392.
International News Service v. *Associated Press* (1918) 248 U.S. 215.
Leather Cloth Co. Ltd. v. *American Leather Cloth Co. Ltd.* (1865) 11
     H.L.Cas. 523, H.L.(E.).
Kark (Norman) Publications Ltd. v. *Odhams Press Ltd.* [1962] 1 W.L.R.
     380; [1962] 1 All E.R. 636 [1962] R.P.C. 163.
Reddaway & Co. Ltd. v. *Banham & Co. Ltd.* [1896] A.C. 199, H.L.(E.).
Slazenger & Sons v. *Feltham & Co.* (1889) 6 R.P.C. 531, C.A.   D
Spalding (A.G.) and Brothers v. *A. W. Gamage Ltd.* (1915) 32 R.P.C. 273;
     84 L.J. Ch. 449, H.L.(E.).
Victoria Park Racing and Recreation Grounds Co. Ltd. v. *Taylor* (1937)
     58 C.L.R. 479.
Warnink (Erven) Besloten Vennootschap v. *J. Townend & Sons (Hull)*
     Ltd. [1979] A.C. 731; [1979] 3 W.L.R. 68; [1979] 2 All E.R. 927,
     H.L.(E.).   E

The following additional cases were cited in argument:

Ash (Claudius) Sons & Co. Ltd. v. *Invicta Manufacturing Co. Ltd* (1911)
     28 R.P.C. 252; 28 R.P.C. 597, C.A.; (1912) 29 R.P.C. 465 H.L.(E.).
Attorney-General for Trinidad and Tobago v. *Eriché* [1893] A.C. 518,
     P.C.
Australian Consolidated Press Ltd. v. *Uren* [1969] 1 A.C. 590; [1967] 3   F
     W.L.R. 1338; [1967] 3 All E.R. 523, P.C.
Australian Woollen Mills Ltd. v. *F. S. Walton and Co. Ltd.* (1937) 58
     C.L.R. 641.
Baxter v. *Commissioners of Taxation, New South Wales* (1907) 4 C.L.R.
     1087.
Bear (Thomas) & Sons (India) Ltd. v. *Prayag Narain & Jagennath* (1940)
     58 R.P.C. 25, P.C.   G
Beaudesert Shire Council v. *Smith* (1966) 120 C.L.R. 145.
Benmax v. *Austin Motor Co. Ltd.* [1955] A.C. 370; [1955] 2 W.L.R. 418;
     [1955] 1 All E.R. 326, H.L.(E.).
Burberrys v. *J. C. Cording & Co. Ltd.* (1909) 26 R.P.C. 693.
Burger King Corporation v. *Registrar of Trade Marks* (1973) 128 C.L.R.
     417.
Cellular Clothing Co. Ltd. v. *Maxton & Murray* [1899] A.C. 326,   H
     H.L.(Sc.).
Chemical Corporation of America v. *Anheuser-Busch Inc.* (1962) 306 F. 2d
     774.
Christy & Co. v. *Tipper & Son* (1904) 21 R.P.C. 97.
Connecticut Fire Insurance Co. v. *Kavanagh* [1892] A.C. 473, P.C.
Con-Stan Industries Pty. Ltd. v. *Satinique Corporation Pty. Ltd.* (1969)
     91 W.N. (N.S.W.) 563.
F.M.C. Engineering Pty. Ltd. v. *F.M.C. (Australia) Ltd.* [1966] V.R. 529.

A   *Fairfax (John) & Sons Pty. Ltd.* v. *Australian Consolidated Press Ltd.*
    [1960] S.R. (N.S.W.) 413.
    Flexitized Inc. v. *National Flexitized Corporation* (1964) 335 F. 2d 774.
    General Electric Co. (of U.S.A.) v. *General Electric Co. Ltd.* [1972] 1
        W.L.R. 729; [1972] 2 All E.R. 507, H.L.(E.).
    Gilbey (W. & A.) Ltd. v. *Continental Liqueurs Pty. Ltd.* (1960) 103 C.L.R.
        406.
B   *Harrods Ltd.* v. *R. Harrod Ltd.* (1923) 41 R.P.C. 74, C.A.
    Hexagon Pty. Ltd. v. *Australian Broadcasting Commission* [1976] R.P.C.
        628.
    Hunter Douglas Australia Pty. Ltd. v. *Perma Blinds* (1970) 122 C.L.R. 49.
    Lansell v. *Lansell* (1964) 110 C.L.R. 353.
    Leahy, Kelly and Leahy v. *Glover* (1893) 10 R.P.C. 141, H.L.(E.).
    Marengo v. *Daily Sketch and Sunday Graphic Ltd.* (1948) 65 R.P.C. 242,
C   H.L.(E.).
    Oertli (T.) A.G. v. *E. J. Bowman (London) Ltd.* [1957] R.P.C. 388, C.A.;
        [1959] R.P.C. 1, H.L.(E.).
    O'Sullivan v. *Noarlunga Meat Ltd.* [1957] A.C. 1; [1956] 3 W.L.R. 436;
        [1956] 3 All E.R. 177, P.C.
    *Perpetual Executors Trustees and Agency Co. (W.A.) Ltd., as Executor
        of the will of Patrick Andrew Conolly, decd.* v. *Maslen and Com-
        monwealth of Australia* [1952] A.C. 215, P.C.
D   *Philco Corporation* v. *Phillips MFG Co.* (1943) 133 F. 2d 663.
    Pioneer Express Pty. Ltd. v. *Hotchkiss* (1958) 101 C.L.R. 536.
    Plomien Fuel Economiser Co. Ltd. v. *National School of Salesmanship Ltd.*
        (1943) 60 R.P.C. 209, Morton J. and C.A.
    Reg. v. *Green; Ex parte Cheung Cheuk To* (1965) 113 C.L.R. 506.
    Samuelson v. *Producers' Distributing Co. Ltd.* [1932] 1 Ch. 201, C.A.
    Schweppes Ltd. v. *Gibbens* (1904) 22 R.P.C. 113, Warrington J. and C.A.
E   *Society of Motor Manufacturers and Traders Ltd.* v. *Motor Manufac-
        turers' and Traders Mutual Insurance Co. Ltd.* [1925] Ch. 675, C.A.
    Southern Cross Refrigerating Co. v. *Toowoomba Foundry Pty. Ltd.* (1954)
        91 C.L.R. 592.
    Triangle Publications Inc. v. *New England Newspaper Publishing Co.*
        (1942) 46 Fed.Supp. 198.
    Vandervell's Trusts (No. 2), In re [1974] Ch. 269; [1974] 3 W.L.R. 256;
F   [1974] 3 All E.R. 205, C.A.
    Warren v. *Coombes* (1979) 53 A.L.J.R. 293.
    Willard King Organisation Pty. Ltd. v. *United Telecasters Sydney Ltd.*
        (unreported) January 12, 1970, Supreme Court of New South Wales.

APPEAL (No. 5 of 1980) from a judgment given on August 8, 1978,
by Powell J. in the Supreme Court of New South Wales, Equity Division
G by which he dismissed an action brought by the plaintiffs, Cadbury-
Schweppes Pty. Ltd., Tarax Drinks Holdings Ltd., Tarax Drinks Pty. Ltd.
and Tarax Pty. Ltd., against the defendant, Pub Squash Co. Pty. Ltd., for
damages in respect of passing off and unfair trading, for an account of
profits, for an order for rectification of the Register of Trade Marks by
expungement of the defendant's trade mark and for an injunction to
restrain the defendant from using the name " Pub Squash " as the name
H for any soft drink produced or sold by it.
    The facts are stated in the judgment.

    L. J. Priestley Q.C. and *P. G. Hely* (both of the New South Wales Bar)
for the plaintiffs.
    C. J. Bannon Q.C. and *S. M. P. Reeves* (both of the New South Wales
Bar) for the defendant.

                                        Cur. adv. vult.

October 13.   The judgment of their Lordships was delivered by LORD A
SCARMAN.

Two questions arise in this appeal from the Supreme Court of
New South Wales, Equity Division.   One, which goes to the merits
of the dispute, is whether the appellants, who are the plaintiffs in the
suit, have established a cause of action in tort against the defendant.
The tort alleged is that which is known to lawyers as passing off one's
own goods as the goods of another.   The second question is whether B
Her Majesty in Council has jurisdiction to entertain the appeal.   The trial
judge, Powell J. found against the plaintiffs on the first question.   He
did not consider, nor was it any part of his duty to consider, the second
question; for it could not arise until the plaintiffs sought leave to appeal
to Her Majesty in Council.   Counsel, for reasons which will later emerge,
developed the case on the merits before they turned to the question of C
jurisdiction.   It will be convenient for their Lordships to take the same
course.

The history

The full story is well and, as counsel admit, accurately told by Powell J.
Their Lordships, therefore, extract from his narrative only the critical
events.   The plaintiffs are members of the Cadbury Schweppes Australian D
group of companies.   The defendant company which was incorporated in
1973, came under control of a Mr. P. R. Brooks in 1974, when he acquired
its shares.   Originally Langeath Pty. Ltd., the defendant company
changed its name, when Mr. Brooks acquired control, to Passiona
Marketers Pty. Ltd.   In 1976 there was another change of name to the
Pub Squash Co. Pty. Ltd. E

In 1973 the plaintiffs decided upon a new strategy to increase their
share of the market in soft drinks in Australia.   They would develop a
new product to compete with Coca-Cola.   It was to be of a different
flavour from Cola.   They selected as their product a lemon squash, which
Powell J. described as " a type of soft drink commonly accepted in hotels
and licensed clubs and restaurants as an occassional alternative to beer."
It was to be presented as a man's drink, fit for, and a favourite with, F
rugged masculine adventurers.   The advertising campaign was to stress
its masculinity and at the same time to awake happy memories of the
sort of squash hotels and bars in the past used to make.   The two themes
of manliness and pubs were reflected in the name of the product and its
get-up.   They named it " Solo " and designed a medallion type of label
very similar to the labels on beer sold in Australia.   It was to be put up G
in cans and bottles, but especially cans, for which they chose a distinctive
greenish yellow colour.

A major feature in launching the new product was a television and
radio advertising campaign.   Their Lordships would not seek to better
Powell J.'s description of this campaign.   They (i.e. the commercials)
were, he said, as follows: H

"(i) *Television Commercial.*   The bulk of this commercial was
devoted to action shots (accompanied by dramatic background music)
of a rugged lone male canoeist shooting the rapids in a single kayak,
attention being focused upon the potential dangers, such as rocky
outcrops, bends, eddies, and the like upon the run down the rapids.
At the conclusion of the run, the canoeist pushes his kayak ashore.
He then reaches into a portable ice-box and, having taken out and

A opened a can of ' Solo,' gulps it down. While he is drinking, a ' voice-over ' announcer says ' You've never tasted a lemon drink like " Solo " before . . . unless it was one of those great lemon squashes that pubs used to make . . . extra tang . . . not too many bubbles . . .'. As he drinks, the canoeist spills some of the liquid down his chin. He finishes his drink with a smile and wipes his chin

B with the back of his hand. The ' voice-over ' announcer says, and, as well, there is flashed on the screen, the words ' " Solo "—a man's drink.' "

" (ii) *Radio Commercials.* Although the first two radio commercials were not precisely identified, it seems that they were in or to the following effect: (A) ' You hear the sound first . . . the hairs on the back of your neck rise. And you're into the white water. It's

C not so much the rocks you see that bother ya. It's the ones ya can't see. You've only a thin skin of fibreglass under you and no time to think. Just react. And all the time you're building up a " Solo " thirst. " Solo " lemon. With all the tang of those great lemon squashes that pubs used to make. " Solo " lemon. A man's drink.' (B) ' Remember those lemon squashes the pubs used to make? Dry, hard extra tang. Today, Tarax have captured that true lemon squash

D in " Solo." " Solo " is the lemon drink you can quaff straight down without too many bubbles getting in the way of your thirst. Just like the lemon squashes you remember. " Solo " lemon. A man's drink.' "

The initial launch was in Victoria and Queensland during the summer months of 1974. Television and radio advertising began in the two states

E in December 1973 and continued, with a break in January 1974, until the end of May 1974. It was backed up by a drive to introduce the product to supermarkets, hotels, and other retail outlets. The advertising material used in the drive including such descriptions as " Great product, research proven, just like the old Pub Squash." By the end of May or June in 1974 the limited initial launch was considered a success and it was decided

F to launch the product nation-wide in the coming spring. Radio advertising was resumed in July 1974 and television advertising in September when the product went on sale. Again, by way of back-up, there was the distribution of advertising material to the trade. The cost of the advertising represented a very substantial investment in the product; television and radio advertising in 1974 alone cost some $300,000. As the national campaign developed, the theme of the lone male adventurer was further

G elaborated. Viewers were introduced to a lone sailor fighting his way through boiling surf in a catamaran, and two virile men battling it out in a squash court. Lone masculine endeavour was the theme supporting the name " Solo." Meanwhile the " audio " in television and the radio broadcasts maintained the other theme, nostalgia for " those great lemon squashes the pubs used to make." The product sold well. The advertising

H programme continued throughout 1975, television cost over $400,000 and radio over $160,000 in that year. New rugged men arrived on television: amongst others, a big-game fisherman, a horse-breaker and wrestlers. The nostalgic pub squash theme continued to sound in the ears of viewers and listeners. The trial judge summed up the success of the campaign in these words:

" . . . the impact of this advertising campaign, and, in particular, of the television advertising campaign, appears to have been quite

remarkable. Nearly every witness who was called, whether by the A
plaintiffs or the defendant, recalled the television advertisements,
particularly the first, and the incident of the canoeist spilling some of
the drink down his chin, and many recalled the slogan ' a great
squash like the pubs used to make ' and ' a man's drink,' although
not all the witnesses associated the former slogan with ' Solo '."

Advertising " Solo " continued along the same lines in 1976 and 1977: B
but in September 1976 the pub motif disappeared, sound as well as vision
now concentrating on " a man's drink " and the word " Solo."

On April 8, 1975, the defendant launched on the market its product
" Pub Squash." Full-scale production did not, however, begin until
June 1975. A television advertising programme, modest when compared
with that of the plaintiffs, began at the end of April. Its theme was, as
was that for " Solo," heroically masculine (" The Million Dollar Man ") C
and the audio was similarly nostalgic, the hero after his endeavours
ripping into a " pub " lemon soda squash. The label on the product was
of a medallion type upon which the name " Pub Squash " appeared in
bold red letters. The cans in which it was sold were of the same size and
the same shade of yellow as those in which " Solo " was put up. On May
6, 1975, the defendant applied to register its " Pub Squash " label as a D
trade mark; and on September 6, 1976, it was registered in class 32
No. B.286,987. The competition from " Pub Squash " and certain other
lemon squashes which entered the market in 1975 had its effect upon the
sales of " Solo ". They were 15 per cent. lower in 1976 than they had
been in 1975. The plaintiffs believed (and the belief was not unreasonable)
that the advent of " Pub Squash," timed as it was to take advantage of
their advertising campaign, put up in not dissimilar cans, and accompanied E
by its own advertising campaign stressing its high favour with stalwart
men and evoking the memory of the pub squashes of the past, was a
substantial cause of the drop in the sales of " Solo." On June 1, 1977,
they instituted these proceedings, claiming damages or an account of
profits and an injunction in respect of passing off, and the expungement
from the register of the defendant's " Pub Squash " trade mark. By a F
later amendment they added a claim in respect of unfair trading.

The appeal on the merits

It is unnecessary to explore the law in any depth, because it is now
accepted by both sides that the issue in the case is whether in promoting
its product the defendant so confused or deceived the market that it
passed its product off as the product of the plaintiffs. Nevertheless the G
case presents one feature which is not to be found in the earlier case law.
The passing off of which the plaintiffs complain depends to a large
extent upon the deliberate adoption by the defendant of an advertising
campaign based on themes and slogans closely related to those which the
plaintiffs had developed and made familiar to the market in the radio
and television advertising of their product. Does confusion or deception, H
if it be shown to arise from such an advertising campaign, amount to a
passing off? To answer the question it is necessary to consider the modern
character of the tort.

In *Erven Warnink Besloten Vennootschap* v. *J. Townend & Sons (Hull)
Ltd.* [1979] A.C. 731 (the *Advocaat* case) the House of Lords formulated,
so far as the law of England is concerned, the modern principle which
governs the tortious liability compendiously described as passing off. The

A facts of that case bear no resemblance to the present case: but the declarations of principle to be found in the speeches of Lord Diplock and Lord Fraser of Tullybelton are of general application. At p. 741 Lord Diplock found a rational basis for the modern tort in the speech of Lord Parker in *A. G. Spalding and Brothers* v. *A. W. Gamage Ltd.* (1915) 84 L.J. Ch. 449, 450, where he identified the right protected by the tort as the " property in the business or goodwill likely to be injured by the

B misrepresentation." The significance of *A. G. Spalding and Brothers* v. *A. W. Gamage Ltd.* Lord Diplock found to lie:

C " . . . in its recognition that misrepresenting one's own goods as the goods of someone else was not a separate genus of actionable wrong but a particular species of wrong included in a wider genus of which a premonitory hint had been given by Lord Herschell in *Reddaway & Co. Ltd.* v. *Banham & Co. Ltd.* [1896] A.C. 199, 211 when, in speaking of the deceptive use of a descriptive term, he said: ' I am unable to see why a man should be allowed *in this way more than in any other* to deceive purchasers into the belief that they are getting what they are not, and thus to filch the business of a rival.' "

D Lord Fraser of Tullybelton at p. 755, stated the principle as being:

" . . . the plaintiff is entitled to protect his right of property in the goodwill attached to a name which is *distinctive* of a product or class of products sold by him in the course of his business." (emphasis supplied).

E The *Advocaat* case was all about a name. But Lord Fraser of Tullybelton did not, any more than did Lord Diplock, limit the principle to the misappropriation of a name. He cited with approval, as also had Lord Diplock, Lord Herschell's speech in *Reddaway & Co. Ltd.* v. *Banham & Co. Ltd.* [1896] A.C. 199, and quoted a passage at p. 209, where Lord Herschell approved the now classic dictum of Lord Kingsdown in *Leather Cloth Co. Ltd.* v. *American Leather Cloth Co. Ltd.* (1865) 11 H.L.Cas. 523, 538 to the effect:

F " The fundamental rule is, that one man has no right to put off his goods for sale as the goods of a rival trader, and he cannot therefore (in the language of Lord Langdale, in the case of *Perry* v. *Truefitt* (1842) 6 Beav. 66, ' be allowed to use names, marks, letters, *or other indicia,* by which he may induce purchasers to believe that the goods which he is selling are the manufacture of another

G person.' " (emphasis supplied).

In *Hornsby Building Information Centre Pty. Ltd.* v. *Sydney Building Information Centre Pty. Ltd.* (1978) 52 A.L.J.R. 392 the High Court of Australia stated the principle in similar terms. Again the case was about a name but Stephen J., with whom Barwick C.J. agreed, formulated the principle in terms which allow of its applicability to " other indicia " than

H the name of the product. But he also sounded a warning as to its application in cases where the descriptive material which the defendant has misappropriated is also applicable to " other like businesses." Stephen J., after referring to the principle that the tort of passing off is essentially an infringement of the " plaintiff's intangible property rights " in the goodwill attaching to his product, went on to say, at pp. 396–397:

" There is a price to be paid for the advantages flowing from the possession of an eloquently descriptive trade name. Because it is

descriptive it is equally applicable to any business of a like kind, its A
very descriptiveness ensures that it is not distinctive of any particular
business and hence its application to other like businesses will not
ordinarily mislead the public. In cases of passing off, where it is
the wrongful appropriation of the reputation of another or that of
his goods that is in question, a plaintiff which uses descriptive words
in its trade name will find that quite small differences in a competitor's
trade name will render the latter immune from action—*Office* B
Cleaning Services Ltd. v. *Westminster Window and General Cleaners
Ltd.* (1946) 63 R.P.C. 39, 42 *per* Lord Simonds. As his Lordship
said at p. 43, the possibility of blunders by members of the public
will always be present when names consist of descriptive words—
' So long as descriptive words are used by two traders as part of their
respective trade names, it is possible that some members of the C
public will be confused whatever the differentiating words may be.'
The risk of confusion must be accepted, to do otherwise is to give
to one who appropriates to himself descriptive words an unfair
monopoly in those words and might even deter others from pursuing
the occupation which the words describe."

He is discussing a name: but what he says about a name may with D
equal force be applied to other descriptive material, if it has given to a
product (or business) a distinctive character.

The width of the principle now authoritatively recognised by the High
Court of Australia and the House of Lords is, therefore, such that the
tort is no longer anchored, as in its early 19th century formulation, to
the name or trade mark of a product or business. It is wide enough to E
encompass other descriptive material, such as slogans or visual images,
which radio, television or newspaper advertising campaigns can lead the
market to associate with a plaintiff's product, provided always that such
descriptive material has become part of the goodwill of the product. And
the test is whether the product has derived from the advertising a
distinctive character which the market recognises. But competition must
remain free: and competition is safeguarded by the necessity for a F
plaintiff to prove that he has built up an " intangible property right "
in the advertised descriptions of his product: or, in other words, that
he has succeeded by such methods in giving his product a distinctive
character accepted by the market. A defendant, however, does no
wrong by entering a market created by another and there competing with
its creator. The line may be difficult to draw: but unless it is drawn, G
competition will be stifled. The test applied by Powell J. in the instant
case was to enquire whether the consuming public was confused or misled
by the get-up, the formula or the advertising of the defendant's product
into thinking that it was the plaintiffs' product. And he held on the
facts that the public was not deceived. Their Lordships do not think that
his approach in law (save in one respect, as will later appear), to the
central problem of the case can be faulted. The real question in the H
appeal is, therefore, one of fact: whether the judge erred in the inferences
he drew from the admitted primary facts.

The plaintiffs' alternative case of unfair trading irrespective of whether
the market was deceived or confused into mistaking the defendant's
product for that of the plaintiffs need not be considered by the Board,
since the plaintiffs now restrict themselves to a case based on such
confusion. For such a case to succeed it would be necessary to show

A that the law of Australia has developed a tort of unfair competition along the lines suggested in the well-known decision of the United States Supreme Court, *International News Services* v. *Associated Press* (1918) 248 U.S. 215, 241–242 in which Pitney J., delivering the majority opinion, said:

B "It is said that the elements of unfair competition are lacking because there is no attempt by defendant to palm off its goods as those of the complainant, characteristic of the most familiar, if not the most typical, cases of unfair competition: *Howe Scale Co.* v. *Wyckoff, Seamans & Benedict*, 198 U.S. 118, 140. But we cannot concede that the right to equitable relief is confined to that class of cases. In the present case the fraud upon complainant's rights is C more direct and obvious. Regarding news matter as the mere material from which these two competing parties are endeavouring to make money, and treating it, therefore, as quasi property for the purposes of their business because they are both selling it as such, defendant's conduct differs from the ordinary case of unfair competition in trade principally in this that, instead of selling its own goods as those of complainant, it substitutes misappropriation D in the place of misrepresentation, and sells complainant's goods as its own."

The development of such a tort has not escaped judicial criticism in the United States of America itself (e.g. Judge Learned Hand, in *Cheney Brothers* v. *Doris Silk Corporation* (1929) 35 F. 2d. 279). It has also been criticised in Australia: see *Victoria Park Racing and Recreation Grounds* E *Co. Ltd.* v. *Taylor* (1937) 58 C.L.R. 479, and, in particular, the criticism offered by Dixon J. at pp. 508–509. Their Lordships prefer to express no opinion on it in a case such as the present where the facts do not require that it be considered.

The hearing before Powell J. occupied some 26 days. Sixty-four witnesses gave evidence, some 30 of whom spoke to the issue of confusion F between the two products. As always in a passing off action the ultimately critical question was one of fact. The critical question in this case proved to be: were customers, or potential customers, led by the similarities in the get-up and advertising of the two products into believing that " Pub Squash " was the plaintiffs' product? Or, if no deception be proved, was there a real probability of deception? Powell J. addressed himself to this question of fact first when considering the claim in passing off, and G secondly when stating his conclusions on the alternative claim of unfair trading. In respect of passing off, he asked himself whether the defendant did sufficiently distinguish its product from " Solo." He answered the question as follows:

". . . it can readily be seen that they are different. This, however, is not necessarily enough, for one must take into account the nature H of the market-place and the habits of ordinary purchasers (see, for example, *Saville Perfumery Ltd.* v. *June Perfect Ltd.* (1914) 58 R.P.C. 147, 174–175; *Tavener Rutledge Ltd.* v. *Specters Ltd.* [1959] R.P.C. 83, 88–89). As I have pointed out earlier, it is not uncommon, albeit that it is not the universal practice, both in supermarkets, and in mixed businesses and milk-bars which have self-selection display refrigerators for products such as ' Solo ' and ' Pub Squash ' to be displayed alongside each other; and in those cases in which they are not, they are, nonetheless displayed in close proximity to A each other. Further, as I have pointed out, the purchase of a soft drink is often a casual transaction. These two features of the market seem to explain most, if not all, of the cases of incorrect selection of which evidence has been given. . . . But even accepting, as I do, that by reason of the nature of the market-place and of the habits of purchasers, mistakes are likely to, and do, in fact, occur, the evidence would seem to demonstrate that in most, although not all, B cases in which there has initially been a wrong selection by a customer, or the wrong product has been offered by the shopkeeper, the error has been recognised before the purchase has been completed. . . . This being so, it seems to me that the defendant has sufficiently differentiated its product from that of the plaintiffs'."

This answer, it is true, related to the effect of get-up as a cause of C confusion and was not addressed to the problems of the advertising campaign. Nor, when he gave it, was the judge directing his attention, let alone making any findings, upon the conduct of Mr. Brooks or any of the other officers of the defendant company in the marketing of their product. When, however, he came to consider the claim of unfair trading, he examined in detail, and made a number of adverse findings upon, their D conduct in the development and marketing of " Pub Squash." He stated his findings and conclusion on this aspect of the case in a remarkable passage which, because it is the key to a full understanding of his judgment, their Lordships quote in full:

" (vii) *Conclusion.* From what I have written above it will appear that it is my view that, as from a time being no later than the later E part of August 1974, the defendant, having by means of one or more of its officers become aware of the successful launch of ' Solo ' in Victoria and of the sale of ' Solo ' in southern New South Wales, and, thus, appreciating that in all probability the Victorian ' launch ' would be followed by a large-scale ' launch ' of ' Solo ' upon the New South Wales market, set out in a deliberate and calculated fashion F to take advantage of the plaintiffs' past efforts in developing ' Solo ' and of the plaintiffs' past and anticipated future efforts in developing a market for a product such as ' Solo,' and that, in particular the defendant, by its officers, sought to copy or to approximate the formula for ' Solo,' and chose a product name and package for the defendant's proposed product derived from, and intended to gain, the benefit of the plaintiffs' past and anticipated advertising campaign, G and the plaintiffs' package for their product.

" Notwithstanding these findings, it is my view, as I have earlier indicated, that, as the facts, as I have earlier found them, do not reveal any relevant misrepresentation on the part of the defendant as to its goods, the plaintiffs have not made out a case for relief based upon the expanded concept of passing off or upon unfair H trading."

Put very shortly, Powell J. concluded that there was no " relevant misrepresentation," no deception or probability of deception. The competition developed by the defendant and its officers took advantage of the plaintiffs' promotion of their own product but never went so far as to suggest that " Pub Squash " was the product of the plaintiffs, or merely another name for " Solo." It might have been expected that he would

A   have inferred from these findings the existence of confusion and the fact of deception: but after a long trial and a detailed examination of the evidence he refused to take the step of drawing the inference. His decision, taken very deliberately and with full awareness of what the defendant and its officers did in promoting their product, is, whether right or wrong, entitled to the greatest respect.

B   Counsel for the plaintiffs accepted that the issue of deception was crucial. In submitting that the judge fell into error, he sought to rely on three points. He submitted first that the judge misled himself by the way in which he " compartmentalised " his judgment; secondly, that he misled himself by an error of law as to the relevant date for establishing the necessary goodwill or reputation of the plaintiffs' product; and thirdly, that his conclusion was contrary to his primary findings of fact.

C   First, the " compartmentalisation " point. The plaintiffs' submission may be summarised as follows. Counsel attributed the error, into which, on his submission, the judge fell, to the structure of the judgment. The judge, as their Lordships have already noted, dealt with the cause of action in passing off first. At that stage he made no findings as to the conduct of the defendant's officers, Mr. Brooks and his colleagues. He found that D   there was no " relevant misrepresentation on the part of the defendant as to its goods " without considering the defendant's intentions. But intention is relevant. Having found no misrepresentation, he then considered the case of unfair trading. He now found as a fact that the defendant set out deliberately to take advantage of the plaintiffs' efforts to develop the market for " Solo "; but this was of no consequence, since he had already found no deception or misrepresentation. Had Powell J. E   appreciated that the case must be considered as a whole, and not in separate compartments, he would have had regard to the defendant's intention in determining whether there was deception or the probability of deception; and, had he done so, only one conclusion was possible: namely, that the defendant was passing off its goods as the goods of the plaintiffs. This is a formidable submission.

F   Where an intention to deceive is found, it is not difficult for the court to infer that the intention has been, or in all probability will be, effective: *Slazenger & Sons* v. *Feltham & Co.* (1889) 6 R.P.C. 531, 538 *per* Lindley L.J. But in dealing with the issue of deception Powell J. directed himself correctly and made the comment, which is also good law, that:

G   " . . . the court must be on its guard against finding fraud *merely* because there has been an imitation of another's goods, get-up, method of trading or trading style (see, for example, *Goya Ltd.* v. *Gala of London Ltd.* (1952) 69 R.P.C. 188)."

After a very careful consideration of the judgment as a whole, their Lordships do not think that in the arrangement of the subject matter of H   his judgment the judge allowed himself to overlook the importance, subject to safeguards, of a defendant's intention when deciding the issue of deception.

        Once it is accepted that the judge was not unmindful of the defendant's deliberate purpose (as he found) to take advantage of the plaintiffs' efforts to develop " Solo," the finding of " no deception " can be seen to be very weighty: for he has reached it, notwithstanding his view of the defendant's purpose. But it is also necessary to bear in mind the nature

of the purpose found by the judge. He found that the defendant did   A
sufficiently distinguish its goods from those of the plaintiffs. The intention was not to pass off the defendant's goods as those of the plaintiffs
but to take advantage of the market developed by the advertising
campaign for " Solo." Unless it can be shown that in so doing the
defendant infringed " the plaintiffs' intangible property rights " in the
goodwill attaching to their product, there is no tort: for such infringement
is the foundation of the tort: see Stephen J., in *Hornsby Building*   B
Information Centre Pty. Ltd. v. *Sydney Building Information Centre Pty.*
Ltd. (1978) 52 A.L.J.R. 392, 396. In their Lordships' view, therefore, the
first submission fails. And, once the conclusion is reached that the judge
did not allow the structure of his judgment to mislead him, the submission
recoils upon itself. The finding of the judge becomes, by its rejection,
immensely strengthened.   C

The second submission is less formidable. Powell J., it is conceded,
misdirected himself in holding that the relevant date for determining
whether a plaintiff has established the necessary goodwill or reputation of
his product is the date of the commencement of the proceedings (i.e.
June 1, 1977). The relevant date is, in law, the date of the commencement of the conduct complained of, i.e. April 8, 1975, when the defendant   D
began to market " Pub Squash ": *Norman Kark Publications Ltd.* v.
Odhams Press Ltd. [1962] 1 W.L.R. 380. Despite his error, the judge
did direct his mind to the facts as they were in " the early months of
1975." He found that by then " Solo " had attained a significant level of
recognition and acceptance in the market and went on to consider, and
make findings upon, " the nature and extent of the goodwill and reputation which ' Solo ' had, *by early 1975* (emphasis supplied,) attained, and   E
which it thereafter maintained." This submission, therefore fails.

Their Lordships now turn to the main attack upon the judge's conclusion. His primary findings, which the plaintiffs accept, should, it is
submitted, have led him to conclude that there was confusion amongst
buyers and deception by the defendant. The judge's analysis of the
nature of the goodwill or distinctive reputation which " Solo " had
acquired by April 1975 cannot, in their Lordships' view, be challenged.   F
The reputation he found to be that of:

> " a lemon squash type of soft drink, marketed under the name of
> ' Solo,' packaged, principally in yellow cans bearing a rondel-like or
> medallion-like device . . ., and widely advertised on television by
> advertisements featuring a rugged masculine figure."
                                                                       G
He was not, however, persuaded that *any of the variants* upon the phrase
" those great old squashes like the pubs used to make " and " a man's
drink " were generally associated with " Solo " (emphasis supplied). He
based his negative conclusion upon his understanding of the evidence of
" the confusion witnessess," especially those members of the consuming
public, who were called, and upon his view of the nature and effect of
the advertisements for " Solo," of which he said that: H

> " he had regard to two particular features . . . namely: the fact that
> television is principally a visual medium so that the ' audio ' tends to
> have less impact than the visual image, and, secondly, the fact that,
> no matter what variation be worked upon it, the phrase ' those great
> old squashes the pubs used to make ' is essentially descriptive of the
> *type* of product advertised—it does not, of itself, *identify,* or denote

A   the origin of, the product being advertised. (cf. and cp. the slogan in issue in *Chemical Corporation of America* v. *Anheuser-Busch Inc.* (1962) 306 F. 2d 433."

The plaintiffs' challenge is to the negative conclusion. In their Lordships' opinion, it fails to displace either the judge's inference, based on his analysis of the nature of the market in which the two products were sold,

B or his finding that the advertising of " Pub Squash," intended though it was to win a share of the market from its competitor " Solo," led to no significant confusion or deception. He accepted that on occasions there was confusion at the point of sale: but he found, and there was plenty of evidence on which he could find, that the confusion was almost always corrected before the moment of sale. Such confusion as there was arose,

C in his view, from the casual attitude of many purchasers in the market to the product offered and not from any failure of the defendant sufficiently to distinguish its product from " Solo." He found that " the principal, if not the only, part of the market in which the wrong product has been selected or given, is in relation to cans." He saw the two cans: he refused to hold that, because " Solo " became known as being sold in yellow cans, it " thereby became entitled to a monopoly " of sale or that the

D mere fact the defendant adopted a yellow can for its product dictated a finding of passing off. He was unable, on the evidence, to find that the consuming public associated yellow cans only with " Solo." Nevertheless, the judge recognised that the similarity in size and shape of can (which was a stock size and shape in the trade), and in colour made it " incumbent " upon the defendant to distinguish its package from that

E of " Solo." He looked at the cans and commented that " it can readily be seen that they are different " and then proceeded to analyse the market and the effect of such confusion as there was in the way already described.

When the judge turned to consider the effect of the radio and television advertising, he rejected the submission that either of the two themes used in these media had become the property of the plaintiffs in the sense in which the word " property " is used in this class of case. They were

F descriptive of the product (perhaps even " eloquently descriptive "), but never became a distinguishing feature. There was ample evidence to support his rejection of this submission, and their Lordships are in no position to substitute for his assessment of the effect of the " Solo " advertising campaign a different assessment or to challenge his analysis of the market, i.e. the character of the buying public.

G In reaching his conclusion of fact that the defendant had " sufficiently " distinguished its product from " Solo," the judge had not only to conduct an elaborate and detailed analysis of the evidence, which he certainly did, but to bear in mind the necessity in this branch of the law of the balance to be maintained between the protection of a plaintiff's investment in his product and the protection of free competition. It is only if a plaintiff can establish that a defendant has invaded his " intangible property right "

H in his product by misappropriating descriptions which have become recognised by the market as distinctive of the product that the law will permit competition to be restricted. Any other approach would encourage monopoly. The new, small man would increasingly find his entry into an existing market obstructed by the large traders already well known as operating in it.

For these reasons their Lordships are of the opinion that the appeal fails, even if it be competent: the question to which they now turn.

Cadbury-Schweppes v. Pub Squash Co. (P.C.)   [1981]

The question of jurisdiction   A

By their statement of claim the plaintiffs raised a question of federal
law, i.e. the validity or otherwise of the defendant's registered trade mark,
and sought the expungement of the trade mark from the register.
Powell J., though a state judge, undoubtedly possessed the necessary
federal jurisdiction to deal with the trade mark question: and, if he did
so, no appeal would lie to Her Majesty in Council. Final appeal in such a   B
case would lie only to the High Court: section 39 (2) of the Judiciary Act
1903–1973. The only exception would be if the High Court itself should
certify (which in this case it has not done) that the question is one which
ought to be determined by Her Majesty in Council: article 74 of the
Constitution. The defendant submits that the judge was exercising his
federal jurisdiction and that no appeal lies, therefore, to Her Majesty
in Council. The judge ruled, it is submitted, upon the question *even*   C
though he did not expressly deal with it.

The propositions of constitutional law, to which their Lordships have
briefly referred, are, of course, not in dispute: nor is it disputed that the
trade mark question was raised upon the pleadings. But the plaintiffs
say that the question was not litigated at trial and that, by consent, the
judge confined himself to the issue of liability, which the judge clearly   D
understood to be that of passing off. The federal question was, therefore,
it is submitted, not adjudicated upon: on the contrary, the judge confined
himself to the issue of passing off, which was within his state jurisdiction.
The very late appearance of the point strongly suggests that neither the
parties nor the judge regarded the trial as directed to any issue other than
that of passing off. If the point were going to be raised, the time to raise
it was when the plaintiffs sought leave to appeal. But the defendant did   E
not raise it until it lodged its written case. The point has no merits and,
were it not one of jurisdiction, would be rejected out of hand.

But, since it goes to the competence of the Board to entertain the
appeal, the submission of the defendant must be considered. The issue is
whether, the trade mark question having been raised and never abandoned,
the trial judge must be held to have been exercising his federal jurisdiction   F
when dealing with the case. The submission that he must be held to have
been doing so largely rested on the decision of the High Court in *Felton* v.
Mulligan (1971) 124 C.L.R. 367, and in particular upon the following
passage in the judgment of Barwick C.J. at p. 374:

> " The critical question in the case is whether the defence did involve
> the exercise of federal jurisdiction by the Supreme Court. It would   G
> do so if the matter before the Supreme Court became or involved
> by reason of the defence raised to the applicant's claim, either wholly
> or partly a matter arising under a law made by the Parliament. . . .
> Further the matter arising under a law of the Parliament will have
> arisen if the suit could have been disposed of by deciding the matter,
> whether or not the suit was so disposed of. . . . It is of course not
> enough that a law made by the Parliament must be construed in the   H
> course of the decision of the case. There must be a matter arising
> under a law of the Parliament."

In their Lordships' view the question is one of legal policy which is
pre-eminently a matter for the High Court to determine. Their Lordships
would not, therefore, express an opinion unless it were necessary for a
decision in the appeal. In the present case the necessity does not arise.

A   For the reasons given in considering the plaintiffs' claim based on passing off their Lordships are able to advise Her Majesty that the appeal be dismissed without having to rule on the point so belatedly raised by the defendant as to its competence.   Accordingly, they humbly advise Her Majesty that the appeal be dismissed with costs.

B   Solicitors: *Stephenson, Harwood; Slaughter & May.*

                                                           T. J. M.

C   [COURT OF APPEAL]

              * ARMAR SHIPPING CO. LTD. *v.* CAISSE ALGERIENNE
                      D'ASSURANCE ET DE REASSURANCE

                            [1979 A. No. 3105]

D   1980   July 17, 18; 31   Megaw, Eveleigh and Oliver L.JJ.

Conflict of Laws—Contract—Proper law—Lloyd's average bond—
  Bond not specifying governing law—Bill of lading specifying
  that general average to be adjusted at such place as shipowners
  might select—Shipowners selecting London—Whether English
  law proper law—Whether shipowners' selection of London rele-
  vant—Whether proper law to be ascertained from circumstances
E   *at time of making of contract—R.S.C., Ord. 11, r. 1 (1) (f) (iii)*

        By a time charterparty dated February 6, 1973, the plain-
    tiffs, Cypriot shipowners, chartered a vessel to a Cuban com-
    pany. The charterparty included a London arbitration clause
    and a provision that general average would be settled and
    adjusted in London according to the York-Antwerp Rules 1950.
    Under the charterparty, parcels of sugar were shipped at
F   Havana for carriage to Santander, Spain, and Mostagenem,
    Algeria. The bills of lading did not incorporate the charter-
    party terms. Clause 10 of each provided that general average
    should be adjusted, stated and settled, according to the York-
    Antwerp Rules, except rule XXII, at such port or place as
    might be selected by the plaintiffs. It was not contended that
    the proper law of the bills of lading was English law. During
    the voyage, the vessel grounded off Santander. The plaintiffs
    contended that they thereby incurred sacrifices and expenditures
G   of a general average nature in order to enable the voyage to
    be completed. At Mostagenem, a Lloyd's average bond in
    English was signed by the master of the vessel on behalf of
    the plaintiffs and by the defendants, an Algerian company, as
    insurers of the Algerian consignees, the defendants adding a
    reservation in French. It was not disputed that the defendants,
    who had not been parties to the bill of lading, thereby became
H   parties to the contract contained in the bond. The bond con-
    tained no express provision as to the law that was to govern
    the contract contained in it, nor any provision for arbitration
    in London or submission to the jurisdiction of the English
    courts. Subsequently, pursuant to clause 10 of the bill of
    lading, the plaintiffs arranged for general average to be adjusted
    in London, and the adjustment was published in London on
    February 14, 1977, showing that a contribution was due to the
    plaintiffs from cargo. They issued a writ against the defendants
    in England claiming £52,420·18 as their contribution. Robert

208

Goff J. granted leave ex parte to serve notice of the writ on the A defendants out of the jurisdiction. The defendants applied for the order to be set aside. Mustill J. declined to do so, holding that the contract between the plaintiffs and the defendants contained in the Lloyd's average bond was, by implication, governed by English law, so that R.S.C., Ord. 11, r. 1 (1) (f) (iii) applied.[1] He said that, in the particular circumstances of the case, where there was a contract of carriage to which the consignees were parties and where pursuant to that contract B English law had become the law of the adjustment, and thence the law governing the liability of the consignees to make contribution in general average, and where the defendants had taken on a primary obligation to pay the sum assessed as the amount for which contribution was to be made, it could properly be said that English law was the system of law with which the bond was most closely concerned: the proper law could be regarded as having been " floating " until the plaintiffs had C selected the place of adjustment.

On appeal by the defendants: —

Held, allowing the appeal, that the proper law of a contract had to be ascertainable at the time of the making of the contract; that the fact that the plaintiffs had subsequently decided, in pursuance of their right under clause 10 of the bill of lading, that general average adjustment should take place in London could not be a relevant factor in determining D the proper law of the contract contained in the Lloyd's average bond; that nothing else in the facts and circumstances of the case, including the use of English and the word " Lloyd's " in the heading of the bond, was sufficient to make English law the governing law of the contract, or to make the English system of law that with which it had its closest and most real connection; and that, accordingly, the order for leave to serve notice of the writ out of the jurisdiction should be set E aside (post, pp. 213C–E, 215H—216C, G–H).

Per curiam. It it were possible, or permissible, to conceive that such a contract might have different governing laws according to which particular contractual provision was relevant to the particular dispute, the English court could not properly treat it—for it must be the whole contract as a single entity—as governed by English law for the purposes of assuming extraterritorial jurisdiction (post, p. 216F–G). F

Decision of Mustill J. reversed.

No cases are referred to in the judgments.

The following cases were cited in argument:

Compagnie Tunisienne de Navigation S.A. v. *Compagnie d'Armement Maritime S.A.* [1971] A.C. 572; [1970] 3 W.L.R. 389; [1970] 3 All G E.R. 71, H.L.(E.).

Rossano v. *Manufacturers' Life Assurance Co.* [1963] 2 Q.B. 352; [1962] 3 W.L.R. 157; [1962] 2 All E.R. 214.

Schothorst and Schuitema v. *Franz Dauter G.m.b.H.* [1973] 2 Lloyd's Rep. 91.

INTERLOCUTORY APPEAL from Mustill J.　　　　　　　　　　　　　　H

On October 5, 1979, the plaintiffs, Armar Shipping Co. Ltd., of Famagusta, Cyprus, obtained leave ex parte from Robert Goff J. in

[1] R.S.C., Ord. 11, r. 1: " (1) . . . service of a writ, or notice of a writ, out of the jurisdiction is permissible with the leave of the court in the following cases, that is to say— . . . (f) if the action begun by the writ is brought against a defendant . . . to enforce, . . . a contract, . . . being . . . a contract which— . . . (iii) is by its terms, or by implication, governed by English law; . . ."

A   chambers under R.S.C., Ord. 11 to issue a writ and to serve notice of it in Algeria on the defendants, Caisse Algérienne D'Assurance et de Réassurance. By the writ, dated October 8, 1979, the plaintiffs' claim was for general average contributions in accordance with the statement of general average prepared by a firm of average adjusters dated London, February 14, 1977, in which general average expenditures and sacrifices arising from the stranding of the m.v. *Armar* off Santander on April 17,

B   1974, had been apportioned between the parties pursuant to the undertaking in the form of a general average bond in which the defendants had undertaken and had wrongly and in breach of the undertaking not paid the sum of U.S.$115,492·15 (£52,420·18) as established in the statement of general average together with interest according to statute and costs.

C   The defendants applied to Mustill J. in chambers for the order of Robert Goff J. to be set aside, on the ground that the plaintiffs' claim did not fall within any of the categories listed in R.S.C., Ord. 11, r. 1 (1) and that in any event the court should not in its discretion choose to exercise discretion over the matter. Mustill J., on April 2, 1980, dismissed the defendants' application.

D   The defendants appealed, on the grounds that the judge had misdirected himself in holding that the contract between the parties was a contract impliedly governed by English law and in holding that the case was a proper one for service of notice of the writ out of the jurisdiction.
        The facts are set out in the judgment of Megaw L.J.

E   *Peregrin Simon* for the defendants.
        Stewart Boyd for the plaintiffs.

Cur. adv. vult.

July 31.   The following judgments were read.

F   MEGAW L.J.   This appeal from an order of Mustill J. of April 2, 1980, is concerned with the question whether leave should be given to the plaintiffs, Armar Shipping Co. Ltd., a shipowning company in Cyprus, to serve notice of a writ out of the jurisdiction on the intended defendants, Caisse Algérienne d'Assurance et de Réassurance, an Algerian company. Mustill J. granted leave. The defendants (I shall for brevity omit the word " intended ") appeal to this court.

G   The issue arises on R.S.C., Ord. 11, r. 1 (1) (*f*) (iii). Leave may be given to serve out of the jurisdiction, under that paragraph, where the action is brought on a contract which " is by its terms, or by implication, governed by English law." The contract here in question is contained in a Lloyd's average bond which was signed on behalf of the plaintiffs and the defendants on May 24, 1974.
        The plaintiffs own a vessel, the *Armar*. By a charterparty dated

H   February 6, 1973, they chartered the *Armar* for 20 months to a Cuban company, Empresa Cubana de Fletes. The charterparty included a London arbitration clause and a provision that general average would be settled and adjusted in London according to the York-Antwerp Rules 1950. It is agreed that those charterparty provisions do not affect the issue with which we are concerned. Perhaps unusually, the charterparty terms were not incorporated into the bill of lading contract, to which I shall refer hereafter. We, therefore, do not have to consider what the decision should

have been in the present case if the charterparty terms had been incor-   A
porated.

Under the charterparty, a cargo of sugar was shipped at Havana for
carriage to Santander in Spain and to Mostagenem in Algeria. There were,
of course, separate bills of lading for the parcels of cargo destined to
those different destinations. The bill of lading which was before the court
was that of the parcel destined to Mostagenem. Mustill J. was prepared   B
to hold that, apart from quantity and destination, there would be no
material difference in the terms of the two contracts of carriage, if and
in so far as those terms might be relevant to the issue which he had to
decide.

A question was raised before us in the submissions on behalf of the
defendants as to the proper law of the bill of lading contract. It would
seem that this had not been raised in the arguments before Mustill J.   C
I do not know what the answer to that question would be; but I do not
think that it matters for the decision of the present issue. No one suggests
that it is English law.

As I have said, the bill of lading did not incorporate the charterparty
terms. The only part of the bill of lading contract which, on the submissions, might be relevant is the first paragraph of clause 10. It reads: D

"General average shall be adjusted, stated and settled, according to
York-Antwerp Rules 1950, except rule XXII thereof, at such port
or place as may be selected by the carrier. Matters not provided for
by these rules to be adjusted, stated and settled according to the laws
and usages at such port or place as may be selected by the carrier."

"The carrier" in this provision is the plaintiff shipowner.   E

On the face of the bill of lading, against "Consignee" appear the
words "To order"; and then, against the printed words "Notify (if con-
signed to shipper's order)," were typed the initials O.N.A.C.O., with an
address in Algeria. It is not in dispute that O.N.A.C.O. are to be regarded
as the consignees and, at the relevant time, the owners of the parcel of
sugar as purchasers, directly or indirectly from the shippers, even though   F
no endorsement appears on the copy of the bill of lading before the court.
They obtained their title, as purchasers, by transfer to them of the bill of
lading.

During the voyage, on April 17, 1974, the vessel grounded off Santander. It is asserted by the owners, the plaintiffs, that they incurred
sacrifices and expenditures of a general average nature in order to enable
the voyage to be completed. The parcel destined to Santander was dis-   G
charged at that port. The vessel went on to Mostagenem.

At Mostagenem, before the cargo was delivered to O.N.A.C.O. and,
no doubt, as a condition of the plaintiffs not exercising a lien in respect
of a claim for general average contribution, a Lloyd's average bond was
signed on May 24, 1974. It was signed by the master on behalf of the
shipowners, the plaintiffs. In the schedule, which contains columns in   H
which are identified (i) the number of the bill of lading, (ii) the description
of quantity of cargo and (iii) the signature and address of consignees, the
consignees were shown as O.N.A.C.O.: but the signature, verifying a
rubber stamp bearing the name of the defendant company, was that of
the defendant company. No doubt they are insurers of O.N.A.C.O. It
is not disputed that the defendants became parties to the contract con-

The Weekly Law Reports, March 6, 1981

211

1 W.L.R.   Armar Shipping Co. v. Caisse Algérienne (C.A.)   Megaw L.J.

A tained in the Lloyd's average bond. Over their stamp and signature there were typed, in the French language, words of reservation as follows: " Sous réserve de discuter tant les principes de l'avarie commune que le taux de la contribution."

The Lloyd's average bond is a printed form with its title " Lloyd's Average Bond " in large print at the top. The first paragraph of the bond reads:

B

"An agreement made this (blank) day of (blank) 19 (blank) between Armar Shipping Co. of Famagusta, Cyprus, owner of the ship or vessel called the *Armar* of the first part and the several persons whose names or firms are set and subscribed hereto being respectively consignees of cargo on board the said ship of the second part Whereas the said ship lately arrived in the port of (blank) on a voyage from (blank) and it is alleged that during such voyage the vessel met with a casualty and sustained damage and loss and that sacrifices were made and expenditure incurred which may form a charge on the cargo or some part thereof or be the subject of a salvage and/or a general average contribution but the same cannot be immediately ascertained and in the meantime it is desirable that the cargo shall be delivered Now therefore these presents witness and the said owner in consideration of the agreement of the parties hereto of the second part hereinafter contained hereby agrees with the respective parties hereto of the second part that he will deliver to them respectively or to their order respectively their respective consignments particulars whereof are contained in the schedule hereto on payment of the freight payable on delivery if any and the said parties hereto of the second part in consideration of the said agreement of the said owner for themselves severally and respectively and not the one for the others of them hereby agree with the said owner that they will pay to the said owner of the said ship the proper and respective proportion of any salvage and/or general average and/or particular and/or other charges which may be chargeable upon their respective consignments particulars whereof are contained in the schedule hereto or to which the shippers or owners of such consignments may be liable to contribute in respect of such damage loss sacrifice or expenditure and the said parties hereto of the second part further promise and agree forthwith to furnish to the owner of the said ship a correct account and particulars of the value of the goods delivered to them respectively in order that any such salvage and/or general average and/or particular and/or other charges may be ascertained and adjusted in the usual manner."

C

D

E

F

G

The second and third paragraphs contain provisions, which were not brought into operation in this case, for the deposit by the consignees of security in joint names. Nothing, therefore, turns in this case on the fact that those paragraphs contain the word " trustees," which in other circumstances might have some bearing on an issue as to the proper law of the contract.

H

The Lloyd's average bond contains no express provision as to the law which is to govern the contract contained therein; nor is there any provision for arbitration in London or for submission to the jurisdiction of the English courts, which, if such provision had been included, would, in English private international law, almost inevitably have made such

an agreement governed by English law. In this respect, the Lloyd's average A
bond differs significantly from two other standard forms of agreement
bearing the name of Lloyd's: the Lloyd's Standard Form of Salvage
Agreement, No Cure—No Pay, and the Lloyd's General Average Bond
and Guarantee, Settlement of Claims Abroad. The texts of these forms
are set out in *British Shipping Laws*, vol. 7, 10th ed. (1975), App. 3.
In their texts, in contrast with the standard form with which we are concerned, there are provisions which might be said to point, at least strongly, B
to English law as being the intended proper law.

After the Lloyd's average bond was signed—how long after we do
not know—the plaintiffs arranged for general average to be adjusted in
London. That, vis-à-vis a bill of lading holder, the plaintiffs were contractually entitled to do by virtue of clause 10 of the bill of lading. The
resulting adjustment was published in London on February 14, 1977. It C
showed that a contribution was due to the shipowners, the plaintiffs, from
cargo. On the basis of that adjustment, the defendants presumably having
refused to pay, the plaintiffs issued a writ in England, claiming against
the defendants the sum of £52,420·18 as the contributions in general
average which the defendants were liable to pay by reason of their promise
contained in the Lloyd's average bond. We are told that the defendants'
refusal to pay is based on their contention that the event which gave rise D
to the general average sacrifice and expenditure was due to the fault of
the plaintiff shipowners. By virtue of rule D of the York-Antwerp Rules
that would not be a matter which would be considered by the average
adjusters. But it could provide a defence to the claim on the adjustment
or a counterclaim. What is " fault " may, as a matter of law, be decided
differently in different systems of law. E

Leave to serve notice of that writ out of the jurisdiction was granted
by Robert Goff J. on October 5, 1979. The defendants applied to set aside
that order. Mustill J. declined to set aside the order. By his judgment of
April 2, 1980, he held that the contract between the plaintiffs and the
defendants contained in the Lloyd's average bond was, by implication,
governed by English law: therefore R.S.C., Ord. 11, r. 1 (1) (*f*) (iii) per- F
mitted the grant of leave to serve notice on the defendants out of the
jurisdiction. The judge rejected the further submission on behalf of the
defendants that, even if English law were the proper law of the contract,
he should exercise his discretion against granting leave.

The defendants appeal on both points. I say at once that, if I had
come to the conclusion that the judge was right in holding that English
law was the governing law of the contract, I should have seen no ground G
for interfering with his view as to the proper exercise of the discretion.

The defendants are not parties to the bill of lading contract. If the
plaintiffs had sued O.N.A.C.O., as being parties to the contract, on the
average adjustment, and if O.N.A.C.O. had objected to the grant of leave
to serve them outside the jurisdiction, different considerations would have
arisen. That does not arise here. The defendants are not contractually H
bound by clause 10 of the bill of lading contract. They have not agreed
with the plaintiffs, as a matter of contract between them, that the plaintiffs
may decide where any average adjustment, arising out of the bill of lading
voyage, is to take place and that the law of that place, so chosen, will
apply.

What, then, is the proper law of the contract contained in the Lloyd's
average bond? For on the answer to that question, by reason of the

The Weekly Law Reports, March 6, 1981

213

1 W.L.R.   Armar Shipping Co. v. Caisse Algérienne (C.A.)   Megaw L.J.

A   provisions of R.S.C., Ord. 11, r. 1 (1) (*f*) (iii), the question whether the English court has jurisdiction depends. It is a contract made in Algeria, between a Cypriot shipowner and two Algerian companies. It is in the English language, though the defendants' signature is conditioned by a reservation in the French language. It provides for the delivery of a cargo of sugar shipped in Cuba, under a bill of lading the proper law
B   of which is not English law, in a ship flying, I imagine, the flag of Cyprus, at a port in Algeria, consequent on the abandonment of a lien which would have been exercisable there, against the payment in that Algerian port of freight, if any, due on the cargo, and against the promise of the consignee and the defendants, the consignee's insurers, to pay the proper proportion of any general average charges which might be payable upon the particular consignment of cargo. Where is there scope for implication
C   that English law governs that contract? Can it be suggested that the intention of the parties is to be inferred that English law shall govern (*Dicey and Morris, The Conflict of Laws,* 9th ed. (1973), r. 146, sub-r. 2, p. 735)? Can it be fairly asserted that the transaction " has its closest and most real connection " with English law (sub-r. 3, p. 742)?

Mustill J. did not place any weight on the use of the English language.
D   I think that in the circumstances that is right. Amongst other considerations the English language is, if I may use the phrase, the lingua franca of commerce; it is the language of the United States of America; and, in the present case, the contractual document included a reservation in the French language inserted at the instance of the defendants. Counsel for the plaintiffs before us sought to place some reliance on the use of the word " Lloyd's " in the heading of the contract form. I do not regard
E   that as a matter of great significance, especially when one observes the absence from this standard form of the indications of English law as the governing law which are to be found in the other two Lloyd's standard forms to which I have referred.

The only way in which, as I see it, an attractive or persuasive argument can be adduced in support of English law as the governing law, by
F   implication, of this contract is the way in which Mustill J., if I may say so, both attractively and persuasively stated the argument which he thought right to accept. That argument is founded on the basis that an important factor—the plaintiffs say that it is a decisive factor—is the place where the average is to be adjusted. If the Lloyd's average bond had provided, expressly or by clear and unambiguous implication, that the general average adjustment was to take place in London, I should have thought
G   that that might well have been decisive. But this contract, in my opinion, did not so provide, either expressly or by clear implication. London, it is stated in an affidavit on behalf of the plaintiffs, is " an important international centre for the adjustment of general average." That fact may unhesitatingly be accepted. " Algeria," it is said, " has no internationally recognised average adjusters." " London," it is said, " . . . is the most com-
H   monly chosen centre for adjustments where the general average is connected with Europe or the Mediterranean." But whether or not it would be chosen in a particular case would obviously depend on many factors affecting the particular case. It is accepted that London is by no means the only possible choice of venue for general average adjustment in respect of a casualty such as gave rise to this claim. General average adjustments are, we are told, by no means uncommonly carried out in, for example, Germany, Belgium and the United States of America. No doubt individual ship-

owners, where it rests with them, or their insurers, have their own   A
individual preferences.

Mustill J. accepted that

"if this had been an ordinary contract, there would have been
strong grounds for arguing that the system of law with which the
contract had the closest connection was the law of Algeria."

But he did not regard this as an ordinary contract. As I understand it,   B
his reasons for regarding it as being out of the ordinary were that it contemplated an adjustment of general average; as the defendants' obligation
to pay under the contract (apart from any initial payment of freight due)
was an obligation to pay the amount of general average chargeable upon
the consignment, so assessed, the place of the average adjustment became
the paramount consideration in ascertaining the proper law of the contract   C
contained in the Lloyd's average bond; and, ultimately, in this particular
case London was the venue for general average adjustment chosen by the
carriers, the plaintiffs, who, so far as the bill of lading contract was concerned, had the contractual option so to decide.

The judge accepted that the defendants, not having been parties to
the bill of lading, "cannot be fixed beyond doubt with notice of the terms   D
of the bill of lading." Counsel for the plaintiffs accepted, before us, that
he could not contend that the defendants were to be treated in this commercial sphere as being affected with constructive notice of those terms.
Mustill J. said:

"But [the defendants] must at least be taken to have foreseen that
there would be a contract of carriage between the persons liable to
contribute and the shipowners, and that this contract might stipulate   E
for a place of adjustment other than Algiers, and expressly or by
inference provide for a law to govern the adjustment which was
not the law of the state of Algeria."

Subject to a caveat as to the words "at least," I should not be disposed
to quarrel with the inference which the judge there states. However,   F
stress must be laid, as counsel for the defendants rightly contends, on
the word "might." But, in my opinion, if it rests there, it falls short, and
far short, of establishing that English law is the law with which this
transaction has the closest and most real connection. It is no more
than this: that the average adjustment *might* take place in England, and
that, if so, this would not be inconsistent with the terms of the bill of
lading contract, as between the plaintiffs and O.N.A.C.O., who were the   G
defendants' assured. That does not, in my judgment, satisfy the standard,
the strict standard, which the courts of this country should maintain in
examining a claim for the assertion of this extraterritorial jurisdiction.

The judge then goes on to say:

"It seems to me that in the particular circumstances of this case,
where there was a contract of carriage to which O.N.A.C.O. were   H
parties and where pursuant to that contract English law became the
law of the adjustment, and hence the law governing the liability of
O.N.A.C.O. to make contribution in general average, and where the
defendants took on a primary obligation to pay the sum assessed as
the amount for which contribution was to be made, it can properly
be said that English law is the system of law with which the bond
is most closely concerned."

A   With very great respect, the only additional matter added in that sentence is the fact that " English law became the law of the adjustment." That is a reference to the fact that at some unknown date, after the contract with which we are concerned, contained in the Lloyd's average bond, had been made, the plaintiffs, as " carriers " under the bill of lading contract, decided that the average adjustment should take place in London. Whether, and if so when, that decision was made or when it was notified B to O.N.A.C.O., or to the defendants, we know not. But, at least, it was something which took place after the contract, the proper law of which we are seeking to ascertain, had already been made and had, almost certainly, already been executed in part.

Mustill J., as one would expect, has not overlooked the possible difficulty which arises in bringing in as a factor for ascertaining the proper C law of a contract an event which has happened after the contract was made. However, he came to the conclusion, for reasons which he expounds attractively in the following paragraph of his judgment:

" the proper law can be regarded as ' floating ' until such time as the exercise of a choice by the carrier had the effect of fixing both governing laws at the same time."

D   (The other governing law to which Mustill J. refers is, I assume, the governing law of the average adjustment provisions in the bill of lading contract introduced by clause 10.)

But can this really be so? Counsel for the defendants submits, with what seems to me to be unanswerable legal logic, that there must be a proper law of any contract—a governing law—at the time of the making of that contract. If, as is the case here, at the time when the contract was E made, the question remained undecided whether the average adjustment was to be in England or in the United States or in Germany or somewhere else, then the fact that it was subsequently decided by one of the parties that the venue should be England cannot be a relevant factor in the ascertainment of the proper law at an earlier date. As a matter of legal logic, I find insuperable difficulty in seeing by what system of law one F is to decide what, if any, is the legal effect of an event which occurs when a contract is already in existence with no proper law: but, instead, with a " floating " non-law.

But in my opinion the difficulty goes beyond mere technicality or legal logic. Under the terms of this Lloyd's average bond contract, things had to be done by the parties forthwith and disputes under the contract might G well, as a matter of commercial reality, arise forthwith. For example, there might be an immediate dispute as to whether freight was payable, or, if so, how much freight. There might be a dispute as to whether the shipowner had duly delivered the right cargo, in the right amount, or at the right time, to the right person. Those disputes, if they were to arise, would be disputes under the terms of this contract, involving, it may be, questions as to the construction and effect of those contractual terms. H It cannot be that the contract has to be treated as being anarchic: as having no governing law which the court, taking jurisdiction in respect of such a dispute under the contract, would apply in deciding the dispute. There must be a governing law from the outset: not a floating absence of law, continuing to float until the carrier, unilaterally, makes a decision.

The governing law cannot fall to be decided, retrospectively, by reference to an event which was an uncertain event in the future at the time when obligations under the contract had already been undertaken, had fallen to be performed and had been performed. Nor is it, I think, an A attractive, or a possible, concept of English private international law that the governing law, initially being, say, the law of Algeria, should thereafter change into the law of England.

If, as I believe, the fact of the carriers' subsequent designation of England as the place of the general average adjustment cannot operate to crystallise a theretofore " floating " proper law (or to fill the gap of a theretofore non-existent proper law), the most that can be said in this case B is that, when the contract was made, there was a possibility that English law might be the place of the general average adjustment. But that, as I have said, cannot, in my opinion, have the effect of making English law the governing law of the contract.

Nothing else in the facts and circumstances of the present case appears to be sufficient to have that effect, or to make the English system of law C the system with which this transaction had the closest and most real connection.

I would add that in the earlier part of his judgment Mustill J. has made a very helpful analysis of what he describes as the " three groups of issues " which may arise. He said that " it does not follow that all three groups are governed by the same system of law." By this, I think, he D means that if, for example, the proper law of the Lloyd's average bond contract were English law, that would by no means necessarily mean that the English court would apply English domestic law to all the different types of issue which might arise by way of dispute under the contract. The English court, applying English law including the English principles of private international law, might, for example, apply the proper law (whatever it may be) of the bill of lading contract in respect of any issues E which involved the interpretation of that contract for purposes relevant to the decision of the dispute under the Lloyd's average bond contract. But I am confident that the judge was not, for one moment, intending to suggest that, on the question whether, for the purposes of R.S.C., Ord. 11, r. 1 (1) (f) (iii), the Lloyd's average bond contract was to be treated as governed by English law, the court might properly reach different decisions according to the nature of the particular dispute under that contract which F it might be anticipated would fall to be decided if the court assumed jurisdiction. If it were possible, or permissible, to conceive that the contract might have different governing laws according to which particular contractual provision was relevant to the particular dispute under the contract, then I should say, without hesitation, that the English court could not properly treat the contract in question—for it must be the whole G contract as a single entity—as governed by English law for the purposes of asserting extraterritorial jurisdiction. Accordingly, on that hypothesis (which I think is an unreal one, at least in this case) the court should refuse jurisdiction.

I would allow this appeal and set aside the order for leave to serve notice of the writ out of the jurisdiction.

H

EVELEIGH L.J. I agree.

OLIVER L.J. I agree.

Appeal allowed with costs.
Leave to appeal refused.

Solicitors: *Ince & Co.; Elborne Mitchell & Co.*

M. G.

A

[QUEEN'S BENCH DIVISION]

* REGINA v. HATFIELD JUSTICES, Ex parte CASTLE

1980 May 22   Waller L.J. and Park J.

B *Justices — Election for trial on indictment — Criminal damage —
Criminal damage under £200 charged with three other offences
all triable only summarily — Criminal damage triable either
way if part of series of "offences of the same or a similar
character" — Whether defendant entitled to elect trial on
indictment—Criminal Law Act 1977 (c. 45), s. 23 (7)*

The defendant was charged with criminal damage to a
C   police officer's uniform, using threatening words and behaviour
whereby a breach of the peace was likely to be occasioned
and assault on and obstruction of a police constable in the
execution of his duty. All the charges arose out of the same
incident. The latter three were triable only summarily. The
value involved in the criminal damage charge was only £23·67,
and, accordingly, by virtue of section 23 (1) and (2) of the
Criminal Law Act 1977,[1] that charge was triable only summar-
D   ily unless it was one of two or more offences which appeared
to form part of a series of two or more offences of the same
or a similar character within the meaning of section 23 (7) of
the Act. The defendant elected trial by jury in respect of the
charge of criminal damage on the ground that it was part of
a series within section 23 (7), and the justices determined that
he was entitled to do so.

On an application by the prosecutor for judicial review
E   by way of prohibition to prevent the justices from sitting
further as examining justices and by way of mandamus to
direct them to hear the charge by way of summary trial: —

Held, granting the application, that in order for section
23 (7) to apply the offences said to be of the same or a similar
character had to display similarity in fact and in law and had
to form part of a series, and that an essential element of the
similarity was that they should all have the characteristics of
F   being triable either way, i.e. summarily or on indictment;
that in the present case it was not necessary to decide whether
the offences were part of a series since none of the other
characteristics was present, and, accordingly, the charge of
criminal damage was triable only summarily.

Reg. v. *Ludlow* [1971] A.C. 29, H.L.(E.) and *In re Prescott (Note)* (1979) 70 Cr.App.R. 244, C.A. applied.

G
The following cases are referred to in the judgment:

Prescott, In re (Note) (1979) 70 Cr.App.R. 244, C.A.
Reg. v. *Ludlow* [1971] A.C. 29; [1970] 2 W.L.R. 521; [1970] 1 All
E.R. 567, H.L.(E.).

No additional cases were cited in argument.

H
APPLICATION for judicial review.

The prosecutor, Douglas Castle, applied for judicial review by way of
prohibition and mandamus directed to the Hatfield justices sitting at
Hatfield, to prevent them from committing the defendant, Stephen James
Mark Healy, for trial on a charge of criminal damage under section 1 (1)

---

[1] Criminal Law Act 1977, s. 23 (7): see post, p. 219A–B.

Reg. v. Hatfield JJ., Ex p. Castle (D.C.)   **[1981]**

of the Criminal Damage Act 1971, and to require that he be charged by A
way of summary trial pursuant to section 23 (2) of the Criminal Law Act
1977.

The facts are stated in the judgment of Waller L.J.

John Howarth for the prosecutor.
James Wadsworth for the defendant.   B

WALLER L.J.   This is an application by the prosecutor for leave to
apply for judicial review of a determination made on March 10, 1980, by
the Hatfield justices sitting at Hatfield magistrates' court. The application
is for an order prohibiting the justices from committing the defendant
for trial on a charge of criminal damage and involves the consideration
of section 23 (7) of the Criminal Law Act 1977.   C

The defendant was charged before the justices with four offences: that
he did, on December 24, 1979, use threatening words and behaviour
whereby a breach of the peace was likely to be occasioned, contrary to
section 5 of the Public Order Act 1936 (as amended); that on the same
day he assaulted Robert Hamblin, a constable, in the execution of his
duty, contrary to section 51 (1) of the Police Act 1964; that on the same D
day, without lawful excuse, he damaged a police uniform, contrary to
section 1 (1) of the Criminal Damage Act 1971; and that on the same day
he wilfully obstructed Robert Hamblin, a constable, acting in the execution
of his duty, contrary to section 51 (3) of the Police Act.

The value of the damage to the police uniform tunic amounted to
£23·67. The justices in their affidavit go on to say, not surprisingly, that
they were of opinion that the damage to the police uniform tunic did not E
exceed £200 and that the provision of section 23 (7) (*a*) applied to the
offence of damaging a police uniform, and that the offence of criminal
damage was suitable for summary trial. It is to be noted that the other
three offences were triable summarily only. When the court proceeded in
accordance with the provisions of section 21 of the Criminal Law Act
1977 the defendant elected to be tried by jury.   F

The justices, having had their attention drawn to an article in the
Justice of the Peace newspaper, came to the conclusion that the defendant was entitled to elect trial by jury, and it is that issue which comes
before us.

Sections 19 to 23 of the Criminal Law Act 1977 deal with procedure
for determining the mode of trial of offences which are triable either
summarily or on indictment. Section 23 (1) deals particularly with certain G
offences which are triable either way but are made triable summarily if
the value involved is small.

Section 23 (1) provides:

". . . subject to subsection (7) below, the court shall, before proceeding in accordance with section 20 above, consider whether, having
regard to any representations made by the prosecutor or the accused, H
the value involved (as defined in subsection (10) below) appears to the
court to exceed the relevant sum."

It was in relation to that that the justices came to the opinion that the
relevant sum was £23·67. As the section goes on to say "For the purposes
of this section the relevant sum is £200," it was below that sum.

Then subsection (2) provides:

The Weekly Law Reports, March 6, 1981

219

1 W.L.R.   Reg. v. Hatfield JJ., Ex p. Castle (D.C.)   Waller L.J.

A

" If . . . the value involved does not exceed the relevant sum, the court shall proceed as if the offence were triable only summarily, and sections 20 to 22 above shall not apply."

But subsection (7) reads as follows:

B

" Subsection (1) above shall not apply where the offence charged— (a) is one of two or more offences with which the accused is charged on the same occasion and which appear to the court to constitute or form part of a series of two or more offences of the same or a similar character; . . ."

C

Mr. Howarth on behalf of the prosecutor submits to this court that the offences here were neither of a similar character nor did they constitute what formed part of a series. They all occurred, submits Mr. Howarth, at virtually the same time. They all occurred in relation to the same officer and therefore they were not part of a series. The time probably was not more than a minute or two. Secondly, they were not offences of a similar character.

D

Threatening words and behaviour whereby a breach of the peace is likely to be occasioned, contrary to section 5 of the Public Order Act 1936, has nothing in common with criminal damage. Assaulting a constable has nothing in common with criminal damage except that the damage was to a constable's uniform, but criminal damage may be done to anything. Criminal damage has nothing in common with wilful obstruction of a constable in the execution of his duty.

E

Mr. Howarth submits that the authority of the Court of Appeal, decided after the article in the *Justice of the Peace* newspaper makes that clear. He referred first to *In re Prescott (Note)* (1979) 70 Cr.App.R. 244, which was a case where the magistrate had refused to give the defendant the right to elect trial by jury. The episode was one where the defendant obstructed a police officer named Robin Finch while he was looking for somebody, and in obstructing him he damaged a pair of his trousers to the value of £12. There was an offence of obstructing a police officer in the course of his duty and of criminal damage to trousers, so that it was similar to at any rate part of the offences charged in this case.

F

Ormrod L.J. said, at p. 246:

G

" When one turns to the nature of the offences charged in this case, one is an offence of obstructing a police officer in the course of his duty and the other is the offence of criminal damage to the officer's trousers. It seems to be plain beyond any question that the two offences were not of the same or similar character, nor can I see on the facts of this case how these two offences could possibly be described as a ' series.' There is no series."

H

He went on to dismiss the appeal.

If one applies that decision to the present case, clearly the obstruction is not similar to criminal damage. In my judgment, equally clearly, insulting behaviour is not similar to criminal damage. Nor is the offence of assault similar to criminal damage. There may be occasions when they are similar in what happens but they are not similar offences.

Mr. Howarth has drawn attention to a passage in the speech of Lord Pearson in *Reg.* v. *Ludlow* [1971] A.C. 29 where Lord Pearson is con-

Waller L.J.   Reg. v. Hatfield JJ., Ex p. Castle (D.C.)   **[1981]**

A

sidering the elements of similarity. The arguments apparently having been on the one side that it was factual similarity and on the other side legal similarity, Lord Pearson expressed the view, at p. 39:

". . . I think the proper conclusion to be drawn from the judgments as a whole is that both the law and the facts have been and should be taken into account in deciding whether offences are similar or dissimilar in character."

B

He is there referring to a number of passages in the judgment of the Court of Appeal which had been cited. Both of those requirements have to be present.

What had happened in this case produced a very extraordinary state of affairs. The offence of criminal damage of an amount of £23 was in many ways rather less serious than the other offences with which this defendant was charged. Assault on a police constable is more serious in the ordinary way than criminal damage of a small amount. The public order offence may well be more serious. Obstructing a police constable in the course of his duty may well be more serious than criminal damage itself.

C

The result of the justices' feeling compelled to send this case for trial (compelled by the article in the *Justice of the Peace*) was that the defendant was being sent for trial certainly for no more serious an offence than the others with which he was charged, and almost certainly for a rather less serious offence, which is a rather extraordinary result. None of those others was triable other than summarily.

D

In my judgment, one of the essentials to comply with this section is that the offences which are said to be of the same or similar character should have the characteristic, among others, of being triable either way. The words of this subsection follow closely the words of rule 9 of the Indictment Rules 1971 (S.I. 1971 No. 1253), which are concerned with offences which can be tried on indictment, and one can understand those words being used to enable offences to be tried together on indictment when they are all triable either way. In my opinion, that is one of the characteristics that should apply.

E

In my judgment, in this case the justices were wrong in the conclusion to which they came, albeit they were misled by an article in the *Justice of the Peace* and that, in order for this subsection to apply, there has to be similarity of fact; there has to be similarity in law; there has to be the characteristic of similarity in that the offences are all triable either way and they must form part of a series. In this particular case it is not necessary to decide whether these offences formed part of a series. It is sufficient to say that none of the other characteristics was present and therefore the court was not obliged to consider section 23 (7), and this offence of criminal damage remained an offence that was triable only summarily.

F

G

PARK J. I agree.

H

Application granted.

Solicitors: *Pellys, Bishop's Stortford; Bretherton & Co., St. Albans.*

R. D.

A

[CHANCERY DIVISION]

* SPECTRUM INVESTMENT CO. AND ANOTHER v. HOLMES

[1979 H. No. 156]

B 1980   June 12, 13, 16, 17, 18;   Browne-Wilkinson J.
         July 9

*Land Registration—Register—Rectification—Squatter registered as
proprietor of leasehold interest with possessory title—Lessee's
title deleted — Whether freeholder entitled to possession —
Whether squatter's title to be deleted and lessee's reinstated
—Purported surrender of lease by lessee—Freeholder's right*
C *to possession—Land Registration Act* 1925 (15 & 16 Geo. 5,
c. 21), *ss.* 11, 69 (1) (4), 75 [1]

In 1939 the lessee of a 99-year registered lease dated
December 24, 1902, granted an oral monthly tenancy of the
demised house to H who lived there with her daughter, the
defendant. The lessee assigned her interest to D in 1944 and
requested H to pay the rent to D's solicitors but the solicitors
D refused to accept it. Between 1947 and 1951 H was required
to pay rent to the local authority for carrying out works under
the Public Health (London) Act 1936. H died in 1951 and
the defendant continued in possession, paying no rent. The
plaintiff acquired the freehold in 1957 and was registered as
proprietor with possessory title. On March 19, 1968, the
defendant applied for registration as proprietor of the leasehold interest. The Land Registry notified D's solicitors of
E that but the solicitors took no action. In June 1968 the
registry closed the register showing D as proprietor and opened
a new register showing the defendant as first proprietor with
possessory title of the leasehold interest. The defendant's
interest was noted on the land certificate issued in 1975 when
the plaintiff's absolute freehold title was registered. By a deed
of surrender dated May 7, 1975, D purported to surrender
the unexpired term of the lease to the plaintiff.
F On the plaintiff's originating summons to which D was
added as the second plaintiff at the hearing, seeking, inter
alia, deletion of the defendant's title from the freehold register,
or alternatively, rectification of the leasehold register by reinstating D as the proprietor: —
Held, (1) that under section 11 of the Land Registration
Act 1925 the plaintiff could only enforce its rights when the
lease had come to an end; that by section 69 (1) and (4) the
G term of the lease had vested in the defendant and only she could
dispose of it; accordingly, the purported surrender by D was
ineffective and the plaintiff's claim failed (post, pp. 228A–C,
231D–E).
(2) That, on the true construction of section 75 (3) the
Land Registrar was under a duty to register the defendant's
title if, on application for registration under section 75 (2),
he was satisfied of her title; accordingly, D was not entitled
H to rectification of the register so as to reinstate herself as
registered proprietor of the lease and could not surrender
the term so as to merge it in the plaintiff's freehold (post,
pp. 230D–H, 231E).
St. Marylebone Property Co. Ltd. v. *Fairweather* [1963]
A.C. 510, H.L.(E.) distinguished.

[1] Land Registration Act 1925, s. 11: see post, p. 227A–B.
S. 69 (1) (*a*) see post, p. 227D–F.
S. 75: see post, p. 226E–H.

Spectrum Investment v. Holmes (Ch.D.)   **[1981]**

The following cases are referred to in the judgment: A

Jessamine Investment Co. v. *Schwartz* [1978] Q.B. 264; [1977] 2 W.L.R. 145; [1976] 3 All E.R. 521, C.A.

St. Marylebone Property Co. Ltd. v. *Fairweather* [1963] A.C. 510; [1962] 2 W.L.R. 1020; [1962] 2 All E.R. 288, H.L.(E.).

Williams & Glyn's Bank Ltd. v. *Boland* [1980] 3 W.L.R. 138; [1980] 2 All E.R. 408, H.L.(E.).

B

The following additional cases were cited in argument:

Bridges v. *Mees* [1957] Ch. 475; [1957] 3 W.L.R. 215; [1957] 2 All E.R. 577.

Claridge v. *Tingey* [1967] 1 W.L.R. 134; [1966] 3 All E.R. 935.

Epps v. *Esso Petroleum Co. Ltd.* [1973] 1 W.L.R. 1071; [1973] 2 All E.R. 465.

Lee v. *Barrey* [1957] Ch. 251; [1957] 2 W.L.R. 245; [1957] 1 All E.R.   C
191, C.A.

Marshall v. *Robertson* (1905) 50 S.J. 75.

Morelle Ltd. v. *Wakeling* [1955] 2 Q.B. 379; [1955] 2 W.L.R. 672.

Tickner v. *Buzzacott* [1965] Ch. 426; [1965] 2 W.L.R. 154; [1965] 1 All E.R. 131.

ORIGINATING SUMMONS   D

The plaintiff, Spectrum Investment Co., was the registered proprietor of the freehold interest in a house and land known as 43 Mount Pleasant Lane, London E5, registered under title no. LN 155216. On the Charges Register of that title a lease dated December 24, 1902, made between William Walter Hayworth and Annie Marie Kelsey had been noted with the defendant, Mary Holmes, as the registered proprietor with possessory title and registered under title no. NGL 65073.   E

The plaintiff issued an originating summons on January 11, 1979, seeking orders that the whole of the entry on the register under title no. NGL 65073 be deleted and that the Charges Register of title no. LN 155216 be rectified by the deletion of the entry which referred to the lease and the defendant's registered title. The plaintiff further sought declarations that the defendant was, and had since May 7, 1977, been,   F a trespasser, that she had no right under the lease, and alternatively, that she was a statutory tenant.

At the hearing Mrs. Louisa David, who had acquired the leasehold interest in 1944, was added as the second plaintiff and she sought rectification of the register by deleting the defendant as the registered proprietor and reinstating her as the proprietor.

The facts are stated in the judgment.   G

Romie Tager for the plaintiffs.
A. W. H. Charles for the defendant.

Cur. adv. vult.

H

July 9.   BROWNE-WILKINSON J. read the following judgment. This case concerns the rights of the defendant in a house, 43, Mount Pleasant Lane, Hackney, London ("the house"). The plaintiff, Spectrum Investment Co. is registered at the Land Registry as proprietor of the freehold with title absolute. The defendant is in possession and claims to be entitled to remain in possession on two alternative grounds: first, she claims on the ground that she is registered

The Weekly Law Reports, March 6, 1981

223

1 W.L.R.   Spectrum Investment v. Holmes (Ch.D.)   Browne-Wilkinson J.

A at the Land Registry as proprietor (with possessory title) of a long leasehold interest which does not expire until 2001; alternatively, she claims as a tenant protected by the Rent Acts. As will emerge, this case is primarily concerned with the first of those grounds.

The material facts are as follows. The freehold interest was first registered on September 20, 1901. By a lease dated December 24, 1902, the freeholder granted a lease of the house for 99 years from December 25, 1902, at a rent of £7 per annum. That leasehold interest was registered on January 2, 1903, and subsequently became vested in a Miss Kelsey.

In 1939 Miss Kelsey granted an oral monthly tenancy to a Mrs. Holmes at a rent of £4 13s. 4d. per month. Mrs. Holmes lived there with her daughter, the defendant, and paid the rent to Miss Kelsey's agent until 1944. In 1944 Miss Kelsey assigned the lease to a Mrs. David, who was registered as proprietor of the lease under title no. LN 66166. Miss Kelsey told Mrs. Holmes to pay the rent in future to a firm of solicitors, Messrs. Gale & Phelps. Mrs. Holmes tried to do this but the tender of rent was refused. She made some efforts to find out to whom she should pay the rent, but without success. The last payment of rent by Mrs. Holmes was in 1944. In 1947 the local authority, having carried out certain works to the house, required Mrs. Holmes to pay the rent to them under the Public Health (London) Act 1936. The last of such payments was made in 1951.

In 1951 Mrs. Holmes died. No grant has been taken to her estate, but the defendant stayed in possession. The plaintiff concedes that, were it not for the defendant's claim to be in possession as registered proprietor of the lease, the defendant is entitled to protection under the Rent Acts as successor to her mother.

In 1957 the plaintiff acquired the freehold interest in the house and was registered as proprietor. It is common ground that by 1963 at the latest, 12 years having expired since the last payment of, or on account of, rent, the defendant had acquired a title to the house by adverse possession as against Mrs. David, the leaseholder, but not as against the plaintiff, the freeholder.

On March 19, 1968, the defendant applied to be registered at the Land Registry as proprietor of the leasehold interest. Notice of this application was given by the Land Registry to Messrs. Gale & Phelps as solicitors for Mrs. David, but they took no action.

In June 1968 the Land Registry gave effect to the defendant's application as follows: (a) they closed the registration of the leasehold title no. LN 66166 on which Mrs. David was registered as proprietor; and (b) they opened a new registration of the leasehold title under title no. NGL 65073 on which the defendant was shown as being registered on March 19, 1968, as first proprietor with possessory title of the leasehold interest. The Property Register describes the property registered as "The leasehold land . . . known as 43 Mount Pleasant Lane," Hackney. It then goes on, under a cross heading "Short particulars of lease under which the land is held," to give a description of the lease dated December 24, 1902.

Until 1975 the freehold title had itself only been a possessory title, but on April 28, 1975, the plaintiff was registered as freehold proprietor with absolute title. There appeared on the land certificate a reference to the defendant's title to the lease registered under title no. NGL

Browne-Wilkinson J.   **Spectrum Investment v. Holmes (Ch.D.)**   **[1981]**

65073.   Either for this or for some other reason, at this stage the plain-   A
tiff and Mrs. David woke up and started to take action.

It appears that Mrs. David is a wealthy lady who during the war
departed to the west country and ignored her properties.   For some
unexplained reason, neither she nor Messrs. Gale & Phelps (who were
her solicitors throughout) seem to have taken any normally prudent
steps to safeguard her position.   She is a member of the family who
are the shareholders in the plaintiff.   Messrs. Gale & Phelps are the   B
solicitors for the plaintiff also.   A Mr. Galinski is related to Mrs. David,
a director of the plaintiff, and was also a solictor with Messrs. Gale &
Phelps.

Having discovered the defendant's claim to a possessory title, Mrs.
David and the plaintiff entered into a transaction which was quite
frankly admitted to be a device designed to defeat the defendant's claim.   C
On May 7, 1975, Mrs. David executed a deed of surrender.   It reads:

> "H.M. Land Registry.   Land Registration Acts 1925 and 1966.
> County of Greater London.   Title No. 66166.   Property 43 Mount
> Pleasant Lane, Hackney.   May 7, 1975.   In consideration of the
> release hereinafter contained I Louisa David care of Messrs. Gale
> & Phelps of 220 Stamford Hill London N16 (hereinafter called
> 'the lessee') as beneficial owner hereby surrender and release to   D
> Spectrum Investment Co. (an unlimited liability company formerly
> known as Spectrum Investment Co. Ltd.) of 220 Stamford Hill
> London N16 (hereinafter called 'the reversioner') the land com-
> prised in the title above referred to for all the unexpired residue
> of the term granted by the registered lease to the intent that the
> said term of years shall forthwith be merged and extinguished   E
> absolutely in the reversion thereof registered under the title
> number LN 155216 of which the reversioner is the registered
> proprietor and the reversioner in consideration of the premises
> hereby releases and discharges the lessee from all and singular the
> covenants agreements and conditions contained in the registered
> lease and on the part of the lessee to be paid performed and
> observed and from all liability in respect thereof and from all claims   F
> demands expenses or proceedings in respect of any breach or non-
> performance or non-observance of the said covenants agreements
> and conditions arising thereunder . . ."

The deed is executed by Mrs. David and by the plaintiff.

It is to be noted that the document purports to be a surrender of a
lease registered in the Land Registry under title no. LN 66166.   At that   G
date there was no such title number, it having been closed in 1968.

It is the plaintiff's case that the surrender by Mrs. David was effective
to merge the leasehold interest in the freehold interest and that accordingly the plaintiff, as freeholder, is now entitled to possession against the
defendant.   For this proposition the plaintiff relies on the decision of
the House of Lords in *St. Marylebone Property Co. Ltd.* v. *Fairweather*   H
[1963] A.C. 510.   Moreover the plaintiff alleges that, the defendant
having been in possession of the house under the possessory title to the
lease, can no longer claim any protection under the Rent Acts.   I
pause only to point out that if the plaintiff is right on both of these
points the law will have achieved a result worthy of Catch 22.   The
defendant and her mother, having tried to pay the rent but being unable
to find anyone to take it due to the landlord's shortcomings, have got

The Weekly Law Reports, March 6, 1981

225

1 W.L.R.   Spectrum Investment v. Holmes (Ch.D.)   Browne-Wilkinson J.

A into a position in which the defaulting landlord and her associated family company are able to evict the defendant from her home, which could not have happened if the landlord had arranged for someone to receive the rent.

Having executed the surrender, the plaintiff applied to the county court claiming possession and mesne profits. The defendant has tendered arrears of rent due under the lease but this has been refused. The county court proceedings have been stood over to enable the questions of title to be decided in these proceedings in the High Court.

B By this originating summons the plaintiff claims (1) rectification of the register by deleting the whole of the defendant's possessory title to the lease and references to that title on the freehold register; (2) a declaration that the defendant has no right under the lease; and (3) a declaration that she is a trespasser or, alternatively, a statutory tenant.

C In the course of the hearing before me the plaintiff's case has been somewhat modified. First, the plaintiff by its counsel has said that the plaintiff will not in any event seek to evict the defendant from the house, but, if successful on all points, will grant her a tenancy at a fair rent to be agreed. Secondly, whilst reserving the right to renew the claim in the Court of Appeal, the plaintiff concedes that before me its claim to a declaration that the defendant is not even a statutory tenant is decided against it by the decision of the Court of Appeal in *Jessamine Investment Co. Ltd.* v. *Schwartz* [1978] Q.B. 264 (another case in which Mrs. David's strange management of her properties raised problems for her tenants).

D Therefore, in the event, the only point that I have to decide is whether, notwithstanding the purported surrender of the lease, the defendant has a good right against the freeholder to remain in possession until the expiry of the lease by reason of her possessory title as against Mrs. David.

E I will first consider the Limitation Act 1939 as it applies to a case such as this, where the freeholder has granted a lease to X (" the documentary lessee ") and Y (" the squatter ") has been in adverse possession for upwards of 12 years. It is common ground that in such a case the squatter acquires no rights against the freeholder under the Act of 1939, since the freeholder's right of action to recover possession does not accrue until the termination of the lease. But under sections 4 (3) and 9 of the Act of 1939 the right of the documentary lessee to recover possession from the squatter is barred. Section 16 of the Act reads:

F

G " Subject to the provisions of section 7 of this Act and of section 75 of the Land Registration Act 1925, at the expiration of the period described by this Act for any person to bring an action to recover land (including a redemption action) or an action to enforce an advowson, the title of that person to the land or advowson shall be extinguished."

H The impact of that section in a case where leasehold land is not registered is now established by the decision of the House of Lords in *St. Marylebone Property Co. Ltd.* v. *Fairweather* [1963] A.C. 510. The facts of that case are for all material purposes incapable of being distinguished from the facts in the present case, i.e. the right of action of the documentary lessee against the squatter was barred, but the documentary lessee had subsequently surrendered the lease to the free-

holder. The House of Lords held that the freeholder was entitled to A
recover possession from the squatter.

The plaintiff claims that the same result should follow in this case,
notwithstanding that in this case both the freehold and the leasehold
interest are registered at the Land Registry. It is therefore important
to analyse exactly what was decided by the House of Lords in *St.
Marylebone Property Co. Ltd.* v. *Fairweather.*

The House of Lords held that the effect of the Limitation Act 1939 B
is not to vest the lease in the squatter by a form of parliamentary conveyance. Although by section 16 of the Act the title of the documentary
lessee is " extinguished," that extinguishment operates only as against
the squatter; the interest is not extinguished for all purposes. In particular, as between the freeholder and the documentary lessee, the
documentary lessee remains the tenant and there is privity of estate C
between them: the documentary lessee continues to hold the term of
years and the estate in it granted by the lease. It follows that, notwithstanding that the documentary lessee's rights against the squatter are
barred, the documentary lessee as holder of the legal estate in the term
can effectively surrender the term to the freeholder so as to cause a
merger. Thereafter the freeholder is entitled to recover possession from
the squatter by virtue of the freeholder's unencumbered interest in the D
property.

Against that background I turn to the provisions of the Land
Registration Act 1925 dealing with title acquired by adverse possession.
It will be remembered that section 16 of the Act of 1939 is expressly
made subject to the provisions of section 75 of the Land Registration
Act. Section 75 provides: E

" (1) The Limitation Acts shall apply to registered land in the same
manner and to the same extent as those Acts apply to land not
registered, except that where, if the land were not registered, the
estate of the person registered as proprietor would be extinguished,
such estate shall not be extinguished but shall be deemed to be held
by the proprietor for the time being in trust for the person who, F
by virtue of the said Acts, has acquired title against any proprietor,
but without prejudice to the estates and interests of any other
person interested in the land whose estate or interest is not extinguished by those Acts. (2) Any person claiming to have acquired
a title under the Limitation Acts to a registered estate in the land
may apply to be registered as proprietor thereof. (3) The registrar
shall, on being satisfied as to the applicant's title, enter the applicant G
as proprietor either with absolute, good leasehold, qualified, or
possessory title, as the case may require, but without prejudice to
any estate or interest protected by any entry on the register which
may not have been extinguished under the Limitation Acts, and
such registration shall, subject as aforesaid, have the same effect
as the registration of a first proprietor; but the proprietor or the H
applicant or any other person interested may apply to the court for
the determination of any question arising under this section . . .
(5) Rules may be made for applying (subject to any necessary modifications) the provisions of this section to cases where an easement,
right or privilege has been acquired by prescription."

If (as in the present case) the squatter is registered under section
75 (3) as first proprietor with possessory title of leasehold land, there are

The Weekly Law Reports, March 6, 1981

227

1 W.L.R.   Spectrum Investment v. Holmes (Ch.D.)   Browne-Wilkinson J.

A important sections stating the effect of such registration. Section 11 reads:

> " Where the registered land is a leasehold interest, the registration of a person as first proprietor thereof with a possessory title shall not affect or prejudice the enforcement of any estate, right, or interest (whether in respect of the lessor's title or otherwise) adverse
B to or in derogation of the title of such first registered proprietor, and subsisting or capable of arising at the time of the registration of such proprietor; but, save as aforesaid, shall have the same effect as registration with an absolute title."

Therefore one has to find what is the effect of being registered with an absolute title. That is provided for by section 9 which reads:

C > " Where the registered land is a leasehold interest, the registration under this Act of any person as first proprietor thereof with an absolute title shall be deemed to vest in such person the possession of the leasehold interest described, with all implied or expressed rights, privileges, and appurtenances attached to such interest, subject to the following obligations, rights, and interests, that is to
D say, . . . (a) Subject to all implied and express covenants, obligations, and liabilities incident to the registered land; . . . but free from all other estates and interests whatsoever, including estates and interests of His Majesty."

Section 69 (1) then provides:

E > " The proprietor of land (whether he was registered before or after the commencement of this Act) shall be deemed to have vested in him without any conveyance, where the registered land is freehold, the legal estate in fee simple in possession, and where the registered land is leasehold the legal term created by the registered lease, but subject to the overriding interests, if any, including any mortgage term or charge by way of legal mortgage created by or under the
F Law of Property Act 1925 or this Act or otherwise which has priority to the registered estate."

I can now shortly state the contentions of the plaintiff. The plaintiff submits that the Land Registration Act 1925 introduces mere machinery for proving title to and transferring land and does not affect the substantive rights which parties enjoy under the general law. Accordingly, it is said that the rights of the plaintiff (as established by *St. Marylebone*
G *Property Co.* v. *Fairweather* [1963] A.C. 510) must be reflected in the provisions of the Act of 1925 and are preserved by the words in section 11 which expressly provide that registration with possessory title " shall not affect or prejudice the enforcement of any estate, right, or interest (whether in respect of the lessor's title or otherwise) adverse to or in derogation of " the proprietor with possessory title. So, it is said, having
H obtained a surrender of the lease from Mrs. David, the plaintiff's right to possession as against the defendant is preserved.

There is in my judgment a short answer to the claim by the plaintiff. Accepting for the moment the broad proposition that the Act of 1925 was not intended to alter substantive rights, it undoubtedly was intended to alter the manner in which such rights were to be established and transferred. The surrender by Mrs. David to the plaintiff is the linchpin of the plaintiff's claim. But in my judgment that surrender has not been

The Weekly Law Reports, March 6, 1981

Browne-Wilkinson J.   Spectrum Investment v. Holmes (Ch.D.)   **[1981]**

effected by the only means authorised by the Land Registration Act   A
1925 for the disposal of a registered leasehold interest by act of the
parties.   At the date of the alleged surrender the lease was registered
under title no. NGL 65073 in the name of the defendant.   Mrs. David was
not registered as proprietor, her title no. LN 66166 having been taken
off the register.   By virtue of section 69 (1) the effect of the registration
of the defendant as proprietor of the lease was, as against Mrs. David,
to vest the term or deem it to be vested in the defendant.   B

Section 69 (4) provides: " The estate for the time being vested in the
proprietor shall only be capable of being disposed of or dealt with by
him in manner authorised by this Act."

In my judgment the effect of these provisions is that, so long as the
defendant is registered as proprietor of the lease, only she can dispose of
it.   Moreover by virtue of sections 21 and 22, even the defendant can   C
only do so by a registered disposition.   Accordingly, in my judgment
there has, as yet, been no valid surrender of the lease and the plaintiff's
claim fails in limine.

Mr. Tager for the plaintiff sought to avoid this result by saying that
a surrender was not a registrable disposition and referred me to section
46 of the Act.   This argument does not meet the point that Mrs. David
was not registered as proprietor when she purported to surrender the   D
lease.   But even if she had been, in my judgment the surrender would
have had to be effected by a registered disposition.   Section 69 (4) makes
it clear that even a registered proprietor only has power to deal with any
estate vested in him in the manner authorised by the Act.   The only
powers of disposition are those conferred by section 21 of the Act which
authorises the transfer of the registered estate.   In my judgment the   E
word " transfer " in this section must include surrendering the term,
otherwise the Act does not authorise a surrender.   Any disposition under
section 21 has to be completed by registration: section 22.   Section 46
on which Mr. Tager relied merely directs the registrar to note on the
register the determination of the lease, however that occurs, which will
include determination by effluxion of time or operation of law.   Section
46 does not purport to lay down the ways in which the determination can   F
be effected by disposition of one of the parties.

Mr. Tager submitted further that there ought to have been two
registered titles to the lease, of which Mrs. David was the proprietor of
one and the defendant was the proprietor of the other.   This suggestion
seems to have no warrant in any provision of the Act and in my judgment
runs contrary to the whole scheme of the Act, which is intended to   G
ensure that there shall be one title for any interest in registered land and
anyone dealing with that land can treat the registered proprietor of that
interest as the owner of that interest.

For these reasons, in my judgment there has, as yet, been no surrender
of the term by Mrs. David to the plaintiff.   Therefore, the plaintiff's claim
fails since, so long as the term exists, it has no immediate right to possession.   However, in order to determine the real issue between the   H
parties I gave leave for Mrs. David to be joined as co-plaintiff.   If she
is entitled to rectification of the register, she may thereafter be able to
execute the necessary registered surrender and, if she can, the plaintiff's
claim to posession would be unanswerable.

Mr. Charles's submissions for the defendant were very far-reaching.
He submitted that the whole scheme of the Land Registration Act 1925
shows that the position of the squatter on registered land is totally

The Weekly Law Reports, March 6, 1981

229

1 W.L.R.   Spectrum Investment v. Holmes (Ch.D.)   Browne-Wilkinson J.

A different from that of a squatter on unregistered land as laid down by
the House of Lords in *St. Marylebone Property Co. Ltd.* v. *Fairweather*
[1963] A.C. 510. He submits that section 75 (2) makes it clear that
the squatter who has obtained title against the documentary lessee is
entitled to apply to be registered as proprietor of the documentary
lessee's registered estate in the land, i.e. as proprietor of the lease itself.
Section 75 (3) then requires the registrar, if satisfied of the facts, to
B effect such registration. Accordingly it is said that what was done in
the present case was quite correct: the defendant is rightly registered as
proprietor of the lease itself. As a result, it is said, the legal term of
years is vested in the defendant by a parliamentary conveyance contained
in section 69 of the Act. By virtue of sections 9 and 11 of the Act the
defendant as registered proprietor is deemed to have vested in her the
C possession of the leasehold interest, subject to the express and implied
obligations in the lease and subject to any rights of the freeholder
adverse to her interest. Therefore, Mr. Charles submits, the scheme
of the Land Registration Act 1925 is to produce exactly the result which
the House of Lords held was not the result in relation to unregistered
land, namely, to make the squatter the successor in title to the documentary lessee by parliamentary conveyance, the squatter taking subject
D to and with the benefit of the covenants in the lease.
    This is a formidable and far-reaching submission. But, on the other
side I was strongly pressed with authority suggesting that squatter's
rights were the same over both registered and unregistered land. In *St.
Marylebone Property Co. Ltd.* v. *Fairweather* [1963] A.C. 510 it emerged
at a late stage in the proceedings that the land there in question was
E registered land. The squatter was not registered as proprietor of the
lease, but contended that the provisions of section 75 (1) of the Act
(which makes the documentary lessee as registered proprietor a trustee
for the squatter) prevented the documentary lessee from surrendering
the term to the freeholder. It was not proved at what date the documentary lessee was registered, and on that ground it was held that
section 75 had no application. But Lord Radcliffe said, at pp. 542–543:
F
    "I do not think, therefore, that the appellant can succeed on this
    point. I only wish to add that at present I am not at all satisfied
    that section 75 (1) does create a trust interest in the squatter of the
    kind that one would expect from the words used. So to hold would
    raise difficulties which I do not now explore; and the trust of the
    dispossessed owner's title under subsection (1) must somehow be
G   reconciled with the provision under subsection (2) for the squatter
    to apply to register his own title, which would presumably be his
    independent possessory title acquired by the adverse possession."

See also *per* Lord Denning at p. 548.
    To similar effect are the remarks of Sir John Pennycuick in *Jessamine
Investment Co.* v. *Schwartz* [1978] Q.B. 264, 275:

H   "I should be very reluctant to introduce a substantive distinction
    in the application of a provision of the Limitation Act to registered
    land and unregistered land respectively, based upon what is plainly
    a conveyancing device designed to adapt that provision to the former
    class of land."

    Although these are obiter dicta, they are obviously of some weight in
supporting the contention that the position of a squatter does not vary
according to whether the land is registered or unregistered.

A   Finally, the words of section 75 (1) itself state that the Limitation Acts shall apply to registered land " in the same manner and to the same extent " as it applies to unregistered land, and then goes on to state exceptions.

On the other hand, I take into account the recent decision of the House of Lords in *Williams & Glyn's Bank Ltd.* v. *Boland* (decided since the conclusion of the argument in this case) [1980] 3 W.L.R. 138 which B shows that, if the words of the Land Registration Act 1925 are clear, they are to be given their natural meaning and not distorted so as to seek to produce uniformity in the substantive law as between registered and unregistered land. I therefore approach this question on the basis that one would expect that substantive legal rights would be the same whether the land is registered or unregistered but that clear words in the Act of 1925 must be given their natural meaning even if this leads to C a divergence.

I do not find it necessary to reach any conclusion on the far-reaching propositions which Mr. Charles put forward, since I think that I can decide this case on quite a narrow ground, leaving it to others to resolve the more fundamental questions. In my judgment, if Mrs. David is to succeed in any claim to have the defendant deleted from the register as proprietor of the lease, she (Mrs. David) must show at least that the D registration of the defendant was not a mandatory requirement of the provisions of the Land Registration Act 1925. It is clear from the references in section 75 (3) that section 75 applies to a leasehold interest. Under section 75 (3) the registrar is under a mandatory duty to register the squatter on the application made by the squatter under section 75 (2) if the registrar is satisfied as to the squatter's title. For what does the E squatter make application? I will read section 75 (2) again: " Any person claiming to have acquired a title under the Limitation Acts to a registered estate in the land may apply to be registered as proprietor thereof."

To my mind the words are clear and unequivocal: the squatter claims to have acquired a title to " a registered estate in the land " (i.e. the leasehold interest) and applies to be registered as a proprietor " *thereof* " F (my emphasis). Therefore under section 75 (2), references to the squatter having acquired title to a registered estate must include the rights which under the Limitation Act 1939 the squatter acquires in relation to leasehold interests. Section 75 (2) then refers to the squatter applying to be registered as proprietor " thereof." This word can, in my judgment, only refer back to the registered estate in the land against which the G squatter has acquired title under the Act of 1939, i.e. the leasehold interest. The clear words of the Act therefore seem to require that, once the 12 years have run, the squatter is entitled to be registered as proprietor of the lease itself, and is bound to be so registered if he applies for registration. It follows that in my judgment the defendant (as the squatter) is correctly registered as proprietor of the lease itself in accordance with the clear requirements of section 75. If that is right, H Mrs. David cannot be entitled to rectification of the register as against the defendant, and she can therefore never get into a position in which she is competent to surrender the lease to the plaintiff.

I am conscious that in so deciding I am reaching a conclusion which produces at least a limited divergence between squatter's rights over registered and unregistered land. Once the squatter is rightly registered as proprietor under section 75 (3) the documentary lessee and the free-

The Weekly Law Reports, March 6, 1981

231

1 W.L.R.   Spectrum Investment v. Holmes (Ch.D.)   Browne-Wilkinson J.

A   holder can no longer defeat the squatter's rights by a surrender.   But I am not deciding anything as to the position during the period between the date when the squatter obtains his title by adverse possession and the date on which he obtains registration of it.   This is the period covered by section 75 (1) which is the subsection on which Lord Radcliffe in *St. Marylebone Property Co. Ltd.* v. *Fairweather* [1963] A.C. 510, 542, and Sir John Pennycuick in *Jessamine Investment Co.* v. *Schwartz* [1978]
B   Q.B. 264, 275, were commenting.   It may well be, as their dicta suggest, that during the period preceding any registration of the squatter's rights, the documentary lessee (as registered proprietor of the lease) and the freeholder can deal with the legal estate without reference to a person whose rights are not recorded on the register.   But once the Act provides for registration of the squatter's title, it must in my judgment follow that
C   the squatter's rights (once registered) cannot be overriden.   The difference between registered and unregistered land in this respect is an inevitable consequence of the fact that the Land Registration Act 1925 provides for registration of the squatter as proprietor and that registered proprietors have rights.

I can summarise my conclusions as follows:

D   (a) The plaintiff cannot, under section 11 of the Act, have any estate right or interest adverse to or in derogation of the title of the defendant (as registered proprietor of the lease with possessory title) unless and until the lease has come to an end.

(b) The lease has not come to an end by virtue of the purported surrender of May 7, 1975, since at that date the leasehold interest was registered land and the surrender was not made in accordance with the
E   provisions of the Act.

(c) Mrs. David is not entitled to rectification of the register reinstating her as registered proprietor of the lease, since the defendant is registered in accordance with the mandatory requirements of section 75 of the Act.

Therefore (d) Mrs. David can never surrender the term so as to merge it in the freehold, and accordingly the plaintiff cannot become entitled
F   to possession by reason of such a surrender.

In these circumstances it is not necessary for me to consider the argument that in exercising my discretion whether or not to rectify the register, I should not in any event order rectification against the defendant, the registered proprietor in possession, at the suit of those whose disregard of their own property interest has led to the defendant's registration.

I therefore dismiss the claim by the plaintiff.

G

Action dismissed with costs.

Solicitors: *Gale & Phelps; G. Houghton & Son.*

A. R.

H

A

[COURT OF APPEAL]

* B.P. EXPLORATION CO. (LIBYA) LTD. *v.*
HUNT (No. 2)

1980   June 3, 4, 5, 6,   Lawton, Bridge and   B
        9, 10, 11, 12; 16   Shaw L.JJ.

> *Contract—Frustration—Remedy—Agreement to develop oil con-*
> *cession—Concession developed into oil field on stream—*
> *Agreement frustrated by Libyan Government expropriating*
> *one party's interest in field and excluding them from field—*
> *Resulting unjust enrichment of other party—Principles to be*   C
> *applied in awarding just sum—Currency of award—Whether*
> *interest payable on sum awarded—Law Reform (Miscellaneous*
> *Provisions) Act 1934 (24 & 25 Geo. 5, c. 41), s. 3—Law*
> *Reform (Frustrated Contracts) Act 1943 (6 & 7 Geo. 6, c. 40),*
> *ss. 1 (2), (3), 2 (3)*

The defendant, who had been granted an oil concession in
Libya, entered into a " farm-in " agreement with the plaintiffs,
under which the plaintiffs received a half-share in the con-   D
cession and agreed in return to transfer to the defendant
certain " farm-in " contributions in cash and in oil, and to
undertake the exploration of the concession and, if oil was
found, the development of and production of oil from the
field.   Under the agreement, the plaintiffs were to provide all
necessary finance until the field came on stream; but once the
field came on stream, the plaintiffs were to take and receive
not only one-half of all oil produced from the field, but also   E
" reimbursement oil " in the form of three-eighths of the
defendant's share of the production until the plaintiffs had
received in reimbursement 125 per cent. of their farm-in
contributions and of one-half of the money expended by them
in the exploration and development of the field before it
came on stream.   After the field came on stream, the cost
of production and development of the field was to be borne
equally by the two parties.   The agreement between the   F
parties was contained in two documents, the operating agreement and the letter agreement, and by clause 6 of the letter
agreement it was agreed that the defendant should have no
personal liability to repay the sums required in the operating
agreement.

The plaintiffs spent many millions of pounds in exploration
and, having found a large oil field, in its development.   The
field came on stream in 1967 and, thereafter, substantial   G
quantities of oil were produced from the field until December
1971, when the Libyan Government expropriated the plaintiffs' interest in the concession.   The plaintiffs had by then
received about one-third of the reimbursement oil to which
they were entitled.   The defendant, under increasingly difficult
conditions, was able to export some oil from the field until
his interest was expropriated by the government in July 1973.
Both parties received compensation from the Libyan Govern-   H

---

[1] Law Reform (Frustrated Contracts) Act 1943, s. 1: " (2) All sums paid . . . to
any party in pursuance of the contract before the time when the parties were so
discharged . . . shall . . . be recoverable from him as money received by him for
the use of the party by whom the sums were paid . . .   (3) Where any party to the
contract has . . . obtained a valuable benefit (other than a payment of money to
which the last foregoing subsection applies) before the time of discharge, there shall
be recoverable from him by the said other party such sum . . . as the court
considers just . . ."

A ment based on the book value of the facilities in Libya but nothing for the loss of the concession.

The plaintiffs claimed a declaration that the contract had been frustrated and an award of a just sum under section 1 (3) of the Law Reform (Frustrated Contracts) Act 1943.[1] The defendant contended that the Act had no application because the contract was not governed by English law and the contract had not been frustrated. In the alternative, he denied that

B the plaintiffs were entitled to an award and he claimed an award under the Act. The judge held that the contract was governed by English law and had been frustrated in December 1971 and, since clause 6 of the letter agreement could not be construed as being intended to apply in the event of frustration, the provisions of section 2 (3) of the Act did not apply to exclude an award under the Act. He further held that the defendant had been adequately compensated for his perform-

C ance under the contract and, therefore, he was not entitled to an award under the Act but the plaintiffs were entitled to a just sum for the valuable benefit the defendant had received as a result of their contractual performance. In assessing the sum, the judge made no allowance for the "time value of money," i.e., the notional benefit derived from the fact that the defendant had had the use of the product of the plaintiffs' contractual performance over a period of time before the

D frustrating event occurred. On the basis that the defendant's benefit was the oil he obtained from the concession and the settlement with the Libyan Government of which half was as a result of the plaintiffs' contractual performance and the other half deriving from the defendant's ownership of the concession, the judge made an award in dollars in respect of the farm-in cash and oil and in sterling for the services rendered by the plaintiffs. He ordered that interest was pay-

E able on the award from June 14, 1974, when the plaintiffs had made it clear that they intended to claim restitution.

On appeal by the defendant and cross-appeal by the plaintiffs: —

Held, dismissing both the appeal and the cross-appeal, (1) that the legal effect of frustration was to bring a contract to an end forthwith; that, accordingly, since on its true con-

F struction clause 6 of the contract was not intended to have effect regardless of frustration, it ceased to apply after the contract had been frustrated and did not operate to deprive the plaintiffs of their right to claim a just sum under the Act of 1943 (post, p. 241A–B, C–D).

(2) That it was for the judge at first instance to assess, under section 1 (3) of the Act, what was a just sum in all the circumstances and an appellate court was not entitled to

G interfere unless the decision was so plainly wrong as to be unjust (post, p. 238A–B); that the section did not require the court at first instance to draw up a balance sheet showing how each party to a contract had benefited and to make an award in favour of the party who had benefited least, but merely to fix a sum which it considered just, and the reimbursement basis used by the judge could not be said to be wrong so as to entitle the court to interfere with his decision (post,

H pp. 242F–G, 243H).

(3) That, on the true construction of section 1 (2) of the Act, sums paid by a party to a contract in pursuance of the contract before the frustrating event were to be recoverable from the other party to the contract, but there was no scope for adding to the sums paid a further sum to represent the "time value of the money" either under subsection (2) or subsection (3) of section 1 (post, p. 244E–H).

(4) That the Act contemplated payment of a just sum in respect of the benefit obtained by the defendant, and, accord-

ingly, it was right that he should pay back dollars in respect   A
of the " farm-in " oil and payments, which he had obtained
in dollars, and that he should pay back sterling in respect of
the money expended in development, which the plaintiffs, an
English company with accounts in sterling operating a contract
governed by English law, had advanced from their sterling
resources (post, p. 245A–C).

(5) That the judge's choice of date for the commencement
of interest on the sum awarded was made in the exercise of   B
his discretion, and there was no ground for interfering with
it (post, p. 245F).

Decision of Robert Goff J. [1979] 1 W.L.R. 783 affirmed.

The following cases are referred to in the judgment of the court:

B.P. Exploration Co. (Libya) Ltd. v. *Hunt* [1976] 1 W.L.R. 788; [1976]
    3 All E.R. 879.
Chandler v. *Webster* [1904] 1 K.B. 493, C.A.   C
Fibrosa Spolka Akcyjna v. *Fairbairn Lawson Combe Barbour Ltd.* [1943]
    A.C. 32; [1942] 2 All E.R. 122, H.L.(E.).
Hirji Mulji v. *Cheong Yue Steamship Co. Ltd.* [1926] A.C. 497, P.C.

The following additional cases were cited in argument:

Aldora, The [1975] Q.B. 748; [1975] 2 W.L.R. 791; [1975] 2 All E.R.   D
    69.
Bank Line Ltd. v. *Arthur Capel & Co.* [1919] A.C. 435, H.L.(E.).
General Tire & Rubber Co. v. *Firestone Tyre & Rubber Co. Ltd.* [1975]
    1 W.L.R. 819; [1975] 2 All E.R. 173, H.L.(E.).
Way v. *Latilla* [1937] 3 All E.R. 759, H.L.(E.).

APPEAL from Robert Goff J.   E

The defendant, Nelson Bunker Hunt, appealed from a judgment of
Robert Goff J. given on March 16, 1979, whereby he ordered the
defendant to pay to the plaintiffs, B.P. Exploration Co. (Libya) Ltd.
(" B.P."), U.S. $15,575,823 (comprising principal of $10,801,534 and
interest thereon) and £8,922,060 (comprising principal of £5,666,399 and
interest thereon) by way of a just sum under section 1 (3) of the Law
Reform (Frustrated Contracts) Act 1943.   F

The grounds of the appeal were, inter alia, that the judge wrongly held
that clause 6 of the letter agreement between the parties dated June 24,
1960, was not " intended to have effect in the event of circumstances
arising which operate, or would, but for the said provision, operate, to
frustrate the contract," or was not " intended to have effect whether
such circumstances arise or not " and wrongly failed to " give effect to
the said provision " and wrongly gave effect to section 1 of the Law   G
Reform (Frustrated Contracts) Act 1943 notwithstanding that to do so
was inconsistent with that provision; that the judge, having correctly held
that it would usually be wrong to identify the discovered mineral as the
benefit of the service of prospecting, then misdirected himself by concluding that the benefit obtained by the defendant was the enhancement
of the concession by the exploration work and the development of the   H
oilfield to commercial production, whereas he should have held that the
benefit obtained by the defendant was the downpayments and advances
of expenditure; that the judge incorrectly valued the benefit gained by the
defendant from the plaintiffs as one-half of the value of the oil which
the defendant received from the concession plus the amount the defendant
received by way of settlement on his own expropriation by the Libyan
Government. That was in effect to treat the profits as the benefit

A provided by the plaintiffs whereas if (as the judge concluded) the correct approach was to take into account the enhancement of the value of the concession that would be achieved by way of valuation not by a calculation of all sums derived from a share in the concession. The judge ought to have concluded that the benefit which the plaintiffs obtained from the defendant was a half share in the concession at a valuation,

B whereas the benefit which the defendant obtained from the plaintiffs was the downpayments and advance payments to the defendant or for the defendant's account subject to the express limitation upon the plaintiffs' right of recovery. Further grounds included that in determining that it was just that the plaintiffs should recover any sum from the defendant the judge failed to take into account: (i) that the defendant had in no way been " unjustly enriched," in that the parties had expressly contem-

C plated and " specifically understood and agreed " that the plaintiffs' entitlement to recover downpayments and advances should be calculated solely by reference to oil produced, saved and delivered and that the plaintiffs had drawn oil in accordance with such entitlement; (ii) that the award of any " just sum " would involve taking away from the defendant part of the benefit expressly conferred by the contract upon him, namely, that

D the entitlement of the plaintiffs to recovery of downpayments and advances should not be more than provided by the agreement as amended calculated by reference to oil drawn by the defendant; (iii) that no sum could ever be just if it deprived a party of part of the consideration for an obligation which that party had executed, and to require the defendant to pay any sum to the plaintiffs imposed a solution which altered the consideration for his executed obligations to the detriment of the defendant

E in a manner contrary to the contemplation of the parties and the express terms of their bargain; (iv) that the award of a sum would compensate the plaintiffs upon a basis fundamentally contradictory to the limitation of the agreements, and would entitle them to improve upon their bargain; (v) that it could not be just to transfer the risk of making a loss, or of making a lesser profit, from the plaintiffs to the defendant where such

F risk had been undertaken by the plaintiffs under the agreement; (vi) that the agreement had specifically excluded any personal liability by the defendant in respect of the downpayments and advances, and failed to consider whether it could be just to impose personal liability after frustration in such circumstances; (vii) that, unlike the position in " entire " contracts, the parties had agreed a careful method of reimbursement by reference to the production of oil and that regular recovery had taken

G place in accordance with the contractual provisions. The judge misdirected himself in holding that the contract was frustrated; the judge erred in failing to conclude that the defendant had given full consideration for the services and downpayments by transferring half the concession to the plaintiffs and granting them the right to take and receive reimbursement oil in accordance with clause 9 (e) of the operating

H agreement; he misdirected himself in holding that a claim under section 1 (3) of the Law Reform (Frustrated Contracts) Act 1943 was a proceeding for the recovery of a debt or, in any event was a claim on which interest could be awarded pursuant to the Law Reform (Miscellaneous Provisions) Act 1934; and he misdirected himself in holding that in all the circumstances interest should be awarded to the plaintiffs either at the rate and for the period awarded or at all and in holding that any award should be in any currency other than sterling.

The plaintiffs cross-appealed on the grounds, inter alia, that the judge   A
erred in law in failing to assess the just sum by reference to or alternatively in failing to give any or any sufficient weight for the purposes
of such assessment to the value of the benefit obtained by the defendant
by reason of what the plaintiffs did in and for the purpose of the
performance of the contractual arrangements which, as the judge held,
was to be identified with the end product of such services; in failing to   B
assess the just sum by reference to or alternatively in failing to give any
or any sufficient weight for the purposes of such assessment to the value
of the reimbursement oil which the plaintiffs would have been entitled
to receive under clause 9 (e) of the operating agreement, as amended,
but for the frustration of the contractual arrangements and/or in disregarding the same on the grounds that it was " too speculative " or
" extraordinarily high," in holding that as a matter of construction it   C
was not open to the court either in assessing the value of the benefit
obtained by the defendant or the just sum to be awarded to the plaintiffs
in respect thereof, to take account of the time value of money, and in
failing to take account thereof notwithstanding, as the judge acknowledged, that this would have led to a more realistic valuation of the
defendant's benefit as at the date of frustration; in assessing the just   D
sum by reference to and by making the award mainly in sterling and
in failing to assess the just sum and to make the award wholly in U.S.
dollars, notwithstanding U.S. dollars was (a) the currency of the defendant
and the currency in or by reference to which the defendant's benefit was
received and/or valued and/or enjoyed by him; (b) the currency of the
plaintiffs, in that the plaintiffs traded in oil in or by reference to that
currency; (c) the currency in or by reference to which the international   E
oil business is and was at all material times conducted; (d) the currency
of payment in respect of the defendant's benefit under the contractual
arrangements; (e) the currency to which oil, being the " currency " of
account in respect of the benefit under the contractual arrangements as
amended at the date of frustration, was to be most closely equated; and
in failing to award interest on the just sum for the whole of the period   F
from December 7, 1971 (the date of frustration) to judgment.

The facts are stated in the judgment of the court.

Peter Curry Q.C., Nicholas Lyell Q.C. and Peregrin Simon for the
defendant.
Kenneth Rokison Q.C., Iain Milligan and R. G. Wood for the
plaintiffs.   G

                                                      Cur. adv. vult.

July 16. LAWTON L.J. read the following judgment of the court.
This case concerns an appeal by the defendant, Mr. Nelson Bunker Hunt,
and a cross-appeal by the plaintiffs, B.P. Exploration Co. (Libya) Ltd.,
against an order made by Robert Goff J. [1979] 1 W.L.R. 783, on March   H
26, 1979, whereby he adjudged that, pursuant to the Law Reform
(Frustrated Contracts) Act 1943, the defendant should pay the plaintiffs
U.S. $15,575,823 and £8,922,060, both sums including interest. The
defendant has submitted, first, that he should not have been ordered to
pay anything, as his contract with the plaintiffs absolved him from having
to pay anything; and, secondly, if anything was payable, he has been
ordered to pay too much because the trial judge assessed his liability on

A the wrong basis. The plaintiffs, by their cross-appeal, have submitted that the judge should have awarded them much more than he did because, first, he made his assessment on a wrong basis; secondly, he failed to take into account the commercial concept of the time value of money (sometimes referred to by accountants as discounted cash flow); and, thirdly, he should have made the whole of the award in U.S. dollars.

B That both parties should allege that the judge had made his assessment on the wrong basis is not surprising as this is believed to be the first case to have come before the Supreme Court of Judicature under the Law Reform (Frustrated Contracts) Act 1943, which, in its relevant provisions, defines in the most general terms the scope of the powers which it confers on the court.

The Act of 1943 was passed shortly after the decision of the House C of Lords in *Fibrosa Spolka Akcyjna* v. *Fairbairn Lawson Combe Barbour Ltd.* [1943] A.C. 32, which overruled *Chandler* v. *Webster* [1904] 1 K.B. 493. The earlier case had been regarded as authority for the proposition that, on the occurrence of an event which frustrates the performance of a contract, the loss lies where it falls and that money paid by one party to the contract to the other party is to be retained by the party in whose hands it is. The object of the Act was to make the operation of the D law more fair when a contract governed by English law (as the one under consideration in this case was found by Kerr J. to be in an interlocutory judgment: *B.P. Exploration Co. (Libya) Ltd.* v. *Hunt* [1976] 1 W.L.R. 788, has become impossible of performance and the parties to it have for that reason been discharged from further performance. This was to be done by adjusting the rights and liabilities of the parties in E the ways set out: see section 1 (1).

Section 1 (2) dealt with payments of money. They were to be recoverable as money received for the use of the payer; but an adjustment could be made for expenses incurred by the recipient before the time of discharge in, or for the purpose of, the performance of the contract. The amount of the adjustment was to be such as the court considered just, having regard to all the circumstances of the case. In F section 1 (3) the Act provided for the case where one party had obtained a valuable benefit (other than a payment of money) before the time of discharge. In such a case there should be recoverable from the party receiving the benefit:

> " such sum (if any), not exceeding the value of the said benefit to the party obtaining it, as the court considers just, having regard to G all the circumstances of the case and, in particular,—(*a*) the amount of any expenses incurred before the time of discharge by the benefited party in, or for the purpose of, the performance of the contract . . . and (*b*) the effect, in relation to the said benefit, of the circumstances giving rise to the frustration of the contract."

Before the court can make an award under this subsection it must H be satisfied that one party to a contract has obtained a valuable benefit by reason of something done by the other. In this case the plaintiffs did a great deal for the defendant and he obtained, before the frustrating events happened, a most valuable benefit from what they had done for him, which was so great that it was incapable of any exact valuation. This part of the problem presented no difficulties for the judge. What was difficult was the assessment of the sum which the court considered just, having regard to all the circumstances of the case. Save for what

is mentioned in paragraphs (a) and (b), the subsection gives no help as A
to how, or upon what principles, the court is to make its assessment or
as to what factors it is to take into account. The responsibility lies with
the judge: he has to fix a sum which he, not an appellate court, *considers*
just. This word connotes the mental processes going to forming an
opinion. What is just is what the trial judge thinks is just. That being
so, an appellate court is not entitled to interfere with his decision unless
it is so plainly wrong that it cannot be just. The concept of what is B
just is not an absolute one. Opinions among right thinking people may,
and probably will, differ as to what is just in a particular case. No one
person enjoys the faculty of infallibility as to what is just. It is with
these considerations in mind that we approach this case.

The facts are complex. They are set out in detail in the lengthy
judgment which is before us. For the purposes of this judgment we set C
them out in the barest outline. Some 30 years ago the Libyan Government had reason for thinking that there might be oil underneath the
Sahara Desert. Without capital and " know how " it could not be got
out of the ground, if it were there. Both would have to come from
outside Libya. To attract those willing to risk their capital in trying to
develop oil fields, the Libyan Government granted concessions at very D
cheap rates. The defendant, who is a Texan, took one up in December
1957. It was no. 65. It was deep in the Sahara and a long way from
the Mediterranean Sea. If it was to remain valid he had to start drilling
for oil within three years of the grant, that is by December 18, 1960.
With his own resources he could not hope to do so. He joined up with
the plaintiffs, who had other concessions in Libya. They made an agreement to develop the concession together, but it was not intended that E
they should be partners. The terms of this agreement were set out in
a letter from the plaintiffs to the defendant dated June 24, 1960. It
incorporated by reference two common forms of agreement, with modifications, used by the plaintiffs in their business. One of them, referred
to as the operating agreement, is of importance in this case. Both
parties, understandably, wanted to arrange their affairs as far as they
properly could so as to avoid the incidence of taxation. The letter F
agreement provided for a working arrangement as follows: the defendant
was to transfer one half of his interest in the concession to the plaintiffs,
who were to provide all the skill, resources and capital for its development subject to reimbursement by the defendant in a particular way of
his share of the development expenses. The plaintiffs were to pay the
defendant $2,000,000 before July 1, 1960; this sum was to be reimbursed G
by him later out of his share of the oil, but after he had made other
reimbursements. The plaintiffs were to deliver to the defendant 4,000,000
barrels of Iranian oil which he was to account for at a later date and
after he had reimbursed the plaintiffs for all other expenses. Payments
and deliveries of this kind and on these sort of terms were common in
the oil industry and were known as " farm-in payments " and " farm-in H
oil." Once oil became available in commercially worthwhile quantities
(in oil industry jargon " on stream ") all operating expenses were to be
shared equally between the plaintiffs and the defendant. What the
defendant was to get for assigning a half share in the concession to the
plaintiffs was half the oil when it came on stream. Provision had to be
made, however, for the defendant to reimburse the plaintiffs for his
share of the development expenses. This was done in clause 6 of the

A letter agreement and clause 9 (e) of the operating agreement. Clause 6 was as follows:

> " It is specifically understood and agreed that Hunt shall have no personal liability to repay the sums required in the operating agreement and this letter agreement to be advanced by B.P. for Hunt's account or paid to Hunt, but B.P.'s right to recover any such sums
B which B.P. is required to pay or advance for Hunt's account shall be limited to recovery solely out of three-eighths ($\frac{3}{8}$) of Hunt's half of the production, and in the manner specified under section 9 of the operating agreement, if, as and when produced, saved and delivered at the Libyan sea terminal."

Clause 9 (e) provided:

C   " *Reimbursement of Payments*
> " B.P. shall be entitled to take and receive three-eighths ($\frac{3}{8}$) of Hunt's share of the oil production from the concession delivered f.o.b. Libyan seaboard until B.P. has received a quantity of crude oil equal to the sum of the following: 1. a quantity equal in value to 125 per cent. . . . of all costs and expenses advanced by B.P. for Hunt's account on exploration, development, or any other work
D performed in or in connection with the concession, then 2. a quantity equal in value to U.S. $2,500,000, and then 3. 5,000,000 barrels."

It is pertinent to point out that under clause 6 the restriction on the defendant's personal liability was limited to repayment of the sums required by the letter agreement to be advanced by the plaintiffs for the
E defendant's account or to him. It did not extend to such liability as he was under to discharge the cost of the " farm-in oil " delivered to him. This clause has an odd structure. The first half is designed to ensure that there is no obligation on the defendant to pay money to the plaintiffs who are required by the second half to look for reimbursement solely to the defendant's share of the oil. There was evidence that this structure
F was insisted on by the defendant for U.S. tax reasons. There was also evidence that the provisions for reimbursement in clause 9 (e) of the operating agreement, with their references to 125 per cent. of all costs and expenses, U.S. $2,500,000, instead of $2,000,000, and 5,000,000 barrels instead of 4,000,000 barrels, were an attempt to reflect an interest element in the repayments. This, submit the plaintiffs, is relevant to the point taken on their behalf about the judge's failure to take the time value of
G money into account.

The plaintiffs started drilling operations before the concession ran out. Oil was found in quantities which seemed to be worthwhile commercially. Development started. By January 11, 1967, oil came on stream at the sea terminal which the plaintiffs had built near Tobruk. By this time the plaintiffs had spent for the defendant's account £30,800,281 on
H development. They could look forward to being reimbursed this amount out of the defendant's share of the oil if there were enough of it. In 1967 it seemed likely that there would be enough. In June 1967, the plaintiffs and the defendant decided to amend the letter agreement and the operating agreement. New terms were agreed for the discharge by the defendant of his liability to reimburse the plaintiffs in respect of expenses incurred by them until oil came on stream, including the " farm-in payments " and the " farm-in oil." His liability was fixed at a total of

50,000,000 barrels of oil. This liability was referred to during the trial as
the first oil debt. The defendant's share of expenses after the oil came
on stream and advanced by the plaintiffs in connection with development
was to be paid out of oil. This was the second oil debt. After July 1,
1967, all reimbursements by the defendant out of his share of the oil
were to be at the rate of 18,750 barrels per day or three-eighths of the
defendant's share of the daily production, whichever should be the less.
As production increased substantially after July 1967, the defendant's
liability to reimburse the plaintiffs was at the specified daily barrelage
rate.

On December 7, 1971, disaster overtook the plaintiffs' Libyan oil
interests. The then Libyan government, which was of a different political
complexion to the one which had granted the concession and under
which it had been developed, expropriated all the plaintiffs' oil interests
in the country. This was done as an act of political retaliation against
H.M. Government. By that date the defendant had made over to the
plaintiffs in discharge of his obligation to reimburse his share of expenses
incurred before January 11, 1967, 33,101,811 barrels, approximately two-
thirds of his total indebtedness in this respect.

The plaintiffs' interest in the concession came under the control of a
Libyan Government agency which operated it with such help as the
defendant could provide. Production went on but at a lower level
than before December 7, 1971. On June 11, 1973, the Libyan Government expropriated the defendant's interest in the concession. Between
December 7, 1971, and June 11, 1973, the defendant had obtained
74,000,000 barrels of oil from the concession.

Both the plaintiffs and the defendant claimed compensation from the
Libyan Government. After some delay they got some, the plaintiffs
being paid theirs in November 1974 and the defendant his in May 1975.

On May 2, 1975, the plaintiffs commenced proceedings against the
defendant in this country. Relief of various kinds was prayed. The
only claim in the writ as issued which is relevant to these appeals was
for a just sum pursuant to the Act of 1943, it being accepted by both
parties that the letter agreement, as amended by the 1967 agreement,
had been frustrated. At the trial the parties and the judge had treated
the " farm-in payment " of $2,000,000 as part of the benefit which the
defendant had obtained from the frustrated contract. In the course of
the hearing before us, it was pointed out by Bridge L.J. that, as this was
a payment of money in pursuance of the contract, it had to be considered
under section 1 (2) of the Act of 1943, not section 1 (3). Mr. Rokison
accepted that this was so and applied to amend the plaintiffs' claim so as
to include a claim for the recovery of the " farm-in payment." We gave
leave to amend.

The first question for decision in this court was whether, having regard
to clause 6 of the letter agreement, the plaintiffs were entitled to be paid
a just sum. The defendant submitted that section 2 (3) of the Act of
1943 applied, the effect of which is to exclude the operation of the Act
if, upon the true construction of the contract, any provision in it is
intended to have effect whether frustration arises or not. Mr. Curry's
argument on behalf of the defendant was that the emphatic opening
words of clause 6—I repeat them: " It is specifically understood and
agreed that Hunt shall have no personal liability to repay "—meant that
in no circumstances of any kind should the defendant be called upon to

A pay the plaintiffs any sum. The clause does not say this: the limitation does not apply to the defendant's liability in respect of "farm-in oil." The delivery of this oil to him in 1961 was a valuable benefit for which a just sum might be recoverable. This is, however, not the effective answer to the defendant's submission. Clause 6 can only be of help to the defendant if it survived the frustrating events. The legal effect of frustration is to bring a contract to an end forthwith, without more and

B automatically: see *Hirji Mulji* v. *Cheong Yue Steamship Co. Ltd.* [1926] A.C. 497, 505, *per* Lord Sumner. It follows that clause 6 ceased to operate after December 7, 1971, unless, on its true construction, it was intended to have effect whether there was frustration or not. We can find no words in it to that effect. It was a clause which provided that the defendant should discharge his obligation to reimburse the plaintiffs

C for sums advanced to his account or paid to him not in money but in oil. The obligation which he was to discharge with oil arose under the contract and it was in respect of that contractual obligation that there was to be no personal liability. In order to sustain the defendant's submission the clause would have to be read as meaning that the defendant should have no personal liability under the contract or otherwise, including under the Act of 1943, to repay. In our judgment there is no

D reason why the clause should be read in these terms; and, if it is not so read, it ceased to have effect when the frustrating events occurred. What the defendant has been ordered to pay under the judgment is not what was due under the contract but what was recoverable from him as a just sum under the Act.

     The judge assessed the just sum on what can be described as a reim-

E bursement basis, that is to say, by ensuring as far as was practicable that the plaintiffs got back what they had paid out on the defendant's behalf before the frustrating events happened. The plaintiffs had provided for the benefit of the joint venture their expertise, their capital resources and the services of their staff. All this had cost them a lot of money. They had advanced money and oil to the defendant in the early days of

F the enterprise; and, for a few months after the oil came on stream, they had spent £440,026 (the second oil debt) on his behalf. Under clause 9 (e) of the operating agreement as varied they were to be reimbursed out of the defendant's share of the oil after it came on stream, up to a limit of 50,000,000 barrels. By the time the frustrating events happened they had been reimbursed with oil to the extent of about two-thirds of the total barrelage due to them. The judge was of

G the opinion that the just sum should be calculated by adding together four items: viz., the cost of development on the defendant's account (£30,800,281, or U.S. $86,180,612), the "farm-in payment" of U.S. $2,000,000, the value of the "farm-in oil" at the date of delivery to the defendant, that is $8,801,534, and the second oil debt of £440,026 or $1,056,062, and subtracting the value of the defendant's share of the oil

H which they had taken over pursuant to the operating agreement as varied, this oil being valued at the dates of receipt by the plaintiffs at $63,367,000. This left a balance of $34,671,208. The "farm-in payment" should not have been included in this calculation of a just sum under section 1 (3) of the Act as it was recoverable under section 1 (2); but the mistaken inclusion is a matter of form, not of substance.

     Both parties have submitted that this method of assessment was wrong. The defendant argued that the judge had failed to take into

account that, under clause 6 of the letter agreement, the plaintiffs had
assumed the risk of untoward events happening, and that the judge had
assumed that the defendant had made substantial profits out of the
74,000,000 barrels of oil which he got out of the concession between
December 7, 1971, and June 11, 1973, whereas his profits had been
modest. The plaintiffs had been willing in the early years of the development to accept the risk that they might expend money without getting
a commercial return; but, by 1971, it was known that the concession
was a very valuable one indeed which was likely to produce enough oil
to enable the defendant within about three more years to reimburse the
plaintiffs out of his share of the oil for all that they had expended on
his behalf in the development—and both of them anticipated in 1971
that oil would probably flow for about another 15 years. In our judgment, the fact that the plaintiffs were willing in the early days of the
joint enterprise to take risks with their money is of little, if any, significance to the assessment of the just sum which has to be fixed with
regard to all the circumstances of the case, particularly those existing
when the frustrating events happened.

The defendant's argument, based on the comparatively unprofitable
working of the concession after December 7, 1971, was put in this
way. The amounts of reimbursement oil received by the plaintiffs from
the defendant before December 7, 1971, represented five-sixths of the
plaintiffs' expenditure on development for the defendant's account. It
followed that only one-sixth at most of the oil recovered after that date
should be brought into account. The defendant had incurred heavy
expenses and Libyan taxes whilst trying to operate the concession with
a Libyan agency after December 7, 1971. During this period operating
conditions had been difficult because of political interference and the
lack of the plaintiffs' expertise. Furthermore, because he had drawn oil
after that date, his interest in the concession had depreciated more than
the plaintiffs'. This was a factor taken into account by the Libyan
Government when fixing his compensation. Against this factor can,
however, be put the sum which he got by way of compensation for his
share of the equipment which had been installed by the plaintiffs in the
course of developing and operating the concession. All these points
might have been relevant had it been the judge's task to draw up a
balance sheet showing on one side how the plaintiffs benefited from the
joint venture, on the other how the defendant did, and making an award
in favour of the plaintiffs if the defendant had benefited more than they
had done. The Act does not require the judge to perform such an
accountancy exercise; and, even if it had done, the use of different, but
professionally acceptable, accountancy methods might have produced
differing results. All the Act requires him to do is to fix a sum which
he considers just.

The defendant also submitted that the judge should have taken
account of the tax and other benefits which the plaintiffs obtained from
arranging their finances as they did and from selling most of their oil
within the B.P. group of companies. In our judgment, all this was too
remote from the assessment of a just sum.

Mr. Rokison, on behalf of the plaintiffs, accepted that there could
be more than one way of assessing a just sum. He pointed out that
there was nothing in the Act to indicate that its purpose was to enable
the judge to apportion losses or profits, or to put the parties in the

A positions which they would have been in if the contract had been fully performed or if it had never been made. This we accept. He submitted that the concept behind the Act was to prevent unjust enrichment. This is what the judge had thought. We get no help from the use of words which are not in the statute. Mr. Rokison's submission came to this— that, in the circumstances of this case, the judge should have assessed the just sum to be awarded to the plaintiffs in one of two ways, either

B by reference to the second oil debt and the value of the 16,900,000 barrels of oil which had not been made over on the dates when they would have been delivered but for the frustration of the contract; or by fixing a sum which would equalise the value of the benefits which were obtained by the parties. Whichever way the judge chose, he should, so it was submitted, have brought into his calculation the time value of

C money. For the purposes of this judgment we do not think it necessary to set out the calculations upon which Mr. Rokison relied. The figures were not in dispute. It suffices to say that, on the basis of the equalisation of benefits, had the time value of money been taken into account the just sum would have been U.S. $87,956,557 and, without it, U.S. $57,350,359. Further, submitted Mr. Rokison, the whole of the award should have been in U.S. dollars and not split into dollars and sterling

D as in the order under appeal.

Valuing the undelivered oil may be one way of assessing the just sum. It is the converse of the judge's approach which was to value the delivered oil as at the dates when it was received by the plaintiffs. The suggested way gives a figure which would have been obtained if nothing had happened to stop the joint venture; the judge's way gives a figure

E which was obtained as a result of deliveries which were made. An assessment based on what happened might commend itself more to many right-minded persons than one based upon what might have happened. The balancing of benefits is another way of assessing a just sum; but it is not the only way. In our judgment, this court would not be justified in setting aside the judge's way of assessment merely because we thought that there were better ways. Mr. Rokison tried to show that the judge's

F way was wrong and palpably wrong. He suggested that the judge started by assessing the just sum by reference to the value of the undelivered oil at the dates when it should have been delivered but was put off continuing with this method because the figure which resulted was greater than the sums which the plaintiffs had expended on development. Assuming this this is a correct interpretation of what the judge said (and we are

G not satisfied that it is) he was entitled to have second thoughts about a particular method of assessment if it did not fit in with his concept that, in the circumstances of this case, a just sum could be assessed by reference to reimbursing the plaintiffs for what they had paid out on behalf of the defendant. This was said to be wrong too because section 1 (3) is not concerned with expenditure. There is, of course, no reference to ex-

H penditure in section 1 (3) nor is there to the balancing of benefits or the valuing of undelivered goods. All these may be relevant to the assessment of a just sum and whether they are will depend upon the circumstances of each case. In our judgment, it cannot be said that the judge went wrong, and certainly not palpably wrong, in assessing a just sum by reference to the concept of reimbursing the plaintiffs.

The plaintiffs went on to submit that, even if the judge's way of assessing a just sum was correct, he misdirected himself by refusing,

when fixing the amount, to take account of the benefit which the A
defendant had obtained from the time value of money. The argument
was that, from 1960 until December 7, 1971, the defendant had had the
benefit of the large sums which the plaintiffs had expended on his behalf.
Without what the plaintiffs had done in this way, he would have been
faced with the choice of either not developing the concession at all or
borrowing the necessary capital; and, had he borrowed it, he would have
had to pay interest at the current commercial rates. The plaintiffs, for B
their part, had tied up over many years large amounts of capital in the
concession for the defendant's benefit as well as their own. The evidence
was that, in commerce and industry, the time value of money was taken
into account when deciding whether an enterprise was likely to be or
had been profitable. On a reimbursement basis, without the time value
factor, the plaintiffs appeared to have made a profit of about U.S. C
$55,000,000 out of operating the concession; but, if it was taken into
account, they had made a loss of about $11,000,000. Commercial men
would regard this as a real loss. In so far as the defendant had benefited
from what they had done, the just sum awarded should, it was submitted,
reflect the time value factor. By clause 9 (e) of the operating agreement
the parties had recognised in 1960 that time had to be paid for by the
defendant when money was paid to him or expended on his behalf. This D
was to be inferred from the provision that the oil to be handed over by
the defendant should be equal in value to 125 per cent. of all costs and
expenses advanced and the " farm-in payment " and the " farm-in oil "
should be increased to the same extent.

The judge stated that, had it been open to him to do so, he would
have considered the time value of money (which is known as the dis- E
counted net cash flow method of accounting) when assessing what benefit
the defendant had obtained from the joint enterprise. He concluded
that, on the true construction of the Act, he was unable to do so. We
are of the same opinion and for the same reasons.

Under section 1 (2) sums paid by a party to a contract in pursuance
of the contract and before the frustrating events are to be recoverable F
from the other party as money received by him for the use of the other
party. This can only mean that what has been paid out must be paid
back. There is no scope in this subsection for adding to the sum paid
something extra to represent the time value of money. Section 1 (3)
deals with the position when one party has obtained a valuable benefit
by reason of anything done by the other party. The doing could include,
and often would include, as in this case, the spending of money for the G
benefit of the other party. It would be odd if, in one section dealing
with the adjustment of rights and liabilities following the frustration of
a contract, the time value of money had to be taken into account if
money were spent by one party for the benefit of the other, but not if it
were paid to the other. In our judgment, the part of section 1 (3) dealing
with the amount of any expenses incurred before the time of discharge H
by the benefited party shows that there is no such distinction. If the
court is to have regard to *the amount of any expenses incurred*, it must
look at the sum paid out as expenses, not at the sum calculated by
reference to the discounted net cash flow method of accountancy.

Having used the reimbursement way of assessing a just sum, the judge
ordered it to be paid partly in sterling and partly in U.S. dollars. He
explained his reasons for doing so at considerable length. The plaintiffs

A submitted that all the sums payable under the order should have been in U.S. dollars because such dollars are the currency of the international oil industry and the defendant obtained dollars for his share of the oil. The Act intended that he should pay a just sum in respect of the benefit he had obtained. As he had obtained dollars in respect of his benefit he should pay dollars back. The judge accepted this argument in relation to the " farm-in payment " and the " farm-in oil." The defendant had been

B paid dollars and had had oil delivered which, on the international market, is valued in dollars. The judge's opinion was that the position with regard to the money expended in development on the defendant's account both before and after the oil came on stream was different. The plaintiffs were an English company, keeping their accounts in sterling and operating under a contract governed by English law. The money they advanced

C came from their sterling resources. The consequence was that they were entitled to be repaid in sterling. We agree with this reasoning.

When making his order, the judge decided to add interest to the just sum he had assessed. He did so pursuant to the provisions of the Law Reform (Miscellaneous Provisions) Act 1934. He ordered that interest should be paid on the amount due as from June 14, 1974, this being

D the date upon which the plaintiffs had made clear to the defendant that they were going to make a claim against him for a sum of £17,000,000. Both parties submitted that this date was wrong. The plaintiffs argued that interest should have been ordered to run from December 7, 1971, that being the date upon which the plaintiffs' right to be paid a just sum arose. The defendant submitted that the right date was that on which the judge delivered the main judgment, namely, June 30, 1978, because,

E until that date, there was no debt which could attract interest within section 3 (1) of the Act of 1934. Both submissions were misconceived. The exercise of the power to award interest on debts and damages is discretionary. The judge chose June 14, 1974, because until then the defendant did not know that the plaintiffs were going to make a claim against him and before then it had not been clear that they would or

F could. The judge's choice of this date was made in the exercise of his judicial discretion. We can see no reason for saying he exercised his discretion wrongly. The defendant's submission could not be supported. His liability to pay the plaintiffs a just sum arose on December 7, 1971. From then onwards he was indebted to the plaintiffs but the amount of his indebtedness could not be known until the judge had assessed it.

The appeal and cross-appeal are dismissed.

G

> *Appeal and cross-appeal dismissed.*
> *Plaintiffs to have two-thirds of their*
>   *costs in Court of Appeal.*
> *Leave to appeal refused.*

H   November 6. The Appeal Committee of the House of Lords (Lord Diplock, Lord Keith of Kinkel and Lord Scarman) allowed a petition by the defendant for leave to appeal to the House of Lords.

[Reported by MISS HENRIETTA STEINBERG, Barrister-at-Law]

[1981]

A

* WHITEHOUSE . . . . APPELLANT

AND

JORDAN AND ANOTHER . . . . RESPONDENTS

1980 Oct. 27, 28, 29, 30;   Lord Wilberforce, Lord Edmund-Davies, B
      Nov. 3;   Lord Fraser of Tullybelton,
      Dec. 17   Lord Russell of Killowen and
                                       Lord Bridge of Harwich

> *Medical Practitioner—Negligence—Standard of care—Obstetrician
> —Use of forceps in delivery—Five or six pulls with forceps—
> Obstruction of ischial spines—Subsequent hospital report*   C
> *stating that infant's head disimpacted prior to Caesarean
> section—Whether evidence establishing negligence—Error of
> clinical judgment—Whether capable of amounting to
> negligence*
> *Evidence—Expert evidence—Medical report—Action for negligence
> against medical practitioner—Joint report prepared by plain-
> tiff's medical experts and settled by counsel—Whether undesir-
> able practice*   D

The plaintiff was born in 1970 with severe brain damage,
and he brought an action against, inter alia, the first defendant,
a senior registrar at the time of his birth, and the hospital
authority claiming that the damage had been caused by
the first defendant's professional negligence. The principal
allegations of negligence were that in the course of carrying
out a " trial of forceps delivery " the first defendant had pulled
too long and too strongly on the plaintiff's head, thereby   E
causing the brain damage, and that he had continued traction
with the forceps after the obstruction of the ischial spines
had been encountered so that the plaintiff's head had become
wedged or stuck. It had been anticipated before the birth
that it was likely to be difficult. At the birth, the first defendant had first used forceps and then proceeded to Caesarean
section. The plaintiff had then been found to be apnoeic and
had only been made to breathe after 35 minutes, after which   F
irretrievable brain damage had occurred. It was accepted that
the Caesarean section had been properly performed. In a
report made after the birth by the consultant in charge of the
maternity unit at the hospital, which was seen by the first
defendant, it was stated:

" A trial of forceps was carried out under epidural anaesthesia . . . Descent, however, did not follow traction and
in the interest of the child the head was disimpacted prior   G
to speedy delivery by Caesarean section."

At the trial, the mother said that, when the forceps had been
applied, it had " felt like a deadened electric shock that lifted
my hips . . . off the [delivery] bed." Both the first defendant
and the doctor who had assisted him denied that she had been
lifted off the bed or that the first defendant had pulled violently
with the forceps. The first defendant denied that the plaintiff's   H
head had been wedged or stuck; he had been able without
difficulty to push it up a little in preparation for Caesarean
section. He said that his trial by forceps, in which he had
pulled with five or six contractions, had been to overcome
what might have been minimal obstruction of the ischial spines
and that he had not tried to pull despite them. Considerable
expert evidence was called as to, inter alia, the meaning of
" impaction." The judge did not express disbelief of the first
defendant's evidence but appraised it in relation to the other

A   evidence. He rejected the mother's account of what had happened to her when the forceps had been applied but said that, though it might not be exact in its clinical detail, he believed her in so far as her description could be taken to be understood as a pulling of her towards the bottom of the delivery bed in a manner and with such force as to have been inconsistent with a trial of forceps properly carried out. In all the circumstances, he was doubtful whether the first

B defendant had in fact been undertaking a trial of forceps as opposed to an attempt at vaginal delivery that had failed and in the course of which the plaintiff's head had been wedged, stuck or jammed, which on anyone's view of the matter would have been unjustified. In any event, if it had been a trial of forceps then the first defendant had pulled too hard and too long so that the plaintiff's head had become wedged or stuck. In getting it wedged or stuck, or unwedged or unstuck, the

C first defendant had caused asphyxia which in its turn had caused the cerebral palsy. In that respect he had fallen below the very high standard of professional competence that the law required of him. He accordingly gave judgment for the plaintiff. The Court of Appeal (by a majority) allowed an appeal by the defendants.

    On appeal by the plaintiff: —

    Held, dismissing the appeal, that, although the judge had

D had the advantage of seeing and hearing the witnesses, including the plaintiff's mother, the Court of Appeal had been entitled to form an opinon on the question whether anything of evidentiary value could be extracted from her evidence, and that they had rightly rejected the judge's finding based on it that she had been pulled toward the bottom of the delivery bed in a manner and with such force as to be inconsistent with a trial of forceps properly carried out; that the

E first defendant's account of what he had done was consistent with sound medical practice and with a possible use of the word " impacted " and the Court of Appeal had been entitled to take his evidence as evidence that he had not got the plaintiff's head wedged or stuck; that they had been justified in concluding that the use of the word " impacted " in the hospital report together with the mother's evidence had not been of sufficient strength to lead to a finding of professional

F negligence; and that they had been entitled, on well-established principles, to reverse the judge's decision (*post,* pp. 249F–H, 253E–G, 254G—255A, 256C–F, G, 257C–D, 260D–F, 261E–G, 262E–H, 263F–H, 265C–F, 266A–C, 268A–B, D–E, F—269A, G—270A, F–G, 271D—272B, 273A–D).

    The Hontestroom [1927] A.C. 37, H.L.(E.) and *The Glannibanta* (1876) L.R. 1 P.D. 283, 287, C.A. applied.

    Per Lord Edmund-Davies, Lord Fraser of Tullybelton and

G Lord Russell of Killowen. It is not correct to say that an error of clinical judgment is not negligent. If the error is one that would not have been made by a reasonably competent professional man professing to have the standard and type of skill that the defendant held himself out as having, and acting with ordinary care, then it is negligent. If it is an error that such a man, acting with ordinary care, might have made, then it is not negligent (*post,* pp. 257G—258D,

H 263D–F, 968C–D).

    Dictum of McNair J. in *Bolam* v. *Friern Hospital Management Committee* [1957] 1 W.L.R. 582, 586 applied.

    Per Lord Wilberforce and Lord Fraser of Tullybelton. While some degree of consultation between experts and legal advisers is entirely proper, it is necessary that expert evidence presented to the court should be, and should be seen to be, the independent product of the expert, uninfluenced as to form or content by the exigencies of litigation (*post,* pp. 256H—257A, 268B).

Whitehouse v. Jordan (H.L.(E.))   **[1981]**

    Decision of the Court of Appeal [1980] 1 All E.R. 650   **A**
affirmed.

The following cases are referred to in their Lordships' opinions:
Bolam v. *Friern Hospital Management Committee* [1957] 1 W.L.R. 582;
    [1957] 2 All E.R. 118.
Chin Keow v. *Government of Malaysia* [1967] 1 W.L.R. 813, P.C.
Clarke v. *Edinburgh and District Tramways Co. Ltd.*, 1919 S.C.(H.L.) 35,   **B**
    H.L.(Sc.).
Glannibanta, The (1876) L.R. 1 P.D. 283, C.A.
Hontestroom, The [1927] A.C. 37, H.L.(E.).
Julia, The (1860) 14 Moo.P.C.C. 210, P.C.
Powell v. *Streatham Manor Nursing Home* [1935] A.C. 243, H.L.(E.).

The following additional cases were cited in argument:
Grunther Industrial Developments Ltd. v. *Federated Employers Insurance*   **C**
    Association Ltd. [1976] 2 Lloyd's Rep. 259, C.A.
Hart v. *Frame, Son & Co.* (1839) 6 Cl. & F. 193, H.L.(Sc.).
Hornal v. *Neuberger Products Ltd.* [1957] 1 Q.B. 247; [1956] 3 W.L.R.
    1034; [1956] 3 All E.R. 970, C.A.
Purves v. *Landell* (1845) 12 Cl. & F. 91, H.L.(E.).

APPEAL from the Court of Appeal.   **D**
    This was an appeal by the plaintiff, Stuart Charles Whitehouse, suing
by his mother and next friend Mrs. Eileen Whitehouse, from the majority
judgment of the Court of Appeal (Lord Denning M.R. and Lawton L.J.,
Donaldson L.J. dissenting) on December 5, 1979, by which they reversed
a judgment given by Bush J. at Birmingham Crown Court on December
1, 1978, in favour of the plaintiff against the defendants, J. A. Jordan   **E**
and the West Midlands Regional Health Authority (sued as the Board
of Governors of the United Birmingham Hospitals (a corporate body)).
    By his writ, dated December 14, 1972, the plaintiff claimed damages
for personal injuries suffered and consequential loss and damage sustained
as the result of the professional negligence of the defendants or one or
other of them, their servants or agents on or about January 7, 1970,
at the Queen Elizabeth Hospital, Edgbaston, Birmingham. The par-   **F**
ticulars of negligence pleaded in the statement of claim included so
carrying out the attempted forceps delivery of the plaintiff and/or the
subsequent disimpaction preparatory to Caesarean section as to interrupt the flow of blood to the plaintiff's brain. The defendants denied
negligence. Bush J. awarded the plaintiff agreed damages of £100,000.
    The defendants appealed, on the grounds that Bush J. had misdirected   **G**
himself in holding that there was any or any sufficient evidence that the
first defendant in the course of delivering the plaintiff had pulled too
hard and too long; that he had failed to consider and find whether, if he
had made any error, it had been an error of clinical judgment as opposed
to negligence; and that his judgment had been against the weight of the
evidence.
    The Court of Appeal refused the plaintiff leave to appeal from their   **H**
decision. On February 21, 1980, the Appeal Committee of the House of
Lords (Lord Diplock, Lord Salmon and Lord Scarman) gave the plaintiff leave to appeal. He appealed.

    Michael Wright Q.C. and *Desmond Perrett* for the plaintiff.
    Ian Kennedy Q.C., Bernard Hargrove Q.C. and *Roy Warne* for the
defendants.

A   Their Lordships took time for consideration.

December 17. LORD WILBERFORCE. My Lords, Stuart Whitehouse
is a boy now aged 10: he was born on January 7, 1970, with severe brain
damage. In these circumstances, tragic for him and for his mother, this
action has been brought, by his mother as next friend, in which he claims
that the damage to his brain was caused by the professional negligence
B of Mr. J. A. Jordan who was senior registrar at the hospital at Birmingham where the birth took place. There were originally also claims against
Professor McLaren, the consultant in charge of the maternity unit to
which Mr. Jordan belonged, and also against the hospital on its own
account. But these have disappeared and the hospital, more exactly the
West Midlands Regional Health Authority, remains in the case only as
C vicariously responsible for any liability which may be established against
Mr. Jordan.

A large number of claims have been made since the event most of
which have now been eliminated or withdrawn. The negligence ultimately
charged against Mr. Jordan is that in the course of carrying out a
" trial of forceps delivery " he pulled too long and too strongly upon the
D child's head, thereby causing the brain damage. The trial judge, after a
trial of 11 days in which eminent medical experts were called on each
side, and numerous issues were canvassed, reached the conclusion, which
he expressed in a most careful judgment, that the plaintiff had made good
his case: he awarded £100,000 damages. His decision was reversed by a
majority of the Court of Appeal (Lord Denning M.R. and Lawton L.J.,
Donaldson L.J. dissenting) which refused leave to appeal to this House.
E Leave was, however, granted by an Appeal Committee. The essential
and very difficult question therefore has to be faced whether, on a pure
question of fact, the Court of Appeal was justified in reversing the
decision of the trial judge.

My Lords, I need not elaborate upon the principles of law which
have to be applied. First, it is necessary, in order to establish liability
F of, and to obtain an award of compensation against, a doctor or a hospital
that there has been negligence in law. There is in this field no liability
without proof of fault. Secondly, there are strict limitations upon this
power of an appeal court to reverse the decision of the judge on an
issue of fact. These have been well and clearly stated notably by Lord
Sumner in *The Hontestroom* [1927] A.C. 37, and by the Court of Appeal
in *The Glannibanta* (1876) L.R. 1 P.D. 283, 287. The Court of Appeal
G had them fully in mind. The main reason why, in the absence of an
error of law, the judgment of the trial judge calls for the utmost respect
is that he has seen and heard the witnesses, often, as in this case, including the rival parties (the mother and Mr. Jordan). The strength of this
consideration will vary from case to case according as conclusions have
to be reached as to credibility, or based on demeanour. In the present
H case they exist but are not compelling. A view had to be and was
expressed as to the credibility of the mother: she was, generally, found
to be incapable, in the understandable circumstances, of giving reliably
precise evidence, but there remains a question whether, though what she
said was unacceptable, something of evidentiary value can be extracted
from it. On this I consider that the Court of Appeal was entitled to
form an opinion.

As to the evidence of Mr. Jordan, no question of credibility arose:

Lord Wilberforce   **Whitehouse v. Jordan (H.L.(E.))**   [1981]

there was no doubt that he was telling the truth as he saw it. The judge A
did not express disbelief of his account: what he did was to appraise it
in relation to such other evidence as was available: this he was entitled
to do, but the Court of Appeal, while bound to attach great weight to
the judge's views, was able to evaluate it for itself.

Thirdly, there was the evidence of Professor McLaren. I think that
his demeanour in the witness box must have had an influence upon the
judge's views, and this calls for complete respect. But, as I shall hope B
to show, the ultimate conclusion to be drawn depends much more upon
the setting in which his evidence was given, and the relation which it
must be thought to have to the events which occurred.

Lastly, there were the expert witnesses. The judge was entitled to be
impressed by the way in which each of them gave evidence, but he gave
no indication how this factor balanced out. In the end, as to the standard C
of skill to be expected of Mr. Jordan, there was little difference of
opinion: such as there was related to what they respectively thought Mr.
Jordan had actually done. This brings us back to the primary issue, as
to what really happened in the critical 25 minutes.

The appeal brought out, very clearly to my mind, that the issue does
not depend upon the endless refinements—for example on the meaning D
of " impaction "—of the experts, but upon one issue: what, if any,
evidence of negligence was provided by (a) the evidence of the mother;
(b) the report and evidence of Professor McLaren; (c) the evidence of
Mr. Jordan. Unfortunately the solution of this issue remains one of
immense difficulty.

Mr. Jordan was at the time a senior registrar, of near consultant
status, esteemed by his professional colleagues. There is no question E
but that he brought the utmost care to bear upon Mrs. Whitehouse's
labour and delivery. If he was negligent at all, this consisted in a departure, in an anxious situation, from a standard accepted by the profession
at the time. Put very briefly, it was said to lie in continuing traction
with the forceps after an obstruction had been encountered so that the
baby's head became " impacted ": I shall not explain this word at this F
stage. It is obvious that the error, if error there was, lay centrally in
the area of the exercise of expert judgment and experienced operation.
Mr. Jordan was a member of the obstetrical unit at the hospital headed
by Professor McLaren, which had a high reputation: Professor McLaren
himself was a distinguished obstetrician, unfortunately ill at the time of
the birth.

Mrs. Whitehouse was accepted as 30 years of age: this was her first G
baby. She was small, only 4 ft. 10½ in. in height. She was a difficult,
nervous and at times aggressive patient. She was unable, or refused, to
agree to vaginal examination during her pregnancy, or to have taken a
lateral X-ray, though urged to do so by Professor McLaren. These
processes would have helped to discover the exact shape of the pelvis.
It is fair to say that, when Mr. Jordan came on the scene, he was not H
greatly handicapped by this, because Mrs. Whitehouse was at that time
under epidural anaesthetic, and he was able to examine her vaginally.
However, he had not the advantage of accurate measurements of the
pelvis or of the ischial spines.

I need say little about the pre-natal history of the case. It is fully
told in the judgments of the trial judge and Lord Denning M.R. The
mother was seen by a number of doctors in the course of her pregnancy

A   including Professor McLaren and Mr. Jordan. I do not think that any criticism can be made of what they did. She was identified clearly as likely to be a difficult case: on December 31, 1969, Professor McLaren recorded that he thought the outlet was tight and that a trial of labour would be needed. The means that labour would be permitted to start and to proceed under close supervision in order to see whether the head could, with safety, proceed down the birth canal.

B   Mrs. Whitehouse was admitted to the hospital at 0200 hours on January 6, 1970, her membranes having ruptured shortly before. The vertex was recorded as engaged at 0230, and this was confirmed by Mr. Kelly, of consultant status, at 1000. He noted " fair sized baby."

So at this point we have a small woman, anxious and distressed, awaiting a baby, for her on the large side, with the head in a favourable
C   position and engaged in the pelvis; noted as being probably a case for " trial of labour." At 1130 she was given an epidural anaesthetic which would prevent her from feeling pain and probably from sensation below the waist.

At 1830 she was seen by Dr. Skinner. He examined her vaginally and abdominally. He reported " Vertex engaged. Foetal heart satisfactory
D   . . . Pelvis seems adequate."

Now comes the period critical for this case. At 2330 Mr. Jordan, who was not on duty, came to talk to Dr. Skinner. On his radio communicator the latter was told that Mrs. Whitehouse was fully dilated. Dr. Skinner thought that this was a case for a more senior man than he, and Mr. Jordan agreed to go: he saw her at 2330 and examined her abdominally and vaginally. He read the notes on the case, which, as
E   the above summary shows, informed him precisely of what he had to deal with: a difficult case calling for great care.

He made a detailed note which I need not copy in full. It gave all the necessary medical details. Against " pelvis " he wrote " small gynaecoid " (i.e., of appropriate female shape) and then " Normal delivery out of the question."

F   He decided to embark on a trial of forceps and did so at 2345. The full expression for this is " trial of forceps delivery " which, as the evidence showed beyond doubt, means that the operator tries to see whether with the use of forceps a delivery per vaginam is possible. This involves two things, first tentative and delicate handling at least at the start; second the necessity of continuously reviewing progress with the obligation to stop traction if it appears that delivery per vaginam cannot
G   be proceeded with without risk. Then delivery will take place by Caesarean section.

Two things must be said at this stage. First—though for the plaintiff it was at one time otherwise contended—the decision to try for vaginal delivery rather than go at once to a Caesarean section was unquestionably the right and correct procedure, in order to avoid if possible the risk to
H   the mother inevitably involved in section. Secondly, for the plaintiff an attempt was made to draw a line between trial of forceps, on the one hand, and delivery by forceps on the other, and to make a case that Mr. Jordan was, unjustifiably, proceeding to the latter. This, to my mind, completely failed. There is no such clear-cut distinction. A trial of forceps (delivery) is what it says: it is an attempt at delivery accompanied by the two special conditions I have mentioned. There can be no doubt that this is what Mr. Jordan was attempting. I take what

happened from his notes. Under " Summary of reasons for operation " **A**
he wrote:

> " Trial of forceps under epidural anaesthesia. Lower segment
> Caesarean section under G.A." Then: " (1) *Forceps* begun at 2345,
> 6.1.70. Head rotated to O-A [with] Kiellands—no problem." (Kiel-
> lands is a kind of forceps used by some operators to rotate the head.
> This procedure was correct.) " A *very tight fit*. No episiotomy." **B**
> (Cutting of the perineum.) " After pulling with five or six contractions
> it was obvious that vaginal delivery would be too traumatic—for
> Caesarean section."

He then recorded the Caesarean section which everyone agrees was
impeccably performed in two minutes. He noted " no apparent [vaginal]
trauma." To complete the history, the baby, extracted apparently un- **C**
harmed, was handed over to the paediatricians, found apnoeic, and made
to breathe after 35 minutes, by which time irretrievable brain damage
had occurred.

Here, with one possible exception, is a record of a birth carried out
with all correct procedures, with, as unhappily occurs in the best managed
hospitals and with the best medical care, tragic results. The possible
exception lies in the reference in Mr. Jordan's own report to " pulling **D**
with five or six contractions." Did Mr. Jordan pass the limits of professional competence either in continuing traction too long, or in pulling
too hard? That is the whole issue. As direct evidence from persons
present there was the evidence of Mr. Jordan, Mrs. Whitehouse and
Dr. Skinner. There was no ward sister present and the two attending
midwives could not be traced. As indirect evidence there was a report **E**
from Professor McLaren made to the hospital administrator some time
between January 22 and March 10, 1970, based upon his reading of the
notes, a conference with Mr. Jordan, and his own experience. On top
of this there was expert evidence on each side as to what Mr. Jordan
ought to have done, and as to the correctness of what he did. What
is clear is that, in a trial of forceps, the operator should not attempt to
pull past an obstruction, or at least not past a bony obstruction. Did **F**
Mr. Jordan do this?

My Lords, at this point it is vital to recall that we are not here
entitled to re-try the case. We have indeed read almost the whole of the
transcripted evidence. But it is not for us to say how we would have
decided the case at trial. What we can properly do is to examine the
judge's findings and to reach a conclusion, difficult though this may be, **G**
whether they can reasonably be supported on the evidence—recognising
his advantages and, as fairly as we can, his difficulties—and whether the
Court of Appeal was justified in reversing them.

One point must be put out of the way: was whatever occurred at the
birth causative of the brain damage?—in itself a very difficult question.
The baby was apparently undamaged at birth: brain damage does occur
for no ascertainable reason, and in normal births. Many alternatives **H**
were considered. The judge was able to find and did so that the probability was that the damage occurred between 2345 and 0010 on January
6/7, that is, during the period in which the forceps were used. Whether
I, or any other judge, would have reached the same conclusion is not
here or there: the finding had evidence to support it and cannot be
disturbed. It does not of itself, of course, prove that the damage arose
from lack of skill: that is a point which must be independently decided.

A   There were three critical pieces of evidence.

First, there was the evidence of the mother—in the abstract the best person to know exactly what happened. In the concrete, the situation was otherwise. She had been in labour for nearly 24 hours: recorded as distressed: there had been vomiting: she was—for understandable reasons connected with her family—intensely anxious and tense: she was in a condition of lack of confidence in the medical procedure. She

B was under epidural anaesthetic, so inhibited from feeling unless very imprecisely what was going on. In these conditions she testified as follows: when the forceps were applied " It felt like a deadened electric shock that lifted my hips off the table, up off the bed." This is also what she told the eminent professors who on this basis prepared their report for the plaintiff. But the judge—inevitably—did not accept this. No

C witness regarded it as possible—any traction must have been downwards. Dr. Skinner, who was standing by her side the whole time, said that nothing like this occurred—he would have seen it and remembered it " for its fantasticness." With all allowance for professional loyalty this evidence is too strong to be totally discounted. But, though rejecting this account, the judge did make some use of it: he said " it could be

D that she was pulled towards the bottom of the delivery bed *depending upon the amount of force used*." But this does not prove that excessive force *was* used, and that is what is required. Again, in the crucial conclusory part of his judgment he says:

> " Though Mrs. Whitehouse's description of what occurred to her when the forceps were applied may not be exact in its clinical detail, I believe her, in so far as her description can be taken to be under-
E > stood, as a pulling of her toward the bottom of the delivery bed in a manner and with such force as to be inconsistent with a trial of forceps properly carried out."

But I must agree with the majority of the Court of Appeal that I cannot accept this as a defensible finding. A process by which, after rejecting the account given by a witness—and it was more than inexact " in clinical

F detail "—that account is reconstructed so as to be evidence not of a general character, but of a precise and critical degree of traction supposed to differ from what would have been quite proper, seems to me with all respect to be illegitimate. If excessive traction is otherwise proved, her evidence might be consistent with that, but it cannot be used itself as evidence of that excess. I think that the Court of Appeal were quite right

G to discard this finding. In this they were unanimous.

The next piece of evidence consists of Mr. Jordan's own testimony. He was examined and cross-examined at length. In his judgment the judge made comparatively little reference to this evidence, relying much more heavily on the second-hand evidence of Professor McLaren. For myself, I would regard Mr. Jordan's first-hand account of the matter as of

H cardinal importance. Parts of it, indeed, may be regarded as the most solid evidence against him. I have anxiously considered it with the reservations proper in a case when a man is defending himself against a serious claim. The tenor of it, read as a whole, was that this was a very tight fit; that with the first few pulls—made (correctly) with the contractions—some progress was made. With the fifth pull he realised that he was not making progress: he tried once more to see if he could ease the head past what might be minimal obstruction. Failing this, he thought that delivery per

vaginam, though possible, would be too traumatic and that a Caesarean   A
section was needed. With a view to this he eased the head slightly upwards
with the forceps.

The attack on this was really twofold. First, it was to say that Mr.
Jordan pulled too hard. There was no direct evidence of this except that
of the mother which I have already discussed. Dr. Skinner—though I
quite accept that not too much weight can be placed on his description—
said that he had never ever (sic) seen Mr. Jordan violently pull forceps   B
in his life.

Then, and this was the critical point, it was said that Mr. Jordan tried
to pull past a bony obstruction—which would be contrary to the best
medical practice—and got the head " wedged " or " stuck " or
" impacted." In his judgment the judge quoted this passage:

> " Q. Perhaps I should end by asking you this: did you try to pull   C
> past any bony part?   A. My trial by forceps was to overcome what
> may be minimal obstruction so one did, as it were, pass the level of
> the ischial spines.   Q. The question was not well phrased. Did you
> try to pull despite them?   A. No."

His comment on it is that " perhaps some clue was given [by it] ."
                                                                        D
But if the first answer is somewhat obscure, the second is a plain
denial that he tried to pull despite (that is, over any resistance of) the
ischial spines.

I would compare with this his final answer given in reply to the learned
judge:

> " Bush J. Mr. Jordan, on that aspect of it that you have been talking   E
> about, what was it that made you believe that to continue the traction
> might be harmful to the baby?   A. Because one is aware from the
> very nature of the forceps delivery that there is some resistance, and
> the aim of a trial of forceps is to ease the baby past whatever resis-
> tance there may be, whether it is the pelvic floor or the side walls of
> the pelvis, and you pull slowly and tentatively and then you form an
> impression that to continue with that rate of progress may take too   F
> long, or too much traction, and I think that is all."

Other passages exist to the same effect. And what I think Mr. Jordan is
trying to explain is that, in a trial of forceps, the operator, who has to work
on feel, and instinct, and experience, is by the nature of things always
working against resistance, just because of the narrowness and irregular
shape of the birth canal. This he has to do, with of course care, and a   G
margin of safety. What he must not do, and what Mr. Jordan denies that
he did, was to pull past a bony obstruction: then he must stop.

This leads on to the issue of whether the head was " stuck " or
" wedged." So far as Mr. Jordan is concerned he firmly denied that it
ever was. It would not, without risk, go any further, but that was all.
At the end he was able without difficulty to push it back up a little in   H
preparation for the Caesarean section. I think that it is possible to carry
this point further. Sir John Dewhurst, Professor at Queen Charlotte's
Hospital and at Chelsea Hospital for Women, and the author of an
important book *Integrated Obstetrics,* gave evidence *after* Mr. Jordan
and *after* hearing the latter's evidence—an advantage not possessed by
the plaintiff's witnesses. He found nothing wrong in the procedure which
Mr. Jordan had followed, including the resort to five or six pulls.

A   I reach the conclusion, then, that here too the Court of Appeal, particularly Lawton L.J., were justified in taking—contrary to the view of the judge—Mr. Jordan's evidence as evidence that he did not get the head wedged or stuck.

    So finally there is Professor McLaren's report and evidence, on which the judge placed much reliance. I have explained that his report was prepared on the basis of the hospital notes and of conference with Mr. Jordan. It is therefore evidence against Mr. Jordan, to the extent, and only to the extent, that it may be taken to incorporate Mr. Jordan's account at the time to his superior. It must be borne in mind that it was written in order to answer a long letter of complaints by Mr. Whitehouse as to the conduct of the birth, one of his complaints relating to the pulls exerted by Mr. Jordan. The tenor of the report was to maintain that Mrs. Whitehouse had received correct and skilled treatment and that no blame attached to anyone for the sad result which followed. Though this was the purpose of the report it was said that nevertheless it " let the cat out of the bag " in two respects revelatory of a failure of skill by Mr. Jordan.

    In a critical passage he wrote:

D   " A trial of forceps was carried out under epidural anaesthesia the head rotating with ease with Kiellands forceps. Descent, however, did not follow traction and *in the interest of the child* the head was disimpacted prior to speedy delivery by Caesarean section. However, there was need to switch from epidural to general anaesthetic for section."

E   The first point is easily disposed of. " Descent did not follow traction " is clearly a statement referring to the whole of the process and is merely saying that the traction did not extract the baby. It cannot be read as saying, as for the plaintiff it was sought to say, that no movement whatever took place. It leads to no conclusion.

    The second point is more difficult. It relates to the word " disimpacted." This involves, it is said, that the head was " impacted "— and " impacted " means " wedged or stuck." This proves therefore that Mr. Jordan pulled too hard. It should be noted that a copy of this report was sent to Mr. Jordan who did not comment on the word: he must therefore, it is said, be taken to have agreed with it.

    Many hours of evidence were devoted to this word. Professor McLaren himself tried to explain it away—he should not have used it—he did not mean to convey that the head required to be " unstuck " or that it was stuck. He pointed out, justly, that the report referred to " a tentative attempt at forceps " . . . " the accepted obstetrical technique of tentative trial of forceps " . . . " satisfactory trial of labour." All of this was inconsistent with getting the head " wedged." But what did he mean by the word—used three times?

H   There was no unanimity among the experts as to the meaning of the word " impacted." The dictionary meaning is:

    " Denoting a foetus that, because of its large size or narrowing of the pelvic canal, has become wedged and incapable of spontaneous advance or recession." (*Steadman's Medical Dictionary,* 23rd ed. (1976).)

No reference here, be it noted, to the result of force.

Lord Wilberforce   **Whitehouse v. Jordan (H.L.(E.))**   **[1981]**

A

Sir John Stallworthy did not disagree with this.
Sir John Peel:

> " I think that an impacted head is one that does not move either up or down without further force or exertion being applied. Either with forceps in pulling it down or the fingers pulling it up."

Sir John Dewhurst:

B

> " It is not a term I use in my medical practice, no. I think it is capable of being used in various ways. I suppose perhaps one reason why I never use it is impaction in the sense solidly wedged has almost disappeared from medical practice in this country."

Dame Josephine Barnes: " I mean the head is in a position where it cannot go any further on."

C

So there is no unanimity, or even balance of opinion, that impaction is something which occurs from or is evidence of excessive or unprofessional pulling. It is a condition, which may arise from many causes.

The learned judge's conclusion was: " . . . I find it difficult to accept Professor McLaren's explanation of his use of the word ' impacted ' "—and this was a critical finding against Mr. Jordan. But with respect I think that the mass of medical evidence had led him to focus on an inessential D question. The argument was not about the meaning of a word, but about what Mr. Jordan did. Mr. Jordan gave a complete and detailed account of what he did. He proceeded to the point when the baby would go no further. He denied that it was " stuck." He said that he easily pushed it up. All of this was consistent with sound medical practice, and with a possible use of the terminology. If Professor McLaren had thought, after E discussing the case with Mr. Jordan, that something had gone wrong, and that the head had become wedged through excessive force, it is incredible that, in the context of a wholly disculpatory report, he would have used a word meaning " wedged by force " without some explanation. It is quite simple to suppose that the word was used to refer to the routine action in preparation for Caesarean section.

In my opinion, the Court of Appeal was justified in concluding that F this, together with the evidence of Mrs. Whitehouse which formed the main pillars of the judgment, was not nearly of sufficient strength to lead to a finding of professional negligence.

My Lords, I could, but will not, comment on other aspects of the evidence. I am, for myself, not happy about the manner in which the judge used the evidence about the foetal heart beat: I understand that others of your Lordships may enlarge upon this point. At the end of G it all, upon the single issue whether during the critical half-hour Mr. Jordan departed from his own high standard of professional competence, I find the judgments of Lord Denning M.R. and of Lawton L.J. convincing, and appreciative as I am—as were the members of the Court of Appeal— of the judge's care and clarity, I must agree that this is a case where an appeal court can and should interfere.

H

One final word. I have to say I feel some concern as to the manner in which part of the expert evidence called for the plaintiff came to be organised. This matter was discussed in the Court of Appeal and commented on by Lord Denning M.R. [1980] 1 All E.R. 650, 655. While some degree of consultation between experts and legal advisers is entirely proper, it necessary that expert evidence presented to the court should be, and should be seen to be, the independent product of the expert,

A uninfluenced as to form or content by the exigencies of litigation. To the extent that it is not, the evidence is likely to be not only incorrect but self-defeating.

I would dismiss the appeal.

B LORD EDMUND-DAVIES. My Lords, I have wrestled long and hard over this appeal. The evidence at the trial occupied 11 days, and the judgment delivered 10 days later by Bush J. is a model of clarity and care. But the fact that this award of £100,000 to the grossly disabled infant plaintiff was reversed by a majority at the conclusion of a four days hearing in the Court of Appeal and that the appeal to this House occupied five days should serve to demonstrate that difficult issues are involved.

C I gratefully adopt the narrative of salient facts prepared by my noble and learned friend, Lord Wilberforce, and I shall add little to it. There arose an acute conflict on many points and between both lay and expert witnesses. It has long been settled law that, when the decision of a trial judge is based substantially on his assessment of the quality and credibility of witness, an appellate court " must, in order to reverse, not merely entertain doubts whether the decision below is right, but be convinced that it is wrong " (*The Julia* (1860) 14 Moo.P.C.C. 210, 235, *per* Lord Kingsdown). And that is so irrespective of whether or not the trial judge made any observation with regard to credibility (*Clarke* v. *Edinburgh and District Tramways Co. Ltd.*, 1919 S.C.(H.L.) 35, 36, *per* Lord Shaw of Dunfermline).

E Certain important matters are not in doubt. The first (as the learned judge himself stressed) is that the delivery of a brain-damaged baby does not necessarily connote negligence by anyone, for such a misfortune can inexplicably occur in circumstances where there are no grounds for suspecting any lack of proper skill. Again, although the obdurate attitude of Mrs. Whitehouse during her pregnancy had created a lack of information regarding the dimensions of her birth canal, before Mr. Jordan started even an exploratory pull on the foetus he contemporaneously noted that he was confronted by " a very tight fit " a situation which Dame Josephine Barnes described as " certainly a high risk case " and one which Sir John Dewhurst said would have occasioned him " considerable concern." On the other hand, it was unchallenged that Mr. Jordan was right to use forceps, for, although vaginal delivery by contraction alone was out of the question, it was inadvisable to proceed directly to Caesarean section.

G The principal questions calling for decision are: (a) in what manner did Mr. Jordan use the forceps, and (b) was that manner consistent with the degree of skill which a member of his profession is required by law to exercise? Surprising though it is at this late stage in the development of the law of negligence, counsel for Mr. Jordan persisted in submitting that his client should be completely exculpated were the answer to question (b) " Well, at worst he was guilty of an error of clinical judgment." My Lords, it is high time that the unacceptability of such an answer be finally exposed. To say that a surgeon committed an error of clinical judgment is wholly ambiguous, for, while some such errors may be completely consistent with the due exercise of professional skill, other acts or omissions in the course of exercising " clinical judgment " may be so glaringly below proper standards as to make a finding of negligence

258

inevitable. Indeed, I should have regarded this as a truism were it not that, despite the exposure of the " false antithesis " by Donaldson L.J. in his dissenting judgment, learned counsel for the respondents adhered to it before your Lordships.

But doctors and surgeons fall into no special legal category, and, to avoid any future disputation of a similar kind, I would have it accepted that the true doctrine was enunciated—and by no means for the first time —by McNair J. in *Bolam* v. *Friern Hospital Management Committee* [1957] 1 W.L.R. 582, 586 in the following words, which were applied by the Privy Council in *Chin Keow* v. *Government of Malaysia* [1967] 1 W.L.R. 813:

> ". . . where you get a situation which involves the use of some special skill or competence, then the test as to whether there has been negligence or not is not the test of the man on the top of a Clapham omnibus, because he has not got this special skill. The test is the standard of the ordinary skilled man exercising and professing to have that special skill.'

If a surgeon fails to measure up to that standard in *any* respect (" clinical judgment " or otherwise), he has been negligent and should be so adjudged.

Mr. Jordan said that, in the situation confronting him, he embarked on a trial of forceps, its object being to establish whether there was any disproportion or obstruction in the birth canal sufficient to put at risk a vaginal delivery. Trial of forceps needs to be carried out gently and tentatively, " progress being observed when reasonable traction is exerted," as Sir John Dewhurst, a defence witness, put it. If progress is achieved, the process of pulling with contractions, opening the forceps when a contraction ceases, then applying them again with the next contraction continues until (in Mr. Jordan's words) " such time as the baby was delivered or it became apparent, as in this case, that further attempts at delivery may be unwise." He accepted that during the trial of forceps the surgeon is *not* embarking on a delivery, but merely exploring the possibility of vaginal delivery being achieved, and that:

> " Before undertaking mid-forceps delivery, the physician's clinical judgment must permit him to conclude unequivocally that he can in fact deliver the baby safely per vaginam, and that this method of delivery places less risk to the mother and baby than Caesarean section."

How far had Mr. Jordan proceeded before he abandoned the notion of a vaginal delivery and decided upon a Caesarean section? He said he had pulled with five or six contractions, and formed the view that the head was making satisfactory progress after the first four pulls. There came a fifth pull with possibly no " movement." When asked: " What conceivable factor can there be which would stop you on the fifth? " his significant reply was: " The spines," that is, the ischia. A little later he said: " If I got difficulty on the fifth, then I would confirm it on the sixth." Asked how in such circumstances he could justify pulling yet once more, Mr. Jordan answered:

> " What one wants to know is, is there at this particular moment— and this is the crucial part as far as the trial of forceps is concerned —or would this little extra pressure or traction deliver this head past that bony obstruction or not? In these circumstances, realising

A   that this was the point at which the decision had to be made finally, as to continue or go back, it is justified to see whether or not a little more—a little extra traction with other contractions—would be enough to overcome the resistance one is feeling."

That answer has to be considered in the light of the directive in a work prepared by Sir John Dewhurst (*Integrated Obstetrics*, p. 500):

B   " *No obstruction below the head.* This is an absolute rule. The head should never be pulled past an area of obstruction. Caesarean section is indicated . . . "

Mr. Jordan insisted that his trial of forceps terminated at the stage when the factor of the *safety* of the baby arose, although he entertained no doubt that vaginal delivery could have been achieved. As to this, and the case generally, the conclusion of the learned judge was expressed in this way:

C

"... I am doubtful whether Mr. Jordan was in fact undertaking a trial of forceps as opposed to an attempt at vaginal delivery which failed, and in the course of which the baby was wedged, stuck or jammed, and which on anyone's view of the matter would be un-justified. However in any event if it were a trial of forceps then he pulled too hard and too long so that the foetus became wedged or stuck. In getting it wedged or stuck, or unwedged or unstuck, Mr. Jordan caused asphyxia which in its turn caused the cerebral palsy. In this respect Mr. Jordan fell below the very high standard of professional competence that the law requires of him."

D

E   In the light of the conflicting evidence, is that a conclusion to which the experienced trial judge was entitled to arrive? With the single exception of Dame Josephine Barnes, the medical witnesses on both sides agree that, as the judge put it:

"... if in fact the trial of forceps proceeded to the lengths where the foetal head was wedged or stuck and had to be unwedged or unstuck with the use of force, then unprofessional force would have been used, both in getting it wedged and in having to unwedge it."

F

His observations on this cardinal issue began with the evidence given by the mother, and he dealt with it in this way:

"According to Mrs. Whitehouse when the forceps were applied, ' I felt like a deadened electric shock that lifted my hips off the table,' and she described her buttocks and hips being lifted upwards off the table. This cannot be an accurate description since the pull is downwards, but it could be that she was pulled towards the bottom of the delivery bed, depending upon the amount of force used. She was a little woman and it would be a question of degree whether this indicated in itself the use of excessive force."

G

H

When Sir John Stallworthy, a plaintiff's witness, was cross-examined to establish that the mother would not be lifted off the bed, he said:

"What very frequently happens, and I would have thought—I don't know—what probably happened from her description was with the forceps she was pulled down to the end of the bed. She is a small woman and it was a big baby, and it would have been perfectly

reasonable with an ordinary, successful forceps delivery for this to   A
have happened."

But two comments on that evidence are called for.   (1) We are not
here concerned with an accomplished forceps delivery, but with what
was described as a trial of forceps which was abandoned at a stage when
it was still open to Mr. Jordan to change his mind and proceed to a
Caesarean section.   (2) Dr. Skinner, who was standing nearby in the   B
operating theatre when the baby was delivered, said that Mr. Jordan never
went further than trial of forceps.   He added that there was no violent
pulling, and spoke of the "fantasticness" of the allegation of Mrs.
Whitehouse being lifted off the bed.   That does not in terms negative a
downward pull, but it controverts the use of force beyond that customary
in a trial of forceps.
                                                                        C
    Regarding this important matter the learned judge said:

    "Though Mrs. Whitehouse's description of what occured to her
    when the forceps were applied may not be exact in its clinical detail,
    I believe her, in so far as her description can be taken to be under-
    stood, as a pulling of her toward the bottom of the delivery bed in a
    manner and with such force as to be inconsistent with a trial of
    forceps properly carried out."   D

My Lords, I have some difficulty in following how anything in Mrs.
Whitehouse's testimony could be "understood" in the sense adopted
by the learned judge.   She was the only witness who in direct terms spoke
adversely of the degree of force exerted by Mr. Jordan, and he had found
her unreliable in several respects.   Once more the learned judge rejected
her evidence, this time in relation to what happened when the forceps   E
were applied.   In its place he "believed" an account which, while to a
degree in conformity with what Sir John Stallworthy said *could* happen
in forceps delivery, was one which she herself did not advance.   It was
accordingly not such a finding as an appellate court, lacking the judge's
advantage of seeing and hearing the witnesses, is normally obliged to leave
undisturbed.   It was in truth a finding without an evidential basis.   F

    I turn to consider another matter which undoubtedly operated power-
fully on the judge's mind, and which, indeed, he described as "perhaps
the strongest piece of evidence that something untoward was done . . ."
It has perplexed me perhaps more than any other part of this worrying
case, and I entertain no strong conviction even now that I have reached
the right conclusion about it.   I have in mind the report prepared by   G
Professor McLaren, head of the unit and himself a defendant to these
proceedings until they were discontinued against him in March 1976.   He
drafted the report after discussions with Mr. Jordan which began a few
days after the baby was delivered.   Each knew that Mrs. Whitehouse
was very upset and angry, and on January 22, 1970, there arrived a
letter from her husband making grave complaints against the unit staff.
The hospital administrator therefore called for a report, and this led to   H
discussions on points which both the professor and Mr. Jordan realised
were of "the utmost importance."   It was in the light of these discussions
and the hospital notes that Professor McLaren prepared his undated
report, and, in due course, showed it to Mr. Jordan before submitting
it to the hospital administrator on March 10.   Judging from the time
factor, accordingly, it does not appear to have been hastily prepared.   It
can, I think, be fairly described as in some respects an odd document for

A   a person with the professional experience and sophistication of Professor McLaren to have prepared, and for Mr. Jordan, in his turn, to have passed without amendment. Certainly one can well understand the learned judge being very troubled by it. But, having said that, what is beyond doubt is that the report set out to be wholly exculpatory of Mr. Jordan and of the entire hospital staff. Thus, it refers to " this well conducted trial of labour and forceps," and to Mrs. Whitehouse's " first-

B   class obstetric care,' and it concluded, ". . . we accept no criticism or implication that in terms of being humane, or in technical skills, we neglected Mrs. Whitehouse." Yet the learned judge found it possible to conclude that the report was actually confirmatory of the charge of negligence made against Mr. Jordan, and this mainly on the strength of the inclusion therein of the following observations:

C   (1) " A trial of forceps was carried out under epidural anaesthesia . . . *Descent, however, did not follow traction,* and *in the interest of the child the head was disimpacted* prior to speedy delivery by Caesarean section."

      (2) In relation to the foetus having sustained a cerebral haemorrhage: " It could be that a congenital weakness of a blood vessel

D   existed *so that the fixing of the head in the pelvis and its disimpaction* for Caesarean section led to a leaking of blood in the skull."

      (3) " Possibly at Caesarean section *the disimpaction of the head* was critical and cerebral haemorrhage followed." (My emphasis added in each case.)

E   For my part, I cannot attach significance to the observation that " Descent . . . did not follow traction," as it is the plaintiff's own case that descent to a point there certainly was. But at the trial, in the Court of Appeal, and again in this House many hours were spent considering the much more important matter of the threefold use of the word " disimpaction." Is " impaction " its converse and what situation or action does each word connote? Mr. Jordan himself, in common with several

F   of the expert witnesses, accepted as accurate the *Steadman's Medical Dictionary* meaning of " impacted ": see ante, p. 255H.

    Professor McLaren, too, accepted that it had the generally accepted meaning of " stuck," but he averred that his repeated use of " disimpaction " had no relation to unsticking or unwedging, or fixation or any state of immovability. He apologised for his misuse of language and explained that in his vocabulary " disimpaction " involves no more than

G   a gentle pushing of the head upwards with one finger before proceeding to a Caesarean section.

    My Lords, the point is important in the light of the expert evidence supportive of the view that, if the head of the foetus had become so stuck as to cause asphyxia, excessive force had been used. I remain mystified why, in the drafting of what was known to be an extremely important

H   report, its author should have used in the sense claimed by him a variant of the word " impaction " which in medical science has such a different meaning, and why Mr. Jordan (who was familiar with that accepted meaning) should have allowed " disimpaction " to go forward without comment.

    I could well understand the McLaren report taking the form it did were the version of events then intended to be advanced that Mr. Jordan had gone past the trial of forceps stage and had decided upon vaginal

delivery; that he had proceeded with proper skill to implement that deci-   A
sion up to the stage when he could with safety go no further and therefore
turned to Caesarean section; and that the misfortune which occurred did
not arise from any negligence on his part.   But the defence presented
to the judge was that Mr. Jordan never went beyond a trial of forceps.
It is true that, if all goes well, there may be no clear line of demarcation
between trial of forceps and actual delivery by forceps, the one merging
into the other.   But that is not to say that there does not arise, however   B
fleetingly, a stage when the operator has to consider whether he can
safely go further.   At one time, however, Mr. Jordan referred in evidence
to his " attempt at forceps delivery, followed by Caesarean section," and
in his pleaded defence it was expressly admitted that he " . . . attempted
but abandoned a forceps delivery and then proceeded to deliver the
plaintiff by Caesarean section," an admission which his learned counsel   C
told this House was due to an oversight and should not have been made.
It could well be that it was on the basis of such material that the learned
trial judge expressed himself as " . . . doubtful whether Mr. Jordan was
in fact undertaking a trial of forceps, as opposed to an attempt at vaginal
delivery which failed . . ."

But the point is a fine one, and it should not of itself lead to the
condemnation of the defendant.   In his dissenting judgment, Donaldson   D
L.J. [1980] 1 All E.R. 650, 665 concluded that the evidence of Mrs.
Whitehouse being " pulled towards the bottom of the bed in the sense
that her body was moved " could not be right, and he added, at p. 666:

> " But having said that, I still have to decide whether the judge's
> conclusion was wrong and I am not satisfied that it was.   Reading
> the judgment as a whole, it seems to me that Mrs. Whitehouse's   E
> evidence was treated as no more than consistent with or, at most,
> confirmatory of Professor McLaren's report and that even if Bush J.
> had put her evidence on one side, he would still have reached the
> same conclusion."

If that is right, as with respect it seems to be, the outcome of these
proceedings was regarded by the learned judge as finally turning on the   F
use of one word.   I daresay that at times even greater issues have turned
on less.   But that word cannot properly be considered out of context, and
I again stress that the whole drift of the lengthy McLaren report was
that the Whitehouse baby had been delivered in accordance with the
highest professional standards.   Such being the setting, to hold that the
threefold use of " disimpaction " should be regarded as establishing that
the complete opposite was the truth is, in my judgment, to impose on it   G
an excessive and insupportable burden.

Such, at least, is my conclusion about this distressing case.   It has
evidently caused me greater difficulty than it has any of my noble and
learned brethren.   But I have at last found myself impelled and compelled
to hold that, despite the great care and ability manifested by the learned
judge, there was lacking the evidence needed to uphold his basic finding   H
that Mr. Jordan " pulled too hard and too long so that the foetus became
. . . stuck."   I therefore concur in holding that the appeal should be
dismissed.

LORD FRASER OF TULLYBELTON.   My Lords, this is an action of damages
for professional negligence against a senior registrar at Birmingham
Maternity Hospital.   After a long trial, the learned judge held negligence

A established against the registrar, but the Court of Appeal by majority (Lord Denning M.R. and Lawton L.J., with Donaldson L.J. dissenting) reversed his decision. They did so not because they considered that the learned trial judge had misstated the relevant law. Clearly he did not; he said, rightly in my opinion, that negligence for the purposes of this case meant

B   "a failure . . . to exercise the standard of skill expected from the ordinary competent specialist having regard to the experience and expertise that specialist holds himself out as possessing."

He added the proviso that the skill and expertise to be considered were those applying in 1969 to 1970. Although that statement was not criticised in the Court of Appeal, Lord Denning M.R. did criticise a later C sentence in the judgment because, in his view, it suggested that the law made no allowance for errors of judgment by a professional man. Referring to medical men, Lord Denning said [1980] 1 All E.R. 650, 658:

      "If they are to be found liable [sc. for negligence] whenever they do not effect a cure, or whenever anything untoward happens, it D would do a great disservice to the profession itself."

That is undoubtedly correct, but he went on to say this: "We must say, and say firmly, that, in a professional man, an error of judgment is not negligent." Having regard to the context, I think that the learned Master of the Rolls must have meant to say that an error of judgment "is not necessarily negligent." But in my respectful opinion, the statement as it E stands is not an accurate statement of the law. Merely to describe something as an error of judgment tells us nothing about whether it is negligent or not. The true position is that an error of judgment may, or may not, be negligent; it depends on the nature of the error. If it is one that would not have been made by a reasonably competent professional man professing to have the standard and type of skill that the defendant held himself out as having, and acting with ordinary care, F then it is negligent. If, on the other hand, it is an error that such a man, acting with ordinary care, might have made, then it is not negligent.

The main reason why the Court of Appeal reversed the judge's decision was that they differed from him on the facts. The question therefore is whether the Court of Appeal was entitled to reverse the judge's decision on a pure question of fact. The view of the judge G who saw and heard the witnesses as to the weight to be given to their evidence is always entitled to great respect. We were reminded particularly of dicta to that effect in *The Hontestroom* [1927] A.C. 37 and *Powell* v. *Streatham Manor Nursing Home* [1935] A.C. 243, and there is other high authority to the same effect. But in this case, unlike cases such as *Powell* and *The Hontestroom,* no direct issue of credibility arises. It is not suggested that any witness, or body of witnesses, was giving H dishonest evidence. The only witness whose reliability is seriously in question is Mrs. Whitehouse, the mother of the plaintiff, and I shall refer to the critical part of her evidence in a moment. Apart from her evidence, the important facts are almost entirely inferences from the primary facts, and in determining what inferences should properly be drawn an appellate court is just as well placed as the trial judge. Accordingly this is a case where the judge's decision on fact is more open to be reassessed by an appellate court than it often is.

264

Whitehouse v. Jordan (H.L.(E.))

A

The learned judge expressed his conclusion as to the primary facts which had been established with admirable clarity and conciseness, as follows:

> "On the balance of probabilities I have come to the conclusion, first that the damage to the brain of Stuart [the infant plaintiff] was not the result of inherent maldevelopment, and secondly that asphyxia or anoxia caused the brain damage, and thirdly that the asphyxia itself was caused by some event between 2345 and 0025— that is between the commencement of the trial of forceps and the delivery of the child by Caesarean section."

B

That passage in the judgment is immediately followed by a repetition of the caution, to be found elsewhere in the judgment, that such damage may be caused by the violent event of birth itself and " may occur without professional fault on the part of those having the care and management of the patient." So the learned judge was evidently on his guard against treating this as a case of res ipsa loquitur.

C

He then turned to consider what evidence there was on the vital question of whether " unprofessional force," by which he evidently meant excessive force, had been applied by Mr. Jordan when using forceps. He relied first on the evidence of Mrs. Whitehouse herself, and secondly on what he regarded as " perhaps the strongest piece of evidence that something untoward was done "—namely the report by Professor McLaren who was the head of the department in which Mr. Jordan worked, and who himself was a distinguished obstetrician. Professor McLaren was ill at the time and was not present at the birth. Thirdly, the learned judge relied on the evidence of Mr. Jordan, the first defendant. I must consider these pieces of evidence.

D

E

The evidence of Mrs. Whitehouse was that when Mr. Jordan pulled on the forceps she had " felt something like a deadened electric shock that lifted my hips off the table." All the medical evidence was that Mrs. Whitehouse was not, and could not have been, lifted up off the table by the pulling on the forceps because the traction would have been in a downward direction. The judge therefore rejected Mrs. Whitehouse's account of what had occurred as being mistaken. He had already rejected her evidence on several points relating to her treatment in the earlier stages of pregnancy. So far as this matter is concerned, it is not surprising that she was mistaken considering her condition at the time to which she was referring. She had been without sleep, according to her own account, for 40 hours by this time. She had not had any food because she had been vomiting, and as she put it herself " I was at the end of the line really." Above all the lower part of her body was under epidural anaesthetic which meant that it was largely without sensation. But the judge, having rejected Mrs. Whitehouse's account, went on to accept an interpretation of it suggested by Sir John Stallworthy, one of the medical experts who gave evidence on behalf of the plaintiff. He said that he interpreted Mrs. Whitehouse's evidence as meaning that she had been pulled down off the bed and then lifted back on to it by the medical staff. That interpretation was never put to Mr. Jordan or to the other medical witness who had been present at the time, Dr. Skinner, although Dr. Skinner was asked about Mrs. Whitehouse's original account of being lifted up off the bed and denied that any such thing had occurred. It would be natural for Dr. Skinner to feel professional and personal

F

G

H

A loyalty towards Mr. Jordan, who was his superior and also his friend, and who had taken charge of the delivery because Dr. Skinner felt that it was beyond his competence. I would therefore have been prepared to discount his evidence to some extent if it had stood alone, but the learned judge does not indicate any doubt about its reliability, and so far as it goes it is entirely consistent with the evidence of the medical experts as to the impossibility of Mrs. Whitehouse's account. The learned judge's

B conclusion about Mrs. Whitehouse's evidence on this matter was expressed thus:

> "Though Mrs. Whitehouse's description of what occurred to her when the forceps were applied may not be exact in its clinical detail, I believe her, in so far as her description can be taken to be understood, as a pulling of her toward the bottom of the delivery
> C bed in a manner and with such force as to be inconsistent with a trial of forceps properly carried out."

In my opinion that conclusion contains two serious flaws, either of which would be enough to make it unacceptable. First I do not consider that it is permissible to accept Mrs. Whitehouse's evidence " in so far as " her description can be taken to mean something different from what she

D said, and something which was not tested by a cross-examination of the witnesses, including the defendant and Dr. Skinner, who could have confirmed or denied it. I agree with Lawton L.J. who said [1980] 1 All E.R. 650, 660:

> "In Lord Sumner's words in the *The Hontestroom* [1927] A.C. 37, 47 the trial judge in this case ' palpably misused his advantage ' in
> E having seen and heard the mother. These advantages could not be used, as the trial judge used them, to turn an account of what had happened which physically could not have taken place, into one which could."

Secondly, even if the interpretation of Mrs. Whitehouse's evidence were

F correct, it would not by itself indicate that the degree of force used was excessive and inconsistent with a trial of forceps delivery properly carried out.

  I come now to Professor McLaren's report. This was written in answer to a request from the hospital administrator for information. It was based partly on the clinical notes and partly on oral discussion with Mr. Jordan, and it was shown to Mr. Jordan before being sent (by Mr.

G Jordan) to the administrator. It can, therefore, be regarded as having been accepted by Mr. Jordan and as having possible evidential value against him. There was one word in the report upon which the learned judge particularly relied for drawing an inference unfavourable to Mr. Jordan. That was the word " disimpacted." It was used, as the judge pointed out, no less than three times in the report. Probably the most

H significant use was in the following sentence which is quoted in the judgment:

> "Descent, however, did not follow traction and in the interest of the child the head was disimpacted prior to speedy delivery by Caesarean section."

The importance attached to the word by the judge arose in this way. He said: " For something to be disimpacted it must first have been impacted,"

Whitehouse v. Jordan (H.L.(E.))   **[1981]**

and he relied upon a definition of the word " impacted " in relation to a   A
foetus given in *Steadman's Medical Dictionary*: see ante, p. 255H.

That definition was accepted by several of the medical experts, though
not by all of them, and the learned judge considered that, if the head
was impacted, that indicated that it had become tightly stuck or wedged
between parts of the bony structure of the pelvis and that it had been
pulled by forceps too long or too hard. I do not think that the latter
part of his conclusion was justified. Professor McLaren in his evidence   B
apologised for using the word. He said that it was not a good word but
it was one that he was accustomed to use, though he did not intend it to
suggest that there had been such wedging that one needed a lot of force
to push the head up again before embarking upon the Caesarean section.
It seems that Professor McLaren's apologetic evidence made an unfavourable impression upon the judge, and his finding on the matter was   C
expressed thus: " It is with regret that I find it difficult to accept
Professor McLaren's explanation of his use of the word ' impacted.' " I
have tried to make proper allowance for the importance to be attached
to the judge's view on this matter but I have reached the opinion that the
Court of Appeal was entitled to differ from it for these reasons. First, the
conclusion of the professor's report was to the effect that Mrs. Whitehouse
had received excellent care while in the hospital, and in particular he   D
said that there was no evidence that she had anything but " first-class
obstetric care." That conclusion would have been been impossible if
the obstetrician concerned, Mr. Jordan, had employed forceps with
excessive force, and it is therefore very unlikely that the professor used
the word " disimpacted " in a sense intended to imply that such force had
been used. It is also unlikely that Mr. Jordan would have passed the   E
report, containing that word, without objection if he had understood the
word in that sense. Secondly, the medical evidence as a whole showed
that the word is used with various shades of meaning, and that it does
not necessarily mean that the foetus is so firmly wedged or stuck as to
require much force to dislodge it. The medical evidence showed also
that the exact degree of force which could properly be used was a
matter for expert judgment by a skilled obstetrician and might vary   F
considerably according to circumstances. Thirdly (and in my opinion
of considerable importance), when the two expert witnesses who gave
evidence for the plaintiff were preparing their joint report (or rather
approving the joint report which was, rather surprisingly, " settled " for
them by counsel), they did not emphasise Professor McLaren's reference
to " disimpaction "; if it was really so fatal to the defendant's case as the   G
learned judge seems to have thought, one would have expected them
to fasten on it at once. It seems to me, therefore, that he attached too
much importance to it.

Apart from the use of that one word, the learned judge evidently
regarded Professor McLaren's report as a whole as indicating that the
defendant had pulled too hard and too long. That may have been partly   H
because he treated the expression " descent did not follow traction " as
meaning that the foetus did not descend at all as a result of traction.
That meaning was urged upon us in argument, but I do not accept it
because if *no* descent took place, that is if the foetus did not move
downwards at all as a result of traction, the impaction (whatever may
be the exact meaning of the word) could not have been caused by the
traction. I read the expression as meaning, what Mr. Jordan said it

A meant, that descent did not continue to the extent of delivery. So read, the statement is correct but throws no light on the question we are considering. I think much of the importance attached by the learned judge to the report was due to the statement it contained that " after a reasonable *attempt at delivery* by forceps a Caesarean section was carried out." (My emphasis.) The significance of the words emphasised is that a distinction was drawn by the medical witnesses between a *trial* of

B forceps delivery (generally abbreviated to a trial of forceps) and an *attempted* forceps delivery. The former should be very tentative and gentle. The latter, in which stronger traction is permissible, should never be embarked upon unless the physician's clinical judgment permits him to conclude unequivocally that he can deliver the patient safely per vaginam. Mr. Jordan in his evidence was insistent that he never got

C beyond the trial stage and that the fact of his having used five or six pulls did not indicate the contrary. He did not profess to remember every detail of what he had done, and his evidence was based on the clinical notes and on his usual practice, but he was quite clear about what he must have done. He said that, taking six pulls as the total, he must have made some progress until the fifth pull. The fifth pull made no progress and the sixth pull would have confirmed that no further

D progress was possible consistent with safety. The learned judge did not in terms reject that evidence nor did he express any reservation about Mr. Jordan's evidence as a whole. What he said, in the decisive paragraph of his opinion, was this:

E "In all these circumstances I am doubtful whether Mr. Jordan was in fact undertaking a trial of forceps as opposed to an attempt at vaginal delivery which failed, and in the course of which the baby was wedged, stuck or jammed, and which on anyone's view of the matter would be unjustified. However in any event if it were a trial of forceps then he pulled too hard and too long so that the foetus became wedged or stuck. In getting it wedged or stuck, or unwedged or unstuck, Mr. Jordan caused asphyxia which in its

F turn caused the cerebral palsy. In this respect Mr. Jordan fell below the very high standard of professional competence that the law requires of him."

It seems to me with respect that the learned judge was seeking to draw too sharp a line between a trial of forceps delivery and an attempted forceps delivery. The former, if it makes progress, will merge into the latter, and may be carried on to a complete delivery. Whether Mr.

G Jordan ever moved from the trial stage to the attempted delivery stage is really a question of words; the important issue is whether there was evidence that, in the learned judge's words, " he pulled too hard and too long so that the foetus became wedged or stuck." He himself denied that it ever became wedged or stuck, and I have already explained why I do not think that Professor McLaren's use of the word " impacted "

H means " stuck." The evidence which seems to me to come nearest to convicting him of negligence in this respect is his own. He explained, what after all is obvious, that the purpose of pulling with forceps is to overcome resistance to the descent of the foetus down the natal canal and that after the fifth pull he would have had to make a decision whether to continue, and whether a " little extra pressure or traction [would] deliver this head past that bony obstruction or not." It was argued that that passage in Mr. Jordan's evidence, and some other passage to the like

effect, showed that he was willing to pull too hard. But the trial judge   A
does not seem to have thought so, and nor do I. The mere fact that he
pulled five or six times is no indication of how hard he pulled. After
he had finished the trial of forceps he pushed the foetal head upwards
to facilitate removal of the foetus by Caesarean section, but that again
does not indicate that it had become wedged; it is a normal preliminary
to Caesarean section, as Dame Josephine Barnes explained. In these   B
circumstances there was in my opinion no sufficient evidence to justify
a finding that he had been negligent.

I would therefore dismiss the appeal.

I respectfully agree with the observations of my noble and learned
friend Lord Wilberforce in the final paragraph of his speech about his
concern as to the manner in which part of the expert evidence for the
plaintiff was organised.   C

LORD RUSSELL OF KILLOWEN. My Lords, I wish at the outset to
emphasis one matter. Some passages in the Court of Appeal might
suggest that if a doctor makes an error of judgment he cannot be found
guilty of negligence. This must be wrong. An error of judgment is not
per se incompatible with negligence, as Donaldson L.J. pointed out. I   D
would accept the phrase " a mere error of judgment " if the impact of
the word " mere " is to indicate that not all errors of judgment show a
lapse from the standard of skill and care required to be exercised to
avoid a charge of negligence.

The details of this case and the reasons for dismissing this appeal have
been so fully canvassed by my noble and learned friends that there is
but little that I can add, without tedious repetition, in saying that I   E
agree to that dismissal.

As has been pointed out, and as Sir John Stallworthy accepted, there
was no indication from the foetal heartbeats that during the trial of
forceps delivery the foetus was in any way distressed. They were normal.

The learned judge, in a passage quoted by your Lordships, which came
immediately before his conclusion of negligence by Mr. Jordan, in that   F
he pulled too long and too hard, inferred from evidence given by the
mother that she was physically pulled down the bed. This I think was
quite without justification on the basis of her evidence which did not
point to that at all. It was not permissible to erect a theory of what
she might have said but did not say, and base a conclusion of negligence
at least in part upon that theory. It may be that the judge borrowed   G
the theory from medical evidence given on behalf of the plaintiff: but
the medical experts were no more entitled than the judge to read the
mother's rejected evidence as intended to mean something totally different. As has been pointed out it was never suggested to Mr. Jordan
that his activities pulled the mother towards him. As to the report
written by Professor McLaren (and shown to Mr. Jordan) two points
were sought to be made. The first was its statement that descent did   H
not follow traction: I see nothing in this: it means not that no progress
at all resulted from the trial of forceps delivery but that there was no
delivery by forceps. The second was the reference to disimpaction.
Much evidence was given as to the meaning of disimpaction and impaction, and what was involved in " stuck " and " wedged." All these
words are words of degree. " Impacted " may simply mean that the
foetus is unable to move either way spontaneously and some assistance

A is required. The mere fact that some assistance was required to
"disimpact" cannot show negligence: if it did, the joint medical report
would not merely have mentioned disimpaction but would surely have
said that it proved negligence.

My Lords, I also would dismiss this appeal.

B   LORD BRIDGE OF HARWICH. My Lords, at 12.25 a.m. on January 7,
1970, the appellant was born at the Birmingham Maternity Hospital.
The mother had been in labour since the early hours of January 6
The possibility of a difficult birth had been anticipated by the medical
authorities at the hospital responsible for her case. By 11.30 p.m. on
January 6, the mother was fully dilated. From that point onwards the
first respondent, now a consultant obstetrician, then a senior registrar in
C Professor McLaren's unit at the hospital, was in charge of the operation
of delivering the child. He concluded from his examination of the
mother that a normal delivery was out of the question. At 11.45 p.m.
he proceeded to undertake a "trial of forceps." In the light of this trial
he decided that delivery per vaginam would be too traumatic for the
mother and the child. Accordingly he proceeded to effect delivery by
D Caesarean section. The child was found to have sustained severe brain
damage.

Bush J., the trial judge, made a finding, which is not challenged, that
the brain damage to the appellant was caused by anoxia occurring at
some time between the beginning of the trial of forceps and the delivery
of the child. This might seem to the layman to suggest some improper
use of the forceps, but any such suggestion is emphatically refuted by
E the evidence. It is common ground that a child may, in the course of
an apparently normal birth, suffer anoxia for which no specific cause can
be assigned and certainly that the mere fact of anoxia occurring when
it did in.the course of the appellant's birth affords no evidence whatsoever
of fault on the part of the first respondent.

The judge's finding of negligence against the first respondent (on which
F the vicarious liability of the second respondent in turn depends) is based
on a finding that in using the forceps "he pulled too hard and too long
so that the foetus became wedged or stuck" and that "in getting it
wedged or stuck, or unwedged or unstuck" the first respondent caused
the anoxia which occasioned the brain damage. In the light of the
direction which the judge had given himself early in his judgment in
defining the criterion to be applied to decide whether the first respondent
G was negligent (a direction which I do not criticise) this finding must be
understood as implying that the first respondent applied traction to the
foetus with the forceps which both in strength and duration exceeded
what any competent obstetrician of the status of senior registrar would
have regarded as the permissible limits in carrying out the procedure of
a trial of forceps. The judge's decision in favour of the appellants having
H been reversed by a majority in the Court of Appeal, the sole question,
as it seems to me, which your Lordships' House has to decide is whether
the judge's finding that the first respondent applied excessive traction to
the foetus in the sense indicated above can be supported on the evidence.

My Lords, I recognise that this is a question of pure fact and that
in the realm of fact, as the authorities repeatedly emphasise, the advantages which the judge derives from seeing and hearing the witnesses
must always be respected by an appellate court. At the same time the

importance of the part played by those advantages in assisting the judge A
to any particular conclusion of fact varies through a wide spectrum from,
at one end, a straight conflict of primary fact between witnesses, where
credibility is crucial and the appellate court can hardly ever interfere,
to, at the other end, an inference from undisputed primary facts, where
the appellate court is in just as good a position as the trial judge to
make the decision. It has been strongly urged, on behalf of the appellant, B
that in this case the judge's assessment of the reliability of the witnesses,
particularly of the first respondent himself and of his superior at the
Birmingham Maternity Hospital, Professor McLaren, was of such critical
importance to his decision as to render it unassailable and this view
prevailed with Donaldson L.J., who dissented in the Court of Appeal,
even though he in terms rejected one of the judge's subordinate findings
on which his ultimate conclusion depended. At first blush I was much C
attracted to this view of the case but a close scrutiny of the judge's
analysis of the evidence and of the particular features of the evidence
on which he relied in support of his finding of negligence persuades me
that that finding was not justified. I will consider in turn the four main
aspects of the evidence on which the judge based his conclusion.

  1. *The mother's evidence.* The mother gave evidence emphatically D
that when the forceps were applied she was lifted up from the bed.
Everyone accepted that this was impossible. Any pulling on the forceps
is downward. The appellant's expert witnesses canvassed the possibility
that the mother might have been pulled off the end of the bed and lifted
back on to it. This was denied by Dr. Skinner, a witness who was
present at the birth, and the suggestion was never even put to the first
respondent in cross-examination. The mother's evidence at every other E
point where it was in controversy had been rejected by the judge. At
the time of the trial of forceps she had been in labour for many hours
and was under an epidural anaesthetic. Yet the judge said of her:

  " Though Mrs. Whitehouse's description of what occurred to her
  when the forceps were applied may not be exact in its clinical detail,
  I believe her, in so far as her description can be taken to be under- F
  stood as a pulling of her toward the bottom of the delivery bed in
  a manner and with such force as to be inconsistent with a trial of
  forceps properly carried out."

  Counsel for the appellant has not sought to support this part of the
judge's judgment and it was rejected by all three members of the Court
of Appeal. I agree with them. The mother's evidence could not be G
understood in the sense suggested and was manifestly incapable of affording any reliable indication of the degree of force applied with the forceps
by the first respondent.

  2. *Professor McLaren's report.* Following complaints by the appellant's parents to the hospital administrator, Professor McLaren, as
head of the unit responsible, prepared a report on the circumstances of H
the appellant's birth. This was based in part on the hospital records,
in part on discussion with the first respondent. In its express terms the
report was wholly favourable to the first respondent. In his summary
Professor McLaren said:

  " Finally an expert obstetrician in my team undertook the accepted
  obstetrical technique of tentative trial of forceps. After a reasonable
  attempt at delivery by forceps a Caesarian section was carried out.

A   The baby, alas, was seriously affected by this well conducted trial of labour and forceps."

In expressing his opinion he added:

B

" My own view is that both Mr. and Mrs. Whitehouse are naturally very distressed although there is no evidence that she had anything but first-class obstetric care. We can appreciate the letter from Mr. Whitehouse of January 22, 1970, but we accept no criticism or implication that in terms of being humane, or in technical skills, we neglected Mrs. Whitehouse."

Despite these passages the judge described the report as " perhaps the strongest piece of evidence that something untoward was done." He based this view on the use more than once in the report of the word

C " disimpaction " to describe the action of the first respondent, having decided to abandon the trial of forceps and proceed to Caesarean section, in pushing the head of the foetus upwards with the forceps to facilitate delivery by Caesarean section.

It was common ground that a trial of forceps is a tentative procedure to discover whether the baby's head can pass safely through the mother's

D pelvis. The obstetrician must proceed gently and not attempt actually delivery unless and until he is satisfied that there is no such bony disproportion between head and pelvis as to present a risk of injury to the baby. Of course, if no significant obstruction is encountered, the trial of forceps will merge into an actual forceps delivery.

Against this background a great deal of evidence was given by the

E expert witnesses on both sides as to the significance, in relation to the conduct of a trial of forceps, of the fact of the foetus becoming " stuck " or " wedged " in the course of it. A definition of " impacted " from *Steadman's Medical Dictionary,* 23rd ed., as

" Denoting a foetus that, because of its large size or narrowing of the pelvic canal, has become wedged and incapable of spontoneous advance or recession "

F

was canvassed with the witnesses.

Now it will be apparent that in any context the words " stuck " or " wedged " are imprecise. An object may be lightly or tightly stuck or wedged. The degree of force required to free it may be great or small. I can find nothing in the expert evidence to suggest that in an obstetric

G context the words as applied to a foetus described as " stuck " or " wedged " in the pelvic canal do not suffer from the same imprecision. If " impacted " is synonymous with " wedged " the same consideration must apply.

The judge, however, has drawn the inference from Professor McLaren's use of the word " disimpaction " that the foetus had become so firmly wedged as to indicate that a degree of force must have been

H used by the first respondent in producing that result which was clearly excessive in a trial of forceps. He rejected Professor McLaren's explanation that he meant no more by " disimpaction " than what could be achieved by gently pushing the head of the foetus up out of the pelvic cavity with one finger.

If Professor McLaren used the word " disimpaction " *intending* it to bear the meaning the judge attributed to it, the implications are twofold. First, Professor McLaren must have appreciated from what the first

respondent told him that the trial of forceps had been misconducted and A
had ended in disaster; it would follow from this that the exculpatory
passages in the report were a dishonest attempt to whitewash a subordinate. But secondly, it also reveals Professor McLaren as not only a
knave but a fool who attempts a whitewash in one part of his report
but gives the game away in another part.

I find it impossible to suppose that the judge appreciated these far-
reaching implications of the significance he was attaching to a single B
word in the professor's report or that, if he had done so, he would have
been prepared to stigmatise the witness in such a manner.

3. *The foetal heart rate.* The respondents relied at the trial, in
support of their case that the trial of forceps was not the cause of the
appellant's anoxia, on readings of the foetal heart rate during the trial
of forceps being within normal limits. At 11.35 p.m. the rate was 140. C
At 11.45 p.m., when the trial of forceps began, it was 130. It was the
same five minutes later. At 12.30 a.m. when the trial of forceps concluded it was 120. After the delivery of the baby at 12.25 a.m. the
rate had fallen to 100 or below. After referring to this evidence the
judge commented:

> " Though all these readings save the one at 100 or below are within D
> normal limits, there is here a steady drop indicating to my mind
> that something was wrong."

I take this comment to indicate that the judge not only rejected the
evidence that the readings during the trial of forceps were inconsistent
with anoxia being caused at that stage but also regarded the fall from
140 before the trial began to 120 when it concluded as affording some E
support for the contrary view. That view, however, was not expressed
by any of the expert witnesses and indeed is contrary to all the expert
evidence on the subject.

4. *The number of pulls.* The first respondent had recorded in his
operation notes: " After pulling with five or six contractions it was
obvious that vaginal delivery would be too traumatic . . . " He accepted F
in evidence that he had probably exerted six pulls coincident with the
mother's uterine contractions. The effect of his evidence was that, so
far as he could remember or reconstruct the occasion, the first pull
was extremely tentative and produced no movement. Thereafter, the
next three pulls achieved some progress, the last two none. Having
encountered difficulty on the fifth pull, he pulled once more to see
whether a little extra traction would overcome the resistance he was G
feeling, but it did not. Sir John Peel, an expert witness called for the
appellant, had based his criticism of the first respondent in part on the
recorded note of five or six pulls but had said that it was " difficult to
be dogmatic " about this.

The judge refers to this issue in the following passage:

> " Sir John Peel, while conceding that the number of pulls may H
> depend on the progress being made, has said that he cannot under-
> stand why it should have needed five or six pulls to test whether
> delivery per vaginam was possible. Mr. Jordan's answer to this is,
> as I have related above, that until say the fifth full he was making
> progress. If, as I have found, the head was engaged it would not
> have all that far to go before the widest part of the head was at
> the ischial spines, and I share Sir John Peel's doubt."

A   The judge added a reference to two cryptic answers given in re-examination by the first respondent, but I refrain from quoting these because I confess that I do not follow what significance the judge attached to them.

  This is perhaps the most difficult part of the case, but I am satisfied that the criticism of the first respondent for exerting six pulls, qualified as it was, could not by itself sustain a finding of negligence against him.

B

  As regards the evidence of the first respondent, the judge records that, according to him, there was nothing unusual that occurred from the commencement of the trial of forceps to the delivery of the child. I appreciate, of course, that the judge's finding involves, by necessary implication, a rejection of this evidence. It is trite to observe, however, that rejection of a defendant's denial provides no material to establish

C the positive case sought to be made against him. On the other hand, if the judge had construed anything in the first respondent's evidence as amounting to an admission of fault on his own part (which the cryptic answers referred to above certainly did not provide), he would surely have made this abundantly clear and put it in the forefront of his reasons for making a finding of negligence against him.

D   In the result I can find no sufficient foundation for this finding and would accordingly dismiss the appeal.

> *Appeal dismissed.*
> *Appellant's costs in House of Lords to be taxed in accordance with provisions of Schedule 2 to Legal Aid Act* 1974.
> *Respondents' costs in House of Lords and Court of Appeal to be paid out of legal aid fund pursuant to section* 13 *of Act of* 1974.

E

F   Solicitors: *Keene, Marsland & Co. for Roper & Co., Birmingham; Hempsons.*

M. G.

G

H

A

[FAMILY DIVISION]

*PRACTICE DIRECTION (DIVORCE REGISTRY: FAILURE TO MAINTAIN)

Husband and Wife—Financial provision—Failure to maintain—Application to High Court—Hearing date in Principal Registry —Matrimonial Causes Act 1973 (c. 18), s. 27 (as amended by Domestic Proceedings and Magistrates' Courts Act 1978 (c. 22), s. 63)

B

As from February 1, 1981, section 27 of the Matrimonial Causes Act 1973 is amended by the Domestic Proceedings and Magistrates' Courts Act 1978, so as to provide that either party to a marriage may apply to the court for an order under that section that the other party has failed to provide reasonable maintenance for the applicant or has failed to provide, or made a proper contribution towards, reasonable maintenance for any child of the family. The revised jurisdiction does not require that the failure should be wilful.

C

The Matrimonial Causes Rules 1977 have been amended accordingly, so as to provide, inter alia, that these applications may be dealt with by a registrar.

D

In the Divorce Registry it will not be the practice to allocate a hearing date on the notice of the application which is served on the respondent. Application for a hearing date should be made by lodging form D270 as in any other application for financial provision in a matrimonial cause proceeding in this Registry.

E

R. L. BAYNE-POWELL
Senior Registrar.

February 14, 1981.

F

[COURT OF APPEAL]

*COMPANIA FINANCIERA " SOLEADA " S.A. AND OTHERS v. HAMOOR TANKER CORPORATION INC. THE BORAG

1980 Dec. 16, 17, 18, 19

Lord Denning M.R., Shaw and Templeman L.JJ.

G

Damages—Remoteness—Foreseeability—Ship's wrongful arrest—Expenses of obtaining release—High interest—Charges on overdraft to provide security—Whether damages or mitigation —Whether recoverable

Shipping—Ship's management—Dedicated pater familias—Agreement between owners and managers—Whether relationship of trustee and beneficiary created—Manager's liability for wrongful arrest—Extent

H

Ships' names—Borag

By an agreement of April 1969, managers agreed to manage the *Borag* on behalf of her owners as if the ship belonged to them and by clause (2) to "watch over the owners' interests as a dedicated pater familias (bon père de famille)." In 1971

1 W.L.R.   **Compania Financiera v. Hamoor Tanker Corp. (C.A.)**

A disputes arose between the parties and the managers caused the *Borag* to be wrongfully arrested at Cape Town for sums alleged to be due to them. The *Borag* was released some two weeks later after the owners had provided a bank guarantee. In subsequent arbitration proceedings in London the owners claimed that they were entitled to recover the heavy bank interest charges which they incurred in obtaining the guarantee because they operated on the basis of a very substantial bank

B overdraft and their bank had debited the full amount of the guarantee to their overdrawn account. The umpire held that the interest charges were not recoverable as damages naturally and foreseeably flowing from the wrongful arrest of the *Borag*. On a special case stated Mustill J. held that the owners could recover the whole of the interest charges which were not to be regarded as expenditure recoverable as damages for a wrongful act but as money expended by way of mitigation of the

C managers' wrongful act.

 On appeal by the owners : —

 Held, allowing the appeal, (1) that the managers were liable to compensate the owners in damages for their breach of duty in the wrongful arrest of the ship and that clause (2) of the agreement did not affect the amount of compensation to which the owners were entitled (post, pp. 280F–G, 283E, G).

D (2) That the owners' expenditure to obtain the release of the ship was to be regarded as damages and not mitigation of damage; and that the bank interest charges were too remote, too unreasonable and too unforseeable to be regarded as damages reasonable and foreseeably flowing from the wrongful arrest and were not recoverable (post, pp. 281C–D, 282G, 284G–H).

 The Liesbosch [1933] A.C. 449, H.L.(E.) applied

E Decision of Mustill J. [1980] 1 Lloyd's Rep. 111 reversed.

The following cases are referred to in the judgments:

Dodd Properties Ltd. v. *Canterbury City Council* [1980] 1 W.L.R. 433; [1979] 2 All E.R. 118; [1980] 1 All E.R. 928, Cantley J. and C.A.
Liesbosch, The [1933] A.C. 449, H.L.(E.).

F *Moore* v. *DER Ltd.* [1971] 1 W.L.R. 1476; [1971] 3 All E.R. 517, C.A.
Parsons (H.) (Livestock) Ltd. v. *Uttley Ingham & Co. Ltd.* [1978] Q.B. 791; [1977] 3 W.L.R. 990; [1978] 1 All E.R. 525, C.A.
Radford v. *De Froberville* [1977] 1 W.L.R. 1262; [1978] 1 All E.R. 33.

The following additional cases were cited in argument:

G *Bunge S.A.* v. *Kruse* [1976] 1 Lloyd's Rep. 357.
Czarnikow (C.) Ltd. v. *Koufos* [1969] 1 A.C. 350; [1967] 3 W.L.R. 1491; [1967] 3 All E.R. 686, H.L.(E.).
Edwards v. *Bairstow* [1956] A.C. 14; [1955] 3 W.L.R. 410; [1955] 3 All E.R. 48, H.L.(E.).
Hickman v. *Kent or Romney Marsh Sheepbreeders' Association* (1920) 37 T.L.R. 163, C.A.

H *Intertradex S.A.* v. *Lesieur-Tourteaux S.A.R.L.* [1978] 2 Lloyd's Rep. 509, C.A.
Livingstone v. *The Rawyards Coal Co.* (1880) 5 App.Cas. 25, H.L.(Sc.).
Quistclose Investments Ltd. v. *Rolls Razor Ltd. (In Liquidation)* [1970] 567; [1968] 3 W.L.R. 1097; [1968] 3 All E.R. 651, H.L.(E.).
Royal Greek Government v. *Minister of Transport* (1949) 83 Ll.L.R. 228.
Victoria Laundry (Windsor) Ltd. v. *Newman Industries Ltd.* [1949] 2 K.B. 528; [1949] 1 All E.R. 997, C.A.

276

APPEAL from Mustill J.

A

The claimant managers, Compania Financiera " Soleada " S.A., Netherlands Antilles Ships Management Corporation Ltd. and Dammers and Van Der Heide's Shipping and Trading Co. Ltd., appealed against that part of the judgment of Mustill J. [1980] 1 Lloyd's Rep. 111 on June 22, 1979, whereby it was adjudged that the amount of damages payable by them to the respondent owners, Hamoor Tanker Corporation Inc., in respect of the arrest of the *Borag* was different from that found by the umpire, Dr. R. E. Kingsley, in his award and refused to remit the award to the umpire for further findings of fact to be made on the issue of mitigation of damages.

B

The grounds of appeal were that the judge (1) erred in law in failing to hold that the correct measure of damages for the arrest of the vessel was those of costs of procuring her release which were in the reasonable contemplation of the parties; (2) erroneously held that the costs of procuring the vessel's release incurred by the owners were costs of mitigating their loss resulting from the arrest and, therefore, not subject to the rules of remoteness of damage; (3) erred in law in failing to hold that the interest charges paid on behalf of the owners to the National Bank of Kuwait were too remote for the reasons set out in paragraphs 11 (36) and (37) of the award; (4) erred in holding that, on the facts found in paragraphs 11 (36) and (37) of the award, the bank interest charges were caused by the arrest of the vessel; (5) if, as the judge held, the bank interest charges were part of the cost of mitigation, the judge ought to have held that the burden of proof that such charges were reasonably incurred was on the owners (in particular in view of the fact that such charges were not in the reasonable contemplation of the parties) and that there was no finding in the award, either express or implicit, that the owners acted reasonably in incurring such charges in addition to the bank charges levied on them for the provision of the guarantee; (6) having held that the issue between the parties turned on mitigation rather than on remoteness or causation the judge ought to have remitted the award to the umpire for further findings of fact to be made on the issue of mitigation, in order that justice might be done between the parties; (7) in declining to remit the award for further findings of fact to be made on the issue of mitigation the judge erred (a) in assuming that it would be necessary, if the award were remitted, to have a whole new arbitration on the issue of mitigation; (b) in failing to give any or sufficient weight to the fact that the issue of mitigation had been raised in the pleadings and had been the subject of evidence and argument before the umpire, that both parties had requested the umpire to make findings of fact relevant to the issue of mitigation, that a transcript of the evidence and argument was available, and that the managers in seeking remission were merely seeking findings by the umpire on the basis of the evidence and arguments already presented to him; (c) in holding that none of the findings of fact on mitigation requested by the managers was sufficiently specific to compel a decision in the managers' favour on mitigation; (d) in regarding the delay by the managers in the service of the notice of motion to remit the award, and/or the managers' failure to serve an affidavit explaining such delay, as a sufficient reason for refusing to remit the award pursuant to the managers' notice of motion; in particular the judge failed to pay any or sufficient regard to the fact that the umpire's award on the question of the bank interest charges was in favour of the managers and that any

C

D

E

F

G

H

A   delay in the service of the notice of motion did not have any effect on the
date at which the application to remit was actually raised before the
court; and (e) in taking into account the question of which side had exercised their right of appeal. If, as the judge held, that question was relevant,
the judge was wrong in deciding that the right of appeal was exercised
by the managers.

B   By a respondents' notice the owners contended that the judgment of
Mustill J. should be upheld on the additional grounds that the umpire
erred in treating the question of foreseeability of the interest charges as a
question of fact and not of law; that the managers must have foreseen that
the incurring of banking expenses (including interest charges) would be
the likely result of the arrest and that such charges were not too remote;
and that the judge failed to hold that the managers had assumed all the
C   obligations of trustees and were accordingly liable as trustees to make
restitution for all loss and damage occasioned to the owners by the arrest
regardless of whether such loss or damage was foreseeable.

The facts are stated in the judgment of Lord Denning M.R. and in the
case stated [1980] 1 Lloyd's Rep. 111, 112–118.

D   *Kenneth Rokison Q.C.* and *Julian Cooke* for the managers.
David Johnson Q.C. and *Peter Rawson* for the owners.

LORD DENNING M.R.   In this case a vessel was wrongfully arrested. It
was afterwards released on the owner providing security. The question is:

The facts of the case are set out in the judgment of Mustill J. [1980]
1 Lloyd's Rep. 111. So I need only state sufficient of them today to set
E   the scene.

The owners of the vessel *The Borag* were a Liberian or Monrovian
company. They were quite inexperienced in the management of vessels of
that type. They therefore employed a company called Compania Financiera
" Soleada " S.A. and two other companies to manage the vessel. A management agreement was made in 1969 whereby the managers were to manage
the vessel with the utmost care, as if they themselves were the owners of
F   it—as if they were managing it in their own interest—managing it (clause
(2)) as a " dedicated pater familias (bon père de famille)."

The managers managed the vessel from 1969 to 1971. They were
financed by the owners, who put them in funds at the beginning of each
month. In addition, when extra expenses had been incurred, the managers
would recoup them, on proper vouchers being produced.

G   Then in 1971 a special situation arose. *The Borag* entered into dry dock
at Cadiz for repairs and survey. The account came to much more than
was anticipated. The managers required to be put in funds to meet these
extra expenses: and, of course, they wanted their monthly payment at
the beginning of each month. But unfortunately, at the beginning of
December, the managers had not been paid anything to meet the expenses.
H   In particular they had not received the monthly advance for December
1971.

The managers were disturbed about this. So they made a demand on
the owners for payment: otherwise, they said, they would take steps on
their own behalf to see that they received payment. That was in December
1971.

I should say that a little time later the owners did pay the agreed sum
of U.S. $55,000 by way of the monthly payment: and said that they would

pay any extra amount against vouchers. But this was too late for the A
managers: because meanwhile the managers decided to protect their
interests as best they could. They did it in a most unfortunate way.

The vessel was at Cadiz. She was due to go round the Cape to the
Gulf. She put in at Dakar on the way. The managers had arranged for one
of their employees, Mr. van Brakel, to sail with the ship to Dakar. He
was subsequently instructed to remain on board while the vessel went
round the Cape. The usual practice was that the vessel would not go into B
the port at Cape Town (because she might be arrested). She would only
stop outside to pick up mail and then continue on her voyage to the Gulf.
Instead on this occasion—on Mr. van Brakel's instructions—the vessel did
put in to the port of Cape Town. The captain kept it quiet. He did not
tell the owners anything about it. Mr. van Brakel told him to keep it
quiet. So the vessel put into the port at Cape Town unbeknown to the C
owners. The managers there applied to the South African courts to arrest
the ship in rem because, they said, they had these moneys due to them.
The vessel was arrested in Cape Town on December 17, 1971.

The owners were very upset. The conduct of the managers was a subterfuge. It was completely unjustified. After the arrest, the owners took
steps to get the vessel released. Their agents at Cape Town took the matter
up: but they were very dilatory about it. Banks in Cape Town, Kuwait D
and the like had to be communicated with. At all events, it was a fortnight before the vessel was eventually released—on December 30, 1971.
So she was held up in Cape Town for 14 days owing to the wrongful
arrest.

As it happened, the 14 days were four days longer than they should
have been. If the owners' agents had acted as promptly and expeditiously E
as they should have, the vessel would only have been under arrest for 10
days. At all events, the vessel was out of action for at least 14 days by
reason of the wrongful arrest.

All sorts of trouble arose—repudiation and cancellation of the arrangement and the like—which we need not go into at all. Those matters were
thrashed out in the course of a London arbitration of tremendous length. F
The hearing lasted 17 days, with leading counsel on both sides, and so
forth. But I need not go into all the details because the umpire who heard
the case (Dr. Kingsley) held—after going through all the accounts—that
the amount due from the owners to the managers was U.S. $113,908.65.
He was ready to award that sum as a final award in favour of the managers.
The managers were entitled to that sum on the final statement of account
—subject to this one point, on which the umpire stated a special case for G
the opinion of the court—what sum should be allowed to the owners as
compensation for the wrongful arrest?

The owners' claim for compensation was put under three main heads.
(1) The first was a perfectly legitimate head. It was the overheads and
expenses thrown away by reason of the arrest and delay while the vessel
was held up in Cape Town. The salaries of the crew, insurance and the H
like, were all clearly expenses consequent on the wrongful arrest. (2) There
was also a claim for the cost of providing the security and obtaining the
release of the vessel. (3) In addition there was a claim for the loss of the
profit the vessel would have made but for the wrongful arrest.

We are not concerned with the claim for overheads and expenses:
because that has been settled in the sum of about $30,000. Nor are we
concerned with loss of profit: because it turned out that this was not a

The Weekly Law Reports, March 13, 1981

279

1 W.L.R.   Compania Financiera v. Hamoor Tanker Corp. (C.A.)   Lord Denning M.R.

A   profit-making concern. What we are concerned about are the expenses of and incidental to obtaining the release of the vessel. They were divided into two main parts. The first was the cost of actually getting the guarantee and the bank charges incurred in doing it. That came to roughly $30,000. We are not concerned with that. We are concerned with an interest charge coming to some $100,000 as part of the expense of getting the vessel released.

B   The way in which the owners say they incurred that expense is very strange. It is so complicated that the umpire had to hear a lot of evidence in an attempt to sort it out. I will read the paragraphs of the award which deal with it.

Paragraph 11, point 34:

C   " The bank guarantee put up to procure the vessel's release from arrest was arranged by owners through the National Bank of Kuwait (' N.B.K.'). The guarantee was actually furnished by the United Bank of Kuwait Ltd. against a counter-guarantee from the N.B.K. The N.B.K. was not required to provide a deposit with the United Bank of Kuwait Ltd. as counter-security for the guarantee."

D   Point 35: " Total commission charges made by the N.B.K. to the owners amount to the agreed figure of Kuwait dinars 9,208.07 or U.S. dollars 32,044.08. . . ."

Then comes point 36 which deals with the point:

" In addition to the bank charges or commission mentioned above under point 35 the N.B.K. raised interest charges against the owners. Most of the December 1977 hearing was taken up with controversy

E   regarding this issue. On the very involved and detailed evidence I find that the interest charges arose from the fact that the owners and their associated companies operated on the basis of a very substantial bank overdraft (finding this method of conducting their business convenient in view of their policy of making long-term investments abroad) and that consequently the N.B.K. found it right and necessary to increase the current overdraft by the amount of the guarantee.

F   The managers were not informed by the owners of the incurring of this interest charge; nor could they reasonably have foreseen that as a result of their demand for the establishment of a bank guarantee the payment of interest charges, in addition to bank charges or commission, would flow as a natural and foreseeable consequence."

G   It sounds very complicated: but the net result of it was that the owners were debited in their overdraft with the full amount of the sum guaranteed, and they had to pay interest on it. Not only simple interest: but compound interest. In other words, they had to pay interest on the full amount involved—in contrast to a small sum of bank charges for giving a guarantee.

The whole question in the case is: can the owners recover this interest

H   charge of such a large amount—it ran from 1971 to 1976—and not merely the cost of providing a guarantee which might never be called upon? That is the real point in the case.

The umpire held that the compound interest was not a consequence of the guarantee which was established to procure the vessel's release from arrest: but it flowed from the owners' financial policy in the conduct of their business. So he knocked that out.

As to the overdraft, he said at paragraph 12 (c):

" The owners are entitled to damages in respect of their reasonable A
foreseeable and naturally flowing costs and expenses of obtaining the
vessel's release from wrongful arrest."

Paragraph 12 (d):

" The interest charges raised by the N.B.K. against owners are not
recoverable as damages naturally and foreseeably flowing from the
wrongful arrest of the vessel and the owners' efforts to secure the B
vessel's release from such arrest."

On those findings, the umpire disallowed the interest charges—he disallowed the compound interest point—and made his award accordingly.

The case was stated by the umpire for the opinion of the court.
Mustill J. [1980] 1 Lloyd's Rep. 111 reversed the decision of the umpire. C
He held that the owners could recover the whole of the interest charges.
That would mean that the managers would get nothing. Their claim on
the final award would be outweighed by the owners' claim for compensa-
tion. Now there is an appeal to us.

Many points have been canvassed. I will try to deal with them shortly.
First, the relationship between the owners and the managers. There was
certainly a breach of duty under that relationship—whatever it was. It was D
said by Mr. Johnson that it was equivalent to a relationship of a trustee
and a beneficiary. The wrongful arrest was a breach of trust by the
managers. Accordingly the compensation should be on the basis on which
a trustee is made liable to account. He referred us to a passage in
Underhill's Law of Trusts and Trustees, 13th ed. (1979), p. 702, where the
author says: " Liability for breach of trust can be more extensive than E
liability for damages for tort or breach of contract." But, if you read the
whole passage, it seems to me plain that the author is dealing with that
special aspect of a trustee's position when the trust funds are depleted or
diminished in some way, and it is a question of the trustee recouping
them. The damages with which we are concerned in this case do not
result from any intermeddling with trust property. There is no question
of recoupment or restitution of money which has been done away with. F
It is simply damages for breach of duty. Whatever the relationship was
—whether it was the special relationship between trustee and beneficiary
or whether it was fiduciary or whether it was breach of contract—the
whole question here is, what is to be the compensation for the wrongful
act of arrest? I do not think any help is to be derived by putting the
relationship into one or other category. The whole question is, what is the G
proper compensation for the wrongful arrest of this vessel and her subsequent release?

The second point which arose was: What is the proper category into
which to put the claim for the overdraft interest? Is its proper heading
" damages for wrongful arrest "? Or is it " moneys expended in mitigation
of damage "? H

The umpire regarded it as a question of damages—expenditure recoverable as damages for a wrongful act. Whereas the judge, in his careful
judgment, refused to treat it as damages. " That is the wrong legal
category," he said in effect [1980] 1 Lloyd's Rep. 111, 125–126. " This is
money expended by way of mitigation of another person's wrongful act to
which different principles apply as to foreseeability, burden of proof, and
the rest of it."

The Weekly Law Reports, March 13, 1981

281

1 W.L.R.   Compania Financiera v. Hamoor Tanker Corp. (C.A.) Lord Denning M.R.

A   I can understand that in some cases that distinction may be useful and valuable: but for myself, when expenditure is incurred as a result of a wrongful act, the common law has always looked upon it as damages. I need not go through all the cases. In a personal injury case the medical expenditure incurred is regarded as damages. In damage to property, if you have a lorry or motor car which has been damaged and put out of action, the cost of providing a substitute is not regarded as sums expended
B   in mitigation. It is always regarded as sums recoverable by way of damages for the wrongful act.

The distinction fades into nothingness in most cases. In *Moore* v. *DER Ltd.* [1971] 1 W.L.R. 1476 a car was damaged beyond repair. The test applied was, what was reasonable expenditure to make good the damage? Oliver J. makes a useful analysis in *Radford* v. *De Froberville*
C   [1977] 1 W.L.R. 1262, 1272. He points out that often there is nothing in it: it is virtually the same inquiry. There is the recent case of *Dodd Properties Ltd.* v. *Canterbury City Council* [1980] 1 W.L.R. 433, where some of the cases were gone into. It seems to me, as a matter of common sense and common law, that expenditure made to obtain the release of a vessel from arrest should be regarded as an item of damages,
D   and not as mitigation. It is the natural way of dealing with it.

The judge admitted that this was an attractive argument: but on the whole he felt that he could not accede to it [1980] 1 Lloyd's Rep. 111, 125. But it seems to me that it is the right way of dealing with it. It is damages, not mitigation.

Next there was the question of causation or remoteness. I would agree that the overdraft interest was in a sense a consequence of the unlawful
E   arrest. It flowed from it in the sense that, if there had been no unlawful arrest, the overdraft would not have been incurred. But, as we all know, it is not every consequence of a wrongful act which is the subject of compensation. The law has to draw a line somewhere. That has nowhere been better stated than by Lord Wright in *The Liesbosch* [1933] A.C. 449, 460:

F   " The law cannot take account of everything that follows a wrongful
        act; it regards some subsequent matters as outside the scope of its
        selection, because ' it were infinite for the law to judge the cause of
        causes,' or consequences of consequences . . . In the varied web of
        affairs, the law must abstract some consequences as relevant, not per-
        haps on grounds of pure logic but simply for practical reasons."

G   That is the question in this case. Although the overdraft interest may be a consequence of the initial unlawful arrest, is it such a consequence that ought to be visited in damages?

Upon this point—I do not care whether you call it " causation " or whether you call it " remoteness "—causation and remoteness are two different ways of stating the same question. Is the consequence sufficiently
H   closely connected with the cause as to be the subject of compensation or not? To my mind causation and remoteness here are the same

Mr. Johnson referred to the recent case of *H. Parsons (Livestock) Ltd.* v. *Uttley Ingham & Co. Ltd.* [1978] Q.B. 791. In that case I drew a distinction at pp. 802–803 between loss of profit cases on the one hand and damage or expenditure on the other This comes into the damage and expenditure line and not into the loss of profit line.

As to the damage and expenditure cases, it seems to me that the rules

282

we have laid down as to causation (whether it is sufficiently proximate to   A
be a consequence or not) or remoteness (whether it is naturally and
reasonably flowing from the breach or not) come down to the same thing.
If applied, the judge himself would say that the managers were not liable.
He said in his judgment [1980] 1 Lloyd's Rep. 111, 127:

> " If it were appropriate to regard the bank interest as a direct item
> of damage, there would be much to be said for the view that it had   B
> reference to some particular arrangements of the owners which were
> unknown to the managers and not communicated to them, and which
> were not therefore in the contemplation of the parties at the time when
> they made the contract, and that accordingly they represent an item
> which must be disallowed."

So on that approach to the case—which I think is the right approach—   C
the judge would have come to the same view as the umpire.

It comes back to what Templeman L.J. said in the first hour or two of
hearing this appeal: They are entitled to all the reasonable expenditure
which they incurred as a result of the wrongful arrest and getting the ship
released: but not " unheard-of " overdraft interest of this kind.

In the circumstances the question of remission to the arbitrator does
not apply. I would only say this: The question of expenses incurred in   D
respect of mitigation was fully argued before the umpire. But he did not
make any findings upon it. He was content to rest himself on the findings
which I have already mentioned. Each of the parties wanted to serve notice
of motion to remit. The managers wanted to put in a notice of motion
saying how unreasonable was the so-called mitigation, and it should not
be allowed. The owners wanted to put in another motion to get a finding   E
that it was reasonable. Pages and pages were taken up in the notices of
motion. The judge refused to go into them. He thought that there had been
too much delay in the matter. But it seems to me that, if the umpire was
at fault in not dealing with mitigation, it was his fault and not that of
either of the parties. If it was necessary—in order to do justice—to have
findings on that point, I should have thought it would have been very   F
desirable to remit the matter to the umpire for him to determine those
outstanding points: especially as in the last paragraph of his case stated
he says in effect that, if anything was wanting, he would ask the court to
remit the award to him so as to enable him to re-draft it.

In the circumstances it seems to me that it is quite unnecessary and
undesirable to remit the award to the umpire. It seems to me that the
umpire directed himself properly. He thought that the interest charges   G
were too remote, too unreasonable, too unforeseeable altogether to be
properly counted as a head of compensation. That seems to me to be
a very sensible and correct way of dealing with it. It is not a matter in
which the court should interfere.

I would therefore allow the appeal and restore the decision of the
umpire.   H

SHAW L.J. I agree; and what I add is only a postscript to the judgment
which has just been delivered by Lord Denning M.R. The arguments
developed before the umpire as to the respective concepts of causation,
foreseeability and mitigation of damage assumed almost the character of
a debate on some philosophical abstraction. It is small wonder that the
umpire in the elucidation of the problems with which he was confronted

The Weekly Law Reports, March 13, 1981

283

1 W.L.R.   Compania Financiera v. Hamoor Tanker Corp. (C.A.)   Shaw L.J.

A made an analysis which enable him to arrive at an award seemingly based on only one of those concepts. After all, he was called upon to deal with a practical commercial situation and not with a hypothetical exercise in jurisprudence elaborated by incursions into the law of trusts. He looked at the whole matter as should a man of business who was sufficiently informed in regard to the broad legal principles involved in breach of contract and the right and reasonable basis for compensation for the
B damage occasioned by a particular breach.

Although the umpire made no express reference to mitigation of damage, he must have recognised the question of reasonableness as intruding itself into the determination of what was the damage arising from the breach. Whether the costs of the guarantee were incurred in mitigation of damage or constituted the actual damage might have some consequence
C as to where lay the burden of proving what was reasonable or unreasonable. But the answer to that problem ought not to affect the ultimate result in any quantitative sense. As I read the award, the umpire had all the material basic considerations in mind when reaching his decision. His resolution of the inter-related problems was not only tenable but just in the light of the facts found by him; and those facts were adequate
D to support a just result in legal as well as in mercantile terms.

With all respect to the judge, whose knowledge and experience in this field can hardly be surpassed, I venture to think that he was deflected from a relatively straight road into a legalistic labyrinth. If one returns to the straight road, there is no need to look for further elucidation of the facts, and therefore no occasion to remit the award to the umpire.

For the reasons which have been stated by Lord Denning M.R. I too
E would allow the appeal and restore the award of the umpire.

TEMPLEMAN L.J. I also agree. The managers, in breach of contract, arrested the owners' vessel to secure payment of the owners' debts. The managers became liable for the reasonably foreseeable damages suffered by the owners as a result of that breach of contract. Mr. Johnson relied
F on clause (2) of the management agreement, which Lord Denning M.R. has read, and which imposes on the managers a particularly onerous standard of duty. Rightly or wrongly the owners were then allowed to call evidence as to what the clause meant and as to the parties' discussions about its meaning when they were negotiating the agreement; and rightly or wrongly the gloss has been put on the clause that it imposed on the managers the duties of trustees. So be it; but that does not mean that the
G contractual laws of measurement of damages or mitigation can be thrown out of the window and that Hamoor Tanker Corporation Inc.—who can only be described as odd beneficiaries under a trust—can play ducks and drakes with the trustees when it comes to running up damages for breach of the duty imposed upon the managers. In my judgment, in the circumstances of this case, clause (2) does not make any difference to the
H amount of money which the managers must find for their now admitted breach of contract.

Approaching the consequences of that breach of contract with the spectacles adopted by the managers, it was reasonably foreseeable that the owners would seek to procure the release of their vessel arrested in breach of contract, and for this purpose they might obtain a guarantee for payment of their debt, and they would incur expense in obtaining a guarantee. That expense, if reasonable, would be recoverable as foreseeable damages.

A   Approaching the case with the slightly different coloured spectacles put on by the owners, the obtaining of a guarantee was a reasonable form of mitigation. The reasonable expenses of obtaining a guarantee must be recoverable whichever pair of spectacles is adopted, either as being foreseeable damages or as being expenses of mitigation.

The owners paid a commission and bank charges to obtain a guarantee from their bankers. The umpire held that the commission and the bank charges were recoverable from the managers. Subsequently to the grant B of the guarantee, the bankers debited an overdraft account of the owners with interest, compounded by quarterly rests, on the maximum sum secured by the guarantee. The owners submitted to and accepted liability for these interest charges down to 1976 but not beyond that date. The umpire held that these interest charges were not recoverable from the managers.

C   The owners had ample opportunity in the course of the arbitration to explain and justify their submission to interest charges in respect of money which they had never borrowed. Paragraphs 79 to 87 of the findings of fact requested by the owners were designed to establish that it was reasonable and necessary for the owners to incur and pay the interest charges. Conversely, the managers had ample opportunity in the course of the D arbitration to establish that the interest charges were wholly unreasonable or, alternatively, partly unreasonable. Paragraphs 56 to 82 of the findings of fact requested by the managers were designed to establish that it was unreasonable for the owners to incur and pay the interest charges.

It is inconceivable that the umpire overlooked the necessity of making up his mind on these problems and overlooked the necessity of deciding in brief whether it was reasonable or unreasonable for the owners to incur E these interest charges.

It was thus the task of the umpire to determine whether or not the interest charges were reasonable. This was not a difficult path for an umpire to follow. Unfortunately the umpire was plunged into a murky pool and was urged to distinguish between the shallow end of mitigation of damages, the middle depths of causation of damages, and the deep end of F remoteness of damages. It is not surprising that the umpire reported the results of his journey, and short-circuited the requests for detailed findings of fact, and avoided the legal arguments to which he had been subjected, and avoided everything except the ultimate answer, namely, that the interest charges were not reasonably foreseeable damages suffered by the owners as a result of the managers' breach of contract. In taking this G shortcut, the umpire exposed himself to the accusations of the owners, to which we have been subjected, that he failed to ask himself the right question.

The judge plunged into the same pool and failed to discern that on any footing the umpire had provided a relevant and decisive answer. That answer is to be found in the umpire's award in paragraph 11(36) and 11(37), in paragraphs 12 (c) and (d), and in the ultimate paragraph 13 (e). H In short, he gave the ultimate answer that the interest charges were not damages naturally and foreseeably flowing from the wrongful arrest of the vessel.

The judge succeeded in holding that the interest charges were recoverable damages, although the only relevant finding of the umpire was that the interest charges were not foreseeable. The judge [1980] 1 Lloyd's Rep. 111, 126, said that the umpire's finding that the interest charges were

The Weekly Law Reports, March 13, 1981

285

1 W.L.R.   Compania Financiera v. Hamoor Tanker Corp. (C.A.)   Templeman L.J.

A unforeseeable did not justify the inference that the incurring of the interest charges " was due to the owners having adopted an unreasonable form of mitigation." In my judgment, the inference of the umpire's award is irresistible that the interest charges were wholly unreasonable and should never have been incurred either as a head of damage or as part of a reasonable form of mitigation. The umpire, who found that the interest charges were not recoverable because they were not foreseeable, must have
B concluded that the bank charges and commission were recoverable because they were foreseeable. The only possible distinction between the bank charges and commission which were recoverable and the interest charges which were irrecoverable lies in the fact that the interest charges were wholly unreasonable and must have been found so by the umpire. The umpire must have thought that the owners could and should have adopted
C a form of mitigation which was reasonable either by refusing to pay the interest charges to their bankers or by seeking a guarantee elsewhere or by some other available form of securing the release of the vessel more cheaply.

The umpire [1980] 1 Lloyd's Rep. 111, 117 (36), found that the owners submitted to the interest charges because, as Lord Denning M.R.
D has quoted, they " operated on the basis of a very substantial bank overdraft (finding this method of conducting their business convenient . . .) ", and he held that " the interest charges . . . are not recoverable as damages naturally and foreseeably flowing from the wrongful arrest." To reach this conclusion, he must have determined that the interest charges were unreasonable and unnecessary; and, although as between the owners and their bank, it may have suited the owners in their business interests and
E having regard to their relationship with their bankers to suffer this interest, nevertheless as between the owners and the managers the interest charges were wholly unreasonable and should not have been incurred.

Whatever principle is invoked—whether it be the principle of causation or mitigation—the acid test in the present circumstances must have been reasonableness; and, if the interest charges were unreasonable, they were
F not damages for which the managers are liable. I agree with Mr. Johnson that in some circumstances different principles may require different tests and produce different results, but in the present case, if the interest charges were unreasonable—they were too remote; they were not caused by the breach; they were not part of a reasonable form of mitigation—all these matters hang together. In view of the fact that the umpire found that the interest charges were not recoverable and were not damages which were
G foreseeable, I have no doubt that he concluded that the interest charges were wholly unreasonable for the purpose of any and every principle which had been canvassed before him. As I said, he avoided all the detailed questions he was asked to find on and all the theoretical aspects of the matter and simply ruled that the interest charges were not recoverable.

I too would restore the umpire's award.

H
Appeal allowed. Umpire's award restored. Managers to have costs in Court of Appeal, half their costs below and half costs of notice of motion. Leave to appeal refused.

Solicitors: *Holman, Fenwick & Willan; Hedleys.*

A. H. B.

[1981]

A

[CHANCERY DIVISION]

* SAFEGUARD INDUSTRIAL INVESTMENTS LTD. v. NATIONAL
WESTMINSTER BANK LTD. AND ANOTHER

[1979 M. No. 2780]

B

1980 April 15, 16;   Vinelott J.
       May 23

Company—Shares—Transfer—Articles of private company restricting transfer of shares—Notice to be given of proposed transfer
—Executor of deceased member holding shares for benefit of
members of family—Whether " transfer " of shares   C

The plaintiff acquired approximately one-sixth of the total
issued shares of a private family company, giving it a strategic
stake in that company. A block of approximately one-sixth of
the issued shares was held by a member of the family, P, until
his death on July 25, 1976, after which those shares were held
by the first defendant, a bank, as the deceased's executor. The
remaining two-thirds of the shares were held by other mem-   D
bers of the family in proportions such that neither of two
branches of the family held sufficient shares to command a
majority of the votes at general meetings. Until 1971, the business of the company was run by two brothers, cousins of P,
who were the respective heads of the two branches of the
family. In 1970, differences of opinion arose between the
brothers as to the way in which the company's business should
be run. In 1971 the brothers ceased to be directors and an   E
associate of the plaintiff joined the board and was appointed
chairman. During his life, P had remained neutral, supporting
neither branch, and after his death the bank, which became
the registered holder of his shares, likewise continued to
maintain a neutral attitude during the administration of the
deceased's estate with the result that the plaintiff had been
able to hold the balance of power between the two opposing
factions, and so long as P's shares did not come under the   F
control of either faction that position could be preserved.
However, by his will P had left his shares to G, who was the
daughter of one of the brothers, and by a deed of family
arrangement G gave effect to a wish which P had expressed
before his death, that G and her brother should each have
one half of his shares.

The company's articles of association contained certain   G
pre-emption provisions, under which shares might be transferred to the other members in proportion to their existing
holdings, but not to a non-member so long as any member was
willing to buy at a fair price. Except where the proposed transfer was to be made to certain close relatives, which did not
include G and her brother, article 7B required notice in writing
to be given to the company by the transferor of his desire to
transfer the shares, in order to ascertain whether any member   H
was willing to purchase them. Fearing that the balance of
control would be upset on the completion of the administration, and that the bank would henceforth exercise its voting
rights as directed by G and her brother, the plaintiff issued an
originating summons, which asked the court to determine,
inter alia, whether on the true construction of the articles the
bank, on the completion of the administration, should give the
company a transfer notice pursuant to article 7B. The bank
filed evidence that the administration was in fact complete,

The Weekly Law Reports, March 13, 1981

287

1 W.L.R.   Safeguard Ltd. v. National Westminster Bank (Ch.D.)

A   and that the bank regarded itself as holding the shares on
trust for G and her brother, but that G and her brother did
not want the bank to transfer the shares to them, and that the
bank did not propose to do so unless so directed.

On the question whether on completion of administration
of the deceased's estate, and having assented or purported to
assent to the vesting of the beneficial interest in the deceased's
shares in G and her brother, the bank was bound to give a
B   transfer notice pursuant to the pre-emption provisions: —

Held, that, on the true construction of article 7B of the
company's articles of association, the word " transfer " meant
a transfer of the legal interest in the shares, and did not refer-
to the transfer of the beneficial interest therein; that article 7B
applied to any person entitled to transfer a share, whether as
a member or as a personal representative or trustee in bankruptcy of a member, and that the desire to transfer a share,
C   such as would give rise to an obligation to serve a transfer
notice on the company, was a desire expressed or implemented
by such person; that the desire of a deceased member, expressed in his will, to transfer his shares to a person who was
not a close relative could not be treated as the desire of his
personal representative and therefore there was no obligation
on the bank to serve a transfer notice on the company (post,
pp. 297E–H, 299D–E).
D   *Lyle & Scott Ltd.* v. *Scott's Trustees*, 1958 S.C. 230; [1959]
A.C. 763, H.L.(Sc.) and *Hunter* v. *Hunter* [1936] A.C. 222,
H.L.(E.) considered.

The following cases are referred to in the judgment:

Greenhalgh v. *Mallard* [1943] 2 All E.R. 234, C.A.
Hunter v. *Hunter* [1936] A.C. 222, H.L.(E.).
E   *Lyle & Scott Ltd.* v. *Scott's Trustees*, 1958 S.C. 230; [1959] A.C. 763;
[1959] 3 W.L.R. 133; [1959] 2 All E.R. 661, H.L.(Sc.).
Scott v. *Frank F. Scott (London) Ltd.* [1940] Ch. 794; [1940] 3 All E.R.
508, C.A.

The following additional cases were cited in argument:

F   *Delavenne* v. *Broadhurst* [1931] 1 Ch. 234.
Hawks v. *McArthur* [1951] 1 All E.R. 22.
Inland Revenue Commissioners v. *Hawley* [1928] 1 K.B. 578.
Moodie v. *W. & J. Shepherd (Bookbinders) Ltd.* [1949] 2 All E.R. 1044,
H.L.(Sc.).
Roberts v. *Letter " T " Estates Ltd.* [1961] A.C. 795; [1961] 3 W.L.R. 176,
P.C.
G   *Smith and Fawcett Ltd., In re* [1942] Ch. 304; [1942] 1 All E.R. 542,
C.A.

ORIGINATING SUMMONS

On July 26, 1979, the plaintiff, Safeguard Industrial Investments Ltd.
which held approximately one-sixth of the 132,003 issued shares of a
private family company, M. Wright & Sons Ltd., issued an originating
H   summons against the first defendant, National Westminster Bank Ltd.
which was the executor of a deceased shareholder, Philip James Rhodes
Wright (" the deceased ") who until his death had held 22,254 shares in
the company (approximately one-sixth), and also against the private
company itself, as second defendant. Until his death, the deceased had
remained neutral in a family dispute, and after his death the bank had
likewise maintained a neutral position during the administration of his
estate, and that had enabled the plaintiff to hold the balance between the

two opposing factions in the family. The plaintiff feared that at the termi- **A** nation of the administration, it would cease to be able to exercise that control, owing to the fact that, by virtue of the deceased's will and a deed of family arrangement the deceased's shares were destined to be transferred to two other members of the family in equal shares, both of whom were in the same branch of the family in the dispute. Accordingly the relief which the plaintiff sought in the originating summons was that **B** it might be determined whether on the true construction of the company's articles of association the defendant bank, as the deceased's executor, on the completion of the administration of his estate (a) should serve a transfer notice pursuant to article 7B of the company's articles of association, which article contained certain pre-emption provisions, in respect of all the shares of which the deceased was the registered holder at his death or (b) should take some other, and if so what, course of action in regard **C** to the shares. The originating summons also contained a request for further or other relief and for provision to be made for costs. After evidence had been filed that the administration was in fact complete and that the defendant bank regarded itself as holding the shares as to 11,127 for Mrs. Georgina Maltby, and as to 11,127 for her brother, Michael Pochin Marius Wright, but that neither of them wanted the shares actually trans- **D** ferred to them, and that the bank did not propose to do so unless so directed, the question which the court was asked to determine was whether on completion of the administration of the deceased's estate, the bank were bound to give a transfer notice pursuant to the pre-emption provisions.

The facts are stated in the judgment.

E

Gerald Godfrey Q.C. and *Elizabeth Gloster* for the plaintiff.
Oliver Weaver for the first defendant bank.
The second defendant was not represented.

Cur. adv. vult.

F

May 23. VINELOTT J. read the following judgment. M. Wright & Sons Ltd. (which I shall call " the company ") is a private company. It was incorporated in 1950. Its share capital is now £200,000 divided into 200,000 shares of £1 each, of which 132,003 have been issued and are fully paid or credited as fully paid. The plaintiff, Safeguard Industrial Investments Ltd. (which I shall call " Safeguard "), is a public investment **G** company. It specialises in acquiring strategic stakes in private companies —that is, blocks of shares which are of a size which would normally give the holder some influence over the way in which the company's affairs are conducted but which are not large enough to carry voting control. In 1961 or thereabouts, Safeguard acquired approximately one-sixth of the issued shares of the company. The business was then run by two brothers, Michael Wright senior and Marius Wright. They continued to run the **H** business until 1971. The brothers, together with Marius Wright's children, Michael Pochin Marius Wright (" Michael Wright junior "), and Mrs. Georgina Maltby, together held approximately two-thirds of the shares of the company. A block of 22,254 shares (approximately one-sixth of the total issued shares) was held by one Philip James Rhodes Wright, who died on July 25, 1976, and to whom I shall refer as " the deceased." He

The Weekly Law Reports, March 13, 1981

289

1 W.L.R.   Safeguard Ltd. v. National Westminster Bank (Ch.D.)   Vinelott J.

A was the son of one Walter Wright, the brother of Sidney James Wright who was the father of Marius Wright and Michael Wright senior.

In 1970 there were differences of opinion between Michael Wright senior and Marius Wright as to the way in which the company's business should be conducted. The company suffered in consequence. Neither Michael Wright senior, on the one hand, nor Marius Wright and his two children, on the other hand, held a sufficient number of shares to command B a majority of votes at general meetings. The votes attaching to the shares held by the deceased and by Safeguard were thus of crucial importance.

In 1971 there was a change in the constitution of the board. A Mr. King joined the board and became chairman. He is still the chairman. He is a director of a company associated with Safeguard and was, I assume, introduced by Safeguard. Michael Wright senior and Marius Wright ceased C to be directors. Since 1971 the business of the company has been conducted by a board consisting of Mr. King, Michael Wright junior and two directors who are not connected with either side of the family. It is said by Safeguard that since this change the business of the company has prospered. Safeguard also claims that while the deceased was alive it effectively held the balance of power between the two warring factions and D was able to ensure that the company did not come under the control of either of them. The details of the family shareholdings are not set out in the evidence but, as I understand the position, Safeguard held the balance of power in this way only so long as the deceased also sat on the fence and supported neither side. As I have said he died on July 27, 1976. His will, which was dated March 25, 1966, was proved on October 4, 1976, by National Westminster Bank Ltd. as successor of Westminster E Bank Ltd., the sole executor named in the will. National Westminster Bank (" the bank ") was registered as the holder of the deceased's shares on or about March 30, 1977. It is said by Safeguard that the bank, since it was registered as the holder of the deceased's shares, has exercised its voting rights " in accordance with its judgment of the best interests of the deceased's estate " and, as I understand it, the bank, in turn, has not F supported either faction so that Safeguard has continued to exercise the same degree of practical control which it was able to exercise during the lifetime of the deceased. The position of Safeguard is now threatened by the events to which I now turn.

By his will, the deceased left his shares in the company to Mrs. Maltby then and therein described as Miss Georgina Wright. Shortly before his death—on May 27, 1976—he wrote to Michael Wright junior inquiring G whether he would be willing to act as his executor. In that letter he expressed his wish that his shares should go to Michael Wright junior and Mrs. Maltby equally. He also expressed uncertainty as to whether under his existing will the shares went to them both equally or to one or other of them. After the death of the deceased, Mrs. Maltby decided to give effect to the deceased's wishes as expressed in that letter and by a deed of H family arrangement, dated April 10, 1978, to which she, Michael Wright junior and the bank were parties, it was declared that the deceased's will should be read and take effect as if his shares in the company had been left to Michael Wright junior and Mrs. Maltby equally. Safeguard feared that on completion of administration of the estate the bank's practice with regard to the exercise of the voting rights attached to the shares would change, that the bank would exercise their rights in accordance with the directions of Michael Wright junior and Mrs. Maltby, and that

Marius Wright and his children would secure control of the company. **A**
That would deprive Safeguard of the influence over the company's affairs
which their strategic stake had previously secured. Safeguard also claimed
that under certain pre-emption provisions in the articles of association of
the company the bank would be bound, on completion of the administration of the estate, to offer the deceased's shares to the other members of
the company pro rata to their shareholdings. That claim having been disputed by Mrs. Maltby and by Michael Wright junior, Safeguard took **B**
out the originating summons which is now before me, joining the bank
and the company as defendants. The originating summons, as originally
framed, asked that it be determined whether on completion of administration of the estate the bank will be bound to give a transfer notice in respect
of the deceased's shares pursuant to the pre-emption provisions. In the
course of these proceedings evidence has been filed on behalf of the bank **C**
in which it is said that administration of the deceased's estate is complete
and that the bank regards itself as holding 11,127 of the deceased's shares
on trust for each of Mrs. Maltby and Michael Wright junior absolutely.
It is said by the bank that Mrs. Maltby and Michael Wright junior have
made it clear that they do not want the bank to transfer the shares to
them, that the bank does not propose to transfer the shares unless directed **D**
so to do and that accordingly " the bank as registered holder of the
said shares neither proposes nor desires to transfer all or any of the said
shares or any interest in them." The significance of this last statement will
appear from the pre-emption provisions. In the light of that evidence by
the bank, Safeguard now asks that it be determined whether " on completion of administration of the deceased's estate and having assented or
purported to assent to the vesting of the beneficial interest " in the **E**
deceased's shares in Mrs. Maltby and Michael Wright junior, pursuant
to the joint effect of the will and the deed of family arrangement, the bank
are bound to give a transfer notice pursuant to the pre-emption provisions.

Article 1 of the articles of association of the company provides that
the regulations in Table A of Schedule 1 to the Companies Act 1948:

> " shall apply to the company save in so far as they are excluded or **F**
> varied hereby: that is to say, the clauses in Part 1 of Table A num-
> bered 24, 30, 31, 53, 75, 77 and 136 shall not apply to the company;
> but in lieu thereof, and in addition to the remaining clauses in Part 1
> of Table A the following shall be the regulations of the company."

Article 2 provides: " The company is a private company, and accordingly
clauses 2, 3, 4, 5 and 6 in Part II of Table A shall apply to the company." **G**
Articles 7 and 8 are headed " Transfer of shares." Article 7A deals
with a class of preference shares which no longer exist. The first two
paragraphs of article 7B read:

> " A member shall not be entitled to transfer an ordinary share except
> subject to clause 3 of Part II of Table A and in accordance with the
> following provisions: (a) An ordinary share may be transferred by a **H**
> member or other person entitled to transfer to the other members in
> the proportions between them (if more than one) as nearly as may
> be to the number of ordinary shares held by them respectively, but
> no ordinary share shall be transferred to a person who is not a
> member as long as any member is willing to purchase the same at
> the fair value. (b) Except where the transfer made is pursuant to
> article 8 hereof, in order to ascertain whether any member is willing

The Weekly Law Reports, March 13, 1981

291

1 W.L.R.   Safeguard Ltd. v. National Westminster Bank (Ch.D.)   Vinelott J.

A   to purchase an ordinary share, the proposing transferor shall give notice in writing (hereinafter called ' the transfer notice ') to the company that he desires to transfer the same. Such notice shall constitute the company his agent for the sale of such share to any member of the company at the fair value."

B   Paragraphs (c), (d), (e) and (f) provide for shares specified in a transfer notice to be offered by the directors at fair value to the other members pro rata, for the machinery for acceptance of such offers, for the execution of transfers on behalf of a proposing transferor who makes default in transferring shares specified in a transfer notice and for the ascertainment of the fair value of the shares. Paragraph (g) provides that if no member is willing to purchase shares comprised in a transfer notice within a specified
C   period the proposing transferor is to be free to sell them to a non-member but at not less than a fair value. Paragraph (h) contains special provisions concerning shares held by employees including those departmental directors who are not directors of the company. Those special provisions are not relevant to the questions I have to decide.

Article 8 I must read in full. It reads:

D   "Any share in the company may be transferred by a member (other than a departmental director) during his life or by his legal personal representatives on his death, as the case may be, to any husband, wife, son, daughter or other lineal descendant, son-in-law, daughter-in-law, father, mother, brother, sister, nephew, niece, widow or widower of any such member or to any trustees appointed by deed or will upon trusts for the benefit of any such person or by such
E   trustees to new trustees or by any such trustees on the termination of the said trusts to any such person as aforesaid and the restrictions contained in article 7 and in clause 3 of Part II of Table A shall not apply to any transfer authorised by this article."

Article 8A contains special provisions relating to Safeguard's shares. It restricts the directors' power to refuse to register transfers to certain
F   companies associated with Safeguard and modifies the pre-emption provisions in article 7 in effect by giving Safeguard the right to specify the price at which shares it wishes to transfer are to be offered to other members.

These articles contain at least two unusual provisions which I should mention before turning to the main arguments which have been addressed to me. First, article 1 adopts Table A, except certain specified clauses.
G   The excepted clause include clauses 30 and 31. Clause 30, so far as material, provides that a person becoming entitled to a share in consequence of the death of a member may be required by the directors to elect to be registered himself or to have some person nominated by him registered as transferee so that in either case the directors are to have the same power to decline or suspend registration as they would have had in
H   the case of a transfer by a deceased member. Clause 31 provides that if a person becoming so entitled shall elect to be registered he shall send to the company a notice stating that he so elects and if he elects to have another person registered shall testify his election by executing a transfer to him. In either case:

"... All the limitations, restrictions and provisions of these regulations relating to the right to transfer and the registration of transfers of shares shall be applicable to any such notice or transfer as afore-

A

said as if the death or bankruptcy of the member had not occurred
and the notice or transfer were a transfer signed by that member."

The effect of the words which I have cited is that upon a personal
representative electing either to be himself registered or to have another
person registered any pre-emption provisions in the articles come into
operation in just the same way as if the deceased member had signed a
transfer. It is common ground that in the present case, clauses 30 and 31   B
having been excluded, the bank, as personal representative of the deceased,
was entitled to be registered as the holder of the shares registered in his
name: see *Scott* v. *Frank F. Scott (London) Ltd.* [1940] Ch. 794.

The second and related point is that upon registration as the holder of
the deceased's shares the bank became a member of the company.
Article 8 permits a share to be transferred by a member or by the per-   C
sonal representatives of a deceased member to a class of close relatives
of the member or deceased member. Literally construed article 8 would
permit a personal representative who became registered as the holder of
the deceased's shares to transfer the shares to his close relatives. Mr.
Weaver, who appeared for the first defendant, went further. He said that
once the personal representative had been registered he was bound by
the article in the same way as if he had been registered as transferee and   D
could no longer transfer the deceased's shares to a close relative of the
deceased. He said that the fact that the personal representative once registered would not be entitled to transfer to the close relatives of the deceased
—unless they also happen to be close relatives of his—was a matter to be
taken into account by the personal representative in deciding whether or
not to apply for registration. While that conclusion follows from a literal   E
construction of article 8, the article is, I think, capable of another construction which produces a more sensible result. The second part of
article 8 permits a transfer to be made ". . . to any trustees appointed
by deed or will upon trusts for the benefit of any " close relatives of a
member " or by such trustees to new trustees or by any such trustees on
the termination of the said trusts to " any such close relative. Those words,
by expressly permitting the transfer of a share by a trustee to a bene-   F
ficiary—being a close relative of the settlor member—impliedly prohibit a
transfer by the trustee to his own close relatives. The same restriction
must, in my opinion, be read into the first part of article 8. It cannot have
been intended that a personal representative who becomes registered as the
holder of a share should be in any different position from that of a trustee
for a close relative of a deceased member to whom the same personal   G
representative might subsequently transfer the share pursuant to directions in the will and who, in turn, might be registered as the holder of
the share. If article 8 is read as a whole it is, I think, clear that the
draftsman intended that a personal representative or a trustee who became
registered as the holder of a share devolving on death or transferred inter
vivos, though becoming a member, would not fall to be treated as a   H
member for the purposes of article 8, but would stand in the shoes of, and
be treated as a representative of, the deceased member or settlor from
whom the shares were derived, and that in the case of a personal representative as in the case of a trustee he would be entitled to transfer the
shares to the close relatives of the deceased member even though he had
himself become registered as the holder of the shares.

The bank, of course, has no relatives. And Mrs. Maltby and Michael

The Weekly Law Reports, March 13, 1981

293

1 W.L.R.   Safeguard Ltd. v. National Westminster Bank (Ch.D.)   Vinelott J.

A Wright junior are not close relatives of the deceased; they are children of a cousin of his. Thus the fact that the bank is registered as the holder of the deceased's shares is irrelevant. The question whether the bank is bound to give a transfer notice would have arisen even if the shares had remained registered in the name of the deceased. Mr. Godfrey, who appeared for Safeguard, did not contend that the bank became bound to give a transfer notice as regards Michael Wright junior's shares, when the deed of family
B arrangement was executed. He argued that the bank became bound to give a transfer notice as regards all the deceased's 22,254 shares as soon as it had completed administration and had informed Mrs. Maltby and Michael Wright junior, that it held 11,127 shares as her or his nominee and would transfer them to her or him as she or he might direct. He based this argument on two grounds. First, he submitted that the reference in
C article 7B to the transfer of a share should be construed as extending to a disposition of the entire beneficial interest in a share, that on completion of administration of the estate the deceased's beneficial interest, which was in suspense during the period of administration, vested in Mrs. Maltby and in Michael Wright junior and that the bank became bound to give a transfer notice at the moment when the bank first informed Mrs. Maltby
D and Michael Wright junior that administration of the estate was complete and that the bank would deal with the shares as directed by them, that being, it is said, an assent by the bank to the vesting of the beneficial interest in Mrs. Maltby and Michael Wright junior.

   The second and alternative submission is that the deceased by his will evinced a desire to transfer his shares to a person who was not permitted transferee of his entire holding—Mrs. Maltby has, of course, been a
E member at all material times but a transfer to a member can be made under paragraph (a) of article 7B only if the shares are offered pro rata to all members—and that that expression of his desire to transfer his shares became on his death an irrevocable direction to his executor to transfer the shares to Mrs. Maltby, subject only to the bank's power as executor to sell the shares or some of them if such a sale should become necessary
F in the course of administration. The deceased's expressed desire to transfer his shares, it is said, must be treated as one expressed on his death. But it was not then such an expression of his desire to transfer his shares as required the bank, as his representative, to give a transfer notice under article 7B; the reason is that the desire evinced by the will was a desire to transfer his shares in the future—that is, on completion of administration of the estate—and was conditional in that the legatee's right to a
G transfer would be subject to the executor's power to sell the shares if necessary in the course of administration. But, it is said, on communication by the bank to Mrs. Maltby and Michael Wright junior, that administration had been completed and that the bank would deal with the shares at their direction, the deceased's expressed desire to make a future and conditional transfer took effect through the executor as his represen-
H tative as an expressed desire to make an immediate and unconditional transfer to Mrs. Maltby and, in effect, through her to Michael Wright junior. At that stage it is said paragraph (b) of article 7B operated in just the same way as if the bank had, at the deceased's direction, entered into a contract to sell the shares to them for a nominal consideration.

   In support of his first submission Mr. Godfrey relied upon the decision of the Court of Session in *Lyle & Scott Ltd.* v. *Scott's Trustees*, 1958 S.C. 230 and on certain observations in the House of Lords in the sub-

sequent appeal from that decision [1959] A.C. 763. In that case the A
articles of association of Lyle & Scott Ltd. prohibited any transfer by
a shareholder holding more than one per cent. of the shares of the company
for a nominal consideration or by way of security and provided that

". . . no transfer of ordinary shares . . . shall take place for an
onerous consideration so long as any ordinary shareholder is willing
to purchase the same . . ."   B

either at a price to be ascertained by agreement between the transferor and
the directors or failing agreement fixed by the auditors. That was the first
and prohibitive part of the article. The article then provided:

". . . any such ordinary shareholder who is desirous of transferring
his ordinary shares shall inform the secretary in writing of the number
of ordinary shares which he desires to transfer, and the price shall   C
immediately be fixed as aforesaid ": see p. 765.

There followed the usual provisions for the shares to be offered by the
company to the other shareholders. An offer was made by a non-member,
Hugh Fraser, for all the shares of the company which offer was accepted
by certain of the shareholders. The offer was initially conditional on
acceptance by 75 per cent. of the members and was to be completed by D
payment against executed transfers in the usual way. Subsequently the
condition was waived. The shareholders who had accepted were paid the
agreed price, which had been increased since the original offer, and each
delivered a share certificate and a form of general proxy. The shareholders
concerned claimed in their evidence that it had also been agreed by Mr.
Fraser at the time of payment of the consideration for the shares that no   E
instruments of transfer would be executed and delivered unless and until
requested by him. Mr. Fraser accordingly did not apply for registration.
It was argued on behalf of the shareholders at first instance that all they
had done was " to sell the beneficial interest in their shares, retaining the
legal title and membership of the company in themselves ": see 1958
S.C. 230, 233. That argument was rejected by Lord Strachan, the Lord   F
Ordinary, on the ground that it had not been averred in the evidence that
the sale was a sale of the beneficial interest alone. He held that the contract
for the sale of the shares was a breach of the first or prohibitive part of
the article. But he refused to order that the shareholders were bound to
give notice to the secretary of their desire to transfer their shares upon
the ground that the second part of the article prescribed the provisions by
which alone a member's shares could be transferred but did not give the G
other members the right to compel a member desirous of transferring his
shares to offer them to the other members. He said, at p. 235:

". . . even if the defenders in this case do desire to transfer shares,
they would be entitled to change their minds after sending the prescribed notification to the secretary, and a fortiori they would be
entitled to do so before they had taken the first step under article 9. H
To find that they are now bound to implement article 9, or to ordain
them to do so, would be to deprive them of their right to change
their mind . . ."

That decision was upheld by the Court of Session upon the same ground.
In the Court of Session the company sought to uphold the Lord Ordinary's
judgment upon the ground that the shareholders had sold and transferred

The Weekly Law Reports, March 13, 1981

295

1 W.L.R.   Safeguard Ltd. v. National Westminster Bank (Ch.D.)   Vineloft J.

A the beneficial interest in the shares and that the second part of the article accordingly applied. It was said, that " the term ' desirous of transferring ' struck at all transfers, not merely technical transfers of shares " : see p. 235. As to that argument Lord Clyde, the Lord President, said, at p. 243:

B " An attempt was made to contend that although the legal title to the shares remained with the defenders they had competently disposed of some equitable or beneficial right in the shares. But whatever may be the validity in Scotland of such a distinction—and upon that matter I reserve my opinion—the contract averred by the pursuers is, by Scots law, either a contract of sale of the shares or nothing. For the essence of the contract in question is that the price is payable against delivery of an effective transfer. As such a transfer cannot be given, no obliga-
C tion has been incurred to convey an interest in the property. No question therefore arises, in my opinion, in the case as presented to us, on the pursuers' averments regarding equitable or beneficial interests."

But Lord Sorn accepted the argument. He said at p. 250:

D " The language of the article thus seems to me to make it clear that what it purports to prohibit is a sale of the shares, and that this includes a prohibition of the sale of the beneficial interest in them. Indeed, when the purpose of the article is regarded, it would be strange if the language had not had this meaning. The article is plainly designed to give members of the company *some* kind of opportunity of keeping the share capital and control of the business in the hands of existing members. If it is read in the way I have suggested, it
E purports to do this effectively. If it is read in the opposite way, it would purport to achieve little or nothing, because it would be left open to a shareholder, prepared to let himself remain on the register as a bare trustee, to sell his shares to an outsider and give him a general proxy. It is difficult to think that the article intended to leave this obvious manoeuvre unprohibited."

F In the House of Lords the late Sir Milner Holland similarly argued, at p. 768, that the article prohibited " transfers of shares, including transfers of the beneficial interest." It was held in the House of Lords that the shareholders were bound to give notice to the secretary in accordance with the second part of the article. But the majority based this conclusion upon the ground that the shareholders who accepted the offer had by contracting to sell their shares shown that they desired to transfer them and that they
G could not be heard to say that they did not desire to transfer them so long as the contract remained on foot. Viscount Simonds, after referring to the distinction which had been made in the court below between the first or prohibitive and the second part of the article, said, as regards this first part of the article, at p. 773:

H " I do not dissent, my Lords, from the opinion expressed by the Lord Ordinary and the Lord President (Lord Clyde) and Lord Russell in the first division that Scott's trustees had been guilty of a breach of this part of the article. The determination of this question rests on the meaning to be assigned to the word ' transfer ' where it there occurs. But I do not think it necessary to express a final opinion upon it, for, as I have said, the question is not whether what has been done is a breach of the first part of the article but whether it demonstrates

with sufficient clearness that Scott's trustees are persons desirous of   A
transferring their ordinary shares."

As I read that passage the question on which Viscount Simonds refrained
from expressing a final opinion was whether there had been a breach of
the first or prohibitive part of the article and not the question whether
the article applied to the sale of a beneficial interest in a share. But Lord
Keith of Avonholm did deal with this question. He said, at p. 785 :   B

"If I may express my view of the article in the most general sense,
I think the prohibitory part of the article is the sanction which prevents
a shareholder from carrying through a transfer of shares without
complying with the machinery of transfer set out in the second part
of the article. And I think a shareholder who has transferred, or
pretended to transfer, the beneficial interest in a share to a purchaser   C
for value is merely endeavouring by a subterfuge to escape from the
peremptory provisions of the article. A share is of no value to anyone
without the benefits it confers. A sale of a share is a sale of the
beneficial rights that it confers, and to sell or purport to sell the
beneficial rights without the title to the share is, in my opinion, a
plain breach of the provisions of article 9. This, I think, is the view   D
which commended itself to Lord Sorn, and I think he is right."

The observations of Lord Keith of Avonholm, of course, lend powerful
support to Mr. Godfrey's first argument but they do not stand alone. In
the earlier case of *Hunter* v. *Hunter* [1936] A.C. 222, which was referred
to by Lord Sorn, Viscount Hailsham L.C. expressed the contrary opinion.
In *Hunter* v. *Hunter* the main question was whether a mortgagee bank's   E
power of sale over shares of a private company had become exercisable
and if it had, whether a purported sale by the bank was in breach of
pre-emption provisions. The first part of the relevant article provided :

"No member shall be entitled to transfer any shares otherwise than
in accordance with the following provisions : (*a*) A member desirous
of selling his shares (hereinafter called 'the selling member') shall   F
give a notice (hereinafter called 'the notice of sale') to the secretary
of the company containing an offer to sell the same, and stating the
number of the shares which he desires to sell and the price which he
is willing to accept for such shares, which price shall be a price to
be fixed and certified by the auditors or auditor of the company for
the time being, and which price when so fixed shall be deemed to be
the fair price and final and binding."   G

There followed provisions for the secretary to give notice of the offer to
the other shareholders and a right for one of the shareholders in certain
circumstances to accept the offer in priority to the other shareholders. The
bank had apparently procured its nominees to be registered as the holders
of the shares in question, in breach of article 17, before it purported to   H
exercise its power of sale.

It was held by the majority in the House of Lords that the power of
sale had not become exercisable and by all their Lordships that the purported sale infringed the article. It had been argued by the bank that the
sale was a sale of an equitable interest only and that the article did not
apply to it. All their Lordships held that the sale was not a sale of an
equitable interest divorced from the legal interest. But Viscount Hailsham

The Weekly Law Reports, March 13, 1981

297

1 W.L.R.   Safeguard Ltd. v. National Westminster Bank (Ch.D.)   Vinelott J.

A L.C., after making it clear that his observations on this latter point were not intended to be binding authority, said at pp. 248–249:

> "I cannot accept the view of the Court of Appeal that the trans- action between the bank and Harry Hunter operated as a valid sale of the equitable interest in the shares. A mortgagee of shares cannot split up the interest of the mortgagor and sell the mortgagor's bene-
B ficial interest while retaining for himself the legal title, any more than a mortgagee of a house can sell the fixtures in the house leaving the mortgagor the equitable owner of what is left: *In re Yates* (1888) 38 Ch.D. 112. If the bank had been selling the equitable interest of the plaintiff in the shares, none of the provisions of article 17 as to the restriction on the possible purchasers, or as to the method of
C fixing a price, would have been effective; it would have been quite a different transaction from a sale of the shares."

As I read the speech of Lord Russell of Killowen he agreed with Viscount Hailsham L.C. on this point, though, again, he made it clear that he was not to be taken as expressing any concluded opinion. He said, at p. 264:

> "Neither am I able to justify to myself the way in which the Court
D of Appeal have upheld what purported to be a sale of the legal and equitable interest in the shares at the restricted price enforced by the articles (and necessarily at that price) as a sale of the equitable interest only *which, if permissible, would not be in any way subject to those restrictions, but open to free competition.*" (my italics)

The references to the judgments in the Court of Appeal suggest that the
E Court of Appeal may have decided that the sale was a sale of the equit- able interest and that the sale did not infringe article 17: see also the first six lines on p. 231. However, this decision of the Court of Appeal is not reported and the record in the House has not been obtained so that this must remain at present a matter of speculation.

Faced with these conflicting observations in the House of Lords I
F must decide which to follow. Although it may seem at first sight unduly restrictive to read the word "transfer" as referring only to a transfer of the legal interest in a share leaving, as Lord Sorn puts it, 1958 S.C. 230, 251, the "obvious manoeuvre" of a sale of the beneficial interest un- prohibited, article 7B seems to me wholly inapt to "catch" transfers of beneficial interests. A "transfer of a share" in the ordinary sense of that expression is a transfer of the legal title to the share with the rights and
G liabilities attaching to it; on registration of the transfer the transferor ceases to be and the transferee becomes a member of the company in right of that share. A member who desires to transfer a share will carry his intention into effect by executing a transfer and lodging it for registration. At that stage the restrictions in the pre-emption provisions come into operation. To treat the references to the transfer of a share as com-
H prehending a transfer or disposition of a beneficial interest in a share is to give the expression "transfer of a share" a meaning wider than it would ordinarily bear. No doubt there are contexts in which that exten- sion would readily be made. But the context of articles 7 and 8 points, if anything, in the opposite direction. Any number of equitable interests can be carved out of the equitable ownership of a share. But it is impos- sible to construe article 7 as applying to any disposition of a beneficial interest in a share however small. And if the article is construed as apply-

ing to a disposition of the entire beneficial interest in a share but not to A
a disposition of part of the beneficial interest it may operate in a way that
is both capricious and which in practice would afford little protection
against the " obvious manoeuvre " of a shareholder determined to defeat
the pre-emption provisions. A shareholder is entitled to transfer a share
to trustees on trust for his infant son contingently on attaining 21 with
remainder to himself or to another close relative if the son dies under 21.
Article 8 clearly permits such a transfer and is not restricted to a transfer B
to trustees as bare trustees for a close relative absolutely entitled; for it
contemplates a transfer to the beneficiary for whose benefit the trust was
created on termination of the trust. On the wider construction of the word
" transfer " a sale by the son after attaining 21 would be a " transfer "
of the share bringing the pre-emption provisions into operation. But a
sale by the son immediately before attaining 21 would not pass the entire C
beneficial interest and would not therefore bring the pre-emption provisions into operation. Similarly, a shareholder might declare himself a
trustee for a purchaser who is not a close relative contingently on the
happening of some future event for instance his survival to a stated date.
The declaration of trust again would not operate as a transfer of the entire
beneficial interest even though it might be practically certain that the event D
would happen. Again, a shareholder might vest a reversionary interest
expectant upon his own death in a purchaser by a declaration of trust
constituting himself a trustee for himself for life with remainder to the
purchaser. The declaration of trust would not amount to a transfer of the
share even on the wider construction. The shareholder might subsequently
sell his life interest to the same purchaser. He would then have divested
himself of the entire beneficial interest in the share in favour of the pur- E
chaser but without at either stage executing a transfer of the entire
beneficial interest. Weighing anomalies may be an uncertain guide to construction. But it is, I think, legitimate to take into account the anomalies
which result from giving an extended meaning to an expression as a ground
for not departing from its ordinary meaning.

It is possible that if a shareholder were to declare himself a trustee F
of a share for a purchaser and were to hand over an irrevocable proxy to
vote the share the court might draw the inference that the parties intended
that the transaction should take effect as a contract for the sale of the
share, and that the owner had sufficiently evinced a desire to transfer the
legal interest in the share. That, as I see it, is the ground of the opinions
expressed by Lord Sorn and Lord Keith of Avonholm, in the *Lyle &
Scott* case, 1958 S.C. 230—though it should be noted that it is inherent G
in the view of the majority in the House of Lords, that the operation
of the article could be avoided by a consensual cancellation of the
contract, that the passing of the equitable interest which resulted from the
arrangements made when the purchase price was paid did not of itself
bring the second part of the article into operation. However, in my judgment, it cannot be said that a member has transferred a share or desires H
to transfer a share if all that is shown is that he has disposed of or agreed
to dispose of an equitable interest in it.

Mr. Godfrey's second argument is at first sight a more formidable one.
He stressed that during the period of administration the beneficial ownership of the deceased's shares was in suspense and that on completion of
administration Mrs. Maltby's and Michael Wright junior's title to the
shares related back to the date of the testator's death. Thus, said Mr.

The Weekly Law Reports, March 13, 1981

299

1 W.L.R.   Safeguard Ltd. v. National Westminster Bank (Ch.D.)   Vinelott J.

A   Godfrey, the transfer must be treated as having been made on the testator's death when his desire to transfer his shares to a person who was not a close relative was first expressed in a document containing directions as to the disposition of his shares which was the precise equivalent of a contract for the sale of the shares albeit subject to the condition that the executor was to have power to sell the shares if necessary for the purpose of administration. But the argument, though persuasively presented, leads

B   again to anomalous results. If a testator gives his shares in the company by will to a person who is not a close relative then on completion of administration, if the argument is well-founded, his executor is bound to give a transfer notice. But if he dies intestate and his sole next of kin is a person who is not a close relative this result does not follow; the deceased cannot be said to have expressed the desire that his shares should be trans-

C   ferred on completion of administration to his next of kin. Indeed it is not easy to see how the argument would apply to the testator's shares in the present case. The testator did not by his will give any of his shares to Michael Wright junior. Michael Wright junior became entitled only under the deed of family arrangement. The argument, if well founded, would seem to lead to the conclusion that on completion of administration the

D   executor would be bound to give a transfer notice in respect of Mrs. Maltby's 11,127 shares, but not in respect of Michael Wright junior's 11,127 shares. The answer to the argument is, I think, that article 7B applies to any person who is entitled to transfer a share whether as a member or as personal representative or trustee in bankruptcy of a member. The desire to transfer a share, the expression or implementation of which gives rise to the obligation to give a transfer notice, is a desire

E   expressed or implemented by such a person. Article 8 excepts the case of a transfer by a member or the personal representative of a member to or to trustees for a close relative of such a member. The desire of a member as expressed in his will that his shares shall be transferred to a person who is not a close relative cannot be attributed to his personal representatives.

F   I reach this conclusion with some regret. I have no doubt that if the draftsman had foreseen this situation he would have found some means of extending the pre-emption provisions in such a way as to impose on the legatee an obligation to serve a transfer notice. But the gap cannot, in my judgment, be filled by construction. It requires a radical re-drafting of the article. And I must bear in mind the observations of Lord Greene M.R. in *Greenhalgh* v. *Mallard* [1943] 2 All E.R. 234 where he said,

G   at p. 237:

    " Questions of construction of this kind are always difficult, but in the case of the restriction of transfer of shares I think it is right for the court to remember that a share, being personal property, is prima facie transferable, although the conditions of the transfer are to be found in the terms laid down in the articles. If the right of transfer,

H   which is inherent in property of this kind, is to be taken away or cut down, it seems to me that it should be done by language of sufficient clarity to make it apparent that that was the intention."

                                        Declaration accordingly.

    Solicitors: *McKenna & Co.; Harvey, Ingram, Leicester.*

                                        T. C. C. B.

A

[COURT OF APPEAL]

* PROPERTY DISCOUNT CORPORATION LTD. *v.*
LYON GROUP LTD. AND OTHERS

1979   July 23, 24; 31

1980   July 30, 31

Goulding J.

B

Buckley, Templeman and Brightman L.JJ.

*Company—Charge—Registration—Company's contingent right to
grant of leases under building agreement—Interest charged to
mortgagee as security for advances—Registration of mortgage
against company under company legislation—No registration
of equitable charge against freeholder—Leases granted and
assigned—Whether leaseholders' interest in land subject to
equitable charge created by mortgage—Companies Act 1948
(11 & 12 Geo. 6, c. 38), s. 95—Land Charges Act 1925 (15
& 16 Geo. 5, c. 22), s. 10 (1) (5)* [1] *—Land Charges Act 1972
(c. 61), s. 3 (1) (7)*

C

By a mortgage dated July 31, 1968, in consideration for
advances up to £80,768 made by the plaintiff company, the
defendant company, L, assigned by way of equitable charge to
the plaintiff all its interest under a building agreement made
on February 27, 1968, with the freeholder of a plot of land
whereby L would enter on the land in order to construct
certain buildings and the freeholder would grant to L leases of
the land as and when buildings had been completed thereon.
L covenanted in the mortgage to execute a proper legal mortgage of the land if any leave under the agreement was granted
while money remained owing to the plaintiff. On August 12,
1968, the mortgage was registered pursuant to section 95 of
the Companies Act 1948. No registration was made under
the Land Charges Act 1925.

D

E

On November 7, 1969, part of the land subject to the
agreement was leased to L and on December 15 another part
of the land was leased. In 1973, L for value assigned the
benefit of both leases, one to the second defendant and the
other to the third defendant.

F

The plaintiff by summons sought the enforcement of the
mortgage and, on the preliminary issue whether the second
and third defendants' interests in the property comprised in
the leases were subject to the charge created by the mortgage,
Goulding J. held that the mortgage created only one charge
capable of registration and that the registration under section
95 of the Companies Act 1948 was sufficient registration so
that the second and third defendants took subject to the mortgage.

G

On appeal by the second and third defendants: —

Held, dismissing the appeal, that the mortgage contained a
charge on a single subject matter, namely, the conditional
right of L to be granted leases when the buildings were
completed and on those leases as and when granted, and,
since the charge was upon a single subject matter, there was
only one charge capable of registration (post, p. 311F–G);
that, although the charge was capable of being registered as
a general equitable charge under section 10 (1) of the Land
Charges Act 1925 against the freeholder, the wording of
section 10 (5) made it clear, as did subsequent provisions under
the Land Charges Act 1972, that registration against L under

H

[1] Land Charges Act 1925, ss. 10 (1) (5): see post, pp. 309F, 310B–C.
S. 20: see post, p. 309H.

A   section 95 of the Companies Act 1948 was sufficient and, therefore, both the second and third defendants as purchasers of L's interest under the leases had notice of that registration and took subject to it (post, pp. 309E, 312E–H, 313D, G).

Decision of Goulding J., post, p. 302c et seq.; [1980] 1 All E.R. 334, affirmed.

B   The following cases are referred to in the judgments of the Court of Appeal:

Barrett v. Hilton Developments Ltd. [1975] Ch. 237; [1974] 3 W.L.R. 545; [1974] 3 All E.R. 944, C.A.
Jackson & Bassford Ltd., In re [1906] 2 Ch. 467.
Williams v. Burlington Investments Ltd. (1977) 121 S.J. 424, H.L.(E.).

C   The following additional case was cited in argument in the Court of Appeal:

Love (Gregory) & Co., In re [1916] 1 Ch. 203.

The following cases are referred to in the judgment of Goulding J.:

Barrett v. Hilton Developments Ltd. [1975] Ch. 237; [1974] 3 W.L.R. 545; [1974] 3 All E.R. 944, C.A.
D   London and South Western Railway Co. v. Gomm (1881) 20 Ch.D. 562.
Pritchard v. Briggs [1980] Ch. 338; [1979] 3 W.L.R. 868; [1980] 1 All E.R. 294, C.A.

The following additional case was cited in argument before Goulding J.:

Eastham v. Leigh London and Provincial Properties Ltd. [1971] Ch. 871; [1971] 2 W.L.R. 1149; [1971] 2 All E.R. 887, C.A.

E

PRELIMINARY ISSUE

By an agreement dated February 27, 1968, Western Ground Rents Ltd. licensed the first defendant company, Lyon Group Ltd. (then known as Ronald Lyon (Estates) Co. Ltd.), for 60 months to enter on land at Penarth Road, Cardiff, in order to construct certain buildings.
F   It was agreed that the first defendant would be granted leases of those parts of the land, where the buildings thereon had been completed, for a term of 99 years from the date of the agreement to build.

By a mortgage dated July 31, 1968, Lyon charged, inter alia, its interest under the agreement to the plaintiff, Property Discount Corporation Ltd., in consideration of certain advances made. On August 12, the charge was registered pursuant to section 95 of the Companies Act
G   1948. No registration was effected under the Land Charges Act 1925.

On November 7, 1969, pursuant to the agreement, Western Ground Rents Ltd. leased to Lyon part of the land (unit 7) and on December 15, 1969, they leased a further part of the land (unit 8) to Lyon. On January 22, 1973, Lyon assigned the benefit of the lease of unit 8 to the second defendant, J. H. Fenner and Co. (Holdings) Ltd., and on July 9,
H   1973, Lyon assigned the benefit of the earlier lease (unit 7) to the third defendant, I.T.T. Distributors Ltd.

On September 25, 1975, certain of the advances secured by the mortgage being outstanding, the plaintiff issued an originating summons for enforcement of the mortgage. On June 11, 1976, the third defendant's summons (as amended on March 19, 1979) asked that the following question be tried as a preliminary point of law: whether the interests of the second and third defendants in the property, comprised in the

302

second and the first lease respectively, were subject to the charge created   A
by the mortgage.

The facts are stated in the judgment of Goulding J.

Donald Rattee Q.C. and *Vivian Chapman* for the plaintiff.
Benjamin Levy for the second defendant company.
Martin Nourse Q.C. and *R. J. Simpkiss* for the third defendant   B
company.

The first defendant company (Lyon) was unrepresented.

Cur. adv. vult.

July 31, 1979. GOULDING J. read the following judgment. The
present application arises in proceedings commenced by originating   C
summons dated September 25, 1975, for the enforcement of an equitable
mortgage dated July 31, 1968, which I shall call simply " the mortgage."
It was made between the first-named defendant company, Lyon Group
Ltd. (by an earlier name) as borrower and the plaintiff, Property Discount
Corporation Ltd., as lender, and it related to property fronting Penarth
Road in Cardiff. Lyon Group Ltd., whom I shall call " Lyon," has not
been represented before me and is, I think, in liquidation. I am required   D
to try, as a preliminary point of law, a particular question raised upon a
statement of facts agreed between the plaintiff and the remaining two
defendant companies.

The statement of facts begins by reciting an agreement in writing,
which I shall refer to as " the building agreement," dated February 27,
1968, and made between Western Ground Rents Ltd. and Lyon. It   E
provided that Lyon should during a specified period enter on land
belonging to Western Ground Rents Ltd. and build and complete on the
site certain factories, warehouses, offices and roads according to plans,
elevations, etc., to be first approved in writing by the surveyor of
Western Ground Rents Ltd., whose approval should not be unreasonably
withheld. The work was to be carried out in conformity with all
statutory requirements and to be varied only as should be mutually agreed   F
by the parties in writing and to be completed to the reasonable satisfaction
of Western Ground Rents Ltd. or its surveyor. The building agreement
contained the usual powers of re-entry on default, and other provisions
usual in such documents. It provided that until the grant of leases the
interest of Lyon in the site should only be that of a tenant at will, and
that Lyon should not assign or deal with its interest under the building   G
agreement except with the consent of Western Ground Rents Ltd.
(which consent was not to be unreasonably withheld) to an assignment
by way of mortgage or charge for the purpose of financing the development. Another clause declared that no interest in the premises could
be acquired by the deposit of the building agreement, with an exception
in favour of any mortgage or charge in respect of which consent should
have been given as aforesaid. The building agreement further provided   H
that on completion of each of the intended buildings without default on
the part of Lyon, Western Ground Rents Ltd. would forthwith grant to
Lyon a lease of the appropriate part of the site with the building thereon
for a term of 99 years from the date of the building agreement at such
a rent and with such provisions as appeared from the building agreement
and from a form of lease identified by contemporaneous signature.
Finally, Western Ground Rents Ltd. agreed with Lyon to make certain

The Weekly Law Reports, March 13, 1981

303

1 W.L.R.   Property Discount Corp. v. Lyon Group (Ch.D.)   Goulding J.

A advances of money in connection with the construction of roads and sewers on the site and the infilling thereof.

The statement of facts then refers to the mortgage between Lyon and the plaintiff. The mortgage began by reciting the building agreement and an agreement on the part of the plaintiff to make advances to Lyon not exceeding a total of £80,768. By clause 1 of the mortgage, Lyon, as beneficial owner, assigned by way of equitable charge to the plaintiff all

B the interest of Lyon under the building agreement and the benefit thereof, together with all buildings to be built on the site, etc., as security for, and charged with the payment to the plaintiff of, all sums to be advanced to Lyon by the plaintiff pursuant to the following covenant, with interest thereon. By clause 2 the plaintiff covenanted with Lyon to make advances not exceeding £80,768 by instalments regulated by

C architect's certificates. Clause 3 contained a series of covenants by Lyon with the plaintiff—(a) to repay the advances with interest, (b) to comply with the terms of the building agreement, (c) to insure the buildings, (d) not to procure the grant of any lease without the plaintiff's consent, such consent not to be unreasonably withheld, and to make payments in reduction of principal on the grant or sale of each lease, and (e) if any lease should be granted to Lyon while money remained owing on the

D security of the mortgage, to execute forthwith a proper legal mortgage of the land comprised in such lease. I need not rehearse the various stipulations contained in clause 4 of the mortgage, but I ought to mention that clause 5 empowered the plaintiff, in the name of Lyon or otherwise, to demand from Western Ground Rents Ltd. the execution of any lease which Lyon might neglect or refuse to take up.

E The statement of facts next shows that on August 12, 1968, particulars of the mortgage were duly registered pursuant to section 95 of the Companies Act 1948, and adds that no registration was effected under the Land Charges Act 1925.

The statement of facts then records the grant by Western Ground Rents Ltd. to Lyon, pursuant to the building agreement, of a lease dated November 7, 1969, of part of the development known as unit 7, the

F assignment of that lease for value on July 9, 1973, by Lyon to the third-named defendant, I.T.T. (Distributors) Ltd., the similar grant to Lyon of a lease dated December 15, 1969, of another part known as unit 8 and the assignment of that second lease for value on January 22, 1973, by Lyon to the second defendant, J. H. Fenner & Co. (Holdings) Ltd. I shall call the second and third defendants together "the leaseholders."

G The statement of facts concludes by stating that certain moneys secured by the mortgage are still due to the plaintiff from Lyon, and that the leaseholders are in possession of the land subject respectively to the two before-mentioned leases.

The question posed for the preliminary decision of the court is, whether on the basis of the facts stated and documents referred to in the statement of facts, the interests of the leaseholders under their respective

H leases in the property comprised therein are subject to the charge created by the mortgage.

The plaintiff's case, as expounded by Mr. Rattee, is quite simply stated. Mr. Rattee says that the building agreement conferred on Lyon an equitable interest in the land. The mortgage thus was, or contained, an equitable charge affecting land, capable of registration as a land charge of class C under section 10 (1) of the Land Charges Act 1925, which was in force at the time the mortgage was executed. That charge

was however by law required to be registered under section 95 of the A
Companies Act 1948, being a charge created by a company registered in
England on land or an interest in land. It was in fact so registered in
due time, as appears from the statement of facts. Now section 10 (5) of
the Land Charges Act 1925 provided that, in the case of a land charge
for securing money created by a company, such registration in the
Companies Registry should be sufficient in place of registration under
the Act of 1925, and should have effect as if the land charge had been B
registered under that Act. Section 3 (7) of the Land Charges Act 1972,
which replaced the Act of 1925, preserves the foregoing provision so far
as regards land charges created, as the mortgage was, before January 1,
1970. Therefore, the mortgage has effect as if registered under the Land
Charges Act 1925. By section 198 of the Law of Property Act 1925, the
registration of any instrument or matter under the provisions of the C
Land Charges Act 1925, is deemed to constitute actual notice of such
instrument or matter to all persons and for all purposes connected with
the land affected. Thus, it is submitted, the leaseholders acquired their
respective leases with actual notice of the mortgage and cannot claim
to be purchasers for value without notice thereof. Accordingly, their
interests are now subject to the charge contained in the mortgage.

The leaseholders attack the plaintiff's contentions on a number of D
alternative grounds. I can state them shortly, as follows. (1) The
building agreement did not confer on Lyon any interest in land, and so
the mortgage did not contain any land charge or other obligation capable
of affecting Lyon's successors in title. (2) Alternatively, the mortgage
contained two separate equitable charges, one on Lyon's right to require
the grant of leases, the other (given by way of covenant to execute a E
legal mortgage) on the leases when granted. The first was spent when
leases were granted and so cannot affect the interests of the leaseholders.
The second was for more than one reason never lawfully registered, and,
therefore, the leaseholders took free from it by virtue of section 13 of
the Land Charges Act 1925, in the case of the second defendant, and
of section 4 of the Land Charges Act 1972, in the case of the third
defendant (the latter Act having come into force on January 29, 1973) F
fortified in each case by section 199 of the Law of Property Act 1925.
(3) In the further alternative, registration under section 95 of the
Companies Act 1948 was not in this instance equivalent to registration
under the Land Charges Act 1925 because Lyon was not at the date of
the mortgage the owner of any legal estate in the land. I will examine
those three arguments one by one.   G

The first point, that the building agreement conferred no interest in
land, was chiefly expounded by Mr. Nourse who represented the third
defendant. As appears from the classical judgment of Sir George Jessel M.R. in *London and South Western Railway Co.* v. *Gomm* (1881)
20 Ch.D. 562, 581 a contract for the sale or lease of a parcel of land gives
the purchaser an interest in the land, because the right to call for a grant
of land is itself an equitable interest in the land. The purchaser, on H
performing his side of the bargain, can demand the promised estate in
the land, and if necessary enforce his claim by an action for the specific
performance of the contract. Now Mr. Nourse says in the first place
that at the date of the mortgage, as appears from its date and from its
terms, the work of development under the building agreement was still
at an early stage, that in those circumstances the court would not have
decreed specific performance against Lyon at the suit of Western Ground

The Weekly Law Reports, March 13, 1981

305

1 W.L.R.   Property Discount Corp. v. Lyon Group (Ch.D.)   Goulding J.

A Rents Ltd., nor by mutuality would it have decreed specific performance against Western Ground Rents Ltd. at the suit of Lyon.

Mr. Rattee says, and in my judgment rightly, that that consideration is not enough to prevent the immediate acquisition by Lyon of an interest in the land at the date of the building agreement. A contract gives an interest in land if it puts it in the purchaser's power to require a grant of land without the further permission of the owner. See what Sir

B George Jessel M.R. said, in the passage that I have cited, about the holder of an option. He said, at p. 581:

"A person exercising the option has to do two things, he has to give notice of his intention to purchase, and to pay the purchase-money; but as far as the man who is liable to convey is concerned, his estate or interest is taken away from him without his consent,

C and the right to take it away being vested in another, the covenant giving the option must give that other an interest in the land."

Again, Sir James Hannen said in the same case, at p. 586:

"... I must say that it appears to me to be a startling proposition that the power to require a conveyance of land at a future time does not create any interest in that land."

D The point is developed at greater length in the judgment of Goff L.J. in *Pritchard* v. *Briggs* [1980] Ch. 338.

Mr. Rattee says that, for present purposes, Lyon may be regarded in the same light as a person who contracts to take a long lease at a fine or premium. The latter has to find the money. Lyon had to do the

E building. In each case, having simply done what he promises, the contracting party can exact execution of the lease.

Mr. Nourse endeavoured to show that the last analogy is a false one. But for the limited purpose for which it was used, I do not think it is. The various requirements of the building agreement for approval by, or for the satisfaction of, Western Ground Rents Ltd. or its surveyor are carefully hedged by such expressions as "not to be unreasonably with-

F held" or "reasonable satisfaction." Variations in the works required by the building agreement are to be such only as shall be mutually agreed by the parties. Changes in the agreed form of lease are limited to those necessary to meet any special circumstances, and so on. It is true that the completion of the building agreement might have been prevented by supervening impossibility outside the control of either party. The

G sub-soil might have proved incapable of bearing the intended buildings, or the planning authority might have refused to permit development of the site. Such chances are not, in my view, relevant. As between the parties, Western Ground Rents Ltd. had parted with dominion over the land and could no longer dispose of it at will. Lyon, on the other hand, had a present right to the future grant of leases on completion of the respective buildings, and so had, in my judgment, acquired an interest in

H the land, an interest which it later assigned by way of charge to the plaintiff.

The leaseholders' second argument was fully deployed by Mr. Levy, who appeared for the second defendant. However, he failed to per-suade me that the contents of the mortgage can be split in the way he wants. When Lyon expressly assigned by way of equitable charge to the plaintiff all Lyon's interest under the building agreement, and the benefit thereof, it gave the plaintiff, in my judgment, a single continuing equitable

charge that operated (as between Lyon and the plaintiff) both on Lyon's   A
chose in action enforceable against Western Ground Rents Ltd. and
on each term of years as granted to Lyon, the leases being in truth the
only real benefit of the building agreement to Lyon. The covenant to
execute legal mortgages I regard as an ancillary or supplemental provision, though no doubt sufficient of itself to constitute an equitable
charge if it stood alone. I think that, if the leaseholders are to be
treated as having had actual notice of the mortgage when the leasehold   B
interests were assigned to them, their consciences are affected by the
charge contained in clause 1 of the mortgage, with or without the
addition of clause 3 (e).

     That conclusion makes it unnecessary for me to examine the
grounds on which Mr. Levy claimed that any land charge constituted by
clause 3 (e) of the mortgage was never validly registered. Such a charge,   C
he said, must have been an estate contract, that is a land charge of class
C (iv) as defined by section 10 (1) of the Land Charges Act 1925, and not
a general equitable charge within class C (iii). He suggested that this
would be so even without the statutory requirement that a class C (iii)
land charge must be an equitable charge not included in any other class
of land charge. However, he also relied on that requirement if necessary,
thus raising the question whether class C (iv) is to be considered a   D
separate class of land charges for this purpose or only a sub-division of
class C. If the charge constituted by clause 3 (e) of the mortgage was
only an estate contract, Mr. Levy said, it could not be eligible as a
charge on land or an interest therein for registration under section 95
of the Companies Act 1948. Alternatively, the charge could only take
effect upon each leasehold term at the moment the respective lease was   E
granted to Lyon; it took effect by operation of equity, not as a charge
created by a company; therefore it could not have been registered under
section 95. If the Act of 1948 required registration at all, it was registration under section 97, not section 95, and even had that been done, it
would not have been equivalent to a land charge registration.

     I think that I ought not to express any opinion upon these far-ranging
submissions, since I have as the ground of my judgment rejected that   F
dissecting construction of the mortgage which alone makes them relevant.

     The leaseholders' third objection to the plaintiff's contentions was
explained to me by Mr. Nourse. It has been common ground in the
debate in this court that an equitable mortgage affecting land, if not
secured by deposit of the legal title deeds, is capable of registration as a
land charge, even though the mortgagor may himself have had only an   G
equitable interest in the land affected. No one, I observe in passing, has
referred in argument to section 137 of the Law of Property Act 1925.
However, in such a case, that is where a merely equitable interest is
mortgaged, section 3 (1) of the Land Charges Act 1972 requires registration in the name, not of the mortgagor, but of the owner of the underlying legal estate. That appears clearly from the observations of the
Court of Appeal, regarding registration of a sub-purchaser's contract, in   H
Barrett v. Hilton Developments Ltd. [1975] Ch. 237, 244. But registration, under section 95 of the Companies Act 1948, is necessarily under the
name of the company which creates the charge: see section 98 of the
same Act. In such circumstances, Mr. Nourse submits that section
10 (5) of the Land Charges Act 1925, or section 3 (7) of the Land
Charges Act 1972, cannot operate to bring about an effective land
charge registration by way of registration under section 95. The result

The Weekly Law Reports, March 13, 1981

307

1 W.L.R.   Property Discount Corp. v. Lyon Group (Ch.D.)   Goulding J.

A would be so anomalous, so inconsistent with the scheme of the 1925
property legislation, so productive of practical difficulties, says Mr.
Nourse, that it cannot have been intended by the legislature. He would
have me read the two subsections as though each ended with the words
" shall have effect as if the land charge had been registered *in the name
of the company* under this Act," thus giving no protection unless the
B company is the owner of the legal estate concerned. I have felt this to be
the most difficult part of the case, for the enactment is not very
satisfactory on either view. If Mr. Rattee is right, it is a potential trap
for purchasers. No difficulty could arise on the assumed facts of the
present case, for Lyon subsequently acquired the legal terms of years, and
the leaseholders, as purchasers thereof from Lyon, must, or ought to,
have made a company search against Lyon's name. But one can imagine
C circumstances wherein a purchaser might be afflicted by statutory notice
of a charge given by a company whose name would not appear on the
title and whose existence he could not possibly discover. On the other
hand, if Mr. Nourse's view is preferred, the enactment is a potential trap
for lenders, since it says in terms that registration under section 95 shall
be sufficient in place of registration under the Land Charges Act.
    Confronted by such a problem, I think it my duty to choose the more
D literal construction of the statutes, that is, to decide in favour of the
plaintiff.
    Accordingly, all the leaseholders' alternative contentions fail, and
my answer to the question formulated by a summons in this action dated
June 11, 1976, as amended on March 19, 1979, and also set out at the
foot of the statement of facts, is " Yes," and I so declare.

E
                                            Declaration accordingly.

    Solicitors: *Linklaters & Paines; Barlow, Lyde & Gilbert; Slaughter
& May.*

                                                    K. N. B.

F   APPEAL from Goulding J.
    The second and third defendants appealed on the grounds that (1)
the judge erred in law in holding that the building agreement dated
February 27, 1968, and made between Western Ground Rents Ltd. of the
one part and Lyon Group Ltd. of the other part conferred on Lyon an equitable interest in land so that the mortgages of July 31, 1968, were or con-
G tained a land charge capable of binding the successors in title of Lyon
to the property comprised in the lease and capable of registration under
the Land Charges Act 1925; (2) in failing to hold that the building
agreement did not confer on Lyon any interest in land, and so that
the mortgage did not contain any land charge or other obligation
capable of affecting Lyon's successors in title to the property; (3) the
judge misdirected himself in holding that the mortgage created a single,
H immediate and continuing equitable charge on Lyon's interest under
the lease in favour of the plaintiffs; (4) the judge erred in law in failing
to hold that any land charge created by the mortgage did not affect
the second and third defendants' interests under the lease by reason
of its not being lawfully registered in the Land Charges Register or
for the purposes of the Land Charges Acts 1925 and 1972 at the date
of the lease; (5) in holding that the registration of the charge created by
the mortgage under section 95 of the Companies Act 1948 as sufficient

in place of registration under the Land Charges Act 1925 in the Land A
Charges Register and should have effect as if the charge had been
registered under the Land Charges Act 1925; (6) in failing to hold that
the charge was not binding on the second and third defendants by
reason of its not being registered as a land charge in the Land Charges
Register.

Richard Scott Q.C. and *Benjamin Levy* for the second and third B
defendants.
Donald Rattee Q.C. and *Vivian Chapman* for the plaintiff.
The first defendant was unrepresented.

BRIGHTMAN L.J. delivered the first judgment. This is an appeal from
a decision of Goulding J. The dispute is between an equitable mortgagee
and assigns of the mortgagor. The issue is whether the assignee took sub- C
ject to or free from the mortgage. The mortgage was registered under
section 95 of the Companies Act 1948, but not under the Land Charges Act
1925. The matter came before the judge on an agreed statement of facts
and copies of the relevant documents. The facts are fully set out in
the judgment of the judge. I do not therefore intend to repeat them,
but to confine myself to a brief summary necessary to enable my D
judgment to be, I hope, understood.

In 1968 Western Ground Rents Ltd. owned the freehold of a six-
acre industrial site in Cardiff. It decided to develop the site through
a company which later became known as Lyon Group Ltd. ("Lyon").
For this purpose it entered into a building agreement with Lyon,
which was dated February 27, 1968. By clause 2 of the building E
agreement, Lyon agreed to erect industrial buildings according to plans
and specifications to be approved by the surveyor of Western Ground
Rents Ltd. The work was to be completed within five years. Pending
completion Lyon was to be a tenant at will. As and when each building
was completed, Western Ground Rents Ltd. was to grant to Lyon or its
nominee a long lease of that part of the site. As part of the financing,
Lyon arranged to borrow money by instalments from the plaintiff, F
Property Discount Corporation Ltd. In order to secure the loan, Lyon
executed a mortgage deed, dated July 31, 1968, in favour of the plaintiff.
By clause 1 of that deed, Lyon assigned to the plaintiff by way of
equitable charge all the interest of Lyon under the building agreement
and the benefit thereof, as security for the money to be advanced.

Clause 3 (e) of the 1968 mortgage provided that if any lease should G
be granted to Lyon of the site or any part thereof while any money
remained owing on the mortgage, it would forthwith execute a proper
legal mortgage in favour of the plaintiff of the land comprised in such
lease, to secure all the money for the time being remaining due under
the mortgage deed.

On August 12, 1968, the mortgage was registered under section 95
of the Companies Act 1948. No registration was effected under the H
Land Charges Act 1925. Lyon proceeded to erect buildings on the site.
Two of the buildings came to be identified as "unit 7" and "unit 8."

On December 15, 1969, Western Ground Rents Ltd. executed a lease
of unit 8 in favour of Lyon pursuant to its obligation under the building
agreement. Lyon, in circumstances which are not known to us, did
not execute a legal mortgage of unit 8 as required by clause 3 (e) of
the 1968 mortgage.

The Weekly Law Reports, March 13, 1981

309

1 W.L.R.   Property Discount Corp. v. Lyon Group (C.A.)   Brightman L.J.

A   On January 22, 1973, Lyon assigned to the second defendant, J. H.
Fenner and Co. (Holdings) Ltd., for value, the benefit of the lease of
unit 8.   That assignment is not before us, but I think it is accepted
that it contained nothing that is material for present purposes.   I shall
deal later with the lease of unit 7 and the assignment thereof to a
company called I.T.T. Distributors Ltd., the third defendants.

B   Money secured by the 1968 mortgage remains due from Lyon to
the plaintiff.   Proceedings were begun in 1975 by the plaintiff against
Lyon and the second and third defendants.   In the course of those
proceedings the third defendant issued a summons for the trial of a
preliminary issue, whether on the basis of an agreed statement of
facts and the documents the interests of the second and third defendants
under the leases were subject to the charge created by the 1968 mort-
C   gage, notwithstanding the absence of any registration under the Land
Charges Act 1925.   Goulding J. decided this issue in favour of the
plaintiff.   The second and third defendants now appeal.   The arguments
in the court below seem to have been, for the most part, the same as
those submitted to us in this court.   I think it would be simpler to
explain first the argument of the plaintiff—for whom Mr. Rattee appears.
I shall still confine myself only to unit 8.

D   The argument is as follows.   Clause 1 of the 1968 mortgage was
expressed to create an equitable charge over the whole interest of Lyon
under the building agreement, and the benefit thereof.   That interest
and benefit included the right of Lyon to occupy the site for the purpose
of putting up the buildings, and the right of Lyon to a lease of each
building as and when completed.   Therefore, when the lease of unit 8
E   was executed, that lease became in equity subject to the charge created
by the 1968 mortgage.   The charge, which was equitable throughout,
attached automatically to the lease when granted.   The 1968 mortgage
created a land charge which was registerable as a class C land charge
under section 10 (1) of the Land Charges Act 1925, though not in fact
so registered.   This subsection provides, so far as material:

F   " The following classes of charges on, or obligations affecting,
land may be registered as land charges in the register of land
charges, namely . . . Class C:—A mortgage charge or obligation
affecting land of any of the following kinds . . . (iii) any other equitable charge, which is not secured by a deposit of documents relating
to the legal estate affected and does not arise or affect an interest
G   arising under a trust for sale or a settlement and is not included
in any other class of land charge (in this Act called ' a general
equitable charge '); . . ."

The 1968 mortgage created a charge.   That charge was a land charge
within the meaning of the Act because it was a charge on land, namely,
a charge on the interest of Lyon in the six-acre site under the terms of
H   the building agreement.   " Land " is widely defined by section 20 of the
Land Charges Act 1925; it includes:

" . . . land of any tenure, and mines and minerals, whether or not
severed from the surface, buildings or parts of buildings . . . and
other corporeal hereditaments . . . and other incorporeal hereditaments, and an easement, right, privilege or benefit in, over or
derived from land. . ."

Section 13 (2) of the Land Charges Act 1925 contains the sanction for   A
failure to register.   It provides that a land charge of, inter alia, class C
shall be void as against a purchaser of the land charged therewith
unless the land charge is registered in the appropriate register before
the completion of the purchase.   Under section 20 " purchaser " means
a person who, for valuable consideration, takes any interest in land.
The second defendant was such a purchaser.   However, the omission   B
to register under the Land Charges Act 1925 does not avoid the charge
as against the plaintiff; the charge is saved, it is submitted, by section
10 (5) of the Act, as amended, which, so far as is material for present
purposes, reads :

> " In the case of a land charge for securing money, created by a
> company . . . registration under section 95 of the Companies Act,
> shall be sufficient in place of registration under this Act and shall   C
> have effect as if the land charge had been registered under this Act."

The words I have omitted in reading the subsection were words inserted
by the Law of Property Act 1969 but in my view they have no relevance
to the argument that we have to consider.

The 1968 mortgage, it was submitted, created a land charge for
securing money.   The charge was created by a company and it was   D
duly registered under section 95 of the Companies Act 1948, which
applies, inter alia, to a charge on land wherever situate or any interest
therein, excluding a rent charge.   In the result, it was argued, registration of the land charge created by the 1968 mortgage under section 95
of the Companies Act was sufficient in place of registration under
the Land Charges Act 1925, and has effect as if the land charge had   E
been registered under the Land Charges Act.   It therefore binds the
interest of the second defendant in unit 8, notwithstanding that the
second defendant was a purchaser of the lease for valuable consideration.

The arguments of Mr. Scott, for the second defendant, against the
validity of the charge are deployed from two directions.   The attack
stems first from a careful analysis of the effect of the 1968 mortgage,
and secondly from what is said to be the true construction and effect   F
of section 10 (5) of the Land Charges Act 1925.   The first attack is
based upon the proposition that the 1968 mortgage does not contain one
single security consisting of a charge on all the interest of Lyon under
the building agreement.   The subject matter of the charge, it was said,
varies from time to time as the development of the site progresses, as
buildings are completed and leases are granted.   This variation of the   G
subject matter of the charge leads to inevitable changes from time to
time in the registrations necessary in order to preserve the priority of the
plaintiff as mortgagee.   Mr. Scott submitted that on a true analysis
the 1968 mortgage contained, first, an assignment by way of charge of
the contractual right of Lyon to be given a lease of each part of the
site upon the completion of a building; and, secondly, a covenant by
Lyon to grant a legal mortgage of each lease as and when it was granted.   H
The 1968 mortgage, it was said, did not, either at the date of execution
or at the date of registration under section 95 of the Companies Act 1948,
create any charge on the leasehold interest of Lyon in unit 8 because that
leasehold interest was not in existence at those times.   The only land
charge which qualified for registration under section 95 of the Companies
Act on August 12, 1968, which was the date of registration, was the *contractual right* of Lyon to be granted a lease on the future completion

The Weekly Law Reports, March 13, 1981

311

1 W.L.R.   Property Discount Corp. v. Lyon Group (C.A.)   Brightman L.J.

A of the building. The effect of the execution of the lease of unit 8 was, inevitably, to discharge Western Ground Rents Ltd.'s obligation under the building agreement to grant such a lease, and thus the charge of Lyon's contractual right quoad unit 8 necessarily disappeared at that stage. All that was then left to the plaintiff quoad unit 8 was the benefit of the covenant of Lyon to execute a legal mortgage over the lease which had been granted. It cannot possibly be said that that covenant at B the date of the 1968 mortgage created a charge on the lease, because the lease was not then in existence.

Reliance was placed on the observations of Buckley J. in *In re Jackson & Bassford Ltd.* [1906] 2 Ch. 467, 477, to the effect that an agreement that in some future circumstances a security shall in the future be created, does not create any present security which qualifies for regis-C tration under the predecessor of section 95 of the Companies Act 1948. Reference was also made to *Williams* v. *Burlington Investments Ltd.* (1977) 121 S.J. 424, which was decided by the House of Lords. The covenant to execute a legal mortgage was not registerable under section 95 of the Companies Act 1948; it was a contract to create a legal estate, and therefore fell to be registered as an estate contract under class C (iv) of the Land Charges Act 1925, section 95 having no relevance to that D contract. In the result, the registration under section 95 falls to be ignored for present purposes and the sanction imposed by section 13 (2) of the Land Charges Act 1925 applies. Accordingly the second defendant is left with the lease of unit 8, free from any charge.

Goulding J. rejected that argument for a reason which he stated quite shortly as follows; indeed, I do not think it is susceptible of much E elaboration. He said, ante, at pp. 305H—306A.

> " When Lyon expressly assigned by way of equitable charge to the plaintiff all Lyon's interest under the building agreement, and the benefit thereof, it gave the plaintiff, in my judgment, a single continuing equitable charge that operated (as between Lyon and the plaintiff) both on Lyon's chose in action enforceable against
F   Western Ground Rents Ltd. and on each term of years as granted to Lyon, the leases being in truth the only real benefit of the building agreement to Lyon. The covenant to execute legal mortgages I regard as an ancillary or supplemental provision, though no doubt sufficient of itself to constitute an equitable charge if it stood alone."

I agree. In my view the 1968 mortgage contained a charge on one G single subject matter, namely, the conditional right of Lyon to be granted leases, and on such leases as and when granted. That was a single subject matter, subjected to a single charge. I intend no disrespect to Mr. Scott if I describe his able arguments on this aspect of the case as artificial, and as introducing a subtlety which I think would be more apt to confuse the system of registration of charges than to contribute to any rational scheme of registration, and I would accede H to his submissions with great regret.

I turn to what I think, as did Goulding J., is the real problem in this case. If the 1968 mortgage had been registered as a general equitable charge, as it could have been and certainly ought to have been in the absence of any registration under section 95 of the Companies Act 1948, it would have been registrable against, and only against, Western Ground Rents Ltd. This follows from section 10 (2) of the Land Charges Act 1925 which, so far as material for present purposes, provides that a land

charge shall be registered in the name of the estate owner whose estate
is intended to be affected.   Registration against the name of a subsequent
estate owner is ineffective: *Barrett* v. *Hilton Developments Ltd.* [1975]
Ch. 237.   Under section 20 of the Land Charges Act 1925, " estate owner "
means, by reference to the Law of Property Act 1925, the owner of a
legal estate.   The only owner of the legal estate in the six-acre site at
the date of the 1968 mortgage and at the date of registration under
section 95 of the Companies Act 1948, was Western Ground Rents Ltd.
The registration under section 95, however, was necessarily against Lyon.

The question therefore arises whether registration of a land charge
under section 95 against company X can, on the true construction of
section 10 (5) of the Land Charges Act 1925, be regarded as an effective
substitute for registration under the Land Charges Act 1925 in the name
of Y.   The obvious purpose of section 10 (2) of the Act of 1925 was to
avoid the necessity of double registration, as indeed is said by the editors
of both the 1972 and the 1932 editions of *Wolstenholme & Cherry, Conveyancing Statutes* 12th ed., vol. 2 (1932), p. 844; 13th ed., vol. 6
(1972), p. 56 in their commentaries on the subsection.   There could,
however, be no double registration in a case where the company creating
the charge on the land is not the estate owner, because the registration
names under the two Acts would in that case be different.   It might be
considered a somewhat odd result if registration under the Companies
Act 1948 against X absolved an encumbrancer from registration under
the Land Charges Act 1925 against Y under the guise of avoiding the
necessity for double registration.   It is possible to construct cases in
which a system of substituted registration so applied could work a real
injustice, as was demonstrated during the course of the argument, though
I think that the likelihood of any such case of injustice would be fairly
remote.

I was at one time disposed to think, on general principles of logic,
that section 10 (5) must somehow be confined to a case where the registration under the Companies Act 1948 is against the same name as
the registration would be if done under the Land Charges Act 1925.   If that
were so in the present case, the appeal of the second defendant must
succeed, for the plaintiff would then have no escape route from the
penalty of invalidity imposed by section 13 (2) of the Land Charges Act
1925.   I have, however, in the end come to the conclusion, as did
Goulding J., that the argument must be rejected.   The wording of
section 10 (5) is too clear, however illogical the result may seem on the
facts of the present case.   The Companies Act registration is to be
sufficient.   It is to be sufficient in place of registration under the
Land Charges Act 1925.   It is to have effect as if the land charge had
been registered under the Land Charges Act 1925.   As the only registration which could have been validly effected under the Land Charges
Act 1925 at the date of the registration under the Companies Act 1948
was registration against the name of Western Ground Rents Ltd., it follows,
in my view, that the registration whose place is taken by the section 95
registration must be registration against the name of Western Ground
Rents Ltd., and the same effect is to follow as if there had in fact been
such a registration.

In the result, therefore, I accept in toto the argument of Mr. Rattee,
which I sought to summarise at the start of my judgment, and I would
dismiss the appeal of the second defendant.

The Weekly Law Reports, March 13, 1981

313

1 W.L.R.   Property Discount Corp. v. Lyon Group (C.A.)   Brightman L.J.

A   The facts in the second defendant's case differ only to the extent that the assignment of the lease by Lyon of unit 7 took place after the date when the Land Charges Act 1972 superseded the Land Charges Act 1925, namely, in January 1973. The provisions of the land charges legislation which apply in the second defendant's case are therefore those of the Act of 1972, but such provisions were repeated in the 1975 legislation in all material respects.

B   I would therefore also dismiss the appeal of the second defendant.

TEMPLEMAN L.J. I agree, and I cannot see that there is any great harm done in the result. The assignee in 1973 of a 99-year lease granted in 1969 should take the precaution of investigating the title of the landlord and the title of the lessee. Investigation of the title of a C lessee company will routinely include a search in the Companies Registry to see if there are any entries under section 95. Such a search in the present case would have disclosed the mortgage entered into by Lyon; the fact that the mortgage preceded the grant of the lease would not, in view of the possibility of the existence of a relevant floating charge, absolve the assignee from inquiring into the terms of the mortgage and from then satisfying himself that the property comprised in the lease D had been released from the equitable charge contained in the mortgage. It is hardly possible to conceive of instances in which a proper investigation of title would not have disclosed the section 95 entry.

For the reasons given by Brightman L.J. I agree that the appeals should be dismissed.

E   BUCKLEY L.J. I also entirely agree with the judgment that Brightman L.J. has delivered. Before the judge in the court below it was treated as common ground that an equitable charge upon an equitable interest in land would fall within class C (iii) of section 10 (1) of the Land Charges Act 1925 as an equitable charge described in that paragraph. Initially Mr. Scott, in the course of his argument in this court, sought to depart from that concession, if it was a concession, in the court below and to F contend that only an equitable charge upon a legal estate in land could fall within class C (iii). However, in the course of his argument in this court he abandoned that point and accepted that the paragraph is apt to extend to an equitable charge upon an equitable interest in land.

I have nothing to add to the reasoning of the judgment delivered by Brightman L.J. and I agree that, for the reasons which he has given, the G appeal fails and should be dismissed.

Appeal dismissed with costs.
Leave to appeal refused.

Solicitors: *Barlow, Lyde & Gilbert; Slaughter & May; Linklaters & H Paines.*

L. G. S.

November 25, 1980. The Appeal Committee of the House of Lords (Lord Diplock, Lord Edmund-Davies and Lord Fraser of Tullybelton) refused petitions by the second and third defendants for leave to appeal.

A

[HOUSE OF LORDS]

* A/S AWILCO OF OSLO . . . . . . RESPONDENTS

AND

FULVIA S.p.A. DI NAVIGAZIONE OF CAGLIARI . APPELLANTS

THE CHIKUMA

B

1981 Jan. 19, 20;   Lord Diplock, Lord Simon of Glaisdale,
    Feb. 19   Lord Edmund-Davies, Lord Scarman,
                                    and Lord Bridge of Harwich

*Shipping—Charterparty—Time charter—Hire—Right to withdraw
ship " failing . . . punctual . . . payment "—Payment of hire* C
*to be made " in cash "—Credit transfer on due date—Interest
not to run until four days later—Whether payment " in cash "
—Whether owners entitled to withdraw ship*
Ships' Names—Chikuma

By clause 5 of a time charterparty the hire of a vessel was
to be paid " in cash in United States currency monthly in
advance." The owners had the right to withdraw the vessel D
" failing . . . punctual . . . payment." Before January 1976
monthly payments of hire had always been made punctually by
credit transfer to the owners' bank. On January 21, 1976, in
respect of the payment due on January 22, the charterers
instructed their Norwegian bank to make the required payment
by credit transfer. By a telex message of 1141 on Thursday,
January 22, there was a credit transfer to the owners' bank of
$68,863·84 representing the sum due. On the same day the E
credit transfer became irrevocable under Italian banking law
and practice and the funds became available to the owners
although interest on those funds would not begin to run in
favour of the owners' bank until Monday, January 26. On
January 22, the owners' bank credited the owners' account
with the equivalent sum of dollars and under Italian banking
law and practice, the owners had the immediate use of the
money even though interest on the sum would not begin to F
run in favour of the owners until January 26. If the owners
had withdrawn that sum they would probably have incurred a
liability to their bank to pay interest until January 26. On
Friday, January 23, the owners instructed their bank to refuse
payment of the hire and accordingly it re-credited the amount
of dollars in question.

On January 24 the owners withdrew the vessel from the
service of the charterers on the ground that they had failed G
to pay the monthly instalment of hire due on January 22. The
charterers disputed the alleged failure and, in due course,
claimed damages for wrongful withdrawal of the vessel.

The dispute was referred to arbitration. The abitrator
reached the conclusion that the owners were not entitled to
withdraw the vessel but stated his interim award in the form
of a special case, the question of law for decision of the court
being that on the assumption that hire in the sum of U.S. H
$68,863·84 was due on or before January 22, 1976, whether
the owners were entitled to withdraw the vessel on January 24,
1976, under clause 5 of the charterparty.

Robert Goff J. gave judgment for the owners holding that
there had not been a payment in cash of the instalment due
and that therefore clause 5 had not been complied with. On
appeal, the Court of Appeal allowed the appeal.

On appeal by the owners:—

A
     Held, allowing the appeal, that when payment was made to
a bank otherwise than literally in cash, i.e., in dollar bills or
other legal tender, there was no " payment in cash " within
the meaning of clause 5 unless what the creditor received was
the equivalent of cash, or as good as cash; that the book entry
made by the owners' bank on January 22 in the owners'
account was plainly not the equivalent of cash, nor was there
any reason why the owners should have been prepared to

B
treat it as the equivalent of cash for it could not be used to
earn interest, e.g., by immediate transfer to a deposit account,
and the owners' bank had the right in the circumstances to
charge interest if it was drawn, since in substance the transaction was the equivalent of an overdraft facility which the
bank was bound to make available; that accordingly, on
January 22, there was no " payment in cash " by the charterers
of the hire then assumed to be due and it followed that the

C
owners, having refused to accept the credit as payment in
accordance with clause 5 were entitled to withdraw the ship,
as they did, on January 24 (post, p. 320A,–B, D–G).
    The Brimnes [1975] Q.B. 929, C.A. applied.
    Per curiam. Where shipowners and charterers embody
in their contracts common form clauses it is of overriding
importance that their meaning and legal effect should be
certain and well understood. The ideal at which the courts

D
should aim, in construing such clauses, is to produce a result,
such that in any given situation both parties seeking legal
advice as to their rights and obligations can expect the same
clear and confident answer from their advisers (post, p. 322A–B).
    Decision of the Court of Appeal [1980] 2 Lloyd's Rep.
409 reversed.

E
    The following cases are referred to in the opinion of Lord Bridge of
        Harwich:
Brimnes, The [1973] 1 W.L.R. 386; [1973] 1 All E.R. 769; [1975] Q.B. 929;
    [1974] 3 W.L.R. 613; [1974] 3 All E.R. 88, C.A.
Empresa Cubana de Fletes v. *Lagonisi Shipping Co. Ltd. (The Georgios
    C)* [1971] 1 Q.B. 488; [1971] 2 W.L.R. 221; [1971] 1 All E.R. 193, C.A.
Mardof Peach & Co. Ltd. v. *Attica Sea Carriers Corporation of Liberia

F
    (The Laconia)* [1977] A.C. 850; [1977] 2 W.L.R. 286; [1977] 1 All
    E.R. 545, H.L.(E.).
Nova Scotia Steel Co. Ltd. v. *Sutherland Steam Shipping Co. Ltd.* (1899)
    5 Com.Cas. 106
Tankexpress A/S v. *Compagnie Financière Belge des Petroles S.A.* [1949]
    A.C. 76 [1948] 2 All E.R. 939, H.L.(E.).

G
    The following additional cases were cited in argument:
China National Foreign Trade Transportation Corporation v. *Evlogia
    Shipping Co. S.A. of Panama* [1979] 1 W.L.R. 1018; [1979] 2 All
    E.R. 1044, H.L.(E.).
Tropwood A.G. v. *Jade Enterprises Ltd.* [1977] 1 Lloyd's Rep. 397.
Vallejo v. *Wheeler* (1774) 1 Cowp. 143.

H
    APPEAL from the Court of Appeal.
    This was an appeal, by leave of the House of Lords, by the appellants,
Fulvia S.p.A. Di Navigazione of Cagliari, from an order dated June 4,
1980, of the Court of Appeal (Lord Denning M.R., Waller and Dunn L.JJ.)
reversing an order dated October 23, 1978, of the commercial judge
(Robert Goff J.) upon an award stated in the form of a special case by
Mr. Donald Davies as sole arbitrator for the decision of the High Court
pursuant to section 21 of the Arbitration Act 1950.

Awilco v. Fulvia (H.L.(E.))   **[1981]**

A   The dispute arose under a time charterparty dated December 18, 1968, made on the standard form of the New York Produce Exchange, which was concluded between Reardon Smith Ltd. as owners and the respondents, A/S Awilco of Oslo. By a novation, the appellants became parties to the charterparty as owners of the vessel, by then named *Chikuma.*

The facts are set out in the opinion of Lord Bridge of Harwich.

B   *Christopher Staughton Q.C.* and *V. V. Veeder* for the appellants, the owners.

Andrew Leggatt Q.C. and *Roger Buckley Q.C.* for the respondents, the charterers.

Their Lordships took time for consideration.

C   February 19. LORD DIPLOCK. My Lords, I have had the advantage of reading in draft the speech prepared by my noble and learned friend Lord Bridge of Harwich. For the reasons he has given I too would allow the appeal.

D   LORD SIMON OF GLAISDALE. My Lords, I have had the privilege of reading in draft the speech prepared by my noble and learned friend Lord Bridge of Harwich. For the reasons he has given I too would allow the appeal.

LORD EDMUND-DAVIES. My Lords, I am in respectful agreement with the reasons advanced in the speech prepared by my noble and learned friend Lord Bridge of Harwich, for concluding that this appeal should be allowed.

E

LORD SCARMAN. My Lords, I have had the advantage of reading in draft the speech to be delivered by my noble and learned friend Lord Bridge of Harwich. For the reasons he gives I would allow the appeal.

F   LORD BRIDGE OF HARWICH. My Lords, this appeal arises from a dispute under the terms of a time charterparty in the New York Produce Exchange form to which at the material time the appellants (" the owners ") were parties as owners of the vessel *Chikuma* and the respondents (" the charterers ") as charterers. By clause 5 of the charterparty payment of the hire was

G   " to be made . . . in cash in United States currency, monthly in advance . . . . otherwise failing the punctual and regular payment of the hire . . . . the owners shall be at liberty to withdraw the vessel from the service of the charterers . . ."

An addendum to the charterparty provided for all freights to be paid to the owners' agents " care of Istituto Bancario San Paolo di Torino—Sede di Genova " (" the owners' bank ").

H   On January 24, 1976, the owners withdrew the vessel from the service of the charterers on the ground that they had failed to pay the monthly instalment of hire due on January 22. The charterers disputed the alleged failure and in due course claimed damages for wrongful withdrawal of the ship. This claim was referred to arbitration by Mr. Donald Davies as sole arbitrator. On a preliminary issue he was requested by the parties and agreed to state an interim award in the form of a special case on the

A   assumption that a monthly instalment of hire fell due on or before January 22, 1976, in the sum of U.S. $68,863·84 (the amount of which was at one time, but may well now no longer be, in issue).

Having set out his findings of primary fact, the arbitrator held that the charterers had paid the appropriate sum on the due date in accordance with the contract and that the owners were accordingly not entitled to withdraw
B   the vessel when they did. This conclusion was reversed by Robert Goff J. [1979] 1 Lloyd's Rep. 367. On appeal by the charterers, the Court of Appeal (Lord Denning M.R., Waller and Dunn L.JJ.) [1980] 2 Lloyd's Rep. 409 unanimously restored the decision of the arbitrator. The owners now appeal to your Lordships' House.

Before January 1976, monthly payments of hire had always been made punctually by credit transfer to the owners' bank. On January 21, 1976,
C   the charterers instructed their Norwegian bank to make the required payment by credit transfer. On Thursday, January 22, at 11.41 a.m., on instructions from the Norwegian bank, Credito Italiano, Genoa sent a telex to the owners' bank to the following effect:

" Pay without expenses for us
U.S. $68,863·84
D   [By] order Christiania Bank O.G. Kredietkasse Oslo
for account A./S. Awilco
in favour S.A.S.D.A. S.p.A. account 16020 c/o yourgoodselves
Re: *Chikuma* stop
[We] telecover you value 26 through Chase Manhattan Bank New York account yours of Turin stop."

E   This text is a translation from the original of the telex but I have added in square brackets words which, it was agreed at the hearing of the appeal, produce a more accurate version than the English text used in the courts below, though I think nothing turns on this. I should add that this telex was not exhibited to the special case by the arbitrator, but it was agreed between the parties at the hearing before Robert Goff J. that it should be treated as an exhibit. This was eminently sensible, for without seeing the
F   telex it would be difficult to understand the arbitrator's crucial findings of fact which are set out in the following two paragraphs:

" 4.   By a telex message of 1141 on Thursday, January 22, there was a credit transfer to the owners' bank of U.S. $68,863·84 representing the 81st payment of hire. At about noon on the same day the said transfer became irrevocable under Italian banking law and practice
G   and the funds representing the 81st payment of hire became available to the owners' bank for payment to the owners although interest on those funds would not begin to run in favour of the owners' bank until Monday, January 26. 5. On January 22, 1976, the owners' bank credited the owners' account with U.S. $68,863·84 (representing the 81st payment of hire) and, under Italian banking law and practice, the owners had the immediate use of the said sum even though interest
H   on the sum would not begin to run in favour of the owners until Monday, January 26. If the owners had withdrawn the said sum from their bank on January 22 (which was not the case although they had the right so to do) they would probably have incurred a liability to their bank to pay interest on the sum until January 26."

It is further found that on the owners' instructions, the owners' bank recredited the amount of the transfer to Credito Italiano on January 23.

At the conclusion of his findings of fact, the arbitrator posed the ques-   A
tion of law for the decision of the court (on the assumption to which I
have referred earlier) in the following terms:

> " Whether the respondent owners were entitled to withdraw the vessel
> on Saturday, January 24, 1976, under clause 5 of the charterparty
> dated December 18, 1968."

Under the heading " Award," the arbitrator wrote: B

> " Subject to the decision of the court, I hold that: — 1. There was a
> payment to the owners, by the charterers, of U.S. $68,863·84, on
> Thursday, January 22, 1976. 2. On the assumption that hire in the
> above sum was due on January 22 the owners were not entitled to
> withdraw the vessel on Saturday, January 24, 1976, under clause 5
> of the charterparty."   C

I have set out these extracts from the special case at some length in
order to point to the conclusion, which seems to me inevitable, that the
arbitrator was treating the question he had to resolve, having found the
relevant primary facts, as a pure question of law depending on the true
construction of the contractual provision applicable. What he held in   D
setting out his award did not purport to be other than a conclusion of law
and, in particular, there is no indication in the case that, either on the basis
of expert evidence or by applying his own knowledge as a very experienced
commercial arbitrator, he was attaching to any of the contractual words
any special technical meaning other than their ordinary meaning.

This is a convenient point at which to make two general observations
about the facts. First, the effect of the telex from Credito Italiano to the   E
owners' bank seems, in the light of the arbitrator's findings in paragraphs
4 and 5, to produce a situation, in accordance with Italian banking law
and practice, which in the eyes of an English banker or lawyer, has some
strikingly unusual features. It is a situation hardly likely to trouble the
English courts again unless as a result of a similar Italian inter-bank
transaction. Secondly, if the owners are right, this is yet another instance   F
of a clause such as clause 5 of the New York Produce Exchange form
operating to produce what appears to be a harsh result. The unexpired
term of the time charter must have been a valuable asset. The Court of
Appeal was told that the charterers' claim for damages was U.S. $3,000,000.
Yet their failure, if there was a failure, to comply with their obligation
under clause 5 was obviously of a very minor character.   G

My Lords, this is not the first time that the clause 5 of the New York
Produce Exchange form of charterparty has been before the courts. In
giving his considered judgment in *The Brimnes* [1973] 1 W.L.R. 386,
Brandon J. said, at p. 400, of this very clause:

> " I consider first the meaning of ' payment . . . in cash ' in clause 5
> of the charterparty. In my view these words must be interpreted   H
> against the background of modern commercial practice. So interpreted
> it seems to me that they cannot mean only payment in dollar bills or
> other legal tender of the United States. They must, as the owners
> contend, have a wider meaning, comprehending any commercially
> recognised method of transferring funds the results of which is to give
> the transferee the unconditional right to the immediate use of the
> funds transferred."

A   In the instant case, the test enunciated in the last sentence of the passage quoted was adopted and applied both by Robert Goff J. and by the Court of Appeal. But it led them to opposite conclusions. Robert Goff J. said [1979] 1 Lloyd's Rep. 367, 374:

B   " Here, the money took the form of a telex transfer and the telex transfer had attached to it, in my judgment, a condition embodied in the words ' value 26.' The effect of that was that the transfer was conditional upon interest not accruing on that money for the benefit of the transferee until a date later than the due date specified in the contract. I can see no escape from the conclusion that the effect of the imposition of that condition was to render it a payment which did not give the transferee the unconditional right to the immediate use

C   of the funds transferred. . . . It is as though the cash was handed over the counter on the Thursday and at the time of its transfer a condition was attached to it—that, if it was made available to the beneficiary immediately, interest was to be payable until the Monday, and if it was not made available to him immediately, interest would not accrue to him until the Monday. . . . In my judgment . . . one cannot ignore the power of money to breed interest. To do so is to ignore an

D   essential attribute of money itself."

All three members of the Court of Appeal reached the conclusion that the owners' right to the immediate use of the funds transferred was unconditional. They naturally expressed themselves in different terms, but I hope I fairly summarise their main grounds as follows: (1) that the last sentence of the telex containing the crucial words " value 26 " was an

E   inter-banking arrangement which did not affect the rights of the owners; (2) that the arbitrator had found as a fact, or on a mixed question of fact and law, that the owners' right was unconditional and there was evidence to support such a finding; (3) that the stipulation as to interest imposed no true condition.

With respect, it seems to me clear that the first two grounds are un-

F   sound. As to the first, Credito Italiano, as sub-agents of the charterers, effected the transfer on terms which deferred the right of owners' bank to the enjoyment of the funds to January 26. It was a plainly foreseeable consequence of the deferment that it would be, as it was, reflected in the terms which the owners' bank would be entitled to impose on the use of funds by the owners between January 22 and 26. As to the second, the word " unconditional " nowhere appears in the special case and, as I have

G   pointed out earlier, the arbitrator treated the question he had to decide as a question of law depending on the construction of clause 5 of the charterparty.

The third ground depends on the interpretation of the word " unconditional " in the context of the statement of principle by Brandon J. in *The Brimnes* [1973] 1 W.L.R. 386, bearing in mind that it is not to be

H   construed as if it were a statute. If the word is understood in its narrow, legal sense as meaning that the transferee's right to the use of the funds transferred is neither subject to the fulfilment of a condition precedent nor defeasible on failure to fulfil a condition subsequent, I can see that the owners' right in this case to the use of the funds on January 22 could be described as unconditional. But Robert Goff J. obviously understood it in a much wider and more liberal sense as equivalent to unfettered or un-restricted. I am bound to say that, before the argument in this appeal

brought to light this ambiguity, it would never have occurred to me that   A
Brandon J.'s formulation of the relevant principle was in any respect either
inaccurate or inadequate. Now that the ambiguity is exposed, I have no
doubt how it should be resolved. The underlying concept is surely this, that
when payment is made to a bank otherwise than literally in cash, i.e. in
dollar bills or other legal tender (which no one expects), there is no " payment in cash " within the meaning of clause 5 unless what the creditor   B
receives is the equivalent of cash, or as good as cash. This is supported
both by the common sense of the matter and by the judgments in the
Court of Appeal affirming the decision of Brandon J. in *The Brimnes*
[1975] Q.B. 929. Edmund-Davies L.J. said, at p. 948:

> " The owners' contention, however, that the tendering of the com-
> mercial equivalent of cash would suffice found favour with Brandon J.
> In particular, he concluded that any transfer of funds to M.G.T. for   C
> the credit of the owners' account so as to give them the uncon-
> ditional right to the immediate use of the funds transferred was good
> payment. In my judgment, that was clearly right . . ."

Megaw L.J. said, at p. 963 :

> " Whatever mode or process is used, ' payment ' is not achieved until   D
> the process has reached the stage at which the creditor has received
> cash or that which he is prepared to treat as the equivalent of cash
> or has a credit available on which, in the normal course of business or
> banking practice, he can draw, if he wishes, in the form of cash."

The book entry made by the owners' bank on January 22 in the owners'
account was clearly not the equivalent of cash, nor was there any reason   E
why the owners should have been prepared to treat it as the equivalent of
cash. It could not be used to earn interest, e.g. by immediate transfer to a
deposit account. It could only be drawn subject to a (probable) liability to
pay interest. In substance it was the equivalent of an overdraft facility
which the bank was bound to make available. I have put the word
" probable " in brackets because I attach no significance to its use in the   F
arbitrator's finding. The finding of a probable liability to pay interest must
connote a right in the owner's bank to charge interest, which is the decisive
factor. It follows, in my view, that on January 22 there was no " payment
in cash " by the charterers of the hire then assumed to be due and accordingly the owners, having refused to accept the credit as payment in accordance with clause 5, were entitled to withdraw the ship, as they did, on
January 24.   G

In the Court of Appeal it was calculated that the interest on the
monthly instalment of hire from Thursday, January 22 to Monday,
January 26 would have been U.S. $70 or $100. This calculation encouraged
Lord Denning M.R. to say [1980] 2 Lloyd's Rep. 409, 412 :

> " It seems to me that that trifling bank charge, if it had been exacted,
> would not have affected the nature of the payment which had already   H
> been made. The credit was available to the owners, in their bank, as
> from mid-day on Thursday, 22 January. The owners had the full use
> of it. It was unconditional. The mere debiting of a trifling bank charge
> would not make it conditional."

I do not know if the emphasis in this passage on the word " trifling " was
intended to invoke and apply the de minimis principle. It was not argued

A for the charterers before your Lordships that if there was a failure to make
punctual payment in cash under clause 5, the owners' right to withdraw the
ship in consequence of that failure could be resisted on the ground that the
failure was de minimis. Accordingly, it is unnecessary to decide in what
circumstances, if ever, the de minimis principle could be invoked to excuse
such a failure. It certainly could not in this case.

B My Lords, earlier exercises of judicial ingenuity to mitigate the rigours
of clauses in charterparties giving to shipowners a right to withdraw their
ships on failure or default in payment of hire or freight have not had a
happy history. One such was the decision of Bigham J. in *Nova Scotia
Steel Co. Ltd.* v. *Sutherland Steam Shipping Co. Ltd.* (1899) 5 Com. Cas.
106. This was overruled by your Lordships' House in *Tankexpress A/S* v.
Compagnie Financière Belge des Petroles S.A. [1949] A.C. 76. In that
C case Lord Wright said, at pp. 94–95:

> " A dictum or decision of Bigham J. in *Nova Scotia Steel Co. Ltd.* v.
> *Sutherland Steam Shipping Co. Ltd.*, 5 Com. Cas. 106, has been relied
> upon as an authority that a certain latitude was permissible so that
> payment made two days after the due date did not constitute a default
> in payment. But I cannot agree that so drastic a departure from the
D specific words of the charter can be supported. In that case the clause
> provided for regular and punctual payment: these adjectives however
> add nothing to the stringency of the simple and unqualified language
> in the charter before this House. I think that so much of Bigham J.'s
> judgment as conceded a latitude as to the date of payment is erroneous
> in law and should be overruled. The importance of this advance pay-
E ment to be made by the charterers, is that it is the substance of the
> consideration given to the shipowner for the use and service of the
> ship and crew which the shipowner agrees to give. He is entitled to
> have the periodical payment as stipulated in advance of his perform-
> ance so long as the charterparty continues. Hence the stringency of his
> right to cancel."

F Another such attempt was the decision of the Court of Appeal in
Empresa Cubana de Fletes v. *Lagonisi Shipping Co. Ltd.* (*The Georgios C*)
[1971] 1 Q.B. 488, which gave rise to much difficulty and uncertainty until
it was overruled by this House in *Mardorf Peach & Co. Ltd.* v. *Attica Sea
Carriers Corporation of Liberia* (*The Laconia*) [1977] A.C. 850. As Lord
Salmon said, at p. 878:

G " Certainty is of primary importance in all commercial transactions.
> I am afraid that ever since 1971 when *The Georgios C* [1971] 1 Q.B.
> 488 was decided a great deal of doubt has been generated about the
> effect of clauses conferring the right upon shipowners to withdraw
> their vessels when charterers fail to pay hire in accordance with the
> terms of the charterparties in the well known New York Produce
> Exchange, Baltime and Shelltime forms. No such doubt existed
H between [1948] (when the *Tankexpress* case [1949] A.C. 76 was
> decided) and 1971. My Lords, I hope that the doubts which have
> troubled the waters since 1971 will now be finally dispelled by this
> decision of your Lordships' House."

It has often been pointed out that shipowners and charterers bargain at
arm's length. Neither class has such a preponderance of bargaining power
as to be in a position to oppress the other. They should be in a position

to look after themselves by contracting only on terms which are acceptable   **A**
to them. Where, as here, they embody in their contracts common form
clauses, it is, to my mind, of overriding importance that their meaning and
legal effect should be certain and well understood. The ideal at which the
courts should aim, in construing such clauses, is to produce a result, such
that in any given situation both parties seeking legal advice as to their
rights and obligations can expect the same clear and confident answer from   **B**
their advisers and neither will be tempted to embark on long and expensive litigation in the belief that victory depends on winning the sympathy
of the court. This ideal may never be fully attainable, but we shall certainly
never even approximate to it unless we strive to follow clear and consistent principles and steadfastly refuse to be blown off course by the
supposed merits of individual cases.

    I would allow the appeal, restore the order of Robert Goff J. and order   **C**
the respondents to pay the appellants' costs in your Lordships' House and
in the Court of Appeal.

Appeal allowed.

  Solicitors: *Richards, Butler & Co.; Sinclair, Roche & Temperley.*   **D**

J. A. G.

[CHANCERY DIVISION]

E

* PRACTICE DIRECTION
(CHANCERY: SETTING DOWN FOR TRIAL)

[No. 1 of 1981]

*Practice—Chancery Division—Trial—Setting action down for trial
—Leave of court not required—R.S.C., Ord. 34, r. 2 (1)*   **F**

    The following direction is made to bring the Chancery practice in line
with the practice in the Queen's Bench Division as set out in *Practice
Direction (Action: Setting Down for Trial)* [1979] 1 W.L.R. 1040.

    1. Subject to compliance with R.S.C., Ord. 3, r. 6 (requirement of
service of notice of intention to proceed after a year's delay), where
applicable, the plaintiff need not obtain the leave of the court or the   **G**
consent of the defendant or defendants, if there are more than one, before
setting an action down for trial after the period fixed by an order under
R.S.C., Ord. 34, r. 2 (1).

    2. The foregoing change in the practice in no way relieves the plaintiff
of his obligation to set the action down for trial within the time fixed by
the order of the court, and his failure to do so may entail the dismissal   **H**
of the action for want of prosecution under R.S.C., Ord. 34, r. 2 (2).

    By direction of the Vice-Chancellor.

EDMUND HEWARD
Chief Master.

February 20, 1981.

A

[EMPLOYMENT APPEAL TRIBUNAL]

* PRACTICE DIRECTION (E.A.T.: PROCEDURE)

Industrial Relations—Employment Appeal Tribunal—Procedure—
B *Appeals and interlocutory applications—Special procedure—*
Directions — Documents and exhibits — Complaints of bias
—Employment Appeal Tribunal Rules 1980 *(S.I. 1980 No.*
2035), r. 3

Practice Direction (E.A.T.: Appeals) [1978] 1 W.L.R. 573 dated
March 3, 1978, as amended by *Practice Direction (E.A.T. : Appeals) (No. 2)*
[1979] 1 W.L.R. 289 of February 22, 1979, is hereby revoked and replaced
C by the following.

1. The Employment Appeal Tribunal Rules 1980 (S.I. 1980 No. 2035)
(hereinafter called " the Rules ") came into operation on February 1, 1981.

2. By virtue of paragraph 17 (2) of Schedule 11 to the Employment
Protection (Consolidation) Act 1978 the appeal tribunal has power, subject
to the Rules, to regulate its own procedure.

D
3. Where the Rules do not otherwise provide, the following procedure
will be followed in all appeals to the appeal tribunal.

4. *Appeals out of time*
(a) By virtue of rule 3 (1) of the Rules every appeal under section 136
of the Employment Protection (Consolidation) Act 1978 or section 4 of
of the Employment Act 1980 to the Employment Appeal Tribunal shall
E be instituted by serving on the tribunal, within 42 days of the date on
which the document recording the decision or order appealed from was
sent to the appellant, a notice of appeal as prescribed in the Rules.

(b) Every notice of appeal not delivered within 42 days of the date on
which the document recording the decision or order appealed from was
sent to the appellant must be accompanied by an application for an exten-
F sion of time, setting out the reasons for the delay.

(c) Applications for an extension of time for appealing cannot be considered until a notice of appeal has been presented.

(d) Unless otherwise ordered the application for extension of time will
be considered and determined as though it were an interlocutory application.

(e) In determining whether to extend the time for appealing, particular
G attention will be paid to the guidance contained in *Marshall* v. *Harland*
& Wolff Ltd. (Practice Note) [1972] I.C.R. 97, and to whether any
excuse for the delay has been shown.

(f) It is not necessarily a good excuse for delay in appealing that legal
aid has been applied for, or that support is being sought, e.g. from the
Equal Opportunities Commission, or from a trade union. In such cases
H the intending appellant should at the earliest possible moment, and at the
latest within the time limit for appealing, inform the registrar, and the
other party, of his intentions, and seek the latter's agreement to an extension of time for appealing.

(g) Time for appealing runs from the date on which the document
recording the decision or order of the industrial tribunal was sent to the
appellant, notwithstanding that the assessment of compensation has been
adjourned, or an application has been made for a review.

(h) In any case of doubt or difficulty, notice of appeal should be A presented in time, and an application made to the registrar for directions.

5. *Institution of appeal*

(a) Subject to rule 3 (2) of the Rules, if it appears to the registrar that a notice of appeal or application gives insufficient particulars or lacks clarity either as to the question of law or the grounds of an appeal, the registrar may postpone his decision under that rule pending amplification B or clarification of the notice of appeal, as regards the question of law or grounds of appeal, by the intended appellant.

(b) An appellant will not ordinarily be allowed to contend that " the decision was contrary to the evidence," or that " there was no evidence to support the decision," or to advance similar contentions, unless full and sufficient particulars identifying the particular matters relied upon have been supplied to the appeal tribunal.   C

(c) It will not be open to the parties to reserve a right to amend, alter or add to any pleading. Any such right is not inherent and may only be exercised if permitted by order for which an interlocutory application should be made as soon as the need for alteration is known.

6. *Special procedure*

(a) Where an appeal has not been rejected pursuant to rule 3 (2) but D nevertheless the appeal tribunal considers that it is doubtful whether the grounds of appeal disclose an arguable point of law, the President or a judge may direct that the matter be set down before a division of the appeal tribunal for hearing of a preliminary point to enable the appellant to show cause why the appeal should not be dismissed on the ground that it does not disclose a fairly arguable point of law.

(b) The respondent will be given notice of the hearing but since it will E be limited to the preliminary point he will not be required to attend the hearing or permitted to take part in it.

(c) If the appellant succeeds in showing cause, the hearing will be adjourned and the appeal will be set down for hearing before a different division of the appeal tribunal in the usual way.

(d) If the appellant does not show cause, the appeal will be dismissed. F

(e) The decision as to whether this procedure will be adopted in any particular case will be in the direction of the President or a judge.

7. *Interlocutory applications*

(a) On receipt of an interlocutory application the registrar will submit a copy of the application to the other side, and will indicate that if it is not intended to oppose the application it may be unnecessary for the parties G to be heard and that the appropriate order may be made in their absence. Where the application is opposed the registrar will also in appropriate cases give the parties an opportunity of agreeing to the application being decided on the basis of written submissions.

(b) Save where the President or a judge directs otherwise, every inter-locutory application to strike out pleadings or to debar a party from taking any further part in the proceedings pursuant to rule 16 or 21 will be heard H on the day appointed for the hearing of the appeal, but immediately preceding the hearing thereof.

8. *Meeting for directions*

On every appeal from the decision of the certification officer, and, if necessary, on any other appeal or application, so soon as the answer is delivered, or if a cross-appeal, the reply, the registrar will appoint a day

A when the parties shall meet on an appointment for directions and the appeal tribunal will give such directions, including a date for hearing, as it deems necessary.

9. *Right to inspect the register and certain documents and to take copies*

B Where, pursuant to the direction dated March 31, 1976, a document filed at the Employment Appeal Tribunal has been inspected and a photographic copy of the documents is bespoken, a copying fee of 25p for each page will be charged.

10. *Listing of cases*

A. *England and Wales*

C (a) When the respondent's answer has been received and a copy served on the appellant, the case will be put in the list of cases for hearing. At the beginning of each calendar month a list will be prepared of cases to be heard on specified dates in the next following calendar month. That list will also include a number of cases which are liable to be taken in each specified week of the relevant month. Parties or their representatives will be notified by recorded delivery. When cases in the list with specified D dates are settled or withdrawn cases warned for the relevant week will be substituted and the parties notified as soon as possible.

(b) A party finding that the date which has been given causes serious difficulties may apply to the listing officer before the 15th of the month in which the case first appears in the list. No change will be made unless the listing officer agrees, but reasonable efforts will be made to accommodate parties in difficulties. Changes after the 15th of the month in which the E list first appears will not be made other than on application to the President of the Employment Appeal Tribunal; arrangements for the making of such application should be made through the listing officer.

(c) Other cases may be put in the list by the listing officer (with the consent of the parties) at shorter notice, e.g., where other cases have been settled or withdrawn or where it appears that they will take less time than F originally estimated. Parties who wish their cases to be taken as soon as possible and at short notice should notify the listing officer.

(d) Each week an up-to-date list for the following week will be prepared including any changes which have been made (in particular specifying cases which by then have been given fixed dates).

(e) The monthly list and the weekly list will appear in the Daily Cause G List and will also be displayed in Room 6 at the Royal Courts of Justice and at no. 4, St. James's Square, London, SW1. It is important that parties or their advisers should inspect the weekly list as well as the monthly list.

(f) If cases are settled or to be withdrawn notice should be given at once to the listing officer so that other cases may be given fixed dates.

H B. *Scotland*

When the respondent's answer has been received and a copy served on the appellant both parties will be notified in writing that the appeal will be ready for hearing in approximately six weeks. The proposed date of hearing will be notified to the parties three or four weeks ahead. Any party who wishes to apply for a different date must do so within seven days of receipt of such notification. Thereafter a formal notice of the date fixed for the hearing will be issued not less than 14 days in advance.

This will be a peremptory diet. It will not be discharged except by the   A
judge on cause shown.

11. *Admissibility of documents*

(a) Where, pursuant to rule 15 or 19, an application is made by a
party to an appeal to put in at the hearing of the appeal any document
which was not before the industrial tribunal, including a note of evidence
given before the industrial tribunal (other than the chairman's notes), the   B
application shall be submitted in writing, with copies of the document(s)
sought to be made admissible at the hearing.

(b) The registrar will forthwith communicate the nature of the application and of the document(s) sought to be made admissible to the other
party and where appropriate, to the chairman of the industrial tribunal,
for comment.

(c) A copy of the comment will be forwarded to the party making the   C
application, by the registrar who will either dispose of it in accordance
with the Rules or refer it to the appeal tribunal for a ruling at the hearing.
In the case of comments received from the chairman of the industrial
tribunal a copy will be sent to both parties.

12. *Complaints of bias, etc.*

(a) The appeal tribunal will not normally consider complaints of bias   D
or of the conduct of an industrial tribunal unless full and sufficient particulars are set out in the grounds of appeal.

(b) In any such case the registrar may inquire of the party making the
complaint whether it is the intention to proceed with the compaint in
which case the registrar will give appropriate directions for the hearing.

(c) Such directions may include the filing of affidavits dealing with the   E
matters upon the basis of which the complaint is made or for the giving
of further particulars of the complaint on which the party will seek to rely.

(d) On compliance with any such direction the registrar will communicate the complaint together with the matters relied on in support of
the complaint to the chairman of the industrial tribunal so that he may have
an opportunity of commenting upon it.

(e) No such complaint will be permitted to be developed upon the   F
hearing of the appeal, unless the appropriate procedure has been followed.

(f) A copy of any affidavit or direction for particulars to be delivered
thereunder will be communicated to the other side.

13. *Exhibits and documents for use at the hearing*

(a) The appeal tribunal will prepare copies of all documents for use
of the judges and members at the hearing in addition to those which the   G
registrar is required to serve on the parties under the Rules. It is the
responsibility of parties or their advisers to ensure that all documents submitted for consideration at the hearing are capable of being reproduced
legibly by photographic process.

(b) In Scotland a copy of the chairman's notes will not be supplied to
the parties except on application to the appeal tribunal on cause shown.   H
In England and Wales copies will only be sent to the parties if in the
view of the appeal tribunal all or part of such notes are necessary for the
purpose of the appeal or on application to the tribunal on cause shown.
Chairman's notes are supplied for the use of the appeal tribunal and not for
the parties to embark on a " fishing " expedition to establish further
grounds of appeal.

(c) It is the duty of parties and their solicitors to ensure that only

A   those documents which are relevant to the point of law raised in the appeal, and which are likely to be referred to, are included in the documents before the tribunal.

(d) It will also be the responsibility of the parties or their advisers to ensure that all exhibits and documents used before the industrial tribunal, and which are considered to be relevant to the appeal, are sent to the appeal tribunal immediately on request. This will enable the appeal tribunal to number and prepare sufficient copies, together with an index, for the judges and members at least a week before the day appointed for the hearing.

(e) A copy of the index will be sent to the parties or their representatives prior to the hearing so that they may prepare their bundles in the same order.

C
                                                          SLYNN J.
                                                          President.

February 17, 1981.

D

                    [SUPREME COURT TAXING OFFICE]

              * PRACTICE DIRECTION (TAXATION: VAT) (No. 3)

                          [No. 1 of 1981]
E
*Costs—Taxation—Value added tax—Solicitor's litigation on matter
    arising from practice—Tax not chargeable—Presentation of bill*

1. A problem has recently arisen on *Practice Direction (Taxation: VAT)* [1973] 1 W.L.R. 438 issued on March 9, 1973 as varied by *Practice Direction (Taxation: VAT) (No. 2)* [1974] 1 W.L.R. 217 issued on January
F   28, 1974, which dealt generally with the incidence of value added tax (VAT) on the taxation of costs.

2. Where a solicitor acts in litigation on his own behalf in a matter arising out of his practice he is not treated for the purposes of VAT as having supplied services and therefore no VAT is chargeable on the bill of that solicitor.

G   3. Consequently where such a bill is presented for agreement or taxation VAT should not be claimed and should not be allowed on taxation.

4. This direction is made with the agreement of the Senior Registrar of the Family Division and the Admiralty Registrar, and is issued with the concurrence of the Lord Chancellor.

                                            E. J. T. MATTHEWS
H   *Chief Taxing Master*

February 19, 1981.

A

[QUEEN'S BENCH DIVISION]

* REGINA v. NORTH DEVON DISTRICT COUNCIL,
Ex parte LEWIS (J. P.)

1980 Sept. 15;
Oct. 6

Woolf J.

B

Local Government—Housing—Homeless persons—Applicant claiming to be homeless with priority need—Previous application by intentionally homeless member of family—Applicant's conduct in acquiescing in decision resulting in family being homeless—Whether applicant " homeless intentionally "—Housing (Homeless Persons) Act 1977 (c. 48), ss. 4, 17

The applicant and her child lived with H in a house that C was provided by H's employer for so long as H worked for him. H gave notice terminating his employment with the result that the employer subsequently obtained an order for possession of the property and the family was made homeless. H applied to the respondent housing authority for accommodation under the Housing (Homeless Persons) Act 1977. The housing authority refused to provide him and the family with permanent housing on the ground that he had become homeless D intentionally within the meaning of section 17 of the Act.[1] The applicant who was pregnant and therefore had a priority need, then applied to the housing authority and her application made it clear that she intended H to share any accommodation which the authority made available for her occupation. The housing authority decided that she had also become intentionally homeless because she had acquiesced in H's decision to terminate his employment knowing that his right to occupy E the property would thereby cease.

On her application for a judicial review of the housing authority's decision: —

Held, (1) that, on an application under the Housing (Homeless Persons) Act 1977, a housing authority had to consider the family unit and where possible to carry out the purpose of the Act which was to keep members of a family together; that to give effect to the purpose of the Act, section 17 had F to be given a literal construction and, therefore, a housing authority had a duty under the Act to provide accommodation for an applicant, who was not homeless intentionally, even though a member of the applicant's family would also be housed who had deliberately caused the family to be homeless (post, pp. 333A, F).

(2) Dismissing the application, that, on an application under the Act, a housing authority was entitled to consider the G conduct of the members of the family and, therefore, could consider whether an applicant was a party to the conduct which rendered the family homeless; that, since there was ample material on which the housing authority could find that the applicant had acquiesced in H's decision to give up his employment, she was a party to H's conduct and, accordingly, the housing authority could properly come to the conclusion that she was intentionally homeless (post, pp. 333F–H, 334C).

H

No cases are referred to in the judgment and none were cited in argument.

APPLICATION for judicial review.

Pursuant to leave granted by Griffiths J. on September 1, 1980, the

[1] Housing (Homeless Persons) Act 1977, s. 17: see post, p. 332C–F.

A applicant, Julie Pauline Lewis, applied for judicial review in respect of a decision made on July 9, 1980, by the respondent housing authority, the North Devon District Council, that she had become homeless intentionally for the purposes of the Housing (Homeless Persons) Act 1977. The applicant sought, inter alia, (1) a declaration that she had not become homeless intentionally within the meaning of section 17 of the Housing (Homeless Persons) Act 1977; (2) an order of certiorari to quash the decision of the housing authority made on July 9, 1980; (3) an order of mandamus directed to the housing authority requiring it to secure that accommodation was available or alternatively did not cease to be available for her occupation in accordance with the provisions of the Act.

B

The grounds upon which the relief was sought were (1) that the housing authority did not properly exercise the discretion vested in it by section 4 of the Act in determining whether the applicant was an intentionally homeless person within the meaning of section 17 of the Act; (2) that there was no material upon which the housing authority could find that the applicant was intentionally homeless within the meaning of section 17 of the Act; (3) that the applicant was not an intentionally homeless person within the meaning of the Act by reason of her giving up possession of premises of which she had no right of occupation, they being held by Martin Hopkins under a service tenancy agreement; and (4) that the decision of the housing authority was contrary to natural justice.

C

D

The facts are stated in the judgment.

Anthony Puttick for the applicant.
David Fletcher for the housing authority.

E

Cur. adv. vult.

October 6. WOOLF J. read the following judgment. This case concerns an application by Mrs. Lewis for judicial review in respect of a decision by the housing authority, the North Devon District Council, that the applicant had become homeless intentionally for the purposes of the Housing (Homeless Persons) Act 1977. Under that Act, if the housing authority are satisfied that an applicant has become homeless intentionally, their duties are more restricted than they would otherwise be.

F

The case involves consideration of the effect upon an application under the Act of a previous application by a person who has been living with the applicant as man and wife, where the housing authority, in respect of the previous application, have lawfully come to a conclusion that the other person had become homeless intentionally, and the applicant intends to go on living with that other person in any accommodation provided by the housing authority.

G

This is a question of general application and one in respect of which both parties invited me to give judgment in open court although as the application was heard during the vacation, it was dealt with in chambers.

H

The housing authority argue that the whole scheme of the Housing (Homeless Persons) Act 1977 is to look at the family unit and to provide accommodation for that unit and it was the manifest intention of Parliament that where one member of that family unit is homeless intentionally the family unit should be treated as homeless intentionally. The result of that approach is that where a man and woman are living together as

man and wife, the housing authority is entitled to reject an application   A
by the woman merely because there has been a previous application by
the man and they have found that that man became homeless intentionally.

The applicant, on the other hand, contends that it is her conduct and
her conduct alone which should be considered and that it is wrong to
take into account any previous decision in respect of the man with whom
she is living. On this approach, in this case, the housing authority's   B
decision should at least be quashed as a decision which was wholly unreasonable, or as one which could only be reached on the basis of the
housing authority wrongfully taking into account the conduct of the man
with whom the applicant is living.

The facts can be stated briefly as follows: the applicant had married
on August 25, 1976, but in January 1979, she became separated from her   C
husband, from whom she is now seeking a divorce on the ground of his
adultery. At the relevant time she had two children, one of whom is
four and the other just three. In February 1979 she formed an association
with Mr. Hopkins, with whom she still lives. In August 1979, Mr.
Hopkins took employment as a farm labourer and was provided with a
farmhouse to enable him to perform his duties and he lived at the farm-
house with the applicant and one of her children.   D

Mr. Hopkins was not happy in the job but according to the applicant
she encouraged him to stay; but the situation got worse and, on November
8, 1979, Mr. Hopkins told her that he intended to give in his notice that
day and he was so unhappy and disappointed about the job that the
applicant says, " his mind was firmly made up to leave and I could not have
changed it."   E

As a result of giving in his notice, the owner of the farm required
possession of the farm-house and eventually brought proceedings against
Mr. Hopkins which resulted in possession of the farm-house being obtained
on March 6, 1980. The applicant was then two months pregnant with
Mr. Hopkins' child.

An application under the Housing (Homeless Persons) Act 1977 was   F
made by Mr. Hopkins but the housing authority considered that both he
and the applicant were intentionally homeless because Mr. Hopkins had
voluntarily given up his job. The family were, however, provided with
temporary accommodation.

On May 23, 1980, Mr. Hopkins and the applicant sought orders
in the Barnstaple County Court restraining the housing authority from
withdrawing temporary accommodation and a declaration that it had   G
misdirected itself in finding that they were intentionally homeless. Those
proceedings were dismissed after the facts had been fully investigated by
Judge Goodall. In giving his judgment, however, the judge said (according to the note which is before me):

" Whether even though the first plaintiff has no redress in action the
    question arises whether the second plaintiff had redress. At first   H
    sight no one could suggest that she has made herself intentionally
    homeless. She was not employed by Mrs. Burton and did not give
    notice. It is clear that discrimination between husband and wife or
    man and common law wife creates appalling problems with the
    administration of the Act, problems I doubt the legislature considered.
    The only duty owed by the local authority under section 4 of the
    Act is to a person who has applied to them for accommodation.

The Weekly Law Reports, March 20, 1981

331

1 W.L.R.   Reg. v. N. Devon Council, Ex p. Lewis (Q.B.D.)   Woolf J.

A   Evidence on this point is scanty. It is clear Mr. Hopkins was the applicant even though [Mrs. Lewis] accompanied him to the housing department. Evidence comes from Mr. Cook that he saw the plaintiffs on March 10 when they visited the Civic Centre. He spoke to Mr. Hopkins and considered it as an application by the household and treated them as a whole family This is illustrated from the

B   application form. The applicant is stated to be Mr. Hopkins; Mrs. Lewis is listed in members of the household. The form which Mr. Cook filled in at the time the plaintiffs visited him shows only one applicant, Mr. Hopkins. There is no suggestion that Mrs. Lewis wanted a place on her own. There is no suggestion that she was an applicant. It it not necessary for me to decide this awkward question, what would happen if she made an application on her own count. I

C   am only concerned with the duty owed by the North Devon District Council to the applicant, Mr. Hopkins, and for the reasons stated they are not in breach of duty.

        If ever there was a deserving case where a man had made himself intentionally homeless, then this is it. For example often in cases of intentional homelessness a couple come from elsewhere to take a job in a hotel and are trying to be given the sack by carrying out

D   their duties poorly. They then apply to the local authority for housing. South Devon are well aware of the situation. However, here is a hard-working deserving man who has always worked and had a reason for giving his notice. An employer should not keep an employee dangling at the end of a string. It is hard that he should be disqualified from the provisions of the Act. From the

E   dates it is clear that the plaintiff had no notice that a child was on the way when he gave up his employment. However, in conclusion, it is easy for a judge not faced with housing on a limited budget to come to such conclusions. No doubt this point did not escape the North Devon District Council. I must say this is the worst possible time to be without accommodation in Devon and it is the hardest case I have yet had to determine. Nevertheless the action fails."

F
        Because of what was said by the judge, the applicant made a fresh application for accommodation under the Act. That application showed her child and Mr. Hopkins as members of her household and it is clear that it was intended that Mr. Hopkins should share accommodation which was provided under the Act.

G   Having investigated the application, a letter dated July 11, 1980, was written to the applicant by the solicitor to the housing authority which begins:

        " Housing (Homeless Persons) Act 1977: Application No. HO349
        Following inquiries made by officers of my department into your application under the above Act, I write to inform you that the

H   council considers that you have become homeless intentionally for the following reason: You rendered yourself and your dependants intentionally homeless within the meaning of section 17 of the Act in that you acquiesced in your common law husband's decision to terminate his employment at Limeslake Farm, knowing that the accommodation which you, your common law husband and your dependants occupied, was tied to your common law husband's employment and that by terminating his employment, you, your

common law husband and your dependants' right to remain in   A
occupation ceased."

It was that decision which gave rise to these proceedings.

In support of their approach, the housing authority contend that an
absurd position would be created if a husband or a man living with a
woman could intentionally make the family homeless and then the wife
or woman concerned could make an application and because she,   B
rather than he, makes the application, the family would be treated differently from the way it would have been treated if he made the application. This would result in his obtaining benefits under the Act which
it was never intended that he should receive because he had rendered
himself intentionally homeless.

The test as to whether a person is intentionally homeless or not is   C
contained in section 17. That section provides:

"(1) Subject to subsection (3) below, for the purposes of this Act
a person becomes homeless intentionally if he deliberately does or
fails to do anything in consequence of which he ceases to occupy
accommodation which is available for his occupation and which
it would have been reasonable for him to continue to occupy.
(2) Subject to subsection (3) below, for the purposes of this Act a   D
person becomes threatened with homelessness intentionally if he
deliberately does or fails to do anything the likely result of which
is that he will be forced to leave accommodation which is available
for his occupation and which it would have been reasonable for
him to continue to occupy. (3) An act or omission in good faith on
the part of a person who was unaware of any relevant fact is not   E
to be treated as deliberate for the purposes of subsection (1) or (2)
above. (4) Regard may be had, in determining for the purposes of
subsections (1) and (2) above whether it would have been reasonable for a person to continue to occupy accommodation, to the
general circumstances prevailing in relation to housing in the area
of the housing authority to whom he applied for accommodation
or for assistance in obtaining accommodation."   F

Section 4 makes it clear that it is not for the applicant to show that he
did not become homeless intentionally, it is for the housing authority
as a result of its inquiries, to satisfy themselves that the applicant
became homeless or was threatened with homelessness intentionally.
Homelessness is defined in section 1 (1):
                                                                          G
"if there is no accommodation . . . (a) which he, together with any
other person who normally resides with him as a member of his
family or in circumstances in which the housing authority consider it
reasonable for that person to reside with him . . ." is available.

That definition and a number of other provisions of the Act make it
clear that in looking into an application under the Act the housing   H
authority has to have regard to what I will loosely describe as the family
unit. I draw attention to section 2 (1) (a) and (c), section 2 (2), section
5 (1) (a) (i) and (ii), and section 16. Of those sections I will read only
section 16 which says:

"For the purposes of this Act accommodation is only available
for a person's occupation if it is available for occupation both by
him and by any other person who might reasonably be expected

The Weekly Law Reports, March 20, 1981

333

1 W.L.R.   Reg. v. N. Devon Council, Ex p. Lewis (Q.B.D.)   Woolf J.

A   to reside with him and any reference in this Act to securing accommodation for a person's occupation shall be construed accordingly."

Those provisions make it clear that it is the policy of the Act to keep families together where possible. Such a policy is not surprising in an Act of Parliament passed in 1977.

B   As it is to the family unit that the housing authority are to have regard, it would be readily understandable if Parliament had provided expressly that the application should be made by the family unit and the question should be whether or not the family should be regarded as having become homeless intentionally. However, as is conceded on behalf of the housing authority, there are no express words which provide that where a man and a woman are living together, if one of the

C   couple becomes homeless intentionally, the other should be treated as being homeless intentionally. The Act does not place any express limitation on who can make an application or as to how many applications can be made.

The main argument on behalf of the authority was that section 17 must be read as though it provided that, for the purposes of the Act, a person becomes homeless intentionally if he, or a person who resides

D   with him or who could reasonably have been expected to reside with him, became homeless intentionally.

Such a construction of section 17, in my view, is not possible. It is inconsistent with the wording of section 17 as a whole.

Clearly Parliament could have chosen to treat a woman who lived with a man who had become homeless intentionally as though she was

E   tainted by his conduct. This would have been hard on her but would have avoided his obtaining benefits to which he was not entitled in his own right. Alternatively, Parliament could adopt the approach that, albeit the man was undeserving, because the woman was not herself homeless intentionally, he was to benefit because she was entitled to the additional rights of a person who was not homeless intentionally

F   and she could only obtain those rights if he benefited as well. The literal wording of section 17 indicates that it was the second alternative that Parliament intended and such a result is not so wholly unreasonable that I feel compelled to read into the Act words which are not there so as to arrive at the opposite conclusion.

This construction does not mean that a housing authority should close its eyes to the conduct of the other members of the family. On

G   the contrary, in my view, the fact that the Act requires consideration of the family unit as a whole indicates that it would be perfectly proper in the ordinary case for the housing authority to look at the family as a whole and assume, in the absence of material which indicates to the contrary, where the conduct of one member of the family was such that he should be regarded as having become homeless intentionally, that

H   was conduct to which the other members of the family were a party.

So, for example, where the husband is a tenant and gives notice in circumstances where he is properly to be regarded as having become homeless intentionally, the wife, even though she was not the tenant and she did not give the notice, can be regarded in the same way. In normal circumstances this would be treated as a joint decision. If, however, at the end of the day because of material put before the housing authority by the wife, the housing authority are not satisfied that she was a party

Woolf J.   **Reg. v. N. Devon Council, Ex p. Lewis (Q.B.D.)**   **[1981]**

to the decision, they would have to regard her as not having become   A
homeless intentionally.

In argument the housing authority drew my attention to the difficulties which could arise in cases where the husband spent the rent on
drink. If the wife acquiesced to his doing this then it seems to me it
would be proper to regard her, as well as him, as having become homeless intentionally. She had failed to do something the likely result of   B
which would be that she would be forced to leave the accommodation
which was available for her occupation as provided by section 17. If,
on the other hand, she had done what she could to prevent the husband
spending his money on drink instead of the rent then she had not failed
to do anything and it would not be right to regard her as having become
homeless intentionally.

Turning therefore to the facts of this case, the finding of the housing   C
authority stated that the applicant had acquiesced in Mr. Hopkins's
decision to terminate his employment knowing the accommodation was
tied to Mr. Hopkins's employment. Having come to that conclusion it
was perfectly proper to take the view that the applicant was herself
intentionally homeless.

It was argued on behalf of the applicant, before me, that they could   D
not reasonably come to a conclusion that she had acquiesced in this
decision of Mr. Hopkins. However, on the material before the authority, I do not regard that contention as being right. There was ample
material before the housing authority on which they could come to the
conclusion which they did and the decision which the housing authority
came to in this case, which I regard as being perfectly proper, indicates
that perhaps the difficulties which the housing authority fear might be   E
caused by what I regard as the proper construction of section 17, are
not quite as great as they fear.

Because the housing authority approached the matter properly by
looking at the applicant's conduct, this application must be dismissed.

Application dismissed.   F
Order for costs not to be executed
without leave.

Solicitors: *Bischoff & Co., for Harding, Rootham & Stallard, Barnstaple; J. G. Bradley, Barnstaple.*

[Reported by MISS ISOBEL COLLINS, Barrister-at-Law]   G

A

[COURT OF APPEAL]

* MANLEY v. THE LAW SOCIETY AND ANOTHER

[1979 M. No. 2230]

B 1980 Oct. 8, 9, 10   Bristow J.
       Nov. 25, 26, 27;   Lord Denning M.R., Ormrod
       Dec. 16   and O'Connor L.JJ.

Legal Aid—Costs—Charge on property—Compromise of action—
Action settled on terms that defendant discharge legally aided
plaintiff's debts to amount of sum offered — Whether sum
C   *property " recovered or preserved " for plaintiff—Whether*
      sum subject to statutory charge—Legal Aid Act 1974 (c. 4),
      s. 9 (6) (7)

The plaintiff, who had incurred debts of more than £30,000
in developing an invention, obtained a legal aid certificate to
bring an action against a company for breach of a contract
to exploit the invention. The interlocutory stages, which
D   involved heavy costs, took six years, and before the trial
started, the parties, anxious to minimise the expenditure,
compromised the action on terms, which had been notified
to The Law Society and were embodied in a consent order,
that the company would pay £40,000 to be held in a joint
account by both parties' solicitors as the company's agents,
that the money would first be used to pay off the debts by
purchasing them for the company and not enforcing them
E   against the plaintiff, and that the balance of the money, if
any, should be paid as a contribution to the plaintiff's costs.
The Law Society informed the solicitors that the legal aid
fund, by virtue of section 9 (6) and (7) of the Legal Aid
Act 1974,[1] had a charge on the £40,000 for the costs, which
were fixed at £17,000. The solicitors retained £17,000 in the
joint account, pending the decision on the plaintiff's claim
for a declaration that the £40,000 was not subject to the
F   statutory charge.
Bristow J., giving judgment for the plaintiff, held that
since the parties' legal advisors had acted with propriety and
candour the scheme could not be regarded as a mere fiction
to avoid the statutory charge, and therefore the court would
not look behind the terms of the agreement to compromise
the action to the purpose of the scheme; and that as the
plaintiff's only right under the compromise was to have his
G   debts discharged from the £40,000 and be paid the balance,
the £40,000 had not been " recovered " for the plaintiff for
the purposes of the section.
On appeal by The Law Society: —
Held, allowing the appeal, that notwithstanding the form
in which the compromise was expressed, the £40,000 was a
payment made for the benefit of the plaintiff, in that it was
to be used in truth and in fact to pay off his debts at his
H   request; that, therefore, it was " recovered . . . for him "
within section 9 (6) and, accordingly, the legal aid fund had
a charge on the £17,000 for the costs (post, pp. 346E–F, 351E–F,
H—352A, 354B).
Hanlon v. *The Law Society* [1980] 2 W.L.R. 756, H.L.(E.)
applied.
Per Lord Denning M.R. (i) Whenever the question of a
settlement comes up, the legal advisers of a legally aided

[1] Legal Aid Act 1974, s. 9 (6) (7): see post, p. 338E–G.

plaintiff should consider any offer on the merits of the case   A
itself, just as if they were acting for a private client of
moderate means, not one who is wealthy enough to go to
any expense, or one who is very much in debt already, against
a defendant who is also of moderate means and will get an
order for costs against the plaintiff if he wins.   Once a
figure is reached which is reasonable, they should settle the
case at that figure.   They should not try to manipulate the
destination of the sum so as to avoid the statutory charge.   B
In particular, they should not make the sum payable to the
creditors of the plaintiff or to anyone other than the plaintiff
(post, p. 346E–F).

(ii) The cases on a solicitor's lien do not directly apply
but the principle of them does.   The matter has gone too
far for the settlement to be set aside but equity can intervene
to hold that, if and in so far as the solicitors have intentionally
deprived the legal aid fund of a charge on their costs, they   C
are themselves precluded from making any claim on the legal
aid fund for those costs (post, p. 347D–F).

Decision of Bristow J., post, p. 337E–F et seq. reversed.

The following cases are referred to in the judgments in the Court of
Appeal:

Customs and Excise Commissioners v. *Pools Finance (1937) Ltd.* [1952]   D
1 All E.R. 775, C.A.
Griffiths v. *J. P. Harrison (Watford) Ltd.* [1963] A.C. 1; [1962] 2
W.L.R. 909; [1962] 1 All E.R. 909, H.L.(E.).
Hanlon v. *The Law Society* [1980] 2 W.L.R. 756; [1980] 1 All E.R.
763; [1980] 2 All E.R. 199, Reeve J., C.A. and H.L.(E.).
Hope, The (1883) 8 P.D. 144, C.A.
Inland Revenue Commissioners v. *Duke of Westminster* [1936] A.C. 1,   E
H.L.(E.).
Margetson and Jones, In re [1897] 2 Ch. 314.
New Zealand Shipping Co. Ltd. v. *Société des Ateliers et Chantiers de
France* [1919] A.C. 1, H.L.(E.).
Welsh v. *Hole* (1779) 1 Doug. 237.

The following additional cases were cited in argument before the Court   F
of Appeal:

Barker v. *St. Quintin* (1844) 12 M. & W. 441.
Cadogan v. *Cadogan* [1977] 1 W.L.R. 1041; [1977] 1 All E.R. 200;
[1977] 3 All E.R. 831, Slade J. and C.A.
Dunthorne v. *Bunbury* (1883) 24 L.R.Ir. 6.
Fuld, decd. (No. 4), In the Estate of [1968] P. 727; [1967] 3 W.L.R.
314; [1967] 2 All E.R. 649.   G
Harrison v. *Harrison* (1888) 13 P.D. 180, C.A.
Neill v. *Glacier Metal Co. Ltd.* [1965] 1 Q.B. 16; [1964] 2 W.L.R. 55;
[1963] 3 All E.R. 477.
Price v. *Crouch* (1891) 60 L.J.Q.B. 767.
Ralli's Will Trusts, In re [1964] Ch. 288; [1964] 2 W.L.R. 144; [1963]
3 All E.R. 940.
Ross v. *Buxton* (1889) 42 Ch.D. 190.
Slater v. *Sunderland Corporation* (1863) 33 L.J.Q.B. 37.   H

No cases are referred to in the judgment of Bristow J.

The following additional cases were cited in argument before Bristow J.:
Cadogan v. *Cadogan* [1977] 1 W.L.R. 1041; [1977] 1 All E.R. 200; [1977]
3 All E.R. 831, Slade J. and C.A.
Hope, The (1883) 8 P.D. 144, C.A.

A   *Foxon* v. *Gascoigne* (1874) L.R. 9 Ch.App.654.
     Hanlon v. *The Law Society* [1980] 2 W.L.R. 756; [1980] 1 All E.R. 763;
          [1980] 2 All E.R. 199, Reeve J., C.A. and H.L.(E.).
     Margetson and Jones, In re [1897] 2 Ch. 314.
     Pinkerton v. *Easton* (1973) L.R. 16 Eq. 490.
     Price v. *Crouch* (1891) 60 L.J.Q.B. 767.
     Sullivan v. *Pearson, In re, Ex parte Morrison* (1868) L.R. 4 Q.B. 153.

B   *Till* v. *Till* [1974] Q.B. 558; [1974] 2 W.L.R. 447; [1974] 1 All E.R. 1096,
          C.A.
     Twynam v. *Porter* (1870) L.R. 11 Eq. 181.

ORIGINATING SUMMONS

     By a summons dated June 15, 1979, the plaintiff, David Michael John
Picton Manley, claimed against The Law Society as administrators of the
C legal aid fund (1) a declaration that the fund of £40,000 paid by Marconi
International Marine Co. Ltd. to their agents, Messrs. Coward Chance and
Messrs. Kennedys, solicitors, under the terms of a consent order made in
the Queen's Bench Division of the High Court of Justice on October 3,
1978, in the action the short title and reference to the record whereof were
Manley v. *Marconi International Marine Co. Ltd.*, 1972 M No. 4245, did
D not stand and never had stood charged for the benefit of the legal aid fund
under and by virtue of the provisions and for the purposes of section 9 (6)
and (7) of the Legal Aid Act 1974; (2) further or other relief; (3) costs.
     By an order of the master, dated April 24, 1980, leave was given to
join Marconi International Marine Co. Ltd. as second defendant, but they
did not appear.
     The facts are stated in the judgment.

E

     Jack Hames Q.C. and *Peter Flint* for the plaintiff.
     Duncan Matheson for The Law Society.

     BRISTOW J. The plaintiff is an inventor. He invented a shallow water
echo sounder for large ships and entered into an agreement with Marconi
F International Marine Co. Ltd. (" Marconi ") for its exploitation.   He
and his corporate alter ego incurred heavy expenditure, met by borrowing, in the development of his invention.   Marconi refused to exploit
it on the ground that it did not meet the requirements of the agreement.
The plaintiff brought an action for damages for breach of contract
against Marconi.   He applied for and obtained a legal aid certificate
for the purpose of the action and prosecuted his action throughout as
G an assisted person.
     The essence of the legal aid scheme in this country is that an assisted
person who brings an action shall have the same services of solicitors and
counsel as he would have if he were not an assisted person and that the
costs of those services, subject to his own contribution, which is assessed
according to his means, will be paid by The Law Society, to whom his
H solicitors render the bill they would otherwise have rendered to him, out
of the legal aid fund of public money which The Law Society administers.
If any fruits accrue to the assisted person as a result of his litigation then
those fruits are available to The Law Society to meet the assisted person's
solicitor's bill or to recoup them for meeting the assisted person's solicitor's
bill, and the machinery by which they are made available is a statutory
first charge upon them in favour of The Law Society. The solicitor of a
litigant not assisted under the legal aid scheme has since the time of Lord

Mansfield had the right to apply to the court, of which he is an officer, for A
an order that the fruits of litigation conducted by him for his client shall
be charged in his favour to meet his costs and the court has a discretion
to make an order to that effect, an order enforceable by effective remedies.

As can be seen from the many reported cases, that discretion was freely
exercised by the court to protect its officers, the basis of the jurisdiction
being that it is in the public interest that the courts should have the assist- B
ance of solicitors and counsel in order to do justice to those who have to
come before the courts to resolve their disputes which they are unable to
resolve for themselves. There is a common thread which runs through all
the cases, that the discretion will be exercised not simply where a solicitor
is at risk of not recovering his costs but where he is at risk of not recovering his costs by reason of a " dirty trick." Sometimes in the cases the word
used to describe the dirty trick is " fraud," sometimes it is " collusion," C
sometimes it is " cheating " and sometimes the facts are described without
any opprobrious label at all. But the common denominator in all the
cases cited to me—and I am told by counsel, as you would expect, that it
is the common denominator of the many cases on the subject which he
did not cite—is the presence of a " dirty trick " of one sort or another.
That, in my judgment, is a factor which leads the court in its discretion D
to charge the fruit of the litigation in favour of the solicitor, and to
give effect to the charge.

The charge on the fruits of litigation of an assisted person in favour of
The Law Society and the remedies to enforce the charge are creatures of
statute, are not discretionary and have nothing to do with " dirty tricks."
The provisions are to be found in section 9 (6) of the Legal Aid Act 1974.
Subsection (6) provides: E

" Except so far as regulations otherwise provide, any sums remaining
unpaid on account of a person's contribution to the legal aid fund in
respect of any proceedings and, if the total contribution is less than the
net liability of that fund on his account, a sum equal to the deficiency
shall be a first charge for the benefit of the legal aid fund on any
property (wherever situated) which is recovered or preserved for him F
in the proceedings."

Subsection (7) provides:

" The reference in subsection (6) above to property recovered or
preserved for any person shall include his rights under any compromise arrived at to avoid or bring to an end the proceedings and any G
sums recovered by virtue of an order for costs made in his favour
in the proceedings (not being sums payable into the legal aid fund
under section 8 above)."

These provisions imposing and dealing with the ambit of the charge are
reinforced by regulation 19 of the Legal Aid (General) Regulations 1971, H
which provides, under sub-regulation (1):

" (1) Any charge on property recovered or preserved for an assisted
person arising under section 3 (4) of the Act shall vest in The Law
Society."

Regulation 19 (2) deals with enforcement. Sub-regulation (3) deals with
the charges affecting land. Sub-regulation (4) provides:

A
" Subject to the provisions of the Land Charges Act 1925, all conveyances and acts done to defeat, or operating to defeat, such charge
shall, except in the case of a conveyance to a bona fide purchaser for
value without notice, be void as against The Law Society."

As was inevitable from the nature of the plaintiff's action, very heavy
costs were incurred by both sides in the preparation of the case for trial,
B and the ultimate outcome was uncertain. As any sensible person would in
the circumstances, the parties and their advisers before trial thought in
terms of compromise. Negotiations took place, and the plaintiff's solicitors
and counsel ascertained that Marconi were prepared to pay him £40,000.
No doubt this was in part to be rid of the continuing cost and uncertainty
of the litigation, especially because of the difficulty in the case brought by
C an assisted person in a defendant getting any significant contribution to his
costs if he wins. But I am told, and readily accept, that Marconi felt a moral
obligation to the plaintiff in respect of the debts incurred in the development
of his invention.

The plaintiff and his advisers then considered whether £40,000 was
acceptable or whether it would be an acceptable risk to refuse and go
forward to trial, with the additional costs which would be involved and no
D certainty of success at any rate to the extent of more than £40,000 or indeed
at all. Messrs. Kennedys, the plaintiff's solicitors, then estimated what
their bill would be for the costs involved to date, and the figure they gave
was £25,000. So the amount payable under the statutory charge in favour
of The Law Society which would immediately attach if the plaintiff
accepted £40,000 in satisfaction of his claim would be £25,000. The
E plaintiff found that the amount of his debts was such that the balance of
the £40,000 would not be sufficient to save him from bankruptcy, so that
from his point of view there was nothing to lose by taking the risk of
refusing the £40,000 and taking the risk of losing his action.

But solicitors and counsel for an assisted person have a duty not only
to their client, not only to the court, but also to the legal aid fund, and it
would be a breach of that duty to continue to act for an assisted person who
F was unreasonably pursuing a course of action likely to be detrimental to
the fund. The plaintiff's advisers took the view that on their assessment
of the prospects of success in the action the probable detriment to the fund
if the plaintiff went on to trial would be very great and that it would not
only be in the interests of their client but also in the interests of the fund
itself if a way could be found of compromising the action at the figure
G which Marconi were prepared to provide which would not involve so
much of the fruit of the litigation going to the fund that the plaintiff
would be bankrupt anyway.

The scheme which the plaintiff's advisers devised, which was acceptable
to the plaintiff and to which solicitors and counsel on the other side were
prepared to agree, was this. The £40,000 was to be paid to Messrs. Kennedys
H and to Messrs. Coward Chance, Marconi's solicitors, jointly. The solicitors
were to be Marconi's agents for the purpose of buying for Marconi the
debts incurred in developing the invention. Marconi were then to write off
the debts. The solicitors were to reimburse themselves from the expenses
properly incurred in the conduct of the operation out of the £40,000. If
there was any balance they were to pay it to the plaintiffs.

The result, of course, would be that the only money in the plaintiff's
hands to satisfy The Law Society's statutory charge in favour of the fund

would be such balance as might be paid to him after the purchase of the   A
debts out of the £40,000 paid to the solicitors by Marconi and after they
had deducted their expenses. So the plaintiff's advisers put the area secretary of The Law Society in the picture. The compromise was arrived at
very shortly before the action was to come on and The Law Society had
very little time to consider what action it could or should take. Nevertheless,
it was informed of what was being done and had the opportunity to apply   B
to the court to stop it. It did not do so, as is perfectly understandable
having regard to the time scale involved.

On October 3, 1978, the plaintiff's action was called on before Tudor
Evans J. The plaintiff's counsel explained the terms of the compromise and
the reasons for the compromise fully to the judge and a consent order was
then made embodying its terms. Marconi paid the £40,000 to the solicitors.
The Law Society claimed that the statutory charge had attached to the   C
£40,000. Kennedys ultimately undertook that their bill to be defrayed by
The Law Society would not exceed £17,000, and that sum therefore is all
that the statutory charge is there to produce, and the solicitors are presently
holding that sum inviolate.

In that state of affairs the plaintiff on June 15, 1979, issued an originating summons claiming a declaration that the £40,000 paid by Marconi to   D
the solicitors under the terms of the consent order is not charged to The
Law Society by section 9 (6) and (7) of the Act of 1974. The Law Society
says that the statutory charge attaches to the £40,000 because (1) it is the
£40,000 which is the property which is recovered for the plaintiff in the
proceedings. It is his money. (2) The form of settlement is a fiction. The
truth of the matter is that the plaintiff recovered £40,000 in respect of
damages and costs. The scheme embodied in the terms of settlement is a   E
" dirty trick " and the court should disregard it and look at the reality.

Counsel for The Law Society, as I would expect, expressly disclaimed
any intention by his clients to attack the plaintiff's counsel, or Kennedys,
or Coward Chance, on the basis that any of them had taken part in a
" dirty trick " or that the solicitors, having been paid the £40,000, would
apply it in any way other than the way in which the consent order requires   F
them to do. In my judgment, this immediately disposes of the second limb
of The Law Society's case. It is, in my judgment, not enough to make the
scheme of the compromise a fiction, or a " dirty trick " which the court
will not allow to defeat the statutory charge, that the object of the exercise
was to defeat the effect of the charge. You cannot hunt the " dirty trick "
line when you say, as counsel for The Law Society does, that the plaintiff's
advisers and both firms of solicitors have acted with complete candour   G
and honesty. If you are doing a " dirty trick " you would be unlikely
to tell the judge all about it in asking him to make a consent order, and
if you did it is unlikely that the order would be made.

Then what was the property recovered for the plaintiff in the action to
which by reason of section 9 (6) of the Act of 1974 the charge in favour of
The Law Society attaches? Certainly the fruit of the compromise was worth   H
£40,000 to the plaintiff. But, in my judgment, it does not follow that £40,000
was what he recovered as fruits of the action. In my judgment, the result of
the compromise embodied in the consent order was that he acquired the
right to have his debts discharged by the machinery which the compromise
provided and the right to be paid any balance remaining. In my judgment,
the effect of section 9 (6) and (7) is that it is that right, and not the £40,000,
to which, for better or for worse, this charge attaches. This result, in my

A   judgment, is produced by the plain words of the Act and the facts of this case. That being so, the provisions of regulation 19 (4) do not affect this problem. It is not what has happened since the charge attached which is the subject matter of attack.

I am told that, when the debts have been bought, out of the £40,000 there is likely to be nothing left, let alone £17,000; so that the charge which the statute imposes will probably produce nothing. Whether the legal aid

B   fund will be better or worse off than it would have been had the action been fought to the bitter end is a matter of speculation but, for better or worse, the impact of the statutory provisions on the facts of this case is, in my judgment, that the charge in favour of The Law Society did not attach to the £40,000 paid by Marconi to the solicitors, and I make the declaration accordingly.

C   There is one further complication in this matter. I am told that in the course of the solicitors buying off a major liability, land which was charged to secure that liability has now been freed from its encumbrance. Mr. Matheson, on behalf of The Law Society, wishes to argue that that land is available just as any balance after payment of the debts would be available, to meet the liability imposed by the charge. This was something raised this morning on the third day of the hearing and it obviously calls for an

D   investigation of fact about what happened. There may be a number of complications of which Mr. Matheson is not aware. Having asked Mr. Hames, on behalf of the plaintiff, what his view of the situation was, he very candidly says that he is not in a position to argue that there may not be a case to be made that that land might be available to discharge the obligations to The Law Society under the charge which has attached to

E   the plaintiff's rights.

In those circumstances, it seems to me that the right way to deal with the problem is to adjourn this summons for that matter to be considered further by both parties, and if they come to the conclusion that the proposition either is or is not well founded, no doubt they will act accordingly; or they may, having investigated the facts, be unable to agree upon it, in which case the summons should be restored and the matter can be decided.

F   It might be that even if they were unable to agree they might conclude that a compromise was the right answer.

As far as I can see, there would not be any point in this case in making an order for costs because The Law Society, with the utmost propriety, has given the plaintiff a legal aid certificate for the purposes of these proceedings, and it seems that they are paying the cost of both sides

G   anyway.

Declaration granted.
No order as to costs.

Solicitors: *Kennedys; Collyer-Bristow.*

H   [Reported by Isobel Collins, Barrister-at-Law]

APPEAL from Bristow J.

The Law Society appealed on the grounds that the judge ought to have held that on the proper construction of the terms agreed between the plaintiff and the second defendant as set out in the schedule to the consent order made by the High Court of Justice, Queen's Bench Division, on October 3, 1978, the plaintiff in truth and in reality recovered the

sum of £40,00 and that the statutory charge in favour of the legal aid   A
fund attached to the sum; alternatively, the judge ought to have held
that the form of agreement, as set out in the schedule to the order, did
not truly state the nature of the agreement or arrangement between the
parties which was that the plaintiff recovered the sum of £40,000 from
the second defendant; the judge ought to have held that the agreement
was one which fell within the provisions of regulation 19 (4) of the Legal
Aid (General) Regulations 1971 and was accordingly void against the   B
first defendant as being an act done to defeat, alternatively operating to
defeat, the statutory charge in favour of the legal aid fund; the judge
ought to have held that in view of the expressed purpose and/or intention
of the agreement, namely, to avoid or to defeat the statutory charge in
favour of the legal aid fund, then even though the agreement itself
would otherwise be fully valid and binding as between the parties thereto,   C
the court had an overriding jurisdiction and/or discretion to order that
so much of the fund as should be equivalent to the net liability of the
legal aid fund on the account of the plaintiff under the civil aid certificate
issued to him in connection with the proceedings between him and the
second defendant (as defined by section 9 (9) of the Legal Aid Act 1974)
should be paid to the legal aid fund or alternatively should be declared
to be the subject of the statutory charge in favour of the legal aid fund,   D
and should exercise such jurisdiction or discretion to make such order;
the judge ought to have held that the constitution of the fund under the
terms of the consent order itself amounted to the " preservation " of
the property for the plaintiff and that, accordingly, the statutory charge
in favour of the legal aid fund attached thereto; and in the premises,
the judge ought to have held that the fund stood charged in favour of   E
the legal aid fund, and should have made a declaration accordingly.

  Duncan Matheson for The Law Society.
  Jack Hames Q.C. and *Peter Flint* for the plaintiff.

                                                    Cur. adv. vult.   F

  December 16. The following judgments were read.

  LORD DENNING M.R. Some 10 years ago the plaintiff invented an
" echo sounder " by which large ships could tell if they were getting
into shallow water. He got the Marconi International Marine Co. Ltd.
interested in it. They agreed to exploit it if it came up to their require-   G
ments. But it failed to come up to their requirements. So they refused
to go on with it. He alleged that they were guilty of a breach of contract.
He claimed damages, huge damages, because of the loss of profit that he
said he would have made. He also claimed to be reimbursed the money
he had spent in developing his echo sounder. It came to £30,000 or
more. He borrowed it from the banks and had charged his house as   H
security for it.
  The plaintiff had no money of his own to bring an action. So he
applied for legal aid and got it. His contribution to the costs was only
£100 payable by 12 monthly instalments of £8·35. He started an action
in 1972 against Marconi. The interlocutory stages took six years.
Marconi paid £8,000 into court. I do not suppose for one moment
that they considered themselves under any liability to the plaintiff: but

A they wanted to get rid of a case in which they would get no costs even if they won—because the plaintiff was legally aided. The plaintiff refused to take out the £8,000. So the proceedings went on until the case was ready for trial. It was fixed to start on Tuesday, October 3, 1978, and was estimated to last for 30 days.

The action was, however, settled. Marconi were ready to pay £40,000 to get rid of it altogether, rather than incur the expense of
B fighting the case over 30 days against a legally aided plaintiff. But here is the crux of the case. The plaintiff was not agreeable to settle for £40,000, if that money was to be paid straight to his solicitors. He was himself already insolvent. He had bankruptcy notices outstanding against him, but they were being held over pending the action. He owed at least £30,000 to his creditors. In addition, his own solicitors estimated
C their own costs on his behalf to be in the region of £25,000, for which the legal aid fund would have a charge on the £40,000 if paid over to him or his solicitors. The legal aid fund would have to insist on its charge and take it out of the £40,000: see *Hanlon* v. *The Law Society* [1980] 2 W.L.R. 756, 802. So there would be only £15,000 left for the plaintiff and he would remain, as he says in his affidavit, " in a bankrupt situation."
D

The pressure brought by the plaintiff

So the plaintiff (with the backing of his solicitors and counsel) said to himself: " I will only settle for £40,000 if that money is used first to pay off my creditors (£30,000 or more), and then any balance (£10,000 or less) can go to my solicitors as a contribution to their costs, and they
E can get the rest of their costs from the legal aid fund." Marconi said: " We don't mind how you deal with the £40,000, as long as you accept that sum in settlement of the action." The plaintiff brought this pressure to bear on all concerned. He said to them in effect: " Unless things can be settled on these lines, I insist on the action going on for trial for the 30 days—and that will put Marconi and the legal aid fund to
F enormous expense in costs."

Faced with this problem, the plaintiff's legal advisers put their thinking caps on and brought forward a solution which was eventually agreed between the counsel and solicitors for both sides.

Terms simplified

G 1. Marconi were to pay £40,000 into a joint account in the names of Kennedys (the solicitors for the plaintiff) and Coward Chance (the solicitors for Marconi); then those two firms were to hold the £40,000 *as agents* for Marconi. 2. Kennedys (as agents for Marconi) were to negotiate with the creditors of the plaintiff and to pay them off—out of the £40,000 in the joint account belonging to Marconi. But in those negotiations Kennedys were not to disclose to the creditors that the
H money was coming from the account of Marconi. The creditors might then be induced to accept less than their full amount. 3. The payment-off of the creditors should be made in the form of a purchase by Marconi of the debts which the plaintiff owed to the creditors. The creditors were to assign to Kennedys (as undisclosed agents for Marconi) the benefit of the debts. But Marconi undertook not to enforce the debts against the plaintiff. 4. After the payment-off of the creditors, then if there was any balance left of the £40,000, it was to be paid to Kennedys

(as the plaintiff's solicitors) as a contribution to his costs. On that being A done, all claims of the plaintiff against Marconi were to be extinguished.

The information to The Law Society

The legal advisers thought that those terms would deprive the legal aid fund of its charge. They thought that Kennedys would not have " recovered " the £40,000 for the plaintiff. They would only have " recovered " for him the right to have the terms enforced. That was B only a chose in action which was worth little or nothing in money. It only sufficed to keep him out of bankruptcy. The legal advisers thought that Kennedys could still recover their costs from the legal aid fund, despite having deprived it of the charge. Their justification for this advice was that, by settling on these terms, they would save the legal aid fund all the expense of a 30-day trial. C

But the legal advisers felt that they ought to tell The Law Society about the terms of settlement and get their opinion on it. I must say that it was a very rushed affair. The case was due to start on the morning of Tuesday, October 3, 1978. It was only the day before, at 9.30 a.m. on Monday, October 2, 1978, that Mr. Hames, counsel for the plaintiff, telephoned the offices of the area secretary of The Law Society. He outlined the proposed terms of settlement and said he thought that D the charge would not apply to the £40,000. The reply was that, in the opinion of the legal aid fund, the charge would apply. Later that day there were further discussions. In the result the legal aid fund felt itself unable to commit itself on such short notice to any firm view: and that Mr. Hames must exercise his own judgment on the right course to follow. E

I must say that I think The Law Society acted with complete propriety. They could not possibly be expected, at such short notice and on such meagre information, to look into this complicated matter and express any view upon it.

The settlement is announced

On the morning of Tuesday, October 3, 1978, the case of *Manley* F v. *Marconi International Marine Co. Ltd.* was in the list for hearing. As soon as it was called on Mr. Hames rose and gave a short explanation. He asked for a consent order in the Tomlin form. The judge did not approve or disapprove. The terms were set out in a schedule to the order. It was all over in 19 minutes.

The follow-up G

On October 17, 1978 Marconi paid the £40,000 into the joint account. The plaintiff's debts have been found to be, not £30,000, but £48,000. So if the terms of settlement were implemented, the whole of the £40,000 would be used up in " purchasing " his debts. But the terms of settlement have been held up. The reason is because the legal aid fund is H liable to pay Kennedys their costs of the action against Marconi, when taxed on a legal aid taxation. Kennedys put their costs at £25,000, but they have agreed to limit them to £17,000. The legal aid fund says that it has a charge on the £40,000 for that £17,000. Kennedys dispute it. They say that the legal aid fund has no such charge. These proceedings have been brought to resolve the issue. Pending the decision, the £17,000 has been retained in the joint account. The remaining £23,000

A   has been used—or will be used—to pay off some of the plaintiff's debts. In particular, £20,000 of it has been used to pay a debt to a bank and release some land which was given by the plaintiff to the bank as security.

The issue

Kennedys say that the £40,000 is not subject to the statutory charge.
B   They say that the whole of the £40,000 should be used to clear off the plaintiff's debts—as far as possible—and that Kennedys themselves should be paid their own costs (fixed at £17,000) by the legal aid fund. The legal aid fund admits that it is liable to pay Kennedys the £17,000, but claims to recoup itself out of the £40,000, because it has a statutory charge on the money or, alternatively, it has an equitable claim to the
C   money.

The statutory provisions

The clause which gives Kennedys their right to have their costs paid is section 10 (1) of the Legal Aid Act 1974, which says:

D   "... a solicitor who has acted for a person receiving legal aid shall be paid for so acting out of the legal aid fund, and any fees paid to counsel for so acting shall be paid out of that fund."

The clause which gives the statutory charge is section 9 (6) which says (omitting unnecessary words) that the net liability of the fund to the solicitor:

E   "shall be a first charge for the benefit of the legal aid fund on any property (wherever situated) which is recovered or preserved for him in the proceedings."

But when there is a compromise (as happened here) there comes into play section 9 (7) which says:

F   "The reference in subsection (6) above to property recovered or preserved for any person shall include his rights under any compromise arrived at to avoid or bring to an end the proceedings . . ."

The judge's ruling

The judge pinned his faith on section 9 (7). There was here a compromise arrived at so as to bring to an end the proceedings. The charge was on "his rights under [the] compromise." The judge said
G   that the plaintiff:

"acquired the right to have his debts discharged by the machinery which the compromise provided and the right to be paid any balance remaining . . . it is that right, and not the £40,000, to which, for better or for worse, this right attaches."

H   Good faith

Everyone accepted that, in making this compromise, all the legal advisers acted honestly and in good faith and with the desire to act fairly by the legal aid fund. That is why they told the area committee about it before they concluded it. They say that, if they had not settled the case on these terms, it would have gone on for 30 days—at a great expense to the legal aid fund. So it was, they say, to the advantage of the legal aid fund to do this. They were entitled, they say, to draw up

the terms of settlement, so as to express the rights of the plaintiff under A
the compromise as being a right to have his debts discharged (a chose
in action) and not the £40,000. They say that the written terms should
be given their legal effect just as were the terms of the covenants in
Inland Revenue Commissioners v. *Duke of Westminster* [1936] A.C. 1.

The truth of the transaction

B

I can see the force of that argument. The judge accepted it. But
I think it is erroneous. This case comes under another and better
principle which I stated simply in *Customs and Excise Commissioners*
v. *Pools Finance (1937) Ltd.* [1952] 1 All E.R. 775, 780: " [The parties]
cannot assert that black is white and expect the courts to believe it." It
is the same as that which Lord Reid and I applied in *Griffiths* v. *J. P.
Harrison (Watford) Ltd.* [1963] A.C. 1. The court should always look C
for the truth of the transaction. It should not let itself be deceived by
the stratagems of lawyers, or accountants. It should not allow them to
pull the wool over its eyes. It should not allow them to dress up a
transaction in clothes that do not belong to it.

Now the plain truth of this transaction is that the £40,000 was to
be used to pay off the plaintiff's debts. Kennedys were to supply D
particulars of his debts. They were to negotiate the payment without
disclosing that they were acting for anyone else but the plaintiff. The
payment-off was to be described as a " purchase " of his debts, but the
purchasers (Marconi) undertook not to enforce their purchase against
him. So, although it was in form a purchase, it was in fact a payment-
off of the creditors by the plaintiff's solicitors on the best terms that
they could arrange, on the appearance that they were acting for the E
plaintiff.

To my mind, once we pull aside the curtain of words, and the
supposed rights, the truth is that this £40,000 was to be used to pay off
the plaintiff's debts at his request. It is, therefore, the subject of the
statutory charge in favour of the legal aid fund. When money is paid
to a party, or at his request to his creditors, it is plainly " recovered . . . F
for him " within section 9 (6) of the Act of 1974. The legal aid fund
has, therefore, a charge for the costs (£17,000) on the money in the
joint account. It should be paid out to the fund. The fund should pay
it to the solicitors. But the fund should pay nothing out of its own
pocket.

Other provisions

G

If I am wrong, however, in looking behind the curtain—if the transaction is to be taken at its face value—then I doubt whether it would
be defeated by the other provisions which were put before us. Regulation 19 (4) may not help: if the charge is only on the chose in action,
the settlement does not defeat it. Regulation 18 (3) (*b*) may not help:
the £40,000 was not received by the plaintiff's solicitors as his solicitors, H
but as agents for Marconi. Regulation 18 (4) (*c*) may not help because
the first charge would be on the chose in action and not on the £40,000.

Equity

Mr. Matheson referred us to a very interesting line of cases on a
solicitor's lien. A typical instance is when a man is owed £100 by
another. He goes to a solicitor who issues proceedings. If the defendant

A settles the action by paying £75 to the plaintiff's solicitor, then the solicitor has a lien on the £75 for his costs. These amount to £25. So that the plaintiff only receives £50 clear. Now suppose the plaintiff, behind the back of his solicitor, goes to the defendant and agrees to take £70 in settlement, and spends it all in riotous living. The settlement is binding. The solicitor has been deprived of his lien for costs. Has he any recourse against the defendant? It is clear that if the defendant

B had notice of the solicitor's lien, and made the agreement with the plaintiff collusively so as to deprive the solicitor of his lien, then the solicitor can recover from the defendant his costs of £25. That is clear from a series of cases from *Welsh* v. *Hole* (1779) 1 Doug. 237 to *In re Margetson and Jones* [1897] 2 Ch. 314. But there is a question as to what constitutes " collusion " for this purpose. On this point I am

C content to go by the observation of Brett M.R. in *The Hope* (1883) 8 P.D. 144, 145: " . . . The plaintiffs' solicitors must show that both the plaintiffs and the defendants entered into the compromise with the intention of depriving them of their lien."

Those cases do not apply directly to our present case. The plaintiff's solicitors had no lien for their costs. They looked to the legal aid fund for payment of them. The legal aid fund had no lien for costs. They

D had only a charge on any property when it was " recovered." Marconi had no intention to defeat the legal aid fund. They left everything to Kennedys to arrange.

Now, although those cases do not directly apply, I am of opinion that the principle of them does. It is clear beyond doubt that the object of the plaintiff and his solicitors was to deprive the legal aid fund of

E any charge on the £40,000. That was the be-all and end-all of this elaborate transaction. The solicitors wanted to make the legal aid fund pay all their costs, and at the same time deprive the legal aid fund of any charge in respect of those costs. I do not think they should be permitted to succeed in this. I do not think the settlement itself can be set aside. It has gone too far to do that. But I think that equity can

F intervene so as to hold that, if and in so far as the solicitors have intentionally deprived the legal aid fund of a charge on their costs, they are themselves precluded from making any claim on the legal aid fund for those costs. It is a very old principle laid down by Lord Coke that a man shall not be allowed to take advantage of a condition that he himself has brought about: see *per* Lord Finlay L.C. in *New Zealand Shipping Co. Ltd.* v. *Société des Ateliers et Chantiers de France* [1919]

G A.C. 1, 8.

Conclusion

My conclusion is that the £17,000 now in the joint account should be released to the legal aid fund: because the fund has a charge on it to secure the costs of £17,000 which the legal aid fund has to pay to

H the solicitors for the plaintiff. Alternatively, if the £17,000 is released to the solicitors they are precluded in equity from recovering anything from the legal aid fund. In short, the solicitors get the £17,000, but the legal aid fund pay nothing.

In parting from this case I cannot forbear from saying that I think the legal advisers of the plaintiff were ill-advised to try to circumvent the statutory charge. Either the settlement at £40,000 was good or it was bad—on the merits of the action itself. If it was good, it should have been accepted without any manipulation of the destination of the **A** £40,000. If it was bad, it should have been rejected. It was quite wrong for the plaintiff to say " You must go ahead with the action unless my creditors are paid off." That was a quite inadmissible threat by a legally aided person, who was not paying the costs of going on. It was most unfair to put the defendants to all the great expense of contesting the case. If the £40,000 was reasonable on the merits of the case, and the plaintiff refused to accept it, his refusal should have been reported to **B** the area committee for them to decide whether his certificate should be continued or not.

This case brings out vividly the responsibility which attaches to legal advisers who conduct an action for a legally aided person. They must remember that they are funded at the expense of the state, and that they are putting the defendant (who is not legally aided) to a great deal **C** of worry and expense in contesting the case—a defendant who will not recover any of his costs even if he wins. This puts the legal advisers for the plaintiff in an extremely strong bargaining position. There is inequality of bargaining power. They should not abuse it at the expense of the defendant. Nor should they abuse it at the expense of the legal aid fund. Whenever the question of a settlement comes up, the legal advisers for the plaintiff should consider any offer on the merits of the **D** case itself, just as if they were acting for a private client of moderate means, not one who is wealthy enough to go to any expense, or one who is very much in debt already, against a defendant who is also of moderate means and will get an order for costs against the plaintiff if he wins. Once a figure is reached which is reasonable, they should settle the case at that figure. They should not try to manipulate its destination so as **E** to avoid the statutory charge. In particular, they should not make the sum payable to the creditors of the plaintiff or to anyone other than the plaintiff. If they should do so, they will find, as in this case, that they will incur the displeasure of the court, which will see that their manipulations do not succeed.

I would allow the appeal accordingly.   **F**

ORMROD L.J. It is right to say at the outset of this judgment that I accept unreservedly that Mr. Hames and those who helped him to draw up the terms of the compromise agreement believed that they were acting in the best interests of all concerned, including that of The Law Society as administrators of the legal aid fund. On the other hand, I think that they misapprehended the position of The Law Society. **G**

The situation as they saw it was that the plaintiff had reasonable grounds for pursuing his claim for very substantial damages against Marconi, but that the action, which was estimated to last for six weeks, and which would involve heavy costs, particularly in respect of expert witnesses, might very well fail in the end. The consequences would be that the plaintiff recovered nothing and a very heavy liability in respect **H** of his costs would fall on the legal aid fund.

Marconi were prepared to offer £40,000 in full settlement of all the plaintiff's claims and costs, but the plaintiff, who was under a threat of bankruptcy, insisted upon his outstanding debts being paid out of this sum, which would not be enough to meet both his debts and his costs to date. It was assumed, erroneously in my opinion, that he was in a position, vis-à-vis The Law Society, to insist upon going on with his

A action unless he received a sufficient proportion of the sum of £40,000 to clear his debts. Consequently, it would be to the advantage of The Law Society in the long run if terms of compromise could be so arranged that no effective charge in favour of The Law Society under section 9 (6) and (7) of the Legal Aid Act 1974 fell upon the sum of £40,000. The Law Society would be compensated by the substantial savings if the action did not proceed to judgment. This assumes that the plaintiff was

B in control of the situation. In my opinion he was not.

Under regulation 12 (3) and (6) of the Legal Aid (General) Regulations 1971 the area committee could have discharged the plaintiff's legal aid certificate. Regulation 12 (3) provides that they

" shall discharge a certificate from such date as they consider appropriate if— . . . (b) . . . (i) the assisted person no longer has reasonable
C   grounds for asserting or disputing the claim or for taking, defending or being a party to the proceedings; or (ii) the assisted person has required the claim to be asserted or disputed or the proceedings to be conducted unreasonably so as to incur an unjustifiable expense to the fund; or (iii) it is unreasonable in the particular circumstances that the assisted person should continue to receive legal aid: . . ."

D This, and many other provisions of the legal aid scheme, show that, although the scheme is designed to interfere as little as possible with the traditional relationship between counsel and solicitors and client, and is administered in such a way as to keep interference to a minimum, nonetheless it has altered this relationship in important, and sometimes subtle, ways. The existence of the legal aid fund has introduced a
E third party into what was formerly a one to one relationship, and this new relationship is governed by the Legal Aid Act 1974 and the regulations made under it. It was, in my opinion, the duty of the plaintiff's solicitors to inform and consult the area committee of The Law Society before entering, on the plaintiff's behalf, into the compromise agreement of October 3, 1978. Some attempt was made on October 2 by Mr. Hames to consult the officers of the area committee, but they were given a
F wholly inadequate time in which to consider the complex and difficult issues involved. In retrospect at least, it is difficult to appreciate the reasons for the apparent urgency.

The extent to which the position of solicitors and counsel has been changed by the introduction of legal aid is shown by the facts of this case. Had the plaintiff not been an assisted person, the terms of compromise would have been inconceivable unless his solicitors were prepared
G to forgo their lien or charge on the £40,000. Had they refused to do so they would have declined to continue to act for the plaintiff until he had put them in funds.

Mr. Hames submitted that all rights and obligations relating to the legal aid fund are statutory in origin and must be found in the Legal Aid Act 1974 or in the regulations made under it. They are, therefore,
H dependent upon the construction of the relevant statutory provisions. I accept that submission, from which it follows that the rules of common law or equity affecting the rights of solicitors are relevant only in so far as they may throw light on the true construction of the relevant provisions in the Act or in the regulations. The answer to the question raised in the originating summons in this case, therefore, depends first upon the construction of section 9 (6) and (7) of the Act of 1974, which create The Law Society's statutory charge on the proceeds of the litigation as

350

security for the costs of the assisted person which ultimately fall on the   A
fund and, secondly, upon the true construction of the written agreement
of compromise dated October 3, 1978.   Section 9 provides:

> "(6) Except so far as regulations otherwise provide, any sums
> remaining unpaid on account of a person's contribution to the legal aid
> fund in respect of any proceedings and, if the total contribution is
> less than the net liability of that fund on his account, a sum equal   B
> to the deficiency shall be a first charge for the benefit of the legal
> aid fund on any property (wherever situated) which is recovered or
> preserved for him in the proceedings.   (7) The reference in sub-
> section (6) above to property recovered or preserved for any person
> shall include his rights under any compromise arrived at to avoid
> or bring to an end the proceedings and any sums recovered by
> virtue of an order for costs made in his favour in the proceedings   C
> (not being sums payable into the legal aid fund under section 8
> above)."

The crucial words for present purposes in subsection (6) are "any
property (wherever situated) which is recovered or preserved for him in
the proceedings."   Subsection (7) extends subsection (6) to "rights under
any compromise," but does not restrict the charge to such rights.   This   D
is made clear by the use of the word "include" in subsection (7).

Mr. Hames submitted that the property recovered for the plaintiff
under the compromise was limited to the bundle of rights or choses in
action which he acquired, i.e. a right to compel Marconi to pay £40,000
to their agents, the respective firms of solicitors for the parties; a right
to require Marconi to purchase such of his debts for up to £40,000 as   E
he chose; a right to insist on Marconi not enforcing such debts against
him, and so on.   This is property in one sense, but it is valueless to
support The Law Society's charge as security for the costs paid on the
plaintiff's behalf.   Mr. Matheson, for The Law Society, argued that the
statutory charge attached to so much of the £40,000 as was required to
meet the net liability of the legal aid fund, after deducting any contribution paid by the plaintiff as a term of his legal aid certificate.   F

Mr. Hames's submission requires that the word "property" be
construed in the sense in which lawyers use it as a term of art; Mr.
Matheson urged that it should be given its ordinary meaning in the
English language.   This question was fully considered (though in a
different context) by the House of Lords in *Hanlon* v. *The Law Society*
[1980] 2 W.L.R. 756.   Lord Scarman and Lord Lowry favoured the   G
broader construction.   Lord Scarman said, at p. 806:

> "The subsection must be construed so that in matrimonial as in
> other proceedings the legal aid fund has the security of its charge.
> The words 'recovered or preserved' are apt to cover ordinary civil
> litigation in which a plaintiff recovers or a defendant preserves an
> asset: but they are not so apt to cover a transfer of property   H
> ordered by a court in the exercise of its discretion under sections 24
> and 25 of the Matrimonial Causes Act 1973.   Nevertheless, they
> can be read as covering such an order without any very great dis-
> tortion of their ordinary meaning.   A woman who obtains an order
> transferring to her the matrimonial home will be seen, by herself
> and by others, to have 'got' the house: and it is not difficult to
> construe 'property recovered' as property obtained."

A Lord Lowry said, at p. 809:

> " The purpose, after all, of creating a charge on property is to give the legal aid fund or the solicitor, as the case may be, a security, if the assisted person or the client has gained financially as a result of the proceedings; the way in which that result has been achieved should not matter."

B Lord Simon of Glaisdale, however, at p. 796E, thought a " liberal approach to construction is not appropriate in a measure imposing a charge for a social service." It is, however, clear on the facts of that case that the House did not adopt the strict legal meaning of the word " property " or of " recovered," but instead came to the conclusion that Mrs. Hanlon had substantially recovered the whole of the former matrimonial home C to which, accordingly, the statutory charge attached.

In reaching their conclusion, the House held that it was permissible to look at the regulations made under the Legal Aid Act 1974 as an aid to the construction of the Act itself: see in particular *per* Lord Lowry at p. 811 et seq. There is one regulation which is useful in the present case, namely, regulation 18 (4) of the Legal Aid (General) Regulations 1971, which reads:

D

> " Where in any proceedings to which an assisted person is a party —(*a*) an order or agreement is made providing for the recovery or preservation of property for the benefit of the assisted person and, by virtue of the Act, there is a first charge on the property for the benefit of the fund; . . ."

E This is a clear indication that the statutory charge is not limited to property recovered by the assisted person, but extends to property recovered for his benefit.

In my judgment, therefore, the court should adopt the broader approach and construe the phrase " property . . . recovered or preserved " for the assisted person as including property recovered for his benefit, looking at the reality of the matter rather than concentrating exclusively F on the form of the transaction, particularly when the court is concerned with a compromise. Judgments deal in realities: compromises provide scope for an infinite variety of forms, limited only by the ingenuity of the draftsman. It would be wrong, in my view, to extend the formalistic approach adopted in revenue cases, e.g. *Inland Revenue Commissioners* v. *Duke of Westminster* [1936] A.C. 1, to other branches of the law.

G I now turn to consider the terms of the compromise as finally agreed. The concept underlying it is in the last degree artificial. There could be no conceivable reason, or at least there is no evidence at all of any reason, why Marconi should wish to purchase unspecified debts from unspecified creditors of the plaintiff at his option. Still less when Marconi undertake not to enforce them against the plaintiff. There can equally be no sensible reason why the plaintiff's solicitors should be H involved in the purchase of such debts, or why they should be made joint agents of Marconi with Marconi's solicitors except to avoid receipt of the £40,000 by the plaintiff's solicitors which would have instantly brought regulation 18 (3) (*b*) of the Regulations of 1971 into force, and required them to pay over to The Law Society any sum so received. In my view the compromise was expressed in this form solely for the benefit of the plaintiff, in order that the whole sum of £40,000 would be available to him to pay his debts and nothing would be available to The Law Society

as security for their costs. In truth and in fact, the plaintiff was clearly A
in effective control of the distribution of this fund and was the sole
beneficiary of it. I would, therefore, hold that the statutory charge
attached to the fund of £40,000 to the extent necessary to cover the net
liability of The Law Society for the plaintiff's costs.

On this view of the case the only remaining question is that of
enforcement of the statutory charge, but fortunately a sum of £17,000 B
has been retained by the solicitors, at the instance of The Law Society,
pending the outcome of this appeal, which is sufficient to cover the net
liability of the legal aid fund. So this problem does not arise. Had it
been necessary to consider it, as the judge in the court below felt
obliged to do, the line of cases cited to us by Mr. Matheson dealing
with solicitors' liens and charges might have been helpful. They show
the lengths to which the court has been prepared to go in its equitable C
jurisdiction to protect solicitors who have been deprived of their lien
or charge under the Solicitors Acts. An analogous situation might
have arisen in this case if the whole of the £40,000 had been put out
of reach of the statutory charge, e.g. by a simple agreement that Marconi
would pay the plaintiff's debts direct to the creditors up to a total of
£40,000. It is unnecessary to say more than this: there is no case in D
the books in which a solicitor who has been a party to such an arrangement, which deprives himself of his own lien or charge, has recovered
his costs from a third party. That is not, however, to say that a solicitor
for an assisted party puts his costs at risk if he is a party to a compromise in which the other party, for reasons of his own, offers terms
which do not include the payment of money or the transfer of property,
but some other less tangible form of benefit to the assisted person. E

I too would allow this appeal.

O'CONNOR L.J. This case is concerned with legal aid in civil proceedings. Where a person qualifies for legal aid, solicitors and counsel act
for him but are paid by the legal aid fund. The Act gives to the fund
a first charge on all property recovered or preserved for the assisted F
person in the proceedings. These provisions cause no difficulty in any
case where the assisted person loses the case. They can be troublesome
where the assisted person wins his case and very often raise serious
problems when a compromise is under discussion.

The present case is a classic example of the compromise difficulty. The
plaintiff is an inventor who alleged that Marconi were in breach of a
contract to exploit his invention. The matter was highly technical and G
the damages claimed for loss of royalties on world-wide sales of very
expensive equipment were large. The case was due to start on October
3, 1978, and the parties estimated that the hearing would take 30 days.
This is very expensive litigation. Marconi knew that, if they succeeded,
they would have to pay their own costs and, if they lost, in addition
they would have to pay to the plaintiff both damages and costs. That H
was a situation which was ripe for compromise.

The plaintiff gave firm instructions. He had incurred debts in producing a working prototype of his invention of the order of £30,000,
although no accurate figure was known on October 3, 1978. His creditors
were threatening to make him bankrupt. He said that so long as
Marconi paid enough to pay his debts he was content; if not, the case
must go on. Negotiations took place and Marconi made a final offer

A of £40,000, inclusive of costs, to be rid of the litigation at that time. Mr. Hames asked the plaintiff's solicitors for an estimate of their costs to date and got the answer £25,000. It was obvious that if the legal aid charge attached to this money there would not be enough to discharge the plaintiff's debts.

B Mr. Hames certainly, and possibly others of the plaintiff's legal advisers, did not take a rosy view of the plaintiff's chances of success in this litigation. They calculated that if the trial ran for the estimated 30 days the plaintiff's costs would rise to £60,000. Marconi would pay no more. So it was that they decided to devise a scheme so as to avoid the charge to the legal aid fund. The scheme proposed would leave any balance of £40,000, after payment of the plaintiff's debts, available for the legal aid fund, and as at October 3 this was thought to be of the

C order of £10,000. The legal aid fund was being asked to buy a potential liability of £60,000 for £15,000.

The scheme devised was simple. Marconi were to pay £40,000 into an account in the joint names of the plaintiff's and Marconi's solicitors who were declared to be agents for Marconi for this purpose. The plaintiff's solicitors as undisclosed agents for Marconi were to buy the

D plaintiff's debts for Marconi. Marconi undertook not to have recourse to the plaintiff for such debts. The solicitors were to recover their own charges for this work from the £40,000. Thereafter, if there was any money left, it would be paid to the plaintiff's solicitor who would hold it for the legal aid fund.

On October 2 The Law Society were told of the scheme on the telephone and asked to approve it and to agree not to claim the legal

E aid fund charge against the £40,000. This The Law Society would not and did not do. On October 3, 1978, the case was settled on the terms of the scheme now embodied in a Tomlin order. It was fully mentioned in open court to the judge. It is not and never has been suggested that the plaintiff's legal advisers acted other than openly and in good faith, believing that they were acting in the best interests of their client and

F the legal aid fund.

The Law Society claimed the charge on the fund of £40,000. The plaintiff's solicitors quantified their costs and agreed to limit their claim against the fund to £17,000. That sum is held pending the outcome of these proceedings; the balance was released for the purposes of this scheme. The plaintiff commenced these proceedings against The Law Society by originating summons asking for a declaration that the fund

G of £40,000 " does not stand and never has stood charged for the benefit of the legal aid fund under and by virtue of the provisions and for the purposes of the Legal Aid Act 1974." The case was heard by Bristow J. who gave judgment on October 10, 1980, in favour of the plaintiff and made the declaration prayed for. The Law Society appeal to this court.

The Law Society contend that upon the true construction of the

H compromise agreement the fund of £40,000 was " property recovered or preserved for the plaintiff in the proceedings " within the meaning of section 9 (6) of the Legal Aid Act 1974. The crucial words are " property . . . recovered or preserved for him." That the £40,000 was a fruit of this litigation is beyond doubt, but not all fruits of litigation are " property recovered." Mr. Hames, on behalf of the plaintiff, submits that the property recovered in this case was the right to force Marconi to carry out the terms of the compromise which included a contingent

354

right to any balance of the £40,000 that might remain, and he submits A
that that was the property to which the charge attached. I cannot agree.
Under the terms of the compromise the plaintiff had the right to specify
which of his debts were to be discharged out of the £40,000. Marconi
had no interest in what debts the plaintiff chose to have paid off. The
provision in the compromise making the plaintiff's solicitors the undisclosed agents of Marconi was solely for the benefit of the plaintiff, in
the hope that his debts could be " bought " for less than their book B
value. I do not think that there can be any doubt that the £40,000
was property recovered for the benefit of the plaintiff. Can it be said
that nevertheless it is not recovered " for him " ? I think not, and I am
fortified in that view when I look at regulation 18 (4) of the Legal Aid
(General) Regulations 1971:

" Where in any proceedings to which an assisted person is a party C
—(a) an order or agreement is made providing for the recovery or
preservation of property for the benefit of the assisted person and,
by virtue of the Act, there is a first charge on the property for the
benefit of the fund; . . . The Law Society may take such proceedings in its own name as may be necessary to enforce or give effect
to such an order or agreement."
D

For these reasons I hold that the £40,000 was property recovered for
the plaintiff and the charge in favour of the legal aid fund attaches.

In the present case no problem of enforcement arises and I do not
wish to add anything of my own to what Lord Denning M.R. and
Ormrod L.J. have said were the position to be that the money had all
gone, save that I agree with them. E

I too would allow the appeal.

> *Appeal allowed with costs in Court*
> *of Appeal and below not to be*
> *enforced except by application to*
> *a judge in chambers.*
> *Legal aid taxation of plaintiff's costs.* F
> *Declaration in terms sought.*

Solicitors: *Collyer-Bristow; Kennedys.*

B. O. A.
G

A

[COURT OF APPEAL]

* REGINA *v.* LANDY

REGINA *v.* WHITE

REGINA *v.* KAYE

B

1980   Dec. 4, 5, 8, 9, 10, 11, 12;   Lawton L.J., Michael Davies
1981   Jan. 12   and Bingham JJ.

*Crime—Fraud—Conspiracy to defraud—Bank director and
employees using banking irregularities and malpractices
followed by loss—Count to contain clear and concise particulars
—Essential ingredient of offence—Whether dishonesty in mind
or intention of person charged—Whether to be stressed in
directing jury*

C

*Crime—Practice—Pre-trial review—Papers in complicated case—
Whether to be provided to judge well before review hearing*

The appellants, who included the chairman of a bank which
stopped payments and was liquidated involving loss to creditors,
were charged with conspiring together to defraud customers of

D

the bank. The case for the prosecution was that the appellants
had used banking irregularities and malpractices in siphoning
money from the bank, must have known what was going on
and were actively engaged in ensuring that the money went to
where it was siphoned for purposes which put the bank's
customers at risk, and in concealing what was happening. The
appellants' defence was, in effect, a plea of confession and
avoidance in that they were honest but careless. At no stage

E

of the summing up were the jury directed clearly and precisely
that they had to be sure that each appellant had agreed to act
dishonestly. The appellants were convicted.

On appeal against conviction:—

Held, allowing the appeals, that dishonesty, which was the
all-important ingredient of an offence of conspiracy to defraud,
had to be stressed in a direction to the jury and not minimised
in any way (post, p. 365c); and that, since the jury had not

F

been clearly and correctly directed as to the meaning of defraud
and thereby each of the appellants had lost his chance of
having his defence fairly put to the jury, they had not had a
fair trial and the verdicts were unsatisfactory and would be
quashed (post, pp. 368B–D).

Per curiam. (i) In a complicated case papers for a judge
conducting a pre-trial review should be supplied to him well
before the review hearing and in time for him to read and

G

analyse them (post, p. 361D–E). (ii) A count charging conspiracy
to defraud should set out concise and clear particulars in
order to inform the defendants and court of the prosecution's
allegations; the words " and by divers other false and fraudulent devices " are a relic of the past and should not be used
post, p. 362A–C). (iii) A proper direction to a jury on
a charge of conspiracy to defraud is that they may say to
themselves: " We are sure he was acting dishonestly because

H

we can see no reason why a man of his intelligence and experience would not have appreciated, as right minded people would
have done, that what he was doing was dishonest " (post,
p. 365G).

Reg. v. Feely [1973] Q.B. 530, C.A. explained.

The following cases are referred to in the judgment:

Reg. v. Feely [1973] Q.B. 530; [1973] 2 W.L.R. 201; [1973] 1 All E.R.
341, C.A.

Reg. v. *Moon* [1969] 1 W.L.R. 1705; [1969] 3 All E.R. 803, C.A.   A
Reg. v. *Sinclair* [1968] 1 W.L.R. 1246; [1968] 3 All E.R. 241, C.A.
Stafford v. *Director of Public Prosecutions* [1974] A.C. 878; [1973] 3
    W.L.R. 719; [1973] 3 All E.R. 762, H.L.(E.).
Welham v. *Director of Public Prosecutions* [1961] A.C. 103; [1960] 2
    W.L.R. 669; [1960] 1 All E.R. 805, H.L.(E.).

The following additional cases were cited in argument: B
Boggeln v. *Williams* [1978] 1 W.L.R. 873; [1978] 2 All E.R. 1061, D.C.
Reg. v. *Allsop* (1976) 64 Cr.App.R. 29, C.A.
Reg. v. *Badjan* (1966) 50 Cr.App.R. 141, C.C.A.
Reg. v. *Barnes* (1970) 55 Cr.App.R. 100, C.A.
Reg. v. *Cordrey; Reg.* v. *Cervello* (unreported), March 14, 1980.
Reg. v. *Diggin* [1980] Crim.L.R. 656, C.A.   C
Reg. v. *Greenfield* [1973] 1 W.L.R. 1151; [1973] 3 All E.R. 1050, C.A.
Reg. v. *Greenstein* [1975] 1 W.L.R. 1353; [1976] 1 All E.R. 1, C.A.
Reg. v. *Griffiths* (1974) 60 Cr.App.R. 14, C.A.
Reg. v. *Hallatt* (unreported), February 26, 1980, C.A.
Reg. v. *Lawrence* (unreported), May 20, 1980, C.A.
Reg. v. *Mansell* (unreported), June 6, 1980, C.A.
Reg. v. *Muff* (unreported), November 1, 1979, C.A.   D
Reg. v. *Penny* (unreported), October 3, 1980, Talbot J., C.C.C.
Reg. v. *Prater* [1960] 2 Q.B. 464; [1960] 2 W.L.R. 343; [1960] 1 All E.R.
    298, C.C.A.
Reg. v. *Scott* [1975] A.C. 819; [1974] 3 W.L.R. 741; [1974] 3 All E.R. 1032,
    H.L.(E.).
Reg. v. *Sheppard* (unreported), January 14, 1974, C.A.
                                                                                E
APPEALS against conviction.

On July 25, 1979, at the Central Criminal Court (Judge Abdela), after
a trial occupying 90 days, the appellants, Harry Landy, Arthur Malcolm
White and Charles Kaye, were all convicted on count 1 of conspiracy to
defraud depositors with the Israel British Bank (London) Ltd. between
September 30, 1968, and July 12, 1974, and the appellants Landy and   F
White were convicted also on counts 2 and 3 of conspiracy to utter forged
documents between November 1, 1971, and July 12, 1974. Landy was
sentenced on count 1 to five years' imprisonment, fined £350,000 with
12 months' imprisonment consecutive in default, and was ordered to pay
£100,000 costs, and on each of counts 2 and 3 to three years' imprisonment concurrent. White was sentenced on count 1 to four years' imprisonment, fined £5,000 with 12 months' imprisonment consecutive in default   G
and was ordered to pay £2,000 towards the costs of the prosecution, and
on each of counts 2 and 3 to three years' imprisonment concurrent. Kaye
was sentenced on count 1 to 12 months' imprisonment suspended for two
years and was ordered to pay £2,500 towards the legal aid costs of his
defence; he was acquitted on both counts 2 and 3. They appealed against
conviction on the grounds, inter alia, that the judge misdirected the jury   H
on the mental element involved in the offence of conspiracy to defraud,
on issues of fact, and that the summing up, which occupied six days, was
diffuse and confusing.

On December 12, 1980 Lawton L.J. announced that the convictions
would be quashed and that the court would give their reasons at a later
date.

The facts are stated in the judgment.

A   *John Hazan* Q.C. and *James Goudie* for the appellant Landy.
       John Alliott Q.C. and *Robin Laurie* for the appellant White.
       Richard Du Cann Q.C. and *Henry Grunwald* for the appellant Kaye.
       Allan Green and *Robert Rhodes* for the Crown.

Cur. adv. vult.

B
       January 12. LAWTON L.J. read the following judgment of the court.
These appellants, Harry Landy, Arthur Malcolm White and Charles Kaye,
appeal by leave of this court against their convictions at the Central
Criminal Court on July 25, 1979, after a trial lasting 90 days before
Judge Abdela. All three were convicted on a count charging them with
conspiracy to defraud; Landy and White were also convicted on two counts
C charging them with conspiracy to utter forged documents. Kaye was
acquitted on those counts. Landy was sentenced to five years' imprisonment for the conspiracy to defraud. He was also fined £350,000 for that
offence with a further 12 months' imprisonment in default of payment
and ordered to pay £100,000 towards the legal aid costs of his defence. He
was also sentenced to concurrent terms of three years' imprisonment on
D each of the counts of conspiracy to utter forged documents. White was
sentenced to four years' imprisonment for the conspiracy to defraud and
concurrent terms of three years for the conspiracies to utter forged documents. He was also fined £5,000 on the count charging conspiracy to
defraud and was ordered to pay £2,000 towards the costs of the prosecution. Kaye was sentenced to 12 months' imprisonment suspended for two
years and ordered to pay a contribution of £2,500 towards the legal aid
E costs of his defence.
       On December 12, 1980, we adjudged that the convictions of all three
appellants should be quashed on the ground that the verdicts had been
unsatisfactory. We stated that we would give our reasons later and we
are today doing so.
       The case centred round Landy. He was born in 1911. In 1935 he
F married the daughter of a wealthy man named Williams, who had extensive interests, including one in banking acquired later known as the
Palestine British Bank. Soon after his marriage Landy became involved
in his father-in-law's business interests and by about 1968 he was a director
of 156 companies and had himself become a wealthy man. He became
a managing director of the Palestine British Bank in 1953. This bank
had been founded in Palestine in 1942 and had a London branch. From
G 1962 onwards its premises were on two floors of the Williams National
House in Holborn Viaduct. In 1968 the London branch was incorporated
as the Israel British Bank (London) Ltd. It was a wholly owned subsidiary of the parent bank which was from about 1962 known as Israel
British Bank (Tel Aviv). This bank was managed by another of Williams'
sons-in-law named Bension. We shall refer to the Tel Aviv bank as
H "IBBTA" and the London bank as "IBBL." Until his death in 1971
Williams was chairman of both banks. During the period with which
this case is concerned IBBL was primarily a bankers' bank, that is to
say, most of its business was international and consisted of borrowing
from and lending to other banks but it had a few private depositors,
mostly charities and members of, or connected with, the Williams family
or the Williams' group of companies. Outwardly IBBL was run like any
other secondary bank based in London. It was recognised as an autho-

rised bank and depository by the Bank of England for the purposes of A
the Exchange Control Act 1947. Without this recognition it could not
have carried on its international banking business.

IBBTA was run differently. It had its international banking side but
it dealt in commodities, futures, securities, gold and silver on what was
described later by the liquidator of IBBL as an enormous scale. Indeed
such was the scale of its dealing activities that the Bank of Israel, which B
in that country occupies a position and performs a function akin to that
of the Bank of England, was displeased with what was going on as being
inconsistent with normal banking activities and took steps, seemingly
unsuccessfully, to stop Bension doing what he was doing which was to
do IBBTA's dealings through a group of companies which had been
formed mostly in Liechtenstein from the late 1940's onwards by Williams
or persons connected with him. Two companies, Mobilia and Investment C
and Building Trust (IBT), had been founded by Landy, the first in 1951,
the other in 1962. The beneficiaries of IBT were stated to be Landy and
Williams' four daughters. Why Bension wanted to do IBBTA's dealings
through these Liechtenstein companies was never established. During the
period covered by the indictment, that is from September 30, 1968, to
July 12, 1974, he may have wanted to hide what he was doing from the D
Bank of Israel.

Bension used IBBL as a source of finance for these dealings. He
would borrow money from IBBL, asking that it should be credited to
IBBTA's account with another bank outside the United Kingdom. He
would then use this money for dealing in the name of one of the Liechtenstein companies. IBBL, however, would debit not IBBTA but the Liechtenstein companies of Bension's choice. The full details of Bension's E
dealings and of the profits and losses made have never been discovered.
Attempts by IBBL's liquidator to find out have been unsuccessful. It is
known, however, that substantial profits were made from dealings in gold
and silver through a Liechtenstein company called Denver Finance Establishment. IBBL debited the Liechtenstein companies with the interest
payable on the loans requested by Bension in their names but the liquidator F
was unable to find any evidence that any profits which may have been
obtained from Bension's dealings, and there were probably substantial
ones from some of them, ever reached IBBL, Landy, his wife or any of
the Williams group of companies based in Great Britain. There was a
lot of documentary evidence showing that over many years and particularly
between 1968 and 1974 Landy gave instructions to the so-called trustees
of the Liechtenstein companies, who were little more than registrars. G
These instructions were mostly of a formal kind and were usually given
at Bension's request. Landy never went to Liechtenstein and there was
no evidence that he took an active part in Bension's dealings.

He did, however, know that Bension was managing IBBTA in a way
which met with the disapproval of the Bank of Israel. On January 12, 1969,
Landy had been present at a meeting in Israel which had been attended H
by the Governor of the Bank of Israel, Dr. Heth, who was an examiner
of that bank, Bension and others connected with IBBTA. The Governor
and Dr. Heth made it clear to the two joint managing directors of IBBTA,
who were Landy and Bension, although the latter was the active one,
that the Bank of Israel was disturbed first by the size of the indebtedness
of the Williams group of companies to IBBTA as the security for loans
seemed to be inadequate, secondly by various management deficiencies

A for which Bension carried responsibility, and, thirdly, by auditing deficiencies which had concealed IBBTA's true liquidity position and showed
that bank as being stronger than it was. IBBTA's position was serious.
At the end of 1968 there had been a deficiency of Israeli £ 37,000,000 in
collateral securities. The Williams group of companies owed I£ 28,000,000,
which was covered by no more than a guarantee.

B The Bank of Israel's expressions of disapproval did not curb Bension's
activities nor stop IBBL from providing finance for them. By 1970 IBBTA
required help from the Bank of Israel. A loan of I£ 12,000,000 by that
bank to IBBTA was arranged on terms, the important one for the purposes
of this case being that no credit whatsoever should be given to the Williams
group of companies, which included IBT and Mobilia which Landy had
established, without Dr. Heth's prior authority. This agreement was dis-
C regarded. IBBL continued to finance IBBTA through the Liechtenstein
companies.

In October 1972 the Supreme Court in Israel, when dismissing an
appeal by IBBTA in a civil case (referred to in the evidence as "the
Gutwirth case") had stated that IBBTA was unfit to act as a bank or
trustee. On November 7, 1972, the Governor of the Bank of Israel, accom-
D panied by Dr. Heth, had a meeting with Landy and Bension. At the trial
there was some difference of recollection as to what had been said at this
meeting. The details may not be all that important; but what is clear is
that Landy left the meeting knowing that the Governor disapproved of
Bension and the way he was running IBBTA. On November 15, 1972,
Landy had a private meeting with the Governor. According to Landy
the Governor said that Bension had not acted fraudulently but he had
E gone as far as he could within the law, he was too speculative and needed
restraining. After this conversation Dr. Heth joined them and, according
to his recollection, Landy said the agreement made in December 1970
would be honoured. It was not. The only step which IBBL seems to
have taken to safeguard its position in relation to the advances to the
Liechtenstein companies was to ask IBBTA for guarantees, and letters of
F pledge, in respect of two Liechtenstein companies. They were given. The
guarantees were not in the usual form used by banks and it is probable
that they would not have been enforceable in law. The pledges were
nothing more than pieces of paper. At one stage, one of the Liechtenstein
companies did deposit some securities but they were no longer available
when IBBL's liquidator took over. None of the usual banking inquiries
were made as to what was being pledged and about the supporting titles.

G Even if the guarantees given by IBBTA had been enforceable the
loans made to the Liechtenstein companies exceeded them and were at
a higher level in 1973 than they had been in 1971, $80,000,000 as against
$40,000,000.

Apart from the kind of transaction to which we have referred and
which were the core of the prosecution's case there was evidence of a
H number of banking malpractices. There was an inadequate spread of risk.
Some Liechtenstein companies were debited with large loans without
evidence that they were the borrowers. IBBTA's account was credited
with repayments when those of Liechtenstein companies should have been.
These wrong creditings were no mere bookkeeping errors or even malpractices. They operated, and probably were intended to operate, to
improve IBBTA's appearance of liquidity. IBBL's balance sheet was made
to give a better impression than the true figures did by means of end of

year transfers—the so-called window dressing of accounts. Substantial   A
loans were made or overdrafts allowed to Landy and to members of the
Williams family or Williams companies without interest being charged or
security given. By July 1974 two-thirds of IBBL's sterling advances, nearly
£5,000,000, were to the Williams family or the Williams companies. The
advances were concealed in the accounts on audit dates by temporary
credits. Landy's own indebtedness in July 1974 on an interest-free overdraft was £1,000,000. We do not consider it necessary for the purposes   B
of this judgment to give any more details of these banking irregularities.
In our opinion the trial would have been easier for the judge to conduct
and the issues clearer for the jury if the prosecution had omitted some of
them from their case.

We must, however, refer specifically to one kind of banking transaction
which had irregular features, namely, the discounting of bills of exchange   C
in respect of what purported to be a series of dealings in diamonds. These
dealings were part of the evidence on the conspiracy to defraud count, and
the subject of the conspiracy to utter forged document counts. Landy was
the director of a small Williams company called E. Posen & Co. Export
Ltd. (" Posen "). During 1972, 1973 and the first half of 1974 two Israeli
companies, S. J. Birmback and I. Sussman and Syndiam purported through
Posen to sell diamonds to two Liechtenstein companies, named Nargin and   D
Secmex, which were Williams companies. Bills of exchange were drawn
and discounted by IBBL. No diamonds were sold. The first of the Israeli
companies had gone out of business and the second did not exist. The
invoices which were used for the purposes of getting Bank of England
authorisation for the discounting were forged. All these dealings looked
odd commercially because they were always for about the same weight   E
of diamonds and the amounts of the bills were always much the same,
varying between £48,000 and £42,000. IBBL got little out of these transactions and on occasions waived the discount charges. Between March
and July 1974, 45 bills matured and payment became overdue. Not until
July 10, 1974, was anything done to get payment on these bills. They
were never met. IBBL lost over £2,000,000.

All through 1973 and the first half of 1974 the Bank of Israel became   F
more and more concerned about the way IBBTA was being conducted.
On July 9, 1974, with the consent of the Israeli Government, they seized
it, whatever that may mean in Israeli law. This put IBBL in difficulty.
On July 11, 1974, IBBL suspended all payments. Various investigations
were carried out. In August 1974 IBBL presented its own petition for
winding up. The official receiver was appointed provisional liquidator   G
and partners in Messrs. Price Waterhouse & Co. were appointed special
managers. On December 2, 1974, a compulsory winding up order was
made and in January 1975 joint liquidators were appointed from the same
firm of accountants.

When IBBL stopped payments it owed £37,100,000 to 85 banks,
£4,000,000 to members of the Williams family and to companies in the   H
Williams group, and £1,800,000 to other depositors. It was owed
£31,000,000 by four Liechtenstein companies and one Swiss company,
£2,000,000 on bills of exchange discounted by Posen and £5,000,000 by
members of the Williams family and companies in the Williams group.
Most of these debts were thought to have, and indeed proved to have,
little value. The deficit in July 1974 was about £38,000,000; but since
then considerable sums have been obtained from Landy and the Williams'

A   interests. All small depositors and charities have been repaid in full. The larger creditors are likely to be paid a dividend of about 40p in the £.

    Landy, White and Kaye were arrested in April 1977. After committal proceedings which lasted 31 days, the appellants were committed for trial at the Central Criminal Court together with one Peter Lynn, who had been a partner in IBBL's auditors and who was acquitted on the indict-

B ment, and one Joseph Bloomberg who died before the trial started on March 1, 1979.

    Before the trial started there was a pre-trial review before Judge Abdela. A full scale review was certainly needed. However it was only a day or two before the review that the judge was provided with the papers, which were massive, and a copy of the opening speech of leading counsel before the committing justices. The review produced no worth-

C while result. This was not the fault of the judge. He could not be expected to master this complicated case in the time available to him. Had he been able to do so we have no doubt that he would have done some extensive pruning. That should be an important object of a pre-trial review in cases of this kind. Prosecuting counsel who have been immersed in the details of a case for months sometimes do not appreciate the diffi-

D culty which a judge and a jury may have in assimilating the evidence. At the pre-trial review the judge (and he should normally be the one who is going to try the case) should be ready and willing to take the initiative to ensure that all unnecessary detail is omitted. This he cannot do unless he is given the papers well before the review hearing and has time to read and analyse them. If he is not he may think it right to postpone the review. We are sure that a robust pre-trial review in this case would

E have resulted in a shorter and more satisfactory trial.

    The particulars set out under count 1 of the indictment were as follows:

    " Harry Landy, Arthur Malcolm White, Charles Kaye, Joseph Bloomberg and Peter Lynn on divers days between September 30, 1968, and July 12, 1974, conspired together and with the late Walter Nathan Williams, Joshua Bension and the late Isaac Cohen [an officer of
F   IBBTA] to defraud such corporations, companies, partnerships, firms and persons as might lend funds to or deposit funds with Israel British Bank (London) Ltd. by falsely representing that the business of Israel British Bank (London) Ltd. was being conducted in an honest and proper manner, by knowingly employing such funds to the prejudice of the said lenders and depositors and contrary to the best interests
G   of the Israel British Bank (London) Ltd., by fraudulently concealing that the said funds were being so supplied, and by divers other false and fraudulent devices."

    Mr. Alan Green, on behalf of the prosecution, told us that he drafted this indictment with that used in *Reg.* v. *Sinclair* [1968] 1 W.L.R. 1246 in mind. It is a form which is commonly used, particularly at the Central
H Criminal Court. In simple cases it may be adequate but in a complicated case it is not because it lacks particularity. There was nothing to show how the false representations were made or how the funds were employed to the prejudice of IBBL and its customers or what was the nature of the concealment. Junior counsel for Landy asked for particulars at the beginning of the committal proceedings, the committal charge being the same as count 1 of the indictment. He was told that he would get all the information he needed from leading counsel's opening speech. Attempts to

get particulars at later stages of the case were met with the same answer. A
We were told by counsel that this is the answer almost always given by
prosecuting counsel. In our judgment particulars should have been given
and for these reasons: first, to enable the defendants and the trial judge
to know precisely and on the face of the indictment itself the nature of
the prosecution's case, and secondly, to stop the prosecution shifting their
ground during the course of the case without the leave of the trial judge
and the making of an amendment. The words "and by divers other false B
and fraudulent devices" are a relic of the past and should never again
appear in an indictment. In criticising the form of indictment used in
this case, we should not be taken to be adjudging that particulars of conspiracies to defraud should be set out in the same kind of detail as would
be required in a statement of claim in an action for damages for conspiracy
to defraud. What is wanted is conciseness and clarity.   C
    In our opinion the particulars of the count charging conspiracy to
defraud should have been in some such terms as these:

Particulars of Offence

> Harry Landy, Arthur Malcolm White, Charles Kaye and Peter Lynn
> on divers days between the 30th day of September 1968 and the 12th D
> day of July 1974 conspired together and with the late Walter Nathan
> Williams, Joshua Bension and the late Isaac Cohen to defraud such
> corporations, companies, partnerships, firms and persons as might
> lend funds to or deposit funds with Israel British Bank (London)
> Ltd. ("the bank") by dishonestly
>
> (i) causing and permitting the bank to make excessive advances
> to insubstantial and speculative trading companies incor- E
> porated in Liechtenstein and Switzerland, such advances being
> inadequately secured, inadequately guaranteed and without
> proper provision for payment of interest
>
> (ii) causing and permitting the bank to make excessive advances
> to its parent company in Tel Aviv, such advances being
> inadequately secured, inadequately guaranteed and without F
> proper provision for payment of interest
>
> (iii) causing and permitting the bank to make excessive advances
> to individuals and companies connected with the said Walter
> Nathan Williams and his family, such advances being inade-
> quately secured, inadequately guaranteed and without proper
> provision for payment of interest
>
> (iv) causing and permitting the bank's accounts and Bank of G
> England returns to be prepared in such a way as (a) to con-
> ceal the nature, constitution and extent of the bank's lending
> and (b) to show a false and misleading financial situation as
> at the ends of the bank's accounting years
>
> (v) causing and permitting the bank to discount commercial bills
> when (a) there was no underlying commercial transaction (b)
> the documents evidencing the supposed underlying transac- H
> tions were false and (c) the transactions were effected in order
> to transfer funds to the bank's parent company in Tel Aviv.

Such particulars would have avoided such terms as "falsely representing"
and "to the prejudice" which are imprecise and likely to confuse juries
and would have made everyone aware of what the prosecution were
alleging.

A   The first 73 days of the trial were taken up with prosecuting counsel's opening speech, submission and evidence. The last days of winter passed into high summer. By the beginning of July the jury must have had the evidence well in mind. What they wanted at that stage of the case was a clear and concise summary of what each party was putting forward. What they got was 11 days of counsels' speeches followed by six days of
B   summing up. Prosecuting counsel's speech went on for four days, the speeches of defending counsel taking up seven days. We have no reason for thinking that counsel were unduly prolix by the standards of present day forensic fashion. The fault lies partly in the fashion, but also in the present tendency to overload cases. The great advocates of the past did not find it necessary to address juries at such great length. We can see no good reason for such prolixity nowadays. If the object of a closing speech
C   is to ensure that the jury keep in mind when considering their verdict the points which counsel wish to bring out, they are unlikely to do so if, as in the case of Mr. Green's speech on behalf of the prosecution, they heard it three weeks before.

The case which the judge had to sum up came to this. For some six years, IBBL siphoned money to IBBTA which was used by Bension for
D   speculative dealings through the Williams' Liechtenstein companies. In the case of the Posen transactions there was not even speculation, just fraud. The inference was that Bension was behaving as he did partly for his own benefit and partly for that of the Williams' interests, which included Landy's. In order to effect the siphoning various banking malpractices were used, together with much concealment of what was going on. The prosecution submitted that all three appellants must have known
E   what was going on and were actively engaged first in ensuring that money did go to IBBTA for what they must have known were purposes which put at risk IBBL's customers, and secondly in concealing what was happening. Landy was in charge of IBBL. From 1971 he had been the chairman of both IBBTA and IBBL. During the period covered by the indictment, and at a time when he knew of the disquiet felt by the Bank
F   of Israel about the way Bension was behaving and managing IBBTA's business, he attended board meetings in Tel Aviv. He took no effective steps to ensure that IBBTA performed the agreement made with the Bank of Israel in December 1970 and connived at its breach. He knew that some of IBBL's staff were disturbed about the irregularities and that one of them, an accountant named Coxall, disapproved so strongly at what was going on that he resigned his appointment as from December 31, 1972.
G   Further Landy took advantage of his position to get an interest-free and unsecured overdraft from IBBL of about £1,000,000.

The case against White was of the same general kind as that against Landy but was not as strong. He had joined the London branch of IBBL in 1964. He was then 32. He had had several years of experience of merchant banking in London behind him. He became a director of
H   IBBTA in 1967 and of IBBL in 1968 when it was incorporated. He did not attend board meetings in Tel Aviv. He was in charge of IBBL's foreign exchange department and in that capacity he gave instructions relating to the raising of the finance which was debited to the Liechtenstein companies but went to IBBTA. His department was also concerned with discounting bills of exchange. He knew that some members of IBBL's staff, in particular Coxall, were disturbed about the banking irregularities and accounting malpractices which were going on but continued to allow

them to do so. The prosecution submitted that he was willing to further A the fraudulent aims of both Landy and Bension because they had made it worthwhile for him to do so. Besides his salary, which in 1974 was £12,000 per annum, he had been given various facilities, including one for share dealing in Tel Aviv and a Swiss Bank account into which IBBTA paid between £90,000 and £100,000 as commission based on IBBL's net profits and a percentage of all funds remitted to IBBTA from IBBL including the money which was debited to the Liechtenstein accounts. B

The prosecution's case against Kaye was much the same in nature as that against White but he was lower down the executive ladder in IBBL. He had started his working career as a clerk. After war service he got a job as a book-keeper and cashier with the London branch of the Palestine British Bank. He was made a director of IBBL in July 1970 and by 1974 was earning about £5,200 per annum. At all material times he was in C charge of IBBL's general banking business. In that capacity he knew what was being lent to the Williams family interests and that the Posen bills were being discounted. Although he had no professional qualifications as an accountant, after Coxall's resignation in December 1972 he became IBBL's chief accountant and in that capacity signed Bank of England "returns of foreign currency positions" which inaccurately described the advances to the Liechtenstein companies as "deposits with and D advances to banks abroad." Coxall, who was Kaye's predecessor as chief accountant, had refused to sign returns in this form and his concern over this deception of the Bank of England had been one of the reasons for his resigning his position with IBBL. Kaye knew of the irregularities and malpractices which had caused Coxall to be disturbed and to resign but he was prepared to go on helping Landy to manage IBBL in a way E which led to the closing of the bank. One of the strongest pieces of evidence against Kaye was his own admission when giving evidence about a "window dressing operation" to which he was a party that it could be considered dishonest and disgraceful conduct on the part of an authorised bank. A little earlier he had said that "window dressing" was "certainly unethical and technically improper."

Landy's defence can be summed up in a short phrase. He claimed to F have been honest but careless. He said that at the material times he was a very wealthy man, which was true. He trusted Bension, who was his brother-in-law, and had no reason not to do so. The Bank of Israel had had its suspicions about Bension's behaviour as a banker but had not suggested before July 1974 that he should be stopped operating as such. Further it had had far better opportunities than he had had to learn G what was going on because from 1973 onwards it had had its officers supervising inside IBBTA. Neither he nor the Williams' interests in the United Kingdom had made anything out of Bension's dealings. There had been no risk for IBBL in making unsecured loans to either him or the Williams' interests because all the borrowers were well able to repay and after the crash did so. Landy claimed that he had given little of his H time to the affairs of either IBBTA or IBBL. He had many other interests, both business and charitable, which occupied most of his working hours. He knew little about banking being by training and experience a dealer in property.

White's defence was that he had been honest, loyal and over-trusting. Although he was a director of IBBTA he knew little about what was going on in Tel Aviv. Whenever queries arose about the regularity of transactions

A   between IBBL and IBBTA he had spoken to Landy and had accepted whatever he had been told. He had had no concern with the preparation of the yearly accounts and balance sheets and only signed them after Landy had agreed them with the auditors.

Kaye's defence was much the same. He was able to say, with truth, that he knew far less than White about what was going on. Unlike White he received nothing more than his salary which was modest.

B

All three defences can be described as " confessions and avoidance." Few of the primary facts were in issue: the documents spoke for themselves. What was in issue was the honesty of the three defendants. There could be no doubt that all three defendants, particularly Landy, had failed lamentably to perform their duties as directors with the result that IBBL had crashed. Had they been sued in misfeasance proceedings it is

C   probable, indeed almost certain, that judgment would have been given against them. Misfeasance, however, is not necessarily dishonesty; but may be evidence from which dishonesty can be inferred.

What the prosecution had to prove was a conspiracy to defraud which is an agreement dishonestly to do something which will or may cause loss or prejudice to another. The offence is one of dishonesty. This is the

D   all important ingredient which must be stressed by the judge in his directions to the jury and must not be minimised in any way. There is always a danger that a jury may think that proof of an irregularity followed by loss is proof of dishonesty. The dishonesty to be proved must be in the minds and intentions of the defendants. It is to their states of mind that the jury must direct their attention. What the reasonable man or the

E   jurors themselves would have believed or intended in the circumstances in which the defendants found themselves is not what the jury have to decide; but what a reasonable man or they themselves would have believed or intended in similar circumstances may help them to decide what in fact individual defendants believed or intended. An assertion by a defendant that throughout a transaction he acted honestly does not have to be accepted but has to be weighed like any other piece of evidence. If that

F   was the defendant's state of mind, or may have been, he is entitled to be acquitted. But if the jury, applying their own notions of what is honest and what is not, conclude that he could not have believed that he was acting honestly, then the element of dishonesty will have been established. What a jury must not do is to say to themselves: " If we had been in his place we would have known we were acting dishonestly so he must have known he was." What they can say is: " We are sure he was acting

G   dishonestly because we can see no reason why a man of his intelligence and experience would not have appreciated, as right minded people would have done, that what he was doing was dishonest." In our judgment this is the way Reg. v. Feely [1973] Q.B. 530 should be applied in cases where the issue of dishonesty arises. It is also the way in which the jury should have been directed in this case but, unfortunately, they were not.

H   There were three basic defects in the summing up: first, the trial judge failed to direct the jury clearly that they have to be sure that each of the defendants had agreed dishonestly to act in the way the prosecution alleged; secondly, on occasions he treated inferences from the evidence as if they were rules of law; and, thirdly, the summing up was so diffuse that it was likely to confuse the jury. As the prosecution accepted in this court that the summing up was seriously defective, and contested the appeal largely on the question whether the proviso to section 2 (1) of the Criminal

Appeal Act 1968 should be applied, it is unnecessary to set out in detail **A**
the passages in the summing up about which complaint has been made
on behalf of the appellants. A few examples will suffice. Early in his
summing up the judge said:

> " . . . I think it is only right that I should try and help you if I can
> in relation to the approach that I invite you to make about the words
> ' to defraud ' and ' prejudice,' because to defraud is in fact to act to **B**
> the prejudice of another's right. If anyone may be prejudiced in any
> way by the fraud that is enough to constitute the intent to defraud.
> If anyone may be prejudiced and it is important to remember this:
> that an intent to risk possible injury to another's right is sufficient
> intent to prejudice . . ."

More followed on the same lines. By this direction dishonesty was **C**
taken out of the concept of defrauding and that which could be evidence
of defrauding, as by acting to the prejudice of another's right, was treated
as if it *constituted* (the judge's word) an intent to defraud. Prosecuting
counsel understandably was concerned about this direction. The next
day, when the court sat, and in the absence of the jury, he invited the
judge's attention to *Reg.* v. *Sinclair* [1968] 1 W.L.R. 1246 and the
approval by this court in that case of the trial judge's use of the words **D**
" deliberate dishonesty." Judge Abdela seemed somewhat reluctant to
accept what was being suggested to him. He concluded this interruption
by saying: " Very well, and I will certainly deal with it in the appropriate
time." He went on with his summing up all that day. The next day,
which was now two days after he gave what was clearly a misdirection
in law to the jury, he said this: **E**

> " I am indebted to learned counsel, who have pointed out to me that
> a part of my direction to you at the outset of this case may have led
> you to apply probably an unsatisfactory test of the defendants' state
> of mind when considering whether or not their conduct, or the con-
> duct of any one of them, was dishonest. Let me make it clear. To
> prove fraud it must be established that the conduct was deliberately **F**
> dishonest."

The words " may have led you to apply probably an unsatisfactory test "
were inapt to describe what had happened. He had directed the jury to
apply a wrong test and should have said so specifically and have gone on
there and then in clear terms which would have been incapable of being
misunderstood to direct them what the law was: see *Reg.* v. *Moon* **G**
[1969] 1 W.L.R. 1705. What he did do was to continue as follows:

> " Now what sort of test should be applied as to whether the conduct
> was dishonest? It is fraud if it is proved that there was a taking of
> a risk which there was no right to take, which would cause detriment
> or prejudice, and you will ask and inquire: have the prosecution
> proved and established that? Because the test of dishonesty is what **H**
> we call a subjective one, that is to say, it is a question of the state
> of mind of the accused person."

What the judge was doing was making the same mistake as he had made
earlier in his summing up, treating evidence from which fraud could be
inferred as if it were proof of fraud; and he made his direction more
confusing by tacking on to the end of it a reference to a subjective test,

A which may have been a new and strange concept for many, probably most, of the jurors and which had no connection with what he had just said to them. At the very end of his summing up, in what he intended to be a helpful summary of the issues, he once again left the jury with the impression that they could find each of the appellants guilty on the first count if they had taken a risk with the assets of IBBL, in a manner

B which they knew to be contrary to the best interest of that bank and to the prejudice of lenders or depositors and the jury thought that such conduct was dishonest.

During this long summing up the jury were never told in clear and precise terms that they had to be sure that each of the appellants had agreed to act dishonestly. The complaint about the diffuseness of the summing up arises from its length, the lack of an obvious structure and

C the judge's propensity to instruct the jury on the law relating to peripheral matters such as the duties of directors and the recording in accounts of loans to directors. A summing up should be clear, concise and intelligible. If it is overloaded with detail, whether of fact or law and follows no obvious plan, it will not have any of the attributes it should have. This summing up suffered from the fact that the judge was over conscientious.

D He seems to have decided that the jury should be reminded of nearly all the details of the evidence and directed as to every facet of the law which applied. He must have spent hours preparing his summing up but in the end he got lost in the trees and missed the wood.

We turn to the directions given by the judge on the two counts charging conspiracy to utter forged documents—the Posen counts. There was much overlap between these counts and that charging conspiracy to

E defraud. The Posen transactions were part of the means by which Bension got money from London to Tel Aviv. We doubt whether any useful purpose was served by adding the Posen counts to the indictment. On their face there was nothing to show whom the alleged conspirators intended to defraud. The prosecution's case based on *Welham* v. *Director of Public Prosecutions* [1961] A.C. 103 was that the intention was to

F defraud the Bank of England by inducing that body to give permission for the remission of funds to Israel by producing forged invoices as evidence of genuine commercial transactions. If there were a conspiracy it could also have been to defraud IBBL. When the judge started his summing up on these counts, he seems to have thought that the conspiracy alleged was one to defraud IBBL and directed the jury accordingly. At the end of the day, and in the absence of the jury, Mr. Green on behalf

G of the prosecution pointed out that the prosecution were alleging an intent to defraud the Bank of England. The next day the judge invited the jury's attention to the limited way in which the prosecution had put their case. The judge gave a new direction but it fell somewhat short of what this court in *Reg.* v. *Moon* [1969] 1 W.L.R. 1705 said should be done when a judge has to make a correction but in other respects it was satis-

H factory. Had this part of the summing up stood by itself we should have upheld the convictions of Landy and White on these two counts. They were, however, not much more than part of the prosecution's case on count 1. The judge himself referred to " a considerable amount of overlap." It follows, in our judgment, that the defects in the summing up on count 1 were bound to spill over on to the Posen counts so as to make convictions on those counts unsatisfactory if that on count 1 was adjudged unsatisfactory.

Most of the argument in this court was directed to the application of A
the proviso to section 2 (1) of the Criminal Appeal Act 1968. Mr. Green
took us through the evidence in detail and invited us to adjudge, following
the dictum of Viscount Dilhorne in *Stafford* v. *Director of Public Prosecutions* [1974] A.C. 878, 893 that if the jury had been properly directed
it would inevitably have come to the same conclusion. Mr. Hazan, on
behalf of Landy, submitted that when there has been a fundamental misdirection, as he said there had been in this case, the proviso should never   B
be applied. We do not intend in this judgment to express any opinion as
to when the proviso can be applied and when it cannot. We are concerned
with the facts of this case and nothing more. The appellants were entitled
to a fair trial. Nowadays that means that they were entitled to have the
jury clearly and correctly directed as to the law to be applied and to have
all defences fairly open to them put to the jury. In this case, for the   C
reasons we have stated, the jury were not directed correctly or clearly as
to the law, and this was not on a minor matter but on the issue which
went to the heart of the case, namely, what was meant by " defraud."
Because of this, each of the defendants lost his chance of having his
defence (honest but careless) fairly put to the jury. It follows that two
essentials of a fair trial were missing. In such circumstances the verdicts
must be unsatisfactory and if they are, it cannot be said that no mis-   D
carriage of justice has actually occurred.

It was for these reasons that we allowed the appeals and quashed the
convictions.

Appeals allowed.
Convictions quashed.   E

Solicitors: *D. J. Freeman & Co.; Harold Stern & Co.; Whitelock
& Storr; Director of Public Prosecutions.*

L. N. W.

1 W.L.R.

A

[COURT OF APPEAL]

* BEARD v. BEARD

1980   Nov. 5   Cumming-Bruce, Dunn and Griffiths L.JJ.

B

*Minor — Custody — Interim order — Mother having custody of
children sole tenant of council house—Breakdown of mother's
health—Father moving into house at mother's request to look
after children—Application by father for interim care and
control and for injunction to exclude mother from house—
Court's jurisdiction in emergency situation to interfere with
tenant's right of occupation*

C

Four children, whose parents were divorced, lived with
their mother in a council house of which she was sole tenant.
Following a breakdown of the mother's health, their father
moved into the house to look after the children at the
mother's request while she received treatment in hospital.
The mother returned home for a short time before returning
to hospital again for further treatment, but eventually she discharged herself. On an application to the High Court by the
father to restrain the mother from entering the house, the
judge, dealing only with the emergency in the children's lives
arising from the mother's breakdown of health, made interim
orders in favour of the father for care and control of the
children and for the injunction sought.

On appeal by the mother : —

E

Held, dismissing the appeal, that for the purpose of protecting the children of a family in an emergency, the court
had power to make an order for interim care and control of
the children if no suitable person was presently in care and
control of them, and also to order that the person to whom
it confided their interim care and control should have the
right to enter a council house in which they lived, whether
or not the tenant agreed, and stay there for the period of
the emergency, unless the local authority took steps to intervene on the ground that its rights as landlord had been
infringed; that, consequential upon that order, the court had
power to make an order preventing the tenant from returning
to the house if it was necessary to do so in order to avoid
putting the children temporarily at risk, and, accordingly,
the judge's order, made for the temporary protection of the
children during an emergency, was correct.

F

G

No cases are referred to in the judgment or were cited in argument.

APPEAL from Judge Monier-Williams sitting as a judge of the Family
Division.

In 1979, the parents of four children were divorced and on September
26, 1980, Judge Monier-Williams, sitting as a High Court judge, in
chambers, made an order that the children of the family should remain
in the interim care and control of the father, and an order that the mother
be restrained until December 26, 1980, or the hearing of the father's
summons for custody of the children from molesting or interfering with
the father and the children of the family, and entering or attempting to
enter the house where the children lived without the leave of the court
or the prior authority from the father or his solicitors.

H

The mother appealed on the grounds that the judge misdirected him- A
self in holding (1) that he had jurisdiction to make an order restraining
the mother from returning to the house where the children lived after the
decree absolute, the house being a council house in the sole name of
the mother which had been acquired by her after the breakdown of the
marriage and in which the parties had never lived together as man
and wife; and (2) that he had jurisdiction to make an order affecting the
rights of occupation of a council house in the absence of any notice to B
the local authority, or any evidence from the local authority as to their
practice and as to their intentions in the case; that the judge failed
properly to take account of the evidence; and that the judgment was
against the weight of the evidence.

The facts are stated in the judgment of Cumming-Bruce L.J.

C

Robert Sich for the mother.
J. C. J. Tatham for the father.

CUMMING-BRUCE L.J. This is an appeal by a mother against the order
of Judge Monier-Williams when on September 26, 1980, it was ordered
that, upon the respondent father undertaking to file a summons for D
custody, the children of the family should remain in the care and control
of the respondent father; the petitioner mother be restrained from returning to the house where the children lived; there was to be reasonable
access; there should be a court welfare report; the injunction was to
remain in force until December 26, or the hearing of the application for
custody, whichever was to be the sooner; an existing supervision order was
to continue in force; and the petitioner's application that the respondent E
leave the house and that he should not enter the property or interfere
with the petitioner's occupation should be dismissed.

In the circumstances that have arisen it is unnecessary to explain the
facts, save in the barest details. As custody proceedings are on foot and it
is hoped to resolve them in a matter of weeks, the less that is said in this
court about the merits of the respective cases for custody, care and control F
the better.

The parties were married in January 1964. They are now 36 and 31.
There are now four children. The eldest boy was born in March 1964
and the next son was born in 1965; then there is a boy born in 1970 and
the youngest son was born in 1974. Proceedings for the dissolution of the
marriage, which had been unhappy for some time, began in September G
1975. An order was made then excluding the husband from the then
matrimonial home, which, we are told, was a council house. The judge
found that from that time onwards the marriage was effectively at an
end and the parties have not since lived together as husband and wife.
Eventually the marriage was dissolved. The decree absolute was in
October 1979 and after contested proceedings the mother was granted
custody, care and control of all four children. About three years ago H
the mother moved into another council house, of which she is the sole
tenant. Of course she moved into that house with the children. That
has been the children's home ever since.

It appears from the findings of the judge, who made an interim order
for care and control in favour of the father, that in the summer of 1979 a
crisis arose in the children's lives flowing from a combination of two
main factors. The mother had a major breakdown of health and had to

A resort to hospital treatment as an in-patient, leaving the children high and
dry unless she made some other arrangements for their care, which she very
properly did by inviting her former husband to come into her house and
look after the children during her temporary absence. There was another
factor which the judge dwelt on in his judgment, that the mother had
made friends with a young man whom she brought to live with her. The
B two elder boys did not get on with that young gentleman and there were
alleged to have been features of the young gentleman's behaviour which
gave rise to anxiety. The mother decided to give up the treatment being
advised and she came back home and there was a short period when the
mother and the father were living with the children under the same roof.
On August 27 there was some trouble which the judge referred to, and
the mother went to hospital again but discharged herself. She had not
C before the judge's decision been back to live in the home.

The judge heard evidence and considered a welfare report of a kind
on the subject of who should look after the children on an interim basis,
having regard to the emergency that had arisen as a result of the mother's
apparent two successive breakdowns in health. It is perfectly clear from the
judge's judgment that—and he says it in terms—all that he was deciding on
D September 26 was what to do for the children in the emergency that had
arisen. He decided that it was not practicable for him to attempt to reopen
the custody proceedings proper, if only because there was no such application at that time. The father gave an undertaking to issue a summons for
variation of the existing custody order. The judge gave directions—it is
clear from his order—for a welfare report and evidently contemplated that
the custody proceedings would come on in December, so that he was
E focusing his attention on the practical arrangements for the care of the
children during the period that would elapse between September 26 and
the determination of the custody proceedings, which, with any luck, it was
anticipated would come on in December. That was all that the judge
expressly was dealing with and he came to the conclusion that he was
quite clear that during that tiding-over period until the custody proceedings
F could be launched and heard the father ought to look after the children.

I may say that meanwhile the mother is living in accommodation provided for her by her employers at her place of employment which, we are
told, is a caravan which is manifestly—unless it is a very exceptional caravan—not an ideal kind of accommodation as the winter approaches. She
would like to come home of course.

Mr. Sich has exercised characteristic judgment in the way in which he
G has handled this appeal. Having had a chance of reading the judge's very
clear and emphatic findings of fact on the material then before him, Mr.
Sich rightly did not seek any longer to challenge in this court the judge's
decision that the interim care and control of the children should be confided to the father. That is the basis on which we now approach the appeal.
The other grounds of appeal raised questions that might, if it was necessary
H to grapple with them, give rise to some rather interesting and nice questions
in relation to the power of the court under the Matrimonial Causes Act
1973 to intervene and interfere with the common law rights of the mother
as tenant of a local authority and entitled thereby to occupation of her
home.

The question of jurisdiction was canvassed before the judge. His
approach was to exercise his powers under the Matrimonial Causes Act
1973 on an emergency basis for the protection of the children in the

emergency that had arisen. In his findings of fact he explained what the A
emergency was and it is unnecessary for me to repeat it, save to say that
it is not challenged in this court that there was an emergency in the lives of
the children so that the judge had to deal with it. What the judge decided
to do was, having regard to his powers conferred under the Matrimonial
Causes Act 1973 in relation to custody, care and control and protection
of children, to make an order that the person to whom he confided interim
care and control of the children should remain in the house which was the B
children's home in the absence of the mother because of the background
history which showed quite clearly that it was no longer feasible for the
former husband and the former wife to attempt to live together in amity
in the house. That it was not practicable is demonstrated by the fact
that the mother, on seeking to return to her home, has not, I think,
suggested on a long term basis that it would be sensible for her former C
husband to be there too.

The judge heard a discussion in argument of cases which discussed the
problems of transfer of property and considered also some obiter dicta
in cases which did not actually have to decide the extent of the jurisdiction
of the court when it is called upon to interfere with the exercise of common
law rights in order to exercise appropriately the power conferred for the D
protection and care of children in the Matrimonial Causes Act 1973. It
may be that after the custody proceedings have been concluded—one hopes
in December—that some of those problems may arise. It is perfectly possible that they will not arise at all. There are all kinds of permutations and
combinations. The mother may find that she is restored to the care and
control of the children. Alternatively the father may find that the interim
order for care and control made in September is translated into an order E
that he, for the immediately forseeable period, is to be the custodian of the
children with care and control. As the children are living in their mother's
council house the local authority is closely involved and if there is a
transfer of custody from mother to father it may very well be that it will
be necessary for the parties to approach the local authority and invite the
local authority to make up their minds whether to make any change in the F
present allocation of council tenancy to the mother or not. What they will
do it is pointless to speculate. The situation may not arise at all. But it
may arise and the experience of courts has been that these problems,
where children are living in council property, can only be satisfactorily
resolved by means of close co-operation between the courts exercising the
jurisdiction under the Matrimonial Causes Act 1973 and the local authority with a responsibility for housing the grown-up and the children. G
All those matters may fall for argument and decision after the custody
proceedings have been decided. They are wholly hypothetical at the
moment.

Mr. Sich has expressed an anxiety that the judge in his judgment
expressed himself in terms that might be interpreted by another judge as
suggesting that the judge had formed a view about the jurisdiction of the H
court to interfere with the common law rights of the mother other than on
an emergency basis to deal with an emergency situation facing the children.
Having read the way in which the judge expressed himself, I find no reason
for sharing Mr. Sich's apprehension, but I have such confidence in Mr.
Sich's judgment that, if there really was absolutely no ground for apprehension, I would not expect him to have any anxiety at all and so I respect
the fact that he has announced an anxiety. The passage in the judgment

A   that matters is: " The point is that I have to consider an emergency situation." That sentence follows a passage in which the judge expressly shows that he is not looking beyond the present emergency and its resolution in the custody proceedings which will take place in or about December.   All that I say is this, for the removal of doubt: nothing in my judgment is to be interpreted as throwing any light at all upon the question whether in any situation other than the emergency considered by

B   the judge the court has jurisdiction to intervene for the protection of the children by making the orders that the judge made. In connection with those orders I state the following propositions.   If children of a family are in an emergency which requires action on the part of the court for their protection, the court has power to decide whether, if there is no suitable person presently in care and control under an order of the court,

C   to make an order for care and control of the children to protect them during the emergency. If, as on the facts in the instant case, the children's home is the home in which they have lived for some years which it would be quite wrong to disturb on an interim basis, then, when the judge has made an order deciding who is the grown-up who should on an interim basis come into the children's lives to exercise care and control in the

D   emergency, the court has power to order, for the protection of the children, that the person selected as the person appropriate for interim care and control shall have the right, on the order of the court, to enter the children's house—the house where the children are living—whether the council tenant agrees or not, and the court has jurisdiction for the period of the emergency to order that the interim custodian shall stay in the council house unless the local authority takes steps to intervene on the ground that

E   the landlord's rights have been infringed, which appears to me an extremely outside chance. Consequential upon such an order for the protection of children during the continuance of the emergency, the court has power to order the tenant not to return to the house in which she is a tenant if the court takes the view, as the judge decided in this case, that her presence in the home would put the children temporarily at risk.

E   For those reasons I would affirm the judge's order and dismiss this appeal, having made it perfectly clear that this court, like the judge, has only been considering the temporary protection of the children during the continuance of an emergency situation.

    DUNN L.J.   I agree.

G   GRIFFITHS L.J.   I agree.

Appeal dismissed.
No order as to costs save legal
aid taxation.

H   Solicitors: *Berry & Berry, Tunbridge Wells; Cripps, Harries, Hall & Co., Tunbridge Wells.*

B. O. A.

A

[QUEEN'S BENCH DIVISION]

* REGINA v. SOUTHAMPTON JUSTICES, Ex parte DAVIES (NEIL)

1980 Nov. 4; 7   Donaldson L.J. and Forbes J.

B

Justices—Committal warrant—Non-payment of fines—Applicant in arrears—Justices' order fixing term of imprisonment for each fine—Warrant issued to total of periods fixed—Period in excess of period applicable to total amount of fines—Validity of warrant—Magistrates' Courts Act 1952 (15 & 16 Geo. 6 & 1 Eliz. 2, c. 55), ss. 64 (1) (3), 65 (2), Sch. 3, para. 1 (as amended by Criminal Law Act 1977 (c. 45), s. 59)

C
The justices ordered the applicant to pay £232·63 in fines, costs and compensation in June 1979. In January 1980, he appeared again before the justices and was convicted of seven motoring offences and fined a total of £245. By February a substantial part of the fines still remained unpaid and a means inquiry was held. The justices, pursuant to sections 64 and 65 of the Magistrates' Courts Act 1952,[1] fixed the period of imprisonment for each fine outstanding under the January order, which in each case complied with the period prescribed by the table in paragraph 1 of Schedule 3 to the Magistrates' D Courts Act 1952 and made a committal order suspended on payment of £15 a week. By September, when the applicant defaulted, he had paid off the total amount under the June order and £81·37 of the January order. By calculating the number of days fixed for each fine still unpaid, the warrant was issued for a period of 59 days and the applicant was committed to prison for that period. E

On an application for judicial review and the remedy of an order of certiorari to quash the order on the ground that the justices had acted in excess of jurisdiction: —

Held, granting the order of certiorari, that where one warrant was issued for non-payment of a number of fines, the period could not exceed the maximum for the total amount of the fines outstanding; that, accordingly, since the total outstanding did not exceed £200, the maximum period in F accordance with section 64 (1) and the table in paragraph 1 of Schedule 3 to the Act of 1952 could not exceed 30 days and, therefore, the order would be quashed and an order for a period of 30 days would be substituted.

The following case is referred to in the judgment of Forbes J.:

Reg. v. *Metropolitan Stipendiary Magistrate for South Westminster, Ex* G *parte Green* [1977] 1 All E.R. 353, D.C.

The following additional case was cited in argument:

Reg. v. *Clerkenwell Stipendiary Magistrate, Ex parte Mays* [1975] 1 W.L.R. 52; [1975] 1 All E.R. 65, D.C.

H
APPLICATION for judicial review.

The applicant, Neil Osborne Davies, applied for a judicial review of an order made by the Southampton Magistrates Court on October 8, 1980, that the applicant, in default of payment of fines imposed by the court on January 21, 1980, should be committed to prison for a period

---

[1] Magistrates' Courts Act 1952, s. 64 (1) (3): see post, pp. 377H—378A.
  Sch. 3, para. 1: see post, p. 376C–D.

A of 59 days; and the remedy of an order of certiorari to quash the order.
The grounds upon which the application was made were that the order
was made in excess of the jurisdiction afforded by the provisions of
section 64 of and Schedule 3 to the Magistrates' Courts Act 1952; that
the order was wrong in law; and that the order was contrary to established principles of justice.

B   The facts are stated in the judgment of Forbes J.

   Peter Towler for the applicant.
   The respondent did not appear and was not represented.

                                                Cur. adv. vult.

C   November 7. FORBES J. read the following judgment. In this case
Mr. Towler moves on behalf of the applicant to bring up and quash an
order of the Southampton justices committing him to prison for 59 days.
The case raises a novel point about justices' powers to impose terms
of imprisonment for non-payment of fines.
       The facts are these. On June 20, 1979, the applicant appeared before
D the Southampton justices and was ordered to pay a total of £232·63 in
respect of a fine, costs and compensation. On January 22, 1980, he
appeared before the same justices in respect of a number of motoring
offences. He was convicted of them and sentenced as follows: (1)
driving without insurance—£60; (2) using a vehicle with a defective
tyre—£25; (3) driving without due care and attention—£60; (4) driving
without "L" plates—£15; (5) driving unsupervised—£25; (6) using a
E vehicle with defective brakes—£25; (7) using a vehicle with a defective
tyre—£25. In addition the justices disqualified him from driving,
ordered him to pay £10 costs in respect of the first offence and made
an instalment order for the payment of the total of £245 at the rate of
£5 per week.
       On February 13, 1980, the applicant appeared again before the same
F court on a means inquiry. At that date there was still outstanding
£173·63 from the June order and the full sum of £245 from the January
1980 order. He was accordingly committed to prison by the justices
for 30 days in respect of the amount outstanding on the earlier order
and a total of 95 days in respect of the sum of £245. Each of these
committal orders was suspended on payment of the sum of £15 a week,
starting on February 18, 1980.
G   The period of 95 days was made up as follows: (1) £60 and costs—
30 days; (2) £25—7 days; (3) £60—30 days; (4) £15—7 days; (5) £25—7
days; (6) £25—7 days; (7) £25—7 days. Each of these periods was made
to run consecutively, making a total of 95 days. On September 24,
1980, it became clear to the justices' clerk's staff that the instalment
payments, as a condition of which the justices had suspended his com-
H mittal, had not been paid. Accordingly a warrant was issued for his
committal to prison for 59 days, the balance of the total of 95 days.
This period of 59 days was arrived at in a manner I shall refer to in a
moment. In fact before the warrant was executed the applicant of his
own volition appeared before the Southampton justices on October 8,
1980, asking them to order that the warrant be withdrawn; the justices
declined and the applicant was accordingly conveyed to prison on the
authority of that warrant. The applicant in his affidavit suggests that

the justices committed him to prison on that day but it seems clear to me   A
that the correct way of looking at what occurred on October 8, is as I
have set out.

By September 24, 1980, the applicant had in fact paid off the whole
of the sum due under the June order and £81·37 towards the sum of
£245 due for the convictions in January.   The justices' clerk had applied
that £81·37 to the outstanding sum of £245 in this way.   The first £70
was applied to cancel the first period of 30 days for non-payment of the   B
£60 fine and costs; the balance of £11·37 was used to reduce the second
period of 30 days, that is for offence no. (3), by 6 days, because £11·37
bears the same relationship to £60 as does 6 days to 30 days.

It is now necessary to consider the provisions of Schedule 3 to the
Magistrates' Courts Act 1952, as amended by section 59 of the Criminal
Law Act 1977.   This Schedule reads: C

"Subject to the following provisions of this Schedule, the periods
set out in the second column of the following table shall be the
maximum periods applicable respectively to the amounts set out
opposite thereto, being amounts due at the time the imprisonment
is imposed."

There then follows a table starting with: D

"An amount not exceeding £25—7 days.   An amount exceeding
£25 but not exceeding £50—14 days.   An amount exceeding £50
but not exceeding £200—30 days " and finishing up with " An
amount exceeding £5,000—12 months."

It will be seen that the periods of imprisonment fixed by the justices   E
on February 13, 1980, were in fact the maxima permitted under this
table.   Paragraph 2 of Schedule 3 reads:

"Where the amount due at the time imprisonment is imposed is
so much of a sum adjudged to be paid by a summary conviction as
remains due after part payment, the maximum period applicable to
the amount shall be the period applicable to the whole sum reduced
by such number of days as bears to the total number of days therein   F
the same proportion as the part paid bears to the whole sum:
Provided that in calculating the reduction required under this paragraph any fraction of a day shall be left out of account and the
maximum period shall not be reduced to less than five days."

Mr. Towler's main argument is that, when imposing terms of   G
imprisonment under section 65 (2) of the Magistrates' Courts Act 1952,
Schedule 3 to that Act must be read as if the justices in imposing a
term of imprisonment for non-payment of fines were subject to the
maxima applicable to the aggregate of the fines imposed.   He says this is so
for three main reasons.   First, the application of the Schedule produces
anomalies if it is not so construed.   Secondly, the Act of 1952 is a consolidating Act (except for amendments detailed by the Lord Chancellor   H
to Parliament, and there are none relevant here); that its predecessor,
the Summary Jurisdiction Act 1879, section 5, can be read as indicating that at any rate partial aggregation was intended by Parliament; and
that therefore the Act of 1952 provisions must be assumed to adopt the
same approach as those of 1879.   And, thirdly, in any event the period of
imprisonment ordered by the justices ran counter to well established
principles affecting the imposition of consecutive sentences and, as there

The Weekly Law Reports, March 27, 1981

377

1 W.L.R.   Reg. v. Southampton JJ., Ex p. Davies (Neil) (D.C.)   Forbes J.

A is no appeal to the Crown Court against sentences of imprisonment imposed by the justices for non-payment of fines, the applicant is entitled to come to this court for redress under this procedure for judicial review.

Before turning to examine these contentions it would be as well to be clear about two points. First, the powers of the justices are derived B from section 64 and section 65 of the Magistrates' Courts Act 1952. Section 64 (1) gives the power, where default is made in payment of sums due by conviction or order, to issue a distress warrant or a warrant committing the defaulter to prison. By section 64 (3) the period for which a defaulter may be sent to prison is limited to the appropriate maximum set out in Schedule 3. Section 65 (2) empowers the justices to fix a term of imprisonment and postpone the issue of the warrant until C such time and on such conditions as the court thinks just. It is clear to me that on February 13, 1980, the justices here decided to fix the appropriate terms of imprisonment and to postpone the issue of the warrant so long as the applicant paid £15 a week. This they did under section 65 (2) and it meant that on failing to pay the £15 in any one week the warrant would then and there issue, unless, of course, before its D issue the justices took steps, as, say, on an application by the defaulter, to stay the warrant. It is accordingly the decision of the justices on February 13, 1980, which is before us and not their decision not to recall the warrant, assuming they had power to do so, on October 8.

The second point is that there can be no doubt that it is competent to the justices to impose consecutive terms of imprisonment in default of payment of fines imposed on separate offences; this is clear from a E perusal of section 108 of the Act of 1952. The broad effect of sub-sections (1) and (2) of that section, as amended by Schedule 12 to the Criminal Law Act 1977, is to impose overall maxima of six months and 12 months respectively for consecutive sentences in respect of summary offences and offences triable either way tried summarily. Subsection (5) reads:

F   " For the purposes of this section a term of imprisonment shall be deemed to be imposed in respect of an offence if it is imposed as a sentence or in default of payment of a sum adjudged to be paid by the conviction . . ."

Mr. Towler does not challenge that there is power to impose con-secutive sentences in respect of default in payment of fines imposed for G two or more offences; he says, as I have indicated, that Schedule 3 must be read as involving maxima for the aggregate of the sums unpaid and not for each of the constituent sums.

Mr. Towler made his submissions with great skill and persuasiveness, and as a result I have changed my original attitude to his application. But it is not necessary, I think, to consider his submissions in detail H because I believe that there is another and more fundamental objection to the course the justices adopted.

What the justices purported to do on February 13, 1980, was to fix a term of imprisonment under section 65 (2) and postpone the issue of the warrant. But these powers themselves derive from section 64. On turning to that section it will be seen that under subsection (1) where there is " default . . . in paying a sum adjudged to be paid . . . the court may . . . issue a warrant committing the defaulter to prison." Sub-

Forbes J.   Reg. v. Southampton JJ., Ex p. Davies (Neil) (D.C.)   [1981]

section (3) brings in the maxima " The period for which a person may be A
committed to prison *under such a warrant* . . . shall not . . . exceed the
period applicable to the case under Schedule 3. . . ."

It seems plain to me from these provisions that where a warrant is
issued for an outstanding sum the period must be not more than the maximum for the aggregate sum found on the warrant. If separate periods for
non-payment for separate fines are to be fixed, then separate warrants would B
have to be issued. In coming to this conclusion I am not to be taken
as encouraging the issue of many separate warrants where a number of
separate fines is outstanding. Each case will clearly have to be decided
by the justices on its own facts. In doing so they should, it seems to me,
adopt the approach which formed the subject matter of Mr. Towler's
third and most eloquent submission; the fixing of consecutive sentences
of imprisonment for non-payment of fines is still the imposition of con- C
secutive sentences and as such is subject to certain well-known principles.
These include that, usually, consecutive sentences are inappropriate
where several offences arise out of the same incident, and that, even
when they are appropriate, the sentencer should consider whether the
totality of the sentence is not excessive having regard to the totality of
the criminal activity.

But having said that, I have no doubt that in fixing the term of D
imprisonment for which the warrant was to issue the justices should
have considered the maximum period applicable to the aggregate of the
sums outstanding. We have not been shown the warrant but it is clear
from the affidavit of the justices' clerk that in this case only one warrant
for the total of 59 days' imprisonment was issued. Accordingly the
maximum period in this case is 30 days. The order fixing the period of E
imprisonment at 59 days should therefore be quashed and there should be
substituted an order fixing the period as 30 days.

Before leaving this case I should mention *Reg.* v. *Metropolitan
Stipendiary Magistrate for South Westminster, Ex parte Green* [1977] 1
All E.R. 353, because we have been referred to it. All I need say is
that it was argued on wholly different submissions, namely, that section F
108 of the Act prevented the justices from imposing terms of imprisonment of more than six months in the aggregate, and that the significance
of the wording of section 64 was not brought to the court's attention.

DONALDSON L.J. I agree.

Application granted. G
*Committal order for
30 days substituted.
Legal aid taxation.*

Solicitor: *Gregory, Rowcliffe & Co. for Abels, Southampton.*

[Reported by MISS LESLEY HEWLETT, Barrister-at-Law] H

A

[COURT OF APPEAL]

* *In re* C.B. (A MINOR) (WARDSHIP: LOCAL AUTHORITY)

1980 May 22   Ormrod and Bridge L.JJ.

B *Minor — Ward of court — Jurisdiction — Child in care of local*
  authority—Mother seeking custody of child—Local authority
  making child ward of court—No exceptional circumstances
  making it undesirable for mother to have care of ward—
  Whether correct test where local authority plaintiff to pro-
  ceedings—Family Law Reform Act 1969 (c. 46), s. 7 (2)

C   In 1977, mother voluntarily placed her child, then aged nine
      months, in the care of a local authority and that authority
      placed the child with a short term foster parent. The following
      year the mother indicated that she wished her child to be
      returned to her and the local authority issued a summons
      making the child a ward of court. The registrar made an
      interim order committing the care and control of the child
      to the local authority. It considered that the child should be
      placed with long term foster parents and in September 1979,
D   without reference to the court, it placed the child with eminently
      suitable long term foster parents and the child began to form
      a secure relationship with them. Both the child's mother and
      her previous foster parent sought to have the care and control
      of the child and the matter was referred to the court. The
      judge considered that he was bound to grant the mother care
      and control of the child as there were " no exceptional circum-
      stances making it impracticable or undesirable " for the ward
E   to be under the care and control of her parents within the
      meaning of section 7 (2) of the Family Law Reform Act 1969.[1]
        On appeal by the local authority, to which the ward's
      present foster parents were joined as appellants: —
        Held, allowing the appeal, (1) that where a local authority
      was the plaintiff in wardship proceedings and was seeking an
      order giving care and control of the child to itself, section
      7 (2) of the Family Law Reform Act 1969 had no application
F   and the court had an unfettered jurisdiction to commit the
      care and control of the child to any suitable person; accord-
      ingly, the judge erred in law in considering that he was bound
      by section 7 (2) of the Act to grant the care of the ward to
      the mother in the absence of exceptional circumstances making
      it impracticable or undesirable for the ward to be cared for
      by her mother (post, pp. 387A–E, 388C–F, 389G—390A).
        (2) That in wardship proceedings, the court's duty was to
G   consider the paramount interest of the ward and where, on a
      local authority's application, the court decided to grant care
      and control of the ward to a local authority, the local authority
      exercised that care and control under the supervision of
      the court and not as if a care order had been made under the
      Children Acts 1948 and 1975; that in the present case the
      circumstances were such that it was not in the child's interest
      to be returned to her natural parents or to her previous foster
H   parent and, therefore, the court would order that the present
      foster parents should be given care and control of the child
      with a supervision order to the local authority (post pp. 387F–H,
      388G—389D, 390E—391A).

---

[1] Family Law Reform Act 1969, s. 7: " (2) Where it appears to the court that
there are exceptional circumstances making it impracticable or undesirable for a
ward of court to be, or to continue to be, under the care of either of his parents or
of any other individual the court may, if it thinks fit, make an order committing
the care of the ward to a local authority; . . ."

In re C.B. (Wardship: Local Authority) (C.A.)   **[1981]**

> *Per* Ormrod L.J. When a child is made a ward of court, A
> the court order means what it says. The child is a ward of
> court and it is for the court to decide all serious issues relating
> to the child. The court takes the major decisions. That is
> equally the case whether the care and control is granted to
> either parent or to some other individual or to a local authority
> (post, pp. 387H, 388C).
> Decision of Bush J. reversed.

B

The following case is referred to in the judgment of Ormrod L.J.:

J. v. *C.* [1970] A.C. 668; [1969] 2 W.L.R. 540; [1969] 1 All E.R. 788,
H.L.(E.).

No additional cases were cited in argument.

C

APPEAL from Bush J.

On June 15, 1978, Mr. Registrar Kenworthy made an order committing the interim care and control of a child, who had been made a
ward of court, to a local authority. On September 28, 1979, the local
authority, who had placed the child with a foster parent, transferred
the child to new foster parents. By an order of May 8, 1980, Bush J.
committed the care and control of the child to her natural mother. D

The local authority appealed on the grounds that the judge erred in
finding that there were not exceptional circumstances which made it
unreasonable for the minor to be returned to the mother within the
meaning of section 7 (2) of the Family Law Reform Act 1969; failed
to give sufficient weight to the welfare of the minor; erred in finding
that by making the minor a ward of court that the local authority had E
"blocked" the mother's request for the return of the minor from
voluntary care, in that the mother could have pursued the request in
the proceedings; and erred in law in finding that an order for an interim
care and control only gave the local authority the right to maintain the
status quo, in that the order placed a duty on the local authority to
safeguard the welfare of the minor as a paramount consideration within
section 12 (1) of the Children Act 1948 as re-enacted by section 59 of F
the Children Act 1975.

On the hearing of the appeal, the court granted leave to join the new
foster parents as plaintiffs and appellants.

The facts are stated in the judgments.

Shirley Ritchie Q.C. and *Mhairi McNab* for the local authority. G
Anita Ryan for the new foster parents.
Lionel Swift Q.C. and *Pamela Scriven* for the mother.
Brian Capstick Q.C. and *Elizabeth Szwed* for the former foster parent.

ORMROD L.J. This is an appeal by the local authority in wardship
proceedings concerning a little girl whom I will call Claire. It is a very
sensitive case and one which should be reported in such a way as to avoid H
identifying the child or any of the persons concerned in the case because
it would be extremely sad if any of them were subjected to any kind of
publicity to add to the distresses that they have already suffered in the
case one way and another. It is an important case from the point of view
of local authorities, because it raises at least two points under the wardship jurisdiction which require to be made clear, and I will come to them
in due course.

The Weekly Law Reports, March 27, 1981

381

1 W.L.R.   In re C.B. (Wardship: Local Authority) (C.A.)   Ormrod L.J.

A   At the beginning of the appeal, Miss Ryan, on behalf of the present foster parents of the child, applied for them to be joined as plaintiffs in the originating summons and appellants in this court. We decided that it was most desirable that they should be joined, and in fact had that application not been made, it is probable that the court itself would have suggested it. At present, for obvious reasons, they have been described in the application by their Christian names, but it seems to me, subject to

B   anything that counsel may subsequently say, that so far as the court record itself is concerned their surnames must appear on the court record. There is no necessity, as I see it at present, for any documents or any copies of documents to be circulated. It would be quite enough if the court record showed their true names because they must be capable of being identified in the event of any subsequent application.

C   Before I come to deal with the important points, I will give a brief summary of the facts. The judge, in his judgment, summarised them in great detail. The child was born on January 23, 1977, so she is 3½ years now. She was an illegitimate child and, at the time of her birth, her mother was only 17, having been born on January 20, 1960. The mother had had a very turbulent life herself; she had been in care, had had

D   experience of a good deal of difficulty and violence in her own family, and she had had school problems which led to her being put into care. She became pregnant as a result of intercourse with the father of the child, and when her pregnancy was discovered the father and mother, who were then very, very young, ceased to see one another. The mother was living with her mother (Claire's grandmother), and the grandmother was living with a man who, it is said, was a violent person.

E   Claire's mother, not surprisingly, with her background and faced with this child, was in a very difficult position. It is said that she often went out (not surprising at her age), leaving the child in the care of the grandmother, and the mother's situation in her mother's home was obviously one of great stress and difficulty. So much so that when Claire was about three months old, her mother left home, taking the child with her, and

F   went to stay with friends for a while, a matter of some two or three months. She then moved back into her mother's house.

But on October 23, 1977—the child was then nine months old—she left the child altogether in the care of the grandmother. In a matter of a few days, less than a week later, the grandmother asked for the child to be taken into voluntary care by the local authority. The local authority were able to contact the mother and she agreed.

G   So that on October 31, 1977, Claire was placed with a lady (" Mrs. R ") who became her first foster mother. Mrs. R was one of the local authority's short-term foster parents whom they used with great success from time to time and on whom they relied. She was a divorced lady with three children, who were teenagers at that time aged 16, 13 and 11, and she had one other foster child with her who was, we are told, about

H   the same age as Claire. There is no doubt whatever that Mrs. R made an admirable home for this baby, and she is certainly entitled to every credit for what she did for the child, and no one could have anything but sympathy for her in what later happened.

It is the fate of foster mothers to become attached to their foster children (that is what they are there for) and for the foster children to become fond of the foster mothers. Then sooner or later, and so often,

a break has to be made with all the distress and trauma which is inevitable   A
in that situation.

It was contemplated by both Mrs. R and the local authority that the
child's stay with her would be essentially a short-term fostering. The
local authority have other people whom they call "long-term" foster
parents and whom they choose, I suppose, on some rather different basis
from that for choosing the "short-term" foster parents.
                                                                            B
In the early stages the mother occasionally visited the child; Miss
Ritchie, who appears for the local authority in this court, gave us six
dates between November 7, 1977, and May 25, 1978, but it is said—and
one can well understand it and certainly would not make any criticism
of it—that the mother found these visits distressing.

In April 1978, the mother married a man (not the father or the puta-
tive father of the child) and went to live with him with his parents. Very   C
soon after the marriage, she indicated that she wanted Claire back. As
the child was in voluntary care, subject only to giving the necessary 28
days' notice because the child had been in care so long, the mother would,
prima facie, be entitled to have had the child back. But she did not give
the 28 days' notice, so that the local authority's care under the Children
Act 1948 continued.
                                                                            D
A social worker, Mr. Gilding, who was in charge of the case and who
was a very experienced person, as everyone agrees, had become anxious
about the situation which had developed. The mother then was pregnant
with another child, the local authority did not know anything about her
new husband, and they did not know anything about the accommodation
or what arrangements she could possibly make for Claire if Claire ceased
to be in their legal care.
                                                                            E
So in those circumstances, faced with the difficulties which local authorities have to contend with in this area of their duties, owing to the
difficulties of the legislation which they have to operate, it was decided
that the right thing, in the interests of Claire, was to make her a ward of
court. The object of doing that is to fill a serious gap in the local authorities' powers where children are concerned, when a period of voluntary   F
care looks as if it is going to be brought to an end by the withdrawal of
the consent of the relevant parent. This produces a situation of great
difficulty for the local authorities; they have obviously a very important
and serious duty to the child in such cases, and it is all too easy to see
how the interests of the child may clash with the wishes of the parent.

So the local authority's social workers—and we all should recognise
this—are in an invidious position: they have great responsibility, great   G
moral responsibility but, as some would say, inadequate legal powers, to
discharge those responsibilities. And so it has become customary, or perhaps not customary but quite frequent, for the local authorities nowadays
to resort to the ward of court procedure to help them over their difficulties.
This court has never said, and I hope never will say, anything to discourage that practice. It has always seemed to me that when a serious   H
dispute arises about the welfare of a child, it is asking too much for the
social workers to be made to be judges as well as social workers in the case,
and that it is to the advantage of all parties, including the local authority,
to resort to the court in order that a judge may take the responsibility for
the decision.

So that was what was decided to be done, and on May 26, 1978, the
originating summons was issued, and the matter came before Mr. Registrar

The Weekly Law Reports, March 27, 1981

383

1 W.L.R.   In re C.B. (Wardship: Local Authority) (C.A.)   Ormrod L.J.

A Kenworthy on June 15, 1978, for directions and a preliminary order. He directed that the mother file an affidavit within 28 days, and made an order granting what is called interim care and control to the local authority. I will come back to that later.

    At that stage, the mother instructed solicitors and they entered an appearance on her behalf, but no affidavit was filed by her and thereafter

B she seems to have lost touch with her solicitors. About the same time, that is in July 1978, she left her husband and returned to live with her mother; but she did not get in contact with her solicitors and they did not seem to be able to find her, with the result that in October 1978 they applied for their legal aid certificate to be discharged because they could not get instructions, and that was done.

    In June 1978 the mother did pay a visit to the child, but thereafter

C she did not see the child again that year. Also about the same time, that is July 1978, the long-term problem of Claire was coming to the surface so far as the local authority social workers were concerned. Mr. Gilding, who was in charge of the case, was beginning to think of long-term fostering for the child, with a view ultimately to adoption, on the footing that the mother had in fact dropped out of the child's life altogether or

D almost.

    At that time, Mrs. R, the short-term foster mother, was anxious that some such step should be taken, but most tragically for all concerned in this case, the local authority's social workers' strike began. It is not for this court to make any comment on that, except to note its consequences. The strike continued from August 1978 until June 1979, a very long time in the lives of the children who were in the charge of the social workers

E in that area. But, very conscientiously, Mr. Gilding, in spite of the strike, paid a visit to see how this child was getting on.

    In January 1979, the mother did pay another visit to the child, and that was the last time that she saw the child. It is not clear why she did not visit; there seems to have been no physical difficulty and no obstruction put in her way by Mrs. R, but she did not. She said to the judge

F that it was a matter which caused her great distress and she found it difficult to do. I think that all of us can understand that aspect of it, and it is certainly no part of the court's duty to criticise her in any way at all. It is a mistake, I think, in these cases for parties to criticise one another as to what they did or did not do in relation to the people concerned. The only relevant question is what effect did the conduct have on the child?

G   The effect it had on the child, of course, is obvious. The child has never formed any kind of relationship with her mother so that from the point of view of the child, the mother is a stranger. Parents may have some sense of blood ties, but the one thing that a three-year-old child does not have is any sense of a blood tie to an absent mother or father. Without any criticism of the mother, she has brought about a situation,

H so far as this little girl is concerned, which is unalterable and with which the court has to deal as best it can. It is part of the facts; and its significance is to be assessed in terms of its effects on the child now and in the future.

    In February 1979, Mr. Gilding paid his unofficial visit, and there is no doubt that he was, as he said, alarmed by what he found. The situation had changed with regard to Mrs. R in an important way. She had formed an association with a man of more or less, I think, her own age but not

at all in good health, who had parted from his wife and who had two A
children who were aged 12 and 9. He and the two children had moved
into Mrs. R's house, and about that time, I think, her eldest daughter
left the house; she moved out but I do not suggest anything was wrong
in her leaving. There is no doubt Mr. Gilding found the situation in
Mrs. R's house disturbing. In June 1979, when the strike ended, there
were discussions about this and Mr. Gilding was in a position to take
action. The situation was that he felt the household was overcrowded, B
although it is true that head-counting made them only one more than
they had been in the past. Neither Mrs. R nor her co-habitee was in
good health—not in bad health to any significant extent, I think—but what
disturbed Mr. Gilding was the child. He thought her attitude had changed
and he described her as " clinging to Mrs. R, banging her head and rock-
ing about;" and generally Mr. Gilding was disturbed by what he found. C
    It is always difficult to describe why an experienced person like Mr.
Gilding is disturbed by what he finds, and it may be that a description of
the child's behaviour is not all that convincing to a court, but the court
should, I think, take note of the fact that a very experienced social worker
was seriously disturbed by what he found.
    At that stage, according to Mr. Gilding—it is probable it may have D
been in issue—he saw the mother and there was a discussion about the
possibility of adoption, and arrangements were made for the mother to see
an adoption officer. Unfortunately, the mother again, I think, was pregnant, and on June 26 she was seen when she was in hospital. She was
living in temporary council accommodation with her child, another little
girl, who had been born on December 5, 1978. The mother agreed that
she was not in a position to take over Claire, but she would not agree to E
an adoption, as she was perfectly entitled to do.
    But, meanwhile, the social workers involved had come to the conclusion
that in those circumstances long-term arrangements would have to be made
for Claire. They did not think that Mrs. R was in a position to provide
long-term fostering care for the child, or perhaps able to do it satisfactorily.
At any rate, they came to the conclusion—and there was the usual con- F
ference on the matter—that a move of the child was necessary. Mrs. R
was told about this and as one can understand, she was extremely upset.
The child had been with her so long that obviously they had become very
fond of each other, and a break could be nothing but painful on both
sides. Not surprisingly, her co-habitee was very upset and angry, but
Mrs. R did her best to help and there is no doubt she did honestly try her
best, in spite of the distress which this caused her. G
    Attempts were made, at that stage, to get in touch with the mother,
but they were not successful. The judge said that he did not think sufficient effort had been made by the local authority; he thought that they
could have got in touch with the mother if they had tried harder. So on
September 28, 1979, Claire was transferred to her new foster parents, that
is, the persons whom we have just given leave to join in these proceedings, H
and she has been with them since then.
    On October 3, both the mother and Mrs. R were distressed and upset
about this change and they both went to see one of the social workers,
a Mrs. Hill. The mother asked to see Claire although at that stage she
did not give any clear indication that she was going to ask for the child
back. What the local authority did not do was to tell the court, the
registrar, of the change to new foster parents before it was made, and

The Weekly Law Reports, March 27, 1981

385

1 W.L.R.   In re C.B. (Wardship: Local Authority) (C.A.)   Ormrod L.J.

A the judge, in my view rightly, criticised the local authority for failing to take that step because it is fundamental in wardship jurisdiction that no serious change in the arrangements for a ward should be made without reference to the court. It is true that this wardship had not proceeded further than the preliminary stages, but there is no doubt that in law the duty of the local authority was to inform the court and obtain the sanction of the registrar to make the move. It would almost certainly have given
B the mother and Mrs. R an opportunity to make representations to the court if either or both of them wished to do so. The local authority did inform the court, on October 11, by letter, of the change, but that was after it had happened and it was too late then to take any active step.

About the same time, the mother seems to have got in touch again with the child's father, and the two of them went to see Mr. Gilding.
C What she was wanting at that stage is not very clear. Mr. Gilding said she did not want the child herself but wanted the child returned to Mrs. R, and indicated that she was prepared to fight all and sundry at that stage over the child.

Mrs. R, by this time, had taken advice, and she applied on November 8 to intervene in the proceedings, and on November 22 she was joined as
D a defendant in the proceedings by the registrar, who ordered a welfare officer's report. Thereafter, the father and mother seemed to have seen a lot of one another and in March or April they went to live together and they are at present living together, though they have not been together very long.

It was in that state of affairs that the matter came before Bush J., whose order is the subject matter of this appeal. Having heard the evidence
E and having had the advantage of hearing all the social workers concerned and having an extremely full and detailed welfare report, Bush J. made an order that the care of Claire should be transferred to her mother. That order was a few days later stayed by this court pending appeal, and now the appeal comes before us. The local authority are the first appellants; the present foster parents are the second and third appellants; the first
F respondent is the mother and the second respondent is Mrs. R.

Now on the facts of the case, the position is quite simple. Stated baldly, the facts are these. This child had known one stable home up to September 1979, and only one stable home, and that was with Mrs. R. The mother is a virtual stranger to her; the father is a total stranger to her. But since September she has begun to make, and it appears from all the evidence, particularly the welfare report and the short affidavit which
G has been filed today by the present foster parents that she is making, a successful relationship with the present foster parents. There she is alone with no other children; they are described as eminently suitable foster parents. It is obvious from reading their brief affidavit that they are sensitive, responsible and reliable people, and from the evidence (such as it is and it is strong from the welfare officer and from the foster parents
H themselves) that the child is extremely well placed with them and is forming a secure relationship with them.

So the judge, in practice, had three possible alternative solutions to this problem: one was to leave the child where she is with her present foster parents; another was to send her back to her pseudo-mother, her mother substitute, Mrs. R; and the third was to hand her over to her own mother.

The indications for the first, that is leaving the child where she is with

her present foster parents, are first, that she has settled down with them;   A
second, that they are in a position to offer her the very highest standard
of care; and third, any further changes in the child's life are bound to
add to her intense insecurity and are bound to be very upsetting to her,
if not in the short term then in the long term. There are all sorts of
psychological problems which might or might not arise from sending her
back or moving her away from her present foster parents.

    The attraction of Mrs. R, of course, is that the child is going back   B
to an environment with which she is familiar and where she might feel
equally secure. But against that, the court has to bear in mind the views
of the social workers concerned that this arrangement was not going to be
viable in the long term and might have to be changed later, but it was
clearly an alternative which was a practical alternative.

    The third proposition that Claire should be handed over to her own   C
mother and father, although emotionally attractive, in my judgment has
very little to support it. It is absolutely vital in these cases that we look
at reality and look at it through the eyes of the child. It is clear that the
child would be grossly disturbed by being handed over to yet a third
couple, a third couple with whom she has had no contact at all, although
she may have some vague memory of her mother. So it would require,   D
I think, a very, very strong case to justify taking this child of three and
handing her over to total strangers simply because they are her blood
mother and blood father.

    Now the judge did not, as I see it, approach the case in the way I
have just indicated. Having set out the facts very fairly in his judgment,
he said:

    " This decision does not turn upon the relative merits of [the present   E
    foster parents] and the mother in the ideal parents' stakes. No doubt
    the mother would come off second best, particularly as she has not
    been given a chance to show what she can do with Claire. The ques-
    tion turns upon whether the local authority have shown that it is
    undesirable that the child should be or continue to be under the care
    of either of her parents. The court must look at the totality of the   F
    circumstances, bearing in mind that Parliament intended that children
    should remain with their parents if at all possible, and bearing in
    mind also that the welfare of the child is the paramount considera-
    tion."

    With respect to the judge, I think he was wrong and misdirected him-
self there in that passage because the decision *does* turn upon what he   G
called " the relative merits " of the present foster parents and the mother
" in the ideal parents' stakes."

    It may be that the judge was confused by the form of the relief which
was sought by the originating summons. In it the local authority asked,
first, that the child should remain a ward of court during her minority
or until further order, and, secondly, that the care and control of the child   H
should be committed to the plaintiffs, that is, to themselves. As I have
already said, the registrar made an order for interim care and control to
the local authority. It seems to have got into the mind of the judge that
the whole case was dominated and controlled by section 7 (2) of the
Family Law Reform Act 1969. That subsection, which is in identical
terms with the corresponding section, section 43 (1), of the Matrimonial
Causes Act 1973, reads:

The Weekly Law Reports, March 27, 1981

387

1 W.L.R.   In re C.B. (Wardship: Local Authority) (C.A.)   Ormrod L.J.

A   " Where it appears to the court that there are exceptional circumstances making it impracticable or undesirable for a ward of court to be, or to continue to be, under the care of either of his parents or of any other individual the court may, if it thinks fit, make an order committing the care of the ward to a local authority; and thereupon Part II of the Children Act 1948 (which relates to the treatment of children in the care of a local authority) shall, subject to the next

B   following subsection, apply as if the child had been received by the local authority into their care under section 1 of that Act."

That is the subsection which the judge treated as controlling the whole of the case. So, instead of considering who was going to look after this child and considering, as he ought to have done, what the welfare of the

C   child, as the paramount consideration, required, he was led to consider whether or not there were exceptional circumstances making it " impracticable or undesirable " for the ward to be under the care of either of her parents. He treated the matter as one of law. He felt that he had to find first that the circumstances were exceptional; and secondly he had to decide whether it was impracticable or undesirable for the ward to continue to be in the care of either of her parents or any other individual.

D   In fact, of course, the subsection never applied at all in this case because at all times the proposal of the local authority was that the child should remain in the care of the present foster parents, that is, " any other individual " within section 7 (2). Nor is it at all difficult, in a case like this, to find exceptional circumstances. No one, I venture to think, would dream of making an order committing the care of a ward to a local authority unless the circumstances were exceptional. Nor would they contem-

E   plate doing it unless it was the only practical solution open to the court at the time.

It was a mistake to treat this case as if it was a section 7 (2) case because the local authority were the plaintiffs. This is the first point to be made so far as the wardship jurisdiction is concerned. It is an unfettered jurisdiction to place the ward in the care and control of any person

F   who can best look after him or her. Ever since *J. v. C.* [1970] A.C. 668 in the House of Lords, the principles are absolutely clear; the court in its discretion must decide what the paramount interests of the child require. It is not concerned with allocating blame or adjusting rival claims. It has to make a decision sufficiently difficult in all conscience, but the decision it has to make is what is in the best interests of this child at this stage.

G   Looking as far ahead as is possible to look, and making as wise a decision about the child's future as it is possible for the court to make, if the court thinks that it would be desirable or in the interests of the child to make an order committing the child to the care and control of the local authority, so be it. But that is not a care order under the children legislation; it is an order which has some similar effects, in the sense that the local authority has powers over the child and is entitled to exercise them but

H   subject always to the court's supervision.

Now so far as wardship is concerned, this should be said at the outset, I think—and I say it with all sympathy for local authorities and social workers because I know the difficulties under which they work—that when a child is made a ward of court the order means what it says. The child is a ward of the court and it is for the court to decide all the serious issues relating to the child. That is why in orders made in the wardship jurisdiction the court never grants custody to anybody. It used to be

388

said in the old days that the court " retained custody in itself," which was A
only a form of words to emphasise the fact that the court remains in
control of the child, and it grants care and control to somebody to look
after the child in the ordinary day-to-day way and, although I do not
want to make too much of this, if the child is a ward of the court in that
sense, it is only reasonable that the persons who have the actual control
of the child under the order of the court should not make any major
change in the child's way of life without getting the approval of the court. B
This may be an inconvenience, but this case illustrates very well how
important it is to observe these sometimes tiresome routine rules because
there is no doubt that the whole course of this case would have been
different if the matter had come before the court in, say, August or
September 1979 before the change to new foster parents was made.

I am most anxious to emphasise that once the child is a ward of the C
court, the major decisions relating to that child are for the court to take.
That is equally the case whether the care and control is granted to either
parent or to some other individual or to a local authority.

The judge, unfortunately, did not approach the matter, as I think, in
the right way. He was side-tracked by considering whether he had the
necessary jurisdiction under section 7 (2). But in this case the local autho- D
rity were themselves the plaintiffs in the originating summons asking for
" care and control," not for an order under section 7 (2). Had he had
the present foster parents before him as parties, I do not think that this
error would have crept in. The result is that, with respect to the judge,
the conclusion is inescapable that he exercised his discretion on an entirely
wrong basis. He did not, at any stage, compare the mother's proposals
for the child with the present foster parents' proposals. He did not weigh E
one against the other and make any assessment of the advantages to the
child in regard to one course or the other, in the short term or the long
term. He was almost wholly concerned with deciding whether the local
authority had made out their case under section 7 (2), but as I have
already said, if a local authority takes the initiative of making a child a
ward, I do not think that section 7 (2) comes into the case at all. Section F
7 (2) was passed to give the court power, in proceedings between parents
or between a parent and a third party, to make an order committing the
child to the care of the local authority, or to make it clear that the court,
in wardship proceedings, had these same powers as it has under the
Matrimonial Causes Act 1973.

That being the case, it is for this court to exercise its discretion on
the material as it is before it. From what I have said already, it is obvious G
what view I take. To my mind, it would be entirely wrong and contrary
to this child's best interests to hand her over to her natural parents who,
as I have said before, are total strangers to her. If they were not her
natural parents, no one could imagine for a moment making such an
order. So the real issue is whether she should be in the care and control of
her present foster parents, or whether she should go back to Mrs. R. H

I hope I have said enough to make it plain to Mrs. R that I feel very
sorry for and sympathetic towards her. She has had a tragic experience
with this child, but once the break has been made between her and the
child, it would be wrong, in my view, to try to go back, unless there was
some pretty powerful indication that that would be the best course. If
the present foster parents were not able to get on terms with the child,
or the child was fretting for Mrs. R, then there might have been a strong

The Weekly Law Reports, April 3, 1981

389

1 W.L.R.   In re C.B. (Wardship: Local Authority) (C.A.)   Ormrod L.J.

B

case for saying that she should go back to Mrs. R; but the evidence is really all the other way. Although the trauma of that break from Mrs. R is going to be with the child, I should think for a very long time indeed, it has been incurred; but I think it is going to be possible to repair that damage. It may well be that the step having been taken, it has been taken for the best; I am not suggesting for a moment that the child would be better off with Mrs. R than she will be with her present foster parents. I do not, however, think it is possible to say that it will be in her interests to try to go backwards in her development, and in view of the admirable reports as to the proposed adopters contained in the welfare officer's report, I think that the right course is to follow the strong recommendation of the welfare officer, not only because it is made by the welfare officer, but because it seems to me to be plain and good common sense, looked at from the point of view of this child.

C

I would like to finish where I began by saying that what we are concerned with is the child's future. We are not concerned with the natural parents' position. We have to judge the situation as it is at the moment, no matter how it has come about and answer the question: where does the future of this child best lie? I answer that without any hesitation by saying: with her present foster parents.

D

In those circumstances, I would allow the appeal and make the order in that form.

BRIDGE L.J. I agree. In the proceedings below, this case, as it seems to me, was bedevilled by the attention which was directed to, and the proposition which was derived from, section 7 (2) of the Family Law Reform Act 1969. The judge said of that section:

E

" . . . the section emphasises that, if at all possible, it was the intention of Parliament that parents should not lose their children to the care of local authorities except for good cause and in exceptional circumstances."

Then in a passage which has already been referred to by Ormrod L.J., he said:

F

" The court must look at the totality of the circumstances, bearing in mind that Parliament intended that children should remain with their parents if at all possible, . . ."

Those two propositions, thought to be derived from section 7 (2), seem to me to have dominated the judge's approach to this whole problem.

G

Now the situation with which section 7 (2) is dealing is a situation where it is impracticable or undesirable for a ward of court to be under the care of either of his parents or any other individual—and I emphasise those concluding words " or any other individual "—and once that is appreciated, it becomes apparent that section 7 (2) had nothing whatever to do with this case. No one could possibly have suggested that it was either impracticable or undesirable in this case for Claire to continue in the care of the new foster parents or to be returned to the care of the previous foster parent or of the natural parents.

H

The reason why section 7 (2) seems to have loomed so large was that by what seems to have been a purely procedural accident, the new foster parents were not parties before the court, so it was the local authority who, in form, were applying for an order to be made in their favour. But in substance nobody could have been in any doubt that the issue was

whether the little girl should be in the care of her natural parents, or one A
or other of the sets of foster parents who were " other individuals " within
the meaning of section 7 (2).

In fact section 7 (2) indicates no parliamentary a priori preference
for giving the care of a child to natural parents as against giving it to
anybody else. The paramount consideration in a simple case like this, and
the sole consideration, is what will best serve the welfare of the child. E
Once the misapprehension derived from section 7 (2) is cleared out of
the way, and the case is approached on the basis of what will best serve
the welfare of this little girl of now just over three years old, the solution
to the problem, to my mind, stands out so as to be unmistakable.

Here is a little girl who, in her short life, has already been disturbed
by a number of traumatic experiences. Now for the last eight months
she has been in what, from all accounts, appears to be an ideal home, in C
the care of the new foster parents of whom the welfare officer in her report
speaks in glowing terms. From the evidence before us, it is apparent that
signs of disturbed behaviour which were apparent when the child first
went to the new home are greatly improved, and that in the eight months
she has been with them, the new foster parents and the little girl have
formed extremely strong bonds of mutual affection. So strongly did the D
welfare officer feel about the matter that she concluded her report by
saying:

> " I feel that it would be disastrous for Claire to be uprooted yet again,
> and for the fine progress which " the new foster parents " have made
> with her to be interrupted."

Against that background, when one considers the possibility of the E
child being returned to the care of her natural mother and father, it seems
to me clear that would be a course which would not serve the welfare of
the child. As Ormrod L.J. has pointed out, the father is a total stranger
to the little girl, and the mother, through no fault of her own but inescap-
ably in fact, has now become a virtual stranger. If one were to ask the
question whether it would be in the interests of this child, at the impres-
sionable age of just over three, to be removed yet again from the home F
where she has settled and to be transferred to total strangers who were
not related to her by blood, the answer would be so obvious that one
would laugh the suggestion out of court. The sole argument before this
court, and the argument which misled the trial judge, as I think, is the
argument that the tie of blood in some way supersedes other considerations
and determines what the child's future must be unless there is some over- G
whelming consideration to the contrary.

Accordingly, I reach, without hesitation, the conclusion that the judge's
order was erroneous. I think the question whether the child should stay
with the new foster parents or return to Mrs. R, where she was for so
long, is a much more difficult question, but on that the judge came to the
conclusion that if it were not for the involvement of the natural mother, H
the balance of the decision would be to leave the child with the new
foster parents rather than risk returning her to Mrs. R, and he explained
what he thought the risk involved in that course would be. So for the
reasons he gave, and for the reasons given in the judgment of Ormrod
L.J., I agree that the decision should be to leave the child with the new
foster parents rather than to return her to Mrs. R.

A   I accordingly agree that this appeal should be allowed and I agree with the order proposed by Ormrod L.J.

> *Appeal allowed: care and control to new foster parents with supervision to local authority.*
> *Adoption proceedings to be started before another High Court judge.*
> *Legal aid taxation.*
> *Leave to appeal refused.*

B

C   Solicitors: *H. D. Cook; Denton Hall & Burgin; Breeze, Benton & Co.; Alexander Johnson.*

B. O. A.

[FAMILY DIVISION]

D

* GREEN *v.* GREEN AND ANOTHER

1980   Oct. 3   Eastham J.

Husband and Wife—Property—Transfer of property—Avoidance of transaction—Land conveyed for valuable consideration to company—Company charging land to bank—Divorce—Wife seeking to set conveyance aside—Whether power to set aside bank's charge—Matrimonial Causes Act 1973 (c. 18), *s.* 37 (3)

E

During the subsistence of the marriage, the parties lived in a large house with extensive grounds. The property had been conveyed into the joint names of husband and wife. In December 1977, they sold 10½ acres of the grounds for £20,000 to an Isle of Man company. The company then charged the land to a bank as security for a loan to the company of more than £60,000. In ancillary proceedings, following divorce, the wife sought to set aside the conveyance to the company under section 37 of the Matrimonial Causes Act 1973 [1] and also sought to set aside the subsequent charge to the bank.

F

G   On the preliminary question whether if, after hearing the evidence, the court found that there were grounds for avoiding the transaction, there was power to set aside the bank's charge under section 37 (3): —

Held, that, as it was conceded that the court had no jurisdiction to set aside the bank's charge under section 37 (1) and (2) of the Matrimonial Causes Act 1973, the court, in giving consequential directions under subsection (3) if minded to set aside the conveyance, could not set aside the charge because the terms of subsection (3) were not wide enough to set aside a transaction that could not be set aside under subsections (1) and (2) and defeat the bank's defence under subsection (4) that the disposition was made for valuable consideration, in good faith and without notice of any intention on the part of the husband to defeat the wife's claim for financial relief.

H

---

[1] Matrimonial Causes Act 1973, s. 37 (3): see post, p. 393E–F.

No cases are referred to in the judgment.   A

The following case was cited in argument:

Whittingham v. Whittingham (National Westminster Bank Ltd., inter-
    vener) [1979] Fam. 9; [1978] 2 W.L.R. 936; [1978] 3 All E.R. 805;
    Balcombe J. and C.A.

                                                               B

SUMMONS
On July 9, 1980, the former wife made application to set aside the
conveyance to a company of property situated in Norfolk which had
been held in the joint names of the husband and wife and also to set aside,
under section 37 (3) of the Matrimonial Causes Act 1973, a legal
charge executed on September 21, 1978, in favour of Barclays Bank Ltd.
by the company on the property. Notice of the wife's application was   C
served on the bank. The bank was joined in the suit.
The application was heard and judgment on the preliminary point
of law delivered in chambers. The judgment is reported with the
permission of Eastham J.
The facts are stated in the judgment.

                                                               D
Joseph Jackson Q.C. and Bruce Blair for the wife.
Margaret Puxon and John Akast for the husband.
Michael Oppenheimer for the bank.

EASTHAM J.   At the request of Barclays Bank Ltd., which is interested
in these proceedings in a manner which I will describe later, and without objection by the other parties to this litigation, I have been asked   E
to determine a point of law relating to section 37 of the Matrimonial
Causes Act 1973.
The former wife (whom I shall call "the wife" hereafter) is in
these proceedings claiming financial relief against her former husband.
Before the break down of the marriage, the matrimonial home was a
very large and pleasant property near Norwich in Nolfolk. The present   F
value of that house with the grounds which existed during the marriage
until December 1977 is £165,000, that being an agreed valuation. The
property was in joint names and still is in the joint names of the husband
and wife.
On December 28, 1977, the husband and wife conveyed approximately
10½ acres of the grounds of that house to an Isle of Man company for
a consideration of £20,000. The wife received no part of that sum.   G
In these proceedings, the wife contends that she was induced to enter
into that conveyance partly because of her fear for her husband and
partly because she was told that it was a necessary transaction in order
to avoid taxation.
The value of the house without those 10½ acres of land is somewhere
between £75,000 and £80,000. In the proceedings before me there is   H
an application at the instance of the wife to set aside that conveyance
under section 37 of the Matrimonial Causes Act 1973.
After that conveyance, on September 21, 1978, the Isle of Man
company, charged those 10½ acres to Barclays Bank Ltd., and Barclays
Bank Ltd., in respect of that security and other security, have advanced
to the company sums in excess of £60,000. Notice has been given to
Barclays Bank Ltd. of the application by the wife to set aside the

A   conveyance under section 37 of the Act, and they attend here by counsel.

It is conceded and accepted by Mr. Jackson, on behalf of the wife, that it is not possible, having regard to the wording of section 37 (1) and (2), for the wife to attack the charge between the Isle of Man company and Barclays Bank Ltd. under those subsections. If it were

B   possible, the bank would be able to avail itself of the defence set out in section 37 (4), which provides that a disposition which would otherwise be reviewable ceases to be reviewable if it was made for valuable consideration:

"to a person who, at the time of the disposition, acted in relation to it in good faith and without notice of any intention on the part

C   of the other party to defeat the applicant's claim for financial relief."

But in these proceedings Mr. Jackson says, first of all, that, as a result of irregularities between the company and the bank and violations of the provisions of the articles of association and as a result of defective minutes, the charge, in his submission, was invalid ab initio; secondly,

D   and more importantly, as a legal point he submits that, even though the wife cannot under the provisions of section 37 (1) and (2) make a direct attack on the charge, he maintains that if I come to the conclusion that the conveyance which preceded the charge can be successfully attacked under section 37 (1) and (2) as against the husband, then under the provisions of subsection (3) I can under an absolute discretion, as he submits, vested in me give directions to give effect to the order setting

E   aside the conveyance which would include setting aside the charge or reducing it, if I thought right.

Section 37 (3) of the Matrimonial Causes Act 1973 reads:

"Where the court makes an order under subsection (2) (b) or (c) above setting aside a disposition it shall give such consequential directions as it thinks fit for giving effect to the order (including

F   directions requiring the making of any payments or the disposal of any property)."

Mr. Jackson submits that those are very wide words and that they are not confined to any particular property but extend to any property. Mr. Oppenheimer, on behalf of the bank, says, first of all, that he disagrees with Mr. Jackson's submission that the subsection is in wide

G   terms, and he lays particular emphasis on the words "consequential directions," submitting that that restricts very largely or entirely the subsection to directions requiring, for example, the repayment of any money which had been paid under the conveyance which had been set aside.

He also submits that, if Mr. Jackson's submissions are correct, it

H   would deprive his client, the bank, entirely of the statutory defence set out in subsection (4) which it could rely on if it were possible for the proceedings to be brought against the bank under section 37 (1) and (2).

I have been asked to decide the point of law because it has been submitted to me that it may save a good deal of inquiry into fact if the bank's submissions are correct. I have come to the conclusion that Mr. Oppenheimer's submissions are correct and that I have no discretion or power under section 37 (3) of the Act of 1973 to attack the charge

394

A

under the provisions of that subsection. That, however, does not end the matter, because by virtue of section 43 of the Supreme Court of Judicature (Consolidation) Act 1925 it is provided:

> "The High Court . . . in exercise of the jurisdiction invested in them by this Act, shall, in every cause or matter pending before the court, grant, either absolutely or on such terms and conditions as the court thinks just, all such remedies whatsoever as any of the parties thereto may appear to be entitled to in respect of any legal or equitable claim properly brought forward by them in the cause or matter, so that, as far as possible, all matters in controversy between the parties may be completely and finally determined, and all multiplicity of legal proceedings concerning any of those matters avoided."

B

C

In relation to Mr. Jackson's first submission, namely, that the charge was invalid ab initio, quite clearly that argument must lie outside the scope of section 37 of the Act of 1973, and in relation to that matter, without objection from the bank, I have already directed that points of claim setting out the grounds of the alleged invalidity shall be served on the bank by Monday. It seems to me, having regard to the provisions of that section and having regard to the fact that it may be that the bank has continued to advance money after having full knowledge of the wife's claims against her former husband and to get rid of all matters in controversy between the parties, I should also in relation to the second line of argument direct that, within a time to be discussed with counsel, points of claim should be served setting out the grounds upon which it is contended that the charge should be reduced, partially or entirely, as a result of conduct or misconduct on the part of the bank. But on the point raised by the bank I am quite satisfied for myself that I cannot do as the wife requests me to do—attack the charge under the provisions of section 37 (3) of the Matrimonial Causes Act 1973.

D

E

Declaration accordingly.

F

Solicitors: *Mills & Reeve, Norwich; Hill & Perks, Norwich; Durrant Piesse.*

M. B. D.

G

H

A

[PRIVY COUNCIL]

* ATTORNEY-GENERAL OF HONG KONG . . APPELLANT

AND

HO PUI-YIU . . . . RESPONDENT

B

[APPEAL FROM THE COURT OF APPEAL OF HONG KONG]

1980 Nov. 19;   Lord Wilberforce, Lord Elwyn-Jones,
     Jan. 12   Lord Keith of Kinkel, Lord Roskill and
                                     Lord Bridge of Harwich

C

*Hong Kong—Crime—Bribery—Control of assets disproportionate
to official emoluments—Proof of cost of acquisition—Whether
prosecution to prove value of assets at charge date—Prevention of Bribery Ordinance (Laws of Hong Kong, 1974 rev.,
c. 201), s. 10 (1) (b)*

D

     The defendant, a Crown servant, was charged under section
10 (1) (b) of the Prevention of Bribery Ordinance [1] with being
on December 3, 1973 (the charge date) in control of pecuniary
resources and property disproportionate to his then present and
past official emoluments. At his trial the prosecution adduced
evidence of the defendant's official emoluments up to the
charge date, of his possession of assets at that date and of the
cost of their acquisition. The prosecution did not lead evidence
of the value of the assets at the charge date. The trial judge
found that at the charge date the defendant was in control of

E

property amounting to $124,650, that no satisfactory explana-
tion had been given and that the amount was disproportionate
to the defendant's official emoluments. The defendant was convicted and appealed. The Court of Appeal held that because
there had been no evidence before the trial judge as to the
value of the assets at the charge date, proper comparison with
total emoluments had been impossible and it allowed the

F

appeal.
     On the prosecutor's appeal to the Judicial Committee:—
     Held, allowing the appeal, that to establish the dispropor-
tion required to constitute an offence under section 10 (1) (b)
of the Prevention of Bribery Ordinance the prosecution had to
show that the defendant could not have afforded the assets
which were under his control at the charge date out of his
official emoluments and for that purpose the cost of acquiring

G

the assets had necessarily to be before the court but there was
no rule of law which required the prosecution to lead evidence
of the value of the assets at the charge date; and that, accordingly, the trial judge had been in a position to make the
comparison necessary for a finding of disproportion and there
had been no error in the prosecution not having adduced
evidence of the value of the assets at the charge date.
     Decision of the Court of Appeal of Hong Kong reversed.

H

The following cases are referred to in the judgment of their Lordships:

Mok Chuen v. *The Queen* [1977] H.K.L.R. 605.
Reg. v. *Chung Cheong* (unreported) December 22, 1977, Victoria District
    Court of Hong Kong.
Sturgeon v. *The Queen* [1975] H.K.L.R. 677.

---

[1] Prevention of Bribery Ordinance, s. 10 (1) (b): see post, p. 396D–F.

The following additional case was cited in argument: A

Hunt v. *The Queen* [1974] H.K.L.R. 31.

APPEAL (No. 13 of 1980) by the Attorney-General of Hong Kong
against a judgment (January 22, 1979) of the Court of Appeal of Hong
Kong (Briggs C.J., Huggins and Pickering JJ.A.) by which it allowed the
appeal of the defendant, Lawrence Ho Pui-yiu, against his conviction on
April 27 by Garcis D.J. in the Victoria District Court of Hong Kong of an   B
offence under section 10 (1) (*b*) of the Prevention of Bribery Ordinance.

The facts are stated in the judgment of their Lordships.

Anthony Scrivener Q.C. and *C. Warwick Reid* (Deputy Principal Crown
Counsel, Hong Kong) for the Attorney-General.

John Hazan Q.C. and *Doreen Le Pichon* (of the English and Hong   C
Kong Bars) for the defendant.

Cur. adv. vult.

January 12. The judgment of their Lordships was delivered by LORD
KEITH OF KINKEL.

This is an appeal by the Attorney-General, with special leave, from a   D
judgment of the Court of Appeal of Hong Kong, whereby that court
allowed the defendant's appeal against his conviction in the Victoria
District Court of an offence under section 10 (1) (*b*) of the Prevention of
Bribery Ordinance. Section 10 (1) enacts:

" Any person who, being or having been a Crown servant—(*a*) maintains a standard of living above that which is commensurate with his   E
present or past official emoluments; or (*b*) is in control of pecuniary
resources or property disproportionate to his present or past official
emoluments, shall, unless he gives a satisfactory explanation to the
court as to how he was able to maintain such a standard of living or
how such pecuniary resources or property came under his control, be
guilty of an offence."
                                                                         F
The defendant was for many years in the revenue service of the Hong
Kong government, latterly as acting assistant superintendent of the Customs
and Excise Service. On September 29, 1977, he was charged as follows:

" *Statement of Offence*: Being a Crown Servant in control of pecuniary resources or property disproportionate to his then present or past
official emoluments, contrary to section 10 (1) (*b*) of the Prevention of   G
Bribery Ordinance, c. 201 Laws of Hong Kong.

" *Particulars of Offence*: Ho Pui-yiu, Lawrence, a Crown Servant, was
on December 3, 1973, in control of pecuniary resources totalling
$15,516·09 and property namely: [there followed a list of assets com-
prising a flat in Kowloon, a Volkswagen motor car, and a number of
blocks of shares] which pecuniary resources and property were disproportionate to his then present or past official emoluments."   H

The defendant was tried before Garcia D.J. in the Victoria District
Court. The Crown led evidence about his official emoluments throughout
his period of government service up to December 3, 1973, and also about
the sums at credit of various bank accounts in his own name or that of
his wife as at that date. As regards the items of property specified in the
charge, the Crown led evidence indicating that these were owned by the

A defendant or his wife at December 3, 1973, but no evidence as to their value on that date. Evidence was led, however, about the dates of acquisition of the various items, and of payment therefor (all these dates being between mid-1972 and December 1973), and also as to the amount of the consideration paid in each case. At the close of the Crown case, it was submitted for the defendant that he had no case to answer, upon the ground inter alia that, since there was no evidence about the value of the
B items of property specified in the charge as at the charge date, there was no basis upon which a disproportion with the defendant's official emoluments could properly be held to exist. The trial judge rejected this submission. After hearing evidence led for the defendant, he examined the evidence as a whole, and concluded that the defendant was in control on the charge date of property amounting to $124,650 of which no satisfactory
C explanation had been given. He went on to find that the total amount of unexplained property under the defendant's control on the charge date was disproportionate to his net official emoluments up to that date. He therefore, on April 28, 1978, convicted the defendant and sentenced him to 15 months' imprisonment and a fine of $75,000.

The defendant appealed to the Court of Appeal on a number of grounds
D including the following:

"That the learned district judge erred on a point of law in holding that the prosecution need not adduce evidence as to the value of the assets at the charge date as opposed to the values at the dates of purchase to prove that the assets at the charge date were disproportionate to the official emoluments received by the [defendant] from the commencement of government service up to the charge date."
E
On January 22, 1979, the Court of Appeal (Briggs C.J., Huggins and Pickering JJ.A.) accepting that ground as valid and finding it unnecessary to deal with the other grounds, quashed the conviction and set aside the sentence. Pickering J.A., delivering the judgment of the court, said:

"In the present case no evidence was given of the value of the
F defendant's total assets as at the charge date so that comparison of that total value with total emoluments as at the charge date was impossible. On this ground alone the appeal must be allowed . . ."

The Attorney-General argues that the Court of Appeal have fallen into error in that they appear to have laid down a rule of law, unwarranted by the terms of the statute, that in proceedings under section 10 (1) (b) the
G prosecution can in no circumstances establish a disproportion in the statutory sense if they do not lead evidence as to the values at the date of the charge of the items of property specified therein as being under the control of the defendant. The Court of Appeal have also erred, so it is maintained, in holding the acquisition costs of the various items of property to be irrelevant for the purpose of establishing the requisite disproportion.

In the normal case the nature of the evidence requisite to prove a par-
H ticular statutory offence is entirely at large. While it is possible that the statute creating an offence might impose some limitation on the nature of the evidence admissible to prove it, that would require to be done by express words or necessary implication. Section 10 (1) (b) of the Prevention of Bribery Ordinance does not expressly impose any such limitation as is contended for by the defendant. The question is whether it does so by necessary implication. It is to be observed at the outset that section 10 (1) (b) does not refer directly as it might have done, to the value of any

property of which the defendant may be in control. It is an essential   A
ingredient of the offence thereby created that the defendant should, at a
particular date, be in control of certain pecuniary resources or property, or
both. The amount of the pecuniary resources as at the date in question can
obviously be expressed only in terms of money. But the description of other
items of property does not require any resort to money terms. All that is
needed initially is to look and see what particular items of property are
under the control of the defendant at the date specified in the charge.   B
Having proved the amount of pecuniary resources and the other assets in
the defendant's control at that date, the prosecution must go on to prove
his total official emoluments up to the same date, and finally it must
establish a disproportion between the two. The word " disproportionate
to " convey the idea that the acquisition of the total assets under the defendant's control at the relevant date could not reasonably, in all the circum-   C
stances, have been afforded out of the total official emoluments up to that
date. To put it another way, the question is whether such official
emoluments were or were not sufficient to finance the acquisitions which
resulted in the particular assets being under the defendant's control on the
relevant date. An answer to that question necessarily involves that the cost
of each acquisition should be examined. A mere comparison as at the
charge date of the then monetary value of the assets with the monetary   D
total up to that date of the official emoluments could not in itself, in a great
many cases, enable a satisfactory answer to be given, because the value of
certain types of asset can fluctuate widely from time to time.

The view that evidence of the acquisition cost of particular assets may
be relevant to establish disproportion derives support from a consideration
of certain other provisions of the Prevention of Bribery Ordinance. In the   E
first place, the provision in the latter part of section 10 (1) regarding satisfactory explanation by the defendant of how the pecuniary resources or
property came under his control plainly contemplates that the circumstances of acquisition should be gone into. That necessarily involves, in the
case of acquisitions for value, that the amount of the consideration paid
should be put in evidence. If the amount of the consideration is to be
relevant for the purpose of showing that any disproportion between assets   F
and emoluments is reasonable, it could hardly be irrelevant for the purpose
of proving the existence of an unreasonable disproportion. Then section 14
of the Ordinance, relating to the power of the commissioner to obtain
information where an offence under inter alia section 10 (1) (b) is alleged or
suspected, enables him, by subsection (1) (a) (i), to require any person to
specify the date upon which he acquired any particular property and, in   G
the event of acquisition by purchase, the consideration paid therefor. This
plainly indicates a statutory contemplation that evidence of such consideration may be relevant in proceedings under section 10 (1) (b).

In the result, their Lordships are of opinion that the terms of section
10 (1) (b) afford no warrant for the view that any artificial restriction has
been imposed as to the nature of the evidence which is admissible and   H
relevant for the purposes of proving an offence thereunder. In particular,
there is no rule of law to the effect that evidence of the market value as
at the charge date of the assets then under control of the defendant must in
all cases be led, nor rendering irrelevant evidence as to the acquisition cost
of such assets or, where appropriate, as to their value at the date of
acquisition. Evidence of the latter could obviously be important where

A property may have been acquired at an under-value under circumstances of corruption.

Their Lordships were referred to two cases as bearing on the point at issue, one in the Full Court and one in the Court of Appeal of Hong Kong. These are *Sturgeon* v. *The Queen* [1975] H.K.L.R. 677 and *Mok Chuen* v. *The Queen* [1977] H.K.L.R. 605. Their Lordships have no reason to suppose that either of these cases may have been wrongly decided, and neither
B of them touches so closely on the point at issue here as to call for any comment or criticism. Their Lordships were also referred to *Reg.* v. *Chung Cheong* (unreported), Victoria District Court (Hooper D.J.), December 22, 1977. The transcript of the judgment with which their Lordships were provided contains certain observations which are at variance with the view taken by them, and which must be regarded as erroneous.

C For these reasons their Lordships will humbly advise Her Majesty that the appeal should be allowed. The case will be remitted to the Court of Appeal to deal with the grounds of appeal which they left undecided. Since the appeal raised a point of principle of considerable importance to the criminal authorities in Hong Kong, there will be no order for costs.

D Solicitors: *Charles Russell & Co.; Bower, Cotton & Bower.*

T. J. M.

E
[QUEEN'S BENCH DIVISION]

* CLEAR v. SMITH

1980   Feb. 4   Lord Widgery C.J. and Wien J.

Social Security—Supplementary benefit—False statement or repre-
F *sentation—Dishonest statement by claimant that not working*
—Claimant dealing in scrap metal for no pecuniary reward—
Whether " work "—Whether finding of dishonesty sufficient
mens rea of offence—Supplementary Benefits Act 1976 (c. 71),
s. 21

During a period in which the defendant was in receipt
of unemployment and supplementary benefit, he frequently
used his motor vehicle and trailer to deliver scrap metal to
G dealers' yards for the benefit of others, including relatives
and friends. He received no payment for his services but
he was sometimes reimbursed for the petrol used. Each week
he completed a DHSS form stating that he had done no
work that week and signed a declaration that his statements
were true. Informations were preferred against him that for
the purposes of obtaining benefit he had made representations
that he knew were false, namely, that he had done no work
H whereas he had dealt in scrap metal, contrary to section 21
of the Supplementary Benefits Act 1976. The justices convicted the defendant of the offences, finding that, although
there was no evidence that he had received remuneration, he
was dealing in scrap as an almost full time occupation; he
himself considered that he was working and had dishonestly
made the statements to the contrary.
On appeal by the defendant: —
Held, dismissing the appeal, that there was no general
proposition that there had to be remuneration before an

Clear v. Smith (D.C.)   [1981]

A activity qualified as work and whether that activity did so qualify was a matter of fact and degree (post, pp. 405H—406A); that there was no requirement that the prosecution had to prove, under section 21 of the Supplementary Benefits Act 1976, that a false statement was made with the intention to defraud and, therefore, since the justices had found that the defendant had worked and acted dishonestly, he had correctly been convicted of making statements which he knew to be false (post, pp. 407E–F).

B

The following case is referred to in the judgment of Lord Widgery C.J.:

Moore v. *Branton* (1974) 118 S.J. 405, D.C.

No additional cases were cited in argument.

C CASE STATED by West Sussex justices sitting at Chichester.

On October 5, 1977, informations were preferred by the prosecutor, against the defendant, Michael Vernon Clear, that he (a) on or about November 8, 1976, at Chichester, for the purpose of obtaining for himself benefit under the Supplementary Benefit Act 1966, made a representation which he knew to be false, that was to say that he had done no work on any day in the week ending November 6, 1976, whereas during
D that week he had worked dealing in scrap, contrary to section 29 of the Supplementary Benefit Act 1966; (b) on or about November 15, 1976, at Chichester, the defendant, for the purpose of obtaining for himself benefit under the Supplementary Benefits Act 1976, made a representation which he knew to be false, that was to say that he had done no work on any day in the week ending November 13, 1976, whereas
E during that week he had worked dealing in scrap, contrary to section 21 of the Supplementary Benefits Act 1976; and (c) on or about January 10, 1977, at Chichester, the defendant, for the purpose of obtaining for himself benefit under the Supplementary Benefits Act 1976, made a representation which he knew to be false, that was to say that he had done no work on any day in the week ending January 8, 1977, whereas during that week he had worked dealing in scrap, contrary to section 21
F of the Supplementary Benefits Act 1976.

The justices heard the informations on December 20, 1977, and found that the defendant had been unemployed since 1975 and was still unemployed on January 22, 1977. His last employment had been as a farm worker. He lived with his wife and four children in temporary accommodation at Budgenor Lodge, Midhurst, during the relevant
G period from October 17, 1976, until January 22, 1977. Supplementary benefit was paid to the defendant during the period October 18, 1976, to January 20, 1977. On October 21, 1976, the defendant owned motor vehicle registration number NRV 660, scrapping that vehicle on November 16, 1976, replacing it by a motor vehicle registration number 7213 PJ. The defendant also owned a trailer which he used with those vehicles. The defendant had experience as a car breaker and knew how
H to dispose of scrap. During the week ending November 6, 1976, the defendant made ten separate deliveries of scrap to the scrap yard of C. D. Joiner & Son at Portsmouth, on five days, twice a day. During the week ending November 13, 1976, the defendant made three similar deliveries to the same scrap yard. During the week ending January 8, 1977, the defendant made two similar deliveries to the same scrap yard, both on January 7, 1977. During the period of 14 weeks from October

A 17, 1976, to January 22, 1977, the defendant made 25 similar deliveries to the same scrap yard on occasions other than those mentioned above. Twelve of the deliveries were made, two a day, on six separate days. The 40 deliveries of scrap made by the defendant were by means of either vehicle NRV 660 or 7213 PJ, on every occasion using his trailer on which to carry the loads. The scrap metal the defendant delivered comprised

B of old vehicle bodies or light iron. On each occasion the defendant made a delivery his journey would have been from Midhurst to Portsmouth via the point where the load was to be collected. Some of those collection points were Cocking, Boxgrove, Bepton and Angmering. The shortest journey would have been Midhurst to Portsmouth and return, approximately 64 miles. The journey via Boxgrove, approximately 66 miles, via Angmering—the longest journey—well under 100 miles. Each

C journey would take over two hours. The deliveries made by the defendant were for the benefit of others, including friends and relatives, to whom he gave the money he had been paid for the scrap. The money collected by the defendant amounted to £522.45. The defendant was voluntarily given quantities of petrol or sums of money to buy petrol up to about £2.50 per delivery by those whose scrap he had delivered.

D On some occasions the sums might not have covered the cost of the petrol actually used on the journeys.

The defendant made a declaration on DHSS form UB88P(S) on 14 occasions between October 23, 1976, and January 22, 1977, each declaration being in respect of a full week, including Sunday. That form was for use by a claimant for unemployment benefit and for supplementary allowance who was living six miles or more from the nearest

E unemployment benefit office. On each of the 14 occasions the defendant made a declaration on form UB88P(S) he wrote against each day of the week " unemployed " and signed p. 3. The defendant had had DHSS leaflet UBL 18 read to him by his wife because he could not read. He was aware of its contents.

The justices found that the defendant had expected official offers

F of employment to be sent to him by post. He had made no other arrangements as to how he could be contacted during the day if, for example, he was on a journey delivering scrap. That, the justices found, did not comply with Part III of explanatory leaflet UBL 18. There were 12 days during the period October 1976 to January 1977, when the defendant was fully engaged for the whole day delivering scrap during which time he could not be contacted immediately should an offer of

G employment have been made to him. The defendant was bored with unemployment, his wife was unwell and their accommodation was cramped. The evidence of the defendant, his witnesses and prosecution witness Stent and Merry appeared to be rather well-rehearsed, their recollections fitted in too neatly with the common defence story, being slightly vague on detail perhaps to escape detection when pressed on inaccuracies. The

H justices were not convinced of the truthfulness of the defendant's evidence and not impressed by the innocent interpretation he placed on the regular and almost full time work he had done. The justices found the defendant to be a man of average intelligence.

[The case stated then set out notes of the evidence and continued:] It was contended by the defendant that the deliveries he made of scrap metal was not " work " dealing in scrap, but he was doing favours for friends and relatives because he was bored. The money he received

for the deliveries he made was not remuneration but reimbursement of   A
the cost of petrol. The defendant also contended that the evidence did
not prove he had made a false declaration for the purpose of obtaining
supplementary benefit knowing it to be false.

It was contended by the prosecutor that the regularity of the
defendant's deliveries to Portsmouth with scrap metal showed that he was
doing " work " dealing in scrap; that he was not available for offers of   B
employment whilst making those deliveries and could not be contacted
when away from home. The prosecutor further contended that the
defendant was receiving payment for his services and that there were
other transactions which had not been explained; the defendant was
working during times when he was claiming supplementary benefit
and declaring that he was not working, that he therefore made false
representations knowing them to be false.   C

The justices' opinion set out in the judgment of Lord Widgery C.J.,
post, pp. 404H—405C, E–H, stated that the defendant knew that he was
doing work dealing in scrap.

The justices were satisfied that he knowingly made false declarations
on the three occasions covered by the informations, and accordingly they
convicted the defendant of the three informations, fined him £20 on each,   D
ordered him to pay £35 prosecutor's costs and £20 legal aid contribution.

The defendant appealed. The questions for the opinion of the High
Court were (a) whether the justices' definition of " work " was correct in
law, and (b) whether the evidence put before the justices justified their
finding as a fact that the defendant had made a false declaration to the
Department of Health and Social Security knowing it to be false or
not believing it to be true.   E

Robert Seabrook for the defendant.
Simon D. Brown for the prosecutor.

LORD WIDGERY C.J. Before giving judgment in this case I would
like to draw attention to the very long statement of evidence which   F
the stated case includes. Rule 65 of the Magistrates' Courts Rules 1968
tells an appellant what he should do in this regard, and those who tax
costs will soon have to consider reacting in cases where an unnecessary
statement of the evidence has been given.

To come back to the case before us, this is an appeal by case stated
by West Sussex justices sitting at Chichester on December 20, 1977.   G
On that occasion the justices were dealing with three charges all brought
by the respondent prosecutor against the appellant defendant, and it
suffices if I read the details of the first. It was:

" On October 5, 1977, informations were preferred by the prosecutor
against the defendant that he: (a) on or about November 8, 1976,
at Chichester for the purpose of obtaining for himself benefit under
the Supplementary Benefit Act 1966, made a representation which he   H
knew to be false, that is to say, that he had done no work on any
day in the week ending November 6, 1976, whereas during the said
week he had worked dealing in scrap, contrary to section 29 of the
Supplementary Benefit Act 1966."

The other two charges, as I say, are of a similar kind charged under the
equivalent section of the Supplementary Benefits Act 1976, section 21,

A   and it is evident what the case is all about. It was said below that the defendant in claiming supplementary benefit had made a false representation to support his application.

The facts are quite brief but they are all important. The defendant had been unemployed since 1975, and he gave evidence that he had become bored by his inactivity and was looking for ways of employing
B   himself. He was unemployed in January 1977 and his last employment had been as a farm worker. He had a wife and four children. He lived in Sussex in temporary accommodation throughout the period relevant to this case, which is from October 17, 1976, until January 22, 1977. Supplementary benefit was paid to the defendant during the period October 1976 to January 1977.

On October 21, 1976, the defendant owned a motor vehicle and it had
C   a trailer. He used this vehicle and trailer to carry scrap metal of various kinds to Portsmouth on behalf of persons in his neighbourhood in Sussex who had scrap to dispose of and who would welcome the opportunity of having it transported. The work which it is alleged to have been done by the defendant and the reference to which his declaration is said to be false was the work of carrying scrap to the scrap merchants with the
D   use of these vehicles.

The defendant, in a sense, was specially suited to dealing with these activities, because he had been a car breaker. He knew how to dispose of scrap. He was also a keen grass track racer, and obviously had the eye and nose for motors which those two activities suggest.

In the week ending November 6, 1976, he made 10 separate deliveries
E   of scrap to a scrap yard at Portsmouth. He went on five days during the week, and he went twice a day during those five days. In the next week he made three similar deliveries, as against 10 in the week ending November 6, 1976. Then during the next week, referred to ending January 8, 1977, the defendant made two similar deliveries to the same scrap yard, both on January 7, 1977.

The case goes on to find that during the period of 14 weeks, October
F   17, 1976, to January 22, 1977, the defendant made 25 similar deliveries to the same scrap yard on occasions other than those mentioned above. Twelve of the deliveries were made, two a day, on six separate days. The 40 deliveries of scrap made by the defendant were by means either of the vehicle I have already referred to or another, on every occasion using the same trailer. The scrap metal, the justices find, which the
G   defendant delivered comprised of old vehicle bodies or light iron.

They go on to describe the nature of the route which had to be followed by the defendant when making these deliveries, and they disclose that the shortest journeys were 64 miles return and the longest journeys were up to 100 miles return, these journeys being done, as I have already recited, up to twice in a day.

The most interesting finding of the justices at this stage is the finding
H   in the case stated:

"The deliveries made by the defendant were for the benefit of others, including friends and relatives, to whom he gave the money he had been paid for the scrap. The money collected by the defendant amounted to £522.45."

Now one sees the nub of the case. What is alleged is that he has been carrying this scrap gratuitously for friends and relatives, and that substantially supports the argument brought by Mr. Seabrook that there A was no work being done at the relevant time.

The justices find that the defendant was given petrol by the friends or relatives from time to time. Obviously he was not intended to suffer in his pocket by reason of doing this, but whether or not the petrol given to him balanced that which was expended on the journeys we do not know.

The documentation of the case comes in this wise. There is a form B UB88P(S) which contains declarations that an applicant is required to complete if he is claiming supplementary benefit and is a man who would normally work. We find in looking at these papers that the first form to be filled up by the applicant who wants supplementary benefit is a form which requires him to say every day of the week whether he was unemployed or whether he was working. The defendant—and it is not C disputed—on every day of the relevant weeks entered the word " Unemployed." The fact that he must not do that if he is working is stressed on the next page of the pamphlet which requires the defendant to declare:

" (1) I have read and understand the leaflet ' responsibilities of claimants ' (UBL 18) and I have reported everything that I am D required to report and (2) on each day on p. 2 against which I have written ' Unemployed ' (a) I was unemployed and did no work; (b) I was able and willing to do any suitable work but was unable to get any."

There is his declaration in the clearest terms that on the days in question (and I have identified them already) he was unemployed and E did no work. In point of fact, on the days in question he went to Portsmouth once or twice a day.

One focuses attention on what is really the point of the case. We have to decide whether his trips to Portsmouth once or twice a day, carried out as he says for the benefit of friends and relatives, prevented him from certifying for himself on this supplementary benefit literature F that he had not worked and was unemployed.

The word " work " in this context does not come from any statute. It comes from the terms of the pamphlet to which I have specifically referred. We were not, therefore, concerned with looking for Parliamentary intention in regard to these matters in this case; we are concerned with looking to the declaration which the defendant unquestionably signed and considering whether by so doing he made the G false representation which is alleged against him.

The justices give a fairly extensive statement of their opinion, and I think it is almost necessary to read the whole of it. They say:

" We were of opinion that the regular use by the defendant of his own vehicles with which to dispose of scrap involving journeys in excess of 60 miles, and the effort, energy and time he expended on the H deliveries and also the employment of his knowledge of cars and the scrap business was clear evidence that he was engaged, albeit on a casual basis, on work dealing in scrap. Moreover the scrap merchants at Portsmouth were clearly of the opinion that they were dealing with the defendant as the principal and not as the agent. The three informations before us were only specimen offences. The whole of the evidence, which included all the scrap deliveries made

A by the defendant over a relatively short period, showed a clear pattern, illustrating to us that the defendant was involved in an almost full time occupation. He was following a line of work which he had knowledge of and experience in and not, significantly, another perhaps less arduous pursuit to relieve boredom he suffered during the time he was unemployed. The first of the three informations dealt with the week ending November 6, 1976. During that week . . ."

B

and then they set out the journeys during the week to which I have referred. Then there is this very important finding of the justices at this point in their case. They say:

C "We were of opinion that there was no doubt in the defendant's mind that he was working. The declaration he made for the purpose of claiming unemployment benefit was that he was unemployed and did no work every day of that week. That declaration was false and he was dishonest in making it."

Later on the justices accept, as the evidence clearly required them to do, that the statement of the defendant that he was doing this gratuitously for his friends and relatives could not be upset, but it is quite obvious that the justices, in the passages I have read, together with another passage in which they describe the defendant as being somewhat over-rehearsed, were not impressed with his truthfulness and found him to be dishonest in the regards to which I have referred.

Those matters being the facts upon which the court has to rely and the views of the justices having been duly recorded, further findings of the justices are expressed in this way:

"We were of opinion that the word 'work' in the context of this case had a special connotation. It was special because the defendant was receiving state unemployment benefit and he had been warned that he must not claim benefit unless he was unemployed and did no work on the days in respect of which he claimed. This would, we were of opinion, put the defendant on inquiry, that is to examine carefully any activity he was engaged in and, if he had any doubt about whether the authorities would class it as work or not, to declare it. No intelligent man could mislead himself as to the nature of the work which the defendant was engaged upon. We were of opinion that the defendant, although he could not read, was a man of average intelligence and that he knew that he was doing work dealing in scrap. We were satisfied that he knowingly made false declarations on the three occasions covered by the informations, and accordingly we convicted the defendant of the three informations . . ."

It cannot be doubted, in my judgment, that, if the defendant had been carrying out this activity for reward, that activity would have been work. The word "work" has to be given its ordinary meaning in this context, and it would be satisfied by showing that the defendant, with his car and trailer, was carrying scrap if the scrap had been carried for remuneration.

The whole question here on the first argument in this case is whether it makes any difference that the work should be done not for remuneration but done in the manner in which I have described. I think this is,

above all, a point for the justices as a question of fact and degree. A
One cannot possibly lay down as a general proposition that an unpaid
activity is not work. As was suggested in argument, no housewife would
be ready to accept that proposition with equanimity. On the other
hand, it does not follow that every activity which is backed up by
remuneration is work. It is a question of fact and degree for the
justices to give the word a commonsense meaning in its context as part
of a declaration.   B

Therefore, looking at the matter objectively, one would say that the
justices' decision was based upon factors and facts which they were
entitled to base it upon and, looking at the matter objectively, the
justices were entitled to find that the work was work and thus to get one
step at all events towards convicting the defendant.

But the matter does not necessarily stop there, because we have C
been given a transcript of the judgment in *Moore* v. *Branton* (1974) 118
S.J. 405. It is a decision of this court of May 7, 1974, and it is concerned with a matter very close to the present case because it is
concerned with a declaration made by a person in receipt of supplementary benefit which was said later on to be false and to have produced
the same criminal responsibility which is produced in the instant case D
before us.

What had happened in *Moore's* case, in a word or two, was that
the husband and wife had parted and then they had had what was
described in the case as a trial reconciliation. They had come back
together to some degree to see if they could make a fresh start. The
regulations required that the factor be disclosed if the husband came
back to live with his wife or wife came back to live with her husband, E
and in this case it was not disclosed.

The case is reported in a footnote in *Stone's Justices' Manual*, 112th
ed. (1980) vol. 2, p. 4188 and Mr. Brown tells us it has been giving a
great deal of trouble from time to time. If that is so, it is worth noting
that the case was not decided upon any of the issues of fact which are
canvassed in the instant case; on the contrary, there was not enough F
evidence to show that the husband had returned to his wife. The
basic proposition that the parties had come together again was not made
out. That being the case, of course the authority is of no value as an
authority at all. It is to be hoped that it will be put in a place appropriate to its value accordingly.

That does not mean of course that the question of mens rea is
wholly outside this case. It seems to me, I must say, to have a very G
limited application. But Mr. Brown submits, and I would not be disposed to quarrel with him, that if the objective test is satisfied in this
case, as it is, all that is further necessary is to prove that the defendant
knew when he signed the declaration that it was false.

There can be no doubt to my mind that that requirement is also
satisfied because of the finding of dishonesty in the text of the case H
itself. If the finding of dishonesty is made out, as it was, then I have
no trouble in satisfying myself that the defendant knew of the nature
of the falsity in his declaration when he signed it. Accordingly, I would
dismiss this appeal.

WIEN J. The main submission on behalf of the defendant was that
the word " work " in the declaration which the defendant signed of

A necessity means remunerative work, that is that either the defendant received some sort of payment or received something in kind to reward him for the work that he undoubtedly did.

In my view, that is stretching the meaning of the word too far. It does not of necessity follow that the word " work " has to denote some reward for a declaration of this nature to be false.

B The two questions which to my mind have to be posed are these: did the defendant's activities come within the meaning of " work " in the declaration? If they did, then did the defendant know that his declaration was false?

I think the answer to the first question is clear. His activities consisted of almost full time work over the relevant periods. The justices were perfectly entitled to come to the conclusion on the evidence C that his activities did come within the meaning of the word " work."

If that be so, then the only other question that had to be answered in order to convict this defendant was: did he know that his declaration was false in this respect? He knew what the meaning of the word " work " was because that work covered his activities, and he also knew that that declaration was false. That is all covered by the findings of the D justices who said quite explicitly:

"We were of opinion that there was no doubt in the defendant's mind that he was working. The declaration he made for the purpose of claiming unemployment benefit was that he was unemployed and did not work every day of that week. That declaration was false and he was dishonest in making it."

E That being so, it seems to me that there is no scope for the contention that in this case the justices were wrong.

It was submitted on behalf of the defendant that the mens rea in this case was an intention to defraud. I venture to disagree. All that had to be proved was that for the purpose of obtaining for himself benefit under the Supplementary Benefit Act 1966, this defendant made F a representation which he knew to be false, namely, that he had done no work on some particular days. What that means is that he knowingly made a declaration that was false. It would also follow of course that he could not know that it was false unless he were dishonest. That finding has in fact been made.

It seems to me immaterial that the justices at some part of the case concerned themselves with availability for work in accordance with the G words used in one of the pamphlets. To my mind, that is irrelevant and the justices need not have concerned themselves with that aspect of the case. For the reasons given by Lord Widgery C.J., I agree that this appeal fails.

Appeal dismissed.
No order for costs.

H

Solicitors: *Thomas Eggar & Son, Chichester; Solicitor, Department of Health and Social Security.*

H. J.

[1981]

A

[QUEEN'S BENCH DIVISION]

* BARRASS v. REEVE

1980 May 20   Waller L.J. and Park J.

Social Security—Sickness benefit—False representation—Untrue B
statement made to deceive employer—No intention to obtain
extra benefit — Whether offence — Social Security Act 1975
(c. 14), s. 146 (3)

On March 4, 1977, the defendant completed and signed
a form claiming sickness benefit under the Social Security
Act 1975, declaring that he last worked on February 25,
1977, and that he became unfit for work on February 28, C
1977. He knew that the statement as to the date on which he
last worked was false, since unknown to his employer he had
been engaged by a company between February 28 and March
2, 1977, to assist in the boarding of a ship. The defendant
believed that his claim for benefit was from March 4 and
was unaware that waiting days would count from February
28, and he made the false statement not for the purpose of
obtaining benefit to which he was not entitled, but in order D
to deceive his employer so that he would not lose his job.
An information was preferred against him that he knowingly
made a false representation for the purpose of obtaining
benefit, contrary to section 146 (3) of the Act of 1975.[1] The
justices found that, while the defendant's deception of his
employer was reprehensible, he lacked the necessary mens
rea of the offence under section 146 (3), and accordingly
they dismissed the information.   E

On appeal by the prosecutor: —

Held, allowing the appeal, that the ingredient of the
offence under section 146 (3) of the Act was the making of
a statement that was known to be untrue and not the
intention to obtain benefit to which the claimant was not
entitled; that, accordingly, the fact that the false statement
was made solely to deceive the defendant's employer was F
irrelevant and he had committed an offence under the subsection (post, pp. 411c–e, 413c–d).

Stevens & Steeds Ltd. v. *King* [1943] 1 All E.R. 314,
D.C. and *Clear* v. *Smith* [1981] 1 W.L.R. 399, D.C. applied.

The following cases are referred to in the judgment of Waller L.J.:

Clear v. *Smith* [1981] 1 W.L.R. 399, D.C.
Moore v. *Branton* (1974) 118 S.J. 405, D.C.   G
Stevens & Steeds Ltd. v. *King* [1943] 1 All E.R. 314, D.C.

No additional cases were cited in argument.

CASE STATED by Humberside justices sitting at Grimsby.

On March 2, 1978, an information was preferred by the prosecutor, H
Maureen Barrass, against the defendant, George William Reeve, that
he on March 7, 1977, at Grimsby, for the purpose of obtaining for
himself benefit under the Social Security Act 1975, knowingly made a
false representation, namely, that he last worked on February 25, 1977,
whereas he worked on subsequent days assisting in the boarding of

[1] Social Security Act 1975, s. 146 (3): see post, p. 410e–f.

A   *M.T. Globtik Venus,* contrary to section 146 (3) of the Social Security
Act 1975.

The justices heard the information on May 24, 1978, and found the
following facts. The defendant signed and completed a benefit claim
form on March 4, 1977, declaring that he became unfit for work on
Monday, February 28, 1977, and that he last worked on Friday, February
25, 1977. The defendant was engaged by Globtik Management Ltd.
B   between February 28, 1977, and March 2, 1977, and was paid for his
services. The defendant knew the statement as to the last date on which
he worked on the claim form was false. The defendant completed the
claim form on March 4, 1977, on which date the doctor examined him
and advised that he should refrain from work for ten days.

It was contended by the prosecutor that having completed the
C   declaration on the claim form, which was admitted to contain a false
statement which was made knowingly, albeit to deceive his employer,
and not having shown any way in which he intended to prevent benefit
being paid to him wrongly, the justices should conclude that he had
knowingly made the false representation for the purpose of obtaining
benefit for himself.

It was conceded by the defendant that he had made a false statement,
D   but that it was only to deceive his employer, and it was contended that
mens rea had to be shown to exist for the purpose alleged in the
information.

The justices were of the opinion that the defendant, on completing
the form, believed his claim for benefit was from March 4, 1977, and
was ignorant of the fact that waiting days would count from February
E   28, 1977; that the defendant completed the form in the way he did to
deceive his employer so that he would not lose his job; that that deception,
whilst reprehensible, did not amount to mens rea as far as the offence
was concerned, i.e. it was not made for the purpose of obtaining benefit
for himself under the Act of 1975; and that, being satisfied that the
defendant believed what he had put could not affect the date from
which he would be paid benefit, they should follow the ruling in *Moore*
F   v. *Branton* (1974) 118 S.J. 405 and, accordingly, they dismissed the
information.

The prosecutor appealed. The question for the opinion of the High
Court was whether, on the facts, the justices were entitled to conclude
that the defendant was not guilty of the offence.

G   *Simon D. Brown* for the prosecutor.
Peter Morrell for the defendant.

WALLER L.J. This is an appeal by way of case stated from Humberside justices sitting at Grimsby. On May 24, 1978, they heard an
information which had been preferred on March 2, 1978, alleging that
for the purpose of obtaining for himself benefit under the Social Security
H   Act 1975, the defendant knowingly made a false representation, namely,
that he had last worked on February 25, 1977, whereas he worked on
subsequent days assisting in the boarding of the vessel *Globtik Venus,*
contrary to section 146 (3) of the Social Security Act 1975.

The situation was that the defendant was regularly employed by
one employer and had worked for him up to and including Friday,
February 25, 1977. On February 28, 1977, the defendant did some
other work assisting in the boarding of the vessel *Globtik Venus* and

410

he took part in assisting in the boarding on March 2. Then two days   A
later, on March 4, 1977, he filled in a form claiming benefit. The form
said: " When did you become unfit to work? On Monday February 28.
On what day did you last work? On Friday February 25 " and then
finished stating the time he had finished. That form was signed by the
defendant on March 4, 1977, the Friday.

    The justices, having heard the case (and I do not think it is necessary
to refer to any other of the facts), found that the defendant conceded   B
that he had made a false statement but that he had only made it to
deceive his employer. As it was submitted that mens rea had to be
shown to exist for the purpose alleged in the information, that is to say
for the purpose of obtaining benefit, they were of the opinion that he,
completing the form, believed his claim for benefit was from March 4
and was ignorant of the fact that waiting days would count from   C
February 28. In other words, he did in fact obtain slightly more benefit
than he would otherwise have done, but he was ignorant of that. As
they found that he believed that what he had put could not affect the
date from which he would be paid benefit, they followed the ruling in
Moore v. Branton (1974) 118 S.J. 405 and accordingly dismissed the
information. The question they ask is whether or not they came to a
correct conclusion.   D

    The issue which has been argued before this court is whether or not
there is a third ingredient in the offence or whether it consists only of
two. The first ingredient is: was there a false representation? The
second is: was the false representation known to be false? The third
(and this is the one in issue) is: was it falsely made for the purpose of
obtaining benefit?   E

    Section 146 (3) of the Social Security Act 1975 provides:

    " If a person—. . . (c) for the purpose of obtaining any benefit
    or other payment under this Act, whether for himself or some
    other person, or for any other purpose connected with this Act—
    (i) knowingly makes any false statement or false representation . . .
    he shall be liable on summary conviction to a fine not more than   F
    £400, or to imprisonment for a term not more than 3 months, or
    to both."

The justices in their finding, having come to the conclusion that the
falsity of the declaration by the defendant was not made for the purpose
of obtaining extra benefit, acquitted him.

    It is submitted on behalf of the prosecutor by Mr. Brown on behalf   G
of the Department of Health and Social Security that in doing so the
justices were in error. He relied first on Stevens & Steeds Ltd. v.
King [1943] 1 All E.R. 314, where a case under article 42 of the
Rationing Order 1939 was considered by this court. That article said:

    " A person shall not: for the purpose of obtaining any rationed
    food make any statement which he knows to be false in a material
    particular or recklessly make any statement which he knows to   H
    be false in a material particular . . ."

The only difference between the form of that article and the subsection
with which we are concerned is the part which deals with a reckless
statement.

    The court came to the conclusion there that, where statements were
made which were false, the fact that the falsity did not in itself achieve

A any benefit from the regulations was not something which made any difference to the offence. Viscount Caldecote C.J., in giving judgment, said, at p. 315:

> " Therefore, in the ordinary sense of the words, it seems to me that these documents were made for the purpose of obtaining rationed food, although it is possible that the evidence would not
> B have justified a finding that they attempted to obtain any rationed food by means of such a reckless statement. It is of obvious importance to the food department to have accurate returns for the purpose of distributing available supplies and of estimating the supplies which will be required in the future. I have come to the conclusion, therefore, that in respect of those three articles of food, as well as in the case of the cheese, there was evidence upon
> C which the magistrates could come to the conclusion that an offence had been committed under article 42."

The effect of that decision was that the court came to the conclusion that it was not an ingredient of the offence that the representation should be falsely made in order to achieve a greater benefit from the rationing restrictions.

D   That authority would appear to show that when similar words are used in the Social Security Act 1975 the same consequences would follow; in other words " for the purpose of obtaining any benefit or other payment under this Act . . . knowingly makes any false statement or false representation." In other words, the form is " for the purpose of obtaining benefit " and if in that form a false representation is
E knowingly made the offence would have been committed. The prosecutor submits that one does not have to go further and show that it was actually falsely made with the object of obtaining extra benefit.

The difficulty in the way of that construction, which I am bound to say strikes me as the correct construction, is the decision of *Moore* v. *Branton,* 118 S.J. 405 which was referred to by the justices in this case. That was a case where the appellant was claiming benefit under the
F Supplementary Benefit Act 1966 (formerly the Ministry of Social Security Act 1966) and she had to make a regular declaration as to the state in which she was living. She was obtaining benefit because she was separated from her husband and was living alone. There was a week-end when, in an effort to obtain a reconciliation, the husband spent either one or two nights in the house. The form warned the appellant
G that if any part of the declaration was not true it would be a criminal offence. One of the things that she was required to state was whether there was a change of circumstance, including the question of whether somebody had come to live in the house or whether anybody now living in the house had gone away. She did not disclose that. The allegation was that she failed to disclose something which under the provisions of the allowance book she was required to disclose and represented—this was
H her representation—that she was entitled to the sum of £18·10 whereas this was not true because she had become reconciled with her husband.

The justices came to the conclusion that there was a trial reconciliation, but this court came to the conclusion that in reality there was no reconciliation. What they found in terms is that her failure to make a disclosure about the trial reconciliation was not a dishonest failure with the object of swindling the Department of Social Security, and there is no doubt whatever that that was true.

The difficulty arises in this way: that this court came to the conclusion that there was no misstatement that there had been no change of circumstances. Bristow J. came to the conclusion it was very doubtful whether as a matter of law her husband coming at the weekend was within the paragraph at all. But in the course of his judgment he said that, in his view, section 29 created a criminal offence which involved mens rea in the true sense. In explaining what the true sense was, he said:

"In my judgment the evil aimed at by section 29 is getting money out of the Department of Social Security by dishonesty. In this case the justices find specifically that Mrs. Moore was not dishonest in what she did; she did not think, and they found that her evidence to that effect was true, that what happened in her case would have affected the amount of her benefit."

If that were the end of what Bristow J. said, that would be inconsistent with the view that I have just expressed, but he went on:

"Indeed, when one looks at the terms of paragraph 6 of the coloured pages of the allowance book, it is doubtful whether as a matter of law her husband's coming for weekends falls within paragraph 6 (5) (c) at all. Whether it does or not, the justices' findings are that she genuinely did not believe that her failure to disclose that partial reconciliation was something which could affect the amount of the social security she was receiving."

The note of that, we are told, in Stone's Justices' Manual, 112th ed. (1980), vol. 2, p. 4188, does not fully represent the decision of the court. This court in Clear v. Smith [1981] 1 W.L.R. 399 had to consider again similar words in relation to section 29 of the Supplementary Benefit Act 1966. There the false statement was that the appellant had done no work on any day in a week when in fact he had been doing work for which he had not been paid. Lord Widgery C.J. in the course of his judgment said, ante p. 406c:

"But the matter does not necessarily stop there, because we have been given a transcript of the judgment in Moore v. Branton (1974) 118 S.J. 405. It is a decision of this court of May 7, 1974, and it is concerned with a matter very close to the present case because it is concerned with a declaration made by a person in receipt of supplementary benefit which was said later on to be false and to have produced the same criminal responsibility which is produced in the instant case before us."

Then Lord Widgery C.J. sets out briefly the facts and says, ante, p. 406G:

"That does not mean of course that the question of mens rea is wholly outside this case. It seems to me, I must say, to have a very limited application. But Mr. Brown submits, and I would not be disposed to quarrel with him, that, if the objective test is satisfied in this case, as it is, all that is further necessary is to prove that the defendant knew when he signed the declaration that it was false."

Wien J. says, ante, p. 407E–F:

"It was submitted on behalf of the defendant that the mens rea in this case was an intention to defraud. I venture to disagree. All that had to be proved was that for the purpose of obtaining

1 W.L.R.   Barrass v. Reeve (D.C.)   Waller L.J.

A for himself benefit under the Supplementary Benefit Act 1966, this defendant made a representation which he knew to be false, namely, that he had done no work on some particular days. What that means is that he knowingly made a declaration that was false. It would also follow of course that he could not know that it was false unless he was dishonest. That finding has in fact been made."

B As it seems to me, that decision of the court, which was given on February 4, 1980, and of which we have a transcript, is wholly in line with the earlier decision on the defence regulation in *Stevens & Steeds Ltd.* v. *King* [1943] 1 All E.R. 314. If it is inconsistent with *Moore* v. *Branton,* 118 S.J. 405, I would think it was right to follow the later case of *Clear* v. *Smith* [1981] 1 W.L.R. 399. But, as Mr. Brown has indicated, there is a difference in the facts of *Moore* v. *Branton* in that the representation which was the basis of the case was that she was entitled to the sum of £18.10 which was rather different to the factual representations with which we are concerned.

In my judgment, the plain words of this subsection are covered if a person, for the purpose of obtaining any benefit or other payments under this Act, knowingly makes any false statement or false represen-
D tation. There are no words to say " with intent to obtain money " or anything of that sort. In my judgment, the offence is committed when there is a false representation made which the person claiming benefit knows to be false. I would, therefore, allow this appeal.

E PARK J. I agree.

Appeal allowed.
Case remitted to justices with direction to convict.
Leave to appeal refused.

F Solicitors: *Solicitor, Department of Health and Social Security; John Barkers, Grimsby.*

H. J.

G

[QUEEN'S BENCH DIVISION]

* REGINA *v.* WORTHING JUSTICES, *Ex parte* NORVELL AND ANOTHER

H 1980 Oct. 17   Donaldson L.J. and McNeill J.

Justices—Summons—Application for—Clerk to justices refusing application—Whether justices required to reconsider application—Justices' Clerks Rules 1970 (S.I. 1970 No. 231), r. 3, Sch., para. 2

The applicants applied to the magistrates' court for the issue of summonses against two named individuals for perjury. The clerk to the justices, acting under the Justices' Clerks

Rules 1970,[1] heard their application in a hearing which lasted   A
over two hours. After considering the evidence he exercised
his judicial discretion and, without giving reasons, declined
to issue the summonses.

On an application for an order of mandamus requiring the
justices to issue a summons: —

Held, refusing the application, (1) that, although the
justices could give reasons for their decision, it was neither
usual nor obligatory for a magistrates' court to do so.   B

(2) That, where a justices' clerk acted under rule 3 of
the Justices' Clerks Rules 1970, his position was that of a
single justice, and, therefore, since the justices could not be
required to consider an application for the issue of a summons
which had already been dismissed by justices of the same
bench, they could not be required to reconsider the application
dismissed by their clerk.

C

The following case is referred to in the judgment of Donaldson L.J.:

Reg. v. *Battier* (1880) 44 J.P. 490.

No additional cases were cited in argument.

APPLICATION for judicial review.   D

The applicants, Patricia Audrey Norvell of Worthing, Sussex, and
George James Abbot of Harrowby Street, London, a private investigator,
applied for a judicial review of the refusal of the clerk to the Worthing
justices to issue a summons and sought an order of mandamus directed to
the Worthing justices, requiring them to hear and determine a charge by
the applicants of perjury which they alleged had been committed by a
solicitor and a solicitor's managing clerk.   E

The facts are stated in the judgment of Donaldson L.J.

The applicants in person.
Simon D. Brown for the justices.

DONALDSON L.J. This is an application for judicial review brought   F
by the applicants in respect of a decision of the Worthing justices refusing to issue a summons against two named individuals for perjury.

What happened was that the applicants applied to the magistrates'
court for the issue of the summonses and they were seen by the clerk
to the justices. He heard their application in the ordinary way and did
so at very considerable length, as was right because, as has been stressed   G
by the applicant, Mr. Abbot, this is a very serious matter, serious not
only for the applicants but equally serious for the two people to whom
the summonses would be addressed if they were issued. I can think of
few things more serious than to be served with summonses alleging
perjury. The clerk to the justices considered the evidence which the
applicants put before him and the hearing lasted over two hours. In
the end he declined to issue the summonses. In that he was exercising   H
a judicial discretion.

The applicants complain that he did not give reasons for his refusal,
but there are a number of spheres of judicial activity where reasons are

---

[1] Justices' Clerks Rules 1970, r. 3: "The things specified in the Schedule to
these Rules, being things authorised to be done by, to or before a single justice
. . . may be done by, to or before the justices' clerk . . ."
Sch., para. 2: "The issue of any summons, including a witness summons."

The Weekly Law Reports, April 10, 1981

415

1 W.L.R.   Reg. v. Worthing Justices, Ex p. Norvell (D.C.)   Donaldson L.J.

A not given. In this court itself it is not usual to give reasons when refusing ex parte applications for leave to bring proceedings. It is not usual in magistrates' courts to give reasons for finding a case proved. It is not usual to give reasons for declining to issue summonses, although it is always open of course to any court to give reasons, particularly where the giving of reasons would be helpful. For example, if somebody

B applies for the issue of a summons but they fail to supply an essential piece of evidence which has to be put before the justice before a summons can be issued, it is helpful if a justice says " But you have forgotten to bring evidence on this point. If you come back with that evidence, it may be you can have your summons." But there is no obligation to give reasons.

    Then I move on to what is the essential point, because the applicants

C want an order requiring the justices to issue a summons notwithstanding that there is already a decision by their clerk that the summonses shall not issue.

    The real point in this case, and I do not doubt the point in respect of which leave to apply was given, is whether a decision by the clerk to justices that a summons shall not issue in any way binds the justices in

D the same way as would a decision of one of the justices themselves.

    Mr. Brown has helped us by taking us to the authorities, and it is quite clear that where a clerk acts under the Justices' Clerks Rules 1970 in respect of any of the matters set out in Schedule 1, which includes dealing with the laying of an information or the making of a complaint, he is acting as a justice. That is made clear beyond peradventure by section 28 of the Justices of the Peace Act 1979, which is in some ways a

E consolidating statute. This provides:

> " (1) Rules made in accordance with section 15 of the Justices of the Peace Act 1949 may (except in so far as any enactment passed after October 25, 1968, otherwise directs) make provision enabling things authorised to be done by, to or before a single justice of the peace to be done instead by, to or before a justices' clerk. (2) Any enact-
>
> F ment (including any enactment contained in this Act) or any rule of law regulating the exercise of any jurisdiction or powers of justices of the peace, or relating to things done in the exercise or purported exercise of any such jurisdiction or powers, shall apply in relation to the exercise or purported exercise thereof by virtue of subsection (1) above by the clerk to any justices as if he were one of those
>
> G justices."

    The position here is that the clerk has decided in exactly the same way as a single justice could have decided that these summonses should not issue. Once one gets to that position and it is appreciated that the clerk is not in a different position from that of a single justice, the question arises of whether there are any possible grounds requiring us

H to issue an order ordering the justices to issue these summonses.

    It may be doubtful whether it is proper for justices to decide, as a matter of discretion, to entertain a second application on exactly the same material as has been considered by other justices of the same bench, but we do not have to decide that definitively in this case. Suffice it to say that it would be wholly impossible, in my judgment, for this court to require justices to reconsider an application which had already been dismissed by their fellow justices. If authority be required for so

Donaldson L.J.   **Reg. v. Worthing Justices, Ex p. Norvell (D.C.)**   **[1981]**

obvious a proposition, it is to be found in *Reg.* v. *Battier* (1880) 44 J.P.   A
490. Accordingly, I would refuse this application.

McNEILL J.   I agree.

Application refused.

Solicitor: *Treasury Solicitor.*

R. D.

────────────

C

[COURT OF APPEAL]

* REGINA *v.* HUSSAIN

1980 Oct. 30;   Eveleigh L.J., Cantley and Lloyd JJ.
      Nov. 19
                                                                              D

*Crime—Firearms—Possession—Pen gun used as toy gun—No
certificate—No knowledge that gun lethal weapon—Whether
absolute offence—Firearms Act* 1968 (c. 27), s. 1 (1) (a)

  The police found in the defendant's house a metal tube
eight inches in length with a striker pin activated by a spring
which the defendant claimed was a toy gun and at one time   E
used by his young son to fire corks. Ballistic tests showed that
the gun was capable of firing ·32 cartridges. The defendant
was charged with possessing a firearm without a certificate,
contrary to section 1 of the Firearms Act 1968. The judge
directed the jury that if they found that the gun was a lethal
weapon, it would be a firearm and the defendant would be
guilty of the offence if they found that he was in possession
of the article, even though he might not know it was a   F
firearm. The defendant was convicted.
  On the defendant's appeal against conviction: —
  Held, dismissing the appeal, that the offence created by
section 1 of the Firearms Act 1968 was the possession of a
firearm without a certificate; that it was immaterial that the
defendant did not know the nature of the article in his
possession and, therefore, the jury had arrived at their verdict
on a correct direction by the judge.
                                                                              G
  Reg. v. *Warner* [1969] 2 A.C. 256, H.L.(E.) applied.

The following cases are referred to in the judgment:

Reg. v. *Howells* [1977] Q.B. 614; [1977] 2 W.L.R. 716; [1977] 3 All
  E.R. 417; 65 Cr.App.R. 86, C.A.
Reg. v. *Warner* [1969] 2 A.C. 256; [1968] 2 W.L.R. 1303; [1968] 2
  All E.R. 356, H.L.(E.).
                                                                              H

The following additional cases were cited in argument:

Thorne v. *Motor Trade Association* [1937] A.C. 797; [1937] 3 All E.R.
  157, H.L.(E.).
Sweet v. *Parsley* [1968] 2 Q.B. 418; [1968] 2 W.L.R. 1360; [1968] 2
  All E.R. 337, D.C.; [1970] A.C. 132; [1969] 2 W.L.R. 470; [1969]
  1 All E.R. 347, H.L.(E.).

A   APPEAL against conviction.

On July 10, 1979, the defendant, Iftikhar Hussain, was charged at Snaresbrook Crown Court (Judge Mason) that, on March 22, 1978, he not being a person exempted under the Firearms Act 1968 had in his possession a firearm, namely, a pen gun without holding a firearm certificate in force at the time. He was convicted and fined £100.

B   The defendant appealed against conviction on the ground, inter alia, that the judge was wrong in law to direct the jury that the defendant would be guilty of the offence even if he did not know that the object was a firearm, provided he knew he had the object in his possession.

The facts are stated in the judgment.

C   *Nina Stranger* for the defendant.
Christopher Nutt for the Crown.

Cur. adv. vult.

November 19. EVELEIGH L.J. read the judgment of the court. On
D   July 10, 1979, at the Snaresbrook Crown Court the defendant was convicted of possessing a firearm without holding a firearms certificate. He was fined £100 and was ordered to pay the full costs of his defence. He now appeals against conviction.

On March 22, 1978, a police officer went to the defendant's house and in a box containing motor cycle parts he found an article which the prosecution alleged was a firearm. The defendant did not have a cer-
E   tificate. The article was a metal tube about 8 inches long. It had a striker pin which was activated by a spring. The defendant said: " It is a small gun. Kids use them in my country."

An expert witness from the Metropolitan Police Forensic Science Laboratory gave evidence that he clamped the tube to a table and fired from it .32 Smith and Wesson cartridges. A London telephone directory
F   was penetrated to about three-quarters of its thickness, indicating a potentially lethal force. The defence called an expert witness who expressed the opinion that the article was not an effective firearm. He said that if held in the hand that penetration would be considerably less than when clamped to the table, that it would not fire certain cartridges, and that if the tube was held in the hand it would penetrate a quarter of an inch of wood at 15 inches whereas a standard Smith and Wesson revolver
G   would go through something like $3\frac{1}{2} \times \frac{7}{8}$ inch boards. The defendant himself said that the article was a toy which his son had once used to fire corks.

Section 57 of the Firearms Act 1968 reads:

"(1) In this Act, the expression ' firearm ' means a lethal barrelled weapon of any description from which any shot, bullet or other
H   missile can be discharged. . . ."

In summing up to the jury the judge told them the meaning of the expression " firearm " and in effect directed them that if the article was a firearm the accused would be guilty of the offence if they found that he was in possession of that article, even though he might not know that it was a firearm. On behalf of the defendant it is submitted that this direction was wrong and that, as counsel put it, it is necessary for the

prosecution to prove that the accused had the knowledge of the nature A
of the article in order to establish the mens rea required for the offence.
Section 1 (1) of the Firearms Act 1968 reads:

"Subject to any exemption under this Act, it is an offence for a
person—(a) to have in his possession, or to purchase or acquire, a
firearm to which this section applies without holding a firearm
certificate in force at the time, or otherwise than as authorised by B
such a certificate."

The subsection makes no reference to the state of knowledge of the
accused. It is drafted in absolute terms and can be contrasted with
other sections of the Act where the accused's state of mind is specifically
referred to. For example, section 24 (1) provides: "It is an offence to
sell or let on hire any firearm or ammunition to a person under the age C
of 17," but in section 24 (5) it is stated:

"In proceedings for an offence under any provision of this section
it is a defence to prove that the person charged with the offence
believed the other person to be of or over the age mentioned in
that provision and had reasonable ground for the belief."

Again, section 25 reads: D

"It is an offence for a person to sell or transfer any firearm or
ammunition to, or to repair, prove or test any firearm or ammunition
for, another person whom he knows or has reasonable cause for
believing to be drunk or of unsound mind."

However, we do not think it is necessary to deal with this matter at
length for in our opinion the reasoning of their Lordships in *Reg.* v. E
Warner [1969] 2 A.C. 256 which case was referred to in *Reg.* v. *Howells*
[1977] Q.B. 614, in relation to section 1 of the Drugs (Prevention of
Misuse) Act 1964 is applicable to this case. That section reads:
"(1) . . . it shall not be lawful for a person to have in his possession a
substance . . . specified in the Schedule to this Act . . ." It was held
that the offence created by that subsection is an absolute offence and F
proof of mens rea is not required.
In *Reg.* v. *Warner* [1969] 2 A.C. 256 Lord Morris of Borth-y-Gest
stated the way in which the construction of the Act of 1964 should be
approached and said, at p. 295:

"For the reasons that I have earlier given I think that before the
prosecution can succeed they must prove that a person knowingly
had in his possession something which in fact was a prohibited G
substance."

In the present case the prosecution proved that the appellant knowingly
had in his possession an article which was in fact a lethal weapon, in
other words a firearm. Lord Morris went on to say:

"Was it, however, for the prosecution to prove that the appellant
knew the nature and quality of that which he had? In my view H
it was not. The evidence proved that what the appellant had in
his possession was B-aminopropylbenzine or a salt of that substance."

Lord Guest said at p. 301:

"Absolute offences are by no means unknown to our law and have
been created, inter alia, in relation to firearms (Firearms Act 1937)

A   and shotguns (Criminal Justice Act 1967, section 85), which Acts
     create serious offences. A common feature of these Acts and the
     Drugs Act is that they all deal with dangerous substances where the
     object is to prevent unauthorised possession and illegal trafficking
     in these articles."

       In our opinion *Reg.* v. *Warner* provides a short answer to the
B   defendant's submission.

       It was also submitted that the judge wrongly influenced the jury in
     relation to the question whether the article was a lethal weapon. It is
     true that during the examination of the expert witnesses for the prose-
     cution he used expressions which indicated that the article appeared to
     be a lethal weapon but in this he was in no way misrepresenting the
     effect of the prosecution evidence. It is also true that he used
C   expressions which indicated that he considered the article to be lethal,
     but in summing up to the jury he said:

          " Counsel was absolutely right when she said to you last evening and
          today that if I, as presiding judge, in the course of the case make
          any comment about it, or in the course of this summing up make any
          comment about it, and those comments relate to the facts, which
D   are your province, you must disregard entirely what I say unless
          the comments I have made and the views I have expressed happen
          to tally with your views because this case, so far as the facts are
          concerned, is being tried by you, the jury, no one else."

       We do not think that the jury were wrongly influenced.

E   *Appeal dismissed.*
                                   Certificate that point of law of public
                                      importance involved in decision
                                      refused.
                                   Prosecution's costs to be paid out of
                                      central funds.
F
       Solicitors: *Maurice Nadeem & Co.; Solicitor, Metropolitan Police.*

          [Reported by MISS LESLEY HEWLETT, Barrister-at-Law]

       _____

G   [COURT OF APPEAL]

                     * REGINA v. BARRINGTON

     1980 Nov. 13; 28   Dunn L.J., Phillips and Drake JJ.

     Crime—Evidence—Corroboration—Similar facts—Indecent assaults
H   *on girls—Circumstances similar to those leading to commission*
        of offences—Evidence not disclosing offence—Whether ad-
        missible

          The appellant and the co-defendant had induced the three
       complainants, girls aged 11, 13 and 15, to come to the co-
       defendant's house on the pretext of being employed as baby
       sitters and there the appellant committed acts of indecency
       upon them. He was charged, inter alia, with three offences of
       indecency and an offence of having sexual intercourse with a

girl under 16. He denied the offences and in cross-examination   A
it was suggested to one complainant that they had concocted
their evidence between them. The prosecution was given leave
to call three other girls whose evidence did not disclose the commission of similar offences but disclosed circumstances similar
to those leading to the commission of the offences against the
complainants. The appellant was convicted of indecent assault
and an attempt to have sexual intercourse with a girl under
16. He appealed against conviction.   B
    On the question whether the evidence of the three girls
was admissible: —
    Held, dismissing the appeal, that, although the evidence
of the three girls did not disclose the commission of similar
offences, their evidence was admissible to rebut the appellant's
defence that the complainants had been brought to the house
for the innocent purpose of baby sitting (post, p. 429E–F); that
the evidence was also admissible on the ground that the   C
circumstances of the girls' relationship with the appellant were
so similar to the circumstances leading to the commission of
the offences against the complainants that the similarity could
properly be described as " striking " and, since it could not be
explained on the basis of coincidence, the evidence was of
positive probative value in determining the guilt of the appellant and was admissible as being evidence of similar facts
(post, pp. 429F–H, 430F).   D
    Dicta of Scarman L.J. in *Reg.* v. *Scarrott* [1978] Q.B.
1016, 1025, 1026, C.A. applied.

The following cases are referred to in the judgment:
Reg. v. *Boardman* [1975] A.C. 421; [1974] 3 W.L.R. 673; [1974] 3 All E.R.
    887, H.L.(E).
Reg. v. *Doughty* [1965] 1 W.L.R. 331; [1965] 1 All E.R. 560, C.C.A.   E
Rex v. *Horry* [1949] N.Z.L.R. 791.
Reg. v. *Johannsen* (1977) 65 Cr.App.R. 101, C.A.
Reg. v. *Kilbourne* [1973] A.C. 729; [1973] 2 W.L.R. 254; [1973] 1 All E.R.
    440, H.L.(E).
Reg. v. *Novac* (1976) 65 Cr.App.R. 107, C.A.
Reg. v. *Scarrott* [1978] Q.B. 1016; [1977] 3 W.L.R. 629; [1978] 1 All E.R.
    672, C.A.   F
Rex v. *Smith* (1915) 11 Cr.App.R. 229.

No additional cases were cited in argument.

APPEAL against conviction.
    On November 15, 1979, at Bristol Crown Court (Milmo J.), the appel-
lant was convicted of three offences of indecent assault and one offence   G
of attempted sexual intercourse with a girl under 16. He appealed on the
ground that the evidence of three girls, other than the complainants, did
not amount to " similar fact " evidence, and should not have been admitted.
    The facts are stated in the judgment.

    David Lane (assigned by the Registrar of Criminal Appeals) for the
appellant.   H
    Patrick Whelon for the Crown.

    November 28. DUNN L.J. read the following judgment of the court.
This appeal once again raises the question as to the admissibility of what
is called " similar fact " evidence, especially in sexual cases. In particular
it raises the question of whether evidence of similar facts falling short of
similar offences with which an accused is charged can ever be admissible.

A   On November 15, 1979, at Bristol Crown Court, before Milmo J., the
appellant and Constance May Meredith were arraigned on an amended
indictment containing ten counts. The appellant was involved in nine of
the counts. Three counts charged him with rape; two counts charged
him with unlawful sexual intercourse with a girl under 13 years of age;
one count (10) charged him with unlawful sexual intercourse with a girl
under 16 years of age, and three counts charged him with indecent assault.
B   The counts charging unlawful sexual intercourse were alternatives to the
counts charging rape. He pleaded not guilty to all the counts. He was
found guilty on three charges of indecent assault; not guilty as charged,
but guilty of attempt, on count 10, and not guilty on the remaining counts.

    On November 29 he was sentenced as follows: count 4—indecent
assault on a girl aged 11 years—three years' imprisonment; count 7—
C   indecent assault on a girl aged 13 years—18 months' imprisonment concurrent; count 9—indecent assault on a girl aged 13 years—12 months'
imprisonment concurrent; count 10—attempted sexual intercourse with a
girl under 16—nine months' imprisonment concurrent. Total imprisonment—three years. The appellant was also ordered to pay the prosecution
costs not exceeding £500 and to pay the whole of the defence costs.

D   He now appeals against conviction by leave of the single judge, who
observed for the attention of counsel and the full court: " I have given
leave because I think the full court should consider the directions on
corroboration. But for that issue I would have refused leave." The single
judge refused the appellant's application for leave to appeal against sentence and his renewal of that application has been refused by the full court.

    Constance May Meredith (aged 29) was indicted jointly with the appel-
E   lant on three counts of indecent assault and by herself on a single count
charging assault occasioning bodily harm (she beat one girl, Sally, with a
cane, causing weals). Meredith pleaded guilty to all the counts against
her and she was sentenced to a total of 18 months' imprisonment. She
has not applied for leave to appeal. After her arrest she eventually made
a full confession and volunteered to give evidence for the prosecution,
which she did.
F
    The case for the Crown at the trial was that the appellant and Meredith
combined together to induce young girls to go into Meredith's house,
ostensibly for the purpose of baby sitting, but in reality for the sexual
purposes of the appellant. For that purpose they operated and put into
effect a system which emerged through the evidence.

    In her evidence Meredith said that at the end of 1978 she was work-
G   ing as a casual waitress at a hotel. She there met the appellant who was
a travelling salesman engaged in the sale of heating apparatus. He told
her that he was in fact Terry Nation and that he was the script writer of
the TV series " Dr. Who." She believed him and became sexually
involved with him. Within a few days he moved from the hotel to her
house, even though the house was described as a dirty, squalid and ill-
H   furnished place. He asked Meredith to procure young girls for him for
sexual purposes, the younger the better. He assured her that if they were
under 16 years of age he would not have sexual intercourse with them,
but would only play with them. He offered to give her £50 per girl and
in addition he said that he would take out £30,000 computer shares for
her daughter (then aged 2½ years) whom he would also send to a private
school. At the time Meredith was very short of money and heavily in
debt and she agreed to his request. He suggested also that Meredith train

as a masseuse so that she could persuade the girls to allow her to massage A
them.

Anita, aged 15 years, gave evidence. She was the first girl to be procured and was readily available. She had been employed by Meredith
as a baby sitter since the summer of 1978. She was still so employed
and she was sexually experienced. The appellant told her that he was
the writer of books, like "Dr. Who," under the name Terry Nation. He B
showed her a number of pornographic books. One evening after Meredith
left the room the appellant committed various acts of indecency upon
Anita, and attempted to have intercourse with her. She struggled and he
did not succeed. Anita's evidence was the basis of his conviction on count
10. Anita said that she returned to baby sit once after that. The appellant offered her £200 if she would pose for some photographs. He did
not say what kind of photograph, but from what he had done to her she C
had a good idea what type he wanted.

Early in 1979 Susan (aged 11) took over the job of baby sitting from
Anita. She was paid £1 a night for her services. Susan said that one
evening Meredith fell asleep and the appellant then took her, Susan,
upstairs to Meredith's bedroom. He told her to take her skirt and jumper
off and, although she did not want to, she did so, because she was D
frightened. He then pushed her onto the bed and got on top of her. She
tried to push him off but she could not. He then committed various acts
of indecency upon her. When giving evidence she did not mention sexual
intercourse. She did not say that the appellant had had, or had tried to
have, sexual intercourse with her, neither did she say that he had not.
She was not cross-examined about it but merely asked general questions
on the basis that all her evidence was untrue. The incident ended when E
Meredith came upstairs. Meredith said that when she arrived upstairs,
Susan was lying across the bed with her pants and socks off and the
appellant was on top of her, moving up and down as if he were trying
to have intercourse with her. Susan appeared to be upset and after she
had gone home, the appellant apologised.

Despite his apologies, the same sort of thing occurred on another F
evening, the only difference being that on the later occasion Susan did
not seem upset. She continued to baby sit for a week or two and during
that time she frequently had her bottom smacked and caned by the
appellant. On one occasion after a bath Meredith massaged Susan's back,
and while she was doing so the appellant came into the room and took
over the massage. He turned her onto her face and massaged her back.
He then turned her onto her back and there followed various acts of G
indecency by both the appellant and Meredith upon Susan.

Sally, aged 13, succeeded her sister Susan as Meredith's baby sitter.
On an occasion, after she had had a bath, Meredith massaged her and
while she was doing so the appellant came into the room. Sally was
frightened and the appellant went downstairs. Later that same day Sally
had another bath by request and afterwards the appellant took photo- H
graphs of her in the nude, in various poses, including indecent ones. He
told her that she would get £200 for them. When she later saw the photographs she was scared that someone else might see them, or that they
might be put in books. Frequently she, Meredith and the appellant were
together in the bedroom, nude, and indulging in sexual practices. This
happened on more than one occasion and afterwards when she went
downstairs the appellant would smack or cane her bottom. Similar acts

A occurred on every occasion that she went baby sitting for Meredith. On one occasion in the bedroom she took a photograph of Meredith and the appellant in the nude.

It was suggested in cross-examination of Meredith and each of the three girls that the whole of their evidence was a tissue of lies and that the three girls had put their heads together to concoct a false story against the appellant, whose conduct had been such that it should not have excited B any criticism at all. At the conclusion of their evidence, there was an application by counsel for the Crown to call three other girls, whose statements were annexed to a notice of additional evidence. The submissions of counsel for the Crown in support of his application are set out in the transcript:

C "It was put to Sally, the last girl, I think, in effect, that the girls had put their heads together and knew what each was saying and that each had their own private motives for making up these lies. The prosecution say that is not right and the truth of what the girls say can be judged by seeing the picture as a whole. It was a course of conduct which occurred with three further girls who, I suggest, were in the pipeline for further offences had not the matter blown D up early in March. Certainly, they were being introduced to the house, shown sexual matters, introduced to sexual matters, in this course of conduct hoping that the girls would be amenable."

Counsel for the defence objected and his objections appear in the transcript. He said:

E "My Lord, I respectfully submit that the evidence of Bernadette and of the two other girls should be excluded. I have analysed their respective witness statements and may I state my conclusions first and then show your Lordship how I arrive at them. My first proposition is this and if I call Anita and the two sisters the complainants and if I call Bernadette and the two other sisters the girls, for shortness and brevity of distinction: my Lord, the evidence of the three F girls, Bernadette and the two other sisters, and it is their witness statements as they stand, do not corroborate the evidence of the three complainants in the material allegations of rape and or indecent assault. . . . If these girls were to give evidence the prejudicial effect of their evidence would outweigh their probative value."

After further argument the judge ruled the evidence of the three other G girls as admissible, giving his reasons in the following terms:

"In my judgment this evidence is admissible and it is admissible on two grounds which can be stated quite shortly. One is that it is evidence, and it is for the jury to say what weight is to be given to it, it is evidence that to the knowledge of the defendant, girls were being recruited for immoral purposes—as one tests that by showing H them these photographs—for immoral purposes under the cover of being required for baby sitting. It is evidence for the jury to consider whether it was not for the immoral gratification of the defendant that these girls were being recruited for that alleged purpose. Secondly, because the leave was given and the court was pressed to give leave for the girls to be interrogated, or for one of the girls to be cross-examined, on matters which would not otherwise have been allowed under the Sexual Offences Amendment Act 1976 to be cross-

examined, because the suggestion was that the allegations which A
these girls were making about this man were emanations of their
own dirty minds, fabrications which had nothing to do with anything
with which he was connected or that he had in any way taken any
part in the matters complained of. I admit this evidence on these
grounds."

The three other girls accordingly gave evidence. Their names were B
Bernadette, aged 13, and two sisters, Shirley, aged 15, and Anne, aged 16.
It appeared that whilst Sally was still employed as baby sitter by Meredith,
the appellant and Meredith saw the three girls in a cafe in Gloucester
with a view to engaging a new baby sitter. They were obviously school
girls, dressed in school uniform. The appellant asked them what they
were doing and they told him that they were playing truant. He went out
to buy some film and when he returned he drove them all back to the C
house in his car.

Bernadette said that the appellant told them that he was Terry Nation.
He was smartly dressed. When they got to the house they were shown
photographs of nude women by the appellant and by Meredith and they
were asked if they would like to have their photographs taken. At that
stage, she, Bernadette, went out to keep an appointment with a social D
worker. When she came back she was shown photographs, decent ones,
of Shirley and Anne clothed. She went to the bedroom with Meredith
to have her photograph taken. One was taken of her fully clothed and
then she agreed to have photographs of her taken in the nude. Four were
taken of her in indecent positions and they were shown to the appellant.
She was paid £2 for them. She was shown photographs of girls being
whipped and other photographs, including an obscene one of part of the E
appellant's body. She was offered a job as a baby sitter and she was
paid £5 for two days' work.

Anne said that at the house they were shown by the appellant magazines containing pornographic photographs. They were also shown other
photographs by both Meredith and the appellant, including the obscene
one of the appellant. It was suggested that she, Anne, should be photo- F
graphed. She agreed to be photographed with her clothes on but she
refused to be photographed in the nude, even though she was told that
there was a prize of £200 and both the appellant and Meredith tried to
persuade her that she could do with the money. Baby sitting was not
mentioned to her at the house, although that was supposed to be why
they had gone there, and she was not offered a job as a baby sitter.

Shirley gave evidence which did not differ in any essential way from G
that of her sister. She said that the appellant told them that he produced
films like " The Persuaders " and " The Saint " and talked about the film
stars he knew. At the house she also was shown the indecent photographs.
She had her photograph taken clothed, but she refused to have any nude
photographs taken although she was told about the £200 prize. She, like
her sister, heard nothing more about the baby sitting. No photographs H
of any of the girls were found by the police. Meredith said that they
had been destroyed when the investigation started.

The appellant did not give evidence and no other evidence was called
by the defence. It was submitted that all the allegations against the appellant were lies. He had not done any of the things alleged against him
and he had not indulged in any improper behaviour. He did not show
the girls any improper books or photographs. If they had seen any they

A   must have obtained them themselves. The whole case was a wicked
conspiracy by the girls.

The judge said in his summing up:

"No evidence as we know was called by the defence, but I think I
can fairly summarise what the defence in this case has been as indicated by the speech from counsel. It is that the defendant never
B   committed any of the offences charged, and that the evidence given
in respect of those offences are lies from start to finish. He never
indulged in any improper behaviour or did any of the things which
are alleged against him as having taken place in that house, number
49. So far as the pictures are concerned, it is said that the girls could
have got their hands on these pictures, and I say: 'How did they get
to know what was in these pictures?'; and then, members of the
C   jury, it is further suggested and it is for you to say whether there is a
vestige of support for this or not that this is a gigantic conspiracy,
a wicked diabolical conspiracy by these girls for some ulterior reason
which I think that counsel said it was not for him to suggest a motive
and he could not do so and was not going to do so."

D   The judge, dealing with the " similar fact " evidence, said:

"There is a body of evidence which you have had in this case which
can be described and called 'similar fact' evidence, evidence of
system. It relates, members of the jury, primarily to the evidence
of Bernadette and the two other sisters, coupled with the evidence of
the three girls against whom offences are alleged. Bernadette and
the other sisters do not give any direct evidence of the charges in the
E   indictment, and moreover, members of the jury, the evidence they
give does not pretend to prove that the accused committed or even
attempted to commit on them the offences charged in the indictment.
. . . These girls' evidence is relevant in so far as it goes to show that
Brian Barrington was at the material time using the same technique
and methods of luring girls into number 49 for the purpose of per-
F   forming acts of physical indecency with them."

The judge then listed six pieces of evidence which he left to the jury as
capable of constituting similar fact evidence. First the baby sitting
proposition. Secondly, the boasting claims to the girls about his position
as a script writer of well-known television programmes, and a friend of
the stars. Thirdly, Meredith was described as a professional photographer.
G   Fourthly, the evidence about the £200 prize for nude photographs. Fifthly,
the evidence that all the girls were shown pornographic pictures and
pornographic magazines. And sixthly, the technique, as the judge described it, that was employed to try to get the girls to strip eventually for
nude photographs. "And you may think," the judge concluded, "that
the nude photographs were merely part of the leading to what is said to
H   be the eventual indecent assaults of various kinds and descriptions."

The judge then went on to deal with the question of corroboration,
saying:

"If you are satisfied that the evidence of these girls, coupled with
the other girls or even taken by themselves—it is really taken by themselves I ought to say—taken to prove that there was an intention on
the part of this defendant to get these girls into the house, one after
the other, for indecent purposes that could amount to corroboration.

It is for you to say whether it does or whether it does not. . . . There   A
is what I will refer to as the similar fact evidence, the evidence of
system, and that is the evidence of Bernadette and the two other
sisters. You know what I am referring to, and that, I have directed
you, could be corroboration. It is for you to decide whether it is in
fact corroboration, and members of the jury, the prosecution have
submitted to you or they have not put that matter before you as
corroboration; they have only put it as evidence of similar facts."   B

Mr. Lane for the appellant made no complaint about the direction as to
the evidence of the three other girls being capable of corroborating the
evidence of the complainants if the evidence of the three other girls was
admissible. Indeed in the light of the remarks of Lord Cross of Chelsea
in *Reg.* v. *Kilbourne* [1973] A.C. 729, 760, it would have been impossible   C
for him to have done so. Lord Cross said:

"Once the 'similar fact' evidence is admitted—and it was common
ground that it was properly admitted in this case—then of necessity
it 'corroborates'—i.e. strengthens or supports—the evidence given
by the boy an alleged offence against whom is the subject of the
count under consideration."   D

But Mr. Lane submitted that the evidence of the other girls should not
have been admitted at all. None of the other girls gave evidence of an
indecent assault, or any other act of indecency upon their person. Indeed
their evidence related to events after Susan and Sally had been in the
house. It was accordingly incapable of amounting to "similar fact"
evidence. Although other grounds were put forward in the notice of appeal,   E
this was the only ground relied on in this court.

Mr. Lane referred us first to *Reg.* v. *Doughty* [1965] 1 W.L.R. 331,
334–335, where Lord Parker C.J. said:

"It is to be observed in the present case that while it might be said
that there was evidence capable of being treated in a sinister respect
and held to be indecent assault, the acts to which the small girls   F
had spoken were certainly equally consistent with what one might
call a paternal or avuncular interest. It is not without interest that
neighbours came, and in particular the mother of Carol said that she
knew the defendant, that he was highly respected, that she absolutely
trusted her children with him, and that he undoubtedly was very fond
of children. That there was evidence of familiarity in the sense of a
paternal or avuncular interest is undoubted. The evidence that it was   G
not merely for that but in order to satisfy lust was tenuous to a
degree. Further, it is to be observed that even if the acts complained
of were capable of being interpreted as indecent it was quite a
different form of indecency in regard to physical acts from that spoken
to by the two girls who were the subject of the counts.

"In the circumstances, this court is satisfied that where the evidence   H
of indecency is tenuous to a degree and where even if held to be
indecent it is a different form of indecency, then the court can only
exercise its discretion in one way, by excluding that evidence, the
reason being that its prejudicial value is quite overwhelming. It is
well known that this court is very reluctant ever to interfere with
the discretion of a trial judge. They will in the ordinary way only do
so if he has erred in principle. The court feels, however, that in the

A   circumstances as I have indicated them, this discretion could properly
     only be exercised in one way, by excluding the evidence. That being
     so, and this evidence being clearly directed to both counts—both
     that dealing with Carol as well as that dealing with Shirley—the only
     proper course the court can take is to quash both convictions."

     Nobody could say that the evidence of the three other girls in this case
B   disclosed no more than a paternal or avuncular interest on the part of
     the appellant and we do not feel that we are assisted by *Reg. v. Doughty.*
        Mr. Lane also referred us to more recent and well known authorities
     on the admissibility of " similar fact " evidence. They are *Reg. v.
     Boardman* [1975] A.C. 421; *Reg. v. Johannsen* (1977) 65 Cr.App.R. 101;
     Reg. v. Novac (1976) 65 Cr.App.R. 107 and *Reg. v. Scarrott* [1978] Q.B.
C   1016. He also referred to *Cross on Evidence*, 5th ed. (1979), p. 356 and
     to *Rex v. Horry* [1949] N.Z.L.R. 791, 792. In that case:

        " The evidence the admission of which was complained of was, first,
        that of two women, who, as well as [the] complainant, had each
        replied to [the] accused's newspaper advertisement and had
        (separately) met him by appointment; each had had an interview
D   with him broadly similar to that between [the] accused and [the]
        complainant, except that in the case of these two women there was
        no suggestion of any attempt to kiss or to assault; and, secondly,
        the evidence of a detective-sergeant (to whom [the] accused was well
        known as one who had many convictions), who saw him meet and
        converse with one of these two women. It was contended that the
E   evidence of the two women served merely to show that they, too,
        had been deceived, which was not an offence, and was irrelevant;
        that such evidence merely created in the minds of the jury prejudice
        against [the] accused; and that the evidence of the detective-sergeant,
        in so far as it revealed [the] accused was known to him and that the
        detective-sergeant troubled to keep him under observation, implied
F   previous offences, and so prejudiced [the] accused from obtaining a
        fair trial. The admissibility of the two young women's evidence was
        argued in chambers before trial, when it was sought to justify its
        being led on the grounds (i) that it was indicative of system, and
        (ii) that it assisted in the establishment of the identity of [the]
G   accused as the person against whom [the complainant's] allegations
        were directed. The learned judge ruled that the evidence was admis-
        sible on the latter ground."

     On appeal to the Court of Appeal, Gresson J. said, at p. 793:

        " Dealing first with the question as to whether this evidence was
        properly admitted: in order to be admissible, it must be relevant.
H   It contributed nothing towards establishing that [the] accused
        improperly kissed or assaulted [the complainant], which was the
        offence with which he was charged, and, in so far as it revealed
        deception practised upon other young women, it was prejudicial. But
        it had relevance on the question of identity, and this, on the depo-
        sitions, was in issue no less than whether a kiss was forced on an
        unwilling recipient."

At p. 798, having cited a large number of authorities, the judge said: A

"It was in the light of these authorities that Callan J. had to rule.
As the matter then stood, the evidence, being relevant to the issue
of identity, was admissible, but, from counsel's assurance that identity
would not be disputed, it became clear that identity would not in fact
be the subject of contention. Evidence that goes to an issue not
really in contest, and merely prejudices [the] accused, should be   B
excluded."

The judge then referred to the decision of the Privy Council in *Noor
Mohamed* v. *The King* [1949] A.C. 182 and said, at pp. 798–799:

"[That decision] has established beyond all question that there is
such a discretionary power. But in this case the question goes
deeper, and is whether the evidence is admissible at all, since the   C
issue to which it relates no longer exists. Its sole justification is to
establish identity, and that the Crown is no longer called upon
to do. . . . Our view is, therefore, that the learned judge should
have disallowed the evidence, not as a matter of discretion, but
because it was inadmissible as irrelevant."

So if the question of identity had remained in issue, the evidence would   D
have been relevant to that issue and would have been admitted notwithstanding that it did not disclose the commission of any offence.

In all the cases so far cited, except *Reg.* v. *Doughty* [1965] 1 W.L.R.
331 and *Rex* v. *Horry* [1949] N.Z.L.R. 791, the evidence of similar facts
included evidence of the commission of an offence similar to that with
which the accused was charged. Counsel could find no case in which   E
it did not, and the evidence was held admissible.

Finally counsel relied on a passage in *Archbold Criminal Pleading
Evidence & Practice*, 40th ed. (1979), para. 1324, under the heading
"Proximity," which is in the following terms:

"The decisions of the Court of Appeal are not consistent on another
point, namely whether the 'striking similarity' must relate to the   F
commission of the offence as opposed to the surrounding circumstances.

In *Reg.* v. *Novac*, 65 Cr.App.R. 107, the facts were very like
those in *Reg.* v. *Johannsen*, 65 Cr.App.R. 101, but (at p. 112) the
court said: 'If a man is going to commit buggery with a boy he
picks up, it must surely be a commonplace of such an encounter   G
that he will take the boy home with him and commit the offence
in bed. The fact that the boys may in each case have been picked
up by Raymond' (one of the appellants) 'in the first instance at
amusement arcades may be a feature more approximating to a
"unique or striking similarity." . . . It is not, however, a similarity
in the commission of the crime. It is a similarity in the surrounding   H
circumstances and is not, in our judgment, sufficiently proximate to
the commission of the crime itself to lead to the conclusion that the
repetition of this feature would make the boys' stories inexplicable
on the basis of coincidence.'

"In *Reg.* v. *Scarrott* [1978] Q.B. 1016 the court were faced with
the apparent conflict between the approach of the differently con-

A   stituted courts in *Reg.* v. *Johannsen* and *Reg.* v. *Novac* to barely
distinguishable facts. After referring to the use by the court in
Reg. v. *Novac* of ' the rather strange word . . . " proximate " ' the
court made it plain that they preferred the approach of the court
in *Reg.* v. *Johannsen.* They said that ' it would be wrong . . . to
elevate the passage ' [cited above] ' . . . into a statement of law.'

B   They also pointed out that ' in one of the most famous of all cases
dealing with similar fact evidence, the brides in the bath case, *Rex*
v. *Smith* (1915) 11 Cr.App.R. 229 the court had regard to the facts
that the accused man married the women, and that he insured their
lives. Some surrounding circumstances have to be considered in order
to understand either the offence charged or the nature of the similar

C   fact evidence which it is sought to adduce and in each case it must
be a matter of judgment where the line is drawn.' "

Counsel submitted that evidence to be admissible must be probative of
an indecent assault, not merely of an intention to commit an indecent
assault. And in as much as none of the three other girls had in fact said
that they had been indecently assaulted their evidence was not probative

D   of the charges of indecent assault on the three complainants.
Mr. Lane submitted that evidence of similar facts to be admissible
must relate to the facts of an offence similar to that with which the appellant was charged, and not to the surrounding circumstances, which he
submitted were too remote. He conceded however that if the evidence
of the three other girls had included evidence of indecent assault, then

E   their evidence, including the evidence of surrounding circumstances, would
have been admissible, even though Susan had not been introduced by
photographs, although Sally was photographed in the nude.
Counsel for the Crown sought to support the ruling of the judge that
the evidence of the three other girls was admissible on the basis that the
principal issue in the case was whether the appellant had lured all six

F   girls to the house for a sexual purpose, or whether, as the defence alleged,
the purpose was an innocent one, namely baby sitting, and that the evidence
tended to rebut that defence. In our judgment the admission of the evidence can certainly be supported on that ground. But admission of the
evidence can be supported on another and wider ground.

It is well established that although evidence of a disposition or propen-

G   sity to commit the offence with which the accused is charged is not admissible, evidence may in certain circumstances be led of similar facts tending
to show that the accused is guilty of the offence charged. Such evidence
has it appears hitherto only been admitted where it has disclosed the
commission of similar offences although it has also included the surrounding circumstances. In some cases the similarity of the surrounding cir-

H   cumstances has been stressed more than the similarity of the mode of
commission of the offences themselves. Surrounding circumstances include
the preliminaries leading up to the offence, such as the mode and place
of the initial approach and the inducement offered or words used.

The two sets of facts must be looked at as a whole. In *Reg.* v.
Scarrott [1978] Q.B. 1016 the very point with which we are concerned
was raised although it was not necessary for the decision because there

was evidence of the commission of an offence. Scarman L.J., giving   A
the judgment of the court, said, at p. 1025:

"Mr. Fallon has based a submission . . . that, to be admissible,
the similar fact evidence must reveal features of a striking similarity
with the offence itself, not its surrounding circumstances. He submits that is all that the rather strange word that Bridge L.J. used
[in *Reg.* v. *Novac*, 65 Cr.App.R. 107] 'proximate' means. In our   B
view, we are here in that area of judgment upon particular facts from
which the criminal law can never depart. Plainly some matters,
some circumstances may be so distant in time or place from the
commission of an offence as not to be properly considered when
deciding whether the subject matter of similar fact evidence displays
striking similarities with the offence charged. On the other hand,
equally plainly, one cannot isolate, as a sort of laboratory specimen,   C
the bare bones of a criminal offence from its surrounding circumstances and say that it is only within the confines of that specimen,
microscopically considered, that admissibility is to be determined.
Indeed, in one of the most famous cases of all dealing with similar
fact evidence, the brides in the bath case, *Rex* v. *Smith* (1915) 11
Cr.App.R. 229, the court had regard to the facts that the accused   D
man married the women, and that he insured their lives. Some
surrounding circumstances have to be considered in order to understand either the offence charged or the nature of the similar fact
evidence which it is sought to adduce and in each case it must be
a matter of judgment where the line is drawn. One cannot draw
an inflexible line as a rule of law."   E

Then Scarman L.J. said, at p. 1026:

"We therefore have to reach a judgment upon the evidence of this
particular case, and to determine whether the evidence adduced,
that is the similar fact evidence adduced, possesses such features that
it is a proper exercise of judgment to say that the evidence is   F
logically probative, that it has positive probative value in assisting
to determine the truth."

We accept and follow the reasoning of Scarman L.J. in *Reg.* v.
Scarrott. The various facts recited by the judge in this case as constituting
" similar facts " were so similar to the facts of the surrounding circumstances in the evidence of the complainants that they can properly be   G
described as " striking." That they did not include evidence of the commission of offences similar to those with which the appellant was charged
does not mean that they are not logically probative in determining the
guilt of the appellant. Indeed we are of opinion that taken as a whole
they are inexplicable on the basis of coincidence and that they are of
positive probative value in assisting to determine the truth of the charges   H
against the appellant, in that they tended to show that he was guilty of
the offences with which he was charged.

In deciding whether or not to admit similar fact evidence the judge
will always assess whether the prejudice caused outweighs the probative
value of the evidence. In this appeal counsel has not suggested that if
the evidence is admissible it should be excluded on the ground that it is

A prejudicial. We are satisfied that the evidence was properly admitted and accordingly, for the reasons we have given, the appeal is dismissed.

> *Certificate that point of law of general public importance involved, namely:*
> *"Whether evidence of similar facts falling short of similar offences with which an accused is charged can ever be admissible?"*
> *Leave to appeal refused.*

Solicitor: *Director of Public Prosecutions.*

[Reported by MISS KATE O'HANLON, Barrister-at-Law]

February 26. The Appeal Committee of the House of Lords (Lord Diplock, Lord Keith of Kinkel and Lord Bridge of Harwich) dismissed a petition by the appellant for leave to appeal.

[CHANCERY DIVISION]

* McCARNEY (INSPECTOR OF TAXES) *v.* FREILICH

1980 Nov. 14   Goulding J.

Revenue—Income tax—Assessment—Notional income arising on sale of assets cum dividend—Basic rate of tax—Whether chargeable—Income and Corporation Taxes Act 1970 (c. 10), s. 30 (4) (as amended by Finance Act 1971 (c. 68), s. 37 (1), Sch. 6, Pt. I, para. 13)

In 1979, a taxpayer was assessed to income tax under section 30 of the Income and Corporation Taxes Act 1970, in respect of notional income of £10,015, arising on the sale of assets cum dividend. The charge of £8,604·85 consisted of £3,505·25 of basic rate tax, £3,597·35 higher rate tax, and £1,502·25 investment income surcharge. The taxpayer did not dispute the figures or his liability to pay tax at the higher rates or the investment income surcharge, but appealed against the assessment so far as it related to the charge to tax at the basic rate, on the ground that the charge to tax under section 30 (4), as amended by Schedule 6 to the Finance Act 1971,[1] did not extend to tax at the basic rate. The special commissioners allowed his appeal.

On appeal by the Crown: —

Held, dismissing the appeal, that if Parliament had intended, on the abolition of surtax, to amend section 30 (4), of the Income and Corporation Taxes Act 1970 so as to extend the charge to tax to cover tax at the basic rate, it would have expressed so radical a change in clearer words; and, on its true construction, section 30 (4) as amended plainly pointed to an intention to counteract avoidance of " excess liability," and nothing more (post, pp. 437H, 438B–E, F–H, 439G—440A).

Dictum of Lord Buckmaster in *Greenwood* v. *F. L. Smidth & Co.* [1922] 1 A.C. 417, 423, H.L.(E.) considered.

-----

[1] Income and Corporation Taxes Act 1970, s. 30 (4), as amended: see post, p. 436F–G.

McCarney v. Freilich (Ch.D.)   **[1981]**

The following cases are referred to in the judgment: A

Greenwood v. *F. L. Smidth & Co.* [1922] 1 A.C. 417, H.L.(E.).
Schaffer v. *Cattermole* [1979] S.T.C. 670.
Wigmore v. *Thomas Summerson & Sons Ltd.* [1926]] 1 K.B. 131.

No additional cases were cited in argument.

CASE STATED by the Commissioners for the Special Purposes of the   B
Income Tax Acts.

On March 19, 1979, assessment to income tax for the year 1975–76
was made on the taxpayer, Jeffrey Freilich, under section 30 of the
Income and Corporation Taxes Act 1970 in respect of notional income
of £10,015 deemed to arise on the sale of assets cum dividend. The tax
charged was £8,604·85 made up as follows: income tax at basic rate   C
£3,505·25, income tax at higher rates £3,597·35 and £1,502·25 investment
income surcharge.

Mr. Freilich appealed against the assessment on the ground that the
amount of tax charged under section 30 of the Act, as amended, was
limited to income tax at the higher rates and the additional rate on
investment income and that it did not extend to basic rate tax. He did
not dispute that the amount of income assessable was £10,015. The   D
special commissioners heard the taxayer's appeal on October 5, 1979, and
on November 16, 1979, gave their decision, allowing the appeal and
reducing the amount of tax payable to £5,099·60, being the total of the
higher rates and the additional rate.

The Crown appealed.

The facts and the decision of the special commissioners are set out   E
in the judgment.

Michael Hart for the Crown.
The taxpayer did not appear and was not represented.

GOULDING J. In 1979 an assessment to income tax for the year   F
1975–76 was made on a taxpayer, Jeffrey Freilich. The income assessed
was described as " section 30 charge, £10,015." The tax charged, before
setting off an overpayment of capital gains tax, was £8,604·85, and it was
divided into three portions: income tax at basic rate, £3,505·25; income
tax at higher rates, £3,597·35; and investment income surcharge,
£1,502·25, making the total that I have already mentioned.

The sum charged, the £10,015, was notional income from assets sold   G
cum dividend which the taxpayer was deemed to have received by
virtue of section 30 of the Income and Corporation Taxes Act 1970,
as amended. The taxpayer did not dispute his liability to pay the
assessed tax at the higher rates or the investment income surcharge; but
he claimed that the notional sum of £10,015—which amount, again,
he did not dispute—was not liable to be taxed at the basic rate. Accor-   H
dingly, he appealed against the assessment to the special commissioners,
and they, on October 5, 1979, heard his appeal, which they decided in
his favour. They accordingly reduced the tax payable under the
assessment to £5,099·60, being the sum of the second and third items
into which it was broken up, as I have already mentioned.

The Crown appeals to this court against the special commissioners'
decision in favour of the taxpayer. The taxpayer has not appeared,

A either in person or by counsel. Nonetheless, the special commissioners' decision must stand unless counsel on behalf of the Crown can persuade me that it is wrong. That he has failed to do. In my view the case stated, if I may say so with respect, is an admirable document, and I am tempted simply to say that in my judgment the special commissioners came to the right conclusion for the right reasons. However,
B in deference to the very fair and lucid argument that I have heard from Mr. Hart on behalf of the Crown, I will go over the ground in my own way and comment on the decision accordingly.

The legislation in question arose from the circumstances that in the ordinary way income does not arise for the purposes of income tax until it is received by the taxpayer. Accordingly, if one person sells a security cum dividend, in due course the purchaser receives the next
C payment of dividend, which is then taxable, as to the whole, as his income, and the vendor does not pay tax in respect of any part of that dividend, which he never had any right to receive. That that was the law appeared from the decision of *Wigmore* v. *Thomas Summerson & Sons Ltd.* [1926] 1 K.B. 131. Accordingly, there was an opportunity for individuals with a large income to diminish their liability to surtax by acquiring investments, allowing them to become big with accrued divi-
D dend not yet payable and then selling them cum dividend. In that way, what might have been income was in effect turned into capital. Parliament countered that operation by section 33 of the Finance Act 1927, which in due course passed into the Income and Corporation Taxes Act 1970, as section 30, the section under which the assessment now in question was made.

E I must read the whole of section 30 as it appeared on the passing of the consolidation Act of 1970:

"(1) Any individual upon whom notice is served by the board requiring him to furnish a statement of and particulars relating to any assets in which, at any time during the period specified in the notice, he has had any beneficial interest, and in respect of
F which, within such period, either no income was received by him or the income received by him was less than the sum to which the income would have amounted if the income from such assets had accrued from day to day and been apportioned accordingly, shall, whether an assessment to surtax in respect of his total income has or has not been made for the relevant year or years of assessment, furnish such a statement and such particulars in the form and
G within the time (not being less than 28 days) required by the notice. (2) The board may serve further notices whenever they consider it necessary for the purposes of this section until complete particulars have been furnished to their satisfaction. (3) If it appears to the board by reference to all the circumstances in relation to the assets of any such individual (including circumstances with respect to
H sales, purchases, dealings, contracts, arrangements, transfers or any other transactions relating to such assets) that the individual has thereby avoided, or would avoid, more than 10 per cent. of the amount of the surtax for any year which would have been payable in his case if the income from those assets had been deemed to accrue from day to day and had been apportioned accordingly and the income so deemed to have been apportioned to him had been treated as part of his total income for the purposes of surtax, then

434

those assets shall be deemed to be assets to which subsection (4) A
below applies. (4) For the purposes of assessment to surtax in the
case of any such individual, the income from any assets to which
this subsection applies shall be deemed to accrue from day to day
and, in the case of the sale or transfer of any such assets by or to
him, shall be deemed to have been received as and when it is
deemed to have accrued: Provided that an individual shall not be B
liable to be assessed to surtax under this section in respect of any
such income if he proves to the satisfaction of the board that the
avoidance of surtax was exceptional and not systematic, and that
there was not in his case in any of the three next preceding years
any such avoidance of surtax as is described in the provisions of
subsection (3) above. (5) If any individual fails to furnish any
statement or particulars required under this section, or if the board C
are not satisfied with any statement or particulars furnished under
this section, they make an estimate of the amount of the income
which, under the preceding provisions of this section, is to be
deemed to form part of his total income for the purposes of surtax.
(6) For the purposes of this section ' assets ' means—(a) stocks or
securities entitled to interest or dividend at a fixed rate only, not D
being stocks or securities the interest or dividend on which is
dependent on the earnings of a company, and (b) any other stocks
or securities and any shares, if transactions in relation thereto have
been effected by the individual otherwise than through a stock
exchange in the United Kingdom and by a transfer on which ad
valorem duty has been paid under the heading ' Conveyance or
transfer on sale ' in Schedule 1 to the Stamp Act 1891."   E

There was in the consolidation Act of 1970 a converse provision aimed
at giving relief from surtax where an individual had purchased assets
carrying a right to already accrued income. That was section 32, and
while I am referring to the Act I will read it:

" If any individual, on a claim made to the board under this section, F
proves to the satisfaction of the board that, in consequence of the
sale or transfer to him of any assets, the amount of surtax payable
by him for any year of assessment exceeds by more than 10 per
cent. the amount of the surtax which would have been payable by
him for that year if the income from those assets and from any
assets sold or transferred by him were deemed to have accrued
from day to day, then, for the purposes of surtax in the case of G
that individual for that year, the income from all such assets as
aforesaid shall be deemed to have accrued from day to day and to
have been received by him as and when it is deemed to have
accrued."

Such were the provisions on the consolidation of income tax law in H
the Act of 1970. Not very long afterwards a new system of charging tax
on larger incomes came into force. That was the system introduced
by the Finance Act 1971, to come into operation for 1973–74 and
subsequent years of assessment. The old dichotomy of income tax at
the standard rate and surtax at further rates was swept away. Instead,
section 32 (1) of the Finance Act 1971, laid down the following scheme
for the future:

A   " Income tax shall be charged—(a) in respect of any income not
falling within paragraph (b) below, at such rate, to be known as
the basic rate, as Parliament may determine, and (b) in respect of
so much of an individual's total income as exceeds such amount
as Parliament may determine, at such higher rate or rates as
Parliament may determine; and where an individual's total income
B   includes investment income and that investment income exceeds
such amount as Parliament may determine, income tax shall also
be charged in respect of the excess at such additional rate or rates
as Parliament may determine."

That, of course, is a quite different system from the system of
standard rate and surtax previously in force, leading to a considerable
acceleration of the payment of tax by those with larger incomes.
C   Now, the change made by section 32 of the Finance Act 1971
required considerable adjustments in those parts of the Income Tax Acts
which dealt with surtax, and in the Finance Act 1971, we find section
37. The side note to that section reads, " Consequential amendments
and repeals." I am content to accept the submission that marginal
notes cannot be taken into account in construing a statute, though it
has sometimes been authoritatively done. But an examination of the
D   contents of section 37 confirms, in my view, that the marginal note
is at any rate broadly accurate. The section is divided into two subsections:

" (1) The enactments mentioned in Schedule 6 to this Act shall
have effect subject to the amendments specified therein. (2) The
E   enactments mentioned in Part II of Schedule 14 to this Act are
hereby repealed to the extent specified in the third column of that
Part."

Section 30 of the Act of 1970 was not repealed, but it was amended,
and the amendments are in Schedule 6, referred to in section 37 (1).
Schedule 6 is headed, " Schedule 6—Amendments consequential on
F   new method of charging tax." Then comes the further heading, " Part
I—Amendment of Income and Corporation Taxes Act 1970." In paragraph 13 of that Part I are the amendments to section 30. In subsection
(1) the words between commas, ". . . whether an assessment to surtax
in respect of his total income has or has not been made for the relevant
years or years of assessment . . ." were simply deleted. So there is now
G   no reference to any particular form of tax in subsection (1); it simply
enables the board to require a return in the circumstances specified.
Subsection (2), relating to the service of further notices, required no
amendment.

In subsection (3), the test of tax avoidance was reworded. Instead
of being a test that the individual avoided

H   " . . . more than 10 per cent. of the amount of the surtax for any
year which would have been payable in his case if the income . . .
had been deemed to accrue from day to day, . . ."

the new test was that the individual avoided

" . . . more than 10 per cent. of what would have been his excess
liability for any year if the income . . . had been deemed to accrue
from day to day."

That new formula is explained by an addition at the end of subsection A
(3):

> "In this subsection ' excess liability' means the excess of liability
> to income tax over what it would be if all income tax were charged
> at the basic rate to the exclusion of any other rate."

So far, then, the amendment seems simply to reflect the new system of
taxation.   B

But then comes subsection (4) of section 30, on which the argument
has centred before me. It will be remembered that subsection (4)
began, " For the purposes of assessment to surtax in the case of any
such individual..." The new wording is, " For the purpose of assessing
any individual to tax in pursuance of this section ..."; and in the proviso
to subsection (4) the word " surtax " is three times altered to " tax." C
I shall have occasion later to read straight through subsection (4) as
amended; I will leave it for the moment.

Finally, subsection (5), which authorises the board to make an estimate of income if they do not get satisfactory returns, ended, it will be
remembered, with the words "... deemed to form part of his total
income for the purposes of surtax." There, the words " for the purposes D
of surtax " have simply been deleted.

The Inland Revenue Commissioners have taken the view—and I am
told that they have over a period of years already acted on it—that the
amendments to subsection (4) not only took account of the necessary
consequences of the changes in the system of taxation but also extended
the taxation of the notional apportioned income under section 30 to
include all income tax: not merely the higher rates and the additional E
rate known as investment income surcharge, but also tax at the basic
rate, even though previously there had been no liability to tax at the
old standard rate. It is submitted on behalf of the Crown that, if you
simply read subsection (4) in its natural meaning, it is perfectly clear,
and, it is said, there is no room to cut it down by reference to the
context.   F

I will now read subsection (4), as amended, straight through:

> " For the purpose of assessing any individual to tax in pursuance
> of this section, the income from any assets to which this subsection
> applies shall be deemed to accrue from day to day and, in the case
> of the sale or transfer of any such assets by or to him, shall be
> deemed to have been received as and when it is deemed to have G
> accrued: Provided that an individual shall not be liable to be
> assessed to tax under this section in respect of any such income
> if he proves to the satisfaction of the board that the avoidance of
> tax was exceptional and not systematic, and that there was not in
> his case in any of the three next preceding years any such avoidance
> of tax as is described in the provisions of subsection (3) above."

                                                                      H
Now, say the representatives of the Crown, " tax " in the context
of a section dealing with income tax, unless it is restrained by some words
of exception, must mean the whole income tax: basic rate, higher rates,
additional rates—all that is " tax." I have been referred, at my request,
to section 526 (3) of the Act of 1970 as containing the only relevant
definition of the word " tax." That says merely:

> " Except in so far as the context otherwise requires, in this Act,

A   and in any enactment passed after this Act which by any express provision is to be construed as one with the Tax Acts, 'tax,' where neither income tax nor corporation tax is specified, means either of those taxes."

I do not myself find that that interpretation provision throws any light on the point now in question.

B   The special commissioners heard argument on both sides. Some of the taxpayer's arguments were clearly untenable, but the special commissioners were impressed by others and, in the end, the taxpayer prevailed. I will now read the reasons they give for their decision, and I will afterwards comment upon them to explain why I approve of them. They said:

C   "We do not find this an easy question. Before the Finance Act 1971 was enacted section 30 was directed at the avoidance of surtax but not at income tax at the standard rate. Now, say the Inland Revenue, it is directed not only at avoidance of 'excess liability' but it is also directed at avoidance of basic rate income tax. We see force in Mr. Blair's argument as to the meaning of 'tax' on 'total income.' But if such a radical extension of the section had
D   been intended one might have expected clearer wording expressing the new charge. For example, section 35 of the Finance Act 1971 expressly abolishes certain reliefs relating to surtax including the relief afforded by section 32 of the Income Tax Act 1970 in the case of purchase cum dividend—the other side of the coin from section 30. By contrast, the amendment to section 30 is relegated
E   to a Schedule containing no fewer than 93 groups of 'amendments consequential on new method of charging tax.' Moreover unlike, it would seem, any other provision in the Income Tax Acts, the charge to basic rate income tax (if there is one) is not assigned to any Schedule. We note that subsection (3), which Mr. Blair dismisses as no more than setting out the conditions of the imposition
F   of a charge, takes percentage avoidance of 'excess liability' (as opposed to percentage avoidance of total income tax) as the criterion. We do not think it unreasonable to suppose that if avoidance of basic rate tax as well as avoidance of excess liability is to be countered all components of the income tax should be brought into account in fixing the threshold for liability. With basic rate tax being charged at a flat rate and excess liability at progressive rates,
G   there can obviously be cases where liability under section 30 would arise where comparison is made by reference to excess liability but would not arise if comparison were made by reference to total income tax. Taking account of the various considerations, we think on balance that section 30, as amended by the Finance Act 1971, should be construed as imposing a charge which is limited to excess liability and we so hold."

H   It will be observed that those reasons fall into three branches. First of all, the special commissioners say that the change contended for on behalf of the Crown involves a radical extension of the section and they would have expected clearer words. There is no doubt to my mind that the extension is a radical one. Supposing a security with accrued dividend not yet payable is sold cum dividend to a person paying tax, then the part that will be apportioned under section 30 to the vendor

will bear tax at the basic rate twice over, because there is no exemption A
in the hands of the purchaser. True it is, of course, that if a person
with a large income buys from another such person an investment cum
dividend there will be a duplication in any case of tax at the higher rates.
Section 32 of the Act of 1971, which gave relief to a purchaser of an
investment cum dividend, has been repealed.

That new burden on the taxpayer, however, as the special com- B
missioners point out, has not been left to mention in the Schedule referred
to in section 37 of the Finance Act 1971—the Schedules which appear
on the face of them to be mainly, at any rate, dealing with consequential
matters. In Part II of Schedule 14, containing enactments repealed in
connection with the new method of charging tax, we find that section 32
of the Act of 1970 is listed, but the Finance Act 1971 does not make the
change merely in that obscure way. The repeal of section 32 of the C
Act of 1970 and certain other increases of fiscal burden, not merely
consequential, are enumerated in a substantive section, section 35 of
the Finance Act 1971, which is in these terms:

"Sections 31 (relief where income for longer period is received in
    one year) 32 (relief in case of purchases cum dividend) and 35
    (expenses of Crown servants abroad) of the Taxes Act shall cease to D
    have effect."

So the special commissioners thought, and in my opinion rightly
thought, that, looking at the scheme of the Finance Act 1971, and the
way in which substantial changes are separated from merely consequential
provisions, it is unlikely that it was intended to extend assessment under
section 30 to tax at the basic rate.

A counter argument was put forward by Mr. Hart. He took me E
through Schedule 6 and referred to several paragraphs amending other
sections of the Act of 1970. Those amended sections are sections 34,
36, 287, 296, 297, 399 and 457. They are sections dealing with a
diversity of topics. What is common to all the amendments in Schedule
6 relating to them is that it is made perfectly clear that the changes
relate only to the substitution of higher rate income tax for surtax, F
and that there is to be no effect on tax at the basic rate. The technique
of drafting used for that purpose is not uniform throughout the Schedule,
but Mr. Hart is right, I think, in saying that in all those cases the intention is made quite explicit.

I am unable, however, to feel the force of the inference drawn
therefrom: that if in the case of section 30 the intention is not entirely
clear, therefore it must have been meant to impose liability to basic G
tax. I am unable to follow that. I think it is neutral. Section 30, so
far as the language of the Schedule is concerned, may have been intended
to be altered in substance as well as in machinery, or it may not. I
have to judge from the language of the amendments, I think, not from
the fact that other amendments dealing with other sections may have
been clear. So I agree with the first branch of the special commissioners' H
reasoning, that one would have expected clearer language for such a
major change.

The second branch was that in many places in the Income Tax Acts
one finds some deeming provision, either bringing a hypothetical income
into existence or deeming the income of one person to be that of another,
or otherwise artificially imposing a liability to tax; in those provisions
again and again one finds that there is a direction as to the Schedule—

A among the six Schedules of the income tax legislation—whereunder tax at the basic rate is to be levied; and it is remarkable, if it was intended to bring the notional apportioned income into charge to basic rate tax, that there was not here also a direction indicating the appropriate Schedule. Mr. Hart submits that since income from the different classes of assets that might come within section 30 of the Act of 1970 will of its own nature be taxable under one or other of the cases of Schedule

B D—or, as I think he should have added, also possibly under Schedule C in some cases—there was no need to allot a particular Schedule in the amending legislation.

    I do not propose to express any opinion on that submission. I am not entirely persuaded by it; but even if it is correct, it remains, so far as I know, unique in the Income Tax Acts, that in such circumstances

C there should not be a direction specifying a Schedule. Accordingly, this is a second point—not perhaps of as much weight as the first one, but a second point—in favour of the taxpayer.

    The third point turns on the language of subsection (4) of the amended section 30 itself, because that is the section on which the Crown relied as the charging section. It is said, " You really do not need to

D look at anything else; here is a direction that the notional apportioned income is to be charged to tax; meaning income tax generally." But in my judgment there is little or no force in that submission if one reads carefully the whole subsection. It is not self-contained. It does not just begin " Income from any assets to which this subsection applies shall be deemed," etc. What it says is, " For the purpose of assessing any individual to tax in pursuance of this section, the income . . . shall be

E deemed to accrue . . . and . . . to have been received," etc. The whole matter is governed by the words, " For the purpose of assessing any individual to tax in pursuance of this section . . ." So you have to look at what has preceded, and what has preceded points plainly to an intention to counteract the avoidance of what is called in the new words added to subsection (3) " excess liability," and nothing more. Therefore,

F one starts reading subsection (4) with at any rate an expectation of finding that the charge is going to be to tax at the higher and additional rates, not at the basic rate. It is building too much on the one word " tax," I think, to say that that must point to a different conclusion.

    Moreover, the word " tax " itself occurs in the amended subsection four times: once in the main body of the subsection—the words I have already read, " For the purpose of assessing any individual to tax in

G pursuance of this section . . ."—and then three times in the proviso. In the first place where it occurs in the proviso the word " tax " is in a similar context to that in which it occurs in the earlier part of the subsection; namely, in the words, " Provided that an individual shall not be liable to be assessed to tax under this section." But in the other two places in the proviso the word " tax " occurs in the expression

H " avoidance of tax." The first is, ". . . the avoidance of tax was exceptional and not systematic . . ." and the second is, ". . . any such avoidance of tax as is described in the provisions of subsection (3) above." The avoidance of tax which has been described is, of course, avoidance of the " excess liability," and that alone is referred to where avoidance of tax is mentioned in the proviso to subsection (4). That again leads one to think that the word " tax " throughout subsection (4) may indeed be directed only at the tax in excess of the basic rate.

I therefore reach the conclusion, as did the special commissioners, that A
the contentions of the Crown are not well founded. Were the taxpayer
present, he would no doubt have recited the observations of Lord Buckmaster in *Greenwood* v. *F. L. Smidth & Co.* [1922] 1 A.C. 417, 423,
where he said:

> " It is, I think, important to remember the rule, which the courts
> ought to obey, that, where it is desired to impose a new burden by B
> way of taxation, it is essential that this intention should be stated
> in plain terms. The courts cannot assent to the view that if a
> section in a taxing statute is of doubtful and ambiguous meaning,
> it is possible out of that ambiguity to extract a new and added
> obligation not formerly cast upon the taxpayer."

Lord Buckmaster went on to say that the subsection there under C
scrutiny was at best of an extremely doubtful character, and that if it
had been designed to impose an additional liability some clearer and
better reference should have been made.

However, though that passage would no doubt have been invoked
by the taxpayer had he been here, it is I think true to say that the
attitude of the courts to taxing legislation has to some extent been
modified and that it is no longer popular to say that a tax is to be D
imposed only in clear terms. I will therefore make it quite plain that I
do not myself rely on any such doctrine in the present case. I have
endeavoured to look at the amendments made by the Finance Act 1971,
quite neutrally in their context, and I agree with the special commissioners entirely—indeed, I do not think that I find it so hard a
question as they seem to have felt—that they were right in allowing E
the taxpayer's appeal as presented to them.

My attention has been directed by Mr. Hart to *Schaffer* v. *Cattermole*
[1979] S.T.C. 670, which is a case I decided last year. In my judgment
I said of the Finance Act 1971, at p. 676:

> " The anti-avoidance provisions, which had become section 30 of
> the Income and Corporation Taxes Act 1970, were adapted and
> re-enacted and were made, as I think, somewhat more severe; but F
> the relieving enactment, then section 32 of the Act of 1970, was
> simply repealed."

Mr. Hart, who appeared for the Crown in *Schaffer* v. *Cattermole* and
remembers more of the case, I think, than I do, tells me that both
sides there were inclined to favour the view now contended for by the G
Crown, but that the effect of the amendment of section 30 was not in
immediate question and was not fully argued. The reference to that
case shows once again the great danger of even a single superfluous
word in a judgment on a point of law, and therefore I say no more
than that the present appeal is dismissed.

> *Appeal dismissed.*   H
> *No order as to costs.*
> *Liberty to apply as to interest on*
> *repaid tax.*

Solicitor: *Solicitor of Inland Revenue.*

T. C. C. B.

A

[COURT OF APPEAL]

* CARGILL v. GOTTS

1980   Nov. 12, 13, 14;   Lawton, Brandon and
B   Dec. 18   Templeman L.JJ.

*Easement—Right to draw water—Statutory restriction—Use of
   water from mill pond forming part of river—Occupier of
   dominant tenement having no statutory licence to abstract
   water—Increase of user during prescriptive period—Whether
   bar to prescription—Right to damages for interference with
   right—Effect of statute—Water Resources Act 1963 (c. 38),
C   ss. 23 (1), 24 (1), 135 (8)*

Since before 1927 water had been abstracted for the purposes of a 400-acre farm, mainly for watering cattle, from a
mill pond forming part of a river some 500 yards from the
southern boundary of the farm. In 1928 the plaintiff became
the tenant of the farm and had been in continuous occupation
of it ever since. In 1942 he purchased the freehold. At first
D   he or his employees drew water from the mill pond by means
of a water cart with a capacity of 200 gallons but in 1942 he
began to spray crops and the amount of water abstracted
increased. By the 1950s the crop spraying had become a
practice and the plaintiff was using a "bowser" with a
capacity of 900 gallons, to which a further 500 gallon tank
was subsequently added. By 1977 the quantity of water
abstracted had increased tenfold, 4,000 gallons sometimes being
E   abstracted in one day. The plaintiff did not obtain a licence
from the river authority (now the water authority by virtue
of the Water Act 1973) under section 23 (1) of the Water
Resources Act 1963,[1] and therefore from July 1, 1965, under
section 24 (1) of that Act the quantity of water he was entitled
to abstract was limited to 1,000 gallons a day provided that it
did not form "part of a continuous operation or of a series
of operations." In 1977 the mill pond came into the owner-
F   ship of the defendant who, in February of that year, forcibly
prevented the plaintiff's employee from drawing water from the
mill pond. The plaintiff claimed a declaration that he had an
easement to draw water from the mill pond for the more
convenient occupation of his farm, an injunction restraining the
defendant from preventing him from so doing, and damages.
The defendant denied that the plaintiff had acquired any easement and further pleaded that since July 1, 1965, the plaintiff
G   had been prevented by the Water Resources Act 1963 from
drawing water from the mill pond. The deputy judge held

[1] Water Resources Act 1963, s. 23: "(1) Subject to the following provisions
of this Part of this Act, as from the end of the period of three months beginning
with the second appointed day . . . [April 1, 1965] no person shall abstract water
from any source of supply in a river authority area, or cause or permit any other
person so to abstract any water, except in pursuance of a licence under this Act
H   granted by the river authority [now the water authority by virtue of the Water Act
1973] and in accordance with the provisions of that licence."
   S. 24: "(1) The restrictions imposed by subsection (1) of the last preceding section
does not apply to any abstraction of a quantity of water not exceeding 1,000 gallons,
if it does not form part of a continuous operation, or of a series of operations,
whereby in the aggregate more than 1,000 gallons of water are abstracted."
   S. 135: "(8) Except in so far as this Act otherwise expressly provides, and
subject to the provisions of section 33 of the Interpretation Act 1889 . . . the
restrictions imposed by sections 23, 36, 72 and 78 of this Act . . . shall not be
construed as . . . (c) derogating from any right of action or other remedy (whether
civil or criminal) in proceedings instituted otherwise than under this Act."

that prior to 1963 the plaintiff had acquired an easement to   A
draw water from the mill pond for the purposes of his farm
and that the Act of 1963 did not extinguish that right but
merely controlled the exercise of it. He made the declaration
and granted the injunction and awarded the plaintiff £50
damages for interference with his rights.

On appeal by the defendant: —

Held, allowing the appeal in part, (1) that on the facts of
the present case, each abstraction of water by the plaintiff   B
formed part of a series of operations the object of which was
to help to meet the water requirements of his farm and
accordingly the plaintiff was not entitled to the benefit of
the exception contained in section 24 (1) of the Act of 1963
so that every time he abstracted water after June 30, 1965,
he acted illegally, and could not rely on any abstraction of
water after that date to establish an easement by prescription
(post, pp. 446F, G–H, 449C–E, 451F–G, 452B).   C

Per Templeman L.J. Section 24 (1) is not apt to authorise
and was not intended to authorise any one person to abstract
as much water as he pleases from any source of supply provided only that each abstraction does not exceed 1,000 gallons
(post, p. 446F–G).

(2) That the Act of 1963 did not, however, affect an easement acquired before 1963; that the right which the farm had
begun to acquire in or about 1927 was to take water from the   D
mill pond for all farming purposes and such right had ripened
into an easement and that the improvement of farming methods
by crop spraying and the increased quantity of water employed
for that purpose was not sufficient to destroy or alter the
nature of the right asserted or the easement acquired; that, on
the evidence, the right asserted in 1977 was no different from
the right asserted in 1927 and the introduction of crop spraying
had not affected a radical change in the dominant tenement   E
and that, accordingly, the plaintiff was entitled to an easement at common law to draw water from the mill pond for
the purposes of farming his farm but he would only be able
to exercise his easement when he had obtained a licence under
the Act of 1963 and in accordance with the terms of that
licence (post, pp. 447E—448A, C, 451H, 452B).

Williams v. *James* (1867) L.R. 2 C.P. 557 and *R.P.C. Holdings Ltd.* v. *Rogers* [1953] 1 All E.R. 1029 applied.   F

Rugby Joint Water Board v. *Walters* [1967] Ch. 397
distinguished.

Hulley v. *Silversprings Bleaching and Dyeing Co. Ltd.*
[1922] 2 Ch. 268 considered.

(3) (Templeman L.J. dissenting) that, on its true construction, section 135 (8) of the Act of 1963 did not affect the
plaintiff's right to sue for damages for interference with his
right to abstract water from the mill pond notwithstanding   G
that such abstraction was prohibited by section 23 (1) and
accordingly the award of £50 damages should stand (post, pp.
451H—452B, B–C).

Decision of H. E. Francis Q.C. sitting as a deputy judge
of the Chancery Division [1980] 1 W.L.R. 521; [1980] 2
All E.R. 49 reversed in part.

H

The following cases are referred to in the judgment of Templeman L.J.:

British Railways Board v. *Glass* [1965] Ch. 538; [1964] 3 W.L.R. 913; [1964]
    3 All E.R. 418, C.A.
Hulley v. *Silversprings Bleaching and Dyeing Co. Ltd.* [1922] 2 Ch. 268.
Millington v. *Griffiths* (1874) 30 L.T. 65.
R.P.C. Holdings Ltd. v. *Rogers* [1953] 1 All E.R. 1029.
Rugby Joint Water Board v. *Walters* [1967] Ch. 397; [1966] 3 W.L.R.
    934; [1966] 3 All E.R. 497.

A   *Williams* v. *James* (1867) L.R. 2 C.P. 577.
     Woodhouse & Co. Ltd. v. *Kirkland (Derby) Ltd.* [1970] 1 W.L.R. 1185;
          [1970] 2 All E.R. 587.

     The following additional cases were cited in argument:

     Neaverson v. *Peterborough Rural District Council* [1902] 1 Ch. 577, C.A.
     Attorney-General v. *Cohen* [1937] 1 K.B. 478; [1937] 1 All E.R. 27, C.A.

B

     APPEAL from H. E. Francis Q.C., sitting as a deputy judge of the
Chancery Division.
     By a writ dated December 6, 1977, the plaintiff, David Cargill, the
owner and occupier of Grove Farm, Gimingham, Norfolk, sought (1) a
declaration that he was entitled either at common law or under section
C 2 of the Prescription Act 1832 to draw water for use appertaining to the
dominant tenement, Grove Farm, from the mill pond at Gimingham,
which was owned by the defendant, Brown Gordon Gotts; (2) alternatively, a declaration that he was entitled to the right to draw water by
virtue of the doctrine of lost modern grant; (3) an injunction restraining
the defendant from preventing the plaintiff from drawing water from the
mill pond; and (4) damages.
D   The defendant denied that the plaintiff was entitled to the declaration,
the injunction, or damages. He denied that the plaintiff had an easement
to draw water from the mill pond and contended, further or alternatively,
that the plaintiff had since July 1, 1965, been prohibited by virtue of
sections 23 (1) and 24 (1) of the Water Resources Act 1963 from extracting water in excess of the limit therein specified.
E   H. E. Francis Q.C. held that the plaintiff had been entitled to an
easement at common law to draw water from the mill pond for use on
his farm for agricultural purposes immediately prior to the Water
Resources Act 1963; that that Act had not extinguished his right but
merely controlled its exercise by precluding the abstraction of water
otherwise than in accordance with a licence granted by the river authority
and within the limits imposed by section 24 (1) of the Act but that the
F servient owner as such had no right to enforce the restrictions imposed by
the Act. He held further that in the present case the increase of user of
water was no bar to prescription and that, in the absence of evidence that
the increase in the quantity of water abstracted had materially affected the
level or flow of water in the mill pond, the plaintiff was entitled to the
declaration and injunction sought and to £50 damages for interference
with his right.
G
     The defendant appealed on the grounds that the deputy judge had
erred (1) in finding that the plaintiff had established a prescriptive right
at common law to an easement to abstract water for agricultural purposes
on the farm because on the evidence of user which the deputy judge
accepted of a tenfold increase in abstraction between the 1950s and 1977
the same did not amount to a sufficiently definite and continuous user on
H which to establish a prescriptive right; (2) that the deputy judge should
have found that in addition to the numerous occasions when the plaintiff's employees took away a full load in the plaintiff's bowser in breach
of the provisions of the Water Resources Act 1963 on all occasions after
June 30, 1965, upon which one or more loads were abstracted either on
a single day or on separate days, that constituted breaches of the Water
Resources Act 1963 and as such were illegal; (3) that the deputy judge
should have found that it was impossible to sever the illegal extraction

of water after June 30, 1965, from any extraction operations there may   A
have been which did not infringe the Water Resources Act 1963;
(4) that the deputy judge should have held that the abstraction of water
for crop spraying which commenced in 1953 comprised a separate and
additional burden upon the servient tenement which if established as an
easement would have constituted a separate right from any right based
upon the use for general agricultural purposes prior to 1953 such as the
watering of stock and the operation of steam driven machinery and that   B
in the light of the illegality affecting the enjoyment after 1965 there was
no sufficient lawful exercise of any such separate right for the plaintiff
to establish a prescriptive right thereto at common law; and (5) that the
deputy judge had erred in awarding damages and issuing an injunction
against the defendant because the extraction operations on behalf of the
plaintiff with which the defendant interfered were unlawful in that (a)   C
they were in contravention of the provisions of the Water Resources
Act 1963 and (b) they were not severable from the extraction of water
for use on certain other farms other than Grove Farm in respect of
which a right to draw water was neither pleaded nor proved.

The facts are stated in the judgment of Templeman L.J.

John Knox Q.C. and *Sonia Proudman* for the defendant.   D
Vivian Chapman for the plaintiff.

Cur. adv. vult.

December 18. The following judgments were read.

E
TEMPLEMAN L.J. read the first judgment. This is an appeal from a
decision of Mr. H. E. Francis, Q.C., sitting as a deputy High Court judge
in the Chancery Division and delivered on October 26, 1979. The deputy
judge held that the plaintiff, Mr. David Cargill, was entitled at common
law to an easement to draw water from the defendant's mill pond at
Gimingham in Norfolk for the purpose of farming the plaintiff's Grove
Farm. The defendant, Mr. Gotts, appeals to this court.   F

The River Mun flows in a south-easterly direction from Clapham
Dams and south of Grove Farm under the highway which runs north
and south through the village of Gimingham. After crossing the highway,
the river flows east to the sea at Mundesley. West of the highway the
river broadens to the Gimingham mill pond which is separated from the
highway by a narrow strip of land. The mill pond and the narrow strip   G
of land which allows access from the highway to the mill pond are
owned by the defendant. The plaintiff's Grove Farm comprises 400 acres
and its southern boundary is 500 yards from the defendant's mill pond.

Since before 1927 water was drawn from the mill pond by a water
cart for use on Grove Farm, mainly for the purpose of watering horses
and cattle. At first, the water cart carried a barrel with a capacity
variously estimated at between 50 and 100 gallons. The water cart drew   H
water from the mill pond at intervals of time which varied according to
the seasons and according to the recollection of the witnesses from four
times a week to two or three times a day. In winter the mill pond was
not used so much by Grove Farm because sufficient water was available
from another source. At threshing times and possibly at other times
water from the mill pond was or may have been used to operate steam
driven machinery on Grove Farm.

A   About 1942 the plaintiff began to use water from the mill pond to
spray crops on Grove Farm. The water barrel was replaced by a tank
which held 250 to 300 gallons. Crop spraying which was originally
carried out in April and May was progressively extended and intensified.
By 1953 crop spraying was described as a practice and, in the late 1950s,
the 250 gallon tank was replaced by a 900 gallon tanker called a bowser.
This was later augmented by a second tank of 500 gallons so that 1,400
B gallons in all could be drawn from the mill pond by means of a pump
attached to the bowser at any one time. Between the middle 1950s and
1977 the quantity of water abstracted by the plaintiff from the mill pond
increased tenfold, but this increase was partly due to the fact that the
plaintiff by 1977 was taking water not only for Grove Farm but for
three other farms as well. Occasionally, the plaintiff drew 4,000 gallons
C in a single day. In February 1977 the defendant forcibly prevented the
plaintiff from drawing water from the mill pond and, by the writ in
these proceedings dated December 6, 1977, the plaintiff claimed a declaration that he was entitled to draw whatever water he required from the
mill pond for the more convenient occupation of Grove Farm by virtue
of the Prescription Act 1832 or, alternatively, by common law or, alternatively again, by the operation of the doctrine of lost modern grant.
D The plaintiff also claimed an injunction restraining the defendant from
preventing the plaintiff from drawing water from the mill pond and the
plaintiff asked for damages. The defendant by his defence denied that
the plaintiff had acquired any easement and further pleaded that, since
July 1, 1965, the plaintiff had been prevented by the Water Resources
Act 1963 from drawing water from the mill pond.
E   By section 23 (1) of the Water Resources Act 1963 and orders made
under that Act, it became illegal on and after July 1, 1965, subject to
certain exceptions, for any person to abstract water from any source of
supply except in pursuance of a licence under the Act granted by the
appropriate river authority.[2] The mill pond is such a source.
      By section 24 (1) the restriction imposed by section 23 (1):

F   " does not apply to any abstraction of a quantity of water not
      exceeding 1,000 gallons, if it does not form part of a continuous
      operation, or of a series of operations, whereby in the aggregate
      more than 1,000 gallons of water are abstracted."

      By section 24 (2) the restriction imposed by section 23 (1) does not
apply to any abstraction from an inland water by or on behalf of an
G occupier of land contiguous to that water at the place where the abstraction is effected, in so far as the water is abstracted for use on a holding
consisting of that land and is abstracted for use on that holding for
inter alia agricultural purposes other than spray irrigation. This exception does not avail the plaintiff because Grove Farm is not contiguous
to the mill pond.
H   By section 27 an application for a licence to abstract water may be
made by the occupier of land contiguous to the supply or by anyone
who has a right of access to the supply. The plaintiff had a right of
access to the mill pond if he acquired an easement before July 1, 1965,
but he did not apply for a licence prior to these proceedings.
      By section 33 where any person abstracted water from a source of

      [2] By the Water Act 1973 the functions of river authorities were transferred to
the water authorities which were set up by the Act of 1973.

supply at any time within a period of five years ending with June 30,   A
1965, he was, on application made to the river authority before June 30,
1965, entitled to a grant of a licence under the Act. The plaintiff was
thus entitled to a licence of right under the Act, a licence which would
have been limited to the amount of water and the purposes for which
he had used the water from time to time during the preceding five years:
see section 35. The plaintiff did not apply for a licence of right under
the Act.   B

In the result, the plaintiff acted illegally on every occasion when he
abstracted water from the mill pond after June 30, 1965, unless he is
entitled to the benefit of the exception contained in section 24 (1) and
can establish that, every time his bowser abstracted 1,000 gallons or
less from the mill pond, that abstraction did not " form part of a continuous operation, or of a series of operations." The deputy judge held   C
[1980] 1 W.L.R. 521, 527:

> " it is open to the plaintiff to abstract water from the mill pond
> consistently with the provisions of the Act of 1963 provided he does
> not draw more than 1,000 gallons on any one occasion."

I am unable to agree. If the plaintiff planned to abstract 10,000
gallons by 10 instalments of 1,000 gallons for the purpose of filling a   D
swimming pool, then clearly each abstraction would form part of a series
of operations designed to fill the pool, whether the instalments were
abstracted on the same day or on 10 separate days or at irregular intervals.
If the plaintiff planned to abstract as much water as was needed to fill
and maintain a swimming pool and employed a 1,000 gallon tank for
that purpose, again each abstraction would form part of a series of   E
operations designed to fill and maintain the swimming pool, whether the
capacity of the pool was known or not, whether the pool leaked at an
unknown rate or not and whether or not the 1,000 gallon tank was
filled once per day or on irregular days. Similarly, if the plaintiff planned
to abstract 10,000 gallons to spray his crops or planned to abstract as
much water as was necessary to spray his crops and employed a 1,000
gallon tank for that purpose, again each filling of the tank formed part   F
of a series of operations designed to spray the crops. In my judgment,
on the facts of the present case, each abstraction of water by the plaintiff formed part of a series of operations, the object of which was to
help meet the water requirements of Grove Farm for agricultural purposes. Section 24 (1) is not apt to authorise and was not intended to
authorise any one person to abstract as much water as he pleases from   G
any one source of supply provided only that each abstraction does not
exceed 1,000 gallons.

I conclude that every abstraction of water by the plaintiff from the
mill pond after June 30, 1965, was illegal. It follows, in my judgment,
that the plaintiff cannot rely on any abstraction of water carried out
after June 30, 1965, in order to establish an easement by prescription.
The court will not recognise an easement established by illegal activity.   H
The Act of 1963, however, does not contain any provision which destroys
an easement already acquired. An easement of water acquired before
July 1, 1965, may not lawfully be exercised without a licence, but does
not cease to be an easement if a licence is not obtained nor does it
cease to be an easement until a licence has been obtained. The easement
remains an easement but cannot be exercised without committing an
offence under the Act of 1963.

A   If the plaintiff can establish that, before July 1, 1965, he acquired an
easement to take water from the mill pond, then he will be entitled to
apply for a licence and, if he is granted a licence, may thereafter lawfully exercise the easement to the extent justified by the easement but
subject to any limitations and provisions imposed by the terms of the
licence or any modification or renewal of the licence from time to time.

B   The plaintiff claims that the evidence established that, before July 1,
1965, Grove Farm acquired by more than 20 years user the right to water
from the mill pond for agricultural purposes. The deputy judge was
right to declare that the plaintiff, as the owner of Grove Farm, is
entitled at common law to an easement to draw water from the mill
pond for the purpose of farming Grove Farm.

The defendant claims that, down to 1953, the evidence only estab-
C   lished user of water from the mill pond to the extent of 300 gallons a
day for the purpose of watering stock and operating steam machinery
on Grove Farm. Between 1953 and 1965 the quantity of water abstracted
was increased and the purpose for which the water was used was altered.
The plaintiff cannot demonstrate 20 years' definite and continuous user
necessary to found any prescriptive right. Alternatively, if the plaintiff
D   began to establish a separate easement to use water for crop spraying in
1953 that did not ripen into an easement before 1965 when the user
became illegal.

The argument is that the introduction of crop spraying made a substantial change in the rights claimed by the dominant tenement and
imposed a substantial additional burden on the servient tenement.

In my judgment, it is a mistake to concentrate on gallonage and
E   detailed user. When Grove Farm, in or before 1927, took 100 gallons
from the mill pond to water 100 bullocks, Grove Farm did not begin to
acquire an easement to take 100 gallons to water 100 bullocks but began
to assert a right which, after 20 years, ripened into an easement to take
water from the mill pond for the benefit of Grove Farm for all purposes
according to the ordinary and reasonable use to which Grove Farm
F   might be applied at the time when the right was and continued to be
asserted.

To state the obvious, Grove Farm was and at all times remained a
farm. The right to take water from the mill pond was and at all times
remained a right to take water for farm purposes. If bullocks were
replaced by sheep, if pasture became arable, if beetroot was substituted
for barley, the right was asserted for the benefit of Grove Farm, provided
G   that the right asserted over the requisite period of 20 years, was a right
to take water for farm purposes and that right did not cease to be
asserted by fluctuations from time to time in the amount and application
of the water, fluctuations which were attributable to changes in the type
and method of farming currently pursued at Grove Farm. Water used
for crop spraying is just as much used for agricultural purposes as water
H   used for bullocks and the fact that more water may be required for crop
spraying than for watering bullocks is not sufficient to destroy or alter
the nature of the right asserted or the easement acquired. The principle
in relation to prescriptive rights of way was enunciated in *Williams* v.
James (1867) L.R. 2 C.P. 577, 580 and applied in *R.P.C. Holdings Ltd.*
v. *Rogers* [1953] 1 All E.R. 1029. The principle is

" When a right of way to a piece of land is proved, then that is,
unless something appears to the contrary, a right of way for all

purposes according to the ordinary and reasonable use to which   A
that land might be applied at the time of the supposed grant."

In my judgment, the same principle must apply to a right to take water.
The right to take water for the benefit of Grove Farm is a right to take
water for farming purposes, that being the ordinary and reasonable use
to which Grove Farm has at all times been applied.

There may in other cases be some scientific developments which   B
completely change the character of the right asserted. Thus in *Rugby
Joint Water Board* v. *Walters* [1967] Ch. 397 the right of a riparian owner
to take water for ordinary purposes, including agricultural purposes, did
not extend to taking 60,000 gallons a day for the purposes of spray irrigation. In the present case the improvement of farming methods by crop
spraying and the quantity of water employed for that purpose do not
jointly or separately amount to the assertion of a new right or the   C
excessive exercise of an ancient right. On the evidence in this case,
the right asserted in 1977 was no different from the right asserted in 1927,
namely, the right to use the water in the mill pond for the agricultural
purposes of Grove Farm. The introduction of crop spraying did not
effect a radical change in the dominant tenement.

Mr. Knox, who appeared for the defendant, referred to *Millington* v.   D
Griffiths (1874) 30 L.T. 65. In that case a prescriptive right to pollute
was not established because, over the alleged prescription period, the
amount of pollution had gone on increasing. If a plaintiff claims a
prescriptive right to pollute a stream he must show that he has, for a
20 year period, asserted the right to introduce polluting material of a
kind and quantity which produces the effect on the stream which he
claims to be entitled to continue. No such principle applies or needs   E
to be applied to a prescriptive right to take water from a stream if, as
in the present case, the right claimed has no material effect on the stream.
The defendant in the present case is not defending the stream; he is
seeking, for understandable reasons, to prevent the plaintiff from introducing a vehicle on the defendant's property.

In *Hulley* v. *Silversprings Bleaching and Dyeing Co. Ltd.* [1922] 2 Ch.   F
268 it was held that the progressive increase in plant in a mill which
polluted water taken from a stream and in the volume of water subsequently polluted was destructive of that certainty and uniformity essential
for the measurement and determination of the user by which the extent
of the prescriptive right claimed was to be established. That is another
pollution case in which the plaintiff could not establish the extent of the
right which he had asserted for 20 years. It was not sufficient for him   G
to show that he had put some polluting material in the stream throughout
the 20 year period. He must justify the extent of the pollution which he
was causing at the date of the proceedings. In the present case the
plaintiff does not claim a prescriptive right to extract any particular
volume of water from the mill pond. He claims he has asserted for
20 years and more the right to take such water as he requires from the mill   H
pond for agricultural purposes connected with Grove Farm. Easements
to take water, whether express or prescriptive, are rarely if ever defined
by reference to quantity as well as or instead of by reference to the
purposes for which the water may be abstracted.

A mere increase in the enjoyment of the right asserted does not throw
into confusion the nature of the right asserted, nor does it destroy the
right. Thus, in *British Railways Board* v. *Glass* [1965] Ch. 538, the right

A asserted during the 20 year prescriptive period was a right of way to a field used from time to time as a caravan site. During the period the number of caravans on the site increased from six to 30. This did not prevent the owner of the field from obtaining a prescriptive right of way for caravans without limitation on numbers. There had been no change in the character of the dominant tenement. In the present case the increase from 300 gallons to a maximum of 4,000 gallons without any
B change in the character of the dominant tenement did not affect the nature or quality of the right asserted during the prescriptive period.

In *Woodhouse & Co. Ltd.* v. *Kirkland (Derby) Ltd.* [1970] 1 W.L.R. 1185 increased user, as distinct from user of a different kind or for a different purpose, did not affect or prejudice the acquisition of a prescriptive right of way. Plowman J. at p. 1192 refrained from considering
C "whether an increase in user, if very great, can ever of itself amount to excessive user." It is equally unnecessary to decide the point in the present case because, in the circumstances, the increase in user cannot be described as being very great, measured, as it must be measured, by the effect of the user on the stream and on riparian owners.

In the result I agree with the deputy judge that the plaintiff is entitled
D at common law to an easement to draw water from the defendant's mill pond for the purpose of farming Grove Farm.

But, contrary to the views expressed by the deputy judge, I do not consider that it has been lawful for the plaintiff to exercise his rights since July 1, 1965.

I would accordingly declare that the plaintiff is entitled to the easement but also declare that it has not been lawful since July 1, 1965, and
E remains unlawful for the plaintiff to abstract water from the mill pond for the purpose of farming Grove Farm except in pursuance of a licence under the Water Resources Act 1963 and in accordance with the provisions of such licence.

The deputy judge granted the plaintiff an injunction restraining the defendant from preventing the plaintiff from drawing water from the
F mill pond in exercise of the plaintiff's easement. I do not consider that the injunction is now necessary or appropriate. So long as the plaintiff is not in possession of a licence and cannot lawfully exercise his easement, he will not draw water from the mill pond. When the plaintiff obtains a licence the defendant will not, in view of the outcome of this appeal, seek to prevent the plaintiff from drawing water from the mill pond.
G
The deputy judge also awarded the plaintiff £50 damages for interference with his easement. Mr. Chapman, who appeared for the plaintiff, argued that the plaintiff remained entitled to damages because, by section 135 (8) of the Water Resources Act 1963, the restrictions imposed by section 23 of the Act shall not be construed as derogating from any
H right of action or other remedy (whether civil or criminal) in proceedings instituted otherwise than under the Act. In my judgment, section 135 (8) confirms, if such confirmation is necessary, that the plaintiff, despite the provisions of the Water Resources Act 1963, remains entitled to a declaration concerning the easement which he has proved at common law. But, though the plaintiff is entitled to the easement, he has not suffered damage from any interference with his exercise of the rights constituting that easement because such exercise was illegal at the time of the interference.

In my judgment, the plaintiff does not suffer damage by being prevented   A
from doing something which it was illegal for him to do.

It does not follow, as Mr. Knox claimed, that the defendant was
entitled forcibly to prevent the plaintiff from taking water from the mill
pond. Section 49 of the Water Resources Act 1963 provides that any
person who contravenes section 23 (1) shall be guilty of an offence and
shall be liable on conviction, on indictment or on summary conviction
to a fine. Section 180 provides that it shall be the duty of a river authority   B
[now the water authority] to enforce the provisions of the Act in relation
to the area of the authority and that no proceedings for any offence
under the Act shall be instituted except by a river authority [now the
water authority] or by or with the consent of the Director of Public
Prosecutions. Section 135 (8) provides that the restrictions imposed by
section 23 shall not be construed as conferring a right of action in any   C
civil proceedings in respect of any contravention of those restrictions.
Mr. Knox submitted that the defendant, as the owner of the mill pond,
had the right to prevent any illegality happening on his property and to
exercise the right of self help to prevent any such illegality. In my
judgment, as between the plaintiff and the defendant, the plaintiff has
the right to come on to the defendant's land and to take water from the
mill pond. If the defendant knows or suspects that the plaintiff is com-   D
mitting an offence under the Water Resources Act 1963 (as amended),
the defendant may report the matter and make representations to the
relevant water authority or the Director of Public Prosecutions.

At a late stage of this appeal the defendant asked to amend his pleadings to allege that the plaintiff was, in 1977, extracting water from the
mill pond not only for Grove Farm but also for three other farms. This   E
allegation corresponds with the evidence, but the plaintiff never had the
opportunity to demonstrate at the trial, if he could, that he had become
entitled to a prescriptive right to take water for one or more of those
three farms, and, accordingly, I do not think the amendment should now
be allowed.

At the trial, as between the plaintiff and the defendant, the sole real   F
issue was whether the plaintiff could establish an easement at common
law to take water from the mill pond for the purposes of Grove Farm.
On this issue the plaintiff succeeded below and succeeded in this court.
The defendant was never entitled to interfere with the exercise of this
easement. It has not been established whether the defendant was entitled
to require the plaintiff to desist from taking water for the purposes of any
farm other than Grove Farm and the defendant only interfered with the   G
plaintiff's rights in order to prevent water being taken for Grove Farm.
This interference was not justified. The defendant attempted and failed
to rely on the Water Resources Act 1963 to prove that the plaintiff was
not entitled to an easement for Grove Farm. The defendant has succeeded
in this court in getting rid of an injunction which was, in my view, in any
event unnecessary once the court decided an easement existed.   H

I would declare that the plaintiff is entitled at common law to an
easement to take water from the mill pond for the farming purposes of
Grove Farm and I would add a declaration that the plaintiff is only
entitled to exercise his easement when he has obtained a licence under
the Water Resources Act 1963, as amended, and in accordance with the
terms of that licence.

A   LAWTON L.J. I too am satisfied that before July 1, 1965, being the second appointed day for the purposes of section 23 (1) of the Water Resources Act 1963, the plaintiff as the owner of Grove Farm acquired by more than 20 years use the right to take water from the mill pond for agricultural purposes on that farm. When, in or before 1927, water from the mill pond first came to be used on Grove Farm, it was for the needs of that farm at that date. Those needs were principally for water-

B   ing cattle and providing water for steam driven farm machinery such as a threshing machine. The probabilities were, as Mr. Knox accepted, that from time to time small quantities were used for other farm purposes.

A farm's needs for water can change with the seasons, with changes in the demand for agricultural produce and with improvements in agricultural methods. What is wanted in a dry summer may not be needed

C   in a wet one. At one time it may be worthwhile fattening store cattle on arable land which has been turned into pasture. A fews years later it may be more profitable to change from raising beef to growing corn and when this is done less water will be needed. Crop spraying is an example of the improvements in agricultural methods which have come about since 1927. In those days farmers often dressed their seed corn with chemicals which were reputed to deter birds, field mice and other rodents but they had

D   few, if any, means of protecting their crops from insects and plant diseases. Now, by means of spraying, they can give their crops this kind of protection but such spraying has to be done with water based chemicals. When water is so used it is for a normal agricultural purpose just as in 1927 water was used on farms to generate steam in threshing machines. The fact that spraying is a new way of protecting growing crops whereas

E   threshing machines are now more often seen in museums than on farms does not confine the user of the easement of water appertaining to Grove Farm to the purpose for which water was used in or about 1927 or to the quantities which were used before 1953, when large scale spraying started. The legal position would be different if water were used on Grove Farm for some abnormal agricultural purpose as might happen, for example, if part of the farm were turned into a trout hatchery.

F   Whether a particular purpose was a normal or abnormal agricultural use would be a question of fact.

What has affected the use of this easement is the Water Resources Act 1963. I agree with Templeman L.J. that the plaintiff will not be able to take advantage of the exception contained in section 24 (1) by limiting each abstraction of water to 1,000 gallons or less. In the past he has

G   sent his bowser to the mill pond for his farming purposes at Grove Farm. Each abstraction has been, or should have been, for such purposes and amounted to an operation with an end in view and it was always the same end, namely, the agricultural purposes of that farm. It follows, in my judgment, that his abstractions since 1965 have formed part " of a series of operations whereby in the aggregate more than 1,000 gallons of

H   water (have been) abstracted."

Although I agree generally with the reasoning in Templeman L.J.'s judgment I find myself unable to agree with him on the issue of damages. This is because of the unusual wording of section 135 (8) of the Act of 1963 which provides that the restrictions imposed by a number of sections, including section 23, " shall not be construed as . . . (c) derogating from any right of action or other remedy (whether civil or criminal) in proceedings instituted otherwise than under this Act." These proceedings

were by way of a civil action for nuisance. To deny the plaintiff a remedy   **A**
in damages because his abstraction of water was prohibited by section 23
would be to run counter to the provision of section 135 (8). The intention
of Parliament appears to have been to leave the enforcement of the
restrictions imposed by the Act entirely to the river authority concerned,
leaving the rights of individuals as between themselves unchanged. It
follows in my judgment that the award of £50 damages should stand.
This may seem a strange result but I cannot find any other way of con-   **B**
struing the Act.

BRANDON L.J. I agree in general with the judgment of Templeman
L.J. With regard to the issue of damages, however, I agree with the
different view expressed by Lawton L.J. and with the reasons given by
him for that view.   **C**

> *Appeal allowed to extent that injunc-*
> *tion discharged.*
> *Declaration that the plaintiff entitled*
> *at common law to easement to take*
> *water from mill pond for farming*
> *purposes of Grove Farm but only*   **D**
> *entitled to exercise it after obtain-*
> *ing licence under Water Resources*
> *Act 1963, as amended, and in*
> *accordance with terms of that*
> *licence.*
> *Plaintiff to have three-quarters of costs*
> *in Court of Appeal and below.*   **E**
> *Leave to appeal refused.*

Solicitors: *Collissons for Keefe Forman & Co., Norwich; Daynes,
Chittock & Back, Norwich.*

E. M. W.   **F**

[CHANCERY DIVISION]

* FROST (INSPECTOR OF TAXES) *v.* FELTHAM   **G**

1980 Nov. 21, 24   Nourse J.

> *Revenue—Income tax—Loan interest relief—Licensee of public*
> *house acquiring mortgage to purchase house—Tenancy agree-*
> *ment requiring him to reside at licensed premises—Monthly*
> *visits to house—Whether house " only or main residence "—*
> *Whether entitled to relief for mortgage interest—Finance Act*   **H**
> *1974 (c. 30), Sch. 1, para. 4 (1) (a)*

The taxpayer had for many years been the tenant and
licensee of a public house in Essex. His tenancy could be
terminated at any time by the brewers giving 12 months'
notice. A further term of his tenancy provided that he should
reside on the premises. However that requirement was not
rigidly adhered to and in 1976, jointly with his wife, he purchased a house in Wales. A part of the purchase price was

A   provided by a building society mortgage that was also in their
joint names. The house was fully furnished and equipped as
a home and the taxpayer and/or his wife spent some time
there each month. It was the only house he had ever
purchased. His claim for income tax relief in respect of
the mortgage interest for the years 1975–76 and 1976–77
was refused by the inspector of taxes. His appeal against
that refusal was allowed by the general commissioners on the
B   ground that the interest qualified for the relief under Schedule
9 of the Finance Act 1972 because the house was used by
him as " his only or main residence " within paragraph 4 (1)
(a) of Schedule 1 to the Finance Act 1974.[1]
      On appeal by the Crown: —
      Held, dismissing the appeal, that as the taxpayer lived for
much of the time at the public house his house in Wales was
not used as his " only " residence; that a person's " main "
C   residence was his " principal " or " more important " one and
that issue could not be decided solely by the way in which
he divided his time between two residences but depended on
all the circumstances of the case; that, although the taxpayer
and/or his wife probably spent only two or three days each
month at the house in Wales, on the evidence the commissioners were entitled to conclude that it was his " main "
residence in respect of which tax relief on the mortgage
D   interest was allowed.

The following cases are referred to in the judgment:

Byrne v. Rowbotham (1969) 210 E.G. 823, C.A.
Edwards v. Bairstow [1956] A.C. 14; [1955] 3 W.L.R. 410; [1955] 3
    All E.R. 48, H.L.(E.).
Fowell v. Radford (1969) 21 P. & C.R. 99, C.A.

E
The following additional case was cited in argument:

Brimelow v. Price (1965) 49 T.C. 41.

CASE STATED by the Commissioners for the General Purposes of the
Income Tax for the Division of Harlow.
F   The taxpayer, Bryan Kaye Bruce Feltham, was the publican tenant
and licensee of the White Horse Inn, Roydon, Essex. In March 1976
he purchased jointly with his wife and with the assistance of a mortgage
a house at Llanidloes, Powys. His claim for income tax relief in respect
of the mortgage interest of £150 for 1975–76 and of £1,395 for 1976–77
was refused by the inspector of taxes.
      The commissioners having considered the evidence and the con-
G   tentions of the parties decided to allow the appeal.
      The Crown appealed.
      The facts are set out in the judgment.

Robert Carnwath for the Crown.
Christopher Sokol for the taxpayer.

H
NOURSE J. This is an appeal by way of case stated from a decision
of the general commissioners for the Harlow division of Essex given on
October 16, 1978. At that hearing the taxpayer, Mr. Feltham, appealed
against the refusal by the inspector of taxes to allow him income tax
relief for mortgage interest for the years of assessment 1975–76 and 1976–

[1] Finances Act 1974, Sch. 1, para. 4 (1) (a): see post, p. 454c.

77 in respect of a property known as Mount Severn, Llanidloes, Powys,   A
in Wales. The amounts of the mortgage interest in question for the two
years of assessment are £150 for the year 1975–76 and £1,395 for the
year 1976–77. The question for the determination of the commissioners
was whether Mount Severn was used by the taxpayer during the period
covered by the two years of assessment as his " only or main residence "
within paragraph 4 (1) (a) of Schedule 1 to the Finance Act 1974. The
commissioners answered that question in the affirmative, and the   B
inspector of taxes now appeals to this court.

The material provisions of Schedule 1 to the Act of 1974 constituted
a restriction on the relief for loans for the purchase or improvement of
land which had been granted by the Finance Act 1972. So far as
relevant to the present case paragraph 4 (1) (a) of Schedule 1 to the Act
of 1974 is in these terms: C

> " Subject to the following provisions of this Part of this Schedule,
> Part I of Schedule 9 to the Finance Act 1972 shall not apply unless
> the land . . . referred to therein either—(a) is at the time the interest
> is paid used as the only or main residence of the person by whom it
> is paid . . ."

The facts found by the commissioners were based entirely on the   D
evidence given by the taxpayer himself, which they accepted. Those
facts were as follows. The taxpayer was in 1978, and I believe still is,
the tenant and licensee of a public house known as the White Horse Inn,
Roydon, in Essex. He had been the tenant and licensee of that house for
some 17 years previously. It was a term of his tenancy agreement with
the brewers that he should reside on the premises, but that requirement   E
was not rigidly enforced. More important is the fact that the tenancy
could be terminated at any time by the brewers on giving 12 months'
notice. That, of course, is a provision which is often found in tenancies
of tied houses.

Turning to Mount Severn, that had been purchased in March 1976 in
the joint names of the taxpayer and his wife with the assistance of a   F
mortgage, also in their joint names, from a building society. It was the
only house that the taxpayer had ever purchased. Mount Severn was
fully furnished and equipped as a home. During the period from March
1976 to April 1977 (that is the material period for present purposes) the
taxpayer and/or his wife visited the property and spent some time each
month there, and all outgoings on the property, such as general and water
rates, were paid as they fell due. Finally, the taxpayer considered Mount   G
Severn to be his only or main residence.

On the basis of those facts, the general commissioners expressed
their conclusion in these terms: " We the commissioners who heard the
appeal having considered the evidence and the contentions of the parties
decided to allow the appeal." It is to be noted, first, that the commissioners did not say whether the ground of their decision was that   H
the taxpayer used Mount Severn as his only residence or as his main
residence, or as both; and, secondly, that they gave no reasons for their
decision. However, they could hardly have thought that Mount Severn
was the taxpayer's only residence. And one of the contentions which
had been advanced on his behalf and considered by them was that the
Concise Oxford Dictionary defined " main " as " principal " or " most
important." I therefore think I must assume that the commissioners

A were of the opinion that Mount Severn was used by the taxpayer as his principal or more important residence, and I propose to treat that as having been the ground of their decision.

Returning to the words of paragraph 4 (1) (*a*) of Schedule 1, I observe that before the taxpayer could obtain tax relief for mortgage interest it had to be shown that Mount Severn was used as his only or main residence during the material period. The question, therefore, is

B not whether it was his only or main residence during that period, but whether it was used as such. At one stage in the argument I thought it might be of some importance that the word found in this statutory provision is " used " and not " occupied." There is a comparable provision in section 1 (2) of the Leasehold Reform Act 1967 which in certain circumstances enables a tenant of a house held on a long lease to purchase

C the freehold. In that subsection the right of the tenant to purchase the freehold applies only where the tenant is, in right of the tenancy, " occupying it as his only or main residence (whether or not he uses it also for other purposes)." It occurred to me that " used " might be a word which, although it required a substantial degree of association with the house in question, prima facie required one less substantial

D than the word " occupied." However, neither side took up that point and I propose to discuss it no further.

As I have already said, it seems to me that the commissioners could hardly have thought that Mount Severn was used as the taxpayer's only residence. A residence is a place where somebody lives, and it is clear that the taxpayer lived for the greater part of the year at the White Horse Inn, Roydon. Therefore, he could not have used Mount Severn

E as his only residence. But that does not at all mean that he could not have used it as his principal or more important residence, even though he spent very little time there. If someone lives in two houses the question which does he use as his principal or more important one cannot be determined solely by reference to the way in which he divides his time between the two. I can test that by reference to an example

F far removed from the facts of this case and the conditions of our own times. In his *Lives of the Lord Chancellors, 3rd series* (1847), vol. 7, Lord Campbell tells how Lord Eldon was often prevented by the burdens of his office from visiting his estate at Encombe in Dorset for long periods at a time. Sometimes he was only able to get down there for three weeks or so in the year, for the partridge shooting in September. True it was that Lord Eldon also had a good house in Hamilton Place, but it could

G not really have been suggested that he did not use Encombe as his principal or more important residence.

The question is essentially one of fact and degree for the tribunal of first instance, in this case the commissioners. If authority is needed for that, it can be found in two decisions of the Court of Appeal on section 1 (2) of the Leasehold Reform Act 1967. The first of these was

H *Byrne* v. *Rowbotham* (1969) 210 E.G. 823, where Salmon L.J., in delivering the principal judgment, said:

> " It would be wrong to regard the case before the court as a decision on a point of law. There was an infinity of variations of circumstances to take into account in deciding which was a man's main home. Each case would differ from the other; there might be cases where it was very difficult to decide the question."

The second case was *Fowell* v. *Radford* (1969) 21 P. & C.R. 99. At A
p. 100. Lord Denning M.R. in delivering the principal judgment and
having referred to the findings of the judge in that case, pointed out that
the judge had preferred to look at

> "The whole of the history and the circumstances, the value of the
> residences, the purposes for which they are used, the time they have
> been used and the amount of time spent during the course of the year B
> at each." Then he said: "I think that he was right in so doing."

I must therefore examine the facts found by the commissioners in
order to see whether they can support the conclusion at which they
arrived. Mr. Carnwath for the Crown said that they cannot. He said
that the true and only reasonable conclusion on the facts found by the
commissioners is that the taxpayer did not use Mount Severn as his C
main residence, and he went on to say that there was indeed no evidence
on which they could have based the contrary conclusion. In other words,
he said that this case is one of the same order as the well-known case
of *Edwards* v. *Bairstow* [1956] A.C. 14. And he referred in particular
to a passage in the speech of Lord Radcliffe at p. 36 in which, as one of
the possible ways of expressing the test for upsetting a decision of the
commissioners, general or special, Lord Radcliffe said that it must be D
shown that the true and only reasonable conclusion contradicts their
determination. Mr. Carnwath said that this is a case where, on the
basis of that test, I can and ought to reverse the decision of the commissioners. Mr. Sokol, on the other hand, for the taxpayer said that
the test for upsetting their decision is higher than that to which I have
just referred. And he pointed to other passages in the speeches of Lord E
Simonds and Lord Radcliffe in support of that proposition.

In my judgment, there is only one test to be extracted from the
decision of the House of Lords in *Edwards* v. *Bairstow,* and it is correctly
stated in the passage on which Mr. Carnwath relied. But even if that
is not so, it seems to me that whatever test is to be extracted from that
decision it is not satisfied in the present case. In order to give my F
reasons for that view I must return to certain of the facts found by the
commissioners. First I refer to the fact that the taxpayer's tenancy of
the White Horse Inn could be terminated at any time by the brewers on
giving 12 months' notice. That is a real power of determination, because
a tenancy of a tied house is an exception from any form of statutory
protection. So it could be said that, although the taxpayer had already
been there for some 17 years, he nevertheless had no real security of G
tenure. Secondly, I refer to the fact that Mount Severn is a property
which was purchased in the joint names of the taxpayer and his wife,
and that it is the only house which the taxpayer has ever purchased.
Mr. Carnwath said that those are neutral facts, and viewed in isolation
they may well be so. But they are certainly facts which the commissioners were entitled to take into account, and when combined with H
the other facts they may well have carried some weight. Thirdly, I
refer to the fact that Mount Severn was fully furnished and equipped as
a home. Mr. Sokol relied on that as showing, first, that further
expenditure had been incurred by the taxpayer and his wife and
secondly, and I think more importantly, that the commissioners regarded
the property as being not merely a residence but a home. Fourthly,
there is the finding that the taxpayer and/or his wife visited the property

A and spent some time each month there. I might have wished that the commissioners had expressed themselves with a little more particularity in this respect, but I have to take that finding as it stands. In my judgment it amounts to this. I bear in mind that Powys is a long way from Essex. It seems to me therefore that the taxpayer and/or his wife, on the visits to Mount Severn in each month, must have spent longer than a day or so there on each occasion. Equally, it seems to me that it

B would be unrealistic to think that the taxpayer and/or his wife spent a great deal of time there. In the light of the geographical separation between the two properties and the fact that the taxpayer, at all events, would have had to devote the greater part of his time and attention to the running of the White Horse Inn. I think that I must take the expression " some time in each month " to mean that the taxpayer and/or

C his wife spent periods of two or three days in each month at Mount Severn. Of course, viewed in isolation those are not long periods of time to spend at a house which can properly be described as the principal or more important residence of the persons concerned. But the question what was the correct view of the facts as a whole was essentially one for the decision of the commissioners. It may not have been an easy one. At this stage I must quote another passage from the judgment

D of Lord Denning M.R. in *Fowell* v. *Radford* (1969) 21 P. & C.R. 99, where he said, at p. 101:

"Very often a couple have two residences, a town residence and a country residence, so that it is almost impossible to say which is the main residence. In such a case, the judge has to come down on one side of the line or the other."

E It seems to me that I must assume that this is exactly what the commissioners did. To put it the other way round, I see no reason for not assuming that they took all the material facts into account, including the question of how much time was spent at Mount Severn, and gave due weight to each. Although in other circumstances it might well

F have been that the facts were not sufficient to justify a finding that that was the principal or more important residence of the taxpayer, it seems to me that it would be quite impossible for me to say that that was a conclusion at which the commissioners could not properly arrive on the evidence which was actually before them in this case, taking all the material facts together.

I have left to the end the commissioners' finding that the taxpayer

G considered Mount Severn to be his only or main residence. By that they must have meant that he considered it to be his main residence. Mr. Carnwath said, in my view quite rightly, that it was not enough for the taxpayer to take the view that it was his principal or more important residence. The matter must be decided objectively. Mr. Sokol, on the other hand, said that it was something which the commissioners were

H entitled to take into account as part of the picture as a whole. I agree with both those contentions. It seems to me that on its own the taxpayer's view could not carry much weight. But again it seems to me that it is something which can be thrown into the balance. I see no evidence from the commissioners' finding as a whole that they gave any undue weight to that particular consideration. Therefore I must assume that they took due account of it and no more. In my judgment Mr. Carnwath has failed to show that this is a case in which the true and only

reasonable conclusion was that the taxpayer did not use Mount Severn   A
as his main residence during the period in question, and that means
that the appeal must be dismissed.

Appeal dismissed with costs.

Solicitors: *Solicitor of Inland Revenue; Hatchett, Jones & Kidgell.*

B

[Reported by MRS. HARRIET DUTTON, Barrister-at-Law]

[CHANCERY DIVISION]

C

** STAFFORD WINFIELD COOK & PARTNERS LTD. v. WINFIELD

[1978 S. No. 5363]

1980 March 10, 21; 31   Sir Robert Megarry V.-C.

Practice—Jury, civil action—Right to jury—Proceedings in   D
Chancery Division—Allegation of fraud—Litigant requesting
trial by jury—Application to transfer action to Queen's Bench
Division—Court's discretion to transfer case to another
division—Whether " fraud " in issue—Administration of
Justice (Miscellaneous Provisions) Act 1933 (23 & 24 Geo. 5,
c. 36), s. 6 (1)[1]—R.S.C., Ord. 4, r. 3 (1)[2]

In an action in the Chancery Division the plaintiff (a   E
company in liquidation) claimed that the defendant and her
late husband, both directors, had wrongfully mis-applied the
company's moneys in purported payment of consultancy fees
or for services rendered by her but that in reality she had
rendered no such services to the company and the moneys
were intended by both the defendant and her husband to be
for the provision of maintenance for her by the husband.
The company further claimed that the payments were made
ultra vires and in breach of the fiduciary duties owed to the   F
company by the defendant and her husband and that the
defendant knew or ought to have known that the money paid
to her belonged to the company. There was a charge of
conspiracy between the defendant and her husband and of
conversion by the defendant, and the relief sought included
a claim for "damages for fraud."
On the defendant's summons for an order transferring the
action to the Queen's Bench Division under R.S.C., Ord. 4,   G
r. 3 so that she could claim trial by jury under the provisions
of section 6 (1) of the Administration of Justice (Miscellaneous
Provisions) Act 1933 : —
Held, dismissing the summons, (1) that a litigant charged
with fraud in the Chancery Division had no right by statute
or the rules to trial by jury and no right to require the
action to be transferred to the Queen's Bench Division so
that he could exercise the right of a litigant in that division,   H

---

[1] Administration of Justice (Miscellaneous Provisions) Act 1933, s. 6: "(1) . . .
if, on the application of any party to an action to be tried in the King's Bench
Division of the High Court . . . the court or a judge is satisfied that—(a) a charge of
fraud against that party . . . is in issue, the action shall be ordered to be tried
with a jury. . . ."
[2] R.S.C., Ord. 4, r. 3: "(1) A cause or matter may, at any stage of the proceedings therein, be transferred from one division to another by order of the court
made in the division in which the cause or matter is proceeding."

A   under section 6 (1) of the Act of 1933, to apply for trial by
jury but it was open to the court under R.S.C., Ord. 4, r. 3 (1)
to transfer the proceedings in a suitable case (post, pp. 465F—
466A).

        International Producers Ltd. v. *Forbes* [1922] W.N. 76
considered.

      (2) That " fraud " in section 6 (1) of the Act of 1933 meant
an intentional misrepresentation or concealment of fact induc-

B ing the other party to act on it to his detriment; that there
was no such allegation against the defendant and therefore
fraud was not in issue within the meaning of the subsection;
and that, since the defendant would not be entitled to trial by
jury and the nature of the action was not suitable for such
a trial, the court would not exercise its discretion under
R.S.C., Ord. 4, r. 3 (1) to order the action to be transferred
to the Queen's Bench Division (post, pp. 466B–E, 467B–F).

C   *Barclays Bank Ltd.* v. *Cole* [1967] 2 Q.B. 738, C.A.
applied.

        Jenkins v. *Bushby* [1891] 1 Ch. 484, C.A. and *Williams* v.
Beesley [1973] 1 W.L.R. 1295, H.L.(E.) considered.

The following cases are referred to in the judgment:

Back v. *Hay* (1877) 5 Ch.D. 235.

D   *Barclays Bank Ltd.* v. *Cole* [1967] 2 Q.B. 738; [1967] 2 W.L.R. 166;
     [1966] 3 All E.R. 948, C.A.

Clarke v. *Cookson* (1876) 2 Ch.D. 746.

Davy v. *Garrett* (1878) 7 Ch.D. 473, C.A.

Derry v. *Peek* (1889) 14 App.Cas. 337, H.L.(E.).

Duport Steels Ltd. v. *Sirs* [1980] 1 W.L.R. 142; [1980] I.C.R. 161;
     [1980] 1 All E.R. 529, Kenneth Jones J., C.A. and H.L.(E.).

E   *Everett* v. *Islington Guardians* [1923] 1 K.B. 44.

Hope v. *Great Western Railway Co.* [1937] 2 K.B. 130, C.A.

International Producers Ltd. v. *Forbes* [1922] W.N. 76.

Jenkins v. *Bushby* [1891] 1 Ch. 484, C.A.

Pacaya Rubber and Produce Co. Ltd., In re [1913] 1 Ch. 218, C.A.

Reese River Silver Mining Co. Ltd. v. *Smith* (1869) L.R. 4 H.L. 64,
     H.L.(E.).

F   *Ruston* v. *Tobin* (1879) 10 Ch.D. 558, Malins V.-C. and C.A.

Warner v. *Murdoch* (1877) 4 Ch.D. 750, C.A.

Williams v. *Beesley* [1973] 1 W.L.R. 1295; [1973] 3 All E.R. 144,
     H.L.(E.).

The following additional cases were cited in argument:

Baring Bros. & Co. v. *North Western of Uruguay Railway Co.* [1893] 2
     Q.B. 406, C.A.

G   *Forrester* v. *Jones* [1899] W.N. 78.

Gould and Co. Ltd. v. *Houghton* [1921] 1 K.B. 509.

National Coal Board v. *Gamble* [1959] 1 Q.B. 11; [1958] 3 W.L.R.
     434; [1958] 3 All E.R. 203, D.C.

Rex v. *Atwell* (1801) 2 East's Pleas of the Crown, 768.

Reg. v. *Kelly* (1847) 2 Car. & K. 379.

Tunstall v. *Steigmann* [1962] 2 Q.B. 593; [1962] 2 W.L.R. 1045; [1962]

H   2 All E.R. 517, C.A.

Wells v. *Smith* [1914] 3 K.B. 722.

PROCEDURE SUMMONS

      In proceedings begun by writ dated November 28, 1978, in the
Chancery Division, the plaintiff company, Stafford Winfield Cook &
Partners Ltd. (in liquidation), claimed inter alia a declaration that
between 1971 and 1976 the defendant, Wendy Madeleine Helen Styles

Winfield, and her late husband wrongfully misapplied moneys belonging A
to the company to their own use in purported payment by the company
for services rendered to the company by the defendant.

The statement of claim alleged, inter alia, that the defendant and
Mr. Winfield, as directors of the company, owed it fiduciary duties,
including a duty to act in all respects and to deal with the company's
property in good faith in the company's interests. The defence dated
November 13, 1979, was a denial of any misapplication of the company's B
moneys.

By summons dated November 16, 1979, the defendant applied to
have the action transferred to the Queen's Bench Division for trial with
a jury. The summons was adjourned into court as a procedure
summons.

The facts are stated in the judgment.   C

Christopher Allen for the defendant.
R. C. B. McCombe for the plaintiff company.

Cur. adv. vult.

March 31. SIR ROBERT MEGARRY V.-C. read the following judgment. D
This is a summons by the defendant to have the action transferred
to the Queen's Bench Division, there to have a trial by jury. The
action is brought by a company called Stafford Winfield Cook &
Partners Ltd. which went into liquidation in April 1976: I shall call it
" the company." The defendant is a widow. Her late husband was
a director of the company from 1962 until it went into liquidation, and E
the defendant, too, was a director from February 1975. The dispute is
in respect of sums amounting to rather over £12,500 paid by the company
to the defendant during the period from July 1971 to December 1975.
The sums originally claimed were a little over £10,000, and the receipt of
these has been admitted. The larger figure was subsequently inserted
in the statement of claim by way of amendment, and I have not seen
any amended defence. There is also an alternative claim for rather F
over £3,000 (which originally was for a little over £1,100) for mistaken
overpayments; but nothing at this stage turns on this or on the precise
figures.

What is in issue is the company's allegation that whereas the payments
purported to have been made against invoices rendered to the company
by the defendant for consultancy fees or services rendered by her to the G
company, in fact the defendant did not perform, and was never intended
to perform, any services in respect of the invoices. The payments were
made for no consideration, says the company, were made ultra vires and
in breach of the fiduciary duties of the defendant and her husband, and
were made, and were intended by the defendant and her husband to be
made, as a provision by him for her maintenance; they had admittedly
ceased to live together in about March 1972. The defendant, says the H
company, knew or ought to have known that the money belonged to
the company and was improperly paid from the company's assets, and
that the husband paid it dishonestly in breach of his duties to the
company. There is an allegation of conspiracy between the defendant
and her husband, and of conversion by the defendant, and that the
defendant is liable to account as a constructive trustee. The relief
sought is a declaration that the defendant and her husband wrongfully

The Weekly Law Reports, April 17, 1981

461

1 W.L.R.   Stafford & Partners v. Winfield (Ch.D)   Sir Robert
                                                                  Megarry V.-C.

A misapplied the company's moneys, an order for the defendant to pay the
company the larger sum as representing money received by her as a
constructive trustee for the company, damages, an alternative claim for
an order to pay the smaller sum of a little over £3,000 as money had and
received to the company's use, interest, and various consequential
relief. From first to last the word " fraud " is not used, though in
the writ there was a claim for " damages for fraud."

B
The defence is basically a denial of most of the allegations in the
statement of claim, and an assertion that the invoices were rendered
in respect of design consultancy work carried out by the defendant at
the company's request from time to time. In essence, the central issue
is whether or not the invoices were genuine invoices for work genuinely
done by the defendant for the company, or whether they are shams,
C designed to conceal payments improperly procured by the husband out
of the company's assets in order to maintain the defendant. On that,
two main questions have been admirably argued by Mr. McCombe on
behalf of the company and Mr. Allen on behalf of the defendant. The
first is whether this is a case in which " a charge of fraud " against the
defendant " is in issue " within the meaning of the Administration of
Justice (Miscellaneous Provisions) Act 1933, section 6 (1), and the
D second is whether, if it is, the discretion of the court under R.S.C.,
Ord. 4, r. 3 (1) to transfer the case to the Queen's Bench Division,
where the defendant may claim trial by jury as of right, ought to be
exercised. Mr. Allen accepted that if he did not succeed on the first
point, his claim to a transfer must fail.

It was common ground that if there was to be a trial by jury, the
E action must be transferred to the Queen's Bench Division, since there
is no machinery for jury trial in the Chancery Division. Indeed, *Clarke*
v. *Cookson* (1876) 2 Ch.D. 746, 748, shows that Sir George Jessel M.R.
and all three Vice-Chancellors considered that the terms of the Supreme
Court of Judicature Act 1873 precluded trial by jury in the Chancery
Division; and in *Warner* v. *Murdoch* (1877) 4 Ch.D. 750 this was approved
by the Court of Appeal. On one view, the first point to decide is
F whether there is in fact a charge of fraud; but before I do that I think
that it is desirable to consider what provision has been made by statute
for trial by jury where fraud is charged. This has changed considerably
over the years, as Mr. McCombe demonstrated in his careful survey.

Under R.S.C., Ord. 36, set out in the Supreme Court of Judicature
Act (1873) Amendment Act 1875, Schedule 1, the mode of trial was to
G be specified in the notice of trial by the party giving the notice, with
the right for the other party, if trial by jury had not been specified,
then to give notice requiring trial by jury; and the court had a discretion
to direct trial without a jury in certain respects: see rules 2, 3, 4 and 26.
Fraud was not specially mentioned, and no special rule was laid down
for the Chancery Division.

H
This provision was varied by Rules of the Supreme Court 1883.
Ord. 36, r. 2 allowed either party, by notice, to require a jury in cases
of slander, libel, false imprisonment, malicious prosecution, seduction
or breach of promise of marriage. This rule, too, made no mention of
fraud. Causes or matters assigned to the Chancery Division by the
Supreme Court of Judicature Act 1873 (see section 34, and also section
35, and section 11 of the Act of 1875) were directed, by the new
provisions of R.S.C., Ord. 36, r. 3, to be tried by a judge without a jury

462

unless the court or a judge otherwise ordered; and rule 4 repeated the A
previous discretion of the court to direct trial without a jury in certain
respects. Rule 5 introduced a new power for the court or a judge to
direct trial without a jury of any cause, matter or issue requiring any
prolonged examination of documents or accounts, or any scientific or
local investigation, which could not conveniently be made with a jury.
Rule 6 then, a little surprisingly, provided that in any other cause or
matter any party could on application insist on trial by jury. That, of B
course, left untouched the Chancery Division (rule 3: see *Jenkins* v.
Bushby [1891] 1 Ch. 484), and the matters under rule 5; but I say
that it seems a little surprising because rule 2 provided for the right
to a jury in the six specified cases of libel, slander and so on, and
this hardly presaged the general right to trial by jury which rule 6
gave. The only difference seems to be that under rule 2 the litigant C
exercised his right to a jury by giving notice, and under rule 6 he did
it by making application. In the absence of any exercise of the right to
a jury, or an order for jury trial, rule 7 provided for a trial without a
jury.

It seems to have been the Juries Act 1918, which introduced fraud
for the first time into this subject; at any rate, no earlier provision has
been cited to me. This was professedly an Act " to limit the right to a D
jury in certain civil cases "; and section 1 provided that all trials " in the
High Court " should be by a judge alone. There were then certain
provisos, one of which, proviso (*b*), enabled any party to claim trial by
jury as of right if " fraud is alleged ", or there was a claim for libel,
and so on. On this, Mr. McCombe commented that it would be a
little strange if in limiting the right to a jury the Act had in fact E
extended it by enabling the litigant in the Chancery Division in a case
in which fraud was alleged to claim a jury as of right, whereas previously
the trial would have been by a judge alone unless it had been otherwise
ordered. The Act, indeed, made no separate mention of the Chancery
Division, but spoke generally of the High Court. Proviso (*c*) to section
1, however, empowered the court to direct trial by jury if a party applied
for it, and the matter was " more fit " to be tried with a jury.   F

This enactment came before Peterson J. in *International Producers
Ltd.* v. *Forbes* [1922] W.N. 76. The action had been commenced in
the Chancery Division, and there were allegations of fraudulent misrepresentation and corrupt bargain. The defendant claimed the right
to a jury under proviso (*b*), and also under the court's discretion under
proviso (*c*) and generally. The case is somewhat shortly reported (I was G
told that the only other report was in 66 S.J. 333 and was equally brief),
but it is plain that the judge did not accept the contention that proviso
(*b*) applied to the Chancery Division. He rejected the idea that matters
assigned to the Chancery Division such as dissolution of partnerships,
setting aside deeds, and specific performance, in which allegations of
fraud were common, would entitle the defendant to demand a jury and
have the action which statute had assigned to the Chancery Division H
transferred to the King's Bench Division. The Act showed an intention
to limit the right to a jury, and not to extend it to the Chancery Division
where the right to a jury had never existed before. What proviso (*b*)
contemplated was an application for a jury, and not an application for
transfer to another division in which a jury could be obtained; it was
restricted to cases where, apart from the Act, the court had power to
direct trial by jury. Further, the judge saw no reason for exercising

A his power to transfer the case to the King's Bench Division, or for thinking that it would be tried more satisfactorily there; and so he refused the application.

At the time of that decision, the Administration of Justice Act 1920 had been enacted, but section 2 of it had not been brought into force. Section 2 dealt with trial by jury in civil cases. Subsection (1) gave the court power to direct trial without a jury " in the High Court " if either B party applied for it and the court was satisfied that the matter " cannot as conveniently be tried with a jury as without a jury." Proviso (a), however, prohibited trial without a jury if fraud was alleged, or there was a claim for libel and so on, unless both parties consented. These provisions were superseded by the Administration of Justice Act 1925, section 3. This provided that section 2 of the Act of 1920 should cease C to have effect, and that rules of court could prescribe which trials in the High Court were to be with a jury and which without. Until then, the rules of court which were in force immediately before the Act of 1918 was passed were to have effect.

Fraud thus lost the position which the Act of 1918 had conferred on it. This was, however, restored by the Administration of Justice (Miscellaneous Provisions) Act 1933, section 6. This is in force today, D save that as a result of the Law Reform (Miscellaneous Provisions) Act 1970 breach of promise of marriage has disappeared from the familiar list of six causes of action, beginning with libel. Seduction, abolished by the same Act, still remains; I know not why, but it does not matter. Section 6 of the Act of 1933 provides that on the application of any party to an action " to be tried in the King's Bench Division of the E High Court," if the court or a judge is satisfied that a charge of fraud against that party, or a claim for libel and so on, is in issue, the action must be tried with a jury, unless the court or judge is of opinion that the trial " requires any prolonged examination of documents or accounts or any scientific or local investigation which cannot conveniently be made with a jury." Subject to this, any " action to be tried in that division " may, in the discretion of the court or a judge, be ordered to be F tried either with or without a jury. For some while after the Act of 1933 was passed, the ancestors of the rule which now stands as Ord. 33, r. 5, repeated the substance of much of section 6 of the Act; the present rule avoids this, though like the section it is specifically confined to actions " to be tried in the Queen's Bench Division."

I pause there. Section 1 of the Act of 1918 had conferred the right G to a trial by jury in a case " in the High Court " if fraud was alleged. *International Producers Ltd.* v. *Forbes* [1922] W.N. 76 had shown that this gave no right to demand a jury in actions in the Chancery Division; and then, in 1933, the section in the Act which gave a litigant charged with fraud the right to demand a jury was in terms confined to an action " to be tried in the King's Bench Division of the High Court." In those circumstances, there is plainly much force in the contention H that Parliament meant what it said, and did not intend to confer any right to a jury on a litigant charged with fraud in the Chancery Division by the indirect method of making it obligatory for the Chancery Division to transfer any such case to the Queen's Bench Division in order to give him a statutory right to a jury. I should certainly be surprised if a charge of fraud in a matrimonial cause were held to give a right to trial by jury despite rule 43 (1) of the Matrimonial Causes Rules 1977. The power to transfer a case from one division to another given by

R.S.C., Ord. 4, r. 3 appears to be purely a matter for the discretion A
of the court (to be exercised, of course, on proper principles), for the
verb is "may," without more. Is it right to say that a party charged
with fraud who has been given no right to a jury is entitled to require
the power to transfer the case to be exercised in order to confer on
him the right to a jury which Parliament has refrained from giving
him? Alternatively, can it be said that because the right to a jury has
been given to a party charged with fraud in the Queen's Bench Division, B
that is a strong or compelling reason for the court to exercise its
discretion to transfer to the Queen's Bench Division a case in the
Chancery Division in which that party has no right to a jury?

Questions such as these plainly lead to others. In particular, what is
the reason for not giving the right to litigants in the Chancery Division?
May not a party charged with fraud legitimately ask why the right to C
the jury that he seeks should depend on whether the division in which
the plaintiff has issued the writ is the Queen's Bench Division or the
Chancery Division? Does anything turn on whether the assignment
to the Chancery Division is obligatory or optional? In other words,
does anything turn on whether the proceedings have been assigned to
the Chancery Division by force of the Supreme Court of Judicature
(Consolidation) Act 1925, section 56, which specifically assigns certain D
types of action to that division, or whether the action is of a kind which,
although it could have been commenced in either the Chancery Division
or the Queen's Bench Division, has in fact been assigned to the Chancery
Division by the plaintiff exercising his right under section 58 to assign
it to that division simply by marking the writ with the name of that
division? Section 56, I may say, replaced section 34 of the Act of 1873, E
and section 58 replaced section 35 of the Act of 1873 and section 11 of
the Act of 1875, the old and the new provisions being substantially to
the same effect in what is material.

In considering these questions, it seems plain that many of the
matters specifically assigned to the Chancery Division by section 56 of
the Judicature Act 1925 are inherently unlikely to be suitable for trial
by jury. Further, nobody can practise or sit in this division for long F
without being well aware that many allegations of fraud are made and
tried by a judge sitting alone. I have already referred to what Peterson
J. said in *International Producers Ltd.* v. *Forbes* [1922] W.N. 76;
and there are a number of older authorities to the same effect, even if
one does not go the whole way with Sir Richard Malins V.-C. in saying
that "questions of fraud have always been considered to be peculiarly G
within the jurisdiction of the Court of Chancery": *Back* v. *Hay* (1877)
5 Ch.D. 235, 240, and see p. 241. In *Ruston* v. *Tobin* (1879) 10 Ch.D. 558,
the action was brought in the Chancery Division to have an agreement
induced by the fraudulent misrepresentations of the defendant set aside
and cancelled, for repayment of the money paid under the agreement,
and damages. The plaintiff required trial by jury, and the defendant H
thereupon moved for trial by a judge alone. One obvious point against
the plaintiff was that if he had wanted a jury, he should have issued his
writ in one of the common law divisions of the High Court, instead of
coming into Chancery. The plaintiff sought to meet this by saying that
he had been forced to come into Chancery because actions for cancellation of written instruments were assigned to the Chancery Division by
the Judicature Act 1873, section 34; but Sir Richard Malins V.-C. held

The Weekly Law Reports, April 17, 1981

465

1 W.L.R.   Stafford & Partners v. Winfield (Ch.D)   Sir Robert
                                                                  Megarry V.-C.

A that as cancellation was not essential to the relief claimed, there was no
need for the plaintiff to have sued in the Chancery Division.

That aspect of the case is not, of course, directly in point in the
present case; but at p. 562 the Vice-Chancellor went on to rest his
decision on a further ground. " Independently of these considerations,"
he said, the case was one of setting aside a transaction on the ground
that it was brought about by fraud. As he had pointed out in many
B cases

> " that is peculiarly, and always has been considered peculiarly the
> jurisdiction of the Court of Chancery when that court existed, and
> is the jurisdiction and business of this court now that it is simply
> called the Chancery Division. There are no cases of that nature,
> however complicated, however difficult, however lengthy, which
C this court has not been in the habit of dealing with, and which it
> does not deal with almost constantly. It is therefore, and always
> has been, considered the peculiar tribunal for trying these questions,
> and being so, I could not send such a case to be tried by a jury
> unless I was absolutely satisfied that justice could not be obtained
> here, or that there is an absolute right on the part of the plaintiffs
D to take the defendant to a jury."

In the Court of Appeal Sir George Jessel M.R. observed at p. 565 that
there must be a " very strong case " before the Court of Appeal would
interfere with the discretion of a judge as to the way in which a case
before him should be tried. He then said that the Vice-Chancellor

> " went on the ground that this was a kind of case which had always
E been tried in Chancery, and never at common law; not a case
> turning on a single misstatement, but on a series of representations,
> so that there was no single question of fact which could be con-
> veniently submitted to a jury. It is no part of my duty to say what
> I should have done if this case had come before me in the first
> instance, but I do unhesitatingly say that I should have done what
F the Vice-Chancellor has done."

With this, James and Bramwell L.JJ. concurred.

Both on the authorities and on principle it seems to me that the
position may be summarised as follows. (1) A litigant who is charged
with fraud has been given by statute the right to demand a jury if the
action is brought in the Queen's Bench Division, but not if the action
G is brought in Chancery. (2) Such a litigant has been given no right to
require the action to be transferred from the Chancery Division to the
Queen's Bench Division simply in order to obtain the jury to which,
ex hypothesi, he has no right. (3) These consequences flow from the
language of the statute and the rules; but if reasons for them are sought,
one reason may well be that many of the matters proceeding in the
Chancery Division are of a nature which makes them inherently unsuit-
H able for trial by jury, irrespective of fraud; and the inclusion of a charge
of fraud does not make suitable for jury trial proceedings which are
unsuitable. Another reason may lie in the long experience that the
Chancery Division has had in hearing cases of fraud which arise in the
types of case usually to be found in that division. (4) The power to
transfer proceedings from (inter alia) the Chancery Division to the
Queen's Bench Division which is given by Ord. 4, r. 3 (1), provides
something of a safety-valve. It would be open to the court to exercise

466

the power in a case in which fraud is charged which (a) is suitable for   A
trial by jury, and (b) is of a nature such that the interests of justice
sufficiently require that the transfer should be made. (5) Any contention that the plaintiff has deliberately issued his writ in the Chancery
Division in order to deprive the defendant of the right to a jury which
he would have had if the writ had been issued in the Queen's Bench
Division can be dealt with adequately under the court's power to transfer   B
the action. This may occur when the assignment of the case to the
Chancery Division was made by the plaintiff exercising his option under
the Judicature Act 1925, section 58, in a case where there is no obligatory
assignment to the Chancery Division under section 56, especially where
the subject matter of the action has no particular Chancery element.

With these considerations in mind, I turn to the other main head,
i.e., whether in fact in this case "a charge of fraud against that party"   C
(namely, the defendant) "is in issue" within the meaning of those
words in the Administration of Justice (Miscellaneous Provisions) Act
1933, section 6 (1) (a). Certain matters are clear. First, the word
"fraud" is used not in any general sense of dishonesty, but as meaning
an intentional misrepresentation (or in some cases concealment) of fact
made by one party with the intention of inducing another party to act   D
on it, and thereby inducing the other party to act on it to his detriment.
In other words, "fraud" means "fraud" in the sense of *Derry* v. *Peek*
(1889) 14 App.Cas. 337: see *Barclays Bank Ltd.* v. *Cole* [1967] 2 Q.B.
738, especially at pp. 744, 745, where robbery was held not to be fraud
for this purpose. Second, it is plain that a charge of fraud may be made
without using the word "fraud." This is so where a defendant is said
to have made representations to the plaintiff on which he intended the   E
plaintiff to act, and the representations were untrue, and were known
to the defendant to be untrue: see *Davy* v. *Garrett* (1878) 7 Ch.D. 473,
489. Third, it is settled that a mere superadded allegation of fraud
will not suffice: there must be a charge of fraud which will have to be
decided in order to determine the rights of the parties. Thus if the
only issue is whether or not goods have been paid for, an allegation that
the defendant was fraudulent does not give him the right to a jury: see   F
Everett v. *Islington Guardians* [1923] 1 K.B. 44, 46. That case
depended on the action being one "in which fraud is alleged," so that
the present requirement that fraud should be "in issue" strongly
reinforces the decision.

Mr. McCombe's contentions on the point really fell under two
main headings. First, he said that the essence of the company's case   G
was to recover money from the defendant which she had received as
a constructive trustee, and that success in such a claim in no way
depended on proving fraud against the defendant. However fraudulent
the defendant's husband may have been, fraud on the defendant's part
was not a necessary ingredient for success by the company. Second,
he said that there was plainly no question of the defendant having deceived
the representative of the company with whom she dealt (namely, her   H
husband), since the company's case was that the two of them were
acting in concert, with the husband probably the prime mover.

Now the claim in respect of the alleged constructive trust obviously
does not depend on the company establishing fraud against the defendant,
and the same applies to the claim for money had and received to the
company's use. There is, indeed, a claim for damages; but since the

The Weekly Law Reports, April 17, 1981

467

1 W.L.R.   Stafford & Partners v. Winfield (Ch.D)   Sir Robert
                                                                  Megarry V.-C.

A Misrepresentation Act 1967, section 2, such a claim may succeed without
proving that the misrepresentation was fraudulent; and the charge of
conspiracy to pay the money in breach of duty to the company is not
a charge of fraud. It seems to me that the company could succeed in
all that is claimed without establishing that the defendant is guilty of
Derry v. *Peek* fraud. Obviously the company's claims against the
defendant involve grave imputations against her; but that is not enough
B to bring the case within the statute. Mr. Allen took me on an interesting
tour of a number of criminal and other authorities on aiding and
abetting, on accessories before the fact, on imputing an agent's knowledge
to his principal, and on lifting the corporate veil; but I do not think I
need discuss them. For the reasons that I have given I do not consider
that this is a case in which a charge of fraud against the defendant is
C in issue. Accordingly, even if the case were to be transferred to the
Queen's Bench Division, the defendant would have no right to a jury.

If I am wrong in that, and a charge of fraud against the defendant
is in issue, then there is the question whether I ought to transfer the
case to the Queen's Bench Division. First, as I have mentioned, R.S.C.,
Ord. 4, r. 3 (1) simply provides that the proceedings " may " be transferred, without more; and this, I think, gives the court a discretion, to
D be exercised on proper principles. Second, I think that, on ordinary
principles, it is for the litigant who seeks the transfer to make out a
sufficient case for the power to be exercised. Certainly the onus rests
on an applicant who asks for a discretionary power to order trial by
jury to be exercised: *Jenkins* v. *Bushby* [1891] 1 Ch. 484. Third, the
fact that the transfer will give the defendant the right to claim a jury,
E and that that is what she wants, is only one of the factors to be borne
in mind. Others include the nature of the case, the suitability or
otherwise of the Chancery Division for deciding the case as compared
with the suitability of trial by jury (and this includes the probability
of a trial by judge alone being shorter and cheaper), as well as the
wishes of the other party to the litigation. In deciding whether there
should be trial by jury, the court must act fairly to all parties: see
F *Williams* v. *Beesley* [1973] 1 W.L.R. 1295.

Mr. Allen advanced a contention that the cases in which the
suitability of the Chancery Division for trying cases of fraud had been
asserted were cases where the fraud was mere equitable fraud, and not
those where there was *Derry* v. *Peek* fraud. I do not think that he made
good this proposition. Thus *Ruston* v. *Tobin* (1879) 10 Ch.D. 558, which
G I have already discussed, seems to me to be a plain case in which *Derry*
v. *Peek* fraud was charged. However, in the course of his submissions
Mr. Allen cited *In re Pacaya Rubber and Produce Co. Ltd.* [1913] 1
Ch. 218; and it was a dictum of Kennedy L.J. in that case which
perhaps helped him most. The case was one in which an order for
transfer to the Chancery Division had been made in respect of an action
in the King's Bench Division for fraudulent misrepresentations in the
H prospectus of a company which was being wound up by the Companies
Court. Both Neville J. and the Court of Appeal held that the transfer
had been rightly made; and at p. 223 Neville J. reiterated the view that
the Chancery Division was not unfitted to deal with allegations of fraud,
because both that division and the old Court of Chancery were largely
concerned with cases of that kind. That, of course, was a case in which
the transfer would take away the right to a jury, and not a transfer
which, like the transfer sought in the present case, would confer the

468

right to a jury.   At p. 225 Kennedy L.J. said that if the directors of   A
the company had taken up the position that the charge of fraud " was
a serious charge," which they wished to have tried by a jury, he would
have come to a different conclusion, since it would be right to have a
trial by jury in such a case.   Mr. Allen, of course, strongly relied on
this dictum.   He linked it with a reference to some words of Lord
Cairns in *Reese River Silver Mining Co. Ltd.* v. *Smith* (1869) L.R. 4   B
H.L. 64, 79, another case of an allegedly fraudulent company prospectus.
There, Lord Cairns refrained from entering into any question regarding
" fraud in the more invidious sense," and said that it was quite possible
that the directors were ignorant of the untruth of the statements in
their prospectus, though they would still be civilly liable for them.

Now I would accept that one of the factors to be borne in mind in
considering a transfer is the degree of gravity of the charges made   C
against the defendant, and especially that of any charges of fraud.   But
that is only one of the factors.   It has to be weighed against all the
other factors in the case.   Here, the claim is based on a whole series
of invoices, and whether the work alleged in them to have been done
by the defendant had in fact been done or not.   This comes close to
the words in the judgment of Sir George Jessel M.R. in *Ruston* v. *Tobin*
(1879) 10 Ch.D. 558, 565 that I have already quoted, that of a case   D
not " turning on a single misstatement, but on a series of representations,
so that there was no single question of fact which could be conveniently
submitted to a jury."   Furthermore, I cannot see any circumstances of
especial gravity in the charge of fraud made against the defendant in
this case, nor anything which makes it unsuitable for trial in the
Chancery Division.   Indeed, there is force in Mr. McCombe's contention   E
that a case about the doctrine of constructive trusts in relation to a
company, and the fiduciary duties of directors, with an allegation of
ultra vires to boot, is not very suitable fare for a jury, even though
there are also allegations of fraud and dishonesty.   The natural home for
such a case may well be said to be the Chancery Division, where such
matters are almost a commonplace, so that the case ought to stay where
it is.   I should add that there is indeed a sizeable bundle of invoices to   F
be examined; but although I do not accept Mr. McCombe's contention
that the trial requires a " prolonged examination of documents or
accounts which cannot conveniently be made with a jury " so as to
satisfy the statutory requirement for excluding trial by jury even in
cases of fraud, I think that the invoices make a small contribution
towards preferring trial by a judge alone.   G

Looking at the case as a whole, it seems to me that not only is
there no strong case for a transfer, but there is, on balance, no case at
all: the factors in favour of a transfer are outweighed by those in favour
of the case remaining where it is.   The matter is an anxious one
because as I understand it, both on the older authorities (to which may
be added *Hope* v. *Great Western Railway Co.* [1937] 2 K.B. 130) and   H
also on the recent statement of the House of Lords in *Duport Steels
Ltd.* v. *Sirs* [1980] 1 W.L.R. 142 (a case on a quite different point), in
discretionary matters the discretion is that of the judge at first instance,
and it will not readily be interfered with on appeal.   I have tried to
express the major considerations in this judgment in accordance with
the submissions put before me, but of course it is not practicable to set
forth every single matter that is of any possible relevance.   I can only

The Weekly Law Reports, April 17, 1981

469

1 W.L.R.   Stafford & Partners v. Winfield (Ch.D)   Sir Robert
                                                                  Megarry V.-C.

A say that, looked at as a whole, the case appears to be entirely appropriate
to the Chancery Division; and even on the assumption that a charge of
fraud against the defendant is in issue, no case has been made out which
would justify the case being transferred to the Queen's Bench Division.
Accordingly, the application fails, and the summons will be dismissed.

B
                                                    Order accordingly.

Solicitors: *Gregsons; W. F. Prior & Co.*

                                                            K. N. B.

C
                              [PRIVY COUNCIL]

* RAGHO PRASAD .   .   .   .   APPELLANT
                              AND
D THE QUEEN .   .   .   . RESPONDENT

                [APPEAL FROM THE COURT OF APPEAL OF FIJI]

1980 Oct. 13, 14;   Lord Hailsham of St. Marylebone L.C.,
      Nov. 17   Lord Diplock, Lord Edmund-Davies, Lord
                                Russell of Killowen and Lord Roskill

E
*Fiji — Crime — Evidence — Confession — Issue of admissibility —
    Whether issue for trial judge or assessors
Privy Council—Jurisdiction—Criminal matter—Appeal from Fiji
    —Basis for reviewing decision of local appellate court*

        The defendant was tried for murder before a judge and
F   five assessors. The only evidence against him was a con-
    fession statement. The defendant challenged the admis-
    sibility of the statement on the ground that it was a
    fabrication and that he had been forced to sign it. The
    judge held on a voire dire (in the absence of the assessors)
    that the statement was voluntary and he admitted it in
    evidence. In his summing up to the assessors the judge
    directed them:
        " It was suggested to you that you have to be satisfied
G   that the confession is voluntary, but that it not so. All
        you have to consider is whether the [defendant] made
        that statement and whether it is true."
    The judge also referred to some inadmissible hearsay evidence.
    The assessors gave their unanimous opinion that the defendant
    was guilty of murder. He was convicted and appealed. The
    Court of Appeal decided that the judge's direction on the
    issue of the voluntariness of the confession was a correct
H   statement of the law and that, notwithstanding some criticism
    of the summing up, taken as a whole it was adequate and
    any defects were not such as to justify allowing the appeal.
        On the defendant's appeal to the Judicial Committee: —
        Held, dismissing the appeal, that the judges of the Fiji
    Court of Appeal being aware of local conditions and social
    attitudes, were in a better position to assess the effect of a
    misdirection or irregularity on the assessors and the Judicial
    Committee would only interfere with a decision of a Court of
    Appeal where a defendant had been deprived of the substance

of a fair trial or of the protection of the law or where the
decision would, in general, tend to create a bad precedent
(post, p. 471E–G); and that since there was no authority which
required that the issue of the voluntariness of a confession
should be decided by the assessors and the summing up had
been correct in that regard and since, in the context of the
summing up, there was no substance in the defendant's complaint that he had been prejudiced by the judge's passing
reference to the inadmissible hearsay evidence, there was no
ground to the inadmissible hearsay evidence, there was no
ground on which the Judicial Committee would be justified
in examining the general adequacy of the summing up which
was a matter entirely for the Court of Appeal (post, pp. 473A–E,
H—474A).

> *Ibrahim* v. *The King* [1914] A.C. 599, P.C. applied.
> Dictum in *Reg.* v. *McCarthy* (1980) 70 Cr.App.R. 270,
> 272, C.A. explained.
> Decision of the Court of Appeal of Fiji affirmed.

The following cases are referred to in the judgment of their Lordships:

Chan Wei Keung v. *The Queen* [1967] 2 A.C. 160; [1967] 2 W.L.R.
552; [1967] 1 All E.R. 948, P.C.
Ibrahim v. *The King* [1914] A.C. 599, P.C.
Reg. v. *Burgess* [1968] 2 Q.B. 112; [1968] 2 W.L.R. 1209; [1968] 2
All E.R. 54, C.A.
Reg. v. *McCarthy* (1980) 70 Cr.App.R. 270, C.A.

The following additional cases were cited in argument:

Dillet, In re (1887) 12 App.Cas. 459, P.C.
McGreevy v. *Director of Public Prosecutions* [1973] 1 W.L.R. 276;
[1973] 1 All E.R. 503, H.L.(N.I.).
Reg. v. *Sykes* (1913) 8 Cr.App.R. 233, C.C.A.
Reg. v. *Thompson* [1893] 2 Q.B. 12, C.C.R.
Wong Kam-ming v. *The Queen* [1980] A.C. 247; [1979] 2 W.L.R. 81;
[1979] 1 All E.R. 939, P.C.

APPEAL (No. 32 of 1979) by the defendant, Ragho Prasad s/o Ram
Autar Rao, from a judgment (July 22, 1977) of the Fiji Court of Appeal
(Gould V.-P., Marsack and Henry JJ.A.) whereby it dismissed the
defendant's appeal against his conviction of murder on December 1,
1976, in the Supreme Court of Fiji (Western Division) (Criminal Jurisdiction) before Stuart J. and five assessors.

The facts are stated in the judgment.

Anthony Scrivener Q.C. and *Nigel Murray* for the defendant.
George Newman for the Crown.

Cur. adv. vult.

November 17. The judgment of their Lordships was delivered by
LORD DIPLOCK.

At a trial in the Supreme Court of Fiji, held before Stuart J. and
five assessors, Ragho Prasad (the defendant) was convicted of murder-
ing his father, and sentenced to life imprisonment. He appealed to the
Fiji Court of Appeal against his conviction, on the ground of various
alleged errors and other defects in the judge's summing up to the
assessors, whose unanimous opinion, with which the judge concurred,
was that the defendant was guilty of murder. The Court of Appeal gave

A thorough detailed consideration to these criticisms. They are dealt with in the judgment of the court delivered by Gould V.-P. who concluded by saying:

"We have expressed some criticism of the summing up but do not consider, in the light of the whole, that the learned judge went beyond permissible limits in permitting his opinions of some facts to be seen, and do not find any of the other criticisms urged by counsel are justified to such an extent as would induce us to allow the appeal."

The practice of the Judicial Committee in the exercise of its appellate jurisdiction in criminal matters was authoritatively stated by Lord Sumner in *Ibrahim* v. *The King* [1914] A.C. 599, 614–615. The practice remains unchanged, and the whole passage bears repetition:

"Leave to appeal is not granted ' except where some clear departure from the requirements of justice ' exists: *Riel* v. *The Queen* (1885) 10 App. Cas. 675; nor unless ' by a disregard of the forms of legal process, or by some violation of the principles of natural justice or otherwise, substantial and grave injustice has been done ': *Dillet's* case (1887) 12 App. Cas. 459. It is true that these are cases of applications for special leave to appeal, but the Board has repeatedly treated applications for leave to appeal and the hearing of criminal appeals as being upon the same footing: *Riel's* case; *Ex parte Deeming* [1892] A.C. 422. The Board cannot give leave to appeal where the grounds suggested could not sustain the appeal itself; and, conversely, it cannot allow an appeal on grounds that would not have sufficed for the grant of permission to bring it. Misdirection, as such, even irregularity as such, will not suffice: *Ex parte Macrea* [1893] A.C. 346. There must be something which, in the particular case, deprives the accused of the substance of fair trial and the protection of the law, or which, in general, tends to divert the due and orderly administration of the law into a new course, which may be drawn into an evil precedent in future: *Reg.* v. *Bertrand* (1867) L.R. 1 P.C. 520."

To this their Lordships would only add that courts of appeal composed of judges more familiar than members of this Board can hope to be with local conditions and social attitudes, are in a better position than their Lordships to assess the likely effect of any misdirection or irregularity upon a jury or other deciders of fact in a criminal case. This is all the more so where, as in Fiji, the mode of trial is not the same as in England or Scotland. There is no jury; the trial is before a judge and assessors to the number of not less than four in capital cases. The judge sums up to them; each then states his individual opinion as to the guilt of the accused; although permitted to consult with one another they are not obliged to do so; and the ultimate decider of fact (as well as law) is the judge himself who need not conform to the opinions of the assessors, even though they be unanimous, if he thinks that their opinions are wrong. The field of comment upon evidence that is proper to a judge in summing up to a jury in a trial in which they are collectively the exclusive deciders of fact is not necessarily the same as in summing up to assessors whose function it is to help the judge in making up his own mind as the sole ultimate determiner of fact.

472

A

Adherence to their settled practice, as described in *Ibrahim* v. *The King* [1914] A.C. 599, makes it unnecessary in the instant case for their Lordships to do more than state in bare outline the case against the defendant, of which a full account is to be found in the judgment of the Court of Appeal. On July 27, 1976, there had been a party attended by members of an extended Hindu family of which the deceased, the father of the defendant, was the head. It was held at premises in the compound where most of the extended family lived to celebrate the completion of the cane harvest by one of the defendant's brothers. The defendant, the deceased and some eight others were present, including one called Jai Raj. The deceased had left the party before it ended in order to go home to bed. His body was discovered some time later near a toilet in the compound. He had received some 13 cuts from a sharp instrument of which four were very severe and were the cause of his death.

B

C

For reasons into which it is unnecessary to enter the only evidence of the defendant's guilt that was available at his trial was a confession. If he had made it and it was true, it was conclusive of his guilt. The prosecution's case was that he had made it to a police inspector when he had been confronted with Jai Raj who had said to the defendant: " When grandfather went to sleep, after some time when the dogs started barking, you went and came back after 10 to 15 minutes."

D

When asked by the inspector if what Jai Raj had said was true, the defendant replied:

> A. " Yes, sir, now, this is true. My brother Sohan Lal said to get rid of this problem. My father went towards the house. A little after, I went and I was annoyed and struck him with a knife."
> Q. " How many times did you strike with a knife?"
> A. " Three or four times."
> Q. " What did you do with the knife?"
> A. " I kept the knife at home washing it and the police took it from me."

E

This dialogue was recorded in the inspector's notebook and initialled by the defendant.

F

At the trial the admissibility of this confession was challenged on a voire dire before the judge in the absence of the assessors. The defendant gave evidence on oath. He alleged that what purported to be recorded in the note book was a complete fabrication; he had never said it, it had never been read over to him: he had been forced to initial it as a result of violence inflicted upon him by the police. The judge disbelieved the defendant's evidence on the voire dire. He held the confession to be voluntary and admitted it in evidence. At the trial in the presence of the assessors, the defendant again gave evidence on oath and made the same sort of allegations of fabrication and violence as he had made on the voire dire. Nevertheless the assessors were unanimous in their opinion that he was guilty beyond reasonable doubt, and so was the judge.

G

H

Of the complaints made in the Court of Appeal about the judge's summing up, it was sought on behalf of the defendant to re-argue two before this Board. The first was that the judge did not sufficiently stress to the assessors the danger of convicting on the evidence of the confession alone. Having admitted the confession on the voire dire he instructed the assessors:

A
" It was suggested to you that you have to be satisfied that the confession is voluntary, but that is not so. All you have to consider is whether the defendant made that statement and whether it is true."

He went on, however, to point out that if they thought that the defendant had been forced to make it they might think it was a very good reason why it was not true. The Court of Appeal were of opinion that the
B first sentence in the passage that their Lordships have reproduced verbatim correctly stated the law as laid down by this Board in *Chan Wei Keung* v. *The Queen* [1967] 2 A.C. 160, and that the summing up upon the confession and the weight to be attached to it when taken as a whole was adequate. Before their Lordships, however, it was contended that, since the decision of the Fiji Court of Appeal in the instant
C case, the Court of Appeal in England had decided in *Reg.* v. *McCarthy* (1980) 70 Cr.App.R. 270 that the question whether a confession that had been admitted on the voire dire was voluntary was for the jury to decide. Their Lordships have considered the passage in *McCarthy's* case that was relied upon. It consists of the few words italicised hereunder in a single sentence of the judgment, at p. 272:

D
" If he (the judge) allows the evidence to be given, then it is for the jury to consider whether or not there was an inducement *and whether or not it was voluntary,* and it is for the jury, after a proper direction, to assess its probative value: . . ."

Looked at in their context the words italicised may be equivocal, but the authorities cited for the proposition are *Chan Wei Keung's* case itself and *Reg.* v. *Burgess* [1968] 2 Q.B. 112, a decision of the Court of Appeal
E of England in which *Chan Wei Keung's* case was followed and applied. In their Lordships' view all that the words italicised should be understood to mean is that the jury should take into consideration all the circumstances in which a confession was made, including allegations of force, if it thinks they may be true, in assessing the probative value of a confession. So, in their Lordships' view, there is no fresh authority in
F this particular field of criminal law that would justify this Board in re-examining the sufficiency of the summing up as respects the reliability of the confession, since this is a matter that was peculiarly the province of the Fiji Court of Appeal. The same applies to the criticisms advanced against the way in which the judge in his summing up permitted his own views of the credibility of the defendant and of other witnesses to become apparent to the assessors.
G
Finally, their Lordships must deal briefly with a point on which they have not had the benefit of the views of the Fiji Court of Appeal, for the point was not taken before them. At an early stage in his summing up, when he was in the course of narrating how the prosecution put their case, the judge mentioned that they alleged that when the defendant rejoined the family party after 10 to 15 minutes' absence (during which
H he was alleged to have killed his father) he had changed his clothes. Jai Raj had in fact said this but not in the presence of the defendant. That Jai Raj had so informed the police inspector at a previous interview was extracted from the inspector in the course of cross-examination on behalf of the defendant. It was, however, hearsay and did not constitute evidence to which the deciders of fact were entitled to have regard in determining the guilt of the defendant. Apart from this passing reference the judge never mentioned changing of clothes again. He

Ragho Prasad v. The Queen (P.C.)   **[1981]**

never suggested that there was any evidence that the defendant had A
changed his clothes. He emphasised to the assessors that the only
evidence against the defendant was the alleged confession; and the only
subsequent reference that he made to clothes of the defendant was to
suggest to the assessors that they did not help at all in determining
whether or not the confession was true.

In their Lordships' view there is nothing in this fresh point. They
are fortified in this view by the fact that despite what had obviously B
been a meticulous analysis of each sentence in the summing up, it had
never occurred to anyone to take the point in the notices of appeal
(original and supplementary) to the Court of Appeal or at the hearing
in that court or even in the defendant's written case before this Board.
It was advanced for the first time at the oral hearing. Their Lordships
will, accordingly, humbly advise Her Majesty that this appeal must be C
dismissed.

Solicitors: *Philip Conway Thomas & Co.; Charles Russell & Co.*

T. J. M.

D

[CHANCERY DIVISION]

* PRACTICE NOTE (BANKRUPTCY: AFFIDAVIT OF SEARCH)

E

*Bankruptcy—Bankruptcy notice—Bankruptcy notice file—Duty to
search file before presenting petition—Requirement for affidavit
of results of search*

Hitherto the practice has been that where a bankruptcy petition is
presented which is founded upon a bankruptcy notice, an affidavit showing
the result of a search of the bankruptcy notice file has been required to F
be filed on behalf of the creditor. Where the bankruptcy notice has been
issued by the court to which the petition is presented, this requirement
serves no useful purpose.

Directions have already been given by the Chief Registrar that no such
affidavit will in future be required on the creditor's behalf in such cases.
It will, however, continue to be the responsibility of persons filing bankruptcy petitions to inspect the bankruptcy notice file in order to ascertain G
whether there has been any application to set aside the bankruptcy notice.

By the direction of the judges of the Chancery Division exercising
bankruptcy jurisdiction.

RICHARD HUNT,
Chief Bankruptcy Registrar. H

March 25, 1981.

A

[CHANCERY DIVISION]

* WICKS v. FIRTH (INSPECTOR OF TAXES)

JOHNSON v. FIRTH (INSPECTOR OF TAXES)

B 1980 Nov. 4, 5, 6   Goulding J.

Revenue—Income tax—Employment—Benefits of directors and higher-paid employees—Employers settling funds on trustees —Trustees awarding scholarships to employees' children— Whether " benefits " accruing to employee—Income and Corporation Taxes Act 1970 (c. 10), s. 375—Finance Act 1976 (c. 40), s. 61 (1)

C

In 1977 a company executed a trust deed settling funds on trustees to make discretionary awards to the children of employees of the company and of certain of its subsidiary companies to assist them in their further education. Since the formation of the trust, the trustees awarded scholarships regularly at a rate in excess of 2,000 each academic year. Once a scholarship had been awarded to a beneficiary it

D remained payable even if his parent ceased to be an employee of the company. The only relevant criterion to an award being made was whether the educational attainments of a child entitled him to attend a course of further education which in accordance with the trust deed the trustee determined as eligible for awards. Initially the Inland Revenue accepted that no liability to income tax was imposed on the parents of children receiving the awards because of the ex-

E emption in section 375 of the Income and Corporation Taxes Act 1970.[1] However in 1978 it was announced that in relation to directors or higher-paid employees of the company, the cost of providing such awards would henceforth be regarded as benefits in kind accruing to them and taxable under section 61 of the Finance Act 1976.[2]

The taxpayers, both being higher-paid employees of the company, were assessed to income tax for 1978–79 in respect

F of the awards made under the scheme to their children of £600 and £460 respectively. They appealed against the assessments to the special commissioners who held that the sums were taxable under section 61 of the Finance Act 1976 and that the exemption in section 375 of the Income and Corporation Taxes Act 1970 did not apply.

On appeal by the taxpayers: —

Held, allowing the appeals, (1) that section 375 of the

G Income and Corporation Taxes Act 1970 provided an unqualified exemption from income tax for scholarship income and that, in the absence of any express indication, section 61 of the Finance Act 1976 should not be construed as nullifying that exemption by imposing on the taxpayers a liability to tax on the " cash equivalent " of the scholarship awards received by their children (post, p. 483c–e).

H (2) That the breadth of the exemption in section 375 was not to be curtailed by relating it merely to the income of the scholarship holders themselves and, since section 375 precluded the taking of scholarship income into account in computing any taxpayer's income, the assessments made on the taxpayers should not have taken into account income arising from their children's scholarship awards (post, pp. 483e–484c).

[1] Income and Corporation Taxes Act 1970, s. 375: see post, p. 480g–h
[2] Finance Act 1976, s. 61: see post, p. 479c–d.

Mapp v. *Oram* [1969] 1 Ch. 293, C.A. considered.   A

Quaere. Whether the discretionary scholarship awards paid to the employees' children out of the educational trust fund were provided by reason of the employment of their parents for the purposes of section 61 (1) of the Finance Act 1976 (post, p. 484c–e).

The following case is referred to in the judgment:

Mapp v. *Oram* [1969] 1 Ch. 293; [1968] 3 W.L.R. 442; [1968] 3 All   B
     E.R. 1, C.A.; [1970] A.C. 362; [1969] 3 W.L.R. 557; [1969] 3 All
     E.R. 215; 45 T.C. 651, H.L.(E.).

The following additional cases were cited in argument:

Barty-King v. *Ministry of Defence* [1979] 2 All E.R. 80.
Brumby v. *Milner* [1976] 1 W.L.R. 1096; [1976] 3 All E.R. 636; 51 T.C.   C
     583, H.L.(E.).
Hochstrasser v. *Mayes* [1960] A.C. 376; [1960] 2 W.L.R. 63; [1959]
     3 All E.R. 817; 38 T.C. 673, H.L.(E.).
Hughes v. *Bank of New Zealand* [1938] A.C. 366; [1938] 1 All E.R. 778;
     21 T.C. 510, H.L.(E.).
Inland Revenue Commissioners v. *Educational Grants Association Ltd.*
     [1967] Ch. 993; [1967] 3 W.L.R. 41; [1967] 2 All E.R. 893; 44
     T.C. 93, C.A.   D
Income Tax General Purposes Commissioners for City of London v.
     Gibbs [1942] A.C. 402; [1942] 1 All E.R. 415, H.L.(E.).
Maughan v. *Free Church of Scotland* (1893) 3 T.C. 207.
Metropolitan Water Board v. *St. Marylebone Assessment Committee*
     [1923] 1 K.B. 86.

CASE STATED by the Commissioners for the Special Purposes of the   E
Income Tax Acts.

By a trust deed dated January 13, 1977, Imperial Chemical Industries Ltd. established an educational trust. Under the trust, the trustees were directed to exercise their discretion in paying scholarships to such of a defined class of beneficiaries as they sought fit in respect of full-time instruction at establishments of further education. The Inland Revenue   F
initially accepted that the scholarship awards were exempt from income tax under section 375 of the Income and Corporation Taxes Act 1970. By a press release dated June 14, 1978, however, the Inland Revenue announced that from that date they would regard the cost of providing such scholarship awards as benefits in kind taxable, in appropriate cases, under section 61 of the Finance Act 1976.

In November 1978 the trustees of the Imperial Chemical Industries   G
Educational Trust awarded a scholarship of £600 to Martin Wicks who was about to start his first year at King's College, Cambridge, reading natural sciences. His father, the taxpayer, Malcolm James Wicks, was an employee of Imperial Chemical Industries Ltd. and was assessed to income tax for the year 1978–79 in the sum of £11,413. The assessment included the sum of £600 for his son's scholarship. During the same   H
month the trustees awarded £460 to Christine Johnson, starting her first year at Newcastle University reading medicine. Her father, the taxpayer, Maurice Johnson, an employee of the same company, was assessed to income tax for the year 1978–79 in the sum of £10,168. The assessment included the sum of £460 received by his daughter. Both taxpayers appealed against the assessments on the ground that they were not liable to be taxed in respect of the awards made to their children from the

A educational trust. It was agreed that the appeals would be regarded as a test case in the sense that the outcome would determine the Inland Revenue's policy in respect of such awards.

The commissioners heard both appeals together, dismissing them in principle and confirming the two assessments. The taxpayers appealed.

The facts are set out in the judgment.

B
Frank Heyworth Talbot Q.C. and *G. R. Aaronson* for the taxpayers. *Robert Carnwath* for the Crown.

GOULDING J. I have before me two appeals by taxpayers from decisions of the special commissioners given in favour of the Crown. Both taxpayers are in the employment of Imperial Chemical Industries
C Ltd., which I shall refer to by the well known abbreviation of " ICI." The subject matter of the appeals is the taxation of certain scholarships, coming from a fund known as the ICI Educational Trust, which was set up in 1977 by ICI, in cases where the scholarship is given to the child or dependant of a director or of what is known in the legislation as " a higher-paid employee " of ICI. The trust, as I have said, was
D established in 1977. It is constituted under a trust deed dated January 13, 1977. The initial trust fund mentioned in the deed is £15,000, but it has been subsequently augmented by very large payments, all made by ICI. The commissioners found that at the date with which they were concerned no other contributions had been made to the fund, although it had of course received additions by way of interest on money awaiting use.
E
I am content to take from the case stated by the commissioners, without reading the deed, a sufficient indication of its character. They said:

"Under the trust deed the trustees are directed to exercise their discretion in paying what the trust deed terms scholarships to such of the class of beneficiaries as they think fit. Scholarships are
F limited ... to awards only in respect of full-time instruction at a university or other comparable establishment of further education, with preference to be given to undergraduate courses."

The class of beneficiaries is defined under the deed to mean the children of all employees and officers of ICI and of certain nominated subsidiaries of ICI. " Children " for this purpose includes adopted
G children, stepchildren and illegitimate children. It is expressly provided by the deed that once a scholarship has been awarded to a beneficiary it remains payable normally even if he or she ceases to be a beneficiary as a result of the parent employee ceasing to be employed by ICI or one of the nominated subsidiaries. It is further provided that such an individual remains eligible for certain future awards. The trustees,
H according to the case stated, have been awarding scholarships regularly since the foundation of the trust at the rate of something over 2,000 in each academic year.

The facts as regards the particular cases before the court are these. A son of one of the taxpayers received in November 1978 from the trustees the award of a scholarship of £600. He was about to start his first year at King's College, Cambridge, reading natural sciences. Subsequently, when the trustees came to consider the renewal of the award

for a second academic year, they continued a part of the £600—namely, A
what they called a basic award of £400—but did not renew the additional
£200, which was originally described as a merit award, because of the
contents of his college report.   The other case is that of a daughter of
the other taxpayer.   She also, in November 1978, was about to start
her university career, in her case reading medicine at the University of
Newcastle.   Her initial award was £460, consisting of a basic award of
£260 and a merit award of £200—the merit award as in the boy's case, B
being based on her previous record, particularly her A-levels.   However,
the lady, when she completed her first year at college, had a quite
exceptionally distinguished report, and so in her case, not only was the
basic award continued for a second year but the merit award was also
continued and, indeed, increased.

In both cases income tax assessments for the year 1978–79 were C
made on the respective fathers of the scholarship holders—that is, on the
two taxpayers—in respect of their emoluments from ICI, and in each
case a figure was included as a benefit from the ICI Educational Trust,
the figure being that of the first year's scholarship award—£600 in the
case of the boy's father, £460 as regards the girl's father.   The commissioners received oral as well as documentary evidence of the practice D
of the trustees in exercising their discretion under the trust deed.   They
accepted evidence that the trust fulfilled a valuable educational and
social purpose in helping to bridge the gap between the financial
resources available to university students and their real needs for money
sufficient to get the maximum benefit from the university.   Evidence was
also given (at considerable length, I am told) about the selection of
candidates by the trustees.   The commissioners found these facts: E

" The trustees in deciding whether to make an award were in no
way influenced by the position of the applicant's parent vis-à-vis his
employer.   The only criteria were whether the applicant was eligible
under the terms of the trust deed and whether his educational attainments were such that he had been accepted for a course which in
accordance with the trust deed the trustees had determined as F
eligible for awards.   Indeed, when the question whether the award
should be renewed for a subsequent year came before the trustees
they would not know whether his parent was still an employee of
ICI (or one of its nominated subsidiaries, as the case might be).
Broadly speaking, however, awards were made to all eligible applicants for eligible courses."
                                                                         G

The commissioners stated that they:

" inferred that ICI had made and would continue to make (if the
present appeals were to succeed) sufficient contributions to the
educational trust to enable the trustees to continue their existing
policy in this respect."
                                                                         H

The commissioners also found that applicants for awards usually
learned about the trust from their parents, who knew of the scheme
from notice boards and other publicity inside ICI and obtained their
application forms from ICI's personnel officers.   Then the commissioners
said:

" After the applicant had made his application, his parent had no
further standing in the matter and the trustees dealt only with the

A   applicant himself and, if he was successful, sent him the cheque:
they would refuse to tell the parent of the amount of any award
to his child.   No award would be made until the trustees had seen
a copy of the letter stating the amount of the local education
authority's award to the applicant.   The scheme of awards was
sufficiently flexible to meet special circumstances and special
B   hardship."

Such being, in outline, the facts of the case as found by the commissioners, I now turn to the legislation under which the revenue has
assessed the two taxpayers in respect of the sums here in question.
It is section 61 of the Finance Act 1976 subsection (1) of which I will
now read, though, as will appear in a moment, it is necessary in order to
understand it to look at several other subsections in the same Act.
C   Section 61 (1) reads:

"Where in any year a person is employed in director's or higher-
paid employment and—(a) by reason of his employment there is
provided for him, or for others being members of his family or
household, any benefit to which this section applies; and (b) the cost
of providing the benefit is not (apart from this section) chargeable
D   to tax as his income, there is to be treated as emoluments of the
employment, and accordingly chargeable to income tax under
Schedule E, an amount equal to whatever is the cash equivalent of
the benefit."

The phrase " director's or higher-paid employment " is defined in section
69 (1) of the Act, subject to certain qualifications, as employment as a
E   director of a company or employment with emoluments at a particular
rate per year or more, the figure having been modified from time to
time.   It was originally £5,000; it was £7,500 in the year 1978–79; and
it was subsequently raised to £8,500.   There is no question in this
case as to the meaning of the term: it is accepted that both the taxpayers
are in " director's or higher-paid employment."   Then, section 61 (1)
F   (a) starts off with the words " by reason of his employment there is
provided " a benefit.   The phrase " by reason of his employment " has
an extended meaning, because in section 72 (3) of the Act we find:

"For the purposes of this Chapter, all sums paid to an employee
by his employer in respect of expenses, and all such provision as is
mentioned in this Chapter which is made for an employee, or for
G   members of his family or household, by his employer, are deemed
to be paid to or made for him or them by reason of his employment."

Thus, a benefit is material for the purposes of section 61 if it is either,
on a proper construction of the words, provided by reason of the taxpayer's employment or in fact provided by his employer.   Either of
H   those alternatives, which of course must often coincide, will bring the
benefit within section 61.

The next phrase explained is " members of his family or household,"
benefits to whom are to rank in the same way as benefits to the employee
himself.   That is explained in section 72 (4), which is in these terms:

"References to members of a person's family or household are to
his spouse, his sons and daughters and their spouses, his parents
and his servants, dependants and guests."

Then there is a provision in section 61 (3) to identify the person who **A**
provides the benefit. That says:

"For the purposes of this section and sections 62 and 63 below, the
persons providing a benefit are those at whose cost the provision is
made."

"Benefit" receives a highly extended meaning by section 61 (2),
which, as amended by paragraph 5 of Schedule 8 to the Finance Act **B**
1977 reads:

"The benefits to which this section applies are accommodation
(other than living accommodation), entertainment, domestic or
other services, and other benefits and facilities of whatsoever nature
(whether or not similar to any of those mentioned above in this
subsection), excluding however those taxable under sections 64 to 68 **C**
below in this Chapter, and subject to the exceptions provided for by
the next following section."

The subsection thus makes a number of special exceptions, but it is not
necessary for me to go through them here.

Finally, in order to understand what section 61 is doing, it is necessary
to see what is meant by the phrase "the cash equivalent of the benefit," **D**
because at the end of subsection (1) what is to be chargeable to tax
under Schedule E is "an amount equal to whatever is the cash equivalent of the benefit." That is defined in section 63 (1), which reads:

"The cash equivalent of any benefit chargeable to tax under section
61 above is an amount equal to the cost of the benefit, less so much
(if any) of it as is made good by the employee to those providing the **E**
benefit."

Mr. Heyworth Talbot and Mr. Aaronson, on behalf of the taxpayers,
made, I think, five alternative points in answer to the claim by the Crown
under section 61 of the Finance Act 1976. I can deal with the matter
most conveniently if I enumerate the five points at once and afterwards
return to two of them which require further observations not convenient **F**
to make in a short survey. The first point—and, in the submission of
Mr. Heyworth Talbot, at any rate, the primary or main point—was that
the claim is answered by a specific exemption relating to scholarship
income contained in section 375 of the Income and Corporation Taxes
Act 1970. It is necessary for me to read only the first two of the three
subsections in section 375:

G

"(1) Income arising from a scholarship held by a person receiving
full-time instruction at a university, college, school or other educational establishment shall be exempt from income tax, and no
account shall be taken of any such income in computing the amount
of income for income tax purposes. (2) In this section 'scholarship' includes an exhibition, bursary or any other similar educational endowment."

H

That, as I have said, was Mr. Heyworth Talbot's primary submission, and
I shall return in a moment to deal with it in detail.

The second point was that when one looks at the provisions of section
61 of the Act of 1976 and the neighbouring ancillary sections one sees that
the emphasis is entirely on benefits in kind, and they are not apt to cover
cash payments such as that made by the trustees to the children of the

A two taxpayers. It was pointed out that there is a long enumeration of benefits in kind in section 61 (2), which I have read, and that section 62, which I have not read, contains exceptions relating to different species of benefit in kind. It was also submitted that the very words of charge, if you read the definition of " cash equivalent " back into section 61 (1)— that is, tax is chargeable on " an amount equal to whatever is an amount equal to the cost of the benefit, less so much (if any) of it as is made good

B by the employee "—are really only sensible in relation to benefits in kind, and not in cash. I may say at once that I have not been persuaded by that submission. The words " of whatsoever nature (whether or not similar to any of those mentioned above in this subsection) " are to my mind too strong to admit of the inference which I have been invited to draw. It is also not immaterial, I think, that one of the specific

C exceptions in section 62—namely, in subsection (6)—is a benefit consisting in the provision of a pension, annuity or the like on the employee's death or retirement. At least that makes it clear that, but for the words of exception, provisions for future cash sums would be within the scope of section 61, thereby making it all the harder, I think, to limit the words " benefits and facilities of whatsoever nature " by reference to

D what has gone before. Accordingly, without further ado I can reject that second submission.

The third point is this. The taxpayers challenge the assertion of the Crown that the scholarships (or the benefit of the scholarships, if preferred) have been provided by reason of the taxpayers' employment. That, of course, requires two propositions to be made good: first, that on the proper construction of the words in the statute the benefits were

E not in fact provided by reason of the employment; and, secondly, bearing in mind the extended provision in section 72 (3), that the provision was not in fact made by ICI. It is said that, on the one hand, the employment of the parent was a necessary qualification for the child, as was, on the other, the attainment by the child of a sufficient academic standing to benefit from or be eligible for a university or college course.

F But those are qualifications. The benefits, it was submitted, were *provided* by reason of the decision of the trustees as an independent act, quite independent, as the special commissioners have found, of ICI, in the exercise of their fiduciary discretion under the trust deed. It was contended, secondly, on a consideration of the same facts, that the provision was made not by ICI but by the trustees out of the trust fund under their sole control. Those submissions raise matters of difficulty

G on the interpretation of the Finance Act 1976 and I leave them for the moment.

The fourth point is really conceived, I think, as reductio ad absurdum. The Finance Act 1976 inserted a fresh version of section 15 into the Taxes Management Act 1970. That is the section which requires employers to make returns to the inspector of taxes relating to their

H employees; and in its revised form it provides also for returns to state, in respect of an employee, whether any benefits have been provided " for him (or for any other person) by reason for his employment, such as may give rise to charge to tax under," among other provisions, sections 61 to 68 of the Finance Act 1976. Various details may be required, and there is also provision for the inspector to require information from any person who appears to him to have been concerned " in providing benefits to or in respect of employees of another."

I need not go into detail, but Mr. Heyworth Talbot submitted, **A**
putting it shortly, that when one looks at that section and also at the
general machinery for obtaining information for the purposes of assessment to income tax, the charge introduced under section 61 is simply
unworkable if construed so widely as to bring in the scholarship payments made, not by an employer but by the trustees, not to an employee
but to the child of an employee, in the present case. He said that
without information that they perhaps could not get, it would be **B**
impossible for employees to make correct returns of their own income;
it would be impossible for employers to comply with their statutory
obligations because they would be required to have knowledge in the
possession of people like the trustees in the present case, whom they
might not be able to compel to disclose the facts; and section 61 would
present, it may be, an impossible task to the officers of the Inland **C**
Revenue themselves. That submission is another that I can dispose of
shortly. I am not convinced by it. It is of course possible that, in
spite of the endeavour of Parliament to extend the field of section 15
of the Taxes Management Act 1970 to dimensions commensurate with
the new legislation in the Finance Act 1976, great difficulties will arise
in particular cases, both for the taxpayer and for the revenue. Nevertheless, such difficulties cannot to my mind affect the construction of the **D**
Act to such an extent as to curtail the natural meaning of the terms
employed in section 61 and its appended ancillary sections.

I can likewise dismiss shortly the fifth and last of the points made
on behalf of the taxpayers, as I understand them. That again is an
appeal to possible difficulty in the application of the 1976 legislation if
given the wide construction favoured by the Crown. The particular **E**
difficulty emphasised was that a payment might be made to an individual
who had a double qualification, so that two or more employees of the
same employer might be assessable. For example, the child of one
employee of ICI might be the dependant of another, or might be the
wife of a child of the other. In those cases, who is to be assessed, or
is there to be a double charge to tax? It is even conceivable that a **F**
director or higher-paid employee might himself be a scholar under the
educational trust. Those are interesting and difficult problems which
may or may not arise in practice, but, once again, I do not think there are
any answers to the proper construction of the charging section itself.

After that survey I return to what was described on behalf of the
taxpayers as the primary submission—that based on the exemption contained in section 375 (1) of the Income and Corporation Taxes Act **G**
1970. It has two limbs. The first says that " Income arising from a
scholarship held by a person receiving full-time instruction at a university, college, school or other educational establishment shall be exempt
from income tax;" and the second limb is that " no account shall be
taken of any such income in computing the amount of income for income
tax purposes." Both limbs were relied on by counsel for the taxpayers, **H**
and both have been debated at some length. On the first limb—that
income arising from a scholarship should be exempt—it was not disputed that the awards under the ICI Education Trust are scholarships;
nor was it disputed for the purposes of these cases that the sums received
by the taxpayers' children are " income arising from a scholarship."
In their decision the special commissioners relied on the distinction
between the income received by the scholarship holder and the cash

A equivalent which is to be taxed as emoluments of the parent employee under section 61 of the Finance Act 1976. They say:

"The charge under section 61 is on the cash equivalent of the benefit provided not on the benefit itself. The cash equivalent is not of itself income but is to be treated as an emolument. A notional sum so treated is not, in our judgment, covered by the words income arising from a scholarship."

B

I think that at one time I should have found that reasoning more conclusive than I do at present. I think there is no doubt that, perhaps under continental influences, in recent years the court, in interpreting recent statutes, has tended to be less literal and to look a little more at the purposes of a particular enactment, as disclosed by the words of the

C enactment itself. Considered in that way, although I do not find the point free of difficulty, I cannot think that Parliament, without giving an express indication, intended in effect to nullify or impair an unqualified exemption of this kind of scholarship income under section 375 by introducing, in relation to a very much wider class of benefit, a scheme of assessing notional sums, that scheme (which is really in the nature of machinery) being necessary because in general the benefits aimed at

D are given not in cash but in kind. Accordingly, although I see the force of the distinction drawn by the special commissioners between a purely notional sum and actual income, when one looks at the purposes of section 375 in giving an exemption and at the reason for introducing the fiction of a notional sum in section 61 of the later Act, I do not think it would be right to infer that the generality of the exemption was

E impaired. Accordingly, it seems to me that on the first limb the taxpayers should succeed.

I now turn to the second limb. There are really two points, I think, on that. When the Act says that no account shall be taken of income arising from the scholarship in computing the amount of income for income tax purposes, does it relate only to the scholarship holder

F or does it forbid the taking of scholarship income into account in computing any taxpayer's income? The main argument about that for the Crown was that if section 375 receives such a construction that its latter part is not limited to the income of the scholarship holder, then the proviso to section 10 (5) of the Income and Corporation Taxes Act 1970 would be otiose. Of course, one hesitates to make inferences of

G that kind from a consolidation statute drawn from many sources, but any such objection was removed when it was shown that both the present section 10 (5) and the present section 375 are derived from the same original statute; namely, the Finance Act 1920.

However, a similar argument was developed before the Court of Appeal in *Mapp v. Oram* [1969] 1 Ch. 293, 309, 314 and 319, and it was

H not found persuasive by any of the members of the court, divided though they were on the result of the appeal in that case. It afterwards went to the House of Lords [1970] A.C. 362, but the particular argument was not, as I understand it, used there, so no further light can be found in the speeches of their lordships. There is, I think, no other sufficient ground for curtailing the literal breadth of the second limb, so I decline to limit it to the income of the scholarship holder himself.

The other point is directed to the words " computing the amount of   A
income for income tax purposes." The relevant computation, as it
seems to me, of the amount of income for income tax purposes is
of the emoluments taxable under Schedule E of the scholarship holder's
parent. Mr. Carnwath, for the Crown, submitted that in making that
computation you do not take account of the scholarship income: it is
only taken into account, if it is proper to use such words at all, at the
earlier stage of ascertaining the relevant benefit received by the child of   B
an employee from his employer which is afterwards converted into a
cash equivalent by the Act of 1976, the cash equivalent but nothing else
entering into the computation of the amount of income for income tax
purposes. That, I think, is too narrow an interpretation. Trying to use
the words in their ordinary sense, it seems to me that account has been
taken in the present case of the income arising from the taxpayers'   C
children's scholarships in computing the amount of the taxpayers'
respective emoluments for income tax under Schedule E. Accordingly,
in my judgment they succeed on the second limb of section 375 as well as
on the first.

That leaves the third point, as I called it in my general survey, which
relates to the construction of the provisions in section 61 and also   D
section 72 of the Finance Act 1976 requiring the relevant benefits to be
provided by reason of the employment of the taxpayer. As I said, those
questions are difficult. They apply not only to scholarships but to the
whole field of operation of section 61. It would not assist an appellate
court, if this case should go further, to know what was my opinion on
these pure matters of law. Accordingly, though I must not be thought
in any way ungrateful or discourteous in regard to the excellent argu-   E
ments I heard on both sides, I think it better that I should not give any
judgment on that question; I have found in favour of the taxpayers'
main contention, that they can rely on the specific exemption in section
375 of the Income and Corporation Taxes Act 1970.

> *Appeals allowed with costs.*   F
> *Assessments remitted to commis-*
> *sioners for adjustment.*

Solicitors: *V. O. White, Solicitor Imperial Chemical Industries Ltd.;*
Solicitor of Inland Revenue.

[Reported by MRS. HARRIET DUTTON, Barrister-at-Law]   G

A

[COURT OF APPEAL]

* CHANEL LTD. *v.* F. W. WOOLWORTH & CO. LTD.
AND OTHERS

[1979 C. No. 2107]

B

1980 Oct. 13, 14; 23   Foster J.

1980 Nov. 3, 4   Buckley, Shaw and Oliver L.JJ.

*Practice—Consent order—Application to discharge—Undertakings
given until judgment or further order—Subsequent decision of
Court of Appeal—Whether sufficient grounds for setting aside
order*

C

The plaintiffs, an English company, brought an action for
infringements of trade marks of which they were the registered
proprietors and for passing-off against the importers and
retailers of foreign products bearing the plaintiffs' trade marks.
On April 6, 1979, a motion by the plaintiffs for interlocutory
relief was stood over until trial by consent on undertakings by
the defendants until judgment or further order, inter alia, not
to deal in goods bearing the plaintiffs' marks which were not
the plaintiffs' goods. In October 1979 the Court of Appeal, in
deciding a similar case, held that every company in a group
of multinational companies must be taken to have consented
to the use by other companies in the group of a trade mark
which had become distinctive of products of the group as a
whole.

D

E

On a motion by the second defendants to be discharged
from their undertakings, contending, inter alia, that in view
of the subsequent Court of Appeal decision and recently
obtained evidence suggesting the existence of a group structure
embracing the plaintiffs and the foreign suppliers of the goods
complained of, the plaintiffs had no reasonable prospect of
obtaining at the trial relief in the nature of that afforded by
the undertakings : —

F

Held, dismissing the motion and refusing leave to appeal,
that a subsequent change in the law was not a sufficient reason
for setting aside an order made by consent; that, even if the
consent order could be set aside, there was insufficient evidence
to show that the present case was indistinguishable from the
Court of Appeal decision (post, p. 490D); and that, therefore,
it had not been shown that the plaintiffs had no real prospect
of obtaining a permanent injunction at the trial and there
were no grounds for discharging the undertakings.

G

Revlon Inc. v. *Cripps & Lee Ltd.* [1980] F.S.R. 85, C.A.
considered.

Regent Oil Co. Ltd. v. *J. T. Leavesley (Lichfield) Ltd.*
[1966] 1 W.L.R. 1210 distinguished.

On an application by the second defendants to the Court of
Appeal for leave to appeal against the decision of Foster J. : —

H

Held, dismissing the application, that the point raised by
the Court of Appeal decision had been open to the defendants
on April 6, 1979, notwithstanding that the Court of Appeal
had not then decided that case and the relevant evidence could
have been obtained earlier; and, accordingly, that there had
been no change in the potential ability of the defendants to
resist the plaintiffs' motion sufficient to justify the discharge or
modification of the undertakings and leave to appeal should
not be granted (post, p. 493A–B).

Chanel Ltd. v. Woolworth & Co. (Ch.D.)   **[1981]**

A

Per curiam. (i) An order or undertaking to the court expressed to be until further order by implication gives a right to the party bound by the order or undertaking to apply to have the order or undertaking discharged or modified if good grounds are shown. Such an application is not an application to set aside or modify any contract implicit in the order or undertaking. It is an application in accordance with such contract (post, p. 492D–E).

B

(ii) The judge's refusal to discharge the undertakings is not analogous to the grant or refusal of an injunction, appeal from which requires no leave, and leave to appeal is required (post, p. 493C–D).

Decision of Foster J. affirmed in part.

The following cases are referred to in the judgment of Buckley L.J.:

C

Purcell v. *F. C. Trigell Ltd.* [1971] 1 Q.B. 358; [1970] 3 W.L.R. 884; [1970] 3 All E.R. 671, C.A.
Revlon Inc. v. *Cripps & Lee Ltd.* [1980] F.S.R. 85, C.A.

The following additional cases were cited in the Court of Appeal:

Attorney-General v. *Tomline* (1877) Ch.D. 388.
G.C.T. (Management) Ltd. v. *Laurie Marsh Group Ltd.* [1973] R.P.C. 432; [1972] F.S.R. 519.

D

The following cases are referred to in the judgment of Foster J.:

American Cyanamid Co. v. *Ethicon Ltd.* [1975] A.C. 396; [1975] 2 W.L.R. 316; [1975] 1 All E.R. 504, H.L.(E.).
G.C.T. (Management) Ltd. v. *Laurie Marsh Group Ltd.* [1973] R.P.C. 432; [1972] F.S.R. 519.
Purcell v. *F. C. Trigell Ltd.* [1971] 1 Q.B. 358; [1970] 3 W.L.R. 884; [1970] 3 All E.R. 671, C.A.

E

Regent Oil Co. Ltd. v. *J. T. Leavesley (Lichfield) Ltd.* [1966] 1 W.L.R. 1210; [1966] 2 All E.R. 454.
Revlon Inc. v. *Cripps & Lee Ltd.* [1980] F.S.R. 85, C.A.

The following additional cases were cited in argument before Foster J.:

F

Attorney-General v. *Tomline* (1877) 7 Ch.D. 388.
Brister v. *Brister* [1970] 1 W.L.R. 664; [1970] 1 All E.R. 913.
Dunhill (Alfred) Ltd. v. *Sunoptic S.A.* [1979] F.S.R. 337, C.A.
Lonrho Ltd. v. *Shell Petroleum Co. Ltd.* [1980] Q.B. 358; [1980] 2 W.L.R. 367, C.A.
Wenlock v. *Moloney* [1965] 1 W.L.R. 1238; [1965] 2 All E.R. 871, C.A.

G

MOTION

By a writ dated March 29, 1979, the plaintiffs, Chanel Ltd., brought an action claiming, inter alia, an injunction restraining the second defendants, Three Pears Wholesale Cash and Carry Ltd., from infringing the plaintiffs' registered trade marks by the parallel importation and sale of similar products supplied by an American company and bearing the plaintiffs'

H

trade marks. By a notice of motion of the same date the plaintiffs sought, inter alia, an interlocutory injunction in similar terms. On April 6, 1979, the second defendants gave undertakings until judgment or further order not to part with possession of or deal with products bearing the plaintiffs' trade marks, not being the plaintiffs' products, or otherwise infringe the plaintiffs' trade marks or pass off such products as those of the plaintiffs and by consent the motion was stood over until trial.

A   By notice of motion dated June 5, 1980, the second defendants applied
to be released or discharged from their undertakings.

Terence Cullen Q.C. and *John Baldwin* for the second defendants.
Charles Sparrow Q.C. and *Bruce Spalding* for the plaintiffs.

B   *Cur. adv. vult.*

October 23. FOSTER J. read the following judgment. I have before
me a motion which seeks to discharge an undertaking given by the second
defendants, Three Pears Wholesale Cash and Carry Ltd., by consent on
the footing that there has been a change of law since that date. Before I
go further I should say that both parties have relied to a very limited
C extent on delay. I have carefully examined the dates in this case but I do
not think that the delays which have occurred are unusual in such a
difficult action as the present. I therefore propose to disregard any question
of delay in deciding this motion.

Chanel Ltd.
D   The plaintiffs, Chanel Ltd., are an English company which sell in the
United Kingdom and Ireland the well known marks of perfumery, scent
and sprays under the names Chanel No. 5, Chanel No. 19 and Chanel
No. 22. They are the registered holder of the trade mark in those countries.
They discovered that the second defendants were importing from Belgium
and selling to retailers similar products which had been imported into
E Belgium from the United States which were sold to it by Chanel Inc., a
United States company. All of the distinctive marks were on both, the only
difference being that on the back of the United States product it showed
" Chanel Inc. New York " and the formula used, which was necessary
under United States law.

The parent company seems to be a Swiss company called Fibo A.G.
F There is also another English company called Bourjois Ltd., which is also
a subsidiary of Fibo A.G. It is not known who are the shareholders in the
French company, Chanel S.A. There is another Swiss company Pamerco,
but there is no information as to its shareholders either, and there is no
information as to who are the shareholders in Chanel Inc., the United
States company. It seems that the plaintiffs mainly market goods from
France and the United States company either purchases the goods from
G France or itself manufactures them. No doubt the interconnection between
these companies and the degree of control exercised by whichever company
is the parent will emerge at the trial.

The writ was issued on March 29, 1979, and on that date an *Anton
Piller* order was obtained against the second defendants. The order was
served on the second defendants on April 2, 1979, the goods being seized
H on April 3, 1979, and on April 5, 1979, the plaintiffs brought a motion for
committal for breach of that order. The main motion came on for hearing
on April 6, 1979, and a consent order was made on that date. On April 24,
1979, the motion for committal of the second defendants and two of the
directors was heard and Walton J. held that there was a contempt and
ordered that the directors should pay the costs on an indemnity basis. The
present position of the action is that it was set down for hearing on
September 15, 1980, though there is still outstanding a request by the second

defendants for further discovery. If the parties are willing to allow the A
action to float it could well be heard early in 1981 though if they wanted a
date to be fixed a date could not be obtained before October or
November 1981.

The present motion

On April 6, 1979, as I have said, a consent order was made in these B
terms:

" Upon motion for an injunction this day unto this court by
counsel . . . and upon reading the order dated March 29, 1979, and
the plaintiffs and the defendants by their counsel consenting to this
order "—then there is the usual undertaking as to damages and the
order goes on—" And the defendants by their counsel undertaking C
until after judgment in this action or until further order in the meantime that they will not do (whether by their directors officers servants
or agents or any of them or otherwise howsoever) the following acts
or either of them that is to say (i) part with possession power custody
or control of or in any way deal with perfume eau de toilette eau de
cologne bath oil bath powder and other toiletries (hereinafter referred
to as ' products ') not being the plaintiffs' or any cartons boxes or D
other packaging therefor not being the plaintiffs' bearing on or in
relation thereto the words or marks Chanel or Chanel No. 5 or any
words or marks colourably similar thereto (ii) otherwise infringe the
plaintiffs' registered trade marks "—and the numbers of five are
given—" or any of them or otherwise pass off products not being the
plaintiffs' as or for the plaintiffs'. And the defendants by their counsel E
undertaking until after Friday, April 13, 1979, or until further order
in the meantime that they will not do . . . the following act that is to
say disclose without the leave of the plaintiffs the subject matter of
this action or the plaintiffs' interest herein to any person save for the
purpose of obtaining legal advice. This court doth order that the said
motion do stand to the trial of this action."
F
The notice of motion for committal had not then been heard.

On November 22, 1979, the Court of Appeal gave judgment in *Revlon
Inc.* v. *Cripps & Lee Ltd.* [1980] F.S.R. 85. The present motion by the
second defendants is dated June 5, 1980, and came on for hearing on
June 10, 1980, when it was stood over to be heard as a motion by order
on October 13, when it came before me. The present motion is in these
terms: G

" By counsel on behalf of the second defendants for an order that
the second defendants be released or discharged from their undertakings given to this court on April 6, 1979, not to "—and then there
goes in the two undertakings which they gave—" on the grounds that
the plaintiffs have no real prospect of obtaining relief of such a nature
at the trial herein, alternatively that the balance of convenience is in H
favour of such discharge or release, alternatively that it is just that
there be such discharge or release " and for further or other relief and
for costs.

As I have said, the second defendants seek to have the consent order
of April 6 set aside pending the hearing of the action. Two questions arise.
First, can a consent order be set aside where there is no allegation that the

A order was made by fraud or by mistake when it was made? Secondly, does the effect of the *Revlon* decision mean that the plaintiffs have no reasonable chance of succeeding at the hearing of the action?

The consent order

In *Purcell* v. *F. C. Trigell Ltd.* [1971] 1 Q.B. 358 the Court of Appeal
B decided that a consent order could not be set aside even in an interlocutory matter unless there were grounds which would justify the setting aside of a contract entered into with knowledge of the material matter by a legally competent person: see Winn L.J. at p. 365.

In *G.C.T. (Management) Ltd.* v. *Laurie Marsh Group Ltd.* [1973] R.P.C. 432 an undertaking was offered by the defendant company until judgment or further order and accepted by the plaintiffs. The plaintiffs
C brought a second interlocutory motion as they said confusion between the names of the two cinemas was still causing confusion. Whitford J. says, at p. 434:

"The point of interlocutory relief is basically to protect the position of the plaintiffs who fear that unless some interlocutory relief be granted to them they will suffer damage and will not be adequately
D compensated in damages if they eventually succeed in the action. When they made their first application the plaintiffs were in fact prepared to accept that the possibility of serious damage pending the final determination of the action would be sufficiently obviated if they accepted the undertaking which the defendants offered, and they accepted the undertaking upon this basis. It seems to me that, in
E those circumstances, it would be wholly wrong for them now if perhaps they feel, or circumstances would appear to indicate, that they wrongly estimated what the result of the change of name would be, to re-open the matter."

The second defendants rely on *Regent Oil Co. Ltd.* v. *J. T. Leavesley (Lichfield) Ltd.* [1966] 1 W.L.R. 1210. In that case the plaintiff was granted
F an injunction to restrain the defendant from breaking a solus agreement until a certain date and on that date the defendant consented to the injunction being extended to the trial. Meantime two decisions of the Court of Appeal had held that the doctrine of restraint of trade did have a place in commercial agreements which limited the restraint to a particular property, reversing a previous decision. The defendant company brought another motion to have the injunction discharged. This case was of course
G prior to the House of Lords decision in *American Cyanamid Co.* v. *Ethicon Ltd.* [1975] A.C. 396 and the test then was whether the plaintiff made out a prima facie case for the continuance of the injunction. Stamp J. said [1966] 1 W.L.R. 1210, 1216:

"For the reasons I have given, if the plaintiff company were today applying for interlocutory relief, I should be constrained reluctantly
H to refuse it—reluctantly because this court is reluctant on an interlocutory application not to hold a party bound to the very words of his covenant—and I would have to hold that there ought not to be an injunction from today until the trial. Taking the view I do, that the plaintiff company has no built-in rights to the continuance of the injunction it obtained, after it has become apparent that it was founded on a decision wrong in law, I ought in my view to discharge the injunction, and this I do."

Foster J.   **Chanel Ltd. v. Woolworth & Co. (Ch.D.)**   **[1981]**

In that case the original injunction was not made by consent but the defendant consented to its continuing until trial. The point before me was never argued in that case. In the *Revlon* case [1980] F.S.R. 85 all the facts were before the court and were adjudicated upon. In the present case all the facts are by no means before the court and the consent order provided that there should be no hearing of the motion at all until trial. As I have said, the test is now different. The first test is: have the plaintiffs any real prospect of succeeding in their claim for a permanent injunction at the trial? The second defendants admit that their evidence is incomplete in attempting to prove what the actual Chanel group control in fact amounts to but say that the court should draw inferences to show that there is sufficient group control to bring it within the *Revlon* case. It is interesting to note that the House of Lords in refusing leave to appeal in the *Revlon* case said that it would be better if the action went for trial.

In my judgment, I do not have proper evidence to decide whether the undertaking given should be now discharged as the plaintiffs have not answered the second defendants' evidence on this motion other than to answer the allegation of delay. The second defendants do not allege any mistake when the consent order was made. They rely on a subsequent change of the law. In my judgment a subsequent change of the law is insufficient to upset a consent order. Even if I am wrong in that and I should hear the motion on the evidence before the court, it is clearly insufficient in showing that the *Revlon* case completely covers the present case.

The Revlon decision

In my judgment, there are many facts in the present case which would enable the plaintiffs to distinguish this case from *Revlon Inc.* v. *Cripps & Lee Ltd.* [1980] F.S.R. 85. To mention just a few: (a) in that case the English company was not the registered holder of the trade mark as in the present case; (b) in the *Revlon* case the following words were on the register:

> " The trade mark is to be used by the registered user in relation to the goods only so long as the registered proprietor and the registered user are controlled by Revlon Inc."

(c) On all the Revlon products sold in the United Kingdom were the words " Revlon, New York, Paris and London ". In this case on the plaintiffs' products sold there are usually the words " Chanel, Paris " and some have also the words "Made in France." On the United States products the words always used are " Chanel Inc., New York, N.Y. 10019." (d) There is no specific evidence as to the control imposed on the English company by the French or any other company in the group.

In those circumstances I cannot conclude that the plaintiffs have no real prospect of succeeding in obtaining a permanent injunction at the trial. It follows that the motion fails and I propose to dismiss it.

Motion dismissed with costs.
Leave to appeal refused.

Solicitors: *Sharpe, Pritchard & Co.* for *Philip Baker, King & Co.,* Birmingham; *Wilkinson, Kimbers & Staddon.*

[Reported by G. B. PURVES, ESQ., Barrister-at-Law]

A   APPLICATION for leave to appeal.
      On November 3, 1980, the second defendants moved the Court of
Appeal for leave to appeal from the decision of Foster J.
      The facts are stated in the judgment of of Buckley L.J.

      Terence Cullen Q.C. and *John Baldwin* for the second defendants.
      Charles Sparrow Q.C. and *Bruce Spalding* for the plaintiffs.
B

      BUCKLEY L.J. This is an application by the second defendants for leave
to appeal against refusal by Foster J. to discharge or modify undertakings
given by those defendants until judgment or further order in the following
circumstances.
      By their writ issued on March 29, 1979, the plaintiffs sued for relief
C of a normal character for alleged infringement of trade marks and alleged
passing-off. They moved ex parte for interlocutory relief by way of an
Anton Piller order and injunctions, and obtained ex parte relief on
March 29, 1979. Before the motion came on inter partes the second
defendants, Three Pears Wholesale Cash and Carry Ltd., believing that
the only defence available to them was one under European Community
law, felt constrained to give undertakings until judgment or further order
D in the terms of the notice of motion. Accordingly, when the motion came
before the court inter partes, the defendants tendered such undertakings.
The plaintiffs were content, upon the defendants' giving those undertakings,
to their motion being stood over until the trial. Accordingly, on April 6,
1979, the motion was disposed of in that manner by consent without its
being opened to the court and without the evidence being read.
E   Subsequently the defendants made certain company searches on
May 2 to 10. These disclosed certain apparent organisational links between
the plaintiff company and the other companies (which were in fact foreign
companies) through whom the goods which are the subject matter of the
alleged infringements and passings-off were acquired by the defendants.
These links suggest that there may exist a group structure embracing both
F the plaintiff company and the foreign companies from or through whom
the defendants acquired the goods. The defendants also discovered other
evidence, in the form of advertising material and the like, suggesting the
existence of a group structure of that kind.
      In November 1979 this court decided an appeal in *Revlon Inc.* v.
Cripps & Lee Ltd. [1980] F.S.R. 85. In that case the plaintiff companies
formed part of a group of companies in which all save the parent company
G were wholly owned subsidiaries, or wholly owned sub-subsidiaries, of that
parent company. The plaintiff company sued for passing-off Revlon goods
manufactured in the United States of America by a Revlon company
operating in the United States as Revlon goods manufactured in the
United Kingdom by another Revlon company operating in the United
Kingdom. This court held that the marks, or get-up, in that case had been
H developed as a house mark distinctive of the whole group and that every
company in the group must be taken to have consented to the mark's
being used by every other company of the group to designate the products
so marked as products of the group as a whole.
      The second defendants in the present case contend that that decision
threw a new light on the legal position of the parties in this case, and that
this, in conjunction with the additional evidential material which they had
acquired since they gave their undertakings, created a new state of affairs,

in which they were entitled to ask the court to discharge the undertakings. **A**
They accordingly moved Foster J. for such relief. The judge refused it on
two grounds: first, that the order of April 6, 1979, being a consent order,
had contractual effect and could not be set aside unless there were grounds
which would justify the setting of it aside as a contract (*Purcell* v. *F. C.
Trigell Ltd.* [1971] 1 Q.B. 358); and, secondly, that the evidence was insufficient to establish that the case was covered by *Revlon Inc.* v. *Cripps
& Lee Ltd.* [1980] F.S.R. 85.   **B**

The defendants have submitted that the consent order, or rather the
undertakings associated with it, was only to bind them until judgment or
further order in the meantime. The plaintiffs contend that their motion was
stood over until the trial in consideration of the undertakings, and that the
defendants are contractually bound by it until the trial unless grounds are
adduced for rescinding or modifying it which would be effective grounds   **C**
for rescinding or modifying a contract. I shall assume in the plaintiffs'
favour, as I think is probably the case, that the consent order has contractual force as between the parties. Nevertheless, it was a term of that
contract that the undertakings should only bind the defendants until judgment or further order in the meantime.

In my judgment, an order or an undertaking to the court expressed   **D**
to be until further order by implication gives a right to the party bound by
the order or undertaking to apply to the court to have the order or undertaking discharged or modified if good grounds for doing so are shown.
Such an application is not an application to set aside or modify any
contract implicit in the order or undertaking. It is an application in accordance with such contract, being an exercise of a right reserved by the
contract to the party bound by the terms of the order or undertaking.   **E**
Accordingly, with deference to Foster J., I take a different view from that
which he took on his first ground for rejecting the defendants' application.

When the motion for an injunction came before the judge inter partes,
the defendants did not seek any adjournment to permit them to put in
evidence in answer to the plaintiffs' evidence. They might then have asked
for a sufficiently long adjournment to permit them to make the company   **F**
searches which they made in May, and possibly to search for corroborative
evidence in the form of advertising material and so forth, to build up a
case for saying that a relevant group structure existed in this case. They
did not do so, probably because it had not then occurred to their advisers
that evidence of this kind might assist them in accordance with the reasoning on which the *Revlon* decision was based. The fact that the *Revlon*
decision had not then taken place is, in my view, no ground for saying that   **G**
the defendants might not have succeeded in resisting the motion successfully on parallel reasoning. Let me assume (which I am not deciding) that
the evidence now available would have enabled the defendants to succeed
on those lines if such evidence had been adduced before Foster J. in April
1979 and they had resisted the motion on *Revlon* lines. Ought they to be
allowed to reopen the matter six months later, having armed themselves   **H**
with evidence which they could have obtained on the earlier occasion but
failed to do so? In my judgment, the answer should be "No."

The defendants are seeking a rehearing on evidence which, or much
of which, so far as one can tell, they could have adduced on the earlier
occasion if they had sought an adequate adjournment, which they would
probably have obtained. Even in interlocutory matters a party cannot
fight over again a battle which has already been fought unless there has

A been some significant change of circumstances, or the party has become aware of facts which he could not reasonably have known, or found out, in time for the first encounter. The fact that he capitulated at the first encounter cannot improve a party's position. The *Revlon* point was open to the defendants in April 1979, notwithstanding that this court had not then decided that case. Some at least of the new evidence was readily available to them at that time.

B   In my judgment, there has been no change, since April 6, 1979, in the potential ability of the defendants to resist the plaintiffs' motion successfully, sufficient to justify a court in discharging or modifying the undertakings which the defendants then offered and gave.

    The defendants have contended that the order of the judge from which they seek leave to appeal is analogous to the grant or refusal of an C injunction, being in effect a refusal to discharge an injunction or an undertaking having the same effect as an injunction. No leave is required to appeal from an order granting or refusing an injunction. So, they say, we should give leave in the present case.

    I feel unable to accept this. The defendants freely offered their undertaking in April 1979. They now seek to escape from it. The D position, in my view, is not analogous to the grant or refusal of an injunction. Leave to appeal is required.

    For the reasons I have indicated, I do not consider that this is a case in which we should give leave. I would consequently dismiss this motion.

    SHAW L.J. I agree.

E   OLIVER L.J. I agree.

Motion dismissed with costs.

    Solicitors: *Sharpe, Pritchard & Co. for Philip Baker, King & Co., Birmingham; Wilkinson, Kimbers & Staddon.*

F   C. N.

[CHANCERY DIVISION]

G   * *In re* WOODHAMS, DECD.

LLOYDS BANK LTD. *v.* LONDON COLLEGE OF MUSIC AND OTHERS

[1978 W. No. 2034]

1980 May 8;   Vinelott J.
      July 23
H

Charity—Cy-près doctrine—Impracticability of part of intention—
    Bequests to found musical scholarships for absolute orphans
    from homes run by named charities—Refusal of bequests if
    restricted to absolute orphans from named charitable homes
    —Whether bequests to be applied cy-près

        By his will dated November 2, 1956, and codicil, the testator
    bequeathed one moiety of his residuary estate, after an initial
    life interest, to each of the " London College of Music " and the

A "Curwen Memorial College (Tonic Sol-fa College of Music)," to found annual scholarships commemorating his name "for the complete musical education of a promising boy who is an absolute orphan and only of British nationality and birth from any one of Dr. Barnardo's homes or the Church of England Children's Society homes." By an earlier clause in his will the testator had given certain very detailed pecuniary specific legacies, with gifts over, in some cases, to charity, with an expressed preference for Dr. Barnardo's homes or the

B Church of England Children's Society. At the date of the testator's death on November 18, 1968, the London College of Music and the Curwen Memorial College could have provided a complete musical education as intended by the testator but they would not have been willing to accept the bequest if the applicants for scholarships were to be confined to boys who were absolute orphans coming from one or other of the charitable homes named in the will.

C On an originating summons taken out by the executor and trustee named in the will, the court was asked to determine, inter alia, whether on the true construction of the will and in the events which had happened the trusts declared to take effect after the determination of the life interest in respect of the residuary estate, were valid and effectual or were invalid for impracticability or otherwise: —

D *Held,* that the testator's intention was to further musical education and to do so by founding scholarships at the two colleges; that, although the testator had chosen absolute orphans from the homes run by the two charities named in the will as being those most likely to be in need of assistance, it was not an essential part of his intention that the scholarships should be so restricted; and that, therefore, the trusts of residue did not fail, since at the date of the testator's will they could have

E been carried into effect by a modification deleting the requirement that the boys entitled to benefit must be absolute orphans from those homes and the case would, therefore, be referred to the Charity Commissioners for the settlement of a suitable cy-près scheme (post, pp. 504H—505c).

In re Lysaght, decd. [1966] Ch. 191 and *Attorney-General for New South Wales* v. *Perpetual Trustee Co. Ltd.* (1940) 63 C.L.R. 209 applied.

F
The following cases are referred to in the judgment:

Attorney-General for New South Wales v. *Perpetual Trustee Co. Ltd.* (1940) 63 C.L.R. 209.

Crowe decd., In re (unreported), October 3, 1979, Slade J.

Dalziel, In re [1943] Ch. 277; [1943] 2 All E.R. 656.

Lysaght, decd., In re [1966] Ch. 191; [1965] 3 W.L.R. 391; [1965] 2 All

G E.R. 888.

Mills v. *Farmer* (1815) 19 Ves.Jun 483.

Mitchell's Will Trusts, In re (1966) 110 S.J. 291.

Monk, In re [1927] 2 Ch. 197, C.A.

Rymer, In re [1895] 1 Ch. 19, C.A.

Tacon, In re [1958] Ch. 447; [1958] 2 W.L.R. 66; [1958] 1 All E.R. 163; C.A.

Willis, In re [1921] 1 Ch. 44, C.A.

H *Wilson, In re* [1913] 1 Ch. 314.

No additional cases were cited in argument.

ORIGINATING SUMMONS

By an originating summons, dated September 6, 1978, the plaintiffs, Lloyds Bank Ltd., as executor and trustee under the will of Herbert

A George Woodhams, who died on November 18, 1968, sought against the defendants, London College of Music, the Curwen Institute, Henry George Payne and the Attorney-General, the following relief: (1) that it might be determined whether upon the true construction of the testator's will and in the events which had happened the trusts declared in the will over the testator's residuary estate to take effect after the death of Helen Amy Dear (a) were valid and effectual so that the first and second defen-

B dants were each entitled to receive and give a good receipt for a moiety thereof, or (b) were invalid for impracticability or otherwise; (2) if the trusts declared over the whole or a moiety of the testator's residuary estate were held to be invalid, that it might be determined whether the property thereby affected (a) fell to be applied cy-près or (b) was subject to the trusts affecting property in respect of which the testator died

C intestate; (3) that if necessary a scheme be directed for the application of the testator's residuary estate; (4) that the defendant, Henry George Payne, be appointed to represent for the purposes of the present application the persons entitled to property in respect of which the testator died intestate; (5) if and so far as necessary, administration of the testator's estate; (6) further or other relief, and (7) that the costs of the application be provided for.

D On December 4, 1978, the summons was amended pursuant to the order of Master Heward, dated November 29, 1978; the Tonic Sol-fa Association Ltd., a registered charity, was substituted for the Curwen Institute as second defendant and it was recorded that the first defendant, London College of Music, was likewise a registered charity.

The facts are stated in the judgment.

E *John Weeks* for the plaintiff bank.
Robert Ham for the first and second defendants.
Charles Turnbull for the third defendant Henry George Payne.
John Mummery for the Attorney-General.

F   *Cur. adv. vult.*

July 23. VINELOTT J. read the following judgment. The testator, Herbert George Woodhams, died on November 18, 1968. His will, which he made on November 2, 1956, was proved on January 17, 1969, by Lloyds Bank Ltd. ("the bank"), as sole executor and trustee named therein. In his will the testator described himself as "musician and

G teacher of music." By clause 4 of his will he gave a number of small pecuniary and some very detailed specific legacies; there were 21 pecuniary and specific legacies in all. Some were given on charitable trusts and have been relied on as throwing light upon the questions before me, which relate to the testator's residuary estate.

They are as follows. First, by paragraph (a) of clause 4 the testator

H gave £200 to the vicar and church wardens of the church where he should hold the appointment as organist and choirmaster at his death to be spent in the purchase of a piece of furniture which was to bear a tablet with an inscription commemorating him and his family. Secondly, by paragraph (b) he gave the bank £200 conditionally upon his holding the appointment of organist at a church at the time of his death on trust to invest the same and pay the income to the vicar and church wardens of the church to be applied by them for charitable purposes for the

The Weekly Law Reports, April 17, 1981

496

Vinelott J.   In re Woodhams, decd. (Ch.D.)   [1981]

benefit of the parish, so long as the vicar and church wardens should A
out of the income provide an annual tea and entertainment for the choirboys, with a gift over to a charity to be selected by his trustee, but with
preference for Dr. Barnardo's homes, in the event that the vicar and
church wardens should fail to provide an annual tea and entertainment.
Thirdly, by paragraph (c) he gave to the London College of Music of
Great Marlborough Street his textbooks on musical subjects and his
pianoforte music for use in their library, and his licentiate and other B
certificates to be hung in the college building; and he gave his licentiate
cap, gown, and hood for use by a deserving male student taking the
licentiate for the pianoforte. Fourthly, by paragraph (d) he gave to " the
Curwen Memorial College (Tonic Sol-fa College of Music), 9, Queens-
borough Terrace " his pianoforte, his textbooks on tonic sol-fa and his
licentiate and membership certificates, expressing the wish that they C
should be hung in the college building, and he gave his licentiate hood
for the use of a deserving male student taking the licentiate for singing;
and he gave his copies of services, cantatas, and oratorios for use in the
college library. Lastly, by paragraph (u) he gave to the bank £300 on
trust to invest the same and to pay the income to the vicar and church
wardens of the church where he should hold the appointment of organist
and choirmaster at his death to be applied for charitable purposes, and D
he directed that the trust should continue for so long as the vicar and
church wardens should " out of the said income " keep in good order
and repair a family grave, keeping the lettering on the gravestone legible
and that on failure to observe these conditions the gift should determine and the fund be paid and transferred to a charitable institution
selected by the trustee with a preference for Dr. Barnardo's homes or E
the Church of England Children's Society.

The validity both of the trusts of the income of this last legacy
and of the gift over must be open to serious doubt: see *In re Dalziel*
[1943] Ch. 277. There may also be a question whether the provision of a
tea and entertainment for choirboys is a charitable purpose and, if it is
not, whether the trusts of income in paragraph (b) and the gift over in
that paragraph are not also void. The validity of these gifts is not one F
of the questions raised in the originating summons. The amount of the
legacies would hardly support the cost of deciding these questions, even
if the income were sufficient to maintain the family grave and provide
tea and entertainment for the choir. But reliance is placed on the
identity of the institutions named as beneficiaries under the gifts over.

The testator gave his residuary estate on usual administrative trusts G
and directed that the income of the net residue, defined as " the trust
fund ", should be paid to one Helen Amy Dear. Clause 7 reads:

" After the death of the said Helen Amy Dear as to both capital
and income to divide the same (in equal shares) between the London
College of Music Great Marlborough Street London W.1. and the
Curwen Memorial College (Tonic Sol-fa College of Music) 9, Queens- H
borough Terrace Bayswater London W.2. and at each college to
found a scholarship to be known as the Herbert G. Woodham's [sic]
scholarship for the complete musical education of a promising boy
who is an absolute orphan and only of British nationality and birth
from any one of the Dr. Barnardo's homes or the Church of England
Children's Society homes at the London College of Music to enable
such boy to be educated for the teacher's licentiate diploma in piano-

The Weekly Law Reports, April 17, 1981

497

1 W.L.R.   In re Woodhams, decd. (Ch.D.)   Vinelott J.

A   forte playing and at the Curwen Memorial College for the associate and licentiate diploma (singing) in both notations (music and tonic sol-fa) one boy to each college annually and in each case when the boys have taken their respective diploma to have the right to state that they are Herbert G. Woodhams' scholars the selection of boys in each case must rest with the college authorities."

B   The testator made a codicil to his will dated October 6, 1961, whereby after revoking a small pecuniary legacy he confirmed his will.

The gross value of the testator's estate was sworn for the purposes of probate at £12,712. After payment or satisfaction of funeral and testamentary expenses and death duties, and specific and pecuniary legacies, the net residue amounted to £11,437. Helen Amy Dear died on November 2, 1973. No death duties were payable on her death. At her C death the value of the trust fund did not differ significantly from its value at the testator's death. It is now worth approximately £15,700.

The London College of Music was founded in 1887 and was incorporated in 1939. It has at all material times provided full-time courses in musical education. It also holds examinations for its own diplomas. One diploma awarded is the licentiate teacher's diploma in a musical D subject including the pianoforte. The course leading to the diploma is of two or three years' duration. There is evidence in an affidavit by Mr. John Paul Pelham Burn, the warden of the London College, and in correspondence between the London College and the Treasury Solicitor, exhibited to an affidavit filed on behalf of the Attorney-General, which is sufficient to justify the inference that in the circumstances known or foreseeable at the death of the testator a half share of his residuary estate E would probably have sufficed at the time when it might have been expected to fall into possession to found a scholarship which could have been administered by the London College strictly in accordance with the terms of the will.

So far no difficulty arises. However, the London College have made it clear that they would not have been willing to accept the bequest of F a half share of the testator's residuary estate at or at any time after the testator's death if the college would thereby have become bound to use the bequest to found and administer a scholarship to be awarded strictly in accordance with the directions in the testator's will. While the London College would have been and would now be prepared to accept the bequest and to found and administer a scholarship to assist a G male of British nationality and birth to study for the teacher's licentiate diploma in the pianoforte, it would not then have been willing and is not now willing to found and administer such a scholarship if subject to a further condition restricting it to absolute orphans coming from one of Dr. Barnardo's homes or the Church of England Children's Society's homes. The reason given in Mr. Burn's affidavit and in correspondence with the Treasury Solicitor, as elaborated in argument by Mr. Ham, H who appeared for the London College, is that in the post-war world there has been a decrease in the number of absolute orphans brought up in those homes and at the same time an increase in public moneys available for the musical education of promising boys. Local authority grants are mandatory for the college's music school courses and discretionary in the case of the professional courses; but even in the field of discretionary grants an absolute orphan from one of the named homes, who proved to have musical ability, would be a strong candidate for a

498

grant. The advantage to the London College of a scholarship to be A
awarded by it would be to enable the college to make a discretionary
award to a promising boy who does not qualify for a full grant or who
for some other reason might not be able to complete his course without
assistance. In these circumstances, the London College feel that the
creation of a scholarship strictly in accordance with the conditions in the
testator's will would create problems which would more than outweigh
any practical benefit which might be derived from it.   B

The position of the institution described as " the Curwen Memorial
College (Tonic Sol-fa College of Music) " is more complex. At the dates
of the will, the codicil, and the testator's death there was in existence a
company originally called " the Tonic Sol-fa College " which later
changed its name to " the Tonic Sol-fa College of Music " and which I
will call " the old Tonic Sol-fa College." It had been founded in 1863 C
and incorporated in 1875. Its purpose was to propagate the method of
teaching music, devised and advocated in the writings of a Mr. John
Curwen. The testator was a long-standing member of the council of the
old Tonic Sol-fa College. After the war the old Tonic Sol-fa College
carried on its activities under the name " the Curwen Memorial College,"
the name of the old Tonic Sol-fa College carrying, it was thought, an
old-fashioned image. The Curwen Memorial College has never had any D
separate existence. There can be no doubt that the old Tonic Sol-fa
College is the body described by the testator of " the Curwen Memorial
College (the Tonic Sol-fa College of Music)."

The activities of the old Tonic Sol-fa College included the holding of
examinations and the awarding of certificates, scholarships, and diplomas.
It also held subsidised summer schools for students. In 1950 or there- E
abouts the council decided that it would try to accommodate full time
students, but this project was not a success. The old Tonic Sol-fa College
ceased to provide regular tuition for an enrolled student body in 1966,
that is after the testator made his codicil but before his death. The old
Tonic Sol-fa College finally abandoned the project of providing a full
time musical education in 1970 and in 1971 it formally resolved that F
" general music teaching at the college will cease as from the end of the
present term (July, 1971)." However, returning to the position at the
testator's death, an affidavit has been filed on behalf of the defendant,
the Tonic Sol-fa Association Ltd.—which, as I shall later explain, has
taken over the assets of the old Tonic Sol-fa College—by one Bernarr
Rainbow, the chairman of the association and formerly for many years
the chairman of the old Tonic Sol-fa College. Mr. Rainbow's evidence G
is that at the testator's death the old Tonic Sol-fa College—under the
name of the Curwen Memorial College—could have provided a complete
musical education, including tuition in a wide variety of instrumental
playing, singing, harmony, counterpoint and sight singing, by means of
the conventional and the tonic sol-fa notations, though that education
would have been provided on the basis of individual teaching or coaching H
and not to a full time enrolled student body, and that at that time the
old Tonic Sol-fa College still examined for and awarded—to cite from the
will—" the associate and licentiate diploma (singing) in both notations
(music and tonic sol-fa)." The evidence of Mr. Rainbow, as amplified
in correspondence between the Treasury Solicitor and the solicitors for
the association, and as elaborated by Mr. Ham on behalf of the association, is that, in the light of the circumstances known or reasonably fore-

The Weekly Law Reports, April 17, 1981

499

1 W.L.R.   In re Woodhams, decd. (Ch.D.)   Vinelott J.

A seeable at the testator's death, the old Tonic Sol-fa College would have
expected that a half-share of the testator's residuary estate when it fell
into possession would be sufficient to found a scholarship which could
then have been administered by the old Tonic Sol-fa College in accordance
with all the conditions in the testator's will. However, like the London
College, the old Tonic Sol-fa College would not then or at any time
thereafter have been willing to accept the bequest on terms that it
B should be used to found a scholarship confined to applicants who were
absolute orphans from one of Dr. Barnardo's homes or the Church of
England Society's homes, though it would have accepted the bequest
and have founded and administered a scholarship to be awarded to a
promising boy of British nationality and birth.

In 1975 the defendant association was incorporated, and in 1976 the old
C Tonic Sol-fa College was dissolved and its assets transferred to the association. The association carries on two activities. First, under the name
" the Curwen Institute " it organises and disseminates a new tonic Sol-fa
method of music teaching using a new notation recommened by a working
party set up by the old Tonic Sol-fa College. Secondly, it continues under
the name " the Tonic Sol-fa College " to cater for the needs of those who
wish to continue to use the old notation. Although the old college
D ceased to provide any general musical education in 1971 the association
has revived the summer schools which were one of the original and
central features of the old Tonic Sol-fa College activities. A summer
school was started under the name of the Curwen Institute in conjunction
with Britten Pears School of Advanced Musical Studies at Snape in 1979.
These developments are, of course, irrelevant to the question which I
E have to decide, which is whether the bequest of a half share of the
testator's residuary estate failed to take effect ab initio. They are relevant
to the further question as to the way in which this moiety should be
applied, if a cy-près application is possible. The association propose that
a half share of the residuary estate be used to endow the summer schools
so as to enable free places to be made available, preference being given
to suitable candidates presented by Dr. Barnardo's homes and the Church
F of England Society's homes.

It is clear that the testator intended that on the death of Helen Amy
Dear a half share of his residuary estate should be transferred to both the
London College and the old Tonic Sol-fa College and intended that the
scholarships which he wanted to provide should be founded and administered by the London College and the old Tonic Sol-fa College and by
G no one else. Thus each bequest was, in effect, conditional on the London
College and the old Tonic Sol-fa College, as the case may be, being
willing to accept the bequest as trustee on trust to found a scholarship
in accordance with the terms of the will. The willingness of the London
College or the old Tonic Sol-fa College to accept the bequest on those
terms must, of course, be determined at the date of the testator's death
H when the bequest first vested in interest and in the light of circumstances
and reasonable expectations at that time: see In re Tacon [1958] Ch. 447.
The question which I have to decide is whether the fact that both the
London College and the old Tonic Sol-fa College would have refused to
accept a reversionary interest in a half share of the residuary estate on
terms that they would be bound when the interest fell into possession to
found and administer scholarships restricted to absolute orphans from one

500

of the named homes, has the consequence that the residuary gift fails A
altogether.

A similar question, but without the complication of an intervening life
interest arose in *In re Lysaght, decd.* [1966] Ch. 191. In that case a
testatrix gave a legacy to the Royal College of Surgeons on trust to
apply the income in establishing and maintaining scholarships of a specified amount tenable for a term of one to five years. She set out detailed
conditions restricting the class of persons to whom studentships might be B
awarded and governing the courses of study to be followed by the holders
of studentships and conferred wide discretions on the council of the
college to revoke studentships and to call on students for reports. One
of the qualifications was that a student must be " a British born subject
and not of the Jewish or Roman Catholic faith." The college refused
to accept the bequest if it bound them to restrict the class of persons C
amongst whom it might award studentships to those who were not of
the Jewish or Roman Catholic faith. The college was willing to accept
the bequest if that restriction was deleted. Buckley J. held that the court
could, by way of scheme, modify the terms of the trust by deleting that
restriction. In reaching this conclusion he made some general observations as to the meaning of the " general charitable intent " which has
to be shown before the court can modify the terms of a charitable gift D
which would otherwise fail for impracticability. He took the example of
four imaginary testators, at pp. 201–202:

" The first bequeathes a fund for charitable purposes generally, the
second for relief of poverty, the third for relief of poverty in the
parish of ' X,' the fourth for the relief of a particular class of poor
(for example, of a particular faith or of a particular age group) in E
the parish of ' X.' Each of them couples with his bequest an indication of a particular manner in which the gift should be carried
into effect, say, by paying the fares of poor persons travelling by rail
from the village of ' X ' to the town of ' Y ' to obtain medical advice
and attention. Between the dates of the wills and of the deaths of the
four testators the railway between ' X ' and ' Y ' is closed so that it F
becomes impossible for anyone to travel by rail from the one to the
other. In each case the court must consider whether it was an essential
part of the testator's intention that his benefaction should be carried
into effect in all respects in the particular manner indicated and no
other, or whether his true intention was, in the first case to make
a gift for charitable purposes without qualification; in the second,
to relieve poverty; in the third, to relieve poverty in the parish of G
' X '; and in the fourth, to relieve the poverty of the particular
class of persons in the parish of ' X '; the specification of a particular
mode of giving effect to such an intention being merely an indication
of a desire on his part in this respect: see the well known passage in
the judgment of Parker J. in *In re Wilson* [1913] 1 Ch. 314, 320, 321.
If on the true construction of any of the wills the latter is the H
true view, the court will, if it can, carry the testator's true intention
into effect in some other way cy-près to the impracticable method
indicated by the testator. In so doing the court is not departing
from the testator's intention but giving effect to his true paramount
intention. Such an intention is called a general, charitable intention.
It is not general in the sense of being unqualified in any way or as
being confined only to some general head of charity. It is general

The Weekly Law Reports, April 17, 1981

501

1 W.L.R.   **In re Woodhams, decd. (Ch.D.)**   Vinelott J.

A   in contrast with the particular charitable intention which would have been shown by any of the four supposed testators who upon the true construction of his will intended to benefit poor people by paying their railway fares when travelling by rail between ' X ' and ' Y ' to obtain medical advice and attention and in no other way. Such a general intention would not avail if the court could find no practical or legal method of giving effect to it—if, for instance, it could be shown in respect of the bequest of the fourth testator that at the relevant time there were no poor people of the particular class specified in his will to be found in the parish of ' X ' and there was no reasonable likelihood of there being any such at any foreseeable time in the future. The question would then arise whether the testator's true intention was restricted to benefiting this particular class of poor people or whether he had some yet more general charitable intent to which the court could give effect.

B

"A general charitable intention, then, may be said to be a paramount intention on the part of a donor to effect some charitable purpose which the court can find a method of putting into operation, notwithstanding that it is impracticable to give effect to some direction by the donor which is not an essential part of his true intention —not, that is to say, part of his paramount intention.

C

D

"In contrast, a particular charitable intention exists where the donor means his charitable disposition to take effect if, but only if, it can be carried into effect in a particular specified way, for example, in connection with a particular school to be established at a particular place, *In re Wilson* [1913] 1 Ch. 314, or by establishing a home in a particular house: *In re Packe* [1918] 1 Ch. 437."

E

This passage is criticised in *Tudor, Charities,* 6th ed. (1967). After referring to the penultimate paragraph of the passage I have cited, the editors say, at p. 247:

"It is suggested, with diffidence, that this formulation does not accord with the usual understanding of a ' general charitable intention ' discussed above. Furthermore, there would seem to be considerable difficulty, in view of the detailed provisions in the will, in the way of the construction which was made, and it is respectfully suggested that the learned judge's view of the will was, as a matter of construction, erroneous. Although a ' liberal spirit ' may perhaps in some circumstances be commendable, it should not be applied in such a way as to defeat a testator's intention."

F

G

That criticism is, I think, ill-founded. In a well known passage in *In re Wilson* [1913] 1 Ch. 314, 320–321, Parker J. stresses that the jurisdiction of the court to direct a scheme for the carrying out of the trusts of a charitable gift which has otherwise failed through impracticability is founded upon the fact that:

H

"... the gift is given for a particular charitable purpose, but it is possible, taking the will as a whole, to say that, notwithstanding the form of the gift, the paramount intention, according to the true construction of the will, is to give the property in the first instance for a general charitable purpose rather than a particular charitable purpose ..."

But in earlier cases what is stressed is the distinction between, on the one hand, the case where the scheme prescribed by a testator can be regarded

The Weekly Law Reports, April 17, 1981

502

Vinelott J.   **In re Woodhams, decd. (Ch.D.)**   [1981]

as the mode by which a charitable purpose is to be carried into effect A
and where " the court does not hold, that the mode is of the substance
of the legacy; but will effectuate the gift to charity, as the substance ":
see *per* Lord Eldon L.C. in *Mills* v. *Farmer* (1815) 19 Ves.Jun. 483, 486;
and, on the other hand, the case where no part of the scheme prescribed
by the testator can be disregarded as inessential without frustrating the
testator's evident intention. The distinction was explained by Lindley L.J.
in *In re Rymer* [1895] 1 Ch. 19, 35 in these terms: ". . . you have to B
consider whether the mode of attaining the object is only machinery, or
whether the mode is not the substance of the gift." And in *In re Willis*
[1921] 1 Ch. 44, Younger L.J., in a passage cited by Buckley J. in *In re
Lysaght, decd.* [1966] Ch. 191, 203 expresses the principle in these terms,
at p. 54:

> " The problem which in this case we have to solve is to say by which C
> of two different principles the construction of this gift has to be
> controlled. The first of these principles is that if a testator has
> manifested a general intention to give to charity, whether in general
> terms or to charities of a defined character or quality, the failure of
> the particular mode in which the charitable intention is to be
> effectuated shall not imperil the charitable gift. If the substantial D
> intention is charitable the court will substitute some other mode of
> carrying it into effect. The other principle, which I paraphrase from
> the judgment of Kay J. in *Biscoe* v. *Jackson* (1887) 35 Ch. D. 460, 463
> is this. If on the proper construction of the will the mode of appli-
> cation is such an essential part of the gift that you cannot distinguish
> any general purpose of charity but are obliged to say that the pre-
> scribed mode of doing the charitable act is the only one the testator E
> intended or at all contemplated, then the court cannot, if that mode
> fails, apply the money cy-près."

The distinction between these two categories of cases is expressed in the
joint judgment of two very distinguished Australian judges, Dixon J. and
Evatt J., in *Attorney-General for New South Wales* v. *Perpetual Trustee
Co. Ltd.* (1940) 63 C.L.R. 209, 225 as a distinction: F

> ". . . between, on the one hand, cases in which every element in the
> description of the trust is indispensable to the validity and operation
> of the disposition and, on the other hand, cases where a further and
> more general purpose is disclosed as the true and substantial object
> of the trust, which may therefore be carried into effect at the expense
> of some part of the particular directions given by the trust instrument." G

These are, of course, all different ways of expressing the same distinction.
I have referred to what Sargant L.J. once, in *In re Monk* [1927] 2 Ch. 197,
212 called " the long bead-roll of cases on the subject "—to which some
recent cases have been added—because if the well known passage in the
judgment of Parker J. in *In re Wilson* [1913] 1 Ch. 314 which I have
cited is read in isolation, it may mislead the reader into looking at the H
testator's will or at the document by which a disposition of property on
charitable trusts is made, to see whether there can be discovered a paramount or dominant charitable purpose served by the specific directions
made by the testator or settlor. To search for such a paramount or
dominant charitable purpose or intention is in many cases to follow a
will-o'-the-wisp. Of course, there are cases where a particular disposition
is prefaced by general words which state expressly the object which the

The Weekly Law Reports, April 17, 1981

503

1 W.L.R.   In re Woodhams, decd. (Ch.D.)   Vinelott J.

A testator or settlor desires to achieve and make it clear that the particular
scheme prescribed is only a means of achieving that more general end.
Such cases are rare. In most cases the charitable intention can only be
inferred from the particular scheme directed by the testator or settlor.
And as was pointed out in *Attorney-General for New South Wales* v.
Perpetual Trustee Co. Ltd., 63 C.L.R. 209 by Dixon J. and Evatt J. in
B the joint judgment to which I have referred, at p. 227:

" . . . the construction of the language in which the trust is expressed
seldom contributes much towards a solution. More is to be gained
by an examination of the nature of the charitable trust itself and
what is involved in the author's plan or project."

Dixon J. and Evatt J. also observe at p. 225 that the distinction " . . .
C however clear in conception, has proved anything but easy of application."
As I see it, one way of approaching the question whether a prescribed
scheme or project which has proved impracticable is the only way of
furthering a charitable purpose that the testator or settlor contemplated
or intended, is to ask whether a modification of that scheme or project,
which would enable it to be carried into effect at the relevant time, is one
which would frustrate the intention of the testator or settlor as disclosed
D by the will or trust instrument interpreted in the light of any admissable
evidence of surrounding circumstances. Two cases where such an interpretation would have frustrated the testator's intention may serve to
illustrate this. In *In re Mitchell's Will Trusts* (1966) 110 S.J. 291, a
testator gave a three-quarter share of her residuary estate in reversion
after a life interest on trust to be applied

E " . . . to the providing of four beds in the Barnsley Beckett hospital,
for the use of injured workmen from the Mitchell Main and Darfield
Main collieries,"

to be known by the names of four members of the Mitchell family. At
her death the income of three-quarters of her residuary estate was insufficient to maintain four beds at the hospital. At the date of her will
F and at the date of her death the hospital had a scheme for the naming
of cots and beds in perpetuity in return for gifts of stated amounts, the
money given being invested and applied for the general purposes of the
hospital. There was evidence that assuming that four beds had been
reserved exclusively for injured workmen in the main collieries, the beds
would have been very much under used; that the hospital committee would
not have accepted the gift if it required them to set aside the four beds
G for the exclusive use of men from the named collieries and that they could
not or would not have accepted the gift if it required them to guarantee
that, even if no beds were set aside exclusively for the workmen, up to four
beds would always be available. Cross J. held that the gift failed. There
the gift could not be construed as a gift for the benefit of the hospital
alone; to treat it as a mere endowment of the hospital would have frustrated
H the testator's evident intention to benefit miners from the named pits.
Equally the gift could not be construed as a gift for the benefit of miners
from the named pits, otherwise than by the provision of special facilities
in the named hospital. It is clear from the judgment of Cross J. that he
did not take the view that the scheme prescribed by the testatrix could
not be modified in any particular. He said, at p. 292:

" Had the evidence been that, although the hospital would not provide
four beds for the exclusive use of the workmen, it would nevertheless

504

guarantee that there would always be four beds available, the position A might be different . . ."

But any modification of the terms of the gift which would have made the scheme practicable would have frustrated the testatrix's intention to benefit workmen from the named pits and to do so by the provision of special facilities at the named hospital.

In the unreported decision of Slade J. in *In re Crowe,* October 3, 1979, B a testatrix gave her residuary estate on trust to arrange for

" . . . the creation of a scholarship at the Royal Naval School for officers' daughters to be used for the best student (such student must be a naval officer's daughter) in the Spanish and Russian languages in memory of my father."

Slade J. construed the gift as a gift to provide a single scholarship, such C scholarship to be awarded in both Spanish and Russian. The school did not teach Russian and was not willing to provide a course at or outside the school. On the construction of the will adopted by Slade J. the foundation of a scholarship in Spanish alone, or in Spanish and some language other than Russian, or the creation of a scholarship in Spanish and Russian otherwise than for pupils at the named school, would equally have frus- D trated the testatrix's intention. No modification was possible which would have made the gift practicable without frustrating her evident intention.

On the other side of the line stands the *Attorney-General for New South Wales* v. *Perpetual Trustee Co. Ltd.,* 63 C.L.R. 209. In that case a testatrix whose home was a farming property known as " Milly Milly " gave it on trust to be used as a training farm for orphan lads in Australia. The farm was too small, the plant was too old-fashioned, and the income would E not have sufficed to meet the expenses of the supervisory staff needed. It was held by the majority of the High Court of Australia that the intention that " Milly Milly " should be the actual place of training was not an essential part of the gift, so that the property could be sold and the proceeds applied for the purpose of training Australian orphan boys in farming without frustrating her intention. F

Returning to the residuary gift in the instant case Mr. Turnbull, who argued the case for intestacy on behalf of the representative next of kin, stressed that apart from small legacies to individuals and gifts designed to perpetuate his own and his family's reputation the testator devoted his whole estate to the furtherance of two charitable objects, namely, music and the welfare of orphans cared for by Dr. Barnardo's or the Church G of England Society's homes. He pointed out that the gifts over of the legacies settled or purportedly settled by paragraphs (b) and (u) of the will were in favour of or with a preference for those bodies. Thus, said Mr. Turnbull, the gifts of the two half shares of the residuary estate are designed to further two ends: first, the activities of the London College and the old Tonic Sol-fa College, and, secondly, the welfare of orphans brought up in one of Dr. Barnardo's or the Church of England Society's H homes. To delete the requirement that persons to whom scholarships might be awarded should be absolute orphans from one of these homes would be to frustrate the testator's intention as surely as to transfer either bequest to some body other than the London College or the old Tonic Sol-fa College.

I do not take that view. The testator has in clause 7 of his will set out in very considerable and, in view of the modest value of his estate

The Weekly Law Reports, April 24, 1981

505

1 W.L.R.   In re Woodhams, decd. (Ch.D.)   Vinelott J.

A and the indefinite duration of the trusts, somewhat excessive detail a scheme for the foundation of scholarships. But as I see it the intention which can be discerned from the bequest is two-fold. The testator wanted to further musical education and to do so by means of founding scholarships at colleges with which he had a long and, as is apparent from paragraphs (c) and (d) of clause 4 of the will, a valued connection. He chose absolute orphans from homes run by well known charities as those most likely to need assistance. But it was not, as I see it, an essential part of this scheme that the scholarships should be so restricted, whatever needs might present themselves in changed circumstances. That being so, that part of the scheme or mode of achieving a charitable purpose can be modified without frustrating his intention.

C In my judgment, therefore, the trusts of residue do not fail. At the date of the testator's will the trusts could have been carried into effect by a modification of the trust of each moiety, deleting the restriction to absolute orphans from the named homes. There have been further changes of circumstances as regards the old Tonic Sol-fa College since the testator's death and a more radical scheme may be required. I will therefore refer to the Charity Commissioners the settlement of a scheme.

D
                                              Order accordingly.

Solicitors: *Latter & Willett; Norton Rose, Botterell & Roche; Warmingtons & Hasties; Treasury Solicitor.*

                                              T. C. C. B.

E

[COURT OF APPEAL]

* THOMAS BATES AND SON LTD. *v.*
WYNDHAM'S (LINGERIE) LTD.

F 1980 Nov. 13, 14, 17, 18, 19, 20, 21   Buckley, Eveleigh and
                                              Brightman L.JJ.

Equity—Rectification—Lease—Rent revision clause failing to provide for default of agreement—Common intention that rent to be fixed by arbitrator in default of agreement—Execution of lease by tenant knowing omission due to landlord's mistake—Whether landlord entitled to rectification

G *Landlord and Tenant—Rent—Revision—Revised rent to be fixed by arbitrator in default of agreement—Whether rent to be market rent or reasonable rent—No provision in event of failure to agree revised rent—Whether reasonable rent to be implied*

In 1970 negotiations took place between the plaintiff landlords and the defendant tenants for a new lease of 14 years, pursuant to a renewal clause in the existing lease which provided that the rent should be agreed between the parties or, in default of agreement, fixed by an arbitrator. The parties agreed a rent for the first five years of the new term and agreed that the rent should be reviewed at the end of the fifth and tenth years of the term. The new lease, which was drawn up by the landlords, provided for the rents payable during the review periods to be such "as shall have been agreed between the lessor and the lessee" but made no provision in default of agreement. When executing the lease

Thomas Bates Ltd. v. Wyndham's Ltd. (C.A.) [1981]

on behalf of the tenants, the tenants' officer noticed that the
rent review clause was defective but did not bring it to the
attention of the landlords. In 1975 the parties were unable
to agree a revised rent, and the landlords brought an action,
inter alia, for rectification of the lease. The judge's order
declared that the rent during the review periods should be
the market rent for the premises and required the lease to
be rectified to provide for the revised rents, in default of
agreement, to be determined by an arbitrator.

On appeal by the tenants: —

Held, affirming the judge's order in regard to rectification
but deleting the declaration, that where one party to a document was aware that it did not give effect to the common
inention of the parties due to a mistake on the part of the
other party and executed the document without telling the
other party and where (*per* Buckley L.J.) the mistake was one
calculated to benefit him, or (*per* Eveleigh L.J.) the mistake
was detrimental to the other party, he was precluded from
resisting rectification on the ground that the mistake was not, at
the time of execution of the document, mutual (post, pp. 515H
—516B, 520H—521A, E); that, as, on the evidence, those
requirements were satisfied in regard to the omission from the
rent review clause of any reference to arbitration, the judge
was right in ordering rectificaion of the lease; and that an
arbitrator, when fixing a revised rent pursuant to the rectified
clause, would have to assess what rent it would have been
reasonable for the landlords and the tenants to have agreed
under the lease having regard to all the circumstances relevant
to any negotiations between the parties for a new rent from
the review date (post, pp. 519D, 521E).

A. Roberts & Co. Ltd. v. *Leicestershire County Council*
[1961] Ch. 555 and *Beer* v. *Bowden (Note)* [1981] 1 W.L.R.
522, C.A. applied.

Ponsford v. *H.M.S. Aerosols Ltd.* [1979] A.C. 63, H.L.(E.)
distinguished.

Observation of Russell L.J. in *Riverlate Properties Ltd.* v.
Paul [1975] Ch. 133, 140 C.A. considered.

Per Buckley L.J. If the court were wrong on rectification,
then on construction and by implication, the court would
ascertain by inquiry what rent the landlords and the tenants,
as willing negotiators anxious to reach agreement, would
arrive at for each of the review periods (post, p. 519E–G).

Decision of Michael Wheeler Q.C., sitting as a deputy
of the Chancery Division, varied.

The following cases are referred to in the judgments:

Beer v. *Bowden (Note)* [1981] 1 W.L.R. 522, C.A.
Hornal v. *Neuberger Products Ltd.* [1957] 1 Q.B. 247; [1956] 3 W.L.R.
1034; [1956] 3 All E.R. 970, C.A.
Ponsford v. *H.M.S. Aerosols Ltd.* [1979] A.C. 63; [1978] 3 W.L.R. 241;
[1978] 2 All E.R. 837, H.L.(E.).
Riverlate Properties Ltd. v. *Paul* [1975] Ch. 133; [1974] 3 W.L.R. 564;
[1974] 2 All E.R. 656, C.A.
Roberts (A.) & Co. Ltd. v. *Leicestershire County Council* [1961] Ch.
555; [1961] 2 W.L.R. 1000; [1961] 2 All E.R. 545.
Sykes (F. & G.) (Wessex) Ltd. v. *Fine Fare Ltd.* [1967] 1 Lloyd's Rep.
53, C.A.

The following additional cases were cited in argument:

Bottomley v. *Ambler* (1877) 38 L.T. 545, C.A.
British Bank for Foreign Trade Ltd. v. *Novinex Ltd.* [1949] 1 K.B. 623;
[1949] 1 All E.R. 155, C.A.

A   *Brown* v. *Gould* [1972] Ch. 53; [1971] 3 W.L.R. 334; [1971] 3 W.L.R. 334; [1971] 2 All E.R. 1505.

    Churchward v. *Ford* (1857) 2 H. & N. 446.

    Collins v. *Collins* (1858) 26 Beav. 306.

    Courtney & Fairbairn Ltd. v. *Tolaini Brothers (Hotels) Ltd.* [1975] 1 W.L.R. 297; [1975] 1 All E.R. 716, C.A.

B   *Dempster (R. & J.) Ltd.* v. *Motherwell Bridge and Engineering Co. Ltd.*, 1964 S.L.T. 353.

    Dungey v. *Angove* (1794) 2 Ves.Jun. 304.

    Foley v. *Classique Coaches Ltd.* [1934] 2 K.B. 1, C.A.

    Hillas & Co. Ltd. v. *Arcos Ltd.* (1932) 147 L.T. 503, H.L.(E.).

    Joscelyne v. *Nissen* [1970] 2 Q.B. 86; [1970] 2 W.L.R. 509; [1970] 1 All E.R. 1213, C.A.

C   *Kenilworth Industrial Sites Ltd.* v. *E. C. Little & Co. Ltd.* [1975] 1 W.L.R. 143; [1975] 1 All E.R. 53, C.A.

    King v. *King* (1980) 255 E.G. 1205.

    King's Motors (Oxford) Ltd. v. *Lax* [1970] 1 W.L.R. 426; [1969] 3 All E.R. 665, D.C.

    Liverpool City Council v. *Irwin* [1976] Q.B. 319; [1975] 3 W.L.R. 663; [1975] 3 All E.R. 658, C.A.; [1977] A.C. 239; [1976] 2 W.L.R. 562; [1976] 2 All E.R. 39, H.L.(E.).

D   *Moorcock, The* (1889) 14 P.D. 64, C.A.

    Prenn v. *Simmonds* [1971] 1 W.L.R. 1381; [1971] 3 All E.R. 237, H.L.(E.).

    Stylo Shoes Ltd. v. *Wetherall (Bond Street) Ltd.* (1974) 237 E.G. 343, C.A.

    Trollope & Colls Ltd. v. *North West Metropolitan Regional Hospital Board* [1973] 1 W.L.R. 601; [1973] 2 All E.R. 260, H.L.(E.).

E   *United Scientific Holdings Ltd.* v. *Burnley Borough Council* [1978] A.C. 904; [1977] 2 W.L.R. 806; [1977] 2 All E.R. 62, H.L.(E.).

APPEAL from Michael Wheeler Q.C., sitting as a deputy judge of the Chancery Division.

By writ issued on October 31, 1977, and amended February 27, 1978, the plaintiffs, Thomas Bates and Son Ltd., claimed, inter alia, (1) a
F declaration that on the true construction of a lease dated December 17, 1970, and made between the plaintiffs and the defendants, Wyndham's (Lingerie) Ltd., comprising factory premises at Church Road, Harold Wood, in the London Borough of Havering, the rents during the rent review periods therein provided should be the market rents for the premises; (2) rectification of the lease to provide for the rents for the rent review periods to be determined by a single arbitrator in default
G of agreement between the parties; (3) alternatively, a declaration that the lease was void and/or rescission of the lease; and (4) further or alternatively, a declaration that the defendants were liable to pay a proper sum for the use and occupation of the premises from November 15, 1975. On June 6, 1979, Michael Wheeler Q.C., sitting as a deputy High Court judge, inter alia, declared that upon the true construction
H of the lease the rents during the period of five years from November 15, 1975, and the period of four years from November 15, 1980, should be the market rent for the premises and ordered that the lease be rectified so that in the reddendum thereof after the words " such rents as shall have been agreed between the lessor and lessee " there be inserted the words " or shall in default of such agreement be determined by a single arbitrator to be appointed by the president for the time being of the Royal Institution of Chartered Surveyors."

Thomas Bates Ltd. v. Wyndham's Ltd. (C.A.)   [1981]

By notice dated February 22, 1980, the defendants appealed on the A
grounds, inter alia, that (1) the judge was wrong in law in holding that
it was an implied term of the lease that " rent " in the rent review clause
meant " market rent "; (2) the judge erred in law in holding (by implication) that a reasonable rent and the market rent were one and the same
thing; (3) the judge erred in law in holding (by implication) that " rent "
in the rent review clause meant " reasonable rent "; (4) the judge erred
in law in applying to the provision in the rent review clause for the B
payment of " such rents as shall have been agreed between the lessor
and the lessee " the doctrine of The Moorcock (1889) 14 P.D. 64; (5)
the judge erred in law in both making a declaration as to the implied
term and ordering rectification of the lease; (6) the judge erred in law
and found against the weight of the evidence in holding that the defendants through Mr. Avon were guilty of sharp practice; (7) the judge C
found against the weight of the evidence and was wrong in fact in
holding that a provision [as to the rent being fixed in default of agreement by a single arbitrator] had been mistakenly omitted by the plaintiffs
from the rent review clause; (8) the judge found against the weight of
the evidence and was wrong in fact in holding that Mr. Avon deliberately
allowed such omission to go uncorrected; (9) the judge was wrong in D
law in failing to apply, or properly to apply, the test as to the burden
of proof applicable to a claim for rectification; and (10) the judge erred
in law in holding that the plaintiffs' burden of proof in a claim for
rectification had been discharged.

By respondent's notice dated March 18, 1980, the plaintiffs gave
notice of their desire to contend that (1) in the event of the Court of
Appeal finding that the judge was wrong in holding that " rent " in the E
rent review clause meant " market rent " then the Court of Appeal
ought to hold that it was implied in the clause that " rent " meant
" reasonable rent " on the ground that such a term was implied in law;
(2) in the event of the Court of Appeal finding that the judge was wrong
in holding that the lease ought to be rectified so as to include a provision
for arbitration, then the rents under the lease for the review periods F
should be referred to an inquiry for determination by the court what was
a market rent, or alternatively a reasonable rent, for the premises during
those periods; and (3) in the event of the Court of Appeal finding that
there was no obligation on the defendants to pay rent for each of the
review periods, or that the rent for each of those periods could not be
reviewed, then the Court of Appeal ought to hold that the lease was
void ab initio, or alternatively ought to be set aside. G

The facts are stated in the judgment of Buckley L.J.

E. G. Nugee Q.C. and J. C. Harper for the appellant defendants.
Robert Wakefield for the respondent plaintiffs.

BUCKLEY L.J. This is an appeal from a decision of Mr. Michael H
Wheeler Q.C., sitting as a deputy judge in the Chancery Division on
June 6, 1979. The issues in the case relate to a rent review clause
contained in a lease dated December 17, 1970, and made between the
plaintiffs, Thomas Bates and Son Ltd., as lessors and the defendants,
Wyndham's (Lingerie) Ltd., as lessees. The subject matter was some
factory premises at Hornchurch in Essex. In order to understand the
issues it is necessary to go back in history a little while.

The Weekly Law Reports, April 24, 1981

509

1 W.L.R.   Thomas Bates Ltd. v. Wyndham's Ltd. (C.A.)   Buckley L.J.

A   In the year 1956, by a lease dated August 20, 1956, the plaintiffs (whom I will call "the landlords") let to predecessors of the defendants (and I will call the defendants "the tenants") the factory premises in question for a term of seven years from September 1, 1956, at a yearly rent of £650. That lease contained, in clause 5, an option provision in the following terms:

B   "That the lessor will on the written request of the lessees made six months before the end of the term hereby created and if at the time of such request there shall not be any existing breach or non-observance of any of the covenants on the part of the lessees hereinbefore contained at the expense of the lessees grant to the lessees a lease of the demised premises for a further term of seven or fourteen years from the expiration of the said term at a rent to be agreed between the lessor and the lessees but in default of such

C   agreement at a rent to be fixed by a single arbitrator appointed by the President for the time being of the Royal Institution of Chartered Surveyors and containing the like covenants and provisos as are herein contained."

     The term under that lease was in due course assigned to the tenants,
D   and when the time for the exercise of the option drew near Mr. Bates, the managing director of the landlords, wrote a letter to the tenants, for the attention of a Mr. Avon, who was the director of the tenants who at all times has handled matters relating to this leasehold property on behalf of the tenants, a letter drawing attention to the fact that the time had come to consider a renewal of the lease, and Mr. Bates said
E   in that letter that the landlords would require an addition of £125 per annum, bringing the rent up to £775 per annum for the seven years from the expiration of the then current lease.
     Stimulated by that communication, Mr. Avon, on behalf of the tenants, gave a formal notice exercising the option on February 19, 1963, requesting the landlords to grant to the tenants a renewed lease of the premises for the further term of 14 years from the expiration of the
F   current term:

     "at a rent to be agreed between us but in default of such an agreement at a rent to be fixed by a single arbitrator appointed by the President . . . of the Royal Institution . . ."

     In response to that Mr. Bates wrote in reply saying that in fact the landlords would require rather more rent than he had stated in his
G   earlier letter, £850 a year; in consequence of which there were some oral communications, and on March 11, 1963, Mr. Bates wrote to Mr. Avon confirming offers which he had made orally for a further seven-year term at £800 a year, and proposing that the landlords should construct certain additional buildings on the property, in consideration of which there would be a further rent of another £800 a year during the ensuing
H   seven-year period.
     Those terms were accepted by the tenants, and on November 29, 1963, the parties entered into a new lease for a term of seven years from November 15, 1963, at a yearly rental of £1,600; and that lease contained an option clause in precisely the same terms as the option clause in the 1956 lease, save that it only granted an option for a further seven years and not for seven or 14 years as had been the case in the 1956 lease.

510

Time went by and the year 1970 arrived when the time was approach- A
ing for the exercise of the option in the 1963 lease, and on April 14,
1970, the landlords wrote a letter to the tenants drawing their attention
to this fact, in consequence of which Mr. Avon, on May 4, signed and
sent to the landlords a formal notice exercising the option contained in
the 1963 lease, and by that notice he requested the landlords to grant
a renewed lease of the premises for a further term of seven years
from the expiration of the then current term: B

> " at a rent to be agreed between us but in default of such agree-
> ment at a rent to be fixed by a single arbitrator appointed by the

> President for the time being of the Royal Institution . . ."

The language of that notice followed the language of the option clause
contained in the 1963 lease.   C
As has been pointed out in argument, the effect of that notice was
to change the legal relationship between the parties and to bring into
existence a contract for the grant of a further term of seven years at a
rent to be agreed or, in default of agreement, to be fixed by an arbitrator.
The landlords wrote back to the tenants on May 7, 1970, indicating
that the rent they would require would be £2,600 per annum for the first
three years of the new term of seven years, the rental thereafter to be D
reviewed and agreed for the remainder of the term. Those words are
taken from the letter of May 7, 1970. So being then under a contractual
obligation to grant a new lease for seven years at a rent to be agreed
or in default of agreement to be fixed by an arbitrator, they proposed
agreeing the rent for part of that term only, leaving the remainder of
the term the subject of a further review and agreement at a later date. E
On August 3—that is to say, rather later than the letter I have
just referred to of May 7—there having been some oral communications
in the meantime and Mr. Avon having paid a visit to the landlords'
offices to discuss the matter, the landlords wrote saying that they were
prepared to grant a lease for a further period of 14 years from the
expiration of the then current term, with a clause for rent reviews at
the end of the fifth and tenth years of the term, the rental for the first F
period of five years to be £2,350 per annum exclusive of rates.
To that letter Mr. Avon replied on August 17, 1970, that the tenants
were reluctantly prepared to accept the figure of £2,350, but he said that
they were not in agreement with rent reviews after five and ten years
but were willing to accept a clause for a rent review at the end of the
seventh year. That was, in effect, a counter offer to the offer which had G
been put forward in the letter of August 3, 1970.
The landlords replied on August 18 insisting upon rent reviews after
five and ten year intervals, and on August 20, following some telephonic
communication, they again wrote insisting upon the rent reviews, and
that letter has a postscript:

> " Whilst your present lease provides for a further seven years'
> renewal, the question of the rent review period is something quite H
> separate and distinct."

It seems to me that the landlords there are saying: we recognise your
right under the exercise of the option; you are entitled to a term of
seven years at a rent to be agreed or in default of agreement to be
fixed by an arbitrator, but we are not at the moment prepared to agree
any rent beyond the first five years.

The Weekly Law Reports, April 24, 1981

511

1 W.L.R.   **Thomas Bates Ltd. v. Wyndham's Ltd. (C.A.)**   Buckley L.J.

A   On September 22 the tennant's solicitors, Messrs Nabarro Nathanson, wrote indicating that the tenants, subject to formal exchange of the lease, accepted the offer of a new lease for a term of 14 years from November 15, 1970, at the exclusive rent of £2,350 per annum, subject to review at the expiration of the fifth and tenth years of the new term.

B   It seems to me that it is implicit in that that the rent, at any rate in respect of the two years next following the initial five years of the term under the new lease, would be fixed by agreement or, in default of agreement, by an arbitrator appointed under the provisions to that effect in the option clause.

The lease and counterpart were then executed and exchanged. The lease had not been prepared by the landlords' legal advisers; it was C   prepared under the instructions of Mr. Bates and was typed by Mr. Bates' secretary Miss Cannon. The lease so prepared and executed demised the property to the tenants for a term of 14 years from November 15, 1970, and now I quote from the document itself:

D   "Yielding and paying therefor during the first five years of the said term unto the lessor the yearly rent of £2,350 and for the next period of five years of the said term and the final period of four years of the said term such rents as shall have been agreed between the lessor and the lessee such rents to be paid clear of all deductions by equal monthly payments on the first day of each month in advance..."

E   and then there is a provision that the tenants should also pay the costs of insurance but we are not concerned with that.

The lease contains an option clause in, I think, the same terms as the option clause which was contained in the 1963 lease except that any further lease to be granted under the option in the 1970 lease was not to be required to contain an option clause. It will be observed that in the reddendum there is no reference to arbitration in default of agreement.

F   At a later stage when the time for fixing the rent from the end of the first five years of the term onwards became imminent, the landlords became aware of this and wrote a letter, signed by Mr. Foley who was the property manager for the landlords, to the tenants as follows:

"As you will be aware under the terms of your lease the rent of this property is due to be reviewed, effective from November 15, G   1975, and this letter is intended to be a formal notice advising you of our intention to review the rent. The lease has no specific note how the rent may be settled should your company and ourselves fail to agree upon a figure and I suggest that the matter be settled by an independent arbitrator. I therefore enclose an agreement in duplicate and shall be obliged if you will sign the top copy and return it to me."

H   As a result of that, and a hastener written on May 2, 1975, a telephone conversation took place on May 6, 1975, in the course of which Mr. Avon said he was not prepared to sign any such agreement. Mr. Foley then got into contact with the landlords' own solicitors, who advised him that because the rent review clause did not contain some means of definitely settling the new rent, e.g. by arbitration following appointment by the President of the Royal Institution of Chartered Sur-

512

A

veyors, should the parties to the lease not agree, the review clause would be unenforceable at law and the rent could remain the same until the lease expired.

Nothing further seems to have taken place immediately with regard to that, but there was later a telephone conversation between Mr. Avon and Mr. Foley, to which I shall have to refer again later, in which Mr. Avon said—or is said by Mr. Foley to have said—that he had been aware of the implications of the clause from the day the lease was signed; that he might be prepared to pay a slightly higher rent, but not nearly so high a rent as the landlords were in fact then proposing.

B

It seems to me clear that the omission of any reference to arbitration in default of agreement in the reddendum of the lease of 1970 must have been due to a mistake on the part of Mr. Bates, under whose instructions, as I have said, that lease was prepared. The omission was one which was clearly contrary to the landlords' interests. The only possible legal consequences which have been suggested in the course of arguments are: first, that no rents having been agreed in respect of any period after the first five years of the 14-year term, no rent would be payable after the end of that five-year period. Mr. Nugee, appearing for the tenants, although he did not in the course of his argument altogether abandon the idea that that might be the legal consequence of the omission, frankly and very properly admitted that it could not have been in the contemplation of the parties that there would be any period during the term of this lease when no rent would be payable at all, and it is inconceivable that that could have been the parties' real intention.

C

D

Secondly, it has been suggested that as no rent other than the rent of £2,350 per annum would have been agreed, that rent should continue in force until some other rent should be agreed by the parties. It seems to me that such a proposition is absolutely contrary to the clear intention of the rent review provision. The rent review provision was clearly a provision insisted upon by the landlords because they wanted the matter reviewed at the end of five years and wanted a new rent to be then arrived at. If merely by withholding consent or agreement to a new rent the tenants could stultify the revision clause and ensure that the original rent of £2,350 should continue to be payable, the whole purpose of the rent revision clause would be destroyed or frustrated. I cannot believe that it could have been Mr. Bates' intention that the lease in the form in which he framed it should have had that effect.

E

F

Thirdly, it has been suggested that in respect of the period after the first five years, and in default of agreement between the parties, the rent would have to be fixed by a process of litigation involving implication of the parties' intentions, and it has been suggested that by implication the rent ought either to be the market rent, that is to say the rent for which this property would be let in the open market, or such rent as these particular landlords and these particular tenants would agree having regard to all the matters which would affect them in arriving mutually at a rent which the one was content to accept and the other was content to pay, which would very possibly be markedly different from a market rent, and it seems to me inconceivable that a landlord would have been content to rely on fixing a rent by a process of implication in that way without it being at all clear in what way the court would view the matter and how the rent to be so ascertained should be assessed.

G

H

The only other possible legal consequence of the omission that has

The Weekly Law Reports, April 24, 1981

513

1 W.L.R.   Thomas Bates Ltd. v. Wyndham's Ltd. (C.A.)   Buckley L.J.

A been suggested at all, either in the course of argument or in the course of the evidence given before the judge, was that the clause was entirely inoperative because of the omission and because either it amounted to no more than an agreement to agree, or it amounted to a provision which contained such defective machinery that it could not be carried into practical effect. It will be seen that advice on those lines was what was

B received by Mr. Foley. It seems also to have been the advice received by Mr. Avon.

Mr. Foley gave evidence before the judge, but Mr. Avon did not. The judge was somewhat critical of Mr. Avon for not giving evidence. That was, no doubt, a matter which rested not so much in Mr. Avon's discretion as in the discretion of those who were conducting the case on the part of the tenants. The judge, in the course of his judgment, makes

C the following finding:

"In evidence before me Mr. Foley amplified this note."—He is referring to a note written on the letter of September 23, 1975, to which I have already referred.—"I think it probable that in his oral evidence Mr. Foley may to some extent have telescoped two tele-phone conversations with Mr. Avon into one. His evidence—which

D was given with care and which I accept without hesitation—was to the following effect. He said that he quoted a new rent to Mr. Avon of (he thought) about £5,000 per annum: that Mr. Avon seemed amused and, when asked what he thought, said he might pay £100 or £200 more. Mr. Foley said he realised that Mr. Avon's figure bore no relation to the market value but he felt that he (Mr. Foley) was in a slightly ticklish position and said he would refer the position

E to [the landlords'] solicitors; that Mr. Avon then said that he (Mr. Foley) must be aware as he (Mr. Avon) was that the rent revision clause as drawn was inoperative and that he (Mr. Avon) had been aware of this at the time the lease was entered into because it had been brought to his notice by [the tenants'] solicitors."

F The judge spoke critically of Mr. Avon in that respect and said that, in his judgment, Mr. Avon's conduct amounted to sharp practice. As the judge had not heard any evidence from Mr. Avon we cannot tell in what circumstances or under what advice Mr. Avon acted as he did. It is clear that he was at that time in contact with and receiving advice from the tenants' solicitors, and for my part I do not feel it necessary to associate myself with that stricture on the part of the judge upon Mr.

G Avon's conduct. Nevertheless the fact emerges that when the tenants executed the 1970 lease they did so realising the omission of any reference to arbitration in default of agreement in the review clause and without drawing the attention of the landlords to that omission in any way.

The only reasonable conclusion, it appears to me, that can be drawn from the documents is that the lease was executed in the form in which

H it was with regard to the terms of the review clause as a consequence of a mistake on Mr. Bates' part, for at the time when the lease was prepared and put forward the tenants had a contractual right to have the rent, at any rate in respect of the sixth and seventh years of the term, agreed or, in default of agreement, determined by an arbitrator appointed by the President of the Royal Institution of Chartered Surveyors. No doubt the grant of the lease displaced the contract which had arisen as a result of the exercise of the option, but the terms of that contract relating to

fixing the rent in respect of the first seven years of the term which was A
granted by the 1970 lease remained in force up to the execution of the
lease and that, in my judgment, affords a strong indication that until, at
any rate, Mr. Avon realised the omission of any reference to arbitration,
it was the mutual intention of both parties that the rent to be paid under
the lease after the first five years should be a rent which was agreed
between the parties or, in default of agreement, ascertained by arbitration.   B

Mr. Bates did not give evidence because unhappily he had died in
January 1973. That was a date a considerable number of months after
the issue of the writ but before the trial. No written statement of Mr.
Bates made during his lifetime was adduced in evidence under the Civil
Evidence Act 1968. We are told by counsel, but we have got no other
evidence of the fact, that Mr. Bates did not make any written statement. C
So there was no evidence of any kind emanating from him.

But there was the evidence of Miss Cannon. Miss Cannon's evidence,
in my view, in no way negatives the possibility or probability that the
omission of a reference to arbitration was due to a mistake on Mr. Bates'
part. Her evidence, taking it quite shortly and generally, is to the effect
that she typed the lease; that she did it in accordance with instructions   D
which she received from Mr. Bates; but there is nothing in her evidence
which establishes one way or the other whether Mr. Bates, in giving his
instructions, was himself labouring under a mistake. If, as Mr. Avon
thought was the position, the clause in the way in which it was drawn
was an inoperative clause, it seems to me to be absolutely manifest that it
must have been so framed as the result of a mistake, for one cannot
believe that any landlord would put into a lease a clause which he   E
intended to be inoperative.

Mr. Nugee has said that there is no evidence as to what Mr. Bates'
intention was, and he stressed that in cases of rectification a high standard
of proof is required by the court. Indeed, in some cases the standard
has been equated with the criminal standard of proof " beyond all
reasonable doubt." I think that the use of a variety of formulations to   F
express the degree of certainty with which a particular fact must be
established in civil proceedings is not very helpful and may, indeed, be
confusing. The requisite degree of cogency of proof will vary with the
nature of the facts to be established and the circumstances of the case. I
would say that in civil proceedings a fact must be proved with that degree
of certainty which justice requires in the circumstances of the particular
case. In every case the balance of probability must be discharged, but   G
in some cases that balance may be more easily tipped than in others.

In *Hornal* v. *Neuberger Products Ltd.* [1957] 1 Q.B. 247, 258
Denning L.J. said:

> " The more serious the allegation the higher the degree of probability
> that is required: but it need not, in a civil case, reach the very high
> standard required by the criminal law."   H

That, in my judgment, encapsulates the law about the standard of proof
required in civil proceedings applicable to all civil proceedings, and as
applicable to cases of rectification as to any other kind of civil action.

The landlords claim rectification in the present case on the basis of a
principle enunciated by Pennycuick J. in *A. Roberts & Co. Ltd.* v.
Leicestershire County Council [1961] Ch. 555, 570 where he said:

The Weekly Law Reports, April 24, 1981

515

1 W.L.R.   Thomas Bates Ltd. v. Wyndham's Ltd. (C.A.)   Buckley L.J.

A

"The second ground rests upon the principle that a party is entitled to rectification of a contract upon proof that he believed a particular term to be included in the contract, and that the other party concluded the contract with the omission or a variation of that term in the knowledge that the first party believed the term to be included. . . .

B

"The principle is stated in *Snell on Equity*, 25th ed. (1960), p. 569 as follows: 'By what appears to be a species of equitable estoppel, if one party to a transaction knows that the instrument contains a mistake in his favour but does nothing to correct it, he (and those claiming under him) will be precluded from resisting rectification on the ground that the mistake is unilateral and not common.'"

C

Of course if a document is executed in circumstances in which one party realises that in some respect it does not accurately reflect what down to that moment had been the common intention of the parties, it cannot be said that the document is executed under a common mistake, because the party who has realised the mistake is no longer labouring under the mistake. There may be cases in which the principle enunciated by Pennycuick J. applies although there is no prior common intention,

D

but we are not, I think, concerned with such a case here, for it seems to me, upon the facts that I have travelled through, that it is established that the parties had a common intention down to the time when Mr. Avon realised the mistake in the terms of the lease, a common intention that the rent in respect of any period after the first five years should be agreed or, in default of agreement, fixed by an arbitrator.

E

The principle so enunciated by Pennycuick J. was referred to, with approval, in this court in *Riverlate Properties Ltd.* v. *Paul* [1975] Ch. 133, where Russell L.J., reading the judgment of the court, said, at p. 140:

"It may be that the original conception of reformation of an instrument by rectification was based solely upon common mistake: but certainly in these days rectification may be based upon such knowledge on the part of the lessee: see, for example, *A. Roberts & Co.*

F

Ltd. v. *Leicestershire County Council* [1961] Ch. 555. Whether there was in any particular case knowledge of the intention and mistake of the other party must be a question of fact to be decided upon the evidence. Basically it appears to us that it must be such as to involve the lessee in a degree of sharp practice."

G

In that case the lessee against whom the lessor sought to rectify a lease was held to have had no such knowledge as would have brought the doctrine into play. The reference to "sharp practice" may thus be said to have been an obiter dictum. Undoubtedly I think in any such case the conduct of the defendant must be such as to make it inequitable that he should be allowed to object to the rectification of the document.

H

If this necessarily implies some measure of "sharp practice", so be it; but for my part I think that the doctrine is one which depends more upon the equity of the position. The graver the character of the conduct involved, no doubt the heavier the burden of proof may be; but, in my view, the conduct must be such as to affect the conscience of the party who has suppressed the fact that he has recognised the presence of a mistake.

For this doctrine—that is to say the doctrine of *A. Roberts & Co. Ltd.*

v. *Leicestershire County Council*—to apply I think it must be shown: A
first, that one party A erroneously believed that the document sought
to be rectified contained a particular term or provision, or possibly did
not contain a particular term or provision which, mistakenly, it did
contain; secondly, that the other party B was aware of the omission or
the inclusion and that it was due to a mistake on the part of A; thirdly,
that B has omitted to draw the mistake to the notice of A. And I think
there must be a fourth element involved, namely, that the mistake must B
be one calculated to benefit B. If these requirements are satisfied, the
court may regard it as inequitable to allow B to resist rectification to give
effect to A's intention on the ground that the mistake was not, at the
time of execution of the document, a mutual mistake.

   Mr. Nugee has drawn attention to a number of other departures in
the language of the 1970 lease from the language of the corresponding C
clauses of the 1963 lease, and he says that this lease was not, or should
not be regarded as having been, granted in pursuance of the exercise of
the option, but as a newly negotiated lease, the negotiations no doubt
being prompted by the exercise of the option, but the new lease not
flowing from the exercise of the option. I, with respect to Mr. Nugee's
argument, do not find very much force in that contention. The parties D
were of course at liberty to modify the terms of their lease in any way
they mutually agreed and none of these variations to which I am now
referring has any bearing upon the review clause or the language
employed in it. It seems to me, as I have already said, that the omission
from the review clause of any reference to arbitration was one which was
clearly contrary to the landlords' interests, one which must have occurred
as a result of a mistake, and one which Mr. Avon, on his own evidence, E
recognised, and must I think be taken to have recognised, as having been
the result of a mistake on the part of Mr. Bates.

   The judge disposed of the matter on this aspect in three numbered
paragraphs:

   "... (i) that I cannot regard Miss Cannon's evidence as proving
   that Mr. Bates was not making a mistake in omitting a longstop pro- F
   vision for arbitration of some sort; (ii) that although Miss Cannon
   said that she thought there had been other leases [of the landlords]
   which contained the same type of rent review provision as the 1970
   lease none was produced, and I cannot accept that any reasonable
   businessman would deliberately have adopted such a potentially
   defective provision; and (iii) that the provision for an option to G
   renew the 1970 lease in clause 5 which was in similar terms to the
   options in [the tenants'] earlier leases showed perfectly clearly that
   the parties recognised the necessity for a longstop for rent fixing
   purposes and that it is reasonable to suppose that it was a provision
   in these terms which [the landlords] mistakenly omitted and which
   [the tenants], through Mr. Avon, deliberately allowed to go
   uncorrected." H

   I have already dealt with Miss Cannon's evidence. With regard to
the judge's second numbered paragraph, I agree that it is highly improbable that Mr. Bates would have purposely adopted a form of clause
which was so disadvantageous as the review clause is with the omission
of any reference to arbitration.

   With regard to the third paragraph, I would myself prefer to relate

The Weekly Law Reports, April 24, 1981

517

1 W.L.R.   Thomas Bates Ltd. v. Wyndham's Ltd. (C.A.)   Buckley L.J.

A this point, not to clause 5 of the 1970 lease, but to the exercise of the option under the 1963 lease and the contract which arose from its exercise. The point is, I think, precisely the same point. It is that the parties must have had present to their minds the desirability, and indeed the obligation of the landlords in relation at any rate to the first seven years of the new term, to arrive at a rent which was not necessarily a rent which had to be at the same rate throughout the term, but

B they had to arrive at a rent which was agreed between them or, in default of agreement, was one determined by arbitration.

There was no precedent for a review clause contained in the 1963 lease, for the 1963 lease did not provide for any rent review; and it is not difficult to believe that a layman like Mr. Bates, in preparing the 1970 lease, failed to detect the shortcoming of the review clause as he

C had framed it, and failed to apply his mind to the difficulties which would arise if no provision was made for reference to arbitration.

On those findings the judge rectified the lease. The form of the order provides:

D "This court doth declare·that upon the true construction of the lease dated December 17, 1970, and made between the plaintiffs and the defendants comprising factory premises at Church Road Harold Wood in the London Borough of Havering the rents during the period of five years from November 15, 1975, and the period of four years from November 15, 1980, should be the market rent for the said premises. And this court doth order that the said lease be rectified so that in the reddendum thereof after the words

E 'such rents as shall have been agreed between the lessor and the lessee' there shall be inserted the words 'or shall in default of such agreement be determined by a single arbitrator to be appointed by the President for the time being of the Royal Institution of Chartered Surveyors.'"

F So far as rectification is concerned, the language which the judge has adopted follows the language used in the option clauses in this case, except that he used the word "determined" instead of "fixed," and perhaps it would have been better if the word had been "fixed."

If the lease is so rectified the question arises: by what measure is an arbitrator to fix the rent if the parties do not agree? Mr. Wakefield, for the landlords, initially contended that the arbitrator so-called would act not as an arbitrator but as a valuer. He based that argument upon

G the use of the words "shall have agreed" and the word "fixed" in the review clause. On that basis he submitted that the rent should be the market rent for the property, on the authority of a decision of the House of Lords in *Ponsford* v. *H.M.S. Aerosols Ltd.* [1979] A.C. 63. Subsequently he conceded that the clause must be read as an agreement to arbitrate and not as an agreement to abide by a valuation. Upon that

H footing he agreed that, upon the true construction of the clause, the rent should be such as it would have been reasonable for these landlords and these tenants to have agreed under the lease. It would consequently be proper for the arbitrator to take into account all considerations which would affect the mind of either party in connection with the negotiation of such a rent, as, for example, past expenditure by the tenant on improvements.

In my judgment, Mr. Wakefield was right to make that concession A
and to have accepted that the present case falls within the reasoning of
the minority of the House of Lords in *Ponsford* v. *H.M.S. Aerosols Ltd.*
and not within the reasoning of the majority in that case. The review
clause which was there under consideration was a review clause in a
lease which provided for a yearly rent of £9,000:

> " during the first seven years of the said term and during the second B
> and third seven years of the term... the sum of £9,000 aforesaid
> or such sum whichever be the higher as shall be assessed as a
> reasonable rent for the demised premises for the appropriate period
> such assessment to be made in the following manner that is to say:
> (a) Such assessment as shall be agreed between the parties hereto in
> writing "—and there were certain provisions as to the date by which
> that agreement should be reached—" (b) In the event of the parties C
> hereto failing to reach such agreement as aforesaid on or before
> the date appointed... then the reasonable rent for the second and
> third periods shall be fixed or assessed by an independent surveyor:
> ..." (see [1977] 1 W.L.R. 1029, 1031)

That form of clause, as it seems to me, focuses attention upon what is
there described as " a reasonable rent for the demised premises " for D
the appropriate period, and that expression is first used without any
reference to agreement between the parties to the lease at all. It
then goes on to provide that such assessment—that is to say, the fixing
of the amount of the rent so to be charged—shall be either agreed
or, in default of agreement, arrived at by valuation by an independent
surveyor. That form of wording, in my judgment, certainly affected E
the views of the majority in the House of Lords in that case. Viscount
Dilhorne said, at p. 77:

> " The rent payable by the lessees will of course be rent for the
> demised premises but as I see it, the task of the surveyor is not
> to assess what would be a reasonable rent for the lessees to pay but
> what is a reasonable rent for the premises." F

Lord Fraser of Tullybelton said, at p. 83:

> " In my opinion the words point unambiguously to the result conten-
> ded for by the landlords... and they mean the reasonable rent
> assessed on an objective basis, without reference to the particular
> landlord or the particular tenant or to the history of how the
> premises came to be built or paid for." G

Lord Keith of Kinkel, at p. 86:

> " In my opinion the words ' a reasonable rent for the demised
> premises ' simply mean ' the rent at which the demised premises
> might reasonably be expected to let.' "

The other two Lords, Lord Wilberforce and Lord Salmon, took a con- H
trary view. They thought that what had to be ascertained was what
would be reasonable between the particular parties to the transaction.
However, they were in the minority upon the construction of that
particular rent review clause. But it appears to me that the terms of the
clause there under consideration were noticeably different in important
respects from the clause which we have, which refers to nothing other
than such rent as the parties shall have agreed. Consequently I think

The Weekly Law Reports, April 24, 1981

519

1 W.L.R.   Thomas Bates Ltd. v. Wyndham's Ltd. (C.A.)   Buckley L.J.

A   that Mr. Wakefield was well advised in making the concession which
he made.

Mr. Nugee, on the other hand, who had argued in the earlier stages
of the appeal that in default of agreement the rent should continue
after the review date at the original rate of £2,350 per annum, conceded
that in the light of a decision of this court in *Beer* v. *Bowden* (*Note*),
post p. 522, he could no longer support that argument. That again was

B   a concession which I think he was constrained to make. *Beer* v. *Bowden*
was only brought to the attention of counsel and, through counsel, to
the attention of the court late in the course of the argument.

So the parties are now at one, that on the true construction of the
clause as rectified, the rent is to be fixed by the arbitrator at such
amount as it would be reasonable for the parties to agree having regard

C   to all such considerations as I have mentioned. This was not the
construction adopted by the judge, who, as appears from the terms of
his order, implied a term that the rent to be agreed should be the
market rent. His attention had not, of course, been drawn to the
decision of this court in *Beer* v. *Bowden*. As I understand the position,
neither party now contends that the judge's view in that respect is

D   right, and I myself am satisfied that the market rent would not provide
a proper standard to adopt in the present case. In my judgment, in
default of agreement between the parties, the arbitrator would have to
assess what rent it would have been reasonable for these landlords
and these tenants to have agreed under this lease having regard to all
the circumstances relevant to any negotiations between them of a new
rent from the review date.

E   If I were wrong on a point of rectification, then, on construction
and by a process of implication, the rent to be ascertained in default of
agreement must, I think, be a fair rent as between the landlords and
the tenants. It would be most unjust that the landlords should receive
no rent because of failure of the parties to agree. The landlords have
granted a 14-year term and the court must endeavour to fill any gap
in the terms of the lease by means of a fair and reasonable implication as

F   to what the parties must have intended their bargain to be. See in this
connection the decision of this court in *F. & G. Sykes* (*Wessex*) *Ltd.* v.
Fine Fare Ltd. [1967] 1 Lloyd's Rep. 53, which was a case very different
on its facts from the present, but in which the court explained the
function of any court of construction where parties have embarked upon
any commercial relationship but under terms that are not altogether

G   adequate to cover the eventualities. The court would ascertain by
inquiry what rent the landlords and the tenants, as willing negotiators
anxious to reach agreement, would arrive at for each of the two rent
review periods. In short, the standard would be the same, as I see
it, as would have to be adopted by an arbitrator under the clause if it
is rectified in the way in which I consider that it should be rectified.

H   For these reasons I think that the judge, while he came to the wrong
conclusion on the matter of market rent, reached the right conclusion
on the matter relating to rectification. I would accordingly uphold
that part of his order which directed rectification, though I would
substitute the word " fixed " for " determined," purely, as a matter
of pedantry, I think. It is for consideration whether, in those circumstances, any declaration is really required to be included in the order

at all. That is a matter upon which, perhaps, we can hear submissions A
at a later stage. I would dispose of the matter in that way.

EVELEIGH L.J. The correspondence beginning with May 4, 1970,
contained references to rent reviews. The first reference specifically
was

" at a rent to be agreed between us but in default of such an agree- B
ment at a rent to be fixed by a single arbitrator appointed by the
President for the time being of the Royal Institution of Chartered
Surveyors."

The letter of September 22, 1970, from the tenants' solicitors accepting
the proposed lease for 14 years said merely " at the exclusive rent of
£2,350 per annum subject to review at the expiration of the fifth and C
tenth years of the new term." Quite clearly that letter was written
upon the basis that the nature of the review was understood. It is
inconceivable that a solicitor would confirm an agreement and ask for
a draft lease which would, of course, reflect that agreement, as they in
fact did, if such an important matter had not been resolved. The word
" review " was clearly shorthand. I take the letter of May 7 from the
landlords to the tenants in the same way. The phrase there used is D
" thereafter to be reviewed and agreed for the remainder of the term."
If anyone had asked the parties at that time how the review would take
place, I am quite convinced that the answer would have been that the
machinery contemplated had already been put forward by Mr. Avon in
his letter of May 4, to which the letter of May 7 was a reply.

I see nothing in the words of the other letters written in the course E
of negotiations between the parties to indicate that the review machinery
first referred to was being abandoned in favour of something else. I
find it particularly difficult to conclude, as the tenants contend, that
it was being replaced by a vague gentlemen's agreement. The fact that
the parties ultimately agreed upon a lease of different duration from
that originally agreed, and containing other terms not in the lease of F
1963, in no way alters my conclusion. Certain important changes were
specifically discussed. The machinery for rent review as opposed to the
length of the period was treated without further discussion. The only
reasonable conclusion, in my opinion, must be that the parties were
negotiating upon the basis that rent review in default of agreement was
to be as indicated in the letter of May 4, 1970, I therefore think that
there was a common intention that the rent should be fixed by a single G
arbitrator in default of agreement.

I also think that the evidence established that Mr. Avon knew that
the lease did not contain the appropriate clause and knew that Mr. Bates
intended that it should. Where a party is aware that the instrument
does not give effect to the common intention of the parties as communicated each to the other, there may well be an inference of sharp H
practice or unfair dealing. In my opinion, this will not always be so.
I do not think that it is always necessary to show sharp practice. In a
case like the present if one party alone knows that the instrument does
not give effect to the common intention and changes his mind without
telling the other party, then he will be estopped from alleging that
the common intention did not continue right up to the moment of the
execution of the clause. There is no need to decide whether his conduct

The Weekly Law Reports, April 24, 1981

521

1 W.L.R.   Thomas Bates Ltd. v. Wyndham's Ltd. (C.A.)   Eveleigh L.J.

A amounted to sharp practice. I think he might at that time have had no intention of taking advantage of the mistake of the other party. I do not think that it is necessary to show that the mistake would benefit the party who is aware of it. It is enough that the inaccuracy of the instrument as drafted would be detrimental to the other party, and this may not always mean that it is beneficial to the one who knew of the mistake.

B   I agree that the lease should be rectified in the way indicated by Buckley L.J. and I agree with the order which he proposes. I should just add that I, too, regard this case as being different from *Ponsford* v. *H.M.S. Aerosols Ltd.* [1979] A.C. 63. There the reference was specifically to the demised premises and that is an important difference. Lord Keith of Kinkel said, at p. 85:

C   " At first impression the words ' reasonable rent for the demised premises ' suggest that what has to be ascertained is simply the rent that is reasonable for the premises as such in their actual state, the situation being viewed entirely objectively. ' The demised premises ' must mean the demised premises as improved, by virtue both of the ordinary law and of the passage I have quoted from

D   the licence agreement. So upon this view any contribution the improvements might have made to rental value would have to enter into the assessment."

He also clearly attached importance to the words " demised premises " in the passage which Buckley L.J. has read.

       For those reasons I agree that the lease should be rectified in the

E terms stated, and I further agree with the interpretation of " reasonable rent " that Buckley L.J. has given.

       BRIGHTMAN L.J. I agree that the order of the judge should stand, subject to minor variation, for the reasons given by Buckley L.J. I wish to say a few words only on two points. First as regards the standard of

F proof. The standard of proof required in an action of rectification to establish the common intention of the parties is, in my view, the civil standard of balance of probability. But as the alleged common intention ex hypothesi contradicts the written instrument, convincing proof is required in order to counteract the cogent evidence of the parties' intention displayed by the instrument itself. It is not, I think, the standard of proof which is high, so differing from the normal civil

G standard, but the evidential requirement needed to counteract the inherent probability that the written instrument truly represents the parties' intention because it is a document signed by the parties.

       The standard of proof is no different in a case of so-called unilateral mistake such as the present. The mistake in the instant case was unilateral and not mutual only because the tenants became aware of the

H implications of the review clause on the eve of the execution of the new lease. That consideration, as it seems to me, leads to no different conclusion in relation to the standard of proof required in a rectification action.

       The other point I want to touch on briefly is this. In his judgment the judge said:

       " . . . the parties recognised the necessity for a longstop for rent fixing purposes and . . . it is reasonable to suppose that it was a

A

provision in these terms which Mr. Bates mistakenly omitted and which [the tenants], through Mr. Avon, deliberately allowed to go uncorrected. In my judgment, this was sharp practice. . ."

I would not be prepared to assume, on the evidence, that Mr. Avon was consciously guilty of sharp practice. Nor is such an assumption necessary for the landlords' case. As I indicated, I take the view that there was a common intention on both sides to extend to the new B lease the rent assessment arrangements contained in the covenant for renewal in the expiring lease. The discrepancy between the formula in the expiring lease and the formula in the engrossment of the new lease was not observed by Mr. Avon until it was pointed out by his solicitor. I am not willing to assume that the reputable firm of solicitors acting for him would have allowed him to execute the lease in any circumstances which they saw to be dishonest. If the judgment C is intended to contain a finding of sharp practice on the part of Mr. Avon, I would respectfully wish to disagree with the judge on such a finding. I do not think this would be justified.

As I have said, I agree that the judge's order should, with the slight variation mentioned, stand.

D

> *Order varied by deleting declaration*
> *and substituting " fixed " for " de-*
> *termined " in the direction for*
> *rectification.*
> *Plaintiffs' costs of appeal.*

Solicitors: *Chethams* (instructed on appeal only); *Tolhurst & Fisher,* E
Southend-on-Sea.

C. N.

F

NOTE

[COURT OF APPEAL]

* BEER AND OTHERS v. BOWDEN

1976 April 2   Buckley, Geoffrey Lane and Goff L.JJ. G

Landlord and Tenant—Rent—Revision—No provision in event of
failure to agree revised rent—Whether fair rent to be implied

By a lease dated July 17, 1968, premises were demised by the plaintiff landlords, Anthony Wilders Beer, William Paul Elliott de Beer and Michael Wills de Beer, to the defendant tenant, Harold Herbert Bowden, for a term H
APPEAL from Foster J.
of 10 years, the tenant:

" . . . paying therefor as follows: — until March 24, 1973, . . . the rent of £1,250 per annum and from March 25, 1973, such rent as shall thereupon be agreed between the landlords and the tenant but no account shall be taken of any improvements carried out by the tenant in computing the amount of increase, if any, and in any case not less than the yearly rental payable hereunder . . ."

A The landlords issued an originating summons to determine whether on the true construction of the rent revision provision the rent payable was a reasonable and proper rent having regard to the market value of the premises on March 25, 1973. Foster J. held that the tenant was liable to pay a rent representing what the demised premises were reasonably worth on March 25, 1973, on a demise for a term of five years therefrom.

The tenant appealed.

B The facts are stated in the judgment of Goff L.J.

The following cases are referred to in the judgments:

Foley v. Classique Coaches Ltd. [1934] 2 K.B. 1, C.A.
Kenilworth Industrial Sites Ltd. v. E.C. Little & Co. Ltd. [1974] 1 W.L.R. 1069; [1974] 2 All E.R. 815; [1975] 1 W.L.R. 143; [1975] 1 All E.R. 53, C.A.

C King's Motors (Oxford) Ltd. v. Lax [1970] 1 W.L.R. 426; [1969] 3 All E.R. 665, D.C.

Geoffrey Jaques for the tenant.
Ellen Solomons for the landlords.

D GOFF L.J. delivering the first judgment. This is an appeal from a judgment of Foster J. dated June 12, 1975, given in proceedings commenced by originating summons, raising questions as to the effect of the provision as to rent in a lease, dated July 17, 1968, of premises known as 54 and 56, Torbay Road, Paignton, in the county of Devon.

The appellant was the defendant in the proceedings and tenant under the lease. It is not necessary, I think, to read any part of the lease other than some parts of clause 1, by which clause the premises were demised for a
E term of 10 years from March 25, 1968. The clause then reads:

". . . paying therefor as follows: —until March 24, 1973, (yearly and proportionately for any fraction of a year) the rent of £1,250 per annum and from March 25, 1973, such rent as shall thereupon be agreed between the landlords and the tenant but no account shall be taken of any improvements carried out by the tenant in computing the amount of increase, if any, and in any case not less than the yearly rental payable
F hereunder such rent to be paid in advance by four equal quarterly payments on the four usual quarter days."

The term of 10 years was increased in 1971 to 14 years by a memorandum endorsed on the lease which reads:

"Memorandum. In consideration of the covenants on the part of the tenant contained in the within-written lease the landlords agree that the terms of years contained in clause 1 of the within-written lease shall be
G read and construed as if the term of 14 years were substituted therein in the place of 10 years and the reference in the said clause to a rent review in respect of the rent to be charged for the said premises from March 25, 1973, shall be read and construed as if there were also inserted reference to a rent review for the rent to be charged for the said premises from March 25, 1978, but that in all other respects the covenants conditions and agreements in the within-written lease shall remain in
H full force."

At the end of the first five years, the parties failed to agree on a new rent. In these circumstances, the landlords issued an originating summons, which was amended before the hearing, and, in its amended form, posed two questions in these terms:

"1. Whether upon the true construction of clause 1 of a lease made July 17, 1968, between the plaintiffs as landlords and the defendant as tenant of premises known as 54 and 56 Torbay Road, aforesaid and of

the memorandum to the said lease dated May 17, 1971, the rental payable A
under the said lease (subject only to the provisions of Part II of the
Counter Inflation Act 1973 and orders made thereunder) between the
25th days of March 1973 and 1978 is a proper and reasonable rental
having regard to the market value of the said premises on March 25, 1973.
2. If yes, whether the sum of £2,850 per annum represents such a proper
and reasonable rental."

It is not absolutely plain what happened at the hearing, because the judge B
came to the conclusion that he had decided something which was not in
accordance with the submissions of either party, and on that account he
made no order as to costs. But, as far as I can gather, except that he
imported the restriction that one should not take account of tenant's improvements in ascertaining the market value of the premises, he did in fact (though
perhaps by a different route) accept the submission which was being made on
behalf of the landlords, or at any rate arrived at the same result.   C

In reply, it appears to have been suggested on behalf of the landlords
that if the true view were that no rent was reserved at all for the second five
years, then the lease was or had become void for uncertainty. That submission arose in that way only, and it was not submitted on behalf of the
tenant, nor has it been submitted before us, that the lease was or became void.

The actual order which the judge made was as follows:

"This court doth declare upon the true construction of clause 1 of the D
said lease "—then it is described by its date and parties—" and of a
memorandum "—which is also described—" that the defendant is liable
to pay to the plaintiffs (a) between March 25, 1973, and March 24, 1978,
(subject only to the provisions of Part II of the Counter-Inflation Act
1973 and orders made thereunder) a rental representing what the demised
premises at 54 and 56 Torbay Road Paignton Devon were reasonably
worth on March 25, 1973, on a demise for a term of five years therefrom E
provided that (i) in computing such amount no account shall be taken
of any improvements carried out by the defendant and (ii) the said rental
shall not be less than £1,250 per annum and (b) between March 25, 1978,
and March 24, 1982, a rental representing what the said premises are
reasonably worth on March 25, 1978, on a demise for a term of four
years therefrom subject to the same provisos as are set out in sub-
paragraphs (i) and (ii) of paragraph (a) of this order."   F

The expression used there, " what the demised premises were reasonably
worth," must, I think, mean what would be a fair rental value for the premises.
I cannot see any other meaning which could be attributed to it. I think one
should also point out that, of course, so far as paragraph (b) of that order
is concerned, it will only become operative subject to any agreement which
the parties may make with regard to the rent for the last four years.

The landlords are content to stand on the order, but they have served a G
respondents' notice in which, should this court be of opinion that the order
ought to be reversed or varied, they seek to make certain submissions as to
the proper order and to revive the alternative contention that the lease might
be void.

Mr. Jaques, who has taken every point here which could be taken on
behalf of the tenant, has put forward as his first submission an argument
that the words in clause 1, " and in any case not less than the yearly rental H
payable hereunder," upon their true construction, mean " and in default of
agreement the yearly rental payable hereunder;" that is, £1,250. He says
that clause 1 is really in three parts: first, it reserves a rent of that amount
for the first five years; secondly, it provides that the rent for the second five
years shall be as the parties agree; and, thirdly, so construing the words I
have mentioned, he says it provides that in default of agreement the rent
shall continue to be £1,250. He treats the words " but no account shall be
taken of any improvements carried out by the tenant in computing the

A   amount of increase, if any " as if they were in parenthesis, but he does not take into that parenthesis the further words " and in any case not less than the yearly rental payable hereunder."

I think, for my part, that that is an impossible construction. It is not, on the scheme of the clause as a whole, in my view, the natural meaning of the words; and, if one is to treat any part of it as in parenthesis, I think the provision about rent is as much in the parenthesis as the provision about
B   tenant's improvements. But, secondly, that construction would make the clause futile, because, if in default of agreement the rent was to continue to be £1,250, obviously the tenant would never agree to pay more, however much the premises might appreciate in value, and conversely, in the unlikely event of them depreciating, the landlords clearly would not agree to accept less. All that that clause was doing, as it seems to me, was setting out the basis upon which it was contemplated that the parties would seek to agree upon the rent to become payable at the end of the first five years.
C   I think " such rent as shall thereupon be agreed " must be " such fair rent." It does not make sense otherwise. So the basis was that it was to be a fair rent, not taking into account improvements made by the tenant himself, and in the perhaps unlikely event of depreciation, the rent was not to be reduced below £1,250. Accordingly, in my judgment, that submission fails.

Then Mr. Jaques seeks to obtain the same result by a different method, by implying a covenant that in the absence of an agreement the rent shall
D   be £1,250. In approaching that argument, it must be observed first, as I have said, that the tenant does not suggest that the lease ever was or has become void for uncertainty. If he had done so, I think he would have been in difficulties, but it is not necessary to pause to consider that further, because he has not done so, and the court has to approach this problem on the footing that there is a subsisting lease. Secondly, he concedes (and, in my judgment, rightly) that he cannot stay on there and pay no rent at all.
E   Quite apart from the fact that one would naturally lean towards that conclusion, he has quite fairly indicated that there are provisions in the lease which support it and indeed render it inevitable. He has referred us to the covenant for quiet enjoyment and the provision about cesser or suspension of rent in the event of damage to the premises by fire.

That being so, we have to imply some term defining what the rent is to be. Mr. Jaques submits that there are two alternatives; one £1,250, the other a fair
F   market rent for the premises—of course, subject to the qualification about tenant's improvements. Given, therefore, that some implication has to be made, I asked him upon what in the lease he founded the implication that the rent should be £1,250. His answer was: " I say, look at the two alternatives, look at such authorities as there are, and where market rent is implied they show that there must be something in the nature of an arbitration clause to fix a rent. Here there is nothing to justify implication of market rent." He said: " If the landlords want to get an increased rent, there must
G   be something in the lease clearly giving them the right to that advantage." My Lord has suggested that that might be improved upon in this way: clause 1 shows there must be at least £1,250 and there is no clear machinery for imposing a higher rent. Whichever way you look at it, I can see no justification whatever for accepting the alternative implied term which crystallises and fixes the rent for the residue of the 14 years at the £1,250.

The authorities upon which Mr. Jaques relied were, first, *King's Motors*
H   *(Oxford) Ltd.* v. *Lax* [1970] 1 W.L.R. 426. But that case, in my judgment, is wholly distinguishable and does not really assist at all. That was a case of an option to renew, and the exercise of the option could operate, if at all, only to create a contract. Valid contract it could not be, because an essential term—namely, the rent—was neither agreed nor ascertainable. That, in my judgment, poses an entirely different problem from that which arises where one starts with the premise that there is a subsisting lease which creates an estate in the land and with the premise that the court must imply some term, because it is conceded that rent is payable.

The second authority, *Foley* v. *Classique Coaches Ltd.* [1934] 2 K.B. 1,   A
in fact is relied upon by both sides. The landlords in the court below relied
upon it in support of implying a fair rent by analogy with what was there
implied, a reasonable price. But Mr. Jaques relies upon it because he
says it shows that one could only make an implication of that character
if assisted by the presence of an arbitration clause. It is fair to say that
if one looks only at the judgment of Maugham L.J. at p. 16, he did appear
to be relying substantially upon the arbitration clause in arriving at his   B
conclusion. But I do not think that is the true ratio of the case. Where you
have got an arbitration clause, then if you imply a term that there shall be
a reasonable price (as it was in that case) or a fair rent (as it would be in
this), any dispute as to what is reasonable or fair falls within the arbitration
clause; and, if you have not got one, it falls to be resolved by the court.
But, in my judgment, the presence or absence of an arbitration clause does
not matter. I would refer to a passage in the judgment of Scrutton L.J.
where, whilst it is true he referred to an arbitration clause, he put the   C
matter as one of general principle. He said, at p. 10:

> " In the present case the parties obviously believed they had a contract
> and they acted for three years as if they had; they had an arbitration
> clause which relates to the subject matter of the agreement as to the
> supply of petrol, and it seems to me that this arbitration clause applies
> to any failure to agree as to the price."—That is what it applies to.   D
> Then he goes on—" By analogy to the case of a tied house there is to
> be implied in this contract a term that the petrol shall be supplied at
> a reasonable price and shall be of reasonable quality. For these reasons I
> think the Lord Chief Justice was right in holding that there was an
> effective and enforceable contract, although as to the future no definite
> price had been agreed with regard to the petrol."

Then again, Greer L.J. said, at p. 11:   E

> " I think the words of Bowen L.J. in *The Moorcock* (1889) 14 P.D. 64, 68
> are clearly applicable to a case of this kind, and that in order to give
> effect to what both parties intended the court is justified in implying
> that in the absence of agreement as to price a reasonable price must
> be paid, and if the parties cannot agree as to what is a reasonable price
> then arbitration must take place."

So, again, one implies a term on general principles, and then only turns to   F
the arbitration clause to resolve any dispute arising upon the implied term.
     The third and last authority on which Mr. Jaques relied was *Kenilworth
Industrial Sites Ltd.* v. *E. C. Little & Co. Ltd.* [1974] 1 W.L.R. 1069, and
in particular a passage on p. 1071, where Megarry J. said:

> " First, the lease reserves no rent beyond the first five years. The
> question is not one of the landlord having an option to displace an   G
> agreed rent for the later years of the term. If no new rent is ever
> ascertained, then as a matter of obligation under the terms of the lease,
> no rent at all is reserved for the last 16 years of the term. Mr. Prince
> repudiated any idea that the tenant could remain rent free after the first
> five years, and accepted and asserted that the tenant must pay rent at
> the rate initially reserved, namely, £2,980 a year. This, however, is
> not what the lease says, and Mr. Prince had to rely upon a term to this   H
> effect being implied in the lease. Such a term, however, would be
> entirely contrary to the mechanism laid down by clause 5, and would
> have to be a term implied if, and only if, the landlord failed to operate
> clause 5 according to its tenor. There seem to me to be considerable
> difficulties in implying a conditional term of this kind."

But, of course, Megarry J. did not have before him the problem of whether
anything should be implied and, if so, what because there was a clause which

A   gave the landlord a right to require an increase in rent to be ascertained in accordance with certain prescribed machinery. The point in *Kenilworth's* case was that the landlord failed to serve notice to start that machinery working within the time prescribed. The question at issue was whether time was of the essence and he was therefore too late or not. The judge held that he was within time. Therefore, the machinery operated, and there was no necessity to imply anything, or room for doing so.

B   That case went to the Court of Appeal [1975] 1 W.L.R. 143, and it is unnecessary to refer to the judgments there except for one passage, where what I have just been saying is clearly pointed out by Megaw L.J. He said, at p. 146:

"But, says Mr. Prince, it is proper and necessary to imply into this lease the provision that if the landlord fails within the stated time to give the notice seeking agreement or arbitration then the rent which was
C   payable in the preceding period shall continue to be the rent to be paid during the succeeding five years. For myself, I am quite unable to see that there is any valid basis for implying such a term in this lease. It would, in my judgment, be inconsistent with the express provisions of clauses 1 and 5, whether read separately or together. Moreover, the provisions of the second proviso cannot, in my judgment, be ignored, and if they are not ignored there is no reason for implying such a term."

D   That was because the proviso said that the landlord was not to fail in the exercise of ascertainment of the new rent merely because he was out of time.
        Therefore, as it seems to me, the authorities do not assist Mr. Jaques. On the contrary, they are against him, because the nearest case to the present one is *Foley's* case [1934] 2 K.B. 1, where the court did imply a reasonable price, and did so, as I think, quite clearly without having to rely upon the arbitration clause. At all events, in my judgment, such a clause is not
E   essential. Therefore, one is left with the two alternatives which have been posed.
        Now, the court must imply a term in order to give business efficacy to the contract, and I ask myself: why should it choose the alternative which is inconsistent with the basis which the parties showed they contemplated, rather than the one that implements it? Really, Mr. Jaques is attempting by implied term to get himself back into the first submission, that of an
F   implied agreement fixing a rent in default of agreement, and his second argument produces the same futility. It is quite obvious from clause 1 that the parties intended that the rent should be increased if the premises appreciated in value, and none the less so although they used the words " if any." They clearly contemplated also, as it seems to me, that the rent should be increased to such amount as would be a fair rent for the premises excluding tenant's improvements. They failed to agree. There is a hiatus. As the
G   judge rightly held, that hiatus has to be filled by an implied term, and it seems to me quite obvious that one must imply the alternative which gives effect to that clearly expressed intention of the parties.
        In my judgment, therefore, the judge was right; and I would dismiss the appeal.

        GEOFFREY LANE L.J. I agree. Had this been a contract of sale or an
H   ordinary commercial contract of some sort, there would be a great deal to be said for the view that from the date of the first rent review in March 1973 the contract was void for uncertainty, the parties having failed to agree on a vital term of the contract. But here there is a subsisting estate, and a subsisting estate in land, the lease, which is to continue until 1982, 14 years from the date of the lease itself. It is conceded by the tenant that some rent must be paid in respect of these premises by the tenant, and therefore it follows that the court must imply something, some term which will enable a rent to be fixed.

Mr. Jaques, on behalf of the tenant, submits that on the face of the   A
agreement and upon the true construction of it, the landlords have failed to
stipulate for anything more than the original rent of £1,250 per annum, and
that therefore the court should fix that amount as the proper rent for the
next period. Mr. Jaques concedes that if that is the case, then upon the
further review which is due to take place in 1978, exactly the same thing will
happen and the tenant will be in the happy position of paying a rent for
the whole of the rest of the term which is well below the market value.
That is plainly a highly undesirable result on any view, because it would   B
mean in effect that the court would be implying an unfair rent. But, for
the reasons which have been set out by Goff L.J., that is not a tenable
construction of the terms of the lease.

The court should, if it can, give effect to the intention of the parties as
exhibited from the terms of the agreement itself. That intention was quite
clearly to fix at these moments of review a fair rent by agreement between
the parties, subject to the provisos which they set out.   C

In the absence of such agreement, the court, as is made quite clear from
the decision of this court in *Foley* v. *Classique Coaches Ltd.* [1934] 2 K.B. 1,
must try to produce the same effect for the parties. It seems to me that
the judge's order in this case produces precisely that desirable effect.

For those reasons, as well as those already advanced by Goff L.J., I too
would dismiss this appeal.

                                                                          D

BUCKLEY L.J. I agree. It appears to me that the introduction by
implication of a single word in the clause in the lease relating to the rent to
be payable solves the problem of this case; that is, the insertion of the word
" fair " between the words " such " and " rent." If some such implication
is not made, it seems to me that this would be a completely inoperative rent
review provision, because it is not to be expected that the tenant would agree
to an increase in the rent if the rent to be agreed was absolutely at large.   E
Clearly the parties contemplated that at the end of five years some adjustment
might be necessary to make the position with regard to the rent a fair one,
and the rent review provision with which we are concerned was inserted
in the lease to enable such an adjustment to be made. The suggestion that
upon the true construction of the clause it provides that the rent shall
continue to be at the rate of £1,250 a year unless the parties otherwise agree
would, in my opinion, render the provision entirely inoperative, because, as   F
I say, one could not expect the tenant voluntarily to agree to pay a higher
rent.

For the reasons which have been developed by Goff L.J. and Geoffrey
Lane L.J. in the judgments which they have delivered, I am in agreement
that this appeal should be dismissed, the judge having, I think, arrived at the
right conclusion.

                                                                          G

                                        Appeal dismissed with costs.

Solicitors: *Boxall & Boxall for R. Hancock & Sons, Callington; Scott,
Son & Chitty, Epsom.*

                                                        C. N.

                                                                          H

A

[HOUSE OF LORDS]

* SANTILLO . . . . PETITIONER

AND

SECRETARY OF STATE FOR THE

B   HOME DEPARTMENT . . . . . . RESPONDENT

1981 April 9   Lord Russell of Killowen, Lord Scarman
and Lord Bridge of Harwich

PETITION by the applicant for leave to appeal to the House of Lords
from the decision of the Court of Appeal in *Reg.* v. *Secretary of State*
C *for the Home Department, Ex parte Santillo* [1981] 2 W.L.R. 362.
The Appeal Committee dismissed the petition.

R. C. W.

D

[HOUSE OF LORDS]

* HARMAN . . . . PETITIONER

AND

HOME OFFICE . . . . RESPONDENT

E   1981 April 9   Lord Russell of Killowen, Lord Scarman
and Lord Bridge of Harwich

PETITION for leave to appeal to the House of Lords from the decision
of the Court of Appeal in *Home Office* v. *Harman* [1981] 2 W.L.R. 310.
The Appeal Committee allowed the petition.

F

R. C. W.

[COURT OF APPEAL]

G * GREAT ATLANTIC INSURANCE CO. *v.* HOME INSURANCE CO.

AND OTHERS

1981 Jan. 14, 15; 28   Templeman and Dunn L.JJ.

*Practice—Discovery—Privilege—Professional privilege—Communi-
cation between plaintiffs and legal advisers—Part of communi-
H   cation read by counsel in opening trial—No intention to waive
any privilege—Whether communication severable for purposes
of privilege—Whether privilege waived*

When preparing documents for trial the plaintiff's solicitors
disclosed a document which comprised the first two paragraphs
of a memorandum sent to the plaintiffs by American attorneys
in their capacity as legal advisers to the plaintiffs. The solicitors
regarded the remainder of the memorandum as privileged but
failed to make it clear that the memorandum contained

additional matter in respect of which privilege was claimed. **A**
In opening the trial counsel for the plaintiffs read the document
to the judge, unaware that it was incomplete and without any
intention of waiving any privilege. When later in the trial it
emerged that the document did not represent the whole of the
memorandum the third defendants applied for disclosure of
the additional matter. The judge ordered the plaintiffs to disclose the whole of the memorandum.

On appeal by the plaintiffs: —   **B**

Held, dismissing the appeal, that the whole of the memorandum, being a communication to the plaintiffs from their
legal advisers, was privileged (post, p. 534B); that the memorandum dealt with a single subject matter and so was not
capable of being divided into two separate and distinct memoranda; that, accordingly, privilege could not be waived as to
part and asserted as to the remainder (post, p. 536A–C); that the
deliberate introduction by the plaintiffs' counsel of part of the **C**
memorandum into the trial record effectively waived privilege
with regard to the whole memorandum (post, pp. 537H, 540E–F);
and that there was no discretion by which the court could
restore and enable the plaintiffs to assert privilege in respect
of the whole or part of the memorandum (post, pp. 540G—
541A).

Wilson v. *Northampton and Banbury Junction Railway
Co.* (1872) L.R. 14 Eq. 477; *Churton* v. *Frewen* (1865) 2 **D**
Drew & Sm. 390 and *Burnell* v. *British Transport Commission*
[1956] 1 Q.B. 187, C.A. applied.

Decision of Lloyd J. affirmed.

The following cases are referred to in the judgment of Templeman L.J.:

Anderson v. *Bank of British Colombia* (1876) 2 Ch.D. 644, C.A.
Ashburton (Lord) v. *Pape* [1913] 2 Ch. 469, C.A.   **E**
Belsham v. *Harrison* (1846) 15 L.J.Ch. 438; sub. nom. *Belcham* v. *Percival*
     7 L.T. O.S. 300.
Burnell v. *British Transport Commission* [1956] 1 Q.B. 187; [1956] 2 W.L.R.
     61; [1955] 3 All E.R. 822, C.A.
Butler v. *Board of Trade* [1971] Ch. 680; [1970] 3 W.L.R. 822; [1970] 3
     All E.R. 593.
Buttes Gas and Oil Co. v. *Hammer (No. 3)* [1980] 3 W.L.R. 668; [1980] 3 **F**
     All E.R. 475, C.A.
Causton v. *Mann Egerton (Johnsons) Ltd.* [1974] 1 W.L.R. 162; [1974] 1
     All E.R. 453, C.A.
Churton v. *Frewen* (1865) 2 Drew. & Sm. 390.
Doland (George) Ltd. v. *Blackburn Robson Coates & Co.* [1972] 1 W.L.R.
     1338; [1972] 3 All E.R. 959.
Goldstone v. *Williams, Deacon & Co.* [1899] 1 Ch. 47.
Griffiths v. *Evans* [1953] 1 W.L.R. 1424; [1953] 2 All E.R. 1364, C.A.   **G**
Lyell v. *Kennedy* (1884) 27 Ch.D. 1, C.A.
Macfarlan v. *Rolt* (1872) L.R. 14 Eq. 580.
Matthews v. *Munster* (1887) 20 Q.B.D. 141, C.A.
Minter v. *Priest* [1930] A.C. 558, H.L.(E.).
Nea Karteria Maritime Co. Ltd. v. *Atlantic & Great Lakes Steamship
     Corporation* (unreported), December 11, 1978, Mustill J.
Procter v. *Smiles* (1886) 55 L.J.Q.B. 527, C.A.   **H**
Wheeler v. *Le Marchant* (1881) 17 Ch.D. 675, C.A.
Wilson v. *Northampton and Banbury Junction Railway Co.* (1872) L.R.
     14 Eq. 477.

The following additional cases were cited in argument:

Cameron's Coalbrook, etc. Railway Co., In re The (1857) 25 Beav. 1.
Calcraft v. *Guest* [1898] 1 Q.B. 759, C.A.

A
Davis v. *Spurling* (1829) 1 Russ. & M. 64.
Humphery v. *Humphery and Wake* (1917) 33 T.L.R. 433.
Jones v. *Jones* [1970] 2 Q.B. 576; [1970] 3 W.L.R. 20; [1970] 3 All
E.R. 47, C.A.
Lodge v. *Prichard* (1851) 4 De G. & Sm. 587.
Prince v. *Samo* (1838) 7 Ad. & El. 627.
Randle v. *Blackburn* (1813) 5 Taunt. 245.

B
Reg. v. *Leverson* (1868) 11 Cox C.C. 152.
Waugh v. *British Railways Board* [1980] A.C. 521; [1979] 3 W.L.R. 150;
[1979] 2 All E.R. 1169, H.L.(E.).

INTERLOCUTORY APPEAL from Lloyd J.

In the course of the trial of an action by the plaintiffs, Great Atlantic
Insurance Co., the third defendants, C. E. Heath & Co. (International)
C Ltd., applied for the disclosure of certain plaintiffs' documents for which
the plaintiffs claimed privilege. On December 16, 1980, Lloyd J. ordered,
inter alia, that in respect of a memorandum dated May 2, 1980, and
entitled " Great Atlantic Insurance Co. Dispute with Elger " the entire
memorandum should be disclosed to the third defendants.

By notice of appeal dated December 19, 1980, the plaintiffs appealed
D on the grounds that (1) the judge was wrong in law to hold that the first
two paragraphs of the memorandum were privileged when in fact they
merely summarised and passed on information to the plaintiffs; (2) in
disclosing the first two paragraphs, neither the plaintiffs nor their legal
advisers were intending to waive privilege, nor did they do so; (3) at no
time did any competent officer of the plaintiffs authorise their legal
advisers to disclose any privileged document; (4) even if the first two
E paragraphs of the memorandum were privileged and such privilege had
been waived, there had been no waiver of privilege as to the remaining
part of the document which dealt with a separate and distinct subject
matter; and (5) in the circumstances in which the plaintiffs had disclosed
the first two paragraphs, no rule of the law of evidence or any requirement of fairness demanded that the whole document be disclosed.

F
The facts are stated in the judgment of Templeman L.J.
At the conclusion of the hearing of the appeal Templeman L.J.
announced that the appeal would be dismissed for reasons to be given
later.

Patrick Phillips Q.C. and *Paul Walker* for the plaintiffs.
Johan Steyn Q.C. and *Jeffrey Gruder* for the third defendants.

G
Cur. adv. vult.

January 28. TEMPLEMAN L.J. read the following judgment. This is
an appeal from an order made by Lloyd J. on the 14th day of a trial
which is still progressing whereby he ordered the plaintiffs to give
discovery of parts of a memorandum for which the plaintiffs claim
H privilege. In granting leave to appeal the judge made observations
deprecating any appeal in the course of a trial but he considered that
he was constrained in the exceptional circumstances to grant leave. I
agree wholeheartedly that appeals in the course of a trial should be
firmly prevented or discouraged save in the most exceptional circumstances. Such appeals cause difficulties for the litigants, for the trial
judge and for this court. In the present case, for example, this court
has been inevitably hampered, notwithstanding the assistance of experi-

enced counsel, by a necessarily brief and incomplete recital of the facts, A
some of which remain in dispute, and by the necessity for a speedy
resolution of this appeal. I intend no criticism. Indeed it is a credit
to all concerned that the plaintiffs' cause of action in a matter of great
complexity with large sums of money at stake only arose on June 11,
1980, and trial of the action began before Lloyd J. on November 24,
1980.

By an underwriting agency agreement dated June 2, 1977, the second B
defendants, Afia, authorised the third defendants, C. E. Heath & Co.
(International) Ltd., to enter into re-insurance agreements as agents for
and on behalf of the first defendants, Home Insurance Co. In November
1977, in exercise or in purported exercise of their authority, Heath entered
into an agreement with the plaintiffs, Great Atlantic Insurance Co., which
are insurers, and the fourth to eight defendants, which are companies C
carrying on marine insurance broking business under the inspiration of
Mr. Elger. The agreement of 1977 was replaced by a quota share marine
and aviation re-insurance agreement dated January 9, 1978, whereby
marine insurance sought by clients of, and negotiated by, Mr. Elger and
his companies would be accepted by the plaintiffs while Home would
re-insure to the extent of 90 per cent. of the risk. On March 29, 1978, D
Heath confirmed to the plaintiffs that the re-insurance agreement made
on January 9, 1978, was effective and was binding on Home by reason
of the authority vested in Heath by the underwriting agency agreement
dated June 2, 1977.

In 1980 the plaintiffs became worried about the results of insurance
business negotiated by Elger, accepted by the plaintiffs and re-insured
by Home. The plaintiffs sent out an insurance expert, a Mr. Alexander, E
to investigate Elger's business and he made a written report commenting
very adversely on the conduct and results of Elger's business. This report
is not a document for which privilege against disclosure in legal proceedings can be claimed by the plaintiffs or has been claimed by the plaintiffs.

About the same time as he made his report, Mr. Alexander orally
reported the results of his investigation and discussed the results of his F
visit to Elger's offices with a representative of the firm of American
attorneys who were acting for the plaintiffs as their lawyers. No privilege
can be claimed for what Mr. Alexander said to the American representative because litigation was not at the time in prospect in the present
proceedings: see *Wheeler* v. *Le Marchant* (1881) 17 Ch.D. 675. Heath
could for example subpoena Mr. Alexander and the American representative to give evidence of what was said between them. G

By a memorandum dated May 2, 1980, the American attorneys wrote
to the plaintiffs setting out in the first two paragraphs of that memorandum an account of the discussions between Mr. Alexander and the
representative of the American attorneys. The memorandum then continued with additional matter which, according to the sworn affidavit of
a partner in the plaintiffs' English firm of solicitors, dealt with " questions
of strategy affecting both the Elger and Marlow matters." For present H
purposes the " Marlow matters " need no explanation; they are connected
with the difficulties which had arisen over the Elger matters.

In this appeal the plaintiffs argue that the first two paragraphs of the
memorandum are not privileged because they are merely an account of a
discussion which was itself not privileged. They argue that the additional
matter was privileged. Heath claim that the whole of the memorandum

The Weekly Law Reports, April 24, 1981

533

1 W.L.R.   Gt. Atlantic Insurance v. Home Insurance (C.A.)   Templeman L.J.

A   was privileged and that the privilege has been waived in the circumstances which I shall shortly narrate and that Heath are entitled to see the whole of the memorandum including the additional matter for which privilege is asserted. The judge agreed with Heath.

In June 1980 Home and Afia repudiated the 1977 re-insurance agreement and also the substituted re-insurance agreement dated January 9, 1978. Home and Afia denied that Heath had authority to bind either
B   Home or Afia to the 1978 agreement. The plaintiffs in the present proceedings are seeking a declaration that both Home and Afia are bound by the 1977 and 1978 agreements. If the plaintiffs fail in any respect because Heath did not possess the necessary authority to bind Home and Afia, then in the same action the plaintiffs seek damages from Heath for breach of warranty of authority.

C   It is part of Heath's reamended defence that the plaintiffs connived with Home and Afia in connection with the repudiation by Home and Afia of the 1977 and 1978 re-insurance agreements. The report by Mr. Alexander and the memorandum from the plaintiffs' American attorneys dated May 2, 1980, are said to be relevant to this defence in that they support the plaintiffs' case as to the reason for a meeting held in London
D   in June 1980 between representatives of the plaintiffs and Afia at which it is said by Heath that the connivance between the plaintiffs and Home and Afia took place.

The plaintiffs' English solicitors intended to give discovery of the first two paragraphs of the memorandum dated May 2, 1980, and intended to claim privilege for the additional matter contained in that memorandum. The plaintiffs' solicitors did not intend and the plaintiffs did
E   not intend to waive any privilege in respect of any document. By mishap, no doubt due to the speed with which this litigation has been conducted, the plaintiffs' solicitors failed to claim privilege or to make clear that they were claiming privilege in respect of the additional matter contained in the memorandum. The plaintiffs' solicitors, however, only provided to the defendants and for use in the trial copies of the memorandum limited to
F   the first two paragraphs and excluded the additional matter for which privilege was intended to be claimed and is now claimed. In the result none of the defendants is aware of the contents and terms of the additional matter.

In the course of his opening speech in the first days of the trial which began on November 24, 1980, the plaintiffs' counsel read to the judge in open court the first two paragraphs of the memorandum dated May 2,
G   1980, which formed part of a bundle of agreed documents. At that stage the plaintiffs' counsel was not aware that the two paragraphs only represented part of the contents of the memorandum and he had no knowledge of the additional matter and he had no intention of waiving privilege in respect of the whole or part of the memorandum or any other privileged document.

H   A few days later the plaintiffs' counsel and Heath's counsel discovered that the memorandum as read to the judge was incomplete and did not include the additional matter which the plaintiffs' solicitors believed to be privileged and for which they intended to claim privilege. Heath's counsel on behalf of Heath asked for disclosure of the additional matter on the ground that part of a document having been put before the court by the plaintiffs, Heath were entitled to see the whole of the document whether or not that document had originally been privileged. The plain-

A

tiffs declined to disclose the additional matter in the memorandum on
the grounds that the first two paragraphs were not privileged and had
been disclosed for that reason, but that the additional matter was privileged and that privilege had not been waived. Lloyd J. decided in favour
of Heath, and ordered disclosure of the whole of the memorandum. With
leave of the judge, the plaintiffs appeal to this court.

B

The first question is whether the whole of the memorandum dated
May 2, 1980, was privileged or, as the plaintiffs' English solicitors thought,
the first two paragraphs were not privileged and therefore were bound
to be disclosed. In my judgment, the whole of the memorandum was
privileged because it was a communication by the plaintiffs' American
attorneys to the plaintiffs relating to a matter, namely the Elger matter,
upon which the American attorneys were instructed to act as legal
advisers to the plaintiffs. The fact that the memorandum included an

C

account of a conversation between Mr. Alexander and a representative
of the American attorneys, which conversation was not privileged, does
not alter the confidentiality attaching to the memorandum as a whole
by virtue of the relationship between the Amercian attorneys in their
capacity as legal advisers and the plaintiffs in their capacity as clients of
those legal advisers.

D

In *Anderson* v. *Bank of British Columbia* (1876) 2 Ch.D. 644,
658 Mellish L.J. drew a distinction between privileged communications
between solicitor and client and information which is obtained by a
solicitor from a third party, which information is not necessarily connected with litigation, is not obtained for the purpose of litigation and
is not privileged.

E

In *Wheeler* v. *Le Marchant,* 17 Ch.D. 675 this distinction was affirmed.
Sir George Jessel M.R., at p. 681, said that information obtained by
a solicitor from a third party was only protected where it had " come
into existence after litigation commenced or in contemplation . . ." But
the protection afforded to communications between a solicitor and his
client is wider. The protection is applied and is, said Sir George Jessel
M.R., at p. 682:

F

" . . . restricted to the obtaining the assistance of lawyers, as regards
the conduct of litigation or the rights to property. It has never gone
beyond the obtaining legal advice and assistance, and all things
reasonably necessary in the shape of communication to the legal
advisers are protected from production or discovery in order that
that legal advice may be obtained safely and sufficiently. . . . a

G

communication with a solicitor for the purpose of obtaining legal
advice is protected though it relates to a dealing which is not the
subject of litigation, provided it be a communication made to the
solicitor in that character and for that purpose. . . . It is a rule
established and maintained solely for the purpose of enabling a man
to obtain legal advice with safety."

H

Similarly Brett L.J. said, at p. 683:

" The rule as to the non-production of communications between
solicitor and client is a rule which has been established upon grounds
of general or public policy. It is confined entirely to communications
which take place for the purpose of obtaining legal advice from
professional persons."

The Weekly Law Reports, April 24, 1981

535

1 W.L.R.   Gt. Atlantic Insurance v. Home Insurance (C.A.)   Templeman L.J.

A   In *Minter* v. *Priest* [1930] A.C. 558 the House of Lords affirmed that a communication between solicitor and his client is privileged provided that the relationship of solicitor and client is established and that the communication is " such as, within a very wide and generous ambit of interpretation, must be fairly referable to the relationship . . . : " *per* Lord Buckmaster at p. 568.

B   The clearest authority relevant to the present point is to be found in *Wilson* v. *Northampton and Banbury Junction Railway Co.* (1872) L.R. 14 Eq. 477 where in a specific performance action the plaintiffs sought disclosure of inter alia correspondence between the defendants and their solicitors subsequent to the contract but previous to the commencement of litigation and before the litigation was in contemplation. Malins V.-C. said, at pp. 482–483:

C   " I think cases of this kind are better decided upon principle. Here is a contract entered into which has led to litigation, and how is it possible for anybody to point out the precise moment between the date of the contract and the filing of the bill when the dispute arose? . . . It is of the highest importance . . . that all communications between a solicitor and a client upon a subject which may
D   lead to litigation should be privileged, and I think the court is bound to consider that . . . almost any contract entered into between man and man . . . may lead to litigation before the contract is completed. Any correspondence passing between the date of the contract which afterwards becomes the subject of litigation and the litigation itself is, in my opinion, on principle, within the privilege extended to the non-production of communications between solicitors and clients . . .
E   it is absolutely essential to the interests of mankind that a person should be free to consult his solicitor upon anything which arises out of a contract which may lead to litigation; that the communications should be perfectly free, so that the client may write to the solicitor, and the solicitor to the client, without the slightest apprehension that those communications will be produced if litigation
F   should afterwards arise on the subject to which the correspondence relates."

Finally, at p. 484, Malins V.-C. repeated the principle:

    " . . . all correspondence between solicitors and clients relating to the subject matter of a contract which has been entered into, and which may lead to litigation—whether it has done so or may do so,
G   which may lead to litigation—whether it has done so or may do so, whether it is probable or improbable that it will do so—ought certainly to be privileged."

In the present case the correspondence between the American attorneys and the plaintiffs related to the Elger matter and to the re-insurance contract which had been entered into and which, as history
H   relates, have led to litigation. Such correspondence " ought certainly to be privileged."

In the present case the relationship of solicitor and client between the American attorneys and the plaintiffs is undoubted. The plaintiffs were seeking and the American attorneys were proffering advice in connection with a business transaction. The fact that litigation was not then contemplated is irrelevant. This appeal may serve a useful purpose

if it reminds the profession that all communications between solicitor   A
and client where the solicitor is acting as a solicitor are privileged subject
to exceptions to prevent fraud and crime and to protect the client and
that the privilege should only be waived with great caution. This principle
applies equally to communications between a client and his foreign
lawyers or attorneys: *Macfarlan* v. *Rolt* (1872) L.R. 14 Eq. 580.

The second question is whether, the whole of the memorandum being   B
a privileged communication between legal adviser and client, the plaintiffs may waive the privilege with regard to the first two paragraphs of
the memorandum but assert privilege over the additional matter. In my
judgment, severance would be possible if the memorandum dealt with
entirely different subject matters or different incidents and could in effect
be divided into two separate memoranda each dealing with a separate
subject matter. The judge, with the experience of 14 days of the trial   C
and after reading the whole of the memorandum, came to the conclusion
that the first two paragraphs of the memorandum and the additional matter
dealt with the same subject matter. Knowing far less about the circumstances, I would be slow to come to a different conclusion. Having
read the whole memorandum, I agree with him. Indeed the affidavit
of Mr. Williams, of the plaintiffs' English solicitors, makes this plain.
                                                                          D
Mr. Phillips who appeared for the plaintiffs argued that severance is
permissible where the part disclosed is only an account of a discussion
which itself is not privileged. But once it is decided that the memorandum
deals with only one subject matter, it seems to me that it might be or
appear dangerous or misleading to allow the plaintiffs to disclose part
of the memorandum and to assert privilege over the remainder. In the
present case the suspicions of Heath which have not unnaturally been   E
aroused by the disclosure of only part of the memorandum can only be
justified or allayed by disclosing the whole. It would be undesirable for
severance to be allowed in these circumstances. In my judgment, the
simplest, safest and most straightforward rule is that if a document is
privileged then privilege must be asserted, if at all, to the whole document
unless the document deals with separate subject matters so that the document can in effect be divided into two separate and distinct documents   F
each of which is complete.

Support for this simple method of dealing with the matter is to be
found in *Churton* v. *Frewen* (1865) 2 Drew. & Sm. 390. In that case a
privileged report contained copies of, extracts from and references to
documents and records which had been culled from a public registry
and for which no privilege could be asserted. The plaintiffs sought   G
discovery of so much of the report as consisted of " copies or extracts
from or references to documents or records in the Bishop's Registry at
Lewes . . ." Disclosure was refused on the grounds, stated at p. 394:

"... it would be very dangerous, and trench very much upon the
principle which protects the report itself, if that were permitted;
for it would be hardly possible to seal up and effectually protect   H
from inspection those parts which constitute the report, and which
it is admitted there is no right to see. Such a report would most
probably (indeed, from its nature, almost necessarily) be not merely
a collection of extracts from, and copies of ancient records, with a
distinct and separate report referring to them; but the extracts and
copies would be so interspersed with . . . observations and comments
. . . as to render it quite impossible to separate the different portions."

The Weekly Law Reports, April 24, 1981

537

1 W.L.R.   Gt. Atlantic Insurance v. Home Insurance (C.A.)   Templeman L.J.

A   It is true that in the present case the first two paragraphs can be divided from the remainder of the memorandum but they deal with the same subject matter. Waiver of part of a document is bound to lead to grave difficulties for all parties and to many unjustified suspicions.

Mr. Phillips relied on *Belsham* v. *Harrison* (1846) 15 L.J. Ch. 438, reported under the name of *Belcham* v. *Percival* in 7 L.T. O.S. 300. In that case the personal representative of a deceased defendant filed a
B   defence referring to a draft answer prepared for the deceased and setting out parts of the contents of the draft answer. The plaintiffs were refused disclosure of the whole of the draft answer. No reasons were given for the decision which may be bound up with the niceties of pleading. I derive no assistance from this case. Mr. Phillips referred to *Lyell* v. *Kennedy* (1884) 27 Ch.D. 1, 24 and to *Buttes Gas and Oil Co.*
C   v. *Hammer* (*No. 3*) [1980] 3 W.L.R. 668, 683, 687–688, 703 but these citations do not assist him to show that where a document refers to one subject matter privilege may be waived with regard to part of that document and asserted with regard to the remainder.

The third question is whether privilege in respect of the memorandum dated May 2, 1980, was in fact waived by or on behalf of the plaintiffs.
D   Neither the plaintiffs nor any of the plaintiffs' legal advisers intended to waive any privilege. The plaintiffs' English solicitor intended to disclose the first two paragraphs of the memorandum which he wrongly but excusably considered must be disclosed. The plaintiffs' counsel, who read the memorandum in open court, did not know that the memorandum which he read was an incomplete part of a document. The plaintiffs in so far as they were in attendance by their directors and officers knew
E   nothing of what was going on. The plaintiffs and all their legal advisers never intended to waive any privilege.

The plaintiffs' legal advisers introduced and intended to introduce before the judge in open court during the trial a document which proved to be part of the memorandum. It is true that the plaintiffs now say that the first two paragraphs of the memorandum are of no
F   assistance to them and of no harm to the defendants and could have been omitted and would have been omitted if they had realised that they were introducing part of a privileged document. But the plaintiffs' legal advisers did not read the first two paragraphs of the memorandum as a result of a mistake induced by any of the defendants, and it is difficult to see how the mistake which the plaintiffs did make could fairly be rectified after the first two paragraphs of the memorandum had been
G   read to the judge.

In interlocutory proceedings and before trial it is possible to allow a party who discloses a document or part of a document by mistake to correct the error in certain circumstances. Where a document has been disclosed as a result of misconduct by the defendants, against the will of the plaintiffs and in any event not by the deliberate act of the plaintiffs,
H   then remedial action both before and during the trial may be possible. But in my judgment the plaintiffs deliberately chose to read part of a document which dealt with one subject matter to the trial judge, and must disclose the whole. The deliberate introduction by the plaintiffs of part of the memorandum into the trial record as a result of a mistake made by the plaintiffs waives privilege with regard to the whole document. I can see no principle whereby the court could claim to exercise or could

fairly and effectively exercise any discretion designed to put the clock   A
back and to undo what has been done.

In *Burnell* v. *British Transport Commission* [1956] 1 Q.B. 187 counsel
for the defendant cross-examining a witness put to the witness certain
observations made by the witness in a written statement. Denning L.J.
said, at p. 190:

> "... although this statement may well have been privileged from   B
> production and discovery in the hands of [the defendants] at one
> stage, nevertheless when it was used by cross-examining counsel in
> this way, he waived the privilege, certainly for that part which was
> used; and in a case of this kind, if the privilege is waived as to the
> part, it must, I think, be waived also as to the whole. It would be
> most unfair that cross-examining counsel should use part of the
> document which was to his advantage and not allow anyone, not   C
> even the judge or the opposing counsel, a sight of the rest of the
> document, much of which might have been against him."

In *George Doland Ltd.* v. *Blackburn, Robson Coates & Co.* [1972]
1 W.L.R. 1338 the deliberate waiver of privilege of certain communications between solicitor and client relating to two particular subject
matters before litigation became pending or contemplated involved   D
waiver of any other communications relating to those two subject matters
but did not involve waiver of the further privilege which applied to
documents which were brought into existence after litigation was pending or contemplated. In *Nea Karteria Maritime Co. Ltd.* v. *Atlantic and
Great Lakes Steamship Corporation* (unreported) decided by Mustill J.
on December 11, 1978, Mustill J. succinctly summarised the position as   E
follows:

> "I believe that the principle underlying the rule of practice exem-
> plified by *Burnell* v. *British Transport Commission* is that where a
> party is deploying in court material which would otherwise be privi-
> leged, the opposite party and the court must have an opportunity
> of satisfying themselves that what the party has chosen to release   F
> from privilege represents the whole of the material relevant to the
> issue in question. To allow an individual item to be plucked out of
> context would be to risk injustice through its real weight or meaning
> being misunderstood. In my view, the same principle can be seen
> at work in *George Doland Ltd.* v. *Blackburn, Robson Coates & Co.*
> in a rather different context."

I agree and would only add that it would not be satisfactory for the   G
court to decide that part of a privileged document can be introduced
without waiving privilege with regard to the other part in the absence
of informed argument to the contrary, and there can be no informed
argument without the disclosure which would make argument unnecessary.

Mr. Phillips attempted to distinguish the decisions in *Burnell* v.
British Transport Commission [1956] 1 Q.B. 187 and *George Doland*   H
Ltd. v. *Blackburn Robson Coates & Co.* [1972] 1 W.L.R. 1338 on the
ground that it was necessary in those cases for the whole statement to
be disclosed in order that the consistency of the testimony of a witness
could be scrutinised. In my judgment, however, the rule that privilege
relating to a document which deals with one subject matter cannot be
waived as to part and asserted as to the remainder is based on the
possibility that any use of part of a document may be unfair or mis-

The Weekly Law Reports, April 24, 1981

539

1 W.L.R.   Gt. Atlantic Insurance v. Home Insurance (C.A.)   Templeman L.J.

A leading, that the party who possesses the document is clearly not the person who can decide whether a partial disclosure is misleading or not, nor can the judge decide without hearing argument, nor can he hear argument unless the document is disclosed as a whole to the other side. Once disclosure has taken place by introducing part of the document into evidence or using it in court it cannot be erased.

B The fourth question is whether the introduction of the memorandum into the trial record by the plaintiffs' counsel was effective to waive the privilege which belonged to the plaintiffs personally and which the plaintiffs did not wish to waive.

The general principle is that " a solicitor is the agent of his client in all matters that may reasonably be expected to arise for decision in the cause:" *per* Denning L.J. in *Griffiths* v. *Evans* [1953] 2 All E.R.
C 1365, 1371. In *Matthews* v. *Munster* (1887) 20 Q.B.D. 141 the defendant's counsel in the absence of the defendant and without his express authority in open court consented to a verdict for the plaintiff for £350 and costs and agreed that all imputations should be withdrawn against the plaintiff. This settlement was held to be a matter within the apparent general authority of counsel and was binding on the defendant. Lord Esher
D M.R. said, at p. 143:

"But when the client has requested counsel to act as his advocate
. . . he thereby represents to the other side that counsel is to act for him in the usual course, and he must be bound by that representation so long as it continues, so that a secret withdrawal of authority unknown to the other side would not affect the apparent
E authority of counsel. The request does not mean that counsel is to act in any other character than that of advocate or to do any other act than such as an advocate usually does. The duty of counsel is to advise his client out of court and to act for him in court, and until his authority is withdrawn he has, with regard to all matters that properly relate to the conduct of the case, unlimited power to do that which is best for his client. I apprehend that it is not
F contended that this power cannot be controlled by the court. It is clear that it can be, for the power is exercised in matters which are before the court, and carried on under its supervision. If, therefore, counsel were to conduct a cause in such a manner that an unjust advantage would be given to the other side, or to act under a mistake in such a way as to produce some injustice, the court has authority
G to overrule the action of the advocate."

The provisions of the last paragraph of Lord Esher M.R.'s judgment do not avail the plaintiffs in the present case because the action of the plaintiffs' counsel in disclosing part of the memorandum in open court cannot be overruled. What is done is done.

To this general rule, there is, according to Mr. Phillips, an exception
H in the case of waiver because the privilege belongs to the client and not to the solicitor. For this proposition he cited *Procter* v. *Smiles* (1886) 55 L.J.Q.B. 527 and other authorities which establish that a solicitor in an action to which a client is not a party or in which the solicitor is not representing a client cannot waive the client's privilege. In *Procter* v. *Smiles* the client was not a party to the action and did not confer any express or implied authority on the solicitor to waive privilege. The solicitor was a defendant to a libel action and pleaded justification. The

solicitor objected to answering certain interrogatories administered by A
the plaintiffs on the ground that the answers would involve the solicitor
in disclosing information of a confidential nature procured by the solicitor
as solicitor for a third party for the purpose of litigation pending or
threatened against that third party. Lord Esher M.R. refused to order
the solicitor to disclose the privileged information notwithstanding that
the solicitor might already have disclosed part. Different considerations B
apply in the present case in which as in *Matthews* v. *Munster,* 20 Q.B.D.
141 the plaintiffs who are entitled to the privilege have instructed solicitors
and counsel to represent them for all the purposes of the action and are
bound by the decisions made by their legal advisers within the scope
of their ostensible authority including authority to conduct the case in
such manner as they think in the interests of the clients, involving
decisions as to waiver of privilege and other matters connected with the C
proceedings.

In *Causton* v. *Mann Egerton (Johnsons) Ltd.* [1974] 1 W.L.R. 162
Lord Denning M.R. in a dissenting judgment held that the defendant's
solicitors had entered into a binding agreement with the plaintiff's
solicitors for the exchange of certain medical reports including medical
reports for which the defendant could claim privilege. This agreement D
amounted to waiver of privilege and came within the authority of the
solicitor to conduct litigation on behalf of his client. Stamp and Roskill
L.JJ. decided that there was no agreement. In the absence of such an
agreement it was not necessary for them to express and they reserved
their views on the question of whether a waiver can be affected by a
solicitor without the authority of his client. In my judgment this
authority does not assist the plaintiffs in the present case. It certainly E
does not establish the principle for which Mr. Phillips contends, that
the waiver of privilege is an exception to the general rule that the legal
advisers of a client have ostensible authority to bind him in any matter
which arises in or is incidental to litigation. In my judgment when
counsel in the course of a trial introduces into the record a document
or part of a document he thereby effectively waives any privilege attach- F
ing to that document which could otherwise be asserted by his client.

That proposition is supported by *Goldstone* v. *Williams, Deacon &
Co.* [1899] 1 Ch. 47 to which Dunn L.J. referred in the course of
argument. Stirling J. said, at p. 52:

"It has been decided that notes of proceedings in open court . . .
are, as a rule, not privileged, but must be produced. . . . on the G
ground . . . that the administration of justice in this country is a
matter of public interest, and to be conducted (again as a general
rule) in public, and, consequently, that there can be nothing privileged or confidential which passes in open court."

The fifth question is whether there is any general or special discretion
equitable or otherwise which will enable the court in this instance to H
restore and enable the plaintiffs to assert privilege in respect of the
whole of the memorandum or in respect of that part which has not
been introduced in evidence so far. In the instant case Lloyd J. decided
that if there was such a discretion it would not be proper for him to exercise
it in favour of the plaintiffs. The experienced judge who, as I have said,
had already endured 14 days of the trial and who had read the whole
of the memorandum decided that this was not a case in which he should

The Weekly Law Reports, May 1, 1981

541

1 W.L.R.   Gt. Atlantic Insurance v. Home Insurance (C.A.)   Templeman L.J.

A exercise any discretion vested in him. There being no grounds for saying that the judge did not properly consider the exercise of his discretion, this court will not interfere.

In any event I am not persuaded that any discretion exists. Mr. Phillips relied on *Lord Ashburton* v. *Pape* [1913] 2 Ch. 469. The court granted an injunction to restrain the use of stolen privileged documents.
B A man who is entitled to assert privilege over a document does not waive that privilege by suffering the misfortune of the theft of those documents from his custody or from the custody of his solicitor. In *Butler* v. *Board of Trade* [1971] Ch. 680 the Board of Trade through the Official Receiver obtained a copy of a letter written by the plaintiff's solicitor to the Official Solicitor in connection with the affairs of a company which subsequently went into compulsory liquidation. The Board of Trade were therefore
C innocent recipients of privileged information. Goff J. was of the opinion that the principles to be found in *Lord Ashburton* v. *Pape* [1913] 2 Ch. 469 applied not only where documents were stolen but where documents were innocently conveyed in breach of confidence. He nevertheless held, at p. 690:

D "... it would not be a right or permissible exercise of the equitable jurisdiction in confidence to make a declaration at the suit of the accused in a public prosecution in effect restraining the Crown from adducing admissible evidence relevant to the crime with which he is charged."

. These two authorities have no relevance to the present case. The court has no jurisdiction to relieve the plaintiffs from the consequences
E of their own mistakes particularly as those consequences cannot be wholly eradicated; part of the memorandum has in fact been read to the trial judge.

For these reasons I would dismiss the appeal.

DUNN L.J. I entirely agree with the judgment of Templeman L.J.
F and have nothing to add.

Appeal dismissed with costs.

Solicitors: *McKenna & Co.; Ince & Co.*

C. N.

G

H

A

* HOWARD v. DEPARTMENT FOR NATIONAL SAVINGS

1980   Oct. 13, 14   Lord Denning M.R., Ackner
                                                   and Griffiths L.JJ.

B

*Employment—Unfair dismissal—Excluded classes—Normal retiring
age—Civil servant—Minimum retirement age of 50—Discretionary retention beyond minimum age—Civil servants usually
allowed to complete 20 years' service—Civil servants in one
department dismissed if 60 or over—Whether claim for unfair
dismissal excluded—Trade Union and Labour Relations Act
1974 (c. 52), Sch. 1, para. 10 (b)*

C

The employee was a district commissioner employed by
the Department for National Savings. As a district commissioner he ranked as a higher executive officer in the Civil
Service and the employment was subject to the rules now
contained in the Civil Service Pay and Conditions of Service
Code. The rules, which were subject to review, provided
that the minimum age of retirement was between 60 and 65
and, although retention beyond 60 was discretionary, the
intention was that civil servants should be allowed to stay until
they had achieved 20 years' service or reached 65, subject to
fitness. The Civil Service support for the voluntary savings
movement was to be withdrawn on March 31, 1978, and the
plans for the civil servants in the department were either
their transfer to other work or retirement. The employee
came within the category of those who were to be retired
and he was given 12 months' notice that his employment
would terminate on March 31, 1978, when he would be 61 and
have completed 19 years' service. The employee applied to
an industrial tribunal for compensation for unfair dismissal.
The tribunal held that he was excluded from bringing the
complaint under paragraph 10 (b) of Schedule 1 to the Trade
Union and Labour Relations Act 1974 [1] because he had
attained the age of 60 which was the normal retiring age in the
undertaking in which he was employed for an employee
holding the position which he held.

D

E

F

The Employment Appeal Tribunal dismissed his appeal,
holding that because it was permissible for the department not
to extend the period of employment of officers aged 60 and
over the industrial tribunal had been entitled to conclude that
the normal retiring age was 60. —

On appeal by the employee: —

G

Held, dismissing the appeal, that the normal retiring age of
an employee was to be found by looking at the provisions of
his contract of employment, express or implied, and it was the
age at which it was specified that he could be compulsorily
retired, even though he might be retained thereafter by mutual
agreement; that, in the present case, the employee's normal
retiring age was 60 and, accordingly, he was precluded from
bringing a claim for unfair dismissal.

H

Dictum of Lawton L.J. in *Nothman* v. *Barnet London
Borough Council* [1978] I.C.R. 336, 346, C.A. applied.

Department of Health and Social Security v. *Randalls*
[1981] I.C.R. 100, E.A.T. considered.

Decision of the Employment Appeal Tribunal [1979] I.C.R.
584 affirmed.

[1] Trade Union and Labour Relations Act 1974, Sch. 1, para. 10: see post, p.
544F–G.

The Weekly Law Reports, May 1, 1981

543

1 W.L.R.   Howard v. Dept. National Savings (C.A.)

A   The following cases are referred to in the judgments:

Department of Health and Social Security v. Randalls [1981] I.C.R. 100, E.A.T.

Nothman v. Barnet London Borough Council [1978] 1 W.L.R. 220; [1978] I.C.R. 336; [1978] 1 All E.R. 1243, C.A.; [1979] 1 W.L.R. 67; [1979] I.C.R. 111; [1979] 1 All E.R. 142, H.L.(E.).

Post Office v. Wallser (unreported), July 3, 1980; Court of Appeal (Civil
B   Division) Transcript No. 556 of 1980, C.A.

No additional cases were cited in argument.

APPEAL from the Employment Appeal Tribunal.

The employee, Ronald James Clarke Howard, appealed from a decision
C   of the Employment Appeal Tribunal (Slynn J., Mr. M. L. Clement-Jones
and Mr. J. D. Hughes) given on March 23, 1979, upholding the decision of
an industrial tribunal that he had no right to claim compensation for
unfair dismissal against his employer, the Department for National
Savings, by reason of the fact that he had attained the normal retiring
age for an employee holding the position that he held as an officer of
the National Savings Committee before the effective date of termination
D   of his employment. The grounds of the appeal were (1) that the Employment Appeal Tribunal had misdirected themselves in holding that the
normal retiring age in the employee's employment was 60 and in reaching
that conclusion had failed to take sufficient cognisance of the effect of
provisions of the Civil Service Pay and Conditions of Service Code which
provided that, subject to fitness, a civil servant should be retained until
E   he had completed 20 years' reckonable service or reached 65 and that
officers with short service generally had special claims to retention; (ii)
the fact that the employee had not completed 20 years' service or reached
65; (iii) the fact that the rules of the code were mandatory so that, by
implication, they were minimum rules which could be improved upon but
not diluted; and (2) that upon a true construction of " normal retiring
age " within the meaning of paragraph 10 (b) of Schedule 1 to the Trade
F   Union and Labour Relations Act 1974 and of the contractual provisions
relating to retirement applicable to the employee the Employment Appeal
Tribunal had erred in holding that there was a normal retiring age for
an employee holding the position held by the employee and that that
age was 60.

The facts are stated in the judgment of Lord Denning M.R.

G
Alexander Irvine Q.C. and Elizabeth Slade for the employee.
Simon D. Brown and David Blunt for the department.

LORD DENNING M.R. This case will be of interest to those in the Civil
Service—and elsewhere—who are approaching retirement age. Unlike me!
To understand it, you must realise that, under the statute, when you are
H   compulsorily retired, you are to be regarded as having been dismissed by
your employers. The question of compensation depends on whether or not
there is a normal retiring age for a man in your position. If there is a
normal retiring age—let us say at 60—and you stay on at work afterwards
—say till 63—you cannot claim for unfair dismissal. But if there is no
normal retiring age, you can claim up till the age of 65.

The contest in this case is whether there was a normal retiring age for
Mr. Howard. He held a position with the National Savings Committee for

The Weekly Law Reports, May 1, 1981

544

Lord Denning M.R.   Howard v. Dept. National Savings (C.A.)   [1981]

many years. His rank was said to be rather equivalent to that of a higher A
executive officer in the Civil Service. He was compulsorily retired at the
age of 61¾—that is 3¼ years short of 65. He claimed that, in the circumstances, it was equivalent to an unfair dismissal. But the department say
that he cannot claim at all: because the normal retiring age for a man in
his position is 60. That is the whole question in the case. Was the normal
retiring age for a man in his position age 60? In which case he cannot
claim. Or was there no normal retiring age for a man in his position? In B
which case he can claim. That is the question. It has come before the
industrial tribunal and before the Employment Appeal Tribunal, each of
which held that the normal retiring age for Mr. Howard was 60. And so
each held that he cannot claim. Now there is an appeal to this court.

First, I will give Mr. Howard's dates. He was born on July 2, 1916. He
joined the Civil Service on January 5, 1959, when he was 42. He was C
appointed to the National Savings Committee. In 1977 the department in
which he was employed virtually closed down. He was then 61 years of age.
Steps were taken to transfer as many employees as possible to other departments. But, so far as employees aged 60 or over were concerned—and Mr.
Howard was one of them—they were given notice that their employment
would be determined in March 1978. This is the letter to him of March 15, D
1977:

> "It is with regret that I write to advise you that, because of the
> Government's decision to withdraw Civil Service support staff from
> the Voluntary Savings Movement, it will not be possible to retain
> mobile grades over the age of 60 beyond March 31, 1978. There will
> however be employment for you up to this date but I now give you 12
> months' formal notice that your appointment will be terminated on E
> grounds of redundancy on March 31, 1978, which will be regarded as
> your last day of service."

That was the notice terminating his employment. He claims compensation
for unfair dismissal. But he cannot succeed if the normal retiring age was
60, even though he went on working afterwards.

F

The Statute and regulations

The right to compensation for unfair dismissal is given by paragraph 4
of Schedule 1 to the Trade Union and Labour Relations Act 1974. But
paragraph 10 provides:

> ". . . paragraph 4 above does not apply to the dismissal of an employee
> from any employment if the employee . . . (b) on or before the effective G
> date of termination attained the age which, in the undertaking in
> which he was employed, was the normal retiring age for an employee
> holding the position which he held, or, if a man, attained the age of 65,
> or, if a woman, attained the age of 60."

The question is, what was the normal retiring age for a person holding the H
position which Mr. Howard held?

The Civil Service generally

So far as the Civil Service generally is concerned, there are provisions
dating back to 1952 which say that a person can be compulsorily retired
at the age of 60. Thereafter he may be kept on but it is a matter entirely
within the discretion of the head of the department. The " minimum "

The Weekly Law Reports, May 1, 1981

545

1 W.L.R.   Howard v. Dept. National Savings (C.A.)   Lord Denning M.R.

A   retiring age—as it is put—is age 60 in the Civil Service as a whole: but a man can be retained afterwards at the discretion of the head of the department.

But there is a provision—which would apply to people like Mr. Howard —who had not completed a full 20 years' service. At the time Mr. Howard left, he had only served 19¾ years. I will read from the general Civil Service provisions, the Civil Service Pay and Conditions of Service Code, B   paragraph 10442:

> " Any officer who has not completed 20 years' reckonable service on reaching age 60 should, provided he is fit, efficient and willing to remain in service, be allowed to continue until he has completed 20 years' reckonable service or has reached age 65, whichever is the earlier . . ."

C
The word " should " has been canvassed before us. It was suggested that it means " must." I do not agree. I think it means should normally be allowed. It still leaves the compulsory retirement age at 60—with a potential extension.

Mr. Howard's department
D
So far as Mr. Howard's department is concerned, there was a special provision about retirement. It was introduced in 1970. It contemplated that several officers should be called upon to retire at the age of 60. But there was to be an exception under paragraph 7 (c) of that document. This exception is very much relied upon by Mr. Howard. It was:

> " Subject to reasonable efficiency and physical capacity any officer who E   would have less than 20 years' reckoned service to his credit at age 60 will be allowed to stay on until he has completed 20 years or reached age 65 whichever is the earlier."

At the age of 60 Mr. Howard had not completed 20 years' service at all. He had only served about 17 years. The department agree that that provision did apply to him in 1970: and that, at that time, if he had served F   less than 20 years, he would have been allowed to stay on until he had completed 20 years' service. But it is important to notice that, in the 1970 statement of retirement policy, there is an overriding clause. It is clause 13, which says: " All the above arrangements are subject to review from time to time as occasion may require and are specifically subject to alteration if general Civil Service rules make that necessary."

G   Some years later it was necessary to review the arrangement. It was necessary by the year 1977. In that year a different policy was adopted whereby the staff of the National Savings Committee were to be withdrawn and placed elsewhere. So in 1977 an amendment was made. By circular 44/77 dated March 10, 1977, it was announced:

> " In the new situation created by the decision to withdraw the staff of the National Savings Committees by March 31, 1978, officers of the H   N.S.C.'s with the dispensation provided in the D.N.S. Agreement of 1970 will by that date:— . . . having reached age 60 (including those who are already 60) be allowed to continue in D.N.S. employment up to March 31, 1978 . . ."

What was the effect of this policy change? Did it mean that there was a return to the compulsory retirement age of 60 with an allowable extension to March 31, 1978? Or, as Mr. Irvine has contended before us this morning,

does it do away with the normal retiring age of 60 for people like Mr. A
Howard? In which case, it would mean that there was no normal retiring
age.

The law

It remains to consider the law on the matter, particularly the meaning
of " normal retiring age." There are several authorities about it. In the
early days Sir John Donaldson, when he was sitting in the National Indus- B
trial Relations Court, suggested that " normal retiring age" means the
usual age at which men retired. That has now been held to be incorrect. It
was departed from in this court in *Nothman* v. *Barnet London Borough
Council* [1978] 1 W.L.R. 220, affirmed by the majority in the House of
Lords [1979] 1 W.L.R. 67. The contest there was whether there was a
fixed age of retirement for both men and women at the age of 65, or C
whether there was no normal retiring age. The evidence showed that
teachers up and down the country retired at varying times between ages
55 and 65. So you could not find any " usual " retiring age. It was
held by this court and by the House of Lords that the normal retiring
age was that which was fixed by the conditions of the contract. Lord
Salmon said [1979] 1 W.L.R. 67, 72:
                                                                          D
> ". . . that paragraph sets up two different upper age limits for basically
> different classes of people, one for those who have a normal retiring
> age fixed by their conditions of service and the other for those who do
> not."

Then the next question arises. What is the position when, as in many
cases, there is an age at which a person *can* be retired compulsorily accord- E
ing to their contract, but which can be departed from at the discretion of
the head of the department? For instance, a circuit judge can be retired
compulsorily at age 72, but he may be allowed to stay on for another year
or two. In *Nothman's* case Lawton L.J. said [1978] 1 W.L.R. 220, 229:

> " It follows that the normal retiring age of teachers employed by the
> council is the age at which they would have to retire unless their
> service was extended by mutual agreement."   F

That one sentence places stress on the age at which they would have to
retire under their contract, unless their service was extended by mutual
agreement.

That observation was applied by this court last July in *Post Office* v.
Wallser (unreported), July 3, 1980; Court of Appeal (Civil Division) G
Transcript No. 556 of 1980. The contract with the Post Office said:
" Officers may be compulsorily retired on age grounds at or after the age
of 60." That was a term of the contract. It was held that 60 was the normal
retiring age. Evidence was brought before this court that a lot of people
did not retire at the age of 60 in the Post Office. Hardly any people were
retired compulsorily at the age of 60 from the years 1975 to 1978. Many
were allowed to stay on some years longer. The court held that that H
evidence did not affect the position. People could be compulsorily retired
at age 60. So 60 was the normal retiring age.

I find some of the observations in the judgments difficult to follow.
Lawton L.J. said: ". . . the concept of a normal retiring age does not
depend exclusively, or indeed at all, on the terms of a contract." Bridge
L.J. said that the normal retiring age is not necessarily to be discovered
in the contract of employment.

The Weekly Law Reports, May 1, 1981

547

1 W.L.R.   Howard v. Dept. National Savings (C.A.)   Lord Denning M.R.

A   It seems to me that those observations only apply when there is no term in the contract fixing the time of retirement. As I read the authorities, the normal retiring age is to be found by looking at the provisions of the contract. If they specify an age at which the man can be compulsorily retired, that is the normal retiring age: even though he may be retained thereafter by mutual arrangement. It would be the same if there was no express term in the contract: but it was imported by custom and practice that a man

B   could be compulsorily retired, say, at age 60.

But when there is nothing of that kind—nothing in the contract, or in custom and practice—then there is no " normal retiring age " at all. You revert to the statutory age, 65 for men, 60 for women.

This ruling brings certainty into the law. It is fair enough. If a man is being retired at the age at which he can be compulsorily retired, he ought

C   not to be able to complain of unfair dismissal. He is being retired at the allotted age which he understood when he entered the employment. In the same way as a circuit judge can be dismissed at the age of 72: or he may be allowed to stay on. But, if he is dismissed at the age of 72, he cannot claim for unfair dismissal. That seems to me to be the underlying notion of the statute.

D   We have had before us a very interesting and important judgment by the Employment Appeal Tribunal in a case which seems to be of general application throughout the Civil Service, *Department of Health and Social Security* v. *Randalls* [1981] I.C.R. 100. It was only given on July 4, 1980: but the same point arises now. In that case Slynn J. put it quite succinctly in a passage which I should like to read, at p. 108:

E   " Nor does the fact, relied upon by the employee, that many civil servants may be kept on beyond 60, affect the position. It will be very relevant to the question: what is the usual age of retirement? That is not now the test and it seems to us that the matter must, as we have said, be approached on the basis of the conditions of his employment. It is only if the conditions themselves do not make the position clear

F   that it might be necessary to look to what happens in practice to see whether a condition of service is to be implied or has been established by conduct and practice over the years."

The appeal tribunal go on to say that they were satisfied that the normal retiring age appropriate to the employee was age 60. That goes back to what I said in the very first part of this judgment: that, in the

G   Civil Service, the minimum retiring age from the year 1952 has been 60. That is the age at which he could be compulsorily retired. Even though in many cases that is extended, it still remains the compulsory retiring age. Therefore, on the authorities, it is the normal retiring age. In the latest provision, paragraph 10442, as I have indicated, the word " should " ought not to be read as altering the fact that the normal retiring age is the age of 60.

H   Those are the general Civil Service provisions. They do not directly arise in this case. We are only concerned with one particular department, the National Savings Committee. For the reasons which I have given, it seems to me that the normal retiring age at the time when Mr. Howard retired—that is, from 1976 onwards—was 60.

I would therefore uphold the decision of the tribunal and dismiss the appeal.

The Weekly Law Reports, May 1, 1981

548

Howard v. Dept. National Savings (C.A.) [1981]

ACKNER L.J. *Nothman* v. *Barnet London Borough Council* [1979] A
1 W.L.R. 220 decides that "normal retiring age" does not mean the
usual or average retiring age as had previously been thought to be the case.
The question to ask is: at what age would an employee have to retire unless
his service was extended by mutual agreement?

It was submitted by Mr. Irvine, in his powerful address to us, that in
Nothman's case the contract came automatically to an end on the retiring
age, but that here the contract does not come to an end at 60, but con- B
tinues. Therefore there was no need for there to be any extension by
mutual agreement when Mr. Howard reached the age of 60. However—on
the basis that the *Nothman* test is correct, and I must so treat it—that is
too artificial a distinction. In a case where the contract, unlike the *Nothman*
contract, does not come to an end specifically on the age intended to be
the retiring age, one asks the question: when would he have to retire if C
the employers so wished? This means, perhaps surprisingly, that often the
normal retiring age is the minimum retiring age in the sense that it is the
earliest date at which there is a contractual liability to retire, even though
in practice it may be that the vast majority of employees holding the
relevant position retire much later.

In order to apply the Nothman test, it seems to me that you must look D
at the conditions of service (see in particular the speech of Lord Salmon
cited by Lord Denning M.R.); because, if the employee does not have to
retire at a given date, then there is no normal retiring age. The conditions
of service may of course not be only in writing; the contract may be partly
oral, partly in writing or wholly oral. Moreover, terms may have to be
implied by reason, for instance, of a custom, or by virtue of some long-
standing practice. But I too, like Lord Denning M.R., am puzzled by E
the observations made by this court, to which he has made reference, in
Post Office v. *Wallser* (unreported), July 3, 1980.

Mr. Simon Brown submits that, if a normal retiring age cannot be found
in the contract, then there is no normal retiring age. On the basis of the
authority of *Nothman's* case I accept his submission, and I too would
therefore dismiss this appeal for the reasons given by Lord Denning M.R. F
as well as for the reasons which I have set out above.

GRIFFITHS L.J. I agree that the normal retirement age must be ascertained by looking at the terms of the contract of service whether they be
express or implied. If this matter were free from authority, I doubt if I
should have construed "normal retiring age" as the minimum retiring age
in the sense of it being the earliest age at which an employer could impose G
compulsory retirement.

Suppose a contract provided both a minimum and a maximum retiring
age, and the fact was that employees were in practice kept on until the
maximum retiring age, why should not the maximum retiring age in those
circumstances be considered to be the normal retiring age? It appears to
me that ordinary use of language would drive one to the conclusion that the H
maximum retiring age was in such a case the normal retiring age.
If against this practice, one employee finds himself singled out for compulsory retirement at the minimum retiring age, I can well understand him
having a real sense of grievance and believing that he has been unfairly
dismissed. Furthermore—although perhaps it is a somewhat unlikely contingency—Mr. Irvine points out that such a construction would enable an
unscrupulous employer to evade the protection given to employees in the

The Weekly Law Reports, May 1, 1981

549

1 W.L.R.   Howard v. Dept. National Savings (C.A.)

A Act by inserting in the contract of service a wholly unrealistic minimum compulsory age of retirement.

The matter is not, however, free from authority. In *Nothman* v. *Barnet London Borough Council* [1979] 1 W.L.R. 220 the normal retiring age was construed as the age at which an employee must retire if required to do so, and that decision was followed by this court in *Post Office* v. *Wallser* (unreported), July 3, 1980. *Nothman* v. *Barnet London Borough Council* can be distinguished on its facts from this case because there the contract provided for a fixed date of retirement, but I can find no such distinguishing feature in *Post Office* v. *Wallser*; and I regard those two authorities of this court as conclusive on the main point which arises in this appeal.

C I agree that the narrow construction of circular 44/77 advanced by Mr. Irvine is not the correct one; and for the reasons given on that point by Lord Denning M.R., I agree that this appeal must be dismissed.

> *Appeal dismissed with costs not to be enforced without leave of the court.*
> *Leave to appeal.*

D

Solicitors: *Simmonds Church Rackham; Treasury Solicitor.*

R. C. W.

E

[COURT OF APPEAL]

* JOYCE *v.* YEOMANS

[1973 J. No. 6042]

F

1980 Dec. 4, 5, 8, 9   Waller, Brandon L.JJ. and
                                                Sir David Cairns

Evidence—Expert evidence—Appellate court—Conflict of opinion between medical experts at trial—Judge preferring opinion of one expert—Extent of appellate court's powers of review

G *Damages—Earnings, loss of—Future earnings—Boy injured in accident—Future earning capacity impaired—Approach to assessment of damages*

Some months after an accident for which the defendant was responsible, the plaintiff, who was aged nine at the time and who sustained a head injury, a rupture of the spleen and a fracture of the clavicle, began to suffer epileptic seizures which continued when he went to grammar school, to the detriment of his performance there and future employment prospects. At the trial, on quantum of damages only, of the plaintiff's action against the defendant, there was a difference of opinion between Dr. E, the medical expert who gave evidence for the defendant, who thought that the plaintiff had had a predisposition to epilepsy whose advent was merely accelerated by the accident, and the two experts called by the plaintiff, who considered that the seizures were caused solely by the accident. Thompson J. preferred the evidence

H

of Dr. E, and awarded general damages of £7,500 with **A**
interest, without appropriating sums to particular heads of
damage.

On the plaintiff's appeal on the grounds that the judge had
erred in preferring the evidence of Dr. E to that of the
plaintiff's experts, and that the figure for general damages was
too low having regard to the effect of the injury on the
plaintiff's earning capacity: —

Held, (1) that even in the case of evidence given by experts, **B**
the trial judge, who had observed the demeanour of the witnesses, was in a significantly better position than an appellate
court to assess the value of the evidence given, and accordingly the appellate court should be slow to interfere with the
judge's findings, although not to the same extent as where
evidence had been given by witnesses of fact; and since there
were ample grounds for the judge's findings, and nothing to
indicate that he had adopted a wrong approach, his con- **C**
clusion that Dr. E's evidence was to be preferred should not
be disturbed (post, pp. 553E–F, 554B–C, 556G–H, 557E–F, G–H).

Stojalowski v. *Imperial Smelting Corporation (N.S.C.)
Ltd.* (1976) 121 S.J. 118, C.A. distinguished.

(2) That (*per* Waller L.J. and Sir David Cairns) in a case
such as the present where, in regard to damages for loss of
earning capacity, there were many imponderables and the **D**
assessment of the damages was necessarily a matter of guesswork, it was inappropriate to apply a multiplier and multiplicand and make a mathematical calculation, and the correct
approach was to select a global figure which seemed to represent fair compensation (post, pp. 555A, 556A–B, 558C).

Per Brandon LJ. While a court is not bound to arrive at
a multiplier and multiplicand in a case of this kind in order
to assess the damages, it would not be erring in law if it **E**
attempted to do so. If that method is adopted, however, then
the court should take a very careful look at the ultimate
result in the round in order to see whether it seems a sensible
figure in general terms (post, p. 557B–C).

(3) Allowing the appeal, that the judge's overall figure of
£7,500 could not have included a sufficient sum for loss of
future earning capacity, and there would be substituted sums **F**
of £6,000, with interest, for pain and suffering, loss of amenity,
embarrassment from the attacks of epilepsy and the physical
injuries, and £7,500, without interest, for loss of earning
capacity (post, pp. 555H, 556B–D, 558A–B, C).

Clarke v. *Rotax Aircraft Equipment Ltd.* [1975] 1 W.L.R.
1570, C.A. applied.

Order of Thompson J. varied.

G

The following cases are referred to in the judgments:

Clarke v. *Rotax Aircraft Equipment Ltd.* [1975] 1 W.L.R. 1570; [1975]
 I.C.R. 440; [1975] 3 All E.R. 794, C.A.
Stojalowski v. *Imperial Smelting Corporation (N.S.C.) Ltd.* (1976) 121
 S.J. 118, C.A.
Watt (or Thomas) v. *Thomas* [1947] A.C. 484; [1947] 1 All E.R. 582,
 H.L.(Sc.).   **H**

The following additional cases were cited in argument:

Moeliker v. *A. Reyrolle & Co. Ltd.* [1977] 1 W.L.R. 132; [1976] I.C.R.
 253; [1977] 1 All E.R. 9, C.A.
Pickett v. *British Rail Engineering Ltd.* [1980] A.C. 136; [1978] 3 W.L.R.
 955; [1979] 1 All E.R. 774, H.L.(E.).
Smith v. *Manchester Corporation* (1974) 17 K.I.R. 1, C.A.

A   APPEAL from Thompson J.

By a writ dated June 9, 1973, the plaintiff, Michael Joyce, an infant
suing by Michael Joyce his father and next friend, claimed from the
defendant, Derek Yeomans, damages for injury, loss and damage caused
by the defendant's negligent driving of his car. Liability having been
admitted, Thompson J. awarded £7,500 general damages. The plaintiff
B   appealed, on the grounds (1) that the judge misdirected himself in, and
failed to give any or any sufficient reason for, preferring the evidence of
the medical expert called by the defendant to that of the two experts
called by the plaintiff, and the decision was against the weight of the
evidence, and (2) that the amount awarded by way of general damages
was manifestly inadequate by reason of the effect of the plaintiff's injuries
on his education and the consequent loss of earning capacity.

C   The facts are stated in the judgment of Waller L.J.

Roger Titheridge Q.C. and *Maura Logan* for the plaintiff.
Richard Clegg Q.C. and *Michael Brompton* for the defendant.

WALLER L.J. This is an appeal from a decision of Thompson J. given
D   on July 5, 1979, when he awarded £7,500 to the plaintiff. The plaintiff was
a boy who was born in 1963 who had a serious accident in February
1973, when he was a few months short of his tenth birthday. The accident
happened when he was watching the snow in the evening, and a car
skidded into a garden, causing him a head injury, some six inches in
length, a rupture of the spleen and a fracture of the clavicle, and he was
in hospital for only a few weeks. He recovered at that stage well, but he
E   did complain of some dizzy spells. By October 1973 he was getting visual
disturbance and hallucinations, and in February 1974 an electroencephalograph revealed a focal abnormality of a temporal lobe, and temporal lobe
epilepsy was diagnosed.

At that stage the plaintiff was about to start at grammar school, and
he did start at grammar school in September 1974 when he was 11 years
F   of age. The attacks that he was having then were such that he was put on
to phenobarbitone, and during the first three years that he was at grammar
school, his general performance and behaviour were poor to bad. During
that period, he had four or five grand mal attacks, and in 1975 there was
another electroencephalograph which confirmed an earlier one, although
later there were two others which showed no abnormality.

G   In February 1975 he was seen by Dr. Evans. There was a claim
against the defendant at this time, and Dr. Evans was asked to examine
the boy and make a report, and he did so in February 1975. His conclusion was that the plaintiff was suffering from epilepsy. He said in his
report:

"It seems that since the accident Michael has developed attacks of
H   minor epilepsy which arise, in all probability, from an epileptic focus
in the posterior temple region of the brain. It is unlikely, in my
opinion, that the epileptic focus was due to the head injury that
occurred in the accident in question. In all probability the epileptic
focus has been present since birth and the head injury in question had
the effect of bringing out epileptic attacks which would, in any case,
have developed in the next few years . . ."

and he thought that that would have been probably before the age of 14.

The contrary view was expressed in July 1975 by Dr. Gordon who, having described the epileptic seizures, said:

"As they have only occurred since the accident, and as I was unable to obtain any history of a possible cause prior to the accident, I feel it must be presumed that the minor seizures have resulted from the head injury."

There was then an exchange of reports, but neither doctor accepted the view of the other.

At the trial, evidence was given by Dr. Evans for the defendant, and by Dr. Neary and Dr. McKinlay for the plaintiff. Dr. Neary was called into the case at a late stage because Dr. Liversedge, who appears to have been the best qualified medical witness of the plaintiff, had unfortunately died. Thompson J. accepted the evidence of Dr. Evans. He said:

"Dr. Evans is in the minority amongst the doctors whose opinions I have before me. Nonetheless, I accept his view as correct. What the accident did in the case of the plaintiff was, in my judgment, to bring on attacks of epilepsy earlier than, had there been no accident, they would have been likely to manifest themselves."

Mr. Titheridge on behalf of the plaintiff has submitted that the judge was wrong in preferring the evidence of Dr. Evans. He submitted, in a very persuasive argument, that Dr. Evans in the course of his evidence had said that in his experience one third to one half of his patients who had temporal lobe epilepsy did not have a history of any disturbance or occurrence at birth or before the epilepsy started. Therefore, Mr. Titheridge submitted, when considering this case, at the most it was only an even chance that there was some previous pre-disposing factor and that accordingly there was insufficient evidence to upset what he submitted was the primary inference that the epilepsy was caused by the accident. He further submitted that in cross-examination Dr. Evans agreed that it was one of the factors which he took into consideration which could have happened without a pre-disposing cause. He submitted that this was a case in which the judge's finding of fact could be interfered with.

As I have said, Dr. Evans, a consultant neurologist and a Fellow of the Royal College of Physicians, expressed the view quoted above at the beginning. He told the defendant's solicitors to send his opinion to those representing the plaintiff because he thought that they might agree it. They did not. The plaintiff then went to Dr. Liversedge, another consultant neurologist and a Fellow of the Royal College of Physicians, and he said in his report, expressing the view that this was probably a result of the accident:

". . . it is extremely difficult to support the view that his epilepsy was in any way constitutional and I would be inclined to agree with the opinion expressed by Dr. Gordon that these attacks are post-traumatic, particularly in view of the focal abnormality on the electro-encephalograph. In short, therefore, I would disagree with Dr. Evans' conclusions. This is clearly a very important case and for this reason I think we must carry out one of the new E.M.I. scans, which will be most helpful in establishing the presence or the absence of any focal change due to trauma."

A   So an E.M.I. scan was done, and it was negative. Dr. Liversedge said that that was encouragement for the future but did not alter his opinion, but one cannot help having the impression that Dr. Liversedge thought that the E.M.I. scan would be decisive in his favour.

At the trial, as I have already said, Dr. Neary gave evidence instead of Dr. Liversedge, and Dr. Evans also gave evidence. I think that I should quote just one or two of Dr. Evans's answers because it is his evidence that
B   is being attacked. Dealing with the E.M.I. scan, in answer to the judge's question: " You would expect it to be shown in the temporal region if there had been brain damage caused by the accident?" he said " That is what I mean, yes." And so he was attaching some importance to that particular factor. He also said that he would expect post-traumatic amnesia of more than 24 hours as being the kind of factor he was looking
C   for if it was to be attributed to the accident; and in this case the post-traumatic amnesia was said to be 12 to 24 hours.

He also said that he would have looked for a history of complications, such as a depressed fracture or a blood clot or, he said, " a history of epilepsy within seven days of the impact, but none of those arose." He thought that the symptoms of post-traumatic epilepsy should have developed earlier than in fact they did. He said that about 50 per cent.
D   of patients developed this within 12 months, and he was apparently excluding such symptoms as appeared within 11 months in this case. He also relied on the head injury as not being the kind of head injury which he would expect to cause temporal lobe epilepsy. He agreed, as I have already said, that each one of those things might not have happened with epilepsy caused directly by the accident, but he was relying on all of
E   them.

Mr. Titheridge sought to rely on *Stojalowski* v. *Imperial Smelting Corporation (N.S.C.) Ltd.* (1976) 121 S.J. 118 where this court reversed the view of a medical witness which had been formed by the judge. The abbreviated report is accurate so far as it goes, but a perusal of the transcript reveals a totally different situation from the present case in
F   that there were a number of factors in the case which were impossible to reconcile with the evidence of the witness.

The demeanour of a medical expert giving evidence is probably not so important as other witnesses of fact when the value of his evidence is being assessed, but in my opinion the observations of Lord Thankerton in the well known case of *Watt (or Thomas)* v. *Thomas* [1947] A.C. 484, 487, where he was considering the position of an appellate court when
G   dealing with a finding of fact by the judge, should be borne in mind. He set out two principles which I will quote:

" I.   Where a question of fact has been tried by a judge without a jury, and there is no question of misdirection of himself by the judge, an appellate court which is disposed to come to a different conclusion on the printed evidence, should not do so unless it is
H   satisfied that any advantage enjoyed by the trial judge by reason of having seen and heard the witnesses, could not be sufficient to explain or justify the trial judge's conclusion; . . . III.   The appellate court, either because the reasons given by the trial judge are not satisfactory, or because it unmistakably so appears from the evidence, may be satisfied that he has not taken proper advantage of his having seen and heard the witnesses, and the matter will then become at large for the appellate court."

In this case the judge had three medical witnesses of high qualifica- A
tions. There was no question of other credible witnesses giving evidence
contradicting the facts on which the experts gave their opinion. There was
no dispute about the basic facts, and on those basic facts two different
opinions were expressed. I do not know how the judge made his decision,
but the care with which Dr. Evans examined the facts and the opinions
which he expressed about them were very much matters for the trial
judge. I can only say that reading the reports, the view of Dr. Evans is B
more convincingly put forward. Furthermore, it seems reasonably clear
that Dr. Liversedge expected the E.M.I. scan to confirm his view, but it
did not.

In his evidence, Dr. Evans explained in detail how he arrived at his
opinion, and having heard the argument of Mr. Titheridge and having
read all the evidence relevant to this issue, I see no reason to fault the C
finding of the judge. Dr. Evans had obviously given careful consideration
to his view and to the contrary view, and there were ample grounds on
which he could so find. Accordingly, this ground of appeal fails.

The second ground of appeal by Mr. Titheridge is against the amount
of damages awarded. The judge awarded £7,500 on a total award covering the head injury, the loss of the spleen, the fractured clavicle and the
accelerated onset of epilepsy. It also covered the injury to the plaintiff's D
earning capacity.

It was submitted on behalf of the plaintiff that the judge's figure was
inadequate and did not truly reflect the damage suffered by the plaintiff.
On the basis of the evidence of Dr. Evans, the plaintiff was someone who
would probably suffer from temporal lobe epilepsy and in any event it
would most likely occur in his teens—that is to say at 14 or 15. It might E
not happen at all but that was very unlikely. As a result of the accident
the plaintiff had epilepsy starting at the age of 10 and the attacks were
very much worse and more frequent than they would otherwise have been.
There were, as I have already mentioned, four or five grand mal attacks
which, the evidence was, would have been unlikely had it not been for
the accident. F

The effect of the attacks on the plaintiff's education was serious.
He missed a number of days at each of his first three years at grammar
school: 20 per cent. of the days in the first year, 16 per cent. of the days
in the second year and 10 per cent. of the days in the third year. His
behaviour was not good. He was difficult and troublesome. He had
done well in his 11-plus examination and might have done quite well at
grammar school, but probably not up to university standard. G

The effect of the epilepsy was such that he could not pass any O levels.
Dr. Evans, in his report, described it in this way: " The emotional
problems of settling into a grammar school where the standards are high
and the competition is greater " were factors that had disturbed the
plaintiff's behaviour. Those problems were aggravated by the loss of time
on account of fits and the fact that the plaintiff was receiving pheno- H
barbitone, which in itself has the effect of causing behavioural disturbances in children. Those difficulties continued until the end of 1976. At
the time of the hearing he had not had any fits for about six months and
had no behavioural disturbance whatsoever and was settling in well at his
new job.

In evidence, in answer to the judge, Dr. Evans said: " A substantial
part of his failure in grammar school can be laid at the door of his

A epilepsy." Then later he said that was true to a considerable extent. He explained that he thought that the falling off of the plaintiff's behaviour between his primary school and grammar school was largely attributable to the epilepsy.

I agree with the judge that the assessment of damage is an exercise in guesswork. The judge assessed the damage at £7,500 but he did not divide that figure between pain and suffering and loss of amenity on the one hand, and injury to earning capacity on the other. He awarded, with the consent of Mr. Russell for the defendant, interest on the whole figure.

Mr. Titheridge submitted on behalf of the plaintiff that the figure of £7,500 was such that there was very little margin for injury to earning capacity. The plaintiff's injuries consisted of the ruptured spleen, the removal of which, it is said, does not do any harm, but nevertheless the cases show that a figure in the region of £1,500 or £2,000 would not be excessive for this alone; the fractured clavicle, which would add a little, but not very much to that figure; and the onset of epilepsy which would probably have occurred one day but might not, and which was worse in its effect than it would otherwise have been. When all these matters are taken into account, the total figure must be getting near the £7,500 mark, leaving therefore a very small margin for injury to earning capacity.

Mr. Titheridge has submitted that the injury to earning capacity should be calculated on a multiplier/multiplicand basis and he suggested figures of very considerable size. He submitted that the average weekly earnings should be a basis, and arrived at a weekly loss of very considerable sums.

I agree with Mr. Clegg that the multiplier/multiplicand basis is inappropriate in a case of this sort, although I do not accept his submission that the figure could properly be contained in the balance of the figure which the judge found. The plaintiff has, in my opinion, sustained a very real and substantial injury to his earning capacity by reason of the onset of epilepsy just as he was starting at grammar school; his education has been seriously interfered with. Instead of being a boy with three, four, or even five O levels but not quite good enough to go to university, he has no O levels at all. Instead of being a boy with a remote chance of never having epilepsy, he has had it in a serious form and in any event sooner than he otherwise would.

In the doctor's view he was always, with that remote exception, going to be ineligible for those jobs which bar an epileptic—the police, which he favoured, jobs involving moving machinery, and so on. On the other hand, he has lost the educational advantages which might well have helped to minimise the limitations imposed on a known epileptic. He may be able to do something to repair that loss by adult education—but that is a possibility, not a probability.

In my opinion, the figure which should be awarded for this is, with great respect to the judge, much greater than could be contained in the margin to which I referred earlier. I would therefore consider separately the two figures.

In my judgment a fair figure for the pain and suffering, loss of amenity and the general embarrassment resulting from the earlier and more serious attacks of epilepsy, and the loss of the spleen and the fractured clavicle which I have already mentioned, would be £6,000. The injury to his earning capacity resulting from the serious educational loss is, as I have already said, a serious one and should include something for being deprived of the remote chance of never having epilepsy at all. A

I have already said that I do not accept the multiplier/multiplicand method of calculation. There are so many imponderables. For example, how long will the plaintiff live? What job will he in fact get? What sort of job would he have got if he had had the epilepsy later in his life? All of those are capable of a wide variety of answers.

I therefore would assess a figure which in my judgment would properly compensate the plaintiff for all those matters, and the figure I would award would be one of £7,500 for this part of the damage. Having regard to the decision of this court in *Clarke* v. *Rotax Aircraft Equipment Ltd.* [1975] 1 W.L.R. 1570, this figure for loss of earning capacity is in the same situation as damages for loss of future earnings, and does not carry interest.

I would therefore allow this appeal and substitute for the figure of C £7,500 with interest (which was accepted by the defendant in the court below), a figure of £6,000, together with interest, and a further £7,500 without interest, up to the date of judgment.

BRANDON L.J. I agree that the appeal should be allowed and that damages should be awarded in accordance with the judgment which Waller L.J. has just given. D

The appeal raises two questions of some general importance. The first question is the extent to which it is legitimate for an appellate court to interfere with the findings of fact of a trial judge based upon the evidence of expert witnesses—in this case, medical expert witnesses.

It has been suggested in argument, and there is some support for the suggestion derived from *Stojalowski* v. *Imperial Smelting Corporation* E *(N.S.C.) Ltd.* (1976) 121 S.J. 118, that, where expert witnesses are concerned, the trial judge has no significant advantage over an appellate court in forming a correct judgment between conflicting views. I do not think that that authority goes, or was intended to go, as far as that.

In my judgment, even when dealing with expert witnesses, a trial judge has an advantage over an appellate court in assessing the value, the F reliability and the impressiveness of the evidence given by experts called on either side. There are various aspects of such evidence in respect of which the trial judge can get the " feeling " of a case in a way in which an appellate court, reading the transcript, cannot. Sometimes expert witnesses display signs of partisanship in a witness box or lack of objectivity. This may or may not be obvious from the transcript, yet it may be quite plain to the trial judge. Sometimes an expert witness may refuse to make G what a more wise witness would make, namely, proper concessions to the viewpoint of the other side. Here again this may or may not be apparent from the transcript, although plain to the trial judge. I mention only two aspects of the matter, but there are others.

I do not think that the authorities on the right of an appellate court to interfere with the findings of fact of a trial judge based on witnesses of H simple fact are entirely applicable to cases where the finding is based on expert evidence, but I certainly would not go to the other extreme and say that the trial judge has no advantage over an appellate court because the witnesses are expert. I think he has certain advantages—not perhaps so great as those applicable where witnesses are witnesses of fact, but nevertheless significant advantages which an appellate court ought not to ignore.

A   The second matter of general interest is whether and to what extent in a case of this kind the loss of future earning capacity should be calculated on some kind of mathematical basis, that is to say by taking a multiplier and multiplicand. Waller L.J. has expressed the view that, on the facts of this particular case, any attempt to arrive at a figure for damages on a basis of a multiplier and a multiplicand would be inappropriate because of the very great number of imponderables which exist.

B   I feel it right to express my view that, while a court is not bound to arrive at a multiplier and a multiplicand in a case of this kind in order to assess the damages, it would not be erring in law if it attempted to do so. The basis for finding a multiplicand is slender but judges are often faced with having to make findings of fact on evidence which is slender and much less convincing than would be desirable. Therefore it seems
C   to me to be open to the court to approach the problem by putting a figure upon the loss of earning capacity on a weekly or annual basis and applying a multiplier to that figure. I do however think that, if that method is adopted, then the court should take a very careful look at the ultimate result in the round in order to see whether it seems a sensible figure in general terms or not.

D   In this case, having approached the matter perhaps from a slightly different angle from that of Waller L.J., I nevertheless agree entirely with the figure of £7,500 at which he has arrived by a more general approach.

        SIR DAVID CAIRNS. I agree that this appeal should be allowed and that the judgment should be varied in the manner indicated by Waller L.J.
        On the issue as to whether the head injury resulting from the accident
E   was the cause of epilepsy in a boy who up to the time of the accident had no tendency to epilepsy, or was rather the agent activating a latent epilepsy which would probably have become active without any such injury within the next few years, I am of opinion that Thompson J. was entitled to prefer the evidence of Dr. Evans to that of other medical witnesses, and that no sufficient reason is shown why we should reverse his finding.

F   I do not consider that anything that was said in *Stojalowski* v. *Imperial Smelting Corporation (N.S.C.) Ltd.* (1976) 121 S.J. 118 meant, or was intended to mean, that the court of appeal is in every case in as good a position as the trial judge to assess the value of an expert evidence given before him. It is clear from what Waller L.J. has said in his judgment today, that that was not the intention. If I had thought that it was so intended at the time when the judgments were delivered in the *Stojalowski*
G   case, I should have expressed my dissent from it, though recognising that the other two members of the court had far greater experience than I had had in evaluating oral evidence of doctors.
        In *Stojalowski* the effect of a whole body of written and oral evidence was such as to convince the court that the evidence of a witness whom the judge had accepted as reliable was in fact untrue. In the present case,
H   the evidence seems to me to be very finely balanced. Dr. Evans expressed his opinion firmly and gave several reasons for it. I do not accept the submission made in this court that his reasons were demolished in cross-examination. The transcript of the opposing evidence has not convinced me that the judge was wrong in his finding on that matter, and in the circumstance I am of opinion that that finding cannot be disturbed.
        I am, however, satisfied that the judge must have under-estimated the effect on the plaintiff's prospects, of the interference with his education

by the occurrence of epilepsy when it did occur. The effects, other than **A** those which relate to earnings, of the injuries that he had—the initial pain and suffering, the probability that epileptic fits were more frequent and more severe than they would have been if the epilepsy had become active later, the possibility that it would never have become active, and the probable loss of some pleasure in his employment as well as loss of earnings, must be regarded as represented by most of the £7,500 award. I do not think that left to myself I would have attributed as much as £6,000 **B** to those other elements, but I do not feel strongly enough about that matter to dissent from that assessment.

If then only £1,500 out of the £7,500 is to be considered as representing loss of earning capacity, I am satisfied that despite all the uncertainties of the case, that figure is substantially too small.

I do not find it useful in this case to make any attempt to work out a **C** multiplier and a multiplicand. I regard it as essentially a case in which the best approach is that of going straight to estimating in the round what the figure should be and I agree that that figure should be £7,500.

I further agree, following *Clarke* v. *Rotax Aircraft Equipment Ltd.* [1975] 1 W.L.R. 1570, that the interest, while payable on the £6,000, is not payable on the £7,500.

D

> *Appeal allowed.*
> *Judge's order varied.*
> *Leave to appeal refused.*

Solicitors: *Lickfolds, Wiley & Powles for Taylor, Hindle & Rhodes, Manchester; James Chapman & Co., Manchester.*

E

[Reported by MICHAEL HAWKINGS, ESQ., Barrister-at-Law]

F

[CHANCERY DIVISION]

* CICUTTI *v.* SUFFOLK COUNTY COUNCIL

[1979 C. No. 8715]

1980 July 22; 25   **G**
                                    Sir Robert Megarry V.-C.

Education—Students' grants—Overseas students—Student entering United Kingdom to attend school—Student forming intention to remain in United Kingdom—Application to education authority for award for university course—Whether " ordinarily resident" in United Kingdom—Education Act 1962 (10 & 11 Eliz. 2, c. 12), s. 1 (1) (a)—Local Education Authority Awards Regulations 1979 (S.I. 1979 No. 889), reg. 13 (a)

H

An Italian student was sent by his parents in 1969 at the age of 10 to a boarding school in England as they wished him to be educated in this country. By October 1976, he had formed an intention to live and work in England and at some stage he applied for naturalisation. During the next three years he remained in England except for one summer holiday and three Christmas holidays spent in Italy. He applied to

A   the local education authority for an award for the purpose
of reading history at a university. In June 1979, the authority
refused him an award on the ground that he did not fulfil
the ordinary residence qualifications in their area, required
by section 1 of the Education Act 1962,[1] and in the United
Kingdom, required by regulation 13 of the Local Education
Authority Awards Regulations 1979.[2] The student sought a
declaration that he was entitled to such an award.

B   On the question whether the student's presence in the
local education authority's area and in the United Kingdom
for the required three year period had the quality necessary
to make him " ordinarily resident " within the meaning of the
two statutory provisions: —

     Held, that, since " ordinarily resident " within the mean-
ing of section 1 (1) (*a*) of the Education Act 1962 and regulation 13 of the Local Education Authority Awards Regu-

C   lations 1979 meant a person who resided in the country for
a general purpose as opposed to one who resided here only
for a specific or limited purpose, a local education authority
had to ascertain the reason for a person coming to this
country and his intention in coming and remaining here; that
although a person might come to this country for a specific
or limited purpose, he was not precluded from changing his
intention provided his intention at the time the award was

D   made (and by regulation 13, during the three year period
preceding the course for which the award was sought) was
an intention to remain for the general purpose of living here;
that providing the intention was genuine it did not have to
be supported by physical indicia such as a home or bank
account in this country or severance from a previous residence
abroad, especially when it was the family home, although
the sojourn in this country had to be of sufficient length and

E   continuity to show the quality of ordinariness in the residence;
that accordingly, since the student throughout the material
three year period had lived, and had a genuine intention to
remain, in the United Kingdom and had been acting in
accordance with that intention, he was ordinarily resident for
the purposes of the statutory provisions and entitled to an
award (post, pp. 563G–H—564A–B, 565A–D, E–H, 566F–H).

     Reg. v. *Barnet London Borough Council, Ex parte Nilish*
F   *Shah* [1981] 2 W.L.R. 86, D.C. applied.

The following cases are referred to in the judgment:

Clarke v. *Insurance Office of Australia Ltd.* [1965] 1 Lloyd's Rep. 308.
Cunliffe v. *Goodman* [1950] 2 K.B. 237; [1950] 1 All E.R. 720, C.A.
Inland Revenue Commissioners v. *Lysaght* [1928] A.C. 234, H.L.(E.).
Levene v. *Inland Revenue Commissioners* [1928] A.C. 217, H.L.(E.).
G   *Reg.* v. *Barnet London Borough Council, Ex parte Nilish Shah* [1981]
     2 W.L.R. 86; [1980] 3 All E.R. 679, D.C.
Stransky v. *Stransky* [1954] P. 428; [1954] 3 W.L.R. 123; [1954] 2 All
     E.R. 536.

No additional cases were cited in argument.

H

ORIGINATING SUMMONS

     By summons dated December 12, 1979, the plaintiff, Ambrose
Cicutti, an Italian student aged 19 years, sought inter alia a declaration
that he was entitled to have an award bestowed on him by the defen-

---

[1] Education Act 1962, s. 1 (1) (*a*): see post, p. 560E.
[2] Local Education Authority Awards Regulations 1979, reg. 13 (*a*): see post,
p. 560E–F.

A

dants, the Suffolk County Council, in respect of his attendance at a course at Warwick University pursuant to the provisions of section 1 of the Education Act 1962, and regulation 13 of the Local Education Authority Awards Regulations 1979; further, that at the material time he was ordinarily resident in the defendants' area and had been so resident for the three years immediately preceding the first year of the course within the meaning of the Act and the Regulations.

B

The facts are stated in the judgment.

Michael Beloff for the plaintiff.
Anthony Dinkin for the defendants.

Cur. adv. vult.

C

July 25. SIR ROBERT MEGARRY V.-C. read the following judgment. This case turns on the complex meaning of the simple term " ordinarily resident " in relation to awards by local education authorities for courses leading to a first degree at a university. The plaintiff applied to the defendants, a county council, for such an award on May 15, 1979; and on June 1, 1979, the defendants refused the award on the ground that the plaintiff did not meet the statutory requirements of residence. The plaintiff accordingly seeks a declaration which will establish his right to an award. There is no dispute about any other requirements for an award; the only question is on the expression " ordinarily resident."

D

That term comes into the matter in two ways. First, there are the words of qualification in section 1 (1) (*a*) of the Education Act 1962. Subsection (1) enacts that it is the duty of every local education authority, subject to and in accordance with regulations made under the Act, " to bestow awards on persons who—(*a*) are ordinarily resident in the area of the authority . . ." Second, there are the words of disqualification in regulations made under the Act, the Local Education Authority Awards Regulations 1979. By regulation 13 (*a*), an authority is under no duty to bestow an award in respect of a person's attendance at a course

E

F

" upon a person who has not been ordinarily resident, throughout the three years preceding the first year of the course in question, in the United Kingdom . . ."

There is then a reference to the E.E.C. in the alternative which it is agreed has no application in the present case. At the time of the refusal of the award, the Regulations in force were S.I. 1978 No. 1097; but so far as is relevant to this case, the corresponding provisions in those Regulations, though worded a little differently, are the same in substance. The questions before me are thus (1) whether at the time of the decision on or about June 1, 1979, (for that, I think, must be the relevant time) the plaintiff was " ordinarily resident " in the defendants' area, and so was entitled to an award, and (2) if he was, whether during the three years prior to the beginning of the plaintiff's university course in October 1979 the plaintiff had not throughout been " ordinarily resident " in the United Kingdom, and so was disqualified from requiring the award to be made.

The facts are relatively simple, and are not in dispute. The plaintiff has sworn two affidavits, the second being in answer to certain questions

G

H

A put to him by the defendants; and the defendants have been content to argue the case on the contents of these two affidavits and their exhibits, without putting in evidence of their own. The plaintiff was born in Rome on March 10, 1961, so that he is between 19 and 19½ years old. His father is an Italian citizen and lives in Rome. His mother died in 1969. He himself is still an Italian citizen, though he has applied for naturalisation here; I do not know when. His parents wished him to

B have an English education, and so in September 1971, when he was 10½, he was sent as a border to the preparatory section of a college in Ipswich; and shortly afterwards he was moved to the college itself. He continued there until the end of the summer term in June 1979. In October 1979 he began reading for a history degree at Warwick University. During the three years from October 1976 to October 1979, he

C spent one summer and three Christmas holidays in Rome, and three Easter and two summer holidays in England, working during the last of these, but otherwise staying with friends. Save for the holidays in Rome, he has remained throughout in this country.

Apart from the question of intention, about which there was much argument, those are the basic facts. It was accepted that there was no difference as regards being " ordinarily resident " between the plaintiff's

D position on June 1, 1979, and his position throughout the three year period which began in October 1976, or, for that matter, his position today. Nor was it contended that the plaintiff was resident in the area of any local education authority other than that of the defendants. The whole question is whether the plaintiff's presence in the defendants' area and in the United Kingdom had the quality required to make him

E " ordinarily resident " within the meaning of the two statutory provisions.

The argument between Mr. Beloff for the plaintiff and Mr. Dinkin for the defendants naturally centred on the recent decision of a Divisional Court of the Queen's Bench Division in *Reg.* v. *Barnet London Borough Council, Ex parte Nilish Shah* [1981] 2 W.L.R. 86. In that case, there

F was an extended consideration of the meaning and effect of the term " ordinarily resident " in the statutory provisions which are now before me. The court consisted of Ormrod L.J. and Kilner Brown and McNeill JJ., and it was Ormrod L.J. who delivered the judgment of the court. The facts were materially different from those in the case before me. There were two applications for judicial review of the refusal of the local education authority in question to make awards.

G Each applicant had been born in Kenya and came to England in August 1976, aged some 17 years. One of them, a citizen of Kenya, came with his parents, and was admitted for an indefinite period to settle here. After 5 weeks, his parents returned to Kenya; he remained here, living with relations but returning to Kenya for the summer holidays each

H year. In his case, the court quashed the local education authority's decision to refuse an award, and directed that authority to reconsider the award. The court held that there was no evidence to support the local education authority's refusal of the award. In the other case, the applicant, a citizen of the United Kingdom and Colonies who had no right of entry here, came here alone with a student's entry certificate, and was given leave to enter for two months, a leave which was extended from time to time. He became a student at a technical college and lived

with his brother; nothing is said about visits to Kenya or anywhere else.   A
In his case the application for judicial review was dismissed.

Both Mr. Beloff and Mr. Dinkin argued the case on the footing that
the *Barnet* case, as I shall call it, was binding on me, though Mr. Beloff
delicately indicated an alternative line of argument that he would otherwise have pursued. I do not propose to analyse the case in detail,
though I must consider the ratio. After quoting from the judgment of   B
Smith J. in the Australian case of *Clarke* v. *Insurance Office of Australia
Ltd.* [1965] 1 Lloyd's Rep. 308, 310, 311, Ormrod L.J. said, at pp. 92–93:

> " We think that the most significant point which emerges from this
> analysis is that the concept of ' ordinary residence ' embodies a
> number of different factors, such as time, intention, and continuity,
> each of which may carry a different weight according to the context
> in which, and the purpose for which, the phrase ' ordinarily resident '   C
> is used in a particular statute."

He then said, at p. 93, that in regulation 13 (*a*) " ordinarily resident "
was " used to distinguish between those who are resident for general (i.e.
ordinary) purposes, and others who are resident for a specific or special
or limited purpose."
                                                                           D
After considering a variety of decisions, many on income tax, and
concluding that there was nothing in them, when carefully examined,
which was inconsistent with this conclusion, Ormrod L.J. concluded, at
p. 95:

> " . . . an important, though not the only, element to be considered
> in ascertaining whether an individual is ' ordinarily resident ' in the
> United Kingdom for the purposes of regulation 13 (*a*), is the purpose   E
> of, or the reason for, his presence in the United Kingdom, and his
> intention in coming and remaining here. ' Why is he in this
> country? ' is a relevant question. If the answer is for a specific
> or limited purpose, rather than the general purposes of living here
> he will not be ' ordinarily resident ' within the meaning of this
> regulation."   F

The court, I should say, rejected the " real home " test based on
Stransky v. *Stransky* [1954] P. 428.

These principles were then applied to the two individual cases, with
the result that in the first of them it was held, at p. 97, that the applicant,
who was referred to as " Nilish," had come to the country " for the
purpose of settling here, i.e. for all ordinary purposes of living, and not   G
for the specific purpose of being educated here, and has been so residing
here since August 1976." The other applicant, who was referred to
as " Jitendra," had come " as a student, for a limited period only, and
for a specific or limited purpose, namely to study, and if possible, obtain
a professional qualification " (see p. 98); and the terms on which he was
permitted to enter were strong evidence of his purpose in coming here   H
and his reasons for remaining here. Ormrod L.J. said, at p. 98:

> " The contrast between these two cases brings out very clearly the
> difference between ' resident ' and ' ordinarily resident ' in the legis-
> lative context of regulation 13 (*a*). Nilish's answer to the question,
> ' Why are you here? ', would be, ' To live, to study, and to remain.'
> Jitendra's answer could only be, ' To study, to qualify if possible,
> and then to leave.' "

A On this, it might perhaps be questioned whether Jitendra's answer might not have added to it the additional phrase " To live," since he had resided in England for over three years, and if asked where he was living it is not easy to see why he should not say that he was living in England. However special and limited the purpose in going to another country, a man may still say that he lives there if he has gone there for any sub-stantial period. He who goes as a visiting professor to Harvard for a

B year surely lives in Cambridge for that year. The real difference between the two hypothetical answers seems to me to lie in the contrast between the concluding phrases, between " to remain " and " then to leave."

      With that, I can turn to the question of intention in the case now before me. This was at the centre of the argument. On the evidence, it is clear that the plaintiff initially came to England for the purpose

C of being educated here. It is not disputed that subsequently he formed the intention of remaining here, and living and working here. It does not appear precisely when or how or why he formed that intention, but the defendants accept that it occurred at some time before October 1976, when the three year period began to run. They also accept that it is a perfectly genuine intention and not a spurious intention asserted for

D the purpose of obtaining an award. As a student of Italian nationality the plaintiff is subject to immigration control, and his passport shows that when on January 7, 1979, he returned to England from his last Christmas holiday in Rome, he was given leave to remain here for six months; and doubtless this leave has been duly renewed from time to time. In any case, Mr. Dinkin accepted that no significance could be attached to the restriction of the leave to remain to six months. He

E also accepted that when the plaintiff left Warwick University he would, as a citizen of an E.E.C. country, be entitled under the right of establish-ment to remain here to work even if he had not by then become naturalised here. His intention is to pursue a career in the Civil Service, though counsel were not able to tell me whether for this British nationality is requisite.

F   The case accordingly raises questions not only of the effect of a person's intentions on the quality of his residence here, but also of the result of a change of intention after the initial entry into the country. Mr. Dinkin said that the Barnet case [1981] 2 W.L.R. 86 made it plain that the plaintiff would have failed if his intention on first entering the country had remained unchanged, since that intention was to come here merely for the specific limited purpose of being educated here. Every-

G thing therefore depended on the effect of the plaintiff's change of inten-tion. A mere intention to remain here was not enough, Mr. Dinkin said, even though it was a perfectly genuine intention to remain here permanently. There must be more than a mere state of mind: there must be some translation of that state of mind into physical facts which demonstrated a change in the character of the residence. Pressed for

H examples of such facts, Mr. Dinkin suggested the acquisition of a home here, even if it was merely a single room in a boarding house or the home of a friend. Another indication would be the existence of a place in which to keep personal belongings, or some arrangements for this pur-pose; and yet another would be the making of financial arrangements here, as by opening a bank account. A further example would be the severance of connections with all previous places of residence.

I found these contentions unconvincing. I can well see that in   A
deciding whether or not an asserted intention is genuine, the presence
or absence of indicia such as these may well be a matter of some
importance. But once it is accepted, as it has been in this case, that
the intention is perfectly genuine, I do not see why the presence or
absence of such indicia should affect the matter. Furthermore, in the
case of somebody who at all material times has been a schoolboy, I can
see little reality in suggesting that he ought to have acquired a home   B
here. There would be no sense in paying rent or some equivalent for
even a single room when for three-quarters of the year he was boarding
at school. Indeed, if somebody did that, it might suggest that he was
attempting to manufacture evidence to bolster up an intention of dubious
genuineness. As for personal belongings, those of most schoolboys are
usually of modest bulk, and those which are not left at school for the   C
holidays may readily be taken to wherever the boy spends his holidays.
Nor is there anything in the question of bank accounts and other
financial arrangements, for, on instructions, Mr. Beloff told me, without demur by Mr. Dinkin, that the plaintiff had long had an account
with both a bank and a building society here. Lastly, I cannot see why
the severance of connections with all previous places of residence should
be a requisite of holding the plaintiff to be ordinarily resident here,   D
especially when his only previous place of residence is his father's home.
Many an adult retains close connections with his parent's home without thereby doing anything to suggest that he is not ordinarily resident
elsewhere. The idea of such a severance comes, I think, from the
judgment of Smith J. in *Clarke* v. *Insurance Office of Australia* [1965]
1 Lloyd's Rep. 308, 311; and there it was used for the quite different   E
purpose of indicating a way in which a man may be said to be " ordinarily resident " at a new place as soon as he begins to reside there.

For his part, Mr. Beloff at first accepted that a mere intention to
remain here was not enough, as there must in addition be the ability to
carry out that intention. However, in view of the celebrated passage
in the judgment of Asquith L.J. in *Cunliffe* v. *Goodman* [1950] 2 K.B.
237, 253, I suggested that such an ability was implicit in the word   F
" intention " itself, and distinguished it from mere matters of hope or
desire. A man cannot truly be said to " intend " something unless he has
at least a reasonable prospect of bringing it about by his own act. On
that footing, Mr. Beloff ultimately contended that a genuine intention
sufficed per se, and alternatively that such an intention must be
supplemented by the taking of such steps as the person concerned could   G
reasonably be expected to take. Here, the person was a schoolboy, and
the change in where he spent his holidays sufficed for the purpose.

I propose to consider the matter by stages. (1) From the *Barnet*
case [1981] 2 W.L.R. 86 it seems clear that " ordinarily resident " is a
concept which requires the examination of a variety of factors, including
time, intention and continuity, and that the weight to be given to those   H
factors depends on the context in which the phrase appears, and the
purpose for which the statute uses the phrase.

(2) The purpose for which the phrase is used in section 1 of the Act
of 1962 and regulation 13 (a) of the Regulations is, I think, to define the
local education authority which is required to make the award, to define
the applicants who are entitled to such awards, and to exclude those
who lack a sufficient connection with the particular local education

A authority, or with the United Kingdom, thereby preventing abuses of the system of awards. Quoad the applicant, the statutory provisions are enacted in relation to the conferring of a benefit, as contrasted with provisions imposing a burden, as under legislation for taxation or national service.

(3) The *Barnet* case establishes that the test is not one of what is the
B "real home" of the applicant. Instead, the dividing line is between those who are in this country for some specific or limited purpose, and those who on the other hand are present for the general purposes of living here. What must be ascertained is the purpose or reason for that presence, and the intention of the person in coming here, and also in remaining here. These are matters which cannot be determined without ascertaining the intention of the person concerned.

C (4) The *Barnet* case indicates that in the term " ordinarily resident," the word " ordinarily " is primarily directed not to duration but to purpose. The question is not so much where the person is to be found " ordinarily," in the sense of " usually " or " habitually," and with some degree of continuity (as opposed to " unusually " or " extraordinarily "), but whether the quality of the residence is " ordinary " and general, rather than merely for some special or limited purpose. No doubt there
D must be residence for a sufficient length of time and with a sufficient degree of continuity to be capable of supporting the contention that the residence is ordinary in its quality; but it is that quality of ordinariness which is of the essence, and not the duration or continuity. The Divisional Court rejected indications to the contrary which may be found in revenue cases, such as *Levene* v. *Inland Revenue Commissioners* [1928]
E A.C. 217, 225 and *Inland Revenue Commissioners* v. *Lysaght* [1928] A.C. 234, 243; and on the footing that I was bound by the *Barnet* case, no submissions were put before me on these cases.

(5) It seems to me that the intention to be considered is the intention that exists at the time in question. Under section 1 (1) (*a*) of the Act, that time is, I think, the time of the decision by the local education
F authority, both for general reasons and by reason of the use of the present tense; the verb is " are." Under regulation 13 (*a*), the time is the whole of the three year period. I say nothing about fluctuations of intention during that period, for no such point arises in this case. Intentions which existed previously, or came into being subsequently, do not seem to me to be relevant except so far as they throw some light on the intention at the relevant time. A person who comes to this country
G with one intention and then asserts that at the relevant time a different intention had come into being may well find it harder to convince the local education authority or the court than a person whose case is based on his original intention having remained unchanged throughout.

(6) I do not think that there is any requirement that for this purpose an intention must be supported by any particular physical or other mani-
H festation. Provided an intention is genuine, and is a true intention in the sense that the person concerned has at least a reasonable prospect of carrying out what he says that he intends, I think that it can suffice for this purpose. As I have suggested, physical or other manifestations of the intention may play their part in supporting or detracting from the existence of a genuine intention; but I do not regard their presence or absence as being of the essence.

If those are the correct principles, then it is plain that some appli- A
cants for awards will have a strong motive for asserting that they have
an intention which will entitle them to an award, and so, it may be said,
the door to an abuse of the system will stand ajar. As this contention
was not advanced in argument I shall not say much about it; but it may
assist those concerned if I say something. First, it is clear that motive
and intention are distinct; an intention is not vitiated merely because
the person forming it has a self-interest in doing so. Indeed, the B
stronger the motive for forming the intention, the more likely it is that
it will truly be formed. The question is whether the intention does exist,
and not why it was formed. Second, nobody can form a genuine intention to live in this country for general purposes if he has no right to be
here save for a limited time and purpose, and no real expectations of
having these limitations removed. Third, I would regard it as an C
important part of the functions of a local education authority to scrutinise with care any such asserted intention, and to investigate any that
appear to be doubtful or suspicious. Fourth, in any case I am bound
by the statutory language and, it seems, by the construction put on it
by the Divisional Court. If that language, so construed, is considered
to be too relaxed, no doubt it will be amended or qualified by a further
statutory instrument. D

I return to the facts of the case before me. Mr. Dinkin understandably stressed the plaintiff's Italian origin and connections. His
father and his father's home are in Italy; he has no home over here,
apart from what has been provided by his school and then his university;
he is an Italian citizen with an Italian passport which states his residence
to be Rome; he is being maintained from Italy by his father; and until in E
1977 he began to spend most of his school holidays here, he spent all of
them in Italy. Further, he had no connection with the United Kingdom
until he came here, and then he came only for the special and limited
purpose of being educated here. I agree that if you look to the past,
Italy plainly predominates. But look, as one must, at the three year
period, and look at his intentions and his daily life then, and Italy F
retreats into the background. It is obviously probable that he will be
able to remain here to finish his degree course, and after that the right
of establishment will enable him to work here, as he intends. Not only
is his intention of remaining here admittedly genuine, and capable of
being put into effect, but also, in spending most of his school holidays
here and in applying for naturalisation, the plaintiff has been acting in G
accordance with that intention. The old pattern of his life has been
superseded by the new; and in my judgment that new pattern was and
is a pattern of being here for the general purpose of living here. The
mere existence of foreign connections seems to me to be per se of small
importance in considering where a person is " ordinarily resident "; what
matters far more is where he moves and dwells and has his being, and
for what purposes he does so. His centre of gravity, once in Rome and H
Italy, came to be in Ipswich and the United Kingdom.

It therefore seems to me that Mr. Beloff's contentions are right in
their essentials. As the action is for a declaration and not merely for
certiorari, the question is not whether there was or was not sufficient
evidence to support the decision of the defendants, but what the relevant
rights of the plaintiff are. I shall therefore make a suitable declaration
in his favour: the precise terms are for consideration. I will add that

1 W.L.R.   Cicutti v. Suffolk C.C. (Ch.D.)

A   if, contrary to the *Barnet* case, " ordinarily " had to be construed in the sense of " usually " or " habitually," my present impression is that I would have reached the same conclusion on the facts of this case, unless, indeed, Mr. Dinkin had been able to put before me some authority or contention that at the moment I cannot envisage.

B
                          Declaration that plaintiff was ordi-
                          narily resident within the area of
                          the defendants both at the time
                          of his application for an award and
                          at the time of the decision by the
                          defendants in respect of such appli-
C   *cation; further, that he was ordi-*
                          narily resident within the United
                          Kingdom throughout the period of
                          three years preceding the first year
                          of his university course.

      Solicitors: *Iliffe & Edwards for Prettys, Ipswich; Sharpe, Pritchard & Co. for K. O. Hall, Ipswich.*
D
                                                                    K. N. B.

_____

                    [QUEEN'S BENCH DIVISION]

E   * VEATER *v.* G. AND OTHERS

  1981   Jan. 26, 27;   Lord Lane C.J. and Lloyd J.
         Feb. 16

Justices — Peace — Recognisance to keep — Juveniles' refusal of
*   consent to binding over—Jurisdiction to imprison for refusal*
F *   —Whether power to bind over without juveniles' consent—*
*   Powers of Criminal Courts Act 1973 (c. 62), s. 19 (1)*

      A complaint was preferred by the prosecutor against the defendants, six youths aged between 14 and 15, that they had behaved in a manner whereby a breach of the peace was likely to be occasioned, contrary to common law. At the hearing of the complaint in the magistrates' court the defendants admitted the allegation. The justices, who were minded to exercise
G   their powers of preventive justice under the Justices of the Peace Act 1361 [1] and to bind the defendants over in their own recognisance of £100 to keep the peace for one year, asked the defendants if they would consent to be so bound, but each of them refused. The justices were of the opinion that they could not exercise the sanction which was normally available to them and commit the defendants to prison for their refusal to enter into the recognisances, because section 19 (1) of
H   the Powers of Criminal Courts Act 1973 [2] prohibited them from imposing imprisonment on persons under 17 years of age, and that they were not authorised to impose any other custodial sentence upon them. They further considered that they had

_____

[1] Justices of the Peace Act 1361: ". . . [justices] shall have power . . . to take of all them that be [not] of good fame, where they shall be found, sufficient surety and mainprise of their good behaviour towards the King and his people. . . ."
[2] Powers of Criminal Courts Act 1973, s. 19: "(1) Neither the Crown Court nor a magistrates' court shall impose imprisonment on a person under 17 years of age."

no power to impose on the defendants an obligation to be   A
bound in the sum suggested without their consent, and ordered
the defendants to leave the court.

On appeal by the prosecutor: —

Held, dismissing the appeal, (1) that the essence of a binding over order was that a person acknowledged that he was
indebted to the Queen; that by that acknowledgment he became
bound to pay the sum fixed by the court if he failed to keep
the peace and, therefore, the justices could not bind over a   B
person unless he acknowledged the debt and, if he refused to
do so, their only sanction was to commit him to prison (post,
pp. 577c–d).

(2) That whether the justices were exercising a civil or
criminal jurisdiction under the Act of 1361, section 19 of the
Powers of Criminal Courts Act 1973 applied and the clear,
comprehensive and imperative terms of subsection (1) had
abrogated the justices' powers to commit to prison a person   C
under the age of 17 and, accordingly, the justices had no
effective power in the matter (post, pp. 574g—575a, 576e–f,
578c–d).

Morris v. *Crown Office* [1970] 2 Q.B. 114, C.A. considered.

The following cases are referred to in the judgment:

Everett v. *Ribbands* [1952] 2 Q.B. 198; [1952] 1 All E.R. 823.   D
Lansbury v. *Riley* [1914] 3 K.B. 229.
Morris v. *Crown Office* [1970] 2 Q.B. 114; [1970] 2 W.L.R. 792; [1970]
      1 All E.R. 1079, C.A.
Reg. v. *Aubrey-Fletcher, Ex parte Thompson* [1969] 1 W.L.R. 872; [1969]
      2 All E.R. 846, D.C.
Reg. v. *Greenwich Justices, Ex parte Carter* [1973] Crim.L.R. 444, D.C.
Reg. v. *Southampton Justices, Ex parte Green* [1976] Q.B. 11; [1975]   E
      3 W.L.R. 277; [1975] 2 All E.R. 1073, C.A.
Rex v. *London County Quarter Sessions Appeals Committee, Ex parte
      Metropolitan Police Commissioner* [1948] 1 K.B. 670; [1948] 1 All
      E.R. 72, D.C.

The following additional cases were cited in argument:

Reg. v. *Cork Justices* (1882) 15 Cox C.C. 149.   F
Reg. v. *Marquis* [1974] 1 W.L.R. 1087; [1974] 2 All E.R. 1216, C.A.
Reg. v. *Woking Justices, Ex parte Gossage* [1973] Q.B. 448; [1973] 2
      W.L.R. 529; [1973] 2 All E.R. 621, D.C.

CASE STATED by Bristol Justices.

On April 11, 1980, complaints were preferred by the prosecutor against
the defendants, who were all juveniles, that they on February 22, 1980, in   G
the City of Bristol, did behave in a manner whereby a breach of the peace
was likely to be occasioned, contrary to common law. In the light of the
defendants' conduct and demeanour on February 22, 1980, the prosecutor
applied for the justices to exercise their powers of preventive justice and
bind each of the defendants over to keep the peace for the future in some
suitable sum for a suitable period.

The justices heard the complaints on July 25 and 31, 1980, and found   H
the following facts. At 12.50 p.m. on February 22, 1980, Police Constables
Lerpiniere and Allsop, of the Avon and Somerset Constabulary, were
directed to Park Road, Stapleton, in Bristol, because the six defendants,
and another had reportedly been behaving in a disorderly manner. When
the officers arrived in Park Road, they saw a group of seven youths
walking along that road, two of whom were carrying sticks and one of
whom was wearing a stocking mask. The group were all arrested and

A taken to a police station. They were later interviewed and made statements in which they all admitted that they had left their own locality to walk together to a school some distance away with the express intention of assaulting some pupils at that school, if they could find them. The defendants had all at some stage been armed with sticks and two had stocking masks with them. By the time they were arrested by the police most of the group had discarded their sticks. Having been to the school B and having failed to find the pupils, they were returning in the general direction of their homes.

No evidence was led by the defendants as all admitted that their behaviour was such that a breach of the peace was likely to be occasioned.

The justices considered the evidence and decided that each of the defendants should be bound over in his own recognisance of £100 to keep C the peace for one year. Each of the defendants was asked if he would acknowledge himself bound in the sum of £100 and enter into the recognisance. Each refused.

It was contended by the prosecutor that (i) the justices were acting under their common law powers derived from their Commission of the Peace and the Justices of the Peace Act 1361. They were not acting under the power given to them by section 91 of the Magistrates' Courts D Act 1952. Section 91 was intended to deal with " inter-party " disputes, whereas orders under the Act of 1361 and Commission were much wider in scope, involving as they did an eventual recognisance towards " the King and his people." (ii) Under the powers given by their Commission and the Act of 1361, the justices could " oblige " the defendants to enter into a recognisance; that is, the order to be bound over was a unilateral order E directed by the court to the defendants and needed no consent or acknowledgment. It was not open to the defendants to decide if they would accept the order, their obligation was to keep the peace for the period of 12 months specified by the justices, and if they failed in that obligation the justices could forfeit all or part of the sum of £100. (iii) The effect of " consent " was merely to relieve the prosecutor of the burden of adducing evidence and was not a necessary prerequisite for making the order of F binding over. (iv) The Magistrates' Court's (Appeals from Binding Over Orders) Act 1956, gave a right of appeal to the Crown Court against a binding over. There was, however, no such right against the binding over of a parent under section 7 (7) of the Children and Young Persons Act 1969, or under section 12 of the Powers of Criminal Courts Act 1973— presumably because under those statutes the consent of the defendant was G required. (v) Other statutory provisions, that is, section 91 of the Magistrates' Courts Act 1952 and section 1 (7) of the Justices of the Peace Act 1968, although not appropriate in this case, used the words " ordered by a magistrates' court . . . to enter into a recognisance " and " by requiring him to enter into his own recognisances. . . ." Those provisions indicated that the order was mandatory and could be imposed unilaterally by the justices. (vi) The justices, in dealing with juveniles, would otherwise be H placed in an impossible situation. Imprisonment not being available as a sanction for non-compliance, the justices would have no power to enforce their decision. (vii) It was a rule of statutory interpretation that statutes should be construed to give effect to them rather than to nullify them. If two interpretations were open to a court it should not choose the one that would enable the juveniles to escape the provisions of the Act of 1361. To do so would result in no sanction being available to the court when dealing with antisocial behaviour which fell short of a criminal offence. (viii) The

sanction of imprisonment for non-compliance was an option open to the A
justices in the case of an adult and not a compulsory course of action.
Therefore, the argument that because sanctions were available a person
had to acknowledge himself bound was fallacious. In any event, acting
under their powers at common law the justices had no specific power to
imprison as a sanction for non-compliance with a binding over order.

It was contended by the defendants that (i) it was necessary for a
binding over order to be effective that the defendants acknowledged their B
obligation and agreed to enter into the recognisance in the sum of £100
as ordered by the justices. (ii) The language used in the Act of 1361 was
difficult: ". . . and to take of all them that be [not] of good fame, where
they shall be found, sufficient surety and mainprise of their good behaviour
towards the King and his people . . ." but the words " to take of them . . .
surety and mainprise " meant that the taking of a recognisance as expressed C
in later statutes was the intention of the statute. This concept reappeared
in later statutes such as (a) section 91 of the Magistrates' Courts Act
1952—a person could be ordered to enter into a recognisance and if he
was so ordered and failed to comply, he could be committed to custody
for up to six months or until he sooner complied; (b) section 1 (7) of the
Justices of the Peace Act 1968, which stated that a court of record had the
power to bind over a person by requiring him to enter into his own D
recognisance or to find sureties or both, and committing him to prison if
he did not comply. (iii) The use of the word " recognisance " indicated a
consensual undertaking. Its dictionary definition of " a bond or obligation
entered into and recorded before a court or magistrate by which a person
engages himself to perform some act or observe some condition " meant
that there must be consensus. Although justices might order a person to E
be bound over in a certain sum for a certain period, it was still open to
him to refuse to enter into the recognisance. (iv) The result of such a
refusal if the court was dealing with an adult was that he would be liable
to imprisonment as a sanction for non-compliance. There would be no
provision for sanctions for non-compliance if a person could have a binding
over order imposed on him unilaterally as suggested. (v) The justices had
an inherent power at common law to imprison as a sanction if a person F
refused to enter into a recognisance as ordered by the court. That had been
the case for many centuries and was the established practice of the courts.
If a person refused to acknowledge his obligation it was explained to him
that he might be imprisoned until he agreed to enter into his recognisance.
(vi) There were different meanings for the word " consent " in the context
of binding over cases. " Consent " at a preliminary stage meant the G
person was admitting that his conduct was such that a breach of the peace
was likely, that is, that person did not wish to show cause why an order
should not be made. However, it was still open to that person, if and
when the justices decided to order him to be bound over, to refuse to
" consent " or " acknowledge " himself bound in his own recognisance in
the amount ordered by the court. (vii) The appeals provision in section 1 H
of the Magistrates' Courts (Appeals from Binding Over Orders) Act
1956 as amended: " Where . . . a person is ordered by a magistrates'
court . . . to enter into a recognisance with or without sureties to keep the
peace . . . he may appeal to the Crown Court . . ." supported the concept
of entering into a recognisance as the object and raison d'etre of a binding
over. (viii) The justices were in a difficult position when dealing with
juveniles who refused to acknowledge themselves bound in their own

A recognisances in the sum fixed by the court, in that apparently no sanctions were available. However, if this was an anomaly, Parliament would have to rectify it.

    The justices were of the opinion that (a) a distinction had to be made between a magistrates' court acting under its common law powers derived from the Justices of the Peace Act 1361, and the Commission of the Peace, and a court acting under the statutory power given by section 91

B of the Magistrates' Courts Act 1952. The justices were acting under the authority of the former and therefore the provisions of section 91 did not directly apply to the application. (b) The cases referred to by the prosecutor did not deal with the issue before the court. The court was being asked to decide (i) whether a binding over can be imposed unilaterally, or (ii) whether, to be effective, a binding over required an acknowledgment

C and acceptance of the recognisance ordered. *Reg.* v. *South West London Magistrates' Court, Ex parte Brown* [1974] Crim.L.R. 313 dealt with " consent " but the justices felt that this was used in the context of the preliminary stages of such proceedings, that is, the defendants were admitting their conduct and the prosecution were relieved of their duty of calling evidence because there was material before the justices to enable them to exercise their powers of preventive justice. *Reg.* v. *Hendon*

D *Justices, Ex parte Gorchein* [1973] 1 W.L.R. 1502 and *Reg.* v. *North London Metropolitan Magistrate, Ex parte Haywood* [1973] 1 W.L.R. 965 appeared to the justices to be concerned with the rules of natural justice, that is, whether or not it was necessary (depending on the circumstances of the case) for a person before the court to be given the opportunity to show cause why an order should not be made. (c) *Reg.* v. *Woking*

E *Justices, Ex parte Gossage* [1973] Q.B. 448 was concerned with " natural justice." However, the point in issue in the present case was referred to in that a person before the court asked what would happen if he did not acknowledge his obligation (having been ordered to be bound over to keep the peace for two years in his own recognisance of £100). It was explained to him that a prison sentence might result. That information having been

F given he entered into the recognisance. Although that was only reciting what had happened before the Woking justices, no adverse comment was made on the procedure by the court which appeared to the justices to have been the established practice of courts for many years. (d) the justices were acting under their Commission of the Peace which provided:

> " . . . Know ye that We have assigned you and every of you jointly and
> severally Our justices to keep Our peace in and throughout the City
> G and County of Bristol and to keep and cause to be kept all ordinances
> and statutes made for the good of Our peace and for the conservation
> of the same and for the quiet rule and government of Our people in
> all and every the articles thereof in the said City and County according
> to the form and effect of the same and to chastise and punish all
> persons that offend against the form of those ordinances or statutes or
> H any one of them in the aforesaid City and County as it ought to be
> done according to the form of those ordinances and statutes and to
> cause to come before you or any one of you all those who to any one
> or more of Our people have used threats to find sufficient security for
> the peace or their good behaviour towards Us and Our people and if
> they shall refuse to find such security then them in our prisons until
> they shall find such security to cause to be safely kept. And therefore
> We command you that you diligently apply yourselves to the keeping

Our peace, ordinances statutes and all and singular other the premises A
and perform and fulfil the same in form aforesaid doing therein what
to justice appertains according to the laws and customs of
England ..."

and the Act of 1361 which again referred to the justices taking
" sufficient surety and mainprise." The whole concept of a binding over,
therefore, involved the taking of a recognisance and the acknowledg- B
ment by a person that he was bound in that recognisance in the sum fixed
by the court and for the period stated and that a " unilateral " bind over,
that is, one imposed on a person, was not in the justices' view possible.
(e) The fact that sanctions were available to a court if a person refused
to acknowledge his obligation gave credence to the justices' view. The
power to imprison as a sanction had always been an inherent power of C
justices at common law. It seemed that there was no limit to the period
of imprisonment they could impose (apart from the years 1853–1892 when
by statute there was a maximum period of one year) but Everett v.
Ribbands [1952] 2 Q.B. 198, to which they referred, supported the general
practice of a six months' limit on imprisonment for refusing to enter into
a recognisance to be bound over or failing to find sureties. That was
analogous to the power given to justices by section 91 of the Magistrates' D
Courts Act 1952. (f) When dealing with juveniles no sanctions were available if they refused to acknowledge themselves bound in their own recognisance to keep the peace. The justices were not minded to follow the
example of Mr. Recorder Whelon, who ordered a 14 year old prosecution
witness to be remanded until she agreed to be bound over as they could
find no statutory provision enabling that to be done. (g) As an analogy
the justices considered section 91 (3) of the Magistrates' Courts Act 1952, E
which stated that if a person ordered to enter into a recognisance to keep
the peace failed to comply with the order, the court might " commit him
to custody " for a period of six months or until he sooner complied with
the order. Section 126 of the Magistrates' Courts Act 1952 defined
" commit to custody " as " commit to prison or, where any enactment
authorises or requires committal to some other place of detention instead F
of committal to prison, to that other place; . . ." Section 19 (1) of the
Powers of Criminal Courts Act 1973, stated that imprisonment must not
be imposed on a person under 17 years. The only alternative for a
juvenile, therefore, was a detention centre, where that was authorised by
any enactments. However, having considered section 4 of the Criminal
Justice Act 1961, the justices felt they were not passing " sentence "on a
young " offender " and, therefore, had no authority to take that course G
under that or any other enactment.

In view of their opinion in (d) above, the justices felt that each defendant
had to acknowledge and enter into a recognisance fixed by them in the
sum of £100 to keep the peace for one year, in order that the binding over
should be effective. The justices, therefore, again asked each defendant
if he would acknowledge himself bound in the sum of £100 and keep H
the peace for one year. Each again refused.

In view of their opinion in (f) and (g) above, the justices felt that
they could not secure compliance with their order as no sanctions were
available to them when dealing with juveniles. The authority of the
court had been undermined by the refusal of the defendants to acknowledge
the recognisance and the justices were thus in the humiliating position of
not being able to impose unilaterally an order that they had made, and

A of having no sanctions available to enforce their decision. The defendants
were accordingly ordered to leave the court.

The prosecutor appealed. The questions of law for the opinion of the
High Court were as follows. (i) Were the justices correct in holding that a
defendant had to acknowledge the recognisance before they could bind him
over to keep the peace under the Justices of the Peace Act 1361, or their
Commission of the Peace? (ii) Were the justices correct in holding that
B they had no power to order unilaterally a defendant (whether adult or
juvenile) to be bound over to keep the peace in some specified sum, when
acting under the Act of 1361 or their Commission? (iii) If a juvenile refused
to acknowledge the recognisance did the justices have power to order him
to be detained in a remand or detention centre pending his entering into
that recognisance, analogous to the power to imprison an adult?

C
James Black Q.C. and *Ian Glen* for the prosecutor.
Ian Bullock for the defendant, W.
The other defendants did not appear and were not represented.

Cur. adv. vult.

D
February 16. LORD LANE C.J. read the judgment of the court. This
is an appeal by way of case stated from a decision of the Bristol justices
given on July 31, 1980. The facts are very simple. On February 22,
1980, six youths aged 14 and 15, were reported as behaving in a disorderly
manner in Park Road, Stapleton, Bristol. When the police arrived on the
scene they found two of the youths carrying sticks and a third wearing a
E stocking mask. All six were arrested, and taken to the police station.
Subsequently they all made statements in which they admitted that they had
been on an expedition with the object of assaulting pupils at the neighbouring school, but had not been able to find them. They had all at some
stage been armed with sticks. The police preferred a complaint against
them that they were behaving in a manner whereby a breach of the peace
F was likely to be occasioned, contrary to common law.

When the matter came before the justices, the facts were admitted.
The justices were minded to bind over each of the defendants in his own
recognisance of £100 to keep the peace for one year. They asked each of
the defendants whether he would acknowledge himself bound, and each
refused. The justices then heard legal argument as to their powers.
They took the view that they could not, in law, impose a binding over
G order unilaterally. To be effective each of the defendants had to acknowledge his indebtedness in the amount fixed. So the justices asked them
all again whether they would acknowledge their indebtedness. Once again
they all refused. The justices then found themselves in what they
described as a humiliating position. They felt that they had no sanction
to secure compliance with their order; that they had no alternative but
H to let the defendants go, which they did. The question for the court is
whether they were right.

Mr. Black, who appeared for the prosecutor, took two main points.
In the first place he argued that the justices were wrong to conclude that
they had no sanction. They were entitled to send the defendants to prison
until they agreed to be bound. Secondly, he argued that the justices were
in any event entitled to impose a binding over order unilaterally. Such an
order would have had exactly the same effect as if the defendants had

acknowledged their indebtedness and entered into their own recognisance A in the amount fixed. It is convenient to take each of these points in turn.

By section 91 (1) of the Magistrates' Courts Act 1952 a magistrates' court has power, on complaints, to order a person to enter into a recognisance, with or without sureties, to keep the peace or to be of good behaviour. If the person fails or refuses to comply with the order, then by section 91 (3) the court may commit him to prison for a period not B exceeding six months, or until he sooner complies. The power under section 91 must be distinguished from the somewhat similar power under the Justices of the Peace Act 1361. Unlike the powers under the Act of 1952, the powers under the Act of 1361 are exercisable by a single justice; and they are exercisable not by reason of any offence having been committed, but as a measure of preventive justice, that is to say, where the person's conduct is such as to lead the justice to C suspect that there may be a breach of the peace, or that he may misbehave: see *Blackstone's Commentaries,* 16th ed. (1825), Book IV, p. 251; *Lansbury* v. *Riley* [1914] 3 K.B. 229; *Rex* v. *London County Quarter Sessions Appeals Committee, Ex parte Metropolitan Police Commissioner* [1948] 1 K.B. 670; *Reg.* v. *Aubrey-Fletcher, Ex parte Thompson* [1969] 1 W.L.R. 872 and see also *Everett* v. *Ribbands* [1952] 2 Q.B. 198, 204–206, D *per* Denning L.J. The sanction in the case of a failure or a refusal to enter into a recognisance under the Act of 1361 is the same as under the Act of 1952, namely, imprisonment.

By section 19 (1) of the Powers of Criminal Courts Act 1973 Parliament provided that neither the Crown Court nor a magistrates' court should impose imprisonment on a person under 17 years of age. Section 19 (4) is a definition section. It provides as follows: E

" In this section ' impose imprisonment ' means pass a sentence of imprisonment or commit to prison in default of payment of any sum of money, or for want of sufficient distress to satisfy any sum of money, or for failure to do or abstain from doing anything required to be done or left undone."

On the face of it, section 19 (1) of the Act of 1973 has taken away the F power of the justice to impose imprisonment on a person under 17 who has failed to enter into a recognisance when required. Mr. Black submits that it is not so. He submits that the powers of the justices under the Act of 1361 are part of their civil jurisdiction, and have been left intact by subsequent criminal legislation, including section 19 of the Act of 1973. He argues that Parliament cannot have intended to take away from G justices their only sanction under the Act of 1361.

We cannot accept that argument. Even if one assumes that the power of justices to bind over under the Act of 1361 is part of their civil, and not their criminal, jurisdiction, we would still hold that the prohibition on imprisonment of persons under 17 years of age applies. The language of section 19 (1) of the Powers of Criminal Courts Act 1973 is clear, H comprehensive and imperative. We see no reason to suppose that Parliament intended to make an exception in the case of the justices' civil jurisdiction. It would indeed be an odd result if, in the case of persons under 17, Parliament had intended to take away the power to commit under section 91 of the Magistrates' Courts Act 1952 where an offence had actually been committed, but had left unaffected the power to commit under the Act of 1361 where no offence had been committed.

A   It is therefore unnecessary to decide whether the premise to Mr. Black's argument is correct. At first sight however there is much to be said for the view, contrary to his argument, that the power to bind over to keep the peace is part of the justices' criminal jurisdiction. Certainly the occasion on which it was exercised in the present case was a criminal proceeding. *Reg.* v. *Southampton Justices, Ex parte Green* [1976] Q.B. 11 is a very different case. In that case a man was granted bail on terms that he B provide sureties. One of his sureties was his wife, who duly entered into a recognisance. The man failed to appear at the committal proceedings, and the justices estreated the wife's recognisance. She applied for leave to move the Divisional Court, but her application was refused. On appeal to the Court of Appeal it was held that the court had jurisdiction, because it was not a criminal cause or matter. The debt created by the recognis-C ance was a civil debt. But in that case there was no question of the exercise of any powers under the Act of 1361. The facts of the case are so removed from the present that it affords no real help.

    Mr. Black submitted as a last resort that there had not been a " failure " to do anything here within section 19 (4) of the Powers of Criminal Courts Act 1973—merely an outright refusal. That is a distinction without a difference.

D   Mr. Black further relied heavily on a decison of the Court of Appeal in *Morris* v. *Crown Office* [1970] 2 Q.B. 114. In that case a number of Welsh students created a disturbance in the High Court in the course of a hearing of a libel action. Eleven of them refused to apologise and were sentenced to three months' imprisonment for contempt of court. They were all, save one, under 21. They appealed to the Court of Appeal. E There were two points. First, it was said that a sentence of imprisonment should not have been imposed on those under 21 by reason of section 17 (2) of the Criminal Justice Act 1948, which corresponds to section 19 (2) of the Act of 1973. The Court of Appeal held that the judge was entitled to take the view that no other method of dealing with the students was appropriate, and that the second half of section 17 (2) is directory F and not mandatory. What was said on that point does not help the prosecutor.

    But there was a second point. It was argued that the sentence of imprisonment, being for only three months, should have been suspended under section 39 (3) of the Criminal Justice Act 1967. It was held by the Court of Appeal that section 39 of the Act of 1967 did not apply to a sentence of imprisonment for contempt. Davies L.J. said, at pp. 126–127:

G   " What may loosely be called the criminal law statutes apply in my view to the ordinary process of criminal prosecution, whether in a court of summary jurisdiction or at assizes or quarter sessions. Quite apart from the difficulty, to which Lord Denning M.R. adverted, in the way of enforcing a suspended sentence, if such were passed for a criminal contempt, there are a number of provisions in the criminal law H statutes, as I am calling them, which obviously have no application whatsoever to proceedings for contempt. Take probation: it would be quite impossible, I think, for a judge dealing with a case of contempt to make a probation order. Yet such a course is possible in all criminal cases. I cannot see for myself that it would be possible for the judge committing for contempt to send the offender, if he were of the appropriate age, to a detention centre. What it comes to, in my mind, is that the code—the procedure, if that is the apt

expression—is entirely different in cases of criminal contempt from **A**
that which applies in ordinary criminal cases."

Salmon L.J. said, at p. 129:

" This power to commit for what is inappropriately called ' contempt
of court' is sui generis and has from time immemorial reposed in
the judge for the protection of the public. Although the point is by
no means free from difficulty, I agree with my Lords that Parliament **B**
cannot be taken to have intended that this power should be fettered
by the Criminal Justice Acts of 1948 and 1967. To my mind it is
plain that Parliament never intended these Acts to apply to proceedings such as these. For one thing, the Act of 1967 supplied no
machinery whereby a suspended sentence for contempt of court could
ever be made effective if the culprit repeated his offence. Therefore **C**
the point that the judge's power was limited by section 39 (3) of
the Act of 1967 to imposing only suspended sentences fails."

Mr. Black argued that by the same process of reasoning the " criminal
law statutes " do not apply to the power of justices to commit to prison
for refusal to enter into a recognisance under the Act of 1361.

There are two reasons why we cannot accept that argument. In the **D**
first place the Court of Appeal clearly regarded the power to commit for
contempt as sui generis: see the successful argument of Sir Elwyn Jones
at p. 118 and the judgment of Salmon L.J. at p. 129. If the powers of
the court in the case of contempt are indeed sui generis, it follows that
they cannot provide any useful analogy in any other case. The powers
of the justices under the Act of 1361 may also be regarded as sui generis.
But that does not make them ejusdem generis. **E**

Secondly, the ratio of Lord Denning M.R.'s judgment (with which
Davies L.J. agreed) is the quite narrow ground that the Act of 1967 read as
a whole does not contain any provision for giving effect to a suspended
sentence in the case of contempt. Therefore section 39 cannot have been
intended to apply to such a case. There is nothing in section 19 of the
Powers of Criminal Courts Act 1973, or anywhere else, which makes it **F**
inapplicable to the power of justices to commit under the Act of 1361.

For the reasons which we have given we hold that the justices have
no power to impose a sentence of imprisonment for failure or refusal to
enter into a recognisance in the case of persons under 17.

We note in passing that in *Reg.* v. *Greenwich Justices, Ex parte
Carter* [1973] Crim.L.R. 444, the Divisional Court seems to have assumed **G**
that the justices would likewise have no power to impose a sentence of
imprisonment on a person under 17 for failing to comply with a witness
summons.

It was common ground that the justices had no power to impose any
other custodial sentence. The reason is that the power to order a person
under 21 to be detained in a detention centre or remand home is purely
statutory. By section 4 of the Criminal Justice Act 1961 the court is **H**
given power to make a detention order in the case of a person under 21
in lieu of passing a sentence of imprisonment. But it only applies in
the case of " an offender," which these persons, ex hypothesi, were not.
Moreover, by section 38 (1) a " sentence " is defined as excluding committal for default, which is in turn defined by section 39 (1) as including
a failure to do anything required to be done. So it is clear that detention
in a detention centre or remand home is not available as an alternative

A sanction in the case of a failure by a person under 17 to enter into a recognisance.

We now turn to Mr. Black's second main submission. Were the justices entitled to impose a binding over order unilaterally?

At first sight there is much to be said for the view that an order that a person be bound over to keep the peace or to be of good behaviour
B is like any other order imposed by a court. To suggest that such an order requires consent before it is effective is almost a contradiction in terms. Moreover, a consent which can be compelled, in the case of a person over 17, by the threat of imprisonment, is hardly the sort of consent which, in other circumstances, the court looks on with favour. But counsel has taken us through the whole history of the matter, starting with *Dalton's Countrey Justice* (1697), described by Lord Goddard in *Rex*
C v. *London County Quarter Sessions Appeals Committee, Ex parte Metropolitan Police Commissioners* [1948] 1 K.B. 670, 675, as a work of the highest authority. As a result we have been convinced first, that the essence of a binding over is that the person bound over acknowledges his indebtedness to the Queen, and thereby becomes bound in the sum fixed by the court, and secondly, that the court cannot, as it were, force such an acknowledgement upon a person behind his back, or treat him as being
D bound when he is not. The court's only remedy where a person refuses to acknowledge his indebtedness, and thereby becomes bound, is put him in prison until he does.

The process of binding over to keep the peace is described in *Dalton's Countrey Justice* (1697), at p. 263, as follows:

E   " Surety for the Peace, is the acknowledge of a Recognisance (or Bond) to the King (taken by a competent Judge of Record) for the keeping of the Peace: and it is called Surety, of the word *Securitas,* because the party that was in fear, is thereby the more secure and safe."

From this and subsequent passages it apears that the " security " offered by the process of binding over consists in the recognisance, or bond,
F entered into either by the principal or by his sureties or both. In *Blackstone's Commentaries,* 16th ed. (1825), Book IV, pp. 252–253, there is this passage:

    " This security consists in being bound, with one or more securities, in a recognisance or obligation to the King, entered on record, and taken in some court or by some judicial officer; whereby the parties
G   acknowledge themselves to be indebted to the crown in the sum required, (for instance £100) with condition to be void and of none effect, if the party shall appear in court on such a day, and in the meantime shall keep the peace; either generally, towards the King, and all his liege people; or particularly also, with regard to the person who craves the security."

H Then, at p. 254:

    " Wives may demand [such security] against their husbands: or husbands, if necessary, against their wives. But femes covert, and infants under age, ought to find security by their friends only, and not to be bound themselves: for they are incapable of engaging themselves to answer any debt; which, as we observed, is the nature of these recognisances or acknowledgments."

578

A similar point is made in *Hawkins' Pleas of the Crown*, 8th ed. (1824), A vol. I, p. 479 as follows: " But infants and femes covert ought to find security by their friends, and not to be bound themselves."

These last passages seem to us particularly significant, for they show that the essential element in the process of binding over is that the person binds himself. If the court could impose an obligation to be bound, then there would be no difference between the case of femes B coverts and infants and any other case.

There is nothing in any of the books to which we were referred which suggests that justices have any power to impose an obligation to be bound, except indirectly by threatening imprisonment. If they have such a power, then it seems strange that the much more drastic sanction of imprisonment should have become so firmly rooted in our law at such an early stage. The form of recognisance into which a person is required to C enter has remained in substantially the same language for centuries. By that language the person acknowledges that he is indebted to the Queen in the sum fixed. In our judgment, it is now far too late to argue that the acknowledgment can be treated as a mere formality, which can be dispensed with when occasion demands. Acknowledgment of the indebtedness is an essential ingredient in the binding over process. We would D therefore reject Mr. Black's second main submission.

That disposes of the present appeal. Though we have every sympathy with the justices in the position in which they found themselves, they reached the right conclusion in law. The appeal is accordingly dismissed.

We would add this. It is clear from what we have said that the law is in an unsatisfactory state. The justices should not be left powerless as they are. E

Appeal dismissed.
Prosecution costs out of central funds.

Solicitors: *Blyth, Dutton, Holloway, for R. O. M. Lovibond, Bristol; Gerald Davey & Co., Bristol.* F

[Reported by ISOBEL COLLINS, Barrister-at-Law]

[QUEEN'S BENCH DIVISION] G

* KAUR *v.* CHIEF CONSTABLE FOR HAMPSHIRE

1981 Jan. 29   Lord Lane C.J. and Lloyd J.

Crime — Theft — Dishonest appropriation — Selection of goods in H *store with two different price labels — Intention to obtain goods at lower price—Cashier charging lower price—Whether contract of sale void — Whether appropriation of property belonging to another—Theft Act* 1968 *(c.* 60*), s.* 1 (1)

Shoes were displayed in a store on two racks, shoes on one rack being priced at £6·99 and on the other at £4·99. The defendant selected a pair of shoes from the £6·99 rack and noticed that one shoe bore a price label to that effect and the

The Weekly Law Reports, May 8, 1981

579

1 W.L.R.   Kaur v. Chief Constable for Hants. (D.C.)

A   other had a £4·99 label. Without concealing either label, she
took the shoes to the cashier with the intention of obtaining
the advantage of the lower price, and on being asked for £4·99
she paid and left the store with the shoes. Outside the store
she was stopped and later charged with theft contrary to
section 1 (1) of the Theft Act 1968. The justices held that
the cashier had no authority to accept an offer to pay £4·99 and
that, since the defendant knew that that was not the correct
B   price, the contract was void and the defendant had appropriated
property belonging to the store and was guilty of theft.
     On appeal by the defendant: —
     Held, allowing the appeal, that the cashier had authority
to charge the price marked on the shoes, and the fact that she
chose the lower of two prices so marked did not mean that
she was acting without authority; that a mistake as to the
price induced by wrong marking was not so fundamental as to
C   destroy the validity of the contract of sale, but merely rendered
it voidable, and, accordingly, since the contract had not been
avoided by the time that the defendant left the store, property
in the shoes passed on payment and the defendant had not
appropriated property belonging to another (post, p. 583B–G).

     The following cases are referred to in the judgment of Lord Lane C.J.:
D   *Anderton* v. *Wish* [1980] Crim.L.R. 319, D.C.
     Hartog v. *Colin and Shields* [1939] 3 All E.R. 566.
     Lacis v. *Cashmarts* [1969] 2 Q.B. 400; [1969] 2 W.L.R. 329, D.C.
     Pilgram v. *Rice-Smith* [1977] 1 W.L.R. 671; [1977] 2 All E.R. 658, D.C.
     Reg. v. *Lawrence (Alan)* [1972] A.C. 626; [1971] 3 W.L.R. 225; [1971]
          2 All E.R. 1253, H.L.(E.).

E
     No additional cases were cited in argument.

     CASE STATED by Hampshire justices sitting at Southampton.
     On October 18, 1979, a charge was preferred by the prosecutor against
the defendant, Dip Kaur, that she on September 1, 1979, at Southampton,
stole a pair of shoes valued at £6·99, the property of British Home Stores
F   Ltd., contrary to section 1 (1) of the Theft Act 1968.
     The justices heard the case on August 29, 1980, and September 12,
1980, and found the following facts. On September 1, 1979, the defendant was present in the retail shop of British Home Stores Ltd., Above
Bar, Southampton. Among the goods displayed in the shop were two
adjacent racks of shoes. The defendant saw that one of the racks bore
a notice indicating that the price of each pair of shoes displayed on that
G   rack was £6·99, and that the other rack bore a notice similarly indicating
a price of £4·99 for each pair of shoes displayed thereon.
     The defendant took one pair of shoes from the rack priced £6·99,
noticing that to one of those shoes was attached a price label marked
" £6·99 " but that to the other shoe was attached a similar label marked
" £4·99." The correct price of the pair of shoes selected by the defendant
H   was £6·99. She realised that, having observed that the shoes priced £4·99
per pair were displayed on the adjacent rack. She did not interfere with
any price label. She placed both shoes she had selected on a counter in
front of a cashier, without concealing either price label, but intending if
possible to take advantage of the retailer's mistake in pricing one of the
shoes. The cashier asked her to pay £4·99 for the pair of shoes and, on
receiving payment in that sum from the defendant, issued a receipt
accordingly and delivered the shoes to her in a bag supplied by the

The Weekly Law Reports, May 8, 1981

580

Kaur v. Chief Constable for Hants. (D.C.)   [1981]

retailer. The defendant believed that it would be wrong to take the shoes   A
out of the shop in these circumstances, but nevertheless did so, and was
accosted by a store detective.   At the conclusion of the case for the prosecution on August 29, 1980, the defendant submitted that there was no
case to answer.   The justices rejected the submission and the defendant
gave evidence contradicting several major points of the prosecution evidence.   After legal argument the justices adjourned the case to September   B
12, 1980, for research into authorities.

At that hearing no further evidence was called but further legal argument took place.   It was conceded by the defendant that if, as the prosecutor alleged, both shoes had initially borne price labels marked " £6·99 "
and the defendant had exchanged one of those labels for a label marked
" £4·99," the justices would be entitled, following *Anderton* v. *Wish*
[1980] Crim.L.R. 319, to convict her on the charge of theft.   It was, how-   C
ever, contended by the defendant that if she had not interfered with any
price label but had found one shoe of the pair with a label marked
" £4·99 " already attached and had tendered the pair of shoes to the
cashier without comment (i) she had not, prior to her arrival at the cash
point, done anything capable of amounting in law to an appropriation of
the shoes; (ii) at the cash point she in effect offered to buy the shoes for   D
£4·99 and the cashier's acceptance of that offer bound the retailer to a
contract of sale at that price; (iii) such a contract would not be void on
the principle contained in *Hartog* v. *Colin and Shields* [1939] 3 All E.R.
566, because the defendant could not know the price of the shoes until
the cashier stated a price of £4·99.   Any mere belief she might have
formed up to that point concerning a higher price would not suffice to
avoid the contract; (iv) on payment of the price fixed at £4·99 the shoes   E
became in all respects the property of the defendant and could not thereafter be stolen by her; and (v) the defendant's conduct had been outwardly impeccable, and she could not be guilty of theft by virtue of a
mere belief that she was not entitled to buy the shoes for £4·99 or was
committing an offence.

It was contended by the prosecutor that, even if the defendant had   F
not interfered with any price label, provided she knew that the sum of
£4·99 demanded by the cashier was less than the price fixed by the retailer
(i) it was open to the justices to find, following *Hartog* v. *Colin and
Shields* [1939] 3 All E.R. 566, that any contract appearing to be formed
at the cash point was void, and (ii) if so, the shoes remained in all respects
the property of the retailer and on removing them from the shop the
defendant dishonestly appropriated them within the meaning of the Theft   G
Act 1968.

The justices were of the opinion, on the basis of the facts they found,
that the cashier had no authority to accept on behalf of the retailer an
offer by the defendant to buy the shoes for £4·99 and, since the defendant
knew that was not the correct price, the apparent contract made at the
cash point was void; the transaction at the cash point did not therefore   H
convey ownership of the shoes to the defendant, so that on leaving the
shop she appropriated property belonging to British Home Stores Ltd.;
and it was right to describe as dishonest the state of mind in which the
defendant appropriated the shoes.   They accordingly convicted the defendant on the charge and adjudged that she pay a fine of £25.

The defendant appealed.   The question for the opinion of the High
Court was whether upon the facts found by the justices they were right

The Weekly Law Reports, May 8, 1981

581

1 W.L.R.   Kaur v. Chief Constable for Hants. (D.C.)

A in law to conclude that the defendant had dishonestly appropriated property belonging to British Home Stores Ltd. so as to be guilty of theft contrary to section 1 (1) of the Theft Act 1968.

Stephen Alexander for the defendant.
Nigel Mylne for the prosecutor.

B

LORD LANE C.J. This is an appeal by way of case stated from the justices for the County of Hampshire acting for the petty sessional division of Southampton. It arises in this way. On October 18, 1979, the prosecutor preferred a charge against the defendant, that she had stolen a pair of shoes in September 1979, valued at £6·99, the property of British Home Stores Ltd.

C The facts of the alleged theft were these. On September 1, 1979, the defendant went to British Home Stores at Southampton. Amongst other goods displayed, there were two racks of shoes, one alongside the other. One of the racks contained shoes which were said to be priced at £6·99 and the other, adjacent rack contained shoes marked at £4·99. The defendant took a pair of shoes from the £6·99 rack and she noticed

D that the pair were not identically marked; one of the shoes was marked £6·99 and the other was marked £4·99. The correct price in fact of the shoes she had selected was £6·99 and the justices found as a fact that the defendant realised this. She did not, as is regrettably sometimes done, interfere in any way with the price labels on the shoes. She took the pair of shoes to the check-out. She placed them on the desk in front

E of the cashier. She made no attempt to conceal either of the price labels, but she hoped that the cashier would select the wrong label and would charge her £4·99 instead of £6·99. She was going to buy the shoes whichever price was demanded. She was lucky. She must have thought so, at any rate, because the cashier rang up £4·99. That sum was handed over by the defendant to the cashier, who put it in the till and, all that having happened, the shoes were then placed in a bag. They were

F handed to the defendant who left to go home.

The justices found as a fact " The defendant believed that it would be wrong to take the shoes out of the shop in these circumstances, but nevertheless did so, and was accosted by a store detective." These proceedings were then launched. It seems, from what we have been told, that initially the suspicion was that this lady had in fact switched the

G labels on the shoes, but that was not the case.

The justices came to the conclusion that the cashier had no authority to accept, on behalf of the retailer, an offer by the defendant to buy the shoes for £4·99, and, since the defendant knew that this was not the correct price, the apparent contract made at the cash point was void. Secondly, they were of the opinion that the transaction at the cash point

H did not convey ownership to the defendant, so that on leaving the shop she appropriated the property belonging to British Home Stores Ltd. Finally, they concluded, it was right to describe as dishonest the state of mind with which the defendant appropriated the shoes. Accordingly the justices convicted the defendant on the charge and adjudged that she be fined £25. They ask this court to say:

"Whether upon the facts found by us we were right in law to
conclude that the defendant had dishonestly appropriated property

The Weekly Law Reports, May 8, 1981

582

Lord Lane C.J.   Kaur v. Chief Constable for Hants. (D.C.)   [1981]

belonging to British Home Stores Ltd. so as to be guilty of theft   A
contrary to section 1 (1) of the Theft Act 1968."

It is sometimes of advantage to reduce this sort of problem to its
ingredients. In order to bring the charge home to the defendant the
prosecution had to prove the following matters: first of all, that the
defendant acted dishonestly; secondly, that she appropriated the shoes,
that is to say, she assumed over the shoes the rights of an owner; thirdly,   B
that at that moment those shoes belonged to somebody else; and fourthly
and finally, that she intended permanently to deprive the owner of them.

It was found by the justices that she realised that the correct price
of the shoes selected by her was £6·99, and that she believed it would be
wrong to take the shoes out of the shop in the circumstances. They
came to the conclusion that it was right to describe that as dishonest.   C
She certainly assumed the rights of an owner when, having paid, she took
the shoes in the paper bag from the cashier in order to go home. I do
not pause to inquire at the moment whether " appropriation " is an accurate description of what she did. There is no doubt that she intended
permanently to deprive the owner of the shoes. So the only matter in
issue in this case is whether the prosecution had proved that at the
moment she took the shoes out of the shop the ownership of the shoes   D
was still in the shop. If so, the offence was proved; if not, it was not
proved.

There is ample authority for the proposition that, so far as supermarkets, at any rate, are concerned, and in so far as an ordinary transaction in a supermarket is concerned, the intention of the parties, under
section 18 of the Sale of Goods Act 1979, is that the ownership of the   E
goods should pass on payment by the customer of the price to the cashier.
It also seems to accord with good sense, and if any authority is needed
for that, it is to be found in Lacis v. Cashmarts [1969] 2 Q.B. 400.

Prima facie, then, when the defendant picked up the shoes to take
them home, she was already the owner of the shoes. They did not then
belong to somebody else, and she was not intending to deprive the owner
of them.   F

But the prosecutor contends that the apparent contract between the
shop and the defendant was no contract at all, was void, and that therefore, despite the payment made by the defendant, the ownership of the
shoes never passed to the defendant, and the offence was accordingly
made out. Mr. Mylne puts it with very great simplicity: she never paid
the price, he says, and so there was never any contract at all. He went   G
so far as to suggest that if this lady had been given 10p too much by way
of change and realised that she had been given 10p too much by way
of change and had walked out of the shop with the shoes, in those circumstances she would likewise have been guilty of theft of the shoes.

The first thing to note, as indeed the justices did, is that this was not
a case where there was any deception at all perpetrated by the defendant.
She had not switched the price labels, as happened in Anderton v. Wish   H
[1980] Crim.L.R. 319, in which it was held that the property was appropriated when the price tickets were changed. There is no need to comment on that decision, although it has been the subject of adverse
criticism.

The prosecution, before the justices, as they did here, relied upon
the decision in Hartog v. Colin and Shields [1939] 3 All E.R. 566. In
that case there had been extensive negotiations between the parties, both

The Weekly Law Reports, May 8, 1981

583

1 W.L.R.   Kaur v. Chief Constable for Hants. (D.C.)   Lord Lane C.J.

A oral and in writing, about the sale by the defendants to the plaintiffs of hare-skins. All those negotiations had been based on a price of so many pence per piece. The final offer by the defendants to sell was mistakenly quoted in so many pence per pound. Skins worth 10¾d. each were on this basis being offered at 3¾d. On discovering their obvious mistake, the defendants refused to deliver the skins and the plaintiffs claimed damages. The report of the extempore judgment of Singleton J. is not

B altogether clear, but the facts are so far divorced from those on the present case that they provide little assistance. We were also referred to *Pilgram* v. *Rice-Smith* [1977] 1 W.L.R. 671. That was a case where the shop assistant and the customer agreed together to defraud the shop-owners, and likewise does not provide any guidance.

The justices based their conclusion primarily on the fact that the

C cashier had no authority to accept on behalf of the retailer an offer by the defendant to buy the shoes for £4·99. In my judgment they were in error. The cashier had the authority to charge the price which was marked on the ticket on the goods. The fact that there were two different prices marked and that she chose the lower one does not mean that she was acting without authority. No false representation was made by the

D defendant. This is not one of those cases where the true offence was really obtaining by deception under section 15, and where the prosecution should, accordingly, have alleged that offence, and have resisted the temptation to charge theft. This was either theft or nothing.

It seems to me that the court should not be astute to find that a theft has taken place where it would be straining the language so to hold, or where the ordinary person would not regard the defendant's acts, though

E possibly morally reprehensible, as theft. In essence here, as I have already said, the problem is, whether the ownership of the shoes passed to the defendant, or whether the apparent contract was void by reason of mistake. Where questions of mistake are involved there will always be great difficulty in deciding where the line is to be drawn and what renders a contract void and what renders a contract merely voidable.

F The mistake here was the cashier's, induced by the wrong marking on the goods as to the proper price of these goods. It was not to the nature of the goods or the identity of the buyer. Speaking for myself, I find it very difficult to see how this could be described as the sort of mistake which was so fundamental as to destroy the validity of the contract. It was in essence, as Lloyd J. pointed out in argument, very little, if at all, different from a mistake as to quality. A mistake as to quality

G has never been held sufficiently fundamental so as to avoid a contract. The cashier was in effect thinking that these were £4·99 quality shoes, when in fact they were £6·99 quality shoes. Consequently in my judgment the prosecution failed to prove that this alleged contract was void. If it was merely voidable it had certainly not been avoided when the time came for the defendant to pick up the shoes and go.

H Happily in this case we are not concerned with the difficulties raised by the decision in *Reg.* v. *Lawrence (Alan)* [1972] A.C. 626, because here the ownership of the goods had passed on payment, and the appropriation was at a later stage, when the shoes were put in the bag and carried away by the defendant. Nor is it necessary to discuss the vexed question of whether the true owner, albeit in a voidable contract, can properly be said to " appropriate " his own property or to " assume the rights of an owner " over it when he takes possession of it. At first sight those

584

words would appear to imply some action which was adverse to the in-   A
terests of another. Nor do I pause to consider whether the justices'
finding of dishonesty on the part of the defendant can be justified;
whether in other words this is the sort of dishonesty which is envisaged
by the Theft Act. I should also add, for the sake of completeness, that
section 5 (4) of the Theft Act has no application here, because the defendant was not under an obligation to make restitution of the shoes at   B
the material time. For these various reasons I would allow this appeal
and would answer the justices' question, namely whether upon the facts
found by them they were right in law to conclude as they did, in the
negative.

  LLOYD J. I agree.
                                                                            C
                     Appeal allowed with costs.
                     Conviction quashed.
                     Prosecutor's costs out of central funds.

  Solicitors: *Plumer Price & Beswick, Southampton; R. N. Bourne,
Winchester.*
                                                                            D
  [Reported by MISS LESLEY HEWLETT, Barrister-at-Law]

                                                                            E

                          [COURT OF APPEAL]

* REGINA *v.* SECRETARY OF STATE FOR THE ENVIRONMENT   F
            AND ANOTHER, *Ex parte* POWIS

1980 Oct. 22, 23, 27, 28, 29;   Stephenson and Dunn L.JJ.
      Nov. 6   and Sir David Cairns

        *Landlord and Tenant—Business premises (security of tenure)—
        Certificate of Secretary of State—Local authority applying   G
        for certificate of change of use—Local authority wishing to
        store highways materials on site of premises—Local authority
        of use and occupation "requisite" for purposes of landlord
        —Landlord and Tenant Act* 1954 (2 & 3 Eliz. 2, c. 56), s. 57 (1)

            The appellant held about an acre of land, adjacent to a
        local authority refuse tip, under a lease from the county coun-
        cil. On it he carried on the business of a car breaker and scrap   H
        metal dealer. The county council's development plans for the
        area involved obtaining possession of the land occupied by the
        tenant for use as a store for highways materials. In 1975 the
        county council served notice on the tenant under the Landlord
        and Tenant Act 1954 to obtain possession of the land in order
        to carry out substantial reconstruction works. The tenant's
        defence that that notice had been waived by acceptance of
        rent was upheld by the judge in the county court. In 1977 the
        county council applied to the Secretary of State for the

A   Environment for a certificate under section 57 (1) of the Landlord and Tenant Act 1954 [1] to obtain possession of the land, and both parties made written submissions to him. In 1978 the Secretary of State granted a certificate, stating that it was requisite for the purpose of the county council that the use and occupation of the land should be changed by February 1979. The tenant was thereby precluded from applying to the court for a new tenancy under the Act. In his reasons the

B   Secretary of State said that the county council genuinely intended to carry out the proposals and that the public need to repossess the land justified the grant of the certificate. The tenant applied for judicial review by way of certiorari on the grounds, inter alia, that the Secretary of State had misdirected himself as to the meaning of " requisite " and should not have relied on the assertion of the county council to establish the fact that the use of the tenant's land was requisite for the

C   council's purposes. He also sought to adduce fresh evidence. The Divisional Court refused the application holding that " requisite " in section 57 (1) meant " required by circumstances," and refused to admit the fresh evidence.

On the tenant's appeal: —

Held, dismissing the appeal, (1) that on its true construction " requisite " in section 57 (1) of the Landlord and Tenant Act 1954 meant " reasonably necessary," which was compatible

D   with its ordinary and natural meaning of " required by circumstances " and its context in Part IV of the Act; that the Secretary of State, in giving reasons for his decision, had been entitled to say that, although " requisite " meant genuinely required, the tenant's site was in any event reasonably necessary for the county council's purposes, and had not erred in law; that the material on which the Secretary of State could rely in reaching a decision depended on the statutory provi

E   sions applicable to, and the circumstances of, each case, and where there was no public hearing he had to assess the submissions and reach a decision on the material before him after weighing the statements submitted; that it was impossible to say that the Secretary of State had been wrong in taking into account the material put before him or that he had failed to take into account any relevant factors, and, accordingly, the Divisional Court had been right to refuse the application for

F   certiorari (post, pp. 591E, 592D–E, 593E—594A, G–H, 595D).

Robinson v. Minister of Town and Country Planning [1947] K.B. 702 and Coleen Properties Ltd. v. Minister of Housing and Local Government [1971] 1 W.L.R. 433, C.A. considered.

(2) That fresh evidence should be admitted on an application for judicial review only in order to show what material was before the Secretary of State or tribunal, to decide a

G   question of fact where jurisdiction depended on it, to inquire into a procedural error or where proceedings were tainted by misconduct of the Secretary of State or inferior tribunal; that the fresh evidence sought to be admitted in the present case did not come within any of those categories, and accordingly should be excluded (post, pp. 595G—596A, 597D–F).

Ashbridge Investments Ltd. v. Minister of Housing and

H   Local Government [1965] 1 W.L.R. 1320, C.A. and Reg. v. West Sussex Quarter Sessions, Ex parte Albert and Maud Johnson Trust Ltd. [1974] Q.B. 24, C.A. applied.

Secretary of State for Education and Science v. Tameside Metropolitan Borough Council [1977] A.C. 1014, H.L.(E.) considered.

Decision of Divisional Court of the Queen's Bench Division affirmed.

---

[1] Landlord and Tenant Act 1954, s. 57 (1): see post p. 587A.

The following cases are referred to in the judgment of the court: A

Ashbridge Investments Ltd. v. *Minister of Housing and Local Government*
[1965] 1 W.L.R. 1320; [1965] 3 All E.R. 371, C.A.

Associated Provincial Picture Houses Ltd. v. *Wednesbury Corporation*
[1948] 1 K.B. 223; [1947] 2 All E.R. 680, C.A.

Coleen Properties Ltd. v. *Minister of Housing and Local Government*
[1971] 1 W.L.R. 433; [1971] 1 All E.R. 1049, C.A.

Reg. v. *West Sussex Quarter Sessions, Ex parte Albert and Maud Johnson*   B
Trust Ltd. [1974] Q.B. 24; [1973] 3 W.L.R. 149; [1973] 3 All E.R.
289 C.A.

Robinson v. *Minister of Town and Country Planning* [1947] K.B. 702.

Secretary of State for Education and Science v. *Tameside Metropolitan
Borough Council* [1977] A.C. 1014; [1976] 3 W.L.R. 641; [1976] 3 All
E.R. 665, C.A. and H.L.(E.).

X.L. Fisheries Ltd. v. *Leeds Corporation* [1955] 2 Q.B. 636; [1955] 3   C
W.L.R. 393; [1955] 2 All E.R. 875, C.A.

No additional cases were cited in argument.

APPEAL from the Divisional Court of the Queen's Bench Division.

On May 23, 1980, the Divisional Court (Shaw L.J. and Kilner Brown J.)
refused an application for an order of certiorari made by the tenant,   D
Arthur Glyn Powis, to quash the certificate granted by the Secretary of
State for the Environment on August 7, 1978, under section 57 of the
Landlord and Tenant Act 1954 and refused an application for a declaration that the tenant's land, in respect of which the certificate was granted,
was not " requisite " for the purposes of the respondents, Buckinghamshire
County Council. The tenant sought an order that the Secretary of State's   E
certificate should be quashed or, alternatively, that his land should be
declared not to be " requisite " for the county council's purposes on the
grounds, inter alia, (1) that the Divisional Court had misdirected itself
as to certain facts as a result of which it had misdirected itself as to the
issues in the case; (2) that it erred in law in finding that the Secretary
of State had acted reasonably; (3) that the court had erred in law in
holding that " requisite " in section 57 (1) of the Landlord and Tenant   F
Act 1954 did not mean " essential for " or " necessary," and in so
holding the court failed to consider that, since the section conferred
executive power, its construction should favour the subject; (4) that the
court had erred in law in that it refused to receive new evidence, which
consisted of notes of the planning inquiry concerning the land; and
(5) that the court had erred in law in holding that the county council   G
were not unfairly or improperly motivated against the tenant.

The facts are stated in the judgment of the court.

R. G. Rougier Q.C. and *R. G. Marshall-Andrews* for the tenant.
Simon D. Brown for the Secretary of State.
Nicholas Huskinson for the county council.

H

November 6. DUNN L.J. read the following judgment of the court.
This is an appeal by leave from the refusal of the Divisional Court on
judicial review to grant an order of certiorari to bring up and quash a
certificate of the Secretary of State for the Environment given under
section 57 (1) of the Landlord and Tenant Act 1954.

The material statutory provisions are as follows—and I read the
material words of section 57:

A   " (1) Where the interest of the landlord or any superior landlord in the property comprised in any tenancy belongs to or is held . . . by a local authority, . . . the Minister or Board in charge of any government department may certify that it is requisite for the purposes of the first-mentioned department, or, as the case may be, of the authority, . . . that the use or occupation of the property or a part thereof shall be changed by a specified date. (2) A certificate under the last fore-

B   going subsection shall not be given unless the owner of the interest belonging or held as mentioned in the last foregoing subsection has given to the tenant a notice stating—(a) that the question of the giving of such a certificate is under consideration by the Minister or Board specified in the notice, and (b) that if within 21 days of the giving of the notice the tenant makes to that Minister or Board repre-

C   sentations in writing with respect to that question, they will be considered before the question is determined, and if the tenant makes and such representations within the said 21 days the Minister or Board shall consider them before determining whether to give the certificate."

Section 57 (3) and (4) provides in effect that the section has no immediate
D   effect on the rights of a contractual tenant of business premises. But once the contractual tenancy is validly determined by a landlord's notice under section 25 of the Act, then where a certificate has been given the tenant is precluded from applying for a new tenancy and the court has no power to grant the tenant a new tenancy expiring later than the date specified in the certificate. Section 59 of the Act provides for compensation to a tenant in respect of whose property a certificate has been given. Such compensation
E   is in accordance with section 37 of the Act.

The result of these provisions is that business tenants of local authorities and other public bodies may be deprived by certificate under section 57 of the Act of the rights which they would otherwise have had of applying to the county court to obtain a new tenancy. They are deprived of the opportunity of testing in court any objection by the landlord under section
F   30 of the Act to a grant of a new tenancy, with the advantage of a public hearing, discovery of documents and cross-examination of witnesses. The decision under section 57 is a ministerial decision which can only be challenged in the courts on the well established principles laid down in *Associated Provincial Picture Houses Ltd.* v. *Wednesbury Corporation* [1948] 1 K.B. 223 and other similar cases. As Lord Evershed M.R. said in *X.L. Fisheries Ltd.* v. *Leeds Corporation* [1955] 2 Q.B. 636, 648,
G   section 57 confers certain particular privileges on public authorities.

The appellant is the tenant of about one acre of land at High Heavens Wood, Marlow Bottom, Buckinghamshire. He held originally under a lease from the High Wycombe Borough Council dated June 1, 1964. The lease comprised, in addition to the land, a right of way to afford access. It was a yearly tenancy determinable by a quarter's notice given by either party
H   and the yearly rent was £5. Amongst the tenant's covenants there was a covenant " not to use or permit the said piece of land to be used in connection with any trade or business other than that of breaking up derelict motor vehicles." The demised site was immediately adjacent to a large rubbish tip owned by the borough council at High Heavens Wood and extending to some 64 acres. On December 11, 1972, a new lease in the same terms was entered into between the borough council and the tenants. The tenant also had an agreement with the borough council for the dis-

588

posal of abandoned vehicles which had been removed by the borough A
council pursuant to their powers and duties under section 21 (1) of the
Civic Amenities Act 1967, and in addition he carried on a general business
on the site of a car breaker and scrap metal dealer with the concurrence
of the borough council. At that time there were two other traders, a Mr.
Jackman and a Mr. Bowan, carrying on similar businesses at different
sites. Mr. Jackman was a tenant of the borough council, Mr. Bowan was
not. As a result of the local government reorganisation in 1974 the Bucking- B
hamshire County Council took over the relevant functions of the High
Wycombe Borough Council. The agreement for the disposal of vehicles
with the tenant was terminated, and on April 1, 1974, the reversion of the
lease vested in the county council and they then became the tenant's landlords.

On August 4, 1975, outline planning permission for two and a half C
acres of land immediately north of the refuse tip was granted by the
county council to itself for use as a gipsy caravan site. This permission
provides:

" (4) a landscaping scheme shall be submitted to and approved by the
county council . . . including the planting of trees and shrubs where
necessary . . . in order to preserve the amenities of the neighbourhood." D

The southern part of this site encroached onto the northern part of the
tenant's land. In fact the county council did not use the northern part of
the land because it was in other ownership and would have required a
compulsory purchase order. So the limits of the caravan site were confined to the southern portion.

In March 1976 the county council as they were entitled to do also E
granted themselves planning permission for the erection of a refuse
pulverisor and transfer station for the treatment of refuse and salvage at
the High Heavens refuse tip. Final planning permission was granted on
March 23, 1976. The permission was subject to the following condition:

" (1) The screen bank along the south side of the transfer station shall
be completed and landscaped within one year of the station being
brought into operation, and shall be constructed so as to effectively F
screen the buildings, treatment area, highway depot and car breaking
areas from the south, and the trees shall be planted in the first planting
season following completion of any section of the bank.
" The reasons for imposing the above conditions are: To minimise
the effect that the development is likely to have on the amenities of
the locality." G

It was not surprising that that condition was inserted because High
Heavens Wood was scheduled as an area of outstanding beauty.

There was no other condition attached to the planning permission
although, according to the county council in representations which they
subsequently made to the Secretary of State, the planning permission was
granted on the understanding that the area to be used for waste disposal H
purposes would be kept to the minimum, that the rest of the site would
be restored to an agricultural use, and that the appearance of the waste
disposal facility would be as tidy as the nature of the business would
allow. Two banks of earth were erected by the county council to mark the
southern limit of the refuse treatment area and to screen it from the
south.

Thus the tenant's site was sandwiched between the proposed gipsy

A   caravan site to the north and the refuse treatment area to the south. Meanwhile on August 27, 1975, the county council served notice on the tenant under section 25 of the Landlord and Tenant Act 1954. That notice stated that on the termination of the current tenancy the county council intended to demolish or reconstruct the whole or a substantial part of the premises or to carry out substantial work of construction on the whole or part of them, and that they could not reasonably do so without obtaining posses-
B   sion of the premises. This constituted reliance on section 30 (1) (f) of the Act. The tenant did not serve a counter-notice under section 26 but filed a defence alleging that the section 25 notice had been waived by subsequent acceptance of rent by the county council. The judge upheld that defence and gave judgment for the tenant on May 5, 1977. So the tenant still holds under the tenancy of December 11, 1972.

C   Certainly by 1976 the county council had decided to reduce the number of car breakers from three to one. They sent out invitations to tender for the lease of the site occupied by Mr. Jackman, opposite the tenant's site to the west of the access road to the tip. The tenant duly tendered on July 23, 1976, but his tender was not accepted. Mr. Jackman also tendered but his tender was not accepted and the successful tenderer was a Mr. Powell. Mr. Jackman had by then given up his site pursuant
D   to a possession order against him in the county court on October 30, 1975. The third breaker, Mr. Bowan, remained in occupation of his site just to the south of the tenant's site but he has now also given up his site and left the area.

       In May 1977 shortly after the county court judgment, the county council caused the tenant's telephone to be cut off at the site. We mention
E   this because it is relied on as evidence of bad faith on the part of the county council. The tenant at once issued a writ in the Queen's Bench Division and obtained an interim injunction on June 3, 1977, which was discharged on June 16, on undertakings by the county council in effect not to take any steps to remove the telephone. The tenant was granted his costs in any event.

F   On July 15, 1977, the county council applied to the Secretary of State for a certificate under section 57 of the Act. The application was supported by reasons which were sent to the Secretary of State under a covering letter, although the county council at first refused to send their reasons to the tenant. However these were later sent to him by the Secretary of State. On August 4, the tenant submitted written representations to the Secretary of State and there were further represenations and reasons
G   by both parties including a report from a surveyor instructed by the tenant. All this material was put before the Secretary of State in writing.

       The reasons given by the county council in support of their application were that the site was required: (1) partly for a gipsy caravan site, (2) for a store for highways material and (3) for the erection of fencing round the pulverisor and transfer stations. The tenant, having agreed to surrender
H   the northern part of his site for incorporation into the gipsy caravan site, and the proposed fencing having been shown to be unnecessary, the only ground finally relied on by the county council was that the site was required for use as a store for highways materials.

       On August 7, 1978, the Secretary of State issued his decision by letter. Paragraph 2 of that letter reads:

       " The Secretary of State, having considered the representations of the tenant, is satisfied that it is requisite for the purposes of the council that the use and occupation of the property should be changed by A February 23, 1979, and hereby certifies accordingly."

On October 31, 1979, in reply to a request by the tenant, the Secretary of State gave his reasons for his decision although, as he said, he was not bound to do so. He set out the nature of the application, the submissions of both parties and his conclusion which was in the following terms:

"5. The Secretary of State carefully considered the submissions of both B parties. It was noted that the pulveriser complex proposals had gone ahead, apparently without [the tenant's] land being required in connection with preparatory work for fencing, and account was taken of [the tenant's] willingness to give up part of his land for the proposed gypsy site. However, the evidence showed that only a very small area was required in connection with the fencing proposals and it was not C accepted that the council's decision not to proceed in accordance with the permission granted for a gypsy caravan site in 1975 indicated that they did not really require [the tenant's] land. The majority of [the tenant's] land was, in fact, required in connection with the council's proposals for a highways materials store; and the council's submission was accepted that the land was suitable for this purpose and that, whilst they did not necessarily have to show that this was the case, D no alternative site was available, either within the area covered by planning permission or elsewhere. [The tenant's] personal reasons for opposing the grant of a certificate were taken into account but, on the evidence as a whole, the Secretary of State was satisfied that it was requisite for the purposes of the council that the use or occupation of the land should be changed by the date specified in the certificate. He E was satisfied that the council genuinely intended to carry out their proposals, to which there was no obstacle such as a refusal of planning permission; and that the public need to repossess the land in question justified taking [the tenant's] tenancy out of the normal operation of the provisions of Part II of the Act of 1954."

In summary form the tenant's case may be put in this way. The county F council had available a refuse tip extending to 64 acres. They had voluntarily reduced the available area of that tip to about 10 acres described as " refuse treatment area " by using the southern part of the tip for forestry, which was a limitation not imposed on them by the planning permission of March 23, 1976. But even with the remaining 10 acres there was ample room for the county council to store the highways materials for which less than one acre was needed. As Mr. Bowan had given up his G site the existing highways material store could remain in its present position without interfering with the activities of the county council in the refuse treatment area, and it was not necessary to use the tenant's site for the storage of highways materials. It was said that no reasonable Secretary of State could have come to any other conclusion.

It was submitted on behalf of the tenant that the history of the matter H showed that the application of the county council was not made bona fide but for the purpose of evicting the tenant from his site for a purpose unconnected with the application, namely, so that the tenant could not compete with Mr. Powell, the successful tenderer on the site opposite.

Secondly, it was submitted that the Secretary of State misdirected himself in law as to the meaning of the words " requisite for the purposes of . . . the authority " in section 57 (1). It was said that those words meant

A more than "required" or "reasonably required" and that the word "requisite" was synonymous with "necessary" or "reasonably necessary" for the purposes of the county council. The Divisional Court held that the word "requisite" meant "required by circumstances" and it was submitted on behalf of the tenant that the Divisional Court, having given that meaning to the word "requisite," should have held that the Secretary of State had misdirected himself in the phraseology he used in paragraph 5 of his letter of October 31, 1978.

B   Thirdly, it was submitted that whether or not the use of the tenant's site was requisite or necessary for the purposes of the county council was a question of fact not planning policy, and that there was no evidence apart from the bald assertion of the county council to establish that fact. It was said that the Secretary of State should not have based his decision

C on that assertion. Reliance was placed on the decision of this court in *Coleen Properties Ltd.* v. *Minister of Housing and Local Government* [1971] 1 W.L.R. 433. It was submitted that the Divisional Court in upholding the Secretary of State's decision on the evidence misdirected itself as to certain important issues of fact, and made findings of fact which were unsupported by the evidence.

D   It was finally submitted that the court should consider fresh evidence considered de bene esse by the Divisional Court, and that the Divisional Court were wrong to refuse to allow such evidence to be admitted on judicial review.

       We were told that this was the first case in which the decision of a minister to give a certificate under section 57 (1) has been the subject of judicial review, and we consider first the meaning of the word "requisite"

E in the subsection. Taken by itself the natural and ordinary meaning of the word "requisite" is "required by circumstances" or "necessary" as used in the Book of Common Prayer in the phrase "to ask those things which are requisite and necessary as well for the body as the soul." But it is said on behalf of the Secretary of State and the county council that a looser and more subjective meaning should be put on the word in the context of this particular Act of Parliament. It is said that in that context

F the word means "reasonably wanted for a purpose which the local authority genuinely and bona fide intends to carry out."

       Section 57 appears in Part IV of the Act of 1954. Part II of the Act enables certain tenants of business premises to obtain new tenancies in certain cases. Some business tenancies, e.g. agricultural tenancies which are covered by other legislation, are excluded from Part II. The material

G sections of Part II are expressed to be subject to Part IV, which contains a group of sections giving any minister power to give a certificate in effect excluding the tenant from his rights under Part II. Different language is used in each of these sections as to the circumstances in which the minister may give a certificate of change of use. The words in subsection (1) of section 57 are, as I have already quoted, "requisite for the purposes of the first-mentioned department." The words in subsection (5) of section

H 57 are that the minister "may certify that it is necessary in the public interest . . . ." In subsection (7) are the following words:

       "Where the interest of the landlord . . . belongs to the National Trust the Minister of Works may certify that it is requisite, for the purpose of securing that the property will as from a specified date be used or occupied in a manner better suited to the nature thereof."

   In section 58, which is concerned with "Termination on special grounds

of tenancies to which Part II applies," subsection (1) provides that the   A
Minister may certify " that for reasons of national security it is necessary
that the use or occupation of the property should be discontinued or
changed." Subsection (3) of that section provides:

> " Where the landlord's interest . . . is held by statutory undertakers,
> nothing in this Act shall invalidate an agreement to the effect—(a)
> that where the minister . . . certifies that possession of the property   B
> comprised in the tenancy or a part thereof is urgently required for
> carrying out repairs (whether on that property or elsewhere) which
> are needed for the proper operation of the landlord's undertaking,
> the tenancy may be terminated . . ."

Section 60, which deals with " Special provisions as to premises provided
under Distribution of Industry Acts," provides:
C
> ". . . the Board of Trade certify that it is necessary or expedient for
> achieving the objects of the said Acts that the use or occupation of the
> property should be changed . . ."

These different words were described by counsel in *X.L. Fisheries* v. *Leeds
Corporation* [1955] 2 Q.B. 636, as " the rising scale of urgency," and in
this case by Mr. Huskinson, for the county council, as a " hierarchy of   D
terms," and it was submitted that the word " requisite " comes low in the
hierarchy and that it must mean something less than necessary. We
accept that in the context of Part IV of the Act the word " requisite "
should be given a less exacting meaning than " necessary " in the sense
of " indispensible " and that the word " necessary " must be qualified so
as to give effect to that. We would say that " reasonably necessary " was
compatible both with the ordinary and natural meaning of the word   E
" requisite " and the context of the section in which it appears in this
part of the Act.

Little assistance is to be derived from the construction given by courts
to the same word used in other statutes. The only case which has been
cited to us in which the word " requisite " has been construed in anything
like the present context was *Robinson* v. *Minister of Town and Country   F
Planning* [1947] K.B. 702, in which the word " requisite " in section 1 (1)
of the Town and Country Planning Act 1944 fell to be construed. Lord
Greene M.R. said, at p. 713:

> " The words " requisite " and " satisfactorily " clearly indicate that
> the question is one of opinion and policy, matters which are peculiarly
> for the minister himself to decide. No objective test is possible."
G
It is important to observe the context in which the word " requisite "
appears in section 1 (1) of the Town and Country Planning Act 1944.
Section 1 provides:

> " (1) Where the Minister of Town and Country Planning . . . is satis-
> fied that it is requisite, for the purpose of dealing satisfactorily with
> extensive war damage in the area of a local planning authority, that a
> part or parts of their area, consisting of land shown to his satisfaction   H
> to have sustained war damage or of such land together with other
> land contiguous or adjacent thereto, should be laid out afresh and
> redeveloped as a whole, an order declaring . . . such . . . land subject
> to compulsory purchase . . . may be made by the minister . . ."

The case affords little if any assistance as to the meaning of the word
itself, though it is valuable as to the nature of the minister's decision.

A   In *Coleen Properties Ltd.* v. *Minister of Housing and Local Government* [1971] 1 W.L.R. 433 the court had to consider the words " reasonably necessary " which is the meaning we have put on the word " requisite." Lord Denning M.R., at p. 438, described it as an inference of fact. Sachs L.J. said, at p. 439:

B   " The question before [the minister] was not, to my mind, one of policy: it was in essence a question of fact that had to be established as a condition precedent to the exercise of the powers to take away the subject's property. It was no less a question of fact because it involved forming a judgment on matters on which expert opinion can and indeed ought to be given. (I rather doubt whether there is much material difference between the view I have just expressed and that of Mr. Slynn who has argued that the question was simply a matter of C   planning judgment which had to be based on evidence.)"

We agree with the words of Sachs L.J. which I have just read, which appear in brackets in the last sentence, as referable to this case. We think it matters not whether the decision of the Secretary of State is described as one of opinion and planning policy or as forming a judgment on matters of fact and opinion. In either case the Secretary of State has to arrive at a D   value judgment based on facts. If in arriving at that decision the Secretary of State asks himself the wrong question and so errs in law, or if he takes into account matters he should not have taken into account or fails to take into account matters he should have taken into account, or if there is no evidence to support his decision so that it is contrary to all the evidence before him, then the court can interfere with his conclusion.

E   Did the Secretary of State err in law by putting the wrong meaning on the word " requisite? " If he did, his decision cannot stand. The answer to this question depends on the terms of the Secretary of State's reasons of October 31, 1978, and in particular paragraph 5. Although the Secretary of State used the word " required " in three different places in that paragraph in the sense of " wanted " which is different from " reasonably necessary," he ended the paragraph in this way:

F   ". . . and the council's submission was accepted that the land was suitable for this purpose and that, whilst they did not necessarily have to show that this was the case, no alternative site was available, either within the area covered by planning permission or elsewhere. [The tenant's] personal reasons for opposing the grant of a certificate were taken into account but, on the evidence as a whole, the Secretary of G   State was satisfied that it was requisite for the purposes of the council that the use or occupation of the land should be changed by the date specified in the certificate. He was satisfied that the council genuinely intended to carry out their proposals, to which there was no obstacle such as a refusal of planning permission; and that the public need to repossess the land in question justified taking [the tenant's] tenancy out H   of the normal operation of the provisions of Part II of the Act of 1954."

What the Secretary of State was there saying was: " I think that the word requisite means genuinely required, but if I am wrong about that and if I have to consider whether alternative sites were available so that I can be satisfied that the tenant's site was reasonably necessary for the purposes of the county council, then I am satisfied that it was." Despite the submissions of Mr. Rougier for the tenant, there is nothing wrong

A in the Secretary of State expressing himself in this way. It is a type of
formula commonly used by judges and we cannot find that the Secretary
of State erred in law in using it.

But then it was said that the only evidence before the Secretary of
State was the bald assertion of the county council that no alternative sites
were available and that, accordingly, the tenant's site was reasonably necessary for their purposes. It was said that the Secretary of State should not
B have acted on that bald assertion in the light of the evidence on behalf of
the tenant and especially the statement of the surveyor which was before
him. It was said that the county council made no attempt to put before
the Secretary of State evidence of the acreage required for each of their
activities within the refuse treatment area, so as to demonstrate that it
was reasonably necessary for them to use the tenant's site for a highways
material store.   C

Reliance was placed on the statement of Lord Denning M.R. in
Coleen Properties Ltd. v. *Minister of Housing and Local Government*
[1971] 1 W.L.R. 433, 437:

    " At any rate, I am quite clear that the mere ipse dixit of the local
    council is not sufficient. There must be some evidence to support their
    assertion. And here there was none."   D

It is said that that statement exactly reflects the situation in this case in
that the only evidence before the Secretary of State was the ipse dixit of
the county council. It is important to see the facts of *Coleen Properties
Ltd.* v. *Minister of Housing and Local Government.* There had been a
public inquiry. Evidence had been called before the inspector. Witnesses
had been examined and cross-examined. The inspector had made a report E
containing his findings of fact, conclusions and recommendations. The
minister reversed his recommendations. There was no evidence on which
he could do so except the statement of the advocate for the local authority
that the land was reasonably necessary for the proposed redevelopment.

The situation here is quite different. Subsection (2) of section 57 does
not envisage an inquiry or other hearing and no inquiry or hearing was
held. The tenant was entitled to make representations in writing which he F
did. There is not even a provision in the subsection for reasons to be given
by the local authority although reasons were in fact given. And there were
counter-reasons and counter-representations by both parties. All this
material was before the Secretary of State and it amounted to considerably
more material than was envisaged by the subsection.

The nature of the material on which a minister is entitled to rely in G
reaching a decision must depend on the statutory provisions and the circumstances of each case. It may well be that, where there is a public hearing, the Secretary of State should not rely on bare assertions unsupported
by evidence. But where as here there was no public hearing, the Secretary
of State must assess the submissions and reach his conclusion as best he
can on the material put before him. It is a matter for him to weigh the H
statements submitted to him and reach his decision in accordance with
them.

The Secretary of State summarised the submissions of the county council, in paragraph 3 of his letter, in this way:

    " The council submitted that it was essential that the materials store
    be between the pulveriser complex and gypsy site for the pulveriser
    complex to remain secure and this would also facilitate use of the

A   containers and the movement of vehicles in and around the pulveriser. An earth-bank screen was being constructed south of the transfer station and treatment area, in accordance with the planning consent, beyond which only forestry would be undertaken and the council argued that, for that reason, the treatment area could not be moved further south. Because a number of activities would be concentrated in the treatment area, it was stated to be impossible for highways

B   materials to be stored there as well, and it was said to be impracticable to locate a highways depot on the far side of the waste disposal complex. The council submitted that the depot at High Heavens Wood was used by Wycombe District Council, as agent authority for the county council, to keep materials for use on roads within the boundaries of the former borough of High Wycombe and had to be easily

C   accessible in times of emergency: . . ."

Then the Secretary of State deals with alternative depots at different sites which were not relied on in this court by the tenant.

The Secretary of State accepted those submissions in paragraph 5. It was not necessary for the minister to go further and insist on evidence of acreage of each activity proposed by the county council in order to check

D   its submissions. There were other relevant considerations than mere acreage, e.g. the access to the various sites and the security of the pulveriser installation. It is impossible to say that the Secretary of State was wrong in taking into account the material put before him by the county council or that because he failed to take into account the exact acreage of the various sites his decision was thereby vitiated.

E   The Secretary of State and the Divisional Court both rejected the submission of bad faith on the part of the county council. Bad faith was, however, relied on but not pressed in this court and we think the Divisional Court were right to reject it. At the same time we cannot help thinking that it was foolish of the county council to threaten to cut off the tenant's telephone and unwise of them not to serve another notice under section 25

F   after the dismissal of the county court proceedings, and seek to obtain possession under Part II of the Act as they did in the case of Mr. Jackman. But those matters were all before the Secretary of State and it is impossible on judicial review to disturb his finding that the county council genuinely required this site for their purpose.

Finally there was an application on behalf of the tenant to admit fresh evidence which the Divisional Court had refused to admit. Like the Divi-

G   sional Court we considered the evidence de bene esse. What are the principles on which fresh evidence should be admitted on judicial review? They are (1) that the court can receive evidence to show what material was before the minister or inferior tribunal: *Ashbridge Investments Ltd.* v. *Minister of Housing and Local Government* [1965] 1 W.L.R. 1320, 1327, *per* Lord Denning M.R.; (2) where the jurisdiction of the minister or

H   inferior tribunal depends on a question of fact or where the question is whether essential procedural requirements were observed, the court may receive and consider additional evidence to determine the jurisdictional fact or procedural error: see *de Smith's Judicial Review of Administrative Action*, 4th ed. (1980), at pp. 140, 141 and cases there cited; and (3) where the proceedings are tainted by misconduct on the part of the minister or member of the inferior tribunal or the parties before it. Examples of such misconduct are bias by the decision making body, or fraud or perjury by

a party. In each case fresh evidence is admissible to prove the particular   A
misconduct alleged: see *Reg.* v. *West Sussex Quarter Sessions, Ex parte
Albert and Maud Johnson Trust Ltd.* [1974] Q.B. 24, 39, 43 *per* Orr and
Lawton L.JJ.

There was discussion at the Bar as to the situation where a party
deliberately suppressed material facts with the intention of misleading the
Secretary of State. If that were the situation then it would be for the   B
court to consider whether the conduct of that party could be described as
fraudulent so as to permit the admission of fresh evidence.

It is said that there is a distinction between cases such as the *West
Sussex* case where an order of certiorari was sought to quash the decision
of an inferior tribunal after a hearing and cases such as the present where
it is sought to quash the decision of the Secretary of State where there
has been no hearing. We can find no such distinction and the remarks of   C
the majority in the *West Sussex* case are quite general in their application
to certiorari.

Reliance was placed by Mr. Rougier, for the tenant, on *Secretary of
State for Education and Science* v. *Tameside Metropolitan Borough
Council* [1977] A.C. 1014. In that case fresh evidence was admitted to
the Court of Appeal by consent. Certain passages in the judgment of   D
Scarman L.J. in the Court of Appeal (at p. 1030E) and in the speeches of
Lord Wilberforce (at p. 1047D) and Lord Diplock (at p. 1064) were particularly relied on by Mr. Rougier. It was said that those statements support
the proposition that if the Secretary of State is misled by the failure of
one party falling short of fraud to put before him evidence which should
have been put before him, and on which he would probably have come to   E
a different conclusion from that to which he came on the evidence which
was put before him, then the court on judicial review should admit that
evidence as fresh evidence. It was said that to fail to do so would be a
breach of natural justice.

The *Tameside* case was a very special case. In effect the minister was
himself reviewing the decision of the local authority and his decision was   F
analogous to the position of the court on judicial review. The evidence
was admitted in the Court of Appeal by consent. The case is not
authority for the proposition relied on by Mr. Rougier. Indeed there are
indications in the speeches in the House of Lords to the contrary: see *per*
Lord Wilberforce, at p. 1052:

> " To rephrase the question: on June 11, 1976 (this is the date of the   G
> direction, and we are not entitled to see what happened thereafter),
> could it be said that the authority was acting unreasonably in proceed-
> ing with a selection procedure which was otherwise workable in face
> of the possibility of persistent opposition by teachers' unions and indivi-
> dual teachers, or would *the only* (not ' the more ') reasonable course
> have been for the authority to abandon its plans? This is, I think, the
> ultimate factual question in the case. And I think that it must be   H
> answered in the negative—i.e., that it could not be unreasonable, in
> June 1976, and assuming that the Secretary of State did not interfere,
> for the authority to put forward a plan to act on its approved
> procedure."

And Lord Russell of Killowen said, at p. 1076:

> " The question whether the Secretary of State was justified in his

A   conclusion that the proposals of the local authority were unreasonable falls to be decided at the date of his conclusion, June 11: that is common ground. I would not however subscribe to the view that facts subsequently brought forward as then existing can properly be relied upon as showing that the proposals were not unreasonable unless those facts are of such a character that they can be taken to have been
B   within the knowledge of the department."

If there is doubt as to the construction of those words of Lord Russell, we agree, save in one respect, with the construction put upon them by the reporter in the headnote, at p. 1016:

   " Facts subsequently brought forward as existing on June 11 could not properly be relied on as showing that the authority's proposals were
C   not unreasonable unless they were of such a character that they could be taken to have been within the knowledge of the Secretary of State."

The words " the department " used by Lord Russell at the end of his speech are distinguishable from the words " the Secretary of State " used by the reporter at the end of the headnote, unless those words are to be interpreted as meaning " the Secretary of State or his department." The
D   converse of Lord Russell's proposition as stated by him is that fresh evidence may be admitted of facts within the knowledge of the department though unknown to the Secretary of State at the time of his decision. This is an example of one of the classic reasons for interfering with the ministerial decision within *Associated Provincial Picture Houses Ltd.* v. *Wednesbury Corporation* [1948] 1 K.B. 223 namely, that such facts are
E   plainly facts which the Secretary of State should have taken into account. If he failed to do so fresh evidence of the facts within the knowledge of the department could be admitted as a ground for quashing his decision.

    This court is bound by the majority judgments in *Reg.* v. *West Sussex Quarter Sessions, Ex parte Albert and Maud Johnson Trust Ltd.* [1974] Q.B. 24 which formed the ratio decidendi of the case. *Secretary of State*
F   *for Education and Science* v. *Tameside Metropolitan Borough Council* [1977] A.C. 1014 is not authority for the proposition that the circumstances in which fresh evidence on judicial review may be admitted can be extended beyond the categories laid down in the *West Sussex* case.

    There is nothing in the fresh evidence in this case to bring it within any of the categories of evidence which may be admitted on judicial
G   review. We agree with the Divisional Court that the fresh evidence is not admissible. But we do not agree with the following test proposed by the Divisional Court:

   " so long as a minister or a tribunal has balanced the factors and weighed the evidence before him or it, no superior court should intervene unless it is plain that there has been such manifest failure to
H   administer justice that the decision is perverse."

We have already stated the principles on which fresh evidence may be admitted on judicial review.

    Although it is true that there are certain mistakes in the statements of fact in the judgment of the Divisional Court, we do not think that those mistakes affected the conclusion at which the court arrived. We think that they were right to refuse the application for a writ of certiorari, although

Reg. v. Environment Sec., Ex p. Powis (C.A.)   **[1981]**

A

for the reasons which we have stated in this judgment; the appeal is accordingly dismissed.

Appeal dismissed.
Appellant to pay half costs of each
respondent.

B

Solicitors: *A. Banks & Co.; Treasury Solicitor; Sharpe, Pritchard & Co. for D. U. Pullen, Aylesbury.*

[Reported by MISS HENRIETTA STEINBERG, Barrister-at-Law]

C

[COURT OF APPEAL]

* WADSWORTH *v.* LYDALL

D

1981 Jan. 15, 16   Ormrod and Brightman L.JJ.
                                                     and Reeve J.

Damages—Contract—Breach—Non-payment of money due under
contract—Loss suffered by reason of non-payment—Whether
recoverable as special damages

E

The defendant, the owner of a dairy farm, entered into an informal partnership agreement with the plaintiff under which the partnership was granted an agricultural tenancy and the plaintiff lived in the farm house and ran the farm. On the dissolution of the partnership, an agreement was made which provided inter alia that the plaintiff would give up possession of the farm on or before May 15, 1976, and on that event would receive £10,000 from the defendant. On May 10, the plaintiff, expecting to receive £10,000 in five days time and having no other capital, entered into an agreement for the purchase of a property from G., by which £10,000 of the purchase price was to be paid on completion. On May 15 the plaintiff gave up possession of the farm but the defendant did not pay him the £10,000. On July 21, G.'s solicitors served a 28-day notice to complete. In October the defendant paid the plaintiff £7,200. The plaintiff passed that sum on to G. and raised the balance of the sum due on completion by taking out a mortgage from G., of which he had to pay the legal costs.

F

G

In an action brought against the defendant, the plaintiff claimed as special damages £335 in respect of interest that he had had to pay G. for late completion, and £16·20 in respect of the mortgage costs. Smith J. awarded the plaintiff damages, but disallowed the two items of special damage on the ground that they were too remote. The plaintiff appealed.

H

On the question whether the two items of damages disallowed by the judge were recoverable: —

Held, allowing the appeal, that a party to a contract was entitled to special damages in respect of loss suffered by him as a result of the failure by another party to the contract to pay moneys due to him under the contract, provided that the loss was not too remote; that since the defendant knew or ought to have known that the plaintiff would need to acquire another farm or smallholding, using the £10,000 payable under

A   the contract for the purpose, and that if the £10,000 was not paid the plaintiff would be compelled to incur expense in arranging alternative finance and paying interest, the claims for £335 and £16·20 were not too remote and were payable by the defendant (post, pp. 602E–F, 603F–G, 605A–F).

London, Chatham and Dover Railway Co. v. South Eastern Railway Co. [1893] A.C. 429, H.L.(E.) distinguished.

Dicta of Denning and Romer L.JJ. in Trans Trust S.P.R.L.

B   v. Danubian Trading Co. Ltd. [1952] 2 Q.B. 297, 306, 307, C.A. applied.

Order of Smith J. varied.

The following cases are referred to in the judgments:

Hadley v. Baxendale (1854) 9 Exch. 341.

London, Chatham and Dover Railway Co. v. South Eastern Railway Co.

C   [1893] A.C. 429, H.L.(E.).

Parsons (H.) (Livestock) Ltd. v. Uttley Ingham & Co. Ltd. [1978] Q.B. 791; [1977] 3 W.L.R. 990; [1978] 1 All E.R. 525, C.A.

Trans Trust S.P.R.L. v. Danubian Trading Co. Ltd. [1952] 2 Q.B. 297; [1952] 1 All E.R. 970, C.A.

No additional cases were cited in argument.

D

APPEAL from Smith J.

By a writ dated May 24, 1978, the plaintiff, David Howard Wadsworth, alleged that the defendant, Frank B. Lydall, had failed on or before May 15, 1976, to pay the plaintiff £10,000, in breach of a contract between the parties dated January 16, 1976. The plaintiff claimed, inter alia, £335 in respect of interest charges that he had had to pay for

E   late completion of his purchase of a farm and £16·20 in respect of the legal costs of a mortgage he took out from the vendor of the farm. Smith J. awarded the plaintiff damages of £2,303·96, but disallowed those two inter alia items of claim.

The plaintiff appealed on the ground, that the judge erred in holding that the sums of £335 and £16·20 were irrecoverable under the rule in

F   Hadley v. Baxendale (1854) 9 Exch. 341.

The facts are stated in the judgment of Brightman L.J.

John Behrens for the plaintiff.

Timothy Hirst for the defendant.

G   BRIGHTMAN L.J. delivered the first judgment. This is an appeal from an order made by Smith J. in an action by one partner to recover money said to be due from the other partner on the dissolution of the partnership.

In 1972 the defendant, Mr. Lydall, bought a dairy farm known as Cherry Tree Farm near Sheffield. His purpose was to accommodate his race horses rather than to farm the land himself. He entered into an informal partnership agreement with the plaintiff, Mr. Wadsworth, under

H   which the partnership was granted by the defendant an agricultural tenancy and the farm was to be run by the plaintiff and his wife at a salary for each of them. The capital of the partnership was £6,000 contributed by them in equal shares in cash or kind. The net profits of the partnership business were to be divided between the two partners equally.

Three years later the defendant decided to determine the partnership so that he could sell the farm, as he was entitled to do. The plaintiff had nowhere else to live and no other occupation and—not unnaturally—

sought to protect his position. He had the advantage of a partnership A
share in an agricultural tenancy and that no doubt gave him a bargaining
counter. Negotiations ensued between the plaintiff and the defendant.
The defendant made arrangements to sell the farm by auction on January
22, 1976. The first dissolution agreement made between the parties
proved abortive because the farm did not sell at the auction. A second
bargain was struck. It is contained in a letter dated January 16, 1976,
written by the defendant's solicitors to the plaintiff's solicitors and altered B
in manuscript by the plaintiff and the defendant shortly after the auction.
The agreement as recorded in this letter was as follows:

" 1. Mr. Lydall will pay £10,000 to Mr. Wadsworth on vacant possession, on or before May 15, 1976, being given of Cherry Tree
Farm, house, land and buildings, time being of the essence. 2.
Mr. Wadsworth will do all that is necessary to facilitate the giving up C
of possession of the land and farm buildings (other than the house
itself) prior to May 15, 1976, if so required. 3. Mr. Wadsworth will
be entitled to no part of the partnership assets or the proceeds of
sale thereof, all of which shall belong to Mr. Lydall. 4. The partnership now subsisting between our respective clients shall be treated
as determined on [January 22, 1976,] the date of the auction sale D
of the farm. 5. Notwithstanding the contents of paragraph 4 above,
Mr. Wadsworth shall be entitled (a) to his salary of £35 per week until
the sale of the live and dead stock, which is to be agreed between
himself and Mr. Lydall, but is anticipated to be around mid-February
1976; (b) to any underdrawn salary from the date of the commencement of the partnership's current financial year to the above mentioned date of termination, [January 22, 1976], but if such salary E
(at the rate of £35 per week) shall have been overdrawn, Mr. Wadsworth shall repay to Mr. Lydall the amount overdrawn. 6. Mr.
Lydall's prior approval shall be required to the sale prices of all
partnership assets sold."

That agreement was subject to a term arranged between the parties
themselves that the amount due to the plaintiff under paragraph 5 (b) F
should be referred to the parties' respective accountants for agreement.
In fact I understand that one firm of accountants acted for both sides.
The partnership business continued down to March 31, and not to the
date referred to in the agreement which I have read.

The plaintiff scrupulously fulfilled his part of the agreement. On May
15, he gave up possession of the farm house as the agreement required.
At about the same time a bargain was struck between the plaintiff and G
the defendant that the plaintiff should take over from the partnership
five items of farm equipment at an agreed total sum of £1,563. They consist of a pump valued at £1,015, a bottle filler valued at £140, a chain
saw valued at £18, a tractor valued at £190 and a van valued at £200.
On May 10, the plaintiff, in anticipation of the receipt in five days' time
of £10,000 from the defendant under the express terms of the contract, H
entered into an agreement to purchase a property known as Overton
Farmhouse near Wakefield from a Mr. Gascoigne. I take the details
from the correspondence, the contract not being before us. The price
was £16,000. £10,000 was to be paid on completion. The balance of
£6,000 was to be paid three years later.

Unfortunately the defendant defaulted on his obligation to pay the
£10,000 on May 15 under clause 1 of the agreement. On July 16, the

A plaintiff's solicitors wrote to the defendant's solicitors demanding payment, which they correctly stated was then already two months overdue. On July 21 Mr. Gascoigne's solicitors served on the plaintiff a 28-day notice to complete in accordance with the general conditions of sale incorporated in the contract for the purposes of Overton Farmhouse. The defendant was informed of this. The effect of the notice to
B complete was that, on the plaintiff's default, Mr. Gascoigne would be entitled to forfeit the deposit paid under the contract, to resell the property and to charge the plaintiff with any loss on the resale. The defendant remained in default. The plaintiff's position became desperate.

In October the plaintiff succeeded in extracting £7,200 from the defendant. This sum was immediately paid over to Mr. Gascoigne. Mr. Gascoigne had stayed his hand under the notice to complete. The
C sale was completed on October 18, on the basis that the balance shown due by the completion statement, namely £2,861·20, should remain outstanding on second mortgage until December 1, 1976. The first mortgage comprised the balance of £6,000 to which I have already referred and which was to remain outstanding for three years. The figure of £2,861·20, which I mentioned as due on the completion date, included a sum of £16·20 representing the legal costs of the second mortgage.
D The defendant declined to pay the balance of £2,800 due under the agreement until the partnership accounts to March 31, 1976, were signed. It was not until October 1977, for some reason or another, that the accountants were able to complete the accounts. These showed that a sum of £246·33 was due to the plaintiff as at March 31, 1976. Accordingly, on October 20, the plaintiff's solicitors wrote to the defendant's
E solicitors asking for payment by the defendant of the outstanding £2,800 plus interest, and the amount of £246·33 shown by the accounts as due to the plaintiff. By this time the plaintiff was almost 10 months in arrear in discharging the second mortgage and he was threatened with legal proceedings.

On May 24, 1978, the plaintiff, having exhibited exemplary patience, issued a writ against the defendant. He claimed £2,800, the balance of
F the £10,000; £246·33, the balance shown as due to him on the partnership accounts; £335 in respect of interest payable by the plaintiff to Mr. Gascoigne by reason of the delayed completion of the purchase of Overton Farmhouse; and £16·20 legal costs of the second mortgage.

The plaintiff succeeded in the action to the extent that the judge found that the plaintiff was entitled to receive £10,000 under the terms
G of the dissolution agreement, whereas he had only been paid £7,200. The judge expressed himself as follows:

"In my judgment the defendant was liable by the terms of the agreement to pay £10,000, to which must be added an agreed sum of £200 in respect of the electric cooker . . . To the total I should add to that a further agreed sum of £246·33 for profits, a figure which has been agreed and which emerges from the accounts which have
H been exhibited in the annexe in this case. From the total of £10,446·33 is to be deducted the payment of £7,200 and from the balance is to be deducted the aforementioned sum of £1,563 in respect of the items of equipment which the plaintiff bought from the defendant. If my mathematics are correct the plaintiff is accordingly entitled to judgment for £1,683·33."

That paragraph contains the error which the plaintiff submits has been

made by the judge. It is the principal matter arising on this appeal. The A
plaintiff submits that the sum of £1,563 ought not to be treated as a
deduction because it had already been taken into account by the accountants in arriving at the figure of £246·33.

In my view the plaintiff is correct in his submission. [His Lordship
considered the accounts and continued:] In my view the accounting
position is absolutely clear beyond any possibility of doubt. It must follow
therefore that the judge was mistaken when he deducted the sum of B
£1,563 from the balance which he was calculating in his judgment as
due to the plaintiff. On this issue of the appeal—which is the primary
issue—it seems to me clear that the plaintiff is entitled to succeed.

The second question on the appeal is a little more difficult. It is
whether the plaintiff is entitled to recover as special damages the loss
which he has suffered as a result of the defendant's failure to pay his C
debt under the contract on the due date. To put the matter shortly, the
plaintiff incurred under his contract with Mr. Gascoigne an interest
charge of £335 as a result of the delayed completion, the interest being
calculated for the period from the date fixed for completion until actual
completion on October 18, 1976. He also incurred an expenditure of
£16·20 legal costs of the second mortgage for the sum of £2,800-odd in
respect of the balance due on completion. Neither of those charges D
would have been incurred if the defendant had fulfilled his part of the
contract by paying £10,000 on the due date, namely, May 15, 1976. The
judge dismissed this claim on the ground that it was too remote. He
made an award of interest on the amount recovered under the judgment.

In my view the damage claimed by the plaintiff was not too remote.
It is clearly to be inferred from the evidence that the defendant well E
knew at the time of the negotiation of the contract of January 1976 that
the plaintiff would need to acquire another farm or smallholding as his
home and his business, and that he would be dependent on the £10,000
payable under the contract in order to finance that purchase. The defendant knew or ought to have known that if the £10,000 was not paid to
him, the plaintiff would need to borrow an equivalent amount or would F
have to pay interest to his vendor or would need to secure financial
accommodation in some other way. The plaintiff's loss in my opinion
is such that it may reasonably be supposed that it would have been in
the contemplation of the parties as a serious possibility, had their attention been directed to the consequences of a breach of contract.

The defendant sought to escape from this conclusion by relying on
the decision of the House of Lords in *London, Chatham and Dover* G
Railway Co. v. *South Eastern Railway Co.* [1893] A.C. 429. In that
case the appellants had brought an action against the respondent for an
account of money due under a joint traffic agreement. The account
was taken before an official referee who found that a considerable sum
was due to the appellants. He included in the sum found due £36,000
interest under Lord Tenterden's Act. To recover interest under that H
Act, so far as material for present purposes, it was necessary to show
that there was a debt or sum certain payable at a certain time by virtue
of some written instrument. It was held by the Court of Appeal and by
the House of Lords that the claim did not satisfy that condition. So the
appellants sought interest by way of damages as alternative relief. Lord
Herschell L.C. said, at p. 437:

"... the appellants contended that even although they might not

A   under the terms of Lord Tenterden's Act be entitled to interest, yet interest might be given by way of damages in respect of the wrongful detention of their debt. I confess that I have considered this part of the case with every inclination to come to a conclusion in favour of the appellants, to the extent at all events, if it were possible, of giving them interest from the date of the action; and for this

B   reason, that I think that when money is owing from one party to another and that other is driven to have recourse to legal proceedings in order to recover the amount due to him, the party who is wrongfully withholding the money from the other ought not in justice to benefit by having that money in his possession and enjoying the use of it, when the money ought to be in the possession of the other party who is entitled to its use. Therefore, if I could see my

C   way to do so, I should certainly be disposed to give the appellants, or anybody in a similar position, interest upon the amount withheld from the time of action brought at all events. But I have come to the conclusion, upon a consideration of the authorities, agreeing with the court below, that it is not possible to do so, although no doubt in early times the view was expressed that interest might be given under such circumstances by way of damages."

D   The defendant contends that we are bound to follow that principle and that, although interest can be awarded nowadays under the Law Reform (Miscellaneous Provisions) Act 1934, damages cannot be awarded in respect of unpaid indebtedness. The plaintiff is confined, the defendant says, to such interest as he is able to claim under the Act of 1934, but is not entitled to damages. The interest which can be claimed under

E   the Act of 1934 is not sufficient to cover the damage suffered by the plaintiff if as the plaintiff concedes it cannot be awarded on the sum of £7,200 paid before the action was started.

In my view the court is not so constrained by the decision of the House of Lords. In *London, Chatham and Dover Railway Co.* v. *South Eastern Railway Co.* [1893] A.C. 429 the House of Lords was not con-

F   cerned with a claim for special damages. The action was an action for an account. The House was concerned only with a claim for interest by way of general damages. If a plaintiff pleads and can prove that he has suffered special damage as a result of the defendant's failure to perform his obligation under a contract, and such damage is not too remote on the principle of *Hadley* v. *Baxendale* (1854) 9 Exch. 341, I can see no logical reason why such special damage should be irrecoverable merely

G   because the obligation on which the defendant defaulted was an obligation to pay money and not some other type of obligation. I derive support for this view from obita dicta in *Trans Trust S.P.R.L.* v. *Danubian Trading Co. Ltd.* [1952] 2 Q.B. 297. I refer first to a paragraph in the judgment of Denning L.J., at p. 306:

H   " It was said that the breach here was a failure to pay money and that the law has never allowed any damages on that account. I do not think that the law has ever taken up such a rigid standpoint. It did undoubtedly refuse to award interest until the recent statute: see *London, Chatham and Dover Railway Co.* v. *South Eastern Railway Co.* [1893] A.C. 429; but the ground was that interest was ' generally presumed not to be within the contemplation of the parties ': see *Bullen & Leake,* 3rd ed., at p. 51. That is, I think, the only real ground on which damages can be refused for non-

604

payment of money. It is because the consequences are as a rule A too remote. But when the circumstances are such that there is a special loss forseeable at the time of the contract as the consequence of non-payment, then I think such loss may well be recoverable. It is not necessary, however, to come to a firm conclusion on this point, because I regard the provision of a credit as different from the payment of money and not subject to the special rules, if any B there are, relating thereto."

Romer L.J. said, at p. 307:

". . . I am not, as at present advised, prepared to subscribe to the view that in no case can damages be recovered for non-payment of money; I agree with Denning L.J. that in certain circumstances such damages might well be recoverable provided that the loss C occasioned to the plaintiff by the defendant's default was reasonably within the contemplation of the parties when the bargain between them was made."

In my view the plaintiff in the instant case ought to have been allowed the £335 and £16·20 damages which he claimed. Those damages are pleaded as special damages. They are not, for the reasons which I have given, too remote. I think that they are recoverable under the ordinary D principles upon which this court proceeds in the case of damages. I do not think that the present case is concluded by the *London, Chatham and Dover* case. I would adopt as the law the view tentatively expressed by Denning and Romer L.JJ. in the passages I have read.

The last issue on the appeal is whether this court ought to interfere with the trial judge's decision to reserve the costs of the trial to the E district registrar. The basis of the judge's decision was that, by agreement between the parties, one item on the partnership accounts which related to milk sales receipts was to be referred to the district registrar. The judge thought that the result of that inquiry might deprive the plaintiff of any substantial benefit from the judgment. I do not myself think that the judge was justified in delegating that decision to the registrar. He ought, in my view, to have dealt with the costs himself and he ought F to have awarded them to the plaintiff. The judge's conclusion was that the defendant was liable, by the terms of the agreement of January 1976, to pay £10,000 to the plaintiff. That was the principal claim of the plaintiff when he started his action. It seems to me that the plaintiff clearly succeeded in his action. He obtained the major part of the relief he sought. The fact that the taking of an account on one particular aspect G of the partnership might lead to a cross-payment by the plaintiff to the defendant was not, in my opinion, any sufficient reason for omitting to give the plaintiff the costs of the action there and then. All that ought to have been referred to the district registrar was the costs of the inquiry relating to the milk sales.

In the result, I would allow the appeal on all the points.

H

REEVE J. I agree.

ORMROD L.J. I too agree but, as we are differing from the judge, I shall add a few words of my own. [His Lordship considered the question whether the judge was correct in deducting £1,563 from the sum payable to the plaintiff, and continued:] It is perfectly plain that the plaintiff is owed—one way or the other—the sum of £1,563. I would

A   allow the appeal on that item for those reasons as well as for those much more fully given by Brightman L.J.

On the interesting question of damages for the cost to which the plaintiff was put as a result of the non-payment of the £10,000, I would just say this. The first question it seems to me is, is this alleged damage too remote? The test as set out in the judgments of this court in *H. Parsons (Livestock) Ltd. v. Uttley Ingham & Co. Ltd.* [1978] Q.B. 791

B   gives the test for remoteness. Taking it very shortly, Lord Denning M.R. said, at p. 801:

> " In the case of a *breach of contract,* the court has to consider whether the consequences were of such a kind that a reasonable man, at the time of making the contract, would *contemplate* them as being of a very substantial degree of probability."

C   Scarman L.J. made the same point in a slightly different way. He said, at p. 807:

> " The court's task, therefore, is to decide what loss to the plaintiffs it is reasonable to suppose would have been in the contemplation of the parties as a serious possibility had they had in mind the breach when they made their contract."

D

To use the language of objective/subjective, it is an objective test. The court has to look not at what this particular defendant knew or contemplated but what a reasonable person in his position would have contemplated. I find it inconceivable that this particular defendant did not contemplate and fully understand the plaintiff's position. He must

E   have known as a fact that the plaintiff was dependent upon this £10,000 to make arrangements for alternative accommodation for himself and his family. Moreover, if he did not know, no reasonable person in 1976 looking at the facts could come to any other conclusion but that £10,000 was vital to the plaintiff and that, if he could not get the £10,000 immediately, he was bound to be put to expense in arranging alternative sources of finance—assuming that he could do so. On remoteness, I find no

F   difficulty in disagreeing with the judge.

A more important and more difficult point arises on *London, Chatham and Dover Railway Co. v. South Eastern Railway Co.* [1893] A.C. 429. As to that, I entirely agree with all that Brightman L.J. has said and I do not find it necessary to say anything more than that. It would seem to me the most extraordinary conclusion to reach, and one has the advantage of knowing that in 1893 Lord Herschell L.C. regarded the

G   statement of the law he felt obliged to make as profoundly unsatisfactory. This case is not on all fours with—and can be distinguished from—the *London, Chatham and Dover* case and clearly ought to be so distinguished.

I agree that this appeal should be allowed.

Appeal allowed with costs in Court of Appeal and below.

H

Solicitors: *Dransfield & Hodgkinson, Penistone; Eaton Smith & Downey, Huddersfield.*

[Reported by MICHAEL HAWKINGS, ESQ., Barrister-at-Law]

[1981]

A

[QUEEN'S BENCH DIVISION]

* TAYLOR v. CHIEF CONSTABLE OF KENT

1981 Jan. 14   Donaldson L.J. and Forbes J.

B

*Crime—Drugs—Occupier of premises—Cultivation of cannabis
plants on premises—Whether occupier permitting production
of controlled drug—Misuse of Drugs Act 1971 (c. 38), ss. 8,
37 (1) (as amended by the Criminal Law Act 1977 (c. 45), s. 52)*

The defendant, who was the occupier of premises, was
aware that another person was growing cannabis plants in a
bedroom in that property. He was charged that he, being
the occupier of the premises, permitted or suffered the produc-   C
tion of a controlled drug, cannabis, contrary to section 8 of
the Misuse of Drugs Act 1971.[1] The justices were of the
opinion, that by virtue of the definition of " produce " in
section 37 (1) of the Act, cultivation of the cannabis plants
amounted to the production of a controlled drug within the
meaning of section 8 and they convicted the defendant.

On the defendant's appeal: —

D

Held, dismissing the appeal, that since the definition of
" cannabis " in section 37 (1) of the Misuse of Drugs Act 1971
had been extended by section 52 of the Criminal Law Act 1977
from the flowering and fruiting tops of the plant to virtually
the whole plant and the definition in the subsection of
"produce" included cultivation, the offence of knowingly permitting the production of a controlled drug in section 8 of the
Act included the growing of the plant cannabis; that, accord-   E
ingly, since the defendant knew that plants were being cultivated
in the bedroom of the premises, he had been rightly convicted
under the section as the occupier of the premises.

Per Donaldson L.J. Reputable horticulturists, who have
licences to cultivate the plant and are, thereby, protected from
a charge under section 6 of cultivating the plant, may now in
theory, as a result of the amendment, be liable to prosecution
for producing the drug contrary to section 4 of the Act of 1971   F
(post, p. 609D–E).

No cases are referred to in the judgments and none were cited in
argument.

CASE STATED by Kent justices sitting at Ashford.

On October 2, 1979, a charge was preferred by temporary Detective   G
Constable Alan James Palmer against the defendant, Howard Peter Taylor,
that at Ashford, Kent on July 25, 1979, he being the occupier of certain
premises at 83, Quantock Drive did permit or suffer the production of a
certain controlled drug, namely, cannabis, contrary to section 8 of the
Misuse of Drugs Act 1971.

The justices heard the charge on April 10, 1980, and found the   H
following facts. The defendant was the occupier of 83, Quantock Drive.

[1] Misuse of Drugs Act 1971, s. 8: " A person commits an offence if, being the
occupier or being concerned in the management of any premises, he knowingly
permits or suffers any of the following activities to take place on those premises,
that is to say—(*a*) producing or attempting to produce a controlled drug in contravention of section 4 (1) of this Act; . . ."

S. 37 (1), as amended: see post, pp. 608H—609A.

A   Five cannabis plants in individual pots were on the premises in an upstairs bedroom which was not that occupied by the defendant. The
medium in which the plants were growing was damp. The presence of
the plants in that condition on the premises was known to the defendant.
The plants had been cultivated by another occupant of the premises who
had been convicted under section 6 of the Misuse of Drugs Act 1971.

B   It was contended by the defendant that there was no production of
a controlled drug under section 8 of the Misuse of Drugs Act 1971; that
the activity in question was cultivation of plants of the genus cannabis
under section 6 of the Act which was not an activity proscribed by
section 8; that by bringing the prosecution under section 8 the prosecution were equating section 6 (cultivation) with section 4 (producing)
of the Act, as a result of the amendment to the Act by section 52 of
C   the Criminal Law Act 1977 and that the amendment was not intended
to have that effect. In support of that contention it was argued that
the distinction between sections 4 and 6 subsisted because regulations
5 and 12 of the Misuse of Drugs Regulations 1973 still differentiated
between authorisation to cultivate cannabis and authorisation to produce
drugs; and the evidence did not support a finding that there had been
cultivation of the plants on July 25, as no specific act had taken place
D   that day in furtherance of the plants' growth.

     It was contended by the prosecution that the definition of "produce"
was contained in section 37 (1) of the Misuse of Drugs Act 1971. It
specifically referred to producing by means of cultivation and that embraced
the cultivation of the five cannabis plants found upon the premises; and
the definition applied to the word "cultivation" by the defendant was
E   erroneous.

     The justices were of the opinion that by virtue of the definition of
"produce," cultivation of the five cannabis plants amounted to production
of a controlled drug within the meaning of section 8 of the Misuse of
Drugs Act 1971, and that there did not have to be evidence of a specific
act on July 25, 1979, for them to find that the plants were being cultivated
F   —the evidence of dampness around the plants showed that there had been
recent attention to them and when plants which needed to be grown in a
protected environment were grown in a bedroom they could not survive
without such necessary attention as amounted to cultivation. The justices
accordingly convicted the defendant and on May 8, 1980, ordered that he
be discharged conditionally for one year and further ordered that he pay
G   £25 towards the costs of the prosecution within 21 days.

     The questions for the opinion of the High Court were whether the
justices were right in finding that the cannabis plants were being cultivated
on July 25, 1979, and if so, whether such cultivation was a production of
a controlled drug within the meaning of section 8 of the Misuse of Drugs
H   Act 1971.

     Anthony Shaw for the defendant.
     Seddon Cripps for the prosecutor.

     DONALDSON L.J. In this case the defendant appeals by case stated
against his conviction by Kent justices sitting at Ashford of an offence
under section 8 of the Misuse of Drugs Act 1971.

608

That section makes it an offence for the occupier of premises knowingly A
to permit or suffer any of certain specified activities to take place on those
premises, including " (a) producing or attempting to produce a controlled
drug in contravention of section 4 (1) of this Act." If one goes to section
4 (1) of the Act, one finds that the offence is simply producing a controlled
drug, and at one stage I could not understand why there was any need
for section 8 to refer to section 4 (1). The reason in fact is that section B
4 (1) is introduced with the words: " Subject to any regulations under
section 7," which are exempting regulations enabling people to be licensed
to produce controlled drugs. While I am bound to say I think there would
have been easier ways of drafting section 8, that is the way it is drafted.
No regulations under section 7 have any application to this case, so for
practical purposes in the context of this case section 8 provides that it is
an offence for an occupier to permit or suffer the production of a controlled C
drug.

The facts upon the basis of which this conviction has been recorded
are simply these: the defendant was the occupier of a house at Ashford.
There were five cannabis plants in individual pots on the premises in an
upstairs bedroom which was not occupied by the defendant but by somebody else. When the matter was investigated the plants were found to be D
damp. That was relevant to the defendant's contention that no one had
been cultivating these plants, but that now has been abandoned. He knew
of the presence of these plants, and it is apparently common ground that
another occupant of the premises has been convicted under section 6 of
the Act of 1971, which is a section which makes it an offence for anybody
to cultivate any plant of the genus cannabis. Mr. Shaw submits on the
defendant's behalf that no offence is committed in this case. E

I have already said that section 8 makes it an offence to permit or
suffer the producing of a controlled drug on the premises. " Produce " is
defined in section 37 (1) as follows: ". . . where the reference is to producing a controlled drug, means producing it by manufacture, cultivation or
any other method, . . ." One can substitute in section 8 for the word
" produce " the words " produce by cultivation." He was charged with F
knowingly permitting or suffering the production by cultivation of a
controlled drug. The controlled drug alleged was cannabis, and under the
original Misuse of Drugs Act 1971 " cannabis " was defined as meaning

" . . . the flowering or fruiting tops of any plant of the genus cannabis
from which the resin has not been extracted, by whatever name they
may be designated; . . ." G

Under the Act in its original state this charge would have amounted to a
charge against the defendant that he had suffered the production by
cultivation of the flowering or fruiting tops of a plant of the genus
cannabis, and of course there is no evidence of that at all. The evidence
related simply to the plants with or without flowering or fruiting tops, that
not being specified. H

But the prosecution say that that does not matter because the definition
of " cannabis " has been altered by section 52 of the Criminal Law Act 1977
which is in these terms:

" In section 37 (1) (interpretation) of the Misuse of Drugs Act 1971,
for the definition of ' cannabis ' there shall be substituted—' " Cannabis " (except in the expression " cannabis resin ") means any plant of

The Weekly Law Reports, May 15, 1981

609

1 W.L.R.   Taylor v. Chief Constable of Kent (D.C.)   Donaldson L.J.

A   the genus cannabis or any part of any such plant (by whatever name designated) except that it does not include cannabis resin or any of the following products after separation from the rest of the plant, namely—(a) mature stalk of any such plant, (b) fibre produced from mature stalk of any such plant, and (c) seed of any such plant.' "

B   The prosecution, represented by Mr. Cripps, say that when one writes in all the definitions what was here being charged was knowingly permitting or suffering the production by cultivation of a cannabis plant.

Mr. Shaw for the defendant says that cannot be right. That would be to equate section 4 of the Act of 1971—the production of a drug—with section 6—the cultivation of a plant. Parliament cannot have intended to produce the same offence in almost consecutive sections.

C   The answer to that was given by Forbes J., namely, that, while that is a very good argument in relation to an original Act of Parliament, it loses much of its force when applied to an amendment to an Act of Parliament. Parliament could of course have removed section 6 if it had wanted to. But there is not much point in removing section 6 even if it overlaps section 4. I can see no answer to this contention by the prosecution.

D   The only thing which has disturbed me is a point to which Forbes J. drew attention, namely, that you may well find that there are reputable horticulturists who have licences to cultivate the cannabis plant, licences granted under regulations made under section 7, which would protect them against a charge under section 6. Following the amendment by the Criminal Law Act 1977 they may, in theory at any rate, now be open to a charge under section 4 or possibly under section 8 of the Misuse of Drugs Act

E   1971, as occupiers of premises on which cannabis is being cultivated and therefore the cannabis drug is being produced contrary to section 4. They would need special authorisation to protect them in respect of that activity, which is the same activity but could be impugned under a different section.

Mr. Cripps says that we do not have to worry about that because the police will be sensible about their prosecutions. That may be, but it is not

F   a very happy approach to the situation. If any person has a licence to cultivate the cannabis plant, it would be well that they should ensure that it is a licence which authorises not only cultivation, which would otherwise be prohibited by section 6, but also the production of a drug, which would also be prohibited under section 4.

I would therefore, dismiss the appeal.

G   FORBES J. I agree and would just like to add this. What does disturb me about this case can be put in this way. As I understand it, before the amendment produced by the Criminal Law Act 1977 no offence was committed by an occupier of premises even though he knew that somebody was cultivating cannabis on the premises, an offence under section 6: aliter if he knew that a drug was being produced.

H   If the argument for the prosecution here is right, the effect of the amendment made by section 52 of the Act of 1977 is now to make it an offence by an occupier to do that which was no offence before that amendment. One would have expected that, if that had been the intention of Parliament, something would have been said, some reference would have been made in the Act, to the fact that a new offence was being created which affected the occupiers of premises in those circumstances, and nothing of the kind is included in the Act.

610

But doing as Donaldson L.J. has done, writing in to section 8 the   A
various pieces of the various definitions in section 37 of the Act of 1971
as amended, we get the situation that a person commits an offence if,
being the occupier of premises, he knowingly permits or suffers the producing by cultivation or the attempting to produce by cultivation any
plant of the genus cannabis or any part of such plant. That seems to me
to be the inevitable result of the definitions as amended by section 52.   B

That being the perfectly clear result, in my opinion, from the words used
by Parliament, and there being no escape unless there is an ambiguity in
that wording, it seems to me that one must follow the matter through and
say that the offence is in fact in those circumstances committed; a new
offence has been created by a side wind without any specific reference to
it in the Act of Parliament which creates it, but there it is.   C

> *Appeal dismissed.*
> *Legal aid taxation.*
> *Prosecutor's costs out of central funds.*

On January 27, 1981, the court refused the defendant leave to appeal   D
to the House of Lords, but certified the following question to be a point
of law of general public importance: Whether, by virtue of the amendment of the definition of cannabis effected by section 52 of the Criminal
Law Act 1977, the cultivation of any plant of the genus cannabis is
not only an offence under section 6 of the Misuse of Drugs Act 1971
(cultivating cannabis plants) but is also an offence under section 4 of the   E
Act (producing a controlled drug).

Solicitors: *Girling, Wilson & Harvie, Canterbury; R. A. Crabb,
Maidstone.*

[Reported by ISOBEL COLLINS, Barrister-at-Law]   F

March 19. The Appeal Committee of the House of Lords (Lord
Wilberforce, Lord Roskill and Lord Bridge of Harwich) dismissed a
petition by the defendant for leave to appeal.

G

H

A

[HOUSE OF LORDS]

*REGALIAN SECURITIES LTD. . . . . RESPONDENTS AND
CROSS-APPELLANTS

AND

B RAMSDEN . . . . APPELLANT AND
CROSS-RESPONDENT

1981 March 16, 17;   Lord Wilberforce, Lord Salmon,
April 9   Lord Russell of Killowen,
Lord Keith of Kinkel and Lord Roskill

C *Landlord and Tenant—Rent restriction—Personal occupation—
Long tenancy at low rent—Penthouse comprising maisonette
with self-contained flat attached—Original use as family home
—Assignment of long lease—Subsequent sub-letting of
maisonette for term of head lease less less one day—Sub-tenant
in unlawful occupation after term date—Tenant in occupation
of flat—Tenant's intention to use whole premises as family
home—Whether protected in respect of whole—Whether*
D *penthouse let as one separate dwelling—Landlord and Tenant
Act 1954 (2 & 3 Eliz. 2, c. 56), ss. 1, 2 (1) (2), 22 (3) [1]—Rent
Act 1977 (c. 42), s. 2 (3) [2]*

By a lease dated September 29, 1936, R took for a term
of 42 years at a rent of £300 a year a penthouse consisting of
a maisonette for himself and his family and a flat for his
domestic servants. The door to the flat adjoined a door to
E the maisonette but there was no internal connection between
them. On March 9, 1973, R assigned the lease to his son,
the present tenant. Although the son wished to preserve the
family home (the penthouse) for his own family home in the
future at that time he had no use for such a large property
and, accordingly, on March 15, 1973, he granted an under-
lease of the maisonette to B for the remainder of the term
of the head lease less one day, the son retaining residential
F occupation of the flat. Subsequently the unexpired residue
of the term granted by the under-lease was assigned to C who
was occupying the maisonette as his residence when the term
granted by the under-lease expired on September 28, 1978,
and he remained in occupation thereafter claiming initially
to be protected by the Rent Act 1977.
The present head landlords applied to the county court
under section 2 (2) of the Landlord and Tenant Act 1954,
G for an order declaring that the son's tenancy of the penthouse
was not to be treated for the purposes of Part 1 of the Act
of 1954 as a tenancy to which section 1 of that Act applied
on the ground that the penthouse was not let as a separate
dwelling at the relevant time, and that, in any event, the son
was not occupying it as a residence. The judge dismissed the
action. On the landlords' appeal the Court of Appeal allowed
the appeal in respect of the maisonette but not in respect of
H the flat.
On appeal by the son and cross-appeal by the landlords: —
Held, allowing the appeal and dismissing the cross-appeal,
(1) that in determining whether there had been abandonment
of intention it was necessary to distinguish between the land-

[1] Landlord and Tenant Act 1954. s. 1: see post, p. 618F–G.
S. 2 (1) (2): see post, pp. 618G—619B.
S. 22 (3): see post, p. 619C–E.
[2] Rent Act 1977, s. 2 (3): see post, 619G–H.

A

lords and the son as tenant under the head lease on the one
hand, and the position between the son as lessor and C as
lessee under the under-lease on the other, and that for the
purposes of the Act of 1954 it was the former relationship
and not the latter which was of prime importance (post, pp.
613B–C, 615D).

(2) That on the term date, the penthouse was let to the
son as a separate dwelling because (a) there had initially been
a single letting of the penthouse at a single rent for residential   B
purposes; (b) the under-lease had expired by effluxion of time;
(c) the sub-tenant's occupation thereafter was unlawful; (d) the
only person entitled to lawful possession of the whole premises
on the term date was the tenant; (e) it was on that date the
tenant's settled intention to occupy the penthouse as a family
home as soon as he could move there; (f) notwithstanding
the sub-tenant's unlawful occupation, the tenant was
in possession of the penthouse on the term date with that   C
settled intention, that, accordingly, in the circumstances the
son as tenant was entitled to the protection afforded by the
Rent Acts in respect of the whole premises (post, pp. 613B–C,
614H—615B, D).

Haines v. Herbert [1963] 1 W.L.R. 1401, C.A. and
Herbert v. Byrne [1964] 1 W.L.R. 519, C.A. approved.

Per Lord Wilberforce, Lord Salmon, Lord Keith of Kinkel
and Lord Roskill. The effect of section 2 (3) of the Rent Act   D
1977 is to preserve the judge-made law relating to the predecessors of that provision. Accordingly, a statutory tenant
may be a statutory tenant of only a part of what he has
hitherto been the contractual tenant (post, pp. 613B–C, 615D,
620B–F).

Decision of the Court of Appeal [1980] 2 All E.R. 497
reversed.

E

The following cases are referred to in their Lordships' opinions:

Crown Lodge (Surbiton) Investments Ltd. v. Nalecz [1967] 1 W.L.R.
    647; [1967] 1 All E.R. 489, C.A.
Haines v. Herbert [1963] 1 W.L.R. 1401; [1963] 3 All E.R. 715, C.A.
Herbert v. Byrne [1964] 1 W.L.R. 519; [1964] 1 All E.R. 882, C.A.
Horford Investments Ltd. v. Lambert [1976] Ch. 39; [1973] 3 W.L.R. 872;   F
    [1974] 1 All E.R. 131, C.A.

The following additional cases were cited in argument:

Baron v. Phillips (1978) 38 P. & C.R. 91, C.A.
Barrell v. Fordree [1932] A.C. 676, H.L.(E.).
Langford Property Co. Ltd. v. Goldrich [1949] 1 K.B. 511; [1949] 1 All
    E.R. 402, C.A.   G
Wolfe v. Hogan [1949] 2 K.B. 194; [1949] 1 All E.R. 570, C.A.

APPEAL from the Court of Appeal.

This was an appeal and cross-appeal by leave of the House of Lords
by the appellant, Jack R. Ramsden, and the respondents, Regalian
Securities Ltd., respectively, from an order dated April 1, 1980, of the   H
Court of Appeal (Lord Denning M.R., Bridge and Oliver L.JJ.) allowing an appeal by the respondents, from the order dated September 24,
1979, of Judge Rowland whereby the respondents' application for a
declaration under section 2 (2) of Part 1 of the Landlord and Tenant Act
1954 was dismissed.

The question in this appeal related to the circumstances in which a
residential tenant of flats demised by a long lease might fail to be

A protected by Part 1 of the Landlord and Tenant Act 1954 in respect of the whole property comprised in his letting.

The facts are stated in the opinions of Lord Russell of Killowen and Lord Roskill.

Patrick-Garland Q.C. and *Mark Blackett-Ord* for the appellant.
Robert Pryor and *Nicholas Dowding* for the respondents.

B

Their Lordships took time for consideration.

April 9. LORD WILBERFORCE. My Lords, I have had the benefit of reading in advance the speech prepared by my noble and learned friend, Lord Roskill. I agree with it and would allow the appeal and dismiss
C the cross-appeal.

LORD SALMON. My Lords, I have had the advantage of reading in draft the speeches prepared by my noble and learned friends Lord Russell of Killowen and Lord Roskill. For the reasons they have given I too would allow the appeal and dismiss the cross-appeal.

D
LORD RUSSELL OF KILLOWEN. My Lords, in 1936 the father of the appellant persuaded the builder of a block of flats in Petty France, S.W.1. to change in part the plans so as to constitute a penthouse which he wished to lease as a residence for his family. This having been done a lease of the penthouse was granted to the father for a term expiring on September 29, 1978, and for the next 37 years the father made it his family
E home. The penthouse consisted of a maisonette on the eighth and ninth floors and an adjacent flat on the ninth floor intended primarily for staff of the household. The front door of the flat was conveniently disposed beside a door leading into the maisonette. It is common ground that notwithstanding the form of construction of the penthouse this was a lease of one dwellinghouse.

F In 1973 the father, being of a good age, wished to retire and to live in the country. In March 1973 he assigned the lease of the penthouse to the appellant for a payment of £10,000. The appellant's employment was then largely out of London but he wished, as the judge found, to preserve the family home (the penthouse) for his own family home in the future. Shortly after the assignment, the appellant subleased the maisonette to a friend, Mr. de Bye, for the rest of the term less one day. The appellant
G lived from time to time thereafter in the flat. In 1975, de Bye assigned the sublease of the maisonette to one Carter. Under the sublease it was, of course, the duty of Carter to vacate the maisonette 24 hours before the term date of the lease and make it available for occupation by the appellant. He did not in fact do so, asserting without justification in law that he had a right to stay there. Carter could not be evicted by the appellant
H without a court order, and remained in de facto occupation of the maisonette until after the lease term date. In fact, the appellant made no attempt to secure Carter's eviction until after the conclusion of the case (next mentioned) before the county court judge, when he established a right against the reversioners to remain after the lease term date as tenant under Part I of the Landlord and Tenant Act 1954: any earlier attempt would have been fruitless had the appellant failed against the reversioner.

Part I of the Act of 1954 contains provisions whereby a tenant under

a particular type of tenancy is afforded the protection of the Rent Acts,   A
and the tenancy is continued beyond the term date of the tenancy, though
with a number of provisions affecting the terms of the continued tenancy.
It was and is the contention of the appellant that his lease of the penthouse fulfilled the requirements of the Act of 1954 in this regard, and the
judge so held. The Court of Appeal [1980] 2 All E.R. 497 reversed the
judge as to the maisonette, but (apparently without objection by the present
respondent reversioner) held that the appellant was entitled under the Act   B
to a continuation of the lease so far as concerned the flat. The Appeal
Committee of this House gave leave to the appellant to appeal to your
Lordships, and to the respondent to cross-appeal as to the flat. It is convenient here to notice that it was accepted for the respondent that if the
appeal were to succeed the cross-appeal must fail. There is provision
(section 2 (2)) for application to the court for decision of such questions   C
before the term date of the tenancy in question. On April 3, 1978, the
respondent applied for an order declaring that the tenancy of the penthouse is not to be treated for the purposes of Part I of the Act of 1954
as a tenancy to which section 1 of the Act applies. That application
was, on September 24, 1979, dismissed.

Section 1 of the Act is the section which if applicable confers on a   D
tenant protection of the Rent Acts.

Section 2 (1) requires the tenancy to be a long tenancy at a low rent.
The lease of the penthouse was such. It also requires the tenancy to be
one as respects which for the time being the " qualifying condition " is
fulfilled. The qualifying condition requires that the circumstances (as
respects the property comprised in the tenancy, the use of the property,
and all other relevant matters) are such that on the coming to an end of   E
the tenancy at that time the tenant would, if the tenancy had not been
a long tenancy at a low rent, be entitled by virtue of the Rent Acts to
retain possession of the whole or part of the property comprised in the
tenancy.

Section 22 (3) of the Act is also to be noted. In effect it provides that
in considering the " nature of the property " at the time of the creation
of the tenancy it is to be deemed to have been the same as its nature at   F
the time in relation to which the question arises—here the term date: and
secondly that the purpose for which the property was let under the tenancy
is deemed to have been the purpose for which the property is used at that
time.

It appears to me that section 22 (3) operates and operates only in relation to the first part of the qualifying condition under section 2 (1), and   G
that in the instant case there was no such operation. The nature of the
property—the penthouse—remained the same: there had been no structural alteration: the purpose for which the penthouse was used was and
remained the same—residential use.

I come back, then, to the question of the second branch of the qualifying condition. There is I apprehend ample authority for the proposition   H
that a tenant entitled to the protection of the Rent Acts in respect of a
dwelling-house does not lose that protection if he sublets part of the
dwelling comprised in the tenancy provided that he does not mean to
abandon for the future all intention of ever occupying the sublet part as
his residence. And this approach has been carried through into consideration of the Act of 1954: see *Herbert* v. *Byrne* [1964] 1 W.L.R. 519
which in my opinion was rightly decided. There was ample evidence

A upon which the county court could find that the appellant intended to occupy the whole penthouse when it should become available, as in law it would have before the term date had Carter vacated the maisonette in accordance with his obligations under the sublease. Had Carter fulfilled his obligations, and had the appellant promptly moved in a bed, table and chair, the matter would not have allowed doubt: and I cannot think that Carter's obduracy (based on an erroneous view of his legal rights) can affect the situation under the Act.

B

The Court of Appeal admitted evidence designed to show that the judge's findings of the intentions of the appellant were, or might have been erroneous. The respondent sought in the alternative a new trial. In common with your Lordships I did not find the new evidence at all cogent, and declined to order a new trial.

C   Accordingly I would allow the appeal, dismiss the cross-appeal, and restore the order of the county court judge, the costs in the Court of Appeal and in this House to be paid by the respondent.

LORD KEITH OF KINKEL. My Lords, for the reasons given in the speech to be delivered by my noble and learned friend Lord Roskill, which I have had the advantage of reading in draft and with which I agree, I too would allow the appeal and dismiss the cross-appeal.

D

LORD ROSKILL. My Lords, this appeal concerns a penthouse on the eighth and ninth floors of Vandon Court, Petty France, Westminster, S.W.1. That penthouse comprised a maisonette on the eighth and ninth floors, the flat numbers of which were 83 and 84, and a self-contained flat on the ninth floor, the flat number of which was 85. To avoid confusion, I shall call that self-contained flat on the ninth floor (85) "the flat," and numbers 83 and 84 on the eighth and ninth floors "the maisonette." When I refer to "the penthouse" I shall use that phrase to describe the totality of these premises.

E

The appellants claims the protection accorded to residential tenants by Part I of the Landlord and Tenant Act 1954 in respect of the penthouse. The respondents (whom I shall call "the landlords") dispute that claim. They took advantage of the provisions of section 2 (2) of the Act of 1954 to start proceedings against the appellant on April 3, 1978, in Westminster County Court for an order that the appellant's tenancy of the penthouse was not to be treated as a tenancy to which Part I of the Act of 1954 applied. For the reasons given in a careful reserved judgment dated September 24, 1979, the county court judge (Her Honour Judge Rowland) dismissed the landlords' application. The landlords appealed to the Court of Appeal (Lord Denning M.R., Bridge and Oliver L.JJ.) who on April 1, 1980, allowed the landlords' appeal in relation to the maisonette but affirmed the decision of the learned judge in relation to the flat. The Court of Appeal refused the appellant leave to appeal to your Lordships' House. But such leave was granted by an Appeal Committee on June 5, 1980, who also gave the landlords leave to appeal against that part of the Court of Appeal's order which related to the flat. Hence the landlords' cross-appeal with which I shall deal later.

F

G

H

The history of the penthouse and of the lease which became vested in the appellant is fully set out in the learned judge's judgment. I can summarise the main facts as follows.

Lord Roskill   **Regalian Securities v. Ramsden (H.L.(E.))**   [1981]

1. Vandon Court was being built in 1936. Its owner was a Mr. Griggs, A
who was a friend of the appellant's father. He became interested in the
construction, and in the result, with Mr. Grigg's agreement, he employed
his own architect to re-design the top of Vandon Court so as to create
what ultimately became the penthouse. The penthouse was a single family
home, the flat being intended for domestic staff. I need not trouble your
Lordships with the details of the accommodation. Suffice it to say that
at no time between 1936 and the end of 1978 were any structural altera- B
tions made to any part of the penthouse.

2. On October 1, 1936, Mr. Griggs granted the appellant's father a
lease of the penthouse for 42 years from September 29, 1936, at the yearly
rate of £300. It was common ground that from that day until March 9,
1973 (that is for some 37 years), the penthouse was occupied by the
appellant's father, and his family, as a single family home or, to use the C
language used by Russell L.J. in *Horford Investments Ltd.* v. *Lambert*
[1976] Ch. 39, 46H, as " one unit of habitation." In the language of the
Rent Acts, the penthouse was throughout that period of some 37 years,
let and used as " a separate dwelling." The lease contained in clause 2 (9)
a covenant against user for trade, professional or business purposes.

3. In 1973, the appellant's father, then 81 years of age, decided to
live in the country. On March 9, 1973, he assigned the residue of the D
term of years created by the 1936 lease of the penthouse to the appellant
for the sum of £10,000. But the appellant had no immediate need of the
penthouse. On March 15, 1973, he granted to a Mr. de Bye (who was a
friend of the appellant's father) an under-lease of the maisonette for a
sum of £8,600 and a yearly rental of £228. The term of that under-lease
was for the residue of the term of the 1936 lease, less one day. But before E
and after the 1936 lease became vested in the appellant, he had used the
flat for his own purposes, and he continued to do so after he married
in 1965, when he was in London on business, or for visits with his wife.
The details of his movements over this period will be found in the learned
judge's judgment. Since July 1978—that is, since the present proceedings
were begun—the appellant has been working mainly in London and since F
then has used the flat for some two to three days each week. At about
the same time as the appellant acquired the 1936 lease from his father,
he spent some £5,500 modernising the flat.

4. On March 25, 1975, Mr. de Bye assigned the residue of his under-
lease of the maisonette to a Mr. Carter. The under-lease contained no
prohibition against assignment. The under-lease thus expired by effluxion
of time on September 28, 1978. The 1936 lease expired by effluxion of G
time on September 29, 1978. Mr. Carter did not, however, leave the
maisonette on September 28, 1978. Though he could not, of course, on
or after that date, have been evicted from the maisonette without an
order of the court, it was common ground that thenceforth he had no
legal entitlement to possession of the maisonette. A possession order was
ultimately obtained against him, and your Lordships were told that he H
finally left the maisonette in March 1980, having seemingly continued to
occupy it for some months as a trespasser.

5. Though certain of the facts which I have summarised have been
in dispute at the trial, the landlords expressly accepted before your Lordships' House that: (i) until the assignment in March 1973 the appellant's
father had occupied the penthouse as a separate dwelling; (ii) on the term
date of the 1936 lease, that is to say, September 29, 1978, the appellant

A   was in occupation of the flat as a residence; (iii) after the term date of the under-lease, that is September 28, 1978, Mr. Carter had no contractual or statutory right to remain in possession of the maisonette save that he could not be lawfully evicted without a court order.

At the conclusion of her judgment, the learned judge made the following findings:

B   "I take the following view: I reject the contention on behalf of the applicant" (that is, the landlords) "that the subletting changed the character of the original single unit into two separate dwellings. There are no physical structural alterations. It is not a case of a home subsequently converted into separate flats. In my view the premises remain the same single unit as when built and let as such and used by one family for 37 years until 1973. I find the purpose of the respondent" (that is, the present appellant) "in purchasing the remainder of the lease of the penthouse was to keep the family home. He sublet the maisonette because he had no immediate use for more than the domestic flat. I find that he had and retained an intention to reoccupy the penthouse as a family home and that the terms of the sublease were designed to preserve the penthouse for such future occupation when required. The family furniture remained and still remains in the maisonette. His work commitments now require a family home in London. I find his original intention crystallised into an immediate intention before the relevant term date through the exigencies of his employment and his large family and domestic staff requirements. I am satisfied that he intends to occupy the whole penthouse as a family home in the near future and that it is a settled intention. . . . On the issue of occupation of the domestic flat I find that the respondent never abandoned his occupation of it. He always retained it, never let it and in 1973 spent £5,500 modernising it. He spent occasional nights there, sometimes with his wife. It was his only home for eight months in 1976. Since July 1978 with the transfer of his employment to London publishers he has occupied it several days each week. In my view whatever his past use of it, it was his London home at the relevant term date. I find that the respondent at the relevant term date had a settled intention to occupy the whole penthouse as a family home as soon as he could move his family there, was in regular personal residence of the domestic flat which I find constitutes a part of the penthouse and that he thus satisfies the requirements of the qualifying condition under the Act of 1954."

C

D

E

F

G

In the Court of Appeal the landlords sought to challenge (among other matters) the learned judge's findings regarding "the family furniture" having remained and still remaining in the maisonette. To this end it was sought to produce further evidence regarding the furniture. It was said that not only had the learned judge made a wrong finding of fact in this connection, as the new evidence was alleged to show, but that this alleged error vitiated her finding regarding the appellant's "settled intention" regarding the penthouse. The landlords, by amendment of their notice of appeal to the Court of Appeal, asked for a new trial because of this new evidence. But in view of their partial success in that court, that submission was understandably not

H

Lord Roskill   **Regalian Securities v. Ramsden (H.L.(E.))**   **[1981]**

pursued. The same request was, however, made of your Lordships' House **A**
—indeed learned counsel for the landlords made this his first submission
at the outset of his address.

Lord Denning M.R. observed in his judgment in the Court of Appeal
[1980] 2 All E.R. 497, that it was not altogether clear to whom the furniture belonged. He added, at p. 500J: "At all events, no help can be
gained from the furniture." My Lords, I respectfully agree with this view.
Your Lordships were, however, invited to examine, and did examine, the **B**
new evidence placed before the Court of Appeal. Much reliance was placed
upon exhibit DJS 5 to an affidavit by a Mr. Sheahan, a legal executive
with the landlords' solicitors. This exhibit is described in the affidavit as
a "draft letter" from Mr. de Bye to the appellants' then solicitors. How
the landlords' solicitors acquired this document is not explained, and I
am quite unable to see how this document could possibly be admissible **C**
evidence against the appellant. But whatever the arrangements were
regarding the furniture, this so-called new evidence leaves a very clear
impression on my mind that those arrangements were informal. Certainly
I can see nothing which casts sufficient doubt upon the foundation of the
learned judge's findings regarding the appellant's intention, which is the
important matter which would justify your Lordships taking the extreme **D**
step, after proceedings which have now occupied the time of three tribunals,
of ordering a new trial. As I have already said, I respectfully agree with
the observations made by Lord Denning M.R. on this point. In my opinion,
this appeal must be decided upon the basis of the learned judge's findings
of fact which I have already stated. I would therefore, without hesitation,
refuse that application by the landlords.

Part I of the Act of 1954 gave to certain residential tenants the protec- **E**
tion of the Rent Acts to which, apart from those statutory provisions, such
tenants would not have been entitled. The Rent Acts were defined in
section 22 (1) of the Act of 1954 as meaning the Rent and Mortgage
Interest (Restrictions) Acts 1920 to 1939 and the Landlord and Tenant
(Rent Control) Act 1949. To secure Rent Act protection for such residential
tenants the following provisions were enacted in the Act of 1954. I should **F**
perhaps explain that I quote these provisions as originally enacted and
ignore any subsequent amendments and re-amendments which are presently
irrelevant:

"1. On the termination in accordance with the provisions of this
Part of this Act of a tenancy to which this section applies the tenant
shall be entitled to the protection of the Rent Acts subject to and **G**
in accordance with those provisions.

"2 (1) The foregoing section applies to any long tenancy at a
low rent, being a tenancy as respects which for the time being the
following condition (hereinafter referred to as 'the qualifying condition') is fulfilled, that is to say that the circumstances (as respects
the property comprised in the tenancy, the use of that property,
and all other relevant matters) are such that on the coming to an **H**
end of the tenancy at that time the tenant would, if the tenancy
had not been one at a low rent, be entitled by virtue of the Rent
Acts to retain possession of the whole or part of the property
comprised in the tenancy. (2) At any time before, but not more than
12 months before, the term date application may be made to the
court as respects any long tenancy at a low rent, not being at the time

A   of the application a tenancy as respects which the qualifying condition
is fulfilled, for an order declaring that the tenancy is not to be treated
for the purposes of this Part of this Act as a tenancy to which the foregoing section applies; and where such an application is made—
(a) the court, if satisfied that the tenancy is not likely, immediately
before the term date, to be a tenancy to which the foregoing section
applies, but not otherwise, shall make the order; (b) if the court
B   makes the order, then notwithstanding anything in subsection (1) of
this section the tenancy shall not thereafter be treated as a tenancy
to which the foregoing section applies. . . .

    " 3 (1) A tenancy which is current immediately before the term
date and is then a tenancy to which section 1 of this Act applies
shall not come to an end on that date except by being terminated
C   under the provisions of this Part of this Act, and if not then so
terminated shall subject to those provisions continue until so terminated and shall, while continuing by virtue of this section, be
deemed (notwithstanding any change in circumstances) to be a
tenancy to which section of this Act applies. . . .

    " 22 (3) In determining, for the purposes of any provision of this
D   Part of this Act, whether the property comprised in a tenancy, or any
part of that property, was let as a separate dwelling, the nature of the
property or part at the time of the creation of the tenancy shall
be deemed to have been the same as its nature at the time in
relation to which the question arises, and the purpose for which it
was let under the tenancy shall be deemed to have been the same
as the purpose for which it is or was used at the last-mentioned
E   time."

    When the landlords began the instant proceedings, the relevant provi-
sions regarding Rent Act protection were no longer to be found in the
statutes originally referred to in section 22 (1) of the Act of 1954, but
in the Rent Act of 1977. The most relevant provisions of the Act of 1977
F   are as follows:

    " 1. Subject to this Part of this Act, a tenancy under which a
dwelling-house (which may be a house or part of a house) is let as
a separate dwelling is a protected tenancy for the purposes of this
Act. Any reference in this Act to a protected tenant shall be construed accordingly.
G   " 2 (1) Subject to this Part of this Act—(a) after the termination of a protected tenancy of a dwelling-house the person who,
immediately before that termination, was the protected tenant of
the dwelling-house shall, if and so long as he occupies the dwelling-
house as his residence, be the statutory tenant of it; . . . (3) In
subsection (1) (a) and in Part I of Schedule 1, the phrase ' if and
H   so long as he occupies the dwelling-house as his residence ' shall be
construed as it was immediately before the commencement of this
Act (that is to say, in accordance with section 3 (2) of the Rent Act
1968). (4) A person who becomes a statutory tenant of a dwelling-
house as mentioned in subsection (1) (a) above is, in this Act,
referred to as a statutory tenant by virtue of his previous protected
tenancy."

Schedule 23, paragraph 16 reads :

A

"In section 22 (1) of the Landlord and Tenant Act 1954, in the definition of ' the Rent Act,' for ' the Rent Act 1968 ' . . . substitute . . . ' the Rent Act 1977 ' . . ."

I should explain in connection with this last citation that the reference to the Rent Act 1968, which was deleted by paragraph 16 of Schedule 23, was inserted by Schedule 15 to the Rent Act 1968, which had in this respect substituted a reference to that Act for the original definition in section 22 (1) of the Act of 1954. Thus, by 1978 when the instant proceedings were begun, the relevant protection accorded by the Act of 1954 has to be determined by reference to the Rent Act 1977. But, as already stated, section 2 (3) of the Act of 1977 enjoined that the phrase in section 2 (1) (*a*) " if and so long as he occupies the dwelling-house as his residence " should be construed in accordance with section 3 (2) of the Rent Act 1968. Reference back to that subsection shows that it provided that that same phrase

B

C

"shall be construed as requiring the fulfilment of the same, and only the same, qualifications (whether as to residence or otherwise) as had to be fulfilled before the commencement of this Act to entitle a tenant, within the meaning of the Increase of Rent and Mortgage Interest (Restrictions) Act 1920, to retain possession, by virtue of that Act and not by virtue of a tenancy, of a dwelling-house to which that Act applied."

D

Thus, one is taken right back to the Increase of Rent and Mortgage Interest (Restrictions) Act 1920. I think I need only refer to sections 12 (2) and 15 (1) of the Act of 1920. The purpose of this convoluted series of references back, both in the Acts of 1977 and 1968, and thence to the Act of 1920, must, I think—and indeed Mr. Garland Q.C. so submitted for the appellant—have been to preserve, unchanged, that vast body of judge-made law on the sufficiency or insufficiency of residence in this context. That body of case law will be found collected in *Megarry, The Rent Acts,* 10th ed. (1967), p. 184 et seq.

E

F

It is against this complex statutory background that I turn to consider the application of the facts found by the learned judge to the requirements of the Act of 1954 which have to be complied with before the protection accorded by that Act can be successfully claimed by a tenant. The structure and intention of sections 1 and 2 of the Act of 1954 seem reasonably plain. The provisions are designed to give Rent Act protection to tenancies otherwise excluded from such protection, because they are long tenancies at low rents. If they are long tenancies at low rents, then " the qualifying condition " has to be satisfied before protection is accorded. The qualifying condition is :

G

"that the circumstances (as respects the property comprised in the tenancy, the use of that property, and all other relevant matters) are such that on the coming to an end of the tenancy at that time the tenant would, if the tenancy had not been one at a low rent, be entitled by virtue of the Rent Acts to retain possession of the whole or part of the property comprised in the tenancy."

H

There is no question that the terms of the head lease satisfied the requirements of being a long tenancy at a low rent. The crucial question

A is, therefore, whether on the term date, September 29, 1978, the appellant would as a tenant have been entitled to retain possession of the whole or part of the property comprised in the tenancy.

The effect of section 2 (1) of the Act of 1954 has been fully considered in three decisions of the Court of Appeal, *Haines* v. *Herbert* [1963] 1 W.L.R. 1401; *Herbert* v. *Byrne* [1964] 1 W.L.R. 519 (the court consisted of Lord Denning M.R. and Russell and Salmon L.JJ.) and *Crown Lodge*
B *(Surbiton) Investments Ltd.* v. *Nalecz* [1967] 1 W.L.R. 647. In each of the two last-mentioned cases Lord Denning M.R., at pp. 525–526 of the former report, and pp. 650–651 of the latter, analysed the structure of this section, and on both occasions emphasised the importance of looking at " the whole house "—at p. 526 of the former report, the Master of the Rolls italicised the word " whole." I respectfully agree with him and adopt his analysis.
C The court has to concern itself with the position as between landlord and tenant, and not—at least at the outset of its inquiry—look into the position between the tenant and any sub-tenants. The court must look at the totality of that which was the subject matter of the letting, section 22 (3) enjoining it to treat the factual situation at the term date regarding the nature of the property and the purpose for which the property was let as
D that nature and purpose which had subsisted at the beginning of the tenancy. In passing, I would observe that—as my noble and learned friend Lord Russell of Killowen pointed out during the hearing—section 22 (3) plays little if any part in the determination of this appeal since the nature of the property was the same in 1978 as in 1936 (there had been no structural alteration whatever) and the purpose for which that property was let was the same (namely residential). Moreover, as the first of the two
E cases which I have mentioned shows, the fact that there is a sub-letting of one or more parts of the property in question, does not of itself mean that the tenant has ceased to occupy the whole property as his residence: see in particular the judgment of Lord Denning M.R. in *Herbert* v. *Byrne* [1964] 1 W.L.R. 519, 525–526.

Mr. Pryor, for the landlords, founded much of his argument upon the
F supposed irrelevancy of the learned judge's finding as to the appellant's intention regarding the occupation of the penthouse. Any relevant intention must, he argued, be capable of being put into practical effect during the term of the tenancy, and what was found to have been the appellant's intention on September 29, 1978, could never have been put into effect on or before that date, since Mr. Carter was then still in occupation of
G the maisonette albeit as a trespasser. It was only present intention that was relevant, and not intention as to the future after the term date. The appellant as lessor to Mr. Carter was responsible for that which Mr. Carter did or omitted to do, and he must bear the consequences of Mr. Carter's trespass which involved that there was no practical possibility of the appellant gaining possession of the maisonette and thus possession of the penthouse as distinct from his existing possession of the flat, on the
H one crucial day, namely, September 29, 1978. Mr. Pryor described that one day reversion as a conveyancing device to prevent the conversion of an under-lease into what, in the absence of such a single day, would be an assignment. Too much weight was not to be attached to its existence.

My Lords, the decisions of the Court of Appeal in both *Haines* v. *Herbert* [1963] 1 W.L.R. 1401 and *Herbert* v. *Byrne* [1964] 1 W.L.R. 519 militate strongly against the landlords' submissions on the question of

Lord Roskill   **Regalian Securities v. Ramsden (H.L.(E.))**   **[1981]**

intention. In the former case, the tenant had " the intention of reconvert- A
ing the whole messuage into one dwelling-house "—I quote from Harman
L.J. at p. 1407—but had not done so before the term date. That did not
prevent there being a single occupation on the term date. In the latter,
the tenant " had formed the intention to make the new premises in the
fullest sense his home, at least as soon as they were fully fit for occupation as such . . ."—I quote from Russell L.J. at p. 527. Salmon L.J. at
p. 529 emphasised the same point. B

But, my Lords, I do not think it would be possible to accept this part
of the argument by the landlords without disapproving at least a part of
the reasoning in *Haines* v. *Herbert* [1963] 1 W.L.R. 1401, and in truth
the decision in *Herbert* v. *Byrne* [1964] 1 W.L.R. 519. My Lords, even if
I had any doubt as to the correctness of those decisions, and of the
reasoning which led to them, which I emphatically do not, I would not C
willingly have suggested that your Lordships' House should overrule those
decisions nearly 20 years after they were given. In the interval many
cases must have been decided in county courts on the foundation there
laid by the Court of Appeal, and it would be wrong now to disturb that
secure foundation.

The Court of Appeal reached their decision in the present case by, D
in effect, treating the existence of the under-lease of the maisonette to
Mr. Carter as determinative of the crucial issue whether the penthouse
was, on the term date, let to the appellant as a separate dwelling. But,
quite apart from the fact that the term date of the under-lease was one
day earlier than the term date of the lease to the appellant, the decisions
to which I have referred, and in particular, the decision in *Herbert* v.
Byrne [1964] 1 W.L.R. 519, show that the existence of sub-letting, even E
of protected sub-letting, is in no way determinative of the issue. Mr.
Pryor did not shrink from inviting your Lordships' House to say that
Herbert v. *Byrne* was wrongly decided in this respect. In my view, if I
may respectfully say so, *Herbert* v. *Byrne* is in this respect, too, correctly
decided, and for the reasons I have already given, I would not, even if I
had thought otherwise, have been prepared to suggest that it should be F
overruled. Of course, if in a particular case, a landlord could show
abandonment by the tenant of his right to possession (for example) by
reason of one or more sub-lettings so that there was clearly no intention
at any time thereafter to resume possession, the position might well be
different. Where I respectfully differ from the Court of Appeal, is that I
think they failed sufficiently to distinguish between the landlords and
the appellant as tenant under the 1936 lease on the one hand, and the G
position between the appellant as lessor and Mr. Carter as lessee under
the under-lease on the other. They directed attention to the latter rather
than to the former, which as the cases show is what the Act of 1954
enjoins the court to do. Indeed, I venture to think that the decision of the
Court of Appeal in the present appeal is inconsistent with its previous
decision in *Herbert* v. *Byrne*, to which Lord Denning M.R. and Bridge L.J. H
referred, but which was not discussed in detail in their judgments.

My Lords, I am clearly of the view that on the term date, one day
after the expiry of the under-lease, the penthouse was let to the appellant
as a separate dwelling-house because (1) there had initially been a single
letting of the penthouse at a single rent for residential purposes; (2) the
under-lease had expired by effluxion of time on September 28, 1978;
(3) Mr. Carter's occupation on September 29, 1978, was unlawful; (4) the

A only person entitled to lawful possession, not only of the flat but also of the maisonette, and therefore of the penthouse, on September 29, 1978, was the appellant; (5) it was on that date, the term date, the appellant's settled intention to occupy the penthouse as a family house as soon as he could move here; (6) notwithstanding Mr. Carter's unlawful occupation, the appellant was in possession of the penthouse on the term date with that settled intention.

B It follows that I find myself in general agreement with the very clear judgment of the learned county court judge and I would allow the appeal and restore her decision, dismissing the landlords' application under the Act of 1954.

Mr. Pryor conceded that if the appellant's appeal should succeed, the landlords' cross-appeal must fail. I agree that this is so. Strictly, there-

C fore, it is unnecessary for your Lordships to express any view upon the cross-appeal. But your Lordships may, nevertheless, think it right to do so in order to dispose of the argument skilfully advanced in its support, less otherwise it reappears in some later case. The submission proceeded upon the footing that, as the Court of Appeal held, there was not one separate dwelling-house, the maisonette and the flat were each so

D separately let. But since the flat was only a part of what had been let in 1936, the Rent Act 1977 (which had become the relevant statute to write into sections 1 and 2 of the Act of 1954 as I have already said), does not allow protection of a part of a tenancy. Only the whole tenancy can now be protected under the Act of 1954. This ingenious argument was, your Lordships were told, advanced in the Court of Appeal but not pressed, since it seemingly found little favour in that court. The landlords, content

E with victory in respect of the maisonette did not seek to press their victory to the point of gaining possession of the flat as well. But your Lordships were also told that when the appellant obtained leave to appeal to your Lordships' House, it was ordered that the landlords should be at liberty to cross-appeal if they so wished notwithstanding what had happened in the Court of Appeal. Your Lordships have not, therefore, had the advan-

F tage of the views of the Court of Appeal upon the subject matter of the cross-appeal.

My Lords, the argument is admirably stated in paragraphs 20 to 23 of the landlords' printed case, and I shall not repeat what is there fully set out. It depends for its validity upon the fact that section 1 of the Act of 1977 attaches protection to the tenancy under which the dwelling-house is let as a separate dwelling, and not to the dwelling-house itself, as in the

G earlier statutes. It seems that this change of language was first made in section 1 of the Rent Act 1965. It was continued in section 1 of the Rent Act 1968, a consolidating Act, and in effect repeated in section 1 of the Rent Act 1977, also a consolidating Act. My Lords, legislative accidents can happen, but it would be strange indeed if the effect of the changes made in 1965, and continued in 1968 and 1977, which were designed to

H increase the protection accorded to tenants by restoring to them the right to retain possession of certain premises—see the long title of the Act of 1965—were to have the inadvertent result when those provisions are written in to the Act of 1954 of depriving persons admittedly up to 1965 entitled to protection in respect of part of the tenancy falling within the Act of 1954, of that protection. Those who gained protection in 1965 can, if this argument be right, only have gained it at the expense of others who lost protection which had existed between 1954 and 1965.

The landlords' submissions involve that the relevant provisions of the   A
Act of 1977 must be treated as so inconsistent with those of the Act of
1954 that the former must be regarded as impliedly repealing the latter.
My Lords, I freely confess that I would only accept this argument if I saw
no escape from it as a matter of construction, for I find it impossible to
believe that the framers of the Act of 1977 and its predecessors can
possibly have intended this result.
                                                                          B
My Lords, a close examination of the relevant provisions has led me
to the conclusion that this argument is, in truth, ill-founded. Mr. Garland
drew your Lordships' attention to section 2 (3) of the Act of 1977 and its
predecessors. I have already traced the legislative history of this subsection through to its source, and I shall not repeat it again. I see no need
to trace through the judicial history of the phrase which is also long and
complex. Suffice it to say that under the law, as so preserved, a statutory   C
tenant may be a statutory tenant of only a part of what he has hitherto
been the contractual tenant. On that view the problem disappears. I
would, therefore, dismiss the cross-appeal in addition to allowing the
appeal.

Appeal allowed.
Cross-appeal dismissed.
                                                                          D

Solicitors: *Watkins, Pulleyn & Ellison*; *Thornton, Lynne & Lawson.*

J. A. G.

                                                                          E
[CHANCERY DIVISION]

* EXXON CORPORATION AND OTHERS *v.*
EXXON INSURANCE CONSULTANTS INTERNATIONAL LTD.

[1980 E. No. 696]
                                                                          F
1981   Jan. 13, 14, 16; 22   Graham J.

Copyright—Infringement—Literary work—Invented word—Whether
" original literary work "—Copyright Act 1956 (4 & 5 *Eliz.* 2,
c. 74), *s.* 2

The plaintiffs claimed copyright in an invented word,   G
" Exxon," which formed part of the corporate names of three
of the four plaintiff companies, as being an " original literary
work " entitled to copyright protection within the meaning of
section 2 of the Copyright Act 1956. They sought, inter alia,
an injunction to restrain the defendant company from infringing
their copyright in the word, an injunction to restrain the defendant company from using the word " Exxon " or any name   H
confusingly similar thereto so as to pass off its business, goods,
or services as and for those of the plaintiffs or as being connected or associated therewith, and an order directing the
defendant company to change its corporate name and omit
the word " Exxon " therefrom. The defendant company, which
had no connection with any of the plaintiffs failed to put in a
defence.
On the plaintiffs' motion for judgment in default of
defence: —

A   *Held*, (1) that the plaintiffs were entitled to an injunction
and ancillary relief to restrain passing off by the continued
use of the word " Exxon " together with costs relating to that
issue (*post*, p. 630G–H); that Exxon, though invented and therefore original, had no meaning and suggested nothing in itself;
that, since to give the word substance and meaning it had to
be accompanied by other words or be used in a particular
context or juxtaposition, it did not qualify for copyright
B   protection as an " original literary work " within the meaning
of section 2 of the Copyright Act 1956 and, therefore, the
plaintiffs were not entitled to an injunction restraining an
infringement of copyright (*post*, pp. 634E–635A, F—636A).
       University of London Press Ltd. v. *University Tutorial
Press Ltd.* [1916] 2 Ch. 601 and *Ladbroke (Football) Ltd.* v.
William Hill (Football) Ltd. [1964] 1 W.L.R. 273, H.L.(E.)
considered.
C   (2) That the plaintiffs were entitled to an injunction to
restrain the defendant company from allowing its corporate
name incorporating the word Exxon to remain on the register
of companies (*post*, p. 636B–D).
       Anciens Etablissements Panhard et Levassor S.A. v.
Panhard Levassor Motor Co. Ltd. [1901] 2 Ch. 513 applied.

D   The following cases are referred to in the judgment:
Anderson (D. P.) & Co. Ltd. v. *Lieber Code Co.* [1917] 2 K.B. 469.
Charles v. *Shepherd* [1892] 2 Q.B. 622, C.A.
Dicks v. *Yates* (1881) 18 Ch.D. 76, C.A.
Francis Day and Hunter Ltd. v. *Twentieth Century Fox Corporation Ltd.*
       [1940] A.C. 112; [1939] 4 All E.R. 192, P.C.
Gibbings v. *Strong* (1884) 26 Ch.D. 66, C.A.
E   *Graves* v. *Terry* (1882) 9 Q.B.D. 170, D.C.
Ladbroke (Football) Ltd. v. *William Hill (Football) Ltd.* [1964] 1 W.L.R.
       273; [1964] 1 All E.R. 465, H.L.(E.).
Life Music Inc. v. *Wonderland Music Co.* (1965) 241 Fed.Supp. 653.
Panhard et Levassor Anciens Etablissements S.A. v. *Panhard Levassor
       Motor Co. Ltd.* [1901] 2 Ch. 513.
Suhner & Co. A.G. v. *Suhner Ltd.* [1967] F.S.R. 319.
F   *University of London Press Ltd.* v. *University Tutorial Press Ltd.* [1916]
       2 Ch. 601.
Wallersteiner v. *Moir* [1974] 1 W.L.R. 991; [1974] 3 All E.R. 217, C.A.
Walter v. *Lane* [1900] A.C. 539, H.L.(E.).

The following additional cases were cited in argument:
Ager v. *Collingridge* (1886) 2 T.L.R. 291.
G   *Ager* v. *Peninsular and Oriental Steam Navigation Co.* (1884) 26 Ch.D.
       637.
Broemel v. *Meyer* (1912) 29 T.L.R. 148.
Burberrys v. *J.C. Cording & Co. Ltd.* (1909) 26 R.P.C. 693.
Day v. *Brownrigg* (1878) 10 Ch.D. 294, C.A.
Exchange Telegraph Co. Ltd. v. *Central News Ltd.* [1897] 2 Ch. 48.
Karo Step Trade Mark [1977] R.P.C. 255.
Kelly v. *Byles* (1880) 13 Ch.D. 682, C.A.
H   *Kirk* v. *J. & R. Fleming Ltd.* [1928–35] Mac.C.C. 44.
Lamb v. *Evans* [1893] 1 Ch. 218, C.A.
Licensed Victuallers' Newspaper Co. v. *Bingham* (1888) 38 Ch.D. 139, C.A.
Mack v. *Petter* (1872) L.R. 14 Eq. 431.
Maxwell v. *Hogg* (1867) L.R. 2 Ch.App. 307.
Metzler v. *Wood* (1878) 8 Ch.D. 606, C.A.
Sinanide v. *La Maison Kosmeo* (1928) 139 L.T. 365, C.A.
Taverner Rutledge Ltd. v. *Trexapalm Ltd.* [1977] R.P.C. 275.

The Weekly Law Reports, May 15, 1981

Exxon Corpn. v. Exxon Insurance Ltd. (Ch.D.)   [1981]

Tett Bros. Ltd. v. *Drake & Gorham Ltd.* [1928–35] Mac.C.C. 492.   A

Walter v. *Steinkopff* [1892] 3 Ch. 489.

Weldon v. *Dicks* (1878) 10 Ch.D. 247.

Wombles Ltd. v. *Wombles Skips Ltd.* [1977] R.P.C. 99.

MOTION

By a writ dated March 21, 1980, and a statement of claim served on June 19, 1980, the plaintiffs, Exxon Corporation, Esso Petroleum Co. Ltd., B Exxon Ltd. and Exxon International Ltd., sought against the defendants, Exxon Insurance Consultants International Ltd., (1) specific performance of an alleged agreement between the parties, contained in correspondence between their respective solicitors, of which an express term was that the defendant would change its corporate name so as to delete therefrom the word " Exxon " and not include therein any other word similar C to or resembling the word Exxon, in consideration of which the plaintiffs promised to pay to the defendant the sum of £40 on production of a copy of the certificate of incorporation showing such change of name; (2) damages for breach of contract; and/or (3) an injunction to restrain the defendant whether by its directors, servants, agents or otherwise howsoever from infringing the plaintiffs' copyright in the name Exxon; (4) an order that the defendant be directed to change its corporate name D and omit the word Exxon therefrom; (5) an injunction to restrain the defendant whether by its directors, servants, agents or otherwise howsoever from using the word Exxon or any name confusingly similar thereto so as to pass off its business goods or services as and for those of the plaintiffs or as being connected or associated with the plaintiffs; (6) destruction or delivery up of all infringing copies and of any other E matter the use whereof would offend against the provisions of the foregoing injunctions; (7) damages in respect of the defendant's acts of infringement, passing off and conversion or at the plaintiffs' option an account of profits and payment of any sum found due together with interest to the plaintiff; (8) additional damages pursuant to section 17 (3) of the Copyright Act 1956; (9) costs and (10) further or other relief.

By a notice of motion dated July 24, the plaintiffs sought an order F that judgment be granted against the defendant in default of defence under the provisions of R.S.C., Ord. 19, r. 7, in accordance with attached minutes of order.

The facts are stated in the judgment.

Vivian Price Q.C. and *J. V. Fitzgerald,* for the plaintiffs.   G

John F. Mummery for the Attorney-General, as amicus curiae.

The defendant was not present or represented.

Cur. adv. vult.

January 22. GRAHAM J. read the following judgment. This is a H motion for judgment against the defendant in default of defence. Only the plaintiffs were represented at the hearing. The principles applicable on the motion are to be found in R.S.C., Ord. 19, and particularly in rule 7 of that Order. No evidence is permissible and judgment must be given in accordance with the pleadings alone; and the court will give such judgment as the plaintiffs appear entitled to on the statement of claim. At the same time, the note to rule 7 in *The Supreme Court Practice*

The Weekly Law Reports, May 15, 1981

627

1 W.L.R.   Exxon Corpn. v. Exxon Insurance Ltd. (Ch.D.)   Graham J.

A (*1979*), p. 333 states that, although expressed to be mandatory, the rule is that the judgment on the motion is in fact discretionary, as for example when, instead of giving judgment, the court extends the defendant's time for pleading.

The leading case is *Wallersteiner* v. *Moir* [1974] 1 W.L.R. 991 and there are two passages in that case which I would like to mention. First of all, Lord Denning M.R. said, at p. 1007:

B

"According to R.S.C., Ord. 19, r. 7 (1): 'on the hearing of the application the court shall give such judgment as the plaintiff appears entitled to on his statement of claim.' Likewise with a counterclaim: see R.S.C., Ord. 19, r. 8. Although the word 'shall' is used in that rule, it is clear from the authorities that it is not imperative but directory. The court will not enter a judgment which it would afterwards set aside on proper grounds being shown: see *Graves* v. *Terry* (1882) 9 Q.B.D. 170 and *Gibbings* v. *Strong* (1884) 26 Ch.D. 66. A judge in chambers has a discretion which he will exercise on the same lines as he will set aside a judgment in default. He will require the party to show that he has 'a good defence on the merits'."

C

D The second passage is in the judgment of Scarman L.J. This was an appeal from Geoffrey Lane J. After referring to the cases, Scarman L.J. said, at p. 1029: "In my opinion the judge went too far. R.S.C., Ord. 19 declares the consequences of a default of pleading"; and then he deals with rules 2 to 6; and when he gets to rule 7, he says, at p. 1030:

"Rule 7 makes provision for all other descriptions of claim (of which claims for declaratory relief are one). R.S.C., Ord. 19, r. 7 (1) provides that in all such cases the consequence of a failure to serve a defence within the proper time shall be that the claimant 'may . . . apply to the court for judgment, and . . . the court shall give such judgment as [he] appears entitled to on his statement of claim.' Notwithstanding the word 'shall,' the case law has established that the court retains the right to refuse the claimant judgment even when upon his pleading he appears entitled to it. If the court 'should see any reason to doubt whether injustice may not be done by giving judgment,' it may refuse judgment at this stage":

E

F

and then there is a reference to the judgment of Lord Esher M.R. in *Charles* v. *Shepherd* [1892] 2 Q.B. 622, 624. Then Scarman L.J. continues: "This discretion is a valuable safeguard in the hands of the court." Then he takes the case and explains why in that case Geoffrey Lane J. in the court below had gone too far. *Gibbings* v. *Strong*, 26 Ch.D. 66 and *Graves* v. *Terry*, 9 Q.B.D. 170, referred to by Scarman L.J. were cases where time for pleading was extended.

G

As I read it, *Wallersteiner* v. *Moir* [1974] 1 W.L.R. 991 is deciding that the rule means that the court should prima facie give judgment if justified on the pleadings, but there may be some good reason why it should not do so, such as doubt whether injustice may not be done by doing so, and in such a case there is clear discretion to refuse. Now, in a case where, as here, only the party asking for relief is present, it seems to me that, if the relief claimed is far-reaching in its consequences and may, if granted, affect the public interest adversely in other cases, before giving judgment the court is entitled to be sure that it has heard full and proper argument both for and against the correctness of the law upon which

H

the statement of claim is founded and as to the propositions alleged to   A
establish the relief asked for.

Here, if the plaintiffs' argument is right, all invented words which
might be registrable as trade marks could be argued to be the subject
of copyright whether they were also registered or not. The consequences
would be far-reaching and probably in many cases objectionable, as will
be seen hereafter; and in such circumstances it seemed right to me to   B
ask for the assistance of the Attorney-General so that I could be sure
that I received argument on both sides. I am grateful to the Attorney-
General for nominating Mr. Mummery to represent him here and to
help the court in its task; but I should also make it clear that, as one
would expect, there is no question that Mr. Price, for the plaintiffs, in
the first instance did not deal with the case fully and fairly in the
absence of any opponent.   C

The facts are very simple as disclosed in the statement of claim.
Paragraphs 2 to 7 are not relied upon and need not be referred to, but
I think that I should read some of the following paragraphs, starting
with paragraph 8:

" (8) Further and/or alternatively to the matters set out in paragraphs 2 to 7 above, the plaintiffs allege that until November 1, 1972,   D
the first plaintiff was known as the Standard Oil Co. (New Jersey),
which is directly and/or through its associates or subsidiaries concerned in the business of production, transportation and marketing
of petroleum and petroleum products and other energy resources,
together with all goods and services connected therewith and incidental thereto. Moreover it is concerned as aforesaid in the promotion and sale of a wide variety of goods including electronic   E
equipment, office machines, sporting products and in the manufacture, promotion and sale of numerous chemical products.

" (9) Prior to 1970, the first plaintiff set up a committee to devise
and select a new name and trade mark for itself and which could
also be used by overseas associates and subsidiary companies when
appropriate. The said committee concluded that the said new name   F
must satisfy the following three basic conditions, namely: (a) was
capable of being readily identified with the first plaintiff and its
associates or subsidiary companies, their goods and services, (b) was
invented and was devoid of any meaning in English or in any other
language spoken in any place in which the goods and/or services
of the first plaintiff and/or its associates and/or subsidiary companies
were marketed or likely to be marketed, (c) was short, distinctive   G
and easily memorised.

" (10) Following considerable research and testing the said committee selected the word Exxon, devised by them.

" (11) Accordingly, on November 1, 1972, the first plaintiff
adopted the name Exxon and the name of Standard Oil Co. (New
Jersey) was formally changed to Exxon Corporation. A number of   H
its associate or subsidiary companies similarly adopted Exxon as
their company or trade name.

" (12) The first plaintiff carries on business throughout the United
States of America and has associate or subsidiary companies in
almost 100 countries. All or almost all of the said associates or
subsidiary companies used the word Exxon as a trade mark. In
particular and by way of example, firstly a United Kingdom sub-

The Weekly Law Reports, May 15, 1981

629

1 W.L.R.   Exxon Corpn. v. Exxon Insurance Ltd. (Ch.D.)   Graham J.

A   sidiary of the first plaintiff, namely Esso Chemical Ltd., carries on
the business of manufacturing and marketing in the United Kingdom
and exporting therefrom chemical goods, the majority of which are
sold under the plaintiffs' Esso and Exxon brand names; secondly,
a Bermudan (associate) company of the first plaintiff, namely, Exxon
Insurance Services Ltd., carries on the business of performing
management services, in the field of insurance for associate or
B   affiliated companies of the plaintiffs.

" (13) The second plaintiff is engaged inter alia in the business
of producing, transporting, refining and marketing through inter alia
motor garage outlets, petroleum products in all parts of the United
Kingdom, together with all goods and services connected therewith
and a wide variety of other goods displaying the name Exxon
C   together with the name Esso.

" (14) The first plaintiff is the registered proprietor of the trade
mark Exxon in Part A of the register in the United Kingdom in
respect of goods in every class and in each case the second plaintiff
is the registered user thereof. Further, the first plaintiff is the
registered proprietor of the trade mark Exxon in many other
D   countries throughout the world.

" (15) The third plaintiff was incorporated on February 25, 1969,
to carry on business as set out in the memorandum and articles of
association of the said third plaintiff.

" (16) The fourth plaintiff was incorporated on May 14, 1973, to
carry on business as set out in the memorandum and articles of
association of the said fourth plaintiff.

E   " (17) The plaintiffs have either by themselves or through their
associated or subsidiary companies made extensive and considerable
use of the name Exxon in numerous countries throughout the
world in connection with their business and numerous goods have
been sold and services have been supplied under or by reference to
the name Exxon.

F   " (18) The plaintiffs have either by themselves or through their
subsidiaries and associated companies expended considerable sums
on promoting their diverse business activities, goods and services by
reference to the name Exxon in numerous countries of the world
including the United Kingdom by almost every promotional means.
Moreover the business goods and/or services of the plaintiffs or
their associated companies and subsidiaries have under the name
G   Exxon been the subject of numerous references on radio, television
and in the press in many countries of the world, including the United
Kingdom."

The statement of claim then comes to the question of copyright, and
paragraph 19 reads:

H   " (19) The word Exxon is an original literary work falling within
the provisions of section 2 (1) of the Copyright Act 1956 and the
first plaintiff is the owner of the copyright therein and the second,
third and fourth plaintiffs licensees thereof.

" (20) Further by reason of the matters referred to above the plain-
tiffs have acquired a substantial reputation and goodwill in the name
Exxon inter alia amongst the relevant trade and public in the
United Kingdom so that, when used in relation to any business, goods

or services, the word Exxon means the business goods or services of   A
the plaintiffs and none other. Further and/or alternatively, the name
Exxon when used in connection with any business goods or services
indicates to the relevant trade and public a connection or association
with the plaintiffs' large and substantial multinational business and
related goodwill."

The statement of claim then goes on to deal with the formation of the   B
defendant, and says, in paragraph 22:

" (22) Further the defendant has, without the licence or consent of
the plaintiffs, reproduced and/or authorised the reproduction of the
plaintiffs' copyright work Exxon in the defendant's corporate name,"

that it has adopted the name Exxon, and, by paragraphs 23 and 24:

" (23) By reason of the matters referred to in paragraphs 1 and 8–22   C
the defendant has infringed the plaintiffs' copyright in the word
Exxon, and threatens to continue to do so. (24) Further and/or
alternatively, the defendant has, by reason of matters referred to in
paragraphs 1 and 8 to 22 above, used the word Exxon in connection
with its business so as to be likely to cause confusion and deception
and pass off its business and/or services as and for the business   D
and/or services of the plaintiffs and further or alternatively as
being connected or associated with the business or services of the
plaintiffs."

From the statement of claim, it is seen that the Exxon corporation came
into being as a result of the change of name by the Standard Oil Co. in
the U.S.A. in November 1972. There are no reasons given for this change   E
and it is, I think, anyway irrelevant for present purposes. After the
change of the corporation's name in the U.S.A. and of its adoption by
many subsidiaries throughout the world, Exxon appears to have become
their main trade mark and it is registered for goods in every class of the
classification of goods in the Register.

It seems, however, that the plaintiffs' previous trade mark Esso, which
was also part of their name in many of their companies, is still being   F
used, certainly in this country; and that the word Exxon is really a
substitute for wider use throughout the world in place of the previous
mark Esso. The defendant has no connection with the plaintiffs or any
of them, but none the less it has adopted the plaintiff's name Exxon as
part of its corporate name.

It will be seen from the statement of claim that the plaintiffs make   G
two claims for relief and say that they have two independent rights of
action against the defendant. The first is passing off, and as to this
the statement of claim alleges, inter alia, that the use by the defendant
of Exxon is bound to lead to passing off and in particular to suggest
that the defendant company has some connection with or is a subsidiary
of the plaintiffs and in particular the parent corporation. This I think
must be so; and I have already indicated in argument, and I now confirm,   H
that the plaintiffs are, in my judgment, entitled to an injunction and
ancillary relief to restrain such passing off by continued use by the
defendant of the word Exxon.

In addition, however, the plaintiffs claim to have copyright in the
name Exxon and to be entitled to an injunction to restrain infringement
of such copyright. This, if correct, would give a number of advantages
to the plaintiffs in establishing their rights in their name and mark. The

The Weekly Law Reports, May 15, 1981

631

1 W.L.R.   Exxon Corpn. v. Exxon Insurance Ltd. (Ch.D.)   Graham J.

A argument in support is short and simple. It is said, first, that considerable time and labour was expended in arriving at the name Exxon,
which had to fulfil all the special requirements set out in paragraph 9
of the statement of claim. Though I must accept this for present purposes
I do so with some reservation as to the extent and nature of the literary
or research work involved. Secondly, it is said that the word having
been devised after the expenditure of such effort, qualified therefore as
B an "original literary work" within the meaning of section 2 of the
Copyright Act 1956.

It was argued strongly that it is, and it was said that the size of a
literary work is immaterial; there is logically no reason why one word
which is written should not be a literary work just as much as a work
of greater length; if otherwise qualified because of labour expended on
C it, then it can be a literary work. The definition of "literary" in the
Shorter Oxford English Dictionary, 3rd ed. (1944), is: "Pertaining to the
letters of the alphabet"—that is an earlier meaning—and "Of or pertaining to, or of the nature of, literature . . . or books. . . ."

A number of cases were referred to by Mr. Price. In *University of
London Press Ltd.* v. *University Tutorial Press Ltd.* [1916] 2 Ch. 601
he referred in particular to an important passage in the judgment of
D Peterson J. which comes at the start of the judgment and reads, at p. 608:

"The first question that is raised is, are these examination papers
subject of copyright? Section 1 (1) of the Copyright Act of 1911
provides for copyright in 'every original literary dramatic musical
and artistic work,'"—the relevant words are therefore the same as an
the Act of 1956—"subject to certain conditions which for this purpose
E are immaterial, and the question is, therefore, whether these examination papers are, within the meaning of this Act original literary works.
Although a literary work is not defined in the Act, section 35 states
what the phrase includes; the definition is not a completely comprehensive one, but the section is intended to show what, amongst other
things, is included in the description 'literary work,' and the words are
F '" Literary work " includes maps, charts, plans, tables, and compilations'. It may be difficult to define 'literary work' as used in
this Act, but it seems to be plain that it is not confined to 'literary
work' in the sense in which that phrase is applied, for instance, to
Meredith's novels and the writings of Robert Louis Stevenson. In
speaking of such writings as literary works, one thinks of the quality,
the style, and the literary finish which they exhibit. Under the
G [Copyright Act 1842] which protected 'books,' many things which
had no pretensions to literary style acquired copyright; for example,
a list of registered bills of sale, a list of foxhounds and hunting days,
and trade catalogues; and I see no ground for coming to the conclusion that the present Act was intended to curtail the rights of authors.
In my view the words 'literary work' cover work which is expressed
H in print or writing, irrespective of the question whether the quality
or style is high. The word 'literary' seems to be used in a sense
somewhat similar to the use of the word 'literature' in political or
electioneering literature and refers to written or printed matter.
Papers set by examiners are, in my opinion, 'literary work' within
the meaning of the present Act."

It is clear from that definition that Peterson J., dealing with the matter
in 1916, felt that the words "literary" and "original" must be treated

reasonably broadly; and I think it follows from what he said that, if a   A
word is invented, it must, for practical purposes, be considered as original.

I also, while I have the report before me, should refer to a short
statement on p. 609–610, where he says:

"The objections with which I have dealt do not appear to me to
have any substance, and, after all, there remains the rough practical
test that what is worth copying is prima facie worth protecting."   B

The longer passage in the judgment of Peterson J. which I have just
read was quoted with approval by Lord Pearce in *Ladbroke (Football)
Ltd.* v. *William Hill (Football) Ltd.* [1964] 1 W.L.R. 273 where he says,
at p. 291:

"My lords, the question whether the plaintiffs are entitled to copyright in their coupon "—this was a football coupon case—" depends   C
on whether it is an original literary work. The words ' literary work '
include a compilation. They are used to describe work which is
expressed in print or writing irrespective of whether it has any
excellence of quality or style of writing."

Then he refers to what Peterson J. said in *University of London Press
Ltd.* v. *University Tutorial Press Ltd.* [1916] 2 Ch. 601, 608 and continued: D

"The word ' original ' does not demand original or inventive thought,
but only that the work should not be copied but should originate
from the author. In deciding therefore whether a work in the nature
of a compilation is original, it is wrong to start by considering
individual parts of it apart from the whole, as the appellants in
their argument sought to do. For many compilations have nothing   E
original in their parts, yet the sum total of the compilation may be
original."

Then he refers as an example to *Palgrave's Golden Treasury*, and goes
on:

"In such cases the courts have looked to see whether the compilation of the unoriginal material called for work or skill or expense.   F
If it did, it is entitled to be considered original and to be protected
against those who wish to steal the fruits of the work or skill or
expense by copying it without taking the trouble to compile it themselves. So the protection given by such copyright is in no sense a
monopoly, for it is open to a rival to produce the same result if
he chooses to evolve it by his own labours."   G

Then Lord Reid in the same case, in dealing with the question
of infringement, at p. 279, referred to the "rough practical test" of
Peterson J., which I have already read, with approval.

However, I still have to come back to the basic question whether it is
proper to construe "original literary work" in the Copyright Act 1956,
section 2, as covering a single invented word even if considerable time   H
and work were expended on it and, if so, whether the word "Exxon"
here is such a work. There are, I think, no decided cases which deal
specifically with the precise point that I have to decide. The answer,
therefore, must in the end depend upon the proper construction of the
words in the Act according to general principles and on the facts of the
case.

The history of copyright legislation shows that prior to 1911, when

The Weekly Law Reports, May 15, 1981

633

1 W.L.R.   Exxon Corpn. v. Exxon Insurance Ltd. (Ch.D.)   Graham J.

A the Act of that year was passed and in section 1 first used the words "original literary work," the protection given by copyright before that time was limited to books; and the Act of 1842 did not require originality as a necessary qualification: see *Walter* v. *Lane* [1900] A.C. 539. Cases before 1911 and also *Francis Day and Hunter Ltd.* v. *Twentieth Century Fox Corporation Ltd.* [1940] A.C. 112, a Privy Council appeal from Canada, must be read with these qualifications in mind. In 1911 and

B again in the present Act of 1956, the words used are "original literary work," but there is no definition in the Act of what is meant by this phrase though section 48 does specify that "literary work" includes any written table or compilation.

On general principles of construction, the words must be treated as having their ordinary English meaning as applied to the subject matter

C with which they are dealing. There is, as I see it, no necessity to read the words in any sense which is not their ordinary sense in the English language as so applied, though the definition in section 48 and cases such as *University of London Press Ltd.* v. *University Tutorial Press Ltd.* [1916] 2 Ch. 601 and *Ladbroke (Football) Ltd.* v. *William Hill (Football) Ltd.* [1964] 1 W.L.R. 273 show that the word "literary" is not to be

D read in the Act in a narrow sense so as to be confined, for example, to material having a high intellectual quality or style of writing. The words of Peterson J. in the *University of London* case [1916] 2 Ch. 601 were, as I have shown, approved, and the "rough practical test" is prayed in aid by Mr. Price as a justification for the plaintiffs' contention.

Mr. Price also referred to the so-called "code" cases, of which *D. P. Anderson & Co. Ltd.* v. *Lieber Code Co.* [1917] 2 K.B. 469 is perhaps

E the best example as showing that meaningless words can be the subject of copyright. In these cases, however, it is of course the whole compilation of many thousands of such words designed for use in coded messages which is the subject of copyright and the question whether a particular meaningless word infringed the copyright is a different question, which was not considered. It is fair to say that Mr. Price did not put

F the case forward as establishing that a single word qualified as a "literary work."

He did emphasise, of course, that in the *Francis Day and Hunter* case [1940] A.C. 112, it was the title of the song, "The man who broke the bank at Monte Carlo," for which copyright was claimed, and that Lord Hodson in the *Ladbroke* case [1964] 1 W.L.R. 273, 286 had made it clear that the appellants' submission in the case before him, that "titles

G could not be protected" was based on *Dicks* v. *Yates* (1881) 18 Ch.D. 76 and the *Francis Day* case [1940] A.C. 112, neither of which supported the proposition as a matter of law. The primary reason was no doubt because the question in those cases was not whether a title was a "literary work," but whether it came within the definition of "book" within the Act of 1842.

H Mr. Mummery's argument, as amicus curiae, was similarly short and to the point. He contended that a single word such as Exxon here could not fairly and properly be considered to be a "literary work" within section 2 of the Copyright Act 1956. Even if such a word were invented so as to qualify for originality, it could not in any normal English sense be considered as "a literary work." It was, of course, capable of being written and in that sense is literary, as being something identified by letters and the subject of writing. This meaning, incidentally, corresponds

with the early meaning of " literary " in the *Shorter Oxford English* **A**
Dictionary already mentioned. It was not, however, a work which was
literary in the normal sense of constituting or concerned with literature
or books.

He also pointed out, and I agree that there is force in the contention,
that, if the plaintiffs are right, it would have extremely inconvenient
consequences as far as the public are concerned, in that no one could **B**
refer to any of the plaintiff companies or to any of their goods bearing
the name Exxon without having the plaintiffs' licence expressly or
impliedly to do so. There is nothing in section 6, which deals with
general exceptions from protection, which would exclude the necessity
for such a licence, since the exceptions relate only to literary, reporting
and similar more specialised activities. One may well ask also whether
the Bishop of Exeter can continue to use the word " Exon " as part **C**
of his name, albeit when spelt with one " x."

Mr. Mummery also contended that, on a fair reading of the Act,
it cannot really have been intended to give further rights of property in
words or names which would naturally and properly qualify for excellent
protection as registered trade marks or as the subject of passing-off
actions. There was no need to give any further protection, which, though **D**
it might assist a plaintiff in proving his case against a user of his name
or mark, would be limited to the period of copyright—a thing quite
inappropriate to a trade mark or name, whether registered or a common
law mark, neither of which are so limited. Such protection as such is
inappropriate to a single word or name such as Exxon, having no meaning in itself.

The counter-argument is thus equally short and simple, and neither **E**
of them admits of much elaboration.

As I have already stated, the question that I have to decide is,
shortly stated, whether Exxon is an " original literary work " within
section 2? I do not think it is. What is it then?, one may ask. It is
a word which, though invented and therefore original, has no meaning
and suggests nothing in itself. To give it substance and meaning, it must **F**
be accompanied by other words or used in a particular context or juxtaposition. When used as part of any of the plaintiffs' corporate names,
it clearly has a denominative characteristic as denoting the company in
question. When used, as I assume it is, with the plaintiffs' goods, it
would clearly have the effect of denoting origin or quality. It is in
fact an invented word with no meaning, which is a typical subject for
trade mark registration, and which no doubt, with adequate user, is **G**
capable also of becoming, if it has not already become, distinctive of
the plaintiffs and their goods at common law. It is not in itself a title
or distinguishing name and, as I have said, only takes on meaning or
significance when actually used with other words, for example indicating
that it is the name of a company, or in a particular juxtaposition as, for
example, upon goods. **H**

Nothing I have said above is intended to suggest that I consider that
a word which is used as a title can, as a matter of law, never in any
circumstances be the subject of copyright, and I would disagree with
dicta in previous cases to the contrary effect. Such a word would, however, I think, have to have qualities or characteristics in itself, if such a
thing is possible, which would justify its recognition as an original literary
work rather than merely as an invented word. It may well turn out not

The Weekly Law Reports, May 15, 1981

635

1 W.L.R.   Exxon Corpn. v. Exxon Insurance Ltd. (Ch.D.)   Graham J.

A to be possible in practice, but, as at present advised, I consider that the mere fact that a single word is invented and that research or labour was involved in its invention does not in itself, in my judgment, necessarily enable it to qualify as an original literary work within section 2 of the Act.

By analogy nobody really would suggest that there would be an infringement of Edward Lear's copyright—ignoring the fact that the author of

B "Nonsense Songs" died in 1888 and copyright no longer subsists—in calling one's home " Chankly Bore " or in selling new toy products called " Jumblies," even if the latter had green heads and blue hands.

The point is a narrow one, and it may well be thought difficult to decide between the two arguments, but my view is clear. At the risk of losing my way in the " tulgey wood " and becoming bogged in the " slithy toves," my view can perhaps best be illustrated by consideration

C of Lewis Carroll's fantasy " Jabberwocky." The whole poem was, during the appropriate period, undoubtedly properly part of Lewis Carroll's copyright in the book *Through the Looking-Glass.* As such, the poem itself, if copied, would certainly be regarded as an infringement of the copyright in the book. The poem, it will be remembered, " seemed very pretty " to Alice, but was " rather hard to understand." The subject,

D as illustrated so vividly in John Tenniel's drawings, was the awesome Jabberwock, an invented monster with an invented name. The title of the poem, " Jabberwocky " with a " y " at the end, seems to be used by the author adjectivally to mean a story about a Jabberwock. Undoubtedly the whole composition of the poem and the suggestive and invented words which form its essence and make it so memorable is, just as in the " code " cases, worthy of copyright, and that copyright could properly

E be held to be infringed by the copying to a greater or lesser extent, as the case might be, of its invented words.

Assuming the poem had been recently written and was the subject of the Act of 1911 or 1956, it is I suppose just conceivable that the use in some literary context of either of the single words " Jabberwock " or " Jabberwocky " alone might also be held to be an infringement as being

F a substantial part of the whole poem. But could Lewis Carroll, if he had merely invented the word " Jabberwock " and had never written the poem of which it is a part, have successfully contended that he had copyright in the word alone? In the absence of its registration as a trade mark, could he, by virtue of copyright, prevent a commercial company adopting it as part of such company's corporate name? I think not, the legal reason being that the word alone and by itself cannot properly be con-

G sidered as a " literary *work*," the subject of copyright under the Act. It becomes part of a " literary work " within the Act when it is embodied in the poem, but it is the poem as a composition which is a work within the Act and not the word itself. The American case, *Life Music Inc.* v. *Wonderland Music Co.* (1965) 241 Fed.Supp. 653, was referred to by Mr. Mummery. Copyright was claimed in the word " Supercalafajalistick-

H espeealadojus," infringement being alleged by the defendants' use of the word " Supercalifragilisticexpialidocious " but the case does not really carry the matter any further. The refusal there of an interlocutory injunction turned on the failure of the plaintiff to make out a prima facie case of infringement and, although it could be said that the possibility of copyright in the word was assumed, there was no real argument on the copyright aspect of the matter and the case has really no persuasive authority on this point.

I therefore conclude that the plaintiffs cannot, for the reasons given A above, succeed on the ground of copyright in their word Exxon.

[Argument was then addressed to the court on the question whether the defendants could be directed to change their corporate name on the Register of Companies.]

GRAHAM J. As a result of the judgment which I gave this morning B the plaintiffs ask me inter alia to grant an injunction in the form for which they ask in their statement of claim, which reads: " (4) An order that the defendant be directed to change its corporate name and omit the word Exxon therefrom."

Having listened to the arguments on both sides and having been referred to *Anciens Etablissements Panhard et Levassor S.A.* v. *Panhard Levassor Motor Co. Ltd.* [1901] 2 Ch. 513 and to *Suhner & Co. A.G.* v. C *Suhner Ltd.* [1967] F.S.R. 319, where Plowman J., who had also been referred to the previous *Panhard et Levassor* case [1901] 2 Ch. 513, decided that the injunction should be in the form of that granted by Farwell J. in the *Panhard et Levassor* case, I agree that, in the circumstances, that is the right injunction to make, namely, an injunction to restrain the company from allowing its name to remain on the register in D its present form, using the word Exxon.

This case is slightly different from the two previous cases, because there is no defendant here except the company itself. Under section 18 (1) of the Companies Act 1948, a company is empowered to change its name by special resolution, employing the mechanism that is there set out; and therefore it does seem to me that there is nothing wrong in preventing it continuing to have its name on the register if the conclu- E sion is that the company is doing something which is unlawful by so doing. If it continues to do it, the act of so doing, if not fraudulent, is at least more unlawful and is clearly damaging to the plaintiffs. If that is the situation, I think that a court would be shutting its eyes to realities unless it did the best that it can to prevent any such thing happening in the future.

For my own part, I am prepared therefore to grant an injunction F against the company itself in the terms of the *Panhard et Levassor* case, as near as may be.

> *Injunction to restrain passing off.*
> *Obliteration on oath of any infringing matter in respect thereof.*
> *Inquiry as to damages and payment* G *of any sum found due.*
> *Costs on issue of passing off but not on issue of copyright.*
> *Injunction to restrain defendant from allowing any name incorporating word Exxon in its corporate name* H *remaining on Register of Companies.*

Solicitors: *Needham & Grant; Treasury Solicitor.*

T. C. C. B.

A

[CHANCERY DIVISION]

* INLAND REVENUE COMMISSIONERS v. METROLANDS
(PROPERTY FINANCE) LTD.

B
1980 Nov. 25, 26;
      Dec. 11

Nourse J.

Revenue—Development land tax—Compulsory acquisition—
Purchase notice for sale of land served and accepted by local
authority—Introduction of tax—Subsequent agreement as
to compensation—Date of " disposal and acquisition " of land
—Whether deemed compulsory purchase—Whether trans-
C   action chargeable to tax—Town and Country Planning Act
1971 (c. 78), s. 181 (2)—Development Land Tax Act 1976
(c. 24), s. 45 (1) (2) (4)

In May 1974 the taxpayer company was refused planning
permission for houses to be built on 4·31 acres of land it owned
near Bolton. The reason for the refusal was that the local
council required the land for use for educational purposes.
D   Accordingly in October 1974 the taxpayer company served a
purchase notice on the council under the provisions of section
180 of the Town and Country Planning Act 1971. The notice
stated that the land had become incapable of reasonably
beneficial use and required the council to purchase it from the
taxpayer company. In December 1974 the terms of the notice
were accepted by the council but it was not until August 11,
1976, that the amount of compensation to be paid for the land
E   was finally agreed at £64,650. The taxpayer company was
assessed to development land tax in the sum of £29,085 in
respect of the disposal. It appealed against the assessment on
the ground that by virtue of the provisions of section 45 (2)
of the Development Land Tax Act 1976 [1] the land had been
disposed of when the council accepted the terms of the purchase notice in December 1974, and that was before the Act
came into force. The special commissioners allowed the appeal,
F   rejecting the Crown's case that because of the deeming provision in section 181 (2) of the Town and Country Planning Act
1971 [2] the disposal had, in accordance with the provisions of
section 45 (4) of the Act of 1976, to be determined as having
taken place on the date when the compensation was finally
agreed, that being 11 days after the Act took effect to impose
the charge.
    On appeal by the Crown: —
G   Held, allowing the appeal, that the provisions of section
181 (2) of the Town and Country Planning Act 1971 were to
be applied to all cases of compulsory acquisition so that it
was to be deemed that the relevant authority had been
authorised to acquire the owner's interest in land by compulsory purchase and had served a notice to treat; that, since the
application of those provisions to section 45 of the Development Land Tax Act 1976 would not lead to unjust, anomalous
H   or absurd results, there had been a deemed compulsory purchase of the land for the purposes of the section and, accordingly, the land was disposed of under the provisions of section
45 (4), when the purchase price was agreed, on August 11,
1976, with the result that the taxpayer company had been
properly assessed to tax (post, pp. 647B–D, H—648B, 649H—
650B).

[1] Development Land Tax Act 1976, s. 45: see post, p. 642A–C.
[2] Town and Country Planning Act 1971, s. 181 (2): see post, p. 640F–G.

638

I.R.C. v. Metrolands Ltd. (Ch.D.) [1981]

Ex parte Walton (1881) 17 Ch.D. 746, C.A.; *East End* A
Dwellings Co. Ltd. v. *Finsbury Borough Council* [1952] A.C.
109, H.L.(E.) and *Murphy* v. *Ingram* [1974] Ch. 363, C.A.
considered.

The following cases are referred to in the judgment:

Capital Investments Ltd. v. *Wednesfield Urban District Council* [1965]
Ch. 774; [1964] 2 W.L.R. 932; [1964] 1 All E.R. 655.   B
East End Dwellings Co. Ltd. v. *Finsbury Borough Council* [1952] A.C.
109; [1951] 2 All E.R. 587, H.L.(E.).
Harding v. *Metropolitan Railway Co.* (1872) L.R. 7 Ch.App. 154.
Haynes v. *Haynes* (1861) 1 Dr. & Sm. 426.
Hill v. *East and West India Dock Co.* (1884) 9 App.Cas. 448, H.L.(E.).
Leitch v. *Emmott* [1929] 2 K.B. 236; 14 T.C. 633, C.A.
Murphy v. *Ingram* [1974] Ch. 363; [1974] 2 W.L.R. 782; [1974] 2 All   C
E.R. 187; 49 T.C. 410, C.A.
W. & S. (Long Eaton) Ltd. v. *Derbyshire County Council* (1975) 29
P. & C.R. 522; (1976) 31 P. & C.R. 99, C.A.
Walton, Ex parte (1881), 17 Ch.D. 746, C.A.
West Midland Baptist (Trust) Association (Inc.) v. *Birmingham Corpora-
tion* [1970] A.C. 874; [1969] 3 W.L.R. 389; [1969] 3 All E.R. 172,
H.L.(E.).   D

The following additional cases were cited in argument:

Grice v. *Dudley Corporation* [1958] Ch. 329; [1957] 3 W.L.R. 314;
[1957] 2 All E.R. 673.
Munton v. *Greater London Council* [1976] 1 W.L.R. 649; [1976] 2 All
E.R. 815, C.A.

E

CASE STATED by the Commissioners for the Special Purposes of the
Income Tax Acts.

On October 9, 1974, the taxpayer company, Metrolands (Property
Finance) Ltd., served a purchase notice on the Bolton Metropolitan
Borough Council requiring it to purchase 4·31 acres of land at Westhoughton, in respect of which planning permission had been refused. On F
December 11, 1974, the council accepted the purchase notice. On August
11, 1976, it was finally agreed that compensation of £64,650 would be paid
by the council to the taxpayer company. The taxpayer company appealed
against an assessment to development land tax in the sum of £29,085 made
on it in respect of the disposal of the land. The commissioners allowed the
appeal and discharged the assessment on the ground that the disposal took
place before August 1, 1976, the date on which the tax first became   G
chargeable.

The Crown appealed.

The facts are set out in the judgment.

Robert Carnwath for the Crown.
D. C. Potter Q.C. and *R. M. K. Gray* for the taxpayer company. H

Cur. adv. vult.

December 11. NOURSE J. read the following judgment. This is the first
case in which the court has been asked to decide a question on the development land tax which was introduced in 1976 by the Act of that name. The
expressed intention of the Act was to impose a new tax on the realisation

A of the development value of land. That was the fifth occasion on which Parliament had sought to impose such a tax during the present century. Dealing only with more recent times, there was the betterment levy which was introduced by the Land Commission Act 1967. That was abolished in 1971. But in December 1973 the then Conservative administration made proposals, having immediate effect, for the introduction of a tax on development gains. Those proposals had not been published in the form of a bill before the change of government in March 1974, but a tax which became known as development gains tax was brought into being by the Finance Act 1974 and it remained in effect until replaced by the Development Land Tax Act 1976. Apart from a reduction in rates, there has been no significant change since that date.

The new tax first became chargeable on August 1, 1976. It is not
C chargeable on disposals made before that date. In the present case the disposal was made under what can broadly be described as the compulsory purchase legislation. But it was not the normal case where the acquiring authority takes the land against the will of the owner. It was a species of what are sometimes known as reverse compulsory purchases. The owner, having been refused planning permission for the development of the land,
D required the authority to purchase it pursuant to the provisions contained in Part IX of the Town and Country Planning Act 1971. The question which I have to decide is whether in the light of those provisions and those of the Act of 1976 the disposal took place before or after August 1, 1976. If it took place before, no tax will be chargeable; if after, the tax will be £29,085. This then, is a case of a transitional nature. But it is likely to result in a determination of the more general question what is the time
E at which a disposal is made in this type of reverse compulsory acquisition.

The question comes to the court as an appeal by way of case stated from a decision of the special commissioners dated August 22, 1979. The land in question is 4·31 acres at Westhoughton, near Bolton, and the owner is the taxpayer company, Metrolands (Property Finance) Ltd. The acquiring authority was the Bolton Metropolitan Borough Council. The
F commissioners held that the disposal took place on December 20, 1974, before the tax became chargeable. They accordingly discharged an assessment which had been made on the taxpayer company. But the Crown contend that the disposal and acquisition took place on August 11, 1976, 10 days too late from the taxpayer company's point of view, and that is the basis of its appeal to this court.

The facts are fully and carefully set out in the case stated. This was in
G part made necessary so that the commissioners might resolve a dispute of fact which is no longer in issue. The facts which are still material can be stated with comparative brevity. On May 9, 1974, the local council refused the taxpayer company planning permission for houses to be built on the land. That was because they themselves required it for educational purposes. Accordingly, on October 9, 1974, the taxpayer company served on
H the local council a purchase notice under section 180 of the Town and Country Planning Act 1971 claiming that the land had become incapable of reasonably beneficial use in its existing state and that it could not be rendered capable of such use by the carrying out of any other permissible development, and requiring the council to purchase it accordingly. On December 20, 1974, the council wrote to the taxpayer company's solicitors for the purpose of informing them that the council had determined to accept the taxpayer company's purchase notice. It is clear that that was a

statement that the council were willing to comply with the purchase notice A
within section 181 (1) (a) of the Act of 1971. The letter enclosed a form
of claim "for completion and return to me on behalf of your clients so
that negotiations as to purchase price can begin." As I have already
indicated, the taxpayer company contend and the special commissioners
held that the council's statement that they were willing to comply with the
purchase notice effected a disposal of the taxpayer company's interest in
the land for the purposes of the Development Land Tax Act 1976 on that B
day. Negotiations as to the purchase price did indeed take place subsequently, but they took a long time to come to fruition. It was not until
August 11, 1976, the date for which the Crown contends, that a figure
of £64,650 was finally approved by the council. It is now agreed that it
was not until that approval was given that the purchase price or, more
accurately, the compensation, was fixed. The Development Land Tax Act C
1976 had reached the statute book on July 22, and August 1 had been
prescribed as the appointed day for the purposes of the Act. If, contrary
to the view of the commissioners, the taxpayer company is liable for the
tax, then it may be said that it is very hard luck that the compensation was
not fixed a fortnight or so earlier. But that is something which cannot
enter into a decision of this case.

I must now refer in greater detail to the material provisions of Part IX D
of the Town and Country Planning Act 1971, to certain principles of the
law of compulsory acquisition and to the material provisions of the Act
of 1976, and in particular to section 45. As to the Act of 1971, I have
already sufficiently referred to section 180. Section 181 (1), in addition to
enabling the council to state that they are willing to comply with the
purchase notice, gives them two other courses of action. First, they can E
serve a notice stating that another local authority or statutory undertakers
have agreed to comply with the purchase notice in their place. Secondly,
they can serve a notice stating that, for reasons which must be specified
in the notice, they are not willing to comply with the purchase notice, have
not found anyone else who will agree to comply with it in their place, and
have transmitted a copy of it to the Secretary of State. I will return to
him later, but I must now read section 181 (2), which is of great importance F
to the present case, in full. It says:

"Where the council on whom a purchase notice is served by an owner
have served on him a notice in accordance with subsection (1) (a) or
(b) of this section, the council, or the other local authority or statutory
undertakers specified in the notice, as the case may be, shall be deemed
to be authorised to acquire the interest of the owner compulsorily in G
accordance with the relevant provisions, and to have served a notice
to treat in respect thereof on the date of service of the notice under
that subsection."

That, then, is a deeming provision, the effect of which has been much
debated in argument before me.

Section 182 sets out the procedure on transmission of a purchase notice H
to the Secretary of State. Shortly stated, the position is that the Secretary
of State can either confirm the purchase notice or take certain other action
of a kind which is specified in section 183. For example, he can grant
planning permission for the relevant development for which permission has
been refused by the council. The next section I should refer to is section
186, which deals with cases where the Secretary of State either (1) confirms
the purchase notice or (2) neither confirms it nor takes any other action

A on it. In either of those events there are deeming provisions similar to that contained in section 181 (2). The only other section of the Act of 1971 to which I need refer at this stage is section 208, which provides:

". . . the power conferred by section 31 of the Land Compensation Act 1961 to withdraw a notice to treat shall not be exercisable in the case of a notice to treat which is deemed to have been served by B virtue of any of the provisions of this Part of this Act."

I refer next to the principles of the law of compulsory acquisition relating to the effect of a notice to treat. These are conveniently summarised in *Halsbury's Laws of England,* 4th ed., vol. 8 (1974), para. 136. I will read that paragraph so far as material to the present case. The paragraph heading is, " Relation of parties as vendor and purchaser after C notice to treat." It reads:

"The effect of serving a notice to treat is to establish a relation analogous in some respects to that of vendor and purchaser, a relation which binds the owner of the land to give up the land subject to his being paid compensation, and which binds the undertakers or acquiring authority to take the land, but there is no contract of sale until the D price is ascertained and the land remains the property of the landowner. Both parties have the right to have the price ascertained and the purchase completed in manner provided by the Lands Clauses Acts or the Compulsory Purchase Act 1965 or any Acts modifying those Acts. . . . When the price has been ascertained the relationship of vendor and purchaser exists between the parties as if there had been an ordinary agreement for sale, and . . . the parties' rights and duties E are the same as those arising out of an ordinary contract for the sale of land including the right to have the contract enforced by specific performance, and the owner's interest then, but not before, becomes an interest in personalty."

It is also material to note that where the landowner has notified the F acquiring authority of the amount he claims by way of compensation the authority has six weeks to withdraw the notice to treat, if it wishes to do so. That power is given by section 31 of the Land Compensation Act 1961, to which reference has already been made. I should also mention that the authority may normally enter on the land after service of a notice to treat on not less than 14 days' notice. It is not necessary for the compensation to have been agreed or assessed before entry is made.

G I now come to the Development Land Tax Act itself. Section 1 (1) provides that the tax shall be charged in accordance with the provisions of the Act in respect of the realisation of the development value of land in the United Kingdom. Subsection (2) provides that, subject to the provisions of the Act, a person shall be chargeable to the tax on " the realised development value," determined in accordance with the Act, which accrues H to him on the disposal by him on or after the appointed day of an interest in land in the United Kingdom. Subsection (3) provided that, subject to section 13, the rate of the tax should be 80 per cent. Section 13 provided for a reduced rate of 66⅔ per cent. up to a certain limit, and that is the rate which would be applicable in the present case. I can ignore sections 2 and 3. Sections 4 and 5 tell you how to get at the realised development value; and then I can go straight to section 45. I will read subsections (1), (2) and (4) in full, subsection (3) being immaterial to the present case:

" (1) The provisions of this section shall have effect for determining the A
time at which, for the purposes of liability to development land tax,
an interest in land is to be taken to be disposed of or acquired.
(2) Subject to subsections (2) and (3) of section 3 above and the following provisions of this section, where under a contract an interest in
land is disposed of and that interest or, in the case of a part disposal,
the granted interest is acquired, then, (a) if the contract is conditional
(and, in particular, if it is conditional on the exercise of an option) the B
time at which the disposal and acquisition is made is the time when
the condition is satisfied; and (b) in any other case, the time at which
the disposal and acquisition is made is the time the contract is made
and not, if it is different, the time at which the interest is conveyed or
transferred. . . . (4) Subject to subsections (5) and (8) below, where
an interest in land is acquired compulsorily by an authority possessing C
compulsory powers, the time at which the disposal and acquisition is
made is the time at which the compensation for the acquisition is
agreed or otherwise determined (variations on appeal being disregarded
for this purpose), or, if earlier, the time when the authority enter on
the land in pursuance of their powers."

I must also read subsection (8), which is in these terms: D

" Subject to subsection (9) below, where an interest in land is disposed
of on or after the appointed day to an authority possessing compulsory
powers then, if notice to treat in respect of that interest was (or is by
virtue of any enactment deemed to have been) served before September
13, 1974 on the person making the disposal, the disposal shall be
treated for the purposes of this Act as having been made before the E
appointed day."

Shortly stated, the decision of the special commissioners was to the
following effect. First, they rejected the Crown's contention that the
disposal and acquisition fell within section 45 (4). Secondly, they accepted
the taxpayer company's contention that the disposal and acquisition fell
within section 45 (2) (b). The meat of their decision on these points was F
expressed in these terms:

" There was in this case no compulsory acquisition at all. By serving
the purchase notice the company indicated its willingness to sell and
by accepting that notice the council indicated its willingness to buy.
It is common ground that neither party was able to withdraw from
that situation and that the only thing that remained to be done was G
the fixing of the amount of compensation. It is also common ground
between the parties that there was no uncertainty as to this amount
because it would be fixed either by agreement or failing agreement by
reference to the Lands Tribunal. We, therefore, accept Mr. Gray's
submission, on behalf of the company, that there was a contract
between the parties as from December 20, 1974, and that their
relationship under that contract was that of vendor and purchaser." H

The commissioners then went on more particularly to reject the Crown's
argument that the deeming provision in section 181 (2) of the Act of 1971
required an assumption that the only thing that had happened was the
service of a notice to treat following a compulsory purchase order. As
to this, they expressed the view that there was no justification for the
contention that they must ignore the purchase notice and its acceptance

A and regard the transaction in question as one of compulsory purchase pure and simple. They discharged the assessment accordingly. They then added that they had been helped in reaching their decision by the fact that section 45 (8) expressly referred to a deemed service of a notice to treat. In this connection they observed that if Parliament had intended section 45 (4) to apply to a deemed compulsory acquisition they would have expected to find a similar express reference in that subsection. Finally, they held,
B in case their decision should be wrong and the true view was that the transaction fell within section 45 (4), that the disposal and acquisition did not take place until August 11, 1976, when the amount of the compensation received the approval of the council. That finding of fact is the one from which there has been no appeal to this court.

Whatever else may be said about this case, it seems to me that once
C you have studied the material legislation and the relevant principles of the law of compulsory acquisition there is no obvious answer to the question what is the time at which, for the purposes of liability to development land tax, an interest in land is to be taken to be disposed of and acquired in the case of a purchase notice with which a council have stated that they are willing to comply pursuant to section 181 (1) (a) of the Act
D of 1971. On the arguments which I have heard, three possibilities have been suggested. First, that the transaction falls within section 45 (4). That was the contention of Mr. Carnwath on behalf of the Crown. Secondly, that it falls within section 45 (2). That was the contention of Mr. Potter on behalf of the taxpayer company. Thirdly, that it does not fall within section 45 at all. That was an alternative contention advanced by Mr. Carnwath, and it is, I think, accepted that it would result in the question
E falling to be determined by reference to the date of the " disposal " for the purposes of section 1 (2) of the Act.

Mr. Carnwath, in arguing for subsection (4), said, first, that the transaction cannot fall within subsection (2) because it is not a " contract." He said that where a party, in this case the council, accepts the undertaking of a statutory obligation, that does not amount to a contract; and he said
F that the council's letter of December 20, 1974, was nothing more than an acceptance of that nature. He then referred to section 181 (2) of the Act of 1971 and pointed out that a council which has accepted a purchase notice is deemed to have served a notice to treat. He said that the mere service of a notice to treat does not in itself create a contract, because at that stage the compensation has not been fixed. For that well established proposition he referred amongst other cases to Capital Investments Ltd. v.
G Wednesfield Urban District Council [1965] Ch. 774, 794, per Wilberforce J. He then said that, even if the transaction did amount to a " contract " within section 45 (2), it did not become such until, in accordance with the rule which was settled in cases of true compulsory purchase by the House of Lords in West Midland Baptist (Trust) Association (Inc.) v. Birmingham Corporation [1970] A.C. 874, the amount of the compensation was fixed
H on August 11, 1976. And he pointed to the fact that the same rule has now been applied to transactions of this nature by the Court of Appeal in a case to which I will refer.

Turning to subsection (4), Mr. Carnwath accepted that the sole question is whether the transaction was one by which it can be said that the land was acquired compulsorily. He accepted that it was not in reality so acquired. He relied entirely on the deeming provision in section 181 (2) of the Act of 1971. He said that the effect of that provision is to transmute

the transaction into one where the land is acquired compulsorily, not   A
perhaps necessarily for all purposes, but at least for the purposes of subsection (4). He also said that if I were to hold that the transaction in the
present case does not fall within subsection (4) it would follow that a
significant class of other reverse compulsory purchases under enactments
containing similar deeming provisions would not fall within subsection (4)
either, and that at least one of them would by its nature be incapable of
falling within subsection (2). He therefore said that Parliament must have   B
intended that subsection (4) should apply to all cases of compulsory
acquisition, both true and reverse. Finally, he said that it would be very
dangerous to attach, as the special commissioners did, too much weight to
section 45 (8).

    Mr. Potter, in arguing for subsection (2), said, first, that the events
which culminated in the council's letter of December 20, 1974, constituted   C
a " contract " within the subsection. He said that many arrangements are
entered into by statutory or other bodies or individuals who owe duties to
others, but that does not mean that those arrangements do not have the
consensual element necessary to constitute a contract. He relied on *Haynes*
v. *Haynes* (1861) 1 Dr. & Sm. 426 and on *Harding* v. *Metropolitan Railway
Co.* (1872) L.R. 7 Ch.App. 154. In the latter case, Lord Hatherley L.C.,   D
sitting as the Court of Appeal in Chancery, said, in reference to a true
compulsory purchase, at p. 158:

    " But the case is different when the price is ascrtained, for you have
    then all the elements of a complete agreement, and, in truth, it
    becomes a bargain made under legislative enactment between the
    railway company and those over whom they were authorised to
    exercise their power."   E

Mr. Potter accepted that if the council had been bound to accept the
purchase notice the consensual element would have been lacking and there
would have been no contract. But he pointed to the various courses of
action available to the council under section 181 (1) and said that their
decision to comply with the purchase notice was an act of will which did   F
give the transaction the necessary consensual element. He said that the case
is different from that where a notice to treat is served. He accepted that
the notice itself creates no consensus. If it is followed by an agreement
as to compensation then at that stage, but not before, there is a consensus.
If, on the other hand, there is no such agreement there is never a consensus
at all. Although both parties are bound to proceed to an assessment by the
Lands Tribunal and to carry out the other steps in the compulsory purchase   G
procedure, those are obligations originating not in a consensus but in
statute.

    Turning to section 45 (4), Mr. Potter first examined the deeming
provision in section 181 (2) of the Act of 1971. He said that the Crown's
argument necessarily involves the proposition that the provision undoes
the whole effect of the previous service and acceptance of the purchase   H
notice. Mr. Potter said that that goes too far and that the provision is
necessary only for the purpose of supplying the element which is still
lacking, namely, the ascertainment of the compensation. Mr. Gray, in
following Mr. Potter, said that there was another reason for the deeming
provision, and that was to make it clear that in a case, like the present,
where planning permission had been refused because the council wanted
the land for educational purposes, the acquisition could and should be

A made under the compulsory purchase legislation and not under any other
powers. Mr. Potter then went on to submit, both as a matter of common
sense and on authority, that deeming provisions must be construed to have
effect only for the purposes for which they were enacted. Those purposes
were the two that he and Mr. Gray had mentioned. He said that it would
be absurd to think that Parliament intended to give to this transaction a
character which it would not otherwise own for the purposes of a taxing
B statute unheard of in 1971. He also relied on section 45 (8) and on the
point which appealed to the commissioners. He said that the express
reference in subsection (8) to a deemed service of a notice to treat suggested
that the exclusion of such a reference from subsection (4) was deliberate.

I have found this a difficult case, and my mind fluctuated from one side
to the other during the course of the arguments. Had it not been for their
C clarity and economy I would have had greater difficulty still in arriving
at the clear conclusion to which I have now come. I will start with
section 45 (4). Mr. Potter's general submission that deeming provisions
must be construed to have effect only for the purposes for which they were
enacted is based on the judgment of the Court of Appeal in *Murphy* v.
Ingram [1974] Ch. 363. In that case, Russell L.J., in delivering the judg-
D ment of the court, said at p. 370 that it had been remarked upon high
authority that in considering " deeming " provisions in statutes it was
important to have in mind what appeared to be the purpose of their enactment. For that the court referred to some earlier authorities to which I shall
come in a moment. But it must first be noted that at p. 371 the Court of
Appeal expressed themselves to be of the view that not only anomalies but
also absurdities would follow if the deeming provisions which were there
E under review were extended to the point for which the taxpayer had successfully argued before Megarry J. The Court of Appeal declined to go that far.

The earlier authorities on deeming provisions started with *Ex parte
Walton* (1881) 17 Ch.D. 746. That was a case on section 23 of the Bankruptcy Act 1869 (the predecessor of section 54 of the Act of 1914), which
enabled a trustee in bankruptcy to disclaim, amongst other things, a lease
F belonging to the bankrupt, whereupon it was deemed to have been
surrendered on that date. It was held by the Court of Appeal that such
a disclaimer operated as a surrender only so far as was necessary to relieve
the bankrupt and his estate and the trustee from liability, and did not
otherwise affect the rights or liabilities of third parties in relation to the
property disclaimed. At the end of the judgment of James L.J. there
appears this passage, at pp. 756–757:

G   " When a statute enacts that something shall be deemed to have been
        done, which in fact and truth was not done, the court is entitled and
        bound to ascertain for what purposes and between what persons the
        statutory fiction is to be resorted to. Now, the bankruptcy law is a special
        law, having for its object the distribution of an insolvent's assets equit-
        ably amongst his creditors and persons to whom he is under liability,
H   and, upon this cessio bonorum, to release him under certain conditions
        from future liability in respect of his debts and obligations. That
        being the sole object of the statute, it appears to me to be legitimate
        to say, that, when the statute says that a lease, which was never
        surrendered in fact (a true surrender requiring the consent of both
        parties, the one giving up and the other taking), is to be deemed to
        have been surrendered, it must be understood as saying so with the
        following qualification, which is absolutely necessary to prevent the

most grievous injustice, and the most revolting absurdity, ' shall, as   A
between the lessor on the one hand, and the bankrupt, his trustee and
estate, on the other hand, be deemed to have been surrendered.' "

That passage was approved by all the members of the House of Lords in
Hill v. *East and West India Dock Co.* (1884) 9 App.Cas. 448, which was
another case on the same section. The first part of it was also relied on
by Sankey L.J. in *Leitch* v. *Emmott* [1929] 2 K.B. 236, 248. That was   B
another case where the Court of Appeal did not allow a deeming provision
the extended effect contended for. But it is not of much assistance in the
present case. The deeming provision took the form of a proviso to a
substantive provision. The decision turned not on any injustice, anomaly
or absurdity which would have flowed from the contrary view, but on a
construction of the enactment as a whole.
                                                                           C
On the other side I was referred to *East End Dwellings Co. Ltd.* v.
Finsbury Borough Council [1952] A.C. 109, where the relevant enactment
provided that, in ascertaining the appropriate payment under the War
Damage Act 1943, the value of the interest in question for the purposes
of a compulsory purchase should " be taken to be " the value which it would
have had if the whole of the damage had been made good before the date
of the notice to treat. In 1944 a block of dwellings let on rent-controlled   D
tenancies was demolished by enemy action. In 1948, no rebuilding having
been done, a notice to treat was served. The House of Lords held that,
the original building having been totally destroyed, if the whole of the
damage had been made good before the date of the notice to treat the new
building would have had a different identity and would not have been
subject to the Rent Acts; and that accordingly the value of the interest   E
must be arrived at on that basis. None of the earlier cases to which I have
been referred appears to have been cited to their Lordships, but nothing
turns on that. Mr. Carnwath relied in particular on the following passage
in the speech of Lord Asquith, at pp. 132-133 :

> " If you are bidden to treat an imaginary state of affairs as real, you
> must surely, unless prohibited from doing so, also imagine as real
> the consequences and incidents which, if the putative state of affairs   F
> had in fact existed, must inevitably have flowed from or accompanied
> it. One of these in this case is emancipation from the 1939 level of
> rents. The statute says that you must imagine a certain state of affairs;
> it does not say that having done so, you must cause or permit your
> imagination to boggle when it comes to the inevitable corollaries of
> that state of affairs."
                                                                           G
Those were the only authorities to which I was referred on the extent
to which deeming provisions or the like can be carried. From them I
deduce these principles. When considering the extent to which a deeming
provision should be applied, the court is entitled and bound to ascertain for
what purposes and between what persons the statutory fiction is to be
resorted to. It will not always be clear what those purposes are. If the   H
application of the provision would lead to an unjust, anomalous or absurd
result then, unless its application would clearly be within the purposes
of the fiction, it should not be applied. If, on the other hand, its application
would not lead to any such result then, unless that would clearly be outside
the purposes of the fiction, it should be applied. In order to apply these
principles to the present case I must start by examining section 181 (2)
of the Act of 1971 with some care. That which is to be deemed in the

A   case of a purchase notice accepted by the council is, first, that they are
" authorised to acquire the interest of the owner compulsorily in accordance
with the relevant provisions," and, secondly, that they " have served a
notice to treat in respect thereof " on the date of service of the purchase
notice. The relevant provisions are defined by section 181 (4) to mean
those of Part VI of the Act. That Part is entitled "Acquisition and
Appropriation of Land and Related Provisions," and it is clear that, as
B   with other similar provisions in other acts, they must themselves be
supplemented by resort to the general principles of the law of compulsory
acquisition. It seems to me, therefore, that the arguments of Mr. Potter
and Mr. Gray that the purposes of the deeming provision are at the most
twofold cannot be right. Indeed, it might have been enough for the main
purpose of ascertaining the compensation if the second part of section 181
C   (2) had merely said " shall be deemed to have served a notice to treat in
respect thereof on the date of service of the notice under that subsection,"
but I do not attach much weight to that as an individual point. What does
seem clear to me is that it was intended that the statutory fiction should
be resorted to at least for all the purposes of the law of compulsory
acquisition. Having got that far, I observe that there is nothing in the
D   provision itself which requires that resort should be made to it for those
purposes and for none other. And so it can be said that resort should
prima facie be made to it for all purposes. At the lowest it seems to me that
it is a provision where the purposes for which the statutory fiction is to be
resorted to are not clear.

   I must next consider whether the application of the deeming provision
for the purposes of section 45 (4) would lead to any of the results to which
E   I have referred. Mr. Potter said that it would be absurd to apply it for
the purposes of a taxing statute unheard of in 1971. But is that so? On
one view there is a big step to be taken between the two Acts. And it
must be said that in all the earlier cases what was in question was whether
a deeming provision or the like should be applied to a state of affairs
which did not involve the application of a later statute dealing with a
F   different subject matter; whereas what I have to decide is whether a
deeming provision in the compulsory purchase legislation should be applied
for the purposes of a later statute which is not part of that legislation. In
spite of these objections, I cannot on consideration see that any unjust,
anomalous or absurd result would follow from applying the deeming
provision in section 181 (2) for the purposes of section 45 (4). The object
of section 45 is to determine the time at which, for the purposes of the
G   tax, an interest in land is to be taken to be disposed of or acquired. It
may be that its provisions are not exhaustive. Mr. Carnwath gave the
example of a case where the parties to a sale by private treaty proceeded
to conveyance without a prior contract. In that case it would appear that
the matter would be governed by the general provision in section 1 (2), and
that the disposal would occur on the execution of the conveyance. Never-
H   theless, I think I ought to proceed on the assumption that section 45 was
intended to be exhaustive so far as concerns cases where the parties
become subject to an obligation to complete, contractual or otherwise, prior
to conveyance. On that footing I can see nothing unjust, anomalous or
absurd in saying that the transaction in this case falls within subsection (4)
rather than within subsection (2). If it is right to assume that it falls
within one or the other, there is no a priori reason for preferring either.

   I can at this stage summarise my provisional view of section 45 (4) as

follows. The purposes for which the statutory fiction created by the deem- A
ing provision in section 181 (2) are to be resorted to are either general or,
at the lowest, not clear. Since its application for the purposes of section 45
(4) would not lead to any unjust, anomalous or absurd result, and since
its application would not clearly be outside the purposes of the fiction, it
should be so applied. I must now see whether my provisional view of
subsection (4) is either confirmed or displaced by a consideration of three
other matters. First, I will consider the other reverse compulsory purchases B
under enactments containing similar deeming provisions. Mr. Carnwath
referred me to two of these: section 196 (1) of the Act of 1971 (blight
notices) and section 11 of the New Towns Act 1965. He also told me that
there were similar provisions in the current legislation dealing with forestry,
agriculture and housing. I think it important that I should say as little
as possible about these other provisions, which were not fully explored or C
debated in argument. Nevertheless, Mr. Carnwath has I think shown clearly
enough, first, that the decision in this case may have wide results for the
purposes of section 45, and, secondly, that his argument would have the
virtue of applying subsection (4) to most, and perhaps all, of the reverse
compulsory purchase cases, whereas Mr. Potter's might leave some of them
in a no-man's land between subsections (2) and (4). In regard to the latter D
point, I will mention section 11 of the New Towns Act 1965. That is a
provision which obliges the acquiring authority to accept the landowner's
purchase notice. Even though, as I believe to be the position, the power
conferred by section 31 of the Land Compensation Act 1961 to withdraw
the deemed notice to treat would there be available to the acquiring
authority, I understood Mr. Potter to accept that that was a case where the
consensus necessary to bring the transaction within subsection (2) was E
lacking. On Mr. Potter's argument that would be a transaction which fell
within neither subsection. On the whole, therefore, it seems to me that a
consideration of this point confirms my provisional view of subsection (4).

Secondly, I must look more closely at section 45 (2). I find it helpful
to approach it in this way. I start by assuming that subsection (4) was not
there. If that were the position, then, applying *Haynes* v. *Haynes* (1861) F
1 Dr. & Sm. 426 and *Harding* v. *Metropolitan Railway Co.* (1872) L.R. 7
Ch.App. 154, I would have little difficulty in concluding that a true compulsory acquisition where the compensation had been agreed fell at that
stage within subsection (2) (*b*). And limiting myself only to the case of a
purchase notice accepted by a council under section 181 (1) (*a*), I can
see a strong case for saying that the same could be said of that transaction,
even though the compensation remained to be agreed or assessed. However, G
on the authorities, such as they are, that latter proposition is by no means
established. It appears that the only authority which touches on this point
is *W. & S. (Long Eaton) Ltd.* v. *Derbyshire County Council* (1975) 29
P. & C.R. 552; (1976) 31 P. & C.R. 99 which was the case which applied the
rule settled in *West Midland Baptist (Trust) Association (Inc.)* v.
Birmingham Corporation [1970] A.C. 874 to transactions of this nature. H
But in the judgments both of the Lands Tribunal, of which Sir Douglas
Frank Q.C. was a member, and of the Court of Appeal (Buckley and
Orr L.JJ.) there are passages which bear on the question whether the
transaction constitutes a contract or not. In the judgment of the Lands
Tribunal, 29 P. & C.R. 522, 524–525, there is this passage:

  " In our view the two notices, coupled with the statutory procedures
    for determining the price, do constitute a contract for sale. But is the

A   contract, at that stage, an enforceable one? We think not. It is well settled that the court does not order specific performance of a contract until the price is fixed."

As I read that passage the Lands Tribunal were saying that the transaction constituted a contract in the sense that there were mutual obligations which had originated in a consensus, but that the contract was not at that stage

B enforceable by specific performance. I do not however read the passage as meaning that the Lands Tribunal were necessarily of the view that the contract was not enforceable in damages. For example, in a case where a council went back on their acceptance of the purchase notice and the landowner had in the meantime lost an opportunity for a private sale to a third party at a favourable price, it might be—I do not know—that

C the landowner would have an action for damages in contract. But whether that is right or not I would myself think that there was a lot to be said for the view that a transaction of this nature would fall within subsection (2) if subsection (4) was not there. However, in *W. & S.* (*Long Eaton*) *Ltd.* v. *Derbyshire County Council* (1976) 31 P. & C.R. 99 Buckley L.J., in delivering the judgment of the Court of Appeal, said, at p. 104:

D   " It is also true that, when the acquiring authority accepts the purchase notice, a consensual situation arises. The Lands Tribunal expressed the opinion that this, coupled with the statutory procedures for determining the price, constitutes a contract for sale, but not, at that stage, an enforceable one. We do not think that it is necessary for us to decide that question. We are inclined to doubt whether the consensual situa-tion amounts to more than an agreement that the case is a proper one

E   for a purchase notice. At any rate, it is clear that ownership of the land and the title to it remain at that stage both at law and in equity in the party serving the purchase notice."

Although the court did not think it necessary to decide the question, that passage shows that it is by no means clear that the transaction would fall within subsection (2) if subsection (4) was not there. And, more important,

F it does I think show that even if it could be a contract for the purposes of subsection (2) it is one which would not sit there with any great comfort. And that returns me from the hypothetical to the actual contents of section 45, and to the conclusion that a consideration of subsection (2) does not displace my provisional view of subsection (4).

          Thirdly and finally, I must consider section 45 (8). One thing which is clear about subsections (4) and (8) is that the former is a permanent

G provision and the latter is a transitional one. On a superficial level I can see the attractions of the argument which appealed to the special com-missioners. But I think that it would be very dangerous, in trying to get to the effect of the permanent provision, to attach too much weight to the particular wording of the transitional one. September 13, 1974, was the date on which the White Paper was published. That, then, was a crucial

H date for the purposes of the new tax. It seems to me that the probable explanation of the express reference to a deemed notice to treat in sub-section (8) is that it was intended to make it absolutely clear that the crucial date was to be the same in the cases of both actual and deemed such notices. In my judgment there is nothing in subsection (8) which displaces my provisional view of subsection (4).

          In the result my clear conclusion is that the transaction did fall within section 45 (4). I derive great comfort from the fact that this means that

subsections (2) and (4) ought for the most part to have a tidy working A
relationship between them. That may be something which will make the
answer to the question in this case appear more obvious to some minds than
it has to mine. But it will, I think, be clear from the lengthy, perhaps
laborious, process of reasoning by which I have arrived at my conclusion
that it is a consideration on which I have not found it necessary to rely.
It follows that the disposal and acquisition in the present case did not take
place until August 11, 1976, when the amount of the compensation received B
the approval of the council. That means that the Crown's appeal must be
allowed.

Appeal allowed with costs.
Case remitted to special commissioners
    for determination in accordance
    with judgment.   C
Certificate under section 12 of Admin-
    istration of Justice Act 1969 to
    appeal to House of Lords.

Solicitors: *Solicitor of Inland Revenue; Henry Fallows & Co., Bolton.*

[Reported by MRS. HARRIET DUTTON, Barrister-at-Law]   D

[COURT OF APPEAL]

                                                                  E

* HARRISON *v.* HAMMERSMITH AND FULHAM
         LONDON BOROUGH COUNCIL

HARINGEY LONDON BOROUGH COUNCIL *v.* MOSNER

WATSON *v.* HACKNEY LONDON BOROUGH COUNCIL
                                                                  F

1980 Dec. 9, 10, 11, 15;   Waller and Brandon L.JJ.,
1981 Jan. 21   Sir David Cairns

*Landlord and Tenant — Secure tenancy — Housing Act 1980 —
Notices to quit served on local authority tenants—Proceedings for possession brought before legislation coming into
effect—Whether premises " let under a secure tenancy"—*   G
*Whether tenants having licence to occupy—Housing Act 1980
(c. 51), ss. 28 (1), 33 (1), 34 (1), 48 (1)*

Three tenants of flats held on periodic tenancies from
local authority landlords were served with notices to quit but
they remained in possession of the premises after the notices
had expired. The landlords brought proceedings for possession
in county courts before the provisions as to security of tenure H
for council tenants in Chapter II of Part I of the Housing
Act 1980 came into force on October 3, 1980. In two of the
actions, the judge made an order for possession holding that
the Act did not apply because secure tenancies had not come
into being under the provisions of section 28 (1) of the Act,[1]

_____

[1] Housing Act 1980, s. 28 (1): see post, p. 654B–C.
S. 33 (1): see post, p. 655A.
S. 34 (1): see post, p. 655C–D.
S. 48 (1): see post, p. 655D–E.

A   and the premises were not so " let " within the meaning of
sections 33 (1) and 34 (1) at the commencement of the proceedings and at the time of the hearing. In the third action,
the judge refused to make an order for possession.
        On appeal by the tenants in the first two actions and by
the landlord in the third action: —
        Held, dismissing the appeals by the tenants and allowing
the appeal by the landlord, that giving the ordinary and
natural meaning to the words " is let as a secure tenancy "
B   in section 28 (1) and " let under a secure tenancy " in sections
33 (1) and 34 (1) of the Act they could not apply to premises
which had ceased to be let under a periodic tenancy by
October 3, 1980; that, although the purpose of the Housing
Act 1980 was to give to public sector tenants a similar protection as tenants in the private sector had under the Rent Acts,
the factors requiring the courts to interpret the early Rent
C   Acts so that effect was given to the purpose of that legislation
by making the Acts retrospective did not apply to the Act
of 1980; that, accordingly, the ordinary and natural meaning of the subsections should prevail and, therefore, as the
periodic tenancies had been terminated before the relevant
provisions of the Act came into effect, secure tenancies had
not been created and the landlords were entitled to possession
(post, pp. 660H—661B, E, 662F—663A, G—664A, C—E, 665F—H,
D   666G—667A).
        Remon v. *City of London Real Property Co. Ltd.* [1921]
1 K.B. 49, C.A.; *Hutchinson* v. *Jauncey* [1960] 1 K.B. 574,
C.A. and *Jonas* v. *Rosenberg* [1950] 2 K.B. 52, C.A. distinguished.
        Held, further, that it could not be inferred from the fact
that after the notice to quit had expired and pending the
hearing of the actions the landlords had given the tenants
E   licences to remain in the properties and, therefore, the tenants
could not claim security of tenure as being licensees under
the provisions of section 48 of the Act (post, pp. 663D—G,
666G, 667A).

        The following cases are referred to in the judgments:

Athlumney, In re [1898] 2 Q.B. 547.
F   *Hutchinson* v. *Jauncey* [1950] 1 K.B. 574; [1950] 1 All E.R. 165, C.A.
Jonas v. *Rosenberg* [1950] 2 K.B. 52; [1950] 1 All E.R. 296, C.A.
Remon v. *City of London Real Property Co. Ltd.* [1921] 1 K.B. 49, C.A.

        The following additional cases were cited in argument:

American Economic Laundry Ltd. v. *Little* [1951] 1 K.B. 400; [1950]
        2 All E.R. 1186, C.A.
G   *Barras* v. *Aberdeen Steam Trawling and Fishing Co. Ltd.* [1933] A.C. 402,
        H.L.(Sc.).
Dobson v. *Richards* [1919] W.N. 166.
McPhail v. *Persons, Names Unknown* [1973] Ch. 447; [1973] 3 W.L.R.
        71; [1973] 3 All E.R. 393, C.A.
National Real Estate and Finance Co. Ltd. v. *Hassan* [1939] 2 K.B. 61;
        [1939] 2 All E.R. 154, C.A.
H   *Thomas* v. *Sorrell* (1673) Vaugh. 330.
Welby v. *Parker* [1916] 2 Ch. 1, C.A.

        APPEALS from Judge Stucley, Judge Tibber and Judge Willis sitting
at West London, Edmonton and Shoreditch County Courts respectively.
        On June 28, 1976, the plaintiffs in the first action, the Hammersmith
and Fulham London Borough Council, let to the defendant, George
Harrison, on a weekly tenancy a flat known as Hall Floor, 81 Brackenbury

Road, Hammersmith, London S.W.6, the rent for which at the time of   A
the action was £11·66. On June 23, 1980, the local authority served on
the defendant notice to quit the flat on July 21, 1980. The defendant did
not comply with the notice and on August 5, 1980, the local authority
began an action in the West London County Court to recover possession
of the flat. On October 13, 1980, Judge Stucley gave judgment for the
local authority, ordering the defendant to give up possession on November 10, 1980.   B

The defendant appealed by notice dated October 30, 1980. The grounds
of the appeal were (1) that the judge ought to have held that on the
expiry of the notice to quit the defendant became and remained a tenant
at sufferance; (2) that the judge erred in holding that on the expiry of the
notice to quit the defendant became a trespasser; (3) that the judge erred
in not holding that on the commencement of sections 33 and 34 of the   C
Housing Act 1980, on October 3, 1980, the defendant was a tenant under
a tenancy to which those sections applied; (4) that the judge erred in
holding that the Act of 1980 could not be invoked retrospectively, in so
far as he held that it did not apply to tenancies created before the commencement of Chapter II of Part I of the Act; (5) that the judge misdirected himself in law in holding that on the expiry of the notice to quit   D
the defendant became a trespasser in the absence of evidence that the
parties contemplated a new tenancy; (6) that in determining the status of
the defendant the judge failed to have any or any sufficient regard to the
local authority's evidence that they were under a duty to house him
pursuant to the Housing (Homeless Persons) Act 1977; and (7) that the
judge ought to have held that the defendant was a secure tenant within
the meaning of section 28 of the Act of 1980 in respect of whom the   E
local authority had to prove one of the grounds for possession set out in
Part I of Schedule 4 to the Act in order for an order for possession
to be made.

On April 9, 1979, the plaintiffs in the second action, Haringey London
Borough Council, let to the defendant, Ellen Mosner, a flat known as 206,
The Sandlings, Pelham Road, London N.22, the rent for which at the time   F
of the action was £13·88 per week. On June 6, 1980, the local authority
served on the defendant notice to quit the flat on July 7, 1980. The defendant did not comply with the notice and on August 29, 1980, the local
authority began an action in the Edmonton County Court to recover
possession. On October 29, 1980, Judge Tibber dismissed the action.

The local authority appealed by notice dated November 21, 1980. The
grounds of appeal were (1) that the judge misdirected himself in holding   G
that the defendant's occupation of the premises was protected by the
provisions of the Housing Act 1980; (2) that the judge was wrong in holding that he was bound by *Remon* v. *City of London Real Property Co.
Ltd.* [1921] 1 K.B. 49 to hold that the defendant's occupation was protected by the Acts of 1980; (3) that the judge misconstrued the Act of
1980 and in particular sections 28, 47 and 48; (4) that the judge failed to   H
give effect to the consideration that the local authority could not have
served a notice complying with section 33 of the Act at the time the
notice to quit was served; (5) that the judge wrongly treated the provisions of the Rent Acts as analogous to the provisions of the Act of 1980;
and (6) that the judge wrongly construed the Act of 1980 so as to give it
retrospective effect.

The plaintiffs in the third action, Hackney London Borough Council,

A   let to the defendant, Mrs. Jenny Watson, on a weekly tenancy a flat known as 50, Corbiere House, Balmes Road, London N.1, the rent for which at the time of the action was £19·08. On June 5, 1980, the local authority served on the defendant notice to quit the flat on July 7, 1980. The defendant did not comply with the notice and on September 12, 1980, the local authority began an action in the Shoreditch County Court to recover possession. On October 15, 1980, Judge Willis tried as a preliminary

B   issue the question whether, having regard to the provisions of the Housing Act 1980, the particulars of claim disclosed any cause of action. He decided that issue in favour of the local authority.

By notice dated October 21, 1980, the defendant appealed. The grounds of the appeal were that the judge erred or misdirected himself in law in that he (1) misconstrued the effect of the Housing Act 1980; (2) misdirected himself by adopting an interpretation of the Act of 1980 which failed to give effect to the policy of the Act; (3) misdirected himself by

C   seeking to interpret the Act of 1980 in isolation from existing law, and/or failed to give due weight to existing law; and (4) misconstrued the effect on the position of the defendant of sections 1 to 3 of the Protection from Eviction Act 1977.

D   The appeals were heard together.

Andrew Bano for Mr. Harrison.
Colin Braham for Hammersmith and Fulham London Borough Council.
Simon Goldblatt Q.C. and *Anna Worrall* for Haringey London Borough Council.

E   *Andrew Arden* for Mrs. Mosner.
Andrew Arden for Mrs. Watson.
Simon Goldblatt Q.C. and *Anna Worrall* for Hackney London Borough Council.

Cur. adv. vult.

F   January 21. The following judgments were read.

BRANDON L.J. read the first judgment. The court has before it three appeals from the decisions of three different circuit judges in possession actions brought by local authority landlords against persons who were in any case formerly, and claim still to be, council tenants. The three appeals raise the same question on the construction of those

G   provisions of the Housing Act 1980 which relate to security of tenure for public sector tenants and have accordingly been heard together.

[His Lordship stated the facts, and continued:] The Act of 1980 was passed on August 8, 1980. The provisions relating to security of tenure for public sector tenants are contained in Chapter II of Part I of the Act. Section 153 (2) provided that Chapter II of Part I should come into

H   operation on such day as the Secretary of State might by order appoint or, if no such order should have been made, on the expiry of the period of eight weeks beginning with the day on which the Act was passed. No order was made by the Secretary of State for the coming into operation of Chapter II of Part I, and that Chapter accordingly came into operation eight weeks after the passing of the Act, that is to say on October 3, 1980.

The question of law raised by the three appeals can therefore be

formulated as follows. Where a local authority landlord has (a) brought
a tenant's periodic tenancy to an end by service and expiry of a valid
notice to quit, and (b) subsequently begun, but not yet obtained judgment
in, a possession action against the tenant, all before October 3, 1980,
when the provisions of the Act of 1980 relating to security of tenure for
public sector tenants came into operation, can the tenant rely on those
provisions as a defence to the action? In the three cases now on appeal
before us, two of the judges concerned have answered that question of
law in the negative, while the third has answered it in the affirmative.

The sections of Chapter II of Part I of the Act of 1980 relating to
security of tenure for public sector tenants provide, so far as material, as
follows:

" 28. – (1) A tenancy under which a dwelling house is let as a separate
dwelling is a secure tenancy at any time when the conditions described
below as the landlord condition and the tenant condition are satisfied . . . (2) The landlord condition is that—(a) the interest of the
landlord belongs to one of the bodies mentioned in subsection (4)
below . . . (3) The tenant condition is that the tenant is an individual
and occupies the dwelling house as his only or principal home . . .
(4) The bodies referred to in subsection 2 (a) above are—(a) a local
authority . . ."

" 29. – (1) Where a secure tenancy (in this section referred to as ' the
first tenancy') is a tenancy for a term certain and comes to an end by
effluxion of time or by an order under section 32 (2) below, a periodic
tenancy of the same dwelling house arises by virtue of this section,
unless the tenant is granted another secure tenancy of the same
dwelling house (whether a tenancy for a term certain or a periodic
tenancy) to begin on the coming to an end of the first tenancy.
(2) Where a periodic tenancy arises by virtue of this section—(a) the
periods of that tenancy are the same as those for which rent was last
payable under the first tenancy; and (b) the parties and the terms
of the tenancy are the same as those of the first tenancy at the end
of it; except that the terms are confined to those which are compatible
with a periodic tenancy and do not include any provision for re-
entry or forfeiture."

" 32. – (1) A secure tenancy which is either—(a) a weekly or other
periodic tenancy; or (b) a tenancy for a term certain but subject to
termination by the landlord; cannot be brought to an end by the landlord except by obtaining an order of the court for the possession of
the dwelling house or an order under subsection (2) below; and where
the landlord obtains an order for the possession of the dwelling
house the tenancy ends on the date on which the tenant is to give up
possession in pursuance of the order. (2) Where a secure tenancy is
a tenancy for a term certain but with a provision for re-entry or
forfeiture, the court shall not order possession of the dwelling
house in pursuance of that provision; but in any case where, but for
this section, the court would have made such an order it shall instead
make an order terminating the secure tenancy on a date specified in
the order. (3) Section 146 of the Law of Property Act 1925 (restriction on and relief against forfeiture) . . . and any other enactment or
rule of law relating to forfeiture shall apply in relation to proceedings for an order under subsection (2) above as if they were proceedings to enforce a right of re-entry or forfeiture."

The Weekly Law Reports, May 22, 1981

655

1 W.L.R.   Harrison v. Hammersmith Council (C.A.)   Brandon L.J.

A
" 33. – (1) The court shall not entertain proceedings for the possession of a dwelling house let under a secure tenancy . . . unless the
landlord has served on the tenant a notice complying with the
provisions of this section and, if the tenancy is a periodic tenancy—
(a) the proceedings are begun after the date specified in the notice;
and (b) the notice is still in force at the time the proceedings are
begun. (2) A notice under this section must be in a form prescribed
B
by regulations made by the Secretary of State and must specify the
ground on which the court will be asked to make an order for
the possession of the dwelling house or for the termination of
the tenancy and give particulars of that ground. (3) If the secure
tenancy is a periodic tenancy the notice—(a) must also specify a date
after which proceedings for the possession of the dwelling house may
C
be begun; and (b) ceases to be in force 12 months after the date
specified in it; and the date specified in it must not be earlier than
the date on which the tenancy could, apart from this Act, be brought
to an end by notice to quit given by the landlord if the notice to quit
were given on the same date as the notice under this section . . ."
" 34. – (1) The court shall not make an order for the possession of a
dwelling house let under a secure tenancy except on one or more of
D
the grounds set out in Part I of Schedule 4 to this Act . . ."
" 47. – This Chapter applies to tenancies granted before as well as
tenancies granted after the commencement of this Chapter."
"48. – (1) Where a person who is not the tenant of a dwelling house
has a licence (whether or not granted for a consideration) to occupy
the dwelling house and the circumstances are such that, if the licence
E
were a tenancy, it would be a secure tenancy, then, subject to subsection (2) below, this Part of this Act applies to the licence as it
applies to a secure tenancy and, as so applying, has effect as if
expressions appropriate to a licence were substituted for ' landlord,'
' tenant,' ' tenancy ' and ' secure tenancy.' (2) Subsection (1) above
does not apply to a licence which was granted as a temporary ex-
F
pedient to a person who entered the dwelling house or any other land
as a trespasser (whether or not before the grant another licence to
occupy that or another dwelling house had been granted to him)."
" 50. – (1) In this Chapter— . . . 'local authority' means . . . the
council of a London borough . . . (2) For the purposes of this
Chapter—(a) a dwelling house may be a house or part of a house . . ."

G
In connection with section 33 (2), paragraph 62 of Part II of
Schedule 25 to the Act of 1980, entitled " Transitional Provisions and
Savings," provides:

" For the purposes of section 33 of this Act a notice served at any
time after regulations are first made for the purposes of subsection (2)
of that section, but before the commencement of that section shall be
treated as duly served under that section if it would have been so
H
treated had Chapter II of Part I of this Act then been in force."

The Secretary of State availed himself of the power conferred on him by
paragraph 62 of Part II of Schedule 25 by making, in advance of the
coming into operation of Chapter II of Part I, anticipatory regulations
of the kind authorised by that paragraph. These regulations are the Secure
Tenancies (Notices) Regulations 1980 (S.I. 1980 No. 1339). They were
made on September 4 and came into operation on September 5, 1980.

Brandon L.J.   **Harrison v. Hammersmith Council (C.A.)**   **[1981]**

The latter date was 28 days before October 3, 1980, when Chapter II of   A
Part I came into operation, and the inevitable inference is that the Secretary of State was of the opinion that, if a notice in the form prescribed by
those regulations was served on the first day on which they came into
operation, it would be an effective notice for the purpose of any action
brought 28 days later when the restrictions relating to the entertainment
by the court of actions for possession of dwelling houses let on secure
tenancies first came into operation.   B

The following matters were not in dispute. First, that, by virtue of the
definition of the expression "dwelling house" contained in section
50 (2) (a), all the flats concerned in these three appeals were dwelling
houses for the purposes of sections 28, 29, 33 and 34 of the Act of 1980.
Secondly, that, prior to the termination, by the service and expiry of notices
to quit, of the tenancies of the three flats concerned, the conditions   C
prescribed in section 28 (2) and (3) as the landlord condition and the
tenant condition respectively were satisfied. Thirdly, that none of the
three local authority landlords concerned had served on their tenants
notices of the kind required by section 33 in the form prescribed by the
Secure Tenancies (Notices) Regulations 1980. Fourthly, that none of the
three local authority landlords concerned had based their claims to possession on any of the grounds specified in Part I of Schedule 4 to the   D
Act of 1980, whether they would have been able to do so or not. On the
contrary, they based such claims, and based them solely, on the service
on their respective tenants of notices to quit in the ordinary form, which
had expired before their respective actions were begun.

It follows from those matters that, if at the dates when the actions for
possession were begun, or the dates on which such actions were heard and   E
adjudicated on, or both, the flats concerned were "let under a secure
tenancy" within the meaning of that expression as used in sections 33 (1)
and 34 (1), the landlords' claims for possession must fail and be dismissed.
This is because section 33 (1) prohibits the court from entertaining proceedings for the possession of a dwelling house let under a secure tenancy,
unless the landlord has previously served on the tenant a notice of the   F
kind required by section 33 (2), that is to say a notice in the form
prescribed by the Secure Tenancies (Notices) Regulations 1980; and
section 34 (1) further prohibits the court from making an order for the
possession of a dwelling house let under a secure tenancy except on one
or more of the grounds set out in Part I of Schedule 4.

For the local authority landlords it was contended that, since valid
notices to quit had been served in each case, and had expired before the   G
date on which the relevant action for possession had been begun, and a
fortiori before the date on which such action had been heard and adjudicated on, it was impossible to say that, at either of these two dates, which
were the material dates for the purposes of sections 33 and 34, the flats
concerned were let by the landlords to the tenants at all, let alone that
they were let to them on secure tenancies.   H

In support of this contention much reliance was very properly placed
on the use of the present tense in the expression " is let "in section 28 (1),
the section in which the nature and characteristics of a secure tenancy
are defined and explained. In view of the use of the expression " is let "
in section 28 (1), it was the duty of the court, it was said, so far as
section 33 (1) is concerned, to ask itself this simple question as at the date
on which each of the three actions for possession was begun: " Is this

The Weekly Law Reports, May 22, 1981

657

1 W.L.R.   Harrison v. Hammersmith Council (C.A.)   Brandon L.J.

A flat presently let by the landlords to the tenant at all? " And the answer to
that simple question which the court would be bound to give itself, having
regard to the prior service and expiry of a valid notice to quit, would be:
" No, the flat was formerly let by the landlords to the tenant, but it is no
longer presently so let." Similarly, so far as section 34 (1) is concerned,
it was the duty of the court to ask itself the same simple question as at
the date on which the action was heard and adjudicated on, and the answer

B which the court would be bound to give itself would be the same.

These contentions are based on the ordinary and natural meaning of
the words used in sections 28, 33 and 34, and, as such, must necessarily
carry great force. The result of the contentions, if correct, is that, since
in each of the three cases concerned the relationship of landlord and tenant
had been brought to an end before the relevant action for possession was

C begun, the defendant who had ceased to be a tenant had no defence to
the claim, and the court was bound to make the order for possession
sought.

For the tenants, it was not disputed that the expression " let under a
secure tenancy " as used in sections 33 (1) and 34 (1) included the meaning contended for by the local authority landlords. It was, however, con-

D tended that the expression as so used was an elastic one, which included
also the extended meaning " was previously, prior to the service and
expiry of any otherwise valid notice to quit, let under a secure tenancy, as
defined and explained in section 28." In support of this contention,
reliance was placed on a series of authorities on certain of the earlier Rent
Acts, with which it was said that Chapter II of Part I of the Act of 1980
was in pari materia, and in conformity with which it was said that ques-

E tions of construction on analogous provisions in the Act of 1980 should
be decided.

The first, and by far the most important, of the authorities relied on
was Remon v. City of London Real Property Co. Ltd. [1921] 1 K.B. 49.
In that case the defendants had in December 1915 let to the plaintiff two
rooms for business purposes. In February 1920 the defendants gave the

F plaintiff a valid notice to quit expiring on June 24, 1920. The plaintiff did
not comply with the notice, nor with a solicitor's letter requiring him to
give up possession immediately. On July 2, 1920, the Increase of Rent
and Mortgage Interest (Restrictions) Act 1920 came into operation. On
the same day, after the plaintiff had finished work, and had locked up the
premises and gone home, the defendants took advantage of his absence
to have the locks broken and take possession. The plaintiff then brought

G an action against the defendants in the High Court, in which, relying on
the protection given to him by the Act of 1920, he claimed an injunction
restraining the defendants from interfering with his possession.

The relevant provisions of the Act of 1920 were these. By section
12 (2), the Act applied to any house or part of a house " let as a separate
dwelling . . ." subject to certain specified limits with regard to the annual
amount of the standard rent or the rateable value. By section 5 (1) no

H order or judgment for the recovery of possession of any dwelling house
to which the Act applied, or for the ejectment of a tenant therefrom, was
to be made or given, except in a number of specified circumstances. By
section 15 (1) a tenant who, by virtue of the provisions of the Act, retained
possession of any dwelling house to which the Act applied, was, so long
as he retained possession, to observe and be entitled to the benefit of all
the terms and conditions of the original contract of tenancy, so far as the

same were consistent with the provisions of the Act. By section 13 (1) the A
Act applied also, subject to certain modifications which are not material,
to premises used for business purposes.

It was not in dispute that the Act applied to the premises which had
been occupied by the plaintiff, nor did the defendants suggest that there
existed any of the various circumstances specified in section 5 (1) which
would have entitled the court to make an order for possession against the
plaintiff. McCardie J., treating by agreement a summons in chambers by B
the plaintiff for an interlocutory injunction as the hearing of the action,
without prejudice to an appeal, held that the plaintiff was entitled to the
protection of the Act of 1920 and granted him the injunction which he
sought. On an appeal by the defendants to the Court of Appeal, consisting of Bankes, Scrutton and Atkin L.JJ., the plaintiff's right to
the injunction was upheld. The decision of the Court of Appeal is C
summarised in the headnote [1921] 1 K.B. 49 as follows:

> " Held, that although the agreement of tenancy had come to an end
> by the notice to quit, the rooms were ' let ' within the meaning of
> section 12 (2), and the plaintiff was a tenant who by virtue of the
> provisions of the Act retained possession within the meaning of
> section 15 (1) of the Act, and that the landlords could not lawfully D
> disturb him in his possession."

The reasoning of the court appears from the judgments of Bankes
and Scrutton L.JJ., with which Atkin L.J. agreed. Bankes L.J. said, at
p. 54 :

> " In no ordinary sense of the word was the respondent a tenant of the
> premises on July 2. His term had expired. His landlords had E
> endeavoured to get him to go out. He was not even a tenant at
> sufferance. It is however clear that in all the Rent Restrictions Acts
> the expression ' tenant ' has been used in a special, a peculiar sense, and
> as including a person who might be described as an ex-tenant, some-
> one whose occupation had commenced as tenant and who had con-
> tinued in occupation without any legal right to do so except possibly F
> such as the Acts themselves conferred upon him. The respondent
> therefore on the coming into operation of the new Act was a tenant
> within the meaning of that expression in the Act, and as the Act for
> the first time included business premises within its protection, the
> premises were not excluded on the ground that they were business
> premises only."

Later, dealing with the expression " let " in section 12 (2), Bankes L.J. G
said, at p. 56:

> " I have already explained the meaning which must necessarily be
> given to the expression ' tenant ' as used in the Act. I consider that
> a similar construction must be placed upon the expression ' let ' in
> section 12 (2). The subsection cannot be confined to premises in
> respect of which a letting is in existence at the time when the protec- H
> tion of the Act is claimed. The expression must be read as suffi-
> ciently elastic to include the letting under which the tenant who claims
> the protection of the Act became tenant."

Scrutton L.J. said, at p. 58:

> " Whom did they mean to include in the term ' tenant?' If a tenant
> by agreement whose tenancy had expired was not within those terms,

The Weekly Law Reports, May 22, 1981

659

1 W.L.R.   Harrison v. Hammersmith Council (C.A.)   Brandon L.J.

A   the whole purpose of the Act would have been defeated, for it was obviously intended to allow former tenants who were willing to carry out the terms of their old tenancy, as modified by any permissible statutory increases of rent, to stay on. If this was not so every weekly or monthly tenant, the small tenant for whose benefit the Acts were obviously framed, was outside the Act. Unless ' tenant ' includes a former tenant by agreement holding over against the will

B   of the landlord, and ' letting ' includes the landlord's relation to such a tenant, the whole object of the Acts is defeated."

Then, after saying that the persons under consideration could not properly be described as tenants at sufferance, he continued, on the same page: " Yet I think it is clear Parliament has intended to confirm these people

C   in a statutory tenancy and to speak of their position as a ' letting.' " Finally, dealing with the argument that the words of the Act should be given their ordinary and natural meaning, Scrutton L.J. said, at p. 59:

" . . . I feel that I am straining language in speaking of a person whose tenancy has expired, and who stays in against the active protest of the landlord, as a ' tenant,' and of the landlord's relation to him as a ' letting,' but such a person appears to be within the clear

C   intention of the legislature . . ."

The second authority relied on for the tenants was *Hutchinson* v. *Jauncey* [1950] 1 K.B 574. In that case the tenant of a house within the protection of the Rent Acts had sublet two rooms in it, sharing the use of the scullery for cooking with a subtenant. Later the subtenant pur-

E   chased the house subject to the tenancy, and in his capacity as landlord served on the tenant notice to quit expiring on April 25, 1949. The tenant failed to comply with the notice and on May 25, 1949, the landlord began an action in the Edmonton County Court claiming possession.

As the law stood before the coming into operation of the Landlord and Tenant (Rent Control) Act 1949, a tenancy which involved the sharing of part of the accommodation let to a tenant with a subtenant

F   was not within the protection of the Rent Acts. On June 2, 1949, however, the Act of 1949 came into operation, and by section 9 extended the protection of the Rent Acts to tenancies involving sharing of this kind. The action came on for hearing in the county court on June 22, 1949, and the question arose whether the change in the law effected by the Act of 1949 was of such retrospective effect as to give the tenant a good defence

G   to the action. It was held by the Court of Appeal, consisting of Sir Raymond Evershed M.R. and Cohen and Asquith L.JJ., that the law applicable was that in force at the date of the hearing, rather than that which had been in force at the date of the expiry of the notice to quit or the commencement of the action, and that the county court judge accordingly had no jurisdiction to make an order for possession against

H   the tenant.

The court accepted the general rule that a statute should not, in the absence of express provision, be construed as depriving persons of accrued rights. They considered, however, on the authority of *Remon* v. *City of London Real Property Co. Ltd.* [1921] 1 K.B. 49, that the Rent Acts, in so far as they provided tenants with protection, or additional protection, against eviction, constituted an exception to that general rule. In this connection Sir Raymond Evershed M.R. said [1950] 1 K.B. 574, 579:

" The question, therefore, really is : since a summons had been issued   A
before the Act came into force, did the landlord acquire rights pursuant to the law as it stood before the Act was passed, and are those
rights unaffected either by the express language of or by the necessary implication to be drawn from sections 9 and 10 of the Act of
1949? Apart from the decision in *Remon* v. *City of London Real
Property Co. Ltd.* [1920] 1 K.B. 49, I think that the point might have
been one of very serious difficulty, nor do I think that it is an easy   B
one now. But that case seems to me to have laid down the application
of a principle to this class of legislation generally, and I think, therefore, that citations from authorities relating to wholly different subject-
matters may not be so pertinent to cases of this character."

The third authority relied on for the tenants was *Jonas* v. *Rosenberg*
[1950] 2 K.B. 52. That case raised, in substance, the same question as   C
Hutchinson v. *Jauncey* [1950] 1 K.B. 574 had raised with regard to the
retrospective effect of section 9 of the Act of 1949 in relation to a tenancy
involving the sharing of accommodation between a tenant and a sub-
tenant. The only potentially significant difference between the two cases
was that in *Jonas* v. *Rosenberg* the hearing of the landlord's action for
possession was concluded on May 31, 1949, just before the Act of 1949   D
came into operation, but judgment in it was reserved and not given till
August 4, 1949, some two months after the Act of 1949 came into operation. Much of the argument in the case appears to have turned on the
meaning of the words " or anything done " towards the end of section 10
of the Act of 1949. In the result, however, the Court of Appeal held that
the case was indistinguishable from *Hutchinson* v. *Jauncey,* the law applicable being that in force when the county court judge delivered his   E
reserved judgment on August 4, 1949.

The argument for the tenants was founded on the basic proposition
that the provisions for security of tenure for public sector tenants contained in Chapter II of Part I of the Housing Act 1980 were in pari
materia with the provisions for security of tenure for private sector
tenants contained in the earlier Rent Acts, in particular the Increase of   F
Rent and Mortgage Interest (Restrictions) Act 1920, with which *Remon*
v. *City of London Real Property Co. Ltd.* [1921] 1 K.B. 49 was concerned. Relying on this basic proposition, counsel for the tenants argued
that, since the Court of Appeal in *Remon's* case had found it necessary
to give a strained and unnatural meaning to such expressions as " let " in
section 12 (1), and " tenant " in section 15 (1), of the Act of 1920, this
court should interpret the expression " let under a secure tenancy " in   G
sections 33 (1) and 34 (1) of the Act of 1980 as including a comparably
strained and unnatural meaning.

In my opinion this basic proposition, from which counsel for the
tenants sought to derive the result which I have stated, is not, when the
characteristics of the two pieces of legislation are looked at and analysed
as a whole, a correct proposition.   H

It is true that there are certain important similarities between the
relevant provisions of the earlier Rent Acts and those of Chapter II of
Part I of the Act of 1980. The first such similarity is that both pieces of
legislation have as their purpose the provision of security of tenure for
tenants of rented homes. The second similarity is that the legislature has
in both cases achieved this purpose by (a) preventing a landlord from
obtaining possession of the premises which he has let except in pursuance

The Weekly Law Reports, May 22, 1981

661

1 W.L.R.   Harrison v. Hammersmith Council (C.A.)   Brandon L.J.

A of an order of a court, and (b) prohibiting a court from making such an order for possession unless and until it is satisfied by the landlord that certain circumstances exist or certain conditions are fulfilled.

Against these two important similarities, however, there must be set what appear to me to be two even more important differences. The first difference is between the housing situation in which, and the social background against which, the two pieces of legislation were passed. The Act of 1920, in relation to which *Remon's* case was decided, was passed to deal with the critical housing shortage which followed the demobilisation of immense numbers of the armed forces after the end of the first world war. It was necessary that legislation to meet that situation should be passed, and that its remedial qualities should take effect, as quickly as possible.

C By contrast, Chapter II of Part I of the Act of 1980 was not enacted in order to meet any immediate or urgent crisis in housing accommodation. Its purpose was rather the social one of giving to tenants in the public housing sector, so far as reasonably practicable, the same kind of protection from being evicted from their homes without good and sufficient cause as had been enjoyed by tenants in the private housing sector for many decades under the Rent Acts. This assimilation of rights as between public and private sector tenants, though no doubt regarded as desirable in the general interests of social equality and non-discrimination, was not an urgent matter, and no special reason for setting the earliest possible deadline for such assimilation existed. In this connection it is to be observed that, for numerous years past, it had been thought safe and proper to give to local authority landlords a complete discretion with regard to the eviction of public sector tenants, and to rely on them to exercise such discretion fairly and wisely.

The second difference is between the method used by the legislature in order to effect its purpose in the Rent Acts, particularly the Acts prior to 1965, on the one hand, and that used by it to effect its purpose in Chapter II of Part I of the Act of 1980 on the other hand.

F In the earlier Rent Acts the legislature did not seek to interfere with the common law principles on which contractual tenancies, whether periodic or for a term certain, could be brought to an end. In the case of periodic tenancies, the legislature left landlords free to bring them to an end by the service and expiry of valid notices to quit. In the case of tenancies for a term certain, the legislature left such tenancies to come to an end automatically by effluxion of time. What the legislature did, however, in order to protect the person who had been a contractual tenant before his contractual tenancy came to an end, was to create a new relationship between the person and his former contractual landlord, which Scrutton L.J. described, in the second passage from his judgment which I quoted earlier in *Remon* v. *City of London Real Property Co. Ltd.* [1921] 1 K.B. 49, 58, as a " statutory tenancy," the parties to which were the former contractual tenant, from then on described as a " statutory tenant," and the former contractual landlord or his successor in title. The concept of a statutory, as distinct from a contractual, tenancy, having been formulated initially by the court, as a matter of necessary implication from such provisions as section 15 (1) of the Act of 1920, and accepted for many years thereafter as a convenient description of the relationship concerned, was in the end formally recognised by the legislature in section 1 (4) (*b*) of the Rent Act 1965, and still remains, despite subsequent developments

with regard to " controlled " and " regulated " tenancies, ingrained in the A
Rent Acts legislation as a whole.

By contrast, in the Act of 1980 the legislature went about the matter
in quite a different way. It abolished altogether the common law principles
on which contractual tenancies, both periodic and for a term certain, could
be brought or come to an end. It did this by providing, first, that, on the
expiry of a contractual tenancy for a term certain, there should come B
into existence a periodic tenancy in its place, unless a further contractual
tenancy for a term certain should be granted: section 29 (1) and (2); and,
secondly, that a periodic tenancy, whether having that character originally, or coming into being on the expiry of a term certain, should not be
capable of being brought to an end by a landlord except by the latter
obtaining an order of the court for possession: section 32 (1), or, in cases
where provisions for re-entry or forfeiture are relied on, an order terminat- C
ing the secure tenancy: section 32 (2).

The significance of the first difference between the two pieces of legislation to which I have referred above is that, in a situation where the
legislature, having passed the Act of 1980 as a whole on August 8, 1980,
has then seen fit not to bring Chapter II of Part I into operation until eight
weeks later, namely on October 3, 1980, there is no policy reason of any D
kind why the court should seek, by giving a strained and unnatural meaning to certain expressions in the Act, to give retrospective effect to the
provisions of that Chapter.

The significance of the second difference between the two pieces of
legislation to which I have referred is this. Whereas a court interpreting the
earlier Rent Acts, such as the Act of 1920 in *Remon's* case, felt obliged
to fill gaps in the express provisions of the Acts on the basis of neces- E
sary implication from their manifest purpose, the Act of 1980 deals much
more fully and explicitly with the methods by which the purpose of providing security of tenure for public sector tenants is to be achieved. The result
is that gaps in the express provisions of the kind which existed in the
earlier Rent Acts do not exist in the Act of 1980, and do not therefore
require to be filled up by the kind of process of strained and unnatural F
construction to which the Court of Appeal was admittedly driven in
Remon's case.

In my view, when one looks at the differences, as well as the similarities,
between the Rent Acts legislation on the one hand and Chapter II of
Part I of the Act of 1980 on the other, it is impossible to say that the
two pieces of legislation are in pari materia, so that a decision on the
retrospective effect of certain provisions in the first of these two pieces of G
legislation should be regarded as binding this court to reach a similar
decision with regard to the retrospective effect of what are, to some
extent at least, comparable provisions in the second of the two pieces of
legislation.

In *Remon's* case the Court of Appeal felt bound to give strained and
unnatural meanings to perfectly ordinary words, such as " tenant,"
" tenancy," " letting " and " let." It did so for one reason and one reason H
only, namely, that unless those words were given strained and unnatural
meanings, the manifest purpose of the Act of 1920—to protect from eviction persons whose contractual tenancies had been brought or come to an
end—would be defeated.

In the three cases with which these appeals are concerned, I do not
see any compelling reason why the court should follow its predecessor in

The Weekly Law Reports, May 22, 1981

663

1 W.L.R.   Harrison v. Hammersmith Council (C.A.)   Brandon L.J.

A *Remon's* case by giving a strained and unnatural meaning to the expression " let under a secure tenancy " as used in sections 33 (1) and 34 (1) of the Act of 1980.

The ordinary and natural meaning of the expression is " let under a secure tenancy at the date to which each subsection concerned relates," that is to say the date of commencement of an action for possession, in the case of section 33 (1), and the date of deciding whether an order for possession should be made in such an action in the case of section 34 (1).

B

To adopt that ordinary and natural meaning of the expression concerned will not, so far as I can see, in any way defeat the purposes of Chapter II of Part I of the Act of 1980. It will only mean that, since under section 153 (2) of the Act Chapter II of Part I did not come into operation, by the decision of the legislature and the Secretary of State,

C until eight weeks after the passing of the Act, namely on October 3, 1980, only those public sector tenants whose tenancies were not lawfully brought to an end before that date will benefit from the provisions of that Chapter.

What I have said disposes of the primary way in which the case for the tenants was put. It remains, however, for me to deal with a secondary, and very much subsidiary, argument advanced on their behalf. This alter-

D native argument was based on section 48 (1) of the Act of 1980, which deals with the position of persons occupying dwelling houses as licensees, and equates their rights with those occupying them as tenants.

The argument was that if, contrary to the tenants' primary case, they did not have, as a result of the expiry of their respective notices to quit, secure tenancies of the dwelling houses which they occupied, they were nevertheless, as a result of staying on after such notices to quit had

E expired, licensees of the dwelling houses concerned within the meaning of section 48 (1).

I find it impossible to accept this alternative submission. The whole tenor of section 48 makes it clear that it is referring to licences granted by the owner, or other person entitled to the possession, of the dwelling house concerned. It was not open to the local authority landlords to evict

F their tenants except in pursuance of a court order. In these circumstances it is impossible to infer that the local authority landlords, by awaiting the results of their actions for possession, were expressly or impliedly giving their former tenants licences to remain in their flats. It can, I think, be said that the former tenants had a statutory licence or dispensation to remain in occupation of their flats unless and until orders for possession were made by a court against them. Assuming that to be right, however,

G I do not think that the result is to create the relationship of licensors and licensees between the local authority landlords and their former tenants. I would, therefore, reject this alternative argument for the tenants based on section 48.

For the reasons which I have given I have come to the conclusion that, since the local authority landlords (a) terminated their tenants' periodic

H tenancies by valid notices to quit, and (b) subsequently began actions against them for possession, before October 3, 1980, when the provisions of the Act of 1980 relating to security of tenure for public sector tenants came into operation, the tenants are not entitled to rely on those provisions as a defence to their actions.

It follows, in my judgment, that the appeals brought by George Harrison against the judgment of Judge Stucley and by Jenny Watson against the decision of Judge Willis should be dismissed; but that the

appeal brought by Haringey London Borough Council against the judg- A
ment of Judge Tibber should be allowed.

WALLER L.J.   The question which arises for decision in these three
cases is whether the tenant of a local authority upon whom a notice to
quit has been served is entitled after the time of expiry of the notice to
quit to the protection of the Housing Act 1980, even though the notice B
to quit expired in each case before the Act came into effect.

Mr. Arden in his submissions has relied on the phrase in section 28 (1)
of the Act of 1980, " let as a separate dwelling " as a connecting link
between this Act and the Increase of Rent and Mortgage Interest (Restrictions) Act 1920 and subsequent Rent Acts. Founding his submission on
Remon v. *City of London Real Property Co. Ltd.* [1921] 1 K.B. 49, which
was concerned with the Act of 1920, and *Hutchinson* v. *Jauncey* [1950] C
1 K.B. 574, which was concerned with the Landlord and Tenant (Rent
Control) Act 1949, Mr. Arden submitted that expressions in those Acts
which were held to cover the case of ex-tenants remaining in possession
should apply to the Housing Act 1980.

The Act of 1920 was an Act passed to protect tenants after the first
world war from increase of rent and protect them from ejection. There D
were strong reasons for interpreting the phrase " a house . . . let as a
separate dwelling " as including a house where the notice to quit had
expired and the word " tenant " to cover the case of a tenant who had
been given notice to quit on a certain day and was still in possession after
that day. Similarly the Act of 1949 was passed in order to cover conditions arising after the second world war. In that case also it was held E
that " tenant " included ex-tenant holding over.

If the language used in the Housing Act 1980 were similar to that used
in those two Acts I would, for myself, follow those two decisions even
though the circumstances of the passing of the Act of 1980 are very
different from those in 1920 and 1949. Mr. Goldblatt submitted, however,
that the Rent Act 1968 was a consolidating statute which repealed all the F
preceding Rent Acts and replaced the legislation with somewhat different
phraseology. He has also emphasised that the purpose of the Act of 1980
was rather different from the earlier Rent Acts.

In *Remon* v. *City of London Real Property Co. Ltd.* [1921] 1 K.B. 49
the court was concerned with two sections of the Increase of Rent and
Mortgage Interest (Restrictions) Act 1920: section 12 (2), which read:
" This Act shall apply to a house or a part of a house let as a separate G
dwelling . . . ," and section 15 (1): " A tenant who by virtue of the provisions of this Act retains possession of any dwelling house to which this
Act applies . . ." Those two provisions were those which concerned the
court. Bankes L.J. said, at p. 54:

" It is however clear that in all the Rent Restrictions Acts the expression ' tenant ' has been used in a special, a peculiar sense, and as H
including a person who might be described as an ex-tenant, someone
whose occupation had commenced as tenant and who had continued
in occupation without any legal right to do so except possibly such
as the Acts themselves conferred upon him."

Scrutton L.J., after saying that unless the word " tenant " included a
tenant whose tenancy had expired the whole purpose of the Act would

A have been defeated, went on, at p. 58: " Yet I think it is clear Parliament
has intended to confirm these people in a statutory tenancy and to speak
of their position as a ' letting.' "

In *Hutchinson* v. *Jauncey* [1950] 1 K.B. 574 the Act being considered
was the Landlord and Tenant (Rent Control) Act 1949. That Act gave
Rent Act protection to subtenants who were sharing part of the accom-
B modation with the landlord. Sir Raymond Evershed M.R. said, at p. 577 :

> ". . . having regard to the decision in *Remon* v. *City of London Real
> Property Co. Ltd.* [1921] 1 K.B. 49, if it had not been for the issue of
> the plaint before the Act came into operation, the tenant must have
> been entitled to claim the benefit of section 9 of the Act of 1949 not-
> withstanding the service of an effective notice to quit."

C The court went on to hold that the important time at which the matter
had to be considered was the time of the hearing of the case and not the
time of the issuing of the plaint. If therefore those Rent Acts were still in
force and the Housing Act 1980 was simply adding additional provisions
to them, the arguments of Mr. Arden would have great force.

Section 20 of the Rent Act 1965 gave statutory effect to the decision
D in the *Remon* case. Specific provision was made for the transitional stage
and section 20 (1) said :

> " Where the tenancy of a dwelling house has come to an end before
> the commencement of this Act and the tenancy would have been a
> regulated tenancy had this Act been then in force, then—(*a*) no order
> for the possession of the dwelling house shall be made which would
E not be made if this Act had come into force before the termination
> of the tenancy . . ."

That Act was followed by the Rent Act 1968, which repealed most of the
earlier Rent Act legislation and in particular the whole of the Act of 1920,
the whole of the Act of 1939 and the whole of the Act of 1949. It also
repealed the Rent Act part of the Act of 1965, leaving only Part III which
F dealt with harassment.

The Rent Act 1968 adopted different phraseology. Section 1 (1) read:
" A tenancy under which a dwelling house . . . is let as a separate dwelling is a protected tenancy for the purposes of this Act . . . ," and this
phraseology is followed in the Act of 1980. Section 28 (1) of the Act of
1980 provides: " A tenancy under which a dwelling house is let as a
G separate dwelling is a secure tenancy at any time when the conditions
described below . . ." are in existence. While it is possible, with reference
to the Act of 1920, to describe " house . . . let as a separate dwelling " as
including a house which has been let as a separate dwelling and " a tenant
who by virtue of the provisions of this Act retains possession of [a] dwelling house . . ." as still being a tenant when he retains possession after notice
H to quit, more particularly when, as Scrutton L.J. pointed out in *Remon* v.
City of London Real Property Co. Ltd. [1921] 1 K.B. 49, 58, the whole
intention of the Act would be defeated if another interpretation was given,
it is in my opinion very difficult to say that the words " a tenancy under
which a dwelling house is let " should include " a tenancy under which a
dwelling house was or has been let " as a separate dwelling.

Although in the earlier Rent Acts the effect of the decisions that I
have already quoted was to make the Acts retrospective:

" Perhaps no rule of construction is more firmly established than this A —that a retrospective operation is not to be given to a statute so as to impair an existing right or obligation, otherwise than as regards matter of procedure, unless that effect cannot be avoided without doing violence to the language of the enactment." *Per* Wright J. in *In re Athlumney* [1898] 2 Q.B. 547, 551.

And the judge went on: " If the enactment is expressed in language which B is fairly capable of either interpretaiton, it ought to be construed as prospecive only."

In 1920 in the immediate years after the first world war there were strong reasons for preserving as far as possible the restriction on rents and security of tenure. And as Scrutton L.J. pointed out in *Remon* v. *City of London Real Property Co. Ltd.* [1921] 1 K.B. 49, 58: C

" If a tenant by agreement whose tenancy had expired was not within [the terms of the Act], the whole purpose of the Act would have been defeated, for it was obviously intended to allow former tenants who were willing to carry out the terms of their old tenancy, as modified by any permissible statutory increases of rent, to stay on."

Similar circumstances existed after the second world war, circumstances D with which the Act of 1949 was dealing.

The circumstances surrounding the Housing Act 1980 are different and reflect one of two different approaches to public sector housing. One view is that housing associations and local authorities should have a greater power over their tenants and be able to make their own decisions about possession in order to use the housing to best advantage. Another view is E that the courts and only the courts should decide upon these matters. The Act of 1980, which enables tenants to purchase their houses, also gives effect to the latter of these two views regarding possession. However, in my opinion the purpose of the Act of 1980 would in no way be frustrated if the plain meaning of the words in section 28 were adopted. This would mean that the important date would be the date of coming F into effect of the Act.

There was some argument before us as to the status of an ex-tenant —a tenant to whom a notice to quit has been given, but who because of statutes such as the Prevention of Eviction Act 1977 could not be said to be a trespasser. The question of whether he is a tenant at sufferance or whether he is a licensee or whether he has some other status was discussed before us. If it were necessary to decide it I would be of the opinion that G an ex-tenant would not be a tenant at sufferance nor would he be a licensee of the landlord. It is possible that there might be a statutory licence but this would not put the landlord in the position of licensor. Probably the best description is to call him the ex-tenant.

I have come to the conclusion that section 28 of the Act of 1980 has no retrospective effect. The words " a tenancy under which a dwelling H house is let as a separate dwelling " mean one which is let as a separate dwelling at or after the time of coming into force of the Act. It does not mean in the context of this Act " a tenancy under which a dwelling house was formerly let as a separate dwelling but where the ex-tenant remains in possession." Accordingly I would allow the appeal of Haringey London Borough Council and dismiss the appeals of Mr. Harrison and Mrs. Watson.

A   Sir David Cairns. I have had the advantage of reading beforehand the two judgments which have already been delivered. I entirely agree with the reasoning of both of those judgments, and accordingly I agree that the appeal of Haringey London Borough Council should be allowed, and the other two appeals should be dismissed.

B

> *Appeal of Mr. Harrison dismissed.*
> *Appeal of Haringey London Borough*
> *Council allowed.*
> *Appeal of Mrs. Watson dismissed.*
> *Leave to appeal refused.*

C   Solicitors: *Hammersmith and Fulham Community Law Centre; C. T. Mahoney; T. F. Neville; Tottenham Neighbourhood Law Centre; Hackney Law Centre; R. A. Benge.*

[Reported by Michael Hawkings, Esq., Barrister-at-Law]

D

[COURT OF APPEAL]

* ATTORNEY-GENERAL'S REFERENCE (No. 4 of 1979)

E   1980 June 9;   Lord Lane C.J., Boreham and
          July 14   Ralph Gibson JJ.

Crime—Theft—Handling stolen goods—Evidence—Cheques ob-
tained by deception—Cheques paid into bank account with
other moneys—Cheque drawn on balance representing defen-
dant's share of crime—Whether evidence of defendant handling
F *stolen goods—Theft Act* 1968 *(c. 60), ss. 22 (1), 24 (2)* [1]

    Over a period of six months a fellow employee of the defendant dishonestly obtained by deception from their employer cheques totalling £859 and paid them into her bank account. She also paid into that account during the same period cheques lawfully received from her employer representing amounts due to other employees, which she paid to them, and amounts lawfully earned by herself. She gave
G the defendant a cheque for £288·53. The defendant, who stated that she knew that cheques had been obtained by deception, said that she regarded the payment to her as " her share." She was charged with handling stolen goods, contrary to section 22 of the Theft Act 1968. At the end of the prosecution case, the recorder ruled that there was no evidence that the cheque paid to the defendant represented stolen goods and directed the jury to acquit the defendant.
H   On the Attorney-General's reference to the Court of Appeal on the point of law whether, where a payment was made out of a fund constituting money amounting to stolen goods and money not so tainted, or of a bank account similarly constituted, in such a way that the origin of the sum paid could not be identified with either portion of the fund, a jury was entitled to infer that the payment represented stolen goods

[1] Theft Act 1968. s. 24 (2): see post, p. 674G–H.

A.-G.'s Reference (No. 4 of 1979) (C.A.)   [1981]

A   from the intention of the parties that it should represent stolen goods or a share thereof: —

Held, that a cheque obtained by deception constituted stolen goods for the purposes of sections 22 and 24 of the Theft Act 1968 and, under section 24 (2), a balance in a bank account could be stolen goods as directly or indirectly representing the stolen cheque (post, p. 675A–C); that before the defendant could be convicted of handling stolen goods, it

B   had to be shown that she had received the cheque from the balance of the account representing the stolen goods; that, since the defendant was not in a position to know the source of the funds paid into the fellow employee's bank account, she could not give admissible evidence as to whether she had received in whole or in part the proceeds of the theft and, therefore, in the absence of evidence that she had received stolen goods, the case had been properly withdrawn from the

C   jury (post, pp. 675E–G, 676D–G).

Surujpaul v. *The Queen* [1958] 1 W.L.R. 1050, P.C. applied.

The following cases are referred to in the opinion of the court:

Attorney-General's Reference (No. 2 of 1975) [1976] 1 W.L.R. 710; [1976] 2 All E.R. 753, C.A.

Surujpaul v. *The Queen* [1958] 1 W.L.R. 1050; [1958] 3 All E.R. 300, P.C.

D

The following additional cases were cited in argument:

Banque Belge pour l'Etranger v. *Hambrouck* [1921] 1 K.B. 321, C.A.

Cory Brothers and Co. Ltd. v. *Owners of the Turkish Steamship " Mecca "* [1897] A.C. 286, H.L.(E.).

Devaynes v. *Noble (Clayton's Case)* (1816) 1 Mer. 572.

Diplock, In re [1948] Ch. 465; [1948] 2 All E.R. 318, C.A.

E   *Hallett's Estate, In re* (1880) 13 Ch.D. 696, Fry J. and C.A.

Kingston, Ex parte (1871) L.R. 6 Ch.App. 632.

Lupton v. *White* (1808) 15 Ves.Jun. 432.

McCormick v. *Grogan* (1869) L.R. 4 H.L. 82; H.L.(I.).

Oatway, In re [1903] 2 Ch. 356.

Tilley's Will Trusts, In re [1967] Ch. 1179; [1967] 2 W.L.R. 1533; [1967] 2 All E.R. 303.

F

REFERENCE by the Attorney-General under section 36 of the Criminal Justice Act 1972.

The Attorney-General referred a point of law for the opinion of the Court of Appeal in the following terms:

" 1. The Court of Appeal is asked to give its opinion on the following

G   point of law:

' Where a payment is made out of a fund constituted by a mixture of money amounting to stolen goods within the meaning of section 24 of the Theft Act 1968, and money not so tainted, or of a bank account similarly constituted, in such a way that the specific origin of the sum paid cannot be identified with either portion of the fund, is a jury entitled to infer that the payment represented stolen goods

H   within the meaning of section 24 (2) of the Act, from the intention of the parties that it should represent the stolen goods or a share thereof?'

" 2. The material facts of the case which gives rise to this reference are: (a) A fellow employee of the accused ('the thief') had a bank account into which each week over the period from September 13, 1976, to April 11, 1977, she paid cheques paid to her by their employer which

A represented (i) amounts earned by and due to fellow employees, which the thief was required to pay them; (ii) amounts earned by the thief; (iii) amounts dishonestly obtained by the thief's deception of the employer, namely, £859·70. The thief had paid out to fellow employees by cheque the amounts referred to in item (i). Each of the amounts (i), (ii) and (iii) was greater in total than the balance in the account at the relevant date, namely £641·32. (b) At the relevant date the thief handed

B to the accused a cheque drawn on the bank account for a sum less than half the balance, namely, £288·53. The accused in due course admitted knowing of the obtaining by deception of the extra amounts referred to in item (iii). It was open to the jury to conclude that her co-operation or at least acquiescence had been necessary for the deception to succeed. In answer to a question about the cheque paid to her: 'Was that your

C share?' the accused said: 'I suppose it was' and added that she still had the money in her account and: 'I suppose you could call it guilt, but I haven't touched it.' (c) The accused was charged that on the relevant date she dishonestly received certain stolen goods, namely, the cheque handed to her by the thief, knowing or believing the same to be stolen goods. (d) The prosecution wished to invite the jury to conclude

D that the thief and the accused intended the cheque as a share of the amounts dishonestly obtained by deception ('stolen' goods by virtue of section 24 (4) of the Theft Act 1968), and that it accordingly 'represented' what was originally obtained, as defined in section 24 (2) (a) of the Act. (e) At the close of the prosecution case the learned recorder withdrew the case from the jury and directed an acquittal. In his ruling he equated direct representation with conversion of goods into cash or

E other goods. Here there was no such direct representation. He rejected the prosecution submission that it was open to the jury to find that the cheque represented stolen goods if the parties so intended it, tempting though he said it was, since in his judgment the Act did not say or imply it. The Act would have said so if Parliament intended it, and it had to be strictly construed in favour of the defendant.

F   " 3. It is contended that the ruling was wrong in law. The effect of section 24 (2) (a) of the Act is easy to see in dealing with 'goods' in the ordinary meaning of the word. Thus in the example given in *Smith and Hogan, Criminal Law,* 4th ed. (1978), p. 605 of a thief who exchanges a stolen Austin for a Bentley, exchanges the Bentley for a Citroen, and sells the Citroen for £500, plainly all the cars are, for the purposes of handling, 'stolen goods.' So is the £500. If the thief hands part of the

G £500 to another, the latter is receiving stolen goods. But suppose the thief puts the £500 into his pocket, which already contains some honest money. If he takes a sum from that pocket, and hands it to another, both of them intending it as a share of the proceeds of the crime, is the sum 'stolen goods'? Of course, if it exceeds the amount of honest money, some of the payment must be part of the 'stolen' £500 in

H specie—and no problem arises; and the same applies if the 'stolen' £500 consists of identifiable notes. But suppose it is otherwise. Does it really matter which notes from the mixed fund are handed over? It is contended that common sense rebels against it. If the parties so intend, the money handed over 'represents' the stolen money in the ordinary meaning of the word. If the thief hands the £500 to a friend to keep for him, and the friend returns to him £500, then even if what he hands back is a different £500, it is contended that this is 'stolen goods' in exactly the same way as the Bentley and Citroen. There is no difference A in principle if it is the thief himself who substitutes one set of notes for another. Finally, it is contended that it does not alter the case when the transactions are made through the medium of rights of action against the bank instead of cash.

" 4. An additional argument is that the rules of common law and equity relating to tracing and the rules of equity relating to the right of a B beneficiary under a trust to trace trust assets which have passed through the bank account of a trustee to a volunteer confirm the contentions set out above.

" 5. A person who obtains the property of another by means of fraud becomes a constructive trustee of the property for the party who is injured by the fraud: *McCormick* v. *Grogan* (1869) L.R. 4 H.L. 82, 97.

" 6. Where an employee drew in his own favour a number of his C employer's cheques, forged his employer's signature on them, paid them into his own account and thereafter drew a cheque in favour of a volunteer, the employer was held to be entitled to recover the amount of the cheque from the volunteer: *Banque Belge pour l'Etranger* v. *Hambrouck* [1921] 1 K.B. 321.

" 7. Where, however, a trustee pays the trust assets into his own bank D account, where they are mixed with his own, the onus is upon the trustee to distinguish the separate assets. To the extent that he fails to do so, they belong to the trust: *In re Tilley's Will Trusts* [1967] Ch. 1179, 1183 and *Lupton* v. *White* (1808) 15 Ves.Jun. 432.

" 8. Where a trustee, who has mixed trust assets with his own in a bank account, draws a cheque on that account, with the intention of ' unmix- E ing' the trust assets from his own, that intention will have effect (*Ex parte Kingston* (1871) L.R. 6 Ch.App. 632 and *In re Diplock* [1948] Ch. 465, 552, 560–561) and will displace any presumption to the contrary (*In re Oatway* [1903] 2 Ch. 356 and *Cory Brothers and Co. Ltd.* v. *Owners of the Turkish Steamship 'Mecca'* [1897] A.C. 286).

" 9. The rule in *Devaynes* v. *Noble* (*Clayton's Case*) (1816) 1 Mer. 572, F that on a current account between banker and depositor each payment is impliedly appropriated to the earliest debt that is not statute-barred (in the absence of any express appropriation), is a rule for determining the intention of the parties.

" 10. The rule in *In re Hallett's Estate* (1880) 13 Ch.D. 696, whereby a trustee who draws for his own purposes on funds in a bank account containing a mixed fund of trust assets and his own, is, so far as is G possible, deemed to draw on his own assets first, even if they were the more recently paid into the account, is, likewise, a ruling for determining the intention of the trustee.

" 11. Accordingly, it is submitted that (a) the thief was at all material times a trustee of the ' stolen ' money, having a duty to keep it separate from her own; (b) the thief mixed the ' stolen ' money with her own in H her bank account, thereby impressing the whole of the funds in her account with the trust; (c) accordingly, the cheque drawn by the thief in favour of the accused transferred ' stolen ' money to the accused; (d) if the application of the rules in *Clayton's Case* and *In re Hallett's Estate* enable a distinction to be made between the ' stolen ' money and the thief's money in the thief's account, the intention of the thief to pass the property in the ' stolen ' money to the accused is evidence from

A which the jury can draw the inference that the cheque represented the
' stolen ' money or a part of it."

   Anthony Nicholl for the Attorney-General.
   Malcolm Lee for the defendant.

                                                      Cur. adv. vult.

B
       July 14. LORD LANE C.J. read the following judgment of the court.
   This reference by the Attorney-General arises out of a case in which the
   defendant was indicted on one count which alleged that she dishonestly
   received certain stolen goods, namely, a cheque for £288·53, knowing
   or believing the same to be stolen goods.
       After a submission on behalf of the defendant at the end of the
C prosecution case, the trial judge directed the jury to acquit. There was
   no issue as to the receipt by the defendant of the cheque, nor was it in
   dispute that the person who paid the cheque had previously obtained
   sums of money by dishonest deception, but the judge ruled that there
   was no evidence that the cheque so paid to the defendant was in law
   stolen goods.
D   The facts of the case were these. Over a period of six months in
   1976 and 1977, a fellow employee of the defendant obtained by deception
   from their employer certain cheques. It is convenient, for a brief reference, to refer to that fellow employee as " the thief." The thief paid
   those fraudulently obtained cheques into her bank account. During the
   same period the thief also paid into her bank account other cheques
   which she had lawfully received from her employer and which repre-
E sented, first, amounts earned by and due to fellow employees which she
   was required to pay on to those employees; and, secondly, sums lawfully
   earned by the thief. The total of the sums paid into the bank account
   by the thief as sums dishonestly obtained by deception from the employer
   was £859. The thief had duly paid out to the other employees the
   amounts she had received for such payments. On the date when the thief
F handed to the defendant the cheque for £288·53, the state of the thief's
   bank account was a credit balance of £641·32. The total amount lawfully
   received into the account by the thief for payment to other employees,
   which had been paid out to them, exceeded that balance of £641·32. The
   total amount lawfully received by the thief in respect of her own earnings and paid into the account had also exceeded £641·32. The court
   has no information as to the nature or purpose of other disbursements
G made from the account by the thief and assumes that there was no
   evidence.
       There was evidence that the defendant had admitted that she knew
   of the obtaining by deception of the £859 by the thief. It is said that
   there was evidence from which it would have been open to the jury to
   conclude that, for the continued deceptions of the thief to succeed, the
H co-operation or at least acquiescence of the defendant was necessary.
   Whatever the reason it was thought more appropriate to charge her with
   handling than with obtaining by deception.
       The defendant was asked about the cheque paid to her by the thief.
   One question asked of her was this: " Was that your share?" She
   replied: " I suppose it was." She added, according to the evidence which
   the jury was invited to consider: " I suppose you could call it guilt but
   I haven't touched it." Th e judge at the trial was invited to rule that there

was no evidence upon which the jury could conclude that the cheque   A
given to the defendant by the thief amounted in law to stolen goods
within the meaning of the Theft Act 1968.

Two points were taken on behalf of the defendant by counsel. First,
that the offence of handling stolen goods could not be committed with
reference to a stolen thing in action, or to a thing in action representing
stolen goods; secondly, that on the evidence before the court the offence
of handling stolen goods could not be proved.   B

As to the first point, the judge rejected the submission. As to the
second, the judge ruled that since the thief's bank account had been fed
by payments in the three categories described above, namely, (i) sums
lawfully obtained for payment on to other employees; (ii) sums lawfully
obtained as money earned by the thief; and (iii) the £859·70 dishonestly
obtained by deception, it was impossible for the prosecution to prove that   C
the payment made to the defendant was in law stolen goods. In reaching
his conclusion the judge said:

"I have to consider whether or not the cheque which the thief paid
to the defendant's account indirectly represents the stolen goods in
the hands of the thief. It is very tempting to say that if the drawer
of the cheque and the recipient of the cheque intend that the money   D
represented by the cheque shall represent that part of the choses in
action owed by the bank to the account holder which is stolen
money that that is sufficient for these purposes. But in my view
the Act does not say that. It does not imply it and I consider that
as I have to construe this part and every part of the Act strictly
that if Parliament had intended to provide for such a case it would
have said so."   E

It is from this conclusion on the second point that the point of law
referred to this court arises. The point of law referred to us under
section 36 (1) of the Criminal Justice Act 1972 is as follows:

"Where a payment is made out of a fund constituted by a mixture
of money amounting to stolen goods within the meaning of section   F
24 of the Theft Act 1968, and money not so tainted, or of a bank
account similarly constituted, in such a way that the specific origin
of the sum paid cannot be identified with either portion of the fund,
is a jury entitled to infer that the payment represented stolen goods
within the meaning of section 24 (2) of the Act, from the intention
of the parties that it should represent the stolen goods or a share
thereof?"   G

Before dealing with the substance of the question as it arose in the
instant case as a point of law, it is necessary to emphasise that the
power given to the Attorney-General to refer a point of law to this
court is a power to refer a point of law which actually arose in a real
case. There is no power to refer theoretical questions of law, however
interesting or difficult. As was said in this court by James L.J. in   H
Attorney-General's Reference (No. 2 of 1975) [1976] 1 W.L.R. 710, 714:
"A reference of a point of law under section 36 of the Act of 1972 is
not a reference in the abstract but is in relation to the case in which the
point has arisen."

The point of law as referred begins with reference to a fund constituted by a mixture of money. There was no mixture of money in this
case. The question continues with reference to a bank account consti-

A   tuted by a mixture of money. The court will deal with that part of the question, although we do not suggest that a mixed fund of money in specie would necessarily require to be treated in any different manner.

      The point of law as stated also refers to the fact that the bank account of the thief in this case had been fed with money of the three types stated: sums honestly received for onward payment to other employees; sums honestly received by and for the thief herself; and stolen money,

B   that is, the proceeds of cheques obtained by fraud. At the time of payment of the cheque for £288·53 to the defendant, that sum could not be objectively identified as coming from any one of the three types of money. So much is obvious from the nature of a bank account in which the balance is stated, for the purposes of the banker and of the customer, as the sum of the various credits and debits. At the trial, the attitude

C   of the prosecution was, as stated by the judge, that it was impossible to say what part of the money in the thief's account represented stolen goods, and the prosecution therefore submitted that the intention of the parties, that is of the paying thief and of the receiver of the payment, must be looked at as at the time when the money passed. The question referred to us assumes, in conformity with that attitude, that, apart from proof of what any party to the payment *said* about her intention at the

D   time of payment, it was impossible to demonstrate that the balance in the account at the time of payment, or the particular payment made, was to be regarded, for the purposes of the prosecution, as having originated from any particular type of money in the account.

      The submissions which have been made can be summarised as follows. Mr. Lee, who has appeared to support the ruling made by the judge, has

E   submitted that the offence of handling cannot be committed with reference to a thing in action, at least so far as concerns handling by receiving. He made it clear that this was not the main point of his argument and he did no more than raise the point for the court's consideration. He referred us to passages in *Smith, The Law of Theft,* 4th ed. (1979), and in *Smith and Hogan, Criminal Law,* 4th ed. (1978), in which the point was discussed.

F   The main submission developed by Mr. Lee was that, where a bank account was made up of a mixture of credit, some lawfully obtained and some dishonestly obtained, as in this case, the receipt of a payment of part of that mixed fund cannot be demonstrated as being in law the receipt of stolen goods. Once the identity of the dishonestly obtained or stolen money is destroyed by mixing in the account with untainted money,

G   that identity as stolen money cannot be subsequently revived by any evincing or proof of intention on the part of the holder of the account or of the recipient of a payment. This conclusion was, said Mr. Lee, a consequence in law of the nature of money.

      On behalf of the Attorney-General on the reference Mr. Nicholl has submitted that a chose in action was capable of being stolen goods within the meaning of section 24 (2) of the Theft Act 1968, that is as

H

        " other goods which directly or indirectly represent . . . the stolen
        goods in the hands of the thief as being the proceeds of any disposal
        or realisation . . . of the goods stolen . . ."

Next, he submitted that the receipt of a payment out of a mixed bank account, like that of the thief in this case, could be proved by admissible evidence to constitute the receipt of stolen goods if it could thereby be shown that the intention of the thief, in making payment out of the

674

mixed fund, was to pay to the receiver all or part of that part of the   A
mixed fund which represented the stolen goods in the hands of the thief.

Mr. Nicholl contended that the matter should be approached by
examining first whether, upon the evidence of the payments in and out
of the account, it was possible that, at the date of the payment in
question, that payment could constitute part of the mixed fund which
represented the stolen goods. If that is shown to be possible—he argued
as at the date that the cheque is drawn—then, according to his sub-   B
mission, it is necessary to consider whether by admissible evidence it is
demonstrated that the thief, in paying the money, intended the payment
to be part of the mixed fund which represented the stolen goods. If a
prima facie case to that effect is made out the jury must be allowed to
consider the whole case, and, if they think right, to reach the conclusion
that the payment received represented stolen goods within the meaning   C
of section 24 (2) of the Act of 1968. If they could reach that conclusion,
of course, the jury would have to consider the other essential issues as
to whether the defendant knew or believed the payment to represent
stolen goods and whether she received the payment dishonestly.

Perhaps because it was thought that admissible and effective evidence
of the intention of the thief in making any such payment might rarely
be available, Mr. Nicholl contended that the rules of common law and   D
equity, which relate to the principle of tracing property, and the rules of
equity relating to the right of a beneficiary under a trust to trace trust
assets which have passed through the bank account of a trustee to a volunteer, were of assistance to his submissions. He said that the Theft Act 1968
was enacted by reference to and against the background of the general
law of property; that the rules of common law and equity which relate   E
to tracing and restitution supported the general argument that the nature
of a payment out of a mixed fund could be determined by reference to
the intention of the payer; and that a jury should be directed in such a
case as this to consider those rules of law and equity and have regard to
them in deciding whether the money paid out of the mixed fund bank
account by the thief was proved to have been part of the money dishonestly obtained by the thief. Reference was made to a number of   F
cases (paragraphs 5 to 11 of the reference).

We can begin the statement of our opinion upon the point of law
referred to us by observing that the cheque which the defendant was
alleged to have received was, plainly, not part of the goods originally
stolen or obtained. In order to succeed, therefore, the prosecution had
to bring the case within the terms of section 24 (2) of the Theft Act 1968,   G
which defines the scope of offences relating to the handling of stolen
goods. The relevant provisions are contained in section 24 (2), which
reads:

"... references to stolen goods shall include ... (a) any other goods
which directly or indirectly represent or have at any time represented
the stolen goods in the hands of the thief as being the proceeds   H
of any disposal or realisation of the whole or part of the goods
stolen ..."

By section 24 (4) the reference to "goods which have been stolen"
includes goods which have been obtained by deception.

It was submitted that the language of section 24 (2) (a) afforded some
support for the first point made on behalf of the defendant, namely, that
a thing in action cannot be handled by receiving within section 22 of the

A Theft Act 1968. By section 34 (2) (*b*), however, the interpretation section of this Act, " goods," except where the context otherwise requires, " includes money and every other description of property except land, and includes things severed from the land . . ." Further by the combined effect of section 4 (1) and section 34 (2), " property " includes money and all other property, real and personal, including things in action. In

B our judgment therefore it is clear from that extended definition of " goods " that a cheque obtained by deception constitutes stolen goods for the purposes of sections 22 and 24 of the Act.

Next, it is clear that a balance in a bank account, being a debt, is itself a thing in action which falls within the definition of goods and may therefore be goods which directly or indirectly represent stolen goods for the purposes of section 24 (2) (*a*). Further where, as in the present case,

C a person obtains cheques by deception and pays them into her bank account, the balance in that account may, to the value of the tainted cheques, be goods which " directly . . . represent . . . the stolen goods in the hands of the thief as being the proceeds of any disposal or realisation of . . . the goods stolen . . ." within the meaning of section 24 (2) (*a*).

D If, however, the prosecution is to prove dishonest handling by receiving, it is necessary to prove that what the handler received was in fact the whole or part of the stolen goods within the meaning of section 24 (2) (*a*). To prove that, the prosecution must prove (i) that at the material time, namely, at the time of receipt by the handler, in such a case as this, the thief's bank balance was in fact comprised, at least in part, of that which represented the proceeds of stolen goods; and (ii) that the handler

E received, at least in part, such proceeds. In some cases no difficulty will arise. For example, if the thief opened a new account and paid into it only dishonestly obtained cheques, then the whole balance would constitute stolen goods within the meaning of section 24 (2) (*a*). If then the thief transferred the whole balance to a defendant, that defendant would, in our opinion, have received stolen goods. By the same reasoning, if at

F the material time the whole of the balance in an account consisted only of the proceeds of stolen goods, then any cheque drawn on that account would constitute stolen goods within section 24 (2) (*a*). We have no doubt that when such a cheque is paid, so that part of such a balance in the thief's account is transferred to the credit of the receiver's account, the receiver has received stolen goods because he has received a thing in

G action which " . . . directly . . . represent[s] . . . the stolen goods in the hands of the thief as being the proceeds of . . . realisation of the . . . goods stolen . . ." The same conclusion follows where the receiver directly cashes the cheque drawn on the thief's account and receives money from the paying bank.

The allegation in this case was that the defendant received stolen

H goods when she received the thief's cheque. Mr. Lee, in the course of argument, was disposed to accept a suggestion from a member of the court that a cheque drawn by the thief, directed to her bank, and intended to enable the defendant to obtain transfer of part of the thief's credit balance, or cash, might not itself be stolen goods within the meaning of section 24 (2) (*a*). The point is not necessary for decision on the point of law referred to us and it has not been fully argued. It appears to us that there is much to be said in favour of the proposition that

receipt of such a cheque, drawn in circumstances wherein it is plain that   A
it must serve to transfer the proceeds of stolen goods, would constitute
receiving stolen goods on the ground that such a cheque would directly
or indirectly represent the stolen goods within section 24 (2) (*a*).

The difficulties arise for the prosecution where, as in the present case,
the stolen cheques are paid into a mixed account containing sums honestly
obtained. In our opinion the difficulties are of proof and not of principle.   B
The mere fact that stolen cheques have been paid into a mixed account
will often render more difficult proof that at least part of what was
received by a defendant from that account represented the stolen goods
in the hands of the thief as being the proceeds of the goods stolen. It does
not preclude such proof. In some circumstances proof may be simple.
For example, a particular account, into which it is proved that stolen
cheques were paid, may have been little used with few cheques drawn   C
on it. It might readily be demonstrated that the sum paid to the defendant was in excess of that part of the balance which could possibly
represent the proceeds of honest cheques. In such circumstances the
defendant would be shown to have received stolen goods within section
24 (2) (*a*).

In the present case the prosecution sought such proof, as to the nature   D
of the payment received by the defendant, from the statement which the
defendant made as to her understanding and intention when the payment
was made. She had said that she regarded the payment to her as " her
share." In our opinion, such an admission could not by itself prove
either that part of the thief's bank balance did or could represent
stolen goods within section 24 (2) (*a*), or that part of such stolen goods
was received by the defendant. Her admission was, of course, plainly   E
admissible on the issue of her knowledge that the payment represented
stolen goods, and as to her honestly in receiving the money. On the
issue of fact, however, as to whether the cheque received by her represented stolen goods, the primary rule is that a defendant can only make
a valid and admissible admission of a statement of fact of which the
defendant could give admissible evidence: see *Surujpaul* v. *The Queen*   F
[1958] 1 W.L.R. 1050. It is not necessary in this case to examine the
limits of, or the extent of any exceptions from, that primary rule.

In our opinion Mr. Nicholl was right in his submission when he
acknowledged that the prosecution must, in such a case as this, prove
in the first place than any payment out of a mixed account *could*, by
reference to payments in and out, be a payment representing stolen
goods. Unless she had personal knowledge of the working of the thief's   G
account, the defendant could make no valid admission as to that.

It is to be noted that the point of law referred to us contains the words:
" Is a jury entitled to infer . . . from the intention of the parties . . ."
The use of the plural " parties " is misleading. There was no direct
evidence in this case of what the intention of the thief might have been,
only of that of the receiver. It may perhaps be that a payment can be   H
proved to have been a payment of money representing stolen goods,
even where there was enough honest money in the account to cover
the payment, if there is proof direct or by way of necessary inference
of the intention of the paying thief to pay out the stolen money. That
problem can be decided when it arises. It does not do so here. The
prosecution did not advance their case on such a basis. The only question
arising on the facts here is whether a jury is entitled to infer that the

A payment represented stolen goods within section 24 (2) (*a*) from the intention or belief of the receiver that it should or did. The answer is " no."

Opinion accordingly.

Solicitors : *Director of Public Prosecutions; Pickering & Butters, Stafford.*

B

[Reported by LEO PILKINGTON, ESQ., Barrister-at-Law]

C

[COURT OF APPEAL]

* WESTMINSTER CITY COUNCIL *v.* HAYMARKET PUBLISHING LTD.

1981   Feb. 26, 27;   Lord Denning M.R., Shaw
D   March 2   and Oliver L.JJ.

*Rating—Unoccupied hereditament—Surcharge—Commercial build-
ing unoccupied for more than six months—Legal charge in
favour of mortgagee prior in time to rating authority's charge
—Whether rating authority's charge on all interests in land—
Whether binding on purchasers from mortgagee—General Rate
Act 1967 (c. 9), ss. 17A, 17B (3) (7) (as amended by Local
E   Government Act 1974 (c. 7), s. 16)*

On January 3, 1974, a company acquired certain commercial premises, which it charged by way of legal mortgage in favour of a bank, to secure all moneys and indebtedness present and future owing by the company to the bank. The premises remained empty and unused for a period extending beyond October 24, 1975, and a rating surcharge amounting to £16,940·93 became payable under section 17A (1) of the General Rate Act 1967. By section 17B of the Act [1] a surcharge was to be a " charge on the land comprised in the hereditament " until recovered. On March 19, 1976, the bank served a demand for payment of the amount due under the bank's legal charge. In April 1976 the rating authority demanded payment of the surcharge and registered it in the land charges registry as a local charge. In August 1977 the bank, in exercise of its powers as legal mortgagee, sold the premises to the defendants. In the contract of sale the bank agreed to indemnify the defendants against the rating surcharge, if that charge was binding on them. Dillon J. held that the charge was a charge on the bank's interest as mortgagee and took priority over all interests in the land.

On appeal by the defendants : —

Held, dismissing the appeal, that, on its true construction a " charge on the land " in section 17B meant a charge on all the estates and interests in the land, and, accordingly, the charge took priority over the mortgage debt owing to the bank and was binding on the defendants.

Birmingham Corporation v. *Baker* (1881) 17 Ch.D. 782 and *Paddington Borough Council* v. *Finucane* [1928] Ch. 567 applied.

F

G

H

[1] General Rate Act 1967, s. 17A: see post, p. 679H.
S. 17B (3) (7): see post, p. 680A.

Westminster Council v. Haymarket Publishing (C.A.)   **[1981]**

    Per curiam. Section 17A of the Act contemplates only a   A
single owner on whom the surcharge is to be levied. As
between mortgagor and mortgagee it is quite plain that unless
and until the mortgagee enters into possession, in accordance
with the mortgage law, and takes the rents and profits, the
mortgagor is the person entitled to possession. The " owner "
under section 17A is the person who really has control of the
letting (post, pp. 680B–C, 681C–E).

    Decision of Dillon J. [1980] 1 W.L.R. 683; [1980] 1 All E.R.   B
289 affirmed.

The following cases are referred to in the judgments:

Birmingham Corporation v. *Baker* (1881) 17 Ch.D. 782.
Paddington Borough Council v. *Finucane* [1928] Ch. 567.
Tendring Union (Guardians of) v. *Dowton* [1891] 3 Ch. 265, C.A.

                                                     C

The following additional cases were cited in argument:

Banister v. *Islington London Borough Council* (1972) 71 L.G.R. 239, D.C.
Bristol Corporation v. *Virgin* [1928] 2 K.B. 622.
London Corporation v. *Cusack-Smith* [1955] A.C. 337; [1955] 2 W.L.R.
   363; [1955] 1 All E.R. 302, H.L.(E.).
Tottenham Local Board of Health v. *Rowell* (1880) 15 Ch.D. 378, C.A.

                                                     D

APPEAL from Dillon J.

    The defendants, Haymarket Publishing Ltd., owners of premises at
22 Lancaster Gate, London W.2, appealed against a judgment of Dillon J.
given on October 18, 1979, in which he declared that a rating surcharge
of £16,940·93 payable in respect of those premises to the rating authority,
Westminster City Council, by virtue of sections 17A and 17B of the   E
General Rate Act 1967, and registered on April 22, 1976, under the
provisions of the Local Land Charges Act 1975, had priority over and
bound the defendants' interest in the land and all other interests in the
land.

    The defendants appealed by a notice of appeal dated March 24, 1980,
seeking a declaration that the rating authority's charge (a) took priority   F
according to the date on which it arose and was registered, and therefore
ranked after a legal mortgage of the land dated January 4, 1974, between
the then owners, Shop Investments Ltd., and the National Westminster
Bank Ltd. as mortgagees; and (b) was overridden by the sale to the
defendants under the power of sale in the mortgage.

    The grounds of the appeal were that the judge was wrong in law in
holding that the rating authority's charge on the land was a charge on   G
all the interests in the land, and therefore had priority over the mortgage,
and in failing to hold that the charge affected only the interest of the
owner of the land, namely the freehold interest of Shop Investments Ltd.
subject to the mortgage.

    By a respondent's notice dated September 2, 1980, the rating authority
sought to uphold the judgment of Dillon J. on the additional ground   H
that the National Westminster Bank Ltd., as legal mortgagee, was at all
material times an owner or the owner of the land, whether or not Shop
Investments Ltd. was also an owner.

    The facts are stated in the judgment of Lord Denning M.R.

Peter Millett Q.C. and *Gregory Hill* for the defendants.
W. J. Mowbray Q.C. and *Colin Braham* for the rating authority.

A   March 2.   The following judgments were read.

LORD DENNING M.R.   On the north side of Hyde Park there is an
elegant period property, no. 22, Lancaster Gate.   It was very suitable
for use as offices by high class organisations.   But it remained empty for
many months, like the notorious Centre Point.   The owners did not try
to let it to anyone.   It suited them better, in days of inflation, to let it
B   remain empty, not paying rates.
Parliament did not approve of such goings on.   So in 1974 they
enacted provisions under which the local authority could impose a
surcharge on commercial buildings left empty in this way.   If a commercial building was left empty for 12 months the surcharge would be
double the normal rates.   Treble in the second 12 months.   Quadruple in
C   the third 12 months.   And so forth.
The question in this case is whether the surcharge applies to commercial buildings which are mortgaged up to the hilt.   Is the surcharge
payable by the mortgagor, or by the mortgagee?   If it is not paid, how
can it be enforced?
This building at no. 22, Lancaster Gate was bought on February 3,
D   1974, by a company called Shop Investments Ltd.   That company was a
subsidiary of a holding company Amalgamated Investment and Property
Company Ltd.   Shop Investments Ltd. guaranteed the indebtedness of the
holding company to the National Westminster Bank Ltd.   It came to
over £6 million.   As security, Shop Investments Ltd., mortgaged no. 22,
Lancaster Gate to the bank.   It was by way of a charge of legal mortgage
on February 4, 1974.   A few days later, on February 8, 1974, the Local
E   Government Act 1974 was passed, bringing the surcharge into effect for
empty properties left unused.
Despite the new Act, Shop Investments Ltd. left no. 22, Lancaster
Gate empty.   They left it empty for nearly two years.   They made no effort
to let it.   This came to the notice of the Westminster City Council.   They
decided to levy a surcharge for the period from February 8, 1974, when
the Act came into force, to October 24, 1975, that being the period
F   when the mortgagors had made no effort to let it at all.   The surcharge
came to £16,940·93.   The Westminster City Council registered it in the
Local Land Charges Registry.
In 1977 the holding company went into liquidation, owing the bank
£6 million.   The bank, as mortgagees, sold the property to Haymarket
Publishing Ltd. for £220,000.   The Westminster City Council claim that
G   this surcharge of £16,940·93 takes priority over the mortgage debt.   But
the bank say that the mortgage debt of £6 million takes priority over
the surcharge of £16,940·93.   So the practical question is: who gets the
£16,940·93?   The Westminster City Council or the bank?
It all comes down to the correct interpretation of two sections which
were inserted in the General Rate Act 1967 by section 16 of the Local
Government Act 1974.   It is written in by two supplemental sections, 17A
H   and 17B.   Section 17A says who is to pay the surcharge.   It says:

" (1) If for a continuous period exceeding six months a commercial
building is not used for the purpose for which it was constructed
or has been adapted, its owner shall pay in respect of that period
. . . a surcharge additional to the rates (if any) payable apart from
this section."

So there is the liability to pay put upon the owner.   The meaning of

" owner " is defined in section 17B (7): ". . . ' owner ' means the person   A
entitled to possession. . . ." If the owner does not pay, then section 17B
provides for how it can be enforced. Section 17B (3) says: " A surcharge
imposed under section 17A of this Act in respect of a hereditament shall
until recovered be a charge on the land comprised in the hereditament; . . ."

The first question is: who is liable to pay the rates? Who is the
" owner?" Who is " entitled to possession " when it is a question   B
between mortgagor and mortgagee? It is quite plain to my mind that
unless and until the mortgagee enters into possession, in accordance with
the mortgage law, and takes the rents and profits, the mortgagor is the
person entitled to possession. He is the person who is entitled to put up
advertisements, to let and do all that is necessary to let—unless and until
the mortgagee interferes. It seems to me that the " owner " under section   C
17A is not two, three or more people. It is the one who really has control
of the letting. In this case the " owner " means the mortgagor, Shop
Investments Ltd. They were liable to pay the surcharge. No doubt
Westminster City Council could sue them for it if they were worth suing
—which unfortunately they are not.

Then under section 17B we get the provision that the surcharge is
" a charge on the land." What does that mean? I agree that it is   D
ambiguous. The meaning is difficult to discover from the words of the
statute. But fortunately there has been a series of cases in the courts
which lead inevitably to the interpretation that it means a charge on
" all the estates and interests in the land." I will go through the series
of cases which lead to this result. The first is *Birmingham Corporation*
v. *Baker* (1881) 17 Ch.D. 782. In that case there was a charge on the   E
" premises." Sir George Jessel M.R. said, at p. 786:

" Now, the houses per se being inanimate, they cannot bear the
burden. If there be a charge on the houses it is a charge on the
total ownership—if I may call it so, on the proprietorship; not on
any particular section or portion of the proprietorship, but on the
whole."   F

The next case is the *Guardians of Tendring Union* v. *Dowton* [1891]
3 Ch. 265. That again was a question of a charge on the " premises."
I would pick out the words of Fry L.J., at p. 269: " All the Act does is
to create a charge on the premises—that is, on the land—that is, on all
the interests of the owners of the land."

To finish the citations, I would refer to *Paddington Borough Council*   G
v. *Finucane* [1928] Ch. 567. That was a decision of Russell J., who said
of the Public Health Act 1875, at p. 575:

" . . . when it confers a charge on the premises, [it] means not a
charge only on the interests of the rack-rent owner in the premises,
but a charge upon the entirety of the interests of the premises, the
whole of the proprietary interests of the premises."   H

Having regard to that line of authorities, it seems to me that we
should interpret the words in this statute, " a charge on the land comprised in the hereditament," in the same sense.

It was suggested that it should be confined to cases where the charge
was in respect of improvements or expenses incurred upon the land—
as happened in some of those cases—and that it should not apply to a
charge in respect of a penal provision such as this. That distinction is

The Weekly Law Reports, May 22, 1981

681

1 W.L.R.   Westminster Council v. Haymarket Publishing (C.A.)   Lord Denning M.R.

A not well-founded. The issue depends simply on the interpretation of the words in the statute. It seems to me that " a charge on the land " means a charge on " all the estates and interests in the land."

This conforms with the intention of Parliament. Any other view would mean that it would be open to companies, by manipulation of their affairs between holding and subsidiary companies, to avoid the charge altogether. The land could be bought in the name of a subsidiary
B company with money obtained on mortgage from a holding company: and, lo and behold, the charge would be gone. That cannot be right. The judge was quite right in holding that there was a charge on the land in favour of Westminster City Council, and that it took priority over the mortgage debt which was owing to the bank.

I would dismiss the appeal accordingly.

C
SHAW L.J. I agree. I would only add that support is to be found in the subsection itself for limiting the application of the phrase " person entitled to possession " where it appears in section 17B (7) of the Act to the person who is at material times actually exercising that right. It provides for apportionment between persons who become successively entitled to possession during a period of non-use. This could hardly be
D apt in relation to persons who are in law collaterally and contemporaneously entitled to possession.

I would dismiss the appeal.

OLIVER L.J. I also agree. It is quite clear, in my judgment, that section 17A contemplates, contrary to Mr. Mowbray's submission, only
E one owner—a single individual or persons holding jointly—on whom the surcharge would be levied. But that, of course, is not conclusive of the matter because the question at issue is the ambit of the charge which is imposed by section 17B (3). In section 17B (2) it is said:

" References in section 17A of this Act and this section to a commercial building are references to a hereditament . . . whose net annual value falls to be ascertained under section 19 (2) of this
F Act; . . ."

So quite clearly the hereditament there is the commercial building.

Then one comes to subsection (3), where it is provided: " A surcharge imposed under section 17A of this Act in respect of a hereditament shall until recovered be a charge on the land comprised in the hereditament; . . ." This is a formula which is familiar in other statutes,
G for instance the Public Health Act 1936 and Housing Acts, and Lord Denning M.R. has already referred to cases in which similar words have been construed.

What is there in this statute to restrict the words in section 17B (3) in such a way as to lead to the conclusion that they do not mean exactly what they say? There is the fact, first of all, that this is a charge imposed
H by way of a penalty. It may be argued that the statute should be construed restrictively, but that by itself does not, I think, justify the court in concluding that the section does not mean exactly what it says. Then it is said that it is very unfair that the effect of the charge is to make the recovery of the rates from persons such as mortgagees, tenants and owners who are not in possession and were not under an original liability. But the words of the statute are, as I think, plain and one must start from the position that Parliament must have been aware of how

Oliver L.J.   Westminster Council v. Haymarket Publishing (C.A.)   [1981]

similar words in previous statutes had been construed. If it had been   A
intended to confine the charge to the interest of the owner in the premises,
nothing would have been simpler than to have said so. The legislature
did not do that.

I agree that the judge came to the right conclusion, and I too would
dismiss the appeal.

Appeal dismissed with costs.
Leave to appeal refused.   B

Solicitors: *Wilde Sapte; Solicitor, Westminster City Council.*

R. C. W.

C

[CHANCERY DIVISION]

* *In re* THOMPSON & RICHES LTD. (IN LIQUIDATION)

1981   Jan. 12; 16   Slade J.

D

Company—Register—Restoration to register—Winding up petition
presented before dissolution of company—Winding up order
made and perfected after dissolution—Court's discretion to
declare dissolution void—Companies Act 1948 (11 & 12 Geo.
6, c. 38), ss. 352 (1), 353 (5) (6) [1]

A private company ceased to carry on business in 1973
and, thereafter, no annual returns were filed as required by   E
section 124 of the Companies Act 1948. The petitioner, a
shareholder in the company, presented a petition for the
winding up of the company on August 14, 1979, at a time
when, unknown to the petitioner, the Registrar of Companies,
in the exercise of his powers under section 353 of the Act,
was preparing to dissolve the company. The company's name
was struck off the register and it was dissolved on August 21.
On November 12, the court ordered that the company be   F
wound up and the official receiver was appointed provisional
liquidator. The winding up order was perfected on December 5.

On the petitioner's motion for a declaration that the dissolution of the company was void under section 352 (1) of
the Act: —

Held, that, under section 353 (5) (*b*) of the Companies
Act 1948, the court had power to wind up a company which
had been struck off the register and consequently the winding   G
up order was a valid order even though the name of the
company had not been restored to the register (post, pp. 685H,
686B–C).

that where a company's name had been struck off the register,
a petitioner was entitled to apply to the court for relief either
under section 353 (6) or section 352 (1); and that, since the
petitioner had chosen to apply for relief under section 352 (1),
the court, in the circumstances of the present case, would   H
exercise its discretion under that subsection and declare that
the dissolution of the company was void (post, pp. 687H—
688C, F–H).

In re Test Holdings (Clifton) Ltd. [1970] Ch. 285 and
In re Cambridge Coffee Room Association Ltd. [1952] 1 All
E.R. 112 applied.

[1] Companies Act 1948, s. 352 (1): see post, pp. 683H—684A.
   S. 353 (5) (6): see post, pp. 683G–H, 684A–C.

1 W.L.R.   **In re Thompson & Riches Ltd. (Ch.D.)**

A   The following cases are referred to in the judgment:

Cambridge Coffee Room Association Ltd., In re [1952] 1 All E.R. 112.
Test Holdings (Clifton) Ltd., In re [1970] Ch. 285; [1969] 3 W.L.R. 606;
[1969] 3 All E.R. 517.

No additional cases were cited in argument.

B   MOTIONS

By notice of motion dated August 22, 1980, the petitioner, Michael
Frederick John Thompson, as a contributory of Thompson & Riches Ltd.
(" the company ") applied to the court under section 352 (1) of the Companies Act 1948 for a declaration that the dissolution of the company on
August 21, 1979, was void. By a second notice of motion dated November
C   11, 1980, the petitioner sought an order that he be at liberty to amend the
petition dated August 14, 1979, for the winding up of the company to
include an application for a declaration that the dissolution was void
and that the winding up order dated November 12, 1979, might be amended
by the addition of an order that the dissolution of the company was void
prior to the making of that order.

The facts are stated in the judgment of Slade J.

D

R. D. Hacker for the petitioner.
John Lindsay for the official receiver.

Cur. adv. vult.

January 16. SLADE J. read the following judgment. There are before
E   me two motions issued in somewhat unusual circumstances. In each of
them the applicant is Mr. M. F. J. Thompson, who is a contributory of a
company known as Thompson & Riches Ltd. The first seeks a declaration, under section 352 (1) of the Companies Act 1948, that the dissolution
of the company is void. The second seeks an order that the petitioner
may be at liberty to amend a petition for the winding up of the company
which was presented by him on August 14, 1979, and that a winding up
F   order made by the court in respect of the company and perfected on
December 5, 1979, may be amended by the addition of an order that the
dissolution of the company may be declared void immediately prior to its
winding up.

The company has been struck off the Register of Companies and dissolved by virtue of section 353 (5) of the Companies Act 1948. For ease
of subsequent reference, I shall begin by setting out the relevant statutory
G   provisions. Section 353 (5) so far as material for present purposes provides:

" At the expiration of the time mentioned in the notice the registrar
may, unless cause to the contrary is previously shown by the company,
strike its name off the register, and shall publish notice thereof in the
Gazette, and on the publication in the Gazette of this notice the
company shall be dissolved: provided that . . . (*b*) nothing in this
H   subsection shall affect the power of the court to wind up a company
the name of which has been struck off the register."

Section 352 (1) of the Act of 1948 provides:

" Where a company has been dissolved, the court may at any time
within two years of the date of the dissolution, on an application
being made for the purpose by the liquidator of the company or by
any other person who appears to the court to be interested, make an

684

order, upon such terms as the court thinks fit, declaring the dissolution   A
to have been void, and thereupon such proceedings may be taken as
might have been taken if the company had not been dissolved."

Section 353 (6) provides:

" If a company or any member or creditor thereof feels aggrieved by
the company having been struck of the register, the court on an application made by the company or member or creditor before the expira-   B
tion of 20 years from the publication in the Gazette of the notice
aforesaid may, if satisfied that the company was at the time of the
striking off carrying on business or in operation, or otherwise that it
is just that the company be restored to the register, order the name of
the company to be restored to the register, and upon an office copy
of the order being delivered to the registrar for registration the com-   C
pany shall be deemed to have continued in existence as if its name
had not been struck off; and the court may by the order give such
directions and make such provisions as seem just for placing the
company and all other persons in the same position as nearly as may
be as if the name of the company had not been struck off."

Finally, section 354 provides: D

" Where a company is dissolved, all property and rights whatsoever
vested in or held on trust for the company immediately before its
dissolution (including leasehold property but not including property
held by the company on trust for any other person) shall, subject and
without prejudice to any order which may at any time be made by
the court under the two last foregoing sections, be deemed to be bona   E
vacantia and shall accordingly belong to the Crown, or to the Duchy
of Lancaster or to the Duke of Cornwall for the time being, as the
case may be, and shall vest and may be dealt with in the same manner
as other bona vacantia accruing to the Crown, to the Duchy of
Lancaster or to the Duke of Cornwall."

In the present case the company was incorporated in March 1965   F
under the Act of 1948 as a private company limited by shares. Its nominal
capital is £15,000 divided into 15,000 shares of £1 each. The amount of
its capital paid up or credited as paid up is £14,600. The petitioner holds
5,000 fully paid-up shares in the company, of which he holds one as the
administrator of his late mother. According to his evidence, he has never
been an active participant in the business of the company. The history
of the matter up to February 22, 1978, is conveniently summarised as   G
follows in paragraphs 7 to 13 of the winding up petition, which the
petitioner has verified on oath:

" 7. The company was formed to carry on the business of retail
dealers in milk. The company ceased to carry on business in or about
early 1973. It has not carried on business since and it would appear
unlikely that it will ever resume business. 8. Certain of the milk   H
rounds which were the company's undertaking were sold on or about
March 9, 1973, April 8, 1974, and March 12, 1975, for £5,000, £3,500
and £5,033 respectively. The company has sold and/or is in the
process of selling off its commercial vehicles. 9. No annual return
has been made by the company under section 124 of the Companies
Act 1948 since the return for 1973, which said return was made up to
May 10, 1973. The annual returns of the company for the years

A   1970, 1971 and 1972 were, however, made up to the end of December
or thereabouts of each said year. 10. The company has failed to hold
annual general meetings since in or about 1973 or has failed to give
your petitioner notice of any such meetings as may have been held.
11. On numerous occasions in 1975, 1976 and 1977 your petitioner
made written and oral requests by himself and by his solicitors to
directors of the company for information about the general and finan-
B   cial position of the company and of the application of proceeds of
sale of the company's undertaking. The company has failed or
omitted to furnish any or any adequate information and has not made
up accounts to any date later than January 31, 1972. 12. On February
22, 1978, your petitioner gave notice that he required to be allowed
to inspect the register of, and copies of instruments creating, charges
C   over the company, and books containing the minutes of the proceedings of any general meetings of the company, to be sent copies of
certain said documents, and that he required the directors to hold an
extraordinary general meeting under section 132 of the Companies
Act 1948. 13. On February 22, 1978, the petitioner's agent was
informed by one W. Joice, a director of the company, that all documents referred to in paragraph 12 hereof had been destroyed by fire,
D   and the company has failed to provide your petitioner with copies of
them. The directors have failed to hold the extraordinary general
meeting referred to in paragraph 12 hereof, or have failed to give
your petitioner notice of any such meeting."

On the basis of these facts the petitioner presented a winding up
petition to the court on August 14, 1979. Some months before that date,
E   the Registrar of Companies had taken steps with a view to the dissolution
of the company under the powers conferred on him by section 353 of the
Act of 1948, enabling him to take action in regard to defunct companies.
The petitioner and his solicitors had no knowledge that such steps had
been taken. On August 21, 1979, the company was dissolved under
section 353 (5) of the Act. The fact of the dissolution still did not for the
F   time being come to the notice of the petitioner or his solicitors. He therefore proceeded with his winding up petition in the ordinary way.

In a situation such as this, there is no procedure by which, before the
making of a winding up order, the court will gain knowledge of a prior
dissolution of the company concerned, unless this is brought to its attention
by the parties. Accordingly on November 12, 1979, no doubt in ignorance
of the prior dissolution, Oliver J. made the usual compulsory winding up
G   order in respect of the company under which, inter alia, one of the official
receivers attached to the court was constituted provisional liquidator of the
company's affairs.

In the absence of any authority, it might perhaps have appeared open
to possible question whether the court had power to wind up a company
the name of which had previously been struck off the register. The
H   existence of such power is, however, clearly recognised both by statute
and at least one reported decision of the court. Section 353 (5) (b) of
the Act of 1948 expressly provides that nothing in this subsection shall
affect the power of the court to wind up a company the name of which
has been struck off the register. Furthermore, in *In re Cambridge Coffee
Room Association Ltd.* [1952] 1 All E.R. 112, the name of a company
limited by guarantee had been struck off the register of companies and
the company itself had been dissolved pursuant to section 353 (5). Sub-

sequently two of the directors presented a petition to the court asking A
that (i) the name of the company might be restored to the register
pursuant to section 353 (6) and (ii) the company might be wound up.
Wynn-Parry J. in his judgment pointed out that the only question for
decision was whether or not it was convenient to restore the name of the
company to the register before making a winding up order. He said, at
p. 112:

B

> " In my judgment, it is more convenient to do so, but I do not intend
> to cast doubt on past cases where a compulsory winding-up order
> has been made without the name of the company having been
> restored to the register."

In these circumstances I conclude that the winding up order of November
12, 1979, was a valid order, even though the name of the company had C
not previously been restored to the register, and I shall for the rest of
this judgment proceed on that footing.

However, before leaving *In re Cambridge Coffee Room Association Ltd.*
[1952] 1 All E.R. 112, it should be observed that Wynn-Parry J. reached his
decision because he considered that doubt existed whether a compulsory
winding up order alone would amount to an order " made by the court
under the two last foregoing sections," within the meaning of section 354 of D
the Act of 1948, so as to divest the Crown of the interest in the company's
assets which the Crown would otherwise have under that section, and
so as to re-vest it in the company: see at p. 114. The essential purpose
of the present applications is to resolve the difficulties that would otherwise
arise from the existence of such doubt.

After the making of the winding up order in the present case, the
registrar of the court sent to the official receiver a notice informing him E
of it, pursuant to rule 38 of the Companies (Winding-up) Rules 1949.
As is his practice, the official receiver then proceeded to check the facts
asserted in the petition. This, as in other similar cases, was the first
independent investigation of these facts. During the course of it, he
discovered that the company had been dissolved on August 21, 1979,
that is after the date of the presentation of the petition, but before the F
making of the winding up order. Mr. Lindsay, who has appeared on
his behalf, tells me on instructions that, where the official receiver, during
the investigations following the making of a winding up order, discovers
that the company in question had already been dissolved before the making
of such order, it is his practice to communicate this information both
to the court and to the petitioner's solicitors. He tells me on instructions
that this was done in the present case.

G

The evidence sworn on behalf of the petitioner in support of his
present application suggested that neither he nor his solicitors knew of
the dissolution until after the winding up order was perfected. However,
Mr. Hacker, who appears for the petitioner, now tells he that his instructing
solicitors, after a further search of their files, have discovered that the
official receiver in fact informed them of the dissolution on or about H
November 15, 1979, that is about three weeks before the perfection of
the winding up order.

Following such communication, the course ordinarily adopted by
petitioners in such cases (which I think are not uncommon), is to come
to the court as soon as possible before the winding up order is perfected,
for the purposes of ensuring that the company's assets are vested in it
and not in the Crown, and that the liquidator will be able effectively to

A act as such. If a petitioner follows the common practice which has been adopted in the light of the decision in *In re Cambridge Coffee Room Association Ltd.* [1952] 1 All E.R. 112, he will ask for (1) rescission of the existing winding up order; (2) liberty to amend his petition, so as to include an application for restoration of the name of the company to the register; (3) an order for such restoration; and (4) a new winding up order. In my experience this course usually gives rise to few difficulties.

B   Regrettably, I think, for reasons which are not entirely clear to me, this was not the course adopted by the petitioner's legal advisers in the present case. This is the factor which makes it an unusual one. Instead, without making any further application to the court, they allowed the winding up order to be perfected in the ordinary way and in the common form on December 5, 1979. The subsequent course of events, so far as

C material for present purposes, was as follows. On August 22, 1980, the petitioner issued the first notice of motion which is now before me, seeking a declaration that the dissolution of the company is void, the notice being addressed to the official receiver as respondent. This motion came on for hearing for the first time on October 20, 1980. Mr. Hacker has reminded me that, earlier that day, I made an order in a somewhat similar case, granting relief to a petitioner by way of an amendment of a winding

D up order under the " slip rule ": R.S.C., Ord. 20, r. 11. I recollect making some such order, but do not recall the name or any other particulars of the case.

    On October 20, counsel for the petitioner in the present case informed me that the notice of motion had not yet been served on the official receiver. He asked for, and obtained, an adjournment of 28 days for

E the purpose of such service, and of considering whether relief should be sought in the alternative under the slip rule.

    On November 11, 1980, the petitioner issued the second notice of motion which is now before me. The persons named as respondents to it are the company, the official receiver and the Treasury Solicitor. It seeks liberty for the petitioner to amend the petition in accordance with the terms of the draft annexed to it, and an order that the winding up

F order may be amended by the addition of an order that the dissolution of the company may be declared void immediately prior to its winding up.

    On November 17, 1980, both motions came before me, and the official receiver appeared for the first time, on this occasion in person. I then suggested to him, in effect, that, because the points raised by the motions raised points of law and practice which appeared to be somewhat novel, and not without difficulty, and because my decision might affect similar

G cases in the future with which he might be concerned, he might like to consider instructing counsel. As a result, on his application, the motions were adjourned without opposition from the petitioner. Mr. Lindsay appeared for the official receiver on their final hearing last Monday, January 12. He has given me very valuable assistance for which I am grateful.

H   I shall deal first with the first motion. As Megarry J. said in *In re Test Holdings (Clifton) Ltd.* [1970] Ch. 285, 287: " Prima facie the appropriate mode of proceeding in respect of a company struck off under section 353 is by an application under section 353 (6)." The declaration sought by the petitioner in the first motion is sought not under that subsection but under section 352 (1). In the last-mentioned case it was submitted, inter alia, that any application which can be made under section 353 (6) ought to be made under this subsection, even if it could

also be made under section 352 (1). Megarry J. rejected this argument. **A**
As he said, at p. 288:

> " If upon the true construction of the Act the applicant is entitled
> to proceed under either subsection, it is not for the court to say that
> he ought to have proceeded under what the court considers to be the
> more suitable subsection instead of under what the court considers
> to be the less suitable subsection. It would be wrong for the courts **B**
> to seek to take away a choice which the legislature has decided that
> the applicant should have."

In the light of this decision Mr. Lindsay accepted that the petitioner in
the present case could not properly be criticised for applying to the court
under section 352 (1) rather than adopting the alternative course which
he submitted would have been open to the petitioner, that is an application **C**
under section 353 (6). Furthermore, he accepted (in my judgment correctly) that section 352 (1) by its terms gives the court the jurisdiction to
make the order which is sought by the first motion. The application has
been duly made within two years of the date of the dissolution. It is
made by a person who is manifestly " interested " within the subsection,
as being a contributory of the company.
D
Megarry J. in *In re Test Holdings (Clifton) Ltd.* [1970] Ch. 285 held
that where it is sought under section 352 (1) to revive a company which
has been struck off under section 353, but which is not in liquidation,
the Registrar of Companies ought normally to be made a respondent to
the notice of motion, to this extent assimilating the practice to that under
section 353 (6). Megarry J., however, expressly excepted from this general
statement of principle other applications under section 352 (1): see at **E**
p. 292G.

I myself can see no factors which ordinarily would make the joinder
of the Registrar of Companies necessary, either in his own or in the
public interest, in a case where the company concerned is already in
liquidation. I accept Mr. Lindsay's submission that his joinder is not
necessary in the present case. The Treasury Solicitor has written a letter **F**
stating in effect that no objection is taken on his behalf to the grant of
the declaration sought, so that no difficulty arises on account of the
Crown's possible interest.

Accordingly, the question on the first motion resolves itself into one
for the court's discretion. In the particular circumstances, Mr. Lindsay
has told me that the official receiver does not feel able to resist the making
of the order sought on this motion. If and when it is made, the official **G**
receiver will be in a position for the first time effectively to exercise his
functions without any doubt as to his powers in regard to the company's
assets. Furthermore, on the particular facts, I am told he will be able
to do so without embarrassment, particularly since the company ceased
trading many years ago.

In all the circumstances, I can see no remaining obstacle to the making **H**
of the order sought on the first motion and I propose to make such order.
This makes it unnecessary to consider the second motion, and I do not
propose to do so. I should, however, mention that, in relation to that
motion, Mr. Lindsay submitted that, on the particular facts of the present
case, the court would have no jurisdiction to make the order sought,
essentially on the ground that the slip rule cannot apply in relation to
the winding up order, because, though the court which made it was under

A a misapprehension of fact, the order made by it duly gave effect to its actual intention, which was to wind up the company.

Before leaving the substance of the matter I would make these observations. First, although the petitioner has now succeeded in obtaining relief under section 352 (1), even though the winding up order was perfected many months ago, it should not be concluded that such relief will always be available for the asking in any similar case in the future.

B The court is given a discretion by section 352 (1). I conceive that circumstances could arise in which it would feel bound to refuse to exercise its discretion even in favour of a petitioner who brought himself within the wording of the subsection, for example, if there were to be opposition to the application on reasonable grounds by the official receiver or the Treasury Solicitor, or other persons. Particularly in view of the risk of

C potential embarrassment to the official receiver, which may increase the longer the period of uncertainty subsists, a petitioner who seeks relief under section 352 or 353 in a case such as the present, after a winding up order has been made, should, in my judgment, apply to the court promptly, as soon as reasonably practicable after he becomes aware of the dissolution. If, as will normally be the case, he becomes so aware before the winding up order has been perfected, he will still be well

D advised, without any delay and before the winding up order is perfected, to apply to the court for relief, in accordance with the common practice adopted in the light of the decision in *In re Cambridge Coffee Room Association Ltd.* [1952] 1 All E.R. 112; I have outlined the form of appropriate relief earlier in this judgment. If he fails to take this course, he could be faced with much greater difficulties on a subsequent applica-

E tion.

Secondly, I have already referred to the possible difficulties which could face the official receiver during the awkward twilight period occurring after the making of a winding up order, but before the making of any order under section 352 or section 353—and, indeed, after the latter order has been made, particularly if it was long delayed. I conceive that he himself might well have the locus standi to make an application under

F section 352 (1) (though not section 353) as being a " person interested " within the former subsection. However, in all but the most exceptional cases, the primary responsibility for making any such application will, I conceive, fall on the petitioner rather than the official receiver. If the petitioner wishes practical effect to be given to the winding up order obtained at his instance, it will ordinarily be incumbent on him to take

G all necessary steps to enable this to be done. If, however, he is in any doubt as to the course which he should adopt, the official receiver can always apply to the court for directions under section 246 (3), as indeed, I understand, he did in the present case.

Declaration accordingly.
Petitioner to pay costs of both motions
H   *on party and party basis but official*
receiver to pay petitioner's costs
incurred by adjournment.

Solicitors: *Turner, Peacock* for *Basil D. Laitner & Smythe, Sheffield;* Treasury Solicitor.

[Reported by MISS EILEEN O'GRADY, Barrister-at-Law]

[1981]

A

[COURT OF APPEAL]

* REGINA v. MALCHEREK

REGINA v. STEEL

B

1981 March 17   Lord Lane C.J., Ormrod L.J. and Smith J.

Crime—Homicide—Causation—Victim of assault connected by
doctors to life-support machine—Machine disconnected on
doctors' conclusion of victim's brain death—No evidence of
original wound not being continuing and operating cause of
victim's death—Whether causation issue for jury—Whether
chain of causation broken
Crime—Evidence—Medical evidence—Homicide—Tests for brain
death—Suggestion of tests being insufficiently stringent and
inadequately carried out — Whether admissible — Whether
reception on appeal desirable, expedient or necessary —
Criminal Appeal Act 1968 (c. 19), s. 23 (1) (2)

C

Victims of assaults which necessitated medical treatment
were given normal and conventional medical treatment involving connection with life-support systems. In each case
after a time the doctors decided that the victim was " brain
dead " so that the treatment was otiose, the life-support system
was disconnected and all bodily functions ceased. Each
assailant was tried on a charge of murder. There was no
evidence that, at the time when all bodily functions ceased,
the original wound or injury was other than a continuing,
operating and substantial cause of death. The judge withdrew
from the jury any issue of causation, and the assailant was
convicted.

D

E

On appeal, on the question whether the issue of causation
should have been left to the jury for decision, and on
applications for leave to adduce further medical evidence
as to the sufficiency and adequacy of tests by the doctors to
determine brain death:

Held, dismissing the appeal and refusing the applications,
(1) that the fact that the victim had died despite or because of
the medical treatment given by skilled medical practitioners did
not exonerate the assailant from responsibility for the death,
and the discontinuance of the treatment did not in the circumstances break the chain of causation between initial injury and
death; and that, therefore, the issue of causation had been
properly withdrawn from the jury (post, pp. 696H—697A,
D–E, G).

F

G

Reg. v. Jordan (1956) 40 Cr.App.R. 152, C.C.A.; Reg. v.
Smith [1959] 2 Q.B. 35, Ct.M.A.C. and Reg. v. Blaue
[1975] 1 W.L.R. 1411, C.A. considered.

(2) That, since the additional medical witnesses sought to
be called could say nothing to alter the fact that in each
case the assailant's actions continued to be the operating
cause of the death, their evidence could not afford any ground
for allowing the appeal; and that, therefore, it was neither
necessary nor desirable nor expedient to receive the proposed
evidence (post, p. 697B–C, F).

H

The following cases are referred to in the judgment:

Reg. v. Blaue [1975] 1 W.L.R. 1411; [1975] 3 All E.R. 446, C.A.
Reg. v. Jordan (1956) 40 Cr.App.R. 152, C.C.A.
Reg. v. Smith [1959] 2 Q.B. 35; [1959] 2 W.L.R. 623; [1959] 2 All E.R.
    193, Ct.M.A.C.

A   The following additional cases were cited in argument:

     Reg. v. *Lomas* [1969] 1 W.L.R. 306; [1969] 1 All E.R. 920, C.A.
     Rex v. *Harding* (1936) 25 Cr.App.R. 190.

APPEAL against conviction.
APPLICATIONS.

B   On November 12, 1979, at Winchester Crown Court (Willis J.) the
appellant, Richard Tadeusz Malcherek, was convicted of the murder of the
victim of assault who had been connected to a life-support machine which
had been disconnected by medical practitioners, and he was sentenced to
life imprisonment. On November 30, 1979, at Leeds Crown Court
(Boreham J.) the applicant, Anthony Steel, pleaded not guilty to the murder
of the victim of assault, who had been connected to a life-support
C machine which had later been disconnected by medical practitioners; on
December 13, 1979, he was convicted and sentenced to life imprisonment.
The appellant and the applicant respectively appealed and applied for
leave to appeal against conviction on the ground that the trial judge erred
in withdrawing from the jury the issue of causation. The appellant and
the applicant also applied for leave to call further medical evidence. The
appeal and applications were heard together. The applicant further sought
D leave to appeal on grounds other than causation; they are not material
to the present report.

     The facts are stated in the judgment.

     T. G. Field-Fisher, Q.C. and *Anthony Bailey* for appellant, Malcherek.
     Wilfred Steer Q.C. and *J. S. H. Stewart* for the applicant, Steel.
E   *J. J. Smyth Q.C., Donald Gordon* and *J. M. Meredith* for the Crown.

     LORD LANE C.J. gave the following judgment of the court. These two
appeals, one an appeal and the other an application, raise similar points
and it was accordingly thought convenient that they should be dealt with
together, and that is what has happened.
     The facts of the two cases are as follows. I start with the applicant
F Steel. The applicant, on December 13, 1979, at Leeds Crown Court before
Boreham J. and a jury, was convicted of murder, and he now applies to
this court for leave to appeal against conviction and also to call certain
witnesses—two medical men.
     The victim of the attack was a girl called Carol Wilkinson. She was
20 years of age at the time. She lived in the Ravenscliffe area of Bradford
with her fiancé and worked at a bakery which was situated about a half
G a mile away from her home. The applicant was then aged 21. He lived
not far away in another house on the same Ravenscliffe estate. He was
sharing accommodation with a girl named Pamela Ward, but at the same
time he was carrying on an association with another girl whom he eventually
married. He was employed by the local council as a gardener.
     It was on October 10, 1977, at about 9 a.m. that Carol Wilkinson was
H walking to work from her home to the bakery. At some time on that
morning between about nine o'clock and half-past-nine, she was savagely
attacked by someone who stripped off the greater part of her clothing, and
then battered her about the head with a 50 lb. stone which was found
nearby. She was found shortly afterwards, in a field by the road, unconscious. She was taken as rapidly as could be to hospital. She had
multiple fractures of the skull and severe brain damage as well as a broken
arm and other superficial injuries which need not concern us. She was put

almost immediately on a life-support machine in the shape of a ventilator. **A** On October 12 the medical team in whose charge she was, after a number of tests, came to the conclusion that her brain had ceased to function and that, accordingly, the ventilator was in effect operating on a lifeless body. The life support machine was switched off and all bodily functions ceased shortly afterwards.

The judge withdrew the issue of causation from the jury on the fifth day of that trial, and the jury were accordingly left to decide the issue, hotly **B** contested, of whether they were sure that it was the applicant who had been the girl's assailant. The case for the Crown depended very largely, though not entirely, on admissions which were said to have been made by the applicant, both orally and in writing, to the police during the time in April 1979 when he was being questioned about events of October 10, 1977. Part of the grounds of appeal is based on the allegation that **C** those admissions were wrongly allowed to go before the jury by the judge when the admissions had, it is said, been extracted from the applicant by threats or by oppression or possibly in contravention of the Judges' Rules. That aspect of the application has been left in abeyance until the problem of causation, with which we are concerned now, has been concluded.

D

So far as that issue is concerned, namely, the issue of causation, the following facts are material. Upon admission to the casualty department of the Bradford Royal Infirmary at about 10.15 a.m. on Monday, October 10, Carol was seen by Dr. Nevelos, who found her to be deeply unconscious with no motor activity, her eyes open and the pupils fixed. She was breathing only with the aid of the ventilator. An hour later she was admitted to the intensive care unit of the Royal Infirmary and during the **E** whole of that day she remained deeply unconscious and unresponsive. At 10 p.m. the consultant neuro-surgeon, Mr. Price, examined her. He found her to be in a deep coma, unresponding to any stimulus. He carried out a test for electrical activity in the brain which proved negative. The total absence of any motor activity since the girl had been admitted to hospital and the early fixation of the pupils, which I have already mentioned, led **F** him to the conclusion that there had been an devastating impact injury to the brain. The cerebral function monitor showed no activity. Her eyes were too occluded, so it is said, to allow any caloric testing. The suggestion was made by Mr. Price that her temperature should be raised and that if by the morning her cerebral function remained as it had been up to date, namely, zero, they should declare her brain to be dead. In fact, in the morning shortly after 10 a.m., a cerebral blood flow test was carried out **G** which indicated that there was no blood circulating in the brain. Several electroencephalogram tests were made during that day. None of them had any positive result.

On Wednesday, October 12, two days after the injuries had been inflicted, another electroencephalogram test was made in the morning and another one at 6 p.m. but none of those tests showed any signs of electrical **H** activity at all. After that there was a consultation between the doctors who were in charge of the patient, and it was agreed among them that the continued use of the ventilator was without any purpose. At 6.15 p.m. the patient was withdrawn from the ventilator, and at 6.40 p.m. she was declared to be dead. There is an indication, though we are told it was not part of the evidence at the trial, that on post-mortem 50 minutes later it was found that her brain was already in the process of decomposition.

A   Much of the cross-examination of the medical men was taken up with suggestions that they had failed to conform to certain criteria which have been laid down by the royal medical colleges on the subject of the ascertainment of brain death. The matter which Mr. Steer invites this court to take into consideration as possibly differentiating the case of the applicant from that of the appellant is that he says that two of the suggested tests were not carried out properly, namely, the corneal reflex test and the

B   vestibulo-ocular reflex test. The corneal reflex test consists of touching the cornea of the eye with a piece of cotton wool to see if that creates any reaction in the patient and, as we understand it, the vestibulo-ocular reflex test consists of putting ice-cold water into the aperture of the ear, again to see if that produces any reflex in the patient. Reasons were given for neither of those tests having been carried out.

C   We now turn to the facts in the case of the appellant. On November 12, 1979, this time at Winchester Crown Court before Willis J. and a jury, the appellant was convicted of murder. He appeals against the conviction by leave of the single judge. The victim was Christina Malcherek, his wife, who was then aged 32. It seems that in November 1978 she left the appellant in order to go and live with her daughters at Poole. There was a non-molestation order in force, directed at the appellant, but on the

D   evening of March 26, 1979, he went to her flat where she was living. There was a quarrel and, to cut a long story short, he stabbed his wife nine times with a kitchen knife. One of the stabs resulted in a deep penetrating wound to Mrs. Malcherek's abdomen.

She was taken to Poole General Hospital and there was preliminary treatment in order to try to rectify her very low blood pressure, which was ascertained on admission. The surgical registrar then performed a

E   laparotomy and removed rather more than one and a half litres of blood from the abdomen. There was a section of the intestine which was damaged, and he excised that and joined up the two ends. For several days it seemed as though Mrs. Malcherek was making an uneventful recovery. Indeed, she was clearly confidently expected to survive. However, on April 1 she collapsed and the preliminary diagnosis was that

F   she had suffered a massive pulmonary embolism. She was resuscitated and arrangements were made for her admission to the Western Hospital at Southampton, which was equipped to deal with this type of emergency. She arrived there shortly before midnight. A couple of hours later her condition suddenly deteriorated and her heart stopped. She was taken straight away to the operating theatre and given cardiac massage. The

G   surgeon then opened her chest. He found that her heart was distended and not beating. He made an incision into the pulmonary artery and extracted from the pulmonary artery a large clot of blood some 12 inches long, which had plainly formed in one of the veins of the leg (which, we are told, is a common complication of major abdominal surgery), and had then moved on from the leg to the pulmonary artery with the results already described. When the clot was removed the heart started again

H   spontaneously. It will be appreciated that since the heart was not beating for a period of something like 30 minutes there was a grave danger of anoxic damage to the brain. She was returned to the ward and connected to a ventilator. Throughout the Monday she remained on that machine receiving intensive care, but in the afternoon an electroencephalogram showed that there were indeed symptoms of severe anoxic damage to the brain. The prognosis was poor.

The consultant neurologist saw her at 7 p.m. She was unresponsive

to any stimulus save that her pupils did react to light. He suggested a A
further electroencephalogram because at that stage it was not clear how
much brain damage had been suffered. On the morning of Tuesday, Dr.
Manners decided to dispense with the ventilator if that could possibly be
done. When that was done she was able, first of all, to breathe adequately
by herself, but towards midday she suffered a sharp and marked deterioration and the diagnosis was that she had suffered a cerebral vascular
accident—possibly a ruptured blood vessel, possibly a clot—causing further B
brain damage. In any event, by 1.45 p.m. her attempts to breathe were
inadequate and she was put back on to the ventilator. There was a
continued deterioration and by the following day she was deeply unconscious and seemed to have irreversible brain damage. There was less
electrical activity than before when a further electroencephalogram was
carried out. C
    On April 5 the situation had deteriorated still more, and it was quite
obvious at 1.15 p.m. on that day, when Dr. Lawton made an examination,
that her brain was irretrievably damaged. He carried out five of the six
royal medical colleges' confirmatory tests. The one he omitted was the
" gag reflex " test, again for reasons which he explained. The patient's
relations were consulted and a decision was made to disconnect the
ventilator, which was done at 4.30 p.m. A supply of oxygen was fed to D
her lungs in case she should make spontaneous efforts to breathe but she
did not, and shortly after 5 p.m. she was certified to be dead.
    In these circumstances, as in the earlier case, the judge decided that
the question of causation should not be left for the jury's consideration.
Consequently, the only issue they had to decide was the one of intent,
there being no argument but that the appellant had in fact inflicted the E
knife wound or wounds on Mrs. Malcherek. In this case the principal and,
in effect, the only ground of appeal, as Mr. Field-Fisher has told us, is that
the judge should have left the issue of causation to the jury.
    This is not the occasion for any decision as to what constitutes death.
Modern techniques have undoubtedly resulted in the blurring of many of
the conventional and traditional concepts of death. A person's heart can
now be removed altogether without death supervening; machines can keep F
the blood circulating through the vessels of the body until a new heart
can be implanted in the patient, and even though a person is no longer
able to breathe spontaneously a ventilating machine can, so to speak, do
his breathing for him, as is demonstrated in the two cases before us. There
is, it seems, a body of opinion in the medical profession that there is only
one true test of death and that is the irreversible death of the brain stem, G
which controls the basic functions of the body such as breathing. When
that occurs it is said the body has died, even though by mechanical means
the lungs are being caused to operate and some circulation of blood is
taking place.
    We have had placed before us, and have been asked to admit, evidence
that in each of these two cases the medical men concerned did not comply
with all the suggested criteria for establishing such brain death. Indeed, H
further evidence has been suggested and placed before us that those
criteria or tests are not in themselves stringent enough. However, in each
of these two cases there is no doubt that whatever test is applied the victim
died; that is to say, applying the traditional test, all body functions,
breathing and heart beat and brain function came to an end, at the latest,
soon after the ventilator was disconnected.
    The question posed for answer to this court is simply whether the

A   judge in each case was right in withdrawing from the jury the question of causation. Was he right to rule that there was no evidence on which the jury could come to the conclusion that the assailant did not cause the death of the victim? The way in which the submissions are put by Mr. Field-Fisher on the one hand and Mr. Wilfred Steer on the other is as follows: the doctors, by switching off the ventilator and the life support machine were the cause of death or, to put it more accurately, there was

B   evidence which the jury should have been allowed to consider that the doctors, and not the assailant, in each case may have been the cause of death.

In each case it is clear that the initial assault was the cause of the grave head injuries in the one case and of the massive abdominal haemorrhage in the other. In each case the initial assault was the reason for the medical

C   treatment being necessary. In each case the medical treatment given was normal and conventional. At some stage the doctors must decide if and when treatment has become otiose. This decision was reached, in each of the two cases here, in circumstances which have already been set out in some detail. It is no part of the task of this court to inquire whether the criteria, the royal medical colleges' confirmatory tests, are a satisfactory code of practice. It is no part of the task of this court to decide whether

D   the doctors were, in either of these two cases, justified in omitting one or more of the so called " confirmatory tests." The doctors are not on trial: the applicant and the appellant respectively were.

There are two comparatively recent cases which are relevant to the consideration of this problem. The first is *Reg.* v. *Jordan* (1956) 40 Cr.App.R. 152. That was a decision of the Court of Criminal Appeal,

E   presided over by Hallett J. There the appellant stabbed his victim on May 4, 1956. The victim died in hospital on May 12. At the trial the pathologist who carried out the autopsy gave evidence that the cause of death was bronchopneumonia following a penetrating abdominal injury. The main burden of the appeal was whether fresh medical evidence, which was not called at the trial, should be admitted and considered by the Court of Criminal Appeal.

F   In due course, in what was described as the exceptional or the exceedingly unusual circumstances of the case, that evidence was admitted. Evidence was given, accordingly, by two pathologists who said that in their opinion death had not been caused by the initial stab wound, which had almost healed at the time of the death, but by the introduction of terramycin after the deceased man had shown himself to be intolerant to that drug, and also by the intravenous introduction of huge quantities of

G   liquid, which was an abnormal medical treatment and which, in these circumstances, was quite wrong. The conviction was quashed because the court came to the conclusion, in effect, that the further evidence demonstrated that the death of the victim might not have resulted from normal treatment employed to cope with a felonious injury but that the treatment administered, the terramycin and the intravenous fluid, was an abnormal

H   treatment which was palpably wrong which, in its turn, caused the death at a time when the original wound was in the process of healing and indeed had practically healed.

The other decision is *Reg.* v. *Smith* [1959] 2 Q.B. 35. In that case the appellant had stabbed a fellow soldier with a bayonet. One of the wounds had pierced the victim's lung and had caused bleeding. Whilst being carried to the medical hut or reception centre for treatment, the victim was dropped twice and then, when he reached the treatment centre,

he was given treatment which was subsequently shown to have been A
incorrect. Lord Parker C.J., who gave the judgment of the court, stressed
the fact—if it needed stressing—that *Reg.* v. *Jordan* (1956) 40 Cr.App.R.
152 was a very particular case depending on its own exact facts, as indeed
Hallett J. himself in that case had said. In *Reg.* v. *Smith* [1959] 2
Q.B. 35 counsel for the appellant argued that if there was any other cause,
whether resulting from negligence or not, operating, if something happened
which impeded the chance of the deceased recovering, then the death did B
not result from that wound.

A very similar submission to that has been made to this court by
counsel in the instant case. The court in *Reg.* v. *Smith* was quite unable
to accept that contention. Lord Parker C.J. said, at pp. 42–43:

   " It seems to the court that if at the time of death the original wound
   is still an operating cause and a substantial cause, then the death C
   can properly be said to be the result of the wound, albeit that some
   other cause of death is also operating. Only if it can be said that
   the original wounding is merely the setting in which another cause
   operates can it be said that the death does not result from the wound.
   Putting it in another way, only if the second cause is so overwhelming
   as to make the original wound merely part of the history can it be D
   said that the death does not flow from the wound."

In the view of this court, if a choice has to be made between the decision
in *Reg.* v. *Jordan* (1956) 40 Cr.App.R. 152 and that in *Reg.* v. *Smith*
[1959] 2 Q.B. 35, which we do not believe it does (*Reg.* v. *Jordan* being
a very exceptional case), then the decision in *Reg.* v. *Smith* is to be
preferred.   E

The only other case to which reference has been made, it having been
drawn to our attention by Mr. Steer, is *Reg.* v. *Blaue* [1975] 1 W.L.R.
1411. That was the case where the victim of a stabbing incident was a
Jehovah's Witness who refused to accept a blood transfusion although she
had been told that to refuse would mean death for her—a prophecy which
was fulfilled. The passage that has been drawn to our attention in that
case is the last paragraph of the judgment of Lawton L.J., at p. 1416:   F

   " The issue of the cause of death in a trial for either murder or
   manslaughter is one of fact for the jury to decide. But if, as in this
   case, there is no conflict of evidence and all the jury has to do is to
   apply the law to the admitted facts, the judge is entitled to tell the
   jury what the result of that application will be. In this case the judge
   would have been entitled to have told the jury that the defendant's G
   stab wound was an operative cause of death. The appeal fails."

There is no evidence in the present case that at the time of conventional death, after the life support machinery was disconnected, the
original wound or injury was other than a continuing, operating and indeed
substantial cause of the death of the victim, although it need hardly be
added that it need not be substantial to render the assailant guilty. There H
may be occasions, although they will be rare, when the original injury has
ceased to operate as a cause at all, but in the ordinary case if the treatment is given bona fide by competent and careful medical practitioners,
then evidence will not be admissible to show that the treatment would
not have been administered in the same way by other medical practitioners.
In other words, the fact that the victim has died, despite or because of
medical treatment for the initial injury given by careful and skilled medical

A practitioners, will not exonerate the original assailant from responsibility
for the death. It follows that so far as the ground of appeal in each of
these cases relates to the direction given on causation, that ground fails.
It also follows that the evidence which it is sought to adduce now, although
we are prepared to assume that it is both credible and was not available
properly at the trial—and a reasonable explanation for not calling it at the
trial has been given—if received could, under no circumstances, afford
B any ground for allowing the appeal.

The reason is this. Nothing which any of the two or three medical
men whose statements are before us could say would alter the fact that in
each case the assailant's actions continued to be an operating cause of the
death. Nothing the doctors could say would provide any ground for a
jury coming to the conclusion that the assailant in either case might not
C have caused the death. The furthest to which their proposed evidence
goes, as already stated, is to suggest, first, that the criteria or the confirmatory tests are not sufficiently stringent and, secondly, that in the
present case they were in certain respects inadequately fulfilled or carried
out. It is no part of this court's function in the present circumstances to
pronounce upon this matter, nor was it a function of either of the juries
at these trials. Where a medical practitioner adopting methods which are
D generally accepted comes bona fide and conscientiously to the conclusion
that the patient is for practical purposes dead, and that such vital functions
as exist—for example, circulation—are being maintained solely by mechanical means, and therefore discontinues treatment, that does not prevent
the person who inflicted the initial injury from being responsible for the
victim's death. Putting it in another way, the discontinuance of treatment
E in those circumstances does not break the chain of causation between the
initial injury and the death.

Although it is unnecessary to go further than that for the purpose of
deciding the present point, we wish to add this thought. Whatever the
strict logic of the matter may be, it is perhaps somewhat bizarre to
suggest, as counsel have impliedly done, that where a doctor tries his
conscientious best to save the life of a patient brought to hospital in
F extremis, skilfully using sophisticated methods, drugs and machinery to do
so, but fails in his attempt and therefore discontinues treatment, he can
be said to have caused the death of the patient. For these reasons we do
not deem it either necessary under section 23 (2) of the Criminal Appeal
Act 1968 nor desirable or expedient under section 23 (1) to receive the
proposed evidence of the doctors which, in statement form, has been placed
G before us. Likewise, there is no ground for saying that the judge in either
case was wrong in withdrawing the issue of causation from the jury. It
follows that the appeal of Malcherek is dismissed. It now remains to
consider the application in the case of Steel in so far as it relates to the
matters other than causation. [The court considered the application and
stated that it was dismissed.]

H   *Applications refused.*
                                                Appeal dismissed.

Solicitors: *Trevanion & Curtis, Parkstone; T. I. Clough & Co., Bradford;
Director of Public Prosecutions.*

                                                L. N. W.

A

[COURT OF APPEAL]

* WESTMINSTER CITY COUNCIL *v.* MONAHAN AND OTHERS

[1981 W. No. 46]

1981 Jan. 19

Lawton and Eveleigh L.JJ.
and Sir David Cairns

B

*Practice—Possession of land—Summary proceedings—Short notice
—Freehold owner planning redevelopment of building—
Protesters opposed to redevelopment occupying to stop demolition—Leave to serve short notice—Owner's evidence not
showing urgency—Whether summons to be dismissed or
adjourned—Supreme Court of Judicature (Consolidation) Act
1925 (15 & 16 Geo. 5, c. 49), s. 27 (1)[1]—R.S.C., Ord. 113,
r. 6 (1)[2]*

C

The defendants, who opposed the plaintiff council's plan to
redevelop a site consisting of flats and shops, occupied one
of the shops as a protest, without the council's licence or
consent, after it was vacated by the tenant. The council
issued an originating summons under R.S.C., Ord. 113 for an
order for possession against the defendants. On January 8,
1981, the council applied to Russell J. for leave to serve short
notice for hearing on January 14 which was granted.
Lawson J. heard the summons and, not being satisfied that the
council's evidence disclosed any urgency, he set aside Russell
J.'s order and dismissed the council's summons.

D

On appeal by the council: —

Held, allowing the appeal, (1) that where a summons
issued under R.S.C., Ord. 113 had been properly issued and
the judge was satisfied on the evidence that the plaintiffs had
established a right to an order for possession, the judge could
only make a final order, if less than five clear days had elapsed
from the date of service of the notice, in a case of urgency;
but if there was no evidence of urgency the judge should
adjourn the summons until after the five days had expired
rather than dismiss it (post, pp. 702H, 703A, C–D, F, 704H,
705A).

E

F

Practice Direction (Possession of Land: R.S.C., Ord. 113)
[1970] 1 W.L.R. 1250 applied.

(2) That section 27 (1) of the Supreme Court of Judicature
(Consolidation) Act 1925 gave the Court of Appeal power to
make an order which could have been made at first instance;
and that, accordingly, an order for possession would be made
without remitting the case to the judge, since five days had
elapsed and the defendants had shown no right to be in
possession (post, pp. 704G, H, 705A).

G

The following cases are referred to in the judgment of Lawton L.J.:

Mercy v. *Persons Unknown,* The Times, June 5, 1974; Court of Appeal
(Civil Division) Transcript No. 197 of 1974, C.A.

Practice Direction (Possession of Land: R.S.C., Ord. 113) [1970] 1 W.L.R.
1250; [1970] 3 All E.R. 240.

H

[1] Supreme Court of Judicature (Consolidation) Act 1925, s. 27: "(1) Subject as
otherwise provided in this Act and to rules of court, the Court of Appeal shall have
jurisdiction to hear and determine appeals from any judgment or order of the
High Court, and for all the purposes of and incidental to the hearing and determination of any appeal, and the amendment, execution and enforcement of any
judgment or order made thereon, the Court of Appeal shall have all the power,
authority and jurisdiction of the High Court: ..."

[2] R.S.C., Ord. 113, r. 6 (1): see post, p. 702F–G.

1 W.L.R.   **Westminster Council v. Monahan (C.A.)**

A   The following additional cases were cited in argument:

Greater London Council v. *Jenkins* [1975] 1 W.L.R. 155; [1975] 1 All E.R. 354, C.A.

Orpen Road, Stoke Newington, In re 9 [1971] 1 W.L.R. 166; [1971] 1 All E.R. 944.

B   APPEAL from Lawson J.

The plaintiffs, Westminster City Council ("the council"), were the freehold owners of a building consisting of flats and shops including the shop premises at 51, Charing Cross Road, Westminster, London, W.C.2. They planned to redevelop the building. On January 5, 1981, the tenant vacated the shop and the building was, thus, ready to be demolished.

The defendants, James Monahan, Brian Lake and Ms. G. Kirk and C other persons unknown, as a protest against the council's redevelopment scheme, occupied the shop. The council issued an originating summons under R.S.C., Ord. 113, on January 7 seeking an order for possession of no. 51, Charing Cross Road on the ground that they were entitled to possession and that the persons in occupation were in occupation without licence or consent.

D   On January 8 the council applied to Russell J. for leave to serve short notice for hearing on January 14. Leave was granted. On January 14 the case came before Lawson J. who was not satisfied on the council's evidence that there was any urgency. The judge set aside Russell J.'s order and dismissed the originating summons.

By a notice of appeal dated January 14 the council appealed on the grounds (i) that the judge misdirected himself in law as to the matters E which a court could consider on an application under Ord. 113, r. 1, and in considering matters relating to convenience and policy having regard to the terms of the summons; (ii) that the judge failed adequately to consider the evidence in support of the summons lodged by the council; (iii) that the judge wrongfully admitted evidence by the defendants on matters of convenience, policy and efficacy in relation to the making of F the order; (iv) that the judge failed to find any facts at all relevant to the dismissal of the summons; (v) that there was no evidence served by the defendants to contradict the council's assertion that the defendants had entered into and remained in occupation of the premises without the leave, licence or consent of the council; (vi) that the judge misdirected himself in setting aside Russell J.'s order giving leave to serve short notice to the defendants.

G

Peter Mottershead Q.C. and *Philip Newman* for the council.
David Watkinson for the defendants.

LAWTON L.J. This is an application by the Lord Mayor and citizens of the City of Westminster ("the council") against James Monahan, Brian H Lake, a woman called Kirk, and persons unknown, to expedite the hearing of an appeal from an order made by Lawson J. in chambers on January 14, 1981. The application went on to ask that, if the application to expedite the hearing were granted, the court should hear the appeal forthwith. We do expedite the hearing and we have today heard the appeal. The appeal is one of some importance, because it has revealed some misunderstanding about the effect of R.S.C., Ord. 113.

On the west side of Charing Cross Road, in the City of Westminster,

700

there is a block of property known as Sandringham West. It consisted at A one time of about 200 flats and at street level a number of shops. One of these was known as no. 51 and was the shop of an antiquarian bookseller. The council of the City of Westminster have plans for the redevelopment of the site of Sandringham West. These plans have been the subject matter of acute controversy, not only within the council chamber itself but amongst others who are interested in the development of that part of the B City of Westminster. By a majority, the City of Westminster have resolved to go on with their redevelopment plan. Some of those who were in the minority and some of their supporters outside the council are concerned about the decision to redevelop the site at the present time. No doubt there are many reasons why the redevelopment of the site is being opposed, but one of them is a pragmatic one, that in these days of financial stringency the money is not available to redevelop and, if the first step towards C redevelopment is taken, namely, demolition of the existing building, there will be left on the site in the foreseeable future what has been described by counsel as a hole alongside the road and no doubt an unsightly one.

The defendants in this case were amongst those who were bitterly opposed to the decision of the council to redevelop the site. On or about D January 7, 1981, they occupied the vacant bookseller's shop at no. 51. The tenant of that shop had given up possession to the council earlier that month. During the course of January 7, 1981, the council sent workmen to no. 51 to secure the premises pending demolition. When they arrived they found the defendants in occupation and the defendants intimated to them that they intended to remain there all round the clock. The workmen reported back to the chief executive of the council. As a result, he decided E to start proceedings by way of originating summons under R.S.C., Ord. 113 for an order for possession against the defendants. It was clear to him, and it has been clear to us, that the defendants had no title whatsoever to be in possession of no. 51. They were there as protesters against the decision of the council to go on with the redevelopment of this site. They were not even homeless people seeking somewhere to live. What they were F doing was making a gesture for the purpose of attracting attention to what the council were doing.

An originating summons under Order 113 has to be supported by evidence. A law clerk named Jones was given the task of drafting the necessary affidavits and swearing them. I have some sympathy with Mr. Jones, because he was not fully qualified as a lawyer and he had to take steps to do what he could to get the matter before the court as quickly G as possible. What he did was to deal with the bare essentials of the matter so far as the council were concerned. He did not deal in his affidavit with any of the background matter and in particular he did not give any reasons why it was necessary to act promptly for the purposes of getting possession of no. 51. He took the view, and those behind him took the view, having regard to the wording of Ord. 113, r. 6, that it would be necessary to get H the leave of a judge to give what is commonly known as " short notice " of the originating summons. As a result, an application was made by counsel to Russell J. on January 8, 1981, for leave to serve the originating summons for hearing on January 14, 1981. We have been told in the course of the hearing today that counsel told Russell J. that the demolition contractors would be moving in by the end of the month to start the demolition of Sandringham West. Russell J. gave leave to serve short

The Weekly Law Reports, May 22, 1981

701

1 W.L.R.   **Westminster Council v. Monahan (C.A.)**   Lawton L.J.

A notice of the originating summons. In due course it came on for hearing on Wednesday, January 14, 1981, before Lawson J.

By that time the defendants had obtained affidavits from a number of people, some of whom were members of the council, in which they expressed their opinion about the undesirability of developing Sandringham West and what they considered to be the unlikely chance of the develop-
B ment going ahead in the present financial climate. There was nothing whatsoever in these affidavits to show that the defendants had, or claimed to have, any right or title to be in occupation of no. 51.

When the case was called on before Lawson J. in chambers, it took a somewhat unusual course, because, according to the affidavit of Mr. Jones and, indeed, to the affidavit of Mr. Lake, which was put in on behalf of the defendants, the judge started by dealing with what one might call the
C general merits of the redevelopment scheme of the council. He took the view, on such information as was before him in the affidavits, that there was not much likelihood of this redevelopment scheme going forward, having regard to the difficulties existing at the present time over public finance. In those circumstances, he asked why the council wanted to go on with their originating summons for possession. After some discussion
D with counsel, most of which seems to have been irrelevant, the judge did get down to the point which was for him to deal with, namely, whether there was any evidence on the affidavits which would entitle him, on Wednesday, January 14, 1981, to make a final order. He came to the conclusion that there was no such evidence on the affidavits.

Mr. Mottershead, who today has appeared on behalf of the council, has accepted that the evidence of urgency was inadequate. In those circum-
E stances, the judge clearly was entitled to refuse to make a final order there and then for possession of no. 51. But what the affidavits did disclose and what the judge, from what he said, clearly accepted was that the defendants had no right or title to be in no. 51 at all. In other words, save for the fact that there was no urgency about the matter, the council clearly, on their affidavits, had established a right to an order for possession but not
F a right to have that order made on January 14, 1981.

The judge made an order in these terms: " that the order of Russell J. herein of January 8, 1981, as to short notice be set aside, and the applica-tion under Order 113 be dismissed." It is against that order in that form that the council have appealed to this court. The argument has been that, having regard to the fact that the originating summons was taken out in
G the right kind of case, was properly served and supported by affidavits, and all the evidence therein showed that the council had a right to the order, the judge should not have dismissed the originating summons under Order 113 but should have adjourned the matter in order to ensure that the necessary time elapsed before a final order was made.

The defendants, on the other hand, have submitted that the judge was entitled to dismiss the originating summons altogether; alternatively, if
H he was not entitled to dismiss it altogether, he was entitled to refuse to make any order on January 14, 1981, leaving the council to restore the originating summons before either the same judge or another judge at a later date.

The course of events, as I indicated at the beginning of my judgment, reveals a certain confusion of thought about the way in which Order 113 operates. It is now necessary for me to examine Order 113 in some detail. The jurisdiction given by the order came into existence in 1970 as a result

of the gap in the law which was revealed by a series of squatter cases A
which had occurred in the two or three years before 1970. These cases
had shown that there was difficulty in getting speedy possession of property
when it had been occupied by trespassers. The object of the order was
two-fold. The first was to provide a procedure whereby an order for
possession could be obtained even though the property owner did not know
the names of the trespassers; and the second was so that the time lag
between starting proceedings and getting an order for possession could be B
very considerably shortened. The intention was that the new procedure
should be used in a particular type of case. That type of case is defined
in rule 1, which is in these terms:

"Where a person claims possession of land which he alleges is occupied
solely by a person or persons (not being a tenant or tenants holding
over after the termination of the tenancy) who entered into or remained C
in occupation without his licence or consent or that of any predecessor
in title of his, the proceedings may be brought by originating summons in accordance with the provisions of this order."

As I understand that rule, it means this, that a property owner faced
with squatters can decide for himself whether he wishes to proceed for D
recovery of his property by writ in the ordinary way or whether he wishes
to proceed by way of the summary proceedings described in rule 1. The
summary proceedings described in rule 1 are, however, confined to a
particular type of case and if a property owner decides to use the procedure
prescribed by rule 1 he has to comply with the other provisions of the
order. He must use the form of originating summons prescribed by the
rule. The affidavit in support must contain the matters to which rule 3 E
applies. He must serve the originating summons in accordance with rule 4.
Rule 4 (3) provides: " Ord. 28, rule 3, shall not apply to proceedings under
this order." Ord. 28, r. 3, is a rule which deals with the amount of time
that must be given by way of notice to a defendant. So what rule 4 is doing
is getting rid of the time limits set out in Ord. 28, r. 3. It takes out of the
new procedure that particular rule. It does not take out of the new pro- F
cedure other rules in Order 28, including rule 5 dealing with adjournments.

Then rule 6, which is the relevant one for the purposes of this appeal,
provides:

"(1) A final order shall not be made on the originating summons
except by a judge in person and shall, except in case of urgency and
by leave of the court, not be made less than five clear days after the G
date of service..."

Then sub-rule (2) deals with the form of the order for possession.

It is rule 6 which has caused the difficulty in this case and has seemingly caused difficulty in other cases, because the idea has got around that,
if it is thought necessary to abridge the time for getting an order for
possession because of urgency—and it may well be in some cases that H
an order for possession is required very urgently indeed—what can be
done is to go to a judge before the date of the hearing and ask him to
abridge the time because of urgency. That seems to have been the intention
in this case. The council went to Russell J. If that judge did think he was
abridging time because of urgency (and I doubt whether he did), he would
have been deciding an issue in the absence of the defendants and without
their being heard. But on my reading of rule 6 (1) it is the judge making

A the final order who is concerned with the issue of urgency, no one else. It follows, therefore, save for an administrative purpose to which I shall refer in a moment, that going to another judge, who is not going to hear the summons, to certify that there is urgency, is not the right procedure to follow. But for an administrative reason it may be necessary to go to another judge. The reason is this. In the ordinary way, so we were told, the listing clerks will not accept an originating summons for hearing

B before a judge except with a minimum of five days' notice. They will, however, of course, accept such a summons on less than five days' notice if a judge so orders. It follows, therefore, that when a property owner wishes to bring an originating summons to the attention of the judge before five clear days, it will be necessary for him to go to a judge for the purpose of getting the listing clerks to accept the originating summons

C for listing. That was the real purpose of the application which was made to Russell J.

When the matter comes before the judge on the hearing of the originating summons, he has to decide whether the originating summons has been properly issued, whether the evidence in support of it is adequate, and if he is so satisfied, then he will make the final order. But he must

D not make the final order unless at least five clear days have elapsed, save when the case is one of urgency. It follows that if, in a particular case, the summons is properly constituted, the evidence is clear and there is no possible answer to the summons, but the judge is of the opinion that it is not a case of urgency, what he should do is to adjourn the matter until such time as five clear days have elapsed.

This seems to be the practice in the Chancery Division, according to

E *Practice Direction* (*Possession of Land: R.S.C., Ord. 113*) [1970] 1 W.L.R. 1250 which was issued in 1970. Paragraph 6 of that *Practice Direction* is:

"An application for abridgment of time for the purposes of rule 6 (1) shall be made to the judge at the hearing in court and if the judge does not allow such abridgment the matter shall be adjourned to such date as the judge shall direct."

F It seems to me that the practice in the Queen's Bench Division should be the same as in the Chancery Division; in other words, if everything is in order except that the judge is not satisfied about urgency, he should do what judges in the Chancery Division do, namely, adjourn the matter so that at least five clear days have elapsed before the final order is made.

G In deciding in that way I am not for one moment suggesting that the judge can never dismiss an application under Order 113. He clearly can. If the case does not come within the ambit of Order 113 he can dismiss it. If there is something wrong with the service he can dismiss it. If it is clear that matters have been joined in the summons which ought not to be there he can dismiss it. If there is an issue to be tried and on the trial of the issue it appears that the plaintiff has not got the case which he said he

H had then clearly the judge should dismiss it. But when, as in this case, the plaintiff's case is as clear as anything could be and the defendants have not got the beginnings of an answer, in my judgment it would be wrong to dismiss the summons out of hand. The proper course would be to adjourn it.

It was said on behalf of the defendants, who in this court have made no attempt to make any claim of right to be in possession of these premises,

that Lawson J. could have done what was done in *Mercy* v. *Persons* A
Unknown, The Times, June 5, 1974; Court of Appeal (Civil Division)
Transcript No. 197 of 1974, namely, refuse to make an order, thereby
leaving the plaintiff to restore the summons before the same judge or
another judge. It is necessary now for me to say something about the
decision in *Mercy* v. *Persons Unknown,* because it was a case relied upon
strongly by the defendants in this appeal. That was a case in which a
property owner sought to get squatters out of his property using the B
summary procedure under Order 113. The originating summons was issued
on May 22, 1974. The hearing took place on May 24, 1974. In other words,
seven clear days had not elapsed, as the rules then required. The judge
made an order for possession. There was, in the judgment of this court,
no evidence of urgency and, as a result, the court discharged the order for
possession. The basis upon which it discharged the order for possession is C
clear from one sentence in the judgment of Lord Denning M.R.: " It was
not a proper case for the judge to make a final order on that Friday,
May 24. On that ground I think the appeal should be allowed and the
order of the judge set aside." Stephenson L.J. gave judgment to substantially the same effect. I agreed with the judgments delivered by Lord
Denning M.R. and Stephenson L.J.
     When this case was first brought to our attention I was of the opinion D
that we might find ourselves bound by it for the purposes of this appeal
unless it could be distinguished. In order to make certain what had happened, the court sent for, and looked at, the form of order which was made.
The order was in these terms: " It is ordered that this appeal be allowed
and the order of Bristow J. set aside." It follows that in *Mercy* v. *Persons
Unknown* all that the court was doing was setting aside an order made by E
Bristow J. when there had not been seven clear days between the taking
out of the summons and the making of the final order. It was not a case
where the proceedings for all purposes under Order 113 had been dismissed.
     Mr. Watkinson in this court conceded that in *Mercy* v. *Persons
Unknown* what could have happened would have been for the property
owner to have gone back after seven clear days had passed and asked the
court to reconsider the matter; and, having regard to the fact that there F
was no evidence that the squatters had any right to be on the premises,
it is probable that an order would have been made. Mr. Watkinson asked
us to adopt the same course here: to adjudge that no order should have
been made on January 14, 1981, leaving the council to go back and ask
for an order at some later date. For my part, I can see no sense in taking
that course, because had they gone back all that would have happened G
would have been that they would have got their order. In the circumstances of this case it seems to me that the proper course for this court
to take, bearing in mind the provisions of section 27 of the Supreme Court
of Judicature (Consolidation) Act 1925, is for this court to make the order
which could have been made at first instance once five clear days has
elapsed.
     In those circumstances, I would allow the appeal. H

     EVELEIGH L.J. I agree. Mr. Jones seems to have thought that it was
sufficient to say that the premises were due to be demolished very shortly.
Not surprisingly, particularly in view of the other affidavits filed in the
case, Lawson J. did not regard that information as sufficient to justify him
making an order as a matter of urgency. I agree, for the reasons stated

The Weekly Law Reports, May 29, 1981

705

1 W.L.R.   Westminster Council v. Monahan (C.A.)   Eveleigh L.J.

A by Lawton L.J., that the judge, however, should not have dismissed the case but should have adjourned it.

I too agree, for the reasons stated, that this appeal should be allowed.

Sir David Cairns. I also agree that the appeal should be allowed and the order made as indicated by Lawton L.J. for the reasons which have already been given.

B

> *Appeal allowed.*
> *Order for possession.*
> *No order as to costs.*

Solicitors: *Solicitor, Westminster City Council; Jane Wright, Central London Community Law Centre.*

C

A. R.

[COURT OF APPEAL]

D

* ATTORNEY-GENERAL'S REFERENCE (No. 4 of 1980)

1981 March 26;   Ackner L.J., Tudor Evans
       April 2   and Drake JJ.

E *Crime—Homicide—Manslaughter—Death resulting from one or other act of assailant—Each act if causing death sufficient to establish manslaughter—Whether necessary to identify act causing death—Whether jury to be satisfied of each act being sufficient to establish offence whichever act resulting in death*

The respondent was tried on a charge of manslaughter of a woman whose body was never found and no expert evidence was available about the cause of death; she had died as a result of the respondent pushing her and causing her to fall backwards over a handrail and downstairs head first on to the floor, or by being strangled with a rope used by him for dragging her upstairs or by his cutting her throat. The Crown conceded that it was impossible to prove whether she had died as a result of the fall, or from what the respondent did thereafter. On a submission the judge directed an acquittal on the ground that the Crown had failed to prove the cause of death.

F

G On a reference by the Attorney-General under section 36 of the Criminal Justice Act 1972, on the question whether, if an accused killed another person by one or other of two or more different acts, each of which if it caused the death was a sufficient act to establish manslaughter, it was necessary in order to found a conviction to prove which act caused the death: —

Held that, in the opinion of the court, (1) it was unnecessary in order to found a conviction to prove which act caused the death (post, p. 710c–d).

H

(2) That, since it was common ground that the woman was killed by an act done by the respondent to her and it was conceded that the jury could not be satisfied which act caused the death, they should have been directed to ask themselves questions so framed that they could have resulted in the jury being satisfied that, whichever act killed the deceased, each was a sufficient act to establish the offence of manslaughter (post, p. 710f–h).

The following cases are referred to in the opinion of the court: A

Meli v. *The Queen* [1954] 1 W.L.R. 228; [1954] 1 All E.R. 373, P.C.
Reg. v. *Church* [1966] 1 Q.B. 59; [1965] 2 W.L.R. 1220; [1965] 2 All
   E.R. 72, C.C.A.

The following additional case was cited in argument:

Reg. v. *Ramsey* [1967] N.Z.L.R. 1005.   B

REFERENCE by the Attorney-General under section 36 of the
Criminal Justice Act 1972.

The Attorney-General referred a point of law for the opinion of the
Court of Appeal in the following terms:

" 1.   The Court of Appeal is asked to give its opinion on the
following point of law: ' Whether a person who has committed a series   C
of acts against another culminating in the death of that other person,
each act in the series being either unlawful and dangerous or an act of
gross criminal negligence, is entitled to be acquitted of manslaughter
on the ground that it cannot be shown which of such acts caused the
death of the deceased.'

" 2.   The material facts of the case which give rise to this reference   D
are as follows: (a) the deceased was the fiancée of the accused and for
some months before her death had lived with him in a rented flat
[maisonette]; the flat was on two floors connected by two short flights of
carpeted wooden stairs.   (b) The deceased was employed locally and was
last at work on January 17, 1979.   After she left work that day, at about
5 p.m. no one other than the accused ever saw her alive again.   (c) The   E
deceased met her death on January 18, 1979, though this fact was not
known until February 13, 1979, when the accused so informed a friend.
His account then was that in the course of an argument [on the evening
of January 17] he had slapped her on the face causing her to fall downstairs and bang her head.   He said that he had then put her to bed but
discovered next morning [i.e., January 18] that she was dead and that
he had then taken her body to his home town and buried her.   (d) On   F
February 14, 1979, the accused altered his above account by telling the
same friend that after the incident when the deceased had ' fallen downstairs ' he had dragged her upstairs with a piece of rope tied round her
neck and had subsequently cut up her body with a saw before burying
it.   (e) On February 15, 1979, upon the advice of his friend the accused
went to see a superior and gave an account similar to the one he had   G
given his friend.   (f) On February 27, 1979, having consulted solicitors the
accused, through his legal advisers, contacted the police who saw him at
his solicitor's office.   At first, the accused gave to the police substantially
the same account he had given to his friend and superior but added that,
instead of burying the deceased he had ' dumped ' the various parts of
her body on a tip.   At the police station later that day he amplified this
by saying that the incident when the deceased ' fell downstairs ' occurred   H
at about 7 p.m. on January 17 and that it was the following morning
when he found her motionless, pulled her upstairs by a rope tied round
her neck and then cut up her body in the bathroom.   (g) On February
28, 1979, the accused after much questioning changed his account and
said that everything had happened on Thursday, January 18, at about
7 a.m.   He said that (i) he and the deceased had an argument on the
landing in the course of which each slapped the other, he seized the

A deceased and shook her hard, she dug her nails into him and he pushed
her away instinctively, causing her to fall backwards over the handrail,
down the stairs, head first on to the floor; (ii) he went downstairs
immediately to find her motionless . . . [and on a very cursory examination discovered] no pulse, no sign of breath but frothy blood coming
from her mouth; (iii) almost immediately thereafter he dragged her
B upstairs by a piece of rope tied around her neck, placed her in the bath
and cut her neck with a penknife to let out her blood, having already
decided to cut up her body and dispose of the pieces. He agreed that his
previous account was untrue and he made a detailed voluntary statement along the lines set out at (i), (ii) and (iii) above and describing how
subsequently he had cut up and disposed of her body. (h) In the course
of the above interviews at the police station after the accused had given
C his revised account, the following conversation took place: Officer:
' How long was it from the time that she went backwards over the
handrail to when you started pulling her up the stairs with the piece of
rope around her neck? ' Accused: ' I went straight downstairs when
she went backwards. I looked at her, tried her pulse. I tried to lift
her and she wee'd, so I put her down again. Then the two girls went
D past (the glass fronted door) so I covered the door with the blanket.
Then I got the piece of rope and pulled her up the stairs.' Officer:
' When did you decide you were going to cut the body up and dispose of
it? ' Accused: ' Just before I pulled it up the stairs.' And later . . .
Officer: ' Is it correct that you hauled (her) to the bathroom, put her into
the bath and then cut her neck with a knife to let the blood out and
these were all a continuous series of events? ' Accused: ' Yes, they all
E happened together.' (i) Thereafter the police discovered a body of evidence to corroborate the accused's account of how, where and when he
had cut up the body; they found the saw he had used and the shopkeeper
who sold it to him. (j) The body of the deceased was never found—only
some minute fragments of bone, which were discovered in the flat. In
the circumstances it was [conceded that it was] not possible for the
F Crown to prove whether the deceased died as a result of the ' fall '
downstairs or from what the accused did to her thereafter.
   " 3. The indictment charged the accused with (i) manslaughter;
(ii) obstructing the coroner in the execution of his duty; (iii) preventing
the burial of a corpse. The accused pleaded guilty to the third count; the
Crown offered no evidence upon the second and the trial proceeded upon
the count of manslaughter. At the close of the Crown's case the trial
G judge withdrew the case from the jury and directed an acquittal on the
ground that the Crown had failed to prove the cause of the death of the
deceased. He appears to have been influenced in his decision by questions
of sentencing and the fact that the accused had already pleaded guilty to
count 3.
   " 4. It is submitted that (a) in cases of manslaughter if an accused
H kills another by one or other of two or more different acts, each of
which, if it caused the death, is a sufficient act to prove the offence
charged, it is not necessary in order to found a conviction to prove
which act caused the death; (b) a man is guilty of manslaughter if he
commits a series of acts against another culminating in the death of that
other and if each act in the series is either an unlawful act or an act of
gross criminal negligence, whether or not it is proved which of these acts
caused the death."

Brian Walsh Q.C. (who did not appear below) and *Keith Lawrence* A
for the Attorney-General.

James Chadwin Q.C. (who did not appear below) and *Ashraf Khan*
for the respondent.

Cur. adv. vult.

April 2.   ACKNER L.J. read the following opinion of the court.   This B
is a reference to the court by the Attorney-General of a point of law
seeking the opinion of the court pursuant to section 36 of the Criminal
Justice Act 1972.   It raises yet again the problem of the supposed corpse
and the facts, which I take from the terms of the reference itself, are
inevitably macabre.

The deceased was the fiancée of the accused and for some months
before her death they had lived together in a maisonette, consisting of C
two floors of a house connected by two short flights of carpeted wooden
stairs.   The deceased was employed locally and was last seen at work
on January 17, 1979, at about 5 p.m.   Thereafter no one, other than the
accused ever saw her alive again.

The deceased met her death on January 18, 1979, although this fact
was not known until over three weeks later when the accused so D
informed a friend.   His account (given on February 13), the first of
a number, was that in the course of an argument on the evening of
January 17 he had slapped her on the face causing her to fall downstairs and bang her head.   He said that he had then put her to bed but
discovered next morning that she was dead.   He then took her body to
his home town and buried her.

On the following day (February 14) he gave his second account, E
telling the same friend that after the deceased had "fallen downstairs"
he had dragged her upstairs by a piece of rope tied around her neck.
He subsequently cut up her body with a saw before burying it.   The
next day, upon the advice of his friend, the accused went to see a
superior and gave an account similar to the one he had given his friend.

We now come to the statements which he made to the police.   On F
February 27 having consulted solicitors, the accused was interviewed by
the police at his solicitors' office.   He began by giving the police substantially the same account that he had given to his friend and his
superior but added that instead of burying the deceased he had
"dumped" the various parts of her body on a tip.   At the police station
later that day he amplified his statement by saying that the incident
when the deceased "fell downstairs" occurred at about 7 p.m. on G
January 17 and that it was the following day, when he found her motionless, that he pulled her upstairs by a rope around her neck and then cut
up her body in the bathroom.   On the following day after much
questioning by the police he changed his account stating that everything
had happened on Thursday, January 18, at about 7 a.m.   This is what
he then said happened.   (i) He and the deceased had an argument on the H
landing in the course of which each slapped the other, he seized the
deceased and shook her hard; she dug her nails into him and he pushed
her away instinctively, causing her to fall backwards over the handrail,
down the stairs head-first on to the floor.   (ii) He went downstairs
immediately to find her motionless and on a very cursory examination
discovered no pulse, and no sign of breath but frothy blood coming from
her mouth.   (iii) Almost immediately thereafter he dragged her upstairs

A by a rope tied around her neck, placed her in the bath and cut her neck with a penknife to let out her blood, having already decided to cut up her body and dispose of the pieces.

He agreed that his previous account was untrue and he made a detailed voluntary statement along the lines set out in (i), (ii) and (iii) above describing how subsequently he had cut up and disposed of her body.

B In the course of these interviews at the police station, after the accused had given his revised account, the following conversation took place:

C

> "Officer: 'How long was it from the time that she went backwards over the handrail to when you started pulling her up the stairs with a piece of rope around her neck?'
> "Accused: 'I went downstairs when she went backwards. I looked at her, tried her pulse. I tried to lift her and she wee'd, so I put her down again. Then two girls went past (the glass fronted door) so I covered the door with the blanket. Then I got the piece of rope and pulled her up the stairs.'
> "Officer: 'When did you decide you were going to cut the body
> D up and dispose of it?'
> "Accused: 'Just before I pulled her up the stairs.'"

Later he was asked by the officer:

E

> "Is it correct that you hauled (her) to the bathroom, put her into the bath and then cut her neck with a knife to let the blood out and these were all a continuous series of events?" To this the accused answered: "Yes, they all happened together."

Subsequently the police discovered evidence which corroborated the accused's account of how, where and when he had cut up the body. They also found the saw he had used and the shopkeeper who sold it to him. However, the body of the deceased was never found, only some
F minute fragments of bone, which were discovered in the maisonette. There was thus no expert evidence as to the cause of death. The deceased died either as a result of being pushed and thus caused to fall backwards over the handrail and backwards down the stairs head-first on to the floor, or by being strangled with the rope, or having her throat cut. The Crown conceded that it was not possible for them to prove whether the deceased died as a result of the " fall " downstairs
G or from what the accused did to the deceased thereafter.

The indictment charged the accused with (i) manslaughter, (ii) obstructing the coroner in the execution of his duty, and (iii) preventing the burial of a corpse.

The accused pleaded guilty to the third count, the Crown offered no evidence upon the second and the trial proceeded upon the count of
H manslaughter.

At the close of the Crown's case counsel for the accused stated that he proposed to submit that on the facts proved there was no case of manslaughter capable of going to jury. It is not easy to follow from the transcript the exact basis of his submissions, but what he appears to have been contending was that (a) it was not possible for the jury to be sure what caused the deceased's death and (b) whether the death was caused as a result of her " fall " down the stairs or from what the

710

accused subsequently did, believing her to be dead, in neither event   A
was there a prima facie case of manslaughter.

The judge, although expressing his reluctance to accept that the
accused could be in a better position as a result of his dismembering the
body of the deceased, appeared to have been very concerned at what he
described as " an insuperable problem of sentencing," were the accused
to be convicted of manslaughter. He expressed the view that the real
criminality of the accused's behaviour was in disposing of the body, a   B
view which this court is unable to accept. These views appear to have
influenced his decision, which was to withdraw the case from jury and
to direct an acquittal on the ground that the Crown had failed to prove
the cause of the death of the deceased.

On the above facts this reference raises a single and simple question,
viz: if an accused kills another by one or other of two or more different   C
acts each of which, if it caused the death, is a sufficient act to establish
manslaughter, is it necessary in order to found a conviction to prove
which act caused the death? The answer to that question is " No, it is
not necessary to found a conviction to prove which act caused the
death." No authority is required to justify this answer, which is clear
beyond argument, as was indeed immediately conceded by Mr. Chadwin   D
on behalf of the accused.

What went wrong in this case was that counsel made jury points to
the judge and not submissions of law. He was in effect contending that
the jury should not convict of manslaughter, if the death had resulted
from the " fall," because the push which had projected the deceased
over the handrail was a reflex and not a voluntary action, as a result of
her digging her nails into him. If, however, the deceased was still alive   E
when he cut her throat, since he then genuinely believed her to be dead,
having discovered neither pulse nor sign of breath, but frothy blood
coming from her mouth, he could not be guilty of manslaughter because
he had not behaved with gross criminal negligence. What counsel and
the judge unfortunately overlooked was that there was material available
to the jury which would have entitled them to have convicted the   F
accused of manslaughter, whichever of the two sets of acts caused her
death. It being common ground that the deceased was killed by an act
done to her by the accused and it being conceded that the jury could
not be satisfied which was the act which caused the death, they should
have been directed in due course in the summing up, to ask themselves
the following questions: (i) Are we satisfied beyond reasonable doubt
that the deceased's " fall " downstairs was the result of an intentional   G
act by the accused which was unlawful and dangerous? If the answer
was " No " then they would acquit. If the answer was " Yes " then
they would need to ask themselves a second question, namely: (ii) Are
we satisfied beyond reasonable doubt that the act of cutting the girl's
throat was an act of gross criminal negligence? If the answer to that
question was ' No " then they would acquit, but if the answer was   H
" Yes " then the verdict would be guilty of manslaughter. The jury
would thus have been satisfied that, whichever act had killed the
deceased, each was a sufficient act to establish the offence of manslaughter.

The facts of this case did not call for " a series of acts direction "
following the principle in Melli v. The Queen [1954] 1 W.L.R. 228.
We have accordingly been deprived of the stimulating questions as to

A   whether the decision in *Reg.* v. *Church* [1966] 1 Q.B. 59 correctly
extended that principle to manslaughter, in particular to "constructive
manslaughter" and if so whether that view was part of the ratio
decidendi.

Opinion accordingly.

B   Solicitors: *Director of Public Prosecutions; Sanderson, Kaye &
Martin, Hull.*

L. N. W.

C

[HOUSE OF LORDS]

* BUNGE CORPORATION, NEW YORK .   .   APPELLANTS AND
                                        CROSS-RESPONDENTS
D   AND

TRADAX EXPORT S.A., PANAMA .   .   .   RESPONDENTS AND
                                        CROSS-APPELLANTS

1981 Feb. 23, 24, 25, 26;   Lord Wilberforce, Lord Fraser
E   May 7   of Tullybelton, Lord Scarman,
                                     Lord Lowry and Lord Roskill

*Contract—Condition or warranty—Mercantile contract—Sale of
    goods (f.o.b.)—Buyers to give 15 days' loading notice —
    Whether condition or intermediate term—GAFTA form 119,
    cl. 7*
*Damages—Sale of goods—Construction of contract—F.o.b. con-
F   tract—Whether "default in shipment or delivery" confined
    to default by seller—Whether general principles of assessment
    of damages applicable where buyer defaults—GAFTA form
    119, cl. 22*

        By a contract made on January 30, 1974, the buyers agreed
    to buy from the sellers 15,000 tons, 5 per cent. more or less at
    buyers' option, of U.S. soya bean meal, with shipment of
G   5,000 tons in each of the months May, June, July 1975, at
    U.S. $199·50 a metric ton, f.o.b. one U.S. Gulf port at sellers'
    option. The contract incorporated the terms of the Grain and
    Feed Trade Association Ltd.'s (GAFTA) standard form of
    contract 119, clause 7 of which in respect of the May ship-
    ment provided, "Period of delivery—during [May 1975] at
    buyers' call. Buyers shall give at least [15] days' notice of
    probable readiness of vessel(s) . . ." By notice given by the
H   buyers under clause 8 of GAFTA form 119 the period of
    delivery was extended for one calendar month. In consequence
    the last day upon which the sellers could ship goods in
    performance of the contract was June 30, 1975, and the last
    day for the buyers to give the requisite notice under clause 7
    was June 12. In the event, notice was not given until June 17.
    Subsequently the sellers declared the buyers in default and
    claimed damages for repudiation of the contract on the ground
    that the term as to notice was a condition. Clause 22 of
    GAFTA form 119 provided ". . . In the event of default in

shipment or delivery any damages shall be computed upon the
mean contract quantity."

The dispute was referred to arbitration under the rules of
GAFTA. The two arbitrators disagreed. The umpire awarded
the sellers, inter alia, $317,500 as damages (the market price
having fallen substantially below the contract price) the damages being calculated on the mean contract quantity of 5,000
tons. The Board of Appeal of GAFTA upheld the award
subject to the opinion of the court. Parker J. held, inter alia,
that the term as to time when notice was to be given was
not a condition and in any event there had been no breach
of it and therefore the sellers were not entitled to damages.

On appeal by the sellers the Court of Appeal allowed the
appeal, but held that damages had to be assessed on 5,000
tons less 5 per cent., namely 4,750 tons, the minimum quantity
which the buyers were obliged to take.

On appeal by the buyers and cross-appeal by the sellers: —

Held, (1) that the court required precise compliance with
stipulations as to time wherever the circumstances of the case
indicated that that would fulfil the intentions of the parties,
and that, in general, time was of the essence in mercantile
contracts (post, pp. 716D–F, G—717A, 718E–F, 725A–D).

(2) Dismissing the appeal, that in a mercantile contract
when a term had to be performed by one party as a condition
precedent to the ability of the other party to perform another
term especially an essential term such as the nomination of a
single loading port, the term as to time for the performance
of the former obligation would in general fall to be treated
as a condition; that accordingly, clause 7 was a condition for
until the requisite notice had been given the sellers could not
know for certain which loading port they should nominate
so as to ensure that the contract goods would be available
for loading on the ship's arrival at that port before the end
of the shipment period (post, pp. 714E, 716G—717A, 718C, E–F,
723H, 729E–H).

Hongkong Fir Shipping Co. Ltd. v. *Kawasaki Kisen Kaisha
Ltd.* [1962] 2 Q.B. 26, C.A. and *United Scientific Holdings Ltd.*
v. *Burnley Borough Council* [1978] A.C. 904, H.L.(E.) considered.

(3) Dismissing the cross-appeal, that on its true construction the expression " default in shipment or delivery " in clause
22 applied only to default by the seller, and that, therefore,
damages for default by the buyer were to be assessed on
ordinary principles, namely on the minimum quantity the
buyers were obliged by the terms of the contract to take (post,
pp. 714E, 716G—717A, 718E–F, 731F–G).

Toprak Mahsulleri Ofisi v. *Finagrain Compagnie Commerciale Agricole et Financière S.A.* [1979] 2 Lloyd's Rep. 98,
C.A. approved.

Decision of the Court of Appeal [1980] 1 Lloyd's Rep. 294
affirmed.

The following cases are referred to in their Lordships' opinions:

Behn v. *Burness* (1863) 3 B. & S. 751.

Bentsen v. *Taylor, Sons & Co.* [1893] 2 Q.B. 274, C.A.

Boone v. *Eyre* (1777) 1 Hy.Bl. 273n.

Bowes v. *Shand* (1877) 2 App.Cas. 455, H.L.(E.).

Bremer Handelsgesellschaft m.b.H. v. *J. H. Rayner & Co. Ltd.* [1978]
2 Lloyd's Rep. 73; [1979] 2 Lloyd's Rep. 216, C.A.

Bremer Handelsgesellschaft m.b.H. v. *Vanden Avenne-Izegem P.V.B.A.*
[1978] 2 Lloyd's Rep. 109, H.L.(E.).

Carapanayoti & Co. Ltd. v. *Comptoir Commercial Andre et Cie. S.A.*
[1972] 1 Lloyd's Rep. 139, C.A.

1 W.L.R.   **Bunge Corpn. v. Tradax S.A. (H.L.(E.))**

A   *Cehave N.V.* v. *Bremer Handelsgesellschaft m.b.H.* (*The Hansa Nord*)
       [1976] Q.B. 44; [1975] 3 W.L.R. 447; [1975] 3 All E.R. 739, C.A.
     Comptoir Commercial Anversois and Power, Son & Co., In re [1920]
       1 K.B. 868, C.A.
     Hongkong Fir Shipping Co. Ltd. v. *Kawasaki Kisen Kaisha Ltd.* [1962]
       2 Q.B. 26; [1962] 2 W.L.R. 474; [1962] 1 All E.R. 474, C.A.
     Jackson v. *Union Marine Insurance Co. Ltd.* (1874) L.R. 10 C.P. 125.
B   *McDougall* v. *Aeromarine of Emsworth Ltd.* [1958] 1 W.L.R. 1126;
       [1958] 3 All E.R. 431.
     Mihalis Angelos, The [1971] 1 Q.B. 164; [1970] 3 W.L.R. 601; [1970]
       3 All E.R. 125, C.A.
     Moorcock, The (1889) 14 P.D. 64, C.A.
     Oppenheim v. *Fraser* (1876) 34 L.T. 524.
     Photo Production Ltd. v. *Securicor Transport Ltd.* [1980] A.C. 827; [1980]
C   2 W.L.R. 283; [1980] 1 All E.R. 556, H.L.(E.).
     Reardon Smith Line Ltd. v. *Yngvar Hansen-Tangen* (*trading as H. E.
       Hansen-Tangen*) [1976] 1 W.L.R. 989; [1976] 3 All E.R. 570, H.L.(E.).
     Reuter v. *Sala* (1879) 4 C.P.D. 239, C.A.
     Stach (Ian) Ltd. v. *Baker Bosley Ltd.* [1958] 2 Q.B. 130; [1958] 2 W.L.R.
       419; [1958] 1 All E.R. 542.
     Tarrabochia v. *Hickie* (1856) 1 H. & N. 183.
D   *Toepfer* v. *Lenersan-Poortman N.V.* [1978] 2 Lloyd's Rep. 555; [1980]
       1 Lloyd's Rep. 143, C.A.
     Toprak Mahsulleri Ofisi v. *Finagrain Compagnie Commerciale Agricole
       et Financière S.A.* [1979] 2 Lloyd's Rep. 98, C.A.
     Turnbull (Peter) & Co. Pty. Ltd. v. *Mundas Trading Co. (Australasia) Pty.
       Ltd.* [1954] 2 Lloyd's Rep. 198.
     United Scientific Holdings Ltd. v. *Burnley Borough Council* [1978] A.C.
       904; [1977] 2 W.L.R. 806; [1977] 2 All E.R. 62, H.L.(E.).
E
     The following additional cases were cited in argument:

     Aries Tanker Corporation v. *Total Transport Ltd.* [1977] 1 W.L.R. 185;
       [1977] 1 All E.R. 398, H.L.(E.).
     A/S Awilco of Oslo v. *Fulvia S.p.A. di Navigazione of Cagliari* [1981]
       1 W.L.R. 314; [1981] 1 All E.R. 652, H.L.(E.).
F   *Daulatram Rameshwarlall* v. *European Grain & Shipping Ltd.* [1971] 1
       Lloyd's Rep. 368.
     Even v. *Topp* (1851) 6 Exch. 424.
     Empresa Cubana de Fletes v. *Lagonisi Shipping Co. Ltd.* [1971] 1 Q.B.
       488; [1971] 2 W.L.R. 221; [1971] 1 All E.R. 193, Donaldson J. and
       C.A.
     Federal Commerce & Navigation Co. Ltd. v. *Molena Alpha Inc.* [1979]
G   A.C. 757; [1978] 3 W.L.R. 991; [1979] 1 All E.R. 307, H.L.(E.).
     Federal Commerce & Navigation Co. Ltd. v. *Tradax Export S.A.* [1978]
       A.C. 1; [1977] 3 W.L.R. 126; [1977] 2 All E.R. 849, H.L.(E.).
     Glaholm v. *Hays* (1841) 2 Man. & G. 257.
     Graves v. *Legg* (1854) 9 Exch. 709.
     Hartley v. *Hymans* [1920] 3 K.B. 475.
     Heisler v. *Anglo-Dal Ltd.* [1954] 1 W.L.R. 1273; [1954] 2 All E.R. 770,
       C.A.
H   *Mardorf Peach & Co. Ltd.* v. *Attica Sea Carriers Corporation of Liberia*
       [1977] A.C. 850; [1977] 2 W.L.R. 286; [1977] 1 All E.R. 545, H.L.(E.).
     Plasticmoda Societa Per Azioni v. *Davidsons (Manchester) Ltd.* [1952]
       1 Lloyd's Rep. 527, C.A.
     S.C.C.M.O. (London) v. *Société Générale de Compensation* [1956] 1
       Lloyd's Rep. 290.
     Scandinavian Trading Co. A/B v. *Zodiac Petroleum S.A.* [1981] 1 Lloyd's
       Rep. 81.

Sharp v. *Christmas* (1892) 8 T.L.R. 687, C.A.   A

Trans Trust S.P.R.L. v. *Danubian Trading Co. Ltd.* [1952] 1 K.B. 285;
    [1952] 1 All E.R. 970, C.A.

Tsakiroglou & Co. Ltd. v. *Transgrains S.A.* [1958] 1 Lloyd's Rep. 562.

APPEAL from the Court of Appeal.

This was an appeal by the appellants, Bunge Corporation, New York,
from an order dated December 14, 1979, of the Court of Appeal (Megaw   B
Browne and Brightman L.JJ.) allowing an appeal by the respondents,
Tradax Export S.A., Panama, from an order dated April 11, 1979, of
Parker J., setting aside an award of the Board of Appeal of the Grain
and Free Trade Association Ltd. (GAFTA) dated November 7, 1978.

The questions raised by the appeal were (i) by what criteria should
the court determine whether a provision in a mercantile contract that   C
one party should perform some obligation by a stated time was a strict
condition or an " innominate " or " intermediate " term; (ii) was the
provision in an f.o.b. contract incorporating the terms and conditions of
GAFTA form 119 whereby the buyer was to give to the seller 15 days'
notice of probable readiness of the buyer's vessel to load a strict condition
or an intermediate term?

The facts are set out in the opinion of Lord Roskill.   D

Roger Buckley Q.C. and *Nicholas Merriman* for the appellants, the
buyers.

Christopher Staughton Q.C. and *Mark Havelock-Allan* for the respondents, the sellers.
                                                                        E
Their Lordships took time for consideration.

May 7. LORD WILBERFORCE. My Lords, I have had the advantage of
reading in advance the speech to be delivered by my noble and learned
friend, Lord Roskill. I agree entirely with it and desire only to add a few
observations on some general aspects of the case.   F

The appeal depends upon the construction to be placed upon clause 7
of GAFTA form 119 as completed by the special contract. It is not
expressed as a " condition " and the question is whether, in its context and
in the circumstances it should be read as such.

Apart from arguments on construction which have been fully dealt
with by my noble and learned friend, the main contention of Mr. Buckley   G
for the appellant was based on the decision of the Court of Appeal in
Hongkong Fir Shipping Co. Ltd. v. *Kawasaki Kisen Kaisha Ltd.* [1962]
2 Q.B. 26, as it might be applied to clause 7. Diplock L.J. in his seminal
judgment illuminated the existence in contracts of terms which were neither,
necessarily, conditions nor warranties, but, in terminology which has
since been applied to them, intermediate or innominate terms capable of
operating, according to the gravity of the breach, as either conditions or   H
warranties. Relying on this, Mr. Buckley's submission was that the buyer's
obligation under the clause, to "give at least [15] consecutive days'
notice of probable readiness of vessel(s) and of the approximate quantity
required to be loaded," is of this character. A breach of it, both generally
and in relation to this particular case, might be, to use Mr. Buckley's
expression, " inconsequential," i.e. not such as to make performance of
the seller's obligation impossible. If this were so it would be wrong to

A   treat it as a breach of condition: *Hongkong Fir* would require it to be treated as a warranty.

This argument, in my opinion, is based upon a dangerous misunderstanding, or misapplication, of what was decided and said in *Hongkong Fir.* That case was concerned with an obligation of seaworthiness, breaches of which had occurred during the course of the voyage. The decision of the Court of Appeal was that this obligation was not a condition, a breach

B   of which entitled the charterer to repudiate. It was pointed out that, as could be seen in advance the breaches, which might occur of it, were various. They might be extremely trivial, the omission of a nail; they might be extremely grave, a serious defect in the hull or in the machinery; they might be of serious but not fatal gravity, incompetence or incapacity of the crew. The decision, and the judgments of the Court of Appeal, drew

C   from these facts the inescapable conclusion that it was impossible to ascribe to the obligation, in advance, the character of a condition.

Diplock L.J. then generalised this particular consequence into the analysis which has since become classical. The fundamental fallacy of the appellants' argument lies in attempting to apply this analysis to a time clause such as the present in a mercantile contract, which is totally different

D   in character. As to such a clause there is only one kind of breach possible, namely, to be late, and the questions which have to be asked are, first, what importance have the parties expressly ascribed to this consequence, and secondly, in the absence of expressed agreement, what consequence ought to be attached to it having regard to the contract as a whole.

The test suggested by the appellants was a different one. One must consider, they said, the breach actually committed and then decide whether

E   that default would deprive the party not in default of substantially the whole benefit of the contract. They invoked even certain passages in the judgment of Diplock L.J. in the *Hongkong Fir* case [1962] 2 Q.B. 26 to support it. One may observe in the first place that the introduction of a test of this kind would be commercially most undesirable. It would expose the parties, after a breach of one, two, three, seven and other numbers of days to an

F   argument whether this delay would have left time for the seller to provide the goods. It would make it, at the time, at least difficult, and sometimes impossible, for the supplier to know whether he could do so. It would fatally remove from a vital provision in the contract that certainty which is the most indispensable quality of mercantile contracts, and lead to a large increase in arbitrations. It would confine the seller—perhaps after arbitra-

G   tion and reference through the courts—to a remedy in damages which might be extremely difficult to quantify. These are all serious objections in practice. But I am clear that the submission is unacceptable in law. The judgment of Diplock L.J. does not give any support and ought not to give any encouragement to any such proposition; for beyond doubt it recognises that it is open to the parties to agree that, as regards a particular obligation, any breach shall entitle the party not in default to treat the

H   contract as repudiated. Indeed, if he were not doing so he would, in a passage which does not profess to be more than clarificatory, be discrediting a long and uniform series of cases—at least from *Bowes* v. *Shand* (1877) 2 App.Cas. 455 onwards which have been referred to by my noble and learned friend, Lord Roskill. It remains true, as Lord Roskill has pointed out in *Cehave N.V.* v. *Bremer Handelsgesellschaft m.b.H. (The Hansa Nord)* [1976] Q.B. 44, that the courts should not be too ready to interpret contractual clauses as conditions. And I have myself commended, and continue to commend, the greater flexibility in the law of contracts to which *Hongkong Fir* points the way (*Reardon Smith Line Ltd. v. Yngvar Hansen-Tangen (trading as H. E. Hansen-Tangen)* [1976] 1 W.L.R. 989, 998). But I do not doubt that, in suitable cases, the courts should not be reluctant, if the intentions of the parties as shown by the contract so indicate, to hold that an obligation has the force of a condition, and that indeed they should usually do so in the case of time clauses in mercantile contracts. To such cases the " gravity of the breach " approach of the *Hongkong Fir* case [1962] 2 Q.B. 26 would be unsuitable. I need only add on this point that the word " expressly " used by Diplock L.J. at p. 70 of his judgment in *Hongkong Fir* should not be read as requiring the actual use of the word " condition ": any term or terms of the contract, which, fairly read, have the effect indicated, are sufficient. Lord Diplock himself has given recognition to this in this House: *Photo Production Ltd. v. Securicor Transport Ltd.* [1980] A.C. 827, 849. I therefore reject that part of the appellants' argument which was based upon it, and I must disagree with the judgment of the learned trial judge in so far as he accepted it. I respectfully endorse, on the other hand, the full and learned treatment of this issue in the judgment of Megaw L.J. in the Court of Appeal.

I would add that the argument above applies equally to the use which the appellants endeavoured to make of certain observations in *United Scientific Holdings Ltd. v. Burnley Borough Council* [1978] A.C. 904, a case on which I do not need to comment on this occasion.

In conclusion, the statement of the law in *Halsbury's Laws of England,* 4th ed., vol. 9 (1974), paras. 481–482, including the footnotes to paragraph 482 (generally approved in the House in the *United Scientific Holdings* case), appears to me to be correct, in particular in asserting (1) that the court will require precise compliance with stipulations as to time wherever the circumstances of the case indicate that this would fulfil the intention of the parties, and (2) that broadly speaking time will be considered of the essence in " mercantile " contracts—with footnote reference to authorities which I have mentioned.

The relevant clause falls squarely within these principles, and such authority as there is supports its status as a condition: see *Bremer Handelsgesellschaft m.b.H. v. J. H. Rayner & Co. Ltd.* [1978] 2 Lloyd's Rep. 73 and see *Turnbull (Peter) & Co. Pty. Ltd. v. Mundas Trading Co. (Australasia) Pty. Ltd.* [1954] 2 Lloyd's Rep. 198. In this present context it is clearly essential that both buyer and seller (who may change roles in the next series of contracts, or even in the same chain of contracts) should know precisely what their obligations are, most especially because the ability of the seller to fulfil his obligation may well be totally dependent on punctual performance by the buyer.

I would dismiss the appeal, and for the reasons given by my noble and learned friend, Lord Roskill, the cross-appeal.

LORD FRASER OF TULLYBELTON. My Lords, I have had the advantage of reading in draft the speeches of my noble and learned friends, Lord Wilberforce and Lord Roskill, and I agree with them. For the reasons stated by them I would dismiss the appeal and cross-appeal.

LORD SCARMAN. My Lords, I have had the advantage of reading in draft the speeches of my noble and learned friends, Lord Wilberforce and

A   Lord Roskill. I agree with both of them, and would, therefore, dismiss the appeal and the cross-appeal.

    I wish, however, to make a few observations upon the topic of " innominate " terms in our contract law. In *Hongkong Fir Shipping Co. Ltd.* v. *Kawasaki Kisen Kaisha Ltd.* [1962] 2 Q.B. 26, the Court of Appeal rediscovered and reaffirmed that English law recognises contractual terms which, upon a true construction of the contract of which they are part, are

B neither conditions nor warranties but are, to quote my noble and learned friend Lord Wilberforce's words in *Bremer Handelsgesellschaft m.b.H.* v. *Vanden Avenne-Izegem P.V.B.A.* [1978] 2 Lloyd's Rep. 109, 113, " intermediate." A condition is a term, the failure to perform which entitles the other party to treat the contract as at an end. A warranty is a term, breach of which sounds in damages but does not terminate, or entitle the

C other party to terminate, the contract. An innominate or intermediate term is one, the effect of non-performance of which the parties expressly or (as is more usual) impliedly agree will depend upon the nature and the consequences of breach. In the *Hongkong Fir* case the term in question provided for the obligation of seaworthiness, breach of which it is well known may be trivial (e.g. one defective rivet) or very serious (e.g. a hole in the bottom of the ship). It is inconceivable that parties when including

D such a term in their contract could have contemplated or intended (unless they expressly say so) that one defective rivet would entitle the charterer to end the contract or that a hole in the bottom of the ship would not. I read the *Hongkong Fir* case as being concerned as much with the construction of the contract as with the consequences and effect of breach. The first question is always, therefore, whether,

E upon the true construction of a stipulation and the contract of which it is part, it is a condition, an innominate term, or only a warranty. If the stipulation is one, which upon the true construction of the contract the parties have not made a condition, and breach of which may be attended by trivial, minor or very grave consequences, it is innominate, and the court (or an arbitrator) will, in the event of dispute, have the task of deciding whether the breach that has arisen is such as the parties

F would have said, had they been asked at the time they made their contract: " it goes without saying that, if that happens, the contract is at an end."

    Where, therefore, as commonly happens, the parties do not identify a stipulation as a condition, innominate term, or warranty, the court will approach the problem of construction in the way outlined by Upjohn L.J. [1962] 2 Q.B. 26, 63, 64. As the Lord Justice put it:

G   " Where, however, upon the true construction of the contract, the parties have not made a particular stipulation a condition, it would in my judgment be unsound and misleading to conclude that, being a warranty damages is necessarily a sufficient remedy."

    Unless the contract makes it clear, either by express provision or by necessary implication arising from its nature, purpose, and circumstances

H (" the factual matrix " as spelt out, for example, by Lord Wilberforce in his speech in the *Reardon Smith* case [1976] 1 W.L.R. 989, 995–997), that a particular stipulation is a condition or only a warranty, it is an innominate term, the remedy for a breach of which depends upon the nature, consequences, and effect of the breach.

    When the Court of Appeal had taken the logical step of declaring that the *Hongkong Fir* analysis applied to contracts generally (*Cehave N.V.* v. *Bremer Handelsgesellschaft m.b.H.* [1976] Q.B. 44), the law was back

where it had been left by Lord Mansfield in *Boone* v. *Eyre* (1777) 1 Hy.Bl.   A
273n and the judgment of Bramwell B. in *Jackson* v. *Union Marine Insurance Co. Ltd.* (1874) L.R. 10 C.P. 125. Section 11 (1) (*b*) of the Sale
of Goods Act 1893 can now be seen to be no more than a statutory guide
to the use of the terms " condition " and " warranty " in that Act. It is not
to be treated as an indication that the law knows no terms other than
conditions and warranties. This fallacy was exposed in the *Hongkong Fir*
case [1962] 2 Q.B. 26. To read the subsection as a guide to a compre-   B
hensive classification of contractual terms is to convert it into a will-o'-the-
wisp leading the unwary away from the true path of the law.

The difficulty in the present case is, as Mr. Buckley's excellent argument for the appellants revealed, to determine what is the true construction
of the completed clause 7 of GAFTA form 119, which the parties incorporated in their contract. After some hesitation, I have concluded that   C
the clause was intended as a term, the buyer's performance of which
was the necessary condition to performance by the seller of his obligations.
The contract, when made, was, to use the idiom of Diplock L.J. [1962]
2 Q.B. 26, 65 and *Demosthenes* (Oratt. Attici, Reiske 867.11), " synallag-
matic," i.e. a contract of mutual engagements to be performed in the future,
or, in the more familiar English/Latin idiom, an " executory " contract. The
seller needed sufficient notice to enable him to choose the loading port: the   D
parties were agreed that the notice to be given him was 15 days: this was
a mercantile contract in which the parties required to know where they
stood not merely later with hindsight but at once as events occurred.
Because it makes commercial sense to treat the clause in the context and
circumstances of this contract as a condition to be performed before the
seller takes his steps to comply with the bargain, I would hold it to be not   E
an innominate term but a condition.

LORD LOWRY. My Lords, I have had the advantage of reading in draft
the speeches of my noble and learned friends Lord Wilberforce and Lord
Scarman, as well as the comprehensive review of the facts and the relevant
law contained in the speech about to be delivered by my noble and learned   F
friend Lord Roskill. I respectfully agree with their opinions, which taken
together leave little of value to be said.

If I venture to add a few words of my own (which gives me an
opportunity to acknowledge the excellent arguments on both sides), it is
because I wish to refer to two points of general interest and then to state
shortly why I would hold the term breached by the buyers to have been a
condition.   G

As your Lordships have observed, the appellants based themselves on
Hongkong Fir Shipping Co. Ltd. v. *Kawasaki Kisen Kaisha Ltd.* [1962]
2 Q.B. 26, but they sought from that case a degree of support which it
could not give them by citing it for the proposition that a term of a contract is not a condition unless a breach of it is seen to have deprived the
party not in default of substantially the whole benefit which he was   H
intended to obtain from the contract. By this argument the appellants were
saying that in *Hongkong Fir* Diplock L.J. had adopted a new criterion for
deciding by means of hindsight whether a term was a condition or not.

This was wrong. In the first place, the term in question in *Hongkong Fir*
was one relating to seaworthiness, and the entire court agreed that it was
not a condition but a term the remedy for a breach of which might be
rescission (with or without damages) or merely damages for the breach.

A   Secondly, at p. 70 Diplock L.J. introduces the discussion by saying that
there are many contractual undertakings of a more complex character
which cannot be categorised as being conditions or warranties. And the
description which has since been applied to this kind of term provides a
conclusive answer to the appellants' contention. It is " intermediate "
because it lies in the middle *between* a condition and a warranty (just as
the remedy for its breach lies somewhere between the remedies for breach
B   of a condition and breach of a warranty), and it is " innominate " because
it is not *called* a condition or a warranty but assumes the character of
each in turn.

It is by construing a contract (which can be done as soon as the contract is made) that one decides whether a term is, either expressly or by
necessary implication, a condition, and not by considering the gravity of
C   the breach of that term (which cannot be done until the breach is
imminent or has occurred). The latter process is not an aid to construing
the contract, but indicates whether rescission or merely damages is the
proper remedy for a breach for which the innocent party might be recompensed in one way or the other according to its gravity. The approach of
Diplock L.J. in the *Hongkong Fir* case [1962] 2 Q.B. 26, 69–70 is absolutely consistent with the classic statement of Bowen L.J. in *Bentsen* v.
D   *Taylor, Sons & Co.* [1893] 2 Q.B. 274, 281 which Sellers L.J. cited at
p. 60.

The " wait and see " method, or, as my noble and learned friend Lord
Wilberforce has put it, the " gravity of the breach " approach, is not the
way to identify a condition in a contract. This is done by construing the
contract in the light of the surrounding circumstances. By his illuminating
E   analysis Diplock L.J. shed a new light on old and accepted principles: he
did not purport to establish new ones.

The second general point which I desire to mention concerns stipulations as to time in mercantile contracts, in regard to which it has been said
that, broadly speaking, time will be considered to be of the essence. To
treat time limits thus means treating them as conditions, and he who
F   would do so must pay respect to the principle enunciated by Roskill L.J.
in *Cehave N.V.* v. *Bremer Handelsgesellschaft m.b.H.* [1976] Q.B. 44,
71A, that contracts are made to be performed and not to be avoided.

The treatment of time limits as conditions in mercantile contracts does
not appear to me to be justifiable by any presumption of fact or rule of
law, but rather to be a practical expedient founded on and dictated by the
experience of businessmen, just the kind of thing which Bowen L.J. could
G   have had in mind when framing his classic observations on the implied
term in *The Moorcock* (1889) 14 P.D. 64, 68:

"Now, an implied warranty, or, as it is called, a covenant in law, as
distinguished from an express contract or express warranty, really is in
all cases founded on the presumed intention of the parties, and upon
reason. The implication which the law draws from what must
H   obviously have been the intention of the parties, the law draws with
the object of giving efficacy to the transaction and preventing such a
failure of consideration as cannot have been within the contemplation
of either side; and I believe if one were to take all the cases, and they
are many, of implied warranties of covenants in law, it will be found
that in all of them the law is raising an implication from the presumed
intention of the parties with the object of giving to the transaction
such efficacy as both parties must have intended that at all events it

720

should have. In business transactions such as this, what the law A
desires to effect by the implication is to give such business efficacy to
the transaction as must have been intended at all events by both
parties who are business men; not to impose on one side all the perils
of the transaction, or to emancipate one side from all the chances of
failure, but to make each party promise in law as much, at all events,
as it must have been in the contemplation of both parties that he
should be responsible for in respect of those perils or chances. Now B
what did each party in a case like this know? For if we are examining
into their presumed intention we must examine into their minds as to
what the trasaction was."

This passage has stood the test of time and I commend it to all lawyers
who undertake to advise their clients on mercantile affairs.

C

In order to identify an implied term (concerning which both parties to
the contract, being men of business, would say, " of course; it goes without
saying ") one must construe the contract in the light of the surrounding
circumstances and, to understand how that is done, we cannot do better
than read the passage from Lord Wilberforce's speech in the *Reardon
Smith* case [1976] 1 W.L.R. 989, 995E–997C to which my noble and learned
friend, Lord Scarman, has already referred your Lordships.

D

The law having been established, why should we regard the term here
in question as a condition? I start by expressing my full agreement with
the reasons given in your Lordships' speeches. Among the points which
have weighed with me are the following: (1) There are enormous practical
advantages in certainty, not least in regard to string contracts where today's
buyer may be tomorrow's seller. (2) Most members of the string will have E
many ongoing contracts simultaneously and they must be able to do
business with confidence in the legal results of their actions. (3) Decisions
would be too difficult if the term were innominate, litigation would be rife
and years might elapse before the results were known. (4) The difficulty of
assessing damages is an indication in favour of condition: *McDougall* v.
Aeromarine of Emsworth Ltd. [1958] 1 W.L.R. 1126, 1133. (5) One can at F
least say that recent litigation has provided indications that the term is a
condition. Parties to similar contracts should (failing a strong contra-
indication) be able to rely on this: *The Mihalis Angelos* [1971] 1 Q.B. 164,
199F *per* Edmund-Davies L.J. (6) To make " total loss " the only test of
a condition is contrary to authority and experience, when one recalls that
terms as to the date of sailing, deviation from a voyage and the date of
delivery are regarded as conditions, but that failure to comply with them G
does not always have serious consequences. (7) Nor need an implied condition pass the total loss test: see (6) above. (8) If the consequences of
breach of condition turn out to be slight, the innocent party may treat the
condition as an innominate term or a warranty. (9) While the sellers could
have made time of the essence, if it were not so already, this would require
reasonable notice, which might well not be practical either in a string H
contract or at all. (10) In *Tarrabochia* v. *Hickie* (1856) 1 H. & N. 183, 188
upon which the appellants strongly relied, Bramwell B. said:

" No doubt it is competent for the parties, if they think fit, to declare
in express terms that any matter shall be a condition precedent, but
when they have not so expressed themselves, it is necessary for those
who construe the instrument to see whether they intend to do it.
Since, however, they could have done it, those who construe the

A   instrument should be chary in doing for them that which they might, but have not done for themselves."

But in that very case both Pollock C.B. and Bramwell B., without the benefit of any express term, said that, where the agreement was that a ship should sail on a particular day, that was a condition precedent. (11) To accept the argument that conditions ought not to be implied " because the parties themselves know how to describe a term " would logically condemn

B the entire doctrine of implied terms. (12) Arbitrators and courts might if the term were innominate, give different answers concerning the effect of a breach in very similar transactions, and parties could never learn by experience what was likely to happen in a given situation. So-called string contracts are not made, or adjudicated on, in strings.

C   The only arguments against treating the term as a condition appear to me to be based on generalities, whereas the considerations which are peculiar to this contract and similar contracts tell in favour of its being a condition. For these reasons, and for the reasons given by my noble and learned friends, I would concur in dismissing both the appeal and the cross-appeal.

D   LORD ROSKILL. My Lords, the appellants (Bunge Corporation, New York) were the buyers and the respondents (Tradax Export S.A., Panama) the sellers under a contract concluded on January 30, 1974, through their respective brokers in Antwerp and Rotterdam for the sale and purchase of 15,000 long tons, 5 per cent. more or less in vessel's option, of United States soya bean meal, shipment of 5,000 long tons in each of May, June

E and July 1975 at a price of U.S. $199·50 per metric ton, f.o.b. one United States Gulf port at sellers' option. The respondents through their associated German company issued a contract note bearing that date for 5,000 long tons, 5 per cent. more or less for May 1975 shipment and the present appeal arises out of that May 1975 shipment. The appellants' brokers in Antwerp issued a single contract note for the entire quantity of 15,000 tons already referred to. The two contract notes were not in identical terms but

F nothing now depends upon the differences.

     The contract incorporated the terms and conditions of GAFTA form 119. The relevant extracts from the two contract notes are as follows:
The respondents' contract note:

     " *Quantity*: 5,000 (five thousand) tons of 2,240 lbs, 5 per cent. more

G   or less in vessel's option at contract price, to be declared latest when nominating the vessel. . . . *Shipment*: May, 1975—buyers to give 15 days' loading notice f.o.b. one Gulf port at seller's option, stowed/ trimmed."

The appellants' contract note:

     " *Quantity*: 15,000 L.T. of 1,016 kilos, 5 per cent. more or less at

H   vessel's option at contract price, quantity to be declared latest when nominating vessel. . . . *Other Conditions*: . . . Buyers to give 15 days' preadvice of readiness of steamer."

The most relevant clauses in form 119 are as follows:

     " 7. *Period of Delivery*. During .... at buyers' call. Buyers shall give at least .... consecutive days' notice of probable readiness of vessel(s), and of the approximate quantity required to be loaded. Buyers shall keep sellers informed of any A changes in the date of probable readiness of vessel(s).

"8. *Extension of Delivery.* The contract period of delivery shall, if desired by buyers, be extended by an additional period of one calendar month, provided that buyers give notice in accordance with the notices clause not later than the next business day following the last day of the delivery period. In this event sellers shall carry the goods at buyers' account and all charges for storage, interest, insur- B ance and other such normal carrying expenses shall be for buyers' account. Should buyers not have taken delivery by the end of this extension period, sellers shall have the option of declaring the buyers to be in default or shall be entitled to demand payment at contract price plus such charges as stated above, less current f.o.b. charges, against warehouse warrants and such tender of warehouse receipts C shall be considered complete performance of the contract on the part of the sellers. . . .

"20. Notices. Any notices received after 1600 hours on a business day shall be deemed to have been received on the business day following. A notice to the broker or agent shall be deemed a notice under this contract. All notices given under this contract shall be D given by letter or by telegram or by telex or by other method of rapid written communication. In case of resales all notices shall be passed on without delay by buyers to their respective sellers or vice versa. . . .

"22. Default. In default of fulfilment of contract by either party, the other, at his discretion shall, after giving notice by letter, telegram or telex, have the right to sell or purchase as the case may be, against the defaulter and the defaulter shall make good the loss, if any, on E such purchase or sale on demand. If the party liable to pay be dis- satisfied with the price of such sale or purchase or if the above right is not exercised and damages cannot be mutually agreed, any damages, payable by the party in default shall be settled by arbitration. In the event of default by sellers entitling buyers to damages, such damages shall be based upon the actual or estimated value of the goods on date F of default, to be fixed by arbitration unless mutually agreed, and nothing contained in or implied under this contract shall entitle buyers to recover any damages in respect of loss of profit upon any sub- contracts made by themselves or others unless the arbitrators or Board of Appeal, having regard to any special circumstances, shall in their sole and absolute discretion award such damages. In the event of G default in shipment or delivery, damages, if any, shall be computed upon the mean contract quantity."

My Lords, since it was agreed that there was no material difference between the two important clauses regarding the giving of the 15 days' notice to which those clauses refer, it is clear that the two blanks in clause 7 of form 119 have to be treated as completed with the words " during May H 1975 " in the first blank and the figures " 15 " in the second blank, so that clause 7 thus completed reads:

"Period of delivery—during May 1975 at buyers' call. Buyers shall give at least 15 consecutive days' notice of probable readiness of vessel(s), and of the approximate quantity required to be loaded. Buyers shall keep sellers informed of any changes in the date of probable readiness of the vessel(s)."

A   It was found by the Board of Appeal of GAFTA, in paragraph 6 of the special case, that extensions were claimed under clause 8 of form 119 so that the relevant delivery period became June 1975. The Board of Appeal also found in paragraph 11 of the special case, that the appellants' nomination of the vessel concerned to load what had thus become a June shipment was given to the respondents at 08.46 on June 17, 1975, when it was received by the respondents' brokers in Rotterdam, less than 15

B   consecutive days before the end of the extended shipment period. It is not necessary to detail the passing on of this notice until it reached the respondents on June 18, 1975. On June 20, 1975, the respondents claimed default because of the alleged lateness of the appellants' notice. The relevant details will be found in paragraphs 12, 13, and 14 of the special case. As is found in paragraph 19 of the special case, the market price

C   had by then fallen by over U.S. $60 per metric ton. The respondents claimed damages from the appellants. The dispute was referred to arbitration in accordance with clause 26 of form 119. The umpire awarded the respondents U.S. $317,500 as damages, this figure being based on the mean contract quantity of 5,000 long tons together with certain other sums not now immediately relevant. The appellants appealed to the Board of Appeal of GAFTA and that board consisting of five members dismissed

D   their appeal in all respects but stated a special case for the decision of the court. Upon the hearing of that special case by Parker J., that learned judge reversed the decision of the Board of Appeal and upheld their alternative award. The respondents thereupon appealed to the Court of Appeal (Megaw, Browne and Brightman L.JJ.) who restored the award of the Board of Appeal on liability but varied the quantum of damages

E   holding that these should be measured by the minimum quantity the appellants would have been obliged to take. Leave to appeal to your Lordships' House was granted by the Court of Appeal.

     My Lords, your Lordships' House is the fifth tribunal before whom this dispute has been heard. I understand all your Lordships are agreed that the appeal and also the cross-appeal on quantum fail in substance

F   for the reasons given by Megaw L.J. in, if I may respectfully say so, a powerful and closely reasoned judgment in the Court of Appeal. It follows that the same view upon the main issue involved in this dispute has been formed by six members of GAFTA, three learned Lords Justices and five members of your Lordships' House, a total of 14 with only the learned judge taking the opposite view on that main issue. My Lords, I intend no disrespect to the learned judge in pointing this out. I do so merely for

G   the purpose of expressing regret that, notwithstanding repeated adverse comments in your Lordships' House, in a simple case of this kind there should be a succession of no less than four appeals from the decision of an umpire well versed in disputes of this kind and that this is still possible. I derive some comfort however from the fact that with the passing of the Arbitration Act 1979 this multiplicity of appeals should soon be a thing

H   of the past.

     My Lords, the central question in this appeal is whether the appellants' obligation under clause 7 completed as I have completed it, are of such a character that a breach of them by the appellants such as, in my view, undoubtedly took place, entitled the respondents forthwith to rescind and claim damages. Put into lawyers' language—is the appellants' obligation to give the required 15 days' notice a condition or not? If it is, this appeal fails. If it is not, this appeal must succeed. As already stated, at all stages

of these proceedings, save one, this obligation has been held to be a condi- **A**
tion. The learned judge not only held that it was not a condition but also
held that there was no breach by the appellants of clause 7. The Court of
Appeal disagreed and this latter submission which found favour with the
learned judge was not—rightly in my view—pursued in argument before
your Lordships' House.

My Lords, the relevant phrase " give at least 15 consecutive days'
notice " consists only of six words and two digits. But the able arguments **B**
of which your Lordships have had the benefit have extended over three
full days. The appellants' arguments may be summarised thus. They submitted that this term was not a condition but was what has come to be
described since the *Hongkong Fir* case [1962] 2 Q.B. 26, as an " innominate " obligation—neither a condition nor a warranty, and that when a
term is an innominate obligation the question whether or not a breach **C**
gives the innocent party the right to rescind depends upon whether the
innocent party was thereby deprived " of substantially the whole benefit
which it was intended that he should obtain from the contract." This last
quotation is from the judgment of Diplock L.J. in the *Hongkong Fir* case
[1962] 2 Q.B. 26, 70. It was further argued that since the respondents
accepted that they could not show the now admitted breach by the **D**
appellants in giving a late notice had deprived them of substantially the
whole benefit which it was intended they should obtain from the contract,
the respondent had no right to rescind on account of that late notice. Much
reliance was also placed by Mr. Buckley for the appellants upon the
ensuing passage in Diplock L.J.'s judgment, also at p. 70: " and the legal
consequences of a breach of such an undertaking, *unless provided for
expressly in the contract* [my emphasis], depend upon the nature of the **E**
event to which the breach gives rise." There was, Mr. Buckley argued, no
such " express " provision in this contract. Mr. Buckley also placed
reliance upon the application of the principle enunciated in the *Hongkong
Fir* case, which was a case of time charterparty relating to an unseaworthy
ship, to contracts for the sale of goods, such as the present, by the Court
of Appeal in *Cehave N.V.* v. *Bremer Handelsgesellschaft m.b.H.* [1976] **F**
Q.B. 44, a decision approved in your Lordships' House in the *Reardon
Smith* case [1976] 1 W.L.R. 989. The principles enunciated in the first
two cases mentioned were, he said, of general application and pointed the
way to a new and now correct approach to the question how a term
in a contract alleged on the one hand to be a condition and on the other
hand to be an " innominate term " should be approached.

My Lords, it is beyond question that there are many cases in the books **G**
where terms, the breach of which do not deprive the innocent party of
substantially the whole of the benefit which he was intended to receive from
the contract, were nonetheless held to be conditions any breach of which
entitled the innocent party to rescind. Perhaps the most famous is *Bowes*
v. *Shand*, 2 App.Cas 455. *Reuter* v. *Sala* (1879) 4 C.P.D. 239 is another
such case. Both these cases were decided before the Sale of Goods Act **H**
1893 was enacted. But that Act only codified the relevant common law.
I think Mr. Buckley was entitled to say that these two, and other similar
cases, largely turned upon the fact that the breach complained of was
part of the description of the goods in question and that would therefore
today be a statutory condition under section 13 of the Sale of Goods Act.
But there are many other cases, modern and less modern, where terms in
contracts for the sale of goods have been held to be conditions any breach

A of which will give rise to a right to rescind. Though section 10 (1) of the Sale of Goods Act 1893 provides that, unless a different intention appears, terms as to the time of payment are not deemed to be of the essence of a contract of sale, there are many cases, notably those in connection with the opening of bankers credits and the payment against documents, where the relevant obligations have been held to be a condition a breach of which will entitle the innocent party to rescind. No useful purpose will be served

B by listing all those cases cited in argument on either side. Many are usefully collected in the judgment of Diplock J. in *Ian Stach Ltd.* v. *Baker Bosley Ltd.* [1958] 2 Q.B. 130, 139–144, and I would emphasise in this connection the need for certainty in this type of transaction to which that learned judge referred at pp. 143 and 144 of his judgment. Parties to commercial transactions should be entitled to know their rights at once and should not, when possible, be required to wait upon events before

C those rights can be determined. Of course, in many cases of alleged frustration or of alleged repudiatory delay it may be necessary to await events upon the happening or non-happening of which rights may well crystallise. But your Lordships' House has recently reiterated in a series of cases arising from the withdrawal of ships on time charter for non-payment of hire the need for certainty where punctual payment of hire is required

D and has held that the right to rescind automatically follows a breach of any such condition.

My Lords, I find nothing in the judgment of Diplock L.J. in the *Hongkong Fir* case [1962] 2 Q.B. 26 which suggests any departure from the basic and long standing rules for determining whether a particular term in a contract is or is not a condition and there is much in the judgment of

E Sellers L.J. with which Upjohn L.J. expressly agreed, to show that those rules are still good law and should be maintained. They are enshrined in the oft quoted judgment of Bowen L.J. in *Bentsen* v. *Taylor, Sons & Co.* [1893] 2 Q.B. 274, 281:

F " There is no way of deciding that question except by looking at the contract in the light of the surrounding circumstances, and then making up one's mind whether the intention of the parties, as gathered from the instrument itself, will best be carried out by treating the promise as a warranty sounding only in damages, or as a condition precedent by the failure to perform which the other party is relieved of his liability."

G That well-known passage will be found quoted by Sellers L.J. in the *Hongkong Fir* case [1962] 2 Q.B. 26, 60. I would add a reference in this connection to the judgment of Scrutton L.J. in *In re Comptoir Commercial Anversois and Power, Son & Co.* [1920] 1 K.B. 868, 899, where he added to the statements of the same principle in the Exchequer Chamber in *Behn* v. *Burness* (1863) 3 B. & S. 751 and in *Oppenheim* v. *Fraser* (1876) 34 L.T. 524 his own great authority.

H My Lords, the judgment of Diplock L.J. in the *Hongkong Fir* case is, if I may respectfully say so, a landmark in the development of one part of our law of contract in the latter part of this century. Diplock L.J. showed by reference to detailed historical analysis, contrary to what had often been thought previously, that there was no complete dichotomy between conditions and warranties and that there was a third class of term, the innominate term. But I do not believe Diplock L.J. ever intended his judgment to afford an easy escape route from the normal consequences of rescission to a

contract breaker who had broken what was, upon its true construction, A
clearly a condition of the contract by claiming that he had only broken
an innominate term. Of course when considering whether a particular
term is or is not a condition it is relevant to consider to what other class
or category that term, if not a condition, might belong. But to say that is
not to accept that the question whether or not a term is a condition has to
be determined solely by reference to what has to be proved before rescission
can be claimed for breach of a term which has already been shown not to B
be a condition but an innominate term. Once it is appreciated that the
whole of the passages on pp. 69 and 70 of Diplock L.J.'s judgment are
directed to the consequences of a term which is not a condition but an
innominate term and not to the question of whether or not a particular
term is a condition, the difficulties mentioned by Megaw L.J. in his
judgment if the passages in question are read too literally, and as the C
appellants invite your Lordships to read them, disappear. The only criticism
I would respectfully venture of these passages is the use of the adverb
" expressly " in the passage I have already quoted from the middle of
the full paragraph on p. 70. Surely the same result must follow whether
the legal consequences of the breach are also " impliedly " provided for
in the contract upon that contract's true construction? In venturing D
this amendment to what Diplock L.J. said, I derive comfort from the
fact that my noble and learned friend, Lord Diplock himself in *Photo
Production Ltd.* v. *Securicor Transport Ltd.* [1980] A.C. 827, 849 speaks
of the case where the contracting parties have agreed

> " *whether by express words or by implication of law* " (my emphasis)
> that " *any* " (Lord Diplock's emphasis) " failure by one party to
> perform a particular primary obligation (' condition ' in the nomen-   E
> clature of the Sale of Goods Act 1893), irrespective of the gravity of
> the event that has in fact resulted from the breach, shall entitle the
> other party to elect to put an end to all primary obligations of both
> parties remaining unperformed."

Thus I think it legitimate to suggest an amendment to the passage in [1962]
2 Q.B. 26, 70 either by deleting the word " expressly " or by adding the   F
words " or by necessary implication."

My Lords, your Lordships' House had to consider a similar problem in
relation to a different clause (clause 21) in a different GAFTA contract in
Bremer Handelsgesellschaft m.b.H. v. *Vanden Avenne-Izegem P.V.B.A.*
[1978] 2 Lloyd's Rep. 109. In passing I would observe the text of that
clause is inaccurately quoted in the headnote of the report but will be found   G
correctly quoted in the speech of Viscount Dilhorne at p. 121. My noble
and learned friend Lord Wilberforce said, at p. 113 :

> " Automatic and invariable treatment of a clause such as this runs
> counter to the approach, which modern authorities recognise, of
> treating such a provision as having the force of a condition (giving
> rise to rescission or invalidity), or of a contractual term (giving rise   H
> to damages only) according to the nature and gravity of the breach.
> The clause is then categorised as an innominate term. This doctrine
> emerged very clearly in *Hongkong Fir Shipping Co. Ltd.* v. *Kawasaki
> Kisen Kaisha Ltd.* [1962] 2 Q.B. 26 in relation to the obligation of
> seaworthiness, and was as applied to a contract for sale of goods
> made on GAFTA form 100 in *The Hansa Nord* [1976] Q.B. 44, a
> decision itself approved by this House in *Reardon Smith Line Ltd.* v.

A
Yngvar Hansen-Tangen [1976] 1 W.L.R. 989. In my opinion the clause may vary appropriately and should be regarded as such an intermediate term: to do so would recognise that while in many, possibly most, instances, breach of it can adequately be sanctioned by damages, cases may exist in which, in fairness to the buyer, it would be proper to treat the cancellation as not having effect. On the other hand, always so to treat it may often be unfair to the seller, and unnecessarily rigid."

B

The passage I have just quoted was directed to clause 21 of the contract there in question. All members of your Lordships' House were of the opinion that that clause was not a condition because it was insufficiently definitive or precise: see the speeches of my noble and learned friends,

C
Lord Salmon at p. 128 and Lord Russell of Killowen at p. 130. But it is important to observe that your Lordships' House had also to consider clause 22 of that contract. All members of your Lordships' House held that clause 22 was a condition: see the speeches of my noble and learned friends, Lord Wilberforce at p. 116 and Lord Salmon at p. 128. I venture to emphasise the statement in the former passage that accurate compliance

D
with the stipulation in question was essential to avoid commercial confusion in view of the possibility of long string contracts being involved, a point of especial importance in the present case.

In short, while recognising the modern approach and not being over-ready to construe terms as conditions unless the contract clearly requires the court so to do, none the less the basic principles of construction for determining whether or not a particular term is a condition remain as

E
before, always bearing in mind on the one hand the need for certainty and on the other the desirability of not, when legitimate, allowing rescission where the breach complained of is highly technical and where damages would clearly be an adequate remedy. It is therefore in my opinion wrong to use the language employed by Diplock L.J. in the *Hongkong Fir* case [1962] 2 Q.B. 26 as directed to the determination of the question which

F
terms of a particular contract are conditions and which are only innominate terms. I respectfully agree with what Megaw L.J. [1980] 1 Lloyd's Rep. 294, 307–308 said in the passage in his judgment in the instant case. The explanation of the passage which he quotes is that which I have just given.

My Lords, Mr. Buckley founded much of this part of his argument

G
upon the decision of your Lordships' House in *United Scientific Holdings Ltd. v. Burnley Borough Council* [1978] A.C. 904 when your Lordships' House, unanimously reversing two separate decisions of the Court of Appeal, held that the time table specified in rent review clauses for the completion of the various steps for determining the rent payable in respect of the period following the review was not of the essence. Naturally,

H
Mr. Buckley relied upon a passage in the speech of my noble and learned friend, Lord Diplock, at p. 928. I quote the passage in full:

"My Lords, I will not take up time in repeating here what I myself said in the *Hongkong Fir* case, except to point out that by 1873:

"(1) Stipulations as to the time at which a party was to perform a promise on his part were among the contractual stipulations which were not regarded as 'conditions precedent' if his failure to perform that promise punctually did not deprive the other party of substantially

the whole benefit which it was intended that he should obtain from A
the contract;

"(2) When the delay by one party in performing a particular
promise punctually had become so prolonged as to deprive the other
party of substantially the whole benefit which it was intended that he
should obtain from the contract it did discharge that other party from
the obligation to continue to perform any of his own promises which
as yet were unperformed;   B

"(3) Similar principles were applicable to determine whether the
parties' duties to one another to continue to perform their mutual
obligations were discharged by frustration of the adventure that was
the object of the contract. A party's ability to perform his promise
might depend upon the prior occurrence of an event which neither
he nor the other party had promised would occur. The question   C
whether a stipulation as to the time at which the event should occur
was of the essence of the contract depended upon whether even a
brief postponement of it would deprive one or other of the parties
of substantially the whole benefit that it was intended that he should
obtain from the contract."

Read literally, the passage might be thought to be of universal D
application and to suggest that by 1873 terms in contract as to time,
whatever their character, were not to be construed as conditions any
breach of which would give rise to a right to rescind unless the several
prerequisites specified in this passage were fulfilled. My Lords, I do not
think that my noble and learned friend can possibly have intended this
passage to be so read. In the immediately preceding pages he had been
dealing with the manner in which the Courts of Chancery had been   E
developing the equitable principles which he describes and explaining how
contemporaneously the courts of common law were reaching the same
result though by a different route. But to read the passage I have just
quoted as of universal application and in particular as of application to
stipulations as to time in mercantile contracts would be to misread it,
for it would be quite inconsistent with many earlier authorities such as F
Behn v. *Burness,* 3 B. & S. 751 as well as later authorities such as *Bowes*
v. *Shand,* 2 App.Cas. 455, *Reuter* v. *Sala,* 4 C.P.D. 239 and *Bentsen* v.
Taylor, Sons & Co. [1893] 2 Q.B. 274 to which I have already referred.
That this is so is strongly reinforced by the fact that Mr. Hugh Francis
whose argument for the appellants was unanimously accepted by your
Lordships' House, expressly conceded that the doctrine that my noble
and learned friend, Lord Diplock, ultimately so clearly expounded [1978] G
A.C. 904, 926–928 did not apply in three classes of case of which the
second was "where the courts may infer from the nature of the contract
or the surrounding circumstances that the parties regard time stipulations
as of the essence of their bargains: mercantile contracts . . ."—see p. 908,
a concession which I think was clearly rightly made.

In reply to this part of Mr. Buckley's argument Mr. Staughton drew H
your Lordships' attention to *Halsbury's Laws of England,* 4th ed., vol. 9
(1974), paras. 481 and 482. He was able to show that the penultimate full
paragraph in paragraph 481 had been expressly approved by no less than
three of your Lordships in the *United Scientific Holdings* case [1978] A.C.
904, by Viscount Dilhorne at p. 937, Lord Simon of Glaisdale at pp.
941 and 944, and by Lord Fraser of Tullybelton at p. 958, while Lord
Salmon at p. 950 stated the law in virtually identical terms though without

A an express reference to this particular passage in *Halsbury*. The passage in question reads:

"The modern law, in the case of contracts of all types, may be summarised as follows. Time will not be considered to be of the essence unless: (1) the parties expressly stipulate that conditions as to time must be strictly complied with; or (2) the nature of the subject matter of the contract or the surrounding circumstances show that time should be considered to be of the essence; or (3) a party who has been subjected to unreasonable delay gives notice to the party in default making time of the essence."

The relevant passage in para. 482 reads:

"Apart from express agreement or notice making time of the essence, the court will require precise compliance with stipulations as to time wherever the circumstances of the case indicate that this would fulfil the intention of the parties. Broadly speaking, time will be considered of the essence in 'mercantile' contracts and in other cases where the nature of the contract or of the subject matter or the circumstances of the case require precise compliance."

D A footnote, no. 3, refers among other cases to *Reuter* v. *Sala*, 4 C.P.D. 239 and to *Bowes* v. *Shand*, 2 App.Cas. 455. My Lords, I agree with Mr. Staughton that the express approval of the passage in paragraph 481 cannot be taken as involving implied disapproval of the passage I have just quoted from paragraph 482.

My Lords, I venture to doubt whether much help is necessarily to be derived in determining whether a particular term is to be construed as a condition or as an innominate term by attaching a particular label to the contract. Plainly there are terms in a mercantile contract, as your Lordships' House pointed out in *Bremer Handelsgesellschaft m.b.H.* v. *Vanden Avenne-Izegem P.V.B.A.* [1978] 2 Lloyd's Rep. 109, which are not to be considered as conditions. But the need for certainty in mercantile contracts is often of great importance and sometimes may well be a determining factor in deciding the true construction of a particular term in such a contract.

To my mind the most important single factor in favour of Mr. Staughton's submission is that until the requirement of the 15-day consecutive notice was fulfilled, the respondents could not nominate the "one Gulf port" as the loading port, which under the instant contract it was their sole right to do. I agree with Mr. Staughton that in a mercantile contract when a term has to be performed by one party as a condition precedent to the ability of the other party to perform another term, especially an essential term such as the nomination of a single loading port, the term as to time for the performance of the former obligation will in general fall to be treated as a condition. Until the 15 consecutive days' notice had been given, the respondents could not know for certain which loading port they should nominate so as to ensure that the contract goods would be available for loading on the ship's arrival at that port before the end of the shipment period.

It follows that in my opinion the umpire, the Board of Appeal and the Court of Appeal all reached the correct conclusion and for the reasons I have given I would dismiss the appellants' appeal. It will have been observed that I have reached this conclusion as a matter of the construction of the relevant clause. I have thus far paid no regard to the finding in

paragraph 5 of the special case that " This term in an f.o.b. contract is   A
regarded in the trade as of such great and fundamental importance that
any breach thereof goes to the root of the contract." Naturally, though
the crucial question of construction is a matter of law for the court, the
court will give much weight to the view of the trade tribunal concerned.
Though I question whether on the argument of a special case it is
permissible to look outside the findings of fact in that special case to
findings of fact in other special cases, Mr. Buckley was able to point to a   B
contrary finding of fact by a different Board of Appeal of the same
association in *Bremer Handelsgesellschaft m.b.H.* v. *J. H. Rayner & Co.
Ltd.* [1978] 2 Lloyd's Rep. 73, 81 :

> " Failure of an f.o.b. buyer to indicate to his seller the demurrage/
> despatch rate with the nomination of a vessel or at any time is *not*
> [my emphasis] customarily treated by the trade as being a term of   C
> great or fundamental importance to the contract such as to give a
> seller the right to reject the nomination or to refuse to ship the goods."

The relevant clause 7 in that case will be found in the judgment of
Mocatta J., at p. 85 :

> " 7. Nomination of Vessel. Buyer to give nomination of vessel to
> seller, in writing, in time for seller to receive with minimum 15 days'   D
> notice of earliest readiness of tonnage at first or sole port of loading."

Mocatta J. held at p. 89 of his judgment that the finding which I have just
quoted did not preclude his reaching the conclusion that that clause was as a
matter of construction a condition, a breach of which entitled the innocent
party to rescind. His decision was reversed on appeal on a different point :
see [1979] 2 Lloyd's Rep. 216. But Bridge L.J. at p. 224 was at pains   E
to say that as then advised he was not persuaded that on this question the
learned judge had reached the wrong conclusion : see also the judgment of
Megaw L.J. at p. 229. With respect, I think that Mocatta J. was plainly
correct in his conclusion on this question.

Mr. Staughton also relied upon a number of cases where the argument
presently urged by Mr. Buckley might have been but was not advanced.   F
They included *Turnbull (Peter) & Co. Pty. Ltd.* v. *Mundas Trading Co.
(Australasia) Pty. Ltd.* [1954] 2 Lloyd's Rep. 198 (a decision of the High
Court of Australia which included Dixon C.J.) and *Carapanayoti & Co.
Ltd.* v. *Comptoir Commercial Andre et Cie. S.A.* [1972] 1 Lloyd's Rep. 139
—a decision of the Court of Appeal. With respect I doubt whether past
omissions, whether for good or bad reasons, greatly advance the solution
of the present problem.   G

My Lords, I would only add in conclusion that it seems clear from the
argument and indeed from the judgment of Parker J. in the present case
that certain passages in the judgment of Diplock L.J. in the *Hongkong Fir*
case [1962] 2 Q.B. 26 and in the speech of my noble and learned friend
Lord Diplock in *United Scientific Holdings Ltd.* v. *Burnley Borough
Council* [1978] A.C. 904 have been read out of context and thus misunder-   H
stood. An excellent illustration of this misunderstanding is shown by the
argument advanced and unanimously rejected in *Toepfer* v. *Lenersan-
Poortman N.V.* [1978] 2 Lloyd's Rep. 555 (Donaldson J.) and [1980] 1
Lloyd's Rep. 143 (Court of Appeal). There the sellers attempted on the
strength of the decision in the *Hongkong Fir* case to argue that the sellers'
obligations regarding time for presentation of the documents against which
the buyers had to pay not later than 20 days after the bill of lading date

A was not a condition a breach of which entitled the buyers to rescind but was only an innominate term. I find myself in complete agreement with the observations of Donaldson J. pointing out how the *Hongkong Fir* case had been misunderstood. I would, therefore, dismiss this appeal with costs.

My Lords, I turn to deal briefly with the respondents' cross-appeal. Both the umpire and the Board of Appeal awarded the respondents damages on the basis of the mean contract quantity of 5,000 long tons.

B They clearly reached this conclusion on the strength of the last sentence of clause 22 of GAFTA form 119. The Court of Appeal reduced the damages payable to the respondents by assessing them by reference not to 5,000 long tons but to 4,750 long tons being 5 per cent. less than the mean contract quantity, this being the minimum quantity the appellants would have been obliged to take. As a result of the Court of Appeal deci-

C sion, the Board of Appeal subsequently made a supplementary award in the respondents' favour for a lesser amount based upon the figure of 4,750 long tons.

It was common ground that the reference in the contract " at vessel's option " meant " at buyers' option." My Lords it was also common ground that the Court of Appeal was bound to reach this conclusion by reason of an earlier decision of that court, *Toprak Mahsulleri Ofisi* v.

D *Finagrain Compagnie Commerciale Agricole et Financière S.A.* [1979] 2 Lloyd's Rep. 98 to which I was a party. In that case the court held that the relevant sentence in the contract applied only to default of shipment by the seller or default of delivery by the seller and not to default by the buyer. In the latter case damages fell to be assessed on ordinary principles.

My Lords the respondents urged that in this context " default " bore

E its primary dictionary meaning of " failure " or " want " or " absence " and that since there had been a " failure " or " want " or " absence " of shipment by the sellers that was sufficient to enable the last sentence of clause 22 to be invoked so as to require the respondents' damages to be assessed on the mean contract quantity.

My Lords, no doubt in some contexts the word " default " may bear this particular dictionary meaning. But in determining the meaning of the

F word in any case, the context in which the word is used is of crucial importance. One has only to see the number of times that the word " default " or " defaulter " is used in clause 22 to see that the context is one of a breach of contract sounding in damages and not of non-performance without breach. My Lords, I am clearly of the view that " default " in the last sentence of clause 22 means default by the sellers

G in breach of their contractual obligations. That sentence has no application to the present case. Accordingly with all respect to the umpire and the Board of Appeal in the present case I think that the *Toprak* case was correctly decided. If the trade wishes to have the same result where the relevant default is by the buyer and not by the seller the terms of GAFTA form 119 and other similar terms will require to be altered. For these

H reasons I would dismiss the cross-appeal with costs.

Appeal and cross-appeal dismissed.

Solicitors: *William A. Crump & Son; Sinclair, Roche & Temperley.*

J. A. G.

A

* GOLD STAR PUBLICATIONS LTD. . . . . APPELLANTS

AND

DIRECTOR OF PUBLIC PROSECUTIONS . . . RESPONDENT

B

[On appeal from GOLD STAR PUBLICATIONS LTD. v. COMMISSIONER
OF POLICE OF THE METROPOLIS]

1981 March 9, 10;   Lord Wilberforce, Lord Simon
     May 7   of Glaisdale, Lord Russell of Killowen,
                                      Lord Keith of Kinkel and Lord Roskill

C

*Crime—Obscene libel—Forfeiture—Articles destined for publica-
tion abroad—Whether " kept for publication for gain "—
Obscene Publications Act 1959 (7 & 8 Eliz. 2, c. 66), s. 3 (1) (3)*[1]

Acting under section 3 of the Obscene Publications Act
1959, police seized 151,877 magazines in the appellants' export
warehouse. Subsequently, magistrates made an order under
section 3 (3) for their forfeiture. The appellants appealed to   D
the Crown Court, contending, inter alia, that the power of
forfeiture did not extend to material destined for publication
abroad and that there was no evidence that the magazines
were obscene within the meaning of the Act. The Crown
Court found that 391 of the magazines had been destined
for home consumption and that 6,609 had been packed for
export to the United States. The precise destination of the
remaining 144,877 was unknown, but the appellants exported   E
their publications to Europe, America, Africa and elsewhere
abroad. The Crown Court took the view that the magazines,
which consisted of photographs and written matter in English,
were clearly obscene; that they could properly infer that they
were intended to be published to persons who had some
standard of literacy in English and who would comprehend
them; and that their effect would be such as to tend to
deprave and corrupt those persons. They dismissed the appeal,   F
and the Divisional Court of the Queen's Bench Division, on
further appeal by the appellants, upheld their decision, certifying as a point of law of general public importance the question
whether in proceedings for forfeiture under section 3 of the
Act of 1959 where articles had been seized in a warehouse in
England but were destined for export and publication overseas
having regard to the definition of obscenity in section 1 (1) an
English court was both competent and entitled in law to hold   G
that those articles were obscene. They refused the appellants
leave to appeal.

On appeal by the appellants by leave of the House of
Lords: —

Held, dismissing the appeal (Lord Simon of Glaisdale dissenting), that the words " kept for publication for gain " in
section 3 (1) and (3) of the Obscene Publications Act 1959
were quite general and there was no reason to confine the   H
powers of seizure and forfeiture to articles intended for
publication in England and Wales (post, pp. 734F—735B, G–H,
739A–B, 742H—743A).

Per Lord Wilberforce, Lord Russell of Killowen, Lord
Keith of Kinkel and Lord Roskill. In a case where the
magistrates are unable to form any opinion on the question

[1] Obscene Publications Act 1959, s. 3 (1) (3): see post, p. 740B–E.

A   under section 1 (1) of the Act of 1959 whether the effect of
an article intended for publication abroad is such as to
tend to deprave and corrupt persons likely to read, see or
hear the matter contained or embodied in it, they will have
to release it.   If a defence of public good is raised, they
must deal with it on the evidence.   The word " overseas " in
the question certified should properly be " outside the jurisdiction of the English courts " (post, pp. 735c–e, h, 739a–b,
B   743b–c, f).
        Decision of the Divisional Court of the Queen's Bench
Division (1980) 71 Cr.App.R. 185 affirmed.

        The following cases are referred to in their Lordships' opinions:
        Attorney-General's Reference (No. 2 of 1975) [1976] 1 W.L.R. 710;
            [1976] 2 All E.R. 753, C.A.
C   *Director of Public Prosecutions* v. *Whyte* [1972] A.C. 849; [1972] 3
            W.L.R. 410; [1972] 3 All E.R. 12, H.L.(E.).
        Handyside v. *United Kingdom* [1980] 1 E.H.R.R. 737.
        Reg. v. *Henn* [1980] 2 W.L.R. 597; [1980] 2 All E.R. 166, E.C.J. and
            H.L.(E.).
        Reg. v. *Jordan* [1977] A.C. 699; [1976] 3 W.L.R. 887; [1976] 3 All
            E.R. 775, H.L.(E.).
D   *Transport Publishing Co. Pty. Ltd.* v. *Literature Board of Review* (1956)
            99 C.L.R. 111.

        The following additional cases were cited in argument:
        Burke v. *Copper* [1962] 1 W.L.R. 700; [1962] 2 All E.R. 14, D.C.
        Cox v. *Stinton* [1951] 2 K.B. 1021; [1951] 2 All E.R. 637, D.C.
        Drucker, In re (No. 2) [1902] 2 K.B. 210.
E   *Reg.* v. *El-Hakkaoui* [1975] 1 W.L.R. 396; [1975] 2 All E.R. 146; 60
            Cr.App.R. 281, C.A.
        Reg. v. *Jameson* [1896] 2 Q.B. 425.
        Reg. v. *Treacy* [1971] A.C. 537; [1971] 2 W.L.R. 112; [1971] 1 All
            E.R. 110, H.L.(E.).
        Thomson v. *Chain Libraries Ltd.* [1954] 1 W.L.R. 999; [1954] 2 All
            E.R. 616, D.C.

F
        APPEAL from the Divisional Court of the Queen's Bench Division.
        The appellants, Gold Star Publications Ltd., appealed from the
judgment of the Divisional Court (Eveleigh L.J. and Watkins J.) on
April 2, 1980, dismissing their appeal by case stated from a decision of
the Croydon Crown Court (Judge David Thomas Q.C. and justices) on
G   May 2, 1979.   By that decision, the Crown Court dismissed the appellants'
appeal against an order made by Croydon justices on December 12,
1978, for the forfeiture under section 3 of the Obscene Publications Act
1959 of 151,877 magazines belonging to the appellants.   The Divisional
Court on April 30, 1980, certified that their decision involved a point of
law of general public importance, viz.:

        " whether in proceedings for forfeiture under section 3 of the
H   Obscene Publications Act 1959 where articles have been seized in a
        warehouse in England but are destined for export and publication
        overseas having regard to the definition of obscenity in section 1 (1)
        of the Act an English court is both competent and entitled in law
        to hold that these articles are obscene,"

but refused the appellants leave to appeal.   On July 3, 1980, the Appeal
Committee of the House of Lords (Lord Diplock, Viscount Dilhorne and

734

Lord Russell of Killowen) granted the appellants leave to appeal. They A appealed.

Louis Blom-Cooper Q.C. and *Geoffrey Robertson* for the appellants. *David Tudor Price* and *Timothy Davis* for the Crown.

Their Lordships took time for consideration.   B

May 7. LORD WILBERFORCE. My Lords, section 3 of the Obscene Publications Act 1959 entitles the police, upon warrant issued by a magistrate, to seize and remove obscene articles from premises in which they are " kept for publication for gain." By subsequent proceedings, the articles so seized may be forfeited. In the appellants' export ware- house at Whyteleafe, Surrey, the police found a large number of maga- C zines which were, according to standards applied in England, undoubtedly " obscene articles "—viz. hard pornography. Of these the great majority, some 150,000 in all, were, according to the appellants' contentions, which the justices and the Crown Court must have accepted, for export to Europe, America, Africa and elsewhere abroad, though there were a few destined for sale in this country by mail order. This has given rise D to the certified question of law whether the Act applies not only to material published in this country but to material destined for publica- tion overseas. The issue depends entirely upon the scope to be given to the words " kept for publication for gain," in, of course, their context. I do not think, though the contrary was submitted, that the case raises any question as to the territoriality or extraterritoriality of United Kingdom legislation—the property in question is located in this country, E and the disposal of it by the police is to take place in this country. Nor are authorities as to composite crimes, that is, crimes of which some elements may occur within and some outside the jurisdiction, of any help or relevance. Nor is the fact, if it be so, that property interests of foreigners may be affected by the seizure of any relevance. Foreigners may be, and commonly are, interested as importers, or indeed as F publishers, of obscene literature or articles, but within the United Kingdom they are totally subject to our laws against obscenity.

The relevant words are quite general, but it is necessary to consider the implications of holding that they apply to articles intended for export. The question is quite a legitimate one whether Parliament intended this piece of legislation to apply to articles which could not deprave or corrupt the British public, but were being sent to places G outside the jurisdiction of English courts.

There were two objections against ascribing this intention to Parlia- ment. First it may be said that to do so would be a kind of moral imperialism, or at least paternalism. The answer to this is that Parlia- ment's intentions cannot be limited in this way. Parliament may well have desired to prevent this country becoming the source of a flourishing H export trade in pornography, and may have thought that profits made by exports could help to sustain domestic trade. The words " for gain " seem to me significant. Further, the Act does not apply to Scotland or Northern Ireland, so it would follow from the appellants' argument that articles destined for those parts of the United Kingdom could not be seized. It seems to me most unlikely that Parliament can have intended this, and if not, it must follow that articles destined for export to other

A   countries must be capable of seizure.   One may add that to exempt articles intended for export would offer an easy pretext for avoiding the application of the section.   So I cannot accept that Parliament must be supposed to have intended to confine this power to articles intended for publication in England or Wales.

B   But, secondly, it may be said that to extend the Act to articles destined for export would make the Act unworkable.   Obscenity—viz. tendency to deprave or corrupt persons likely to read the relevant matter (section 1 of the Act)—is relative: what may deprave or corrupt some may have no effect, or, theoretically, a beneficial effect, on others: see *Director of Public Prosecutions* v. *Whyte* [1972] A.C. 849, *Reg.* v. *Jordan* [1977] A.C. 699 and *Handyside* v. *United Kingdom* [1980] 1 E.H.R.R. 737 decided by the European Court of Human Rights.   How,

C   it may be asked, can magistrates decide upon the likely effect of this material upon foreigners of different attitudes and mores?   How (still less) can they decide upon a defence of the public good if this is raised under section 4 of the Act?

In my opinion it has to be accepted that in some cases the magistrates will not be able to form any opinion on this matter: in such cases, since

D   the court has to be satisfied that the articles are obscene (section 3 (3)), it would have to release them.   In other cases there might be evidence before them either way: that the articles would not tend to deprave or corrupt likely readers in the country of destination, or that they would. Then they would have to decide on the evidence.   In still other cases they would be justified in taking the view that, having regard to the likely readers, the articles were so clearly obscene that evidence was not

E   needed.   As was said in *Transport Publishing Co. Pty. Ltd.* v. *Literature Board of Review* (1956) 99 C.L.R. 111, 118—High Court of Australia— there is such a thing as ordinary human nature which is not a subject for proof by evidence.   If a defence of public good is raised, they must deal with it on the evidence.

In the present case, the Crown Court took the view that the articles

F   were clearly obscene.   The decision shows that the members of the court perused agreed samples; they found that they consisted of photographs and written matter in the English language; the price of the articles was given in United States, Canadian, or Australian dollars:

" They are plainly not intended for publication to some remote and primitive tribe who would not comprehend them.   We can properly

G   infer and do infer that they were intended to be published to persons . . . who have some standard of literacy in English and who would comprehend them and that the effect of them would be such as to tend to deprave and corrupt those persons."

These findings to my mind show both that the Act is workable as regards exports, and that the court properly applied its mind to the probable

H   effect of the articles upon likely readers.   The Divisional Court so found, and I agree with their judgment.   In my opinion, therefore, the certified question should be answered in the affirmative with the rider that the word " overseas " should properly be " outside the jurisdiction of the English courts," and the appeal dismissed.

LORD SIMON OF GLAISDALE.   My Lords, I have the misfortune to differ from my noble and learned friends.   I venture a few words in

deference to the argument by which I was convinced and because con- A
sideration of the Williams Report on Obscenity and Film Censorship (1979)
(Cmnd. 7772) might embrace the question how far English law really wishes
to concern itself with the morals of foreign nationals.

I do not think that the instant issue can be resolved merely by
fastening on the words " publication for gain ": " publication " cannot
here be construed as an abstraction. With publication to whom was
Parliament was concerned? It seems to me inherently unlikely that B
Parliament was concerned with the effect of obscene publications on
anyone outside the United Kingdom.

It would be mere officiousness in any case to seek to impose our own
rules and standards and forensic judgments for the moral welfare of
foreign nationals. And this is a field in which cultural standards and
legislative policies are notoriously diverse. C

The inherent unlikelihood of Parliament being concerned with the
morals of foreign nationals, and therefore with publication abroad, is
borne out when the Act of 1959 is purposively construed. It had two
objectives: first, to enable serious literary, artistic, scientific or scholarly
work to draw on the amplitude of human experience without fear of
allegation (which was implicit in the previous law) that it could con- D
ceivably have a harmful effect on persons other than those to whom it
was in truth directed; and, secondly, by hiving off such work, to enable
effective action to be taken against the exploitation of " hard pornography "—obscene articles without pretension to any literary, artistic,
scientific or scholarly value.

These twin objectives are, indeed, indicated in the long title of the
Act: E

"... to amend the law relating to the publication of obscene matter;
to provide for the protection of literature; and to strengthen the law
concerning pornography."

It is, incidentally, a mistake to suppose that the phrase " strengthen
the law concerning pornography " in the long title involves any artificial
construction of the powers of search, seizure, and forfeiture in section 3 F
of the Act. There were such powers in the Obscene Publications Act
1857. The changes made in 1959 as regards such powers were as follows:
(1) certain interested persons other than the person summoned became
entitled to be heard by the court; (2) the operation of the powers was
extended to cover articles on a stall or vehicle; (3) a search warrant
empowered the police to seize documents related to a business; (4) it was G
no longer necessary for the complainant to swear that there had already
been a publication; (5) the defence of " public good " under section 4
became available in forfeiture proceedings. These changes sufficiently
explain everything in the long title so far as it relates to the powers
of search, seizure and forfeiture. They give no warrant for the construction of section 3 to protect the morals of foreign nationals living
in foreign countries. I can well believe that not a few people hold H
that, notwithstanding any difficulty in defining internationally acceptable
standards of what is obscene, it is the moral duty of the British legislature
to inhibit international trade in pornographic material. But if so high-
minded an objective had really been one of the purposes of the Act of
1959, it would certainly have been stated in the long title. Its absence
is clamant when it comes to a purposive interpretation of the enacting
provisions.

A   The inherent unlikelihood of Parliament legislating to safeguard from moral pollution foreign nationals in foreign countries, regardless of the policies of their own respective legislatures; the confirmation of such self-restraint by scrutiny of the long title; and the absence of any contra-indication in the enacting provisions—these considerations are borne out by a further one: the nature of the tasks imposed on the justices in the forfeiture jurisdiction.   They have in the first place to determine

B whether the material liable to forfeiture is likely to deprave and corrupt a significant proportion of the persons likely to be exposed to it.   They have, secondly, to determine whether publication was nevertheless justified as being for the public good on the grounds of its literary, etc., value. English justices are capable of making such judgments in respect of their fellow citizens in the United Kingdom.   To form such a judgment

C for the benefit of, say, Danes (even those who can read English), not to mention the Ik people of East Africa or Rastafarians in the Caribbean (who, incidentally, can presumably read English), seems an unlikely task to be imposed by Parliament.

          In my respectful submission the argument reduced itself to absurdity when counsel for the respondent candidly accepted that in principle it had to extend to a publication in Arabic for export to an Arab-speak-

D ing country—and presumably even if the owner of the material and prospective publisher was himself a national of the country to which the export was proposed.

          But the difficulty facing the justices on the construction contended for by the respondent is not limited to the task of determining what will deprave and corrupt people with whom they might well have no cultural

E standards in common.   By section 4 of the Act of 1959 they have to go on to determine in respect of such people whether the deleterious tendency of the material is outweighed by the benefits conferred by its literary, artistic, scientific, etc., value.   This balancing task is difficult enough of performance by English justices as regards fellow-citizens; it seems to me so impossible of performance as regards exotic peoples as to constitute

F yet further indication that Parliament was not concerned at all with publication in foreign countries.

          Counsel for the appellant put in the forefront of his argument the undoubted principle that it is only exceptionally (and then by clear words) that United Kingdom legislation operates extraterritorially.   I do not think that this rule assists the appellant's case directly; since, although the material in question was destined for abroad, it was seized and declared to

G be forfeited within the jurisdiction.   But two concepts lie behind this rule. First, that Parliament does not legislate where it has no effective power of enforcement: this does not assist the appellant, since enforcement here is within the jurisdiction.   But the second concept does indeed further the appellant's argument: the rule is also based on international comity. Other than quite exceptionally, sovereigns do not meddle with the

H subjects of foreign sovereigns within the jurisdiction of those foreign sovereigns—a consideration inherently potent in matters where international standards vary greatly.   It is in this indirect way that the presumption against extraterritoriality avails the appellant.

          Counsel for the appellant sought to support his argument based on extraterritoriality by reference to the fact that the Act does not extend to Scotland or Northern Ireland.   I do not think this helps the appellant. In so far as the presumption against extraterritoriality assists the appel-

738

A

lant, it is because sovereigns do not legislate for foreign subjects; and
Scots and Northern Irish are not foreign subjects.   But if the argument
that the Act does not extend to Scotland or Northern Ireland does not
help the appellant, neither does it avail the respondent.   It is said that,
if the forfeiture provisions of the Act do not extend to material destined
for publication in foreign countries, neither can they apply to material
designed for publication in Scotland or Northern Ireland.   I do not think
that this follows at all.   Legislation of this type is characteristically cast
in separate English and Scottish (and sometimes Northern Irish) enactments: this merely reflects the several systems of law which operate
within the United Kingdom.   But an Act which does not extend beyond
England and Wales (or Scotland) is still passed by a parliament consisting
of representatives of England, Wales, Scotland and Northern Ireland.
If such a parliament passes an Act limited to England and Wales it does
not imply that Scotland is regarded as a foreign country.   A parliament
in which the people of Scotland and Northern Ireland are represented
may be legitimately concerned with material in England which would
deprave and corrupt people in Scotland or Northern Ireland, without its
being an inevitable conclusion that such a parliament legitimately has
an equivalent concern to impose its domestic standards of morality on
foreign people.   Equally, the fact that Parliament does not concern
itself with the morals of the people of Denmark does not imply that
it must necessarily show unconcern for the welfare of the people of
Scotland.

As for " export," which is the word which appears in the point of law
certified for your Lordships' consideration, not since the Act of Union
has the traffic of goods across the Scottish border been described as
" export "; and not since the days of Canute has traffic from England
to Denmark been otherwise described.   This is no mere verbal point: it
indicates the fallacy of arguing that, if Parliament did not intend " publication " to extend to publication to persons for whom it has no political
concern, then Parliament must equally be credited with unconcern as
to the effect of publication in Scotland or Northern Ireland.

There is one further matter which I think reinforces the interpretation
I venture to put on the Act—namely, that " publication " was not intended
to extend to publication in foreign countries.   Parliament has not only
legislated generally in this field by the Act of 1959; it has also legislated
particularly within the field by the Protection of Children Act 1978.   That
is an Act to prevent the exploitation of children by making indecent photographs of them; and to penalise the distribution, showing and advertisement
of such indecent photographs.   The Act contains provisions for entry,
search, seizure and forfeiture similar to those in the Obscene Publications
Act 1959.   But the significant feature of the Act of 1978, in contrast to the
Act of 1959, is that it contains a provision whereby offences under it are
to be included in the list of extradition crimes contained in Schedule 1 to
the Extradition Act 1870.   The effect of this is that the British Government
can negotiate treaties with foreign powers providing for the mutual extradition of persons who have committed the extradition crime.   The Act of
1978 thus shows the different way in which Parliament proceeds when it
evinces concern for offences against decency which might affect the nationals
of foreign powers.

For these reasons I would allow the appeal, holding that section 3 of the

B

C

D

E

F

G

H

A Obscene Publications Act 1959 does not apply in respect of articles which are " destined for export and publication overseas."

LORD RUSSELL OF KILLOWEN. My Lords, I have had the advantage of reading in draft the speeches prepared by my noble and learned friends, Lord Wilberforce and Lord Roskill. I agree with them and concur in the answer proposed to the question posed and the dismissal of this appeal.

B

LORD KEITH OF KINKEL. My Lords, I have had the benefit of reading in draft the speech of my noble and learned friend, Lord Wilberforce. I agree with it, and for the reasons which he gives I too would answer the certified question in the manner which he proposes, and dismiss the appeal.

C   LORD ROSKILL. My Lords, the appellants, Gold Star Publications Ltd., appeal to your Lordships' House against an order of the Divisional Court (Eveleigh L.J. and Watkins J.) made on April 2, 1980, dismissing an appeal by way of case stated from an order by Croydon Crown Court (Judge David Thomas Q.C. sitting with justices) on May 2, 1979. That Crown Court had dismissed an appeal by the appellants from an order made by justices sitting at Croydon Magistrates' Court on December 12, 1978, pursuant to the powers conferred upon them by section 3 (3) of the Obscene
D Publications Act 1959. That order was for the forfeiture of no less than 151,877 magazines published by the appellants and seized on April 21, 1978, in the appellants' export warehouse, pursuant to a warrant issued under section 3 (1) of the Act of 1959 on April 18, 1978. The total market value of those magazines is found by the Crown Court to have been of the order of £150,000. The Divisional Court certified this question for your
E Lordships' House as a point of law of general public importance:

"whether in proceedings for forfeiture under section 3 of the Obscene Publications Act 1959 where articles have been seized in a warehouse in England but are destined for export and publication overseas having regard to the definition of obscenity in section 1 (1) of the Act an English court is both competent and entitled in law to hold
F   that these articles are obscene."

The Divisional Court refused leave to appeal to your Lordships' House but that leave was granted on July 3, 1980.
      The appeal indeed raises a point of general interest under the Act of 1959 in relation to magazines and the like found by justices to be " obscene "
G but which are destined for export and thus for publication overseas, for it is submitted on the appellants' behalf that in such a case it is not within the power of an English court of otherwise competent jurisdiction to make a forfeiture order such as was made in the present case. Whether this submission is well founded depends solely on the true construction of the Act of 1959. For ease of reference I set out in full the several relevant parts of that statute. The long title reads thus:
H
"An Act to amend the law relating to the publication of obscene matter; to provide for the protection of literature; and to strengthen the law concerning pornography."

The following sections are the most relevant.
      "1 (1) For the purposes of this Act an article shall be deemed to be obscene if its effect or (where the article comprises two or more distinct items) the effect of any one of its items is, if taken as a whole,

such as to tend to deprave and corrupt persons who are likely, having   A
regard to all relevant circumstances, to read, see or hear the matter
contained or embodied in it.   (2) In this Act 'article' means any
description of article containing or embodying matter to be read or
looked at or both, . . .   (3) For the purposes of this Act a person
publishes an article who—(a) distributes, circulates, sells, lets on hire,
gives, or lends it, or who offers it for sale or for letting on hire; . . .
" 3 (1) If a justice of the peace is satisfied by information on oath   B
that there is reasonable ground for suspecting that, in any premises
in the petty sessions area for which he acts, or on any stall or vehicle
in that area, being premises or a stall or vehicle specified in the
information, obscene articles are, or are from time to time, kept for
publication for gain, the justice may issue a warrant under his hand
empowering any constable to enter (if need be by force) and search   C
the premises, or to search the stall or vehicle, within 14 days
from the date of the warrant, and to seize and remove any articles
found therein or thereon which the constable has reason to believe to
be obscene articles and to be kept for publication for gain. . . .(3) Any
articles seized under subsection (1) of this section shall be brought
before a justice of the peace acting for the same petty sessions area
as the justice who issued the warrant, and the justice before whom   D
the articles are brought may thereupon issue a summons to the
occupier of the premises or, as the case may be, the user of the stall
or vehicle to appear on a day specified in the summons before a
magistrates' court for that petty sessions area to show cause why the
articles or any of them should not be forfeited; and if the court is
satisfied, as respects any of the articles, that at the time when they   E
were seized they were obscene articles kept for publication for gain,
the court shall order those articles to be forfeited : Provided that if
the person summoned does not appear, the court shall not make an
order unless service of the summons is proved.   (4) In addition to
the person summoned, any other person being the owner, author or
maker of any of the articles brought before the court, or any other
person through whose hands they had passed before being seized,   F
shall be entitled to appear before the court on the day specified in
the summons to show cause why they should not be forfeited. . . .
(7) For the purposes of this section the question whether an article
is obscene shall be determined on the assumption that copies of it
would be published in any manner likely having regard to the circumstances in which it was found, but in no other manner. . . .   G
" 4 (1) A person shall not be convicted of an offence against section 2
of this Act, and an order for forfeiture shall not be made under the
foregoing section, if it is proved that publication of the article in
question is justified as being for the public good on the ground that
it is in the interests of science, literature, art or learning, or of other
objects of general concern.   (2) It is hereby declared that the opinion
of experts as to the literary, artistic, scientific or other merits of an   H
article may be admitted in any proceedings under this Act either to
establish or to negative the said ground.
" 5 (3) This Act shall not extend to Scotland or to Northern Ireland."

My Lords, it is important to observe that, as already mentioned, the
present proceedings arise under section 3 of the Act of 1959. That section,
unlike section 2 (1) which was later amended by section 1 of the Obscene

A Publications Act 1964, does not create a criminal offence and a person
whose property is seized or forfeited under section 3 is not for that reason
alone guilty of a criminal offence. Section 3 is concerned with prevention
and not with punishment and is one of the provisions in the Act of 1959
which is designed, as the long title of that Act shows, " to strengthen the
law concerning pornography." No prosecution of the appellants has taken
B place. My Lords, the Crown Court made the following findings of fact
relevant to the present appeal.

" The forfeited magazines fall into three groups: (1) In the first
group are 391 magazines which were found in the mail order department of the appellants' premises. These were destined for home
consumption. (2) The second group consists of 6,609 magazines which
were packed in crates ready for export to the U.S.A. (3) The third
C group consists of 144,877 magazines. These were found in the export
warehouse at the appellants' premises. We do not know the precise
destination of any of them, but we have been told that the appellant
company exports its publications to Europe, America, Africa and
elsewhere abroad."

D Nothing turns in the present appeal upon the first of those three groups.
My Lords, the first question to determine is the true construction of the
relevant words in section 3 (1) of the Act of 1959. The condition precedent to the right of a justice to issue a warrant is that he is satisfied that
in the area in question " obscene articles are, or are from time to time, kept
for publication for gain. . . ." It was strenuously argued that these words
mean " kept for publication in England and Wales for gain in England
E and Wales " and that any other construction would involve giving extraterritorial effect to these provisions of the Act of 1959 when not only
was there no clear provision to that effect but it could not have been the
intention of Parliament in this statute to concern itself with the morals
of persons outside the jurisdiction. It was further argued that the construction contended for by the Crown could not be correct since to accept
F that construction would or might involve the forfeiture of property, rights
or interests within the jurisdiction of persons outside the jurisdiction. My
Lords, this last point though argued first may be quickly disposed of. Not
only is there no finding that any property, rights or interests within the
jurisdiction or persons outside the jurisdiction are presently involved, but
even if there were such a finding there could be no objection to such
property, rights or interests being subjected to legislative control by
G Parliament.
My Lords, there are no express words of limitation upon the relevant
words in section 3 (1). Moreover the Act of 1959 has no application to
Scotland or Northern Ireland. Though the certified question is stated to
relate to export " overseas," the appellants' argument if sound must apply
equally to obscene articles (as defined in section 1 (2)) kept in England
H not for export overseas, as in the present case, but for despatch—" export "
is hardly the right word—to Scotland or Northern Ireland. My Lords,
there being no express words of limitation in section 3 (1), the limitation
contended for by the appellants must be deduced, if at all, from other
provisions of the Act of 1959. In my view no question of the extraterritorial effect of legislation in the proper understanding of that phrase
arises in this appeal. The magazines in question are within the jurisdiction.
The place of their seizure was within the jurisdiction. The appellants are

a limited company amenable to the jurisdiction. No question of extra-   **A**
territoriality arises in connection with section 3.

The crucial question is whether, because of the definition of obscenity
in section 1 (1) and also because of the provisions of section 4, a narrow
meaning must be given to the all-important words in section 3 (1), notwithstanding the absence of any words of limitation in that subsection.
The strongest way in which the appellants' case can be put arises from
  B
the fact that, since the passing of the Act of 1959, there is no longer any
" abstract " concept of obscenity. As my noble and learned friend, Lord
Wilberforce, pointed out in *Director of Public Prosecutions* v. *Whyte*
[1972] A.C. 849, 860 and again in *Reg.* v. *Jordan* [1977] A.C. 699, 717,
section 1 is directed to " relative obscenity "; that is, obscenity relative to
likely readers or other likely recipients of the article in question. It has
thus become important to these cases to determine who are the likely   **C**
readers or customers, for it is only when that class or those classes have
been sufficiently identified that the next question arises, namely whether
the allegedly offending article will " tend to deprave and corrupt persons "
who form a significant part of that class or of those classes. Only if that
further condition is satisfied will the article in question then be " obscene "
within section 1 (1). This being the true construction of this subsection,
the question is naturally forcefully asked on the appellants' behalf how an   **D**
English magistrates' court can possibly answer these questions in relation
to persons of no known or readily identifiable class or propensity in different
countries throughout the world. It is further asked why Parliament should
have concerned itself with the protection of the morals of such persons
whoever they may be. Standards of morality vary immensely in different
countries and what is forbidden or is obscene in one country may even be   **E**
thought to be therapeutic in another. Reliance was placed in this connection upon the opinion of Mr. Advocate-General Warner in *Reg.* v. *Henn*
[1980] 2 W.L.R. 597, 604 quoting from the judgment of the European
Court of Human Rights in *Handyside* v. *United Kingdom* [1980] 1
E.H.R.R. 737 and also upon the passage in the judgment of the European
Court of Justice, at p. 629:

  F

> " In principle, it is for each member state to determine in accordance
> with its own scale of values and in the form selected by it the require-
> ments of public morality in its territory."

My Lords, these are powerful arguments and they can be reinforced
by consideration how the defence of " public good " introduced by section
4 of the Act of 1959 could be effectively raised in such circumstances as
  G
those now under consideration. But powerful as these arguments are, they
seem to me to overlook the fact that the Act of 1959 was concerned
amongst other matters to strengthen the law concerning pornography and
that one of its objectives in section 3 (1) is to stop persons in England and
Wales " publishing for gain." " Publish," so far as presently relevant, is
defined in section 1 (3) (*a*) and if a person in this country, for example,
offers an article for sale he is publishing that article. If that article is   **H**
obscene, he is publishing an obscene article for sale and if he does so for
valuable consideration he is publishing an obscene article for gain. On a
fair reading of section 3 (1) I am unable to see why he ceases so to publish
an obscene article for gain because its ultimate destination is in Scotland,
Northern Ireland or anywhere else in the world, for Parliament may very
well have intended that England and Wales should not become a source
from which unrestricted supplies of obscene articles should flow unchecked

A not only to other parts of the United Kingdom but also to other countries throughout the world.

My Lords, I fully recognise that this conclusion may face a magistrates' court with difficult practical and evidential problems. But their task in administering the Act of 1959 and the later amending legislation on this subject has long been recognised as difficult, unenviable, and a matter for

B sympathy. It is not correct to say that a magistrates' court grappling with this problem will be asked to apply English standards of morality to allegedly offending articles destined elsewhere. The court will be asked to do its best to decide whether those articles will have a tendency to deprave or corrupt a significant number of people in the country to which they are destined. It would be open to those objecting to forfeiture, and thus exercising their rights under section 3 (3) and (4), to adduce evidence to

C show that the conditions specified in section 1 (1) have not in relation to the particular destination in question been satisfied. Moreover, I see no reason in principle why, if it is desired in a particular case to raise the " public good " defence, it should not be possible to do so. In principle I see no objection to seeking to show by admissible evidence that a particular article is to be regarded in a particular country to which it is destined as of (for example) literary merit even though it might not be so regarded

D in this country.

Two other matters shall be mentioned for the sake of completeness. First, reliance was placed on the appellants' behalf on the Protection of Children Act 1978 and in particular upon the extradition conditions in section 1 (6) of that statute, a provision omitted from the Act of 1959. My Lords it cannot be right to interpret the Act of 1959 by reference to

E another Act passed nearly 20 years later on a different subject matter. The presence of an extradition provision in the Act of 1978 or the absence of such a provision in the Act of 1959 are not aids to the construction of section 3 (1) of the latter statute. Secondly, much reliance was placed on the decision of the Court of Appeal in *Attorney-General's Reference (No. 2 of 1975)* [1976] 1 W.L.R. 710. With respect, I have not found that decision of assistance in determining the present appeal. In the result I

F would answer the certified question in the affirmative, subject to the amendment proposed by my noble and learned friend, Lord Wilberforce, and I would dismiss this appeal for substantially the same reasons as those given in the Crown Court and in the Court of Appeal in their clear and succinct judgments.

G

> *Certified question answered in affirmative with qualification that " overseas " means " outside the jurisdiction of the English Courts."*
> *Appeal dismissed with costs.*

H Solicitors: *Offenbach & Co.; Director of Public Prosecutions.*

M. G.

[1981]

A

[HOUSE OF LORDS]

* THOMPSON . . . . APPELLANT

AND

BROWN AND ANOTHER . . . . RESPONDENTS

B

1981 March 17, 18;   Lord Diplock, Lord Elwyn-Jones,
     May 7   Lord Fraser of Tullybelton, Lord Scarman
                                   and Lord Bridge of Harwich

*Limitation of Action—Personal injuries—Time limit, power to
override—Writ not issued within three-year period due to
negligence of solicitors—Plaintiff having unanswerable claim
against solicitors—Whether jurisdiction in court to allow action
to proceed—Whether plaintiff suffering no prejudice if action
barred—Limitation Act 1939 (2 & 3 Geo. 6, c. 21) (as amended
by Limitation Act 1975 (c. 54), s. 1), s. 2D (1)* [1]

C

On March 4, 1976, the plaintiff, a bricklayer's labourer,
was injured by a collapse of scaffolding at his place of work.
He consulted solicitors, and negotiations followed. Subsequently, however, the solicitors' file became mislaid and
forgotten, and in consequence a writ was not issued until
April 10, 1979. In their defence, the scaffolders pleaded the
Limitation Act 1939 and denied that it would be equitable
to allow the action to proceed under section 2D notwithstanding the expiry of the three-year limitation period under section
2A. That matter was tried as a preliminary issue by Phillips J.,
who held that he was bound by the decision of the Court of
Appeal in *Browes* v. *Jones & Middleton* (unreported) to
hold that, since if the action were not allowed to proceed
the plaintiff would have an unanswerable claim in negligence
against his solicitors, he had not been prejudiced by the
provisions of section 2A and that, accordingly, the court
had no jurisdiction under section 2D to direct that those
provisions should not apply. He granted the plaintiff a certificate under section 12 of the Administration of Justice Act
1969 for appeal direct to the House of Lords, and the House
of Lords subsequently granted leave under section 13.

On appeal by the plaintiff: —

Held, allowing the appeal, that even in a case where, if
the action were not allowed to proceed, the plaintiff would
have an unanswerable claim against his solicitors for negligence in which the damages would be no less than those
that he would be able to recover against the defendant if it
were allowed to proceed, he would suffer some prejudice,
albeit only minor, in that he would be obliged to find and
instruct new and strange solicitors, there was bound to be
delay, he would incur a personal liability for costs of the
action up to the date of the court's refusal to give a direction
under section 2D and he might prefer to sue a stranger who
was a tortfeasor with the possible consequences that that
might have on the tortfeasor's insurance premiums rather
than to sue his former solicitors with corresponding consequences on their premiums; that the court's discretion to
make or refuse an order under section 2D, if it considered
it equitable to do so, was unfettered; and that, accordingly,
the case should be remitted to Phillips J. for further consideration (post, pp. 750F–G, 752E, 753B–E).

Per curiam. When weighing what degree of prejudice the

D

E

F

G

H

---

[1] Limitation Act 1939, as amended, s. 2D (1): see post, p. 748G–H.

A   plaintiff has suffered, the fact that if no direction is made under section 2D he will have a claim over against his solicitor for the full damages that he could have recovered against the defendant if the action had proceeded must be a highly relevant consideration (post, pp. 752c–d, 753b–e).

    Firman v. *Ellis* [1978] Q.B. 886, C.A.; *Walkley* v. *Precision Forgings Ltd.* [1979] 1 W.L.R. 606, H.L.(E.) and *Browes* v. *Jones & Middleton* (unreported), June 15, 1979; Court of B   Appeal (Civil Division) Transcript No. 377 of 1979, C.A. considered.

    Decision of Phillips J. reversed.

The following cases are referred to in the opinion of Lord Diplock:

Browes v. *Jones & Middleton* (unreported), June 15, 1979; Court of Appeal (Civil Division) Transcript No. 377 of 1979, C.A.
C   *Firman* v. *Ellis*, The Times, July 7, 1977; [1978] Q.B. 886; [1978] 3 W.L.R. 1; [1978] 2 All E.R. 851, C.A.
Smith v. *Central Asbestos Co. Ltd.* [1973] A.C. 518; [1972] 3 W.L.R. 333; [1972] 2 All E.R. 1135, H.L.(E.).
Walkley v. *Precision Forgings Ltd.* [1979] 1 W.L.R. 606; [1979] 2 All E.R. 548, H.L.(E.).

D   The following additional cases were cited in argument:

Chappell v. *Cooper* [1980] 1 W.L.R. 958; [1980] 2 All E.R. 463, C.A.
Deeming v. *British Steel Corporation* (1978) 123 S.J. 303, C.A.
Finch v. *Francis* (unreported), July 21, 1977, Griffiths J.
Mann v. *Bournemouth District Council* (unreported), December 20, 1979, Michael Davies J.
Simpson v. *Norwest Holst Southern Ltd.* [1980] 1 W.L.R. 968; [1980] E   2 All E.R. 471, C.A.

APPEAL from Phillips J.

    By writ dated April 10, 1979, the plaintiff, James Thompson, claimed against the defendants, George Albert Brown (trading as George Albert Brown (Builders) & Co.) and Scaffolding (Great Britain) Ltd., damages for losses and injuries sustained and expenses incurred as the result of F   an accident that had occurred on March 4, 1976, at British Steel Corporation, Ebbw Vale, Gwent, which accident he alleged had been due to the negligence and breaches of statutory duty of the first defendants, their servants or agents, or of the second defendants, their servants or agents, or of both of them. By their defences, the defendants pleaded that the plaintiff's action was statute-barred by virtue of the provisions of the Limitation Act 1939 and denied that it would be equitable for G   the limitation period to be waived. On October 18, 1979, Master Warren ordered that the defence as raised by the second defendants be tried as a preliminary issue. On May 16, 1980, Phillips J., having tried the issue, ordered that judgment be entered for both defendants. On July 16, 1980, he certified pursuant to section 12 of the Administration of Justice Act 1969 that a point of law of general public importance was involved in H   his decision and that that point of law was one in respect of which he was bound by a decision of the Court of Appeal in previous proceedings and that had been fully considered by the Court of Appeal in those previous proceedings. The Appeal Committee of the House of Lords subsequently granted the plaintiff leave to appeal pursuant to section 13 (3) of the Act of 1969.

    The plaintiff appealed.

    The facts are set out in the opinion of Lord Diplock.

746

Michael Turner Q.C. and *Charles Welchman* for the plaintiff.   A

Piers Ashworth Q.C. and *Roderick Denyer* for the second defendants.

Their Lordships took time for consideration.

May 7. LORD DIPLOCK. My Lords, on March 4, 1976, scaffolding
that had been erected by the second respondents (" the scaffolders ") at   B
the Ebbw Vale works of the British Steel Corporation collapsed and
injured the appellant (Mr. Thompson), a bricklayer's labourer employed by
the first respondents (" the builders "). Through his trade union Mr.
Thompson was put in touch with solicitors who took up his claim against
the scaffolders and the builders for damages for personal injuries caused
by their negligence. The solicitors acted promptly; as early as April 27,   C
1976, the claim was notified to both intended defendants who referred it
to their respective insurers. The scaffolders were clearly liable to Mr.
Thompson, so it was their insurers who conducted the negotiations for
settling the case. On March 17, 1977, these insurers wrote to Mr. Thompson's solicitors saying that they had completed their inquiries and were
prepared to put forward an offer in settlement of the case. They asked
for particulars of Mr. Thompson's earnings and a medical report. The   D
solicitors encountered considerable delay in obtaining the medical report
and, at some date after August 1977, their file dealing with Mr. Thompson's
claim became mislaid and forgotten. It was not rediscovered until the
spring of 1979, and the writ was not issued until April 10, 1979—37 days
after the expiration of the three-year limitation period under section 2A of
the Limitation Act 1939, as amended by the Limitation Act 1975. The   E
sections of that Act that fall to be construed in this appeal have since been
replaced by sections 11 to 14 and 33 of the Limitation Act 1980, but the
relevant words remain the same.

The statement of claim followed three days after the writ. The builders
as well as the scaffolders were made defendants; but since it is undisputed
that the accident was entirely due to the negligence of the scaffolders, the
fact that the builders are also parties to the action may now be ignored.   F
In their defence the scaffolders pleaded the Act of 1939 and denied that
it would be equitable to allow the action to proceed under section 2D
notwithstanding the expiry of the three-year limitation period under
section 2A. The issue raised by this defence was tried as a preliminary
issue by Phillips J. on May 16, 1980. That learned judge was of opinion
that if the action were not allowed to proceed Mr. Thompson would have   G
a " cast-iron " case in an action for negligence against his own solicitors
in which the damages recoverable would be at least as much as, and, it
may be, more than, those which would have been recoverable against the
scaffolders if the action against them had been allowed to proceed.
Although it was disputed by counsel for Mr. Thompson at the hearing
before Phillips J. it has been conceded before your Lordships' House that
this is indeed so.   H

The judge was of opinion that in these circumstances he was bound
by an unreported decision of the Court of Appeal in *Browes* v. *Jones &
Middleton*, June 15, 1979; Court of Appeal (Civil Division) Transcript
No. 377 of 1979 to hold as a matter of law that the provisions of section 2A
had not prejudiced Mr. Thompson and that the court had no jurisdiction
under section 2D to direct that those provisions should not apply to his
cause of action against the scaffolders. So he gave the appropriate cer-

A tificate under section 12 of the Administration of Justice Act 1969 to enable an appeal from his decision to come direct to your Lordships' House by the "leap-frog" procedure.

My Lords, the unreported case of *Browes* was one in which the early history of the matter was similar to the instant case. The plaintiff, Browes, had been injured in a traffic accident by the undoubted negligence of a lorry driver employed by H. Camm Ltd. He went to solicitors, Jones & Middleton, who conducted the negotiations with Camm's insurers but allowed the three-year limitation period under section 2A to expire before they had issued a writ. On learning that the limitation point would be relied upon by Camm if a writ should be issued, Jones & Middleton advised Browes to consult other solicitors. He did so and, on their advice, started an action against Jones & Middleton claiming damages for their negligence as solicitors. That action had gone on for a year against Jones & Middleton alone before Camm was added as a second defendant. Camm pleaded section 2A as a defence and this was tried as a preliminary issue. Paradoxically notwithstanding that it was the plaintiff, Browes, who had joined Camm as a defendant it was his counsel who was arguing strenuously that the plaintiff had *not* been prejudiced by his former solicitors' failure to issue the writ within the time limited by section 2A, and it was counsel for his former solicitors who was arguing strenuously that he had. There were additional complications into which it would not be profitable to go. Suffice it to say that the Court of Appeal felt compelled by the reasoning in the speeches of Viscount Dilhorne and myself in *Walkley* v. *Precision Forgings Ltd.* [1979] 1 W.L.R. 606 to hold that section 2D did not apply in the circumstances of that case.

E My Lords, I shall have to refer brieflly to *Walkley* in connection with the construction of sections 2A and 2D; but in view of the very special facts of *Browes* and the bizarre course that the argument took the law reporters, in my opinion, exercised a wise discretion in consigning it to the limbo of unreported cases. For reasons I shall endeavour to develop it ought not to be treated as authority for the proposition of law that Phillips J. treated it as laying down.

In approaching the construction of sections 2A and 2D of the Act of 1939 (now sections 11 and 14 and section 33 of the Act of 1980) account must be taken of the legislative history of these sections. The Act of 1939 by section 2 re-enacted the limitation period of six years from the date on which the cause of action accrued for actions founded in tort. The Law Reform (Limitation of Actions, etc.) Act 1954, section 2 (1), reduced this period to three years in actions for damages for personal injuries. This shortened period led to what was felt to be injustice, particularly in cases of long-maturing industrial diseases; and the somewhat complicated provisions of Part I of the Limitation Act 1963 were passed in the hope that they would provide an equitable solution. These proved to be unsatisfactory in application and gave rise to considerable differences of judicial opinion as to their true interpretation, particularly as to whether a plaintiff's ignorance that acts or omissions by the defendant that were known to him gave him in law a cause of action had the effect of extending the limitation period: cf. *Smith* v. *Central Asbestos Co. Ltd.* [1973] A.C. 518.

Section 1 of the Act of 1975 represented the next attempt by Parliament to solve the problem. It did so by adding four new sections 2A, 2B, 2C and 2D to the Act of 1939. The sections relevant to the instant case were 2A and 2D, and for the purpose of seeing how they apply to it it is

convenient to set out most of their provisions in extenso leaving out only   A
those which deal with cases when the person injured has died.

" 2A (1) This section applies to any action for damage for negligence,
nuisance or breach of duty (whether the duty exists by virtue of a
contract or of provision made by or under a statute or independently
of any contract or any such provision) where the damages claimed
by the plaintiff for the negligence, nuisance or breach of duty consist   B
of or include damages in respect of personal injuries to the plaintiff
or any other person.   (2) Section 2 of this Act shall not apply to an
action to which this section applies.   (3) Subject to section 2D below,
an action to which this section applies shall not be brought after the
expiration of the period specified in subsections (4) and (5) below.
(4) Except where subsection (5) applies, the said period is three years
from— (a) the date on which the cause of action accrued, or (b) the   C
date (if later) of the plaintiff's knowledge. . . .   (6) In this section,
and in section 2B below, references to a person's date of knowledge
are references to the date on which he first had knowledge of the
following facts—(a) that the injury in question was significant, and
(b) that that injury was attributable in whole or in part to the act or
omission which is alleged to constitute negligence, nuisance or breach   D
of duty, and (c) the identity of the defendant, and (d) if it is alleged
that the act or omission was that of a person other than the defendant,
the identity of that person and the additional facts supporting the
bringing of an action against the defendant, and knowledge that any
acts or omissions did or did not, as a matter of law, involve negligence,
nuisance or breach of duty is irrelevant.   (7) For the purposes of this
section an injury is significant if the plaintiff would reasonably have   E
considered it sufficiently serious to justify his instituting proceedings
for damages against a defendant who did not dispute liability and was
able to satisfy a judgment.   (8) For the purposes of the said sections
a person's knowledge includes knowledge which he might reasonably
have been expected to acquire—(a) from facts observable or ascertainable by him, or (b) from facts ascertainable by him with the help of   F
medical or other appropriate expert advice which it is reasonable for
him to seek, but a person shall not be fixed under this subsection with
knowledge of a fact ascertainable only with the help of expert advice
so long as he has taken all reasonable steps to obtain (and, where
appropriate, to act on) that advice. . . .

" 2D (1) If it appears to the court that it would be equitable to
allow an action to proceed having regard to the degree to which—(a)   G
the provisions of section 2A or 2B of this Act prejudice the plaintiff
or any person whom he represents, and (b) any decision of the court
under this subsection would prejudice the defendant or any person
whom he represents, the court may direct that those provisions shall
not apply to the action, or shall not apply to any specified cause of
action to which the action relates. . . .   (3) In acting under this section   H
the court shall have regard to all the circumstances of the case and
in particular to—(a) the length of, and the reasons for, the delay on
the part of the plaintiff; (b) the extent to which, having regard to the
delay, the evidence adduced or likely to be adduced by the plaintiff
or the defendant is or is likely to be less cogent than if the action had
been brought within the time allowed by section 2A or as the case
may be 2B; (c) the conduct of the defendant after the cause of action

A arose, including the extent if any to which he responded to requests reasonably made by the plaintiff for information or inspection for the purpose of ascertaining facts which were or might be relevant to the plaintiff's cause of action against the defendant; (d) the duration of any disability of the plaintiff arising after the date of the accrual of the cause of action; (e) the extent to which the plaintiff acted promptly and reasonably once he knew whether or not the act or
B omission of the defendant, to which the injury was attributable, might be capable at that time of giving rise to an action for damages; (f) the steps, if any, taken by the plaintiff to obtain medical, legal or other expert advice and the nature of any such advice he may have received. (4) In a case where the person injured died when, because of section 2A, he could no longer maintain an action and
C recover damages in respect of the injury, the court shall have regard in particular to the length of, and the reasons for, the delay on the part of the deceased. (5) In a case under subsection (4) above, or any other case where the time limit, or one of the time limits, depends on the date of knowledge of a person other than the plaintiff, subsection (3) above shall have effect in particular as if references to the plaintiff included references to any person whose date of knowledge is or was
D relevant in determining a time limit. . . . (7) In this section ' the court ' means the court in which the action has been brought. . . .''

At common law there was no time limit upon a person's right to bring an action for tort. So a Limitation Act takes the form of a statutory prohibition upon bringing an action after the expiry of a specified time. In
E the case of actions for damages for personal injuries section 2A (3) imposes such a prohibition after the expiry of a period of three years from the date of the accrual of the plaintiff's cause of action, or his knowledge of the material facts specified in subsection (6) if that is later. But the prohibition is not absolute; it is expressed to be subject to section 2D, which creates exceptions to the general rule laid down in section 2A (4). During this primary limitation period the plaintiff has an indefeasible right to bring
F his action; until it has expired section 2A has no effect upon him or his cause of action at all.

Section 2A (6) provides a statutory answer to the question that divided this House in *Smith* v. *Central Asbestos Co. Ltd.* [1973] A.C. 518 under the Act of 1963. A plaintiff's ignorance that in law he had a cause of action against the defendant is not to prevent the limitation period from
G starting if knows the other facts referred to in subsections (6) and (7) or has imputed knowledge of them under subsection (8). In section 2D (3) (e), when one comes to it, will be found an indication that the draftsman contemplated that such ignorance of law on the plaintiff's part might be a common reason why he would need to have recourse to section 2D.

Walkley v. *Precision Forgings Ltd.* [1979] 1 W.L.R. 606 was a case in which the plaintiff had issued and served his writ within the primary
H limitation period; so section 2A had not affected him at all. No further steps were taken in the action within the primary limitation period and it was ripe to be dismissed for want of prosecution. In an attempt to avoid this fate a second writ founded on the same cause of action was issued by the plaintiff's new solicitors. Considerable procedural manoeuvring by both parties followed, in the course of which application was made under section 2D to allow the action started by the second writ to proceed. This House took the view that, the plaintiff having brought within the

750

primary limitation period an action for damages for the very negligence A
which constituted the cause of action alleged in the second writ, he had
not been affected by section 2A at all, let alone prejudiced by it. In my
own speech in that case, however, there is a sentence, at p. 618H, that
needs to be amended in the light of the arguments addressed to the House
in the instant case.

Section 2D empowers the court to direct that the primary limitation
period shall not apply to a particular action or cause of action. This is B
by way of exception, for unless the court does make a direction the
primary limitation period will continue to apply. The effect of such a
direction, and its only effect, is to deprive the defendant of what would
otherwise be a complete defence to the action, viz. that the writ was issued
too late. A direction under the section must therefore always be highly
prejudicial to the defendant, for even if he also has a good defence on the C
merits he is put to the expenditure of time and energy and money in
establishing it, while if, as in the instant case, he has no defence as to
liability he has everything to lose if a direction is given under the section.
On the other hand if, as in the instant case, the time elapsed after the
expiration of the primary limitation is very short, what the defendant
loses in consequence of a direction might be regarded as being in the
nature of a windfall.   D

Section 2D appears to be drafted on the further assumption that the
expiry of a limitation period before his action has been started must
always prejudice the plaintiff in some degree. With great respect to the
opposite view taken by the Court of Appeal in *Browes* v. *Jones & Middleton,* June 15, 1979, this too seems to me self-evident, unless the plaintiff's
prospects of success in the action if it is allowed to proceed are so hopeless E
as to deprive it even of nuisance value—which is very far from being the
instant case. The degree to which the plaintiff would be prejudiced by
being prevented from proceeding with his action will be affected by how
good or bad would have been his prospects of success; so too it will be
affected by the extent to which the plaintiff will be able to recover in an
action for negligence against his own solicitor the value of his lost prospects of success. But even where, as in the instant case, and as in *Browes,* F
if the action were not allowed to proceed the plaintiff would have a cast-
iron case against his solicitor in which the measure of damages will be no
less than those that he would be able to recover against the defendant if
the action were allowed to proceed, some prejudice, although it may be
only minor, will have been suffered by him. He will be obliged to find and
to instruct new and strange solicitors; there is bound to be delay; he will G
incur a personal liability for costs of the action up to the date of the
court's refusal to give a direction under section 2D; he may prefer to sue
a stranger who is a tortfeasor with the possible consequences that may
have on the tortfeasor's insurance premiums rather than to sue his former
solicitors with corresponding consequences on their premiums. It was
suggested that it might be more advantageous to a plaintiff to sue his own
solicitor rather than the original tortfeasor since he could recover in an H
action against the solicitor interest on damages from the date on which the
writ against the tortfeasor would have been issued if reasonable diligence
had been shown, whereas against the tortfeasor he could only recover
interest on damages from the later date, after the expiry of the primary
limitation period, at which the writ was actually issued. This, however,
is fallacious; he can recover the difference in the interest on damages
between the earlier and the later date in a separate action against his

A solicitor for negligence even if the action against the first tortfeasor is allowed to proceed.

In *Walkley* v. *Precision Forgings Ltd.* [1979] 1 W.L.R. 606 the primary period of limitation had not expired when the plaintiff had started his action against the tortfeasor. That was the only reason why section 2D did not apply to his case. Whenever section 2D does apply, however, what the court has to decide is whether it would be " equitable " to allow

B the action to proceed. The section goes on to specify the matters to which the court must have regard in deciding whether it would be equitable. Those matters are contained not only in subsection (1) itself but also, and importantly for the purposes of the instant case, in subsection (3). In *Walkley*, at p. 618, I referred incorrectly to the degree of prejudice to plaintiff and defendant respectively which is referred to in subsection (1)

C as the only two matters to which the court must have regard. Although reference to these two matters was all that was necessary for the decision that in *Walkley* section 2D did not apply, I ought either to have omitted the word " only " or to have mentioned the matters referred to in subsection (3) as other matters to which the court would also have had to have regard if section 2D had applied.

D Subsection (3) requires the court to have regard to " all the circumstances of the case," but singles out six matters for particular mention. These six present a curious hotchpotch. " The delay " referred to in paragraph (a) must be the same delay as in paragraph (b); so it means the delay after the primary limitation period expired. It is the length of this delay (in the instant case 37 days) and the reasons for it that matter under paragraph (a). Paragraph (b) refers to the extent to which the

E cogency of evidence likely to be adduced by either the plaintiff or the defendant is likely to be less as a result of the delay. So far as the diminished cogency affects the defendant's evidence it increases the degree of prejudice he will suffer if the action is allowed to be brought despite the delay; but so far as diminished cogency affects the plaintiff's evidence and so reduces his chances of establishing cause of action if the action is allowed to be brought it lessens the degree of prejudice the plaintiff will

F suffer if he is not allowed to bring the action at this late stage.

Paragraphs (a) and (b) are the only two paragraphs which appear to be dealing with matters that affect the extent to which the plaintiff and the defendant will be prejudiced according to whether or not the action is allowed to proceed. Paragraphs (c), (e) and (f), on the other hand, deal with the conduct of the parties—a matter that is always relevant

G when considering whether it is " equitable " to give a direction granting a benefit to one party at the expense of the other party. Paragraph (d) is restricted to cases where plaintiffs have been under a disability, a class of persons that equity has always been zealous to protect.

Paragraph (c) requires the court to take into account the defendants' conduct ever since the action arose—not, be it noted, from what in the absence of knowledge by the plaintiff of material facts may be the later

H date when the primary limitation period started to run. The reference in this paragraph to response to reasonable requests by the plaintiff for information recognises an obligation on a potential defendant not to be obstructive in enabling a potential plaintiff to obtain relevant information, though not imposing any obligation to volunteer such information; but in this paragraph the conduct of the defendant must, I think, be understood as including the conduct of his solicitors and his insurers by whom in the ordinary course of things any requests for information will be dealt.

Paragraphs (e) and (f), which deal with the conduct of the plaintiff, **A** appear to be chronologically in the wrong order, at any rate so far as the latter deals with the obtaining of legal advice. Until he has obtained legal advice a plaintiff (unless he is himself a barrister or solicitor) will not know whether or not he has a cause of action for damages against the defendant, although under section 2A (6) the lack of this knowledge will not prevent the primary limitation from starting to run. The steps he has taken up to the point when he receives advice that he has a possible **B** cause of action are dealt with in paragraph (f), whereas how promptly and reasonably he acted after receiving that advice is dealt with in paragraph (e).

In contrast to paragraph (c) I think it is apparent that paragraphs (e) and (f) are referring to the conduct of the plaintiff himself, as well as that of his lawyers after he has consulted them for the first time. If he has **C** acted promptly and reasonably it is not to be counted against him, when it comes to weighing conduct, that his lawyers have been dilatory and allowed the primary limitation to expire without issuing a writ. Nevertheless, when weighing what degree of prejudice the plaintiff has suffered, the fact that if no direction is made under section 2D he will have a claim over against his solicitor for the full damages that he could have recovered **D** against the defendant if the action had proceeded must be a highly relevant consideration.

My Lords, when the court makes a direction under section 2D that the provisions of section 2A should not apply to a cause of action, it is making an exception to a general rule that has already catered for delay in starting proceedings that is due to excusable ignorance of material facts by the plaintiff as distinct from his lack of knowledge that the facts which **E** he does know may give him a good cause of action in law. The onus of showing that in the particular circumstances of the case it would be equitable to make an exception lies upon the plaintiff; but, subject to that, the court's discretion to make or refuse an order if it considers it equitable to do so is, in my view, unfettered. The conduct of the parties as well as the prejudice one or other will suffer if the court does or does not make **F** an order are all to be put into the balance in order to see which way it falls. I do not think that this House with its minimal experience of appeals which have involved directions under section 2D ought to attempt itself to lay down guidelines for the High Court judges who are familiar with the typical kinds of circumstances in which applications are made. In matters of practice and discretion if guidelines are needed they are better **G** laid down by the Court of Appeal.

It follows that I agree with what was said about the unfettered nature of the discretion by the Court of Appeal in *Firman* v. *Ellis* [1978] Q.B. 886, although the actual decision in that case must be regarded as having been overruled by *Walkley* v. *Precision Forgings Ltd.* [1979] 1 W.L.R. 606. The writ in *Firman* v. *Ellis* and in the other three cases that were heard with it had been issued before the expiry of the primary limitation **H** period. The trouble was that they had been neither served nor renewed within a year. It may seem anomalous that a defendant should be better off where, unknown to him, a writ has been issued but not served than he would be if the writ had not been issued at all; but this is a consequence of the greater anomaly too well-established for this House to abolish that, for the purposes of a limitation period, an action is brought when a writ or other originating process is issued by the central office of the High

A Court and not when it is brought to the knowledge of the defendant by service upon him.

Phillips J. considered that as a matter of law he had no jurisdiction to make a direction under section 2D. He accordingly did not exercise his discretion, nor did he say how he would have exercised it if he had felt free to do so. Since for the reasons I have given I am of opinion that he had an unfettered discretion, I would allow the appeal and remit the case to him for further consideration as to whether it would be equitable to direct that the provisions of section 2A of the Limitation Act 1939 shall not apply to this action.

LORD ELWYN-JONES. My Lords, I have had the advantage of reading in draft the speech prepared by my noble and learned friend Lord Diplock and I agree with it.

For the reasons he gives, I would allow the appeal and remit the case to Phillips J. for further consideration, as Lord Diplock has proposed.

LORD FRASER OF TULLYBELTON. My Lords, I have had the advantage of reading in draft the speech prepared by my noble and learned friend Lord Diplock and I agree with it.

For the reasons given by him, I would allow the appeal and remit the case to Phillips J. for further consideration, as Lord Diplock has proposed.

LORD SCARMAN. My Lords, I have had the advantage of reading in draft the speech of my noble and learned friend, Lord Diplock. I agree with it. For the reasons he gives I would allow the appeal and remit the case to the judge for further consideration, as my Lord proposes.

LORD BRIDGE OF HARWICH. My Lords, I have had the advantage of reading in draft the speech of my noble and learned friend Lord Diplock. I agree with it and with the order he proposes.

> *Appeal allowed with costs in House of Lords.*
> *Cause remitted to High Court for further consideration.*
> *Costs in High Court reserved for decision of that court on determination of remission.*

Solicitors: *O. H. Parsons & Partners; Hextall, Erskine & Co. for Cartwrights, Bristol.*

M. G.

754

A

[COURT OF APPEAL]

* PAYNE v. LORD HARRIS OF GREENWICH AND OTHERS

1981 Feb. 23, 24, 25;   Lord Denning M.R., Shaw,
       March 12; 19   and Brightman L.JJ.

B

*Prisons—Prisoners' rights—Release on licence—Application for
release—Recommendations to Secretary of State by Parole
Board and local review committee of prison—Refusal to
release on licence—Whether prisoner entitled to be given
reasons for refusal—Criminal Justice Act 1967 (c. 80), ss. 59,
62*

*Natural Justice—Statutory board—Duty to be fair—Whether
Parole Board and local review committee of prison obliged
to give reasons for refusal of release on licence of prisoner*

C

The plaintiff was convicted of murder in 1968 and sentenced to life imprisonment. He was well-behaved in prison,
being described as a " model prisoner," and was in the lowest
security category. He sought release on licence, which, after
periodic reviews in accordance with the Criminal Justice Act
1967 and the Local Review Committee Rules 1967, had been
refused. With the object of being better able to prepare
representations for the next review he sought declarations
against the defendants, representatives of the Parole Board
and the local review committee of the prison where he was
detained and the Home Secretary, that, in effect, he was
entitled to know the reasons for refusing to release him on
licence. McNeil J. refused the declarations sought.

D

On appeal by the plaintiff: –

Held, dismissing the appeal, (1) that the Criminal Justice
Act 1967 and the Local Review Committee Rules 1967 formed
a comprehensive code setting out the procedure for release
of a prisoner on licence, specifying the occasions when he was
entitled to make representations or to be told reasons; that a
prisoner could not require something to be done where no
specific obligation was placed on the Parole Board or a local
review committee, and, since there was no specific provision
requiring that a prisoner should be informed of the reasons
for refusal to release him on licence, the defendants were
under no obligation to supply such reasons (post, pp. 757D–E,
762D–E, H, 763A, 765C–D, F–G, 766H—767A, H).

E

F

(2) That the scope of the duty to act fairly imposed on all
administrative bodies by the rules of natural justice depended
upon the subject matter and circumstances of each case; that
the duty did not require the disclosure to a prisoner of reasons
for refusal of release on licence, and, accordingly, the plaintiff was not entitled to the declarations sought (post, pp. 757F–G,
759B–D, 764A–C, 766D–G).

G

Reg. v. *Gaming Board for Great Britain, Ex parte Benaim
and Khaida* [1970] 2 Q.B. 417, C.A. applied.

The following cases are referred to in the judgments:

Cinnamond v. *British Airports Authority* [1980] 1 W.L.R. 582; [1980]
2 All E.R. 368, C.A.

Golder case, February 21, 1975, Publications of the European Court of
Human Rights, Series A no. 18.

Heywood v. *Board of Visitors of Hull Prison* [1980] 1 W.L.R. 1386;
[1980] 3 All E.R. 594.

Kanda v. *Government of Malaya* [1962] A.C. 322; [1962] 2 W.L.R.
1153, P.C.

McInnes v. *Onslow-Fane* [1978] 1 W.L.R. 1520; [1978] 3 All E.R. 211.

H

A   *Pergamon Press Ltd., In re* [1971] Ch. 388; [1970] 3 W.L.R. 792;
       [1970] 3 All E.R. 535, C.A.
    Reg. v. Gaming Board for Great Britain, Ex parte Benaim and Khaida
       [1970] 2 Q.B. 417; [1970] 2 W.L.R. 1009; [1970] 2 All E.R. 528,
       C.A.
    Reg. v. Secretary of State for the Home Department, Ex parte Santillo
       [1981] 2 W.L.R. 362, D.C. and C.A.

B   *Wiseman v. Borneman* [1968] Ch. 429; [1968] 2 W.L.R. 320; [1967]
       3 All E.R. 1045; [1971] A.C. 297; [1969] 3 W.L.R. 706; [1969] 3
       All E.R. 275, C.A. and H.L.(E.).
    Thompson v. Goold & Co. [1910] A.C. 409, H.L.(E.).

    The following additional cases were cited in argument:
    De Verteuil v. Knaggs [1918] A.C. 557, P.C.
C   *Fairmount Investments Ltd. v. Secretary of State for the Environment*
       [1976] 1 W.L.R. 1255; [1976] 2 All E.R. 865, H.L.(E.).
    H.K. (An Infant), In re [1967] 2 Q.B. 617; [1967] 2 W.L.R. 962;
       [1967] 1 All E.R. 226, D.C.
    Howarth v. National Parole Board [1976] 1 R.C.S. 453.
    K. (Infants), In re [1965] A.C. 201; [1963] 3 W.L.R. 408; [1963] 3 All
       E.R. 191, H.L.(E.).
    Payne v. Home Office (unreported), May 2, 1977, Cantley J.
D   *Reg. v. Board of Visitors of Hull Prison, Ex parte St. Germain* [1979]
       Q.B. 425; [1979] 2 W.L.R. 42; [1979] 1 All E.R. 701, C.A.
    Ridge v. Baldwin [1964] A.C. 40; [1963] 2 W.L.R. 935; [1963] 2 All
       E.R. 66, H.L.(E.).

    APPEAL from McNeill J.

E   By specially indorsed writ dated October 10, 1977, as subsequently amended, the plaintiff, Roger John Payne, a prisoner serving a life sentence in Maidstone Prison following his conviction for murder on May 24, 1968, claimed certain declarations against the first defendant, Lord Harris of Greenwich, the chairman of the Parole Board, sued on his own behalf and as representing all other members of the board, the second defendant, Peter Timms, the chairman of the local review
F   committee of Maidstone Prison, sued on his own behalf and as representing all other members of the committee, and the third defendant, the Secretary of State for the Home Department. The declarations sought were (1) that the defendants were bound to apply the rules of natural justice in deciding whether to recommend the plaintiff for early release on licence; (2) that the first and second defendants' decisions, on various dates between January 1977 and June 1977, declining to recommend the
G   plaintiff for early release on licence were null and void; (3) that the plaintiff was entitled to make representations to the first and second defendants as to his case for early release, and they were bound to acquaint him with the nature of the case for declining to recommend it when his sentence was last reviewed; and (4) that the third defendant was bound to acquaint the plaintiff with any reason for not complying
H   with any recommendation made by the Parole Board or the local review committee for the plaintiff's early release on licence and to consider the plaintiff's representations thereon. On July 24, 1979, McNeill J. refused the declarations sought.

    The plaintiff appealed on the grounds (1) that the judge erred in deciding that fairness did not require a prisoner to be informed shortly of the reasons why his application for parole had failed; (2) that the judge failed to give sufficient weight to the argument that a right to make

representations was only properly and adequately effective if the person A
having such right knew enough about the case which he had to meet to
be able to make cogent representations directed thereto; (3) that the
judge misconstrued the effect of sections 59 to 61, and section 62 of the
Criminal Justice Act 1967; (4) that the judge wrongly held that if natural
justice applied that would necessarily require such a full statement of
reasons as would involve the full panoply of particularisation, discovery,
interrogatories, etc. and a breach of judicial confidentiality; and (5) that B
the judge failed sufficiently to consider whether the Local Review
Committee Rules 1967 had been applied fairly in the circumstances.

The facts are stated in the judgment of Lord Denning M.R.

David Turner-Samuels Q.C. and *Brian Langstaff* for the plaintiff.
Simon D. Brown and *John Laws* for the defendants.   C

Cur. adv. vult.

March 19.   The following judgments were read.

LORD DENNING M.R.   Nearly 13 years ago, on May 24, 1968, Roger D
John Payne—being then aged about 26—was convicted of the murder of
a woman and was sentenced to life imprisonment. (He had two previous
convictions when he was about 18 and 23 years old.   Each of them
involved an assault on a woman).

On December 4, 1968, he was placed in prison in category A as being
a man whose escape would be highly dangerous to the public.   He was
in that category for seven years until July 7, 1975, when he was placed in E
category B as being a man for whom escape must be made very difficult.
Three years later, on March 23, 1978, he was placed in category C as
one for whom simple basic precautions would be sufficient.   He is now
in category D.   He is still in prison in that category.   Throughout his
time in prison he has been exceptionally well-behaved.   He is described
as a " model prisoner."   He is in the " blue band " allocated to the F
educational department at Maidstone Prison.

Being a life-sentence prisoner, Roger Payne does not qualify for
remission.   Whereas, a prisoner who is given a determinate sentence may,
if he is well-behaved, get one-third of his sentence remitted—in which
case he is released unconditionally without being liable to recall.   Yet
even a life-sentence prisoner may be released on licence—subject always
to conditions, and in particular to being liable to recall.   It is so provided G
in section 61 of the Criminal Justice Act 1967.

Roger Payne has sought to be released on licence ever since he had
completed six years in prison.   But he has never been granted a licence.
His case has been reviewed from time to time, but he has never been let
out on parole.   He has asked to be told the reasons for refusal.   He
wants them, he says, so as to be able to prepare his representations for H
the next review.

Now he has brought an action in the High Court seeking a declaration
that he is entitled to know the reasons.   McNeill J. rejected his claim.
He appeals to this court.   I would like to say that, instead of seeking a
declaration, it would have been more appropriate to proceed by judicial
review: see *Heywood* v. *Board of Visitors of Hull Prison* [1980] 1
W.L.R. 1386.   But, as the case is before us, we will deal with it.

A *The procedure*

The procedure is governed by sections 59 to 62 of the Criminal Justice Act 1967 and the Local Review Committee Rules 1967. The stages are as follows.

The prisoner (if he is willing) is interviewed by a member of the local review committee. At that interview " he shall be given a reasonable
B opportunity to make any representations he wishes to be considered by the committee ": rule 3 (2). The member writes a report of the interview. He includes it in any representations made by the prisoner. The local review committee considers the report of their member. They then make a report to the Secretary of State of the suitability of the prisoner for release on licence. The Secretary of State then refers the case to the Parole Board. The Parole Board advises the Secretary of
C State. If they recommend that the man should be released on licence, the Secretary of State may then release a life-sentence prisoner—but only after consultation with the Lord Chief Justice and the trial judge. If the Parole Board do not recommend that he be released on licence, that is the end of the matter—until his case comes up for a further review.

D *The interpretation of the provisions*

It seems to me that the statute and the rules together form a comprehensive code. They set out the procedure in such detail that there is nothing more needed to supplement it. They set out the occasions when a man is entitled to make representations: and when he is to be informed of reasons. In particular, it is specifically provided in
E section 62 (3) of the Act of 1967 that, if he is recalled, he " shall on his return to prison be informed of the reasons for his recall." There is no corresponding provision when he is refused a licence. That goes to show that the legislature did not think that reasons were necessary.

But I hesitate to decide this case on that simple ground. In a parallel case when we thought it sufficient to go by the procedure laid down by the statute (see *Wiseman* v. *Borneman* [1968] Ch. 429), the House of
F Lords said that natural justice was still to be considered: see *Wiseman* v. *Borneman* [1971] A.C. 297, especially by Lord Wilberforce, at p. 317.

Natural justice

No doubt it is the duty of all those concerned—from the member of the local review committee, to the Parole Board, to the Secretary of
G State—to act fairly. That is the simple precept which now governs the administrative procedure of all public bodies. But the duty to act fairly cannot be set down in a series of set propositions. Each case depends on its own circumstances. As Sachs L.J. said, in *In re Pergamon Press Ltd.* [1971] Ch. 388, 403:

" In the application of the concept of fair play, there must be real
H flexibility, so that very different situations may be met without producing procedures unsuitable to the object in hand."

Sometimes fairness may require that the man be told the outline of the case against him. As in *Reg.* v. *Gaming Board for Great Britain, Ex parte Benaim and Khaida* [1970] 2 Q.B. 417, 431, I said:

" . . . without disclosing every detail, I should have thought that the board ought in every case to be able to give to the applicant sufficient

indication of the objections raised against him such as to enable him   A
to answer them."

That is what Mr. Turner-Samuels urged here.

At other times it may not be necessary to have a hearing or even to
tell the man the case against him, because it must be obvious to him.
As, for instance, in *Cinnamond* v. *British Airports Authority* [1980] 1
W.L.R. 582, 590–591; and *Reg.* v. *Secretary of State for the Home*   B
Department, Ex parte Santillo [1981] 2 W.L.R. 362, 374–375.

Submissions on behalf of Roger Payne

Mr. Turner-Samuels submitted that, in the case of life-sentence
prisoners at any rate, it was only fair that they should be given the
reasons, at any rate in outline, why they were refused to be let out on   C
licence. One reason was because he would be better able to make
adequate representations on the next occasion when his case was reviewed.
Another reason was that it would be beneficial to the man, as a human
being, to be told the reasons for refusal. In support of this view, Mr.
Turner-Samuels called Mr. Louis Blom-Cooper Q.C., who said:

> " It can only be beneficial in helping the prisoner grapple with the   D
> problems of perhaps long confinement or even to grapple with the
> probability of a release which may be some years away."

Mr. Blom-Cooper also said that James L.J. was very much in favour of
giving reasons in the parole system, and he quoted Lord Hunt, the first
chairman of the Parole Board as saying: " It is a moral right that cannot
be indefinitely denied and it is a failure of natural justice which has lasted   E
for far too long."

Only a few days ago Mr. Turner-Samuels drew to our notice the
Golder case, February 21, 1975, Publications of the European Court
of Human Rights, Series A no. 18. Golder complained that it was a
wrong statement in his prison record that prevented him being recommended
for parole.

  F

Submissions to the contrary

There are equally strong submissions to the contrary. The first is
the practical difficulty of giving the reasons of a body of five members.
One or two may have a different reason from the other three or four.
Some may be spoken. Other unspoken. The next is the danger that the
reasons, if given, would tend to become short and stereotyped, rather   G
than full and informative. So they would be of little avail. If they were
full and informative, they would give the prisoner an opening with which
he could challenge the refusal. He could lodge an application for
judicial review complaining that the board took things into account
which they should not have done—or that their decision was
unreasonable. If he were refused judicial review, he would harbour a   H
grievance which would become obsessive—just as much as if he is refused
parole without reasons being given.

Apart from these practical considerations, I would suppose that in
most cases the man will know the reasons well enough himself. He will
have known the gravity of his crime. He will know whether he is
thought to be a danger or not. He will know whether he has behaved
well in prison or not. He will be able to deal with all these points in the

A   representation which he is allowed to make. If there should be any new factor adverse to him—of which he is unaware—the Parole Board might well arrange for one of their members to interview him so as to ascertain his reaction to it. This is contemplated by section 59 (4) (b) of the Act of 1967. Thus fairness will be ensured here just as we envisaged in the *Santillo* case [1981] 2 W.L.R. 362, 374.

B   *On balance*

In the end I think the problem comes down to this: what does public policy demand as best to be done? To give reasons or to withhold them? This is more a matter for the Secretary of State than for the courts. But, so far as I can judge of the matter, I should think that in the interests of the man himself—as a human being facing indefinite
C   detention—it would be better for him to be told the reasons. But, in the interests of society at large—including the due administration of the parole system—it would be best not to give them. Except in the rare case when the board itself think it desirable, as a matter of fairness, to ask one of the members to interview him. That member may then think it appropriate to tell him.

D   This is not a case for any declaration. I would dismiss the appeal.

SHAW L.J. The Criminal Justice Act 1967 introduced what was, in the United Kingdom, a new and dramatic concept in our penal system. Part III of the Act under the heading "Treatment of Offenders" made provision for the possible release of prisoners on licence. The concept was not a novel one. It had, in differing forms, been applied in other
E   countries for some years. Their experience was known and had been studied. The impulse which led to the adoption of a system of parole in this country was of a complex nature. It derived from considerations which were humanitarian, sociological, moral and practical and which in combination made early release a justifiable expedient. If the reformation of a prisoner appeared to have been securely achieved before
F   the expiry of his sentence, that circumstance might (though not necessarily if it stood alone) justify his earlier release. So too might his need (and his capacity) to make his own way and meet his own responsibilities, domestic and general, in an open society to which he had the ability to make a useful contribution. It may be added without any cynical inflexion that by the end of the 1960's prisons had become very overcrowded with a resultant deterioration in conditions and standards.
G   If it was possible, without involving an undue threat of some detriment to society as a whole, to relieve the pressure on the walls of prisons by a system providing for the premature release of prisoners that system was worth pursuing though with due caution and always bearing in mind the general well-being of society.

I have embarked on this preamble as it seems to me important to set
H   the scene for a consideration of the rights and responsibilities which are created by the provisions of Part III of the Act of 1967. Those provisions relate to persons who, ex hypothesi, are in the process of serving custodial sentences lawfully imposed. Those sentences are primarily to be served in designated institutions, namely prisons, and for their full term subject only to remission for good conduct. When a prisoner is so discharged his sentence is exhausted and he cannot be recalled even though he commits a further offence during the period represented by remission.

At common law there was no power to release a prisoner before the due   A
expiry of his sentence otherwise than by the exercise of the Crown's
prerogative of mercy to which recourse was appropriate only in
exceptional situations.

The object and effect of Part III of the Act of 1967 is to empower the
Secretary of State for the Home Department to release a prisoner on
licence before the expiry of his sentence. This power is exercisable only   B
on the recommendation of the Parole Board set up under section 59 (1).
In the absence of such a recommendation the Secretary of State cannot
order a release on licence. On the other hand, he is not bound to follow
such a recommendation if it should be made though in practice he
generally does. If, following a recommendation in that regard, release
on licence is directed, the duration of the sentence is unaffected. The
effect of the licence is that, subject to the power of recall vested in the   C
Secretary of State if recommended by the Parole Board, the residue of
the sentence is served (that is to say, worked out) free from confinement.

The mechanics of the operation whereby the Secretary of State may
release a prisoner on licence are prescribed in sections 59 to 60 of the
Act and in the Local Review Committee Rules 1967 made under it.
Nowhere in the Act or in the rules is there any reference to " granting   D
parole " though this is the phrase generally heard in colloquial usage.
The statutory expression is simply " release on licence." The Secretary
of State does not, in directing release on licence, accede to a claim by a
prisoner to the benefit of the statute. As I see it, he is doing an executive
act which is considered to be justified in the immediate interests of the
prisoner and, no less importantly, in the general interests of society when
those interests appear to coincide. Whether they do so or not, it is the   E
responsibility of the Parole Board to determine and to make their
recommendation to the Secretary of State in accordance with their
determination.

To ensure so far as practicable that all aspects of a prisoner's situation
may be duly considered by the Parole Board called upon to decide whether
to recommend release on licence, the constitution of the board is   F
prescribed by Schedule 2 to the Act. It is there provided that among its
members (of whom there must be not less than five) there shall be
included:

" (a) a person who holds or has held judicial office; (b) a registered
medical practitioner who is a psychiatrist; (c) a person appearing to
the Secretary of State to have knowledge and experience of the   G
supervision or after-care of discharged prisoners; and (d) a person
appearing to the Secretary of State to have made a study of the
causes of delinquency or the treatment of offenders."

I reproduce these requirements not merely to emphasise the breadth of
the disciplines involved as safeguards for the interests of a candidate for
parole but as indicating also the wide area in which members trained in   H
different disciplines may travel in arriving at their respective conclusions.
In the result, whether they agree or differ, they may assign different
reasons for the view they reach.

The Local Review Committee Rules 1967, to which I have referred,
provide for the creation of a local review committee for every prison.
The constitution of these committees is also prescribed. They must
include a probation officer who is not a prison welfare officer and a

A member of the board of visitors, but no prison officer other than the governor. It is their function to meet at least once a year to review prisoners' cases in accordance with the rules.

In regard to any individual prisoner, no review of his case may proceed until he has been interviewed by a member of the committee (not being the prison governor) if he is willing to be interviewed. Rule 3 (2) provides: " When a prisoner is interviewed he shall be given a reasonable
B opportunity to make any representations which he wishes to be considered by the committee." The interviewing member is required to make a report of the interview for the consideration of the local review committee and a copy of the report must be sent to the Secretary of State together with the committee's report on the prisoner's suitability for release.

The interviewing member of the local review committee is thus the
C only direct link between a prisoner whose case is to be reviewed and the ensuing parole process. Counsel for the plaintiff has contended that this is too precarious a means of communication and that it might in practice be inadequate and unrevealing. The prisoner might be inarticulate or illiterate or both so that some matter of consequence in relation to his prospect of parole might not become known or fully understood.

D This contention may have some substance but it ignores practicalities. A full scale system of interviewing by the local review committee as a body or by the Parole Board would perhaps be the ideal method of inquiry, but such a procedure would be unworkable and the parole scheme would succumb. In any case a prisoner can seek assistance not only from the interviewing member but in advance of the interview from the prison welfare officer or the chaplain or from the prison doctor or a
E prison visitor. Not even the most obtuse prisoner is bereft of all resource when he sees a hope of freedom. For those who can read, the Home Office provides easily understood pamphlets dealing comprehensively with all material questions which may arise in relation to parole.

This argument was put forward as reinforcing what was the main contention of the plaintiff, namely that where a prisoner is not
F recommended for parole he should be told why. Without surrendering the generality of this proposition, Mr. Turner-Samuels argued that in the case of a prisoner serving a sentence of imprisonment for life it was imperative that he should be informed of the matters which militated against his release on parole. Unlike a prisoner serving a finite sentence, he could not assess his prospect of release on any scale of time. If the obstacle to parole was remediable, how could a life prisoner set about
G meeting the requirements of the parole board if he was left to conjecture and to speculate as to what were the factors which influenced the board against recommending parole.

The argument is not without substance. It has been the subject of much debate by experienced and informed protagonists of divergent views. Ethical and moral considerations play their part, but so also does
H expediency and the well-being of the law-abiding section of society. The courts are concerned with the legalities, that is to say, with rights and obligations which have their source in the law or in its proper administration. It is requisite, therefore, to begin with the statutory provision as to the release on licence of a person serving a sentence of life imprisonment. Section 61 of the Act of 1967 enacts that the Secretary of State may, if recommended to do so by the Parole Board, release such a prisoner on licence but shall not do so except after

consultation with the Lord Chief Justice together with the trial judge if **A** available.

Although the issue as to whether parole should be recommended assumes a different dimension in the case of a prisoner sentenced to life imprisonment, the essential problem remains the same. It will generally speaking involve a more onerous responsibility. Whether the sentence was imposed on a conviction for murder or for some other grave crime, the prospect of releasing such a prisoner into society must be fraught with **B** very great anxiety. The validity of parole may be called in question if a person so released commits murder again—as has indeed happened. Unlike the case of a person serving a fixed term whose case is reviewed after he has been detained for a third of his sentence or for one year, whichever is the longer, the case of a prisoner sentenced to life imprisonment is reviewed only when the Secretary of State directs it. **C** This is not to say that such a direction will be captiously withheld but at what stage it will be given must depend in part on the circumstances of the crime itself. It will not be until after the lapse of some years from conviction.

It is now necessary to look back to discover what legal rights, if any, are conferred on persons serving sentences of imprisonment by the Act of **D** 1967 or by the rules made under it.

In relation to the release of a prisoner on licence, I cannot deduce from the statute itself any right with which a person serving a sentence of imprisonment can claim to be invested. The Act, as I read it, sets up an administrative procedure in accordance with which the Secretary of State is empowered to release such a person before the natural expiry of his sentence. In this regard what the Act does is to invest the Parole **E** Board with responsibilities which it owes to the Secretary of State and to no one else.

The Local Review Committee Rules 1967, in giving shape to the parole procedure, do confer certain rights on a prisoner. If he is serving a determinate sentence and does not indicate that he does not wish to be considered for parole, the local review committee is under a duty to **F** review his case. Rule 3 (1) then requires that before such review the prisoner, if willing, shall be interviewed by a member of the committee. By rule 3 (2), a prisoner being interviewed must be given a reasonable opportunity to make any representations he wishes to be considered by the committee. Rule 4 provides that, before the review, a prisoner must be told that he has a right to make written representations to the committee. The duties so imposed in regard to incidental matters of **G** substance confer corresponding rights on the prisoner concerned; he is entitled to complain if those duties are not observed and to insist that they should be duly carried out. What he cannot do is to require something to be done where there is no specific obligation placed upon the Parole Board or the local review committee to do something to or with the prisoner. There is nowhere any reference to informing any **H** prisoner of the reasons for not recommending release on licence. This situation is in sharp contrast to the position created under section 62 of the Act which deals with the revocation of a licence by the Secretary of State on the recommendation of the Parole Board. Where such a revocation does occur, it is provided by section 62 (3):

"A person recalled to prison . . . may make representations in writing with respect to his recall and shall on his return to prison be

A   informed of the reasons for his recall and of his right to make such representations."

There is no equivalent statutory requirement that the Parole Board should give to a prisoner information as to the reasons for not recommending his release on licence; nor is there any such requirement that the Secretary of State should do so. The actual decision is, of
B   course, his, though it is related to the recommendation of the Board. By a late re-amendment of the statement of claim there was added to the relief sought a prayer for

"a declaration that on the occasion of any interview by a member of the local review committee under rule 3 of the Local Review Committee Rules 1967, or by a member of the Parole Board under
C   section 59 (4) (b) of the Criminal Justice Act 1967 matters which may weigh against the recommendation of a release on licence should be put to the plaintiff except to the extent that the same are against public interest."

The difficulties to which I have already referred do not disappear by using the interviewing member of the local review committee as the
D   means of communicating the reasons. He will not know them save in so far as they are expressed in some cryptic formula such as "not recommended on account of nature and circumstances of offence" or "risk of re-offending unacceptable."

It is not easy, even if it were desirable, to give expression to or to define the subjective reasons in the minds of the members of the board;
E   it is often virtually impossible to communicate them in exact terms via a third party. Not only is there no statutory requirement to disclose to a prisoner the reasons for an adverse recommendation as to release on licence, but I doubt whether there is any statutory authority to make such a disclosure.

Notwithstanding what I think is a statutory inhibition against disclosing reasons for not recommending parole, Mr. Turner-Samuels advanced a
F   powerful argument founded on the principle of natural justice or fairness in the exercise of administrative functions. If no disclosure is made to a prisoner, it may be that some adverse factor which should not in truth relate to him at all may have affected the board's decision; and the error may survive in records and affect the next consideration of the case and any succeeding one. He cited the Golder case, February 21, 1975,
G   Publications of the European Court of Human Rights, Series A no. 18, as an illustration of how matters may go wrong so that injustice results. However, in the best of regulated procedures something may sometimes go awry; the question is whether the safeguards against possible error may not bring greater risks of injustice than what is prevented. A prisoner might find in being told the reason for refusal a specious and insincere means of creating a totally misleading impression by his conduct thereafter.
H   A person sentenced to imprisonment could not expect to be released before the due expiry of his sentence. Since the introduction of parole he may hope that part of his sentence may be served outside prison. If his offence was of a heinous kind, even that hope will be a frail one. When he seeks release on licence, he cannot undo the past. No doubt he will strive to convey to the Parole Board all the redeeming and more favourable aspects of his history. He needs no special information to

enable him to do this; nor is the case he puts forward one to be argued. A It will make its impact one way or the other. Of course the board must act fairly as must any body discharging a public duty which affects the interests of individuals. In the well-known case of *Reg.* v. *Gaming Board for Great Britain, Ex parte Benaim and Khaida* [1970] 2 Q.B. 417, 430, Lord Denning M.R. said:

> " It is not possible to lay down rigid rules as to when the principles B of natural justice are to apply: nor as to their scope and extent. Everything depends on the subject matter . . ."

In a context in which the public interest may be put at risk by the inopportune release of a prisoner on licence, no constraints or pressures should weigh upon the Parole Board in coming to what must in the end be a decision in which expediency must be an important influence. C

I agree with the conclusion of McNeill J. I would dismiss the appeal.

BRIGHTMAN L.J. This appeal involves the proper construction and application of sections 59 to 62 of the Criminal Justice Act 1967 and the Local Review Committee Rules 1967. The parole procedure can be summarised as follows. (1) A prisoner can only be released on licence by D a decision of the Secretary of State. In the case of a person imprisoned for life, the decision of the Secretary of State must be preceded by consultation with the Lord Chief Justice and the trial judge if available: sections 60 (1) and 61 (1). (2) Every such decision of the Secretary of State must be preceded by a " recommendation " of the Parole Board to that effect, unless the case is in the special category to which section 35 of the Criminal Justice Act 1972 applies; if in that category, the Home E Secretary may reach his decision upon the " recommendation " of the local review committee instead of the Parole Board. (3) Every such " recommendation " of the Parole Board must be preceded by a " report " of the local review committee to the Secretary of State; rule 3 (3). This " report " is not a " recommendation." The statutory function exercised by the committee in relation to prisoners is " to report to the Secretary F of State on their suitability for release on licence ": see rule 1 (1). The distinction drawn between a " recommendation " and a " suitability report " clearly emerges from the language of section 59 (6) (*a*) of the Act of 1967 and rules 1 (1) and 3 (3), which refer to suitability reports of the local review committee, and sections 60 (1), 61 (1) of the Act of 1967 and section 35 of the Act of 1972 which refer to recommendations of the G Parole Board. The local review committee does not make a " recommendation " except in a section 35 case. The plaintiff does not fall into the section 35 category. We are not therefore concerned with any " recommendations " by the local review committee but only with " suitability reports " by that body. I shall omit hereafter any reference to the section 35 procedure, although my conclusions would equally apply to a section 35 case. (4) The " recommendation " of the Parole Board is H also preceded by an interview between a member of the board and the prisoner if the board consider such an interview necessary: section 59 (4) (*b*). (5) Every " suitability report " of the local review committee must be preceded by an interview between a committee member and the prisoner, if the prisoner is willing: rule 3 (1). On this occasion the interview depends not on the decision of the authority but on the decision of the prisoner. (6) On the occasion of his interview by a member of

A the local review committee (if the interview takes place) the prisoner is to be given " a reasonable oppportunity to make any representations which he wishes to be considered by the committee ": rule 3 (2). (7) Rule 4 gives the prisoner a further right, independent of any interview taking place, to make written representations to the committee.

B The plaintiff was informed in 1975 and 1977 that the Parole Board had decided not to recommend his release on licence. As will be seen from my analysis of the Act and the Rules, each such adverse recommendation will have been preceded by a suitability report by the local review committee. I have laboured the distinction between a "recommendation" and " a suitability report " because the Act and the Rules clearly draw that distinction, but it is overlooked in the pleaded case. A suitability report will not necessarily contain any C recommendation at all. It could properly consist, and for all I know may in this case consist, only of an assessment of the pro's and con's.

The rights which the plaintiff possesses under the Act and the rules therefore include the following: (i) a right to be considered for release on licence if his case is referred by the Secretary of State to the local review committee: see rule 5; (ii) a right, prior to such consideration, to be D interviewed by a member of the local review committee: rule 3 (1); (iii) a right on the occasion of such interview to be given a reasonable opportunity to make any representations which he wishes to be considered by the committee: rule 3 (2); and (iv) a right independently of such interview to make written representations to the committee before it reviews his case: rule 4.

E The plaintiff's purpose in these proceedings is to establish his right to know the reasons, or the gist of the reasons, why he has not in the past been recommended for release on licence, in order to assist him in the exercise of his statutory right to make representations for his future release on licence. The case has proceeded in the pleadings and to some extent in argument on the basis that the local review committee as well as the Parole Board has declined to recommend the plaintiff for F release on licence. So far as the Parole Board is concerned, that is correct. The plaintiff does not know, nor do we know, what recommendations (if any) the local review committee has made. That is not its statutory function in the plaintiff's case.

A " right to know " is not expressly given to a prisoner in the plaintiff's situation by any statute or statutory instrument. Nor is there any G general principle of law which imposes on a decision-maker a duty to make known the reasons for his decisions. I agree with what was said by Sir Robert Megarry V.-C. in this respect in *McInnes* v. *Onslow-Fane* [1978] 1 W.L.R. 1520, 1531 et seq.

To succeed in this action, therefore, the plaintiff must rely either on the application of some principle of natural justice, or on an implication which ought to be made into the Act or the Rules as a matter of H construction. No other foundation for the plaintiff's claim has been suggested.

So far as natural justice is concerned, both the board and the committee accept that they are under a duty to act fairly in the exercise of their statutory functions. So the question that has to be asked is whether fairness requires that a prisoner in the situation of the plaintiff ought to be apprised of the reasons why he has not heretofore been recommended by the board for release on licence, or at least the gist of A the reasons, or of matters which may tend to weigh against him.

In *Kanda* v. *Government of Malaya* [1962] A.C. 322 the plaintiff, an inspector of police, had under the constitution of the Federation a right to be heard before being dismissed from the police service. The Judicial Committee observed, at p. 337: " If the right to be heard is to be a real right which is worth anything, it must carry with it a right in the accused B man to know the case which is made against him." That is the basis of the plaintiff's claim in this present action. In my judgment there is no close comparison between the two cases. The function of the Parole Board is to make a recommendation and of the local review committee to make a suitability report. In neither case is it to investigate charges. The board and the committee will each, no doubt, make an assessment of the prisoner's character and his likely reaction to a free environment; C and also, perhaps more importantly, an assessment of the public interest. According to the undisputed evidence, the committee's suitability report, and the board's recommendation, will be based on a consideration of the prisoner's file, including all reports which have been made from time to time by prison staff and reports specially prepared for the review, and also the representations (if any) made by the prisoner. The suitability report D of the local review committee and the representations of the prisoner form part of the material placed before the Parole Board to enable it to exercise an advisory function. I can see no principle of fairness which requires that the prisoner should be informed, even in outline, of the reasons which accompanied previous suitability reports of the local review committee or recommendations of the Parole Board, or of the adverse E matters which may weigh against him. Indeed, the prisoner will be only too well aware of the adverse factors likely to feature in reports made about him. He will not be better able to formulate effective representations because he has been told of the character assessments and the assessments of the public interest which may also feature in the file.

The scope and extent of the principles of natural justice depend on F the subject matter to which they are sought to be applied: see *Reg.* v. *Gaming Board for Great Britain, Ex parte Benaim and Khaida* [1970] 2 Q.B. 417, 430. They apply to the present case, as conceded, to the extent that they impose on the board and the committee, and each member of it, a duty to act fairly. That duty does not, in my judgment, require that any disclosure is made to the prisoner of adverse material which the board and the committee have in their possession to assist them in their G advisory and reporting functions.

There are other problems in applying the principles of natural justice so as to produce the result which the plaintiff seeks. One problem would be to define in legally intelligible language the limits of the disclosure which must be made if the plaintiff is right. The local review committee's report will be a report on the plaintiff's suitability for release on licence. H It is not claimed that he is to be given a copy of that report. Is he to be given a précis of it? If so, why not the whole report? If not a précis, how is one to define in legal language what has to be given? Much the same questions must be asked in relation to disclosure of the Parole Board's conclusions upon which its recommendation is founded.

Once the conclusion is reached that natural justice, i.e., fairness, does not require disclosure to be made, it is difficult to see how the same goal

A   can be reached as a matter of construction of the Act and the Rules. As I have said, there is nothing in the Act or the Rules which expressly requires disclosure to be made. So the duty, if it exists, must be an implied duty. The law is, I think, correctly expressed in *Maxwell on Interpretation of Statutes,* 12th ed. (1969), p. 33:

B   ' It is a corollary to the general rule of literal construction that nothing is to be added to or taken from a statute unless there are adequate grounds to justify the inference that the legislature intended something which it omitted to express."

The authority cited for that proposition is an observation in the speech of Lord Mersey in *Thompson* v. *Goold & Co.* [1910] A.C. 409, 420: " It is a strong thing to read into an Act of Parliament words which are not
C   there, and in the absence of clear necessity it is a wrong thing to do."

It was submitted that rule 3 (2) by necessary implication imposed on the interviewing member of the committee the obligation to make known to the prisoner the matters which might weigh against him. The prisoner is to be given " a reasonable opportunity " to make representations; that reasonable opportunity is to be given at the interview; therefore it is to
D   be implied, so the argument runs, that the interviewer is under a duty to direct the prisoner's attention to those aspects of his case which need to be answered; it is not easy to plead to an undisclosed case. The statement of claim was amended during the argument in order to raise this point. Clearly the interviewing member of the committee should brief himself in advance of the interview. So he is likely to know the probable impediments to release on licence if impediments exist. I found this
E   approach attractive at one time, and not inconsistent with the common sense of the situation. However on reflection I feel no doubt at all that such an implication, even if it could be formulated with sufficient precision, is unjustified in the absence of necessity. There is no " necessity " that such an inference should be made, particularly if I am right in concluding that natural justice does not so require. The system
F   has apparently worked for the last 10 years or more without disclosure being made. I can understand the argument that disclosure might be helpful to a prisoner who wishes to exercise his statutory right to make effective representations, but it is not " necessary." As Lord Mersey said, it is a strong thing to imply what Parliament has omitted. Furthermore, we have in section 62 (3) of the Act an express provision that a person who is recalled to prison shall be informed of the reasons for his recall.
G   He, too, has a statutory right to make representations. As the duty to give reasons is expressly imposed where recall to prison is in issue, but not where release on licence is in issue, it seems fairly obvious that the duty was not intended to be imposed in the latter case.

When this case was restored for further argument, we were referred to the *Golder case,* February 21, 1975, Publications of the European Court
H   of Human Rights, Series A no. 18. Mr. Golder was serving a term of imprisonment for robbery. In 1969 a prison riot took place. It was thought that Mr. Golder had taken part. Charges were prepared against him for offences against prison discipline. The charges were dropped but his prison record referred to their existence and to the fact that they were not proceeded with. In due course Mr. Golder was considered for parole but was not recommended. He complained to the European Commission of Human Rights in relation to stoppage of mail

768

and refusal of access to a solicitor.   Later the abandoned charges were   A
expunged from his prison record.   As I understand it, we were referred
to this case merely to illustrate the truism that misleading material is
capable of finding its way into a prisoner's record.   This might be an
argument for disclosing to a prisoner the factual matters which appear on
his record, so that he can check their accuracy, but is not an argument
for disclosing to him the assessments, reasons, opinions and   B
recommendations on his file, which are the material the plaintiff is
seeking.   The case is not therefore in my opinion illustrative of anything
relevant to this appeal.

I, too, would dismiss the appeal.

Appeal dismissed.
No order for costs save legal aid   C
taxation of appellant's costs.
Leave to appeal refused.

Solicitors: *Gulland & Gulland, Maidstone; Treasury Solicitor.*

R. C. W.   D

[QUEEN'S BENCH DIVISION]
E
*REGINA v. HEREFORD AND WORCESTER LOCAL
EDUCATION AUTHORITY, *Ex parte* JONES

1981 Feb. 25   Forbes J.

Education—School—Education authority, statutory duties of—   F
Individual music tuition—Proposal by authority to charge fees
—Whether instrumental tuition part of education—Whether
authority entitled to charge—Education Act 1944 (7 & 8 Geo.
6, c. 31), ss. 8, 61 (1)

Two girls who attended schools maintained by the local
education authority, each received individual tuition in a
musical instrument during school hours as part of the curricu-   G
lum free of charge. The local education authority notified
parents that it intended to charge fees for individual and group
music tuition. On application by the father of the two girls
by way of judicial review for a declaration that the local
education authority by reason of section 61 (1) of the Education Act 1944 [1] was not entitled to charge him with any fee
for the individual music tuition provided in school for his
daughters: —
Held, granting the application, that inclusion of individual   H
instrumental music tuition could properly be regarded as education and capable of forming part of the curriculum of any
school maintained by a local education authority; that where
an authority had decided that such tuition should be included
in the curriculum, then as long as it remained part of the
curriculum provided in the schools, the mandatory terms of

[1] Education Act 1944, s. 61 (1): see post, p. 771E.

The Weekly Law Reports, May 29, 1981

769

1 W.L.R.   R. v. Hereford Education Authority, Ex p. Jones (D.C.)

A   section 61 (1) precluded any fees from being charged (post, p. 773B, C–D).
         Semble. If the authority had decided that they could no longer afford to deploy scarce resources in money and teachers on individual music tuition at all the court could not interfere (post, p. 773H).

B   The following cases are referred to in the judgment:

         Associated Provincial Picture Houses Ltd. v. *Wednesbury Corporation* [1948] 1 K.B. 223; [1947] 2 All E.R. 680, C.A.
         Watt v. *Kesteven County Council* [1955] 1 Q.B. 408; [1955] 2 W.L.R. 499; [1955] 1 All E.R. 473, C.A.

         The following additional case was cited in argument:

C   *Inland Revenue Commissioners* v. *McMullen* [1981] A.C. 1; [1980] 2 W.L.R. 416; [1980] 1 All E.R. 884, H.L.(E.).

         APPLICATION for judicial review.
         The parent, Eric William Jones, applied for a declaration that the Hereford and Worcester Local Education Authority was by reason of
D   section 61 (1) of the Education Act 1944 not entitled to charge him with any fee for clarinet tuition provided in the Pershore High School in the County of Worcester and Hereford for his daughter Helen Elizabeth Jones or for violin tuition provided in the St. Nicholas Church of England Middle School in Pinvin in that county for his daughter Ruth Hannah Jones. The grounds of the application, inter alia, were that both schools were provided by the local education authority in accordance with its
E   duty under the Education Act 1944; for several years until the end of the spring term 1980 the local education authority had in accordance with its duty provided music instrumental tuition free of charge as part of the curriculum at both schools; on or about February 1980 the local education authority by its county general inspector of music notified the parent that it intended charging fees in respect of the instrumental tuition provided for
F   his two daughters as from the beginning of the summer term 1980; and the imposition of such a charge was contrary to the provisions of section 61 (1) of the Education Act 1944.
         The additional applications for an order of mandamus and for an injunction were not pursued.
         The facts are stated in the judgment.

G   *R. H. Tucker Q.C.* and *M. P. Reynolds* for the parent.
         Alan Fletcher for the local education authority.

         FORBES J. In this case Mr. Tucker moves for judicial review in the form of an order for mandamus, an injunction and a declaration against the respondents, the Hereford and Worcester Local Education Authority. The
H   matter is concerned with the provision of individual tuition on musical instruments. Mr. Jones, the applicant parent who, coincidentally, is deputy headmaster of the Pershore High School, has two daughters, one of whom is, in fact, at the Pershore High School and the other is at another school maintained by the local education authority, called the St. Nicholas Church of England Middle School, Pinvin. Both the girls, apparently, have some musical aptitude; Helen, who is at the High School, is receiving tuition on the clarinet and Ruth, at St. Nicholas, tuition on the violin.

Until very recently those individual instrumental lessons were provided A
free of charge. Recently, however, the local education authority—and I
will come to the reasons in a moment—decided that parents should be
charged modest sums (I think it is £10 a term) for the individual tuition
provided on musical instruments of this kind. The applicant parent maintains that the authority is not entitled to do that because it is not entitled
to charge for education.
                                                                        B
It is necessary, I think, to start by looking at some of the sections of
the Education Act 1944. Section 7 sets out the three stages of education,
primary, secondary and further education. Section 8 is important:

"(1) It shall be the duty of every local education authority to secure
that there shall be available for their area sufficient schools—(a) for
providing primary education "—and then there is a description of
what primary education is all about—" (b) for providing secondary C
education "—and there is a similar explanation of secondary education,
and the section goes on—" and the schools available for an area shall
not be deemed to be sufficient unless they are sufficient in number,
character, and the equipment to afford for all pupils opportunities for
education "—and these, I think, are the important words—" offering
such variety of instruction and training as may be desirable in view D
of their different ages, abilities, and aptitudes, and of the different
periods for which they may be expected to remain at school, including
practical instruction and training appropriate to their respective needs."

The next section to which I should turn is section 23. That provides
for the control of what is called " secular instruction." There is a distinction made in the Act of 1944 between religious education and secular E
instruction. Section 23 deals with secular instruction, and it says under
subsection (1) that in every county school, and so on, the secular instruction
to be given to the pupils shall be under the control of the local education
authority. Subsection (3) says that the power to control the secular
instruction provided in any county school:

"shall include power to determine the times at which the school F
session shall begin and end on any day, to determine the times at
which the school terms shall begin and end, to determine the school
holidays, and to require that pupils in attendance at the school shall
attend any class not conducted on the school premises for the purpose
of receiving instruction or training included in the secular curriculum
of the school."
                                                                        G
It will be seen, I think, from what I have read from those sections
that the statute is dealing with education as if it were synonymous with
instruction and training. It may be—it probably is—the position that
education is a word which is susceptible of a very much wider interpretation
than that, but it seems to me, at any rate for the purposes of the matters
I have to decide in this case, that what is being talked about under the H
term " education " in this Act is instruction and training, including, as
section 8 makes clear, practical instruction and training.

I should read section 53, or refer to it, at any rate, because Mr. Fletcher
relied upon it. That is the section headed, " Provision of facilities for
recreation and social and physical training ", and says:

"(1) It shall be the duty of every local education authority to secure
that the facilities for primary secondary and further education pro-

The Weekly Law Reports, May 29, 1981

771

1 W.L.R.   R. v. Hereford Education Authority, Ex p. Jones (D.C.)   Forbes J.

A   vided for their area include adequate facilities for recreation and social and physical training, and for that purpose a local education authority . . . may establish maintain and manage, or assist the establishment, maintenance, and management of camps, holiday classes, playing fields, play centres, and other places (including playgrounds, gymnasiums, and swimming baths not appropriated to any school or college), at which facilities for recreation and for such training as

B   aforesaid "—that is social and physical training—" are available for persons for whom primary secondary or further education is provided . . . and may organise games, expeditions and other activities for such persons, and may defray or contribute towards the expenses thereof."

So that provides that in certain circumstances the local education authority

C   may defray, or contribute towards, the expenses of providing facilities for recreation and social and physical training.

I think there is the clearest distinction between "facilities," which is being spoken of in section 53, and "instruction and training" which is being talked about in section 8. Section 53 is dealing with the question of facilities, parallel bars in the gymnasium or the gymnasium itself, or, if one can translate it into orchestral terms, the provision of a cello, or

D   something of that kind, so that somebody can play the instrument. It is not dealing with the provision of tuition or training. I very much doubt whether in any event, having regard to the subject in this case, one could possibly say that orchestral instruments were "facilities for recreation and social and physical training" any more than one would think the provision of bunsen burners were for somebody who had a bent for chemistry.

E   Then section 61, which is the important section, says:

"(1) No fees shall be charged in respect of admission to any school maintained by a local education authority, or to any county college, or in respect of the education provided in any such school or college."

If I may extract from that the relevant words so far as this case is concerned, they are simply these: "No fees shall be charged . . . in respect

F   of the education provided in any such school." Those are the words, it seems to me, I have to interpret in this case.

I do not think that section 76, to which reference has been made, is of great importance in this case. That is the section which indicates that, other things being equal, pupils should be educated in accordance with the wishes of their parents. I say "other things being equal" because it is plain from

G   the decision of the Court of Appeal in *Watt v. Kesteven County Council* [1955] 1 Q.B. 408 that that really is the effect of the section.

That being the position in law, what was the position in fact? The fact is that these two children have been receiving individual instrumental tuition in their respective schools for some time. Helen began in September 1975 to be taught the clarinet and Ruth started receiving her violin lessons in September 1979. It is plain from one of the documents exhibited to the

H   parent's affidavit that the local education authority were, if I can say so with respect, taking a very proper and sensible view about the provision of this kind of individual tuition. They—when I say "they," this is a document which emanated from the Pershore High School but no doubt the same position obtained at St. Nicholas—made it clear that tuition was available on the full range of brass instruments and, with one or two exceptions, all of the orchestral instruments, and they deal with the way in which these lessons can be given and taken by the pupils. They are given

772

by the county peripatetic music staff, to take place during normal lesson   A
times. There were timetables arranged so that, in fact, the pupils having
such individual instruction did not miss the same period every time they
had a lesson. They were switched around so that they would only miss
one period, and a different period, as it were, each week. There was
provision for the pupils to make up the lost time in the lessons which they
missed owing to the instrumental tuition.

The document makes it clear, I think, that there is a limited supply   B
of instruments, there is a limited supply of teachers and that, therefore, they
will only pick out for this type of tuition prospective pupils showing
musical potential. Further, if they want to learn a second instrument it
may be, in fact, very difficult to do so because of the limited supply of
instruments and teachers and of the fact that the upset in the other lessons
would be multiplied. As I say, it seems to me a very proper and sensible   C
approach to the problem of providing instrumental tuition on an individual
basis.

The brochure from the Pershore High School seems to me to make it
perfectly clear that such individual tuition was, indeed, part of the
curriculum offered by the school. There is a short passage saying:

"Musical Instrument: Pupils who wish to study a particular musical   D
     instrument, individually or in small groups, may do so by special
     arrangement."

What happened, as I said, was that everything went on swimmingly
until February 25, 1980, when Mr. Polybank, who is the county general
inspector of music, sent out to all parents, a letter saying that from the
commencement of the summer term charges would be levied at the rate   E
of £10 per term for individual lessons and less for group lessons. It goes on:

"If your child is at present receiving music lessons from a county
     peripatetic instrumental music teacher and you wish him or her to
     continue receiving lessons, it will be necessary for you to complete
     the attached application form ..."

F
It was that proposal to charge which brought this parent to launch these
proceedings on the grounds that this instrumental music tuition was part
of the education provided in the Pershore High School and, for that matter,
in St. Nicholas School as well, and that therefore no fees should be charged.

I have also had affidavits from Mr. Hosier, who is the principal of
the Guildhall School of Music and Drama, and Mr. Fletcher, who is the
principal music adviser for the Leicestershire education committee, and   G
principal of the Leicestershire School of Music. The burden of those two
affidavits, if I may condense them without any disrespect to their authors,
is that the study of an instrument, that is training in the ability to play
an instrument, can properly be regarded as education and, indeed, can,
in certain circumstances, be a very important part of the individual education of a particular pupil. But they also say—and I have been shown   H
examples—that there are at least three of the examining boards—the
London University Board, the Cambridge University Board, and the
Associated Examination Board—who provide O and A level certificates
for performing musicians.

Taking this quite shortly, by looking at one, the "London University
Board A Level: Practical Music 509," I need only read the first sentence
of the introductory aims:

The Weekly Law Reports, June 5, 1981

773

1 W.L.R.   R. v. Hereford Education Authority, Ex p. Jones (D.C.)   Forbes J.

A   " The syllabus is intended to develop, in some depth, the practical,
        aural and historical awareness of the performing musician in ways
        particularly relevant to the executant's situation."

In other words, it is plain that that is an A level paper designed for the
executant and not the theoretician. It is clear that it requires a very high
degree of competence in the actual playing of musical instruments in order
B that the entrant should pass his A level paper in music. I need not deal
with the other two but the same kind of thing is available from the other
boards.

        I have no doubt at all that practical tuition in playing an instrument
is not only educative and part of education but is certainly something which
an education authority is entitled to include in the curriculum if it wishes.
C I have no doubt that there are many education authorities who, in their
particular situations, will do so. If it is possible for a pupil to get an
A level as a performing musician, or an O level, that is a qualification
towards which a school curriculum might well aim. For this purpose there
seems no logical reason for distinguishing between an O level in physics
and one in piano playing. I find no difficulty in coming to the conclusion
that individual instrumental music tuition is capable of forming part of
D the curriculum of any school provided and maintained by local education
authorities.

        If it is provided as part of the curriculum it seems to me that, having
regard to the terms of section 61, it is education provided in that school
and, as such, no fees may be charged for it. On the other hand, I am
bound to say that, having regard to the provisions of section 23 (3), the
E question of whether such tuition is to be included in the curriculum is a
matter within the competence of the local education authority to decide.
Subject to the rules in *Associated Provincial Picture Houses Ltd.* v.
Wednesbury Corporation [1948] 1 K.B. 223, one could not challenge their
decision in the courts if taken properly and without running counter to any
of the matters which are set out in Lord Greene M.R.'s judgment in
F that case.

        The position here—and I have the deputy education officer's affidavit—
is that it is plain that this local education committee was faced, as no doubt
most education committees are, with a very difficult task. They were required
to review the provision of education in their schools against the background
of financial limitations which meant, in effect, that something would have to
go. In any situation like this it seems to me that an administrative
G authority, faced with the problem of carrying out its statutory duty by the
deployment of scarce resources, is entitled to say, " Much as we regret it
we have got to cut something " and unless, as I say, that is an unreasonable
way of looking at it under the *Wednesbury* case, no court is going to
interfere. What this local education authority did was to look at the problem
and to say that they took the view that what they called " the basic
H statutory provision of education " must be maintained, and what they
regarded as matters which were to some extent extraneous to the basic
statutory provision of education would have to be paid for.

        That it seems to me, is where they fell into error. I could not say that
if they had decided they could no longer afford to deploy scarce resources
in money and teachers on individual music tuition at all, that would be
something which this court could interfere with. But, short of that, if the
subject remains part of the education provided in the school, it seems

to me that they are not entitled to charge for it. I have no doubt at all, **A** reviewing the facts of this case, that the individual instrumental tuition provided to these two girls is part of the education provided in these schools. That being so, it seems to me that section 61 (1) is mandatory and no fee can be charged.

Mr. Tucker does not seek, as I understand it, to ask this court that an order of mandamus should go, and, indeed, he might be in very great difficulty as the request for that relief is set out in the statement filed **B** pursuant to R.S.C., Ord. 53, because what he is asking for is an order for mandamus requiring the local education authority to provide clarinet instrumental tuition free. That would be an order which I do not think I could possibly accede to in any way. It involves and subsumes the proposition that it is the duty of the authority to provide clarinet instrumental tuition anyway, and I am not persuaded that the authoriy is under **C** any such duty. So he is not really pursuing that, or the injunction, and, again, I would not be disposed, where one has (as one has here) a sensible and reputable authority which would obviously follow and feel itself bound by any declaration this court made, to grant an injunction where a declaration will do. So that all I will do, having regard to what I have said earlier about the situation, is to say that Mr. Tucker is entitled to a declaration in the terms which were amended during the course of argu- **D** ment, namely, that the local education authority is by reason of section 61 of the Education Act 1944 not entitled to charge the parent with any fee for clarinet tuition provided in the Pershore High School for his daughter Helen, or violin tuition provided in St. Nicholas School for his daughter Ruth. With those amendments I think the declaration should be made.

E

Declaration granted with costs.

Solicitors: *H. Pierce; J. W. Renney, Worcester*

[Reported by MISS STELLA SOLOMON, Barrister-at-Law]

F

[COURT OF APPEAL]

* REGINA *v.* MARCUS

G

1981 March 23;   Shaw L.J., Tudor Evans
April 9   and Sheldon JJ.

*Crime—Attempt—Causing noxious thing to be taken by another
—Drugs from sedative and sleeping tablets in milk—Little
harm arising from toxicity of drugs—Danger to person carrying
out potentially hazardous operation with faculties impaired—* **H**
*Whether " noxious thing"—Offences against the Person Act
1861 (24 & 25 Vict., c. 100), s. 24*

Section 24 of the Offences against the Person Act 1861
provides:

" Whosoever shall . . . cause to be . . . taken by any other
person any poison or other destructive or noxious thing,
with intent to injure, aggrieve, or annoy such person, shall
be guilty of [an offence]."

A   The defendant put into a milk bottle delivered to her
neighbour's home eight sedative and sleeping tablets. She
was tried on a count charging that she attempted to cause
to be taken by the neighbour or another a noxious thing
with intent to injure, aggrieve or annoy the neighbour or
another. Expert opinion was that the drugs comprised a dose
which would be likely to cause sedation and even sleep, and
that little harm was likely to arise from the toxicity of the
B   drugs themselves, but there was a danger to someone carrying
out normal but potentially hazardous operations such as
driving a car. The jury were directed that it was a matter of
fact and degree for them to decide whether the drugs in the
milk were noxious. The defendant was convicted.
          On appeal against conviction on the ground that the sub-
stance being intrinsically harmless it could not become noxious
or harmful because it was given in excess quantity: —
C   *Held*, dismissing the appeal, that for the purposes of
section 24 of the Offences against the Person Act 1861, the
concept of the " noxious thing " involved not only the quality
or nature but also the quantity of the substance administered
or sought to be administered and it was a question of fact
and degree in all the circumstances whether a thing was
noxious; that, on the true construction of section 24 " noxious "
meant something less in importance than, and different in
D   quality from, poison or other destructive things and that,
accordingly, the jury had been properly directed (post, pp.
779G, H—780A, D).
          Reg. v. *Hennah* (1877) 13 Cox C.C. 547 and *Reg.* v.
Cramp (1880) 5 Q.B.D. 307 applied.
          Reg. v. *Cato* [1976] 1 W.L.R. 110, C.A. distinguished.

E   The following cases are referred to in the judgment:

Donoghue v. *Stevenson* [1932] A.C. 562, H.L.(Sc.).
Reg. v. *Cato* [1976] 1 W.L.R. 110; [1976] 1 All E.R. 260, C.A.
Reg. v. *Cramp* (1880) 5 Q.B.D. 307.
Reg. v. *Hennah* (1877) 13 Cox C.C. 547.

The following additional case was cited in argument:

F   *Reg.* v. *Perry* (1845) 2 Cox C.C. 223.

APPEAL against conviction.
          On December 13, 1979, at the Central Criminal Court (Judge Buzzard),
the defendant, Lily Marcus, was convicted on an indictment charging that
she on May 15, 1978, attempted maliciously to cause to be taken by
Mary Ann Laskey or another a noxious thing, namely, a quantity of
G nitrazepan and dichloralphenasone with intent to injure, aggrieve or annoy
Mary Ann Laskey or another. On February 7, 1980, the defendant
was made subject to an order to enter into her own recognizance in
the sum of £300 to come up for judgment if called upon within three
years, and she was ordered to pay a contribution of £150 towards the
legal aid costs of her defence.
H   The defendant appealed against conviction on the grounds that the
judge wrongly decided that a quantity of nitrazepan and dichloralphenazone, the chemical constituents of Mogadon and Welldorm, proprietary
brands of sleeping tablets frequently prescribed and in common use, was
or was capable of being a noxious thing; that the judge wrongly disregarded and wrongly failed to apply the dicta of Lord Widgery C.J.
in *Reg.* v. *Cato* [1976] 1 W.L.R. 110, 119; that the judge drew an incorrect or unjustifiable inference from the evidence of William David

Reg. v. Marcus (C.A.)   [1981]

Campbell Wilson that " little harm is likely to arise from the toxicity of A
the drugs themselves but there is obvious danger to someone carrying out
normal but potentially hazardous operations (e.g. driving) whilst their
faculties are impaired," in relying on that evidence in support of a ruling
that a quantity of nitrazepan and dichloralphenazone was or was capable
of being a noxious thing; and that, in all the circumstances, the verdict
of the jury was unsafe or unsatisfactory in that (a) the drugs, the sole
subject matter of the count, were impacted at the bottom of a bottle of B
milk; (b) unless the bottle was shaken the drugs would remain in impacted
powder form at the bottom of the bottle, where they were unlikely to be
used for or liable to human use or consumption; (c) that when the drugs
first appeared in the bottle the members of the Laskey family, for whose
household the bottle was supplied, had left home for work and were in
no position to use or consume all or any of the contents until several C
hours later on their respective return to their home; (d) by reason of
alleged previous mishaps during the previous week with bottles of milk
none of the Laskey family was likely to use or consume the bottle's
contents; and (e) that, therefore, the drugs were unlikely to cause all or
any of the Laskey family any harm.

The facts are stated in the judgment.
                                                                          D

Hugh Torrance (assigned by the Registrar of Criminal Appeals) for
the defendant.
Arthur French for the Crown.

                                                        Cur. adv. vult.
                                                                          E

April 9. TUDOR EVANS J. read the following judgment of the court.
This is an appeal against conviction on a point of law. On December
13, 1979, the defendant was convicted at the Central Criminal Court of
an attempt to cause to be taken a noxious thing with intent to injure,
aggrieve or annoy contrary to section 24 of the Offences against the Person
Act 1861. On February 7, 1980, the defendant was made subject to an
order to enter into her own recognizance in the sum of £300 to come up F
for judgment if called upon within three years. She was also ordered
to pay £150 towards the legal aid costs of her defence.

The defendant lived very close to a family named Laskey. There had
been trouble between them for a number of years. For some days before
May 15, 1978, the Laskey family had noticed that there was something
wrong with the milk that was being delivered to their house. At first they G
blamed the dairy, but eventually they became suspicious and informed the
police. On May 12, one of the milk bottles was handed in for analysis.
On the morning of May 15 a police officer started to keep watch. He
first saw the defendant with some children in the yard area between her
house and the Laskeys' house. At 8.40 a.m. a milkman delivered two
bottles of red top milk at the Laskeys' back door leaving them in a
basket. By that time the Laskeys had left home for the day. The police H
officer who was concealed in a ground floor room then saw the defendant
hurry over to the Laskeys' back door and remove the two bottles of milk.
She took them into her own house. Very shortly afterwards she was seen
to emerge from her own house carrying two bottles of red top milk. She
replaced them in the basket at the Laskeys' back door. The red top on
one of the bottles was found to be intact. The top of the other bottle
was slightly loose.

A   A toxicologist, Mr. Wilson, was called to give evidence on behalf of
the Crown. He analysed the contents of the bottle, which the Laskeys
had handed in on May 12, as well as the bottle which had been found
to have a slightly loose top. The bottle handed in on May 12 gave a
positive test for some type of household detergent. Mr. Wilson was of the
opinion that the detergent present could not be harmful. The incident
of May 12 did not form part of the indictment. However, Mr. Wilson
B   found that the contents of the other bottle were contaminated by two
powdered substances which he identified as nitrazepan and dichloralphenazone. These chemical substance were used in the preparation of
well-known types of sedative and sleeping tablets. The former was sold
only under the trade name Mogadon. The latter was used in sleeping
tablets sold under a number of trade names but most commonly under
C   the name Willdorm. Mr. Wilson found that the powdered drugs were
impacted up to a level of half an inch from the bottom of the bottle.
He also found, in the contents of the bottle, a trace of a well known
pain killer called paracetamol. The presence of paracetamol in the milk
could have been explained if the person who had put the sleeping tablets
into the milk had just been handling a drug containing paracetamol.
D   Mr. Wilson and Mr. Tozeland, a toxicologist called for the defence,
were agreed that there were three to four doses of each of the sleeping
tablets in the bottle. Mr. Tozeland thought that at least eight tablets had
been put into it. They were also agreed that the dose of the drugs would
be likely to cause sedation and even sleep. The speed at which the drugs
would operate would depend upon the amount taken and upon the contents of the stomach at the time. The greater the amount of food in the
E   stomach, the longer it would take for the drugs to have effect; if taken
on an empty stomach, the effect would be more immediate and deeper.
Mr. Wilson said in evidence that in his opinion little harm would arise
from the toxicity of the drugs themselves but that there was a danger
to someone carrying out potentially hazardous operations, for example,
driving a car. He said that he would never describe a drug as harmless
since the object of a drug is to affect the physiology of the person who
F   takes it. Although this may operate in an appropriate case beneficially,
there may be concurrent adverse side effects. Mr. Tozeland substantially
agreed with him.
      According to the defendant, on the morning of May 15, she had seen
two bottles of red top milk on her draining board. She was unable to
remember if she had brought the bottles into her house. At some stage,
G   because she had had a bad night, she had in her hands a couple of tablets
known as Solpdene. These were pain-killing tablets containing paracetamol, a trace of which was subsequently found in the bottle containing
the sleeping tablets. The defendant said that she had pushed the top
of one of the bottles down but then, because of the colour of the top,
she realised that the milk was not hers and she then put them outside
the Laskeys' back door.
H   There was evidence before the jury that the defendant had previously
taken sleeping tablets (including Mogadon but not Willdorm), but that
she did not have sleeping tablets at the time of the alleged offence. When
interviewed by the police, the defendant denied putting anything into the
milk but later she said that she had been upset and annoyed by the
Laskeys and had put two Solpdene tablets into their milk.
      There was ample evidence before the jury upon which they could find

Reg. v. Marcus (C.A.)   **[1981]**

that the defendant had put at least eight tablets into the milk bottle and   A
that, when she did so, she intended to injure, aggrieve or annoy the
Laskeys. But counsel for the defendant contends that an offence was
not committed because the tablets were not a " noxious thing " within
section 24 of the Offences against the Person Act 1861.

Two submissions are made. First, it is said that for a thing to be
noxious within the meaning of section 24, it must be noxious in itself.
A thing which is intrinsically harmless cannot become noxious or harmful   B
because it is given in excess quantity. In support of this submission,
counsel relies upon obiter dicta of Lord Widgery C.J. in *Reg.* v. *Cato*
[1976] 1 W.L.R. 110. Secondly, it is submitted that the word " noxious "
means harmful and that the meaning is necessarily confined to injury to
bodily health. The word cannot mean harm involving an impairment of
faculties. Counsel submits that on the undisputed evidence there was in   C
fact no risk of injury to bodily health. If any one member of the Laskey
family had drunk the milk, or any part of it, he or she would have been
sedated or at most would have been caused to fall asleep.

In *Reg.* v. *Cato* the appellant had been convicted of manslaughter
and of an offence under section 23 of the Offences against the Person Act
1861, by the administration of heroin. Section 23 is in language similar
to section 24, but concerns the endangering of life or the causing of   D
grievous bodily harm. Lord Widgery C.J., speaking of section 23,
observed, at p. 119:

> " The thing must be a ' noxious thing ' and it must be administered
> ' maliciously.' What is a noxious thing, and in particular is heroin
> a noxious thing? The authorities show that an article is not to be
> described as noxious for present purposes merely because it has a   E
> potentiality for harm if taken in an overdose. There are many articles
> of value in common use which may be harmful in overdose, and
> it is clear on the authorities when looking at them that one cannot
> describe an article as noxious merely because it has that aptitude.
> On the other hand, if an article is liable to injure in common use,
> not when an overdose in the sense of an accidental excess is used   F
> but is liable to cause injury in common use, should it then not be
> regarded as a noxious thing for present purposes? "

It was then held that heroin was a noxious thing for the purposes of
section 23. Counsel for the defendant, relying upon those observations,
submits that the sleeping tablets, being harmless in themselves, could not
be regarded as noxious within section 24 simply because the defendant   G
had attempted to administer or cause to be administered an excess quantity
of them.

The question whether a thing could be noxious within the Act of 1861
if administered in excessive quantity was considered in a number of
authorities in the last century. It was held in cases to which we shall
refer that, although a substance may be harmless if administered in small
quantities, it may nevertheless be noxious if administered in excessive   H
quantities. In *Reg.* v. *Hennah* (1877) 13 Cox C.C. 547 the defendant
was charged with administering cantharides, contrary to section 24 of the
Act. In his judgment, Sir Arthur Cockburn C.J. clearly envisaged that,
although a substance may be harmless in small quantities, it may be
noxious within the section, if a sufficient quantity were administered. He
is reported as saying, at p. 549:

A
" Upon the medical evidence before us, cantharides, or, as it is
commonly called, Spanish Fly, is administered medicinally, and in
small quantities, and up to a certain extent, is incapable of producing
any effect. What is important to the present case is that the quantity
administered was incapable of producing any effect. The statute
makes it an offence to administer, although not with the intention of
taking life or of doing any serious bodily harm, any noxious thing
B
with intent to cause injury or annoyance. But unless the thing is a
noxious thing in the quantity administered, it seems exceedingly
difficult to say logically there has been a noxious thing administered.
The thing is not noxious in the form in which it has been taken;
it is not noxious in the degree or quantity in which it has been given
and taken. We think, therefore, the indictment will not hold. It
C
would be very different if the thing administered, as regards either
its character or degree, were capable of doing mischief."

In *Reg* v. *Cramp* (1880) 5 Q.B.D. 307, the defendant was convicted of
an offence under section 58 of the Act of 1861, which, inter alia, makes it
an offence to procure or attempt to procure an abortion by administering
or causing to be administered any poison or other noxious thing. The
D
poison or noxious thing administered was a half ounce of juniper. It
was submitted on behalf of the defendant, as it is in this case, that the
offence consists of administering a thing in itself noxious and that the
statute does not make it an offence to administer harmless substances
even in excessive doses. The submission was unanimously rejected by
a court of five judges. We need refer only to two passages. Lord
Coleridge C.J. said, at p. 309:
E

" The intent with which the oil of juniper was given was proved
and it was further proved that it was noxious in the quantity
administered. What is a poison? That which when administered
is injurious to health or life, such is the definition of the word
poison. Some things administered in small quantities are useful,
which, when administered in large quantities, are noxious."
F

Denman J. said, at p. 309:

" Where a person administers with the improper and forbidden intent
large quantities of a thing which so administered is noxious, though
when administered in small quantities it is innocuous, the case falls
within the statute."

G
We are of the opinion that for the purposes of section 24 the concept
of the " noxious thing " involves not only the quality or nature of the
substance but also the quantity administered or sought to be administered.
If the contention of the defendant is correct, then, on the assumption
that the drugs were intrinsically harmless, it would follow that if the
defendant had attempted to administer a dose of 50 tablets by way of the
H
milk, an amount which, if taken, would have been potentially lethal, she
would have committed no offence. We do not consider that such a
result can follow from the language of section 24. The offence created
by the section involves an intention to injure, aggrieve or annoy.
We consider that the words " noxious thing " mean that the jury
has to consider the very thing which on the facts is administered or
sought to be administered both as to quality and as to quantity. The
jury has to consider the evidence of what was administered or attempted

to be administered both in quality and in quantity and to decide as a   A
question of fact and degree in all the circumstances whether that thing
was noxious.   A substance which may have been harmless in small
quantities may yet be noxious in the quantity administered.   Many illustrations were put in the course of the argument: for example, to lace
a glass of milk with a quantity of alcohol might not amount to administering a noxious thing to an adult but it might do so if given to a child.

　We do not consider that Lord Widgery C.J. in *Reg.* v. *Cato* [1976]   B
1 W.L.R. 110, 119 was intending to lay down the general proposition that
a substance harmless in itself and in small quantities could never be
noxious within section 24 of the Act if administered in large quantities.
Reg. v. *Cato* was a very different case from the present.   The court was
concerned with heroin, plainly a dangerous substance.   *Reg.* v. *Cramp*
(1880) 5 Q.B.D. 307 was not cited to the court.   C

　We shall now consider the second submission for the appellant, that
the word " noxious " means harmful in the sense of injury to bodily
health.   Counsel took us through the relevant sections of the Act.   In a
number of sections (including section 24) the words " poison or other
destructive or noxious thing " appear.   It was submitted that the meaning
of the word " noxious " must take colour from the preceding words.   We   D
do not accept that construction.   It seems to us, looking at the relevant
sections, that the statute is dealing with offences in a declining order of
gravity and that by " noxious " is meant something different in quality
from and of less importance than poison or other destructive things.

　On this part of his argument, counsel relies upon evidence from the
toxicologists on both sides that the dose would do no more harm than
cause sedation or possibly sleep and was therefore harmless.   In fact,   E
the evidence was not so confined.   In the course of his summing up, the
judge, having referred to the evidence relating to sedation and sleep,
continued:

　　" Mr. Wilson said that little harm is likely to arise, in his opinion,
　　from the toxicity of the drugs themselves, but there is a danger to
　　someone carrying out normal but potentially hazardous operations,   F
　　for example, driving, whilst their faculties are impaired.   You may
　　think that it would not have to be driving, it might be crossing a
　　London street, for example; one could think of a lot of things."

　There was therefore evidence before the jury that the drugs in the
quantity in which they were present in the milk were potentially harmful
in the sense of being capable of causing injury to bodily health.   The   G
result of the evidence was that the milk might have had a direct physical
effect on the victim.   But we do not consider that the word " noxious "
bears the restricted meaning for which counsel contends.

　In the course of his summing up, the judge quoted the definition of
" noxious " from the *Shorter Oxford English Dictionary,* where it is
described as meaning " injurious, hurtful, harmful, unwholesome."   The   H
meaning is clearly very wide.   It seems to us that even taking its weakest
meaning, if for example, a person were to put an obnoxious (that is
objectionable) or unwholesome thing into an article of food or drink
with the intent to annoy any person who might consume it, an offence
would be committed.   A number of illustrations were put in argument,
including the snail said to have been in the ginger beer bottle (to adapt
the facts in *Donoghue* v. *Stevenson* [1932] A.C. 562).   If that had been

A done with any of the intents in the section, it seems to us that an offence would have been committed.

The judge, when summing up to the jury, reminded them fully of the evidence and directed them that it was a matter of fact and degree for them to decide whether the drugs in the milk were noxious. His direction in law was unexceptionable. The appeal must be dismissed.

B Solicitor: *Solicitor, Metropolitan Police.*

Appeal dismissed.

L. N. W.

C

[CHANCERY DIVISION]

* PILKINGTON BROTHERS LTD. *v.*
INLAND REVENUE COMMISSIONERS

D 1980 Nov. 27, 28;   Nourse J.
        Dec. 19

Revenue—Corporation tax—Group relief—Tax avoidance scheme
to provide relief by purchase of surplus capital allowances
from shipping company—Whether "arrangements" in exist-
ence enabling purchasing company to be treated as a member
E *of same group of companies as surrendering company—*
Whether group relief available—Income and Corporation
Taxes Act 1970 (c. 10), s. 528 (1) [1]*—Finance Act 1973 (c. 51),*
s. 29 (1) [2]

In 1974 the taxpayer company negotiated a scheme to enable it to obtain substantial group relief from corporation tax by purchasing from M. Ltd., a ship-owning company, excess capital allowances arising from the purchase of a con-
F tainer ship. Had M. Ltd. simply commissioned and paid for the ship, the first year capital allowances would have consider-ably exceeded that company's liability to tax. The scheme was thus designed to benefit both the taxpayer company and M. Ltd. —the taxpayer company being able, by virtue of the company group relief provisions, to reduce its own liability to tax by purchasing M. Ltd.'s excess capital allowances at a discount. The scheme involved making use of two dormant subsidiaries
G of the taxpayer company, H. Ltd. and V. Ltd., and of G.C.L. Ltd., a subsidiary of M. Ltd. On September 26, 1974, H. Ltd. adopted amended objects clauses to carry on business as a general investment holding company, and V. Ltd. adopted simi-larly amended objects clauses, and amended its articles of association; its two issued shares were redesignated as "A" shares and two ordinary shares designated as "B" shares were issued for cash to M. Ltd. The articles of association of
H G.C.L. Ltd. were also amended. The results of those arrange-

---

[1] Income and Corporation Taxes Act 1970, s. 258: " (1) Relief for trading losses and other amounts eligible for relief from corporation tax may in accordance with the following provisions of this Chapter be surrendered by a company (called the ' surrendering company ') which is a member of a group of companies and, on the making of a claim by another company (called ' the claimant company ') which is a member of the same group, may be allowed to the claimant company by way of relief from corporation tax called " ' group relief.' "

[2] Finance Act 1973, s. 29 (1): see post, p. 787D–F.

The Weekly Law Reports, June 5, 1981

782

Pilkington Bros. Ltd. v. I.R.C. (Ch.D.)   [1981]

ments were that (i) M. Ltd. together with the taxpayer com-   A
pany had equal shareholdings and equal voting rights in V.
Ltd.; (ii) the taxpayer company had all the shares and voting
rights in H. Ltd., and (iii) H. Ltd. and V. Ltd. had equal
shareholdings in G.C.L. Ltd., H. Ltd. having twice as many
votes but no preponderance of voting power because of an
article requiring resolutions to be approved by both H. Ltd.
and V. Ltd. Under a sale and purchase agreement dated
September 30, 1974, M. Ltd. agreed to sell half of its share-   B
holding in G.C.L. Ltd. to H. Ltd. and half to V. Ltd., those
two companies thereby being placed in a dead-lock situation
regarding the control of G.C.L. Ltd. The scheme at no time
required any amendments to be made to either the taxpayer
company's or M. Ltd.'s articles of association. By a further
agreement dated September 30, 1974, G.C.L. Ltd. contracted
to purchase a containerised cargo vessel and containers at a
basic price of £11,070,000. The final step in the scheme was   C
the execution of a group relief agreement dated December
31, 1974, whereby, for accounting periods ending March 31,
1975, 1976 and 1977, G.C.L. Ltd. would claim capital allowances to produce sufficient " available loss " not exceeding
£13,000,000 for companies in the taxpayer company's group
and that such companies would pay M. Ltd. 87½ per cent. of
the corporation tax thereby saved.

The inspector of taxes refused to allow the taxpayer com-   D
pany's claim for group relief for its accounting period to
March 31, 1975. On appeal by the taxpayer company the
special commissioners upheld the inspector's refusal on the
ground that G.C.L. Ltd. was to be treated as not being a
member of the same group of companies as the taxpayer
company because the provisions in section 29 (1) (b) of the
Finance Act 1973 had not been complied with.

On appeal by the taxpayer company:—   E

Held, allowing the appeal, that to establish the taxpayer company's entitlement to relief under section 258 of the Income
Corporation Taxes Act 1970 it had to circumvent the restriction
contained in section 29 (1) (b) (ii); that on the true construction of that subsection " arrangements " referred to a combination of things or a disposition of measures for a purpose (post,
pp. 787c–d, 791d); that no " arrangements " existed whereby, during or after the relevant accounting period, either the   F
taxpayer company and M. Ltd. together, or the shareholders of
those two companies, had control of G.C.L. Ltd. but not of the
taxpayer company; and that since the scheme did not involve
amending the taxpayer company's articles of association, no
" arrangements " existed during the relevant period whereby
the shareholders of the taxpayer company controlled the taxpayer company but not G.C.L. Ltd.; accordingly the restriction
in section 29 (1) (b) (ii) had been overcome, the taxpayer com-   G
pany was to be treated as being a member of the same group of
companies as G.C.L. Ltd. and was thus entitled to reduce its
liability to corporation tax by the acquisition of the excess
capital allowances accruing to G.C.L. Ltd. (post pp. 791d–e,
792d–e).

The following cases are referred to in the judgment: H

Greenberg v. *Inland Revenue Commissioners* [1972] A.C. 109; [1971] 3
    W.L.R. 386; [1971] 3 All E.R. 136; 47 T.C. 240, H.L.(E.).
Inland Revenue Commissioners v. *Joiner* [1975] 1 W.L.R. 1701; [1975]
    3 All E.R. 1050; 50 T.C. 449, H.L.(E.).
Inland Revenue Commissioners v. *Parker* [1966] A.C. 141; [1966] 2
    W.L.R. 486; [1966] 1 All E.R. 399, H.L.(E.).
Inland Revenue Commissioners v. *Plummer* [1980] A.C. 896; [1979] 3
    W.L.R. 689; [1979] 3 All E.R. 775, H.L.(E.).

The Weekly Law Reports, June 5, 1981

783

1 W.L.R.   Pilkington Bros. Ltd. v. I.R.C. (Ch.D.)

A The following additional cases were cited in argument:

  British Basic Slag Ltd. v. *Registrar of Restrictive Trading Agreements*
   (1963) L.R. 4 R.P. 116; [1963] 1 W.L.R. 727; [1963] 2 All E.R. 807,
   C.A.

  Foss v. *Harbottle* (1843) 2 Hare 461.

B CASE STATED by the Commissioners for the Special Purposes of the
Income Tax Acts.

  In 1974 Manchester Liners Ltd. put to the taxpayer company, Pilkington Brothers Ltd., a proposal whereby both companies were to benefit
under the provisions giving group relief from corporation tax by the
utilisation of capital allowances on a container ship. Transactions thereafter took place that culminated in the taxpayer company, through two
C of its subsidiary companies, purchasing at a discount capital allowances
accruing to a subsidiary company of Manchester Liners Ltd.

  The taxpayer company appealed against the refusal by the inspector
of taxes to allow its claim for group relief from corporation tax for the
accounting period to March 31, 1975.

  The commissioners dismissed the appeal for the following reasons.
(1) It seemed to them that the words " power ... to secure ..." in sec-
D tion 534 require complete and ultimate control, de jure and de facto, not
merely the ability to produce deadlock, i.e. to obstruct by veto. On that
view control of Golden Cross Line Ltd. (G.C.L. Ltd.) lay, by virtue of
the arrangements, in the taxpayer company and Manchester Liners Ltd.
together, not in the one or the other by itself. To put it another way, the
control was shared or joint. (2) They saw nothing in the wording of
E section 29 (1) (*b*) (ii) that prevented the taxpayer company as the second
company from also being one of the joint controllers of G.C.L. Ltd.
Indeed, the word " any " prima facie suggested absence of exclusion,
limitation or restriction. (3) It could not be said that the taxpayer company and Manchester Liners Ltd. together had " control " of the taxpayer company in the ordinary meaning of that word. The whole of the
control of the taxpayer company was vested in its shareholders, and no
F part had been transferred by virtue of any arrangement or otherwise to
Manchester Liners Ltd. or the latter's shareholders. (4) They drew no
material distinction between the taxpayer company and Manchester
Liners Ltd. as persons on the one hand and their respective shareholders
as bodies of persons on the other. It seemed to them that the shareholders were as much bound by the arrangements as the companies them-
G selves.

  In the result, they acceded to the Crown's main submissions, but they
had been specifically asked to deal with its alternative or " de facto "
submission, which they could do quite shortly. The supervision and
management agreements were agency agreements entered into in the
ordinary course of business, having nothing to do with the matters mentioned in section 534 (*a*) and (*b*) and did not therefore decide the control
H of G.C.L. Ltd. The shipbuilding expertise of the two G.C.L. Ltd.
directors nominated by Manchester Liners Ltd. was no doubt essential
to the proper functioning of G.C.L. Ltd., and perhaps an indication of
where one might have expected to find the control if the words in (*a*)
and (*b*) of section 534 had not been enacted. Even if the expertise, together with the supervision and management agreements, amounted to
de facto control that would not in the commissioners' view have satisfied the test propounded by section 534. Accordingly they held that

The Weekly Law Reports, June 5, 1981

784

Pilkington Bros. Ltd. v. I.R.C. (Ch.D.)   **[1981]**

G.C.L. Ltd. was to be treated for the purposes of group relief as not be-   A
ing a member of the taxpayer company's group, and they postponed final
determination of the assessments for one month to enable the parties to
agree figures if possible.

The taxpayer company appealed. At the hearing of the appeal the
Crown, pursuant to a notice served under R.S.C., Ord. 91, r. 4, contended that in the accounting period ended March 31, 1975, arrangements existed (namely the share structure of Villamoor Ltd. and G.C.L.   B
Ltd. and the arrangements subsisting within each company under its
articles of association as to the powers of its directors) such that for the
purposes of section 29 (1) (*b*) (ii) of the Finance Act 1973 the shareholders of the taxpayer company had control of the taxpayer company
but did not have and could not have obtained control of G.C.L. Ltd.

The facts are set out in the judgment.   C

C. N. Beattie Q.C. for the taxpayer company.
Allan Heyman Q.C. and *Robert Carnwath* for the Crown.

Cur. adv. vult.

December 19, 1980. NOURSE J. read the following judgment. The ques-   D
tion in this case is whether group relief from corporation tax which would
otherwise have been available to the taxpayer company under section 258
of the Income and Corporation Taxes Act 1970 has been denied it by the
restrictions on that relief which were introduced by the Finance Act 1973.
The particular provision of the Act of 1973 with which this case is concerned is section 29 (1) (*b*) (ii). Broadly stated, that says that the relief   E
is not to be available as between two companies in a group where arrangements are in existence by virtue of which, at some time during or after
the expiry of a relevant accounting period, any person or persons control
or could obtain control of one of the companies but not the other. The
question comes to the court as an appeal by way of case stated from a
decision of the special commissioners given on March 13, 1979. The
effect of their decision was to confirm the inspector of taxes' refusal to   F
allow the taxpayer company the group relief which had been claimed for
the accounting period to March 31, 1975. The taxpayer company now
appeals against that decision.

Before turning to the facts of the present case I should like to say
something about group relief in general terms. It was first introduced in
1967. Its broad purpose was to allow one company in a group to deduct   G
the trading losses and other amounts eligible for relief from corporation
tax—for example, capital allowances—of another company in the same
group in computing its own profits for the purposes of that tax. Two
companies could claim to be members of the same group for this purpose
only if one was a 75 per cent. subsidiary of the other or both were 75 per
cent. subsidiaries of a third company. A company was treated as being
a 75 per cent. subsidiary of another if and so long as not less than 75 per   H
cent. of its ordinary share capital was owned directly or indirectly by that
other. There were further provisions dealing with what was meant by
ownership, direct or indirect. The ordinary share capital of a company
was so defined as to exclude capital the holders whereof had a right to
a dividend at a fixed rate but had no other right to share in the profits
of the company. One of the results of that last definition was that participating preference shares, by carrying rights to share in the profits of

The Weekly Law Reports, June 5, 1981

785

1 W.L.R.   Pilkington Bros. Ltd. v. I.R.C. (Ch.D.)   Nourse J.

A the company, ranked as ordinary share capital for the purposes of group relief.

Mr. Beattie, who appeared for the taxpayer company, told me that before 1973 advantage was taken of the then provisions, in particular of the definition of ordinary share capital, for the purpose of obtaining group relief in circumstances where Parliament might well not have intended it to be available. He illustrated that by an example, not so far removed B from the present case, of a shipping company which wanted to buy a new ship but could do so only by incurring losses during the period of construction. It was a member of a group which made overall losses or at least had insufficient profits to take full advantage of the shipping company's losses for the purposes of group relief. Some clever lawyer or accountant then conceived the idea of getting round this difficulty by C obtaining group relief in another way. This was how they did it. Suppose that the shipping company had an issued capital of £100 divided into 100 ordinary shares of £1 each. All it had to do was to issue for cash at par 300 participating preference shares of £1 each to a profitable company outside the group. The shipping company thus became a 75 per cent. subsidiary of the outside company, which took a surrender of the losses and put in a claim for group relief. In return for this the outside D company agreed to pay to the shipping company an amount equivalent to the corporation tax saved by it, less an appropriate discount. Once the ship had been built and was available for charter the operation was put into reverse. The shipping company was returned to its old group and its profits on chartering became available to absorb the losses there. Mr. Beattie said—and he may be right—that it was in order to defeat E this sort of device that sections 28 to 32 of the Finance Act 1973 were enacted. And he said that of those sections it is section 28 which is the most important. Subsection (2) of that section introduced two new requirements before one company could be treated as being a subsidiary of another for the purposes of group relief. In the case of a 75 per cent. subsidiary it requires first, that the parent company should be beneficially entitled to not less than 75 per cent. of any profits available for distribu- F tion to equity holders of the subsidiary company, and, secondly, that the parent company should be beneficially entitled to not less than 75 per cent. of any assets of the subsidiary company available for distribution to its equity holders on a winding up. Those, said Mr. Beattie, were the two additional requirements which were needed to defeat, and did defeat, the sort of device to which I have referred. He then said that if Parlia- G ment had also intended that there should be some overriding requirement as to voting control, then that is something which one would have expected to find in section 28 (2) and not in section 29. He then went on to advance a broadly based argument to the effect that section 29 is concerned with arrangements for some change to take place and not with a static state of affairs.

The material facts in the present case are these. In July 1974 another H company, Manchester Liners Ltd., put a proposal to the taxpayer company which was intended to benefit both companies by the utilisation of capital allowances on container ships. Manchester Liners Ltd. is a company of shipowners in the Furness Withy Group, and it wanted a new ship. If Manchester Liners Ltd. had simply gone ahead and commissioned and paid for the building of the ship, first year allowances would have considerably exceeded the amount of the group's liability to corporation tax. Accordingly, those allowances would not have been fully

786

Nourse J.   Pilkington Bros. Ltd. v. I.R.C. (Ch.D.)   [1981]

utilised. So far as the taxpayer company was concerned, the proposal A
would have the advantage of reducing its own liability to corporation tax
by the purchase of the excess allowances from Manchester Liners Ltd. at
an appropriate discount. Negotiations proceeded between both sides
during the summer of 1974 and the resultant scheme, so far as now
material, had been agreed and implemented by the end of the year.

In the light of a considerable narrowing of the issues in dispute it is
unnecessary for me to deal with the scheme in the detail in which it had B
to be looked at by the special commissioners. The essentials of the
scheme, so far as material for present purposes, were these: the taxpayer
company had two wholly owned dormant subsidiaries called Hello T.V.
Ltd. and Villamoor Ltd. On the other side, Manchester Liners Ltd. had
a wholly owned subsidiary called Golden Cross Line Ltd. whose main
object was to undertake and carry on all or any of the trades or businesses C
of carriers by sea. On September 26, 1974, (i) Hello T.V. Ltd. amended
its objects so as to carry on business as a general investment holding
company; (ii) Villamoor Ltd. amended its objects in like manner and also
its articles of association; its two issued ordinary shares were redesignated
as " A " shares and two more ordinary shares designated as " B " shares
were issued for cash to Manchester Liners Ltd.; and (iii) Golden Cross
Line Ltd. amended its articles of association. On September 30, 1974, D
Manchester Liners Ltd. agreed to sell half the issued share capital of
Golden Cross Line Ltd. to Hello T.V. Ltd. and half to Villamoor Ltd.

As a result of these dealings with the share capital of Villamoor Ltd.
and Golden Cross Line Ltd. and the material amendments to the memoranda and articles of association of those two companies and Hello T.V.
Ltd., the position was as follows. The taxpayer company retained 100 E
per cent. of the issued share capital of Hello T.V. Ltd. and 50 per cent.
of the issued share capital of Villamoor Ltd. (the " A " shares). Manchester Liners Ltd. had acquired the other 50 per cent. of the issued
share capital of Villamoor Ltd. (the " B " shares). (It was agreed that
in spite of apparent differences between the voting rights attaching to
the " A " and " B " shares there was deadlock between the taxpayer F
company and Manchester Liners Ltd. in regard to Villamoor Ltd., so
that neither controlled or could control it). Hello T.V. Ltd. and Villamoor Ltd. had each acquired 50 per cent. of the issued share capital of
Golden Cross Line Ltd., but again there was deadlock between them, so
that neither controlled or could control Golden Cross Line Ltd. This
latter deadlock, at all events, was intentional and was thought desirable
for commercial reasons, but it is the admitted inability of Hello T.V. G
Ltd. and therefore of the taxpayer company to control Golden Cross
Line Ltd. which is perhaps the most crucial issue in the determination of
the taxpayer company's claim to be allowed group relief in the present
case. Also on September 30, 1974, an agreement was entered into by
which a firm of shipbuilders agreed to build and deliver to Golden Cross
Line Ltd. a containerised cargo vessel and containers at a basic price of H
£11·7 million.

The final step in the scheme which is material for present purposes
was an agreement dated December 31, 1974, between the taxpayer company and Golden Cross Line Ltd., by which it was agreed that for the
accounting periods ending March 31, 1975, 1976 and 1977 Golden Cross
Line Ltd. would claim capital allowances so as to produce sufficient
" available losses " not exceeding £13 million for companies in the tax-

The Weekly Law Reports, June 5, 1981

787

1 W.L.R.   Pilkington Bros. Ltd. v. I.R.C. (Ch.D.)   Nourse J.

A payer company's group and that such companies would pay Manchester Liners Ltd. 87·5 per cent. of the corporation tax thereby saved. I have been told that the target of £13 million was fully reached, and may have been exceeded. On a figure of £13 million the saving to the taxpayer company of corporation tax at 52 per cent. would be £6·76 million. Accordingly, if the scheme worked the taxpayer company would have to pay £5·915 million to Manchester Liners Ltd. and would be able to retain
B a saving of £845,000 for itself.

I should emphasise, for the purposes of the argument of Mr. Heyman for the Crown, that the whole scheme and every stage of it required and was conditional upon the approval of the boards of the taxpayer company anl Manchester Liners Ltd. On the other hand, and for the purposes of the argument of Mr. Beattie, I should emphasise that although the
C scheme required and involved amendments to the objects of Hello T.V. Ltd. and Villamoor Ltd., and to the articles of Villamoor Ltd. and Golden Cross Line Ltd., it did not require and it did not involve any amendments to the memoranda or articles of association of either the taxpayer company or Manchester Liners Ltd.

It has been common ground throughout that the taxpayer company satisfied all the requirements of sections 258 and 259 of the Income and
D Corporation Taxes Act 1970, and also all the further requirements of sections 28, in particular the two additional requirements of subsection (2), and 29 of the Finance Act 1973, except those of section 29 (1) (b) (ii), which, when suitably abstracted, reads as follows:

> " 29 (1) If, apart from this section, two companies (in this section referred to as ' the first company ' and ' the second company ') would
E be treated as members of the same group of companies and—(a) in an accounting period which ends on or after March 6, 1973 . . . (b) arrangements are in existence by virtue of which, at some time during or after the expiry of that accounting period,—. . . (ii) any person has or could obtain, or any persons together have or could obtain, control of the first company but not of the second . . . then, for the purposes of the enactments relating to group relief, the first company
F shall be treated on and after March 6, 1973, as not being a member of the same group of companies as the second company."

Section 29 (5) gives to " control " the meaning assigned to it by section 534 of the Income and Corporation Taxes Act 1970. I need not refer to that, because it has not given rise to any debate before me. Section
G 32 (6) of the Act of 1973 defines " arrangements " to mean arrangements of any kind, whether in writing or not. I need not refer to any of the other statutory provisions.

I should like to make two observations on section 29 (1) (b) (ii) at this stage. First, as between two companies in the same group either can be " the first company " or " the second company ", and vice versa. Secondly, on what I conceive to be the natural reading of sub-paragraph
H (ii) that provision contemplates that the person or persons there referred to is or are a third party or third parties distinct from the first and second companies.

It is not entirely clear from the case stated how the matter proceeded before the commissioners, or what were the precise grounds of their decision in favour of the Crown, but my understanding of the position is as follows. For the purposes of the Crown's arguments Golden Cross Line Ltd. was the first company and the taxpayer company the

The Weekly Law Reports, June 5, 1981

788

Nourse J.   Pilkington Bros. Ltd. v. I.R.C. (Ch.D.)   [1981]

second. The Crown's primary argument was that arrangements were in A existence by virtue of which, at some time during or after the expiry of the relevant accounting period, the taxpayer company and Manchester Liners Ltd. together had control of Golden Cross Line Ltd. but not of the taxpayer company. That argument was accepted by the commissioners as the main ground for their decision. The Crown's secondary argument was that arrangements were in existence by virtue of which, etc., the shareholders of the taxpayer company and the shareholders of B Manchester Liners Ltd. together had control of Golden Cross Line Ltd. but not of the taxpayer company. Mr. Beattie said—and I agree with him—that the commissioners appear, somewhat obliquely, to have accepted this argument as an alternative basis for their decision in favour of the Crown.

In opening the taxpayer company's appeal to this court, Mr. Beattie C dealt first with the two arguments which had been advanced by the Crown before the commissioners and then with an entirely new point which had been raised by the Crown pursuant to a notice under R.S.C., Ord. 91, r. 4. But when Mr. Heyman came to argue on behalf of the Crown he confined himself to this new point. With regard to the other two points he did no more than formally adopt the reasoning and decision of the commissioners so far as necessary. I think that means that Mr. Heyman D left it to me to see whether I thought that the commissioners' decision could be supported on either of the grounds on which they appear to have founded themselves. I cannot, without some enlightenment, see my way to doing that. It seems to me that the first ground involves the doubtful proposition that the persons referred to in sub-paragraph (ii) can include the first or second company. It also involves the curious, even comical, E notion that a company (in this case the taxpayer company) might in certain circumstances be said to control itself. As to the second ground, that involves the different but equally curious notion that when considering who controls the taxpayer company you can bring into the reckoning the shareholders of Manchester Liners Ltd., whose presence at any meeting of the shareholders of the taxpayer company, even if it were welcome, would nevertheless be superfluous. F

I turn therefore to the new argument which has been advanced on behalf of the Crown. The companies are now reversed, the first being the taxpayer company and the second Golden Cross Line Ltd. Mr. Heyman said that arrangements were in existence by virtue of which, at some time during or after the expiry of the accounting period ending March 31, 1975, the shareholders of the taxpayer company together had G control of the taxpayer company but not of Golden Cross Line Ltd. On that footing he said that paragraph 29 (1) (b) (ii) is satisfied and that, for the purposes of the enactments relating to group relief, the taxpayer company is to be treated as not being a member of the same group of companies as Golden Cross Line Ltd. It will at once be seen that the Crown's new argument does not involve the doubtful proposition or either of the curious notions which appear to me to have infected its earlier H arguments. But Mr. Beattie has advanced a number of submissions to the contrary, including his broadly based argument as to the concern of section 29.

The first, and in my view the crucial question is: what are the "arrangements" contemplated by section 29 (1) (b)? Mr. Heyman said that in the present case they were the share structure of Villamore Ltd.

The Weekly Law Reports, June 5, 1981

789

1 W.L.R.   Pilkington Bros. Ltd. v. I.R.C. (Ch.D.)   Nourse J.

A and Golden Cross Line Ltd., and the arrangements subsisting within each
of those companies and the other companies concerned, including the
taxpayer company, under their respective articles of association.   He
pointed in particular to the articles of the taxpayer company, which admittedly enable the shareholders of that company to control it, and said that
they are part of the arrangements contemplated by the provision.
Although Mr. Beattie was prepared to accept that the dealings with the
B share capital of Villamoor Ltd. and Golden Cross Line Ltd. and the
material amendments to the memoranda and articles of those two companies and Hello T.V. Ltd. were part of the arrangements, he emphatically denied that status to the articles of the taxpayer company. He said,
correctly, that they have been in existence for very many years, and the
scheme did not require and did not involve any amendments to them.
C He said, therefore, that they cannot be part of the arrangements which
are contemplated by the provision, particularly when it is borne in mind
that the shareholders were not parties to the scheme and in all probability knew nothing about it, at all events until after it had been implemented. He then cited an anomaly which would flow from the Crown's
argument and to which I shall refer in due course. In reply to this Mr.
D Heyman said that all the provision requires me to ask is what arrangements were in existence at the material time. Why should they not
include the articles of association of a company, which embody the
arrangements between the shareholders for the governance of the company, albeit that they have been in existence for very many years and
did not require any alteration for the purposes of the scheme?

    Mr. Heyman also submitted that I must adopt a similar approach to
E the interpretation of these provisions as that now adopted for the purposes of the legislation enabling the Crown to counteract the tax advantages of certain transactions in securities under section 460 of the Income
and Corporation Taxes Act 1970. For that he referred to a well known
passage in the speech of Lord Wilberforce in *Inland Revenue Commissioners* v. *Joiner* [1975] 1 W.L.R. 1701, 1705–1706, where he said:

F   " Upon the enactment of the original section 28 of the Finance Act
     1960 it was possible to contend, and it was contended, that this sec-
     tion (and its associated sections) was directed against a particular type
     of tax avoidance known generally under such descriptions as dividend
     stripping, asset stripping and bond washing and that the sections
     and particular expressions used in them, amongst others ' transactions
     in securities ', should be interpreted in the light of this supposed
G   purpose. But this line of argument became unmaintainable after
     the decisions of this House in *Inland Revenue Commissioners* v.
     Parker [1966] A.C. 141 and *Greenberg* v. *Inland Revenue Commis-
     sioners* [1972] A.C. 109. It is clear that all the members of this House
     who decided those cases were of opinion that a wide interpretation
     must be given to the sections and to the expressions used in them.
H   More than this, it appeared from the opinion of Lord Reid in *Green-
     berg* v. *Inland Revenue Commissioners* that the sections called for a
     different method of interpretation from that traditionally used in
     taxing Acts. For whereas it is generally the rule that clear words
     are required to impose a tax, so that the taxpayer has the benefit of
     doubts or ambiguities, Lord Reid made it clear that the scheme of
     the sections, introducing as they did a wide and general attack on
     tax avoidance, required that expressions which might otherwise have

The Weekly Law Reports, June 5, 1981

790

Nourse J.   **Pilkington Bros. Ltd. v. I.R.C. (Ch.D.)**   [1981]

been cut down in the interest of precision were to be given the wide A
meaning evidently intended, even though they led to a conclusion
short of which judges would normally desire to stop."

Mr. Heyman submitted that those observations apply to any legislation
which mounts a wide and general attack on tax avoidance, and he said
that sections 28 to 33 of the Finance Act 1973 are enactments of that
character. I have no hesitation in rejecting that argument, which, if B
correct, would be the thin edge of a substantial wedge. I find it impossible to read the words of Lord Wilberforce, or of Lord Reid in *Greenberg* v. *Inland Revenue Commissioners* [1972] A.C. 109, as having been
intended to go further than to prescribe an approach to the legislation
which was there under consideration. In the circumstances, I approach
the interpretation of sections 28 to 33 by the traditional route which has C
to be followed in the construction of a taxing statute. I think that means
that, just as the taxpayer has the benefit of doubts or ambiguities in
deciding whether a tax has been imposed on him, so does he have that
benefit in deciding whether a relief which was formerly available to him
has been restricted. However, I do not find it necessary to rely on that
principle for the purpose of determining what are the arrangements contemplated by section 29 (1) (*b*) in the present case. D

As to that question, I start from the position that "arrangements"
means arrangements of any kind, whether in writing or not, and that it is in
both ordinary and statutory parlance a word of wide import by no means
confined to relationships having contractual force and effect. But that is not
to say that anything which in isloation or in another context can be described
as arrangements are necessarily arrangements or part of the arrangements E
for the purposes of the provisions now in question. They must in
my judgment be arrangements by virtue of which both the control of
the first company is had and the control of the second is lacking. The
articles of association of the taxpayer company were in themselves
arrangements by virtue of which the control of that company was had.
The provisions of the scheme were in themselves arrangements by virtue
of which the control of Golden Cross Line Ltd. was lacking. Do the F
arrangements contemplated by the provision include both? Unless they
do the provision does not operate.

I think that my general approach to the meaning of "arrangements"
must be dictated by a passage in the speech of Lord Wilberforce in *Inland
Revenue Commissioners* v. *Plummer* [1980] A.C. 896, where his Lordship
was considering the definition of "settlement" which is to be found in G
section 454 (3) of the Act of 1970. That reads, "any disposition, trust,
covenant, agreement or arrangement." Lord Wilberforce said at p. 911:

"But it still becomes necessary to inquire what is the scope of the
words 'settlement' and 'settlor' and of the words which are included in 'settlement' in the context in which they appear. If it
appears, on the one hand, that a completely literal reading of the H
relevant words would so widely extend the reach of the section that
no agreement of whatever character fell outside it, but that, on the
other hand, a legislative purpose can be discerned, of a more limited
character, which Parliament can reasonably be supposed to have intended, and that the words used fairly admit of such a meaning as
to give effect to that purpose, it would be legitimate, indeed necessary, for the courts to adopt such a meaning."

The Weekly Law Reports, June 5, 1981

791

1 W.L.R.   Pilkington Bros. Ltd. v. I.R.C. (Ch.D.)   Nourse J.

A   If, therefore, I felt that a completely literal reading of " arrangements " in section 29 (1) (b) (ii) would so widely extend the reach of the provision that no arrangements of whatever character and however dissociated from each other fell outside it, then I would have to pay close attention to Mr. Beattie's argument as to the concern of section 29 in order to see whether I could discern a legislative purpose of a more limited character which Parliament could reasonably be supposed to have intended. How-

B   ever, I do not find that necessary in the present case, which in my judgment can be decided on no more than the ordinary meaning of the word. The material dictionary meanings of " arrangement " are: " a structure or combination of things for a purpose "; " disposition of measures for a particular purpose: see the *Shorter Oxford English Dictionary*, 3rd ed. (1944), p. 99. Both those definitions require that the individual elements of an

C   arrangement should be combined or disposed for a particular purpose, and I do not think that, unless there is a context to the contrary, that requirement is displaced by the use of the plural as opposed to the singular. All that that adds is the possibility that there may be more than one combination of things or more than one disposition of measures. But without a context it would, as it seems to me, be unnatural to read the plural as dispensing with the need for some unifying link between each

D   of the combinations or dispositions. I therefore construe this provision in the expectation that it is intended to refer to things or measures which are combined or disposed for a particular purpose. On that footing it is at the least difficult, and in my view impossible, to see how it can include the articles of association of the taxpayer company, whose nature and effect remained unchanged throughout and cannot in any ordinary sense

E   be said to have been things or measures which were combined or disposed with the provisions of the scheme. The unifying link is just not there. That point seems to me to be emphasised by a consideration of the fact that the shareholders of the taxpayer company, who are the persons between whom the articles have effect as the arrangements for the governance of the company, were not parties to the scheme. It was said on behalf of the Crown that the shareholders were " brought into the

F   arrangements " by the board of the taxpayer company, alternatively that they " were as much bound by the arrangements " (those were the special commissioners' words) as the taxpayer company itself, but vague concepts of that kind are not really an aid to statutory construction.

I can perhaps best express my own view of the meaning of " arrangements " by reference to the so-called Aristotelian or dramatic unities of

G   action, time and place. Just as the European drama outside the French 17th century in general ignored the unities of time and place (there are notable exceptions, such as *The Alchemist* and *John Gabriel Borkman*), so it seems to me that they are unnecessary requirements of " arrangements," which can be enacted over a considerable period of time and in a number of different places. But on the unity of action both the drama and the language have insisted. It seems to me that " arrangements "

H   cannot sensibly include the script of another piece played out at a second theatre, normally not more than once a year, by actors not only not booked to appear on the stage of the first, but unaware that the performance was on.

I must now refer to the anomaly which Mr. Beattie said would result from the Crown's new argument. Mr. Beattie took the simple example of three companies, A, B and C, where A is the parent company, B is a wholly owned subsidiary of A and C is a wholly owned subsidiary of B. That, he said, is an entirely straightforward and familiar type of company structure. There can be no doubt that before the Act of 1973 C could have surrendered its losses to A, which could then have claimed group relief. But on the Crown's new argument that would no longer be so for these reasons. C is the first company and A the second for the purposes of section 29 (1). B is a person who has control of C, by virtue of C's articles of association, but not of A. On the Crown's argument section 29 (1) (b) (ii) is satisfied, and that means that A cannot claim group relief on a surrender to it of C's losses. That, said Mr. Beattie, would be a most anomalous and far-reaching result of the Crown's new argument. Mr. Heyman accepted this as an inevitable result of the argument, but he sought to counter the difficulty by saying that it would be open to the three companies to take simple and inoffensive steps to remedy the position. That may well be so, but that again is not an aid to statutory construction. It seems to me that an anomaly of this kind, unless it can be answered, is one which, if it was necessary to do so, would again have to be taken very seriously in discerning the legislative purpose which Parliament can reasonably be supposed to have intended in regard to this provision. However, I wish to emphasise that I have not found it necessary to rely on it for the purpose of arriving at a conclusion on this point.

In the circumstances, my conclusion on what in the end is a short point is that the " arrangements " for the purposes of section 29 (1) (b) (ii) in the present case did not include both the articles of association of the taxpayer company and the provisions of the scheme. That is enough to dispose of the Crown's new argument, and I propose to say nothing further about Mr. Beattie's alternative submissions to the contrary. The appeal must be allowed.

> *Appeal allowed with costs.*
> *Certificate under section 12 of*
> *the Administration of Justice*
> *Act 1969 to appeal to the*
> *House of Lords.*

Solicitors: *Norton, Rose, Botterell & Roche; Solicitors of Inland Revenue.*

[Reported by MRS. HARRIET DUTTON, Barrister-at-Law]

A

[HOUSE OF LORDS]

* INLAND REVENUE COMMISSIONERS . . . APPELLANTS

AND

GARVIN . . . . RESPONDENT

B 1981 March 23, 24, 25;   Lord Wilberforce, Lord Russell
          May 14   of Killowen, Lord Keith of Kinkel,
                          Lord Scarman and Lord Bridge of Harwich

*Revenue—Income tax—Tax avoidance—Transaction in securities
—Tax advantage—Relationship between transaction and
receipt of dividend—Transaction "whereby" other person
subsequently receives abnormal amount by way of dividend*
C *—Distribution of profits where company under "control" of
not more than five persons—Date for determination—Income
and Corporation Taxes Act 1970 (c. 10), s. 461, para. C (1),[1]
para. D (1)[2]*

Prior to April 3, 1969, the taxpayer owned beneficially 50
per cent. of the shares in five companies, ABCFS, which
owned valuable freehold and leasehold properties. On April
D 3, 1969, the taxpayer and his two co-shareholders sold all their
shares in the five companies to Excalibur, the sale price for
the taxpayer's shares being £235,999. With a view to spread-
ing liability to capital gains tax over a long period of time
the price was made payable by instalments over 200 years,
the first instalment of £50 being payable in 1968–69 and the
remaining instalments yearly thereafter with a very substantial
final instalment payable on April 3, 2169, interest at 10¼ per
E cent. per annum being payable on the amount from time to
time outstanding. On April 14, 1969, he sold his right to
the instalments to Greave for £235,949. The taxpayer thus
obtained his sale price in full with negligible immediate
liability to capital gains tax. Subsequently, however, pursuant
to section 116 (3) of the Finance Act 1972, he paid the
capital gains tax which he had avoided. At the time of the
sale of the shares ABCFS had between them profits of £176,453
F available for distribution by way of dividend. The properties
then held by those companies, if sold at then market value,
might have been expected to produce additional profits aggre-
gating £382,527, which with the aforementioned profits would
have produced total available profits of £558,980. Excalibur
having purchased the shares in ABCFS put into operation in
April 1969 a scheme enabling those companies to dispose of
their properties in such a way as to spread liability to corpor-
G ation tax on the profits arising from such disposals over a
long period by granting leases at premiums payable by instalments over periods of 999 years (or shorter periods in the case
of leasehold properties having a shorter term to run). The
taxpayer was not a party to those arrangements nor was he

---

[1] Income and Corporation Taxes Act 1970, s. 461, para. C (1): see post, p.
802G–H.
   [2] S. 461, para. D: " (1) That in connection with the distribution of profits of a
H company to which this paragraph applies, the person in question so receives as is
mentioned in paragraph C (1) above such a consideration as is therein material. (2)
The companies to which this paragraph applies are:—(a) any company under the
control of not more than five persons, and (b) any other company which does not
satisfy the condition that its shares or stocks or some class thereof (disregarding
debenture stock, preferred shares or preferred stock), are authorised to be dealt in
on a stock exchange in the United Kingdom, and are so dealt in (regularly or from
time to time), so, however, that this paragraph does not apply to a company under
the control of one or more companies to which this paragraph does not apply. (3)
Subsections (2) to (6) of section 302 of this Act (definition of control) shall apply for
the purpose of this paragraph."

aware that Excalibur intended to cause ABCFS so to avoid cor-   A
poration tax, though the special commissioners informed that
his professional advisers knew from the price offered for the
taxpayer's shares that Excalibur intended in some way to avoid
corporation tax. The only part that the taxpayer played in
the subsequent transactions carried through, by, or at the
instance of the purchaser of his shares was to arrange for a
company called Central in which he was a 50 per cent. shareholder to buy back the properties. The special commissioners   B
found that in April 1969 the directors of Excalibur had not
decided whether to procure the payment of a dividend by
ABCFS and that it remained an open question for about a
year. On April 13, 1970, ABCFS paid an aggregate amount
of £554,000 to Excalibur by way of dividend. It was not
disputed that the dividend so received by Excalibur was
abnormal in amount within the meaning of section 467 (3)
of the Income and Corporation Taxes Act 1970.   C

The revenue served a notice on the taxpayer under section
460 (3) of the Act of 1970 alleging that he obtained a tax advantage by not causing the companies ABCFS, to pay out their
profits, actual and potential by way of dividend before the sale
of the shares to Excalibur, and that the taxpayer obtained that
advantage either in the circumstances mentioned in paragraph C of section 461 or in those mentioned in paragraph D
thereof. The taxpayer appealed to the special commissioners   D
who allowed the appeal. Their decision was affirmed by
Slade J. and by the Court of Appeal (by a majority).

On appeal by the revenue: —

Held, dismissing the appeal, (1) that the word " whereby " in
paragraph C was equivalent to " by which " and connoted
some causal connection, albeit of a somewhat loose nature,
between the transactions in question and the subsequent receipt
of the abnormal dividend; that although the transactions of   E
April 1969 were a sine qua non the declarations of dividend
in April 1970 would have been made that was not a sufficient
connection to satisfy the language of paragraph C and that
accordingly, the claim under that paragraph failed (post, pp.
798F–H, 801A–B, D, H—802A, 803F–H).

(2) That the " control " postulated by paragraph D must
be shown to have existed at the date either when there was a
distribution of profits or a realisation of assets, and that   F
therefore, in the circumstances, the relevant company for
consideration was Excalibur and that since there was no
evidence that Excalibur was a close company the claim under
paragraph D also failed (post, pp. 798A–C, 800G, 801H—802A, F).

Per Lord Wilberforce, Lord Keith of Kinkel, Lord Scarman
and Lord Bridge of Harwich. Relief from double taxation
should be a right not a privilege (post, pp. 799G, 801H—802A,
D–E, 804E–F).   G

Quaere (*per* Lord Russell of Killowen and Lord Bridge
of Harwich). Whether it was open to the Crown having
levied a tax on the basis that the transaction was a dealing
in capital, then to assert that it can indirectly, by counteraction, be treated as giving rise to taxable income (post, pp.
801F–G, 804F–G).

Decision of the Court of Appeal [1980] S.T.C. 295   H
affirmed.

The following cases are referred to in their Lordships' opinions:

Greenberg v. *Inland Revenue Commissioners* [1972] A.C. 109; [1971]
    3 W.L.R. 386; [1971] 3 All E.R. 136; 47 T.C. 240, H.L.(E.).
Inland Revenue Commissioners v. *Joiner* [1975] 1 W.L.R. 1701; [1975]
    3 All E.R. 1050; 50 T.C. 449, H.L.(E.).

The Weekly Law Reports, June 5, 1981

795

1 W.L.R.   I.R.C. v. Garvin (H.L.(E.))

A   The following additional cases were cited in argument:
Anysz v. *Inland Revenue Commissioners* [1978] S.T.C. 296.
Emery v. *Inland Revenue Commissioners* [1981] S.T.C. 150.
Inland Revenue Commissioners v. *Cleary* [1968] A.C. 766; [1967] 2
W.L.R. 1271; [1967] 2 All E.R. 48; 44 T.C. 399, H.L.(E.).
Inland Revenue Commissioners v. *Parker* [1966] A.C. 141; [1966] 2
W.L.R. 486; [1966] 1 All E.R. 399; 43 T.C. 396, H.L.(E.).
B   *Inland Revenue Commissioners* v. *Wiggins* [1979] 1 W.L.R. 325; [1979]
2 All E.R. 245.
Ramsey (W. T.) Ltd. v. *Inland Revenue Commissioners* [1981] 2 W.L.R.
449; [1981] 1 All E.R. 865, H.L.(E.).
Williams v. *Inland Revenue Commissioners* [1980] 3 All E.R. 321,
H.L.(E.).

C   APPEAL from the Court of Appeal.
This was an appeal by the appellants, the Inland Revenue Commissioners, from an order dated February 27, 1980, of the Court of Appeal (Buckley and Donaldson L.JJ.; Templeman L.J. dissenting) affirming the order dated July 28, 1978 of Slade J. who had dismissed an appeal by way of case stated from a decision of the Commissioners for the Special Purposes of the Income Tax Acts who had found in favour of the
D   respondent, Louis Garvin.
The appellants had served on the respondent a notice under section 460 (3) of the Income and Corporation Taxes Act 1970, seeking to counteract a tax advantage alleged to have been obtained by him in circumstances mentioned in section 461 of the Act and in consequence of the combined effect of transactions in securities. The respondent appealed
E   to the special commissioners against that notice and against the consequential income tax and surtax assessments made for the year 1968–69 each in the sum of £235,941. The special commissioners had allowed the appeal.
The facts are set out in the opinion of Lord Wilberforce.

F   *Donald Rattee Q.C.* and *Christopher McCall* for the appellants.
C. N. Beattie Q.C. for the respondent.

Their Lordships took time for consideration.

May 14. LORD WILBERFORCE. My Lords, this case arises under sections 460 to 468 of the Income and Corporation Taxes Act 1970, a
G   group of sections passed in order to deal with certain types of tax avoidance. These include, broadly, transactions by which individuals holding shares in companies having accumulated profits obtain the equivalent of such profits in a form which does not expose them to income tax. The revenue is empowered in such cases to counteract this "tax advantage" by assessing the individual to income tax. This they have done as
H   regards the respondent, Mr. Garvin, for a sum of £235,949 in respect of the year of assessment 1968–69. Mr. Garvin has appealed against this assessment and he has been successful in all instances up to this House.
The revenue's claim is directed to sums arising under a tax-avoidance scheme devised and provided for the respondent by Mr. Bradman, a well-known practitioner in this business. Mr. Garvin, together with two other gentlemen, owned all the share capital in five companies, referred to in the proceedings as ABCFS, which companies owned valuable freehold and

leasehold properties capable, if sold, of producing substantial distributable A
profits. The object of the scheme was to make these profits or part of them
available to the shareholders in a tax-free form.

The scheme was complicated and involved 25 transactions. Many of
these, consisting of circulating money round a number of companies in
which the taxpayers had no interest, were of concern only to Mr. Bradman
and his associates. Those which concerned the taxpayers were summarised B
by Buckley L.J. in his judgment in the Court of Appeal. As I cannot
improve upon it, I reproduce this summary verbatim:

"The salient features are that immediately before April 3, 1969,
Mr. Garvin, Mr. Rose ('the taxpayers') and Mr. Philip Rose between
them owned all the shares in five companies referred to in the case
as ABCFS. On April 3, 1969, they sold all the shares in those five
companies to a company called Excalibur, in which they had no C
interest, for £471,998 payable by 200 yearly instalments of £150 and
a final instalment of £441,898 payable on April 3, 2169, with interest
at 10¼ per cent. per annum on the amount from time to time outstanding in the meantime. ABCFS owned freehold and leasehold
properties of substantial value, on the realisation of which substantial
profits could have been obtained which would have been available D
for distribution by way of dividends. These sales were the first step
in an admitted scheme comprising the transactions numbered 1 to 8
in annexure 2 to the case stated and a loan of £472,000 by the three
vendors to a company called Central, of which they were the only
shareholders.

"Paragraph 5 (3) of the case contains the following important findings by the special commissioners: E

"'At the time of the sale the directors of Excalibur intended that
the properties owned by ABCFS should be sold. Pursuant to the
admitted scheme both they and [the taxpayers and Mr. Philip Rose]
hoped and expected that the latter would reacquire the properties
but there was no agreement to that effect. At the time of the sale
of the shares the directors of Excalibur had not decided whether to F
procure the payment of a dividend by those companies: it remained
an open question for about a year, a decision being reached only in
the spring of 1970 when a dividend was paid. . . . None of [the
taxpayers and Mr. Philip Rose] was aware at the time of the sale of
his shares of any tax avoidance scheme intended to be carried out
by the purchaser and no such scheme was discussed between the
purchaser and the professional advisers of [the taxpayers and Mr. G
Philip Rose]. But the commissioners inferred from the amount of the
sale price that the professional advisers knew that Excalibur intended
in some way to avoid corporation tax.'

"On April 8, 1969, ABCFS leased all their properties to a company called Geltan for the term of 999 years for premiums amounting
to £982,862 payable by small instalments over 997 years and a very H
substantial final instalment payable in April 2968 with interest in the
meantime at 10¼ per cent. per annum on the balance from time to
time outstanding. Each lease, however, contained a break clause
under which the lessee could determine the lease at the end of 49
years of the term. This was intended to avoid a liability to corporation
tax.

"On April 14, 1969, ABCFS sold the reversions on the leases to

A   a company called County in consideration of £100 payable to each of the five companies. On the same day Geltan sold and assigned the leases to County for valuable considerations, thus effecting a merger of the long leasehold terms. County on the same day sold the properties, free from the leases, to Central for £989,095.

B   "Also on April 14, 1969, Excalibur for consideration assumed the obligation to pay the instalments of the premiums due to ABCFS and a company called Greave, out of moneys lent by Excalibur, bought from the taxpayers and Mr. Philip Rose the right to receive the instalments of the purchase price of the shares at the price of £471,848. Central borrowed the £989,095 as to £472,000 from the taxpayers and Mr. Philip Rose and as to £517,095 from other sources.

C   "In the outcome (a) the taxpayers and Mr. Philip Rose sold their shares in ABCFS to Excalibur for £471,998 payable by instalments, which were converted into £471,848 received from Greave; (b) ABCFS sold their properties for £928,862, payable by instalments, and £500 paid for the reversions; (c) Central bought all the properties for £989,095, part of which was provided by the taxpayers and Mr. Philip Rose lending £472,000 to Central. Before the inception of the scheme the taxpayers and Mr. Philip Rose owned ABCFS, who owned D   all the properties, but the taxpayers and Mr. Philip Rose could not get any money out of ABCFS except by way of dividends which would attract tax. At the close the taxpayers and Mr. Philip Rose owned Central who owned all the properties; ABCFS no longer owned any of the properties, but had received £983,362 for them, payable mainly by very small instalments and a long delayed final payment; the tax-E   payers and Mr. Philip Rose were creditors of Central in a sum of £472,000 which they could recover from Central on demand and which Central would or could raise out of the properties.

F   "The only transaction comprised in the scheme to which the tax-payers and Mr. Philip Rose were parties, either directly or through Central, were (1) the sale of the shares, (2) the sale to Greave of the right to the instalments of the purchase price, (3) the purchase by Central of the properties, and (4) the loan to Central, but they were participants in the scheme as a whole."

    The companies called "Excalibur," "Geltan," "County" and "Greave" were owned or controlled by Mr. Bradman. On April 13, 1970 (viz. about a year later) Excalibur caused ABCFS, which were then G   wholly owned by Excalibur, to pay dividends amounting to £555,000 to Excalibur. These dividends were made exempt from income tax by section 256 of the Act, and were admittedly abnormal dividends.

    The revenue's assessment relates to the above-mentioned sum of £471,848, i.e. the sum paid by "Greave" to the taxpayers for the instalments of the purchase price of the shares in ABCFS: the respondent's share of this was £235,949. It is based, in the alternative on two of the H   "circumstances" stated in section 461 of the Act, namely, C or D.

    I will deal first with D, since this can be shortly disposed of. The condition for the application of D is that the taxpayer shall have received consideration of a specified kind (and it is not disputable that he did) "in connection with the distribution of profits" of (relevantly) a company under the control of not more than five persons. Distribution of profits is elsewhere (section 467 (2)) defined so as to include realisation of assets. The question is as to the date at which the company must be under the

control of not more than five persons. The revenue contends that it is A
sufficient if this control exists at any time in the period covered by the
relevant transactions. If this is right, the condition would be satisfied,
since it could be applied to ABCFS, all of which were initially controlled
by the three taxpayers.

The respondent on the other hand says that the control must be shown
to exist at the date when either there is a distribution of profits or a
realisation of assets. If this is so, then the relevant company would be B
Excalibur. There is, however, no evidence that Excalibur was controlled
by not more than five persons, and in the absence of such evidence the
revenue must fail.

In my opinion, the taxpayer is right on this point. The language is
plain. The words " in connection with the distribution of profits of a
company . . ." must contemplate distribution by that company (and C
similarly as to realisation of assets), and so inevitably a state of control
at that date. It is impossible to relate them to the receipt of the consideration or to any other transaction. I think, therefore, that the claim
under paragraph D must fail.

I deal next with paragraph C. In order for the revenue to succeed,
it is necessary to show that the taxpayer received, in consequence of a
transaction whereby Excalibur subsequently received an abnormal amount D
by way of dividend, a consideration of a specified type, and so received
it that he did not pay tax on it as income. It is clear that the taxpayer
did receive a consideration of the type specified (sc. in the purchase price
for the shares in ABCFS), that he so received it as not to pay tax on it as
income, and that Excalibur did, on April 13, 1970, receive an abnormal
amount by way of dividend from ABCFS. E

The first question to ask, then, is what, if any, was a transaction
whereby Excalibur received the dividend. Then the second question is
whether the taxpayer received the consideration in consequence of that
transaction.

I do not think that the word transaction can be limited to the immediate cause of the dividend being received, *viz.* the declaration of the
dividend by ABCFS, even if it is gramatically capable of bearing such a F
meaning: see *Greenberg* v. *Inland Revenue Commissioners* [1972] A.C.
109. The word must be capable of including some anterior step in the
scheme which led to the declaration being made. The connection between
that step and the declaration of the dividend is denoted by " whereby."
This must be the equivalent of " by which " and must connote some
causal connection, though—and here I agree with Buckley L.J.—this may G
be of a fairly loose character.

There are only two possible transactions which can be considered as
qualifying, namely, (i) the sale by the taxpayer of his shares to Excalibur,
or (ii) the realisation by ABCFS of their properties. The first put
Excalibur in a position, if and when it so decided, to cause dividends to
be declared: the second provided ABCFS with the resources with which to
declare and pay them. Each of these transactions took place in April H
1969, a year before the dividends were declared. Obviously each was
something sine qua non the declarations would have been made: but is
the connection closer than that? I find this a difficult question, but on the
whole I come to the conclusion that the majority of the Court of Appeal
were right in holding that it is not. I accept, as one must, the finding of
the special commissioners, that in April 1969 the directors of Excalibur
had not decided whether to produce the payment of a dividend by

A ABCFS: "it remained an open question for about a year." Mr. Bradman and his associates had, no doubt, their own preoccupations as regards tax, and it is clear from an examination of the intervening transactions from April 1969 to April 13, 1970, which were numerous, that a number of decisions had to be made and inter-company adjustments effected before the distribution was ultimately made. I cannot detail them, but they are set out in tabular form in exhibit 2 to the case stated. From these I feel
B forced to the conclusion that there is not sufficient connection between either of the events of April 1969 and the declaration of the dividends to satisfy the words "a transaction whereby" even giving a wide meaning to "whereby." I would add that if I had found it possible to decide that the sale of the shares in ABCFS or the realisation of their proprieties was such a transaction, I should not find much difficulty in reaching the conclusion
C that the taxpayer received his consideration (substantially on April 14, 1969) in consequence of that transaction, but, on the view which I take, this becomes immaterial.

In my view, therefore, the revenue fails on paragraph C as well as on paragraph D, and this entails failure of the appeal.

This makes it unnecessary to decide whether, if either paragraph applied, the taxpayer obtained any tax advantage in the year of assessment
D 1968–69 (as claimed) other than £150, or any tax advantage at all. However, on the latter point I think it right to express agreement with the conclusion of the Court of Appeal that the taxpayer did, in whichever year, obtain a tax advantage, and disagreement with the argument for the taxpayer that he did not obtain a tax advantage because he never contemplated taking a (taxable) dividend. To limit section 460 in this way would
E be to emasculate it.

Finally, I must comment on one other matter. The relevant sections were first enacted by the Finance Act 1960, i.e. before the creation of the capital gains tax in 1965, and were therefore drafted without regard to possible cumulation of these two taxes. In the present case, it is clear that a charge to capital gains tax might arise. In fact, the taxpayer has been assessed for capital gains tax as regards the sale of his shares. To
F charge the proceeds of these shares with capital gains tax as disposals of capital assets and also with income tax under section 460, amounts to manifest double taxation—indeed, the total amount chargable would exceed the amount which the taxpayer received. We were told that, by way of concession, if the revenue succeeded in the present appeal, it would give credit for the capital gains tax paid. This would certainly be fair, but it
G is not satisfactory that the matter should rest on concession. The interaction of these two taxes seems to require consideration with a view to avoiding double taxation, which should be a right and not merely a privilege.

I would dismiss the appeal.

LORD RUSSELL OF KILLOWEN. My Lords, others of your Lordships,
H in agreeing upon dismissal of this appeal by the Crown, have set out the facts of this case in a manner which enables me to be brief.

At the outset I would remark that the very multiplicity of transactions, in most of which the taxpayers were not participants, and the apparently nonsensical introduction of moneys payable by relatively small instalments with a final large instalment payable well into the next century, tend to raise suspicions in the mind: but their transactions had as their aim the minimising of corporation (capital gains) tax by a method then successful

The Weekly Law Reports, June 5, 1981

800

Lord Russell
of Killowen

I.R.C. v. Garvin (H.L.(E.))

[1981]

but subsequently made unsuccessful by later legislation. They do not assist   A
in the solution of this appeal.

What is required to enable the Crown to take the counteraction which
it sought to do in this case?

(1) There must be a transaction in securities: this requirement is
satisfied by the sale to Excalibur by the taxpayers of the shares in ABCFS
companies: and—
                                                                              B
(2) as a consequence of that transaction the taxpayer is in a position
to obtain or has obtained a tax advantage: and—

(3) that the circumstances set out in either paragraph C or paragraph D
of section 461 exist: and—

(4) the tax advantage is such as is defined in section 466:

  " a relief or increased relief from . . . or the avoidance of a possible
  assessment [to tax], whether the avoidance . . . is effected by receipts   C
  accruing in such a way that the recipient does not pay or bear tax on
  them . . ."

These references to tax are to tax on income—i.e. to income tax. Such
profit as the taxpayers made on the sale to Excalibur of the ABCFS would
(apart from successful counteraction) be liable only to capital gains tax:
and indeed they were assessed on that basis and paid accordingly. To that   D
I will recur.

I turn at once to consideration of circumstances C and D. If neither
embraces the facts in this case that is the end of the Crown's case for
counteraction.

Under paragraph D the following are the requirements:

(i) The taxpayer receives a consideration which either is or represents   E
the value of assets of a company which are available for distribution by
way of dividend or is or represents the value of trading stock of the
company: the consideration for the sale of the ABCFS shares to Excalibur
would fall under one or other of those heads.

(ii) The receipt of the consideration must be " in connection with the
distribution of profits of a company " to which paragraph D applies—i.e.   F
as a convenient label, a close company.

On the facts of this case there can be no doubt that each of them,
ABCFS, was a close company when their shares were held by the taxpayers: and I would be prepared to find that there was a " connection "
of some sort between the receipt of that consideration and the declaration
some time later of the abnormal dividends by those companies. But
there is no evidence to show that, at the time of the declarations of   G
dividends, ABCFS were close companies, that question depending on the
" make up " of Excalibur. The question must, in my opinion, clearly fall
to be resolved in the light of the situation at the time of the distribution
of profits, and the Crown adduced no evidence on the point, no doubt
because the Crown before the commissioners never thought of relying on
paragraph D. Thus the Crown fails on paragraph D.
                                                                              H
The other circumstance said by the Crown to exist is paragraph C.
The requirements of that paragraph are these:

(i) The taxpayer receives a consideration which I have summairsed
under my reference above to D (i).

(ii) The receipt of that consideration must be " in consequence of a
transaction."

(iii) The transaction in question must be " a transaction whereby any

A other person—(a) subsequently receives . . . an abnormal amount by way of dividend."

The transaction here in consequence of which the taxpayer received the relevant consideration was the sale of the ABCFS shares to Excalibur. The sole question is whether that transaction was a transaction " whereby " Excalibur subsequently received the abnormal amounts by way of dividend from ABCFS. What is intended by " whereby? " I believe the word to

B be primarily a version of " by which ": it can also be used in the sense of " by means of which." But to treat the word as introducing the concept that all that is required is that the transaction should be a causa sine qua non of the subsequent abnormal dividend goes in my opinion too far. Counsel for the Crown was unwilling to say that it could be followed through a succession of sales by Excalibur of the shares and by subsequent

C purchasers of the shares to a final abnormal dividend reaped by some final purchaser. In the instant case it was no part of the transaction, so far as the taxpayers were concerned, that these abnormal dividends should be distributed: and indeed the evidence was accepted that Excalibur itself at the time of the transaction had not decided at all on such a dividend. The fact that the taxpayers' advisers may well have thought that some saving of corporation tax was a possibility can be referred to the attempt (which

D largely failed to spread out consideration for corporation (capital gains) tax purposes.

All in all, my Lords, I am of opinion that " whereby " is not satisfied in the present case, and would reject the Crown's case under paragraph C.

The result is that the appeal must fail.

I do not propose to enter upon the " tax advantage " point, on which I

E incline to agree with what has fallen from your Lordships.

I have previously referred to the fact that the taxpayers have been assessed to capital gains tax—and have paid it—on the consideration received on the sale to Excalibur of the share in ABCFS. The Crown say that if they were successful in this appeal they would as a concession bring the amount so paid into credit against the attempted counteraction.

F However " fair " that would have been I doubt whether such a concession could have been made. After all, the capital gains tax has been levied and paid, and remains perfectly valid. Rather do I venture to doubt the ability of the Crown (according to the taxpayer's case to this House), having levied a tax on the basis that the transaction was a dealing in capital, then to assert that it can indirectly, by counteraction, be treated as giving rise to taxable income. But no argument was advanced for the taxpayers that

G the Crown was debarred from thus blowing hot and cold—or perhaps I should say warm and hot—and I say no more on this.

I have referred sometimes to " the taxpayers " and sometimes to " the taxpayer." The appeal concerns only one taxpayer, but the others are in like case.

Accordingly I would dismiss the appeal.

H

LORD KEITH OF KINKEL. My Lords, I have had the advantage of reading in draft the speech prepared by my noble and learned friend, Lord Wilberforce. I agree with it, and would accordingly concur in the dismissal of the appeal.

LORD SCARMAN. My Lords, I agree with the speech delivered by my noble and learned friend, Lord Wilberforce. I am troubled by the

Lord Scarman   I.R.C. v. Garvin (H.L.(E.))   [1981]

"double taxation" aspects of the case, to which my Lord refers at the   A
very end of his speech.

It is unclear whether the law as it now stands authorises the cumulation
of capital gains tax and income tax on the one receipt: and the House
heard no argument on the point. The Revenue, it seems, take the view
that it does not: the taxpayer alleges that it does. I express no opinion.
But, if the taxpayer be right, the law is anomalous.

The figures are disturbing. The assessed income tax and surtax total   B
£214,681·51. If the capital gains tax already paid is added, the total tax
exigible would exceed the receipt (£235,941) upon which it is charged. The
Revenue, very properly, have disclaimed an intention to insist on the payment of the full amount of the income tax in addition to the capital gains
tax already paid. But this is a precarious, and therefore unacceptable
basis, for the voidance of double taxation. Those who use the services of   C
an inventor and purveyor of tax avoidance schemes" (Templeman L.J.'s
phrase) can expect no mercy: but they are entitled, like the rest of us, to
justice. If the law is such that they are put at the mercy of the Crown
(who, through its agent, the Board of Inland Revenue, may, or may not,
feel disposed to make a concession), they are denied justice at the hands
of the court.

I would surmise that, when the capital gains tax was introduced in   D
1965, its relationship with the income tax avoidance provisions, which
section 28, Finance Act 1960, had introduced into the law, was not fully
appreciated. Prior to 1965 a capital gain was not taxable. If, therefore,
income could be transmuted into a capital gain, no tax was then payable.
Since 1965 both types of receipt are taxable: hence the risk, which this
case shows is a real one, of double taxation. The law requires review   E
so that the possibility of double taxation is unambiguously excluded.

I would dismiss the appeal.

LORD BRIDGE OF HARWICH. My Lords, the facts arising for consideration in this appeal are set out in the speech of my noble and learned
friend, Lord Wilberforce. I respectfully agree with him that, for the
reasons he gives, the Crown cannot successfully invoke the provisions of   F
paragraph D of section 461 of the Income and Corporation Taxes Act
1970, as applicable to the circumstances of this case.

I have been much troubled by the problem that arises on the construction of paragraph C of section 461. Sub-paragraph (1) of that
paragraph provides, so far as material:

"That the person in question receives, in consequence of a transaction   G
whereby any other person—(a) subsequently receives, or has received,
an abnormal amount by way of dividend; or (b) . . . a consideration
which either—(i) is, or represents the value of, assets which are (or
apart from anything done by the company in question would have
been) available for distribution by way of dividend, or . . . (iii) is, or
represents the value of, trading stock of the company, and the said
person so receives the consideration that he does not pay or bear   H
tax on it as income."

It is now well established that the provisions of sections 460 to 468,
being aimed at "the multiplicity of ingenious schemes which are constantly
being devised to evade taxation," should not be construed on the principle
that the subject is not to be taxed except by plain words but by giving such
a wide interpretation to the language used as may be necessary to give

A   effect to the evident intention of Parliament: see *Greenberg* v. *Inland Revenue Commissioners* [1972] A.C. 109, *per* Lord Reid at p. 137; *Inland Revenue Commissioners* v. *Joiner* [1975] 1 W.L.R. 1701, *per* Lord Wilberforce at pp. 1705, 1706.

I do not think it is very difficult to visualise the kind of tax avoidance scheme at which the language of paragraph C which I have quoted above is directed. A and B ("the persons in question"), individual income tax

B   and surtax payers, between them hold all the shares in a company X, which has large undistributed profits available for distribution by way of dividend. If X pays a large dividend to A and B, they will incur heavy liabilities to income tax and surtax. If they can find a buyer, company Y ("any other person"), which will be in a position, for one reason or another, having acquired company X, to extract the profits in the form of an abnormal

C   dividend without incurring any tax liability, they may be able to sell their shares for a price which substantially represents the value of the undistributed profits. This will be a capital receipt which, apart from paragraph C of section 461 and assuming that no other paragraph of the section applies, will attract no liability to income tax or surtax in the hands of A and B. If the quoted provisions of paragraph C can never apply to counteract the tax advantage which A and B obtain in such circumstances

D   as I have indicated, I find it difficult to see how they serve any useful purpose at all in the scheme of the Act.

If I have correctly identified the statutory target, how can the statutory language be construed to give it the intended effect? The difficulty arises from the use of the words "transaction" and "whereby." In my example, if "transaction" is given its ordinary meaning, the sale by A

E   and B of their shares in company X to company Y is one transaction, the declaration and payment of an abnormal dividend by company X to company Y is quite another. In the context in which it is used in paragraph C, I do not think it is possible to construe the word "transaction" as equivalent to "series of transactions," or to stretch its meaning to embrace both the sale of shares and the subsequent payment of a dividend in a single transaction. This would introduce more problems than it would

F   solve. If the reasoning is sound so far, it must follow that "whereby" cannot be used in its narrowest sense, since, on that reading, the only transaction whereby Y receives the abnormal dividend, would be the declaration and payment of the dividend itself. Accordingly, "whereby" must at least be wide enough to denote some kind of causal connection between the transaction of sale and purchase of shares in X, in consequence

G   of which A and B receive a tax-free consideration of the kind to which paragraph C applies, and the subsequent receipt of an abnormal dividend by Y. The kernel of the problem is to determine what kind of causal connection is contemplated. It cannot, in my opinion, be required that one should find that the receipt of the abnormal dividend is a necessary consequence of the share transaction, for this requirement could seldom,

H   if ever, be satisfied. I was at one time much attracted to the view that there was a sufficient causal connection if the purchase of the shares by Y enabled Y to procure the subsequent payment of an abnormal dividend by X. But on further reflection I appreciate that this would make the liability of A and B potentially dependent on an event which was outside their knowledge or control. This can hardly have been intended. Counsel for the respondent submitted that the taxpayer could not be liable under paragraph C unless he was a "party" to payment of the abnormal divi-

dend. I do not accept this formula, but I accept, at least in part, what I   A
take to be the idea underlying the submission. To revert to the charac-
terisation used in my example, to establish that the sale of shares by A
and B to Y was a transaction " whereby " Y subsequently received an
abnormal dividend, it would be necessary, in my opinion, to show that
Y's purpose or one of Y's purposes, in purchasing the shares was to
procure in due course the payment of an abnormal dividend by X to Y,
and that A and B were, at the time of the sale, aware of this purpose.   B
These are, of course, matters which will seldom be susceptible of direct
proof but will often be plain by inference from circumstances.

In the instant case the special commissioners were specifically invited
to draw just such inferences as would have satisfied the criteria of causation which I have suggested above, and, perhaps surprisingly, but equally
specifically and emphatically, declined to do so. It has never been suggested   C
that the commissioners' findings in this regard were open to challenge on
appeal. It follows, in my view, that the Crown's case under paragraph C
of section 461 fails.

Had the Crown been able to show that paragraph C of section 461
applied, I should have had no doubt that a " tax advantage," as defined
in section 466, was obtained. It is unnecessary to express any opinion on
the difficult question as to whether that advantage (leaving aside the   D
instalment of £150 paid on April 3, 1969) was obtained in the fiscal year
1968–69 or 1969–70.

As my noble and learned friend, Lord Wilberforce, has pointed out, the
respondent has paid capital gains tax on the gain accruing upon the sale
of his shares in ABCFS to Excalibur. The Crown accepted that if they
succeeded in this appeal they should give credit against the liability to   E
income tax and surtax for the capital gains tax paid. No issue of estoppel
was raised, but it is not clear whether the Board of Inland Revenue's
willingness to treat the taxpayer's liability in respect of the same receipt
to capital gains tax on the one hand and to income tax and surtax on the
other hand as alternative rather than cumulative is regarded by them as a
matter of concession or a matter of right. I agree with others of your
Lordships who have expressed the view that it would be most unsatisfactory   F
that the avoidance of such double taxation should be dependent on a
concession. If any doubt on the point is removed by statute, so much the
better. But, if an attempt were to be made to levy both taxes in respect of
a single receipt—a contingency which can, I hope, be regarded as remote
—I can see a powerful argument being mounted to the effect that, if a
receipt falls to be treated as income and taxed as such under one code,   G
it must, by necessary implication, be exempt from liability to taxation as
a capital receipt under another code.

I would dismiss the appeal.

Appeal dismissed.

Solicitors: *Solicitor of Inland Revenue; Berwin Leighton.*   H

J. A. G.

A

* PAULINE BURNES . . . . APPELLANT

AND

TRADE CREDITS LTD. . . . . . . RESPONDENT

B

[APPEAL FROM THE SUPREME COURT OF NEW SOUTH WALES
COURT OF APPEAL]

1981 Jan. 28;   Lord Diplock, Lord Simon of Glaisdale,
      March 4   Lord Edmund-Davies, Lord Keith of Kinkel
                                     and Lord Scarman

C

*Guarantee—Debt—Mortgage securing loan—Variation of mortgage
without guarantor's consent — Mortgagee and mortgagor's
agreement increasing mortgage interest rate and extending
time for repayment of principal sum — Guarantee covering
further advances—Whether variation "further advance"—
Whether guarantor discharged from liability*

D
    In 1972 land was sold to a hotel company. It was agreed
between the vendor and the company that a part of the
purchase price should remain unpaid and should be secured
as a loan from the vendor to the company by a mortgage on
the land at an interest rate of 9 per cent. The due date for
payment of the principal was October 12, 1975. By a deed
of guarantee executed at the same time as the mortgage the
defendant (" the guarantor ") and her husband guaranteed the
E
company's debt. Clause 14 of the guarantee provided that
"any further advance or advances" by the vendor to the
company were to be covered by the guarantee unless the
guarantor gave notice that they were not to be so covered.
Clause 18 of the guarantee provided that the guarantor's
consent was not necessary for any grant by the vendor to
the hotel company of time or "any other indulgence or
consideration." The vendor assigned the mortgage to the
F
plaintiff. On November 25, 1975, the plaintiff and the company
varied the mortgage and without the guarantor's consent agreed
to an increase in the interest rate to 16 per cent. and an
extension of the time for payment of the principal sum to
October 12, 1976. The vendor thereafter assigned the benefit
of the guarantee to the plaintiff. The company defaulted on
the payments of interest on the loan and the plaintiff sued
on the guarantee claiming the amount of interest outstanding.
G
In the Sydney District Court the judge found that there had
been a material variation of the mortgage to which the
guarantor had not consented and that the variation had discharged her liability. He dismissed the claim. The Court of
Appeal allowed the plaintiff's appeal on the ground that the
variation of the mortgage was covered by the words "further
advance" used in clause 14 of the guarantee.
    On the guarantor's appeal to the Judicial Committee: —
H
    Held, allowing the appeal, that the word "advance"
normally meant the furnishing of money for a specific purpose
and that the phrase "further advance" as used in clause 14
of the guarantee referred to the furnishing of an additional
principal sum by way of loan and did not cover an extension
of time for the repayment of the original principal sum;
that the agreement for an extension of time coupled as it
had been with the increased rate of interest could not be
considered an "indulgence or consideration" so as to bring
it within the terms of clause 18; and that, accordingly, since

Burnes v. Trade Credits Ltd. (P.C.)   **[1981]**

the mortgage had expressly provided that the interest rate was   A
to be 9 per cent. for however long the principal sum remained
outstanding, the agreement for an increase in the rate to
16 per cent. was a substantial alteration of the mortgage
and, therefore, the guarantor's liability under the guarantee
had been discharged (post, pp. 808c–E, H—809c).

    Payton v. *S. G. Brookes & Sons Pty. Ltd.* [1977] Cr.A.R. 91
distinguished

    Decision of the Supreme Court of New South Wales Court   B
of Appeal reversed.

The following case is referred to in the judgment of their Lordships:

Payton v. *S.G. Brookes & Sons Pty. Ltd.* [1977] W.A.R. 91.

The following additional cases were cited in argument:

A.J.S. Bank v. *Costello* (1890) 6 W.N.(N.S.W.) 94.   C
Armco (Australia) Pty. Ltd. v. *Federal Commissioner of Taxation* (1948)
    76 C.L.R. 584.
Hancock v. *Williams* (1942) 42 S.R.(N.S.W.) 252.
London Financial Association v. *Kelk* (1884) 26 Ch.D. 107.
M'Kune v. *Joynson* (1858) 5 C.B.N.S. 218.
Parr's Banking Co. Ltd. v. *Yates* [1898] 2 Q.B. 460, C.A.
Queensland Investment and Land Mortgage Co. Ltd. v. *Hart* (1894) 5   D
    Q.L.J. 186.
Smith, In re [1918] 2 Ch. 405.
Trade Indemnity Co. Ltd. v. *Workington Harbour and Dock Board* [1937]
    A.C. 1; [1936] 1 All E.R. 454, H.L.(E.).
Treadwell v. *Hitchings* [1925] N.Z.L.R. 519.

APPEAL (No. 29 of 1980) with leave of the Supreme Court of New   E
South Wales by the defendant, Pauline Burnes (the guarantor), against a
judgment (August 7, 1979) given by the Supreme Court of New South
Wales Court of Appeal (Street C.J., Samuels and Mahoney JJ.A.) by
which it allowed an appeal by Trade Credits Ltd. (the plaintiff) from a
judgment (February 3, 1978) of Judge Geoffrey-Smith in the Sydney District Court dismissing the plaintiff's action against the guarantor on her
guarantee given on October 12, 1972, in respect of a debt incurred by   F
Civic Hotel Pty. Ltd.

The facts are stated in the judgment.

Paul Flannery Q.C. and *Colin O'Connor* (both of the New South
Wales Bar) for the guarantor.

Richard Southwell Q.C. and *Peter Moss* (of the New South Wales Bar)   G
for the plaintiff.

                                      Cur. adv. vult.

March 4. The judgment of their Lordships, was delivered by LORD
KEITH OF KINKEL.

This appeal is concerned with the proper construction of certain   H
provisions in a deed of guarantee. On July 12, 1972, a company called
D. G. Hogan Pty. Ltd. (" the vendor ") contracted to sell certain land
to Civic Private Hotel Pty. Ltd. (" the hotel company "). It was agreed
that the sum of $100,000, part of the purchase price, should remain
outstanding, being secured by a mortgage on the subjects of sale. So
the hotel company on October 12, 1972, executed in favour of the vendor
a memorandum of mortgage securing payment of $100,000, with interest

A at the rate of 9 per cent. per annum until payment, payable monthly, the principal sum being repayable on October 12, 1975. On the same date the appellant ("the guarantor") and her then husband, who were associated with the hotel company, executed in favour of the vendor a deed of guarantee of the debt. On October 18, 1973, the vendor assigned the mortgage to the plaintiff, the respondent in this appeal. The due date for payment of the mortgage debt passed without such payment

B being made by the hotel company, and on November 25, 1975, it and the plaintiff entered into a memorandum of variation of the mortgage. This provided that the rate of interest payable under the mortgage should be increased from 9 per cent. to 16 per cent. per annum as from October 12, 1975, and that the term of the mortgage should be extended to October 12, 1976. The guarantor was not asked to and did not consent

C to this variation. Finally, on March 25, 1976, the vendor assigned to the plaintiff the benefit of the guarantee by the guarantor and her husband.

It appears that the hotel company defaulted in the payment of interest under the mortgage as varied, and on June 16, 1976, the plaintiff commenced proceedings against the guarantor and her husband in the District Court at Sydney, claiming payment by them as guarantors of the sum

D of $8,583.31 by way of interest then due and unpaid by the hotel company. Default judgment was entered against the guarantor's husband, but on February 3, 1978, Judge Godfrey-Smith entered judgment for the guarantor. He held that the variation of the terms of the mortgage, which was agreed to be a material one, had been entered into without the consent of the guarantor, that on a proper construction of the

E relevant conditions of the guarantee the variation was not such as might consistently therewith be entered into without her consent, and that accordingly its effect was to discharge the guarantor's liability under the guarantee. The plaintiff appealed to the Supreme Court of New South Wales, and by order dated August 7, 1979, the Court of Appeal (Street C.J., Samuels and Mahoney JJ.A.) set aside the order of Judge Godfrey-Smith and entered judgment against the guarantor for the sum of

F $8,583.31. Against that judgment the guarantor now appeals to Her Majesty in Council.

It is common ground between the parties that the variation of the term of the mortgage effected by the memorandum dated November 25, 1975, was a material one, and, if not authorised by some provision of the guarantee, of such a nature as to bring about the legal result of

G discharging the whole of the obligations thereunder. The provision of the guarantee upon which the plaintiff principally relies as having authorised the variation is clause 14. This provides, so far as material:

"It is hereby expressly provided that any further advance or advances which may be made by the lender to the borrower shall be included in this guarantee unless the guarantor shall have given to the lender

H notice in writing . . . clearly stating that no further advances shall be covered under the terms of this guarantee . . ."

The main argument for the plaintiff which was accepted by the Court of Appeal, was that the transaction embodied in the memorandum dated November 25, 1975, amounted in substance to a "further advance" within the meaning of this provision. It was pointed out that clause 1 of the guarantee provided that it was to be a continuing one, while clause 5 contained reference to the guarantor's obligation to pay interest,

in the event of failure by the borrower, not only on the principal sum A
but also on " any other moneys which may bear interest under the terms
of the loan," and clause 11 mentioned " any security or other document
taken by the lender." The position was the same, so it was maintained,
as if the original principal sum had been repaid and re-advanced to the
borrower.

In accepting this argument Mahoney J.A., whose opinion was concurred in by the other members of the Court of Appeal, said: B

> " In my opinion ' further advance ' as used in clause 14 should be
> held to include the subsequent transaction. I do not think that
> ' advance ' according to its ordinary meaning is limited to transactions
> under which money or goods are, as part of the particular transaction,
> handed over or delivered to the debtor. The term is, in my opinion,
> wide enough to include a transaction under which, money being C
> already available to a debtor, he becomes entitled to retain it for a
> period beyond that for which otherwise it would have been available
> to him. According to ordinary parlance, it would be proper to
> describe that money as having been ' advanced ' for a further term."

In their Lordships' opinion that view is erroneous and the argument
for the plaintiff is unsound. While the meaning of the word " advance " D
may be shaded somewhat by the context, it normally means the furnishing
of money for some specified purpose. The furnishing need not necessarily
be by way of loan, but clearly that is what was in contemplation here.
When clause 14 refers to " a further advance " it appears to their
Lordships to be referring to the furnishing of an additional principal
sum. Where the term for repayment of the original principal sum is E
extended, it is true to say that that sum remains advanced for a further
term, but it is a distortion of language to say that a further advance
has been made. In reaching the conclusion which their Lordships have
quoted Mahoney J.A. referred to a considerable number of decided
cases. Their Lordships have examined these, but have not found any
of them to support his conclusion, or indeed to be of any assistance at
all for present purposes. F

In considering the true substance and effect of the memorandum
dated November 25, 1975, it is important to keep in view the provisions
of the first and second clauses of the mortgage. These are:

> " Firstly—That the mortgagor will pay to the mortgagee the principal
> sum, or so much thereof as shall remain unpaid on October 12, 1975.
> " Secondly—That the mortgagor will pay interest on the principal G
> sum or on so much thereof as for the time being shall remain unpaid
> and upon any judgment or order in which this or the preceding
> covenant may become merged, at the rate of nine per cent. per
> annum as follows, namely—By equal monthly payments . . . until
> the principal sum shall be fully paid and satisfied . . ."

It is thus clearly agreed that the interest payable is to be at the rate of H
9 per cent. per annum, however long the principal sum may be outstanding.

Under the memorandum of November 25, 1975, it was agreed that
the rate of interest was to be increased to 16 per cent. from October 12,
1975. That cannot be regarded as anything but an alteration of what
was previously agreed, irrespective of the circumstance that at the same
time the term of the mortgage was extended for one year. Their

A Lordships are unable to find anywhere in the provisions of the guarantee any indication of an intention that the guarantors should be required to undertake, without their specific consent, liability for such increased interest as mortgagor and mortgagee might subsequently agree upon.

The plaintiff relied upon the subsidiary argument that what was agreed by the memorandum of November 25, 1975, was authorised by clause 18 of the guarantee. This provide for the lender, without the
B consent of the guarantor, granting to the borrower time or " any other indulgence or consideration," without thereby affecting the liability of the guarantors. Their Lordships are of opinion that, while the agreement for the extension of the term of the mortgage might, if it stood alone, be authorised by this provision, the superadded agreement for an increased rate of interest goes beyond anything which was thereby contemplated.
C The granting of an indulgence to a debtor may have the effect of pre-judicing the rights of the guarantor vis-à-vis the debtor, and accordingly, in the absence of a provision such as this one, it has the effect of releasing the guarantor from liability. The purposes and effect of the provision in question is merely to safeguard the creditor against that eventuality. It does not enable the debtor and creditor, by agreement between themselves, to require the guarantor to shoulder an added liability.
D   Their Lordships were referred upon this branch of the appeal to the Western Australia case of *Payton* v. *S.G. Brookes & Sons Pty. Ltd.* [1977] W.A.R. 91. This decision, which might at first sight appear to be in point, turns out on closer examination not to be so. The granting of time to the debtor under a hire purchase agreement was there held to be covered by a provision similar to that presently under consideration,
E notwithstanding that the agreement entered into had the result of the debtor being required to pay additional sums by way of interest. That liability, however, arose from a provision of the hire purchase agreement itself, regarding the payment of interest on overdue instalments, and did not flow directly from the later agreement granting time. The case is therefore distinguishable.

For these reasons their Lordships will humbly advise Her Majesty
F that the appeal should be allowed and the order of Judge Godfrey-Smith restored. The plaintiff will be liable for costs before this Board and in the Court of Appeal.

Solicitors: *Ingledew, Brown, Bennison & Garrett; Clifford Turner.*

G
                                                                    T. J. M.

H

A

[FAMILY DIVISION]

* DENNIS v. McDONALD

1981 Jan. 16, 19;
      Feb. 19   Purchas J.

B

*Tenants in Common—Realty—Family home—House purchased as
family home by man and woman living together—Woman
leaving home with children because of man's violent behaviour
—Man continuing to occupy house with some of children—
Woman's application for order directing sale—Jurisdiction to
make orders other than order for sale—Whether woman excluded from premises—Whether entitled to occupation rent—*   C
Law of Property Act 1925 (15 & 16 Geo. 5, c. 20), s. 30
Tenants in Common—Ouster—Occupation rent—Assessment

In January 1970 the plaintiff and defendant, having lived
together as man and wife since 1962, bought a dwelling-house
with the intention that it would be the family home. Each
contributed in equal shares towards the purchase price of
£3,200. £2,000 was obtained on a mortgage. The property   D
was conveyed and regestered in both their names as tenants
in common in equal shares. During the twelve years of co-
habitation the relationship was stormy and the plaintiff left on
several occasions because of the defendant's violence towards
her. In 1974 she left permanently, taking with her the five
children of the family.

The defendant continued to occupy the property and later
that year the three older children returned to live with him.   E
The two younger children remained with the plaintiff in
rented property. The defendant continued to make the
mortgage repayments, and from March 1980 the property was
unencumbered.

On the plaintiff's application under section 30 of the Law
of Property Act 1925 for an order for the sale of the property
and further or other relief : —

Held, (1) that since the circumstances in which the trust   F
for sale originated had envisaged as one of the primary objects
the provision of a home for the family, it would not be right
in the exercise of the court's discretion under section 30 to
make an order for sale (post, p. 814D–E, F).

In re Evers' Trust [1980] 1 W.L.R. 1327, C.A. followed.

(2) That, although a tenant in common in sole occupation
of premises was not liable to pay an occupation rent where
the other tenant in common voluntarily chose not to exercise   G
a right of occupation, if the non-occupying tenant had been
excluded from the premises the court would order payment of
an occupation rent if it was necessary to do justice between
the parties; that it was unreasonable to expect the plaintiff
to exercise her right of occupation as she had done before the
breakdown of her relationship with the defendant and thus,
she was, for practical purposes, excluded from occupation and   H
prevented from enjoying her rights as a tenant in common
and accordingly she was entitled to an occupation rent from
1974 (post, pp. 816H—817C, 819F–G).

M'Mahon v. *Burchell* (1846) 2 Ph. 127 and dictum of
Stirling J. in *Hill* v. *Hickin* [1897] 2 Ch. 579 applied.

Jones (A. E.) v. *Jones (F. W.)* [1977] 1 W.L.R. 438, C.A.
considered.

(3) That although section 30 of the Law of Property Act
1925 had been passed for conveyancing purposes and did not

A   confer any power on the court to make orders where no order for sale was made, on general principles it was open to the court to make an order for payment of an occupation rent; that for the years 1974–1976, since the major element in the early years of mortgage repayments was interest, justice could be done by ordering that no credit should be given for the plaintiff's share of the mortgage repayments in fact paid by the defendant; that for the years 1977–1980, since the defen-

B   dant's right to occupy the property was similar to that granted to a statutorily protected tenant, the proper way to assess the occpation rent would be a " fair rent " as assessed by a rent officer for an unfurnished letting of the whole property to a protected tenant and that, after an inquiry to assess the sum, the plaintiff would be entitled to receive half of such sum (post, pp. 820A, F—821A).

    Leake (formerly Bruzzi) v. *Bruzzi* [1974] 1 W.L.R. 1528,
C   C.A. and *Suttill* v. *Graham* [1977] 1 W.L.R. 819, C.A. applied.

    Per curiam. Although section 30 does not grant a power to the court to order the payment of an occupation rent it certainly could be used to indicate that unless an undertaking to pay an occupation rent was forthcoming from the defendant then an order for sale would be made (post, pp. 819H—820A).

D
    The following cases are referred to in the judgment:

Evers' Trust, In re [1980] 1 W.L.R. 1327; [1980] 3 All E.R. 399, C.A.
Henderson v. *Eason* (1846) 10 Jur. 821; (1851) 17 Q.B. 701.
Hill v. *Hickin* [1897] 2 Ch. 579.
Jones (A. E.) v. *Jones (F. W.)* [1977] 1 W.L.R. 438; [1977] 2 All E.R. 231, C.A.
E   *Leake (formerly Bruzzi)* v. *Bruzzi* [1974] 1 W.L.R. 1528; [1974] 2 All E.R. 1196, C.A.
M'Mahon v. *Burchell* (1846) 2 Ph. 127; 1 Coop.t.Cott. 457.
Suttill v. *Graham* [1977] 1 W.L.R. 819; [1977] 3 All E.R. 1117, C.A.
Turner v. *Morgan* (1803) 8 Ves.Jun 143.
Williams (J. W.) v. *Williams (M. A.)* [1976] Ch. 278; [1976] 3 W.L.R.
F   494; [1977] 1 All E.R. 28, C.A.

    The following additional case, supplied by the courtesy of counsel, was cited in argument:

Kennedy v. *De Trafford* [1897] A.C. 180, H.L.(E.).

ACTION
G   By her summons dated November 14, 1978, issued in the Chancery Division under sections 30 and 203 (5) of the Law of Property Act 1925, the plaintiff sought (1) an order that the former family home be sold; (2) a declaration that she was entitled to receive one-half of the net proceeds of sale; (3) an order that the trusts affecting the property be carried out with all the necessary accounts and inquiries, including an account of
H   rents from part of the property received by the defendant; and (4) further or other relief.

    On March 6, 1980, the plaintiff issued a summons in the Family Division under the Guardianship of Minors Act 1971 seeking an order that the custody of the five children of the family be granted to her.

    On April 10, 1980, the action which had been commenced in the Chancery Division was transferred to the Family Division. Both proceedings were heard by Purchas J. sitting in chambers. Judgment on the

application under the provisions of section 30 of the Law of Property Act A
1925 was given in open court.

The facts are stated in the judgment.

Andrew Walker for the applicant.
T. A. C. Coningsby and *David Van Hee* for the respondent.

Cur. adv. vult.   B

Feb. 19. PURCHAS J. read the following judgment. This is an originating summons commenced in the Chancery Division which by order of
Master Cholmondeley Clarke of April 10, 1980, has been transferred to
this division to be dealt with as if it were originally assigned to the
Family Division. The purpose of the transfer was to enable the matter C
to be considered by the judge who considered an application under the
Guardianship of Minors Act 1971 which had been made in relation to the
five children who were the issue of the plaintiff. Immediately prior to
the hearing of this summons I heard evidence in the guardianship of
minors application and delivered judgment. With the consent of the
parties I ordered that the evidence in the guardianship of minors application shall be evidence where relevant in this application. A transcript D
of my judgment in the guardianship of minors application is filed with
the papers in this case.

The plaintiff seeks an order for the sale of property in accordance
with the trust for sale under which it is held in the joint names of the
plaintiff and the defendant as tenants in common. She applies under
the provisions of section 30 of the Law of Property Act 1925 for such E
an order or, alternatively, for such other order as the court may think
fit. In the further alternative the plaintiff seeks " such further or other
relief " in support of which application, according to Mr. Andrew Walker
(her counsel) she relies upon the general principles applied by the courts
in doing justice between tenants in common.

Both the plaintiff and the defendant are of Jamaican origin. They
have lived in this country since at least 1962. In that year they started to F
cohabit. Apart from three or four occasions upon which the plaintiff
left the respondent for periods of varying length the parties lived together
until early in 1974, i.e. for about 12 years. On the occasions when she
did leave, the plaintiff took with her such children as had, at the time,
been born.

In 1974 the plaintiff left the defendant for the last time and per- G
manently. Again she took with her the five children who formed the
family at that time. Apart from the final separation the last substantial
departure of the plaintiff from the home occurred in the summer of
1969 when she left with the four children who were then living. In
January 1970 the plaintiff and the defendant together bought the premises making more or less equal financial contributions towards its
purchase. Thereafter the plaintiff, who was then pregnant with the fifth H
child of the family, whose paternity the defendant does not admit,
returned to live with the defendant. Here they established a home for
themselves and the five children which lasted until the final breakdown of
the association about four years later. The defendant accepted the fifth
child as a member of the family.

It is common ground that the house was purchased and registered in
the joint names of the plaintiff and the defendant as tenants in common

A in equal shares. At one stage during these proceedings, prior to the
discovery of a solicitor's attendance note recording the instructions given
by the defendant in relation to the purchase of the property and its conveyance into the joint names, there was an issue on this matter. Since
that document was discovered the defendant has admitted the plaintiff's
contention that the property is held by the parties as tenants in common
in equal shares.

B   At the time of the final separation early in 1974 the plaintiff took
all five children with her. Shortly thereafter (i.e., within a matter of
months and certainly not more than a year later) the two older children
returned to live with the defendant. Later the third child returned to
live with his father. These three children have remained living with the
defendant at the family home. Apart from a comparatively short period
C during which the fourth child lived with his father, the fourth and fifth
children have remained with the plaintiff and still remain with her. The
result of the orders which I have made in the guardianship of minors
application stabilises this position. The three older children will remain
with the defendant in the erstwhile family home whilst the remaining two
children will remain with the plaintiff in a home which she has established
in a council house. The ages of the children now living with the defen-
D dant range from 16 to 14 years. The two children living with the
plaintiff are aged 13 years and 11 years.

The purchase price of the house including the costs of the purchase
was £3,220. Of this sum £2,000 was obtained on a mortgage. In very
rough terms the balance of £1,220 was provided by the parties paying a
sum of approximately £610 each. The defendant has throughout paid
E the instalments on the mortgage. These were regular payments of £36·67
per month over a period of ten years. The last such payment was made in
March 1980. The property now stands unencumbered.

The defendant is employed by the Thames Water Board. He earns
something in the region of £7,400 gross per annum although this varies
with the amount of overtime available. He says that he has no savings
and gave evidence as to his means and financial commitments. I treat
F his evidence with some reservation, however. I think that he may well
have more assets than he cares to disclose. In any event the means of
the parties are not, in my judgment, relevant. The plaintiff is also in
employment earning a little over £2,000 per annum gross. There is no
regular overtime available for her. Again, she has dealt with her means
and declared that she has some very modest savings in the region of
G £300. As with the defendant I do not think that these matters are relevant; but I accept the plaintiff as an honest and reasonably accurate
witness.

Evidence has been produced in the form of letters from two firms of
chartered surveyors. This establishes, in my judgment, that a fair market
value at the date of the hearing of the freehold property with the benefit
H of full vacant possession would be £19,000. The defendant has given
evidence, which I accept, that he has been offered by the appropriate
housing authority an improvement grant of £3,500 on condition that he
contributes a further £1,000 towards repairs and improvements to the
premises which will cost £4,500. He would only have to repay this grant
if he sold the property during the ensuing five years. He has, however,
been warned that the improvement in the property would be reflected in
an increase in the rates of some undetermined amount. Depending on

the outcome of these proceedings the defendant would like to take up **A**
this offer. He sees no difficulty in meeting his side of the bargain.

This case raises some interesting questions relating to the rights as
between parents who have established a home but who are not married.
Apart from the recent provisions of the Domestic Violence and Matrimonial Proceedings Act 1976 the law gives no rights to a mistress arising
out of her relationship with her lover per se except as the father of her
children (see the Guardianship of Minors Acts 1971 and 1973). She **B**
receives no recognition by way of analogy either under the Married
Women's Property Act 1882 or under the Acts which culminated in the
Matrimonial Causes Act 1973.

On the other hand, she does not lose any rights at law or in equity
which she would otherwise enjoy merely because she is a mistress. She
is, therefore, to be treated in exactly the same way as any other tenant **C**
in common in relation to the joint property. Mr. Coningsby, who
appeared for the defendant, submitted that no order should be made
under section 30 of the Law of Property Act 1925 but alternatively submitted that if any order were to be made under that section then I should
take into account all the financial liabilities and capabilities of the parties
much as the court is required to do under the provisions of section 25
of the Matrimonial Causes Act 1973. To do this, however, would be **D**
inconsistent with the position enjoyed in relation to the property by the
plaintiff as a tenant in common and I am, therefore, unable to accede to
Mr. Coningsby's alternative submission.

In support of his first contention Mr. Coningsby relied, inter alia, on
In re Evers' Trust [1980] 1 W.L.R. 1327. This case is a clear authority
for the proposition that where the circumstances in which the trust for sale **E**
originated envisaged as one of the primary objects the provision of a home
for the family rather than an immediate sale, then the proper approach to
the exercise of the discretion granted by section 30 of the Law of Property
Act 1925 is not to make an order for sale: see also the dictum of Lord
Denning M.R. in *Williams (J. W.)* v. *Williams (M. A.)* [1976] Ch. 278, 285.
There is no doubt that this is such a case. Subject to what follows hereafter in this judgment it would not be proper to make an immediate order **F**
for the sale of the property; nor would it be either convenient or appropriate to make such an order suspended during any specific period, e.g.,
the minority of the youngest of the children enjoying the property as his
home. Mr. Walker, whilst keeping his options open, has not seriously
argued against this proposition.

The main argument has revolved around the right or otherwise of the **G**
plaintiff to receive an occupation rent as a co-tenant who is excluded
from the property. Mr. Coningsby has referred me to a judgment of Lord
Denning M.R. in *Jones (A. E.)* v. *Jones (F. W.)* [1977] 1 W.L.R. 438, 441:

> " First the claim for rent. It is quite plain that these two people
> were in equity tenants in common having a three-quarter and one-
> quarter share respectively. One was in occupation of the house. **H**
> The other not. Now the common law said clearly that one tenant
> in common is not entitled to rent from another tenant in common,
> even though that other occupies the whole . . . As between tenants in
> common, they are both equally entitled to occupation and one cannot
> claim rent from the other. Of course, if there was an ouster, that
> would be another matter: or if there was a letting to a stranger for
> rent that would be different, but there can be no claim for rent by

A　one tenant in common against the other whether at law or in equity."

In *Jones (A. E.)* v. *Jones (F. W.)* the plaintiff failed not only on the ground that no occupation rent could be claimed by one tenant in common from another but also upon, the ground of equitable estoppel. Lord Denning M.R. had been referred to *M'Mahon* v. *Burchell* (1846) 2 Ph. 127. In that

B　case the issue as pleaded involved the simple question whether or not a tenant in common by the mere fact of his occupation of the property became liable to pay an occupation rent to any other tenant in common of that property. It had been submitted to Lord Cottenham L.C. that there was a ruling by Sir Launcelot Shadwell V.-C. in *Henderson* v. *Eason* (1846) 10 Jur. 821 to the effect that such a liability existed. In his judgment Lord Cottenham L.C. said, 2 Ph. 127, 134:

C　" . . . I cannot think that Sir Launcelot Shadwell V.-C. can have laid down any such doctrine; for the effect would be, that one tenant in common, by keeping out of the actual occupation of the premises, might convert the other into his bailiff; in other words, prevent the other from occupying them, except upon the terms of paying him rent. There is nothing in the Acts of Parliament (Statute 4 Anne c.

D　16, section 27) to lead to that conclusion, which is contrary to the law as clearly established from the time of Lord Coke downwards. I cannot think, therefore, that Sir Launcelot Shadwell V.-C. intended to lay down such a proposition. Indeed, it has hardly been contended for at the Bar; for the argument has been, that there is enough in the answer to raise a claim to rent which may have arisen in some other manner. There may, no doubt, be various modes of occupation,

E　which would make the party occupying liable for rent to other tenants in common; but there is nothing in these pleadings to entitle the defendant to an inquiry, whether the plaintiff's occupation was in one of those modes, beyond the statement in the answer to which I have referred."

F　The same case is reported in rather more detail in (1846) 1 Coop.t.Cott. 457. Both in argument and in the judgment the expression "exclusion" is used. Submissions made by counsel for the appellants involved the proposition, at p. 464:

" There must be either exclusion, or some contract, to make the occupying tenant in common liable. In the present case the house had been open to all the tenants in common; it was clear that there

G　was no exclusion. As to contract, none was alleged by the answer."

Passing to the judgment, I cite the following extract, at pp. 467–468:

" With regard to exclusion it was plain there was none. The answer alleged that the plaintiff, William M'Mahon, and one of his brothers and two of his sisters, had occupied the house during certain periods: but it nowhere alleged that the other brothers and sisters might not

H　have occupied the house if they had thought fit . . . The plaintiffs say, it is very true that the plaintiff, William M'Mahon, occupied the house, but he never occupied it to the exclusion of the other tenants in common. This the defendants do not think fit to contest. The case set up by the defendants, therefore, was neither contract, nor exclusion, nor anything else except simple occupation."

Lord Cottenham L.C. went on to deal later with this suggestion at p. 469:

"There were, no doubt, various modes of occupation which would A
make the tenant in common occupying liable to rent to the other
tenants in common,—but those other modes ought not to be the
subject of discussion in the master's office."

And then later, at p. 471:

"The question then was, the house being open to all the tenants in
common, and the plaintiff, William M'Mahon, having been in the occu- B
pation, but there being no exclusion of the other tenants in common,
and there being an absence of all contract, was the plaintiff, William
M'Mahon, liable to rent."

The report then continues as does the report in 2 Phillips 127 that in
these circumstances no occupation rent could be claimed by the tenants
in common not in occupation, unless by agreement the occupying tenant in C
common became bailiff for another tenant in common and thereby liable
to pay.

Mr. Walker submitted that when one refers to *M'Mahon* v. *Burchell,*
which was the basis of the comment by Lord Denning M.R. in *Jones (A. E.)*
v. *Jones (F. W.)* [1977] 1 W.L.R. 438 it is clear that in citing the instances
of "ouster" and "letting to a stranger for rent" Lord Denning M.R. was D
instancing but two of the occasions upon which the courts would hold
that a tenant in common might be liable for an occupation rent. In any
event the old meaning of the word "ouster' was probably wider than the
sense of expulsion which the word carries today. The right of a tenant
in common to claim his fair share of rent received from a stranger, to
which Lord Denning M.R. referred, was granted by Statute, 4 Anne c. 16,
section 27, which was considered in *Henderson* v. *Eason* (1851) 17 Q.B. E
701. Lord Denning M.R. did not mention, for instance, the situation
mentioned in *M'Mahon* v. *Burchell,* 2 Ph. 127, where, by agreement,
one tenant in common became the bailiff for another or other tenants in
common and in that way was liable for occupation rent or alternatively
an agreed rent. The reference by Lord Cottenham L.C. to "other modes
of occupation" which might give rise to an occupation rent is clearly
much wider than this. The Court of Chancery was ever ready to inquire F
into such matters: see the judgment of Stirling J. in *Hill* v. *Hickin* [1897]
2 Ch. 579, 580, where the description of the issue is as follows:

"The writ was issued in 1890, and judgment given in 1892, and one
of the inquiries thereby directed was what sum was due from the
defendant James Hickin in respect of his occupation of the heredit-
ments since September 29, 1890 (he having been in occupation during G
that period without payment of rent), having regard to any previous
tenancy thereof."

In his judgment Stirling J. said, at p. 580:

"The defendant James Hickin not having been tenant or bailiff of
his co-owners, nothing could have been recovered from him at law; H
nor does the Statute of Anne (4 Anne c. 16 section 27) apply: see
Henderson v. *Eason* (1851) 17 Q.B. 701. It has, however, long been
the practice of the Court of Chancery and of the Chancery Division
to direct such inquiries as have been directed in the present case: see
as to occupation rent, *Turner* v. *Morgan* (1803) 8 Ves.Jun. 143, 145."

Mr. Walker submitted, I think correctly, that when one looks at
the judgment in *M'Mahon* v. *Burchell,* 2 Ph. 127 together with the

A extract from the judgment of Stirling J. in *Hill* v. *Hickin* [1897] 2
Ch. 579 the true position under the old authorities was that the Court
of Chancery and Chancery Division would always be ready to inquire
into the position as between co-owners being tenants in common either
at law or in equity to see whether a tenant in common in occupation of
the premises was doing so to the exclusion of one or more of the other
tenants in common for whatever purpose or by whatever means. If
B this was found to be the case, then if in order to do equity between the
parties an occupation rent should be paid, this would be declared and
the appropriate inquiry ordered. Only in cases where the tenants in
common not in occupation were in a position to enjoy their right to
occupy but chose not to do so voluntarily, and were not excluded by
any relevant factor, would the tenant in common in occupation be en-
C titled to do so free of liability to pay an occupation rent.

In the instant case the plaintiff is clearly not a free agent. She was
caused to leave the family home as a result of the violence or threatened
violence of the defendant. In any event, whatever might have been the
cause of the breakdown of the association, it would be quite unreasonable
to expect the plaintiff to exercise her rights as a tenant in common to
occupy the property as she had done before the breakdown of her
D association with the defendant. In my judgment she falls into exactly the
kind of category of person excluded from the property in the way
envisaged by Lord Cottenham L.C. in *M'Mahon* v. *Burchell*, 2 Ph. 127.
Therefore, the basic principle that a tenant in common is not liable to
to pay an occupation rent by virtue merely of his being in sole occupation
of the property does not apply in the case where an association similar
E to a matrimonial association has broken down and one party is, for
practical purposes, excluded from the family home.

I should add that I have thought it proper to consider the wider
implications of what I believe to be the wide ambit of the meaning of
the word " exclusion " in the context of joint tenants because I am
reluctant to see any extension of the concept of " constructive desertion "
F after it has to a large extent been successfully eliminated by the provisions
of section 1 (2) (*b*) of the Matrimonial Causes Act 1973. On the particular facts of this case, however, I am satisfied that by his acts of
violence and threats of continuing violence the defendant forced the
plaintiff to leave the home and thereafter prevented her returning to
it in circumstances amounting to constructive desertion. Whatever may
be the true test of " expulsion " or " ouster " I have no doubt that the
G plaintiff in this case was expelled by the conduct of the defendant from
the property and prevented by him from enjoying her rights as a tenant
in common.

Mr. Walker pointed out that the court in effect ordered the tenant in
common in occupation to pay the equivalent of an occupation rent in
some of the other cases which were cited in argument. In *In re Evers'*
H *Trust* [1980] 1 W.L.R. 1327, whilst dismissing the appeal, the court
altered the order made by the judge. Ormrod L.J. said, at p. 1134:

" For these reasons the judge was right not to order an immediate
sale but the form of his actual order is not satisfactory. Under
section 30, the primary question is whether the court should come
to the aid of the applicant at the ' particular moment and in the
particular circumstances when the application is made to it ' . . . see
In re Buchanan-Wollaston's Conveyance [1939] 1 Ch. 738, 747. In

the present case, at the present moment and in the existing circum- A
stances, it would be wrong to order a sale. But circumstances may
change unpredictably. It may not be appropriate to order a sale
when the child reaches 16 years—a purely arbitrary date—or it may
become appropriate to do so much sooner, for example on the
mother's remarriage, or on it becoming financially possible for her
to buy the father out. In such circumstances it will probably be
wiser simply to dismiss the application while indicating the sort of B
circumstances which would, prima facie, justify a further application.
The ensuing uncertainty is unfortunate but, under this section, the
court has no power to adjust property rights or to re-draft the terms
of the trust. Ideally, the parties should now negotiate a settlement
on the basis that neither of them is in a position to dictate terms.
We would therefore, dismiss the father's appeal, but would vary the C
order to dismiss the application on the mother's undertaking to
discharge the liability under the mortgage, to pay the outgoings and
maintain the property, and to indemnify the father so long as she
is occupying the property."

Mr. Walker points out that the terms upon which the court declined
to make an order included an undertaking by the mother who was occupy- D
ing the premises to discharge the liability under the mortgage. This
included not only capital but also interest elements and, therefore, in effect
required her to pay an occupation rent for the privilege of continuing to
occupy as a tenant in common the whole property adversely to the father.
   In *Leake (formerly Bruzzi)* v. *Bruzzi* [1974] 1 W.L.R. 1528, which
was an application under section 17 of the Married Women's Property Act
1882, the question arose as to what relief the husband who had paid all E
the mortgage instalments should get for having, in effect, paid the wife's
share for which she would otherwise be liable. The court ordered that the
husband should have relief only in respect of the capital element of those
payments. In effect, by depriving him of relief in respect of the wife's
liability for the interest element of the mortgage repayments, the court was
charging him indirectly with an occupation rent. Mr. Walker submitted, F
in answer to a question put by me, that had the wife not availed herself of
the relief afforded by section 17 of the Married Women's Property Act
1882 she could just as well have proceeded under section 30 of the Law
of Property Act 1925. I cannot see any fallacy in this submission. It
would not be satisfactory if differing results could be obtained depending
upon which cause of action was adopted. *Leake (formerly Bruzzi)* v.
Bruzzi [1974] 1 W.L.R. 1528 therefore is support for Mr. Walker's con- G
tentions notwithstanding that it was a case brought under the Married
Women's Property Act 1882, and not the Law of Property Act 1925. In
another case under the Married Women's Property Act 1882—*Suttill* v.
Graham [1977] 1 W.L.R. 819—the husband and wife bought a house on
mortgage as a matrimonial home and it was conveyed to them jointly in
equal shares. The parties separated and each remarried but the husband H
continued to occupy the home and pay the mortgage instalments. In an
action under section 17 of the Married Women's Property Act 1882 and
the Matrimonial Proceedings and Property Act 1970 for a declaration that
she was entitled to half the beneficial interest of the home and for an order
for sale, the husband contended that he should be credited with one-half
of the mortgage instalments which he had paid, including both capital and
interest, and that the sum claimed by the wife should be reduced accord-

A ingly.   The judge held that the husband should be credited with one-half
of the capital repayments only since they had reduced the principal sum
owing and increased pro tanto the value of the property.   On appeal
Stamp L.J. said, at p. 821 :

"It must be emphasised at this point that this is not a case where
the husband, nor for that matter the wife, is claiming in the divorce
suit ancillary relief in the form of a property adjustment order or
B   lump sum payment.   The matter has throughout been dealt with under
the machinery laid down in the Married Women's Property Act 1882
as amended. Accordingly it would be open to the wife, who was not
represented and did not appear on this appeal, to submit, first, that
applying *Pettitt* v. *Pettitt* [1970] A.C. 777 and *Gissing* v. *Gissing*
[1971] A.C. 886, the rights of the parties must be judged on general
C   principles in considering questions of title to property; and second, that
applying those principles a beneficiary entitled to an equal share in
equity of property in which he is a trustee, and which he himself
occupied, is to be charged with at least an occupation rent; so that
if as here he seeks to charge his co-beneficiary trustee with half the
outgoings, he should be charged with half the occupation rent.   That
is not precisely the way in which such a situation has been approached
D   in the cases to which attention has been called by counsel on behalf of
the husband.   But in *Leake (formerly Bruzzi)* v. *Bruzzi* [1974] 1
W.L.R. 1528 this court arrived at a similar conclusion by regarding
the mortgage interest paid by the husband while in possession as
something equivalent to rent or payment for use and occupation.
That will normally produce a fair result and save costs; and where,
E   as here, the husband in possession does not submit to be charged with
an occupation rent, it must be wrong that he should seek to charge the
wife with half the mortgage interest which he has paid while living in
the property rent free and resisting a sale of the property."

Since early 1974 the defendant has occupied the property in circumstances in which he should pay an occupation rent to the applicant.   I now
F turn to consider section 30 of the Law of Property Act 1925.   Mr. Walker
submitted that I can make appropriate orders by virtue of the provision
in section 30.   After considering the wording of this section I have come to
the conclusion that it does not confer any power upon the court to this
effect.   As was said in argument, the section was really passed for conveyancing purposes to help to deal with the flood of equitable tenants in
common holding under trusts for sale which resulted from the passing
G into law of the Law of Property Act 1925.   I do not think that this section
enables the court to make orders where an order for sale is not made. Only
orders ancillary to an order for sale which are necessary to implement
the sale are envisaged by the words of the section.   The words are "*and*
the court may make such order as it thinks fit" and not "*or* the court
may make such other orders" etc.   As is explained in *Megarry and Wade,*
H *The Law of Real Property,* 4th ed. (1975), p. 427, section 30 of the Law
of Property Act 1925 is the successor to the old Partition Acts and in
particular the power of sale granted under the Partition Act 1868.   In
Turner v. *Morgan* (1803) 8 Ves.Jun. 143, 145 Lord Eldon L.C. held the
threat of making a partition order over the parties in order to bring them
to terms.   Although section 30 does not grant a power to the court to order
the payment of an occupation rent it certainly could be used in a manner
similar to that adopted by Lord Eldon, by means of indicating that unless

an undertaking to pay an occupation rent was forthcoming from the   A
defendant then the order for sale would be made.

However, such an indirect method may not be necessary. I think that
on the general principles of the law set out in this judgment it is open to
the court to make an order that an occupation rent should be paid. If
I am wrong about this then the course outlined immediately above should
be adopted.

Mr. Walker put the matter in an alternative way which out of   B
respect for his able argument I refer to here. He submitted that the
defendant was seeking equity and, therefore, under the old maxim, must
himself do equity. This argument has its attractions. It is based on the
proposition that in resisting an order for sale under section 30 the defendant is seeking equitable relief. This would be so if the trust for sale had
as its sole object the sale of the property and if its postponement was a   C
matter of seeking the indulgence of the court. In this case, as I have
already said, it is clear that the prime object of the trust was to provide a
home. Whilst it is still being used for this purpose, as without doubt it
still is, then I do not think that it is right to describe the defendant as
someone who is seeking equity to protect him from the due execution of
the trusts for sale. Whilst the family occupy the house the sale is
secondary to the trust to provide a home for the family.   D

Mr. Coningsby submitted that if I came to the conclusion that the
defendant was liable to pay an occupation rent then I should not make
an order that was retro-active. The main plank of his argument was that
if I made such an order it would impose a heavy financial burden on the
defendant and might well prejudice him in taking advantage of the offer
made by the housing authority to pay an improvement grant. It is   E
obviously important for both parties that the value of their joint investment
should be enhanced and that this offer is taken up. I do not think that
I can accede to Mr. Coningsby's submission. I am by no means satisfied
that the defendant was wholly frank about either his means or his capital
assets. There is in any event a valuable property here which at the moment
is unencumbered.

Mr. Walker submitted that I should deal with the question of occupa-   F
tion rent to date in two stages. He submitted that between the years 1974
and 1976 inclusive there should not be any inquiry but that I should order
that for this period no credit should be given either for the capital or
interest elements of the plaintiff's share of the mortgage payments which
have in fact been paid by the defendant. This would be in line with
the approach of Stamp L.J. in *Suttill* v. *Graham* [1977] 1 W.L.R. 819
and Ormrod L.J. in *Leake (formerly Bruzzi)* v. *Bruzzi* [1974] 1 W.L.R.   G
1528. The basis of his submission is that during the early years the
major element in the mortgage repayment is interest on the capital advanced
and that half of the sums would be broadly equivalent to an occupation
rent. This would in my judgment do rough justice between the parties.

As to the years 1977 to 1980 inclusive, Mr. Walker submitted that an
occupation rent would be noticeably higher than half the mortgage pay-   H
ments which would otherwise be due to be paid by the plaintiff. During
this period Mr. Walker suggested that there should be an inquiry as to
what the occupation rent ought to be with an order for the payment of
such sums subject to the defendant's entitlement to set off any amount
paid in redemption of the mortgage on behalf of the plaintiff. Since 1980,
of course, no question of mortgage repayment arises and the liability of the
defendant to pay an occupation rent must be a payment to half the

A   appropriate rent for the property. The question arises whether such a rent ought to be assessed as a normal rack rent, as the interest to be paid on a sum equivalent to the value of the property, or should the rent be assessed as " a fair rent " such as would be assessed by a rent officer?

I indicated in argument that I did not think that the occupation rent ought to be assessed in relation to the value of the capital asset involved— or, rather, half of it—as this was not the concept behind an occupation
B   rent. Although Mr. Walker again kept his options open on this score he did not pursue the argument.

The question then reverts to whether it should be a rack rent assessed on the basis that there is not a protected tenancy involved or whether it should be a fair rent to be assessed in the ordinary way as with a protected tenancy. There is room for argument here. The approach which I adopt
C   is that as each party has a right to occupy the property but the occupation rent arises as a result of the exclusion of the plaintiff in the manner already described in his judgment, then the plaintiff's rights as against the defendant must envisage that the respondent himself has a right to occupy the property akin to the sort of protection given to a protected tenant. For these reasons I think that the proper way to assess the amount of the occupation rent for which the defendant is liable is that this should
D   be half the fair rent which would be assessed by the rent officer for a letting unfurnished of the whole of the property to a protected tenant. An inquiry should be ordered, therefore, to assess this figure for the years 1977 to 1980 inclusive. In such an inquiry the defendant should be entitled to credit for any sums paid in respect of the property which enhances its capital value but not for any sums paid in the ordinary
E   maintenance and repair of the property.

If the defendant gives an undertaking to pay the amount found due by such an inquiry for the years 1977 to 1980 inclusive and for the year 1981 and thereafter undertakes to pay such amount by way of occupation rent as shall be agreed between the parties or otherwise to be determined by the rent officer, then I shall not make an order under section 30 of the Law of Property Act 1925. As to the exact form of the order, I will leave it
F   to counsel to draft minutes of order for my approval to carry out the effect of this judgment.

Order accordingly.

Solicitors: *Eric Hauser & Co.; Robert Thompson & Partners.*

G
M. B. D.

H

A

* GRAPPELLI AND ANOTHER v.
DEREK BLOCK (HOLDINGS) LTD. AND ANOTHER

1981 Jan. 19, 20

Lord Denning M.R., Templeman
and Dunn L.JJ.

B

*Libel and Slander — Pleadings — Innuendo — Extrinsic facts in
support of innuendo occurring after publication — Whether
original words having defamatory meaning alleged in innuendo
— Failure to plead names of individuals with knowledge of
secondary meaning of statement — Whether cause of action
complete on publication or on subsequent damage*

C

The plaintiffs were musicians, the first named having an
international reputation. The defendants were promoters of
concerts who at one time were agents for the plaintiffs. In or
about June 1976 the defendants purported to arrange concerts
for the plaintiffs at, inter alia, Tameside, near Manchester, on
November 26, 1976, and Milton Keynes, on December 4, 1976.
On September 21, 1976, the defendants told the managers of
the Tameside and Milton Keynes concert halls that the plain-   D
tiffs' concerts had been cancelled because the first-named plaintiff was " very seriously ill in Paris " and it would be surprising
" if he ever toured again." The information given by the
defendants was passed on to the managers' staff and to members of the public who inquired about the two concerts. On,
about and after November 12, 1976, by advertisements and a
press release in Manchester, and on November 28, 1976, by an
advertisement in " The Sunday Times " an announcement was   E
made of concerts to be given by the plaintiffs at Hanley on
December 2, at Manchester on December 3 and at other places
on December 4, 5 and 6, 1976.

The plaintiffs said that the defendants acted without their
authority, that the statement about the first-named plaintiff's
health was false and they claimed damages for injurious falsehood; and for libel and slander alleging that the facts gave
rise to an innuendo that the plaintiffs had given a reason for   F
cancelling the concerts which they knew to be false. The plaintiffs' pleadings did not identify any members of the public who
were alleged to have knowledge of the extrinsic facts supporting the innuendo. Hodgson J. dismissed the defendants' appeal
from the master's order refusing to order that (a) the allegations of libel and slander be struck out or (b) the plaintiffs
give particulars of individuals who understood the words complained of to bear the meaning alleged.   G

On appeal by the defendants: —

Held, allowing the appeal, (1) that in defamation, whether
libel or slander, the cause of action was complete when the
words alleged to be defamatory of the plaintiff were published
to a person who then knew all the material, extrinsic facts;
and that inferences put on the statements published on
September 21, 1976, by facts learned subsequently did not   H
make those statements defamatory when published (post,
pp. 825B–D, H, 826D–E, 831B–C).

Dictum of Blair J. in *Simons Proprietary Ltd.* v. *Riddell*
[1941] N.Z.L.R. 913, 932 applied.

(2) That, further, in defamation there was a general rule
that a plaintiff who relied on a legal innuendo must specify
the persons who had the particular knowledge from which
they drew a defamatory meaning; and that, accordingly, the
plaintiffs' allegations of libel and slander would be struck out

A

on both grounds leaving them to rely on the allegation of injurious falsehood (post, pp. 826B, D–E, 829H—830A).

Fullam v. *Newcastle Chronicle and Journal Ltd.* [1977] 1 W.L.R. 651, C.A. followed.

Per Dunn L.J. There may be an exception to the general rule in the case of a national newspaper with a very wide circulation where the only reasonable inference is that some of its readers must have knowledge of the facts giving rise to the innuendo (post, p. 830A–B).

B

Decision of Hodgson J. reversed.

The following cases are referred to in the judgments:

Astaire v. *Campling* [1966] 1 W.L.R. 34; [1965] 3 All E.R. 666, C.A.

Bata v. *Bata* [1948] W.N. 366, C.A.

Cassidy v. *Daily Mirror Newspapers Ltd.* [1929] 2 K.B. 331, C.A.

C

Consolidated Trust Co. Ltd. v. *Browne* (1948) 49 S.R.(N.S.W.) 86.

Fullam v. *Newcastle Chronicle and Journal Ltd.* [1977] 1 W.L.R. 651; [1977] 3 All E.R. 32, C.A.

Hayward v. *Thompson* (unreported), November 9, 1979, O'Connor J.

Hough v. *London Express Newspapers Ltd.* [1940] 2 K.B. 507; [1940] 3 All E.R. 31, C.A.

Russell v. *Kelly* (1872) 13 Am.Rep. 169.

Sadgrove v. *Hole* [1901] 2 K.B. 1, C.A.

D

Simons Proprietary Ltd. v. *Riddell* [1941] N.Z.L.R. 913.

The following additional case was cited in argument:

Hulton (E.) & Co. v. *Jones* [1910] A.C. 20, H.L.(E.).

INTERLOCUTORY APPEAL from Hodgson J.

E

By writ of November 9, 1977, the plaintiffs, Stephane Grappelli and William Charles Disley, claimed damages for injurious falsehood, slander and libel against the defendants, Derek Block (Holdings) Ltd. and Ray Nedas.

The defendants applied for leave to appeal from the order of Hodgson J. on December 1, 1980, dismissing their appeal against the order of Master Waldman on July 9, 1980, who had refused to order

F

that (a) the allegations of libel and slander in the amended statement of claim should be struck out or (b) the plaintiffs within 14 days give particulars of individuals who understood the words complained of to bear the meanings alleged.

The grounds of appeal (if leave to appeal were granted) were that the judge was wrong in law in holding that (1) the plaintiffs were entitled in support of claims for libel and slander based upon a legal innuendo to

G

rely upon extrinsic facts where such facts occurred or the knowledge thereof was acquired by the publishers of the words complained of after the date of publication of those words; (2) their causes of action in libel and slander need not be complete at the time of publication of the words complained of; and (3) the judge should have ordered the plaintiffs to give particulars of individuals who understood the words complained of

H

to bear the meaning alleged in the amended statement of claim.

The application for leave to appeal was treated as the hearing of the substantive appeal.

The facts are stated in the judgments of Lord Denning M.R. and Dunn L.J.

Peter Bowsher Q.C. and *Adrienne Page* for the defendants.

Richard Rampton for the plaintiffs.

824

LORD DENNING M.R. Mr. Grappelli is a professional jazz violinist with   A
an international reputation. Mr. Disley is a professional guitarist. He is
the leader of a trio which accompanied Mr. Grappelli as part of his team.
It appears that they had as their managers or agents at one time a
company called Derek Block (Holdings) Ltd. About June 1976 these
managers or agents purported to book concerts for Mr. Grappelli and
his team at various places in England. They were fixed for some months
ahead. For instance, in June a concert was fixed at Milton Keynes to   B
be held on December 4, 1976. At Tameside an arrangement was made
for a concert to be held on November 26. 1976. And so forth.

Mr. Grappelli says that the agents acted without his authority when
they booked him for those engagements. The agents had to cancel the
bookings they had made. So on September 21, 1976, they telephoned
the people concerned, and put forward this excuse: " The Stephane   C
Grappelli concert has been cancelled because Stephane Grappelli is very
seriously ill in Paris and I would be surprised if he ever toured again."

Mr. Grappelli says that that was an entirely false statement about his
health: it was known by the agents to be false. They put it forward as
an excuse to get themselves out of the unauthorised engagements. If it
was a false statement, maliciously made, which would cause damage, it   D
would give rise to a cause of action for injurious falsehood. A cause of
action has been brought accordingly.

Not content with a cause of action for injurious falsehood, Mr.
Grappelli and Mr. Disley also allege that the statement was a slander
as being defamatory of Mr. Grappelli. It is obviously not defamatory as
it stands. It is not defamatory of a person to say that he is seriously ill.
But Mr. Grappelli says that it became actionable thereafter. He says   E
that on November 28 there was a notice in " The Sunday Times " (and
other papers) saying that Mr. Grappelli was performing in various concert
halls. Not at the concert halls previously arranged but at others. For
instance, the notice in " The Sunday Times " said that he was going to
appear at St. Albans on December 4. Not at Milton Keynes. It also
said that he was going to appear at Manchester on December 3.   F

It is said on behalf of Mr. Grappelli that when people read on
November 1976 in " The Sunday Times " that these other new engagements had been made for him, they would read an innuendo into the
the statement made in September 1976. They would say to themselves,
" That was a put-up job. He was not really ill. He gave a reason which
he knew to be false." It is said that that subsequent knowledge would
lead people to think that the original statement about Mr. Grappelli   G
being ill was a put-up job. The plaintiffs allege a legal innuendo that
the words were understood to mean that the plaintiffs had given a reason
for cancelling the concerts which they knew to be false.

That is the pleading as it stands. An application was made by the
defendants—not to strike out the malicious falsehood part of the claim
—but to strike out the claim in regard to slander on the ground that   H
there was no cause of action in defamation.

The case raises two quite interesting points on the law of libel. I
summarised the law about innuendo in *Fullam* v. *Newcastle Chronicle
and Journal Ltd.* [1977] 1 W.L.R. 651. There is a cause of action for
words in their natural and ordinary meaning. That is not alleged here.
The other cause of action is one which is based on a legal innuendo.
In it the plaintiff relies on special circumstances which convey to some

The Weekly Law Reports, June 5, 1981

825

1 W.L.R.   Grappelli v. Derek Block Ltd. (C.A.)   Lord Denning M.R.

A particular person or persons, knowing those circumstances, a special defamatory meaning other than the natural and ordinary meaning. That is a separate cause of action.

The question which arises in this case is as to legal innuendo. When the plaintiff relies on special circumstances known to another person, have those special circumstances to be in his knowledge *at the time* when he reads or hears the words? Or is it sufficient that—because of

B some later facts—he puts a defamatory meaning upon them?

Upon this point we heard an interesting discussion on both sides. I would go by the principle, which is well-established, that in defamation— be it libel or slander—the cause of action is the *publication* of defamatory words of and concerning the plaintiff. The cause of action arises when those words are *published* to the person by whom they are read or

C heard. The cause of action arises then: and not later.

Mr. Rampton urged us to say that in slander it may be different. He suggests that the cause of action there does not arise until there is damage—like actions in negligence and the like.

I prefer to go by the principle that in defamation a cause of action arises (and a writ can be issued) as soon as the words are published to a person *then* knowing all the material facts. If there are extrinsic facts,

D he must know them *then*—at the time of publication. That is when a cause of action arises. It cannot be made into a cause of action by reason of facts subsequently coming to the knowledge of the reader or hearer.

We were referrd to a New Zealand case, which was not cited to the judge below. It is *Simons Proprietary Ltd.* v. *Riddell* [1941] N.Z.L.R.

E 913. Blair J. seemed to me to put the position quite accurately when he said, at p. 932:

" On the authorities—see *Cassidy* v. *Daily Mirror Newspapers* ([1929] 2 K.B. 331) and *Tolley* v. *J. S. Fry and Sons Ltd.* ([1930] 1 K.B. 467; [1931] A.C. 333)—innocent matter may be given a defamatory meaning by readers with knowledge of facts not known to the writer. But

F those cases do not lay down that a writer of innocent matter can by reason of certain facts coming into existence subsequent to publication of his innocent matter become liable in damages for libel because persons learning of that subsequent material are able to read into the innocent matter a defamatory meaning."

That seems to me to be correct. He emphasised it by saying that, if the

G person was liable in damages in those circumstances, it would mean a great extension in the law of libel. He said at p. 933 it would be extending it much too far

" to ascertain whether the next day or the next week or the next year some one may not say or do something that will enable a defamatory meaning to be given to otherwise innocent statements."

H That principle seems to me to be applicable here. The inferences which were put upon the statements *after* the publication (by facts subsequently learnt) do not render them defamatory in the beginning.

The second point arises on the pleadings. The plaintiffs do not identify any of the readers of " The Sunday Times ", or other publications, who—by reason of the later facts—may have put a defamatory meaning upon the statement. The question is whether particulars should be given identifying the persons concerned. Again, on this point it seems

Lord Denning M.R.   **Grappelli v. Derek Block Ltd. (C.A.)**   **[1981]**

to me that it can be dealt with in principle. I ventured to put it myself A
in *Fullam* v. *Newcastle Chronicle and Journal Ltd.* [1977] 1 W.L.R. 651,
655, in the case of secondary meanings:

> " . . . he must in his statement of claim specify the particular person
> or persons to whom they were published and the special circum-
> stances known to that person or persons . . . there is no exception
> in the case of a newspaper: . . ."

B

It seems to me that that general principle of pleading applies here.
In the case of these secondary meanings—even innuendos—the plaintiffs
ought to specify the persons who have the particular knowledge from
which they drew a defamatory meaning.

So on both these points it seems to me that we ought to give leave
to appeal. I can understand the judge's difficulty: he was not referred
to all the cases to which we were referred. He was referred to a ruling C
of O'Connor J. at first instance, *Hayward* v. *Thompson* (unreported),
November 9, 1979. That seems to me to be understandable on other
grounds, but of no assistance here. I would give leave to appeal, allow
the appeal, and strike out the causes of action in so far as they rely on
defamation: but leave intact completely the causes of action in relation
to malicious or injurious falsehood: because it seems to me that that is D
really what the plaintiffs should depend upon.

I would allow the appeal accordingly.

TEMPLEMAN L.J. I have had the advantage of some discussion with
Lord Denning M.R. and Dunn L.J. For the reasons given by Lord
Denning M.R. and for the reasons which Dunn L.J. is about to give, E
I too would allow the appeal, and cannot usefully add anything.

DUNN L.J. I agree that the appeal should be allowed. The judge,
in giving leave to appeal, said that this appeal raised a novel point of
law. The principal question of law is whether, when extrinsic facts are
relied on in support of an innuendo which arose after the publication,
the original words, not defamatory in their ordinary and natural mean- F
ing, can have the defamatory meaning alleged in the innuendo. Both
the master and the judge held that they could. The defendants in this
appeal have submitted that they could not.

For the purposes of the appeal we must assume that all the facts
alleged in the statement of claim are proved. The statement of claim
is complicated and only parts of it are material to this appeal. The first
plaintiff is a well-known jazz violinist with an international reputation. G
The first defendants are promoters of concerts. In May or June 1976,
without the authority of the plaintiffs, they purported to arrange a
number of concerts by the first plaintiff and the second plaintiff, his
accompanist. The only concerts to which I need refer in this judgment
are those fixed at Milton Keynes eventually on December 4, 1976, and
at Tameside fixed for November 26, 1976. H

On September 21, or perhaps just before, the second defendant, who
was an employee of the first defendants, told a Miss Collard, who was
the manager of the Milton Keynes entertainment authority, that (and I
quote from paragraph 4 of the statement of claim): " The Stephane
Grappelli concert has been cancelled because Stephane Grappelli is very
seriously ill in Paris and I would be surprised if he ever toured again."
Miss Collard passed on that information to a subordinate of hers, a Mrs.

A Gormly; and between September 21 and December 4, 1976, Mrs. Gormly informed over the telephone a large number of members of the public both of the cancellation and the reason for it. A substantial number of members of the public were informed before November 28 and some after. The importance of the date November 28 will appear in a moment. According to a letter sent by the plaintiffs' solicitors to the defendants' solicitors on November 18, 1980, between the end of September 1976 and

B the date of the concert, December 4:

"Mrs. Gormly answered no less than 100 and possibly as many as 250 inquiries from members of the public about the concert. On each occasion, she told the person concerned that the concert had been cancelled because Stephane Grappelli was seriously ill and would probably never tour again. She was still answering inquiries

C in that way during the week before the concert (i.e., the week beginning November 28, 1976), but she is unable to be precise about the number of inquiries she received during that week."

The relevance of the date November 28 is that on that day there appeared in the issue of "The Sunday Times" an advertisement announcing that concerts would be given by "the legendary Stephane Grappelli with the

D Diz Disley trio" led by the second plaintiff "at the following venues on the following dates: Odeon Theatre, Hanley, December 2, 1976"— and this is the material one—"Royal Exchange Theatre, Manchester, December 3, 1976." Then there were other concerts advertised: at the City Hall, St. Albans, on December 4; the Central Hall, Chatham, on December 5; and the Civic Hall, Guildford, on December 6.

E What is alleged in the action as a result of those facts is that they give rise to an innuendo that the plaintiffs had given a reason for cancelling the concert which they knew to be false. That is the allegation which is alleged to be defamatory and upon which this action so far as it relates to slander and libel is based.

It will be observed that in the case of Milton Keynes some members of the public were informed of the cancellation before "The Sunday

F Times" advertisement and others after "The Sunday Times" advertisement, and consequently different considerations may apply to each of these two categories.

The other concert which illustrates the points of law which arise in the case is the Tameside concert. In that case the same words, namely, that the concert had been cancelled because Stephane Grappelli was very

G seriously ill and the second defendants would be surprised if he ever toured again, were published to a Mr. Booth, who was the manager of the Tameside Theatre in Ashton-under-Lyme on or before September 21. Mr. Booth republished those words to a Mr. Clark, who was his assistant manager; and Mr. Clark passed on the information to a number of members of the public who had inquired when the concert was going to take place.

H The plaintiffs' concert at the Royal Exchange Theatre, Manchester, for December 3 had been advertised in the weeks prior to that concert by posters in Manchester, by a press release dated November 15, and in programmes for forthcoming events in Manchester, which of course is quite close to Tameside and Ashton-under-Lyme, for the four weeks before the concert. There had also been advertisements in the "Manchester Evening News" of November 12, 18 and 19 and December 3.

The relevance of the Tameside example is that knowledge of the special

circumstances about the Tameside slander existed, it is said, before **A**
" The Sunday Times " advertisement and probably from early November.
In that respect, by further and better particulars, which were subsequently
delivered, of the innuendo, it was said that on a date in November one
of the members of the public to whom Mr. Clark had republished the
said words informed Mr. Clark:

> " that she had seen an advertisement in the ' Manchester Evening **B**
> News ' for a concert by the plaintiffs at the Royal Exchange Theatre
> on December 3, 1976. Thereafter, Mr. Clark republished the said
> words to members of the public on about six occasions and on each
> occasion he informed the member of the public concerned that,
> although the plaintiffs' concert at Tameside had been cancelled for
> the reason given, it nonetheless appeared that the plaintiffs were due
> to give a concert at the Royal Exchange Theatre on December 3." **C**

And the same innuendo was alleged as for the previous allegation.

On that basis of fact Mr. Bowsher for the defendants submitted, first,
that at the time of the publication or republication to Mrs. Gormly and
Mr. Clark there was no slander because the extrinsic facts constituting the
innuendo were not known to the public. Secondly, he submitted that any
republication by Mrs. Gormly or Mr. Clark to members of the public at **D**
the time before information was available that the reason given by the
plaintiffs for cancelling the concert was false was likewise no slander
in the case of Milton Keynes before November 28 and in the case of
Tameside before early November when the Royal Exchange concert was
first publicised. He submitted accordingly that the paragraphs alleging
libel and slander based on those new publications before those dates **E**
should be struck out.

He submitted in the alternative, and in any event, that the paragraphs
alleging libel and slander should be struck out because the pleadings did
not identify those members of the public who were alleged to have knowledge of the extrinsic facts supporting the innuendo. He submitted that
the plaintiffs should be left to their remedy for damages for injurious **F**
falsehood in respect of the false statement by the defendants.

As to his first submission, Mr. Bowsher submitted that publication
was an essential ingredient of the torts of libel and slander. Once there
was publication, he submitted, the cause of action was complete and the
relevant knowledge of the publishees to support the innuendo was their
knowledge at the date of the publication and not thereafter acquired
knoweldge. In support of that submission he cited to us *Bata* v. *Bata* **G**
[1948] W.N. 366; *Sadgrove* v. *Hole* [1901] 2 K.B. 1; *Astaire* v. *Campling*
[1966] 1 W.L.R. 34, 41, *per* Diplock, L.J. and in particular *Simons Proprietary Ltd.* v. *Riddell* [1941] N.Z.L.R. 913. That was a case in which
the appellants were a brewery company, and the manager published in a
newspaper on June 6 an advertisement that H and R " are no longer
in our employ and are not authorised to canvass for us or collect cash **H**
or empties on our behalf." Then in a later issue—a week later—there
was a report of the conviction of H on a charge of issuing a valueless
cheque with intent to defraud. It was held by the whole Court of
Appeal, first, that the words of the advertisement were not by themselves capable of a defamatory meaning. It was also held by the whole
court that the news item published a week later was inadmissible, and
accordingly they ordered a new trial. Lord Denning M.R. has read

A extracts from the judgment of Blair J. who dealt with the matter most
fully and concluded his judgment with these words, at p. 932:

"If that be a correct summary of the law as it now stands, then,
with respect, I venture to say that it would be widening the net of
liability of writers too far by enunciating the doctrine that the
inquiry . . . must go still further by looking into the future to
ascertain whether the next day or the next week or the next year
B some one may not say or do something that will enable a defamatory
meaning to be given to otherwise innocent statements."

As to his second point—the pleading point—Mr. Bowsher adopted
as part of his argument a statement in *Duncan & Neill, Defamation*
(1978), p. 37, para. 8.04, where it is said:

C "Where the plaintiff relies on a true innuendo meaning"—sometimes called a legal innuendo—" the general rule is that it is necessary for the plaintiff to plead and prove: (*a*) that the words were
published to a specific publishee or to specific publishees; and (*b*)
that the publishee or publishees knew of specific facts which would
enable them to understand the words in the innuendo meaning or
to understand the words to refer to the plaintiff."

D He relied on two cases mentioned in *Duncan & Neill: Hough* v. *London
Express Newspapers Ltd.* [1940] 2 K.B. 507, and an Australian case
Consolidated Trust Co. Ltd. v. *Browne* (1948) 49 S.R.(N.S.W.) 86. He
submitted accordingly that, the plaintiffs having said in the statement of
claim in terms that they could not identify the members of the public
with the special knowledge, those paragraphs should be struck out.

E As to that second point, Mr. Rampton for the plaintiffs has said,
first, that *Fullam* v. *Newcastle Chronicle and Journal Ltd.* [1977] 1
W.L.R. 651, to which Lord Denning M.R. has referred, was a very
special case; and, in any event, this case falls within the exception stated
by Scarman L.J. when he said, at p. 659:

"... the facts may be very well known in the area of the news-
F paper's distribution—in which event I would think it would suffice
to plead merely that the plaintiff will rely on inference that some
of the newspaper's readers must have been aware of the facts which
are said to give rise to the innuendo."

Counsel submitted that that was this case; that there was the allegation
that Mr. Clark had passed on the information to a number of persons
G who had rung up asking for the date of the original Tameside concert,
and that from the pleading point of view was sufficient. Difficult questions
might arise on questions of admissibility of evidence when it came to
trial, but Mr. Rampton submitted that this court should not adopt the
draconian course of striking out the allegations at this stage because he
was unable to identify the persons with special knowledge.

H I agree with Lord Denning M.R. that the law is fully set out in
Fullam v. *Newcastle Chronicle and Journal Ltd.* [1977] 1 W.L.R. 651,
especially in the passage of Lord Denning M.R.'s judgment, to which
he has referred, at p. 655, and at p. 656 where he said:

"In such cases as those "—that is to say, cases of innuendo—" the
identity of the person (who has knowledge of the special circumstances) is a most material fact in the cause of action. It is the
publication to him which is the very foundation of the cause of

action. So he should be identified in the pleading itself or in   **A**
particulars under it."

I agree that that is the general rule as stated by *Duncan & Neill,*
Defamation, p. 37, in the passage which I have quoted.

I would only add this, that I agree also with Scarman L.J. that there
may be cases which are exceptions to that rule, such as the cases that
he refers to at p. 659 of the report, where the publication is in a national   **B**
newspaper with a very wide circulation, and the only reasonable inference
is that some of the readers of that newspaper must have knowledge of
the facts which are said to give rise to the innuendo.

But that is not this case. In this case there was a very much more
limited publication to a very much more limited number of publishees.
It involved them connecting up in the first instance the reason given
for the cancellation with either the advertisement in "The Sunday   **C**
Times" or one of the advertisements which appeared in Manchester.
In circumstances of that kind, I agree with Lord Denning M.R. that
the general rule should prevail and that those persons should be identified
in the pleadings.

That would be sufficient to dispose of this case by allowing the appeal;
but, so far as the general question is concerned, Mr. Rampton submitted   **D**
that the cause of action for libel or slander was complete when all the
facts were in existence and not before. He submitted that it was one
thing to say that once all the facts were in existence the cause of action
was complete, but another thing to say that once there was publication
the cause of action was complete, and that it was impossible for further
facts to arise which might give rise to a cause of action subsequent to
publication. He pointed out that there are three elements in a cause of   **E**
action. There must be publication; the publication must refer to the
plaintiff; and the words must have a defamatory meaning. Mr. Rampton
submitted that there was no cause of action until the necessary meaning
had been supplied. Once that occurred, then the cause of action was
complete.

He relied in support of that submission on the American case of   **F**
Russell v. *Kelly* (1872) 13 Am.Rep. 169. That was a case in which in
the orginial publication the name of the plaintiff had not been mentioned.
Evidence was called, including a subsequent publication by the defendant,
in which the plaintiff's name was mentioned; and it was held that that
evidence was admissible so as to make the original publication referable
to the plaintiff and so defamatory. Crockett J. referred at p. 171 to
G
"The rule as laid down in 2 Starkie on Slander, p. 51, is that the
application of the slanderous words to the plaintiff, and the extrinsic
matters alleged in the declaration, may be shown ' by the testimony
of witnesses who knew the parties and circumstances, and who can
state their judgment and opinion on the application and meaning of
the terms used by the defendant '."
H
Holding that the evidence was admissible, he said, at p. 172:

"It is equally clear that the subsequent publication was admissible
for the same purpose, and this was the only purpose for which it
was offered or admitted."

Mr. Rampton said that there was no English authority directly in
point apart from a ruling of O'Connor J. in *Hayward* v. *Thompson*

A (unreported), November 9, 1979, in which in the course of the trial before the jury he allowed to stand an allegation that a second article had been published referring by name to the plaintiff, who had been the subject of an article the previous week which did not refer to him by name. The judge appears to have relied upon *Russell* v. *Kelly,* 13 Am.Rep. 169, he referred to it as the most useful case which had been cited to him—but at the end of the notes of his judgment, with which

B we have been helpfully provided, he appears to have dealt with the case as a re-publication of the original defamatory statement; and certainly it appears from the transcript of his summing up to the jury that that indeed was how he dealt with it. Speaking for myself, I do not derive a great deal of assistance from that case.

Like Lord Denning M.R., I would prefer to deal with this on principle.

C I agree that a publication is an essential part of the cause of action; that once there is publication the cause of action is complete, and there is no room for the doctrine that the cause of action can, so to speak, be allowed to be inchoate or lie dormant until such time as some fact emerges which would transform an otherwise innocent statement into a defamatory one. That I believe to be the principle underlying the

D judgment of Blair J. in *Simons Proprietary Ltd.* v. *Riddell* [1941] N.Z.L.R. 913; and on that ground I too would hold that these paragraphs alleging libel and slander cannot stand. I think the plaintiffs should rely upon the allegation of injurious falsehood, and I would allow the appeal.

Leave to appeal.
Appeal allowed with costs in
Court of Appeal and below.

E

Solicitors: *Ingledew, Brown, Bennison & Garrett; Marsh Regan.*

A. H. B.

F

[QUEEN'S BENCH DIVISION]

* PLUMMER *v.* P. W. WILKINS & SON LTD.

G
1980   June 10, 11, 12;   Latey J.
       July 8

Damages—Earnings, loss of—Supplementary benefit allowance—
Self-employed man injured in industrial accident—Cessation
of unemployment benefit—Receipt of supplementary allow-
ance—Whether benefit deductible from special damages

H

The plaintiff, a self-employed ceiling fixer, was injured when a trestle platform, erected by the defendants and from which he was working, collapsed. He claimed damages for negligence or breach of statutory duty against the defendants who admitted liability. As a result of his injury, the plaintiff was unable to work and therefore received unemployment benefit for the statutory period and thereafter supplementary benefit allowance under the provisions of the Supplementary Benefit Act 1966.

Plummer v. Wilkins Ltd. (Q.B.D.)   **[1981]**

A

On the question whether the amount of £3,424 which the plaintiff had received in supplementary benefit should be deducted from the special damages for loss of earnings: —

Held, that, since the purpose of damages was to compensate the victim for loss and suffering as a result of the act of the tortfeasor and not to confer a windfall and as supplementary benefit, like unemployment benefit, was receivable as of right by those suitably qualified and was not discretionary, supplementary benefit, as well as unemployment benefit, was to be regarded as compensation for loss of earnings and thus deductible from the amount of special damages to be awarded to the plaintiff (post, pp. 834H—835A, 836H—837A).

B

Parsons v. *B.N.M. Laboratories Ltd.* [1964] 1 Q.B. 95, C.A. and *Nabi* v. *British Leyland (U.K.) Ltd.* [1980] 1 W.L.R. 529, C.A. applied.

Foxley v. *Olton* [1965] 2 Q.B. 306 distinguished.

Basnett v. *J. & A. Jackson Ltd.* [1976] I.C.R. 63 not followed.

C

Dicta of Lord Reid in *Parry* v. *Cleaver* [1970] A.C. 1, 14, 19, H.L.(E.) considered.

Per curiam. Another and perhaps wholly acceptable solution might be for the tortfeasor to pay the full amount and when the amounts were met, the benefits to be repaid to public funds. But that would require legislation (post, p. 837B–C).

D

The following cases are referred to in the judgment:

Basnett v. *J. & A. Jackson Ltd.* [1976] I.C.R. 63.

Cackett v. *Earl,* The Times, October 15, 1976.

Elridge v. *Videtta* (1964) 108 S.J. 137.

Foxley v. *Olton* [1965] 2 Q.B. 306; [1964] 3 W.L.R. 1155; [1964] 3 All E.R. 248.

E

Nabi v. *British Leyland (U.K.) Ltd.* [1980] 1 W.L.R. 529; [1980] 1 All E.R. 667, C.A.

Parry v. *Cleaver* [1970] A.C. 1; [1969] 2 W.L.R. 821; [1969] 1 All E.R. 555, H.L.(E.).

Parsons v. *B.N.M. Laboratories Ltd.* [1964] 1 Q.B. 95; [1963] 2 W.L.R. 1273; [1963] 2 All E.R. 658, C.A.

F

Shaw v. *Cape Insulation Co. Ltd.* (unreported), July 18, 1977, Hollings J. (Manchester).

No additional cases were cited in argument.

ACTION

G

By writ dated December 6, 1976, the plaintiff, Eddy Hardwick Plummer, claimed damages against the defendants, P. W. Wilkins and Son Ltd., for personal injuries and other losses and expenses incurred as a result of an accident which occurred on or about March 5, 1975, at the Imperial Hotel, Torquay, Devonshire arising out of the negligence and/or breach of the statutory duty of the defendants. The defendants admitted liability. The issue between the parties was whether supplementary benefit allowance should be deducted from the special damages.

H

The facts are stated in the judgment.

Colin F. Sara for the plaintiff.
William Crowther Q.C. and *Stephen Archer* for the defendants.

Cur. adv. vult.

A   July 8, 1980.   LATEY J. read the following judgment.   This is an action
for damages for personal injury.   The plaintiff, for much of his life, has
been a skilled carpenter and joiner employed by others.   In 1965 he set
up his own business specialising in ceiling fixing.   New materials and new
systems were being introduced.   He did well, and, what was just as
important to him as his financial success, he was his own master.

      On March 5, 1975, came the accident which caused the injury to his
B   shoulder and which has given rise to this action.   A trestle platform,
erected by the defendants, from which he was working, collapsed.   There
is no need to go into more detail—liability is accepted by the defendants.
He fell and injured his shoulder.   The injury did not at first appear
serious.   It turned out to be serious and disabling.   He cannot raise his
arm above shoulder level and this continues to be so although a variety
C   of treatments, including surgery, have been carried out.   It has meant the
end of his business, that is his livelihood, since 1975.

      There are three heads of damages.   First, special damages, that is what
he has lost to date.   Secondly, general damages, that is to say compensation for pain, suffering and loss of amenity since the accident to the
present, and in the future.   Thirdly, loss of earnings in the future.   I took
time after the end of the hearing to consider my judgment for this reason:
D   after the accident the plaintiff received unemployment benefit for the
statutory period: when that expired he began to receive, and has continued
to receive, supplementary allowance under the Supplementary Benefit Act
1966: the defendants claim that the amounts, both of unemployment benefit and supplementary allowance, which the plaintiff has received, should
be deducted from the compensation to which he would otherwise be
E   entitled.

      For the plaintiff, it is accepted that as the law stands the amount of
unemployment benefit must be deducted because in Nabi v. British Leyland (U.K.) Ltd. [1980] 1 W.L.R. 529, the Court of Appeal has so laid
down.   Though in that case, the Court of Appeal so held because it was
bound by precedent, but said that the matter should be considered by the
F   House of Lords.   Counsel for the plaintiff, Mr. Sara, informed me that
inquiries had been made and that there was not going to be an appeal in
that case to the House of Lords.   He said that were it open to him he
would argue that that decision, and earlier cases which the Court of
Appeal had felt bound to follow, were wrongly decided and that unemployment benefit should not be deducted.   But the Court of Appeal has never
been called upon to decide whether supplementary allowance, and its
G   predecessor national assistance, should or should not be deducted.   That
question has fallen to be considered at first instance in the High Court.
It has been differently decided by different judges.   Unfortunately, in
some of these cases there is a report only of the conclusion and not of the
reasons.

      In this case the amount of supplementary allowance is a substantial
H   amount, £3,424, and whether or not it should be deducted from the
damages to which the plaintiff would otherwise be entitled is of importance
both to him and the defendants.   Counsel have advanced their arguments
on the point fully and helpfully and I think it is convenient to decide
that matter first.   It is unfortunate that it has not been decided by the
Court of Appeal so that all concerned know where they stand. Counsel
think, I suspect rightly, that in many cases the amount at stake in each
is not sufficient to justify the expense of an appeal.   They further think

834

that in the aggregate of cases over a year a large amount of money is A
at stake. As already mentioned, in *Nabi's* case the Court of Appeal gave
a clear indication that the question whether or not unemployment benefit
should be deducted should be considered by the House of Lords. After
hearing the full and careful arguments by counsel in the instant case and
the review of such authorities as there are, one hopes that there will soon
be a suitable case taken to the House of Lords for a decision both as to
unemployment benefit and supplementary allowance in this context, so B
that the existing judicial doubts and dichotomy may be resolved.

In *Parsons* v. *B. N. M. Laboratories Ltd.* [1964] 1 Q.B. 95, the question for present purposes was whether the damages should be reduced by
the amount of unemployment benefit which the plaintiff had received.
The Court of Appeal held that they should. Pearson L.J. posed the
question in this form, at p. 141: C

"Are the sums of unemployment benefit received by the plaintiff
to be brought into account in reduction of the damages for wrongful
dismissal, or are they too remote to be brought into account for this
purpose?"

The answer to that question, at pp. 143–144, is in these terms:
D
"The common-sense answer is that of course it is not too remote.
It is not 'completely collateral.' The dismissal caused the plaintiff
to become unemployed, and therefore entitled, as a matter of general
right under the system of state insurance and not by virtue of any
private insurance policy of his own, to receive unemployment benefit.
The effect of the dismissal was not to deprive him of all income but
to reduce his income by substituting unemployment benefit for his E
salary. It would be unrealistic to disregard the unemployment benefit,
because to do so would confer on the plaintiff . . . a fortuitous
windfall in addition to compensation."

In this context is there any real distinction to be drawn between
unemployment benefit, which ceases after the prescribed period has
expired, and supplementary allowance, or its predecessor national assis- F
tance, which begins after unemployment benefit ceases? Were the matter
at large, my view would have been, and, anticipating, is, that there is no
valid distinction, but other judges have reached the contrary view. In
Eldrige v. *Videtta* (1964) 108 S.J. 137, Veale J. held that national assistance
benefit should not be deducted from the special damages. The report is
a very short one. The case was decided on February 3, 1964. Whether G
Veale J. was referred to the decision of the Court of Appeal in *Parson's*
case does not appear. He is reported as saying that no authority justifying
the deduction of national assistance benefit had been cited to him. Such
a deduction appeared to be wrong in principle and he was not prepared
to make it.

In *Foxley* v. *Olton* [1965] 2 Q.B. 306, John Stephenson J. held that
national assistance grants were not deductible from the damages. He H
observed, at p. 312: "It is difficult to draw the line between what is too
remote and what is not remote enough, and between the collateral and
the completely collateral." He held that the national assistance grants
were too collateral and remote because of the discretionary nature of
those grants. It is to be observed that unlike national assistance grants,
supplementary allowances are not discretionary. A qualifying recipient
is entitled to them as of right. Anticipating my own concluded view,

A unemployment benefit is receivable as of right: provided the claimant
is otherwise qualified, as this plaintiff has been, he is entitled to supplementary allowances as of right. If unemployment benefit is a deduction
from damages, how can supplementary benefit not be? I can see no
grounds for distinguishing one from the other in this context.

In *Parry* v. *Cleaver* [1970] A.C. 1, the plaintiff was a police constable.
He had made compulsory contributions to a police pension fund which
B entitled him as of right to a pension, on being discharged from the force,
for disablement. He was severely injured by a motor car driven negligently
by the defendant and he was discharged owing to disablement resulting
from his injuries. The House of Lords by a majority of three to two,
held that the police pension should be ignored in assessing the damages
under the head of financial loss. In his speech Lord Reid said, at p. 14:

C   " It would be revolting to the ordinary man's sense of justice, and
     therefore contrary to public policy, that the sufferer should have his
     damages reduced so that he would gain nothing from the benevolence
     of his friends or relations or of the public at large, and that the only
     gainer would be the wrongdoer. We do not have to decide in this
     case whether these considerations also apply to public benevolence
D   in the shape of various uncovenanted benefits from the welfare state,
     but it may be thought that Parliament did not intend them to be
     for the benefit of the wrongdoer."

And, after referring to *Foxley* v. *Olton* [1965] 2 Q.B. 306 and *Eldrige* v.
Videtta, 108 S.J. 137 he said, at p. 19:

     " I find it difficult to draw a distinction between unemployment benefit
E   and national assistance. The former could be regarded as a com-
     bination of insurance and national benevolence while the insurance
     element is absent from the latter. But there are here other considera-
     tions beside those with which I have dealt. There has been no full
     argument about them and I do not propose to express any concluded
     opinion on this matter."

F Those dicta of Lord Reid were obiter, but coming from such a source
they of course merit the most careful consideration and it is upon the
tenor of them that Mr. Sara founds the main thrust of his argument.

In *Basnett* v. *J. & A. Jackson Ltd.* [1976] I.C.R. 63, the plaintiff was
made redundant and received a redundancy payment. He further received
unemployment benefit and, after that, supplementary benefit. The defendants accepted that the plaintiff was wrongly dismissed and most of the
G judgment is devoted to the argument whether or not the redundancy payment should be deducted from the damages. It was not apparently drawn
to Crichton J.'s attention that while national assistance grants were discretionary, supplementary benefit allowances are not. Crichton J. followed
what John Stephenson J. said in *Foxley* v. *Olton* [1965] 2 Q.B. 306 and
held that the amount of the supplementary benefits should not be deducted
H from the damages.

In *Cackett* v. *Earl,* The Times, October 15, 1976, the report merely
records that Milmo J. in a claim for damages for personal injuries held
that unemployment benefit, industrial rehabilitation allowance and supplementary benefits must all be deducted. Hollings J.'s decision in *Shaw* v.
Insulation Co. Ltd. was decided in July 1977. It has not apparently been
reported but part of his judgment is quoted in *Nabi* v. *British Leyland
(U.K.) Ltd.* [1980] 1 W.L.R. 529, 537. Hollings J. held that unemploy-

ment benefit should be deducted but that supplementary benefits should A
not. In the passage quoted he says that he will quote briefly his reasons
for the distinction but the statement of those reasons is not quoted. *Nabi*
v. *British Leyland (U.K.) Ltd.* [1980] 1 W.L.R. 529 was concerned only
with the question whether unemployment benefit should be deducted, and
in their judgment their Lordships expressed no view about supplementary
benefit allowances.

 Those are the authorities to which counsel referred. Mr. Sara, for B
the plaintiff, contended that a distinction might be made on the ground that
there are contributions from both employer and employee in the nature of
insurance in the case of unemployment benefit, whereas supplementary
benefits are not directly linked to any contribution made by employer and
employee. Yes, says Mr. Crowther, for the defendants, but supplementary
benefits come from public funds, to which both plaintiff and defendants C
contribute as taxpayers. Mr. Sara accepted realistically that it is difficult
to distinguish between unemployment benefit and supplementary benefit
in any way which can matter in this context. His main argument was
along these lines: Lord Reid's observations in *Parry* v. *Cleaver* [1970]
A.C. 1 suggest that were the deductibility of unemployment benefit,
national assistance, and supplementary benefits, payments from public
benevolence to be considered in the House of Lords, the decision would D
probably be that they should not be deducted. There are similar indications, he says, in the judgment of the Court of Appeal in *Nabi* v. *British
Leyland (U.K.) Ltd.* [1980] 1 W.L.R. 529. Accepting, as he must, that
at the levels of a court of first instance and of the Court of Appeal,
unemployment benefit must be deducted, there is no such binding decision
regarding supplementary allowance, and so, he argues, the court can and E
should follow the indications of Lord Reid and the Court of Appeal and
not deduct supplementary allowances; and of course he urges that other
judges have taken this view, though one, Milmo J., has not. I cannot
myself accept this argument. Lord Reid's indications are no more than
indications and he points out that the matter was not fully argued in the
House. In *Nabi's* case the Court of Appeal go no further than suggesting
that the point is ripe for decision by the House of Lords, as no doubt it F
is, in view of the dichotomy which has developed.

 At first instance if one kind of benefit, unemployment, must be
deducted, so, in my opinon, must the other, supplementary, unless the
character of the one is different from the other in the relevant context of
damages. I have been unable to discern any such difference in character
explained in the reported cases, nor have counsel in the instant case been G
able to suggest any. Indeed, in my respectful opinion, there was no such
difference of character between unemployment benefit and national assistance. To adopt the words of Pearson L.J. in *Parsons* v. *B.N.M. Laboratories Ltd.* [1964] 1 Q.B. 95, 143, " neither is too remote or completely
collateral." Moreover after hearing counsel's very full and careful arguments I am by no means persuaded that it is probable that the House of
Lords would decide that these payments of either kind should not be H
deducted. Leaving aside exemplary damages to which essentially different
considerations apply, the purpose of damages is to compensate the victim
for what he has suffered and lost as a result of the tortious act of the
tortfeasor. It is not to fine the tortfeasor: it is not to put the victim in a
better position than he would have been had there been no tortious act:
it is to put him in the same position he would have been in had there been
no tortious act. Unless the payments concerned are deducted he would

A be in a better position than if there had been no tortious act. I add, parenthetically, that very different considerations apply in the case of a pension or charitable gifts or the like. As Mr. Crowther cogently put it, " Would it be unfair to the plaintiff to deduct these payments? " Not in the slightest. From one source or another he has received all the compensation to which he is entitled to put him in the position he would have been had the accident not occurred. Is it unfair to him not to confer on

B him a windfall profit? Why should he receive double compensation?

For these reasons in my judgment, the payments of supplementary allowance as well as those of unemployment benefit should be deducted from the otherwise agreed figure of special damages. Parenthetically, I suppose yet another and perhaps wholly acceptable solution might be for the tortfeasor to pay the full amount and, when the amounts were met,

C the benefits to be repaid to public funds. But that would require legislation.

[His Lordship assessed general damages, future loss of earnings, and, having made the appropriate deductions from the agreed figure of special damages, gave judgment for £27,206·70 with interest and costs.]

Judgment for the plaintiff for
£27,206·70 with costs.

D

Solicitors: *James Mason, Tucker & Son, Newton Abbot; Ashford, Sparkes & Harward, Exeter.*

M. B. D.

E

[HOUSE OF LORDS]

* CLOWSER   .   .   .   .   APPELLANT

AND

CHAPLIN   .   .   .   .   RESPONDENT

F

FINNIGAN   .   .   .   .   APPELLANT

AND

SANDIFORD   .   .   .   .   RESPONDENT

1981   April 13;   Lord Hailsham of St. Marylebone L.C.,
       May 14   Lord Diplock, Lord Keith of Kinkel,
G   Lord Scarman and Lord Roskill

Road Traffic—Arrest—Validity—Breath test—Police officers acting lawfully when requesting motorist to provide specimen of breath — Motorist refusing to provide specimen — Officers entering without permission on motorist's property to arrest for such refusal—Whether arrest unlawful—Whether invali-
H *dating subsequent request for specimen—Road Traffic Act 1972 (c. 20), s. 8 (5)* [1]

The power to arrest without warrant conferred by section 8 (5) of the Road Traffic Act 1972 on a constable does not

[1] Road Traffic Act 1972, s. 8 (5): " If a person required by a constable under subsection (1) or (2) above to provide a specimen of breath for a breath test fails to do so and the constable has reasonable cause to suspect him of having alcohol in his body, the constable may arrest him without warrant except when he is at a hospital as a patient."

838

authorise him to enter private premises as a trespasser for the   A
purpose of arresting a person from whom he has lawfully
required a specimen of breath under subsection (1) or (2) of
the section and who has failed to provide one.
    Morris v. *Beardmore* [1980] 3 W.L.R. 283, H.L.(E.)
applied.

The following case was referred to in the opinions: B
Morris v. *Beardmore* [1980] 3 W.L.R. 283; [1980] 2 W.L.R. 753,
    H.L.(E.).

The following additional cases were cited in argument:
Davis v. *Lisle* [1936] 2 K.B. 434; [1936] 2 All E.R. 213, D.C.
Reg. v. *Porter* [1973] 1 W.L.R. 866; [1973] 2 All E.R. 800, H.L.(E.).
Reg. v. *Waterfield* [1964] 1 Q.B. 164; [1963] 3 W.L.R. 946; [1963] 3   C
    All E.R. 659, C.C.A.
Swales v. *Cox* [1981] 2 W.L.R. 814; [1981] 1 All E.R. 1115, D.C.

APPEALS from the Divisional Court of the Queen's Bench Division.

CLOWSER v. CHAPLIN

The defendant, Clive Norman Chaplin, was the driver of a motor car   D
involved in a collision at Brighton at 9 p.m. on May 18, 1980. At 10 p.m.
two police constables entered the private driveway of the residence, rang
the door bell, which was answered by his wife and asked to speak to him.
She told them they were not allowed into the house and must wait at the
door which was then closed. Eventually the defendant appeared and
acknowedged that he was the driver of the car in question. One of the   E
constables having requested him to give a specimen of breath, he twice
refused, stating that he was in his own house and the constables had no
power to act. He then started to retreat into the hallway. One of the
constables reached out to prevent him from withdrawing stating that he
was being arrested for refusing to supply a specimen of breath. A struggle
ensued in the hallway and finally the defendant was taken to the police
station. At the police station the police went through the correct breath-   F
alyser procedure but the defendant failed to provide a specimen of blood
or urine. He was charged with failing to provide a specimen of breath
for a breath test contrary to section 8 (3) of the Road Traffic Act 1972
and also with failing to provide a specimen of blood or urine contrary to
section 9 (3) of the Act.

At Brighton Magistrates' Court on August 14, 1980, the justices dis-   G
missed the informations on the ground that the constables had unlawfully
entered on the defendant's land and the arrest was therefore unlawful.

On appeal by way of case stated by the prosecutor, Bruce John
Clowser, a detective constable of the Sussex Constabulary, the Divisional
Court of the Queen's Bench Division (Donaldson L.J. and Bingham J.)
dismissed the appeal. Donaldson L.J. reading the reserved judgment of the
court, on February 20, 1981, said that *Morris* v. *Beardmore* [1980] 3   H
W.L.R. 283 decided that in enacting the relevant part of the Road Traffic
Act 1972 Parliament did not intend to authorise a constable to require a
specimen of breath when he himself was acting unlawfully by trespassing
on the defendant's property. The reason underlying their Lordships'
speeches was that Parliament should not be presumed to have authorised
any greater invasion of privacy than was expressly mentioned and that no
right of entry was to be inferred when none was granted. As regarded the

A charge under section 8 (3), Parliament intended the constable's authority
or lack of authority to be determined once and for all in the circumstances
prevailing when the request for a specimen was made. The defendant
had no lawful excuse for failing to provide a specimen of breath since the
request was lawful and he should have been convicted on that charge.
As regarded the charge under section 9 (3), the constable had no right to
enter the defendant's house even though he had refused to comply with
B the lawful request for a specimen of breath and the constable was a
trespasser when he arrested him. Therefore the justices were right to
dismiss the charge under section 9 (3).

FINNIGAN *v.* SANDIFORD

C   On May 10, 1980, the defendant, Anthony Victor Sandiford, drove a
motor car in excess of the speed limit at Ellesmere Port. At the time
he had consumed alcohol in excess of the prescribed limit. He failed to
provide a specimen of breath following a lawful request to do so made by
a police sergeant at the door of his home. The sergeant entered his home
without permission and, while a trespasser, arrested him. On September 16,
1980, at Ellesmere Port Magistrates' Court the defendant was charged with
D driving a motor car having consumed alcohol in such quantity that the
proportion thereof in his blood exceeded the prescribed limit contrary to
section 6 (1) of the Road Traffic Act 1972. The justices dismissed the
information on the ground that the sergeant was a trespasser at the time
of effecting the arrest, which was therefore unlawful.
       On appeal by the prosecutor Dennis Finnigan, an inspector of the
Cheshire Constabulary, by way of case stated, the Divisional Court of the
E Queen's Bench Division (Donaldson L.J. and Bingham J.) held, on
February 20, 1981, that since in *Clowser* v. *Chaplin* the court had just
decided that a constable was not empowered to enter a house without
invitation and as a trespasser to effect an arrest under section 8 (5) of the
Road Traffic Act 1972, following a failure to provide a specimen of breath,
it followed that that appeal also had to be dismissed.
F   The respective prosecutors in both cases appealed to the House of Lords.

   Desmond Fennell Q.C. and *Richard Carr* for the appellant, Clowser.
   Desmond Fennell Q.C. and *Roger Bell* for the appellant, Finnigan.
   Michael Beckman Q.C. and *Charles Taylor* for the respondent, Clive
Norman Chaplin.
   B. A. Hytner Q.C. and *D. M. Evans* for the respondent, Anthony
G Victor Sandiford.

   Their Lordships took time for consideration.

   May 14. LORD HAILSHAM OF ST. MARYLEBONE L.C. My Lords,
having read in draft the opinion about to be delivered by my noble and
H learned friend, Lord Keith of Kinkel, I find its reasoning to be unanswerable, and it therefore follows that, for the reasons he gives, these two
appeals must be dismissed. Whether, from the point of view of policy,
the results of these or several of the earlier decisions arrived at by the courts
under the peculiar jurisprudence of the breathalyser are desirable in the
public interest is something which only Parliament in its legislative capacity
can now determine.
   In my view, the analysis of the law contained in the speeches in *Morris*

840

v. *Beardmore* [1980] 3 W.L.R. 283 is clearly correct, and I agree with A
my noble and learned friend that this analysis implies a general principle,
and that the exact point in these appeals, although technically left open in
Morris v. *Beardmore,* is covered by that principle. The conclusion is
therefore inescapable.

LORD DIPLOCK. My Lords, the reasoning in the speech of Lord Keith
of Kinkel, which I find unanswerable, leads ineluctably to the conclusion B
that once again the way in which the " breathalyser " provisions of the
Road Traffic Act 1972 are drafted has enabled motorists to " cock a
snook " at the law. These provisions, at first enacted in the Road Safety
Act 1967, were controversial. They represented a novel intrusion on the
liberty of the motorist to drive a potentially lethal vehicle on a public
road when there was a risk that his judgment or co-ordination had been C
impaired by the alcohol he had consumed; and consequently the means
available to a constable to ascertain whether such was the case were hedged
around with restrictions. The many loop-holes in the law that the ingenuity
of defence lawyers has brought to light are, in my view, doing more to
bring the criminal law of this country into disrepute than any other legislation. The revision of the " breathalyser " provisions is under consideration
in the Transport Bill now before Parliament. It is for Parliament to make D
up its mind whether it wants this lamentable state of affairs to continue.

LORD KEITH OF KINKEL. My Lords, these appeals represent a sequel
to the decision of this House in *Morris* v. *Beardmore* [1980] 3 W.L.R.
283. It was there held, upon a consideration of section 8 (2) of the Road
Traffic Act 1972, that Parliament had not thereby authorised a police E
constable in uniform lawfully to require a person to undergo a breath test
under circumstances where the constable was in a position to make the
requirement only because he was present, without any right to be so, upon
premises occupied by the person concerned. Accordingly, a person who
refused to comply with a requirement made under such circumstances was
not guilty of an offence under section 8 (3).

The two instant cases present the common feature that in each of them F
the requirement to undergo a breath test was lawfully made. In Mr.
Sandiford's case it was made under section 8 (1) and in Mr. Chaplin's
case under section 8 (2). The police officer in each case was lawfully
present just outside the main door of the defendant's dwelling house, and
the defendant was standing just inside the main door. The defendant
heard and understood the requirement, but he refused to comply with it and
retreated further inside the house. Police officers advanced inside after the G
defendant, although they had no permission to enter the house, arrested
him, and took him to a police station. Mr. Sandiford there supplied a
specimen of blood which proved positive, and in due course he was
charged with a contravention of section 6 (1) of the Act of 1972. Mr.
Chaplin, having subsequently refused to supply a specimen of blood or
urine for a laboratory test, was charged with offences under section 8 (3) H
and 9 (3) of the Act. In each case the justices dismissed the information
upon the ground that the arrest of the defendant, following his refusal to
undergo a breath test, was unlawful. The respective prosecutors appealed
by way of stated case, and both appeals came before a Divisional Court
consisting of Donaldson L.J. and Bingham J. As regards Mr. Chaplin's
appeal, they held that he should have been convicted of the offence under
section 8, in respect that nothing which happened after his failure to com-

A ply with the requirement to undergo a breath test invalidated the legality of the requirement, but they dismissed the appeal in respect of the section 9 charge, upon the ground that the police officers were trespassing in Mr. Chaplin's house where they arrested him, and that this invalidated all that followed. The court dismissed the appeal in Mr. Sandiford's case for the same reason.

B In relation to each appeal the Divisional Court, while refusing leave to the prosecutor to appeal to this House, certified that their decision involved the following point of law of general importance:

"Whether a constable in uniform who is lawfully within the curtilage of a house and at the door of such premises being the home of a person to whom the constable makes a lawful requirement for a specimen of breath pursuant to section 8 (1) " section 8 (2) in Mr. Chaplin's case
C " Road Traffic Act 1972 is empowered to enter the said house without invitation and as a trespasser and effect an arrest under section 8 (5) Road Traffic Act 1972 following a failure to provide a specimen of breath."

In connection with the appeal in Mr. Chaplin's case the Divisional Court certified a further question relating to the effect upon the legality of the
D requirement to undergo a breath test of excessive force employed by the police officers in arresting Mr. Chaplin. In view of the course which the hearing upon the main question followed before your Lordships, no argument was advanced upon this second question, and it need not be considered.

So the only issue which your Lordships have to decide turns upon the
E proper construction of section 8 (5) of the Act of 1972, which provides:

"If a person required by a constable under subsection (1) or (2) above to provide a specimen of breath for a breath test fails to do so and the constable has reasonable cause to suspect him of having alcohol in his body, the constable may arrest him without warrant except while he is at a hospital as a patient."

F The procedures described by section 9 of the Act as regards the making of a requirement to provide a specimen of blood or urine for laboratory test, which upon compliance may lead to a charge under section 6 (1) or, upon non-compliance, to a charge under section 9 (3), are applicable only to a person who has been arrested under section 8 (or possibly under section 5 (5), relating to driving when unfit to drive through drink or drugs). It
G follows that, if a person has not been lawfully arrested under the relevant enactment, the section 9 procedures cannot validly be applied to him and the results of the purported application are inept to form the basis of any conviction. Counsel for the appellants, quite rightly, made no attempt to argue the contrary. The question accordingly comes to be whether the power to arrest without warrant conferred by section 8 (5) carries with it the power lawfully to enter, by force if need be, the dwelling house of the
H person whom it is intended to arrest, for the purpose of carrying out that intention.

It may confidently be stated as a matter of general principle that the mere conferment by statute of a power to arrest without warrant in given circumstances does not carry with it any power to enter private premises without the permission of the occupier, forcibly or otherwise. Section 2 of the Criminal Law Act 1967 creates a category of " arrestable offences " in respect of which the power of arrest without warrant may be exercised.

Such offences are extremely serious, being those punishable by five years' **A**
imprisonment on first conviction, and attempts thereat. Subsection (6)
specifically provides:

> " For the purpose of arresting a person under any power conferred
> by this section a constable may enter (if need be, by force) and search
> any place where that person is or where the constable, with reasonable
> cause, suspects him to be."
B

Apart from the category of arrestable offences, there are a considerable
number of instances where a specific power of arrest without warrant is
conferred in relation to particular statutory offences. In some instances
power of entry is also conferred, for example by section 50 (2) of the
Firearms Act 1968. In a great many others, no power of entry is conferred.
The proper inference, in my opinion, is that where Parliament considers it **C**
appropriate that a power of arrest without warrant should be reinforced
by a power to enter private premises, it is in the habit of saying so
specifically, and that the omission of any such specific power is deliberate.
It would rarely, if ever, be possible to conclude that the power had been
conferred by implication. Counsel for the appellants maintained that in
the present case such an implication was properly to be drawn from the
circumstance that the penalty under section 8 (3) for failing to provide a **D**
specimen of breath was a minor one compared with that under section 9 (3)
for failing to provide a specimen of blood or urine, or under section 6 (1)
in the event of the specimen proving positive. It was therefore to be
inferred, so it was argued, that Parliament did not contemplate the
possibility of any interruption in the sequence of events from the making
of a lawful requirement for a breath test to the formulation of charges **E**
under section 6 (1) or section 9 (3). But that consideration does not offer
any sufficient foundation for the implication claimed to be necessary.
There can be no question of the legislative scheme being unworkable in its
absence. It is also to be observed that, as noticed above, section 9 is tied
in with section 5 (5) as well as with section 8 (5). It would be strange if
the latter were held to confer power to enter for the purpose of effecting
an arrest, but not the former. The proper conclusion, in my opinion, is **F**
that Parliament did not intend to confer such power in either case.

This conclusion is consistent with the principle upon which the decision
in *Morris* v. *Beardmore* [1980] 3 W.L.R. 283 proceeded, namely that in
this particular piece of legislation Parliament cannot be taken to have
authorised any further inroads upon the rights of individual citizens than
it specifically enacted. The conclusion does, however, have a wider signi- **G**
ficance, in respect that it must be of general application in cases where a
statute has conferred a power of arrest without warrant, but no specific
power of entry on private premises for the purpose of effecting the arrest.

My Lords, for these reasons I would deal with each of these appeals by
answering the certified question in the negative and dismissing the appeal.

LORD SCARMAN. My Lords, I have had the advantage of reading in **H**
draft the speech delivered by my noble and learned friend, Lord Keith of
Kinkel. I agree with it, and would dismiss each appeal. I also agree with
his comment that the House's conclusion has a wider significance than the
mere interpretation of section 8 (5) of the Road Traffic Act 1972. It is
that, as a general rule, the courts will not construe an enactment conferring
a power of arrest without warrant as impliedly authorising a power of entry
into private premises for the purpose of effecting the arrest. If it be

A Parliament's intention to confer a power of entry, the draftsman must ensure that the power is expressly conferred. Parliament is not to be presumed, in the absence of express words, so to intend, unless the implication is irresistible, which would be rare indeed.

B LORD ROSKILL. My Lords, I too have had the advantage of reading in draft the speech of my noble and learned friend, Lord Keith of Kinkel. For the reasons which are there set out, I agree that these appeals must be dismissed. It would seem that the problems to which the decision of your Lordships' House in *Morris* v. *Beardmore* [1980] 3 W.L.R. 283 and the instant appeals have given rise had not previously been appreciated. I venture to echo the hope that in the light of these decisions the matter may now be reviewed by Parliament.

C *Appeals dismissed.*

Solicitors: *Sharpe, Pritchard & Co. for T. Lavelle, Lewes; Sharpe, Pritchard & Co. for E. C. Woodcock, Chester; David M. Laing & Co., Brighton; Kenwright & Cox for Blain, Boland & Co., Ellesmere Port.*

D F. C.

E [CHANCERY DIVISION]

* *In re* MARQUESS OF ABERGAVENNY'S ESTATE ACT TRUSTS

MARQUESS OF ABERGAVENNY *v.* RAM AND ANOTHER

[1980 A. No. 2266]

F 1980 Dec. 2   Goulding J.

Trusts—Distribution of fund—Appropriation to beneficiary—Life tenant's entitlement to one half—Half share paid to life tenant —Retained half share appreciating in value—Whether trustees having power to make further appropriation—Marquess of Abergavenny's Estate Act 1946 (9 & 10 Geo. 6, c. 1), Sch. 7,
G *Pt. I, para. 2 (ii)*

By the Marquess of Abergavenny's Estate Act 1946, trustees were directed to hold a settled fund on trust for the plaintiff as tenant for life with remainders over in strict settlement and an ultimate remainder to the plaintiff himself. The trustees were given a wide continuing discretionary power to raise and pay to the plaintiff or any other life tenant from time to time
H during his life, and on his written request, " any part or parts not exceeding in all one half in value of the settled fund of which he becomes tenant for life in possession." For that purpose, the trustees could " compute and decide the value of the settled fund or any part thereof " as they thought proper. In 1965 the trustees exercised their power to its full extent in favour of the plaintiff. Since then, the money value of the retained half share of the fund had considerably appreciated, partly because they had bought from the plaintiff the family estate which had gone up in value.

In re Abergavenny (Ch.D.)   **[1981]**

On the question whether the discretionary power given to   A
the trustees by the Act of 1946 would enable them to make
further payments to the plaintiff on an upward revaluation of
the settled fund:—

Held, that the only true conclusion from the evidence put
in by the plaintiff was that the half share of the assets already
paid out under the terms of the power given to the trustees
represented the full extent of what the settlor had authorised,
and therefore no further exercise of their power in favour of   B
the plaintiff on an appreciation of assets was possible (post,
pp. 847B, F).

In re Richardson [1896] 1 Ch. 512 and *In re Gollin's
Declaration of Trust* [1969] 1 W.L.R. 1858 considered.

The following cases are referred to in the judgment:

Gollin's Declaration of Trust, In re [1969] 1 W.L.R. 1858; [1969] 3 All   C
    E.R. 1591.
Richardson, In re [1896] 1 Ch. 512.

No additional cases were cited in argument.

ORIGINATING SUMMONS

By summons dated June 2, 1980, the plaintiff, John Henry Guy, the   D
Marquess of Abergavennny, tenant for life under the trusts declared by
Part I of Schedule 7 to the Marquess of Abergavenny's Estate Act 1946,
sought determination by the court of the question whether, on the true
construction of the trust's powers and provisions contained in Schedule 7
to the Act, and in the events which had happened (*a*) the defendants,
Edward David Abel Ram and Anthony West Ponder, the trustees of the
trusts, could, upon an upward revaluation of the assets comprised in the   E
trust fund, exercise further in favour of the plaintiff their discretionary
power to raise and pay to him any part or parts of the trust fund; or (*b*)
the power had already been exercised to the full.

The facts are stated in the judgment.

M. C. B. Buckley for the plaintiff.   F
R. H. W. Marten for the defendant trustees.

GOULDING J. The Marquess of Abergavenny's Estate Act 1946 c. 1
of the personal Acts of Parliament of that year, was enacted on a bill
which was prepared, as I believe, by the most eminent draftsman of his
day. I also have reason to believe that he regarded the bill as one of his
choicest pieces of work. Nevertheless, such is the difficulty of the con-   G
veyancer's art, the variety of supervening events, and the ingenuity of
the learned, that I have before me today a short question of construction
upon one of the provisions contained in the statute.

The orginating summons on which I am now giving judgment was
taken out by the present Lord Abergavenny, who was Earl of Lewes at
the time the statute was passed. The defendants to the summons are the   H
present trustees of a certain settlement provided for thereby. Lord Abergavenny himself is tenant for life of the settled property.

I go at once to the relevant legislative provisions. The Act of 1946
removed from the family estates an unbarrable statutory entail dating
from Tudor times and it made a number of provisions for members of
the Nevill family. By section 5 of the Act the then trustees for the
purposes of the Settled Land Act 1925 of the settlement of the entailed

A　estate were directed by sale, mortgage or other means to raise certain sums of money, one of which was a sum of £230,000 referred to in Part IV of Schedule 4 to the Act of 1946. The trustees were by the same section directed to hold that sum on the trusts and with and subject to the powers and provisions set forth in Schedule 7 to the Act. Reference to Schedule 7 shows that the said sum of £230,000 is governed by trusts, powers and provisions set out in Part I of Schedule 7. The first trust is

B　for the plaintiff during his life with remainders over in strict settlement and an ultimate remainder to the plaintiff himself. Then there are a number of provisos, of which the one that has given rise to the present question is set out in paragraph 2 (ii). It provides:

C　" In the case of each tenant for life for the time being in possession under the foregoing trusts the trustees of the settlement shall have power in their discretion from time to time during his life and upon his request in writing to raise and pay to him for his own use and benefit any part or parts not exceeding in all one half in value of the settled fund of which he becomes tenant for life in possession. And they may for that purpose compute and decide the value of the settled fund or any part thereof in such manner and upon such

D　evidence as they shall think proper; . . ."

I should have said that the expression " the settled fund " is defined near the beginning of Schedule 7 as meaning the sum of £230,000 or the investments and property for the time being representing it.

In 1965 the trustees of the settled fund determined to exercise their power under paragraph 2 (ii) to its full extent in favour of Lord Aber-

E　gavenny. They took into account certain payments or transfers of assets that had already been made to him in exercise of the power. No question arises as to the values they put on such previously released assets. Nor does any question arise as to the figure which in 1965 they determined would represent the balance of one half share of the settled fund. Nor is it in doubt that in that year, or at any rate very shortly afterwards,

F　Lord Abergavenny received such balance to the full. However, the money value of the retained fund, after giving Lord Abergavenny a half at the time I have mentioned, has very considerably appreciated. The trustees subsequently bought the family landed estate from Lord Abergavenny and, like most land in the south of England, it has gone up a great deal in value. Accordingly, the suggestion is made on behalf of the plaintiff that the trustees, if in their discretion they think fit, should

G　now make over to him a sufficient part of the assets in their hands to bring him up to half the sum of the present value of the property retained by the trustees in 1965 (or what now represents it) plus the value in 1965 put on the half share then made over to the plaintiff himself. The trustees say that they would be minded to make at any rate some further payment to the plaintiff if the court thinks they have power to do so.

H　It is well known to those who advise on family trusts that a variety of accounting problems arise where there is a power of appointment or advancement exercisable over a fund of fluctuating value and limited by a fractional maximum. It is difficult to lay down any general principles that will solve all such problems. No doubt the learned draftsman of the bill for the Act of 1946 felt that he had done the best he could by giving the trustees a wide discretionary power to compute and decide the value of the settled fund or any part thereof in such manner and on such evidence

846

as they should think proper when exercising their power to benefit the A
tenant for life. However, it is not suggested on either side that that discretionary power of valuation enables the trustees to decide the question
of construction that is now placed before me.

The point is a short one. It is not, so far as the researches of counsel
have revealed, the subject of any express judicial authority. Mr. Buckley
for the plaintiff, Lord Abergavenny, has referred me to cases that he
submits are applicable by analogy, namely, cases where appropriation is B
necessary to constitute a fractional share of a fund and a partial appropriation has been made in the first place. There the approved practice
is, when the balance of the share comes to be appropriated, to require
the beneficiary to bring in what he has previously received at a money
valuation as at the date when it was previously allocated to him. That is
brought into account and the fund still retained by the trustees or other C
holders of the fund is valued as at the date of the further appropriation.
The cases cited to illustrate that principle are *In re Richardson* [1896]
1 Ch. 512, a decision of North J., and *In re Gollin's Declaration of Trust*
[1969] 1 W.L.R. 1858, decided by Buckley J. The principle regarding
successive appropriations being as I have stated, Mr. Buckley says that
it really should make no difference whether a limit has been completely D
reached or nearly reached. If the remainder of the fund appreciates,
why should the person previously paid out be entitled to get his benefit
from it if he has had almost the whole of his share and yet be debarred
from reopening the matter just because the limit has been reached? It
is offensive to logic, Mr. Buckley submits. In the present case, as long
as the remaining assets in the trustees' hands remain in settlement, it
is submitted that Lord Abergavenny should be entitled to come back, E
being himself of course life tenant, see what they are worth, and say
" Well, taking into account what I have already received, I have not had
a half yet; consider giving me some more if you think fit." I put to Mr.
Buckley an illustration suggested to me by *In re Richardson* [1896] 1 Ch.
512 but on much simpler facts: supposing that a testator gives his residue,
half to his son absolutely and half in settlement for his daughter and her F
children, and the son's share is fully paid out in one operation shortly
after the testator's death, would anyone suppose that he could at any time
thereafter during his sister's life require a valuation of the half retained
for her and her children and, if it had appreciated since the original
appropriation, require some more? I think that Mr. Buckley did not
feel able to resist my suggestion that in such a case the son could not
reopen the appropriation, but he did draw a distinction between a simple G
appropriation case and one like the present where there is a continuing
discretionary power, intended to be available for repeated exercise during
the whole of a life. The power here is that the trustees in their discretion may raise and pay assets to Lord Abergavenny, or any other life
tenant, from time to time during his life and on his request in writing.
Another distinction drawn by Mr. Buckley was that in the case I put of H
the appropriation between the two children's shares the son would by
some express receipt, or at any rate by conduct in taking what was given
to him, accept it and agree it as satisfying his whole entitlement under the
residuary bequest, and there is no such requirement at any point, says
Mr. Buckley, in the provisions now under scrutiny. I am not persuaded
by that distinction. Looking at the account which has been put in
evidence by the plaintiff himself to show what was done in 1965, it does

A   seem to me that he must have accepted it in full satisfaction of what could be given to him under the settlement. Had the question been asked at that time I think he would have unhesitatingly agreed. However, that may be thought speculative and I do not put my judgment on it.

    Mr. Hedley Marten for the trustees, although they are sympathetic, as I have said, to Lord Abergavenny's request, has none the less per-

B formed his duty of putting the other side of the argument on construction. He suggests, and I agree, that the only true conclusion from the evidence is that Lord Abergavenny received a full one half of the trust fund as valued in 1965. Then, Mr. Hedley Marten says, as a matter of law, that amounted to an exhaustive exercise of the power which ceased to be exercisable for the future, whatever might happen to the retained assets, that is, whether they went up or down in value. In my judgment

C that is right. I do not think that the authorities on a partial appropriation followed by a supplemental appropriation really assist in the present matter one way or the other. The judges who have had to consider that question have never, so far as I know, had the present point drawn to their attention. Buckley J. said in the *Gollin* case [1969] 1 W.L.R. 1858, 1861 :

D   " I treat the first defendant as having received in specie one-third of the fund in 1947. Having regard to the decision I have reached on the first question in the summons, her entitlement at that time was not one-third of the fund but five-ninths of the fund and that appropriation was insufficient to satisfy her whole absolute entitlement."

E It was against that background that he considered how as a matter of account the first defendant in that case was obliged to bring in what she had previously received. I do not think that on a fair consideration of the questions decided in that and in the earlier *Richardson* case [1896] 1 Ch. 512 they really help the present controversy one way or the other.

    I think myself that the reason why there is no direct authority on the

F question is because the answer has always seemed plain. Any layman, and any lawyer I think, without such special and persuasive advocacy as I have heard this morning, would feel that where there is a power to make successive payments to a person up to a limit of a certain fraction of a fund and at a certain date, he, the beneficiary, has received assets then fully reaching the prescribed limit, thereafter no further exercise of the power is possible. All that the settlor authorised has been done. It

G would be to my mind strange and unexpected if the object of the power as such retained an interest or possibility of interest in the fund still in settlement, so that he could require accounts from the trustees and demand reconsideration of his position whenever there should be an appreciation of assets. It is perfectly true that even in the partial appropriation cases the beneficiary who has received something early may do

H very well because he may keep what has been given to him in some asset that appreciates while he only has to bring a cash sum, fixed once for all, into account; it may of course go the other way. But some such possibility of good or ill fortune is inherent in the very nature of payments made under a duty or a power on successive occasions up to an aggregate limit. There is no reason that I can see why such inequality, or exposure to fortune, should be continued to the possible disadvantage of other beneficiaries after the limit has been reached.

Goulding J.   In re Abergavenny (Ch.D.)   **[1981]**

I have endeavoured to give reasons for my view on what is really a A
very short point and, as I say, it does not seem to me a very difficult one
when one looks at the terms of the power. Accordingly. I must answer
the question asked by the originating summons by declaring that on the
true construction of the Act of 1946 and in the events which have happened the power has already been exercised to the full. Unless anyone
is going to submit the contrary, I should have thought that it was a case
in which the usual order as to costs could be made directing the plain- B
tiff's costs on the common fund basis and the defendants' costs as trustees
to be taxed and to be raised and paid out of the capital of the trust fund.

Orders accordingly.

Solicitor: *Withers.*

                                                                    C

K. N. B.

[QUEEN'S BENCH DIVISION]

                                                                    D

* BARNETT *v.* FRENCH

1980 Dec. 10, 11; 19   Donaldson L.J. and Kilner Brown J.

> *Road Traffic—Tyres—Defects—Vehicle owned by government
> department—Government employee nominated for purpose of
> proceedings relating to government vehicles—Whether crimi- E
> nally liable—Road Traffic Act* 1972 (c. 20), *s.* 188 (8) (9)
> *Crown—Crown vehicles—Road traffic offences—Nominated person
> —Practical advantages in nominating John Doe—Road Traffic
> Act* 1972, *s.* 188 (8)

The defendant was the principal transport officer of the
Department of the Environment with an office in London, and
in overall control of 3,500 vehicles in various parts of the
country. He was nominated under section 188 of the Road F
Traffic Act 1972 [1] as the person responsible for proceedings in
relation to vehicles in the service of the department. One of
the department's vehicles was found parked with a defective
tyre at the side of the road. The driver was an employee of
the department. The defendant, as the department's nominee,
was convicted of using a motor lorry with a worn tyre on the
highway.
        On appeal by the defendant against conviction: — G
        Held, dismissing the appeal, that since it was not shown that
the driver alone was responsible for using the vehicle with a
defective tyre, the defendant, being the nominee under section
188, was deemed by the statute to be the person actually
responsible for so using it, and accordingly the justices were
right to convict him (post, p. 851G–H).
        Per curiam. Pending any change in the law the court can H
see no legal, constitutional or ethical objection and very real
and practical advantages if government departments were to
nominate John Doe under section 188 of the Act of 1972. It
would probably be convenient that service of proceedings
should be accepted on his behalf by the solicitor to the
department concerned or by the Treasury Solicitor (post,
pp. 853H—854B).

[1] Road Traffic Act 1972, s. 188: see post, p. 851B–C.

A   The following cases are referred to in the judgment:

Afromar Inc. v. *Greek Atlantic Cod Fishing Co.* [1980] 2 Lloyd's Rep. 17, C.A.

Levy v. *Levy* (unreported), November 9, 1979, C.A.

The following additional cases were cited in argument:

Crawford v. *Haughton* [1972] 1 W.L.R. 572; [1972] 1 All E.R. 535, D.C.

B   *Garrett* v. *Hooper* [1973] R.T.R. 1, D.C.

CASE STATED by South Molton justices.

On August 1, 1979, an information was preferred by the prosecutor, Anthony Gerald French, against the defendant, H. G. Barnett, that on May 2, 1979, in a certain highway called East Street, South Molton, he did use on the road a motor lorry, the tread pattern of the rear nearside tyre not having a depth of at least one millimetre throughout at least three quarters of the breadth of the tread and round the entire outer circumference of the tyre, contrary to regulation 107 (F) of the Motor Vehicles (Construction and Use) Regulations 1978 and section 40 of the Road Traffic Act 1972. The justices heard the information on Wednesday, November 7, 1979.

D   The defendant contended that he had not been nominated in accordance with section 188 (8) of the Road Traffic Act 1972 and that although he had said to the police officer he was the nominated person, that was not correct since he had not been officially nominated. Further, the nomination in the letter produced was in respect of the case in Nottingham only. He also contended that even if it was held that he was the nominated person he still relied on section 188 (8) of the Road Traffic

E   Act 1972 in that the driver was the responsible person, he being responsible for checking the vehicle for tyres on the day it was in use; and therefore he, the defendant, was not the responsible person. The notice in the vehicle quite clearly instructed the driver regarding his duties in respect of tyres.

The prosecutor contended that it was obvious that the defendant was

F   the person who was to be proceeded against and that was made clear by what he had said to the police officer; the terms of the letter to Nottingham were sufficiently wide to embrace all prosecutions; and the defendant had said he had overall responsibility for all the department's vehicles and he had some 3,500 vehicles under his control. Also it mattered not about the notice in the vehicle. Whereas the driver might have been responsible for driving the vehicle with a defective tyre, equally the defendant

G   was in the same position as any other employer and therefore liable to prosecution for permitting the vehicle to be used in the course of business with a defective tyre.

After hearing the evidence and the arguments advanced on behalf of both the defendant and the prosecutor, the justices made the following findings of fact. The vehicle did have a defective tyre; it was being used

H   on the public highway at the relevant time on the business of the Department of the Environment; and the defendant was the person nominated for the purpose of section 188 (8) of the Road Traffic Act 1972.

The justices found, as a matter of law, that the defendant was in the same position as any other employer accused of that offence and they convicted him, despite the consideration that his employee might well have contributed to the commission of the offence. The justices fined him £15 and ordered him to pay prosecution costs of £20. They did not order the endorsement of the defendant's driving licence, since they found that there were special circumstances which made it inappropriate to do so.

The defendant appealed. The question for the opinion of the High Court was (a) whether on the facts found proved, the justices were correct in ruling that the defendant used the motor vehicle in question and (b) what should be done in those premises.

Simon D. Brown for the defendant.
R. W. G. Threlfall for the prosecutor.

Cur. adv. vult.

December 19. DONALDSON L.J. read the following judgment of the court.

Mr. Barnett is and was the principal transport officer of the Department of the Environment, Property Services Agency, with an office in central London. As such, he is a senior civil servant in overall control of 3,500 vehicles operated by the department in the public service of the Crown. In the nature of things he can have no personal control over these vehicles, which are distributed all over the country.

Now Mr. Barnett has a grievance and, in our judgment, it is a very legitimate grievance. Solely because of the position which he holds, he is at risk of becoming the citizen with the longest record of motoring convictions ever known. Indeed he has made a start, for on November 7, 1979, he was convicted by the justices of the petty sessional division of South Molton in the County of Devon. The offence was one of using a motor lorry on the highway when one tyre was worn and defective contrary to regulation 107 (*f*) of the Motor Vehicles (Construction and Use) Regulations 1978 and section 40 of the Road Traffic Act 1972. He was fined £15 and ordered to pay £20 towards the costs of the prosecution. Happily the justices refrained from also ordering an endorsement of his driving licence. Had they done so, he might have had difficulty in explaining to any court which subsequently convicted him that it " did not count " when it was there on his driving licence for all to see. And were it to happen on three or more occasions within two years, he would risk the loss of his licence. He now appeals by way of case stated.

The facts can be simply stated. The Public Services Agency has duties throughout the country and its vehicles operate out of different bases. The particular vehicle concerned in this offence operated out of Bristol where there were three supervisory officers of different grades, some or all of whom might have been expected to have had close control over the state of this vehicle's tyres. In addition, every vehicle carried a notice in the cab reminding the driver that it was his duty to report any tyres which might be defective. However, on May 2, 1979, one of these vehicles was stopped on the road by the police and its rear nearside tyre was found to have less than the minimum tread required by the law. In such circumstances either or both the driver and the owner of the vehicle may be guilty of an offence. But Mr. Barnett was neither. The driver was Mr. Lewis, who was in fact warned that he might be prosecuted, although no prosecution took place. The owner was not Mr. Barnett but the Crown which, for historic, constitutional and procedural reasons can never be prosecuted.

It was no doubt Parliament's recognition of the immunity of the Crown from prosecution, coupled with an understandable wish that

A   " government " should not be able to offend against the law with impunity, which led as early as the Lights on Vehicles Act 1907 to the unusual concept that, in the case of Crown vehicles, proceedings should be brought against a nominated defendant. The current version of section 5 of that Act is contained in section 188 of the Road Traffic Act 1972, subsections (8) and (9) of which provide as follows:

B   " (8) For the purpose of proceedings for an offence under this Act (except an offence under section 81) in connection with a vehicle in the public service of the Crown, being proceedings against a person other than the driver or rider of the vehicle, the person nominated in that behalf by the department in whose service the vehicle is used shall be deemed to be the person actually responsible unless it is shown to the satisfaction of the court that the driver or rider only

C   was responsible. (9) For the purposes of sections 68 to 81 of this Act in their application to vehicles in the public service of the Crown, the person whom the department in whose service any such vehicle is used names as the person actually responsible shall be deemed to be the person who causes or permits the vehicle to be on the road."

D   Before the justices Mr. Barnett was minded to contend that, while he had in the past enjoyed the doubtful distinction of being the department's nominee, there could be no general nomination and he had not been effectively nominated in this instance. The justices ruled against him and, since the point is no longer pursued, we need say no more about it.

   The physical condition of the tyre was not in dispute. Nor was the fact that at the relevant time the vehicle was being used on the public
E   highway on the business of the Department of the Environment. On these facts, the justices held that Mr. Barnett, as the person nominated under section 188 (8) of the Road Traffic Act 1972, " was in the same position as any other employer accused of this offence and we convicted him, despite the consideration that his employee may well have contributed to the commission of the offence." The justices ask us whether,
F   on the facts found, they were correct to rule that Mr. Barnett used the vehicle and, if so, what they should have done.

   The difficulties to which the section gives rise are well illustrated by the justices' own finding. Mr. Lewis, the driver, was not Mr. Barnett's employee. He was not even an employee of the Secretary of State. He was a servant of the Crown. So confusing is this concept of a nominated defendant that in another case in which Mr. Barnett was concerned in
G   that capacity, the Nottingham City justices managed to convict the Secretary of State himself. This conviction had to be quashed and we so ordered immediately before hearing the present appeal.

   For our part we can see no ground upon which the decision of the South Molton justices can be impugned. If the vehicle was used with a defective tyre, as it was, Mr. Barnett as the nominee under section 188
H   (8) is deemed to be the person actually responsible for so using it, unless it can be shown that only the driver was responsible. This was not shown and on the facts it probably never could have been shown because one or other of the Bristol supervising officers must have had some responsibility in addition to that of the driver. If Mr. Barnett had in fact been responsible for using the vehicle, he would properly have been convicted. As the statute provides that he is deemed to have been actually responsible, the magistrates were right to convict him.

The second question asked by the justices concerns penalty and, in A
particular, the decision not to endorse Mr. Barnett's licence. This was
clearly right. Under the appropriate part of Schedule 4 to the Road
Traffic Act 1972, endorsement is obligatory and disqualification discretionary for the offence of using a vehicle with defective tyres unless the
offender proves that he did not know and had no reasonable cause to suspect that the facts of the case were such that the offence would be committed. Whether a nominated defendant can ever bring himself within B
the exception when he is deemed to have been *actually* responsible may
be open to doubt. But this does not matter because there were " special
reasons " for not endorsing. In argument it was suggested that these
related to Mr. Barnett's personal position rather than the offence. We
do not agree. They related to both. Mr. Barnett's special position is
obvious. However, so is the circumstance that the offence was not in C
reality committed by Mr. Barnett, but is only deemed by statute to have
been committed by him. In the absence of any culpability on the part
of Mr. Barnett any endorsement of his licence and, a fortiori, any disqualification would have been a travesty of justice.

So much for the appeal, but the problem of the nominated defendant
still remains and we were asked whether we could suggest a solution. D

In our judgment, it is a serious problem and not one which can be
brushed aside by saying, " Oh well, if Mr. Barnett in his personal capacity is ever convicted of a motoring offence, he will be able to explain
how he came to have such a record of convictions." The fact that such
a situation could have arisen at any time since 1907 is nothing to the
point, since we are told that it is only recently that prosecuting authorities have started to ask government departments to nominate a defendant. E
Nor would it be right to ask these authorities to desist, since Parliament
clearly intended that, in the case of road traffic offences involving Crown
vehicles, it should be possible to institute proceedings analagous to those
which in other cases would be brought against the owner. Similarly we
reject the suggestion that government departments should refrain from
nominating defendants, since to do so would again involve frustrating the F
intentions of Parliament.

A further idea which was mooted in argument is that justices should
impose an absolute discharge when convicting a nominated defendant.
However, this also would frustrate the intention of Parliament which
clearly was that where a fine is the appropriate penalty in the case of
other owners, the same penalty should be imposed when the vehicle concerned is owned by the Crown. But something must be done to safe- G
guard the position of the unfortunate Mr. Barnett and others like him.
One solution would be for Parliament to provide by statute that a conviction as a nominated defendant was not to be treated for any purpose
as a conviction of the individual concerned, that a nominated defendant
could not be disqualified from holding or obtaining a driving licence or
have a conviction endorsed upon his driving licence and that he should H
be indemnified by his department in respect of any monetary penalty.
However, Parliamentary time is at a premium and some interim solution
must, if possible, be provided.

It was faintly suggested that the department should only nominate an
official who was in some way culpable, but this is wholly objectionable
since it involves the department in trying the issue of culpability before
making a nomination. It is also far from clear whether the department

A is entitled to nominate someone without their consent. We therefore reject this suggestion. Neither Mr. Barnett nor the department put forward any other ideas, but it seems to us that it would be a grave reflection upon the flexibility and ingenuity of a common law system if what is essentially a procedural problem were to be accepted as insoluble. And we do not think that it is.

B A little over 300 years ago a not dissimilar problem arose in connection with proceedings for the recovery of land. The accepted forms of action made it difficult for a plaintiff to prove that he was a freeholder entitled to possession. Mr. John Doe came to the rescue, sometimes assisted by Mr. Richard Roe. These two gentlemen were conceived, in an intellectual rather than a biological sense, about the year 1656, and are said to have been the brain children of Rolle C.J. (see *Potter's His-*
C *torical Introduction to English Law*, 3rd ed. (1948), p. 498). John Doe's function was to become the tenant under fictitious leases granted by claimant freeholders. The courts did not permit the fiction to be challenged, but confined the issue to the right of the claimant freeholder to grant the lease, thus indirectly and simply determining his title as a freeholder.

Following the modernisation of the court's procedures, both these
D gentlemen retired, so far as this country is concerned, but we understand that they have continued to assist in proceedings in the United States of America. We are also told that John Doe recently made a brief reappearance in the context of actions to evict squatters before the new R.S.C., Ord. 113 was introduced. He also reappeared before a Court of Appeal consisting of Lord Denning M.R. and myself in *Levy* v. *Levy* (unreported), November 9, 1979. There were problems over granting an
E injunction against an individual who was clearly identifiable, but refused to disclose his name. Unfortunately the proceedings have not been reported, but as I recollect the matter, an injunction was granted against John Doe with provision for service on the defendant, coupled with a liberty to either party to apply to amend if it appeared that there had been a misnomer and that this was not in fact the gentleman's name.

F So far as we know, John Doe's services to the law have thus far been confined to the civil jurisdiction of the courts and he has never been called upon to serve the Crown. However, we see no reason why he should be unable or unwilling to assist the courts with this new problem. If Parliament's obvious intentions are to be fulfilled, what is required is " a person " who will stand in the shoes of the department for the purposes of criminal proceedings, but who cannot be prejudiced personally
G by performing this very important function. A juridical person would fill the bill, and of course, proceedings are often taken against employers who are juridical persons. Accordingly, at one time we canvassed the suggestion that departments should nominate " Crown Defendants Ltd.," a company with a nominal share capital to be held by the Permanent Secretaries. However, this did not appeal to Mr. Simon Brown, who has
H appeared both on behalf of Mr. Barnett and of the Department of the Environment. In his submission, there would be considerable difficulty in drafting the company's principal objects.

If a " natural " person is to be nominated, it is clear that only John Doe, Richard Roe or one of his relations fills the bill. John Doe would have been particularly well qualified in the instant case since the Department of the Environment is known to its intimates as " DoE." Pending any change in the law, we can see no legal, constitutional or ethical ob-

jection and very real and practical advantages if government departments A
were to nominate John Doe under subsections (8) and (9) of section 188
of the Road Traffic Act 1972. As Lord Denning M.R. said in *Afromar
Inc.* v. *Greek Atlantic Cod Fishing Co.* [1980] 2 Lloyd's Rep. 17, 19:

" . . . the law is quite accustomed to the use of fictions to give jurisdiction in those cases where it ought to be had. The shades of John
Doe and Richard Roe will bear me out, see Blackstone III 201." B

It would probably be convenient that service of proceedings should be
accepted on his behalf by the solicitor to the department concerned or
by the Treasury Solicitor and we suggest that prosecuting authorities
throughout the country should be informed of whatever arrangements
are made.

Of course, the name John Doe is not unknown in real life, but we do C
not think that any confusion could arise between the departmental John
Doe and any others. For the purposes of criminal records, people with
the same name are usually distinguished by their date of birth and John
Doe's is " circa 1657." We trust that our suggestion will not lead to
John Doe acquiring any considerable criminal record, but if he does it
will be for the government department concerned and not for John Doe
to offer an explanation and he will have the consolation of having yet D
again rendered a signal service to the law.

Appeal dismissed.

Solicitors: *Treasury Solicitor; N. B. Jennings, Exeter.*

R. D.

E

[COURT OF APPEAL]

* ATTORNEY-GENERAL *ex rel.* TILLEY *v.* F
WANDSWORTH LONDON BOROUGH COUNCIL

[1979 T. No. 1504]

1981 Feb. 4 Lawton, Brandon and Templeman L.JJ.

G

*Children and Young Persons—Care of—Intentional homelessness—
Families with young children—Local authority resolving that
assistance with alternative housing be not provided—Whether
resolution ultra vires—Children and Young Persons Act 1963
(c. 37), s. 1 (1)*

A local authority resolved that, in those cases where intentional homelessness had been determined by it in respect of
a family with young children and subsequently an approach H
was made to its social services department, assistance with
alternative housing should not be provided under the provisions
of the Children and Young Persons Act 1963 [1] although consideration should be given to the reception into care of the
children should their circumstances warrant it. The plaintiff,
who claimed that the resolution was unlawful, brought an

---

[1] Children and Young Persons Act 1963, s. 1 (1): see post, p. 857B–C.

The Weekly Law Reports, June 12, 1981

855

1 W.L.R.   Att.-Gen. ex rel. Tilley v. Wandsworth L.B.C. (C.A.)

A   action against the local authority for declarations, and the
     deputy judge declared that the resolution was unlawful and
     that the local authority was not entitled to implement it or
     give effect to it.
        On appeal by the local authority: —
        Held, dismissing the appeal, that on the true construction
     of section 1 (1) of the Children and Young Persons Act 1963
     the power to provide " assistance " included the power to
B   provide or pay for accommodation; that in exercising that
     power a local authority was under a duty to consider each
     case individually; and that a resolution by which it ordered
     its committees or officials not to provide alternative housing
     in the case of children of parents who were intentionally
     homeless unlawfully fettered its discretion and the performance
     of its duties and was accordingly ultra vires (post, pp. 857F—
     858c).
C   *Per* Templeman L.J. I am not myself persuaded that even
     a policy resolution hedged around with exceptions would be
     entirely free from attack (post, p. 858G).
        Per Lawton and Brandon L.JJ. An opinion on that ques-
     tion should be reserved until it arises for decision (post, p.
     859A).
        Decision of Judge Mervyn Davies sitting as a deputy judge
     of the Chancery Division affirmed.
D

     No cases are referred to in the judgments and none were cited in argument.

     APPEAL from Judge Mervyn Davies sitting as a deputy judge of the
Chancery Division.
        By specially indorsed writ dated July 30, 1979, as subsequently amended,
E   the plaintiff, the Attorney-General at the relation of Mrs. Tracey Sandra
Helen Tilley, sought a declaration that the defendants, the Wandsworth
London Borough Council, were not entitled to exclude consideration of
the provision of housing or cash to provide housing in order to promote
the welfare of children by diminishing the need to receive them into care
pursuant to section 1 of the Children and Young Persons Act 1963 on the
F   ground that such children were living with persons determined by the
defendants to be " intentionally homeless " within the meaning of section 17
(1) of the Housing (Homeless Persons) Act 1977 and a declaration that
a resolution passed by the defendants' social services committee on July 4,
1979, and notified to the defendants on July 24, 1979 (post, p. 856F–G), was
unlawful and that the defendants were not entitled to implement or give
effect to it.
G   By their defence, the defendants pleaded, inter alia, that their social
services department and/or they had at all material times since the notification of the resolution implemented, and continued to implement, the policy
contained in it but had been and were prepared to listen to any applicant
for assistance from them as to why an exception should be made to the
policy in the case of the applicant. They denied that the resolution was
H   unlawful and that the plaintiff was entitled to the relief claimed.
        In a reserved judgment delivered on March 17, 1980, the deputy judge
held that the resolution was invalid. He made an order declaring that it
was unlawful and that the defendants were not entitled to implement or
give effect to it.
        The defendants appealed, on the grounds that the deputy judge had
erred in holding that the resolution and/or the implementation thereof was
ultra vires the powers of the defendants; that they had a power under

section 1 of the Act of 1963 to make available assistance by way of A
accommodation and/or cash for accommodation; that the phrase " assistance in kind " in section 1 included assistance by way of accommodation;
that the phrase " assistance . . . in cash " in section 1 included assistance
by way of cash for accommodation; that the words " assistance in kind
or . . . in cash " in section 1 were explanatory or enlarging of the word
" assistance " in the opening clause of the section and/or failed to dis- B
tinguish between what assistance a local authority had a duty to give and
what assistance it had a power to give thereunder; that the defendants had
bound themselves by the resolution to make future decisions in individual
cases under the Act without taking into account some of the considerations
that under the Act ought to be taken into account; and that they were
obliged under section 1 to consider in the case of every child whether to
make available to such child and/or the family thereof assistance by way C
of accommodation and/or cash for accommodation and/or to make such
assistance available to such child for the purpose of promoting the welfare
of such child by diminishing the need to receive such child into care; and
that he ought to have held that the defendants were entitled to take into
account factors referred to in a report by the chairman of their social
services committee and/or the factor of economy in deciding whether and D
if so how to exercise their power to give assistance under section 1.

Michael Beloff for the defendants.
John Macdonald Q.C. and *Andrew Bano* for the plaintiff.

TEMPLEMAN L.J. delivered the first judgment. This is an appeal from E
a decision of Judge Mervyn Davies sitting as a deputy judge of the Chancery
Division delivered on March 17, 1980. The deputy judge declared ultra
vires a resolution that was passed by the social services committee of the
Wandsworth London Borough Council on July 4, 1979, and confirmed
by the full council on July 24, 1979. The resolution was:

> " That in those cases where intentional homelessness had been deter- F
> mined by the council in respect of a family with young children and,
> subsequently, an approach is made to the social services department,
> it be decided that assistance with alternative housing be not provided
> under the provisions of the Children and Young Persons Act 1963
> although consideration be given to the reception into care of the
> children should their circumstances so warrant it and that the whole G
> matter be reviewed by committee in three months' time."

The deputy judge decided that it was not open to the council to lay
down that certain discretions and duties that were available and were
imposed on it by the Act of 1963 should not be carried out.

The Housing (Homeless Persons) Act 1977 introduces the notion of
intentional homelessness. Under this Act local authorities are under a duty H
to provide accommodation for families with children, and their duties vary
according as the homelessness of the parents is intentional or unintentional.
In the case of unintentional homelessness, a local authority is under a duty
to provide permanent accommodation. In the case of intentional homelessness—and this could occur, for example, if a parent rashly gave up
property that he owned or of which he had a lease, or behaved so badly

The Weekly Law Reports, June 12, 1981

857

1 W.L.R.   Att.-Gen. ex rel. Tilley v. Wandsworth L.B.C. (C.A.)   Templeman L.J.

A that he was evicted as being a nuisance or in breach of covenant—then the duty of the council is much more limited. The council need not provide permanent accommodation. It must give the parent advice and assistance to find somewhere else for himself, and it has to give him temporary accommodation while he can look round and find some place for himself and his family.

B   The Act of 1963 deals with individual children. Section 1 (1) says:

"It shall be the duty of every local authority to make available such advice, guidance and assistance as may promote the welfare of children by diminishing the need to receive children into or keep them in care under the Children Act 1948, . . .; and any provisions made by a local authority under this subsection may, if the local authority think fit, include provision for giving assistance in kind or, in exceptional
C circumstances, in cash."

    Under the Act of 1948 a child may be taken into care where it appears to a local authority, inter alia, that his parents, through incapacity or any other circumstances, are prevented from providing for his proper accommodation, maintenance and upbringing. So in the case of a child, if his
D parents cannot provide him with proper accommodation, maintenance and upbringing the local authority can take that child into care—in other words, remove him from his parents and put him with foster parents or in a home. The Act of 1963 imposes on the council a duty diminishing the need to take a child into care—in other words a duty to see, if possible, that the child can stay with his parents or, perhaps, with some other relations, by such advice, guidance and assistance as the council may think appropriate.
E The resolution that is now in question says that alternative housing should be not provided under the provisions of the Act of 1963 but that consideration should be given to taking the children of intentionally homeless parents into care.

    Mr. Beloff, who appears for the council, seeks to uphold this resolution in two ways, one oblique and one direct. His oblique way is to say that,
F as a matter of construction, it is not open to a council under the Act of 1963 to provide assistance by way of housing because the express powers that are conferred on a local authority refer to the "giving [of] assistance in kind or, in exceptional circumstances, in cash." Mr. Beloff says that assistance in "kind" does not include providing accommodation and that, therefore, cash cannot be provided to pay for accommodation. In my judgment, however, that is a misconstruction of the Act. The Act is
G dealing with children who are taken into care under the Act of 1948. This can happen, as I have already indicated, if the parents are unable to provide accommodation for the child, and the Act of 1963 provides that, if there is lack of accommodation, the council must try to deal with the situation by some other method than taking the child into care. To my mind, the word "assistance" in section 1 (1) of the Act of 1963 clearly
H includes the provision of accommodation and then provides that the general powers of a local authority shall include specific powers. The specific powers do not cut down the general powers of the local authority in the way that Mr. Beloff argues and that would prevent that authority from diminishing the need to receive children into care by providing them with accommodation or by paying for accommodation.

    Construction being out of the way, we have to consider whether the

858

council can properly order its committees and its officials not to provide A
alternative housing under the Act of 1963 in the case of children of parents
who are intentionally homeless. On well recognised principles public
authorities are not entitled to fetter the exercise of discretion or to fetter
the manner in which they are empowered to discharge the many duties
that are thrust on them. They must at all times, in every particular case,
consider how to exercise their discretion and how to perform their duties.
    Although the resolution appears to be mandatory and to prevent alter-   B
native housing being provided under the Act of 1963, nevertheless Mr.
Beloff said, and the judge accepted that there was evidence, that exceptions
were in practice made to the resolution. On a question of ultra vires the
practice of making exceptions is irrelevant, but, for my part, even if the
resolution had provided for exceptions and even if, as Mr. Beloff urged,
this was a general policy and not a mandatory order, the resolution would   C
not get rid of the vice that a local authority, dealing with individual
children, should not make a policy or an order that points towards fettering
its discretion in such a way that the facilities offered to the child do not
depend on the particular circumstances of that child, or of the child's family,
but follow some policy that it expressed to apply in general cases. The fact
of the matter is that intentional homelessness can take many forms and   D
can be arrived at for a great many reasons. Children's needs, and their
welfare, depend on a variety of factors. When the council are considering
the exercise of their powers and duties under the Act of 1963 one of the
factors that they must take into account is the history of the family,
including any history of intentional homelessness. The council must not
take intentional homelessness into account for the purpose of punishing
the child or punishing the parents of the child, but must take it into account   E
in asking: " What is the best way, in the interests of this child, of exercising
the powers which are given to us? " If, of course, there is a history of a
parent who continually changes homes and causes great stress and worry
to a child it may be that the council will say " In those circumstances,
we think that we had better take the child into care." On the other hand,
if the intentional homelessness still enables the family to be brought up   F
as a family under one roof, or does not require the child to be taken into
care, the council may come to a different conclusion.
    In what was, if I may say so, a careful and lucid judgment, the deputy
judge dismissed the construction of the Act for which Mr. Beloff contended; he correctly applied the principle that local authorities are not
allowed to fetter their discretions and duties, and he reached a conclusion   G
that I cannot fault save for this: that I am not myself persuaded that
even a policy resolution hedged around with exceptions would be entirely
free from attack. Dealing with children, the discretion and powers of any
authority must depend entirely on the different circumstances of each
child before them for consideration.
    Accordingly, I would dismiss this appeal.   H

    BRANDON L.J. I agree with the judgment just delivered by Templeman
L.J., but I would like to make one reservation. I am satisfied that this
resolution lays down a policy without any exceptions at all and is invalid.
Whether a resolution that laid down some general policy with a number
of specified exceptions would also be invalid is not a question that falls

The Weekly Law Reports, June 12, 1981

859

1 W.L.R.   Att.-Gen. ex rel. Tilley v. Wandsworth L.B.C. (C.A.)   Brandon L.J.

A for decision by this court today, and I would prefer to reserve my opinion
in respect of such a resolution to a case where it does arise for decision.

   LAWTON L.J. I agree that the appeal should be dismissed, and I share
Brandon L.J.'s reservation on the point that he has mentioned.

                    Appeal dismissed with costs on common fund basis.

B

   Solicitors: *Mrs. S. G. Smith; Wilford McBain.*

                                                              M. G.

C   [COURT OF APPEAL]

                          * REGINA *v.* BLOXHAM

   1981 Feb. 10; 20   Dunn L.J., Kilner Brown and Taylor JJ.

D *Crime—Theft—Handling stolen goods—" Realisation by or for the
     benefit of another person "—Innocent purchase of stolen goods
     —Subsequent suspicion of theft and realisation of goods by sale
     —Whether " for the benefit of " buyer—Theft Act 1968 (c. 60),
     s. 22 (1)*

            In January 1977 the defendant agreed to buy a car for
         £1,300, not knowing that it had been stolen and fitted with
         false number plates. He paid £500 on account, the balance
E   to be paid on receipt of registration documents, which were
         never produced. In December he sold it for £200 to a man
         he did not know, who was prepared to buy it without docu-
         ments. He admitted to the police that by May 1977 he sus-
         pected that the car had been stolen. He was charged with
         handling stolen goods contrary to section 22 (1) of the Theft
         Act 1968,[1] in that he had dishonestly undertaken or assisted
         in the disposal or realisation of the stolen vehicle by or for the
F   benefit of the unknown purchaser. The trial judge rejected a
         submission that the charge did not, in the light of the facts,
         reveal an offence known to the law and ruled that the realisa-
         tion was for the benefit of the unknown buyer. The defendant
         thereupon pleaded guilty to the offence.
            On the defendant's appeal against conviction: —
            Held, dismissing the appeal, that an offence of dishonest
         handling of stolen goods under section 22 (1) of the Theft Act
G   1968 was committed when an innocent purchaser of stolen
         goods after he had come to believe them to be stolen realised
         them by selling on to another person who derived some bene-
         fit from the transaction; accordingly, the judge's ruling was
         justified on the basis that the ultimate purchaser's benefit was
         the use of the car at a cheap price even though no title passed
         (post, p. 862c–d).

H   The following cases are referred to in the judgment:
      Reg. v. *Deakin* [1972] 1 W.L.R. 1618 ; [1972] 3 All E.R. 803, C.A.
      Reg. v. *Sloggett* [1972] 1 Q.B. 430 ; [1971] 3 W.L.R. 628 ; [1971] 3 All E.R.
         264, C.A.

      No additional cases were cited in argument.

      [1] Theft Act 1968, s. 22 (1): see post, p. 860f–g.

Regina v. Bloxham (C.A.)   **[1981]**

A

APPEAL against conviction.

On November 27, 1979, at Southampton Crown Court (Judge McCreery), the defendant, Albert John Bloxham, was charged on an indictment containing two alternative counts of handling stolen goods contrary to section 22 (1) of the Theft Act 1968. Count 1 alleged that he had received a stolen Ford Cortina motor car knowing or believing it to have been stolen; count 2 alleged that he dishonestly assisted in the disposal or realisation of the car by or for the benefit of another, namely an unknown purchaser. The jury were discharged from returning a verdict on count 1 and on January 16, 1980, after the judge had rejected a submission that count 2 did not, in the light of the facts, reveal an offence known to the law, the defendant pleaded guilty to that count. He was conditionally discharged for 12 months and ordered to pay £250 towards the costs of the defence.

B

C

The defendants applied for leave to appeal against conviction on the ground that the judge was wrong in ruling that section 22 covered this offence in that the admitted disposal of the car was not by or for the benefit of another but solely for the benefit of the defendant. The hearing of the application was treated by the court as the hearing of the appeal.

The facts are stated in the judgment of the court.

D

David Griffiths and *S. W. Watkins* (assigned by the Registrar of Criminal Appeals) for the defendant.
Neil Butterfield and *Claudia Ackner* for the Crown.

Cur. adv. vult.

E

February 20. KILNER BROWN J. read the following judgment of the court. This application for leave to appeal against conviction raises a point of law and has been treated by the court as an appeal. The defendant Bloxham was convicted on his plea of guilty on January 16, 1980, at Southampton Crown Court before Judge McCreery after the judge had ruled against a submission that the facts did not disclose an offence within the statutory provisions relied upon in the indictment. The alleged offence was charged as being contrary to section 22 (1) of the Theft Act 1968, the relevant parts of which read as follows:

F

" A person handles stolen goods if (otherwise than in the course of stealing) knowing or believing them to be stolen goods he ... dishonestly undertakes or assists in their ... realisation by or for the benefit of another person ... "

G

The meaning and application of these words in the context of the facts of this case has not, so far as we are aware, come up for consideration by the Court of Appeal although this section of the Act was considered in differing circumstances in *Reg.* v. *Sloggett* [1972] 1 Q.B. 430 and *Reg.* v. *Deakin* [1972] 1 W.L.R. 1618. Neither case dealt with the interpretation to be put upon the words " for the benefit of another." The situation disclosed by the facts of this case has, however, been considered hypothetically in the academic field and has given rise to obvious difference of opinion.

H

The facts can be summarised in a sentence or two. In January 1977 the defendant agreed to buy a Ford Cortina motor car for the sum of £1,300 which in fact, though unknown to him, had been stolen and fitted

The Weekly Law Reports, June 12, 1981

861

1 W.L.R.   Regina v. Bloxham (C.A.)

A with false number plates. He paid £500 on account and the balance of £800 was to be paid on production of the registration documents. No such documents were forthcoming and the defendant admitted to the police that by May 1977 he suspected that the car might be stolen. He drove it until August 1977 when the tax expired. Desiring to be rid of it and to avoid further possession of a car which might be stolen he sold

B it in December 1977 for £200 to a man he did not know who was prepared to buy it without the appropriate documents. It was this act in the month of December 1977 which gave rise to the offence alleged against him. By his ruling the judge decided that this was a dishonest realisation of the car for the benefit of another person, namely the unknown buyer. The benefit was the use of the car at a cheap price even though he had no title to it. The judge ordered a conditional discharge but added to the

C net loss of £300 a further sum of £250 by way of payment of prosecution costs.

On behalf of the defendant it was argued before us, as it was before the trial judge, that the section as a whole is intended to link the dishonest receipt of goods or assistance given by realisation thereof with a theft by another person or a prior dishonest handling by another person. Thus

D the "another" who gets a benefit would often be the thief. The section, so it is said, was drafted in this fashion to prevent conviction for dishonest handling as well as theft being registered against the thief. In this counsel has the support of *Smith, The Law of Theft,* 4th ed. (1979), para. 420 and *Smith and Hogan, Criminal Law,* 4th ed. (1978), p. 611. That being so, it was further submitted that if the realisation of the goods was to a genuine innocent purchaser, such realisation was not intended by the

E legislature to be applied so as to cover the transaction in this case because the innocent purchaser derives no benefit from the sale, since he has no title to the goods. The only person to benefit was the defendant who received the cash consideration for the sale and because of the inclusion of the words "for the benefit of another" he has committed no offence under the section.

F On behalf of the Crown it is argued that whatever the intention of Parliament may have been, the words "for the benefit of another" are plain and unambiguous and the innocence or otherwise of the "another" is irrelevant. Nevertheless it has to be recognised that the convoluted terminology of the section as a whole can give rise to a variety of interpretations. In *Griew, The Theft Acts 1968 and 1978,* 3rd ed. (1978), it says, at p. 147: "Realisation for the benefit of another typically occurs

G when an agent sells on behalf of a principal." We recognise that the use in the section of the words "assists in" contemplates that the accused is playing a subsidiary role to a principal and that the alternative word "undertakes" also implies that it is to do something for a principal. So the question is whether the section has to be limited in its application to the situation where there is a relationship of principal and agent.

H Professor Smith concentrates, in the paragraph of his book to which reference has been made, upon the thief who sells to an innocent purchaser and asserts that the thief cannot be guilty of handling unless merely performing the contract with the purchaser amounts to acting for the benefit of another. Perhaps wisely, he does not advert to the situation, as in the instant case, where it is not the thief but a purchaser with knowledge or belief in the stolen nature of the goods who then sells on to another. On the other hand the precise situation was con-

sidered by L. W. Blake in an article, "The Innocent Purchaser and   A
section 22 of the Theft Act" [1972] Crim.L.R. 494. He recognised
that despite the confusion of thought in the association of "by . . .
another person" with "for the benefit of another person," the words of
the section do not allow for the contention that "If a purchaser for
value discovers that he has bought stolen goods, he may be guilty of
obtaining property by deception if he resells them, but he does not become
a handler." He plainly recognises that the resale situation is covered by   B
the terminology of the section which makes it a dishonest handling.

We have come to the same conclusion as Mr. Blake, not so much on
academic and metaphysical grounds as on pragmatic grounds. The mischief at which the section is aimed is a dishonest handling. If the words
permit of a simple approach capable of being readily understood by a jury
this is to be preferred. In this case, although the defendant received the   C
car innocently, there came a time when he believed it to be stolen. He
then realised the car by selling it. Although he undoubtedly received a
benefit so did the buyer. He had the use of the car for which he had
paid less than its true value. No one can tell what he might have done
with it. The section does not require that in realising the car the buyer
should have got the better transaction, or that the seller should have no
benefit. It simply requires that the buyer should have derived some bene-   D
fit. In the view of this court he did derive a benefit and, it being accepted
that the appellant, in realising the car believing it to be stolen, acted dishonestly, all the elements of the offence are complete. The appeal is
dismissed.

                                        Appeal dismissed.
                                        Certificate under section 33 (2) of   E
                                           the Criminal Appeal Act 1968
                                           that point of law of general
                                           public importance was involved
                                           in decision, namely: " Does a
                                           bona fide purchaser for value
                                           commit an offence of dis-   F
                                           honestly undertaking the dis-
                                           posal or realisation of stolen
                                           property for the benefit of
                                           another if when he sells the
                                           goods on he knows or believes
                                           them to be stolen? "
                                        Leave to appeal refused.   G
                                        Legal aid to defendant for solici-
                                           tors and counsel to petition for
                                           leave to appeal.

Solicitor: *R. N. Bourne, Winchester.*

                                                                                H
[Reported by MISS EIRA CARYL-THOMAS, Barrister-at-Law]

April 9. The Appeal Committee of the House of Lords (Lord Russell
of Killowen, Lord Scarman and Lord Bridge of Harwich) allowed a petition
by the defendant for leave to appeal.

A

* BRIKOM INVESTMENTS LTD *v.* SEAFORD

1981 Feb. 18, 19;   Ormrod and Griffiths L.JJ.
B   March 5

*Landlord and Tenant—Repairs—Covenant implied by statute—
Lease for seven years—Tenant covenanting to carry out
internal repairs—Landlords' statutory obligation if lease for
less than seven years—Entry into possession on date lease
expressed to commence—Lease delivered 14 days later—
Whether lease for seven years or less—Landlords accepting*
C *rent assessed by rent officer on basis of their liability for
repairs—Tenant doing repairs and withholding part of rent—
Landlords' claim for arrears of rent—Whether landlords
estopped from denying liability for repairs—Housing Act 1961
(9 & 10 Eliz. 2, c. 65), ss. 32 (1), 33 (1) (3) (5)*

A lease of a flat expressed to be for a term of seven years
from November 1, 1969, contained a tenant's covenant to
D carry out all internal repairs. The tenant moved into the flat
on November 1 and paid rent in advance as from that date.
The lease was executed on or about November 12 and was
delivered on November 15. In 1975 the landlords applied to
the rent officer to determine a fair rent of the flat. The rent
officer made his assessment on the footing that the landlords
were liable for the repairs specified in section 32 (1) of the
Housing Act 1961 [1] and registered a higher rent than if the
E tenant were liable, and the landlords accepted the rent on
that basis. Further assessments by the rent officer, on the
same basis, were made in 1977 and 1979. In the event the
tenant did the repairs himself and withheld a proportion of
the rent to cover the cost.

In November 1979 the landlords brought an action against
the tenant for possession and arrears of rent. In his defence
the tenant claimed to set off the cost of the repairs against the
F arrears of rent. The landlords disputed their liability and
claimed that the lease was for a term of seven years, and
accordingly was not within section 33 (1) of the Act of 1961
and therefore they were not liable for the section 32 repairs.
Judge Honig gave judgment for the landlords.

On appeal by the tenant: —

Held (1) that on its true construction " lease " in section
33 (1) included an agreement for a lease as well as a lease,
G and for the purpose of that section the term of any lease as
so defined began at the point of time at which the tenant
was in a position to say that he was entitled to remain in the
premises thereafter as tenant either at law or in equity; that
that date was November 1, 1969, since all the terms of the
lease had been agreed and there was part performance on that
date by entry into possession and payment and acceptance of
rent; and accordingly that the tenant's term was one of seven
H

[1] Housing Act 1961, s. 32: (1) In any lease of a dwelling-house, being a lease
to which this section applies, there shall be implied a covenant by the lessor . . .
(b) to keep in repair and proper working order the installations in the dwelling-
house—(i) for the supply of water, gas and electricity, and for sanitation . . . and
any covenant by the lessee for the repair of the premises . . . shall be of no effect
so far as it relatets to the matters mentioned in paragraphs (a) and (b) of this
subsection . . ."

S. 33: " (1) Section 32 of this Act applies . . . to any lease of a dwelling-house
. . . being a lease for a term of less than seven years . . ."

years and the landlords were therefore not in principle liable A
for section 32 repairs (post, 867A–E, H).

Dictum of Russell L.J. in *Roberts* v. *Church Commissioners
for England* [1972] 1 Q.B. 278, 284, C.A. applied.

(2) But, allowing the appeal, that since the landlords had
throughout accepted rent at an enhanced rate on the basis
that they were liable for section 32 repairs, they were estopped
from subsequently denying responsibility for the repairs while
at the same time claiming rent at the enhanced rate, and the B
tenant could only be made liable for the repairs under his
covenant if the registered rent was corrected to reflect the
tenant's liability (post, pp. 868G–H, 869C–D).

The following cases are referred to in the judgment:

Bradshaw v. *Pawley* [1980] 1 W.L.R. 10 ; [1979] 3 All E.R. 273.
Cadogan (Earl) v. *Guinness* [1936] Ch. 515 ; [1936] 2 All E.R. 29.   C
Kai Nam v. *Ma Kam Chan* [1956] A.C. 358 ; [1956] 2 W.L.R. 767 ; [1956]
1 All E.R. 783n., P.C.
Roberts v. *Church Commissioners for England* [1972] 1 Q.B. 278 ; [1971]
3 W.L.R. 566 ; [1971] 3 All E.R. 703, C.A.
Territorial and Auxiliary Forces Association of the County of London v.
Nichols [1949] 1 Q.B. 35 ; [1948] 2 All E.R. 432, C.A.

D

The following additional cases were cited in argument:

Baxter v. *Eckersley* [1950] 1 K.B. 480 ; [1950] 1 All E.R. 139, C.A.
Brikom Investments Ltd. v. *Carr* [1979] Q.B. 467 ; [1979] 2 W.L.R. 737 ;
[1979] 2 All E.R. 753, C.A.
Campden Hill Towers Ltd. v. *Gardner* [1977] Q.B. 823 ; [1977] 2 W.L.R.
159 ; [1977] 1 All E.R. 739, C.A.
Colton v. *Becollda Property Investments Ltd.* [1950] 1 K.B. 216, C.A.   E
Harnham Singh v. *Jamal Pirbhai* [1951] A.C. 688, P.C.
*Hooley Hill Rubber and Chemical Co. Ltd. and Royal Insurance Co. Ltd.,
In re* [1920] 1 K.B. 257, C.A.
Morgan v. *Liverpool Corporation* [1927] 2 K.B. 131, C.A.
Parker v. *O'Connor* [1974] 1 W.L.R. 1160 ; [1974] 3 All E.R. 257, C.A.
Regor Estates Ltd. v. *Wright* [1951] 1 K.B. 689 ; [1951] 1 All E.R. 219,
C.A.   F
Walsh v. *Lonsdale* (1882) 21 Ch.D. 9, C.A.
Wilchick v. *Marks and Silverstone* [1934] 2 K.B. 56.
Williams v. *Staite* [1979] Ch. 291 ; [1978] 2 W.L.R. 825 ; [1978] 2 All E.R.
928, C.A.

APPEAL from Judge Honig sitting at Willesden County Court.

The tenant, David Seaford, appealed from an order of Judge Honig   G
granting to the landlords, Brikom Investments Ltd., possession of premises known as flat 72, Herga Court, Sudbury Hill, Harrow-on-the-Hill,
arrears of rent and mesne profits. The grounds of the appeal were that
the judge erred in law (1) in holding that the provisions of section 32 of
the Housing Act 1961 were not to be implied into the relationship
between the landlords and the tenant, and (2) in failing to hold that the   H
landlords were estopped from denying that the obligations set out in
section 32 of the Act of 1961 fell upon them.

By a respondent's notice the landlords sought to uphold the judgment
on the grounds, inter alia, that if, which was denied, the lease was for
a term of less than seven years by reason of the date of execution being
on November 12, 1969, the date should be rectified to November 1, 1969,
from which date it was the common intention of the parties to the lease

A that the lease should commence; that it being the common intention of both parties that the lease should be for a term of seven years from November 1, 1969, the judge rightly held that section 32 of the Housing Act 1961 did not apply; and that the plaintiff's not having made any representation to the Rent Assessment Committee that section 32 of the Act of 1961 applied there could not be any estoppel nor in any event could there be any such estoppel since the question was a question of law.

B

The facts are stated in the judgment.

Isaac Jacob for the tenant.
Norman Primost for the landlords.

Cur. adv. vult.

C

March 5. ORMROD L.J. read the following judgment of the court. This appeal concerns the liability, as between the tenant and the landlords, for certain internal repairs, as defined in section 32 (1) (*b*) of the Housing Act 1961, in respect of flat 72, Herga Court, Sudbury Hill, a block of flats owned by the landlords, Brikom Investments Ltd.

D The tenant puts his case in two alternative ways. First, he relies upon section 32 of the Housing Act 1961 under which there is to be implied into any lease to which the section applies a covenant by the landlord, inter alia, to keep certain installations in the dwelling house for the supply of water, gas, electricity, etc. in repair and working order, notwithstanding a covenant by the tenant in the lease to the contrary. Alternatively he says that the landlords, in the events which have hap-

E pened, are estopped from disputing their liability for the repairs referred to in the defence and counterclaim. The first point, which raises a difficult question of construction of sections 32 and 33 of the Act of 1961, was decided against the tenant by Judge Honig, sitting at Willesden County Court, on June 27, 1980. The second point was not specifically dealt with by the judge.

F By section 33 (1) of the Act of 1961, section 32 applies, subject to the provisions of the section, to " any lease of a dwelling-house granted after the passing of this Act, being a lease for a term of less than seven years." So the question is whether the tenant had a lease for not less than seven years. He contends that his lease was for less than seven years; the landlords contend that the lease was for seven years.

G The dates in the case are, therefore, important. It is common ground that this flat was vacant in October 1969 and that the landlords' letting agents, Stackpole & Co., introduced the tenant to the flat in that month. He was shown a specimen lease for a term of seven years, which was the standard form used by the landlords. He decided to take the flat on the proposed terms. His references had to be approved by the managing agents, Waite & Sons, on behalf of the landlords, who approved

H them in due course, and on November 1, 1969, he was allowed into possession and paid in advance a proportion of the quarterly rent in respect of the period November 1 to December 25, 1969. He also signed the counterpart of the lease on that day. The landlords did not immediately execute the lease and it is not known precisely when they did so, but the lease itself bears the date November 12, 1969. It was sent by post to the tenant, who received it on November 15, 1969. The evidence was that the date on the lease was filled in by the landlords' solicitors but

that it was " somewhat fortuitous," depending upon the conveyancing A
clerk's arrangements for stamping.

The habendum of the lease provides that the tenant is to hold the
premises from November 1, 1969, for a term of seven years at an annual
rent of £385 payable by equal quarterly instalments, but it is clear that
the lease was not executed by the landlords until some days after November 1, and not delivered until November 15, 1969. So, once again, the
problem arises of determining, for the purposes of a statutory definition, B
the length of the term of a lease.

It has been held in many cases, of which *Earl Cadogan* v. *Guinness*
[1936] Ch. 515, *Roberts* v. *Church Commissioners for England* [1972] 1
Q.B. 278 and *Bradshaw* v. *Pawley* [1980] 1 W.L.R. 10 are examples
(arising, however, in connection with different statutes), that a term,
defined in a deed as beginning from a date prior to the delivery of the C
deed, say for 10 years from such date, is not a term of 10 years. It is
a shorter term beginning from the date of delivery of the deed and ending 10 years from the earlier date specified in the lease: see *per* Clauson
J. in *Earl Cadogan* v. *Guinness* [1936] Ch. 515, 518, or, as Stamp L.J.
put it in *Roberts* v. *Church Commissioners for England* [1972] 1 Q.B.
278, 285:
D
> " It is well settled that the habendum in a lease only marks the
> duration of the tenant's interest, and that the operation of the
> lease as a grant takes effect only from the time of its delivery: , , ,"

Mr. Jacob, for the tenant in this case, accordingly submits that, although
the habendum refers to a term of seven years from November 1, 1969,
the actual term created by the lease is two weeks short of seven years, E
and is, accordingly, a lease for a term of less than seven years and,
therefore, falls within section 32.

The question to be decided, however, is what does the phrase " being
a lease for a term of less than seven years " mean in the context of
section 33. Mr. Primost, for the landlords, drew attention to section 33
(5), which reads:
F
> " In the application of this section to a lease granted for a term
> part of which falls before the grant, that part shall be left out of
> account and the lease shall be treated as a lease for a term
> commencing with the grant."

Mr. Primost submitted that if section 33 (1) is construed in accordance
with the principle laid down in the cases cited, subsection (5) is wholly
unnecessary because in any event the term cannot start before the grant. G
So, he says, section 33 (1) must refer to the term as described in the
habendum, namely, seven years from November 1, 1969; the term in the
present case is therefore not a term of less than seven years. This
submission, however, does not help him because if he is right such a
lease is caught later by the same subsection (5); the part falling before
the grant must be left out of account, and the term computed from the H
date of the grant. So, he is back to square one!

This is obviously an unsatisfactory conclusion. It is difficult to
believe that Parliament intended that the application of section 32,
which seriously affects the rights of landlords and tenants, should depend
on something so essentially fortuitous as the date of the delivery of the
lease. Fortunately, there is another way of approaching the problem
which the judge in the court below in substance adopted.

A   This Act (unlike the Acts with which this court was concerned in other cases) contains a definition section which defines the word " lease " in relatively broad terms. Section 32 (5) provides that " lease " includes, inter alia, " an agreement for a lease . . . and any other tenancy," and the word " term " is to be construed accordingly. In the present case there was, undoubtedly, an agreement for a lease of seven years beginning on November 1, 1969, made by the parties on or before that date, because B by that time the terms of the lease as set out in the specimen lease or in the counterpart had been agreed and there had been part performance by entry into possession and payment and acceptance of rent.

    In *Roberts v. Church Commissioners for England* [1972] 1 Q.B. 278 there was, as Russell L.J. emphasised, no agreement for a lease of the length required to satisfy the terms of section 3 (1) of the Leasehold C Reform Act 1967, namely, a tenancy for a term of years certain exceeding 21 years. " Tenancy " in that Act means a " tenancy at law or in equity ": section 37 (1) (*f*). Russell L.J. suggested at p. 284 a test which the tenant must pass to fulfil that definition, namely, that he

> " must at some point of time be, or have been, in a position to say
> that, subject to options to determine, rights of re-entry and so forth,
> D   he is entitled to remain tenant for the next 21 years, whether at law
> or in equity."

The tenant in the present case is in a position to fulfil that test, substituting seven years, which is the relevant period under the Act of 1961. So if this is the right approach to the Act of 1961, as we think it is, we are entitled to hold that for the purposes of section 33 (1) there was an E agreement for a lease, and therefore a " lease " as defined, for a term which was not less than seven years.

    But the landlords have still to get over section 33 (5), the language of which is not very apt to agreements for a lease unless the words " granted " and " grant " are to be read as equivalent to " made." If this is permissible the subsection will still be effective to prevent the mis- F chief at which it was presumably directed, that is, to prevent a landlord granting or agreeing to grant a lease for less than seven years and backdating the term so as to make it seven years from some anterior date. We do not think that such a construction does undue violence to the language of these sections read as a whole.

    If this goes beyond the limits of construction we think the same result follows from the application of section 33 (3), which deals with consecu- G tive leases. The tenant in this case was a person who immediately before the lease was granted—that is, delivered—was the lessee under another lease, i.e. under the agreement for the lease which for the purpose of these provisions is to be regarded as a lease. So he is within section 33 (3) (*a*). The other lease—that is, the agreement for the lease—was not a lease to which section 32 applies because it was for not less than seven years; so H section 33 (3) (ii) is satisfied and, accordingly, section 32 does not apply.

    In our judgment, therefore, an agreement for a lease for a term of seven years is not caught by section 32, provided that the term begins on or after the date of the agreement, whether or not it is followed by a formal lease. Accordingly we would hold, in agreement with the judge in the court below, that section 32 does not apply to the lease in the present case, and that the liability for internal repairs is governed by the terms of the original lease.

That, however, does not dispose of this appeal because if the tenant A is right on the estoppel point he will still be entitled to succeed in this action. The alleged estoppel arises in a curious way. In 1975 the land-lords applied under the terms of the Rent Act 1968 to the rent officer to register the rent of this flat. The application itself has not survived, but on September 23, 1975, the rent officer determined the rent at the sum of £555 exclusive of rates with effect from May 16, 1975, and duly registered it. In the notification of registration of rent the rent officer B set out very clearly the basis of his determination. Under the heading " Allocation of liability for repairs " he referred to the lease and added the words " and subject to the provisions of sections 32 and 33 of the Housing Act 1961," plainly indicating that his assessment of the rent was made on the basis that the landlords were liable for the repairs specified in section 32 (1) (b) and that the tenant's covenant in the lease C did not apply to such repairs. This, of course, resulted in the registration of a higher rent than would have been the case if the liability had been on the tenant.

The landlords did not object and thereafter demanded and received rent at the enhanced rate. In June 1977 the landlords applied again for the registration of a fair rent. After a full hearing, at which the land-lords' representative and several tenants gave evidence, the rent assess- D ment committee on January 30, 1978, determined the fair rent of this and other flats in Herga Court. In the case of flat 72 it was accepted by both sides that sections 32 and 33 applied, that is, that the landlords were liable for the section 32 repairs. On that basis the fair rent for flat 72 was assessed at £671·92 exclusive. Again the enhanced rent was demanded and paid. Another application was made in 1979 resulting in E the registration of a fair rent in the sum of £930, still on the same basis.

About the same time correspondence took place between the parties on the subject of repairs, and it is clear that throughout the landlords accepted that they were liable for the section 32 repairs, but in the event the tenant did the repairs, paid for them, and withheld a proportion of F the rent. Eventually the landlords brought the present action for posses-sion and arrears of rent at the enhanced rate, and the tenant filed a defence claiming to set off the cost of the repairs against the rent. Then, for the first time, the landlords disputed their liability and claimed that section 32 did not apply to this lease. Thus, in the same proceedings, they are seeking to recover arrears of the rent fixed on the basis that they were liable for those repairs and claiming that they were not liable G for them.

In our judgment it would clearly be inequitable to hold that the tenant was liable for the full amount of the arrears of a rent which reflects, in part, that the landlords were liable for the repairs, and at the same time that the tenant was liable for the cost of such repairs. This is the classic situation which the doctrine of estoppel was designed to H meet.

Mr. Jacob put his case in alternative ways. Either the landlords, by demanding a rent fixed on the basis of the rent officer's allocation of liability for repairs, represented that they accepted liability accordingly, or the landlords, by not taking steps to have the registered rent changed so as to reflect the true position and by suing for the enhanced rent, had

A made their election and could not be heard, in these proceedings, to assert a claim inconsistent with the position they had adopted.

Mr. Primost, however, contended that the representation was a representation of law and not of fact and, therefore, could not give rise to an estoppel, and that the tenant was seeking to use the estoppel as a sword, that is, to recover the cost of the repairs, and not, in the classic phrase, as a shield. He relied upon two cases, *Territorial and Auxiliary*
B *Forces Association of the County of London* v. *Nichols* [1949] 1 Q.B. 35 and *Kai Nam* v. *Ma Kam Chan* [1956] A.C. 358, in neither of which had the party alleging estoppel acted to his detriment, nor had the other party gained any advantage from the representation.

These dichotomies are dangerously neat and apt to mislead. Representations of fact shade into representations of law, and swords, with a
C little ingenuity, can be beaten into shields, or shields into swords. In this case the shield may have quite a sharp edge but it is nonetheless a shield and the representation was essentially one of fact, i.e., that the landlords accepted liability for the section 32 (1) (*b*) repairs to the tenant's flat in return for the enhanced rent. We would hold that so long as the enhanced rent is claimed the landlords cannot put the burden of the section 32 repairs on the tenant. But they can take immediate
D action to have the fair rent corrected so as to reflect the true position in regard to repairs, and will then be entitled to the benefit of the tenant's covenant. The tenant, therefore, succeeds on this point.

The judge in the court below attempted to deal with the matter on broad common sense lines by assessing the amount of excess rent paid by the tenant under the rent officer's assessments and allowing credit
E accordingly. But he had insufficient material on which to estimate the amount of the overpayment and, in our opinion, no jurisdiction to make such an adjustment, although he may have been under the impression that the parties were consenting to his taking this course. In fact, it seems clear from a letter from the tenant's solicitors written shortly after judgment was given that he had not agreed to it. This appeal must, therefore, be allowed.
F

> *Appeal allowed with costs.*
> *Case remitted to judge.*
> *Leave to appeal refused.*

Solicitors: *J. E. Kennedy & Co., Harrow; A. E. Hamlin & Co.*

G
[Reported by MICHAEL HAWKINGS, ESQ., Barrister-at-Law]

H

A

[QUEEN'S BENCH DIVISION]

* NEW ZEALAND GOVERNMENT PROPERTY
CORPORATION v. H.M. & S. LTD.

1980 Oct. 29, 30; 31   Woolf J.

B

*Landlord and Tenant—Surrender—Surrender by operation of law
—Grant of new tenancy—Whether terminating tenant's right
to remove tenant's fixtures*

When the term of an underlease of a theatre was due to
expire, the tenants did not remove their fixtures but entered
into an agreement with their landlords for the grant of a new
underlease. The new underlease contained a rent review
clause under which the rent for the second seven years of
the term was to be the " open market rental value " of the
premises. The parties could not agree a new rent. The
dispute was referred to an arbitrator who held that the open
market rental was to be determined on the basis that the
lease had ended, that the tenants had vacated the premises,
had removed any tenant's fixtures that they could lawfully
remove at the end of the term, and that they had removed
only those fixtures annexed after the date on which the parties
had agreed the material terms for the grant of a new lease.
On a special case stated to the High Court: —

Held, that the situation where a tenancy came to an end
by normal effluxion of time, and a new tenancy was entered
into immediately, differed from that of an express surrender
in that the parties intended to grant new rights and not to
take away old rights except in so far as they were inconsistent
with the new rights; that where, as in the present case, there
was a clear inference that the tenants did not intend to give
up their right to remove fixtures, the " open market rental
value " as defined by the new underlease was to be determined on the basis that the tenants had removed all tenant's
fixtures whether they were annexed to the premises during
the term of the old or the new underlease (post, pp. 874E–H,
880A–C).

Leschallas v. *Woolf* [1908] 1 Ch. 641 and *Smith* v. *City
Petroleum Co. Ltd.* [1940] 1 All E.R. 260 applied.

C

D

E

F

The following cases are referred to in the judgment:

Leschallas v. *Woolf* [1908] 1 Ch. 641.
Slough Picture Hall Co. Ltd. v. *Wade* (1916) 32 T.L.R. 542.
Smith v. *City Petroleum Co. Ltd.* [1940] 1 All E.R. 260.

G

No additional cases were cited in argument.

SPECIAL CASE stated by an arbitrator.

The lease of a theatre by the landlords, New Zealand Government
Property Corporation, to the tenants, H.M. & S. Ltd., expired by effluxion
of time on October 1, 1970. On July 1, 1971, the parties agreed the
material terms for the grant of a new underlease which was executed on
February 8, 1973, for a term of 21 years from October 1, 1970. A rent
review clause provided that the rent for the second seven year period of
the lease was to be the " open market rental value."

By an interim award dated August 24, 1979, Judge Hawser sitting as
an arbitrator appointed by consent under section 11 of the Arbitration

H

The Weekly Law Reports, June 19, 1981

871

1 W.L.R.   New Zealand Govt. Corpn. v. H.M. & S. Ltd. (Q.B.D.)

A Act 1950 and R.S.C., Ord. 36, held that the " open market rental value "
of the demised premises as defined by the terms of the underlease was to
be determined on the basis that the lease had ended, that the tenant had
vacated and that the tenant had removed any tenant's fixtures that he
could lawfully remove at the end of the term, such fixtures being those
which had been annexed after July 1, 1971.

B   The facts are stated in the judgment.

   Raymond Sears Q.C. and *Anthony Porten* for the claimant landlords.
   Ronald Bernstein Q.C. and *Kirk Reynolds* for the respondent tenants.

Cur. adv. vult.

C   October 31. WOOLF J. The issue in this case is as to the effect of a
surrender of a tenancy by operation of law on the grant of a new tenancy,
on the tenants' right to remove fixtures under the old tenancy. The issue
comes before the court in somewhat unusual circumstances and by an
abnormal route.
        The respondents are tenants of Her Majesty's Theatre in the Hay-
D market and the claimants are their landlords. The respondents are tenants
under an underlease made on February 8, 1973, which I will call the
" new lease." That new lease has a rent review clause which provided
that the rent for the second seven years of the term was to be the open
market rental value of the demised premises, and defined " open market
rental value " as :

E   " The annual rental value of the demised premises in the open market
        which might reasonably be demanded by a willing landlord on a lease
        for a term of years certain equivalent in length to the residue un-
        expired at the review date of the term of years hereby granted with
        vacant possession at the commencement of the term but upon the
        supposition (if not a fact) that the lessee has complied with all the
        obligations as to repair and decoration . . . and there being disregarded
F   (if applicable) those matters set out in paragraphs (*a*) (*b*) and (*c*) of
        section 34 of the Landlord and Tenant Act 1954."

After the procedure for rent review prescribed in the new lease had been
instituted, the parties failed to agree upon a new rent and they therefore
entered into an agreement dated August 28, 1978, whereby they referred
their disputes and differences and all matters of fact and law arising there-
G in to the award of a circuit judge discharging the functions of an official
referee.
        On August 24, 1979, Judge Hawser made an interim award in the
form of a special case for the decision of this court, Judge Hawser sitting
as an arbitrator appointed by consent under section 11 of the Arbitration
Act 1950 and R.S.C., Ord. 36.
H   By the interim award the judge gave answers to three questions as
follows :

        " Question 1 : Is the open market rental value to be determined on
        the basis that the lease has ended, that the tenant has vacated and
        that the tenant has removed any tenant's fixtures that he could law-
        fully remove at the end of the term?
        Answer : Yes.

The Weekly Law Reports, June 19, 1981

872

Woolf J.   New Zealand Govt. Corpn. v. H.M. & S. Ltd. (Q.B.D.)   [1981]

Question 2: If the answer to question 1 is Yes is the open market A
rental value to be determined on the basis that upon vacating the
tenant removed

(a) all the said fixtures whenever annexed or

(b) such of the said fixtures as were annexed after July 1, 1971, or

(c) none of the said fixtures?

Answer: (b)."

  B

Then question 3 in an amended form:

" In respect of each of the said fixtures which added to the letting
value of the premises, is it to be treated as an improvement made
immediately before July 1, 1971, or as an improvement made when
it was annexed to the premises?"

and the answer was: " When it was annexed to the premises."   C

Before me, the parties accepted that the judge's answer to question 1
is correct, and most of the argument has turned on question 2. The
reference to July 1, 1971, in question 2(b) is because that was the date
at which the parties agree they had agreed the material terms for the
grant of a new lease. Were it not for that agreement the critical date,
subject to the provisions of the Act of 1954, would be the date on which D
the new lease was made, namely, February 8, 1973.

The reason why the answer to the second question is important in
order to resolve the issues between the parties is that prior to the new
lease there had been an earlier lease of the premises and the landlords
contend that on the new lease being entered into the tenants lost the
right which previously existed during the currency of the old tenancy to
remove the tenant's fixtures. If, but only if, this was right would their E
value have to be taken into account in determining the increase of rent
payable as a result of the review?

The old lease was made on July 11, 1899, between the Carlton Hotel
Ltd., as lessors, and Herbert Beerbohm Tree and Playhouse Ltd., whereby
in consideration of the expense incurred by the said Herbert Beerbohm
Tree in erecting the theatre, the lessors, at the request of the said Tree, F
demised the theatre to Playhouse Ltd. for 72 years from October 10,
1898 (less 10 days) so that the term was due to expire at the end of
September 1970. By an agreement dated December 29, 1952, G. C. Dobell
& Co. Ltd. being the then lessees agreed first to assign to the respondent
tenants the premises demised by the lease for the residue of the term
thereby created and second to sell to the tenants " the fixtures fittings
carpets curtains seating and other contents and equipment as now in and G
about the said theatre and belonging to the vendors " for the price of
£30,000.

By the date on which the terms granted by the underlease was due
to expire, the reversion had become vested in the claimant landlords
who in due course served notice on the tenants to determine the old
tenancy under section 25 of the Landlord and Tenant Act 1954. The H
tenants served the appropriate counter-notice and commenced proceedings
in the Chancery Division for a new tenancy. Those proceedings were
adjourned pending negotiations between the parties which on February 8,
1973, resulted in the new lease. The new lease was for a term of 21 years
from October 1, 1970, that being the date the term of the old lease
expired; the old tenancy having been continued in the interim by section 24
of the Act of 1954. The new lease described the premises demised as:

The Weekly Law Reports, June 19, 1981

873

1 W.L.R.   New Zealand Govt. Corpn. v. H.M. & S. Ltd. (Q.B.D.)   Woolf J.

A   "All that piece of land situate in the Parish of St. James in the
said City of Westminster and being on the west side of The Haymarket and the south side of King Charles II Street together with
the buildings erected thereon and known as Her Majesty's Theatre
which land and buildings are delineated on the plan annexed hereto
and are thereon edged red and are hereinafter called 'the demised
B   premises '."

The new lease contained a covenant to repair which was in these terms :

"The lessee . . . covenants . . . to put and keep the demised premises
and the appurtenances thereof including the landlord's fixtures doors
windows and window frames and all fitting pipes and the sanitary
and water apparatus and the painting papering and decoration thereof
C   in good and substantial repair and condition and properly fitted up
and decorated in a state in every respect fit for theatrical representations of a high class character (damage by fire and other insured risks
save where the insurance moneys shall be irrecoverable in consequence of any act or default of the lessee only excepted)."

D   The tenants also covenanted:

"Not at any time during the said term to use the demised premises
for any other purposes than those of a theatre used for the production of plays concerts, . . ."

and covenanted:

E   "To yield up the demised premises with the fixtures and fittings and
additions thereto (tenant's fixtures only excepted) at the expiration
or sooner determination of the said term in good and substantial
repair and condition (landlord's fixtures and fittings being duly
renewed and replaced) in accordance with the several covenants
hereinbefore contained."

F   There was also a collateral agreement dated February 8, 1973, whereby,
in consideration of the tenants having that day exchanged the new
underlease and having incurred or been about to incur substantial
expenditure estimated as shown in the schedule thereto to fulfil their
repairing obligations under the lease, the landlord agreed that they would
during the first four years of the term grant to the tenants in each of
those years an allowance of £5,000 as a deduction from rent subject to
G   the production of certified receipts. The schedule included items which
would appear to be tenant's fixtures in normal circumstances and subject
to the questions in issue in this case.
       The tenants have never sought to remove the tenant's fixtures which
were attached to the premises during the old tenancy. However this does
not affect the importance of the answer given by the judge to the second
H   question since in carrying out the hypothetical exercises involved in fixing
the rent, although those fixtures have not in fact been removed, if they
are still removable by the tenants they would have to be ignored in fixing
the increased rent. If they cannot be removed they would be treated as
being included in the demise and would have to be taken into account
subject to the correct answer to the third question which I will deal with
as a separate matter.
       In considering the effect of surrender by operation of law of the old

The Weekly Law Reports, June 19, 1981

874

Woolf J.   New Zealand Govt. Corpn. v. H.M. & S. Ltd. (Q.B.D.)   [1981]

tenancy which was continued under the Act of 1954 it is convenient to   A
begin by stating certain general principles which are not in dispute.

Tenant's fixtures are normally only removable by the tenant during
the term and for such longer period of possession which is (and I quote
from *Hill and Redman's Law of Landlord and Tenant*, 16th ed. (1976),
p. 529) " in such circumstances that he is entitled still to consider himself as tenant." So the right to remove continues while a business
tenancy is continued under the Act of 1954.   B

It is always open to the parties to make special provisions as to the
right of removal, subject to such a special agreement not being inconsistent with rights of third parties.

There is a qualification to these general principles where the tenancy
terminates in such circumstances that the tenant would not have time to
remove fixtures. Then the right of removal continues for a reasonable   C
time after the expiration of the term. I would refer in that connection to
Smith v. *City Petroleum Co. Ltd.* [1940] 1 All E.R. 260.

In accord with the general principles if there is an express surrender
of a tenancy by a tenant, the right to remove subject to the terms of the
surrender ends with the surrender. Furthermore, I regard myself as being
bound by the authorities to which I will have to refer hereafter, to take   D
the same view where there is an express surrender followed by an express
grant of a new lease between the same parties of the same premises.

There is however, no clear authority on what is to be the position
where a tenancy comes to an end by normal effluxion of time and there
is a new tenancy entered into immediately following the termination of
the old tenancy. Where the tenant holds over as a yearly tenant, however,
the position appears to be that the right to remove continues in accord-   E
ance with the general principles which I have stated above.

Before turning to the authorities, it is right that I should make it clear
that it is my view that the ordinary tenant, untutored in the intricacies of
the law of landlord and tenant, would never expect that by taking a new
tenancy he could, if nothing was said, lose the right, which could be of
considerable value, to remove tenant's fixtures. In this respect I can see   F
very real differences in practical terms between an express surrender and
a surrender by operation of law. In the case of an express surrender
which is silent about what is to happen to fixtures, I can well understand
why the courts have taken the view that the tenant has given up all his
rights to what is then part of the premises. Where, however, there is no
express surrender, it seems to me the position is different because what the
parties have in mind is the granting to the tenant of new rights and not   G
of taking away of old rights except in so far as they are inconsistent with
the new rights. I mention this because it is clear from the reasoning set
out in the case by the judge, that he was influenced in giving the answer
which he did to the second question by the fact that he regarded the
authorities, as I do, as binding on him in respect of express surrender,
and took the view that there was no logical basis for differentiating   H
between the effect of an express surrender and of a surrender by
operation of law.

Turning to the authorities, I start with *Foa's General Law of Landlord
and Tenant*, 8th ed. (1957). I do so because Mr. Bernstein, appearing
on behalf of the tenants, found this his most embarrassing hurdle because
in fact he was one of the editors responsible for the relevant edition of
this authoritative textbook. I refer first of all to para. 1975, p. 706:

The Weekly Law Reports, June 19, 1981

875

1 W.L.R.   New Zealand Govt. Corpn. v. H.M. & S. Ltd. (Q.B.D.)   Woolf J.

A   "The mere fact that the tenant retains possession of the demised premises after the expiration of his interest does not extend the period during which he may sever fixtures, even though the reason for his holding over is that his successor in the tenancy has failed to pay him an agreed price for them. And where the continuance in possession is under a new lease or agreement, his right to carry away the fixtures is determined, and he is in the same situation as if the

B landlord, being seised of the land together with the fixtures, had demised both to him; so that if a tenant taking a fresh lease of the demised premises wish to preserve his right to remove fixtures they must be made the subject of a special agreement. So, where the old lease has come to an end by surrender, the transaction being what is

C usually termed one of surrender and renewal; though where such a surrender is one by operation of law upon the taking of a new lease, it may, in certain circumstances, be inferred that what are surrendered and re-demised are, not the premises in their actual condition, but the premises minus the tenant's fixtures. But if nothing be said about the fixtures at all, there would seem to be no ground for drawing such an inference, and the general rule will not be displaced. It

D is thought, however, that the ordinary case where a tenant holds over by arrangement after the expiration of a lease, and pays rent on a tenancy from year to year, is not a continuance in possession under a 'new agreement' within the meaning of the above rule, and that the right to remove fixtures when he gives up possession being one of the terms of the lease applicable to his new holding, the special

E agreement here spoken of would be implied."

And then paragraph 1076, p. 707:

      "The general principle appears equally to apply (apart from cases of fresh holding) where the tenant by his own act puts an end to the term, as where it expires by effluxion of time; so that after a surrender, for instance, the tenant's right to sever fixtures is gone. In

F the case indeed of surrender, it has been said that the right does not survive the time when the agreement upon which it is founded is made: the tenant as from that time being in the same position as if he had contracted to sell his lease. Upon a forfeiture, in spite of a somewhat guarded dictum of the Court of Appeal [In re Roberts, Ex parte Brook (1878) 10 Ch.D. 100, 109] that possibly the tenant

G may have a reasonable time afterwards, when he remains in possession, to sever his fixtures, it has more than once been decided that he has no such right, and that a person claiming under him is in no better position than himself."

The only part of the passages to which I have referred from which Mr. Bernstein can get any comfort at all is the qualification which is made in

H respect of surrenders by operation of law, at p. 706:

      ". . . it may, in certain circumstances, be inferred that what are surrendered and re-demised are, not the premises in their actual condition, but the premises minus the tenant's fixtures."

However, that passage has to be read in conjunction with the following sentence which indicates that if nothing is said about fixtures at all there would be no ground for drawing such an inference.

The Weekly Law Reports, June 19, 1981

876

Woolf J.   New Zealand Govt. Corpn. v. H.M. & S. Ltd. (Q.B.D.)   [1981]

The next textbook to which I shall refer is *Hill and Redman's Law* A
of Landlord and Tenant, 16th ed. (1976), p. 529, para. 425:

"Time for removal. – Where fixtures are removable by a tenant he
is only entitled to exercise this right during the term, and if he omits
to do so they become the absolute property of the reversioner, save
that if the tenant remains in possession after the term in such circumstances that he is entitled still to consider himself as tenant, his right B
to remove fixtures continues as long as this state of things lasts; and
if he is a tenant holding on an uncertain tenancy, then his right to
remove fixtures continues for a reasonable time after the determination of the tenancy. This rule applies in whatever manner the term
comes to an end, whether by effluxion of time or by surrender or
forfeiture; save that, in case of surrender or forfeiture, a third party,
such as a mortgagee of the fixtures from the tenant, is entitled to a C
reasonable time within which to remove them. A tenant, who is
entitled to remove fixtures under the stipulations of the lease, can
remove them within a reasonable time after the determination of the
term. From the principle that the tenant is not at liberty to remove
fixtures after the determination of the term, including a determination
by surrender, it follows that where there is a surrender, followed D
by the grant of a new lease to the same lessee, the new lease includes
the former tenant's fixtures as part of the demised premises, and in
the absence of express stipulation, any right which he had to remove
them is gone. Similarly, tenant's fixtures left by a former tenant
do not become tenant's fixtures of the subsequent tenant."

As I read that passage, there is not the same difficulty in Mr. Bernstein's E
way because that passage is at least open to the interpretation that it is
referring to a situation where there is an express surrender followed by a
re-grant; and it is not dealing with the question of surrender by operation
of law.

The third textbook is *Woodfall, Landlord and Tenant*, 28th ed.
(1978), vol. 1, and in relation to *Woodfall* I refer to paras. 1572 and F
1573. Without setting out the paragraphs in full in this judgment, it
is sufficient if I draw particular attention to this statement in para. 1573,
p. 678:

"On negotiating a renewal, a tenant must be careful to preserve his
right to fixtures, for without some express stipulation he may lose his
right of removal."
                                                                         G

It is right to say that with regard to *Woodfall*, like *Hill and Redman*, it
does not expressly close the door to the right of removal continuing notwithstanding a surrender by operation of law, as opposed to an express
surrender.

Mr. Bernstein took me through all the authorities which were relevant,
which are cited in *Foa's General Law of Landlord and Tenant*, so as to H
support his contention that in the case of a surrender by operation of
law, it is still open to the court to take the view which he submitted
was in accord with the commercial realities of the situation, namely,
that such a surrender does not automatically bring to an end the right
of removal of tenant's fixtures. In the end, the result turns on three
cases which I must now examine.

The first of those cases is *Leschallas* v. *Woolf* [1908] 1 Ch. 641. I do

The Weekly Law Reports, June 19, 1981

877

1 W.L.R.   New Zealand Govt. Corpn. v. H.M. & S. Ltd. (Q.B.D.)   Woolf J.

A   not think it is necessary to extend this judgment by reading the headnote.
It will suffice if I indicate that that was a case where there were three
parties involved, landlord, tenant and subtenant. The tenant surrendered
and there was a new tenancy granted direct to the subtenant. The decision
was one of Parker J. and he said, at p. 650:

"Assuming, however, that I am wrong in this, I will pass to the
B   second point in the case . . . Now it seems to me that a tenant who
contracts for the surrender of his lease to his landlord is in the same
position as if he had contracted to sell the lease, and cannot as
against the surrenderee, any more than he could as against a purchaser, remove fixtures which were upon the freehold at the date of
the contract, even though they might be of the nature of tenant's
or trade fixtures. No contract for the surrender of the lease would,
C   however, affect his sub-tenants or alter their rights without their
consent, though, if a sub-lessee stepped in and rightfully removed
fixtures after such a contract to surrender, the lessee might be unable
to complete the surrender which he had contracted to make, or might
be bound to make compensation for breach of his contract. I also
think that a contract to surrender a lease is a contract to surrender
D   in possession free from sub-tenancies, and is not a contract to surrender subject to such sub-tenancies as may have been created by the
surrenderor. "This position appears to have been accepted by the
solicitors for both parties."

He is there referring to that case and continues later on, at p. 651:

"On the construction of the surrender I am of opinion that all
E   fixtures are included in the premises surrendered. If, as I think is at
any rate arguable, the defendant was a consenting party to this
surrender, his tenancy would be determined thereby, and any right
he might have to remove fixtures would be gone . . . The defendant
[that is the sub-tenant] claims now, not only that he had the right
to remove during those three days the fixtures which had been affixed
F   by him to the freehold during his tenancy under [the former tenant],
but that the right continued after the determination of such tenancy
by the acceptance of a new tenancy under the agreement of August 7.
It seems to me that there is no precise authority deciding that a
tenant loses his right to remove tenant's fixtures by the surrender of
his tenancy to, and the acceptance of a new tenancy from, his landlord.
G   "It is quite clear that he loses the right by a surrender alone, but
it is said that this applies only when he ceases to be the tenant, and
not to cases where the tenancy is merely surrendered in order that a
new tenancy on the same or different terms may be created so that he
does not go out of possession of the property at all. In my opinion,
however, if the tenant upon the surrender of his lease in order that a
H   new lease may be granted makes no stipulation to the contrary, he
does lose his right to remove tenant's fixtures, for the surrender of
the demised premises prima facie includes fixtures, and the subject
of the new lease is prima facie what is surrendered in order to be
re-demised. Furthermore, it may well be that the value of the fixtures
the right to remove which is thus abandoned is a material consideration in settling the terms of the new lease. The right to remove fixtures
erected during the term is, I think, a right coupled with and depen-

The Weekly Law Reports, June 19, 1981

878

Woolf J.   New Zealand Govt. Corpn. v. H.M. & S. Ltd. (Q.B.D.)   [1981]

dent upon the termor's interest. Prima facie when this interest ceases A the right is gone, though there are, no doubt, exceptional cases in which, where the termor has remained in possession after the expiration of his term under such circumstances that the period of such possession can be looked upon as a mere prolongation of the term, he has been allowed to exercise the right after the term is ended."

Then he says that that seems to him to be the effect of a number of B decisions, and adds :

"The law on the subject is summed up more or less by Thesiger L.J. in *Ex parte Brook* (1878) 10 Ch.D. I will read the following passage in his judgment: 'The general presumption of law with reference to tenant's fixtures remaining affixed to the freehold when a term comes to an end is, that "they become a gift in law to him in C reversion," and are, therefore, not removable.'"

Pausing there: so far as an express surrender is concerned, it seems to me that that statement by Parker J. is clearly binding upon me and should be given effect to by me in coming to my conclusion about this case. In saying that it is binding upon me I do have regard to the fact that that is a decision which has been referred to thereafter by the Court of Appeal, D and by other courts, and has never been doubted as an expression of the law, subject to one matter which I will refer to hereafter in a later case. The judge later on goes on to say, at p. 653 :

"'But, however that may be, we are clearly of opinion that the case of a surrender of a lease by a tenant, while tenant's fixtures remain affixed to the freehold, does not, either upon principle or the E authority of decided cases, give any right to the tenant subsequently to remove such fixtures. At the date of the surrender they form part of the freehold, and the law has no right to limit the effect of the surrender by excluding from it that which legally passes by it, and which has not been excluded from it by the bargain of the parties.' Possibly, where the surrender is a surrender by operation of law upon the taking of a new lease, it may, under certain circumstances, be F inferred that what is surrendered and re-demised is not the premises in their actual condition, but the premises minus the tenant's fixtures. Possibly also, parcel or no parcel being a question of fact, evidence might be admitted under this head. There may, too, be cases where the terms of the existing tenancy are varied only without the creation of a new tenancy: but in the present case I am of opinion that G what [the tenant] contracted to surrender, and did surrender, included all fixtures; that what was agreed to be let to the defendant under the agreement of August 7, 1907, was what [the tenant] agreed to surrender, and subsequently did surrender; and that, by accepting the tenancy commencing on August 12, 1907, the defendant himself surrendered such tenancy as he might have had in the premises, and with it any right which he might have had to H remove fixtures as an incident of the tenancy. This, indeed, seems to me to be the only conclusion consistent with the surrounding facts."

So far as that second passage of the judgment of Parker J. is concerned, and particularly his reference to surrenders by operation of law, it could be said, and said with justification, that that passage is in fact obiter.

The Weekly Law Reports, June 19, 1981

879

1 W.L.R.   New Zealand Govt. Corpn. v. H.M. & S. Ltd. (Q.B.D.)   Woolf J.

A   Nonetheless, I think it is right to approach this case on the basis that that passage should be regarded as setting out the appropriate approach to the law and one which I propose to adopt.

    The next case to which I should refer is *Slough Picture Hall Co. Ltd.* v. *Wade* (1916) 32 T.L.R. 542. The facts of that case are complicated, and again, I do not propose to read those facts or indeed read B the headnote. Certain of the effects of the judgment can, however, be understood from a passage at p. 543. That refers to the fact that on April 14, 1915, a series of events took place, the legal effect of which the judge, Scrutton J., said was of great importance. He then refers to that series of events and goes on: " Both Wilson " (the tenant) " and his sublessee thus surrendered their interest in the premises to the landlords, who let to Mrs. Wade, who relet to the Picture Hall Co." What is C being described in that passage is a situation whereby what was originally a letting by a landlord to a tenant, and a letting by a tenant to a subtenant, is replaced by a situation where the subtenant enters into a new agreement with a new tenant after the original tenant has given up its tenancy. The judge refers to the case which I have just cited, *Leschallas* v. *Woolf*, and then recites what Parker J. held, and goes D on, at p. 544:

>   " I have come to the conclusion that this is a precise authority on the point before me and I must follow it. Wilson must have surrendered his tenancy to the brewers when he sold his interest to Mrs. Wade and consented to her granting a tenancy to the Slough Picture Hall Co. The Picture Hall Co. surrendered their sub-
> E   tenancy when they accepted a new sub-tenancy from Mrs. Wade, who had acquired her tenancy from the brewers. As a general rule fixtures cannot be removed after the end of the term except by express agreement. In cases where the tenancy determines on an uncertain event, as in a lease for lives, the tenant may have a reasonable time to remove fixtures after the end of the last life. I have considered the suggestion of Parker J., at p. 654, that ' possibly where the
> F   surrender is by operation of law upon the taking of a new lease it may under certain circumstances be inferred that what is surrendered and re-demised is not the premises in their actual condition, but the premises minus the tenant's fixtures. Possibly also parcel or no parcel being a question of fact evidence might be admitted under this head.' But in this case nothing was said about the fixtures at all, and I can
> G   find no ground for implying an exception out of the ordinary consequences of a surrender or for treating the premises demised to and sublet by Mrs. Wade as anything less than the whole premises."

    That case does create a difficulty from the tenants' point of view in this case, over and above that created by the words of Parker J. in the first case that I cited, because it indicates that, on the facts before H Scrutton J., he was not prepared to make an inference which Parker J. envisaged as a possibility. However it is to be noted that there is a distinction between that case and this in that unlike this case, there was not in that case a straightforward grant of a new tenancy which operated as the surrender of the earlier tenancy, the new tenancy being between the same parties as the previous tenancy and, although on different terms, in practical effect a continuation of the old tenancy.

I propose now to approach this case relying on the same words as were A
considered by Scrutton J. from the judgment of Parker J. Basing myself
on those words I have come to the view that in this case there is a clear
inference that it was not the tenants' intention to give up their right to
remove the fixtures. It is correct that the demise did not refer to fixtures
and the lease expressly reserved the right to remove tenant's fixtures at
the end of the term granted by the new lease without indicating that B
tenant's fixtures meant other than tenant's fixtures attached to the
premises after the commencement of that lease. However, so far as old
fixtures are concerned, while I would accept that the lease can be regarded
as being neutral, there is a firm inference, even in the case of a neutral
lease, that the tenant was not intending to give up the right to his old
fixtures when he enters into a new lease with the same landlord. If the
parties turned their minds to the question I feel confident that that is what C
they intended. If, not having turned their minds to it, they had been asked,
I feel confident that the parties would have agreed that the tenants' rights
should not be given up. Certainly that, in my view, would be the reaction
of an objective bystander. I do not regard the collateral agreement as
being inconsistent with this approach although I accept that there is a
technical argument to be based on the use of the word " repair ". D

I regard my view as being confirmed by the fact that in Mr. Bernstein's long experience in this field, he has never seen a new lease which
resulted in the surrender of an old lease by operation of law, which contained any provision to protect a tenant's right to remove fixtures. The
very experienced solicitors acting for the landlords were unable to find
any lease for which they had been responsible which protected a tenant's E
rights in such circumstances. I cannot believe that the very many tenants,
of whom those practitioners can speak, whose old tenancies must have
been terminated by operation of law on the grant of a new tenancy wanted
to give up their right to remove the fixtures.

It may well be that there are leases where there is an express reference
by the lawyers who were responsible for the drafting, to what was to happen
on the taking of a new lease. Such an express reference would indeed be F
desirable because, as I have already indicated so far as the effects of a
surrender by operation of law is concerned on the right to remove fixtures,
the law is certainly far from clear. The authorities do not deal with the
matter precisely and, apart from Foa's General Law of Landlord and
Tenant, the textbooks, so far as my investigations have revealed, and
those of counsel who placed the relevant textbooks before me have G
revealed, do not deal with the matter in clear language.

It follows from what I have already said that, unlike Judge Hawser,
I do not consider myself bound to follow alternative (b) in a situation
as here where there is only a surrender by the operation of law, and
not a surrender by express agreement. Accordingly, it follows that my
answer to question 2 would be (a) instead of (b) which was the answer H
of the judge.

So far as question 3 is concerned, I can deal with the matter shortly,
and I will do so by repeating as part of this judgment the reasons of the
judge, upon which I do not feel I can improve, for rejecting the tenants'
contention that the limitation contained in section 34 (2) on disregarding
improvements made by the tenant, ran for 21 years in the case of tenant's
fixtures from the date on which the tenant's fixtures became irremovable

The Weekly Law Reports, June 19, 1981

881

1 W.L.R.   New Zealand Govt. Corpn. v. H.M. & S. Ltd. (Q.B.D.)   Woolf J.

A and not 21 years from the date on which they were affixed. It follows that in respect of the third question, I would reject the tenants' contentions which were argued before me.

Award upheld in part.

Solicitors: *Allen & Overy; Nicholson, Graham & Jones.*

B

R. D.

[QUEEN'S BENCH DIVISION]

C   * REGINA *v.* CAMDEN LONDON BOROUGH RENT OFFICER
Ex parte EBIRI AND ANOTHER

1980 Oct. 27   Donaldson L.J. and Forbes J.

Landlord and Tenant—Rent restriction—Rent assessment—Jurisdiction—Application by tenant to register fair rent—Issue
D   whether protected tenant—Rent officer so satisfied—Adjournment of application to register fair rent pending court proceedings to determine nature of tenancy—Whether rent officer
under duty to register fair rent prior to ruling of court

In May 1980 an application was made to the rent officer
by occupiers of premises whose tenancy agreement described
their occupation as a holiday letting to have a fair rent
E   registered. The landlords contended that the rent officer had
no jurisdiction to determine and register a fair rent as the
tenancy was a holiday letting and not a protected tenancy. The
tenants commenced county court proceedings to determine
whether or not their tenancy was protected. On July 28, 1980,
at a preliminary consultation between the parties, the rent
officer, having heard evidence, decided that the tenancy was
not a holiday letting and that he had jurisdiction to proceed.
F   He fixed August 12, 1980, as the date when representations
were to be made as to the amount of rent to be fixed. In the
interim the landlords wrote to the rent officer contending that
since tenancy was described as a holiday letting in the tenancy
agreement the rent officer was acting ultra vires in proceeding
with the application for registration of a fair rent before the
court had decided whether the tenancy was protected. The
rent officer adjourned the meeting of August 12 sine die and
G   postponed the registration of a fair rent.
On an application by the tenants for a judicial review in
the form of an order of mandamus directing the rent officer to
determine and register a fair rent: —
Held, granting the application, that when an application to
register a fair rent depended on the disputed question whether
the agreement between a landlord and a tenant amounted to a
protected tenancy, although the rent officer had no jurisdiction
H   to make a final decision, he was under a duty to consider it
by inquiring into the facts; that once he was satisfied that there
was a protected tenancy he was obliged to proceed to determine
and register a fair rent, and a discretion not to proceed would
normally only arise when there was doubt whether there was a
protected tenancy; that, accordingly, since the rent officer was
satisfied that there was a protected tenancy, he was under a
duty to determine and register a fair rent.
Reg. v. *Kensington and Chelsea (Royal) London Borough
Rent Officer, Ex parte Noel* [1978] Q.B. 1, D.C. considered.

The following cases are referred to in the judgment: A

Reg. v. *Brent London Borough Rent Officer, Ex parte Ganatra* [1976]
    Q.B. 576; [1976] 2 W.L.R. 330; [1976] 1 All E.R. 849, D.C.
Reg. v. *Kensington and Chelsea (Royal) London Borough Rent Officer,
    Ex parte Noel* [1978] Q.B. 1; [1977] 2 W.L.R. 797; [1977] 1 All E.R.
    356, D.C.
Rex v. *Fulham, Hammersmith and Kensington Rent Tribunal, Ex parte
    Zerek* [1951] 2 K.B. 1; [1951] 1 All E.R. 482, D.C.   B

The following additional case was cited in argument:

Reg. v. *Croydon and South West London Rent Tribunal, Ex parte
    Ryzewska* [1977] Q.B. 876; [1977] 2 W.L.R. 389; [1977] 1 All E.R.
    312, D.C.

APPLICATION for judicial review.   C
    The applicants, Cyril Ifeanyi Ebiri and Bekky Ebiri, sought an order
of mandamus directed to J. McW. Smith, a rent officer for the London
Borough of Camden, requiring him to determine a fair rent and register it
as the rent for Flat 3, 105, York Way, London, N.7 in accordance with
paragraph 5 of Schedule 11 to the Rent Act 1977. The grounds of the
application were that in accordance with paragraph 4 of Schedule 11 of   D
the Act, the rent officer held a consultation on August 12, 1980, and
considered what rent ought to be registered, but adjourned the consultation sine die without registering the rent; that by letter of August 18, 1980,
the solicitor for the applicants requested the registration of a fair rent
within seven days and the rent officer had failed to register a rent; that, in
the circumstances, the rent officer had failed to fulfil his duties under
paragraph 5; and that further or in the alternative, the rent officer by   E
having regard to irrelevant or incorrect facts failed to hear and determine
the application for registration of a fair rent according to law.
    The facts are stated in the judgment of Donaldson L.J.

David Watkinson for the applicants.
Simon D. Brown and *John Laws* for the respondent.   F

DONALDSON L.J. In this matter the applicants, Mr. and Mrs. Ebiri,
apply for judicial review in the form of an order of mandamus addressed
to the rent officer for the London Borough of Camden. The relief which
the applicants seek is to require the rent officer to determine and to
register a fair rent for certain premises within his area.
    The history of the matter is this. The two applicants took a tenancy of   G
the premises at Flat 3, 105, York Way, London N.7, in November 1979.
In May 1980 they applied to have a fair rent registered. A copy of the
application was forwarded by the rent officer in the usual and required
way to the landlords, Sherman Securities Ltd., and the landlords by a
letter dated June 18 took the point that this was not a protected tenancy
but was a holiday let and so was outwith the jurisdiction of the rent   H
officer.
    As soon as that letter was received by the applicants or very shortly
afterwards they started proceedings in the county court in order to determine whether or not this was a protected tenancy, the applicants of course
contending that it was and the landlords contending that it was not.
    The rent officer meanwhile had arranged for a preliminary consultation
between the parties to take place on July 28 and at that meeting he went

The Weekly Law Reports, June 19, 1981

883

1 W.L.R.   R. v. Camden Rent Officer, Ex p. Ebiri (Q.B.D.)   Donaldson L.J.

A into the question of whether or not this was a protected tenancy. It was not a case, as was the position in *Reg.* v. *Kensington and Chelsea (Royal) London Borough Rent Officer, Ex parte Noel* [1978] Q.B. 1 of merely having submissions from agents or representatives of the parties. The parties gave evidence. There was a statement from the tenants. A Mr. Sherman represented the landlords and cross-examined the tenants. At the end of the proceedings the rent officer said:

B

"In the light of what I have heard this afternoon, I have come to the conclusion that this is not a holiday let, but an ordinary regulated tenancy. In the light of the reference and Mr. Ebiri's statement, I feel I have jurisdiction to proceed. I have cases where I decide straight away that there is a holiday let and adjourn them sine die for the tenant to prove it in court. Sometimes I have never heard any more,

C   or the courts have confirmed it. In this instance there is no doubt in my mind, and I do feel that I can proceed."

Having done that, he then proceeded to fix August 12 as being the date for the consultation when representations were to be made by both parties as to the amount of the fair rent, rather than proceeding straight away to determine that rent. He adopted this course in order to give the landlords

D opportunity to apply for judicial review if they wished to prevent him proceeding further and also to prepare any arguments they might want to advance to him about the exact level of rent.

The landlords took no steps to prohibit him from proceeding, and the parties met again before the rent officer on August 12. Meanwhile the landlords had written to the rent officer on August 4, saying:

E

"You will recall that despite the pending county court proceedings to decide whether the occupancy of the above flat is a protected tenancy, you made your own decision that it is so. The fact that the letting agreement describes the tenancy as '. . . a holiday letting only,' is prima facie evidence that it is until the court decides otherwise under section 141 of the Rent Act 1977. We feel that you are pre-empting the decision of the court and acting beyond your powers in proceeding

F   with the application for the registration of a fair rent until the court has determined whether a protected tenancy exists. In those circumstances we feel that the consultation proposed for August 12 should not be proceeded with."

On August 12, the rent officer referred to that letter. He said that in his view the letter constituted " new evidence " and that in the light of that

G and other factors he considered that it would be wiser for him not to register a rent. He said he would adjourn the consultation sine die. The representative of the tenants argued that that was not the right course and that the rent officer ought to register a rent. The rent officer said that he still thought he had jurisdiction to do so but that he would not in fact register a rent. He did not say so, but clearly he thought he was acting

H within the scope of his discretion and he said, somewhat incorrectly, that no one could compel him to register a rent.

The proceedings then went on by the tenants' representative urging the rent officer to give detailed reasons and drawing his attention to the fact that there might be rights vested in the tenants which would be lost if there was any delay as a result of orders being made bringing parts of the Housing Act 1980 into operation. I need not pursue exactly how that could operate. No orders have yet been made and it is unlikely that they

will be made until the end of November. But it clearly was a factor which **A**
he was entitled to take into consideration if and in so far as he had a
discretion in the matter.

The rent officer adhered to his view that he could not register the rent,
but he did proceed to hear argument on what should be the level of rent
which would be fixed if and when he was prepared to register it. The
facts end with a letter from the rent officer to the tenants' representative **B**
simply saying:

> " Following the meetings held at this office on July 28 and August 12
> last, from the information made available to me and in view of the
> fact that application has been made to the court for a declaration
> I am adjourning this case pending the decision of the court. No doubt
> you will let me know the outcome."

 C

In my judgment, it is the duty of a rent officer to consider what his
jurisdiction is in cases in which he has an application which depends on
a disputed question whether the particular contractual arrangement between
landlord and tenant or landlord and licensee is or is not a protected
tenancy. He has to consider it but he cannot determine it. He has no
jurisdiction to determine it on a final and binding basis, subject to appeal as **D**
between the parties. His jurisdiction is like that of an arbitrator. It stems
from an assumption, namely, in the case of an arbitrator that there is an
agreement to refer; in the case of a rent officer determining a fair rent on
an assumption that there is a protected tenancy. Somebody else has to
decide whether that assumption is valid, if the matter is to be determined
in a final and binding way. But this is very far from meaning of course
that every case where there is a doubt is to be referred to the courts. The **E**
duty of the rent officer, I think it is clear from such cases as *Noel's* case,
to which I have referred, and *Reg. v. Fulham, Hammersmith and
Kensington Rent Tribunal, Ex parte Zerek* [1951] 2 K.B. 1, which is
referred to in *Noel's* case, is to inquire as to the facts. If he is satisfied
that there is not a protected tenancy he has no problem. He just does not
proceed further until it has been determined by a court of competent **F**
jurisdiction that there is a protected tenancy. If he is satisfied that there
is a protected tenancy (and, note, I say " satisfied " and not " decided "
because he has no jurisdiction to decide), in my judgment, he must
proceed. It is only if he is in doubt whether there is or is not a protected
tenancy that he has a discretion whether to proceed or not to proceed.
That is putting the position, I accept, in somewhat black and white terms,
and his discretion might extend to not proceeding in a case in which he is **G**
certain or virtually certain in his own mind that there is a protected
tenancy, but within 24 hours he knows it is going to be decided by a court
of competent jurisdiction. I would not dissent from the view that in that
highly unusual and marginal case he may have a discretion to postpone
deciding the matter for 48 hours to get beyond the decision. But the
broad position, as I see it, is that he is obliged to proceed if he is satisfied. **H**

What is unusual about this case is that the rent officer was satisfied.
He expressed himself as being satisfied that this was a protected tenancy.
He remained satisfied at all times and it is not possible to attack his satisfaction, as it was possible in *Noel's* case. There it was said that the rent
officer could not be satisfied because he did not have any evidence on
which to be satisfied. There was evidence in this case and he was satisfied.
Let me make it clear in order that nobody should be influenced by any-

The Weekly Law Reports, June 19, 1981

885

1 W.L.R.   R. v. Camden Rent Officer, Ex p. Ebiri (Q.B.D.)   Donaldson L.J.

A   thing that I say that he may have been wholly wrong in being so satisfied. That is a matter which the judge in the county court will have to determine eventually, but he was satisfied and, being satisfied, I think it was his duty to go ahead and register this rent. If he does not do so and there is any delay in the county court deciding the matter, it looks as if these applicants will suffer a real diminution in their rights. But quite apart from that, I think that was the rent officer's duty. Accordingly, I would B   let an order go requiring him to determine and to register whatever fair rent he determines.

FORBES J. I agree and I would only desire to add one short point because of a matter which arose in the course of argument. Of course in these cases the rent officer is often asked to determine a preliminary issue C   of fact: is this a protected tenancy or not? Such a determination is not conclusive, as Donaldson L.J. has pointed out. The attitude which the rent officer ought to adopt is, I think, very shortly set out in the judgment of Slynn J. in *Reg.* v. *Kensington and Chelsea (Royal) London Borough Rent Officer, Ex parte Noel* [1978] Q.B. 1, 8, explaining the decision in *Reg.* v. *Brent London Borough Rent Officer, Ex parte Ganatra* [1976] D   Q.B. 576:

> " What I understand Park J. to have said was that if the rent officer, having gone into the matter, found that he was in doubt as to whether there was jurisdiction, so that he was not himself able to determine the matter, he should leave it so that the parties could take the matter to the county court if they so chose."

E   Originally on behalf of the rent officer it was argued in this case that, although the rent officer initially decided on this preliminary issue that it was in fact a protected tenancy, he subsequently changed his mind, but this argument has now been abandoned. The argument now is that the rent officer was indeed satisfied that it was a protected tenancy but nevertheless decided it was inappropriate to proceed at once to determine to F   register the rent. In my judgment, he was wrong about that, as Donaldson L.J. has said. However, during the course of the original discussion on the argument whether he had changed his mind, the effect of *Noel's* case was said to be this: that the rent officer was precluded from deciding the question of whether it was a protected tenancy or not whenever the allegation was made that the tenancy documents were a sham; and in all those cases, so it was argued or said, he should always leave it to the county G   court. In my view, *Noel's* case cannot be so read. It is clear to me that when one looks at the judgment of Slynn J. what he started with was that the rent officer was entitled to conclude that there was a protected tenancy, but that in *Noel's* case he went about it the wrong way. He attempted to decide that issue on submissions. Slynn J. said [1978] Q.B. 1, 9–10:

H   > " In my judgment it is quite impossible to resolve a matter of this kind merely on the basis of submissions made and arguments put before a rent officer by the solicitors for the parties. An allegation was made that this document was a cloak or a sham, a device to avoid the effect of the Rent Acts. That is a matter which could only properly be dealt with by the hearing of oral evidence, and if required, by subsequent cross-examination . . . In my judgment the procedure which was adopted on this occasion is not at all satisfactory and the

886

rent officer was not, because of the procedure adopted, in a position   A
to come to a determination of this kind in the way that he did."

As I say, I read that as simply an indication that in that particular case
the rent officer went about it the wrong way because he attempted to deal
with a question which involved fraud or something of that kind, at any
rate that the document was a sham, not on oral evidence at all but on
submissions by solicitors, and one could not determine a matter of that   B
kind merely on such submissions. But where the rent officer goes into the
matter and hears evidence, as he did in this case, and hears cross-
examination of the applicants, it seems to me there is nothing in *Noel's*
case which prevents him, if he wishes, from determining that question, as
indeed he did in this case. I agree with Donaldson L.J. that the order
should go in the way he has indicated.

Application granted.   C

Solicitors: *Nicholas J. Madge; Treasury Solicitor.*

[Reported by MISS EILEEN O'GRADY, Barrister-at-Law]

D

[QUEEN'S BENCH DIVISION]

* REGINA *v.* STATUTORY COMMITTEE OF THE
PHARMACEUTICAL SOCIETY OF GREAT BRITAIN,
Ex parte PHARMACEUTICAL SOCIETY OF GREAT BRITAIN   E

1980   Nov. 10, 11   Lord Lane C.J. and Webster J.

> *Tribunal — Statutory — Disciplinary proceedings — Complaints of
> misconduct following criminal convictions — Effect of con-
> ditional discharge—Whether tribunal precluded from hearing
> evidence of facts which led to convictions — Powers of   F
> Criminal Courts Act 1973 (c. 62), s. 13*
>
> The first respondents, when students, were involved in a
> fracas at the London School of Pharmacy in which another
> student was injured.   They were convicted of unlawfully
> wounding the student, contrary to section 20 of the Offences
> against the Person Act 1861.   On being conditionally dis-
> charged, they were each ordered to pay compensation to the   G
> victim and a proportion of the prosecution costs. Following
> their convictions, complaints of misconduct were made by the
> society to its disciplinary tribunal, the statutory committee,
> that the first respondents were guilty of such misconduct as
> to render them unfit to be on the Register of Pharmaceutical
> Chemists.   The chairman of the statutory committee, on a
> preliminary consideration of the complaints, ruled that the
> committee had no jurisdiction to hear the complaints on the   H
> ground that section 13 (3) of the Powers of Criminal Courts
> Act 1973 [1] required the statutory committee to disregard con-
> victions, in respect of which the offenders had been con-
> ditionally discharged, for the purposes of any disqualification
> or disability.   He further held that to hear evidence of the
> facts which led to the convictions would amount to violating
> the maxim " nemo debet bis puniri pro uno delicto."

---

[1] Powers of Criminal Courts Act 1973, s. 13: see post, p. 889B–D.

The Weekly Law Reports, June 19, 1981

887

1 W.L.R.   Reg. v. Statutory Cttee., Ex p. Pharmaceutical (D.C.)

A   On an application by the society for judicial review and
orders of certiorari and mandamus directed to the statutory
committee requiring them to hear the complaints: —
          Held, allowing the application, (1) that, on the assumption
that the removal of a name from the register was a disqualification or disability within the meaning of section 13 (3) of
the Act, the prohibition in the section was against relying on
a conviction as evidence of professional misconduct; that the
B   section did not affect a finding of misconduct supported by
proof of facts which had been adduced before a criminal court
and, therefore, since the allegation against the first respondents
did not rely on the convictions but on the circumstances
leading up to those convictions, the section had no application
(post, p. 891A–B).
          Rex v. *Harris* [1950] 2 All E.R. 816, C.C.A. applied.
          (2) That since the offence and findings of a disciplinary
C   tribunal differed from those of a criminal court and such a
tribunal was not a court of competent jurisdiction, the maxim
nemo debet bis puniri pro uno delicto did not preclude the
statutory committee from hearing and determining the complaints (post, p. 893G–H).

          The following cases are referred to in the judgment:

D   *Connelly* v. *Director of Public Prosecutions* [1964] A.C. 1254; [1964] 2
              W.L.R. 1145; [1964] 2 All E.R. 401, H.L.(E.).
          Lewis v. *Mogan* [1943] 2 All E.R. 272.
          Medical Practitioner, In re A [1959] N.Z.L.R. 784.
          Reg. v. *Hogan* [1960] 2 Q.B. 513; [1960] 3 W.L.R. 426; [1960] 3 All
              E.R. 149, C.C.A.
          Rex v. *Harris* [1950] 2 All E.R. 816, C.C.A.
E   *Simpson* v. *General Medical Council,* The Times, November 9, 1955,
              P.C.

          No additional cases were cited in argument.

          APPLICATION for judicial review.
          The Pharmaceutical Society of Great Britain applied for judicial
F review by way of orders of certiorari and mandamus directed to the
Statutory Committee of the Pharmaceutical Society of Great Britain,
the second respondents, requiring them to hear complaints under section 8
of the Pharmacy Act 1954 made by the society against the first respondents, Michael Richard Shutt, Jerome Frederick Brookman and Keith
Frank Martin. The complaint stated that it appeared that the first
respondents had pleaded not guilty before the Central Criminal Court
G on August 3, 1978, of grievous bodily harm and they had been made the
subject of a conditional discharge and it alleged that they were guilty of
such misconduct as to render them unfit to be on the Register of Pharmaceutical Chemists. The ground on which relief was sought was that the
statutory committee erred in law in holding that section 13 of the Powers
of Criminal Courts Act 1973 and the maxim " nemo debet bis puniri
H pro uno delicto " deprived the committee of jurisdiction to inquire into
the complaints.
          The facts are stated in the judgment of Lord Lane C.J.

          Richard Du Cann Q.C. and *Robert Webb* for the society.
          John Toulmin Q.C. for the second respondent, the statutory com-
mittee.
          The three respondent members of the society in person.

888

LORD LANE C.J. delivered the judgment of the court. This is an appli- A
cation for judicial review by way of certiorari and mandamus. It arises
in the following way. The first respondents, Mr. Shutt, Mr. Brookman
and Mr. Martin, are three young men, who at the time of the events I am
about to describe were students at the London School of Pharmacy. They
are not represented before us here in this court, but they have put in
a document which we have considered.

The case arose out of an incident on March 12, 1977, in which those B
three respondents were concerned. It was a fracas at a student disco-
thèque at the London School of Pharmacy. As a result of that fracas
another student, apart from the three I have mentioned, was seriously
injured. Among other injuries he suffered a fractured skull.

As a result of that incident criminal proceedings were instituted against
these three at the Central Criminal Court under section 18 of the Offences C
Against the Person Act 1861. In the upshot they were acquitted of the
section 18 offence and convicted of the lesser offence under section 20
of that same Act. Judge Buzzard, having heard the records of their
antecedent history, imposed upon them a conditional discharge. He also
ordered them to pay £50 compensation and £50 towards the prosecution
costs. D

Those matters were considered by the ethics committee of the Pharmaceutical Society, of which the three were student members. The ethics
committee resolved to refer the matter to the disciplinary committee which
is called the statutory committee, in order for them to consider the matter,
the suggestion being that the conduct exhibited by the three on that
occasion rendered them unfit to be on the Register of Pharmaceutical
Chemists. E

There was a gap in the proceedings, time elapsed, and by the time the
proceedings came to be heard Shutt and Brookman had become qualified,
so the suggestion was that the names of those two should be removed
from the register.

In November 1978 there was a letter directed to the statutory committee, and in due course, on February 9, 1979, the secretary wrote to the F
three young men making it clear what was the allegation against them.
I read the letter which was directed to the respondent Shutt, because all
the letters were in the same form. It read as follows:

"On behalf of the Statutory Committee of the Pharmaceutical Society
of Great Britain, I give you notice that the committee have received
a complaint from the Council of the Pharmaceutical Society of Great G
Britain, 1, Lambeth High Street, London S.E.1, from which it appears
that on August 3, 1978, you were before the Central Criminal Court
in London on a charge of causing grievous bodily harm to a Mr.
David Thompson. You pleaded not guilty. You were made subject
to a conditional discharge order for two years, and ordered to pay
£50 compensation and £50 costs towards the cost of the prosecution.
The council allege that you may have been guilty of such misconduct H
as to render you unfit to be on the Register of Pharmaceutical
Chemists."

It is to be noted that in that letter there was no mention at all of the word
" conviction ", a point which will become of importance in a moment.

The statutory committee sat on March 12, 1979. It was, as the
Pharmacy Act 1954 requires, presided over by a legally qualified chairman

The Weekly Law Reports, June 19, 1981

889

1 W.L.R.   Reg. v. Statutory Cttee., Ex p. Pharmaceutical (D.C.)

A   in the shape of Sir Gordon Willmer. Counsel there on behalf of the three respondents raised the question of whether the committee was entitled to receive as evidence of misconduct the same evidence as that on which these three young men had been found guilty under section 20 at the Central Criminal Court. The argument was that section 13 of the Powers of Criminal Courts Act 1973 prohibited that. Section 13 reads as follows:

B   " (1) Subject to subsection (2) below, a conviction of an offence for which an order is made under this Part of this Act placing the offender on probation or discharging him absolutely or conditionally shall be deemed not to be a conviction for any purpose other than the purposes of the proceedings in which the order is made and of any subsequent proceedings which may be taken against the offender under the preceding provisions of this Act. (2) Where the offender was of or over 17 years of age at the time of his conviction of the offence in question and is subsequently sentenced under this Part of this Act for that offence, subsection (1) above shall cease to apply to the conviction. (3) Without prejudice to the preceding provisions of this section, the conviction of an offender who is placed on probation or discharged absolutely or conditionally under this Part of this Act shall in any event be disregarded for the purposes of any enactment or instrument which imposes any disqualification or disability upon convicted persons, or authorises or requires the imposition of any such disqualification or disability."

C

D

The point raised by counsel in that way was certainly a novel point, and it is certainly a point which, if correct, would have some remarkable effect E upon disciplinary proceedings before statutory professional bodies, be they bodies of dentists, or bodies of veterinary surgeons, bodies of doctors, medical men, or bodies of pharmacists.

Sir Gordon Willmer reserved his judgment in the matter. There had been cited before him no authority on the matter, which, in retrospect, was perhaps unfortunate. On March 14 he gave his judgment, the material F part of which reads as follows:

       " I accordingly rule that in the light of section 13 (3) of the Act of 1973 this committee is without jurisdiction to hear and pronounce upon the complaint now put forward by the council. In my judgment, to allow evidence to be adduced before this committee as to the same facts as led to the decision of the criminal court would be a viola-G   tion of the well known maxim nemo bis vexari debet. It follows that, without proceeding any further, the present complaint by the council against these three parties must be dismissed."

The chairman seems to base himself upon two foundations—first of all, the provisions of section 13 of the Powers of Criminal Courts Act 1973 and secondly, the maxim, a truncated version of which he gave in H that passage in his judgment.

The contents of that judgment, and particularly the passage which I have read, caused some considerable concern to the Pharmaceutical Society, and consequently they wished the matter to be determined by this court as to whether that ruling is correct or not. They were concerned, says Mr. Du Cann, who appears for the society, for a number of reasons. If that judgment is right it might very well be better for the society not to prosecute breaches, for example, of the Pharmacy Act 1954 at all, on

the basis that it would be preferable to ensure that the member or   A
student no longer practised or belonged to the society than that he should
have a conviction recorded against him, a finding of guilt, which might
be simply followed by an absolute or conditional discharge or a probation
order.

As a matter of practice the society deals with cases either as "conviction cases" or misconduct cases, the latter including cases where a
probation order, or an order of absolute discharge, or an order of con-   B
ditional discharge is made. This instant case, as the letter which I read
indicates, was expressly alleged as a misconduct case.

There are, as Mr. Du Cann rightly pointed out to us, three questions
to be asked. First of all, does section 13 apply at all in the present circumstances? Secondly, if it does, how does it affect such proceedings, as
opposed to criminal proceedings? Thirdly, is the Latin maxim relevant?   C

First of all, it is right to point out, on the third point, that the full
version of the maxim is not as the chairman cited it, but is: "nemo debet
bis vexari, si constat curiae quod sit pro una et eadem causa", or in its
alternative form, "nemo debet bis puniri pro uno delicto"—"no one
ought to be twice punished for the same offence".

It is necessary, first of all, to read the relevant sections of the Pharmacy   D
Act 1954. Section 7 sets up the statutory committee:

"For the purposes of this Act there shall be appointed a committee
of the society (to be known as 'the statutory committee'), and the
provisions of Schedule 1 to this Act shall have effect in relation to
the statutory committee."

Section 8, which is the important section reads, so far as is material: E

"(1) Where—(a) a person applying to have his name registered, or
(b) a registered pharmaceutical chemist or any person employed by
him in the carrying on of his business, or (c) a person whose name
has been removed from the register under section 12 of this Act or
any person employed by him as aforesaid, has been convicted of any
such criminal offence or been guilty of such misconduct (being in a   F
case falling within paragraph (c) of this subsection a conviction or
misconduct which took place either before or after the removal of the
name) as in the opinion of the statutory committee renders the convicted or guilty person unfit to have his name on the register, the
committee may, after enquiring into the matter . . ."

and then it sets out the powers of the committee in those circumstances.   G

It is clear from those sections and subsections that whatever the
criminal offence or whatever the punishment has been the committee is
required and bound to inquire and to consider whether it is such as to
render the offender unfit to have his name on the register. In other
words they must inquire into the matter, and they cannot simply take
the conviction on its own, simpliciter, as being the basis of whatever   H
determination they choose to make.

The Powers of Criminal Courts Act 1973 was a consolidating Act. It
replaced section 12 of the Criminal Justice Act 1948, without making any
significant alteration to the wording. Section 12 of the Act of 1948 was new
for two reasons. First of all, prior to 1948 there was no such thing as an
absolute discharge or a conditional discharge at all. They did not exist
and at that stage probation orders could be made without any conviction

A being recorded against the subject of the order. Therefore, when the Act of 1948 came into force the position with regard to probation orders had to be preserved, and also new provisions had to be made in respect of orders of absolute and conditional discharge, those being new forms of order, hence section 13 of the Powers of Criminal Courts Act 1973.

B One can assume for the purposes of argument that the removing of a name from the register is a disqualification or disability within the provisions of section 13 (3) of the Act of 1973, although it is perhaps a somewhat tortuous way of describing it, but it seems to us clear that whatever section 13 may do, it does not purport to prevent a tribunal such as this one from acting upon the facts which underly the finding of guilt.

This indeed was the view taken by the Privy Council in a case under the Medical Act 1858, *Simpson* v. *General Medical Council*, The Times,
C November 9, 1955, before Viscount Simonds, Lord Keith of Avonholm and Lord Somervell of Harrow. The reasoning of their Lordships was given by Viscount Simonds. The relevant passage from the judgment reads as follows. His Lordship first quoted section 29 of the Medical Act 1958, which read:

D " If any registered medical practitioner shall be convicted in England or Ireland of any felony, or misdemeanour, or in Scotland of any crime or offence, or shall after due inquiry be judged by the general council to have been guilty of infamous conduct in any professional respect, the general council may, if they see fit, direct the registrar to erase the name of such medical practitioner from the register."

and Viscount Simonds continued:

E " The relevant facts are not in dispute and can be briefly stated. The appellant was at Chelmsford Assizes in November 1954, charged with, and pleaded guilty to, a number of very grave offences against his female patients which clearly constituted infamous conduct in a professional respect unless effect is given to the plea now advanced on his behalf. Having pleaded guilty he was duly convicted, but the
F learned judge, having heard medical evidence, did not pass any sentence upon him but placed him on probation, the condition of the probation order being that he should submit to treatment as a resident patient at the Runwell Mental Hospital, Wickford, Essex, for 12 months or such less period as the superintendent might direct and should thereafter submit to treatment by and under the direction of the superintendent of the said hospital. The result of these proceed-
G ings was that by virtue of section 12 of the Criminal Justice Act 1948, the appellant's conviction could not be deemed to be a conviction for any purpose other than for the purposes of these proceedings and must be disregarded for the purposes of any enactment which imposes any disqualification or disability on convicted persons or authorises or requires the imposition of any such disqualification or disability.

H " It was therefore not open to the committee whose duty it was to review the conduct of the appellant to proceed upon the footing that he had been convicted of a crime. It was for them to determine after due inquiry whether he had been guilty of infamous conduct in any professional respect and, if they so determined, then, if they saw fit, to direct the registrar to erase his name from the register. It was agreed by the appellant before the hearing by the committee that the depositions of certain witnesses taken at the magistrates'

court should be put in as evidence and at the hearing the facts alleged A
in the charge agreed and admitted on his behalf."

Then finally his Lordship said:

" The Medical Acts are designed at the same time to protect the
public and to maintain the high professional and ethical standards of
an honourable calling. If a practitioner, having committed the grave
offences of which the appellant has been guilty, can upon such a plea B
successfully resist the charge of infamous conduct and the erasure of
his name from the register, the public will lack their proper protection and the honour of the profession may be endangered by the
continued practices of one who can still claim to be of their number."

On that basis their Lordships humbly advised Her Majesty that the appeal
of the practitioner should be dismissed. The point was not specifically C
argued in that case, but nevertheless that judgment demonstrates clear
approval of the arguments addressed to this court by Mr. Du Cann.

The situation under the Medical Acts is not precisely the same as it is
under the Pharmacy Act 1954. We have not overlooked that point. Nevertheless, that seems to us to be powerful persuasive authority that what the
committee did here was incorrect.
D
We were referred to a decision of the Court of Criminal Appeal in
Rex v. *Harris* [1950] 2 All E.R. 816. The Court of Criminal Appeal was
composed of Humphreys, Morris and Sellers JJ. The headnote reads:

" Under section 12 (1) of the Act of 1948 the conviction of December 13, 1949, was not to be regarded for the purpose of another case
as a conviction, and, therefore, the certificate of conviction should
not have been accepted in evidence, but evidence would have been E
admissible by a witness who had heard the appellant confess in court
to the charge of having been found in possession of housebreaking
implements or had heard him convicted of that offence and conditionally discharged."

Humphreys J., delivering the judgment of the court, said, at p. 181: F

" In the present case the offence was under the Vagrancy Act 1824,
section 4, which was amended by the Prevention of Crimes Act
1871, section 15 (headed ' Amendment of criminal law in certain
cases '). Section 15 of the Act of 1871 provides that: '. . . in proving
the intent to commit a felony it shall not be necessary to show that
the person suspected was guilty of any particular act or acts tending
to show his purpose or intent, and he may be convicted if from the G
circumstances of the case, and from his known character as proved
to the justice of the peace or court before whom or which he is
brought, it appears to such justice or court that his intent was to
commit a felony. . . .'

" That section obviously renders admissible in such a case that
which would otherwise, according to the common law of England, be H
inadmissible, viz., evidence of the previous bad character of the
accused person although he has not himself put his character in
issue. No possible objection, in our view, could have been taken to
the procedure adopted in this case if the detective constable, whose
deposition I have read, had been present at the trial and had given
evidence to the following effect: ' I was present at the court on the
day named when the accused was there. I heard him confess to a

The Weekly Law Reports, June 19, 1981

893

1 W.L.R.   Reg. v. Statutory Cttee., Ex p. Pharmaceutical (D.C.)

A   charge of having been found in possession of certain implements of
housebreaking, and he was then discharged subject to the condition
that he commit no offence during the period of 12 months thereafter.'
That would have been, not merely proof of a previous conviction,
but proof of the appellants 'known character' in that he was a
person who had admitted in a court of justice that he had committed
a certain offence. What was done was merely to produce a docu-
B   ment which purported to be a record of a conviction in regard to the
appellant, and no other evidence was given in regard to the matter.
In any future case we think that courts—whether courts of summary
jurisdiction or courts trying a case on indictment with a jury—should
be careful to see that evidence is given, not that the accused has
been previously convicted, because the conviction itself is not to be
C   regarded for the purpose of any other case as a conviction, but that
he was seen doing this, that, or the other, which showed that he is
a person of bad character."

That citation from *Rex* v. *Harris* seems to us to put precisely the contention of Mr. Du Cann in this case and to demonstrate its correctness.
    Mr. Toulmin, on behalf of the statutory committee, submits that
D   although the word " conviction " was not used in the letter of complaint
which I have read yet nevertheless it was clear that the conviction was to
be relied upon. We respectfully disagree with that contention. What was
to be relied upon—and the letter makes it perfectly plain—were the facts
which lay behind the conviction, namely, the use by these young men of
disastrous force upon the body of the injured student.
E   My conclusion is that on the wording of section 13 there was nothing
to prevent the allegation of misconduct being supported by the proof of
facts which were adduced in the first instance at the Central Criminal
Court before Judge Buzzard. There is nothing in section 13 to suggest
that the underlying facts in that way should be disregarded. Apart from
any other reasons, it seems to me, if it had been intended that not only
F   the conviction but the facts underlying the conviction should be disregarded
in any future proceedings, then the Act should have said so and it did
not.
    We have had our attention drawn to an Act which does make
specific provision to that effect. That is the Rehabilitation of Offenders
Act 1974, and particularly section 4 and its various subsections. There
is no need for us to read those particular provisions. So much for the
G   first point arising under the terms of section 13.
    Our attention has been drawn to a number of authorities in respect
of the second issue, that is to say the maxim: *Lewis* v. *Mogan* [1943]
2 All E.R. 272; *Reg.* v. *Hogan* [1960] 2 Q.B. 513; *Connelly* v. *Director
of Public Prosecutions* [1964] A.C. 1254 and a New Zealand case, *In re
A Medical Practitioner* [1959] N.Z.L.R. 784. I can, however, deal with
H   this matter very briefly because Mr. Toulmin has not sought to argue
against the contention advanced by the society here that the maxim, in
whatever form one chooses to relate it, has no reference to tribunals
such as this one at all. First of all, although the facts might be the same
before the criminal court and before the tribunals, the offence and the
findings are totally distinct. Secondly, it is plain on the authorities that
a tribunal such as this is not a court of competent jurisdiction to which
the maxim applies.

Reg. v. Statutory Cttee., Ex p. Pharmaceutical (D.C.)   **[1981]**

A   In those circumstances it is enough for me to say that the second leg of the argument based on the so-called maxim fails. The result is that the request that certiorari and mandamus should issue in this case is good, and they must issue. What the penalty may be when the case goes back, in all the circumstances, is none of our affair, though doubtless the committee will take fully into account the matters which have been urged upon us in the document I have mentioned, which was put before us by the three young men. The appeal must, in the circumstances, be allowed.

B

Application allowed.
No order as to costs.

Solicitors: *Walker, Martineau & Co.; Le Brasseur & Bury.*

C

[Reported by G. B. PURVES ESQ., Barrister-at-Law]

D

[QUEEN'S BENCH DIVISION]

* SEAROSE LTD. *v.* SEATRAIN U.K. LTD.

1981 Feb. 13, 16   Robert Goff J.

E

Injunction — Interlocutory — Mareva injunction — Conditions — Application to restrain removal by defendant of any money in any bank account at specified branch—Whether plaintiff entitled to injunction—Whether plaintiff to pay bank's reasonable costs

F   The plaintiffs issued a writ against the defendants claiming damages for breach of contract. The following day they applied, ex parte, for a *Mareva* injunction to restrain the defendants from removing from the jurisdiction or otherwise disposing of any of their assets within the jurisdiction, in particular any moneys in any bank account of the defendants at a specified branch, save in so far as such assets or moneys exceeded £44,000.

On the application: —

G   *Held,* that third parties such as banks risked proceedings for contempt if they acted contrary to the terms of *Mareva* injunctions of which they were given notice, and they were therefore obliged to determine whether any assets to which the injunctions applied were within their possession or control; that it was not reasonable to expect third parties to bear the cost of such investigations without being reimbursed by the plaintiff, except where, in the case of a bank, the injunction identified a particular bank account; that, accordingly, the appropriate course was to grant the injunction sought on condition that the plaintiffs undertook to pay any reasonable costs so incurred by any person, other than the defendants, to whom notice of the injunction was given (post, pp. 895G, 896A–C).

H

Dictum of Lord Denning M.R. in *Prince Abdul Rahman Bin Turki Al Sudairy* v. *Abu-Taha* [1980] 1 W.L.R. 1268, 1273, C.A. applied.

A   The following case is referred to in the judgment:

Rahman (Prince Abdul) Bin Turki Al Sudairy v. Abu-Taha [1980] 1 W.L.R. 1268; [1980] 3 All E.R. 409, C.A.

No additional cases were cited in argument.

Ex parte application

B   By a writ issued on February 12, 1981, the plaintiffs, Searose Ltd. (trading as European Container Services), claimed damages against the defendants, Seatrain U.K. Ltd., for breach of a written contract or contracts made between the parties in or about or since 1975 and/or to be implied from a course of dealing between the parties since 1975.

On February 13, the plaintiffs applied, ex parte, for a *Mareva* injunc-
C   tion to restrain the defendants from removing from the jurisdiction or otherwise disposing of any of their assets within the jurisdiction save in so far as such assets exceeded the sum of £44,000. They further asked that the injunction should specify, in particular, any moneys in any bank account of the defendants with Williams & Glynn's Bank Ltd. at their branch at 38 Moseley Street, Manchester, M60 2BE.

The application was heard and judgment given in chambers on
D   February 13, but on February 16 Robert Goff J. redelivered part of the judgment in open court.

David Hunt for the plaintiffs.

February 16. Robert Goff J. read the following judgment. On
E   Friday, February 13, 1981, the plaintiffs applied ex parte in chambers for a *Mareva* injunction to restrain the defendants from disposing of their assets within the jurisdiction, save in so far as such assets exceeded the sum of £44,000, which was the amount of the plaintiffs' claim against the defendants for damages for breach of contract. I granted the injunction; but since the application raised one matter which may be of general interest concerning this rapidly developing jurisdiction, I propose
F   to repeat my judgment, so far as it concerns that matter, in open court. The plaintiffs have agreed to my taking this course.

The matter in question is this. The plaintiffs asked that the *Mareva* injunction should specify, in particular, any moneys in any bank account of the defendants with Williams & Glynn's Bank Ltd., 38 Moseley Street, Manchester, M60 2BE. I informed the plaintiffs that, in the circumstances,
G   I was only prepared to grant the injunction if they gave an undertaking to pay the reasonable costs incurred by any person (other than the defendants) to whom notice of the terms of the injunction was given, in ascertaining whether or not any asset to which the order applied was within his possession or control. I did so for the following reasons.

In *Prince Abdul Rahman Bin Turki Al Sudairy* v. *Abu-Taha* [1980]
H   1 W.L.R. 1268, 1273, Lord Denning M.R. said: " . . . when there is a *Mareva* injunction of this kind, if the people who are notified of it are put to any expense in regard to it, that expense must be paid by the plaintiff." Now it may well be that, in giving this guidance, Lord Denning M.R. had particularly in mind the effect of *Mareva* injunctions upon banks. It is well known to the judges who sit in the Commercial Court that, as *Mareva* injunctions have come to be granted more frequently, the banks in this country have received numerous notices of injunctions which have been granted. Sometimes the injunction identifies the bank account in question;

896

sometimes it identifies the branch of a bank, at which the defendant is said   A
to have a bank account; sometimes it identifies the bank and no more;
sometimes it does not even identify the bank. Now where the particular
account is identified, I do not think the bank can reasonably complain.
Every citizen of this country who receives notice of an injunction granted
by the court will risk proceedings for contempt of court if he acts inconsistently with the injunction; and a bank, like any other citizen, must avoid
any such action. But where the particular account is not identified, the   B
situation is somewhat different. I do not think it is right that the bank
should incur expense in ascertaining whether the alleged account exists,
without being reimbursed by the plaintiff for any reasonable costs so
incurred. Banks are not debt-collecting agencies; they are simply, in this
context, citizens who are anxious not to contravene an order made by the
court, an order which has been obtained on the application of, and for the   C
benefit of, the plaintiff. Even where the particular branch of the bank is
identified, some expense is likely to be incurred in ascertaining whether the
defendant has an account at the branch. But where the branch is not
identified, the bank will be put in a very difficult position. It is, I think,
well known that Barclays Bank has over 3,000 branches in this country,
and Lloyds Bank has over 2,000 branches. Are they to circulate all their   D
branches? If they did so, it would involve them in great expense; moreover such an exercise cannot, in ordinary circumstances, reasonably be
expected of them.

It seems to me that this problem can be solved, in accordance with the
guidance given by Lord Denning M.R. in *Prince Abdul Rahman Bin Turki
Al Sudairy* v. *Abu-Taha* [1980] 1 W.L.R. 1268 by requiring the plaintiffs
to give an undertaking in the terms which I have indicated. The effect   E
of this undertaking will be that a bank to whom notice of an injunction
is given can, before taking steps to ascertain whether the defendants have
an account at any particular branch, obtain an undertaking from the
plaintiffs' solicitors to pay their reasonable costs incurred in so doing.
The bank will then be protected; moreover the plaintiffs' solicitors will no
doubt be encouraged to limit their inquiry to a particular branch, or to   F
certain particular branches.

It is possible that a practice may develop under which, in ordinary
circumstances, the clearing banks charge a standard fee where the branch
of the bank is identified, and charge another standard fee per branch to be
searched if no branch is identified. If reasonable standard fees can be
established to the satisfaction of the taxing masters, a great deal of time and
money may be saved thereafter on the taxation of costs.   G

I have certain other comments to make. First, the cost of the search
must in the first instance be borne by the plaintiff, on whose ex parte
application the injunction has been granted. Whether he will be able to
obtain an indemnity from the defendant will depend upon any order as to
costs which is thereafter made between the parties to the litigation.

Secondly, the undertaking required of the plaintiff must be so drawn   H
as to affect only costs incurred by a person other than the defendant (to
whom notice of the injunction is given) but not costs incurred by the
defendant himself (upon whom the order is served).

Thirdly, although I have in this judgment dwelt upon the position of
banks, because they are most likely to be affected, the undertaking so given
could, if appropriate, be equally effective to protect other third parties
similarly affected.

The Weekly Law Reports, June 19, 1981

897

1 W.L.R.   Searose Ltd. v. Seatrain Ltd. (Q.B.D.)   Robert Goff J.

A   Lastly, may I say this. It is, I believe, now generally recognised that the *Mareva* jurisdiction has filled a gap in the court's powers which badly needed to be filled. In the Commercial Court, certainly, a very large number of these injunctions is granted each year. But care must be taken to ensure that such injunctions are only given for the purpose for which they are intended, viz. to prevent the possible abuse of a defendant removing assets in order to prevent the satisfaction of a judgment in pending pro-

B   ceedings: and likewise, care must be taken to ensure that such injunctions do not bear harshly upon innocent third parties. If these principles are not observed, a weapon which was forged to prevent abuse may become an instrument of oppression.

It follows that, first, an order for a *Mareva* injunction should not be sought in terms wider than are reasonably required in the circumstances of

C   the case. Secondly, any asset in respect of which an order for a *Mareva* injunction is sought should be identified with as much precision as is reasonably practicable. Thirdly, as regards any asset to which the order applies but which has not been identified with precision in the form of order proposed, e.g. money held in an unidentified bank account, the plaintiff may be required to give an undertaking to pay reasonable costs incurred by any person (other than the defendant) to whom notice of the terms of the

D   injunction is given, in ascertaining whether or not any asset to which the order applies, but has not been identified in it, is within his possession or control.

Of course in many cases (for example where, as is usually the case, the plaintiff is unable to identify assets of the defendant which are known to be greater in value than the sum in respect of which he seeks a *Mareva*

E   injunction), it will be appropriate for the court to give the *Mareva* injunction in the now hallowed form, under which the defendant is restrained from removing from the jurisdiction or otherwise disposing of any of his assets within the jurisdiction, and in particular a specific asset or assets, save in so far as the value of such assets exceeds a certain sum. But if an injunction is given in such terms, the court may require—and indeed in my judgment should ordinarily require—that the plaintiff gives an undertaking

F   in the form I have indicated.

In the present case, I have required the plaintiffs to give such an under-taking as a condition of the grant of the injunction. It is right that I should record that the plaintiffs made no objection to this; indeed they regarded it as entirely reasonable.

Finally I should state that I have not considered in this case the position

G   which may arise where a third party incurs expense by reason of the fact that, through the imposition of a *Mareva* injunction of which he is given notice, he is unable to part with the possession of a chattel, e.g. an air-craft, which has been entrusted to him by the defendant. This point will no doubt be considered in some future case, in which it arises for decision.

Order accordingly.

H

Solicitors: *Lawrence Jones & Co.*

[Reported by ISOBEL COLLINS, Barrister-at-Law]

[1981]

A

[QUEEN'S BENCH DIVISION]

* A. LAMBERT FLAT MANAGEMENT LTD. *v.* LOMAS

1980 Dec. 11; 19   Ackner L.J. and Skinner J.

B

Public Health—Nuisance—Abatement notice—Noise made by lifts in block of flats—Validity of abatement notice unchallenged —Failure to comply with notice—Whether common law defences to allegation of nuisance "reasonable excuse" for non-compliance—Control of Pollution Act 1974 (c. 40), s. 58 (1) (4)

The defendant company was the lessee of a block of self-contained flats and a party to separate but identical leases   C
between the freeholder and the tenants of the flats. Under the terms of those leases, it managed the property and the tenants were liable to reimburse the defendant for the expenses incurred. The premises contained two lifts and each lift motor was situated in the roof above an upper storey flat, which was adjacent to the lift shaft. The residents of those two flats complained to the local authority of the noise made by the lifts and the local authority, being satisfied that the noise   D
amounted to a nuisance, served notices on the defendant, under section 58 of the Control of Pollution Act 1974,[1] requiring it to abate the nuisance and to execute certain works for that purpose. The defendant neither appealed against the notices under section 58 (3) of the Act nor complied with the terms of the notices. Informations were preferred against the defendant alleging contravention of the notices, contrary to section 58 (4). The justices convicted the defendant. On the   E
defendant's appeal, the Crown Court found that the noise emanating from the lifts amounted to a nuisance but they allowed the appeal on the ground that the defendant had a "reasonable excuse" within the meaning of section 58 (4) for not complying with the notices by establishing that the residents, being lessees of a portion of the premises, had to take the premises as they found them. The prosecutor appealed.

On the question whether section 58 of the Act applied   F
where the activity complained of arose in pursuance of a covenant in a lease between the defendant and the lessees and where the defendant would have defences in a common law action in nuisance brought by the lessees of the flats: —

Held, allowing the appeal, that once the level of noise was such that it interfered with the use and enjoyment of land then there was a nuisance to which section 58 of the Act applied and it was irrelevant that a recipient of a notice served   G
under the section had no liability for the nuisance in contract or tort (post, pp. 905F–G, 906F); that, although it was a defence to a prosecution brought under the Act to prove a reasonable excuse for non-compliance with the notice, "reasonable excuse" within the meaning of subsection (4) did not include matters that should have been raised on an appeal challenging the validity of the notice; and that, accordingly, since the defendant was challenging the validity of the notice by relying   H
on common law defences, the Crown Court erred in law and should have dismissed the defendant's appeal (post, pp. 904H, 906,F, 907C–F).

The following cases are referred to in the judgment:
Ager v. *Gates* (1934) 151 L.T. 98.

---

[1] Control of Pollution Act 1974, s. 58: see post, pp. 902H—903C.

A   *Francis* v. *Yiewsley and West Drayton Urban District Council* [1958]
       1 Q.B. 478; [1957] 3 W.L.R. 919; [1957] 3 All E.R. 529, C.A.
     Kiddle v. *City Business Properties Ltd.* [1942] 1 K.B. 269; [1942] 2 All
       E.R. 216.

     The following additional cases were cited in argument:

     Mason v. *Smith* [1953] C.P.L. 493, C.A.

B   *Sedleigh-Denfield* v. *O'Callaghan* [1940] A.C. 880; [1940] 3 All E.R. 349,
       H.L.(E.).

     CASE STATED by the Bournemouth Crown Court.
        On March 15, 1979, the Bournemouth justices convicted the defendant,
     A. Lambert Flat Management Ltd., of ten offences under section 58 of
   C the Control of Pollution Act 1974 in respect of premises known as
     Kernella Court, 51/53, Surrey Road, Bournemouth, Dorset. An appeal
     against the convictions by the defendant to the Bournemouth Crown Court
     was heard on June 28, 1979, and the convictions were set aside.
        The Crown Court found that Kernella Court consisted of a block of
     24 self-contained flats owned by A. Lambert Investments Ltd. (called
     the freeholder) and leased by the freeholder to individual lessees
   D for terms of 99 years—flat 23, situated on the top floor of the building,
     was at all material times leased to Mr. and Mrs. Thomas as assignees of
     the original lessees; flat 11, also situated on the top floor, was at all
     material times leased to Mrs. Price. In each instance the defendant, in
     the capacity of manager was party to the lease, the powers and duties of the
     manager being defined in identical terms in each lease. In particular,
   E the manager's duties related to parts of the building not demised to the
     individual lessees, the parts not so demised being referred to as the reserved
     property. Inter alia, the defendant covenanted by clause 4 and paragraph
     5 (8) of the sixth schedule with the freeholder and the individual lessees
     to keep the halls, stairs, lifts, landings and passages forming part of the
     reserved property clean and in good order. The individual leases further
     provided, inter alia, that, in addition to paying into a common fund annually
   F a certain sum towards the costs of the defendant in carrying out its duties,
     the lessees must indemnify the defendants against all costs, charges and
     expenses incurred by the defendant in carrying out its obligations. By a
     lease made September 28, 1976, the freeholder granted to the defendant
     a lease for 99 years, at a peppercorn rent, from June 24, 1974, of the
     block of flats and outbuildings together with the roof and rafters, the
   G foundations, common entrances passageways, stairs, exterior walls and
     interior walls adjoining all commonways. The reserved property included
     two passenger lifts, situated some distance from each other, the liftshafts,
     extending from ground floor to top floor. The shaft of one lift adjoined
     flat 11; the shaft of the other adjoined flat 23. The motors of each lift
     were sited, in the case of the one lift, in the roof immediately above
     flat 11, and in the case of the other in the roof immediately above flat 23.
   H   As a result of complaints made to the Bournemouth Borough Council
     as the local authority for the area in which Kernella Court was situated
     by the lessees of flat 11 and flat 23, investigations were carried out by the
     environmental health officer employed by the local authority. On January
     23, 1978, notices under section 58 of the Control of Pollution Act 1974
     were served upon the freeholder and the defendant by the prosecutor,
     Keith Lomas, who was the chief executive and town clerk of the local
     authority, on behalf of the authority. The notices were in the following

terms. The Bournemouth Borough Council being satisfied that noise   A
amounting to a nuisance existed and was likely to recur at Kernella Court,
51/53, Surrey Road, Bournemouth arising from the lift motors and associated equipment serving the two lifts in those premises required the
defendant within six months (a) to abate the noise and for that purpose
(i) to acoustically isolate the motors and associated equipment from the
building structure, in such a manner as to prevent noise amounting to a
nuisance in living accommodation, namely flat 11 and flat 23 (informations   B
1 and 7 respectively); (ii) to modify the landing gate mechanism in such a
manner as to prevent noise amounting to a nuisance in living accommodation, namely, flat 11 (information 2); (iii) to carry out such works as
might be necessary to prevent noise from the lift motors and other
associated equipment from generating noise amounting to a nuisance in
living accommodation, namely, flat 11 and flat 23 (informations 3 and 8   C
respectively); and (b) to prevent its recurrence and for that purpose to
(i) acoustically isolate the motors and associated equipment from the building structure in such a manner as to prevent noise amounting to a nuisance
in living accommodation, namely, flat 11 and flat 23 (informations 4 and
9 respectively); (ii) modify the landing gate mechanism to prevent noise
amounting to a nuisance in living accommodation, namely, flat 11 (information 5); (iii) carry out such works as might be necessary to prevent noise   D
from the lift motors and other associated equipment from generating noise
amounting to a nuisance in living accommodation, namely flat 11 and flat
23 (informations 6 and 10 respectively).

No appeals were lodged against the section 58 notices and no work of
modification or otherwise was carried out to the lift machinery or allied
equipment, or, in the case of flat 11, to the landing gate mechanism. On   E
December 13, 1978, the prosecutor on behalf of the local authority, laid
informations in the Bournemouth Magistrates' Court alleging in ten
instances contravention by, in one series, the freeholder, and in another
series, the defendant, of the requirements of the section 58 notices. The
Bournemouth justices subsequently dismissed the informations against the
freeholder.

The lessee of flat 11 and the lessees of flat 23 complained of nuisance   F
by noise. In the case of flat 23 the lessees were seriously disturbed by a
shrieking noise each time the lift was used, followed by a hum as the lift
travelled, and a banging each time the landing gates opened and shut,
with rattling and vibration in the lift doors. The lessee of flat 11 was
seriously disturbed by a shrieking noise each time the lift was used followed
by clattering when the landing gates opened and shut.

It was contended by the defendant that the nuisance which the Control   G
of Pollution Act 1974 was intended to remedy fell into the categories
either of public or private nuisance; that any liability of the defendant in
relation to nuisance created by the lift mechanism arose in contract, not
in tort; that there was no evidence of negligence by the defendant nor
evidence of public nuisance; alternatively, that the defendant had reasonable excuse for not complying with the notices served under section 58 of   H
the Control of Pollution Act 1974 if there was no legal nuisance or if in a
civil action based on the alleged nuisance it would have had a defence;
that the nuisance alleged by the prosecutor consisted of noise and vibration
experienced in flats 11 and 23, Kernella Court which were, in the block,
the closest to the motors of the lifts; that the lifts were operated by the
defendant for the benefit of the whole block of flats and were so operated
for no other reason than that the defendant was bound to do so by the

A covenant with the lessees of each flat in the block including the lessees of flats 11 and 23. Therefore the defendant's obligations in respect of the lifts vis-à-vis the occupants of the block arose in contract and were governed by contract, not tort; that only the occupants of flats within the building had been affected; that a nuisance at common law could not arise if it affected only the people occupying the premises where the nuisance was said to have taken place; that the block of flats constituted one set of B premises of which the individual flats formed part; that the lessees of flat 11 and flat 23 had full knowledge of the existence of the lifts before entering into their respective leases and must be taken to have given implied consent to their presence and that the defendant was only bound to take reasonable care to prevent a nuisance.

It was contended by the prosecutor that by failing to appeal against C the section 58 notices the defendant was estopped from denying that the matters complained of were a nuisance within the provisions of the Control of Pollution Act 1974; that each part of the building constituted separate premises; that the reserved property leased by the freeholder to the defendant must by the nature of things be separate premises from flat 11 or flat 23; the lessees of neither of those flats could, under the terms of their leases, occupy the reserved property nor each other's property; that the D excessive noise complained of by the lessees of flat 11 and flat 23 in no way resulted from the use and occupation of, nor emanated from, those flats; that the implied consent to taking premises as one found them, which could be raised as a defence in a civil action could not be a defence to proceedings from an offence under section 58 of the Control of Pollution Act 1974.

E The Crown Court found that the noise level emanating from the two lifts was excessive and caused the residents of the two flats, flat 11 and flat 23, distress and would amount to a nuisance by noise, and, further, that no work had been done by the defendant to comply with the section 58 notices and/or to abate the nuisances. The court held that it was bound by the authorities and in particular by *Kiddle* v. *City Business Properties Ltd.* [1942] 1 K.B. 269 which in effect meant that the lessees at Kernella F Court had to take the premises as they found them, and the Crown Court allowed the appeal.

The prosecutor appealed. The questions for the opinion of the High Court were (1) whether the implied consent to taking premises as one found them was a valid defence to proceedings for an offence under the Control of Pollution Act 1974. (ii) Whether volenti non fit injuria could be a G defence in such proceedings on the grounds that (a) there was then no nuisance, or (b) there was then a reasonable excuse, and if so whether on the facts found the defence was made out. (iii) Whether there could be a legal nuisance within the meaning of the Control of Pollution Act 1974 when (a) the activities complained of were undertaken in a block of flats by a management company in pursuance of a covenant between the management company and the lessee of the flats in the block and (b) the H noise caused by the activities was experienced only in the flats in the block. (iv) Whether proof of the facts set forth in question (iii) (a) and (b) above could amount to a reasonable excuse within section 58 of the Control of Pollution Act 1974; if not, whether such proof together with proof that the cost of complying with the statutory notices would ultimately fall on the lessees of each flat could amount to such reasonable excuse. (v) Did the provisions of section 58 of the Control of Pollution Act 1974 apply where,

as in the case of Kernella Court, the property was divided into flats on A
the one part and property reserved to the management on the other part,
so that there were a number of separate legal entities within the exterior
walls of the building. (vi) Whether the Crown Court was wrong in allowing the appeal of the defendants.

David Keene Q.C. and *Deirdre McKinney* for the prosecutor.   B
Michael Norman for the defendants.

                                                Cur. adv. vult.

December 19. The following judgments were read.

    SKINNER J. read the first judgment. This is an appeal by way of
case stated from a decision of the Bournemouth Crown Court presided C
over by Judge Blaker. The Crown Court allowed an appeal from Bournemouth Magistrates' Court against convictions of the defendant on ten
summonses alleging contraventions of section 58 of the Control of Pollution Act 1974 in respect of a block of flats known as Kernella Court in
Bournemouth.

    The Crown Court found that Kernella Court consisted of a block of 24 D
self-contained flats owned by A. Lambert (Investment) Ltd., the freeholder. All the flats were leased on 99-year leases to which the defendant
was a party. In each lease the hall, stairs, lifts, landings and passages
were referred to as " reserved premises " and the defendant covenanted
both with the freeholder and the lessees to keep the reserved property
clean and in good order. Subsequently in 1976 the freeholder granted the
defendant a lease of the whole building at a peppercorn rent for 99 years. E

    In the block of flats were two lifts. By the top of each lift was one
flat and above each flat was the lift motor. It is these flats, no. 11 and
no. 23, which are the subject of the proceedings in this case. The Crown
Court found:

> " In the case of flat 23 the lessees were seriously disturbed by a
> shrieking noise each time the lift was used, followed by a hum as the F
> lift travelled, and a banging each time the landing gates opened and
> shut, with rattling and vibration in the lift doors. The lessee of flat 11
> was seriously disturbed by a shrieking noise each time the lift was
> used followed by a clattering when the landing gates opened and shut."

The residents complained, the local authority investigated the matter, and
on January 23, 1978, served notices under section 58 of the Control of G
Pollution Act 1974 on the defendant.

    Section 58 lies in Part III of the Act, which provides an entirely new
code for the control of noise. Previous legislation had been contained in
the Noise Abatement Act 1960 which had applied the provisions of the
Public Health Act 1936 to noise as a " statutory nuisance." Section 57
provides:

> " It shall be the duty of every local authority to cause its area to be H
> inspected from time to time—(a) to detect anything which ought to
> be dealt with under the following section; . . ."

Section 58 provides:

> " (1) Where a local authority is satisfied that noise amounting to a
> nuisance exists, or is likely to occur or recur, in the area of the local

A　authority, the local authority shall serve a notice imposing all or any of the following requirements—(a) requiring the abatement of the nuisance or prohibiting or restricting its occurrence or recurrence; (b) requiring the execution of such works, and the taking of such other steps, as may be necessary for the purpose of the notice or as may be specified in the notice; and the notice shall specify the time or times within which the requirements of the notice are to be complied

B　with. (2) The notice shall be served on the person responsible for the nuisance or, if that person cannot be found or the nuisance has not yet occurred, on the owner or occupier of the premises from which the noise is emitted or would be emitted. (3) The person served with the notice may appeal against the notice to a magistrates' court within 21 days from service of the notice. (4) If a person on

C　whom a notice is served under this section without reasonable excuse contravenes any requirement of the notice, he shall be guilty of an offence against this Part of this Act."

The procedure on appeals under section 58 (3) is contained in section 70 of the Act which provides that they shall be made by way of complaint and gives the Secretary of State power to make regulations as to appeals

D　under Part III of the Act. These regulations are contained in the Control of Noise (Appeals) Regulations 1975 (S.I. 1975 No. 2116) which came into force on the same day as Part III of the Act, that is January 1, 1976.

Regulation 4 (2) deals comprehensively with the grounds of appeal available including at paragraph (a): " that the notice is not justified by the terms of section 58." Regulation 4 (5) gives the magistrates' court wide powers on the hearing of the appeal, to quash the notice, vary it in favour

E　of the appellant or to dismiss the appeal, and goes on to provide: " a notice which is varied . . . shall be final and shall otherwise have effect, as so varied, as if it had been so made by the local authority." Section 73 (1) of the Act defines the " person responsible " for the purpose of section 58 (2) as " in relation to the emission of noise . . . the person to whose act, default or sufferance the noise is attributable; . . ."

F　Returning to the history, the effect of the notices served upon the defendant was to require it within six months to abate the noise and for that purpose to acoustically isolate the motors and associated equipment of the lift from the building structure, to modify the landing gate mechanism in such a manner as to prevent noise amounting to a nuisance arising, and to carry out such works as to be necessary to prevent noise from the lift motors and other associated equipment from generating noise amounting

G　to a nuisance in the living accommodation concerned. They also required the defendant to take similar steps to prevent the recurrence of the nuisance.

The defendant did not appeal against the notices under section 58 (3) nor did it do anything to abate the nuisance in accordance with the notices or at all. Thus on December 13, 1978, the prosecutor laid informations in the magistrates' court alleging " contraventions " of the section 58

H　notices contrary to subsection (4). The justices convicted. The defendant appealed to the Crown Court and the Crown Court found, in addition to the facts I have already mentioned, that the noise level emanating from the two lifts was excessive and caused the residents of the two flats, no. 11 and no. 23, distress and would amount to a nuisance by noise, and further that no work had been done by the defendant to comply with the section 58 notices and/or to abate the nuisance. The court went on to hold that it was bound by certain authorities which had been quoted to it and, in particular, *Kiddle* v. *City Business Properties Ltd.* [1942] 1 K.B. 269, **A** which in effect meant that the lessees at Kernella Court had to take the premises as they found them. The Crown Court thereupon allowed the appeal. The basis of the Crown Court's decision was that any defence that would have been open to the defendant if used by the occupier of premises affected by the nuisance in a civil action was available to it in proceedings brought by the local authority under section 58 (4).

This the prosecutor challenges. It was common ground before this **B** court that, on the Crown Court findings, the defendant had contravened requirements of the notices and the only question this court has to consider is whether, in law, the facts disclosed could amount to a " reasonable excuse " which would exempt it from liability under section 58 (4).

Mr. Keene, in his clear and helpful argument, submitted that a reasonable excuse must be limited to an excuse for non-compliance with the **C** notice and cannot include a challenge to its validity. He gave as an instance an owner who was not an occupier who had difficulty in gaining access to the premises. An excuse cannot be reasonable, he goes on to submit, if it involves matters which could have been raised on appeal under section 58 (3). He cited in support of that proposition *Ager* v. *Gates* (1934) 151 L.T. 98, a decision under the Public Health Act 1875, **D** where the question at issue was whether a person served with a nuisance order under that Act had acted with due diligence. Against that Mr. Norman, for the defendant cited *Francis* v. *Yiewsley and West Drayton Urban District Council* [1958] 1 Q.B. 478, a decision under the provisions of sections 23 and 24 of the Town and Country Planning Act 1947.

Mr. Norman objected that since section 58 involves an invasion into private rights of property, and creates criminal offences, Parliament cannot **E** have intended that the onus of challenging the local authority's right to interfere should be placed upon the " person liable " and that, since there is no provision for extension of the time for appealing, he should lose his right to challenge after 21 days. What, he asked, if the " person liable " did not receive the notice because he was ill or abroad? The answer, says Mr. Keene, and I agree with him, is that these are matters which can, and would, constitute a " reasonable excuse " within section 58 (4): the contra- **F** vention proceedings would be defeated and the local authority could then, if it wished, commence fresh proceedings in which the " person liable " would have his right of appeal.

For my part I do not derive assistance from either of the cases cited by counsel: each is a decision on its own special facts and its own special statute. I prefer to look at the scheme laid down in this Act and its **G** associated Regulations. A comprehensive right of appeal is given by section 58 (3) which was not available under the Noise Abatement Act 1960. Regulation 4 (2) (*a*) of the Control of Noise (Appeals) Regulations 1975, permits an appeal on the ground that the notice is not justified by the terms of section 58.

In my judgment an excuse cannot be " reasonable " under section 58 (4) **H** if it involves matters which could have been raised on appeal under section 58 (3) unless such matters arose after the appeal was heard or, if there was no appeal, after the time for appeal had expired.

Mr. Keene next submitted that the Crown Court was wrong in holding in any event that a defence inter parties in a civil action based on the tort of nuisance could be a defence to a charge under section 58 (4). The burden of this submission was that, save in one respect, the concepts

A involved in a civil action in tort are foreign to sections 57 and 58. He makes four points.

First, the one respect in which the tort of nuisance is relevant is in dealing with the question whether " noise amounting to a nuisance " exists within section 58 (1). The subsection does not require that noise amounting to a nuisance actionable at common law by a party who has suffered damage should exist. Mr. Norman replies that to be " noise amounting
B to a nuisance " it must be tortious, that is, wrongful and unlawful, and it cannot be wrongful or unlawful if a defence at common law is available.

Mr. Keene countered that argument in advance by his third submission, viz. the defences upheld by the Crown Court only exist between certain identifiable parties who are ex hypothesi different from the parties to proceedings under section 58. What is more, whereas liability at common
C law rests with the person who created the nuisance, or the land owner if he knew or ought to have known the facts constituting the nuisance, liability under the statute is determined by section 58 (2) and the definition of " person responsible " in section 73 (1). I need not repeat the words of section 58 (2). Suffice it to say that a notice requiring the abatement of the nuisance and the execution of works may be served on the owner
D of the premises from which the noise is emitted even though he is not the " person liable " and may know nothing about it. The Act, says Mr. Keene, has its own code of who takes proceedings, who is liable and what are the defences available, and the only relevance of the common law is in deciding the question whether the noise amounts to a nuisance. He justifies this interpretation in part by his second submission, viz. that this is an Act concerned with the public good and the cure of nuisances at the
E initiative of the local authority under the duty imposed by section 57. It is not concerned with the consents of individuals or the complex questions which can arise in actions between individuals. Finally, he submitted that on the facts of the present case, the Crown Court had no difficulty in concluding that " a noise amounting to a nuisance " existed within section 58 (1) and that was the only relevant question for them to decide.

F I accept Mr. Keene's submissions. The only relevance of the tort of nuisance in proceedings under section 58 is to establish the level of noise which exists: it is a measure or standard. Once that level has been established to the satisfaction of the local authority, the procedure laid down by section 58 comes into play. The " person liable " may contest that the noise amounts to a nuisance under regulation 4 (2) (a) of the Control of Noise (Appeals) Regulations 1975, but any defence based on
G his duties in tort or contract to any person affected by the nuisance is not open to him.

This last sentence answers the first five questions raised in this case. The sixth and last asked whether the Crown Court was wrong in allowing the appeal of the defendant. In my judgment it was and I would remit the case to the Crown Court with a direction to restore the convictions.

H
ACKNER L.J. I agree. On January 1, 1976, Part II of the Control of Pollution Act 1974 was brought into operation. There was also brought into operation on the same day the Control of Noise (Appeals) Regulations 1975, made by the Secretary of State for the Environment in the exercise of the powers conferred upon him by section 70 (2) of the Act of 1974. Thus from the date mentioned above it became the duty of every local authority under section 57 of the Act to inspect its area from time to time

and to detect anything which ought to be dealt with under section 58. A
Section 58 (1) provides that where a local authority is satisfied that noise
amounting to a nuisance exists, it shall serve a notice which may require
the abatement of the nuisance or the execution of necessary works.

The first question to decide is the proper interpretation of the words
"noise amounting to a nuisance." It is common ground that the noise
must amount to a nuisance in the ordinary legal case. Mr. Keene for the
appellant contends that although this must mean that the noise must   B
amount to the undue interference with the use or enjoyment of the relevant
flats, the local authority does not have to be satisfied that a civil action in
respect of such nuisance would necessarily succeed.

Mr. Norman for the defendant contends that the local authority must
be satisfied that the noise constitutes an actionable nuisance at common
law. In my judgment it is clear that section 58 is not concerned, given   C
that the noise unduly interferes with the use or enjoyment of land, with
whether or not there is a sound cause of action in respect of that noise.
Subsection (2) provides that the notice shall be served on the person
responsible for the nuisance or, if he cannot be found, on the owner or
occupier of the premises from which the noise is emitted. The "person
responsible" in relation to the emission of noise is defined by section   D
73 (1) as meaning "the person to whose act, default or sufferance the noise
is attributable." It by no means follows that he must of necessity be a
tortfeasor.

Moreover, if the legislature was concerned to restrict the local authority's activities to actionable nuisances, then it seems odd indeed that the
owner or occupier, who ex hypothesi, on the wording of subsection (2),
is not the "person responsible for the nuisance," should be a proper   E
recipient of the notice. To make such a person who is innocent of all
civil liability guilty of a criminal offence for not complying with the notice
would seem an odd result indeed to achieve, if an actionable nuisance,
that is, one to which there was no defence, has to be established before the
notice could issue.

To my mind section 58 is concerned with what can conveniently be   F
labled a statutory nuisance, that is a nuisance where the conduct complained of unduly interferes with the use or enjoyment of the land of
another, but in regard to which the various common law defences are
irrelevant.

The person served with a notice may appeal against the notice to a
magistrates' court within 21 days of the service of the notice: section
58 (3). The regulations to which I have referred at the outset of this   G
judgment make detailed provision for such appeal. They provide for the
grounds of appeal, which are many and various, they also provide for the
quashing or variation of the notice as well as, of course, for the dismissal
of the appeal. On the hearing of the appeal the court may make such
order as it thinks fit with respect to the person by whom any work is to
be executed and the contribution to be made by any person towards the   H
cost of the work, or as to the proportions in which any expenses which
may become recoverable by the local authority are to be borne by the
appellant and any other person. The magistrates' courts are specifically
enjoined in exercising the powers to which I have just referred, to have
regard as between an owner and an occupier to the terms and conditions,
whether contractual or statutory, of any relevant tenancy in the nature
of the work required. There are, of course, the ordinary rights of appeal

A from the magistrates' court to the Crown Court or to this court by case stated.

Section 58 (4) provides that if a person on whom a notice is served under the section without reasonable excuse contravenes any requirement of the notice, he shall be guilty of an offence against this Part of this Act. In this case no appeals were lodged against the notices and no work

B of modification or otherwise was carried out to the lift machinery or allied equipment or to the landing gate mechanism of flat 11. In those circumstances can the defendant urge, as a reasonable excuse for failing to comply with the notice, that the same was invalid for one or more of the reasons provided by the Regulations as permissible grounds of appeal? I am assuming, which assumption is wholly justified on the facts of this case, that there was no special reason such as illness, non-receipt of the

C notice or other potential excuse for not entering an appeal.

The answer to my mind is clearly in the negative. As stated above, not only is the right of appeal given by the statute but very detailed provisions have been made by the Regulations for the prosecution of such appeals. Section 58 (4) was not designed, in my judgment, to give the recipient of the notice a choice of forum in which to mount his attack on the notice.

D It was designed to provide a defence to a criminal charge where he had some reasonable excuse, such as some special difficulty in relation to compliance with the notice. It does not provide an opportunity, when prosecuted, to challenge the correctness and justification of the notice where the defendant has not availed himself of his statutory opportunity to do this by way of appeal.

In my judgment the Crown Court had no jurisdiction to inquire into the

E question as to whether the noise amounted to a nuisance. However, if I am wrong about that, the Crown Court, having found that the noise level emanating from the two lifts was excessive and caused the residents of the two flats distress, and that no work had been done by the defendant to comply with the notices, had no alternative but to dismiss the appeals against the convictions by the Bournemouth justices on March 15, 1979.

F The Crown Court were therefore wrong in allowing the appeal and I accordingly agree with the order proposed.

Appeal allowed with costs.

Solicitors: *S. J. C. Chappell, Bournemouth; E. W. Marshall Harvey & Dalton, Bournemouth.*

G

[Reported by ISOBEL COLLINS, Barrister-at-Law]

H

[CHANCERY DIVISION]

* MALLALIEU v. DRUMMOND (INSPECTOR OF TAXES)

1981   March 2, 3; 12   Slade J.

B

Revenue—Income tax—Expenses of trade or profession (Schedule D)—Barrister—Expenditure on replacing and cleaning professional clothes required to be worn in court—Whether incurred wholly and exclusively for purposes of profession—Whether deductible expense—Income and Corporation Taxes Act 1970 (c. 10), s. 130

Section 130 of the Income and Corporation Taxes Act 1970 provides:

C

" Subject to the provisions of the Tax Acts, in computing the amount of the profits or gains to be charged under Case I or Case II of Schedule D, no sum shall be deducted in respect of—(a) any disbursements or expenses, not being money wholly and exclusively laid out or expended for the purposes of the trade, profession or vocation . . . "

The Bar Council's notes for guidance on dress in court issued in its Annual Statement for 1973–74 provide:

D

"1. The dress of barristers appearing in court should be unobtrusive and compatible with the wearing of robes. 2. Suits and dresses should be of dark colour. Dresses or blouses should be long-sleeved and high to the neck. Men should wear waistcoats. Shirts and blouses should be predominantly white or of other unemphatic appearance. Collars should be white and shoes black."

E

The taxpayer, a practising barrister, was called to the Bar in 1970 and by 1976 had a practice that ensured she appeared in court on most days. It would have been virtually impossible for her to practice unless she complied with the Bar Council's notes for guidance on dress in court. A barrister appearing in court improperly dressed could be told by a judge that he could not be heard or he could be reprimanded by a more senior member of the profession. During the year of assessment 1977–78 the taxpayer spent £564·38 on items of clothing for wearing in court, laundry and cleaning. She preferred to wear coloured clothes of a more adventurous style than those she was required to wear in court. She had a private wardrobe of clothes and shoes that was sufficient to keep her clothed in comfort and she would not have bought any of the disputed items had it not been for the requirement of her profession that she should comply with the notes for guidance when appearing in court. In the evening if she went direct from chambers to a social engagement she would normally first change from her court clothes into coloured, more stylish clothes. Although by wearing court clothes she saved wear and tear on her private wardrobe that was not a consideration when she bought the relevant items of clothing, nor was the preservation of warmth and decency.

F

G

H

She appealed against an assessment to Schedule D, Case II income tax for 1977–78 in the sum of £6,000 on the ground that the expenditure of £564 on the replacement and laundry of her professional clothes had been incurred by her wholly and exclusively for the purposes of her profession and was deductible from her taxable profits. The general commissioners held that she had a dual purpose in making the expenditure, namely to enable her to earn profits in her profession and also to enable her to be properly clothed during the time she was

A   engaged in her professional activity, and refused to allow the deduction.

     On appeal by the taxpayer: —

     Held, allowing the appeal, that there was no broad principle that one purpose of the purchase of an item that would in part meet a basic human need, must always be deemed to be the partial satisfaction of that need; that there was no evidence to support the commissioners' decision that the taxpayer had

B   a dual purpose, both professional and personal, in incurring the expenditure on her professional wardrobe for she did not incur it in order to be warm and properly clad, since she had an adequate private wardrobe, but solely for the purpose of enabling her to be properly clothed in accordance with the requirements of her profession as a barrister, and accordingly it was expenditure incurred wholly and exclusively for the purposes of the taxpayer's profession and deductible in com-

C   puting her taxable income (post, pp. 917E—918A, 920D, 921F–G).

     Bentleys, Stokes & Lowless v. *Beeson* [1952] 2 All E.R. 82, C.A. applied.

     The following cases are referred to in the judgment:

Bentleys, Stokes & Lowless v. *Beeson* [1951] 2 All E.R. 667; [1952] 2 All E.R. 82; 33 T.C. 491, C.A.

D   *Caillebotte* v. *Quinn* [1975] 1 W.L.R. 731; [1975] 2 All E.R. 412; 50 T.C. 222.

Hillyer v. *Leeke* (1976) 51 T.C. 90.

Murgatroyd v. *Evans-Jackson* [1967] 1 W.L.R. 423; [1967] 1 All E.R. 881; 43 T.C. 581.

Norman v. *Golder* [1945] 1 All E.R. 352; 26 T.C. 293, C.A.

E   *Prince* v. *Mapp* [1970] 1 W.L.R. 260; [1970] 1 All E.R. 519; 46 T.C. 169.

Robinson v. *Scott Bader Co. Ltd.* [1980] 1 W.L.R. 755; [1980] 2 All E.R. 780.

Ward v. *Dunn* (1978) T.C. Leaflet No. 2710.

     The following additional cases were cited in argument:

Baker v. *E. Longhurst and Sons Ltd.* [1933] K.B. 461, C.A.

F   *Harrods (Buenos Aires) Ltd.* v. *Taylor-Gooby* (1964) 41 T.C. 450, C.A.

Meredith v. *Roberts* (1968) 44 T.C. 559.

Morris v. *Luton Corporation* [1946] K.B. 114; [1946] 1 All E.R. 1, C.A.

Sargent v. *Barnes* [1978] 1 W.L.R. 823; [1978] 2 All E.R. 737; T.C. Leaflet No. 2683.

Strong & Co. of Romsey Ltd. v. *Woodifield* [1906] A.C. 448; 5 T.C. 215, H.L.(E.).

G

     CASE STATED by the Commissioners for the General Purposes of the Income Tax for the Division of the Middle Temple.

     The taxpayer, Miss Ann Mallalieu, a barrister with a substantial court practice, incurred during the year of assessment 1977–78 expenditure of £564·38 on the replacement and laundry of her professional clothes. She

H   appealed against an assessment made on her under Case II of Schedule D for that year in the sum of £6,000 in respect of the profits of her profession on the ground that the £564·38 should be deducted in computing her taxable profits as it had been expended wholly and exclusively for her professional purposes within the meaning of section 130 of the Income and Corporation Taxes Act 1970. The commissioners dismissed the appeal and confirmed the assessment in the agreed amount of £4,605. The taxpayer appealed.

Mallalieu v. Drummond (Ch.D.)   **[1981]**

The facts and the decision of the commissioners are set out in the   **A**
judgment (post, pp. 910E—912B, 914E—915H).

Andrew Park Q.C. and *David Milne* for the taxpayer.
Robert Carnwath for the Crown.

Cur. adv. vult.

  B

March 12. SLADE J. read the following judgment. This is an appeal
by way of case stated against a decision of the general commissioners.
The taxpayer, Miss Mallalieu, is a practising barrister. During her
accounting year 1976–77 she expended a total sum of £564·38 on the
replacement, cleaning and laundering of certain items of clothing. She
claims that this expenditure was incurred wholly and exclusively for the   **C**
purposes of her profession. An assessment was made on her for income
tax under Case II of Schedule D for the year of assessment 1977–78 in
respect of the profits of her profession as a barrister. She appealed
against this assessment to the commissioners. She contended that in
computing the profits of her profession for this year of assessment (which
were based on the profits for her accounting year 1976–77) she was
entitled to deduct the sum of £564·38.   **D**

The commissioners disallowed her claim in a written decision delivered
on April 24, 1980. On her requirement they subsequently stated a case
for the opinion of this court pursuant to section 56 of the Taxes Management Act 1970. In paragraph 4 of the case, the commissioners set out
the following facts, which they found admitted or proved:

"(a) The [taxpayer] is a practising barrister having been called to   **E**
the Bar by the Inner Temple in 1970. She commenced practice in
October 1970 and became a member of the South Eastern Circuit.
At all material times her practice was a mixed common law practice
of which about 60 per cent. of the work was criminal and most of
the rest was personal injury work.

"(b) During the year with which we are concerned her practice   **F**
had become such that it was a rare day when she was not in court
somewhere. The majority of her court appearances were in courts in
and around London. On days when she went to her chambers in the
morning because she was not then retained to go into court that day
it often happened that before the day was out she found herself
required to go to court later in the day as the result of some emergency
or situation that had arisen at short notice.   **G**

"(c) Notes for guidance on dress in court were issued by the Bar
Council in its Annual Statement for 1973–74. A copy of the relevant
paragraph is [set out below]. Though the rules laid down in the
notes for guidance were issued by the Bar Council, the sanction which
ensures that they are complied with is that they are enforced by the
judiciary. A barrister who is improperly dressed may be told by   **H**
the judge that he cannot be heard or may receive a message from the
judge's clerk or may receive a reprimand from a more senior member
of the profession. The rules for guidance are thus normally complied
with and it would be virtually impossible for a lady barrister to
practice unless she complied with the rules laid down.

"(d) In the accounting period for the year of assessment 1977–78
the [taxpayer] spent a total of £564·38 on the following items of

A

expenditure: black tights, £50·00; black shoes, £65·97; black suits, £133·79; black dresses, £73·44; shirts, £134·18; replacement collar, £7·00; laundry and cleaning, £100·00 [making a total of] £564·38.

" (e) The [taxpayer] prefers to wear coloured clothes rather than black ones and prefers clothes of a more adventurous design and style than is compatible with the notes of guidance which require that the dress should be unobtrusive. She considers that black clothes

B

are ageing and do not suit her blonde colouring. None of the disputed items of clothing was of the sort that she would wear for going out in the evening or for other social occasions.

" (f) At all material times the [taxpayer] had a private wardrobe of clothes and shoes which was amply sufficient to keep her clothed and shod in comfort and decency, without having to resort to any

C

of the disputed items. She would not have purchased any of the disputed items had it not been for the requirement of her profession that she should comply with the notes for guidance when appearing in court.

" (g) The [taxpayer] normally drives when going to and from court or her chambers. On such journeys she wears her court clothes even on those occasions when she is going to her chambers and is

D

not already booked to go to court on that day, as she has always to be ready to go to court at short notice. On the relatively rare occasions when she wishes to spend the day in chambers reading papers and has asked her clerk not to arrange for her to go to court she would normally wear clothes such as she wore at the hearing before us, that is to say smart clothes from her non-court wardrobe

E

not suitable for wearing in court.

" (h) The [taxpayer] prefers to wear high-heeled shoes but finds that in court they are not suitable as she may have to stand for long periods. She therefore wears black court shoes with lower heels in court. Such shoes are suitable to wear when driving her car while high-heeled shoes are not suitable for that purpose. The nature of her practice takes her to courts in many places away from her chambers,

F

and she has to drive considerable distances in the course of a year for that reason.

" (i) When in the evening the [taxpayer] goes direct from her chambers to a social engagement she normally changes from her court clothes into the coloured and more stylish type of clothes that she prefers.

G

" (j) Though it must be the case, and she agreed, that by wearing her court clothes for a large part of her working lifetime she saves the clothes of her private wardrobe from wear and tear, we accept that this fact was not a consideration in her mind when she bought the disputed items. She bought such items only because she would not have been permitted to appear in court if she did not wear, when in court, them or other clothes like them. Similarly the preservation

H

of warmth and decency was not a consideration which crossed her mind when she bought the disputed items.

" (k) The white blouses and black clothing bought by the [taxpayer] were items of ordinary civilian clothing readily available for purchase by anyone at many clothing stores.

" (l) Over the last five years the average percentage of garments stocked by Marks & Spencers Ltd. in its ladies' wear departments

which are black were: skirt department, 15 per cent.; dress depart- A
ment, 10 per cent.; suit department, 10 per cent. Black clothing is
always very acceptable whether it is in fashion or not because it is
a good colour with which to team other colours or white. Black
velvet jackets are one of the most successful lines and are a perennial
favourite. The standard basic colours for ladies' blouses are white
and cream and these represent between 15 per cent. and 25 per cent.
of the range in stock at Marks & Spencers."   B

The notes for guidance on dress in court issued by the Bar Council which
are referred to in the case read as follows:

" 1. The dress of barristers appearing in court should be unobtrusive
and compatible with the wearing of robes. 2. Suits and dresses
should be of dark colour. Dresses or blouses should be long-sleeved C
and high to the neck. Men should wear waistcoats. Shirts and
blouses should be predominantly white or of other unemphatic
appearance. Collars should be white and shoes black. 3. Wigs should,
as far as possible, cover the hair, which should be drawn back from
the face and forehead, and if long enough should be put up. 4. No
conspicuous jewellery or ornaments should be worn."
                                                                     D
At least five points have been common ground before me, as I think
they were before the commissioners. First, with one possible trivial
exception relating to collars, no distinction falls to be drawn between the
relevant expenses incurred by the taxpayer in replacement of clothes and
those incurred by her in laundering and cleaning. With that possible
exception, all of them stand or fall together. Secondly, since the clothes E
were purchased by way of replacement of existing clothes, all the expenses
are of a revenue rather than a capital nature. Thirdly, if they are to be
allowable as deductions, they must fall outside the ambit of section 130 (a)
and (b) of the Income and Corporation Taxes Act 1970 by virtue of which
no sum falls to be deducted in respect of:

" (a) any disbursements or expenses, not being money wholly and F
exclusively laid out or expended for the purposes of the trade, profession or vocation, (b) any disbursements or expenses of maintenance
of the parties, their families or establishments, or any sums expended
for any other domestic or private purposes distinct from the purposes
of the trade, profession or vocation . . ."

Fourthly, all the relevant expenses either fall within both subsections or G
fall outside both of them. In the event, therefore, the argument centred
wholly on section 130 (a). Fifthly, it was common ground that, in determining whether these expenses have been wholly and exclusively laid out
or expended for the purpose of the taxpayer's profession of a barrister,
it is necessary to ascertain what purpose or purposes was or were in her
mind at the date when they were incurred: see *Bentleys, Stokes & Lowless*
v. *Beeson* [1952] 2 All E.R. 82, 84–85 *per* Romer L.J. Walton J. in H
Robinson v. *Scott Bader Co. Ltd.* [1980] 1 W.L.R. 755, having reviewed
this and earlier authorities relating to the predecessors of section 130 (a),
said, at p. 761:

" It follows from all this that (i) the test is a subjective, not an
objective one—i.e., the relevant question is, ' What was the object of
the person making the disbursement in making it?', not, ' What was

A   the effect of the disbursement when made?'—and (ii) that this is, in all cases, a pure question of fact."

The correctness of this statement of the law, with its reaffirmation of the subjective test of intention and of the critically important distinction between the purpose and the incidental results of expenditure, has not been challenged before me.

B   Not even every foreseeable result of expenditure necessarily amounts to its purpose. In the context of section 130 (*a*), a crucial distinction falls to be drawn between (a) expenditure incurred solely for the purpose of a taxpayer's profession which happens to produce benefits to him in his personal capacity, and (b) expenditure incurred partly for the purposes of the taxpayer's profession and partly for the purpose of producing benefits to him in his personal capacity. It is obvious that expenditure

C   falling within category (b) (often referred to as "dual purpose expenditure") is disqualified from deduction by section 130 (*a*) because it is not exclusively laid out for the purposes of the profession. The distinction between dual purpose expenditure and expenditure falling within category (a) (which I will call "single purpose professional expenditure") can be well illustrated by a reference to one case. In *Prince* v. *Mapp* [1970]

D   1 W.L.R. 260 an engineering draughtsman played the guitar in his spare time, both as a hobby and for payment. As a result of an accident he suffered an injury to his left hand, which interfered with his guitar playing. He underwent an operation which restored partial flexibility to his hand. On an appeal against an assessment to income tax under Schedule D in respect of his profits as a dance musician, he sought to deduct the costs of the operation as being wholly and exclusively expended for the

E   purposes of his profession. The special commissioners disallowed the cost. In the course of the case stated by them, they said, at p. 262:

F   "The operation to the taxpayer's left hand hereinbefore referred to was undergone to enable the taxpayer to continue to play the guitar not solely so that he could make money by exploiting his skill professionally but equally to enable him to continue to enjoy and practise his hobby of playing that instrument."

On an appeal to the High Court, Pennycuick J. said in relation to this passage, at p. 266:

G   "That is a clear and express finding of a dual purpose and assuming there was evidence to support that finding, it concludes the case against the taxpayer. On that footing, paragraph (*a*) is directly applicable because the expense of the operation would not be money wholly and exclusively expended for the purposes of his profession; it would be expended partly for the purposes of his profession and partly for the purposes of his hobby."

H   Having found that there was material upon which the commissioners could have reached their conclusion of fact, he dismissed the appeal. This was, therefore, a clear example of dual purpose expenditure failing to qualify for a deduction. In the course of his judgment, however, Pennycuick J., at p. 263, referred to a further finding of fact in the case stated, that: " . . . the operation was a complex one and he [the taxpayer] would not have undergone it had he not wished to continue to play the guitar." He observed in this context, at p. 267:

"If the finding had included the word 'professionally' (i.e. if it had   A
read 'He would not have undergone it had he not wished to continue
to play the guitar professionally') the result might, I think, have been
otherwise. However, that word 'professionally' is not there."

Even if the taxpayer in that case had undergone the operation solely with
the intention of enabling himself to exploit his skill professionally, it must
still in addition have produced some incidental benefit to him in his   B
personal, non-professional capacity. Yet, Pennycuick J.'s observation
indicates that he would not have regarded this readily foreseeable incidental benefit as necessarily disqualifying him from receiving tax relief,
provided that it did not form part of the purpose itself.

   This distinction between dual purpose expenditure and single purpose
professional expenditure is illustrated by many other decisions and is at   C
the heart of the dispute in the present case. However, it is perhaps easier
to state than to apply to the particular facts of individual cases, where
the true intention of the taxpayer, viewed subjectively, may not always be
easy to ascertain. Even on the application of a subjective test, its ascertainment may involve a degree of inference on the part of the tribunal
of fact, as I think it plainly did in the present case. The ultimate question
for my decision here will, I think, be whether, having regard to their   D
primary findings of fact as set out in paragraph 4 of the case stated, there
was evidence to support the inference ultimately drawn by the commissioners that the expenditure was incurred by the taxpayer with dual
purposes in mind.

   The process of thought which led the commissioners to their final
conclusion adequately appears from the following extracts from their   E
decision. In paragraph 2 they said (inter alia):

   "We accept that she had during the accounting period with which
   this appeal is concerned (the year to April 5, 1977) ample clothing
   of the type that conformed to her natural taste and that there was no
   need for her to, and she virtually never did, wear the clothes that she
   bought for wearing in court when she was not in court except when   F
   in chambers when applying herself to paper work or conferences and
   when travelling to and from her work and on other occasions when
   she did not find it necessary or desirable that she should change out
   of her court clothes. When she wished to go straight from chambers
   to some function or party at which she would prefer more becoming
   clothes she would change before going there."
                                                                           G
I infer, however, from the findings in paragraph 4 (e) of the case that the
taxpayer would almost invariably change before going out in the evening
or for other social occasions. Paragraphs 7, 8, 9 and 10 of the decision
read as follows:

   "7. The problem with which we are faced is, therefore, whether
   when [the taxpayer] bought the clothes in question or had them   H
   cleaned or laundered the expenditure of so doing was laid out wholly
   and exclusively for the purposes of her profession as a barrister. The
   decision of the Court of Appeal in *Bentleys, Stokes & Lowless* v.
   Beeson [1952] 2 All E.R. 82 is, in our view, authority for the proposition that in determining the purpose of expenditure we must
   consider, as a subjective matter, the state of [the taxpayer's] mind
   and decide as a question of fact what her purpose was.

A

" 8. We consider that the evidence shows that when she bought the clothes she bought them to wear in court and that she would not have bought them but for the exigencies of her profession. She had no intention of wearing them except when in court or chambers or in the other circumstances mentioned in paragraph 2 above.

B

" 9. Does that mean that she laid out the money spent in purchasing them wholly and exclusively for the purposes of her profession? It is clear from the reasoning of Romer L.J. in *Bentleys, Stokes & Lowless* v. *Beeson* that the purpose for which a particular sum has been laid out does not necessarily cease to be the purpose of the profession simply because some incidental effect is achieved by the payment which may be said to be non-professional and which it was no part of the purpose of the taxpayer to achieve. In *Bentley's*

C

case the incidental effect which the court held, on the facts of that case, did not deprive the expenditure of its character of expenditure for professional purposes was the fact that the payment for the clients' lunch not only helped to earn profits for the firm of solicitors but also inevitably provided hospitality for the clients. It was no part of the purpose of the solicitors when incurring that expenditure that it should achieve that latter effect which was an inevitable result

D

of the expenditure.

" We consider, in the present case, that when [the taxpayer] laid out money on clothes for wearing in court her purpose in making that expenditure was to enable her to earn profits in her profession and also to enable her to be properly clothed during the time she was on her way to chambers or to court and while she was thereafter

E

engaged in her professional activity, and in the other circumstances indicated in paragraph 2. We do not consider that the fact that her sole motive in choosing the particular clothes was to satisfy the requirements of her profession or that if she had been free to do so she would have worn clothes of a different style on such occasions altered the purpose of the expenditure which remained the purpose of purchasing clothes that would keep her warm and clad during the

F

part of the day when she was pursuing her career as well as the purpose of helping her to earn profits in that career. We think, therefore, that the expenditure had a dual purpose, one professional and one non-professional, and we, therefore, hold that, subject to one matter which we mention hereafter, she is not entitled to deduct the sums claimed.

G

" 10. The exception to what we have said above is the cost of a replacement collar of a special sort which enable bands to be worn conveniently. The revenue concedes that the cost of this is deductible and we think it is right to take that view. This, like the wig and gown that barristers are required to wear, is more in the nature of a badge of the profession and it serves no purpose of

H

clothing and is not intended to be worn out of court. The money expended on its purchases was laid out for no purpose other than the purpose of [the taxpayer's] profession. It seems to us that the purpose of the expenditure on items of this sort is to show that the wearer is a qualified barrister and just as the expenditure on a licence to practice, were such a thing necessary, would be deductible so the expenditure of this particular item is deductible."

This being the form of the commissioners' decision and of the case   A
stated, Mr. Carnwath, on behalf of the Crown, submitted that they applied
the correct test on a question of fact which is not open to challenge.   The
crux of their decision, he contended, is to be found in the sentence in
paragraph 9 of their decision, in which they said:

> " We consider, in the present case, that when [the taxpayer] laid out
> money on clothes for wearing in court her purpose in making that   B
> expenditure was to enable her to earn profits in her profession and
> also to enable her to be properly clothed during the time she was
> on her way to chambers or to court and while she was thereafter
> engaged in her professional activity, and in the other circumstances
> indicated in paragraph 2."

That, Mr. Carnwath submitted, was a clear finding of fact by the com-   C
missioners that the taxpayer, in incurring the relevant expenditure, had
a dual purpose in mind, namely, (i) that of enabling her to earn profits
in her profession, and (ii) that of enabling her to be properly clothed
during the time she was on her way to chambers or to court and while
she was thereafter engaged in her professional activity, and in the other
circumstances indicated in paragraph 2 of the decision, that is to say,
the " other occasions when she did not find it necessary or desirable that   D
she should change out of her court clothes."   The commissioners did not
further particularise these " other occasions," but, in view of the findings
in paragraph 4 (e) of the case, I think it clear that these did not include
any social functions or parties, though they did include certain occasions
in the evening, when she was not going to social functions or parties and
did not think it necessary or desirable to change out of her court clothes.   E
   I accept that, as Romer L.J. said in *Bentleys, Stokes & Lowless* v.
Beeson [1952] 2 All E.R. 82, 86:

> " . . . it is a firm rule in tax cases that, if the tribunal of fact has
> found the fact, the court will not disturb its conclusion unless it
> is clear either that the tribunal has misapplied the law to the
> facts found or that there was no evidence whatever to support the   F
> finding."

The ultimate conclusion as to the taxpayer's purpose, expressed in paragraph 9 of the commissioners' decision, cannot therefore be lightly
disturbed.   For, though Mr. Park submitted to the contrary, I think this
did amount to a finding of fact.
   Nevertheless, no doubt bearing in mind the principles which govern   G
appeals from their decisions, the commissioners, in fairness to both sides,
have, by the form of their decision and case stated, given the court every
opportunity to trace the process of thought which led them to their
ultimate decision on the crucial question of intention.   Thus paragraphs
2, 3 and 4 of the decision and paragraph 4 of the case set out the primary
facts which, after having heard the taxpayer give evidence on her own
behalf, they regarded as admitted or proved by direct evidence.   In   H
contrast, paragraphs 8, 9 and 10 of their decision, as I read them, set out
the inferences of fact which they drew from those primary facts.   I think,
therefore, that I am at liberty, and indeed am bound, to consider whether
there was sufficient evidence to justify these inferences, particularly in the
face of their primary findings of fact, as set out in paragraph 4 of the case.
   I will now extract verbatim from paragraph 4 certain of those primary
findings of fact which I think particularly relevant in the present context:

A   " At all material times the [taxpayer] had a private wardrobe of clothes and shoes which was amply sufficient to keep her clothed and shod in comfort and decency, without having to resort to any of the disputed items."

    " She would not have purchased any of the disputed items had it not been for the requirement of her profession that she should comply with the notes for guidance when appearing in court."

B   " None of the disputed items of clothing was of the sort that she would wear for going out in the evening or for other social occasions."

    " . . . It would be virtually impossible for a lady barrister to practise unless she complied with the rules laid down."

    " Though . . . by wearing her court clothes for a large part of her working lifetime she saves the clothes of her private wardrobe from

C   wear and tear, we accept that this fact was not a consideration in her mind when she bought the disputed items."

    " Similarly the preservation of warmth and decency was not a consideration which crossed her mind when she bought the disputed items."

    " She bought such items only because she would not have been

D   permitted to appear in court if she did not wear, when in court, them or other clothes like them."

    I think it a fair assumption that the commissioners, in preparing their decision and case stated, would have referred to any evidence which they regarded as tending to support their ultimate decision as to the taxpayer's intentions. In the light of all the evidence referred to by them, I ask

E   myself three questions, which seem to me of crucial importance: (1) Was there any evidence at all to support the conclusion that part of the purpose of the taxpayer's expenditure was to enable her to be properly clothed " during the time she was on her way to her chambers or to court "? My answer to that question must be no. She had, as the commissioners found, an ample private wardrobe of clothes. She would not have worn any of them during these journeys, but for the require-

F   ments of her profession. The preservation of warmth and decency did not enter into her mind when she bought them. Considerations of convenience no doubt required that, after the clothes had been purchased, she would, as an incidental result, wear them during these journeys. In my view, however, to infer that she bought them partly for the purpose of keeping herself clothed during these journeys would be to confuse

G   purpose and incidental effect. (2) Was there any evidence before the commissioners to support the conclusion that part of the purpose of her expenditure was to enable her to be properly clothed " while she was thereafter engaged in her professional activity "? My answer to that question would be yes, if " properly clothed " means " properly clothed in accordance with the particular requirements of her profession." This, however, would not, in my judgment, render the relevant expenditure

H   dual purpose expenditure. If by " properly clothed " is meant " warm and decently clad," my answer must be no. Considerations of warmth and decency did not enter her mind. (3) Was there evidence before the commissioners to support the conclusion that part of the purpose of her expenditure was to enable her to be properly clothed " in the other circumstances indicated in paragraph 2 "? My answer to this question on the evidence must again be no. True it is that she did on occasions, as a matter of convenience, continue to wear her court clothes after court hours. However, to infer that she purchased them for the purpose of A continuing to wear them after court hours would, I think, be wholly inconsistent with all of the seven findings of the commissioners which I have extracted from paragraph 4 of the case stated. So to infer would once again be to confuse purpose and incidental effect.

The very experienced commissioners were themselves clearly alive to the distinction between purpose and incidental effect, as appears from the B first few sentences of paragraph 9 of their decision. If my ultimate conclusion be correct and theirs be incorrect, it is relevant to consider what process of inference may have ultimately led them into error. As to this I can only speculate, but I think the answer to this question may be found in paragraph 6 (b) and (c) of the case. From these sub-paragraphs it would appear that, before the commissioners, the Crown in effect was submitting the broad proposition that where a taxpayer incurs C expenditure on any item, such as clothes, which supplies an ordinary basic human need, it can never, in any circumstances, be said to be incurred wholly and exclusively for the purposes of the taxpayer's profession, even if the particular manner in which that basic human need is to be met may be dictated by the requirements of the profession. If this contention had been correct, it would clearly have disqualified the taxpayer from claim- D ing the deductions now in question. Some superficial support for this broad proposition might be found in a passage from the judgment of Lord Greene M.R. in *Norman* v. *Golder* [1945] 1 All E.R. 352. In that case a shorthand writer appealed against an assessment to income tax under Schedule D in respect of his professional earnings. He had suffered from a severe illness, which he stated was the direct result of working in un-favourable conditions. He incurred medical expenses, which he claimed E should be deducted in computing his liability to tax in respect of his earnings, as being expenditure wholly and exclusively incurred in con-nection with his professional work. The Court of Appeal rejected his claim. Lord Greene M.R. said, at p. 354:

"It is quite impossible to argue that a doctor's bills represent money wholly and exclusively laid out for the purposes of the trade, F profession, employment or vocation of the patient. True it is that if you do not get yourself well and so incur expenses to doctors you cannot carry on your trade or profession, and if you do not carry on your trade or profession you will not earn an income, and if you do not earn an income the revenue will not get any tax. The same thing applies to the food you eat and the clothes that you wear. But G expenses of that kind are not wholly and exclusively laid out for the purposes of the trade, profession or vocation. They are laid out in part for the advantage and benefit of the taxpayer as a living human being."

For obvious reasons, in any case where part of the effect of expenditure is to supply what may be regarded as a basic human need of the taxpayer H —whether for clothes, food, medical attention or otherwise—the com-missioners or any other tribunal of fact will be slow to hold that at least part of the purpose of such expenditure is not to satisfy such need. The decisions of Goulding J. in *Hillyer* v. *Leeke* (1971) 51 T.C. 90, and of Walton J. in *Ward* v. *Dunn* (1978) T.C. Leaflet No. 2710 (both relating to tax under Schedule E) are examples of cases where the taxpayer's ex-penditure on clothes had an obvious dual purpose.

A   Mr. Carnwath relied strongly on *Murgatroyd* v. *Evans-Jackson* [1967] 1 W.L.R. 423. In that case a trade mark agent suffered an accident for which he was advised to have treatment in hospital. He was offered a bed in a hospital under the National Health Service, but could not have carried on his business there owing to the lack of a telephone and restricted facilities for visting. Instead, therefore, he entered a nursing

B   home as a private patient, where he was provided with the necessary facilities for carrying on his business. On appeal against an assessment to income tax under Schedule D he contended that 60 per cent. of his total expenses at the nursing home should be allowed as a business expense in respect of the use of his room there as an office. Plowman J. rejected his claim, saying, at p. 431:

C   " It seems to me that the claim by the taxpayer for 60 per cent. of his expenses is really fatal to his case, because implicit in a claim for only 60 per cent. of the expenses must be an admission that the expenses involved a dual purpose, namely as to 60 per cent. expenses of conducting an office and as to 40 per cent. something else."

D   Plowman J. then observed that the taxpayer's claim would have been more plausible had he claimed the whole of his expenses in the nursing home. However, he continued, at p. 431:

"But even had he claimed the whole of the expenses, it seems to me that it would not really be a rational view of the situation to conclude that the whole of his expenses in the nursing home were incurred wholly and exclusively for the purposes of his business. The whole object of going into the nursing home in the first place was to receive

E   treatment for the injury which he had sustained, and it seems to me that it would offend common sense to say that at any rate one of his motives or purposes in going into the nursing home was not to receive treatment for that injury—treatment which would enure to his benefit, not merely during the time when he was carrying on his business, but, as Lord Greene M.R. said in the passage I have already read

F   from *Norman* v. *Golder* [1945] 1 All E.R. 352, 354, ' as a living human being.' "

In my judgment, however, the decision of the Court of Appeal in *Bentleys, Stokes & Lowless* v. *Beeson* [1952] 2 All E.R. 82 (which was subsequent to that in *Norman* v. *Golder*) clearly shows that the broad propositions advanced before the commissioners and set out in paragraph

G   6 (b) and (c) of the case were too widely stated. In that case, in the court of first instance, Roxburgh J. [1951] 2 All E.R. 667, held that, on the facts as found in the case stated, the expenses incurred by a firm of solicitors in entertaining clients were expenses wholly and exclusively laid out or expended for the purpose of their profession within Schedule D. Significantly for present purposes, however, the expenses claimed and allowed included not only the costs of the meals of the clients but also

H   the costs of the meals of the solicitors themselves, consumed during the course of this hospitality. Roxburgh J., at p. 671, accepted the submission that the transaction was one single transaction which was embarked upon for business or professional purposes solely and exclusively and in which the partners' lunches were essential ingredients. He pointed out at the same page that the partner who actually attends the lunch gets a separate and personal benefit to the extent (and only to the extent) that he gets

his mid-day sustenance without the obligation to pay for it. He concluded, A
however, that

> " The mere circumstance that the partner gets that degree of gratuitous
> sustenance cannot, in my judgment, be a sufficient reason for holding
> that a transaction, which is from every other point of view a business
> transaction, lacks that characteristic in any degree whatever."

The Court of Appeal affirmed the decision of Roxburgh J. Romer L.J. B
delivering the judgment of the court, expressed the opinion, at p. 84, that
Roxburgh J.'s view on the question of the cost of the partners' own
lunches was " clearly right." Furthermore, in that case both Roxburgh J.
and the Court of Appeal were prepared to go behind the finding in paragraph 6 of the case that " the expenses claimed were primarily and
principally, but not purely, for business purposes," and a similar finding
in paragraph 11.   C

In the present case the commissioners, while referring to the *Bentleys'*
case [1952] 2 All E.R. 82, did not refer at all to the cost of the partners'
own lunches in that case. They only mentioned the cost of the clients'
lunches. I am not therefore sure that they fully appreciated what I regard
as the main significance of that decision of the Court of Appeal in the
present context. In my judgment it illustrates decisively that there is D
no broad principle that one purpose of the purchase of food to be consumed by the purchaser, or of any other item such as clothes, which will
in part meet a basic human need of the purchaser, must always be deemed
to be the partial satisfaction of that need. No irrebuttable presumption of
law arises to this effect. An incidental effect of a purchase may still
constitute no more than an incidental effect, even though it consists of a
readily foreseeable personal benefit to the spender. Similarly, as to E
medical expenses, I have already referred to a passage from the judgment
in *Prince* v. *Mapp* [1970] 1 W.L.R. 260, 262, in which Pennycuick J.
accepted in principle that, in the special hypothetical circumstances referred
to by him, medical expenses could have constituted deductible expenses for
Schedule D purposes.

In relation to clothes, an illuminating illustration of the relevant prin- F
ciples is to be found in the judgment of Templeman J. in *Caillebotte* v.
Quinn [1975] 1 W.L.R. 731. In that case a carpenter, who worked on
sites some distance from his home and could not go home for lunch on
a working day, purchased for himself more expensive lunches than he
would have eaten at home. He attributed the additional cost to the
need to eat a more substantial meal, in order to maintain the energy expended in carrying out physical work and to keep warm during the winter. G
The general commissioners allowed that additional cost as a deduction
from his profits under Schedule D. On appeal, it was held that the cost
of the lunches could not be apportioned, and that no part of it was
exclusively expended for the purposes of the taxpayer's trade as a
carpenter. Templeman J., however, observed, at p. 733: " The cost of
tea consumed by an actor at the Mad Hatter's tea party is different, for H
in that case the quenching of a thirst is incidental to the playing of the
part." In other words, he considered the purpose of the purchase of the
tea in such circumstances would be to enable the actor to play the part,
rather than to satisfy a human need. He went on to observe:

> " The cost of protective clothing worn in the course of carrying on
> a trade will be deductible, because warmth and decency are inci-
> dental to the protection necessary to the carrying on of the trade."

A   In other words, the purpose of the purchase of protective clothing to be worn in the course of carrying on a trade is to be regarded as that of providing the protection necessary to carry it on, rather than to provide warmth and decency.

   I put to Mr. Carnwath in the course of argument the hypothetical case of a repertory actress who found herself obliged to purchase black B   clothes so as adequately to play the part of a lady barrister in a theatrical production.   He did not, as I understood him, dispute that the expense of such purchases, by way of replacement, would in principle be well capable of qualifying for deduction.   Nor, as I understood him, did he advance such broad propositions on behalf of the Crown as are to be found summarised in paragraph 6 (b) and (c) of the case stated.   He did, however, submit that, notwithstanding their primary findings of fact C   set out in paragraph 4 of the case, the commissioners' ultimate finding as to the taxpayer's intention could be justified on the basis that, on the evidence, she needed the clothes as a human being and it made no difference that the choice of the particular clothes was governed by her professional requirements.   He sought to draw an analogy with *Murgatroyd v. Evans-Jackson* [1967] 1 W.L.R. 423, on the grounds that, just as the D   taxpayer in that case needed the medical attention as " a living human being," so did the taxpayer need the clothes in the present case.   If the evidence had shown her to be a penniless barrister with an empty wardrobe, this submission and analogy would have been well founded. With all respect to Mr. Carnwath's excellent argument, however, the fallacy seems to me to lie in one short but fundamental point.   On the facts as found by the commissioners, the taxpayer, as a human being, neither E   needed nor wanted the clothes in question.   In incurring the expenditure on them, she had no thought of warmth and decency.   As the com- missioners found, she bought them " only because she would not have been permitted to appear in court if she did not wear, when in court, them or other clothes like them."   In the circumstances, I think that, with all respect to the commissioners, there was no evidence to support the inference which they finally drew to the effect that she had a dual purpose F   in mind.   On the evidence, I am driven to the conclusion that the relevant expenditure in the present case was incurred by her solely for the purpose of carrying on her profession and that the benefits of warmth and decency, which she would enjoy while wearing the clothes during the various times referred to by the commissioners in paragraph 9 of their decision, were purely incidental to the carrying on of her profession.   In these circum- G   stances the expenses are, in my judgment, deductible.

   I conclude by making a few general observations.   One obvious distinction between the clothes under discussion in the present case (other than the replacement collars) and the wig and gown which the taxpayer, like any other barrister, is required to wear, lies in the fact that the clothes in question were perfectly suitable for wearing on social occasions H   and, on the evidence, were from time to time worn by her outside the strict course of her profession, though she would not ordinarily have chosen to do so.   Factors such as these would, I conceive, be very relevant when any tribunal of fact such as the commissioners had to ascertain the true intentions of the taxpayer at the date of purchase.   In particular, they would be relevant in determining whether they could accept a taxpayer's evidence that she bought the clothes solely because of the requirements of her profession, and not partly in order to keep herself properly clad outside ordinary working hours. In the present case, A however, I think that the commissioners' primary findings of fact, set out in paragraph 4 of the case stated, show that they did accept her evidence to this effect.

I accordingly emphasise that this is a decision on the particular facts of the present case. It is not intended to imply that all lady practising barristers (or, for that matter, all male practising barristers) who purchase black suits, dresses or shoes suitable for use in the course of their B profession and by way of replacement should be entitled to deduct the expense of the purchase for Schedule D tax purposes. Everything must depend upon the available evidence as to the purpose of the particular taxpayer in effecting the particular purchase. If, as must be the case in many instances, a lady barrister buys her black clothing, partly for the purpose of using it during the course of her profession and partly for C the purpose of using it when she is not pursuing her profession, then the expenditure will be truly dual purpose expenditure and will not qualify for a deduction. Similar principles apply mutatis mutandis in relation to cleaning and laundry.

I appreciate that this decision, if correct, may give rise to some uncertainty in some individual cases, which may not be very satisfactory either for the Inland Revenue or for members of the Bar. This, however, D seems to me the inevitable result of the wording of section 130 (a), coupled with the principle illustrated by Bentleys' case [1952] 2 All E.R. 82, that in applying the subsection the purpose of any expenditure must be determined subjectively. This principle inevitably makes the application of any "rules of thumb" much more difficult, save in those cases where the purpose of the relevant expenditure is obvious (for E example, the purchase by a practising barrister of a wig and gown). However, the particular facts as found by the commissioners in the present case, save for their ultimate inference, could hardly have been more favourable to the taxpayer. On the basis of these particular facts she has, in my judgment, brought herself outside the ambit of section 130 (a) and (b). I must accordingly allow this appeal.

F

> *Appeal allowed with costs.*
> *Assessment to be reduced to an*
>   *amount to be agreed.*
> *Any excess tax to be repaid with*
>   *interest at a rate to be agreed.*
> *Liberty to apply.*

G

Solicitors: *Penningtons; Solicitor of Inland Revenue.*

[Reported by MRS. HARRIET DUTTON, Barrister-at-Law]

H

A

[CHANCERY DIVISION]

* E.M.I. RECORDS LTD. *v.* RILEY AND OTHERS

[1978 E. No. 1778]

B 1981 March 13

Dillon J.

Practice—Parties—Representative action—Infringement of copy-
right—Member suing in personal capacity and on behalf of
class—Admissions by defendant—Whether member entitled to
injunction and to inquiry as to damages in representative
capacity

C
The plaintiffs were members of B.P.I. whose members
were all involved in the business of producing, manufacturing
and distributing sound recordings. The defendant was a
market trader. In 1978, the plaintiffs commenced an action
against the defendant who they believed to be involved in
the manufacture and sale of " pirate records " made directly
or indirectly from sound recordings in which B.P.I. members
D owned the copyright. Their claim, made on behalf of themselves and on behalf of all B.P.I. members was for an injunction to prevent further infringements of their copyright and
an inquiry as to damages. The defendant admitted the sale
of pirate records.

On the plaintiffs' application for judgment on admissions,
for an order restraining the defendants from infringing their
copyright and an inquiry as to the damage suffered as a result
E of previous infringements: —

Held, (1) that, since the defendant had admitted the sale
of pirate records, the plaintiffs were entitled on their own
behalf and on behalf of all B.P.I. members, to an injunction
restraining the defendant from ordering, selling or parting
with any pirate records (post, p. 925E–H).

(2) That, since nearly all recordings in this country were
produced by members of B.P.I. and the defendant had
F admitted that most of her pirate records had been recordings
of discs, records and tapes produced, made and distributed
by members of B.P.I., the plaintiffs, suing in a representative
capacity in which they could claim an injunction, could also
recover damages suffered as a result of any infringement of
the members' copyright and, therefore, avoid the unnecessary
complications of establishing what damage had been suffered
individually by members if the court required each member to
G commence proceedings on his own behalf (post, p. 926E, G–H).

Prudential Assurance Co. Ltd. v. *Newman Industries*
Ltd. [1980] 2 W.L.R. 339 distinguished.

The following cases are referred to in the judgment:

Prudential Assurance Co. Ltd. v. *Newman Industries Ltd.* [1980] 2
W.L.R. 339; [1979] 3 All E.R. 507.

H
No additional cases were cited in argument.

MOTION

On October 19, 1979, the plaintiffs, E.M.I. Records Ltd. (" E.M.I."),
members of the British Phonographic Industry Ltd. (" B.P.I."), acting
on their own behalf and representing all other members of B.P.I., issued
a writ claiming infringement of their copyright, inter alios, by the

924

defendant, Grace Riley, a market trader, who had been selling pirate　A
records copied from recordings in which the B.P.I. members owned
copyright. On November 19, 1979, in her defence, the defendant
admitted the infringements. Having regard to those admissions, E.M.I.
issued a motion for judgment in their action on March 13, 1981, claiming
an order, inter alia, that the defendant be restrained from making or
selling any record made directly or indirectly from a sound recording
the copyright in which was owned by any member of B.P.I. and an　B
inquiry as to the damages sustained by members of B.P.I. by reason
of the defendants' infringements of their copyright.

P. R. K. Prescott for the plaintiffs.
The defendant appeared in person.

C

DILLON J. This is a motion for judgment on admissions. The action
is brought by E.M.I. Records Ltd., suing on behalf of themselves and
on behalf of and as representing all other members of the British Phonographic Industry Ltd., against a Mrs. Riley, as first defendant. There
were a number of other defendants originally named in the proceedings,
and the proceedings remain on foot against one of them, Mr. Patrick　D
Buckley, but no claim against him is before me today.

The action was started in 1978, and the statement of claim was
served on June 8, 1979. The admissions by the defendant, Mrs. Riley,
which are relied on are contained in two documents. One is called
" Reply to plaintiff's statement of claim " and it is signed by the
defendant and dated November 19, 1979. This was, I think, intended
to represent the defendant's defence to the action, but it was not　E
accepted as satisfactory in form, and accordingly a little later she served
a document which is substantially to the same effect, headed "Defence
of Grace Riley first defendant," which is signed and dated November
22, 1979.

The action concerns the sale of pirate cassettes. The statement of
claim sets out in paragraph 1 certain definitions. The definition of　F
" pirate record " is a " record made directly or indirectly from a sound
recording without the licence of the United Kingdom copyright owner
or exclusive licensee, being a member of the class," and the " class " is
all members of the British Phonographic Industry Ltd. (" B.P.I.") a
company limited by guarantee. The statement of claim then sets out in
paragraphs 2 and 3 that the plaintiffs are a legitimate record company
and members of the B.P.I. and they sue on behalf of and representing　G
and for the benefit of the class, and that nearly all records in this
country are produced, made or distributed by members of the class,
and in her defence the defendant agrees both those paragraphs. Paragraph 4 of the statement of claim sets out that the members of the class
are continually and frequently producing, making or distributing records
embodying new sound recordings. The member of the class respon-　H
sible for each sound recording owns the copyright therein or is the
exclusive licensee thereunder. The defendant in her defence expressly
does not deny the existence of copyright.

Paragraph 8 of the statement of claim (I shall have to come back
to paragraph 7 of the statement of claim) asserts that the defendants
and each of them had been concerned in a business in this country of
making pirate records and/or authorising them to be made and/or selling

A and/or distributing for trade purposes records which to their knowledge were pirate and the said business, the paragraph asserts, occurred on a massive scale and over a considerable period, and particulars are served separately with the statement of claim.

As to that the defendant Mrs. Riley denies ever making a pirate record in her life, but she says that she did order them to be made and she did authorise her daughter to sell them for her. She denies that the

B business occurred on a massive scale over a considerable period, but she does say that the business was conducted for some 25 weeks on 25 Saturdays in Portobello Market, 12 days in Carnaby Street, and 32 days in Oxford Street, and she says that the total number of the tapes sold was approximately 2,980, and that the probable quantity affecting members of the class was 2,900 tapes on the assumption that

C her sales affected members of the class. She claims that her sales were too small to affect the large record companies, but I take this to mean that she is accepting that 2,900 out of the 2,980 tapes she admits selling were pirated versions of recordings made by members of the class.

Paragraph 7 of the statement of claim asserts that the members of the class have consented to all pecuniary remedies granted in respect

D of actions for inter alia infringement of copyright in sound recordings and selling counterfeit records and all sums paid in settlement of such actions being actions conducted by the solicitors to the B.P.I. being paid to the B.P.I. in order to defray the expenses of detecting and suppressing the pirate and counterfeit record and like trades, and it asserts further that the action is being conducted by the solicitors to the B.P.I. The

E defendant in her defence says that she has no comment on that, by which I take her to mean that she does not dispute it. She has also said that she does not want this action complicated and extended by massive inquiries.

It seems to me that on the admissions in the defendant's defence and in the reply to the statement of claim, which is to the same effect and on the further admissions in a sworn statement by the

F defendant which is dated November 17, 1978, which she has put before me, the plaintiffs are entitled to an injunction against the defendant. They are entitled to relief in respect of goods seized under an *Anton Piller* order, and they are entitled to the costs of the action, but the entitlement is not entirely in the form of the draft minutes of order, because the draft minutes of order set forth a form of injunction which

G would restrain the defendant, for instance, from making or assisting in the making of pirate records, and she has expressly denied that she has ever made such a record or assisted in the making of such a record. I think that the plaintiffs are entitled to an injunction restraining her from ordering or selling or exposing for sale or inviting offers to acquire or parting with any pirate record, that is to say, any record made directly or indirectly from a sound recording without the licence of the United

H Kingdom copyright owner or exclusive licensee being a number of the class.

I think the plaintiffs are also entitled to an order that their solicitors may deliver to the plaintiffs or to their order all pirate records, including the packaging thereof, which are currently in the custody of the solicitors as a result of the *Anton Piller* order which was executed at the inception of the proceedings, but there should be an order that the

solicitors release to the defendant all genuine cassettes which are in   A
their possession as a result of the *Anton Piller* order.

The minutes of order then ask for an inquiry as to what damages
the members of the class have sustained by reason of the defendant's
infringements of copyright and conversion of infringing copies, the
costs of the inquiry to be reserved and that the plaintiffs do recover
judgment for such sums as are found due together with interest thereon   B
without prejudice to the plaintiffs' obligations to hold or apply the said
sums in such manner if any as may be required of them at law or in
equity.

Mr. Prescott for the plaintiffs has taken me to the judgment of
Vinelott J. in *Prudential Assurance Co. Ltd.* v. *Newman Industries
Ltd.* [1980] 2 W.L.R. 339, where the judge expressed the view that it
was not appropriate to award damages to a plaintiff in a representative   C
capacity. A plaintiff in a representative capacity might be entitled to
relief by way of declaration or injunction, but not to relief by way of
damages. Mr. Prescott has submitted that that case is distinguishable
on its facts from the present case, and he has referred me to orders made
by Foster J. and Whitford J. who on motions for judgment in default
of defence directed inquiries as to damages suffered by the plaintiffs   D
or any other member of the B.P.I.

I think that the fundamental factor is the special position in this
particular trade of the B.P.I. This is not a case of a small number of
manufacturers getting together as a self-constituted association where
there would be a serious likelihood that other pirate cassettes which the
defendant may have sold would have nothing to do with the members
of the association, because she herself has admitted that nearly all records   E
in this country, and "record" includes discs or tapes or similar con-
trivances for reproducing sound, are produced, made or distributed by
the members of the B.P.I. The matter of substance that underlies this is
that if the plaintiffs can only recover damages in respect of tapes in
which they individually own the copyright they will have considerable
difficulty in establishing which pirate E.M.I. tapes were sold by the   F
defendant among the 2,980 tapes which she admits having sold or among
whatever higher number it is found she had sold, but given the admission
that nearly all records including tapes are produced, made or distributed
by members of the B.P.I., on an inquiry as to damages suffered by all
members of the B.P.I. the task will be much simpler since it will be
clear and seems to be admitted that nearly all the tapes which the
defendant had sold were tapes the copyright in which belongs to members   G
of the B.P.I.

In the circumstances of the B.P.I. and the pleaded allegations,
including paragraph 7 of the statement of claim, and I have already
referred to the defence to these, it seems to me that it is appropriate
that damages should be recoverable by the plaintiffs in the representative capacity in which they are entitled to sue for an injunction, and   H
it would be a wholly unnecessary complication of our procedure if the
court were to insist that for the purposes of the inquiry as to damages
all members of the B.P.I. must be joined as co-plaintiffs, or alternatively,
all members except for E.M.I. Records Ltd. must issue separate writs
and apply for them to be consolidated with the claim for damages of
E.M.I. Records Ltd.

Therefore, in my judgment, it is appropriate that the inquiry as

A to damages should be in the form set out in the draft minutes of order, but it must be clear that there is to be no duplication of damage in so far as there are claims outstanding as against other defendants. That is a matter which Mr. Prescott mentioned at an early stage in his submissions, but did not in fact elaborate as the argument proceeded.

   Finally, the plaintiffs must be entitled as against the defendant to
B their costs of the action to date, including the costs of obtaining and executing the *Anton Piller* order, such costs to be taxed if not agreed, but the costs of the inquiry and all future further costs after today's date are reserved.

> *Injunction granted.*
> *Order for inquiry as to damages.*
> *Plaintiffs' costs to date to be taxed*
C > *if not agreed.*
> *All further costs reserved.*

   Solicitors: *A. E. Hamlin & Co.*

   [Reported by MISS EILEEN O'GRADY, Barrister-at-Law]
D

[COURT OF APPEAL]

E * FAITH PANTON PROPERTY PLAN LTD. *v.*
   HODGETTS AND ANOTHER

[1979 F. No. 519]

1980 Dec. 15, 16, 17, 18;   Waller and Brandon L.JJ.
1981 Jan. 21   and Sir David Cairns
F

Injunction—Interlocutory—Jurisdiction to grant—Interlocutory order for payment of taxed costs — Order unenforceable pending taxation—Intention to defeat enforcement of order by disposal of assets—Injunction restraining disposal of assets before trial—Supreme Court of Judicature (Consolidation) Act 1925 (15 & 16 Geo. 5, c. 49), s. 45 (1)

G   The plaintiffs, in a claim restraining the defendants from doing certain acts calculated to harm their business, including passing off their goods or business as the goods or business of the plaintiffs, moved for interlocutory relief and, in those proceedings, the defendants gave undertakings to the court until trial. On motions to commit the first defendant for breaches of the undertakings, Foster J. ordered him to pay the costs of the motions to be taxed on the basis of a
H full indemnity. Those costs, assessed at £12,000, had not yet been taxed and due to the delay before taxation could take place, it was unlikely that they would be taxed for another four or five months. The plaintiffs, anxious about the enforcement of the order for costs as the first defendant had stated that he intended to sell his business assets and make himself bankrupt, applied for an injunction restraining the defendants from assigning, selling or otherwise dealing with moulds and any rights they might have in the copyright and letters patent relating to a design of bathroom and sanitary

Faith Panton Ltd. v. Hodgetts (C.A.)   **[1981]**

ware. Vinelott J. refused the injunction and the plaintiffs   A
appealed.

On the question whether the court had jurisdiction to
grant an injunction under section 45 (1) of the Supreme Court
of Judicature (Consolidation) Act 1925 [1] or on the authority
of the *Mareva* decisions: –

Held, allowing the appeal, that prior to the development
of the *Mareva* injunction, on an application for an interlocutory injunction to restrain a person from dealing with   B
property, the court had only exercised its jurisdiction under
section 45 (1) of the Supreme Court of Judicature (Consolidation) Act 1925 in cases where the applicant had a judgment
of the court in his favour; that where there had been a
judgment which could not be executed because there had
been no taxation, the court had exercised its jurisdiction under
the subsection by appointing a receiver, and, accordingly, the
authorities did not preclude the court from granting an in-   C
junction in the present circumstances, and, in the exercise of
its discretion, the court would grant the injunction under
section 45 (1); and that therefore it was unnecessary to decide
whether it would be a proper case in which to grant a
Mareva injunction (post, pp. 933A–E, 936A–C).

Cummins v. *Perkins* [1899] 1 Ch. 16, C.A. applied.

Lister & Co. v. *Stubbs* (1890) 45 Ch.D. 1, C.A. dis-   D
tinguished.

Decision of Vinelott J. reversed.

The following cases are referred to in the judgments:

Allen v. *Jambo Holdings Ltd.* [1980] 1 W.L.R. 1252; [1980] 2 All E.R.
502, C.A.

Barclay-Johnson v. *Yuill* [1980] 1 W.L.R. 1259; [1980] 3 All E.R. 190.   E
Beddow v. *Beddow* (1878) 9 Ch.D. 89.

Blunt v. *Blunt* [1943] A.C. 517; [1943] 2 All E.R. 76, H.L.(E.).

Brewis v. *Brewis* [1893] W.N. 6.

Bullus v. *Bullus* (1910) 26 T.L.R. 330.

Burmester v. *Burmester* [1913] P. 76.

Chartered Bank v. *Daklouche* [1980] 1 W.L.R. 107; [1980] 1 All E.R.
205, C.A.   F

Cummins v. *Perkins* [1899] 1 Ch. 16; [1898] W.N. 166, C.A.

Gebr Van Weelde Scheepvaart Kantoor B.V. v. *Homeric Marine Services
Ltd.* [1979] 2 Lloyd's Rep. 117.

Gillet v. *Gillet* (1889) 14 P.D. 158.

Jagger v. *Jagger* [1926] P. 93, C.A.

Lister & Co. v. *Stubbs* (1890) 45 Ch.D. 1, C.A.

Mareva Compania Naviera S.A. v. *International Bulkcarriers S.A.* (*Note*)   G
[1980] 1 All E.R. 213; [1975] 2 Lloyd's Rep. 509, C.A.

Newton v. *Newton* (1885) 11 P.D. 11.

Newton v. *Newton* [1896] P. 36; [1895] W.N. 152.

Nippon Yusen Kaisha v. *Karageorgis* [1975] 1 W.L.R. 1093; [1975]
3 All E.R. 282, C.A.

Rahman (Prince Abdul) bin Turki al Sudairy v. *Abu-Taha* [1980] 1
W.L.R. 1268; [1980] 3 All E.R. 409, C.A.

Rasu Maritima S.A. v. *Perusahaan Pertambangan Minyak Dan Gas*   H
Bumi Negara (Government of the Republic of Indonesia intervening)
(Pertamina) [1978] Q.B. 644; [1977] 3 W.L.R. 518; [1977] 3 All
E.R. 324, C.A.

Scott v. *Scott* [1951] P. 193; [1950] 2 All E.R. 1154, C.A.

Sidney v. *Sidney* (1867) 17 L.T. 9.

[1] Supreme Court of Judicature (Consolidation) Act 1925, s. 45 (1): see post,
p. 931c.

A   *Siskina (Owners of cargo lately laden on board)* v. *Distos Compania
          Naviera S.A.* [1979] A.C. 210; [1977] 3 W.L.R. 818; [1977] 3 All
          E.R. 803, H.L.(E.).
     Ward v. *James* [1966] 1 Q.B. 273; [1965] 2 W.L.R. 455; [1965] 1 All
          E.R. 568, C.A.
     Waterhouse v. *Waterhouse* [1893] P. 284, C.A.
     Wright v. *Wright* [1954] 1 W.L.R. 534; [1954] 1 All E.R. 707.

B
     The following additional cases were cited in argument:
     A. v. *C. (Note)* [1981] 2 W.L.R. 629; [1980] 2 All E.R. 347.
     Anton Piller K.G. v. *Manufacturing Processes Ltd.* [1976] Ch. 55;
          [1976] 2 W.L.R. 162; [1976] 1 All E.R. 779, C.A.
     Bankers Trust Co. v. *Shapira* [1980] 1 W.L.R. 1274; [1980] 3 All E.R.
          353, C.A.
C   *Carter* v. *Carter* [1896] P. 35.
     Cretanor Maritime Co. Ltd. v. *Irish Marine Management Ltd.* [1978]
          1 W.L.R. 966; [1978] 3 All E.R. 164, C.A.
     Fanshawe v. *Fanshawe* [1927] P. 238.
     Lloyds Bank Ltd. v. *Marcan* [1973] 1 W.L.R. 1387; [1973] 3 All E.R.
          754, C.A.
     Mills v. *Northern Railway of Buenos Ayres Co.* (1870) 5 Ch.App. 621.
D   *Norwich Pharmacal Co.* v. *Customs and Excise Commissioners* [1974]
          A.C. 133; [1973] 3 W.L.R. 164; [1973] 2 All E.R. 943, H.L.(E.).
     Robinson v. *Pickering* (1881) 16 Ch.D. 660, C.A.
     Stewart Chartering Ltd. v. *C. & O. Managements S.A. (Practice Note)*
          [1980] 1 W.L.R. 460; [1980] 1 All E.R. 718.
     Third Chandris Shipping Corporation v. *Unimarine S.A.* [1979] Q.B.
          645; [1979] 3 W.L.R. 122; [1979] 2 All E.R. 972, Mustill J. and
E   C.A.
     Twentyman v. *Twentyman* [1903] P. 82.

     INTERLOCUTORY APPEAL from Vinelott J.
     In an action brought by the plaintiffs, Faith Panton Property Plan
Ltd., alleging, inter alia, passing off of certain bathroom and sanitary
F   ware by the first defendant, Alan Charles Hodgetts, and his wife, the
second defendant Sheila Hodgetts, trading together as Dekor Bathroom
Laminates, the defendants gave undertakings to the court on April 10,
August 8 and 29, 1979. On November 3, 1980, Foster J. ordered the
first defendant to pay the costs of several motions for his committal
for breaches of the undertakings and those costs to be taxed on an
indemnity basis. Taxation of the bill of costs, assessed at approximately
G   £12,000, could not take place for some four or five months. The first
defendant informed the plaintiffs' solicitors that he would be unable
to pay the costs when taxed and that he intended to sell his business
assets.
     On December 9, 1980, the plaintiffs applied for an injunction to
restrain the defendants from assigning, selling or dealing with the copy-
H   right and letters patent relating to and moulds for bathroom and sanitary
ware of a certain design, formerly manufactured by the defendants for
the plaintiffs. Vinelott J. refused the application.
     By notice of appeal dated December 11, 1980, the plaintiffs appealed
on grounds that (1) the judge was wrong in holding that the jurisdiction to
grant an injunction restraining the first defendant from disposing of his
assets or some of his assets to defeat the plaintiffs' rights either generally
or after judgment obtained by the plaintiffs was restricted to the granting

of an injunction restraining the defendant from disposing of his assets A
outside the jurisdiction; and (2) the judge was wrong in holding that
the discretion conferred on the court by section 45 (1) of the Supreme
Court of Judicature (Consolidation) Act 1925 should not be exercised
so as to prevent the dissipation by the defendants of assets within the
jurisdiction.

The facts are stated in the judgment of Waller L.J.

B

Colin Brodie Q.C. and *Malcolm Warner* for the plaintiffs.
The first defendant in person.
The second defendant did not appear and was not represented.

Cur. adv. vult.

C
January 21. The following judgments were read.

WALLER L.J. This is an appeal from a judgment of Vinelott J.
in which he refused an injunction against both defendants. The plaintiffs have a business of interior decorators, designers and suppliers of
bathroom equipment. The defendants also manufacture fibreglass baths
and other bathroom equipment. In 1978 and early 1979 there was an D
agreement between the plaintiffs and either the first defendant or both
defendants concerning the manufacture of bathroom equipment. In
March 1979 that agreement was determined and there followed a number
of proceedings in the High Court. The plaintiffs brought proceedings
alleging passing off, procuring breaches of contract, slander of goods
and malicious falsehood and moved for interlocutory relief as a result E
of which a number of undertakings were given to the court until trial.
There was also a counter claim in the same proceedings raising claims to
copyright and the ownership of the patent and alleging infringement of
the copyright and patent. There was also a reply and defence to that
counter claim. Those were proceedings in the Chancery Division and
there was also an action in the Queen's Bench Division.

On November 8, 1979, the plaintiffs obtained judgment in the Queen's F
Bench Division for £9,679·23 but a stay of execution was granted
pending the determination of the Chancery proceedings. On January 23,
1980, both defendants were ordered to pay costs which were subsequently
taxed at £526·24 on a motion to set aside a subpoena on Mrs. Faith
Steedman, the majority shareholder in the plaintiffs' company. On
November 3, 1980, the first defendant was ordered to pay the costs of G
four motions before Foster J. The judge directed that the costs were
to be taxed on an indemnity basis and paid forthwith. They have not
yet been taxed and it is estimated that they will not be taxed for some
four or five months but they will be assessed at approximately £12,000.

The first defendant has said that he intends to go bankrupt, and has
said falsely that he had an offer from a substantial company for his assets. H
He then said after that, that he received another offer and accepted it
and that he has spent the purchase money. He has told the plaintiffs'
solicitors that he intends to sell his copyright and patents to a substantial
company; he also has said that moulds which are estimated to be worth
£1,000 each are in his possession but that he had sold them in March
1979 on terms that he was allowed to remain in possession of them.

A   The plaintiffs are anxious about the enforcement of the order for costs of approximately £12,000 and in this application they apply to restrain the defendants from dealing in any rights that they may have in the alleged copyrights, patent or in the moulds, and they also seek an order that each of the defendants disclose upon oath the names of the persons to whom they have assigned or transferred the copyrights, letters patent or moulds.

B   The plaintiffs claim that they are entitled to the injunction under section 45 of the Supreme Court of Judicature (Consolidation) Act 1925 and on the authority of the *Mareva* decisions.

   Section 45 of the Supreme Court of Judicature (Consolidation) Act 1925 reads:

C   " (1) The High Court may grant a mandamus or an injunction or appoint a receiver by an interlocutory order in all cases in which it appears to the court to be just or convenient so to do."

Mr. Brodie submits that the discretion given to the court is one which is unfettered and relies on *Beddow* v. *Beddow* (1878) 9 Ch.D. 89; *Blunt* v. *Blunt* [1943] A.C. 517 and *Ward* v. *James* [1966] 1 Q.B. 273. In D the latter case Lord Denning M.R. said, at p. 295:

        " The cases all show that, when a statute gives discretion, the courts must not fetter it by rigid rules from which a judge is never at liberty to depart. Nevertheless the courts can lay down the considerations which should be borne in mind in exercising the discretion, and point out those considerations which should be ignored."

E   Where however a plaintiff is asking for an injunction in proceedings which are pending Cotton L.J. in *Lister & Co.* v. *Stubbs* (1890) 45 Ch.D. 1 said, at p. 13:

        " I know of no case where, because it was highly probable that if the action were brought to a hearing the plaintiff could establish that a debt was due to him from the defendant, the defendant has F   been ordered to give security until that has been established by the judgment or decree."

   We have been referred to a number of matrimonial cases both in the 19th century and the first half of this century in which injunctions were granted or refused and it would seem that in practice an injunction was only granted where the sum due was a liquidated sum which had G been ordered by the court: see, for example, *Newton* v. *Newton* (1885) 11 P.D. 11; *Jagger* v. *Jagger* [1926] P. 93; *Scott* v. *Scott* [1951] P. 193 and a number of other cases. These cases are no longer good law because as Brandon L.J. pointed out in the course of argument Parliament has reversed them in matrimonial cases.

   Cummins v. *Perkins* [1899] 1 Ch. 16 (which was not a matrimonial H case) showed that an order for costs could be the subject of an order for a receiver of a married woman's separate estate even though those costs had not been taxed. Sir Nathaniel Lindley M.R. made the order for a receiver on the ground that the court was " dealing with equitable estates and a judgment that a debt [was] to be paid out of a particular equitable estate." He said, at p. 20:

        " That is the principle on which the learned judge has acted here— a perfectly sound principle, even without invoking the aid of section

25 of the Judicature Act [1873]. But the introduction of that A
section does not curtail the power of the court to grant injunctions
or to appoint receivers: it enlarges it. It has not revolutionised the
law, but it has enabled the court to grant injunctions and receivers
in cases in which it used not to do so previously. I will not say
where it had no jurisdiction to do so, that would be going too far,
but where in practice it never did so . . ."

B

Mr. Brodie has also relied on the *Mareva* line of cases: *Nippon
Yusen Kaisha* v. *Karageorgis* [1975] 1 W.L.R. 1093; *Mareva Compania
Naviera S.A.* v. *International Bulkcarriers S.A.* (*Note*) [1980] 1 All E.R.
213; *Rasu Maritima S.A.* v. *Perusahaan Pertambangan Minyak Dan Gas
Bumi Negara* (*Government of the Republic of Indonesia intervening*)
[1978] Q.B. 644; *Siskina* (*Owners of cargo lately laden on board*) v.
Distos Compania Naviera S.A. [1979] A.C. 210 and *Prince Abdul Rahman
bin Turki al Sudairy* v. *Abu-Taha* [1980] 1 W.L.R. 1268 and others as
altering the practice which had hitherto governed such cases. He has
submitted that although the *Mareva* line of cases all concerned either
foreign defendants who had assets in this country which were liable to
be removed or, as in *Prince Abdul Rahman bin Turki al Sudairy*
v. *Abu-Taha*, a foreign defendant apparently living in this country in D
similar such circumstances, the only logical explanation of the exercise
of the jurisdiction was on the basis of jeopardy. That unless some such
order was made the plaintiff would be jeopardised by being deprived of
the fruits of any judgment that he might get. It was submitted that
jeopardy does not depend solely on the risk of assets being removed out
of the jurisdiction and reliance was placed on the judgment of Lord
Denning M.R. as showing that the *Mareva* injunction is not to be con- E
fined to cases where assets are likely to be removed out of the jurisdiction.
Lord Denning M.R. said, at p. 1273:

"So I would hold that a *Mareva* injunction can be granted against
a man even though he is based in this country if the circumstances
are such that there is a danger of his absconding, or a danger of
the assets being removed out of the jurisdiction or disposed of F
within the jurisdiction, or otherwise dealt with so that there is a
danger that the plaintiff, if he gets judgment, will not be able to
get it satisfied."

Emphasis was placed on the words "disposed of within the jurisdiction."
It was submitted that removal out of the jurisdiction was logically only
one way in which jeopardy could occur. In *Rasu Maritima S.A.* v. G
Perusahaan Pertambangan Minyak Dan Gas Bumi Negara [1978] Q.B.
644, Orr L.J. said, at p. 644:

"Whether it is right or just to exercise this particular jurisdiction
must depend on all the circumstances of a given case and not, in
my judgment, on any single factor."

H

And then Orr L.J. went on to enumerate the factors such as the
apparent strength or weakness of the plaintiff's case, whether it is
restricted to money, the effect on the defendant and so on. For myself
I see the force of this argument but to accept it would, in my opinion, be
a considerable extension of the *Mareva* doctrine and I would wish to
reserve my opinion until the facts of the case make it necessary so to
consider.

A   I find it unnecessary to make the decision as to whether or not a *Mareva* injunction would apply in the circumstances suggested by Mr. Brodie. All of the authorities before the *Mareva* cases go to show that injunctions will not be granted before judgment. This is an intermediate case. It is not a case where it is highly probable that if the action is brought to a hearing the plaintiffs would be able to establish a debt as Cotton L.J. was considering in *Lister & Co.* v. *Stubbs*, 45 Ch.D. 1.
B It is a case where the defendant has been ordered to pay the costs of a hearing of several motions on an indemnity basis: a hearing that took four days. It is only because of the delay which must inevitably take place before the taxation that the plaintiffs have not been enabled to execute the judgment. The principle in *Lister & Co.* v. *Stubbs* depends on there being no order or judgment. In this case there is a judgment
C which cannot be enforced for some months because of the difficulties of taxation. In *Cummins* v. *Perkins* [1899] 1 Ch. 16 an order for costs which had not been taxed was treated as an order which could be enforced by appointing a receiver. In my opinion there is nothing in any of the authorities which would make it wrong to grant an injunction in this case.

D   Are the circumstances of this case such that an injunction should be granted? The defendant has shown by his behaviour that he intends to divest himself of his assets if he can. He has shown a lack of frankness to the court in not disclosing to whom he has sold some of his assets when asked by this court. The hearing before Foster J. was for contempt of court and more serious consequences might have followed. In my judgment this is a case where the court should ensure so far as
E possible that its orders are not thwarted, and I would grant an injunction as prayed until after the costs have been taxed and paid.

          I have arrived at this conclusion differing from Vinelott J. with reluctance. He accepted that where there was a substantial judgment, not finally quantified, an injunction might be granted but came to the conclusion that this was not such a case. There has, however, been
F fuller argument before this court and in particular we have been referred to a number of cases which were not before Vinelott J. Furthermore as I have mentioned above there has been before this court a lack of frankness.

          With regard to the prayer for the disclosure of the names of the persons to whom the defendants have assigned or transferred the copyright, letters patent or moulds, this appears to me to be an inquiry of a
G fishing nature. The case put forward by the plaintiffs is based largely on the suspicion that the first defendant had transferred the assets to the second defendant. On this basis the plaintiffs are adequately protected without any further order. The possibility of the assets having been transferred elsewhere is remote and is based on suspicion rather than evidence. If any have been transferred the difficulties of tracing
H them would be almost insuperable. I would therefore refuse this part of the application.

          BRANDON L.J. The facts which constitute the background of this case have been stated in the judgment of Waller L.J. and it is not necessary that I should repeat them.

          By their notice of motion dated December 2, 1980, and amended on December 9, 1980, the plaintiffs applied for two orders in respect of (a)

934

Brandon L.J.   Faith Panton Ltd. v. Hodgetts (C.A.)   [1981]

the defendants' alleged copyright relating to moulds for " Palace Bath- A
room " furniture, (b) the moulds themselves and (c) Patent No. 1541444
relating to an allegedly original design of water closet. In paragraph
(i) of the notice of motion the plaintiffs asked, on the basis that the
defendants had not already assigned or otherwise disposed of the
alleged copyright, moulds, and patent owned by them, for an injunction restraining them from doing so. In paragraph (ii) of the notice of
motion the plaintiffs asked, on the basis that the defendants had already B
assigned or otherwise disposed of the alleged copyright, moulds and
patent owned by them, for an order that they do disclose on oath within
seven days the person, persons, firm or company to whom they made any
such dispositions.

The reason why the plaintiffs asked for these two alternative kinds
of relief in this way was that the first defendant had claimed to have C
sold the moulds in March 1979, although on terms which allowed him to
keep them in his possession, and to have assigned the copyright and
patent on November 5, 1980, but that, due to discrepancies, omissions
and ambivalence in the first defendant's various accounts of these transactions, there was a serious doubt whether his claim to have made such
sale and assignments was true.

So far as the first kind of relief asked for is concerned, namely, an D
injunction against dealing with the copyright, moulds or patent, the
appeal appears to me to raise two questions, each primarily of law. The
first question is whether to grant the injunction asked for would be in
accordance with the practice in such matters established over many
years prior to the development, from 1975 onwards, of the doctrine of the
Mareva injunction. The second question is whether, if the answer to E
the first question is in the negative, to grant the injunction would be in
accordance with the recently developed doctrine to which I have
referred.

I shall consider first what may conveniently be called the pre-Mareva
practice. The basic tenet of that practice was expressed by Cotton L.J.
in Lister & Co. v. Stubbs (1890) 45 Ch.D. 1 where he said, at p. 13: F

  " I know of no case where, because it was highly probable that
  if the action were brought to a hearing the plaintiff could establish
  that a debt was due to him from the defendant, the defendant has
  been ordered to give security until that has been established by
  the judgment or decree."

The practice as so stated was applied mainly in matrimonial cases, G
in which a basic distinction was drawn between cases in which a wife
had obtained against her husband an order for the payment of a
specific sum of money by way of alimony, maintenance, costs or security
for costs on the one hand, and cases in which she had applied for such
an order but not yet obtained it on the other hand. Examples of the
first category of cases are Sidney v. Sidney (1867) 17 L.T. 9; Gillet v. H
Gillet (1889) 14 P.D. 158; Waterhouse v. Waterhouse [1893] P. 284;
Brewis v. Brewis [1893] W.N. 6; Newton v. Newton [1896] P. 36 and
Bullus v. Bullus (1910) 26 T.L.R. 330. Examples of the second category of cases are Newton v. Newton (1885) 11 P.D. 11; Burmester v.
Burmester [1913] P. 76; Jagger v. Jagger [1926] P. 93; Scott v. Scott
[1951] P. 193 and Wright v. Wright [1954] 1 W.L.R. 534.

A   In *Jagger* v. *Jagger* Scrutton L.J. said, at p. 102:

"I am not aware of any statutory or other power in the court to restrain a person from dealing with his property at a time when no order against him has been made."

The distinction between the two categories of cases referred to above operated unjustly to wives, who often had little control over the speed
B   with which their applications for financial relief were carried through to judgment, especially having regard to the manifold opportunities available to husbands to delay that process. This injustice was recognised by Parliament, which dealt comprehensively with the prevention of wives' being deprived of their just dues by their husbands' disposal or other dissipation of their assets before proceedings for financial relief
C   were concluded in the Matrimonial Causes (Property and Maintenance) Act 1958, section 2. These provisions have since been re-enacted in later Matrimonial Causes Acts, and are presently to be found in section 37 of the Act of 1973.

The present case does not fall clearly into either of the two categories of cases discussed above. On the one hand it is a case when an
D   order was made on November 3, 1980, that the first defendant should pay to the plaintiffs their costs of the applications for committal for contempt to be taxed by the taxing master on the basis of a full indemnity. On the other hand taxation of the costs has not yet taken place, and we have been told that, due to the delays presently occurring in such matters, it is unlikely to take place for another five months or so. The amount ultimately payable is, however, by no means at large,
E   for there is evidence before the court, which I see no reason not to accept as reasonably reliable, that the amount is likely to be in the region of £12,000.

How should the court, acting in accordance with the pre-*Mareva* practice, deal with an intermediate case of this kind? Assistance on this is, in my view to be found, first, in common sense, and, secondly,
F   in a further authority on the practice of the court to which I have not yet referred.

First, as to common sense. It seems to me to verge on the absurd that, if the costs had already been taxed at £12,000, the court would have power to grant an injunction against the defendants restraining them from dealing with their assets (if they still hold them); but that, because the costs have not yet been taxed, although there is sufficient evidence
G   that they will in fact amount to about £12,000, the court has no power to grant such an injunction.

Second, as to further authority. This is to be found in *Cummins* v. *Perkins* [1899] 1 Ch. 16. In that case an action brought by a married woman had been dismissed with costs, to be paid out of her separate estate. The defendants' solicitor had brought in a bill of costs
H   amounting to £270. The plaintiff had no, or virtually no, separate estate, except a share in the estate of her deceased sister which was due to her but had not yet been paid. It was held that, in such circumstances, the court had power to appoint a receiver of the share of the plaintiff's deceased sister's estate which was coming to her, and an order for the appointment of such a receiver was made. It is to be observed that the order against the plaintiff was that the defendant's costs should

be paid out of her separate estate, not out of any particular fund A which might constitute such estate.

It is true that this case is complicated by the fact that the court was dealing with a married woman and ordering the costs to be paid out of her separate estate. For myself, however, I cannot see any significant distinction between that situation and the situation in an ordinary modern case like the present one, in which costs are ordered to be paid by a defendant, whether male or female. The order will not, B of course, direct payment out of any separate estate, because there is no need for it to do so. But the effect is in practice the same. Further, assuming that the court could properly appoint a receiver in such a case, I see no reason why it should not afford protection to the party in whose favour the order for costs has been obtained by the alternative method of granting an injunction. C

I am further of the opinion that, having regard to the peculiar, inconsistent and ambivalent conduct of the first defendant with regard to what dispositions, if any, he has made of the alleged copyright, moulds and patent, the court should exercise its discretion by granting the first injunction asked for by the plaintiffs in the present action.

On the footing that the court has power, under the pre-*Mareva* D practice, to grant the first kind of injunction asked for by the plaintiffs, and that it would be right, in the circumstances of this case, to exercise such power, it is not necessary to examine the plaintiffs' alternative case based on the recent development of the doctrine of *Mareva* injunctions. Since, however, considerable argument was addressed to us on the subject, I think it would be right for me to make some observations on it. E

Originally *Mareva* injunctions were granted only in cases where the defendants were foreigners with assets in the jurisdiction, which they could easily remove in time to avoid execution of any money judgment which might subsequently be obtained by the plaintiffs: see *Nippon Yusen Kaisha* v. *Karageorgis* [1975] 1 W.L.R. 1093; *Mareva Compania Naviera S.A.* v. *International Bulkcarriers S.A.* [1980] 1 All E.R. F 213; *Rasu Maritima S.A.* v. *Perusahaan Pertambangan Minyak Dan Gas Bumi Negara (Government of the Republic of Indonesia intervening) (Pertamina)* [1978] Q.B. 644. These were all commercial cases, but the same principle was later applied in an action for personal injuries: see *Allen* v. *Jambo Holdings Ltd.* [1980] 1 W.L.R. 1252.

In *Gebr Van Weelde Scheepvaart Kantoor B.V.* v. *Homeric Marine* G *Services Ltd.* [1979] 2 Lloyd's Rep. 117, Lloyd J. held that there was a settled practice against granting *Mareva* injunctions against defendants resident within the jurisdiction. In *Chartered Bank* v. *Daklouche* [1980] 1 W.L.R. 107, however, this court held that mere residence here did not prevent the grant of a *Mareva* injunction against a defendant of foreign nationality, when her residence here might well be temporary only, and a serious risk of removal of assets from the jurisdiction H existed.

Similarly in *Barclay-Johnson* v. *Yuill* [1980] 1 W.L.R. 1259 Sir Robert Megarry V.-C. granted a *Mareva* injunction against an English defendant who, although he had previously been ordinarily resident within the jurisdiction, had since taken himself off abroad for an indefinite period. The Vice-Chancellor stressed in that case that the

A crucial factor justifying the grant of an injunction was the risk of the
defendant removing assets from the jurisdiction in order to defeat the
plaintiff's claim. That decision was approved by this court in *Prince
Abdul Rahman bin Turki al Sudairy* v. *Abu-Taha* [1980] 1 W.L.R.
1268, where an injunction was granted against foreign defendants who
claimed to be resident within the jurisdiction, but, in the affidavits
which they filed, failed to disclose their " place of residence " as required
B by R.S.C., Ord. 41, r. 1 (4).

It is right to observe, I think, that, although the modern doctrine
of the *Mareva* injunction has developed rapidly since it was first applied
by this court in 1975, it has never yet been applied to a case like the
present one in which no foreign element of any kind exists. It was
argued by Mr. Brodie for the plaintiffs that there was no logicality in
C insisting on the presence of a foreign element, and that the only issue
on which the grant of a *Mareva* injunction should depend was that of
jeopardy, by which he meant a real risk that a defendant, whatever his
nationality, domicil or residence might be, against whom a plaintiff
had a good claim, might dispose of or dissipate his assets, either abroad
or here, in such a way as to prevent the plaintiff from executing any
D judgment which he might later obtain.

I see the force of this argument, and indeed it was fully recognised
by Lord Hailsham of St. Marylebone L.C. in *Siskina* (*Owners of cargo
lately laden on board*) v. *Distos Compania Naviera* [1979] A.C. 210,
when he said in what I may perhaps be permitted to describe as a
particularly prescient passage in his speech, at p. 26:

E   " I believe the truth to be that sooner or later the courts or the
legislature will have to choose between two alternatives. Either
the position of a plaintiff making a claim against an English based
defendant will have to be altered or the principle of the *Mareva*
cases will have to be modified."

It now seems highly likely that it will be the first of the two alterna-
F tives referred to by Lord Hailsham in that passage which will be chosen,
namely, the alteration of the position of a plaintiff making a claim
against an English-based defendant, and further that it will be the
legislature which will before long be making the choice. In this connection I refer to the Supreme Court Bill, recently introduced in the
House of Lords in its legislative capacity. Clause 37 of this Bill, which
is designed to replace section 45 of the Supreme Court of Judicature
G (Consolidation) Act 1925, is in these terms:

       " (1) The High Court may by order (whether interlocutory or
final) grant an injunction or appoint a receiver in all cases in which
it appears to the court to be just and convenient to do so.
       " (3) The power of the High Court under subsection (1) to grant
H   an interlocutory injunction restraining a party to any proceedings
from removing from the jurisdiction of the High Court, or otherwise dealing with, assets located within that jurisdiction shall be
exercisable in cases where that party is, as well as in cases where
he is not, domiciled, resident or present within that jurisdiction."

With fresh legislation of this kind in the offing, I think that it would
be undesirable for this court to express a judicial opinion on what the
law would have been without it, unless it was necessary to do so. Since

938

I am of opinion, for the reasons which I gave earlier, that the plaintiffs   A
in the present action are entitled to the grant of the first injunction
sought by them in accordance with the pre-*Mareva* practice, I do not
propose to express any opinion on the question whether they could, on
the law as it exists at present, obtain such injunction on the basis of
the *Mareva* doctrine as well.

I turn now to the second order asked for by the plaintiffs. That   B
order was, as I indicated earlier, that the defendants, on the assumption
that they had assigned or otherwise dealt with the copyright, moulds or
patent, should disclose on oath within seven days to whom such
assignment or other disposition had been made.

I cannot see any good reason for making such an order. As I
understand the plaintiffs' case, they are not, at present at least, asserting
any proprietary interest, legal or equitable, in the three assets concerned,   C
that is to say the copyright, the moulds and the patent. That being
so, even if there has been an assignment of one or more of these
assets to a third party or parties, I do not see how knowledge of the
identity of such third party or parties will assist the plaintiffs at this
stage. The assets would not be traceable by the plaintiffs in the hands
of their present holders, and knowledge of the identity of such holders   D
would not therefore assist the plaintiffs in obtaining security for the
enforcement of their judgment on costs in the motions for contempt
when these have finally been taxed.

There is the further point in this connection that the defendants
were earlier ordered to pay to Mrs. Faith Marian Steedman, the
managing director of the plaintiffs, costs later taxed at £526.24 in respect
of a successful application by her to set aside a subpoena served on her by   E
them. In relation to this judgment debt an order has been made under
R.S.C., Ord. 48, r. 1 (1), for the attendance of the defendants for oral
examination on January 20, 1981, and it should be possible to elicit
from them in the course of that examination the kind of information
which the plaintiffs seek.

For these reasons I agree with Vinelott J. that the court should   F
not make the second order asked for by the plaintiffs.

I recognise that, in coming to a different conclusion from that of
the judge with regard to the first order asked for by the plaintiffs, I am
disagreeing with him in a matter which involved an exercise of discretion
by him. I think, however, that this court has had the advantage of a
much fuller exposition of the relevant authorities than the judge had,   G
and that, in the light of that fuller exposition, we are entitled, even
though an exercise of discretion is involved, to take a different view of
the matter from that which he took.

For the reasons which I have given I would allow this appeal so far
as it relates to the order asked for in paragraph (i) of the notice of
motion, and dismiss it so far as it relates to paragraph (ii).
                                                                          H

SIR DAVID CAIRNS. I agree that the appeal against the refusal of
an injunction restraining the defendant from disposal of assets should
be allowed, and that the injunction be granted in the terms indicated
by Waller L.J.

I also agree that the appeal against the refusal of an order for the
discovery of certain names should be dismissed.

A   In both cases my agreement is for the reasons given in the judgments already delivered, to which I have no further reasons of my own
to add.

Appeal allowed.
Plaintiffs' costs in cause below.
Defendant to pay four-fifths of
B   *plaintiffs' costs in Court of*
Appeal in any event.

Solicitors: *Dawson & Co.*

[Reported by Mrs. Maria Fleischmann, Barrister-at-Law]

C

[CHANCERY DIVISION]

* *In re* CLEAVER, decd.

D   CLEAVER and Another *v.* INSLEY and Others

[1979 C. No. 5500]

1980 Dec. 15, 16, 17, 18, 19   Nourse J

Will — Mutual wills — Constructive trust — Husband and Wife
making wills in similar terms—Wife taking under husband's
E   *will—Wife making new will—Whether wife under legal obli-*
gation to bequeath her estate in terms of former will —
Whether wife's executors holding estate on terms of former
will

In October 1967, the testator, who was then aged 78, and
the testatrix, then aged 74, were married. The testator had
three children by a previous marriage. The testatrix had no
F   children, but she did have two nieces. In December 1967,
and also in 1970, they both simultaneously made wills in
substantially identical terms. On February 7, 1974, the testator and the testatrix again made wills in almost identical
terms. The testator gave each of his three children a legacy
of £500, and his residuary estate to the testatrix absolutely,
subject to her surviving him for one month, but if she
did not, then his residuary estate was to be divided into
three equal parts, one third each to go to his two younger
G   children, the plaintiffs, absolutely, and the remaining third to
be held in trust for his eldest daughter M for life, with
remainder to the plaintiffs absolutely, with a gift over if the
plaintiffs should predecease M. The testatrix's will was in
identical terms, save that in lieu of the legacies of £500 to
the testator's children, she gave legacies of £500 to each of
her two nieces. The testator died in 1975, and the testatrix
H   duly received the whole of the testator's net residue. On
June 23, 1977, the testatrix made her last will, and in this
she gave her net residuary estate to M and her husband, or
the survivor, in equal shares, absolutely, thus making no provision either for the plaintiffs or for the testatrix's two nieces.
The testatrix died on May 30, 1978.
    On the plaintiffs seeking a declaration that the executors
held the testatrix's estate on trust to give effect to the
testatrix's will dated February 7, 1974, and an order to
administer and distribute the estate accordingly: —

In re Cleaver, decd. (Ch.D.)   [1981]

Held, that for two wills to be enforceable as mutual wills   A
it must be established by satisfactory evidence that the makers
of the wills had agreed between themselves and intended that
they should be bound by the agreement; that the fact that
the wills were made simultaneously and were to the same
effect, although a relevant circumstance, was not by itself
sufficient proof but, in the present case, the court was satisfied
by sufficient extrinsic evidence that the 1974 wills made by
the testator and the testatrix were executed in pursuance of   B
such an agreement, thus imposing on them mutual legal obligations as to the disposal of their property; and that, since
the testatrix had had the benefit of the agreement, a constructive trust was created and the executors were bound
to administer and distribute the estate of the testatrix in
accordance with her will dated February 7, 1974, and not
in accordance with her will of June 23, 1977 (post, pp. 945F–G,
947C–F, H, 948C–D, 949F).

      Birmingham v. *Renfrew* (1937) 57 C.L.R. 666 applied.   C
      Gray v. *Perpetual Trustee Co. Ltd.* [1928] A.C. 391, P.C.
considered.

The following cases are referred to in the judgment:

Birmingham v. *Renfrew* (1937) 57 C.L.R. 666.
Dufour v. *Pereira* (1769) 1 Dick. 419.   D
Gray v. *Perpetual Trustee Co. Ltd.* [1928] A.C. 391, P.C.
Oldham, In re [1925] Ch. 75.
Ottaway v. *Norman* [1972] Ch. 698; [1972] 2 W.L.R. 50; [1971] 3 All
    E.R. 1325.
Pearson Fund Trusts, In re (unreported), October 21, 1977.
Walpole (Lord) v. *Lord Orford* (1797) 3 Ves.Jun. 402.

  E
The following additional cases were cited in argument:

Adams and the Kensington Vestry, In re (1884) 27 Ch.D. 394, C.A.
Gillespie, In re (1868) 69 D.L.R. (2nd) 368.
Green, decd., In re [1951] Ch. 148; [1950] 2 All E.R. 913.
Hagger, In re [1930] 2 Ch. 190.
Heys, decd., In the estate of [1914] P. 192.
Stone v. *Hoskins* [1905] P. 194.   F
Szabo v. *Boros* (1966) 60 D.L.R. (2d) 186; (1967) 64 D.L.R. (2d) 48.

ACTION

By a writ dated August 20, 1979, the plaintiffs, Arthur Cleaver and
his sister, Florence Zetterberg, claiming as legatees under the will dated
February 7, 1974, of Flora Cleaver, deceased (" the testatrix ") who was
the third wife of their father, Arthur Cleaver senior (" the testator "),   G
sought, inter alia, against the first defendants, George Ernest Insley and
David Richard Aldersey, executors of the testatrix under her last will
dated June 23, 1977, and against certain beneficiaries under that will,
being the second to seventh defendants, a declaration that the first
defendants held the estate of the testatrix upon trust to give effect to
her will dated February 7, 1974, and an order that they administer and   H
distribute the estate accordingly. The second to seventh defendants
were respectively, Martha Noble, the plaintiffs' elder sister; Desmond
Noble, her husband; Nigel Noble, the son of Martha and Desmond Noble;
Elizabeth Noble, who was Nigel's wife, and Joanne and Katie Noble,
who were the children of Nigel and Elizabeth Noble.

The first plaintiff, Arthur Cleaver, gave evidence, inter alia, that on
the evening after the testator's death, the testatrix had asked him to

The Weekly Law Reports, June 26, 1981

941

1 W.L.R.   In re Cleaver, decd. (Ch.D.)

A   read both the testator's will and her own will of February 7, 1974, and
had said to him " I want you to see that our wills are exactly the same.
You will also notice that Martha does not come off very well in that,
because your dad was very cross with her because of the way she got
hold of Emma's money." Emma was the testator's sister. The testatrix
had added that the testator had wanted to put it right with the first
plaintiff and his sister, Mrs. Zetterberg.

B   The first plaintiff also gave evidence that he had visited the testatrix
at the end of June 1977, after she had just returned from staying for
two weeks with the Nobles, and that he remembered the testatrix saying
that her solicitor had been to see her, and that a couple of days later he
had asked the testatrix why she had needed her solicitor and that she
had replied " Your father only left me £1,500, and I have had to live
C on my own savings. Martha told me I can leave my money to whom
I like, I do not have to worry about promises made to dad, he is dead
now and can do nothing about it."

  Mr. Gray, a friend and neighbour of the Cleavers, gave evidence of
an occasion some time after the execution by the testator and the testatrix
of their 1974 wills, when Mr. Gray and his wife were taking the testator
D and the testatrix to Southampton in their car, and the testator had asked
Mr. Gray to make a diversion so that he, the testator, could drop his
and the testatrix's wills in at the solicitors. Mr. Gray said in evidence
that after the testator got back into the car he was smiling all over his
face and said " That has settled " or " that has cooked his hash." He
stated that nothing more was said but that it was obvious to everybody
what the testator meant, namely, that he was referring to Mr. Desmond
E Noble, whom the testatrix disliked. Mr. Gray said that his understanding was that the testatrix, though she said nothing, agreed with what
the testator had said.

  Mrs. Zetterberg gave evidence of an occasion at the end of January
or the beginning of February 1974 when the testator, the testatrix
and herself were sitting round the fire, and the testator said he was
F going to tell her " what we have put in our wills," and that if he died
first the testatrix was to have the " use " of his money, and he gave
her the other details of his will, mentioning the restrictions on Mrs.
Noble's interest. The testator, she said, had explained the reason for
the restrictions as being that he thought Mrs. Noble had very unfairly
got her aunt Emma's money, and so that if Mrs. Noble died first, her
G husband and their children should not receive anything. Mrs. Zetterberg
also said that later the same day, when she was alone with the testatrix,
the testatrix had said " You know I did not marry your father for his
money " and " I really do love him, but you need not be afraid that I
shall take any money away from you children, you will get your share."

  Further facts are stated in the judgment.

H

  J. C. Hicks Q.C. for the plaintiffs.
  D. J. Campion for the first defendants.
  M. N. Keenan for the second and third defendants.
  The fourth to seventh defendants were not present or represented.

  NOURSE J. This is a case in which it is alleged that mutual wills are
enforceable. By that I mean that it is one where it is alleged that two

persons—in this case husband and wife—made an enforceable agreement   A
as to the disposal of their property and executed wills in substantially
identical terms in pursuance thereof. The husband died first without
having revoked his will. The wife accepted benefits under the husband's
will and later made her last will in substantially different terms. She is
now dead. The question is whether the persons who would have been
the beneficiaries under the wife's original will can claim that her estate
should be held on the trusts of that will and not of her last will.   B

The persons concerned and the state of their families are as follows.
The testator was Arthur Cleaver and the testatrix was Flora Cleaver.
They were married in about October 1967. It was the testator's third
marriage, his second wife having died in 1966. The testator had had
three children by his first marriage which was dissolved in about 1918.
In order of seniority they are the second defendant, Martha Noble, the   C
second plaintiff, Florence Zetterberg, and the first plaintiff, Arthur
Cleaver junior. There are two years between each of them and Mr.
Arthur Cleaver is now 64. The testatrix never had a child but two
nieces of hers play a minor role in the story. Mrs. Martha Noble's
husband is the third defendant, Desmond Noble. The fourth defendant
Nigel Noble is their son and the fifth Elizabeth Noble is Nigel's wife.   D
The sixth and seventh defendants, Joanne and Katie Noble, are two young
children of theirs. I should also mention that the testator had a sister,
Emma Cleaver, who died in 1959 leaving a net estate sworn for probate
of about £8,500. She left legacies of £100 to the testator, and of £500
to Mr. Arthur Cleaver, and three legacies amounting to £700 to others.
Then she left legacies of £100 each to two sons (Nigel and Adrian) of
Mrs. Martha Noble and her residuary estate to Mrs. Martha Noble   E
absolutely. That would appear to have been worth £7,000 or thereabouts.

At the time of their marriage the testator was aged 78 and the
testatrix about 74. A few days beforehand the testator purchased Flat
No. 4, Basing House, Wilderton Road, Poole, which is just over the
boundary from Bournemouth. They lived there until about November
1971, when they took a lease of Flat 3, Albany House, Balcombe Road,   F
Poole, which was only about 50 yards away from Basing House, a corner,
property, on the other side of the road. In May 1972 the flat at Basing
House was sold for £6,300 and the net proceeds were paid to the testator.

On December 19, 1967, the testator and testatrix each made a will
primarily in favour of the other in substantially identical terms. The
testator gave everything to the testatrix, subject to her surviving him for
a period of one month, in default of which he gave pecuniary legacies   G
to the two nieces of the testatrix and directed his net residue to be
equally divided between Mrs. Martha Noble, Mrs. Zetterberg and Mr.
Arthur Cleaver or the survivor or survivors absolutely. The testatrix's
will was in the same form mutatis mutandis except that she gave one
of her nieces some specific items of property instead of a pecuniary
legacy. Instructions for these wills were taken by Mr. John Ernest   H
Insley, then a partner in the firm of Greenwood & Insley of Bournemouth. The testator and the testatrix visited him together for that
purpose, and he was handed instructions for both wills written out in
what he believes to have been the testator's handwriting.

On June 12, 1970, the testator and the testatrix each made a further
will. On this occasion however there was a difference between the two
gifts over of residue. If the testator was the survivor then his residue

The Weekly Law Reports, June 26, 1981

943

1 W.L.R.   In re Cleaver, decd. (Ch.D.)   Nourse J.

A was to go as before to his three children or the survivors or survivor of them, in equal shares, but if the testatrix was the survivor then her two nieces, if surviving, were to come in and share equally with the testator's three children or the survivor or survivors of them. There is no evidence worth talking of as to the circumstances in which these two wills were made.

B On February 7, 1974, the testator and the testatrix made the allegedly enforceable mutual wills with which this case is concerned. The testator's will gave a legacy of £500 to each of his three children. It then gave his residuary estate to the testatrix absolutely, subject to her surviving him for a period of one month. If she did not so survive him then the residue was directed to be divided into three equal parts, with one going to Mrs. Zetterberg absolutely and the second to Mr.

C Arthur Cleaver absolutely. The third part was settled on trust for Mrs. Martha Noble for life with remainder to Mrs. Zetterberg and Mr. Arthur Cleaver absolutely in equal shares with two provisos, one immaterial and the other to the effect that if Mrs. Zetterberg and Mr. Arthur Cleaver should pre-decease Mrs. Martha Noble then her share should go to Maureen Cleaver, the adopted daughter of Mr. Arthur Cleaver,

D absolutely. The testatrix's will was in identical terms mutatis mutandis except that she gave legacies of £500 to each of her two nieces instead of legacies of the same amount to each of the testator's three children.

The testator died on February 27, 1975, and his 1974 will was duly proved by the testatrix as sole executrix on April 25, 1975. Apart from the legacies of £500 to each of the testator's three children, she thus became absolutely entitled to the whole of the testator's net estate which

E in due course was paid or transferred to her. The net value of the testator's residuary estate was about £6,500. The principal assets were a sum of about £3,500, including accrued interest, standing to his credit with a building society and a Bournemouth bond of £4,000. He also owned a freehold house, 48, Pytchley Road, Rugby. That was subject to a rent controlled tenancy and its value was sworn for probate at a

F figure of £500.

It appears that on May 15, 1975, less than three months after the testator's death, the testatrix gave someone in the firm of Messrs. Greenwood & Insley instructions to make her a new will and on June 2 she did indeed execute a new will. Except for the natural disappearance of all reference to the testator and the reduction of one of her nieces' legacies from £500 to £100 that will was in identical terms to those of

G her 1974 will. On November 13, 1975, the testatrix made a further will by which she gave each of her two nieces a legacy of £500 and directed her residuary estate to be divided in equal shares absolutely between Mrs. Martha Noble, Mrs. Zetterberg and Mr. Arthur Cleaver or the survivors or survivor of them. That was a return to her first will of December 19, 1967, but it clearly involved a breach of the alleged

H agreement between the testator and the testatrix, if such there was, in so far as it restored Mrs. Martha Noble's interest to an absolute one. On January 27, 1976, the testatrix made a codicil to her will which is not material for present purposes. On June 23, 1977, the testatrix made what was to be her last will. By that she gave pecuniary legacies to the fourth to seventh defendants and her net residuary estate to Mrs. Martha Noble and her husband Desmond Noble or the survivor of them if more than one in equal shares absolutely. That will made no

944

provision for Mrs. Zetterberg, Mr. Cleaver or either of the testatrix's **A**
two nieces.

There is no evidence worth talking of as to the circumstances in
which any of the testatrix's testamentary dispositions between her will
of February 7, 1974, and the codicil of January 27, 1976, came to be
made. There is some evidence as to the circumstances in which her
last will came to be made and I will deal with that in due course.

      B

After the testator's death the testatrix continued to live on at the
flat in Albany House, but in about February 1976 she moved to a
nursing home about three-quarters of a mile away. I believe that she
returned home for a period but her second visit was a permanent one.
She was certainly there when she made her last will on June 23, 1977.

The testatrix died on May 30, 1978. Her last will was duly proved
on October 9, 1978, by Mr. Insley and his partner Mr. David Richard **C**
Aldersey, who are the first defendants in this action. The net value of her
estate was sworn for probate at just over £18,000. The principal assets
were sums standing to her credit with two building societies of an aggregate
amount of about £13,500, about £550 in the National Savings Bank, and
the house in Rugby which had formerly belonged to the testator and was
now sworn at a figure of £4,000. On June 7, 1978, about a week after **D**
the testatrix's death, Mr. Arthur Cleaver informed Mr. Insley's firm by
telephone that he would be contesting the last will of the testatrix. By
the beginning of January 1979 that claim had been effectively formulated
by solicitors acting on behalf of Mrs. Zetterberg and Mr. Arthur Cleaver.
That caused Mr. Insley and Mr. Aldersey to commence proceedings in this
division for leave to distribute the testatrix's estate in accordance with the
terms of the 1977 will. When those proceedings came before the master **E**
he very rightly took the view that Mr. Arthur Cleaver and Mrs. Zetterberg
should commence an action against the Noble family; Mr. Insley and Mr.
Aldersey would also be necessary parties. He stayed the administration
proceedings accordingly.

The writ in this action was issued on August 20, 1979. Mr. Arthur
Cleaver and Mrs. Zetterberg claim a declaration that Mr. Insley and Mr. **F**
Aldersey hold the estate of the testatrix upon trust to give effect to the
provisions of her 1974 will, and an order that they administer and distribute the estate accordingly. Mr. Insley and Mr. Aldersey have very
properly submitted to act as the court shall direct, but Mr. and Mrs.
Noble have appeared by counsel and have throughout contested the plaintiffs' claim. The fourth to seventh defendants have entered appearances
and served a defence but they have not appeared and have not been **G**
represented at the hearing before me.

Before I deal with further facts of a more controversial nature it will
be convenient for me to deal with the principles of law which are applicable
to a decision of this case. There cannot now be much doubt about the
nature of those principles, but there is no modern authority in England in
which they have been fully explored.

      H

The foundation of the plaintiffs' claim is the well-known case of *Dufour*
v. *Pereira* (1769) 1 Dick. 419 which was decided by Lord Camden L.C.
in 1769. That case is fully discussed in *Hargrave's Juridical Arguments*
(1799) vol. 2, pp. 304 et seq. That was a case where Lord Camden L.C.
relying as it appears only on the terms of a joint will executed by a husband
and wife concluded that there had been a prior agreement. There have not
been so very many cases on the subject since, but in one of them, *Gray* v.

The Weekly Law Reports, June 26, 1981

945

1 W.L.R.   In re Cleaver, decd. (Ch.D.)   Nourse J.

A *Perpetual Trustee Co. Ltd.* [1928] A.C. 391, the Privy Council decided in clear terms that the mere simultaneity of the wills and the similarity of their terms are not enough taken by themselves to establish the necessary agreement. I will read what appear to me to be the material passages in the judgment of the Board, which was delivered by Viscount Haldane. The first passage reads, at p. 399:

B   " In *Dufour* v. *Pereira* (1769) 1 Dick. 419 the conclusion reached was that if there was in point of fact an agreement come to that the wills should not be revoked after the death of one of the parties without mutual consent, they were binding. That they were mutual wills to the same effect was at least treated as a relevant circumstance, to be taken into account in determining whether there was such an agreement. But the mere simultaneity of the wills and the similarity of

C   their terms do not appear, taken by themselves, to have been looked on as more than some evidence of an agreement not to revoke. The agreement, which does not restrain the legal right to revoke, was the foundation of the right in equity which might emerge, although it was a fact which had in itself to be established by evidence, and in such cases the whole of the evidence must be looked at."

D Their lordships then proceeded to mention two authorities, the second of which was the decision of Astbury J. in *In re Oldham* [1925] Ch. 75. The judgment of the Privy Council continues, at p. 400:

      " Their lordships agree with the view taken by Astbury J. The case before them is one in which the evidence of an agreement, apart from that of making the wills in question, is so lacking that they are unable

E   to come to the conclusion that an agreement to constitute equitable interests has been shown to have been made. As they have already said, the mere fact of making wills mutually is not, at least by the law of England, evidence of such an agreement having been come to. And without such a definite agreement there can no more be a trust in equity than a right to damages at law."

F As to the penultimate sentence of that passage it must, in the light of the earlier passage, to be read as meaning that the mere fact of making mutual wills is not by itself sufficient evidence of such an agreement having been come to.

      It is therefore clear that there must be a definite agreement between the makers of the two wills; that that must be established by evidence; that the fact that there are mutual wills to the same effect is a relevant

G   circumstance to be taken into account, although not enough of itself; and that the whole of the evidence must be looked at.

      I do not find it necessary to refer to any other English case, but I have derived great assistance from the decision of the High Court of Australia in *Birmingham* v. *Renfrew* (1937) 57 C.L.R. 666. That was a case where the available extrinsic evidence was held to be sufficient to establish the

H necessary agreement between two spouses. It is chiefly of interest because both Sir John Latham C.J. and more especially Dixon J. examined with some care the whole nature of the legal theory on which these and other similar cases proceed. I would like to read three passages from the judgment of Dixon J. which state, with all the clarity and learning for which the judgments of that most eminent judge are renowned, what I believe to be a correct analysis of the principles on which a case of enforceable mutual wills depends. The first passage reads, at pp. 682–683:

The Weekly Law Reports, June 26, 1981

946

Nourse J.   In re Cleaver, decd. (Ch.D.)   [1981]

"I think the legal result was a contract between husband and wife. The contract bound him, I think, during her lifetime not to revoke his will without notice to her. If she died without altering her will, then he was bound after her death not to revoke his will at all. She on her part afforded the consideration for his promise by making her will. His obligation not to revoke his will during her life without notice to her is to be implied. For I think the express promise should be understood as meaning that if she died leaving her will unrevoked then he would not revoke his. But the agreement really assumes that neither party will alter his or her will without the knowledge of the other. It has long been established that a contract between persons to make corresponding wills gives rise to equitable obligations when one acts on the faith of such an agreement and dies leaving his will unrevoked so that the other takes property under its dispositions. It operates to impose upon the survivor an obligation regarded as specifically enforceable. It is true that he cannot be compelled to make and leave unrevoked a testamentary document and if he dies leaving a last will containing provisions inconsistent with his agreement it is nevertheless valid as a testamentary act. But the doctrines of equity attach the obligation to the property. The effect is, I think, that the survivor becomes a constructive trustee and the terms of the trust are those of the will which he undertook would be his last will."

Next, at p. 689:

"There is a third element which appears to me to be inherent in the nature of such a contract or agreement, although I do not think it has been expressly considered. The purpose of an arrangement for corresponding wills must often be, as in this case, to enable the survivor during his life to deal as absolute owner with the property passing under the will of the party first dying. That is to say, the object of the transaction is to put the survivor in a position to enjoy for his own benefit the full ownership so that, for instance, he may convert it and expend the proceeds if he choose. But when he dies he is to bequeath what is left in the manner agreed upon. It is only by the special doctrines of equity that such a floating obligation, suspended, so to speak, during the lifetime of the survivor can descend upon the assets at his death and crystallise into a trust. No doubt gifts and settlements, inter vivos, if calculated to defeat the intention of the compact, could not be made by the survivor and his right of disposition, inter vivos, is, therefore, not unqualified. But, substantially, the purpose of the arrangement will often be to allow full enjoyment for the survivor's own benefit and advantage upon condition that at his death the residue shall pass as arranged."

Finally, at p. 690:

"In In re Oldham [1925] Ch. 75 Astbury J. pointed out, in dealing with the question whether an agreement should be inferred, that in Dufour v. Pereira, 1 Dick. 419 the compact was that the survivor should take a life estate only in the combined property. It was, therefore, easy to fix the corpus with a trust as from the death of the survivor. But I do not see any difficulty in modern equity in attaching to the assets a constructive trust which allowed the survivor to enjoy the property subject to a fiduciary duty which, so to speak,

The Weekly Law Reports, June 26, 1981

947

1 W.L.R.   In re Cleaver, decd. (Ch.D.)   Nourse J.

A   crystallised on his death and disabled him only from voluntary dispositions inter vivos."

I interject to say that Dixon J. was there clearly referring only to voluntary dispositions inter vivos which are calculated to defeat the intention of the compact. No objection could normally be taken to ordinary gifts of small value. He went on:

B   "On the contrary, as I have said, it seems rather to provide a reason for the intervention of equity. The objection that the intended beneficiaries could not enforce a contract is met by the fact that a constructive trust arises from the contract and the fact that testamentary dispositions made upon the faith of it have taken effect. It is the constructive trust and not the contract that they are entitled to enforce."

C   It is also clear from Birmingham v. Renfrew, 57 C.L.R. 666 that these cases of mutual wills are only one example of a wider category of cases, for example secret trusts, in which a court of equity will intervene to impose a constructive trust. A helpful and interesting summary of that wider category of cases will be found in the argument of Mr. Nugee in Ottaway v. Norman [1972] Ch. 698, 701–702. The principle of all these D   cases is that a court of equity will not permit a person to whom property is transferred by way of gift, but on the faith of an agreement or clear understanding that it is to be dealt with in a particular way for the benefit of a third person, to deal with that property inconsistently with that agreement or understanding. If he attempts to do so after having received the benefit of the gift equity will intervene by imposing a constructive trust on the property which is the subject matter of the agreement or understanding. E   I take that statement of principle, and much else which is of assistance in this case, from the judgment of Slade J. in In re Pearson Fund Trusts (unreported), October 21, 1977. The statement of principle is at p. 52 of the official transcript. The judgment of Brightman J. in Ottaway v. Norman [1972] Ch. 698 is to much the same effect.

I would emphasise that the agreement or understanding must be such F   as to impose on the donee a legally binding obligation to deal with the property in the particular way and that the other two certainties, namely, those as to the subject matter of the trust and the persons intended to benefit under it, are as essential to this species of trust as they are to any other. In spite of an argument by Mr. Keenan, who appears for Mr. and Mrs. Noble, to the contrary, I find it hard to see how there could be any difficulty about the second or third certainties in a case of mutual G   wills unless it was in the terms of the wills themselves. There, as in this case, the principal difficulty is always whether there was a legally binding obligation or merely what Lord Loughborough L.C. in Lord Walpole v. Lord Orford (1797) 3 Ves.Jun. 402, 419, described as an honourable engagement.

Before turning in detail to the evidence which relates to the question H   whether there was a legally binding obligation on the testatrix in the present case or not I must return once more to Birmingham v. Renfrew, 57 C.L.R. 666. It is clear from that case, if from nowhere else, that an enforceable agreement to dispose of property in pursuance of mutual wills can be established only by clear and satisfactory evidence. That seems to me to be no more than a particular application of the general rule that all claims to the property of deceased persons must be scrutinised with very great care. However, that does not mean that there has to be a

departure from the ordinary standard of proof required in civil proceedings.   **A**
I have to be satisfied on the balance of probabilities that the alleged agreement was made, but before I can be satisfied of that I must find clear and satisfactory evidence to that effect. [His Lordship then considered certain of the background facts and surrounding circumstances. He also reviewed the oral evidence in detail, including the passages set out above. He referred to the two conversations which the testatrix had had with   **B**
Mr. Arthur Cleaver, on the evening of the testator's death and at the end of June 1977 at about the time that the testatrix made her last will. His Lordship expressed the view that what the testatrix said on both those occasions pointed strongly towards obligation rather than mere honourable engagement. His Lordship continued:] I have now reviewed what appear to me to have been the main features of the evidence in the present case, but there was of course a lot of other evidence which I have not   **C**
mentioned. I must look at the whole of the evidence. Having done that as fully and carefully as I can, I find that I am satisfied on what I believe to be clear and satisfactory evidence that the testator and the testatrix did make an agreement which they intended should impose mutual legal obligations as to the disposal of their property; that the 1974 wills were executed in pursuance of that agreement, and that the 1974 wills correctly reproduced its terms. I have already indicated a number of matters   **D**
which have led me to this conclusion but I can summarise my view of the evidence as a whole as follows. Within three months of their marriage at the ages of 78 and 74 respectively the testator and the testatrix, who each had assets of their own, had made mutual wills under which the ultimate residuary beneficiaries were to be the testator's three children. The pattern of identity continued down to and included the 1974 wills with   **E**
a variation only in the case of the testatrix's June 1970 will, which is not in my view of any great significance. In every case the survivor was to take absolutely the bulk of the estate of the first to die. They kept their finances separate, there being no suggestion that they had a joint banking account or anything like that. I am satisfied on the evidence that it was at the beginning of 1974 that the testator gave £2,000 to the testatrix, as he said to even things up but with the intention that the testatrix should pay   **F**
some of the rent. All this suggests to me that they dealt with their joint financial affairs on a more commercial basis than is sometimes the case with other, particularly younger, married couples, but it also suggests that the testator recognised that the testatrix might need capital to live on after his death. That I think is strongly confirmed by what he said to Mrs. Zetterberg at the beginning of 1974. He said that in the event of his   **G**
dying first he wanted the testatrix to have the " use " of his money. I should have said that Mrs. Zetterberg confirmed on two occasions that that was the word which he used. To my mind when one is considering persons in the circumstances of the testator and testatrix that means that the testator wanted the testatrix to have the security after his death which a free power of disposal over his estate would give her. At the same   **H**
time he was a very determined man and everything suggests that he would, so far as he could, have wanted to ensure that anything which was left at her death should go back to his side of the family. I therefore start by approaching the crucial period of January and February 1974 in the belief that it is at the least possible that the testator did do a deal with the testatrix at the beginning of that year. I think he may well have said that he would leave his estate to her if she, as survivor, would leave hers

The Weekly Law Reports, June 26, 1981

949

1 W.L.R.   In re Cleaver, decd. (Ch.D.)   Nourse J.

A back to his children. I think that the £2,000 may very well have been part of an overall arrangement to this effect. As Mr. Hicks pointed out, the testator did by that stage, if not before, have a particular motive for wishing to tie things up in that he wanted Mrs. Noble to have no more than a life interest and Mr. Noble to have no interest at all and, as I think Mr. Keenan accepts, the testatrix at that time clearly looked on the Nobles in the same way as the testator did. However, although I do not have to decide this point, I think that had the matter rested on these considerations alone it would have been difficult for the plaintiffs to make out their case. And I am not certain that what was said to Mrs. Zetterberg at the end of January or the beginning of February 1974, both in the three-sided conversation round the fire, and by the testatrix to her alone afterwards, would necessarily have carried the plaintiffs home. But to the later events

C I do attach considerable importance. First there was the "That has settled" or "That has cooked his hash" incident. That suggests to me that the testator did think that he had tied everything up and that that did have the testatrix's tacit agreement. Then there are the events after the testator's death, in particular the two conversations which the testatrix had with Mr. Arthur Cleaver, the first on the evening of the testator's death and the second at the end of June 1977. I have already dealt with

D those conversations at some length. Having added them to all the other evidence in the case I find that I am in the end fully satisfied as to the existence of an enforceable agreement. I should, however, add that I do also attach some importance to the fact that within three months after the testator's death the testatrix did make a fresh will which faithfully followed her 1974 will in every material respect. There was no need for

E her to make a fresh will. It could perhaps be partly explained as a tidying up operation and I can understand that she might not have wished to have a will which made any mention of her deceased husband. However, in the absence of any evidence as to the circumstances in which that will was made it must I think be of some significance that the testatrix apparently regarded herself as being under more than a moral duty to dispose of her estate in accordance with her 1974 will.

F   In the result, and perhaps contrary to my expectation when the case was opened, I am driven to the conclusion that the plaintiffs are entitled to succeed in this action. Subject to any point which counsel may have on the wording of the relief sought I propose to make a declaration in the terms of paragraph 1 of the prayer for relief and an order in the terms of paragraph 2.

G   *Declaration and order accordingly.*

    Solicitors: *R. Nichols Marcy, Walton-on-Thames; Sharpe, Pritchard & Co.; Le Brasseur & Bury.*

                                                    T. C. C. B.

A

[EUROPEAN COURT OF JUSTICE]

* WORRINGHAM AND ANOTHER v. LLOYDS BANK LTD.

(Case 69/80)

1980 Oct. 29;	Judge J. Mertens de Wilmars (President),
Dec. 11;	Judges P. Pescatore, Lord Mackenzie Stuart
1981 March 11	and T. Koopmans (Presidents of Chambers),
	A. O'Keefe, G. Bosco and A. Touffait
	J.-P. Warner (Advocate-General)

B

Discrimination, Sex — Equal pay — Pension scheme — Male bank C
clerks contributing to pension scheme — Women not contri-
buting to scheme—Men receiving extra salary equivalent to
contribution — Whether additional sum " pay " — Whether
provision as to equal pay directly enforceable in member
states—E.E.C. Treaty (Cmnd. 5179–II), art. 119—Council
Directive (75/117/E.E.C.), art. 1

The employer provided two compulsory contracted-out D
retirement benefit schemes for all permanent staff, one for
men and one for women. To qualify for retirement benefit
under either scheme, an employee must have completed five
years' service and have attained the age of 26. Employees
who left the employer's service before fulfilling either condition were entitled either to the transfer of accrued rights
to another scheme, or to payment by the employer to the
state of the " contributions equivalent premium." All employees were required to contribute 5 per cent. of their salary E
but the two schemes differed in that men were required so
to contribute from the commencement of their employment,
while women were only required to contribute on reaching
the age of 25. Men under 25 received an additional salary
of 5 per cent. equal to their contribution with the result that
men leaving before completing five years' service or attaining
the age of 26 were entitled to benefits not available to women F
in the same position, namely, the refund of contributions
subject to deductions, with interest, as well as certain indirect
advantages.

The applicants, two female employees, brought proceedings
claiming relief from the alleged contravention of the equality
clause incorporated in their contracts of employment by
section 1 (2) (*a*) of the Equal Pay Act 1970 as amended. The
industrial tribunal rejected that claim, and the applicants G
appealed to the Employment Appeal Tribunal which upheld
their appeal without considering the effect of Community
law. The employer appealed. The Court of Appeal held
that since the problem in question involved provisions of
Community law, a reference should be made to the European
Court of Justice under article 117 of the E.E.C. Treaty.

On the reference to the European Court of the questions, H
inter alia, whether contributions paid by an employer to a
retirement benefit scheme were " pay " within the meaning
of article 119 of the E.E.C. Treaty, and whether article 119
or article 1 of the Council Directive of February 10, 1975
(75/117/E.E.C.) had direct effect in member states so as to
confer enforceable Community rights upon individuals in the
present circumstances: —

Held, (1) that a contribution to a retirement benefits
scheme which was paid by an employer in the name of

A   employees by means of an addition to the gross salary and which therefore helped to determine the amount of that salary constituted " pay " within the meaning of the second paragraph of article 119 of the E.E.C. Treaty (post, p. 971D).

     (2) That the national courts had a duty to ensure the protection of the rights which article 119 of the E.E.C. Treaty vested in individuals, in particular in a case where, because of the requirement imposed only on men or only

B   on women to contribute to a retirement benefits scheme, the contributions in question were paid by the employer in the name of the employee and deducted from the gross salary whose amount they determined (post, p. 971D–E).

The following cases are referred to in the judgment:

Defrenne v. *Belgian State* (Case 80/70) [1971] E.C.R. 445, E.C.J.

C   *Defrenne* v. *Sabena* (Case 43/75) [1976] I.C.R. 547; [1976] E.C.R. 455, E.C.J.

Defrenne v. *Sabena* (Case 149/77) [1978] E.C.R. 1365, E.C.J.

Macarthys Ltd. v. *Smith* (Case 129/79) [1981] Q.B. 180; [1980] 3 W.L.R. 929; [1980] I.C.R. 672, E.C.J. and C.A.

The following additional cases were cited in the opinion of Mr. Advocate-

D   General J.-P. Warner:

Caisse Régionale d'Assurance Maladie (C.R.A.M.), Lille v. *Palermo* (Case 237/78) [1979] E.C.R. 2645, E.C.J.

Commission v. *Ireland* (Case 61/77) [1978] E.C.R. 417, E.C.J.

de Cavel v. *de Cavel* (Case 120/79) [1980] E.C.R. 731, E.C.J.

Garland v. *British Rail Engineering Ltd.* [1979] I.C.R. 558; [1979] 1

E   W.L.R. 754; [1979] 2 All E.R. 1163, C.A.

Sotgiu v. *Deutsche Bundespost* (Case 152/73) [1974] E.C.R. 153, E.C.J.

REFERENCE by the Court of Appeal.

     Lloyds Bank Ltd. appealed from a decision of the Employment Appeal Tribunal [1979] I.C.R. 174 allowing an appeal by its employees, the applicants Susan Worringham and Margaret Humphreys, from a

F   decision of an industrial tribunal that they were doing like work but the additional salary paid to men employed by Lloyds Bank were paid to the men by way of " provision made in connection with death or retirement " within the meaning of section 6 (1A) (*b*) of the Equal Pay Act 1970.

     The Court of Appeal referred to the European Court of Justice the

G   questions, inter alia, whether the additional salary was " pay " within the meaning of article 119 of the E.E.C. Treaty and whether the provisions of article 119 and article 5 of the Council Directive (76/207/E.E.C.) had direct effect in member states so as to confer enforceable Community rights on individuals.

     The facts and the questions referred are stated in the judgment.

H

     Anthony P. Lester Q.C. and *Christopher Carr* for the applicants.

     David Hunter Q.C. for Lloyds Bank Ltd.

     Peter Scott Q.C. for the United Kingdom Government.

     Armando Toledano-Laredo and *Michael Beloff* for the Commission.

     March 11. The following judgment was delivered in open court in Luxembourg.

FACTS AND ISSUES

I. *Facts and written procedure*

(1) Lloyds Bank Ltd., hereinafter referred to as "Lloyds," whose headquarters are in the United Kingdom, provides in respect of all permanent staff two retirement benefit schemes, one for men and the other for women. Membership of these schemes, which are contracted-out retirement schemes, is compulsory for both male and female employees at the commencement of their employment.

In both schemes, the trust funds are controlled and administered by trustees to whom the contributions payable to the fund are paid and by whom all benefits payable under the fund are paid.

The same conditions apply for both men and women to qualify upon retirement for benefit under the pension scheme: the employee must have completed five years' service and have attained the age of 26. Moreover, the main benefits provided under the two schemes are essentially the same. Thus the retirement age is 60 for those members in service on or first employed by Lloyds since July 1, 1974, in both cases and both sexes' entitlement to pension benefit is 1/720th of annual salary at retirement for each completed month of service. However, there are differences from other points of view: for example, the men's scheme but not the women's scheme provides for the payment of pensions to the surviving spouse and dependent children.

Male and female employees who leave Lloyds' service before completion of five years' service or attaining the age of 26 are entitled either to the transfer of the accrued rights to another approved retirement benefits scheme; or to the payment by Lloyds to the state of the "contributions equivalent premium," which places the employee in the same position that he or she would have been in the state scheme had he or she been a member of the state scheme instead of a member of the particular retirement benefits scheme. In the latter case, where the employer pays the contributions equivalent premium, the employee is entitled to a refund of his or her past contributions to the particular scheme with interest. However, precisely on this point differences arise between the two schemes in question.

By the terms of the men's retirement benefits scheme all male staff are required to contribute 5 per cent. of their salary to the fund from the commencement of their employment and regardless of their age: the amount of that contribution is considered as part of the employee's "salary." By the terms of the women's retirement benefits scheme all female staff are required to contribute 5 per cent. of their salary to the fund but only upon attaining the age of 25.

Thus in the case of an employee leaving Lloyds' service before completing five years' service or attaining the age of 26, the consequences under the two schemes in question are not the same according to whether the employee is male or female.

A male employee who has paid contributions to the fund from the commencement of his employment before having attained the age of 25 receives those contributions back subject to deductions, with interest, whereas a female employee who has paid no contributions before attaining the age of 25 receives no sum by way of refund of contributions in respect of employment under that age.

A   Moreover, since the amount of the 5 per cent. increment is incorporated in the total amount of " a week's pay," a man receives indirect
advantages which are not enjoyed by a woman. In fact, in so far as
collateral benefits are calculated on the basis of " a week's pay " (unemployment benefits, redundancy payments, credit facilities, etc.), the
fact that the 5 per cent. contribution is incorporated in that pay gives
a man under 25 higher benefits than those to which a woman under 25
B is entitled.

     In May and September 1977, two Lloyds' employees, the applicants
Susan Jane Worringham and Margaret Humphreys, commenced proceedings before an industrial tribunal under the provisions of section 1 (2) (a)
of the Equal Pay Act 1970, as amended, seeking relief from the alleged
contravention of the equality clause incorporated in their contracts of
C employment by virtue of the provisions of that Act.

     When that claim was rejected by the tribunal, the two applicants
appealed to the Employment Appeal Tribunal, which allowed the appeal,
holding that in this case there was an inequality of pay within the
meaning of the Equal Pay Act 1970, without further examining the
arguments put forward by the parties under Community law.

D   In its turn, Lloyds appealed against that decision to the Court of
Appeal, London. That court, pointing out that the problem in question
involves provisions of Community law, submitted to the Court of Justice
under article 177 of the Treaty questions for a preliminary ruling worded
as follows. 1. Are (a) contributions paid by an employer to a retirement
benefits scheme; or (b) rights and benefits of a worker under such a
scheme " pay " within the meaning of article 119 of the E.E.C. Treaty?
E 2. Are (a) contributions paid by an employer to a retirement benefits
scheme; or (b) rights and benefits of a worker under such a scheme
" remuneration " within the meaning of article 1 of the Council Directive
of February 10, 1975 (75/117/E.E.C.)? 3. If the answer to question 1
or 2 is in the affirmative, does article 119 of the E.E.C. Treaty or article
1 of the said directive, as the case may be, have direct effect in member
states so as to confer enforceable Community rights upon individuals in
F the circumstances of the present case? 4. If the answers to questions 1
and 2 are in the negative: (i) are (a) contributions paid by an employer
to a retirement benefits scheme; or (b) rights and benefits of a worker
under such a scheme within the scope of the principle of equal treatment
for men and women as regards " working conditions " contained in article
1, paragraph 1 and article 5, paragraph 1 of the Council Directive of
G February 9, 1976 (76/207/E.E.C.)? (ii) If so, does the said principle have
direct effect in member states so as to confer enforceable Community
rights upon individuals in the circumstances of the present case?

     The order for reference was entered on the Court Register on March
3, 1980.

H   Written observations were submitted pursuant to article 20 of the
Protocol on the Statute of the Court of Justice of the E.E.C. by the
applicants, represented by Anthony Lester Q.C., and Christopher Carr,
barrister, instructed by Lawford & Co., solicitors, by Lloyds, represented
by D. Hunter Q.C., instructed by G. N. Johnson, solicitor, Lloyds Bank
Legal Department, by the Government of the United Kingdom, represented by Peter Scott Q.C., instructed by R. D. Munrow of the Treasury
Solicitor's Department, acting as agent, and by the Commission of the

European Communities, represented by its legal adviser, A. Toledano- A
Loredo, acting as agent, assisted by Michael Beloff, barrister.

After hearing the report of the judge-rapporteur and the views of
the advocate general, the court decided to open the oral procedure without
any preparatory inquiry.

II. *Written observations submitted to the court*

B

The applicants in the main proceedings observe that the immediate
issue raised by this reference is whether the principle of equal pay
laid down in article 119 of the Treaty and article 1 of Directive
(75/117/E.E.C.) and the principle of equal treatment laid down in
articles 1, 2 and 5 of Directive (76/207/E.E.C.) entitle female employees
to be paid the same refund of pension contributions as male employees
engaged in the same work are paid, but that underlying this issue is a C
broader question: whether those principles require that contributions
paid under retirement benefits schemes on behalf of male and female
employees or benefits received by them under such schemes should be
equal.

According to the applicants, by excluding retirement benefits schemes
from the requirement of equality without sex discrimination despite D
the fact that United Kingdom courts and successive governments have
recognised that pensions are an aspect of pay, the law of the United
Kingdom violates the principles of equal pay and other aspects of employment which it has nevertheless expressly recognised. Although this discrimination is completely unjustified, it is however specifically permitted
by the Equal Pay Act 1970 and the Sex Discrimination Act 1975.
Consequently, the only means of overcoming such discrimination is to E
prove that it is incompatible with Community law.

The applicants consider that questions 1 and 2 are closely linked
and that it is therefore convenient to consider them together. If the
principle of equal pay were not applied to protect the rights of workers
under occupational pension schemes, the double aim of article 119 would
be frustrated; that aim consists on the one hand in guaranteeing equal F
conditions of competition for the undertakings of the various member
states and, on the other, in improving the living and working conditions
of female workers.

The concept of pay to which the principle of equality applies is a
broad one under Community law. Retirement benefits are clearly covered
by this concept. In fact, they are funded by contributions paid by the
employer which, in any case, are part of the consideration which the G
employee indirectly receives in the form of a right to specified benefits
under the retirement benefits scheme. The employee's rights under the
scheme are earned by him as part of the reward for his service and are
therefore consideration received in respect of his employment.

In modern economic conditions, many of the benefits of employment are received in forms other than cash. It is no doubt because the H
draftsmen of article 119 recognised the realities of the modern concept
of pay that it also means consideration in kind; article 1 (1) of Directive
(75/117/E.E.C.), with its reference to " all aspects and conditions of
remuneration," moreover confirms this.

It follows from the judgment of the Court of Justice in *Defrenne*
v. *Belgian State* (Case 80/70) [1971] E.C.R. 445 (hereinafter referred
to as " *Defrenne No. 1* "), that a retirement pension established within

A the framework of a social security scheme laid down by legislation does not constitute consideration which the worker receives indirectly in respect of his employment from his employer, within the meaning of article 119. That judgment was fully consistent with the opinion of Mr. Advocate General Dutheillet de Lamothe that retirement benefits schemes with the following characteristics come within article 119.
(a) The pension benefit is paid to the worker because he has a particular
B post in the employment of a particular employer and not because of his status as a worker generally. (b) The management and funding of the scheme are organised on an occupational basis independent of the state social security system. (c) The pension benefit is linked to the contributions payable by the employer, so that it is not payable if the employer defaults in making those contributions. (d) The pension scheme is volun-
C tary in origin and the subject of collective agreement between the employer and the trade union.

    According to the applicants, when a retirement benefits scheme is considered in the light of these criteria the clear conclusion is that such schemes are not part of the social security system and that the rights enjoyed under such a scheme are part of the consideration which the
D worker receives, in respect of his employment, from his employer. In fact, those schemes have all the above characteristics.

    The judgment in *Defrenne No. 1* [1971] E.C.R. 445 was consistent with the above-mentioned opinion of the Advocate General that social security schemes, including pension schemes, do not fall within article 119 if (a) they are directly governed by legislation; (b) they are obligatorily applicable to general categories of workers; and (c) they are established
E and operated without any element of agreement within the undertaking or the occupational branch concerned. However, the retirement benefits schemes operated by British undertakings do not satisfy any of these criteria. Moreover, the contributions to those schemes are determined by the rules of the pension scheme and the amount of the contributions is frequently stated in the contract of employment, whereas, in the judg-
F ment in *Defrenne No. 1,* the court held that the contributions to schemes which do not fall within article 119 are determined more by considerations of social policy than by the employment relationship between the employer and the worker.

    The rights of a worker to benefits under a retirement benefits scheme operated by his employer are part of the consideration the worker receives in respect of his employment and hence are " pay " within article 119.
G
    In fact, a worker does not receive these benefits as a result of his status as a worker or as a result of his membership of a particular occupational category but solely by virtue of his contract of employment. Numerous factual considerations (for example, the differences between the schemes, their voluntary origin, the fact that membership is sometimes voluntary and that benefits are not guaranteed by the state) reinforce
H the conclusion that rights under a retirement benefits scheme arise from contract and not from status.

    As regards the practical application of the principle of equality, this may be achieved in two different ways: either by guaranteeing both equal contributions and similar rights and benefits for men and women, which would be possible by using unisex actuarial tables, or else by guaranteeing only equal benefits, which implies the payment of higher contributions by or on behalf of workers of the relevant sex to produce equal benefits. The second solution is permissible provided that the higher contributions payable by the workers of one sex are paid by the employer and not by the workers concerned.

As regards question 3 the applicants consider that the circumstances of the present case clearly fall within the scope of the direct application of article 119, as defined by the case law of the court. It is in fact accepted by Lloyds that the applicants were at all material times employed on equal work with men in the same establishment and that there are differences based on sex between the treatment of men and women who leave Lloyds' service before attaining the age of 26. There is therefore a form of direct and overt discrimination which may be identified solely with the aid of the criteria of equal work and equal pay referred to in article 119.

If the court does not accept this argument, contrary to the applicants' primary submissions, the applicants submit in the alternative that it is necessary to rely on article 1 (1) of Directive (75/117/E.E.C.) which requires the elimination of all discrimination on the ground of sex " with regard to all aspects and conditions of remuneration." By that expression article 1 plainly includes also the rights and benefits of a worker under a retirement benefits scheme in the circumstances of the present case. In such circumstances, the principle of equal pay outlined in article 119 of the Treaty and further defined in article 1 of Directive (75/117/E.E.C.) has direct effect in member states so as to confer enforceable rights upon individuals.

As regards Directive (75/117/E.E.C.), the applicants submit that it contains a standard aimed at facilitating the practical application of the principle of equal pay laid down in article 119. This aim cannot be effectively attained if individuals are prevented from relying upon the provisions of the directive in national courts. Article 1 (1) of the directive is sufficiently clear and precise to have direct effect, so that since the expiry of the period for compliance, it has become completed and unconditional.

In the judgment in *Defrenne* v. *Sabena* (Case 149/77) [1978] E.C.R. 1365 (hereinafter referred to as "*Defrenne No. 3*"), the court implied moreover that once the period for compliance had expired some provisions of the Equal Treatment Directive would have direct effect. By parity of reasoning article 1 of the Equal Pay Directive now has direct effect in the circumstances of the present case.

With regard to question 4, the applicants consider that if the principle of equal pay does not apply to the contributions paid by an employer to or to the rights and benefits of a worker under a retirement benefits scheme, the principle of equal treatment as defined in Directive (76/207/E.E.C.) applies to such contributions, rights and benefits and has direct effect in member states. They observe that the fourth paragraph of the preamble to that directive refers to " working conditions, including pay," which shows that the phrase " working conditions " encompasses more than the term " pay " in article 119 of the Treaty and in article 1 of Directive (75/117/E.E.C.) even if the latter is understood in the broadest sense. Moreover, as indicated by article 5 (1) of the same directive, working conditions also include the " conditions governing dismissal." It follows a fortiori that they also include the contributions paid by an employer to a retirement benefits scheme and the rights and

A benefits of a worker under such a scheme. Indeed, working conditions include all terms and conditions of employment other than pay.

Article 1 (1) of the directive is sufficiently clear and precise to have direct effect.

Lloyds first of all makes several general remarks as an introduction to the examination of the questions. It begins by explaining the charac-
B teristics of the occupational pension schemes existing in the United Kingdom and points out that the benefits in fact received under one of those schemes can never be exactly the same for two people except purely by accident since they vary in each case according to a variety of personal factors including the options taken up by the person concerned, family circumstances and the age to which he or she lives. For the same reasons, actual receipts cannot be known until after the interests of the member
C and, where applicable, of his or her dependants, cease. It is therefore necessary to consider that even if the sex of members were not taken into account it would in any case be impossible to achieve equality of benefits between them or to fix a priori the total amount of benefits which will be paid to a member.

The pension funds set up by retirement benefits schemes are admin-
D istered on the basis, inter alia, of actuarial statistics on the life expectation of members. It is a group calculation reflecting a group average and not the behaviour of any individual member, and it cannot be otherwise. It is however necessary to make a distinction according to sex for the purposes of that calculation since the result is necessarily influenced by differences of sex and sexual behaviour patterns. In fact, a woman's greater expectation of life means that the cost to the fund of providing
E identical benefits is greater in the case of a woman than in that of a man. Since, as has been seen, the benefits received by the person concerned can only be known after, and in many cases years after, the relevant employment ends, the same applies to the contributions necessary to maintain those benefits.

Moreover, the contributions paid by a worker do not correspond to
F the benefits that he will receive in the future. The contributions are received and administered by the trustees of the pension fund. There is and can be no apportionment between members or actual or notional attribution to any particular member.

Finally, the difference between contributory and non-contributory schemes is irrelevant in the present case since the contributions of Lloyds'
G workers are funded by Lloyds.

On the basis of these considerations, it may therefore be concluded that it is impossible to calculate the value to him or her of membership of a retirement benefits scheme of the type established in the United Kingdom and that the value of the benefits can never, save by pure chance, be identical or equal. The value of prospective benefits could only be ascertained on the basis of an actuarial assessment of an
H "average" person but the apparent equality which might well be pro-
duced if the scheme terms were identical would not be produced in fact. Consequently, if either "pay" or "consideration" are sought to be construed as embracing pension benefits or pension contributions those words would have to be read as extending to such an actuarial assessment of value and as requiring a comparison not of true but of apparent value.

As regards question 1 Lloyds observes that the expression "wage or

salary and any other consideration, whether in cash or in kind, which A
the worker receives directly or indirectly " in article 119 intends to bring
into account also benefits which are akin to pay which are known and
received or enjoyed at the time when the (assumed) like work is being
performed and which are capable then of being calculated, quantified
and compared. In fact, the purpose of the definition contained in article
119 is to identify the constituents of pay in order to enable such comparison readily and simply to be made by employers and workers of both B
sexes and therefore to identify, quantify and correct any inequality.

There are however other terms of a contract of employment which
might become or develop into a source of financial advantage or disadvantage to either sex but the effects of which depend upon future
events or contingencies. In such cases quantification is only possible
after the happening and in the light of such events. If the word C
" consideration " were widely construed to include such elements the
purpose of the definition would be frustrated because contemporary
comparison would become either impracticable or impossible.

Moreover, according to the case law of the court in *Defrenne No. 3*
[1978] E.C.R. 1365, the field of application of article 119 must be
determined within the context of the system of the social provisions of
the Treaty which are set out in the chapter formed by article 117 et seq. D
Articles 117 and 118 provide for a programme to be implemented through
subordinate legislation. They are supplemented but not contradicted or
duplicated by article 119, provided that the criteria therein provided are
strictly construed. In the present case the fact of differential nominal
pay scales and like work is present, but the scales are the product of
the different fund rules and if article 119 were applied, which could E
only be done by equalisation of those scales alone, this would, as the
facts demonstrate, produce even more glaring inequality. In fact, the
discrimination in this case is " indirect " or " disguised " and could only
be abolished by amending one or other of the pension schemes.

Broaching point (a) of question 1, Lloyds observes that the contributions paid by the employer or by the worker to the pension schemes F
cannot constitute pay within the meaning of article 119 since they are
received by the trustees of the pension fund and are not receivable by
the worker himself.

In support of this interpretation, it may be recalled that the court in
its judgment in *Defrenne No. 1* [1971] E.C.R. 445 held that the part due
from the employers in the financing of state pension schemes does not
constitute a direct or indirect payment to the worker. It follows from G
the same judgment that this characteristic is also shared by " special
schemes which . . . relate in particular to certain categories of workers."
This ruling is precisely applicable to retirement benefits schemes in
general and to the instant schemes in particular.

That conclusion is confirmed by the consistent case law of the court
and by the wording of Directive (75/117/E.E.C.) on equal treatment H
and of Directive (79/7/E.E.C.) on social security (Official Journal, 1979,
L.6/24). In fact, a wide construction of the word " pay," which
would cover many of the matters dealt with in the Equal Treatment
Directive, has been expressly rejected by the court. Moreover, article
1 (2) of the Equal Treatment Directive excludes from the scope of that
directive " matters of social security," whereas article 3 (3) of the Social
Security Directive leaves the principle of equality in " occupational

A schemes " in matters of social security to be implemented by subsequent rules. These provisions are consistent only with the view that " occupational schemes," in particular occupational pension schemes, are matters of social security, not pay, are not yet the subject matter of any Community provision and fall to be dealt with in the future under the provisions of article 118.

B With particular reference to the judgment in *Defrenne No. 1* [1971] E.C.R. 445, Lloyds states that the only difference between the pension scheme operated by Sabena (the *Defrenne* case) and those operated by Lloyds is that the former was established by Royal Decree and the latter by trust deeds: this is a matter of form and not of substance. In fact, the applicability of article 119 should not turn upon differences of domestic law or practice in any member state or upon the means by **C** which any particular scheme is in consequence established. The characteristics of the scheme and not its mode of creation should be decisive.

Lloyds asks moreover whether the phrase " within the framework of a social security scheme laid down by legislation " used by the court in the judgment in *Defrenne No. 1* [1971] E.C.R. 445 should be read as descriptive of the scheme before the court or as laying down an essential **D** pre-condition for the exclusion of a pension scheme from the scope of article 119.

It replies as follows. (1) This phrase is simply descriptive. (2) Alternatively, any pre-condition should be satisfied all the same if the relevant scheme is validly established under the relevant domestic law taking into consideration the fact that, for example, in the United Kingdom the statutory creation of such schemes is very rare. (3) Even if a scheme **E** can only be excluded from the application of article 119 if it comes with a national legislative framework, this is the case in the United Kingdom where private schemes must be approved under the Finance Act 1970 and certified under Part III of the Social Security Pensions Act 1975. (4) The categorisation of schemes suggested by Mr. Advocate General Dutheillet de Lamothe was not accepted or approved by the **F** court and is not therefore authoritative.

According to Lloyds, the construction contended for confines the meaning of the word " pay " within clear, manageable, practicable limits, understandable to employers and workers alike, and avoids conflicts or overlaps between article 119 and articles 117 and 118.

With regard to point (b) of question 1, Lloyds observes first of all that it follows from the judgment in *Defrenne No. 1* [1971] E.C.R. 445 **G** that " the worker will normally receive the benefits legally prescribed not by reason of the employer's contribution but solely because the worker fulfils the legal conditions for the grant of benefit." These words apply equally both to a typical state scheme and to a typical occupational scheme.

These benefits are not consideration paid directly or indirectly by **H** the employer. The funds arising under the pension schemes are vested in the trustees of the pension fund who act independently of the bank. No person entitled to any benefit under the scheme has any claim in respect of such benefit except against the fund. Thus it is clear that benefits are received from the fund and not from the employer.

The benefits received by a worker from the trustees of the fund are in no way dependent upon a term in the contract of employment for remuneration or otherwise, or upon any calculation made under such

contract but wholly and fundamentally upon the rules of the particular   A
scheme. The nature and amount of the benefit depend upon a variety
of factors personal and peculiar to the individual worker. The benefit
is receivable only after the termination of the employment and may
continue after the death of the person concerned. There is therefore
no "close connection" between the nature of the services provided and
the benefit received. The receipt is quite unrelated to any particular
work done or past contribution. Equality of benefits between workers   B
is quite unattainable. Further it may be asked how sums received after
retirement and not calculated until death or later can be treated for
comparative purposes as pay earned during a working life and how such
total receipts are to be apportioned over such working period. All that
a worker receives in consequence of his employment is the benefit of
membership of a pension scheme, the benefit of a package of rights and   C
expectations which remain contingent until the employment ceases. Any
attempt to treat the benefits actually received by the worker or his
dependants as "pay" or "consideration" with a resultant requirement
of equality is an attempt to achieve the impossible.

It should moreover be recalled that the equalisation of the terms of
retirement benefits schemes for men and women raises highly complex   D
problems for the solution of which the provisions of article 119 are
inadequate and inappropriate but are reserved by articles 117 and 118
to the discretion of the authorities referred to therein. These problems
require solution in principle by the legislators. The first problem is that
created by the woman's greater expectation of life. There are at least
two schools of thought as to how equality between sexes should be
measured or defined. The approach consisting of fixing identical terms   E
and provisions for men and women seems however unfair because it
can never neutralise the natural female advantage. The other view is
on the other hand that true equality can only be reached by providing
a package of benefits of equal value to men and women, which would
involve the definition of precise actuarial standards. Each of these solutions could, moreover, be modified.   F

However, in addition to resolving this fundamental issue, the legislation
should consider and determine what is to constitute equality over a wide
field of problems including maternity provisions, differences in retirement
age, the position of the surviving spouses of members and differences in
career patterns and so forth.

The difficulties in the above fields could explain both the terms of
article 3 (3) of the Social Security Directive and the absence as yet of the   G
provision therein referred to.

Article 119 can operate directly upon pay clauses in individual contracts
of service but is not intended to meet and cannot be construed as meeting
the essential requirements specified in the preceding paragraphs.

As regards question 2, Lloyds considers that the intent and effect of
Directive (75/117/E.E.C.) was to extend the concept of equal pay to   H
cover both the same work and "work to which equal value is attributed"
but not by the use of the phrase "all aspects and conditions of remuneration" to vary or extend the scope or meaning of the definition of pay in
article 119 itself.

Article 4 of the directive, according to which the member states must
take all necessary measures to declare null and void or amend any provisions appearing "in collective agreements, wage scales, wage agreements

A or individual contracts of employment " shows the absence of any intention to extend the concept of pay and in particular the absence of any intention to cover pension schemes in that directive.

In these circumstances, there is no need to reply to question 3. With regard to question 4, Lloyds observes that the express exclusion of matters of social security by article 1 (2) of Directive (76/207/E.E.C.), coupled with the absence of any reference to pension schemes in article 5 (2) (b),
B show that the general provisions of that directive were not intended to affect pension schemes.

Alternatively, assuming that question 3 or the second part of question 4 are relevant, Lloyds maintains that article 119 of the Treaty, Directive (75/117/E.E.C.) and Directive (76/207/E.E.C.) are each insufficiently precise to have direct effect, both as regards pension contributions and
C in respect of the rights and benefits under retirement benefits schemes. Moreover, with regard to Directive (76/207/E.E.C.), the period for the implementation of that directive in the United Kingdom expired in August 1978, so that the question of direct effect cannot arise in proceedings commenced in 1977.

Finally, also in the alternative, Lloyds draws attention to the conse-
D quences which would be likely if the court were to uphold the applicants' argument. As Lloyds annually employs in the order of 21,500 women, of whom about 13,800 are under the age of 25, such claims for the retrospective adjustment of pay scales covering a period of years could run into milions of pounds altogether. Lloyds therefore suggests that the court, as it has already done in *Defrenne* v. *Sabena* (Case 43/75) [1976] I.C.R. 547, should limit the power to rely upon the direct effect of Community
E provisions in support of claims relating to periods prior to the date of the judgment which it delivers to workers who have already brought legal proceedings or made an equivalent claim.

The United Kingdom considers, with regard to question 1, that neither contributions to a retirement benefits scheme nor rights or benefits enjoyed under such a scheme are, as such, " pay " within the meaning of article 119.

F It observes first of all that the order for reference refers solely to " contributions paid by an employer " without making a distinction between sums compulsorily deducted from the employee's pay, other sums paid on the employee's behalf, sums which the employer is required to pay in order to enable the scheme to function (" the employer's contribution ") or a mixture of these. It is, at least at first sight, surprising that the Court of Appeal and/or the parties see no relevant distinction between these types
G of contribution.

Under the system applied by Lloyds, the problem is whether the 5 per cent. described as forming part of the " salary " of male employees under 25 and paid direct by Lloyds to the trustees of the pension scheme is " pay " or not. If the 5 per cent. is pay, it is pay precisely because it can be identified as such without regard to any terms related to death or
H retirement or to any provision made in connection with death or retirement. It is therefore necessary to concentrate solely on the relationship between employer and employee. The conclusion that the 5 per cent. is pay would seem to involve finding that on the facts the 5 per cent. forms part of the sum due to the employee but is notionally handed back to the employer to be paid on the employee's behalf to the trustees of the scheme. On the facts, such an approach presents certain difficulties since the employee is at no time entitled to insist on the sum being paid to him by the employer.

The question whether in all the circumstances the sum is pay is one   A
primarily for the national court. The United Kingdom expresses no view
on the facts of the present case beyond pointing out that, whichever view
prevails, the answer will not depend on the consequences of the payment
to the trustees but upon the nature of the sum in terms of a payment by
the employer to the employee (or to his order) for a given amount of work.

With regard to the rights and benefits under a retirement benefits
scheme, the arguments against such rights and benefits being " pay " are   B
a fortiori those relating to " contributions paid by the employer." The
extent and amount of such rights and benefits are not related to the work
done but are the product of a number of different factors (contributions,
income from the trustees' own investments and other factors). There is no
difference in principle between such a scheme and that to which public
authorities may contribute. As follows from the case law of the court (the   C
judgment in *Defrenne No. 1* [1971] E.C.R. 445), the part due from an
employer in the financing of a social security scheme does not constitute a
direct or indirect payment to the worker: the latter receives the benefits
legally prescribed solely by reason of the fact that he fulfils the legal
conditions required for their being granted. The rights and benefits are
related to such matters as length of service, wage or salary at retiring age,
attainment of retiring age, age at time of death and so forth. They are   D
paid by the trustees of the scheme, not the employer.

There are differences in terms of the value and amounts of such
benefits as between men and women, for example the retiring age, life
expectancy and the pattern of working life, which are far more complex
than simple questions of equal pay for equal work. These factors are
relevant to the construction of a retirement benefits scheme, though they   E
are irrelevant to simple comparisons of the amount of pay for a given
amount of work.

There is a further objection to treating either the employer's contribution or the rights or benefits as " pay " in any general sense. In the United
Kingdom, there is in fact a state pension scheme and occupational schemes
supplementary to the former which must now fulfil certain detailed statutory
criteria which ensure that the benefits received by workers are adequate   F
in terms of the social policy pursued by the legislation of the United
Kingdom. It would be odd if the legal requirements imposed by Community law on the occupational pension schemes were different from those
imposed on the United Kingdom state scheme to which some 13 million
employees have to look for the entirety of their benefits.

With regard to question 2, the United Kingdom considers, that Council   G
Directive of February 10, 1975 (75/117/E.E.C.), is not concerned to
widen the meaning of the principle of equal pay, still less to widen the
meaning of the word " pay." That directive in fact makes no mention
whatsoever of pensions, retirement benefits schemes, or the like.

The intention to deal with matters of social security separately from
pay is moreover confirmed by the recitals of the preamble to Directive
(76/207/E.E.C.) which contrasts pay and matters of social security, and   H
by article 1 (2) of the same directive which contemplates the progressive implementation by other measures of the principle of equal treatment
in matters of social security.

After putting forward these considerations, the United Kingdom
observes that if these submissions are correct, it is unnecessary to reply
to question 3. For the sake of completeness it, however, also examines that
question.

A In the opinion of the United Kingdom it is clear that if, contrary to its submissions, article 119 applied to pensions, it could not have direct effect. The forms of discrimination in question cannot be identified solely with the aid of criteria based on equal work and equal pay. It is not clear how equality is to be achieved in this field since it is possible to achieve it either by equal benefits or by equal contributions but not by both solutions together so long as retiring ages and life expectancies vary as between

B men and women.

The need thus established to define through appropriate measures at the Community or national level detailed criteria for the attainment of the principle of equality therefore precludes article 119 from having any direct effect.

In this respect, it is necessary to recall that according to the case law

C of the court: " it is . . . impossible to widen the terms of article 119 to the point . . . of jeopardizing the direct applicability which that provision must be acknowledged to have in its own sphere."

With regard to Directive (75/117/E.E.C.) it is necessary to take into account the fact that a provision of a directive can only have direct effect if it is clear, unconditional, and leaves no discretion to the member

D state as to the substance of its implementation.

Where the indefinite nature of the concepts used by a provision leaves the member states a margin of discretion on matters of substance, a discretion of that kind precludes any possibility of according direct effect to the provision in question. However, this would be exactly the situation, as already seen in relation to article 119, if article 1 of Directive (75/117/E.E.C.) applied also to pensions. The need to produce criteria

E with a view to equality in occupational pension schemes has been recognised, moreover, by the Council and by the Commission. The Commission is engaged in drafting a new directive dealing only with those schemes.

The United Kingdom then draws attention to the consequences which the recognition of direct effect would have in the United Kingdom. First

F of all, the pattern of employment could be severely disturbed if the relationship between private schemes and the state scheme were to be destroyed. The direct financial consequences would also be substantial for employers and the administrators of occupational pension schemes. If for example the retirement age of men were reduced from 65 to 60, as for women, the cost to be borne by the pension funds would immediately increase by up to £1,200 million a year, reducing to about half this figure

G after several years, in addition to £100 million for benefits for surviving spouses, regardless of the cost of any payments made to recompense male workers who have already retired. Employers would have to face a massive financial burden of immediate impact. Many of them would then be prompted to discontinue occupational pension schemes or reduce their benefits to a substantial extent.

H With regard to question 4, the United Kingdom considers that Directive (76/207/E.E.C.) on equal treatment as regards working conditions cannot relate to social security since it expressly excludes matters of social security from its field of application.

With regard to direct effect, the arguments against the direct effect of Directive (75/117/E.E.C.) are valid a fortiori with regard to Directive (76/207/E.E.C.). It is possible to add that article 5 of the directive shows that detailed legislation is contemplated to give effect to the general

principle of equal treatment. Finally, the time limit for the implementation A
of the directive in the United Kingdom expired on August 12, 1978, in
other words after proceedings were commenced by the applicants.

The Commission of the European Communities considers, as regards
questions 1 and 2, that contributions paid by an employer to a retirement
benefits scheme are paid within the meaning of article 119 of the Treaty
and remuneration within the meaning of article 1 of Directive (75/117/
E.E.C.) on equal pay.   B

In this case, the additional sum received by male workers for Lloyds
below the age of 25 is described as salary and it is treated as salary for
the purpose of calculating certain collateral benefits. It is thus part of
the " ordinary . . . salary " of a worker within the meaning of article 119.

The additional sum, however, has certain distinctive features since it is
paid by Lloyds only because of the requirements of the retirement benefits C
scheme for the workers concerned and is paid not to these workers themselves but to the trustees of the fund. Strictly speaking, it is not an employer's
contribution but rather a worker's contribution in respect of which he is
indemnified by the employer. It is therefore a contribution paid by an
employer on the worker's behalf. On this analysis it also falls within the
definition of pay in article 119. It is in fact consideration which the worker D
receives, directly or indirectly, in respect of his employment from his
employer.

The question submitted to the Court of Justice by the Court of Appeal
however relates to employers' contributions strictly so-called. According
to the Commission, such contributions fall as a matter of language within
the definition of pay in article 119.

The Commission, moreover, considers that the case law of the court E
favours an affirmative answer to questions 1 and 2. In its opinion, the
retirement benefits scheme in the present case and schemes of which it is
an example fulfil the conditions laid down by Mr. Advocate General
Dutheillet de Lamothe in *Defrenne No. 1* [1971] E.C.J. 445 and do not
display any of the factors which, according to the judgment delivered by
the court in that case, exclude state social security schemes from the ambit F
of article 119. It should be noted that in that judgment the court approached
the question precisely from the standpoint of employers' contributions.

An interpretation of article 119 that construed pay and remuneration
as embracing contributions of employers to pension schemes might promote the economic and social aims of that article, in other words the
promotion of fair competition and the advancement of living and working
conditions of people within the Community, particularly for that sector G
made up of female workers and their dependants.

With regard to the second part of the two questions, the Commission
considers that workers' rights and benefits are pay within the meaning of
article 119 of the Treaty and remuneration within the meaning of article 1
of Directive (75/117/E.E.C.).

In this case, the refund of contributions to male workers of Lloyds H
before the age of 25 falls within the definition of article 119. Moreover,
such rights and benefits generally fall within that definition. The arguments
advanced in relation to " employers' " contributions are repeated mutatis
mutandis with regard to benefits under a retirement benefits scheme. Benefits under such a scheme are commonly and properly considered to be
" deferred pay " and the court itself held in *Defrenne No. 1* [1971] E.C.R.
445 that future pay falls within the scope of article 119.

A   With regard to question 3 the Commission considers that article 119 and article 1 of Directive (75/117/E.E.C.) have direct effect in member states.

According to the case law of the court article 119 is directly effective where direct as opposed to indirect discrimination is involved. The Commission is of the opinion, as it has already said, that the additional sum in question forms part of the salary and that accordingly the pre-condition of

B   direct discrimination is satisfied in this case. With regard to the directive, article 1 (1) thereof in fact constitutes a definition of the concept in article 119. If, therefore, article 119 is directly effective the same must apply to article 1 of the directive.

With regard to question 4, the Commission is of the opinion that it is not necessary to reply to it since that question is only put on the premise

C   that questions 1 and 2 have been answered negatively.

In the light of the foregoing considerations, the Commission submits that the answers to the questions put by the Court of Appeal should be as follows:

"*Question* 1: Contributions paid by an employer to a retirement benefits scheme *and* rights and benefits of a worker under such a

D   scheme are 'pay' within the meaning of article 119 of the E.E.C. Treaty.

"*Question* 2: Contributions paid by an employer to a retirement benefits scheme *and* rights and benefits of a worker under such a scheme are 'remuneration' within the meaning of article 1 of the Equal Pay Directive.

E   "*Question* 3: (i) Article 119 of the Treaty (ii) article 1 of the directive have direct effect in member states so as to confer enforceable Community rights upon individuals in the circumstances of the present case.

"*Question* 4: No answer need be given."

F   III. *Oral procedure*

The applicants, represented by Anthony Lester Q.C. and Christopher Carr, barrister, Lloyds, represented by David Hunter Q.C., the United Kingdom, represented by A. D. Preston, acting as agent, and the Commission of the European Communities, represented by A. Toledano-Laredo, acting as agent, and by M. Beloff, barrister, presented oral

G   argument at the hearing on October 29, 1980.

During the hearing Lloyds completed the statement of facts in this case as follows:

"Since 1968 in the United Kingdom wage scales for junior staff have been agreed nationally. Exceptionally, amongst the banks, Lloyds pension schemes were not only contributory but also provided for

H   men to contribute at the start of their pensionable employment whereas the women started to contribute from the age of 25.

"Accordingly because of the difficulties involved in altering the fund rules and for the sole purpose of producing as nearly as possible equality of take-home pay within Lloyds and between Lloyds staff and the staff of other banks, Lloyds adjusted their salary scales by increasing the national scale by 5 per cent. for all contributory members, i.e. all men and women over 25.

A

"In this way Lloyds provided all contributions required by the fund rules for men and women over 25 and as between itself and these members in substance converted a contributory into a non-contributory scheme.

"Under the existing rules of the two pension schemes to have paid the same nominal salaries to men and women under 25 would have produced glaring inequalities. It was recognised by Lloyds and by the staff that the only step towards equal treatment between men and women was to alter the scheme rules or to amalgamate the two schemes. This process which was started was not within the power of the bank and the staff representatives alone but required the consent of the trustees, the Inland Revenue, the Occupational Pensions Board and a 75 per cent. vote of any affected class of member."

B

The Advocate General delivered his opinion at the sitting on December 11, 1980.

C

DECISION

1. By order of February 19, 1980, which was received at the court on March 3, 1980, the Court of Appeal, London, referred to the Court of Justice under article 117 of the E.E.C. Treaty several questions for a preliminary ruling on the interpretation of article 119 of the E.E.C. Treaty, Council Directive of February 10, 1975 (75/117/E.E.C.) on the approximation of the laws of the member states relating to the application of the principle of equal pay for men and women (Official Journal, 1975, L.45/19) and Council Directive of February 9, 1976 (76/207/E.E.C.) on the implementation of the principle of equal treatment for men and women as regards access to employment, vocational training and promotion, and working conditions (Official Journal, 1976, L.38/40).

D

E

2. These questions have been raised within the context of proceedings between two female workers and their employer, Lloyds Bank Ltd. (hereinafter referred to as "Lloyds"), which they complain was in breach of the clause guaranteeing equal pay for men and women incorporated in their contracts of employment with the bank by virtue of the provisions of section 1 (2) (a) of the Equal Pay Act 1970. The applicants in the main proceedings have claimed in particular that Lloyds has failed to fulfil its obligations under the Equal Pay Act 1970 by not paying female staff under 25 years of age the same gross salary as that of male staff of the same age engaged in the same work.

F

3. It is clear from the information contained in the order making the reference that Lloyds applies to its staff two retirement benefit schemes, one for men and one for women. Under these retirement benefits schemes, which are the result of collective bargaining between the trade unions and Lloyds and which have been approved by the national authorities under the Finance Act 1970 and certified under the Social Security Pensions Act 1975, the member contracts out of the earnings-related part of the state pension scheme and this part is replaced by a contractual scheme.

G

H

4. It follows from the same order that although the two retirement benefits schemes applied by Lloyds do not essentially involve a difference in the treatment of men and women as regards the benefits relating to the retirement pension, they lay down different rules as regards other aspects not related to that pension.

5. The unequal pay alleged in this case before the national court

A originates, according to the applicants in the main proceedings, in the provisions of these two retirement benefits schemes relating to the requirement to contribute applicable to staff who have not attained the age of 25. In fact, it is clear from the order making the reference that men under 25 years of age are required to contribute 5 per cent. of their salary to their scheme whereas women are not required to do so. In order to cover the contribution payable by the men, Lloyds adds an additional 5 per cent. to

B the gross salary paid to those workers which is then deducted and paid directly to the trustees of the retirement benefits scheme in question on behalf of those workers.

6. The order making the reference also shows that workers leaving their employment who consent to the transfer of their accrued rights to the state pension scheme receive a " contributions equivalent premium " which

C entitles them to the refund, subject to deductions in respect of a part of the cost of the premium and in respect of income tax of their past contributions to the scheme of which they were members, with interest; that amount includes, in the case of men under the age of 25, the 5 per cent. contribution paid in their name by the employer.

7. Finally, as follows from the information provided by the national

D court, the amount of the salary in which the above-mentioned 5 per cent. contribution is included helps to determine the amount of certain benefits and social advantages such as redundancy payments, unemployment benefits and family allowances, as well as mortgage and credit facilities.

8. The industrial tribunal, before which proceedings were brought at first instance, dismissed by decision of September 19, 1977, the applicants' claim on the ground in particular that the unequal pay for men and women

E complained of in this instance was the result of a difference in the rules of the bank's retirement benefits schemes for men and women and therefore fell within the exception contained in section 6 (1A) (b) of the Equal Pay Act 1970 which excludes from the operation of the principle of equal pay for men and women terms related to death or retirement or any provision made in connection with death or retirement.

F 9. The applicants appealed to the Employment Appeal Tribunal, contending that the payment of an additional 5 per cent. gross salary to male employees of Lloyds aged under 25 raised a problem of discrimination between men and women in respect of pay which fell outside the exception contained in section 6 (1A) (b) of the Equal Pay Act 1970. They also argued that in any case that section could not be interpreted and applied so as to be contrary to Community law, which overrides the

G provisions of the Equal Pay Act 1970.

10. The appeal tribunal allowed the appeal on the grounds that (a) there was inequality of pay for men and women under the age of 25 in that instance; (b) the terms or provisions in the contract of employment with reference to pay had to be kept separate from terms or provisions with reference to pensions; and (c) the relevant clause in the contract

H of employment was not a provision relating to death or retirement as contemplated by section 6 (1A) (b) of the Equal Pay Act 1970.

11. In view of this legal problem, the Court of Appeal, before which an appeal was brought by Lloyds against the decision of the appeal tribunal, decided to refer to the Court of Justice questions on the interpretation of article 119 of the E.E.C. Treaty, article 1 of the Council Directive of February 10, 1975 (75/117/E.E.C.) and articles 1 and 5 of Council Directive of February 9, 1976 (76/207/E.E.C.).

The first question

A

12. The first question submitted by the national court is worded as follows:

" 1. Are (a) contributions paid by an employer to a retirement benefits scheme; or (b) rights and benefits of a worker under such a scheme; ' pay ' within the meaning of article 119 of the E.E.C. Treaty? "

B

13. It is clear from the information supplied by the national court that the first question asks essentially, first, under (a), whether sums of the kind in question paid by the employer in the name of the employee to a retirement benefits scheme by way of an addition to the gross salary come within the concept of " pay " within the meaning of article 119 of the Treaty.

C

14. Under the second paragraph of article 119 of the E.E.C. Treaty, " pay " means, for the purpose of that provision:

" the ordinary basic or minimum wage or salary and any other consideration, whether in cash or in kind, which the worker receives, directly or indirectly, in respect of his employment from his employer."

D

15. Sums such as those in question which are included in the calculation of the gross salary payable to the employee and which directly determine the calculation of other advantages linked to the salary, such as redundancy payments, unemployment benefits, family allowances and credit facilities, form part of the worker's pay within the meaning of the second paragraph of article 119 of the Treaty even if they are immediately deducted by the employer and paid to a pension fund on behalf of the employee. This applies a fortiori where those sums are refunded in certain circumstances and subject to certain deductions to the employee as being repayable to him if he ceases to belong to the contractual retirement benefits scheme under which they were deducted.

E

16. Moreover, the argument mentioned by the British Government that the payment of the contributions in question by the employer does not arise out of a legal obligation towards the employee is not in point since that payment is in fact made, it corresponds to an obligation by the worker to contribute and is deducted from his salary.

F

17. In view of all these facts, it is therefore necessary to reply to question 1 (a) that a contribution to a retirement benefits scheme which is paid by the employer in the name of the employees by means of an addition to the gross salary and which helps to determine the amount of that salary is " pay " within the meaning of the second paragraph of article 119 of the E.E.C. Treaty.

G

18. In view of this reply, there is no need to examine the second part of the first question, question 1 (b), which is subsidiary to question 1 (a).

H

The second question

19. In its second question, which is almost identical to the first, the national court puts the same problem to the court with reference to article 1 of Council Directive (75/117/E.E.C.).

20. Since the interpretation of Directive (75/117/E.E.C.) was requested by the national court merely subsidiarily to that of article 119

A of the E.E.C. Treaty, examination of the second question is purposeless, having regard to the interpretation given to that article.

21. Moreover, Directive (75/117/E.E.C.), whose objective is, as follows from the first recital of the preamble thereto, to lay down the conditions necessary for the implementation of the principle that men and women should receive equal pay, is based on the concept of " pay " as defined in the second paragraph of article 119 of the Treaty. Although
B article 1 of the directive explains that the concept of " same work " contained in the first paragraph of article 119 of the Treaty includes cases of " work to which equal value is attributed," it in no way affects the concept of " pay " contained in the second paragraph of article 119 but refers by implication to that concept.

C *The third question*

22. The national court asks further in its third question whether, if the answer to question 1 is in the affirmative, " article 119 of the E.E.C. Treaty . . . [has] direct effect in the member states so as to confer enforceable Community rights upon individuals in the circumstances of the present case."
D 23. As the court has stated in previous decisions (judgment of April 8, 1976, in *Defrenne* v. *Sabena* (Case 43/75) [1976] I.C.R. 547 and judgment of March 27, 1980, in *Macarthys Ltd.* v. *Smith* (Case 129/79) [1981] Q.B. 180, article 119 of the Treaty applies directly to all forms of discrimination which may be identified solely with the aid of the criteria of equal work and equal pay referred to by the article in question, without national or Community measures being required to
E define them with greater precision in order to permit of their application. Among the forms of discrimination which may be thus judicially identified, the court mentioned in particular cases where men and women receive unequal pay for equal work carried out in the same establishment or service, public or private. In such a situation the court is in a position to establish all the facts enabling it to decide whether a woman
F receives less pay than a man engaged in the same work or work of equal value.

24. This is the case where the requirement to pay contributions applies only to men and not to women and the contributions payable by men are paid by the employer in their name by means of addition to the gross salary the effect of which is to give men higher pay within the
G meaning of the second paragraph of article 119 than that received by women engaged in the same work or work of equal value.

25. Although, where women are not required to pay contributions, the salary of men after deduction of the contributions is comparable to that of women who do not pay contributions, the inequality between the gross salaries of men and women is nevertheless a source of discrimination contrary to article 119 of the Treaty since because of that in-
H equality men receive benefits from which women engaged in the same work or work of equal value are excluded, or receive on that account greater benefits or social advantages than those to which women are entitled.

26. This applies in particular where, as in this instance, workers leaving their employment before reaching a given age are, in certain circumstances, refunded in the form of a " contributions equivalent premium "

at least a proportion of the contributions paid in their name by the   A
employer and where the amount of the gross salary paid to the worker
determines the amount of certain benefits and social advantages, such
as redundancy payments or unemployment benefits, family allowances
and mortgage or credit facilities, to which workers of both sexes are
entitled.

27. In this case the fact that contributions are paid by the employer
solely in the name of men and not in the name of women engaged in   B
the same work or work of equal value leads to unequal pay for men
and women which the national court may directly establish with the aid
of the pay components in question and the criteria laid down in article
119 of the Treaty.

28. For those reasons, the reply to the third question should be that
article 119 of the Treaty may be relied upon before the national courts   C
and that these courts have a duty to ensure the protection of the rights
which this provision vests in individuals, in particular in a case where,
because of the requirement imposed only on men or only on women to
contribute to a retirement benefit scheme, the contributions in question
are paid by the employer in the name of the employee and deducted
from the gross salary whose amount they determine.
                                                                          D

The temporal effect of this judgment

29. In its written and oral observations, Lloyds has requested the
court to consider the possibility, if the answer to the third question is
in the affirmative, of limiting the temporal effect of the interpretation
given by this judgment to article 119 of the Treaty so that this judgment
" cannot be relied on in order to support claims concerning pay periods   E
prior to the date of the judgment."

30. It maintains for this purpose, first, that the problem of the com-
patibility of the national law with Community law was raised only at
the stage of the appeal brought before the Employment Appeal Tribunal
and, secondly, that acknowledgment by the court of the direct effect of
article 119 of the Treaty would lead, in a case such as the present, to   F
" claims for the retrospective adjustment of pay scales covering a period
of years."

31. As the court acknowledged in its above-mentioned judgment of
April 8, 1976, although the consequences of any judicial decision must
be carefully taken into account, it would be impossible to go so far as
to diminish the objectivity of the law and thus compromise its future   G
application on the ground of the repercussions which might result, as
regards the past, from such a judicial decision.

32. In the same judgment the court admitted that a temporal restriction on the direct effect of article 119 of the Treaty might be taken into
account exceptionally in that case having regard, first, to the fact that
the parties concerned, in the light of the conduct of several member
states and the views adopted by the Commission and repeatedly brought   H
to the notice of the circles concerned, had been led to continue, over a
long period, with practices which were contrary to article 119 and having
regard, secondly, to the fact that important questions of legal certainty
affecting not only the interests of the parties to the main action but also
a whole series of interests, both public and private, made it undesirable
in principle to reopen the question of pay as regards the past.

A   33. In this case neither of these conditions has been fulfilled, either in respect of the information available at present to the circles concerned as to the scope of article 119 of the Treaty, in the light in particular of the decisions of the court in the meantime on this subject, or in respect of the number of the cases which would be affected in this instance by the direct effect of that provision.

B *The fourth question*

34. As the fourth question was only submitted to the Court of Justice by the national court in case the first two questions were answered in the negative, examination of it has become purposeless.

Costs

C   The costs incurred by the Government of the United Kingdom and the Commission of the European Communities, which have submitted observations to the court, are not recoverable. As these proceedings are, in so far as the applicants and Lloyds are concerned, in the nature of a step in the proceedings pending before the national court, the decision on costs is a matter for that court.

D   On those grounds, the court in answer to the questions referred to it by the Court of Appeal, London, by order of February 19, 1980, hereby rules: 1. A contribution to a retirement benefits scheme which is paid by an employer in the name of employees by means of an addition to the gross salary and which therefore helps to determine the amount of that salary constitutes " pay " within the meaning of the second paragraph of article 119 of the E.E.C. Treaty. 2. Article 119 of the Treaty may be relied upon

E before the national courts and these courts have a duty to ensure the protection of the rights which this provision vests in individuals, in particular in a case where, because of the requirement imposed only on men or only on women to contribute to a retirement benefits scheme, the contributions in question are paid by the employer in the name of the employee and deducted from the gross salary whose amount they determine.

F
Solicitors: *Lawford & Co.; G. N. Johnson, Lloyds Bank Legal Department; Treasury Solicitor.*

[Reported by LIONEL PILKINGTON, ESQ., Barrister-at-Law]

G

H

A

* JENKINS v. KINGSGATE (CLOTHING PRODUCTIONS) LTD.

(Case 96/80)

B

1980 Nov. 26;   Judge J. Mertens de Wilmars (President),
1981 Jan. 28; March 31   Judges P. Pescatore, Lord Mackenzie
                         Stuart and T. Koopmans (Presidents of
                         Chambers), Judges A. O'Keeffe, G.Bosco,
                         A. Touffait, O. Due and U. Everling
                         J.-P. Warner (Advocate-General)

C

Discrimination, Sex—Equal pay—Variation due to material difference—Hourly rates of pay—Full-time employees receiving higher rates than female part-time employees—Whether variation due to material difference other than sex—Effect of Community law on municipal law—E.E.C. Treaty (Cmnd. 5179–II), art. 119—Council Directive (75/117/E.E.C.), art. 1

A company employed full-time and part-time workers but, D
to discourage absenteism and to encourage greater productivity,
it paid the full-time employees 10 per cent. more an hour than
part-time employees. All part-time employees except one
were female. The applicant was a part-time employee and she
brought a complaint that the difference in pay between herself
and a full-time male employee contravened the equality clause
in her contract of employment. The industrial tribunal dismissed the complaint holding that, although she was employed E
on like work with the man, the fact that the man was full-time
was a material difference other than the difference of sex
within the meaning of section 1 (3) of the Equal Pay Act 1970.
She appealed.

The appeal tribunal referred to the European Court of
Justice, inter alia, the questions whether the principle of equal
pay in article 119 of the E.E.C. Treaty and article 1 of Council F
Directive (75/117/E.E.C.) required the same hourly rate
of remuneration irrespective of the number of hours worked
and the commercial benefit to an employer to encourage the
maximum number of hours of work, and whether those two
articles were directly applicable in member states: —

Held, (1) that the purpose of article 119 of the E.E.C.
Treaty was to ensure the application of the principle of equal G
pay for men and women for the same work and, therefore, the
prohibition in the article to differences in rates of pay were to
differences based exclusively on the sex of the employee; that,
accordingly, a difference in rates of remuneration between full-
time and part-time employees did not offend the article provided
the difference was attributable to factors which were objectively
justified and did not relate directly or indirectly to discrimination based on sex (post, pp. 982G—983A, 984F–G).

H

(2) That, using the criteria of equal pay for equal work,
without the operation of Community or national measures, to
establish that the payment of lower hourly rates of remuneration for part-time work represented discrimination based on
sex, article 119 of the Treaty applied directly to the situation
(post pp. 983G—984A); that article 1 of Council Directive
(75/117/E.E.C.) was designed to facilitate the practical application of article 119 and in no way altered the content or
scope of article 119 (post, p. 984B–D, G–H).

A   The following cases are referred to in the judgment:
Clay Cross (Quarry Services) Ltd. v. *Fletcher* [1978] 1 W.L.R. 1429;
    [1979] I.C.R. 1; [1979] 1 All E.R. 474, C.A.
Defrenne v. *Sabena* (Case 43 /75) [1976] I.C.R. 547, E.C.J.
Defrenne v. *Sabena (No. 3)* (Case 149/77) [1978] E.C.R. 1365, E.C.J.
Griggs v. *Duke Power Co.* (1971) 401 U.S. 424.
Macarthys Ltd. v. *Smith* (Case 129/79) [1980] 3 W.L.R. 929; [1980]
B   I.C.R. 672; [1980] 1 All E.R. 111, E.C.J. and C.A.
Mazzalai v. *Ferrovia del Renon* (Case 111/75) [1976] E.C.R. 657, E.C.J.
Worringham v. *Lloyds Bank Ltd.* (Case 69/80) [1981] 1 W.L.R. 950,
    E.C.J.

The following additional cases were cited in the opinion of Mr. Advocate-
    General J.-P. Warner:
C   *Commission* v. *Ireland* (Case 61/77) [1978] E.C.R. 417, E.C.J.
Caisse Régionale d'Assurance Maladie (C.R.A.M.), Lille v. *Palermo* (Case
    237/78) [1979] E.C.R. 2645, E.C.J.
Dothard v. *Rawlinson* (1977) 433 U.S. 321.
Sotgiu v. *Deutsche Bundespost* (Case 152/73) [1974] 1 E.C.R. 153, E.C.J.

D   REFERENCE by the Employment Appeal Tribunal.
    The applicant, Jeanette Pauline Jenkins, complained that the em-
ployers, Kingsgate (Clothing Productions) Ltd., were in breach of the
equality clause in her contract of employment by paying her 10 per cent.
less an hour than a male employee, Mr. Bannan.   The industrial tribunal
held that, although she was employed on like work with Mr. Bannan, the
difference in pay was due to a material difference other than sex within
the meaning of section 1 (3) of the Equal Pay Act 1970.   The applicant
E   appealed.
    The Employment Appeal Tribunal referred to the European Court of
Justice questions relating to whether a different rate of pay for part-time
work contravened article 119 of the E.E.C. Treaty and article 1 of
Council Directive (75/117/E.E.C.) and whether those two articles were
directly applicable in member states.
F   The facts and questions referred to the European Court are stated in
the judgment.

    Anthony Lester Q.C. and *John Hand* for the applicant.
    R. D. Munrow for the Government of the United Kingdom.
    J. Dufour for the Government of the Kingdom of Belgium.
    J. Forman for the Commission.
G
    March 31, 1981.   The court delivered the following judgment.

FACTS AND ISSUES

I. *Facts and written procedure*

    1. Kingsgate (Clothing Productions) Ltd. (hereinafter referred to as
H   " Kingsgate "), manufacturers of ladies' clothing, have a factory in
Harlow, Essex, where 89 people are employed, of whom 35 are male and
54 female.   All the male employees except one work full-time (40 hours
per week); of the female employees, however, five work part-time.   The
employees who work full-time are graded into six categories.
    In November 1975, shortly before the entry into force of the Equal
Pay Act 1970, Kingsgate fixed the hourly pay for full-time work at the
same rate for both men and women.   It considered, however, that there

was a fundamental difference between part-time work and full-time work, **A**
independently of the sex of the worker, which justified a difference in
pay. The pay for part-time work was therefore fixed at a rate 10 per cent.
lower than that applicable to full-time work. That difference was not
based on either the characteristics of the worker or the quality of the
work. It was motivated by the need (a) to discourage absenteeism; (b)
to ensure that the expensive machinery in the factory was being used to
its fullest extent; and (c) to encourage greater productivity. **B**

Among the male employees at Kingsgate the *only* one who works half-
time is a worker who was recently retired and who was subsequently and
exceptionally re-engaged to work part-time (16 hours per week) on work
classed in Grade 1.

2. Mrs. Jeanette Pauline Jenkins, an employee of Kingsgate, works
part-time, or to be more precise " more or less 30 hours per week." She **C**
was engaged as a special machinist and does work classed in Grade 2.
Mrs. Jenkins took the view that she was unfairly prejudiced by the fact
that, although she was engaged to perform the same work as that performed by one of her male colleagues, Mr. Bannan, employed full-time,
she drew an hourly rate of pay lower than that drawn by her colleague;
she therefore brought proceedings before an industrial tribunal. In **D**
support of her complaint she alleged that the difference in pay contravened
the equality clause incorporated into her contract and the provisions of
section 1 (2) (*a*) of the Equal Pay Act 1970, according to which the
principle of equal pay for men and women applies in every case: " where
the woman is employed on like work with a man in the same employment."

The employer acknowledged that Mrs. Jenkins had been engaged **E**
to perform like work with that of Mr. Bannan. Nevertheless, the
employer maintained that there was " a material difference, other than
the difference of sex " between her case and his.

The industrial tribunal rejected the complaint and held that working
for a period representing 75 per cent. of the full working hours (30 hours
= 75 per cent. of 40 hours) constituted a " material difference, other **F**
than the difference of sex," sufficient to justify, in Mrs. Jenkins's case, an
hourly rate of pay 10 per cent. lower than that of her male colleague, in
accordance with section 1 (3) of the Equal Pay Act 1970 (as amended),
which reads:

" An equality clause shall not operate in relation to a variation
between the woman's contract and the man's contract if the employer **G**
proves that the variation is genuinely due to a material difference
(other than the difference of sex) between her case and his."

3. Mrs. Jenkins appealed against that decision to the Employment
Appeal Tribunal, which, by an order of February 25, 1980, referred the
following questions to the court for a preliminary ruling:

" 1. Does the principle of equal pay, contained in article 119 of the **H**
E.E.C. Treaty and article 1 of the Council Directive of February 10,
1975, require that pay for work at time rates shall be the same,
irrespective: (a) of the number of hours worked each week; or (b) of
whether it is of commercial benefit to the employer to encourage the
doing of the maximum possible hours of work and consequently to
pay a higher rate to workers doing 40 hours per week than to workers
doing fewer than 40 hours per week?

A

" 2. If the answer to question 1 (a) or (b) is in the negative, what criteria should be used in determining whether or not the principle of equal pay applies where there is a difference in the time rates of pay related to the total number of hours worked each week?

" 3. Would the answer to question 1 (a) or (b) or 2 be different (and, if so, in what respects) if it were shown that a considerably smaller proportion of female workers than of male workers is able to perform the minimum number of hours each week required to qualify for the full hourly rate of pay?

B

" 4. Are the relevant provisions of article 119 of the E.E.C. Treaty or article 1 of the said Directive, as the case may be, directly applicable in member states in the circumstances of the present case? "

C

In accordance with article 20 of the Protocol on the Statute of the Court of Justice of the E.E.C., written observations were submitted by Mrs. Jenkins, represented by Anthony Lester Q.C. and John Hand, barrister, instructed by Messrs. Mills Curry, Gaskell, solicitors; by the Government of the United Kingdom, represented by R. D. Munrow, Treasury Solicitor's Department; by the Government of the Kingdom of Belgium, represented by J. Dufour, Conseiller Adjoint, Ministry of Foreign Affairs; and by the Commission of the European Communities, repre-

D

sented by J. Forman, a member of its Legal Department, acting as agent.

Upon hearing the report of the Judge-Rapporteur and the views of the Advocate General, the court decided to open the oral procedure without any preparatory inquiry. However, it requested the Commission to give a written reply by November 1, 1980, to the following question: " Do any of the member states other than Belgium and the United Kingdom

E

have legislation requiring the pay of part-time workers to be proportional to the pay of full-time workers? " The Commission replied to the question in a letter dated October 28, 1980.

II. *Written observations submitted to the court*

Mrs. Jenkins observes that the issue raised in this case is whether,

F

and if so in what circumstances, the principle of equal pay contained in article 119 of the Treaty and article 1 of Council Directive (75/117/ E.E.C.) applies to part-time workers in the European Community.

She submits that it might be helpful at the outset to place this issue within its wider context, recalling that by far the majority of part-time workers in the Community are women and that in the United Kingdom the proportion of women in part-time work is even greater than in the

G

other member states.

Section 1 (3) of the Equal Pay Act 1970 provides that a variation between a woman's contract and that of a man is justifiable if the employer proves that it is due to a material difference (other than the difference of sex) between her case and his. In certain cases before the Employment Appeal Tribunal, which the Court of Appeal has not had to consider, it

H

has been held that a difference in the number of hours worked does fall within the concept of a material difference.

As against those decisions, Mrs. Jenkins maintains that they are, in any event, incompatible with the principle enunciated by the Court of Appeal in *Clay Cross (Quarry Services) Ltd.* v. *Fletcher* [1978] 1 W.L.R. 1429 according to which the number of hours worked per week and the intentions of the employer are extrinsic circumstances of little relevance as regards proof of the absence of discrimination based on sex. Mrs.

Jenkins also refers to the principle enunciated by the Supreme Court of A
the United States in *Griggs* v. *Duke Power Co.* (1971) 401 U.S. 424,
according to which what must be prohibited are not merely practices which
are intended to discriminate, but equally those which are discriminatory
in their effect, irrespective of the intentions of their authors.

Having thus reviewed the current legislation and case law in the United
Kingdom touching on the present issue, Mrs. Jenkins proceeds to consider
questions 1, 2 and 3 which, in her opinion, are closely linked and may B
conveniently be examined together. She observes that the answers to those
questions are needed irrespective of the answer to question 4 regarding
the direct effect in member states of the principle of equal pay. That is
because, as a matter of national law, if section 1 (3) of the Equal Pay Act
1970 is held by the courts and tribunals of the United Kingdom to be
ambiguous in the circumstances of the present case the answers to the first C
three questions will be relevant for the purpose of resolving any such
ambiguity: cf. *Mazzalai* v. *Ferrovia del Renon* (Case 111/75) [1976]
E.C.R. 657, 665 (paras. 7–11).

She recalls, first, the double aim, economic and social, of article 119
and asserts that that aim would be frustrated if the principle of equal pay
were effectively confined to full-time workers. Such a conclusion would
create competitive disadvantages both for undertakings in countries which D
apply the principle of equal pay equally to part-time workers and for those
in states where the proportion of available part-time workers is lower.
It would also discriminate against women, who are generally prevented
by their family obligations and circumstances from being able to work
as many hours as men doing the same work.

Such a restrictive interpretation of the principle of equal pay would E
not only have absurd consequences (for example, different hourly rates
of pay for persons working 40 and 39 hours per week), but, what is more,
would facilitate widespread misapplication of the principle to the detriment
of women, who constitute the great majority of part-time workers.

If an employer wished to encourage his employees to work longer
hours, he should pay a suitable overtime rate and not reduce the pay of F
those working part-time.

Sub-paragraph (b) of the third paragraph of article 119, states that
". . . pay for work at time rates shall be the same for the same job."
What decides whether the job is the same is the nature of the work performed by the workers concerned, and not the number of hours worked
each week. The fact that it may be advantageous for the employer to
pay a higher basic rate to those working 40 hours per week than to those G
working fewer hours is an extrinsic and irrelevant consideration as regards
the principle of equal pay. Indeed, if that were not the case, the employer
would be able to pay women less than men for equal work, not on the
ground that they were women but because they could be recruited for less
pay than men and that this was to the employer's commercial benefit.

It is not contested by Mrs. Jenkins that in certain situations the H
difference in hourly rates of pay between a female part-time worker and
a male full-time worker may be objectively justified by the operation of
factors which are unconnected with any discrimination on the ground of
sex. It might be the case, for example, that the male worker has superior
skill or qualifications or longer service. That exception to the principle
of equal pay must be strictly confined, however, to real and relevant differences which are personal to the workers concerned, and cannot include

A the employer's motives where they are not related to the personal qualities
of the particular workers.

   In Mrs. Jenkins's opinion the reply to be given to question 1 should
therefore be in the affirmative, which makes it unnecessary to consider
question 2.

   As regards question 3, Mrs. Jenkins submits that the principle of equal
B pay is violated not only where an employer intends to discriminate against
a woman on grounds of sex but also where the effect of his policy on pay
is to discriminate against her on such grounds. If a condition or requirement which must be met in order to obtain equal pay for equal work
operates so as to exclude women and cannot be shown to have a manifest
relationship to the services involved, the application of such a condition
or requirement must be considered to be contrary to the principle of equal
C pay. That is in application of the principle of " adverse impact "
enunciated by the Supreme Court of the United States in *Griggs* v. *Duke
Power Co.*, 401 U.S. 424 and by the British Parliament in section 1 (1) (*b*)
of the Sex Discrimination Act 1975.

   Finally, as to the question of the direct effect of article 119 and
article 1 of the Council Directive (75/117/E.E.C.), it may be recalled
D that, as the court held in its decision of April 8, 1976, in *Defrenne* v.
Sabena (Case 43/75) [1976] I.C.R. 547, these provisions are directly
applicable to all forms of direct and overt discrimination which may be
identified solely with the aid of the criteria of equal work and equal pay,
including unequal pay for equal work carried out in the same establishment or service. The circumstances of this case clearly fall within the
scope of the direct application of article 119: it has been shown that Mrs.
E Jenkins carried out like work with the male worker with whom she com-
pares herself and there is no difficulty in establishing whether she received
lower pay.

   Although " adverse impact " is defined in the legislation of the United
Kingdom as " indirect discrimination," it should not be confused with the
" indirect and disguised discrimination " which has been described by the
F court as falling outside the scope of the direct application of article 119.
Here, " indirect discrimination " is used in such a manner as to exclude
any practice which, although not founded on any discriminatory motives,
nevertheless has a discriminatory effect, and not as meaning discrimination
which can only be suppressed by national or Community legislative
measures more detailed than the provisions referred to above.

   If, contrary to Mrs. Jenkins's submissions, the circumstances envisaged
G by question 3 are held to fall outside the scope of the direct application
of article 119, it will be necessary to rely on article 1 of Council Directive
(75/117/E.E.C.), which requires the elimination of all discrimination
on grounds of sex " with regard to all aspects and conditions of remuneration." That definition of discrimination extends to any condition which
is capable of creating " indirect discrimination " (" adverse impact ") in
H the sense already described. In such circumstances the principle of equal
pay outlined in article 119 of the Treaty and further defined in the first
paragraph of article 1 of the Directive has direct effect in member states
so as to confer on individuals rights which the national courts are bound
to protect.

   As to Council Directive (75/117/E.E.C.) itself, Mrs. Jenkins observes
that it lays down standards aimed at facilitating the practical application of the principle of equal pay set out in article 119. That aim

cannot be effectively attained if individuals are prevented from relying upon   A
the provisions of the Directive in national courts. The first paragraph
of article 1 of the Directive is sufficiently clear and precise to have direct
effect, so that on the expiration of the period allowed to member states
for complying with the Directive, it became complete and unconditionally
applicable.

In its judgment of June 15, 1978, in *Defrenne* v. *Sabena* (Case 149/77)
[1978] E.C.R. 1365 the court implied, moreover, that on the expiration of   B
the period allowed to member states for complying with Council Directive
(76/207/E.E.C.) on equal treatment, some provisions of that Directive
would have direct effect. By analogy it must therefore be conceded that
article 1 of Council Directive (75/117/E.E.C.) now has direct effect in
the circumstances of this case.

The Government of the United Kingdom observes, first, that the pro-   C
visions of Community law referred to it in the request for a preliminary
ruling are concerned solely with discrimination on the ground of sex. It
follows that those provisions are not applicable if a difference in pay is the
consequence of factors unconnected with any discrimination on grounds
of sex. Whether the difference may be so explained in any particular
case is a question of fact for the national court to decide. In performing   D
that duty, the national court may legitimately have regard to the considerations mentioned in question 1 (or to considerations of a similar
nature), not as considerations which are in themselves determinative, but
in so far as the inference may properly be drawn from them that the
difference in treatment is not, in reality, a discrimination based on sex.

The correctness of those submissions is fully supported by the practical
application of them to cases such as this. In this case it has been contended   E
before the national court that the difference between the rates of pay
depended solely upon the number of hours worked; that the fact that
Mrs. Jenkins was paid less than Mr. Bannan was purely a coincidence
and did not depend in any way on her sex; and that indeed there would
have been the same difference in remuneration, but in favour of Mrs.
Jenkins, if she had worked full-time and Mr. Bannan part-time.   F

According to the Government of the United Kingdom these are questions
of fact which the national court must be able to decide without being
fettered by a reply in the affirmative to question 1 (a) or (b).

Thus it is maintained by the Government of the United Kingdom that
the principle of equal pay contained in article 119 of the Treaty and in
article 1 of Council Directive (75/117/E.E.C.) is only applicable where the   G
difference in pay between a male employee and a female employee is the
result of discrimination based on sex; that where it is the consequence of
other factors, ex hypothesi it is not " based on sex " and therefore not
within the ambit of either of those articles; that whether in any particular
case discrimination is based on sex or other factors is a question of fact
for the national court to determine; and, in particular, that the principle of
equal pay does not require that pay for work at time rates shall be the same   H
irrespective of the circumstances described in sub-paragraphs (a) and (b)
of question 1.

As regards question 2 it is of the opinion that the only criterion
which should be employed to determine whether the principle of equal
pay applies in these circumstances is whether the difference in rates of
pay is the result of a discrimination on the ground of sex. The application
of that criterion is a matter for the national courts which alone are in a

A position to undertake the detailed examination of the particular facts of individual cases.   Furthermore, it considers that there is no criterion other than that of whether or not the difference in treatment is a result of discrimination based on sex which may be identified or implied from or read into the wording of article 119 of the Treaty or of article 1 of Council Directive (75/117/E.E.C.).

B As to question 3, the Government of the United Kingdom states that it cannot discern the precise scope of it.   It observes, however, that even if the circumstances described in that question in fact obtained and were the result of discrimination based on sex, that would still constitute indirect and disguised discrimination, which falls outside the sphere of application of the provisions referred to above.

C In regard to question 4, the Government of the United Kingdom concedes that in the event of the court's replying to question 1 in the affirmative, the direct effect of article 119 could not be disputed in a case such as the present.

If the court considers it necessary to interpret article 1 of Council Directive (75/117/E.E.C.) as applying irrespective of the circumstances defined in sub-paragraphs (a) and (b) of question 1, the Government D of the United Kingdom submits that that article, so applied, does not have direct effect.

The Government of the Kingdom of Belgium explains that in Belgium the remuneration of part-time workers may be based on collective employment agreements or, as is more often the case, individual agreements.   If the agreements are silent on the subject, part-time workers might nevertheless be given the right to remuneration in proportion to that laid down E for full-time workers, and has been accepted, moreover, in some decided cases and by the Conseil National du Travail (National Labour Board). It should, however, be emphasised that a difference in pay for part-time work as opposed to full-time work does not constitute a breach of the principle of equal pay in so far as there is no discrimination between male and female workers.

F The Commission of the European Communities notes that the court which has made the reference has asked the Court of Justice to examine the questions referred to it exclusively on the basis of a comparison between the remuneration of a female part-time employee and that of a male full-time employee, although in this case there is an exceptional circumstance that Kingsgate also employed one (and only one) part-time male worker.   However, in the Commission's view, the interpretation G which it would propose for article 119 must apply in the same way to a situation in which not only women, but also men, perform like work on a part-time basis.

The first question which arises is whether the expression " the same job " may only apply where a male employee and a female employee work the same number of hours per week.   The Commission sets out, first, the H arguments which may be used in favour of excluding equal pay in such a case, namely, (a) that it is not " the same job "; (b) that it is in reality the same job, but that the fewer hours worked entail additional charges (principally financial) for the employer which may be taken into consideration to give the female part-time employee a lower time rate.

Next, it sets out the arguments which might be advanced in reply. As to the view that the job is not the same, the language versions other than English would seem to suggest that it is in fact the " post " (slags

arbejde, Arbeitsplatz, poste de travail, posto di lavoro, functie) and not **A**
the number of hours worked which determines whether or not the two
jobs are the same. Reference might also be made to the view of the
court in its recent judgment of March 27, 1980, in *Macarthys Ltd.* v.
Smith [1980] 3 W.L.R. 929, that in deciding whether a female worker is
performing the same work as a male worker regard must be had to the
nature of her services.

B
If, in accordance with sub-paragraph (a) of the third paragraph of
article 119, pay for the same work at piece rates is to be calculated on
the basis of the same unit of measurement, pay for the same work at time
rates should obviously be established on the basis of the same time rate.

From a practical point of view, moreover, it might appear somewhat
artificial, in the case of a reduction in the standard working week, for a
job considered previously as different from another to become by virtue of **C**
that consideration alone " the same job." The same artificial element
might be found in the issue whether women working part-time do the
same work as men who also work part-time, but for a different number
of hours.

As to the extra cost, the position of the Commission has always been
(and it refers in that regard to its recommendation of July 20, 1960, **D**
Bulletin of the European Economic Communities 1960, vol. 6/7, p. 46)
that " factors affecting the cost or the yield of female labour shall not
be taken into consideration in case of work paid by time."

Any other approach, unless it were based, in each case, on an objective,
expert and detailed analysis, would, by its subjective nature, continue to
leave the door open to discrimination based on sex. Moreover, practical
experience would seem to show at present that part-time work, as such, **E**
is in fact neither more nor less costly for the employer than full-time work.

In support of its views the Commission cites in addition the Resolution
of the Conference of the Member States of December 30, 1961, of
equalisation of rates of pay for men and women, and an opinion of June 1,
1978, of the Economic and Social Committee, both to the effect that pay
for part-time work must be proportional to that for full-time work. **F**

In the Commission's opinion, its conclusions remain applicable even
if it is shown that there are male workers who work part-time and are
paid in the same way as female part-time workers, since female part-time
workers are no less discriminated against by comparison with male full-time
workers performing the same work. Of course, that does not exclude
the possibility that a difference between two workers occupying the same **G**
post may be explained by the operation of factors which are unconnected
with any discrimination on grounds of sex. Whether that is the case is a
question of fact.

A reply to questions 2 and 3 being therefore unnecessary, the Commission turns to question 4, concerning the direct effect of article 119 or of
Council Directive (75/117/E.E.C.).

It observes that once it is accepted that the concept of equal work **H**
contained in article 119 extends to part-time work, any difference in rates
of pay between the remuneration of male full-time employees and female
part-time employees must be considered, on the criteria of interpretation
expressed in the decisions of the court, as direct and overt discrimination.
In such circumstances there can be no doubt that article 119 has direct
effect. It thus becomes unnecessary to consider whether Council Directive
(75/117/E.E.C.) has direct effect or not.

A   In conclusion, the Commission therefore suggests that the following reply be given to the question raised by the Employment Appeal Tribunal:

> " 1. The principle that men and women should receive equal pay for equal work enshrined in article 119 of the E.E.C. Treaty implies that the basic pay for work at time rates shall be the same for all employees doing the same job irrespective of the number of hours worked per week.
>
> " 2. Should any amounts additional to the basic time rate be paid to full-time (or part-time) employees in respect of their employment such amounts must depend on factors totally unconnected with the sex of the employees."

III. *Oral Procedure*

Mrs. Jenkins and the Commission of the European Communities presented oral argument at the sitting on November 26, 1980. The Advocate General delivered his opinion at the sitting on January 28, 1981.

DECISION

1. By an order dated February 25, 1980, which was received at the court on March 12, 1980, the Employment Appeal Tribunal of the United Kingdom referred to the court for a preliminary ruling under article 177 of the E.E.C. Treaty several questions as to the interpretation of article 119 of the E.E.C. Treaty and article 1 of Council Directive of February 10, 1975 (75/117/E.E.C.) on the approximation of the laws of the member states relating to the application of the principle of equal pay for men and women (Official Journal, 1975, L.45/19).

2. The questions were raised in the court of a dispute between a female employee working part-time and her employer, a manufacturer of womens' clothing, against whom she claimed that she was receiving an hourly rate of pay lower than that paid to one of her male colleagues employed full-time on the same work.

3. Mrs. Jenkins took the view that such a difference in pay contravened the equality clause incorporated into her contract of employment by virtue of the Equal Pay Act 1970, section 1 (2) (a) of which provides for equal pay for men and women in every case where " a woman is employed on like work with a man in the same employment."

4. The industrial tribunal, hearing the case at first instance, held in its decision of February 5, 1979, that in the case of part-time work the fact that the weekly working hours amounted, as in that case, to 75 per cent. of the full working hours was sufficient to constitute a " material difference " between part-time and full-time work within the meaning of section 1 (3) of the Act of 1970, according to which:

> " An equality clause shall not operate in relation to a variation between the woman's contract and the man's contract if the employer proves that the variation is genuinely due to a material difference (other than the difference of sex) between her case and his."

5. Mrs. Jenkins appealed against that decision to the Employment Appeal Tribunal, which decided that the dispute raised problems concerning the interpretation of Community law and referred a number of questions to the court for a preliminary ruling.

6. According to the information in the order making the reference, prior to 1975 the employer did not pay the same wages to male and female

employees but the hourly rates of pay were the same whether the work was A
part-time or full-time. From November 1975 the pay for full-time work
(that is to say, the pay for those working 40 hours per week) became the
same for male and female employees but the hourly rate for part-time
work was fixed at a rate which was 10 per cent. lower than the hourly
rate of pay for full-time work.

7. It also appears from the order making the reference that at the B
time of the proceedings before the industrial tribunal the part-time workers
employed by the employer in question were all female with the exception
of a sole male part-time worker who had just retired and who at the time
had been authorised to continue working, exceptionally and for short
periods, after the normal age of retirement.

8. On the basis of those facts the Employment Appeal Tribunal referred
the following questions to the court: C

" 1. Does the principle of equal pay, contained in article 119 of the
E.E.C. Treaty and article 1 of the Council Directive of February 10,
1975, require that pay for work at time rates shall be the same,
irrespective: (a) of the number of hours worked each week; or (b) of
whether it is of commercial benefit to the employer to encourage the
doing of the maximum possible hours of work and consequently to pay D
a higher rate to workers doing 40 hours per week than to workers
doing fewer than 40 hours per week?

" 2. If the answer to question 1 (a) or (b) is in the negative, what
criteria should be used in determining whether or not the principle
of equal pay applies where there is a difference in the time rates of
pay related to the total number of hours worked each week?

" 3. Would the answer to question 1 (a) and (b) or 2 be different E
(and, if so, in what respects) if it were shown that a considerably
smaller proportion of female workers than of male workers is able
to perform the minimum number of hours each week required to
qualify for the full hourly rate of pay?

" 4. Are the relevant provisions of article 119 of the E.E.C. Treaty
or article 1 of the said Directive, as the case may be, directly appli- F
cable in member states in the circumstances of the present case? "

First three questions

9. It appears from the first three questions and the reasons stated in the
order making the reference that the national court is principally concerned
to know whether a difference in the level of pay for work carried out part-
time and the same work carried out full-time may amount to discrimination G
of a kind prohibited by article 119 of the Treaty when the category of
part-time workers is exclusively or predominantly comprised of women.

10. The answer to the questions thus understood is that the purpose of
article 119 is to ensure the application of the principle of equal pay for men
and women for the same work. The differences in pay prohibited by that
provision are therefore exclusively those based on the difference of the sex H
of the workers. Consequently the fact that part-time work is paid at an
hourly rate lower than pay for full-time work does not amount per se to
discrimination prohibited by article 119 provided that the hourly rates are
applied to workers belonging to either category without distinction based
on sex.

11. If there is no such distinction, therefore, the fact that work paid at
time rates is remunerated at an hourly rate which varies according to the

A number of hours worked per week does not offend against the principle of
equal pay laid down in article 119 of the Treaty in so far as the difference
in pay between part-time work and full-time work is attributable to factors
which are objectively justified and are in no way related to any discrimination based on sex.

12. Such may be the case, in particular, when by giving hourly rates
of pay which are lower for part-time work than those for full-time work
B the employer is endeavouring, on economic grounds which may be objectively justified, to encourage full-time work irrespective of the sex of the
worker.

13. By contrast, if it is established that a considerably smaller percentage of women than of men perform the minimum number of weekly
working hours required in order to be able to claim the full-time hourly
C rate of pay, the inequality in pay will be contrary to article 119 of the
Treaty where, regard being had to the difficulties encountered by women
in arranging to work that minimum number of hours per week, the pay
policy of the undertaking in question cannot be explained by factors other
than discrimination based on sex.

14. Where the hourly rate of pay differs according to whether the work
is part-time or full-time it is for the national courts to decide in each
D individual case whether, regard being had to the facts of the case, its
history and the employer's intention, a pay policy such as that which is
at issue in the main proceedings although represented as a difference
based on weekly working hours is or is not in reality discrimination based
on the sex of the worker.

15. The reply to the first three questions must therefore be that a
E difference in pay between full-time workers and part-time workers does
not amount to discrimination prohibited by article 119 of the Treaty unless
it is in reality merely an indirect way of reducing the level of pay of part-
time workers on the ground that that group of workers is composed
exclusively or predominantly of women.

F *Fourth question*

16. In the fourth and last question, the national court asks whether
the provisions of article 119 of the Treaty are directly applicable in the
circumstances of this case.

17. As the court has stated in previous decisions (judgment of April
8, 1976, in *Defrenne* v. *Sabena* [1976] I.C.R. 547; judgment of March
27, 1980, in *Macarthys Ltd.* v. *Smith* [1980] 3 W.L.R. 929 and judgment
G of March 11, 1981, in *Worringham* v. *Lloyds Bank Ltd.* [1981] 1 W.L.R.
950), article 119 of the Treaty applies directly to all forms of discrimination which may be identified solely with the aid of criteria of equal
work and equal pay referred to by the article in question, without
national or Community measures being required to define them with
greater precision in order to permit of their application. Among the
H forms of discrimination which may be thus judicially identified, the court
mentioned in particular cases where men and women receive unequal
pay for equal work carried out in the same establishment or service,
public or private.

18. Where the national court is able, using the criteria of equal work
and equal pay, without the operation of Community or national measures,
to establish that the payment of lower hourly rates of remuneration for
part-time work than for full-time work represents discrimination based

on difference of sex the provisions of article 119 of the Treaty apply A
directly to such a situation.

Article 1 *of Council Directive* (75/117/*E.E.C.*)

19. The national court also raises with regard to article 1 of Council
Directive of February 10, 1975 (75/117/E.E.C.) the same questions
of interpretation as those examined above in relation to article 119 of B
the Treaty.

20. As may be seen from the first recital in the preamble the primary
objective of the above-mentioned Directive is to implement the principle
that men and women should receive equal pay which is " contained in
article 119 of the Treaty." For that purpose the fourth recital states
that " it is desirable to reinforce the basic laws by standards aimed at
facilitating the practical application of the principle of equality."   C

21. The provisions of article 1 of that Directive are confined, in the
first paragraph, to restating the principle of equal pay set out in article
119 of the Treaty and specify, in the second paragraph, the conditions
for applying that principle where a job classification system is used for
determining pay.

22. It follows, therefore, that article 1 of Council Directive (75/117/ D
E.E.C.) which is principally designed to facilitate the practical application of the principle of equal pay outlined in article 119 of the Treaty
in no way alters the content or scope of that principle as defined in
the Treaty.

Costs   E

The costs incurred by the Government of the Kingdom of Belgium,
the Government of the United Kingdom of Great Britain and Northern
Ireland and the Commission of the European Communities, which have
submitted observations to the court, are not recoverable. As this case is,
in so far as the parties to the main proceedings are concerned, in the
nature of a step in the proceedings before the national court, the decision
as to costs is a matter for that court.   F

On those grounds, the court, in answer to the questions referred to it
by the Employment Appeal Tribunal by an order dated February 25,
1980, hereby rules:

1. A difference in pay between full-time workers and part-time
   workers does not amount to discrimination prohibited by article
   119 of the Treaty unless it is in reality merely an indirect way of G
   reducing the pay of part-time workers on the ground that that
   group of workers is composed exclusively or predominantly of
   women.

2. Where the national court is able, using the criteria of equal work
   and equal pay, without the operation of Community or national
   measures, to establish that the payment of lower hourly rates of H
   remuneration for part-time work than for full-time work represents
   discrimination based on difference of sex the provisions of article
   119 of the Treaty apply directly to such a situation.

Solicitors: *Mills Curry, Gaskell; Treasury Solicitor.*

H. J.

A

[QUEEN'S BENCH DIVISION]

* REGINA v. LANDS TRIBUNAL,
Ex parte CITY OF LONDON CORPORATION

B
1980 Nov. 10, 11; 18

Judge Newey sitting as a judge of the
Queen's Bench Division

*Lands Tribunal—Case stated by—Interlocutory order—Application
for discovery at hearing of appeal—Dismissal of application—
Refusal of tribunal to state case on determination of application
for discovery—Whether determination final " decision "—Lands
Tribunal Act 1949 (12 & 13 Geo. 6, c. 42), s. 3 (4)*

C
Rating assessments were made by the valuation court in
respect of three public houses in the City of London. The
City of London Corporation, the rating authority for the area,
appealed to the Lands Tribunal against the method of assessment adopted, contending that a different method involving
closer examination of profits of public houses was more appropriate in the City. At the commencement of the hearing of the
D
appeal the corporation applied, under rule 40 of the Lands
Tribunal Rules 1975, for disclosure of certain documents
including records of deliveries of alcohol to the public houses
and the owners' and occupiers' profit and loss accounts. The
application was considered and dismissed. The tribunal
refused the corporation's request to state a case on the
question of discovery for the decision of the Court of Appeal,
pursuant to section 3 (4) of the Lands Tribunal Act 1949,[1] on
E
the ground that it had no jurisdiction to do so, because the
determination of the application was not a final decision within
the meaning of section 3 (4) as it involved only a procedural
matter which arose during the course of proceedings.
On an application by the corporation for judicial review
by way of an order of mandamus requiring the tribunal to
state and sign a case for the decision of the Court of Appeal
under section 3 (4):—
F
Held, granting the application, that section 1 (3) (*e*) of
the Lands Tribunal Act 1949, which provided for the referral
of questions to the Lands Tribunal for determination, conferred jurisdiction on the tribunal to decide not only questions expressly referred to it for determination but also any
interlocutory matter which arose during the course of proceedings and the tribunal, when granting or refusing an
interlocutory application, was making a final decision on
G
that application; that the scope of section 3 (4) was not
limited to decisions bringing the whole reference to an end,
but that the natural and ordinary meaning of " decision " included a decision on an interlocutory matter, and, accordingly,
the tribunal could be required to state a case on the issue of
discovery (post, pp. 990G–H, 991G–H).
Norwich Rating Authority v. *Norwich Assessment Committee* [1941] 2 K.B. 326, D.C. and *Becker* v. *Marion City
Corporation* [1977] A.C. 271, P.C. considered.

H
The following cases are referred to in the judgment:

Atkinson v. *United States of America Government* [1971] A.C. 197;
[1969] 3 W.L.R. 1074; [1969] 3 All E.R. 1317, H.L.(E.).
Becker v. *Marion City Corporation* [1977] A.C. 271; [1976] 2 W.L.R.
728, P.C.

[1] Lands Tribunal Act 1949, s. 3 (4): see post, p. 988A–B.

Magdalen College, Oxford v. *Howard (Valuation Officer)* [1960] 7 R.R.C.   A
    123, C.A.
Norwich Rating Authority v. *Norwich Assessment Committee* [1941]
    2 K.B. 326; [1941] 3 All E.R. 225, D.C.
Science Research Council v. *Nassé* [1980] A.C. 1028; [1979] 3 W.L.R.
    762; [1979] 3 All E.R. 673, H.L.(E.).
Watney Mann Ltd. v. *Langley* [1966] 1 Q.B. 457; [1964] 2 W.L.R. 858;
    [1963] 3 All E.R. 967.   B

No additional cases were cited in argument.

APPLICATION for judicial review.
    The applicant, the City of London Corporation, the rating authority
for the City of London, sought judicial review by way of an order of
mandamus directed to a member of the Lands Tribunal, Mr. J. H.   C
Emlyn Jones, requiring him to state and sign a case for the decision
of the Court of Appeal, pursuant to section 3 (4) of the Lands Tribunal
Act 1949. The respondents to the application were the owners of the
public houses, Watneys London Ltd., Truman Ltd. and Chef & Brewer
Ltd.; the occupiers of the public houses, Goodhews Ltd.; and the valuation officer, R. Burrows. The grounds of the application were that the   D
Lands Tribunal's refusal to state and sign a case upon the ground that
it had no jurisdiction to do so, since it had not given a decision for the
purposes of section 3 (4) of the Lands Tribunal Act 1949, was erroneous
in law.
    The facts are stated in the judgment of Judge Newey.

Bernard Marder Q.C. and *Jeremy Sullivan* for the corporation.   E
Gerald Moriarty Q.C. and *Susan Hamilton* for the owners and occu-
piers of the public houses.
Alan Fletcher for the valuation officer.

Cur. adv. vult.

November 18. JUDGE NEWEY read the following judgment. In 1973   F
entries were made in the rating valuation list for the City of London in
respect of three public houses, known as the Sir Christopher Wren, the
Cock Tavern and the Magogs. Subsequently proposals were made by the
owners and occupiers of the public houses, for reductions in the assessments.
    In 1978 the proposals came before divisions of the London Valuation
Court, when valuations which had been agreed between the valuers acting   G
for the owners and occupiers and the licensed property valuer, acting on
behalf of Mr. R. Burrows, the valuation officer for the City, were put
forward and resulted in orders providing for assessments which were
substantially lower.
    The corporation of the city of London, which is the rating authority
for the city, had not been a party to any of the agreements between
valuers, and it appealed to the Lands Tribunal against all three assess-   H
ments. The assessments had been made in accordance with what is
known as the " direct method " of assessing public houses, described by
Thompson J. in *Watney Mann Ltd.* v. *Langley* [1966] 1 Q.B. 457; and
the gist of the corporation's appeals is that other methods of assessment
involving closer examination of a public house's profits is more appropriate in the city of London. A public house is often comparable with
licensed restaurants and wine bars.

The Weekly Law Reports, June 26, 1981

987

1 W.L.R.   Reg. v. Lands Tribunal, Ex p. London Corpn. (D.C.)   Judge Newey

A   On December 20, 1979, Mr. J. H. Emlyn Jones F.R.I.C.S., a member of the Lands Tribunal, held an informal "pre-trial review" to determine how the appeals should be heard.   Neither at the pre-trial review nor by application to the registrar of the Lands Tribunal under rule 45 (1) of the Lands Tribunal Rules 1975 (S.I. 1975 No. 299), made under section 3 (6) of the Lands Tribunal Act 1949, did the corporation
B apply for disclosure of documents under rule 40 of the Rules of 1975 as amended by the Lands Tribunal (Amendment) Rules 1981 (S.I. 1981 No. 105).   If the corporation had applied to the registrar and had then been refused, the corporation would have had a right of appeal to the president of the tribunal under rule 45 (8).

At the commencement of the hearing of the appeals by Mr. Emlyn Jones, on October 1, 1980, Mr. Bernard Marder applied under rule 40,
C on behalf of the corporation, that the tribunal should require the other parties to disclose certain documents, and it was agreed by all that the application should be dealt with as a preliminary issue.   After reading an affidavit by Mr. E. C. Payne, the valuer advising the corporation on licensed property matters, and hearing argument, Mr. Emlyn Jones adjourned the hearing.   On October 7, 1980, Mr. Emlyn Jones issued a
D document, 15 pages long, refusing to order the production of any of the documents, save for some which the respondents had agreed to produce voluntarily; expressing the opinion that he had no power to state a case at that stage; and refusing a stay of the proceedings.

The documents in respect of which orders for discovery were refused, included the valuations which led to the existing list entries and the owners' and occupiers' records of deliveries of beer, wines and spirits,
E and their profit and loss accounts.

Mr. Emlyn Jones held that the original valuations were irrelevant. He was not prepared to reach a similar conclusion with regard to the other documents; and after quoting Lord Wilberforce in Science Research Council v. Nassé [1980] A.C. 1028, stated that he had a discretion, in the exercise of which he had to weigh the balance of advantage between
F the parties and the degree of relevance.

Mr. Emlyn Jones decided that the profit and loss accounts would not be of any real help to him; that he was not prepared to extend the information which a valuation officer reasonably requires to include profit and loss accounts; and that it would not be in the public interest to require traders to produce such confidential information. Mr. Emlyn Jones expressed willingness to hear further argument as to records of
G deliveries, if, later, detailed examination of return forms showed that answers were incomplete; and with that qualification he dismissed the application.

Mr. Emlyn Jones stated that while he appreciated that the ruling which he had given could be described as a decision, if every time the tribunal gave a ruling, for example, on the admissibility of evidence, an
H appeal arose, the consequences could be that there might be any number of appeals during the same case.   He thought that he had not given a " decision " within the meaning of the Act of 1949, but on a procedural matter arising during the course of the hearing.

The corporation applied without delay to the Divisional Court of the Queen's Bench Division for leave to apply for an order that the Lands Tribunal should state and sign a case for the decision of the Court of Appeal.   Leave to apply was granted with the result that this application

The Weekly Law Reports, June 26, 1981

988

Judge Newey   Reg. v. Lands Tribunal, Ex p. London Corpn. (D.C.)   [1981]

came before me. The corporation also applied to the Divisional Court A
for a stay of proceedings in the Lands Tribunal which was also granted.
The provision in the Lands Tribunal Act 1949 which refers to the
stating of a case is section 3 (4), which, omitting the last part, reads:

"A decision of the Lands Tribunal shall be final: Provided that
any person aggrieved by the decision as being erroneous in point of
law may, within such time as may be limited by rules of court, require B
the tribunal to state and sign a case for the decision of the court . . ."

The time limited by R.S.C., Ord. 61, r. 1 is six weeks.
In order that Mr. Emlyn Jones may be ordered to state a case, it is
necessary therefore, that he should have made a decision which was final
and that that decision should have concerned law and not fact.
Dealing first with the question of what is a decision which is final C
within section 3 (4) of the Act of 1949, all counsel agreed that it had
never previously been considered directly by the courts.
Mr. Marder, for the corporation, however, referred me to three cases,
the first two of which he relied upon as being persuasive, and the third
he sought to distinguish. The first case, *Norwich Rating Authority* v.
Norwich Assessment Committee [1941] 2 K.B. 326 had arisen under the
Rating and Valuation Act 1925. In it the recorder of Norwich had, after D
deciding as a preliminary point of law, that the method of valuation
proposed by the rating authority was unlawful, dismissed its appeal.
On the recorder stating a case for the opinion of the Divisional Court,
the occupier objected on the grounds that the court would not entertain
a case stated by quarter sessions unless the court's decision would finally
dispose of the matter in issue. The occupier argued that the recorder E
should have heard evidence and made an assessment before stating a
case. The Divisional Court held that it had jurisdiction to entertain the
appeal by cases stated. Viscount Caldecote C.J. said, at p. 330, that the
rule for which the occupier contended "was never more than a question
of practice." Tucker J. said, at p. 332, that although the recorder had
come to his decision on the basis that the appellant's proposal was bad
in law, he "nonetheless came to a determination." F
The second case was *Magdalen College, Oxford* v. *Howard (Valuation officer)* (1960) 7 R.R.C. 123, in which the Lands Tribunal, acting as
arbitrator under a reference by consent under section 50 of the Local
Government Act 1948, gave, at the request of the parties, an interim
decision as to the appropriate method of rating colleges and then, on the
application of the valuation officer, stated a case. At the beginning of G
the argument the Court of Appeal raised the question whether an appeal
lay to the court where the tribunal had acted as arbitrator, to which
counsel for the valuation officer replied that the interim decision was a
decision of the Lands Tribunal within section 3 (4) of the Lands Tribunal
Act 1949. Lord Evershed M.R. said, at p. 126, that he would "assume for
the purposes of this judgment that that is so." The Master of the Rolls's
assumption related solely to the court's jurisdiction where the tribunal H
was acting as arbitrator under the Act of 1948; the question of whether
the court had jurisdiction when the decision was "interim" was not
raised.
Mr. Marder's third case, *Atkinson* v. *United States of America Government* [1971] A.C. 197 was concerned with extradition proceedings.
In it the House of Lords decided, inter alia, that section 87 of the
Magistrates' Courts Act 1952, which provides:

The Weekly Law Reports, June 26, 1981

989

1 W.L.R.   Reg. v. Lands Tribunal, Ex p. London Corpn. (D.C.)   Judge Newey

A   " Any person, who . . . is aggrieved by the conviction, order, determination, or other proceeding of the court may question the proceeding on the ground that it is wrong in law . . . by applying to the
justices . . . to state a case . . ."

did not apply to committal proceedings, since they did not lead to a final
decision. Lord Reid said, [1971] A.C. 197, 235:

B   " . . . it frequently happens that a court has to make a decision in the
course of the proceedings—e.g., whether certain evidence is admissible—but it cannot have been intended that the proceedings should
be held up while a case on such a matter is stated and determined
by the superior court."

The basis of the decision was, however, that it was settled law under
C earlier Acts that examining justices had no power to state a case and that
since the Act of 1952 was a consolidation statute there was a strong
presumption that it did not alter the existing law.
          Mr. Marder submitted that even if a decision did not dispose of the
case before the tribunal, but was of an interlocutory nature, it could still
be a final decision. He said that any other construction of section 3 (4)
D could lead to great inconvenience and waste of costs.
          In the present case, if as a result of a case being stated, the opinion
of the Court of Appeal could be obtained, the tribunal and the parties
would know how to proceed. Otherwise the corporation would have to
present its case before the tribunal as best it could and afterwards ask
for a case to be stated. If eventually the Court of Appeal held that the
corporation had been right about the documents, proceedings in the
E Lands Tribunal would have to begin again, possibly before another member of the tribunal.
          Mr. Gerald Moriarty, for the owners and occupiers, said that the
Lands Tribunal's powers in the present case are derived solely from
section 1 (3) (e) of the Act of 1949, which provides that there should be
referred to and determined by the tribunal:

F   " any question on which, but for this provision, an appeal or reference to the county court would or might be made by virtue of section
49, 62 or 87 of the Local Government Act 1948."

He said that only a determination by the tribunal of the question referred
and resulting in the giving of directions within section 77 of the General
Rate Act 1967, could be a final decision within section 3 (4) of the Act
G of 1949.
          Mr. Moriarty conceded, however, that when the president of the
tribunal has heard an appeal from the registrar concerning an interlocutory matter under rule 45 (8), the president can be required to state
a case. Mr. Moriarty submitted that if rulings given during the course
of proceedings before the Lands Tribunal could be the subject of cases
H stated, the result would be likely to be long delays and waste of costs.
He submitted that even if Mr. Emlyn Jones had given a decision, it was
not final; for example, he himself had stated that he would reconsider
disclosure of records of deliveries in certain circumstances.
          Mr. Fletcher, for the valuation officer, adopted Mr. Moriarty's sub-
missions, except that he said that the risk of inconvenience played little
part in his case. He submitted that a decision upon an interlocutory
matter, such as discovery of documents, could not of its nature be a final

decision, because it could always be renewed.   He said that to be final,   A
an order had to decide the rights of the parties.   He said that the words
of section 31 (5) of the Rating and Valuation Act 1925, involved in *Norwich Rating Authority* v. *Norwich Assessment Committee* [1941] 2 K.B.
326 were different from those in section 3 (4) of the Act of 1949.   Mr.
Fletcher cited *Becker* v. *Marion City Corporation* [1977] A.C. 271, in
which the Privy Council, on an appeal from the Supreme Court of South
Australia decided that a decision that a plan did not comply with the   B
requirements of planning legislation, with the result that the appellant
had not been able to have the proposals considered was a final order
entitling her to appeal to the Privy Council without leave.   Mr. Fletcher
said that the corporation was not entitled to have a case stated, but that
if the Lands Tribunal went wrong in law at any stage of its proceedings,
an application for judicial review of its conduct could be made.   Mr.   C
Fletcher further submitted that since section 3 (6) (*c*) of the Act of 1949
expressly provided that rules might apply to the tribunal provisions of the
Arbitration Acts and since rule 38 had applied some of them, including
section 12 of the Arbitration Act 1950, the corporation could apply under
section 12 (6) (*b*) of the Arbitration Act 1950 to the High Court direct
for an order for discovery.   Mr. Fletcher's final submission was that
Parliament had by section 3 (10) of the Act of 1949 expressly preserved   D
to the rule-making body the ability to make rules conferring a right to
require the stating of cases in circumstances in which official arbitrators
could have been required to state them as the result of various statutes
existing prior to 1949.   The power had not been exercised, but it might
be inferred from its existence that Parliament had intended that any
power to state a case under section 3 (4) should be limited and that any   E
alternative power should be conferred by the rules.

In reply Mr. Marder said that if the formula used in section 3 (4)
had been the same as that used in section 31 (5) of the Rating and Valuation Act 1925, namely:

" On the determination of an appeal under this section any party
to the appeal may, if dissatisfied with the decision of the court as   F
being erroneous in point of law, make an application for . . . a case
stated."

it would have been much more difficult for him to have contended that
Mr. Emlyn Jones's decision was final.   Mr. Marder agreed with Mr.
Fletcher that under section 12 of the Arbitration Act 1950, a party to
proceedings before the Lands Tribunal could apply to the High Court   G
for discovery.   He said that if I were against him he would immediately
issue an originating summons and request me to hear it.

I think that section 1 (3) (*e*) of the Act of 1949, when providing that
certain questions should be referred to and determined by the Lands
Tribunal conferred jurisdiction upon it, not merely to decide those express questions, but also others of an interlocutory nature arising during   H
the course of the proceedings.   The fact that rule 45 of the Rules of 1975
made under the Act of 1949 provides a method whereby the registrar may
determine interlocutory applications subject to appeal to the president, does
not take away the power of a member of the tribunal to make such decisions.

A member of the tribunal when granting or refusing an application
made to him is, in my view, making a decision about it, which in ordinary
language can only be described as final.   The fact that it may be open

The Weekly Law Reports, June 26, 1981

991

1 W.L.R.   Reg. v. Lands Tribunal, Ex p. London Corpn. (D.C.)   Judge Newey

A to a party in changed circumstances to make a further application, for example as envisaged by Mr. Emlyn Jones in the present case with regard to records of deliveries, does not prevent the decision upon the application from being final.

If Parliament had intended that section 3 (4) should be limited to decisions bringing the whole reference to an end, I would have expected it to have used a form of words similar to that in section 31 (5) of the

B Rating and Valuation Act 1925, or possibly included in the Act provisions of the type contained in the Planning Acts and in the Highways Acts.

The recorder's decision in *Norwich Rating Authority* v. *Norwich Assessment Committee* [1941] 2 K.B. 326 had in fact determined the proceedings, but I think that Viscount Caldecote C.J.'s words are persuasive

C as indicating the court's willingness to consider interlocutory questions on case stated in suitable circumstances. I have not derived assistance from the *Magdalen College* case, R.R.C. 123, nor from *Atkinson's* case [1971] A.C. 197. The latter was dealing with the construction of a particular statute and with matters very different from those in the present case. In *Becker* v. *Marion City Corporation* [1977] A.C. 271, the decision

D with regard to the plan had disposed of the whole case.

If on a proper construction of section 3 (4) it does not provide a method of avoiding inconvenience, or it gives rise to delays and to expense, the parties must bear the consequences. If, however, the meaning of the section is ambiguous, since Parliament is unlikely to have intended to create hardship, consequences likely to result from alternative constructions may, I think, be taken into account. In my view, to construe

E section 3 (4) as giving a right to require a case to be stated is likely to save inconvenience and costs in most cases. If a party were to make repeated interlocutory applications and repeated requests for cases to be stated, the courts could deal with such conduct by refusing to stay proceedings before the tribunal and by appropriate orders as to costs.

The right of a party to obtain discovery by an order under the Arbitra-

F tion Act 1950 is not, I think, a reason why a case should not be stated under section 3 (4) particularly as an appeal lies in an interlocutory matter, admittedly with leave, from a single judge to the Court of Appeal. I attach no weight to the fact that rules could have provided for cases to be stated in situations where they could have been prior to 1949. Theoretically the rule makers may have thought that there was less need for such provision because a wide construction could be placed on

G section 3 (4).

I think that Mr. Moriarty was right to concede that a party may require the president to state a case in relation to a decision under rule 45, but I think that that right exists more generally.

In my judgment the natural and ordinary meaning of section 3 (4) is that it includes decisions upon interlocutory matters. If it be necessary

H to take into account inconvenience and other considerations to determine the intention of Parliament, I think that they point to the same construction. I find that Mr. Emlyn Jones made a decision which was final.

As to the question of whether the decision related to law, Mr. Moriarty submitted that it did not, and referred in particular to Mr. Emlyn Jones's statement that the profit and loss accounts would be of little help to him. Mr. Fletcher said that the corporation was only seeking the earlier valuation documents from the valuation officer and that Mr. Emlyn Jones's decision that they were not relevant was a decision of fact. Mr. Marder said that Mr. Emlyn Jones's decision contains many decisions upon law.

I have no doubt that while Mr. Emlyn Jones's decision involved some considerations of fact and exercise of discretion, it also involved substantial questions of law, such as those relating to relevance and non-disclosure of documents because of confidentiality.

In the result I make an order requiring the Lands Tribunal to state a case for the Court of Appeal under section 3 (4) of the Lands Tribunal Act 1949.

> *Application granted.*
> *Half applicant's costs to be paid by*
> *valuation officer and half by owners*
> *and occupiers of properties.*

Solicitors: *Stanley F. Heather; C. Cullum Smith; Solicitor of Inland Revenue.*

[Reported by MRS. MARIA FLEISCHMANN, Barrister-at-Law]

[HOUSE OF LORDS]

* COMPANIA FINANCIERA
"SOLEADA" S.A. AND OTHERS . . . . RESPONDENTS

AND

HAMOOR TANKER CORPORATION INC. . . PETITIONERS

1981 June 11   Lord Diplock, Lord Russell of Killowen
                                      and Lord Keith of Kinkel

Petition by the petitioners for leave to appeal from the decision of the Court of Appeal in *Compania Financiera "Soleada" S.A.* v. *Hamoor Tanker Corporation Inc.* [1981] 1 W.L.R. 274.

The Appeal Committee dismissed the petition.

J. A. G.

A

[COURT OF APPEAL]

* McCORMICK *v.* HORSEPOWER LTD.

1981 March 5, 6;
     April 13

Lawton, Templeman and
O'Connor L.JJ.

B

*Employment—Unfair dismissal—Strike—Boilermakers on strike
for more pay—Fitter refusing to cross picket line—Fitter
returning to work before end of strike but subsequently dismissed for redundancy—Boilermaker on strike dismissed—
Complaint of unfair dismissal—Whether fitter "relevant employee"—Employment Protection (Consolidation) Act 1978
(c. 44), s. 62 (2) (4)*

C

The employee was one of a number of boilermakers who
went on strike for more pay. B, who was employed in a
different department which was not involved in the strike,
did not wish to cross the picket line and stayed away from
work although at no time did he tell the employers that he
was on strike. He returned to work during the strike and
crossed the picket line daily before being dismissed for redundancy. At about the same time as B was dismissed, the
employee and other boilermakers, who were still on strike,
were dismissed. On the employee's complaint of unfair dismissal, an industrial tribunal considered whether they had
jurisdiction to hear the case pursuant to section 62 of the
Employment Protection (Consolidation) Act 1978.[1] They
found, by a majority, that, since there was no common
understanding between B and the employers not to continue
to work, B was not in dispute with the employers and was
not on strike; and, therefore, as he was not a "relevant
employee," they had no jurisdiction to hear the employee's
complaint.

On the employee's appeal, the Employment Appeal
Tribunal held that B was taking part in the strike and, therefore, he was a "relevant employee" within the meaning of
section 62 (2) of the Act; and that, although B had been
dismissed on the ground of redundancy after he had returned
to work, at the time of the hearing before the industrial
tribunal he was a relevant employee who had been dismissed
and, therefore, the industrial tribunal had no jurisdiction to
hear the employee's complaint.

On the appeal by the employee: —

Held, dismissing the appeal, that, giving the ordinary
meaning to the wording of section 62 of the Employment
Protection (Consolidation) Act 1978, there was no requirement that a relevant employee had to be dismissed while he
was taking part in the strike; that under section 62 (2) there
was no jurisdiction to hear a complaint of unfair dismissal
by an employee, who had been dismissed while on strike, if
it was shown at the time of the hearing before the industrial
tribunal that all other employees who had taken part in the
strike had been dismissed; and that, accordingly, even if B
had taken some part in the strike and was therefore a relevant
employee, the industrial tribunal had no jurisdiction to hear
the complaint because the employee had failed to show that
not all relevant employees had been dismissed (post, pp.
996c–e, 997d–f, 998a–e, 999b–c).

Stock v. *Frank Jones (Tipton) Ltd.* [1978] 1 W.L.R. 231,
H.L.(E.) applied.

D

E

F

G

H

---

[1] Employment Protection (Consolidation) Act 1978, s. 62: see post, p. 996a–b.

Held, further, that, before an employee could be a relevant **A**
employee within the meaning of section 62, he had to have
taken part in the same strike as the complainant employee;
that B in deciding not to cross the picket line was neither
acting in concert with the boilermakers nor with any one else
and, therefore, he was not taking part in a strike and could
not be a relevant employee for the purposes of the section
(post, pp. 997F—998A, F, 999A–B).

Decision of the Employment Appeal Tribunal [1980] I.C.R. **B**
278 affirmed in part.

The following case is referred to in the judgment of Templeman L.J.:

Stock v. *Frank Jones (Tipton) Ltd.* [1978] 1 W.L.R. 231; [1978] I.C.R.
347; [1978] 1 All E.R. 948, H.L.(E.).

The following additional cases were cited in argument: **C**

Beswick v. *Beswick* [1968] A.C. 58; [1967] 3 W.L.R. 932; [1967] 2
All E.R. 1197, H.L.(E.).

Heath v. *J. F. Longman (Meat Salesmen) Ltd.* [1973] I.C.R. 407; [1973]
2 All E.R. 1228, N.I.R.C.

Wimpey (George) & Co. Ltd. v. *British Overseas Airways Corporation*
[1955] A.C. 169; [1954] 3 W.L.R. 932; [1954] 3 All E.R. 661, **D**
H.L.(E.).

APPEAL from the Employment Appeal Tribunal.

The employee, James McCormick, appealed from a decision of the
industrial tribunal on February 20, 1979, that they had no jurisdiction to
hear his complaint of unfair dismissal against the employers, Horsepower
Ltd., on the ground that the industrial tribunal had erred in the inter- **E**
pretation of section 62 of the Employment Protection (Consolidation)
Act 1978. The appeal tribunal dismissed the appeal.

By a notice of appeal dated February 8, 1980, the employee appealed
on the grounds (i) that the appeal tribunal misconstrued the section by
holding that the date at which to ascertain whether a " relevant employee "
had been dismissed was the date of hearing before the industrial tribunal;
(ii) that the correct date at which to ascertain whether a "relevant **F**
employee " was the last date before the employee ceased to participate in
the material strike; and (iii) that, alternatively, the correct date was the
date of the employee's own dismissal and, accordingly, the appeal tribunal
erred in law in holding that the evidence and/or the findings of the
industrial tribunal established that the dismissal of the material " relevant
employee " had preceded the date of the employee's dismissal.

The facts are stated in the judgment of Templeman L.J. **G**

David Turner-Samuels Q.C. and *Stephen Sedley* for the employee.
Alan Pardoe for the employers.

Cur. adv. vult.

H

April 13. The following judgments were read.

TEMPLEMAN L.J. read the first judgment. This appeal raises two
problems in connection with section 62 of the Employment Protection (Consolidation) Act 1978, which debars an industrial tribunal from determining
whether a dismissed striker has been unfairly dismissed if all the strikers
have been dismissed. The first problem is whether the jurisdiction of the

A tribunal is ousted if a striker resumes his employment in the course of the strike but is dismissed before an application is made by another dismissed striker to the tribunal. The second problem is whether in the events which happened in the present case an employee who was not one of the original strikers took part in the strike when he refused to cross the strikers' picket lines.

B Section 62 provides that where an employee who claims that he has been unfairly dismissed by his employers was at the time of his dismissal taking part in a strike, an industrial tribunal shall not determine whether the dismissal was fair or unfair unless it is shown that one or more of the employees of the same employer who took part in the strike have not been dismissed.

   In the present case the employers, the respondents Horsepower Ltd.,
C employed boilermakers and engineers represented by different unions. On October 2, 1978, the boilermakers, who included the appellant employee, went on strike. The engineers took no industrial action. One of the engineers, a Mr. Brazier, was on holiday when the boilermakers began their strike. When Mr. Brazier returned from holiday on October 9, 1978, he declined to cross the boilermakers' picket lines and was absent from work
D until November 13, 1978, when he crossed the picket lines and resumed work for the employers. Between November 21, 1978, and December 5, 1978, the employers dismissed all the striking boilermakers, including the employee, Mr. McCormick. On November 27, 1978, the employers dismissed Mr. Brazier on the ground of redundancy. The employee applied to the industrial tribunal on December 7, 1978, claiming that he had been unfairly dismissed. The employers replied that the tribunal could not
E determine whether the employee had been unfairly dismissed because section 62 applied.

   The employee's application came before the industrial tribunal on February 20, 1979. The employers argued that Mr. Brazier had not taken part in the boilermakers' strike and, even if he had, he had been dismissed and all the strikers had been dismissed, so that the employee's claim was
F barred by section 62. The employee contended that Mr. Brazier had taken part in the boilermakers' strike, that he had not been dismissed while he was on strike and that all the other strikers, including the employee, who had been dismissed while they were on strike, were not barred by section 62 and were entitled to require the industrial tribunal to determine whether in all the circumstances they had been unfairly dismissed within the meaning of the Act.

G The industrial tribunal, by a majority, decided that Mr. Brazier had not taken part in the boilermakers' strike and that section 62 therefore barred the employee's claim.

   The Employment Appeal Tribunal (Talbot J., Mr. Goff and Mr. Rogers) decided that Mr. Brazier had been on strike but, since Mr. Brazier and all the other strikers had been dismissed by the time the employee's application
H came before the tribunal, section 62 barred the tribunal from determining whether the employee had been unfairly dismissed.

   The employee appeals to this court repeating that Mr. Brazier had taken part in the strike and had not been dismissed while he was on strike and arguing that section 62 does not debar the industrial tribunal unless each and every striker is dismissed at a time when he is on strike.

   The employers contend that Mr. Brazier did not take part in the strike and alternatively that the employee's claim was barred because all

the strikers and Mr. Brazier had been dismissed before the contrary could A
be shown to the tribunal.

Section 62, provides, inter alia:

"(1) . . . in relation to an employee who claims that he has been
unfairly dismissed by his employer where at the date of dismissal
. . . (b) the employee was taking part in a strike . . . (2) . . . an industrial
tribunal shall not determine whether the dismissal was fair or unfair B
unless it is shown—(a) that one or more relevant employees of the same
employer have not been dismissed, . . . (4) . . . (b) ' relevant employees '
means— . . . (ii) in relation to a strike . . . employees who took part
in it . . ."

The employee was at the time of his dismissal taking part in a strike.
If Mr. Brazier was one of the " relevant employees " nevertheless it was C
shown to the tribunal that all the relevant employees had been dismissed.

On behalf of the employee, Mr. Turner-Samuels argued that since
section 62 deals with a claim for unfair dismissal by a striker who was on
strike "at the time of his dismissal" it must be implied as a matter of
construction that a claim by such a striker for unfair dismissal should be
determined by the tribunal unless " it is shown " to the tribunal that " one D
or more relevant employees of the same employer have not been dismissed "
while they were on strike at the times of their respective dismissals.
Mr. Brazier had been dismissed, but not whilst he was on strike.

In my judgment, this construction is inadmissible because it limits
the apparent ambit and alters the ordinary meaning of the words used in
section 62 by the addition of a non-existent requirement that all the
relevant employees shall have been dismissed while they were on strike. E

Mr. Turner-Samuels pointed out that the object of section 62, in
the words of Viscount Dilhorne in Stock v. Frank Jones (Tipton) Ltd.
[1978] 1 W.L.R. 231, 234:

" . . . was to prevent victimisation by an employer of persons who
took part in a strike or other industrial action. The dismissal of all
who took part in such action was not to be regarded as unfair, but dis- F
crimination between those who took part either by not dismissing
some of those who took part or by re-engaging some, but not the
claimant for compensation, of those who had been dismissed rendered
the dismissal unfair if it was for an inadmissible reason."

The speech of Viscount Dilhorne was directed toward the provisions of
legislation which has been repealed and replaced by the Act of 1978, with G
some amendments, but that part of Viscount Dilhorne's speech upon which
Mr. Turner-Samuels relies applies equally to the Act of 1978.

If there is a strike and there comes a time when some strikers are
willing to resume work on terms which they find acceptable but other
strikers reject those terms and remain out on strike, the employer is not
guilty of discrimination if he allows those who wish to resume work to H
do so. The employer will be guilty of discrimination if he subsequently
dismisses those strikers who remain out, without dismissing the strikers
who have resumed employment, and it will then be for the tribunal to
determine whether the dismissed strikers have been unfairly dismissed.
The dismissals of strikers and employees may well take place on different
dates and section 62 fixes the date of the hearing before the industrial
tribunal as the date upon which discrimination must be shown by demon-

A strating that some strikers have been dismissed while others have not been dismissed.

It is said that if the date for demonstrating discrimination is the date of the hearing before the industrial tribunal there will be anomalies and uncertainties. I do not agree. In the first place an employer will not escape from section 62 if he has been guilty of discrimination, which can be demonstrated to the tribunal by reference to the facts existing on that date.

B In the second place, if all that the employer has done is to allow some strikers to resume work on terms offered to all strikers, it is unlikely that the employer will be willing to dismiss the employees who have rejoined before the date of the hearing before the tribunal in order to rely on section 62. The employer is much more likely to retain those employees who have rejoined and to argue that those strikers who stayed

C out and were ultimately dismissed were not unfairly dismissed. In the third place, the procedure for making claims for unfair dismissal will prevent uncertainty in practice. An applicant to the tribunal will serve his complaint of unfair dismissal. The employer must then determine whether to resist the claim and if so whether the employer wishes to rely on section 62 or wishes to contend that the dismissal was a fair dismissal.

D If the employer wishes to rely on section 62 he will make this clear in his reply to the complaint and he will make sure that all strikers have been dismissed before the date of the hearing before the tribunal.

In *Stock* v. *Frank Jones (Tipton) Ltd.* [1978] 1 W.L.R. 231 the House of Lords reaffirmed the principle that, if the words used by Parliament are plain, the circumstances in which they can be departed from by the courts are severely limited. In the present case it was not shown to the

E tribunal, as expressly required by the plain words of section 62, that " one or more . . . employees of the same employer " who took part in the boilermakers' strike " have not been dismissed." In my judgment, that concludes the matter so far as this court is concerned. In the present case no possible injustice can be shown because when Mr. Brazier changed his mind and decided to cross the picket line the employers were not guilty

F of discrimination or strike-breaking or any other unfair industrial action.

This appeal must accordingly fail and it is strictly unnecessary to determine whether Mr. Brazier was a relevant employee. For my part, I do not consider that Mr. Brazier was a relevant employee because, although he may be said to have gone on strike, he did not take part in the same strike as the employee. Section 62 requires that the employee and all relevant employees shall have taken part in the same strike. The

G boilermakers went on strike and agreed or were instructed to come out together and they were under a mutual obligation to stay out together and go back together. Mr. Brazier did not become under any obligation to come out or stay out with the boilermakers. Mr. Brazier did not take part in any sympathetic strike by the engineers or any other body of persons because there was no sympathetic strike. Mr. Brazier did not agree with

H any other person or become under any obligation to come out or stay out with the boilermakers, the engineers or any other person. Mr. Brazier was an individual who voluntarily decided not to work on October 9, 1978, because the boilermakers were on strike and voluntarily decided to resume work on November 13, 1978, although the boilermakers were still on strike. Mr. Brazier did not take part in the boilermakers' strike and for the purposes of section 62 he was an irrelevancy. The employers would not have been guilty of discrimination or victimisation between fellow

strikers taking part in the same strike if, having allowed Mr. Brazier to A
resume work on November 13, 1978, they had continued to employ him
until after the date of the hearing before the industrial tribunal, having
dismissed all the strikers who took part in the boilermakers' strike.

For these reasons I would dismiss the appeal.

O'CONNOR L.J. I agree with Templeman L.J. that this appeal should B
be dismissed. Like him, I can find no ground for reading into the clear
words of section 62 (2) (a) of the Act of 1978 the additional words " while
on strike " as contended for by the employee. I have had more difficulty
in concluding that the time for deciding whether a relevant employee has
not been dismissed is the time of the hearing before the industrial tribunal.

It will be seen that section 62 (1) provides, " The provisions of this
section shall have effect in relation to an employee who claims that he has C
been unfairly dismissed by his employer . . ." Subsection (2) provides,
" In such a case an industrial tribunal shall not determine . . ." That is
in the case of " an employee who claims that he has been unfairly dismissed." An employee becomes " an employee who claims " when he
notifies the claim to the employer. This would appear to point to the time
of making the claim as the time when it must be shown that " one or more D
relevant employees . . . have not been dismissed." Such a construction
would avoid the anomaly created by taking the time of the hearing, namely,
that it enables an employer to deprive the industrial tribunal of jurisdiction
after a claim is made, indeed at any time up to the hearing of the complaint,
by dismissing any strikers who have not been dismissed.

However, the time when " it is shown " to the industrial tribunal must
be the same for both section 62 (2) (a) and (b). Paragraph (b) reads E
" unless it is shown—. . . (b) that one or more such employees have been
offered re-engagement."

The anomalies that would be created by taking the time when a claim
is made are quite unacceptable. If all strikers were not dismissed at the
same time but at different times during the strike, as happened in this case,
then if the first dismissed made a claim at once there would be jurisdiction F
but not for the last. The re-engagement provision would be wholly
uncertain in its incidence.

For these reasons I agree that the time must be the time of the hearing.
Lastly, I agree with Templeman L.J. that Mr. Brazier was not a relevant
employee.

LAWTON L.J. The employee, as a boilermaker who had been on strike, G
was not entitled to have an industrial tribunal determine whether his dismissal by his employers was unfair unless it was shown that Mr. Brazier,
who was employed by the same employers as an engineer, was a relevant
employee within the meaning of section 62 (2) (a) and (4) (b) of the Act
of 1978. He was not a relevant employee unless he took part in the same
strike as the employee. The statutory words " who took part in it " (that H
is, the strike) mean giving help by acting in concert with each other and
in withdrawing their labour for a common purpose or pursuant to a dispute which they or a majority of them or their union have with their
employers and staying away from work as long as the strike lasts. Some
help by standing on picket lines or by doing organising work in committee
rooms. Evidence of Mr. Brazier's refusal to cross the boilermakers'
picket lines even though, as the industrial tribunal found, his refusal was

A not brought about by fear, was not in my judgment enough to prove that he was taking part in the boilermakers' strike. He was not shown to have had a common purpose with them or any interest in their dispute with their employers. He was not acting in concert with them as was shown by the fact that he returned to his work on November 13, 1978, whilst they were still on strike. In my judgment there was evidence upon which the indus-
B trial tribunal could find, as it did, that he was not taking part in the strike and in consequence was not a relevant employee.

Even if Mr. Brazier had been such an employee, he had been dismissed by the relevant time which I adjudge to be when the industrial tribunal started to hear the employee's application. There was no jurisdiction to determine whether his dismissal had been fair or unfair unless it was shown that a relevant employee had not been dismissed. The showing
C had to be to the industrial tribunal and without a showing there was no jurisdiction. The words " have not been dismissed " must relate to a period before the time when the showing is done. There are no statutory words to indicate how long before or whether the dismissal should have been for any reason connected with or relevant to the strike. The meaning of the words is plain and must be applied by the courts even though results might follow which some, perhaps many, may consider undesirable. In my
D opinion, undesirable results may follow from the application of the plain meaning. For example, an employer who had enticed back to work one or more strikers could defeat claims for unfair dismissal by the other strikers by dismissing those he had taken back a day or so before the hearings. In such a case he might have to face damages for wrongful dismissal but in industry such damages would probably be small compared
E to what might be awarded by way of compensation for unfair dismissal. This, however, is my opinion and it remains an opinion even if others may share it. Parliament, for all I know, may have weighed these consequences against others which they thought beneficial for good labour relations and fairness to workers. The only safe and correct way of construing statutes is to apply the plain meaning of the words.

F   I too would dismiss the appeal.

> *Appeal dismissed.*
> *Legal aid taxation of employee's costs.*
> *Leave to appeal refused.*

Solicitors: *Seifert, Sedley & Co. for Casson & Co., Salford; Barlow,*
G *Lyde & Gilbert.*

A. R.

H

A

[COURT OF APPEAL]

* REGINA v. HOLT AND ANOTHER

1981 March 3; 13   Griffiths L.J., Lawson and Balcombe JJ.

B

Crime—Theft—Evading liability by deception—Diners in restaurant falsely claiming to have put money on table in payment of bill—Whether attempt to induce creditor to " forgo payment" with intent to make permanent default—Theft Act 1968 (c. 31), s. 2 (1)

The Theft Act 1978 provides by section 2:

C

" (1) . . . where a person by any deception—(*a*) dishonestly secures the remission of the whole or part of any existing liability to make a payment, whether his own liability or another's; or (*b*) with intent to make permanent default in whole or in part on any existing liability to make a payment, or with intent to let another do so, dishonestly induces the creditor or any person claiming payment on behalf of the creditor to wait for payment . . . or to forgo payment; or (*c*) dishonestly obtains any exemption from or abatement of liability to make a payment; he shall be guilty of an offence."

D

The defendants, while eating in a restaurant, planned to evade paying for their meals by pretending that a waitress had removed a £5 note which they had placed on the table. An off-duty police officer, also eating there, overheard them. When they were presented with their bill for £3·65 they advanced this deception to the manager and declined to pay. The police officer prevented them from leaving the restaurant and they were arrested and charged with attempting to evade liability by deception. The particulars of the offence stated that the defendants attempted to induce the creditor's agent " . . . to forgo payment of £3·65 by falsely representing that payment had been made by them to another servant of the [creditor]." At the close of the prosecution case it was submitted that the offence should have been charged under section 2 (1) (*a*) of the Theft Act 1978 instead of under section 2 (1) (*b*), since, had the attempt succeeded, liability to pay would have been " remitted " and not merely " forgone." The judge rejected the submission and ruled that the charge fitted the case put forward by the prosecution. The defendants were convicted.

E

F

On the defendants' applications for leave to appeal against conviction:—

Held, allowing the applications but dismissing the appeals, that, although there were substantial differences in the elements of the three offences defined in section 2 (1) they had common features in the use of deception to a creditor in relation to a liability, in dishonesty in the use of deception and in the use of deception to gain some advantage in time or money; that the relevant elements of the offence defined by section 2 (1) (*b*) were, first, and unique to paragraph (*b*), the intent to make permanent default on the whole or part of an existing liability, secondly, the use of deception and, thirdly, dishonest practice of the deception to induce the creditor to forgo payment; that, accordingly, since the evidence showed that the conduct of the defendants constituted an attempt to evade liability by deception and the jury concluded that it was motivated by the intent to make permanent default on their liability, all the elements needed to establish an attempt to commit the offence were present and the defendants had been rightly convicted as charged.

G

H

A   No cases are referred to in the judgment or were cited in argument.

APPLICATIONS for leave to appeal against conviction.

On July 15, 1980, at Liverpool Crown Court (Judge J. E. Jones) the
defendants, Victor Reginald Holt and Julian Dana Lee, were charged with
attempting to evade liability by deception, the particulars of the offence
being that they " by deception with intent to make permanent default on
B   an existing liability did attempt to induce Philip Parkinson, servant of
Pizzaland Restaurants Ltd., to forgo payment of £3.65 by falsely representing that payment had been made by them to another servant of the said
Pizzaland Restaurants Ltd." At the close of the case for the Crown a
submission was made in the absence of the jury that the count of the
indictment charged an attempt to commit an offence contrary to section
C   2 (1) (b) of the Theft Act 1978 when it should have charged an attempt to
commit an offence contrary to section 2 (1) (a) of the Act of 1978.   The
judge ruled that the charge fitted the case put forward by the prosecution.
On July 16, 1980, the defendants were convicted.   They applied for leave
to appeal against conviction on the grounds that (1) the judge was wrong in
law in refusing to withdraw the count from the jury at the close of the
prosecution case; and (2) the judge failed to give the jury any direction on
D   the standard of proof required before they could convict the defendants.

On March 3, 1981, Griffiths L.J. announced that the applications would
be granted, the appeals would be dismissed and that the court would give
its reasons in writing at a later date.

The facts are stated in the judgment.

E   P.C. Reid and Brian Pryor (assigned by the Registrar of Criminal
Appeals) for the defendants.
John Leach for the Crown.

Cur. adv. vult.

March 13.   LAWSON J. read the following judgment of the court.   Victor
F   Reginald Holt and Julian Dana Lee apply to the full court for leave to
appeal against their convictions at Liverpool Crown Court, on July 16, 1980,
of attempting, contrary to the common law, to evade liability by deception,
that is to say, an attempt to commit an offence contrary to section 2 (1) of
the Theft Act 1978.   This court granted leave to appeal and treated the
hearing of the application as the hearing of the appeal.

The charge upon which they were convicted was as follows.   The
G   statement of the offence was attempted evasion of liability by deception,
contrary to common law.   The particulars of the offence were that the
defendants, on December 9, 1979, by deception with intent to make
permanent default on an existing liability, did attempt to induce Philip
Parkinson, servant of Pizzaland Restaurants Ltd., to forgo payment of
£3·65 by falsely representing that payment had been made by them to
H   another servant of the said Pizzaland Restaurants Ltd.

From the use of the expressions " with intent to make permanent
default " and " to induce [the creditor's agent] to forgo payment," it is
clear that the attempt charged was one to commit the offence defined by
section 2 (1) (b) of the Act of 1978.

The facts of the case were that in the evening of December 9, 1979,
the defendants consumed meals costing £3·65 in the Pizzaland Restaurant
in Southport.   There was a police officer off-duty also having a meal in the

restaurant and he overheard the defendants planning to evade payment for   A
their meals by the device of pretending that a waitress had removed a
£5 note which they had placed on the table. When presented with their bill,
the defendants advanced this deception and declined payment. The police
officer concerned prevented them from leaving the restaurant and they
were shortly afterwards arrested and charged.

At the close of the prosecution case in the Crown Court, Mr. Reid,
who has also conducted this appeal, made a submission which was over-   B
ruled, the main point of which was that assuming the facts as we have
recounted them to be correct, the attempt to evade thus emerging was
an attempt to commit an offence not under section 2 (1) (b) as charged but
under section 2 (1) (a) of the Act of 1978 since, he submitted, had the
attempt succeeded, the defendants' liability to pay for their meals would
have been " remitted " and not just " forgone," to use the contrasting   C
terms contained in the respective subsections.

Mr. Reid further developed his submission before us. As we understand
it, he submits that the vital differences between the two offences defined
in the first two paragraphs of section 2 (1) of the Act of 1978 are that
" remission " involves that, first, the creditor who " remits " the debtor's
existing liability must communicate his decision to the debtor and, secondly,   D
the legal consequence of the " remission " is to extinguish the debt,
whereas the " forgoing of an existing liability," to use the words of
section 2 (1) (b), need not be communicated to the debtor and has not the
consequence in law of extinguishing such liability. We find great difficulty
in introducing these concepts into the construction of the subsection. We
will later return to the matter.

Mr. Reid further submitted that the effect of section 2 (1) of the Act of   E
1978 was to create three different offences but conceded that there could be
situations in which the conduct of the debtor or his agent could fall under
more than one of the three paragraphs of section 2 (1).

The elements of the offence defined by section 2 (1) (b) of the Act of
1978 relevant to the present case are clearly these: first, the defendant must
be proved to have the intent to make permanent default on the whole or   F
part of an existing liability. This element is unique to section 2 (1) (b); it has
no application to the offences defined in section 2 (1) (a) or (c). Secondly,
given such intent, he must use deception. Thirdly, his deception must be
practised dishonestly to induce the creditor to forgo payment.

It must always be remembered that in the present case, whatever offence
was being attempted, the attempt failed. The creditor was not induced by
the dishonest deception and did not forgo payment. It is clear on the   G
evidence that the defendants' conduct constituted an attempt to evade
liability by deception, and the jury, who were properly directed, clearly
concluded that the defendants' conduct was motivated by the intent to
make permanent default on their supper bill. Thus, all the elements needed
to enable an attempt to commit the offence defined in section 2 (1) (b) were
found to be present, so that the defendants were rightly convicted as   H
charged.

Reverting to the construction of section 2 (1) of the Act of 1978, as to
which the commentators are not at one, we are not sure whether the choice
of expressions describing the consequences of deception employed in each
of its paragraphs, namely, in paragraph (a) " secures the remission of . . .
an existing liability," in paragraph (b) " induces the creditor . . . to forgo
payment " and in paragraph (c) " obtains any exemption from . . . liability "

A are simply different ways of describing the same end result or represent conceptual differences.

   Whilst it is plain that there are substantial differences in the elements of the three offences defined in section 2 (1), they show these common features: first, the use of deception to a creditor in relation to a liability, secondly, dishonesty in the use of deception, and thirdly, the use of deception to gain some advantage in time or money. Thus the differences

B between the offences relate principally to the different situations in which the debtor-creditor relationship has arisen.

   The practical difficulty which Mr. Reid's submissions failed to confront is strikingly illustrated by cases of attempting to commit an offence under section 2 (1) (a) or section 2 (1) (b). If, as he submits, section 2 (1) (a) requires communication of remission to the debtor, whereas section 2 (1) (b)

C does not require communication of the " forgoing of payment " but, as the case is mere attempt, the matter does not *end* in remission of liability or forgoing of payment, then the prosecution would be in a dilemma since it would either be impossible to charge such an attempt or the prosecution would be obliged to charge attempts in the alternative in which case, since any attempt failed, it would be quite uncertain which of the alternatives

D it was.

   These appeals are accordingly dismissed.

Applications for leave to appeal granted.
Appeals dismissed.

E Solicitor: *R. H. Nicholson, Liverpool.*

[Reported by MISS EIRA CARYL-THOMAS, Barrister-at-Law]

[PRIVY COUNCIL]

F
* CALTEX OIL (AUSTRALIA) PTY. LTD.   .   .   APPELLANT

AND

PAUL LESLIE FEENAN AND OTHERS   .   .   .   RESPONDENTS

[APPEAL FROM THE SUPREME COURT OF NEW SOUTH WALES COURT OF APPEAL]

G
1981 Feb. 2;   Lord Diplock, Lord Edmund-Davies,
      March 5   Lord Keith of Kinkel, Lord Scarman
                                     and Sir John Megaw

Australia—New South Wales—Contract—Unfair contract—Indus-
trial Commission declaring voil solus agreement granting licence
to operate motor service station—Whether jurisdiction—
H *Whether contract " whereby a person performs work in any*
industry "—Industrial Arbitration Act 1940 (1980 reprint),
s. 88F (1)

   Section 88F (1) of the Industrial Arbitration Act 1940 provides:
   " The commission may make an order or award declaring void . . . either ab initio or from some other time any contract . . . whereby a person performs work in any industry. . ."

In 1975 an oil company, representing that its motor service   A
station was capable of making an annual profit of about
$24,000, entered into an agreement with the defendants which
provided that in return for a monthly sum to be paid by the
defendants to the company, the company would grant to the
defendants the goodwill of the station and a licence to conduct
the business of supplying petroleum products and other services
on the premises during all lawful hours.   Under the contract
all petroleum products sold at the service station were to be   B
obtained from the oil company. The defendants operated the
station for five months during which time it made a profit at
a rate substantially below that represented by the company.
The defendants gave up the station and in 1979 brought proceedings against the company in the Industrial Commission.
The Industrial Commission made an order under section 88F
(1) of the Industrial Arbitration Act 1940 declaring the agreement void ab initio and ordering the oil company to pay   C
various sums to the defendants. The oil company applied to
the Court of Appeal for a declaration that the Industrial
Commission's order was void for want of jurisdiction in that
the agreement was not one whereby the defendants had been
performing work in industry and for an injunction restraining
the defendants from enforcing the order.   The Court of Appeal
dismissed the application.

On the oil company's appeal to the Judicial Committee: —   D
Held, dismissing the appeal, that since on a proper construction of section 88F (1) of the Industrial Arbitration Act
1940 a person performed work in industry who did anything
which a person employed in the same occupation for hire or
reward might be obliged to do under a contract of employment and a contract " whereby " a person performed such
work was one in consequence of, or in fulfilment of which, he
did it, in operating the service station the defendants had, on   E
the facts, been performing work in industry and the agreement
was a contract whereby they did so; and that, accordingly,
the agreement fell within the ambit of section 88F (1) and the
Industrial Commission had had jurisdiction to make the order
complained of.

Decision of the Supreme Court of New South Wales Court
of Appeal [1980] 1 N.S.W.L.R. 724 affirmed.

F

The following case is referred to in the judgment of their Lordships:

Stevenson v. *Barham* (1977) 136 C.L.R. 190.

The following additional cases were cited in argument:

Becker and Harry M. Miller Attractions Pty. Ltd., In re [1972] A.R.
(N.S.W.) 298.   G

*Haulage Services (V.G.) Pty. Ltd., Ex parte; In re the Industrial Com-
mission of New South Wales* [1972] 2 N.S.W.L.R. 81.

Manning v. *Thompson* [1979] 1 N.S.W.L.R. 384, P.C.

APPEAL (No 52 of 1980) by Caltex Oil (Australia) Pty. Ltd. with
leave of the Supreme Court of New South Wales Court of Appeal from
an order (July 11, 1980) of that court (Moffitt P., Hope and Hutley JJ.A.)   H
dismissing the oil company's application by a summons directed to Paul
Leslie Feenan, Marie Therese Feenan and the Industrial Commission of
New South Wales as defendants for a declaration that a judgment and
order of Macken J. dated September 3, 1979, in proceedings No. 200 in
the Industrial Commission made in favour of Paul and Marie Feenan
were void and of no effect on the ground that they had been made
without jurisdiction and for an injunction restraining the defendants

A   from enforcing the order. The Industrial Commission did not appear before the Judicial Committee.

In proceedings No. 200 Paul and Marie Feenan had applied to the Industrial Commission to avoid a licence agreement made between themselves and the oil company for the operation by them of the oil company's service station at Hexham, Newcastle, New South Wales. In B those proceedings Macken J. ordered (1) that the licence agreement was void in whole and ab initio; and (2) that the oil company should pay $3,600 to Paul and Marie Feenan, $8,000 to Paul Feenan and $6,000 to Marie Feenan.

The facts are stated in the judgment.

C   *T. R. Morling Q. C.* and *R. J. Peterson* (both of the New South Wales Bar) for the oil company

J. S. Coombs Q.C., T. J. Thomas and *H. J. Mater* (all of the New South Wales Bar) for the defendants Paul and Marie Feenan.

Cur. adv. vult.

D   March 5. The judgment of their Lordships was delivered by LORD DIPLOCK.

This is an appeal from an order of the Court of Appeal of New South Wales dismissing an application by the appellant (" Caltex ") for a declaration that an order that the Industrial Commission of New South Wales had purported to make under section 88F of the Industrial Arbitration Act 1940 was made without jurisdiction, and for an injunc-E tion restraining the respondents (" the Feenans ") from enforcing it.

The order of the Industrial Commission, which was made by Macken J. related to an agreement of September 26, 1975 (" the solus contract "), between Caltex and the Feenans setting out the terms on which the Feenans were to operate a service station for the sale of petroleum products supplied exclusively by Caltex at premises at Hexham owned by F Caltex. His Honour's order declared that agreement void ab initio and ordered Caltex to pay to the Feenans various sums of money totalling $17,600.

Section 88F of the Industrial Arbitration Act 1940 is in the following terms:

"(1) The commission may make an order or award declaring void in whole or in part or varying in whole or in part and either G ab initio or from some other time any contract or arrangement or any condition or collateral arrangement relating thereto whereby a person performs work in any industry on the grounds that the contract or arrangement or any condition or collateral arrangement relating thereto—(a) is unfair, or (b) is harsh or unconscionable, or (c) is against the public interest. Without limiting the generality of the words 'public interest' regard shall be had in considering H the question of public interest to the effect such a contract or a series of such contracts has had or may have on any system of apprenticeship and other methods of providing a sufficient and trained labour force, or (d) provides or has provided a total remuneration less than a person performing the work would have received as an employee performing such work, or (e) was designed to or does avoid the provisions of an award, industrial agreement, agreement

registered under Part VIIIA or contract determination. (2) The A
commission, in making an order or award pursuant to subsection
(1), may make such an order as to the payment of money in connection with any contract, arrangement, condition or collateral
arrangement declared void, in whole or in part, or varied in whole
or in part, as may appear to the commission to be just in the
circumstances of the case."

B

Although the order of the Industrial Commission that is appealed against
referred not only to the solus contract, which is in writing, but also to
collateral arrangements between the parties to the contract, the facts
found by Macken J. do not disclose any agreement, understanding or
course of conduct which conflicted with or extended beyond the terms
of the written contract; and the appeal to their Lordships has been
argued on the basis that the terms that regulated the relationship C
between Caltex and the Feenans are to be found in the solus contract
alone.

Macken J. found the solus contract to be harsh, unfair and unconscionable and also contrary to section 88F (1) (d) inasmuch as it provided a total remuneration to the Feenans that was less than persons
who performed the work the Feenans in fact did pursuant to the con- D
tract would have been paid for doing it as employees. These findings
are open neither to appeal nor to review by the Supreme Court or
by their Lordships. The only question open to review is whether the
Industrial Commission had *jurisdiction* under the section to entertain
an application to declare the solus contract void upon those grounds;
and this turns upon whether it was a " contract . . . whereby a person
performs work in any industry."

E

The solus contract was made on Caltex's standard printed form of
contract by which it licences persons to use and operate, for the sale of
petroleum products supplied by Caltex, service stations of which Caltex is
the actual owner or lessee. This is one of the methods most commonly
used by Caltex for marketing its products. It has been found to be more
economical to Caltex than running the service stations with its own F
employees. In the case of the Hexham service station itself, this had
been run by a previous licensee who had terminated his licence in February 1975. Caltex advertised for a successor, representing that a profit
of $20,000 per annum could be gained by its operation. No takers
appeared in response to the advertisements until the Feenans came along
in July 1975, and, as a result of negotiations in the course of which
Caltex's estimate of the potential annual profits rose to $24,000, the G
Feenans were persuaded to enter into the solus contract which took
effect from November 1, 1975. In the meantime from February to
October Caltex had been running the service station directly by its
own employees.

Before turning to the terms of the contract itself, it is convenient to
complete the history. The Feenans ran the service station for five H
months until the end of March 1976. Although both worked very long
hours, Mr. Feenan 85 to 90 hours per week and Mrs. Feenan, who
also ran a snack bar which formed part of the premises, 75 hours per
week, they soon found that they were unable to make anything like the
promised profit of $20,000 to $24,000 per annum. In the five months
during which they were running it they made a cash profit of only
$1,500 each (i.e., at the rate of $7,200 per annum) though they also

A had the benefit of free (two-bedroomed) accommodation on the premises and some saving of expense on food bought at wholesale prices for the snack bar and used for family consumption. Disappointed in their hopes of a reasonable return for the hard work they were putting in, the Feenans gave up the service station in March 1976; and eventually, in March 1979, they started these proceedings in the Industrial Commission.

B   The solus contract, which bore the heading " Licence," recited that Caltex was the owner of the premises on which the service station was situated and of the plant, equipment and facilities thereon and was also owner of the goodwill of the business of a service station conducted on those premises. It went on to grant to the Feenans a licence to use the premises in common with Caltex, its workmen, servants and agents for a

C period of 12 months subject to earlier determination as provided in later clauses. The fee payable for this non-exclusive licence was to be $600 per month. The contract also granted what it described as a lease of the goodwill of the business at a monthly rental of $100, the lease to be co-terminous with the licence. Their Lordships find the concept of a " lease " confined to goodwill a highly artificial one; but presumably it was designed to give to the Feenans protection against Caltex selling its

D own petroleum products on the premises in competition with the Feenans, which the non-exclusive character of the licence might otherwise have permitted it to do.

       A number of other clauses in the contract call for mention. Although the term of the licence was expressed to be for 12 months, Caltex reserved the right to terminate it at any time on giving 30

E days' notice without assigning any reason. If the Feenans held over after the expiry of the first 12 months it became a licence from year to year terminable by the Feenans by three months' notice expiring at the end of any 12 months' period, but continuing to be terminable by Caltex on 30 days' notice at any time. Caltex also retained a right of termination without notice if any debt owing by the Feenans to Caltex

F remained unpaid for seven days.

       The Feenans undertook to conduct the business on the premises during all lawful hours and to use their best endeavours to secure any necessary authority or permission to secure that those lawful hours should be as long as possible. If they should fail to carry it on for any period during lawful trading hours, Caltex could terminate the licence immediately without notice. In fact while the Feenans were running it,

G the service station was open from 7 a.m. to 10.30 p.m. each day and from 8 a.m. to 10.30 p.m. on Sundays, or 107½ hours a week. Needless to say, the Feenans were required to purchase all petroleum products sold at the service station from Caltex only although no price was specified. They also undertook not to be concerned in the sale of petroleum products from any other place within a five-mile radius of the service

H station.

       With these features of the contract in mind their Lordships turn to the crucial question of jurisdiction. Was this a " contract whereby a person performs work in any industry?" As a result of numerous decisions in the Industrial Commission of New South Wales, the Supreme Court of New South Wales and in the High Court itself, it is well established that the phrase is to be treated as broad and comprehensive in its scope. Their Lordships do not find it necessary to refer to any of the earlier authorities, which were helpfully cited in the cases lodged by A the parties on the appeal to their Lordships' Board. The argument at the hearing was largely concentrated on the latest relevant authority in the High Court, *Stevenson* v. *Barham* (1977) 136 C.L.R. 190. In that case, which was about a share-farming agreement, their Honours were split three to two; the majority (Barwick C.J., Mason and Jacobs JJ.) were of opinion that the agreement was caught by section 88F of the Industrial Arbitration Act 1940, the minority (Stephen and Aickin JJ.) B were of opinion that it was not. The share-farming agreement bore no resemblance to the solus contract with which their Lordships are presently concerned. It bore many of the features of a partnership; and on whichever side of the borderline of section 88F it fell, it lay very close to it, as the division of opinion in the High Court shows. The majority and the minority used somewhat different language to express their C understanding of the meaning of the crucial phrase: " any contract whereby a person performs work in any industry," and it has formed the main burden of the argument by Caltex that the way that the minority put it is to be preferred, and that the language that they used in doing so, if properly " construed," excludes the solus contract from the ambit of section 88F. Their Lordships, it was submitted, D unlike Macken J. and the Court of Appeal, were not bound by any gloss placed upon the section by the majority in *Stevenson* v. *Barham*. Their Lordships were invited to say that it was wrong.

To speak of " construing " the words in which judges have chosen to express the reasons for their judgments involves, in their Lordships' view, a misuse of language that is all too common and reflects a mistaken approach to the use of judicial precedent. The only words that require E to be " construed " are those of the statute itself. The language used by judges to explain the reasons why they think the statutory words do, or do not, apply to the particular circumstances of the case under consideration, is chosen with those particular circumstances in mind and is not intended as a paraphrase of the statutory words that is necessarily appropriate to all other circumstances. F

Stevenson v. *Barham*, 136 C.L.R. 190 itself is illustrative of this. The majority, after referring to the judgments in some previous cases, said, at p. 201: " It follows, then, that if the contract is one which leads directly to a person working in any industry it has the requisite industrial character—it is a contract ' whereby a person performs work in any industry ' . . ." Speaking of the expression " performs work " in section 88F of the Industrial Arbitration Act 1940 Stephen J. in his dissenting G judgment said, at p. 193: " . . . the sense it conveys is, I think, that of work being performed for another," while Aicken J. put it, at p. 211: " . . . the basic concept is of a contract whereby one person performs work in an industry for another . . ." The emphasis laid by the minority on the necessity of the work being performed *for another* was because of the view they took that the share-farming agreement was H in all essential features a partnership agreement under which the applicant, who was the working partner, was performing work not for another individual but for the partnership of which he himself was part. In their Lordships' view it does not follow that even the minority in *Stevenson* v. *Barham* would have held that the solus contract, under which no question of partnership arises, fell outside the ambit of section 88F.

A   Their Lordships accordingly turn to what is the only real question of construction in this appeal. Was the solus contract a " contract whereby a person performs work in any industry," *within the meaning of that phrase in section 88F of the Industrial Arbitration Act?* " Industry " is defined in section 5 to mean " craft, occupation, or calling in which persons of either sex are employed for hire or reward."

B It covers, therefore, the occupation of supplying petroleum products and other services to motorists at a service station. Performing work in industry, in their Lordships' view, covers doing anything which a person employed in the same occupation for hire or reward might be expected to be required to do under a contract of employment. So the Feenans when running the service station by their own labours were performing work in industry. The remaining question of con-

C struction is whether the solus contract was a contract " whereby " they did so. In their Lordships' view this provision in the context of contract or arrangement bears its ordinary meaning of " in consequence of which " or " in fulfilment of which." Either meaning is sufficient to bring the solus contract within the description of contracts to which section 88F applies. The Feenans were required to carry on the task of supply-

D ing petroleum products to motorists throughout all lawful working hours. In doing so they were fulfilling their contractual obligations to Caltex. The total remuneration which they received (to use the expression used in section 88F (*d*) was the difference between the prices at which they were able to sell those products and the prices which Caltex chose to sell the products to them, together with licence fee and the so-called rental of goodwill. The benefit obtained by Caltex from the solus

E contract in addition to the licence fee and rental of goodwill, was an assured and profitable outlet for their products without incurring the expense of paying wages to employees for doing what, under the solus contract, the Feenans had bound themselves to do instead.

    In their Lordships' view the solus contract falls fairly and squarely within the ambit of section 88F. The industrial Commission had juris-

F diction to hear and determine the Feenans' application, and since it had jurisdiction no appeal lies against the orders that it made.

    Their Lordships will humbly advise Her Majesty that this appeal should be dismissed with costs.

    Solicitors: *Linklaters & Paines; Charles Russell & Co.*

G

                                                    T. J. M.

H   ————

A

[FAMILY DIVISION]

* PRACTICE DIRECTION (PRE-TRIAL REVIEW:
ANCILLARY RELIEF)

*Husband and Wife—Financial provision—Pre-trial review—Pro-
cedures—Discontinuance of pre-trial review—Continuance of*
procedures incidental to review

B

The experiment in operation from April 1, 1980, to secure the settlement of financial applications at a pre-trial review has resulted in a success
rate so low as not to justify its continuance. Consequently pre-trial reviews
on such applications will not take place as from July 1, 1981.

Nevertheless the following procedures laid down by the registrar's
direction of February 12, 1980, *Practice Direction (Pre-Trial Review:*
Financial Provisions) [1980] 1 W.L.R. 245, are still useful and should
be continued.

C

(a) After affidavits have been filed mutual discovery should take place
without order 14 days from the last affidavit, unless some other period is
agreed, with inspection 7 days thereafter.

D

(b) Where a dispute arises as to the value of any property, a valuation
should be made without order by an agreed valuer, or in default of agreement, by an independent valuer chosen by the President of the Institution
of Chartered Surveyors. The valuation should be produced to the registrar
at the hearing.

(c) If a dispute arises as to the extent of discovery or as to answers in a
questionnaire, an appointment for directions should be taken out. Where
the registrar considers that to answer any question would entail considerable expense and that there is doubt whether the answer would provide
any information of value, he may make the order for the question to be
answered at the questioner's risk as to costs. The registrar may refuse to
order an answer to a question if he considers that its value would be small
in relation to the property or income of the party to whom the question is
addressed.

E

F

(d) Where an issue of conduct is raised on the affidavits, an appointment
for directions should be taken out at which the registrar will inquire
whether the issue is being pursued and, if so, will order particulars to be
given of the precise allegations relied on.

The registrar's direction of February 12, 1980, is hereby cancelled.

G

R. L. BAYNE-POWELL,
Senior Registrar.

June 4, 1981.

H

A

[COURT OF APPEAL]

* CAM GEARS LTD. *v.* CUNNINGHAM

1981 Feb. 16, 17   Cumming-Bruce, Templeman and
                                                         Oliver L.JJ.
B

Landlord and Tenant—Business premises (security of tenure)—
Landlord's intention to occupy—Premises consisting of vacant
site—Landlord intending to erect building before occupying—
Whether intention to occupy " the holding "—Landlord and
Tenant Act 1954 (2 & 3 Eliz. 2, c. 56), s. 30 (1) (g)

C
The tenant held a lease of business premises which was
due to expire in January 1979. The premises consisted of a
vacant site with a concrete surface which the tenant used as
a car park in conjunction with an adjoining business. In July
1978 the landlord served a notice to terminate the tenancy
stating that he required the premises for his own business
purposes. The landlord proposed to erect a commercial building on the site in order to expand his business. The tenant
applied to the county court pursuant to Part II of the Land-
D
lord and Tenant Act 1954 for the grant of a new tenancy.
The application was opposed by the landlord on the ground,
provided by section 30 (1) (g) of the Act, [1] that he intended
to occupy the holding for the purposes of a business to be
carried on by him. The judge refused to grant a new tenancy.
On appeal by the tenant: —
Held, dismissing the appeal, that since " holding " in section
30 (1) (g) was defined as " the property comprised in the
E
tenancy " and as the landlord intended to occupy the whole
of the demised land for the purposes of his business, he did
intend to occupy the holding within the meaning of section
30 (1) (g) and the fact that he intended to erect a commercial
building on the site did not mean that the holding was to be
incorporated into a wider scheme.
Nursey v. *P. Currie (Dartford) Ltd.* [1959] 1 W.L.R. 273,
C.A. distinguished.
F

The following cases are referred to in the judgments:

Method Development Ltd. v. *Jones* [1971] 1 W.L.R. 168; [1971] 1 All
E.R. 1027, C.A.
Nursey v. *P. Currie (Dartford) Ltd.* [1959] 1 W.L.R. 273; [1959] 1 All
E.R. 497, C.A.

G

The following additional case was cited in argument:

McKenna v. *Porter Motors Ltd.* [1956] A.C. 688; [1956] 3 W.L.R. 658;
[1956] 3 All E.R. 262, P.C.

APPEAL from Judge Kingham sitting at Luton County Court.

H
The tenant, Cam Gears Ltd., held a seven year lease of land at
Selbourne Road and Covent Garden Close, Luton, which terminated
on January 1, 1979. On July 3, 1978, the landlord, David Lawrence
Cunningham, served a notice on the tenant under section 25 of the
Landlord and Tenant Act 1954, stating that he would oppose the grant
of a new tenancy on the ground that he wished to occupy the holding
for his own business purposes. The tenant applied to the court, by

[1] Landlord and Tenant Act 1956, s. 30 (1) (g): see post, p. 1012G.

notice dated October 30, 1978, for the grant of a new tenancy under **A**
Part II of the Act of 1954 which on January 11, 1980, was refused by
Judge Kingham.

By a notice of appeal dated February 20, 1980, the tenant appealed
on the grounds that the judge misdirected himself in holding (1) that
the landlord was entitled to rely on the grounds of opposition contained
in section 30 (1) (*g*) of the Act of 1954 as opposed to those contained in
section 30 (1) (*f*) because the landlord's intended use of the premises as a **B**
motor vehicle testing station would necessitate the carrying out on the
premises of a substantial work of construction within the meaning of
section 30 (1) (*f*); and (2) that the landlord intended to occupy "the
holding" for the purpose of his business within the meaning of section
30 (1) (*g*) of the Act and in construing the phrase "the holding" as
meaning anything other than the premises in their existing state as a **C**
car park.

The facts are stated in the judgment of Oliver L.J.

Nicholas Patten for the tenant.
Allan Levy for the landlord.

OLIVER L.J. delivered the first judgment. This is an appeal by a **D**
tenant of business premises from a decision of Judge Kingham, which
was given on January 11, 1980, refusing the grant of a new tenancy
under the provisions of the Landlord and Tenant Act 1954.

The premises with which the application is concerned consist of a
vacant site—that is to say, a site unencumbered by buildings but with
a concrete surface—constituting a car park and situate on the corner **E**
of Selbourne Road and Covent Garden Close in Luton. The tenant
carried on business nearby, and the premises have been at all material
times used as a car park in connection with that business. The premises
were originally let by the landlord to the tenant on a lease dated May
5, 1972, for a term of seven years from January 1, 1972; that term
expired in 1979.

The proper notice under the Act was given by the landlord in July **F**
1978, and there is no dispute that the correct sequence of events envisaged
by the Act has taken place; I need not go through its various stages.

The present dispute arises out of the landlord's opposition to the
grant of a new tenancy which, in the notice served on the tenant, he
put on the ground set out in section 30 (1) (*g*) of the Act of 1954; that
is: **G**

"... that on the termination of the current tenancy the landlord
intends to occupy the holding for the purposes, or partly for the
purposes, of a business to be carried on by him therein, or as his
residence."

The landlord, Mr. Cunningham, has been in business for some time,
originally, I think, in partnership, but more recently through the medium **H**
of a limited company, Technical Brakes Ltd., of which he is a director
and in which he holds 74 out of the 99 issued shares. That company
runs a garage business and, as I understand it, the principal facet of
that business is the provision of Ministry of Transport testing facilities
for vehicles which are more than three years of age. In the course of
its business, at present carried on in Wingate Road, Luton, it tests about
10,000 vehicles a year.

A   What the landlord wishes to do is to expand his business. The lease of the present business premises expired in, I think, June 1980, and he needs two new test lanes.

      As I have mentioned, the premises the subject matter of this appeal are used at present as a car park. They consist simply of a vacant site with no buildings on it, and the landlord's project, if he can get possession,
B   is to have erected on the site what is known as a Banbury prefabricated commercial building, which will cover about one-third of the total area of the site and will furnish a workshop, an office, a waiting room, toilet facilities and inspection pits for vehicles. The total cost of that building is likely to be in the order of £16,000, the total cost of the operation, including erection, being estimated by the landlord before the judge at £20,000. His evidence, which was accepted by the judge, was
C   that facilities would be made available to him by his bankers. The judge accepted the landlord's evidence in toto and he found as a fact that he was bona fide in forming his intention and that the intention was a practicable one, albeit that he would have to get a detailed planning permission, satisfy the building regulations and obtain a Ministry of Transport licence. The judge was satisfied that these were not problems
D   which would stand in the way of a successful outcome of the project.

      The tenant's contention before the judge and in this court was that since the only ground of opposition to the grant of a new tenancy under the Act specified in the landlord's notice was that which appears in section 30 (1) (g), the landlord had to show that his intention was not just to occupy the site, but that he was to occupy " the holding "; that the holding consisted of the present vacant site used as a car park and
E   that the proposed erection on that site of a new building to be used for the purpose of a testing workshop constituted the erection of a new and different holding and that therefore the landlord was not proposing to occupy " the holding " for the purposes of the business.

      The erection of the proposed building was, no doubt, a major work of construction, which could only be carried out if the landlord obtained
F   possession, and it might indeed have justified opposition to the grant of a new tenancy under section 30 (1) (f); but that was not the ground that was specified, and since the only ground relied upon was the ground in paragraph (g), that is the ground upon which the landlord must rely.

      The judge rejected that contention, which was based upon the decision of this court in Nursey v. P. Currie (Dartford) Ltd. [1959] 1 W.L.R. 273.
G   That was a case which bears a superficial resemblance to the present case, in that the landlord's notice in that case was confined to the ground specified in section 30 (1) (g), and what the landlord company proposed to do was to demolish the existing buildings, which were standing in a yard which was occupied by the landlord, and redevelop the site as part of a petrol station which it proposed to carry on there. The Court of Appeal held that the ground of opposition was not made out; and it
H   did so because of the limiting definition of the word " holding " in section 23 (3) of the Act.

      That subsection defines the word " holding " as meaning " the property comprised in the tenancy "—I close the quotation there; there is some more but is not material for present purposes. The court held in that case that that definition included the existing buildings. The landlord, since it intended to remove the existing buildings and replace them with others, did not therefore intend to occupy " the holding " but

intended to occupy the new buildings to be erected on the land forming $\quad$ A
part only of " the holding " viewed as a totality—at any rate, that is
what I apprehend is the ratio of the decision in the *Nursey* case, and
that is the view of it which was adopted by this court in *Method Development Ltd.* v. *Jones* [1971] 1 W.L.R. 168; I refer particularly to the
judgment of Salmon L.J. in that case.

I confess that the *Nursey* decision [1959] 1 W.L.R. 273 is one which
I find it far from easy to understand. The only argument, so far as can $\quad$ B
be deduced from the report at p. 275, had been that since the landlord
intended to demolish the buildings, it could not be intending to occupy
" the holding " which included the buildings. But Wynn-Parry J., who
delivered the first judgment, seems to have taken the view, at any rate
on one reading of his judgment, that it was fatal to the landlord's claim
that the holding was to be occupied as part of a larger complex and not $\quad$ C
as a separate holding on its own. He said, at p. 277:

> " It seems to me that that language circumscribes the use of the
> phrase ' the holding ' in that paragraph "—that being paragraph (g)—
> " and makes it necessary to concentrate the whole of one's attention
> on the particular piece of land, whether it has buildings on it or
> not, which is the subject matter of the tenancy in question. So $\quad$ D
> viewed, it appears to me that the contention for the landlords in the
> present case is too wide, and that when one is looking at the material
> time at ' the holding ' under paragraph (g), it is not permissible to
> take into account the wider scheme which the landlords had in
> mind, and merely to treat the land comprised in the holding as land
> which, in one way or another, will be used for the purpose of the
> wider undertaking." $\quad$ E

I cannot think that the judge can have intended to do more than
to answer the question, which is: is the holding which the landlord
intends to occupy the same holding as that comprised in the tenancy?
Construed in the wide sense that I have indicated, it would follow that
a landlord who carried on a business next door to the demised premises
and who wanted to occupy those premises as one with his existing shop $\quad$ F
for an expanding business, would be unable to rely upon section 30 (1) (g),
and would be able to resist a new lease only if he intended to reconstruct.
For my part, I cannot ascribe so eccentric an intention to the legislature.
Certainly, Willmer L.J. confined his judgment to the narrow ground that
the definition of " the holding " simply involved reading into the subsection, in place of the words " the holding," the parcels of the lease—a $\quad$ G
ratio which hardly helps the present tenant since the lease in the present
case merely refers to " all that piece or parcel of land delineated for
the purposes of identification only on the plan annexed hereto and thereon
edged red," and that is precisely what the landlord intends to occupy.

But even if I am wrong in the limits within which, as I think, the
judgment of Wynn-Parry J. must be read, and even assuming that the
concurrence in that decision of Hodson L.J. renders the wider construc- $\quad$ H
tion binding upon us, it still does not seem to me to help the tenant in
the instant case. There is no wider scheme here in which the holding is
proposed to be incorporated. The landlord simply intends to place a
building on the site and to use the whole site, together with the new
building, for the purposes of his business.

Mr. Patten, who has argued this appeal, if I may say so, with conspicuous frankness and acumen, seeks to steer a course midway between

A the construction of Wynn-Parry J.'s judgment to which I have referred, and the very limited ratio adopted by Willmer L.J. He suggests that the ratio of the *Nursey* case [1959] 1 W.L.R. 273 is that you have to look at the holding as it is at the termination of the tenancy and to ask yourself the question: does the landlord intend to occupy the holding for the purposes of *his* business in substantially the identical condition as it was at the date of termination? If he intends to occupy the whole B of it, but to make any material alteration to its condition, then he is intending to occupy a different holding.

For my part, I find myself unable to follow Mr. Patten through the gap which he thus seeks to make between the prongs of Morton's fork. Whatever may be the true ratio of the *Nursey* case, I am unable to extract that from it and indeed to do so would, I think, be to attribute C a wholly irrational and capricious intention to the legislature. Accepting as I must that *Nursey* is binding upon this court, I certainly do not feel disposed to strain it beyond the narrowest limits within which it is capable of being confined.

I think that the determining feature of the *Nursey* decision was not the *purpose* for which the holdings were occupied by the tenant, or the D particular condition at the time of the determination of the tenancy, but the fact that the holding consisted of the buildings which, under the landlord's proposals, were to be demolished. That may or may not have been a logical or reasonable construction of the section, and I bear in mind Salmon L.J.'s reservation in *Method Development Ltd.* v. *Jones* [1971] 1 W.L.R. 168 as to whether it was correctly decided, E although the combined industry of counsel has not succeeded in unearthing the inconsistent unreported case in the Court of Appeal to which Salmon L.J. referred. But it cannot in any event, in my judgment, have any possible application to a case such as the present, where " the holding " consists solely of a vacant site upon which the landlord proposes to erect a building, so that what he will occupy is " the holding " plus something else. He proposes to occupy everything that is there at the F moment, with the sole exception of two lengths of topsoil and subsoil which will be removed to sink the inspection pits. *Nursey* v. *P. Currie (Dartford) Ltd.* [1959] 1 W.L.R. 273 is, in my judgment, of no assistance to the tenant in such circumstances.

The judge rejected the tenant's submission. So do I, and I would dismiss the appeal.

G

TEMPLEMAN L.J. I agree. By a lease dated May 5, 1972, the landlord demised to the tenant " All that piece or parcel of land edged in red on the plan annexed hereto." The tenant convenanted to use the demised premises only for the purposes of a car park and not to erect on the demised land or any part thereof any buildings or structures other H than those necessary for the parking of vehicles and, should the tenant so require, for providing shelter for vehicles.

The landlord proposed to occupy the demised premises for the business of a Ministry of Transport car testing centre, and for that purpose, needed and planned to erect a building on part of the land.

By section 30 (1) (g) of the Act of 1954, the landlord, having duly determined the lease by notice, is entitled to resist the tenant's present application for a new lease if the landlord, on the determination of the current tenancy, intends to occupy the holding for the purpose of a business to be carried on by the landlord thereon.

By section 23 (3) " the holding " means the property comprised in the tenancy. The lease will determine at the expiration of three months after the final refusal of the tenant's application for a new lease. If there is no appeal from this court the lease will determine three months from today.

Unassisted by authority, it seems to me that the judge in the county court having found that the landlord in fact intends to occupy the whole of the demised land for the purposes I have mentioned, and has the financial resources and the ability and the will to do so, it follows that the landlord made good his opposition under the Landlord and Tenant Act 1954.

We were pressed by the decision of this court in *Nursey* v. *P. Currie (Dartford) Ltd.* [1959] 1 W.L.R. 273 of which I make the melancholy observation that two bad reasons do not make one good reason although both may be binding on this court. It is plain, however, that the facts of the present case are distinguishable. Taking the test adumbrated by Wynn-Parry J.: is this a case where the holding which is to be developed is the same as the holding demised? The answer is Yes; it does not form part of any larger undertaking. Taking the test adumbrated by Willmer L.J., what was comprised in the demise in the present case is a piece of land, and the landlord's business will be carried on upon that piece of land. The fact that for the purposes of enhancing that business, or enabling it to be carried on, the landlord intends to put a workshop on part of the land is neither here nor there. The object of paragraph (*g*) is not to hand the land back to the landlord in a sterilised form, so that he has to put his hand on his heart, saying in effect: " I do not intend to make any alteration." The purpose of the subsection is to hand the land back to the landlord if he wants to carry on his own business there, and that indeed is what this landlord intends to do and that is what he is entitled to do.

Accordingly, I would dismiss the appeal.

CUMMING-BRUCE L.J. I agree with both judgments, hoping that such agreement does not give rise to the difficulties which have arisen as a result of Hodson L.J.'s similar agreement in *Nursey's* case.

Appeal dismissed with costs.
Leave to appeal refused.

Solicitors: *Slaughter & May; John Photiades & Co., Luton.*

L. G. S.

A

[COURT OF APPEAL]

* REGINA *v.* NATIONAL INSURANCE COMMISSIONER,
Ex parte SECRETARY OF STATE FOR SOCIAL SERVICES

B
1981 April 3; 14   Lord Denning M.R.,
                                                Dunn and O'Connor L.JJ.

Social Security—Supplementary benefit—Attendance allowance—
Cooking for severely disabled person—Whether " attention
. . . in connection with . . . bodily functions "—Social Security
Act 1975 (c. 14), s. 35 (1) (a) (i)

C
        The claimant, a severely disabled old lady, was able to
    manage the majority of functions connected with her daily
    living without assistance but her daughter had to do the
    cooking and shopping for her. She applied for a daytime
    attendance allowance under section 35 (1) (*a*) (i) of the Social
    Security Act 1975 [1] in respect of her daughter's " attention
    throughout the day in connection with her bodily functions."
    The delegated medical practitioner on behalf of the Attendance
D
    Allowance Board held that inability to carry out domestic
    duties was not a factor which could be taken into account in
    assessing need for attention in connection with bodily func-
    tions.   On appeal a national insurance commissioner held
    that cooking was an attention in connection with the bodily
    function of eating. Forbes J. dismissed an application by the
    Secretary of State for Social Services for an order of certiorari
    to quash the national insurance commissioner's decision.
E
        On the Secretary of State's appeal: —
        Held, allowing the appeal, that the words " attention . . .
    in connection with . . . bodily functions " in their context in
    section 35 (1) (*a*) (i) of the Social Security Act 1975 connoted
    personal service in the presence of the disabled person in
    connection with functions which fit people normally per-
    formed for themselves and that cooking was too remote to
    fall within the ambit of the words (post, pp. 1022B, H, 1023 F,
F
    G–H, 1026G–H).
        Per curiam. Where there are conflicting decisions by
    national insurance commissioners, the High Court should give
    a ruling (post, pp. 1022E, 1023H—1024A).
        Reg. v. *National Insurance Commissioner, Ex parte Strat-*
    ton [1979] Q.B. 361, C.A. applied.
        Decision of Forbes J. reversed.

G
    The following case is referred to in the judgments:
    Reg. v. *National Insurance Commissioner, Ex parte Stratton* [1979] Q.B.
        361; [1979] 2 W.L.R. 389; [1979] 2 All E.R. 278, C.A.

    No additional cases were cited in argument.

    APPEAL from Forbes J.
H
    By notice of motion of April 14, 1980, the Secretary of State for
Social Services applied to the Divisional Court for an order of certiorari
to remove into the High Court for the purpose of its being quashed
a decision of a national insurance commissioner, Mr. I. O. Griffiths
Q.C., on January 15, 1980, ordering that the determination on review
of the Attendance Allowance Board (" the board ") dated June 7, 1979,

[1] Social Security Act 1975, s. 35 (1): see post, p. 1019A–c.

given by a medical practitioner on behalf of the board be set aside on A
the ground that it was erroneous in law and that the application of Martha
Packer for a review of the decision of a medical practitioner on behalf
of the board of October 3, 1978, that one of the conditions under section
35 (1) (*b*) (the night condition) of the Social Security Act 1975 was satisfied but that neither of the day conditions was satisfied be remitted to
the board.

Forbes J., sitting alone, held that the commissioner's decision was B
right and dismissed the application on the ground that cooking was an
activity which consisted of the application of a number of bodily functions to a particular task and if a disabled person could not perform the
requisite bodily functions himself then someone who performed them on
his behalf was rendering attention in connection with those bodily functions and accordingly the delegated medical practitioner was wrong to C
exclude from his consideration the fact that the disabled person needed
to be cooked for.

The Secretary of State appealed on the grounds (1) that the judge
erred in law in holding that the expression " bodily functions " as used
in section 35 (1) (*a*) (i) of the Act included every mode of action of which
the body was capable at the dictate of the brain but ought to have limited
the expression to such functions as were necessary to keep a person alive D
or healthy; (2) that the judge erred in law in deciding that the intention
of the Act, which he ought to take into account, was to assist a person
to maintain a particular quality of life; (3) that the judge ought in the
circumstances of the case to have considered that the only relevant bodily
function was that of eating and to have decided that cooking was too remote
from that function to constitute or to be capable of constituting attention E
in connection therewith; (4) that, if the judge was correct to define " bodily
functions " as he did and in any event, he erred in deciding that cooking for
a person was attention in connection with that person's bodily function,
because such attention was required in connection with the particular
activity, viz. cooking, resulting from the bodily function, and not in connection with the bodily function itself; (5) that in deciding whether
cooking was capable of constituting an attention within the meaning F
of section 35 (1) (*a*) (i), the judge ought to have considered whether
cooking was an activity which fit persons invariably did for themselves
and/or was a sufficiently immediate or personal act to qualify.

The facts are stated in the judgments of Lord Denning M.R. and
O'Connor L.J.

G

Simon D. Brown for the Secretary of State.
David Latham as amicus curiae.

Cur. adv. vult.

April 14. The following judgments were read.

LORD DENNING M.R. It seems a small matter to bring to this court. H
It is whether an old lady of 83 should get an " attendance allowance "
of £14 a week or £21 a week. But there are many old ladies in a
similar position. So it is desirable to have the matter cleared up.
Especially as there have been conflicting decisions about it by the
national insurance commissioners. The case comes well within what
we said in *Reg.* v. *National Insurance Commissioner, Ex parte Stratton*
[1979] Q.B. 361, 368–369.

The Weekly Law Reports, July 3, 1981

1019

1 W.L.R.   Reg. v. N.I. Comr., Ex p. Soc. Services Sec. (C.A.)   Lord Denning M.R.

A   Under our social security system, an " attendance allowance " is paid
to a person who is so disabled that he needs help to cope with his disability.
The relevant provision is in section 35 (1) of the Social Security Act 1975
which I will set out in full :

> " A person shall be entitled to an attendance allowance if he satisfies
> prescribed conditions as to residence or presence in Great Britain
> B   and either—(a) he is so severely disabled physically or mentally that,
> by day, he requires from another person either—(i) frequent attention
> throughout the day in connection with his bodily functions, or (ii) con-
> tinual supervision throughout the day in order to avoid substantial
> danger to himself or others; or (b) he is so severely disabled physically
> or mentally that, at night, he requires from another person either—
> (i) prolonged or repeated attention during the night in connection
> C   with his bodily functions, or (ii) continual supervision throughout the
> night in order to avoid substantial danger to himself or others."

You will see that (a) covers " by day " and (b) " by night." If the
person requires a good deal of attention both by day and night he or she
gets £21 a week. If only by day or only by night, he or she gets £14 a
week.

D   Our old lady Mrs. Martha Packer used to get only £14 a week because
it was said that she only required attention by night. Her daughter now
says she ought to get £21 because she requires attention by day as well
as by night. Strange to relate, after all is said and done, the point depends
on the cooking of her meals. She cannot cook her own meals. Her
daughter has to cook them for her. Does " cooking " come within the
E   words " attention in connection with her bodily functions? "

The facts of the case

I take the facts from the report of the Attendance Allowance Board.
The board acted through a delegated medical practitioner. He said that
Mrs. Martha Packer was entitled to an attendance allowance for the
F   night :

> " With regard to the night conditions, I note from the medical report
> . . . that attention was required twice a night, for 5 to 10 minutes at
> at time, seven nights a week when she was helped out of bed to go
> to the toilet and given a drink to help her back to sleep . . . I accept
> that she requires repeated attention during the night in connection
> G   with her bodily functions."

But the delegated medical practitioner rejected her claim for an allowance
for the daytime. He said :

> " Before, however, I can . . . issue a certificate for the higher rate of
> attendance allowance I must be satisfied that in addition to fulfilling
> the night requirement, Mrs. Packer also satisfies one of the day
> H   conditions. . . . In this connection I note that Mrs. Packer was
> watched when getting into bed. She could, however, without assist-
> ance from another person get out of bed, walk, use stairs although
> she came down backwards, dress and undress, wash, bathe, eat, drink
> and go to the toilet. She was able to be up for 15 hours during the
> day and was not dependent upon any apparatus. She was not
> incontinent of bowels or bladder, needed no help with adjusting her
> clothes or wiping herself at the toilet . . . Miss Packer says in her

signed statement . . . ' I have to do all the washing and prepare all the meals for my mother. I do all the shopping and see to all the accounts.' "

The delegated medical practitioner then directed himself on the law:

"However, Mrs. Packer's inability to carry out domestic duties is not a factor which I can take into account in assessing her need for attention in connection with her bodily functions. It is clear that she is able to manage the majority of functions connected with daily living and I do not accept that she requires frequent attention through-out the day in connection with her bodily functions."

The commissioner's view

The daughter appealed to a national insurance commissioner. The discussion turned on the question of cooking. He held that it was " attention," etc. He said:

"It seems to me that the personal service of an active kind involved in cooking is immediately and not remotely connected with the bodily function of eating. Indeed preparing food for an invalid cannot reason-ably be regarded as having any purpose other than satisfying the bodily function of eating. The fact that the statute uses the phrase ' in connection with ' (which connotes a wider concept than ' with ') means in my judgment that there must be a sufficient nexus between the personal service and the bodily function it is intended to satisfy. I reject the contention of the Secretary of State that cooking is too remote from the bodily function of eating. In my judgment cooking is an attention in connection with the bodily function of eating."

So the commissioner held that eating is a bodily function: and that cooking is attention in connection with it.

The judge's view

The judge seems to have gone much further than the commissioner. He seems to have interpreted the phrase " bodily functions " as including cooking. He said that the phrase " would include every mode of action of which the fit body is capable at the dictate of the normal brain." He explained this by saying:

"A man must eat and drink, and keep clean. In the normal way he could buy his food and drink, cook it and consume it; he could wash his dishes and his clothes as well as himself. If he is disabled and cannot do some of these things, they may have to be done for him. They involve bodily functions in connection with which attendance may be required."

So the judge held that " cooking " itself is a bodily function. He said:

"that cooking is an activity which consists of the application of a number of bodily functions to a particular task and that if a disabled person cannot perform the requisite bodily functions himself then someone who performs them on his behalf is rendering attention in connection with those bodily functions."

The divergent views

So we have these divergent views. The judge held that *cooking* is a " bodily function." So that if a disabled person cannot cook for him-

The Weekly Law Reports, July 3, 1981

1021

1 W.L.R.   Reg. v. N.I. Comr., Ex p. Soc. Services Sec. (C.A.)   Lord Denning M.R.

A   self—and someone has to do it for him—it is attention which qualifies for an attendance allowance.

    The commissioner held that *eating* is a " bodily function ": and that cooking is sufficiently closely connected with it that, if anyone has to do it for a disabled person it is attention which qualifies.

    The department submit that eating is a " bodily function," but say that cooking is too remote from it for it to be considered as " attention in connection with it."

B

Previous decisions

    We were given a selection of previous decisions which illustrate the difference of opinion.

    1. Mr. Robert Lazarus Q.C. on September 25, 1972 (Decision C.A.

C 6/72):

> " In my judgment, the word ' attention ' denotes a concept of some personal service of an active nature; for example, helping the disabled person to bath or to eat his food, cooking for him, or dressing a wound."

    2. Mr. J. G. Monroe on October 23, 1974 (Decision C.A. 60/74):

D

> " Although it might perhaps be argued that, as eating is a bodily function and as there is an obvious connection between cooking and eating, the person who needs to be cooked for requires attention in connection with one of his bodily functions. I do not consider that there is any substance in such an argument. It is wholly unnatural to say of a man whose wife regularly cooks his meals, that his wife

E

> gives him attention in connection with his bodily functions. I consider that the words of the section refer to a person who needs the relevant degree of attention in connection with the performance of his bodily functions, and that they are directed primarily to those functions which the fit man normally performs for himself."

    3. Mr. Robert Lazarus Q.C. on July 8, 1975 (Decision C.A. 77/74):

F

> " . . . I find myself unwilling to go so far as to say that the preparation of food or drink for a disabled person can never be regarded as an attention in connection with his bodily functions. . . . In my view, it is open to the determining authority to hold that the heating of liquids in order to have a hot drink is an activity in connection with bodily functions."

G   4. Sir Rawden Temple Q.C. on August 27, 1979 (Decision C.A. 2/79):

> " No doubt it is a question of fact and degree whether in any particular case the service performed for a disabled person can be said to be attention in connection with a bodily function." He (the Chief Commissioner) rejected the narrow interpretation " of confining attention to actual physical assistance given to a disabled person . . .

H

> ' attention . . . in connection with . . . bodily functions ' should be broadly interpreted."

    His decision was that cooking was an attention in connection with the bodily function of eating.

The meaning of the words

    The statute contains no definition of the words in controversy. I will first take them separately.

In order to qualify at all, the person must be " so severely disabled **A** physically or mentally " that he requires attention. This conveys the thought that the attention must be required so as to enable him to cope with his disability, whatever it is.

In order to get the allowance, the " attention " must be required frequently " throughout the day " or " prolonged or repeated " during the night. " Frequently " connotes several times—not once or twice. " Prolonged " means some little time. " Repeated " means more than once at **B** any rate.

" Attention " is different from " activity " or " attendance." It connotes something personal to the disabled person.

" Bodily functions " include breathing, hearing, seeing, eating, drinking, walking, sitting, sleeping, getting in or out of bed, dressing, undressing, eliminating waste products—and the like—all of which an ordinary **C** person—who is not suffering from any disability—does for himself. But they do not include cooking, shopping or any of the other things which a wife or daughter does as part of her domestic duties: or generally which one of the household normally does for the rest of the family.

It is the words " in connection with " which give rise to the difficulty. They are very uncertain. Some kinds of attention are closely connected **D** with " his bodily functions " : other kinds are too remote. It is a question of degree upon which different minds may reach different conclusions. As Terence said long ago: " Quot homines tot sententiae; suus cuique mos," which may be translated: " So many men, so many opinions; his own a law to each." In the very question before us, I might say: " So many commissioners, so many opinions: his own a law to each."

Such a situation should not be allowed to continue. These provisions **E** have to be applied, day in and day out, by delegated medical practitioners all over the country. They should be applied uniformly. Else there will be many complaints. " Why should she get it and not me? " To dispel these complaints—as far as possible—I think the courts should lay down rules for guidance. I would hold that ordinary domestic duties such as shopping, cooking meals, making tea or coffee, laying the table or the **F** tray, carrying it into the room, making the bed or filling the hot water bottle, do not qualify as " attention . . . in connection with [the] bodily functions " of the disabled person. But that duties that are out of the ordinary—doing for the disabled person what a normal person would do for himself—such as cutting up food, lifting the cup to the mouth, helping to dress and undress or at the toilet—all do qualify as " attention . . . in connection with [the] bodily functions " of the disabled person. **G**

It will then be for the delegated medical practitioner to add up those items of attention which qualify and decide whether the answer is " frequent attention throughout the day."

Conclusion

So far as the present case is concerned, I would take a different view **H** from the commissioner. I should have thought that the services rendered by the daughter in buying the food at the shops and cooking it was not " attention . . . in connection with [the] bodily functions " of the mother. I see no misdirection by the Attendance Allowance Board: I would, therefore, allow the appeal and restore its decision. But I would add this. It would appear that the daughter gave up her work in order to be at home to look after her mother. She would therefore be entitled to

The Weekly Law Reports, July 3, 1981

1023

1 W.L.R.   Reg. v. N.I. Comr., Ex p. Soc. Services Sec. (C.A.)   Lord Denning M.R.

A receive an " invalid care allowance " under section 37 of the Act: payable to her and not to her mother. In that way she will, I hope, be well treated: and everything will be fair all round.

DUNN L.J.   This appeal raises a short point of construction of section 35 (1) of the Social Security Act 1975 which is set out in full in the judgment of Lord Denning M.R.

B
The judge held in a closely reasoned judgment that cooking and the preparation of food involved bodily functions within the meaning of the section, so that a seriously disabled person who required frequent attention in connection with cooking was entitled to an attendance allowance. Mr. Latham as amicus curiae did not feel able to support the judge's formulation, but he did seek to uphold the reasoning of the national
C insurance commissioner who held that eating was a bodily function and that cooking was an attention in connection with that bodily function.

Mr. Latham submitted that on its true construction the attention to be provided under the section must be required because of the disability, and must be in connection with a bodily function. He accepted the definition of the word " attention " in Decision C.A. 6/72 on the com-
D missioner's file as denoting a concept of some personal service of an active nature. He said cooking fell within that definition and that it was a question of fact and degree in each case whether the cooking was done in connection with the disabled person's bodily functions. While conceding that shopping or growing vegetables were too remote, he submitted that once the food had been brought into the disabled person's house, there was or might be a sufficient nexus between the
E cooking and the bodily function of eating. He pointed out that the words " in connection with " in the section were wide in scope and should be construed broadly.

I look first at the section without regard to authority. To my mind the word " functions " in its physiological or bodily sense connotes the normal actions of any organs or set of organs of the body, and so the
F attention must be in connection with such normal actions. The word " attention " itself indicates something more than personal service, something involving care, consideration and vigilance for the person being attended. The very word suggests a service of a close and intimate nature. And the phrase " attention . . . in connection with . . . bodily functions " involves some service involving personal contact carried out in the presence of the disabled person.

G
Attractive as were Mr. Latham's submissions, it seems to me that they would in practice cause more difficulties than they solved. In each case it would be necessary for the delegated medical practitioner to ascertain whether the claimant usually cooked for himself, because if he did not the attention would not be required because of his disability.

In my view on the construction of the section as a whole, cooking
H including the preparation of a special diet is not as a matter of law capable of being an attention in connection with bodily functions because it is too remote from them. I reach this conclusion on the construction of the section itself. But there have been conflicting decisions of the commissioners on the question whether cooking is or is not an attention in connection with bodily functions and, before finally deciding the question, it is right to look at those decisions. As Lord Denning M.R. said in *Reg.* v. *National Insurance Commissioners, Ex parte Stratton*

[1979] Q.B. 361, 369B: "where there is a difference of opinion between   A
commissioners," then the High Court should give a ruling.

We are told that until 1979 it was the universal practice of delegated
medical practitioners to exclude cooking as too remote. Then in 1979
came a decision of Sir Rawden Temple Q.C., chief commissioner,
Decision C.A. 2/79. The commissioner said:

"... The logical result of confining attention to actual physical   B
assistance given to a disabled person is, for example, that he would
be receiving attention of the required character whilst being bathed,
but not whilst the bath was being prepared for him, and be receiving
attention when his food was being cut up to enable him to eat it, but
not whilst it was being prepared to enable it to become edible.

"Such fine distinctions wholly unintelligible I would suppose to
those for whose benefit the legislation exists, and which fragment   C
the course of personal services given to the severely disabled in
regard to their bodily functions, do not attract me. In my opinion
'attention . . . in connection with bodily functions' should be
broadly interpreted, so to include not only any physical assistance
ultimately given to enable the disabled person to eat (or drink), but
also to include the necessary steps taken by the attendant to prepare   D
the food (or drink) which is to be consumed, with or without later
physical assistance to do so. For myself, I do not doubt that a
disabled person waiting for food or drink to be prepared, if asked
whether he was being attended to, or receiving attention, would
answer that he was, and such answer to my mind would accord
both with common sense and with the fact. I do not believe that
Parliament intended that a disabled person, waiting whilst an   E
attendant prepared a meal or special diet, which he was unable to
do for himself because of his disability, should be held not to be
receiving attention in connection with his bodily function.

"I am fortified in my approach to the scope of 'attention' by
the observation of the commissioner in the Decision C.A. 6/72 . . .
There the commissioner wrote 'In my judgment, the word "atten-   F
tion" denotes a concept of some personal service of an active nature;
for example, helping the disabled person to bath, or to eat his food,
cooking for him . . . or dressing a wound.' The then chief commissioner in Decision R(A) 3/74 . . . said 'This description of attention
is correct,' and [later] he repeated his endorsement of the description
as correct, and found no reason to dissent from the example of   G
cooking as constituting 'attention.'

"I have well in mind that in a decision on commissioner's file
C.A. 60/74 . . . another commissioner expressed the view that the
words in the section, referring to a person who needs 'attention in
connection with his bodily functions,' are directed primarily to those
functions which the fit man normally performs for himself, and that
'it is wholly unnatural to say of a man whose wife regularly cooks   H
his meals that his wife gives him attention in connection with his
bodily functions.' However, in the context of a service to a disabled person who cannot prepare food to eat (whether by cooking
or not) because of his disabilities, the observation (with respect to
the author) has no real application or validity. It was considered in
the Decision C.A. 77/1974 by the author of the Decision C.A. 6/72
and he then expressed himself as unwilling to go so far as to say

The Weekly Law Reports, July 3, 1981

1025

1 W.L.R.   Reg. v. N.I. Comr., Ex p. Soc. Services Sec. (C.A.)   Dunn L.J.

A   that the preparation of food or drink for a disabled person can never be regarded as an attention in connection with his bodily functions. At paragraph 10 he held in terms that it is open to the determining authority to hold that the heating of liquids in order to have a hot drink is an activity (i.e. attention) in connection with bodily functions."

B   Decision C.A. 60/74 was a decision of Mr. Munroe.

With great respect to the care with which Sir Rawden Temple set out his decision and considered all the previous decisions, and indeed to Mr. Griffiths who followed him in this case, for the reasons that I have given upon the construction of the section itself I prefer the decision of Mr. Monroe. In particular I think that his concluding words are useful. They are:

C

" I consider that the words of the section refer to a person who needs the relevant degree of attention in connection with the performance of his bodily functions and that they are directed primarily to those functions which the fit man normally performs for himself."

That seems to me to provide a useful practical approach for the delegated
D   medical practitioners. The line must be drawn somewhere. I think it should be drawn to exclude cooking which is essentially a domestic duty. Domestic duties such as cooking, housework and the like do not constitute attention within section 35. Indeed, as O'Connor L.J. pointed out in the course of the argument, the claimant's daughter in this case could probably claim under section 37 of the Act for invalid care allowance which would cover the kind of domestic duties such as cooking and
E   cleaning which she at present carries out for her mother.

In my judgment the delegated medical practitioner was right to exclude cooking as a factor to be taken into account in considering whether the claimant was entitled to attendance allowance. I would allow the appeal and restore the decision of the delegated medical practitioner.

F   O'CONNOR L.J. There are many people in the community who are so disabled physically or mentally that they cannot look after themselves. Parliament on behalf of the community has made various provisions to make money available so that they can be cared for in the home. This case is concerned with attendance allowance as provided for by section 35 (1) of the Social Security Act 1975. It is payable to the disabled person. The section has been set out and I need not repeat it. It is
G   said by the claimant Mrs. Packer that she " requires from another person frequent attention throughout the day in connection with her bodily functions."

When a claim is made it is assessed by the Attendance Allowance Board, in practice that is by a medical practitioner to whom the duty is lawfully delegated. In the present case the delegated medical practitioner
H   in rejecting a claim for daytime allowance under section 35 (1) (a) (i) said:

" Before, however, I can revise the decision of October 3, 1978, and issue a certificate for the higher rate of attendance allowance I must be satisfied that in addition to fulfilling the night requirement Mrs. Packer also satisfies one of the day conditions overleaf. In this connection I note that Mrs. Packer was watched when getting into bed. She could, however, without assistance from another person get out of bed, walk, use stairs although she came down backwards,

dress and undress, wash, bathe, eat, drink and go to the toilet. She   A
was able to be up for 15 hours during the day and was not dependent
upon any apparatus. She was not incontinent of bowels or bladder,
needed no help with adjusting her clothes or wiping herself at the
toilet. The medical report dated March 19, 1979, substantially
agrees with the earlier report. Miss Packer says in her signed statement in this report 'I have to do all the washing and prepare all the
meals for my mother. I do all the shopping and see to all the   B
accounts.' However, Mrs. Packer's inability to carry out domestic
duties is not a factor which I can take into account in assessing her
need for attention in connection with her bodily functions. It is
clear that she is able to manage the majority of functions connected
with daily living and I do not accept that she requires frequent
attention throughout the day in connection with her bodily functions,   C
or that she has required such attention throughout the period relevant
to the claim. So far as supervision is concerned, there is nothing
in the medical evidence before me to indicate that Mrs. Packer has
any disturbances of behaviour or dangerous tendencies. Miss Packer
says that her mother is nervous but I note from her signed statement in the medical report dated September 14, 1978, that she is
able to leave her for up to two hours. Moreover, I do not accept   D
that the wish to have someone nearby, although perfectly understandable in an old person, constitutes the need for continual supervision for the avoidance of danger. The latest medical report states
that Mrs. Packer is not mentally deranged and is aware of common
danger. She is able to do a bit of cooking and I have no evidence
that she gets into dangerous situations. It is stated that she might   E
fall but I consider that the risk of falls occur at predictable times,
i.e., when she is moving about and in my opinion she could be safely
left for periods seated in a chair with her immediate needs to hand.
The medical report dated September 14, 1978, states that she can
be safely left unsupervised for one to two hours at a time and, having
regard to the evidence as a whole, I do not accept that she requires
continual supervision throughout the day in order to avoid substantial   F
danger to herself or others or that she has required supervision
throughout the period relevant to the claim."

An appeal was made to the commissioner, the claimant contending
that the delegated medical practitioner had erred in law in excluding
from his consideration her inability to cook as being capable of making
the cooking done for her " attention in connection with her bodily func-   G
tion " of eating. The commissioner upheld that contention. He reviewed
a number of decisions by commissioners. The Secretary of State asked
for judicial review of the decision. The judge upheld the decision but
for an entirely different reason. He held that the bodily function involved
was not eating but the physical movements needed for cooking. Like
Lord Denning M.R. and Dunn L.J. I cannot agree with that approach and   H
the question is that asked by the commissioner. With great respect to the
commissioners who have decided that cooking is capable of being attention
in connection with the bodily function of eating, I do not think that it is.
It was suggested in argument that a distinction should be drawn between
ordinary cooking and the preparation of a special diet. I do not think
it right to make any such distinction. I think that cooking is too remote
from the proximity that " attention in connection with a bodily function "

The Weekly Law Reports, July 3, 1981

1027

1 W.L.R.   Reg. v. N.I. Comr., Ex p. Soc. Services Sec. (C.A.)   O'Connor L.J.

A necessarily requires: cutting up food for a person and/or feeding it to a person are clearly within the words. Shopping for food is equally clearly not within the words. The line must be drawn somewhere and I think work in the kitchen is outside the ambit of the section.

Separate provision is made in the Act for paying for the care of a severely disabled person which includes domestic work like cooking: see section 37 of the Act. The payment under section 37 is in addition to B any payment made under section 35. I appreciate that the money is payable to the person providing the service and not the disabled person, but it is part of the scheme to promote the care of the disabled in the home.

I would allow the appeal and restore the decision of the delegated medical practitioner.

C
Appeal allowed.
No order for costs.
Commissioner's decision quashed.
Decision of board restored.

Solicitors: *Solicitor, Department of Health and Social Security; Treasury Solicitor.*
D
A. H. B.

E   [HOUSE OF LORDS]

* DODDS . . . . Appellant

AND

WALKER . . . . Respondent

F 1981 May 21;   Lord Diplock, Lord Edmund-Davies,
        June 18   Lord Fraser of Tullybelton, Lord Russell
                                  of Killowen and Lord Roskill

Landlord and Tenant—Business premises (security of tenure)—
Application for new tenancy—Notice to quit served on
September 30—Tenant's application for new tenancy made on
January 31—Whether application made within statutory four
G *month period—Landlord and Tenant Act 1954 (2 & 3 Eliz. 2,*
c. 56), s. 29 (3)

By section 29 (3) of the Landlord and Tenant Act 1954:
" No application [for a new tenancy] under section 24 (1)
of this Act shall be entertained unless it is made not less
than two nor more than four months after the giving of
the landlord's notice under section 25 of this Act . . ."
H   On September 30, 1978, the landlord, under Part II of the
Landlord and Tenant Act 1954, gave notice to the tenant to
determine his tenancy of business premises. Under section 29
(3) of the Act, the tenant had " four months after the giving
of the landlord's notice " to apply to the county court for a
new tenancy. The tenant applied on January 31, 1979. The
registrar dismissed the application on the basis that it was out
of time and, on appeal, the judge held that, in computing the
four months' period under section 29 (3), the day the landlord
gave notice was to be excluded but, notwithstanding that

September was a 30 day month, the period elapsed on the   **A**
corresponding day in the fourth month, namely, January 30,
and therefore the tenant's application made on the last day
of January was made one day too late. The Court of Appeal
affirmed that decision.

On appeal by the tenant: —

Held, dismissing the appeal, that in construing section 29 (3)
of the Act the corresponding date rule applied, so that in
calculating the period which had elapsed after the giving of the   **B**
landlord's notice and excluding that day, the relevant period
was the specified number of months thereafter which ended on
the corresponding day of the appropriate subsequent month,
and accordingly the tenant had made his application out of
time.

Decision of the Court of Appeal [1980] 1 W.L.R. 1061;
[1980] 2 All E.R. 507 affirmed.

  C

The following cases are referred to in their Lordships' opinions:

Freeman v. *Read* (1863) 4 B. & S. 174.
Lester v. *Garland* (1808) 15 Ves.Jun. 248.

The following additional case was cited in argument:

Migotti v. *Colvill* (1879) 4 C.P.D. 233, Denman J. and C.A.

  D

APPEAL from the Court of Appeal.

This was an appeal from a decision of the Court of Appeal (Stephenson
and Templeman L.JJ., Bridge L.J. dissenting) dated February 29, 1980,
affirming a decision of Judge Whitehead in Grantham County Court.

The issue on this appeal was whether the appellant Robert William
Dodds, the tenant, could rely on section 29 (3) of the Landlord and Tenant   **E**
Act 1954 as authority for the court to entertain his application for a new
tenancy under section 24 of the Act. The respondent Kenneth Edward
Walker, the landlord, sought to rely on the Act as authority for the court
to dismiss the tenant's application for a new tenancy on the ground that it
had been made out of time by virtue of section 29 (3) of the Act. The
respondent contended in effect that by reason of section 29 (3), the tenant's
application could not be entertained by the court as the application was   **F**
made " more than four months after the giving of the landlord's notice
under section 25 of the Act."

Mathew Thorpe Q.C. and *Michael Barnes Q.C.* for the appellant.
The respondent appeared in person but was not called upon.

  G

Their Lordships took time for consideration.

June 18. LORD DIPLOCK. My Lords, Part II of the Landlord and
Tenant Act 1954 entitles a tenant of business premises, whose tenancy has
been terminated by notice given to him by his landlord in accordance with
the provisions of that Act, to apply to the court for a new tenancy. By
section 29 (3) the application must be made " not less than two nor more   **H**
than four months after the giving of the landlord's notice." In the instant
case the respondent landlord's notice was given on September 30, 1978;
the appellant tenant's application to the court for a new lease was made
on January 31, 1979. The only question in this appeal is: Was that one
day too late?

The registrar and the judge of Grantham County Court both thought
that it was too late. They dismissed the tenant's application on the ground

A that the court had no jurisdiction to entertain it.   In the Court of Appeal opinion was divided.   Stephenson and Templeman L.JJ. agreed that it was one day too late; Bridge L.J. thought that it was just in time: and leave was given by that court to appeal to your Lordships' House.

My Lords, reference to a " month " in a statute is to be understood as a calendar month.   The Interpretation Act 1889 says so.   It is also clear under a rule that has been consistently applied by the courts since *Lester*
B v. *Garland* (1808) 15 Ves.Jun. 248, that in calculating the period that has elapsed after the occurrence of the specified event such as the giving of a notice, the day on which the event occurs is excluded from the reckoning. It is equally well established, and is not disputed by counsel for the tenant, that when the relevant period is a month or specified number of months after the giving of a notice, the general rule is that the period ends upon
C the corresponding date in the appropriate subsequent month, i.e. the day of that month that bears the same number as the day of the earlier month on which the notice was given.

The corresponding date rule is simple.   It is easy of application.   Except in a small minority of cases, of which the instant case is not an example, all that the calculator has to do is to mark in his diary the corresponding date in the appropriate subsequent month.   Because the number of days
D in five months of the year is less than in the seven others the inevitable consequence of the corresponding date rule is that one month's notice given in a 30 day month is one day shorter than one month's notice given in a 31 day month and is three days shorter if it is given in February. Corresponding variations in the length of notice reckoned in days occur where the required notice is a plurality of months.

E This simple general rule which Cockburn C.J. in *Freeman* v. *Read* (1863) 4 B. & S. 174, 184 described as being " in accordance with common usage . . . and with the sense of mankind," works perfectly well without need for any modification so long as there is in the month in which the notice expires a day which bears the same number as the day of the month on which the notice was given.   Such was the instant case and such will be every other case except for notices given on the 31st of a 31 day month
F and expiring in a 30 day month or in February, and notices expiring in February and given on the 30th or the 29th (except in leap year) of any other month of the year.   In these exceptional cases, the modification of the corresponding date rule that is called for is also well established: the period given by the notice ends upon the last day of the month in which the notice expires.

G My Lords, I do not personally derive assistance from pursuing metaphysical arguments about attributing to the one day or the other the *punctum temporis* between 24.00 hours on September 30 and 0.00 hours on October 1 at which time began to run against the tenant.   These seem to me quite inappropriate to the determination of the meaning of a statute which regulates the mutual rights of landlords and tenants of all business
H premises and is intended to be understood and acted on by them.   It refers to periods to be reckoned in months and was passed at a time when the corresponding date rule had been recognised for more than a century as applicable in reckoning periods of a month after the occurrence of a specified event.   In agreement with the majority of the Court of Appeal, I would not construe the Act as calling for any departure from the familiar corresponding date rule where this rule can be applied nor as calling for any greater modification in the general rule than was already recognised as

applicable where there is no corresponding date in the month in which the   A
notice expires because it is shorter than the month in which the notice was
given.

In the instant case the corresponding date rule presents no difficulty.
I would apply it and dismiss this appeal.

LORD EDMUND-DAVIES. My Lords, I am in respectful agreement with
the views expressed in the speeches of my noble and learned friends, Lord   B
Diplock and Lord Russell of Killowen, which I have read in draft, and I
would accordingly dismiss the appeal.

LORD FRASER OF TULLYBELTON. My Lords, I have had the advantage
of reading in draft the speeches prepared by my noble and learned friends,
Lord Diplock and Lord Russell of Killowen. I agree with them, and for   C
the reasons stated therein I too would dismiss this appeal.

LORD RUSSELL OF KILLOWEN. My Lords, it is common ground that
in this case the period of four months did not begin to run until the end
of the date of the relevant service on September 30—i.e. at midnight
September 30/October 1. It is also common ground that ordinarily the
calculation of a period of a calendar month or calendar months ends upon   D
what has been conveniently referred to as the corresponding date. For
example in a four month period, when service of the relevant notice was
on September 28, time would begin to run at midnight September 28/29
and would end at midnight January 28/29, a period embracing four calendar
months. It is to be observed that the number of *days* in the four month
period in that example is in one sense inevitably limited by the fact that   E
September and November each contains but 30 days. But the application
of the corresponding date principle inevitably produces variation in the
number of days involved, depending upon the date upon which a four
month notice is served and the irregular allotment of days to different
months. Sometimes it is not possible to apply directly the principle, for
instance if a four month notice is served on October 30 (the time beginning
to run at midnight October 30/31), there being in February but 28 (or 29)   F
days it is not possible to find a corresponding date in February and plainly
a corresponding date cannot be sought in March: the application of the
corresponding date principle in such case can only lead to termination of
the four month period at midnight February 28/March 1 (or midnight
February 29/March 1 in a leap year). That is an inevitable outcome.

Bridge L.J. in his dissenting judgment in this case adopted a simple
stance. Time he said (correctly) began to run at midnight September   G
30/October 1. Stretching ahead were the four calendar months of
October, November, December and January: the tenant was allowed the
whole of those four calendar months including the whole of January:
therefore the application made on January 31 was made in time. I am
with respect unable to accept this departure from the corresponding date
principle simply because the period starts to run at the outset of the first   H
of a month: a departure from the sound and well established rules is not
required in that one instance, as it is required in the example given of
there being no corresponding date in February. For the appellant it was
submitted that Templeman L.J. had fallen into the error of including the
whole of September 30 in the period. I am clearly of opinion that the
language used by him was not to that effect.

Accordingly I am of opinion that the corresponding date principle is

A applicable in this case, that the four month period expired at midnight January 30/31, and that the application made on January 31 was out of time and could not be entertained. Consequently I also would dismiss this appeal.

B LORD ROSKILL. My Lords, I have had the advantage of reading in draft the speeches of my noble and learned friends, Lord Diplock and Lord Russell of Killowen. For the reasons they give, I agree that this appeal fails and should be dismissed.

Appeal dismissed.

Solicitors: *Radcliffes & Co. for Norton & Hamilton, Grantham.*

C   F. C.

D   [QUEEN'S BENCH DIVISION]

* REGINA *v.* GOVERNOR OF PENTONVILLE PRISON,
Ex parte SINGH (HARMOHAN)

1980 Dec. 18;
1981 Jan. 21   Ackner L.J. and Skinner J.
E

*Extradition—Treaty—Construction—Provision for admission of
" sworn depositions or statements of witnesses " in extradition
proceedings—Accomplices' unsworn statements—Acknowledgment of truth of statements on subsequent occasion in court
after being told of penalties for perjury—Whether acknowledgment amounting to affirmation—Whether affirmation admissible
under treaty—Extradition Treaty (Sweden and Norway),*
F   *Order in Council, September 30, 1873, art. X—Extradition Act
1873 (36 & 37 Vict. c. 60), s. 4*

The Extradition Treaty of June 26, 1873, between the United Kingdom and the Kingdom of Sweden and Norway as ratified on August 28 and set out in the Order in Council dated September 30, 1873, applied the Extradition Acts of 1870 and 1873 to the Kingdom of Sweden and Norway. It G was continued in relation to the Kingdom of Norway alone by an agreement dated February 18, 1907 (S.R. & O. 1907 No. 545). Article X of the treaty provided:
    " In the examinations which they have to make . . . the authorities of the state applied to shall admit as entirely valid evidence the sworn depositions or statements of witnesses taken in the other state . . ."
The Extradition Act 1873 which received the Royal Assent H on August 5, 1873, provided by section 4 that the provisions of the Extradition Act 1870 relating to depositions and state-ments on oath taken in a foreign state and copies thereof extended to affirmations and copies of affirmations.
    The Norwegian government sought the extradition of the applicant for alleged offences of conspiracy to supply, supply-ing and dealing in prohibited drugs in Norway. The evidence before the chief metropolitan magistrate included unsworn statements of the applicant's alleged accomplices given before a Norwegian court. Since the Norwegian Penal Code pre-

cluded the giving of evidence on oath by accomplices, the   A
statements had been read in court in Norway to their makers,
and having been accepted as true were incorporated into the
court record. Within a few days that acceptance was repeated
in court after the witnesses had been reminded of the provisions of the Penal Code relating to false evidence. Having
heard the evidence the magistrate found that there was a case
to answer and committed the applicant to prison to await
extradition.   B

On an application for a writ of habeas corpus: —
Held, refusing the application, (1) that since treaties were
to receive a liberal interpretation and their words were to be
given their ordinary international meaning, taking into account
the fact that the Extradition Act 1873 admitting evidence on
affirmation had come into effect before the treaty in question
was ratified, and as one of its objects was to avoid the necessity of bringing witnesses from overseas, it was justifiable to   C
construe the words of article X as extending to affirmations
(post, pp. 1034A—1035D, 1037B–F).

(2) That to constitute an affirmation it had to be shown
that the statement had been adopted in circumstances which
recognised the gravity and importance of the truth being told
on that particular occasion and that was a matter of fact
and degree dependent upon the particular circumstances of
each case; that while an affirmation did not need to be made   D
prior to the making of the statement to which it related,
the mere acknowledgment before a judicial authority that
what had been previously said was the truth did not amount
to an affirmation, but that since the alleged accomplices had
been brought back before the court within a short time after
their initial appearance and had acknowledged the truth of
their evidence after the terms of the Norwegian Penal Code
relating to false evidence had been drawn to their attention,   E
their evidence was properly before the magistrate and, accordingly, a prima facie case had been made out against the
applicant (post, pp. 1036C–F, 1038A–C, E).

The following cases are referred to in the judgments:

Arton (No. 2), In re [1896] 1 Q.B. 509, D.C.
Reg. v. *Governor of Brixton Prison, Ex parte Twena* (unreported),   F
November 27, 1980, D.C.
Reg. v. *Governor of Pentonville Prison, Ex parte Ecke* (unreported),
December 3, 1973, D.C.

The following additional cases were cited in argument:

Reg. v. *Governor of Gloucester Prison, Ex parte Miller* [1979] 1 W.L.R.
537; [1979] 2 All E.R. 1103, D.C.   G
Reg. v. *Governor of Pentonville Prison, Ex parte Kirby (Note)* [1979]
1 W.L.R. 541; [1979] 2 All E.R. 1094, D.C.

APPLICATION for a writ of habeas corpus.

The applicant, Harmohan Singh, applied for a writ of habeas corpus
directed to the Governor of Pentonville Prison, where he was detained   H
consequent on an order made on October 23, 1980, at the Bow Street
Magistrates' Court by the chief metropolitan magistrate (Mr. E. Russell)
under the Extradition Acts 1870 and 1873 pending removal to Norway
on charges of conspiring to supply a dangerous drug; supplying a dangerous
drug; and being knowingly concerned in carrying, removing, depositing,
harbouring, keeping, or concealing or in any manner dealing with a
dangerous drug in respect of which a prohibition on importation was in

A force in Norway. The applicant applied for the writ on the grounds that the committal order was unlawful in that some of the evidence was inadmissible in that it was not taken in accordance with the requirements of the Extradition Acts 1870 and 1873 that such evidence be on oath or affirmation, and that the remainder of the evidence was insufficient to warrant committal.

The facts are stated in the judgment.

B

Richard Du Cann Q.C. and *Andrew Trollope* for the applicant.
David Tudor Price and *Clive Nicholls* for the Government of Norway and the Governor of Pentonville Prison.

Cur. adv. vult.

C

January 21. The following judgments were read.

ACKNER L.J. Harmohan Singh applies for a writ of habeas corpus in respect of a warrant of committal issued by the chief metropolitan magistrate at Bow Street on October 23, 1980. The Government of Norway allege that the applicant is accused of the commission of the crimes of conspiring to supply a dangerous drug; supplying a dangerous drug; and being knowingly concerned in carrying, removing, depositing, harbouring, keeping, or concealing or in any manner dealing with a dangerous drug in respect of which a prohibition on importation is, for the time being, in force within the jurisdiction of the Government of Norway. The drugs involved are alleged to be morphine and heroin.

E The chief metropolitan magistrate, having heard evidence produced by the Government of Norway and submissions on behalf of both the applicant and that government, held that there was a case to answer, and committed the applicant to prison to await his extradition to Norway.

Mr. Du Cann in his most helpful, clear and concise submissions has pointed out that the evidence fell into four different classes. These were:

F (1) evidence on oath before the court in Oslo; (2) statements by four persons, two Norwegians and two Indians, who were accomplices to the alleged crimes. They had all been arrested in Norway prior to signing their statements; (3) evidence on oath by witnesses who gave evidence before a court in Copenhagen; (4) evidence of English police officers given under section 9 of the Criminal Justice Act 1967.

G Mr. Du Cann submitted that the material in class numbers (2) and (3) was not admissible evidence in extradition proceedings in England, and the remaining evidence was not sufficient to justify the committal. He made four submissions. These were: (1) the Extradition Acts of 1870 and 1873 read together with the relevant treaty required that the evidence taken in the requesting state, that is Norway, has to be taken on oath if it is to be admissible in the courts in this country. (2) alternatively, if the above

H proposition is too wide and evidence can be taken on affirmation, then the procedure which took place in Norway was deficient to such a degree as to make the material inadmissible in this country. The procedure was deficient because (a) it did not comply with the Acts and the treaty; (b) it did not comply with United Kingdom rules as to competence of witnesses or admissibility of evidence. (3) In relation to the evidence given in the court in Copenhagen, the treaty did not permit evidence, whether on oath or otherwise, given in a third state to be admissible in a holding state.

(4) Upon the assumption that the above three submissions were correct, A
alternatively the first two submissions were correct, the remaining evidence
was insufficient to justify the committal.

It is convenient to deal first of all with the third submission. The treaty
relied on, concluded on June 26, 1873, in respect of Sweden and Norway
and continued in respect of Norway alone on February 18, 1907, was the
subject matter of Orders in Council made on September 30, 1873, and
July 6, 1907. It provided in Article X: B

> " In the examinations which they have to make, in accordance with
> the foregoing stipulations, the authorities of the state applied to shall
> admit as entirely valid evidence the sworn depositions or statements
> of witnesses taken in the other state, or copies thereof, and likewise
> the warrants and sentences issued therein, provided such documents
> are signed or certified by a judge, magistrate, or officer of such state, C
> and are authenticated by the oath of some witness, or by being sealed
> with the official seal of the Minister of Justice, or some other Minister
> of State."

Mr. Du Cann submits, and Mr. Tudor Price for the Government of
Norway concedes, that the words " taken in the other state " make   D
inadmissible the sworn depositions or statements taken in Denmark.
However, it is common ground that the exclusion of the evidence given
in Copenhagen leaves an adequacy of material to establish a prima facie
case, and I therefore turn to deal with the first two submissions.

As to the first submission, section 14 of the Extradition Act 1870
provides:
                                                                         E
> " Depositions or statements on oath, taken in a foreign state, and
> copies of such original depositions or statements, and foreign certifi-
> cates of or judicial documents stating the fact of conviction, may, if
> duly authenticated, be received in evidence in proceedings under
> this Act."

Lord Brougham's Act 1850, whose worthy object is entitled " An Act   F
for shortening the language used in Acts of Parliament " provided in
section 4, inter alia,

> " That in all Acts . . . the words ' oath,' ' swear,' and ' affidavit ' shall
> include affirmation, declaration, affirming, and declaring, in the case
> of persons by law allowed to declare or affirm instead of swearing."

Nevertheless shortly before the Order in Council referred to above, namely, G
on August 5, 1873, the Extradition Act 1873 was passed, and this provided
by section 4:

> " . . . the provisions of the principal Act relating to depositions and
> statements on oath taken in a foreign state, and copies of such original
> depositions and statements, do and shall extend to affirmations taken
> in a foreign state, and copies of such affirmations."   H

Mr. Du Cann rightly points out that Lord Brougham's Act only applies
to Acts of Parliament and not to treaties. Article X makes no reference
to affirmations and he therefore contends that there is no justification for
construing the words " sworn depositions or statements of witnesses " to
include affirmations.

In relation to the interpretation of treaties, Mr. Tudor Price reminded

The Weekly Law Reports, July 10, 1981

1035

1 W.L.R.   Reg. v. Gov. of Pentonville, Ex p. Singh (D.C.)   Ackner L.J.

A us of the well-known observation of Lord Russell of Killowen C.J. in
In re Arton (No. 2) [1896] 1 Q.B. 509, 517, where he said:

> "In my judgment these treaties ought to receive a liberal inter-
> pretation, which means no more than that they should receive their
> true construction according to their language, object and intent."

In *Reg.* v. *Governor of Pentonville Prison, Ex parte Ecke* (unreported),
B December 3, 1973, Lord Widgery C.J., after reciting that part of the judgment of Lord Russell of Killowen C.J. referred to above, emphasised that
an extradition treaty is not to be construed as though it were a domestic
statute. He said:

> "The words used in a treaty of this kind are to be given their general
> meaning, general to lawyer and layman alike. They are to be given,
C as it were, the meaning of the diplomat rather than the lawyer, and
> they are to be given their ordinary international meaning and not a
> particular meaning which they may have attracted in England or in
> certain branches of activity in England."

Bearing in mind that the Act of 1873 came into effect before the
first Order in Council and, further, that one of the intents of the treaty
D was to avoid the necessity of bringing witnesses from overseas, I consider
that a justifiable liberal interpretation of the treaty involves construing the
words "sworn depositions or statements of witnesses" as extending to
affirmations.

I therefore turn to the second submission, namely, that the statements
of the four accomplices did not amount to affirmations.

E Under section 186 of the Norwegian Penal Code, an oath must not be
taken by a witness who has been found guilty of the act, or guilty of
complicity in the act which is the subject of the investigation, or who is
under suspicion of such guilt. Thus, there could be no question of any
of the four accomplices taking the oath. All four alleged accomplices were
willing to give evidence. What took place in each case was that their
previous statements, or one or more of them, was read and each accepted
F before the court that it was accurate, subject in one case to certain
corrections. These verbal acceptances were dictated by the judges into the
court record which was then signed by these witnesses.

It is provided by section 168 of the Norwegian Penal Code:

> "Anybody who by false accusation, report, or testimony before a
> court, the prosecution or any other public authority, by distortion or
G removal of evidence or by establishment of false evidence, or otherwise
> against his better conscience, attempts to cause somebody else to be
> charged with or convicted of an offence, or is accessory thereto, shall
> be punished by imprisonment from six months to eight years if the
> offence concerned is a felony, and by imprisonment up to four years
> if the offence is a misdemeanour."

H Within two to three days of giving their evidence it was apparently
thought desirable by the authorities to remind the alleged accomplices of
the provisions of this section. They were accordingly brought back before
the judge and informed of the terms of the code. Three of them stated that
in giving their evidence they were each aware that they would be liable
to punishment if they gave "perjurious evidence in court." One of the
Indians, Mr. Hardial Singh, declared that he did not know of the provision
when he gave his evidence, but declared that his evidence would be the

1036

same even if he had known of the provision. He repeated that he had told A
the whole and full truth.

Mr. Du Cann submits that there are three requirements for a valid
affirmation. These are: (1) a solemn undertaking has to be given to the
judicial authority; (2) it must be given prior to the giving of evidence to
the court; (3) the undertaking ought to include some reference to a promise
to tell the truth—however expressed.

The right to affirm was introduced in 1838 for the benefit of Quakers B
and Moravians and the essential part of the declaration is still retained
today, namely, " I . . . do solemnly, sincerely, and truly declare and
affirm." Although neither party suggests that this or any closely comparable formula has to be used, it is agreed that the mere signature to a
document or the verbal acknowledgment that its contents are correct cannot
amount to an affirmation. Where then is the line to be drawn? C

The answer cannot be precise; it must be a matter of fact and degree
dependent upon the particular circumstances of the case. I do not consider
that the affirmation need take place prior to the making of the statement.
What is required, where the statement has been made, is its adoption in
circumstances which recognise the gravity and importance of the truth
being told on the particular occasion. I would not necessarily accept that
the mere acknowledgment, albeit before a judicial authority, that what D
has been previously said is the truth would amount to an affirmation. But
in this case, the acknowledgment before the judicial authority was made
after the terms or the substance of section 168 of the Norwegian Penal
Code was drawn to the attention of each of the alleged accomplices. The
fact that the provisions of this section were not drawn to their attention
initially when they appeared before the judge does not seem to me, in the E
circumstances of this case, to make any material difference. They were
brought back before the court within a very short time of their initial
appearance and their subsequent acknowledgment in the circumstances
which I have described of the truth of what they had previously said
amounted, in my judgment, to a sufficient acknowledgment.

It is conceded that, if the evidence of the alleged accomplices was F
properly before the chief stipendiary magistrate, there was sufficient
evidence to justify his conclusion that a prima facie case had been made
out by the Norwegian Government. I would accordingly refuse this
application.

SKINNER J. Of the four submissions made so clearly by Mr. Du Cann
and referred to by Ackner L.J., I need only consider two. G

The first is that the committing magistrates can only act on sworn
testimony in deciding whether the evidence is such as would, in the words
of section 10 of the Extradition Act 1870:

" according to the law of England, justify the committal for trial of
the prisoner if the crime of which he is accused had been committed
in England . . ." H

This argument depends first on the treaty of 1873 and, in particular, on
Article X which provides that

" the authorities of the state applied to shall admit as entirely valid
evidence the sworn depositions of statements of witnesses taken in
the other state or copies thereof."

Any domestic legislation has to be read in the light of those words. The

A   relevant domestic legislation lies in the Oaths Act 1838, Lord Brougham's Act 1850, section 14 of the Extradition Act 1870 and section 4 of the Extradition Act 1873 to all of which Ackner L.J. has already referred. Mr. Du Cann submits that, however inconvenient or out of date it might be, and whatever the position may have been in English law either in 1873 or now, sworn statements alone can be received.

B   Mr. Tudor Price concedes that the treaty is the determining factor. He relies on the well-known words of Lord Russell of Killowen C.J., in *In re Arton* (*No. 2*) [1896] 1 Q.B. 509, 517:

> ". . . treaties ought to receive a liberal interpretation, which means no more than that they should receive their true construction according to their language, object and intent."

C   Lord Widgery C.J., in *Reg.* v. *Governor of Pentonville Prison, Ex parte Ecke* (unreported), helpfully put the correct approach in the following words:

> " The words used in a treaty of this kind are to be given their general meaning, general to lawyer and layman alike. They are to be given, as it were, the meaning of the diplomat rather than the lawyer, and
> D   they are to be given their ordinary international meaning and not a particular meaning which they may have attracted in England, or in certain branches of activity in England."

Mr. Tudor Price asks us to look at this treaty in the light of events at the time it was signed and ratified. It was concluded on June 26, 1873. On August 5, 1873, the Extradition Act 1873 received the Royal Assent,
E   thereby widening the scope of section 10 of the Act of 1870 to include affirmations, despite the fact that the English courts could only hear affirmed evidence if given by a Quaker or Moravian. On August 28, 1873, the treaty was ratified. Lord Brougham's Act 1850, though not directly relevant to interpretation of the treaty, had been in force for nearly a quarter of a century. In the light of this, what is the general meaning,
F   general to lawyer and layman alike of " sworn depositions or statements of witnesses " in the treaty? Does it include an affirmation? In my judgment it does.

Thus Mr. Tudor Price's argument succeeds on the first point, and as to the second he concedes that, to be within the treaty, the evidence submitted must either be on oath or affirmation: unsworn or unaffirmed evidence cannot be received.

G   That brings me to Mr. Du Cann's second submission that the crucial statements in this case, namely, those given by four alleged accomplices of the applicant, were not affirmations. What is meant by an affirmation in this context? Ackner L.J. has recited what in fact occurred in the Norwegian court and the relevant sections of the Norwegian Penal Code. The difference between the parties is a narrow one. They agree that an
H   affirmation need not follow the wording of the Oaths Act 1838 (which has remained unchanged since 1838); and that there must be a solemn undertaking given to the court to tell the truth. Mr. Du Cann would add that it ought to contain a promise to tell the truth, and that the promise ought to be given before the evidence is recorded.

In my judgment, there has been some confusion caused by failure to differentiate between the verb " to affirm " and the noun " affirmation." Within the context of the Extradition Act 1873 an affirmation must be a

1038

document like a deposition or statement on oath: see *per* Donaldson L.J.   A
and Hodgson J. in *Reg.* v. *Governor of Brixton Prison, Ex parte Twena* (unreported), November 27, 1980. I do not accept Mr. Du Cann's submission
on this point that that court wrongly made a differentiation. In my judgment the document put forward as an affirmation must contain, or show
on its face, a solemn declaration by the witness before a judicial authority
that its contents are true. The document might consist of a record of what
the witness has said or might refer to a record of something said on   B
another occasion and acknowledged or adopted in solemn form before
the judicial authority. The vital constituent is the solemn declaration of
the truth which might be expressed in a number of different ways. For
example, in the present case, the reference in the case of each witness
to section 168 of the Norwegian Penal Code clearly emphasises the
solemnity of what the witness is adopting and accepting in the document.   C

Here, each of the witnesses appeared in court before a judge on May
20 and 21, 1980. Because he was an accomplice Norwegian law precluded
him from taking the oath. Each was informed of his right to refuse to
give evidence. He then accepted or confirmed earlier statements he had
made and this was recorded. The two Indian witnesses are both recorded
as saying that their statements were in accordance with the truth. On   D
May 23, because it was felt that perhaps all the formalities had not
been observed, each was brought back to the court before the judge and
informed (in one case) and reminded (in the other three cases) of the
provisions of section 168. The three " reminded " all said that they had
been aware of the section at the previous hearing. The one " informed "
said that, had he been aware, he would have given the same evidence and
it was the truth. In order to decide whether there was an affirmation in   E
any particular case, the documents recording the witnesses' evidence have
to be looked at as a whole. Doing so here, I have no hesitation in saying
that, in each of these cases, the documents reveal a solemn declaration,
reinforced by penal sanctions, that their contents are true and they amount
to affirmations within section 4 of the Act of 1873. For these reasons I
agree that this application should be refused.   F

> *Application refused*
> *Leave to appeal refused.*

Solicitors: *Hallinan, Blackburn Gittings & Co.; Director of Public
Prosecutions.*
                                                                        G

[Reported by MISS LESLEY HEWLETT, Barrister-at-Law]

May 12. The Appeal Committee of the House of Lords (Lord Fraser
of Tullybelton, Lord Scarman and Lord Roskill) dismissed a petition by the
applicant for leave to appeal.   H

A

[COURT OF APPEAL]

* REGINA *v.* GALBRAITH

1981 May 12; 19   Lord Lane C.J., Peter Pain and Stuart-Smith JJ.

B *Crime—Practice—Submission of no case to answer—Evidence of*
person charged committing crime alleged—Strength or weak-
ness of evidence depending on view taken of witnesses—
Whether for jury to determine

The applicant was charged with having fought and made an
affray. The prosecution evidence showed that there had been
an affray in a bar in which at least three men were stabbed,
C one fatally. There were passages in the evidence of two
witnesses which tended to show that the applicant had taken
an active part in the affray, although in a statement to the
police the applicant had maintained that at the time the affray
was in progress he had not been in the bar but downstairs in the
lavatory. At the close of the prosecution evidence a submission of no case to answer was rejected. The applicant, who
made a statement from the dock reiterating the self-exculpatory
D statement which he had made to the police, was convicted.

On an application for leave to appeal against conviction : —
Held, refusing the application, that when a submission of
no case was made the case was to be stopped when there was
no evidence that the person charged had committed the crime
alleged and was also to be stopped if the evidence was tenuous
and the judge concluded that the prosecution's evidence taken
at its highest was such that a properly directed jury could not
E properly convict on it ; but that, where the prosecution's evidence was such that its strength or weakness depended on the
view to be taken of the reliability of a witness or other matters
which were, generally speaking, within the province of a jury
and one possible view of the facts was that there was evidence
on which they could properly conclude that the person charged
was guilty, the matter was to be tried by them ; that borderline cases were in the judge's discretion ; and that, in the
F circumstances, the applicant's submission of no case to answer
was properly rejected.
Reg. v. *Barker* (*Note*) (1975) 65 Cr.App.R. 287, C.A.
approved.
Reg. v. *Mansfield* [1977] 1 W.L.R. 1102, C.A. explained.

The following cases are referred to in the judgment :

G *Reg.* v. *Barker* (*Note*) (1975) 65 Cr.App.R. 287, C.A.
Reg. v. *Mansfield* [1977] 1 W.L.R. 1102 ; [1978] 1 All E.R. 134, C.A.
Reg. v. *Tobin* [1980] Crim.L.R. 731.

The following additional cases were cited in argument :

Reg. v. *Falconer-Atlee* (1973) 58 Cr.App.R. 348, C.A.
Reg. v. *Hipson* [1969] Crim.L.R. 85, C.A.

H

APPLICATION for leave to appeal against conviction.
On November 13, 1979, at the Central Criminal Court (Mars-Jones
J.) the applicant, George Charles Galbraith, was convicted on an indictment charging that he fought and made an affray. He was sentenced to
four years' imprisonment. He applied for leave to appeal against conviction on the grounds that the judge wrongly rejected a submission at
the end of the prosecution's case that the case against him should be

withdrawn from the jury and that the verdict was unsafe and unsatis-   A
factory. An application for leave to appeal against sentence does not call
for report. At the conclusion of the argument Lord Lane C.J. announced
that the application for leave to appeal against conviction was refused
for reasons to be given at a later date.

The facts are stated in the judgment.

Robin Simpson Q.C. and *Howard Godfrey* for the applicant.   B
Allan Green and *Susan Edwards* for the Crown.

Cur. adv. vult.

May 19. Lord Lane C.J. read the following judgment of the court.
On November 13, 1979, at the Central Criminal Court, the applicant   C
was convicted by a majority verdict of affray and was sentenced to four
years' imprisonment. He now applies for leave to appeal against that
conviction, the application having been referred to this court by the
single judge.

The facts of the case were these. On November 20, 1978, at the
Ranelagh Yacht Club, Putney Bridge, in the early hours of the evening   D
a fight broke out in the bar. There were a number of people present,
amongst them being Darke, Begbe, Bohm, Dennis and Bindon. Knives
were used. At least three men were stabbed, Darke fatally, Bindon
seriously, and Dennis less so. There was in these circumstances no doubt
that there had been an affray. The only question for the jury to decide
was whether it had been established with a sufficient degree of certainty
that the applicant had been unlawfully taking part in that affray.   E

At the close of the prosecution evidence, a submission was made by
counsel for the applicant that there was no case for him to answer. The
judge rejected that submission. The principal ground of appeal to this
court is that he was wrong in so doing. There are other subsidiary
grounds of appeal which we shall have to examine in due course.

We are told that some doubt exists as to the proper approach to be   F
adopted by the judge at the close of the prosecution case upon a submission of " no case ": see *Archbold, Criminal Pleading Evidence &
Practice,* 40th ed. (1979), 6th Cumulative Supplement, para. 575 and
Reg. v. *Tobin* [1980] Crim.L.R. 731.

There are two schools of thought: (1) that the judge should stop the
case if, in his view, it would be unsafe (alternatively unsafe or unsatisfactory) for the jury to convict; (2) that he should do so only if there is   G
no evidence upon which a jury properly directed could properly convict.
Although in many cases the question is one of semantics, and though
in many cases each test would produce the same result, this is not
necessarily so. A balance has to be struck between on the one hand a
usurpation by the judge of the jury's functions and on the other the
danger of an unjust conviction.   H

Before the Criminal Appeal Act 1966, the second test was that which
was applied. By section 4 (1) (*a*) of that Act however the Court of Appeal
was required to allow an appeal if they were of the opinion that the verdict should be set aside on the grounds that " under all the circumstances
of the case it is unsafe or unsatisfactory." It seems that thereafter a
practice grew up of inviting the judge at the close of the prosecution
case to say that it would be unsafe (or sometimes unsafe or unsatisfac-

A   tory) to convict on the prosecution evidence and on that ground to withdraw the case from the jury. Whether the change in the powers of the
Court of Appeal can logically be said to justify a change in the basis of
a " no case " submission, we beg leave to doubt. The fact that the Court
of Appeal have power to quash a conviction on these grounds is a slender
basis for giving the trial judge similar powers at the close of the prosecution case.

B   There is however a more solid reason for doubting the wisdom of
this test. If a judge is obliged to consider whether a conviction would be
" unsafe " or " unsatisfactory," he can scarcely be blamed if he applies
his views as to the weight to be given to the prosecution evidence and as
to the truthfulness of their witnesses and so on. That is what Lord
Widgery C.J., in *Reg.* v. *Barker* (*Note*) (1975) 65 Cr.App.R. 287, 288, said
C   was clearly not permissible :

        " . . . even if the *judge* "—our emphasis—" has taken the view that
        the evidence could not support a conviction because of the incon-
        sistencies, he should nevertheless have left the matter to the jury.
        It cannot be too clearly stated that the judge's obligation to stop
        the case is an obligation which is concerned primarily with those
D   cases where the necessary minimum evidence to establish the facts of
        the crime has not been called. It is not the judge's job to weigh the
        evidence, decide who is telling the truth, and to stop the case merely
        because he thinks the witness is lying. To do that is to usurp the
        function of the jury . . ."

Although this was a case where no submission was in fact made, the
E   principle is unaffected.
     Some of the difficulties have arisen from the subsequent case of *Reg.*
v. *Mansfield* [1977] 1 W.L.R. 1102. Lawton L.J. said, at p. 1106:

        " Unfortunately since this practice started . . ."—sc. withdrawing a
        case from the jury on the ground that a conviction on the evidence
        would be unsafe—" there has, it seems, been a tendency for some
        judges to take the view that if they think that the main witnesses for the
F   prosecution are not telling the truth then that by itself justifies them
        in withdrawing the case from the jury. Lord Widgery C.J. in his
        judgment in *Reg.* v. *Barker* pointed out that this was wrong. . . ."

He then cited part of the passage we have already quoted. Lawton L.J.
then went on to say :

G   " Mr. Cockburn intended to submit to the judge that some of the
        evidence was so conflicting as to be unreliable and therefore if the jury
        did rely upon it the verdict would be unsafe. In our judgment he was
        entitled to make that submission to the judge and the judge was not
        entitled to rule that he could not."

On one reading of that passage it might be said to be inconsistent both
H   with *Reg.* v. *Barker* (*Note*) 65 Cr.App.R. 287 and with the earlier part of
the judgment itself. It is an illustration of the danger inherent in the use
of the word " unsafe "; by its very nature it invites the judge to evaluate
the weight and reliability of the evidence in the way which *Reg.* v. *Barker*
(*Note*) forbids and leads to the sort of confusion which now apparently
exists. " Unsafe," unless further defined, is capable of embracing either
of the two schools of thought and this we believe is the cause of much
of the difficulty which the judgment in *Reg.* v. *Mansfield* has apparently

given. It may mean unsafe because there is insufficient evidence on which   A
a jury could properly reach a verdict of guilty; it may on the other hand
mean unsafe because in the judge's view, for example, the main prosecution witness is not to be believed. If it is used in the latter sense as the
test, it is wrong. We have come to the conclusion that if and in so far
as the decision in *Reg.* v. *Mansfield* [1977] 1 W.L.R. 1102 is at variance
with that in *Reg.* v. *Barker* (*Note*) 65 Cr.App.R. 287 we must follow the
latter.   B

How then should the judge approach a submission of " no case "?
(1) If there is no evidence that the crime alleged has been committed by
the defendant, there is no difficulty. The judge will of course stop the
case. (2) The difficulty arises where there is some evidence but it is of a
tenuous character, for example because of inherent weakness or vague-
ness or because it is inconsistent with other evidence. (a) Where the judge   C
comes to the conclusion that the prosecution evidence, taken at its
highest, is such that a jury properly directed could not properly convict
upon it, it is his duty, upon a submission being made, to stop the case.
(b) Where however the prosecution evidence is such that its strength or
weakness depends on the view to be taken of a witness's reliability, or
other matters which are generally speaking within the province of the   D
jury and where on one possible view of the facts there *is* evidence upon
which a jury could properly come to the conclusion that the defendant is
guilty, then the judge should allow the matter to be tried by the jury. It
follows that we think the second of the two schools of thought is to be
preferred.

There will of course, as always in this branch of the law, be borderline
cases. They can safely be left to the discretion of the judge.   E

We turn now to the evidence in this case. It was admitted that the
applicant had gone to the club with Darke and Begbe and, using a false
name, had signed them in. They had later been joined by Bohm. It was
further not disputed that at the conclusion of the fighting the applicant
was in the bar and, much to his credit, was helping a dying Darke. He
did not go into the witness box, but the account of events which he gave   F
in a self-exculpatory statement to the police, reiterated in a statement
from the dock, was that he had at the material time when the affray was
in progress not been in the bar at all but had been downstairs in the
lavatory.

There were two principal pieces of evidence called by the prosecution
which tended to disprove that assertion and to show that he was in the
bar taking an active part in the affray. The first was a witness called John   G
Gilette. He said that Darke had attacked Bindon and that at that time
there were three men with Darke. They all had knives. He then described
the three men. One description plainly referred to Begbe, another to Bohm
and the third was an accurate description of the applicant. These men
were described by Gilette as standing by the fight watching with knives
out in a threatening way. He had attended an identification parade on   H
February 19, 1979. On that parade the applicant was standing. Gilette
however said he was not able to point out anyone on that parade whom
he recognised as having been in the club that night.

The second piece of evidence was from a witness called Cook. He was
the doorman of the club and was a very reluctant witness. Leave was
eventually given to treat him as hostile. Cook described how the applicant,
or a man who, from the description given by Cook, was plainly and

A admittedly the applicant, had signed Darke and Begbe into the club at about 4.15 p.m. At 6.15 p.m. he heard glass breaking and people shouting in the bar, so he went upstairs. When he got there Dennis had told him that he had been stabbed and pointed to a group of people standing by the juke box. This group was described by Cook as being " John Darke's party, the man with the beard, the fair-haired chap and the bloke with the twisted nose." The reference to the fair-haired chap was
B plainly intended to be a reference to the same person as had signed the other two in at the door two hours previously, namely, the applicant. In cross-examination he said that he could have been mistaken in thinking that the fair-haired man with Darke by the juke box was the same blonde man who signed them in.

In addition to these two pieces of evidence there was a further witness
C called Stanton who gave evidence that when Darke was attacking Bindon as Bindon lay on the floor, a little guy went up to Darke and said " stop it John, you'll kill him." This man was described by Stanton in a way which would fit the applicant. However, in cross-examination, Stanton said the little guy was not the applicant. There was a body of evidence which seemed to indicate that there had been some form of agreement between the witnesses that they would, so far as possible, back-pedal from
D the statements which they had made to the police immediately after the incident had taken place.

In these circumstances it seems to us that this was eminently a case where the jury should be left to decide the weight of the evidence upon which the prosecution based their case. It was not a case where the judge would have been justified in saying that the prosecution evidence
E taken at its highest was such that the jury properly directed could not properly convict upon it.

Of the remaining subsidiary grounds which the applicant advances in his perfected grounds of appeal, the only one that has any substance is the complaint that the judge misdirected the jury in directing them that they could regard Bindon's evidence of having shaken hands with the co-defendants Bohm and Galbraith and having said to them " let bygones be
F bygones " in a cell at the magistrates' court as evidence against the applicant. We are inclined to agree that strictly speaking that was a misdirection. The evidence was certainly part of the background of the case and an important part of the background, but it could not properly be said to be evidence against the applicant. However this minor error on the part of the judge can have had no possible effect on the outcome
G of the case and can safely be disregarded.

There is nothing in the other grounds of appeal which makes it necessary to comment upon them.

Accordingly, as indicated at the close of the argument before us, the application for leave to appeal against conviction is refused. We have already dealt with the question of sentence.

H
Application refused.

Solicitors: *Henry Milner & Co., Director of Public Prosecutions.*

L. N. W.

[COURT OF APPEAL]

* REGINA v. MELLOR

1980 Oct. 28;
Dec. 5

Eveleigh L.J., Cantley and Kilner Brown JJ.

B

Crime—Court of Appeal—Sentence, appeal against—Offence committed by young offender after release on licence on parole recommendation—Whether " serving a sentence of imprisonment "—Criminal Justice Act 1961 (9 & 10 *Eliz.* 2, *c.* 39), *s.* 3 (1) (2) (3)—*Criminal Justice Act* 1967 (*c.* 80), *s.* 60

The defendant, who was under 21 years of age and had been sentenced to three years' imprisonment and released on licence on parole recommendation, committed further offences and was sentenced in respect of them to a total period of 18 months' imprisonment.

C

On appeal against sentence on the grounds that it was unlawful by reason of the limitation on sentences in section 3 (1) of the Criminal Justice Act 1961 [1] and that he was not " a person . . . serving a sentence of imprisonment " within section 3 (2) because he had been released on licence at a time when the court passed the sentence: —

D

Held, dismissing the appeal, that a person under 21 years of age who was released on licence on parole recommendation was still a person "serving a sentence of imprisonment" within section 3 (2) of the Criminal Justice Act 1961 ; that, therefore, the restrictions on sentencing the defendant imposed by section 3 (1) did not apply ; and that, in the circumstances, the sentence of 18 months' imprisonment was correct.

E

No case is referred to in the judgment or was cited in argument.

APPEAL against sentence.

On February 29, 1980, at Warwick Crown Court, the defendant, Gary Mellor, pleaded guilty to an offence of taking a conveyance without the consent of the owner or other lawful authority, and to an offence of theft of a car radio. On April 9, 1980, at the same court, before Judge Harrison-Hall, the defendant pleaded guilty to a count of dishonestly receiving stolen goods knowing or believing them to be stolen. He was sentenced to 12 months' imprisonment for the first offence, six months for the second to run concurrently, and six months for the third to run consecutively, making a total period of imprisonment of 18 months.

F

G

The defendant applied for leave to appeal against the sentences on the grounds that he was aged 20 when the sentences were passed and accordingly the court was subject to the provisions of section 3 of the Criminal Justice Act 1961; that section 3 (1) barred intermediate sentences for young offenders and a period of 18 months came within that category; that he had been sentenced to a period of three years' imprisonment in 1978 but he was not a person serving a sentence of imprisonment within section 3 (2) because supervision and licence were excepted categories and a person released on licence on a parole recommendation was therefore excepted. The single judge referred the application to the full court,

H

[1] Criminal Justice Act 1961, s. 3: see post, p. 1045E–F.

A who granted leave to appeal and treated the hearing as the hearing of an appeal.

The facts are stated in the judgment.

Anthony Engel (assigned by the Registrar of Criminal Appeals) for the defendant.

B *Stephen Waine* for the Crown.

Cur. adv. vult.

Dec. 5. EVELEIGH L.J. read the following judgment of the court. This case was referred by the single judge to the full court, which treated that reference as an appeal against sentence and gave the necessary leave.

C On April 9, 1980, at Warwick Crown Court, the defendant was sentenced to a total period of 18 months' imprisonment. That sentence was made up of 12 months' imprisonment for taking a vehicle without consent, six months' imprisonment concurrent for theft and six months' imprisonment consecutive for handling. Two offences were taken into consideration. He was 20 years of age at that time.

D On June 16, 1978, the defendant had been sentenced to three years' imprisonment. He had been released on parole on November 14, 1979, and his licence was due to expire on April 23, 1981. The first two offences were committed on November 27, 1979, two weeks after his release from prison, when he was staying at a probation hostel. He was arrested that very same day but was granted bail. The third offence was committed on December 5, 1979, while he was on bail.

E It is however submitted that the court had no power to pass a sentence of 18 months' imprisonment because of the restrictions placed upon the sentencing of young offenders by section 3 (1) of the Criminal Justice Act 1961. That subsection reads:

"Without prejudice to any other enactment prohibiting or restricting the imposition of imprisonment on persons of any age, a

F sentence of imprisonment shall not be passed by any court on a person within the limits of age which qualify for a sentence of borstal training except—(a) for a term not exceeding six months; or (b) (where the court has power to pass such a sentence) for a term of not less than three years."

G The case is clearly covered by those words, but the question now arises whether or not it falls within the provisions of section 3 (2), which reads:

"Subsection (1) of this section shall not apply in the case of a person who is serving a sentence of imprisonment at the time when the court passes sentence; and for the purpose of this subsection a person sentenced to imprisonment who has been recalled or returned to prison after being released subject to supervision or on licence, and

H has not been released again or discharged, shall be treated as serving the sentence."

Were it not for the second half of that subsection, we would be of the opinion that a person released on parole was serving a sentence of imprisonment. Upon revocation of the parole licence by the Secretary of State or by the court, section 62 of the Criminal Justice Act 1967 provides that the offender shall be liable to be detained in pursuance of his

sentence. However his sentence has not been suspended while on licence   A
on recommendation for parole, as it is for example in the case of a person discharged temporarily on account of ill health (see section 28 of the
Prison Act 1952); and he will be required to serve the time remaining
from the date of revocation to the end of the sentence (with remission)
or 30 days, whichever is the greater: *Practice Direction (Crime: Sentence)*
[1976] 1 W.L.R. 122, paragraph 4. A person released on licence on   B
parole recommendation or otherwise is not free to do exactly as he wishes,
but is under some constraints by virtue of his prison sentence. In such
circumstances, that is the progressive reduction of the period to be served
and the lack of total liberty, he is in fact serving his sentence but doing
so " in the community." He is not behind the prison walls but he is
still subject to his prison sentence.

It is submitted however that the second half of section 3 (2) of the   C
Act of 1961, by making special provision in relation to supervision or
licence, indicates that a person released on supervision or on licence is
not serving a sentence of imprisonment. By analogy it is said that a person released on licence on recommendation for parole is also not serving
a sentence of imprisonment. It therefore becomes necessary to see why
the references to supervision and licence were made in the Criminal
Justice Act 1961.   D

Section 20 of the Act of 1961 * made provision for supervision of
certain prisoners after release. That section reads:

> " (1) The provisions of Part I of Schedule 3 to this Act shall have
> effect with respect to the supervision after release from prison of
> persons to whom this section applies, and the return to prison of   E
> such persons in the event of failure to comply with the require-
> ments of their supervision. (2) This section applies to persons
> serving the following sentences of imprisonment (being sentences
> commencing after such date as may be prescribed by order of the
> Secretary of State), that is to say—(a) a sentence for a term of four
> years or more; (b) a sentence for a term of six months or more
> passed on a person who has served at least one previous sentence,   F
> being a sentence of imprisonment for a term of three months or
> more or a sentence of corrective training, preventive detention or
> borstal training; and (c) a sentence for a term of six months or more
> passed on a person appearing to the Prison Commissioners to have
> been under the age of 26 at the commencement of the sentence, but
> does not apply to a person serving a sentence of imprisonment for   G
> life."

By paragraph 1 of Schedule 3 the period of supervision is 12 months
from the date of release. Paragraph 5 provides for the return to prison
for a term

> " not exceeding whichever is the shorter of the following, that is to
> say—(a) a period equal to one third of the term of imprisonment to   H
> which he was originally sentenced, or, if that period exceeds six
> months, a period of six months; (b) a period equal to so much of the
> period of supervision as was unexpired at the date of the laying of
> the information by which the proceedings were commenced."

---

* This section was repealed by sections 60 (7), 103 (2) of and Schedule 7, Part I
to the Act of 1967.

A   There are various situations which could result in a person being detained in a prison after the date of the expiration of his original sentence. Not every person detained in prison is "serving a sentence of imprisonment;" for example a person on remand. The status of a person returned to prison in case of breach of supervision might be thought to be equivocal. This difficulty is recognised in para. 16 of Schedule 3, for it provides:

B
      "For the purposes of Part III of this Act, a person who has been sent back to prison under paragraph 5 or paragraph 10 of this Schedule, and has not been released again, shall be deemed to be serving part of his original sentence, whether or not the term of that sentence has in fact expired."

C   However while that paragraph was treating such a person as serving part of his original sentence, it was doing so only for the purposes of Part III of the Act of 1961. Section 3 (1) is contained in Part I of the Act. In order to remove any ambiguity with regard to section 3 (2), a special reference was necessary to the position of a person under supervision.

      Section 25 of the Prison Act 1952 † provided for remission for good conduct. The relevant subsections read:

D
      " (2) If it appears to the Prison Commissioners that a person serving a sentence of imprisonment was under the age of 21 years at the commencement of his sentence, they may direct that instead of being granted remission of his sentence under the rules he shall, at any time on or after the day on which he could have been discharged if the remission had been granted, be released on licence
E   under the following provisions of this section. (3) A person released on licence under this section shall until the expiration of his sentence be under the supervision of such society or person as may be specified in the licence and shall comply with such other requirements as may be so specified . . . (6) Where the unexpired part of the sentence of a person released under subsection (2) of this
F   section is less than six months, subsections (3) to (5) of this section shall apply to him subject to the following modifications— (a) the period for which he is under supervision under subsection (3) and is liable to recall under subsection (4) shall be a period of six months from the date of his release under the said subsection (2); (b) if he is recalled under subsection (4) the period for which he may be detained thereunder shall be whichever is the shorter of the
G   following, that is to say—(i) the remainder of the said period of six months; or (ii) the part of his sentence which was unexpired on the date of his release under the said subsection (2), reduced by any time during which he has been so detained since that date; and he may be released on licence under subsection (5) at any time before the expiration of that period."

H
      Thus again it was possible for a person to be detained at a time when his original sentence would have expired. While section 25 (3) spoke of such a person as being under supervision, strictly speaking he was released on licence under subsection (2). The marginal note to section 25 read "Remission for good conduct and release on licence of persons

      † Section 25 (2) to (6) was repealed by section 103 (2) of and Schedule 7, Part I to the Act of 1967.

sentenced to terms of imprisonment." Thus we find a reference to licence A
in section 3 (2) of the Criminal Justice Act 1961.

In our opinion therefore the references in section 3 (2) were necessitated by the provisions of section 20 of the Criminal Justice Act 1961
and section 25 of the Prison Act 1952. The references were dealing with
those special cases and the reasons for doing so can have no application
to the position of a person on parole by virtue of the provisions of a B
subsequent Act of Parliament in 1967 [i.e. section 60 of the Criminal
Justice Act 1967]. The defendant in the present case therefore was a
person serving a sentence of imprisonment and the restrictions imposed
in section 3 (1) do not apply.

We now turn to the sentence of 18 months itself. That matter can
be shortly dealt with. He had been sentenced on June 16, 1978, to three
years' imprisonment for robbery. That sentence had not expired by the C
time the sentence of 18 months' imprisonment now appealed against was
imposed. One has only to say in this case that he was on parole at the
time of the commission of the first of the offences for which he was sentenced on April 9, and one of those, the third offence, was committed, as
has been said, while he was on bail. It is quite obvious that this defendant had no intention whatsoever of observing the law, and this court D
is of the view that the sentence of 18 months was correct in every way.

This appeal therefore is dismissed.

Appeal dismissed.

Solicitors: *Field & Sons, Leamington Spa.*

[Reported by MISS LESLEY HEWLETT, Barrister-at-Law] E

F

* REGINA *v.* ORPWOOD

REGINA *v.* BROOKER

1981 Feb. 12   Lord Lane C.J., Thompson and Glidewell JJ.

Crime—Court of Appeal—Sentence, appeal against—Young offender G
released on licence committing offence—Whether " serving a
sentence of imprisonment "—Criminal Justice Act 1961 (9 &
10 Eliz. 2, c. 39), s. 3 (1) (2) (3)

The appellant, who was aged 20 and had been sentenced
to three years' imprisonment and released on licence as a
young person, committed an offence while he was still on
licence. He was sentenced to 15 months' imprisonment. H
On appeal against sentence in reliance on section 3 (1) and
(2) of the Criminal Justice Act 1961 [1]:—

---

[1] Criminal Justice Act 1961, s. 3 (1): see post, p. 1050B–C.
S. 3 (2): see post, p. 1050D–E.
S. 3 (3): " In relation to a person who has served a previous sentence of
imprisonment for a term of not less than six months . . . subsection (1) of this
section shall have effect as if for the reference to three years there were substituted
a reference to 18 months . . ."

A   *Held,* allowing the appeal, that, since the appellant was a
young person who was sentenced to imprisonment and released
on licence, he was not " serving a sentence of imprisonment "
within section 3 (2) of the Criminal Justice Act 1961 ; that,
therefore, he did not fall within section 3 (2) and the court's
sentencing power was restricted by section 3 (1) and (3) to
passing a sentence of a term not exceeding six months' or not
less than 18 months' imprisonment ; that, accordingly, the
B   sentence of 15 months' imprisonment was passed without
jurisdiction and, in the circumstances, a sentence of six months'
imprisonment would be substituted.
      Reg. v. *Mellor* [1981] 1 W.L.R. 1044, C.A. not followed.

The following case is referred to in the judgment:
Reg. v. *Mellor* [1981] 1 W.L.R. 1044, C.A.

C
No additional cases were cited in argument.

APPEAL against sentence.
On September 22, 1980, the appellant, Arthur Keith Orpwood, and the
appellant, Gary Patrick Brooker, aged 20, having pleaded guilty before
justices to a joint charge of attempted burglary, were committed for sen-
D   tence to Canterbury Crown Court. On October 21, 1980, at Canterbury
Crown Court each appellant was sentenced to 15 months' imprisonment.
They applied for leave to appeal against sentence and the appellant Brooker
also sought an extension of time of 87 days in which to apply for leave to
make the appeal. His grounds of appeal were that, in view of his age at
the date when he was sentenced, the sentence imposed was passed without
E   jurisdiction under section 3 of the Criminal Justice Act 1961. The hearing
of the application was treated as the hearing of the appeal.
The facts are stated in the judgment.

Greville Davis for the appellants.

LORD LANE C.J. gave the following judgment of the court. On Sep-
F   tember 22, 1980, at Dartford Magistrates' Court, the appellants, as they
now are leave having been given, pleaded guilty to a joint charge of
attempted burglary. They were committed for sentence. They appeared
at the Crown Court at Canterbury on October 21, 1980, and were
sentenced to 15 months' imprisonment each. They now both appeal
against that sentence, Brooker also applying for an extension of time
G   of 87 days, which we grant.
The facts of the case are these. On July 18, 1980, shortly after midnight, a 72-year old man was in bed at his home in Swanley, when he
was awakened by the two appellants knocking at his front door. They
had equipped themselves with stockings, which they had pulled over
their heads in order to conceal their features. They went round to the
back of the house. They removed a piece of plastic which in fact
H   covered a ventilator. They apparently thought it covered a whole pane
of glass. By removing it, they thought, they would have been enabled
to enter the house. That was wrong. They went round to the front
of the house once again, knocked on the door. The elderly gentleman
opened the door and saw the appellants. They ran off. He slammed the
door and shouted to his neighbours. The police were called and they
arrested these two appellants very shortly afterwards. They prevaricated
for a time but eventually admitted the offence. They said that they

were trying to get into the house in order to steal money from the meter. A
They said that they knocked on the door to see whether the house was
empty—it seems unnecessary to have equipped themselves with masks
if that had been the case—and that they had been drinking.

The burden of this case is a technical one, and it arises in this
way. At the time of the sentence the appellant Brooker was 20 years
of age. Thus the power to pass a sentence of imprisonment upon him
was governed by section 3 (1) of the Criminal Justice Act 1961, the B
section which has given this court so much trouble in the past; it provides:

" Without prejudice to any other enactment prohibiting or restricting the imposition of imprisonment on persons of any age, a sentence of imprisonment shall not be passed by any court on a person
within the limits of age which qualify for a sentence of borstal train- C
ing except—(a) for a term not exceeding six months; or (b) (where
the court has power to pass such a sentence) for a term of not
less than three years."

That upper limit of three years is in certain circumstances reduced to 18
months, but in this case there is no doubt that Brooker's record would
lead the court, had it been so minded, to pass a sentence of 18 months D
or more. But the problem arises thus. Section 3 (2) of the same Act
provides:

" Subsection (1) of this section shall not apply in the case of a
person who is serving a sentence of imprisonment at the time when
the court passes sentence; and for the purpose of this subsection
a person sentenced to imprisonment who has been recalled or E
returned to prison after being released subject to supervision or on
licence, and has not been released again or discharged, shall be
treated as serving the sentence."

Brooker's position was this. He had been sentenced in 1977 to three
years' imprisonment for robbery and wounding with intent at Maidstone
Crown Court. That sentence was imposed on him on November 7, 1977. F
He was then a young person and, owing to the various provisions which
it is not necessary for this court to read, young persons are not given
remission, but are released on licence subject to supervision, and indeed
that had happened to Brooker. At the time when the instant offence was
committed he was on licence.

The question is, can it be said that he was serving a sentence of G
imprisonment at the time when the court, that is to say the court we are
considering, passed sentence? It appears to this court prima facie that
the second half of that subsection, which I will read again in a moment,
makes it clear that he was not serving a sentence. The words are:

" . . . and for the purpose of this subsection a person sentenced to
imprisonment who has been recalled or returned to prison after
being released subject to supervision or on licence, and has not H
been released again or discharged, shall be treated as serving the
sentence."

We have had our attention drawn to a decision of this court on
December 5, 1980, Reg. v. Mellor [1981] 1 W.L.R. 1044, where a person
had been released on parole licence. It seems to us that, whatever may
have been the situation in Reg. v. Mellor, the words of section 3 (2) of

A the Criminal Justice Act 1961 must mean that a person who has, as a young person, been released on licence and not recalled is not serving a sentence of imprisonment. Had it been intended that such a person should be regarded as serving a sentence, the section would have read as follows: "and for the purpose of this subsection a person sentenced to imprisonment who has been released subject to supervision or on licence, whether or not he has been recalled or returned to prison there-
B after, shall be treated as serving the sentence". But it does not so read.

Consequently, we have reluctantly come to the conclusion that the sentence imposed upon Brooker of 15 months was not a sentence which was open to the court to pass. It should have been a sentence either of six months or less or 18 months or more, in accordance with section 3 (1) and (3). Consequently so far as Brooker is concerned, although we
C are reluctant to do so, we are forced to reduce his sentence from 15 months to six months.

That leaves the problem of Orpwood. May we say immediately that in the view of this court, for the sort of offence they have committed, 15 months was a lenient sentence, and this court, if left to its devices at the trial, would have sentenced each of the appellants to 18 months' imprisonment at a minimum. But once again the tentacles of section
D 3 (2) have grasped the court. We have been forced to reduce Brooker's sentence against our better judgment. The question is whether justice demands that Orpwood should have his sentence likewise reduced.

Mr. Davis disclaims that there would be any feeling of unfairness in Orpwood's mind were we to leave his sentence, which was perfectly legal, at 15 months. We feel however, in the light of their respective records,
E Brooker being much the more serious criminal according to his previous record, that it would be unfair were we to leave Orpwood at 15 months, having been forced to reduce Brooker's sentence. Consequently, Orpwood, who should consider himself exceedingly lucky in at least three respects, as a matter of fairness should likewise have his sentence reduced.

F Consequently each of these appeals is allowed to the extent that the sentence of 15 months' imprisonment in each case is reduced to six.

Appeals allowed.
Sentences varied.

Solicitors: *Chancellor & Ridley, Dartford.*

G

L. N. W.

H

[CHANCERY DIVISION]

* NABI (GHULAM) v. HEATON (INSPECTOR OF TAXES)

1981   Feb. 27   Vinelott J.

Revenue—Income tax—Personal relief—Polygamous marriage— B
Husband having domicile in Pakistan contracting second
marriage under Muslim law—Husband maintaining second wife
during subsistence of first marriage—Whether entitled to relief
for maintenance of second wife—Income and Corporation
Taxes Act 1970 (c. 10), s. 8 (1)

Section 8 (1) of the Income and Corporation Taxes Act
1970 provides: C
" . . . the claimant shall be entitled—(*a*) if he proves—(i)
that for the year of assessment he has his wife living with
him, or (ii) that his wife is wholly maintained by him
during the year of assessment . . . to a deduction . . ."
The taxpayer came to the United Kingdom from Pakistan
in 1965 and in 1968 married under English law. The marriage
was not successful and the spouses separated the following
year. Thereafter the taxpayer neither lived with nor maintained   D
his wife. The marriage was eventually dissolved in 1975. In
1969 he went back to Pakistan and married again, under
Muslim law. He then returned to live in England but maintained his second wife in Pakistan until 1978 when she came
to live with him. It was agreed that the taxpayer was domiciled
in Pakistan at the time of the second marriage ceremony. The
taxpayer appealed to the general commissioners against assessments to income tax under Schedule E for the years from   E
1970 to 1976, claiming relief under section 8 (1) in respect of
his second wife. The appeal was dismissed, the commissioners
holding that the taxpayer's second marriage was not valid
according to English law.
On appeal by the taxpayer: —
Held, dismissing the appeal, that section 8 (1) was intended
to apply only to a claimant who could show that he had one
wife who was either living with him or being maintained by   F
him and that, even if the taxpayer's second marriage should
be regarded as valid according to English law, he was not
entitled to personal relief from income tax in respect of the
maintenance of his second wife, since during the years to
which the claim related he was still married to his first wife
(post. p. 1058A–B, F–H).
Imam Din v. *National Assistance Board* [1967] 2 Q.B. 213,
D.C. distinguished.   G

The following cases are referred to in the the judgment:

Alhaji Mohamed v. *Knott* [1969] 1 Q.B. 1 ; [1968] 2 W.L.R. 1446 ; [1968]
2 All E.R. 563, D.C.
Attorney-General of Ceylon v. *Reid* [1965] A. C. 720; [1965] 2 W.L.R.
671; [1965] 1 All E.R. 812, P.C.   H
Baindail (orse. Lawson) v. *Baindail* [1946] P. 122; [1946] 1 All E.R. 342,
C.A.
Chaudhry v. *Chaudhry* [1976] Fam. 148; [1975] 3 W.L.R. 559; [1975]
3 All E.R. 687; (Note) [1976] 1 W.L.R. 221; [1976] 1 All E.R. 805,
C.A.
Imam Din v. *National Assistance Board* [1967] 2 Q.B. 213; [1967] 2
W.L.R. 257; [1967] 1 All E.R. 750, D.C.
Sehota, decd., In re [1978] 1 W.L.R. 1506; [1978] 3 All E.R. 385.

A   The following additional cases were cited in argument:

    Henning v. *Church of Jesus Christ of Latter-Day Saints* [1964] A.C. 420;
       [1963] 3 W.L.R. 88 ; [1963] 2 All E.R. 733, H.L.(E.).
    Rex v. *Hammersmith Superintendent Registrar of Marriages, Ex parte*
       Mir-Anwaruddin [1917] 1 K.B. 634, C.A.

      CASE STATED by the Commissioners for the General Purposes of the
B   Income Tax Acts for the Division of Bolton.

      The taxpayer, Ghulam Nabi, married his first wife, Amir, in the
United Kingdom in 1968. They separated in 1969, but remained married
until 1975, when the marriage was finally dissolved. In 1969 the taxpayer
returned to Pakistan and married Suria Begum at a Muslim ceremony.
He returned to the United Kingdom and maintained his second wife in
C   Pakistan until she came to the United Kingdom in 1975. He appealed
against assessments to income tax under Schedule E for 1970–71 of
£1,030, for 1973–74 of £792, for 1974–75 of £2,741 and for 1975–76 of
£2,729, and against the refusal by the inspector of taxes to allow him relief
under section 8 (1) of the Income and Corporation Taxes Act 1970 in
respect of his second wife. The commissioners dismissed his appeal
D   deciding that his second marriage was not valid according to English law.
      The taxpayer appealed.
      The facts are stated in the judgment.

    J. W. Shock for the taxpayer.
    Robert Carnwath for the Crown.

E   VINELOTT J. This appeal raises a short but interesting point of law,
The facts are shortly as follows. The taxpayer, Mr. Nabi, came to the
United Kingdom from Pakistan in 1965. He married his first wife, Amir
(" the first wife "), on August 5, 1968, while he was still in England.
Although not specifically so found by the commissioners, it was common
ground that the marriage was a civil ceremony conducted in accordance
F   with English law. He and his wife separated in August 1969 and since
then he has not lived with or maintained her. The marriage was dissolved
by decree absolute pronounced by the Bolton County Court in October
1975. In the meantime, in 1969, the taxpayer returned to Pakistan. During the course of that year he married one Suria Begum (" the second
wife ") at a Muslim ceremony. It is not clear from the case stated
whether at that time he was divorced from his first wife in accordance
G   with Muslim law; nor is it clear whether, under Muslim law, his English
marriage would have been recognised as valid, though it is common
ground that under Muslim law he could validly have been married to
both wives. However, it seems to me implicit in their findings that the
commissioners were satisfied that there was no divorce under Muslim
law of the first wife at the time of the second marriage. The taxpayer
H   has lived here ever since he returned, which he did in 1969, shortly after
his second marriage. His second wife remained in Pakistan until 1975,
and while she was there the taxpayer maintained her.
      It was contended before the commissioners that the taxpayer had not
abandoned his domicile of origin in Pakistan when he married his second
wife. There was no direct evidence in support of that contention, and
the commissioners do not deal specifically with it. However, the Crown
agreed that for the purposes of this appeal the taxpayer should be treated

1054

as domiciled in Pakistan at the time of his second marriage. The tax- A
payer claimed that for the years of assessment 1970–71 to 1975–76 he
was entitled to the higher personal allowance available under section 8
(1) of the Income and Corporation Taxes Act 1970 to a taxpayer who
can show either that during the relevant year of assessment he had his
wife living with him or that his wife was maintained by him. A deduction
under section 8 (1) having been refused by the inspector, the taxpayer
appealed to the general commissioners. They dismissed his appeal on the B
ground that his second marriage "was not valid according to English
law." From that decision the taxpayer appeals.

Mr. Shock, who appeared for the taxpayer, has referred me to a
number of cases which show that for certain purposes potentially polygamous marriages may be recognised as valid under English law. In
Baindail (orse. Lawson) v. *Baindail* [1946] P. 122 a husband domiciled in C
India married a Hindu woman according to Hindu rites. Later while that
marriage was still subsisting, he went through a ceremony of marriage with
an English woman in London. It was held by Barnard J. and the Court of
Appeal that notwithstanding its polygamous nature the Hindu ceremony
gave him the status of a married man under the law of his domicile, and that
the subsequent pretended marriage was null and void. Lord Greene M.R.
specifically left open the question whether the man would have fallen D
to be treated as married for the purposes of the bigamy law.

In *Imam Din* v. *National Assistance Board* [1967] 2 Q.B. 213, the
appellant married in Pakistan, where both he and his wife were domiciled.
He already had a living wife, but the law of his domicile permitted polygamous marriages. In 1961 he came here with his second wife and children, and later abandoned them. They received national assistance. Section E
42 (1) (*a*) of the National Assistance Act 1948 provides that a man is
liable to maintain his wife and his children. The board sought to recover
part of the assistance given to the wife under section 43 (1), which permits the board to make a complaint against a person who, for the purposes of the Act, is liable to maintain the person assisted. Salmon L.J.,
with whom Widgery J. and Lord Parker C.J. agreed, said, at p. 218:

> "When a question arises of recognising a foreign marriage or of F
> construing the word ' wife ' in a statute, everything depends upon
> the purpose for which the marriage is to be recognised and upon
> the objects of the statute. I ask myself first of all: is there any good
> reason why the appellant's wife and children should not be recog-
> nised as his wife and children for the purpose of the National Assis-
> tance Act 1948? I can find no such reason, and every reason in G
> common sense and justice why they should be so recognised."

In *Alhaji Mohamed* v. *Knott* [1969] 1 Q.B. 1, the appellant, a Nigerian
Muslim, entered into a potentially polygamous marriage in Nigeria with
a Nigerian girl aged 13. Both were domiciled in Nigeria, and the marriage
was valid in accordance with Nigerian law. Subsequently, they came to
England. A complaint was preferred before justices sitting as a juvenile H
court that the girl was in need of care, protection or control, and they found
the complaint proved. On appeal it was held that for the purposes of
ascertaining the girl's status the court would recognise the marriage as
valid and as conferring on her the status of the man's wife, and that it
could not be said that she was exposed to danger because she carried out
her wifely duties. Lord Parker C.J. cited with approval a passage in
Dicey's Conflict of Laws, 7th ed. (1958), p. 278, which reads as follows:

A   " A marriage which is polygamous under rule 34 and not invalid under rule 35 or 36 will be recognised in England as a valid marriage unless there is some strong reason to the contrary."

I should observe that that passage appears in the current edition of *Dicey & Morris, The Conflict of Laws,* 10th ed. (1980), as rule 38. Lord Parker C.J. went on to say, at p. 14:

B   " The editor then goes on to refer to certain cases where there is some strong reason to the contrary, they all being cases which involve the construction in a statute of some such words as ' marriage,' ' wife,' ' husband,' and where one has to decide whether those statutes have in mind merely a monogamous marriage, in which case for the purposes of that statute the polygamous marriage will not C   be recognised; or whether they are statutes which clearly cover marriages whether monogamous or polygamous. In my judgment the justices came to a wrong conclusion in this case, and for the purposes of ascertaining the status of this wife, the courts here will recognise the marriage as a valid marriage giving her that status."

In *Chaudhry* v. *Chaudhry* [1976] Fam. 148, again a husband and wife D were married under Islamic law in Pakistan and later moved to England, although the husband retained his Pakistani domicile. In 1972, while in London, he obtained a divorce by pronouncing talaq at the Pakistani Embassy. The wife sought relief under the Married Women's Property Act 1882. The husband took the preliminary point that the Act did not apply to the parties to a polygamous or potentially polygamous marriage. E   At that time the Matrimonial Causes Act 1973 had come into force. Section 11 of that Act (which re-enacts provisions in the Nullity of Marriage Act 1971 and the Matrimonial Proceedings (Polygamous Marriages) Act 1972) provides:

     " A marriage celebrated after July 31, 1971, shall be void on the following grounds only, that is to say—. . . (*d*) in the case of a polygamous marriage entered into outside England and Wales, that either F   party was at the time of the marriage domiciled in England and Wales. For the purposes of paragraph (*d*) of this subsection a marriage may be polygamous although at its inception neither party has any spouse additional to the other."

Dunn J. said, at p. 153:

G   " In my judgment, the parties having been married according to the law of their domicile, the English court would regard them as husband and wife for the purpose of deciding any application by either of them under section 17 of the Married Women's Property Act 1882. Any other conclusion would, in my judgment, be most impractical and an affront to common sense, because one would have the highly inconvenient situation that parties to a polygamous marH   riage could apply for transfers and settlement of property under the Matrimonial Causes Act 1973 but could not apply for their rights to be determined or for sale under section 17 of the Married Women's Property Act 1882."

Lastly, in *In re Sehota, decd.* [1978] 1 W.L.R. 1506, a husband and wife were validly married under Indian law while both were domiciled in India; the marriage was then potentially, but not actually, polygamous.

The husband later married under Indian law another Indian woman, both   **A**
being again domiciled in India. Later, all three came to England and
acquired an English domicile. Following the husband's death the first
wife made an application under the Inheritance (Provision for Family
and Dependants) Act 1975, on the grounds that she was his wife. Foster
J. said, at p. 1511:

> " I do not think that the Act of 1975 was merely a consolidating Act   **B**
> so that I must construe the words in the same way as I might have
> done in construing the words in the Inheritance (Family Provision)
> Act 1938. The Act of 1975 considerably extended the persons who
> could claim under the Act of 1938 as amended. There is no difficulty
> in practice under the Act of 1975 in there being more than one
> person seeking relief. One often finds cases where there are two or
> more claimants, for instance a widow and infant children. If for   **C**
> instance the deceased had left all his estate to charity, both widows
> would be entitled to claim. In any event I do not think that the
> plaintiff is asking for matrimonial relief in this application. Her hus-
> band is dead and she seeks reasonable provision from his estate. In
> my judgment this is a question of the law of succession and therefore
> never came within the ambit of the rule in *Hyde* v. *Hyde and*   **D**
> *Woodmansee* (1866) L.R. 1 P. & D. 130. I also respectfully agree
> with the decision of Dunn J. in the *Chaudhry* case [1976] Fam. 148
> that the Act of 1972 abolished entirely the rule in *Hyde* v. *Hyde and*
> *Woodmansee*."

Mr. Shock submitted that these cases show that since the war the
courts and the legislature have moved a long way towards recognising   **E**
at least a potentially polygamous marriage as valid. He relied in particular
on the fact that in *Imam Din* v. *National Assistance Board* [1967] 2 Q.B.
213 the Court of Appeal looked at the underlying policy of the National
Assistance Act 1948 in order to decide whether for the purposes of that
Act the court should recognise a polygamous marriage, and that the
court did recognise a polygamous marriage notwithstanding that the
obligation imposed by section 42 (1) (*a*) of the Act is an obligation by a   **F**
man to maintain *his* wife. He submitted that there is no ground of policy
which should prevent the court from similarly recognising a potentially
or actually polygamous marriage for the purposes of section 8 (1), and
that even if a man is for this purpose treated as married to two women
he can only claim relief in respect of one of them, and then only if he is
living with or maintaining one of them.
                                                                          G
Logically, the first question that arises is whether the second marriage
was a valid marriage. It is said in *Dicey & Morris, The Conflict of
Laws*, 10th ed. (1980), at p. 309:

> " It is now settled that the nature of the ceremony according to the
> lex loci celebrationis, and not the personal law of either party, deter-
> mines whether a marriage is monogamous or polygamous. Or, to
> adopt a more sophisticated statement, it is for the lex loci celebra-   **H**
> tionis to determine the nature and incidents of the union and then
> for English law to decide whether the union is a monogamous or
> polygamous marriage."

The commissioners decided that, the first marriage having been solem-
nised in England in English form, the second marriage was not under
English law a valid marriage. As I have pointed out it is inherent in this

A finding that at the time of his second marriage the taxpayer's first marriage was not dissolved by a divorce under Muslim law. However, Mr. Carnwath, who appeared for the Crown, did not seek to support the commissioners' decision upon that ground. He accepted, as I understand it, that there may be a doubt whether, having regard to the decision of the Privy Council in *Attorney-General of Ceylon* v. *Reid* [1965] A.C. 720,

B if a man, domiciled in a country which permits polygamous marriage, marries here and therefore contracts a monogamous marriage, goes back to the country of his domicile and while there marries again, he can contract a subsequent polygamous marriage, the first being, as it were, converted by his return to the country of his domicile into a potentially polygamous marriage within the view of English law. The point has not been fully argued before me, and I do not think it would be right for me to

C express an opinion on it—though I should observe in passing that *Attorney-General of Ceylon* v. *Reid* was concerned solely with the law of Ceylon which, as Lord Upjohn pointed out, at p. 733 " is a country of many races, many creeds and has a number of Marriage Ordinances." The editors of the current edition of *Dicey* state, at p. 313, that: " It is uncertain what the effect on such a marriage "—that is a marriage cele-

D brated in England in monogamous form—" would be if the husband entered into a valid polygamous marriage abroad " and do not express any opinion on the point. Mr. Carnwath invited me to decide this case upon the broader ground that even if the second wife was the taxpayer's wife in the eyes of English law nonetheless he is not entitled to the higher personal allowance under section 8 (1) during the years of assessment in question.

E   Mr. Carnwath's submission was that, even on this hypothesis, the taxpayer is not entitled to the higher personal allowance under section 8 (1) because under section 8 (1) a claimant must show that he has *his* wife living with him or that *his* wife is maintained by him. He submitted that the language of section 8 (1) shows that the legislature assumed that a claimant could only be married to one wife, and intended that relief

F should be available only in that case. Accordingly, he said, as the taxpayer had two wives he could not claim a deduction under section 8 (1) because he lived with or maintained one of them, and indeed would not be entitled so to claim even if he lived with and maintained both of them.

     The phrase " his wife " is, of course, the phrase used in section 42 (1) (*a*) of the National Assistance Act 1948; and, as I have said, in *Imam Din* v. *National Assistance Board* [1967] 2 Q.B. 213 the Court of Appeal

G held that where a man married under a system which allowed polygamy and deserted his wife, the board could claim that he was liable to maintain her on the footing that she was his wife. In that case, although the appellant at one time had two wives, at the time when the board gave assistance he had only one; his first wife, one Nawaa Bibi Din, died before he deserted the second. Salmon L.J. did not consider whether the Act

H would apply to a case where a person or persons assisted by the board was a wife, or were two or more wives, of a man with more than one wife recognised as such by English law. It may be that the National Assistance Act could have applied in such a case on the footing that in the context of section 42 (1) the singular " wife " should be read under section 6 of the Interpretation Act 1978, as including the plural " wives." The observations of Salmon L.J., at p. 218, as to the underlying policy, it may be said, could equally meet the situation where a husband with more than

one wife deserts one or more of them and the National Assistance Board   A
has to spend public money on her or their maintenance. But it is not
easy to see how the phrase " his wife " could sensibly be read in section
8 (1) as including " his wives," since section 8 (1) refers to cases where
the claimant shows that he has his wife living with him or that his wife
is maintained by him. What, one may ask, if he has one living with him
and he maintains the other, who is not living with him? Further, such a
construction would not in any event assist the taxpayer, whose first wife   B
neither lived with nor was maintained by him; and it seems to me that to
read the expression " his wife " as meaning " a wife " or " any wife "
would be to do too great violence to the language of the section.

   Moreover, there are other indications in the Act of 1970 and in
subsequent amending legislation which seem to me to support the construction that Mr. Carnwath put on section 8 (1). Section 8 (1A), which   C
was introduced by section 31 (1) of the Finance (No. 2) Act 1975, gives a
larger deduction " (a) in relation to a claim by a person who proves that he
or his wife was at any time within the year of assessment of the age of 65 or
upwards," and it seems to me difficult to see how that subsection can sensibly
apply to a man with more than one wife. Similarly, section 15A, which was
added to the Act of 1970 by the Finance Act 1980, gives a widow's
bereavement allowance in cases where a man dies in a year of assess-   D
ment during which he was entitled to the higher personal allowance
under section 8 (1). The allowance is given to " his widow." Again, it
cannot have been intended that that section should apply where a man
was recognised by English law as married to more than one wife and
accordingly left more than one widow. These provisions were not part of
the Act of 1970 as originally enacted and it may be that they should be   E
ignored in construing section 8 (1). But section 18, which is part of the
Act of 1970 as originally enacted, gives certain relief to blind persons.
Relief is given to a claimant who can prove " (a) that he is a married
man who for the year of assessment has his wife living with him, and that
one of them was, and the other was not " throughout the year a registered blind person, " or (b) that, not being such a married man, he was "
throughout the year a registered blind person. Again, in my view the   F
legislature quite clearly contemplated only the case where a man had
" a " wife and it could be said of one or other that he or she was blind.

   In my judgment, therefore, the higher personal relief under section
8 (1) would not be available to the taxpayer even if he were to establish
that under English law his second marriage was recognised as a valid
marriage—though, as I have said, I must not be taken as in any way   G
deciding that English law would recognise the second marriage as a valid
marriage. The result is to some extent anomalous, because if the taxpayer
had married both wives in India so that both would have been recognised
as wives, and had come here to live with and maintain both of them,
then the construction which I feel constrained to adopt would have the
result that he would not be entitled to the higher personal relief in respect   H
of either of them.

   Mr. Carnwath also submitted that if and so far as there is doubt as
to the construction of section 8 (1) I am entitled to look at the history
of the section, and he pointed out that it had its origin in section 18 of the
Finance Act 1920 and submitted that as at that time English law took a
very restricted view as to the nature of the marriage of a person domiciled
abroad which would be recognised as valid by English law, the legislature

A must have intended that relief should be given only to persons who contracted a monogamous marriage. I am not persuaded that that is the
right approach to the construction of section 8 (1). It seems to me that
there is much to be said for the view that the question whether a man is
recognised by English law as having a wife (and, if I am right, only one
wife) with whom he lives or whom he maintains should be answered in
B relation to the period to which the claim relates. Further, in 1970 potentially polygamous marriages were recognised for many purposes, and
for my part I can see no reason why a potentially polygamous though
factually monogamous marriage should not be recognised for the purposes of section 8 (1). Indeed, I understand that the revenue have in
practice always allowed the higher personal allowance in the case of a
person domiciled in a jurisdiction which permits polygamous marriages,
C who married there and who at all material times had only one wife. For
the reasons I have given, I think I must dismiss this appeal.

Appeal dismissed.
No order as to costs.

D Solicitors: *Gregory, Rowcliffe & Co. for Haworth & Nuttall, Blackburn; Solicitor of Inland Revenue.*

[Reported by MRS. HARRIET DUTTON, Barrister-at-Law]

E

PRACTICE NOTE

[CHANCERY DIVISION]

* In re A COMPANY (No. 003324 of 1979)

F
1981   March 2, 3   Vinelott J.

*Company — Oppression — Compromise — Application to enforce
purchase of shares by company or directors—Action compromised—Whether order in Tomlin form appropriate—
Companies Act 1948 (11 & 12 Geo. 6, c. 38), s. 210*

G
PETITION
The petitioner, a contributory in the company, brought a petition under
section 210 of the Companies Act 1948 seeking an order to compel the company or its directors to purchase the petitioner's minority shareholding at a
fair price. The petition was compromised and a scheme was agreed between
the parties, the terms of which were embodied in a Tomlin order. The parties
H sought a determination whether an order in Tomlin form was appropriate
where an application under section 210 was compromised.

Ralph Instone for the petitioner.
Eben Hamilton for the company.

VINELOTT J. This is a petition under section 210 of the Companies Act
1948. It does not seek the winding up of the company, and accordingly it
has not been advertised. The only relief sought is an order requiring the

A

company or its directors, who are also majority shareholders, to purchase the shares of the petitioners at the fair value prescribed by the articles but on the footing that the profits of the company are treated as increased by the addition of certain sums which it is said were either wrongly charged against profits or wrongly diverted to another company. The petitioners are supported by the trustees of the will of a former shareholder. The petitioners and the supporting trustees together own approximately 28 per cent. of the shares of the company. The differences between the shareholders have now been resolved. A scheme has been agreed which provides amongst other things for the distribution of exceptional dividends by the company during the current fiscal year and in the early weeks of the next fiscal year and for the purchase of the minority shareholding. In order to mitigate capital gains tax that purchase will take place over a three-year period. These terms have been embodied in a Tomlin order, and I have to decide whether this is a form of order appropriate to be made where an application under section 210 is compromised.

B

C

I can see no reason why this form of order should not be employed in such a case provided that the petitioner does not seek an order for the compulsory winding up of the company. If the petitioner does seek such an order, then it is clearly wrong that the proceedings should be stayed while the terms of compromise are carried into effect since if an order for the compulsory winding up of the company were to be subsequently made it would relate back to the service of the petition. I understand that no order in Tomlin form has been made on the compromise of an application under section 210. The explanation may well be that such petitions commonly do seek an order for the compulsory winding up of the company as an alternative to an order under section 210. In the present case there are clear advantages to the parties in embodying the agreed terms of compromise in an order in Tomlin form so that if any dispute arises in carrying out the terms of the compromise, the matter can be expeditiously and inexpensively referred to the court. I can see no possible prejudice to any other persons concerned with the company, in particular creditors, if the petition remains on the file during the period required to complete the sale and transfer of the minority shareholding. On the other hand I think it would be undesirable that the petition should remain on the file indefinitely, and I shall ask the petitioner for an undertaking to apply to dismiss the petition when the terms of compromise have been fully implemented.

D

E

F

Form of order approved.

Solicitors: *Dibb Lupton & Co., Leeds; Harrison, Leeds.*

[Reported by MISS EILEEN O'GRADY, Barrister-at-Law]

G

H

A

[HOUSE OF LORDS]

* PASCOE . . . . APPELLANT

AND

NICHOLSON . . . . RESPONDENT

B

1981 June 10; Lord Diplock, Lord Fraser of Tullybelton,
    July 2   Lord Russell of Killowen, Lord Keith
               of Kinkel and Lord Roskill

Road Traffic—Laboratory test—Specimen—Provision—Require-
ment for specimen made at one police station — Specimen
C   *taken at another police station — Whether specimen to be*
taken at same police station as requirement and breath test
—Road Traffic Act 1972 (c. 20), ss. 9 (1), 11 [1]

The defendant who had been arrested under section 8 of
the Road Traffic Act 1972, after a positive breath test and
had been taken to a police station, was there given an opportunity to provide a specimen of breath for a breath test, which
D   also proved positive. Thereupon he was required, in accordance with section 9 (1), to provide a specimen for a laboratory
test. On a request to supply a specimen he agreed to do so.
For that purpose he was taken to another police station
where a specimen of blood was taken from him which on
analysis showed a proportion of alcohol exceeding the prescribed limit. He was charged with contravening section 6 (1)
of the Act. Before the justices it was submitted for the
E   defendant that there was no case to answer because the
evidence of the result of the analysis was inadmissible in
view of *Butler* v. *Easton* [1970] R.T.R. 109. The justices
upheld the submission and dismissed the information. The
Divisional Court dismissed the prosecutor's appeal.
On appeal by the prosecutor: —
Held, that there was nothing in the provisions of the Road
Traffic Act 1972, in particular sections 6 to 12, which required
F   that the provisions of a specimen of breath for a breath test
at a police station, the request for a sample of blood or urine
and the giving of such sample, must all take place at the
same police station; and that, accordingly, the appeal must
be allowed.
Butler v. *Easton* [1970] R.T.R. 109, D.C. overruled.
Milne v. *M'Donald,* 1971 J.C. 40 approved.
Decision of the Divisional Court of the Queen's Bench
G   Division reversed.

The following cases are referred to in the opinion of Lord Roskill:

Butler v. *Easton* [1970] R.T.R. 109, D.C.
Milne v. *M'Donald,* 1971 J.C. 40.

No additional cases were cited in argument.
H

APPEAL from the Divisional Court of the Queen's Bench Division.
On August 9, 1979, an information was preferred by the prosecutor,
Chief Inspector Peter Pascoe, of Penzance, against the defendant, David
Ralph Nicholson, that he on June 30, 1979, at the A349 road, Marazion

---

[1] Road Traffic Act 1972, s. 9 (1): see post, pp. 1064H—1065A.
S. 11: see post, p. 1065G.

1062

Pascoe v. Nicholson (H.L.(E.))   [1981]

in the county of Cornwall, did drive a motor cycle on that road he having   A
consumed alcohol in such quantity that the proportion of alcohol in his
blood as ascertained from a laboratory test for which he subsequently
provided a specimen under section 9 of the Road Traffic Act 1972,
exceeded the prescribed limit at the time he provided the specimen
contrary to section 6 (1) of the Road Traffic Act 1972.

On November 5 and 19, 1979, the Penzance justices heard the information which they dismissed. The prosecutor appealed. The Divisional   B
Court of the Queen's Bench Division (Donaldson L.J. and Forbes J.)
dismissed the appeal. The prosecutor appealed to the House of Lords.

The facts are stated in the opinion of Lord Roskill.

Michael Hutchison Q.C. and Claudia Ackner for the appellant.
J. Hampden Inskip Q.C. and Christopher Jervis for the respondent.   C

Their Lordships took time for consideration.

July 2. LORD DIPLOCK. My Lords, I have had the advantage of
reading in draft the speech prepared by my noble and learned friend,
Lord Roskill, with which I am in full agreement.   D

LORD FRASER OF TULLYBELTON. My Lords, I have had the advantage
of reading in draft the speech prepared by my noble and learned friend,
Lord Roskill. I agree with it and for the reasons stated in it I would
allow this appeal, and dispose of the case as he proposes.

LORD RUSSELL OF KILLOWEN. My Lords, I have had the advantage   E
of reading in draft the speech about to be delivered by my noble and
learned friend, Lord Roskill. I agree with it and with the adoption of
the course that he proposes.

LORD KEITH OF KINKEL. My Lords, I have had the benefit of reading in draft the speech of my noble and learned friend, Lord Roskill. I   F
agree with it, and would accordingly allow the appeal and answer the
certified question as he proposes.

LORD ROSKILL. My Lords, all the events giving rise to this appeal,
except the last, took place within less than two hours early on the morning of June 30, 1979. At 12.55 a.m. that morning, two police officers
suspected that the respondent was driving his motor cycle with alcohol   G
in his body. Their suspicions were aroused by the manner of his driving
near Marazion in Cornwall. They stopped the vehicle. They smelt
alcohol on his breath. At 1.00 a.m. one of the officers required the
respondent to provide a specimen of breath. At 1.10 a.m. this specimen
was provided. It was positive. The respondent was arrested and taken
to Penzance Police Station. There, at 1.33 a.m. he provided a second   H
specimen of breath. It, too, was positive. At 1.37 a.m. at Penzance
Police Station, the respondent was required to provide a specimen for a
laboratory test and, pursuant to section 9 (7) of the Road Traffic Act
1972 ("the Act of 1972"), was warned of the consequences of any failure
to provide a specimen of blood or of urine. At 1.39 a.m. a police officer
requested the respondent to supply a sample of blood. The respondent
then agreed to do so. The respondent was thereupon taken from

A Penzance Police Station to Camborne. A specimen of blood was there taken from him by a doctor. On laboratory testing (the admissibility of the result of which was in issue) that specimen was found to contain not less than 164 milligrammes of alcohol in 100 millilitres of blood—more than twice the permitted quantity.

My Lords, on August 9, 1979, an information was preferred by the appellant against the respondent for an offence contrary to section 6 (1) B of the Act of 1972. That information was heard by the Penzance justices on November 5 and 19, 1979. At the close of the case for the prosecution, it was submitted on behalf of the respondent that there was no case to answer because the evidence of the result of the analysis of the specimen of blood, to which I have already referred, was inadmissible. The appellant conceded that, if that evidence were inadmissible, there C was no case to answer. The justices upheld the submission and dismissed the information. They stated a case for the opinion of the High Court, asking the following question:

> " Whether the provisions of the Road Traffic Act 1972 and in particular sections 6 to 12 thereof require that the provisions of a specimen of breath for a breath test at a police station, the request for a sample of blood or of urine and the giving of such sample of D blood or urine, must all take place at the same police station."

My Lords, this submission for the respondent was founded upon a decision of the Divisional Court (Lord Parker C.J., Ashworth and Cantley JJ.) in *Butler* v. *Easton* [1970] R.T.R. 109, decided on October 22, 1969. The attention of the justices was, however, properly drawn to a later decision of the High Court of Justiciary, *Milne* v. *M'Donald,* 1971 E J.C. 40, decided on May 27, 1971, in which that court (Lord Justice-General Clyde and Lords Migdale and Johnston) in a reserved judgment followed an earlier unreported decision of their own and reached the opposite conclusion from that which had been reached by the Divisional Court, and expressly declined to follow that earlier decision.

My Lords, the difference of opinion arose on a single issue, namely, F whether upon the true construction of section 3 (1) of the Road Safety Act 1967 (" the Act of 1967 "), which was the statutory predecessor of section 9 (1) of the Act of 1972, it was essential for the provision of the specimen of blood or of urine to take place at the same police station as that at which the requirement to provide that specimen had been made. The Divisional Court had held that it was essential for that requirement to provide the specimen and its actual provision to take place at the same G police station. The High Court of Justiciary held that it was not.

My Lords, the justices sitting at Penzance rightly held that they were bound to follow the decision of the Divisional Court, though they were referred to and recognised the persuasive authority of the decision of the High Court of Justiciary. It was for this reason that they held that the evidence of the result of the analysis of the specimen of blood taken H from the respondent at Camborne Police Station was inadmissible. They accordingly, and rightly on this view of the law, dismissed the summons.

When the present appeal by the appellant came before the Divisional Court by way of case stated on October 30, 1980, that court was also bound by its earlier decision. Indeed, the proceedings of the Divisional Court are recorded to have lasted only five minutes. But the Divisional Court certified the following question as raising a point of law of general public importance, namely:

" Whether the provisions of the Road Traffic Act 1972 and in A
particular sections 6 to 12 thereof require that the provision of a
specimen of breath for a breath test at a police station, the request
for a sample of blood or of urine and the giving of such sample of
blood or urine, must all take place at the same police station . . ."

thus inviting your Lordships to answer the same question as that which
the justices had asked in their case stated.   B
    The Divisional Court refused leave to appeal but that leave was
granted by your Lordships' House on December 18, 1980.
    My Lords, thus, after an interval of some ten years, your Lordships'
House is invited, for the first time, to decide which of the two decisions
to which I have already referred is right. Those two decisions are in
principle indistinguishable, and indeed, the present case is, upon its facts,
also in principle indistinguishable from those earlier cases.   C
    My Lords, as I have already said, the determination of this appeal
depends upon the true construction of section 9 (1) of the Act of 1972.
But since both learned counsel invited attention to, and indeed sought
support for their respective submissions from, other sections of the statute,
I set out for ease of reference those parts of the several sections upon
which reliance was thus placed: D

" 8 (1) A constable in uniform may require any person driving or
attempting to drive a motor vehicle on a road or other public place
to provide a specimen of breath for a breath test there or nearby,
if the constable has reasonable cause—(a) to suspect him of having
alcohol in his body, or (b) to suspect him of having committed a
traffic offence while the vehicle was in motion; but no requirement
may be made by virtue of paragraph (b) above unless it is made as   E
soon as reasonably practicable after the commission of the traffic
offence. (2) If an accident occurs owing to the presence of a motor
vehicle on a road or other public place, a constable in uniform may
require any person who he has reasonable cause to believe was
driving or attempting to drive the vehicle at the time of the accident
to provide a specimen of breath for a breath test—(a) except while F
that person is at a hospital as a patient, either at or near the place
where the requirement is made or, if the constable thinks fit, at a
police station specified by the constable; (b) in the said excepted case,
at the hospital; but a person shall not be required to provide such
a specimen while at a hospital as a patient if the medical practitioner
in immediate charge of his case is not first notified of the proposal G
to make the requirement or objects to the provision of a specimen
on the ground that its provision or the requirement to provide it
would be prejudicial to the proper care or treatment of the patient.
(3) A person who, without reasonable excuse, fails to provide a
specimen of breath for a breath test under subsection (1) or (2)
above shall be guilty of an offence. . . . (7) A person arrested under
this section, or under the said section 5 (5), shall, while at a police H
station, be given an opportunity to provide a specimen of breath
for a breath test there . . ."

" 9 (1) A person who has been arrested under section 5 (5) or
8 of this Act may, while at a police station, be required by a constable to provide a specimen for a laboratory test (which may be a
specimen of blood or of urine), if he has previously been given an
opportunity to provide a specimen of breath for a breath test at that

A   station under subsection (7) of the said section 8, and either—(a) it appears to a constable in consequence of the breath test that the device by means of which the test is carried out indicates that the proportion of alcohol in his blood exceeds the prescribed limit, or (b) when given the opportunity to provide that specimen, he fails to do so.   (2) A person while at a hospital as a patient may be required by a constable to provide at the hospital a specimen for a laboratory

B   test—(a) if it appears to a constable in consequence of a breath test carried out on that person under section 8 (2) of this Act that the device by means of which the test is carried out indicates that the proportion of alcohol in his blood exceeds the prescribed limit, or (b) if that person has been required, whether at the hospital or else- where, to provide a specimen of breath for a breath test, but fails

C   to do so and a constable has reasonable cause to suspect him of having alcohol in his body; but a person shall not be required to provide a specimen for a laboratory test under this subsection if the medical practitioner in immediate charge of his case is not first notified of the proposal to make the requirement or objects to the provision of a specimen on the ground that its provision, the require- ment to provide it or a warning under subsection (7) below would

D   be prejudicial to the proper care or treatment of the patient.   (3) A person who, without reasonable excuse, fails to provide a specimen for a laboratory test in pursuance of a requirement imposed under this section shall be guilty of an offence. . . .   (5) A person shall not be treated for the purposes of subsection (3) above as failing to provide a specimen unless—(a) he is first requested to provide a

E   specimen of blood, but refuses to do so; (b) he is then requested to provide two specimens of urine within one hour of the request, but fails to provide them within the hour or refuses at any time within the hour to provide them; and (c) he is again requested to provide a specimen of blood, but refuses to do so. . . . (7) A constable shall on requiring any person under this section to provide a specimen for a laboratory test warn him that failure to provide a specimen of blood

F   or urine may make him liable to imprisonment, a fine and disqualifi- cation, and, if the constable fails to do so, the court before which that person is charged with an offence under section 6 of this Act or this section may direct an acquittal or dismiss the charge, as the case may require.   In this subsection 'disqualification' means dis- qualification for holding or obtaining a licence to drive a motor

G   vehicle granted under Part III of this Act . . ."

   " 11. Any person required to provide a specimen for a laboratory test under section 9 (1) of this Act may thereafter be detained at the police station until he provides a specimen of breath for a breath test and it appears to a constable that the device by means of which the test is carried out indicates that the proportion of alcohol in that person's blood does not exceed the prescribed limit."

H
   My Lords, it was urged for the appellant that nowhere in section 9 (1) was there any express limitation upon the place where the specimen for a laboratory test was to be provided.   The subsection properly inter- preted contrasted the requirement to provide such a specimen with its actual provision.   The requirement to provide had to be made at the same police station as that where the opportunity to supply the specimen of breath for the second breath test had been given pursuant to section

Lord Roskill   Pascoe v. Nicholson (H.L.(E.))   **[1981]**

8 (7). Only those two events had to take place at the same police station, but not the third event referred to in section 9 (1), namely, the actual provision of the specimen for the laboratory test.

My Lords, your Lordships' attention was drawn to the provisions of sections 8 (1) and (2) and of section 9 (2) as showing that where the statute intended to limit or define the place at which a particular event, or events, were to take place, it so provided in specific terms. Thus the breath test provided for in section 8 (1) had to take place "there or nearby," that is to say, there or nearby on the road or other public place referred to earlier in that subsection. A similar provision, subject to the stated exception, is included in section 8 (2) in the case of an accident. Moreover, section 9 (2) opens with the words "A person while at a hospital . . ." may be requested in certain circumstances to provide "at the hospital" a specimen for a laboratory test, words of limitation or restriction as to the place where the requirement can be made and the specimen provided which are not to be found in section 9 (1). Attention was also drawn to the provisions in section 9 (7) regarding warning and to the absence of any words of limitation or restriction in that subsection as to where the warning should be given.

My Lords, these were in substance the submissions which found favour with the High Court of Justiciary. But that court did not in its judgment refer to section 11 (formerly section 4 of the Act of 1967) which provides for detention "at *the* police station" (I italicise the definite article), after the specimen for the laboratory test has been provided, in effect, until the motorist is fit to drive. It was this section which had impressed the Divisional Court, and led that court to its conclusion. Lord Parker C.J. said [1970] R.T.R. 109, 111H: "That . . . clearly shows that it is contemplated that he shall be kept throughout at one and only one police station." My Lords, I find it difficult to believe that the High Court of Justiciary overlooked this section, for they clearly considered, but disagreed with, the decision of the Divisional Court which was based upon its provisions. I think the High Court of Justiciary must have thought that the statutory predecessor of section 11 was not, of itself, enough to lead to a different conclusion from that to which the other relevant sections of the Act of 1967 pointed.

Learned counsel for the respondent in his argument founded much upon section 11. He argued that the provisions of this part of the statute, while restricting the liberty of the individual, were designed to see that those liberties were not unduly restricted. He urged that the argument for the appellant had precisely the result of imposing undue restrictions upon those liberties. If a motorist were taken to a police station after the first breath test were positive and then after any second breath test, were required to provide a specimen for a laboratory test, and to that end might be taken many miles to another police station for the provision of that specimen, and there detained until fit to drive, the motorist would be likely when fit to have to go back to the first police station to regain possession of his car in order to go home. It was urged that the appellant's argument ignored the use of the definite article in section 11. If those submissions were sound, it was said that the indefinite article could equally well have been used, as it was used in section 9 (1).

My Lords, as my noble and learned friend, Lord Keith of Kinkel, pointed out during the argument, if upon arrival at a police station the

A motorist sought a second breath test and there was then no suitable breathalyser available at that police station, there is nothing in the statute which would prevent the police at that juncture taking the motorist to another police station where proper equipment was available. If that be permissible, as like my noble learned friend I think it clearly would be, I see no logical reason why in the absense of express statutory provision,

B the motorist should not, after being required to supply the specimen for a laboratory test immediately following any second breath test, be taken to another police station where a doctor is more easily available in order to take from him the specimen of blood. It is not difficult to visualise many parts of the United Kingdom where it might be extremely difficult to obtain the services of a doctor at some isolated police station.

C My Lords, learned counsel for the respondent also founded an elaborate argument upon section 9 (5). Suppose, he contended, that the motorist first volunteered to provide a specimen of blood and to that end was taken to a second police station, and then was unable, or unwilling, perhaps for some understandable reason to provide that specimen, and sought to fall back upon his alternative option, to provide a specimen of urine. The motorist might then have to be taken back to the first

D police station. My Lords, this argument, if I understood it correctly, is based upon a misunderstanding of section 9 (5), which is concerned with and only with the offence created by section 9 (3). A motorist must, before being liable to conviction for an offence against that subsection, namely, of failing to provide a specimen for a laboratory test, be shown to have been given but to have failed to have availed himself of the successive opportunities required by section 9 (5) to have been accorded

E to him. That subsection is, to my mind, irrelevant in the present case and sheds no light upon the true construction of section 9 (1).

My Lords, apart from the provisions of section 11, I would have no doubt that the language of section 9 (1) read in isolation and without regard even to section 9 (2), imposes no restriction which makes it essential that the specimen for the laboratory test must be provided at

F the same police station as that at which the requirement that it be provided is made. But I think this conclusion is strongly reinforced by the provisions of section 9 (2) and also of section 9 (7) regarding the insistence upon warning. With profound respect to Lord Parker C.J. I do not regard the language of section 11 as strong enough to require a contrary conclusion, for in the context I think " *the* police station " in that section can be legitimately construed as meaning " *the* police station

G where he is." It follows that, in my view, *Butler* v. *Easton* [1970] R.T.R. 109 was wrongly decided and the decision of the High Court of Justiciary in *Milne* v. *M'Donald,* 1971 J.C. 40 is to be preferred. I would, therefore, allow the appeal and answer the certified question in the negative.

My Lords, the question also arose whether your Lordships' House should remit this case to the justices with a direction to continue the

H hearing, for as I have already said, the respondent succeeded upon a submission, now held to be wrong but correct when made, of no case to answer. Learned counsel for the respondent told your Lordships that it had been proposed to raise by way of substantive defence an issue whether or not the respondent had been properly told of the reason for his arrest. My Lords, learned counsel for the appellant did not ask your Lordships to remit the case, being content to succeed in the appeal solely upon the question of law raised. In view of this generous attitude by the prose-

1068

Lord Roskill   Pascoe v. Nicholson (H.L.(E.))   [1981]

cution, I think it might leave a sense of injustice in the respondent were   A
he now, some two years after the events in question, to be put in peril
afresh of losing his licence as well as of some financial penalty. Your
Lordships were told that he is a man with no previous convictions. My
Lords, if your Lordships agree, I would propose that exceptionally, and
possibly fortunately for the respondent, your Lordships' House should
only allow the appeal and answer the certified question in the negative,
for this appeal was brought to clarify the law rather than to punish   B
the respondent.

Appeal allowed.

Solicitors: *Robbins Olivey & Lake, for Cornish & Birtill, Penzance;
Burton Yeates & Hart, for Vivian Thomas & Jervis, Penzance.*
                                                                    C

J. A. G.

[QUEEN'S BENCH DIVISION]   D

* CARMEL EXPORTERS (SALES) LTD. *v.*
SEA-LAND SERVICES INC.

1980 Oct. 7, 8, 9;   Robert Goff J.
     Nov. 7
                                                                    E

*Practice—Stay of proceedings—Application—Summons to set writ
aside issued and served within 14 days—Failure to give grounds
of application and serve affidavit within time limit—Whether
procedural irregularity or nullity—Whether submission to
jurisdiction—R.S.C., Ord. 2, r. 1 (1)[1]; Ord. 12, r. 8[2]*

The plaintiffs, intending to issue a writ claiming damages   F
for breach of contract and misrepresentation arising from a
bill of lading, wrote to the defendants' solicitors inquiring
whether they were instructed to accept service on behalf of
the defendants, who were a foreign company. The defendants'
solicitors replied that they had no doubt that they would be
instructed to accept service and, therefore, the writ should be
directed to them. On receipt of the writ, the defendants'
solicitors completed and returned the acknowledgment of   G
service stating that the defendants intended to contest the
proceedings. They then issued and served a summons within
14 days for an order that the writ be set aside on the ground
that the court had no jurisdiction in the matter, pursuant to
the new R.S.C., Ord. 12, r. 8. The defendants failed to state
the grounds of the application or serve the affidavit in support
within the period as required by Ord. 12, r. 8 (3) and (4),
although they did later re-serve the summons with an affidavit.   H
     On the question whether the defendants had submitted to
the jurisdiction of the court in failing to comply with the
requirements of Ord. 12, r. 8 (3) and (4) or by their solicitors'
letter stating they would accept service of the writ: —
     Held, granting the application, (1) that the defendants'
failure to state the grounds of the application as required by

[1] R.S.C., Ord. 2, r. 1: see post, p. 1075E–H.
[2] Ord. 12, r. 8: see post, pp. 1072H—1073H.

A   rule 8 (3) and to serve the affidavits in support as required
by rule 8 (4) within the 14 day period were procedural errors
which should be treated as irregularities to which Ord. 2, r. 1
applied and, therefore, the defendants' failure to comply with
rule 8 (3) and (4) did not nullify the proceedings; that, although
the defendants had not complied with the proper procedure,
they had issued and served a summons within the time limit
and therefore did not need to apply for an extension of time
B   by an application which, in accordance with Ord. 12, r. 8 (2),
had to be made within the 14 day period; that, accordingly,
Ord. 12, r. 8 (2) did not prevent the court from exercising
its wide discretion under Ord. 2, r. 1 and, having in the
exercise of that discretion given the defendants leave to amend
their summons and proceed with it despite the late affidavit,
the court would make the order setting aside the writ (post,
pp. 1074F–H, 1075H—1076A, E—1077B).

C   Dictum of Lord Denning M.R. in Harkness v. Bell's
Asbestos and Engineering Ltd. [1967] 2 Q.B. 729, 735, C.A.
applied.
      (2) That the letter of the defendants' solicitors, stating that
they expected to be instructed to accept service and, on that
basis, proceedings should be directed to them, did not constitute a submission by the defendants to the jurisdiction of
the court (post, pp. 1077H—1078A).
D   Per curiam. The courts will probably construe " apply to
the court " in Ord. 12, r. 8 (1) as requiring a defendant to
issue the summons within 14 days and not as requiring service
of the summons within the time limit. It is desirable for the
point to be drawn to the attention of the Rules Committee so
that they can, if they think fit to do so, clarify or amend the
words of the rule. The Rules Committee might also like to
consider the inflexible fetter in rule 8 (2) that an application
E   for an extension of time under Ord. 3, r. 5 be made with the
14 day period (post, pp. 1078G—1079A, E–F).

The following cases are referred to in the judgment:
Bonnell v. Preston (1908) 24 T.L.R. 756, C.A.
Harkness v. Bell's Asbestos and Engineering Ltd. [1967] 2 Q.B. 729;
      [1967] 2 W.L.R. 29; [1966] 3 All E.R. 843, C.A.
F
The following additional cases were cited in argument:
Brayhead (Ascot) Ltd. v. Berkshire County Council [1964] 2 Q.B. 303;
      [1964] 2 W.L.R. 507; [1964] 1 All E.R. 149, D.C.
Howard v. Secretary of State for the Environment [1975] Q.B. 235;
      [1974] 2 W.L.R. 459; [1974] 1 All E.R. 644, C.A.
G   Keymer v. Reddy [1912] 1 K.B. 215, C.A.
Revici v. Prentice Hall Inc. [1969] 1 W.L.R. 157; [1969] 1 All E.R. 772,
      C.A.
Schafer v. Blyth [1920] 3 K.B. 140.

SUMMONS
      By a summons dated July 2, 1980, the defendants, Sea-Land Services
H   Inc., a foreign company, applied pursuant to R.S.C., Ord. 12, r. 8 (1), for
an order that a writ issued on June 11, 1980, by the plaintiffs, Carmel
Exporters (Sales) Ltd., an English company, claiming damages against
them for breach of contract and/or misrepresentation in respect of bills of
lading relating to the contractual goods, six containers of Iranian cumin
seeds, be set aside on the ground that the court did not have jurisdiction
in the matter.   The plaintiffs opposed the application on the grounds,
first, that the defendants had not complied with R.S.C., Ord. 12, r. 8

A

and secondly, that the defendants had submitted to the jurisdiction of
the English court through their solicitors. The summons was heard in
chambers and judgment was given in open court.

The facts are stated in the judgment.

Michael Brindle for the plaintiffs.
Peter Gross for the defendants.

B

Cur. adv. vult.

November 7. ROBERT GOFF J. There is before the court an application on behalf of the defendants, Sea-Land Services Inc., for an order
that the writ issued by the plaintiffs, Carmel Exporters (Sales) Ltd., be
set aside on the ground that the court has no jurisdiction in the matter.

C

The application raises some questions of general interest concerning the
new procedure, and in particular concerning the new R.S.C., Ord. 12,
r. 8; and I have therefore agreed, at the request of the parties, to deliver
my judgment in open court.

The matter arises as follows (I take the facts from the affidavit evidence
before me). It appears that the plaintiffs, who carry on business in this

D

country, entered into an agreement on December 15 and 16, 1978, for
the purchase of six containers of Iranian cumin seeds from an Iranian
company, Hassas Export Co. Ltd. of Teheran, at a price of $2,498 per
metric ton c. & f. Rotterdam. The containers were, it seems, to be shipped
from Iran in two instalments—three in December 1978, and three in
January 1979. At about the same time as they entered into their purchase
contract with Hassas Export, the plaintiffs on-sold the goods to a Colombian

E

buyer, f.o.b. Rotterdam, shipment January or, latest, first week February
1979. Bills of lading were issued in respect of the six containers. These
bills were in the defendants' form, and appear to have been signed on
their behalf; the defendants are a company carrying on business in the
Netherlands. Three bills were dated December 24, 1978, relating to carriage
on the *Seabridge* (a feeder vessel) and (as the plaintiffs contend) the

F

San Pedro (an ocean-going vessel); and three bills were dated January 3,
1979, relating also to carriage on the *Seabridge* and (as the plaintiffs
contend) the *Pioneer* (another ocean-going vessel). The bills contain a
demise clause, and are expressly governed by the law of the United States
of America. It seems that the goods were not shipped from Iran in either
December 1978 or January 1979. The plaintiffs took up the documents
and paid for the goods, though they do not appear to have done so until

G

April 1979; however it appears that their buyers must have rejected the
documents, and that the plaintiffs were left with the goods on their hands.
The market having fallen, they are now claiming damages from the
defendants, on the grounds of breach of contract and/or misrepresentation.

A dispute has arisen between the parties with regard to the bills of
lading. The plaintiffs contend that the bills are shipped bills, whereas the

H

defendants contend that they are received for shipment bills. It appears
that the words " on board " are stamped on the bills, but the defendants
contend that this was done without their authority. Furthermore, the
defendants say that the bills relate only to carriage on the *Seabridge,* and
that the *Seabridge* was neither owned by, nor demise chartered to, the
defendants.

On the evidence before the court, it is plain that the only connection

The Weekly Law Reports, July 17, 1981

1071

1 W.L.R.   Carmel Exporters v. Sea-Land Inc. (Q.B.D.)   Robert Goff J.

A which the disputes have with this country is that the plaintiffs happen to be an English company. The plaintiffs put their case against the defendants first of all on the basis of breach of either a written contract or an oral contract. The written contract can only be that evidenced by the bills of lading, which have no connection with this country at all. If there was an oral contract, there is no evidence before the court that any such contract could conceivably have been governed by English law, or have had any

B connection with this country at all. There is no evidence that either contract was broken in this country. In the alternative, the plaintiffs put their case on the basis of an alleged misrepresentation, which apparently relates to the words " on board " having been stamped on the bills; though this can only have taken place in Iran, and there is once again no connection with this country at all. In truth there is no possible basis upon which, in

C the present case, the English court could have asserted jurisdiction over the disputes between the parties; and indeed the plaintiffs have not suggested otherwise.

Even so, the plaintiffs oppose the defendants' application. They do so on two grounds. First, they say that the defendants' application must fail, because they have not complied with the relevant provisions of the new

D Ord. 12, r. 8. Second, they say that the defendants through their solicitors have submitted to the jurisdiction of the court.

Before I turn to consider these two submissions, I must outline the course which the proceedings have taken to date. The write was issued with a general endorsement, on June 11, 1980. This was of course a writ in the new form. Thereafter the defendants' solicitors duly completed and on June 23 returned to the court an acknowledgment of service in the

E new form. The acknowledgment of service identified the defendants, stated that the defendants intended to contest the proceedings, and gave the name and address of the defendants' solicitors. On July 2, the defendants' solicitors issued the summons which is now before me. The return date originally specified in the summons was July 29; the relief asked for was simply:

F   " an order that the writ issued on June 11, 1980, be set aside on the grounds that this honourable court does not have jurisdiction in this matter."

The summons was served on the plaintiffs' solicitors, without any affidavit in support, by post, and was received by the plaintiffs' solicitors on July 4. So both issue and service of the summons took place within 14 days of

G the defendants' acknowledgment of service, in which their solicitors gave notice of their intention to defend the proceedings. The affidavit in support of the defendants' application was not in fact served on the plaintiffs' solicitors until September 17, having been posted to them the day before: on September 23, the summons and affidavit together were re-served on the plaintiffs' solicitors. On October 7, the revised return date for the

H hearing of the summons, the matter came before the court for argument.

I shall consider first the plaintiffs' submission that the defendants' application must fail, on the ground that they have not complied with the relevant provisions of Ord. 12, r. 8. For this purpose, it is necessary for me to set out in outline the new procedure, and in detail the relevant provisions of Ord. 12, r. 8.

Under the old procedure, once a writ had been served upon a defendant, if a defendant failed to enter an appearance within the time limited for

appearance the plaintiff was entitled (subject to certain exceptions) to   A
enter final judgment against the defendant for a sum not exceeding that
claimed in the writ and for costs. On the other hand, if the defendant did
enter an appearance, he thereby not only showed his intention to defend
the suit but also submitted himself to the jurisdiction of the court. If a
defendant wished to challenge the jurisdiction of the court, there were two
courses open to him. First he might, with the leave of the court, enter a
conditional appearance in the action. This had the effect of preventing   B
the plaintiff from entering judgment in default of appearance, while
maintaining the defendant's right to object to the jurisdiction of the court,
or indeed to any irregularity in the issue or service of the writ. However,
subject to that right, a conditional appearance was a complete appearance
to the action for all purposes. Accordingly, on the expiration of the
relevant time, if no application had been made by the defendant to set   C
aside the proceedings, or he had made such an application and it had
been dismissed, the appearance stood as unconditional and the plaintiff
could proceed with the action. So, if a defendant wished to avoid submitting to the jurisdiction, his safer course was not to enter a conditional
appearance, but to take the second course open to him, which was to
apply before entering an appearance for an order setting aside the
proceedings. This was of course the usual application made by a party   D
outside the jurisdiction, served with proceedings by virtue of leave given
under Ord. 11, if that party did not wish to submit to the jurisdiction.

    Such in outline was the old procedure. Under the new procedure,
much has changed; but for present purposes the most important change
is that the step of " appearance " has been abolished. In its place, we now
have the step of " acknowledgment of service "; but the two steps are by   E
no means the same. Nowadays, every writ for service must be accompanied
by a form of acknowledgment of service; and it is the duty of each
defendant who wishes to acknowledge service of the writ, and to defend
the action, to complete (either himself or by his solicitor) the form in
accordance with the directions set out on it, and then to return it to the
appropriate court office. If he fails to do so within the prescribed time,   F
then judgment in default of acknowledgment of service may be entered
against him. But, although the acknowledgment of service may operate
as a statement of intention to defend the proceedings, nevertheless it does
not operate as a waiver of any irregularity in the issue or service of the
writ. This is expressly stated in the new Ord. 12, r. 7, which provides:

    " The acknowledgment by a defendant of service of a writ or notice   G
    of a writ shall not be treated as a waiver by him of any irregularity
    in the writ or notice or service thereof or in any order giving leave
    to serve the writ or notice out of the jurisdiction or extending the
    validity of the writ for the purpose of service."

Moreover, not only has the step of " appearance " been abolished, but the
practice of entering a conditional appearance has likewise been abolished.   H
Instead, we find a new procedure for disputing the jurisdiction of the
court. This procedure is set out in Ord. 12, r. 8, which, since it lies at the
heart of the dispute now before me, I propose to set out in full in this
judgment. Rule 8 provides:

    " (1) A defendant who wishes to dispute the jurisdiction of the court
    in the proceedings by reason of any such irregularity as is mentioned
    in rule 7 or on any other ground shall give notice of intention to

The Weekly Law Reports, July 17, 1981

1073

1 W.L.R.   Carmel Exporters v. Sea-Land Inc. (Q.B.D.)   Robert Goff J.

A   defend the proceedings and shall, within 14 days thereafter, apply to the court for—(a) an order setting aside the writ or service of the writ or notice of the writ on him, or (b) an order declaring that the writ or notice has not been duly served on him, or (c) the discharge of any order giving leave to serve the writ or notice on him out of the jurisdiction, or (d) the discharge of any order extending the validity of the writ for the purpose of service, or (e) the protection

B   or release of any property of the defendant seized or threatened with seizure in the proceedings, or (f) the discharge of any order made to prevent any dealing with any property of the defendant, or (g) a declaration that in the circumstances of the case the court has no jurisdiction over the defendant in respect of the subject matter of the claim or the relief or remedy sought in the action, or (h) such other

C   relief as may be appropriate.

" (2) Ord. 3, r. 5, shall apply in relation to the period of 14 days mentioned in paragraph (1) with the modification that the said period may be extended by the court only on an application made before the expiration of the period.

" (3) An application under paragraph (1) must be made—(a) in an

D   Admiralty action in rem, by motion; (b) in any other action in the Queen's Bench Division, by summons; (c) in any other action, by summons or motion, and the notice of motion or summons must state the grounds of the application.

" (4) An application under paragraph (1) must be supported by an affidavit verifying the facts on which the application is based and a copy of the affidavit must be served with the notice of motion or

E   summons by which the application is made.

" (5) Upon hearing an application under paragraph (1), the court, if it does not dispose of the matter in dispute, may give such directions for its disposal as may be appropriate, including directions for the trial thereof as a preliminary issue.

" (6) A defendant who makes an application under paragraph (1)

F   shall not be treated as having submitted to the jurisdiction of the court by reason of his having given notice of intention to defend the action; and if the court makes no order on the application or dismisses it, the notice shall cease to have effect, but the defendant may, subject to rule 6 (1), lodge a further acknowledgment of service and in that case paragraph (7) shall apply as if the defendant had not made any

G   such application.

" (7) Except where the defendant makes an application in accordance with paragraph (1), the acknowledgment by a defendant of service of a writ or notice of a writ shall, unless the acknowledgment is withdrawn by leave of the court under Ord. 21, r. 1, be treated as a submission by the defendant to the jurisdiction of the court in the proceedings."

H   Now it follows that a defendant who wishes to dispute the jurisdiction of the court under this Order, either by reason of any such irregularity as is mentioned in rule 7, or on any other ground, must take the following steps. First, he must give notice of intention to defend the proceedings. That of course he does by completing in the appropriate manner the form of acknowledgment of service, and by returning it to the appropriate court office. Next, within 14 days thereafter, he must apply to the court for the

order which he seeks; this application must, if made in an action in the   A
Queen's Bench Division (other than an Admiralty action in rem), be made
by summons; and it must in any event state the grounds of the application,
and be supported by an affidavit verifying the facts on which the application
is based, a copy of which must be served with the summons (or notice of
motion) by which the application is made. However, it is important to
remember that, in relation to the period of 14 days after notice of intention   B
to defend the proceedings, within which the defendant has to make his
application to the court, Ord. 3, r. 5 (which enables the court to extend or
abridge the period within which a person is required by the Rules to do
any act in any proceedings) applies, but subject to an important modification, namely, that the period of 14 days may be extended by the court
only on an application made before the expiration of that period. This is
indeed a rigid and draconian provision, which could have very harsh   C
consequences: nobody in court on the argument before me was aware of
any other comparable provision in the Rules of the Supreme Court.

It is against this background that I come to the first submission of the
plaintiffs, viz., that the defendants' application must fail, because they had
not complied with the relevant provisions of Ord. 12, r. 8. They said that
the defendants had failed to comply with the rule in two respects. First,   D
their summons, though issued and served within 14 days of their giving
notice of intention to defend the proceedings, did not state the grounds of
the application as required by rule 8 (3); second, no copy of the affidavit
was served with the summons as required by rule 8 (4). It followed, they
submitted, that the defendants, having failed to make an application as
required by the rule within the specified period of 14 days, and having
failed to apply within that period for an extension of time under Ord. 3,   E
r. 5, could no longer dispute the jurisdiction of the court, and must be
treated as having submitted to the jurisdiction of the court by virtue of
Ord. 12, r. 8 (7).

Now it is clear that, whatever meaning is to be attached to the words
" apply to the court " in Ord. 12, r. 8 (1), the defendants did make such
an application within the specified period of 14 days after they gave notice   F
of intention to defend the proceedings, because they not only issued their
summons but also obtained a return date and served the summons on the
plaintiffs' solicitors within the specified period. But it is equally clear that
they failed to comply both with the requirement that the summons so
issued and served should state the grounds of their application, and with
the requirement that a copy of the affidavit in support should be served
with the summons. The latter point is conceded. As to the former, the   G
only ground stated in the summons is that " this honourable court does
not have jurisdiction in this matter." That is plainly not enough; every
application under Ord. 12, r. 8 (1), is an application whereby the defendant
disputes the jurisdiction of the court, and merely to reiterate that bald
fact cannot constitute the " grounds of the application " required by
rule 8 (3) to be stated in the summons or notice of motion.   H

In these circumstances, Mr. Brindle's submission on behalf of the
plaintiffs was simple. He said that the defendants' failure to comply with
either of these two requirements had the effect that the defendants failed
to do what was required of them within the 14 day period specified in
rule 8 (1); and that it was now too late, because of the requirement of
rule 8 (2), to put the matter right.

Now I must confess that I contemplate the consequences of this submis-

The Weekly Law Reports, July 17, 1981

1075

1 W.L.R.   Carmel Exporters v. Sea-Land Inc. (Q.B.D.)   Robert Goff J.

A   sion with dismay. I put on one side the fact that the plaintiffs' submission in the present case is entirely without merit, since it is conceded that the case has no connection whatsoever with this country and so is not a case in which the English courts could assert any jurisdiction, and there is no evidence of the plaintiffs having suffered any prejudice by reason of the defendants' procedural errors. But looking at the matter simply as a point on the construction of the rules, the effect of the plaintiffs' submission is
B   that, if any mistake is made as to the form of a defendant's application— for example, a notice of motion is issued instead of a summons or vice versa, or the grounds are not stated in the summons (even though the plaintiff may already know what they are) or the copy affidavit is not served with the summons (even though the plaintiff may know all the relevant facts which are to be relied upon)—then once the 14 day period
C   has expired without the matter being put right or at least an application being made under Ord. 3, r. 5, the court is powerless to assist the defendant. The possible injustice can be highlighted by taking extreme examples—for example, where the grounds are stated not in the summons but in a letter with which the summons is enclosed; or where a copy of the supporting affidavit is sent not with the summons, but in a separate letter which reaches the plaintiff's solicitors the day before the summons
D   is served; or where the plaintiff's solicitors notice the procedural error, but lie low and say nothing until the 14 day period expires. That the court should be powerless to intervene to ensure that justice is done in such cases as these is surely unthinkable.

      In my judgment, the short answer to the whole problem lies in the wide powers now conferred on the court under Ord. 2, r. 1. That rule
E   provides:

      " (1) Where, in beginning or purporting to begin any proceedings or at any stage in the course of or in connection with any proceedings, there has, by reason of any thing done or left undone, been a failure to comply with the requirements of these rules, whether in respect of time, place, manner, form or content or in any other respect, the
F   failure shall be treated as an irregularity and shall not nullify the proceedings, any step taken in the proceedings, or any document, judgment or order therein. (2) Subject to paragraph (3), the court may, on the ground that there has been such a failure as is mentioned in paragraph (1), and on such terms as to costs or otherwise as it thinks just, set aside either wholly or in part the proceedings in which the
G   failure occurred, any step taken in those proceedings or any document, judgment or order therein or exercise its powers under these rules to allow such amendments (if any) to be made and to make such order (if any) dealing with the proceedings generally as it thinks fit. (3) The court shall not wholly set aside any proceedings or the writ or other originating process by which they were begun on the ground that the proceedings were required by any of these rules to be begun
H   by an originating process other than the one employed."

      Now it will at once be observed that, on a straightforward reading of Ord. 2, r. 1 (1), there have in the present case been in connection with proceedings, by reason of something left undone, two failures by the defendants to comply with the requirements of Ord. 12, r. 8: and it would appear to follow, first that each of such failures shall be treated as an irregularity; second, that neither shall nullify the step taken by the defen-

1076

dants in the proceedings, that is, their application for an order that the A
plaintiffs' writ be set aside; and third, that the court has a discretion either
to set aside the defendants' application or to exercise its power under the
rules to allow such amendment to be made or to make such order dealing
with the proceedings generally as it thinks fit. Such an approach is supported
by the observations of Lord Denning M.R. in *Harkness* v. *Bell's Asbestos
and Engineering Ltd.* [1967] 2 Q.B. 729, where he said of the then new
Ord. 2, r. 1, at pp. 735–736:   B

> " This new rule does away with the old distinction between nullities
> and irregularities. Every omission or mistake in practice or procedure
> is henceforward to be regarded as an irregularity which the court can
> and should rectify so long as it can do so without injustice. It can at last
> be asserted that ' it is not possible for an honest litigant in Her
> Majesty's Supreme Court to be defeated by any mere technicality,   C
> any slip, any mistaken step in his litigation.' "

On this approach, since the plaintiffs have suffered no prejudice by
reason of the defendants' errors, I would of course not hesitate, in the
exercise of my discretion, to give leave to the defendants to amend their
summons to state the grounds of their application, and to proceed with D
their application despite the late service of their affidavit in support.

Mr. Brindle submitted that this course was not open to me. He first
submitted that the defendants did not apply to the court within 14 days
of giving notice of intention to defend the proceedings (as required by
Ord. 12, r. 8 (1)), because their summons, though issued and served
within that time, stated no grounds (as required by Ord. 12, r. 8 (2));
accordingly, no application for an extension of time having been made E
before the expiry of the 14 day period as required by rule 8 (2), the
court was precluded by the rules from assisting the defendants. In
my judgment, that is not right. The defendants did apply to the court
within the specified time, though their application was in one respect
deficient in point of content. Since the defendants did apply to the court
within the specified time, Ord. 12, r. 8 (2), does not act as a fetter upon F
the court's power to do justice in the present case. Next, Mr. Brindle
sought to invoke the old distinction between mandatory and directory
requirements; and further submitted that, having regard in particular to
the imperative words of Ord. 12, r. 8, both of the requirements with which
the defendants failed to comply were mandatory, with the consequence
that the court either could not or should not exercise its discretion under
Ord. 2, r. 1 (2), in the defendants' favour. Again, I cannot accept this G
submission. I very much doubt if the imperative terms of the relevant
provisions of Ord. 12, r. 8, would even under the old law have led to their
being categorised as mandatory; but even if that were so, Mr. Brindle's
submission would, of course, entirely defeat the purpose of the present
Ord. 2, r. 1 (2), and detract from the breadth of the discretion conferred
by that rule. Mr. Brindle then referred me to a number of situations in H
which the defect in procedure is so fundamental that the court will, he
submitted, always set aside the relevant proceedings or step in the proceedings—for example, where a writ has not been served as required by the
rules, or notice of discontinuance has been given without leave where
leave was needed; or a writ has, without leave to renew, been served more
than 12 months after its issue; or a judgment in default has been irregularly
signed. The present case fell, he submitted, within the same category. Let

The Weekly Law Reports, July 31, 1981

1077

1 W.L.R.   Carmel Exporters v. Sea-Land Inc. (Q.B.D.)   Robert Goff J.

A it be assumed, he submitted, that by virtue of Ord. 2, r. 1 (2), the defendants' application was not a nullity; nevertheless, the court must exercise its discretion under that rule to set the application aside. Again, I cannot accept this submission. I do not doubt that there are defects in procedure so fundamental that the court will invariably exercise its power to set aside the relevant proceedings or step in the proceedings; though even in such a case there is usually no draconian provision of the Rules of the
B Supreme Court, equivalent to Ord. 12, r. 8 (2), to prevent the party in error from curing his mistake by then proceeding in accordance with the rules. But I do not for one moment accept that the defects in procedure in the present case fall into this category. It is only necessary for me to point out that, if the grounds of the defendants' application had been set out in a letter to the plaintiffs' solicitors enclosing the summons, and a
C copy of the affidavit in support had not been served with the summons but had been served the next day but still within the 14 day period, Mr. Brindle's argument could have been precisely the same. Plainly, this cannot be right.

It follows that I am unable to accede to any of the plaintiffs' arguments on this point; I therefore exercise my power to give leave to the defendants to amend their summons to state the grounds of their application, and to
D proceed with it despite the late service of their affidavit in support.

I turn next to the plaintiffs' second submission, which is that the defendants' application should be dismissed on the ground that the defendants, through their solicitors, have submitted to the jurisdiction of the court. In support of this submission, the plaintiffs rely upon certain correspondence, prior to the issue of the writ, which passed between the plaintiffs and the defendants' solicitors, and which culminated in the following
E exchange. On July 30, 1979, the plaintiffs wrote a letter to the defendants' solicitors which ended:

"We must ask you to deal with this matter expeditiously, and if your clients are not willing to settle this on a friendly basis, we must ask you to answer the last paragraph of our letter of July 24, namely, if you are willing to accept service on behalf of your clients, when we
F will instruct our solicitors to issue proceedings. We are leaving this matter open until August 6, which should give you sufficient time to communicate with your clients."

On August 6, the defendants' solicitors replied, still disputing the plaintiffs' claim, and their letter ended:

G "If you wish to serve proceedings we have no doubt that we shall be instructed to accept service of them. Please therefore direct any such proceedings to us."

The writ was issued over 10 months later, on June 11, 1980. By that date, the new procedure had come into force; and the defendants' solicitors then completed the form of acknowledgment of service, as I have indicated.

H In my judgment, the short answer to this point is that on no view could this exchange of correspondence amount to a submission to the jurisdiction. It is not even a case where the defendants' solicitors write, stating (with authority) that they have authority to accept service, and then do so; it is simply a case of an indication by the defendants' solicitors that they themselves expected, indeed had no doubt that, they *would* be instructed to accept service, and proposed that, on that basis, proceedings should be directed to them. On no view, in my judgment, could such an indication

constitute a submission by the defendants to the jurisdiction of the English   A
court. I therefore reject this submission. In these circumstances it is
unnecessary for me to burden this judgment with consideration of other
arguments advanced by the defendants, in particular the argument that
acceptance of service by a defendant's solicitors, even with the authority
of their client, does no more than establish the fact and time of service, and
in no way amounts to a submission to the jurisdiction or precludes the
defendant from thereafter seeking to set aside the proceedings on the   B
ground that the English court has no jurisdiction in the matter. Such
arguments are of course open to the defendants, if the matter should be
taken further.

Before leaving the case, there are two matters to which I wish to draw
attention. First, in the course of the argument before me, it appeared that
there is some doubt as to what is meant by the words " apply to the court "   C
in Ord. 12, r. 8 (1). Does this mean that the defendant should have simply
issued his summons or notice of motion? Or that he should have issued
it and obtained a return date? Or that he should have issued it and served
it? The answer to this question is not altogether clear, and I have to say
that the notes to the new rule in *The Supreme Court Practice* (1979) betray
a somewhat ambivalent attitude. Thus in paragraph 12/7—8/6, when   D
referring to the tight time-scale in Ord. 12, r. 8, it is stated that this is
designed so that the plaintiff should know at an early stage whether or not
the defendant intends to dispute the jurisdiction of the court or to object
to any irregularity and, if so, on what ground. Such a rationalisation is
more consistent with a requirement that a summons or notice of motion
should have been issued and served within the 14 day period; and some
support for this construction is perhaps to be derived from the wording of   E
Ord. 12, r. 8 (4), which requires the copy affidavit in support to be served
with the notice of motion or summons by which the application *is made*.
On the other hand, turning again to paragraph 12/7—8/6, reference is there
made to a defendant applying within the 14 day period for an extension
of time, if he is unable to *issue* his summons or motion within the 14 days.
This more limited requirement is more consistent with the traditional   F
approach, under which a distinction is drawn between an application to
the court, which constitutes the issue of the relevant process, and the
service of that process on the respondent. A clear example of this approach
is to be found in the new Ord. 73, r. 5, concerned with certain applications
relating to arbitration proceedings (to remit or set aside an award, or to
direct an arbitrator to state his reasons), which provides that " An
application to the court . . . must be made, and the summons or notice   G
must be served, within 21 days . . ." Furthermore, it was stated in paragraph 12/8/2 of *The Supreme Court Practice* (1979) (in relation to the old
practice that an application to the court to set aside proceedings, after a conditional appearance, must be made within the time limited by the court—
see the old Ord. 12, r. 7), that the application to the court would be in
time if the notice or summons was *issued* within the specified time. It is   H
true that the authority cited in support of this proposition (*Bonnell* v.
Preston (1908) 24 T.L.R. 756) did not in fact support it; even so, this
appears to have been the accepted understanding of the old practice, and
it was against this background that the new Ord. 12, r. 8, was drafted. The
point does not arise for decision in the present case; but there must be
a likelihood that the requirement in the new Ord. 12, r. 8 (1) of application
to the court within 14 days will be construed in the same sense, i.e. as

The Weekly Law Reports, July 31, 1981

1079

1 W.L.R.   Carmel Exporters v. Sea-Land Inc. (Q.B.D.)   Robert Goff J.

A requiring only that the summons or motion should be issued within that time. Since there is, however, some doubt as to the true construction of these words, and since it was argued before me that such a construction would not achieve the purpose expressed in paragraph 12/7—8/6, I think it desirable for the point to be drawn to the attention of the Rules Committee so that they can, if they think fit to do so, clarify or amend the words of the rule.

B   Second, I wish to return to the requirement in the new Ord. 12, r. 8 (2), that an application under Ord. 3, r. 5, for an extension of the 14 day period within which an application to the court under rule 8 (1) has to be made, must be made before the expiration of the 14 day period. The exceptional rigidity of this requirement contrasts forcibly with the flexibility which is now generally characteristic of the Rules of the Supreme Court, and which

C enables the court to ensure that justice is done. No doubt short time limits are sometimes desirable; a recent example of this is the period of 21 days now required under Ord. 73, r. 5, for the commencement and service of proceedings to challenge arbitration awards. But the imposition of the guillotine in Ord. 12, r. 8 (2), appears to be contrary to the trend in our rules, which is to ensure so far as possible that parties do not fall into

D procedural traps, and to give the court power to deal with the situation if they do so. The widening some years ago of the court's powers under Ord. 2, r. 1, to deal with failures to comply with the rules provides a vivid illustration of this trend. It is not difficult to see how, due to error, oversight or even illness in a busy solicitors' office, the 14 day period in rule 8 (1) might be allowed to pass without an application being made under Ord. 3, r. 5, for an extension of time. I must confess that it seems strange that the

E court should be deprived of any power to remedy the situation, especially where the plaintiff has suffered no prejudice, as for example where the point at issue has already been developed in correspondence. I therefore wish respectfully to suggest to the Rules Committee that reconsideration may be given to the inflexible fetter imposed by Ord. 12, r. 8 (2), upon the court's discretion under Ord. 3, r. 5, bearing in mind that the exercise of

F any discretion which the court has to extend time will always take into account the purpose of the time limit and the need for finality in any particular case.

       In the result, I accede to the defendants' application and order that the plaintiffs' writ issued on June 11, 1980, be set aside.

G   *Application to set writ aside*
                                              granted with costs.
                                              Leave to appeal.

   Solicitors: *Sinclair, Roche & Temperley; Ince & Co.*

       [Reported by MISS LESLEY HEWLETT, Barrister-at-Law]

H

[HOUSE OF LORDS]

* GUILFOYLE . . . . **PETITIONER**

AND

HOME OFFICE . . . . **RESPONDENT**

1981 July 13   Lord Diplock, Lord Russell of Killowen
and Lord Bridge of Harwich

PETITION by the plaintiff for leave to appeal to the House of Lords from
the decision of the Court of Appeal [1981] 2 W.L.R. 223 notwithstanding
that the time limited by Standing Order No. X had expired.

The Appeal Committee dismissed the petition.

M. G.

[QUEEN'S BENCH DIVISION]

* REGINA v. UXBRIDGE JUSTICES, Ex parte DAVIES

1980 July 8   Donaldson L.J. and Comyn J.

> *Extradition—Person surrendered by foreign state—Jurisdiction of
> English court — Extradition of offender on theft charges —
> Prohibition against proceeding against offender for any other
> matter—Non-payment of fine for offence previously committed
> —Imprisonment in default—Whether sentence for offence—
> Whether detention unlawful—United States of America (Ex-
> tradition) Order 1976 (S.I. 1976 No. 2144), art. XII*

> The applicant was convicted of conspiracy to import
> krugerrands. He was sentenced to a fine of £40,000 with 12
> months' imprisonment in default of payment. He emigrated to
> the United States of America without having paid the fine,
> and was extradited from there to the United Kingdom on 32
> charges of theft. He was imprisoned while awaiting trial, and
> was then released on bail to appear at the Crown Court. As he
> left the prison he was rearrested and brought before the
> justices for a means inquiry in connection with the unpaid fine
> of £40,000. The justices decided to activate the alternative
> sentence of 12 months' imprisonment, being unaware of the
> fact that under the terms of article XII of the United States
> of America (Extradition) Order 1976,[1] an extradited person
> could not be detained or proceeded against in the territory of
> the requesting party for any offence other than an extradit-
> able offence established by the facts in respect of which his extradi-
> tion had been granted, or on account of any other matter.
> On an application for judicial review: —

> *Held,* granting the application, that imprisonment in default
> of payment of a fine took effect as a penalty imposed for the
> original offence, and not merely as a method of enforcing
> payment of the fine; and that, accordingly, the detention of
> the applicant was within the prohibition contained in article
> XII of the United States of America (Extradition) Order 1976

[1] United States of America (Extradition) Order 1976, art. XII: see post, pp. 1081H
—1082A.

[A   since it was a detention for the offence of conspiracy, which was not an offence established by the facts in respect of which the extradition was granted, or alternatively it was a detention on account of another matter.

No cases are referred to in the judgments or were cited in argument.

B   APPLICATION for judicial review.
The applicant, David William Martin Davies, applied for judicial review by way of an order prohibiting the Uxbridge justices, who had decided to activate a 12 months' prison sentence in default of payment of a fine of £40,000 imposed on the applicant on his conviction on a charge of conspiracy to import krugerrands, from exceeding or misusing the United States of America (Extradition) Order 1976. The ground on which
C   the applicant sought relief was that under the terms of the Order of 1976, he, as a person extradited to the United Kingdom on charges of theft, could not be detained for an offence other than an extraditable offence established by the facts in respect of which his extradition had been granted.
The facts are stated in the judgment of Donaldson L.J.

D
Patrick Back Q.C. and Peter Shier for the applicant.
The justices did not appear and were not represented.

DONALDSON L.J.   Mr. David Davies applies for judicial review directed to the Uxbridge justices with a view to quashing a decision by those justices that he be imprisoned for default of payment of a fine.
E   The history of the matter is that the applicant was convicted in 1975 on a charge of conspiracy to import krugerrands. The sentence was a fine of £40,000 with 12 months' imprisonment in default. In addition there was an order for costs. For reasons which seemed good to him the applicant emigrated to the United States and while he was there he was the subject of extradition proceedings in respect of 32 charges of theft. The extradition
F   order was made by the United States court and he was returned to this country. The 32 charges have been reduced to six on which he is still awaiting trial at the Knightsbridge Crown Court.
There have been most unfortunate delays. After the applicant had been imprisoned awaiting trial for a period of slightly in excess of a year, he was bailed to appear at the Knightsbridge Crown Court. No sooner did he leave the doors of the prison than he was rearrested and brought before
G   the Uxbridge justices for a means inquiry in connection with the fine of £40,000 on the conspiracy charge. The justices decided to activate the alternative sentence of 12 months' imprisonment.
Nobody pointed out to them that there is a statutory restriction which applies in this case. It arises under the United States of America (Extradition) Order 1976 (S.I. 1976 No. 2144). Article XII of that Order provides:

H   " (1) A person extradited shall not be detained or proceeded against in the territory of the requesting party for any offence other than an extraditable offence established by the facts in respect of which his extradition has been granted, or on account of any other matters, nor be extradited by that party to a third state—(a) until after he has returned to the territory of the requested party ";—in this case the United States of America—" or (b) until the expiration of 30 days after he has been free to return to the territory of the requested party."

Again, the United States of America—" (2) The provisions of para- **A** graph (1) of this article shall not apply to offences committed, or matters arising, after the extradition."

Mr. Back, who has appeared on behalf of the applicant, has given an example of the highest traditions of the Bar in seeking to assist the court, even though that assistance might not be for the benefit of his client. He has pointed out that there are some reported cases under the Extradition **B** Act 1870 which might have required explanation in the absence of the statutory instrument. But there being this statutory instrument, it is quite unnecessary to go into them.

He also has invited the court's attention to a matter which perhaps has slightly more weight. A fine is a debt of record, and Mr. Back says that we have to consider whether, when a court makes an order imprison- **C** ing in default of a payment of fine, it is detaining the person concerned for an offence or whether it is enforcing the payment of the debt. Bearing in mind that the person concerned has an unfettered option whether to pay the fine or to go to prison, it seems to me that the activation of the default sentence, although intended no doubt in most cases to result in the enforce- ment of the liability to pay the fine, is not enforcement per se—it is the imposition of a penalty for the original offence. In those circumstances it **D** seems to me that it is within the prohibition contained in article XII as being a detention for an offence other than an extraditable offence estab- lished by the facts in respect of which his extradition has been granted. Alternatively it is detention on account of another matter. The justices were therefore in error in making this order.

I would quash the order and I would prohibit the justices from making **E** any similar order until the expiration of 30 days after the applicant has been free to return to the United States of America: let it be said at once that that must mean free in terms of English law. The fact that the Americans will not take him does not mean he is never liable for the alternative penalty. When that time will come I do not know, because at the moment he is not free to leave this country as he is awaiting trial before the Knightsbridge Crown Court. **F**

COMYN J. I entirely agree with the judgment that has just been given. I agree with the definitions given by Donaldson L.J. They are sound in law and sound in sense. I believe that article XII of the United States of America (Extradition) Order 1976 extended and intended all fairness for the person extradited. When soundness and fairness combine, the law **G** invariably follows. I am happy to think that it does so in this case.

For the reasons given by Donaldson L.J., I entirely agree with the order proposed.

Application granted.

Solicitors: *Gordon & James Morton.* **H**

R. D.

A

[CHANCERY DIVISION]

* WINDSOR AND MAIDENHEAD ROYAL BOROUGH
COUNCIL v. BRANDROSE INVESTMENTS LTD.

[1979 W. No. 1701]

B

1981 Jan. 22, 23;   Fox J.
        Feb. 6

*Town Planning—Development—Agreement—Grant of planning
permission in accordance with agreement necessarily involving demolition of buildings on site—Subsequent inclusion of*
C   *site in conservation area—Whether planning authority able
to exercise statutory power to prevent demolition of buildings—Town and Country Planning Act 1971 (c. 78), ss. 52 (3),
277A (as amended by Town and Country Amenities Act 1974
(c. 32), s. 1 (1))*

The Town and Country Planning Act 1971 provides by
section 52:
D   " (3) Nothing in this section or in any agreement made
thereunder shall be construed—(a) as restricting the
exercise, in relation to land which is the subject of any
such agreement, of any powers exercisable by any minister
or authority under this Act so long as those powers are
exercised in accordance with the provisions of the development plan, or in accordance with any directions which
may have been given by the Secretary of State as to the
E   provisions to be included in such a plan; . . ."

In 1976 the plaintiffs, the local planning authority, in
accordance with an agreement made under section 52 of the
Town and Country Planning Act 1971, granted the defendants
planning permission for development of a site within the local
planning authority's area. The development necessarily involved the demolition of existing buildings. In March 1979,
F   before the buildings had in fact been demolished, the plaintiffs
extended an existing conservation area, in purported exercise
of powers conferred on them by section 277A of the Town
and Country Planning Act 1971,[1] so as to include the site
in respect of which planning permission had been granted.
When, in the summer of 1979, the defendants started to
demolish the buildings on the site, the plaintiffs issued a writ
seeking a declaration that the defendants were not entitled
G   to demolish the buildings without their consent, and they
obtained an ex parte injunction to restrain demolition. However, when the matter came before Walton J. inter partes on
July 11, 1979, he refused to continue the injunction until
trial. The buildings were demolished. The defendants issued
a summons under R.S.C., Ord. 18, r. 19, seeking to have the
statement of claim struck out, inter alia, as disclosing no
reasonable cause of action.
H   On the defendants' summons, which was treated by agreement as the trial of the action: —
Held, dismissing the action, that where a planning authority

_____

[1] Town and Country Planning Act 1971. s. 277A: " (1) This section applies to
all buildings in conservation areas other than—(a) listed buildings; (b) excepted
buildings within the meaning of section 58 (2) above; and (c) buildings in relation
to which a direction under subsection (4) below is for the time being in force. (2) A
building to which this section applies shall not be demolished without the consent
of the appropriate authority."

entered into an agreement under section 52 of the Act, the A
only powers preserved to it under subsection (3) were powers
that were exercised in accordance with the development plan
or with any directions which might have been given by the
Secretary of State as to the provisions to be included in
any such plan; that there was in principle nothing to prevent
the exercise of a statutory power being limited by the previous exercise of another statutory power, and, since there
was no development plan or relevant direction by the Sec- B
retary of State, the agreement between the plaintiffs and the
defendants operated so as to limit the plaintiffs' powers to
prevent the demolition of buildings on the site and, accordingly, the defendants had been entitled at all times since the
execution of the section 52 agreement to demolish the buildings standing on the site (post, pp. 1088H—1089C, D–G,
1091B–E).

Ransom & Luck Ltd. v. Surbiton Borough Council [1949] C
Ch. 180, C.A. distinguished.

The following cases are referred to in the judgment:

Dowty Boulton Paul Ltd. v. Wolverhampton Corporation [1971] 1 W.L.R.
204; [1971] 2 All E.R. 277.
Ransom & Luck Ltd. v. Surbiton Borough Council [1949] Ch. 180; [1949]
1 All E.R. 185, C.A.   D
Southend-on-Sea Corporation v. Hodgson (Wickford) Ltd. [1962] 1 Q.B.
416; [1961] 2 W.L.R. 806; [1961] 2 All E.R. 46, D.C.

The following additional case was cited in argument:
Ayr Harbour Trustees v. Oswald (1883) 8 App.Cas. 623, H.L.(Sc.).

ACTION   E
In 1976, the plaintiffs, Windsor and Maidenhead Royal Borough
Council, in an agreement made under section 52 of the Town and Country
Planning Act 1971, granted to the defendants, Brandrose Investments Ltd.,
planning permission for the development of property at 107–111, Peascod
Street, Windsor, which involved demolition of existing buildings. On or
about March 29, 1979, the plaintiffs, in purported exercise of their powers F
under section 277A of the Town and Country Planning Act 1971, extended
an existing conservation area so as to include the site at 107–111, Peascod
Street, belonging to the defendants, in respect of which the planning permission had been granted. In the summer of 1979, the plaintiffs issued a
writ seeking a declaration that the defendants were not entitled to demolish
the building without the plaintiffs' consent and an injunction restraining
them from doing so. They obtained from Foster J. an ex parte injunction G
restraining the defendants from proceeding with the demolition without
their consent. When the matter came before Walton J. inter partes on July
11, 1979, he refused to grant an interim injunction until trial and dismissed
the motion. The plaintiffs did not appeal and the defendants demolished
the buildings. On January 30, 1980, the defendants issued a summons to
dismiss the action for want of prosecution, but the plaintiffs were allowed H
to deliver a statement of claim in February 1980, in which the claim for
an injunction was abandoned and the only relief sought was a declaration
that the defendants were not and/or had at no time since the land was
included in a conservation area been entitled to demolish the existing
buildings on the site, without obtaining the plaintiffs' consent as local
planning authority, pursuant to section 277A of the Town and Country
Planning Act 1971. On October 7, 1980, the defendants again applied, by

A   summons, to strike out the statement of claim under R.S.C., Ord. 18, r. 19, (a) as disclosing no reasonable cause of action, (b) as being frivolous and vexatious and (c) as being an abuse of the process of the court. The summons also sought an inquiry as to what damages the plaintiffs should pay pursuant to their undertaking given to Foster J. on July 2, 1979, and costs. By agreement, the summons was treated as the trial of the action.

B   The facts are stated in the judgment.

    Lionel Read Q.C. and Timothy F. M. Stow for the plaintiffs.
    K. R. Bagnall Q.C. and Kirk Reynolds for the defendants.

                                                    Cur. adv. vult.

C   February 6. Fox J. read the following judgment. This is an application by the defendants to strike out the statement of claim as disclosing no cause of action.
        The matter arises out of proposals for the development of property at 107–111, Peascod Street, Windsor. The defendants have been the owners of the site since about 1973. The site adjoins land which is owned by the
D   plaintiffs, who are the local planning authority. In 1976 there was a compulsory purchase inquiry at which the defendants were objectors. A compromise was reached in consequence of which three agreements were entered into between the parties. These were (1) a land exchange agreement; (2) an agreement dated January 22, 1976, under section 52 of the Town and Country Planning Act 1971 (" the section 52 agreement "); and (3) a side letter.
E   In October 1976, planning permission was granted by the plaintiffs to the defendants for the development of 107–111, Peascod Street. On March 29, 1979, the plaintiffs amended the boundaries of the conservation areas in Windsor so as to include 107–111, Peascod Street. In general, if property is lawfully designated as within a conservation area, the consent of the planning authority, the plaintiffs in this case, is necessary for the
F   demolition of buildings thereon under section 277A of the Town and Country Planning Act 1971.
        The defendants commenced to demolish 107–111, Peascod Street in the summer of 1979. On July 2, 1979, the plaintiffs applied for an interlocutory injunction to restrain the defendants from proceeding with the demolition without the plaintiffs' consent. Foster J. granted that injunction.
G   The writ was issued on July 3, 1979. It claimed (1) a declaration that the defendants were not entitled to demolish the premises without the plaintiffs' consent; and (2) an injunction to restrain the defendants from demolishing the premises. A notice of motion by the plaintiffs, to restrain the defendants from demolishing until the trial of the action, was issued on July 3. That motion was heard by Walton J. The defendants resisted the
H   application for an injunction. They contended inter alia that the terms of the section 52 agreement were such that the plaintiffs were not entitled to require the defendants to obtain their consent before demolishing the premises. Walton J. gave judgment on July 11, 1979. He refused to grant an injunction and dismissed the motion. The plaintiffs did not appeal.
        Between July 11, 1979, and January 30, 1980, no step was taken in the action. On January 30, 1980, the defendants issued a summons to dismiss

the action for want of prosecution. In February 1980, the plaintiffs **A**
delivered a statement of claim. The relief sought therein differed from
that sought in the writ in that the claim for an injunction has been abandoned. The only substantive relief sought is a declaration that the
defendants are not and/or have at no time since the land was included in
a conservation area been entitled to demolish the buildings thereon known
as 107–111, Peascod Street, without obtaining the consent of the plaintiffs
as the local planning authority pursuant to section 277A of the Town and   **B**
Country Planning Act 1971.

Upon delivery of the statement of claim the plaintiffs withdrew two
enforcement notices which they had served in respect of the premises in
relation to the demolition. In March 1980, the Secretary of State confirmed
the withdrawal of the enforcement notices and stated that he would be
taking no steps in relation to the premises.   **C**

The present summons to strike out the statement of claim was issued
in October 1980. It is common ground that none of the buildings was of
any historic or architectural interest at all. All the buildings have in fact
now been demolished. The present proceedings are, therefore, of no
practical importance save as to costs and, possibly, the question of liability
on the implied undertaking for damages given on the grant of the ex parte
injunction by Foster J.   **D**

Whether this is a proper case for striking out I need not consider. It
is agreed that, since the parties are before me, it is convenient that I should
determine the question whether the defendants are correct in their contention as to the effect of the section 52 agreement. That in turn will determine whether the plaintiffs have a case for the grant of a declaration as
sought. Section 52 of the Town and Country Planning Act 1971, provides   **E**
as follows:

" (1) A local planning authority may enter into an agreement with any
person interested in land in their area for the purpose of restricting or
regulating the development or use of the land, either permanently or
during such period as may be prescribed by the agreement; and any
such agreement may contain such incidental and consequential provi-   **F**
sions (including provisions of a financial character) as appear to the
local planning authority to be necessary or expedient for the purposes
of the agreement.

" (2) An agreement made under this section with any person
interested in land may be enforced by the local planning authority
against persons deriving title under that person in respect of that land,
as if the local planning authority were possessed of adjacent land and   **G**
as if the agreement had been expressed to be made for the benefit of
such land.

" (3) Nothing in this section or in any agreement made thereunder
shall be construed—(a) as restricting the exercise, in relation to land
which is the subject of any such agreement, of any powers exercisable
by any minister or authority under this Act so long as those powers   **H**
are exercised in accordance with the provisions of the development
plan, or in accordance with any directions which may have been given
by the Secretary of State as to the provisions to be included in such
a plan; or (b) as requiring the exercise of any such powers otherwise
than as mentioned in paragraph (a) of this subsection."

Subsection (4) I need not read.

A   The section 52 agreement is in the following terms so far as material:

"Whereas: (1) The developer"—that is the defendants—"is the owner in fee simple of all that land edged purple on plan no. 1 attached hereto. (2) The corporation"—that is the plaintiffs—"are or shortly will be owners in fee simple of, inter alia, all that land edged blue on the said plan. (3) It is intended that the

B   development of the land of the developer and the incidental development of the corporation's land shall be regulated in accordance with the provisions of section 52 of the Town and Country Planning Act 1971.

"Now therefore it is agreed as follows: 1. For the purposes of this deed it is agreed between the parties hereto that the line marked 'XYZ' on the said plan is the boundary between the respective

C   developments of the corporation and the developer. 2. The corporation and the developer hereby covenant in respect of the following rights and restrictions and by reference to the said plan and plan no. 2 attached hereto as follows: (a) the corporation hereby covenants and agrees with the developer that the developer may build up to the said line XYZ and along its length at levels B, D,

D   and E on the said plan no. 2. (b) The developer hereby covenants and agrees with the corporation that the corporation may build up to the said line XYZ and along its whole length at levels B and D. . . . (c) The corporation hereby further covenants and agrees with the developer that above level E the developer may build as follows: (i) Between points X and Y to a level of 5·3 metres above level E or higher if the point is contained within an angle of 50 degrees

E   measured from a point 5·3 metres above level E along the line XY as shown on section AA of the said plan no. 2. (ii) Between points Y and Z to a height contained within an angle of 50 degrees measured from a point 3 metres from the boundary YZ and at a height of 800 metres above level E as shown in section BB on the said plan no. 2. (3) The developer hereby further covenants and agrees with the

F   corporation that the developer will not build on its land edged purple on plan no. 1 to a height exceeding 16 metres above the present ground level at point X shown on the said plan no. 1."

There are, I think, two questions to be determined. (1) Could the plaintiffs lawfully enter into an agreement which has the effect of disentitling the plaintiffs to require consent under section 277A to the demolition

G   of the buildings? (2) If so, did the section 52 agreement have that effect? As to the first question I was referred by Mr. Read, by way of preliminary, to the decision of the Court of Appeal in *Ransom & Luck Ltd.* v. *Surbiton Borough Council* [1949] Ch. 180. That case related to section 34 of the Town and Country Planning Act 1932, which provides:

H   "(1) Where any person is willing to agree with any such authority as is mentioned in subsection (2) of this section that his land, or any part thereof, shall, so far as his interest in the land enables him to bind it, be made subject, either permanently or for a specified period, to conditions restricting the planning, development, or use thereof in any manner in which those matters might be dealt with by or under a scheme, the authority may, if they think fit, enter into an agreement with him to that effect, and shall have power to enforce

the agreement against persons deriving title under him in the like   A
manner and to the like extent as if the authority were possessed of,
or interested in, adjacent land and as if the agreement had been
entered into for the benefit of that adjacent land."

In *Ransom & Luck Ltd.* v. *Surbiton Borough Council*, the parties had
entered into an agreement under section 34. The action was a claim
by the plaintiffs for damages on the ground that the council had refused   B
liberty to develop their land in breach of the provisions of the section 34
agreement, it being contended that under the agreement the council as
authorised by section 34, assumed a contractual obligation not to exercise
statutory powers to restrict the planning development and use of the land
in accordance with the agreement. The council had refused an application for planning permission. The claim failed. It was held that section   C
34 only enable the landowner to enter into an agreement with the local
authority restricting the user of land so that the local authority could
enforce the restrictions against the successor in title of the landowner,
and that it was not competent to the council to incorporate into a section
34 agreement any restrictions on its statutory powers. Lord Greene M.R.,
at p. 195, made observations, to which I was referred, as to the improb-
ability that Parliament, by such a section, would authorise a local authority   D
to tie its hands with regard to its statutory duties, and to contract itself
out of them.

I bear those observations in mind, but plainly Parliament could by
appropriate language authorise a planning authority to enter into agreements which limit the subsequent exercise of the authority's powers. The
question is whether Parliament has done so in section 52.

It is clear that section 52 is very different in its language from section 34.   E
I observe that while section 34 is only dealing with the case where a landowner is willing to agree to conditions restricting the planning development
or use of the land, section 52, on the other hand, opens with a wide general
authority to the planning authority to enter into any agreement with any
person interested in the land for the purpose of restricting or regulating
the development or use of the land. However, that is by the way. The   F
fundamental difference between the two sections is to be found in the
provisions of section 52 (3) which have no counterpart in section 34.
Subsection (3) (*a*) deals with the restriction of the authority's powers. It
provides that nothing in section 52 or in any agreement entered into under
it shall be construed:

> " . . . (*a*) as restricting the exercise, in relation to land which is the   G
> subject of any such agreement, of any powers exercisable by any
> minister or authority under this Act so long as those powers are
> exercised in accordance with the provisions of the development plan,
> or in accordance with any directions which may have been given by
> the Secretary of State as to the provisions to be included in any such
> plan; . . ."   H

If that provision was intended to operate so as to save fully the right of
the authority to exercise any of its powers and discretions the paragraph
could have stopped after the words " this Act," but the subsequent part,
which begins " . . . so long as " is, it seems to me, quite plainly intended
to place a limitation upon the saving provision. The saving only operates
to a limited extent. The extent is that there is no restriction on the
exercise of the planning authority's powers in relation to the land *so*

A *long as* they are exercised in accordance with the development plan or
the appropriate direction of the Secretary of State, but not further.

It seems to me that the only sensible construction of the wording
of paragraph (*a*) is that an exercise of the authority's power is *not*
preserved, contrary to provisions of the agreement, save to the extent
that the exercise is in accordance with the development plan or a direction of the Secretary of State in relation to the contents of the plan.

B The language of paragraph (*a*) seems to me to be quite inconsistent with
a general saving of the authority's right to exercise its powers contrary to
the provisions of the agreement.

I turn to subsection (3) (*b*). That provides that nothing in the section
or any agreement made thereunder shall be construed—" (*b*) as requiring the exercise of any such powers otherwise than as mentioned in

C paragraph (*a*) of this subsection." In my judgment that provision does
require a positive exercise of the authority's powers in certain circumstances. The circumstances are (i) that the provisions of the relevant
section 52 agreement are such as to require such exercise and (ii) that
the exercise is in accordance with the provisions of the development plan
or a relevant direction of the Secretary of State in relation to the
contents of the plan.

D The result, it seems to me, is that both paragraphs (*a*) and (*b*)
in subsection (3) contemplates the existence, in consequence of a section
52 agreement, of fetters upon the powers of the local planning authority.
I do not think that section 52 is merely concerned with enabling the
authority to enforce the agreement; the section seems to me to go a
long way beyond that.

E Now, so far as the present case is concerned, it is common ground
that there was no development plan or direction by the Secretary of
State. In the circumstances it follows in my view that if, upon its true
construction, the section 52 agreement limits the exercise of the plaintiffs'
powers to take steps to prevent the demolition of 107–111, Peascod Street,
there is nothing in law to prevent the agreement having that effect. It
is, of course, well established that a person on whom a statutory power

F is conferred cannot simply fetter its future exercise. Thus, in *Southend-
on-Sea Corporation* v. *Hodgson (Wickford) Ltd.* [1962] 1 Q.B. 416 Lord
Parker C.J. said, at p. 424:

" There is a long line of cases to which we have not been specifically
referred which lay down that a public authority cannot by contract
fetter the exercise of its discretion."

G
There is nothing, it seems to me, in principle to prevent the exercise of
a statutory power being limited by the previous exercise of another
statutory power. As Sir John Pennycuick V.-C. observed in *Dowty
Boulton Paul Ltd.* v. *Wolverhampton Corporation* [1971] 1 W.L.R. 204,
210:

H " The cases are concerned with attempts to fetter in advance the
future exercise of statutory powers otherwise than by the valid
exercise of a statutory power. The cases are not concerned with
the position which arises after a statutory power has been validly
exercised."

Walton J. in his judgment of July 11, 1979, on the motion for an interlocutory injunction, reached the same conclusion as to the effect of
section 52 (3). He said:

" Before the predecessor of section 52—which I think was section **A**
25 of the Act of 1947—was enacted with equivalent provisions to
those in subsection (3), one of the very obvious difficulties in the
way of effecting any such agreement restricting or regulating the
development or use of the land as a permanent matter or during
such period as may be prescribed by the agreement, from the point
of view of the landowner entering into the agreement, was that the
local planning authority was able in a good many ways to change **B**
the rules of the game in its own favour if it so thought fit. The
reason for that was that it was well established under the old law,
and indeed, apart from special provisions still is, that anybody (and
this includes a planning authority) upon whom statutory obligations
and discretions are conferred in general (because there are exceptions and I am simply talking about the general case) cannot do **C**
either of two things; first of all, contract not to exercise its statutory
powers in the future, or secondly, contract as to the manner in
which it will exercise its statutory powers in the future. Those
restrictions mean, of course, that the attractions from the point of
view of the landowner of entering into any such agreement would
be minimal. It is obviously, within certain general limits, therefore
highly desirable that a local planning authority should be able to do **D**
both of those things, and that is provided for by subsection (3)."

Then, after setting out subsection (3), Walton J. continued: " So that,
although I freely confess it is a rather curious method of legislating,
there can be no doubt really about it." Later on Walton J. continued:

" So that subsection 3 (*b*), in a curiously negative way, provides that **E**
the local planning authority may bind itself to exercise its powers
in the future provided that they are exercised in accordance with
the provisions of the development plan and not otherwise. That is
a very considerable breach in the existing law, and so is paragraph (*a*) . . . So that the situation now is, when a developer enters
into a section 52 agreement, he must be taken to know that any
powers, for example the powers of extending a conservation area, **F**
may properly be exercised against him, provided that they are in
accordance with the provisions of the development plan."

I respectfully agree with the views expressed by Walton J.
The next question is the effect of the section 52 agreement itself.
Walton J. took the view that there was an obvious implied agreement
contained in the section 52 agreement by the plaintiffs to the demolition **G**
of the buildings, and indeed, that it was the foundation of what the
defendants were going to do thereafter. I agree with that, and in fact,
Mr. Read for the plaintiffs accepts that, as he says, the whole premise
of the section 52 agreement was that the buildings should be demolished.
Mr. Read says, however, that it does not follow that there is to be
implied into the agreement any provision by the plaintiffs not to require **H**
their consent under statutory powers to such demolition.
That seems to me to be quite unreal. It is conceded that the basis upon
which the agreement proceeded was that the buildings on the site should
be demolished. A purpose of the agreement was, in the language of
section 52 to regulate the development of the land. One of the parties is
the planning authority. It must have been implied that the plaintiffs so
far as they were entitled to do so would do nothing to impede the demo-

A lition.   I treat the section 52 agreement as if it provided in terms that the
defendants be at liberty to demolish the Peascod Street houses.   In the context of an agreement executed under a section which authorises the local
planning authority to restrict the future exercise of its powers, it does not
seem to me sensible to infer that the authority was doing other than
restricting its power to prevent the very thing that it was authorising and
agreeing to.

B
My conclusion, therefore, is the same as that of Walton J., namely that
in view of section 52 (3) the plaintiffs cannot use any of their statutory
powers against the defendants to prevent the demolition of the buildings,
unless what the plaintiffs are proposing is in accordance with the development plan.   There was not and is not any development plan.   The result,
in my view, is that the plaintiffs could not enforce their powers under
C section 277A in relation to the extension of the conservation area, so as to
prevent the demolition of these Peascod Street buildings.

There are two further matters to which I should refer.   First, the
extension of the conservation area was perfectly lawful; the only question
is whether the plaintiffs were entitled to apply the consequences of that
extension against the defendants in relation to the demolition of the build-
D ings on 107–111, Peascod Street, having regard to the section 52 agreement.
As I have indicated I think they are not.   Secondly, there is nothing in
section 52 to prevent a local planning authority stipulating for the insertion
into a section 52 agreement of a provision preserving all or any of its
powers in full.   How far a landowner would be prepared to enter into a
section 52 agreement on that basis is another matter.

The result, it seems to me, is that the defendants have at all times
E since the execution of the section 52 agreement been entitled to demolish
the buildings standing on 107–111, Peascod Street, at the date of the
section 52 agreement without the consent of the plaintiffs under section
277A of the Town and Country Planning Act 1971.   In the circumstances
it seems to me that the action fails.

F   *Action dismissed with costs.*
                                           Declaration accordingly.

Solicitors: *S. G. Hazelton, Maidenhead; Gamlens.*

                                                            T. C. C. B.

G

H

A

[1981]

[QUEEN'S BENCH DIVISION]

* SOUTH OXFORDSHIRE DISTRICT COUNCIL v. SECRETARY OF STATE FOR THE ENVIRONMENT and Another

1980 Nov. 28;   Woolf J.   B
      Dec. 5

*Town Planning—Planning permission—" Material considerations "
—Renewal of application for planning permission for residential
development—Whether time-expired permission material consideration in determining whether to grant planning permission
—Town and Country Planning Act 1971 (c. 78), s. 29 (1), Sch.*   C
24, para. 19 [1]

The applicants owned a site for which detailed planning
permission had been granted in 1957 for the erection of a
bungalow. Unless development of the site had begun by
April 1, 1974, the planning permission expired under the provisions of paragraph 19 of Schedule 24 to the Town and
Country Planning Act 1971.[1] By April 1, trenches had been   D
dug for the foundations of a bungalow, which the applicants
claimed to be the commencement of development within the
meaning of section 43 (2) (b) of the Act but the trenches dug
were for a bungalow which differed in design from that for
which planning permission had been granted. In 1977 a
builder's hut was erected on the site. The planning authority
served an enforcement notice on the applicants requiring the
removal of the hut. The applicants applied to the planning
authority for planning permission to build a bungalow of a   E
similar design to that of the 1957 planning permission and they
also applied for permission to build one of a different design.
The planning authority refused both applications.

The applicants appealed to the Secretary of State for the
Environment in respect of the enforcement notice and the
refusals of planning permission. The Secretary of State
decided that the 1957 planning permission had expired but he
considered that it was a " vitally material consideration " to be   F
taken into account under section 29 (1) of the Act when
deciding whether to grant an application for planning permission and allowed the appeals.

On the planning authority's application to the High Court
under section 245 of the Act: —

Held, allowing the appeal, that, although a planning
authority was not bound by a planning permission which had   G
expired, a previous grant of planning permission was part of
the planning history of the site and could be taken into
account when considering an application for planning permission, but the weight to be attached to it depended on the
circumstances; that the 1957 planning permission could not in
the circumstances of the present case be a " vitally material
consideration " in deciding whether to grant new planning
permission; and, accordingly, the Secretary of State erred in   H

[1] Town and Country Planning Act 1971, s. 29: " (1) . . . where an application is
made to a local planning authority for planning permission, that authority, in dealing
with the application, shall have regard to the provisions of the development plan, so
far as material to the application, and to any other material considerations . . . "
S. 43: " (1) . . . development shall be taken to be begun on the earliest date on
which any specified operation comprised in the development begins to be carried
out. (2) . . . ' specified operation ' means . . . (b) the digging of a trench which is
to contain the foundations . . . of a building; . . . "
Sch. 24, para. 19: see post, p. 1094H—1095A.

The Weekly Law Reports, July 31, 1981

1093

1 W.L.R.   S. Oxon. Council v. Environment Sec. (Q.B.D.)

A   law and his decision would be quashed (post, pp. 1096E–H,
     1099c, G).
          Spackman v. *Secretary of State for the Environment*
     [1977] 1 All E.R. 257 distinguished.

     The following cases are referred to in the judgment:
     Peak Park Joint Planning Board v. *Secretary of State for the Environment*
B   [1979] J.P.L. 618.
     Pyx Granite Co. Ltd. v. *Ministry of Housing and Local Government*
          [1960] A.C. 260; [1959] 3 W.L.R. 346; [1959] 3 All E.R. 1, H.L.(E.).
     Spackman v. *Secretary of State for the Environment* [1977] 1 All E.R. 257.

     The following additional cases were cited in argument:
     Chris Fashionware (West End) Ltd. v. *Secretary of State for the Environ-*
C   *ment and London Borough of Tower Hamlets* [1980] J.P.L. 678.
     Clyde & Co. v. *Secretary of State for the Environment* [1977] 1 W.L.R.
          926; [1977] 1 All E.R. 333; [1977] 3 All E.R. 1123, Willis J. and C.A.
     Collis Radio Ltd. v. *Secretary of State for the Environment* (1975) 73
          L.G.R. 211, D.C.
     Niarchos (London) Ltd. v. *Secretary of State for the Environment* (1977)
          76 L.G.R. 480.

D
     MOTION
          The applicants, Faherty Brothers Ltd., acquired ownership of a site
     at Hadden Hill, North Moreton, Oxfordshire, with detailed planning per-
     mission, granted on February 8, 1957, for a bungalow. By virtue of the
     provisions of paragraph 19 of Schedule 24 to the Town and Country Plan-
E   ning Act 1971, the planning permission would expire on April 1, 1974,
     unless development had commenced by that date. By April 1, 1974, the
     only construction on the site was the digging of some trenches for the
     foundations of a bungalow. On February 23, 1977, the planning authority,
     the South Oxfordshire District Council, served an enforcement notice on the
     applicants requiring the removal of a temporary builders' hut on the site
     which had been erected without planning permission. The applicants
F   refused to comply with the enforcement notice claiming that as the hut was
     needed for the erection of a bungalow for which planning permission had
     been granted on February 8, 1957, it was a permitted development which
     did not require planning permission. The applicants believed that the
     1957 planning permission was still valid because development on the site,
     namely, the digging of trenches, had commenced before April 1, 1974.
     On March 25, 1977, the applicants submitted to the planning authority two
G   applications for planning permission. The first application was for the
     erection of a bungalow similar in design to that for which planning per-
     mission had been granted in 1957. The second application was for the
     erection of a bungalow of a completely different design. The planning
     authority in a notice dated June 13, 1977, refused planning permission for
     both applications. The applicants appealed to the Secretary of State for the
H   Environment against the enforcement notice and the two refusals of plan-
     ning permission. An inquiry into the matter of the three appeals was
     held on December 6, 1977. The inspector who conducted the inquiry,
     Mr. E. D. Crewe, concluded in his report to the Secretary of State that
     the 1957 planning permission was still valid and recommended that the
     appeals be allowed and that planning permission be granted on the two
     applications. The Secretary of State in his decision dated December 18,
     1978, rejected the inspector's conclusions on the validity of the 1957

The Weekly Law Reports, July 31, 1981

1094

S. Oxon. Council v. Environment Sec. (Q.B.D.)   [1981]

planning permission. He held that the 1957 planning permission had
expired on April 1, 1974, for the reason that the trenches, although dug
before April 1, 1974, were not meant for the foundations of a bungalow
conforming with the design of the 1957 planning permission and, therefore,
did not satisfy the requirements of section 43 (2) (b) of the Act of 1971.
Nevertheless, the Secretary of State allowed the appeals and granted planning permissions for the retention of the temporary hut and the two applications for the erection of a bungalow. The Secretary of State regarded
the history of the case, including the 1957 planning permission which had
in his view expired, as a " vitally material consideration " in deciding
whether or not to grant fresh planning permission.

By notice of motion dated January 26, 1979, the planning authority
applied under section 245 of the Town and Country Planning Act 1971 for
an order that the planning permissions granted pursuant to section 36 of
the Act of 1971 for the erection of a bungalow and the planning permission
granted pursuant to section 88 (5) (a) of the Act of 1971 for the temporary
retention of a building be quashed on the ground, inter alia, that the
Secretary of State had purported to take into account as a " vitally material
consideration " the " history of the case " without identifying what facts
and matters constituted and made up the history, and that, in so far as
the history was intended to include the fact that a planning permission had
been granted on the site in 1957, the Secretary of State took into account
an irrelevant matter as that permission had lapsed pursuant to section 38
of the Town and Country Planning Act 1968 and sections 41 to 42 of the
Town and Country Planning Act 1971, and therefore did not amount to a
consideration properly to be taken into account pursuant to section 29 (1)
of the Act of 1971.

David Latham for the planning authority.
Simon D. Brown for the Secretary of State for the Environment.
R. M. K. Gray for the applicants.

Cur. adv. vult.

December 5. WOOLF J. read the following judgment. In this application under section 245 of the Town and Country Planning Act
1971, the appellants, who are the planning authority for South Oxfordshire, are seeking to quash the decision of the Secretary of State contained
in a letter dated December 18, 1978, in which, in respect of three appeals,
the Secretary of State decided to quash an enforcement notice which the
planning authority had served on the applicants, and to grant conditional
planning permission for the retention of the building which was the subject
matter of the enforcement notice, and to allow the applicant's two appeals
against the refusal of the planning authority to grant them planning
permission.

There is one point of planning law of general application raised, on
which both the planning authority and the Secretary of State indicate they
would welcome guidance. The point arises out of the provisions which
are now contained in Schedule 24 to the Town and Country Planning Act
1971. Paragraph 19 of that Schedule provides subject to exceptions which
are not relevant here:

" (1) . . . every planning permission granted or deemed to have been
granted before April 1, 1969, shall, if the development to which it
relates had not been begun before the beginning of 1968, be deemed

The Weekly Law Reports, July 31, 1981

1095

1 W.L.R.   S. Oxon. Council v. Environment Sec. (Q.B.D.)   Woolf J.

A   to have been granted subject to a condition that the development must
be begun not later than the expiration of five years beginning with
April 1, 1969."

The effect of that provision is that unless the development is begun
before April 1, 1974, the planning permission can no longer be relied upon
as permitting the development to which it referred. It re-enacts, as a
B   transitional provision, the time limit as to the validity of planning permissions first introduced by the Act of 1968. Similar provisions dealing with
planning permissions granted under the Town and Country Planning Act
1971 are contained in sections 41 to 42 of that Act. In particular section 43
defines when a development is to be taken to be begun for the purpose of
section 41 and section 42, and paragraph 19 of Schedule 24.

On behalf of the planning authority it is contended that where develop-
C   ment is not commenced before the time limit expires, on a fresh planning
application the earlier planning permission is no longer a relevant consideration which it is permissible to take into account in deciding whether
or not to grant the fresh application.

In deciding whether or not to grant planning permission, the planning
authority is required by section 29 (1) of the Act of 1971 to " have regard
D   to the provisions of the development plan . . . and to any other material
considerations," and it is submitted that a time-expired planning permission
cannot be a material consideration. In support of this submission Mr.
Latham relies upon the only previous relevant authority which is *Peak Park
Joint Planning Board* v. *Secretary of State for the Environment* [1979]
J.P.L. 618. The transcript of the judgment is before me. The judgment is
that of Sir Douglas Frank Q.C. whose opinion as to planning matters I treat
E   with very great respect because of his unrivalled experience. In that case
Sir Douglas was dealing with a decision by an inspector on behalf of the
Secretary of State in which the inspector, in dealing with an appeal against
the refusal of planning permission, purported to apply Circular 17/69 of
the Ministry of Housing and Local Government in deciding an application
for planning permission where there was a previous time-expired permission.
F   The circular dealt with the position where applications are made to, in effect,
renew planning permissions before they became time-expired and stated:

" As a general rule such applications should be refused only where
(a) there has been some material change of planning circumstances
since the permission was granted, e.g. a change in planning policy for
the area or in relevant highway considerations, (b) continued failure
G   to begin the development will contribute unacceptably to uncertainty about the future pattern of development, or (c) the application is
premature because the permission still has a reasonable time to run."

As Sir Douglas rightly pointed out, the reliance upon the circular on the
facts of that case was misconceived because, unlike the circular, it did not
concern a planning permission which was not time-expired. Sir Douglas
H   did, however, go on to say:

" Of course nobody I would have thought would dispute that the
existing planning permission is something which has to be taken into
account. But the whole purpose of the amendment to the law introduced by section 38 of the Act of 1968, now sections 41 and 42 of the
Act of 1971, is to, as it were, remove stale long-standing planning
permissions from any consideration, to prevent them inhibiting the
planning authority in their decision-making process. I therefore think

1096

Woolf J.   S. Oxon. Council v. Environment Sec. (Q.B.D.)   [1981]

The Weekly Law Reports, July 31, 1981

that paragraph is not a planning policy consideration. If anything it A it is some form of administrative policy unrelated to planning, and if it is unrelated to planning questions, then following the well-known principle enunciated in *Pyx Granite Co. Ltd.* v. *Ministry of Housing and Local Government* [1960] A.C. 260 it is ultra vires. This view I find supported by a reference to section 29 of the Act of 1971 where it is provided that in dealing with a planning application the local plan- B ning authority shall have regard, so far as material to the application, to any other material considerations (that is other than the development plan). But as I have said the consideration must be material to plan- ning, and I do not think that having regard to permissions which no longer have any effect is a planning consideration. And if the matter rested there on the question of planning policy, then I would have had little hesitation in quashing the decision, but in my judgment it does C not end there."

The case Sir Douglas was dealing with was a special one because he dismissed the appeal, taking the view that the inspector, on the way the appeal was argued before him, had no alternative to dealing with the matter in the way in which he did. It may be, therefore, that Sir Douglas did not intend his remarks to be regarded as having general effect. If they D were intended to be of general effect, I am bound to say that I have difficulty in agreeing with the views expressed.

The effect of the changes made by the Act of 1968, now embodied in section 41 and section 42 of the Act of 1971, is to get rid of out of date permissions and to allow a planning authority, if it wants to do so, to prevent development by refusing permission in respect of development for which permission previously existed. A planning authority is thus in no E way bound by a previous planning permission which has expired. How- ever, the fact that it is in no way bound, does not mean that it is forced to wholly disregard that pre-existing permission. That there was a pre-existing permission may still be a relevant or material circumstance which a planning authority is permitted to take into account, though it must do so properly, and, as it is unlikely to be of great moment, not give it more weight than F appropriate. For example, it is not unreasonable for a planning authority to want to be consistent in its consideration of planning applications, and taking into account a planning permission which has expired and considering whether there has been any change of circumstances on a fresh application may assist in achieving consistency. I would regard a planning permission which has expired as still being part of the planning history of the site. In my view, it is not without significance that the planning authority can G impose a special time-limit which will then over-ride the time-limit provided for by the Act. If it does, by the time a fresh application is made there could have been a change of circumstances which made the special time- limit inappropriate. In such circumstances a developer should be entitled to ask the planning authority to take into account on a fresh application the fact that if the original planning authority had known that that would H prove to be the position, that time-limit would not have been imposed and the fresh application would not have been necessary. If it could be relevant to have regard to a planning permission which has expired because of a special time-limit, it should be permissible in the appropriate circumstances to have regard to planning permission which has expired because of a statutory time-limit.

Before leaving *Peak Park Joint Planning Board* v. *Secretary of State*

The Weekly Law Reports, July 31, 1981

1097

1 W.L.R.   S. Oxon. Council v. Environment Sec. (Q.B.D.)   Woolf J.

A *for the Environment* [1979] J.P.L. 618, it is right that I should say that I see no reason why the general policy set out in the circular should be regarded as ultra vires and I would therefore reserve the question as to whether or not the criticism of that policy set out in the *Peak Park Joint Planning Board* case is justified.

B It follows that I do not accept the planning authority's general contention as to the law. This, however, is not sufficient to dispose of the application. It is necessary to consider the specific decision of the Secretary of State on the facts of this case.

The enforcement notice related to a temporary builder's hut which the applicants justified solely on the ground that it was needed for the erection of a bungalow which was the subject of a planning permission granted on February 8, 1957. If that planning permission was still valid, then the C enforcement notice would have to be quashed because the hut would be permitted development under class 4 of Schedule 1 to the Town and Country Planning General Development Order 1977. It was therefore necessary for the Secretary of State to decide whether as a matter of fact the development in respect of which the permission had been granted on February 8, 1957, had been begun before the end of March 1974. The D applicants contended that it had been so begun because trenches had been dug which fulfilled the requirements of section 43 (1) and 2 (*b*). While trenches had been dug, they had unfortunately not been for the bungalow to which the planning permission related but for a different bungalow which had been designed so that " it is possible to re-orientate the trenches actually dug so that one wall more or less coincides with where the corresponding wall of the 1957 bungalow ought to be." The Secretary of State did not E consider this was sufficient for the provisions of section 43. He accordingly decided that the planning permission had expired on April 1, 1974.

The Secretary of State went on to consider the two appeals from the decision of the planning authority to refuse permission for bungalows on the same site, and the deemed planning application for permission to retain the building which is the subject of the enforcement notice. One F of the bungalows which was the subject of the appeal was of the same design as the bungalow which had been the subject matter of the earlier planning permission. The other differed.

In his decision letter the Secretary of State quoted what the inspector had concluded with regard to the planning merits of the section 36 appeals, which was as follows:

G "On the planning merit of section 36 appeals the inspector has concluded: ' Turning to the section 36 appeals, this is an area of largely undeveloped country, well away from any recognisable settlement. Although visually a bungalow here would not be unduly prominent, and when seen from any distance to the south would probably be dominated by the bigger house (Hadden House) standing above and to the north of it, it would certainly intensify such residential development H as there is. Forgetting, temporarily, the history of the site it would be difficult to distinguish a dwelling here from other dwellings nearby which other people might apply to build. It could lead to other applications which could not justly be resisted. However, I conclude that there is already a valid planning permission on the site, and it would therefore be inconsistent to reject the first section 36 appeal because the bungalow concerned is identical with the one for which I consider permission exists. But since this bungalow is in my view

The Weekly Law Reports, July 31, 1981

1098

Woolf J.   S. Oxon. Council v. Environment Sec. (Q.B.D.)   [1981]

banal and unsuitable, every encouragement to build a more suitable   A
dwelling should be given. The bungalow in the second section 36
appeal is, I consider, a major improvement on that for which permission exists. I consider, therefore, that both appeals should be
allowed."

The inspector recommended that permission should be granted.
    The Secretary of State then went on: B

    " 10. These conclusions are not accepted in so far as they relate to the
validity of the planning permission which had already been given on
the site in 1957. It is noted that the 1957 conditional planning permission was granted by the former Wallingford Rural District Council
acting on behalf of the former Berkshire County Council. It is further
noted that following local government re-organisation measures of 1974
the present council took over the administration of planning functions   C
in the former rural district area and adopted the policies of the former
council. An application for a design of dwelling different from that
approved in the 1957 permission was still outstanding and was not
determined by the new council until the changeover date for the new
council which coincided with the expiry date for planning permissions
granted before the passing of the Act of 1968. The development plan   D
for the area had not changed since the 1957 permission and at the
time of these applications remained planning authorities which were
taken over by the new council in 1974. The character of the area too
remains what it was for many years, that is, predominantly rural and
agricultural with the bulk of Hadden House standing on higher ground
above the appeal site when viewed from the south. Taking into account
the history of the case which is considered to be a vitally material   E
consideration in this instance and bearing in mind that the character
of the area has not changed in the intervening years since 1957, the
inspector's conclusion that the bungalows ' would not be unduly
prominent when seen from any distance to the south and would
probably be dominated by the bigger house (Hadden House) standing
above and to the north of it ' is accepted. In the special circumstances   F
of this case the view is taken, in agreement with the inspector that
planning permission should be granted on these appeals.
    " 11. The inspector's remarks on the design and the council's
remarks recorded in the report about their preference for the ' second '
design of bungalow is however drawn to your client's attention."

    The first thing which is to be noted about the Secretary of State's deci-   G
sion is that he has granted a planning permission for a bungalow, the design
of which the inspector concluded was " banal and unsuitable." It is understandable that the inspector should have recommended that permission
should be granted for that bungalow because he took the view that there
was already an existing planning permission for such a bungalow so there
would not be any adverse effect in granting further permission. However,
the Secretary of State had already concluded that there was no longer an   H
existing planning permission and therefore there was not that justification
for granting planning permission in what was largely undeveloped country-
side. As the Secretary of State apparently did not disagree with the
inspector's view of the design of that bungalow, and as the applicants
would have been quite content with planning permission for the second
bungalow, I am bound to say that I am at a loss to understand why planning permission for a building of the original bungalow design was granted.

The Weekly Law Reports, July 31, 1981

1099

1 W.L.R.   S. Oxon. Council v. Environment Sec. (Q.B.D.)   Woolf J.

A   Mr. Simon Brown, with his usual candour, confessed that he was equally surprised. It does suggest that there was some error in reasoning of the person responsible for making the decision of the Secretary of State in this case.

I also find it difficult to understand the reference that the decision should be granted on the appeals in agreement with the view taken by the inspector. It is true that the inspector did recommend that planning permission should

B   be granted but it is reasonably clear that he only did so because of his erroneous conclusion that the original permission was still in existence. The reference by the inspector to largely undeveloped country and intensification of residential development and other applications seems clearly to indicate that the inspector was adverse to the granting of planning permission but for the pre-existing permission which he regarded as still valid.

C   Next it is to be noted that the Secretary of State says that the history is a " vitally material consideration." The reference to history must be because of the expired planning permission; as I have indicated such an expired planning permission can be a relevant consideration but I find it very difficult to see how it could ever be regarded in the context of this case as being a " vitally material consideration." While the weight to be given to a particular consideration is for the Secretary of State such a

D   conclusion indicates that either the person responsible for making the decision on behalf of the Secretary of State misdirected himself, or he was acting perversely. In either event his decision was wrong in law. It is therefore not necessary for me to decide which is the appropriate label to apply. I suspect, however, that the person responsible for the decision has failed to appreciate the distinction between a situation where there is an existing planning permission which is still valid, and the position where there was

E   a former planning permission which is no longer valid because it became time-expired. I say this because the very words " vitally material consideration " appear in Spackman v. Secretary of State for the Environment [1977] 1 All E.R. 257, at the end of the judgment of Willis J. at p. 261. In Spackman it was a previous planning permission which was still in existence, which Willis J. regarded as a " vitally material consideration."

F   I was referred to the Spackman case by counsel on behalf of the applicants because I was asked on behalf of the applicants if the matter was going back to the Secretary of State to indicate the Secretary of State's approach to the question of the trenches was wrong, bearing in mind that decision. I do not, I am afraid, agree. As far as the trenches are concerned, it seems to me that the Secretary of State's decision was a perfectly proper one, and, indeed, probably the only possible one, bearing in mind

G   the facts of this case. Spackman's case is quite different because the trenches which were dug in the wrong position were intended for the house for which permission had been given, and not a property of different design.

It follows that I quash the Secretary of State's decision to grant planning permission for both bungalows and also quash his decision to grant permission for the retention of the hut.

H   *Decision of Secretary of State*
                                                                  quashed.
                                                   Secretary of State to pay plan-
                                                       ning authority's costs.

Solicitors: *Sherwood & Co.* for *B. G. Roberts, Wallingford; Treasury Solicitor; Francis & Parkes, Reading.*

[Reported by MRS. MARIA FLEISCHMANN, Barrister-at-Law]

A

[COURT OF APPEAL]

* BOORMAN AND ANOTHER v. GODFREY

1981 March 6; 11   Donaldson and Ackner L.JJ.

B

*Legal Aid—Certificate—Ambit—Certificate granted to plaintiff
limited to representation at one hearing and thereafter obtaining counsel's opinion—Plaintiff ordered to pay costs of later
interlocutory hearing—Certificate not discharged—Whether
costs of later hearing covered by certificate—Legal Aid Act
1974 (c. 4), s. 8 (1) (e)*

C
The first plaintiff commenced proceedings against the defendant claiming a sum of money being the balance of the price
of goods sold and delivered.   The defendant counterclaimed,
inter alia, for an injunction restraining the plaintiff from
entering the defendant's premises or publishing or making
statements damaging to the defendant's business.   Subsequently, the plaintiff applied for legal aid and was granted
an emergency certificate on June 30, 1980, to cover the defendant's application for an injunction and committal to be heard
D   on July 1, 1980.   On July 22, 1980, the plaintiff was granted
an ordinary certificate with the following limitation: " Limited
to representation on the defendant's application for an injunction and committal to be heard on July 1, 1980.   Thereafter
limited to preparation of papers for counsel and obtaining
counsel's opinion. . .Papers and counsel's opinion to be referred
to the area committee for decision whether certificate to be
amended or discharged."   On September 15, 1980, on the
E   defendant's successful application for delivery of further and
better particulars of the particulars of claim, the plaintiff was
ordered to pay the defendant's costs in any event.   On October
23, 1980, the plaintiff applied for the order for costs to be
amended by the addition of a proviso that it should not be
enforced unless a determination of the plaintiff's means had
been made in accordance with section 8 (1) (e) of the Legal
Aid Act 1974.[1]   Judge McDonnell refused the application
F   holding that the plaintiff was not an assisted person at the
time of the application on September 15, 1980, because of the
limitation on the certificate, and that he was liable for the full
costs of the application without any determination under section 8 (1) (e).
On the plaintiff's appeal: –
Held, allowing the appeal, that where legal aid was granted
in relation to a part only of proceedings, the limitation could
G   be by reference either to a particular period of time or to particular issues in the proceedings; that, in the present case, legal
aid assistance was limited by time, the plaintiff being an assisted
person for the whole of the county court proceedings from the
date the emergency certificate was granted until the date of
discharge; and that, accordingly, the costs of the defendant's
application on September 15, 1980, were incurred while the
plaintiff was an assisted person, and the plaintiff's liability for
H   the costs was to be determined in accordance with section
8 (1) (e) of the Legal Aid Act 1974 (post, pp. 1106A–B, D).
Dugon v. *Williamson* [1964] Ch. 59, C.A. and dictum of
Lord Diplock in *Megarity* v. *D. J. Ryan & Sons Ltd. (No. 2)*
[1981] 2 W.L.R. 335, 343, H.L.(E.) applied.
Mills v. *Mills* [1963] P. 329, C.A. considered.

[1] Legal Aid Act 1974, s. 8 (1): see post, p. 1103B–E.

A   The following cases are referred to in the judgment:

Dugon v. Williamson [1964] Ch. 59; [1963] 3 W.L.R. 477; [1963]
    3 All E.R. 25, C.A.
Herbert (orse. Bridgeman) v. Herbert [1964] 1 W.L.R. 471; [1964] 1
    All E.R. 915.
Megarity v. D. J. Ryan & Sons Ltd. (No. 2) [1981] 2 W.L.R. 335;
    [1981] 1 All E.R. 641, H.L.(E.).

B   Mills v. Mills [1963] P. 329; [1963] 2 W.L.R. 831; [1963] 2 All E.R.
    237, C.A.

No additional cases were cited in argument.

INTERLOCUTORY APPEAL from Judge McDonnell sitting at Lambeth
County Court.

C   On November 14, 1979, the first plaintiff, Edward George Boorman,
brought proceedings in the Lambeth County Court in which he claimed
from the defendant, Maurice Godfrey, the sum of £1,043·65 being the
balance of the price of goods sold and delivered.   The defendant counterclaimed, inter alia, for an injunction restraining the plaintiff from
entering the defendant's premises or publishing or making statements
damaging to the defendant's business.   The plaintiff who was not legally
D   aided at that stage, applied for legal aid and was granted an emergency
civil aid certificate on June 30, 1980, which limited assistance to representation on the defendant's application for an injunction and committal
to be heard on July 1, 1980.   On July 22, 1980, an ordinary civil aid
certificate was granted with the following limitation: " Limited to representation on the defendant's application for an injunction and committal
to be heard on July 1, 1980.   Thereafter limited to preparation of papers
E   for counsel and obtaining counsel's opinion...Papers and counsel's
opinion to be referred to the area committee for decision whether certificate to be amended or discharged."   On September 15, 1980, the
defendant applied for an order requiring the plaintiff to deliver further
and better particulars of the particulars of claim.   The application
succeeded and the plaintiff was ordered to pay the defendant's costs in any
F   event.   On October 23, 1980, Judge McDonnell dismissed the plaintiff's
application for the order for costs to be amended so as to include a proviso
that the order should not be enforced unless a determination as to the
plaintiff's means had been made under section 8 (1) (e) of the Legal Aid
Act 1974.   On the same day Jessie Georgina Mockler was joined as
second plaintiff by order of the judge.

G   The first plaintiff appealed from the dismissal of his application
on the grounds that the judge was wrong in finding that the plaintiff
was not in receipt of legal aid in connection with the proceedings on
September 15, 1980, and in failing to limit the order for costs to such
amount which was a reasonable one for the plaintiff to pay having
regard to all the circumstances including the means of the parties and
their conduct in connection with the dispute as required by section
H   8 (1) (e).

The facts are stated in the judgment of Donaldson L.J.

Robert Beecroft for the plaintiff.
Gordon Murdoch for the defendant.

Cur. adv. vult.

March 11.   DONALDSON L.J. read the following judgment.   This

appeal concerns the position of an assisted litigant against whom an A
order for costs is made when his legal aid certificate is subject to
limitations.

In November 1979 the first plaintiff, Mr. Boorman, began proceedings
in the Lambeth County Court claiming the balance of the price of goods
sold and delivered. He was met with a counterclaim which included a
claim for an injunction restraining him from entering the defendant's
premises. There were a number of interlocutory " activities," to use B
a neutral term, but we are only concerned with two. The first was an
application by the defendant for an injunction and committal which
was to be heard, and may well have been heard, on July 1, 1980. How
the making of the order for an injunction could have been combined
with committal, presumably for its breach, is not explained and does not
matter. The second was an application by the defendant for an order C
requiring the plaintiff to deliver further and better particulars of the
particulars of claim. This application was made on September 15, 1980.
It was successful and the plaintiff was ordered to pay the defendant's
costs in any event.

I now turn to the legal aid situation. On June 30, 1980, the plaintiff
was granted legal aid under an emergency certificate in the following D
terms:

> " Description of legal aid—To continue to take proceedings in the
> Lambeth County Court plaint No. 79 15929 between Edward George
> Boorman, plaintiff, and Maurice Godfrey, defendant. Conditions
> and limitations (if any)—Limited to representation on the defendant's
> application for an injunction and committal to be heard on July
> 1, 1980." E

This was superseded on July 22, 1980, by an ordinary certificate
as follows:

> " Description of legal aid—To continue to take proceedings in the
> Lambeth County Court plaint No. 79 15929 between Edward George
> Boorman, plaintiff, and Maurice Godfrey, defendant. Conditions
> and limitations (if any)—Limited to representation on the defend- F
> ant's application for an injunction and committal to be heard on
> July 1, 1980. Thereafter limited to preparation of papers for
> counsel and obtaining counsel's opinion on evidence, merits and
> quantum after a conference at which the assisted person should
> attend. Papers and counsel's opinion to be referred to the area
> committee for decision whether certificate be amended or dis- G
> charged."

When on September 15, 1980, Judge McDonnell ordered the plaintiff
to pay the defendant's costs of the application in relation to particulars
in any event, he had before him a letter from the plaintiff's solicitors
stating, as was the fact, that they represented the plaintiff under a
limited civil aid certificate which would not cover them for that hearing H
and that for that reason they would not be attending.

On October 23, 1980, the plaintiff applied to the judge to amend
the order of September 15, 1980, by adding a proviso that the order
should not be enforced unless there was a determination made under
section 8 of the Legal Aid Act 1974. Both parties were represented
by counsel, Mr. Beecroft appearing for the plaintiff, and Mr. Murdoch
for the defendant. The judge rejected the application, holding on the

A authority of *Mills* v. *Mills* [1963] P. 329 and *Herbert* (*orse. Bridgeman*) v. *Herbert* [1964] 1 W.L.R. 471 that the plaintiff had not been an assisted person quoad the application of September 15. Unfortunately, he was not referred to *Dugon* v. *Williamson* [1964] Ch. 59, which like *Mills* v. *Mills* is a decision of this court. He thus escaped the problem of having to reconcile these two decisions. This task now falls to us on the plaintiff's appeal from the judge's refusal to amend his order.

B

The key statutory provision is section 8 (1) of the Legal Aid Act 1974, which is in the following terms:

"Where a person receives legal aid in connection with any proceedings—(a) the expenses incurred in connection with the proceedings, so far as they would ordinarily be paid in the first instance
C   by or on behalf of the solicitor acting for him, shall be so paid,
except in the case of those paid direct from the legal aid fund as
provided by section 10 below; (b) his solicitor and counsel shall
not take any payment in respect of the legal aid except such payment as is directed by section 10 below to be made out of the legal
aid fund; (c) he may be required to make a contribution to the
D   legal aid fund in respect of the sums payable out of that fund on
his account; (d) any sums recovered by virtue of an order or agreement for costs made in his favour with respect to the proceedings
shall be paid into the legal aid fund; (e) his liability by virtue of an
order for costs made against him with respect to the proceedings
shall not exceed the amount (if any) which is a reasonable one
for him to pay having regard to all the circumstances, including
E   the means of all the parties and their conduct in connection with
the dispute."

In *Mills* v. *Mills* [1963] P. 329 the legal aid certificate entitled the husband

"to be heard as respondent in the High Court of Justice, Probate,
Divorce and Admiralty Division (Divorce) in proceedings entitled:
F   Rhoda Jean Mills, petitioner, and Thomas Leonard Lanty Mills,
respondent, in respect of the claim in the prayer of the petition
for alimony and maintenance, to include application to determine
liability for costs ": see p. 330.

The appeal turned upon the construction of the Legal Aid and Advice
G Act 1949, but there is no material difference between that Act and the
Act of 1974. This court held, to quote the headnote:

"On its true construction ' proceedings ' in section 2 (2) of the Legal
Aid and Advice Act 1949, had a narrower meaning than the whole
of a cause, action or matter, and an assisted person was not protected
by section 2 (2) (e) from paying the full costs of that part of the
cause, action or matter to which his certificate did not extend.
H   Accordingly, the husband was liable to pay the full costs of the
petition."

In *Herbert* (*orse. Bridgeman*) v. *Herbert* [1964] 1 W.L.R. 471 the legal aid certificate entitled the husband " to legal aid to be represented in a suit... as to the claims made by the prayer of the petition for alimony pending suit, maintenance, a secured provision and costs ": see p. 472. Cairns J. applied *Mills* v. *Mills* [1963] P. 329 and ordered the

husband to pay the full costs incurred by his wife in obtaining the **A**
decree on the basis that that was a separate part of the proceedings.

In *Dugon* v. *Williamson* [1964] Ch. 59, 60 the certificate was " Limited
to obtaining transcript of judgment, preparation of papers for counsel,
and counsel's opinion thereafter on merits and prospects of success of the
appeal ": see p. 60. The papers were in fact referred to the committee
together with counsel's opinion and the committee discharged the certi-   **B**
ficate. This court held, to quote the headnote:

"that it was within the jurisdiction of the area committee to grant a
civil aid certificate for the limited purpose of preparing the papers for
counsel and getting counsel's opinion since, even if counsel's opinion
was adverse, it was reasonable to get it, and that, therefore, the
defendant was an assisted person from the date when the certificate   **C**
was granted until the date when it was discharged; the costs incurred
during that period, accordingly, were incurred while the defendant
was an assisted person within section 2 of the Act so that by virtue
of regulation 13 (6) (b) of the regulations of 1962, section 2 (2) (e)
applied and his liability for costs did not exceed the amount which
was reasonable for him to pay in all the circumstances and, in those
circumstances, it was reasonable to make no order in regard to those   **D**
costs."

At this point it may be convenient to refer to the Legal Aid (General)
Regulations 1971 (S.I. 1971 No. 62 (L. 1)). These regulations were
made under the Act of 1949, but are kept in force and are deemed to
refer to the corresponding provisions of the Act of 1974 by section 42
of that Act. Regulation 13 (6) differs slightly from the corresponding   **E**
regulation under the 1962 regulations referred to in *Dugon* v. *Williamson* [1964] Ch. 59, but the differences are not material. Regulation
13 (6) provides:

"Where a certificate has been discharged, the person to whom
the certificate was issued shall remain liable for the payment of his
maximum contribution, if any, as determined by the appropriate   **F**
committee or as determined or redetermined by the commission
up to the amount paid or payable by The Law Society under paragraph (3) (b) and where he continues to assert or dispute the claim
or to take, defend or be a party to the proceedings to which the
certificate related, section [8 (1) (e) of the Act of 1974] shall apply
in so far as the costs were incurred while he was an assisted person."
                                                                          G
Regulation 14 (1):

"Where, after proceedings have been instituted in any court, any
party becomes an assisted person in regard to those proceedings, the
provisions of section [8 (1) (e) of the Act of 1974] shall apply
only to so much of the costs of the proceedings as are incurred
while a certificate is in force."
                                                                          H
Regulation 15 (9):

"Where a certificate has been issued in connection with any proceedings, the assisted person's solicitor or counsel shall not take any
payment for work done in those proceedings during the currency
of that certificate (whether within the scope of the certificate or
otherwise) except such payments as may be made out of the fund."

A Regulation 20 (1):

"Where proceedings have been concluded in which an assisted
person (including, for the purpose of this regulation, a person who
was an assisted person in respect of those proceedings) is liable or
would have been liable for costs if he had not been an assisted
person, no costs attributable to the period during which his certi-
B ficate was in force shall be recoverable from him until the court
has determined the amount of his liability in accordance with
section [8 (1) (e) of the Act of 1974]: provided that where the
assisted person's certificate does not relate to or has been amended
so that it no longer relates to the whole of the proceedings, the
court shall nevertheless make a determination in respect of that
part of the proceedings to which the certificate relates."
C

Mr. Beecroft for the plaintiff submits that a legal aid certificate can
be limited in two different ways with quite different consequences. First,
it can be limited to part of the proceedings. This was the case in *Mills*
v. *Mills* [1963] P. 329 and in *Herbert (orse. Bridgeman)* v. *Herbert*
[1964] 1 W.L.R. 471. The consequence was that the husbands were
D assisted persons only quoad those parts of the proceedings to which the
certificate extended. Secondly, it can be limited by reference to the
steps or procedures which can be undertaken by the assisted person's
legal advisers. This was the position in *Dugon* v. *Williamson* [1964]
Ch. 59. If this latter course is adopted, the consequences may be surprising. However little the assisted person's legal advisers may be
E authorised to do, until they have done it and the certificate has been
discharged, the assisted person has the benefit of section 8 (1) (e) of the
Act of 1974 in relation to all costs incurred by the other party during
that period.

Mr. Beecroft submits that in this case the legal aid authorities chose
to adopt the *Dugon* v. *Williamson* method of limitation. Legal aid
F extended to the whole of the county court proceedings and the limitation
bit only on what the plaintiff's legal advisers were allowed to do, namely
to represent the plaintiff on July 1 and to advise. It follows, as he
submits, that the plaintiff is entitled to the benefit of section 8 (1) (e)
from June 30, 1980, when the emergency certificate was granted and
in particular in relation to the costs of the defendant's application on
September 15, 1980.
G
It is conceded by Mr. Beecroft that in the light of regulation 20 (1)
of the Legal Aid (General) Regulations 1971, it may well be that there
was no need to amend the judge's order and that the correct course
would have been to resist any attempt to recover the costs at a later
stage. But this would only be to defer the problem which now confronts
us, and both parties ask us to determine the question on this appeal.

H Mr. Murdoch for the defendant submits that *Mills* v. *Mills* [1963]
P. 329 is authority on the meaning of "proceedings" and *Dugon* v.
Williamson [1964] Ch. 59 on "in connection with." The relevant
"proceedings" in the instant case were the application on September 15,
1980, and the plaintiff obtained no assistance in relation to that application. He also points out that if the plaintiff's submissions are correct
and he had wanted to be represented on the hearing of that application,
neither his solicitors nor counsel could have been instructed and paid

Donaldson L.J.   **Boorman v. Godfrey (C.A.)**   **[1981]**

privately: see regulation 15 (9) of the Legal Aid (General) Regulations A
1971.

For my part I accept that this is the consequence of the plaintiff's
submissions, but in the light of *Dugon* v. *Williamson* I am driven to the
conclusion that the plaintiff was an assisted person in relation to the
whole of the county court proceedings notwithstanding that as a result
of the limitation upon the certificate the assistance was conspicuous by its
absence in relation to the application on September 15. If this is not B
right, it is necessary to identify a more limited part of the proceedings
in respect of which the plaintiff was an assisted person. In the present
case it might be arguable that this was the application on July 1, 1980,
but in other cases, of which *Dugon* v. *Williamson* is an example, in
which the only authorised work was of an advisory nature, Mr. Murdoch's
submission would lead to the conclusion that the litigant was not assisted C
in relation to any part of the proceedings. This is clearly fallacious.

While preparing this judgment my attention was drawn to the decision
of the House of Lords in *Megarity* v. *D. J. Ryan & Sons Ltd. (No. 2)*
[1981] 2 W.L.R. 335. That case relates to the liability of the legal aid
fund for the costs of unassisted persons and is not directly material.
However, I note that Lord Diplock, who had given the leading judgment D
in *Mills* v. *Mills* [1963] P. 329, expressed the view [1981] 2 W.L.R. 335,
343, that where legal aid is given in relation to part of the proceedings as
contrasted with the whole proceedings, that part might be defined either
by time or by reference to issues. The legal aid regulations to which I
have referred are drawn on the same assumption. In my judgment, in
the instant case the limitation was by reference to time and not to
issues. E

I would allow the appeal. I am not clear quite what order is asked for,
but that can be discussed.

ACKNER L.J. I agree.

> *Appeal allowed with costs.* F
> *Plaintiff's costs in cause.*
> *Order of September 15, 1980, stayed,*
> *re-direction to first plaintiff to*
> *pay costs, not to be enforced*
> *without leave of judge.*

Solicitors: *Daniel Davies & Co.; Simanowitz & Brown.* G

[Reported by MRS. MARIA FLEISCHMANN, Barrister-at-Law]

H

A

[QUEEN'S BENCH DIVISION]

*REGINA v. IMMIGRATION APPEAL TRIBUNAL,
Ex parte SHAIKH (MUNIR AHMED)

B 1981 Feb. 19
Bingham J.

*Immigration—Limited leave to enter—Application to extend stay
— Student expressing intention to remain in country after
studies if permitted — Whether applicant disentitled to grant
of extension—Statement of Immigration Rules for Control
After Entry: EEC and Other Non-Commonwealth Nationals*
C *(H.C. 82), para. 12*

In October 1973 the applicant, a citizen of Pakistan, was
permitted to enter the United Kingdom with limited leave to
remain as a student for an initial period of 12 months. He
obtained extensions of leave to remain until July 1978. In
June 1978, he applied to the Secretary of State for another
extension to enable him to pursue a further course of study
D in the country. On being asked what his long-term intentions
were he stated that if he was permitted to work in the United
Kingdom, he would be able to attend evening classes, and
that his long-term ambition included service in United Kingdom industries. The Secretary of State was of the opinion
that the applicant had no intention of leaving the country on
completion of the further course of study and refused the
application, purporting to act in accordance with paragraph
12 of the Statement of Immigration Rules for Control After
E Entry: EEC and Other Non-Commonwealth Nationals (H.C.
82),[1] read with paragraph 17 of the Statement of Immigration
Rules for Control On Entry: EEC and Other Non-Commonwealth Nationals (H.C. 81).[2] The applicant appealed to an
adjudicator who, being satisfied that the applicant did intend
to leave the country when he finished the course, allowed the
appeal. On appeal by the Secretary of State, the Immigration
Appeal Tribunal held that the burden rested on the applicant
F to satisfy the Secretary of State that he intended to leave
the country on completing the further course, and that he
had failed to discharge the burden. They accordingly allowed
the appeal.

On the applicant's application for judicial review, inter
alia, by way of an order of certiorari to quash the tribunal's
decision: —

G *Held,* granting the application, that although under the
provisions of paragraph 17 of H.C. 81 an applicant seeking
to enter the United Kingdom as a student had to satisfy the
immigration authorities that he intended to return to his own
country on completion of the course of study, there was no
such requirement under paragraph 12 of H.C. 82; that under
paragraph 12 an applicant for an extension of the period of
his leave had to show that he was pursuing a course of studies
H as a bona fide student and not for a collateral purpose or
with an ulterior motive; and that, accordingly, the applicant's
statement that, if he was permitted, he desired to remain in
this country once he had completed his studies, did not of
itself disentitle him to an extension of the period of leave

[1] Statement of Immigration Rules for Control After Entry: EEC and Other
Non-Commonwealth Nationals (H.C. 82), para. 12: see post, p. 1113F–H.
[2] Statement of Immigration Rules for Control on Entry: EEC and Other
Non-Commonwealth Nationals (H.C. 81), para. 17: see post, pp. 1113H–1114B.

Reg. v. Immigration Tribunal, Ex p. Shaikh (D.C.)   [1981]

and, therefore, the case would be remitted to the tribunal   A
for redetermination (post, pp. 1114D–G, 1115C–E, 1116C–D,
1117A–B).

Reg. v. *Immigration Appeals Adjudicator, Ex parte Perween Khan* [1972] 1 W.L.R. 1058, D.C. considered.

The following cases are referred to in the judgment:
Reg. v. *Immigration Appeals Adjudicator, Ex parte Perween Khan* [1972]   B
    1 W.L.R. 1058; [1972] 3 All E.R. 297, D.C.
Reg. v. *Chief Immigration Officer, Gatwick Airport, Ex parte Kharrazi*
    [1980] 1 W.L.R. 1396; [1980] 3 All E.R. 373, C.A.

The following additional cases were cited in argument:
Harding v. *Secretary of State for the Home Department* (unreported),
    January 7, 1976, Immigration Appeal Tribunal.
Tagbo v. *Entry Clearance Officer, Lagos* (unreported), June 5, 1977,   C
    Immigration Appeal Tribunal.

APPLICATION for judicial review.
By an application dated August 26, 1980, the applicant, Munir
Ahmed Shaikh, a citizen of Pakistan, sought judicial review (1) by way
of an order of certiorari to bring up and quash the decision of the   D
Immigration Appeal Tribunal made on the hearing of an appeal on
May 1, 1980, whereby the tribunal decided that the applicant was not
entitled under the Immigration Act 1971 and Rules made thereunder to
a variation of his leave enabling him to continue his studies, on the
ground that he had not shown that he intended to leave the country
on the conclusion of his studies; (2) by way of an order of mandamus
directed to the tribunal requiring it to dismiss the Secretary of State for   E
the Home Department's appeal against the adjudicator's decision of
January 2, 1980, allowing the applicant's appeal against the Secretary
of State's refusal to vary his current leave; and (3) such further or other
relief as might be just.
The application further stated that (1) the applicant, a citizen of
Pakistan, was duly given leave to enter and remain and at all material   F
times thereafter was a bona fide student in the United Kingdom from
his entry on October 27, 1973. (2) Thereafter the Secretary of State
varied his leave from time to time by allowing him extensions of his
leave to remain, the last such period due to expire on October 27,
1978. (3) On January 24, 1979, the Secretary of State refused the
applicant's application duly made within his current leave for a further
extension for the purposes of study; on the grounds that, " . . . the   G
Secretary of State is not satisfied that you intend to leave when your
studies are complete." (4) On January 2, 1980, before the adjudicator,
Mr. C. P. Rushton, the applicant gave evidence and by his determination allowing the appeal the adjudicator held as a fact that the
applicant had shown that he intended to leave at the conclusion of the
studies. (5) On May 1, 1980, the Immigration Appeal Tribunal, Mr. A.   H
Hooton (Chairman), Dr. S. Torrance and Mr. A. W. Lockwood, upheld
the appeal on behalf of the Secretary of State and held (i) that the
adjudicator's finding of fact that the applicant intended to return on the
completion of his studies had to be overturned since no reasonable
immigration officer could have been so satisfied on the evidence available at that time; (ii) that it was a requirement of an applicant to satisfy
the Home Office of his intention to leave on an application for a variation

A of existing leave for the purposes of study; (iii) that an applicant who has expressed an intention of remaining after completion of his course did not meet the requirement of the Immigration Rules even if he had no intention of remaining illegally; and (iv) that the relevant rule governing the instant case was paragraph 12 of the Statement of Immigration Rules Control After Entry: E.E.C. and Other Non-Commonwealth Nationals (H.C. 82), which stated that the student " may be reminded

B that he will be expected to leave at the end of his studies."

The grounds of the application were (a) that the tribunal erred in law in holding that the applicant had to show that he intended to leave at the conclusion of his studies for the purposes of an application for a variation of his leave; (b) that, in the absence of any proof that the intention was to remain illegally, it was in any event insufficient to base a refusal on

C a bare expression of hope or intention, which was the only evidence in the case; (c) that, even if an intention to leave at the conclusion of a course had to be shown in support of an application to remain, the tribunal erred as a matter of law and fact in reversing the finding of the adjudicator in regard to that matter; and (d) that since the applicant otherwise qualified for a variation of his leave and at no material time

D were any other matters in dispute of which he had to satisfy the Home Office, the applicant was entitled to the relief sought.

The facts are further stated in the judgment.

Ian Macdonald for the applicant.
Simon D. Brown for the Secretary of State.

E   BINGHAM J. Mr. Munir Ahmed Shaikh, the applicant, seeks an order of judicial review, namely, an order of certiorari to quash an order of the Immigration Appeal Tribunal made on June 2, 1980, and an order of mandamus instructing that tribunal to dismiss the Secretary of State's appeal to it. The decision it is sought to challenge before me is the decision of the Immigration Appeal Tribunal, and the essential question which that

F tribunal had to determine was whether the Secretary of State in deciding not to extend the applicant's right to remain in this country as a student made a correct decision reached by a correct procedure on January 24, 1979.

I shall have to recite a little of the history in order to make it clear how this question arises. With effect from October 27, 1973, the applicant was given leave to enter this country for 12 months with a restriction on his

G right to accept employment, in order to attend a three-year course at the University of Essex. In fact, it appears that on attending at the University of Essex he found that the course which he was due to attend there overlapped with a degree course which he had already attended in his own country, and consequently he instead went to the Polytechnic in Manchester and embarked on a Higher National Diploma course in computer studies.

H   In October 1974, his leave was extended until October 27, 1975, and there were subsequent extensions granted until the same date in 1976, and in 1977, and finally until July 31, 1978. The reason that the course took so long, it would appear, was not that the applicant was an idle or frivolous student but just that he was not a very successful one, with the result that the course took longer than it should have done.

On June 22, 1978, notice was given by the Manchester Polytechnic that the applicant had been accepted and was due to embark on a three-year

1110

full-time course leading to the Polytechnic's diploma in printing. At this   A
time the Polytechnic confirmed very much what I have said, namely, that
the applicant's attendance as a student had been good, and the Polytechnic
further said that he was considered to be a good candidate for the printing
course.

The Home Office at that point, on July 26, 1978, wrote to the applicant
a letter directed to ascertain from him what his future intentions were, and
the letter ended up by saying: " In which country do you intend to pursue   B
your career? What are your long-term plans? "

The applicant answered that letter on August 3, 1978, and in the course
of his answer made various statements which are of importance in these
proceedings. He said:

> " This printing diploma deals with computers, printing in way that
> helps me to use computer in printing field as well as in photography.   C
> I intend to start a career in computing field. I like to start my com-
> puter career in this country. If you grant me permission to start work
> in this country, then I can join evening classes in advance computing/
> printing. My long-term ambition lies in a good career in computing
> field and long-term service for United Kingdom industries."

Following the receipt of that letter by the Home Office, an extension of   D
permission to remain in this country as a student was refused on October
4, 1978, and that notification, having gone apparently astray, was repeated
on January 24, 1979, which is being treated as the relevant date for the
purposes of these proceedings.

The grounds upon which the Secretary of State refused permission to
remain emerges, I think, from the Home Office statement which reads: E

> " The Secretary of State now considered the application for further
> leave to remain. The applicant had been treated as a genuine, though
> obviously not particularly talented student since his arrival in 1973.
> He had been admitted for a three-year B.A. course but had evidently
> ' lowered his sights ' and taken a two-year H.N.D. course which he had
> passed successfully after four years study. He had applied to continue   F
> his studies by taking a three-year printing course, but had then made
> it clear that he considered his future lay in the United Kingdom and
> had also said he would like to commence employment and continue
> his studies at evening classes. In these circumstances the Secretary of
> State was not satisfied that the applicant intended to leave the United
> Kingdom on completion of his studies and he decided to refuse his
> application in accordance with paragraph 12 of the Statement of   G
> Immigration Rules for Control After Entry: EEC and Other Non-
> Commonwealth Nationals (H.C. 82) read with paragraph 17 of the
> Statement of Immigration Rules for Control on Entry: EEC and
> Other Non-Commonwealth Nationals (H.C. 81). He originally did so
> on October 4, 1978, but the recorded delivery package was lost in the
> post and a fresh notice of refusal and appeal forms were sent on
> January 24, 1979."   H

Perhaps I may interrupt the narrative to mention one part of that
paragraph that has been the subject of comment. It is quite true that the
applicant had, in his letter, said that he would like to commence employment and continue his studies at evening classes, but the paragraph also
contains the statement that the applicant " had then "—that is in his letter
—" made it clear that he considered his future lay in the United Kingdom,"

The Weekly Law Reports, July 31, 1981

1111

1 W.L.R.   Reg. v. Immigration Tribunal, Ex p. Shaikh (D.C.)   Bingham J.

A and that statement is the subject of some criticism as being something not fairly to be extracted from the letter which the applicant wrote.

The applicant having received notice of refusal appealed by a notice given on January 31, 1979, and on January 2, 1980, very nearly a year later, the adjudicator gave his decision. The adjudicator summarised the history very much in the way that I have done and recorded, as was then agreed, that the applicant's printing course had a direct occupational link
B with the computer course that he had previously done. The adjudicator clearly formed a very favourable view of the applicant, saying that he was a good witness and that he accepted his credibility. He then, in the course of his decision, went on as follows :

"Whilst on this course "—that is the first course—" he was informed by his family that as a result of a change of government policy, many
C fewer computer installations were being imported into Pakistan and in consequence job opportunities were greatly reduced. Employment was being given only to persons with experience and it was for this reason that he referred in his correspondence with the Home Office to his wish to gain experience in employment with computers in this country. He said that by using the expression ' long term service for United
D Kingdom Industries ' he meant service abroad by using computer installations manufactured here. He decided to undertake his present course in computer techniques in the printing industry because he had learnt that this was a field in which there was no shortage of job opportunities in his own country and in consequence through pursuing it the necessity for him to obtain work experience in this country prior to leaving was removed. He assured me that he had no intention of remaining here
E beyond the end of his course. He has no relations here—as he put it ' I am alone.' He has five sisters and two brothers in Pakistan and is the oldest son of the family and was clearly aware of his traditional responsibilities as the eldest son and considered that these required him to return at the end of his course. His testimony satisfied me that he is a genuine student with an intention to return at the end of his
F present course. I, therefore, allow the appeal and direct that he be granted permission to remain until the conclusion of his course subject to his progress being satisfactory."

It is, I think, fair to infer from the terms of this decision that when the adjudicator has set out what he was told by the applicant he believed it to be true, having, as I have pointed out, already indicated his acceptance
G of the applicant's credibility.

From that decision the Secretary of State appealed to the Immigration Appeal Tribunal and their decision is dated June 2, 1980. Again, a careful and accurate summary of the history is set out. There is a reference to the evidence given before the adjudicator, to which I will return subsequently, and the tribunal make reference to the terms of paragraph 17 of H.C. 81 and paragraph 12 of H.C. 82, which have already been referred to.
H The crux of the tribunal's decision, I think, is to be found on the last three pages of it, and I shall read such parts as appear to be necessary whilst omitting quite a lot which is inessential for present purposes. The contention on behalf of the Secretary of State is recorded as having been :

"that the Secretary of State had no option but to refuse the respondent a further extension in the light of the latter's expression in his letter of July 26, 1978, of a wish to start his computer career in this country

and his desire for permission to start work in this country. The
Secretary of State could not possibly be satisfied, having received this
letter, that once the respondent had completed his new course of study,
he would depart from the United Kingdom. The onus was on the
respondent to satisfy the Secretary of State that he would then depart;
he had not discharged that onus. He was not entitled to stay for work
experience on the conclusion of his studies."

There was a criticism of the adjudicator's factual findings. The
applicant's representatives' submissions were summarised and, in particular,
the submission that it was not for the tribunal to substitute their findings of
fact for those of the adjudicator who has seen and heard the applicant.
The tribunal then continued:

"In deciding the appeal to us, it is well to have in mind what was the
essential issue the adjudicator had to decide. It was not whether the
respondent was at the time of the hearing before the adjudicator a
genuine student with an intention to return to Pakistan, but whether the
decision the Secretary of State made was correct or wrong. No question of discretion arises under the relevant Immigration Rules; the
adjudicator's function was to decide judicially whether the Secretary of
States' decision was or was not in accordance with the law and those
rules, and in so deciding he was entitled to review any question of fact
on which that decision was based (section 19 of the Immigration Act
1971). An adjudicator is, as it was emphasised in *Visa Officer, Karachi*
v. *Hassan Mohammad* [1978] Imm.A.R. 168, an appellate authority
and not some kind of super immigration officer. In the present appeal,
the adjudicator's function was to decide whether on the facts in existence at the time of the Secretary of State's refusal he should or should
not have been satisfied, on a balance of probability, by [the respon-
dent] that he would depart on conclusion of his studies. On the
facts as put before the Secretary of State by the respondent in his letter
(and his state of mind and intention are facts) no reasonable officer in
the Home Office could have been satisfied that the respondent so
intended. He expressly stated that he had in mind, if permitted,
staying on to work in the first instance in this country. He had an
intention not to depart but to remain at any rate for a time and the
facts that he had no intention of remaining illegally and that his purpose
was to gain experience do not qualify him to stay: see *Harding* v.
Secretary of State for the Home Department (unreported), January
7, 1976, and *Tagbo* v. *Entry Clearance Officer, Lagos* (unreported),
June 5, 1977." The tribunal must reject Mrs. Lam's submission that
he could, on this evidence, be held to have an intention to depart on
conclusion of his studies. We have noted that in his grounds of appeal
to the adjudicator the respondent reiterated that he had no intention
to remain without permission of the Home Office. Thus the principal
question raised by the grounds of appeal was similar to that raised and
decided in *Harding,* but the adjudicator's determination makes no reference to it. The tribunal has considered the record of the respondent's
evidence to the adjudicator and it is noted that he said that he had
thought he should get a job in the United Kingdom to get experience
to enable him to get a job at home. He thought he would get experience by working during the day and studying at evening classes.

"The tribunal is well conscious of the principle enunciated by the
Court of Appeal in the case to which Mrs. Lam referred us. It is a

The Weekly Law Reports, July 31, 1981

1113

1 W.L.R.   Reg. v. Immigration Tribunal, Ex p. Shaikh (D.C.)   Bingham J.

A   principle which it has consistently followed. It has always been reluctant to disturb a finding of fact made by an adjudicator provided there was sufficient evidence to support it and has always been particularly so reluctant when the finding of fact is based on the adjudicator's judgment of the credibility of a witness whom he has seen and heard, even though on the papers before it the tribunal felt it might have itself reached a different conclusion.

B   " It may be possible that by the time the applicant gave evidence to the adjudicator he had abandoned the intention of remaining in this country after his further studies to gain experience, but the evidence is that he had this intention at the time when the Secretary of State made his decision to refuse him a further extension of his leave to be in this country. It follows that the Secretary of State's refusal was in accordance with the law and the Immigration Rules. Further the tribunal considers that the adjudicator's determination is generally an unsatisfactory one. It does not sufficiently deal with or do justice to the Secretary of State's case.

"The Secretary of State's appeal to the tribunal is allowed and his refusal is affirmed."

D   That, therefore, was the decision which the applicant before me seeks to challenge, and Mr. Macdonald, who appears for the applicant, makes three substantial criticisms of that decision. The first is based on the language of the rules themselves, that is paragraph 17 of H.C. 81 dealing with control of those seeking to enter the country as students and paragraph 12 of H.C. 82, laying down the conditions for control after entry. The effect of Mr. Macdonald's submission is that so far as an intention to leave

E   at the end of a period of study is concerned, while paragraph 17 of H.C. 81 contains a clear requirement that on entry an applicant must show an intention to leave at the end of his studies, he is not required by the language of paragraph 12 of H.C. 82 to prove the same intention at the later stage. The decision was therefore wrong in imposing a burden to prove that fact on the applicant.

F   In order to understand that submission it is necessary to look at the language of the rules, and the entry provision contained in paragraph 17 reads as follows:

" An applicant is to be refused an entry clearance as a student if the officer is not satisfied that the applicant is able, and intends, to follow a full-time course of study and to leave the country on completion of it. In assessing the case the officer should consider such points as

G   whether the applicant's qualifications are adequate for the course he proposes to follow, and whether there is any evidence of sponsorship by his home government or any other official body. As a general rule an entry clearance is not to be granted unless the applicant proposes to spend not less than 15 hours a week in organised day-time study of a single subject or of related subjects, and is not to

H   be granted for the taking of a correspondence course."

The important language in that rule is, of course, the reference to the requirement that the officer should be satisfied that the applicant intends to leave the country on completion of the course of study.

When one looks at paragraph 12 of H.C. 82, the provision reads as follows:

"Applications from students or would-be students for variation of

their leave will consist mainly of applications for extension of stay as A
a student. An extension for an appropriate period, normally up to 12
months, may be granted if the applicant produces evidence, which is
verified on a check being made, that he has enrolled for a full-time
course of day-time study which meets the requirements for admission
as a student; that he is giving regular attendance; and that he has
adequate funds available for his maintenance and that of any dependants. When an extension is granted the student may be reminded that B
he is expected to leave at the end of his studies."

The submission made on behalf of the applicant emerges clearly from
the language of the rules themselves, and rests on the fact that whereas in
paragraph 17 the officer is to refuse entry if not satisfied that the applicant
intends to leave the country on completion of his studies, in paragraph 12
the only express provision is that when an extension is granted the student C
may be reminded that he will be expected to leave at the end of his studies.
In the light of that wording, so it is submitted, it would be quite inconsistent
to infer that the student is required at the later stage to discharge the same
burden of satisfying the authorities of his intention to leave once his course
is completed.

Mr. Brown, in rejecting that submission, argues that one must read the D
rules together in order to make sense of them, and that it would be irrational
to have different rules operating at the two stages at which application may
be made. I entirely agree that the rules must be read together since they
form part of a coherent scheme governing immigration into the country
and permission to remain within it, and it would indeed be absurd to attempt
to read the rules in isolation. I further agree with Mr. Brown's submission that one should not construe these rules as if they were a statute. E
On the other hand, it is, in my judgment, incumbent on anybody seeking
to give effect to these rules to read what they say and, so far as possible,
give effect to the language used, unless of course that leads to absurdity or
inconvenience so gross as to have been clearly outside anyone's contemplation.

It is not, in my judgment, irrational that there should be a burden F
imposed on an applicant seeking to enter the country which is not in terms
imposed on him if he seeks to extend his stay. It is, of course, necessary
for him to satisfy the authorities on the latter occasion that he is a bona fide
student, and if the Secretary of State had real ground for believing either
that he was not a bona fide student, or that he had some ulterior motive
in seeking to stay, even for the purpose of carrying out a course of study,
I can well understand that a different situation entirely would arise. But it G
does seem to me, as a matter of looking at these rules and seeking to give
effect to what they say, that it is reading into paragraph 12 language which
is not there, to read it as if it imposes on an applicant for extension a duty
to satisfy the Home Office of something which does not, in terms, appear
in the paragraph at all.

Accordingly, I, in broad terms, agree with Mr. Macdonald's sub- H
mission and do not think it was incumbent on the applicant to satisfy
the Home Office, at that stage, although, for reasons I have just mentioned, that would by no means necessarily be the end of the matter.

The second submission that Mr. Macdonald made was that, in any
event, the purpose of the rules governing admission and continuing stay
as a student, in so far as the rules were concerned with the student's
intentions, were concerned with those intentions in order to make sure

The Weekly Law Reports, July 31, 1981

1115

1 W.L.R.   Reg. v. Immigration Tribunal, Ex p. Shaikh (D.C.)   Bingham J.

A that leave given for a temporary purpose was not used for a collateral purpose and, in particular, was not used so as to enable the student to remain in the country on a longer-term basis illegally. It is right, I think, to say that in his reply Mr. Macdonald laid more stress on the collateral purpose than the avoidance of illegality.

B The real question that arises in this case is this: if the applicant's intention at the relevant time was to leave at the end of his studies but to remain here, if he was permitted to do so, in order to gain work experience, did the mere fact that he harboured the latter intention— that is, to remain if permitted for the gaining of work experience—of itself disable him as a candidate for extension? Was the mere fact that he acknowledged that desire enough to keep him out? Mr. Macdonald says the rules should be administered with common sense and flexibility

C and, no doubt, a measure of humanity.

It is, I think, quite clear, and indeed scarcely needs stating, that in the case of any applicant whose real ambition is to enter under cover of one nominal purpose and to remain for a much longer term for a different illegitimate purpose, the Secretary of State, under these rules, should have, and clearly has, power to exclude him. But should the

D Secretary of State have power to exclude him, and is it the intention of the rules that he should, if somebody, while having no intention to abuse the rules, or flout them, or disobey them, or breach any condition imposed upon him, does wish, if allowed, to remain for a longer period than the strict period allowed for the course of study on which he is embarked?

This is, I think, a difficult question, and it may very well be that some

E distinction falls to be drawn between what a person intends to do willy-nilly and that which he desires to do but has no intention whatever to do without permission. In this context some assistance is, I think, to be drawn from the judgment of Lord Widgery C.J., in the case of *Reg. v. Immigration Appeals Adjudicator, Ex parte Perween Khan* [1972] 1 W.L.R. 1058, where he said, at p. 1062:

F "The fact that the immigrant has in mind the possibility, amongst other things of being allowed to stay in this country should not, in my judgment, affect his or her right of entry, provided that the course of instruction is the primary purpose with which the entry into this country is made. I think that there should be no real difficulty for immigration officers to distinguish between those two

G cases: the case where the course of instruction, although genuinely intended, is really no more than a convenient key to obtain entry into the country; and the case where the course of instruction is the primary or overriding purpose for which the immigrant seeks to obtain entry. I hesitate to suggest yet another form of test, or yet another construction of the Act, but in many cases it seems to me that much will turn on whether the immigrant attaches so much

H importance to the course that he will come to the course anyway, regardless of whether he can stay in the country afterwards or not, or whether the course played such a relatively minor part in his calculations that he would not dream of coming for the course alone, but merely regards it as a stepping stone to other and more permanent sojourn here."

Mr. Brown points out, quite rightly, that one should approach this decision with caution, since it not only relates to different rules but to a different Act as well, and I fully accept that one cannot apply it as it stands to the present case. It does, I think, nonetheless, give some assistance as disavowing the view that a would-be immigrant, under the provision then in force, must show, at the point of entry, a positive intention to go home again, and the view that he is disbarred if he has in mind the possibility, amongst other things, of being allowed to stay in this country. Mr. Brown contended that if this approach was correct much of the argument and decision in *Reg.* v. *Chief Immigration Officer, Gatwick Airport, Ex parte Kharrazi* [1980] 1 W.L.R. 1396 would have been unnecessary. The issue in that case was, however, quite different from that in this case, and there had in the meantime been a very significant alteration in the wording of the rules.

It has been pointed out that under some circumstances the Home Office can give permission to those lawfully in this country as students to remain for an additional period as trainees, and it would, I think, be both harsh, and in many ways unrealistic, if a student who admitted to a desire to take advantage of those possibilities should be excluded whereas one who kept his hopes dark profited from that concealment. Accordingly, in my judgment, the disclosure and the fact, if it was a fact, that this applicant would have wished to stay in this country after his completion of his course of studies, if his extension were granted, and if he were permitted to do so, should not of itself disentitle him to the extension which he sought. In saying that, I emphasise that in a case where somebody was suspected of having some collateral purpose, and in particular an unlawful purpose, or had any intention of abusing, flouting, or breaching in any way the conditions upon which he was permitted to enter, a different situation entirely would arise.

Mr. Macdonald's third submission was that the Immigration Appeal Tribunal was wrong in law to overturn the adjudicator's finding of fact that the applicant did intend to leave on completion of his studies. This submission was based on the familiar and acknowledged principle that an appellate tribunal will only in very rare circumstances substitute its view of the facts for those of the primary fact-finding tribunal. For my part, I think that the tribunal's criticism of the adjudicator's finding of fact was justified because it does appear to me from the terms of his decision that the adjudicator was concentrating on the applicant's intention at the time that he was giving evidence before the adjudicator, about a year after his notice of appeal, and not on his intention at the earlier and appropriate date. Furthermore, it is to be noted that in his evidence to the adjudicator the applicant did say, " I thought I should get job in United Kingdom to get experience to enable me to get job at home." So it seems to me really quite clear, as the tribunal thought, that whatever the position at the time he was giving evidence before the adjudicator there was, nonetheless, an inference to be drawn that at the earlier stage, that is at the stage when the Secretary of State refused permission, it had been the applicants' desire to remain in this country if permitted.

It seems to me, looking at the letter which he wrote, and accepting the adjudicator's interpretation of what the applicant said about his reference to long term service in United Kingdom industries, that the applicant did betray a desire to remain in this country to gain work experience, if permitted. On the other hand, I think that the qualification " if permitted " was clearly to be read in the letter because he said: " I *like* to

The Weekly Law Reports, July 31, 1981

1117

1 W.L.R.   Reg. v. Immigration Tribunal, Ex p. Shaikh (D.C.)   Bingham J.

A   start my computer career in this country. If you grant me permission to start work in this country, then I can join evening classes in advance computing/printing."

Accordingly, although I think that the tribunal's criticism of the adjudicator's finding of fact was justified, I do not think that there was any material before the adjudicator on which he could have concluded that the applicant intended to stay in this country willy-nilly or had any

B   ulterior or collateral purpose and, indeed, it is acknowledged in the tribunal's decision that the applicant had no intention to remain here unlawfully.

On those grounds, it is my conclusion that the Immigration Appeal Tribunal misdirected itself in certain important respects and its decision should be quashed.

C

> *Application for order of certiorari granted.*
> *Case remitted to Immigration Appeal Tribunal for redetermination.*
> *Legal aid taxation of applicant's costs.*
> *No order as to costs.*

D

Solicitors: *Sushma Lal, Manchester; Treasury Solicitor.*

[Reported by ISOBEL COLLINS, Barrister-at-Law]

E   ————————

[COURT OF APPEAL]

* REGINA v. PHEKOO

F   1981 Jan. 16;   Watkins L.J., Cantley and Hollings JJ.
           Feb. 27

Landlord and Tenant—Harassment—Residential occupier—Mistaken belief that occupier not residential occupier—Mens rea—Whether necessary to show reasonable grounds for belief—Protection from Eviction Act 1977 (c. 43), s. 1 (3) (a)

G

The defendant was charged with doing acts calculated to interfere with the peace and comfort of a residential occupier of premises with intent to cause the residential occupier to give up occupation of the premises, contrary to section 1 (3) (a) of the Protection from Eviction Act 1977.[1] At his trial on indictment it was accepted that the defendant visited a house which he owned and found two men in occupation whom

H   he asked to leave. In evidence the two men alleged that the defendant threatened them with physical harm in order to persuade them to leave. The defendant denied issuing the threats and maintained that he believed the house was unoccupied and that the two men had no right to be there. It

---

[1] Protection from Eviction Act 1977, s. 1: " (3) If any person with intent to cause the residential occupier of any premises—(a) to give up the occupation of the premises or any part thereof; . . . does acts calculated to interfere with the peace or comfort of the residential occupier . . . he shall be guilty of an offence."

Reg. v. Phekoo (C.A.)   **[1981]**

was conceded that the men were residential occupiers of the   A
premises within the meaning of section 1 (1) of the Act but
it was submitted that the alleged offence could not be committed if the defendant honestly believed that they were not
residential occupiers. The trial judge rejected the submission,
ruling that the defendant's belief was irrelevant provided that
the person alleged to have been harassed was in fact a residential occupier. In directing the jury as to the elements of
the offence which the prosecution were required to prove the   B
trial judge made no reference to the defendant's belief. The
jury convicted the defendant.

On the defendant's appeal against conviction: —

Held, allowing the appeal, that the substantial penal consequences provided by section 1 (4) for an offence under
section 1 (3) and the stigma and social obloquy attaching to
a person convicted of an offence under subsection (3) indicated
that it was a truly criminal offence which necessitated proof   C
of mens rea; that, accordingly, it was necessary to prove the
specific intent to harass someone who was known or believed
by the defendant to be a residential occupier and not merely a
" squatter," and, accordingly, the judge had erred in his ruling
and in his summing up (post, pp. 1126F–G, 1127A–B).

Sweet v. *Parsley* [1970] A.C. 132, H.L.(E.) and *Reg.* v.
Smith (*David*) [1974] Q.B. 354, C.A. applied.

Reg. v. *Miller* [1975] 1 W.L.R. 1222, C.A. considered.   D

Per curiam. A defendant has to show that he had reasonable grounds for his honest belief that a person was not a
residential occupier (post, p. 1128D).

The following cases are referred to in the judgment:

Albert v. *Lavin* [1981] 2 W.L.R. 1070; [1981] 1 All E.R. 628, D.C.
Alphacell Ltd. v. *Woodward* [1972] A.C. 824; [1972] 2 W.L.R. 1320;   E
[1972] 2 All E.R. 475, H.L.(E.).
Attorney-General v. *Lockwood* (1842) 9 M. & W. 378.
Bank of New South Wales v. *Piper* [1897] A.C. 383, P.C.
Norton v. *Knowles* [1969] 1 Q.B. 572; [1968] 3 W.L.R. 183; [1967] 3
All E.R. 1061, D.C.
Reg. v. *Davidson-Acres* [1980] Crim.L.R. 50, C.A.
Reg. v. *Gould* [1968] 2 Q.B. 65; [1968] 2 W.L.R. 643; [1968] 1 All E.R.   F
849, C.A.
Reg. v. *Miller* [1975] 1 W.L.R. 1222; [1975] 2 All E.R. 974, C.A.
Reg. v. *Morgan* [1976] A.C. 182; [1975] 2 W.L.R. 913; [1975] 1 All
E.R. 8; [1975] 2 All E.R. 347, C.A. and H.L.(E.).
Reg. v. *Sheppard* [1981] A.C. 394; [1980] 3 W.L.R. 960; [1980] 3 All
E.R. 899, H.L.(E.).
Reg. v. *Smith* (*David*) [1974] Q.B. 354; [1974] 2 W.L.R. 20; [1974] 1   G
All E.R. 632, C.A.
Reg. v. *Tolson* (1889) 23 Q.B.D. 168.
Reg. v. *Twose* (1879) 14 Cox C.C. 327.
Sherras v. *De Rutzen* [1895] 1 Q.B. 918, D.C.
Sweet v. *Parsley* [1970] A.C. 132; [1969] 2 W.L.R. 470; [1969] 1 All E.R.
347, H.L.(E.).
Woolmington v. *Director of Public Prosecutions* [1935] A.C. 462, H.L.(E.).   H

The following additional case was cited in argument:

McCall v. *Abelesz* [1976] Q.B. 585; [1976] 2 W.L.R. 151; [1976] 1 All
E.R. 727, C.A.

APPEAL against conviction.

On May 17, 1979, at Croydon Crown Court (Judge Thomas), the

A defendant, Harold Phekoo, was convicted on an indictment containing, inter alia, two counts which alleged that he had done acts calculated to interfere with the peace or comfort of a residential occupier of premises with intent to cause the residential occupier to give up occupation of the premises, contrary to section 1 (3) (*a*) of the Protection from Eviction Act 1977. He was ordered to pay a fine of £100 on each count, with 21 days' imprisonment in default.

B He applied for leave to appeal against conviction. On the hearing of the application the Court of Appeal granted leave and proceeded to hear the appeal.

The grounds of appeal were (1) that the judge was wrong in holding that the defendant's honest, or honest and reasonable, belief that the persons in the premises were not residential occupiers within the meaning of section 1 (1) of the Protection from Eviction Act 1977 was not a defence to the counts; (2) that the judge was wrong in holding that "intent" in section 1 (3) (*a*) of the Act meant an intent to cause any person actually in the premises, who was in fact a residential occupier, to give up the occupation of the premises, whether or not the defendant knew or believed that such a person was a residential occupier; (3) that the judge was wrong in holding that the defendant's honest, or honest and reasonable, belief that the persons in the premises were not residential occupiers did not (a) negative the intent in section 1 (3) (*a*) of the Act, and/or (b) constituted the defence of mistake of fact; and (4) that on a proper construction of section 1 (3) (*a*) of the Act "intent" meant an intent to cause a person, whom the defendant knew or believed to be a residential occupier, to give up the occupation of the premises.

E The facts are stated in the judgment.

Evan Stone Q.C. and *Michael Segal* for the defendant.
David Van Hee for the Crown.

Cur. adv. vult.

F February 27. HOLLINGS J. read the following judgment of the court. On May 17, 1979, at Croydon Crown Court before Judge Thomas the defendant was convicted on two counts of the indictment of offences under section 1 (3) (*a*) of the Protection from Eviction Act 1977. He was acquitted under a third count of possessing an offensive weapon (a knife) in a public place. He was fined £100 on each count with 21 days' imprisonment in default. The defendant applied for leave to appeal against conviction; leave has been granted and with counsel's agreement this hearing, in which the Crown is represented, is being treated as the appeal.

Section 1 of the Act of 1977 repeals and replaces section 30 of the Rent Act 1965. Section 1 (3) (*a*) makes it an offence for any person, H with intent to cause the residential occupier of any premises to give up his occupation of the premises or any part thereof, to do acts calculated to interfere with the peace or comfort of the residential occupier. Section 1 (1) defines residential occupier as meaning in relation to any premises, a person occupying the premises as a residence, whether under a contract or by virtue of any enactment or rule of law giving him the right to remain in occupation or restricting the right of any other person to recover possession of the premises.

The defendant was the owner of a house, no. 67, Chatham Avenue, **A** Hayes. It was common ground that on the day in question, January 15, 1978, there were two persons in the house, Trevillion, named in the first count, and Broster, named in the second count, and that on that day the defendant called on them and asked each of them to leave. Until the conclusion of the evidence, for prosecution and defence, that was the total extent of the common ground. Trevillion and Broster each alleged that the defendant was abusive and uttered threats to " be back **B** with his friends " or " would bring his mates round " and, in the case of Trevillion, threatened to " carve him up " with a knife which he had in his pocket, part of which was visible, if he did not leave—conduct which, if accepted by the jury, was clearly calculated to interfere with their peace or comfort, and from which the jury could (and did) infer the necessary intent to cause the two men to give up their occupation of the **C** house. The defendant said he uttered no threats and, in effect, that he simply asked them to leave. The jury's verdict showed that they disbelieved him.

Part of the evidence was directed to the question, put in issue by the defence, as to whether these two men were residential occupiers within the meaning of the Act; the defendant's evidence was that on the day in question the only person whom he knew was living in the house was **D** one Agate. He had never seen Trevillion or Broster before. The day before his wife had told him (as she confirmed when she gave evidence herself) that Agate had called, left a set of two keys with her and told her that the house had been vacated, or would be by 6 p.m. that evening. He also told her that other people had keys and the house should be secured. **E**

At the conclusion of the evidence counsel for the defence conceded that Trevillion and Broster had indeed been residential occupiers within the meaning of the Act. There had been evidence that they had been given sub-tenancies by Agate or another former tenant, Cassidy, and it is to be assumed that the concession was based upon the fact that the two men's occupation was protected under the Rent Acts, although effective **F** notices to quit had previously been given to Cassidy and Agate. It was, however, at the same time submitted that, in the words used by the judge in his ruling, " on the wording of the subsection it is a defence for the defendant to say that he lacked the belief that these two men were residential occupiers." The judge ruled against this submission, saying:

" I think it matters not whether the defendant, in this or in any other case, thinks that a person is a residential occupier or squatter. **G** If he is a residential occupier within section 1 then no question of the state of mind of the defendant arises in relation to what he believes the residential occupier to be. The state of mind as to the intent, which relates to the acts set out in subsection (3), is very relevant."

The direction to the jury accordingly made no reference to the defend- **H** ant's belief, the judge saying:

" As far as these two counts are concerned the prosecution must prove first of all that Trevillion, who is mentioned in count 1, or Broster, mentioned in count 2, was a residential occupier within the meaning of the Protection from Eviction Act 1977. We now know, because the defence concede it, that is not an issue. It is accepted

A   they were residential occupiers. The next thing the prosecution must prove is that the defendant did the acts alleged in the counts. The prosecution must prove that those acts were calculated to interfere with the comfort and peace of Trevillion or Broster, and they were done with the intention alleged in the count. That is to say, with intention of causing Trevillion or Broster to give up occupation of 67, Chatham Avenue. The defendant, of course,
B   denies he did those alleged acts at all."

     This forms the basis of the appeal. It is the fact that the defendant stated in evidence that he thought both men were squatters and had no right at all to be in the house. If therefore the judge had ruled and summed up on this issue as the defence submitted that he should there
C   was plainly an issue of fact as to the defendant's belief for the jury to decide. In other words the evidential burden of disproving honest belief would have been upon the prosecution. We prefer to express it in this way for, since *Woolmington* v. *Director of Public Prosecutions* [1935] A.C. 462, the burden would be on the prosecution to negative honest belief and it is incorrect or at least misleading to refer to the " defence " of honest belief. If the defendant's submission is right then plainly the convic-
D   tion cannot stand and it is accepted by the prosecution that this is not a case for the application of the proviso. The question for the court therefore is whether, on a proper construction of the subsection and in the light of the decided cases, where the issue has been raised, the prosecution has to prove that the defendant did not honestly believe that the person " harassed " (to put it shortly) was not a residential occupier. This is
E   quite apart from the specific intent required by the subsection, namely, intent to cause the residential occupier to give up occupation of the premises.

     We will leave for later consideration the question whether the jury should also have been directed that such belief should be on reasonable grounds for, since consideration of the defendant's belief, whether reasonably held or not, was wholly withheld from the jury, it is not strictly
F   material to the appeal. It must be emphasised also that what is in question is not the defendant's ignorance of the law—that of course is no defence or excuse—but his alleged ignorance of the facts relating to the status of the persons he was seeking to evict.

     Counsel for the defendant has supplied the court with a transcript of the judgment in *Reg.* v. *Davidson-Acres* [1980] Crim.L.R. 50. Since that
G   decision concerned an offence under section 1 (2) of the Protection from Eviction Act 1977, it has no direct relevance, but subsection (2) itself has or may have relevance however to the construction of subsection (3). Subsection (2) is as follows:

     " If any person unlawfully deprives the residential occupier of any premises of his occupation of the premises or any part thereof, or attempts to do so, he shall be guilty of an offence unless he proves
H   that he believed, and had reasonable cause to believe, that the residential occupier had ceased to reside in the premises."

     " Unlawfully " clearly refers to the following sections 2 and 3. It is to be observed that in this subsection Parliament has seen fit to provide expressly for a particular defence; but it has also provided that the onus of establishing that defence (no doubt on a balance of probability) is to be upon the defendant—contrary to the general principles. In any event

this defence only relates to one aspect—belief that the occupier has A
ceased to reside. It does not assist in deciding the present question,
which can be posted in respect of this subsection also, i.e., what if the
defendant says he believed the occupier was in fact a squatter? In this
connection there is a relevant passage in the judgment of Wills J. in
Reg. v. *Tolson* (1889) 23 Q.B.D. 168 (a case to which further reference will
be made later).

    The most relevant and authoritative guidance is to be found, we   B
consider, in the decision in the House of Lords of *Sweet* v. *Parsley* [1970]
A.C. 132. There the mens rea of the offence created by section 5 of the
Dangerous Drugs Act 1965 was in question. The decision of the House
rested strictly upon the construction of the words of the section and in
particular upon the meaning and effect of the phrase " permits premises
to be used for the purpose of smoking cannabis resin," but some of the C
Law Lords gave general guidance in respect of mens rea in statutory
offences. Lord Reid said, at p. 148:

    " Our first duty is to consider the words of the Act: if they show a
    clear intention to create an absolute offence that is the end of the
    matter. But such cases are very rare. Sometimes the words of the
    section which creates a particular offence make it clear that mens D
    rea is required in one form or another. Such cases are quite fre-
    quent. But in a very large number of cases there is no clear
    indication either way. In such cases there has for centuries been
    a presumption that Parliament did not intend to make criminals
    of persons who were in no way blameworthy in what they did. That
    means that whenever a section is silent as to mens rea there is a
    presumption that, in order to give effect to the will of Parliament, E
    we must read in words appropriate to require mens rea."

After referring to the words of Alderson B. in *Attorney-General* v.
Lockwood (1842) 9 M. & W. 378, 398, Lord Reid continued, at p. 149:

    " It is also firmly established that the fact that other sections of the
    Act expressly require mens rea, for example because they contain F
    the word ' knowingly,' is not in itself sufficient to justify a decision
    that a section which is silent as to mens rea creates an absolute
    offence. In the absence of a clear indication in the Act that an
    offence is intended to be an absolute offence, it is necessary to go
    outside the Act and examine all relevant circumstances in order to
    establish that this must have been the intention of Parliament. I
    say ' must have been ' because it is a universal principle that if a G
    penal provision is reasonably capable of two interpretations, that
    interpretation which is most favourable to the accused must be
    adopted.

        " What, then, are the circumstances which it is proper to take
    into account? In the well known case of *Sherras* v. *De Rutzen*
    [1895] 1 Q.B. 918 Wright J. only mentioned the subject matter with H
    which the Act deals. But he was there dealing with something which
    was one of a class of acts which ' are not criminal in any real sense,
    but are acts which in the public interest are prohibited under a
    penalty ' (p. 922). It does not in the least follow that when one is
    dealing with a truly criminal act it is sufficient merely to have regard
    to the subject matter of the enactment. One must put oneself in
    the position of a legislator. It has long been the practice to recog-

A   nise absolute offences in this class of quasi-criminal acts, and one
can safely assume that, when Parliament is passing new legislation
dealing with this class of offences, its silence as to mens rea means
that the old practice is to apply. But when one comes to acts of a
truly criminal character, it appears to me that there are at least two
other factors which any reasonable legislator would have in mind.
In the first place a stigma still attaches to any person convicted of
B   a truly criminal offence, and the more serious or more disgraceful
the offence the greater the stigma. So he would have to consider
whether, in a case of this gravity, the public interest really requires
that an innocent person should be prevented from proving his
innocence in order that fewer guilty men may escape."

C   Lord Pearce said, at p. 156:

" Before the court will dispense with the necessity for mens rea
it has to be satisfied that Parliament so intended. The mere absence
of the word ' knowingly ' is not enough. But the nature of the crime,
the punishment, the absence of social obloquy, the particular mischief and the field of activity in which it occurs, and the wording
of the particular section and its context, may show that Parliament
D   intended that the act should be prevented by punishment regardless
of intent or knowledge."

Lord Diplock said, at p. 162:

" But only too frequently the actual words used by Parliament to
define the prohibited conduct are in themselves descriptive only of
a physical act and bear no connotation as to any particular state
E   of mind on the part of the person who does the act. Nevertheless,
the mere fact that Parliament has made the conduct a criminal
offence gives rise to *some* implication about the mental element of
the conduct proscribed. It has, for instance, never been doubted
since *M'Naghten's* case (1843) 10 Cl. & F. 200, that one implica-
F   tion as to the mental element in any statutory offence is that the
doer of the prohibited act should be sane within the M'Naghten
rules; yet this part of the full definition of the offence is invariably
left unexpressed by Parliament. Stephen J. in *Reg.* v. *Tolson* (1889)
23 Q.B.D. 168 suggested other circumstances never expressly dealt
with in the statute where a mental element to be implied from the
G   mere fact that the doing of an act was made a criminal offence
would be absent, such as where it was done in a state of somnam-
bulism or under duress, to which one might add inevitable accident.
But the importance of the actual decision of the nine judges who
constituted the majority in *Reg.* v. *Tolson*, which concerned a
charge of bigamy under section 57 of the Offences Against the
Person Act 1861, was that it laid down as a general principle of
H   construction of any enactment, which creates a criminal offence,
that, even where the words used to describe the prohibited conduct
would not in any other context connote the necessity for any particular mental element, they are nevertheless to be read as subject
to the implication that a necessary element in the offence is the
absence of a belief, held honestly and upon reasonable grounds, in
the existence of facts which, if true, would make the act innocent.
As was said by the Privy Council in *Bank of New South Wales* v.

Piper [1897] A.C. 383, 389, 390, the absence of mens rea really   A
consists in such a belief by the accused.

" This implication stems from the principle that it is contrary to
a rational and civilised criminal code, such as Parliament must be
presumed to have intended, to penalise one who has performed his
duty as a citizen to ascertain what acts are prohibited by law
(ignorantia juris non excusat) and has taken all proper care to
inform himself of any facts which would make his conduct lawful.   B

" Where penal provisions are of general application to the conduct of ordinary citizens in the course of their every day life the
presumption is that the standard of care required of them in informing themselves of facts which would make their conduct unlawful,
is that of the familiar common law duty of care. But where the
subject matter of a statute is the regulation of a particular activity   C
involving potential danger to public health, safety or morals in
which citizens have a choice as to whether they participate or not,
the court may feel driven to infer an intention of Parliament to
impose by penal sanctions a higher duty of care on those who choose
to participate and to place upon them an obligation to take whatever measures may be necessary to prevent the prohibited act, without regard to those considerations of cost or business practicability   D
which play a part in the determination of what would be required
of them in order to fulfil the ordinary common law duty of care.
But such an inference is not lightly to be drawn, nor is there any
room for it unless there is something that the person on whom the
obligation is imposed can do directly or indirectly, by supervision
or inspection, by improvement of his business methods or by ex-   E
horting those whom he may be expected to influence or control,
which will promote the observance of the obligation (see *Lim Chin
Aik* v. *The Queen* [1963] A.C. 160, 174)."

In *Sherras* v. *De Rutzen* [1895] 1 Q.B. 918 referred to by Lord Reid,
Wright J., at pp. 921 and 922, gave examples of the kind of offences
which might truly be considered " absolute " (or perhaps more properly   F
of strict liability, see, e.g., *Smith and Hogan, Criminal Law, 4th ed.* (1978),
pp. 79 and 92) in the sense of the mens rea not being an essential ingredient
and suggests that there are three possible classes: acts not criminal
in any real sense but which in the public interest are prohibited under
penalties; acts which are public nuisances; and cases in which, although
the proceeding is criminal in form it is really only a summary mode of
enforcing a civil right.   G

The maximum punishment for an offence under section 1 of the
Protection from Eviction Act 1977 is, on summary conviction, a fine of
£400 or six months' imprisonment or both or, on indictment, a fine
without express limit or two years' imprisonment or both; in neither case
can the sanction be said to be light.

In *Reg.* v. *David Smith* [1974] Q.B. 354, an appeal to this court, it was   H
held that no offence is committed under section 1 (1) of the Criminal
Damage Act 1971, when a person damages property belonging to another
if he does so in the honest though mistaken belief that the property was his
own. The offence created by this statute includes, as James L.J. said
in the judgment of the court, the elements of intention or recklessness
and the absence of lawful excuse (sections 1 and 5 of the Act). The
court, in arriving at its decision that the issue of honest belief that the

A property was his own should have been left to the jury, expressly gave
as its reason that the actus reus of the offence was " destroying or damaging property belonging to another " and said that it was not possible
to exclude the words "belonging to another," which described the
property, and so, applying the ordinary principle of mens rea, the
intention of recklessness and the absence of lawful excuse required to
B constitute the offence have reference to property belonging to another,
so that no offence is committed if the defendant honestly but mistakenly
believes that the property is his own. It is true that in that case there
were earlier cases and earlier Acts indicating that this had been the law
before the Act of 1971: see *Reg.* v. *Twose* (1879) 14 Cox C.C. 327 and
section 13 of the Malicious Damage Act 1861. No reference seems to
have been made to *Sweet* v. *Parsley* [1970] A.C. 132.

C   In *Reg.* v. *Miller* [1975] 1 W.L.R. 1222 (James L.J. again giving
judgment) it was held in this court that section 99 of the Road Traffic
Act 1972 created an " absolute " offence which did not require proof of
mens rea and which was proved when the prosecution established that
there was a driving of a motor vehicle on a road by a person who was
disqualified at the time, so that the judge ruled correctly that the defend-
D ant's state of mind as to the nature of the place upon which he was
admittedly driving, namely, his belief that the place was not a " road "
within the meaning of the Act, i.e., a place to which the public had access,
was irrelevant. *Sweet* v. *Parsley* was considered but the court concluded
that offences under the Road Traffic Act came within the category of
" absolute " or " strict liability " offences. James L.J. said, at p. 1224:

E   " Secondly, we observe that the offence created is in an Act of
      Parliament dealing with the regulation of road traffic, and we ask
      ourselves whether that offence created in that statute by this section
      is one that would properly be called a truly ' criminal ' offence as
      distinct from an offence which is prohibited under the sanction of
      penalties in the interests of the safety of the public. The answer to
      that question appears quite clearly, and Mr. Simpson would not
F   argue strenuously to the contrary, that this does not create what
      would normally be called a truly criminal offence, but does make
      provision for safeguarding the safety of the public by prohibiting an
      act under sanction of a penalty."

Cases under earlier Road Traffic Acts to similar effect were followed;
other provisions of the Act of 1972 itself were also deemed relevant
G (see p. 1226G–H).
      In *Alphacell Ltd.* v. *Woodward* [1972] A.C. 824, a case concerning
pollution of a river contrary to the Rivers (Prevention of Pollution) Act
1951, Viscount Dilhorne said, at p. 839:

      " This Act is, in my opinion, one of those Acts to which my noble
      and learned friends, Lord Reid and Lord Diplock, referred in *Sweet*
H   v. *Parsley* [1970] A.C. 132, 149, 163 which, to apply the words of
      Wright J. in *Sherras* v. *De Rutzen* [1895] 1 Q.B. 918, 922, deals
      with acts which ' are not criminal in any real sense, but are acts
      which in the public interest are prohibited under a penalty.' "

Lord Pearson, at p. 844, also referred to the passage in Lord Diplock's
speech and to Lord Pearce's speech, at p. 156, and Lord Salmon said, at
p. 848:

"The offences created by the Act of 1951 seem to me to be proto- A
types of offences which ' are not criminal in any real sense, but are
acts which in the public interest are prohibited under a penalty ':
Sherras v. *De Rutzen* [1895] 1 Q.B. 918, *per* Wright J. at p. 922,
referred to with approval by my noble and learned friends, Lord Reid
and Lord Diplock, in *Sweet* v. *Parsley* [1970] A.C. 132, 149, 162."

We have been referred to a further, more recent, decision in the B
House of Lords, *Reg.* v. *Sheppard* [1981] A.C. 394 concerning an offence
under section 1 (1) of the Children and Young Persons Act 1933—wilful
neglect of a child. Lord Diplock said, at p. 407 :

"The climate of both parliamentary and judicial opinion has been
growing less favourable to the recognition of absolute offences over
the last few decades, a trend to which section 1 of the Homicide C
Act 1957 and section 8 of the Criminal Justice Act 1967 bear witness
in the case of Parliament, and, in the case of the judiciary, is illustrated by the speeches in this House in *Sweet* v. *Parsley* [1970] A.C.
132."

We refer also to Lord Edmund-Davies's speech, at 411.

It is of interest finally on this aspect to consider *Norton* v. *Knowles* D
[1969] 1 Q.B. 572, which concerned the identical offence of harassment
under section 30 of the Rent Act 1965. Here the complainant lived in
his own caravan on land owned by the defendant. The defendant (the
appellant in the Divisional Court) contended that since the complainant
did not occupy his, the defendant's, land as a residence but only the
caravan, in respect of which there was no contract, the complainant was
not a "resident occupier." This submission failed. We refer to this E
case only to illustrate the distinction between a mistaken belief as to fact
and a mistaken belief as to the law, which is of course not relevant or
available as a "defence"—for the appellant in that case was under no
mistake as to the facts and so it could not be and was not put forward
as a ground of defence or appeal.

We return to the circumstances of the present appeal. Counsel for F
the Crown has submitted that this Act is in essence an adjunct to "social
legislation" relating to the protection of tenants and so is really in the
category of quasi-criminal offences or offences which are not truly
criminal, such as were referred to in the speeches in *Sweet* v. *Parsley*
[1970] A.C. 132 and by this court in *Reg.* v. *Miller* [1975] 1 W.L.R. 1222.
We cannot take that view. Not only are substantial penal consequences
provided for by the section but also conviction for such an offence must G
in our view be considered as a conviction of a truly criminal offence and
as attaching serious stigma to the offender. Nor is there absence of
social obloquy. It is true that the gravity of an offence of harassment
can vary very greatly; at one end of the scale the relevant acts may be
no more than intermittent but persistent withdrawal by the landlord of
services (specifically referred to in the subsection). At the other end of H
the scale however the acts may amount to more serious threats which
are tantamount to the statutory crime of blackmail though not chargeable
as such. We consider that these factors far outweigh the other factors
mentioned in the passages quoted above.

Further, the specific intent required by subsection (3) is an intent to
do certain acts in relation to "the residential occupier." Counsel for
the Crown has argued that the use of "the" rather than "a" gives an

A indication of the meaning that should be attached to this section, namely, that all that suffices is that the person harassed should be " the " residential occupier, whatever the belief of the alleged offender. We consider this too fine a point to be of real assistance. We consider that, general principle apart, the requirement of this specific, guilty intent does, or ought to, when the issue is raised, comprise proof of intent to harass someone who is known or believed by the offender to be a person who, in effect, is not just a " squatter." This, in our judgment, is consistent with the decision in *Reg.* v. *Smith (David)* [1974] Q.B. 354. For these reasons, based upon general principles and upon the construction of the section, we consider that the judge was in error in ruling and summing up as he did.

B

As has been said earlier it is not strictly necessary for the purposes
C of this appeal to decide whether, in his summing up, the judge should have ruled that honest belief, whether reasonably held or justified on the facts or not, had to be disproved by the prosecution, or whether he should have ruled that such belief should have been held reasonably and on reasonable grounds. Although reference was made in the course of the appeal to this aspect, no argument was in fact addressed to us upon this point. We consider however that, having reached the decision which
D we have, we ought to give guidance on this aspect.

Reg. v. *Tolson* (1889) 23 Q.B.D. 168, until the decision of the House of Lords in *Reg.* v. *Morgan* [1976] A.C. 182, has generally been accepted by the court as governing this aspect of mens rea. In that case Cave J. in concurring with the majority of the judges that a belief on reasonable grounds that the first spouse is dead is a good defence to bigamy said,
E at p. 181:

"At common law an honest and reasonable belief in the existence of circumstances, which, if true, would make the act for which a prisoner is indicted an innocent act has always been held to be a good defence. This doctrine is embodied in the somewhat uncouth maxim ' actus non facit reum, nisi mens sit rea.' Honest and reasonable
F mistake stands in fact on the same footing as absence of the reasoning faculty, as in infancy, or perversion of that faculty, as in lunacy. Instances of the existence of this common law doctrine will readily occur to the mind. So far as I am aware it has never been suggested that these exceptions do not equally apply in the case of statutory offences unless they are excluded expressly or by necessary implication."

G
Strong support was given for this view by Lord Diplock in his speech in *Sweet* v. *Parsley* [1970] A.C. 132, 162A–165B: see also *Bank of New South Wales* v. *Piper* [1897] A.C. 383 and *Reg.* v. *Gould* [1968] 2 Q.B. 65.

Reg. v. *Morgan* [1976] A.C. 182, concerned the offence of rape and whether belief that the complainant was consenting should be upon
H reasonable grounds or whether the test was subjective. The majority decided that in the case of rape the prosecution must disprove an actual belief, however, unreasonable it appeared, but it seems to us clear that this decision was confined and intended to be confined to the offence of rape—e.g., Lord Cross of Chelsea, at pp. 199–201, Lord Hailsham of St. Marylebone, at pp. 214–215, Lord Fraser of Tullybelton, at pp. 237–238. Lord Cross (who was otherwise in agreement with the other two who with him made the majority), and Lord Simon of Glaisdale and Lord Edmund-

Davies, who dissented, all confirmed the general application of the principle   A
of *Reg.* v. *Tolson,* 23 Q.B.D. 168.

Reg. v. *Morgan* [1976] A.C. 182 was considered by the Divisional
Court in *Albert* v. *Lavin* [1981] 2 W.L.R. 1070. That case concerned a
charge of assaulting a constable in the course of his duty. The Divisional
Court answered the question whether a belief that the person resisted
by the appellant was not a constable must be held on reasonable grounds
for there to be an acquittal in the affirmative.   B

The Divisional Court refused leave to appeal but certified a point of
law of general public importance:

" Whether a person charged with an offence of assault may properly
be convicted if the court finds that he acted in the belief that facts
existed which if true would justify his conduct on the basis of self-
defence but that there were in fact no reasonable grounds for so   C
believing."

The Appeal Committee of the House of Lords on February 19, 1981,
gave leave to appeal. We do not think it necessary to defer this judgment for the decision of the House of Lords since for the reasons already
given it would not affect the result of this appeal.

In considering therefore, as we do, that there must be a reasonable   D
basis for the asserted belief, we also have regard to the nature and object
of the statutory offence, and, though of lesser influence, to the fact that
in subsection (2) where the onus is placed to the defence Parliament has
deemed it right to provide that the defendant must show reasonable
cause for his belief.

For these reasons we allow the appeal and the conviction is quashed.
                                                                             E

> *Appeal allowed.*
> *Conviction quashed.*
> *Costs of both parties to be paid*
> *out of central funds.*

Solicitors: *Judge & Priestley, Bromley; Solicitor, Metropolitan Police.*   F

[Reported by ISOBEL COLLINS, Barrister-at-Law]

[HOUSE OF LORDS]
                                                                             G

* HAMILTON AND OTHERS   .   .   .   .   .   .   PETITIONERS

AND

HADMOR PRODUCTIONS LTD. AND OTHERS   .   .   RESPONDENTS

1981   July 23   Lord Diplock, Lord Russell of Killowen
                                          and Lord Bridge of Harwich   H

PETITION by the defendants for leave to appeal to the House of Lords
from the decision of the Court of Appeal in *Hadmor Productions Ltd.* v.
Hamilton [1981] 3 W.L.R. 139.

The Appeal Committee allowed the petition.

A

[QUEEN'S BENCH DIVISION]

* PRACTICE DIRECTION
(JURIES: LENGTH OF TRIAL)

1981   June 26   Lord Lane C.J. and Michael Davies J.

B
*Practice—Jury, civil action—Jurors—Inconvenience or hardship
of lengthy trial—Necessity for accurate estimates*

LORD LANE C.J.   The recent trial in *Orme* v. *Associated Newspapers Group Ltd.* (unreported), March 31, 1981, demonstrates the importance of ensuring that all possible steps are taken to prevent unnecessary hardship to the jury in civil actions.   Judges in such cases inquire of prospective
C jurors whether they will suffer inconvenience or hardship by having to serve for the estimated length of the trial and excuse those who will be so affected.

If the estimate of length is inaccurate, the jurors are misled and may suffer great hardship.   It is therefore essential that such estimates should be realistic.   The court must be informed immediately if, at any time
D after the action has been set down for trial, there is any change of circumstances likely to alter the probable length of the trial.

[Reported by ISOBEL COLLINS, Barrister-at-Law]

E

* *In re* ST. MARGARET'S, EARTHAM

1980   July 5   Edwards Ch.
1981   Feb. 3   Owen, Dean of Arches

*Ecclesiastical Law—Faculty—Memorial tablet—Mural tablet in
memory of benefactor of church and parish—Whether faculty
F   to be granted—Relevant considerations*

> The vicar and churchwardens of a village church sought a
> confirmatory faculty authorising the erection of a memorial
> tablet in the church. The tablet commemorated the wife of
> one of the petitioning churchwardens who, together with her
> husband, had contributed considerably towards improving and
> maintaining the church and the village.   The memorial was also
> in accordance with a 200-year-old tradition of memorials to
G > the occupants of a local house in which the deceased and her
> husband had lived but which was no longer in private occupa-
> tion and unlikely to be the source of any further applications
> for memorials. The chancellor refused to grant a faculty.
>   On appeal by the petitioners: —
>   *Held,* allowing the appeal, that, as the deceased had given
> quite exceptional and outstanding service to the village and the
H > church and as the memorial would be in accordance with the
> tradition of memorials to the occupants of the local house in
> regard to which there was no apparent possibility of a similar
> future application, the special privilege of a faculty permitting
> the memorial tablet should be granted (post, pp. 1134G—
> 1135A).
>   *In re St. Nicholas, Brockenhurst* [1978] Fam. 157 approved.
>   *Per curiam.* The grounds for claiming exceptional circum-
> stances for the privilege of erecting a memorial, in future,
> should be stated in the petition (post, p. 1134c–D).

1130

In re St. Margaret's (Const. Ct.)   **[1981]**

The following cases are referred to in the judgment of Owen, Dean of A
    Arches:

St. Edburga's, Abberton, In re [1962] P. 10; [1961] 3 W.L.R. 87; [1961] 2
    All E.R. 429.
St. Nicholas, Brockenhurst, In re [1978] Fam. 157; [1978] 3 W.L.R. 96;
    [1977] 3 All E.R. 1027.

No additional cases were cited in argument before the Court of Arches.   B

The following case is referred to in the judgment of Edwards Ch.:
St. Nicholas, Brockenhurst, In re [1978] Fam. 157; [1978] 3 W.L.R. 96;
    [1977] 3 All E.R. 1027.

PETITION   C
By a petition dated October 7, 1979, the vicar and churchwardens of
St. Margaret's Church, in the parish of Eartham, the Reverend Harold
Reginald St. George Gray, Leonard Thomas Spencer Hawkins and Michael
Desmond Sugden, sought a faculty authorising the erection of a Portland
stone tablet in the church to the memory of Mrs. Annie Hawkins, wife
of the petitioner Leonard Hawkins and a benefactor of the church and
village. Without any faculty having been granted a memorial tablet was D
subsequently erected in the church bearing the inscription:

" Remember with love
ANNIE HAWKINS
1897–1979
Church Councillor
beloved wife of   E
LEONARD HAWKINS
Benefactor of this Church & Village "

Accordingly, when the petition came on for hearing in the Chichester
Consistory Court the petitioners sought a confirmatory faculty.
    The petition, which was unopposed, was heard together with similar
petitions relating to the churches at Lynchmere and Coleman's Hatch, and F
a judgment was given by Edwards Ch. dealing with all three petitions.
    The facts are stated in the judgments of Owen, Dean of Arches, and
Edwards Ch.

    Bernard Williamson, solicitor, for the petitioners.

EDWARDS Ch. I am grateful to all who have appeared before me in G
these cases, none of which have been at all easy to decide. I have arranged
that all these petitions should be heard together because all involved the
application of certain principles which are of some importance. All three
petitions relate to the erection of memorials by way of wall tablets in
churches.
    I have indicated to all petitioners the principles which guide this court H
in deciding petitions for such faculties and I certainly do not want to pro-
long this judgment by recapitulating them at length; they are set out in
In re St. Nicholas, Brockenhurst [1978] Fam. 157 in the Winchester Consistory Court in the judgment of Phillips Ch. He refers, at p. 159, to a
passage in *Halsbury's Laws of England*, 4th ed., vol. 14 (1975), para. 1316,
which was part of the directions of the late and much lamented Wiggles-
worth Ch. in the Diocese of Bath and Wells, of which he was chancellor

The Weekly Law Reports, August 7, 1981

1131

1 W.L.R.   In re St. Margaret's (Const. Ct.)   Edwards Ch.

A in 1966. These principles can perhaps all be summarised in this way, that since there are other methods of commemorating the dead, and particularly by giving of some object to the church or the adornment of some part of the church, the discretion of the court in granting a faculty for the erection of mural tablets will be sparingly exercised. The circumstances when such discretion could be exercised have been mentioned by each of the petitioners or their advocates and is unnecessary for me to repeat them, but I

B can just summarise them by saying that such factors as notable service to the church or country of those to be commemorated by the memorial, the terms of the inscription, the support in the parish for the proposal, the significance of the memorial in recording local history are all to be considered. But it is perhaps worth mentioning that in this diocese in particular the considerations I have mentioned are all especially important. The

C reason being there are in the Diocese of Chichester a large number of small humble churches and Lynchmere Church, in which we sit, is an example of such a church, a small hill church which has been enlarged by additions to it so becoming a small parish church. Coleman's Hatch is very much bigger. This, however, may be taken as a fairly typical Sussex church and one can see how important it is that the court should be reluctant to grant faculties for memorials in such churches, even though they all differ. Here we have

D two small village churches and small churches will in some cases have so many memorials that they will be overloaded by them and be not so much places of worship for the living as places for the remembrance of the dead.

As chancellor it is my duty to be guardian of consecrated churches in this diocese. It may be a very painful duty to refuse faculties of this kind. Nevertheless it is a duty the chancellor may have to perform and he may

E in the process of ecclesiastical law be the only person who can in a particular case refuse an application that some person should be so commemorated. [The chancellor dealt with the Lynchmere and Coleman's Hatch petitions and continued:]

Eartham

F This is an unhappy petition. The decision of the court was anticipated as, on the orders of the incumbent, the memorial has been erected. The Revd. Gray has apologised to the court for his actions and said that he had no intention of flouting the court's authority. I accept his apology but I fail to see any excuse for his action. It seems to me to have been the simplest thing to have inquired from the Diocesan Registry whether the faculty had been issued. In my judgment I should not let the erection of

G the monument influence my decision. If I were to do that I should be encouraging the thwarting of due procedure.

I turn to the amended petition on its own merits and what I have to consider is the memorial as it has been erected, rather than the design of any proposed memorial.

The considerations of which I take account are first the interior of the

H church itself. The church is old, but has been extended and improved and is well maintained. It can only be described, in terms of memorials, as a very crowded church, and in one space only had no memorial been erected. That is the space in which that now under consideration has been placed. Eartham Church has almost become a place of memorials of the dead rather than a place fitted for the living to visit for worship week by week. Secondly, there is the actual memorial itself. I have to take into account the words in the inscription which are intended to describe the late Mrs.

1132

Hawkins as " benefactor of this church and village." I am told it is   A
proposed that, after Mr. Hawkins' death, which must in the course of
nature occur, the dates of his birth and death should be placed immediately above these words. If so, the memorial will contain a simple error
and not be in accordance with the evidence before me, viz. that both
the late Mrs. Hawkins and her husband were benefactors of the church
and village.

    I entirely accept that Mr. Hawkins and also Mrs. Hawkins, during her   B
life, have been popular with the inhabitants of the village. I note that the
petition has the unanimous support of the parochial church council, of
which Mr. Hawkins is a member. I feel bound, however, to say that such
support must carry less weight than might otherwise be the case, if one of
those to be commemorated, and one of the petitioners, is a member of the
council.   C

    As I say, I have taken into account the size of the church and the
availability of space for this memorial within it, the design of the memorial
and the terms of the inscription and the philanthropy, generosity and
kindness of Mr. and Mrs. Hawkins, but, in my judgment, this is not a
case in which, on due application of the principles I have mentioned, a
confirmatory faculty should be granted. Moreover, although it is painful   D
to say so, I cannot accede to the proposition that this court should grant
a faculty at the behest of a living person for the erection of a tablet in a
church recording him as a " benefactor of this church and village; " that
would be an exceptional departure from ordinary practice which I am not
prepared to take.

    I am not saying that Mr. and Mrs. Hawkins have not been good and
kind and generous; they have done much for church and village; but I do   E
not consider that their circumstances are of such an exceptional nature as
to justify the erection of a tablet on the walls of this particular church.

    Accordingly I do not grant the confirmatory faculty sought. I regret
the pain which this decision must cause, the disturbance to the fabric of
the church which the placing and removal of the tablet will cause and the
expense which has been wasted, but the memorial will have to be removed   F
and the wall made good.

    I direct the fees of the court in connection with these hearings be
divided into three and that each of the petitioners do pay one third.

Order accordingly.

    APPEAL from EDWARDS Ch. sitting at the Chichester Consistory Court.   G

    The petitioners appealed by notice of appeal dated December 23, 1980,
on the grounds that (1) the chancellor failed to apply and give proper
weight to *In re St. Nicholas, Brockenhurst* [1978] Fam. 157; (2) the judgment was based on an erroneous evaluation of the facts and evidence
taken as a whole and in particular failed (a) to give due weight to the
notable extent of the service to the church and the community given by   H
Annie Hawkins and Leonard Hawkins over a period of 30 years or so and
to recognise that that service was quite exceptional, (b) to give due weight
to the significance of the memorial in recording local history and completing a tradition going back over about 200 years and a family record going
back over about 75 years, (c) to appreciate and give due weight to the
support in the parish for the memorial, (d) to appreciate that the memorial
had had no noticeable effect on the general appearance of the church,

The Weekly Law Reports, August 7, 1981

1133

1 W.L.R.   In re St. Margaret's (Const. Ct.)

A (e) to give due weight to the evidence that the design of the memorial had, after discussion and revision, been expressly approved by the Diocesan Art Council, and (f) to appreciate and give due weight to the fact that there was no risk of the memorial establishing a precedent or continuing ad infinitum a family record; and (3) the chancellor erred in finding that (a) the church was very crowded in terms of memorials, (b) there was only one space left in the church where no memorial had been erected, (c) the church had almost ceased to be a place fitted for the living to visit for
B worship week by week, (d) (bearing in mind the very small size of the community at Eartham) the unanimous support of the parochial church council should carry less weight than might otherwise be the case if one of the petitioners was himself a member of the council, and (e) the memorial tablet recorded Leonard Hawkins as a benefactor of the church
C and village.

At the conclusion of the hearing of the appeal the Dean of Arches announced that the appeal would be allowed for reasons to be given later.

Sir John Wordie for the petitioners.

Cur. adv. vult.
D

OWEN, Dean of Arches. This is an appeal from the judgment of Edwards Ch. given on July 5, 1980. By his judgment the chancellor refused to grant a confirmatory faculty sought by the petitioners to allow a memorial wall tablet to remain affixed to a wall of the church of St. Margaret in the parish of Eartham in the Diocese of Chichester. The tablet
E which was placed in the church without any lawful authority, for which appropriate apologies have been made by and on behalf of the vicar, commemorates the life of Annie Hawkins who died in 1979 and was the wife of Leonard Hawkins who is, and has been for many years, a church-warden of Eartham Church and is one of the petitioners.

It is now submitted to me on behalf of the petitioners that the
F chancellor exercised his discretion on a basis which was an erroneous evaluation of the facts taken as a whole. If I am satisfied that this sub-mission is correct I shall allow this appeal: see *In re St. Edburga's, Abberton* [1962] P. 10.

The history of the matter makes it necessary for me to emphasise that a faculty is always necessary before a memorial tablet is placed in a church. Failure to realise this is likely to lead to hardship, heartache and
G financial waste as no doubt has happened in this case. Incumbents have a responsibility to prevent breaches of this rule.

Neither the incumbent, nor the parochial church council, nor the Diocesan Advisory Committee has any power to grant a faculty. A faculty can initially only be granted or refused by the chancellor of the diocese. He is the person appointed to consider all the relevant and available
H evidence and argument and then to decide. He will, of course, consider the recommendations of the incumbent, the parochial church council, the Diocesan Advisory Committee and other interested bodies before applying the law and making his decision.

How should he come to this decision? The law requires him to exercise a judicial discretion and in so doing to bear in mind: (i) faculties for memorials cannot be freely or extensively granted for, if they were, the walls of a church might soon become so crowded as seriously to detract

from the church's appearance. (ii) A faculty for a memorial should be   A
regarded as a special privilege reserved for very exceptional cases: see
In re St. Nicholas, Brockenhurst [1978] Fam. 157, a decision of Phillips Ch.
with which I fully agree. The reasoning of that case requires the chancellor
to ask himself the questions (a) is this case so exceptional that the special
privilege of a faculty could properly be granted, and (b), if so, are the
circumstances such that a faculty should be granted?   (iii) Factors which   B
may show exceptionality are for example the character of, or outstanding
service to church, country or to mankind by the person, to be commemorated by the memorial, a desire to record by the memorial some important
or significant aspect of local or national history and some family history
or tradition of such memorials especially, but not necessarily, if any future
application based on the family connection would be impossible. (iv) The
burden of showing that the case is exceptional and that a faculty should   C
be granted is on the petitioner. The chancellor will need clear evidence
and, of necessity, will need to rely greatly on the submissions of the
incumbent, the parochial church council and the Diocesan Advisory Committee. Whatever the grounds of exceptionality claimed, in future they
should be stated in the petition for the benefit of the chancellor, and those
supporting the petition should also explain why the case is considered   D
exceptional and why it is claimed that the special privilege of a faculty
should be granted. (v) Even when exceptionality to an extent which could
justify a faculty is shown, such a faculty will not be granted as a matter
of course as petitioners should be warned by incumbents and registrars.
Factors which may persuade a chancellor not to grant a faculty despite
the exceptional nature of the case would include for example the character
of the church, the number of memorials already in the church, the   E
inappropriate design of the proposed memorial tablet and any lack of
support or, a fortiori, opposition in the parish, the parochial church
council, the Diocesan Advisory Committee or other interested bodies.

No doubt if the grounds of exceptionality were the character or service
to the local church and community of the person to be commemorated a
chancellor would find it difficult to reject the joint opinion of the incum-   F
bent, the parochial church council and the Diocesan Advisory Committee,
provided that he could be sure that the answers given by these bodies were
only given after consideration of the questions which I have set out above.

In this case, the chancellor was given information of the views of the
incumbent, the parochial church council and the Diocesan Advisory
Committee, but he could not be sure that the right questions had been
asked before their support was tendered. I am in no better position.   G

However, I am satisfied that Mrs. Hawkins together with Mr. Hawkins
has given quite exceptional and outstanding service to the village and
church of Eartham. As examples of their beneficent actions I cite their
bringing water and electricity into the village, setting up an endowment
fund to provide for the maintenance of Halnaker Mill, a local landmark,
restoring and endowing the village hall, paying for repairs to the church   H
over many years, providing heating for the church and providing considerable other financial support for the church.

I am also satisfied that the provision of a memorial to Annie Hawkins,
who with her husband at one time lived at Eartham House, will be in
accordance with a tradition of memorials to the occupants of Eartham
House, extending over some 200 years, the last 75 of which have seen
members of Mr. Hawkins's family occupying the house. Mr. and Mrs.

A Hawkins have no descendants, Eartham House is now a school and there
is no apparent possibility of a similar future family application.

   In view of my findings set out above, I am quite satisfied that this case
is so exceptional that the special privilege of a faculty permitting the
memorial tablet could be granted.

   I am told and accept that the incumbent, the parochial church council,
B the village and the Diocesan Advisory Committee all favour and support
the petition. Although I do not know whether they asked the appropriate
questions before giving their support, it is clear that such support should
be a factor in this case even if only to convince me that whilst the
chancellor apparently considered the church to be already overcrowded
with memorial tablets, the incumbent, the parochial church council and
the Diocesan Advisory Committee do not appear to have any such
C reservations.

   On the evidence and the arguments addressed to me I have been
convinced that in this case the chancellor made an erroneous evaluation of
the facts taken as a whole and it was upon this evaluation that he exercised
his discretion. I have also come to the clear decision that not only could
a faculty have been granted but it should have been granted. Accordingly
D I allow this appeal.

Appeal allowed.
Faculty granted.

Solicitors: *Bird & Bird.*

C. N.

E

[COURT OF APPEAL]

* ROBINSON (INSPECTOR OF TAXES) *v.*
SCOTT BADER CO. LTD.

F

1981 May 7, 8; 19   Waller, Oliver and Fox L.JJ.

*Revenue—Corporation tax—Expenses of trade—Parent company
   seconding employee to work for overseas subsidiary—Expenditure incurred by parent company in its own interest—Subsidiary benefiting from expenditure — Whether expenditure
G " wholly and exclusively " for purposes of parent company's
   trade—Whether capital payment—Income and Corporation
   Taxes Act 1970 (c. 10), s. 130 (a) (f)*

   Section 130 of the Income and Corporation Taxes Act 1970
provides:
      " . . . in computing the amount of the profits or gains
   to be charged under Case I or Case II of Schedule D,
   no sum shall be deducted in respect of—(a) any disburse-
H ments or expenses, not being money wholly and exclusively laid out or expended for the purposes of the trade,
   profession or vocation, . . . (f) any capital withdrawn
   from, or any sum employed or intended to be employed
   as capital in, the trade, profession or vocation . . ."
   The taxpayer company manufactured chemicals and
synthetic resins for the glass fibre industry. It had three
subsidiary companies in Europe including a French company
in which it had a 50 per cent. interest and which was making

losses and showing marked lack of success. At a board   A
meeting of the taxpayer company in November 1974 it was
resolved to give strong support and financial backing to the
French subsidiary for the purpose of furthering its own business
in France and in Europe. Towards that end it decided to send
one of its employees to act as manager in France to provide
the subsidiary with the necessary technical and marketing
expertise. Following that meeting the taxpayer company   B
acquired the remaining 50 per cent. interest in the French
subsidiary. During its accounting period ending in July 1976
the taxpayer company expended a total of £16,354 on the
salary, expenses and social costs of its employee whilst he was
working abroad. It appealed against an assessment to corporation tax made on it for that period seeking to deduct that
sum from its taxable profits. The general commissioners
allowed the appeal on the ground that section 130 (a) of the
Income and Corporation Taxes Act 1970 did not preclude the   C
deduction of £16,354 from the taxpayer company's profits.
Walton J., dismissing an appeal by the Crown, held that the
section had no application because the exclusive object of the
taxpayer company in making the expenditure was to further
its own business and not to benefit the subsidiary.

On appeal by the Crown: —

Held, dismissing the appeal, (1) that the test to be applied
under section 130 (a) of the Income and Corporation Taxes   D
Act 1970 to determine whether the taxpayer company had
incurred the expenditure wholly and exclusively for the purposes of its trade was a subjective and not an objective one;
and that although an inevitable result of sending an employee
to work for the subsidiary company was to benefit that
company's running and thus its financial position, the commissioners were entitled to conclude that the taxpayer company
had incurred the expenditure solely for its own trading pur-   E
poses and should be allowed to make the deduction (post, pp.
1140A–D, F–H, 1141B).

(2) That the expenditure, having been incurred for trading
purposes, was of a revenue and not of a capital nature and,
accordingly, was not disallowed under section 130 (f) of the
Act (post, p. 1141B–C).

Decision of Walton J. [1980] 1 W.L.R. 755; [1980] 2 All
E.R. 780 affirmed.   F

The following cases are referred to in the judgments:

Bentleys, Stokes & Lowless v. *Beeson* [1952] 2 All E.R. 82; 33 T.C. 491,
C.A.
Edwards v. *Bairstow* [1956] A.C. 14; [1955] 3 W.L.R. 410; [1955] 3
All E.R. 48, H.L.(E.).
Smith's Potato Estates Ltd. v. *Bolland* [1948] A.C. 508; 64 T.L.R. 430;   G
[1948] 2 All E.R. 367; 30 T.C. 267, H.L.(E.).

The following additional cases were cited in argument:

Marshall Richards Machine Co. Ltd. v. *Jewitt* (1956) 36 T.C. 511.
Mills v. *Inland Revenue Commissioners* [1975] A.C. 38; [1974] 2 W.L.R.
325; [1974] 1 All E.R. 722; 49 T.C. 367, H.L.(E.).
Milnes v. *J. Beam Group Ltd.* (1975) 50 T.C. 675.   H
Morgan v. *Tate & Lyle Ltd.* [1955] A.C. 21; [1954] 3 W.L.R. 85; [1954]
2 All E.R. 413; 35 T.C. 367, H.L.(E.).
Odhams Press Ltd. v. *Cook* [1940] 3 All E.R. 15; 23 T.C. 233, H.L.(E.).

APPEAL from Walton J.

During its accounting period ended July 2, 1976, the taxpayer company, Scott Bader Co. Ltd., whose registered office was Wollaston Hall,

A Wollaston, Northamptonshire, expended £16,354 on seconding one of its employees to work as manager of its French subsidiary company, Scott Bader Sturge S.A., during the first period of its 100 per cent. ownership of that company. The taxpayer company appealed to the Wellingborough General Commissioners against an assessment to corporation tax of £486,000 for that accounting period claiming to deduct the £16,354

B from its taxable profits. The commissioners found that, notwithstanding the provisions of section 130 (a) of the Income and Corporation Taxes Act 1970, the expenditure was an allowable deduction having been made " wholly and exclusively for the purpose of the taxpayer company's trade." They accordingly determined the taxpayer company's taxable profits in the sum of £485,910.

On appeal by the Crown, Walton J. [1980] 1 W.L.R. 755 affirmed

C the commissioners' decision holding that since the exclusive object of the taxpayer company in making the expenditure was to further its own overseas business, the incidental benefit received by the subsidiary in consequence of its parent company's actions did not alter the fact that the expenditure was incurred solely for the purposes of the taxpayer company's trade.

D The Crown appealed on the grounds (1) that the sum of £16,354 paid by the taxpayer company to its employee in the accounting period ended July 2, 1976, for services rendered by him to the French subsidiary company was not money wholly and exclusively laid out or expended for the purposes of the taxpayer company's business; (2) that the judge erred in upholding the commissioners' determination that the sum was so laid out or expended; (3) that the only legitimate inference to be drawn from the

E findings of fact made by the commissioners was that the sum was laid out or expended wholly and exclusively for the purposes of the business carried on by the French subsidiary and partly for the purposes of the taxpayer company's business; (4) that the judge further erred in rejecting the Crown's contention that the taxpayer company's expenditure of the sum was not a permissible deduction by reason of section 130 (e) and/or (f) and/or that

F it was a capital sum.

The facts are stated in the judgment of Waller L.J.

D. C. Potter Q.C. and Michael Hart for the Crown.
J. M. Tallon for the taxpayer company.

Cur. adv. vult.

G

May 19. WALLER L.J. read the following judgment. This is an appeal from a decision of Walton J. dismissing an appeal from the general commissioners. The taxpayer company had claimed to deduct the sum of £16,354 from an assessment to corporation tax but the inspector had not allowed the deduction. The appeal to the commissioners was allowed and

G Walton J. dismissed an appeal from their decision.

The accounting period with which the case is concerned was a period of 53 weeks ending on July 2, 1976. The principal activity of the taxpayer company during that period was the manufacture and marketing of chemical intermediates and synthetic resins. In addition to its subsidiary and associated companies the taxpayer company derives royalty income from licensees in Germany, Italy, Switzerland, South Africa, United States of America and Australia. It trades in a specialised field dealing with the manufacture

1138

and supply of synthetics for glass fibre making. It provides its synthetics A
as raw materials for its subsidiary and associated companies, licensees and
other customers for their manufacturing trades. It also furnishes technical
and marketing expertise by means of its own personnel, to its subsidiary
and associated companies.

At the beginning of that accounting period the taxpayer company had
acquired the whole of the share capital of the French subsidiary having
previously owned 50 per cent of it. After acquiring the 100 per cent., an B
employee of the taxpayer company, Mr. S. Fearon, was seconded to the
French company on the basis that the taxpayer company would pay his
salary and expenses whilst he was in post in France. The sum of £16,354
represents the payments made to him over a period of six months. At the
end of that period of six months Mr. Fearon became the managing director
of the French company, paid directly by it. The decision of the com- C
missioners was that the deduction should be allowed as coming within
section 130 (a) of the Income and Corporation Taxes Act 1970. That
paragraph prohibited the deduction of any disbursements " not being money
wholly and exclusively laid out or expended for the purposes of the trade,
profession or vocation."

It is not necessary to set out the whole of the facts in the case stated,
but I shall start with a board meeting held on November 25, 1970, at which D
a number of representatives of the taxpayer company were present. The
case finds that the taxpayer company's determination to continue activities
in France was minuted as follows :

"Papers were before the meeting from Mr. Trueman setting out
the position and from Mr. Broom itemising the points for and
against the continuing operations in France." And there followed E
an account of how the French subsidiary was being operated in
France " in a very lean manner as far as staff were concerned and
output was high, the margin on sales was low and if these margins
could not be increased added throughput would be needed to get
above break even level." And the minutes went on: " After further discussion, particularly on the desirability for our continuing F
operation in Europe it was unanimously agreed to go ahead with
Scott Bader Sturge S.A. with strong support and backing from
Woolaston."

The case stated went on:

"(h) On March 31, 1975, the [taxpayer company] acquired 100
per cent. interest in the French company and following the departure G
of the managing director of the French company, Mr. S. Fearon,
an employee of the [taxpayer company], acted as manager, which
provided the French company with necessary technical and marketing
expertise."

Mr. Fearon was seconded to the French company on the basis that the
taxpayer company would pay his salary, expenses and social costs whilst H
he was in post in France. This was done and as I have already said, he
was paid £16,354 in respect thereof. There followed in the case certain
findings of fact:

"(j) There is another firm in France named Wauquier S.A., which
is not a subsidiary or associated company of the [taxpayer com-
pany] and with which the [taxpayer company] deals at arm's
length as an ordinary customer. Primarily the [taxpayer company's]

A   business and trading in France is served directly through the French company. (k) Direct sales by the [taxpayer company] to Wauquier S.A. were of specialist products for use only with prerequisite basic products. These basic products were supplied by the French company because substantial transportation costs ruled out supply from the U.K. Without the French company to supply the basic products, sales by the [taxpayer company] of specialist products to Wauquier

B   S.A. would have been lost. (1) The position of the French company vis-à-vis the [taxpayer company] was unique, the rescue operation being undertaken to further the [taxpayer company's] business in France and in Europe."

The only other part of the case stated that I need quote is paragraph
C 9, which said:

"We decided on the evidence that (a) the [taxpayer company] and the French company contribute to and are dependent upon an international unitary business. (b) The nature of that business includes marketing and extension of markets. (c) The deduction of £16,354 from the [taxpayer company's] profits should be allowed."

D   The Crown submitted that the only reasonable conclusion from the findings of fact made by the commissioners was that there were two purposes for the payment of Mr. Fearon, namely, that the money was laid out or expended for the purposes of the subsidiary company as well as the purposes of the taxpayer company. Mr. Potter submitted that the judge was wrong in regarding the test as a subjective one and submitted to this court that it was an objective test. Quoting from the

E case, he submitted that there were four facts of importance: (1) that the taxpayer company owned the entire share capital of the French company and that their trades were separate; (2) that by providing Mr. Fearon as manager, the taxpayer company gave the French company technical and marketing expertise; (3) that the French company had to provide basic products to enable the taxpayer company to sell their products to

F Wauquier S.A.; and (4) that the use of the word "business" in the sentence dealing with the rescue operation included the whole of the business of the subsidiary as well as the taxpayer company. He summarised his argument by saying that the test being objective, the purpose of the expenditure was partly to increase the value of the assets in the French company and partly to prevent loss of the English company's products in Wauquier S.A.

G   The circumstances in which this court can interfere with the findings of commissioners set out in a case stated were considered in *Edwards* v. *Bairstow* [1956] A.C. 14. Lord Radcliffe set out the principles on which the court can interfere, at p. 36:

"When the case comes before the court it is its duty to examine the determination having regard to its knowledge of the relevant

H law. If the case contains anything ex facie which is bad law and which bears upon the determination, it is, obviously, erroneous in point of law. But, without any such misconception appearing ex facie, it may be that the facts found are such that no person acting judicially and properly instructed as to the relevant law could have come to the determination under appeal. In those circumstances, too, the court must intervene. It has no option but to assume that there has been some misconception of the law and that this has

been responsible for the determination. So there, too, there has A
been error in point of law."

Against the background of this test I will consider first the argument
that the test is objective and not, as the judge found, subjective. The
phrase with which the case is concerned is " for the purposes of." In my
judgment " purpose " contains an ingredient of " intention." It is very
difficult, but perhaps not impossible, to determine this without some B
element of subjectivity. Indeed, in many cases the test will be wholly
subjective. When deciding whether or not a solicitor is entertaining a
client to lunch, the test must be wholly subjective. The solicitor is entertaining; it may be because it is an old client; it may be because it is the
only opportunity to discuss the business. The court has to decide the
real purposes, if it is for the trade, vocation or profession, and whether
it is independent, i.e. independent of the business purposes to be served: C
see *Bentleys, Stokes & Lowless* v. *Beeson* [1952] 2 All E.R. 82, 85–86.
It would be impossible in such a case to do other than make the decision
subjectively. In considering the purposes of a company there may be
room for some objectivity, but it will normally be to assist in making
the subjective decision. There may be a case where the evidence shows
that something was done in a different capacity altogether, e.g. *Smith's* D
Potato Estates Ltd. v. *Bolland* [1948] A.C. 508, where it was held that
something done as a taxpayer could not be for the purposes of the trade,
profession or vocation. In my opinion, in spite of Mr. Potter's submission
to the contrary, that does not arise in this case.

In the present case the payment made to Mr. Fearon could not
possibly be solely for the benefit of the subsidiary company. There were
therefore two possibilities which had to be considered by the commis- E
sioners: either the payments were made partly for the purposes of the
subsidiary and partly for the purposes of the taxpayer company; or the
real purposes for which they were made were the purposes of the taxpayer company.

In considering the findings of fact which I have quoted above, it seems
to me that sub-paragraph (l) describing the rescue operation being taken F
to further the taxpayer company's business in Europe is a finding strongly
in favour of the real purpose being for the trade, profession or vocation
of the taxpayer company. And while I am not prepared to say that
" business " could not include the business of the subsidiary, in my opinion
it could certainly be construed as meaning the taxpayer company's trading
operation and, although it is irrelevant, this, in my view, would be the
right construction in this case. Furthermore, the findings at sub-para- G
graphs (k) and (j) both point in the same direction. " The [taxpayer company's] business and trading in France " is important and the French
company's supply of basic products is necessary to support the taxpayer
company's trading. In my judgment this finding also tends to support
the finding that the real purpose was for the taxpayer company. The
inevitable result of sending Mr. Fearon, at the taxpayer company's ex- H
pense, to France would be to improve the running of the French company
and no doubt this would improve that company's financial position. But
it does not follow that that was the real purpose of making the payments.
It was one of the results, albeit it may well be an inevitable result. It
was vis-à-vis the taxpayer company in much the same position as the
provision of lunch by the solicitor in the case referred to above.

I have considered whether in this case there was any positive evidence

A which would tend to show that the commissioners were wrong. The only possible finding is that at paragraph 9 (a), a finding not very happily worded. In my judgment, however, the phrase " international unitary business " in the context of all the findings in this case cannot be construed to indicate that it was the group as a whole which was being considered. This was the commissioners' phrase to describe what had been described earlier in the paragraphs I have already quoted. In my
B judgment it is quite impossible to say that the facts found are such that no person acting judicially and properly instructed as to the relevant law could have come to the determination under appeal. On the contrary, it appears to me to be a perfectly reasonable conclusion at which to arrive.

I should add that an alternative submission was that this was capital,
C and that accordingly it would come within section 130 (f); but in my opinion it is quite impossible to say that this was capital. It was being expended for the purposes of the trading of the company and could not be described as capital. I would dismiss this appeal.

OLIVER L.J. For the reasons given in the judgment which has just
D been delivered by Waller L.J., I agree that the appeal should be dismissed.

Fox L.J. I also agree.

Appeal dismissed with costs.
Leave to appeal refused.

E Solicitors: *Solicitor of Inland Revenue; Jaques & Co.*

[Reported by MRS. HARRIET DUTTON, Barrister-at-Law.]

F [PRIVY COUNCIL]

* HANG WAH CHONG INVESTMENT CO. LTD.   .   APPELLANT

AND

ATTORNEY-GENERAL OF HONG KONG   .   .   RESPONDENT

G [APPEAL FROM THE COURT OF APPEAL OF HONG KONG]

1981 Feb. 5, 9, 10;   Lord Wilberforce, Lord Edmund-Davies,
      March 23   Lord Keith of Kinkel, Lord Scarman
                              and Sir John Megaw

Hong Kong — Town planning — Director of Works — Tenants of
H   *Crown land seeking approval of Director for development —*
           Approval conditional on payment of premium — Whether
           abuse of power

The applicants were the tenants of Crown land in Hong Kong which they held as successors in title to a company which had purchased the right to a 75-year lease at public auction in 1931. The special conditions of the sale specified the type of building permitted on the land and provided that the consent of the Director of Public Works had to be obtained for the erection of blocks of flats and of their

design, height and disposition. No lease was ever executed.   A
In 1973 the applicants made plans to redevelop the land by
building four blocks of flats and applied to the Director of
Public Works for a modification of the special conditions
of sale to allow for the proposed redevelopment. The Director
advised the applicants that the Crown would agree to the
modifications asked for on the payment of a premium. The
applicants did not pay the premium. In 1976 they submitted
plans for the redevelopment to the Director as building   B
authority for his approval. The Director approved the plans
but qualified his approval by stating in effect that it was subject to the applicants' obtaining the necessary modification of
their lease. The applicants applied to the Supreme Court for
a declaration, inter alia, that the Crown was not entitled to
exact any premium in respect of the proposed redevelopment.
The court dismissed the application. The Court of Appeal
dismissed the applicants' appeal.   C
   On the applicants' appeal to the Judicial Committee: —
   Held, dismissing the appeal, that since no lease had been
executed, the conditions of sale operated in lieu of the terms
of the proposed lease and the Crown was entitled to charge
a premium for agreeing to any modification of the conditions;
and that since the Director's responsibilities included both
those of building authority and those of land agent to the
Crown, he had not abused his power by acting as land agent   D
when he made his approval of the redevelopment plans conditional on the payment of a premium to obtain the Crown's
consent to the modification of the conditions.
   Viscount Tredegar v. *Harwood* [1929] A.C. 72, H.L.(E.)
applied.

The following case is referred to in the judgment of their Lordships: E
Tredegar (Viscount) v. *Harwood* [1928] Ch. 59, C.A.; [1929] A.C. 72,
   H.L.(E.).

The following additional cases were cited in argument:
Chinachem Investment Co. Ltd. v. *Chung Wah Weaving and Dyeing
   Factory Ltd.* [1978] H.K.L.R. 83.   F
Dallman v. *King* (1837) 4 Bing.N.C. 105.
Doe d. Baker v. *Jones* (1848) 2 Car. & K. 743.
Gibson v. *Doeg* (1857) 2 H. & N. 615.
Hall & Co. Ltd. v. *Shoreham-by-Sea Urban District Council* [1964] 1
   W.L.R. 240; [1964] 1 All E.R. 1, C.A.
Hepworth v. *Pickles* [1900] 1 Ch. 108.
Newbury District Council v. *Secretary of State for the Environment*
   [1980] 2 W.L.R. 379; [1980] 1 All E.R. 731, H.L.(E.).   G
Panamena Europea Navigacion (Compania Limitada) v. *Frederick Leyland
   & Co. Ltd. (J. Russell & Co.)* [1947] A.C. 428, H.L.(E.).
Reg. v. *Birmingham Licensing Planning Committee, Ex parte Kennedy*
   [1972] 2 Q.B. 140; [1972] 2 W.L.R. 939; [1972] 2 All E.R. 305, C.A.
Reg. v. *Bowman* [1898] 1 Q.B. 663, D.C.
Reg. v. *Hillingdon London Borough Council, Ex parte Royco Homes Ltd.*
   [1974] 2 Q.B. 720; [1974] 2 W.L.R. 805; [1974] 2 All E.R. 643, D.C.   H
Wong Bei-nei v. *Attorney-General* [1973] H.K.L.R. 582.

APPEAL (No. 16 of 1980) with leave of the Court of Appeal of Hong
Kong by Hang Wah Chong Investment Co. Ltd. (the applicants) from
a judgment and order of the Court of Appeal of Hong Kong (Huggins
J.A., Cons and Zimmern JJ.) given on October 31, 1979, dismissing the
applicants' appeal from an order of Yang J. made on August 18, 1978,

A   by which he dismissed the applicants' originating summons claiming various declarations against the Attorney-General (as representing the Crown, the applicants' landlords). The applicants claimed a declaration that as owners of Kowloon Inland Lot, No. 2657, sections Dss 1 and 2 and the remaining portion, they were entitled to proceed with redevelopment of the lot and, inter alia, that the Crown was not entitled to charge the applicants a premium in respect of the redevelopment.

B   The applicants were the lessees of the land which they held as successors in title to a company which had purchased the right to a 75-year lease from the Crown at public auction in 1931. Clauses 6 and 7 of the special conditions of the sale by auction specified the type of building permitted on the land and provided that the consent and approval of the Director of Public Works had to be obtained for the erection of blocks

C   of flats and of their design, height and disposition. No lease was ever executed. In 1973 the applicants made plans to redevelop the land by building four blocks of flats and applied to the Director of Public Works for a modification if necessary of clauses 6 and 7 of the special conditions of sale to allow for the redevelopment. The Director advised the applicants that the Crown would agree to the modifications asked for on the payment of a premium of $3,216,000. The applicants did not pay the

D   premium. In 1976 the applicants submitted plans for the proposed redevelopment to the Director of Public Works as building authority for his approval. The Director formally approved the plans subject to section 14 (2) of the Buildings Ordinance which provides:

"Neither the approval of any plans nor the consent to the commencement of any building works or street works shall be deemed . . .

E   to act as a waiver of any term in any lease or licence."

He also stated that it was necessary for the applicants to obtain the modifications of their lease before proceeding with the redevelopment.

   Mark Littman Q.C., Michael Miller Q.C., Raymond Jack and *Patrick Fung* (of the Hong Kong Bar) for the applicants.

F   *Gerald Godfrey Q.C.* and *Barrie Barlow* (Senior Crown Counsel, Hong Kong) for the Attorney-General.

Cur. adv. vult.

March 23. The judgment of their Lordships was delivered by LORD EDMUND-DAVIES.

G   This appeal is from an order of the Court of Appeal of Hong Kong dismissing the appeal of Hang Wah Chong Investment Co. Ltd. (" the applicants ") from a decision of Yang J. in the High Court of the Supreme Court whereby he dismissed the applicants' originating summons seeking declarations concerning their proposed development of a piece of land off Kadoorie Avenue, Kowloon. This was part of a lot sold by

H   the Crown at an auction in 1931 to the Hong Kong Engineering and Construction Co. (" Hong Kong Engineering "), and the conditions of sale provided for the grant of a Crown lease but none was in fact ever executed.

The following special conditions of sale are of great importance and must be quoted in full:

"6. Save as provided herein the purchaser shall not erect on the lot any buildings other than detached or semi-detached residential

premises of European type or such other buildings of European type   A
as the Director of Public Works may approve of with garages and all
proper outbuildings thereto.   Provided that, subject to the provisions
of special conditions 7 and 8, the purchaser shall be at liberty to
erect flats, with or without shops or self-contained garages on the
ground floor, fronting to Argyle Street and Waterloo Road on that
part of the lot hatched red on the sale plan and having a frontage
of approximately 350 feet to Argyle Street and approximately 125   B
feet to Waterloo Road.   Save as herein provided no buildings erected
on the lot shall be used otherwise than as a private dwelling-house
without the written consent of the Governor.   7. The design of the
exterior elevations plans height and disposition of any buildings to
be erected on the lot shall be subject to the special approval of the
Director of Public Works and no building shall be erected on the   C
lot save in accordance with such approval. . . . 21. Where under these
conditions the consent or approval of the Governor or of the Director
of Public Works is required the grant or withholding of such consent
shall be in the absolute discretion of the person named."

[His Lordship outlined the history of the development of the land
and the correspondence between the Director of Public Works and both   D
the applicants' predecessors in title and the applicants and continued:]
It follows from the foregoing that the extensive redevelopment now
contemplated by the applicants cannot proceed without the consent of the
Director of Public Works, and that, by virtue of special condition 21,
the grant or withholding of that consent is in his absolute discretion.
Even so, as he indicated on October 26, 1976, approval of the building   E
plans (albeit " subject to section 14 (2) of Buildings Ordinance "), can
payment of a premium of *any* amount be exacted as the condition of
granting final permission to proceed?   As the hearing of the appeal
progressed, this proved the most troublesome of all the points raised.
The applicants submitted that, were some modification of the terms of a
lease involved, a landlord could legitimately extort a premium. But no
lease was ever granted and, the appeal turning on the contract of sale and   F
the necessity of obtaining thereunder merely the Director's *approval* and
no modification of a lease, it was submitted that no premiums may be
demanded.   In their Lordships' opinion, however, this question cannot
so simply be answered.   It is necessary to consider carefully the terms
of the contract of sale.

The applicants' next submission was that any discretion as to the   G
granting of approval under special condition 6 possessed by the Director
must relate to matters relevant to the contract and particularly to his
control over the *type* of buildings, whereas in the present case the demand
for a premium is wholly unconnected with any such consideration.   The
argument presented in the applicants' printed case was that

"... the Director is not entitled to take into account matters which   H
are wholly extraneous to the purpose of conditions 6 and 7, such as
the raising of revenue (any more than he could do so in the exercise
of any of his other functions under the conditions) and that if he
does so and such a matter is the sole reason for the withholding of
approval, the applicants are entitled to act as if his approval had
been granted."

A   This submission is in substance similar to that upheld by the Court of
Appeal in *Viscount Tredegar* v. *Harwood* [1928] Ch. 59, but rejected by
the House of Lords [1929] A.C. 72. There Lord Shaw of Dunfermline
rejected the Court of Appeal's implication of a new clause in a lease to
the effect that the lessor's consent to insurance of the leased property
with any responsible insurance company was not to be withheld unreasonably, and added, at p. 80:

B

"... the [Court of Appeal] then proceeds to attach to these terms
and to this contract ... that the lessor must furnish a justification for
his refusal, and further that such a justification must be something
incidental to the individual contract itself and also to the financial
standing or responsibility of the alternative insurance company. I
am humbly of opinion that this process of piling implication upon

C   implication is not a legitimate mode of construing a very simple and
plain condition. It is clogged neither by the one implication nor
the other."

In the same way and for a like reason, their Lordships reject the objection
taken in the present appeal that a premium is not exigible because it is
" wholly extraneous to the purpose of conditions 6 and 7."

D   Somewhat more formidable than the foregoing is the point (scarcely
hinted at in the applicants' printed case, but nevertheless spaciously
developed by their learned counsel) relating to the role assigned to the
Director of Public Works under the contract and particularly in relation
to special conditions 6 and 7. It has already been observed that he is by
definition also the building authority, and he is charged with many duties

E   falling within the public domain, in relation to which it might well amount
to an abuse of power were he to demand a premium as a condition
precedent to acceding to a suppliant's request. Was the Director, ask the
applicants, not operating in the public domain when saddling his approval
of the applicants' building plans in 1976 with a demand for an extremely
high premium which bore no apparent relation to the terms of the
applicants' application? And, in consequence, was he not therefore

F   imposing an insupportable condition on his compliance amounting to an
abuse of power?

It has to be observed in the first place that it is common ground that
the conditions of sale operate in lieu of the terms of the contemplated
Crown lease which was never granted. Secondly, no difference relevant
to the present appeal can be drawn between a lease granted by a public
body, or indeed the Crown, and a private lease: *Wade, Administrative*

G   *Law*, 4th ed. (1977), p. 644. Thirdly, the view expressed by Huggins J.A.
in the Supreme Court that " The Director of Public Works has many
responsibilities besides those imposed by the Buildings Ordinance "
appears well established, one of those responsibilities being that of acting
as the Crown's land agent. And applicants' counsel did not challenge the
conclusion of Huggins J.A. that "... the Director of Public Works can

H   bind himself in his capacity as the building authority without binding
himself in his capacity as land agent and vice versa."

The various conditions of sale well illustrate the wide range of roles
played by the Director in exercising his discretion. As regards some of
the conditions, the Director's role may, almost certainly, be that of
protector of the public interest. The vital question is whether for the
purposes of special conditions 6 and 7 he can properly be regarded as
being entitled to act in his capacity of land agent for the Crown. It is not

open to serious doubt that those conditions relate directly to the land-   A
lord's interests, economic and otherwise, and their Lordships conclude that
the Director was entitled to act, and did act, in that role when granting
·   his qualified approval to the applicants' plans in 1976. On that view, can
it properly be said that it is for the Crown to establish the reasonableness
of the demand for a premium? In the light of *Viscount Tredegar* v.
Harwood [1929] A.C. 72, their Lordships are of the opinion that the ques-   B
tion requires a negative answer. But they must not thereby be taken as
holding that the requirement was capriciously advanced (and, indeed, applicants' counsel expressly disclaimed any such suggestion) or that, were it incumbent upon the Attorney-General to justify the requirement, he would
be unable to adduce good reasons for demanding a premium. It is sufficient,
for present purposes, simply to say that, the applicants' seeking a concession from their landlords in relation to the development of land leased,   C
the landlords were entitled to make the granting of that concession
conditional upon the payment of a premium.

It follows that in their Lordships' opinion the unanimous decision of
the Court of Appeal to uphold Yang J.'s dismissal of the applicants'
originating summons should in its turn be upheld. They will therefore
humbly advise Her Majesty The Queen that the appeal should be dismissed. The applicants must pay the Attorney-General's costs of the   D
appeal.

Solicitors: *Linklaters & Paines; Macfarlanes.*

T. J. M.

E

─────────

[COURT OF APPEAL]

* REGINA *v.* LITTELL

F
1981   Jan. 22, 26;   Watkins L.J., Cantley
        March 6   and Hollings JJ.

> *Road Traffic—Breath test—Alcotest ®80/A—Manufacturer's in-*
> *structions to inflate bag fully in single breath—Bag inflated*
> *by series of short breaths—Breath test negative—Whether test*
> *valid—Whether subsequent evidence of blood analysis admis-*
> *sible—Road Traffic Act 1972 (c. 20), s. 12 (1) (3)* [1]   G

> The defendant, who had been arrested for driving a car
> whilst unfit through drink, agreed to provide a specimen of
> breath for a breath test. He was instructed to inflate the
> breathalyser bag fully in one breath. The defendant took
> 10 short puffs of breath and fully inflated the bag to give a
> negative result. He was given three further opportunities to
> provide a specimen and, on each of those occasions he took   H
> short puffs and failed to inflate the bag fully. He was then
> required to provide a specimen of blood or urine for a labora-
> tory test in accordance with section 9 of the Road Traffic Act
> 1972 and told that if he failed to do so he might be liable to
> a penalty. The defendant agreed to provide a specimen of
> blood which, when analysed, indicated excess alcohol. Sub-
> sequently he was charged with driving a motor vehicle with

[1] Road Traffic Act 1972, s. 12 (1): see post, p. 1148D–E.

A a blood alcohol concentration above the prescribed limit contrary to section 6 (1) of the Road Traffic Act 1972, to which he pleaded Not Guilty. On the judge ruling that the defendant had failed to provide a proper specimen of breath and that the evidence of the result of the blood analysis was admissible, the defendant admitted the charge and was sentenced accordingly.

On appeal against conviction on the ground that the
B evidence of the blood specimen had been unfairly obtained: —

Held, dismissing the appeal, that the definition of a " breath test " in section 12 (1) of the Act showed that its purpose was to obtain an indication of the proportion of alcohol in a person's blood; that by providing the quantity of breath asked for, but in such a way that it was of a quantity which did not indicate the proportion of alcohol in his blood, the defendant had failed to provide a specimen of breath for the test and,
C accordingly, the police officer had properly required a specimen for a laboratory test and the evidence of the result of the analysis of the blood sample had been properly admitted (post, pp. 1150c–d, 1153a–c).

Dicta of Lord Pearson and Lord Diplock in *Webber* v. *Carey* [1970] A.C. 1072, 1090, 1096, H.L.(E.) and Lord Diplock and Lord Kilbrandon in *Walker* v. *Lovell* [1975] 1 W.L.R. 1141, 1147, 1167, H.L.(E.) applied.

D
The following cases are referred to in the judgment:

Attorney-General's Reference (No. 1 of 1978) [1978] R.T.R. 377; 67 Cr.App.R. 387, C.A.
Brennan v. *Farrell*, 1969 J.C. 45.
Reg. v. *Chapman* [1969] 2 Q.B. 436; [1969] 2 W.L.R. 1004; [1969] 2 All E.R. 321, C.A.
E *Reg.* v. *Holah* [1973] 1 W.L.R. 127; [1973] 1 All E.R. 106, C.A.
Walker v. *Lovell* [1975] 1 W.L.R. 1141; [1975] 3 All E.R. 107, H.L.(E.).
Webber v. *Carey* [1970] A.C. 1072; [1969] 3 W.L.R. 1169; [1969] 3 All E.R. 1662, H.L.(E.).

The following additional cases were cited in argument:

Reg. v. *Thorpe (Thomas)* [1974] R.T.R. 465, C.A.
F *Rendell* v. *Hooper* [1970] 1 W.L.R. 747; [1970] 2 All E.R. 72, D.C.
Shepherd v. *Kavulok* [1978] R.T.R. 85, D.C.

APPEAL against conviction.

On July 25, 1979, at Chelmsford Crown Court the defendant, Ronald Arthur Littell, was charged on the first count with driving a motor vehicle when unfit through drink contrary to section 5 (1) of the Road
G Traffic Act 1972 and on the second count with driving a motor vehicle when he had a blood alcohol concentration above the prescribed limit contrary to section 6 (1) of the Act of 1972. He pleaded Not Guilty to both counts but after Judge Hill-Smith had ruled that the result of an analysis of the sample of the defendant's blood was admissible in evidence, he changed his plea to Guilty on the second count. The jury were dis-
H charged from returning a verdict on the first count. The defendant was disqualified for 12 months, his licence was endorsed and he was fined £50 and ordered to pay £75 prosecution costs and a legal aid contribution.

The defendant appealed against conviction on the ground that the judge erred in ruling that he had failed to provide a proper specimen for a breath test and that the evidence of the result of the blood test was admissible.

The facts are stated in the judgment.

Reg. v. Littell (C.A.)   **[1981]**

The defendant in person.   A

Justin Philips for the Crown.

Cur. adv. vult.

March 6. CANTLEY J. read the judgment of the court. This appeal
directly raises for decision yet another entirely technical point in the
lamentable jurisprudence of the breathalyser law.   B

Section 5 (1) of the Road Traffic Act 1972 provides that a person who
when driving a motor vehicle on a road or other public place is unfit to
drive through drink or drugs shall be guilty of an offence. Section 5 (5)
provides that a constable may arrest without warrant a person committing
an offence under this section. Section 8 (7) provides that a person arrested
under section 5 (5) shall while at a police station be given an opportunity   C
to provide a specimen of breath for a breath test there.

Section 9 (1) provides that a person who has been arrested under
section 5 (5) may while at a police station be required by a constable to
provide a specimen for a laboratory test (which may be a specimen of
blood or urine) if he has previously been given an opportunity to provide
a specimen of breath for a breath test at that station under section 8 (7)   D
and either: (a) it appears to a constable in consequence of the breath
test that the device by means of which the test is carried out indicates that
the proportion of alcohol in his blood exceeds the prescribed limit, or
(b) when given the opportunity to provide that specimen he fails to do so.

Section 12 (1) states:

> " . . . 'breath test' means a test for the purpose of obtaining an   E
> indication of the proportion of alcohol in a person's blood carried
> out by means of a device of a type approved for the purpose of such
> a test by the Secretary of State, on a specimen of breath provided
> by that person; . . ."

Section 12 (3) provides that references in sections 8 and 9 of the Act to
providing a specimen of breath for a breath test are " references to pro-   F
viding a specimen thereof in sufficient quantity to enable that test to be
carried out."

On the evening of January 20, 1978, a police constable off duty and in
plain clothes was driving his motor car along Barking Road, London E.6
when he noticed a motor car ahead of his being driven in a markedly
erratic manner. He drew alongside, caused the driver to stop and showed
him his warrant card. The driver was the defendant. He smelled of   G
drink, was unsteady and appeared to be under the influence of alcohol.
The constable arrested him pursuant to the provision of section 5 (5) of
the Road Traffic Act 1972 as being unfit to drive through drink or drugs
and the defendant was taken to Barking police station. At the police
station the defendant as is required by section 8 (7) was given an opportunity to provide a specimen of breath for a breath test and agreed to do   H
so. The official Alcotest equipment was duly assembled and the defendant was told, in accordance with the manufacturer's instruction issued
with the equipment, to inflate the bag in one breath in not less than 10
or more than 20 seconds. It was emphasised that the bag had to be
inflated in one breath. The defendant then took 10 short puffs of breath
and fully inflated the bag. The result was negative: it did not indicate
alcohol above the prescribed limit. The inspector did not regard this

A as a proper test. He gave the defendant further opportunities. On the second attempt the defendant took eight short puffs. The bag was not fully inflated. At the third attempt the defendant took seven short puffs and at the fourth attempt five short puffs. In none of these was the bag fully inflated. The inspector decided that the defendant had failed to provide a specimen of breath for the purposes of the Act and accordingly required him under section 9 to provide a specimen of blood or urine
B for a laboratory test. The defendant provided a specimen of blood which subsequent analysis showed contained not less than 152 milligrammes of alcohol in 100 millilitres of blood. The legal limit is 80.

The defendant elected trial by jury and eventually appeared at the Crown Court at Chelmsford. He pleaded not guilty to an indictment containing two counts under the Act of 1972. The second alleged that
C he drove a motor vehicle when he had a blood alcohol concentration above the prescribed limit contrary to section 6 (1).

During the trial counsel for the defendant asked the judge to exclude the evidence of the result of the analysis of the blood sample on the ground that it had been unlawfully or unfairly obtained. His submission was that the defendant had not failed to provide a specimen of breath nor had the specimens he had provided indicated that the proportion of
D alcohol in his blood exceeded the prescribed limit and accordingly there was no power under the Act to require him to provide the specimen of blood, which it was said was unfairly obtained because the defendant had been warned under section 9 (7) that his failure to provide a specimen of blood or urine would make him liable to prosecution.

The judge ruled that on the undisputed evidence the defendant had
E failed to provide a proper specimen of breath for a breath test by failing to inflate the bag in one breath and the evidence of the analysis of the blood test was therefore admissible. That ruling effectively deprived the defendant of his only defence to the charge under section 6 (1). He therefore withdrew his plea of not guilty to that charge and admitted it and was sentenced accordingly. He now appeals against his conviction
F on the ground that the judge's ruling was wrong.

In *Reg.* v. *Chapman* [1969] 2 Q.B. 436 it was held that if the bag was not fully inflated in one breath that in itself constituted a failure to provide a specimen of breath for a breath test as required by the Act, with the result that the consequences of such failure prescribed by the Act would follow. A more practical view of the purpose of this legislation has since prevailed and it can now be taken as finally settled, despite some
G powerful dissent to the contrary on the way, that if a specimen of breath is provided which indicates a proportion of alcohol above the prescribed limit there has been no failure to provide a specimen of breath in sufficient quantity to enable the test to be carried out even though the bag has not been fully inflated and has been inflated with more than one breath. Failure to comply with the instructions for providing a specimen of breath
H does not of itself invalidate the test if the test result is positive: see *Webber* v. *Carey* [1970] A.C. 1072; *Reg.* v. *Holah* [1973] 1 W.L.R. 127; *Walker* v. *Lovell* [1975] 1 W.L.R. 1141 and *Attorney-General's Reference (No. 1 of 1978)* (1978) 67 Cr.App.R. 387.

In this appeal we have to consider a situation where the test results were negative. At his first attempt this defendant fully inflated the bag but he did not do so in one breath as instructed. At his subsequent attempts he did not fully inflate the bag. None of his attempts produced

a positive result but it was contended that, as he did fully inflate the bag   A
the first time, he did not fail to provide a specimen of breath as required
by the Act although it is clear from the subsequent laboratory test that
the specimen he provided was useless for the purpose of indicating the
proportion of alcohol in his blood. It is said that he filled the bag by
blowing into it and the fact that he took more than one breath to do so
is a mere breach of the manufacturer's instructions and of no legal consequence. The test proved negative. It is claimed that he did not fail   B
the test: he passed it.

So far as we have discovered there is no reported authority directly
dealing with this particular point, although one would expect of this fruit-
ful branch of litigation, where it seems that no arguable defence, however
technical, is ever overlooked or abandoned, that it must have arisen
before.   C

In our view some guidance as to the true meaning of a " breath test "
in the Road Traffic Act 1972 is provided in section 12 (1). A " breath
test " is stated in that subsection to mean a test for the purpose of obtaining an indication of the proportion of alcohol in a person's blood. The
test for this purpose must be carried out by means of an approved device
on " a specimen of breath " provided by that person. By section 12 (3)   D
that person has to provide a specimen of breath in sufficient quantity to
enable the test to be carried out.

Has the stated purpose of all this procedure to be wholly ignored? We
do not think so. Subsection (3) refers to quantity and not to quality;
but if the person provides the quantity he is asked for (one bag full) but,
by ignoring the instructions he has been given, provides it in such a way
that it is of a quality which does not and could not indicate the propor-   E
tion of alcohol in his blood and is no reliable indication of whether the
proportion of alcohol in his blood exceeds the prescribed limit, has the
test contemplated by the Act been carried out? Some would think not,
but judicial opinion has not all been one way.

There are powerful dicta on either side in the speeches in the House
of Lords in *Webber* v. *Carey* [1970] A.C. 1072 and *Walker* v. *Lovell* [1975]   F
1 W.L.R. 1141. In *Webber* v. *Carey,* Viscount Dilhorne at p. 1086
referred to *Reg.* v. *Chapman* [1969] 2 Q.B. 436 and to *Brennan* v.
Farrell, 1969 J.C. 45, a decision to the contrary effect in the High Court
of Justiciary in Scotland, and continued:

"The question which of these two decisions is right does not arise
for decision in this case, but it is to be observed that the only obliga-   G
tion imposed by the Act is to provide a sufficient quantity of breath
to enable the test to be made ... not a sufficient quantity in a single
breath. I do not myself find it easy to see how a breach of the manufacturer's instructions to inflate in a single breath can be regarded
as a failure or refusal to take a test when the Act making it by
section 2 (3) an offence without reasonable excuse to provide a
quantity of breath for the test does not stipulate that it must be in   H
a single breath."

Viscount Dilhorne referred to the question again in *Walker* v. *Lovell*
[1975] 1 W.L.R. 1141, 1156 and said:

"In my opinion these statutory provisions make it clear that a
sufficient quantity of breath to enable a test to be carried out means
in relation to the Alcotest a sufficient quantity to inflate the bag."

A Later, he said, at p. 1158:

> " Parliament could have enacted that a failure by the motorist to comply with the maker's instructions rendered him liable to arrest and prosecution. It did not do so. All that it provided was that failure to provide a specimen of breath in sufficient quantity to enable a test to be carried out rendered him liable to arrest and if
>
> B without reasonable excuse, to prosecution. It may well be that in not stipulating that a specimen must be provided in a single breath, Parliament left a lacuna in the Act. If so, it is not one which, in my view, it would be proper for this House in its judicial capacity to attempt to fill."

A different approach to the problem was made by Lord Pearson, Lord
C Diplock and Lord Kilbrandon. In *Webber* v. *Carey* [1970] A.C. 1072, Lord Pearson said, at p. 1090:

> " My opinion is that there is not in this Act any absolute requirement, express or implied, that a test in order to be a " breath test " within the meaning of the Act must be carried out in perfect compliance with the maker's instructions. There is an express require-
>
> D ment that the test must be carried out for the purpose of obtaining an indication of the proportion of alcohol in the blood, and it follows that the police officer must be trying to use the device correctly in order to obtain a true indication. I think also that there probably is an implied requirement (not adding much for practical purposes to the express requirement) that the test must be carried out with such accuracy as is reasonably attainable in the circumstances."
>
> E

In the same case, Lord Diplock said, at p. 1096:

> " The constable conducting the test must do his honest best to see that this instruction is complied with, but it should be treated in a common sense way. In the circumstances in which the first breath test at any rate is carried out little purpose would generally be
>
> F served by telling the suspect that he must take between 10 and 20 seconds to fill the bag, nor can the constable be expected to time him with a stop watch. The sensible thing to do, and it appears to be the common practice, is to tell the suspect to fill the bag with a single deep breath. It is, in my view, sufficient if in the constable's bona fide judgment the way in which the bag is in fact inflated by the suspect does not depart so widely from the instructions that it
>
> G is likely to show a significantly greater proportion of alcohol in the suspect's blood than is actually there. There was no evidence in the present case as to what would be the effect upon the indication given by the device of a departure from this instruction either by taking more than one breath or by taking less than 10 seconds or more than 20 seconds to fill the bag. Any departure, however, which to
>
> H the constable's knowledge would result in the device giving a lower reading of the blood alcohol content than the true reading can be ignored by him if the result of the test is positive, since the test would still provide a sufficient indication that the proportion of alcohol exceeds the prescribed limit. If, on the other hand, the constable is not possessed of this knowledge and the departure is one which he thinks may be sufficient to make the reading given by the device lower than the true reading, he may require the suspect

to repeat the test in accordance with the instructions and if the   A
suspect fails to do so the constable may arrest him under section
2 (5). If the suspect's failure is without reasonable excuse, e.g.
physical disability not due to alcohol, he also commits an offence
under section 2 (3)."

Lord Diplock in that passage was referring to sections in the Road Safety
Act 1967 which contained provisions corresponding with those in the   B
Road Traffic Act 1972.

    In *Walker* v. *Lovell* [1975] 1 W.L.R. 1141, Lord Diplock referred
to the approved form of breathalyser, Alcotest R80, and continued, at
p. 1147:

    " It makes use of the phenomenon that alcohol present in a person's
    blood stream passes into the air in his lungs where, almost but not   C
    quite immediately, it reaches a state of equilibrium at which the
    proportion of vapourised alcohol in that air reflects with a reasonable
    degree of accuracy the proportion of alcohol in his blood. So a
    ' specimen of breath ' to be provided for a breath test as defined in
    section 12 (1) must mean air that has been drawn into and exhaled
    from the lungs of the person undergoing the test."
                                                                          D
He went on to say, at p. 1148:

    " The reason why the constable should communicate this instruction
    to the person on whom the breath test is to be carried out, is because
    the constable does not know in advance whether the proportion of
    alcohol in that person's blood does not exceed or slightly exceeds or
    greatly exceeds the prescribed limit. If the excess is only slight,   E
    failure to provide enough breath to inflate the bag fully may defeat
    the purpose of a ' breath test ' by making it impossible to obtain by
    means of the Alcotest R80 an indication that the proportion of
    alcohol in his blood exceeds the prescribed limit, though such is
    indeed the fact. The same consequence may follow from using more
    than a single breath to inflate the bag; for to take a fresh breath
    may result in the specimen of breath provided containing a larger   F
    proportion of air that has not been drawn into and exhaled from
    the lungs than would be the case if it were provided in a single breath.
    Mere failure by a person on whom a breath test has been carried
    out to have followed the instructions of the constable is not an
    offence under the Act; nor does it, in my view, constitute a failure
    to provide a specimen of breath for a breath test within the meaning   G
    of section 8 (5), unless the result of his departing from those instruc-
    tions has been to defeat the purpose of the breath test by making
    it impossible to obtain by means of the Alcotest R80 a reliable indi-
    cation whether or not the proportion of alcohol in *his* blood exceeds
    the prescribed limit."

Lord Kilbrandon in the same case said, at p. 1167:   H

    " If too little air is put into the bag, and the crystals do not change
    colour, the test has not been properly conducted, because the con-
    clusion to be drawn from the non-change may be either that the
    proportion in the body is less than that forbidden, or that the amount
    of air exhaled has been inadequate to cause the change of colour to
    occur, although the forbidden proportion be present. The same is
    true, mutatis mutandis, if the bag has been inflated in short puffs.

A   In such circumstances a constable would be entitled to arrest the motorist for failing to take the test."

We respectfully agree with the opinions of Lord Pearson, Lord Diplock and Lord Kilbrandon which we believe correctly interpret what is meant by a " breath test " in section 12 (1) of the Act. To hold that the negative specimen of breath, provided in the way it was provided by the defendant
B   in the present case, constituted " a specimen of breath for a breath test " would, in our view, be to ignore the declared purpose which is part of the definition of a " breath test " in section 12 (1).

The inspector was right when he decided that the defendant had failed to provide a specimen of breath for the breath test. Accordingly he was entitled to require the specimen of blood for a laboratory test and the evidence of the result of that test was admissible.
C   The appeal is dismissed.

Appeal dismissed.
Prosecution's costs out of central funds.

Solicitor: *Solicitor, Metropolitan Police.*

D
[Reported by MISS ANGELA HODES, Barrister-at-Law]

[COURT OF APPEAL]

E   * TOWNSEND AND ANOTHER *v.* STONE TOMS & PARTNERS
AND OTHERS

[1979 T. No. 350]

1981   May 6, 7, 11   Eveleigh and Watkins L.JJ. and Sir David Cairns

F   *Practice—Payment into court—Several defendants—Two defendants sued in one action in respect of breaches of separate contracts—Overlapping claims—Payment into court by one defendant accepted by plaintiff — Whether defendants " sued jointly "—Whether action against other defendant to be stayed in respect of overlapping items of claims—R.S.C., Ord. 22, r. 3 (4)*

G   R.S.C., Ord. 22, r. 3 (4) provides:
" On the plaintiff accepting any money paid into court all further proceedings in the action or in respect of the specified cause or causes of action ... to which the acceptance relates, both against the defendant making the payment and against any other defendant sued jointly with or in the alternative to him shall be stayed."

H   The plaintiffs brought an action in which they claimed damages for breaches of contracts from the first defendants, a firm of architects, and the third defendants, who were builders, in respect of work done to the plaintiffs' house. The breaches alleged arose under separate contracts ; the claim against the first defendants included an allegation of failure to supervise the work properly and the claim against the third defendants was for defective performance of the work. The third defendants paid money into court " in satisfaction of all the causes of action in respect of which the plaintiffs claim,"

and the plaintiffs took it out "in satisfaction of the causes of A
action in respect of which it was paid in and in respect of
which" they claimed against the third defendants. By consent, judgment was subsequently entered in their favour against
the third defendants. On their claim against the first defendants a preliminary point was taken by the first defendants to
the effect that, in so far as there were mutual or overlapping
items in the claims against themselves and the third defendants, the action against them should be stayed, on the ground B
that the payment in by the third defendants had been accepted
by the plaintiffs. The judge took the view that R.S.C., Ord.
22, r. 3 (4) applied and ordered that the action against the
first defendants be stayed in respect of overlapping items.

On appeal by the plaintiffs: —

Held, allowing the appeal, that "sued jointly" in R.S.C.,
Ord. 22, r. 3 (4) related to the case of a claim made where
there was one cause of action but more than one defendant C
liable thereon jointly with the other or others; that, where
there were two separate causes of action, satisfaction of the
one was not a bar to proceedings on the other and, accordingly,
the action should not have been stayed against the first
defendants (post, pp. 1159B, 1161F–G).

Parkes v. *Knowles* [1957] 1 W.L.R. 1040; [1957] 3 All
E.R. 600 considered.

D

The following cases are referred to in the judgments:

Brooke v. *Bool* [1928] 2 K.B. 578, D.C.
Holbrow v. *Swan & Moore (Assessors) Ltd.* (unreported), June 13, 1975;
    Court of Appeal (Civil Division) Transcript No. 257 of 1975, C.A.
Parkes v. *Knowles* [1957] 1 W.L.R. 1040; [1957] 3 All E.R. 600.

E

The following additional cases were cited in argument:

Hutchinson v. *Harris* (1978) 10 B.L.R. 19, C.A.
Isaacs & Sons v. *Salbstein* [1916] 2 K.B. 139, C.A.

APPEAL from James Leonard sitting as a deputy circuit judge assigned
to official referees' business.

By writ dated February 20, 1979, the plaintiffs, Colin Michael Victor F
Townsend and Mary Hay McKay Townsend, claimed against the first
defendants, Stone Toms & Partners (a firm), damages for breach of a
contract for the design of works to be carried out at Frith Farm (formerly
Freeze Farm), Frome, Somerset and for the supervision and administration of a building contract between the plaintiffs and the third defendants,
John Laing Construction Ltd.; against the second defendant, A. L. M.
Gough (male), damages for a breach of a contract for design and super- G
vision of plumbing works for the plaintiffs; and against the third defendants damages for breach of a building contract dated July 30, 1973, for
the carrying out of the works in question, the second plaintiff adding
against the first and second defendants a claim in the alternative for
damages for breach of a duty of care in and about the carrying out of
the contracts in question. The first and third defendants filed defences H
and counterclaims. On November 13, 1980, the third defendants gave
notice of payment into court pursuant to R.S.C., Ord. 22, and on
December 4 the plaintiffs gave notice of acceptance of the sum paid in.
On December 17, 1980, Judge Newey ordered by consent of the plaintiffs
and the third defendants that, inter alia, there be payment out to the
first and second plaintiffs' solicitors in full and final satisfaction of all
the causes of action for which the first and second plaintiffs claimed

A against the third defendants the total sum of £30,000 paid into court
by the third defendants in two sums of £7,500 and £22,500 on January 31,
1980, and November 14, 1980, respectively, the third defendants having
taken into account and satisfied the causes of action in respect of which
they counterclaimed in their payment into court; that judgment be given
in favour of the first and second plaintiffs against the third defendants;
and that the third defendants' counterclaim be dismissed. The matter
B of the plaintiffs' claim against the first defendants came on for hearing
before the deputy circuit judge, who gave judgment on April 30, 1981.
By his order, dated May 1, 1981, he ordered that all further proceedings
in the action against the first defendants in respect of the causes of action
pleaded in specified paragraphs of the plaintiffs' re-re-amended statement
of claim be stayed. He gave the plaintiffs leave to appeal.

C   The plaintiffs appealed, on the grounds that their claims against the
first and third defendants had been made pursuant to R.S.C., Ord. 15, r. 4
in respect of several causes of action arising out of the same series of
transactions and that the deputy circuit judge had erred in law in holding
(to the extent that he had so held) that the plaintiffs' claims were made
in respect of causes of action arising against the first and third defendants
jointly or against either the first or the third defendants in the alternative;
D that he had erred in law in holding that the acceptance by the plaintiffs
of the sums paid into court by the third defendants in respect of the
plaintiffs' causes of action against the third defendants resulted, pursuant
to R.S.C., Ord. 22, r. 3 (4), in a stay of the causes of action specified in
his order or any of them; that Ord. 22, r. 3 (4) had no application to
causes of action arising severally from causes of action in respect of
E which a payment into court was accepted, even where the damage claimed
was similarly quantified; and that the substantive rule of law was that,
where concurrent, but several and distinct, breaches of contract produced
the same damage, the plaintiff was entitled to judgment for the full
amount of the damage suffered against each of the parties in breach,
although he might not execute the judgment so as to obtain more than
F a single recovery, and that the Rules of the Supreme Court should be
construed and applied consistently with that rule.

   Anthony Butcher Q.C. and *Donald Valentine* for the plaintiffs.
   David Gardam Q.C. and *Michael Harvey* for the first defendants.

   EVELEIGH L.J. The plaintiffs in this case were building owners who
G sued architects and plumbing contractors and also the main building
contractor in respect of their work in relation to reconstruction of the
plaintiffs' house. The pleadings in the case are, as the deputy circuit
judge stated, complex and voluminous. Fortunately, the point that arises
on this appeal is a short one, and I therefore do not propose to go into
the details of the statement of claim but propose to summarise it in the
way that was done before the deputy circuit judge by counsel and for
H that purpose will quote from his judgment. The deputy circuit judge
said:

   "I think it is sufficient to accept the summary made by Mr. Butcher
   for the plaintiffs, and his summary of claims made against the first
   defendants "—that is to say, the architects—" is as follows: category
   one, defective design; that is a case against the first defendants as
   architects only. The second category is defective supervision by

the first defendants, resulting in bad work, which the third defendants A
had done and were sued for, getting passed and which will have to
be made good. The damage claimed is the same as was claimed
against the third defendants, but the breaches of duty arise from
different contracts. The third category is over-certification by the
architects in various respects, including certification in respect of
bad work. This claim is primarily against the first defendants, but
it may also be recovered from the third defendants. In the latter B
event there is still a claim for interest because the plaintiffs have
been kept out of their money. There is also a fourth category which
Mr. Butcher added and which he specified thus, claim for loss of
amenity which will break down, he says, under one head or another,
though there is likely to be some overlapping."

One may shortly state the position, then, as follows. The second C
defendant does not enter into the picture for the purpose of this appeal.
The first defendants are architects, and against them it is alleged, in so
far as it is relevant for this appeal, that they failed properly to supervise
the work. Against the third defendants, the builders, in so far as is
relevant for this appeal, it is alleged that they did work badly and
are liable therefor to the plaintiffs. In so far as lack of supervision D
is claimed, it is also claimed in the statement of claim that the first
defendants should be liable in respect of loss of amenities suffered by the
plaintiffs. I do not find it necessary for this appeal to go more deeply
into the precise pleading or the causes of action, or whether or not the
second plaintiff is suing in contract or tort or both, because the position
has come down to a quite narrow one, namely: where there is overlapping
of the items of damage alleged as a result of bad workmanship and also E
alleged to be the subject of a failure to supervise, should the action be
stayed when money paid into court by the third defendants has been
taken out?

The third defendants put in a defence denying liability and also
counterclaimed in respect of their charges to the extent to which they
alleged that they had not been paid. They made two payments in, the F
second of which was accompanied by a notice dated November 13, 1980,
and reads as follows:

"Take notice that John Laing Construction Ltd., the third defendants, have increased the payment into court of £7,500 made on
January 31, 1980, and have paid the further sum of £22,500 into
court; the said £22,500 together with the said sum of £7,500 is in G
satisfaction of all the causes of action in respect of which the plaintiffs
claim and after taking into account and satisfying the above-named
defendants' cause of action for £32,363·92 in respect of which it
counterclaims."

By a notice dated December 4, 1980, the plaintiffs took out the £30,000
(and I quote from their notice) "in satisfaction of the causes of action H
in respect of which it was paid in and in respect of which the plaintiffs
claim against that defendant." Subsequently, an application was made
to Judge Newey on December 17, 1980, when he ordered by consent that
there should be payment out in the terms of the notice and the acceptance.
He further ordered that the first and second plaintiffs recover against
the third defendants their costs of the action attributable to the first and
second plaintiffs' claim and that judgment be given in favour of the first

A and second plaintiffs against the third defendants and that the third defendants' counterclaim be dismissed, in accordance with the terms of the payment in.

The matter then came on for hearing before the deputy circuit judge on April 30, 1981, when a preliminary point was taken to the effect that, in so far as there were mutual or overlapping items in the claim against B the first defendants and the third defendants in relation to lack of supervision and bad workmanship, the action against the first defendants should be stayed, on the ground that the payment in by the third defendants had been accepted.

In support of that application—indeed, as the only basis for it—was the wording of R.S.C. Ord. 22, r. 3 (4), which reads as follows:

C   " On the plaintiff accepting any money paid into court all further proceedings in the action or in respect of the specified cause or causes of action, as the case may be, to which the acceptance relates, both against the defendant making the payment and against any other defendant sued jointly with or in the alternative to him shall be stayed."

D It is not wholly clear to me in this case whether it was alleged that the first defendants were sued jointly or in the alternative—that is to say, in the argument before the deputy circuit judge—but, as I understand it, the contention in this court is that the expression " sued jointly " is apt to cover the case against the first defendants because it is said that in respect of certain items, whilst in strict law the cause of action is a E separate one, the same damage is covered by the claim. The deputy circuit judge took the view that R.S.C., Ord. 22, r. 3 (4) did apply, and in consequence counsel worked out in detail the particular items in the statement of claim that would be covered by such a decision. In other words, where there was an overlapping of the claim counsel drafted the appropriate order, which subsequently became the order of the court, to F stay the action against the first defendants in respect of those items. It is against the judgment on that preliminary matter that the plaintiffs now appeal to this court. The point is a short one: what is the meaning of R.S.C., Ord. 22, r. 3 (4), in particular, the words " sued jointly with or in the alternative to him "?

On behalf of the first defendants it has been submitted, as I have G said, that " sued jointly " does not mean " sued in respect of joint liability "; it means simply " joined together in the same proceedings as defendants," or, if any limitation is to be put upon it, " sued together in the same proceedings as defendants in respect of the same damage."

Some support was invoked from a note in The Supreme Court Practice (1979) under R.S.C., Ord. 22, r. 4. Ord. 22, r. 4 (1) (a) reads:

H   " Where a plaintiff accepts any sum paid into court and that sum was paid into court—(a) by some but not all of the defendants sued jointly or in the alternative by him, . . ."—I omit the other subparagraphs—" the money in court shall not be paid out except under paragraph (2) or in pursuance of an order of the court, and the order shall deal with the whole costs of the action or of the cause of action to which the payment relates, as the case may be."

The note to rule 4 under the heading " Several defendants " reads: A

> " The term ' sued jointly' in this rule does not mean the same thing
> as ' joint liability,' but only that other defendants have been joined
> together in the action. . . ."

The authority for that note does not appear, but it is not unreasonable
to assume that it was prompted by *Parkes* v. *Knowles* [1957] 1 W.L.R.
1040 [1957] 3 All E.R. 600 which has been relied on in this court   B
by the first defendants as authority for their contention that " sued
jointly " does not mean " sued in respect of joint liability " but means
" joined together in the same proceedings as defendants." That was a
motor accident case in which an innocent passenger, as he is sometimes
called, sued two defendants, the drivers of the two vehicles involved in
the collision. One made a payment in, which was acceptable to the   C
plaintiff, and counsel appeared before the judge, Lynskey J., at Birmingham Assizes, to inform him that it was the plaintiff's desire to take the
money out and further to ask him to decide the position as to costs in
relation to the other defendant. As the money accepted was within the
jurisdiction of the county court, the question as to whether the costs should
be paid on a county court scale or a High Court scale arose. Counsel
has submitted that that application, being made as it was, recognised   D
that R.S.C., Ord. 22, r. 4 meant that " sued jointly " was not limited to
the case of people sued in respect of joint liability, because in that case
there was no suggestion of joint liability. Further, reliance was placed
on some words of Lynskey J., who, after he had delivered his judgment
saying what the appropriate scale of costs for the other defendant was,
then said [1957] 3 All E.R. 600, 603:   E

> " Under R.S.C., Ord. 22, r. 4, it is not open now, where there are
> two defendants, for the plaintiff to take the money out. He must
> make an application. Therefore, until he comes before the court to
> make the application he cannot take the money out. My order as
> to costs will include not merely costs up to date of payment in, but
> also the costs of this application."   F

However, be that as it may, the decision of Lynskey J. was in relation
to costs. That was the issue that he had to determine, namely, the scale
of costs. He said [1957] 1 W.L.R. 1040, 1041: " The application now
comes before me under rule 4 (3) of Order 22 as to what order as to
costs shall be made." Then he elaborated upon the issue. Nowhere was
it argued that the leave of the court was necessary, or unnecessary, for   G
the payment out, and nowhere did a question arise as to whether the
action could be stayed as against the other defendant. Lynskey J.'s decision was, as I say, concerned solely with the question of costs. I also take
the view that, when it was intimated to the court that the plaintiff was
accepting the liability of one defendant to the exclusion of that of the
other, as was the case, it could rightly be regarded at that stage as a case
where defendants were being sued in the alternative. In a running-down   H
case where two defendants are blamed on facts similar to those in *Parkes*
v. *Knowles,* each defendant is blamed, but in strict pleading the claim is
made severally against them as separate tortfeasors in respect of the same
damage, and also against each in the alternative, because it very often
turns out, as the plaintiff can anticipate, that one defendant alone will be
found liable to him. Therefore, I take the view that *Parkes* v. *Knowles*
[1957] 1 W.L.R. 1040 can be treated as a case of persons sued in the

A alternative, and the obiter dicta at the end of Lynskey J.'s judgment could be regarded as applying to such a case, or the fact of the case then before him. But, however that might be, I do not regard that case as deciding the question that this court has to decide. The principle that is contended for in this case was never in issue and in no way could be said to be the ratio decidendi of Lynskey J.'s decision. So, I look at this problem for the moment, as indeed I think all such problems of construction should

B be treated, by looking at the wording of the rule with which we are concerned. It says: ". . . any . . . defendant sued jointly with or in the alternative to him. . . ." For myself, I would regard the natural meaning of the words "sued jointly" as relating to the case of a claim made where there is one cause of action but more than one defendant liable thereon jointly with the other or others. The presence of the words "or

C in the alternative to him" to my mind strengthens that conclusion, because if "sued jointly" meant, as Mr. Gardam contends, any defendant in the same action there would be no need to refer specifically to one sued in the alternative. A defendant who is sued in the alternative is sued for his own several liability, and if any defendant is covered by this rule because of the words "sued jointly" so would a person sued in the alternative be covered, without need for any special reference to him.

D Mr. Gardam says that we can read into the rule a limitation, which limitation may make it necessary to have specific reference to an alternative defendant, namely the limitation that the defendants must be sued in respect of the same damage. For myself, I ask: if one is going to read into it the limitation "in respect of the same damage," why should not one read into it the limitation "in respect of the same cause of action"—

E in other words, joint liability? If it is to be one or the other, I would prefer the construction that means "in respect of joint liability," because, strictly speaking, one is not reading it into the paragraph at all. It arises from what I regard as the natural meaning of the expression "sued jointly."

I find some assistance for this in R.S.C., Ord. 15, r. 4. Paragraph (1)
F reads:

"Subject to rule 5 (1), two or more persons may be joined together in one action as plaintiffs or as defendants with the leave of the court or where—(a) if separate actions were brought by or against each of them, as the case may be, some common question of law or fact would arise in all the actions, and (b) all rights to relief claimed in the action (whether they are joint, several or alternative)

G are in respect of or arise out of the same transaction or series of transactions."

Then, by paragraph (3):

"Where relief is claimed in an action against a defendant who is jointly liable with some other person and also severally liable, that

H other person need not be made a defendant to the action; but where persons are jointly, but not severally, liable under a contract and relief is claimed against some but not all of those persons in an action in respect of that contract, the court may, on the application of any defendant to the action, by order stay proceedings in the action until the other persons so liable are added as defendants."

That rule clearly to my mind contemplates three different categories of parties to an action, namely where liability is joint, where liability is

several and where liability is in the alternative. Examples are given of A
that in the notes. They are well known. An example of joint liability
is the case of joint contractors or of vicarious liability, master and servant,
or indeed of joint tortfeasors, such as the well-known case of *Brooke* v.
Bool [1928] 2 K.B. 578. Examples of alternative liability are seen in
cases of principal and agent, or in the running-down case where the
plaintiff is uncertain which of two people drove the offending vehicle; and
of several liability, of course, in cases where one cause of action is B
alleged against one person only. The Rules of the Supreme Court were
much affected, when they were originally drafted, by the common law
principles applicable to cases of joint and several liability. They are
well known. They have been affected and modified by the Law Reform
(Married Women and Tortfeasors) Act 1935 and the Civil Liability (Contribution) Act 1978, but the basic common law principle had an influence C
on the drafting of the rules of court.

    Picking up those three categories from R.S.C., Ord. 15, r. 4, and turn-
ing back again to R.S.C., Ord. 22, r. 3, one finds only two categories
mentioned there: " sued jointly . . . or in the alternative." Quite apart,
then, from arriving at my conclusion from a strict reading of the words,
assistance from R.S.C., Ord. 15, if assistance is necessary, leads me to
the conclusion that three categories are envisaged in the rules, and, if D
there are three, " sued jointly " can only mean " sued in respect of joint
liability," leaving the two other cases of alternative and several liability;
and R.S.C., Ord. 22, r. 3 specifically proclaims that it is concerned with
only two of them. In the case with which we are concerned it is conceded, as indeed it must be, that there are separate causes of action sued
upon against the first and third defendants. That being so, I for my E
part am of the opinion that the case is not covered by R.S.C., Ord. 22,
r. 3 (4) and that the action should not have been stayed. If there had
been separate actions and a payment in had been accepted in the action
against the third defendants, it is accepted by counsel on behalf of the
first defendants that there would be no way in which he could obtain a
stay in the action against them. What the result at the end of the day
will be is not a matter for this court to determine at this stage. To what F
extent money paid will have to be taken into account is a question that
may well have to be argued, but I am not concerned to answer it in this
case.

    I should just mention *Holbrow* v. *Swan & Moore (Assessors) Ltd.*
(unreported), June 13, 1975; Court of Appeal (Civil Division) Transcript
No. 257 of 1975, which has been cited to the court. There, a plaintiff G
was injured in a motor accident. He was an infant plaintiff, and his
father on his behalf engaged assessors to make a claim for him on the
terms that the father was not to be liable for costs. Solicitors were
eventually brought in by the assessors, and the father instructed the
solicitors. The son's claim failed, and the father found himself liable for
costs to the defendants. He brought an action against the assessors and H
the solicitors, alleging against the assessors that they were in breach of
contract in that they had undertaken that he would not be liable for costs
and against the solicitors that it was a result of the breach of their professional duty that his liability had been incurred. The solicitors paid in.
An application was made to the court under Ord. 11, r. 10 (1) (*a*) of
the County Court Rules, which reads:

A " Where payment into court is made—(a) by one or more of several
defendants sued jointly or in the alternative, or . . ."—then there
follow other instances—" the money in court shall not be paid out
except in pursuance of an order of the court."

An application was made to the court for the money to be paid out. In
the course of his judgment, Megaw L.J., having recited the facts and
B the state of the pleadings and the action, said, at p. 4 of the transcript:

" Thereafter the plaintiff filed an application to enable him to take
out the £525 which had been paid into court. That application was
necessary by virtue of the County Court Rules. . . ."

He then quoted the rule that I have just read. So, says Mr. Gardam on
C behalf of the first defendants here, the words are the same; it was said
that application was necessary; it could only have been necessary on
the basis of two defendants sued in the same action, and they were in
that case not sued jointly; they were separate causes of action. I myself
have some doubt as to whether the transcript has a word omitted in that
sentence. I do not know, and it is not really necessary to come to any
conclusion on the matter. It could be that what had been said was:
D " That application was thought to be necessary "—or " thought necessary "—" by virtue of the County Court Rules." I know not. The matter
was not in issue. What Megaw L.J. did decide in that case was this: that
the action against the assessors should proceed. He said that it was a
separate cause of action and that, although money had been accepted
and although that would affect the damages recoverable in the action
against the first defendants, the assessors, that action could proceed
E because there was still an issue as to the liability for costs between the
parties. I refer to that case, and refer to it rather cursorily, because it
has been quoted to this court. I do not find it of direct assistance on the
matter that we have to decide. First, as I say, our problem was not in
issue in that case; and, secondly, Megaw L.J. did say, at p. 7: ". . . the
relief claimed against the two parties was not identical and, properly, was
F not claimed as being identical." So, it might be argued that he would
not have come to the same conclusion if there had been precise overlapping of the damages claimed in the case. I know not. I do, however,
regard the case as pointing in the direction in which our decision should
go, namely that, where there are two separate causes of action, satisfaction of the one should not be a bar to proceedings on the other.

G   For those reasons, I am of the opinion that to stay the action against
the first defendants, albeit in respect of the limited number of heads of
claim, was wrong, and that this appeal should be allowed.

WATKINS L.J. I agree.

SIR DAVID CAIRNS. I also agree. I only want to make an observation
H about one further sentence in the judgment of Megaw L.J. in *Holbrow*
v. *Swan & Moore (Assessors) Ltd.*, June 13, 1975. After saying that the
claims against the two parties were not identical, Megaw L.J. went on,
at p. 7:

" It is true, of course, that the plaintiff, having received satisfaction
for the full amount of his claim against the second defendants, would
not have been entitled to recover anything in the way of a judgment

for damages against the first defendants, because in the circumstances A
that would have involved a duplication of damages."

I do not find that sentence, with great respect to Megaw L.J., entirely
free from ambiguity. If he meant that the plaintiff would not be entitled
to have a judgment against the first defendants if he could establish those
defendants' liability, I would respectfully dissent from that. If he meant B
simply that under such a judgment he could not obtain any further
damages than those already recovered, I would respectfully agree with
what he said. That would be where duplication of damages would come
in, there having been in that case no suggestion that any more than £525
would be the appropriate damages against either defendant.

I entirely agree with all that Eveleigh L.J. has said as to the reasons
for allowing the appeal, and I have nothing further to add to them.   C

Appeal allowed with costs.

Solicitors: *Walters Fladgate; Kennedys.*

M. G.   D

[FAMILY DIVISION]

* PRACTICE DIRECTION (DIVORCE: WELFARE REPORT)

E

*Husband and Wife—Divorce—Children—Practice—Welfare offi-
cer's report—Court to specify matters on which report to be
based—Welfare officer attending hearing*

In order to make the best use of welfare officers' reports and of their
time the President draws attention to the following points:

1. The time of the busy Divorce Court Welfare Service will be better F
spent and the time of busy judges saved if the court specifies those matters
on which the report is to be made.

2. Such specification should never prevent the reporting officer from
bringing to the notice of the court any other matters which he considers
that the court should have in mind.

3. If any party considers it desirable that the reporting officer should G
attend the hearing, the proper course is to ask the registrar so to direct
or, if time does not permit, to inform the reporting officer that it is
proposed at the hearing to ask the judge to direct that he attends.

4. Bearing in mind that contested custody cases often take several
days to hear the parties should agree a convenient date and time for the
attendance of the reporting officer in cases where his attendance is
required, so that his valuable time is not wasted.   H

Issued with the concurrence of the Lord Chancellor.

July 16, 1981.

R. L. BAYNE-POWELL
Senior Registrar.

A

[QUEEN'S BENCH DIVISION]

* PRACTICE DIRECTION
(JUSTICES: CLERK TO COURT)

B
Justices—Clerk to justices—Functions—Responsibility of clerk to advise justices on law, practice and procedure—Manner in which functions to be performed

1. A justices' clerk is responsible to the justices for the performance of any of the functions set out below by any member of his staff acting as court clerk and may be called in to advise the justices even when he is not personally sitting with the justices as clerk to the court.

C
2. It shall be the responsibility of the justices' clerk to advise the justices as follows: (a) on questions of law or of mixed law and fact; (b) as to matters of practice and procedure.

3. If it appears to him necessary to do so, or he is so requested by the justices, the justices' clerk has the responsibility to (a) refresh the justices' memory as to any matter of evidence and to draw attention to

D
any issues involved in the matters before the court, (b) advise the justices generally on the range of penalties which the law allows them to impose and on any guidance relevant to the choice of penalty provided by the law, the decisions of the superior courts or other authorities. If no request for advice has been made by the justices, the justices' clerk shall discharge his responsibility in court in the presence of the parties.

E
4. The way in which the justices' clerk should perform his functions should be stated as follows. (a) The justices are entitled to the advice of their clerk when they retire in order that the clerk may fulfil his responsibility outlined above. (b) Some justices may prefer to take their own notes of evidence. There is, however, no obligation on them to do so. Whether they do so or not, there is nothing to prevent them from enlisting the aid of their clerk and his notes if they are in any doubt as to the

F
evidence which has been given. (c) If the justices wish to consult their clerk solely about the evidence or his notes of it, this should ordinarily, and certainly in simple cases, be done in open court. The object is to avoid any suspicion that the clerk has been involved in deciding issues of fact.

5. For the reasons stated in the practice direction of January 15, 1954,

G
Practice Note (Justices' Clerks) [1954] 1 W.L.R. 213, which remains in full force and effect, in domestic proceedings it is more likely than not that the justices will wish to consult their clerk. In particular, where rules of court require the reasons for their decision to be drawn up in consultation with the clerk, they will need to receive his advice for this purpose.

6. This practice direction is issued with the concurrence of the

H
President of the Family Division.

July 2, 1981.

LORD LANE C.J.

[1981]

[LIVERPOOL CONSISTORY COURT]   A

In re ST. MARK'S, HAYDOCK

1980   July 26   Hamilton Ch.

*Ecclesiastical Law — Headstone — Photographic reproduction —
Erection of headstone incorporating photographs—No indication of photographs on approved design—Whether photo-   B
graphs appropriate on headstone—Whether photographs to
be removed*

A headstone erected in the cemetery of a parish church
incorporated two coloured photographs, one of the deceased
and the other of his car. When the design for the headstone
had been submitted to and approved by the vicar there had
been no indication that it was to include photographs. The   C
vicar and churchwardens petitioned the consistory court for
a ruling concerning the unauthorised placing of the photographs on the headstone.

On the petition: —

Held. that the photographs by their very nature did not
harmonise with the rest of the headstone (post, p. 1166B); that
a pleasing and personal touch could be given to the headstone
by etching a replica of the deceased's car in place of the   D
photograph (post p. 1166C); and that the photographs should
be removed from the headstone.

Per curiam. Photographs of other tombstones to be found
in Church of England cemeteries where photographs have
been used do not encourage the view that photographs on
tombstones should become a general practice (post, p. 1166D).

No cases are referred to in the judgment.   E

PETITION

The petition of the vicar, the Reverend Maurice M. H. Jones, and
churchwardens of St. Mark's, Haydock, requested the consistory court
to make an authoritative legal judgment concerning the unauthorised
placing of two coloured photographic plaques on the headstone of the   F
late Terance Anthony Case buried in the cemetery of St. Mark's Church,
Haydock.

The parents of the deceased and the monumental masons who had
designed and erected the headstone were represented at the hearing as
being persons interested in the petition.

The facts are stated in the judgment.
                                                                     G

The petitioners in person.

Humphrey Roberts, solicitor, for the parties interested.

HAMILTON CH. This case arises out of the tragic death of Terance
Anthony Case. I am quite sure that everyone present has the utmost
sympathy with his parents. The circumstances are set out in the words on H
his tombstone which have a very eloquent simplicity:

" TREASURED
MEMORIES OF
a loving son & brother
TERANCE ANTHONY CASE
tragically killed in road accident
Nov. 19th 1979 aged 22 years."

A   Beside that tombstone stands a smaller monument, inscribed: " Remembered always by his workmates at Bold Colliery." They amply demonstrate the esteem in which Terance was held. It is a very great pity that this case had to arise at all, because it has inevitably been very hurtful to the feelings of the parents. No blame attaches to them at all. But this case arises because the tombstone not merely carried the words I have quoted, but also two coloured photographs, one of the deceased, and the other of the

B   car he enjoyed driving before the fatal accident.

There is no dispute about the fact that, when the design for the tombstone was submitted by the monumental masons for the vicar's approval, there was no indication at all that it was to include the two photographs. It is true that, in the ornamental border at the top of the stone, the design indicated an oval; but that seemed to be part of the design, and nobody

C   could have guessed that it would enclose a photograph. As to the oval at the bottom which came to include the photo of the car, that was not indicated at all. So no criticism can be made of the Reverend Maurice Jones, the vicar, for failing to observe these features, nor of the verger, Mrs. Williams, who passed him this design when it was given to her by the monumental masons.

D   It has been suggested by Mr. Case, the father of the deceased, that when the vicar heard that these photographs had been placed on the tombstone, strong and painful words were used. But, as I indicated during the hearing, I make no finding upon that, because whether true or false it cannot affect the real issues in the present case, which are far wider than that. I appreciate, of course, that feelings are very easily hurt in a situation like this.

E   The vicar felt that he had been the victim of deception by the monumental masons. Here again I have no need to accept that a thoroughly reputable firm, which has carried on business for 40 years without complaint, acted in bad faith. But Mr. Rigby of that firm has to take the blame for the fact that the design did not give any indication that photos were to be on the tombstone. If it had been clear, this unhappy situation would

F   never have arisen. Mr. Rigby states that he has always submitted these designs to the vicar, and they have always been accepted; he came to assume that they always would be. But this case shows that such an assumption was not justified. Sometimes, he told me, the design was only submitted when the tombstone was actually erected; this case shows that there is need for a much more formal approach to the submission of designs and the notification of consent or of objections.

G   What is to be done about the situation now? Any alteration to the tombstone will be very distressing for Mr. and Mrs. Case. But I have to consider the wider issues as well. As the vicar put it:

"It places us in a compromised situation. We would have to decide in future between types of photographs. It is not usual to have photographs in parish cemeteries, and there are no others in this cemetery."

H   He is concerned not only for his own position, but about the situation which might arise for future incumbents in the parish, and future members of the parochial church council. He was so concerned about the irregularity of the procedure, that he got in touch with the Archdeacon of Warrington, who advised him to get a ruling from this consistory court.

When I look at the stone itself—I have seen the original in the churchyard and photographs are before me—the photographs do not add to the beautiful design in any way. In fact, they detract from it. The stone is of A polished black marble, and the words well spaced out and engraved with gold lettering. This is a matter of careful, formal design. But the photographs were not special portrait photographs; they are ordinary informal snap-shots. There is a great deal of difference between their nature and quality and that of the rest of the stone. I was considerably worried about the quality of the photographs as such. One knows that photographs can fade, so that in 10 or 20 years time the photographs could be a smudgy B blur, while the rest of the stone remains as it is now. Mr. Rigby tells me that the photographs are transferred to porcelain by a special process which is permanent, so that this problem will not arise. Even so, the photographs do not by their very nature harmonise with the rest of the stone.

If the photographs were not there, what could be done in their place? Mr. Rigby tells me that there will be two small holes where each photo- C graph was affixed to the stone. But can some alternative design be provided? As far as the portrait of Terance is concerned, this cannot be engraved onto the stone in any satisfactory way. Mr. Rigby said that the result would simply " look like anybody." The car is a different matter. It would be perfectly possible to etch a replica of the car, and this would provide a pleasing and personal touch to the stone. I have been given photographs D of a few other tombstones to be found in Church of England cemeteries where photographs have been used. They do not encourage me to accept the view that photographs should become a general practice on tombstones. Indeed, the Reverend Noel Michell, secretary of the diocesan advisory committee, tells me that they are not. Nevertheless one of these examples is very striking; it is the tombstone of a young man of 25 who was killed whilst playing his guitar; and on the stone, beside the wording, E is carved the outline of the guitar. This gives the stone a touching individuality, and there is all the difference in the world between an etched outline on a carved stone, and a photograph.

When Mr. Case gave evidence before me he told me how his wife, who is now blind, takes a particular pleasure in visiting the grave and running her fingers over the photograph on it of her son; she can feel it, but F is unable to see it. Of course I accept his evidence, but I cannot believe that the photograph is the real object of her visit to the stone, or that her ability to touch the photograph is of central importance to her. This is to give the photograph a deeper emotional quality and significance than it ought to have. To visit the grave itself, and to touch the stone if she wishes, is surely far more important than the photograph itself. It cannot outweigh G the other considerations in this case. Nevertheless, I recognise the sincerity of her feelings, and I have a proposal to make which I would like her and Mr. Case to consider at their leisure; it would not be fair to seek a decision from them on it now. I would like them to consider whether, for instance, they would like to have the car etched on the stone; and whether, in the place now occupied by the photo of their son, they would like to have a H design of flowers, or a simple cross, or something of that nature. If upon reflection they do, then it will only be necessary for the design to be submitted to me for my consideration informally; there will be no need for a further hearing of the consistory court.

I have already made it clear that no moral blame attaches to the monumental masons, in that they had no desire to practise any deception upon the vicar. Nevertheless, this case would not have arisen had they

A submitted a design which was fully explicit of their intentions, and the costs of this hearing must therefore be paid by them.

> *Order that photographs be removed from tombstone.*

B Solicitors: *A. E. Tickle & Son, St. Helens.*

C. N.

C

[LIVERPOOL CONSISTORY COURT]

* *In re* ST. MARK'S, HAYDOCK (No. 2)

D 1980   July 26;   Hamilton Ch.
         Sept. 13

Ecclesiastical Law—Headstone—Right to erect—Permission to erect headstone sought by deceased's estranged widow and by woman with whom deceased associating—Appropriate inscription—Proper order

E   Following the death of her estranged husband, a widow submitted to the vicar of the church where he was buried a proposal for a headstone to be erected over his grave. The vicar also received a request for the erection of a headstone from Mrs. Myra P., a woman with whom the deceased had been associating at the time of his death. The inscription proposed by the widow contained no reference to herself,
F whereas that proposed by Mrs. P. referred to the deceased as " A dear friend of Myra and Family." The vicar petitioned the court for a declaration as to who had the right to erect a headstone.
     On the petition: —
     Held, that in recent years courts had come to recognise that mistresses had certain rights and, though the deceased's association with Mrs. P. had not been established to be adulterous,
G it would be curious if her position would have been stronger had it been so (post, pp. 1169A–B, 1170A); but that there should not be any inclusion of one friend or relative to the pointed exclusion of another on headstones in cemeteries and that a controversial headstone would serve no good purpose (post, p. 1170B, D); and that, accordingly, the headstone should be provided out of the estate of the deceased and bear only a brief inscription (post, p. 1171A–B).

H
     No cases are referred to in the judgment.

PETITION
     The petition of the vicar of St. Mark's Church, Haydock, the Reverend Maurice M. H. Jones, prayed that for both technical and pastoral reasons a decision should be made to declare who had the right to erect a memorial headstone over the grave of the late Brian Atkinson. The deceased's widow

and Mrs. Myra Proudlove, with whom the deceased had formed an asso- A
ciation, were represented at the hearing as persons interested.

The facts are stated in the judgment.

The petitioner in person.
J. F. Whitehead, solicitor, for the widow.
E. Howard, solicitor, for Mrs. Proudlove.

B

HAMILTON CH.   This is a petition brought by the vicar in conjunction
with the churchwardens and parochial church council, asking the court to
make a legal ruling on the following grounds:

> " That for both technical and pastoral reasons a decision should be
> made to declare who has the right to erect a memorial headstone over
> the grave of the late Brian Atkinson."

C

The case is not so much unusual as extraordinary, and I pay tribute
to the delicacy shown by both advocates in the case. Both the parties, Mrs.
Atkinson and Mrs. Proudlove, hold sincere and deep views in the case.

It arises out of the death of Mr. Brian Atkinson on December 2, 1978.
Neither of the two ladies, who are really the parties to this case, claims D
a moral superiority over the other. Mrs. Atkinson, the deceased's widow,
became his wife when her first marriage and his broke up; she was cited
as co-respondent on the grounds of her adultery with him. It has not been
shown that the association which Mrs. Proudlove later formed with the
deceased was an adulterous one, but it nevertheless intruded into her own
existing marriage and into his, whosever fault it may have been. It is easy
to suggest that the marriage was broken up because of the failings of Mrs. E
Atkinson as a wife, or the intrusion of Mrs. Proudlove, and this is the view
each takes of the other. But not enough prominence has been given in this
case to the realities of the deceased's working life. He was a man responsible
for opening up and running many warehouses, some of them in the North
of England, and one in particular near Haydock. It is clear from the
evidence both of the widow and the deceased's brother that he was often F
overworked to the point of exhaustion, working morning, noon and night.
He took pills to cope with the strain, and this strain would have had its
effect on any relationship he formed with any woman.

As his widow has told me, and I accept, he had two adulterous affairs
earlier in the marriage. He confessed both of them to her, with some shame,
and she forgave him. However, when he began his association with Mrs.
Proudlove, she felt it was the last straw, and she moved down to Essex. G
She still hoped that he would give up that association and be reconciled
with her. Correspondence took place between her solicitors and his, but
it never reached the stage when any formal divorce petition was issued by
either party. But as any experienced divorce practitioner knows, not every
threatened or impending case comes to fruition. Relations between a
husband and wife are sometimes healed. As I once heard a divorce judge H
say of a marriage in this situation, " it may not have been much of a
marriage, but it was still a marriage."

Of course it is possible that the deceased and his wife might have been
divorced at some time in the future; it may even be probable. But it cannot
be said to have been certain. It has not been shown that the deceased's
association with Mrs. Proudlove was an adulterous one. It was clearly a
loving one. A letter has been produced which he sent to Mrs. Proudlove.

A It is on romantic notepaper, and begins " To MYRA, my most treasured possession."

Perhaps if it had been an adulterous association the physical liaison would have made it all the stronger; if it was not, there was always the risk that he might have begun another adulterous association elsewhere. But where does that take me? I should be forming a curious value judg-
B ment if I decided that Mrs. Proudlove's position would be stronger if she had been committing adultery. The fact is that, in assessing the future of the deceased's marriage, I am dealing with imponderables.

I accept the evidence of the deceased's brother that the deceased had come to hate his wife; he believed, wrongly in my view, that she was encouraging Mr. Proudlove to kill him. This led him to state that she was to have nothing to do with his funeral should he be killed, and I am
C asked to lend great weight to the deceased's expressed intention. But suppose it be that the deceased's opinion was based on a wrong premise—that it was not, in fact, fair to his wife? I accept the widow's evidence that Mr. Proudlove, who was clearly in a very disturbed state of mind, kept ringing her up to say that he was laying wait for the deceased, so as to kill him. I also accept that she rang her husband up in office hours to pass
D on these warnings to him; for there is no doubt that he was aware of these threats.

They were put into action. First of all Mr. Proudlove assaulted the deceased; he was put on probation for that action. But later on he stabbed him to death. The jury's verdict in the trial of Mr. Proudlove for murder was one of manslaughter, and I naturally am not going behind that verdict.

On the very day of his death there was a stormy meeting between the
E deceased and his wife in St. Helens. The widow says he struck her on that occasion; Mr. Howard sought to cross-examine her to show that she struck him, but I have refused to admit evidence on this point, because it does not help me with the question now before me; this is not a summons for common assault in the St. Helens Magistrates' Court. On an occasion when the widow was confronting her husband for associating with another
F woman, one can quite understand one striking the other. It cannot affect my judgment about the right to erect a headstone.

All these matters are now in the past. The following inscription for the headstone has been proposed by Mrs. Proudlove:

" In loving memory of
BRIAN MALCOLM ATKINSON
G Beloved son of Harry and Winnie
Father of Graeme and Scott
Loving brother of Colin
A dear friend of
Myra and family
Taken from us 2nd December, 1978
H ' He loved those who loved him '."

As I indicated in the course of argument, and as the Reverend Noel Michell said in evidence, this epitaph is far too long even for an unusual case. The Reverend Noel Michell, as Secretary of the Diocesan Advisory Committee, frequently has the task of considering the wording on tombstones, and advising me upon their suitability. His advice is not binding upon me, but it is most helpful; and he tells me that the most important quality in the wording upon headstones nowadays is brevity and simplicity.

A

The courts have in recent years come to recognise that mistresses have certain rights. One could write a long and learned essay on the theoretical rights of a mistress against a widow in a case like this—if it was shown that Mrs. Proudlove was a mistress. The case might be almost impossible to resolve on that basis. But I turn instead to broader principles, because this is an ecclesiastical court.

B

It has been said that in heaven there is no marriage, nor giving in marriage. Equally there should not in cemeteries be any inclusion of one friend or relative to the pointed exclusion of another. I could not possibly contemplate allowing the inscription which included Mrs. Proudlove and excluded the widow. It could make the gravestone a subject of sensation, curiosity or scandal. When the deceased was buried, the funeral arrangements were carried out chiefly by his brother; the grave space was purchased by Mrs. Proudlove. The widow was not even aware that the funeral

C

was taking place, though she had made attempts to see that she should be notified of it. She was certainly not absent from the funeral through any indifference on her part, though from the evidence I have heard she certainly would not have been welcome there.

In due course she sent some flowers to be placed on her husband's grave, and received the most cruel anonymous letter to say that they would not be allowed to remain there. I accept Mrs. Proudlove's evidence that

D

she did not send that letter, and indeed had no knowledge of it at all. But it does serve to illustrate the fact that the mischievous-minded are attracted by this case, and that a controversial headstone would serve no good purpose.

I am asked to pay great attention to the deceased's expressions of hostility towards his wife at a time when he knew that his life was

E

threatened. But on this point his will is of great significance. It was drawn up on July 18, 1978, roughly six months before the deceased's death, at a time when his wife had left for Essex, and when he had been threatened by Mr. Proudlove. By that will the deceased bequeathed the sum of £8,000 to his widow, together with the matrimonial home which was in itself a substantial asset. It is true that under that will he also, by indirect means,

F

left an insurance policy to Mrs. Proudlove worth £6,000. He also provided that his funeral and testamentary expenses were to be discharged out of his estate.

In other words, if the deceased had been minded to exclude his wife from benefit under the will, or give her a far smaller share of his assets than he left to Mrs. Proudlove, he could have done so, but he did not. He could have specified in the will that Mrs. Proudlove was to carry out

G

his funeral arrangements; but he did not.

The widow has a different proposal for the inscription on the headstone:

" In Memory of
BRIAN MALCOLM ATKINSON Aged 45
Died tragically on December 2nd 1978
Son of Winifred and Harry Atkinson
and
Father of Graeme and Scott Atkinson."

H

She is quite happy to accept the phrase "He loved those who loved him." Mr. Howard attacks that form of wording as being a deliberate and cynical attempt on her behalf to up-stage Mrs. Proudlove by excluding her name from the headstone. I cannot agree; in omitting her own name from the

A stone the widow strikes me as being self-denying. However, this inscription is also too long.   Accordingly, I direct that the following shall be the inscription on the headstone:

" In loving Memory of
BRIAN MALCOLM ATKINSON
died tragically on December 2nd 1978, Aged 45.

B   ' He loved those who loved him '.' "

The costs of this stone and of the grave space and the court costs of this hearing shall be payable out of the estate of the deceased.   I make no order as to the costs of the widow and of Mrs. Proudlove, which each shall bear.

Order accordingly.

C

Solicitors: *Frank Platt & Fishwick, Wigan; Eric Howard & Co., Wigan.*

C. N.

D

[ARCHES COURT OF CANTERBURY]

* *In re* ST. MARY'S, FAWKHAM

E   1980   July 25   Goodman Ch.
    1980   Dec. 16   Owen Q.C., Dean of Arches

*Ecclesiastical Law—Headstone—Faculty—Petition to erect head-
stone incorporating photographic reproductions—Whether
appropriate memorial*

F   The petitioners sought a faculty for the erection, over the
joint grave of two members of their family, of a headstone
incorporating phototiles made from coloured photographs of
the two deceased.   Though the petition was unopposed, the
opinion of the Diocesan Advisory Committee, given pursuant
to a request under the Faculty Jurisdiction Rules 1967, was
that such a memorial on a headstone would be alien in an
English   country   churchyard.   The   chancellor   refused   a
faculty.

G   On appeal by the petitioners: —
Held, dismissing the appeal, that there had to be some
control of memorials based on aesthetic evaluations, and
memorials in the form of photographic reproductions of the
deceased on the headstone would be quite inappropriate in an
ancient English country churchyard (post, p. 1175E, G–H).

H   The following case is referred to in the judgment of Owen, Dean of
          Arches:

St. Edburga's, Abberton, In re [1962] P. 10; [1961] 3 W.L.R. 87; [1961]
    2 All E.R. 429.

No cases were cited in argument in the Court of Arches.

No cases are referred to in the judgment of Goodman Ch. and no cases
    were cited in argument in the Rochester Consistory Court.

A

PETITION

By petition dated December 13, 1979, the petitioners, Sidney Frank Jones, Perry D. Jones, Lee C. Jones and Tracey V. Cummins, sought a faculty authorising the erection of a headstone over the grave of two members of their family, Daphne Jones and Billie-Sue Jones, in the churchyard of St. Mary's Church in the parish of Fawkham. The design proposed for the headstone included two porcelain tiles containing colour photographs, approximately three inches by four inches, of the deceased.

B

The petition was unopposed.

The facts are stated in the judgment of Goodman Ch.

The petitioners in person.

C

GOODMAN Ch. Fawkham Parish Church is a small, delightful building dating from the 12th or 13th century set in the middle of open country to the south of Dartford. The church stands in a large meadow surrounded by woods. The churchyard nestles round the church, being an area of cut grass which eventually becomes meadowland. The space occupied by graves is in fact fairly small and compact and the churchyard is beautifully kept and well laid out. There are interesting memorial stones from the last three centuries and there is a pleasing absence of any white marble, black granite or green chippings or other memorials not generally thought suitable in an English country churchyard. Some of the existing memorials have kerbs but, save for the grave in question and two kerbs referred to by the rector, none have been introduced since the Diocesan Churchyard Regulations 1975, which I made for the benefit of the whole diocese, came into operation.

D

E

The application here arises following the tragic death of the first petitioner's wife and young daughter in a road traffic accident in July 1978. They were much loved in the family and beyond and, in the case of Mrs. Jones, particularly in the world of drama. Their bodies were buried in the churchyard opposite which the family had lived until about 1973 when they had moved to neighbouring New Ash Green.

F

Mr. Jones made an approach to the rector for a headstone to be put over their joint grave with phototiles inserted in it, namely, tiles with coloured photographs transposed by heat treatment. One tile was to show Mrs. Jones at dinner on the occasion of their son's wedding and I saw the photograph from which it was proposed to produce a phototile of her head and shoulders. There was also to be a photographic representation of the daughter. The rector explained that he had no authority to allow such a memorial under the terms of the Diocesan Churchyard Regulations 1975 and accordingly advised Mr. Jones and other members of the family that if they wished to press for such a memorial, it would have to be by petition for a faculty.

G

At about the same time Mr. Jones placed a number of large stones from his garden around the joint grave in the form of a kerb. He did not ask the rector's permission and says that he did not know he needed to do so. The rector observed what had happened but thought it was best to leave the question of the stones over until the court had dealt with the petition. The rector told me in the evidence, however, that he found the situation embarrassing as he had had to refuse permission for kerbs in a number of other cases since the regulations came into

H

A   force in 1975 and indeed none of the other graves near the grave in question have kerbs around them. I noticed the stones myself when I was looking at the churchyard shortly before I began to hear the petition in the church and after ascertaining the position from Mr. Jones and the rector I decided to leave the question of the stones over until the end of the hearing.

B   As to the application itself, Mr. Jones presented the case on behalf of himself and his co-petitioners and was in receipt of some assistance from a lawyer who sat beside him. He was in fact the only witness to give evidence on behalf of the petitioners taking the view that there was nothing his co-petitioners could add which would be of assistance. He said that he realised that the proposal would create a precedent but he thought such a form of memorial would add to the warmth and
C   togetherness of the churchyard. He also felt the Church of England ought to get up to date. He agreed that he had no knowledge of any churchyard (as opposed to a public cemetery) in England where there were such memorials but he had seen some in Streatham Cemetery and also in Finchley Cemetery. He did not call any expert witness or undertaker or monumental mason although I inquired whether he wished to do so.
D
        I then called the chairman of the Diocesan Advisory Committee, Mr. Philip Toy, in accordance with notice which had been served on the petitioners pursuant to rule 6 of the Faculty Jurisdiction Rules 1967, as amended. A copy of Mr. Toy's proof of evidence which had the unanimous support of the Diocesan Advisory Committee had been supplied to the petitioners. In his view a memorial in the form of a
E   photographic likeness on a headstone would be alien in an English country churchyard. He said that he had never come across such a memorial in any churchyard of which he had knowledge nor had he seen them elsewhere. He felt that such memorials were not appropriate in English churchyards and he felt that if one was allowed it would create a precedent which would make it difficult to say " no " in other
F   cases.

        I accept Mr. Toy's evidence and while I am very sorry for the petitioners and appreciate the distress they feel regarding the deaths of Mrs. Jones and her daughter and the particular circumstances in which those deaths occurred and their feeling that this form of memorial would be appropriate, I must point out that I am not con-cerned solely with the wishes of the petitioners (which would have been
G   all that would have been relevant if this had been a public cemetery) but have to consider this particular churchyard and the interests not only of the present parishioners but past and future parishioners too.

        Although there has been no opposition to the general citation and although the secretary for the parochial church council in response to special citation said that the council would leave it to me, I feel that it
H   is not appropriate in all the circumstances to allow this form of memorial in an English country churchyard and in this churchyard in particular. I accept that tastes change and I refer to memorials which were fashionable during the 18th and 19th centuries and which are no longer thought appropriate—most of these memorials were erected before it became the practice to apply the faculty jurisdiction to church-yards. But in considering the interests of Fawkham churchyard in the 1980s I feel the introduction of this form of memorial, although com-

monly found in Italy as Mr. Jones pointed out, would be an undesirable A
departure here.   With the passage of time and the effect of the climate
most memorials after 50 to 100 years or less tend to weather and fade and
become part of the general background in the churchyard.   Individual
memorials no longer stand out as these photographs would continue to
do, remaining clear, compelling and an attraction, which is not appropriate in the case of a country churchyard.   Sometimes described as
" God's acre," the churchyard and its stones are part of the English B
scene.   They form a setting for the church and reflect it in all its
periods and times.

   In these circumstances I feel obliged to reject the petition.   The
headstone itself is already in position and, although there are spaces for
the photographic tiles, the headstone could exist perfectly well on its
own as it stands.   I adjourn to chambers the question of the stones C
which presently form a kerb round the grave and this matter remains
to be considered.

Petition dismissed.

APPEAL from Goodman Ch. at the Rochester Consistory Court.
   The petitioners appealed by notice dated September 9, 1980, on the
ground that the judgment was biased particularly as the judge sitting D
in the consistory court was a previous chancellor.

   Dennis Gould for the petitioners.

   OWEN Q.C., Dean of Arches.   This is an appeal against the refusal
on July 26, 1980, by the Chancellor of the Diocese of Rochester of a E
faculty to enable the petitioners to erect in Fawkham churchyard
memorials containing photographic representations in ceramic tiles.
   The grounds of appeal stated in the notice of appeal are that the
judgment was biased, particularly as the judge sitting in the consistory
court was a previous chancellor.   In argument it has emerged that the
contention on behalf of the petitioners is not so much that the chan- F
cellor was biased as that it must so appear to the petitioners because in
June 1975 the chancellor drew up the regulations which govern the
erection of new churchyard memorials in the diocese.   It is sufficient
for me to say, first, that I am quite sure that the chancellor was not
in any way biased against the petitioners and, secondly, that the Diocesan
Churchyard Regulations do not seek to prohibit the erection of memorials. They allow incumbents to give permission for the erection of certain G
specified memorials.   For memorials which are not covered by the
regulations it is necessary to apply to the chancellor for a faculty which
may be granted or refused after consideration of the petition upon which
the chancellor will have received advice from the Diocesan Advisory
Committee.

   Although it is not so stated in terms I construe the notice of appeal H
to include the claim that the chancellor's decision was also wrong, being
based on an erroneous evaluation of the facts taken as a whole.   If I
am satisfied that this implicit claim is correct I shall allow the appeal:
see *In re St. Edburga's, Abberton* [1962] P. 10.
   Mr. Gould, in his helpful presentation of the case for the petitioners
has not challenged the relevant facts set out in the chancellor's judgment, ante, p. 1172C–G.

A   At the consistory court hearing Mr. Jones, the first-named petitioner, gave evidence in which he conceded that some memorials, e.g., those with angels depicted, are inappropriate but he contended that memorials such as he sought and still seeks would add warmth and meaning to churchyards. Mr. Toy, the chairman of the Diocesan Advisory Committee, apparently gave evidence that although there were no theo-
B   logical objections it was not right to pick out one particular moment of a deceased's life and seek to provide a memorial to the whole of that life by concentrating on that moment. He also said that the committee was unanimous in considering that the memorials, as proposed, would be alien to a churchyard and should not be allowed. There was no opposition to the general citation and the secretary for the parochial church council said they would express no view but would leave the
C   decision to the chancellor.

      I believe that I can now deal with the appeal quite shortly. Mr. Jones and his fellow petitioners have suffered a grievous loss and I extend to them and to other members of the family my deepest sympathy. Mrs. Jones was clearly an exceptional lady, greatly and rightly loved by a wide circle of friends. Billie-Sue Jones was only 13 years of age when she died. By their deaths many have suffered and I can
D   well understand the petitioners wishing to provide suitable memorials.

      In deciding whether to grant a faculty for the erection of a memorial a chancellor has to consider two interests, which may well conflict; on the one hand, the interest of the individual petitioner and, on the other, the interests of the whole Church and the public generally. Individuals no doubt think that they should be allowed to do what they believe to
E   be right but, as is accepted by Mr. Jones, there must be some controls. Memorials which for example would be blasphemous or otherwise grossly offensive could not be permitted. There must also be some control based on aesthetic evaluations, e.g., there should be a prohibition on certain materials. Indeed Mr. Jones himself contended that the representation of angels should not be permitted although at one
F   time such representations were freely permitted. In Brasenose College Chapel, Oxford, I have seen a memorial showing a cherub weeping, with his tears being dried by a handkerchief held to his eye yet I cannot accept that the erection of such a new memorial should be allowed in a church or churchyard today. Memorials which would have been considered appropriate 100 years ago may well not be appropriate today and vice versa. I believe Mr. Jones would agree with this.

G   My experience as a chancellor has shown that the control of memorials by the faculty procedure is fraught with difficulty because the petitioners have invariably suffered a great loss which is recent and the grief is still tender. The easy course would be to accede with sympathy to the petition but this would not be right. Although I am sympathetic towards the plight of the petitioners I have come firmly
H   to the view that memorials such as those sought by this appeal would be so alien in an English country churchyard, and especially an ancient country churchyard, that they should not be allowed. My decision is based on aesthetic objections. Although theological objections were raised at one time apparently these were not raised in the consistory court and the chancellor did not in any way rely on such objections.

      In so deciding I have no intention of posing as an aesthetic expert or as the sole censor of memorial styles. The Diocesan Advisory Com-

1176

Owen Q.C.,
Dean of Arches   **In re St. Mary's (Arches Ct.)**   **[1981]**

mittee, comprising six clerical members and eleven laymen, unanimously   A
advised against the grant of a faculty. Goodman Ch. agreed with the
committee. I agree with the chancellor. Some may say that the
Church is being stuffy and narrow-minded in rejecting the memorials
sought by the petitioners but this is not so, it is having a proper regard
for the maintenance of its churchyards.

At the end of his address Mr. Gould suggested that if I was against   B
the appeal I should nevertheless grant a faculty for the lifetime of the
last surviving petitioner; he told me that Mr. Jones did not feel that
such a limited faculty would set a precedent. As I understand the notes
of evidence Mr. Jones did recognise at the consistory court that a
faculty would set a precedent and that there could be other applications.
Whether or not this is a correct understanding I am sure that any
faculty would encourage other applications and I reject this secondary   C
submission.

In the circumstances the appeal must be dismissed with costs.

Appeal dismissed with costs.

Solicitors: *Burbridge & Co., Westerham.*

C. N.   D

[QUEEN'S BENCH DIVISION]   E

* WINDSORS (SPORTING INVESTMENTS) LTD. *v.* OLDFIELD

BOULTON *v.* CORAL RACING LTD. AND ANOTHER

1981 Jan. 23; 30   Donaldson L.J. and Forbes J.

F

*Gaming—Betting—Licensed betting office—Advertisement—Posters
  drawing attention to facilities available at betting offices—
  Posters placed inside windows only legible from outside—
  Whether posters published outside — Whether posters advertisements—Betting, Gaming and Lotteries Act* 1963 (c. 2),
  s. 10 (5)

The defendants in two separate cases were bookmakers. In   G
the windows of their licensed betting shops they displayed
posters which drew attention to the availability of facilities
afforded to persons resorting to licensed betting offices. The
posters were placed inside the windows in such a way that they
could only be read from the street outside. The defendants in
both cases were charged with publishing an advertisement other
than in a licensed betting office drawing attention to the
facilities afforded to persons resorting to their offices, contrary   H
to section 10 (5) of the Betting, Gaming and Lotteries Act
1963.[1] The defendants in the first case were convicted of the
offence and the defendants in the second case were acquitted.

On appeal by the defendants in the first case and by the
prosecution in the second case: —

Held, dismissing the appeal in the first case, and allowing
it in the second case, (1) that as the wording on the posters

[1] Betting, Gaming and Lotteries Act 1963, s. 10 (5): see post, p. 1180E–H.

A   was not visible inside the betting offices, but was only visible
from the outside, the posters were " published " outside the
betting office (post, pp. 1182F–H, 1184A).
   Dunsford v. *Pearson* [1970] 1 W.L.R. 222, D.C. and *Reg.*
v. *Newcastle-upon-Tyne Gaming Licensing Committee, Ex
parte White Hart Enterprises Ltd.* [1977] 1 W.L.R. 1135, C.A.
applied.
   Dictum of Lord Parker C.J. in *Robinson (Roy William)*
B   *Ltd.* v. *Cox* (1968) 67 L.G.R. 188, 195, D.C. doubted.
   (2) That to constitute an advertisement for the purposes
of section 10 (5) it was not necessary that the posters should
state that the premises to which they were affixed were a
licensed betting office and the offence was committed wherever
the document was published, provided that it drew attention
to the availability of facilities afforded to persons resorting to
licensed betting offices; and that the second case would be
C   remitted for further consideration (post, p. 1183A–B).

   The following cases are referred to in the judgments:

   Dunsford v. *Pearson* [1970] 1 W.L.R. 222; [1970] 1 All E.R. 282, D.C.
   Reg. v. *Newcastle-upon-Tyne Gaming Licensing Committee, Ex parte
       White Hart Enterprises Ltd.* [1977] 1 W.L.R. 1135; [1977] 3 All E.R.
       961, D.C. and C.A.
D   *Robinson (Roy William) Ltd.* v. *Cox* (1968) 67 L.G.R. 188, D.C.

   No additional cases were cited in argument.

WINDSORS (SPORTING INVESTMENTS) LTD. *v.* OLDFIELD

   CASE STATED by Bradford Crown Court.
E   On April 9, 1979, an information was preferred by the prosecutor
Derek Oldfield, against the defendants, Windsors (Sporting Investments)
Ltd. that (a) on November 6, 1978, at Bradford they were the licensees
of a licensed betting office at 12, The Green, Idle, Bradford, when an
advertisement drawing attention to the facilities afforded to persons resorting to the office, namely " Meet the Greyhound Trapper, every dog has
his day, this could be yours, William Hill where the action is," was
F   published otherwise than in the licensed betting office or in such manner
as was prescribed on premises giving access to the office, contrary to
section 10 (5) of the Betting, Gaming and Lotteries Act 1963; and (b) on
November 6, 1978, at Bradford were the licensees of a licensed betting
office at 12, The Green, Idle, which was managed otherwise than in
accordance with the rules set out in Schedule 4 to the Betting, Gaming and
Lotteries Act 1963 in that it did not comply with the restrictions
G   prescribed by regulation 3 (2) of the Betting (Licensed Offices) Regulation
1960 with respect of the exhibiting of signs on licensed premises in that a
sign was exhibited inside the premises, contrary to section 10 (1) of the
Betting, Gaming and Lotteries Act 1963.
   West Yorkshire justices acting in and for the petty sessional division
of Bradford heard the prosecution's case on the information on June
H   11, 1979. A submission of no case to answer was made on behalf of
the defendants, the decision on which was adjourned to June 15, when
both submissions were rejected. Thereafter on the defendants' calling
no evidence the justices convicted the defendants on the first information
and dismissed the second information. On July 3, 1979, the defendants
appealed against the conviction, the general grounds of such appeal
being: —(a) that the conviction was wrong in law; and (b) that the
defendants were not guilty of the offence.

1178

Windsors Ltd. v. Oldfield (D.C.) [1981]

The appeal was heard at Bradford Crown Court on September 27, 1979, where the appeal was dismissed, and the defendants were ordered to pay the costs of the prosecution. The court found the following facts (all of which were agreed between the parties). The defendants were the holders of a betting office licence in respect of the premises at 12, The Green, Idle, Bradford, which licence related to the whole of the premises within the outermost extremities of the building and included the window areas. On November 6, 1978, an advertisement comprising the words set out in the information was displayed on a poster in the front window of the betting office. It was not possible to see the advertisement from inside the licensed betting office. The advertisement could be seen clearly by persons outside the said licensed betting office. The wording in the advertisement was of a kind prohibited by section 10 (5) (c) of the Betting, Gaming and Lotteries Act 1963.

It was contended by the defendants that since section 10 (5) only forbade publication of advertisements which were not in a licensed betting office (or in the prescribed manner on premises giving access to such an office) the placing of such an advertisement within the premises so licensed was not in breach of the subsection notwithstanding the fact that it could be read by those outside the licensed premises.

It was contended by the prosecutor that the place of publication was the place where the advertisement could be seen and as the advertisement could be seen by persons outside the premises the advertisement was published outside the premises and therefore was in contravention of section 10 (5) of the Act. On behalf of the prosecutor the *Shorter Oxford English Dictionary* was produced in court as to the meaning of the word " publish," namely " to make known."

The court was of the opinion that the advertisement was published outside the licensed betting office because although it was fixed inside it was not visible inside and was clearly visible to anyone outside the premises. The court interpreted the subsection as banning the publication of advertisements visible on the outside to passers-by. The point of publication was not where the advertisement was fixed but where it was read. The court accordingly dismissed the appeal and ordered the defendants to pay the costs of the prosecution which were fixed at the sum of £160·00.

The question for the opinion of the High Court was whether an advertisement which was fixed within a licensed betting office was nevertheless published outside that office if it could be read by persons outside such office.

BOULTON v. CORAL RACING AND ANOTHER

CASE STATED by stipendiary magistrate for mid-Glamorgan sitting at Bridgend Magistrates' Court.

On September 24, 1979, informations were laid by the prosecutor, Chief Superintendent Sidney Boulton, against each of the defendants, Coral Racing and Barbara Ann Howells, alleging that they had on two separate occasions, namely, June 21, 1979, and September 7, 1979, published advertisements in the shop window of a licensed betting office in Market Street, Bridgend, in such a manner as to draw attention to the facilities afforded to persons resorting to such offices, contrary to section 10 (5) (c) of the Betting, Gaming and Lotteries Act 1963. The first defendant was the owner, and the second defendant was the manageress, of the licensed betting office.

A   The following facts were agreed. The premises concerned were a licensed betting office. On June 21, 1979, a poster was affixed to the inside of the clear glass of the shop window of the premises in such a manner that the poster could only be read from outside the premises as indicated in the agreed photographs. On September 7, 1979, a poster was affixed to the inside of the same shop window in a similar manner.

B   It was contended by the prosecutor that the posters in the shop window constituted an advertisement and a publication of each of the posters. The prosecutor did not have to establish that the sign indicated that the premises were a licensed betting office because that was a different offence under section 10 (5) (*a*) of the Act. The geographical position of the sign did not matter. What did matter was the fact that the sign could be seen by members of the public who passed the window.

C   The poster inside the window was clearly as much of a publication as if it had been outside the window.

It was contended by the defendants that the posters themselves did not constitute advertisements because they made no reference to betting activities or to the purpose of, and facilities available at, the premises.

The stipendiary magistrate dismissed the informations. In view of

D   that decision he made no adjudication on whether the actual posters constituted an advertisement.

The questions for the opinion of the High Court were (1) whether an advertisement affixed to the inside of a clear glass window of a licensed betting office and facing outwards, legible from outside but not legible from inside the office, was published outside the premises; and (2) whether to constitute an advertisement for the purposes of section

E   10 (5) (*c*) of the Betting, Gaming and Lotteries Act 1963, an advertisement which draws attention to the facilities provided by licensed premises had to state as a fact that the premises to which it was affixed was a licensed betting office.

F   *John Marriage Q.C.* and *Rodney Smith* for the defendants, Windsors (Sporting Investments) Ltd.

Stephen Williamson for the prosecutor in the first case.

Alan Jones for the prosecutor in the second case.

Gareth Williams Q.C. and *Anthony Evans* for the defendants, Coral Racing Ltd. and Mrs. Howells.

G   *Cur. adv. vult.*

January 30. The following judgments were read.

DONALDSON L.J. Windsors (Sporting Investments) Ltd. are part of the William Hill Group of bookmakers with a licensed betting office at 12, The Green, Idle, Bradford. On April 9, 1979, Chief Inspector Old-

H   field preferred informations charging them (i) with publishing an advertisement drawing attention to the facilities afforded to persons resorting to that office contrary to section 10 (5) of the Betting, Gaming and Lotteries Act 1963, and (ii) with exhibiting signs on licensed premises which did not comply with regulation 3 (2) of the Betting (Licensed Offices) Regulations 1960, contrary to section 10 (1) of the Betting, Gaming and Lotteries Act 1963.

1180

Windsors were acquitted by the Bradford justices of the charge under A
the regulations, but convicted of the charge under section 10 (5). They
appealed unsuccessfully against that conviction to Bradford Crown Court.
They now appeal again, this time by means of a case stated by Bradford
Crown Court.

Coral Racing Ltd., as its name implies, is a part of the Coral group
of companies and has a licensed betting office in Market Street, Bridgend,
Mid Glamorgan. The office was managed by Barbara Ann Howells. On B
September 20, 1979, Chief Superintendent Sidney Boulton laid informations against Coral Racing and their manageress, charging them with
two separate offences of publishing advertisements contrary to section
10 (5) (c) of the Act. The stipendiary magistrate dismissed the charges
and the police now appeal by case stated.

Both appeals are in the nature of test cases and both raise the question C
of whether it is permissible for advertisements to be " put up," to use a
neutral term, *inside* the window of a licensed betting office in such a
way that they cannot, or cannot normally, be read by anyone inside the
betting office, but are fully visible to passers-by and others outside the
office. We have accordingly heard the two appeals together and this
judgment relates to both.

So far as is material, the scheme of the Act appears to be to provide D
two different zones of control, namely, (a) of the betting office itself
and of premises giving access to such an office and (b) elsewhere. Control
in the case of the betting office and of premises giving access to it is by
section 10 (1), rules contained in Schedule 4 to the Act and the Betting
(Licensed Offices) Regulations 1960 which were continued in force by
section 57 (3) of the Act. Control elsewhere is by section 10 (5) of the E
Act. On any view the window of a betting office is on the interface of
these two zones and it is this which has given rise to the problem.

Section 10 (5) of the Act is in the following terms:

" If, save in a licensed betting office or in such manner as may be
prescribed on premises giving access to such an office, any advertisement is published—(a) indicating that any particular premises are a F
licensed betting office; or (b) indicating where any such office may
be found; or (c) drawing attention to the availability of, or to the
facilities afforded to persons resorting to, such offices, then, in the
case of an advertisement in connection with the office or offices of
a particular licensee, that licensee, and in every case any person who
published the advertisement or caused or permitted it to be published, G
shall be guilty of an offence: Provided that it shall be a defence for
any person charged with an offence under this subsection to prove—
(i) that he did not know and had no reasonable cause to suspect that
the advertisement was, and that he had taken all reasonable steps
to ascertain that it was not, such an advertisement as aforesaid; or
(ii) if he is charged by reason only of being a licensee, that the H
advertisement was published without his consent or connivance and
that he exercised all due diligence to prevent the publishing of any
such advertisement in connection with his office or offices."

Regulation 3 of the Regulations provides as follows:

" (1) The holder of a betting office licence shall exhibit in a conspicuous manner and in some conspicuous place inside the licensed

A   premises a notice stating that persons under the age of 18 years are
       not admitted thereto. (2) The holder of a betting office licence shall
       inside the licensed premises exhibit no written matter or sign of any
       description other than the betting office licence and the notice
       required to be exhibited by paragraph (1) of this regulation, except: —
       (a) in such manner that the matter exhibited cannot be read from
       outside those premises, the rules subject to which betting transactions
B   are effected on those premises and information relating to events in
       connection with which betting transactions may be or have been
       effected thereon, and a page containing such information taken from
       a newspaper may be exhibited under this sub-paragraph notwith-
       standing that it does not consist solely of such information; . . ."

C   I do not think I need bother with (b) and (c).
          In *Windsors'* case, it is not now disputed that the posters which were
       displayed constituted an advertisement drawing attention to the avail-
       ability of, or to the facilities afforded to persons resorting to, licensed
       betting offices. That issue has not been decided in the *Coral* case and
       does not arise for our decision. However, in the interests of simplicity
       I shall assume that the Coral posters also constitute such advertisements.
D   This is not the first time upon which section 10 (5) and the Regula-
       tions have been considered by this court. In *Roy William Robinson Ltd.
       v. Cox* (1968) 67 L.G.R. 188 the bookmaker exhibited a facia-like sign on
       the outside wall of the betting office and over its full length bearing his
       name and the words: " Licensed Betting Office. Open 11 a.m. daily."
       He was charged and convicted under section 10 (5). On appeal to the
E   Divisional Court it was held, not surprisingly, that this notice was not in
       the betting office or on premises giving access to the betting office and
       so within the exception to section 10 (5). However, Lord Parker C.J.
       said, at p. 195:

          " I confess that I have fought against coming to that conclusion
          because it seems to me that there can be no harm whatever in
F   having a sign on the outside of the building, as there was in this
          case, when one realises there is nothing in the Act or Regulations to
          prevent a similar sign, indeed not confined in area and size, appear-
          ing on the inside of the plate glass window facing outside, and
          therefore giving exactly the same advertisement from the inside of
          the office as in the present case appears from the outside of the
G   office."

       Ashworth J. and Willis J. agreed.
          In *Dunsford v. Pearson* [1970] 1 W.L.R. 222 the bookmaker who
       may have been familiar with the decision in *Roy William Robinson Ltd.
       v. Cox,* 67 L.G.R. 188 placed two notices reading " Turf Accountant "
       in the window of the betting office in such a way that they were visible
H   from the highway, but not from inside the office. He was prosecuted
       for breach of regulation 3 of the Regulations of 1960. On appeal his
       acquittal was affirmed because this court held that there was no breach
       of regulation 3 unless the notice could be seen by those inside the
       premises. Ashworth J. put it, at p. 227:

          " Really the issue before this court can be confined in the nutshell
          of ' does exhibition inside involve the proposition that what is ex-

hibited must be visible inside? ' [Counsel for the appellant] put it   A
in exactly that form, that in order to render the present licensee
liable for contravention of the regulation, the notice which he
exhibited must have been exhibited in such a form that it was visible
inside. That is the view which was indicated in *Roy William Robinson Ltd.* v. *Cox*, 67 L.G.R. 188, and it is the view which I take here."

Lord Parker C.J. and Cantley J. agreed. Both Lord Parker C.J. and   B
Ashworth J. affirmed the dictum of Lord Parker C.J. in *Roy William
Robinson Ltd.* v. *Cox*, but this affirmation was no more necessary to the
decision than the original dictum since the bookmaker was charged
under the Regulations and not under section 10 (5).

In *Reg.* v. *Newcastle-upon-Tyne Gaming Licensing Committee,
Ex parte White Hart Enterprises Ltd.* [1977] 1 W.L.R. 1135, the Court
of Appeal was concerned with the Gaming Act 1968, under which a   C
notice of intended application for a licence must be " displayed outside
the entrance to the relevant premises." The prospective licensee placed
the notice on the inside of the window of the premises facing outwards
and this was held to constitute displaying the notice outside the premises.

The stipendiary magistrate felt that he should follow the twice affirmed
dictum of Lord Parker C.J. and, in his position, I should unhesitatingly   D
have done the same. Bradford Crown Court felt free to depart from
this dictum. This may have been a bold decision, but if the deputy
circuit judge was convinced that the dictum was wrong, he was right to
do so. He said:

" We were of the opinion that the advertisement was published outside the licensed betting office because although it was fixed inside   E
it was not visible inside and was clearly visible to anyone outside the
said premises. We interpreted the subsection as banning the publication of advertisements visible on the outside to passers-by. The
point of publication is not where the advertisement is fixed but where
it is read."

In this court we have to give great weight to such a dictum, but it is not   F
binding upon us and it is necessary that we should decide the point.

These advertisements were clearly published, exhibited and displayed.
On the binding authority of *Dunsford* v. *Pearson* [1970] 1 W.L.R. 222,
they were not exhibited in the betting offices, because they were not
visible to anyone in the premises. Were it otherwise an offence would
have been committed under regulation 3. On the binding authority of   G
Reg. v. *Newcastle-upon-Tyne Gaming Licensing Committee, Ex parte
White Hart Enterprises Ltd.* [1977] 1 W.L.R. 1135 these posters were
displayed outside the premises. It would in my view be anomalous to
hold that, although they were not exhibited in the betting office, and
were displayed outside it, they were not published outside the betting
office, and I am quite satisfied that, as a matter of law, they were so   H
published. This conclusion is in my judgment fatal to the appeal of
Windsors (Sporting Investments) Ltd. and I would dismiss it.

In the *Coral* case we are also asked " Whether to constitute an
advertisement for the purposes of section 10 (5) (*c*) of the Betting, Gaming
and Lotteries Act 1963, an advertisement which draws attention to the
facilities provided by licensed premises must state as a fact that the

A premises to which it is affixed is a licensed betting office." I would answer that there is no reason whatsoever why the advertisement should state that the premises to which it is affixed is a licensed betting office. The offence is committed if it is affixed to a hoarding deep in the country, provided only that it draws attention to the availability of, or to the facilities afforded to persons resorting to, such offices. However, I imagine that the question is really directed to the fact that the section is only

B concerned with advertising the availability etc. of licensed betting offices, that is offices involved with cash as opposed to credit betting. This is of course correct and the prosecution will have to satisfy the court that the advertisement concerned did extol the virtues of a licensed betting office or offices. The fact that an advertisement is displayed on or near a licensed betting office may well be a potent factor in deciding upon the

C meaning to be attributed to any particular advertisement. But that would be a matter for the court charged with deciding issues of fact and not for this court.

I think therefore that the *Coral* case will have to be remitted to the stipendiary magistrate for him to consider such further issues as whether the posters constituted an advertisement. He may also have to consider

D the proviso to section 10 (5). As to that I would only say that if the defendants did not know that their poster was such as to contravene section 10 (5) (and I do not see how they could have known this in the light of the state of the art) and if they had considered and accepted the advice contained in the dicta in *Roy William Robinson Ltd.* v. *Cox,* 67 L.G.R. 188 or *Dunsford* v. *Pearson* [1970] 1 W.L.R. 222, I should have

E thought that they had an absolutely impregnable defence—on this occasion, but not in future.

FORBES J. Shorn of all irrelevancies the subsection makes it an offence to publish an advertisement otherwise than inside a betting office. To publish an advertisement both inside and outside is thus an offence. The

F sole question is therefore whether in the circumstances of these cases the advertisement were published solely inside the offices.

It is clear that the advertisements could not be read from inside but only from outside the offices. Both these organisations are commercial enterprises. The only possible commercial purpose of placing, to use a neutral term, material of this character in the windows could have been

G to advertise to those outside the offices the name or the activities of these organisations. The primary meaning of to "publish" is to "make public." The proposition that advertisements placed inside the offices in such a way as to be invisible to anyone inside while on the other hand visible to and clearly aimed at persons outside the offices are published inside but not outside does such violence to the common usage of language

H that for myself I could not accept that this is what Parliament intended.

There is nothing in any report of *Robinson's* case to suggest that any argument about the effect of section 10 (5) was ever addressed to this court on that occasion. Had they had the advantage of hearing the arguments addressed to us, I feel no doubt that neither Lord Parker C.J. nor Ashworth J. would have committed themselves to a dictum which can now be seen to be not only obiter but also per incuriam. As such I think this court must be justified in holding itself free not to follow it.

1184

Forbes J. **Windsors Ltd. v. Oldfield (D.C.)** [1981]

For myself I would be content to rule that an advertisement is not pub- A
lished solely inside premises if, as here, it is clearly visible to and intended
to be read by persons outside.

I have used the term " advertisements " as if the material placed in
these windows properly fell within the meaning of that word. The question of whether or not any material is an advertisement will depend, in
individual cases, on what that material is, and will thus be a question of
fact for the justices to decide. I agree that *Coral's* case must go back B
to the magistrate to consider whether the poster in the window was an
advertisement.

If it is objected that this ruling will mean that it is an offence even to
indicate that premises, other than premises in multiple occupation, are in
fact a betting office I would only say that this would appear to conform
to the clear intention of Parliament that these establishments should be C
difficult to find and, when found, should be internally as dreary as possible.

*Appeal in Windsors (Sporting Invest-
ments) Ltd. v. Oldfield dismissed.
Appeal in Boulton v. Coral Racing
Ltd. allowed and case remitted D
to magistrate for further consideration.
Certificate that point of law of public
importance involved, namely,
" Whether, for the purposes of
section 10 (5) of the Betting,
Gaming and Lotteries Act 1963, E
an advertisement affixed to the outside of a clear glass window of a
licensed betting office and facing
outwards, legible from outside but
not legible from inside the office,
is published outside the premises."
Leave to appeal refused.* F

Solicitors: *Gosschalk, Wheldon & Co., Hull; M. D. Shaffner, Wakefield; J. M. Timmons, Cardiff; John Morse & Co., Swansea.*

R. D. G

A

[FAMILY DIVISION]

*PRACTICE DIRECTION
(PROBATE: REPRESENTATION GRANT)

B *Probate — Practice — Representation, grant of — Fee payable on grant—Form of oath—Inland Revenue account not required for excepted estate — Capital Transfer Tax (Delivery of Accounts) Regulations 1981 (S.I. 1981 No. 880), art. 4—Non-Contentious Probate Fees Order 1981 (S.I. 1981 No. 861 (L. 4)), art. 3, Sch.*

C The Inland Revenue have laid before Parliament the Capital Transfer Tax (Delivery of Accounts) Regulations which provide that in certain types of case therein specified, it will no longer be necessary to deliver an Inland Revenue account for the purposes of applying for a grant of representation. It is anticipated that, subject to acceptance, the Regulations will come into force at the beginning of August 1981.

As from August 3, 1981, the Non-Contentious Probate Fees Order 1981 D (S.I. 1981 No. 861) will provide, inter alia, for the payment of a flat fee of £40 on application for a grant of representation in cases in which the net value of the estate passing under the grant exceeds £10,000 but does not exceed £25,000. No fee will be payable if the value does not exceed £10,000.

Consequently as from that date, in those cases in which an Inland Revenue account is not required to be delivered, it will be sufficient to E state in the oath to lead the grant the brackets into which the estate falls. Every oath must contain a statement by the applicant as follows: —

" To the best of my knowledge, information and belief the gross estate passing under the grant does not exceed/amounts to *£
and that the net estate does not exceed/amounts to *£
[and that this is not a case in which an Inland Revenue Account is F required to be delivered] *

The alternatives marked with an asterisk should be deleted as appropriate.

In addition, as from that date, every oath must state the age of the deceased. In those cases in which the exact age is not known, the applicant should give the best estimate he can.

G It is to be emphasised however that inquiries as to whether or not an Inland Revenue account must be delivered in any particular case should *NOT* be made to the Probate Registries, but to the Capital Taxes Office, Minford House, Rockley Road, London W14 0DF.

R. L. BAYNE-POWELL,
Senior Registrar.

H *June* 23, 1981.

[1981]

A

[COURT OF APPEAL]

* ROOTKIN *v.* KENT COUNTY COUNCIL

1980 April 24, 25   Lawton and Eveleigh L.JJ.
                                       and Sir Stanley Rees

B

*Education — School — Education authority, statutory duties of —
Travelling expenses — Pupil mistakenly thought to be living
over three miles away from school—Season ticket granted—
Whether authority entitled to revoke season ticket after discovering mistake in mileage—Whether authority estopped—
Education Act 1944 (7 & 8 Geo. 6, c. 31), ss. 39 (5), 55 (2)
(as amended by Education (Miscellaneous Provisions) Act 1948
(11 & 12 Geo. 6, c. 40), s. 11, Sch. 1, Part I)*

C

In the spring of 1976 the applicant, whose daughter was
then 12 years of age and had been going to a junior school
near her home, was invited by the defendant council, as the
local education authority, to nominate two or more schools
in her order of preference. The applicant gave her two
choices, stating that she had selected the first school because
other schools were some distance from her home and would
mean the daughter using public transport at extra expense.
In July 1976 the applicant was notified that her daughter was
allocated to the school of her second choice. Her appeal
against the decision was unsuccessful. At an interview with
the divisional education officer she was told that the second
school was not more than three miles from her house; thus,
it was within walking distance as defined by section 39 (5) of
the Education Act 1944.[1] But shortly afterwards the distance
was measured and found to be more than three miles. By a
letter dated July 30, 1976, the education officer informed the
applicant of that, and in September 1976, when her daughter
started going to that school, she was given a season ticket
pursuant to section 55 (2) of the Act. At that time the
applicant abandoned any further rights to appeal against
the school allocation. Owing to a complaint by parents of
another pupil who had been refused a season ticket the
relevant distances were re-measured and it was found that
the distance between the applicant's house and the school
was about 175 yards less than three miles. The education
officer informed the applicant that her daughter was not
entitled to a season ticket and withdrew it. The applicant
protested and solicitors made representations on her behalf to
the council. She also sent a medical report by her doctor,
the effect of which was a recommendation that the daughter
should not walk to school. The council's own doctor examined the daughter and came to the contrary conclusion.
The appropriate council committee reviewed the whole matter
and decided not to issue a season ticket. The applicant
applied for leave to apply for judicial review of that decision
but the Divisional Court refused leave. On appeal against
that refusal the Court of Appeal granted leave.

On the hearing by the Court of Appeal of the application
for judicial review: —

Held, dismissing the appeal, (1) that since the applicant
did not have a right, on the relevant facts being established,
but was only entitled to the benefit of the exercise of the
council's discretion under section 55 (2) of the Education Act

D

E

F

G

H

[1] Education Act 1944, s. 39 (5): see post, p. 1193H.
S. 55 (1) (2): see post, pp. 1192H—1193A, B–C, H.

A   1944, the council's decision was not irrevocable; that the
education officer, as a duly authorised officer of the council
entitled to exercise the council's discretion under section 55 (2),
having made his decision to grant the applicant a season ticket
under a mistake of fact, he was duty bound to reconsider the
matter when he found that a mistake about the distance had
been made (post, pp. 1194G—1195A, B–C, 1197B–C).

B   *Livingstone* v. *Westminster Corporation* [1904] 2 K.B.
109 and *In re 56 Denton Road, Twickenham* [1953] Ch. 51
distinguished.

Per Sir Stanley Rees. The letter of July 30, 1976, did not
purport to be an exercise of a discretion under section 55 (2)
but was an acceptance of the statutory obligation on behalf
of the council to pay the fare of this child on the basis that
the distance exceeded three miles (post, p. 1198C–D).

C   (2) That it was a general principle of law that the doctrine
of estoppel could not be used against a local authority for the
purpose of preventing it from using a statutory discretion but
that, in any event, the applicant had not so altered her
position as to entitle her to rely on the doctrine; that the
council were entitled to take the view, as a matter of policy,
that there was a rebuttable statutory presumption that a child
of 12 and upwards could walk to and from school a distance
of up to three miles, and since there was nothing physically

D   wrong with the applicant's daughter and there were no
particular hazards about the route that presumption was not
rebutted, and accordingly the council had acted reasonably
(post, pp. 1195G—1196C, D–F, G—1197A).

Southend-on-Sea Corporation v. *Hodgson (Wickford) Ltd.*
[1962] 1 Q.B. 416, D.C. applied.

Western Fish Products Ltd. v. *Penwith District Council*
(1978) 77 L.G.R. 185, C.A. considered.

E
The following cases are referred to in the judgments:

Associated Provincial Picture Houses Ltd. v. *Wednesbury Corporation*
      [1948] 1 K.B. 223; [1947] 2 All E.R. 680, C.A.
Denton Road, Twickenham, In re 56 [1953] Ch. 51; [1952] 2 All E.R.
      799.
Lever Finance Ltd. v. *Westminster (City) London Borough Council*
F   [1971] 1 Q.B. 222; [1970] 3 W.L.R. 732; [1970] 3 All E.R. 496,
      C.A.
Livingstone v. *Westminster Corporation* [1904] 2 K.B. 109.
Southend-on-Sea Corporation v. *Hodgson (Wickford) Ltd.* [1962] 1 Q.B.
      416; [1961] 2 W.L.R. 806; [1961] 2 All E.R. 46, D.C.
Surrey County Council v. *Ministry of Education* [1953] 1 W.L.R. 516;
      [1953] 1 All E.R. 705.
G   *Western Fish Products Ltd.* v. *Penwith District Council* [1981] 2 All
      E.R. 204; (1978) 77 L.G.R. 185, C.A.

No additional cases were cited in argument.

APPEAL from the Divisional Court of the Queen's Bench Division.

The respondents, the Kent County Council (" the council ") refused to
H   grant the applicant, Mrs. Pamela Patricia Rootkin, an allowance under
section 55 (2) of the Education Act 1944, as amended by section 11 and
Part I of Schedule 1 to the Education (Miscellaneous Provisions) Act
1948, for the cost of the transport for her daughter, Helen, from home
to school on the grounds that the school was within " walking distance "
as defined by section 39 (5) of the Act, that Helen was a healthy child
and that there were no hazards on the way to make it necessary for the
council to make the allowance.

The Divisional Court (Waller L.J. and Parke J.) refused leave for a   A
judicial review on November 20, 1979, and the Court of Appeal (Lord
Denning M.R., Bridge L.J. and Sir David Cairns) gave leave on December
3, 1979.   By her notice of appeal dated December 14 the applicant
appealed on the grounds (1) that the decision of the council in July 1976
that the applicant qualified for the provision of free travel was irrevocable;
(2) that the council was estopped from denying the truth of the facts upon
which the decision was based, namely that the distance between the   B
applicant's home and the school was three miles or more: in the premises
the council was bound to provide free travel under the provisions of the
Education Act 1944 as amended, and, in so far as any subsequent decision
of the council in relation to the provision of free travel was based wholly
or in part on the fact that the distance was less than three miles,
such decision was invalid and of no effect; (3) that without prejudice to   C
the grounds (1) and (2) above, the purported decision of the council on
November 18, 1976, that the applicant was not entitled to the provision
of free travel was in excess of jurisdiction and void in that:—(a) having
found that the distance was less than three miles the council was bound
to exercise its discretion under section 55 (2) of the Act in relation to
the provision of free travel but failed to do so, (b) the decision was made
under a misapprehension by the council that when such distance was   D
under three miles it had no power to provide free transport or to assist
with the cost thereof; alternatively, the decision was wrongfully made
pursuant to a policy that in such circumstances no such provision or
assistance should be given, and (c) the council failed to take into account
matters relevant to the exercise of its discretion under the section 55 (2),
namely the applicant's financial circumstances, and the health of her   E
daughter; (4) that without prejudice to grounds (1) to (3) above, the
purported decision of the council on May 17, 1978, not to give any
assistance with the cost of travel was in excess of jurisdiction and void
in that the council failed properly or at all to take into account the
applicant's financial circumstances or the fact that she had in July 1976
abandoned her objection to her daughter's attending the school she was
allocated to in reliance on the council's decision of July 30, 1976, and   F
the assurance that the provision of free travel would not be withdrawn,
and in that the decision was inconsistent with and contradictory to the
previous decision of July 30, 1976, and was in all the circumstances of
the case unreasonable.

By a respondent's notice dated April 15, 1980, the council sought
to affirm the decision on the following additional grounds: (1) that the   G
council's power to grant a travelling allowance to a pupil under section
55 (2) of the Act of 1944 was exercisable from time to time; (2) that
the council was not bound by the fact that it granted a travel allowance
to the applicant's daughter for the academic year 1976–77 to grant the
daughter a travelling allowance for future years; (3) that the council's
decision to grant a travel allowance to the applicant's daughter was not a
statutory determination and was revocable; (4) that reviewing its decision   H
to grant a travel allowance to the applicant's daughter, the council was
under a misapprehension of fact; (5) that in reaching its decision to grant
a travel allowance to the applicant's daughter, the council mistakenly considered that it was obliged to grant the allowance; (6) that the council did
not purport to exercise its discretionary power under section 55 (2) of the
Act of 1944 to grant a travel allowance to the applicant's daughter before
coming to its decision of July 30, 1976, as the applicant well knew;

A (7) that in the premises, when the council later exercised its discretion and refused to grant to applicant's daughter a travel allowance for later academic years it was not estopped from so doing; (8) that the applicant did not change her position, or did not do so sufficiently to involve the doctrine of estoppel as a result of the council's letter of July 30, 1976; (9) that the applicant did not act to her detriment, or did not do so sufficiently, to invoke the doctrine of estoppel as a result of the council's letter

B of July 30, 1976; (10) that the council did not intend that the applicant should be influenced in any decision regarding the choice of school for her daughter by the letter of July 30, 1976; (11) that in taking its decision on May 17, 1978, not to grant a travel allowance to the applicant's daughter the council (a) considered that it had power to grant a travel allowance although the pupil lived within three miles of the school, (b)

C took into account all relevant circumstances and did not take into account irrelevant circumstances and (c) did not apply a rigid policy; (12) that the council's decision of May 17, 1978, was not irrevocable; (13) that the applicant's sole remedy was by way of complaint to the Secretary of State for Education under sections 68 and 99 of the Act of 1944; (14) that the council did not misuse its powers; (15) that in the premises the council could not be estopped in performing its statutory functions; and (16) that

D the applicant could not use estoppel as a sword to create a cause of action.

The facts are stated in the judgment of Lawton L.J.

John Powles for the applicant, Mrs. Rootkin.
Gregory Stone for the council.

E LAWTON L.J. In form this is an appeal by the leave of this court by the applicant, Mrs. Pamela Patricia Rootkin, against a refusal of the Divisional Court for leave to move for a judicial review of a decision made by the Kent County Council whereby the council refused to grant Mrs. Rootkin an allowance for the cost of the transport for her daughter from home to school. It is accepted by both parties that on the hearing

F of this appeal this court has jurisdiction to consider the merits of the appeal.

Mrs. Rootkin claims that she is entitled to be given a grant for the cost of transport from home to school for her daughter Helen. She says that when she first applied for the cost of transport, the council refused; then they said she could have it and they issued a yearly season ticket for her daughter; after about three months they purported to withdraw

G that season ticket; and thereafter they refused to grant any other season ticket or to reimburse Mrs. Rootkin in any other way for the cost of transport.

The council say that they issued a season ticket under a mistake of fact believing that they had a duty to issue one. When they discovered they were wrong on the facts as they became known to them, they

H exercised their right to withdraw the season ticket and thereafter, in the proper exercise of their discretion, they refused to grant any other season ticket or to reimburse Mrs. Rootkin for the cost of transport for her daughter.

Mrs. Rootkin through her counsel says that once the council had decided to issue a season ticket, they could not go back on that decision. Alternatively, as a result of what they did, Mrs. Rootkin altered her position with the consequence that the council are estopped from saying

1190

that they were entitled to refuse the grant of a season ticket. Alternatively   A
that in any event they exercised their statutory powers unreasonably.

The council for their part say that once they discovered they had made
a mistake of fact they were entitled to revoke their earlier decision and
they have in no way acted unreasonably, and that the doctrine of estoppel
would not apply in this case, first because the law does not allow
estoppel to be used to prevent a local authority exercising their statutory
discretion and, in any event, there was not such a change in circumstances   B
on the part of Mrs. Rootkin on the wrong decision of the council as to
justify the doctrine of estoppel being brought into operation. Those are
the broad issues in this case.

Mrs. Rootkin is what has come to be known as the head of a one
parent family. She is divorced; she has two children of whom one is the
girl Helen who is now 15 years of age. In 1976 that child was 12. Mrs.   C
Rootkin was living with her children in the Gillingham area. Helen had
been to a primary school and at the age of 12 the time had come for her to
move from primary education to secondary education. In the spring of
1976 the council, as the local education authority, had the task of allocating a secondary school for Helen. They also had the duty, as far as was
practicable, to comply with the wishes of her parent. As a result, in the   D
spring of 1976, Mrs. Rootkin in common with a number of other parents
in a similar situation, was told what facilities were available for the
children and she was asked what school she would like her daughter to go
to. Mrs. Rootkin returned a form which she had been sent, saying that
her first choice was for the Rainham Girls Secondary School and her
second choice was for the Upbury Manor Secondary School. On the back
of the form she said: E

"I have selected one school for Helen as the other schools are some
distance from our home and would mean also using public transport.
Being a one parent family it would mean extra expenses for
travelling."

I do not myself think it necessary to go into the details of Mrs.   F
Rootkin's finances; they are very personal to her. It suffices to say that
she is in straightened circumstances and for my part I readily appreciate
that every single penny is of importance to her and if she could save
money in bus fares for Helen, then she was being prudent in trying to
do so.

Her choice, however, could not be met. Rainham Girls Secondary
School, which was near Mrs. Rootkin's house, was over subscribed. It   G
followed that her second choice had to be considered. There was a
vacancy in the Upbury Manor School, and Mrs. Rootkin was told that.
Under the arrangements made by the council in these sort of circumstances, parents are given an opportunity of appealing against any decision
about the allocation of schools. Mrs. Rootkin exercised her right of
appeal and she appeared before an appeal panel. In the course of the   H
presentation of her case she said that one of the reasons why she had
chosen Upbury Manor School was that she understood it was more than
three miles from her home, and in those circumstances, she would be
entitled, as of right, to be reimbursed the cost of travel by public transport for Helen from home to school. She went on to say, rather surprisingly in the circumstances, that although there was another school,
Woodlands, which was nearer her home and to which Helen could have

A gone, she did not want her to go to that school because she felt she would
have to pay bus fares as that school was about one mile from Helen's
home.   There is no reason to think there were any particular hazards
about the route from home to Woodlands School, so it seems a little
unreasonable at first sight for Mrs. Rootkin to have taken the view that
Helen could not be expected to walk a mile to school.   However, that
was her attitude.

B   She was then told by the divisional educational officer, Mr. Evans,
that Upbury Manor School was not more than three miles from her home
and she would not in those circumstances, for reasons to which I shall
refer later in this judgment, be entitled to reimbursement for the cost of
transport from home to school.   She seems however, to have been content
at that stage with sending Helen to Upbury Manor School.

C   Shortly afterwards, Mr. Evans caused the route from Helen's home to
the school to be measured by being driven over by somebody in a motor
car with the distance measured on the ordinary car speedometer.   When
this was done, the reading showed that the difference from home to school
was just over three miles.   That would have entitled Mrs. Rootkin to be
reimbursed for the cost of transport.   She was so informed by letter dated
D July 30, 1976.

At the beginning of September, Helen started attending the Upbury
Manor School and because it was more than three miles from her home,
the council issued her with a bus season ticket which was valid until the
end of July 1977.   Helen seems to have been one of a number of girls
who lived in the same area of Gillingham and they too had been granted
season tickets on the basis that their homes were more than three miles
E from the school.   But another pupil at the school had been refused a
season ticket on the ground that his home was less than three miles away.
Inevitably the parent of that pupil complained, pointing out that some
children in the neighbourhood were getting bus season tickets and
others were not.   The inference was that a mistake had been made by
someone.   As a result, the divisional educational officer, Mr. Evans,
F decided that the proper course would be to have the distance properly
measured in respect of pupils who had been given bus season tickets.   That
was done with an instrument known as a trumeter, and when it was
done the measurement in Helen's case was found to be 175 yards less than
three miles.   As a result of that discovery, Mr. Evans decided that Helen
was not entitled under the law, as he understood it, to be granted a bus
season ticket.   By letter dated November 18, he informed Mrs. Rootkin
G and said that the bus season ticket was withdrawn.

Mrs. Rootkin, understandably, was both upset and annoyed by this.
She was upset because the cost of transport at that time was at about the
rate of £120 per annum and she felt that she could not afford it.
Secondly, she was annoyed because there had been a reversal of a decision
by the council and she did not think that was right.   She had an interview
H with Mr. Evans about the reversal of the decision.   It is not clear from
the affidavit what was discussed at that interview.   It suffices to say that
she was invited to think over the situation which had arisen and there
was evidence before this court that at mid-November Helen could have
been transferred from the Upbury Manor School to Woodlands School.
Whether that was specifically put to Mrs. Rootkin at the meeting with
Mr. Evans in November 1976 is not clear.   Mrs. Rootkin did consider the
matter and she felt aggrieved.   She then consulted solicitors, and from

November 1976 right up to the present time she has been represented by solicitors. From time to time they made representations on her behalf to the council.

One of the reasons why Mrs. Rootkin felt that Helen had to go to school by public transport and not have to walk a distance of just under three miles was that Helen had had bronchitis and Mrs. Rootkin thought with a tendency towards bronchitis, a long walk to and from school, certainly in the winter months, would not be in Helen's interests. She consulted her doctor just before the beginning of the school term in 1977. The doctor wrote a report dated September 2, 1977, the effect of which was that he recommended that Helen should not walk to school. That report was sent to the council. The council asked a doctor in their employment to examine Helen. He came to the conclusion, and so advised the council, that Helen's physical condition was satisfactory and there was no reason, from a health point of view, why she should not walk three miles to and from school.

The result of all that was that the council decided not to issue a season ticket to Helen and she has never since had one.

Mrs. Rootkin's solicitors continued to press for a review of Helen's case. In May 1978 her case was reviewed by the appropriate committee of the council and it was decided not to issue any season ticket to her.

It is against that background of fact that Mrs. Rootkin applied for leave for a judicial review. She was somewhat tardy in making her application to the Divisional Court. She had learned of the decision of the committee of the council in May 1978, but she made no attempt to apply to the Divisional Court until September 1979. When she did apply it was during the long vacation, and the vacation judge decided that her application did not amount to vacation business and stood it over to be dealt with by the Divisional Court in the Michaelmas Term. It was heard by that court in November 1979 and leave to move for a judicial review was refused; we have been informed by counsel that one of the factors which was mentioned as being a ground for refusing leave was the tardiness with which the application had been made. Mrs. Rootkin at once applied to this court for leave to appeal against the refusal and this court granted leave in December 1979.

Mr. Stone, without pressing the matter, invited our attention to the tardiness in which the application had been made. Mr. Powles, on behalf of Mrs. Rootkin, has invited our attention to the provisions of R.S.C., Ord. 53, r. 4 which deals with delay in applying for relief. It seemed to us that under the terms of that rule we ought not to deal with this matter on the basis of delay unless we were satisfied that the delay would be detrimental—and I use the words of the order—" to good administration." There is nothing in this case to lead me to think that the tardiness of the application in any way puts the council in a difficulty. I approach this case solely on the general merits and on the law applicable.

The law applicable is to be found in the Education Act 1944, as amended. Section 55 is the governing provision which enables local educational authorities to make payments for transport for pupils attending school. Subsection (1) reads:

"A local education authority shall make such arrangements for the provision of transport and otherwise as they consider necessary or as the Secretary of State may direct for the purpose of facilitating the attendance of pupils at schools or county colleges or at any course

A   or class provided in pursuance of a scheme of further education in force for their area, and any transport provided in pursuance of such arrangements shall be provided free of charge."

That is the statutory provision which enables local education authorities to provide school buses. The provision of school buses is sometimes inconvenient, and it is found better to provide money so that the pupils can

B get to school and have their bus fares or train fares provided for by the local education authority. The enabling power for such payment is contained in subsection (2) which reads:

> "A local education authority may pay the whole or any part, as the authority think fit, of the reasonable travelling expenses of any pupil in attendance at any school or county college or at any such
C   course or class as aforesaid for whose transport no arrangements are made under this section."

It is relevant to bear in mind that subsection (2) gives the local authority a discretion and a wide one. It is not bound, on the face of that subsection, to pay anybody anything. It is an enabling section and when it does decide to pay, it can use its discretion as to whether it shall pay the whole or any part of the reasonable travelling expenses. It is the

D exercise of that discretion in the circumstances of this case which we have to review.

Oddly, the provision which has attached a good deal of public attention about the distance children have to walk to school comes under a penal section of the statute, namely section 39. A local education authority is bound by statute to provide educational facilities for children, and

E parents are bound to take advantage of those educational facilities for the benefit of their children, and if they do not do so, they become subject to penalties under the provisions of section 39.

Section 39, in its relevant parts reads:

> "(1) If any child of compulsory school age who is a registered pupil at a school fails to attend regularly thereat, the parent of the child
F   shall be guilty of an offence against this section. (2) In any proceedings for an offence against this section in respect of a child who is not a boarder at the school at which he is a registered pupil, the child shall not be deemed to have failed to attend regularly at the school by reason of his absence therefrom with leave or . . . (c) if the parent proves that the school at which the child is a registered pupil is not within walking distance of the child's home, and that no suitable
G   arrangements have been made by the local education authority either for his transport to and from the school or for boarding accommodation for him at or near the school or for enabling him to become a registered pupil at a school nearer to his home."

Section 39 (5) defines what is meant by " walking distance," and the relevant parts of that subsection are:

H

> ". . . and the expression ' walking distance ' means, in relation to a child who has not attained the age of eight years two miles, and in the case of any other child three miles, measured by the nearest available route."

This is why the three mile limit is so important because if the child lives more than three miles from the school, then the parents are provided with a defence under section 39 (2). It is because there was the defence

based upon distance from the school that in *Surrey County Council* v. A
Ministry of Education [1953] 1 W.L.R. 516 it was adjudged that the effect
of section 39 was to impose a duty on a local education authority to
provide transport or to reimburse the cost of reasonable travelling expenses for any child who lived more than three miles from a school.

This provision seems to have been known to Mrs. Rootkin, and
probably to many other parents, and is what led her, when she appeared
before the appeal panel which heard applications for review of allocations, B
to say that she wanted the child to go to Upbury Manor School because
it was more than three miles from her home and that Helen would thereby
become entitled to have her travelling expenses paid by the council.

The council accepts for the purposes of this appeal, that in any case
where the child lives more than three miles from a school they must pay
the reasonable travelling expenses. On the other hand they submit that C
where the child lives less than three miles from the school, there is a
rebuttable presumption that the child is capable of walking to school and
does not require to be reimbursed for the cost of travelling by public
transport. They accept that they must look at the circumstances of each
child. If the child has to walk less than three miles but by a hazardous
route, then it may be appropriate to exercise the discretion given by D
section 55 (2) to pay reasonable travelling expenses. Similarly, if the child
is of a weak constitution and is physically incapable of walking up to three
miles from home to school, that is another reason for paying reasonable
travelling expenses.

But, says the council, as a matter of policy, that as long as the child
is physically capable of walking up to three miles and there are no special
circumstances, such as a hazardous route, in getting to school, then the E
child should walk.

Counsel for the council has informed this court that that is a policy
which is followed not only by the defendant council but by many other
county councils. For my part I can see nothing wrong in the council
following that policy.

In this case there is evidence that when it was submitted to them that F
it might be a strain for Helen to walk to school because of her previous
attack of bronchitis, they did reconsider the matter but came to the conclusion that the evidence before them was insufficient to justify their
changing their policy on that ground.

It is against that background that I now have to look at what happened
in this case. The council, at the end of July 1976, did decide to exercise G
their discretion under section 55 (2). It is accepted that the officer who
so decided , Mr. Evans, was duly authorised by them to make the decision.
He made his decision under a mistake of fact, namely, that the difference
from Helen's home to the school was more than three miles. On the basis
of that mistake of fact, and pursuant to the decision in *Surrey County
Council* v. *Minister of Education,* he, as an officer of the defendant H
council authorised to exercise his discretion, was bound to authorise the
reimbursement to Mrs. Rootkin of the cost of travelling. He performed
his duty by authorising the issue of a yearly bus ticket. But when the
mistake of fact was discovered in November 1976, he was duty bound, as
I see it, to the council to reconsider the matter because, on the facts as he
knew them in November 1976, there was no duty to issue a bus season
ticket to Helen. I can see no reason in law why he should not have

A reconsidered the matter when he found that a mistake had been made about the distance.

It was submitted to us on the authority of a number of cases of which the last in order of time was *In re 56 Denton Road, Twickenham* [1953] Ch. 51 that what Mr. Evans was doing was making a determination, and having once made a determination, he was not entitled to go back on it. In my judgment, that is a misconception.

B It is the law that if a citizen is entitled to payment in certain circumstances and a local authority is given the duty of deciding whether the circumstances exist and if they do exist making the payment, then there is a determination which the local authority cannot rescind. That was established in *Livingstone* v. *Westminster Corporation* [1904] 2 K.B. 109. But that line of authority does not apply in my judgment to a case where

C the citizen has no right to a determination on certain facts being established; but only to the benefit of the exercise of a discretion by the local authority. The wording of section 55 (2) is far removed from the kind of statutory working which was considered in *In re 56 Denton Road, Twickenham* and *Livingstone* v. *Westminster Corporation.* I cannot, for my part, see any basis for the submission that the decision of Mr. Evans in July 1976 was irrevocable when he found out what the true facts were.

D I turn now to the second head of the submission on behalf of Mrs. Rootkin, namely that the council were estopped from revoking their decision. The way that argument was put was as follows: it was said that Mrs. Rootkin was put into a false position in July 1976 when she was told that Helen's travelling expenses would be paid. At that time she decided to abandon any further rights of appeal she might have against the allocation of Helen to Upbury Manor School. She could have appealed to the

E education officer of the council and if she got no satisfaction out of him, she had statutory rights of appeal to the Secretary of State for Education under the provisions of sections 68 and 99 of the Act of 1944.

It was said that relying upon the assurance given to her about reimbursement of travelling expenses, she decided not to exercise any other

F rights she might have had.

Further, it is said that in September 1976 Helen started at this school on the assurance that her travelling expenses would be paid, but by mid-November 1976 she had settled into the school and that it would have been unreasonable for Mrs. Rootkin to have taken Helen away from a school which she liked and had settled into and put her, half-way through the term, into another school. One can see the human side of this. Children

G do not like being uprooted from one school to another.

It seems to me that there are two answers to the submission based upon estoppel. First, it is a general principle of law that the doctrine of estoppel cannot be used against local authorities for the purpose of preventing them from using the statutory discretion which an Act of Parliament requires them to use. That principle was established clearly

H in *Southend-on-Sea Corporation* v. *Hodgson (Wickford) Ltd.* [1962] 1 Q.B. 416.

The cases relating to estoppel as against local authorities were reviewed by this court in *Western Fish Products Ltd.* v. *Penwith District Council* (1978) 77 L.G.R. 185, when judgment in that case was given on May 22, 1978. In the course of that judgment; which was of the court, it was pointed out that the principle in *Southend-on-Sea Corporation* v. *Hodgson (Wickford) Ltd.* [1962] 1 Q.B. 416 was generally applicable, and that the

only exceptions were where there was proper delegation by a local   A
authority of the power to make determinations. Again, for the reasons
I have already given, in my judgment there was no determination in the
sense used in *Western Fish Products Ltd.* v. *Penwith District Council,* 77
L.G.R. 185, by Mr. Evans when he decided to issue a yearly bus season
ticket to Helen.

But even if that were not the position in law, it seems to me that Mrs.
Rootkin had not so altered her position as to entitle her to rely upon the   B
doctrine of estoppel. She had the benefit of legal advice from November
1976 onwards and no doubt she was well advised not to attempt to exercise
any statutory rights of appeal which she had to the Secretary of State.
She was probably advised that the Secretary of State was not likely to
interfere with the discretion exercised by a local authority about a matter
of this kind. In addition, as I have already said, there was not much   C
likelihood of upset so far as Helen was concerned. True it might have
been more satisfactory if Helen could have remained at Upbury Manor
School. On the other hand, it is difficult to see how she would have been
prejudiced in any real way by being moved, if Mrs. Rootkin had decided
to move her, to Woodlands School.

This case in my judgment is a very long way away from the kind of   D
situation where there is prejudice such as to bring into operation the
doctrine of estoppel.

Finally, I come to the question whether in all the circumstances of
this case the council can be said to have used their statutory powers
under section 55 (2) in an unreasonable way, so as to entitle this court
to interfere. This court can only interfere with the exercise of discretion
by statutory bodies on the grounds set out and recognised as being good   E
in law in *Associated Provincial Picture Houses Ltd.* v. *Wednesbury Corporation* [1948] 1 K.B. 223. Here the defendant council had a policy
which, as I have already stated, cannot be faulted. They were entitled
to take the view that there was a rebuttable statutory presumption that a
child of 12 and upwards could walk to and from school a distance of up
to three miles. There was nothing wrong physically with Helen; there
were no particular hazards about the route which she took, and the fact   F
that her mother was apprehensive and would have preferred her to go by
public transport than to walk, was an irrelevant consideration. I can see
nothing unreasonable about the way the council exercised their discretion.
For my part, I can see no reason why this court should interfere.

Accordingly, I would dismiss the appeal.

  G

EVELEIGH L.J. I agree. This appeal does in the end come down to an
attempt to control the discretion of the education authority by reason of
estoppel. If the distance was over three miles, then the Education Act
1944 in effect creates a duty to provide transport: see *Surrey County
Council* v. *Ministry of Education* [1953] 1 W.L.R. 516.

Therefore, if an authority had provided the cost of transport for one   H
year because the distance was in fact over three miles, it would inevitably
renew the grant for the next year because it would be under a duty so to
do.

In the present case, it could not be said that there was a duty to renew
the grant, for the distance was under three miles, and the authority cannot
impose upon itself a duty by a mistaken assumption of facts when that
duty, arises only if in truth the distance is over three miles.

A   There was no doubt a discretion in this case, under section 55 (2) of the Act of 1944; that discretion must be exercised freely and cannot be thwarted by estoppel: see *Southend-on-Sea Corporation* v. *Hodgson (Wickford) Ltd.* [1962] 1 Q.B. 416.

Counsel has argued that the decision to pay the fare was irrevocable, even if mistaken, and he has relied upon the principle in *Livingstone* v. *Westminster Corporation* [1904] 2 K.B. 109. That principle of irrevoca-
B   bility may well be applicable when there is a power or a duty to decide questions affecting existing legal rights. In *Livingstone* v. *Westminster Corporation* itself the council were concerned to assess compensation for loss of office, to which compensation the plaintiff had a right under the Local Government Act 1899. Generally speaking, however, a dis-
cretionary power may be exercised from time to time unless a contrary
C   intention appears. I can see nothing in the Education Act 1944 to prevent the education authority from reviewing its decisions from time to time—when the decision is under section 55 (2) which is claimed to be applicable in this case.

I too would dismiss this appeal.

D   SIR STANLEY REES. In view of the judgments which have been delivered by Lawton and Eveleigh L.JJ., I can state my views very shortly. When the question arose in April 1976 as to the choice of secondary school for the child Helen, the mother, Mrs. Rootkin, made her position very clear in early 1976 in a document which was despatched to the school and which has been read by Lawton L.J. It is plain from that document and from the evidence that Mrs. Rootkin took a very strong
E   view on two points. The first was that it was undesirable for this child, Helen, to walk a distance of three miles, or even up to one and a half miles as appeared from other evidence in the case, and that she attached great importance to that point. The medical evidence of the family doctor has already been read in the judgment of Lawton L.J. and it is plain that both Mrs. Rootkin and the family doctor took the view that there was a
F   bronchitic condition affecting this child which made it desirable that she should not walk a distance of three miles or any distance of that order.

The second was that it was plain to all concerned that Mrs. Rootkin, being a mother having the care and control of two daughters who were then aged about 11 and 9, was attempting to keep herself and the two daughters on an extremely small allowance—and indeed, was seeking to supplement that income by working part time herself as a school meals
G   attendant. Those factors run throughout this case and accordingly for the reasons which she made plain, she would prefer the child to go to a school at Rainham very close to the home, but if that were not possible then to Upbury Manor School which was, as she was led to believe, about three miles away and therefore would qualify for a grant towards the bus fare.

When she learned of the decision in May 1976 that her request that
H   the child should go to the school at Rainham had been turned down and she had been offered her second choice, Mrs. Rootkin was content with the second choice, provided that transport could be paid for by the council but she appealed. She lost her appeal on July 29, 1976, and she was handed a letter on that date, which I need not read, indicating that the child would go to Upbury Manor School.

Up to that stage the distance to the school had been calculated upon a map as being, as I think, within three miles. It was recalculated by means

1198

of a trip in a motor car, and as a result the school authorities then A
accepted that the distance was over three miles. As a result the divisional
education officer wrote the letter of July 30, 1976, in which this sentence
appears:

> ". . . A further distance check has been made from your home to
> the Upbury Manor Secondary School gates, and as the distance has
> been confirmed as three miles, you will qualify for free travel for B
> Helen."

Now that letter and the decision in it, which was conveyed to Mrs.
Rootkin, was made by the divisional education officer and it is plain
from the evidence (and is conceded by counsel on behalf of the council)
that Mr. Evans had had delegated to him the power under section 55 (1)
of the Act of 1944 to make the grant of the payment of the fare for the C
child.

I venture to express the view that that letter did not in fact purport
to be in the exercise of a discretion under section 55 (2) but was an
acceptance of the statutory obligation on behalf of the council to pay
the fare of this child on the basis that the council were obliged to do so
because the distance exceeded three miles—which has been referred to
in section 39. D

Accordingly, upon the receipt of that letter there was, as I venture to
think, an exercise of a power in pursuance of a duty on the basis that
the distance involved exceeded three miles. So that in my respectful view
Mr. Evans was exercising the power delegated to him, and he accepted,
that once the distance exceed three miles he was bound to grant payment
to the mother for this child. There can be no doubt at all that he knew E
from all that had passed, that Mrs. Rootkin would take the view, as
plainly he did also, that so long as the child resided at that address, and
remained at Upbury Manor School, the council would be obliged, in
pursuance of their duty under section 55 (1) (and not under section 55 (2))
to pay the bus fare of this child.

In these circumstances, having received that letter and having taken F
the view that the problem with which she had been faced since April 1976
had at last been resolved in her favour, and before the child went to the
school, she abandoned all further efforts to have the child moved to a
school nearer to Rainham and accepted the offer which had been made.
As a result, it is strongly argued that she altered her position.

Then the letter of November 18, 1976, came and she learnt that the
distance had been measured for a third time—on this occasion by means G
of a meter—and found to be between 300 and 175 yards less than three
miles. The council then required Mrs. Rootkin to return the ticket which
had been issued to her. She was obviously very upset but she took the
view that since she had been misled by the offer made to her that the
school fare would be paid for the whole time that the child was at
the school; that the child had gone to the school and was settling in it,
that she was entitled in the child's interests to allow her to continue at H
Upbury Manor School. Therefore she perfectly understandably refused
to return the season ticket which lasted for one year and the child
continued to attend the school.

There is the factor which disclosed the vital importance she attached
to protecting Helen from a 5½-mile walk to and from school that despite
her exiguous income which ranged over the material time between about

A £32 a week to about £39 a week, for three people to live on, she somehow managed to pay for the fares for her child to travel to school after the period of the season ticket expired. We were not given precise figures, but over the whole period, excluding the first year, it seems that the amount of money involved is something between £400 and £500. Somehow this mother managed to find that money.

B She continued with her efforts to enable the child to receive a free ticket. I need not go at any length into what she did, because the evidence before us is very clear that she appealed to the council and the council then of course were only able to grant the ticket to Mrs. Rootkin if they could properly do so under section 55 (2) as a matter of discretion. That, as Lawton L.J. has pointed out, is a matter with which this court would only interfere in the most exceptional circumstances.

C Accordingly, the case put by Mr. Powles is on the ground that the decision to grant the ticket to Mrs. Rootkin and to pay the fare during the whole of the school life of the child at this particular school was the exercise of a statutory duty arising under a combination of section 55 (2) and the provisions of section 39 of the Act of 1944. He put the case in its simplest form on behalf of Mrs. Rootkin in this way: that the council,

D through its proper delegated officer, decided that as a matter of duty, they were obliged to pay the fares of this child. That was communicated to Mrs. Rootkin, and Mrs. Rootkin rightly understood that that was a decision binding upon the council, and accordingly she acted upon it to her detriment, as it subsequently turned out. Despite all efforts by way of appeal to the council she was not able to achieve the result she thought right for her child, as a matter of discretion, and accordingly in

E those circumstances she came to this court and did not choose to exercise her right of appeal to the Secretary of State under sections 68 and 99 of the Act which we are considering.

Mr. Powles relied upon the decision of this court in *Lever Finance Ltd.* v. *Westminster (City) London Borough Council* [1971] 1 Q.B. 222 and in particular to a passage in the judgment of Lord Denning M.R.

F to which I shall refer in a moment. In the headnote Lord Denning M.R.'s utterance is summarised in these words, at p. 223:

" A public authority may be bound by a representation made by one of its officers within the scope of his ostensible authority on which another acts. As in the case of a company, a person dealing with a local authority is entitled to assume that all necessary internal resolu-

G tions have been passed."

In the instant case the question of ostensible authority did not arise because the authority was accorded to Mr. Evans by his council and he exercised it, and Mrs. Rootkin sent her child to this school in the firm belief that he had the power to grant payment of the fare for the whole time that the child went to this school and for so long as she resided

H at her present address.

Lord Denning M.R. referred to the facts of the case, which was a planning matter, and he said, at p. 230:

" Things may arise which were not foreseen. It should not be necessary for the developers to go back to the planning committee for every immaterial variation. The permission covers any variation which is not material. But then the question arises: Who is to decide whether a variation is material or not? In practice it has been the

Sir Stanley Rees   Rootkin v. Kent C.C. (C.A.)   **[1981]**

planning officer. This is a sensible practice and I think we should   A
affirm it. If the planning officer tells the developer that a proposed
variation is not material, and the developer acts on it, then the
planning authority cannot go back on it. I know that there are
authorities which say that a public authority cannot be estopped by
any representations made by its officers. It cannot be estopped from
doing its public duty: see, for instance, the recent decision of the
Divisional Court of *Southend-on-Sea Corporation* v. *Hodgson (Wick-*   B
ford) Ltd. [1962] 1 Q.B. 416. But those statements must now be
taken with considerable reserve. There are many matters which
public authorities can now delegate to their officers. If an officer,
acting within the scope of his ostensible authority, makes a representation on which another acts, then a public authority may be bound
by it, just as much as a private concern would be."
    C

And, says Mr. Powles, the present case is stronger than that, as Mr. Evans
had the actual authority delegated to him and he granted the right for
this child's transport to be covered. In those circumstances, he argues
that respondents are bound by that decision.

    I have thought it proper to canvass at some length the powerful
arguments addressed to us by Mr. Powles and also to refer to the merits   D
of the matters in favour of Mrs. Rootkin. Nevertheless for the reasons
stated in the judgments of Lawton and Eveleigh L.JJ., but with regret,
I am bound to agree that this court has no power to make the order
sought on behalf of Mrs. Rootkin.

    I therefore also agree that the appeal should be dismissed.

    E

Appeal dismissed, with costs, to be
paid by the legal aid fund.
Order not to be drawn up for eight
weeks to allow the legal aid fund
to be notified of the Court of
Appeal's intention to order costs.
Legal aid taxation.   F

    Solicitors: *Robbins, Olivey & Lake for Booth, Hearn, Stratton &*
Roberts, Chatham; Solicitor, Kent County Council.

    A. R.

    G

A

[PRIVY COUNCIL]

* CHIN CHOY Alias CHIN CHONG KIM
AND Others . . . . APPELLANTS

AND

B COLLECTOR OF STAMP DUTIES . . . . RESPONDENT

[APPEAL FROM THE FEDERAL COURT OF MALAYSIA]

1981 May 5;   Lord Wilberforce, Lord Fraser of Tullybelton.
      June 8   Lord Roskill and Sir Ninian Stephen

C *Malaysia—Land—Stamp duty—Date for assessing market value—
    Contract of sale followed by statutory memorandum of transfer
    —Collector's assessment at date of execution of memorandum
    —Whether proper—Stamp Ordinance 1949 (No. 59 of 1949)
    (as amended by Stamp (Amendment) Act 1967 (No. 60 of
    1967), Sch. 1), s. 12A*

Section 12A of the Stamp Ordinance 1949 (as amended)
D   provides:
        " For the purpose of assessing the value of any property
      which is the subject of transfer . . . such value shall be
      taken to be— . . . (b) the market value, as on the date of
      execution, of the property transferred . . ."
        On October 30, 1971, a purchaser executed a sale and pur-
      chase agreement with a developer to buy land for $49,000.
      That agreement was duly stamped. On June 26, 1973, the
E   developer, complying with the requirements of the National
      Land Code for transferring the legal title to land, executed a
      memorandum of transfer to the purchaser. The purchaser paid
      to the Collector of Stamp Duties ad valorem stamp duty based
      on the purchase price of $49,000 recited in the 1971 sale
      agreement. The collector applying section 12A (b) of the
      Stamp Ordinance 1949 (as amended) assessed the market
      value of the land as it had been on June 26, 1973, at $65,000
F   and demanded ad valorem duty based on that sum. The pur-
      chaser appealed to the High Court which upheld the
      assessment. On the purchaser's appeal the Federal Court dis-
      missed the appeal.
        On the purchaser's appeal to the Judicial Committee: —
        Held, dismissing the appeal, that although " execution "
      bore different meanings according to the context in which it
      was used, in the context of section 12A (b) of the Stamp
G   Ordinance 1949 (as amended) its meaning was unambiguous
      and referred to the instrument of transfer by means of which
      legal title to the land was transferred to the purchaser; accord-
      ingly, the collector had rightly assessed the market value of
      the land as it had been on June 26, 1973, when the developer,
      as transferor, had executed the memorandum of transfer.
        Decision of the Federal Court of Malaysia affirmed.

H
The following cases are referred to in the judgment of their Lordships:
    Brown (Christopher) Ltd. v. *Genossenschaft Oesterreichischer* [1954] 1
      Q.B. 8; [1953] 3 W.L.R. 689; [1953] 2 All E.R. 1039.
    Fothergill v. *Monarch Airlines Ltd.* [1981] A.C. 251; [1980] 3 W.L.R.
      209; [1980] 2 All E.R. 696, H.L.(E.).
    Lewisham London Borough Council v. *Lewisham Juvenile Court
      Justices* [1980] A.C. 273; [1979] 2 W.L.R. 513; [1979] 2 All E.R.
      297, H.L.(E.).

A

The following additional cases were cited in argument:

Black-Clawson International Ltd. v. *Papierwerke Waldhof-Aschaffen-burg A.G.* [1975] A.C. 591; [1975] 2 W.L.R. 513; [1975] 1 All E.R. 810, H.L.(E.).

Kirkness v. *John Hudson & Co. Ltd.* [1955] A.C. 696; [1955] 2 W.L.R. 1135; [1955] 2 All E.R. 345, H.L.(E.).

Lysaght v. *Edwards* (1876) 2 Ch.D. 499.

Russell v. *Scott* [1948] A.C. 422; [1948] 2 All E.R. 1, H.L.(N.I.).

B

APPEAL (No. 26 of 1979) by the applicant purchasers, Chin Choy alias Chin Chong Kim, Hoe Chooi Peng, Loo Kam Fatt, Chia Ah Kon alias Chia Siew Seng, Pong Kim Ho alias Poong Kim Hua, Ng Ah Yam alias Ng Lee Cheng, Koh Chee Lin, Yow See Kow, Au Hong How Kai, Anthonysamy s/o Joseph, Au Ngan Chan, See Tho Meng, Low Kum Seng, Yong Kwai alias Yong Moke Ying, Soo Heng Choong, Ong Cheow Phine alias Ong Chau Phin, Choong Swan See, Wha Yoke Kee, Wong Kok Kuang alias Wong Kok Kion, Loh Yuet Keng, Wong Kok Thye alias Wong Kok Ngang, Wong Yet Soo and Lo Yoke Lin with leave of the Federal Court of Malaysia from a decision (September 25, 1978) of the Federal Court (Lee Hun Hoe C.J., Borneo, Wan Suleiman and Chang Min Tat F.JJ.) by which it dismissed the applicants' appeal from a decision (June 3, 1977) of Abdul Hamid J. in the High Court of Malaysia confirming assessments of value for stamp duty made by the respondent, the Collector of Stamp Duties, Selangor.

C

D

The applicants challenged the collector's assessments by originating motion dated October 9, 1973, stating that they, as transferees under various memorandums of transfer, were dissatisfied with the assessments and that they severally and jointly gave notice of appeal. They required the collector to state a case for the opinion of the High Court pursuant to section 39 (2) of the Stamp Ordinance 1949.

E

The facts are stated in the judgment of their Lordships.

P. S. Gill (of the Bar of West Malaysia) for the purchasers.

Stewart Bates Q.C. and *Stephen Allcock* for the Collector of Stamp Duties.

F

Cur. adv. vult.

June 8. The judgment of their Lordships was delivered by LORD ROSKILL.

Though these appeals are 23 in number, it is common ground that each raises the same question regarding liability to ad valorem stamp duty chargeable in accordance with section 12A of the Stamp Ordinance 1949 of the Federation of Malaya, as amended by the Stamp (Amendment) Act 1967, of Malaysia, and that the decision of their Lordships, as of the courts below in a single appeal, will determine all the appeals. Their Lordships are therefore concerned only with the appeal of the fourth appellant (" the purchaser ") who on October 30, 1971, executed a sale and purchase agreement with a developer to buy certain property in Kuala Lumpur for the purchase price of $49,000. That agreement was properly stamped for $1 in accordance with item 4 of Schedule 1 to the Stamp Duty (Special Provisions) (Malaysia) Act 1967.

G

H

On June 26, 1973, the developer executed a memorandum of transfer of the property so previously agreed to be sold to the purchaser. That memorandum of transfer was in form 14A and in all respects complied

A with the relevant requirements of the National Land Code for the purpose of transferring to the purchaser the legal title to the property which he had previously agreed to buy. Indeed that legal title could be obtained only by registration in accordance with the provisions of that Code.

B The memorandum of transfer was submitted to the Collector of Stamp Duties, together with a copy of the stamped agreement, the relevant information required by section 5 of the Stamp Ordinance 1949, and ad valorem stamp duty of $490 being one per cent. of $49,000, the consideration stated in the memorandum of transfer. The collector however assessed the market value of the property as at June 26, 1973, at $65,000 and accordingly assessed the stamp duty payable at $650, being one per cent. of $65,000. The purchaser thereupon paid the

C difference of $160. Notice of appeal was subsequently filed against this assessment and a case was stated for the opinion of the court pursuant to section 39 (2) of the Stamp Ordinance 1949.

On June 3, 1977, Abdul Hamid J. upheld the assessment made by the collector. An appeal by the purchaser and others to the Federal Court was dismissed on March 22, 1978. Leave to appeal was granted by the

D Federal Court on November 6, 1978.

In their Lordships' opinion the issue raised by this appeal turns upon the true construction of section 12A of the Stamp Ordinance 1949, as amended by Schedule 1 to the Stamp (Amendment) Act 1967. That section which bears the side note " Assessment of the value of property under transfer or settlement " reads:

E " 12A. For the purpose of assessing the value of any property which is the subject of a transfer or settlement, such value shall be taken to be—(a) the money value, if any, mentioned in the instrument of transfer as the consideration for the transfer or settlement; or (b) the market value, as on the date of execution, of the property transferred or settled, whichever be the greater: Provided that the officer before whom the instrument of transfer is tendered for regis-

F tration may accept the consideration mentioned therein as being the market value, unless he shall have reason to believe otherwise."

The principal submission for the purchaser was that in the context of section 12A the words in paragraph (b) " the market value, as on the date of execution, of the property transferred or settled," must be construed as referring to the execution of the sale and purchase

G agreement dated October 30, 1971, and not to the memorandum of transfer dated June 26, 1973, by which time the value of the property in question had substantially appreciated. " Execution," it was said, was a word capable of bearing several meanings. In this context there was an ambiguity in its use and that ambiguity should be resolved in favour of the taxpayer and not the collector. Their Lordships do not doubt

H that the word " execution " can bear different meanings according to the context in which the word is used. In the context in which the word was used in Christopher Brown Ltd. v. Genossenschaft Oester- reichischer [1954] 1 Q.B. 8 Devlin J. thought its use ambiguous. But ambiguity in one context does not of necessity involve that its use in another and widely different context is also ambiguous. In their Lord- ships' view, as already stated, everything turns upon the context.

Much emphasis was laid by counsel for the purchaser in his argument upon the existence in Malaysia of the Torrens system and upon the A differences between that system and conveyancing practice in England. Nonetheless counsel also contended that the effect of the agreement of October 30, 1971, was to transfer the equitable title of the property to the purchaser notwithstanding that the legal title could only be transferred by registration in accordance with the National Land Code. The collector was prepared to concede that the equitable title was transferred on that date and in that manner. However, the principle that once a B valid contract for sale is concluded the vendor becomes in equity a trustee for the purchase of the estate sold is a peculiarity of English land law. But section 6 of the Civil Law Ordinance 1956 of the Federation of Malaya expressly provides that nothing in that part of that statute should be taken to introduce into the Federation " any part of the law of England relating to the tenure or conveyance or assurance of or C succession to any immoveable property or any estate, right or interest therein." It is not, however, necessary for their Lordships further to pronounce upon this question in the present appeal.

Counsel for the purchaser invited their Lordships' attention to the text of the bill which led to the enactment of the Stamp (Amendment) Act of 1967 and thus to the introduction of section 12A. His purpose D in so doing was to draw attention to the relevant part of the explanatory statement dealing with what became section 12A of that Act. That relevant part stated that this provision was designed to prevent evasion by " the common practice of under-valuing the property by showing a false consideration, less than the true consideration, in the instrument of transfer." Counsel asserted that this was the mischief at which the new provision was aimed and accordingly the section should not be E construed as having a wider effect than was necessary in order to achieve that stated purpose. Their Lordships are quite unable to accept this reasoning. Even if it were permissible to have regard to this part of the explanatory statement for the purpose of construing the section, its existence could not properly be used to give to the words of the statute a more restricted meaning than that which those words naturally F bear upon their true construction. It by no means follows that because the relevant provision was aimed at one particular target its effect may not have been more far-reaching.

The submission for the purchaser, in their Lordships' view, involves reading into paragraph (b) of section 12A words which are not to be found in that paragraph. For the paragraph to bear the meaning contended for it would have to read: G

" . . . market value, as on the date of the execution of the agreement of sale, or, if there be no such agreement of sale, of the memorandum of transfer of the property transferred or settled."

Their Lordships can find no justification for so drastically rewriting this paragraph. The language of paragraph (b), it is true, does not include H any express reference to a memorandum of transfer. But its provisions cannot be divorced from the opening words of the section which refer expressly to " transfer or settlement " as does paragraph (a) of the section. Accordingly, it seems to their Lordships clear that the context in which the language of paragraph (b) is used is one expressly related to instruments of transfer by means of which legal title to the property will be transferred to the purchaser. It follows that, in complete agree-

A ment with the courts below, their Lordships are unable to find any ambiguity in the use of the word "execution."

Counsel for the purchaser also relied upon the provisions of section 2 of the Stamp Duty (Remission) Order 1979 made on April 19, 1979. Their Lordships were informed by counsel that the purpose of this provision was to reverse the effect of the decision of the Federal Court in the instant appeal. It was argued that the existence of this Order
B showed that the intention of the legislature in enacting section 12A must have been to limit the incidence of liability in the manner contended for by the plaintiff. In their Lordships' view it is quite impermissible to construe section 12A by reference to this later amending Order: see *Lewisham London Borough Council* v. *Lewisham Juvenile Court Justices* [1980] A.C. 273, 282 *per* Viscount Dilhorne: "The meaning
C of an unamended section of the earlier Act is not altered by amendments made by the later one." See also *Fothergill* v. *Monarch Airlines Ltd.* [1981] A.C. 251, 288, 301.

In the result their Lordships find themselves in complete and respectful agreement with the conclusions reached in both courts below and will advise His Majesty the Yang di-Pertuan Agong that the appeal should be dismissed with costs.
D

Solicitors: *Philip Conway, Thomas & Co.; Stephenson Harwood.*

T. J. M.

E

[COURT OF APPEAL]

In re A DEBTOR (No. 6864 of 1980),
Ex parte THE DEBTOR v. SLATER WALKER LTD.

F 1981 May 18, 19   Eveleigh and Watkins L.JJ. and
                                                      Sir David Cairns

*Bankruptcy—Bankruptcy notice—Application to set aside—
    Debtor's counterclaim, set-off or cross-demand—Affidavit—
    Time for filing—Whether jurisdiction in court to extend
    beyond 10 days from service of bankruptcy notice—Bank-
    ruptcy Act 1914 (4 & 5 Geo. 5, c. 59), ss. 1 (1) (g), 109 (4) (as
G   amended by Insolvency Act 1976 (c. 60), s. 4)[1]—Bankruptcy
    Rules 1952 (S.I. 1952 No. 2113), rr. 137 (b), 138, 139 (as
    amended by Bankruptcy (Amendment) Rules 1977 (S.I. 1977
    No. 364), rr. 1 (3), (2)[2]*

On May 13, 1980, the creditors issued a writ against the debtor claiming the repayment of money lent. By letter dated July 16, 1980, the debtor acknowledged that he had no
H defence to the action and confirmed that, in consideration of the creditors' agreement not to sign judgment in default of defence for three months from June 5, 1980, he would not enter a defence to the action and would take no other steps to defend it and would consent to the creditors entering judgment against him on September 5, 1980, for the full amount

[1] Bankruptcy Act 1914, s. 1 (1) (g): see post, p. 1208c–E.
    S. 109 (4): see post, p. 1209c–D.
[2] Bankruptcy Rules 1952, r. 139: see post, pp. 1207G—1208A.

1206

of their claim, namely £432,702·60 with interest and costs.   A
On September 30, 1980, the creditors signed judgment against
him.   On January 22, 1981, they served a bankruptcy notice
on him in the prescribed form requiring him to satisfy the
debt within ten days or satisfy the court that he had a counterclaim, set-off or cross-demand as prescribed by section 1 (1) (g)
of the Bankruptcy Act 1914.   No affidavit stating that he had
a counterclaim was filed within the seven days prescribed by
the notice pursuant to rules 137 and 138 of the Bankruptcy   B
Rules 1952.   On February 4, 1981, the creditors presented a
bankruptcy petition.   On February 13, 1981, the debtor filed
an affidavit alleging that he had a counterclaim or counterclaims and applied to the registrar to fix a date for the hearing
of his deemed application to set the bankruptcy notice aside.
His affidavit did not specifically aver that the amount of his
counterclaim or counterclaims was equal to or exceeded the
amount of the judgment debt.   The registrar refused to extend   C
the time for filing the affidavit and accordingly dismissed the
debtor's application.
        On appeal by the debtor: —
        Held, dismissing the appeal, that the court had jurisdic-
tion under section 109 (4) of the Bankruptcy Act 1914 to
extend the seven days prescribed by rule 138 of the Bankruptcy Rules 1952 for the filing of the debtor's affidavit and
to do so retrospectively; but that, once the 10 days prescribed   D
by section 1 (1) (g) of the Act of 1914 had expired without
an affidavit being filed, the debtor had committed an act of
bankruptcy and the court had no jurisdiction to extend either
the 10 days or the seven days so as to overcome that consequence.

The following case is referred to in the judgment of Eveleigh L.J.:
                                                                 E
Debtor (No. 138 of 1980), In re A, The Times, January 29, 1981; 125
    S.J. 133, C.A.

The following additional cases were cited in argument:

Dearle, Ex parte, In re Hastings (1884) 14 Q.B.D. 184, C.A.
Foster, In re, Ex parte Basan (1885) 2 Morr. 29, C.A.
Greenwood v. Martins Bank Ltd. [1933] A.C. 51, H.L.(E.).   F
Lennox, In re, Ex parte Lennox (1885) 16 Q.B.D. 315, C.A.

APPEAL from Mr. Registrar Wheaton.
    The debtor appealed from the order of the registrar whereby he
refused either to set aside the bankruptcy notice, no. 6864 of 1980, filed
by the creditors, Slater Walker Ltd., or to extend the time for the filing of
an affidavit by the debtor under rules 137 to 139 of the Bankruptcy   G
Rules 1952 or to fix a time and place for the hearing of the debtor's
application to set aside the notice or to extend the time for complying
with it pursuant to rule 139, seeking an order that the time for filing
the affidavit be extended, that a time and place be fixed for the hearing
of the debtor's application and that the time for complying with the
notice be extended, on the grounds that the registrar had erred in law   H
in failing to hold that he had power under section 109 (4) of the Bankruptcy Act 1914 to extend the time for the service of the debtor's
affidavit under rules 137 to 139 of the Rules of 1952 beyond the date
of prima facie expiry of the bankruptcy notice; that he had erred in
exercising his discretion not to extend the time for service of the affidavit
by holding the debtor's reasons to be insufficient grounds for its
exercise and by failing to give any or any sufficient weight to the debtor's

A grounds and evidence; and that he had erred in holding that the debtor's counterclaim or cross-claim could have been raised in the action in which judgment had been obtained, within the meaning of rules 137 to 139 of the Rules of 1952.

The facts are set out in the judgment of Eveleigh L.J.

B *Gabriel Moss* for the debtor.
Michael Crystal for the creditors.

EVELEIGH L.J. On May 13, 1980, Slater Walker Ltd. issued a specially indorsed writ against the debtor claiming the repayment of money lent. On July 16, 1980, the debtor wrote a letter, addressed to " The Directors, Slater Walker Ltd.," in the following terms:

C "Dear Sirs, High Court Action 1980 S. No. 2866 Yourselves v. Myself. I hereby acknowledge and accept that I have no defence to the above action ('the action'). I further confirm that, in consideration of your agreement not to sign judgment in default of defence for a period of three months from June 5, 1980, I will not enter a defence to the action and will take no other steps to defend the action and I will consent to Slater Walker Ltd. entering
D judgment against me on September 5, 1980, for the full amount of your claim, namely, £432,702·60 together with interest and costs."

On September 30, 1980, judgment was signed against him. On January 22, 1981, a bankruptcy notice was served. That was in the prescribed form and stated that execution had not been stayed and that
E he was required within 10 days to satisfy the debt or to satisfy the court that he had a counterclaim, set-off or cross-demand that " equals or exceeds the sum claimed." The notice concluded by saying:

"If, however, you have a counterclaim, set-off or cross-demand which equals or exceeds the amount claimed by Slater Walker Ltd. in respect of the judgment and which you could not set up in the action or other proceedings in which the said judgment was
F obtained, you must within seven days apply to this court to set aside this notice, by filing with the registrar an affidavit to the above effect."

The 10 days in fact expired, allowing for dies non, on February 3, 1981. The last sentence of the notice that I have just quoted reflects the Bankruptcy Rules 1952, in particular rule 137, which requires every
G notice to be indorsed with an intimation to the effect stated.

The filing of such an affidavit is made to operate as an application to set aside the bankruptcy notice. That is the effect of rule 139 (1), which reads:

"The filing of the affidavit referred to in rule 137 shall operate as an application to set aside the bankruptcy notice, and thereupon
H the registrar shall, if he is satisfied that sufficient cause is shown, fix a time and place for hearing the application, and shall give not less than three clear days' notice thereof to the debtor, the creditor, and their respective solicitors, if known."

Paragraph (2) reads:

"If the application cannot be heard before the time specified in the notice for compliance with its requirements, the registrar shall

extend the time, and no act of bankruptcy shall be deemed to have   A
been committed under the notice until the application has been
heard and determined."

Rule 138 prescribes the time for filing the affidavit, which in the case
of a notice served in England is seven days.

If an affidavit had been filed in time the registrar would have had
to ask himself if he was satisfied that sufficient cause was shown and,   B
on being so satisfied, he would then have had to fix a date for hearing
the application. In fact in this case nothing at all was done. No affidavit
was filed. The debt was not satisfied. Therefore, on February 3, 1981,
the debtor had committed an act of bankruptcy. That is the effect of
section 1 (1) (g) of the Bankruptcy Act 1914. Section 1 (1) begins:
" A debtor commits an act of bankruptcy in each of the following
cases: — . . ." There are then listed a number of cases, and (g) reads: C

   " If a creditor has obtained a final judgment or final order against
   him for any amount, and, execution thereon not having been stayed,
   has served on him in England, or, by leave of the court, elsewhere,
   a bankruptcy notice under this Act, and he does not, within 10 days
   after service of the notice, in case the service is effected in England,
   and in case the service is effected elsewhere, then within the time   D
   limited in that behalf by the order giving leave to effect the service,
   either comply with the requirements of the notice or satisfy the
   court that he has a counterclaim, set-off or cross-demand which
   equals or exceeds the amount of the judgment debt or sum ordered
   to be paid, and which he could not set up in the action in which the
   judgment was obtained, or the proceedings in which the order was   E
   obtained: . . ."

On February 4, 1981, a bankruptcy petition was presented. On
February 13 the debtor filed an affidavit and applied to the registrar to
fix a date for the hearing of his application to set aside the bankruptcy
notice. In his affidavit he alleged that he had a counterclaim or
counterclaims. There is no need for me to list them in detail. Suffice   F
it to say that one related to the selling of his shares by Slater Walker,
which he alleges were sold at too low a price. Another claim related to
an alleged agreement to refund interest to him, which interest was
payable under a separate agreement granting a loan. It was alleged
that interest then had not been paid. It was further alleged in the
affidavit that the debtor was unable to set up the claim in the action.
The reason for that was the letter of July 16, 1980. The affidavit did   G
not specifically aver that the amount of the counterclaim was equal to
or exceeded the amount of the judgment debt. Indeed, for my part,
I find it quite impossible to arrive at any sort of figure for the alleged
counterclaim.

The registrar refused to extend the time for filing the affidavit. He
said that the reasons given by the debtor were insufficient and he added: H
" . . . in any case [it is] doubtful whether I have power to extend time
beyond service of bankruptcy notice." By that he clearly meant beyond
the expiration of the 10 days. He said:

   " If I am wrong, the counterclaim or cross-claim referred to in . . .
   the debtor's affidavit sworn herein on February 13, 1981, and in
   . . . his supplemental affidavit dated February 16, 1981, could have
   been raised in the action in which judgment was obtained. The

A   document dated July 16, 1980, signed by the debtor precluded him from raising [them]."

He concluded by saying: " He cannot rely on his own act now to say that he has a counterclaim or cross-claim which could not be raised in the action."

The debtor appeals to this court on the ground that the registrar was

B influenced or inhibited in arriving at his decision by his doubt as to whether or not he had jurisdiction, and it is submitted that the registrar did in fact have jurisdiction to extend the time. It is said that he should have extended the time for the affidavit and also extended the 10 days —that must of course follow—for compliance in accordance with section 1 (1) (g). It is further said that he should have fixed a time for hearing,

C namely, a day within the extended term. It was also submitted that the registrar was wrong in concluding that the debtor was precluded from raising the counterclaim as stated by the registrar.

In so far as the question of jurisdiction is concerned, Mr. Moss has relied on section 109 (4) of the Act of 1914. That reads:

D   " Where by this Act, or by general rules, the time for doing any act or thing is limited, the court may extend the time either before or after the expiration thereof, upon such terms, if any, as the court may think fit to impose."

He argues that that is a general power that can be exercised retro-spectively and gives power to extend not only the time of seven days for the filing of the affidavit but also the 10 days referred to in section 1 (1) (g) of the Act. He relied also on a decision of the Court of Appeal,

E *In re A Debtor (No. 138 of 1980)*, The Times, January 29, 1981. It is but a short report, and, as there is no other report of the case, I shall read it in full:

" Ormrod L.J., sitting with Brightman L.J. and Reeve J. in the Court of Appeal, said in a judgment of the court that a registrar in bankruptcy had a discretionary power under section 109 (4) of

F   the Bankruptcy Act 1914 to extend the time for allowing a debtor to file an affidavit relating to a counterclaim, set-off or cross-demand against his creditor: rule 137 (b) of the Bankruptcy Rules 1952. The statement to the contrary in *Williams and Muir Hunter on Bankruptcy*, 19th ed. (1979), p. 467, was based on a misunder-standing of *In re A Debtor (No. 10 of 1953), Ex parte The Debtor*

G   v. *Ampthill Rural District Council* [1953] 1 W.L.R. 1050 and was not correct. In the present case the affidavit was filed after the expiry of the seven day period appropriate under rule 138 (as amended) but before the expiry of the 10 day period before an act of bankruptcy was committed under section 1 (1) (g) of the Act. The debtor had asked that the affidavit be admitted as a valid claim although it was filed two days out of time."

H

That case was dealing with an application made within the 10 day period. The judgment indeed, in the words that I have quoted, emphasises that. However, Mr. Moss, on behalf of the debtor, says that the same power must exist in the present case, because the power derives from section 109 (4) and that is of general application.

So, in the present case, on February 3, 1981, an act of bankruptcy had been committed. That was a fact. The question is whether this

court has power under section 109 to extend time in such a way as to
cancel that act or to revoke it or to deem it never to have occurred.
That means that the debtor in this case has to satisfy the court that
there is a retrospective power to alter the effect of section 1 of the
Act of 1914.

Turning to section 1 (1) (g), one sees that the time prescribed there
of 10 days relates to a failure of the debtor to satisfy the court. The
words used are " If . . . he does not, within 10 days after service of
the notice, . . . satisfy the court . . . ," etc. Now, " If he does not,"
in my view, is equivalent to saying " If he fails to." Once the 10 days
are up the act that gives rise to the consequential act of bankruptcy has
been completed. That act is his failure. Seen in this way, the court, in
my opinion, is concerned to determine whether a condition has been
fufilled so that an act of bankruptcy has been committed and not to
decide whether there is an act that remains to be done. The act has
been done: his failure is complete. If the court extends the 10 days
after the failure is complete it will be refusing to recognise the consequences that Parliament has said have ensued. In my opinion, we
cannot do this. Once the 10 days have expired the failure within that
period of the debtor to satisfy the court is properly to be seen as a
condition that has been fulfilled and that gives rise to the consequences,
namely, that an act of bankruptcy has been committed.

I accept that the court can extend the seven days in rule 138 and
can do so retrospectively. In the present case, however, the registrar
was asked to do this for the purpose of revoking a condition that had
already been fulfilled, that is to say, for the purpose of extending the
10 days. To grant an extension of time for the seven days would be
of no effect if the 10 day period were not to be extended, and, as I
have said, in my opinion we cannot extend the 10 days retrospectively.
The power to extend the seven days must be exercised for a proper
purpose. It cannot be used for the purpose of extending the 10 days.
In my opinion, the court has no jurisdiction to exercise the power under
section 109 (4) for this purpose.

It is interesting to see the provision contained in section 1 (1) (e) of
the Act of 1914, that is to say, that an act of bankruptcy is committed
in the case stated:

" If execution against him has been levied by seizure of his goods
under process in an action in any court, or in any civil proceeding
in the High Court, and the goods have been either sold or held by
the sheriff for 21 days: . . ."

The holding of goods for 21 days by the sheriff is a condition on the
fulfilment of which an act of bankruptcy is committed. Once the 21
days have expired—I say nothing as to the power of the court before
that time—I would find it difficult, and indeed impossible, to say that
the court could alter that period. In the same way I find it impossible to
say that the court can extend the 10 day period once it has expired.

Consequently, I would hold that the court has no jurisdiction. If I
am wrong on that, however, in my opinion this affidavit so lacks precision and clarity that I would hesitate to say that the registrar or the
court should be satisfied, as rule 139 requires. Indeed, the note in
Williams and Muir Hunter on Bankruptcy, 19th ed. (1979), p. 583,
emphasises the importance of the words " if he is satisfied that sufficient
cause is shown." They were inserted in 1952:

A   "reinforcing earlier decisions that if the affidavit does not show
on the face of it that the counterclaim, set-off or cross-demand
equals or exceeds the judgment debt, the rule does not come into
operation; the debtor must therefore quantify his counterclaim and
give full particulars."

The strict interpretation of those words may be relaxed where "the
B shortness of the time for the filing of the affidavit may not permit the
debtor to state more than the outlines of the case," but in the present
case that cannot apply. The proceedings were commenced in 1980.
The debtor must have known then whether or not he had any counterclaim. There was ample time for him to investigate the matter. The
history of this case indicates to my mind that he was not anxious to
proceed with despatch in any way; for, having served notice of this
C appeal, he then opposed an application by the judgment creditor for
the appeal to be expedited. As there will, or may, be further proceedings in this matter in relation to the validity of the counterclaims and
their value and their effect in bankruptcy proceedings, I feel that I
ought not to comment on whether or not the registrar was right in
saying that the debtor could not set up the counterclaims now because
D he had precluded himself by his own act from doing so in the action.
I prefer to say nothing on that aspect of this case, but for the reasons
that I have stated I would dismiss this appeal.

WATKINS L.J.   I agree and have nothing to add.

E   SIR DAVID CAIRNS.   I also agree. I am satisfied that there is no
jurisdiction under section 109 (4) of the Bankruptcy Act 1914 to extend
the period of seven days within which an affidavit setting up a counterclaim may be filed under rule 138 of the Bankruptcy Rules 1952, as
amended in 1977, beyond the 10 days at the expiration of which an
act of bankruptcy is deemed to have occurred under section 1 (1) (g) of
the Act of 1914 as amended by section 4 of the Insolvency Act 1976.
F There is no provision in the Acts for extending the 10 days. Section
109 (4) does not apply to it, because there is no "act or thing" to be
done within the 10 days. When a bankruptcy notice has been given
and nothing occurs before the expiration of the 10 days to hold up its
operation, then the act of bankruptcy takes place by operation of law.
There is nothing in the Acts or the Rules to suggest that, once there
has been an act of bankruptcy, it can be set aside by proceedings under
G rules 137 to 139. Therefore, extension of the time for filing the
affidavit after the 10th day has passed would be nugatory. Parliament
cannot have intended by section 109 to authorise a futile extension.
    That is the formal reason for saying that there is no such juris-
diction. There are good practical reasons too. If the time could be
extended after the 10th day there is no limit to the possible extensions.
H Mr. Moss conceded that, if his argument is right, there could be an
application for extension at any time in the course of the bankruptcy
proceedings, even after adjudication. This would lead only to inconvenience, expense and delay. Moreover, it has to be remembered that
an act of bankruptcy enures to the benefit not only of the creditor who
has served the bankruptcy notice but also of any other creditor who may
wish to present a petition. It would be unsatisfactory if such a right

could be defeated as a result of an application on which no creditor has A
the right to be heard.

If there were jurisdiction to extend the time in this case I would still
say that there was no ground for extending it. In my view, the letter
signed by the debtor on July 16, 1980, constitutes an agreement by him
not to enter a defence and an acknowledgment that he has no defence
to the action. The only counterclaims set up in the debtor's affidavits B
are claims arising out of the same transaction or series of transactions
as that on which the plaintiffs' claim was based. Therefore, if valid,
they would constitute not only counterclaims but set-offs, and a set-off
is a defence.

Next, I was inclined to agree with the registrar that the words
" counterclaim . . . which he could not set up in the action " were not
apt to include a counterclaim which the debtor had debarred himself C
from setting up in the action. Having regard to the caveat entered by
Eveleigh L.J., I express no final opinion on that matter. Lastly, however, in the affidavits filed by the debtor he did not depose to a counterclaim that equalled or exceeded the amount of the judgment debt.

I mention all these various matters because each of them formed
the subject matter of argument before this court and each separate
ground that I have given is, in my judgment, a sufficient reason for D
dismissing the appeal. The fact that I have mentioned them is not to
be taken as any indication that I have any doubt about the primary
ground for dismissing the appeal, namely, the absence of jurisdiction.

Appeal dismissed. E

*Debtor to pay creditors' costs of
appeal including costs of motion to
expedite hearing. Creditors' costs
to be added to costs of petition.
£75 in court to be paid out.*

Solicitors: *Janzen & Co.; Freshfields.*

M. G. F

G

*** PRACTICE DIRECTION
(ADOPTION: JURISDICTION APPLICATION)**

*Adoption—Adoption order—Applications—Preliminary examination
of jurisdiction—Procedure—Adoption (High Court) Rules 1976
(S.I. 1976 No. 1645 (L. 30)), r. 11*

H

The practice direction of November 17, 1976, *Practice Direction
(Adoption: Applications)* [1976] 1 W.L.R. 1267, which, inter alia, set
out the procedure to be followed for a preliminary examination of the
court's jurisdiction under rule 11 of the Adoption (High Court) Rules
1976 is hereby amended.

The revised procedure under that rule will be as follows:

All applications for adoption in the High Court which appear to be

A governed by rule 11 will be referred to a judge for a preliminary examination only if a registrar considers at any stage, either of his own motion or on the ex parte application of the applicant or the guardian ad litem, that the court may be required to dismiss or not proceed with the adoption proceedings.

B In those cases in which the preliminary examination is referred to a judge, the registrar will fix a hearing date and give notice thereof to the applicant, the guardian and, unless otherwise directed, any parent of the child who is not an applicant.

R. L. BAYNE-POWELL,
Senior Registrar.

August 3, 1981.

C

[HOUSE OF LORDS]

* PRACTICE DIRECTION
(HOUSE OF LORDS: COSTS: SECURITY)

D

House of Lords—Costs—Security for—Increase in amount of security—Revision of forms of bill of costs for taxation

(1) *Security for costs*

The House of Lords has ordered the doubling of all forms of security lodged by appellants in appeals to the House of Lords presented on or after
E October 1, 1981, as follows: (*a*) By payment into the House of Lords' Security Fund Account of the sum of £4,000, such sum to be subject to the order of the House in regard to the costs of the appeal; or (*b*) by payment of the sum of £2,000 into the House of Lords' Security Fund Account, and by entering into a recognisance, in person or by substitute, to the amount of £2,000; or (*c*) by procuring two sufficient sureties, to the
F satisfaction of the Clerk of the Parliaments, to enter into a joint and several bond to the amount of £2,000, and by entering a recognisance, in person or by substitute, to the amount of £2,000.

These increases were approved by the House of Lords' Offices Committee, Fourth Report, July 21, 1981, and subsequently by the House of Lords on July 30, 1981.

G (2) *Forms of bills of costs*

The House of Lords has also ordered a revision of the forms of bill of costs applicable to judicial taxations in the House of Lords.

From October 1, 1981, and until March 31, 1982, bills drawn upon the revised and the 1977 scales will be accepted for taxation but thereafter all bills of costs lodged for taxation in the House of Lords should be drawn in
H accordance with the revised scales.

This revision was approved by the Appeal Committee and agreed to by the House of Lords on July 23, 1981.

PETER HENDERSON,
Clerk of the Parliaments.

July 30, 1981.

A

[EMPLOYMENT APPEAL TRIBUNAL: CARDIFF]

* MEARS v. SAFECAR SECURITY LTD.

1980 Nov. 12; 14   Slynn J., Mrs. D. Lancaster and Mr. J. G. C. Milligan

B

*Employment—Contract of employment—Implied term—Statement
of terms of employment containing no reference to sick pay—
No wages paid during absence from work through ill-health
—Whether term to be implied for payment of wages during
period of sickness—Whether sickness benefit to be deducted
Employment Protection (Consolidation) Act* 1978 (c. 44), s. 1
(3) (d)

C

The employee was absent from work because of ill-health
for two periods totalling seven months out of his 14 months'
period of employment. He received sickness benefit under
the Social Security Act 1975 but he neither applied for nor
received any wages from the employers during his absences.
There was no reference to sick pay in his written contract
but he was told by other employees, who visited him while he
was sick, that the employers did not pay wages during periods   D
employees were off work through sickness. He applied to an
industrial tribunal pursuant to section 11 (1) of the Employment Protection (Consolidation) Act 1978 for a determination
of what particulars relating to payment of wages during sick
leave ought to have been included in the written particulars
of his employment under section 1 (3) (d) of the Act. The
industrial tribunal considered that it was to be assumed that   E
there was an implied term in the contract that the employee
would be paid during illness unless the employers could show
that the opposite was to be implied. The majority of the
tribunal were satisfied that if at the time the employee started
working for the employers, the parties had been asked
whether payment was to be made during illness, the employers would probably have answered that it was not their
practice to do so but neither party would have considered   F
it so obvious that nothing need have been said about the
matter. They considered that not too much importance was
to be attached to the fact that the employee had not asked for
payment because he had been influenced by what other employees had told him and a desire not to imperil his employment. They decided that the employers had not shown that
a term was to be implied that payment would not be made
during a period of sickness and that the written particulars   G
ought to have included a term that the employers would continue to pay the employee's wages during any period of
absence through sickness, but subject to a deduction for any
sickness benefits received.

On the employee's appeal from the decision that deductions
should be made and on the employers' cross-appeal from the
decision that they were obliged to pay him while he was away   H
sick:—

Held, dismissing the appeal and allowing the cross-appeal,
that the industrial tribunal were wrong to apply a presumption that if nothing was expressly said about sick pay in the
contract of employment, wages were payable unless the employer could show that some other term was to be implied;
that the proper approach was to consider all the facts and
circumstances and to see whether from the custom and practice in the industry or from the knowledge and actions of the

A   parties, a term was to be implied that wages should or should
not be paid during periods of absence through sickness; and
that the industrial tribunal had erred in their approach and,
on the facts, they should have found that a term was to be
implied in the particulars of employment that wages would
not be paid during periods of absence due to sickness (post,
pp. 1222c–e, 1223a–c, d).

    Petrie v. *Mac Fisheries Ltd.* [1940] 1 K.B. 258, C.A. and
B   *O'Grady* v. *M. Saper Ltd.* [1940] 3 All E.R. 527, C.A. applied.
    Orman v. *Saville Sportswear Ltd.* [1960] 1 W.L.R. 1055
doubted.

    Held, further, that in decided whether there was an
implied term that full wages should be paid without deduction of the amount of sickness benefit received by the employee under the Social Security Act 1975, it was right for
C   the industrial tribunal to consider the nature of the benefits
received under the Act and the terms and conditions of employment; and that, if wages had been payable, a term would
have been implied that money received under the Act of 1975
would be deducted from those wages (post, pp. 1223g—1224b).

    Sun and Sand Ltd. v. *Fitzjohn* [1979] I.C.R. 268, E.A.T.
distinguished.

D   *Marrison* v. *Bell* [1939] 2 K.B. 187, C.A. considered.

The following cases are referred to in the judgment:

Elliott v. *Liggens* [1902] 2 K.B. 84, D.C.

Hancock v. *B.S.A. Tools Ltd.* [1939] 4 All E.R. 538.

Marrison v. *Bell* [1939] 2 K.B. 187; [1939] 1 All E.R. 745, C.A.

O'Grady v. *M. Saper Ltd.* [1940] 3 All E.R. 527, C.A.

E   *Orman* v. *Saville Sportswear Ltd.* [1960] 1 W.L.R. 1055; [1960] 3 All E.R.
105.

Parry v. *Cleaver* [1970] A.C. 1; [1969] 2 W.L.R. 821; [1969] 1 All E.R.
555, H.L.(E.).

Parsons v. *B.N.M. Laboratories Ltd.* [1964] 1 Q.B. 95; [1963] 2 W.L.R.
1273; [1963] All E.R. 658, C.A.

Petrie v. *Mac Fisheries Ltd.* [1940] 1 K.B. 258; [1939] 4 All E.R. 281,
F   C.A.

Sun and Sand Ltd. v. *Fitzjohn* [1979] I.C.R. 268, E.A.T.

Warburton v. *Co-operative Wholesale Society Ltd.* [1917] 1 K.B. 663, C.A.

Wilson v. *Maynard Shipbuilding Consultants A.B.* [1978] Q.B. 665;
[1978] I.C.R. 376; [1978] 2 W.L.R. 466; [1978] 2 All E.R. 78, C.A.

The following additional case was cited in argument:

G   *Liverpool City Council* v. *Irwin* [1977] A.C. 239; [1976] 2 W.L.R. 562;
[1976] 2 All E.R. 39, H.L.(E.).

APPEAL from an industrial tribunal sitting at Exeter.

    The employee, R. J. Mears, appealed from a decision of the industrial
tribunal on January 21, 1980, on his application for a written statement
H   from his employers, Safecar Security Ltd., as to the terms of his contract
of employment regarding wages payable during absence through ill-health.
He appealed from the tribunal's finding that although his contract ought
to have included a provision for sick pay, it was subject to a deduction
for all sickness benefits received under the Social Security Act 1975. The
employers cross-appealed on the ground that the industrial tribunal had
erred in law in implying a provision for sick pay into the contract of
employment.

The appeal was heard by the appeal tribunal and the judgment was A
delivered at Cardiff.

The facts are stated in the judgment.

Peter Clark for the employee.
Eldred Tabachnik for the employers.

Cur. adv. vult.   B

November 14. SLYNN J. delivered the following judgment of the
appeal tribunal. Section 1 of the Employment Protection (Consolidation)
Act 1978 places upon an employer an obligation to give to an employee a
written statement in accordance with the provisions of the section not
later than 13 weeks after the beginning of the employee's period of em- C
ployment. By subsection (3), one of the particulars which has to be
given of the terms of employment in that statement is " (*d*) any terms
and conditions relating to . . . (ii) incapacity for work due to sickness
or injury, including any provision for sick pay." Under section 4 (1)
of the Act, if changes are made in the terms of employment, the employer
is also required to give a statement of the particulars of the change made. D
If an employer does not give an employee such a statement as required
by section 1 or section 4 (1) of the Act, the employee may require a
reference to be made to an industrial tribunal under section 11 (1) to
determine what particulars ought to have been included or referred to
in a statement so as to comply with the requirements of the relevant
section.

In the present case the employee, Mr. Mears, made such an applica- E
tion to an industrial tribunal on September 24, 1979. He said in that
application that his employment had ended on September 18, 1979. He
did not specify the dates on which he required the particulars of the
terms of his employment to be given. It seems to us that, properly construed, he was asking that he be given the particulars to cover the whole
period of employment. What he was particularly concerned about was F
whether any, and if so what, terms should be in those particulars relating
to the payment of wages to him during any period of absence through
sickness.

An industrial tribunal heard the case, and they came to the conclusion
by a majority that the written statement which had been given to him
on July 12, 1978, and which contained no reference to what was to
happen should he be away sick, should have included the following G
term:

"The company will continue to pay your wages during any period
of absence through sickness, but subject to deduction of all sickness benefits received by you under the Social Security Act 1975 in
respect of such period."
     H

The decision of the tribunal was a majority decision so far as the obligation upon the employers to pay wages during the period of absence
through sickness was concerned, but the members were unanimous that
if such a term were to be implied into the contract it should be subject
to deduction of all sickness benefits received under the Act of 1975.

The employee appeals against the decision of the tribunal that the
payment of his wages during the period of sickness should be subject to

A those deductions. The employers cross appeal on the ground that the tribunal erred in law in implying such a term into the particulars of the terms of employment at all.

The industrial tribunal found that the employee started to work for the employers as a security guard based at their Exeter office on July 9, 1978, and it was round about that time that he was given, and signed, the terms of employment to which we have referred. He became ill and was away from work from December 20, 1978, to January 15, 1979, and he was away again ill from March 26, 1979, to September 18, 1979. On September 17, 1979, he gave notice to the employers that he could not carry out his duties because of incapacity and his employment terminated on September 19, 1979.

C It was agreed between the parties at the hearing that when the employee was interviewed, and when he began work, he was not told anything about what would happen to his wages if he was away due to sickness. Nor did he ask about such matter at any time during the period of his employment. When he was away ill the employers did not pay him his wages, either in whole or in part. He did not ask for the payment of any part of his wages during either of the periods of sick-

D ness. During his illness the employers, at one stage, complained about the fact that medical certificates were not being supplied. It seems clear that there were no certificates, at any rate for part of the period, although there was a dispute as to whether some certificates were supplied during the period. The tribunal found that while the employee was ill his colleagues came to see him and they told him that he would not get paid by the employers while he was sick. It was agreed by him that it could

E be said that he never asked for sick pay because he thought in his own mind that he was not entitled to it. Whatever his attitude to this, the industrial tribunal were quite satisfied that it was not the employers' policy to pay sick pay, and if any employee or applicant for a job inquired about the position he would have been so informed. Although the tribunal talk about it as " the policy " of the company, we read that

F as meaning that it was not the employers' practice to make such payments.

The industrial tribunal were referred to a number of authorities which lay down the approach which a tribunal should adopt when considering whether a term is to be implied into a contract, but the case to which reference was principally made was *Orman* v. *Saville Sportswear Ltd.* [1960] 1 W.L.R. 1055. They thought, on the basis of that decision by

G Pilcher J., that they should start by assuming that there was a term to be implied in the contract of employment that wages would be paid unless the employers could show that a term should be implied that wages should not be paid; and they thought here that since there was no custom, and no question of notice having been given by the employers, the right approach was to ask what both sides would have said, had they been

H asked when the employee began to work, " Will wages continue to be paid during sickness? " The industrial tribunal said that they had to ask the question: " Could it be said with confidence that both would reply: ' No, of course not. It is so obvious you needn't put it in the contract '? "

It was at that stage that members of the tribunal were not able to agree. The minority member thought both sides would have said quite categorically that sick pay would not fall to be paid if the employee was away ill. The majority took a different view. They accepted that the

employers might well have said that wages were not to be paid during   A
illness. They thought that if the employers' representative had been
asked, he would not have agreed that it was so obvious that nothing need
to be said about it; that if the employee had been asked he would not
have agreed that it followed that he would not get wages during a period
of sickness. They should not attach too much importance to the fact
when he was ill he did not ask for sick pay, because they thought he
was influenced by what his colleagues had told him and by a desire   B
on his part not to imperil his position of employment by asking for sick
pay when other people said that he would not get it. So, the industrial
tribunal, by a majority, said that the employers had not shown that there
was to be implied a term that the employee would not be paid. They
then went on to consider whether, on the authorities cited to them, the
wages were to be paid with or without deduction, and they came to the   C
conclusion that they were entitled to imply into the term that there should
be a deduction of social security benefits.

In *Orman* v. *Saville Sportswear Ltd.* [1960] 1 W.L.R. 1055, which was
relied upon by the employee and followed by the industrial tribunal,
Pilcher J. said, at pp. 1064–1065, that the authorities which had been
cited to him established the following proposition:
                                                                      D
"Where the written terms of the contract of service are silent as to
what is to happen in regard to the employee's rights to be paid
whilst he is absent from work due to sickness, the employer remains
liable to continue paying so long as the contract is not determined
by proper notice, except where a condition to the contrary can properly be inferred from all the facts and the evidence in the case. If
the employer—and, of course, it will always be the employer—seeks   E
to establish an implied condition that no wages are payable, it is for
him to make it out, and the court, in construing the written contract,
will not accept any implied term which will not pass the test laid
down by Scrutton L.J., in *Reigate* v. *Union Manufacturing (Rams-
bottom) Co. Ltd.* [1918] 1 K.B. 592, 605."
                                                                      F
That test was that a term should only be implied if it was necessary in
the business sense to give efficacy to the contract, and if both parties
would have agreed, when asked, that the term would of course have to
be implied. Pilcher J., on the basis of the authorities, was of the opinion
that in the contract in that case no implied term in regard to payment
during the period of illness could properly be introduced at all. He continued, at p. 1065: "It follows, therefore, that on the authorities the   G
defendants remain liable to pay the plaintiff from the time when he
ceased work until the contract of service was determined."

Now, it seems to us, as it seemed to the industrial tribunal, that Pilcher
J. in *Orman* v. *Saville Sportswear Ltd.* is assuming that one begins with
an assumption that wages are to be paid unless the employer can show
that a term excluding payment of wages is to be implied. In the course   H
of his judgment Pilcher J. referred to a number of authorities to which
it is necessary that we should turn.

The first is *Marrison* v. *Bell* [1939] 2 K.B. 187. That was a case the
headnote to which has been criticised on a number of occasions. It was
a case in which an employee fell ill and after he returned to work he
was given notice to terminate his employment. He was paid no wages,
but he got benefit under the National Health Insurance Act 1936. He

A then sued to recover his wages, and the answer of the employer was that having received benefit under the National Health Insurance Act 1936 he was not entitled to recover his wages. The Court of Appeal decided that the fact that he had received national insurance benefits under the Act of 1936 did not cut down the right which he had to wages under his contract. In the course of the judgment of Scott L.J., reference was made to a number of propositions which were said to be established by existing

B authority. He said, at p. 198:

> "A long series of decisions has been given in our courts making it quite clear that the common law of this country does not recognise any such rule in contracts of service as is suggested by the county court judge."—That is, that there should be a deduction.—"On the contrary, those cases say, in my opinion quite clearly, that under a
C contract of service, irrespective of the question of the length of notice provided by that contract, wages continue through sickness and incapacity from sickness to do the work contracted for until the contract is terminated by a notice by the employer in accordance with the terms of the contract."

Scott L.J., having referred to cases such as *Elliott* v. *Liggens* [1902] 2
D K.B. 84, went on to say, at p. 200:

> "... there was no implied term suspending the right to wages during incapacity by illness, none the less, if a workman so employed under such a contract claimed compensation under the then Workmen's Compensation Act 1897 and was in receipt of compensation during partial incapacity for work (compensation being based, as is well
E known, upon a comparison with his weekly earnings), the Act must be treated as introducing a modification of the contract of service which had the effect of depriving the workman, whilst claiming from his employer compensation, which roughly may be described as half the weekly wages, from recovering from his employer at the same time his whole weekly wages."

F It was held that, the compensation having been received under the Act, the workman could not then turn round and say he was entitled to have the whole of his wages. Scott L.J. concluded in these terms, at p. 204:

> "... rights"—that is, rights under the various statutes to benefit— "are given as a general principle independently of any relation between the rights and the wages, and there is absent, at any rate
G from most of the earlier Acts and certainly from the Act of 1936, any such ground as there is in the Workmen's Compensation Act for supposing that Parliament intended by the Act which conferred the benefits of health insurance to take away from the workman any rights to wages that he might have."

He said that he saw no ground in the statute, the provisions of which
H the court had considered, for saying that there was to be implied a term modifying all contracts of service of persons who came within the scope of those benefits.

It is clear from that judgment, that it has from time to time been said that at common law a workman who is away sick is entitled to his wages during the period of absence. But what was said in *Marrison* v. *Bell* [1939] 2 K.B. 187, has been considered in a number of other cases in the Court of Appeal to which we must refer.

The first of those is *Petrie* v. *Mac Fisheries Ltd.* [1940] 1 K.B. 258. **A**
In that case, Slesser L.J. said that, as he read *Marrison* v. *Bell*, it was
assumed that wages were payable though there were many cases of servants working by the day and by the week, or for longer periods where
it did not necessarily follow that they were entitled to wages during
temporary sickness. He went on, at p. 261:

B
"The real contention in *Marrison* v. *Bell* was whether, if during
illness the servant receives benefit under the National Health Insurance Act, it does or does not deprive him of his right to wages under
the contract of service while sick, assuming that he is entitled to
them during that period."

du Parcq L.J., at p. 264, considered *Marrison* v. *Bell* and *Warburton* v.
Co-operative Wholesale Society Ltd. [1917] 1 K.B. 663, where Lord **C**
Cozens-Hardy M.R. had said, at p. 665:

"It has been long settled that a contract of service is not terminated
by incapacity to work by reason of temporary illness, and that on
return to work the man can recover his wages during the period of
his absence . . ."

D
du Parcq L.J. continued, at pp. 265, 266:

"It was right to point out in *Marrison* v. *Bell* that no qualification
was . . . introduced or suggested as would have prevented those words
from applying to the particular facts of that case, and I venture to
say with great respect that Lord Cozens-Hardy M.R. said nothing inaccurate in that statement if it is read by somebody who does not **E**
expect to find in a short sentence a complete statement of the whole
law. Lord Cozens-Hardy was stating a general proposition, which I
believe to be accurate, and I think it is clearly this: If you have a
weekly hiring of a servant without more, and with nothing in the
terms of it, whether they are expressed or implied, to suggest that
during temporary absence through illness he is not to be paid, then
you may assume that he is to be paid, and that it was the intention **F**
of the parties that he should be paid. . . . The first thing to remember
is that one must find out what the contract is. It is plain that Lord
Cozens-Hardy did not mean that every contract of service, whatever
terms were contained in it, must result in a liability to pay a workman during the time that he is ill. The terms in the contract may
be express, or they may be implied. You may have a custom. . . .
Apart from express terms, or terms imported through some well **G**
known custom, the terms may obviously have been implied in other
ways. I do not dwell on that, because in this case, when the whole
of the facts are looked at, it seems to me plain—and I think that
if the judge had not attached undue importance . . . to the isolated
passage from *Marrison* v. *Bell* . . . he could have come to no other
conclusion—that there was here, at the material time in 1938, a con- **H**
tract, one of the terms of which was that during absence through
illness the workman was to have no right to any remuneration
whatever."

Atkinson J. said, at p. 268:

"The real question was whether or not it was a term of the plaintiff's contract of employment that his wages should be paid during

A   sickness. The defendants said that it was a term of the contract that wages should not be paid during sickness, but that they were ready, not as a matter of right, but ex gratia, to pay a man half-wages for 21 days."

He then referred to the passage from Scott L.J.'s judgment in *Marrison* v. *Bell* and continued, at p. 269:

B   " It is quite true that that principle is laid down without any reference to, or any limitation depending on, the terms of the contract of employment, but it is quite obvious that there must be read into it some such words as ' subject to any express or implied term in the contract to the contrary.' It cannot be thought that Scott L.J. meant that statement to apply to a contract where there was an express

C   term to the contrary . . ."

He also said that it could not apply to such contracts, for example, as those in the weaving industry, where the amount of wages payable depended on the quantity and quality of the work done, or where the wage was only payable for services.

    So it is clear that in *Petrie* v. *Mac Fisheries Ltd.* [1940] 1 K.B. 258,

D   the Court of Appeal approached the question on the basis that one should really look at all the facts and circumstances to see whether a term was or was not to be implied. It recognised that the statement of Scott L.J. in *Marrison* v. *Bell* [1939] 2 K.B. 187 was not intended to be all-embracing.

    In *Hancock* v. *B.S.A. Tools Ltd.* [1939] 4 All E.R. 538, Atkinson J.,

E   who had been a member of the court in the *Petrie* case, said, at pp. 539–540:

    " The question in every case must be: what were the terms of the employment? Under the contract of employment, was the consideration to be work actually done, or was it to be a readiness and willingness to do work if of ability to do it? "

F   He said that if one looked at *Petrie* v. *Mac Fisheries Ltd.* it would be seen that there it was made clear by du Parcq L.J. that in every case it was a question of ascertaining what the real terms of the contract were. He continued, at p. 540:

    " The only point that had to be decided in *Marrison* v. *Bell* was whether or not the position was affected by the National Health

G   Insurance Act. They said that it was not. The mere fact that a man was getting national health insurance did not deprive him of his right to be paid while he was away ill if he had that right under his contract."

    Then in *O'Grady* v. *M. Saper Ltd.* [1940] 3 All E.R. 527, the Court of Appeal considered the position again, and they, too, looked at what had been said in *Petrie* v. *Mac Fisheries Ltd.* in this context. MacKinnon

H   L.J. said, at p. 529:

    " The whole question in such a case as this is what the terms of the contract between the employer and the servant were and what those terms provided in regard to payment of wages to him during his absence from the service by reason of illness. . . . Was it agreed that the man should be paid when he was ready and willing to work, or that he should be paid only when he was actually working? In this

case, as it seems to me, there was abundant evidence that the terms,   A
not expressed, but no doubt implied, upon which this man was employed were that he should not be paid wages whilst he was sick.
Conclusive evidence of that is furnished by the fact that on at least
three occasions during the time he had been employed he was not
paid wages when he was away sick, and he acquiesced in that
position."
                                                                         B
He thought that what the parties would have said, had they been asked
the question at the time when the contract was made for service by the
employee, was best proved, and, as MacKinnon L.J. thought, was con-
clusively proved, by what the parties did when the event arose. That
case, it seems to us, is entirely consistent with what was said in *Petrie* v.
Mac Fisheries Ltd. and in *Hancock* v. *B.S.A. Tools Ltd.*
                                                                         C
We, of course, attach great weight to the judgment of Pilcher J. in
Orman v. *Saville Sportswear Ltd.* [1960] 1 W.L.R. 1055, although strictly
it is not binding upon us, but it seems to us quite clearly that what is said
in that case must be seen against the background of what had been said
in the other cases following *Marrison* v. *Bell* [1939] 2 K.B. 187.

In the result, it seems to us that it is not a correct approach to begin
with the presumption that, if nothing is expressly said in the contract,   D
wages are to be payable unless the employer satisfies the burden of showing that some other term is to be implied. In our judgment the proper
approach is to look at all the facts and the circumstances to see whether
a term is to be implied that wages shall or shall not be paid during periods
of absence through sickness. Such a term, as the cases show, may be
implied from the custom or practice in the industry. It may be implied   E
from the knowledge of the parties at the time when the contract is made.
The implication may depend upon whether the contract is one where the
payment is due if the servant is ready, willing and able to work. It may
depend, as was suggested in an article by A. T. Denning, " Quantum
Meruit: The case of *Craven-Ellis* v. *Canons Ltd.*" (1939) 55 L.Q.R. 54,
not so much as to whether the employee is willing and ready, or willing
and able to work, but on whether payment of the wages is the considera-   F
tion for faithful service at other times during the contract than during
the period of absence rather than for a particular week's work actually
performed. These are all matters which will have to be taken into
account. So will the nature of the contract itself. The implication to
be drawn in a case where a man is employed on a daily basis may be
different from one to be drawn in a case where a man is employed for a   G
fixed term of years, such as five or ten years, as has been referred to in
some of the cases. It seems to us, on the basis of what was said by Mac-
Kinnon L.J. in *O'Grady* v. *M. Saper Ltd.* [1940] 3 All E.R. 527, that it
is also permissible on occasions to look at what the parties did during
the performance of the contract. We, of course, recognise the dangers
which are inherent in such a course, because evidence of what the parties
did is generally inadmissible evidence in construing the terms of contract,   H
but in *Wilson* v. *Maynard Shipbuilding Consultants A.B.* [1978] Q.B. 665,
Megaw L.J., having regard to the general rule, said, at p. 675:

" There would seem, however, to be an exception to the strictness of
that doctrine where there must be a relevant term, but what that
term is cannot be ascertained otherwise than by looking at what the
parties did: . . ."

A   That seems to us to be in accordance with what was said in *O'Grady* v. *M. Saper Ltd.*; and so it seems to us that, contrary to the approach of the industrial tribunal in this case, and contrary to the approach which we understand Pilcher J. to have taken, the right approach is to ask, on all the facts and circumstances of the case to which it is proper to have regard, what term is to be implied. One does not begin by assuming that the term as to payment is to be implied unless the employer displaces it.

B   On the facts of the present case it is clear that nothing was said at the time when the contract was made, but the industrial tribunal were quite satisfied that had the employer been asked he would have said that no wages would be paid to an employee if he was away ill. He would, on the findings of the tribunal, have said that it was their policy not to pay. We understand that to mean also that it was their practice not to pay.

C   There was evidence that the employee, who was ill some six months after he began working, did not ask for any payment—did not, apparently, send in the sort of sick notes regularly from the beginning which one would have expected had he considered that he was entitled to his wages. He was told by his colleagues that he would not get any sick pay from the employers.

D   It seems to us, accordingly, in this case, if one adopts the approach which we consider it is right to adopt in these cases, that here the term to be implied into this contract is that wages would not be paid during periods of absence due to sickness. In our judgment the industrial tribunal in the present case erred in their approach and they refused to imply a term which really ought to have been implied.

E   It seems to us of importance to note that the general statement of principle which is set out in *Marrison* v. *Bell* [1939] 2 K.B. 187, is really interpreted by the Court of Appeal in other cases as meaning that there has to be a presumption of payment if there is nothing more. That does not decide the question of upon whom the onus lies of showing whether the term is to be implied. It may be, at the end of the day, if there are no factors either way which can properly be relied upon, that the correct inference is that if a man is employed for a period on a wage, then, if

F   nothing else can be found, the presumption will be that the wage is to be paid during the period of employment; but if there are other factors it seems to us that they come in at the beginning of the exercise and not after certain presumptions have been made.

    If we are wrong in our approach to that question, the second question arises as to whether there is to be implied a term that wages shall be paid

G   regardless of whether benefits are received under the Social Security Act 1975. It seems to us to be quite clear that *Marrison* v. *Bell* did not decide that in every case where any money was received under the National Health Insurance Act 1936, wages were also to be paid in full. The cases to which we have referred make it plain that the receipt of benefit under the legislation does not take away the man's right under his contract, but that of itself does not determine what the rights under the contract are,

H   and the first question has to be decided as to what are the rights under the contract.

    In our judgment it is clear that in deciding the implied term it is right to have regard to the nature of the payment which is made under the provisions of the Social Security Act 1975 if someone is away from work through illness. It is right, in our judgment, to take into account the differences between payments under that Act and under the National Health

Insurance Act 1936, to consider the fact that both employer and employee   A
make contributions, the fact that for a period earnings related supplements are paid to someone who is away ill in addition to the flat rate
benefit which may provide for as much as 85 per cent. of the employee's
contractual wages, subject to the upper limit provided from time to time
under the legislation. If regard is had to those matters, and to the
terms and conditions of employment on the facts of this case, it seems to
us that quite plainly the term which would have to be implied as to the   B
payment of wages, if one were implied, would have regard to the moneys
which would be payable to the workman under the Act of 1975.

The employee himself accepted in his evidence that he could not have
it both ways, and that he would have to give credit for any moneys
received under the Social Security Act 1975. It is quite plain that the
employers would have said the same thing. Reliance has, however, been   C
placed by the employee on *Marrison* v. *Bell* [1939] 2 K.B. 187. In our
judgment, *Marrison* v. *Bell* does not say, as is contended on behalf of the
employee, that these moneys under the legislation are always payable in
addition to the payment of full wages. One has to look at what is the
implied term in any case.

Mr. Clark, to whom we are indebted for an able and careful argument   D
in this case, has placed reliance upon the decision of the House of Lords
in *Parry* v. *Cleaver* [1970] A.C. 1. That was a case which decided that in
assessing damages for tortious injury, the payment of a police pension
should be ignored in assessing the financial loss which the injured plaintiff
had suffered. There was, in the speech of Lord Reid at p. 19, reference
to the position in cases like *Parsons* v. *B.N.M. Laboratories Ltd.* [1964]
1 Q.B. 95, which decided that in assessing damages for wrongful dismissal   E
unemployment benefit had to be deducted, but it seems to us that those
cases involving claims for damages for tortious injury or for wrongful
dismissal are quite different from the facts of the present case. We do not
consider that *Parry* v. *Cleaver* assists us at all in our decision as to what
should be the term to be implied to the employee's contract of service.

Finally, reliance is placed upon what was said by the appeal tribunal   F
in *Sun and Sand Ltd.* v. *Fitzjohn* [1979] I.C.R. 268. That was a case
where an employee had been unfairly dismissed, and where compensation
was awarded to cover a period of 13 weeks between the date of dismissal
and the date on which new employment was found. The claim was made
on behalf of the employers, on appeal, that the industrial tribunal had
erred in law in failing to deduct the amount of sickness benefit from the
compensatory award. This appeal tribunal held that the industrial   G
tribunal had come to the right decision and ruled that the employee who
had suffered incapacity to work was entitled to sickness benefit regardless
of whether she was also receiving a payment under her contract of
employment, and therefore, as the headnote reads:

"... since the loss resulting from her unfair dismissal was both
wages and sickness benefit she was entitled to be compensated for   H
both and the industrial tribunal's assessment of compensation was
correct."

The appeal tribunal said, at p. 270:

"Since it is not contended, and in our judgment cannot be contended, that she would have had to account to her employers in any
way for the amount of sickness benefit thus received we can see no

A   ground upon which it would be proper to reduce the compensatory award by the amount of the sickness benefit which she received during the period in question."

We cast no doubt on the actual decision in that case, but it has to be observed that the statement of the appeal tribunal was based upon a concession by counsel for the employers in that case. Moreover, it does

B   not seem to us to really raise the question as to what term is to be implied into the contract. If one assumes full wages are due, then as in *Marrison v. Bell* [1939] 2 K.B. 187 it is right that the moneys to be received under the legislation do not have to be taken into account. But that is not the question in our case. Our case is whether full wages are due and are to be paid, and we are quite satisfied that nothing in the *Sun and Sand Ltd.* decision prevents us from coming to the conclusion to which we have

C   come. If we are wrong about that and there is any difference between our decision and *Sun and Sand Ltd.*, then we consider that since the matter was not fully argued in the *Sun and Sand Ltd.* case we are perfectly free to look at the matter on the basis of the arguments which have been put forward with ability by both sides in the present case. We are satisfied here that if we were wrong on the first point, the industrial

D   tribunal came to a correct conclusion when they ruled that the implied term would provide for the deduction from the amount of wages normally payable, the amount of moneys received under the Social Security Act 1975.

Accordingly, we dismiss the appeal in this case, we allow the cross-appeal and set aside the decision of the industrial tribunal. We give leave to the employee to appeal to the Court of Appeal, and we extend

E   the period for entering a notice of appeal to 42 days from the day when the copy of the transcript of our judgment in this case is sent by the appeal tribunal to the parties.

Appeal dismissed.
Cross-appeal allowed.
Leave to appeal.

F

Solicitors: *Cartridge & Co., Exeter; Gilbert H. Stephens & Sons, Exeter.*

J. W.

G

H

[1981]

A

* REEL v. HOLDER AND ANOTHER

[1979 R. No. 236]

1981   June 26, 29, 30   Lord Denning M.R.,
                                                              Eveleigh and Brandon L.JJ.

B

*Contract—Construction—Rules of unincorporated international
federation—Members of federation associations governing
athletics in any " country "—Only one member permitted for
each country—Taiwan association elected member in 1956
after China association elected—China association withdrawing in protest—China association re-elected as member representing mainland and Taiwan—Whether Taiwan " country "
for purposes of rules—Validity of Taiwan's election*

C

The International Amateur Athletic Federation was an
unincorporated association whose members comprised duly
elected national governing associations which controlled
amateur athletics in their respective countries. By rule 1 of the
federation's rules " only one member for each country " could
be affiliated and the jurisdiction of members of the federation
was limited to the " political boundaries of the countries they
represent." In 1954 the association controlling athletics on the
mainland of China was admitted as a member. In 1956 the
association controlling athletics in Taiwan (then Formosa) was
also admitted by a majority decision of the federation's congress. Both the mainland government and the government of
Taiwan claimed sovereignty over both mainland China and
Taiwan, but Taiwan's claim was not recognised in international
law. In 1958 the mainland China association withdrew from
membership in protest against the Taiwan association's
membership. In 1978 a resolution that the mainland association
should be re-affiliated as the only member for China with
jurisdiction over athletics in Taiwan was carried by 200 votes
to 153 in the congress. That resolution amounted to the exclusion of the Taiwan association from the federation. Forbes J.
granted the plaintiff, the secretary general of the Taiwan
association, declarations against the defendants, the honorary
treasurer and president of the federation, that the Taiwan
association was and remained a member of the federation.

D

E

F

On appeal by the defendants: —

Held, dismissing the appeal, (1) that the word " country "
in the rules delineated the area over which one governing
amateur athletic association exercised authority; that membership of the federation was thus not confined to associations
representing sovereign or national states; and that the Taiwan
association was properly eligible for membership of the
federation (post, pp. 1230H, 1232G—1233A, C).

G

(2) That there being a contractual relationship between the
members of the federation as in a club, questions concerning
the application of the rules by a body such as congress or a
committee could be decided by a majority and accordingly
the decision to admit Taiwan in 1956 had been valid (post, pp.
1231E–F, 1233B–C).

H

(3) That the resolution in 1978 to make the mainland
China association the sole representative for both mainland
China and Taiwan, which amounted to a decision to expel
the Taiwan association, was beyond any power conferred
by the rules and the judge had rightly made a declaration
that the Taiwan association was and remained a member of
the federation (post, pp. 1231G, 1233B–C).

Decision of Forbes J. [1979] 1 W.L.R. 1252; [1979] 3 All
E.R. 1041 affirmed.

A   The following case is referred to in the judgments:

    Shen Fu Chang v. *Stellan Mohlin* (unreported), July 5, 1977, Robert
        Goff J.

The following additional cases were referred to in argument:

    Buttes Gas and Oil Co. v. *Hammer (No. 3)* [1981] Q.B. 223; [1980] 3
B   W.L.R. 668; [1980] 3 All E.R. 475, C.A.

    Kawasaki Kisen Kabushiki Kaisha of Kobe v. *Bantham Steamship Co.*
       Ltd. [1939] 2 K.B. 544; [1939] 1 All E.R. 819, C.A.

    Lee v. *Showmen's Guild of Great Britain* [1952] 2 Q.B. 239; [1952] 1 All
       E.R. 1175, C.A.

    Luigi Monta of Genoa v. *Cechofracht Co. Ltd.* [1956] 2 Q.B. 552; [1956]
       3 W.L.R. 480; [1956] 2 All E.R. 769.

C   APPEAL from Forbes J.

      By originating summons of January 25, 1979, the plaintiff, Cheng Chi
Reel who was secretary general of the Republic of China Track and Field
Association (" R.O.C.T.F.A."), suing on behalf of herself and on behalf
of and as representing all other members of such association claimed
against the defendants, Frederick W. Holder and Adriaan Paulen (the
D honorary treasurer and the president respectively of the International
Amateur Athletic Federation (" the federation ") sued on behalf of themselves and on behalf of and as representing all other members of such
federation except the plaintiff) declarations (a) that the R.O.C.T.F.A.
were and remained members of the federation; (b) that the R.O.C.T.F.A.
were and remained entitled to all the rights and privileges of membership
of the federation; (c) that the resolution dated October 5, 1978, of the
E federation in so far as it purported to deprive or to have the effect of
depriving the R.O.C.T.F.A. of membership or alternatively of the rights
and privileges of such federation was void and of no effect; and an
injunction restraining the defendants from doing any act pursuant to or
in consequence of the resolution dated October 5, 1978, of the congress
of the federation in so far as any such act was inconsistent with the
F R.O.C.T.F.A. being a member of the federation.

      On April 2, 1979, Forbes J. [1979] 1 W.L.R. 1252, 1269, granted the
declarations with liberty to apply for an injunction if necessary.

      The defendants appealed on the grounds that (1) the judge was wrong
in law and/or fact in holding that both mainland China and Taiwan could
be described as a country within the meaning of the rules of the federation
G and ought to have held that there had at no material time been more
than one country of China; (2) that the judge was wrong in law and/or
fact in holding that the defendants were not entitled to deny the continuing membership of the plaintiff of the federation by reason of some
waiver or estoppel; (3) that the judge ought to have held that (a) the rules
of the federation provided that there could only be one member for each
country; (b) it was common ground between the representatives of main-
H land China and the representatives of Taiwan that there was only one
nation or country of China, alternatively that that was the position in
fact; (c) the purported election of the R.O.C.T.F.A. to the federation in
1956 was contrary to their rules and invalid since there was already a
member of China; (d) the fact that the R.O.C.T.F.A. was treated as a
member of the federation from 1956 to 1978 could not validate the
invalid election in 1956 since there had at no material time began unanimity amongst the members of the federation as to the validity of the

election and there had never been fewer than four members of the   A
federation who maintained that the election was in fact invalid; (4) that
the decision of the judge was wrong in law and against the weight of the
evidence.

The facts are stated in the judgment of Lord Denning M.R. and
Forbes J. [1979] 1 W.L.R. 1252.

                                                                    B

Konrad Schiemann Q.C. and *Stephen Ruttle* for the defendants.
Robert Alexander Q.C. and *Brian Davenport Q.C.* for the plaintiffs.

LORD DENNING M.R. In 1912 there was formed the International
Amateur Athletic Federation (" the federation "). The athletic associations of many countries joined together to arrange their activities on an
international scale. They took part in the Olympic Games and in com-   C
petitions between countries, and so forth. For many years the President
was the distinguished athlete Lord Burghley, afterwards the Marquis of
Exeter.

The question which arises for decision in this case is in what circumstances a " country " can be admitted or expelled from the federation.
I use the word " country " because it is the word used in the rules. But it   D
is very ambiguous.

The " China " problem has been with the world since 1949. The
government of mainland China—operating from Peking—claimed to have
sovereignty over the mainland and also the island of Formosa, now called
Taiwan. The Taiwan government claimed to have sovereignty over the
island and also over the whole of mainland China. So both governments   E
claimed to have sovereignty over the whole of the two territories.

I put on one side any thought of international politics. In international
law Taiwan's claim is not recognised. I will read the statement made by
the Foreign and Commonwealth Office in a letter of June 29, 1978, to the
federation's solicitors in this case:

" HMG "—Her Majesty's Government—" do not, and have never   F
    regarded Taiwan as a state. Nor do we regard the Chinese nationalist
    authorities in Taiwan as a government and have not done so since
    1950, when we ceased to recognise them as the Government of China.
       ". . . the Government of the United Kingdom acknowledge the
    position of the Chinese Government that Taiwan is a province of the
    People's Republic of China."
                                                                    G

That is in the international sphere of statehood and sovereignty so
declared by this country as far back as 1950. We are told that in 1971
the United Nations followed suit.

To my mind those considerations have no application whatever to
the problem which we have to decide today under the rules of the federation. As long ago as 1954 an application was made by the government in   H
Peking to become a member of the federation. They were accepted only
as the representative of mainland China. They were told that if Formosa
wished to apply for membership, their application would be considered
separately. That decision was set out quite clearly in letters which passed
at that time. On November 9, 1954, the Secretary-Treasurer of the
federation wrote to the President of the China National A.A.F. in mainland China saying:

A   ". . . I must advise you that the application of the All China Atheletic Association for membership of the I.A.A.F. was considered at the congress in August this year and that association was accepted as a new member.

    " At the same time it was agreed that an application for membership from the controlling body of athletics in Formosa would receive consideration."

B   Two years later in 1956 Formosa (now Taiwan) applied to become a member. There was objection from the Eastern bloc—from Russia, Czechoslovakia, Rumania, and mainland China. It is interesting to note what the President, Lord Burghley, said when Taiwan applied for membership:

C   " The president "—that is, Lord Burghley—" said he himself wished to support this application for affiliation in the same way as he had done for other countries. The young people from a country with a population of 18,000,000 "—that is the population of Taiwan—" were involved, and any question of politics should be left out of any discussion for the aim in view was to bring as many young athletes as possible into the family group of the federation. It was impossible D for the athletic association in Peking to organise athletic matches for the Taiwan athletes as there was no communication between the two countries and he therefore moved from the chair that the application be accepted."

The minutes went on to say:

E   " The delegates from the U.S.S.R., Czechoslovakia and Rumania supported the A.A. of the People's Republic of China in their opposition. On a vote being taken it was agreed, with only four dissentients, that the application of the China National Amateur Athletic Federation be accepted on the understanding that they would compete and be known as ' Taiwan '."

F   From that time onwards Taiwan attended the meetings, paid their subscriptions, and were members of the federation. But mainland China did not approve. Two years later they withdrew their own membership. That was in 1958.

    I will now pass on to the critical year in this case. In 1978 there was to be a meeting of the congress of the federation in Puerto Rico. The agenda looked quite innocent. It simply proposed that Taiwan should G remain as a member but should be referred to only by the name of " Taiwan " in future. Then on the very morning of the meeting a circular was distributed of a proposed amendment. It was proposed that Taiwan should be excluded from membership: and that mainland China should come in as the sole representative of all the territories. I will read the resolution which was put forward. It is what is in dispute in this case:

H   " In connection with the request for affiliation of the A.A. of The People's Republic of China "—that is, mainland China—" and (1) having considered I.A.A.F. rule 4 with particular reference to political boundaries; and (2) having heard from the United Nations that the political boundaries of The People's Republic of China include the island of Taiwan; and (3) having received a guarantee that Taiwan athletes may compete in international competitions under I.A.A.F. Rules, under the jurisdiction of the A.A. of The People's Republic of

China, the council recommends the re-affiliation of The People's A
Republic of China as the only representative in the I.A.A.F. for
China."

That resolution was debated at some length. Eventually, after a long
discussion, the congress proceeded to vote. The vote was in favour of
mainland China by 200 to 153. The final minute said:

"The Athletic Association of The People's Republic of China was, B
therefore, accepted as an I.A.A.F. member, to have jurisdiction also
over that territory where athletics was at present governed by the
existing I.A.A.F. member in Taiwan."

It is quite plain that that amounted to the exclusion of Taiwan from
the federation. Mainland China was to be admitted, exercising jurisdiction
not only over the mainland but also over the island. C

That gave rise to much perturbation as to the validity of the resolution.
An action has been brought in the High Court in England to resolve the
matter. The court has been asked to declare that Taiwan still remains a
member of the federation: that they have been wrongly excluded: and
that the resolution of 1978 is void and of no effect.

The court was faced with a similar problem in relation to badminton D
in 1977: *Shen Fu Chang* v. *Stellan Mohlin* (unreported), July 5, 1977. The
judge, Robert Goff J., took the view, with which I agree, that we are not
concerned with international law or with sovereignty. We are simply concerned with the interpretation of the rules of the federation. The rules are
in English. The head office of the federation is in England. It is right
that, if the rules need to be construed, the matter should come to the
English courts to be decided. At the end of his judgment in the badminton E
case, Robert Goff J. made a declaration that Taiwan could be a member
of the International Badminton Federation. He made an injunction to that
effect.

We now have to construe the rules of the federation. First, we have
to consider whether the application by Taiwan in 1956 was valid: whether
Taiwan was eligible for membership. At that time the rules were not as F
full as they are now. They have been developed in the course of time.
Rule 7 of the handbook of the Federation for 1953 said: "7. The national
governing body for amateur athletics in any country shall be eligible for
membership of the federation." "National" is one of the words which
gives rise to trouble. Rule 1 (2) of the 1953 handbook presents another
problem: "The jurisdiction of members of the federation shall be limited
to the political boundaries of the country they represent." G

But some help is to be derived from rule 9 (7). It said that a "colony"
can be eligible to be affiliated as a member. That shows a departure from
statehood. It shows that places such as Hong Kong and Gibraltar—even
though they are under the sovereignty of the United Kingdom—can be
affiliated as members.

In my opinion the membership of this international association is not H
confined to sovereign states in the international sense. Every athletic
association in any territory is eligible for membership provided that it is
the supreme athletic association for that territory and is not subject to any
control by another athletic association. Take, for instance, the United
Kingdom. We have the Amateur Athletic Association which governs all
amateur athletics in this country—England, Scotland and Wales. So the
Amateur Athletic Association is the association to represent the United

A Kingdom as a member of the federation. But if Wales formed their own independent Amateur Athletic Association and wanted to be separately represented, it seems to me that Wales would be a " country " eligible for membership under the rules of the federation.

In the rule, " The jurisdiction of members of the federation shall be limited to the political boundaries of the country they represent," the governing word is " country." One " *country* " is Taiwan. Another
B " country " is mainland China. The jurisdiction of the Athletic Association of Taiwan is limited to Taiwan. The jurisdiction of the Athletic Association of mainland China is limited to mainland China.

One can argue to and fro on the interpretation of these rules. The people who drew them up could not possibly have envisaged all the problems which would have to be coped with in the future in regard to
C them. The courts have to reconcile all the various differences as best they can. It is interesting to notice rule 3 of the rules of 1978, which are certainly applicable in this case. It says:

" The objects of the federation shall be: 1.—To establish friendly and loyal co-operation between all members for the benefit of amateur athletics throughout the world. 2.—To strive to ensure that no racial,
D religious, political or other kind of discrimination be allowed in athletics, and to take all necessary measures to stop such discrimination."

One would hope there would not be any racial discrimination against Taiwan. That is the point in this case. Was Taiwan eligible for membership when it applied—and was accepted—in 1956 with only four dis-
E sentients? It seems to me that the decision to accept Taiwan—by a majority—was perfectly rightly made.

We have had discussions as to how far rulings should be unanimous. There was no provision in the rules in 1956 for their being altered in any way. It was a membership of a club. There was a contract between the parties. If the rules are to be altered later, that can only be done by
F agreement between all the parties. It has to be unanimous. But, when the rules are not to be altered, and the only question is application of the rules by a committee or a body of that kind, then the ordinary rule applies that the decision can be by a majority. In this case the decision in 1956 to admit Taiwan by a majority was perfectly valid.

If that be right, there is no need to go into the question of an estoppel. That would only arise if the admission of Taiwan were wrong. Even if it
G had been wrong, nevertheless there is a strong case for saying that as everyone—except the People's Republic of China—accepted them as a member for 22 years, it would be too late to say that their admission was not valid. But there is no need to go into that in view of the opinion I have expressed that on the rules they were validly admitted.

That brings me to final point in the case. In 1978 the federation
H resolved to make mainland China the sole representatives of the whole area including Taiwan. That amounted to a decision to expel Taiwan. That was beyond any power conferred on the congress by the rules. If the federation want to have power to expel, then the rules will have to be altered.

I would agree with the judge that Taiwan was validly elected a member in 1956. It was wrongfully excluded in 1978. It is still a member. These courts can and should make a declaration in favour of Taiwan to

that extent. We do not think this should give rise to any international A
complications. We are making a declaration on the meaning of the rules
according to English law, which is the governing law. We grant no injunction. We simply state what we think the rules mean.

I would therefore agree with the judge, and dismiss the appeal.

EVELEIGH J. I agree. Rule 1 of the rules as they were in 1956 B
reads:

> "The title shall be the International Amateur Athletic Federation. It
> shall comprise duly elected national governing associations or federa-
> tions of countries, in control of amateur track and field athletics . . .
> Only one member for each country can be affiliated."

By rule 7 it is provided: "The National Governing Body for amateur C
athletics in any country shall be eligible for membership of the federation."
The question as argued in the court below was whether Taiwan was
eligible for membership in 1956.

Reading the rules, one comes clearly to the conclusion that the
International Amateur Athletic Federation is an affiliation of athletic
governing bodies formed to pursue certain objects. It has been contended
in this court that the word " country " in the rules means that which is D
internationally recognised as a state or at least that the congress of the
federation is entitled so to construe it. What would that involve? It would,
as I see it, involve a different meaning being attached to the rules depending upon which court decided the matter. It would mean a different meaning attached to the rules depending upon whether reliance was placed
upon recognition by this state or that state. For example, in 1950 the E
United Kingdom recognised Peking but other countries did not, and
neither did the United Nations at that time although they now do.

Those who formed the federation were not concerned with international politics; they were concerned to set standards for athletics
throughout the world. They were concerned to collect together people
who would be in a position to exercise control over athletics in various
parts of the world. Unless a governing body of some kind applies for F
membership, the federation is not concerned to determine if a given place
or area is a country. It is only in connection with an application for
membership by an applicant who puts himself forward as a governing
body for a particular place, district or region that it becomes necessary to
consider the meaning of " country " in the rules. One thing that is clear
is that there may only be one member for each country. Therefore, in G
entertaining an application, it has to be seen whether or not there is an
existing member who has control, or a measure of control, over the same
area as that for which the applicant contends. There must be no doubt
who is to speak with authority as the governing body for a particular
group of athletes. The word " country " has been used in the rules in
order to delineate the area of authority. They do not use the word in the H
sense of sovereign state. That is clear from rule 9, paragraph 7, which
reads:

> " In international competitions, members of this federation shall be
> represented only by native born or naturalised subjects of the country
> which the affiliated member represents, except in the case of citizens
> of a colony, when they shall be eligible to represent the mother country
> if such colony is not represented by membership of the I.A.A.F."

A   That rule clearly contemplates that there may be an existing member of the federation which is a colony and not itself a sovereign state. I think that the word is used in the rules in the sense of an area or part of the world where the applicant has authority in relation to athletics and an area to which the word " country " is appropriate because the inhabitants share the right to live there in common as one distinct people. This is a question to be answered broadly and not on a political basis alone.

B Political status may have some relevance. It may perhaps help to see the inhabitants as being one people, but it is not the decisive factor.

For those reasons I agree with the judgment delivered by Lord Denning M.R.

BRANDON L.J. I agree with both the judgments which have been

C delivered.

Appeal dismissed with costs.
Leave to appeal refused.

Solicitors: *Linklaters & Paines; Herbert Smith & Co.*

D   A. H. B.

[COURT OF APPEAL]

E   * POWER CURBER INTERNATIONAL LTD. *v.*
NATIONAL BANK OF KUWAIT S.A.K.

[1981 P. No. 356]

1981   June 15, 16, 17;   Lord Denning M.R., Griffiths L.J. and
F   July 3   Waterhouse J.

Banking—Letter of credit—Proper law—Letter of credit issued by
Kuwaiti bank through North Carolina bank—Buyers' provi-
sional attachment order in Kuwait—Whether letter of credit
enforceable by United States' sellers in England—Lex situs of
debt

G   The plaintiffs, American sellers, agreed to export goods on c.i.f. terms to buyers in Kuwait to be paid for by a letter of credit issued by the defendant bank, which was incorporated in Kuwait with a registered office under Part X of the Companies Act 1948 in London. On September 6, 1979, the defendant bank at the request of the buyers issued a letter of credit addressed to the Bank of America, Florida, Miami, U.S.A., advising their irrevocable credit in favour of the plaintiffs

H   through the North Carolina National Bank in Charlotte, North Carolina, U.S.A., to the extent of U.S. $300,000: 25 per cent. of the ex works value of the goods plus freight and insurance was to be paid against presentation of documents and the remaining 75 per cent. after one year of date of shipment. Goods valued at U.S. $101,059 were shipped on December 26, 1979, and 25 per cent. payment was made on presentation of documents. The credit was expressed to be subject to the Uniform Customs and Practice for Documentary Credits (1974 Revision). On March 4, 1980, the defendant bank informed

the North Carolina National Bank that U.S. $75,794 would be A
remitted through a New York trust company on December 26,
1980.

On November 5, 1980, on the application of the buyers, a
Kuwaiti court made an order of " provisional attachment " of
the sums due to the plaintiffs payable by the defendant bank
under the letter of credit. The Kuwaiti court refused an
application by the defendant bank to discharge the order and
the refusal was upheld by the Court of Appeal in Kuwait. B

After starting and then discontinuing proceedings against
the defendant bank in North Carolina, the plaintiffs, by writ
of January 27, 1981, issued in the High Court in England,
claimed U.S. $75,794 against the bank. Parker J. gave judg-
ment for the plaintiffs on their summons under R.S.C., Ord.
14, for the sum claimed and interest, but imposed a stay upon
execution of the judgment pending further order.

On appeal by the plaintiffs against the stay and cross- C
appeal by the defendant bank against the judgment: —

Held, dismissing the cross-appeal, (1) that the proper law
of the letter of credit, under which the defendant bank were
plainly in default, was the law of North Carolina where payment was to be made against presentation of documents (post,
pp. 1240D, 1242E, 1244A); that (*per* Lord Denning M.R. and
Griffiths L.J.) the lex situs of the debt under the letter of credit
was also in North Carolina (post, pp. 1240F, 1242G); and that D
accordingly the Kuwaiti provisional order of attachment did
not affect either the validity or the existence of the debt and the
judge had rightly given summary judgment against the bank
(post, pp. 1240F, 1242H, 1244D).

Offshore International S.A. v. *Banco Central S.A.* [1977]
1 W.L.R. 399, approved.

(2) Allowing the appeal, that in view of the importance in
international trade that a bank issuing a letter of credit should E
honour its obligations, which should not be nullified by an
attachment order at the suit of a buyer, the court should not
recognise the provisional attachment order of the Kuwaiti
court and the stay upon execution of the judgment should be
removed (post, pp. 1241A–B, E, 1242A–B, 1243B, H, 1244H—
1245A).

Edward Owen Engineering Ltd. v. *Barclays Bank International Ltd.* [1978] Q.B. 159, C.A. applied. F

Per Lord Denning M.R. A branch of a bank which is
situated in a different country to that of its head office is subject
to the orders of the courts of the country where it is situated
and not to the orders of the courts where its head office is
situated (post, p. 1241G–H).

Order of Parker J. varied.

G
The following cases are referred to in the judgments:

Discount Records Ltd. v. *Barclays Bank Ltd.* [1975] 1 W.L.R. 315; [1975]
1 All E.R. 1071.

Hamzeh Malas & Sons v. *British Imex Industries Ltd.* [1958] 2 Q.B. 127;
[1958] 2 W.L.R. 100; [1958] 1 All E.R. 262, C.A.

Harbottle (R.D.) (Mercantile) Ltd. v. *National Westminster Bank Ltd.*
[1978] Q.B. 146; [1977] 3 W.L.R. 752; [1977] 2 All E.R. 862. H

Intraco Ltd. v. *Notis Shipping Corporation of Liberia,* The Times, July 7,
1981, C.A.

MacShannon v. *Rockware Glass Ltd.* [1978] A.C. 795; [1978] 2 W.L.R.
362; [1978] 1 All E.R. 625, H.L.(E.).

Nova (Jersey) Knit Ltd. v. *Kammgarn Spinnerei G.m.b.H.* [1977] 1 W.L.R.
713; [1977] 2 All E.R. 463, H.L.(E.).

Offshore International S.A. v. *Banco Central S.A.* [1977] 1 W.L.R. 399;
[1976] 3 All E.R. 749.

A   Owen (Edward) Engineering Ltd. v. Barclays Bank International Ltd.
              [1978] Q.B. 159; [1977] 3 W.L.R. 764; [1978] 1 All E.R. 976, C.A.
          Reg. v. Grossman, The Times, March 6, 1981; Court of Appeal (Civil
              Division) Transcript No. 97 of 1981, C.A.

          The following additional cases were cited in argument:
          Arab Bank Ltd. v. Barclays Bank [1954] A.C. 495; [1954] 2 W.L.R. 1022;
B   [1954] 2 All E.R. 226, H.L.(E.).
          Helbert Wagg & Co. Ltd., In re Claim by [1956] Ch. 323; [1956] 2
              W.L.R. 183; [1956] 1 All E.R. 129.
          Martin v. Nadel [1906] 2 K.B. 26, C.A.
          Montecchi v. Shimco (U.K.) Ltd. [1979] 1 W.L.R. 1180, C.A.
          Rossano v. Manufacturers' Life Insurance Co. [1963] 2 Q.B. 352; [1962]
              3 W.L.R. 157; [1962] 2 All E.R. 214.
C   Swiss Bank Corporation v. Boehmische Industrial Bank [1923] 1 K.B. 673,
              C.A.
          Trendtex Trading Corporation v. Credit Suisse [1980] Q.B. 629; [1980] 3
              W.L.R. 367; [1980] 3 All E.R. 721, C.A.

          INTERLOCUTORY APPEAL from Parker J.
D   By writ of January 27, 1981, the plaintiffs, Power Curber International
      Ltd., of Salisbury, North Carolina, a corporation incorporated in the
      United States of America, claimed against the defendants, the National
      Bank of Kuwait S.A.K., which was incorporated in Kuwait and whose
      registered office under Part X of the Companies Act 1948 was in London,
      U.S. $75,794·46, alternatively damages, and interest. On February 9, 1981,
      the defendants applied for a stay of the proceedings on the grounds that
E   the defendants were amenable to another and more convenient jurisdiction
      and that the proceedings should be stayed in the exercise of the court's
      discretion. On February 11, 1981, the plaintiffs applied for judgment under
      R.S.C., Ord. 14.   On March 27, 1981, Parker J. dismissed the defendants'
      application and gave judgment for the plaintiffs for U.S. $75,794·46 or
      the sterling equivalent at the time of payment together with interest from
F   December 26, 1980, at the minimum lending rate of the Bank of England
      plus one per cent. amounting to £1,180·08; and he adjudged that execu-
      tion be stayed pending further order.
          The plaintiffs appealed on the grounds that the judge had no jurisdic-
      tion to impose a stay in circumstances involving an irrevocable inter-
      national obligation assumed by the defendant bank to pay money in the
      United States under an irrecovable letter of credit; and that he was wrong
G   in law and/or wrongly exercised his discretion in imposing a stay (a) where
      judgment had been obtained in respect of such an irrevocable letter of
      credit to which (b) the terms of the Uniform Customs and Practice for
      Documentary Credits were subject and where (c) the defendant bank had
      made one payment in spite of the provisional attachment order made by
      a court in Kuwait and when (d) there were no arrangements for the
H   reciprocal enforcement of judgments between Kuwait and the United
      Kingdom and (e) without identifying the circumstances in which the stay
      would be removed.
          The defendants cross-appealed on the grounds (1) that the judge erred
      in holding that there was no arguable defence and should have given the
      defendants leave to defend the action; (2) that the judge ought to have
      held that it was arguable (a) that the debt due to the plaintiffs had been
      transferred by order of the court of Kuwait to the court of Kuwait and/or

Hammoudeh & Al Fulaij General Trading & Contracting Co. W.L.L., and   A
that the defendants' liability to the plaintiffs was completely and/or pro
tanto discharged; and (b) that the decision of Ackner J. in *Offshore International S.A.* v. *Banco Central S.A.* [1977] 1 W.L.R. 399 was distinguishable
and/or wrong, that the letter of credit opened by the defendant bank was
governed by the law of Kuwait and that, by that law, it was and remained
illegal for the bank to make any payment to the plaintiffs; (3) that, there
being an arguable defence on the merits, the proceedings should be stayed   B
according to the principles declared in *MacShannon* v. *Rockware Glass Ltd.*
[1978] A.C. 795 on the basis (i) that the dispute had nothing whatever to
do with England; and/or (ii) that the defendants were amenable to
another forum (viz. Kuwait) in which justice could be done at substantially less inconvenience and expense than in the High Court; and/or
(iii) that the court of Kuwait was a more appropriate forum than the   C
High Court in England for the purpose of determining the effect of its
own order; and/or (iv) that if the stay of execution imposed by the judge
was held to have been wrongly imposed or was, at any time in the future
to be removed, the defendant bank would be placed in the position of
having to choose to which order of which court to submit, one of such
courts being its own national court.

The order for provisional attachment by the court of first instance   D
in Kuwait in favour of Hammoudeh & Al Fulaij General Trading &
Contracting Co. was " for the immediate provisional attachment . . . of
moneys due to " the plaintiffs " from the National Bank of Kuwait in
satisfaction of the amount of U.S. $158,341·26 or the equivalent thereof
in Kuwaiti dinars, being the subject matter of the letter of credit No.
A 02/164018/7 dated September 6, 1979."   E

The facts are stated in the judgment of Lord Denning M.R.

Peter Cresswell for the plaintiffs.
Andrew Longmore for the defendant bank.

Cur. adv. vult.   F

July 3.   The following judgments were read.

LORD DENNING M.R. This case raises an important point in international trade. It has nothing to do with England except that an action
has been brought here. It is brought by plaintiffs, American sellers, who
exported goods from the United States to buyers in Kuwait. They were to   G
be paid by a letter of credit issued by the National Bank of Kuwait
S.A.K., the defendants. The bank wish to honour their obligations. They
wish to pay the sums due under the letter of credit. But the courts in
Kuwait have forbidden the bank to pay. What is the bank to do?

The plaintiff company's name is Power Curber International Ltd. You
might think that it was an English company seeing that its name ends with   H
" Ltd." But it is in fact an American corporation which carries on
business at Salisbury in North Carolina. I will call it " Power Curber." It
exports machinery to countries in the Middle East. It operates through a
firm of distributors in Kuwait called Hammoudeh & Al Fulaij General
Trading & Contracting Co. W.L.L. I will call the firm " Hammoudeh."
The directors have close contacts with America and spend their time
between that country and the Middle East. They are the " distributors "

The Weekly Law Reports, October 9, 1981

1237

1 W.L.R.   Power Curber v. National Bank, Kuwait (C.A.)   Lord Denning M.R.

A   for Power Curber in the Middle East. By which I take it they buy goods on their own account from Power Curber and re-sell them on a commission or other basis in the Middle East.

About July 1979 Power Curber agreed to supply machinery to Hammoudeh to be shipped from the U.S.A. not later than March 1, 1980, on c.i.f. terms and paid as to 25 per cent. on presentation of documents and the remaining 75 per cent. one year after date of shipment. The

B   buyers (Hammoudeh) were to give usance drafts (that is, bills of exchange payable at a later date) for this remaining 75 per cent.

In order to be sure of payment, Power Curber required Hammoudeh to open a letter of credit in their favour. Hammoudeh went to their bank, the National Bank of Kuwait S.A.K., and asked them to issue a letter of credit. No doubt Hammoudeh put the bank in funds or otherwise secured

C   the bank so that the bank would be indemnified against their liability under the letter of credit.

The letter of credit

The letter of credit is dated " Kuwait September 6, 1979." It was issued by the National Bank of Kuwait S.A.K. (the issuing bank) to the

D   Bank of America, Florida, Miami, U.S.A. (the advising bank) through the North Carolina National Bank in Charlotte, North Carolina. It was an irrevocable credit but not a confirmed credit. It is so important that I will set out most of it.

" To Bank of America,   Kuwait
     Florida, Miami, U.S.A.   September 6, 1979

E   Our Irrevocable Credit No. A02/164018/7

" Dear Sirs,

" At the request of Hammoudeh & Al Fulaij General Trading & Contracting Co WLL (A/c 59554-9), please advise our irrevocable credit through North Carolina National Bank in Charlotte, North Carolina in favour of Power Curber International Ltd., P.O. Box

F   1639, Salisbury, North Carolina, 28144, U.S.A. (A/c No. 411003742), to the extent of U.S. $300,000 . . . irrevocably valid in U.S.A. until March 1, 1980, and available by drafts without recourse as shown below drawn on the opener for 100 per cent. of the invoice value and accompanied by the documents marked (X) below . . ." Here were set out invoices, bills of lading, insurance policy, etc.

G   " The value of the usance drafts will be remitted by us at relative maturity dates provided all credit terms should have been fully complied with evidencing current shipment not later than March 1, 1980 . . . from U.S.A. to Kuwait of: — ' Equipments and spare parts ' . . . " Payment terms : 25 per cent. of the Ex-works value . . . to be paid against presentation of documents called for in order as per credit terms. Remaining 75 per cent. of the Ex-works value after

H   one year of the date of shipment . . .

" All drafts drawn under this credit must contain the clause : —

" ' Drawn Under L/C No. (as above) of the National Bank of Kuwait, S.A.K. Dated (dated of this advice).'

" In reimbursement of your negotiations under this credit, please draw on our account with Bank of America (International), New York, in respect of sight payment provided you certify to us that all terms of the credit have been complied with, and forward the

original documents direct to us by first registered airmail, duplicates   A
by following airmail.

"This credit is irrevocable on our part and we hereby undertake
that all drafts drawn in compliance with the terms hereof will be
duly honoured. . . .

"Except as otherwise stated herein, this credit is subject to the
Uniform Customs and Practice for Documentary Credits (1974 Revi-   B
sion) International Chamber of Commerce Publication No. 290.

Yours faithfully,
For the National Bank of Kuwait, S.A.K. . . ."

The goods are shipped

On December 26, 1979, the goods were duly shipped from the U.S.A.
The shipment value was U.S. $101,059·28. 25 per cent. of it was paid   C
against presentation of documents. Hammoudeh drew a usance draft on
the National Bank of Kuwait for the remaining 75 per cent. which was
$75,794·46, maturing on December 26, 1980. It was accepted by the
National Bank of Kuwait who wrote on March 4, 1980, to the North
Carolina National Bank:

"Our Letter of Credit No. A02/164018/7.   D

". . . please note that the relative usance draft for U.S. $75,794·46
maturing on December 26, 1980, has been accepted by our principals.
We shall not fail to remit to you the above mentioned amount
through Morgan Guaranty Trust Co. New York at maturity on
December 26, 1980."

     E

The effect of the letter of credit

The law on the point is clear. I take it first from *Edward Owen
Engineering Ltd.* v. *Barclays Bank International Ltd.* [1978] Q.B. 159,
169:

"It has been long established that when a letter of credit is issued
and confirmed by a bank, the bank must pay it if the documents are   F
in order and the terms of the credit are satisfied. Any dispute between
buyer and seller must be settled between themselves. The bank must
honour the credit. That was clearly stated in *Hamzeh Malas & Sons* v.
British Imex Industries Ltd. [1958] 2 Q.B. 127. Jenkins L.J. giving the
judgment of this court, said, at p. 129: '. . . it seems to be plain
enough that the opening of a confirmed letter of credit constitutes a   G
bargain between the banker and the vendor of the goods, which
imposes upon the banker an absolute obligation to pay, irrespective
of any dispute there may be between the parties as to whether the
goods are up to contract or not. An elaborate commercial system has
been built up on the footing that bankers' confirmed credits are of
that character, and, in my judgment, it would be wrong for this court
in the present case to interfere with the established practice.'   H

"To this general principle there is an exception in the case of
what is called established or obvious fraud to the knowledge of the
bank."

Those words apply not only to confirmed credits but also to irrevocable
credits. To which I would add these provisions of the Uniform Customs
and Practice for Documentary Credits (1974 revision) which I take from

The Weekly Law Reports, October 9, 1981

1239

1 W.L.R.   Power Curber v. National Bank, Kuwait (C.A.)   Lord Denning M.R.

A *Gutteridge and Megrah, The Law of Bankers' Commercial Credits,* 6th ed. (1979), pp. 221–222:

> " (c) Credits, by their nature, are separate transactions from the sales or other contracts on which they may be based and banks are in no way concerned with or bound by such contracts. . . .
>
> " A. Form and notification of credits . . .
>
> " ARTICLE 3
>
> " (a) An irrevocable credit constitutes a definite undertaking of the issuing bank, provided that the terms and conditions of the credit are complied with: (i) to pay, or that payment will be made, if the credit provides for payment, whether against a draft or not; (ii) to accept drafts if the credit provides for acceptance by the issuing bank or to be responsible for their acceptance and payment at maturity . . ."

The order made in Kuwait

It appears that early in November 1980 Hammoudeh filed a claim in the courts of Kuwait against Power Curber for 50,000 Kuwaiti dinars. That is about $180,000. We do not know the nature of the claim but it is thought that it may be a claim for commission. Following on that claim, Hammoudeh applied to the court in Kuwait for an order for " provisional attachment " of the sums payable by the National Bank of Kuwait under the letter of credit to Power Curber. On November 5, 1980, the court in Kuwait ordered the " provisional attachment." This order prevented the bank from making any further payment under the letter of credit in Kuwait or outside Kuwait: and made the bank accountable to the court for the amount involved. The bank lodged a protest against the attachment: and applied to the court in Kuwait to set aside the order for " provisional attachment." But the court refused to set it aside. And its refusal has been upheld by the Court of Appeal in Kuwait.

The steps taken by Power Curber

As Power Curber did not receive payment, they sent a telex to the bank in January 1981, saying:

> " We have not received the payment in the amount of U.S. $75,794·46 which matured for payment on December 26, 1980. You had agreed to honour the draft upon maturity under the rules and regulations of the Uniform Customs and Practices for Documentary Credits (1974 revision) International Chamber of Commerce publication No. 290.
>
> " Unless we receive this payment immediately, we will begin legal proceedings against you for failure to pay the balance legally due us . . ."

Power Curber started proceedings in North Carolina, but afterwards discontinued them: and started proceedings in England.

On January 27, 1981, Power Curber issued a writ in the High Court in England against the National Bank of Kuwait (which was trading here and had a registered address in London). They claimed $75,794·46 and applied for judgment under Order 14.

On March 27, 1981, Parker J. gave judgment in favour of Power Curber against the National Bank of Kuwait for that amount but stayed execution on it until further order. There is now an appeal by Power Curber against the stay and by the bank against the judgment.

The questions debated before us were these: I. Should Power Curber   A
be granted summary judgment? II. Even if granted summary judgment,
should execution be stayed?

By our English law a plaintiff is entitled to have summary judgment
given for him if the defendant has no arguable defence to the claim.
Parker J. gave summary judgment for the plaintiffs. But he stayed execution on it until further order. Each side appeals. I will deal first with
summary judgment.   B

I. *Summary judgment*

On the face of it, the National Bank of Kuwait are in default. They
promised to pay the sums due under the letter of credit at maturity. They
have not paid those sums.

Mr. Longmore submits, however, that the " provisional attachment "   C
gives the bank an arguable defence. He says that the proper law of the
contract was Kuwaiti law and that, by that law, the payment of the sums
was unlawful. Alternatively, he says that the lex situs of the debt was
Kuwait: and it is that law which governs the effect of the attachment. If
the attachment was lawful by Kuwaiti law, he says that all other countries
should give effect to it.   D

I cannot accept Mr. Longmore's submissions. The proper law of the
contract is to be found by asking: With what law has the contract its
closest and most real connection? In my opinion it was the law of North
Carolina where payment was to be made (on behalf of the issuing bank)
against presentation of documents. Mr. Longmore sought to say that
Offshore International S.A. v. *Banco Central S.A.* [1977] 1 W.L.R. 399   E
decided by Ackner J. was either wrongly decided or was distinguishable
on grounds parallel to those canvassed in *Gutteridge and Megrah, The
Law of Bankers' Commercial Credits,* 6th ed., pp. 213–214. But I think
the case was rightly decided and cannot be distinguished on any valid
grounds. The letter of credit, and the payments under it, were certainly
valid by its proper law.

Nor can I agree that the lex situs of the debt was Kuwait. It was in   F
North Carolina. A debt under a letter of credit is different from ordinary
debts. They may be situate where the debtor is resident. But a debt under
a letter of credit is situate in the place where it is in fact payable against
documents. I would hold therefore that Parker J. was right in giving
summary judgment against the National Bank of Kuwait for the sums due.

If it were a case where leave to defend should be given, I would hold   G
that the action should be tried in England. By bringing the action in
England, Power Curber have a legitimate juridical advantage of which it
would not be right to deprive them: see *MacShannon* v. *Rockware Glass
Ltd.* [1978] A.C. 795, 812, *per* Lord Diplock.

II. *Stay of execution*   H

In considering the " provisional attachment " order, it must be remembered that the orders of a foreign court fall into three categories. First,
those which are enforceable in England by our English courts. Second,
those which are recognised in England by virtue of the comity of nations:
so that we will do nothing contrary to them. Third, those which will not
be recognised here in England because they do not accord with the public
policy of our law.

The Weekly Law Reports, October 9, 1981

1241

1 W.L.R.   Power Curber v. National Bank, Kuwait (C.A.)   Lord Denning M.R.

A   On this question of recognition, I must draw attention to the importance of letters of credit in international trade. They are the means by which goods are supplied all the world over. It is vital that every bank which issues a letter of credit should honour its obligations. The bank is in no way concerned with any dispute that the buyer may have with the seller. The buyer may say that the goods are not up to contract. Nevertheless the bank must honour its obligations. The buyer may say that he has a

B   cross-claim in a large amount. Still the bank must honour its obligations. A letter of credit is like a bill of exchange given for the price of goods. It ranks as cash and must be honoured. No set off or counterclaim is allowed to detract from it: see *Nova (Jersey) Knit Ltd.* v. *Kammgarn Spinnerei G.m.b.H.* [1977] 1 W.L.R. 713. All the more so with a letter of credit. Whereas a bill of exchange is given by buyer to seller, a letter of

C   credit is given by a bank to the seller with the very intention of avoiding anything in the nature of a set off or counterclaim. This is borne out by the Uniform Customs and Practice for Documentary Credits which have been adopted by the banks in all, or practically all, the countries of the world—from China to Andorra—from Cuba to Nauru. All subscribe to the Uniform Customs and Practice which declare:

D   " Credits, by their nature, are separate transactions from the sales or other contracts on which they may be based and banks are in no way concerned with or bound by such contracts."

    If the court of any of the countries should interfere with the obligations of one of its banks (by ordering it not to pay under a letter of credit) it would strike at the very heart of that country's international trade. No

E   foreign seller would supply goods to that country on letters of credit—because he could no longer be confident of being paid. No trader would accept a letter of credit issued by a bank of that country if it might be ordered by its courts not to pay. So it is part of the law of international trade that letters of credit should be honoured—and not nullified by an attachment order at the suit of the buyer.

F   Added to this, it seems to me that the buyer himself by his conduct has precluded himself from asking for an attachment order. By opening the letter of credit in favour of the seller, he has implicitly agreed that he will not raise any set off or counterclaim—such as to delay or resist payment. He has contracted under the terms of the Uniform Customs and Practice by which he promises that the bank will pay without regard to any set off or counterclaim: and implicitly that he will not seek an attach-

G   ment order. I gather that, if the court in Kuwait had looked at the case in this way, they would not have granted the " provisional attachment." To my mind, it is implicit in the Uniform Customs and Practice that such an attachment is precluded.

    Yet another consideration occurs to me. Many banks now have branches in many foreign countries. Each branch has to be licensed by the

H   country in which it operates. Each branch is treated in that country as independent of its parent body. The branch is subject to the orders of the courts of the country in which it operates; but not to the orders of the courts where its head office is situate. We so decided in the recent case about bankers' books in the Isle of Man: *Reg.* v. *Grossman*, The Times, March 6, 1981. In this case I think that the order for " provisional attachment " operates against the head office in Kuwait, but not against the branch office in London. That branch is subject to the orders of the

English courts. Only the other day this court held that a Mareva injunc-   A
tion should not be granted to stop payment of a bank guarantee outside
the jurisdiction: see *Intraco Ltd.* v. *Notis Shipping Corporation of
Liberia,* The Times, July 7, 1981.

It is my opinion that the courts of England are not bound by the
comity of nations to recognise the " provisional attachment " issued by
the courts in Kuwait. We should not grant a stay of execution. The judgment here should operate against the branch in London so as to require it   B
to pay the sums due under the letter of credit.

Conclusion

The striking fact is that the courts here in London are asked to
enforce a letter of credit opened by buyers in Kuwait in favour of sellers
in the United States for payment in the United States. But this is because   C
London is an important centre of international trade. Merchants from all
the world come here to settle their disputes. Banks from all the world
over have branches here to receive and make payments. So far as we
can be of service to international trade, we will accept the task and fulfil it
to the best of our ability.

I would approve the judgment of Parker J. in favour of the sellers. I   D
would not grant a stay of execution.

GRIFFITHS L.J. I will deal first with the cross-appeal. The bank submit
that the judge should give leave to defend because payment of the sums
due under the letter of credit is unlawful according to the proper law of
the contract. This submission depends upon the proper law of the letter
of credit being Kuwaiti law. In my view the proper law of the letter of   E
credit was the law of the state of North Carolina. Under the letter of
credit the bank accepted the obligation of paying or arranging the payment of the sums due in American dollars against presentation of documents at the sellers' bank in North Carolina. The bank could not have
discharged its obligation by offering payment in Kuwait. Furthermore the
bank undertook to reimburse the advising bank if they paid on their   F
behalf in dollars in America. In *Offshore International S.A.* v. *Banco
Central S.A.* [1977] 1 W.L.R. 399 Ackner J. held that the place at which
the bank must perform its obligation under a letter of credit determines
the proper law to be applied to the letter of credit. In my view that case
was correctly decided.

Secondly, it was submitted that payment was unlawful according to
the lex situs of the debt which it is said is Kuwait. But this is a debt that   G
is owed in American dollars in North Carolina; I do not regard the fact
that the bank that owes the debt has a residence in Kuwait as any reason
for regarding Kuwait as the lex situs of the debt. The lex situs of the debt
is North Carolina, and this ground for giving leave to defend cannot be
supported.

No other grounds were advanced for resisting judgment under R.S.C.,   H
Ord. 14 and I agree that the cross-appeal should be dismissed.

Now as to the appeal: should the judge have granted a stay of the
judgment? At the time the case was before Parker J. the order of the
Kuwait court was under appeal to the Kuwait Court of Appeal. In those
circumstances, I think I should have been very tempted to grant a short
stay to await the outcome of the decision of the Court of Appeal because
I fear that I should have thought it highly unlikely that the Court of

The Weekly Law Reports, October 9, 1981

1243

1 W.L.R.   Power Curber v. National Bank, Kuwait (C.A.)   Griffiths L.J.

A Appeal would uphold an order that interfered so seriously with the well recognised international obligation of a bank under an irrevocable letter of credit. By granting the stay I should have been relieved of the disagreeable obligation to refuse to recognise the order of a court of a friendly state.

B But now we know the result of the Court of Appeal hearing in Kuwait and must face the choice between enforcing the obligation upon the bank to pay under its irrevocable letter of credit or recognising the order of the Kuwait court.

I have no doubt that we should uphold the obligation to pay under the irrevocable letter of credit and remove the stay. Letters of credit have become established as a universally acceptable means of payment in international transactions. They are regarded by merchants the world

C over as equivalent to cash; they have been rightly described by that most distinguished commercial lawyer Kerr J. as " the life-blood of international commerce ": see *R. D. Harbottle (Mercantile) Ltd.* v. *National Westminster Bank Ltd.* [1978] Q.B. 146, 155. The bankers' promise to pay the seller is wholly independent of the underlying contract of sale between the seller and the buyer, or of any contractual dispute that may arise

D between them. The whole purpose of this form of payment is that a seller should not be kept out of his money by litigation against him at the suit of the buyer. In the absence of fraud the seller is entitled to be paid on presentation of genuine documents.

In the present case we do not even know with certainty the nature of the buyer's claim in Kuwait because he obtained his provisional attachment order at an ex parte hearing and has never served the American

E seller with any documents specifying the claim. It may be in respect of commission, or it may arise in respect of the goods in respect of which the letter of credit was issued. There is no suggestion of fraud and in the absence of fraud an English court would not have interfered with the banker's obligation to pay under the letter of credit: see *Discount Records Ltd.* v. *Barclays Bank Ltd.* [1975] 1 W.L.R. 315; *R. D. Harbottle (Mer-*

F *cantile) Ltd.* v. *National Westminster Bank* [1978] Q.B. 146 and *Edward Owen Engineering Ltd.* v. *Barclays Bank International Ltd.* [1978] Q.B. 159.

We should do the Bank of Kuwait a grave disservice if we were not to remove this stay for it would undoubtedly seriously damage their credibility as an international bank if it was thought that their paper was not worth holding because an ex parte application to their domestic courts could

G prevent payment under an expressedly irrevocable obligation.

There is no recognised rule of international law that compels this court to recognise this ex parte order of the Kuwaiti court. It is of course entitled to be treated with respect and wherever possible this court will in the interests of comity seek to recognise and uphold the order of the court of a friendly state. But unhappily in this case the approach of the

H Kuwaiti court appears to be so out of step with that of our own courts and the courts of other trading nations that I fear we cannot recognise it. The choice lies between upholding the world-wide practices of international commerce or the order of the Kuwaiti court. I choose the first option and would remove the stay.

WATERHOUSE J. (read by Griffiths L.J.). I agree that this appeal should be allowed and that the cross-appeal should be dismissed. Despite the

forceful argument of counsel for the bank, I am unable to accept that $\quad$ A
leave to defend the action should have been granted. On the issue as to
the proper law of the letter of credit, I respectfully agree with what has
been said by Lord Denning M.R. and Griffiths L.J. about the correctness
and the application to the instant case of the reasoning of Ackner J. in
Offshore International S.A. v. *Banco Central S.A.* [1977] 1 W.L.R. 399.
The more difficult issue for me has been that relating to the lex situs of
the debt. $\quad$ B

A debt is generally to be looked upon as situate in the country where
it is properly recoverable or can be enforced and it is noteworthy that the
sellers here submitted voluntarily to the dismissal of their earlier proceedings against the bank in North Carolina. We have been told that they did
so because of doubts about the jurisdiction of the North Carolina court,
which was alleged in the pleadings to be based on the transaction of $\quad$ C
business by the bank there, acting by itself or through another named
bank as its agent. As for the question of residence, the bank has been
silent about any residence that it may have within the United States of
America. In the absence of any previous binding authority, I have not
been persuaded that this debt due under an unconfirmed letter of credit
can be regarded as situate in North Carolina merely because there was
provision for payment at a branch of a bank used by the sellers in $\quad$ D
Charlotte: and I do not regard the analogy of a bill of exchange or a
security transferable by delivery as helpful.

Nevertheless, Parker J. was right, in my judgment, to refuse the bank
leave to defend because the Kuwaiti provisional order of attachment did
not affect the existence of the debt. Counsel for the bank has submitted
that the effect of that order was to alter the debt from one due to the $\quad$ E
sellers to a debt due to the court or held to the order of the court awaiting
a decision as to whom it should be paid. I agree with Parker J. that this
submission is based upon a single sentence in an affidavit and that it
does not bear that weight. There is no acceptable evidence that, according to the law of Kuwait, the debt has ceased to be due to the sellers.
There is no ground, therefore, for granting leave to defend and counsel $\quad$ F
for the bank has not sought to argue that a stay of proceedings is justified
if leave to defend was properly refused. If there had been arguable defence,
I would have held that the action should be tried in England because
there is a legitimate juridical advantage to the sellers in proceeding here,
which outweighs any disadvantage to the bank.

The sellers' appeal against the stay of execution granted by Parker J.
has to be considered in the changed circumstance that the bank's appeal $\quad$ G
to the Court of Appeal in Kuwait against the provisional order of attachment has failed. Although a further appeal to the Cour de Cassation there
is proceeding, we have been told that it will not be heard until the end of
the year. I agree, therefore, that the overwhelming balance of the argument now is in favour of removal of the stay of execution. Part of the
argument for the bank on this issue has been that it is inexpedient for the $\quad$ H
court to permit execution to proceed pending resolution of the dispute
between Hammoudeh and the sellers: it is suggested that the bank may
be exposed to the risk of proceedings for contempt in Kuwait or of double
payment. One has sympathy with the bank in its dilemma, and its good
faith is not in doubt, not least because it has already paid to the plaintiffs
$82,546·80 due earlier on November 7, 1980, in respect of the same letter
of credit, despite the provisional attachment order. However, the action

A of the opener, Hammoudeh, and the reasoning of the Kuwait Court of
Appeal appear to me to strike at the essential foundations of the international acceptability of letters of credit so that the stay ought not to
continue.

> *Appeal allowed with costs.*
> *Cross-appeal dismissed with costs.*
B
> *Leave to appeal refused.*

Solicitors: *Jaques & Co.; Allen & Overy.*

A. H. B.

C

---

* SUEDECLUB CO. LTD. *v.* OCCASIONS TEXTILES LTD.

D [1979 S. No. 1014]

1981   May 18;   Nourse J.
       June 3; 19

*Practice—Notice of intention to proceed—Validity—Notice served
  less than one year after last proceeding—Whether valid—*
E *R.S.C., Ord. 3, r. 6*

Early in 1979, the plaintiffs issued a writ for breach of
copyright against the defendants. After interlocutory proceedings, resulting in the giving of certain undertakings until trial,
there was a period of inactivity until the service of the statement of claim on February 29, 1980. On February 18, 1981,
no defence having been served, the plaintiffs' solicitors wrote
to the defendants' solicitors purporting to give notice of
F intention to proceed under R.S.C., Ord. 3, r. 6.[1] Their letter,
although properly served by post never in fact arrived and on
April 3, 1981, the plaintiffs entered judgment in default of
defence for damages, interest to be assessed, and costs.
      On the defendants' summons to set aside the judgment
on the ground that it was irregular by reason of the plaintiffs'
failure to give valid notice of their intention to proceed after
a year's delay pursuant to R.S.C., Ord. 3, r. 6: —
G
      Held, that a notice of intention to proceed under R.S.C.,
Ord. 3, r. 6 could not be validly given until a year or more
had elapsed since the last proceeding in the cause or matter;
and that, accordingly, as the plaintiffs' notice of intention to
proceed was served less than a year after service of the statement of claim, it was invalid, and the judgment entered on
April 3 must be set aside (post, pp. 1247H—1248A).
H   Dictum of Lindley L.J. in *Webster* v. *Myer* (1884) 14
Q.B.D. 231, 234, C.A. considered.

The following case is referred to in the judgment:
Webster v. *Myer* (1884) 14 Q.B.D. 231, C.A.

No additional cases were cited in argument.

---

[1] R.S.C., Ord. 3, r. 6: see post, p. 1247A.

Suedeclub Ltd. v. Occasions Textiles Ltd. (Ch.D.) **[1981]**

A

SUMMONS

By a writ dated February 27, 1979, the plaintiffs, Suedeclub Co. Ltd., commenced a copyright action against the defendants, Occasions Textiles Ltd. The statement of claim was served on February 29, 1980. No defence was served and on February 18, 1981, the plaintiffs' solicitors purported to give notice by letter of intention to proceed in accordance with R.S.C., Ord. 3, r. 6. On April 3, 1981, the plaintiffs entered judgment in default of defence for damages, interest to be assessed and costs under R.S.C., Ord. 19, r. 3. By a summons dated April 8, 1981, the defendants applied to have the judgment set aside and for leave to defend, on the ground, inter alia, that the judgment was irregular.

The facts are stated in the judgment.

B

Christopher Floyd for the defendants.
E. B. H. Bragiel for the plaintiffs.

C

Cur. adv. vult.

June 19. NOURSE J. read the following judgment. This is an application to set aside a judgment entered in default of defence in a copyright action. It has given rise to a short but difficult question on R.S.C., Ord. 3, r. 6. That is the well known rule which requires notice of intention to proceed to be given after a year's delay in the proceedings.

D

The question arises in this way. The writ in the action was issued on February 27, 1979. In March 1979 there were interlocutory proceedings, which led to certain undertakings by the defendants pending trial. There was then a period of inactivity which lasted for nearly a year. The statement of claim was served on February 29, 1980, that being the last proceeding in the action for the purposes of R.S.C., Ord. 3, r. 6.

E

In March and April 1980 there were inconclusive negotiations between the two sides and the matter then went to sleep. No defence was served. On February 18, 1981, the plaintiffs' solicitors wrote to the defendants' solicitors in these terms: " We hereby give you notice of intention to proceed in this matter as we have not received your clients' defence." That was certainly a notice of intention to proceed, but it was given some 10 days before the expiry of one year after the service of the statement of claim. In fact the letter never arrived, but the defendants now accept that it was properly served by post under R.S.C., Ord. 65, r. 5. On April 3, 1981, the plaintiffs entered judgment in default of defence for damages and interest to be assessed, and costs, under R.S.C., Ord. 19, r. 3, the other claims in the action having been abandoned.

F

G

The defendants' application to set the judgment aside was originally based solely on the ground that it was irregular by reason of the plaintiffs' alleged failure to give a valid notice pursuant to R.S.C., Ord. 3, r. 6. In case the judgment should be held to have been regular the application has now been amended to raise an alternative claim for leave to defend based on the ground that the defendants have shown that they have a defence to the action which ought to be tried. It is agreed on both sides that the defendants' alternative claim is a good one, but that if they are forced to rely on that they will have to pay the costs of this application. Therefore, the defendants have argued that their original claim is a good one in order, if they can, to better their position with regard to costs.

H

The Weekly Law Reports, October 9, 1981

1247

1 W.L.R.   Suedeclub Ltd. v. Occasions Textiles Ltd. (Ch.D.)   Nourse J.

A   R.S.C., Ord. 3, r. 6, which is headed, "Notice of intention to proceed after year's delay," is in these terms:

"Where a year or more has elapsed since the last proceeding in a cause or matter, the party who desires to proceed must give to every other party not less than one month's notice of his intention to proceed. A summons on which no order was made is not a pro-
B   ceeding for the purpose of this rule."

Mr. Floyd, who appears for the defendants, argued that the letter of February 18, 1981, was not a notice pursuant to the rule on the ground that it was given less than a year after the service of the statement of claim. He said that the wording of the rule, scilicet: "Where a year or more *has* elapsed ... the party who *desires* to proceed *must give* ..."
C   etc. contemplates, and contemplates only, the giving of a notice after the year has elapsed. He said that if it was intended that a notice could be given before the year had elapsed the rule would have read "the party ... *must give or have given* ..." etc.

On a literal construction of the rule, Mr. Floyd's argument must be correct, but it was said that it would lead to an anomalous result. On
D   Mr. Floyd's argument, the plaintiffs could have entered judgment at any time up to and including February 28, 1981, without notice, and at any time on or after April 1, 1981, with notice, but they could not have entered judgment at any time between March 1 and 31, either with or without notice.

I was at one time impressed by that argument, but Mr. Floyd referred me to the judgment of Lindley L.J. in *Webster* v. *Myer* (1884) 14 Q.B.D.
E   231, 234, where he said:

"The fact of more than a year having elapsed since the last pro-ceeding, seems to show that the plaintiff had intended to abandon the prosecution of the action, and it might be very unjust to allow him to sign judgment without giving the defendant an opportunity of establishing to the satisfaction of the court that the plaintiff is not
F   entitled to proceed further."

That shows that the lapse of a year since the last proceeding is taken to demonstrate that the plaintiff intends to abandon the action. Con-versely, until the year is up his assumed intention is to proceed. If during the year he gives notice of his intention to proceed, he does so
G   unnecessarily. If he gives notice, however late in the year, but does not then proceed within it, he must still be taken to intend to abandon the action. That was the position in the present case and it seems to me that Mr. Floyd is right in saying that before the plaintiffs could enter judgment on April 3 they ought, after February 28, to have given the defendants not less than one month's notice of their intention to proceed.

H   I should add that the suggested anomaly caused by this construction of the rule is at the least balanced, if not outweighed, by another anomaly which would flow from the contrary construction. Mr. Floyd contends that if a notice can be given before the year has expired, the plaintiffs in this case could have given it on March 1, 1980, the day after the service of the statement of claim, and could still have relied on that notice to secure their judgment on April 3, 1981. It seems to me that there is no answer to that contention and that its consequences are

more startling than those which flow from Mr. Floyd's construction **A**
of the rule.

In all the circumstances it seems to me that the only safe course is
for me to apply the literal construction of the rule and to hold that the
letter of February 18, 1981, was not a notice pursuant to it.   That means
that the defendants' claim that the judgment was irregular was a good
one and that the judgment must be set aside on that ground.

B

Judgment set aside with costs.

Solicitors: *Whitelock & Storr; E. D. C. Lord & Co., Southall.*

T. C. C. B.

C

_____

[FAMILY DIVISION]

* LEWISHAM LONDON BOROUGH COUNCIL *v.* M.   **D**

1981   Feb. 23, 24, 25, 26   Hollings J.

*Minor—Ward of court—Jurisdiction—Children in care of local
authority—Mother seeking custody of children—Local authority making children wards of court—Children with foster
parents—Whether their care and control to be committed to
local authority—Family Law Reform Act 1969 (c. 46), s. 7 (2)*   **E**

A local authority had taken into care five illegitimate
children, who had been born between 1972 and 1977. During
the few short periods they had been with their mother, she
had neglected them despite the support she had received from
social workers. By June 1978, the mother demonstrated little
interest in the children. The local authority, who had placed   **F**
the three eldest children with a long-term foster parent and
the two youngest with a short-term foster parent, passed a
resolution, under section 2 of the Children Act 1948, assuming
parental rights and duties over the children. The mother
objected. The local authority then made the children wards of
court and in the proceedings, in which the mother was a
defendant but the children's foster parents were not parties,
the local authority sought an order for the care and control   **G**
of the children. They asked that the care and control order
should be made under section 7 (2) of the Family Law
Reform Act 1969[1] so that the authority would be enabled to
make payments for the maintenance and financial support of
the children under the provisions of Part II of the Children
Act 1948.

On the question whether the court should make an order
under section 7 (2) of the Family Law Reform Act 1969:—   **H**

Held, that section 7 (2) of the Family Law Reform Act
1969 gave the court power to commit a ward of court to the
care of the local authority where it was impracticable or
undesirable for the ward to be in the care of either parent or
" any other individual "; that, since the mother was unsuitable
to have the care of the children, the foster parents were the
only individuals who could be considered as being possible

[1] Family Law Reform Act 1969, s. 7 (2): see post, p. 1252B–D.

A   persons to be granted the care and control of the children;
that although the three eldest children were living with a
foster parent who was another individual within the meaning
of the subsection, it was impracticable to grant her care and
control because she required an allowance in order to provide
for the children's needs and, since the youngest children's
foster parent had indicated that she did not wish to foster them
in the long term, she was not, within the subsection, " any
B   other individual "; and that, therefore, since there was no
" other individual " to care for the children, an order would
be made under the subsection committing the children to the
care and control of the plaintiff local authority (post, pp.
1255G—1256A, C–F).

    In re C.B. (A Minor) (Wardship: Local Authority) [1981]
1 W.L.R. 379, C.A. considered.

C   The following cases are referred to in the judgment:

    C.B. (A Minor) (Wardship: Local Authority), In re [1981] 1 W.L.R. 379;
        [1981] 1 All E.R. 16, C.A.

    J. v. C. [1970] A.C. 668; [1969] 2 W.L.R. 540; [1969] 1 All E.R. 788,
        H.L.(E.).

    Y. (A Minor) (Child in Care: Access), In re [1976] Fam. 125; [1975] 3
        W.L.R. 342; [1975] 3 All E.R. 348, C.A.

D

    No additional cases were cited in argument.

SUMMONS

    The five illegitimate children of the defendant, who was now aged 27
and of West Indian origin, were in the care of the Lewisham London
Borough Council under section 1 of the Children Act 1948. The eldest
E   children were twin boys, born on October 5, 1972; the third child was a
surviving twin girl born on April 5, 1974, and the youngest children were
twin boys, born on October 30, 1977. Each set of twins had been
fathered by a different man.

    The children had spent the greater part of their lives in the care of
the local authority. Before the birth of the youngest twins the mother
F   had had the care of the three elder children but she had left them alone
on a number of occasions. On February 2, 1977, with the mother's
agreement the local authority took the children into care under section 1
of the Children Act 1948 and the boys were placed with a foster mother,
Mrs. B. The children were returned to their mother in the summer but
by October they were back in care and all three were placed with Mrs. B.

    For a short period in the early part of 1978 the mother had the care
G   of all five children but despite help from social workers the children were
neglected and, thereafter, from May 17, 1978, they had been in the
continual care of the local authority.

    The local authority passed a resolution assuming parental rights and
duties in respect of the five children under section 2 of the Children Act
1948. The mother objected to the resolution. On July 24, 1979, by
H   originating summons the local authority made the five children wards of
court and invited the court to grant the care and control of the children
to them. The mother also sought care and control of the children.
By an interim order made by Mr. Registrar Holloway care and control of the children was granted to the local authority. The two elder
boys and the girl were still living with Mrs. B. The two younger boys
were with a short-term foster mother and the local authority proposed
that they should be adopted if suitable adopters could be found.

A

The above statement of facts has been extracted from the judgment of Hollings J., which was delivered in chambers after a hearing in chambers. The case is only reported on the question of the relevance of section 7 (2) of the Family Law Reform Act 1969 and is reported with the permission of Hollings J.

B

Anita Ryan for the local authority.
Judith Parker for the mother.
Mary Hogg for the Official Solicitor, the guardian ad litem.

HOLLINGS J. This is an application by Lewisham London Borough Council, the plaintiffs in wardship proceedings, relating to the care and control of five children. There were three sets of twins: first, twin boys born on October 5, 1972, now aged eight years and four months; then C twin girls born on April 5, 1974, one of whom sadly died soon after birth, the survivor now aged six years and ten months; and twin boys born on October 30, 1977, and now aged three years and four months. They are all the illegitimate children of the defendant. [His Lordship stated the facts and continued:] In the circumstances I am quite satisfied that in the case of the three eldest children they should continue in the long-term fostering care of the foster mother with whom they had D been since 1977; and that there should be no access at this stage by the mother to those children. I by no means rule out access at a later stage, if circumstances permit and the best interests of the children dictate. I think that by all means the mother should be allowed to send letters and should be kept informed of the welfare of her children if she wishes to know. So far as the youngest children are concerned, because of the E comparatively high rate of break-down in fostering, and because of the great confidence expressed by Mrs. Lawson, who is in charge of the local authority's adoption agency, as to her ability to place the children— albeit in all probability with white parents—I think it is right that I should authorise the adoptive process to be commenced.

I had not fully dealt with the argument or discussion about black F adoptive parents. Suffice it to say, I do not think from what I have been told that there is any real prospect of obtaining parents of the right cultural background. But the effort should be made to find such parents because there is a slight advantage in having them as parents. But even if such parents are not available, I am quite satisfied that it is in the interests of the children that they should be with white adoptive parents.

I now come to the form of order, and this is where Miss Ryan, on G behalf of the plaintiff local authority, in particular has asked me to consider a decision in the Court of Appeal and its effect upon local authorities. As I said earlier in this judgment, the foster mother is not a party; and so far as the youngest twins are concerned, there is no relevant foster parent because the short-term foster parent will fade out of the picture in due course. And so all the local authority can do is ask for an order that H care and control in one way or another should be committed to them generally.

In the past it has been quite usual, to my knowledge, where plaintiffs are local authorities for an application to be made that the ward should be committed to their care under section 7 (2) of the Family Law Reform Act 1969; and it has been to my knowledge quite usual for judges to make orders under that section in favour of the plaintiffs local authority.

A In those circumstances it has not been necessary, even if there has been a foster parent or parents caring for or intending to care for the children to make the foster parents themselves parties to the proceedings.

In *In re C.B. (A Minor) (Wardship: Local Authority)* [1981] 1 W.L.R. 379; [1981] 1 All E.R. 16, the Court of Appeal had to consider a decision of Bush J. in relation to an illegitimate child, I think it is
B useful if I set out the facts more or less as they are set out in the head-note [1981] 1 All E.R. 16, because I think they are important in relation to the decision which was actually made in that case:

"In October 1977 an illegitimate child then aged eight or nine months who had been left by her 17-year-old mother in the care of the child's grandmother was taken into voluntary care by the local authority with the mother's consent. The local authority placed the
C child with a short-term foster mother, Mrs. R., who provided a good home for her. The mother occasionally visited the child. In April 1978 she married a man who was not the father of the child and told the local authority that she wanted the child back. The local authority was not satisfied with the mother's proposed arrangements for the child and decided to make her a ward of court. Accordingly,
D the local authority, as plaintiff, took out an originating summons, dated May 26, 1978, to which the mother was the defendant, asking (i) that the child remain a ward of court during her minority and (ii) that care and control of her be committed to the local authority. An interim order was made granting care and control to the local authority and the child remained with Mrs. R. The mother visited the child in June 1978 but thereafter did not see her again until
E January 1979, which was the last time she saw her. Consequently the child did not form any relationship with the mother, and both she and the child's father were strangers to her. In February 1979 the local authority decided that the situation at Mrs. R.'s home was disturbing for the child and that she should be transferred to long-term foster parents. On September 28, without referring the matter
F to the court, the local authority transferred the child from Mrs. R. to the new foster parents who were eminently suitable and with whom the child was forming a secure relationship."

I interpose here to say that it appears from the judgment of Ormrod L.J., at p. 25c, that these new foster parents were proposed adopters.
G I continue:

"Mrs. R. was distressed at the transfer. The court was informed of the change in the foster parents on October 11. The mother, who had left her husband, went back to live with the child's father and wanted the child to be returned to Mrs. R., who was therefore made second defendant to the originating summons. The local authority's view was
H that the child should remain in the care of the new foster parents. The judge, however, having ordered that the child should remain a ward of court, ordered that the mother should have care and control of her, since he thought that the matter was governed by section 7 (2) of the Family Law Reform Act 1969 and he found that there were 'no exceptional circumstances making it impracticable or undesirable,' within that subsection, for the child to be under the mother's care so as to justify an order under that subsection

committing the child to the care of the local authority. The local A
authority appealed."

Now, before I consider the judgment in particular of Ormrod L.J.,
I should say this. The particular concern of the local authority, and indeed
of local authorities, is that if a simple order under the inherent jurisdiction
is made giving care and control of a ward to the local authority, and not
an order under section 7 (2) of the Act of 1969 to which I have yet to B
refer, there may be no power in the local authority to provide for the
maintenance of that ward placed in their control if that ward is placed
with a foster parent or parents. Section 7 (2) of the Family Law Reform
Act 1969 provides:

"Where it appears to the court that there are exceptional circumstances making it impracticable or undesirable for a ward of court to C
be, or to continue to be, under the care of either of his parents or of
any other individual the court may, if it thinks fit, make an order
committing the care of the ward to a local authority; and thereupon
Part II of the Children Act 1948 (which relates to the treatment of
children in the care of a local authority) shall, subject to the next
following subsection, apply as if the child had been received by the D
local authority into their care under section 1 of that Act."

That is, the Children Act 1948. Part II of the Children Act 1948 contains
provisions relating to the general duty of local authorities in care cases,
and in particular section 13 provides for the provision of accommodation
and maintenance for children in care. And so, if a care order is made
under section 7 (2) of the Family Law Reform Act 1969, the local auth- E
ority to whom the care of the ward is committed, would be enabled,
without risk of surcharge by their district auditor, to make payments for
the maintenance and other financial support of any ward placed in their
care under that section. But, as I have said, it is greatly doubted that they
have such power without such a care order.

Now I turn to In re C.B. (A Minor) (Wardship: Local Authority)
[1981] 1 W.L.R. 379. The decision of the Court of Appeal was that F
Bush J. erred in basing his decision upon the requirements and wording
of section 7 (2) of the Family Law Reform Act 1969, the Court of
Appeal holding that the proper approach in considering where the care
and control of a child should be is that laid down in the Guardianship of
Minors Act 1971 and in J. v. C. [1970] A.C. 668 in the House of Lords.
That is, the court in its discretion must decide what the paramount G
interests of the child required, to quote Ormrod L.J.'s words at p. 387F
and that Bush J. was wrong in saying that the words of section 7 (2)
enabled him or directed him to decide whether it was impracticable or
undesirable for the ward to continue to be under the care (in this case)
of his mother; Bush J. had decided that in the circumstances of the case
it was right, having regard to the provisions of section 7 (2), that the
child in question should be with its mother rather than with either of H
the pairs of foster parents. As Ormrod L.J. said, at p. 385:

"So the judge, in practice, had three possible alternative solutions to
this problem: one was to leave the child where she is with her present
foster parents; another was to send her back to her pseudo-mother,
her mother substitute, Mrs. R.; and the third was to hand her over
to her own mother."

A   And he sets out the pros and cons in the case of each. Then Ormrod
L.J. continues, at p. 386:

"Now the judge did not, as I see it, approach the case in the way
I have just indicated. Having set out the facts very fairly in his
judgment, he said: 'This decision does not turn upon the relative
merits of [the present foster parents] and the mother in the ideal
B   parents' stakes. No doubt the mother would come off second best,
particularly as she has not been given a chance to show what she can
do with Claire. The question turns upon whether the local authority
have shown that it is undesirable that the child should be or continue
to be under the care of either of her parents. The court must look
at the totality of the circumstances, bearing in mind that Parliament
intended that children should remain with their parents if at all
C   possible, and bearing in mind also that the welfare of the child is
the paramount consideration.'"

Ormrod L.J. continued:

"With respect to the judge, I think he was wrong and misdirected
himself there in that passage because the decision *does* turn upon
what he called 'the relative merits' of the present foster parents and
D   the mother 'in the ideal parents' stakes.' It may be that the judge
was confused by the form of the relief which was sought by the
originating summons. . . . It seems to have got into the mind of the
judge that the whole case was dominated and controlled by section
7 (2) of the Family Law Reform Act 1969."

E   And he sets it out the subsection. He continues, at p. 387:

"That is the subsection which the judge treated as controlling the
whole of the case. So, instead of considering who was going to look
after this child and considering, as he ought to have done, what the
welfare of the child, as the paramount consideration, required, he
was led to consider whether or not there were exceptional circum-
F   stances making it 'impracticable or undesirable' for the ward to be
under the care of either of her parents. He treated the matter as one
of law. He felt that he had to find first that the circumstances were
exceptional; and secondly he had to decide whether it was impracticable or undesirable for the ward to continue to be in the care of
either of her parents or any other individual." And I stress those
words "any other individual." "In fact, of course, the subsection
G   never applied at all in this case because at all times the proposal of
the local authority was that the child should remain in the care of
the present foster parents, that is, 'any other individual' within
section 7 (2). Nor is it at all difficult, in a case like this, to find exceptional circumstances. No one, I venture to think, would dream of
making an order committing the care of a ward to a local authority
H   unless the circumstances were exceptional. Nor would they contemplate doing it unless it was the only practical solution open to
the court at the time."

Pausing there, in *In re C.B.* (*A Minor*) as I have stressed in reading
the headnote, the parents to whom the Court of Appeal in the end gave
care and control were the last foster parents, the proposed adopters.
They were parties to the wardship proceedings; and ex hypothesi because

they were prospective adopters they were prepared to assume full res- **A** ponsibility, including financial responsibility, for the child. So there was, in *In re C.B.* (*A Minor*) " another individual " which the ward could be under the care of; and it was not impracticable or undesirable for the ward to be in the care of that individual (or those individuals in that case). Indeed, that was never in issue.

And so, in examining the decision in *In re C.B.* (*A Minor*) at this stage one sees two reasons given by the Court of Appeal: one, that the **B** judge misdirected himself when saying that the decision does not turn on the relative merits of the prospective adopters and the mother in the ideal parent stakes, and misdirected himself indeed in being guided by the terms of section 7 (2); and secondly, on the ground that section 7 (2) was in any event irrelevant or inappropriate because the conditions of section 7 (2) were not fulfilled. But Ormrod L.J. went on in two **C** other passages to say something in more general terms, and it is these other passages which have given rise to concern. Continuing from the passage which I have just quoted, Ormrod L.J. said, at p. 387: " It was a mistake to treat this case as if it was a section 7 (2) case because the local authority were the plaintiffs." Taking those words as they are set out, they do not perhaps take the argument much further. One can **D** understand from that that Ormrod L.J. was assuming that Bush J. treated it as a section 7 (2) case because the local authority were the plaintiffs. Well, that may be so. He goes on, at p. 387:

" This is the first point to be made so far as the wardship jurisdiction is concerned. It is an unfettered jurisdiction to place the ward in the care and control of any person who can best look after him or her."

E

Then he stresses the difficulties that local authorities are under and how the local authorities are not to be discouraged from making applications in wardship proceedings, and emphasises, at p. 388:

" I am most anxious to emphasise that once the child is a ward of the court, the major decisions relating to that child are for the court to take. That is equally the case whether the care and control is **F** granted to either parent or to some other individual or to a local authority. The judge, unfortunately, did not approach the matter, as I think, in the right way. He was side-tracked by considering whether he had the necessary jurisdiction under section 7 (2). But in this case the local authority were themselves the plaintiffs in the originating summons asking for ' care and control,' not for an order **G** under section 7 (2). Had he had the present foster parents before him as parties, I do not think that this error would have crept in. The result is that, with respect to the judge, the conclusion is inescapable that he exercised his discretion on an entirely wrong basis. He did not, at any stage, compare the mother's proposals for the child with the present foster parents' proposals. He did not weigh **H** one against the other and make any assessment of the advantages to the child in regard to one course or the other, in the short term or the long term. He was almost wholly concerned with deciding whether the local authority had made out their case under section 7 (2), but as I have already said, if a local authority takes the initiative of making a child a ward, I do not think that section 7 (2) comes into the case at all."

A   And this is the passage which particular concern is felt about:

"Section 7 (2) was passed to give the court power, in proceedings between parents or between a parent and a third party, to make an order committing the child to the care of the local authority, or to make it clear that the court, in wardship proceedings, had these same powers as it has under the Matrimonial Causes Act 1973."

B   That sentence, in my judgment, has to be taken in context with the immediately preceding sentence; and that is that Ormrod L.J. was seeking to show how he thought that Bush J. had been led into considering in the first place the terms of section 7 (2), basing his decision upon the wording of section 7 (2). But what Ormrod L.J. is saying there is much wider in its implications than the two reasons for the decision of the
C   Court of Appeal to which I have already adverted, and it is that which has caused concern.

Section 7 (2) is an extension of a valuable tool that was given to the court in divorce legislation under section 43 of the Matrimonial Causes Act 1973. I say a valuable tool—it is plainly there for the court (a judge of the court) to make use of in the interests of a child or children if he thinks it necessary to do so. There is no restriction, as Miss Hogg for
D   the Official Solicitor has pointed out, in the section itself as to the circumstances in which use of section 7 (2) may be made. Parliament has not thought fit to make any express restriction, and there is no restriction under the original section 43. And there is no restriction in a similar power which is granted under the later Act, section 2 (2) (b) of the Guardianship Act 1973, which has also been considered by Parliament in the Children
E   Act 1975, where an amendment is proposed but it has not yet come into force to that section, an amendment which does not itself again make any restriction upon the use of section 7 (2).

Were it not, therefore, for the words of Ormrod L.J. one would have, I think, no hesitation in saying that the present case is plainly one where it is desirable that there should be an order under section 7 (2),
F   whether the local authority have asked for such an order in their summons or not—because it is, as I say, a tool available to the court who has considered what is necessary in the interests of the children.

I look to the judgment of Bridge L.J. in *In re C.B.* (*A Minor*) [1981] 1 W.L.R. 379 to see if there is any further assistance to be found. This was a two-judge Court of Appeal. One sees that Bridge L.J., having referred to the words of the judge at first instance and section 7 (2),
G   says, at p. 389:

"Now the situation with which section 7 (2) is dealing is a situation where it is impracticable or undesirable for a ward of court to be under the care of either of his parents or any other individual—and I emphasise those concluding words ' or any other individual '—and once that is appreciated, it becomes apparent that section 7 (2) had
H   nothing whatever to do with this case. No one could possibly have suggested that it was either impracticable or undesirable in this case for Claire to continue in the care of the new foster parents or to be returned to the care of the previous foster parent or of the natural parents. The reason why section 7 (2) seems to have loomed so large was that by what seems to have been a purely procedural accident, the new foster parents were not parties before the court, so it was the

local authority who, in form, were applying for an order to be made   A
in their favour. But in substance nobody could have been in any
doubt that the issue was whether the little girl should be in the care
of her natural parents, or one or other of the sets of foster parents
who were ' other individuals ' within the meaning of section 7 (2).
In fact section 7 (2) indicates no parliamentary a priori preference for
giving the care of a child to natural parents as against giving it to
anybody else. The paramount consideration in a simple case like this,   B
and the sole consideration, is what will best serve the welfare of the
child. Once the misapprehension derived from section 7 (2) is cleared
out of the way, and the case is approached on the basis of what will
best serve the welfare of this little girl of now just over three years
old, the solution to the problem, to my mind, stands out so as to be
unmistakable."
                                                                        C

And he deals thereafter with the merits. One notes that he does not make
the general observation as to applicability of section 7 (2) where the local
authority are the plaintiffs; and stresses that in that case there was
" another individual."

Here, in the case of the three elder children, as I have said already,
there is the foster parent who is " another individual " who in this case,   D
unlike in *In re C.B. (A Minor)*, it is impracticable to give care and
control to because she does not have enough money to look after the
children. In the case of the youngest twins there is nobody effectively
able at the moment to have day to day, physical control of them for
anything like a significant length of time. Their stay with the foster
mother is purely temporary. So again in the case of those two there is,   E
subject to the desirability of the mother having the children, no " other
individual " to whom it is practicable to commit the care of those
children. So this is a case where the conditions of section 7 (2) are
complied with.

I have, as I said earlier, found that it is undesirable that any of these
children should go to the care of their mother. That satisfies the other
condition in section 7 (2) of the Act of 1969.   F

I also bear in mind, as I am told by Miss Ryan (who was in *In re
C.B. (A Minor)*) that in fact no argument was addressed to the question
as to whether section 7 (2) could or could not be used if the local
authority was a plaintiff in the proceedings.

In the circumstances, I think I am justified, with the greatest respect
to Ormrod L.J., in assuming that when he made the references to which   G
I have referred it was in the context of explaining how the judge at first
instance had come to deal with the matter in the way in which he did,
and that it was for that reason only that Ormrod L.J. was giving expression to that view. In any event, I think in the circumstances that
it is right to consider that observation as obiter.

I add that although a care order under section 7 (2) gives the local   H
authority the powers contained in Part II of the Children Act 1948, which
include control of access, nevertheless because it is an order made in
wardship proceedings, if, as here, the wardship continues, the court retains
the power to make such directions as to access as it thinks fit—as well, of
course, as the power to discharge the care order: see *In re Y. (A Minor)*
(Child in Care: Access) [1976] Fam. 125.

For those reasons I order that there should be a care order under

A   section 7 (2) in relation to each of these five children. The order, therefore, will be on that basis with provision for care and control and access as I have already indicated.

Order accordingly.

Solicitors: *Robert A. Joy; Gillian A. Butler; Official Solicitor.*

B
M. B. D.

C
[VISITORS TO GRAY'S INN]

* *In re* H. (A BARRISTER)

1981   Feb. 23;   Latey J., Sir Robert Megarry V.-C.
      June 25   and Ralph Gibson J.

D   *Barrister — Discipline — Disciplinary tribunal — Sentencing — Conviction for importuning in public place—Conduct unbecoming a barrister admitted before disciplinary tribunal—Sentence of suspension from practice — Whether not guilty plea to be taken into account in sentencing—Whether sentence in proportion to misconduct—Whether reprimand more appropriate*

    The appellant, a practising barrister of eight years' stand-
E   ing, was convicted by a jury after pleading not guilty to a charge of persistently importuning for immoral purposes in a public lavatory and fined £250. His conviction received considerable publicity in the area in which he lived and practised. As a result of the conviction a complaint was made by the Professional Conduct Committee of the Senate of the Inns of Court and the Bar, and the matter was heard before the disciplinary tribunal of the Senate. The appellant admitted to
F   conduct unbecoming a barrister, and counsel on his behalf asked the tribunal to consider taking a course which would allow him to continue in practice with no suspension and no disbarment. The tribunal were referred to two cases in which barristers had received reprimands for similar misconduct, having pleaded guilty before the criminal court. The tribunal took the view that as the appellant had pleaded not guilty before the Crown Court, and the jury had rejected his
G   evidence, they had no alternative but to impose a sentence of suspension. Accordingly they sentenced him to three months' suspension from practice and from the enjoyment of all rights and privileges as a member of his Inn of Court.

    On the appellant's petition of appeal against sentence, heard by three High Court judges sitting as visitors to Gray's Inn:—

    Held, allowing the appeal, that in its approach to sentencing the tribunal should draw a distinction between professional mis-
H   conduct and misconduct outside the profession, and should impose a sentence in proportion to the misconduct proved; that an unsuccessful plea of not guilty in the Crown Court was a proper factor for the tribunal to take into account but, in the absence of aggravating circumstances, it should not be the predominant factor leading to the very heavy sentence of suspension from practice, where otherwise the lighter sentence of reprimand would have been imposed; that having regard to the facts that the appellant's conduct did not amount to professional misconduct, that there were no aggravating circum-

In re H. (A Barrister)   [1981]

A

stances, and that the conviction had already received local
publicity, the appropriate sentence was a reprimand without
publication.

In re a Solicitor [1956] 1 W.L.R. 1312, D.C. applied.

Per curiam. It is desirable that sentences in comparable
cases should be consistent, and accordingly the record of a
decision ought to state matters such as the penalty imposed
by the criminal court, the approximate length of the barrister's
standing at the Bar, whether or not he is a practising barrister,
and any other matters material to the sentence which can
readily be stated (post, p. 1261B–D).

B

The following case is referred to in the judgment:

Solicitor, In re a [1956] 1 W.L.R. 1312; [1956] 3 All E.R. 516, D.C.

No additional cases were cited in argument.

C

APPEAL from the Disciplinary Tribunal of the Senate of the Inns of
Court and the Bar.

On October 13, 1980, the appellant, H., a barrister and a member of
Gray's Inn, was convicted of persistently importuning in a public place for
immoral purposes, contrary to section 32 of the Sexual Offences Act 1956,
and was fined £250. On February 23, 1981, he admitted one charge of
conduct unbecoming a barrister before the Disciplinary Tribunal of the
Senate. The sentence imposed by the tribunal was that he should be
suspended from practice as a barrister and from the enjoyment of all rights
and privileges as a member of Gray's Inn for three months. He appealed
against that sentence on the grounds that (i) the tribunal was wrong in
imposing a sentence of suspension on the basis that the barrister was
convicted of importuning for immoral purposes after pleading not guilty,
whereas in two previous cases barristers had been reprimanded for the
offence after pleading guilty at their trial; (ii) the tribunal was wrong in the
absence of aggravating circumstances, in imposing a sentence of suspension
for an offence which did not affect the integrity of a barrister in the exercise
of his profession; (iii) the sentence was excessive in all the circumstances
of the case.

D

E

F

John Hazan Q.C. for the appellant.
Nicholas Davidson for the Professional Conduct Committee.

Cur. adv. vult.

G

June 25. LATEY J. read the following decision of the visitors. Gibson J.
is unable to be present today. The statement of reasons which I am about
to read are the reasons of the Panel of Visitors.

Mr. H., a practising barrister of some eight years' standing, was convicted on an offence of persistently importuning for immoral purposes in
a public lavatory on one occasion. The case for the prosecution was not
that he importuned by words or by any direct physical approach, but
that it should be inferred from certain gestures that he was doing so. He
pleaded not guilty and gave evidence. After a lengthy retirement the jury
returned a verdict of guilty, and he was fined £250.

Before the Disciplinary Tribunal of the Senate he admitted one charge
of conduct unbecoming a barrister arising from the conviction. He was
sentenced to a period of suspension for three months from practice as a

H

A barrister and from the enjoyment of all rights and privileges as a member
of his Inn of Court. The tribunal's retirement also was a lengthy one.
From that sentence he appeals to Her Majesty's Judges as Visitors to the
Inns of Court. Before the tribunal he did not seek to go behind the
conviction, nor has he sought to do so before us. Mr. Hazan, who represented him, and Mr. Davidson, who represented the Senate, appeared
also before us. This has been helpful as they have been able to inform us
B of some matters which do not appear in the papers.

Moreover, material—some of it important—has been put before us
which the tribunal did not have. Examples are a comparable case which
has been heard by the tribunal since the instant one, and the approach
and practice of The Law Society concerning solicitors in comparable cases.
The Senate, through counsel, not only did not object to this new material
C being put before us but is anxious that the Visitors should be supplied
with all material which might help them reach a just result. This is
consistent with the jurisdiction and role of the Visitors. Their powers are
not restricted. It is not necessary, for example, that they should find that
the tribunal has erred in principle as a condition precedent of allowing an
appeal or altering a sentence. We emphasise that in saying this we do not
D mean that the decision of the tribunal should be ignored. Far from it. The
tribunal is chaired by a High Court judge and comprises a lay representative and three members of the Bar. It is there to have regard to the
interests of the public and is in close touch with the Bar. As such, its
findings and views should be and are important factors to be weighed
as such with all else.

E Mr. Hazan submitted that the case raises matters of moment and
principle important to the Bar generally. Mr. Davidson said that the
Senate is anxious for any guidance which we may feel able to give as to
the approach to be adopted so that consistency can be achieved so far
as possible in cases of this nature. Rule 5 of the Hearings before the
Visitors Rules 1980 provides:

F   " (3) In an appeal against sentence the petition may refer to any
       factors which it is contended make the sentence unduly severe in
       relation to the appellant's record or to sentence in other similar cases."

On counsel's invitation, and because we agree that it is the right course in
this case, we are stating our reasons in public.

At the heart of the matter are three general questions regarding the
approach to sentencing. First, is there a distinction to be drawn between
G misconduct by a barrister in his professional practice and misconduct in
his private life? Secondly, where the misconduct is in the commission of a
criminal offence, to what extent should the fact that he has unsuccessfully
pleaded not guilty affect the sentence of the disciplinary tribunal? Thirdly,
to what extent should the disciplinary tribunal have regard to sentences
imposed in comparable cases?

H   As to the first question, we are in no doubt that a distinction should
be drawn between professional misconduct and misconduct outside the
profession. In In re a Solicitor [1956] 1 W.L.R. 1312, a solicitor had been
convicted of two indecent assaults and sentenced to three months' imprisonment. The disciplinary committee under the Solicitors Act 1932
ordered his name to be struck off the roll of solicitors. He appealed to
the Divisional Court. Giving the judgment of the court Lord Goddard C.J.,
said at p. 1314:

In re H. (A Barrister)   [1981]

"This court is, and always has been, very loth to interfere with the   A
findings of the Disciplinary Committee either on a matter of fact, or
with regard to the penalties . . . If it is a matter of professional misconduct, it would take a very strong case to induce this court to
interfere with the sentence passed by the Disciplinary Committee,
because obviously the Disciplinary Committee are the best possible
people for weighing the seriousness of professional misconduct. There
is no suggestion of professional misconduct in this case. That being so,   B
I think this court is bound to consider, as the Court of Criminal
Appeal would have to do, whether or not the sentence is in proportion
or out of proportion to the misconduct which has been proved."

That, in our opinion, lays down the approach today as correctly as it did
in 1956, and is equally appropriate to the Disciplinary Tribunal of the   C
Senate, and to the Visitors, though the sentence which the Divisional
Court imposed in that case (suspension from practice for two years) in
what counsel have aptly described as the pre-Wolfenden era would in the
ordinary run of cases be inappropriate in the changed climate of the
post-Wolfenden era.

As to the second question (the unsuccessful plea of not guilty), this,
Mr. Hazan submits, is of major importance to any barrister who is   D
charged with an offence against the law. In the instant case, as counsel
are agreed and as is plain from the statement of decision and sentence
of the chairman of the tribunal, the facts that Mr. H. unsuccessfully
pleaded not guilty and that his evidence was evidently rejected by the
jury caused the tribunal to pass a sentence of suspension instead of
imposing a reprimand, which would have been the sentence had he   E
pleaded guilty.

This, in Mr. Hazan's submission, is of general concern to barristers
who may find themselves charged with a criminal offence outside the
bounds of their professional practice, who may wish to contest the charge
and plead not guilty, and who then have to consider the effect of failure
not only on the sentence passed upon them by the court but also, and
later, on that imposed by the disciplinary tribunal.   F

The relevant ground of the petition of appeal appears to contend that
the tribunal should pay no attention at all in any case to the barrister's
choice of plea in the court. Mr. Hazan does not put it so high. He accepts
that it is a factor which the tribunal is entitled to give weight to. He accepts
that there may be cases where it may be weighty, indeed decisive, and he
instanced the case where the accused barrister fabricates a false alibi.   G
But, he says, such cases apart—cases where the defence advanced is
scandalous or without merit—the disciplinary tribunal should be cautious
about the weight to be attached to a plea of not guilty. He suggests that,
if the approach adopted by the disciplinary tribunal in the instant case is
correct, it places improper pressure upon a barrister who is innocent to
plead guilty and so preserve his right to practise. It would put a barrister   H
defendant in a worse position than any other member of the public. As
to this last point, Mr. Davidson suggests that a barrister is not in a
unique position. In weighing the consequences of pleading guilty or not
guilty, members of other professions and occupations are faced with
somewhat similar pressure for the reason, among others, that a contested
trial usually attracts more publicity.

We agree that in this context a barrister cannot expect to be put in a

A special position. But that does not destroy the generality of Mr. Hazan's submission. We agree with it. An unsuccessful plea of not guilty is a factor which it is proper for the disciplinary tribunal to weigh with all others, but it should not be the predominant factor leading to the very heavy sentence of suspension from practice where otherwise there would have been the lighter one of reprimand, unless there are aggravating circumstances.

B   We may add that in the instant case the weight to be attached to the plea of not guilty was raised by a member of the disciplinary tribunal at the very end of the hearing, and so the tribunal did not have the benefit of the full and researched submissions which we have had from counsel.

   As to the third question, namely, the extent to which the Disciplinary Tribunal should have regard to sentences imposed in comparable cases,
C in general it is desirable that there should be consistency, and rule 5 (3), already quoted, underlines that desirability. For this purpose we think that the record of the decisions ought to state matters such as the penalty imposed by the criminal court, the approximate length of the barrister's standing at the Bar, whether or not he is a practising barrister, and any other matters material to the sentence which can readily be
D stated. We say this because in the records of the three comparable cases put before us, only one stated the penalty imposed by the criminal court, only one disclosed the barrister's standing at the Bar, and none stated whether or not he was practising. In fact, two were practising and one was not; and in deciding whether or not to impose a sentence of suspension the tribunal must obviously bear in mind the greater severity of such a sentence in the case of a practising barrister as compared with a non-
E practising barrister. No doubt in many cases some of these matters could be discovered by consulting the Bar List; but decisions which are to be used as precedents ought to be self-contained.

   Is there yet an established pattern or norm for barristers in this type of case? Of the three comparable cases, one was decided after this case was heard. One of the three was a case of importuning and the other two
F were cases of gross indecency. In all three cases the sentence imposed was a reprimand, with no recommendation for publication. There were, as there always are, some differences between one case and another, and Mr. Davidson says that there is not yet an established pattern. Mr. Hazan suggests that there is already something of a pattern. We agree and consider that it is the appropriate one.

G   But the matter does not stop there. Mr. Hazan has made inquiry of the Law Society and is authorised to inform us that in this category of case where solicitors are involved it is the established practice not to suspend the solicitor from practice but to impose a reprimand or a fine, or both. (The Senate tribunal has no power to impose a fine, as distinct from ordering fees to be repaid or forgone.) In this context we can see no reason in logic or principle to draw a distinction between members of the
H two branches of the profession, and Mr. Davidson accepted this.

   Finally, the mitigation in the instant case was described by the tribunal as impressive. Indeed it is. Mr. H. is spoken of in the highest terms by judges before whom he practises, by the head and all members of his chambers, by leading counsel who was his pupil-master and by solicitors regularly instructing him. Mr. H.'s offence, isolated though it is, is not trivial. But neither is a reprimand a trivial penalty, and we consider it the appropriate one to meet and mark the offence.

In re H. (A Barrister)   **[1981]**

A We have then had to consider whether, having decided that the appropriate penalty is a reprimand and not suspension, the reprimand should be with or without publication. It is to be noted that the original offence of importuning received, in the neighbourhood where this barrister lives and practises, the considerable publicity that such convictions commonly receive in the case of a professional man. The solicitors who normally employ his professional services, or are likely to do so, or who may be B opposed by him in legal proceedings, have undoubtedly learned about the conviction and, in professional circles, that knowledge will persist. Unlike a case of misconduct in professional practice, where the profession and public may hear nothing of the wrongdoing unless the profession publishes it, this conviction has been fully reported.

The function of these proceedings in bringing home to the barrister the fact that the conduct, which brought about the conviction, will not be C passed over or tolerated by the profession has been achieved in this case without the accentuation of the penalty of reprimand by publication of it. Further, all that we have heard of the conduct of this barrister since the offence, and of the continued confidence in him expressed by both clients and colleagues, has persuaded us that publication is not necessary either as a warning and deterrent to him or as a marking by the profession of its view of the commission of such an offence by a barrister. On the facts D of this case the reprimand alone is sufficient.

For all these reasons we have allowed the appeal, set aside the sentence, and substituted for it a reprimand without publication.

Appeal allowed.

E Solicitors: *Darlington & Parkinson.*

R. D.

F

[QUEEN'S BENCH DIVISION]

* CLIPPER MARITIME CO. LTD. OF MONROVIA *v.*
MINERALIMPORTEXPORT

1981 June 17, 19, 23, 29   Robert Goff J. G

Injunction—Interlocutory—Mareva injunction—Conditions—Application to restrain removal by defendant of cargo laden on ship —Effect of injunction on port authority—Court's protection of interests of third parties

The Commercial Court will impose conditions when granting a *Mareva* injunction so that the interests of innocent third H parties will be protected (post, p. 1264E–F).

Where, therefore, plaintiffs sought an injunction restraining the defendant from removing from the jurisdiction cargo on board a vessel in the port of Barry: —

Held, that the injunction would be granted on condition that the plaintiffs undertook to reimburse the port authority for the loss of income and the administrative costs incurred as a consequence of the grant of the injunction; and that the port authority should have a discretion for operational reasons

A   to move or order the ship to be moved within the jurisdiction and, if necessary, in the event of danger to move her outside the jurisdiction of the High Court.

> *Searose Ltd.* v. *Seatrain U.K. Ltd.* [1981] 1 W.L.R. 894 applied.
>
> *Per curiam.* It is of great assistance if the Commercial Court can be kept informed of any adverse effect which *Mareva* injunctions are having upon third parties, as in the

B   case of clearing banks and port authorities so that steps can be taken, where possible, to protect their interests. If other bodies wish to make representations, it would be appropriate to address them to the Secretary of the Commercial Court Committee (post, pp. 1264G—1265A).

The following case is referred to in the judgment:

C   *Searose Ltd.* v. *Seatrain U.K. Ltd.* [1981] 1 W.L.R. 894; [1981] 1 All E.R. 806.

No additional cases were cited in argument.

EX PARTE APPLICATION
The plaintiffs, Clipper Maritime Co. Ltd. of Monrovia, issued a writ
D   claiming damages against the defendants, Mineralimportexport of Bucharest, Rumania, for breach of contract.

On June 17, 1981, the plaintiffs applied, ex parte, for a *Mareva* injunction to restrain the defendants from removing from the jurisdiction or otherwise disposing or dealing with their assets within the jurisdiction so as to reduce the value below U.S. $123,026·40. The application particularly related to the defendants' property on board the vessel *Marie Leonhardt*
E   in the port of Barry, South Wales.

The application was heard and judgment given in chambers on June 17. The injunction was granted for two days and renewed on June 19 and again on June 23. On June 29 Robert Goff J. redelivered part of the judgment in open court.

F   *Christopher C. Russell* for the plaintiffs.

ROBERT GOFF J. On June 17, I made an order in this case for a *Mareva* injunction on the ex parte application of the plaintiffs. Since, however, the case raises one point which is of some importance in this developing jurisdiction, I propose, with the consent of the plaintiffs, to repeat
G   part of my judgment in open court.

The injunction which I granted restrained, on certain undertakings and other terms, the defendants from disposing of or dealing with their assets within the jurisdiction or from removing such assets from the jurisdiction, and in particular cargo or bunkers being the property of the defendants loaded on board a vessel called the *Marie Leonhardt*, so as to reduce the value of those assets below the sum of U.S. $123,026·40.

H   The evidence before the court at the time of the application was that the *Marie Leonhardt* was on time charter to the defendants, and that the defendants were likely to be loading her at the port of Barry in Wales with a cargo of coke for discharge at Constanza. In these circumstances, there was a danger that the injunction might have some effect upon the movements of the ship within the port, and might also have some adverse effect upon the port authority of Barry, which is, of course, a third party having no interest in the dispute between the plaintiffs and the defendants.

In these circumstances, consistent with the recent decision of this A
court in *Searose Ltd.* v. *Seatrain U.K. Ltd.* [1981] 1 W.L.R. 894, I imposed
certain conditions upon the grant of the injunction with a view to preventing it bearing harshly upon the port authority. The particular matters
I had in mind were as follows. (1) The vessel may be docked at a heavily
used and high income producing berth; and, until the port authority can
make satisfactory arrangements to move the vessel without infringing the
terms of the injunction, income from that berth may be lost. (2) The port B
authority may in any event incur administrative costs as a consequence
of the granting of the injunction. (3) It may be necessary for the port
authority to move the vessel in the ordinary course of good administration
of the port; and in cases of danger it may be necessary for the port authority to move her outside the confines of the port, and possible even outside the jurisdiction of the court.   C

To take account of these contingencies I required, as a condition of
granting the injunction, an undertaking by the plaintiffs to pay the actual
income lost to the port authority controlling the port of Barry in South
Wales and the administrative costs incurred by that port authority as a
consequence of the granting of the injunction; and I also qualified the
injunction by making it subject to the proviso that the port authority D
should always have a discretion for operational reasons to move or order
the movement of the vessel within the area of the jurisdiction of the High
Court or, in the event of danger, to move or order the movement of the
vessel outside the jurisdiction of the High Court if a place within the
jurisdiction was not available, and that the defendants should have liberty
to comply with such an order.

It is right that I should record that the plaintiffs have made no E
objection to the imposition of these terms; and further that when, on an
application by the plaintiffs to continue the injunction on June 19, a
representative of the port authority was present in court, it was accepted
by the port authority that such terms were satisfactory to them.

This court will in future, on other ex parte applications for *Mareva*
injunctions which may affect ships in port, impose similar terms, subject F
always, of course, to the particular circumstances of the case. Indeed, I
have imposed the same terms, again without opposition from the plaintiffs,
on the grant of a *Mareva* injunction on another ex parte application last
week.

I wish it to be known that the court has taken this course as a result
of representations made to it by solicitors acting for the British Ports
Association; and that the undertaking imposed in *Searose Ltd.* v. *Seatrain* G
U.K. Ltd. [1981] 1 W.L.R. 894 was imposed as a result of representations
made to the Commercial Court Committee on behalf of the clearing banks.
The Commercial Court is very anxious to provide a service to the commercial community which is sensitive to its needs: and in particular it is
anxious that the *Mareva* jurisdiction, in the administration of which the
Commercial Court plays so substantial a part, should be implemented in H
a manner which takes account of the interests of innocent third parties.
Since initially *Mareva* injunctions are almost invariably granted on ex
parte applications, orders may be made which affect third parties who are
unrepresented at the hearing of the initial application. It is, therefore, of
great assistance if the court can be kept informed of any adverse effect
which these injunctions are having upon third parties, as in the case of
the clearing banks and port authorities, so that steps can be taken, where

The Weekly Law Reports, October 23, 1981

1265

1 W.L.R.   Clipper Maritime v. Mineralimportexport (Q.B.D.)   Robert Goff J.

A possible, to protect their interests. If any other bodies wish to make representations on this point, it would be most appropriate for them to address their representations to the secretary of the Commercial Court Committee at the Royal Courts of Justice, in which event they will immediately be drawn to the attention of the judge in charge of the commercial list.

B
Order accordingly.
Order for substituted service of summons for costs.

Solicitors: *William A. Crump & Son.*

[Reported by Miss Lesley Hewlett, Barrister-at-Law]

C

D

[COURT OF APPEAL]

* HABIB BANK LTD. *v.* HABIB BANK A.G. ZURICH

[1977 H. No. 4426]

1980   Dec. 3, 4, 5, 8, 9, 10, 11, 15, 16, 17, 18   Stephenson, Oliver and Watkins L.JJ.

E

Passing Off—Risk of confusion—Use of family name—Banks in-corporated by well known banking family—Banks in Pakistan and Switzerland closely associated with substantial business—Nationalisation of banks in Pakistan—Whether Swiss bank passing off in carrying on independent trading—Whether good-will and reputation exclusive—Whether nationalised banks' claim barred by acquiescence, laches and estoppel

F

In 1941 a well known banking family incorporated a bank in Bombay under their family name " Habib ". In 1947, on the partition of the Indian sub-continent, the bank moved to Pakistan where it became very well known and developed a very substantial business both internally and inter-nationally and had numerous branches. In 1952 another bank was incorporated in Pakistan, under the name Habib Bank (Overseas) Ltd., who took over all the international business, including the business in the United Kingdom. Both the banks remained closely associated. In 1967 when nationalisation of banks began to be discussed in Pakistan, the Habib family's, after obtaining the necessary permission from the State Bank of Pakistan, incorporated the defendants in Zurich. In May 1973 the defendants opened a branch in London. The arrangements for that and necessary permissions from the Bank of England was handled by the staff of the overseas bank. The defendants' London office opened in a very modest way and was manned by the overseas bank's staff as and when necessary. On January 1, 1974, all the banks in Pakistan were nationalised, including the two Habib banks. They became merged into a new state corporation and their business and goodwill was vested in the plaintiffs. The Habib family's control of those banks ceased. But the plain-tiffs' attempts to gain management control of the defendants was resisted and litigation to resolve that matter was pending

G

H

1266

Habib Bank Ltd. v. Habib Bank A.G. (C.A.)   [1981]

in Switzerland. Between 1974 and 1977 the parties entered A
into various agency arrangements. The plaintiffs issued a
writ on September 23, 1977, seeking an injunction restraining
the defendants, inter alia, from passing off their business as
and for the plaintiffs' and trading under any name containing
the name Habib. The judge dismissed the action.

On appeal by the plaintiffs: —

Held dismissing the appeal, that since the defendants were
set up under the name "Habib" with the express consent B
and co-operation of the plaintiffs' predecessors and had
carried on the business since nationalisation of the two
banks, with their constitution, management, business style
and their motto unchanged there had been no misrepresentation on their part giving rise to a claim for passing off; that,
on the facts, the goodwill and reputation attaching to the
family name "Habib" was such that an organisation established by that family under their name immediately acquired C
the family's goodwill and reputation which attached equally
to any local branch set up in the same place; that the establishment in London of the defendants' office merely showed
that they were loosely associated with the Habib banks and
could not import representation that the responsibility for
the defendants' management vested in those banks and that
there were no agreed or understood limitations on the defendants' activities in London; that, accordingly, the judge did D
not err in principle in concluding that the evidence disclosed
no passing off because there was no misrepresentation (post,
pp. 1275G–H, 1278G–H, 1279D–H, 1280H, 1281B–C, 1287F–G).

Held, further that, even if there had been misrepresentation, the plaintiffs had failed to establish any damage and,
since the defendants were founded and carried on business
with the active concurrence of the plaintiffs' predecessors and
the business co-operation of the plaintiffs since nationalisa- E
tion, the plaintiffs' claim, would be barred on the ground of
acquiescence, laches and estoppel (post, pp. 1281F–H, 1282B,
F–G, 1287F–G).

Per curiam. A broad approach is required in considering
the doctrine of laches or acquiescence and not one based on
the archaic and arcane distinctions between the assertion of
equitable rights and the enforcement by equitable means of
legal rights (post, pp. 1284H—1285C, 1287F–G). F

Decision of Whitford J. affirmed.

The following cases are referred to in the judgments:

Amalgamated Investment & Property Co. Ltd. v. *Texas Commerce International Bank Ltd.* [1981] 2 W.L.R. 554; [1981] 1 All E.R. 923.

Bulmer (H.P.) Ltd. v. *J. Bollinger S.A.* [1978] R.P.C. 79, C.A.

Crabb v. *Arun District Council* [1976] Ch. 179; [1975] 3 W.L.R. 847; G
[1975] 3 All E.R. 865, C.A.

Erlanger v. *New Sombrero Phosphate Co.* (1878) 3 App.Cas. 1218,
H.L.(E.).

Greasley v. *Cooke* [1980] 1 W.L.R. 1306; [1980] 3 All E.R. 710, C.A.

Inland Revenue Commissioners v. *Muller & Co.'s Margarine Ltd.* [1901]
A.C. 217, H.L.(E.).

Inwards v. *Baker* [1965] 2 Q.B. 29; [1965] 2 W.L.R. 212; [1965] 1 H
All E.R. 446, C.A.

Jelley, Son, and Jones' Application, In re (1878) 46 L.T. 381n.

Lindsay Petroleum Co. v. *Hurd* (1874) L.R. 5 P.C. 221, P.C.

Marengo v. *Daily Sketch and Sunday Graphic Ltd.* (unreported) May
17, 1946, C.A.; [1948] W.N. 92; [1948] 1 All E.R. 406, H.L.(E.).

Pirie (Alex) and Sons Ltd.'s Application, In re (1933) 50 R.P.C. 147,
H.L.(E.).

Saunders v. *Sun Life Assurance Co. of Canada* [1894] 1 Ch. 537.

A   *Spalding (A. G.) and Brothers v. A. W. Gamage Ltd.* (1915) 84 L.J.Ch.
          449; 32 R.P.C. 273, H.L.(E.).
      Taylors Fashions Ltd. v. Liverpool Victoria Trustees Co. Ltd. (Note)
          [1981] 2 W.L.R. 576; [1981] 1 All E.R. 897.
      *Warnink (Erven) Besloten Vennootschap v. J. Townend & Sons (Hull)
          Ltd.* [1979] A.C. 731; [1979] 3 W.L.R. 68; [1979] 2 All E.R. 927,
          H.L.(E.).
B   *Willmott v. Barber* (1880) 15 Ch.D. 96.

      The following additional cases were cited in argument:
      Adrema Ltd. v. Adrema-Werke G.m.b.H. [1958] R.P.C. 323.
      Banks v. Gibson (1865) 34 Beav. 566.
      Barr's Patent, In re (1948) 65 R.P.C. 327.
      Brestian v. Try [1958] R.P.C. 161, C.A.
C   *Brinsmead (John) & Sons Ltd. v. Brinsmead* (1913) 30 R.P.C. 493, C.A.
      British Legion v. British Legion Club (Street) Ltd. (1931) 48 R.P.C. 555.
      Burgess v. Burgess (1853) 3 De G.M. & G. 896.
      Cluett Peabody & Co. Inc. v. McIntyre Hogg Marsh & Co. Ltd. [1958]
          R.P.C. 335.
      Coles (J.H.) Proprietary Ltd. (In liquidation) v. Need (1933) 50 R.P.C.
          379, P.C.
D   *Dent v. Turpin* (1861) 2 Johns. & H. 139.
      Draper v. Trist and Tristbestos Brake Linings Ltd. (1939) 56 R.P.C.
          429, C.A.
      Electrolux Ltd. v. Electrix Ltd. (1953) 71 R.P.C. 23, C.A.
      Ewing v. Buttercup Margarine Co. Ltd. (1917) 34 R.P.C. 232, C.A.
      General Electric Co. (of U.S.A.) v. General Electric Co. Ltd. [1972] 1
          W.L.R. 729; [1972] 2 All E.R. 507, H.L.(E.).
E   *Guimaraens (M.P.) & Son v. Fonseca & Vasconcellos Ltd.* (1921) 38
          R.P.C. 388.
      Holder v. Holder [1968] Ch. 353; [1960] 2 W.L.R. 237; [1968] 1 All
          E.R. 665, C.A.
      Jamieson and Co. v. Jamieson (1898) 15 R.P.C. 169, C.A.
      Kammins Ballrooms Co. Ltd. v. Zenith Investments (Torquay) Ltd.
          [1971] A.C. 850; [1970] 3 W.L.R. 287; [1970] 2 All E.R. 871,
          H.L.(E.).
F   *Lecouturier v. Rey* [1910] A.C. 262, H.L.(E.).
      Music Corporation of America v. Music Corporation (Great Britain Ltd.)
          (1946) 64 R.P.C. 41.
      Parker-Knoll Ltd. v. Knoll International Ltd. [1962] R.P.C. 265,
          H.L.(E.).
      Reddaway v. Banham [1896] A.C. 199, H.L.(E.).
      Roberts Numbering Machine Co. v. Davis (1935) 53 R.P.C. 79.
G   *Sayers v. Collyer* (1884) 28 Ch.D. 103, C.A.
      Southorn v. Reynolds (1865) 12 L.T. 75.
      Turton v. Turton (1889) 42 Ch.D. 128, C.A.
      Tussaud v. Tussaud (1890) 44 Ch.D. 678.

      APPEAL from Whitford J.
          The plaintiffs, Habib Bank Ltd., issued a writ on September 23, 1977,
H   seeking an injunction to restrain the defendants, Habib Bank A.G.
      Zurich (" H.B.Z."), inter alia, from (i) trading in this country under the
      names of Habib Bank Zurich, Habib, any name containing the name
      Habib or any name colourably similar to the plaintiffs' name Habib
      Bank, (ii) trading in any manner likely to cause the business of H.B.Z.
      to be confused with the business of the plaintiffs, (iii) trading in any
      manner which did not sufficiently differentiate or distinguish the plain-
      tiffs' bank or their branches from H.B.Z's, (iv) otherwise passing off the

business of H.B.Z. as and for the plaintiffs' business, or (v) trading under- A
the name of Habib Bank A.G. Zurich, Habib Bank, or any name containing the name Habib or any name colourably similar to the plaintiffs'
name so as to represent that H.B.Z. were connected or associated in
business with the plaintiffs or were their branch or a business under the
effective control of the plaintiffs. On October 12, 1979, Whitford J.
dismissed the action.

By a notice of appeal dated February 11, 1980, the plaintiffs appealed B
on the grounds, inter alia, (1) that the judge wrongly held as a matter
of fact and/or law that the reputation in the name Habib built up in the
United Kingdom prior to nationalisation of the plaintiffs was a shared
reputation, that when H.B.Z. commenced business in the United Kingdom they immediately assumed part of such shared reputation, that
H.B.Z. could continue to share that reputation after nationalisation, that C
prior to nationalisation neither Habib Bank (Overseas) Ltd. (" H.B.O.")
nor Habib Bank Ltd. (" the original H.B.L.") had acquired a reputation
in the name Habib to the exclusion of H.B.Z.; (2) that the judge
wrongly failed to find that prior to nationalisation H.B.Z. could only
trade in this country under the designation " Habib " so long as (a)
such trading was limited to such activities as were strictly related to D
the business of H.B.Z. in Switzerland and (b) H.B.Z. was under the
same effective control as H.B.O., that after nationalisation H.B.Z. no
longer so acted, that after nationalisation the use by H.B.Z. of the name
Habib in this country constituted a misrepresentation, and that H.B.Z.'s
actions complained of constituted passing off; (3) that the judge failed
to take into account or, alternatively, failed to give sufficient weight to
the uncontested evidence of the plaintiffs that prior to nationalisation E
H.B.Z. had no reputation in this country; (4) that the judge's decision
that there was a shared reputation was based on an argument that was
not pleaded or advanced before him by H.B.Z.; (5) that the judge
wrongly held that H.B.Z.'s activities complained of had not caused
substantial damage nor were they likely to cause substantial damage to
the plaintiffs and, thereunder the judge failed to take into account or F
failed to give sufficient weight to the evidence of the plaintiffs; that
the confusion by reason of H.B.Z.'s acts complained of that had
occurred and was likely to occur in the future was not great despite
the plaintiffs' evidence to the contrary; that the plaintiffs were barred
from obtaining relief by reason of acquiescence and estoppel and in
particular (i) wrongly interpreted the law as to the requirements necessary for those defences to succeed, (ii) wrongly inferred findings of fact G
of H.B.Z.'s favour, (iii) made incorrect findings of fact as to the plaintiffs' knowledge as to their legal rights, as to H.B.Z.'s belief as to their
rights, as to whether the plaintiffs encouraged H.B.Z. to carry out the
acts complained of and that the expansion of H.B.Z.'s business after
nationalisation was to a substantial extent due to the co-operation of
the plaintiffs, (iv) failed to take into account or gave insufficient weight H
to the fact that the onus to prove the defence was on H.B.Z. and
that H.B.Z. did not produce any evidence to discharge such onus.

By a respondent's notice dated February 22, 1980, H.B.Z. sought to
affirm the judge's judgment on the additional grounds (1) that on the
facts H.B.Z. were not doing anything more than honestly to trade under
their own name which was a defence in law; (2) that by reason of the
absence of any fraudulent intent on the part of H.B.Z. the plaintiffs'

A claim could lie only in equity.   Accordingly, the principles of estoppel
by conduct, laches or acquiescence as they applied to equitable claims
were applicable and, on the facts, applied; (3) that the plaintiffs
on the evidence failed to show any or any significant damage or likelihood of damage; (4) that the only type of confusion shown by the
plaintiffs (namely that arising in inter-bank dealings and in the post)
was irrelevant to passing off in that it did not and could not lead to any
B loss of custom by either party; (5) that the plaintiff showed no damage
or likelihood of damage to their goodwill, which was a necessary ingredient of the tort of passing off; (6) that if, contrary to the finding of
the judge, H.B.Z. had been guilty of passing off relief by way of
injunction was inappropriate because the plaintiffs did not show any
likelihood of significant damage.

C   The facts are stated in the judgment of Oliver L.J.

    William Aldous Q.C. and *Anthony Watson* for the plaintiffs.
    Julian Jeffs Q.C. and *Robin Jacob* for the defendants.

    OLIVER L.J. delivered the first judgment.   This is an appeal from a
D judgment of Whitford J. delivered on October 12, 1979, in which he
dismissed the plaintiffs' action for passing off.   The title to these proceedings indicates the close similarity of the names of the parties and it
is the plaintiffs' contention that in carrying on their business under
their corporate name in the United Kingdom the defendants are either
directly passing off their business as that of the plaintiffs or at least
holding out to the public that they are a company controlled by or
E associated with the plaintiffs.   And indeed, so far as association goes,
they *are* to some extent associated as the history of the matter shows,
although Mr. Aldous submits that that factual association does not
justify what his clients claim to be, effectively, a representation by the
defendants that their business forms part of the plaintiffs' banking
business.

F   The history of the matter goes back to the period before the partition
of the Indian sub-continent into India and Pakistan.   The Habibs were
and are a well known banking family and in 1941 they incorporated a
banking company in Bombay.   That company bore the same name as
the plaintiffs in the action and I will refer to it as " the original H.B.L."
Upon the partition of India in 1947 the seat of this company was moved
to Karachi.   The business of the original H.B.L. was both substantial
G and international and in 1952 it was decided to incorporate a further
company in Pakistan to handle the overseas business.   That company
was Habib Bank (Overseas) Ltd.—which I refer to as " H.B.O." for
short—and it was owned as to 40 per cent. by the original H.B.L. and
as to 60 per cent. by individual members of the Habib family.   The
affairs of the two companies were, throughout their joint corporate
H lives, very closely intertwined.   The original H.B.L. dealt with all
business in Pakistan whilst foreign business was undertaken and
branches in foreign countries were operated by H.B.O.   But the separation was more theoretical than real, because there seems to have been no
practical separation of banking staffs who were treated as freely interchangeable between the two companies and there can be no doubt that
the two companies were known to the general public as " the Habib
Bank" without differentiating between the two corporate entities.

From 1970 onwards the two companies operated under the shadow A
of threatened nationalisation. In 1970 the elections in West Pakistan
were won by Mr. Bhutto's People's Party whose manifesto included a
policy of nationalisation of, inter alia, the banks, but war with India
and the formation of the separate state of Bangladesh intervened and
no immediate nationalisation took place. The writing was, however,
very clearly on the wall and there was an obvious danger of government
interference or supervision, a danger which became more acute when B
certain major industries were nationalised in 1972. It had, in fact, been
on the wall, albeit perhaps in rather fainter characters, since early 1967
when Mr. Bhutto had formed his party and the directors of the bank
saw the merit—no doubt in the bank's own interest as well as in that
of its customers—in forming a branch or affiliate abroad in a country
whose laws prohibited the disclosure of banking information, so that any C
attempted interference or inquiry could effectively be blocked. In July
1967 application was made to the State Bank of Pakistan for permission
to establish a branch in Switzerland. That was approved in principle
and on August 9, 1967, the defendants (to which I will refer as
" H.B.Z.") were established in Zurich. The attitude of the Swiss
authorities was such that the establishment was much facilitated if the D
new bank was established with local capital and accordingly H.B.O.
had only a minority of the shares (45 per cent. initially) the remainder
being issued to a Swiss company called Thesaurus. H.B.Z. formally
opened for business on October 12, 1967. Thereafter until 1974
H.B.Z.'s business was in fact run by the original H.B.L. and H.B.O. as
part of the Habib Bank business, even though H.B.O. was only a
minority shareholder. A member of the Habib family, Mr. Rashid E
Habib, was chairman of the board and another, Mr. Hyder Habib, was
a vice-chairman and the staff of the bank were freely interchangeable
with the staff of H.B.O. and the staff of the original H.B.L. H.B.Z.
was, effectively, the Zurich branch of the Habib bank. Contemporary
internal correspondence at the time of its formation indicates that the
primary purpose of establishing the Swiss bank was to provide a haven F
for customers who desired to place their funds in a hard-currency area
without fear of disclosure.

In May 1973 the board of H.B.Z. decided to open a branch in
London. H.B.O. was already operating there with a small head office in
Finsbury Pavement and a substantial number of branches outside London
in cities where there was a substantial immigrant population from Pakistan. The arrangements for the opening of the London branch of H.B.Z. G
were handled in London by H.B.O. Powers of attorney were given to
two senior executives of H.B.O. in London, Mr. Pirbhai and Mr.
Padiyar, and the latter negotiated the necessary permission from the
Bank of England. It did not really make commercial sense to establish,
in effect, a competitor in the United Kingdom with the same group but
Mr. Padiyar's letter to the Bank of England dated June 5, 1973, indi- H
cated, perhaps rather surprisingly, that the Swiss bank " find considerable scope for expansion of their business here and they desire to
participate in the banking activities of the City of London and the
United Kingdom." The primary business of H.B.O. was the remittance
to Pakistan of funds received from immigrants of Pakistani origin and
one cannot help doubting whether in fact the opening of a branch of
the Zurich business was intended to do more than provide on the spot

The Weekly Law Reports, October 23, 1981

1271

1 W.L.R.   Habib Bank Ltd. v. Habib Bank A.G. (C.A.)   Oliver L.J.

A facilities for remittance to hard-currency areas without the risk of
disclosure which would have existed if they were channelled through a
branch directly controlled from Pakistan. This is consistent with the
object which the then board of the original H.B.L. had in mind when
H.B.Z. was formed as it appears from a letter from Mr. Pirbhai (an
executive of H.B.O. in London) to Mr. Rashid Habib dated February
24, 1967. Nevertheless, a contemporary note of a meeting held on
B February 15, 1974 (that is after nationalisation) of representatives of
both H.B.O. and H.B.Z. with H.B.O.'s auditors, Messrs. Thompson
McLintock, indicates that both H.B.O. and H.B.Z. then had it in contemplation that H.B.Z. would expand into a general banking business
in London.

In so far as any conclusion can be drawn from this it seems to me
C to be merely this, that it bears out the plaintiffs' case that the Swiss
branch in London was treated simply as a branch of the international
business of the Habib Bank and that it was really a matter of indifference at that time by which corporate entity the actual business was
conducted. The whole group was under the management of members
of the Habib family.

The London office of H.B.Z. opened for business in November 1973
D in a very modest way. It consisted of a room adjoining the offices of
H.B.O. in 12, Finsbury Pavement. It had an independent entrance to
the outside corridor but was also accessible through the telex room in
H.B.O.'s office and in practice it consisted of a room, a desk and a
telephone which was manned by one of the members of the staff of
H.B.O. as occasion required. Up to March 1974 it had done very little
E business in the United Kingdom. By that time it had only three
accounts, so that apart from such reputation as it may have enjoyed as
part of the Habib banking group it had had very little time or opportunity to build up any independent goodwill of its own in London. On
January 1, 1974, the Damoclean sword fell. The Pakistan Government
announced the nationalisation of all the banks in Pakistan, which
included both the original H.B.L. and H.B.O. Subsequently in the
F summer of 1974 both the original H.B.L. and H.B.O. were merged in
a new state corporation, the present plaintiffs, and it is not disputed that
the effect of this, as a matter of law, was to vest in the plaintiffs all the
goodwill and rights of the original H.B.L. and of H.B.O.

The effect of nationalisation, however, was to produce a radical
change in the management of the business. All the existing chief
G executives and directors of H.B.L. and H.B.O. were removed, so that
from the beginning of January 1974 the Habib family ceased to have
any say in the banks' operations. But, of course, that did not apply
to H.B.Z. which was not susceptible to control from Pakistan, since
H.B.O. had only a minority shareholding. That in fact had been cut
down to 22½ per cent. as a result of a further issue of shares in November 1973. Matters came to a head in March 1974. Mr. Rashid Habib
H and Mr. Hyder Habib were persuaded to transfer their own nominee
shareholdings to the direction of the Government of Pakistan in July
1974 and this resulted in their vacating office as directors of H.B.Z. for
want of the essential share qualification. They actually resigned in
October 1974. The plaintiffs had, in March 1974, written to H.B.Z.
seeking to appoint their own nominees and had been firmly told that the
composition of the board was a matter for the majority shareholders
and on July 12 H.B.Z. refused to appoint the directors nominated by

1272

the plaintiffs. Thereafter in 1976 the proportionate holding of H.B.O. **A**
in the equity of H.B.Z. was further reduced by a rights issue in which
the plaintiffs were not allowed to participate and in May 1976 litigation
ensued in Switzerland which is still proceeding and in which the plaintiffs are seeking (so far unsuccessfully) to establish control of or increase
their shareholding in H.B.Z.

The important thing for present purposes is the effect of these
upheavals on H.B.Z. in London. In January 1974 Mr. Hyder Habib **B**
came to London to discuss the setting up of an office of H.B.Z. separate
from that of the now nationalised H.B.O. There is a clear history of
assistance and co-operation on the part of H.B.O. in this venture but
the evidence indicates that at this time there was considerable confusion
among the London staff because nobody knew what was going on or
exactly what the effect of nationalisation was going to be. Certainly **C**
normal banking transactions between the nationalised H.B.O. and
H.B.Z. carried on and in May 1974 H.B.Z. moved to 8 City Road with
the active co-operation and help of the management and staff of H.B.O.
They stayed there for a little over a year and in August 1975 moved to
10, Throgmorton Avenue. There was no hint or murmur of any protest
or dissatisfaction on the part of the plaintiffs until August 1977 just
after H.B.Z. had moved its office once more. The new office was at **D**
92, Moorgate just round the corner from H.B.O's office It took place
in July 1977 and on August 22 the plaintiffs' solicitors wrote demanding
that H.B.Z. discontinue the use of its corporate name in the United
Kingdom. The writ followed on September 23.

The basic ingredients of a passing off action are not in dispute
between the parties. Nor could they be for they have been well settled **E**
for years. They are set out in the speech of Lord Parker in *A. G.
Spalding and Brothers* v. *A. W. Gamage Ltd.* (1915) 84 L.J.Ch. 449:

> "This principle is stated by Turner L.J. in *Burgess* v. *Burgess*
> (1853) 3 De G.M. & G. 896, 904–905 and by Lord Halsbury in
> *Reddaway* v. *Banham* [1896] A.C. 199, 204, in the proposition that
> nobody has any right to represent his goods as the goods of some-
> body else. It is also sometimes stated in the proposition that nobody **F**
> has the right to pass off his goods as the goods of somebody else.
> I prefer the former statement, for, whatever doubts may be sug-
> gested in the earlier authorities, it has long been settled that actual
> passing off of the defendant's goods for the plaintiff's need not be
> proved as a condition precedent to relief in equity either by way
> of an injunction or of an inquiry as to profits or damages . . . Nor **G**
> need the representation be fraudulently made. It is enough that
> it has in fact been made, whether fraudulently or otherwise, and
> that damages may probably ensue, though the complete innocence
> of the party making it may be a reason for limiting the account of
> profits to the period subsequent to the date at which he becomes
> aware of the true facts."

H

There is a useful passage with regard to evidence, at p. 452. In particular
it was with regard to advertisements in that case that Lord Parker said:

> "It was also contended that the question whether the advertise-
> ments were calculated to deceive was not one which your Lordships
> could yourselves determine by considering the purport of the
> advertisements themselves, having regard to the surrounding circum-
> stances, but was one which your Lordships were bound to deter-

The Weekly Law Reports, October 23, 1981

1273

1 W.L.R.   Habib Bank Ltd. v. Habib Bank A.G. (C.A.)   Oliver L.J.

A   mine upon evidence directed to the question itself. I do not take this view of the law. There may, of course, be cases of so doubtful a nature that a judge cannot properly come to a conclusion without evidence directed to the point, but there can be no doubt that in a passing-off action the question whether the matter complained of is calculated to deceive—in other words, whether it amounts to a misrepresentation—is a matter for the judge, who,
B   looking at the documents and evidence before him, comes to his own conclusion, and, to use the words of Lord Macnaghten in *Payton & Co. Ltd.* v. *Snelling, Lampard & Co. Ltd.* [1901] A.C. 308, 311, ' must not surrender his own independent judgment to any witness whatever '."

C   More recently the principles have been reiterated in the following passages from the speech of Lord Diplock in *Erven Warnink Besloten Vennootschap* v. *J. Townend & Sons (Hull) Ltd.* [1979] A.C. 731, 742:

" My Lords, *A. G. Spalding and Brothers* v. *A. W. Gamage Ltd.*, 84 L.J.Ch. 449, and the later cases make it possible to identify five characteristics which must be present in order to create a valid cause of action for passing off: (1) a misrepresentation, (2) made
D   by a trader in the course of trade, (3) to propsective customers of his or ultimate consumers of goods or services supplied by him, (4) which is calculated to injure the business or goodwill of another trader (in the sense that this is a reasonably foreseeable consequence) and (5) which causes actual damage to a business or goodwill of the trader by whom the action is brought or (in a quia timet
E   action) will probably do so."

The difficulties, as always, arise in applying these well known principles to the facts of the individual case. Mr. Aldous's case is a very simple one. Up to November 1973 the only Habib Bank presence in the United Kingdom was H.B.O. and its branches. H.B.O. (either alone or in conjunction with its associated company the original H.B.L.) had a
F   substantial goodwill in connection with the banking business carried on from London. H.B.Z. was introduced to London by the original H.B.L. and H.B.O. as a bank operating under the same management and it was allowed to participate in the goodwill generated by H.B.O. but had no goodwill here of its own. It was simply held out or allowed to hold itself out as part of the Habib Bank—that is, as a banking organisation substantially under the same management as that of the existing and
G   established business. In March 1974, however, it ceased in fact to be under the same management as the organisation known as the Habib Bank, not because its management had changed, but because the management of the Habib Bank had changed and H.B.Z. had refused to accept the nominees of the now nationalised Habib Bank. It had, therefore, as Mr. Aldous graphically put it, " left the club." From
H   that moment on, it ceased to be entitled to hold itself out as a member of the club by using the Habib name and by continuing to do so it misrepresented to the public that its business was under the same management as the plaintiffs' business and thus passed itself off as or for a part of the plaintiffs' business when it was not. That, in its essentials, is Mr. Aldous' case, though there are refinements. The case is pleaded as a simple case of an interloper adopting the name of an existing business, but Mr. Aldous has to meet the difficulty that his own

clients were responsible both for the establishment of H.B.Z. in Switzerland and for its introduction to London. He meets this difficulty ingeniously, although without the assistance of any clearly pleaded case of a licence, by suggesting that the only way in which H.B.Z. could become entitled to make use of the existing United Kingdom goodwill of H.B.O. is by a licence from H.B.O. or the original H.B.L., a licence which impliedly endured only so long as the companies remained substantially under the same management. Mr. Aldous skilfully turns the lack of pleading into a weapon by suggesting that the only justification for H.B.Z.'s operation in this country under its own corporate name can be either its possession of a goodwill of its own (and it had none when it commenced business) or an irrevocable licence of some sort from the only company which did have any goodwill, namely H.B.O. And such a licence, he observes, is neither pleaded nor supported by the facts. What was pleaded was that H.B.Z. was established with the active concurrence and support of at least one of the entities now incorporated in the person of the plaintiffs and an open, public and uninterrupted course of business on the part of H.B.Z., in some respects encouraged, in some respects perhaps merely tolerated, but in no respect ever challenged from November 1973 to August 1977—facts which are prayed in aid in support of a plea of acquiescence, laches and estoppel.

Whitford J. in a careful and detailed judgment, reviewed the relevant facts and the evidence and his conclusions may be summarised as follows. (1) The reputation enjoyed by the Habib Bank in this country was a shared reputation, part of which was assumed by H.B.Z. immediately upon entry into the United Kingdom. H.B.Z. thus acquired the right to trade in this country under its corporate name and that right remained unaffected by the nationalisation of H.B.O. and the original H.B.L. or by any refusal on their behalf to accept the plaintiffs' dictates as to their future management. (2) There was, in any event, no misrepresentation. H.B.Z., H.B.O. and the original H.B.L. had a common right to the use of the name Habib and the defendants were doing no more than to trade under the name by which they were incorporated and known and which they were entitled to use. (3) No substantial damage to the plaintiffs had in any event been shown. (4) Although this did not arise on the view which the judge took, any claim by the plaintiffs would in his view have been barred by acquiescence.

Mr. Aldous attacks the first of these conclusions on the ground that, as he submits, there was no evidence which could conceivably support a shared reputation. Up to March 1974, after which time H.B.Z. and the plaintiffs were going their separate ways, there was only one reputation here, that of the Habib Bank, as personified by H.B.O. to whom the reputation adhered. H.B.Z. had substantially no business, it was unknown, its only office was a room in H.B.O.'s office and in so far as it could claim any reputation or goodwill at all it could only be that which it enjoyed by the permissive use of its corporate name here. That permission determined as soon as it threw off the shackles of the new nationalised management. Mr. Jeffs, whilst naturally seeking to support the judgment, ventures to put the matter in a rather different way from that adopted by Whitford J. It is, he submits, not so much a matter of a shared reputation or goodwill, as of an honest and unchallenged concurrent user. There is, he points out, no evidence whatever which can properly support the suggestion that when H.B.Z. came to London there was any limitation of its activities or any condi-

The Weekly Law Reports, October 23, 1981

1275

1 W.L.R.   Habib Bank Ltd. v. Habib Bank A.G. (C.A.)   Oliver L.J.

A   tion as to its management or policy implied, understood, or agreed to. Two companies, both connected with the well known Habib banking family, were perfectly honestly and properly making a concurrent user of that family name just as, for instance, manufacturers of a substance with a well known and recognised trade description, such as champagne, may enjoy the right in common to use that description for their products: see *H. P. Bulmer Ltd.* v. *J. Bollinger S.A.* [1978] R.P.C. 79.

B   In the case of a trade mark section 12 (2) of the Trade Marks Act 1938 enables the registrar to permit registration of a mark in the name of more than one proprietor where an " honest concurrent use " can be shown: see for instance *In re Jelley, Son, and Jones' Application* (1878) 46 L.T. 381n. and *Alex Pirie and Sons Ltd.'s Application* (1933) 50 R.P.C. 147. Now if the statute permits registration of two or more proprietors in the case of trade marks, where there has been honest concurrent use, the case of honest concurrent use of an unregistered name or mark is, Mr. Jeffs argues, a fortiori.

C   I think, if I may say so, that Mr. Jeffs's submissions are too ambitious in this sense, that they seek to elevate into a doctrine dignified by a term of art—" the doctrine of honest concurrent user "—what is, in the sphere of passing off, merely a facet of Lord Diplock's first essential

D   ingredient of misrepresentation in *Erven Warnink Besloten Vennootschap* v. *J. Townend & Sons (Hull) Ltd.* [1979] A.C. 731, 742. As Mr. Aldous has pointed out, section 2 of the Trade Marks Act 1938 expressly provides that nothing in the Act is deemed to affect any rights of action for passing off. The fact therefore that two or more people may be entitled to rely upon honest concurrent user of a mark to achieve registration leaves quite unaffected the question of whether they may

E   be entitled to sue one another in a passing off action. What I think Mr. Jeffs is really saying in propounding his doctrine is really this, that where you find that two traders have been concurrently using in the United Kingdom the same or similar names for their goods or businesses, you may well find a factual situation in which neither of them can be said to be guilty of any misrepresentation. Each represents nothing but the

F   truth, that a particular name or mark is associated with his goods or business.

    It is misrepresentation which lies at the root of the action and Mr. Aldous concedes that if he fails, on the evidence, to demonstrate this, then he fails on this appeal. Whitford J., as I have said, found none, and Mr. Aldous has to submit that that finding was either wrong in

G   law or contrary to the weight of the evidence. It is, therefore, necessary to analyse and examine carefully the major premise upon which Mr. Aldous beguilingly erects the logical structure of his case. We have been treated to a detailed and fascinating guided excursion into the labyrinth of cases relating to the use by traders of their own and other's names, but in the ultimate analysis the question remains, what was the misrepresentation? The Habib Bank A.G. Zurich was set up

H   in London as the Habib Bank A.G. Zurich with the express consent and co-operation of the plaintiffs' predecessors. It is still the Habib Bank A.G. Zurich carrying on the business which it was incorporated to carry on. Its constitution, its management, its business style and its motto remain unchanged. And it is accepted, as it must be accepted on the facts, that when it established its business here there was no misrepresentation.

    I have already outlined in summary the way in which Mr. Aldous

puts his case and it bases itself, on analysis, on a number of axioms—I   A
say axioms advisedly because they are advanced rather as matters which
are self-evident than as matters which can be said to be supported by
the evidence or by the judge's findings. First, it is said that the reputation and goodwill in this country associated with the name Habib was
in November 1973 exclusively the property of H.B.O. because that was
the only company which traded here. Then it is said that H.B.Z. was set
up here and held out as a bank associated with and "*under the same*   B
effective management as"—and these words are crucial to Mr. Aldous's
case—"the existing United Kingdom business of H.B.O." That, the
argument proceeds, was done for the limited purpose of enabling
H.B.O.'s customers in England to make remittances to hard currency
areas. So here, says Mr. Aldous, is the representation imported by the
use by H.B.Z. of the name Habib. "We are under the same   C
effective management as the bank known as Habib Bank Overseas Ltd.
and we are here for the purpose of receiving deposits from customers
of that bank for hard-currency areas."

In the spring of 1974, when the now nationalised Habib Bank Ltd.
sought unsuccessfully to appoint its nominees to the board of H.B.Z.,
Mr. Aldous says that all that changed. The representation remained the
same but it was no longer true. True it is that in the resulting confu-   D
sion H.B.O. and its personnel in London assisted H.B.Z. in finding new
offices and setting up its business. True it is that H.B.O. and H.B.Z.
continued, as they do to this day, to do business together—substantial
business: indeed many thousands of transactions. But they are not
associated together. They are not under the same effective management. Indeed on April 8, 1974, a meeting of the executives of the   E
nationalised bank resolved: "Zurich. We should continue business
relations with them as before. However, rates of interest etc. should
be on competitive basis."

H.B.Z. over the next few years expanded its activities. It received
Bank of England permissions to operate non-resident sterling accounts
in June 1974, to issue and confirm credits (June 1974 and March 1975)
to remit to resident customers' non-resident dependants in the Middle   F
East (September 1975) to open a U.S. dollar account in New York (June
1975) to open a Deutshmark account in Germany (September 1975) and
finally to effect remittances in rupees to resident customers' non-resident
dependent relatives in the Indian sub-continent (September 1978). It
was really only this latter which trespassed in any way on the plaintiffs'
principal business in the United Kingdom which is and has always been   G
that of obtaining remittances for Pakistan.

So, says Mr. Aldous, H.B.Z. "left the club." They eschewed the
same management. They traded on their own in a way quite other than
that contemplated when they were established here. Yet they continued to make use of the plaintiffs' exclusive reputation in the name
Habib for the purposes of their now competing business. From March
1974 onwards therefore Mr. Aldous submits that there was a continuing   H
misrepresentation which entitles him now to an injunction. Now it is
perhaps not surprising that Mr. Aldous seeks to concentrate attention
on March 1974 when his clients' attempt to obtain effective management
of H.B.Z. failed, for it is only thus that he can make out a case for
misrepresentation at all. To some extent it does however obscure the
issue because it ignores the three and a half years of independant trading
which ensued thereafter before the first murmur of discontent was heard

The Weekly Law Reports, October 23, 1981

1277

1 W.L.R.   Habib Bank Ltd. v. Habib Bank A.G. (C.A.)   Oliver L.J.

A which gave rise to this action and the question ultimately is whether there was a cause of action in passing off at the date of the writ and not whether, three years earlier, one party or the other might have succeeded if proceedings had then been commenced.

But granted for a moment Mr. Aldous' hypothesis that this is the relevant moment for testing the matter, and leaving aside all questions of laches and acquiescence, one still has to examine with some care

B whether he can make good his basic factual submissions.

First, let me take his tenet that in March 1974 H.B.O. had the exclusive reputation and goodwill in the United Kingdom in the name, Habib. For this Mr. Aldous relies on two passages in Whitford J.'s judgment which, he claims, constitutes findings in his favour. The judge said:

C   " Although H.B.Z. was and is a separate legal entity, it is clear on the evidence that it in fact operated as if it were another branch of the Habib organisation, just as had been the case with H.B.O. Effectively the control over the operations of H.B.O., H.B.L. and H.B.Z. was the same. . . ."

Later the judge said:

D   " When H.B.Z. entered the United Kingdom, as they did at the instance of and with the approbation and assistance of H.B.L. and H.B.O., they immediately assumed a part in this shared reputation in this country. At this stage H.B.Z. would be taken, as the plaintiffs' witnesses put it, to be the same bank."

E I am unable to put upon these passages the interpretation which Mr. Aldous urges. It seems to me to be perfectly plain that when the judge used the expression " the same bank " he was referring to the whole international banking organisation run by the members of the Habib family whose name was well known to Pakistan's immigrants in this country. That emerges, I think, clearly from these further passages in the judgment. Talking of the action the judge said:

F   " It has only arisen because of the nationalisation on January 1, 1974, of two banking organisations which, together with the defendant bank prior to that date, constituted an international banking network owned and controlled by members of the family bearing the name Habib. I was told by Mr. Tayebi, the plaintiffs' first witness, who is an executive vice-president, chief law officer and secretary of

G   the plaintiffs, that Habib is a not very common name, but it is a name found in Muslim countries. He also told me that, in relation to the business community and in a commercial and banking context the name Habib in Pakistan for many years was associated exclusively with the business of the family who, in 1941, established the Habib Bank Ltd. in Bombay. In the years which followed, up to 1974, this bank remained under the control of the family,

H   but in the years intervening there have been a number of changes."

Later the judge said:

      " Dealing with H.B.L. in Pakistan, or at three overseas branches which H.B.L. ran in Kuala Lumpur, Singapore and New York, and dealing with the branches of H.B.O., the customers would I think proceed upon the basis that they were using the facilities of the Habib Bank without stopping to consider whether or not there were

Oliver L.J.   Habib Bank Ltd. v. Habib Bank A.G. (C.A.)   **[1981]**

A

separate organisations running the different branches in different
parts of the world and without stopping to consider for one moment
who may have held the shares or the majority of the shares in
one or other of these organisations.   There were these two separate
organisations but customers dealing with them could nonetheless be
rightly confident that their interests were safeguarded by reason of
the control exercised by the Habib family, whose reputation in
commercial and banking circles stood and stands very high, as was
said in the evidence of the plaintiffs' witnesses, in particular Mr.
Bukhari . . . I think, on the evidence, the goodwill and repute prior
to 1973 which attached to the name Habib was a goodwill
attaching to the Habib organisation at large and it was no doubt
additionally built up having regard to the confidence felt in the
family which started the bank and the esteem in which they continued to be held."

B

C

The judge said earlier:

"Staff were moved from one company to the other, but always
considered themselves as being servants of the same organisation.
The customers I am sure, whether dealing with H.B.L., H.B.O. or
H.B.Z., thought they were dealing with one and the same organisation—as indeed, so far as any question of effective control is concerned, they were—and the evidence that was called is in support
of this view."

D

That was related to the period before nationalisation.
    The view of the matter expressed by the judge is I think amply borne
out by the evidence.   [His Lordship considered the evidence of the
plaintiffs' witnesses, Mr. Tayebi and Mr. Bukhari and continued:] Of
course, it is perfectly true, as Mr. Aldous submits that the exploitation of
the family name in the United Kingdom had taken place through only
one of the three limited companies founded by the family so that in
one sense the goodwill associated with the name adhered to that company, but it seems perfectly clear from the evidence—and it must be
remembered that the customers were either entirely or substantially
entirely Pakistanis in this country, many of whom were illiterate—the
reputation attached to the family name, so that an organisation established by that family under the family name immediately acquires the
reputation of the family.   The judge has been criticised for his finding
that there was a shared goodwill, which it is said was not a reflection of
the way in which the case had been argued by either side and it may be
that the expression is perhaps less than precise shorthand. But for my
part I cannot see that in the essentials the judge was wrong. Where an
internationally known business establishes a branch in this country
through a limited company, either incorporated here or abroad, it may
be that technically the goodwill and reputation of that business
" belongs " to the limited company in the sense that the company may
be the proper and only plaintiff in an action taken here to protect it.
But it does not cease to be the goodwill and reputation of the international business because it is also the goodwill and reputation of the
local branch.   And that reputation inheres, as it seems to me, equally in
any other local branch which the international business may set up in
the same place.   The expression " goodwill " has been conveniently
defined in the following phrase which is quoted in *Erven Warnink*

E

F

G

H

A *Besloten Vennootschap* v. *J. Townend & Sons (Hull) Ltd.* [1979] A.C. 731, from the speech of Lord Macnaghten in *Inland Revenue Commissioners* v. *Muller & Co.'s Margarine Ltd.* [1901] A.C. 217. Lord Diplock, after referring to Lord Parker in *A. G. Spalding and Brothers* v. *A. W. Gamage Ltd.*, 84 L.J.Ch. 449, said, at p. 741:

> B   " In a speech which received the approval of the other members of this House, he" (that is Lord Parker) " identified the right the invasion of which is the subject of passing off actions as being the ' property in the business or goodwill likely to be injured by the misrepresentation '. The concept of goodwill is in law a broad one which is perhaps best expressed in words used by Lord Macnaghten in *Inland Revenue Commissioners* v. *Muller & Co.'s Margarine Ltd.* [1901] A.C. 217, 223–224: ' It is the benefit and
> C   advantage of the good name, reputation, and connection of a business. It is the attractive force which brings in custom.' "

At the base of Mr. Aldous's submissions there lies the notion that even in the case of an international group in the sense used above, once there has been established here a corporate entity making use of their goodwill, the goodwill becomes a localised asset forming part of the exclusive
D property of the corporate entity, and can be attached to another corporate entity established by the international body only by some transfer from the original user in this country, for instance, by assignment or licence expressed or implied. For my part, I think that that displays an unduly and unjustifiably formalistic approach to the matter and to be an approach which ignores both substance and reality. Essentially the
E evidence and the judge's findings seem to me to justify the proposition that the reputation and that the establishment of a branch in this country, whether as a separate corporate entity or not, imports simply that it is part of that international organisation which is run by the Habib family.

I start therefore from the position that, for my part, I am unable to see that, however he expressed it, the judge went wrong in his rejection
F of Mr. Aldous's first basic assumption of an exclusive goodwill subsisting in H.B.O.

I come then to Mr. Aldous's second axiom, that the establishment here of the defendants' office under the title of H.B.Z. imported a representation that it was a company under the effective management of H.B.O. or the original H.B.L. or under the same effective management as those
G two companies. I do not think it imported anything of the sort save to this extent that all the companies were under the management of members of the Habib family. I can see absolutely no reason why anyone should assume from the name Habib Bank A.G. Zurich that H.B.Z. was a subsidiary of one or the other of H.B.O. or the original H.B.L. or that it was their parent company or indeed anything more
H than it was loosely associated with them by its ties with the same family. It is indeed instructive to see how this was pleaded. In paragraph 5 of the statement of claim it is pleaded as follows:

> " The defendants have passed off and intend to continue to pass off their banking business in this country as and for the business of the plaintiffs or as a business connected or associated with the plaintiffs or a branch thereof or as a business under the effective control of the plaintiffs."

The plaintiffs were asked for particulars of that. They were asked: A

"(a) State what is meant by the plaintiffs' 'effective control' of the defendants. (b) Identify precisely the date when it is alleged that the defendants ceased to be under the effective control of the plaintiffs. (c) State precisely the period during which it is alleged that the defendants were under the effective control of the plaintiffs and all facts and matters relied upon to establish such effective B control. (d) State all facts and matters relied upon to establish that the plaintiffs lost effective control of the defendants. (e) State precisely when the nationalisation and merger are alleged to have taken place."

That request was answered:

"(a) By 'a business under the effective control of the plaintiffs', C the plaintiffs mean a business wherein the majority shareholding is the same as that of the plaintiffs and/or in which the executive decisions are made by the same persons who make such decisions in the plaintiff company. (b) The defendants ceased to be under the effective control of the plaintiffs on the date of nationalisation being January 1, 1974, or shortly thereafter. (c) The defendants D were under the effective control of the plaintiffs at all times prior to the date of nationalisation. In support hereof the plaintiffs, will rely on the fact that prior to January 1, 1974, the majority shareholdings in H.B.Z. and H.B.O. were held by the same persons and that ultimately the executive decisions of the two companies were made by the same persons and in particular by Mr. Hyder Habib." E

(It will be remembered that he remained and still remains to this day one of the controlling persons behind H.B.Z.).

"(d) In support of the allegation that the plaintiffs lost effective control of the defendants, the plaintiffs will rely on the fact that after nationalisation the ownership of H.B.O. and H.B.L. passed to the State of Pakistan and that shortly thereafter the executive F decisions of H.B.O. were taken by persons other than those taking such decisions for H.B.Z."

It then gives the date of nationalisation.

There was never at any time a majority shareholding in H.B.Z. by H.B.O. or by the Habib family and I confess myself wholly unable to see why the mere establishment by a Swiss company of an office in London G where there is already a family company doing business should import any representation at all about who is responsible for the management decisions of either. It seems to me that where you are dealing with Pakistani citizens who are familiar with affairs in Pakistan and well acquainted with the reputation of a well known banking family all that the name imports is "we are a company associated with the Habib H family." That is as true today as it was in 1973.

Then turning to Mr. Aldous's third proposition that there was some agreed or understood limitation on the activities of H.B.Z. in London, which has somehow been transcended by the development of a general banking business, there is, apart from a reference to the original purpose of providing a hard currency haven safe from the prying eyes of an inquisitive government, no evidence to support any such agreement or

The Weekly Law Reports, October 23, 1981

1281

1 W.L.R.   Habib Bank Ltd. v. Habib Bank A.G. (C.A.)   Oliver L.J.

A understanding. H.B.O.'s officers in their answers to the State Bank of Pakistan denied any agreement and simply said that the operations were to be governed by the articles of association (which I should perhaps say cover the carrying on of a general banking business). The Bank of England was informed that H.B.Z. desired to take part in the banking activities of the City of London and Mr. Hussein's evidence was that he was told in Zurich to take over the London branch which would be a general banking business. I find this suggestion of the plaintiffs really wholly unsupported by the evidence, but in any event it seems to me to have relevance only to the question of acquiescence and not to the logically anterior question of whether there was any misrepresentation.

I think that it will have become evident from what I have said so far that I find myself wholly unpersuaded that the judge, however he may have expressed himself, erred in principle in the conclusion at which he arrived that the evidence disclosed no passing off because there simply is not and was not any misrepresentation. That really was sufficient to dispose of the case and it is sufficient, in my judgment, to dispose of this appeal.

The proposition that a nationalisation decree which deprives individuals in a foreign jurisdiction of their control of a foreign company can have the effect of forcing those individuals to give up the use of a name which they have lawfully adopted and are lawfully using in another jurisdiction is one which, in any event, I find a little startling, and Mr. Jeffs has addressed to us, under his cross-notice, an argument that the English court will not prevent a company lawfully incorporated abroad from honestly using its corporate name in connection with a business carried on here. In the view that I take it is unnecessary to decide this interesting point, although it derives some support from the decision of Stirling J. in *Saunders* v. *Sun Life Assurance Co. of Canada* [1894] 1 Ch. 537, and the judgment of Morton L.J. in particular in the Court of Appeal in *Marengo* v. *Daily Sketch and Sunday Graphic Ltd.* (unreported) May 17, 1946, although that decision was subsequently reversed on the facts in the House of Lords [1948] W.N. 92.

But even if I were in doubt about the principal ground for the judge's decision, I think that the judgment can equally be supported on the other grounds which he gave. First, the question of damage. The judge expressed himself in these terms in his judgment, having reviewed the evidence on damage:

G   " Had it been necessary for me to come to a conclusion on the question of damage, I am by no means certain that I could come to the conclusion that the plaintiffs have satisfactorily established their case under this head."

I think that if I have a criticism of the judge's judgment, it is only that in this he did not go far enough. It has to be remembered that damage is of the essence of the claim, although of course it may be inferred. This appears most clearly from the speech of Lord Fraser of Tullybelton in *Erven Warnink Besloten Vennootschap* v. *J. Townend & Sons (Hull) Ltd.* [1979] A.C. 731, 755–756:

" It is essential for the plaintiff in a passing off action to show at least the following facts:—(1) that his business consists of, or includes, selling in England a class of goods to which the particular trade name applies; (2) that the class of goods is clearly defined, and that in the minds of the public, or a section of the public, in A England, the trade name distinguishes that class from other similar goods; (3) that because of the reputation of the goods, there is goodwill attached to the name; (4) that he, the plaintiff, as a member of the class of those who sell the goods, is the owner of goodwill in England which is of substantial value; (5) that he has suffered, or is really likely to suffer, substantial damage to his property in the goodwill by reason of the defendants selling goods B which are falsely described by the trade name to which the goodwill is attached."

But here there really was no evidence of any damage of any significance over the whole period since nationalisation. The witnesses called by the plaintiffs to establish the probability of confusion seem, judging from the transcripts, from the plaintiffs' point of view to have C been disappointingly vague. It has to be remembered that these two banks had been trading together in London for three and a half years before the issue of the writ and nearly six years at the date of the hearing. Yet there was not one atom of evidence of any customer who had opened an account at one in mistake for the other, apart from one case in which a gentleman who had opened an account with H.B.Z. had D subsequently closed it and transferred his business to the plaintiffs. Since he had previously transferred part of the moneys in his account with H.B.Z. to an account opened with the plaintiffs before finally closing his account with H.B.Z. this may import dissatisfaction but it hardly looks like a case of confusion. All the other evidence of confusion related to a decreasing amount of postal confusion (much of which was accounted for by carelessness on the part of the Post Office) E telex confusion by junior banking staff, and a decreasing quantity of credits or debits to the wrong banks, which were swiftly rectified without loss, although this may have caused some slight administrative inconvenience on both sides. But the evidence did indicate that errors of this sort did occur, though much less frequently, even with other banks.

H.B.Z. has 21 branches in various countries, in many of which the F plaintiffs also have branches, sometimes even in the same town. There was no evidence of confusion between the two except in one case of a press report where a guarantee given by the plaintiffs was described as given by the " Zurich based " Habib Bank.

Mr. Aldous says that there is a danger of some malpractice of H.B.Z. rubbing off on his clients. That is a two-way traffic. The judge dismissed this as pure speculation and so it is. Moreover, it is G speculation against the background of some 12 years of concurrent international trading during which there is minimal evidence of any substantial confusion, except of a purely mechanical kind. For my part I would be bolder than the judge. I think that the plaintiffs failed to establish any substantial damage or probability of damage.

Finally I turn to the point of acquiescence, laches and estoppel. The H judge would have held the claim barred on this ground if he had thought that any claim existed; and so would I.

Just consider the facts. It is common ground that H.B.Z. were formed and founded with the active concurrence of the plaintiffs' predecessors and that their staff were used to set them up in London.

After nationalisation H.B.Z. was established in its new office with the help of H.B.O.'s staff in London. It was the evidence of the plain-

The Weekly Law Reports, October 23, 1981

1283

1 W.L.R.   Habib Bank Ltd. v. Habib Bank A.G. (C.A.)   Oliver L.J.

A tiffs' own witnesses that thereafter there were literally thousands of transactions between the two banks every year and that the plaintiffs and H.B.Z. entered into a whole series of agency arrangements which were profitable to both sides.

The relationship after nationalisation is summed up in the following very significant evidence from the plaintiffs' own witness, Mr. Bukhari.
B He was asked:

"Q. Can you tell me, if H.B.O. (subsequently the plaintiffs) had decided to do no business after nationalisation with H.B.Z., what would be the position in relation to H.B.Z.: would they have been able to transact the same business? —A. Not after nationalisation: we could not or did not stop our dealings with Habib Bank Zurich, neither did they stop dealing with us, because there were so
C many transactions, so many accounts mutual and they were so interwoven and so many clients are involved that it was not possible for us or for them to discontinue relationship between the two banks. Q. I do not think you are answering the question I asked but do finish your answer. —A. I was saying that we in London were looking after all the London business of the Habib Bank
D Zurich. All their investments were made to us, all their money was placed or transactions relevant were effected with us. So at that time I believe that Habib Bank A.G. Zurich could not have done without us. Of course, they could make alternative arrangements with other banks, but it would take a lot of time. Q. What about the agency agreements: supposing you had said, ' We will take no agency work ', could they have transacted that with some other
E bank? —A. Yes, it is always possible to make agency arrangements with other banks, but relations being what they were prior to nationalisation, it was easier and more convenient, and particularly they needed Habib Bank with a network of branches in Pakistan, and that is why they approached us and we did make agency arrangements."

F There was also evidence which established that whereas H.B.Z. had from the inception used a logo consisting of a lion, not dissimilar to that used by the original H.B.L. in Pakistan, H.B.O. had right from the outset used in the United Kingdom the insignia of a flying horse. After nationalisation that was abandoned and the plaintiffs elected to use here the original H.B.L. motif thus bringing themselves nearer to
G H.B.Z.—a source of possible confusion compounded by their failure to comply with section 411 of the Companies Act 1948 by specifying in their letterheads that they were incorporated in Pakistan. One's initial reaction, looking at the history of the matter, is that there could hardly be a plainer case of acquiescence than this, but Mr. Aldous says first that there is no properly pleaded case of acquiescence, and, secondly,
H that the essential ingredients of a defence of acquiescence were never proved.

We were again referred to many authorities on this subject and to the debate which has taken place as to whether, in order to succeed in a plea of acquiescence, a defendant must demonstrate all the five probanda contained in the judgment of Fry J. in *Willmott* v. *Barber* (1880) 15 Ch.D. 96: see the recent judgment of Robert Goff J. in *Amalgamated Investment & Property Co. Ltd.* v. *Texas Commerce International*

Bank Ltd. [1981] 2 W.L.R. 554. Whether all five of those probanda A
are necessary or not, Mr. Aldous submits that to succeed H.B.Z. must
at least establish three things. They must show, first, that H.B.Z.
have been acting under a mistake as to their legal rights. That, in the
instant case, must mean that they were unaware that what they were
doing (that is to say, carrying on their business under the name in
which they had been incorporated with the active assistance of the B
plaintiffs' predecessors), constituted any invasion of the plaintiffs' rights.
Secondly, they must show that the plaintiffs encouraged that course of
action, either by statements or conduct. Thirdly, they must show that
they have acted upon the plaintiffs' representation or encouragement to
their detriment.

None of these three essentials, submits Mr. Aldous, has been pleaded
or proved in the instant case. I will consider that submission in a C
moment, but I must first notice Mr. Jacob's submission that in any
event these three allegedly essential ingredients do not constitute the
test for a successful plea of acquiescence or estoppel, at any rate as
the law has now developed. The true principle, Mr. Jacob suggests, is
that to be found in the judgment of the Board in *Lindsay Petroleum Co.*
v. *Hurd* (1874) L.R. 5 P.C. 221, 239, delivered by Sir Barnes Peacock D
and cited with approval by Lord Blackburn in *Erlanger* v. *New Sombrero Phosphate Co.* (1878) 3 App.Cas. 1218, 1279:

"'The doctrine of laches in courts of equity is not an arbitrary or
a technical doctrine. Where it would be practically unjust to give
a remedy, either because the party has, by his conduct done that
which might fairly be regarded as equivalent to a waiver of it, or
where, by his conduct and neglect he has, though perhaps not E
waiving that remedy, yet put the other party in a situation in which
it would not be reasonable to place him if the remedy were afterwards to be asserted, in either of these cases lapse of time and
delay are most material. But in every case if an argument against
relief, which otherwise would be just, is founded upon mere delay,
that delay of course not amounting to a bar by any statute of F
limitations, the validity of that defence must be tried upon principles
substantially equitable. Two circumstances always important in
such cases are the length of the delay and the nature of the acts
done during the interval, which might affect either party and cause
a balance of justice or injustice in taking the one course or the
other, so far as relates to the remedy.'"

G
After quoting that passage Lord Blackburn continued:

"I have looked in vain for any authority which gives a more
distinct and definite rule than this; and I think, from the nature of
the inquiry, it must always be a question of more or less, depending
on the degree of diligence which might reasonably be required, and
the degree of change which has occurred, whether the balance of H
justice or injustice is in favour of granting the remedy or withholding it. The determination of such a question must largely
depend on the turn of mind of those who have to decide, and must
therefore be subject to uncertainty; but that, I think, is inherent
in the nature of the inquiry."

To this Mr. Aldous retorts that that applies only where you are
considering the doctrine of laches or acquiescence in relation to the

The Weekly Law Reports, October 23, 1981

1285

1 W.L.R.   Habib Bank Ltd. v. Habib Bank A.G. (C.A.)   Oliver L.J.

A   assertion of equitable rights and not where you are considering the enforcement by equitable means of legal rights; and we were regaled with authorities on both sides for the purpose of establishing whether a plaintiff in a passing off action is protecting a legal right or an equitable right.

I have to confess that I detect in myself, despite the erudition displayed by both counsel, a strong predilection for the view that such
B   distinctions are both archaic and arcane and that in the year 1980 they have but little significance for anyone but a legal historian. For myself, I believe that the law as it has developed over the past 20 years has now evolved a far broader approach to the problem than that suggested by Mr. Aldous and one which is in no way dependent upon the historical accident of whether any particular right was first recognised by the com-
C   mon law or was invented by the Court of Chancery. It is an approach exemplified in such cases as *Inwards* v. *Baker* [1965] 2 Q.B. 29 and *Crabb* v. *Arun District Council* [1976] Ch. 179. We have been referred at length to a recent judgment of my own in *Taylors Fashions Ltd.* v. *Liverpool Victoria Trustees Co. Ltd.* (*Note*) [1981] 2 W.L.R. 576 in which I ventured to collect and review the authorities. I there said,
D   at p. 593:

"Furthermore the more recent cases indicate, in my judgment, that the application of the *Ramsden* v. *Dyson*, L.R. 1 H.L. 129 principle—whether you call it proprietary estoppel, estoppel by acquiescence or estoppel by encouragement is really immaterial— requires a very much broader approach which is directed rather at ascertaining whether, in particular individual circumstances, it
E   would be unconscionable for a party to be permitted to deny that which, knowingly, or unknowingly, he has allowed or encouraged another to assume to his detriment than to inquiring whether the circumstances can be fitted within the confines of some preconceived formula serving as a universal yardstick for every form of unconscionable behaviour."

F   Whilst, having heard the judgment read by counsel, I could wish that it had been more succinct, that statement at least is one to which I adhere.

But let me, for present purposes, assume in Mr. Aldous's favour the three essentials which he propounds. He says that there was no plea, no assertion, no evidence of H.B.Z.'s innocence in what they did: but,
G   I ask, why should there be? In his statement of claim he asserted that H.B.Z. " intended " to pass off their business as one associated with the plaintiffs and he was asked, in a request for particulars, whether that meant deliberate passing off. That request produced a positive response but it is common ground that the allegation was withdrawn well before the trial. So that the case from thereon proceeded from first to last on the footing that there was no suggestion of male fides. Then, again,
H   before the trial the plaintiffs were asked to make certain admissions and the following facts were all expressly admitted.

It was admitted that H.B.Z. were incorporated under their present name with the consent of H.B.O. It was admitted that clause 2 of H.B.Z.'s statutes translated into English provided:

"The corporation may take up holdings in similar companies, establish branches in Switzerland or abroad and in general transact

any business directly or indirectly connected with realising its   A
objects."

It was admitted by H.P.Z.'s request for admissions:

"By letter dated June 5, 1973, H.B.O. on behalf of H.B.Z. sought
Bank of England consent to open an office in London ... that
H.B.Z. acquired premises at 8 City Road under a lease dated May
22, 1974."   B

It was *not* admitted that the premises were found for H.B.Z. by De
Groot Collis (estate agents) pursuant to instructions given by H.B.O.
officials; but in fact that was proved. And it was admitted: "The
London office of H.B.Z. has maintained an account with H.B.O. and
subsequently the plaintiffs since July 3, 1973."

In paragraph 12 of the reply there was this admission: C

"It is admitted that shortly prior to these proceedings neither
H.B.L. nor H.B.O. objected to the defendants' activities. However
the same does not provide any defence to this action."

There is then a very significant deletion, which was the original pleading:

"Up till that time the defendants' activities in this country had   D
been very limited and had been purely in respect of their Swiss
banking business. The first knowledge the plaintiffs had that the
defendants intended to carry out banking activities in this country
other than as a necessary part of their activities in Switzerland was
when the defendants started preparation to open their new premises
in Moorgate."
                                                                     E
The whole of that was subsequently deleted on amendment before trial.

So here was a company against whom no male fides was alleged, as
to whom it was admitted that its trading name style and objects were
assumed with the consent of the plaintiffs' predecessors, that its offices
were found for it by the plaintiffs' predecessors, that its very consent
from the Bank of England was obtained by the plaintiffs' predecessors,   F
and that up to and after the action it had maintained an account with
the plaintiffs; and in relation to whose user of the name it was never
alleged from first to last that the slightest objection was taken until
about a month before the writ. I am bound to say that it struck me
while Mr. Aldous was addressing us, as it strikes me now, that in these
circumstances the calling of a witness to prove what the facts themselves
seem to me to demonstrate beyond a peradventure, was a work of super-   G
erogation, for there could not, in the proven circumstances, have been
any reason why, in the absence of any adverse claims by the plaintiffs,
anyone should for a moment imagine that there could be the slightest
objection likely to be raised by them to the continuation in business of
what, essentially, had started life as their own creature.

As regards the second of Mr. Aldous' propositions, I challenged   H
Mr. Aldous in the course of the argument to tell us what more the
plaintiffs could have done than what they did to encourage H.B.Z. in
the belief that there was no objection to their trading style and his
answer was that there was more—they could have written a letter
expressly stating that there was no such objection. That answer, I
think, really spoke for itself, although perhaps extracted from counsel
in a moment of exasperation, for really when the facts are examined—

A   and they show a history of continuous mutual trading over the whole period (even including the sale of equipment by the plaintiffs to H.B.Z.) —the case is really unanswerable.

Finally, there was, says Mr. Aldous, neither express allegation nor express proof that H.B.Z. had acted upon the encouragement. There is certainly an allegation in relation to estoppel in paragraph 15 of the defence that H.B.Z. have relied upon the right to use their own name

B   and motif and have been permitted by the plaintiffs to build up a goodwill therein. That goodwill, in fact, was amply proved by the banking documents and by H.B.Z.'s witnesses. I really cannot think that it was necessary formally to call a witness to say " we did this in reliance upon the supposition that we were allowed to use our corporate name." That reliance can be inferred from the circumstances as it was

C   in *Greasley* v. *Cooke* [1980] 1 W.L.R. 1306 (see the judgment of Lord Denning M.R., at p. 1307) and I think that the judge was perfectly justified in inferring it from the evidence before him in this case.

I have to acknowledge my indebtedness to counsel on both sides for some illuminating arguments, but at the end of them I find myself entirely unpersuaded that the judge erred in any material respect. He

D   concluded his judgment in this way on the question of estoppel:

"Of course, estoppel by conduct has been a field of the law in which there has been considerable expansion over the years and it appears to me that it is essentially the application of a rule by which justice is done where the circumstances of the conduct and behaviour of the party to an action are such that it would be wholly inequitable that he should be entitled to succeed in the proceeding."

E   That, to my mind, sufficiently appears on the facts of this case.

I, too, think that it would be wholly inequitable that the plaintiffs should succeed even if, contrary to the view which I have formed, they had established their primary case. I would, therefore, dismiss the appeal.

F   WATKINS L.J.   I agree, and there is nothing I could possibly add to that judgment.

STEPHENSON L.J.   I agree and would like to express my concurrence with what Oliver L.J. has said, both about archaic and arcane distinctions and in his statement in *Taylors Fashions Ltd.* v. *Liverpool*

G   *Victoria Trustees Co. Ltd.* (Note) [1981] 2 W.L.R. 576 which he read from his judgment.

Appeal dismissed with costs.
Leave to appeal refused.

H   Solicitor: *Stones, Porter & Co.; Freshfields.*

A. R.

A

[CHESTER CONSISTORY COURT]

* *In re* ST. MARTIN'S, ASHTON-UPON-MERSEY

1981 April 29   Lomas Ch.

> *Ecclesiastical Law—Faculty—Organ—Petition to install computer*
> *organ—Existing pipe organ unplayable but restorable—*   B
> *Relevance of comparative projected costs of introducing*
> *computer organ or restoring existing organ—Whether pipe*
> *organ to be restored—Whether faculty to be granted*
>
> The churchwardens of a parish petitioned for a faculty to
> install an Allen computer organ in the parish church, the
> existing pipe organ, installed in 1857, having become unplay-
> able due to rain damage. It was proposed that a decision as to   C
> the disposal or restoration of the pipe organ should be made
> at a future date. The relative costs, estimated for a 25-year
> period, of installing and maintaining an Allen organ or restor-
> ing and maintaining the existing pipe organ were comparable.
> The petition was unopposed.
> On the petition: —
> *Held,* dismissing the petition, that, so far as financial con-
> siderations were concerned, it was a proper, even though   D
> problematical, approach to project likely costs over a period of
> 25 years (post, p. 1292A–B); that, on such projections, the com-
> parative costs of introducing the computer organ and of
> restoring the existing pipe organ were finely balanced, but that
> if the projections were inaccurate the church would have
> ceased to have a pipe organ which, once restored would have
> a long life, and would be faced with the cost of replacing the
> computer organ in the future (post, p. 1292D); that in the   E
> circumstances, as the existing pipe organ was capable and
> worthy of restoration, it should be retained and restored (post,
> p. 1292F); and that, accordingly, a faculty to introduce the
> computer organ would be refused.

No cases are referred to in the judgment.

F

PETITION

The churchwardens of the parish of St. Martin, Ashton-upon-Mersey,
petitioned for a faculty to introduce an Allen 201 GB computer organ
into the parish church. The petition was unopposed, and Lomas Ch. requested the Archdeacon of Macclesfield to assist the court.

The facts are stated in the judgment.

G

The petitioners in person.
J. R. Gower-Jones, solicitor, for the archdeacon as amicus curiae.

LOMAS CH. This is a petition seeking a faculty to introduce an Allen
201 GB computer organ into the parish church of St. Martin, Ashton-
upon-Mersey. The petitioners are the churchwardens. No one has entered   H
an appearance in opposition. Mr. Derek Porter, one of the petitioners, has
appeared in person on behalf of himself and his co-petitioners and I would
like to say at once that I received the very greatest assistance from Mr.
Porter in the way he has presented his case. He has presented it with notable
ability and considerable fairness. Mr. Gower-Jones has appeared on behalf
of the Archdeacon of Macclesfield who has intervened at my request in
order that the witnesses might be properly cross-examined where necessary

A and that the evidence of the representative of the Diocesan Advisory Committee might be fully brought out for the benefit of the court and in addition, of course, he has discharged the duty of seeking to assist the court by bringing out the factors which ought to be taken into consideration and I am also grateful to Mr. Gower-Jones for the very fair and balanced way in which he has discharged that difficult task. Difficult because the archdeacon is appearing at my request and he naturally would not wish it to be thought that he was seeking in any way to thwart the parish. This is not his purpose. That is not his objective. It is not the reason for his attendance.

B

     The existing pipe organ was built in 1857 by Kirtland and Jardine. It appears to have been enlarged in 1900 by Jardine and in 1949 the swell organ action was made automatic or pneumatic by W. H. Warrington. That

C is an alteration which was regretted by Mr. David Wickens, the chief organ adviser to the Diocesan Advisory Committee. It suffered rain damage in 1965 and considerable work was done on the organ at that time to repair that damage and to some extent to restore the organ. In the winter of 1979 to 1980 it suffered further rain damage of a more severe and extensive kind as a result of which it is now unplayable.

D   The evidence before me is that the existing organ is capable of repair and restoration. The proposal, however, is that it should be left in its present condition and a decision as to its future or disposal made at a later date. There is a suggestion that it might possibly be restored but I myself am inclined to agree with the archdeacon's view that if restoration does not take place now it is unlikely that it ever will do.

     The evidence I have heard has been on behalf of the petitioners from

E Mr. Parish and Mr. Taylor, both of whom are employees of Crane's who deal with Allen organs in this country, and from Mr. Tracey who is the organist at Liverpool Cathedral. Mr. Wickens has given evidence on behalf of the Diocesan Advisory Committee.

     A great deal of evidence and a considerable amount of argument has been addressed to the question of the comparative costs and expenses

F which will be borne by the parish if either course is taken, that is to say, if the Allen organ is introduced or alternatively the existing pipe organ is restored. These expenses fall into two main groups, first the initial expense of carrying out the work in the case of restoration or introducing the Allen organ if that is the course adopted. Both Mr. Porter for the petitioners and Mr. Gower-Jones for the archdeacon accept that there is little to choose between the two courses at this initial stage. It appears

G that something slightly under £6,000 is expected to be spent in either event. In the case of the restoration of the existing pipe organ it would be necessary or prudent to carry out certain further work to provide a false ceiling over the organ to protect it from a repetition of the rain damage. The cost of that is taken into account in these figures, so that so far as comparative costs are concerned the real decision, and this it appears is

H the view of the parochial church council, turns upon what might be described as the running costs of maintenance and possible replacements over the future span of years and for this purpose Mr. Porter has taken a period of 25 years.

     What Mr. Porter has done is first of all to consider the position in relation to the pipe organ assuming it to have been restored. He has taken certain annual costs for tuning visits and he has sought to estimate the likely increase in such costs over the period of 25 years by adopting an

assumed inflation rate of 12 per cent. per annum so that the total which he A
has produced in relation to that 25-year period amounts to £13,600. Mr.
Porter has then assumed that the organ would require to be cleaned and
overhauled at or towards the end of that 25-year period, and here, of
course, he has a major problem in seeking to estimate the likely cost of
carrying out that work. But adopting the same assumption he has produced a figure of £34,000. Large though that may seem the experience of
the past 10 years would temper anyone's surprise. Over the 25-year period B
Mr. Porter considers that the parish on this basis would have to find some
£48,500. I will return in a moment to another factor which clearly needs
to be considered.

Mr. Porter then considered the position so far as the Allen organ is
concerned over the same period, and here he has assumed that the terms
of the guarantee, which I have not seen, will protect the parish from any C
expense during the first five years. He has then taken the present annual
payment for a maintenance contract which is at present offered by the
Allen Company and he has projected that expense over the remainder
of the 25-year period again taking into acount an inflation rate of 12 per
cent. The outcome of that calculation is that he produces some £9,600 as
payable in this way: a saving of some £4,000 over the period. Mr. Porter D
then considers the possibility of having to replace entirely the Allen organ
at the end of the 25-year period and he has taken the present cost, allowed
12 per cent. per annum inflation but here made a reduction of 25 per cent.
on the following basis. The justification Mr. Porter gives for the reduction
is that in his experience equipment of this kind tends to become relatively
cheaper as it is developed and more extensively used rather than more so
and he instances the well-known case of small calculators. That produces E
a cost of £35,000 at the end of 25 years to replace the Allen organ. That,
it will be seen, is slightly in excess of the computed figure relating to the
pipe organ's cleaning and overhaul at that point in time.

It is fair to say that the witnesses on behalf of the Allen organ, if I
may put it that way, take the view that the Allen organ should not require to be replaced at so early a time, but I think that Mr. Porter is wise F
to make that assumption since there is at present no reliable experience
of the useful life of the model which is proposed to be introduced.

I did say that there was a further factor in relation to the annual costs
of maintenance. This relates to running costs for repairs on the existing
organ assuming it to have been restored. The evidence of Mr. Wickens
was that once the work of restoration had been done the organ ought not
to require further expense other than routine tuning during the 25-year G
period. On the other hand, Mr. Porter does say that the experience of
the parish is that they have annually had to spend sums of material
amount in repairs of this kind in addition to the ordinary costs of tuning.
There is a difficulty here because, of course, as Mr. Wickens said, the
organ would be due for restoration in a further five to 10 years in any
event and, therefore, it could be the case that once the restoration work H
now proposed or now considered was undertaken that much of this
annual cost would be obviated. Mr. Porter did not challenge Mr. Wickens'
view on that particular point. However, there was other evidence from
the organist at Liverpool Cathedral who did mention that there were
occasional faults on the organ at Liverpool and I think Mr. Wickens himself did say when he was speaking of some faults he had experienced on
the Allen organ that, of course, this could occur on a pipe organ as well.

A So that it would be fair at any rate to say that there would be some additional expense apart from the annual tuning costs. My difficulty there is that I have no means of estimating the likely amounts or of knowing whether the parish's existing experience of its expenditure on this particular organ was especially unfortunate or the result of the need for restoration in the near future apart from the accidental damage which has occurred. It is, however, a factor to be taken into account and I cannot disregard the parish's experience with its own organ.

B

   If the figures which have been worked out were the only ones to be taken into account then the saving which the parochial church council has regarded as crucial to its decision, as I am told by Mr. Porter, would be of the order of £4,000 over 25 years. In my view, that figure would as a matter of present decision need to be discounted. Discounted because

C it is not immediately payable and considering the inflationary assumptions which everyone has adopted would represent in real terms a smaller saving over that period than that represented by £4,000 at present values.

   Those are the considerations so far as the financial situation is concerned and I am bound to say that they do seem to be on a fairly fine balance. The second point relates to the question whether the existing pipe organ is worthy of restoration. This I suppose falls into a number of

D aspects of which the first is the intrinsic worth of the organ itself. Here Mr. Wickens took the view that whilst it is not of the first importance it is of historic worth and his reason for saying that was that he took the view that any organ which had been built in the period of this organ and had survived was of historic worth. Mr. Wickens did go further than that on to a second aspect of the matter namely the quality of the instrument.

E Here, asuming it to have been restored, he took the view that there was, in his own words, " a lot of range in this organ." Indeed he felt that the range of the organ was, if anything, greater than was necessary rather than less and I take him to have said that in support of the quality of the instrument. I do not think that Mr. Porter took a fundamentally different view of the quality of the instrument assuming it to have been restored.

F   Mr. Tracey who gave evidence on behalf of the petitioners as organist at Liverpool Cathedral regarded the Allen organ, again in his own words, " to be an acceptable substitute." He thought that for some more intimate kinds of music it had advantages over a pipe organ. That I think was in the context of recitals particularly with smaller groups of singers. But when one analyses Mr. Tracey's evidence he does not appear to dissent in any way from the view taken by Mr. Wickens. His test, as it

G appeared to me, was the same as that of Mr. Wickens for a case of this kind. Mr. Tracey said that where the pipe organ in a church can be restored and it was worthy of restoration then he took the view as an organist that the pipe organ ought to be restored. He excepted the cases where the organ was of poor quality. He said that his reasons for that view were first that pipe organs had been the accepted instrument for over

H 600 years, he then went on to deal with the quality of the sound of the pipe organ and of the range of its notes. These, of course, are statements of opinion and can only be taken into account by me in considering the factors which I ought to weigh in the balance and take into account in arriving at my decision.

   In reaching a decision of this kind I am conscious indeed of the fact that whatever decision I take it is the parochial church council which has to carry the matter through to a conclusion. That must be so whether I grant this petition or whether I reject it in favour of the proposition that the present organ ought to be restored.

So far as the financial aspects are concerned there are some factors which trouble me. There are problems in trying to project likely costs over a short period of time but they are immensely greater over a period of time of 25 years. One is tempted to reject projections, as some courts have, on the basis that the only proper course is to take known factors and costs into account, but for my part I do not regard that as a realistic approach since people do not take business decisions on that basis. They have to make such estimates as they can and are then left to live with them. One of the problems in the present case is the assumption that the maintenance contract which the parochial church council regards as favourable will continue to be available for the Allen organ at comparable rates as at present adjusted for inflation as the organ becomes older. The contract is only an annual contract and there is no assurance of renewal. Mr. Porter said they were more likely to be available on the present models. There is no experience of this since the present type has been produced only for 10 years. The evidence is, however, that Allen will not now enter into maintenance contracts for its earlier types of electronic organs and Mr. Porter's contention must be a matter of judgment and even speculation. On the other side, of course, is the question of the likely costs of maintaining a pipe organ. What troubles me is that the parochial church council has made its decision, as I am told, on the projected expenditure for the future. On these projections the position is finely balanced. If the projections are in any way substantially inaccurate then this church will have ceased to have at its disposal a pipe organ which, on the evidence I have, would have a very long life if it were restored and would be faced for the future with unknown costs of replacing the computer organ with something of a similar kind. On the one hand I have the parochial church council's decision, on the other hand I have a body of opinion which is in favour of retaining pipe organs where possible and suitable based upon their known long life. In this situation I have to decide what is to be done now just as, as Mr. Porter quite rightly says, the parochial church council had to reach its own decision.

As it appears to me, on the evidence which I have heard the existing pipe organ is capable of restoration. It is worthy of restoration and on that basis there must be a substantial case for reaching the conclusion that it ought to be restored and that is the conclusion which I have reached. I am very conscious of the fact that this will be a disappointment to the parochial church council. I am very conscious of the fact that if the advice which has been given as to the future costs of maintaining that organ is inaccurate a substantial burden may well have been cast upon the parochial church council. However, a decision has to be made and it does seem at least likely from the experience which is available that the pipe organ can be restored and ought to be in sufficiently good condition not to require the kind of expenditure on repairs which has been found necessary in the past. In reaching this conclusion I am not making any decision as to the usefulness or worthiness of the Allen organ. I am making a decision on the basis of the evidence as to the situation in this particular case.

Petition dismissed.

Solicitors: *Foysters, Hale.*

C. N.

A

[CHANCERY DIVISION]

* SONY CORPORATION AND ANOTHER *v.* TIME ELECTRONICS

[1981 S. No. 1785]

B 1981 March 17

Goulding J.

Practice—Discovery—Motion for—Undertaking not to use infor-
mation disclosed save for purpose of passing off action—
Execution of order disclosing other counterfeit goods—Test
purchase—Whether fresh cause of action permissible on
evidence of test purchase

C
On evidence given in camera by the plaintiffs in a pending
action of the passing off by the intended defendant firm of
certain of the plaintiffs' cassette tapes as its own, the court
ordered the defendant forthwith, on service of its order, to
disclose to the person serving the order the names and
addresses of the defendant's suppliers and to produce certain
documents and to deliver up to him the apparently improper
D goods. The order was subject to undertakings by the plaintiffs
including an undertaking not without leave of the court to use
any document or information obtained as a result of the
execution of the order save for the purpose of civil proceedings
against the defendant in connection with the subject matter
of the action.

On visiting the defendant's premises, the person serving the
order found there not only goods of the type to which the
E order related but also other goods of a type also manufactured
by the plaintiffs, which he thought might be counterfeit. A test
purchase of goods of the second type was later made by an
employee of the plaintiffs' solicitors which, when examined,
were considered by the plaintiffs to be counterfeit. On the
evidence of the test purchase, the plaintiffs wanted to start
another action in respect of those goods against the defendant
firm and they applied to the court again in camera for an
F order similar to the one already granted them but in respect
of the goods of the second type, found on the defendant's
premises, but not covered by that order: —

Held, that although it was well established that the court
protected a party who made disclosure on discovery and
restricted the use of the material disclosed to the proceedings
in which the discovery took place, the court would not refuse
the order sought by the plaintiffs since their proposed new
G action was founded, not on something the court had ordered
to be disclosed in the earlier order but on evidence provided
by the test purchase of the second type of goods, in respect of
which there was only a collateral connection with the disclosure ordered by the court in the pending action.

Riddick v. *Thames Board Mills Ltd.* [1977] Q.B. 881, C.A.
considered.

H
The following cases are referred to in the judgment:

Home Office v. *Harman* [1981] 2 W.L.R. 310; [1981] 2 All E.R. 349,
Park J. and C.A.

Riddick v. *Thames Board Mills Ltd.* [1977] Q.B. 881; [1977] 3 W.L.R. 63;
[1977] 3 All E.R. 677, C.A.

No additional cases were cited in argument.

MOTION

By notice of motion dated March 11, 1981, the plaintiffs, Sony Corporation and an associated company, Sony (U.K.) Ltd. (incorporated in the United Kingdom), sought an order, until judgment or further order, against the intended defendant, Time Electronics, a firm carrying on business in this country, restraining it or its directors or officers, servants or agents, from, inter alia, selling or disposing of or buying, importing or parting with power, possession, custody or control of, cassette tapes, or advertising material relating thereto, bearing the word " Sony " without the consent of the plaintiffs.

On March 12, 1981, after a hearing in camera, the court made the order on certain undertakings by the plaintiffs and subject to the liberty of the defendant firm to move to discharge or vary the order on notice.

On March 17, 1981, after a further hearing in camera relating to a second type of goods manufactured by the plaintiffs not forming part of the subject matter of the order of March 12, judgment was given in open court.

The facts are stated in the judgment of Goulding J.

Martin Howe for the plaintiffs.
The intended defendant firm was not represented.

GOULDING J.   I am giving judgment in open court, although for reasons that will become obvious, I heard the application in camera. The reason I am giving judgment in open court is that a point of law or practice is involved. The plaintiffs are two companies, one operating internationally in the manufacture and sale of goods, and the other a subsidiary or associated company incorporated in the United Kingdom.

The intended defendant—a writ has not yet been issued—is a firm carrying on business in this country. On March 12, 1981, on evidence of passing off on the part of the defendant firm, I made an order which contained certain injunctions to stop the alleged dishonest trading and ordered the defendant on service of the order forthwith to disclose to the person serving it the names and addresses of the firm's suppliers and to produce certain documents and deliver up the apparently improper goods to the person serving the order, all that being restricted by a certain proviso—which I need not read now—and being, of course, subject to the liberty of the defendant firm to move to discharge or vary the order on notice.

In the course of serving that order of March 12, 1981, a solicitor employed by the solicitors for the plaintiffs visited the defendant firm's premises and found there not only goods of the type to which the order related but also goods of another type quite different, also manufactured by the plaintiffs, which he thought might be counterfeit. He knew that goods of that second type had been the subject of counterfeit production and trade. Accordingly the solicitor to whom I have referred instructed an employee of his firm to make a test purchase of such goods. So far as his draft affidavit goes there was no difficulty in getting them. When brought back they turned out to be, in the opinion of his solicitor, who has had extensive experience of these particular goods, clearly counterfeit. Accordingly, the plaintiffs desire to commence a fresh action against the defendant firm and have applied in camera for an order similar to that of March 12, 1981, but referring to goods of the second class with which, so far as this defendant was concerned, the previous order had nothing to do.

The Weekly Law Reports, October 23, 1981

1295

1 W.L.R.   Sony Corpn. v. Times Electronics (Ch.D.)   Goulding J.

A   The difficulty which has very properly been brought to my attention by counsel results from the fact that the plaintiffs were only in a position to discover the alleged infringement of their rights as regards the second class of goods by entering the defendant firm's premises in the course of serving the order of March 12. The order contains, as I mentioned, obligations to make certain compulsory disclosure of facts and documents relating to goods of the first class. It is well established that a party who makes dis-
B   closure on discovery is entitled to the protection of the court against the facts or documents disclosed being used, otherwise than in the action in which disclosure took place, without special leave of the court given on proper grounds: see *Riddick v. Thames Board Mills Ltd.* [1977] Q.B. 881. The whole subject of the restrictions on the use of material disclosed on discovery has of course been more recently considered by the higher courts
C   in *Home Office v. Harman* [1981] 2 W.L.R. 310. Moreover, in addition to that general principle the order of March 12, contained, among other undertakings, an undertaking by the plaintiffs not without the leave of the court to use any document or information obtained " as a result of the execution of this order " save for the purpose of civil proceedings against the defendant firm or other parties in connection with the subject matter of the action.
D   Accordingly, counsel has invited me to consider whether I can properly make an order in the form of an injunction restraining the alleged improper trade, and requiring disclosure of material facts, against the defendant firm in regard to the second class of goods, their connection with which only became apparent through the visit of the plaintiffs' solicitors to their premises for executing the order of March 12. In my view I ought not to refuse the plaintiffs the relief they seek. The new action is not founded on
E   something that the court ordered to be disclosed in the earlier order. The real foundation of the present action is the evidence obtained on the test purchase. The observation by the solicitor of suspect goods, of the second class, was a merely collateral matter in the execution of the order of March 12 and did not depend on that order for its justification. In other words a solicitor saw something that was there but it was not something that the
F   court had ordered to be disclosed. He then obtained the evidence, which is sufficient in itself, by a test purchase.

    Accordingly, for my part I think that it would be applying too strict a rule to say that this fresh cause of action cannot be pursued because of its collateral connection with disclosure ordered by the court in the pending action. I will therefore make the order desired by the plaintiffs, which was explained to me when the court was sitting in camera.
G

Order accordingly.

Solicitors: *Baker & McKenzie.*

K. N. B.

H

[QUEEN'S BENCH DIVISION]

*PRACTICE DIRECTION
(TRIALS IN LONDON)

*Practice—Trial—Appropriate list—London—Fixed date for hearing
—Vacating list*

All proceedings in the Queen's Bench Division for hearing in London shall be set down in the appropriate list and administered as follows.

1. *The Crown Office list*

(a) Proceedings required to be heard by or applications required to be made to a Divisional Court of the Queen's Bench Division.

(b) Proceedings pursuant to R.S.C., Ord. 53, Ord. 54 and Ord. 56 which may be heard by a single judge.

(c) Actions directed to be set down in the Crown Office list.

(d) Proceedings pursuant to R.S.C., Ord. 55, Ord. 94 and Ord. 111.

(e) Save as is otherwise expressly provided, any other special case or case stated under any statute or order.

2. *Administrative provisions in respect of the Crown Office list*

Without prejudice to any party's right to apply for direction to a judge for the time being hearing matters in the Crown Office list and the right of the Master of the Crown Office to refer such a matter to a judge, the Crown Office list shall be administered by the Crown Office under the direction of the Master of the Crown Office.

3. *The jury list*

Actions ordered to be tried by a judge and jury.

4. *The non-jury list*

(a) Actions other than jury actions or short causes set down under the provisions of R.S.C., Ord. 34, r. 3.

(b) Preliminary questions or issues ordered to be tried under R.S.C., Ord. 33, rr. 3 and 4 (2).

(c) Motions to commit other than those required to be heard by a Divisional Court of the Queen's Bench Division.

(d) Motions for judgment.

5. *The short cause list*

Actions ordered to be tried by a judge alone where the time estimated for the trial does not exceed four hours.

6. *Administrative provisions: jury, non-jury and short cause lists*

(a) All actions in the non-jury list shall in the first instance be set down in a non-jury general list, numbered in sequence and show the setting down date.

(b) Subject to the provisions of paragraph 6 (c), (d) and (e) hereof, non-jury actions shall be liable to come into the warned list (see paragraph 11 below) at any time after the expiration of 28 days from the date of setting down.

(c) (i) As soon as a non-jury action is set down for trial in the general

A list, and within four weeks of such setting down, any party may, on obtaining an appointment from the Clerk of the Lists for this purpose, give notice in writing to the other party or parties of his intention to apply to the Clerk of the Lists to fix a date for the trial of the action. Suitable forms of notice (form B 14d) may be obtained from the forms room (room 278) or from law stationers. (ii) Where an application to fix a date for the trial of the action is not taken out within four weeks of setting down for trial, the parties may, by consent, apply to the Clerk of the Lists to extend the time within which to take out such an application. Any opposed application for such an extension of time must be made to the judge in charge of the non-jury list.

(d) On the hearing of an application for a fixed date the Clerk of the Lists may, after taking into account the wishes of the parties, the circumstances of the case and the state of the non-jury list, (i) fix a date for the trial of the action, or (ii) direct that the case shall come on for trial on a date specified by him, subject to the case or cases already fixed for hearing on that date, or (iii) direct that the case be marked not to come on for trial before a date specified by him, keeping its numerical order in the general list, or (iv) direct that the case be returned to the general list, or (v) direct that the case be placed in the warned list, or (vi) direct that the case be stood over generally, or (vii) direct that the application be referred to the judge in charge of the non-jury list.

(e) If any party is dissatisfied with the date fixed by the Clerk of the Lists or with his direction under sub-paragraphs (ii) to (vi) of paragraph 6 (d) hereof, or with his direction under paragraph 7 (b) hereof, that party may, on giving two days' notice in writing to the other party or parties, apply to the judge in charge of the non-jury list to vary the date so fixed or the direction so given. Such application to the judge shall be made within seven days of the hearing before the Clerk of the Lists, or the date of his decision under paragraph 7 (b) hereof, as the case may be. On the hearing of such application the judge may vary the date fixed, or the direction given by the Clerk of the Lists, or may make such other order or give such other directions on such terms as to costs or otherwise as he shall think fit.

(f) If an application under sub-paragraph (c) of this paragraph be not made the action shall remain in the non-jury general list and be subject to the provisions of sub-paragraph (b) of this paragraph.

(g) When an action or other proceeding in the jury list and the non-jury list is settled, withdrawn, or discontinued, or where the estimate of length of trial is varied, it shall be the duty of the solicitors for the parties so to inform the Clerk of the Lists in writing forthwith.

7. (a) Once an action in the non-jury list has been allocated a fixed date for trial, every opposed application to vacate, alter or otherwise determine the date of trial shall be made to the judge in charge of the non-jury list and be made in accordance with the provisions of paragraph 10 hereof.

(b) Where all the parties to a non-jury action agree to vacate, alter or otherwise determine the date of trial, they may apply to the Clerk of the Lists. The application should be by way of written consent signed by all the parties. The consent shall specify the nature of the application and the grounds thereof. The Clerk of the Lists shall deal with the

application in accordance with the provisions of paragraph 6 (d) hereof, A
and his decision shall be subject to the provisions of paragraph 6 (e)
hereof.

8. (a) On the hearing of the summons for directions the court may, if
it appears that the action ought to have an early trial, give a direction
(to be called " an order for speedy trial ") that an application be made
to the Clerk of the Lists to fix a date for the hearing.   B

(b) Within one week from setting down for trial or within such other
time as may be specified in the order the parties shall apply for a date
to the Clerk of the Lists, who shall deal with the application in accordance with the provisions of paragraph 6 (d) hereof, his decision being
subject to the provisions of paragraph 6 (e) hereof.

9. (a) For each week of each sittings there shall be published a list of C
non-jury action to be called the " Weekly List of Non-Jury Actions."

(b) The weekly list shall be printed on the first day and on every
subsequent Monday of each sittings.

(c) The weekly list shall contain (i) a number of actions in both the
non-jury general list and the non-jury fixture list which are likely to be
tried or have been fixed for trial during the next succeeding week which D
will be listed together under the denomination of the " Week's List ";
(ii) the remaining actions in the non-jury general list which have been
set down on or before the end of the previous week, except actions which
have by order or consent been stood out from the non-jury general list.
The weekly list will, if possible, contain an intimation that actions in the
non-jury general list will not be taken before a date or dates to be   E
specified; (iii) the remaining actions in the non-jury fixtures list fixed for
hearing during the current sittings (or directed to be heard on a particular
day in the sittings subject to fixtures).

10. (a) So far as appropriate the Clerk of the Lists shall administer the
jury and short cause lists in like manner to the non-jury list.

(b) Except in cases dealt with above every application to fix, vacate, F
alter or otherwise determine the date of trial of an action in the jury,
non-jury and short cause list shall be made to the judge in charge of
that list.

(c) Any party making an application under this paragraph shall give
the other party or parties notice of his intention to apply to the judge
in charge of the appropriate list. The notice shall not be less than one
clear day before the date on which such application is proposed to be   G
made and shall specify the nature of the application and the grounds
thereof.

(d) All applications to the judge in charge of the appropriate list shall
be made at the sitting of the court or at such other time or times as may
be specified by such judge for the time being.
                                                                         H
11. (a) A number of actions which are likely to be taken on the following
day will be listed together and printed in the Daily Cause List under the
denomination of the " Warned List." Such actions will be taken from
those standing at the head of the week's list.

(b) No action in the warned list will be removed from it by stay or
postponement or will have its position altered except in accordance with
the provision of paragraphs 7 and 10 hereof.

A 12. *The commercial list*

(a) Actions for trial in the Commercial Court.

(b) Any matter in paragraph 4 hereof which appertains to a matter in the Commercial Court.

13. *The arbitration case list*

B   Proceedings under R.S.C., Ord. 73, r. 2.

14. *Administrative provisions: commercial and arbitration case lists*

Actions or other proceedings in the Commercial Court will be dealt with as follows.

(a) Any party to an action to be tried in the Commercial Court
C may at any stage in the proceedings apply to the commercial judge by summons to fix a date for the trial or to vary or vacate such a date.

(b) An order made by the court fixing the date of hearing will normally also provide for a date by which the cause must be set down for trial in the commercial list.

(c) When a party to an action who has set it down for trial notifies the other parties to the action that he has done so, he should also inform
D the Commercial Court Listing Office to the same effect.

(d) If any action which has been set down for trial in the Commercial Court is settled or withdrawn, or if the estimates of length of trial is revised, it shall be the duty of all parties to notify the court of the fact without delay.

(e) (i) Any proceeding in the arbitration case list shall in the first instance be referred to the judge in charge of the commercial list for
E his consideration as to its suitability for retention in that list. (ii) Where the judge directs that such a matter shall be heard by a commercial judge any party may thereafter apply to fix a date for trial.

15. *The Admiralty list*

Proceedings under R.S.C., Ord. 75.

F

16. *Administrative provisions: Admiralty list*

Actions or other proceedings in the Admiralty Court will be dealt with as follows.

(a) All motions will be listed for hearing by the Admiralty Registry.

(b) In all actions the mode and date of trial will be fixed by the judge
G of the Admiralty Court at the hearing of the summons for directions unless the judge otherwise orders.

17. *General administrative provision*

The lists of actions in the Queen's Bench Division for trial in London shall be kept by the Head Clerk of the Crown Office and shall be included in the general lists of appeals and causes in the Supreme Court of
H Judicature published for each sittings.

18. The directions for London issued by the Lord Chief Justice on December 9, 1958, *Practice Direction* (*Trials in Middlesex*) [1958] 1 W.L.R. 1291, are hereby revoked.

LANE C.J.

July 31, 1981.

[CHANCERY DIVISION]

* *In re* ST. PIRAN LTD.

1981 June 29, July 1;   Dillon J.
      July 7

B

Company — Winding up — Petition — Contributory's petition — In-
spectors' report to Secretary of State—Whether evidence in
support of contributory's petition — Companies Act 1948 (11
& 12 Geo. 6, c. 38), s. 165 (b) [1]*—Companies Act 1967 (c. 81),*
s. 35 (1) [2]

A company was incorporated on June 9, 1970, with a   C
capital of 20,000,000 25p shares of which £2,916,746 was fully
paid. The objects for which it was established were to carry on
tin mining and property development and to invest in similar
companies. In 1973, R became a director of the company and
another company allegedly under his control acquired a substantial shareholding in the company. When difficulties were
experienced in running the company to the satisfaction of all
the shareholders, the Secretary of State for Trade appointed
inspectors to investigate its affairs. The investigation revealed,   D
inter alia, that the company had conducted its affairs in a
manner which was not satisfactory for the majority of its
shareholders and suggested that the Secretary of State might
consider whether it would be in the public interest to petition
the court to wind up the company. The Secretary of State took
no further action but a petition was presented by a contributory
of the company asking that it be compulsorily wound up on   E
the ground that it was just and equitable to do so. The petitioner relied solely on the inspectors' report to support its
petition. The company was solvent and a surplus was available
for shareholders in the event of a winding up.
     On the company's motion to strike out the petition on the
grounds that it was embarrassing, an abuse of the process of
the court and disclosed no reasonable ground for relief: —
     Held, (1) that, since one of the reasons for the appointment   F
of inspectors, under section 165 (b) of the Companies Act 1948,
was the failure of a company to give sufficient information to
the shareholders, the objects of the section could be defeated
if an aggrieved shareholder could not petition and rely on an
inspectors' report establishing that material information had
been withheld in a case where there was insufficient public
interest involved to make it expedient for the Secretary of
State to present a petition; and that, since the inspectors'   G
report was admissible as evidence in support of the petition on
the basis that the inspectors acted in a statutory fact-finding
capacity, there was no reason for confining the report to supporting a petition brought by the Secretary of State and,
accordingly, the petitioner could rely on the report to support
its petition (post, pp. 1306G—1307c).
     In re Travel & Holiday Clubs Ltd. [1967] 1 W.L.R. 711 and   H
In re S.B.A. Properties Ltd. [1967] 1 W.L.R. 799 applied.
     In re Armvent Ltd. [1975] 1 W.L.R. 1679 considered.
     (2) That the petition in its present form was embarrassing
because it relied on the whole of the inspectors' lengthy report;
that, since that was a defect that could be cured by the
petitioner selecting and identifying the matters on which it

[1] Companies Act 1948, s. 165 (b): see post, p. 1306F–G.
[2] Companies Act 1967, s. 35 (1): see post, p. 1303E–F.

A   relied to establish that it was just and equitable to wind up the
company, the motion would be adjourned to allow the
petitioner an opportunity to suggest amendments to the petition
(post, p. 1308A, D–E).

The following cases are referred to in the judgment:

Armvent Ltd., In re [1975] 1 W.L.R. 1679; [1975] 3 All E.R. 441.

B   *Davis Investments (East Ham) Ltd., In re* [1961] 1 W.L.R. 1396; [1961] 3
All E.R. 926, C.A.

Koscot Interplanetary (U.K.) Ltd., In re [1972] 3 All E.R. 829.

Lubin, Rosen and Associates Ltd., In re [1975] 1 W.L.R. 122; [1975] 1
All E.R. 577.

S.B.A. Properties Ltd., In re [1967] 1 W.L.R. 799; [1967] 2 All E.R. 615.

Travel & Holiday Clubs Ltd., In re [1967] 1 W.L.R. 711; [1967] 2 All E.R.
C   606.

The following additional cases were cited in argument:

A.B.C. Coupler and Engineering Co. Ltd., In re [1961] 1 W.L.R. 243;
[1961] 1 All E.R. 354; [1962] 1 W.L.R. 1236; [1962] 3 All E.R. 68.

Allied Produce Co. Ltd., In re [1967] 1 W.L.R. 1469; [1967] 3 All E.R.
399.

D   *Briman Properties Ltd.* v. *Barclays Bank Ltd.* (unreported), November
30, 1978; Court of Appeal (Civil Division) Transcript No. 708 of
1978, C.A.

Willcocks (W.R.) & Co. Ltd., In re [1974] Ch. 163; [1973] 3 W.L.R. 669;
[1973] 2 All E.R. 93.

MOTION

E   The company, St. Piran Ltd., was incorporated on June 9, 1970, under
the Companies Act 1948. Its nominal capital was £5,000,000 made up of
20,000,000 25p shares with £2,916,746 paid up. The company was established with the objects of carrying on tin mining and property development
in the United Kingdom and Malaysia and of investing in similar companies.
In March 1973, John James Raper was made a director of the company
F   and a company acting apparently under his control acquired a substantial
shareholding in the company. Thereafter, the company's affairs were conducted in a manner which the majority of the shareholders, excepting the
principal shareholder, alleged to be unfairly prejudicial to their interests.

On December 18, 1979, the Secretary of State for Trade, pursuant to
the powers under sections 165 (*b*) and 172 of the Companies Act 1948,
appointed Gerald M. Godfrey Q.C. and Alan J. Hardcastle F.C.A. as
G   inspectors to investigate the share ownership and affairs of the company.
The inspectors' report suggested that the Secretary of State might consider
whether it would be in the public interest to petition the court to compulsorily wind up the company under the power conferred by section 35 (1)
of the Companies Act 1967, because the present situation of the company
was not satisfactory for the majority of its shareholders.

H   The Secretary of State took no further action but Runic Nominees Ltd.,
a contributory of the company holding 70,000 shares therein, presented a
winding up petition on May 12, 1981, on the ground that it was just and
equitable that the company should be compulsorily wound up. The whole of
the inspectors' report was relied on to support the petition.

On June 24, 1981, a motion was issued by the company which sought to
have the petition struck out and dismissed on the grounds that it disclosed
no reasonable grounds for ordering the company to be wound up, that it

might prejudice the fair trial of the application to wind up the company   A
and that it was an abuse of the process of the court. The motion was
supported by Gasco Investments (Netherlands) B.V., the principal shareholder in the company.

The facts are stated in the judgment.

   Charles Aldous for the company.
   Ralph Instone for the supporting shareholder.   B
   Alan Steinfeld for the petitioner.

                                      Cur. adv. vult.

   July 7. DILLON J. read the following judgment. I have before me a
motion issued on June 24, 1981, whereby St. Piran Ltd. seeks to have a   C
petition for the compulsory winding up of St. Piran which was presented by
a company called Runic Nominees Ltd. struck out and dismissed on the
grounds that it is embarrassing and an abuse of the process of the court and
discloses no reasonable grounds for the relief claimed. The motion is supported by Gasco Investments (Netherlands) B.V. which is the principal
shareholder in St. Piran.

   The winding up petition was presented on May 12, 1981, by Runic as a   D
contributory. It is common ground that St. Piran is solvent and there would
be a surplus for the contributories in a winding up. Runic is the holder of
70,000 shares at 25p each out of a total issued share capital of St. Piran of
£2,916,746. The basis of the petition is that it is alleged that it is just and
equitable that St. Piran should be compulsorily wound up. The petition also
refers to relief under section 75 of the Companies Act 1980, but Mr.   E
Steinfeld for Runic has made it plain that no form of relief other than a
compulsory winding up order is sought. Had other relief been desired it
would have been incumbent on the petitioner to indicate the nature of the
relief in the petition and that has not been done.

   The petition thus issued on May 12, was mentioned to me in the
ordinary companies list on Monday June 22, that is two days before the   F
present motion was issued, and I then adjourned the petition by consent for
effective hearing on a number of days at the end of July 1981 fixed through
the usual channels. Mr. Steinfeld has, therefore, submitted that the motion
comes too late. Any application to strike out ought to be made at the
earliest opportunity and it is, said Mr. Steinfeld, far too late to apply when
the petition has already been given an agreed date for effective hearing. I do
not take that view. Each case must depend on its own facts and in the cir-   G
cumstances of this present case I have no doubt at all that it is expedient
that the three main points on which St. Piran relies should be considered
by the court in advance of any effective hearing of the petition.

   Before I come to those points, however, I should notice briefly a fourth
point taken by Mr. Instone on behalf of Gasco. Mr. Instone says, no doubt
correctly, that any petitioner who comes to the court seeking to have a   H
company wound up on just and equitable grounds must come with clean
hands, and he submits that Runic does not come with clean hands. He
hints that the petition may have been presented for ulterior and improper
reasons. He puts this forward as a further reason why the petition should
be struck out now. In support he refers to two paragraphs in an affidavit of
Mr. Stone who is a director of St. Piran and also of Gasco in which it is
asserted, and the assertions are admitted, first that the petition was pre-

A   sented and served without any letter before action and secondly, that the filed accounts of Runic show, as indeed its name suggests, that it holds its shares in St. Piran as a nominee for a third party and has only nominal assets of its own. He adds that Runic and its principal have failed to offer any explanation why they seek a winding up order rather than the much less drastic relief of an order under section 75 of the Act of 1980 that their shares be bought by Gasco at a price fixed by the court. This in my judg-

B   ment is altogether too oblique a way of taking such a point as that a petition is not presented in good faith or that the petitioner does not come to the court with clean hands. If it is desired to take such a point the point should be taken fairly and squarely in an affidavit so that the petitioner can direct evidence to the issues it raises. Those issues, like other issues of fact, will then normally be decided on the effective hearing of the petition and not

C   on a motion to strike out. I should add that I am told that Runic, in fact, holds its shares in St. Piran as nominee for its own parent company, a substantial South African mining finance company, and that the parent company, which has no locus standi itself as a petitioner, has offered an undertaking in respect of costs.

I turn to the main issues. The activities of St. Piran and its directors and in particular of a Mr. Raper in relation to the affairs of St. Piran have over

D   recent years attracted a good deal of publicity in the financial press, and on December 18, 1979, Her Majesty's Secretary of State for Trade appointed inspectors, a Queen's Counsel and a chartered accountant, to investigate the affairs of St. Piran under sections 165 and 172 of the Companies Act 1948. The inspectors made their final report on March 31, 1981, and that report has been published by the Secretary of State.

E   Section 35 of the Companies Act 1967 provides so far as material:

> " (1) If, in the case of any body corporate liable to be wound up under the principal Act, it appears to the Board of Trade from any report made under section 168 . . . that it is expedient in the public interest that the body should be wound up, the board may, unless the body is already being wound up by the court, present a petition
>
> F   for it to be so wound up if the court thinks it just and equitable for it to be so wound up. . . ."

In the final sentence of their report the inspectors after referring to section 35 submitted that the Secretary of State might think after considering the report that he had not only the power but the duty to petition the court thus enabling the shareholders to express their views to the court

G   and the court to reach its own conclusion. This invitation the Secretary of State declined to accept. He made his position clear in a letter released on May 7, 1981. He is not willing to present a petition for the winding up of St. Piran or to countenance the expenditure of public money which that would entail. He regards it as no light matter to seek to wind up an active

H   trading company which is solvent and apparently conducting its relations with the outside world without any evidence of criminality.

However, Runic have rushed in where the Secretary of State feared to tread and Runic's petition is very largely founded on the inspectors' report. That report is referred to in paragraph 6 of the petition and the allegations on which Runic submits that it is just and equitable that St. Piran should be wound up by the court are contained in paragraphs 7 and 8 of the petition. These read:

" 7. Since in or about March 1973 when one John James Raper (herein-   A
after called Mr. Raper) became a director of the company and a company or companies acting apparently under his control acquired a
substantial shareholding in the company, the affairs of the company
have been conducted and are continuing to be conducted by or at the
direction of Mr. Raper and his associates as identified in the report in
a manner unfairly prejudicial to the interests of your petitioner and all   B
other shareholders in the company other than those shareholders who
are controlled by Mr. Raper. Full particulars of the manner in which
the affairs of the company have been conducted and are continuing to
be conducted as aforesaid and the manner in which the same is unfairly
prejudicial to the interests of your petitioner and the other said shareholders are contained in the findings of the inspectors in the report, a
copy of which is annexed hereto. Your petitioner adopts as its own   C
allegations all the findings of the inspectors in the report.

" 8. In consequence of the refusal of Mr. Raper, both individually
and through companies controlled by him, to comply with the direction
of the City Panel on Takeovers and Mergers to make an offer to purchase the whole of the issued share capital in the company not already
owned by Mr. Raper and/or any such companies as aforesaid at a price   D
of 85p per share and/or in consequence of the said findings of the
inspectors the quotation of the shares in the company on the Stock
Exchange has been and continues to be suspended and in consequence
of the bid for the whole of the issued share capital of the company by
Gasco Investments (Netherlands) B.V. one of the companies controlled
by Mr. Raper at 60p per share becoming unconditional on Friday, May
8, 1981, and/or in consequence of the findings of the inspectors the   E
quotation on the Stock Exchange of the shares of Milbury Ltd. and
South Crofty Ltd. both subsidiaries of the company were suspended on
May 8, 1981. The marketability of some of the major assets of the
company is thus seriously impaired to the detriment of your petitioner
and other minority shareholders in the company."

By way of evidence these allegations and the rest of the petition are   F
merely supported by the usual statutory affidavit in the form required by
the Companies (Winding-up) Rules 1949 and by an affidavit producing
certain documents. There is also a short affidavit by the chairman of a
company which formerly held shares in St. Piran as to the reasons for
that company's accepting the offer by Gasco referred to in paragraph 8
of the petition. The statutory affidavit, being sworn by an officer of   G
Runic who has no personal knowledge of the matters dealt with by the
inspectors in their report, affords no evidence at all in the normal sense
of that word of the matters recorded by the inspectors or of the validity
of the inspectors' findings and conclusions.

There is no doubt at all that the general rule is that allegations in a
winding up petition must be proved by proper evidence in accordance with   H
the ordinary rules as to the admissibility of evidence in civil litigation and
not by hearsay: see In re Koscot Interplanetary (U.K.) Ltd. [1972] 3 All
E.R. 829. In addition it is a rule of practice, though not an inflexible rule of
law, that a contributory's winding up petition in which allegations of fraud
or serious misconduct are made should be supported by affidavits to prove
the fraud or misconduct in addition to the statutory affidavit. There are
however, two well-established exceptions to the rule about hearsay evidence.

A   The first is that the court is entitled to act on the statutory affidavit, although it is often hearsay, because the statutory affidavit is required by the Companies (Winding-up) Rules 1949. Even so however, it is open to the court in its discretion in an appropriate case to decline to accept a mere statutory affidavit as sufficient to warrant making a compulsory winding up order: see *In re Davis Investments (East Ham) Ltd.* [1961] 1 W.L.R. 1396. The second exception to the hearsay rule is that the court hearing a winding up petition can accept the contents of a report by inspectors appointed by the Secretary of State under the Companies Act 1948 as material which it is proper for the court to take into consideration if, at any rate, the petition has been presented by the Secretary of State under section 35 of the Companies Act 1967 or its predecessor, section 169 (3) of the Companies Act 1948.

B

C   The first point, therefore, taken by St. Piran on this motion is that only the Secretary of State is entitled to rely in support of a petition on the findings in a report of inspectors. Any other petitioner, it is submitted, suing in his own right as a creditor or contributory must make out his case by evidence admissible by the ordinary rules. Therefore, as Runic do not intend to file any further evidence in support of the petition paragraph 7 which depends entirely on the inspectors' report should be struck out. The second point taken is that paragraph 8 alleges no misconduct or breach of legal duty on the part of St. Piran or its management as such. Therefore, it is said, an order for the compulsory winding up of St. Piran could not conceivably be made on the allegations in paragraph 8 and so paragraph 8 also, and therefore, the petition as a whole, should be struck out. The final point taken is that even if St. Piran is wrong on the first point, it is highly embarrassing for the inspectors' report which runs to over 200 pages to be thrown at St. Piran as a whole, as it is by paragraph 7 of the petition without any attempt by way of particulars to classify or pick out the matters canvassed in the report which are said by Runic to warrant the making of a compulsory winding up order.

D

E

     The leading modern authority on the use of an inspector's report on a winding up petition presented by the Secretary of State is the decision of Pennycuick J. in *In re Travel & Holiday Clubs Ltd.* [1967] 1 W.L.R. 711. He there held on an unopposed petition that the court could look at the inspectors' report and being satisfied on the report, in the absence of any evidence to the contrary adduced by the company, that on the basis of the findings in the report it was just and equitable for a company to be wound up, could make the usual compulsory winding up order. He pointed out in the course of his judgment that under section 169 (3) of the Companies Act 1948 there were two requirements. First, it must appear to the Board of Trade, now the Secretary of State, from the report that it is expedient by reason of the specified circumstances to present a winding up petition, and secondly, the court must think it just and equitable to make a winding up order. As to the first requirement under the wording of section 35 of the Act of 1967 which I have already read it must appear to the Secretary of State to be expedient in the public interest that the company should be wound up. That a petition presented by the Secretary of State is presented because a responsible officer of state is of the view that it is in the public interest that the petition should be presented or that the company should be wound up is a factor to which the court always attaches importance in reaching its own decision whether it is just and equitable that the company concerned should be wound up: see *In re Lubin, Rosen and Associates*

F

G

H

Ltd. [1975] 1 W.L.R. 122. Runic cannot, of course, pray that factor in aid   A
in support of this petition. But it is not, as it seems to me, a factor directly
relevant to the question whether or not Runic is entitled to rely on the
inspectors' report at all on this petition.

As I understand the judgments of Pennycuick J. in *In re Travel &*
Holiday Clubs Ltd. [1967] 1 W.L.R. 711 and in *In re S.B.A. Properties*
Ltd. [1967] 1 W.L.R. 799 which was decided shortly afterwards, the reason   B
why he held that the Secretary of State was entitled to rely on the inspectors' report to support his petition was a combination of two factors, first,
that the report was not ordinary hearsay evidence because the inspectors
acted in a statutory fact-finding capacity, and secondly, that it would be
nonsensical if the court could not take the report into consideration in deciding whether it was just and equitable that the company should be wound
up when on the very terms of section 169 (3) of the Act of 1948 as of   C
section 35 of the Act of 1967, it is on the basis of his consideration of
the report that the Secretary of State has concluded that it is expedient
that the winding up petition should be presented or that the company
should be wound up. It would be strange in that context if Parliament
had intended that the Secretary of State should have to rely on entirely
fresh evidence and should not be able to present the report to the court   D
and rely on the findings of the inspectors.

Even if the Secretary of State decides not to present a petition in reliance
on the inspectors' report, the inspectors will still have been acting in a
statutory fact finding capacity in making their report. Inspectors will only
be appointed where facts about some aspect of a company's activities are
not readily available and there appears to be a need for inquiry. The object
of the appointment of inspectors is partly in the public interest, particularly   E
where there is suspicion of criminal activities for instance that the company
has been trading in fraud of the public, and it is the Secretary of State in
particular who is in this field concerned to protect the public interest.
But the object of the appointment may also be to protect the interests
of minority shareholders. The circumstances in which inspectors may
be appointed are set out in section 165 (*b*) of the Companies Act 1948   F
and these include in sub-paragraphs (ii) and (iii) the following:

> " (ii) that persons concerned with its formation or the management of
> its affairs have in connection therewith been guilty of fraud, mis-
> feasance or other misconduct towards it or towards its members; or
> (iii) that its members have not been given all the information with
> respect to its affairs which they might reasonably expect."   G

If inspectors are appointed because there is ground for suspecting that
material information has been withheld from shareholders in a company
and the inspectors by questioning the directors and examining documents
not available to the general body of shareholders establish that this is so and
report accordingly, there may well be little public interest involved to make
it expedient for the Secretary of State to present a petition. A minority   H
shareholder aggrieved by consistent withholding of material information
might, nonetheless, wish to petition, and it would to a considerable extent,
as it seems to me, defeat the object of having the inspectors' inquiry if the
aggrieved shareholder could not rely on their report.

Accordingly I see no valid reason why the inspectors' report cannot be
used to support a contributory's petition to the same extent that it can be
used to support a petition by the Secretary of State. In his judgment in *In re*

A *Travel & Holiday Clubs Ltd.* [1967] 1 W.L.R. 711 Pennycuick J. stated that a different position would arise if the findings in the inspectors' report were to be challenged by evidence adduced on behalf of the company. That aspect was discussed by Templeman J. in *In re Armvent Ltd.* [1975] 1 W.L.R. 1679 where he ruled that the opponents of a petition could not exclude a report of inspectors simply by asserting by counsel that the inspectors' findings were challenged. Any challenge had to be by evidence
B disputing the particular findings which were challenged. If such evidence were adduced then it would be for the judge hearing the petition to weigh all the material before him at the end of the hearing including the report and decide then whether a winding up order should be made: see especially at p. 1685G–H. *In re Armvent Ltd.* [1975] 1 W.L.R. 1679 is in my judgment as applicable to the petition presented by a contributory
C in the present case as it is to any presented by the Secretary of State.

I should add for completeness that it is always open to a company, without filing any evidence to challenge the inspectors' findings, to submit that the findings, even if accepted as wholly correct, are not sufficient to make out that it is just and equitable that the company should be wound up. For the foregoing reasons I reject the first point taken by St. Piran on this
D motion.

I turn to the second point which is directed at paragraph 8 of the petition. It is said for St. Piran that the directions of the City Panel have no legislative sanction and that the failure of Mr. Raper and Gasco or their associates to make a bid for the entire share capital of St. Piran as directed by the panel was not an act or omission, let alone a default or misconduct, on the part of St. Piran itself or on the part of its management as such.
E Therefore, it is said, paragraph 8 could never provide grounds for a winding up order and should be struck out. I do not take such a narrow view. The court has jurisdiction to order the winding up of a company on a contributory's petition if it is just and equitable that the company should be wound up. The words " just and equitable " are wide general words to be construed generally and taken at their face value. The provisions of the City
F Code set out a code of conduct which has been laid down by responsible and experienced persons in the City as being fair and reasonable conduct in relation to companies which, like St. Piran, have obtained the benefit of a public quotation on the Stock Exchange. If the directors of a publicly quoted company or the principal shareholders in such a company choose to flout that code of fair and reasonable conduct and to ignore without good reason the consequent directions of the City Panel, and minority share-
G holders are injured by the withdrawal of the Stock Exchange quotation for the company's shares, then it seems to me that it could very well be just and equitable in the natural sense of those words that the company should be wound up. Whether in any case a winding up order should be made would depend on a full investigation of the facts of the particular case. That is a matter for the hearing of the petition and not for this motion.

H It is sufficient for the present for me to say that paragraph 8, in my judgment, is not demurrable and to say also that as the concept of justice and equity is a very wide concept it must, in my view, be open to St. Piran to show if it can at the hearing of the petition and as a part of the material to be then considered by the court that the panel misdirected itself in making the findings of fact which led to the direction which was disobeyed.

I, therefore, reject Mr. Aldous's second point on behalf of St. Piran and turn to his third point, that the way the whole of the inspectors' report has

been incorporated into paragraph 7 of the petition is highly embarrassing **A**
because it does not make it sufficiently clear what case the petitioners think
they can make out of the report and does not identify the specific matters
in the report on which the petitioners intend to rely. Therefore, St. Piran
cannot wholly know what case it has to meet. Oddly, though this point
loomed large in Mr. Aldous's submissions on behalf of St. Piran it was not
suggested in Mr. Stone's affidavit that the form of the petition is embarrassing for want of particularity. As I have already mentioned, the report runs **B**
to over 200 pages. What the inspectors have done, and given their terms of
reference it is a sensible approach whether their conclusions be correct or
not, is to review the history of St. Piran and its affairs in detail since 1973.
The report ends with a section headed " principal conclusions " which
seems to be a summary of the more important matters that are to be found
in earlier paragraphs. This section itself runs to some 17 pages and even this **C**
section contains many matters as to which I do not as at present advised see
how they can be relevant to the petition. This is not a report which paints
a picture of unmitigated villainy on the part of everyone concerned with
the management of St. Piran. What appears from the report, whether or not
it is enough if unchallenged to warrant a compulsory winding up order, is
a much more complex picture with some former directors exonerated from
all criticism. With such a report it is in my judgment for the petitioner's **D**
advisers to do the necessary work of selection and identify the matters discussed in the report on which the petitioner is really relying to establish, on
the inspectors' findings, that it is just and equitable that St. Piran should be
wound up by the court. I, therefore, find the petition embarrassing in its
present form, but the difficulty may well be capable of being cured by
amendment. **E**

Accordingly, I propose to adjourn the present motion if Mr. Steinfeld
wishes to give him an opportunity of bringing forward suggested amendments to the petition to particularise the complaints in paragraph 7.

Motion adjourned.
F

Solicitors: *Hancock & Willis; Herbert Smith & Co.*

[Reported by MISS EILEEN O'GRADY, Barrister-at-Law]

G

H

A

[HOUSE OF LORDS]

* HAYWARD . . . . RESPONDENT

AND

THOMPSON AND OTHERS . . . . . . PETITIONERS

B

1981 Oct. 12   Lord Diplock, Lord Keith of Kinkel
                                         and Lord Brandon of Oakwood

PETITION by the defendants for leave to appeal to the House of Lords
from the decision of the Court of Appeal [1981] 3 W.L.R. 470.
The Appeal Committee dismissed the petition.

C

M. G.

D

[COURT OF APPEAL]

* G.U.S. MERCHANDISE CORPORATION LTD. *v.* CUSTOMS
AND EXCISE COMMISSIONERS

1981 June 30;   Waller, Donaldson and Ackner L.JJ.
      July 1; 9

E

*Revenue—Value added tax—Gift of goods under £10—Company
operating special retail schemes—Associated mail order company supplying goods without charge to agents under incentive
scheme—Assessment by commissioners including tax on open
market value of incentive supplies—Whether company account-
able to tax on such supplies—Whether such supplies exempt
as gifts—Finance Act 1972 (c. 41), s. 30 (3), Sch. 3, para. 6*

F

The appellant company, G.U.S. was the nominated representative of a value added tax sub-division of a group of companies of which a retail mail order company, B.M.O.C., was a
member. From April 1, 1973, G.U.S. operated special retail
scheme 4 contained in Customs notice 707, and later special
scheme H contained in Customs notice 727, issued pursuant to
regulation 2 (1) of the Value Added Tax (Supplies by Re-
G   tailers) Regulations 1972 [1] and section 30 (3) of the Finance
Act 1972.[2] Under the schemes a company's liability to value
added tax was calculated on the value of its gross receipts
instead of on each taxable supply. B.M.O.C. encouraged the
recruitment of new agents for its mail order business and the
retention of existing agents through an incentive scheme,
which included sending items valued at less than £10 free of
charge to new agents who had placed with the company a first
H   order worth over a certain amount. G.U.S. did not account
for the inducements supplied to agents as outputs in its value
added tax returns in reliance on the inducements being gifts
not exceeding £10 and hence valued at nil for value added tax
purposes by virtue of paragraph 6 of Schedule 3 to the Act.

---

[1] Value Added Tax (Supplies by Retailers) Regulations 1972, reg. 2 (1): see post,
p. 1315H.
[2] Finance Act 1972, s. 30 (3): see post, p. 1315F–G.
Sch. 3, para. 6: see post, p. 1313E.

G.U.S. Merchandise v. Customs & Excise (C.A.)   **[1981]**

G.U.S. further justified its failure to include the value of the   A
inducements in its returns by the contention that the inducements were a supply of goods within the special retail schemes
since there was neither express reference in the schemes to
such inducements nor any requirement to record them
(although the schemes made special provision for certain other
activities). The Customs and Excise Commissioners made two
assessments to output tax on the open market value in respect
of the incentives in accordance with section 10 (3) of the   B
Finance Act 1972. G.U.S., having unsuccessfully appealed
against the assessments to a value added tax tribunal, appealed
to the High Court. Dismissing the appeal, the judge held that
the goods supplied under the incentive scheme were not gifts
within paragraph 6 of Schedule 3 to the Finance Act 1972
since the nature of the transactions was contractual; that on
their true construction the Customs notices were not exhaustive
and were intended to deal with retail sales; and that the supply   C
of goods as incentives was not a sale and accordingly as taxable
supplies they had to be assessed on their open market value in
accordance with section 10 (3) of the Act of 1972.

On appeal by G.U.S.: —

Held, dismissing the appeal, (1) that, since the company
supplied items free as an inducement to make an application
to become an agent for the mail order business and those items
were sent with the goods ordered when an applicant was   D
accepted as an agent, the company was under a contractual
obligation to supply the items and, therefore, it was not a gift
within the meaning of paragraph 6 of Schedule 3 to the Finance
Act 1972 (post, pp. 1314H—1315B).

(2) That, since the purpose of the special schemes was to
permit retailers to calculate their output on sales instead of
keeping the detailed records required under the legislation, the
Customs notices, unless specifically referring to other trans-   E
actions, applied only to a sale of a taxable supply; that the
giving of the inducement to an agent, not being a sale or a
transaction included in the Customs notices, was not a supply
of goods within the terms of the special schemes and, therefore, a separate account had to be kept in respect of such goods
and value added tax had to be paid on their open market value
in accordance with section 10 (3) of the Finance Act 1972   F
(pp. 1316A–B, H—1317C, 1318A–B).

Decision of Woolf J. [1980] 1 W.L.R. 1508 affirmed.

The following case is referred to in the judgment:

Esso Petroleum Co. Ltd. v. *Customs and Excise Commissioners* [1976]
1 W.L.R. 1; [1976] 1 All E.R. 117, H.L.(E.).

G

The following additional cases were cited in argument:

Fickus, In re [1900] 1 Ch. 331.
Grainger & Son v. *Gough* [1896] A.C. 325, H.L.(E.).
Montreal Gas Co. v. *Vasey* [1900] A.C. 595, P.C.
Reg. v. *Secretary of State for Home Affairs, Ex parte Hosenball* [1977]
1 W.L.R. 766; [1977] 3 All E.R. 452, C.A.

H

APPEAL from Woolf J.

G.U.S. Merchandise Corporation Ltd. (" G.U.S. "), the nominated
representative of a value added tax sub-division of a group of companies
of which British Mail Order Corporation Ltd. (" B.M.O.C.") was a member, appealed to the Manchester Value Added Tax Tribunal against two
assessments to value added tax made by the Customs and Excise Commissioners in respect of items supplied free of charge by B.M.O.C. as

A   inducements to mail order agents. On April 10, 1978, the tribunal dismissed the appeal holding, inter alia, that except for certain items of
negligible value, the goods supplied under the incentive scheme were
taxable supplies and not gifts; that they did not come within the special
retail schemes operated by G.U.S.; and that tax was chargeable on them
in addition to the tax liability in respect of the gross receipts of G.U.S. On
B   March 20, 1980, Woolf J. dismissed the appeal by G.U.S. from the
decision of the tribunal.

By notice of appeal dated May 7, 1980, G.U.S. appealed, by leave of
Woolf J., from the judge's order and asked the court for an order (1) that
the judge's order be set aside and that the decision of the tribunal be
reversed or varied; (2) that the judge's order be varied and that the two
C   appeals made by G.U.S. against the assessments dated May 19, 1977, and
June 14, 1977, respectively made by the commissioners be remitted to the
value added tax tribunal for rehearing and determination and the finding
of further facts together with the opinions and directions of the court,
and that the tribunal be given all necessary and consequential directions;
and (3) that the costs of the appeal and of the appeal to the Queen's Bench
D   Division be paid by the commissioners or such other order as to costs be
made as the court might think fit. The grounds of appeal were that (1) the
judge erred in law in affirming the decision of the value added tax tribunal
and holding that the giving of inducements to prospective and existing
selling agents of G.U.S. was a contractual supply and not a gift of goods
within the meaning of paragraph 6 of Schedule 3 to the Finance Act 1972;
(2) the judge erred in law in holding that the special schemes for retailers
E   contained in scheme 4 of Customs notice 707 and scheme H of Customs
notice 727 applied only to goods supplied by a retailer pursuant to cash
sales; (3) the judge erred in law in holding that the giving of inducements
to prospective and existing selling agents of G.U.S. were not supplies of
goods within the terms of the special scheme for retailers; and (4) the
goods given as inducements to prospective and existing selling agents of
F   G.U.S. were acquired as " retail stock " and were acquired within the
terms of the special schemes for retailers.

The facts are stated in the judgment.

Stewart Bates Q.C. and Reginald Nock for G.U.S.
Andrew Collins for the commissioners.
G

July 9. ACKNER L.J. read the following judgment of the court. The
essential facts out of which this appeal arises have the merit of being
both simple and agreed. The appellant company (G.U.S.) is a subsidiary
company of the Great Universal Stores Ltd. Group and is the nominated
representative of a value added tax sub-division of the group. British Mail
H   Order Corporation (B.M.O.C.) with whose activities this appeal is concerned, is a subsidiary of Great Universal Stores Ltd. and the largest
member of the group. As its name indicates it carries on a mail order retail business and issues its catalogues under a number of names. As from
April 1, 1973, the appellant had been operating one of the special schemes
for retailers, initially scheme 4 as contained in Customs notice 707, which
has been renamed scheme H but is otherwise virtually unchanged: see
notice 727.

1312

G.U.S. Merchandise v. Customs & Excise (C.A.)   [1981]

The business   A

It is necessary to give an outline of the nature of the mail order business. Catalogues are issued twice yearly, normally on a seasonal basis in January and July to cover spring/summer and autumn/winter seasons. The catalogues, approaching 1,000 pages in size, are distributed to agents who are normally housewives selling to their relatives and friends on a part-time basis, but also purchasing goods on their own account. B.M.O.C.   B
have over 1,000,000 agents acting in connection with its business. The agents are remunerated by way of 10 per cent. commission upon sales and they are also allowed a 10 per cent. discount on purchases they make for themselves. Having persuaded relatives and friends to agree to purchase goods from the catalogue, the orders are posted by the agent to the mail order house.

An important feature of this business is that the vast majority of sales   C
are on credit and the agent is responsible for collection and remission of the instalments of the purchase price. This makes the financial reliability of a potential agent of prime importance and care is therefore taken in the appointment of persons applying to become agents. Because there is a fairly steady and constant turnover of agencies, a major pre-occupation of all mail order companies is both the recruitment and the retention of   D
good agents. Experience appears to have shown that the provision of what is normally described in the promotional literature as " free gifts " do provide an inducement to persons to apply to become agents, also to continue to act as agents and even to introduce their friends to apply for such an appointment.

E

The appointment of agents

There are two stages in the process of the appointment of an agent. The first stage is for the applicant to complete a simple form applying for a free copy of the catalogue and details of how he or she can obtain his or her free gift. In order to attract applicants there is usually the promise to send with the catalogue some two or three teaspoons as an   F
additional attraction. When this application is received, the applicant is sent a catalogue, the teaspoons and an application form together with a covering letter which explains in detail what must next be done. The covering letter makes it clear to the applicant that in making her application for appointment as an agent she must also place a first order which must be for a minimum amount, currently £10.

Now comes the second stage. When this application form, together with   G
the first order, is completed and received, both the contents of the application form and the nature of the first order are evaluated. So far as the application is concerned, the applicant will receive so many points for living in owner-occupied property, so many for the fact that she is married and so on. Her personal particulars are looked at in the context of the first order she has placed in order to judge her personal circumstances. In   H
addition a first order is required to get the applicant, so it is described, " into the system." There are heavy administrative costs which are incurred in the approval of the appointment of agents and this first order goes some way to offset them.

In all the advertisements there is reserved to the company the right to refuse the application. If the applicant does not score the requisite number of points she is notified that her appointment is not approved and no gift

A   is sent to her. She is requested to return the catalogue (not the spoons) sent to her and for that purpose is provided with a pre-paid addressed label and usually the catalogues are returned. However, if the applicant's application for an agency is approved then her first order will be processed and delivered to her and with the delivery of that merchandise she will also receive her free gift. She will also be sent the documentation necessary for her to run her agency. Where an existing agent is receiving a free gift

B   for recommending a friend who is appointed as an agent, the gift will again normally be delivered at the same time as the merchandise ordered by the new agent.

The " free gifts "

C   It is common ground that not infrequently the mail order house runs out of stock of the particular free gifts offered, in which event the agent is allowed to choose from the current range of free gifts available. The goods are obtained by way of bulk purchase direct from the manufacturer and the cost to the mail order house is in the range of £1 to £4 per item. There has never been a gift where the cost to the company has exceeded £10.

       The first point raised by the appeal is whether or not the free gifts,
D   other than the teaspoons which are accepted certainly for the purpose of this appeal, as being in a special category of their own, were gifts of goods to which paragraph 6 of Schedule 3 to the Finance Act 1972 applies, so that the value of the supply is to be treated as nil with the result that no value added tax is chargeable. Paragraph 6 provides:

E   " Where a supply is a gift of goods . . . the value of the supply shall be taken to be the cost of the goods to the person making the supply; except that if that cost does not exceed £10 and the supply is a gift its value shall be taken to be nil."

In relation to this provision the only issue which was before the value added tax tribunal and on appeal before Woolf J. was whether or not the supply of what was obviously accepted to be inducements, was the supply

F   of gifts or whether the supply was pursuant to a contractual obligation.

       The view of the tribunal was concisely expressed as follows:

       " In our judgment the first stage taken by itself is to encourage a prospective agent to send for the catalogue with a view to making an application to be appointed as an agent. Even if sending for the catalogue and its dispatch could be treated as an offer and an accept-

G   ance with the teaspoons as the consideration relating thereto (which we consider to be doubtful), we do not think at this stage there was any intention to enter into any legal relationship. We therefore hold that the first stage does not constitute a binding contract, and that the three teaspoons (which are at any rate of negligible value) may properly be treated as a free gift within paragraph 6 of Schedule 3.

H   In relation to the second stage, which we think must be considered in conjunction with the first stage, we hold that the completion of the form of application to be appointed as an agent coupled with the placing of her first order constitutes an offer to become appointed as an agent on certain terms; namely, she will be remunerated on a continuing basis at the rate of 10 per cent. on all (of any) merchandise sold by her; and that she will receive the advertised tea set [free gift] on the acceptance by the appellant company of her first order. This

offer is accepted by the appellant company when she is appointed as　A
an agent and when her first order is accepted (both of these are in fact
simultaneous). In our view the tea set is part of the consideration
moving from the appellant company for the contract constituted by
the offer and acceptance . . . The effect of the conclusions which we
have reached is that the teaspoons should be treated as a gift within
paragraph 6 of Schedule 3 to the Finance Act 1972 and that no tax is
chargeable in relation thereto. The tea set, on the other hand, is a　B
taxable supply supplied pursuant to an enforceable contract and
should not be treated as a gift."

The judge accepted the value added tax tribunal's decision so far as
the main gift, which happened to be a tea set, was concerned, although he
expressed grave reservations concerning their decision in relation to the　C
teaspoons, indicating that he probably would have come to a different
conclusion. There is no cross-appeal in relation to the teaspoons and we
need spend no further time upon them.

Mr. Bate's clear and concise submission on behalf of G.U.S. is that
the only offer was to appoint the agent, if considered to be suitable, on the
terms referred to above and the only acceptance occurred when the
agent was approved. In regard to the first order, he submitted that al-　D
though there was an obligation upon his client to supply the goods subject of that order, however since they were supplied on approval, they
could of course be returned. In relation to the " free gift " he said the
offer was too uncertain to result in any contractual obligation. His client
was merely expressing a statement of intention to supply a tea set or
" something else " subject to availability. We have no doubt that G.U.S.　E
could have so expressed itself as to have achieved the result for which Mr.
Bates contended. To have done so would have reduced the power of the
inducement, and seriously detracted from its main intention, which was
not to avoid paying value added tax upon the supply of these goods, but to
recruit and maintain their force of agents. The offer was not in terms, to
supply a tea set or something else. The offer was to provide a specified
item, or on occasion a choice of one out of a number of items or cash　F
in lieu. Mr. Bates stressed that because of the extensive advertising there
was always a risk that the stock of a particular gift would run out and
that there must be implied into the offer, that it was subject to availability
of the goods.

We cannot accept this. G.U.S. having, very understandably, reserved the
right to reject any application to become an agent, could have ensured that　G
it did not accept more applications than it could match with the free gifts.
G.U.S. of course adopted a much more business-like approach and one
which was no doubt quite satisfactory, namely that where it ran out of stock
of a particular article it offered the agent a choice from the then current
range of free gifts. This in practice created no difficulty. Moreover if the
agent had sought to rely upon her strict rights her claim to damages would　H
be nominal, since either she would presumably have been offered the cash
value of the free gift, the supply of which had run out, or it could have been
contended that the substitute was of equal value and any claim in damages
was nominal. We agree with the view expressed by the value added tax
tribunal. The fact that the articles were provided as incentives and indeed
were supplied as " gifts " are not determining factors. We cannot accept
that the circumstances were such as to show that there was no intention to

A create legal relations. The whole scheme was designed to recruit and keep useful agents, and for such a scheme to involve a contractual obligation to supply the very incentive which apparently in practice has proved so effective, seems to us to be in no way surprising. On the contrary, to devise an effective scheme of incentives which involved no binding obligation upon G.U.S. to comply with the very promise upon which the whole scheme was constructed, would inevitably be extremely difficult to devise. Accordingly

B on the first point we would uphold the decision of the judge and dismiss the appeal.

The special scheme for retailers

Before considering the special schemes for retailers and the issue which arises in this appeal relative to such schemes, it is essential first to consider

C the relevant provisions of the Finance Act 1972 and the obligation which it imposes in relation to the payment of value added tax. Section 1 of the Act provides that a tax to be known as value added tax shall be charged on the supply of goods and services in the United Kingdom. Section 2 deals with the scope of that tax. Subsection (2) provides that tax on the supply of goods or services shall be charged only where (a) the supply is a taxable

D supply; and (b) the goods or services are supplied by a taxable person in the course of a business carried on by him; and shall be payable by the person supplying the goods or services. " Taxable supply " means any supply of goods or services in the United Kingdom other than an exempt supply: section 46.

Mr. Bates, for G.U.S., conceded that under section 2 his clients were,

E prima facie, liable to pay value added tax on the " free gifts " and that by virtue of section 10 (3) since the supply was not for a consideration that consisted of money, the value of the supply has to be taken to be its open market value, as defined by the Act. Mr. Bates, however, contended that his client had been exempted from paying value added tax on these goods by virtue of section 30 (3) of the Act and the Regulations made under it. Section 30 (3) provides:

F " Regulations under this section may make special provision for such taxable supplies by retailers of any goods or of any description of goods or of services or any description of services as may be determined by or under the regulations and, in particular,—(a) for permitting the value which is to be taken as the value of the supplies in any prescribed accounting period or part thereof to be determined,

G subject to any limitations or restrictions, by such method or one of such methods as may have been described in any notice published by the commissioners in pursuance of the regulations . . ."

Regulations were made pursuant to section 30 (3) and these are the Value Added Tax (Supplies by Retailers) Regulations 1972. Regulation 2 (1) provides:

H " The commissioners may permit the value which is to be taken as the value, in any prescribed accounting period or part thereof, of supplies by a retailer which are taxable at other than the zero-rate to be determined . . . by any method described in a notice published by them for that purpose; . . ."

A number of notices have been issued pursuant to the regulations and the relevant schemes are scheme 4 of Customs notice 707 and scheme H of

Customs notice 727. These schemes are designed to relieve retailers (that is   A
anyone who is mainly supplying goods or services to the public without tax
invoices) from some of the burden of paper and other work associated with
making the required returns of value added tax payable by them. The
purpose of the special schemes is to enable retailers to calculate output tax
without recording every sale separately. The schemes not only make special
provisions, but also contain explanation and advice. Thus, paragraph 6 of   B
notice 727 which is headed " Special schemes for retailers " states:

" Normally a taxable person has to account for VAT each time he
supplies goods or services to a customer. This is called output tax.
To account for output tax in the normal VAT way, the taxable person
needs to have a record of every separate transaction. . . . But most retailers cannot keep a record of that kind for all their *sales,* because
they do not usually issue invoices to their *customers* or make any   C
written record at the time when *a sale* takes place. So the special
schemes for retailers allow you, as a retailer, to calculate your output
tax (*or most of it*) in other ways, which vary according to the particular
scheme " (emphasis added).

The far less burdensome scheme which G.U.S. was permitted to operate   D
for working out its liability was to calculate the tax on a proportion of its
gross takings. The issue which confronted the tribunal and Woolf J. was
whether, on a proper reading of the schemes, the giving of the free gifts,
the inducements, to prospective and existing selling agents of G.U.S. was a
supply of goods within the terms of the special schemes for retailers, or
whether such supplies should be kept apart from the scheme altogether. In
the former event G.U.S. would be entitled to claim back the value added   E
tax it had paid to its suppliers for goods (input tax) and yet make no
payment of value added tax to the commissioners. If the alternative view
prevails, however, G.U.S. would have to keep a separate account in respect of these goods and pay value added tax on their open market value,
having deducted the input tax.

G.U.S. has protested that in so far as the price of the goods which it   F
sold had to be enhanced to take into account its expenditure on the free
gifts, it was already paying, indirectly, value added tax upon them, since
this was reflected in the gross takings. Accordingly, it would involve G.U.S.
in a measure of double taxation if it was now held liable to treat the supply
of those goods separately and pay value added tax upon them. Mr. Collins
contended that if G.U.S. was held to be exempt from paying value added
tax on the inducements, the revenue would have lost at least part of the   G
tax which they should have received, because in so far as G.U.S. had increased the price of its goods (as to which there was no evidence) by adding
in the cost of obtaining the inducements, this cost would not have included
the value added tax which it paid upon those goods since this would have
been reclaimed. We accept the force of this argument. However, Mr. Collins
was obliged to accept that success in this appeal could mean that the   H
revenue would not only receive the value added tax on the free gifts but
also a greater return from value added tax on the goods which G.U.S. sold,
by virtue of any enhancement in the price to cover the cost of the inducements.

These considerations are not relevant as to whether or not the supply
of the inducements was a supply within the terms of the special scheme.
Mr. Collins's contention, which was accepted by the judge, and indeed was

A the basis of the value added tax tribunal's decision, was that if you examine the schemes in detail the clear implication is that they do not normally cover supplies which are not sales to the public. It was common ground that the transactions with the agents whereby they were supplied with the inducement were not sales. That agreed conclusion was largely based on the majority view in *Esso Petroleum Co. Ltd.* v. *Customs and Excise Commissioners* [1976] 1 W.L.R. 1, a decision of the House of Lords. The judge

B accepted this submission, and in our judgment rightly so, for the following reasons. (1) The schemes are special schemes for *retailers* and therefore would be expected to apply essentially to normal methods of retailing. (2) Paragraph 6 of scheme 727, which I have quoted above but added emphasis, refers specifically to *sales* and *customers.* Moreover it does not purport to be an all-embracing scheme covering all the activities of retailers: ". . . the

C special schemes . . . allow you . . . to calculate your output tax (or most of it) in other ways." (3) Paragraph 30 of notice 707 (revised March 1973) excludes from the special scheme secondary goods purchased by the retailer for linking with main goods sold in the usual way in order to promote his business. It gives, as an example, wine glasses for offer with sales of petrol, although it makes an exception where these are below 10p per item.

D It specifies that an account for output tax in the normal way, that is outside the special scheme, has to be kept for these secondary goods which are given away. True, it is not said that the business promotion scheme described in paragraph 30 can be said to cover the transaction with which we are concerned, that is the recruitment of agents. It is concerned with sales, but it does show that the well recognised form of business promotion involving the purchase by the retailers of goods to be supplied as induce-

E ments to further their retail business, was not to escape the obligation to account for value added tax in the normal way. (4) Paragraph 25 of the same notice relates to goods of a retailer applied by him to his own personal use. These are specifically stated to be taxable supplies and their cost, including value added tax, must be included in the calculation of gross takings. This is yet a further indication that the scheme is not intended to

F exempt the retailer from his ordinary value added tax liability. It is only intended to facilitate its calculation. (5) In paragraph 13 in revised scheme 707:

> " the retailer must split his gross takings for each tax period in proportion to the total amounts, including VAT, which will be payable by customers for standard rate and zero rate goods, respectively."

G The reference to " customers " and the amount payable is inappropriate language to cover the supply of goods without charge to the retailer's agents. (6) The method of calculating the gross takings for the purpose of the schemes contains no provision for a record which would be appropriate to deal with transactions relating to the supply of inducements for agents. Thus the accounting system is inappropriate to record any reference to the

H transaction with which we are concerned. Yet, as the judge correctly observed, the whole framework of the value added tax legislation, including the subordinate legislation and notices, is to require detailed records to be kept. The aim and purpose of these records is of course to enable the commissioners to get, at the end of the day, the ultimate value added tax on the ultimate supply to the ultimate consumer. The result of Mr. Bates's submission must be that, if the inducements proved so effective in the boosting of sales of the main goods that the price of those goods did not

have to be enhanced to carry the cost of the inducements, the retailer would   A
have claimed back the value added tax he paid to his supplier and yet paid
no value added tax directly or indirectly on the inducements, and this
despite the clear statutory obligations to which we have referred.

We accordingly agree with the judge that the clear implication to be
drawn from the notices is that they are intended to deal with retail sales
to customers and are not designed or intended to deal with taxable supplies
in special kinds of transactions which do not involve sales unless they are   B
specifically referred to in the notices. We accordingly dismiss the appeal.

Appeal dismissed with costs.
Leave to appeal refused.

Solicitors: *Paisner & Co.; Solicitor, Customs and Excise.*   C

[Reported by MISS STELLA SOLOMON, Barrister-at-Law]

October 27. The Appeal Committee of the House of Lords (Lord
Wilberforce, Lord Fraser of Tullybelton and Lord Russell of Killowen)
dismissed a petition by G.U.S. Merchandise Corporation Ltd. for leave to   D
appeal.

[CHANCERY DIVISION]   E

* SELIM LTD. *v.* BICKENHALL ENGINEERING LTD.

[1981 S. No. 2776]

1981 May 8; 15   Sir Robert Megarry V.-C.
                                                                        F

Land Charge—Register, vacation of—Pending actions register—
Landlords' notices requiring repairs—Lessees' counter-notices
preventing action for breach of covenant without leave of
court — Cautions entered against houses — Landlords seeking
leave to commence action in county court for breach of
repairing covenants in leases—Whether pending action " relat-
ing to land "—Land Charges Act 1972 (c. 61), s. 17 (1)[1]*—*
Leasehold Property (Repairs) Act 1938 (1 & 2 Geo. 6, c. 34),   G
s. 1 (3)[2]

Two houses were demised by separate leases for 99 years
from June 1890. In May 1980, the landlords served on the
lessees notices under section 146 of the Law of Property Act
1925 requiring them to remedy various wants of repair. The
lessees served on the landlords counter-notices under section 1
of the Leasehold Property (Repairs) Act 1938 having the   H
effect of preventing the landlords without leave of the court
from enforcing any right of re-entry or forfeiture for breach of
the repairing covenants. In October 1980, the leases were

[1] Land Charges Act 1972, s. 17 (1): see post, p. 1320c.
[2] Leasehold Property (Repairs) Act 1938, s. 1: " (3) . . . no proceedings, by
action or otherwise, shall be taken by the lessor for the enforcement of any right of
re-entry or forfeiture under any proviso or stipulation in the lease . . . or for
damages . . . otherwise than with the leave of the court."

A   assigned to the plaintiff company. In December 1980, the landlords applied to the county court for " leave to commence an
action " against the plaintiff in respect of the breaches of the
repairing covenants. In April 1981, the plaintiff instructed
agents to sell at auction the leasehold interest in each of the
houses. Meanwhile, the landlords registered cautions against
the houses in the Land Registry, despite protests by the
plaintiff. Both houses were sold at the auction and in May

B   1981, before completion was due, the plaintiff applied under
section 82 of the Land Registration Act 1925, alternatively
under the inherent jurisdiction, for an order that the cautions
be vacated.

    On the question whether the landlords' application to the
county court for " leave to commence an action " for breach
of the repairing covenants sufficiently " related to " land as to
be a " pending land action " within the meaning of section

C   17 (1) of the Land Charges Act 1972: —

    Held, that although the leave required under section 1 (3)
of the Leasehold Property (Repairs) Act 1938 referred to proceedings for " re-entry or forfeiture " of a lease, and the landlords had merely asked for " leave to commence an action " for
breach of repairing covenants, the probability was that forfeiture would be sought, and the county court proceedings
could fairly be regarded as a preliminary stage in forfeiture

D   proceedings; that further, on any ordinary reading of the
words " relating to land " in section 17 (1) of the Land Charges
Act 1972, forfeiture of a lease, though involving destruction
of an interest in land, would still sufficiently " relate to " land
so as to be a " pending land action " within the definition in
section 17 (1); that, accordingly, the plaintiff's claim for an
order vacating the cautions failed and its application would
be dismissed (post, pp. 1323A–B, B–D, G—1324A).

E   *Heywood* v. *B.D.C. Properties Ltd. (No. 2)* [1964] 1 W.L.R.
267; *Calgary and Edmonton Land Co. Ltd.* v. *Dobinson* [1974]
Ch. 102; and *Whittingham* v. *Whittingham (National Westminster Bank Ltd., intervener)* [1979] Fam. 9, C.A. considered.

The following cases are referred to in the judgment:

Calgary and Edmonton Land Co. Ltd. v. *Dobinson* [1974] Ch. 102; [1974]
F   2 W.L.R. 143; [1974] 1 All E.R. 484.
Greenhi Builders Ltd. v. *Allen* [1979] 1 W.L.R. 156; [1978] 3 All E.R.
1163.
Heywood v. *B.D.C. Properties Ltd. (No. 2)* [1964] 1 W.L.R. 267; [1964]
1 All E.R. 180; [1964] 1 W.L.R. 971; [1964] 2 All E.R. 702, C.A.
Pips (Leisure Productions) Ltd. v. *Walton* (unreported), May 23, 1980,
Sir Robert Megarry V.-C.
G   *Taylor* v. *Taylor* [1968] 1 W.L.R. 378; [1968] 1 All E.R. 843, C.A.
Whittingham v. *Whittingham (National Westminster Bank Ltd., inter-
vener)* [1979] Fam. 9; [1978] 2 W.L.R. 936; [1978] 3 All E.R. 805,
Balcombe J. and C.A.

The following additional cases were cited in argument:

Bellamy v. *Sabine* (1857) 1 De G. & J. 566.
H   *Kanda* v. *Church Commissioners for England* [1958] 1 Q.B. 332; [1957]
3 W.L.R. 353; [1957] 2 All E.R. 815, C.A.
Williams v. *Earle* (1868) L.R. 3 Q.B. 739.

MOTION

    By writ and notice of motion dated May 5, 1981, the plaintiff company,
Selim Ltd., claimed inter alia orders under section 82 of the Law of
Property Act 1925, alternatively under the inherent jurisdiction of the

Selim Ltd. v. Bickenhall Ltd. (Ch.D.)   **[1981]**

court, that registrations in favour of the defendant landlords, Bickenhall   A
Engineering Ltd., of cautions against the proprietorship register of the
plaintiff company's leasehold properties, 58 and 74, Taybridge Road,
Battersea, London, registered under titles no. 308,130 and no. 308,131 at
H.M. Land Registry respectively be vacated.

The facts are stated in the judgment.

M. M. Pascoe for the plaintiff company.   B
William Elland for the defendant landlords.

Cur. adv. vult.

May 15.   SIR ROBERT MEGARRY V.-C. read the following judgment.
This motion raises a single question of law. That question is whether certain   C
proceedings fall within the definition of a " pending land action " in the
Land Charges Act 1972, and so are registrable as a " pending action " under
section 5 of the Act. By section 17 (1), unless the context otherwise requires,
the expression " pending land action " means " any action or proceeding
pending in court relating to land or any interest in or charge on land." The
question is whether this definition includes proceedings in a county court,   D
under the Leasehold Property (Repairs) Act 1938 which seek leave to
commence an action against an assignee of a lease for breach of the repairing covenants.

The matter arises in this way. The two houses in question, nos. 58 and
74, Taybridge Road, Battersea, were demised by separate leases for 99
years from June 24, 1890, each at a rent of £7 a year. On October 17, 1980,
each lease was assigned to the plaintiff company. Some five months earlier   E
the defendant company, the landlords, had served on the assignors notices
under section 146 of the Law of Property Act 1925 in respect of the disrepair of the premises, accompanied by schedules of dilapidations. As over
three years of each lease was unexpired, the assignors were entitled to serve
on the defendant company a counter-notice under the Act of 1938, and this
they did on June 10, 1980, in respect of each house. By section 1 (3) of the   F
Act of 1938, the effect of this was to prohibit the defendant company from
taking any proceedings, by action or otherwise, for the enforcement of any
right of re-entry or forfeiture for breach of the repairing covenants, or for
damages for such breach, without the leave of the court. On December 9,
1980, after the assignment to the plaintiff company, the defendant company
issued originating applications in the Wandsworth County Court in respect
of each house, seeking, inter alia, " leave to commence an action " against   G
the plaintiff company " for breach of the repairing covenants " in the
leases.

The title to each leasehold is registered at the Land Registry with good
leasehold title. By virtue of section 59 (1) and (5) of the Land Registration
Act 1925 a pending action which for unregistered land is required to be
protected under the Land Charges Act 1972 is, for registered land, required   H
to be protected by the entry of a caution against dealings with the land
instead. The plaintiff company wished to sell the leasehold interest in both
houses, and gave instructions for them to be sold at auction on April 27,
1981. However, on April 2, 1981, the defendant company's solicitors wrote
to the plaintiff company's solicitors to say that they had registered cautions
against each of the houses. Despite the protests of the plaintiff company's
solicitors, the defendant company refused to remove the cautions. At the

A auction on April 27 an announcement was made about the service of the schedules of dilapidations and the commencement of proceedings to enforce them; and it was stated that the purchasers would have to deal with all problems relating to these. Despite this, both houses were sold at the auction (one with part vacant possession), and the plaintiff company expects that the purchasers will require the cautions to be vacated before they will complete. The plaintiff company accordingly issued a writ and notice of

B motion on May 5, 1981, seeking in respect of each house, either under section 82 of the Land Registration Act 1925 or the inherent jurisdiction, an order that the cautions be vacated. The writ also claims damages.

On behalf of the plaintiff company and the defendant company respectively, Mr. Pascoe and Mr. Elland were in agreement on every point save the one in dispute. For the purposes of the motion only, Mr. Pascoe

C accepted that there were breaches of the repairing covenants and that leave under the Act of 1938 will be granted by the county court. No question was raised on the power of the court to grant on motion the relief sought by the plaintiff company, or on the jurisdiction (whether inherent or under section 82 of the Land Registration Act 1925) to make the order sought, or on the form of the order, whether personal or impersonal. On both hands it was

D accepted that the only question was whether the application to the Wandsworth County Court was or was not a " pending land action," and so a " pending action," within sections 5 and 17 (1) of the Land Charges Act 1972. Mr. Pascoe, of course, says that it is not, whereas Mr. Elland says that it is.

The meaning of " pending land action " has been discussed in five recent cases to which I should refer. In *Heywood* v. *B.D.C. Properties Ltd.* (*No. 2*)

E [1964] 1 W.L.R. 267, the defendants alleged that the plaintiffs had agreed to sell certain land to them, and registered estate contracts as land charges in respect of the alleged contracts. The plaintiffs then issued a writ seeking vacation of the land charges on the ground that there were no contracts in existence; and on motion they obtained the order that they sought. The defendants then registered the plaintiffs' action as a pending action, and the

F plaintiffs applied for the vacation of this registration. Plowman J. held that the action was not a pending action because neither party was making any claim to land against the other. The plaintiffs were doing no more than seeking a declaration that that was no contract relating to the land between the parties, and there was old authority which showed that a pending action was an action asserting a claim to land or an interest in land. The Court of

G Appeal [1964] 1 W.L.R. 971 reversed this decision on a procedural point, but the decision on the pending action point was not affected. In *Taylor* v. *Taylor* [1968] 1 W.L.R. 378, a wife took out a summons under section 17 of the Married Women's Property Act 1882 in which she sought an order for the sale of the matrimonial home and a declaration that she was entitled to half the proceeds of sale. Both in section 20 (6) of the Land Charges Act 1925 and in section 17 (1) of the Land Charges Act 1972

H " land " is defined as excluding an undivided share in land. The Court of Appeal held that the wife's summons was not a pending action. Then in *Calgary and Edmonton Land Co. Ltd.* v. *Dobinson* [1974] Ch. 102, I followed the *Heywood* case [1964] 1 W.L.R. 267, and held that a summons in the Companies Court to restrain the liquidator from disposing of certain land belonging to a company was not a pending land action, for it claimed no proprietary right in land, and sought merely to restrain a disposition of land.

The other two decisions were on the other side of the line. In A
Whittingham v. *Whittingham* (*National Westminster Bank Ltd., intervener*) [1979] Fam. 9, on a divorce the wife applied for an order
transferring her husband's house to her; and the Court of Appeal,
affirming Balcombe J., held that this application was a " pending land
action " and so was registrable as a pending action. It mattered not that the
wife had no existing proprietary right in the house; it sufficed that she was
seeking an order that would give her such a right. Finally, there was *Greenhi* B
Builders Ltd. v. *Allen* [1979] 1 W.L.R. 156. There, a number of house-
owners brought separate actions against some builders, claiming, inter alia,
that they had easements of support for their houses which were being interfered with by the builders. They sought an injunction to restrain future
interferences, with a mandatory order to make good past interferences,
and damages. Browne-Wilkinson J. held that an action claiming an C
easement was a " pending land action," especially when it included a claim
to the mandatory order sought. I should mention that this case and *Taylor*
v. *Taylor* [1968] 1 W.L.R. 378 were not cited in argument before me.

If one returns to the definition of " pending land action," it seems plain
that in this case the opening words are satisfied, namely " any action or
proceeding pending in court "; and no contention to the contrary has been
put forward. Nor is there much difficulty about the concluding words, " land D
or any interest in or charge on land." " Land," I may say, is given a wide
definition in section 17 (1) of the Act of 1972. The difficulty lies in the two
words " relating to." As was mentioned in a passage in the *Calgary* case
[1974] Ch. 102, 105, which was cited in the *Whittingham* case [1979] Fam.
9, 22, there must be some restriction on the literal width of these words, for
otherwise an action to restrain a nuisance alleged to emanate from X's E
land would be registrable. The question is what that restriction is.

In the *Calgary* case [1974] Ch. 102 I did not seek to lay down any exhaustive definition, and I do not seek to do so now. (In view of what
Stamp L.J. said in the *Whittingham* case [1979] Fam. 9, 23, I may also say
that I certainly did not intend to suggest that only a claim to an existing
interest in land would suffice, so that a claim to have a new right granted F
would not: I would respectfully adopt what Eveleigh L.J. said at p. 24
about this.) What are in question in this case are not proceedings which
merely seek to restrain any disposition of the land, or to obtain a declaration
that no contract to sell it exists. On the other hand, the proceedings do not
seek to obtain a transfer of the land or to assert an easement over it. The
proceedings are a first step towards launching further proceedings which
may merely claim damages or may seek forfeiture of the lease, or may do G
both.

I propose to take the matter by stages. First, if the proceedings were
direct proceedings for forfeiture, would they be registrable as a pending
action? Plainly they would not be proceedings which claim some proprietary right in the land, in any ordinary sense of the words. What they would
seek would be to destroy an estate in the land. Yet I think that one must H
consider the effect of such a distinction. If the immediate reversioner on a
lease purchases that lease, the normal result will be that the lease will perish
by surrender, and the reversion will become an interest in possession; and
if the reversioner sues to enforce the agreement, that plainly would fall
within the authorities as being a pending land action. If instead the reversioner sues for forfeiture, the result, if he succeeds, will be much the same:
the lease will disappear and the reversion will become an interest in pos-

The Weekly Law Reports, November 6, 1981

1323

1 W.L.R.   Selim Ltd. v. Bickenhall Ltd. (Ch.D.)   Sir Robert
                                                            Megarry V.-C.

A   session. Thus although the forfeiture is in one sense an act of destruction, from another aspect it may be regarded as an act of acquisition; for it augments the reversioner's interest in the land.

Even if I am wrong in this view, I have to remember that what I am primarily concerned with is the phrase " relating to land "; and on any ordinary reading of those words, proceedings for the forfeiture of a lease of land seem to me to fall within that expression. I do not think that there
B   is anything in the authorities which precludes me from giving effect to this view. The cases which speak in terms of a claim to specific property, or the recovery or assertion of title to specific property, or a claim to some proprietary right in land (see the *Calgary* case [1974] Ch. 102, 107) do not seem to me to connote that proceedings to destroy an interest in land cannot be a pending land action. After all, the statutory words " relate to " are very
C   general in their meaning, and although there must be some limit to this meaning, I would have thought that proceedings for the destruction of an interest in land " relate to " the land as much as proceedings for the acquisition of an interest in the land. In each case the proceedings directly affect an estate or interest in the land; and without aspiring to any definition, exhaustive or otherwise, I would regard such an approach as providing a
D   helpful guide to proceedings which fall within the statutory definition.

There is a further consideration. In the *Whittingham* case [1979] Fam. 9, 23, and in the *Greenhi* case [1979] 1 W.L.R. 156, 159, there is some discussion of it being material to take into account whether, if the action is not registered, a third party, acquiring the land before judgment in the action and without notice, will take free from the plaintiff's claim. In the case of leaseholds, it seems to me to be important that a purchaser should, by
E   searching, be able to discover pending proceedings for forfeiture, for otherwise he might be purchasing something which, on service of the proceedings for forfeiture, had ceased to exist, Nearly a year ago I had such a case (*Pips (Leisure Productions) Ltd.* v. *Walton* (unreported), May 23, 1980); and it was a striking warning to purchasers of leaseholds. It seems to me that this consideration supports the view that proceedings which, if success-
F   ful, will destroy an interest in land ought, on any fair reading of the words, to be regarded as proceedings which " relate to " that land.

That, however, is not the end of the matter. The present proceedings in the county court are not proceedings for forfeiture of the lease, but at any rate on one view are at best at one remove from such proceedings. Each originating application merely seeks " leave to commence an action " against the plaintiff company " for breach of the repairing covenant " in the
G   lease. Under section 1 (3) of the Act of 1938, such leave is needed both for proceedings for forfeiture and for proceedings claiming damages. There is nothing in the originating application to show that, if leave is given, it is proceedings for forfeiture that will be commenced, with or without a claim for damages. The probability, however, is that forfeiture would be sought, and in any case the affidavit of a solicitor filed on behalf of the defendant
H   company states in terms that the defendant company is seeking leave " to take forfeiture proceedings." The next paragraph, indeed, refers to the prospects " of obtaining forfeiture itself of both leases." In those circumstances, it seems to me that the proceedings in the county court may fairly be regarded as a preliminary stage in the forfeiture proceedings which the defendant company wishes to take. I doubt whether an action for damages for breach of covenant is, by itself, a " pending land action," but I think that proceedings for leave to commence an action which may include a

claim for forfeiture of a lease, and is intended to do so, sufficiently relate to A
the land under lease for them to be a " pending land action." I so hold. It
follows that the claim in the motion for an order vacating the registrations
fails, and so the motion will be dismissed.

Order accordingly.

Solicitors: *L. B. Marks & Co. Slowes.*   B

K. N. B.

[COURT OF APPEAL]   C

* PRACTICE DIRECTION
(CRIME: CROWN COURT BUSINESS) (No. 7)

1981 Oct. 16   Lord Lane C.J., Mustill and McCullough JJ.
                                                                                       D
*Crime—Practice—Crown Court—Distribution of business—Bail—
Courts Act 1971 (c. 23), ss. 4 (5), 5 (4), Sch. 10*

LORD LANE C.J. at the sitting of the court announced the following
direction given by his Lordship with the concurrence of the Lord Chancellor
under sections 4 (5) and 5 (4) of, and Schedule 10 to, the Courts Act 1971.

The following paragraph shall be substituted for paragraph 15 of E
Practice Direction (Crime: Crown Court Business) [1971] 1 W.L.R. 1535.

Applications to the Crown Court for bail

15.—(1) (*a*) Notice of intention to apply for bail shall be given
to the appropriate officer at the location of the Crown Court where
the proceedings in which the application for bail arises took place F
or are pending. (*b*) Where a person gives notice in writing that he
wishes to apply for bail and requests that the Official Solicitor shall
act for him in the application, the application shall be heard by a
judge of the Crown Court in London. (*c*) In any other case, the
application shall be heard at the location of the Crown Court where
the proceedings in respect of which it arises took place or are
pending, or at any other location which the court may direct.   G

(2) Subject to such directions as may be given in any case by or
on behalf of the Lord Chief Justice with the concurrence of the
Lord Chancellor, any application for bail—(*a*) by a person charged
with a Class 1 offence, or in any case where a presiding judge so
directs, shall be heard by a High Court judge or by a circuit judge
nominated by a presiding judge for this purpose; (*b*) by a person H
charged with a Class 2 offence may be heard by a High Court judge
or by a circuit judge or (on the authority of a presiding judge) by
a recorder; (*c*) in any other case may be heard by any judge of the
Crown Court.

L. N. W.

A

[QUEEN'S BENCH DIVISION]

* COVENTRY CITY COUNCIL *v.* DOYLE
COVENTRY CITY COUNCIL *v.* QUINN
CLARKE *v.* COVENTRY CITY COUNCIL

B

1980   Nov. 24; Dec. 17

Donaldson L.J.
and Hodgson J.

Public Health—Nuisance—Complaint by tenant—Statutory nuis-
ance existing when informations laid—Repairs undertaken or
tenants removed to other properties before hearing—Properties
C *left unoccupied—Whether orders to be made—Costs—Public*
Health Act 1936 (26 Geo. 5 & 1 Edw. 8, c. 49), ss. 92 (1),
94 (2) (3), 99

Three tenants of the council laid informations against the
council under section 99 of the Public Health Act 1936 alleging
that the state of the houses they occupied was such that the
houses constituted statutory nuisances within the meaning of
D section 92 (1) (a) of the Act.[1] Prior to the hearing before the
justices, the council moved one tenant to other accommodation
so that the premises could be modernised, the second tenant
was moved to other accommodation during the hearing and,
although the third tenant, C, still occupied her house, the
council had carried out works of repair to the premises. The
justices found that in each case a statutory nuisance had
existed at the time the informations were laid, they made
E nuisance orders requiring the council to carry out certain
works of repair and they ordered the council to pay C's costs
of the proceedings.
    The council appealed against the justices' decision in C's
case. The Crown Court held that, although a statutory nuisance
had existed at the time the information was laid, the relevant
date on which to consider whether there was a statutory nuisance was the date of the hearing before the justices and by
F that date the nuisance had been abated. The court varied the
order for costs to include only those incurred by C before
the date of the hearing.
    On appeal by C against the Crown Court decision and by
the council against the justices' decision in respect of the
other two properties: —
    Held, (1) that on the ordinary and plain meaning of the
wording of section 94 (2) of the Public Health Act 1936, the
G relevant date for determining whether a statutory nuisance
existed was the date of the hearing before the justices and not
the date the information was laid; that, accordingly, in the two
cases where the properties had been vacated by the tenants,
the justices were wrong in law in holding that the relevant date
was the date of the information but they had correctly held
that statutory nuisances existed because at the date of the
hearing the work of repair had not been carried out in those
H unoccupied premises to abate the nuisance (post, pp. 1337H—
1338A, 1340D–F, 1341B–C).
    Northern Ireland Trailers Ltd. v. *Preston Corporation*
[1972] 1 W.L.R. 203, D.C. and *Lambeth London Borough*
Council v. *Stubbs* (1980) 78 L.G.R. 650, D.C. applied.

---

[1] Public Health Act 1936, s. 92 (1): see post, p. 1334F.
S. 94: see post, p. 1335A–F.
S. 99: see post, p. 1336A–B.

Coventry Council v. Doyle (D.C.) [1981]

Per curiam. Although a nuisance has not been abated by A
a house being left unoccupied, different considerations might
apply where property has been effectively rendered incapable
of occupation, e.g. by having all services permanently cut off
and being boarded up prior to demolition (post, p. 1339E–F).

(2) That the mandatory provisions for the payment of costs
in section 94 (3) of the Act was not limited to proceedings
brought by a local authority and any person aggrieved was
entitled to the expenses of the proceedings before the justices B
provided that they established that a statutory nuisance had
existed at the date when the information was laid and, accordingly, the Crown Court was wrong in law to deprive the tenant
C of her reasonable costs of the hearing before the justices
(post, pp. 1338c–f, 1340h—1341a).

The following cases are referred to in the judgment of Hodgson J.: C

Lambeth London Borough Council v. *Stubbs* (1980) 78 L.G.R. 650, D.C.
Northern Ireland Trailers Ltd. v. *Preston Corporation* [1972] 1 W.L.R.
  203; [1972] 1 All E.R. 260, D.C.
Nottingham City District Council v. *Newton* [1974] 1 W.L.R. 923; [1974]
  2 All E.R. 760, D.C.
Reg. v. *Newham East Justices, Ex parte Hunt*; *Reg.* v. *Oxted Justices,
  Ex parte Franklin* [1976] 1 W.L.R. 420; [1976] 1 All E.R. 839, D.C. D
Rex v. *Epping (Waltham Abbey) Justices, Ex parte Burlinson* [1948]
  1 K.B. 79; [1947] 2 All E.R. 537, D.C.

The following additional case was cited in argument:

Salford City Council v. *McNally* [1976] A.C. 379; [1975] 3 W.L.R. 87;
  [1975] 2 All E.R. 860, H.L.(E.).

E

COVENTRY CITY COUNCIL V. DOYLE

CASE STATED by Coventry City justices.

On February 22, 1979, an information was preferred by the respondent
tenant, John William Doyle, against the appellant landlords, Coventry City
Council, that they were the owners/leaseholders of certain premises at 12,
Mason Road, Coventry and that the premises constituted a statutory F
nuisance within the meaning of section 92 (1) (a) of the Public Health Act
1936, namely, the premises were in such a state as to be prejudicial to
health or a nuisance contrary to section 99 of the Public Health Act 1936.

The justices heard the information on May 30 and June 20, 1979, and
found the following facts. On May 2, 1977, the tenant and his family,
comprising his wife and two children, then aged one and two, moved into
premises known as 12, Mason Road, which were owned by the council. G
The property was temporary accommodation for use by a homeless family
and both the council and the tenant accepted that the tenancy was to be
temporary. The premises had been acquired by the council in June 1972
as property affected by highway proposals and used as temporary accommodation ever since. The tenant and his family were moved out of the property
on April 9, 1979, as the council had by that time decided to extend the life H
of the property and to modernise it. On the date the information was laid
the tenant and his family were still residing at 12, Mason Road. Before
the information was heard and determined the tenant and his family had
been moved out to new premises in the ownership of the council. On the
date the information was laid the premises were in a state of disrepair.

It was contended by the council that the relevant date upon which
the tenant must establish the existence of a statutory nuisance was the

A date of the hearing and not the date the information was laid; section 94 (2) of the Public Health Act 1936; that there had been no evidence of the state of the premises at the time of the hearing and in any event the tenant and his family had been moved from the premises before the hearing, thus abating the state of affairs. That meant that it could not be said that any nuisance " exists " at the date of the hearing. Further the words of section 94 (2) were mandatory in that the court " shall " make an order. As the

B tenant no longer resided at the premises there was no order the court could make as the state of affairs was not likely to recur. The correct test was that contained in the speech of Lord Wilberforce in *Salford City Council* v. *McNally* [1976] A.C. 379, 389G, a case relating to proceedings under sections 92 and 99 of the Public Health Act 1936. The council accepted that in proceedings instituted under section 99 of the Public Health Act

C 1936 service of an abatement notice was unnecessary and that the proceedings were of a criminal nature.

It was contended by the tenant that, on the basis of *Reg.* v. *Newham Justices, Ex parte Hunt* [1976] 1 W.L.R. 420, proceedings under section 99 of the Public Health Act 1936 were criminal proceedings. Thus for an offence to be committed the necessary state of affairs must have existed prior to or at the date the information was laid. As in any other criminal

D matter it was not open to the council to avoid conviction by changing the state of affairs between the date of information and the date of hearing, nor could they thereby avoid the ancillary matters which flowed from conviction, namely the liability for compensation and costs. The tenant further contended that it would be correct in law, applying the test put forward by the council, to find on the basis of the evidence that the

E premises constituted a statutory nuisance in that they were prejudicial to health.

The justices were of the opinion that as these were criminal proceedings they should direct their minds to the state of affairs in existence at the date the information was laid. They were further of the opinion that on the evidence they were justified in finding the facts set out above. On those

F facts they considered that at the date the information was laid the property at 12, Mason Road did constitute a statutory nuisance in that it was in such a state as to be prejudicial to health. The continuing dampness, lack of proper ventilation or proper means of heating, risk of organisms and vermin breeding in the crumbling plasterwork, insect life in the area of the skirting boards and the fact that the property was not wind and water tight would be detrimental to the health of any tenant and un-

G doubtedly contributed to the health problems suffered by the tenant and his family. The facts the justices found concerning the property after the date the information was laid, namely, the council's plans for modernisation, were not, in the justices' view, tantamount to defence but factors they could properly take into account when considering the terms of the order.

H There was no evidence before the justices that since the date the information was laid any work had been carried out to abate the nuisance. Hence the justices were of the opinion that the nuisance still existed. They were not persuaded that merely by removing the tenant and his family from the premises was the nuisance abated since it would still be open to the council to relet the property to other tenants before the work they considered necessary had been executed. Accordingly they made a nuisance order directing the council to carry out certain specified works within two

1328

years. The justices imposed no financial penalty on the council and made   A
no order as to compensation. They ordered the council to pay £339·71 by
way of costs to the tenant.

The council appealed. The questions for the opinion of the High Court
were (a) whether the justices were correct as a matter of law in deciding
that the material date for determining whether the premises were in a state
prejudicial to health was the date the information was laid. (b) Whether   B
there was evidence upon which the justices could find as a fact that the
premises were at the relevant date in a state prejudicial to the health of
the tenant. (c) Whether the justices were correct as a matter of law in
making a nuisance order when at the date of the hearing the tenant
ceased to reside in or near the premises. (d) Whether all the terms of the
order the justices made were necessary to abate the nuisance they found
to exist.   C

COVENTRY CITY COUNCIL V. QUINN

CASE STATED by Coventry City justices.

Upon February 22, 1979, an information was preferred by the respondent tenant, Catherine Patricia Quinn, against the appellants, Coventry   D
City Council, that they were the owners/leaseholders of certain premises
at 71, Foleshill Road in the City of Coventry and that the premises
constituted a statutory nuisance within the meaning of section 92 (1) (a)
of the Public Health Act 1936.

The justices heard the information on November 19 and 28 and
December 3, 1979, and found the following facts. The tenant and her
husband and her three children who were then aged four years, two years   E
and 8½ months moved into the premises known as 71, Foleshill Road in
1976. The council were the landlords of the premises. The property
was let to the tenant by the council as temporary accommodation, on
a weekly basis. The state of the property when the tenant took up
residence was of a very sub-standard condition, being in a filthy state,
damp, having crumbling plaster and cracked ceilings as well as a defective   F
roof and unstable rear garden wall, in 1976.

The information was laid on February 22, 1979, and at that time the
tenant and her three children were resident in the premises; her husband
had by that time left her. The tenant had been offered alternative accommodation by the council only a week or two before the commencement of
the hearing of the case (November 19, 1979). She had only moved to   G
alternative accommodation provided by the council on December 2, 1979.
The premises suffered from major defects at the date of the information.
[The case stated then set out the defects in the property and the
contention of the parties and continued.]

The justices were persuaded by the arguments of the tenant with regard   H
to the nature of the proceedings. They were of the opinion that these
were indeed criminal proceedings. Accordingly, they should therefore
ask themselves, " Was the state of the premises such as to be injurious
or likely to cause injury to health at the date alleged in the information,
namely, February 22, 1979? " If the justices were satisfied on the evidence
that a statutory nuisance existed at that date, then they should record a
conviction. Furthermore, only after considering that aspect of the case

A (and of course only if they convicted the council), could they then turn to the question of what order, if any, they should make. In doing that the justices should take into account any evidence adduced as to the state of the premises as at the date of hearing, and its relevance as to the appropriateness of any fine which they had power to impose. In other words, there were two limbs to proceedings brought under section 94: first, the state of affairs existing at the date of the alleged offence recited

B in the information, and secondly, the quasi civil aspect of the case, namely, the terms of the nuisance order, if the principal allegations were proved. In their opinion, an approach along those lines was provided for in section 94 (2), where it said that the powers of the court to make a nuisance order derived from (a) proof that the alleged nuisance existed, or (b) that although abated, it was likely to occur on the same premises; and also

C after having made an order power was afforded to the court to impose a fine not exceeding £200. That approach was underlined by the words of section 99 of the Act as amended by section 42 of the Magistrates' Courts Act 1952, which clearly stamped such proceedings as criminal proceedings, making proof of a statutory nuisance a criminal offence. Again, the justices recognised that the case had been listed for hearing on five previous occasions when it had been adjourned for various reasons. They

D could not overlook the fact that some nine months had elapsed since the information was originally laid and before they started to hear the case. In their opinion that lapse of time should not be allowed to deprive the tenant of her remedy at law, nor afford the council an opportunity to escape the responsibility which Parliament clearly intended landlords should meet.

E   The justices were of the opinion that on the evidence adduced, they were justified in finding that the premises known as 71, Foleshill Road constituted a statutory nuisance within the meaning of section 92 (1) (a) of the Public Health Act 1936 in that they were such as to be injurious or likely to cause injury to health. The defects to the roof, gutterings and flashings, penetrating and rising dampness, rotten windows and perished plaster as well as defects due to condensation and lack of an

F effective damp proof course all contributed to a state which was prejudicial to the health of the tenant and her family as at February 22, 1979.

      The facts the justices found as to the state of the premises at the date of the conclusion of the proceedings led them to make a nuisance order in the terms announced. In making the order the justices took into account all the repairs which the council had executed. The justices did not

G disregard the work carried out by the council since February, but in their view that work was relevant to the terms of the nuisance order and the mitigation of any penalty which the justices could impose, rather than amounting to a defence. (If so much work had been carried out to the premises so that there was no longer any likelihood of causing injury to health then the justices would have declined to make an order under the

H section.)
      The justices were not persuaded that simply by rehousing the tenant and her family did the council escape the ambit of section 92. Nor were they persuaded that simply because the premises were to be used in future for commercial purposes would they cease to be a statutory nuisance because they would continue to be occupied in the condition in which they were found to be. Accordingly, the justices made a nuisance order directing the council to carry out certain work within 12 months from

December 3, 1979. They imposed no financial penalty on the council and   A
made no order as to compensation. They ordered the council to pay £250
by way of costs to the tenant.

The council appealed. The questions for the opinion of the High Court
were (1) whether the justices were correct as a matter of law in deciding
that the premises known as 71, Foleshill Road, Coventry, constituted a
statutory nuisance within the meaning of section 92 of the Public Health
Act 1936, in that they were in such a state to be prejudicial to health at   B
the relevant date. (2) Whether the justices were correct as a matter of law
in deciding that the relevant date for determining whether the premises
were in a state prejudicial to health was the date the information was laid.
(3) Whether there was evidence upon which the justices could find as a
fact the premises were at the date of hearing in a state prejudicial to the
health of the tenant. (4) Whether there was evidence upon which the   C
justices could find as a fact that the statutory nuisance found was likely
to recur. (5) Whether the justices were correct as a matter of law in
making a nuisance order, when at the date of the hearing the tenant and
her family had ceased to reside in and/or near the premises. (6) Whether
the justices were correct as a matter of law in making a nuisance order in
the following terms (i) repair and make good all roofs, gutterings and   D
flashings to the property; (ii) remove all perished and defective plaster
work to walls and ceilings and make good; (iii) carry out all work necessary
to prevent rising damp.

CLARKE V. COVENTRY CITY COUNCIL

CASE STATED by Coventry Crown Court.   E

On February 22, 1979, an information was preferred by the applicant
tenant, Edna May Clarke, against Coventry City Council that they were
the owners/leaseholders of certain premises at 133, Windmill Road in the
City of Coventry, and that the premises constituted a statutory nuisance
within the meaning of section 92 (1) (a) of the Public Health Act 1936
as detailed in a schedule, namely, the premises were in such a state as to   F
be prejudicial to health, contrary to section 99 of the Act.

The justices heard the information on August 22, September 5 and
September 11, 1979, and adjudged that on February 22, 1979, the
premises were prejudicial to health and ordered that the council carry out
certain works at the premises within six months. The justices also ordered
the council to pay the tenant's costs in the sum of £415·80.

The council appealed against the decision and order of the justices   G
and the Crown Court heard the appeal on December 17, 18 and 19, 1979.
The court found the following facts relating to the questions raised by the
tenant in her request for the court to state a case for the consideration of
the Divisional Court. In May 1978 the tenant and her family, consisting
of two children, then aged seven and two moved into the premises known
as 133, Windmill Road, Coventry, which were owned by the council. The   H
tenant gave birth to a third child on May 3, 1979, who had resided at the
premises since that date. The premises were designated by the council as
temporary accommodation to be used by a homeless family or other person
who did not qualify for a regular tenancy and the tenant knew and accepted
that the tenancy of the premises was to be temporary, although no date was
fixed for her departure from the premises. Between May 1978 and February
22, 1979, the tenant made several complaints to the council concerning the

A condition of the premises. The council carried out an inspection of the premises on February 7, 1979, and found them to be in a state of substantial disrepair. As a result of their inspection certain works were carried out to the premises. At the time the information was laid before the justices those works had not been commenced, but they were completed by the date the matter came before the justices in May 1979. The tenant complained that the premises constituted a statutory nuisance at the date when she

B laid the information, namely, February 22, 1979, and also at the date of the hearing before the justices, despite the works that had been carried out by the council.

Prior to the presentation of the evidence the court agreed to hear and determine a preliminary point as to the appropriate date at which it would have to be proved that a statutory nuisance existed for the alleged

C offence to have been committed under the Public Health Act 1936 and for an order to be made under that Act.

For the tenant Mr. King contended that following the decisions in *Reg.* v. *Newham East Justices, Ex parte Hunt; Reg.* v. *Oxted Justices, Ex parte Franklin* [1976] 1 W.L.R. 420 proceedings brought under section 99 of the Act were criminal proceedings. Hence, in this case proceedings

D were commenced by the laying of information and the issue of a summons. Both the summons and information alleged that a criminal offence had taken place and the date of that offence was the day on which the information was laid. *Reg.* v. *Oxted Justices, Ex parte Franklin* stated that it was not necessary for a person taking proceedings under section 99 of the Act to serve an abatement notice before laying information before justices. The matter for the court to decide was not whether the

E council had failed to comply with an abatement notice, but whether "there was a nuisance in existence in fact" (at p. 425). It was argued by the tenant, therefore, that the question was whether at the date of the issue of proceedings there existed in fact a statutory nuisance at 133, Windmill Road, Coventry.

It was further contended by the tenant that, although the law might

F impose a heavy burden on local authorities against whom persons issued proceedings under section 99, such a burden was justified, given the statutory duties and responsibilities of such authorities in relation to housing. It was argued, furthermore, that to reject the tenant's submission as to the appropriate date and to accept as an alternative the date of the hearing before the justices would be in effect to treat the summons as an abatement notice. That would mean that local authorities could escape

G criminal liability by carrying out repairs or rehousing the occupier between the date proceedings were issued and the date of the hearing. That would be contrary to basic principles of the criminal law, as it would be analogous to allowing a burglar to escape criminal liability provided he returned the goods he had stolen before the hearing of his case.

For the council Mr. Taylor referred to the wording of section 94 (2) of

H the Act which stated: "If on the hearing of the complaint it is proved that the alleged nuisance exists . . . the court shall make an order . . ." and submitted that those words clearly stated that the nuisance had to exist at the date of the hearing before the justices to make an order under the section. The council, furthermore, relied upon the judgment in *Northern Ireland Trailers Ltd.* v. *Preston Corporation* [1972] 1 W.L.R. 203 which approved the principle, not in dispute in that case, that it was essential for the complainant to show that the alleged nuisance existed at the date

of the hearing before the justices (at p. 208). It was, therefore, contended **A**
by the council that the appropriate date for the purposes of establishing
whether they should be convicted and whether an order should be made
under section 94 of the Act was the date of the hearing before the justices
and not the date of the issue of proceedings.

Having considered the arguments of Mr. King and Mr. Taylor and
sections 94 to 99 of the Public Health Act 1936, the court was of the
opinion that, although the proceedings were criminal proceedings, the law **B**
and procedure to be applied was that laid down in the Act. The proceedings were different in nature from other criminal proceedings and for
that reason the court was unconvinced by the burglary analogy. The court
were not impressed by the suggestion that local authorities should carry
a heavier burden than a private landlord who was served with an abatement
notice. In the court's view if Parliament had intended that the provisions **C**
of the Public Health Act should have more serious consequences for local
authorities than for private individuals, Parliament would have expressly
made that intention clear in the statute. The court, therefore, determined
that the appropriate date was the date of the hearing before the justices and
that the date of the issue of proceedings was relevant in the present case
only for the purpose of determining whether the council should pay the **D**
tenant's costs and expenses in accordance with section 94 (3). [The case
stated then set out a resume of the evidence and the parties contentions
as to the meaning of " prejudicial to health " in section 92 (1) (a) of the
Act and the definition in section 343. The court then considered the
staircase in the property and the case stated continued:]

The court also dismissed the tenant's allegations concerning other
defects in the repair of the premises, which, she claimed rendered the **E**
premises a statutory nuisance. The court did, however, find that a statutory
nuisance existed at the premises at the date when the information was laid
by the tenant, but that the nuisance had been abated by the council prior
to the hearing of the case before the magistrates' court.

On the question of costs, it was submitted by the tenant that since
the court had found a statutory nuisance to exist at the date of the laying **F**
of the information and issue of proceedings, the court was bound by
section 94 (3) read in conjunction with section 99 of the Act to leave
unaltered the award by the justices of the sum of £415·80, representing
the reasonable expenses incurred by the tenant " in or in connection with
the making of the complaint and the proceedings before the court." The
court, however, was of the opinion that since the council had put in hand,
although not started, the remedial work at, or prior to the time of the **G**
laying of the information and had, moreover, abated the nuisance by the
date of the hearing before the justices, the council should be responsible
only for such of the tenant's expenses as had been incurred before the
matter came before the justices which the court estimated to be £100.

The tenant appealed. The questions of law for the opinion of the
High Court were: (1) Whether the court was correct as a matter of law **H**
in determining that the material date for establishing whether the premises
were prejudicial to health and, therefore, that an offence had been
committed under section 92 (1) (a) of the Public Health Act 1936 was the
date of the hearing before the magistrates' court and not the date of the
laying of information before that court. (2) Whether, having found that a
statutory nuisance existed at the date of the laying of information before
the justices, the court was correct in law in depriving the tenant of the

A   reasonable expenses incurred by her in connection with the hearing before
the magistrates' court and awarded to her by that court under the provisions
of section 94 (3) of the Public Health Act 1936. (3) (a) Whether it was
open to the court to find that the open-sided staircase was not prejudicial
to health within the meaning of the Act. (b) Whether the court was right
to hold that, in the absence of evidence adduced on behalf of the tenant
as to the dimensions, including the height of the rises and steps and the
B   width of the stairs and steps and angles, of the staircase, and in view of
the removal of the handrail of the staircase by the tenant, the tenant had
failed to establish that the staircase was dangerous.

   Keith Simpson for Coventry City Council.
   Stephen Sedley for the tenants.
C
                                                        Cur. adv. vult.

   December 17. HODGSON J. read the first judgment. These three appeals
arise out of litigation between council house tenants and their landlord,
Coventry City Council. Two of them, Doyle and Quinn, are appeals from
decisions of the Coventry City justices who have stated cases; these are
D   brought by the council. The third, Clarke, is an appeal by case stated from
the Coventry Crown Court; this is brought by the tenant from the Crown
Court decision to allow the council's appeal from the adjudication of the
justices. We heard these cases together. They raise questions of some
difficulty and importance.
   The council own a number of houses which are designated as temporary
E   accommodation to be used by homeless families or others who do not
qualify for a regular tenancy. The houses in these cases were short life
property, so that the council was naturally reluctant to spend their scarce
resources upon them. The tenants were members of the Coventry Temporary Tenants Association. Prior to February 22, 1979, each had made
numerous complaints to the council about the condition of their property.
F   On that date all three preferred informations with the justices against the
council under section 99 of the Public Health Act 1936, alleging that the
houses they occupied constituted statutory nuisances within the meaning
of section 92 (1) (*a*) of the Act, namely, that they were in such a state
as to be prejudicial to health.
   The justices heard the informations on the following dates: Doyle on
May 30 and June 20, Clarke on August 22, September 5 and September 11
G   and Quinn on November 19 and December 3. The appeal from the
justices in Clarke's case was heard at the Crown Court on December 17, 18
and 19, 1979.
   The justices found in respect of each house that statutory nuisance
existed at the date of the preferring of the informations, February 22, 1979.
The Doyle family were moved out of their house on April 9, 1979, as the
H   council had decided to extend and modernise their house; at the dates of
the hearing work on the house had begun but was not completed. The
Clarke family was still in occupation at the date of the hearing before the
justices, but the Crown Court found that at that date the nuisance had been
abated. The Quinn family were offered alternative accommodation a week
or two before the date (November 19) fixed for the hearing; they moved
to alternative accommodation on December 2, the day before the third
and final hearing day.

In each case the tenants contended that if they established that a   **A**
statutory nuisance existed at the date the information was laid, then the
justices would have to find that an offence under section 94 had been
committed, whether or not the nuisance had been abated at the date of the
hearing. The council contended that the date upon which the justices had
to find that a nuisance existed was the date of the hearing and that if no
nuisance existed on that date, then the justices could not find that an
offence had been committed, nor make an order unless (and for the purpose   **B**
of these appeals this is not relevant) there was a danger of recurrence.
The only order the court could make, if the nuisance no longer existed at
the date of hearing, was, contended the council, an order as to costs.

Two other questions of law are raised. First, whether, when the
defendant is the council itself, the mandatory provisions as to costs in
section 94 (3) apply or whether the award of costs in such cases is within   **C**
the discretion of the justices. Secondly, whether premises can be prejudicial
to health if there is no one living in them (and, therefore, no actual
prejudice) at the date of hearing. We were also invited to give some
guidance as to the considerations which justices should take into account
in deciding upon the terms of an enforcement order, particularly when
made against the local authority itself.

So far as the first and most important question is concerned, the   **D**
justices' view was that the material date was the date when the information
was preferred; if a statutory nuisance existed at that date, then the council
were guilty of an offence under section 94. In the case that went to appeal
to the Crown Court (Clarke), the Crown Court took the opposite view.

It is with sections 91 to 100 of the Public Health Act 1936 that these
cases are concerned. These sections are primarily concerned with making   **E**
provisions for the local authorities to comply with the duty placed upon
them by section 91: " to cause their district to be inspected from time to
time for the detection of matters requiring to be dealt with ... as being
statutory nuisances."

With the exception of section 99, to which I shall return, the scheme
of this Part of the Act is I think clear. By section 92 (1) it is provided: **F**

> " (1) Without prejudice to the exercise by a local authority of any
> other powers vested in them by or under this Act, the following
> matters may, subject to the provisions of this Part of this Act, be
> dealt with summarily, and are in this Part of this Act referred to as
> ' statutory nuisances ', that is to say: —(a) any premises in such a state
> as to be prejudicial to health or a nuisance; . . ."
>
>   **G**

There then follow a number of other " statutory nuisances " in paragraphs
(b) to (f). The remaining subsections of section 92 are not relevant to
these cases.

Section 93 provides for the service of abatement notices by the local
authority:

> " Where a local authority are satisfied of the existence of a statutory   **H**
> nuisance, they shall serve a notice (hereafter in this Act referred
> to as ' an abatement notice ') on the person by whose act, default or
> sufferance the nuisance arises or continues, or, if that person cannot
> be found, on the owner or occupier of the premises on which the
> nuisance arises, requiring him to abate the nuisance and to execute
> such works and take such steps as may be necessary for that
> purpose: . . ."

A   Section 94 deals with the situation which arises if the abatement notice is not complied with and adds a judicial dimension to the administrative action the local authority is empowered to take under section 93. The section reads:

"(1) If the person on whom an abatement notice has been served makes default in complying with any of the requirements of
B   the notice, or if the nuisance, although abated since the service of the notice, is, in the opinion of the local authority, likely to recur on the same premises, the authority shall cause a complaint to be made to a justice of the peace, and the justice shall thereupon issue a summons requiring the person on whom the notice was served to appear before a court of summary jurisdiction. (2) If on the hearing of the complaint
C   it is proved that the alleged nuisance exists, or that although abated it is likely to recur on the same premises, then, subject to the provisions of subsections (4) and (5) of this section the court shall make an order (hereafter in this Act referred to as 'a nuisance order') for either, or both, of the following purposes—(a) requiring the defendant to comply with all or any of the requirements of the abatement notice, or otherwise to abate the nuisance, within a time specified in the
D   order, and to execute any works necessary for that purpose; (b) prohibiting a recurrence of the nuisance, and requiring the defendant, within a time specified in the order, to execute any works necessary to prevent a recurrence; and may also impose on the defendant a fine not exceeding £5."—That was in 1937; it has now been increased to £200—" Where a nuisance proved to exist is such as to render a building, in the opinion of the court, unfit for human habitation, the
E   nuisance order may prohibit the use of the building for that purpose until a court of summary jurisdiction, being satisfied that it has been rendered fit for human habitation, withdraws the prohibition. (3) Where on the hearing of a complaint under this section it is proved that the alleged nuisance existed at the date of the service of the abatement notice and that at the date of the making of the complaint it either
F   still existed or was likely to recur, then, whether or not at the date of hearing it still exists or is likely to recur, the court shall order the defendant to pay to the local authority such reasonable sum as the court may determine in respect of the expenses incurred by the authority in, or in connection with, the making of the complaint and the proceedings before the court."

G   There is no doubt that section 94 creates an offence: see *Northern Ireland Trailers Ltd.* v. *Preston Corporation* [1972] 1 W.L.R. 203. Therefore, proceedings are properly begun by information, although the Act provides for the institution of proceedings by complaint: section 42 of the Magistrates' Courts Act 1952. It is, however, the tenants' contention that it is section 94 (1) and not section 94 (2) which is the offence creating
H   subsection.

Section 95 provides for penalties for failure to comply with a nuisance order and empowers the local authority to abate a nuisance itself where a nuisance order has not been obeyed, and section 96 provides for the recovery by the local authority of its expenses in abating or preventing the recurrence of a nuisance. Sections 97 and 98 are not relevant to these cases.

Section 99 provides:

> " Complaint of the existence of a statutory nuisance under this Act
> may be made to a justice of the peace by any person aggrieved by
> the nuisance, and thereupon the like proceedings shall be had, with
> the like incidents and consequences as to the making of orders,
> penalties for disobedience of orders and otherwise, as in the case of a
> complaint by the local authority, but any order made in such
> proceedings may, if the court after giving the local authority an
> opportunity of being heard thinks fit, direct the authority to abate
> the nuisance."

It was held in *Rex* v. *Epping (Waltham Abbey) Justices, Ex parte
Burlinson* [1948] 1 K.B. 79 that under this section a local authority may
be made a defendant. When one comes to look carefully at the interaction
between this section and the other sections in this Part of the Act one is
led to suspect that this decision probably came as a surprise to the draftsman. It was under this subsection that the tenants laid informations against
the council.

The submissions made on behalf of the tenants are succintly set out
in the case stated by the Crown Court. For the tenant it was contended
that, following the decisions in *Reg.* v. *Newham East Justices, Ex parte
Hunt; Reg.* v. *Oxted Justices, Ex parte Franklin* [1976] 1 W.L.R. 420,
proceedings brought under section 99 of the Act were criminal proceedings.
Hence, in this case, proceedings were commenced by the laying of
information and the issue of a summons. Both the summons and information alleged that a criminal offence had taken place and the date of
this offence was the day on which the information was laid. *Reg.* v. *Oxted
Justices, Ex parte Franklin* stated that it was not necessary for a person
taking proceedings under section 99 of the Act to serve an abatement
notice before laying information before justices. The matter for the court
to decide was not whether the respondents had failed to comply with an
abatement notice, but whether " there was a nuisance in existence in fact ":
at p. 425. It was argued by the tenant, therefore, that the question in this
case was whether at the date of the issue of proceedings there existed in
fact a statutory nuisance at the house which he occupied.

It was further contended by the tenant that, although the law might
impose a heavy burden on local authorities against whom persons issued
proceedings under section 99, such a burden was justified, given the
statutory duties and responsibilities of such authorities in relation to
housing. It was argued, furthermore, that to reject the tenant's submission
as to the appropriate date and to accept as alternative the date of the
hearing before the justices would be in effect to treat the summons as an
abatement notice. This would mean that local authorities could escape
criminal liability by carrying out repairs or rehousing the occupier between
the date proceedings were issued and the date of the hearing. This would
be analogous to allowing a burglar to escape criminal liability provided
he returned the goods he had stolen before the hearing of his case.

That, I think, also fairly summarises the submissions made to us on
behalf of the tenants by Mr. Sedley. He further pointed out that, if his
argument was rejected, it would mean that a local authority would be
able, by delaying the hearing as much as possible, to give itself more
time to escape liability.

For the council, Mr. Simpson relied upon the wording of section 94 (2)

A and submitted that the plain meaning is that the nuisance must exist at the date of the hearing before the justices and that unless it does exist or, being temporarily abated, is likely to recur, the justices can neither make an order nor impose a fine.

In *Northern Ireland Trailers Ltd.* v. *Preston Corporation* [1972] 1 W.L.R. 203 the question was whether quarter sessions, when hearing an appeal from justices, had to have regard to the situation as it was at the
B date of the hearing before justices or the date they heard the appeal. The court held that the relevant date was the date of the hearing before the justices. In dealing with this part of the case Lord Widgery C.J. said, at p. 208:

"The second point...arises in this way. There had...been a substantial interval of time between the date when the justices made
C the nuisance order... and the date when quarter sessions considered the appeal.... It was not disputed below or before us that when the matter was before the magistrates court it was essential for the complainant to show that the alleged nuisance still existed at that time. The phrase in section 94 (2) is: 'If on the hearing of the complaint it is proved that the alleged nuisance exists' and, accordingly, when
D the matter was before the magistrates' court, proof was directed to the existence of the nuisance at that date."

The same point arose in *Lambeth London Borough Council* v. *Stubbs* (1980) 78 L.G.R. 650. In that case the tenant was in occupation at the date of the hearing before the justices but had been rehoused by the time the appeal was heard. At that date the house was no longer occupied. The
E court decided that the mere fact that the house was empty did not mean that the nuisance had been abated (as to this aspect of the case I shall have to return) but, in giving judgment, Stephen Brown J. used these words, at p. 659:

"The specific ground of appeal which might have resulted, if successful, in the nuisance order being quashed related to the time at which
F the nuisance was alleged to have existed. I think it is clear from the decision in *Northern Ireland Trailers Ltd.* v. *Preston Corporation* [1972] 1 W.L.R. 203 that the relevant date is the date of the information. Accordingly the Crown Court was bound to consider the state of affairs at that date. Of course it was open to it to act upon, and indeed it did act upon, the changed circumstances which had occurred since the original hearing before the justices."
G

The reference to the *Northern Ireland Trailers* case, the fact that it had not been contended that the relevant date was the preferring of the information and the reference at the end of the sentence to the "original hearing before the justices" convinces me that the reference to "the date of the information" was an understandable slip of the tongue and that
H what the judge meant was "the date of the hearing of the information."

I find it a strange argument that the words in an offence creating statute should be construed in a way which is not their natural meaning so as to enlarge the ambit of the offence. In their plain and ordinary meaning the words of section 94 (2) say that the relevant date for the justices to consider is the date of the hearing before them. In the usual case where it is the local authority which is bringing the proceedings there is not the slightest difficulty involved in giving them their natural meaning and the

fact that section 99 was badly drafted does not in my judgment warrant   A
giving the words in section 94 the strained meaning for which the tenants
contend.

I am fortified in my view by the provisions of section 94 (3) which make
an award of expenses to the local authority mandatory in cases where the
nuisance has been abated at the date of hearing. If the relevant date were
the date of the information, no such provision would be necessary. I think
it is clear that it was just because the draftsman realised that if the   B
nuisance was abated at the time of the hearing the justices could make
no order nor convict of any offence that this provision for payment of the
council's costs was included.

I have no hesitation in finding that the relevant date is the date of
the hearing before the justices. It is true that section 99 makes no
provision for the prior service of an abatement notice and that, therefore,   C
its provisions do not fit neatly into the principal scheme, but this does not
seem to me in any way to warrant the forced construction of the plain
words of sections 93 and 94 for which Mr. Sedley contends.

The second question we are asked to consider is whether, where the
council is defendant, the mandatory provision as to costs in section 94 (3)
applies. Section 94 (3) in terms refers to an order that " the defendant to   D
pay to the local authority such reasonable sum as the court may determine
in respect of the expenses incurred by the authority." Section 99 refers to
" the like proceedings " with the like incidents and consequences as to the
making of orders, penalties for disobedience of orders and otherwise, as in
the case of a complaint by the local authority. Obviously these two provisions cannot sensibly be read together. The position contemplated by
section 94 (3) is, as I have pointed out, one where, because the nuisance   E
has been abated at the date of hearing, there is no order or conviction
upon which the justices could hang an order for costs. I think section 99
was intended to put " any person aggrieved " in as nearly as possible the
same position as the local authority when the authority brings proceedings,
and accordingly, I would hold that the mandatory provisions as to payment
of expenses applies to " a person aggrieved " who establishes that at the
date of the information the nuisance (since abated) existed.   F

The last question, whether the premises can be prejudicial to health
if there is no one living in them and, therefore, no actual prejudice to
health at the time of the hearing, arose for consideration in *Lambeth
London Borough Council* v. *Stubbs*, 78 L.G.R. 650, to which I have
referred. In that case at the relevant date, which was the hearing of the
Crown Court appeal, the house was no longer occupied by anyone (it was,   G
in fact, within four months of the hearing demolished). Nevertheless, no
order had been made under section 94 (2) prohibiting the use of the
house for human habitation. Waller L.J. in his judgment said that
" theoretically," therefore, it was possible for the house to be re-let,
though of course it is not suggested that Lambeth London Borough
Council, as a responsible authority, would have done such a thing. But the   H
theoretical position was that it would have been a possibility. Waller L.J.
continued, at p. 656:

> " We have been referred to a number of cases dealing with the various
> problems that have arisen under these sections. As I see it, on that
> very first submission that Mr. Keane has made, it is not a question of
> authority, but a question of the words of the section. Mr. Altaras on
> behalf of the complainants has submitted that there are two sides to the

A   problem which preserve the position of the local authority in a case of this sort without any of the extreme results for which Mr. Keane was contending.

" In my opinion it is not sufficient to say that a nuisance has been abated because the dwelling house has been vacated. Mr. Altaras submits that the whole purport of these sections is to order work to be done; and the words of section 93, which I have already quoted,
B   ' requiring [the owner] to abate the nuisance and to execute such works and to take such steps as may be necessary for that purpose ' indicate that that is the purpose of these provisions. As it seems to me the original finding was that the premises were in such a state as to be prejudicial to health, and if the tenants are removed, nothing has been done to alter the state of the premises.
C   They remain prejudicial to health even if nobody goes and lives in those premises. I should quote one other subsection in dealing with the question of ' prejudicial to health,' because ' prejudicial to health ' is defined in section 343 as meaning ' injurious, or likely to cause injury, to health.' All that is being done by removing the tenants from the house is to reduce the likelihood of injury, but at any time if anybody went back into the house, the likelihood of injury would
D   increase and there would be somebody whose health would be likely to be prejudiced by the state of the house. As it seems to me, in order to abate the statutory nuisance, something must be done to the house. So I would be against Mr. Keane's main submission. Prohibiting occupation simply avoids actual injury to health, the danger remains, and therefore, the nuisance is not affected."

E
In that case it seems that the house, though empty, had had nothing done to it, and the case is clear authority for the proposition that in those circumstances the nuisance has not been abated. If the case ever arises where a house has been effectively rendered incapable of being occupied, e.g. having all services permanently cut off and being boarded up prior to eventual demolition, I think different considerations might apply. But that
F   is not the situation in any of these cases.

As to the considerations which should influence justices in making orders under the Act, I do not think I can do better than refer to the words of Lord Widgery C.J. in *Nottingham City District Council* v. *Newton* [1974] 1 W.L.R. 923. That was a case where there were difficulties as to the precise order which should be made when the final disposition of the
G   house under a clearance order had not been decided at the time of the hearing by the court. Lord Widgery C.J. after referring to the wide discretion in the court as to the order that they made, said, at p. 930:

" In deciding within that wide ambit of detailed discretion just what the terms of the nuisance order should be, I have no doubt it is the duty of the justices, as common sense dictates, to look at the whole
H   circumstances of the case and to try and make an order which is in its terms sensible and just having regard to the entire prevailing situation. They were wrong in my judgment in closing their eyes to the Housing Act proceedings and the imminence of demolition, and had they had regard to those factors as well as all the other relevant factors, it may be that they would have provided for the nuisance to be abated by perhaps March 1974 so that if the demolition proceedings had taken effect meanwhile, the danger of money being spent on the house

1340

abortively in view of the subsequent demolition would be avoided. I   A
think the justices were very nearly right in this case, but I conclude
that they were wrong in restricting the factors to which they had
regard, and I think this appeal should be allowed to the extent that
the case should be sent back to the justices asking them to reconsider
their decision in the light of the discretion within the precise terms of
section 94 (2) and in the light of all the prevailing circumstances, and   B
endeavour to come to what seems to them to be a sensible and just
conclusion."

As Waller L.J. said of this passage in the *Lambeth* case, 78 L.G.R.
650, 657:

"Lord Widgery C.J. was stressing at the beginning of that passage
what common sense dictates. He was stressing the justices should   C
have in mind a decision which will avoid the possibility of public
money being wasted because of the subsequent demolition and saying
that the conclusion should be a sensible and just one."

I now turn to answer the specific questions we are asked in each of
these cases:

                                                                            D

Doyle

(a) The justices were not correct as a matter of law in deciding that
the material date for determining whether the said premises were in a
state prejudicial to health was the date the information was laid.

(b) There was evidence upon which the justices could find as a fact
that the premises were at the date of hearing prejudicial to health (though   E
not to the health of the respondent). At the date of the hearing although
the council intended to modernise the premises, no work had been
begun and, on the authority of the *Lambeth* case, the nuisance, had,
therefore, not been abated although the house was unoccupied.

(c) The justices were, as a matter of law (though for the wrong reason),
correct in making a nuisance order when at the date of the hearing the
respondent ceased to reside in (or near) the premises.   F

(d) The terms of the order made follows the terms of the specification
of work which the local authority said they were actually going to do.
No injustice, therefore, resulted, but as a matter of law it was incorrect,
since some of the work was not necessary for the purpose of abating the
nuisance. If justices feel that they are in some difficulty in proposing or
approving a detailed specification, they can make an order in terms of   G
section 94 requiring the defendant "to execute such works as may be
necessary to abate (or prevent a recurrence of) the nuisance consisting of
(describe the nuisance, e.g. defective roof allowing entry to water, rising
damp etc.)"

Clarke   H

1. The Crown Court was correct as a matter of law in determining that
the material date for establishing whether the premises were prejudicial
to health was the date of the hearing before the magistrates' court and not
the date of the laying of the information before that court.

2. Having found that a statutory nuisance existed at the date of the
laying of the information before the justices, the Crown Court was wrong
in law in depriving the applicant tenant of the reasonable expenses

A incurred by her in connection with the hearing before the magistrates' court and awarded to her by that court under the provisions of section 94 (3) of the Public Health Act 1936.

3 (a) and (b). These questions (which dealt with an open sided staircase) we were not asked to answer.

B *Quinn*

1. and 2. The justices were not correct, as a matter of law, in deciding that the relevant date for determining whether the premises were in a state prejudicial to health, was the date the information was laid, but, as the premises were still in a defective condition and prejudicial to health at the conclusion of the proceedings, the justices were correct as a matter of law

C in deciding that the premises constituted a statutory nuisance within the meaning of section 92 of the Public Health Act 1936, despite the fact that the premises were no longer occupied.

3. There was evidence upon which the justices could so find.

4. Not applicable.

5. The justices were correct in making a nuisance order although at the date of hearing the tenant and her family no longer occupied the

D premises (which were not occupied by anyone).

6. The justices were correct as a matter of law in making the nuisance order they did.

DONALDSON L.J. I agree.

E   *Costs to be paid out of central funds.*
                                          Certificate that point of law of general
                                          public importance involved, namely,
                                          " Whether on a prosecution under sec-
                                          tions 94 and 99 of the Public Health Act
                                          1936 the date at which the existence of a
                                          statutory nuisance must be proved in
F   *order to justify a finding of guilt is the*
                                          date to which the information relates or
                                          the date of the hearing."
                                          Leave to appeal refused.

Solicitors: *Andrew H. Pitts, Coventry City Council*; *Michael J. King,*
G *Leamington Spa.*

[Reported by LEO PILKINGTON, Esq., Barrister-at-Law]

H

A

[COURT OF APPEAL]

* PATEL (MAHENDRAKUMAR) AND ANOTHER v. PATEL (BHARAT)

1981 July 8   Ormrod and O'Connor L.JJ.
                                                              and Sheldon J.

B

*Landlord and Tenant—Rent restriction—Personal occupation—
Personal representatives letting house held on trust for infant
beneficiaries—Personal representatives seeking possession for
occupation with beneficiaries—Whether " landlord " for purposes of application for possession—Rent Act 1977 (c. 42),
s. 98 (1) (b), Sch. 15, Case 9*[1]

C

The plaintiffs were the joint administrators of the estate
of a deceased husband and wife which they held on trust for
the deceased's two infant children. The plaintiffs subsequently
adopted the two children. The plaintiffs granted to the defendant a one-year tenancy of a house which formed part of the
estate. Following the expiry of the tenancy the defendant held
over as a statutory tenant. The plaintiffs instituted proceedings
in the county court for possession of the premises claiming,   D
under Case 9 of Schedule 15 to the Rent Act 1977, that they
as landlords required the premises for occupation as a residence for themselves. The judge, having found that the plaintiffs reasonably required the property for themselves and that
it would be reasonable to make an order for possession, held
that they were not the landlords for the purposes of Case 9
of Schedule 15 as they were personal representatives having no
beneficial interest in the property. He dismissed the claim.   E
On appeal by the plaintiffs : —
Held, allowing the appeal, that although a personal representative, having no beneficial interest in the property could
not usually claim possession of premises under Case 9 of
Schedule 15 because it would be in breach of trust to use the
property for his own purposes, " landlord " in Case 9 had its
normal meaning; that, since the plaintiffs were the legal   F
owners of the property and had let them to the defendant,
they were the landlords and, since they would not be in breach
of trust if they occupied the premises with the infant beneficiaries and they had proved the other requirements of Case
9, they were entitled to an order for possession (post, pp. 1346G
—1347B, H—1348A, D–E, H—1349A, C–D).
Harrison v. *Hopkins* [1950] 1 K.B. 124, C.A.

G

The following cases are referred to in the judgments:

Baker v. *Lewis* [1947] K.B. 186; [1946] 2 All E.R. 592, C.A.
Harrison v. *Hopkins* [1950] 1 K.B. 124; [1949] 2 All E.R. 597, C.A.
Parker v. *Rosenberg* [1947] K.B. 371; [1947] 1 All E.R. 87, C.A.
Sharpe v. *Nicholls* [1945] K.B. 382; [1945] 2 All E.R. 55, C.A.
Smith v. *Penny* [1947] K.B. 230; [1946] 2 All E.R. 672, C.A.
Stratford v. *Syrett* [1958] 1 Q.B. 107; [1957] 3 W.L.R. 733; [1957] 3 All   H
        E.R. 363, C.A.

[1] Rent Act 1977, s. 98: " (1) Subject to this Part of this Act, a court shall not
make an order for possession of a dwelling-house which is for the time being let
on a protected tenancy or subject to a statutory tenancy unless the court considers
it reasonable to make such an order and . . . (b) the circumstances are as specified
in any of the Cases in Part I of Schedule 15 to this Act."
Sch. 15, Case 9: see post, p. 1344c.

A   The following additional cases were cited in argument:

Farrell v. *Alexander* [1977] A.C. 59; [1976] 3 W.L.R. 145; [1976] 2 All
    E.R. 721, H.L.(E.).
Lawrance v. *Hartwell* [1946] K.B. 553; [1946] 2 All E.R. 257, C.A.

APPEAL from Judge Tumin sitting at Willesden County Court.

In December 1977, Mr. and Mrs. H. M. Patel, who owned 9, Garratt
B   Road, Edgware, were killed in an accident. The plaintiffs, Mahendrakumar
Patel and Itadevi Patel, were respectively the brother and sister-in-law of
Mr. H. M. Patel. On July 7, 1978, the plaintiffs were appointed guardians
of the two infant children of the deceased. Letters of administration to
the estate of the deceased were obtained on April 26 and 27, 1979,
respectively. On March 25, 1980, the plaintiffs adopted the two infant
C   children of the deceased. On June 18, 1979, the plaintiffs granted to the
defendant, Bharat Patel, a one-year tenancy of 9, Garrett Road. That
tenancy expired and the defendant held over as a statutory tenant. The
plaintiffs claimed possession of the premises under Case 9 of Schedule 15
to the Rent Act 1977 stating that they reasonably required the premises
for their occupation. On October 31, 1980, Judge Tumin dismissed the
plaintiffs' claim for possession.
D
By notice of appeal dated December 8, 1980, the plaintiffs appealed on
the grounds (1) that the judge erred in law in holding that the plaintiffs
were not " landlords " within the meaning of Case 9 of Schedule 15 to the
Rent Act 1977 when they were the owners of the legal estate immediately
in reversion on the defendant's statutory tenancy; (2) the judge erred in
law in failing to apply the definition of " landlord " in section 152 of the
E   Rent Act 1977 to the provisions of Case 9 and to the facts found by him;
(3) the judge erred in law in holding that the plaintiffs were not the
defendant's landlords for the purposes of Case 9 even though they had
granted the defendant the tenancy of 9, Garratt Road; (4) the judge erred
in law in holding that the plaintiffs did not satisfy the requirements of
Case 9 even though the plaintiffs required 9, Garratt Road for occupation
as a residence for themselves and for their two adopted children and the
F   plaintiffs owned all the legal interest, and the two adopted children owned
all the beneficial interest, immediately in reversion on the defendant's
statutory tenancy.

By a respondent's notice dated December 23, 1980, the defendant
sought to affirm the decision on the following additional ground, namely,
that the plaintiffs failed to serve a valid or any notice terminating the
G   contractual periodic tenancy arising by virtue of a verbal agreement entered
into between the plaintiffs and the defendant in March 1980 before
instituting proceedings to claim possession of 9, Garratt Road.

The facts are stated in the judgment of O'Connor L.J.

Paul Morgan for the plaintiffs.
H   The defendant in person.

O'CONNOR L.J. delivered the first judgment. This is an appeal by the
plaintiffs from an order of Judge Tumin, sitting in Willesden County
Court, refusing their claim for the possession of premises at 9, Garratt
Road, Edgware.

The facts giving rise to this case are tragic and simple. In December
1977, Mr. and Mrs. H. M. Patel, the brother and sister-in-law of the first

1344

plaintiff, were killed in a motor car accident. They left two small children,　A
then aged five and three. They were the joint owners of 9, Garratt Road.
The plaintiffs became guardians to the two children in July 1978. They
became administrators of the estates of both the deceased in April 1979
and in March 1980 they adopted the two children, who are now aged
eight and five. By an agreement in writing, dated June 18, 1979, they let
9, Garratt Road to the defendant (who is not a relative, although he has
the same surname) for one year from April 1, 1979, until March 30, 1980.　B
That agreement expired by effluxion of time and, subject to a matter I will
deal with under the respondent's notice, the defendant held over as a
statutory tenant, as he was entitled to do. Thus it was that the plaintiffs
brought these proceedings for possession of the premises, founding themselves on Case 9 of Schedule 15 to the Rent Act 1977. That provision
reads so far as is material: " Where the dwelling-house is reasonably　C
required by the landlord for occupation as a residence for—(a) himself . . ."
the court may make an order for possession. That provision appears in the
Act of 1977, which is a consolidating statute, effectively re-enacting paragraph (h) in Schedule 1 under section 3 of the Rent and Mortgage Interest
Restrictions (Amendment) Act 1933.

In an admirable and careful judgment the judge directed himself that　D
the issues in the case were:

" (1) Are the plaintiffs landlords for the purposes of Case 9? If they
are not, that is the end of the plaintiffs' case.   (2) If the plaintiffs are
landlords for Case 9, have the plaintiffs established that they reasonably require the property for themselves?   (3) If the plaintiffs reasonably require the property for themselves, has the defendant established
greater hardship?   (4) Is it reasonable to order possession? "　E

First of all the judge considered the last three topics and he found in
favour of the plaintiffs on all three heads.

The defendant, who has appeared in person (and, if I might say, has
conducted his case quite admirably) does not seek to challenge the findings
under (2), (3) and (4) to which I have referred.

In answer to the first question the judge, holding himself bound by the　F
authority of two cases in this court, found against the plaintiffs, and it is
against that that the appeal is brought.

Having looked at the cases I, for my part, have concluded that the
judge did not ask himself the right question. Question (1) should have
stopped at, " Are the plaintiffs the landlords of the premises? "

The reason why he asked the question as he did is undoubtedly due to　G
the way in which the two cases upon which he founded himself, namely,
Sharpe v. Nicholls [1945] K.B. 382 and Parker v. Rosenberg [1947] K.B.
371, have been dealt with in the textbooks. The proposition has found
favour with the textbook writers from those cases that personal representatives cannot be landlords unless they have a beneficial interest in the
premises. As I propose to show, in my judgment, that is not what the　H
cases decide. The question which should be asked is, " Are the plaintiffs
landlords?," and the next question should be, " Have they established that
they reasonably require the premises for themselves? "

Let me get two matters out of the way before I look at the authorities.
The provision in Case 9 that the landlord reasonably requires the dwelling
house for occupation as a resident for himself, " himself " includes his
spouse and children: see Smith v. Penny [1947] K.B. 230.   Secondly,

A " landlord " is to be interpreted, where there are joint owners, as " landlords ": see *Baker* v. *Lewis* [1947] K.B. 186.

Sharpe v. *Nicholls* and *Parker* v. *Rosenberg* are most conveniently
considered in a later decision of this court, *Harrison* v. *Hopkins* [1950] 1
K.B. 124. That case was concerned as to whether a personal representative
tenant was a tenant for the purposes of the Increase of Rent and Mortgage
Interest (Restrictions) Act 1920. Cohen L.J. dealt in his judgment with
B the problems raised by *Sharpe* v. *Nicholls* and *Parker* v. *Rosenberg*. His
judgment sufficiently sets out the facts of the case and I shall read an
extract from it. At p. 132, he said that in those two cases, *Sharpe* v.
Nicholls and *Parker* v. *Rosenberg*:

"... this court had to consider the rights of a landlord to possession.
The question in each case, however, arose not under section 12 (1) (*f*)
C of the Act of 1920, but under section 3 of the Rent and Mortgage
Interest Restrictions (Amendment) Act 1933, and paragraph (*h*) of
Schedule 1 thereto. In the first case proceedings were commenced
by the widow and nephew of the deceased landlord as personal
representatives to recover possession of premises within the Rent
Restrictions Acts for the occupation of the widow. There was no
D evidence to prove that the widow had any beneficial interest in the
estate of the deceased landlord. The actual decision in the case did not
turn on whether personal representatives were landlords within the
meaning of paragraph (*h*), but Morton L.J., expressed an opinion on the
point [1945] K.B. 382, 389, saying: 'The plaintiffs' whole case, as I
have shown from their pleadings, is based upon the allegation that they
were the owners as personal representatives. I cannot find any admis-
E sion at the trial in any shape or form that the widow had any beneficial interest in the house. I do not know in the least who was
entitled to the house. For all I know, Mr. Sharpe may have made a
will leaving it to a nephew or to any other person. In those circumstances, one must consider whether it can be said that the " dwelling-
house is reasonably required by the landlord for occupation as a
F residence for himself or herself," when the plaintiffs are legal personal
representatives suing in that capacity and one of them wants to live
in the house. In my opinion, such a case is not within the terms of
paragraph (*h*) of Schedule 1 at all. Strange results would follow if
that were not so. For instance, you might have four legal personal
representatives, none of whom was related to the testator at all, and
one of them might require the house as a residence for himself or
G herself, having no beneficial interest whatsoever in the property. I am
clearly of opinion that such a case could not possibly be within the
terms of paragraph (*h*). It is also to be observed that the words
" himself or any son or daughter of his ... or his father or mother "
seem to refer to a person who is the landlord not in the sense that he
or she is one of several personal representatives, but in the sense that
H he or she is the sole owner of the property subject to the tenancy.
It seems to me, therefore, that the plaintiffs entirely failed to prove
that they came within paragraph (*h*), and that if they failed to prove
that they came within paragraph (*h*) the words of section 3 of the
Act absolutely precluded the county court judge, and would preclude
this court, from making any order for the recovery of possession.'

" These observations were obiter; but in the second case, that of
Parker v. *Rosenberg* [1947] K.B. 371, they were approved and applied

to a case where legal personal representatives were seeking to recover   A
possession of premises for the occupation of a sister of the testatrix who
was the tenant for life under her will.   Tucker L.J. said, at p. 376: ' It
is clear that neither the definition section of the Act of 1920 nor paragraph (h) of Schedule 1 to the Act of 1933 confer on anyone any right
to an order for possession which he does not otherwise possess. Paragraph (h) is designed to relax in certain cases the previously imposed
statutory restrictions on the right of recovery. In the present case   B
Miss Marsh, apart from the Rent Restrictions Acts, would not have
been entitled to sue in ejectment. She was not a party to the lease
and was not entitled to the reversion. There is nothing in paragraph
(h) of Schedule 1 to the Act of 1933, enabling her to sue or be added
as a plaintiff. As the proper plaintiffs, the trustees, cannot bring
themselves within paragraph (h) and Miss Marsh cannot herself sue,   C
it follows that no order for possession could properly be made in the
present case.'
    " Those decisions lend some colour to Mr. Stabb's argument, but I
would observe that the question in each case before the court was
not as to the meaning of the expression ' landlord ' in the abstract, but
as to the right of the landlord to possession under paragraph (h) of
Schedule 1 to the Act of 1933, and the landlord had therefore to   D
prove not only that he was a landlord but also that he required the
premises for his own occupation, and that greater hardship would be
involved in refusing him possession than in depriving the tenant
of possession, a burden which plainly an executor or administrator
without a beneficial interest in the property would be unable to
discharge. These considerations are not expressly mentioned in the   E
judgments in the cases cited, but they afford a means of reconciling
them with the earlier opinion expressed by Morton L.J. in Lawrance
v. Hartwell [1946] K.B. 553."

It will be seen that, in considering these cases, Cohen L.J. was saying, in
my judgment, correctly, that they are not decisions construing " landlord "
in the abstract. The real reason why it would not be reasonable to make   F
an order in favour of personal representatives who are landlords is because,
in the ordinary course of events, if they claimed possession for their own
occupation, they would be acting in breach of trust. This proposition will
be found in the same case in the judgment of Asquith L.J., where he said,
at p. 135:

    " Further, it is contended, that, on the alternative view, a personal   G
    representative who is a trustee would necessarily, in circumstances
    such as those of the present case, make a profit out of his trust."

    In my view, the true ratio of those cases is that a personal representa-
tive normally cannot claim relief under Case 9, as it now is, because, in
so doing, he would be acting in breach of trust. This is a wholly exceptional case. In the present case the plaintiffs, under the terms of the agree-   H
ment, are quite plainly the landlords of 9, Garratt Road, and, in my
judgment, the defendant is not entitled to challenge that status. There is
nothing in the Act of 1977 which says that personal representatives cannot be landlords. Indeed, section 152 leads one to the contrary conclusion as one would expect. As landlords they are personal representatives
in this case and they are trustees for the two children. In the present case,
in considering whether it is reasonable to make the order on that particular

A ground, they are not acting in breach of trust in seeking to live in the premises with the children.   The children are the beneficial owners of the premises and those exceptional circumstances take this case out of the decisions in *Sharpe* v. *Nicholls* [1945] K.B. 382 and *Parker* v. *Rosenberg* [1947] K.B. 371.

In my judgment, the judge understandably fell into error in considering that he was bound by those decisions to find against the plaintiffs. On the
B main ground of the appeal, therefore, I am satisfied that these plaintiffs were entitled to rely on the provisions of Case 9 and, as all the other requirements were found in their favour, unless there is anything in the respondent's notice I would set aside the judgment and order possession of the premises.

The defendant has submitted in his respondent's notice that the judge
C found facts from which we should infer that he had a further contractual tenancy which had never been determined. It was his case that, in March 1980, just before the written agreement expired by effluxion of time, he agreed with the first plaintiff that he should stay on in the house indefinitely at the same rent. The judge dealt with that proposition in his judgment in this way:

D   " I find that the facts as to what happened in March and April 1980
       do not require a complete finding. The first plaintiff did give an
       indication that the defendant would not be required to move out at
       once. The first plaintiff's recollection is that he went to America on
       business and does not recall seeing the defendant. I also find that at
       some time about then, there was some mention made of the defendant
       buying the premises and of the premises being sold. It took some time
E   for the first plaintiff to make up his mind and discuss it with his family.
       These matters do not affect the first plaintiff's evidence."

In the evidence it is quite plain that the defendant said he went to see the first plaintiff on Sunday, March 30, 1980, and gave him a cheque for £150 for the next month of tenancy and that it was accepted by the first
F plaintiff. The first plaintiff, in his evidence—and the judge held that he was an honest witness and that he accepted his evidence—said that, on the morning of March 30, he left for the United States of America by air, that he never saw the defendant, and never received any cheque. The fact is that the plaintiffs' solicitors sent a cheque dated March 31, 1980, back to the defendant in a letter early in April 1980.   The evidence does not show as to how that cheque came into their possession: it may be that
G it was put through the letter box by the defendant, because he lives within a short distance of the plaintiffs' address at 1, Deansbrook Road.

For my part I can see no reason for inferring that the judge found any facts from which it is possible for this court to say that the defendant had acquired a contractual tenancy by agreement with the first plaintiff by tendering rent and its acceptance, and I would not hold that he is able
H to get that submission on its feet. For these reasons I would allow this appeal and order that the plaintiffs have possession of the house.

SHELDON J. I agree that the appeal should be allowed and that the defendant's contentions in the respondent's notice should be dismissed. The plaintiffs let these premises to the defendant. They created the tenancy agreement. Whatever their title, and even if at the time they had none, by general principles, using the words in their ordinary meaning, as

between themselves and the defendant, they became his landlord. The A
judge, after careful examination of all the relevant facts, found that they
reasonably required the premises for occupation as a residence for themselves and their family. He also decided that the defendant had not
succeeded on the issue of greater hardship and held that it was reasonable to make an order for possession. At first glance, therefore, it is
difficult to understand why such an order should have been refused.

The mistake made by the judge, and the error into which he fell, B
resulted, in my opinion, from a misunderstanding of the real basis on
which *Sharpe* v. *Nicholls* [1945] K.B. 382 and *Parker* v. *Rosenberg* [1947]
K.B. 371 were decided. Nor was such a misunderstanding inexcusable,
having regard to some of the observations made in the course of the
judgments in question. Thus, in *Parker* v. *Rosenberg* Tucker L.J. stated
at p. 376 in terms that the earlier case had decided that:　　　　　　　C

" personal representatives having no beneficial interest in the dwelling-
house in question cannot avail themselves of the provisions of
paragraph (*h*) of Schedule 1 to the Act of 1933."

In other words, that they could not claim possession of the dwelling
house on the grounds that it was " reasonably required by the landlord . . .
for occupation as a residence for himself."　　　　　　　　　　　D

Factually in those cases, although *Sharpe* v. *Nicholls* [1945] K.B. 382
was a case which was sent back to the county court to be re-heard, that
may have been so. It may be that in most such cases the result would be the
same—but, in my opinion, Tucker L.J.'s observation is not properly to be
understood as stating a proposition of law. In my view it is not correct
to say as a matter of law that personal representatives, having no beneficial E
interest in the property, could never be the landlords within the meaning
of paragraph (*h*) of Schedule 1 to the Rent and Mortgage Interest Restrictions (Amendment) Act 1933—a provision which corresponds in terms to
Case 9 of Schedule 15 to the Rent Act 1977.

In my opinion, subject only to one comment, the correct approach to
these cases and to what they decided is set out in the judgment of Cohen F
L.J. in *Harrison* v. *Hopkins* [1950] 1 K.B. 124 to which reference has
already been made but which, for completeness, I will repeat. Cohen L.J.
there said at p. 133 that in *Sharpe* v. *Nicholls* [1945] K.B. 382 and *Parker*
v. *Rosenberg* [1947] K.B. 371:

" . . . the question . . . before the court was not as to the meaning of the
expression ' landlord ' in the abstract, but as to the right of the land- G
lord to possession under paragraph (*h*) of Schedule 1 to the Act of
1933, and the landlord had therefore to prove not only that he was a
landlord but also that he required the premises for his own occupation, and that greater hardship would be involved in refusing him
possession than in depriving the tenant of possession, a burden which
plainly an executor or administrator without a beneficial interest in
the property would be unable to discharge."　　　　　　　　　H

My only criticism of this passage is that the comment that this was
" a burden which plainly an executor or administrator without a beneficial
interest in the property would be unable to discharge," though doubtless
in most cases is true, was an unnecessary addition to the general proposition and, as the facts of the present case have demonstrated, was not
necessarily correct. In my opinion, the question of whether or not per-

A sonal representatives can bring themselves within the provisions of Case 9 is one that has to be answered by applying normal principles of law, using normal canons of construction and in the light of all the facts of each particular case. In the circumstances I have no doubt whatever that, on the findings of fact made by the judge, the plaintiffs are entitled to the order they seek.

B I would adopt, indeed, the direct approach of the court in *Stratford* v. *Syrett* [1958] 1 Q.B. 107, reflecting the closing passage of Lord Evershed M.R. at p. 114. I can see no answer to the simple proposition that being the defendant's landlord, they have succeeded in establishing a ground which entitles the judge to make an order for possession, and that he has thought it reasonable to do. That order, therefore, in my opinion, should have been made.

C

ORMROD L.J. I entirely agree with both the judgments which have been delivered and only add one thing. This case is very exceptional in that the personal representatives, the landlords, are in a position to show that they require the premises for occupation by themselves, they are able to show that they reasonably require the premises because, in occupying D them, they will not in the particular circumstances of this case be in breach of trust, and, consequently, they are able to deal with the other matters as well. They did succeed in showing that it was reasonable for the court to make an order and also they were able to rebut the suggestion that greater hardship fell on the tenant rather than on themselves. If they were in breach of trust, of course, they could not do any of those latter things. They could not show that they reasonably required it or that E it was reasonable to make an order, and they would not have any standing at all on the hardship issue.

For those reasons I agree that the appeal should be allowed and an order for possession made.

Appeal allowed with costs.

F

Solicitors: *Herbert & Gowers & Co.*

[Reported by MRS. MARIA FLEISCHMANN, Barrister-at-Law]

G

[QUEEN'S BENCH DIVISION]

* ASHCROFT *v.* CAMBRO WASTE PRODUCTS LTD.

1981 March 30   Lord Lane C.J., Boreham and Woolf JJ.

H *Public Health—Pollution, control of—Disposal licence—Conditions of licence relating to covering waste—Deposit of waste by company's servants in contravention of conditions—Whether company " knowingly " permitting deposit—Burden of proof —Whether for prosecution to prove knowledge of breach of condition—Control of Pollution Act* 1974 (c. 40), s. 3 (1) (a)

The defendant company operated a waste disposal site under a disposal licence granted by the county council. On August 2, 1980, oil waste deposited on the site was not covered

Ashcroft v. Cambro Ltd. (D.C.)   **[1981]**

with overburden and on August 4, 1980, bags of blue asbestos A
deposited on the site were not covered with incombustible
material in accordance with the conditions of the licence. A
director of the company had overall responsibility for the site,
and although the practical operation was left to the site foreman no functions of management had been delegated to him
by the director. The site foreman was aware of the contraventions of the licence conditions, but the director had no
actual or constructive knowledge of the contraventions. Two B
informations were preferred by the prosecutor, an officer of
the county council, against the company alleging that on the
dates in question the company had knowingly permitted controlled waste to be deposited in contravention of the licence
conditions, contrary to section 3 (1) of the Control of Pollution
Act 1974.[1] The justices were of opinion that knowledge by
the company of the breach of the licence conditions was an
essential element of the offence, and since the site foreman C
was not a directing mind of the company his knowledge was
not sufficient. They accordingly dismissed the informations.

On appeal by the prosecutor : —

Held, allowing the appeal, that on the true construction of
section 3 (1) an offence relating to the deposit of controlled
waste on any land was committed unless such deposit was, in
fact, in accordance with the conditions of a valid licence ; that,
therefore, upon an information laid under section 3 (1) of D
knowingly permitting the deposit of controlled waste in contravention of a licence condition it was for the prosecution to
prove that the deposit had been knowingly permitted, but that
it was unnecessary for the prosecution to prove knowledge
of the breach of condition (post, pp. 1355H—1356A, H—1357B).

The following case is referred to in the judgment of Boreham J.:
E
Tesco Supermarkets Ltd. v. *Nattrass* [1972] A.C. 153 ; [1971] 2 W.L.R.
1166; [1971] 2 All E.R. 127, H.L.(E.).

The following additional case was cited in argument:
Alphacell Ltd. v. *Woodward* [1972] A.C. 824; [1972] 2 W.L.R. 1320;
[1972] 2 All E.R. 475, H.L.(E.).
F

CASE STATED by Derbyshire justices sitting at Chesterfield.

On August 29, 1980, informations were preferred by the prosecutor, Neil
Ashcroft, a duly authorised officer of Derbyshire County Council, against
the defendant company, Cambro Waste Products Ltd., that they: (i) on
August 2, 1980, at Stretton did knowingly permit controlled waste to be
deposited in contravention of condition 19 of waste disposal licence no.
LS44 dated August 10, 1978, by failing to cover solid waste material, G
namely oil residues, with overburden to a depth of not less than 15 centimetres by the end of that day contrary to section 3 (1) of the Control of
Pollution Act 1974; (ii) on August 4, 1980, at Stretton did knowingly permit
controlled waste to be deposited in contravention of condition 28 of the
waste disposal licence no. LS44 dated August 10, 1978, by failing to immediately cover with incombustible material to a depth of one metre fibrous H
asbestos waste, namely bags of blue asbestos, contrary to section 3 (1)
of the Control of Pollution Act 1974.

The justices heard the informations on November 5 and December 9,
1980, and found the following facts.

The company operated a waste disposal site at Morton Road, Stretton,

[1] Control of Pollution Act 1974, s. 3 (1): see post, p. 1353F–G.

A under a waste disposal licence no. LS44 granted by Derbyshire County
Council on August 10, 1978. On August 2, 1980, oil waste deposited on
the site was not covered in accordance with condition 19 of the waste
disposal licence. That oil waste was solid waste within the terms of the
condition. On August 4, 1980, bags of blue asbestos deposited on the
site were not and never had been covered in accordance with condition
28 of the waste disposal licence. The deposits of oil waste and bags of
B blue asbestos were permitted by the company. Miss Joyce Weedon, a
director of the company, had overall responsibility for the site but the
practical operation was left to Richard Thomas Turner, the site foreman. Miss Weedon had not delegated to the site foreman any functions
of management. Miss Weedon had no knowledge actual or constructive
of the contravention of the conditions of the waste disposal licence.
C The site foreman was aware of the contraventions of the conditions of
the waste disposal licence.

It was contended by the appellant that it was necessary only to prove
that the company had knowingly permitted the deposit of controlled
waste; it was then for the company to show that it had a waste disposal
licence and had complied with its conditions; and it need not be proved
that the company had knowledge of the breach of the waste disposal
D licence. If knowledge of the breach of the conditions of the waste disposal licence had to be proved then the knowledge of the site foreman,
was sufficient.

It was contended by the company, inter alia, that it was necessary for
the prosecutor to prove not only that the company had knowingly permitted the deposit of the waste in question but also that the company
E had permitted the breach of the conditions of the licence and it had not
been proved that any person concerned with the management of the
company had knowingly permitted the breach of the conditions of the
licence.

The justices were of the opinion that the company operated a waste
disposal site at Stretton under a licence granted to it by Derbyshire
F County Council. The case arose out of visits to the site by officers of
the county council and subsequent allegations that on two occasions
the conditions of the licence were contravened. It was never in dispute
that the company had authorised the deposits of oil waste and bags of
blue asbestos on the dates in question. The justices approached the matter by first deciding whether the deposits in question had been in accordance with the conditions of the waste disposal licence and having made
G that decision they considered whether any offence had been committed
arising therefrom. On the evidence the justices were satisfied that condition 19 applied to the deposits of oil waste and that it was not appropriately covered. The justices found as a fact, that the asbestos bags
had never been covered in accordance with condition 28 and that the
company could not rely on the defence in section 3 (4) (c) of the Control
H of Pollution Act 1974.

Having ruled that the deposits alleged in the two informations were
not in accordance with the conditions of the licence, the justices went
on to determine what was the mens rea in the offence created by section
3 (1) of the Control of Pollution Act 1974. The prosecutor's view was
that it merely had to be proved that the company knowingly deposited
controlled waste and that it was for the company to show that the deposit was authorised by a waste disposal licence.

A

When the words "knowingly permit" were used, mens rea was clearly required. If the prosecutor's view of the law was correct, the offence would be rendered absolute save for the statutory defences created by section 3 (4) of the Act of 1974. On a true construction of section 3 (1) the culpability required by the Act of 1974 was a knowledge of the unauthorised deposit of controlled waste. There was some support for that view in section 3 (4) (c) of the Act of 1974 in which it was stated that the offence was one of permitting a deposit otherwise than in accordance with the conditions of a waste disposal licence. Accordingly, the prosecutor had to prove that the company permitted the deposits otherwise than in accordance with the licence and knowledge of the breach of the licence conditions was essential.

B

On the evidence, the justices were satisfied that the only conclusion they could draw was that the site foreman either was fully aware of the breach of the conditions or deliberately shut his eyes to that fact. They were satisfied that Miss Weedon, the director on site, was not aware and did not shut her eyes to the unauthorised deposits. On the authorities presented to them they accepted that when dealing with the knowledge of a corporate body, that knowledge had to be imputed to a person who was the directing mind of the company and not merely a servant, or a person to whom functions of management had been delegated as opposed to delegation of a task. They were unable to accept the view that a foreman could be said to be a directing mind of that company. Miss Weedon had said in evidence and it was accepted, that she left the practical operation of the site to the foreman but she retained overall responsibility. The justices considered that to be a normal relationship between a manager and foreman. They could not find that any functions of management had been delegated to the site foreman. It followed therefore, that on the evidence they were unable to find that the company had any knowledge of the unauthorised deposits, and that being an essential element of the offence, they accordingly dismissed the informations.

C

D

E

The appellant appealed. The questions for consideration of the High Court were: (1) whether upon an information laid under section 3 (1) of the Control of Pollution Act 1974 of knowingly permitting the deposit of controlled waste in contravention of a condition of a waste disposal licence it was necessary for the prosecution to prove that the defendant had knowingly permitted the alleged breach of the condition as well as having knowingly permitted the deposit of controlled waste; (2) if the answer to question (1) was affirmative, whether, when an information was laid against a company under section 3 (1) of knowingly permitting the deposit of controlled waste in contravention of a condition of a waste disposal licence it was necessary for the prosecution to prove that a director of the company knowingly permitted the breach of condition or whether proof that it was knowingly permitted by the employee of the company having day to day responsibility for the carrying out of the waste disposal operations (e.g. the site foreman) would suffice; and (3) in the alternative to questions (1) and (2), whether upon an information laid under section 3 (1) of knowingly permitting the deposit of controlled waste in contravention of a condition of a waste disposal licence it was for the defendant to prove the matters specified after the word "unless" in section 3 (1).

F

G

H

Konrad Schiemann Q.C. and *Jeremy Sullivan* for the prosecutor.
James Fox-Andrews Q.C. for the defendant company.

A   BOREHAM J. delivered the first judgment. This is an appeal by way
of case stated from a decision of Derbyshire justices sitting at Chesterfield in respect of an adjudication made by them on December 9, 1980.

On November 5 and December 9, 1980, those justices heard two
informations laid against the defendant company, Cambro Waste Products
Ltd. Those two informations charged, first, that on August 2, 1980, at
B   Stretton they knowingly permitted controlled waste to be deposited in
contravention of condition 19 of waste disposal licence no. LS44 by
failing to cover solid waste material, namely, oil residues, with overburden to a depth of not less than 15 centimetres.

The second information charged a similar offence committed on
August 4, 1980, again at Stretton, again in breach of the conditions of
the same licence, this time in respect of particularly dangerous material,
C   namely, blue asbestos.

The primary facts found by the justices in the course of their hearing
are set out in the case stated and can be shortly referred to. They found
that the company operated a waste disposal site at Morton Road, Stretton, under a waste disposal licence no. LS44 granted by Derbyshire
County Council on August 10, 1978; secondly, that on August 2, 1980,
D   oil waste was deposited on that site and was not covered in accordance
with condition 19 of the licence (the oil waste was solid waste within the
terms of that condition); thirdly, that on August 4, 1980, bags of blue
asbestos deposited on that site were not and never had been covered in
accordance with condition 28 of the waste disposal licence; finally, that
the deposits of oil waste and the bags of blue asbestos were permitted
by the company.

E   They went on to make findings that the director, who had overall
responsibility for the site, had no knowledge, either actual or constructive, of the contravention of the conditions of the waste disposal licence,
though the site foreman had. They found that the practical operation
of the site was left to the site foreman, but there had not been delegated
to him any of the functions of management. They dismissed both in-
F   formations.

The statutory provisions which gave rise to these informations are
to be found in section 3 of the Control of Pollution Act 1974. Section
3 (1), so far as it is relevant to these proceedings, reads:

"Except in prescribed cases,"—and I interpose to say that this is
not a prescribed case—" a person shall not—(a) deposit controlled
G   waste on any land or cause or knowingly permit controlled waste
to be deposited on any land ... unless the land on which the waste
is deposited ... is occupied by the holder of a licence issued in pursuance of section 5 of this Act ... which authorises the deposit ...
and the deposit ... is in accordance with the conditions ... specified
in the licence."

H
Before the justices it was contended on behalf of the prosecutor,
first that it was necessary only for the prosecutor to prove that the company had knowingly permitted the deposit of controlled waste. It was
then for the company to show that it had a waste disposal licence and
that it had complied with the conditions of that licence. In any event
it was not for the prosecutor to prove that the company had knowledge
of the breach of the waste disposal licence.

Secondly, it was contended that, if the first argument was unaccept- A
able and if knowledge of the breach of the conditions of the disposal
licence had to be proved by the prosecutor, the knowledge of the site
foreman was sufficient for that purpose. In other words, the knowledge of the site foreman was, in the circumstances here, to be taken to
be the knowledge of the defendant company.

Before the justices the company took a number of points, but it is
clear from the argument put forward here by Mr. Fox-Andrews on their B
behalf that only one of those points is now relied upon. That is, in
essence, that it was necessary for the prosecutor to prove not only that
the company had knowingly permitted the deposit of the waste in question but also that they had knowingly permitted a breach of the conditions of the licence. It is contended that, if that basic contention is
correct, it had not been proved in current circumstances that any person C
concerned with the management of the company had knowingly permitted a breach of the conditions of the licence. Thus the justices came
to a correct determination.

In the course of the argument in this court two authorities were cited.
It is necessary to refer to but one of them: *Tesco Supermarkets Ltd.* v.
Nattrass [1972] A.C. 153. The judgment to which I make reference is
that of Lord Diplock. He said, at pp. 193–194: D

"Nowadays most business transactions for the supply of goods or
services are not actually conducted by the person who in civil law
is regarded as the party to any contracts made in the course of the
business, but by servants or agents acting on his behalf. Thus, in
the majority of cases the physical acts or omissions which constitute
or result in an offence under the statute will be those of servants or E
agents of an employer or principal on whose behalf the business is
carried on. That employer or principal is likely to be very often
a corporate person, as in the instant appeal. Consumer protection,
which is the purpose of statutes of this kind, is achieved only if the
occurrence of the prohibited acts or omissions is prevented. It is
the deterrent effect of penal provisions which protects the consumer F
from the loss he would sustain if the offence were committed. If
it is committed he does not receive the amount of any fine. As a
taxpayer he will bear part of the expense of maintaining a convicted offender in prison. The loss to the consumer is the same
whether the acts or omissions which result in his being given inaccurate or inadequate information are intended to mislead him,
or are due to carelessness or inadvertence. So is the corresponding G
gain to the other party to the business transaction with the consumer in the course of which those acts or omissions occur. Where,
in the way that business is now conducted, they are likely to be
acts or omissions of employees of that party and subject to his
orders, the most effective method of deterrence is to place upon the
employer the responsibility of doing everything which lies within H
his power to prevent his employees from doing anything which will
result in the commission of an offence." Here comes perhaps the
most important part for present purposes. "This, I apprehend, is
the rational and moral justification for creating in the field of consumer protection, as also in the field of public health and safety,
offences of 'strict liability' for which an employer or principal, in
the course of whose business the offences were committed, is crim-

A inally liable, notwithstanding that they are due to acts or omissions
   of his servants or agents which were done without his knowledge
   or consent or even were contrary to his orders. But this rational
   and moral justification does not extend to penalising an employer
   or principal who has done everything that he can reasonably be
   expected to do by supervision or inspection, by improvement of his
   business methods or by exhorting those whom he may be expected
B to control or influence to prevent the commission of the offence. . . .
   What the employer or principal can reasonably be expected to do
   to prevent the commission of an offence will depend upon the gravity of the injury which it is sought to prevent and the nature of the
   business in the course of which such offences are committed."

C   It is unnecessary to read further. As I understand it, Mr. Schiemann
   on behalf of the prosecutor relies on that as an approach to the construction of the Act in this particular case and urges this court in effect not to
   be surprised to find that the Control of Pollution Act 1974 provides an
   absolute offence so far as defendant company is concerned.
       The contention on behalf of the prosecutor here is, as I have indicated,
   that section 3 (1) lays down an absolute prohibition to this extent, that
D any person who himself deposits controlled waste or causes such a deposit
   or knowingly permits such deposit is guilty of an offence unless it can be
   shown that that deposit was in fact on land which was the subject of a
   licence and that the licence itself authorised the deposit; in other words,
   it was a deposit within and in accordance with a condition of any licence.
   As I have indicated, Mr. Schiemann's contention is that the burden of
E proving that the licence applied to and covered the particular deposit in
   question is upon the company.
       On behalf of the company Mr. Fox-Andrews relies on a number of
   matters in support of his contention that it lies upon the prosecution to
   prove that there was here a permission to breach the terms of the licence.
   He points first to the wording of the informations themselves. I have
   read those and repetition is unnecessary.
F   Secondly, he contends that section 3 (1) is capable of being read in
   the same sense and to the same effect as the informations themselves; in
   other words, he says that the words " knowingly permit " in subsection
   (1) (a) must in effect be imported into or control that which for convenience I call the exception clause, namely, that part of the subsection
   which follows the word " unless." If that is right, then the justices
G certainly, so far as the first point is concerned, came to a correct
   conclusion.
       Another way of putting it, as I understand it, is that section 3 (1) is in
   effect properly and accurately paraphrased in subsection (4) (c); I will
   turn to that in a moment. In other words, this is not the absolute offence
   for which the prosecutor contends.
H   For my part, I find little assistance, save by way of general approach,
   from authorities or decisions which relate to other statutory provisions.
   It seems to me that the meaning of section 3 (1) is clear. Both the
   structure of the section itself and the words themselves impel me to the
   conclusion that they mean what the prosecutor in this case contends
   that they mean, namely, that it is prohibited to deposit or cause to be
   deposited or knowingly permit the deposit of controlled waste on any
   land unless in fact such deposit is in accordance with the conditions of

a valid licence. I do not see how, as a matter of ordinary English, the words " knowingly permit " or their effect can be imported into the exception clause in the present form.

Subsection (4) (*c*), upon which Mr. Fox-Andrews relies heavily, is in these terms:

> " It shall be a defence for a person charged with an offence under this section to prove— . . . (*c*) in the case of an offence of making, causing or permitting a deposit or use otherwise than in accordance with conditions specified in a disposal licence, that he took all such steps as were reasonably open to him to ensure that the conditions were complied with; . . ."

Two things are to be observed. First, that paragraph only becomes relevant when an offence has been prima facie made out; namely, when it has been established that there has been a permitting of a deposit of controlled waste and when it has been shown that the land on which it was deposited was either not the subject of a licence or that the deposit was not in accordance with a condition of that licence—the sort of situation referred to by Lord Diplock in *Tesco Supermarkets Ltd.* v. *Nattrass* [1972] A.C. 153, 193–194.

Secondly, I find it very difficult to understand what could be the purpose or effect of subsection (4) (*c*) if subsection (1) were to have the effect or were to be read in the way for which Mr. Fox-Andrews contends. In any event it would be wrong to import into subsection (1) the sort of paraphrase, if that is the correct word, which appears in subsection 4 (*c*) unless perhaps there were some ambiguity in or difficulty in construing subsection (1)—an ambiguity and a difficulty which I personally do not find. For these reasons I prefer to construe subsection (1) as it stands and not by reference to subsection (4) (*c*).

There has been before us, in addition to the argument as to the proper construction of this subsection, an interesting argument as to where the burden of proof lies in respect of those matters which appear in what I have called the exception clause in subsection (1). In view of the decision that I have reached so far as the meaning of that subsection is concerned, it is unnecessary in present circumstances to decide that interesting question, and I prefer to leave it for another day. I say that for this reason. Wherever the burden lies, in this case the justices have found as facts that the deposits of oil waste and blue asbestos were made in breach of conditions of the licence. No question therefore arises at this stage of the proceedings as to the burden of proof; thus I prefer to leave that matter until it arises for decision.

In these circumstances it follows that I have come to the conclusion that the justices were wrong. I would not wish to leave this case without adding that my conclusion implies no criticism of the justices. I have no doubt that they found it a difficult point and, as is clear from the case itself, they applied their minds to the problem carefully and at some length. In those circumstances, whilst I disagree with the result, I wish to pay tribute to the care they have taken.

It only remains to say that, in my judgment, of the three questions set out in the case only one question requires an answer; that is question (1). It reads:

> " Whether upon an information laid under section 3 (1) of the Control of Pollution Act 1974 of knowingly permitting the deposit

A of controlled waste in contravention of a condition of a waste disposal licence it was necessary for the prosecution to prove that the defendant had knowingly permitted the alleged breach of the conditions as well as having knowingly permitted the deposit of controlled waste."

My answer to that question is " No."

B

WOOLF J. I agree.

LORD LANE C.J. I also agree. I too would like to make mention of the care and clarity with which this case has been prepared by the justices and to pay tribute to that method of presentation which is much to be encouraged.

C The matter therefore will have to be sent back to the justices with a direction to convict and the appeal is accordingly allowed.

Appeal allowed with costs.
Case remitted to justices.
Certificate that point of law of general public importance involved, namely, " Whether upon an information laid under section 3 (1) of the Control of Pollution Act 1974 of knowingly permitting the deposit of controlled waste in contravention of a condition of a waste disposal licence it is necessary for the prosecution to prove that the defendant had knowingly permitted the alleged breach of the condition as well as having knowingly permitted the deposit of controlled waste."
Leave to appeal refused.

July 23. The Appeal Committee of the House of Lords (Lord Diplock, Lord Russell of Killowen and Lord Bridge of Harwich) dismissed a petition by the defendant company for leave to appeal.

Solicitors: *M. W. Ingham, Matlock; Bradley & Clarke, Chesterfield.*

[Reported by MISS STELLA SOLOMON, Barrister-at-Law]

[1981]

A

[CHANCERY DIVISION]

* *In re* MUNRO AND ANOTHER, *Ex parte* SINGER v.
TRUSTEE IN BANKRUPTCY

1981 March 23   Walton J.

B

*Bankruptcy—Trustee in bankruptcy—Release of trustee—Notice
of intention to seek release sent to creditor care of solicitors—
Affidavit in common form stating that notice sent to address
on proof of debt—Whether release to be reversed or discharged
—Bankruptcy Act 1914 (4 & 5 Geo. 5, c. 59), s. 93 (1) (3)—
Bankruptcy Rules 1952 (S.I. 1952 No. 2113), r. 341*

In 1970 a firm of solicitors, of which the applicant was a
client, went bankrupt. Initially the respondent, the trustee
in bankruptcy, took the view that the applicant owed money
to the firm, but later he agreed that the firm was very largely
indebted to the applicant. In 1978 the respondent admitted
the applicant's initial proof for £79,926 10s. 4d. Later that
proof was revised to about £185,000. But the bankrupts'
assets were minimal, so that no dividend of any sort could be
paid out to creditors. The applicant made a claim against
The Law Society's compensation fund and received a payment
of £34,000, without prejudice to any further payment which
might be made out of the fund. On August 5, 1980, the
respondent, in pursuance of rule 341 of the Bankruptcy Rules
1952,[1] swore an affidavit in which he stated that on August
4, 1980, he sent to the debtor and to each creditor who had
proved in the matter a notice of his intention to apply for
release together with a summary of the accounts, and that
such notices were addressed to the debtor at his last known
address and to such of the creditors who had proved their
debts according to the addresses in their respective proofs.
In fact, the notice was sent to the applicant not at the
address given in his proof, but care of his solicitors. On
October 30, 1980, the respondent obtained an order for his
release from his office as trustee in bankruptcy, under section
93 (1) and (3) of the Bankruptcy Act 1914.[2] On November
20, 1980, the applicant, who claimed only to have learnt of
the release on November 13, applied by notice of motion for
an order that the decision of the Secretary of State for the
Department of Trade, granting to the respondent his release
from his office as trustee, might be reversed or otherwise
varied or modified.

On the hearing of the motion: —

Held, that if a trustee in bankruptcy chose to serve notice
of his intention to seek his release on a creditor at an address
other than that given in the creditor's proof of debt, he was
bound to inform the court of precisely what he had done;
that, since the respondent's notice of intention had been sent
to the creditor, not as deposed to in the respondent's affidavit,
at the address given in his proof of debt, but care of his
solicitors, the release had been obtained on evidence which
was in fact untrue; that the purpose of section 93 (3) of the
Bankruptcy Act 1914 was that a release granted under that
section should discharge the trustee from all liability in respect
of any act done or default made by him in the administration of the bankrupt's affairs, and, therefore, if the release
were allowed to stand it would be impossible for the applicant

C

D

E

F

G

H

---

[1] Bankruptcy Rules 1952, r. 341: see post, p. 1360H.
[2] Bankruptcy Act 1914, s. 93 (1) (3): see post, pp. 1360F–H, 1362D–E.

A   to sue the respondent in respect of the administration between 1970 and 1978, and that, accordingly, the order of the Secretary of State granting the release should be reversed.

Per curiam. It is a common fallacy to think that solicitors have an implied authority on behalf of their clients to receive notices. They may have express authority to receive them, but in general a solicitor does not have any authority to accept a notice on behalf of his client (post, p. 1361D).

B

The following case is referred to in the judgment:

Harris, In re, Ex parte Hasluck [1899] 2 Q.B. 97.

No additional cases were cited in argument.

C
MOTION

By a notice of motion, dated November 20, 1980, the applicant, David Mortimer Singer, a creditor in the bankruptcies of Donald Edward Munro and Lionel Rowe, lately practising in partnership as Donald Munro, Tudor and Rowe, solicitors, sought (1) an order that the decision of the Secretary of State for the Department of Trade, granting the release of the respondent, George Albert Auger, trustee in bankruptcy

D   of the bankrupts, might be reversed or otherwise varied or modified; (2) an order that the respondent do pay the costs of and incidental to the motion; and (3) such further or other relief as to the court should seem just.

The facts are stated in the judgment.

E
D. G. M. Marks for the applicant.
The respondent appeared in person.

WALTON J. This is an unusual application by a creditor in bankruptcy of Donald Edward Munro and Lionel Rowe, lately practising in partnership as Donald Munro, Tudor and Rowe, a firm of solicitors, for an order that the decision of the Secretary of State for

F   the Department of Trade granting the release of Mr. Auger, the respondent, from his office as trustee of the property of the said bankrupts may be reversed or otherwise varied or modified; for an order that the respondent do pay the costs of and incidental to this motion, and such further or other relief as to this court shall seem just.

The situation is a little complicated, and I declare to say as little

G   about the complications as I can because in so doing I might be appearing to slant the facts one way or the other. The position is that the applicant, whose address at all material times has been Vieux Cagnes, France, had a very intimate relation with the firm of Donald Munro, Tudor and Rowe in the sense that, apparently, all of his assets were in some way or other looked after by or bound up with that firm. There were a large number of transactions indeed between himself and that firm. When

H   that firm went into liquidation, the trustee in bankruptcy originally took the view that the applicant was largely indebted to that firm, whereas, as we now know, the fact is that the firm was very largely indebted to the applicant. I certainly think that part of the blame is to be found in the fact that that firm did not, apparently, maintain their records in the form that solicitors ought to maintain them; indeed, probably not in the form that any reputable firm ought to maintain them. This may

1360

very well, I know not, have initially put the trustee off the scent.   A
Although the bankruptcy took place as long ago as 1970, it was not
until 1978 that the trustee in bankruptcy finally, as it were, threw in
his hand and admitted the proof of the applicant in the bankruptcy for
the sum of £79,926 10s. 4d. The order of Goulding J., which allowed
that to happen, also allowed the applicant to put in additional claims
either in the bankruptcy of the partnership or in the bankruptcy of the
individuals. I gather that recently he has put in a revised proof of debt   B
of the order of about £185,000. However, he may put in proofs of debt
until he is blue in the face, but the assets of the partnership were absolutely minimal and have not resulted and will not result in any payment
of any dividend to any of the creditors.

The real hope of the applicant recovering any part of his money
lies in the Law Society's compensation fund, which has already paid   C
to him a sum of £34,000 without prejudice to any other payments which
may be made, it being stated in the correspondence with the Law
Society—I have no other evidence so I do not know how true this is—
that the applicant's claim is the largest single claim with which the Law
Society down to the date of its being made had ever had to deal.

In order that there should be no possible get-out, as it were, on any   D
other basis than that the bankrupt firm were thoroughly fraudulent in
their dealings with the applicant, he has commenced proceedings in the
Queen's Bench Division to which, among others, the respondent trustee
in bankruptcy is a party, for the purpose of being able to say that it has
been established by action that the bankrupts were in fact fraudulent.
Whether that is strictly necessary or not, seems to be a matter of some
dispute with the Law Society who appear, and for all I know, quite   E
properly, over a period of time to have changed their stance in that
regard.

However that may be, what has now happened is that the respondent,
the former trustee of the property of the firm, applied to the Department
of Trade for his release under the provisions of section 93 (1) of the
Bankruptcy Act 1914, which reads: F

"When the trustee has realised all the property of the bankrupt,
or so much thereof as can, in his opinion, be realised without
needlessly protracting the trusteeship, and distributed a final dividend, if any, or has ceased to act by reason of a composition having
been approved, or has resigned, or has been removed from his
office, the Board of Trade shall, on his application, cause a report   G
on his accounts to be prepared, and, on his complying with all the
requirements of the Board, shall take into consideration the report,
and any objection which may be urged by any creditor or person
interested against the release of the trustee, and shall either grant
or withhold the release accordingly, subject nevertheless to an appeal
to the High Court."   H

That is, to some extent, fleshed out by rule 341 of the Bankruptcy Rules
1952, which provides:

"Before applying to the Board of Trade for his release, a trustee
shall send notice of his intention so to do, accompanied by a summary of his receipts and payments as trustee to all creditors who
have proved their debt and to the debtor."

A Then there is a proviso which is not material, and I do not read. That rule is quite clearly intended to enable the creditors to know that the trustee is applying for his release and so to take objection against the release if they have any ground upon which they are properly entitled to so object.

B What has happened in the present case it that in all three cases, because the respondent was trustee not only of the property of the firm but also of the individual bankrupts, the common form affidavit was sworn by the trustee in bankruptcy in which he makes oath and says:

C " (1). That I did on August 4, 1980, send to the debtor and to each creditor who has proved in this matter a notice of the trustee's intention to apply for release together with a summary of the accounts in the form hereunto annexed marked 'A.' (2). That such notices were addressed to the debtor at his last known address and to such of the creditors who have proved their debts according to the addresses in their respective proofs."

D As regards the applicant, that last statement just is not true, because his address in his proof was Vieux Cagnes in France. In fact, it transpires that the notice to him was not sent to Vieux Cagnes in France at all but was sent to him care of his solicitors, who at that time were Messrs. Payne, Hicks Beach & Co.

It is, of course, a common fallacy to think that solicitors have an implied authority on behalf of their clients to receive notices. They may have express authority so to receive them, but in general a solicitor does not have any authority to accept a notice on behalf of his client.

E However, if the situation had been that in the affidavit relating to the partnership, the respondent had sworn to that which in fact is said on his behalf did happen, that is to say, that the notice went to the applicant, care of his solicitors, I should at the least have required very detailed explanation from Messrs. Payne, Hicks Beach & Co. as to exactly what they did with that notice when they received it and what

F the applicant's reaction was. But I am here confronted with the fact that half of the evidence upon which the respondent obtained the release from the Department of Trade was just not so. The respondent submitted to me that it was, after all, only a technical slip at the highest and that there are other forms which are in use which show that the trustee can modify the requirements of the affidavit as to service so as to indicate precisely and exactly what he did.

G So far from in any way supporting the respondent's proposition, that evidence is exactly and entirely against him, because it does show that if the trustee in bankruptcy, for whatever reason, and there may very well be in many cases very good reasons why notices have to be served in some peculiar way, serves them upon creditors other than at their respective addresses as set out in their respective proofs, he must

H and is entitled to, indeed is bound to, inform the court of precisely and exactly what he has done. So the position is crystal clear, in that the respondent has obtained his discharge on evidence which, in part, and maybe in vital part, is untrue.

What ought I to do about it? It is quite clear from the provisions of section 93 (1) that there is an appeal to the High Court against the decision of the Department of Trade. It is also clear from rule 8 (1) (d) of the Bankruptcy Rules that the appeal must be heard and determined

in open court. It is also clear that the period is a period of 21 days. **A**
The notice of motion is dated November 20, 1980, and is, indeed, in
time.

If the only matter in issue had been the continuance of the respondent as a defendant in the action in the Queen's Bench Division to which
I have already referred, I do not think that the situation would have
demanded such a drastic alteration as reversal or cancellation of the
decision of the Secretary of State for the Department of Trade, because **B**
it seems to me that quoad that action the official receiver, who now
steps into the shoes of the trustee in bankruptcy as a result of his
release under section 90 (5) of the Bankruptcy Act 1914, would for the
purpose of that action, do just as well as the respondent himself, bearing
more particularly in mind that there are no funds available in the
bankruptcy whatsoever; and that at this stage, when the situation is **C**
pretty well known, nobody is going to supply the trustee in bankruptcy
with any money for the purpose of defending that action which I also
understand is in the event indefensible, and the trustee would not in fact
seek to defend it.

Unfortunately, the matter does not stop there. Section 93 (3) reads:

"An order of the Board"—that is the original wording in the Act **D**
of 1914, but it is now the Department of Trade—". . . . releasing the
trustee shall discharge him from all liability in respect of any act
done or default made by him in the administration of the affairs
of the bankrupt, or otherwise in relation to his conduct as trustee,
but any such order may be revoked on proof that it was obtained
by fraud or by suppression or concealment of any material fact." **E**

Nobody, of course, suggests for one moment that the respondent
has been fraudulent or has intentionally attempted to suppress or conceal
any material fact. The situation, therefore, is that if the order stands it
would be, in my judgment, quite impossible for the applicant to sue the
trustee in respect of his conduct between the time when the order
of adjudication was made in 1970 and the date in 1978 when the trustee **F**
threw in his hand quoad the applicant.

Of course, I know nothing more than an outline of what happened
then, and I have not either practically, judicially or actually the slightest
idea whether there is any possible claim by the applicant against the
trustee or not. What is in my judgment crystal clear is that upon a
true construction of section 93 (3), which interestingly does not ever
appear to have been previously construed, although the proviso thereto **G**
was construed in *In re Harris, Ex parte Hasluck* [1899] 2 Q.B. 97, it
appears to me that the intention of that subsection, and it is a very
right, proper and wholesome intention, is to wipe the slate completely
clean so far as the trustee is concerned, so that he may thereafter pay
no thought to the previous course of his actions as the trustee in
bankruptcy. Of course, that means that if the release is now allowed **H**
to stand, the applicant would be deprived completely of any redress
whatsoever against the trustee in bankruptcy in respect of the whole of
the conduct of the trustee in bankruptcy in relation to the applicant's
own proofs of debt. Having regard to many factors which I need not
go into, the attitude of the trustee to the applicant's proofs may very
well have been, so far as the applicant was concerned, most material
in a large number of respects.

A   It therefore appears to me that at the end of the day in order to enable justice to be done I must carry the fact that the release has been improperly obtained to its logical conclusion and discharge or reverse the order of the Secretary of State for the Department of Trade granting the release of the respondent from his office as trustee of the property of the bankrupt.

B   *Order accordingly.*

Solicitors: *Payne, Hicks Beach & Co.*

T. C. C. B.

C

[COURT OF APPEAL]

* CUMMINS ENGINE CO. LTD. *v.*

DAVIS FREIGHT FORWARDING (HULL) LTD. AND OTHERS

D

[1978 C. No. 4445]

1981 July 16, 17, 20   Eveleigh, Brandon and O'Connor L.JJ.

Practice—Third party proceedings—Service out of jurisdiction— CMR contract for shipment of diesel engines from Scotland
E   *to Amsterdam—Goods shipped to Europoort by English carriers—Dutch carriers responsible for on-carriage of goods to Amsterdam—Accident causing loss while goods in possession, of one carrier—Action for damages in England—Writ served only on English carrier—Whether English carrier entitled to serve third party notices on Dutch carriers—Carriage of Goods by Road Act 1965 (c. 37), Sch., art. 39—R.S.C., Ord. 11, r. 1 (1) (l)*

F *Statute—Construction—International Convention—Enforcement of carriers' right of recovery against other carriers—Competent court or tribunal — Court or tribunal where " one of the carriers concerned " ordinarily resident or carries on business —Meaning—Whether English carrier sued in England entitled to recover from Dutch carriers in English court—Carriage of Goods by Road Act 1965, Sch., arts. 37 (a), 39, para. 2*

G   In May 1977 the plaintiffs and the first defendants, both English companies, entered into a contract to which the Convention on the Contract for the International Carriage of Goods by Road, scheduled to the Carriage of Goods by Road Act 1965, applied. Under the contract the first defendants were to carry, or arrange the carriage of, diesel engines from Scotland to Amsterdam. The first defendants carried the goods by trailer to Hull from where they arranged shipment
H to the Europoort of Rotterdam. The goods arrived in good order and condition on June 13, 1977. The first defendants asked Dutch carriers to arrange on-carriage from the port to Amsterdam. Those carriers passed on the request to another Dutch carrier who in turn asked yet another Dutch carrier to arrange transit to Amsterdam. That carrier took the trailer in tow but on the journey to Amsterdam at 3 a.m. on June 14 the goods were severely damaged by fire when the vehicle carrying them was involved in a road accident. In June 1978 the plaintiffs began an action in the Commercial

1364

Court against the first defendant and the three Dutch carriers, **A**
naming them as second, third and fourth defendants, claiming
£41,452·89 damages, but the writ was served only on the first
defendants, the only defendants within the jurisdiction. On
February 25, 1980, the first defendants applied ex parte pursuant
to R.S.C., Ord. 11, r. 1 (1) (*l*) [1] as applied to third party notices
by Ord. 16, r. 3 (4), for leave to serve out of the jurisdiction
in the Netherlands third party notices on the three Dutch
defendants claiming to be indemnified by each of them against **B**
the plaintiffs' claim. Goff J. made the order and service of
the notices was duly effected in the Netherlands. On March
6, 1981, however, Mocatta J., on the application of the three
Dutch defendants, set aside the order of Goff J. and the third
party notices, holding that, having regard to the agreed facts
and article 37 (*a*) of the Convention, [2] the service of the third
party notices on the second and third defendants must be set
aside and that, in relation to the fourth defendants, the juris- **C**
diction of the English courts was excluded by article 39, paragraph 2, of the Convention and accordingly the third party
notice against the fourth defendants must also be set aside.

On appeal by the first defendants with leave of the judge: —

Held, dismissing the appeal, (1) that, assuming that the
second and third defendants were successive carriers, they were
not responsible for the loss or damage to the goods since that
took place while the goods were being carried by the fourth **D**
defendants, and, therefore, under article 37 of the Convention
the fourth defendants were the only successive carriers from
whom the first defendants were entitled to recover any compensation which they were held liable to pay the plaintiffs;
accordingly the third party proceedings against the second and
third defendants must fail and the order for service out of the
jurisdiction and the service of the third party notices against
them had been properly set aside (post, pp. 1372F–H, 1374F, **E**
1375F–G).

(2) That, on the true construction of article 39, paragraph
2 of the Convention, the expression "the carriers concerned"
when it first appeared, in the context in which it was used,
meant the carriers from whom the carrier primarily liable to a
sender or consignee was seeking to recover the compensation
which he had to pay; that that meaning was reinforced by the
concession which had been made that it was the meaning **F**
given to "the carriers concerned" when it was subsequently
used in article 39, paragraph 2, since it was highly improbable
that the expression would be given two different meanings
when used in two different places in the same paragraph,
accordingly, the first defendants would have to sue the three
Dutch defendants in a court in the Netherlands and would not
be entitled to proceed against them in a court in England;
for that reason also the order and the third party notices **G**
against all three defendants had been properly set aside (post,
pp. 1373A–F, 1375B–E, F–G).

Per Brandon L.J. Although article 39, paragraph 2, only
provides that a carrier "may" make his claim before the
competent court of the country in which one of the carriers
concerned is ordinarily resident or has his principal place
of business, "may" must be interpreted as meaning "must"
for if "may" is interpreted as permissive only there is nothing **H**
in article 39 or any other part of the Convention which permits
actions by one carrier against other carriers for an indemnity

---

[1] R.S.C., Ord. 11, r. 1 (1): ". . . service of a writ, out of the jurisdiction is
permissible with the leave of the court in the following circumstances, that is to
say— . . . (*l*) if the action begun by the writ is brought under the . . . Carriage of
Goods by Road Act 1965 . . ."
[2] Carriage of Goods by Road Act 1965, Sch., art. 37: see post, p. 1370F–H, Art.
39: see post, p. 1371A–D.

A   to be brought in the courts of any countries other than those specified in article 39, paragraph 2 (post, pp. 1373H—1374A).

    Per Eveleigh L.J. I am not prepared to say that " may " in article 39, paragraph 2, is the equivalent of " must," since that article does not contain the words " and in no other courts or tribunals " which appear in article 31. I would leave open the question whether a defendant can claim indemnity or contribution in England against a carrier who has entered an

B   appearance for the purpose of disputing the validity of a payment after receiving notice under article 39. But R.S.C., Ord. 11, r. 1 (1) (*l*) envisages only a claim which can be made according to the procedure specifically permitted by article 39, paragraph 2, and the present claim cannot be covered by that paragraph (post, p. 1375E–G).

    Decision of Mocatta J. affirmed.

C   The following case is referred to in the judgment of Brandon L.J.:

    Ulster-Swift Ltd. v. *Taunton Meat Haulage Ltd.* [1977] 1 W.L.R. 625; [1977] 3 All E.R. 641, C.A.

    The following additional cases were cited in argument:

    Buchanan (James) & Co. Ltd. v. *Babco Forwarding & Shipping (U.K.)*

D   *Ltd.* [1978] A.C. 141; [1977] 3 W.L.R. 907; [1977] 3 All E.R. 1048, H.L.(E.).

    County and District Properties Ltd. v. *C. Jenner & Son Ltd.* [1976] 2 Lloyd's Rep. 728.

    Fothergill v. *Monarch Airlines Ltd.* [1981] A.C. 251; [1980] 3 W.L.R. 209; [1980] 2 All E.R. 696, H.L.(E.).

    Littlewood v. *George Wimpey & Co. Ltd.* [1953] 2 Q.B. 501; [1953] 3

E   W.L.R. 553; [1953] 2 All E.R. 915, C.A.

    McCheane v. *Gyles* [1902] 1 Ch. 287, C.A.

    INTERLOCUTORY APPEAL from Mocatta J.

    On June 7, 1978, the plaintiffs, Cummins Engine Co. Ltd., issued a writ against Davis Freight Forwarding (Hull) Ltd., the first defendants, an

F   English company, and against three Dutch defendants, Charterway Shipping B.V., R.C.A. Van der Graaf and D. Boers B.V., the second, third and fourth defendants, claiming damages for breach of contract and negligence arising out of the carriage of the plaintiffs' goods from Shotts, Lanarkshire, Scotland, to Amsterdam, Holland, in or about June 1977. On February 27, 1979, the writ was served only on the first defendants, they being the only defendants within the jurisdiction.

G   On May 18, 1979, points of claim were served on the first defendants claiming, inter alia, that by the Carriage of Goods by Road Act 1965 the Convention on the Contract for the International Carriage of Goods by Road applied to the carriage of the goods by the first defendants; that by article 17 (1) of the Convention the first defendants were liable for loss of the goods and for damage thereto occurring between the time when

H   they took over the goods and the time of delivery; that it was the duty of the first defendants to deliver the goods in the same good order and condition as they were when they were received and they had failed to exercise reasonable care in the carriage thereof, in particular, because, on or about June 14, 1977, the vehicle in which the goods were being carried crashed on a motorway in Holland and burst into flames and the diesel engines were serious damaged; that the first defendants were liable to the plaintiffs for the damage by virtue of the provisions of the Convention

and/or by virtue of their breach of duty. They also alleged negligence by   A
the first defendants, their servants or agents. They claimed the value of the
engines, which, less salvage, amounted to £41,452·89.

The first defendants served points of defence on July 19, 1979, in which
they admitted entering into the contract and that the Convention applied
to it. They claimed that they had delivered the goods to the second, third
and fourth defendants at the Europoort of Rotterdam in good order and   B
condition and denied that they were responsible for the acts and omissions
of those defendants. They denied that any liability on them had arisen
under article 17 (1) of the Convention.

They admitted that the goods were damaged in transit from the
Europoort to Amsterdam but denied any breach of duty in relation thereto.
They denied that they were liable to the plaintiffs either under the
Convention or by virtue of any other duty owed by them to the plaintiffs   C
or by any negligence on their part or on the part of their servants or agents.

On February 25, 1980, the first defendants had applied ex parte under
R.S.C., Ord. 11, r. 1 (1) (*l*) as applied by Ord. 16, r. 3 (4) for leave to serve
out of the jurisdiction in the Netherlands third party notices on the second,
third and fourth defendants claiming against each defendant to be indemnified against the plaintiffs' claim on the grounds that the defendants had   D
agreed to carry the diesel engines from the Europoort Rotterdam to
Amsterdam and that in breach of such agreement or negligently the
defendants did not carry and deliver them safely and in the condition in
which they had received them for carriage but had caused or were
responsible for their damage during carriage and non-delivery. Robert
Goff J. acceded to the application, made an order giving the first defendants   E
leave to serve the third party notices, and the notices were duly served on
the second, third and fourth defendants at their addresses in the Netherlands.

On August 8, 1980, the fourth defendants, on September 25, 1980, the
third defendants, and on January 29, 1981, the second defendants, issued
summonses supported by affidavits asking that the order of Robert Goff J.
and the service of the third party notices be set aside. Mocatta J. heard the   F
three summonses on March 6, 1981, and made orders setting aside Robert
Goff J.'s order and the service of the three third party notices. He
delivered his judgment in open court and gave the first defendants leave to
appeal against his orders.

The first defendants appealed, seeking to restore the orders of Robert
Goff J. and asking that the third party notices served pursuant thereto
should stand on the grounds, inter alia, that Mocatta J. had erred in law in   G
so construing the provisions of the Carriage of Goods by Road Act 1965
and the Convention set out in the Schedule to that Act as to preclude the
exercise of jurisdiction by the courts in England with respect to the claim
made by the first defendants against the second defendants (the first
third party), the third defendant (the second third party) and the fourth
defendants (the third third party) or, alternatively, in so construing the   H
Act and the Convention as to limit the jurisdiction of the courts in
England and exclude its exercise in the circumstances of that claim; and
that the judge had erred in law or in principle in setting aside the order
made by Robert Goff J. granting leave to issue and serve the third party
notices out of the jurisdiction if, and to the extent that, such decision to set
aside was a matter of discretion.

The facts are stated in the judgment of Brandon L.J.

A
Murray Pickering for the first defendants.
Geoffrey Kinley for the second defendants.
Gavin Kealey for the third defendants.
Richard Aikens for the fourth defendants.

BRANDON L.J. delivered the first judgment. This appeal arises in an action in the Commercial Court in which Cummins Engine Co. Ltd. are
B the plaintiffs, Davis Freight Forwarding (Hull) Ltd. are the first defendants, Charterway Shipping B.V. are the second defendants, R.C.A. Van der Graaf is the third defendant, and D. Boers B.V. are the fourth defendants. I shall refer to these five parties as Cummins, Davis, Charterway, Graaf and Boers respectively.

Cummins is an English company which manufactures and exports
C diesel engines. Davis is another English company engaged in, among other things, the carriage and forwarding of goods from the United Kingdom to the Continent. Charterway and Boers are Dutch companies, and Graaf is a Dutch trader, all engaged in either the forwarding or the carriage of goods by road in the Netherlands.

The appeal raises questions with regard to the true meaning and effect
D of certain provisions of the Convention on the Contract for the International Carriage of Goods by Road made at Geneva on May 19, 1956, which has been part of English law since October 1967. The Convention is commonly known as " CMR " and I shall refer to it by those initials.

The facts giving rise to the action are these. At about the end of May 1977 Cummins and Davis entered into a contract under which Davis
E was to carry, or arrange the carriage of, 14 diesel engines from Shotts in Lanarkshire to Amsterdam. The goods were subsequently loaded by Davis at Shotts into a road trailer belonging to them. They were accompanied by various documents, including invoices and a consignment note of the kind prescribed by articles 4–6 of CMR. In that consignment note Cummins were shown as the sender, N.V. Nederlandsche Ford of Amsterdam as the consignee, and Davis as the carrier. After the goods had been loaded into
F the trailer by Davis, a tractor unit belonging to them hauled the trailer by road to Hull. There Davis arranged for the on-carriage of the trailer by sea to Europoort at Rotterdam, where the trailer and the 14 diesel engines contained in it arrived safely on June 13, 1977.

There remained the further on-carriage of the goods in the trailer to Amsterdam. Davis asked Charterway to arrange this. Charterway asked
G Graaf to do the job. Graaf in turn asked Boers to do it. In the result, Boers sent a tractor unit to Europoort and collected the trailer and the accompanying documents from there. Boers' tractor unit, with the trailer in tow, set out for Amsterdam. Unfortunately, at about 3 a.m. on the morning of June 14, 1977, the tractor and trailer crashed over the side of a bridge at Leiden. As a result of the crash the trailer, and the goods contained in it, were severely damaged by fire. The accompanying documents, however,
H were recovered, although they too had been partly damaged by fire. Those documents included the CMR consignment note.

On June 7, 1978, very shortly before the expiry of the one-year time limit for claims prescribed by article 32 of CMR, Cummins began the action against Davis, Charterway, Graaf and Boers in the Commercial Court to which I referred earlier. The writ was subsequently served on Davis, the only defendants within the jurisdiction, but no attempt appears to have been made to obtain leave to serve notice of the writ on the other

three defendants outside the jurisdiction in the Netherlands. Points of A
claim, points of defence, and further and better particulars of either
pleading were served between May 18, 1979, and July 3, 1980. The amount
claimed by Cummins against Davis for the damage to the diesel engines
was £41,452·89 with interest.

Meanwhile, on February 25, 1980, Davis had made an ex parte application supported by affidavit for leave to serve out of the jurisdiction, in
the Netherlands, third party notices on Charterway, Graaf and Boers, in B
which Davis claimed in each case an indemnity in respect of any liability
to Cummins which might be found against them in the main action. The
ex parte application was heard by Robert Goff J., who acceded to it and
made an order giving Davis the leave for which they had asked. Third
party notices were subsequently served on Charterway, Graaf and Boers
at their respective addresses in the Netherlands. C

On August 8, 1980, Boers, on September 25, 1980, Graaf, and on the
January 29, 1981, Charterway, issued summonses supported by affidavits in
which they asked that the ex parte order of Robert Goff J. made on February
25, 1980, and the service of the third party notices issued and served
pursuant to that order, should be set aside. The three summonses came on
for hearing together before Mocatta J. on March 6, 1981. Because they
involved questions on the meaning and effect of an international con- D
vention, the judge decided to give judgment in open court. He found
against Davis on all three summonses, and made orders setting aside the
order of Robert Goff J. of February 25, 1980, and the service of the three
third party notices issued and served pursuant to that order. He gave
Davis leave to appeal against his orders and it is with that appeal that we
are now concerned. E

The Carriage of Goods by Road Act 1965 was passed on August 5,
1965, and came into force on October 19, 1967. It provides so far as
material:

> Section 1: " Subject to the following provisions of this Act, the
> provisions of the Convention on the Contract for the International
> Carriage of Goods by Road (in this Act referred to as ' the Con- F
> vention '), as set out in the Schedule to this Act, shall have the force
> of law in the United Kingdom so far as they relate to the rights and
> liabilities of persons concerned in the carriage of goods by road under
> a contract to which the Convention applies."

> Section 5: " (1) Where a carrier under a contract to which the
> Convention applies is liable in respect of any loss or damage for which
> compensation is payable under the Convention, nothing in section G
> 6 (1) (c) of the Law Reform (Married Women and Tortfeasors) Act
> 1935, section 16 (1) (c) of the Law Reform (Miscellaneous Provisions)
> Act (Northern Ireland) 1937, or section 3 (2) of the Law Reform
> (Miscellaneous Provisions) (Scotland) Act 1940 shall confer on him
> any right to recover contribution in respect of that loss or damage
> from any other carrier who, in accordance with article 34 in the H
> Schedule to this Act, is a party to the contract of carriage. (2) The
> preceding subsection shall be without prejudice to the operation of
> article 37 in the Schedule to this Act."

> Section 14: " (2) The persons who, for the purposes of this Act,
> are persons concerned in the carriage of goods by road under a
> contract to which the Convention applies are—(a) the sender, (b) the
> consignee, (c) any carrier who, in accordance with article 34 in the

The Weekly Law Reports, November 13, 1981

1369

1 W.L.R.   Cummins Engine Co. v. Davis Freight Ltd. (C.A.)   Brandon L.J.

A   Schedule to this Act or otherwise, is a party to the contract of carriage, (*d*) any person for whom such a carrier is responsible by virtue of article 3 in the Schedule to this Act, (*e*) any person to whom the rights and liabilities of any of the persons referred to in paragraphs (*a*) to (*d*) of this subsection have passed (whether by assignment or assignation or by operation of law)."

B   The effect of section 5 (1) and (2) of the Act of 1965 is to exclude the statutory provisions relating to contribution and indemnity between persons jointly or concurrently liable for the same loss or damage in force in the three parts of the United Kingdom, so leaving the way clear for the operation of the special provisions of CMR relating to those matters to which I shall be referring later. The reference in section 5 to section 6 (1) (*c*) of the Law Reform (Married Women and Tortfeasors) Act 1935 must be taken today to be a reference to the corresponding provisions of the Civil Liability (Contribution) Act 1978. This Act, however, did not come into force until January 1, 1979, well after the casualty here concerned.

C

      CMR, as scheduled to the Act of 1965, is divided into seven chapters. Chapter I, containing articles 1 and 2, is entitled " Scope of Application." Article 1, paragraph 1, provides:

D

      " This Convention shall apply to every contract for the carriage of goods by road in vehicles for reward, when the place of taking over of the goods and the place designated for delivery, as specified in the contract, are situated in two different countries, of which at least one is a contracting country, irrespective of the place of residence and the nationality of the parties."

E

Both the United Kingdom and the Netherlands are contracting parties, and it is not in dispute that CMR applied to the carriage of diesel engines from Shotts to Amsterdam with which this case is concerned.

      Chapter II of CMR, containing article 3, is entitled " Persons for whom the carrier is responsible." Article 3 provides:

F

      " For the purposes of this Convention the carrier shall be responsible for the acts and omissions of his agents and servants and of any other persons of whose services he makes use for the performance of the carriage, when such agents, servants or other persons are acting within the scope of their employment, as if such acts or omissions were his own."

G

      Chapter III of CMR, containing articles 4 to 16, is entitled " Conclusion and Performance of the Contract of Carriage." It is only necessary to refer to article 4, which provides:

      " The contract of carriage shall be confirmed by the making out of a consignment note. The absence, irregularity or loss of the consignment note shall not affect the existence or the validity of the contract of carriage which shall remain subject to the provisions of this Convention."

H

      Chapter IV of CMR, containing articles 17 to 29, is entitled " Liability of the Carrier." Article 17, paragraph 1, provides that the carrier shall be liable for the total or partial loss of the goods or for damage thereto occurring between the time when he takes over the goods and the time of delivery, as well as for any delay in delivery, subject to various defences

1370

set out in article 17, paragraphs 2 and 4, and article 18. Article 27 provides A
for interest on any compensation payable.

Chapter V of CMR, containing articles 30 to 33, is entitled " Claims
and Actions." Article 31 provides:

" In legal proceedings arising out of carriage under this Convention,
the plaintiff may bring an action in any court or tribunal of a contracting country designated by agreement between the parties and, B
in addition, in the courts or tribunals of a country within whose
territory (a) the defendant is ordinarily resident, or has his principal
place of business, or the branch or agency through which the contract
of carriage was made, or (b) the place where the goods were taken
over by the carrier or the place designated for delivery is situated,
and in no other courts or tribunals."

C

Chapter VI of CMR, containing articles 34 to 40, is entitled " Provisions
Relating to Carriage Performed by Successive Carriers." Article 34
provides:

" If carriage governed by a single contract is performed by successive
road carriers, each of them shall be responsible for the performance
of the whole operation, the second carrier and each succeeding carrier D
becoming a party to the contract of carriage, under the terms of the
consignment note, by reason of his acceptance of the goods and the
consignment note."

Article 36 provides:

" Except in the case of a counterclaim or a set-off raised in an action
concerning a claim based on the same contract of carriage, legal E
proceedings in respect of liability for loss, damage or delay may only
be brought against the first carrier, the last carrier or the carrier who
was performing that portion of the carriage during which the event
causing the loss, damage or delay occurred; an action may be brought
at the same time against several of these carriers."

Article 37 provides: F

" A carrier who has paid compensation in compliance with the
provisions of this Convention, shall be entitled to recover such compensation, together with interest thereon and all costs and expenses
incurred by reason of the claim, from the other carriers who have
taken part in the carriage, subject to the following provisions: (a) the
carrier responsible for the loss or damage shall be solely liable for the G
compensation whether paid by himself or by another carrier; (b) when
the loss or damage has been caused by the action of two or more
carriers, each of them shall pay an amount proportionate to his share
of liability; should it be impossible to apportion the liability, each
carrier shall be liable in proportion to the share of the payment for
the carriage which is due to him; (c) if it cannot be ascertained to H
which carriers liability is attributable for the loss or damage, the
amount of the compensation shall be apportioned between all the
carriers as laid down in (b) above."

Article 38 provides:

" If one of the carriers is insolvent, the share of the compensation
due from him and unpaid by him shall be divided among the other

The Weekly Law Reports, November 13, 1981

1371

1 W.L.R.   Cummins Engine Co. v. Davis Freight Ltd. (C.A.)   Brandon L.J.

A   carriers in proportion to the share of the payment for the carriage due to them."

Article 39 provides:

" 1. No carrier against whom a claim is made under articles 37 and 38 shall be entitled to dispute the validity of the payment made by the carrier making the claim if the amount of the compensation was B   determined by judicial authority after the first mentioned carrier had been given due notice of the proceedings and afforded an opportunity of entering an appearance.

" 2. A carrier wishing to take proceedings to enforce his right of recovery may make his claim before the competent court or tribunal of the country in which one of the carriers concerned is ordinarily C   resident, or has his principal place of business or the branch or agency through which the contract of carriage was made. All the carriers concerned may be made defendants in the same action.

" 3 The provisions of article 31, paragraphs 3 and 4, shall apply to judgments entered in the proceedings referred to in articles 37 and 38.

" 4. The provisions of article 32 shall apply to claims between D   carriers. The period of limitation shall, however, begin to run either on the date of the final judicial decision fixing the amount of compensation payable under the provisions of this Convention, or, if there is no such judicial decision, from the actual date of payment."

Article 40 provides: " Carriers shall be free to agree among themselves on provisions other than those laid down in articles 37 and 38."

E   Chapter VII of CMR, containing article 41, is entitled " Nullity of Stipulations Contrary to the Convention." The effect of article 41 is to render void any term of a contract of carriage which is inconsistent with the provisions of CMR except as specially permitted by article 40.

It is clear from the provisions of CMR contained in Chapters V and VI that it contemplates two kinds of legal proceedings arising out of a contract F   of carriage. The first kind of legal proceedings which it contemplates are actions brought by a sender or consignee of goods against one or more carriers. Where successive carriers are involved, the effect of article 31, paragraph 1, combined with article 34, is that the plaintiff can bring a single action against one, more than one, or all the carriers concerned. Article 31, paragraph 1, further requires him to bring his action in certain courts only. These courts are, first, any court of a contracting state which G   has been agreed between the parties; secondly, the courts of the country where any of the carriers sued is ordinarily resident, or has his principal place of business, or the branch or agency through which the contract of carriage was made; and, thirdly, the courts of the place where the goods were taken over for the carriage or the place where they were to be delivered.

H   It is on the basis of these provisions that, in the present case, Cummins issued a writ against four parties, Davis, Charterway, Graaf and Boers, although they have only served such writ on Davis.

The second kind of legal proceedings which CMR contemplates are actions in which one carrier, who has been compelled to pay compensation to a sender or consignee, seeks to recover an indemnity or contribution from one or more other carriers involved in the carriage.

CMR appears to contemplate that these two kinds of legal proceedings

will be separate from each other, the first and main action being followed A
by a second and consequential action. I say this because the opening words
of article 37 are " A carrier who *has* paid compensation in compliance
with the provisions of this Convention, shall be entitled to recover. . . ."
It seems to me, however, that, where the procedure of the court in which
the first and main action is brought allows claims by a defendant for
contribution or indemnity to be added to the main action by way of third
party proceedings, as is the situation in the present case, there is no good B
reason in principle why what is contemplated by CMR as the second and
consequential action should not be brought by way of such third party
proceedings. It is only right to add that none of the defendants who are
respondents to this appeal have sought to contend otherwise.

The application for leave to serve third party notices out of the
jurisdiction was made by Davis under R.S.C., Ord. 11, r. 1 (1) (*l*), as made C
applicable to third party proceedings by R.S.C., Ord. 16, r. 3 (4). Order 11,
r. 1 (1) (*l*) provides for service out of the jurisdiction:

> " if the action begun by the writ is brought under the Carriage by
> Air Act 1961, the Carriage by Air (Supplementary Provisions) Act
> 1962, the Carriage of Goods by Road Act 1965, the Nuclear Instal-
> lations Act 1965, or the Protection of Trading Interests Act 1980." D

The grounds on which Charterway, Graaf and Boers succeeded before
Mocatta J. in having the earlier order of Robert Goff J. and the service of
the third party notices on each of them set aside were as follows. First, so
far as Charterway and Graaf are concerned, that, even assuming that they
are to be regarded as consecutive carriers at all, as the decision in
Ulster-Swift Ltd. v. *Taunton Meat Haulage Ltd.* [1977] 1 W.L.R. 625 E
appears to indicate that they should be, neither was the carrier responsible
for the loss or damage to the goods, so as to entitle Davis to sue them for
an indemnity under article 37. Secondly, so far as all three defendants are
concerned, that, under article 39, paragraph 2, Davis were not entitled to
bring proceedings for an indemnity against them, whether by way of third
party proceedings or separate action, in an English court. F

So far as the first ground relied on by Charterway and Graaf is
concerned, I do not see any answer to it. On the footing that they were
successive carriers, the evidence establishes clearly that the damage to the
goods took place while they were being carried by Boers, with the result
that, under article 37, Boers are the only successive carrier from whom
Davis are entitled to recover over any compensation which they are held
liable to pay to Cummins. It follows that third party proceedings by Davis G
against Charterway or Graaf must fail, and on that ground alone the order
of Goff J. giving leave to Davis to serve third party notices on Charterway
and Graaf out of the jurisdiction in the Netherlands, and the subsequent
service of such notices, must be set aside. It was suggested that, if Boers
became insolvent, Davis would then be entitled to recourse against
Charterway and Graaf under article 38. There was, however, no evidence H
to suggest that Boers were, or were likely to be, insolvent, and, in the
absence of such evidence, I think that the possibility should be disregarded.

I turn to the second ground relied on by all three defendants, namely,
that, under article 39, paragraph 2, Davis were not entitled to bring proceedings for an indemnity against them in an English court. The validity
of this ground depends on the meaning to be given to the expression " the

The Weekly Law Reports, November 20, 1981

1373

1 W.L.R.   Cummins Engine Co. v. Davis Freight Ltd. (C.A.)   Brandon L.J.

A carriers concerned " in line 3 of article 39, paragraph 2. For the defendants it was contended that the expression means, and means only, the carriers from whom the carrier primarily liable to a sender or consignee is seeking to recover the compensation which he has had to pay. I shall call that the first meaning. For Davis it was contended that the expression includes not only the carriers from whom compensation is being sought to be recovered, but also the carrier who is seeking to recover it. I shall call

B that the second meaning.

If the first meaning is correct Davis would have to sue Charterway, Graaf and Boers in a court in the Netherlands and would not be entitled to proceed against them in a court in England. If the second meaning is correct Davis would be entitled to sue the three other carriers either in a court in the Netherlands or in a court in England.

C   In my view, it is necessary to interpret the expression " the carriers concerned " in line 3 of article 39, paragraph 2, in the context in which it is used. That context is a situation in which one carrier, who has been made primarily liable to a sender or consignee, is seeking to recover over against one or more other carriers. That being the context in which the expression is used, I have no doubt at all that it would be given the first

D meaning contended for by the defendants, rather than the second meaning contended for by Davis.

I should reach that conclusion even without considering line 6 of article 39, paragraph 2, where the expression " the carriers concerned " is used a second time. It is used in the last sentence of article 39, paragraph 2, which reads: " All the carriers concerned may be made defendants in the same action." Counsel for Davis conceded, as he was bound to

E do, that in this last sentence the expression " the carriers concerned " has, and can only have, the first meaning, and he was therefore compelled to argue that the expression when used in line 3 had a different meaning from the same expression when used in line 6.

In my view it is highly improbable that those who drafted CMR intended that the same expression, used twice in the same paragraph and in

F the same context, should be given one meaning when used the first time and another meaning when used the second time. This consideration strongly reinforces the view which I should in any case form about the meaning of the expression in line 3, quite independently of its further use in line 6.

Counsel for Davis put forward various arguments against our holding that Davis could not sue Charterway, Graff or Boers for an indemnity in

G England. One argument was that article 31, paragraph 1, applied not only to primary actions brought by a sender or consignee against one or more carriers, but also to secondary actions for an indemnity brought by one carrier against other carriers. That argument is, in my view, quite untenable for two reasons. First, it is inconsistent with the whole way in which the various subject matters in CMR are dealt with successively. Secondly,

H when those who drafted CMR wished to incorporate parts of article 31 into article 39, they said so expressly, as in paragraph 3 of the latter article.

A second argument was that article 39, paragraph 2, only provides that a carrier *may* make his claim in certain countries, not that he *must* do so. I do not think there is anything in this argument either, again for two reasons. The first reason is that I think, having regard to the context, that this is one of those cases where the word " may " must be interpreted, in

1374

effect, as meaning " must." The second reason is that, if the word is in-   **A**
terpreted as permissive only, then there is nothing anywhere else in article
39, or any other part of CMR, which permits actions by one carrier
against other carriers for an indemnity to be brought in the courts of any
countries other than those specified in article 39, paragraph 2.

A third argument was that it was very inconvenient if, in a case like
the present one, both the primary and the secondary proceedings arising
out of the same event could not be dealt with by the same court. I agree   **B**
that it is inconvenient, but that consideration cannot be allowed to distort
what I regard as the clear meaning of article 39, paragraph 2. It may also
be observed that the difficulty would have been avoided if Cummins had
sued all four defendants in the Netherlands, although I recognise that it
is unlikely that they would have chosen to do so.

A fourth argument was that, if Davis were not allowed to serve third   **C**
party proceedings on Charterway, Graaf and Boers out of the jurisdiction
in the Netherlands, there would be no way in which those three parties
could be bound by the result of the main action in the manner contemplated by article 39, paragraph 1. I do not agree with that argument.
There is no reason why Davis, instead of seeking to institute third party
proceedings against Charterway, Graaf and Boers, should not have given   **D**
them notice by letter of the action brought against them by Cummins. If
they had done so, those notified, since they were named as defendants in
the writ, would have been entitled to enter appearances voluntarily under
R.S.C., Ord. 10, r. 1 (3). Or, supposing a different case, where those notified were not already named as defendants, they could, following notice,
apply to be joined as further defendants under R.S.C., Ord. 15, r. 6 (2) (b)
(ii).   **E**

The conclusions at which I have arrived about this case accord with
those expressed in the clear and impressive judgment of Mocatta J. Those
conclusions mean that this appeal, strenuously as it has been argued by
counsel for Davis, fails and must be dismissed.

O'CONNOR L.J. I agree that the appeal must be dismissed. Brandon   **F**
L.J. has set out all the relevant facts and the relevant articles of the CMR
Convention and I need not repeat them. During the course of the case it
seemed to me that, if possible, article 39, paragraph 2, should be construed in such a fashion as to limit the number of places in which litigation arising out of a single casualty had to be heard. So, as Cummins were
entitled to, and did, commence proceedings in England, that meant that, if
possible, the claims for contribution by one carrier against another, if dis-   **G**
puted, should also be heard in England. But, as Brandon L.J. has pointed
out, the provisions of the Law Reform (Married Women and Tortfeasors) Act 1935, in England had been expressly excluded by the Act of
1965, and the sole provision for dealing with claims over by one carrier
against another has to be found in article 39. In order to achieve the result
which, to my mind, would be desirable, it would be necessary to construe   **H**
article 39, paragraph 2 in the way contended for by Davis, namely, that
Davis were themselves a " carrier concerned ' and, therefore, the suit
could be entertained in England.

At first it seemed to me that that might be a viable argument, but in
the end I have been driven to the conclusion that it will not do. It will be
seen that the scheme of the Convention, starting in article 31, is that normally, unless the parties otherwise agree, any legal proceedings are to be

The Weekly Law Reports, November 20, 1981

1375

1 W.L.R.   Cummins Engine Co. v. Davis Freight Ltd. (C.A.)   O'Connor L.J.

A   originated in the jurisdiction of " the defendant " (article 31, paragraph 1 (*a*)), and I am content, under the ordinary rules of interpretation, to read " defendant " for " defendants." The only alternative there given is the place where the goods were taken over or the place designated for delivery. The place where the goods were taken over by the carrier, in my judgment, refers to the place where the contract of carriage commenced (see article 1 of the Convention) and cannot be repeated down the line where successive

B   carriers have participated in the carriage at various stages. That in the present case was Scotland and the place of delivery was Holland. Therefore, Cummins were limited to bringing the action, as far as the jurisdiction of the defendant was concerned, either in England (Davis) or in Holland the other three.

Starting from that and turning back to article 39, paragraph 2, which is

C   providing the machinery for a carrier defined in article 37 as " A carrier who has paid compensation in compliance with the provisions of this Convention," there it will be seen that " A carrier wishing to take proceedings to enforce his right of recovery may make his claim before the competent court or tribunal of the country in which one of the carriers concerned is ordinarily resident." In my judgment, the " carrier concerned " there is the carrier concerned with *making* contribution and not *claiming* contribu-

D   tion. Read in that way, it fits comfortably with the last sentence, of paragraph 2 of article 39: " All the carriers concerned may be made defendants in the same action." That being so, unfortunate as I regard it, it is not possible to construe article 39, paragraph 2, to give effect to what I would regard as a desirable result.

For those reasons and for the reasons given by Brandon L.J., with

E   which I agree, the appeal should be dismissed.

EVELEIGH L.J. I am not prepared to go so far as to say that the word " may " in article 39, paragraph 2, is the equivalent of " must." That article does not contain the words which we read in article 31, " and in no other courts or tribunals." Thus I would leave open the question as to whether a defendant can claim indemnity or contribution in this

F   country against a carrier who has entered an appearance for the purpose of disputing the validity of a payment after receiving notice under article 39. However, I regard R.S.C., Ord. 11, r. 1 (1) (*l*) as envisaging only a claim which could be made according to the procedure specifically permitted or envisaged by article 39, paragraph 2. For the reasons given by Brandon L.J., I do not think that the present claim by Davis can be covered by article 39, paragraph 2. If I am wrong, as a matter of construction, as to the effect of R.S.C., Ord. 11, r. 1 (1) (*l*), then I would say that, in exercising its jurisdiction, the court should act in such a way as to comply with the procedure specifically permitted by the Convention.

In the result then, I too come to the conclusion that this appeal should dismissed.

Appeal dismissed with costs.
Leave to appeal in relation to
D. Boers B.V. refused.

Solicitors: *Clyde & Co., Guildford; Wm. A. Merrick & Co.; Sinclair & Temperley; Ince & Co.*

E. M. W.

63 (2)

A

[QUEEN'S BENCH DIVISION]

* THE JOGOO

[1980 Folio 248]

1981   Jan. 14, 15, 16; 30   Sheen J.   B

> *Admiralty—Mortgage—Priorities—Sale of vessel—Order of priority*
> *of claims—Whether cost of discharging cargo before sale to*
> *become first charge of proceeds*
> *Ships' Names—Jogoo*

In an action in rem by the mortgagees, the vessel *Jogoo*   C
was arrested while berthed at Newport, Gwent. She was laden
with 5,500 tons of mixed cargo and had been on a voyage from
Dar es Salaam to Newport and thence to other European ports.
Prior to the sale of the ship by the Admiralty Marshal the
cargo was discharged at Newport at the expense of the cargo-
owners. The cargo-owners, who were given leave to intervene
in the action, sought a declaration that the cost of discharging
the cargo should rank pari passu with the charges and expenses   D
of the Admiralty Marshal in executing the commission of
appraisement and sale of the *Jogoo* so that those costs would
be a first charge on the proceeds of sale.
On the question whether the court should grant the
declaration: —

Held, refusing the declaration, that in the event of a contract of carriage not being completed by ship-owners the
cargo-owners should pay for the removal of their own cargo   E
and then claim against the ship-owners for the damage suffered.
The Mingren Development [1979] H.K.L.R. 159 considered.

The following cases are referred to in the judgment:

Brave Enterprise, The (unreported), April 4, 1975.
Emilia, The, 1963 A.M.C. 1447.
Mingren Development, The [1979] H.K.L.R. 159.
Myrto, The [1978] 1 Lloyd's Rep. 11, C.A.
Poznan, The, 1927 A.M.C 723.
Ruabon Steamship Co. Ltd. v. *London Assurance* [1900] A.C. 6, H.I
Selina Stanford, The, Shipping Gazette, December 8, 1908.
Unity, The, Shipping Gazette, May 3, 1909.

G

The following additional cases were cited in argument:

Bankers Trust International Ltd. v. *Todd Shipyards Corpor*
        A.C. 221; [1980] 3 W.L.R. 400; [1980] 3 All E.R. 197, P
Carl Hendric, The (unreported).
Fothergill v. *Monarch Airlines Ltd.* [1981] A.C. 251; [198   H
        [1980] 2 All E.R. 696, H.L.(E.).
Gettysburg, The (1885) 52 L.T. 60; 5 Asp. 347.
Medina Princess, The [1965] 1 Lloyd's Rep. 361.
Orion, The (1938) 62 Ll.L.Rep. 33.
Zigurds, The [1932] P. 113.

MOTION
On March 27, 1980, the plaintiffs issued a
against the *Jogoo* as mortgagees claiming D.M.

A arrested at Newport on March 27, 1980. On April 16, 1980, Sheen J. ordered the Admiralty Marshal to permit the cargo-owners (the interveners) to remove their cargo. On June 9, 1980, the plaintiffs obtained judgment in the sum of D.M. 11,025,000, and On August 6, 1980, the *Jogoo* was sold by the Admiralty Marshal for U.S. $4,500,000.

B By motion dated December 23, 1980, the cargo-owners sought a declaration that the costs of discharging the cargo of the *Jogoo* at Newport, Gwent between April 23, and June 2, 1980, should be ranked pari passu with the charges and expenses incurred by the Admiralty Marshal in executing the commission of appraisement and sale of the *Jogoo* and those costs should be a first charge on the proceeds of sale.

The facts are stated in the judgment.

C   *Geoffrey Kinley* for the interveners.
Jonathan Mance for the plaintiffs.

January 30. SHEEN J. read the following judgment. On April 16, 1980, I gave leave to the owners of cargo lately laden on board the ship *Jogoo* to intervene in the action commenced by mortgagees of the vessel against her owners. The court now has before it a motion by the interveners, D which will be more readily understood when I have set out the relevant facts leading up to this motion.

By a memorandum of agreement dated April 28, 1978, the Eastern Africa National Shipping Line Ltd., (a company incorporated in Dar es Salaam, Tanzania), agreed to purchase *Jogoo* from her previous owners E for the sum of D.M.12,250,000. The purchasers paid 10 per cent. of the price in cash on delivery while the balance of 90 per cent. was payable over seven years. As security for the outstanding balance the purchasers provided a first and second mortgage on the vessel. In February 1980 *Jogoo* was engaged in a voyage from Dar es Salaam to Newport and certain ports on the continent of Europe. On February 27, 1980, when *Jogoo* was in Newport she was arrested at the suit of Harding Bros., who claimed that F her owners were indebted to them for various goods supplied to the vessel for her maintenance and upkeep. *Jogoo* was still in Newport under arrest on March 27, 1980, when the writ of this action was issued by the mortgagees. The ship-owners had failed to make payments due under the mortgage deeds. It soon became apparent to Harding Bros. that their claim would be postponed to the rights of the mortgagees and that there was no G point in pursuing their claim against the vessel. *Jogoo* was arrested by the mortgagees on March 27, 1980. On April 16, 1980, I heard a motion by the interveners and after hearing the arguments of counsel and of the Admiralty Marshal, I made the following order:

"(1) The Admiralty Marshal shall permit the discharge of all the cargo presently laden aboard the ship *Jogoo* and deliver to the interveners such portions of the cargo as to which they do produce to him H reasonable evidence of title on their solicitors having undertaken to the court to pay the Admiralty Marshal's costs in relation to the interveners' cargo. (2) The balance of the said cargo to be stored and the owners thereof notified as to its storage. (3) The Admiralty Marshal to be at liberty to apply as to the storage of cargo and disposal of any cargo unclaimed within 30 days after completion of discharge. (4) The costs of this application to be reserved."

Jogoo was laden with 5,500 tons of mixed cargo, about half of which A
was copper destined for Antwerp. There were over 100 different cargo-
owners. All except six of them instructed Messrs. Ince & Co. to act on
their behalf. Only those cargo-owners who have given such instruction to
Messrs. Ince & Co. have intervened in this action. The cargo was discharged from *Jogoo* at the port of Newport between April 23 and June 2,
1980. At that time I had not made an order that *Jogoo* be appraised and
sold.   B

On June 9, 1980, I gave judgment for the plaintiffs in the sum of
D.M.11,025,000 in respect of the principal sum due under both the
mortgages and in the sum of D.M.419,311.46 in respect of interest due
thereon. I further ordered that *Jogoo* be appraised and sold by the
Admiralty Marshal by private treaty and reserved all questions as to priorities. Pursuant to that order *Jogoo* was sold on August 6, 1980, for the C
sum of U.S. $4,500,000. Therefore the mortgagees cannot recover out of
the proceeds of sale the full amount for which they have judgment.

The motion now before the court is a motion by the interveners for a
declaration that the cost of discharging the cargo at Newport, which was
borne by the interveners, should rank pari passu with the charges and
expenses incurred by the Admiralty Marshal in executing the commission D
of appraisement and sale of the vessel, and that that cost should thus become a first charge on the proceeds of sale of *Jogoo;* and for an order that
the interveners should be paid a sum of £148,540·83 and interest thereon
out of the proceeds of sale. It is contended by the interveners that this
sum was the cost incurred by them in discharging the cargo.

The financial collapse of the Eastern Africa National Shipping Line
Ltd. made it impossible for that company (1) to pay its debt to Harding E
Bros., (2) to meet its commitments under the mortgage deeds, and (3) to
finance the completion of the voyage on which *Jogoo* was engaged and its
obligations to discharge the cargo as set out in the bills of lading. Harding
Bros., the mortgagees and the cargo-owners have money claims against the
ship-owners. The first two of them took the opportunity provided by the
presence of *Jogoo* within the jurisdiction of this court to try to make some F
financial recovery. Harding Bros. have now recognised that the mortgagees
will be paid in priority to them and accordingly they have not pursued
their claim. I must now decide the order of priority as between the judgment in favour of the mortgagees and the expense incurred by the interveners in discharging the cargo.

The rival contentions are these. The interveners say that *Jogoo* could G
not have been sold (or could only have been sold for a lower price) while
she remained laden with cargo. Therefore the cargo had to be discharged
and therefore the cost of discharging the cargo is part of the cost of selling
the ship. The interveners contend that as they have borne the cost of discharging the cargo and as they have, to that extent, conferred a benefit on
the mortgagees they are entitled to be reimbursed out of the proceeds of H
sale in priority to the claim of the mortgagees. On the other hand, the
mortgagees say that the cargo-owners have a claim against the ship-owners
for damages for breach of the contract of carriage and that part of the
cargo-owners' claim is for reimbursement of the expense incurred by them
in discharging the cargo. The mortgagees contend that no part of the
cargo-owners' claim can be elevated into the position of a secured claim
having priority over the claim of the mortgagees.

A   Mr. Kinley submitted that when a vessel has been arrested in proceedings in rem any expense reasonably incurred which confers a benefit on the res by enhancing its value should be reimbursed out of the proceeds of sale. He submitted that this is in conformity with a decision of the United States Supreme Court and not contrary to any English decision. It was submitted that any plaintiff who arrests a vessel in order to obtain security for his claim takes the vessel as she is. If she is laden with cargo
B   then the cost of discharging the cargo is part of the cost of realising the security.

Mr. Kinley was unable to find any decision of this court which supported his motion. He drew my attention to a decision of the Supreme Court of the United States in *The Poznan*, 1927 A.M.C. 723 and to the decision of the United States Court of Appeals, Second Circuit, in *The*
C *Emilia*, 1963 A.M.C. 1447. In the latter case the judge of the United States District Court said, at p. 1449:

"The court finds that the presence of cargo aboard has an adverse effect on the sale to the detriment of all parties who have an interest, claim or lien in the vessel. The propriety of charging the cost of discharging the cargo against the proceeds of sale as an administra-
D   tive expense again arises. The court, at the time of the issuance of the order of May 21, 1963, informally expressed its reasons for considering the cost of discharging the cargo as an adminstrative expense and takes this opportunity to formally set them forth. The cargo is lawfully and rightfully aboard ship. The owner of the vessel did not have the right to direct removal of the cargo at the expense of the owners of the cargo. *The St. Paul* (S.D.N.Y., 1921), 227 Fed. 99, 107.
E   The sale of the owner's interest in the vessel cannot serve to vest a greater right than the owner had, nor can it impose an additional liability on the cargo-owners. Discharge of the cargo is a service furnished on authority of the court and should be paid out of the proceeds of the sale as an 'expense of justice.' *The Poznan*, 1927 A.M.C. 723, 726. Since the vessel is in custodia legis the charge against
F   the fund is not a lien. The right of the court to direct payment of such charges before pre-custodial liens is stated in *Gilmore and Black, The Law of Admiralty*, p. 497, as follows: '. . . if equity and good conscience require that they be paid in priority to pre-custodial claimants who do have liens, the admiralty court may properly decree the prior payment.'"

G   This decision was affirmed by the United States Court of Appeals, Second Circuit, with the words, at p. 1448:

"'Service rendered to the ship after arrest, in aid of the discharge of cargo, and afterwards pending the sale, necessarily inured to their [lienor's] benefit, for it contributed to the creation of the fund [now] available to them.' The district court had jurisdiction 'to require that
H   expenses which have contributed to either the preservation or creation of the fund in its custody shall be paid before a general distribution among those entitled to receive it.'"

Mr. Kinley sought to persuade me to give new heart to English Admiralty law and practice by transplanting those decisions from the United States. It seems to me, however, that those decisions are incompatible with the sound body of English case law and must be rejected.

In *The Myrto* [1978] 1 Lloyd's Rep. 11, the question which I now have   A
to decide came before the Court of Appeal on an interlocutory appeal
against an order of Brandon J. The Court of Appeal made an order which
left the point open for decision at a later date, when it could be fully
argued, because of the urgency of the matter and the pressure of time.
Roskill L.J. in the course of his judgment said, at pp. 15–16:

> " I would only add this with regard to the United States authorities to   B
> which we were referred. It is well known that United States Admiralty
> law on priorities is not always the same as English law, and therefore
> while giving the utmost weight to any decision of the United States
> Courts, and particularly to the decision of the Supreme Court in *The
> Poznan* in 1927, I do not think that that affords a certain guide as to
> the course we should follow in the present case, where we are con-
> cerned with priorities to be determined in accordance with the law   C
> prevailing in this country."

At the forefront of Mr. Mance's submissions on behalf of the mortgagees he invited me to consider the contractual relationship between the
cargo-owners and the ship-owners. The cargo was carried in *Jogoo* under
a contract of carriage, one of the terms of which was that freight was pre-
paid at Mombasa. When freight is paid in advance the cargo-owners accept   D
the commercial risk that the voyage will not be completed for whatever
reason. If the contract is frustrated the cargo-owners bear the loss because
the Law Reform (Frustrated Contracts) Act 1943 does not apply to contracts for the carriage of goods by sea: see section 2 (5) (*a*). The ship-
owners repudiated the contract of carriage by failing to pay their creditors
or put up security in order to obtain the release from arrest of their vessel,   E
with the result that the cargo-owners now have claims for damages against
them. The cargo-owners have a right to remove their cargo from the ship,
or they may abandon it.

Mr. Mance pointed out that the cargo-owners applied to intervene in
this action because they were anxious to have the cargo discharged for their
own benefit and primarily with their own interests in mind. Furthermore, I
did not order the cargo to be discharged. My order was that the Admiralty   F
Marshal should permit the cargo-owners to remove their cargo. At the
time when the interveners arranged for the discharge of the cargo the
mortgagees had not obtained judgment and I had not ordered that *Jogoo* be
sold.

I wil assume that one result of the discharge of the cargo was that when
Jogoo was subsequently sold by order of the court, the price paid was   G
higher that it would have been if the cargo had still been on board. Even
on that assumption the interveners have no claim against the mortgagees,
because there is no principle of law which requires a person to contribute
to an outlay merely because he has derived a material benefit from it: see
Ruabon Steamship Co. Ltd. v. *London Assurance* [1900] A.C. 6. Mr.
Kinley did not submit that the interveners had any direct claim for reim-   H
bursement against the mortgagees, but the effect of acceding to his application would be that the expense of discharging the cargo would come out of
the pockets of the mortgagees.

The practice of this court is stated in *Roscoe's Admiralty Practice*, 5th
ed. (1931), p. 287 in these words:

> " When the marshal has in his custody a vessel with a cargo on board,
> and he is ordered to sell the vessel only, the cargo-owners will be given

A   a reasonable time by the court wherein to effect the unlivery of the cargo, but if the unlivery is not effected in the time fixed, the cargo-owners will thereafter be ordered to pay the cost of the detention of the vessel for which they may be responsible: *The Carl Hendric* (1903), Fo. 468; *The Selina Stanford* (Shipping Gazette, December 8, 1908)."

In *The Selina Stanford* Sir Gorell Barnes P. said that he was informed
B   by the Admiralty Marshal:

"it was very desirable the cargo should be transhipped, because if it were landed at Portland under his directions it would be worthless, *and* the cost of landing would probably have to come out of the proceeds of the vessel."

The sense of the report of this case suggests that the word "and" (which
C   I have emphasised) should be read as "and therfore." In *The Unity,* Shipping Gazette, May 3, 1909, Bargrave Deane J. made an order permitting the Admiralty Marshal to discharge and sell the cargo, recouping himself out of the proceeds and paying the balance into court unless the cargo-owners took the cargo from the vessel. In *The Brave Enterprise* (unreported), April 4, 1975, the Admiralty Registrar made an order that the
D   Admiralty Marshal be at liberty to discharge and sell or if necessary destroy the cargo and his expenses incurred in discharge, sale or destruction be paid out of the proceeds of such sale. Any expenses not so recovered to form part of the Admiralty Marshal's expenses in that action.

This same question has recently arisen in Hong Kong in *The Mingren Development* [1979] H.K.L.R. 159, in which case Cons J. decided that the expenses of off-loading and storage of the cargo were to be taken first from
E   the securities lodged by the cargo claimants. In the course of his judgment (with which I entirely agree) Cons J. said, at p. 163:

"It seems to me that the English position derives from the old com-mon law doctrine of frustration. American courts have approached from a different direction. They appear to look at it this way, that from the moment of its arrest a ship is a common fund administered by the
F   court for the common benefit of all those interested in the fund and that any expenses incurred in the administration of that fund should be borne by the fund itself as an 'expense of justice.'"

The judge then referred to *The Poznan,* 1927 A.M.C. 723 and *The Emilia,* 1963 A.M.C. 1447 and continued, at p. 163:

G   "The present position is of long standing. As I see it the position was confirmed in 1943 when contracts for the carriage of goods by sea were deliberately excluded from the operation of the Law Reform (Frustra-ted Contracts) Act. I am not persuaded that the American approach is so much more just or that conditions now are so different from those in 1943 that I should take it on myself to make a general change."

H   Such few cases as have been reported show that in England the Admiralty Court has consistently taken the view that the cargo-owners must pay for removal of their own cargo in the event of the contract of carriage not being completed by the ship-owners, and then make a claim against the ship-owners for the damage which they have suffered. It seems to me that this is correct in principle. For these reasons this motion by the interveners must fail.

In case my decision should be reversed on appeal I must say something

further about the amount claimed. If it should be held hereafter that the A
cost of discharging the cargo should be a first charge on the proceeds of
sale of *Jogoo*, then the amount so charged should be the cost of discharging
the cargo on to the quay and no more. The interveners allege that the cost
of discharging cargo amounted to £148,540·83. That sum appears to include
many items which were of benefit to the cargo-owners but were not incurred
solely for the purpose of freeing the vessel of her cargo. The mortgagees
contend that the amount attributable to discharging alone is less than B
£30,000. It was agreed between the parties that the assessment of the true
discharging costs should be deferred until the question as to who should
bear these costs had been decided.

Declaration refused.

Solicitors: *Ince & Co.; Richards, Butler & Co.*   C

M. B. D.

[HOUSE OF LORDS]

* *In re* DHESI   D
In re HUGHES
In re HILL

1981 Oct. 26   Lord Diplock, Lord Keith of Kinkel
                                                 and Lord Bridge of Harwich E

Petitions by the defendants Gian Singh Dhesi, Stephen Hughes and
Leonard Hill for leave to appeal to the House of Lords from the decision
of the Divisional Court of the Queen's Bench Division in *Reg.* v. *Dartford
Justices, Ex parte Dhesi; Reg.* v. *Edmonton Justices, Ex parte Hughes*
and *Reg.* v. *Manchester Stipendiary Magistrate, Ex parte Hill* [1981] 3
W.L.R. 315.   F
The Appeal Committee allowed the petitions.

F. C.

[HOUSE OF LORDS]   G

* REGINA .   .   .   . RESPONDENT
                          AND
OLUGBOJA .   .   .   . PETITIONER

1981 Oct. 26   Lord Diplock, Lord Keith of Kinkel
                                                 and Lord Bridge of Harwich H

Petition by the defendant for leave to appeal to the House of Lords
from the decision of the Court of Appeal (Criminal Division) [1981] 3
W.L.R. 585.
The Appeal Committee dismissed the petition.

F. C.

A

[COURT OF APPEAL]

* PRACTICE DIRECTION
(COSTS: ACQUITTAL OF DEFENDANT)

B
1981 Nov. 5   Lord Lane C.J. and Skinner J.

*Crime—Costs—Central funds—Crown Court—Acquitted defendant
—Order for costs—Indictments Act* 1915 (5 & 6 Geo. 5, c. 90),
ss. 5, 6—*Costs in Criminal Cases Act* 1973 (c. 14), s. 3

C
LORD LANE C.J. at the sitting of the court handed down the following
practice direction.

Practice Direction (Costs: Successful Defendants) [1973] 1 W.L.R.
718 issued on June 5, 1973, is withdrawn and the following practice
direction substituted.

1. The principal power of the Crown Court to order the payment of
D the costs of an acquitted defendant either out of central funds under
section 3 of the Costs in Criminal Cases Act 1973 or by the prosecutor
under section 4 of that Act is limited to those cases in which the accused
is acquitted on all counts in the indictment.

2. There is a subsidiary and unrestricted power under section 5 of
the Indictments Act 1915 to order the prosecutor or the defendant to
pay any costs incurred as a result of an amendment to or the severance
E of an indictment.

3. The exercise of those powers is in the unfettered discretion of the
court in the light of the circumstances of each particular case.

4. It should be accepted as normal practice that an order should
normally be made for the payment of the costs of an acquitted defendant
out of central funds under section 3 of the Act of 1973 unless there
F are positive reasons for making a different order. Examples of such
reasons are: (a) where the prosecution has acted spitefully or has instituted or continued proceedings without reasonable cause the defendant's
costs should be paid by the prosecutor under section 4 of the Act of
1973; (b) where the defendant's own conduct has brought suspicion on
himself and has misled the prosecution into thinking that the case
against him is stronger than it is the defendant can be left to pay his
G own costs; (c) where there is ample evidence to support a conviction but
the defendant is acquitted on a technicality which has no merit. Here
again the defendant can be left to pay his own costs.

5. This practice direction is to take effect from November 16, 1981.

H
The following notes were handed down with the practice direction.

Practice Direction (Costs: Acquittal of Defendant) was issued by
Lord Lane C.J. on November 5, 1981. The principal change from
Practice Direction (Costs: Successful Defendants) [1973] 1 W.L.R. 718
is that the power to award costs to an acquitted defendant is limited to
cases in which the accused is acquitted on *all* counts in the indictment.
The practice direction also refers to the court's powers under the
Indictments Act 1915.

Lord Lane C.J.   **Practice Direction (Costs: Acquittal of Defendant) (C.A.)**   **[1981]**

The Indictments Act 1915

A

The Indictments Act 1915 empowers the court to make orders for costs under both sections 5 and 6.

Section 5 provides that the court may make such order for costs as it thinks fit where, either before or at the trial, it orders—(i) that a defective indictment be amended under subsection (1); (ii) that the indictment be severed under subsection (3); (iii) that the trial be postponed as a result of (i) and (ii) above. The power is expressed in subsection (6) of this section as being in addition to and not in derogation of any other power.

B

Section 6 empowers the court to make such orders as to the payment of that part of the costs of the prosecution which has been incurred by reasons of the indictment containing unnecessary matter, being of unnecessary length or materially defective in any respect.

C

There is a dearth of authority establishing the principles to be followed in implementing these two sections. It appears, however:

1. Under section 5 the court may—(a) order the prosecution to pay the relevant costs of a defendant whether he is eventually acquitted or convicted; (b) order the defence to pay the relevant costs of the prosecution where severance is ordered, e.g. following a late application by the defence which has unnecessarily increased costs; (c) direct the taxing officer to disallow the relevant costs either out of central funds or inter partes either to the prosecution or to the defendant on a taxation carried out under any order made under section 3 or 4 of the Costs in Criminal Cases Act 1973; (d) make observations for the attention of the taxing officer in respect of legal aid costs.

D

2. Under section 6 the court may (i) direct the taxing officer to disallow the relevant costs of the prosecution on the taxation of his costs out of central funds under section 3 of the Act of 1973; (ii) direct the taxing officer to disallow the relevant costs inter partes on any taxation of the prosecutors as against the defendant under section 4 of the Act of 1973.

E

It is suggested that the court should not make any order, give any directions or make any observations without giving the party or parties concerned an opportunity to show cause, if appropriate, after following the procedure set out in the relevant practice direction: *Practice Direction (Crown Court: Costs)* [1977] 1 W.L.R. 181 and *Practice Direction (Crown Court: Legal Aid Taxation)* [1977] 1 W.L.R. 182.

F

L. N. W.

G

H

A

[FAMILY DIVISION]

* BARNETT *v.* HASSETT

1981 Feb. 9;   Wood J.
B   March 2

Husband and Wife—Matrimonial home—Act of 1967—Registra-
tion of charge under Act—Sale of property owned by wife—
Husband not intending to occupy property—Whether Class F
charge registrable for purpose of freezing wife's assets —
Matrimonial Homes Act 1967 (*c.* 75), *s.* 1 (1) (*b*)

C   The parties were married in February 1980. In November
1979 the husband exchanged contracts for the purchase of a
house in Barnet for £410,000 and paid a deposit. He also
incurred legal and survey fees. In March 1980 he moved into
the wife's house and sold his former house. In May 1980 the
husband informed the vendors of the house in Barnet that he
could not complete the purchase, thus forfeiting his deposit. In
July he moved out of the wife's house, and on July 17 the
D   wife exchanged contracts for the sale of her house. The husband wrote to the purchaser stating that he would not register
a charge against the property under the Matrimonial Homes
Act 1967. In November 1980 the husband instructed new
solicitors, who registered a Class F land charge on the wife's
house. The husband claimed that prior to their marriage the
wife had agreed that the purchase of the house in Barnet
should be in joint names, and that she would provide half the
purchase price; at the end of March 1980 she had repudiated
E   the agreement as a result of which he had suffered losses which
he estimated at £120,000.
             On an application by the wife to set aside the Class F land
charge: —
             Held, that the purpose of the Matrimonial Homes Act 1967
was to protect a spouse who had no proprietary, contractual
or statutory rights of occupation of the matrimonial home and
F   a Class F land charge was intended to protect the right of
occupation created by the Act; that interests other than a right
to occupy were to be disregarded, and, accordingly, since the
husband did not seek to enter into or occupy the whole or
any part of the matrimonial home he was not entitled to ask
the court to freeze part of the proceeds of sale by registering
a Class F land charge, and the charge was an improper use of
G   the procedure under the Act and would be set aside.

The following cases are referred to in the judgment:

Gurasz v. *Gurasz* [1970] P. 11; [1969] 3 W.L.R. 482; [1969] 3 All E.R. 822,
    C.A.
Whittingham v. *Whittingham* (*National Westminster Bank Ltd., inter-*
    vener) [1979] Fam. 9; [1978] 2 W.L.R. 936; [1978] 3 All E.R. 805,
H   Balcombe J. and C.A.

No additional cases were cited in argument.

APPLICATION

The wife, Mrs. C. A. Barnett, made an application to set aside the
registration of a Class F charge placed by the husband, Mr. H. E. Hassett,
on a property owned by her at 2, Spaniards Close, Golders Green, N.W.11.

Barnett v. Hassett (Fam.D.) **[1981]**

A

The application was heard in chambers and judgment was given in open court.

The facts are stated in the judgment.

Scott Baker Q.C. and *Philip Vallance* for the wife.
Nicholas Price for the husband.

Cur. adv. vult.

B

March 2. WOOD J. read the following judgment. The question which I have to decide is whether the use of a Class F charge under the provision of the Matrimonial Homes Act 1967 is proper where its sole purpose is to freeze the assets of a spouse.

This application is made as one of urgency, and I am deciding it upon affidavit evidence alone. In essence the relief sought is to set aside the charge and to permit the sale of a house owned by the applicant wife at 2, Spaniards Close, London, N.W.11. It was her matrimonial home during a previous marriage.

C

Some of the facts are not in dispute and can be summarised. The parties first met in 1976. The marriage took place on February 25, 1980. Each party had been married previously. As a result of the financial provision ordered in October 1979 at the end of her first marriage the wife now owns 2, Spaniards Close. She was also awarded a lump sum of £130,000. She has two children by her former marriage, a boy 14 and a girl 15. They live with her. The respondent husband also has two children by his former marriage. His previous matrimonial home was in Barnet and it was sold for £160,000 on March 22, 1980. He is now living with his two children in rented accommodation. The rent is £375 per week and he pays £75 per week for a housekeeper.

D

E

On November 8, 1979, contracts were exchanged between the husband and the owners of Hadley Hurst, Monken Hadley, Barnet, for the sale of that property to him for the sum of £410,000. The deposit of £41,000 was paid by him.

On March 7, 1980, the husband moved into 2, Spaniards Close with his two children. On July 28, 1980, they left. His belongings were all finally removed during October 1980. Each side claims that he or she has a case upon which to pray for a judicial separation on the grounds of unreasonable behaviour. No petition has yet been filed.

F

At the beginning of May 1980 the husband through his solicitors informed the vendors of Hadley Hurst that he could not complete. In September 1980 that house was sold for £342,000. He has forfeited the deposit of £41,000, and he has spent other sums on surveys and legal fees; they are said to total £80,000—a total loss of about £120,000. I was told that he had been served with a writ by the vendors but I do not know the date. On June 12, he received a bill from solicitors acting in the purchase for £2,557.

G

On July 17, 1980, the wife exchanged contracts with a South American gentleman for the sale of 2, Spaniards Close for the price of £395,000. A deposit of £35,000 was paid on exchange of contracts and two further interim payments of £35,000 have been made on September 30 and November 30, 1980, respectively, a total of £105,000. The balance is payable on completion. The value of the house today is some £145,000 less than the contract price.

H

A   Before exchanging contracts solicitors for the purchaser required a
letter from the husband so as to ensure that no Class F charge would be
placed on the property before completion, and on July 17, 1980, he
signed a letter in the following terms. The letter is addressed from the
address 2, Spaniards Close, London, N.W.11, and dated July 17, 1980; it
is addressed to the purchaser. It says:

B   " Dear Sir,
                    Re 2 Spaniards Close, London N.W.11.
        " In consideration of you today entering into a contract to purchase
    the above freehold property from my wife Carole Hassett I hereby
    confirm that I have not and will not register any charge against the
    said property under the Matrimonial Homes Act and that I will
    vacate the said property on or before the agreed completion date of
C   January 31, 1981.
                                                    Yours faithfully,"

and he signs it.

    Recently the completion date was extended to February 13, and now
finally to February 27, 1981. This has been done for the convenience of
the wife who is negotiating the purchase of the lease of a flat in Regents
D Park for herself and her children. I do not think the husband was aware
of this when he registered the Class F charge.

    In November 1980 the husband instructed his present solicitors,
although it would seem from a letter dated February 2, 1981, that his
former solicitors were still acting in connection with Hadley Hurst. I have
no affidavit from either of them. On December 15, 1980, these new
E solicitors applied to register a Class F charge on 2, Spaniards Close. It was
registered on December 17, 1980, and they were notified of the registration
on December 23, 1980. It is not entirely clear to me whether these solicitors
were at the time aware of the contents of the letter of July 17, 1980, signed
by the husband. The partner dealing with the matter was on holiday from
before Christmas until January 20, 1981, and by letter dated January 22,
1981, he wrote in the following terms. There is obviously no reference for
F the wife's solicitors, and the husband's solicitors' reference is RMP/PS/
and then a number, and it is dated January 22, 1981.

        " Dear Sir,
                        Re Mr. and Mrs. Hassett.
        " We act on behalf of Mr. H. E. Hassett and understand that you act
    on behalf of his wife Mrs. C. A. Hassett (formerly Barnett). We are
G   instructed by our client that unhappily the marriage has broken down.
    We would also notify you that our client has registered a matrimonial
    homes caution in respect of his right of occupation in the matrimonial
    home 2, Spaniards Close, London, N.W.11,"

and it is signed " Yours faithfully " with the signature of the firm of
solicitors.

H   That letter was the first indication to the wife or her advisers that a
Class F charge had been registered on behalf of the husband and it was
the first communication between solicitors on this topic. This present
application dated February 3, 1981, was a reaction to that letter which
must have been anticipated.

    On December 15, or 18, 1980—the husband says the latter—he asked
his wife for a loan of £60,000. This was said to be to try to pay off his
liability to the vendors of Hadley Hurst.

On January 26, 1981, a phone call took place between husband and A
wife. The contents of the conversation are in dispute. It is common
ground only that the husband was demanding £60,000—the wife says that
there were additional demands—and that the conversation ended by the
wife saying that she was not going to be blackmailed.

The husband's case is that prior to their marriage this wife had agreed
that the purchase of Hadley Hurst should be in joint names and that she
would be responsible for half the purchase price. He alleges that at the B
end of March 1980 she repudiated this agreement as a result of which
he has suffered loss which he estimated at £120,000. He claims that he
is therefore justified in acting as he did.

On reading the affidavits it was clear to me that whatever the issues
between the parties and however they were decided the husband's position
would be amply protected if I were to keep control of the purchase C
moneys. On being pressed by me, Mr. Price for the husband agreed that
this was so, but he indicated that the loss had either been agreed or
could only be proved to the amount of £60,000 and that this was the
amount of the proceeds of sale which he now submitted should be frozen.
I have therefore allowed completion to take place on February 27, 1981,
that is last Friday, and give my judgment now as soon as possible thereafter with the knowledge that this wife would not have parted with D
£60,000 prior to my judgment.

Mr. Scott Baker for the wife submits that it would be an abuse
of process for me to make an order freezing any part of the purchase
moneys.

Before turning to the law I analyse the husband's case as follows:
(i) he has rights under section 1 (1) (b) of the Matrimonial Homes Act E
1967 as a spouse not in occupation of the matrimonial home; (ii) he does
not wish to occupy that home or any part of it; (iii) he does not now wish
to prevent its sale (although I doubt whether that was his attitude until
very recently); (iv) he wants to freeze part of the proceeds of sale—
£60,000; (v) he therefore registered a Class F charge to force his wife to
apply to this court to set it aside.

I turn to the Act of 1967 itself. It is unnecessary for me to review the F
history of the rights between husband and wife prior to the passing of
this Act; suffice it to say that the provisions of the Act introduce new
rights.

By section 1 the Act protects a spouse who has no rights to remain
in the matrimonial home. It does not protect a spouse who has proprietary, contractual or statutory rights of occupation: see *Gurasz* v. G
Gurasz [1970] P. 11. If not in occupation the right of a spouse is " with
the leave of the court so given to enter into and occupy the dwelling
house ": section 1 (1) (b). The whole emphasis of the Act is to create and
protect the right to occupation of a spouse not in occupation or a spouse
already in occupation. This is made clear throughout the Act. The right
to occupation must relate to a matrimonial home, and only continues H
during the existence of the marriage. A Class F charge is intended to
protect that right.

One thing is abundantly clear, namely that this husband does not
seek " to enter into and occupy " the whole or any part of the matrimonial
home. Is he entitled to ask the court to freeze any part of the proceeds of
sale? I do not think so. Mr. Price did not draw my attention to any
specific parts of the Act itself, but quite apart from the points to which

A I have already referred, section 3 of the Act seems to me to emphasise that any interest other than a right to occupy is to be excluded or disregarded. By that section a charge can only be registered on one matrimonial home at a time. If the intention of the Act had been to allow a spouse to place his or her hands upon proceeds of sale or to allow the prevention of such a sale then I would have thought that a charge on a matrimonial home not in occupation and when a sale was likely would be

B an obvious source for funds.

When a spouse is applying for a transfer of property order involving the matrimonial home or other land, then it will fall within the definition of " pending land action " in section 17 (1) of the Land Charges Act 1972 and is registerable as such; see *Whittingham* v. *Whittingham* (*National Westminster Bank Ltd., intervener*) [1979] Fam. 9.

C I was informed that the present point is as yet undecided but for the reasons which I have given above and each of them, in my judgment, the registration of this Class F charge in the circumstances of the present case was not a proper use of the process set up by the Act of 1967 and the charge will be set aside. No further order will be made in respect of the proceeds of sale.

Although that is sufficient to explain my decision, I would add that it

D should not be thought that I am satisfied this husband has any valid claim against his wife. I have not found it necessary to decide that issue.

Declaration accordingly.

Solicitors: *S. Rutter & Co.; D. J. Freeman & Co.*

E
[Reported by MISS LESLEY HEWLETT, Barrister-at-Law]

[COURT OF APPEAL]

F
* JANOV *v.* MORRIS

[1980 J. No. 6213]

1981   July 17   Dunn and Watkins L.JJ.

G *Practice—Dismissal of action for want of prosecution—Second action—First action dismissed for failure to comply with peremptory order of court—Second action in respect of same cause of action within limitation period — Whether second action should be struck out—R.S.C., Ord. 18, r. 19 (1) (d)* [1]

In 1978 the plaintiff issued a writ claiming against the defendant damages for breach of contract. The defendant

H delivered particulars of defence and counterclaim pursuant to the plaintiff's request and then no further step was taken in the action for a period of 10 months. On the defendant's application to strike out the action for want of prosecution, the master ordered that the action would be struck out unless the plaintiff served his summons for directions by a specified date. The plaintiff failed to comply with the order or to offer any explanation for his delay in prosecuting the action. In July

[1] R.S.C., Ord. 18, r. 19 (1) (d): see post, p. 1392B.

1980, the master gave judgment on the claim for the defendant. A
In September 1980 the plaintiff issued a second writ pleading
the same cause of action. The defendant successfully applied,
under R.S.C., Ord. 18, r. 19, to strike out the second action as
an abuse of the process of the court. On the plaintiff's appeal,
the judge accepted the plaintiff's contention that he was entitled
to bring a second action at any time within the limitation
period notwithstanding that his original action had been struck
out for failure to comply with a peremptory order of the court B
and he rescinded the master's order striking out the second
action.

On the defendant's appeal: —

Held, allowing the appeal, that on a proper construction of
R.S.C., Ord. 18, r. 19, the court had a discretion to strike out
an action as an abuse of the process of the court where there
had been a failure by a litigant to comply with a peremptory
order of the court in a previous action; that the judge erred in C
principle in not approaching the matter as one of discretion;
that, in the circumstances, the court should uphold the principle
that peremptory orders were made to be complied with and
not to be ignored and, in the absence of any explanation for
the plaintiff's conduct or assurance as to his conduct of the
present action, the court, in the exercise of its discretion,
would order that the action be struck out (post, pp. 1384E,
1395B–F, H–A). D

Dictum of Roskill L.J. in *Samuels* v. *Linzi Dresses Ltd.*
[1981] Q.B. 115, C.A. applied.

Birkett v. *James* [1978] A.C. 297, H.L.(E.) and *Tolley* v.
Morris [1979] I W.L.R. 592, H.L.(E.) considered.

Decision of Smith J. reversed.

The following cases are referred to in the judgment of Dunn L.J.: E

Allen v. *Sir Alfred McAlpine & Sons Ltd.* [1968] 2 Q.B. 229; [1968] 2
W.L.R. 366; [1968] 1 All E.R. 543, C.A.

Birkett v. *James* [1978] A.C. 297; [1977] 3 W.L.R. 38; [1977] 2 All E.R.
801, C.A. and H.L.(E.).

Samuels v. *Linzi Dresses Ltd.* [1981] Q.B. 115; [1980] 2 W.L.R. 836; [1980]
1 All E.R. 803, C.A.

Tolley v. *Morris* [1979] 1 W.L.R. 592; [1979] 2 All E.R. 561, H.L.(E.). F

No additional cases were cited in argument.

INTERLOCUTORY APPEAL from Smith J.

By writ issued on August 7, 1978, the plaintiff, Arthur Janov, claimed
against the defendant, Barry Morris, damages for breach of a contract for
the sale of a yacht. On March 10, 1980, the defendant applied to strike G
out the action for want of prosecution. On March 21, 1980, Master Waldman ordered that the plaintiff serve his summons for directions by April 1,
1980. The order was not complied with and on July 2, 1980, the master
gave judgment on the claim for the defendant. On September 9, 1980, the
plaintiff issued a second writ in respect of the same cause of action. On
March 2, 1981, Master Elton, on the defendant's application under R.S.C., H
Ord. 18, r. 19, struck out the second action on the ground that it was an
abuse of the process of the court. The plaintiff appealed to the judge in
chambers and on April 1, 1981, Smith J. rescinded the master's order.

By notice of appeal dated April 1, 1981, the defendant appealed on
the grounds (1) that the proceedings in the second action should be stayed
as an abuse of process; (2) that the plaintiff's conduct in failing to comply
with the peremptory order dated March 21, 1980, was contumelious, and

A that he was thereby debarred from starting a fresh action in the same subject matter; (3) that, the plaintiff's conduct being contumelious, R.S.C., Ord. 18, r. 19 should apply to stay any fresh action in the same subject matter; (4) that, whereas the judge had to decide between the conflicting dicta of, on the one hand, Lord Diplock in *Birkett* v. *James* [1978] A.C. 297, 321 and *Tolley* v. *Morris* [1979] 1 W.L.R. 592, 603 and, on the other, of Lord Edmund-Davies in *Birkett* v. *James* [1978] A.C. 297, 334 and *Tolley* v.
B *Morris* [1979] 1 W.L.R. 592, 604, he erred in law in allowing the appeal and failing to strike out; and (5) that the judge erred in law in holding that the issue not being time barred under the Statute of Limitations he should follow the ratio in the cases on dismissal for want of prosecution and allow a fresh writ.

The facts are stated in the judgment of Dunn L.J.

C
Robin Miller for the defendant.
Mark Strachan for the plaintiff.

DUNN L.J. This is an appeal from an order of Smith J. made in chambers on April 1, 1981, whereby he allowed an appeal from an order of Master Elton, who had struck out an action on the ground that the
D action was an abuse of the process of the court.

The action, which is 1980 J. No. 6213, arose out of a contract for the sale of a yacht which had been made in April 1978. On August 7, 1978, the plaintiff, the seller of the yacht, had brought an action, 1978 J. No. 4563, claiming damages for non-acceptance of the yacht. A defence was delivered in November 1978, disputing the contract and setting up a counterclaim for
E damages for non-delivery. Various steps were taken in the action, and on May 23, 1979, further and better particulars of the defence and counterclaim were delivered pursuant to a request which had been made on February 1, 1979.

No further step was then taken in the action until March 10, 1980—a period of very nearly 10 months—when the defendant applied to strike
F out the action for want of prosecution. His solicitors swore an affidavit in support of that application. There was no affidavit in reply by the plaintiff, and on March 21, 1980, the master made an order that the action would be struck out unless the plaintiff served his summons for directions by April 1, 1980. There was no appeal by the plaintiff against that order; no explanation was given for the delay and no application was made to extend the time for service of the summons for directions. So accordingly, on July
G 2, 1980, the master gave judgment on the claim for the defendant, but ordered the counterclaim to stand, and directed that proceedings should be issued under R.S.C., Ord. 14 in respect of the counterclaim. On August 13, 1980, the defendant filed an affidavit under R.S.C., Ord. 14, in respect of the counterclaim.

On September 9, 1980, the plaintiff issued a second writ, which is the
H writ with which we are presently concerned, no. 6213, in which he relied on precisely the same cause of action as in the writ, 1978 J. No. 4563 which had been effectively struck out only two months before. The defendant then issued a summons under R.S.C., Ord. 18, r. 19 to strike out that new writ on the ground that it was an abuse of the process of the court.

Meanwhile, in the first action, the plaintiff filed an affidavit in the Order 14 proceedings on November 14, 1980, and was given leave to defend the counterclaim on December 5, 1980. The counterclaim in the first action is

still alive, but if this second action is struck out, then effectively the A
plaintiff is debarred from proceeding with his claim for damages for non-
acceptance.

The defendant's application to strike out came before the master on
March 2, 1981, when the master made the order striking out the second
action, and on April 1, 1981, the judge rescinded that order, and it is
against that order of the judge that the defendant now appeals.

The defendant relies on R.S.C., Ord. 18, r. 19, which provides: B

" (1) The court may at any stage of the proceedings order to be struck
out or amended any pleading or the indorsement of any writ in the
action . . . on the ground that—. . . (d) it is otherwise an abuse of the
process of the court; . . ."

What is said, quite shortly, on behalf of the defendant is that this claim, C
having been struck out once in an action raising an identical cause of
action, it would be an abuse of the process of the court to allow it to be
resurrected.

What is said on behalf of the plaintiff, effectively, is this, that since the
period of limitation for the original cause of action does not expire until
1984, the plaintiff is entitled to bring a second action at any time within
that limitation period, notwithstanding that his original claim was struck D
out by reason of his failure to comply with a peremptory order.

The judge accepted that, and we have been told that he accepted it,
primarily, because he relied on a dictum of Lord Edmund-Davies, in the
well-known case of *Birkett* v. *James* [1978] A.C. 297, 334. The difficulty
in the case arises because there are what were submitted to be inconsistent
obiter dicta in *Birkett* v. *James,* and also in the more recent case of E
Tolley v. *Morris* [1979] 1 W.L.R. 592.

It is important to remember that both *Birkett* v. *James* and *Tolley* v.
Morris were concerned with applications to strike out actions for want of
prosecution on the ground of inordinate and inexcusable delay. They were
not concerned, as in this case, with an application to strike out under
R.S.C., Ord. 18, r. 19, where there had been a failure by the plaintiff to
comply with a peremptory order in a previous action.   F

Ever since *Allen* v. *Sir Alfred McAlpine & Sons Ltd.* [1968] 2 Q.B.
229, it has been accepted that the power of the court to strike out actions
for want of prosecution should be exercised only where the court is either
satisfied that there has been an intentional and contumelious default—for
example, disobedience of a peremptory order of the court—or that there has
been inordinate and inexcusable delay. And although *Birkett* v. *James* G
was dealing with the second ground, there are obiter dicta relating to the
first ground which are, of course, of persuasive authority in this court,
although not binding upon us.

In *Birkett* v. *James* [1978] A.C. 297 Lord Diplock said, at p. 321:

" The court may and ought to exercise such powers as it possesses
under the rules to make the plaintiff pursue his action with all proper H
diligence, particularly where at the trial the case will turn upon the
recollection of witnesses to past events. For this purpose the court
may make peremptory orders providing for the dismissal of the action
for non-compliance with its order as to the time by which a particular
step in the proceedings is to be taken. Disobedience to such an order
would qualify as ' intentional and contumelious ' within the meaning of
the first principle laid down in *Allen* v. *McAlpine.* But where no

A   question of non-compliance with a peremptory order is involved the
court is not in my view entitled to treat as ' inordinate delay ' justifying dismissal of the action in accordance with the second principle in
Allen v. *McAlpine* a total time elapsed since the accrual of the cause
of action which is no greater than the limitation period within which
the statute allows plaintiffs to start that action. To dismiss the action
in such circumstances would, in my view, involve an error in principle
B   in the exercise of judicial ' discretion ' which it is the function of the
appellate court to correct."

Lord Salmon said, at p. 328:

    " I agree with my noble and learned friend Lord Diplock that if an
action is dismissed for want of prosecution or even for the contumelious
C   failure to comply with a peremptory order before the limitation period
has elapsed, this would not empower the court to strike out a writ for
the same cause of action subsequently issued within the limitation
period. The fact that the plaintiff or his solicitor has behaved badly
in the first action does not make him into a vexatious litigant barred
from bringing any further proceedings without permission of the
D   courts. Nor does the dismissal of the first action without any decision
on the merits constitute res judicata."

And Lord Edmund-Davies said, at p. 334:

    " I respectfully concur with my noble and learned friend, Lord Dip-
lock, that, where there appears any likelihood that a plaintiff will issue a
second writ, the case must be quite exceptional (and difficult to
E   imagine) where the court should within the limitation period dismiss an
action simply for want of prosecution. If it be complained that this
places the defendant at the mercy of a dilatory plaintiff, a partial
answer is that in a flagrant case the defendant can always seek
peremptory orders which, if disobeyed, render the plaintiff liable to
have his action struck out on the ground of comtumelious default;
though there, too, a second writ can properly be issued within the
F   limitation period, unless the circumstances are such that it could on
other grounds be regarded as frivolous or vexatious."

    Mr. Miller, for the defendant in this case, having conceded that there
was no other ground upon which this present action could be regarded as
frivolous or vexatious, Mr. Strachan, for the plaintiff, relies strongly on
that obiter dictum of Lord Edmund-Davies, and submits that the mere fact
the first action has been struck out, on the ground of contumelious default,
G   is no reason for the court to strike out this action.

    The matter was adverted to again by their Lordships in *Tolley* v.
Morris [1979] 1 W.L.R. 592 where Lord Diplock, said, at p. 603:

    " Disobedience to a peremptory order would generally amount to such
' contumelious ' conduct as is referred to in *Birkett* v. *James* [1978]
H   A.C. 297 and would justify striking out a fresh action for the same
cause of action, as an abuse of the process of the court."

Lord Edmund-Davies, while agreeing with Lord Diplock on the facts of
the case then before him, said, at p. 604:

    " But I must make one qualification. I am not presently persuaded that
a person who starts an action within the limitation period is liable to
have it struck out as constituting an abuse of the process of the court,

for the sole reason that a previous suit instituted by him in respect of   A
the same cause of action was itself struck out on the ground that his
disobedience to the court's orders (peremptory or otherwise) amounted
to contumelious default. Although not an issue in *Birkett* v. *James*
[1978] A.C. 297, the point was canvassed in the course of argument . . .
and . . . I accordingly expressed obiter the view that even in such circumstances a plaintiff, *not* having been declared a vexatious litigant, could
within the limitation period prosecute to trial a fresh action. Highly un-   B
fortunate though such a conclusion must be regarded, it appeared to
me then to be logically inescapable in the light of our decision in that
case. But the point no more arises for decision in the present appeal
than it did in *Birkett* v. *James,* and a final conclusion on the matter
must await a case in which the point arises directly for determination."

And it is accepted that in this case the point does arise directly for   C
determination.

As was said in the course of argument in this court, one can well understand his Lordship's opinion that the conclusion which he preferred would
be a highly unforunate one, because it was conceded by counsel for the
plaintiff that if it were right, a litigant could disobey and disregard orders
of the court, have his action struck out, and provided he was within the   D
limitation period, he could immediately start another action; and even if
another peremptory order was made in the second action and that action
dismissed, then if the logic of *Birkett* v. *James* [1978] A.C. 297 is taken to
its ultimate, he could start a third or any number of actions provided they
were within the limitation period and none would be regarded as an abuse
of the process of the court.

In view of the difference of opinion of their Lordships we must decide   E
the question according to principle. We are concerned with R.S.C., Ord. 18,
r. 19, and it is plain from the use of the word "may" in that rule, that
the court has a discretion whether to strike out the pleading or not, and
whatever the breadth of the discretion, there is no doubt in accordance with
the rule that it exists.

An analagous though dissimilar situation was considered by this court   F
in *Samuels* v. *Linzi Dresses Ltd.* [1981] Q.B. 115. That was a case where
the defendants had failed to comply with a request for particulars and an
order was made that unless the particulars were delivered by a specified
date, the defence and counterclaim would be struck out—a similar type
of order to the order made in the first action in this case. This court held,
that the court had the power to extend time where an "unless" order had   G
been made, but the mode of exercise of the power was dealt with by
Roskill L.J. He said, at pp. 126–127:

"In my judgment, therefore, the law today is that a court has power
to extend the time where an "unless" order has been made but not
been complied with; but that it is a power which should be exercised
cautiously and with due regard to the necessity for maintaining the   H
principle that orders are made to be complied with and not to be
ignored. Primarily, it is a question for the discretion of the master or
the judge in chambers whether the necessary relief should be granted
or not."

It seems to me that those words are to be applied, by analogy, to a
situation such as this, where an "unless" order has been made and not
complied with, the action has been struck out and a second action started.

A The court then has to consider whether, in the exercise of its discretion under R.S.C., Ord. 18, r. 19, that second action should be struck out. In my view, the court should be cautious in allowing the second action to continue and should have due regard to the necessity of maintaining the principle that orders are made to be complied with and not to be ignored.

We were told that *Samuels* v. *Linzi Dresses Ltd.* [1981] Q.B. 115 was
B not brought to the attention of the judge below, and he appears to have approached the matter on the basis that it was a matter of law and that there was no room for the exercise of discretion, and it was for him to choose between the obiter dicta of Lord Diplock on the one hand, and Lord Salmon and Lord Edmund-Davies on the other.

Speaking for myself, I regard it as a matter of discretion to be exercised, having regard to the circumstances of the particular case. In this case there
C had, from first to last, been no explanation whatever by the plaintiff why there was the 10-month delay before the application to strike out the first action in March 1980. There was no explanation at all why he failed to comply with the " unless " order, and there has been no indication in this present action that he intends to comply with the orders of the court any more than he did in the first action. Indeed he is still in contempt of court.

D In my judgment, the judge was in error in not approaching the matter as one of discretion in that way. His approach, in my view, was wrong in principle. This is a case in which the necessity for maintaining the principle that orders are made to be complied with should be upheld, and in the absence of any explanation as to why the order was not complied with in the previous action or any assurance as to the conduct of this action I would strike out this present action and allow the matter to be litigated on
E the counterclaim in the first action.

Accordingly, I would allow the appeal and restore the order of Master Elton of March 2, 1981.

WATKINS L.J. I agree. A prospective litigant must be deemed to know that upon taking out a writ endorsed with a claim for monetary or
F other relief, his conduct of the action thereby brought into being will be governed thereafter by rules and orders of the court. A failure to conform to any one of these may cause him to be penalised even to the extent of having his action struck out.

In the event of his action being ordered to be struck out for failure to obey a peremptory order, he may appeal against that order seeking, if necessary, an extension of time within which to do so. The outcome of such
G an appeal will to some extent depend upon the excuse for failure preferably set forth in affidavit form provided for the court's consideration. If a litigant neglects to avail himself of that procedure and brings a fresh but precisely similar action to that ordered to be struck out without any explanation then or at any later time for a failure to obey the peremptory order, he should not be surprised that the commencement of the second
H action is found to be an abuse of the process of the court and for that reason it, too, is struck out.

To behave in such a way is in my judgement to treat the court with intolerable contumely. This is a matter which can properly be taken into account in the exercise of the court's discretion. This is how I judge this plaintiff to have conducted himself.

The judge below does not appear to have allowed this consideration to have formed part of the discretion exercised by him in deciding to reverse

the decision of the registrar. If it was, then, like Dunn L.J., I am bound to   A
say that he paid insufficient regard to it in adjudging that this action be
allowed to continue.

For the reasons given by Dunn L.J., and for those briefly expressed by
me, I too would allow this appeal and make the order which Dunn L.J.
proposes.

Appeal allowed with costs.   B
Order of Master Elton of March 2,
1981, restored.
Leave to appeal refused.

Solicitors: *Park Nelson & Doyle Devonshire for Lock, Reed & Lock,*
Dorchester; Myers, Ebner & Deaner.

C

[Reported by Mrs. Maria Fleischmann, Barrister-at-Law]

—————————

[COURT OF APPEAL]   D

* NORTH WEST LEICESTERSHIRE DISTRICT COUNCIL *v.*
EAST MIDLANDS HOUSING ASSOCIATION LTD.

1981   April 10, 13, 14, 15;   Stephenson and Brandon L.JJ.
       May 15   and Sir Stanley Rees   E

Local Government—Contract—Seal—Council's resolution to accept
fixed-price tender—Seal affixed to contract containing price
fluctuation clause — Non-compliance with standing orders in
affixing seal — Validity of contract — Local Government Act
1933 (23 & 24 Geo. 5, c. 51), s. 266 (2)

An urban district council resolved to accept a fixed-price   F
tender by an association for the building of three blocks of
flats. The contract, as drawn up by the clerk to that local
authority, contained a provision for varying the price. The
contract was affixed with the seal of the local authority but
not in accordance with its standing orders. The plaintiff
district council, as the local authority's successor in title,
claimed the recovery of a sum paid under the price fluctuation
clause and the association counterclaimed for moneys due   G
under the clause. The judge held that the proviso to section
266 (2) of the Local Government Act 1933 [1] applied to validate
the contract despite the non-compliance with the local authority's standing orders and he gave judgment for the association
on its counterclaim.

On appeal by the plaintiff: —

Held, allowing the appeal (Brandon L.J. dissenting), that
the clerk had no authority, actual or implied, to agree to the   H
fluctuation clause or to make a contract containing such a
clause; that, since the agreement was not made in accordance
with the local authority's resolution, the parties were not ad
idem and there was no contract; that the proviso to section
266 (2) applied only to contracts which were valid apart from
the failure to comply with the standing orders applicable and
meant that a person entering into a contract with a local

[1] Local Government Act 1933, s. 266 (2): see post, p. 1402B–E.

The Weekly Law Reports, November 20, 1981

1397

1 W.L.R.   North West Leics. D.C. v. East Midlands Ltd. (C.A.)

A   authority was not bound to inquire into whether there had
     been compliance with the local authority's standing orders,
     and, therefore, the proviso did not apply so as to validate the
     contract, and, accordingly, both the claims and the counter-
     claim should be dismissed (post, pp. 1405c–G, 1406B–C,
     1410D–H).
         A. R. Wright & Son Ltd. v. Romford Borough Council
     [1957] 1 Q.B. 431 considered.
B   Per Brandon L.J. The contract would have been invalid
     only if it had been void as being ultra vires or illegal, or void-
     able as having been entered into in reliance on a fraudulent or
     innocent misrepresentation, and, in the result the effect of the
     proviso to section 266 (2) was to make the whole contract, in-
     cluding the additional price fluctuation clause, binding on the
     local authorities concerned (post, pp. 1408H—1409A, B).
         Decision of Swanwick J. reversed.
C
     The following cases are referred to in the judgments:
     Freeman & Lockyer v. Buckhurst Park Properties (Mangal) Ltd. [1964]
         2 Q.B. 480; [1964] 2 W.L.R. 618; [1964] 1 All E.R. 630, C.A.
     L'Estrange v. F. Graucob Ltd. [1934] 2 K.B. 394, D.C.
     Wright (A.R.) & Son Ltd. v. Romford Borough Council [1957] 1 Q.B. 431;
         [1956] 3 W.L.R. 896; [1956] 3 All E.R. 785.
D
     The following additional cases were cited in argument:
     Barned's Banking Co., In re, Ex parte Contract Corporation (1867) L.R.
         3 Ch.App. 105.
     Carlton Contractors Ltd. v. Bexley Corporation (1962) 60 L.G.R. 331.
     Clarke v. Imperial Gas Light and Coke Co. (1832) 1 N. & M. 206.
E   Reuter v. Electric Telegraph Co. (1856) 6 E. & B. 341.
     Royal British Bank v. Turquand (1856) 6 E. & B. 327.
     Staple of England v. Bank of England (1880) 21 Q.B.D. 160, C.A.
     Thames Plate Glass Co. v. Land and Sea Telegraph Co. (1870) L.R. 11
         Eq. 248.

     APPEAL from Swanwick J.
F   By a specially indorsed writ, dated December 9, 1979, the plaintiff,
     North West Leicestershire District Council, claimed, inter alia, a
     declaration that on the true construction of a contract under seal made
     between the plaintiff's predecessor in title, Coalville Urban District
     Council, and the defendant, East Midlands Housing Association (" the
     association "), the contract sum payable thereunder was not and never
     had been adjustable on the index-based formula of the Department of
G   the Environment circular No. 158/73; a declaration that it was not and
     never had been a term of the contract that the sum payable by the
     plaintiff to the association thereunder should be adjusted and/or arrived
     at in accordance with the index-based formula; and an order for the
     payment by the association to the plaintiff of £70,651·39 as money had
     and received to the use of the plaintiff. By their defence and amended
H   counterclaim the association denied that the plaintiff had made an
     overpayment of £70,651·39 or any overpayment, and counterclaimed
     £40,988·88 as the balance due on the association's final account. Swan-
     wick J. dismissed the claim and gave judgment for the association on
     the counterclaim.
         The plaintiff, by a notice of appeal dated October 29, 1979, appealed
     on the grounds, inter alia, that the judge ought to have held that the
     contract of March 18, 1974, between the Coalville Urban District Council

The Weekly Law Reports, November 20, 1981

1398

North West Leics. D.C. v. East Midlands Ltd. (C.A.)   [1981]

and the association was void, alternatively that there was no contract
between the Coalville Urban District Council and the association
because at the time when the seal of that local authority was applied
thereto, that local authority did not intend to make and/or had not
authorised the making of a contract containing a fluctuation clause; that
the judge was wrong in law in holding that section 266 of the Local
Government Act 1933 validated the contract notwithstanding that it had
not been authorised by the Coalville Urban District Council and/or the
standing orders of that local authority had not been complied with and
that the judge ought to have held that the sum of £70,651·39 paid by the
Coalville Urban District Council in purported performance of the contract
was recoverable on the ground that the moneys were paid under a mistake of fact.

By a respondent's notice dated June 17, 1980, the association contended that the judgment should be affirmed on the additional ground
that on the evidence the clerk had usual and/or implied and/or ostensible
authority to agree the insertion of a price fluctuation clause in the
contract.

The facts are stated in the judgment of Stephenson L.J.

Harold Burnett for the plaintiff.
John Dyson for the association.

Cur. adv. vult.

May 15. The following judgments were read.

STEPHENSON L.J. On April 1, 1974, the Coalville Urban District
Council ceased to exist and all its rights and duties were taken over by
the plaintiff council. During the weeks preceding the transfer life in the
offices of the urban district council was, in the words of Mr. Brackenbury,
chief administrative assistant in the department of Mr. Marson, the clerk
to the urban district council, " very, very hectic." One matter under its
consideration in its last year of life was the building of three blocks of flats
for old people. On August 14, 1973, its health and housing committee had
resolved that the council approve in principle the scheme submitted by
the defendant association for the provision of this accommodation and
that the local authority's officers hold discussions with representatives of
the Department of the Environment and the association.

On December 4, 1973, the clerk submitted to a meeting of the urban
district council the association's fixed price tender for its consideration and
the council resolved " that subject to arithmetical check, the tender . . . in
the sum of £467,795·62 . . . be accepted." On December 18, 1973 the
health and housing committee resolved that the fixed price

" tender submitted by the [association] in the revised sum of
£468,985·36 . . . be accepted, subject to written approval . . . with
regard to the housing cost yardstick from the Department of the
Environment."

In the last hectic month before transfer Mr. Marson, the clerk, was no
doubt extremely busy, but only two of his actions concern us. First, on
March 5, 1974, he reported to the finance and general purposes committee of the urban district council that this was the last committee meeting of the council and at his request the committee resolved:

The Weekly Law Reports, November 20, 1981

1399

1 W.L.R.   North West Leics. D.C. v. East Midlands Ltd. (C.A.)

A   " That the chairman of the council be authorised to deal with any
     matter requiring urgent attention during the period up to March 31,
     1974."

Secondly, on March 18, 1974, he met Mr. Elderfield, the secretary and
chief executive of the association, and on a date, not precisely fixed by
the evidence but agreed to be the same day, attested the sealing of a
B printed contract for the building of the flats by the association. That
contract was in one of the standard forms of what used to be called the
R.I.B.A. contract, and it contained manuscript insertions and amendments
by way of deletion, alteration and addition, of which only two are
important.

     First, in the margin of clause 31 B (b) (ii) was written, " (iii) The con-
C tract shall also be adjustable on the index-based formula of the Department of Environment's Circular No. 158/73," subscribed with three sets of
initials " for EMHA " (the association).

     Secondly, the date for completion was amended from 24 months from
the date for possession to 18 and the alteration was signed by Mr. Marson,
" clerk of the council " and Mr. Elderfield, " secretary."

     The effect of incorporating the manuscript clause 31 B (b) (iii) as
D a term of the contract would be to turn a fixed price contract into a
contract with a price fluctuation clause. The plaintiff has paid out
£550,999 on interim certificates of its architect. It was not until the
formula referred to in the fluctuation clause was published that the architect referred to it; he did so in the sixth certificate, and in November 1976
the district auditor took the view that the contract was a fixed price
E contract.

     Hence the plaintiff's action claiming from the association £70,651·39
overpaid as money had and received to the use of the plaintiff if the
contract did not contain the fluctuation clause, and the association's
counterclaim for £40,988·88 due on its final account and not paid if the
contract did contain the fluctuation clause.

F   On July 23, 1979, Swanwick J., in a reserved judgment, held that the
fluctuation clause was incorporated as a term of the contract and so,
dismissing the claim, gave judgment for the association on the counterclaim for £40,988·88 with £10,140·52 interest. From that judgment the
plaintiff appeals.

     The judge reached his conclusion that the fluctuation clause was a
term of the contract by accepting the evidence of Mr. Elderfield, supported
G by the evidence of Mr. Brackenbury, that Mr. Marson agreed the addition
of the fluctuation clause, and by rejecting Mr. Marson's denial that he
agreed it. To that finding of the judge there is no challenge. That finding
also in effect disposed of the association's claim to rectification of the
contract and that claim is not pursued. But there remain two other issues
which the judge had to decide and this court has to decide: (1) Did Mr.
H Marson have authority to agree the clause on behalf of the local
authority? (2) Even if he did not, is the local authority bound by the contract to which its seal is affixed?

     The question of Mr. Marson's authority was raised in the plaintiff's
reply, which alleged that if he did make the agreement pleaded in
the defence as an agreement made at a meeting between Mr. Elderfield
and Mr. Marson that in consideration of a reduction of the contract
period from 24 to 18 months the local authority would accept clause 31

The Weekly Law Reports, November 20, 1981

1400

North West Leics. D.C. v. East Midlands Ltd. (C.A.)   [1981]

B (b) (iii), he had no authority to do so and/or an agreement containing A
this clause was never authorised by the local authority and the local
authority was accordingly not bound by it. That was followed by an
answer to a request for particulars of the agreement pleaded, which
alleged that Mr. Marson made the agreement as agent for the local
authority; but the only particulars which the association could give of the
facts and matters relied on in support of his agency and the local
authority's authorisation of the agreement were none of his actual B
authority at that stage, and of his ostensible authority, three things which
indicated that Mr. Marson held himself out as the local authority's agent
but not that the local authority held him out as its agent. Particulars of
that holding out were not supplied until a late stage of the appeal when
we gave Mr. Dyson leave to add the fact that the local authority placed
Mr. Marson in a position where he could do those three things and/or C
acquiesced in his doing them. Those three things were (a) his correspondence with Mr. Elderfield, (b) his agreement to meet him to discuss
the amendment contained in the clause and (c) his telling Mr. Elderfield
at the meeting that the amendment was acceptable if the contract period
was reduced to 18 months.

The judge found that Mr. Marson and Mr. Elderfield did make the D
agreement pleaded in the defence at their meeting on March 18, 1974,
and he said that he would have held that in striking that bargain with
Mr. Elderfield, Mr. Marson exceeded his authority, actual or ostensible,
had he not found (1) that the bargain embodied in the two amendments
to clause 31 B (b) and the contract period was authorised by the resolution
of March 5, 1974, which I have read, and (2) that the contract as amended
was validated by the proviso to section 266 (2) of the Local Government E
Act 1933, which I shall have to read later.

It is the plaintiff's case put before the judge, and before this court
in Mr. Burnett's notice of appeal and in his helpful submissions, that
the local authority never intended to make or authorised the making of
any contract with the association except a fixed price contract; that Mr.
Marson had no actual authority express or implied, from the resolution F
of March 5, 1974, or any other source, and no ostensible or apparent
authority from the local authority to agree to a fluctuation clause or to
make a contract containing such a clause; and that section 266 did not
have the effect of validating the contract which contained such a clause.
If his submissions are accepted, it would appear to follow that his first
ground of appeal is also correct, namely that the judge ought to have held
that the whole contract was void or there was no contract, but that his G
last ground, that the judge might have held that the sum of £70,051·39
was recoverable as moneys paid under a mistake of fact, would be un-
sustainable.

Mr. Dyson seeks by equally helpful arguments to support the judge's
judgment on the grounds which he gave for it, but also, by a respondent's
notice, on the additional ground that on the evidence Mr. Marson had H
" usual and/or implied and/or ostensible authority to agree the insertion
of a price fluctuation clause in the contract."

The conflict between the two parties has been reduced in one respect.
The terms of the resolution of March 5, 1974, as analysed by Mr. Burnett,
were too clear to support the argument that they gave Mr. Marson the
necessary authority. They gave authority to the chairman, not to the clerk,
and though Mr. Simpson, the chairman, attested the sealing of the con-

The Weekly Law Reports, November 20, 1981

1401

1 W.L.R.   North West Leics. D.C. v. East Midlands Ltd. (C.A.)

A   tract with Mr. Marson, he did not execute the contract in any other manner; to treat his signature as any more than an attestation would be to confuse the party to a written contract who signs it with a witness to his signature. And the matter did not require such urgent attention on March 18, that it could not have been dealt with by a resolution of the council which met for the last time, as was admitted in spite of Mr. Marson's evidence that it did not, on the very next day, March 19.

B   These obstacles led Mr. Dyson to abandon the point.

He did not, however, abandon the point in his respondent's notice that Mr. Marson had actual implied authority. Ostensible authority, he accepted from the judgment of Diplock L.J. in *Freeman & Lockyer* v. *Buckhurst Park Properties (Mangal) Ltd.* [1964] 2 Q.B. 480, 503–507, had to be conferred by the local authority's representing that Mr. Marson had

C   authority to do something which someone in his position of clerk to a local authority would by virtue of that position have authority to do. But though there was nothing in the constitution of the urban district council prohibiting it from giving its clerk authority to contract on its behalf, there was no evidence that clerks to such local authorities ever had that authority or that Mr. Marson had authority to make other contracts like this. Mr. Dyson had, therefore, to rely, and did rely, for Mr. Marson's

D   authority mainly if not solely on actual implied authority.

There he was confronted by Mr. Marson's own emphatic evidence, supported by the equally positive opinion of Mr. Simpson, the chairman, that Mr. Marson had no authority to agree a fundamental change to conditions and contents of this contract with its financial implications. And that was the basis of his denial that he ever agreed to the fluctuation

E   clause which changed the fixed price contract approved by the local authority.

" First of all," he said in evidence, " I had no authority to agree that fluctuating clause myself; secondly, I would have needed the authority of the council for the amendment to the contract in these terms; and, thirdly, it would have been necessary to obtain the ap-

F   proval of the Department of the Environment to the variation of the contract to include the fluctuation clause on the formula laid down in that circular."

Though he retracted in cross-examination the third requirement, he stuck to the first and second; he would have had authority to shorten the contract period but not to agree the fluctuation clause.

G   Mr. Marson had a lifetime's experience in local government and considered himself meticulous in the drafting of documents and in contractual procedures; he became the chief executive of the new local authority until he retired for medical reasons. He had no legal qualifications but his council relied on him for advice on contractual matters. Mr. Dyson was driven to submit that the fact found by the judge of Mr.

H   Marson's agreement to the fluctuation clause spoke louder than his words denying that he agreed it and asserting that it was so fundamental that he would not agree it without reference to his council. I am afraid that I cannot accept that bold submission; in my opinion, the judge was clearly right in concluding that Mr. Marson would have had no authority, actual or ostensible, but for the resolution of March 5, 1974, which is no longer relied on as conferring it, and for section 266 of the Local

The Weekly Law Reports, November 20, 1981

1402

North West Leics. D.C. v. East Midlands Ltd. (C.A.)   **[1981]**

Government Act 1933, on which the whole of the association's case A
must now rest.

Was the judge right to regard that section, when applied to the facts
of this case, as validating an agreement which Mr. Marson had no
authority to make and making that agreement binding on the urban
district council and so on its successor? This was not the ground on which
the main battle was fought below; that was the issue whether the fluctuation clause was agreed by Mr. Marson. So the judge had less argument B
on section 266 than has helped us in this court on what is, in my judgment,
a far from easy matter.

Section 266 enacted:

" (1) A local authority may enter into contracts necessary for the
discharge of any of their functions. (2) All contracts made by a local
authority or by a committee thereof shall be made in accordance with C
the standing orders of the local authority, and in the case of contracts for the supply of goods or materials or for the execution of
works, the standing orders shall—(a) require that, except as otherwise
provided by or under the standing orders, notice of the intention of
the authority or committee, as the case may be, to enter into the
contract shall be published and tenders invited; and (b) regulate the D
manner in which such notice shall be published and tenders invited:
Provided that a person entering into a contract with a local authority
shall not be bound to inquire whether the standing orders of the
authority which apply to the contract have been complied with, and
all contracts entered into by a local authority, if otherwise valid,
shall have full force and effect notwithstanding that the standing
orders applicable thereto have not been complied with." E

The urban district council had a standing order relating to its contracts. It was standing order No. 23, which read:

" (1) The common seal of the council shall not be affixed to any
document unless the sealing has been authorised by a resolution of
the council or of a committee to which the council have delegated
their powers in this behalf, but a resolution of the council (or of a F
committee where that committee has the power) authorising the
acceptance of any tender, the purchase, sale, letting, or taking of any
property, the issue of any stock, the presentation of any petition,
memorial, or address, the making of any rate or contract, or the
doing of any other thing, shall be a sufficient authority for sealing any
document necessary to give effect to the resolution. (2) The seal shall G
be attested by one at least of the following persons present at the
sealing, viz. the chairman or vice-chairman of the council or other
member of the council and an entry of every sealing of a document
shall be made and consecutively numbered in a book kept for the
purpose and shall be signed by a person who has attested the seal."

The sealing of this contract was not authorised by any resolution of H
the council or of a committee. It was never suggested that it was
authorised except by the resolution of March 5, 1974, and that resolution
did not authorise it; and as the only resolution authorising the acceptance
of a tender or the making of a contract was the resolution of December
18, 1973, authorising the acceptance of the association's fixed price tender,
it was an unauthorised sealing.

The evidence as to the sealing, both the affixing of the common seal

The Weekly Law Reports, November 20, 1981

1403

1 W.L.R.   North West Leics. D.C. v. East Midlands Ltd. (C.A.)

A and its attestation, was not completely clear. There was no evidence proving who actually affixed the seal. The judge treated the seals register as proving that the document was, in fact, signed and sealed on March 18, 1974. Mr. Brackenbury arranged for the document, already signed by Mr. Marson and Mr. Elderfield, to be entered in the seals register, but he had no independent recollection of the date when the document was " executed," presumably by affixing and attesting the seal. Nor did Mr. Simpson, the chairman. But he remembered signing the document without reading

B it, when it was already signed by Mr. Marson, in Mr. Marson's office with several other documents. Mr. Marson agreed that he himself signed it and would probably have obtained Mr. Simpson's signature in his office later the same evening. There was no evidence that either Mr. Simpson or Mr. Marson was present at the sealing as required by the standing order, or

C that they signed it when it was already sealed. They probably attested the sealing by signing after it had been sealed in their absence.

Mr. Elderfield was not asked about any seal of the document except the seal of his association. But it is a curiosity of the case that he had been in fact a member of the Coalville Urban District Council from 1971 or 1972. According to his own evidence, though he was not familiar with

D its standing orders, he knew that when it came to make a contract of substance it passed a resolution that contract documents should be prepared and the common seal of the council be affixed to it; and he had received the minutes of the meetings which contained the two resolutions of December 1973 which I have read, but had not read them and after Mr. Marson had told him that the local authority accepted the fluctuation clause assumed that there was a minute delegating him to do so and

E did not question his authority.

The judge must be taken, in accepting Mr. Elderfield's version of his meeting with Mr. Marson on March 18, to have accepted his evidence that he believed Mr. Marson was speaking the truth and had his council's authority to incorporate the fluctuation clause, which Mr. Elderfield regarded as essential to his association's agreeing to build the flats. So we

F must place him and his association, as the judge did, in a position to take advantage of the proviso to section 266 (2).

There is no doubt that standing order No. 23 applied to this contract and was not complied with in two respects: (1) the sealing had not been authorised by the necessary resolution; (2) the seal had not been attested by either the chairman (or the vice-chairman or other member) of the local authority or the clerk (or deputy clerk) of the local authority being

G present at the sealing. But those defects, serious though the first was, did not deprive the contract of its full force and effect " if otherwise valid." Was it otherwise valid? Mr. Burnett submits that it was not. Mr. Dyson that it was. The correct answer to the question would seem to turn on the standing order and whether there was more wrong with the making of this contract complete with fluctuation clause than mere non-compliance

H with the standing order.

Mr. Burnett submits that the contract was made when the seal of the local authority was affixed to the document, or when Mr. Marson instructed someone to affix it, but, although standing order No. 23 had not been complied with, the contract containing the fluctuation clause was not " otherwise valid." This submission was not considered by the judge separately from analogies by which Mr. Burnett sought to support it below but no longer seeks to support it in this court.

1404

Section 266 is not perhaps as clear as section 135 of the Local Govern-   A
ment Act 1972 which replaced it after this contract came into existence.
That later section appears to make standing orders with respect to the
making of contracts generally permissive, but mandatory with respect to
some contracts. However that may be, I would read section 266 (2) as
requiring a local authority to make standing orders relating to contracts
within section 266 (1) including those which are also within section 266
(2). I think that a local authority must make standing orders to apply to a   B
contract for the supply of goods and materials or for the execution of
work (like this contract) because the wording of subsection (2) (*a*) assumes
that there will be standing orders applicable to all such contracts, whatever the position of other contracts within subsection (1). But Standing
orders regulate internal management and procedure. The power to
make them was derived from section 75 and Schedule 3, Part V, para-   C
graph (4), relating to " meetings and proceedings " and " proceedings and
business " respectively. When the Act was passed, sealing was a matter
which standing orders might be expected to deal with, because it was then
the law that a corporation could only contract under seal. So a contract
made by a local authority not under seal could not be " otherwise valid "
within the proviso because it did not comply with a requirement of the
common law: *A. R. Wright & Son Ltd.* v. *Romford Borough Council*   D
[1957] 1 Q.B. 431, 436. In that case there was a standing order authorising
sealing (though its terms are not given), and a standing order which required certain contracts to be in writing, which had been complied with,
but there was non-compliance with the common law so the contract was
invalid. Parliament altered the law, presumably in consequence of that
case, by doing away with the requirement of sealing for a corporation's   E
contracts: see the Corporate Bodies' Contracts Act 1960. So in 1974 a
local authority could make a valid contract in writing or orally. But Mr.
Burnett submits that it must authorise a contract before it can be bound
by it and an agent who has no authority to make contracts for it still
cannot bind it to something it has never agreed. Such a contract is invalid,
not for non-compliance with a standing order authorising sealing but for   F
non-compliance with another requirement of the common law that a
party cannot be bound by a contract made by another without his
authority—unless he ratifies it or is estopped from denying that it is his.

Mr. Dyson submits, in my judgment correctly, that " if otherwise
valid " means " if valid otherwise than by reason of non-compliance with
an applicable standing order," which standing order No. 23 certainly is,
and excludes contracts which are illegal or ultra vires the local authority,   G
or voidable, e.g. for misrepresentation, or which infringe a rule of law, like
that in *A. R. Wright & Son Ltd.* v. *Romford Borough Council* [1957]
1 Q.B. 431. He goes on to submit that this contract is only capable of being
invalidated on the ground that it is unauthorised, and it is only unauthorised
because no resolution authorised it, and that was a breach of standing
order No. 23. But for non-compliance, therefore, with that standing order   H
the contract would be valid and the association can rely on the proviso to
section 266 (2). The council's predecessor having elected to require
authorisation of its contracts by sealing, there is no contract until its seal
is affixed to a contract and it cannot rely on any want of authority, such as
Mr. Marson's, to make this contract, if the association wished to enforce
it; if the local authority wished to enforce it, it would or might be
different.

A   I accept Mr. Burnett's submission in reply that all turns on this standing order and its precise terms on their true construction, including the
negative form of its opening. It does not state that no contract, or rate, can
be made or be valid—or any of the other acts enumerated in the standing
order—unless sealed or unless sealed in pursuance of a resolution: that
may be a natural but is not a necessary assumption, certainly as regards
contracts since the Corporate Bodies' Contracts Act 1960; it deals only
B   with the conditions in which the seal can be affixed, not must be affixed. It
authorises not acts including contracts but the sealing of documents
necessary to give effect to resolutions authorising the acceptance of certain tenders, the presentation of certain things and the making of certain
other things including contracts, all things usually made in documentary
form. It is, as the standing order of the *Romford Borough Council* case
C   [1957] 1 Q.B. 431, 433 was described, an order providing for the sealing
of documents and how the authority for sealing was to be given—not an
order authorising contracts. I suspect that it is in a common form which
was in use before the Act of 1960, but it must be interpreted and applied
against the background of the law as it was when this contract was made.
     If Mr. Marson had made this contract with the association in writing
D   but unsealed, he would not have been in breach of the standing order because it would not have been applicable. He would not have complied with
the December resolutions, but because the contract had ceased to be a fixed
price contract. The association could not enforce it against the local
authority, not because it was not authorised by the order but because it
was made contrary to the resolution. Why should the local authority be
bound by a contract made contrary to the resolution by an unauthorised
E   agent, because it was sealed and the sealing had not been authorised? No
contract, oral or written, with a fluctuation clause was ever entered into or
made by this local authority. The only person who entered into or made
such a contract with the association was Mr. Marson. When he agreed to
Mr. Elderfield's unauthorised alteration of the contract authorised by his
local authority, he and the association were ad idem, but his local
authority and the association were no longer ad idem. There was no con-
F   tract to be sealed. The sealing of the altered contract did not make the
local authority and the association ad idem or make a contract where none
was. It would be extraordinary, in the absence of any plea of estoppel or
ratification, that sealing should have the effect of validating an invalid
contract when all standing order No. 23 lays down is how sealing is to be
authorised and carried out and all the proviso to section 266 (2), as I read
G   it, permits is that a person entering into a contract with a local authority
shall not be bound to inquire into compliance with its standing orders and
such a contract shall have full force and effect if non-compliance is all that
is wrong with it.
     I cannot read the standing order or the proviso as giving to the sealing
of the amended document the effect of making a contract which the local
H   authority did not make or the effect of a signature to a written contract.
The proviso contains the important qualification " if othewise valid." I
accept the submission of Mr. Dyson which I have already referred to, that
" otherwise valid " means " valid otherwise than by reason of non-compliance with an applicable standing order " or, as it is better put by
Brandon L.J., in the judgment which he will deliver, " valid apart from
the failure to comply with the standing order or standing orders applicable." But I regret that I am unable to regard that as meaning " valid if

the standing order or standing orders applicable had been complied with   A
instead of not being complied with," if by that is meant an irrebuttable
presumption that there had been a resolution authorising the particular
contract and it is, therefore, a valid contract. That limits unnaturally the
meaning of the qualifying words, which are, in my judgment, wide
enough to cover not merely voidable or illegal contracts duly authorised
by resolution complying with the standing order, but contracts never
made, agreed to or authorised by any resolution or at all. I do not believe   B
that the proviso has any application to a case where the non-compliance
with a standing order is not just a failure to obtain a resolution required
by the order but is merely incidental to a deliberate contravention of the
will and intention of the local authority expressed in a resolution. Then
more is wrong with the contract than non-compliance with a standing
order; there is also non-compliance with a resolution authorising a different   C
kind of contract and accordingly no contract. Non-compliance with a
resolution is quite different from non-compliance with an order requiring a
resolution by failing, perhaps by mistake, to obtain any resolution. It is the
latter sort of defect in " indoor management," a matter of form, not a
departure from authorised terms of contract, a matter of substance, from
which the proviso protects those who contract with a local authority.
                                                                                   D
    Suppose the local authority had resolved to let some of its houses to
tenants and its clerk, from arrogance or incompetence, had drawn up and
sealed conveyances of the freeholds to them: could it be said that the
sales were otherwise valid at the time when the conveyances were sealed
or the clerk gave instructions to seal them, whatever difficulties there
might be in avoiding the sales later? I think not.

    I would accordingly hold that there is nothing in section 266 and   E
standing order No. 23 which binds the plaintiff to a contract which its
predecessor never intended to make and which purported to be made by
Mr. Marson in circumstances which the judge was unable fully to explain
or understand.

    I would, therefore, allow the appeal and, subject to any further sub-
missions of counsel, dismiss both claim and counterclaim. Though the   F
plaintiff has claimed the recovery of what it has overpaid on the basis of a
fixed price contract unamended to include clause 31B (b) (iii), it has
successfully challenged the validity of the whole document with the consequence, rightly described by the judge if he had found the other way, that
" the plaintiffs cannot recover any moneys paid under it and the defendants
are left to a possible claim on a quantum meruit if they can prove that
they have been paid less than their work was worth."   G

    BRANDON L.J. I have had the advantage of reading in draft the
judgment which Stephenson L.J. has just delivered, and I gratefully adopt
the account of the facts material to this appeal which is contained in it.

    As he has stated, there were at the end of the argument only two
questions left to this court for decision.   H

    The first question is whether Mr. Marson, the clerk of the Coalville
Urban District Council, had the actual or ostensible authority of that
local authority to agree to the addition to the terms of the proposed contract as originally drawn of the new clause 31 B (b) (iii), conveniently
called the price fluctuation clause. That first question is one of fact,
depending on the evidence adduced before the judge in the court below,
and the inferences properly to be drawn from such evidence.

The Weekly Law Reports, November 20, 1981

1407

1 W.L.R.   North West Leics. D.C. v. East Midlands Ltd. (C.A.)   Brandon L.J.

A   The second question is whether, even if Mr. Marson did not have such authority, there nevertheless came into being between the local authority and the association a binding contract including that additional clause as a result of the contractual document to which it had been added being subsequently sealed and delivered on behalf of the local authority. That second question is one of law, depending on the true meaning and effect of the proviso to section 266 (2) of the Local Government Act 1933, and the application of that proviso to the facts of the present case.

B   Stephenson L.J. has expressed in his judgment his conclusion that both the two questions set out above should be answered in the negative. He has expressed the further conclusion that the result of answering both questions in the negative is that no express contract between the council and the association ever came into being.

C   So far as the first question is concerned I agree with the conclusion reached by Stephenson L.J. and with the reasons which he has given for it. So far as the second question is concerned, however, I have reached a conclusion opposite to that of Stephenson L.J., my opinion being that, for reasons which I shall develop, that question should be answered in the affirmative.

D   The manner in which it was contemplated by both parties that the local authority would enter into the contract here in issue was by the contractual document, which had been prepared, being sealed and delivered on behalf of the council.

The sealing of the contractual document on behalf of the local authority was governed by its standing order No. 23. That standing order contained two requirements relevant to the present case. The first requirement was that the seal of the local authority should not be affixed to any document unless such sealing had been authorised by a resolution of the council, or of a committee to which the council had delegated its power to give such authorisation. The second requirement was that the seal should be attested by two persons present at the time when it was affixed, one of whom was to be chairman, vice-chairman or other member of the local authority, and the other the clerk or deputy clerk of the local authority.

F   In the present case the seal of the local authority was affixed to the contractual document concerned after the new clause 31 (B) (b) (iii), the price fluctuation clause, had been added to the terms of that document as originally drawn. The affixing of the seal further appeared on the face of the document itself to have been done in the presence of the chairman of the local authority, Mr. Simpson, and its clerk, Mr. Marson, in that their signatures were written alongside the seal in the spaces provided for them, with a statement that the seal had been affixed in their presence.

In fact, however, neither the affixing of the local authority's seal, nor the attestation of the seal by the two witnesses, complied with the two requirements of the local authority's standing order No. 23 referred to above. The first requirement was not complied with in that there had never been any resolution of the council, or of any committee of the council, with the necessary delegated power, authorising the sealing of the contractual document with the additional price fluctuation clause contained in it. The second requirement was not complied with in that, despite what appeared on the face of the document, the two attesting witnesses were not in fact present at the time when the seal was affixed.

It is a well-established principle of law that, when a person signs a document which he knows to be of a contractual nature, he is bound by all the terms which the document so signed contains, whether he has read, A understood and approved such terms or not: *L'Estrange* v. *F. Graucob Ltd.* [1934] 2 K.B. 394. This is so, moreover, even though the draft of the contract has been prepared by an agent of the person signing it, and contains terms which such agent had no authority from the latter to include in it.

The same principle applies a fortiori to a case where a person, knowing B a document to be of a contractual nature, seals and delivers it as his deed. It is in the light of that principle that I turn to consider the true meaning and effect of the proviso to section 266 (2) of the Local Government Act 1933, and the application of that proviso to the present case.

Section 266 of the Act of 1933 provides, so far as material:

> " (1) A local authority may enter into contracts necessary for the discharge of any of their functions. (2) All contracts made by a local C authority or by a committee thereof shall be made in accordance with the standing orders of the local authority . . . Provided that a person entering into a contract with a local authority shall not be bound to inquire whether the standing orders of the authority which apply to the contract have been complied with, and all contracts entered into by a local authority, if otherwise valid, shall have full force and D effect notwithstanding that the standing orders applicable thereto have not been complied with."

The second part of the proviso deals with cases in which a local authority enters into a contract with a person without complying with one or more of the local authority's standing orders applicable to the making by it of such a contract. It provides that, in such cases, the contract will E be binding on the local authority despite such non-compliance, if otherwise valid.

The question then arises as to what is meant, in the context in which it occurs, by the expression " otherwise valid." In my opinion, that expression means valid apart from the failure to comply with the standing order or standing orders applicable, that is to say, valid if the standing order or F standing orders applicable had been complied with instead of not being complied with.

On the basis that that is the meaning of the expression " otherwise valid," what is the effect of the proviso to section 266 (2) on the facts of the present case? The effect must be that, if the contract would have been binding on the local authority if the two requirements of standing order No. 23 referred to above had been complied with, then it is still binding G on the local authority even though those two requirements were not complied with.

Would the contract then have been binding on the local authority if the two requirements of standing order No. 23 had been complied with? In my view, in accordance with the principles which I discussed earlier, it clearly would have been so binding in respect of all its terms, including H the additional price fluctuation clause, even though Mr. Marson, who acted as the agent of the local authority in preparing the contractual document, did not have the authority of the local authority to include that clause.

The only circumstances which would, on the hypothesis concerned, have made the contract otherwise invalid, and so not binding on the local authority, would in my view have been if it had been void as being ultra

The Weekly Law Reports, November 27, 1981

1409

1 W.L.R.   North West Leics. D.C. v. East Midlands Ltd. (C.A.)   Brandon L.J.

A   vires or illegal, or voidable as having been entered into in reliance on a
fraudulent or innocent misrepresentation. There was no suggestion that
any of these circumstances existed in the present case.

In particular it was not suggested that the local authority, if it had been
minded to do so, could not lawfully have authorised Mr. Marson to agree
to the additional price fluctuation clause on their behalf, as Mr. Elderfield,
B   acting for the association, honestly believed that they had done.

In the result I agree with the view of the judge that the effect of the
proviso to section 266 (2) was to make the whole contract, including the
additional price fluctuation clause, binding on the Coalville Urban District
Council and, therefore, on its successor in title, the North West Leicestershire District Council. It follows that I would affirm the decision of the
judge and dismiss the appeal.

C

SIR STANLEY REES.   I have had the advantage of reading in draft the
judgments delivered by Stephenson L.J. and Brandon L.J.   I respectfully agree with both of them that the trial judge was fully justified upon
the evidence before him in holding that Mr. Marson had neither actual nor
ostensible authority on behalf of the Coalville Urban District Council to
D   agree to the addition of the price fluctuation clause to the proposed
contract.

The only remaining issue, and the one upon which Stephenson and
Brandon L.JJ. have expressed differing opinions, is as to the impact upon
the contract of the provisions of section 266 of the Local Government
Act 1933, which was in force at the time when the contract was made,
although it was replaced by section 135 of the Act of 1972, which came into
E   force shortly afterwards. The relevant provisions of section 266 have been
read by both Stephenson and Brandon L.JJ. and I need not repeat more
than the proviso to subsection (2) which is in these terms:

" Provided that a person entering into a contract with a local
authority shall not be bound to inquire whether the standing orders
of the authority which apply to the contract have been complied
F   with, and all contracts entered into by a local authority, if otherwise
valid, shall have full force and effect notwithstanding that the standing orders applicable thereto have not been complied with."

Stephenson and Brandon L.JJ. have expressed differing views as to the
proper construction of this proviso, Stephenson L.J.'s view is that the vital
words " if otherwise valid " mean " if valid otherwise than by reason of
G   non-compliance with an applicable standing order." Brandon L.J.'s view is
" otherwise valid " means " valid apart from the failure to comply with
the standing order or standing orders applicable, that is to say, valid if the
standing order or standing orders applicable had been complied with
instead of not being complied with."

We were referred to only one reported case in which the provisions of
H   section 266 have been considered. That was a decision of Lord Goddard
C.J. in *A. R. Wright & Son. Ltd.* v. *Romford Borough Council* [1957] 1
Q.B. 431.

In that case the standing orders of a local authority required that the
contract of the kind in issue in that case should be in writing but did not
require it to be sealed. The contract was in writing but was not sealed. At
the relevant time (which was prior to the Corporate Bodies' Contracts Act
1960) the common law required that to be valid such a contract must be

1410

Sir Stanley Rees   North West Leics. D.C. v. East Midlands Ltd. (C.A.)   [1981]

sealed. So the contract complied with the applicable standing orders but
did not comply with the common law. In order to escape liability under the
contract the defendant local authority argued that the contract was not
binding upon them and was not validated by the terms of the proviso to
section 266 (2) because it was not " otherwise valid " in that it was invalid
by the common law. Lord Goddard C.J.'s approach to the interpretation
of section 266 appears from this brief passage taken from his judgment, at
pp. 436–437:

> " Standing orders deal with the internal affairs of the body making
> them and, as the proviso shows, do not affect other persons such as
> those who contract or desire to contract with the corporation. The
> statute requires that the standing orders shall provide for certain steps
> to be taken before contracts are made, and the orders provide for the
> carrying out of these directions. The party contracting or proposing
> to contract with the corporation is not concerned with whether the
> corporation has acted in accordance with their standing orders and, if
> otherwise valid, a contract will be binding though the orders may
> not have been followed, but I can find no words entitling me to say
> that if a corporation does comply with their standing orders the seal
> is no longer necessary either to bind them or to confer contractual
> rights upon them."

I respectfully adopt this approach to the proviso, namely, that regard
must be paid to the relevant provisions of the common law and statute law
when the validity of a local authority's contract is in issue. In the instant
case the terms of standing order No. 23 were not complied with in two
respects: (1) the sealing had not been authorised by any appropriate
resolution and (2) the sealing had not been attested by the chairman (or
the vice-chairman or other member) of the urban district council or its
clerk or deputy clerk being present at the sealing.

But as Stephenson L.J. has pointed out, there was far more wrong with
the contract than mere non-compliance with the standing orders. It is an
inescapable inference from the findings of the trial judge that Mr. Marson
entered into the oral agreement with Mr. Elderfield knowing that he had
no authority of any kind to do so and that the agreement was in direct
conflict with the expressed intentions of his employers. The evidence also
established that it was the intention of Mr. Marson and a direct consequence of this wholly unauthorised oral agreement that the sealing of the
contract took place.

I respectfully agree with the view expressed by Stephenson L.J. that
the proviso should not be so construed as to validate a contract made as a
result of an agreement deliberately and knowingly made by an agent in
contravention of the intention of his principal in a case in which no
estoppel or ratification is or can be relied upon.

Accordingly, I respectfully agree with the decision of Stephenson L.J.
and with the reasons he has given, and would allow the appeal.

Appeal allowed with costs.

Solicitors: *Sharpe, Pritchard & Co.; Whitehouse, Gibson & Alton for
McMorrans, Coalville.*

B. O. A.

A

[CHANCERY DIVISION]

* PERRONS *v.* SPACKMAN (INSPECTOR OF TAXES)

1981   July 1, 2; 6   Vinelott J.

B   *Revenue—Income tax—Employment—Emolument—Local govern-*
ment officer receiving mileage allowance for essential travel
in course of employment—Whether part of emoluments
of employment—Whether cost of providing and maintaining
car allowable deduction—Income and Corporation Taxes Act
1970 (c. 10), ss. 183 (1), 189 (1)

C   The taxpayer was employed by a county council as a rent
officer. In the course of that employment he travelled in his
own car to visit properties for which fair rents had to be fixed.
He drove to and from work each day and on average made
one or two journeys by car on official business. The council
paid him an " essential user allowance " of 11·4 per mile and
a yearly lump sum payment that was calculated by reference
to the engine capacity of his car.   Those allowances were
negotiated at the National Joint Council for local authorities
D   and their officers and were fixed in December each year in
advance for the following calendar year. For the year 1978–79
the taxpayer was assessed to income tax under Schedule E in
the sum of £5,950. He appealed against that assessment claiming a deduction in respect of a mileage allowance of £149 and
a lump sum payment of £220 paid to him by the council in
respect of official journeys made by him in his car during the
year. The special commissioners held that both the mileage
E   allowance and the lump sum were emoluments of his employment and chargeable to tax under section 183 (1) of the
Income and Corporation Taxes Act 1970[1]. However they
allowed him a deduction under section 189 (1) of the Act, of
£64, as being the cost to him of making the official journeys,
and an agreed sum of £51 in respect of capital allowances by
virtue of section 47 (1) and paragraph 5 of Schedule 8 to the
Finance Act 1971.

F   On appeal by the taxpayer against the commissioners' decision regarding the mileage allowance only : —
Held, dismissing the appeal, (1) that although the taxpayer was entitled to a deduction in respect of the actual
cost incurred by him in making official journeys, the mileage
allowance paid to him by his employer included a significant
contribution towards the overhead costs of putting his car on
the road and maintaining it for his private use and thus could
G   not be regarded as mere reimbursement of expenses incurred
by the taxpayer in the course of his employment but was an
emolument of that employment within the meaning of section
183 (1) of the Income and Corporation Taxes Act 1970 (post,
p. 1417F–H).
Pook v. *Owen* [1970] A.C. 244, H.L.(E.) distinguished.
(2) That as it was not a term or condition of the taxpayer's
employment that he should have a car available for his own
H   use on official journeys, he was not necessarily obliged to incur
the expense of running and maintaining his car and that,
accordingly, the whole of that expense was not a permissible

---

[1] Income and Corporation Taxes Act 1970, s. 183 (1): " Tax under Case I, II or
III of Schedule E shall, except as hereinafter mentioned, be chargeable on the full
amount of the emoluments falling under that Case, subject to such deductions only
as may be authorised by the Tax Acts, and the expression " emoluments " shall include all salaries, fees, wages, perquisites and profits whatsoever."
S. 189 (1): see post, p. 1418A–B.

deduction from the taxpayer's emoluments under section 189   A
(1) of the Act (post, pp. 1418H—1419D).

Per curiam. Even if the taxpayer had shown that he was
contractually obliged to provide a car for official use, it would
be impossible to say that the whole cost to him of putting the
car on the road and maintaining it would be one that he would
have been necessarily obliged to incur as part of the expense
of " travelling in the performance of " his duties within section
189 (1) of the Act (post, p. 1420E–G).   B

The following cases are referred to in the judgment:

Brown v. *Bullock* [1961] 1 W.L.R. 1095; [1961] 3 All E.R. 129; 40 T.C. 1,
   C.A.
Hillyer v. *Leeke* (1976) 51 T.C. 90.
Pook v. *Owen* [1967] 1 W.L.R. 679; [1967] 2 All E.R. 579; [1969] 1
   Ch. 535; [1968] 2 W.L.R. 591; [1968] 1 All E.R. 261, C.A.; [1970]   C
   A.C. 244; [1969] 2 W.L.R. 775; [1969] 2 All E.R. 1; 45 T.C. 571,
   H.L.(E.).
Ricketts v. *Colquhoun* [1925] 1 K.B. 725, C.A.; [1926] A.C. 1; 10 T.C. 118,
   H.L.(E.).
Taylor v. *Provan* [1975] A.C. 194; [1974] 2 W.L.R. 394; [1974] 1 All E.R.
   1201; 49 T.C. 579, H.L.(E.).

                                                                D

The following additional cases were cited in argument:

Brumby v. *Milner* [1976] 1 W.L.R. 1096; [1976] 3 All E.R. 636; 51 T.C.
   583, H.L.(E.).
Elwood v. *Utitz* (1965) 42 T.C. 482, McVeigh L.J. and C.A.(N.I.).
Fergusson v. *Noble,* 1919 S.C. 534; 7 T.C. 176.
Hochstrasser v. *Mayes* [1960] A.C. 376; [1960] 2 W.L.R. 63; [1959]   E
   3 All E.R. 817; 38 T.C. 673, H.L.(E.).
Marsden v. *Inland Revenue Commissioners* [1965] 1 W.L.R. 734; [1965]
   2 All E.R. 364; 42 T.C. 326.

CASE STATED by the Commissioners for the Special Purposes of the
Income Tax Acts.

In 1974 the taxpayer, Charles Albert Perrons, was appointed a rent   F
officer by the Nottinghamshire County Council and was so employed
throughout the tax year 1978–79. In the course of his employment he
used his own car to visit properties in respect of which a fair rent had
to be fixed. The council paid him an " essential user allowance " of
11·4p per mile and a yearly lump sum payment calculated by reference
to the engine capacity of his car. He appealed against an assessment
to income tax under Schedule E in the sum of £5,950 for 1978–79   G
claiming a deduction of £149 for the mileage allowance and £220 for
the lump sum payment paid to him by the council in respect of official
journeys made by him in his car during the year. The commissioners
dismissed his appeal on the ground that both the allowance and the
lump sum were emoluments of the taxpayer's employment and chargeable to tax under section 183 (1) of the Income and Corporation Taxes   H
Act 1970. However, they allowed him a deduction under section 189 (1)
of the Act of £40 for the cost of petrol and £24 as an allowable proportion of the cost of car repairs, road tax and insurance. In addition he
was allowed an agreed sum of £51 in respect of capital allowances.
They determined the assessment in the sum of £5,835.

The taxpayer, accepting the commissioners' decision in relation to the
lump sum payment, appealed in respect of the mileage allowance.

1 W.L.R.   Perrons v. Spackman (Ch.D.)

A   The facts are stated in the judgment.

M. B. Musgrave for the taxpayer.
Robert Carnwath for the Crown.

Cur. adv. vult.

B   July 6. VINELOTT J. read the following judgment. This is an appeal
by the taxpayer, Mr. Perrons, against a decision of the special commissioners
who held, first, that a lump sum allowance and mileage allowance paid to
the taxpayer by his employer, the Nottinghamshire County Council, for
making available and using his own car for journeys undertaken in the
course of his employment were emoluments of his office or employment
within the definition of that word in section 183 (1) of the Income and
C Corporation Taxes Act 1970 (" the Taxes Act ") and, secondly, that he was
not entitled to deduct the whole of the expenses incurred in providing and
maintaining his car out of the emoluments of his office or employment
under section 189 (1) of the Taxes Act.
     The facts are fully set out in the very careful and clearly reasoned
decision of the special commissioners. A brief summary will suffice for
D this judgment. At all material times the taxpayer was employed as a rent
officer by the county council. In the course of his employment he had to fix
fair rents for privately rented property in the registration area of the
county council and frequently had to visit a property and discuss matters
arising in the course of fixing a fair rent with the landlord and the tenant.
Initially his duties were confined to the area of the City of Nottingham,
and while his duties were so confined he was entitled under the terms of his
E employment to a " casual user allowance," that is, an allowance payable
to persons " for whom it is merely desirable that a car should be available
when required." In 1976 his area was extended to cover outlying areas
outside the city boundaries, and he became entitled to an " essential user
allowance," that is, an allowance payable to " those whose duties are of such
a nature that it is essential for them to have a motor car at their disposal
F whenever required." The circumstances in which allowances are payable
and the amounts of the allowances are negotiated at the National Joint
Council for Local Authority Administrative, Professional, Technical and
Clerical Services, which is in effect the Whitley Council for local government authorities and their officers and employees. The terms so negotiated
are part of the terms of employment of the officers and employees represented on the council. The allowance is, I understand, fixed in December
G each year in advance for the following calendar year.
     Before turning to describe the way in which the " essential user allow-
ance " is calculated, I should mention that the taxpayer lives about five
miles from the centre of Nottingham in a house which has a garage in
which he keeps his car. His car is an Austin Allegro 1300 c.c. car which he
bought new in 1976. He drives to and from work every day, and on
H average makes one or two trips a day in his car on official business. Two
allowances were payable in 1978 to an essential car user using a car in the
1200 to 1450 c.c. range. First, he was entitled to a lump sum allowance.
That was calculated by adding, first, figures for depreciation and for loss of
interest (at 10 per cent. less tax at 33 per cent.) both ascertained by reference to the cost or the assumed cost of the car, and secondly, an agreed
figure for tax and insurance. The total of those figures in the year 1978 was
£740. They are all described as standing charges. Then there was deducted

A

a notional amount of 30 per cent. for assumed private user, leaving a " net
standing charge " of £518. The lump sum allowance was 45 per cent. of
that figure, that is £233. The lump sum allowance was paid by instalments,
I understand in the taxpayer's case monthly. Then there was an agreed
mileage allowance. That was arrived at by adding together agreed mileage
figures for petrol, for tyres and for service repairs, renewals and oil. Those
agreed figures, which were the assumed running costs, totalled 5·496p per
mile. Then the other 55 per cent. of the net standing charge was apportioned over a mileage of 4,800 miles, giving an additional mileage allowance
of 5·938p and a total mileage allowance of 11·34p. That was the mileage
allowance for the first 9,000 miles travelled on official business. Thereafter
the essential car user was entitled to a mileage allowance of 5·5p that is
the figure of 5·496p running costs rounded up. The explanation of the
figures of 4,800 and 9,000 miles is that it was assumed for the purposes of
the calculation that the average officer would travel 4,800 miles on official
business. The mileage allowance of 11·34p multiplied by 4,800 miles would
reimburse him the whole of the standing charges except those attributable to
the assumed 30 per cent. private use (plus, of course, the running costs
incurred in the use on official business). After 9,000 miles he would have
recovered the whole amount of the standing charges (plus the running costs
attributable to official use) so that after 9,000 miles he only received an allowance equal to the agreed running costs. Of course, this has the result that if
he had travelled 9,000 miles on official business he would be relieved of all
standing charges or overheads in respect of his private use. This basis of
calculation has been used in subsequent years although the actual figures
have varied.

B

C

D

The taxpayer in this case did not in fact travel 4,800 miles on official
business. His total mileage during the fiscal year 1978–79 was 9,988 miles,
of which 1,359 miles were travelled on official business; that is, approximately 14 per cent. of the total mileage. During the fiscal year 1978–79 he
received a lump sum allowance of £220 (slightly less than the lump sum
allowance of £233 payable for the calendar year 1978) and a mileage
allowance of £148·91, a total of £368·91. The commissioners held that the
whole of this sum was an emolument of the taxpayer's office or employment. In this appeal he accepts that the lump sum allowance was an
emolument but claims that the mileage allowance was not.

E

F

Before the commissioners the taxpayer contended that if both
allowances fell to be included in his emoluments he was entitled to deduct
the whole of the cost to him of putting his car on the road and maintaining
it as well as the cost of providing petrol for the 1,359 miles travelled on
official business. The ground of this contention was that it was necessary
for him to incur that cost in order that he should have a car available for
what he and his employer regarded as " essential user." The amount
claimed as the cost of putting his car on the road and maintaining it was
arrived at before the commissioners by adding together an estimated £80 for
servicing and repairs, an estimated £380 for depreciation, £50 for road tax,
£65 for the notional rent for the use of his own garage and £50 for insurance, a total of £625. To that he added £40 for petrol for 1,359 miles
at 30 miles per gallon at a cost of 90p per gallon. The commissioners
disallowed the notional rent for the use of the taxpayer's garage. That that
was properly disallowed is not in dispute. The claim for depreciation of
£380 was not pursued before the commissioners, though the taxpayer
claimed and is admittedly entitled to an apportioned part of a capital

G

H

A   allowance representing the proportion of his total mileage which he
travelled on official business: see section 47 (1) and paragraph 5 of
Schedule 8 to the Finance Act 1971, which specifically provide for capital
allowances to be available to holders of employments, vocations and offices
and provide for apportionment where plant is used partly for business and
partly for other purposes. There was, of course, no dispute about the £40
claimed for the cost of petrol. As regards the other items the commissioners
B   decided:

> " The cost of servicing and repairs is in our opinion properly ap-
> portionable because it can realistically be said that such expense is
> occasioned in part by the private use and in part by the official use.
> The case for apportioning the cost of the licence and insurance is
> perhaps less clear in principle, but the revenue concede it. The ap-
C   > propriate proportion of [the estimated cost of repairs and servicing,
> and the licence and insurance] is agreed to be £24."

They therefore allowed a deduction of £115, including the capital
allowance of £51, but disallowed the whole of the actual cost of providing
and maintaining the car, that is the £665 claimed by him. In this appeal
D   the taxpayer claims that if the lump sum and mileage allowance are both
properly emoluments of his office or employment the commissioners should
have allowed the total cost of repairs and servicing, road tax and insurance,
as well as the £40 for petrol.

The contention that the mileage allowance was not an emolument of the
taxpayer's office or employment was founded on certain observations in
the House of Lords in *Pook* v. *Owen* [1970] A.C. 244. In that case the
E   taxpayer, a Dr. Owen, carried on a general medical practice at the place
where he resided and held a part-time appointment at a hospital 15 miles
away. Under the terms of his employment he was on duty two nights a week
and two weekends a month, when he was required to be accessible by
telephone. On receipt of a telephone call from the hospital it was his usual
practice to instruct the hospital staff and then to go to the hospital by car,
F   though he sometimes advised treatment on the telephone and awaited a
further report. He was paid a travelling allowance at a fixed rate per mile
for travel from his home to the hospital up to a limit of 10 miles for a
single journey. The general commissioners found:

> " (a) that the taxpayer's duties commenced at the moment he was first
> contacted by the hospital authorities. (b) Thereafter his travelling
G   > expenses to and from the hospital or to and from an emergency were
> wholly, exclusively and necessarily incurred or expended in the duties
> of that office."

That decision was reversed by Stamp J. [1967] 1 W.L.R. 679, and on
appeal to the Court of Appeal his decision was upheld [1969] 1 Ch. 535.
In the Court of Appeal it was argued for the first time that the mileage
H   allowance was not part of the taxpayer's emoluments. What had been
argued before was that the expenses were deductible. That argument, that
the mileage allowance was not an emolument, was also relied on in the
House of Lords [1970] A.C. 244. It was throughout assumed without
demur from the Crown that the actual cost to the taxpayer of travelling to
the hospital from his home by car was more than the allowance he was paid,
so that; in the words of Lord Donovan, at p. 260, " it may fairly be assumed
that there was no profit element in the travelling allowances he received in

these two years, but that, on the contrary they left him out of pocket." The **A**
questions argued in the Court of Appeal and in the House of Lords were,
first, whether the car allowance was an emolument; secondly, if it was an
emolument whether the cost of the journeys was a permissible deduction
from his total emoluments under what was then rule 7 of Schedule 9 to the
Income Tax Act 1952 (now section 189 of the Income and Corporation
Taxes Act 1970); and thirdly, if the car allowance was not an emolument
whether the cost of the journeys in excess of the allowance was a permis- **B**
sible deduction. Lord Guest and Lord Pearce held, at pp. 255, 256 and
259, that the car allowance was not an emolument and that any additional
cost incurred by the taxpayer was deductible. Lord Donovan, at p. 260,
agreed that the car allowance was not an emolument but held that any
additional cost incurred by the taxpayer was not deductible. Lord Wilberforce, at p. 263, agreed with Lord Denning M.R., who had dissented from **C**
the majority in the Court of Appeal, that the car allowance was an emolument but that the whole cost of the journeys was deductible ([1969] 1 Ch.
535, 539–541). Lord Denning M.R. based his conclusion that the car allowance was an emolument on the ground that the taxpayer was entitled to the
allowance whether he used his car for a journey to the hospital or went by
bus or bicycle, so that the car allowance could not be treated as a true
reimbursement. Lord Wilberforce, who, as I have said, agreed with Lord **D**
Denning M.R. that the car allowance was an emolument and that the cost
of the journeys was deductible, said, at p. 263:

> " I should add that, if I had not reached this conclusion "— that is,
> that the cost of the journeys was deductible—" I should have difficulty
> in seeing how the appellant could succeed, on his alternative point, in
> establishing that reimbursement of a non-deductible expense is some- **E**
> thing other than an emolument."

Lord Pearson, at p. 266, held that the car allowance was an emolument
and not deductible.

Lord Guest and Lord Pearce based their conclusions that the car
allowance was not an emolument and that any additional cost of the **F**
journeys in excess of the car allowance was deductible, and Lord Wilberforce his conclusion that the actual cost of the journeys was deductible, on
the ground that under the terms of the taxpayer's employment he had two
places of work and that in travelling from his home to the hospital he was,
in the words of Lord Wilberforce, at p. 263, " travelling not to his work but
on his work." They distinguished *Ricketts* v. *Colquhoun* [1926] A.C. 1 **G**
(the well-known case of the barrister practising in London who took an
appointment as recorder in Portsmouth and whose claim to deduct the
expenses of travelling to and from Portsmouth was held by the House of
Lords to be impermissible) on the ground that as the appointment was a
part-time appointment the hospital authorities had no real alternative to
appointing someone with a practice some distance from the hospital and
that anyone appointed would have to be appointed on terms that some of **H**
his duties would be carried out at home and some at the hospital. Lord
Wilberforce said, at p. 263:

> " In this case the hospital management committee required the services
> of doctors on a part-time basis for emergencies: it was found that
> there was difficulty in obtaining suitable men. Unless a suitable retired
> doctor could be appointed (and that case might be different) the com-
> mittee would have to appoint a doctor with a practice of his own and

A also with suitable obstetric and anaesthetic experience: he might live and practise within 15 miles or one mile or 100 yards of the hospital: the choice in the matter, if any exists, does not lie with the doctor, who is there in his practice, but with the committee which decides, however near or far he works, to appoint him and to require him to discharge a part of his duty at his practice premises. A finding that

B expenses necessarily arise from this duality appears to me legitimate and the undemonstrated possibility that a nearer practitioner might have been selected to be irrelevant."

The expenses incurred by Dr. Owen in travelling from his home to the hospital and the expenses incurred by the taxpayer in the instant case in travelling from his office to visit properties in the course of fixing a fair

C rent are precisely analogous. But there, it seems to me, the analogy ends. The opinion of Lord Guest, Lord Pearce and Lord Donovan that the car allowance was not an emolument was clearly based upon the assumption, rejected by Lord Denning M.R. and Lord Wilberforce, that the allowance was no more than the reimbursement of costs actually incurred by the taxpayer in making his way from home to hospital. The assumption is made explicit in the speech of Lord Donovan, who said, at p. 260:

D   " On the footing that the travelling expenses paid to Dr. Owen simply reimbursed what he had spent (or part of what he had spent) on travelling in performance of his duties, I do not think they should be regarded as emoluments of his employment within the meaning of Schedule E."

E The assumption is implicit in the speeches of Lord Guest and Lord Pearce in so far as they refer to the car allowance as an " indemnity " or a " reimbursement."

The conclusion that reimbursement of an actual expense incurred by an employee in the course and for the purposes of his employment is not an emolument is binding on me. Even if it were not, I should myself find difficulty in seeing how any distinction can be drawn for this purpose be-

F tween the case where, for instance, an employee buys a railway ticket for a journey he has to make in the course of his employment and is reimbursed and a case where the ticket is bought for him by the employer or where he buys it and charges it to his employer's account. But in the instant case the mileage allowance as a whole cannot be regarded as mere reimbursement of expenses actually incurred by the taxpayer in making journeys in the course of his duties. The mileage allowance included a significant con-

G tribution to the overhead costs of putting his car on the road and maintaining it for his own private use as well as for use on official journeys. It may be that to the extent that it covered the actual cost of petrol and oil, and possibly a contribution to repairs and replacement of tyres, the mileage allowance could be treated as a reimbursement. But those expenses are admittedly deductible, and it makes no practical difference whether they are

H deducted from the mileage allowance as a reimbursement before the balance is brought in as an emolument or whether the whole of the mileage allowance is brought in as an emolument and the expenses are then deducted under section 189.

I turn, therefore, to consider whether the whole cost of putting the car on the road and maintaining it is a permissible deduction from the tax-payer's emoluments under section 189 of the Income and Corporation Taxes Act 1970. I should, I think, read subsection (1) in full:

"If the holder of an office or employment is necessarily obliged to A
incur and defray out of the emoluments thereof the expenses of
travelling in the performance of the duties of the office or employment,
or of keeping and maintaining a horse to enable him to perform the
same, or otherwise to expend money wholly, exclusively and necessarily in the performance of the said duties, there may be deducted
from the emoluments to be assessed the expenses so necessarily incurred and defrayed."   B

This subsection contains, I think, three distinct limbs. It permits the deduction of "the expenses of travelling in the performance of the duties of
the office or employment" which the holder of the office or employment is
necessarily obliged to incur and defray; it permits the deduction which such
a person is necessarily obliged to incur and defray "of keeping and main-   C
taining a horse to enable him to perform" those duties; and it permits a
deduction where he is obliged "otherwise to expend money wholly,
exclusively and necessarily in the performance of the said duties."
    Before the commissioners it was argued on behalf of the taxpayer that
he was necessarily obliged to incur the whole expense involved in putting
his car on the road and maintaining it within the first limb of section 189
because he needed to have a car available for official use. The com-   D
missioners rejected that argument. I should, I think, read their reasons
for rejecting it in full. They said:

"That argument would have considerable force if the evidence
established that it had been made a condition of his employment, as
it could have been within the terms agreed by the National Joint
Council, that he should provide a motor car for official use. But no E
document was put before us in which that condition was imposed, nor
did [the taxpayer], whom we found to be an entirely honest and
straightforward witness, assert that there was a specific condition to
that effect in his contract of employment. He had formed the impression that he would not have been appointed had he not owned a
car but he was unable to say what would happen if he were un-   F
fortunately to lose his licence to drive. In answer to questions on that
point he said that he presumed that he would have to get about by
other means, possibly confining his visits to properties in the more
easily accessible parts of his area. He did not suggest that he was
likely to forfeit his appointment. It is true that [the taxpayer] received
the 'essential user' car allowance, which means that his employers
considered it essential for the efficient conduct of their business that he G
should be permitted to use his private car on official duty (paragraph
63 (c) (i) of the agreed conditions). But the granting of essential user
status presupposes that the officer has a car available and has applied
for permission to use it on official duty. It does not in itself establish
that the provision of a car was a necessary requirement of the post. On
the evidence we cannot find that [the taxpayer] was necessarily obliged H
to incur the expense of licensing insuring and maintaining his car as
part of the cost of travelling in the performance of his duties and we
must reject his claim to deduct the full cost of those items."

    The finding by the commissioners that it was not a term or condition
of the taxpayer's employment that he should make a car available for use
on his official journeys is clearly a finding of primary fact which the commissioners were entitled to make, if indeed not bound to make on the

A   evidence before them. Mr. Musgrave submitted that the fact that the taxpayer was entitled to the " essential user allowance " showed that the
council regarded it as essential that he should have a car available for use
on official journeys and that it was in the circumstances practically, albeit
not contractually necessary for him to provide his own car for that purpose.
I agree with the commissioners that that conclusion does not follow. If the
B   taxpayer had not himself owned a car and held a driving licence, or if he
had lost his licence the council would have had to have provided a car and,
if the taxpayer had no licence, a driver or to have arranged with the taxpayer to confine his duties to properties within the City or at least to properties in an area accessible by public transport. Mr. Musgrave submitted
that the only reasonable inference is that the council would not have provided a car and, if necessary a driver, but would have arranged with the
C   taxpayer to confine his duties within a smaller area, that he would not then
have been performing the same duties as he performed while a car owner
and that accordingly ownership of a car was a practical necessity if the
taxpayer was to perform the duties actually required of the office or
employment which he actually held at the relevant time. But there was no
evidence before the commissioners as to what course the council would
D   have taken in the circumstances envisaged, and the assumption that they
would not have themselves provided a car and if necessary a driver is no
more than an assumption.

That is sufficient to dispose of this appeal. But it would, I think, be
unsatisfactory to dismiss this appeal simply on the ground that the taxpayer
has not shown that it was a term or condition of his employment, or a
practical necessity imposed by the circumstances of his employment, that
E   he should himself provide a car for use on his official duties. For in my
judgment the appeal fails on another and more fundamental ground. In
Ricketts v. Colquhoun [1926] A.C. 1, 4 Viscount Cave L.C. said that to
fall within the first limb of section 189 (then rule 9 of Schedule E) expenses
must be

F   " expenses which the holder of an office is necessarily obliged to incur
—that is to say, obliged by the very fact that he holds the office and
has to perform its duties—and they must be incurred in—that is, in the
course of—the performance of those duties. The expenses in question
in this case do not appear to me to satisfy either test."

In Taylor v. Provan [1975] A.C. 194, Lord Reid, commenting on this
passage, said, at pp. 207–208:
G
            " Then apparently explaining what he meant by 'in the course of,' he
said that the expenses were incurred because [Mr. Ricketts] travelled
to Portsmouth before he could begin to perfom his duties and travelled
home after concluding them. I have considerable doubt whether Lord
Cave's second test is not too rigid. He does not refer to the fact that
the rule also authorises the deduction of the expenses ' of keeping and
H   maintaining a horse to enable him to perform ' the duties of his office.
The holder of the office would keep his horse at his home, so he would
use it to get from his home to the various places where his duties had
to be performed. So this part of the rule must mean to enable the
holder of the office to get from his home to the place where his duties
are to be performed as well as to enable him to get from one place to
another in the course of performing his duties. There is no suggestion
of a distinction between travelling from his home to the place of work

and travelling between places of work. He can deduct the whole cost   A
of keeping his horse—not merely part of it. Lord Cave recognises
that the holder of an office may have to travel if his duties have to be
performed in several places in succession. I would doubt whether such
travelling is always ' in the course of ' the performance of his duties.
If a part-time officer has to work at A today and at B a week hence
he is not on duty meanwhile and can travel whichever day he chooses.
He is entitled to deduct the expenses of travelling from A to B but it   B
seems to me unreal to say that during the hours he is travelling he is
on duty. He is travelling not in the course of performing his duties but
to enable him to perform his next duty when the time comes."

These observations were clearly obiter and form no part of the actual
decision of the House of Lords in that case. In that case it was held by a
majority that a Canadian businessman who was a director of an English   C
brewery group and who incurred and was reimbursed expenses in travelling
from Canada and Nassau to England, which fell to be treated as emoluments under the special provisions applicable to directors and higher paid
employees, could deduct those expenses (which under those provisions
could be deducted if " expended wholly, exclusively and necessarily in
performing the duties of the office ") from the emoluments. The ground of   D
that decision was that in the very special circumstances of that case the taxpayer was required to work in Toronto and Nassau as well as London, and
that the travelling expenses were incurred in the performance of his duties
and not because he chose to reside at a place far removed from the place
where his duties fell to be performed.

Any observation by Lord Reid must, of course, carry the very greatest
weight. But for my part I cannot see that the fact that the second limb of   E
section 189 (1), which is an anomalous survival, permits the deduction of
the whole cost of keeping a horse if necessary to enable the taxpayer to
perform his duties, albeit that the horse may be used for private purposes,
throws any light on the first limb of section 189 (1). And it would, I think,
be impossible, even if the taxpayer had shown that he was contractually
obliged to provide a car which he could use for his official duties, receiving   F
in exchange the lump sum and mileage allowance, to say that the whole
cost of putting the car on the road and maintaining it would be one he
would have been necessarily obliged to incur as part of the expenses " of
travelling in the performance of " his duties within section 189. The ownership of a car, like the club membership considered in Brown v. Bullock
[1961] 1 W.L.R. 1095, makes officers in the position of the taxpayer more
useful to the council, and that no doubt is why the council are prepared to   G
pay car allowances on a scale which covers part of an officer's overheads
and so reduces the cost to him of maintaining a car which, as the evidence
shows, the taxpayer would have maintained in any event for his private use.
It does not make the expense an expense incurred in the performance of
his duties.

It was accepted by the Crown that the cost of servicing and repairs is   H
apportionable. That an apportionment can be made, at least in a case falling
within the first limb of section 189 (1), has been recognised in a number
of cases (see, for instance, Hillyer v. Leeke (1976) 51 T.C. 90, 93) though
in a case falling within the third limb apportionment may be concessionary.
As the commissioners point out, it is by no means obvious that the cost of
licensing and insuring the car (which the taxpayer would have incurred in
any event since he admitted that he would have maintained the car for his

A own use even if it had not been necessary for him to have it for official use) is similarly apportionable, but the Crown have agreed that these items can also be apportioned, and I accordingly express no opinion on the point.

For the reasons I have given, I think this appeal fails and must be dismissed.

Appeal dismissed with costs.

B

Solicitors: *Legal Officer, National and Local Government Officers Association; Solicitor of Inland Revenue.*

[Reported by MRS. HARRIET DUTTON, Barrister-at-Law]

C

[COURT OF APPEAL]

D ** In re* B. (A MINOR) (WARDSHIP: MEDICAL TREATMENT)

1981   Aug. 7   Templeman and Dunn L.JJ.

Minor—Ward of court—Medical treatment—Newly born mongol child requiring operation to save life—Parents refusing consent —Whether operation in child's best interests

E

A child, who was born suffering from Down's syndrome (mongolism) and an intestinal blockage, required an operation to relieve the obstruction if she was to live more than a few days. If the operation were performed, the child might die within a few months but it was probable that her life expectancy would be 20 to 30 years. Her parents, having decided that it would be kinder to allow her to die rather than

F live as a physically and mentally handicapped person, refused to consent to the operation. The local authority made the child a ward of court and, when a surgeon decided that the wishes of the parents should be respected, they sought an order authorising the operation to be performed by other named surgeons. The judge decided that the parents' wishes should be respected and refused to make the order.

On appeal by the local authority:—

G   *Held*, allowing the appeal, that the question for the court was whether it was in the best interests of the child that she should have the operation and not whether the parents' wishes should be respected; that, since the effect of the operation might be that the child would have the normal span of life of a mongol and since it had not been demonstrated that the life of a mongol was of such a nature that the child should be condemned to die, the court would make an order that

H   the operation be performed.

Decision of Ewbank J. reversed.

No cases are referred to in the judgments.

The following case was cited in argument:

J. v. *C.* [1970] A.C. 668; [1969] 2 W.L.R. 540; [1969] 1 All E.R. 788, H.L.(E.).

1422

In re B. (A Minor) (C.A.)   **[1981]**

APPEAL from Ewbank J.   A

On July 31, 1981, the local authority, Hammersmith and Fulham
London Borough Council, made an ex parte application and, on the local
authority undertaking to file an originating summons that day, Ewbank J.
made an order requiring the child to remain a ward of court during her
minority or until further order, and giving care and control of the child to
the local authority until further order with leave to the local authority to
place the child for adoption and to commence adoption proceedings and   B
to authorise surgery to be performed on the child forthwith. Following
that order, the local authority took out an originating summons naming
the parents as defendants. The Official Solicitor consented to act as
guardian ad litem for the child who was added as a defendant in the
proceedings. By an order of August 7, 1981, the judge revoked that part
of the order of July 31, 1981, authorising surgery to be performed on   C
the child. The local authority appealed.

The facts are stated in the judgment of Templeman L.J.

Anita Ryan for the local authority.
Henry Turcan for the Official Solicitor.
Roger Gray Q.C. and *Mark Cunningham* for the parents.
                                                                         D

TEMPLEMAN L.J. This is a very poignantly sad case. Although we
sit in public, for reasons which I think will be obvious to everybody in
court, and if not will be obvious in the course of this judgment, it would
be lamentable if the names of the parents of the child concerned were
revealed in any way to the general public. The press and people who
frequent these courts are usually very helpful in referring to names by   E
initials, and this is a case where nothing ought to be leaked out to identify
those concerned with the case.

It concerns a little girl who was born on July 28, 1981. She was born
suffering from Down's syndrome, which means that she will be a mongol.
She was also born with an intestinal blockage which will be fatal unless it
is operated upon. When the parents were informed of the condition of the   F
child they took the view that it would be unkind to this child to operate
upon her, and that the best thing to do was for her not to have the operation, in which case she would die within a few days. During those few days
she could be kept from pain and suffering by sedation. They took the view
that would be the kindest thing in the interests of the child. They so informed the doctors at the hospital, and refused to consent to the operation
taking place. It is agreed on all hands that the parents came to that decision   G
with great sorrow. It was a firm decision: they genuinely believed that it
was in the best interests of this child. At the same time, it is of course impossible for parents in the unfortunate position of these parents to be
certain that their present view should prevail. The shock to caring parents
finding that they have given birth to a child who is a mongol is very great
indeed, and therefore while great weight ought to be given to the views of   H
the parents they are not views which necessarily must prevail.

What happened then was that the doctors being informed that the
parents would not consent to the operation contacted the local authority
who very properly made the child a ward of court and asked the judge to
give care and control to the local authority and to authorise them to direct
that the operation be carried out, and the judge did so direct. But when the
child was moved from the hospital where it was born to another hospital

A   for the purposes of the operation a difference of medical opinion developed. The surgeon who was to perform the operation declined to do so when he was informed that the parents objected. In a statement he said that when the child was referred to him for the operation he decided he wished to speak to the parents of the child personally and he spoke to them on the telephone and they stated that in view of the fact that the child was mongoloid they did not wish to have the operation performed. He further
B   stated:

> " I decided therefore to respect the wishes of the parents and not to perform the operation, a decision which would, I believe (after about 20 years in the medical profession), be taken by the great majority of surgeons faced with a similar situation."

C   Therefore the local authority came back to the judge. The parents were served in due course and appeared and made their submissions to the judge, and in addition inquiries were made and it was discovered that the surgeon in the hospital where the child was born and another surgeon in a neighbouring hospital were prepared and advised that the operation should be carried out. So there is a difference of medical opinion.

D   This morning the judge was asked to decide whether to continue his order that the operation should be performed or whether to revoke that order, and the position now is stark. The evidence, as I have said, is that if this little girl does not have this operation she will die within a matter of days. If she has the operation there is a possibility that she will suffer heart trouble as a result and that she may die within two or three months. But if she has the operation and it is successful, she has Down's syndrome, she
E   is mongoloid, and the present evidence is that her life expectancy is short, about 20 to 30 years.

        The parents say that no one can tell what will be the life of a mongoloid child who survives during that 20 or 30 years, but one thing is certain. She will be very handicapped mentally and physically and no one can expect that she will have anything like a normal existence. They make that point
F   not because of the difficulties which will be occasioned to them but in the child's interest. This is not a case in which the court is concerned with whether arrangements could or could not be made for the care of this child, if she lives, during the next 20 or 30 years; the local authority is confident that the parents having for good reason decided that it is in the child's best interests that the operation should not be performed, nevertheless good adoption arrangements could be made and that in so far as any mongol
G   child can be provided with a happy life then such a happy life can be provided.

        The question which this court has to determine is whether it is in the interests of this child to be allowed to die within the next week or to have the operation in which case if she lives she will be a mongoloid child, but no one can say to what extent her mental or physical defects will be
H   apparent. No one can say whether she will suffer or whether she will be happy in part. On the one hand the probability is that she will not be a cabbage as it is called when people's faculties are entirely destroyed. On the other hand it is certain that she will be very severely mentally and physically handicapped.

        On behalf of the parents Mr. Gray has submitted very movingly, if I may say so, that this is a case where nature has made its own arrangements to terminate a life which would not be fruitful and nature should not be interfered with. He has also submitted that in this kind of decision the views of responsible and caring parents, as these are, should be respected, and that their decision that it is better for the child to be allowed to die should be respected. Fortunately or unfortunately, in this particular case the decision no longer lies with the parents or with the doctors, but lies with the court. It is a decision which of course must be made in the light of the evidence and views expressed by the parents and the doctors, but at the end of the day it devolves on this court in this particular instance to decide whether the life of this child is demonstrably going to be so awful that in effect the child must be condemned to die, or whether the life of this child is still so imponderable that it would be wrong for her to be condemned to die. There may be cases, I know not, of severe proved damage where the future is so certain and where the life of the child is so bound to be full of pain and suffering that the court might be driven to a different conclusion, but in the present case the choice which lies before the court is this: whether to allow an operation to take place which may result in the child living for 20 or 30 years as a mongoloid or whether (and I think this must be brutally the result) to terminate the life of a mongoloid child because she also has an intestinal complaint. Faced with that choice I have no doubt that it is the duty of this court to decide that the child must live. The judge was much affected by the reasons given by the parents and came to the conclusion that their wishes ought to be respected. In my judgment he erred in that the duty of the court is to decide whether it is in the interests of the child that an operation should take place. The evidence in this case only goes to show that if the operation takes place and is successful then the child may live the normal span of a mongoloid child with the handicaps and defects and life of a mongol child, and it is not for this court to say that life of that description ought to be extinguished.

Accordingly the appeal must be allowed and the local authority must be authorised themselves to authorise and direct the operation to be carried out on the little girl.

Dunn L.J. I agree, and as we are differing from the view expressed by the judge I would say a few words of my own. I have great sympathy for the parents in the agonising decision to which they came. As they put it themselves, " God or nature has given the child a way out." But the child now being a ward of court, although due weight must be given to the decision of the parents which everybody accepts was an entirely responsible one, doing what they considered was the best, the fact of the matter is that this court now has to make the decision. It cannot hide behind the decision of the parents or the decision of the doctors; and in making the decision this court's first and paramount consideration is the welfare of this unhappy little baby.

One of the difficulties in the case is that there is no prognosis as to the child's future, except that as a mongol her expectation of life is confined to 20 to 30 years. We were told that no reliable prognosis can be made until probably she is about two years old. That in itself leads me to the route by which the court should make its decision, because there is no evidence that this child's short life is likely to be an intolerable one. There is no evidence at all as to the quality of life which the child may expect. As Mr. Turcan on behalf of the Official Solicitor said, the child should be put into

A   the same position as any other mongol child and must be given the
chance to live an existence. I accept that way of putting it.

I agree with Templeman L.J. that the court must step in to preserve
this mongol baby's life. I would allow the appeal and I agree with the
order proposed by Templeman L.J.

B   *Appeal allowed.*
                    Local authority to pay parents' costs of
                              appeal and below.

Solicitors: *C. T. Mahoney; Official Solicitor; Jolliffe & Co., Chester.*

                                                            B. O. A.
C

                            ――――――――

                          [COURT OF APPEAL]

D   * STANTON (INSPECTOR OF TAXES) *v.* DRAYTON
              COMMERCIAL INVESTMENT CO. LTD.

1981   May 20, 21;   Waller, Oliver and Fox L.JJ.
       June 25

E   *Revenue—Corporation tax—Chargeable gains—Allowable deduc-
     tions—Investment company acquiring securities in exchange
     for issue of its own shares—Conditional agreement stipulating
     price of securities and number of shares to be issued in
     exchange—Market value of shares falling before completion
     of agreement—Value of consideration given for securities—
     Finance Act 1965 (c. 25), Sch. 6, para. 4 (1) (a)*

F   In 1972 the taxpayer company entered into a conditional
     agreement with E. Ltd. to purchase from it securities at an
     agreed price of £3,937,962. That purchase price was to be
     satisfied by the allotment by the taxpayer company to E. Ltd.
     of 2,461,226 of its ordinary shares of 25p each, " the issue
     price of each such share for the purpose of satisfying the con-
     sideration being 160p." That price had been agreed by re-
     ference to the middle market quotations for those securities
     on the Stock Exchange as at August 31, 1972. The agreement
G   was conditional on the members of the taxpayer company
     passing a resolution to create the consideration shares and on
     the Stock Exchange granting permission to deal in and quo-
     tation for the consideration shares before October 31, 1972.
     By October 11, 1972, those two conditions were satisfied and
     the securities specified in the agreement were exchanged for
     the shares in the taxpayer company. On the following day
H   the Stock Exchange quoted price for the taxpayer company's
     shares had fallen to 125p. During the taxpayer company's
     accounting periods ending December 1972 and December
     1973 some of the securities that they had acquired under the
     agreement were sold at a profit. In consequence of the sales
     they were assessed to corporation tax in respect of chargeable
     gains for the relevant years on the basis that the amount of
     the gains accruing on the disposals of the securities were to
     be ascertained by reference to the market price of their shares
     at the date when the agreement became unconditional,

1426

namely, 125p and not at the price stated in the agreement of   **A**
160p. An appeal against the assessments was allowed by the
special commissioners who upheld the taxpayer company's
case that the value of the consideration for the purpose of
paragraph 4 (1) (*a*) of Schedule 6 to the Finance Act 1965 [1]
was £3,937,692 being the consideration expressed in the
agreement and based on Stock Exchange quotations on
August 31, 1972, of 160p per share. Vinelott J. allowed an
appeal by the Crown, holding that the value of the considera-   **B**
tion was the Stock Exchange middle market quotation on the
day after the agreement became unconditional of 125p per
share.

On appeal by the taxpayer company: —

Held, allowing the appeal, that the consideration given by
the taxpayer company under the agreement was the issue and
allotment of shares at 160p a share and to credit them as fully
paid up; that, in assessing the value of that consideration for   **C**
the purposes of paragraph 4 (1) (*a*) of Schedule 6 to the Act,
the best evidence of its value was that reached by the parties
to the agreement in a genuine commercial transaction at arm's
length of £3,937,962; and that, accordingly, the amount deductible in computing the gains was 160p per share (post, pp.
1431c–g, 1432f—1433c, e–g).

Osborne v. *Steel Barrel Co. Ltd.* [1942] 1 All E.R. 634,
C.A. and *Craddock* v. *Zevo Finance Co. Ltd.* [1944] 1 All   **D**
E.R. 566; [1946] 1 All E.R. 523, C.A. and H.L.(E.) applied.

Decision of Vinelott J. [1980] 1 W.L.R. 1162; [1980] 3
All E.R. 221 reversed.

The following cases are referred to in the judgment of the court:

Brooklands Selangor Holdings Ltd. v. *Inland Revenue Commissioners*   **E**
    [1970] 1 W.L.R. 429; [1970] 2 All E.R. 76.
Craddock v. *Zevo Finance Co. Ltd.* [1944] 1 All E.R. 566; 27 T.C. 267,
    C.A.; [1946] 1 All E.R. 523; 27 T.C. 267, H.L.(E.).
Crane Fruehauf Ltd. v. *Inland Revenue Commissioners* [1974] 1 All E.R.
    811; [1975] 1 All E.R. 429, C.A.
Osborne v. *Steel Barrel Co. Ltd.* [1942] 1 All E.R. 634; 24 T.C. 293, C.A.

  F

The following additional case was cited in argument:

Aberdeen Construction Group Ltd. v. *Inland Revenue Commissioners*
    [1978] A.C. 885; [1978] 2 W.L.R. 648; [1978] 1 All E.R. 962,
    H.L.(Sc.).

APPEAL from Vinelott J.

  G
On September 21, 1972, the taxpayer company, Drayton Commercial
Investment Co. Ltd. (then called Union Commercial Investment Co. Ltd.),
negotiated a conditional agreement with Eagle Star Insurance Co. Ltd.
to purchase a portfolio of securities for £3,937,962 to be satisfied by the
allotment by the taxpayer company of 2,461,226 of its ordinary shares of
25p. The agreement stated that " the issue price of each such share for
the purpose of satisfying the consideration [is] 160p." By October 11,   **H**
1972, the conditions were satisfied and the agreement completed. On
October 12, 1972, the Stock Exchange middle market quotation of those
shares was 125p. During the accounting periods ended December 31, 1972,
and December 31, 1973, the taxpayer company disposed of some of the
securities comprised in the portfolio. It appealed against assessments to

[1] Finance Act 1965, Sch. 6, para. 4 (1) (*a*): see post, p. 1429f–g.

A corporation tax for those two periods in sums of £178,011 and £440,000 respectively.

The Commissioners for the Special Purposes of the Income Tax Acts upheld its contention that in ascertaining the chargeable gains accruing to the taxpayer company on the disposal of the securities that it had acquired for a price satisfied by the allotment of ordinary shares, the value
B of the shares so allotted was, for the purpose of paragraph 4 (1) (a) of Schedule 6 to the Finance Act 1965, 160p (being their par value plus the premium at which they were allotted) and not their market value of 125p at the time they were first quoted on the Stock Exchange following the allotment. They reduced the assessment for the period ending December 31, 1972, to nil and that for the period to December 31, 1973, to £349,429.

C Vinelott J. reversed the commissioners' determination, holding that paragraph 4 (1) (a) of Schedule 6 to the Finance Act 1965 restricted the sums allowable as deductions in computing the amount of a gain to the market value of the consideration given for the acquisition of the asset and that had to be ascertained by reference to Stock Exchange quotation of the taxpayer company's shares on October 12, 1972, namely 125p.

The taxpayer company appealed on the grounds that (1) the judge
D ought to have held, and was wrong in law in not holding, (a) that in paragraph 4 (1) (a) of Schedule 6 to the Finance Act 1965 the words "the amount or value of the consideration, in money or money's worth, given " by the acquirer of an asset " or on his behalf wholly and exclusively for the acquisition of the asset " were to be construed as referring to the price paid by the acquirer in consideration of the acquisition of the asset and not the market value to the disposer of the consideration
E received for the disposal of the asset; (b) that where a company acquired property in return for the issue of its shares then, unless the contract for the acquisition of the property was merely colourable or fraudulent, the amount or value of the consideration given by the company within the meaning of paragraph 4 (1) (a) was the amount of the credit which it gave to the vendor of the property for the value of the property acquired and
F that that amount fell to be determined by reference to the terms of the contract whereby the asset was acquired; (c) that the sum of £3,937,962 which the judge held was the cost of the portfolio to the taxpayer company and further held was the cost to be entered into the taxpayer company's books to balance the sums which were in part applied to paying up shares at par and in part credited to share premium account was the
G " amount or value of the consideration .. given " by the taxpayer company within the meaning of paragraph 4 (1) (a); (d) that where a company acquired an asset in consideration of the issue of shares in itself the acquisition cost of that asset was determined by reference to the same principles whether the company was a dealing company and the asset was comprised in its trading stock or whether the asset was acquired as a
H capital asset; (e) that in ascertaining the acquisition cost for capital gains tax purposes of an asset acquired by a company in consideration of an issue of its own shares the market value of the shares so issued in the hands of the disposer of the asset was immaterial; (2) the judge misdirected himself and/or was wrong in law in holding, (a) that for the purposes of paragraph 4 (1) (a) " the amount or value of the consideration ... given " by the acquirer of an asset was to be equated with the market value of the consideration received by the disposer of the asset; (b) that

the authorities cited by the judge in his judgment relating to the calcula-   A
tion of the value or price of securities for the purpose of ad valorem
stamp duty had any relevance to the meaning of the words " the amount
or value of the consideration . . . given " in the sub-paragraph; (c) that the
amount or value of the consideration given by the acquirer of an asset for
its acquisition was to be calculated as at the date the contract for the
disposal of the asset became unconditional and not as at the date the   B
contract was entered into.

By a respondent's notice dated June 30, 1980, the Crown gave notice
of its intention to contend that the judge's decision should be affirmed
on the additional ground that the decision of the judge as to the meaning
and effect of paragraph 4 (1) (a) of Schedule 6 to the Finance Act 1965 and
paragraph 10 (2) of Schedule 10 to the Finance Act 1971 was supported by   C
a contrast of those provisions with the corresponding provisions of the
short-term capital gains tax legislation which was not repealed until the
Finance Act 1971.

Michael Nolan Q.C. and *Robert Venables* for the taxpayer company.
C. H. McCall for the Crown.
                                                        Cur. adv. vult.   D

June 25. Fox L.J. delivered the following judgment of the court. This
is an appeal by the taxpayer company from a decision of Vinelott J. concerning, in effect, capital gains tax though the material assessment is to
corporation tax. The facts are (1) by an agreement of September 21, 1972,
and made between Eagle Star Insurance Co. Ltd., of the one part and the   E
taxpayer company (then called Union Commercial Investment Co. Ltd.) of
the other part, Eagle Star agreed to sell and the taxpayer company agreed
to purchase a portfolio of investments at the price of £3,937,962 to be satisfied by the allotment by the taxpayer company to Eagle Star of 2,461,226
ordinary shares of 25p each in the taxpayer company credited as fully paid
up, the issue price of each of such shares for the purpose of satisfying the   F
consideration being 160p. The shares (we will call them the new shares) were
to rank pari passu with the existing ordinary shares of the taxpayer company
save in respect of any final dividend for the year ended December 1972, as
to which Eagle Star was to be entitled to receive certain payments in lieu.
The agreement was expressed to be conditional upon: (i) the shareholders
in the taxpayer company passing the resolution necessary to create the new
shares; (ii) the Stock Exchange granting permission to deal in and quota-   G
tion for such shares subject to allotment before October 31, 1972. The
agreement was to be completed within seven days after those conditions
were satisfied. (2) The price of £3,967,962 (which we will refer to as £3·9
million) was agreed upon by reference to the middle market values of the
portfolio of investments on the Stock Exchange on August 31, 1972. (3)
The resolution of the taxpayer company creating the new shares was   H
passed on October 9, 1972. The Stock Exchange gave permission to deal
in and a quotation for the new shares on October 11, 1972. The agreement, therefore, became unconditional on October 11, 1972. The sale was
completed on October 11, 1972, when the taxpayer company allotted the
new shares to Eagle Star. (4) The agreement of September 21, 1972, was
an arm's length transaction; the Crown did not suggest that the parties
were at any time acting otherwise than in good faith. (5) The middle

A market price of ordinary shares of 25p in the taxpayer company on the following dates were: (i) 142p on August 31, 1972: (ii) 134p on September 21, 1972: (iii) 125p on October 12, 1972, being the day on which the new shares were first quoted. (6) At dates after October 11, 1972, the taxpayer company, sold certain of the investments comprised in the portfolio. (7) The taxpayer company was, at the material times, an investment holding company.

B
The question on this appeal is the basis of the computation of any capital gain by the taxpayer company on those disposals. The revenue made assessments to tax on the footing that, in computing the chargeable gains, the consideration given by the taxpayer company for the acquisitions of the portfolio was to be taken as equal to the market value of the new shares ascertained in accordance with Stock Exchange quoted prices

C on the day on which the shares were first quoted after allotment. The taxpayer company appealed to the special commissioners against those assessments on the ground that the consideration was the price at which the new shares were issued, i.e. par value, plus the premium entered in the taxpayer company's books — which together amounted to the £3·9 million. That figure is based on an issue value per share of 160p (the figure agreed between the parties in the agreement of September 21, 1972).

D The first quoted price of the new shares after allotment, however was only 125p per share. On that basis the aggregate value of the consideration was £3,076,532. The difference between the two bases for valuation is, therefore, about £800,000. The commisioners upheld the taxpayer company's contention. The Crown appealed from the decision of the commissioners. Vinelott J. [1980] 1 W.L.R. 1162 allowed the appeal and re-

E mitted the case to the commissioners for valuation.
We come now to the statutory provisions. Corporation tax is chargeable in respect of chargeable gains of companies computable in accordance with the law relating to capital gains tax: see sections 238 and 265 of the Income and Corporation Taxes Act 1970. One refers, therefore, to the provisions of the Finance Act 1965 dealing with capital gains tax.

F Paragraph 4 (1) of Schedule 6 to that Act provides as follows:

" Subject to the following provisions of this Schedule, the sums allowable as a deduction from the consideration in the computation under this Schedule of the gain accruing to a person on the disposal of an asset shall be restricted to—(a) the amount or value of the consideration, in money or money's worth, given by him or on his behalf wholly and exclusively for the acquisition of the asset, together with the in-

G   cidental costs to him of the acquisition or, if the asset was not acquired by him, any expenditure wholly and exclusively incurred by him in providing the asset. . . ."

We should also refer to paragraph 10 of Schedule 10 to the Finance Act 1971, which is in the following terms:

H   " (1) Subject to section 45 (5) of the Finance Act 1965 and sub-paragraph (2) below, where an asset is disposed of and acquired under a contract the time at which the disposal and acquisition is made is the time the contract is made (and not, if different, the time at which the asset is conveyed or transferred).
" (2) If the contract is conditional (and, in particular, if it is conditional on the exercise of an option) the time at which the disposal and acquisition is made is the time when the condition is satisfied."

Accordingly, in the present case, the disposal and acquisition took place A
on October 11, 1972.

It is clear from paragraph 4 (1) (a) of Schedule 6 to the Act of 1965 that
the allowable deduction is " the amount or value of the consideration, in
money or money's worth, given by " the taxpayer company for the acquisition of the portfolio. The crucial matter is the identification of that
consideration. The Crown say that it was the new shares. The taxpayer
company's contention, in effect, is this: that when a company acquires   B
property in return for an issue of its own shares, the amount or value of
the consideration given by the company, where the bona fides of the
transaction is not in question, is the amount of credit which is given to
the vendor on account of the issue price of the shares. In the present case
the issue price was £3·9 million; Eagle Star were given credit for the
whole of that amount. It is not in dispute between the parties that the   C
taxpayer company's accounts would properly show that the cost to it of
acquiring the portfolio was £3·9 million; and similarly that for the purpose
of computing a trading profit under Schedule D, the cost of the acquisition of the portfolio would be £3·9 million.

The Crown's contention was that the position in relation to the taxation of capital gains is quite different; cost must not be confused with   D
consideration. That was accepted by Vinelott J. The basis of his judgment
is, we think, stated in the report in [1980] 1 W.L.R. 1162, 1169–1170 as
follows:

> " The cost of the portfolio to the taxpayer company was unquestion-
> ably the sum of £3,937,962. It could be nothing else. That was the
> cost that had to be entered into their books to balance the sums   E
> which were in part applied in paying up shares at par and in part
> credited to share premium account. If the taxpayer company had
> been a share dealing company and if the portfolio had been acquired
> as stock in trade, that is the sum that would have been debited
> against sums realised on subsequent disposals in order to ascertain
> its trading profit. But in ascertaining the amount of the gain to be   F
> computed in accordance with Part III of the Finance Act 1965, the
> amount to be deducted in respect of the consideration for the
> acquisition is the amount or value of that consideration. To equate
> the cost to the taxpayer company of issuing the shares in satisfaction
> of the agreed price with the ' amount or value ' of that consideration is
> in my judgment to repeat the fallacy which Lord Greene M.R. found   G
> to underly the arguments of the Crown in the Steel Barrel and
> Craddock cases. To repeat what Lord Greene M.R. said in Craddock
> v. Zevo Finance Co. Ltd. [1944] 1 All E.R. 566, 569: ' In the every-
> day case of reconstruction, the shares in the new company allotted
> to the shareholders of the old company as fully paid will often, if not
> in most cases, fetch substantially less than their nominal value if sold   H
> in the market '."

Vinelott J.'s conclusion was that the Crown's contention was correct
and that the consideration given by the taxpayer company for the portfolio was the new shares. To test that conclusion it is, we think, necessary
to analyse the legal position which arises when a company issues shares
credited as fully paid up for a consideration other than cash. The position

A   is stated by Lord Greene M.R. in *Osborne* v. *Steel Barrel Co. Ltd.* [1942] 1 All E.R. 634, 637 (in a passage referred to by Vinelott J.) as follows:

> " The primary liability of an allottee of shares is to pay for them in cash; but, when shares are allotted credited as fully paid, this pri-
> B   mary liability is satisfied by a consideration other than cash passing from the allottee. A company, therefore, when, in pursuance of such a transaction, it agrees to credit the shares as fully paid, is giving up what it would otherwise have had—namely, the right to call on the allottee for payment of the par value in cash. A company cannot issue £1,000 nominal worth of shares for stock of the market value of £500, since shares cannot be issued at a discount. Accordingly, when fully-paid shares are properly issued for a consideration other than
> C   cash, the consideration moving from the company must be at the least equal in value to the par value of the shares and must be based on an honest estimate by the directors of the value of the assets acquired."

Let us suppose that A.B. Ltd., by a bona fide agreement, contracts to purchase property from X for £100,000 to be satisfied by the issue of
D   100,000 £1 ordinary shares in A.B. Ltd. credited as fully paid. It seems to us that the value of the consideration given by A.B. Ltd. is £100,000. X has committed himself to accept an allotment of the shares and the company has given up its right to call on X for payment of the par value of the shares. But on the Crown's case the consideration is the shares themselves the value of which, on issue, may and probably will be considerably less
E   in the market than their par value of £100,000. That would, in our view, be a quite unreal result. It disregards the commercial reality of the con- sideration moving from the company, i.e., the consideration given by the company, which, as explained by Lord Greene M.R., must be at least equal to the par value of the shares. We are, therefore, led to doubt whether the shares themselves can in truth be regarded as constituting the
F   consideration given by the company. We do not think that the solution is to be found in the proposition that the £100,000 is merely the cost to the issuing company and not the consideration given by the company. It seems to us to be, in the fullest sense, consideration given by the company. It may also be the cost to the company; but it can nevertheless be the consideration. In our judgment the consideration given by the issuing company in such a case is not the shares themselves. And in principle the
G   present case is no different. In *Craddock* v. *Zevo Finance Co. Ltd.* [1944] 1 All E.R. 566 the respondent company purchased a portfolio of invest- ments belonging to another company; both were dealing companies. The investments in the portfolio were purchased by the respondent company at the prices at which they stood in the books of the vendor which was far in excess of their market value on the Stock Exchange. Under the sale
H   agreement the agreed price was to be satisfied in part by the assumption by the respondent company of certain liabilities of the vendor and in part by the allotment of shares in the respondent company credited as fully paid. The Crown claimed that in computing the profits of the respondent company the amount to be debited as the cost of the investments was their market value, and not as the respondent company contended the price paid by the respondent company namely the aggregate of the lia- bilities taken over and the amount credited as paid on the allotted shares.

In rejecting the Crown's argument, Lord Greene M.R. (whose judgment **A** was approved by the House of Lords [1946] 1 All E.R. 523) said [1944] 1 All E.R. 566, 569:

"The fallacy, if I may respectfully so call it, which underlies the argument, is to be found in the assertion that where a company issues its own shares as consideration for the acquisition of property, those shares are to be treated as money's worth as though they were shares **B** in another company altogether, transferred by way of consideration for the acquisition. This proposition amounts to saying that consideration in the form of fully-paid shares allotted by a company must be treated as being of the value of the shares, no more and no less. Such a contention will not bear a moment's examination where the transaction is a straightforward one and not a mere device for issuing shares at a discount." **C**

Lord Greene M.R. then went on to make the observation, cited by Vinelott J. [1980] 1 W.L.R. 1162, 1168 in the passage which we have set out, to the effect that fully paid shares, when issued, will often fetch less in the market than their par value. Lord Greene M.R. continued [1944] 1 All E.R. 566, 569: **D**

"But this does not mean that they are to be treated as having been issued at a discount; or that the price paid by the new company for the assets which it acquires from the old company ought to be treated as something less than the nominal value of the fully paid shares."

We cannot read that passage, which is dealing with the fallacy referred to by Vinelott J. [1980] 1 W.L.R. 1162, 1170, as containing any support **E** for the Crown's contentions. It seems to us to run counter to them. It is, of course, dealing specifically with the argument that the price paid ought to be regarded as something less than the nominal value of the shares— an issue that does not arise in the present case—but the principle with which it is concerned is, we think, in point. The principle is that allotted shares cannot be treated as money's worth as if they were shares **F** in another company and valued accordingly. That proposition is not directed simply to the case of a Schedule D trading computation. Lord Greene M.R. is stating it in general terms as a matter of identifying the nature of the consideration given by way of allotment of shares credited as fully paid. The importance of Lord Greene M.R.'s analysis, we think, is that it emphasises the fact that attention must be given to the value of the credit which the allotting company is providing; it is because **G** of the credit that the value of the consideration given by the allotting company may be in excess of the value of the shares themselves.

In our view the consideration given by the taxpayer company in the present case was the benefit of an agreement by the taxpayer company (i) to issue and allot the shares at 160p per share and (ii) to credit them as fully paid. We should mention here that, as we understand it, the new **H** shares did not exist at the time when the agreement became unconditional and when, therefore, the acquisition took place. They were issued later on the same day. Mr. McCall said that the word "given" is in the past and that therefore there is nothing to value before the issue of the shares. We do not think that is right: the consideration must have existed when the agreement became unconditional. That is consistent with the proposition that the consideration was the benefit of the agreement by the taxpayer com-

A pany to allot the shares and credit them as fully paid. What then is the value of the consideration? The value cannot be less than the par value of the new shares; *Craddock* v. *Zevo Finance Co. Ltd.* [1944] 1 All E.R. 566 is authority for that. But plainly it can be more since shares can be issued at a premium. The parties, in fact, agreed upon a purchase price in the clearest terms. They agreed that the purchase of the portfolio should be at the price of £3·9 million. That price was to be satisfied by the issue

B of the new shares of 160p per share credited as fully paid up. The shares, were, therefore, to be issued at a premium of 135p per share. The agreement of September 21, 1972, was an arm's length transaction. No attack was made by the Crown on its bona fides. No evidence was called before the commissioners to suggest that the figures in the agreement were in any way unreal or uncommercial. In those circumstances, we can see no

C reason for putting on the consideration given by the taxpayer company any value other than that which the parties themselves, a leading insurance company and an investment holding company, honestly chose to put on it. Lord Simonds, in *Craddock* v. *Zevo Finance Co. Ltd.* [1946] 27 T.C. 267, 295, said:

D   "Then the agreement goes on to provide for the consideration moving from the new company. I cannot distinguish between consideration and purchase price, and (using again the language of the Master of the Rolls) I find that, acquiring the investments ' under a bona fide and unchallengeable contract,' they paid the price which that contract required, a price which, whether too high or low according to the views of third parties, was the price upon which these parties agreed."

E

Paragraph 4 (1) of Schedule 6 to the Finance Act 1965 refers merely to the "amount or value of the consideration, in money or money's worth. . ." It seems to us that, on the facts of this case, the best evidence we have of the value of the consideration is the value which the parties themselves, in an arm's length and bona fide transaction, agreed to put on it.

F We see no justification for disturbing that. The result, in our view, is that the value of the consideration given by the taxpayer company for the acquisition of the portfolio was £3·9 million. In business terms we cannot regard that as an unsatisfactory conclusion. Commercial firms agree on a sale and purchase of assets at a specified price. There is nothing to suggest that it is not a wholly genuine arm's length transaction on com-

G mercial terms. In these circumstances, it seems to us realistic that the agreed purchase price should be the value of the consideration given by the purchaser and should provide the base value of the asset for capital gains tax purposes when the purchaser subsequently disposes of the asset.

There are two further matters which we should mention. Reference was made to the stamp duty cases of *Brooklands Selangor Holdings Ltd.*

H v. *Inland Revenue Commissioners* [1970] 1 W.L.R. 429 and *Crane Fruehauf Ltd.* v. *Inland Revenue Commissioners* [1975] 1 All E.R. 429. In the first of these cases Pennycuick J. said at p. 447 that he was unpersuaded that the word " consideration " in section 55 (1) (c) of the Finance Act 1927 meant anything other than the expressed consideration. The language of the enactment is different from that with which we are concerned in the present case, and we do not think the judgment helps either party.

As regards the *Crane Fruehauf* case the point was taken in that case A
that the allotted shares had not been issued at the date of the transfer
which was the relevant date for valuation. It was held, however, that until
the issue of the Crane shares the transfers were escrows. That situation
does not arise here where the effect of Schedule 10 to the Finance Act
1971 is that the contract became unconditional and the disposals took
place before the issue of the new shares. But in any event it was not in
dispute that the property which had to be valued was the *Crane* shares. In B
the present case the identity of the consideration is directly in issue and
we do not think that it was the new shares. Vinelott J. said [1980] 1
W.L.R. 1162, 1174 that *Crane Fruehauf* is inconsistent with the proposition that if shares are issued fully paid as consideration for an acquisition the value of the consideration is the cost to the company. The central
problem in the present case is not whether the value of the new shares C
was necessarily the cost to the company. The problem is to identify the
consideration and then to determine what, upon the facts as found, can
properly be regarded as the value of that consideration. In the circumstances, we do not think that *Crane Fruehauf* is of assistance.

Secondly, Mr. McCall drew our attention to the provisions of the
Finance Act 1962 relating to the short-term capital gains tax. He pointed D
out that by section 13 (1) the computation of the gain is by reference to
Schedule D. The language of paragraph 4 of Schedule 6 to the Act of 1965
is different; it contains no reference to Schedule D. The short-term gains
tax was, however, an income tax on capital gains. It was, therefore, understandable that the draftsmen should have provided for the computation
to be by reference to Schedule D. We do not think that that gives us any
guidance on the present point. We must construe the Act of 1965 on its E
own language.

Accordingly, we allow the appeal.

Appeal allowed with costs.
Determination of the special com-
missioners restored.   F
Leave to appeal on terms that court's
order for costs be not disturbed.

Solicitors: *Ashurst, Morris, Crisp & Co.; Solicitor of Inland Revenue.*

[Reported by MRS. HARRIET DUTTON, Barrister-at-Law]   G

H

A

[PRIVY COUNCIL]

* AYLMER JAMES CROMPTON . . . . . APPELLANT

AND

B
GENERAL MEDICAL COUNCIL . . . . RESPONDENT

[APPEAL FROM THE PROFESSIONAL CONDUCT COMMITTEE OF THE GENERAL
MEDICAL COUNCIL]

1981 July 27;   Lord Diplock, Lord Bridge of
    Aug. 21   Harwich and Sir John Megaw
C

*Medical Practitioner—Professional conduct—Medical reports—
Practitioner suspended for criminal convictions—Fitness to
resume practice—Professional Conduct Committee requiring
evidence of practitioner's mental state—Whether entitled to
confidential medical reports when considering habits and
conduct since suspension—Whether failure to divulge contents*
D   *breach of natural justice—Medical Act* 1978 (c. 12), s. 6,
Sch. 3, *para* 5 (1)—*General Medical Council Disciplinary
Committee (Procedure) Rules Order of Council* 1970 (*S.I.* 1970
No. 596), *Appendix,* r. 47 (*Superseded by General Medical
Council Preliminary Proceedings Committee and Professional
Conduct Committee (Procedure) Rules Order of Council* 1980
(*S.I.* 1980 *No.* 858), *Appendix,* r. 55)

In March 1979 the Disciplinary Committee of the General
E   Medical Council suspended a doctor from practice for 12
months on the ground of his having been convicted of four
criminal offences. In March 1980 the committee extended the
suspension for a further nine months. On August 1, 1980, the
Medical Act 1978 came into force and, accordingly, in compliance with Schedule 3 to that Act the General Medical Council's
reconsideration of the doctor's case was carried out by its
Professional Conduct Committee. In December 1980 that com-
F   mittee suspended the doctor from practice for another three
months and, purporting to act in accordance with rule 47 of the
General Medical Council Disciplinary Committee (Procedure)
Rules 1970,[1] it informed the doctor that before it reconsidered
his case in March 1981 he should furnish it with the names
of professional colleagues including those of two consultants
in adult psychiatry to which the committee could apply for
information to be given in confidence as to his fitness to
G   resume medical practice. The doctor had not previously
consulted a psychiatrist. During the three weeks before
the resumed hearing of his case in order to comply with
the committee's direction he consulted and was examined by
two psychiatrists to whom he was previously unknown. They
sent confidential reports to the committee. On March 9, 1981,
the committee reconsidered the doctor's case. At the hearing
the chairman told the doctor that in deciding on his fitness to
H   resume medical practice the committee was taking into account
the psychiatrists' reports as to his " condition." The doctor
requested that the contents of the reports be disclosed to him.
The committee refused. It directed that the doctor's name be
erased from the register.
     On the doctor's appeal to the Judicial Committee:—

---

[1] General Medical Council Disciplinary Committee (Procedure) Rules 1970, r. 47:
see post, p. 1438B–D.

1436

A

Held, allowing the appeal, that rule 47 of the Rules of 1970 only empowered the Professional Conduct Committee to receive information in disciplinary proceedings in confidence from colleagues and other persons of standing as to how the doctor had behaved since the original hearing and did not enable the committee to obtain medical reports under that rule as to whether the doctor's mental or physical state impaired his fitness to practice; that by refusing to allow the doctor to see the psychiatrists' reports or to inform him of their contents, the committee had failed to observe the rules of natural justice and, accordingly, the direction for erasure was invalid (post, pp. 1438E–F, 1439H, 1441F–G).

B

No case is referred to in the reasons for the report or was cited in argument.

C

APPEAL (No. 24 of 1981) by Dr. Aylmer James Crompton from a determination made by the Professional Conduct Committee of the General Medical Council on March 9, 1981, whereby it ordered that by reason of the proof of convictions for criminal offences in March 1978 and March 1979 Dr. Crompton's name should be erased from the Register of Medical Practitioners.

At the close of the hearing before the Judicial Committee of the Privy Council Lord Diplock announced that their Lordships would recommend that the appeal should be allowed for reasons to be delivered later.

D

The facts are stated in their Lordships' reasons.

Dr. Crompton in person.
Timothy Straker for the General Medical Council.

E

Cur. adv. vult.

August 21. The Registrar of the Judicial Committee handed out the reasons for the report of their Lordships prepared by LORD DIPLOCK.

The disciplinary proceedings in respect of which this appeal is brought were instituted against the appellant, Dr. Crompton, before August 1, 1980, which was the appointed day on which section 6 of the Medical Act 1978 came into operation. It was therefore a pending disciplinary case to which Schedule 3 to the Act applied; and since the Disciplinary Committee appointed under section 32 of the Medical Act 1956 had not completed their inquiry into it, they referred the case under paragraph 5 (1) of Schedule 3 to be dealt with by the Professional Conduct Committee constituted under section 6 of the Act of 1978 with functions broadly similar to those performed by the Disciplinary Committee under the legislation previously in force. Paragraph 5 (2) of Schedule 3, however, provides that in dealing with a case transferred to it in this manner the Professional Conduct Committee " shall have such powers only as would have been available to the Disciplinary Committee under section 33 or 35 of the Medical Act 1956." So Schedule 4 to the Act of 1978, in so far as it confers on the Professional Conduct Committee power to refer to the Health Committee (which is also constituted under section 6 of the Act) the question whether a medical practitioner's fitness to practise may be " seriously impaired by reason of his physical or mental condition," was not applicable in Dr. Crompton's case.

F

G

H

Nevertheless, although the number of cases, such as that of Dr. Crompton, to which Schedule 3 applies will diminish with the passing of time after

A   August 1, 1980, when the Act of 1978 came into operation, the question of law raised by this appeal will continue to be of considerable importance under the new regime established by sections 6 to 14 and Schedule 4 to the Act of 1978, for dealing with criminal offences, professional misconduct and unfitness to practise through mental or physical illness. The question of law turns upon the true construction of rules that formed part of the General Medical Council Disciplinary Committee (Procedure) Rules Order of

B Council 1970 (" the Rules of 1970 ") that were in force up to August 1, 1980, and are reproduced, in language that is identical in all relevant respects, in the General Medical Council Preliminary Proceedings Committee and Professional Conduct Committee (Procedure) Rules Order of Council 1980, (" the current Rules "), that replaced the Rules of 1970 and are presently in force.

C   For a proper understanding of the relevant rules it is necessary to look briefly at the legislative history of the Medical Acts 1956 to 1969 and the Medical Act 1978. The Medical Act 1956 was essentially a consolidation Act, Part V of which, comprising sections 32 to 39, dealt with " erasure and restoration to register." The Disciplinary Committee constituted under section 32 had power under section 33 to direct the erasure from the register

D of the name of any fully registered medical practitioner who had been convicted of a criminal offence by a court in the United Kingdom or the Republic of Ireland or who was judged by the Disciplinary Committee after due inquiry to have been guilty of what is now described as serious professional misconduct. Erasure was the only penalty that the Disciplinary Committee had jurisdiction to impose under the Medical Act 1956. They had no power to suspend a doctor temporarily from practice; but under

E section 34 they did have power to restore a doctor's name to the register upon application made by him not less than 11 months after the date of erasure or, if he had already made an application for restoration that had been refused, not less than 11 months after the date of the last refusal. The power of erasure had existed since 1858. It was a Draconian penalty, and the practice had arisen under which the committee, in cases where they thought that leniency might be justified, instead of delivering their judgment

F at the close of the hearing, would postpone it to some future date, so as to give the doctor an opportunity to redeem himself and show by his good behaviour in the meantime that he was a fit person to remain on the register. Where judgment was postponed in this way it was common practice for the committee to invite the doctor to provide the names of persons, particularly

G professional colleagues, to whom the committee could refer for confidential information as to his behaviour since the original hearing. During the period while judgment was postponed, which was in effect a period of probation, the doctor's name remained upon the register and he was entitled to continue to practise. Until the Medical Act 1969 there was no way of suspending him from practice temporarily. Where temporary suspension would, in

H the Disciplinary Committee's view have been an appropriate penalty, all that they could do was to erase his name and intimate to him that an application for restoration of his name to the register in due course would be likely to receive sympathetic consideration.

    Section 13 of the Medical Act 1969, which substituted new subsections for section 33 (1) of the Medical Act 1956, conferred upon the Disciplinary Committee, as an alternative to ordering erasure, jurisdiction to direct that a doctor's registration be suspended for a period not exceeding 12 months

but with power to extend from time to time for additional periods, not   A
exceeding 12 months at a time, the period specified in the original direction.
The Rules of 1970 made after the passing of the Medical Act 1969 contained provision for continuing the former practice of postponing judgment
in a disciplinary case as well as for the procedure to be followed by the
Disciplinary Committee in exercising its newly-acquired jurisdiction to
direct the suspension of the registration of a doctor's name for a period, or   B
successive periods, of not more than 12 months at a time.

     Rule 47 of the Rules of 1970 provided that in cases both of postpone-
ment of judgment and of suspension:

> " (1) . . . the committee or the president may require the practitioner
> . . . to furnish the registrar with the names and addresses of professional
> colleagues and other persons of standing to whom the council will be
> able to apply for information, to be given confidentially, as to their   C
> knowledge of his habits and conduct since the time of the original
> hearing. (2) Where any practitioner . . . has supplied to the committee
> or to the registrar on their behalf the name of any person to whom
> reference may be made confidentially as to his habits and conduct, the
> committee may consider any information received from such person
> in consequence of such reference without disclosing the same to the   D
> practitioner . . ."

The jurisdiction of the Disciplinary Committee under the Medical Acts
1956 to 1969 was dependent upon the existence of a complaint that a
registered medical practitioner had either been convicted of a criminal
offence by a court of law in the United Kingdom or had been guilty of
serious professional misconduct. There was no power to restrain a doctor   E
from practising simply because he was unfit to do so through mental or
physical illness. It is, in their Lordships' view, quite clear that in rule 47
of the Rules of 1970 the reference to information " as to their knowledge of
his habits and conduct since the time of the original hearing " received
from persons whose names have been furnished by the doctor, is restricted
to information as to how the doctor has behaved himself since the original   F
hearing. It was not open to the Disciplinary Committee under the guise of
acting pursuant to this rule, to obtain medical reports as to his mental state
from psychiatric consultants who were strangers to him; and then to refuse
to disclose the reports to the doctor himself so as to give him an opportunity
of dealing with them.

     The lacuna resulting from the absence of any power to restrain a
doctor from practising because of mental or physical illness which seriously   G
impaired his fitness to practise was filled by the Medical Act 1978; but this
was done, not by extending the jurisdiction of the Disciplinary Committee
but by creating an entirely new committee called the Health Committee
with exclusive jurisdiction to judge whether a doctor's fitness to practise is
seriously impaired by reason of his physical or mental condition; and, if
they so find, to suspend his registration for a period or successive periods,   H
of not more than 12 months at a time, or to make his registration conditional upon his complying with requirements laid down by the Health
Committee. It is to be noted that the Health Committee, unlike the Professional Conduct Committee, has no power of erasure. The only additional
jurisdiction conferred upon the Professional Conduct Committee by the
new Act which had not been enjoyed by the former Disciplinary Committee

A   was the power to make the registration of a doctor who had been convicted of a criminal offence or judged guilty of serious professional misconduct, conditional upon his complying with requirements laid down by the Professional Conduct Committee.

    The Medical Act 1978 provided by Schedule 4, paragraph 4, for the reference and transfer of cases by the Professional Conduct Committee to

B the Health Committee. This provision reads as follows:

> " (1) Where, in the course of inquiring into the case of a practitioner, it appears to the Professional Conduct Committee that his fitness to practise may be seriously impaired by reason of his physical or mental condition, the committee may refer that question to the Health Committee for determination. (2) If, on a reference under this paragraph,
>
> C   the Health Committee determine that the fitness of the practitioner to practise is not seriously impaired by reason of his condition the Health Committee shall certify their opinion to the Professional Conduct Committee. (3) If, on a reference under this paragraph, the Health Committee determine that the fitness of the practitioner to practise is seriously impaired by reason of his condition the Health Committee shall certify their opinion to the Professional Conduct Committee and
>
> D   shall proceed to dispose of the case, and the Professional Conduct Committee shall cease to exercise their functions in relation to the case."

    Reference by the Professional Conduct Committee to the Health Committee of the question of the fitness of the doctor to practise by reason of mental or physical illness is not mandatory. The Professional Conduct

E Committee may consider that the crime of which the doctor was convicted or the professional misconduct of which he has been judged guilty is so grave as to demand the erasure of his name from the register regardless of mental or physical ill-health; but the fact that reference of the question to the Health Committee is discretionary does not permit the Professional Conduct Committee to erase the name of a doctor from the register not

F because of the criminal offence or serious professional misconduct of which he had been guilty but simply because they think that his present fitness to practise is seriously impaired by reason of his physical or mental condition.

    The procedures of the Professional Conduct Committee and of the Health Committee respectively are governed by quite separate rules: the former by the current rules already referred to, the latter by the General Medical Council Health Committee (Procedure) Rules Order of Council

G 1980 (S.I. 1980 No. 859) (" the Health Committee Rules ").

    The passages cited above from rule 47 of the Rules of 1970 are reproduced in rule 55 of the current Rules, and bear the same meaning that their Lordships have already ascribed to them. They authorise the committee to obtain, consider and withhold from disclosure to the doctor information, from persons nominated by the doctor, as to what they know

H about his habits and conduct since the original hearing, that is to say how he has behaved himself during that period. The rule does not authorise the obtaining, consideration and non-disclosure to the doctor of medical reports about his mental condition made by consultants who are strangers to him. Unfortunately it is reports of the latter kind with which the instant case is concerned.

    Dr. Crompton had been convicted in 1975 and 1977 of criminal offences which it is unnecessary to specify. These were the subject of an inquiry by

1440

the Disciplinary Committee in March 1978 who found the convictions   A
proved but postponed their judgment until March 1979. By the time of the
adjourned hearing in March 1979, Dr. Crompton had acquired two more
convictions for which he had served a term of imprisonment. At that hearing the Disciplinary Committee directed that his registration should be
suspended for 12 months. At the resumed consideration in March 1980 the
committee decided to extend the suspension for another nine months. The
hearing of Dr. Crompton's case was next resumed in December 1980 by the   B
Professional Conduct Committee, the Medical Act 1978 being by now in
force. On that occasion the committee suspended the registration for
another three months and told Dr. Crompton's solicitor that:

> " Shortly before that date, the practitioner would be asked to furnish
> the names of professional colleagues *including two consultants in adult
> psychiatry* to whom the council could apply for information, to be   C
> given in confidence, *on his fitness to resume medical practice* "
> (emphasis supplied).

Pursuant to this requirement Dr. Crompton, who had not previously undergone psychiatric treatment, furnished the names of two consultant psychiatrists whom he had seen for the first time in his life during the three weeks
immediately preceding the resumed hearing in March 1981. The name of   D
the second of these, Dr. Fleminger of Guy's Hospital, who examined him
in the week before the hearing, was actually recommended to him by the
registrar of the General Medical Council. The reports of these two consultant psychiatrists were before the Professional Conduct Committee at the
resumed hearing, but the committee refused to tell Dr. Crompton what these
reports said about what the chairman of the committee described as his   E
" condition."

The actual hearing, at which Dr. Crompton insisted on representing
himself in person, was held, at his request, in camera. At the outset, the
chairman made it clear that the purpose of the hearing was to consider
whether the reports received affected the committee's decision as to what
was to happen to Dr. Crompton next. " We are strictly concerned," he
said, " with your present fitness." That this was regarded as the only   F
purpose of the hearing was repeated on several subsequent occasions during
its course. For instance the legal assessor advised the committee: ". . . the
question is whether, in view of the medical evidence and so on, they should
end their suspension," and the chairman on more than one occasion reiterated that what the committee was concerned with was the state of Dr.
Crompton's mental health as it affected his fitness to practise.   G

At the resumption of the public hearing, the chairman announced the
decision of the committee in the following terms:

> Chairman: " Dr. Crompton, the committee have most carefully con-
> sidered everything you have said and also the confidential evidence of
> your condition which is before them today. The committee are bound
> to regard the evidence of your condition as a source of grave and con-   H
> tinuing concern. By reason of the convictions which were proved
> against you in March 1978 and March 1979, the committee have now
> directed the registrar to erase your name from the register."
>
> Dr. Crompton: " May I please ask the condition to which you
> refer? "
>
> Chairman: " This is the evidence that we have had from you and
> from the confidential documents which were put into the committee."

A It is in their Lordships' view quite clear that what the committee were anxious about was Dr. Crompton's mental condition, of which the criminal offences that he had committed might well have been symptoms—an anxiety which what Dr. Crompton had said when he addressed them in camera can have done little to allay. If this situation were to arise in disciplinary pro-ceedings instituted after August 1, 1980, the proper course for the Profes-

B sional Conduct Committee would be to refer the question of the doctor's fitness to practise by reason of his mental condition to the Health Com-mittee under paragraph 4 of Schedule 4 to the Medical Act 1978 which is reproduced in rule 41 of the current Rules. The matter would then proceed in accordance with the Health Committee Rules which, be it noted, contain elaborate provisions for letting the doctor know what is the evidence about his mental or physical condition that is alleged to impair seriously his fitness

C to practise and for enabling him to adduce medical evidence on his own behalf to contradict it. Furthermore, the Health Committee's findings of unfitness to practise for health reasons, as already pointed out, can lead to suspension of registration only, not to erasure.

Their Lordships sympathise with the Professional Conduct Committee in the dilemma in which they found themselves as a result of their inability to refer the question of Dr. Crompton's mental condition to the Health Com-

D mittee because his was a pending disciplinary case governed by Schedule 3 to the new Act and not by Schedule 4. If they had taken the view, upon the expert evidence of psychiatric consultants as to his mental condition, that the criminal offences of which Dr. Crompton had been convicted were symptoms of a persisting mental condition that might well lead him to com-mit further offences, they would have been entitled, if they thought fit, to

E order the erasure of his name from the register. But observance of the rules of natural justice would have demanded that the psychiatric medical evi-dence upon which the committee proposed to act should be disclosed to the doctor and an opportunity given to him to answer it and adduce, if he so wished, expert psychiatric evidence on his own behalf to contradict it. Such expert medical evidence does not fall within the exception of information to

F be given confidentially by professional colleagues and other persons of standing nominated by the doctor, as to their knowledge of his habits and conduct since the time of the original hearing.

On his appeal to their Lordships from the committee's direction to erase his name from the register, Dr. Crompton relied (among various other matters which it is not necessary to mention) upon the committee's failure to

G observe the rules of natural justice by their refusal to let him see the reports by the psychiatric consultants upon which they based their decision, or even to inform him of the general nature of those reports. On this ground their Lordships felt reluctantly compelled to recommend to Her Majesty in Council that this appeal be allowed with the consequence that, the last period of suspension validly fixed by the Professional Conduct Committee

H having now expired, Dr. Crompton's name remains upon the register.

Their Lordships have not thought it right to read for themselves the psychiatric reports relied on by the committee, since they could not in fairness to Dr. Crompton do so without showing them to him and they could not show them to Dr. Crompton without breaking the promise of confidentiality under which the reports were furnished by the consultants.

In these circumstances their Lordships do not consider it to be appro-priate to remit the case to the Professional Conduct Committee for further

1442

Crompton v. G.M.C. (P.C.)   **[1981]**

A

consideration. If there are good reasons, as there may well be, for questioning Dr. Crompton's fitness to practise upon psychiatric grounds, proceedings
may be started de novo under the Health Committee Rules that are now in
force to deal with such a situation.

Solicitors: *Waterhouse & Co.*

T. J. M.   B

[CHANCERY DIVISION]

* HOYE (INSPECTOR OF TAXES) *v.* FORSDYKE

C

1981 July 9   Vinelott J.

> *Revenue—Income tax—Earnings from work done abroad—Relief
> for short or intermittent absences—Qualifying "day"—
> Whether employee working overseas during day but returning
> before midnight entitled to relief—Finance Act 1977 (c. 36),
> Sch. 7, para. 2*

D

> The taxpayer was employed in the United Kingdom but
> was required to perfom the duties of that employment partly
> outside the United Kingdom, for the most part in Europe.
> During the fiscal year 1978–79 he devoted the whole of 31 days
> to working abroad but on nine of them had returned home on
> the same day, arriving back in the United Kingdom before
> midnight. He appealed against an assessment to income tax for
> the year claiming entitlement to a deduction from his emolu-
> ments in respect of duties performed overseas by virtue of the
> provisions of paragraph 2 of Schedule 7 to the Finance Act
> 1977 on the ground that he had spent at least 30 qualifying
> days, within the meaning of paragraph 2 (2), performing the
> duties of his employment outside the United Kingdom. The
> general commissioners held that he came within the qualifying
> provisions and reduced the assessment by £233.

E

F

> On appeal by the Crown: —
> *Held*, allowing the appeal, that in the context of Schedule 7
> to the Finance Act 1977 "day" could only be construed as
> meaning a calendar day of 24 hours from midnight to midnight
> and not as meaning a mere working day, and that since the
> taxpayer had not been absent from the United Kingdom at
> midnight for at least 30 days during the year he was not
> entitled to a deduction in respect of the duties he performed
> overseas.

G

No cases are referred to in the judgment or were cited in argument.

CASE STATED by the Commissioners for the General Purposes of the
Income Tax for the Division of Spelthorne in the County of Middlesex.

H

The taxpayer, John Kenneth Forsdyke, had during the year 1978–79
performed the duties of his employment partly outside the United Kingdom
and had devoted substantially the whole of 31 days to the performance of
such duties. He had, however, been absent from the United Kingdom at
midnight on only 22 days during the year. He appealed against an assessment to income tax made on him under Schedule E in the sum of £10,993,
less expenses of £18, for the year. The grounds of his appeal were that he

A   had been allowed no deduction from the emoluments assessed in respect
of duties performed overseas under paragraph 2 of Schedule 7 to the
Finance Act 1977. The commissioners allowed the appeal and reduced the
assessment by £233. The Crown appealed.

The facts and the determination of the commissioners are set out in
the judgment.

B
    Robert Carnwath for the Crown.
    The taxpayer in person.

    VINELOTT J. This is an appeal from the General Commissioners for the
Division of Spelthorne in Middlesex. The question raised in the appeal is a
pure question of law. The taxpayer, John Kenneth Forsdyke, is employed
C   in the United Kingdom but as part of his work he has to travel abroad
frequently, for the most part to Europe. The question in this case is whether
he is entitled to relief from United Kingdom income tax in respect of a
proportion of his earnings under Schedule 7 to the Finance Act 1977.
Paragraph 1 of that Schedule gives relief in cases where an employee spends
long periods abroad. Paragraph 2 gives relief where he spends short periods
D   abroad but they add up to at least 30 days in any year of assessment. The
relief is governed by reference to what are called " qualifying days," that is
days spent abroad. I should read paragraph 2 (2) in full:

        " For the purposes of this paragraph a qualifying day in relation to an
    employment is a day of absence from the United Kingdom—(*a*) which
    is substantially devoted to the performance outside the United Kingdom
    of the duties of that employment or of that and other employments; or
E   (*b*) which is one of at least seven consecutive days on which the person
    concerned is absent from the United Kingdom for the purpose of the
    performance of such duties outside the United Kingdom and which
    (taken as a whole) are substantially devoted to the performance of such
    duties as aforesaid; or (*c*) on which the person concerned is travelling
    in or for the purpose of the performance of such duties outside the
F   United Kingdom."

That sub-paragraph must be read in conjunction with paragraph 6 which
provides that:

        " For the purposes of this Schedule a person shall not be regarded as
    absent from the United Kingdom on any day unless he is so absent at
G   the end of it."

There are provisions in paragraph 4 which regulate the emoluments eligible
for relief and the proportion of the eligible emoluments in respect of which
a deduction of 25 per cent. can be claimed under paragraph 2, the proportion being, in broad terms, a proportion of the eligible emoluments corresponding to the proportion which the number of " qualifying days " bears to
H   365.

The commissioners found that during the fiscal year 1978–79 the taxpayer performed the duties of his employment partly outside the United
Kingdom and that he had devoted substantially the whole of 31 days to the
performance of his duties outside the United Kingdom. They also found
that he had been absent from the United Kingdom at midnight on only 22
days of the year. Their conclusion was as follows:

" We . . . decided that although the meaning of day in paragraph 6 was   A
ambiguous the interpretation contended for by the taxpayer was more
in conformity with the clear intention of the legislation than that contended for by the inspector of taxes. We took the view that public
policy in this country was to encourage family life not to discourage
it and to insist that the taxpayer stay abroad until after midnight if
he were to obtain the benefit of the relief was nonsense. A normal   B
working day was a more sensible interpretation of the legislation."

And then they say they allow the appeal and reduce the assessment by a
stated figure.

The word " day " can bear any one of a number of different meanings.
In *Halsbury's Laws of England*, 3rd ed., vol. 37 (1962), p. 84, in the chapter
on time the authors say: C

" The term ' day ' is, like the terms ' year ' and ' month,' used in more
senses than one. A day is strictly the period of time which begins
with one midnight and ends with the next. It may also denote any
period of 24 hours, and again it may denote the period of time between
sunrise and sunset."

I doubt whether any one of these possible meanings of " day " is more   D
strict or more accurate than any other. The meaning that word bears
depends wholly upon the context. For instance if a man suggests to his
wife they go to Calais for the day to take advantage of the range and
quality of the goods at the supermarket there, what he would have in mind
would be an early start on the hovercraft and a return in the evening. By
contrast if I were to ask somebody how many days there are in February
next year, I would be understood to ask how many calendar days fall in   E
February next year.

In this instant case I have reached the conclusion, not without regret,
that in Schedule 7 " day " is used in the sense of calendar day. I reach this
conclusion for two reasons. First, the reference in paragraph 6 to a person
being absent at the end of a day, is I think, most naturally read as referring
to midnight, the end of the calendar day. It could mean, as the com-   F
missioners found, the end of a working day, but so read the words convey
a very imprecise concept. The second and more important reason is that
paragraph 2 (2) (*b*) is designed to give relief in the case where a taxpayer is
absent from the United Kingdom for a period of " at least seven consecutive working days " which " (taken as a whole) are substantially
devoted to the performance of " duties outside the United Kingdom. The   G
purpose of sub-paragraph (*b*) is to enable the whole consecutive period to
count notwithstanding that two of the days would necessarily be a Saturday
and a Sunday. In this context it seems to me impossible to read " days " as
meaning anything except calendar days. The taxpayer suggested that
paragraph 2 (2) (*b*) would be satisfied in the case of an employee who
worked abroad Monday to Friday, perhaps commuting each day, who came
home for the weekend and who worked abroad again on Monday and   H
Tuesday. That is, I think, an impossible construction. Days are not consecutive unless they follow the first continuously and without any intervals.
Further the taxpayer's construction renders sub-paragraph (*b*) otiose because
in the case suggested by him the seven working days would, on his construction, rank as qualifying days under sub-paragraph (*a*). I feel, therefore, compelled to the conclusion that a qualifying " day " is a calendar
day or a day from midnight to midnight in relation to which paragraph

The Weekly Law Reports, December 4, 1981

1445

1 W.L.R.   Hoye (Inspector of Taxes) v. Forsdyke (Ch.D.)   Vinelott J.

A   2 (2) (*a*), (*b*) or (*c*) is satisfied and in relation to which the employee in question was absent at midnight at the end of the day.

The taxpayer who appeared in person and argued his case very succinctly and very courteously, made a number of points. I hope I do not deal too briefly with them if I say they were all directed to the unreasonable results which follow from the construction which, as I have said, I feel compelled to adopt. He said that that construction has the result of dis-
B   rupting family life because it provides a fiscal penalty which affects the taxpayer who comes home possibly late at night after a long and active day, in order to spend time with his young family. He said that it is reasonable to construe Schedule 7 in a way which encourages businessmen to go abroad and to get business abroad. He pointed out, I think with great force, that now that we are members of the E.E.C. and now that travel has
C   become very much quicker and aeroplanes so much more frequent than they were, it is becoming increasingly common for businessmen to go abroad and work in Paris, Brussels, perhaps even Frankfurt or Rome, and to depart for home before midnight. He submitted that it would be contrary to the economic interests of this country to construe the relief in a way which either discouraged businessmen from going abroad or encouraged them to spend unneccessary time and money staying overnight
D   with the sole object of clocking-up another qualifying day. These are powerful arguments for modifying the relief, but they do not justify me in construing the legislation otherwise than in the sense which I have indicated, which seems to me to be the only sense which can be fairly attributed to it. It seems to me that in reaching the conclusion that they reached and for the reasons which they expressed, the commissioners were invading the
E   province of the legislature.

For the reason I have given I think I must allow this appeal, but as the taxpayer has been brought here as the respondent and has appeared in person and, as I have said, has put his case moderately and well, I will not, unless I am invited to take a different course, make any orders as to costs.

F   *Appeal allowed.*
No order as to costs.
Assessment determined in the sum of
£10,993.

Solicitor: *Solicitor of Inland Revenue.*

G   [Reported by MRS. HARRIET DUTTON, Barrister-at-Law]

H   ───────────

A

[COURT OF APPEAL]

* REGINA v. DENTON

1981 Oct. 22
Lord Lane C.J., Mustill and
McCullough JJ.

B

Crime—Arson—Destroying or damaging property—Employee setting fire to employer's premises on employer's instructions—
Intention to make fraudulent insurance claim — Whether
employer " entitled to consent " to damage—Whether setting
fire to own premises offence — Whether employee having
" lawful excuse " — Criminal Damage Act 1971 (c. 48), ss.
1 (1) (3), 5 (2) (a)

C

The appellant, who was employed in business by T, set
fire to the business premises and was tried on a count of arson
contrary to section 1 (1) and (3) of the Criminal Damage Act
1971.[1] In reliance on section 5 (2) (a) the appellant gave
evidence that he had been asked to start the fire by T, who
was, as the appellant believed, entitled to consent to the damage
and intended to make a fraudulent insurance claim. On a
submission the trial judge ruled that " entitled " in section 5 (2)
(a) connoted general lawfulness and that T could not be said to
be entitled to consent to damage for a fraudulent purpose, so
that no defence was afforded to the appellant by section 5 (2)
(a). Thereupon the appellant changed his plea to guilty.

D

On appeal against conviction: —
Held, allowing the appeal, that no offence was committed
under section 1 (1) and (3) of the Criminal Damage Act 1971
by a person who set fire to his own premises, and such an
action did not become unlawful because it involved an
inchoate attempt to commit fraud; and that, accordingly, the
judge erred in his ruling and the conviction would be quashed.

E

Semble. The appellant had a " lawful excuse " within
section 1 (1) (post, p. 1449B–C).

No cases are referred to in the judgment or were cited in argument.

F

APPEAL against conviction.
On January 13, 1981, at Wigan Crown Court (Judge Bell) the appellant,
John Thomas Denton, was convicted on a count charging arson contrary to
section 1 (1) and (3) of the Criminal Damage Act 1971 on a change of plea
following a ruling by the judge on the law. He was acquitted by the jury
on a count charging arson with intent contrary to section 1 (2) and (3) of
the Act of 1971. He was sentenced to seven months' imprisonment suspended for two years and a supervision order for one year to the probation
service. He appealed against conviction on a certificate from the trial judge.
The facts and the terms of the certificate are stated in the judgment.

G

Richard Heap (assigned by the Registrar of Criminal Appeals) for the
appellant.
S. J. D. Fawcus for the Crown.

H

LORD LANE C.J. delivered the following judgment of the court. On
January 13, 1981, at the Crown Court at Wigan, the appellant was con-

[1] Criminal Damage Act 1971, s. 1 (1): see post, p. 1448A–B.
S. 5 (2) (a): see post, p. 1488C–D.

A victed on the second count of an indictment laid against him, containing
two counts of arson. The first count alleged arson with intent, contrary to
section 1 (2) and 1 (3) of the Criminal Damage Act 1971; count 2 charged
him with arson contrary to section 1 (1) and 1 (3) of the Criminal Damage
Act 1971, the particulars being that:

B "John Thomas Denton on January 3, 1980, without lawful excuse
damaged by fire a building known as Barnfield Mill belonging to Leslie
Fink & Co. Ltd. and the contents thereof belonging to Albus Products
Ltd. intending to damage such property or being reckless as to whether
such property would be damaged."

He appeals against that conviction on the certificate of the trial judge. He
was, as a matter of history, sentenced to seven months' imprisonment, sus-
C pended for two years, and a supervision order for one year was made in
respect of that sentence.

The facts of the case were somewhat unusual. There is no dispute that
the appellant on January 3, 1980, set light to some machinery in the cotton
mill. The machinery was very badly damaged, and as a result of that con-
flagration damage was also done, to a much lesser degree it is true, to the
building itself. The total damage to stock and building was said to be some
D £40,000.

On Monday March 17, 1980, the appellant presented himself at the
police station and told the police that he had in fact started that fire. He
described how he had done it, and he then made a statement under caution,
in which he gave his reason for having started the fire: that it was for the
benefit of the business, because the business was in difficulties, and,
E although he was going to get no direct benefit from it himself, he thought
he would be doing a good turn to the financial status of the company if he
were to set light to the premises and goods as he did. Hence the charge
against him.

When it came to the trial, by this time of course there were two counts
against him as we have already described, he gave evidence that his employer—to whom we will refer as " T " for obvious reasons—had asked him
F to put the machinery out of action and he had agreed to set light to it. The
reason given to him by the employer for that request was because the company was in difficulties; the way that T put it was: " There is nothing like
a good fire for improving the financial circumstances of a business."

There was then a discussion between counsel and the judge as to the
extent to which those facts, if accepted, could provide a defence to the
G appellant. The judge ruled against the appellant on his counsel's submission. With the appellant pleading guilty to the second count in the light
of the judge's ruling, the trial continued on the first count and he was on
that count acquitted.

The certificate given by the judge reads:

"As to count 2 the defendant's defence was that he believed he had
H not only the permission but the encouragement of the proprietor of
the business for which he worked, to set fire to the goods of that
business with a view to obtaining insurance moneys for that proprietor
by fraud. After hearing submissions of counsel at the conclusion of the
evidence, I ruled the word " entitled " in section 5 (2) of the Criminal
Damage Act 1971, despite the proprietorial basis of the Criminal
Damage Acts, carried a connotation of general lawfulness in addition
to private title. On the basis the proprietor could not be said to be

' entitled ' to consent to damage for a fraudulent purpose the defend- A
ant changed his plea to guilty."

Section 1 (1) of the Criminal Damage Act 1971 provides:

" A person who without lawful excuse destroys or damages any
property belonging to another intending to destroy or damage any such
property or being reckless as to whether any such property would be
destroyed or damaged shall be guilty of an offence."   B

Section 5, which was the section round which the arguments and submissions revolved in the court below, reads:

" (1) This section applies to any offence under section 1 (1) above and
any offence under section 2 or 3 above other than one involving a threat
by the person charged to destroy or damage property in a way which
he knows is likely to endanger the life of another. . . . (2) A person C
charged with an offence to which this section applies shall, whether or
not he would be treated for the purposes of this Act as having a lawful
excuse apart from this subsection, be treated for those purposes as
having a lawful excuse—(a) if at the time of the act . . . he believed
that the person . . . whom he believed to be entitled to consent to the
. . . damage to the property in question had so consented. . . ."   D

It was agreed on all hands for the purpose of this case that T was the
person who, any evil motives apart, was entitled to consent to the damage.
It was likewise conceded that the appellant honestly believed that T
occupied that position and was entitled to consent.

It is plain from the way that the judge put the matter in his certificate,
that he had come to the conclusion that the word " entitled " was in some E
way qualified by a word which does not appear in the section, namely,
" honestly." It is upon that basis that Mr. Fawcus for the Crown here seeks
to support the judge's direction.

In order perhaps to see what the scheme of the Criminal Damage Act
1971 entails, it is necessary to have regard to the earlier Act, namely, the
Malicious Damage Act 1861. Under that Act certainly by section 3, and F
also by two other sections, 13 and 59, a man's right to do what he likes
to his own property was restricted, and it was, amongst other things, an
offence to set fire to certain buildings, if there was an intent to injure or
defraud, even if those buildings were in the possession of the defendant. It
is very striking to observe that the words " with intent to injure or defraud " are absent in the terms of the Act of 1971 which I have just read.
It is quite apparent from that, indeed in this court it is not argued to the G
contrary, that in so far as the Act of 1971 is concerned, it is not an offence
for a man to damage or injure or destroy or set fire to his own premises.

One, therefore, turns to see what the situation would have been had T
made a confession in the same, or similar, terms to that made by the
appellant, and to see what would have happened on the Crown's argument
if the two of them, T and the appellant, stood charged under section 1 (1) H
of the Act of 1971 at the Crown Court at Wigan. It is not an offence for a
man to set light to his own property. So T would have been acquitted. But
if the Crown in correct, the appellant, the man who had been charged with
the task of actually putting the match to the polystyrene and setting the
fire alight, would have been convicted.

Quite apart from any other consideration, that is such an anomalous
result that it cannot possibly be right. The answer is this, that one has to

A decide whether or not an offence is committed at the moment that the acts are alleged to be committed. The fact that somebody may have had a dishonest intent which in the end he was going to carry out, namely, to claim from the insurance company, cannot turn what was not originally a crime into a crime. There is no unlawfulness under the Act of 1971 in burning a house. It does not become unlawful because there may be an inchoate attempt to commit fraud contained in it; that is to say it does not
B become a crime under the Act of 1971, whatever may be the situation outside of the Act.

   Consequently it is apparent to us that the judge, in his ruling in this respect, was wrong. Indeed it seems to us, if it is necessary to go as far as this, that it was probably unnecessary for the appellant to invoke section 5 at all, because he probably had a lawful excuse without it, in that T was
C lawfully entitled to burn the premises down. The appellant believed it. He believed that he was acting under the directions of T and that on its own, it seems to us, may well have provided him with a lawful excuse without having resort to section 5.

   The result is that the plea of guilty to the second count in the indict-ment was based upon a wrong view of the law by the judge. Consequently, despite the plea of guilty, the conviction on the second count must be
D quashed and the appeal allowed.

Appeal allowed.
Conviction quashed.
Legal aid taxation of appellant's costs.
Crown's costs out of central funds.

E
   Solicitor: *D. S. Gandy, Manchester.*

L. N. W.

F

[CHANCERY DIVISION]

* INLAND REVENUE COMMISSIONERS *v.* BERRILL AND ANOTHER

1981 July 13, 14; 23   Vinelott J.
G

*Revenue—Income tax—Additional rate—Settlement—Income of
   fund held on protective trusts for settlors' son—Trustees
   accumulating income in exercise of discretionary power conferred by trust deed—Whether additional rate tax chargeable
   on trust income to which beneficiary entitled subject only
   to trustees' power to accumulate—Finance Act 1973 (c. 51),
   s. 16 (1) (2)*
H
      By deed in 1965 shares were settled on trustees for the benefit of the settlors' son, then 20 years old, giving him a protected life interest for so long as he was alive and under 45, subject to a power to accumulate the whole or any part of the income. Thereafter the capital was to be held for him absolutely. From 1973 to 1975 the trustees accumulated all the income, holding it as accretions to the capital of the fund. The trustees were assessed to income tax at the additional rate at 15 per cent. on dividends and tax credits for 1973–74

in an estimated amount of £35,000 and for 1974–75 in the   A
same estimated amount. On appeal against both assessments,
the special commissioners upheld the trustees' argument that
the provision of section 16 of the Finance Act 1973 [1] charging
additional rate tax on certain trust income, did not apply to
income that was accumulated by trustees pursuant to the
exercise of a discretionary power.

On appeal by the Crown: —

Held, allowing the appeal, that for the purposes of   B
section 16 (1) of the Finance Act 1973, the reference in
section 16 (2) (*a*) to " income which is to be accumulated
or which is payable at the discretion of the trustees " applied
to income from settled property to which a beneficiary was
entitled subject only to the trustees' power of accumulation
and the reference in section 16 (2) (*b*) to income that " is
neither (before being distributed) the income of any person
other than the trustees . . ." did not exclude such income;   C
that accordingly the income from the trust fund that was
accumulated by the trustees was income to which section
16 (1) applied and was chargeable to additional rate income
tax (post, pp. 1455D–F, 1456A–C, E–F, 1459H—1460A).

Dicta of Fox J. in *Pearson* v. *Inland Revenue Commissioners* [1980] Ch. 1, 14–15 considered.

The following cases are referred to in the judgment: D

Allen-Meyrick's Will Trusts, In re [1966] 1 W.L.R. 499; [1966] 1 All
E.R. 740.
Baden's Deed Trusts, In re [1971] A.C. 424; [1970] 2 W.L.R. 1110; [1970]
2 All E.R. 228, H.L.(E.).
Baker v. *Archer-Shee* [1972] A.C. 844, H.L.(E.).
Cory (Wm.) & Son Ltd. v. *Inland Revenue Commissioners* [1965] A.C.   E
1088; [1965] 2 W.L.R. 924; [1965] 1 All E.R. 917, H.L.(E.).
Cunard's Trustees v. *Inland Revenue Commissioners* [1946] 1 All E.R.
159, C.A.
Denley's Trust Deed, In re [1969] 1 Ch. 373; [1968] 3 W.L.R. 457; [1968]
3 All E.R. 65.
Gulbenkian's Settlements, In re (No. 2) [1970] Ch. 408; [1969] 3 W.L.R.
450; [1969] 2 All E.R. 1173.
Locker's Settlement, In re [1977] 1 W.L.R. 1323; [1978] 1 All E.R. 216.   F
Luke v. *Inland Revenue Commissioners* [1963] A.C. 557; [1963] 2 W.L.R.
559; [1963] 1 All E.R. 655; 40 T.C. 630, H.L.(Sc.).
Mangin v. *Inland Revenue Commissioner* [1971] A.C. 739; [1971] 2
W.L.R. 39; [1971] 1 All E.R. 179, P.C.
Nelson v. *Adamson* [1941] 2 K.B. 12; [1941] 2 All E.R. 44; 24 T.C. 36.
Pearson v. *Inland Revenue Commissioners* [1980] Ch. 1; [1979] 2 W.L.R.   G
353; [1979] 1 All E.R. 273; [1980] Ch. 1; [1979] 3 W.L.R. 112; [1979]
3 All E.R. 7, C.A.; [1981] A.C. 753; [1980] 2 W.L.R. 872; [1980] 2
All E.R. 479, H.L.(E.).
Ramsay (W. T.) v. *Inland Revenue Commissioners* [1981] 2 W.L.R. 449;
[1981] 1 All E.R. 865, H.L.(E.).
Stanley v. *Inland Revenue Commissioners* [1944] K.B. 255; [1944] 1 All
E.R. 230; 26 T.C. 16, C.A.   H

The following additional cases were cited in argument:

Baird v. *Lord Advocate* [1979] A.C. 666; [1979] 2 W.L.R. 369; [1979] 2
All E.R. 28, H.L.(Sc.).
Chandos (Marquis) v. *Inland Revenue Commissioners* (1851) 6 Exch. 464.

[1] Finance Act 1973, s. 16 (1) (2): see post, p. 1452F–H.

A   *Corbett* v. *Inland Revenue Commissioners* [1938] 1 K.B. 567; [1937] 4 All
         E.R. 700, 21 T.C. 455, C.A.
     Gardiner, In re [1901] 1 Ch. 697.
     Greenberg v. *Inland Revenue Commissioners* [1972] A.C. 109; [1971] 3
         W.L.R. 386; [1971] 3 All E.R. 136; 47 T.C. 240, H.L.(E.).
     Spens v. *Inland Revenue Commissioners* [1970] 1 W.L.R. 1173; [1970] 3
         All E.R. 295; 46 T.C. 276.

B
     CASE STATED by the Commissioners for the Special Purposes of the
     Income Tax Acts.
         By deed of settlement dated March 19, 1965, the settlors, Henry Ernest
     Kent and Mary Elsie Kent, settled 14,000 ordinary shares of £1 each fully
     paid in Vogue Star Ltd. to be renounced into the names of the trustees,
C   Sir Kenneth Berrill and Alex Gumb. The trustees were to hold the income
     of the fund on protective trusts for the settlors' son, Nicolas, for so long
     as he was living and under the age of 45 and thereafter on trust for him
     absolutely. The trustees exercised the discretion given to them by the
     trust deed and accumulated the whole of the income of the fund. They
     appealed against estimated assessments to income tax in respect of addi-
     tional rate tax at 15 per cent. on dividends and tax credits for 1973–74
D   of £35,000 and for 1974–75 in a like amount. The commissioners allowed
     the appeal holding that the provisions of section 16 of the Finance Act
     1973 did not apply to the trust income that had been accumulated pursuant
     to the trustees exercising their discretionary power. They adjourned the
     proceedings for figures to be agreed between the parties.
         The Crown appealed.
E   The facts and relevant clauses of the trust deed are set out in the
     judgment.

     Edward Nugee Q.C. and *John Mummery* for the Crown.
     Peter Horsfield Q.C. and *Simon Taube* for the trustees.

F   *Cur. adv. vult.*

         July 23. VINELOTT J. read the following judgement. The respondents
     to this appeal, Sir Kenneth Berrill and Mr. Alex Gumb, are the trustees
     of a settlement dated March 19, 1965, and made between Henry Ernest
     Kent and his wife Mary Elsie Kent as settlors, of the one part, and the
     trustees of the other part for the benefit of the settlor's son Nicolas, who
G   was born on January 26, 1945. The settlement contains a usual definition
     of " the trust fund " as including certain shares renounced in favour of
     the trustees by the settlors and any accretions thereto and the investments
     and property for the time being representing the same, and a usual trust
     to retain or sell and reinvest the property from time to time vested in the
     trustees. Clause 3 of the settlement I should read in full:

H   " The trustees shall hold the income of the trust fund upon protective
         trusts for the benefit of the said Nicolas Kent so long as he shall be
         living and under the age of 45 years and if he shall attain that age
         the trustees shall stand possessed of the capital of the trust fund upon
         trust for him absolutely provided always that during the life of the
         said Nicolas Kent or the period of 21 years from the date of the
         execution hereof (whichever shall be the shorter) the whole or any
         part of the income of the trust fund may from time to time be accu-

mulated by investing the same in any investments hereinafter authorised   A
and the accumulations so made shall be held as an accretion to the
capital of the trust fund for all purposes."

Clause 4 contains a trust in the event of the death of Nicolas under 45
for the children of Nicolas who attain 21, and clause 5 contains trusts to
take effect in the event of the failure of the trusts in favour of Nicolas
and his children. By clause 6 the trustees are given power after Nicolas   B
has attained 21 to raise the whole or any part or parts of the trust fund
and to pay it to or apply it for the benefit of Nicolas. There is only one
other provision of the settlement to which I need refer. Clause 9 (b) gives
the trustees power to apply the trust fund in the purchase of and in
making improvements to freehold or leasehold property and in the purchase of chattels for the use of a beneficiary entitled to the income of the
money so applied. Clause 9 (b) (iii) provides that the trustees may " in   C
relation to any leasehold property or other wasting assets effect and maintain sinking fund policies and pay all expenses of keeping up the same
out of the income of the trust fund." It was common ground that this is
a mere administrative power and that to the extent that it is exercised the
exercise diminishes the income of the trust fund. It is not a power or
analogous to a power to accumulate income which operates to divest the   D
right of those entitled to income after it has been ascertained to be income
of the trust fund.

After the date of the settlement the settlors transferred further shares
to the trustees as an accretion to the trust fund. Apart from a payment of
£2,250 net of tax which was made to Nicolas in March 1976 the trustees
accumulated the whole income of the trust fund from the creation of the   E
settlement until at the earliest January 29, 1979, when appeals by the
trustees against assessments to additional rate income tax came before
the special commissioners. Those assessments were made under section 16
of the Finance Act 1973 and were made in respect of income which arose
to the trustees in the fiscal years 1973–74 and 1974–75. The special commissioners allowed the appeals. From that determination the Crown
appeal.   F

I should read section 16 (1) and (2) in full. It reads as follows:

" (1) So far as income arising to trustees is income to which this
section applies it shall, in addition to being chargeable to income tax
at the basic rate, be chargeable at the additional rate. (2) This section
applies to income arising to trustees in any year of assessment so far
as it—(a) is income which is to be accumulated or which is payable   G
at the discretion of the trustees or any other person (whether or not
the trustees have power to accumulate it); and (b) is neither (before
being distributed) the income of any person other than the trustees
nor treated for any of the purposes of the Income Tax Acts as the
income of a settlor; and (c) is not income arising under a trust
established for charitable purposes only or income from investments,   H
deposits or other property held for the purposes of a fund or scheme
established for the sole purpose of providing relevant benefits within
the meaning of section 26 of the Finance Act 1970; and (d) exceeds
the income applied in defraying the expenses of the trustees in that
year which are properly chargeable to income (or would be so chargeable but for any express provisions of the trust)."

A   Subsections (3) and (4) in effect provide for the application of section 16 to income apportioned to trustees under the provisions governing close companies, and subsection (5) provides for the application of section 16 to income derived from building societies with which special arrangements have been made under section 343 of the Income and Corporation Taxes Act 1970. The only other subsection to which I need refer is subsection (8), which provides:

B

"A notice given to trustees under section 8 of the Taxes Management Act 1970 may require a return of the income arising to them to include particulars of the manner in which the income has been applied, including particulars as to the exercise of any discretion and of the persons in whose favour it has been exercised."

C   Section 16 must be read in conjunction with section 17, which deals with the taxation of payments of an income nature made by trustees " in the exercise of a discretion." Section 17 (1) reads as follows:

"Where, in any year of assessment, trustees make a payment to any person in the exercise of a discretion exercisable by them or any person other than the trustees, then, if the sum paid is for all the purposes of the Income Tax Acts income of the person to whom it

D   is paid (but would not be his income apart from the payment), the following provisions of this section shall apply with respect to the payment in lieu of section 52 or 53 of the Taxes Act."

Sections 52 and 53 are, of course, the sections of the Income and Corporation Taxes Act 1970 which deal in the case of the earlier section with

E   the assessment to tax of an annuity or other annual payment made out of profits or gains brought into charge, and in the case of the latter section the deduction of tax on annuities or other annual payments and certain other analogous payments not made out of profits or gains brought into charge by the person making the payment. Section 17 (2) provides:

"The payment shall be treated as a net amount corresponding to a gross amount from which tax has been deducted at a rate equal to the

F   sum of the basic rate and the additional rate in force for the year in which the payment is made; and the sum treated as so deducted shall be treated—(a) as income tax paid by the person to whom the payment is made; and (b) so far as not set off under the following provisions of this section, as income tax assessable on the trustees."

G   I do not need to refer to the remaining subsections of section 17. Section 18 deals with income arising to trustees in respect of which they are entitled to a credit for overseas tax. If on making a payment to a beneficiary the trustees certify that the income out of which the payment was made included taxed overseas income of an amount and from a source stated in the certificate, and that that amount arose to them in or after the year 1973–74 and within six years before the end of the year of

H   assessment in which the payment is made, the beneficiary can claim that the payment up to the amount certified shall be treated as income received from the stated source and in the year in which the payment is made.

Those are the only relevant statutory provisions. The case for the trustees which, as I have said, succeeded before the commissioners is that the language of section 16 (2) which describes the income arising to trustees which is to be subject to additional rate tax is wholly inapt to

include income arising to trustees to which a beneficiary is entitled subject   A
to a power of accumulation.

The differences in trust law between a trust under which a beneficiary
is entitled to income subject to a power of accumulation and a trust under
which a beneficiary is an object of a discretionary trust, whether or not
coupled with a power of accumulation, were analysed by Fox J. in the
recent case of *Pearson* v. *Inland Revenue Commissioners* [1980] Ch. 1,
8–15. In that case a fund was held on trust to pay the income to a   B
daughter of the settlor during her life or until the earlier expiration of a
defined trust period. The trustees had power to accumulate the income
during a period of 21 years from the date of the settlement. Another fund
was held on similar trusts for another daughter of the settlor. Fox J. said,
at pp. 14–15:

" The position as to the trustees' power of accumulation, as I under-   C
stand it, is this: the power is purely permissive. The trustees are not
bound to exercise it. If they do exercise it, they must do so within
a reasonable period after the income has arisen: see *In re Allen-
Meyrick's Will Trusts* [1966] 1 W.L.R. 499 and *In re Locker's
Settlement* [1977] 1 W.L.R. 1323, 1326.

" The result, it seems to me, is that the daughters here would be   D
entitled as of right to income of their shares in each of the following
circumstances: (a) if the trustees decide not to accumulate that
income; (b) if the trustees fail to agree as to whether they should
accumulate or not; (c) if the trustees, having allowed a reasonable
period to elapse after receipt of income, have reached no decision
whether to accumulate or not. In each of those cases the daughter
will be entitled to the income as of right. She will be entitled to it,   E
not because the trustees have decided to give it to her (as would be
the case of Hubert in *Attorney-General* v. *Power* [1906] 2 I.R. 272 or
the discretionary objects in *Gartside* v. *Inland Revenue Commissioners* [1968] A.C. 553) but because she is entitled to it in right of
what is, beyond doubt, her interest in the trust fund. She is entitled
to it by reason of her vested interest—the circumstance that Palles   F
C.B. remarked was lacking in *Power*. In *Power* and in *Gartside* the
beneficiaries got nothing unless the trustees decided to give it to them.
In the present case the daughters are absolutely entitled to income
unless the trustees decide to accumulate.

" There are thus substantial differences between this case, on the
one hand, and *Power* and *Gartside* on the other. A consequence of   G
the fact that what the daughters take they take in right of their
interests is that, as between the daughters, the trustees have no discretion at all. If the trustees decide not to accumulate, they cannot
divert income away from one daughter and give it to another. The
income is captured by the vested interests. The Crown contends that
the position is the same as that of a trust under which, during a
period of 21 years, the trustees have power to pay so much, if any,   H
of the income as they think fit to the three daughters in equal shares
and subject thereto the income is to be held on trust to accumulate
it. That, I think, shows to some extent the artificiality of the attempt
to assimilate the two cases. A power over income which can be
exercised only by distributing income equally among the objects
would, if such a power has ever been created at all, be most unusual;
it is difficult to see any point in such a provision.

A   " There are other differences also between the present case and
cases such as *Power* and *Gartside* (which are cases of discretionary
objects pure and simple). In the present case the daughters have
interests which can be the subject of voluntary assignments; the
objects of a discretionary trust or of a power have not. And the
position as to apportionment of accruing income is quite different in
the case of somebody who becomes entitled in right of an interest from
B   that of a person who merely receives income as a discretionary object.
If a person entitled to an interest, say for life, dies in mid-quarter
there will be apportionment. A discretionary object, on the other
hand, receives only what is appointed to him.
    " The result, in my view, is that while there are similarities, in
that both in *Power* and *Gartside* and in the present case the trustees
C   could prevent income reaching the beneficiaries, the differences between this case, on the one hand, and *Power* and *Gartside*, on the
other, are substantial and not matters of mere form."

Although the actual decision of Fox J., which was approved in the Court
of Appeal, was reversed by a majority in the House of Lords, there is
nothing in the speeches in the House of Lords which casts any doubt on
D   the accuracy or completeness of Fox J.'s analysis on the principles of trust
law in the passage I have cited.
    Turning to section 16 (2), Mr. Horsfield, on behalf of the trustees,
pointed out that the opening words of paragraph (*a*), " income which is
to be accumulated," are apt to describe, and to describe only, income
which trustees are under a positive duty to accumulate. The following
E   words, " or which is payable at the discretion of the trustees or any other
person," are apt to describe and, it is said, apt to describe only, income
arising to trustees who have a discretion as to the selection from among
a class of the person or persons to whom the income is to be paid or as
to the amount to be paid to the members or the selected members of the
class—whether with or without a power of accumulation—or under
which there is a power to pay income to a named person or named
F   persons or selected members of a class with a trust in default of the
exercise of that power, which might be a trust of income or capital for a
beneficiary or a trust for the accumulation of the income. The language
of paragraph (*a*) is, it is said, inapt to describe a trust under which the
only relevant discretion is a power to accumulate. In this connection Mr.
Horsfield relied on the words in parenthesis " whether or not the trustees
G   have power to accumulate it " which, he said, fit naturally if the words
" payable at the discretion of the trustees or any other person " are read
as describing a trust of the former kind but are inapt if the words are
read as including a trust under which the relevant discretion is the power
to accumulate income. This argument impressed the commissioners, who
said that

H   " the phrase ' whether or not the trustees have power to accumulate
it ' is an indication that the power is something different from and
additional to the discretion; it is not an indication that the discretion
includes a decision to accumulate."

    Mr. Horsfield relied on two other features of section 16 in support of
his construction. First, he submitted that if paragraph (*a*) is construed in
the wide sense contended for by the Crown then either paragraph (*a*) or
paragraph (*b*) is otiose because, he said, on that wide construction para-

graph (a) does not add any further qualification beyond that contained
in the first part of paragraph (b) which is by itself apt to include all
income arising to trustees which is not taxable as part of the total income
of a beneficiary, as being income to which he is indefeasibly entitled and
which is not taxable as the settlor's income. I think the answer to this
argument is that given by Mr. Nugee; namely, that even if paragraph (a)
is construed in the wider sense contended for by the Crown, paragraph
(b) is necessary to exclude from section 16 income which is applicable at
the discretion of the trustees in furtherance of a non-charitable purpose
of the kind considered in *In re Denley's Trust Deed* [1969] 1 Ch. 373,
and, possibly, income arising under a trust for creditors. Mr. Horsfield's
second subsidiary argument was founded on the words in parentheses
" before being distributed " in paragraph (b). The argument is that
those words are apt to exclude and must have been intended to exclude
from subsection (2) a trust under which income when it arises to trustees
is income to which a beneficiary is entitled subject to the exercise of a
power to accumulate it. The contrast, it is said, is between income
which, when it arises, is income to which a beneficiary is entitled—albeit
subject to a power to accumulate it—and income which will become the
income of a beneficiary only when it is distributed in pursuance of some
discretion vested in the trustees or in some other person. Again, I accept
Mr. Nugee's explanation of the reason for including these words. There
are cases (although since 1925 they are comparatively rare) where, for
instance, an infant has a vested interest in possession in settled property
and the income so far as not paid to or applied for the maintenance or
benefit of the infant falls to be accumulated but on his death before
attaining full age the accumulations are payable to his or her personal
representatives. In such cases, as Lord Greene M.R. pointed out in
Stanley v. *Inland Revenue Commissioners* [1944] K.B. 255, 261, 262, the
income formerly fell to be included in the infant's total income for surtax
purposes and would now attract additional rate and higher rate tax as
part of his or her total income. The words in parenthesis in paragraph (b)
" before being distributed " are necessary to exclude such income from
the ambit of the charge in section 16 (1) since such income would fall
within paragraph (a)—the trustees having a discretion as to the payment
of the income to or for the maintenance or benefit of the infant—
and unless excluded by paragraph (b) there would have been a double
charge to additional rate tax under section 16 and as part of the infant's
total income under section 32 of the Finance Act 1971.

     Mr. Horsfield's main submission was founded on section 17. He
submitted that the scope of section 17 (1) cannot be narrower than that
of section 16 (2). Otherwise the same income might be chargeable to
additional rate tax twice; once in the hands of the trustees and again in
the hands of a beneficiary. An example will suffice to make this clear. If
an adult beneficiary has a vested interest in income subject to a power
for the trustees to accumulate the whole or part of the income, the power
being expressed to be exercisable within, say, six months after the end
of the year of assessment during which the income arose, then if section
16 (2) (a) is construed in the wide sense contended for by the Crown the
trustees will be liable to additional rate tax under section 16 (1). But as
the beneficiary will be entitled on the expiry of the six-month period to
any income which the trustees have not determined to accumulate, he
will also be liable to additional rate tax under section 32 (1) of the

A Finance Act 1971, unless section 17 (1) also applies and has the effect
that the payment of additional rate tax by the trustees "franks" the
income in the hands of the beneficiary. But, said Mr. Horsfield, it is
impossible to read section 17 (1) as applying to income to which a beneficiary becomes entitled as a result of the expiry of a power of accumulation
or of a decision by the trustees not to exercise such a power or of their
failure to agree to exercise the power within a stated or a reasonable
B period. It cannot be said, for instance, that the payment of the income
to the beneficiary after the time for the exercise of a power of accumulation has expired is a payment in the exercise of a discretion exercisable
by the trustees or any other person; nor can it be said that such income
would not be the income of the beneficiary "apart from the payment"
since it would become his income for the purposes of additional and
C higher rate taxes by reason of the expiry of the power of accumulation
and not by reason of the payment of the income to him by the trustees.
Therefore it is said, if double taxation is to be avoided, section 16 (1)
must similarly be construed as excluding a trust under which a beneficiary
has a vested interest in income subject only to a power of accumulation.

This is a formidable argument, and it was ably developed by Mr.
D Horsfield. But it is not easy to see why additional rate tax should not be
charged in such a case. The anomolous results which flow from this
narrow construction of section 16 (2) can be illustrated by considering
the position that would have obtained on this narrow construction if
sections 16 and 17 had come into force before this settlement was executed.
At the date of the settlement Nicolas was over 20 but under 21 years of
age. It is common ground between Mr. Horsfield and Mr. Nugee that
E while Nicolas was under 21—that is while he was under the law in force
as that time an infant—section 31 of the Trustee Act 1925 applied to
the income of the trust fund. It is common ground that while section
31 applied to the income of the trust fund the income would have fallen
within section 16 (2) (a) because the trustees had a discretion to pay it to
or apply it for the benefit of Nicolas. But if Mr. Horsfield's construction
F of section 16 (2) (a) is correct the income would have fallen outside that
section as soon as Nicolas attained full age—unless or until he forfeited
his right to receive this income—although to someone not versed in the
subtleties of trust law his position before and after he attained 21 would
appear to be substantially the same. Mr. Horsfield did not pretend that
he could find any rational ground for imposing additional rate tax on
income accumulated under the trust in section 31 and not on income
G accumulated under the power in clause 3. He submitted that the failure
to charge additional rate tax in the latter case was an oversight by the
legislature which did not appreciate the niceties of trust law, and that it
was an oversight which can be cured only by legislation and not by construction. He relied on the principle that, in the words of Lord Reid in
Wm. Cory & Son Ltd. v. Inland Revenue Commissioners [1965] A.C.
1088, 1107 "the words of a taxing act must never be stretched against
H a taxpayer." However, this observation must be read in the light of the
earlier decision of the House of Lords in Luke v. Inland Revenue Commissioners [1963] A.C. 557. There the question was whether expenditure
incurred by a company had been incurred in connection with the provision of benefits for a director within section 161 of the Income Tax Act
1952. In the circumstances of that case, if the wide words used in section
161 were given their natural and ordinary meanings, section 161 gave rise

1458

to a charge to tax which was patently unreasonable and unjust. The A
language of section 161 (1) was capable of being read in a way which
avoided injustice to the taxpayer in that case but only at the expense
of so restricting the scope of the section that it would according to Lord
Reid at p. 577 " in many cases defeat the obvious intention of the section."
Faced with this difficulty Lord Reid was prepared to construe section
161 (1) in a way which did some violence to the language used but which
produced a result which avoided injustice to the taxpayer without unduly B
restricting the scope of the section. He said, at p. 577:

> " How, then, are we to resolve the difficulty? To apply the words
> literally is to defeat the obvious intention of the legislation and to
> produce a wholly unreasonable result. To achieve the obvious inten-
> tion and produce a reasonable result we must do some violence to the
> words. This is not a new problem, though our standard of drafting is C
> such that it rarely emerges. The general principle is well settled. It
> is only where the words are absolutely incapable of a construction
> which will accord with the apparent intention of the provision and will
> avoid a wholly unreasonable result, that the words of the enactment
> must prevail."

Then, having reviewed a number of other possible interpretations of D
section 161, Lord Reid said, at pp. 579–580:

> " If it is right that, in order to avoid imputing to Parliament an
> intention to produce an unreasonable result, we are entitled, and indeed
> bound, to discard the ordinary meaning of any provision and adopt
> some other possible meaning which will avoid that result, then what
> I am looking for in examining the obscure provision at the end of E
> section 161 (1) is not its ordinary meaning (if it has one) but some
> possible meaning which will produce a reasonable result. I think that
> the interpretation which I have given is a possible interpretation and
> does produce a reasonable result, and therefore I adopt it."

Mr. Horsfield submitted that the court can depart from the literal F
meaning of the language used in a taxing statute only if the literal construction results in an obvious injustice to the taxpayer, and he relied
on the observations of Lord Reid in *Wm. Cory & Son Ltd.* v. *Inland
Revenue Commissioners* [1965] A.C. 1088, 1107 which I have cited as
authority for that limitation. I do not think that approach is consistent
with the decision of the House of Lords in *Luke* v. *Inland Revenue
Commissioners* [1963] A.C. 557 or with the recent restatement of the G
principles of construction of fiscal statutes by Lord Wilberforce in *W. T.
Ramsay Ltd.* v. *Inland Revenue Commissioners* [1981] 2 W.L.R. 449,
456, where he said:

> " A subject is only to be taxed upon clear words, not upon ' intend-
> ment ' or upon the ' equity ' of an Act. Any taxing Act of Parliament
> is to be construed in accordance with this principle. What are ' clear H
> words ' is to be ascertained on normal principles: these do not confine
> the courts to literal interpretation. There may, indeed should, be
> considered the context and scheme of the relevant Act as a whole,
> and its purpose may, indeed should, be regarded: see *Inland Revenue
> Commissioners* v. *Wesleyan and General Assurance Society* [1946]
> 30 T.C. 11, 16 *per* Lord Greene M.R. and *Mangin* v. *Inland Revenue
> Commissioner* [1971] A.C. 739, 746, *per* Lord Donovan."

A   In the last of the two cases cited Lord Donovan said, at p. 746:

"... the object of the construction of a statute being to ascertain the will of the legislature it may be presumed that neither injustice nor absurdity was intended. If therefore a literal interpretation would produce such a result, and the language admits of an interpretation which would avert it, then such an interpretation may be adopted."

B
Sections 16, 17 and 18 of the Finance Act 1973 form part—a subsidiary part—of one of the revolutionary changes that have transformed the tax system of the United Kingdom since 1965. Until 1971 the system of taxation in the United Kingdom was unusual in combining a high standard rate of tax with a substantial allowance on earned income up to a given limit. This high, and in the case of the vast majority of taxpayers
C   entitled to earned income relief, misleadingly high, standard rate was coupled with an additional tax—surtax—which was payable as a deferred instalment of income tax in the year following the year of assessment in which income was brought into charge to tax at the standard rate. In 1971 a new unified system of taxation was introduced although it did not replace the old system until the year of assessment 1973–74. Under the
D   new unified system tax is charged at a basic rate which in broad terms corresponds to the old rate on earned income reduced by the earned income allowance. Where an individual's total income exceeds a specified figure additional rate tax is charged at 15 per cent. on so much of that income as consists of investment income, which is defined as income which is not earned income. The additional rate tax, in broad terms, restores the old standard rate tax on income other than earned income. Higher rate
E   tax at graduated rates is then charged on an individual's total income in excess of a specified figure. That graduated tax replaces surtax, but, unlike surtax, it is payable in respect of the year of assessment in which income is charged to basic and additional rate tax. Apart from section 16, this new scheme of taxation would have conferred a fortuitous benefit on trust income, necessarily investment income, which did not form part of a beneficiary's income when it arose to the trustees, and which was either
F   accumulated pursuant to some trust or power or simply retained pending the exercise by the trustees of a discretionary trust or power. The trustees would, of course, bear basic rate tax, by deduction or assessment, on income arising to them but not additional or higher rate taxes which are chargeable on the total income to which a person is beneficially entitled.

Looked at in the context of this statutory scheme it is to my mind
G   quite clear that section 16 must have been intended to impose additional rate tax on income which would otherwise not have attracted additional rate tax when it arose to the trustees as part of the total income of a beneficiary, subject, of course, to the specific exceptions in section 16 (2) (b), (c) and (d) (the last of which excepts income applied in defraying the expenses of the trustees notwithstanding that before 1973 such income
H   would have borne standard rate tax). I can see no difficulty in reading section 16 (2) (a) in this sense. The words " income . . . which is payable at the discretion of the trustees " are, I think, as easily applied to income which trustees have power to withhold from a beneficiary entitled in default of the exercise of the power as to income which they have power to apply or which they are bound to apply pursuant to a mandatory discretionary trust. It is true that the words in parenthesis " whether or not the trustees have power to accumulate it " do not fit naturally the case

where the discretion consists of a power to withhold income by accumulating it. That point, as I have said, weighed with the commissioners. But that inelegance of expression does not afford a ground for departing from what appears to me to be the plain intention of the legislature. Mr. Horsfield also stressed that if paragraph (a) is read in this wide sense it largely reproduces the condition stated in the first part of paragraph (b) though, for the reason I have given, it does not render paragraph (b) wholly otiose. But I think Mr. Nugee was right when he said that the purpose of paragraph (a) is to describe in general terms the income to which section 16 (2) is intended to apply, paragraphs (b), (c) and (d) being particular savings or exceptions from that general description.

Mr. Horsfield's main argument was, of course, that founded on section 17. In construing that section there is one other general principle of tax and trust law which must be borne in mind. Under English law a beneficiary entitled to the income of trust property under a trust instrument which contains no power of accumulation is entitled to the income of each asset comprised in the trust property; each asset constitutes a separate source of income. In *Baker* v. *Archer-Shee* [1927] A.C. 844, Lord Wrenbury, describing the life interest of Lady Archer-Shee under a will governed by the law of New York, on the assumption, afterwards shown to be incorrect, that the law of New York was the same in this respect as the law of England, said, at p. 866:

"It is, I think, if the law of America is the same as our law, an equitable right in possession to receive during her life the proceeds of the shares and stocks of which she is tenant for life. Her right is not to a balance sum, but to the dividends subject to deductions as above mentioned. Her right under the will is ' property ' from which income is derived."

The principle applies when the beneficiary is entitled to the income of trust property subject to an annuity (see *Nelson* v. *Adamson* [1941] 2 K.B. 12) or subject to a charge for administrative expenses or the trustees' remuneration, although, of course, a deduction can be made of the amount of the annuity and of the expenses and remuneration in ascertaining the beneficiary's total income. If, on the other hand, a beneficiary has no right to receive income but is paid income (or a sum which for tax purposes falls to be treated as income) in the exercise of a discretion, the exercise of the discretion constitutes a new source of income: see *Cunard's Trustees* v. *Inland Revenue Commissioners* [1946] 1 All E.R. 159, 163, *per* Lord Greene M.R. Mr. Horsfield submitted that if a beneficiary is entitled to income subject to a power of accumulation each asset comprised in the trust property similarly constitutes a separate source of income to which the beneficiary is defeasibly entitled and that if the beneficiary becomes indefeasibly entitled to it by the expiry or the release or abandonment of the power of accumulation, his title to the income relates back to the time when the income arose. That submission, if well founded, would have the startling result that if the power of accumulation were to remain exercisable for more than six years after the income arose to the trustees, as in *In re Gulbenkian's Settlements (No. 2)* [1970] Ch. 408 it might be too late for the revenue to raise an assessment. I think the true position is, as Mr. Nugee submitted, that a new source comes into existence when a power of accumulation expires or is released or abandoned. It was only then that the income formally fell to be included in the beneficiary's

A total income for surtax purposes and would now fall to be included in his total income for purposes of higher rate tax.

If section 17 is construed in the light of these general principles it is to my mind clear that the legislature intended that where income when it arises to trustees is not the income of a beneficiary and later becomes part of the total income of a beneficiary because the trustees exercise a dis-

B cretion in his favour or because his right to it becomes indefeasible on the coming to an end of a power of accumulation or a power to divert the income to some other beneficiary or purpose, the income is to be treated as part of the beneficiary's total income for the purposes of additional rate tax at the date when he becomes indefeasibly entitled to it. Section 18 then extends this principle to the case where the trustees are entitled to a credit for overseas tax in respect of income from a foreign source.

C I accept that this construction does some violence to the language of section 17. It cannot be said that a payment to a person who has become indefeasibly entitled to income in consequence of the expiry or the release or abandonment of a power to accumulate that income or to divert it to another beneficiary is a payment made in the exercise of a discretion or that the income " would not be his income apart from the payment " in

D the natural and ordinary sense of those words. But on any view section 17 cannot be literally construed. Literally construed section 17 does not apply to the case where trustees of a conventional discretionary trust exercise their discretion in favour of a beneficiary by applying income for his benefit, for instance by paying rates on property which he occupies. The sum paid does not become the income " of the person to whom it is paid " but becomes the income of the person for whose benefit it was paid. But

E section 17 must clearly have been intended to apply to such a case. It must, I think, equally clearly have been intended to apply to the case where the trustees of a conventional discretionary trust exercise their discretion in favour of a beneficiary by an irrevocable resolution to pay a given sum to him but at his request retain it in their hands. In both cases there is something analogous to a payment—that is, an irrevocable exercise

F of a discretion—as a result of which income falls to be treated under ordinary principles of tax law as part of a beneficiary's total income. I see no reason why the references to " payment " should not be similarly read as covering the case where a beneficiary becomes indefeasibly entitled to require trustees to pay him income because when it arose he had a vested interest in it subject to a power to accumulate it or to divert it to another person or purpose and the power has expired or has been released

G or abandoned. The difference between a trust for a beneficiary coupled with a power of accumulation and a power to pay income to a beneficiary coupled with a trust for accumulation is of importance in the ascertainment of the rights of a beneficiary and in framing orders for the administration of trusts. But the difference is one which often depends on " a few words and mere straws in the wind " (see, per Harman L.J. in In re

H Baden's Deed Trusts [1969] 2 Ch. 388, 398) and in other contexts is an artificial one.

The commissioners were much influenced by the decision of Fox J. in Pearson v. Inland Revenue Commissioners [1980] Ch. 1, and Mr. Nugee also relied on the decision of the House of Lords in that case [1981] A.C. 753. There, the question was whether a beneficiary entitled to income in default of the exercise of a power had an interest in possession in the trust fund for the purposes of capital transfer tax. Although much light

is thrown in the judgment of Fox J. and in the judgments and speeches A
in the Court of Appeal and House of Lords on the differences in trust
law between the position of a beneficiary who is an object of a discretionary trust or power and one who is entitled to income subject to a power
capable of divesting that entitlement after the income has come into the
hands of the trustees, and on the distinction between a power of accumulation and a power to use income for administrative purposes, the actual
decision in that case to my mind has no bearing and throws no light on B
the very different questions raised by sections 16 and 17.

  For the reasons I have given, I think this appeal must be allowed.

> *Appeal allowed with costs.*
> *Case remitted to the commissioners*
> *for the assessments to be deter-* C
> *mined.*

  Solicitors: *Solicitor of Inland Revenue; Bryden & Williams.*

  [Reported by MRS. HARRIET DUTTON, Barrister-at-Law]

D

[PRIVY COUNCIL]

* TSANG PING-NAM . . . . APPELLANT E

AND

THE QUEEN . . . . RESPONDENT

[APPEAL FROM THE COURT OF APPEAL OF HONG KONG]

1981 July 8;   Lord Diplock, Lord Edmund-Davies,
     Oct. 6   Lord Roskill, Sir John Megaw F
                                and Sir Owen Woodhouse

  Crime—Common law offence—Attempt to pervert course of justice
     —Witness's evidence conflicting with his statement—Witness
     either making false statements or committing perjury but
     neither proved—Whether permissible to charge witness with
     attempt to pervert course of justice G

        The defendant, a police sergeant, was arrested by police
     officers investigating allegations of corruption in the police
     force. He made statements which implicated three other officers.
     He subsequently agreed to make a witness statement based on
     those statements in return for an undertaking given by the
     Crown that, provided he told the truth in the witness statement,
     nothing contained in it would be used in any proceedings H
     against himself. He made the statement. The three officers
     implicated were charged with offences of corruption. Their trial
     took place and the defendant gave evidence. In doing so he
     resiled from his witness statement and denied the officers'
     involvement in the corruption charged. He asserted that he had
     made the statements to ensure immunity from prosecution for
     himself and out of fear that, if he did not, he himself would
     be charged with criminal offences. The three officers were
     acquitted. The defendant was charged with attempting to per-

A   vert the course of public justice contrary to common law in respect of each of the three officers.

No particulars of the charge was requested and, at the trial, the prosecution presented its case on the basis that either the defendant had made false statements or committed perjury. The prosecution conceded that it could prove neither perjury nor an offence, under section 13B of the Independent Commission against Corruption Ordinance,[1] of making a false statement to

B   an investigating officer. The defendant was convicted and appealed. The Court of Appeal dismissed his appeal.

On the defendant's appeal to the Judicial Committee and on the prosecution seeking to support the convictions on the new ground that the defendant had committed the offences charged by obtaining immunity for himself by fraud: —

Held, allowing the appeal, (1) that the prosecution had not complied with its duty to prove every allegation it made by

C   presenting its case in the alternative; and that it was not permissible for the prosecution to allege an attempt to pervert the course of public justice in circumstances where it would circumvent the crucial safeguard for an accused charged with perjury of the requirement that he be convicted on the evidence of more than one witness and where the prosecution could prove neither perjury nor an offence under section 13B of the Ordinance and, accordingly, the convictions should be quashed

D   (post, p. 1466A–B, E–G).

(2) That the Crown, in seeking to uphold the convictions on the basis that the defendant had perverted the course of public justice by seeking immunity against prosecution for himself by fraud, was seeking to introduce offences relating to the defendant himself and not the offences relating to the three police officers that was presented at the trial; that, since that allegation had not been made before the court of trial or the

E   Court of Appeal or raised in the Crown's printed case to the Board, it would be contrary to principle to permit the Crown to introduce that new ground to support the convictions on the appeal to the Board (post, p. 1467A–D).

Decision of the Court of Appeal of Hong Kong reversed.

The following case is referred to in their Lordships' reasons:

F   *Reg.* v. *Rowell* [1978] 1 W.L.R. 132; [1978] 1 All E.R. 665, C.A.

The following additional cases were cited in argument:

Reg. v *Hook* (1858) Dears. & B. 606.
Reg. v. *Kellett* [1976] Q.B. 372; [1975] 3 W.L.R. 713; [1975] 3 All E.R. 468, C.A.
Reg. v. *Wheatland* (1838) 8 C. & P. 238.

G   *Rex* v. *Harris* (1822) 5 Barn. & Ald. 926.
Read and Huggonson, In re (1742) 2 Atk. 469.

APPEAL (No. 37 of 1980) by Tsang Ping-nam, the defendant, with special leave, from a judgment (October 2, 1979) of the Court of Appeal of Hong Kong (Sir Denys Roberts C.J., McMullin J.A. and Leonard J.)

H   whereby that court dismissed the defendant's appeal from his conviction on May 9, 1978, before Bewley D.J. on three charges of attempting to pervert the course of public justice contrary to common law.

At the close of the hearing before the Judicial Committee Lord Diplock announced that their Lordships would advise that the appeal should be allowed for reasons to be delivered later.

---

[1] Independent Commission against Corruption Ordinance, s. 13B: see post, p. 1466c.

The facts are stated in their Lordships' judgment giving the reasons A for their decision.

Harry Ognall Q.C. and *Derek Zeitlin* for the defendant.
Anthony Scrivener Q.C. and *Kevin Egan,* Crown counsel, Hong Kong, for the Crown.

Cur. adv. vult.

B

October 6. The judgment of their Lordships was delivered by LORD ROSKILL.

The defendant appeals by special leave from a judgment of the Court of Appeal of Hong Kong (Sir Denys Roberts C.J., McMullin J.A. and Leonard J.) dated October 2, 1979. By that judgment the defendant's appeal against his conviction on three counts of attempting to pervert the C course of justice was dismissed. That conviction had taken place before Bewley D.J. on May 9, 1979. At the conclusion of the arguments before their Lordships' Board, their Lordships stated that they would humbly advise Her Majesty that the appeal should be allowed and the convictions quashed for reasons to be given later. Their Lordships now give those reasons.

D

Prior to the defendant's arrest on February 1, 1977, in connection with his alleged involvement in grave corruption in the Mongkok Division of the Royal Hong Kong Police Force, he had served as a police sergeant in that division. Following his arrest the defendant made three statements under caution to the investigating authorities respectively dated February 1, 2 and 4, 1977. He then admitted his part in a corruption conspiracy of a grave character in that division. He also implicated, among many others, E three police officers, one an inspector and the other two sergeants in that division. On February 23, 1977, the defendant agreed to make a further witness statement based on those three statements, on condition that, provided he told the truth in that proposed statement, its contents would not be used in any prosecution of himself for any corrupt activities. On April 15, 1977, he made that statement to which he subsequently made certain F additions. It is not necessary for their Lordships to detail the subsequent course of events which led to those three police officers, to whom reference has already been made, and a large number of others being charged on October 25, 1977. They will be found in the long and careful judgment of Bewley D.J.

The Mongkok conspiracy trial, as it became widely known, started in G Hong Kong on April 17, 1978. Three days previously a letter addressed to the defendant dated April 14, 1978, was signed on behalf of the Attorney General. It informed the defendant that, on condition that he gave:

"full and true evidence" in the Mongkok conspiracy trial, "no prosecution will be instituted against you in respect to any offence involving corruption disclosed by you in the course of your testimony in the said proceedings."

H

That letter however was not then given to the defendant. It was only handed to him on June 16, 1978, shortly before he was due to give evidence. He gave evidence in the Mongkok conspiracy trial on June 19 and 20, 1978. He then wholly resiled from all the allegations regarding those three officers. He denied that any of them were true. He also alleged that he had always known the allegation to be untrue but had signed the

A statements in order to ensure immunity for himself from prosecution and from fear that, were he not to do so, he would be charged with various criminal offences. The judge in the Mongkok conspiracy trial gave leave to treat the defendant as a hostile witness and he was cross-examined upon his witness statement. But the defendant throughout that cross-examinaion maintained his denials. Suffice it to say that those three officers and many other of their co-accused were subsequently acquitted.

B Thereafter the detendant was charged with the offences for which he was later convicted and from which the present appeal arises. There were three charges, one in respect of each of the three officers, otherwise the charges were identical. It is therefore sufficient for their Lordships to refer only to one of the charges. I read:

C " Statement of Offence: Attempt to pervert the course of public justice contrary to common law. Tsang Ping-nam, on a date unknown between January 31, 1977, and June 21, 1978, in this colony, attempted to pervert the course of public justice relating to the prosecution of So Siu-kuen, Police Sergeant 6691 of the Royal Hong Kong Police Force, for the offences relating to the involvement of the said So Siu-kuen in a corruption conspiracy in the Mongkok Division of the Royal

D Hong Kong Police Force."

It will be observed that no particulars of this count were ever asked for. Their Lordships find this strange, as did Mr. Ognall who appeared for the defendant before this Board. Had particulars been sought and ordered, the Crown's dilemma must at once have emerged. The Crown conceded that perjury could not be proved against the defendant for there was no affirma-

E tive evidence that the defendant had lied in court let alone any corroboration of any such affirmative evidence. The Crown also conceded that it could not be affirmatively proved that the defendant had given false information to the investigating officers to whom the several statements had been given. But the Crown averred that it was clear that either the defendant had committed perjury or had given false information to the

F investigating officers and that, whichever was the case, he was guilty of an attempt to pervert the course of public justice by his conduct.

It was this submission which the trial judge and the Court of Appeal both accepted though Sir Denys Roberts C.J. at the conclusion of the judgment of the Court of Appeal said that its conclusion had not been reached " without some degree of intellectual discomfort." Their Lordships do not find the existence of this discomfort surprising. Had the

G particulars been asked for, the Crown must have given alternative and mutually inconsistent particulars which could not have been allowed to stand as particulars under the same count. If that pleading difficulty had been surmounted by adding in the case of each of the three officers an additional count, their Lordships are of the clear opinion that, at the close of the case for the prosecution, a submission of no case to answer on both

H of each pair of counts must have succeeded on the ground that the Crown had wholly failed to prove the relevant facts averred in either count.

Mr. Ognall accepted that the relevant law regarding the offence of attempting to pervert the course of justice was correctly stated by the Court of Appeal (Criminal Division) in Reg. v. Rowell [1978] 1 W.L.R. 132. Their Lordships therefore have not found it necessary to consider that decision. But Mr. Ognall urged that an accused person could not be convicted on the basis that one or other of two mutually inconsistent allegations must

be true. The Crown must prove any allegation made. Moreover, once the   A
concession was made that perjury could not be proved, as it was, the
Crown could not be allowed to circumvent the crucial safeguard to an
accused charged with perjury that he must not be convicted solely upon the
evidence of one witness as to the falsity of any statement alleged to be false,
by charging not perjury but an attempt to pervert the course of justice.
Section 43 of the Crimes Ordinance of Hong Kong (c. 200) contains the
same safeguards in this respect as are provided in section 13 of the Perjury   B
Act 1911.

The prosecution authorities in Hong Kong have weapons available
which are not available to prosecution authorities in the United Kingdom
in the case of alleged corrupt activities by public servants. Thus section
13B of the Independent Commission against Corruption Ordinance of
Hong Kong (c. 204) provides: C

" Any person who knowingly—(a) makes or causes to be made to an
officer a false report of the commission of any offence, or (b) misleads
an officer by giving false information or by making false statements
or accusations, shall be guilty of an offence and shall be liable on
conviction to a fine of $10,000 and to imprisonment for one year."

Section 39 of the Crimes Ordinance of Hong Kong provides: D

" Where two or more contradictory statements of fact or alleged fact,
material to the issue or matter in question, have been wilfully made on
oath by one and the same witness in any judicial proceeding or proceedings, whether before the same court or tribunal or person or not,
and whether the respective truth or falsehood of the said statements   E
can be ascertained or not, an indictment may be preferred against
him charging him with having wilfully made the said contradictory
statements, and on conviction thereof, either in whole or in part, such
witness shall be liable to imprisonment for seven years and to a fine."

In the instant case however the requisite affirmative proof was lacking to
support a charge under section 13B while, as respects section 39, the crucial   F
statements had not been made on oath. In their Lordships' view, however
distasteful it may be to allow a self-confessed corrupt police officer to
escape conviction for his gravely corrupt activities, it was wholly illegitimate for the Crown to seek to overcome their difficulties of proof by
charging attempts to pervert the course of justice upon this alternative
basis and their Lordships with respect are therefore unable to accept the
reasoning which led the trial judge to convict the defendant and the   G
Court of Appeal to dismiss his appeal against those convictions. With
commendable frankness, Mr. Scrivener for the Crown, accepted that the
reasoning of the lower courts could not be supported and their Lordships
do not therefore find it necessary to consider the judgments of those courts
further.

But Mr. Scrivener sought to uphold the convictions upon a wholly   H
different basis which he claimed had been submitted to the courts below
but, as he also claimed, had not been dealt with at all by the trial judge
and barely touched upon by the Court of Appeal. It was urged that the
convictions could be supported on the ground that the gravamen of the
offence was the obtaining by the defendant of the immunity for himself by
fraud, fraud conceived at the time that the statements were first made and
persisted in at least until the immunity was granted. Reliance was placed

A　upon a number of answers given by the defendant in cross-examination at his trial in support of this allegation. Their Lordships were given a transcript of part of Crown counsel's opening of the case against the defendant before the trial judge. They have read that transcript with care but they are unable to deduce from that which they have read that the case against the defendant was sought to be advanced in this wholly different way from that dealt with in the judgments of the courts below. This is no doubt why the

B　trial judge made no reference to the submission in his judgment. In a passage relied upon by Mr. Scrivener entitled " Change of Mind " in the judgment of the Court of Appeal Sir Denys Roberts C.J. does not even refer to the grant of immunity. Moreover their Lordships can find no reference to this submission at any place in the Crown's printed case. Their Lordships would observe that this submission involves an alleged attempted perversion

C　of the course of justice as respects the defendant himself. The counts which the defendant faced alleged attempted perversion of the course of justice relating to the prosecution of the three officers. In these circumstances their Lordships are clearly of the view that to allow the Crown at this late stage to seek to support these convictions upon this ground would be against all principle and their Lordships decline to do so. Had the case against the

D　defendant been advanced on this basis at the trial, the trial might well have taken a wholly different course from that which it in fact took. Their Lordships wish to make clear that they express no view whatever whether, had a charge been initially formulated on the basis now suggested by Mr. Scrivener, it might have succeeded.

　　It was for these reasons that their Lordships have humbly advised Her Majesty that the appeal should be allowed and the defendant's three

E　convictions quashed.

　　　Solicitors: *B. M. Birnberg & Co.; Charles Russell & Co.*

　　　　　　　　　　　　　　　　　　　　　　　　　T. J. M.

F

　　　　　　　　　　　　　　[HOUSE OF LORDS]

　　* DAVIS FREIGHT FORWARDING (HULL) LTD. . PETITIONER

　　　　　　　　　　　　　　　　AND

G　D. BOERS B.V. . 　.　　.　　.　　.　　.　　.　　. RESPONDENT

1981 Nov. 12　　　　　　　Lord Wilberforce, Lord Russell of Killowen
　　　　　　　　　　　　　　　　　and Lord Bridge of Harwich

　　PETITION by the first defendants, Davis Freight Forwarding (Hull) Ltd., for leave to appeal to the House of Lords from the decision of the Court

H　of Appeal in *Cummins Engine Co. Ltd.* v. *Davis Freight Forwarding (Hull) Ltd.* [1981] 1 W.L.R. 1363 in which the respondents, D. Boers B.V., were the fourth defendants.

　　The Appeal Committee granted the petition.

　　　　　　　　　　　　　　　　　　　　　　　　　F. C.

A

[HOUSE OF LORDS]

* REGINA . . . . RESPONDENT

AND

HOWELL . . . . PETITIONER

B

1981 Nov. 12   Lord Wilberforce, Lord Russell of Killowen
                              and Lord Bridge of Harwich

PETITION by the defendant, Errol Howell, for leave to appeal to the
House of Lords from the decision of the Court of Appeal [1981] 3 W.L.R.
501.

C

The Appeal Committee dismissed the petition.

F. C.

NOTE

D

[PRIVY COUNCIL]

* ERIC FRATER . . . . APPELLANT

AND

THE QUEEN . . . . RESPONDENT

E

[APPEAL FROM THE COURT OF APPEAL OF JAMAICA]

1981 July 7;   Lord Diplock, Lord Elwyn-Jones,
      Oct. 6   Lord Edmund-Davies, Lord Roskill and
                                    Sir Owen Woodhouse

F

*Privy Council—Appeal as of right—Interpretation of Constitution
—Whether genuine disputable question—Need for vigilance—
Jamaica (Constitution) Order in Council 1962 (S.I. 1962 No.
1550), Sch. 2, ss. 20 (6) (a), 110 (1)*

APPEAL (No. 45 of 1980)

On December 6, 1977, Eric Frater, an attorney-at-law of Jamaica was   G
representing two defendants at their trial before Parnell J. and a jury in the
circuit court at Spanish Town. At the close of Mr. Frater's cross-examination
of a witness the judge asked the witness some questions. Mr. Frater stood
up and objected to the line of questioning. The judge overruled the objection
and told him to sit down. He refused. The judge told him that he was
obstructing the court and he replied: " I am not sitting, I am standing for the
men I am defending. You cite me. You can do anything. You lock me   H
up as well; but I am standing up because that is unfair, that is not justice."
After a short adjournment the judge required Mr. Frater to show cause why
he should not be cited for contempt. A fellow advocate addressed the judge
on his behalf. The judge convicted Mr. Frater of contempt and ordered him
to pay a fine of $500. On his appeal to the Court of Appeal that court by a
majority (Henry and Carberry JJ.A., Kerr J.A. dissenting) on October 12,
1979, dismissed the appeal against conviction but reduced the fine to $200.
He appealed to the Judicial Committee of the Privy Council as of right under

A   section 110 (1) of the Constitution of Jamaica. On July 7, 1981, Lord Diplock announced that their Lordships would advise that the appeal should be dismissed for reasons to be delivered later.

The following cases are referred to in their Lordships' reasons:

Harrikissoon v. *Attorney-General of Trinidad and Tobago* [1980] A.C. 265; [1979] 3 W.L.R. 62, P.C.

B   *Pollard, In re* (1868) L.R. 2 P.C. 106, P.C.

The following additional case was cited in argument:

Maharaj v. *Attorney-General for Trinidad and Tobago* [1977] 1 All E.R. 411, P.C.

C   *Berthan Macaulay Q.C.* (of the Bar of Jamaica) for Mr. Frater.
Ian X. Forte Q.C., Director of Public Prosecutions, Jamaica and *F. Algernon Smith,* Deputy Director of Public Prosecutions, Jamaica, for the Crown.

Cur. adv. vult.

D   October 6. The reasons for the judgment of the Board were delivered by LORD DIPLOCK. [His Lordship, having said that the principle stated in *In re Pollard* (1868) L.R. 2 P.C. 106, 120:

" . . . no person should be punished for contempt of court, which is a criminal offence, unless the specific offence charged against him be distinctly stated, and an opportunity of answering it given to him . . ."

could not be improved upon for brevity and clarity if it were understood that in that context " distinctly stated " meant made known to the contemnor in E   terms which were not reasonably capable of being misunderstood by him, their Lordships were of the view that on the facts of the instant case that requirement had been satisfied and his Lordship continued:] In the result the appeal must fail, but before departing from the matter their Lordships desire to comment upon the grounds upon which the appeal was brought to Her Majesty in Council apparently *as of right* under section 110 (1) of the Constitution of Jamaica. Mr. Frater's application set out three questions F   of law alleged to be of exceptional importance and was expressed to rely on section 35 of the Judicature (Appellate Jurisdiction) Act as bringing it within section 110 (1) (d): " such other cases as may be prescribed by Parliament." But this cannot be so, because section 35 does not apply to proceedings for contempt of court. In the order made by the Court of Appeal upon this application the questions of law were varied so as to include among them questions (2) and (3) which read as follows:

G   " (2) Whether or not a true construction of section 20 (6) (a) of the Constitution, ' the nature of the charge' include the particularisation of the charge. (3) If the answer to (2) above is in the affirmative, whether or not in the instant case there was such particularisation as held by a majority of the Court of Appeal."

Question (2) appears to have been drafted in order to bring the appeal to H   Her Majesty in Council within section 110 (1) (c): " final decisions in any civil, criminal or other proceedings on questions as to the interpretation of this Constitution."

Section 20 (6) (a) of the Constitution reads:

" (6) Every person who is charged with a criminal offence—(a) shall be informed as soon as reasonably practicable, in a language which he understands, of the nature of the offence charged; . . ."

In their Lordships' view it cannot plausibly be suggested that any question of

interpretation of the plain and simple words " informed . . . of the nature of   A
the offence charged " in section 20 (6) (a) arose in the instant case. The
question that did arise, or could have done if in the Court of Appeal reliance
had been placed upon this constitutional provision (as does not appear to have
been the case), was the *application* of these plain and simple words to the
particular facts of Mr. Frater's case. The information required to be given
to an accused by paragraph (a) of section 20 (6) is in order to enable him to
exercise effectively his rights under the immediately following paragraph (b)   B
which provides that he " shall be given adequate time and facilities for the
preparation of his defence."

  In *Harrikissoon* v. *Attorney-General of Trinidad and Tobago* [1980] A.C.
265 this Board had occasion to point out the danger of allowing the value of
the right to apply to the High Court for redress for contravention of his
fundamental rights and freedoms which is conferred upon the individual by
section 6 of the Constitution of Trinidad and Tobago (of which the corre-   C
sponding section in the Constitution of Jamaica is section 25) to become
debased by lack of vigilance on the part of the courts to dispose summarily
of applications that are plainly frivolous or vexatious or are otherwise an
abuse of process of the court. In their Lordships' view similar vigilance
should be observed to see that claims made by appellants to be entitled to
appeal as of right under section 110 (1) (c) are not granted unless they do
involve a genuinely disputable question of *interpretation* of the Constitution   D
and not one which has merely been contrived for the purpose of obtaining
leave to appeal to Her Majesty in Council as of right.

  Solicitors: *Philip Conway, Thomas & Co.; Charles Russell & Co.*

                                                                T. J. M.   E

_____

[QUEEN'S BENCH DIVISION]

* THERMO ENGINEERS LTD. AND ANOTHER *v.*

FERRYMASTERS LTD.   F

[1976 T. No. 3010]

1980 Sept. 8, 9, 10, 11; 22   Neill J.

  Carriage by Land — International carriage of goods by road —   G
    " Other means of transport "—Damage to goods on trailer
    during loading on ship—Liability of carrier—Whether compen-
    sation to be calculated in accordance with law applicable to
    carriage by sea—Carriage of Goods by Road Act 1965 (c. 37),
    Sch., arts. 2, 17

      The defendant carriers agreed to convey machinery manu-
    factured by the plaintiffs at Aylesbury to purchasers in Copen-   H
    hagen. They arranged for the goods to be loaded on a trailer
    at the plaintiffs' premises and taken to their premises at
    Felixstowe and then to the docks for the goods and trailer to
    be loaded on a ship. The loading was carried out by steve-
    dores with the assistance of members of the ship's crew in
    November 1975 who failed to notice the height of the trailer
    and goods. The top of the goods struck the deck head as the
    trailer was being moved and the machinery was damaged. On
    delivery, the purchasers rejected it and it was returned to the

A   plaintiffs so that they could use undamaged parts in similar
machinery. The plaintiffs claimed against the defendants, under
the Convention on the Contract for the International Carriage
of Goods by Road scheduled to the Carriage of Goods by
Road Act 1965,[1] the difference between the value of the
goods and the salvage value, namely, £17,887.

       On the questions whether the defendants were liable as
carriers under the Convention and, if so, whether their liability
B   was to be determined, under article 2, in accordance " with
the conditions prescribed by law for the carriage of goods "
by the " other means of transport ": —

       Held, that, since the damage had occurred to the goods
during loading at a stage when the trailer had passed across
the outboard ramp and across the line of the stern of the
vessel, carriage by sea within the meaning of the Hague Rules
had begun and, therefore, for the purpose of article 2 of the
C   Convention " the other means of transport " had begun; and
that, since the defendants had not been in any breach of their
duty of care and the event that had caused the damage
occurred in the course of, and by reason of, the carriage by
sea, the conditions set out in paragraph 1 of article 2 had been
satisfied and compensation payable to the plaintiffs was to be
calculated in accordance with such conditions as they could
and would have agreed with a carrier by sea in November 1975
D   if a separate contract had been made for the carriage of the
goods from Felixstowe to Copenhagen (post, pp. 1475F–H,
1476H—1477A, B–C, 1478A).

       Per curiam. As the defendants were making use of the
services of those responsible for loading the trailer on the
Orion, they could not escape liability " through circumstances
which the carrier could not avoid," under paragraph 2 of
article 17 of the Convention, even if the standard was one
E   of due diligence. Those words seemed to import a more
limited relief from liability than if the words " by the exercise
of reasonable care " had been used and the words " could
not " should be given their full meaning (post, p. 1478G–H).

       The following cases are referred to in the judgment:

F   *Buchanan (James) & Co. Ltd.* v. *Babco Forwarding & Shipping (U.K.)
       Ltd.* [1977] Q.B. 208; [1977] 2 W.L.R. 107; [1977] 1 All E.R. 518,
       C.A.; [1978] A.C. 141; [1977] 3 W.L.R. 907; [1977] 3 All E.R. 1048,
       H.L.(E.).
       Fothergill v. *Monarch Airlines Ltd.* [1981] A.C. 251; [1980] 3 W.L.R.
       209; [1980] 2 All E.R. 696, H.L.(E.).
       Kühne & Nagel v. *Transports Internationaux Van Miegham* (1974) 9
       E.T.L. 330.
G   *Pyrene Co. Ltd.* v. *Scindia Navigation Co. Ltd.* [1954] 2 Q.B. 402; [1954]
       2 W.L.R. 1005; [1954] 2 All E.R. 158.
       Tatton (William) & Co. Ltd. v. *Ferrymasters Ltd.* [1974] 1 Lloyd's Rep.
       203.

       No additional cases were cited in argument.

H
       ACTION

       By a writ dated November 3, 1976, the first plaintiffs, Thermo Engineers
Ltd., manufacturers of engineering equipment, and the second plaintiffs,
Anhydro A/S, purchasers from the first plaintiffs of a steam heat

_____
[1] Carriage of Goods by Road Act 1965, Sch., art. 2: see post, pp. 1474F—1475A.
Art. 3: see post, pp. 1475H—1476A.
Art. 17: see post, p. 1478C–D.

exchanger, claimed damages, pursuant to the Convention on the Contract   A
for the International Carriage of Goods by Road in the Schedule to the
Carriage of Goods by Road Act 1965, against the defendants, Ferrymasters
Ltd., a transport company, for breach of a contract by which the defendants
agreed to carry the machinery from the manufacturers' premises in Aylesbury to the purchasers in Copenhagen. The second defendants named,
Anglo Overseas Transport Co. Ltd., shipping and forwarding agents, were   B
not served with the writ.

The facts are stated in the judgment.

Richard Aikens for the plaintiffs.
Jonathan Mance for the defendants.

Cur. adv. vult.   C

September 22, 1980. NEILL J. read the following judgment. I am
concerned in this case with the Carriage of Goods by Road Act 1965 and
with the Convention on the Contract for the International Carriage of
Goods by Road set out in the Schedule to that Act.

The action arises out of a contract for the carriage of a steam heat   D
exchanger from the premises of the first plaintiffs, Thermo Engineeers Ltd.,
at Aylesbury to the premises of the second plaintiffs, Anhydro A/S, in
Copenhagen. The contract was made between Thermo Engineers Ltd. and
the defendants, Ferrymasters Ltd. The second defendants named in the
writ, who carry on business as shipping and forwarding agents, have not
been served with the proceedings and it is not necessary for me to say any
more about them.   E

Most of the facts are not in dispute and there has been put before the
court an agreed statement setting out an account of the main events. In
addition I heard oral evidence from three witnesses, Mr. Mitchell who was
called on behalf of the plaintiffs, and Mr. Driver and Mr. Clarke who were
called on behalf of the defendants.

Thermo Engineers Ltd. manufacture heat exchangers. In 1975 they sold   F
a heat exchanger to Anhydro A/S in Copenhagen. The defendants agreed
to transport the heat exchanger to Copenhagen. On October 31, 1975, the
heat exchanger was loaded at Aylesbury onto a trailer belonging to the defendants. A box of spares and some pipes were loaded as well. The trailer
had a superstructure but it was not sheeted. The height from the ground to
the bed of the trailer was 1·05 metres. The height from the bed to the top of
the superstructure was 2·87 metres. The total height of the trailer itself was   G
therefore 3·92 metres. For the purpose of loading, the heat exchanger was
divided into two parts which were loaded one in front of the other. Each
part had dimensions of about 3·7 metres in length by 1·3 to 1·5 metres in
width by 3·265 to 3·33 metres in height. It will be apparent therefore that
the height of the load exceeded the height of the superstructure by about
half a metre. In the agreed statement of facts this excess is stated to be   H
about 1 ft. 3 in. to 2 ft. The total weight of the heat exchanger and the
spares and pipes was 5,100 kg.

The defendants sub-contracted the carriage from Aylesbury to their own
premises at Felixstowe to Eastern Roadways of Norwich. The trailer
reached Felixstowe on October 31. On the next day, Saturday, November
1, the trailer was taken by Mr. Driver, a shunter driver employed by the
defendants, to Felixstowe Docks. Before he left the defendants' premises

The Weekly Law Reports, December 11, 1981

1473

1 W.L.R.   Thermo Engineers v. Ferrymasters Ltd. (Q.B.D.)   Neill J.

A   Mr. Driver was given a shipping note by the yard foreman. This shipping note directed Mr. Driver to go to a compound at the docks. Mr. Driver took the trailer to the compound. He went to the office of the Felixstowe Dock and Railway Co. Ltd. (I shall call that company " the dock company ") and handed in the shipping note. A checker employed by the dock company came out with Mr. Driver and inspected the load. The checker

B   brought with him a document called an equipment condition and receipt form. The checker filled in the form and in the section headed " Damage to Cargo " he wrote these words: " Machinery loaded thro' framework. Too high." The form contained a printed sketch of a trailer which was there to enable the checker to indicate the position of any damage. The checker drew some lines on the sketch and wrote above it the words " 2 foot high up." The form, which was in triplicate, was then initialled by the checker

C   and dated November 1, 1975. Mr. Driver signed his name in the appropriate space on the form. He was then given one of the three copies, which he took back to the defendants. The other copies were kept in the office of the dock company, one copy being intended for the shippers' agents. There was no evidence, however, that that copy reached the shipping company before the ship was loaded.

D   The trailer remained in the custody of the dock company over the week-end. On Monday, November 3, the trailer was taken to be loaded on a ship called the *Orion.* The defendants had made a contract of carriage with Tor Line AB. This contract is evidenced by a bill of loading dated November 3. The *Orion* was a ship which operated between Felixstowe and Denmark during 1975, and the contract between Tor Line AB and the owners of the vessel was produced in court. It is clear that the ship had made a number

E   of journeys from Felixstowe before November 3, 1975, and it is not in dispute that employees of the dock company who acted as stevedores were familiar with the dimensions and layout of the vessel.

    I should refer now to paragraph 10 of the agreed statement of facts. It is there recorded that on November 3, Mr. Ford, an employee of the dock company, driving a Tugmaster vehicle, pushed the trailer in reverse onto

F   the *Orion* on the directions of another employee, Mr. Maule, a dock fore-man with the dock company, with the assistance of other such employees and/or with the assistance of the ship's crew. Mr. Maule had directed Mr. Ford to take the trailer to a space Mr. Maule had selected in the lower cargo deck of the vessel forward of the entrance ramp. The statement of facts continues:

G   " The height between the lower cargo deck and the second cargo deck is shown on the inboard pillar facing the stern of the vessel, in large letter, as 4·2 metres. The top part of the goods struck the deckhead at the lower end of the ramp. The trailer and the goods were taken off the vessel and later reloaded on board the vessel at the after end of the lower cargo deck. The goods and trailer were carried there to

H   Copenhagen, Denmark, without further incident."

And then in paragraph 14: " Because the goods were damaged on arrival in Copenhagen, they were rejected by Anhydro A/S." It is not in dispute that the second plaintiffs were entitled to reject the goods. The statement of facts continues in paragraph 16:

    " Thermo Engineers Ltd. arranged to have the goods returned to their premises at Aylesbury, where they salvaged such parts of the cargo

which were capable of being used by them in the manufacture of A
other similar goods, or otherwise."

The net salved value of the goods was £1,920 and the value of the goods
at the time they were accepted for carriage was £19,807. The primary
claim, therefore, is for £17,887, being the difference between the value
of the goods when accepted for carriage and the net salved value.

The issues to be considered can be listed as follows. (1) Is the liability B
of the defendants to be determined in accordance with the general provisions of the Convention or are some other provisions applicable by reason
of article 2 of the Convention? (2) If the general provisions of the Convention do not apply, how is the liability of the defendants to be
determined? (3) If the general provisions of the Convention do apply, can
the defendants rely on paragraph 2 of article 17 of the Convention? (4) If C
the defendants are liable in accordance with the general provisions of the
Convention what sums can the plaintiffs recover in respect of freight?

It is common ground that unless the general provisions of the Convention are excluded by article 2 the rights of the parties are to be determined
in accordance with those provisions. It is also common ground that in
construing the Convention I should follow the guidance given in the
speeches in the House of Lords in *James Buchanan & Co. Ltd.* v. *Babco* D
Forwarding & Shipping (U.K.) Ltd. [1978] A.C. 141 and in *Fothergill* v.
Monarch Airlines Ltd. [1981] A.C. 251. I must therefore give " a purposive
construction to the Convention looked at as a whole ": see, *per* Lord
Diplock in *Fothergill's* case [1981] A.C. 251, 279. In the context of the
construction of the Convention I was also referred to parts of the English
text of a commentary on it written by Professor Roland Loewe of Austria E
in about 1975. This commentary (" Commentary on the Convention of
May 19, 1956, on the Contract for the International Carriage of Goods
by Road (CMR) ") was mentioned by Roskill L.J. in the *Buchanan* case
[1977] Q.B. 208, 216 and is printed in (1976) 11 E.T.L. 311. In addition
my attention was drawn to four cases concerning the Convention decided
in Germany, Holland and Belgium, and I was provided with translations
of the relevant reports in European Transport Law. Finally, I should F
mention that I had the benefit of being given a copy of the French text
of the Convention.

I turn now to article 2 of the Convention, which is in these terms:

" 1. Where the vehicle containing the goods is carried over part of the
journey by sea, rail, inland waterways or air, and, except where the
provisions of article 14 are applicable, the goods are not unloaded G
from the vehicle, this Convention shall nevertheless apply to the whole
of the carriage. Provided that to the extent that it is proved that any
loss, damage or delay in delivery of the goods which occurs during the
carriage by the other means of transport was not caused by an act or
omission of the carrier by road, but by some event which could only
have occurred in the course of and by reason of the carriage by that H
other means of transport, the liability of the carrier by road shall be
determined not by this Convention but in the manner in which the
liability of the carrier by the other means of transport would have been
determined if a contract for the carriage of the goods alone had been
made by the sender with the carrier by the other means of transport
in accordance with the condition prescribed by law for the carriage
of goods by that means of transport. If, however, there are no such

The Weekly Law Reports, December 11, 1981

1475

1 W.L.R.   Thermo Engineers v. Ferrymasters Ltd. (Q.B.D.)   Neill J.

A   prescribed conditions, the liability of the carrier by road shall be determined by this Convention.

"2. If the carrier by road is also himself the carrier by the other means of transport, his liability shall also be determined in accordance with the provisions of paragraph 1 of this article, but as if, in his capacities as carrier by road and as carrier by the other means of transport, he were two separate persons."

B

It will be seen that the first sentence of article 2 establishes the general rule that where goods remain on the same vehicle for the whole journey the provisions of the Convention will apply even though the journey involves, for example, a sea crossing. This general rule, however, does not cover cases of loss, damage or delay in delivery of the goods where the following
C   cumulative conditions are satisfied: (a) the damage, etc. occurred during the carriage by the other means of transport; (b) the damage, etc. was not caused by an act of omission of the carrier by road; and (c) the damage etc. was caused by some event which could only have occurred in the course of and by reason of the carriage by that other means of transport.

In the present case counsel for the plaintiffs contended that the general provisions of the Convention apply and that none of these con-
D   ditions has been satisfied. I must therefore examine the conditions in turn.

It will be remembered that the damage occurred at the moment when the upper part of the heat exchanger struck the deckhead of the lower 'tween deck of the *Orion*. Mr. Aikens, for the plaintiffs, argued that at that moment the carriage by sea had not yet begun, and that it was only when the effective means of carriage had ceased to be by the wheels of the
E   trailer, and the trailer and its load were secured in the ship, that the carriage by road could be said to have ceased. Mr. Mance for the defendants, on the other hand, argued that carriage by sea includes the operation of loading. He referred me to the Hague Rules (see the Schedule to the Carriage of Goods by Sea Act 1924, and the Schedule to the Carriage of Goods by Sea Act 1971) and the decision of Devlin J. in *Pyrene Co. Ltd.* v. *Scindia Navigation Co. Ltd.* [1954] 2 Q.B. 402.
F   With respect, I am unable to accept the argument of Mr. Aikens that the road transport continued until the trailer and its load were secured in the ship. There is force in the submission of Mr. Mance that the Convention was intended to fit in with other conventions, and I incline to the view that as a general rule the first condition of article 2 will be satisfied where it is proved that sea carriage as understood in the Hague Rules has begun.
G   I recognise, however, that there may be cases where the exact line between two successive means of transport will be difficult to draw. I must concern myself with the facts of the present case. Here I am satisfied that the damage occurred during the carriage by the other means of transport. At the relevant time the loading was well advanced, and, as can be seen from the sketch plan drawn by Mr. Clarke, the trailer had already passed across
H   the outboard ramp and across the line of the stern.

I turn to the second condition. In reaching a decision about this condition it is necessary to have regard to the terms of article 3 of the Convention. Article 3, under the heading "Persons for whom the Carrier is Responsible," provides:

"For the purposes of this Convention the carrier shall be responsible for the acts and omissions of his agents and servants and of any other

persons of whose services he makes use for the performance of the A
carriage, when such agents, servants or other persons are acting within
the scope of their employment, as if such acts or omissions were his
own."

I am satisfied on examination of the Convention as a whole that as a
general rule a carrier by road who has undertaken to carry goods by a
vehicle from this country to a place abroad will be liable for the acts or B
omissions of sub-carriers who perform the sea carriage or air carriage, or
as the case may be. This conclusion is consistent with sections 1 and 14 (2)
of the Act of 1965. I consider, however, that in article 2 the words " carrier
by road " have to be construed in such a way as to impose a narrower responsibility. A construction which imposed a wide responsibility on the
carrier by road would, in my view, be contrary to the purposes which
paragraph 1 of article 2 seeks to achieve. It would also be inconsistent with C
paragraph 2 of that article.

The main argument of Mr. Aikens on the second condition, however,
was put forward on the basis that the words " act or omission of the
carrier by road " did not include any default by a sub-carrier by another
means of transport. He submitted (a) that the defendants were negligent in
failing to warn the stevedores and the ship's officers that the load was of an D
unusual height and that it projected above the frame of the trailer. Such
a warning, he said, should have been given in the loading list or by some
other means, (b) that the dock company, who knew of the excess height,
were the agents of the defendants (in their capacity as carriers by road) for
the purpose of receiving and marshalling the goods to be shipped, and that
they failed in their duty to pass on their knowledge, both within their own E
organisation and to third parties, to those who carried out the loading. In
my view there are simple and commonsense answers to both these
submissions.

The stevedores and the ship's officers knew the height of the lower
deck. Indeed, the height " 4·2 metres " was displayed in large letters on an
inboard pillar facing the stern. It is to be remembered that the *Orion* had
been sailing from Felixstowe nearly every week since the previous May. F
According to the evidence of Mr. Clarke the height of the lower deck on the
Orion was less than the average height of decks used for this kind of traffic.
It was also established that though most trailers, including 12-metre trailers
such as the trailer used in the present case, are less than 4·2 metres in height
there is no standard height for the framework of a trailer. Moreover,
though, in Mr. Clarke's words, it is " not too common " for out-of-gauge G
goods to be loaded on this sort of trailer, it is not unknown. It is to be
noted that the loading list had no column in which to show the height of
any trailer or of any load. Furthermore, the trailer itself with its frame had
a height of 3·92 metres, and this height might well have been increased
during loading by reason of the adjustment of the fifth wheel. Unfortunately
the stevedores and the ship's officers involved in the loading did not give H
adequate attention to the fact that this was a low deck. The height of the
trailer and its load (which was not covered in any way) was obvious. The
top of the load was flat and quite broad. I am not concerned here with a
narrow or barely visible projection. Looking at all these circumstances I
do not see that the defendants or the dock company, in any capacity other
than as stevedores, were in breach of any duty of care or that any act or
omission of these companies, as persons involved in the carriage by road,

The Weekly Law Reports, December 11, 1981

1477

1 W.L.R.   Thermo Engineers v. Ferrymasters Ltd. (Q.B.D.)   Neill J.

A caused the damage. The damage was caused by those directly involved in the loading.

I come to the third condition. The wording of this part of article 2 is not easy to construe. Mr. Aikens submitted that this condition would be satisfied only by an event which was peculiar to the relevant means of transport, for example, the wetting of goods by sea water in the case of carriage by sea. An overhead obstruction, said counsel, is not a peril peculiarly
B associated with the sea; a similar incident could have occurred on land if, for example, the trailer had collided with a low bridge or the entrance to a garage. I see the force of this argument but I am not persuaded by it. One is concerned to consider not whether the loss or damage could only have occurred in the course of the other means of transport but whether the event could only have so occurred. It seems to me that any adequate des-
C cription of the relevant events in this case would have to include a statement to the effect that a collision with the bulkhead of a ship had taken place in the course of loading the ship. Such an event could only have occurred in the course of, and by reason of, the carriage by sea. I therefore consider that the third condition is satisfied.

I must turn now to the second issue. Where the conditions set out in
D the proviso in paragraph 1 of article 2 are satisfied the liability of the carrier by road is determined not by the Convention but

> " in the manner in which the liability of the carrier by the other means of transport would have been determined if a contract for the carriage of the goods alone had been made by the sender with the carrier by the other means of transport in accordance with the conditions pres-
E > cribed by law for the carriage of goods by that means of transport."

Mr. Mance argued that in the context of the present case the liability of the defendants is to be determined in accordance with the Hague Rules as being the conditions prescribed by law in force in November 1975. Mr. Aikens, on the other hand, relied on the fact that article 5 of the Hague Rules allows a carrier to increase his responsibilities and liabilities under
F the rules provided such increase is embodied in the bill of lading. I was referred to the bill of lading and, in particular, to clauses 11 and 13. At this stage I am not asked to determine what the plaintiffs can recover if the general provisions of the Convention do not apply. The parties may be able to agree a figure. But if they cannot do so the determination of the compensation recoverable may involve the consideration of a number of
G arguments, for example, as to the meaning of " gold value " in article 9 of the Hague Rules, and whether or not the free market value of gold is the appropriate yardstick, arguments which, so far, have been merely adumbrated. For the moment I am being asked to decide only the preliminary question: is the compensation to be determined in accordance with article 4, rule 5, and article 9 of the Hague Rules, or do the " conditions pre-
H scribed by law " in paragraph 1 of article 2 of the Convention extend to such conditions as the sender and the sea carrier could legally, and would, have agreed in November 1975?

I have come to the conclusion that, having regard to article 5 of the Hague Rules and the terms of the bill of lading, the argument of Mr. Aikens is to be preferred. Accordingly, in determining the compensation payable, it will be necessary to consider what conditions could and would

1478

A

have been agreed. I can therefore summarise my findings as follows: (1) that the conditions set out in paragraph 1 of article 2 of the Convention have been satisfied and (2) that the compensation payable to the plaintiffs is to be calculated in accordance with such conditions as they could, and would, have agreed with a carrier by sea in November 1975 if a separate contract for the carriage of the heat exchanger alone from Felixstowe to Copenhagen had been made.

B

It is therefore unnecessary for me to express a view on the other issues. Nevertheless, I think it is right that I should state my conclusion on the arguments directed to articles 17, 23 and 25 of the Convention.

Mr. Mance argued that if the provisions of the Convention applied to the plaintiffs' claim, the defendants were relieved from liability by reason of paragraph 2 of article 17. I should read the first two paragraphs of article 17. This article is in Chapter 4 under the heading "Liability of the Carrier":

C

"1. The carrier shall be liable for the total or partial loss of the goods and for damage thereto occurring between the time when he takes over the goods and the time of delivery, as well as for any delay in delivery.
"2. The carrier shall however be relieved of liability if the loss, damage or delay was caused by the wrongful act or neglect of the claimant, by the instructions of the claimant given otherwise than as the result of a wrongful act or neglect on the part of the carrier, by inherent vice of the goods or through circumstances which the carrier could not avoid and the consequences of which he was unable to prevent."

D

It is clear from paragraph 1 of article 17 that prima facie the liability of the carrier by road extends throughout the period of carriage, that is, in the present case, from Aylesbury to Copenhagen. The question for consideration is whether the defendants are relieved from liability under paragraph 2 by being able to prove that the damage was caused through circumstances which they could not avoid and the consequences of which they were unable to prevent.

E

F

Mr. Mance argued that the concluding words of paragraph 2 mean that a carrier can escape liability if he proves that he used due diligence. Mr. Aikens, on the other hand, contended that the words were equivalent to a force majeure. He drew my attention in support of this contention to one of the four cases to which I referred earlier in general terms, *Kühne & Nagel v. Transports Internationaux Van Mieghem* (1974) 9 E.T.L. 330, a decision of the Tribunal de Commerce in Brussels. I have already said that I consider that the general effect of article 3 when considered in the light of the Act of 1965 and the Convention as a whole is to make the carrier by road responsible for the acts of sub-carriers. The damage here was caused by those responsible for loading the trailer on the *Orion*. In my view these persons were plainly persons of whose services the defendants were making use for the performance of the carriage. I am therefore satisfied that, even if the standard envisaged by paragraph 2 of article 17 is one of due diligence, the defendants would not be able to escape liability. I am inclined to the view, however, that the words "through circumstances which the carrier could not avoid" allow a more limited relief from liability than would have been the case if words such as "by the exercise of reasonable care" had been added. Both the English and the French texts show that

G

H

The Weekly Law Reports, December 11, 1981

1479

1 W.L.R.　　　　Thermo Engineers v. Ferrymasters Ltd. (Q.B.D.)　　　Neill J.

A the court is concerned to inquire: was the damage caused through circumstances which the carrier *could not* avoid? The words I have emphasised should be given their full meaning.

I come finally to submissions based on articles 23 and 25. Mr. Mance argued (a) that as the heat exchanger retained a scrap value the sum recoverable for the carriage to Copenhagen (£580) should be reduced proportionately in accordance with paragraph 4 of article 23 and paragraph 1
B of article 25, and (b) that the plaintiffs could not recover the cost of transporting the damaged goods back from Denmark to Aylesbury because such a charge was not incurred in respect of the relevant carriage. I can deal with these arguments quite shortly. In my judgment, it is important to have regard to the fact that though the heat exchanger had some scrap value the damage was such as to render the whole unit unacceptable. The loss of part
C of a consignment does not provide a satisfactory parallel. I therefore consider that if the compensation were to be calculated in accordance with the Convention the whole £580 would be recoverable.

The claim for the return freight involves different considerations, but in my judgment this sum also is recoverable in principle, though it would be necessary for the plaintiffs to prove that the sum claimed was a proper and
D reasonable charge. In *James Buchanan & Co. Ltd.* v. *Babco Forwarding & Shipping (U.K.) Ltd.* [1978] A.C. 141, 154, Lord Wilberforce approved Master Jacob's decision that customs duty was recoverable because it was chargeable having regard to the way in which the goods had been carried. Moreover in the Court of Appeal in that case Lord Denning M.R. expressed the view that return carriage is recoverable and disapproved of the decision by Browne J. on this point in *William Tatton & Co. Ltd.* v.
E *Ferrymasters Ltd.* [1974] 1 Lloyd's Rep. 203. Roskill L.J. agreed with Lord Denning M.R.: see [1977] Q.B. 208, 215, 220. If, therefore, I had held the Convention to apply I would have allowed in principle the claims for return freight set out in paragraph 6 of the amended points of claim.

Order accordingly.

F
Solicitors: *Clyde & Co.; Herbert Smith & Co.*

R. D.

G

————

H

[1981]

A

[COURT OF APPEAL]

* REGINA v. HERON and Others

1981 April 14;   Shaw L.J., Mais and Tudor Evans JJ.
      July 31
                                                                                        B

Crime—Coinage—Counterfeit coins—Copies of current coinage—
   Whether intent to defraud necessary ingredient of offence—
   Coinage Offences Act 1936 (26 Geo. 5 & 1 Edw. 8, c. 16),
   s. 1 (1)

The defendants were seen going to and from premises
which, when raided by the police, were found to contain
articles including a hydraulic press, a metal-cutting machine,   C
copper coins (some plated with gold) and a number of counterfeit half-sovereigns. The defendants were charged on two
counts alleging that between specified dates they conspired
together (1) " to falsely make or counterfeit coins resembling
current gold coins namely half-sovereigns," contrary to section
1 (1) of the Coinage Offences Act 1936 [1] and (2) " to defraud
such persons as might be induced to purchase false or counter-   D
feit half-sovereigns by false representation that they were
genuine." At the close of the prosecution case, the judge ruled
that the substantive offence to which count 1 related required
no specific intent beyond an intention " to falsely make or
counterfeit any current coin." The defendants thereupon
changed their pleas to guilty on count 1 and the jury was
discharged from giving a verdict on count 2.
      On appeal against conviction: —   E
      Held, dismissing the appeals, that the necessary intent to
constitute an offence under section 1 (1) of the Coinage
Offences Act 1936 was an intent to produce coins resembling
current coinage; that it was the act of counterfeiting itself
which constituted the offence and there was no requirement
to prove a dishonest or fraudulent intent (post, pp. 1482G–H,
1484B–C).

                                                                      F

The following cases are referred to in the judgment:
Reg. v. Selby [1972] A.C. 515; [1971] 3 W.L.R. 647; [1971] 3 All E.R.
   810, H.L.(E.).
Reg. v. Sutton (1841) 5 J.P. 195.

The following additional cases were cited in argument: G
Reg. v. Hermann (1879) 4 Q.B.D. 284.
Reg. v. Lawrence (Stephen) [1981] 2 W.L.R. 524; [1981] 1 All E.R. 974,
   H.L.(E.).
Reg. v. McMahon (1894) 15 N.S.W.L.R. 131.
Reg. v. Phekoo [1981] 1 W.L.R. 1117, C.A.
Reg. v. Sheppard [1981] A.C. 394; [1980] 3 W.L.R. 960; [1980] 3 All E.R.
   889, H.L.(E.).   H
Reg. v. Warner [1969] 2 A.C. 256; [1968] 2 W.L.R. 1303; [1968] 2 All E.R.
   356, H.L.(E.).
Sweet v. Parsley [1970] A.C. 132; [1969] 2 W.L.R. 470; [1969] 1 All E.R.
   347, H.L.(E.).
United States v. King (Henry) (1851) U.S.Rep. (7th Circuit) 5 McLean
   208.

[1] Coinage Offences Act 1936, s. 1 (1): see post, p. 1482G.

A   APPEALS against conviction.

On September 8, 1980, at the Central Criminal Court the defendants,
David Heron, Peter Edwin Storey and Christopher Robin Thomas, pleaded
not guilty to two counts of an indictment alleging that between January 1,
1978, and September 22, 1978, they conspired together " to falsely make or
counterfeit coins resembling current gold coins namely half-sovereigns "
(count 1) and " to defraud such persons as might be induced to purchase
B   false or counterfeit half-sovereigns by false representations that the same
were genuine " (count 2). At the close of the prosecution case, submissions
were made on behalf of the defendant Heron that count 2 should not be
left to the jury as the evidence did not demonstrate that the defendants
intended to use the counterfeit half-sovereigns for the purpose of defrauding
anyone, and that in the absence of any such intention the substantive
C   offence on which count 1 was founded was not intended or envisaged and,
accordingly, that count was not supported by the evidence before the jury.
Judge Abdela Q.C. rejected those submissions and held that the substantive
offence to which count 1 related required no specific intent beyond an intention " to falsely make or counterfeit any current coin." The defendants
changed their pleas to guilty on count 1 and the jury was discharged from
D   giving a verdict on count 2.   The defendant Heron was sentenced to 3½
years' imprisonment, the defendant Storey to three years' imprisonment
and the defendant Thomas to 2¼ years' imprisonment.   The defendants
appealed against conviction on the ground that the judge erred in ruling
that the offence under section 1 of the Coinage Offences Act 1936 was
an absolute offence.   They also appealed against sentence.

After hearing the appeals against conviction, the Court of Appeal
E   announced that the appeals would be dismissed but the judgment giving
the reasons for the decision would be reserved.

The facts are stated in the judgment of the court.

Louis Blom-Cooper Q.C. and *Paul Dodgson* (assigned by the Registrar
of Criminal Appeals) for the defendants.
F   *Michael Sayers* and *Andrew Macrae* for the Crown.

Cur. adv. vult.

July 31. SHAW L.J. read the following judgment of the court. These
are the reasons for the judgment of the court given at the hearing of this
appeal. The defendants appeared at the Central Criminal Court in Septem-
G   ber 1980 to answer an indictment which charged them on two counts. The
first count alleged that between January 1, 1978, and September 22, 1978,
they conspired together " to falsely make or counterfeit coins resembling
current gold coins namely half-sovereigns." The second count charged them
with having conspired together between those dates " to defraud such
persons as might be induced to purchase false or counterfeit half-sovereigns
H   by false representations that the same were genuine."

The circumstances which brought them before the court were stark and
telling. At some time in 1978 the defendant Heron procured the use of
premises at 60, Southgate Road, in North London. With the help of the
defendant Thomas and a man named Barry he conveyed a die-stamping
machine from an address of a co-defendant, George Henry Santi, to those
premises.   Thereafter all the defendants as well as other persons were
seen in July, August and September 1978 going to and coming from no. 60.

On September 21, 1978, the police made concerted raids at that address　A
as well as at The Jolly Farmers public-house in the same road, where
Storey was the licensee, and at an address in East London where Santi was
then living. At 60, Southgate Road they found a hydraulic press, a number
of dies and a quantity of copper discs.　There were also some antique coins,
a metal-cutting machine and about 1,000 copper coins, of which half that
number had been plated with gold. In addition there were a number of
counterfeit half-sovereigns. Thomas was in the premises at the time. Asked　B
about the various items there, he said: " You know Heron organised it,"
and in reply to a question about how many coins had been made he said:
" Only those you found. We'd only just started." He later amended this
to " about 1,000 plus what's on the premises."

Heron was arrested outside The Jolly Farmers. At first he denied any
involvement with the activities at No. 60. When told that he had been seen　C
assisting in the taking of the die-stamping machine to that address he was
more forthcoming and said: " I gave them the chance to make a lot of
money and they do this to me."

Storey was seen inside The Jolly Farmers. He told the police that
Heron owed him money and that he hoped to get his money back by taking
part in a scheme for making (counterfeit) half-sovereigns. He also admitted　D
that he had arranged for the use of 60, Southgate Road.

When Santi was seen he admitted his connection with the enterprise
described by Storey, but said that he had played only a minor part in the
matter.

The account of the police observation, supplemented and augmented
by the admissions attributed to the respective defendants, left little room for　E
the defendants to manoeuvre.　On their arraignment Santi pleaded guilty
to count 1. The others pleaded not guilty. At the close of the prosecution
case it was submitted on behalf of Heron that count 2 ought not to be left
to the jury as the evidence did not demonstrate that the defendants intended
to use the counterfeit half-sovereigns for the purpose of defrauding anyone.
A further submission was developed to the effect that, in the absence of any　F
intention to commit the fraud envisaged by count 2, the substantive offence
on which count 1 was founded was not intended or envisaged, and that
accordingly that count was not supported by the evidence before the jury.

The judge ruled against these submissions, holding that the substantive
offence to which count 1 related required no specific intent beyond an
intention " to falsely make or counterfeit any current coin." That substantive offence is concisely defined in section 1 (1) of the Coinage Offences Act　G
1936 in these terms: " Every person who falsely makes or counterfeits any
coin resembling any current coin shall be guilty of [an offence]." No particular intent is required as a constituent element of the offence by the
terms of the subsection; but it is inherent in the nature of the activity
described that there should be an intent to produce coin which simulates
current coin. It is hardly conceivable that a person could produce coins　H
which were imitations of current coins otherwise than purposefully, that is
to say, with the intention of making his products resemble current coin.

Counsel for the defendants contended that in order to give rise to an
offence under section 1 (1) there must also exist a dishonest intention to
utter the spurious coins so as to pass them off as genuine. The only
authority advanced in support of this proposition was Reg. v. Sutton (1841)
5 J.P. 195. The recital of the facts reads:

A   " The prisoner who had every appearance of being a most respectable
person, was a native of Canada, and along with many others was
engaged in the fur trade with the native Indians, inhabiting the rocky
mountains and the banks of the Columbia river. The persons engaged
in this traffic with the Indians do not pay them for those commodities
in money, but give in exchange for the furs, beads, knives, or other
articles of a similar description. The prisoner was sent over to this
B   country for the purpose of procuring articles to traffic with the native
Indians, and amongst other things he was directed to procure a
quantity of medals. The prisoner sent to a tradesman in Sheffield, and
showed him a medal with a ring through the upper part of the medal,
and requested to have a number made similar to the one he exhibited.
The tradesman consented to make the medals, and the prisoner gave
C   him an order for 2,500 of these medals. It appeared that the medals
could not be struck from the die with a hole through the top as the
prisoner desired, and therefore the medals were struck in a perfect
state. After a number of the medals had been made, but before
the order was completed, the person at Sheffield from some information he received, discovered that the medals he was making were an
exact representation of a Mexican dollar; he therefore refused to
D   proceed with his work, and caused the prisoner to be apprehended.
There are certain signs and letters upon the Mexican dollars denoting
the value of the coin and the mint at which it is coined, these were all
faithfully represented upon the medals that had been struck."

The indictment was laid under the statute 37 Geo. 3, c. 126, which is
E   entitled:

    " An Act to prevent the counterfeiting any copper coin in this realm
    . . . or any foreign gold or silver coin; and to prevent the bringing
    into this realm, or uttering, any counterfeit foreign gold or silver coin."

The report concludes with the ruling of Rolfe B., at p. 195, which was
in these terms:

F   " . . . the facts and circumstances of the case, together with the conduct
    of the prisoner, proved to his mind that there was no intention on the
    part of the prisoner to use these medals as coin, but merely as orna-
    ments to gratify the taste of the Indians, and to be given in exchange
    for their furs. He was also of opinion that upon his construction of
    the statute on which the prisoner had been indicted, the jury must be
G   satisfied that the intention of the prisoner in procuring these medals to
    be made, was to defraud and cheat the people of this country."

This direction had the immediate result of a verdict of acquittal.
    Mr. Blom-Cooper, while acknowledging that the statutory context was
different from the present case, urged that by analogy a corresponding construction should be put on the provisions of section 1 (1) of the Act of
H   1936. Section 2 of the Act of 1797 enacted:

    " . . . that if any person or persons shall, from and after the passing of
    this Act, make, coin or counterfeit, any kind of coin not the proper
    coin of this realm, nor permitted to be current within the same, but
    resembling, or made with intent to resemble or look like, any gold or
    silver coin of any foreign . . . country, or to pass as such foreign coin,
    such person or persons . . . shall be . . . guilty of felony . . ."

Section 3 went on to make uttering such counterfeit coin an offence if the A utterer knows it to be "false or counterfeit."

The interpretation of Rolfe B. of those provisions may have been influenced by the reputation and standing of the accused, who had wanted the reproduction Mexican dollars made with a hole punched through them so that they could be used as medals. However that may be, the case is not one which affords any real guidance in the construction of the modern B statute.

Two considerations are important. The first is that section 1 is concerned with the preservation of the integrity of current coin of the realm. It is manifest that this is put at risk as soon as spurious coins are brought into existence, for they may, whether by accident or design, pass into circulation. There is an immediate threat to the purity of the coinage, and it seems clear that the object of section 1 (1) is to obviate even the latent C threat by making the very act of counterfeiting an offence in itself. If reinforcement for this view were necessary it is to be found in section 1 (2), which in effect provides that an offence under section 1 (1) shall have been committed although the coin made or counterfeited has not been finished or perfected. This subsection contemplates a situation in which the counterfeited coin may not be in a fit state to be uttered with D any confident prospect of passing it off as genuine. Thus the intent so to pass it off is clearly not an ingredient of the offence of counterfeiting per se.

Counsel for the defendants placed some reliance on the phrase "falsely makes" in subsection (1). He submitted that "falsely" imported a fraudulent intent. This does not appear to this court to be a valid argument. It may be that those words were necessary to cover the situation where an E employee at the mint goes beyond his authority to mint coins of the realm.

A further argument was that, so far as the protection of the purity of the currency was concerned (in contradistinction to actually putting counterfeit coin into circulation), it was section 8 of the Act of 1936 that made provision in that regard; so that it was superfluous to look to section 1, which dealt with a more advanced activity involving a F prospective uttering with intent to defraud.

This is a misconception of the object and design of section 8. What is there enacted is that selling or having in possession articles in the form of "any medal, cast, coin . . . made wholly or partially of metal . . ." which have some element of resemblance to current coin shall be an offence. Under this section an offence is committed even though the article cannot G be said to counterfeit current coin inasmuch as there is only one or some remote factor or factors of resemblance. Section 8 extends the net cast by section 1; it does not displace it. Furthermore, section 8 affords to a person charged under it a possible defence of lawful authority or excuse. No such defence is available to a charge under section 1.

Reliance was also placed on the decision of the House of Lords in H Reg. v. Selby [1972] A.C. 515. That case was, however, concerned with the construction and operation of section 5 of the Coinage Offences Act 1936. The question which there fell to be decided was whether the offence of uttering counterfeit coin involved not only knowledge of its character but also an intent to pass it off as genuine. The opinion of the majority was that such an intent was a necessary ingredient of the offence defined by section 5. The objective of that section was to discourage not the making of

A counterfeit coin but its circulation. Section 1 seeks to strike at the mischief
at source and condemns the first stage in despoiling the currency of the
realm.

For those reasons we dismiss the appeals against conviction.

The court heard submissions on the appeals against sentence, allowed
the appeals and substituted sentences of 2½ years' imprisonment on the
B defendant Heron, two years' imprisonment on the defendant Storey and
1¼ years' imprisonment on the defendant Thomas.

> *Appeals against conviction dismissed.*
> *Appeals against sentence allowed.*
> *Certificate that point of law of public*
> *importance involved, namely,*
C > *" whether or not the offence of*
> *counterfeiting under section 1 (1) (a)*
> *of the Coinage Offences Act 1936*
> *is an absolute offence which re-*
> *quires no element of dishonest*
> *intent."*
D > *Leave to appeal refused.*

Solicitor: *Director of Public Prosecutions.*

[Reported by MISS EIRA CARYL-THOMAS, Barrister-at-Law]

November 12. The Appeal Committee of the House of Lords (Lord
E Wilberforce, Lord Russell of Killowen and Lord Bridge of Harwich)
allowed a petition by the defendants for leave to appeal.

F
[EMPLOYMENT APPEAL TRIBUNAL]

* JENKINS v. KINGSGATE (CLOTHING PRODUCTIONS) LTD.

1981   June 18, 19;   Browne-Wilkinson J.,
       July 3   Mrs. D. Ewing and Mr. J. D. Hughes
G

Discrimination, Sex—Equal pay—Variation due to material differ-
ence—Hourly rates of pay—Full-time employees receiving
higher rates than female part-time employees—Whether varia-
tion due to material difference other than sex—Effect of Com-
munity law on municipal law—Equal Pay Act 1970 (c. 41),
s. 1 (3) (as amended by Sex Discrimination Act 1975 (c. 65),
s. 8 (1))—E.E.C. Treaty (Cmnd. 5179–II), art. 119—Council
H *Directive (75/117/E.E.C.), art. 1*

The employers paid full-time workers 10 per cent. more
per hour than part-time employees in order to discourage
absenteeism in their factory and to achieve a more efficient use
of their machinery. All but one of the part-time workers were
women. The applicant, a woman part-time worker, complained
to an industrial tribunal that the difference in pay between
herself and a full-time male employee contravened the equality
clause in her contract of employment. The industrial tribunal

Jenkins v. Kingsgate Ltd. (E.A.T.) **[1981]**

A dismissed the complaint on the ground that although she was employed on like work as the man, the fact that the man was full-time was a material difference other than the difference of sex within the meaning of section 1 (3) of the Equal Pay Act 1970,[1] which justified a different rate of pay. The industrial tribunal made no finding as to whether the pay differential did in fact reduce absenteeism or increase business efficiency.

On her appeal, the appeal tribunal referred to the European Court of Justice the questions, inter alia, whether the principle B of equal pay in article 119 of the E.E.C. Treaty[2] and article 1 of Council Directive (75/117/E.E.C.) required the same hourly rate of pay irrespective of the number of hours worked and the commercial benefit to an employer to encourage the maximum number of hours worked, and whether those two articles were directly applicable in member states. The European Court of Justice held that a difference in rates of remuneration between full-time and part-time employees did not offend article 119, C provided that the difference was attributable to factors which were objectively justified and did not relate directly or indirectly to discrimination based on sex. They further held that article 119 of the E.E.C. Treaty applied directly where, using the criterion of equal pay for equal work, it was established that the payment of lower rates for part-time work represented discrimination based on sex.

On the reference back to the appeal tribunal:— D

Held, allowing the appeal, that, in accordance with the decision of the European Court of Justice, a difference between full-time and part-time work was a relevant consideration which could sometimes justify a differential in pay; that, in construing the Equal Pay Act 1970 in accordance with article 119 of the E.E.C. Treaty, such a differential could only be a material difference within the meaning of section 1(3) of the Act if the E employers showed that they had no intention to discriminate and that the differential was in fact an effective or necessary way to reduce absenteeism and increase utilisation of their machinery; and that, therefore, the case would be remitted to the industrial tribunal to consider whether the differential in rates was in fact reasonably necessary to achieve greater business efficiency (post, pp. 1491H—1492c, H, 1493H—1494B, 1495G—1496A). F

The following cases are referred to in the judgment:

Clay Cross (Quarry Services) Ltd. v. *Fletcher* [1978] 1 W.L.R. 1429; [1979] I.C.R. 1; [1979] 1 All E.R. 474, C.A.

Durrant v. *North Yorkshire Area Health Authority* [1979] I.R.L.R. 401, E.A.T.

Griggs v. *Duke Power Co.* (1971) 401 U.S. 424. G

Handley v. *H. Mono Ltd.* [1979] I.C.R. 147, E.A.T.

Kearns v. *Trust Houses Forte Catering Ltd.* (unreported), June 15, 1978.

Macarthys Ltd. v. *Smith* (Case 129/79) [1981] Q.B. 180; [1980] 3 W.L.R. 929; [1980] I.C.R. 672; [1980] 1 All E.R. 111, E.C.J. and C.A.

Shields v. *E. Coomes (Holdings) Ltd.* [1978] 1 W.L.R. 1408; [1978] I.C.R. 1159; [1979] 1 All E.R. 456, C.A. H

The following additional cases were cited in argument:

Dothard v. *Rawlinson* (1977) 433 U.S. 321.

Dugdale v. *Kraft Foods Ltd.* [1976] 1 W.L.R. 1288; [1977] I.C.R. 48; [1977] 1 All E.R. 454, E.A.T.

[1] Equal Pay Act 1970, s. 1 (3) as amended: see post, p. 1490E.
[2] E.E.C. Treaty, art. 119: see post, p. 1490E–G.

A   *Electrolux Ltd.* v. *Hutchinson* [1977] I.C.R. 252, E.A.T.
National Coal Board v. *Sherwin* [1978] I.C.R. 700, E.A.T.
Panesar v. *Nestlé Co. Ltd.* (*Note*) [1980] I.C.R. 144, C.A.
Singh v. *Rowntree MacKintosh Ltd.* [1979] I.C.R. 554, E.A.T.
Worringham v. *Lloyds Bank Ltd.* [1979] I.C.R. 174, E.A.T.

B   APPEAL from an industrial tribunal sitting at London.

The applicant, Jeanette Pauline Jenkins, complained that the employers, Kingsgate (Clothing Productions) Ltd., were in breach of the equality clause in her contract of employment by paying her 10 per cent. less per hour than a male employee. The industrial tribunal dismissed her complaint, holding that although she was employed on like work with the male employee, the difference in pay was due to a material difference other than

C   sex within the meaning of section 1 (3) of the Equal Pay Act 1970. The applicant appealed.

The Employment Appeal Tribunal referred to the European Court of Justice questions relating to whether a different rate of pay for part-time workers contravened article 119 of the E.E.C. Treaty and article 1 of Council Directive (75/117/E.E.C.) and whether the two articles were

D   directly applicable in member states.

The European Court of Justice held that a difference in rates of pay between full and part-time workers did not contravene article 119 provided that the difference did not relate either directly or indirectly to discrimination based on sex, and that article 119 applied directly to the situation: see [1981] 1 W.L.R. 972; [1981] I.C.R. 592. The case was referred back to the Employment Appeal Tribunal for the determination

E   of the applicant's appeal in the light of the European Court's judgment.

The facts are stated in the judgment.

Anthony Lester Q.C. and *John Hand* for the applicant.
B. J. Clayman, director, for the employers.

F   *Cur. adv. vult.*

July 3. BROWNE-WILKINSON J. read the following judgment of the appeal tribunal. In this case, the applicant, Mrs. Jenkins, a part-time worker, is claiming that she ought to be paid the same hourly rate as that paid to full-time male employees of Kingsgate (Clothing Productions)

G   Ltd., the employers. Her claim was originally brought solely under the Equal Pay Act 1970, but, as will appear, she now also relies on article 119 of the E.E.C. Treaty.

Her claim was dismissed by an industrial tribunal sitting in London. The industrial tribunal gave their reasons very shortly. However, this case was referred by the appeal tribunal to the European Court of Justice for their ruling and the order making that reference sets out many more

H   facts than are contained in the findings of the industrial tribunal. We understand that the statement of facts set out in the order was agreed by the parties. They must therefore now be taken to be the established facts. They are as follows.

The employers are manufacturers of ladies' clothing at a factory in Harlow, Essex, where they employ 90 workers. Prior to 1975 the employers paid their male and female workers at different rates but there was no difference in the hourly rate of pay of full-time and part-time workers,

whether male or female. By November 1975, the full-time rate of pay, that   **A**
is the rate for those working 40 hours per week, was equalised for male
and female workers. However, part-time workers, that is, those working for
fewer than 40 hours per week, were paid 10 per cent. less than the full-
time rate. The difference between the full-time and the part-time rates
was introduced as a result of negotiations between representatives of the
employers and representatives of the relevant trade union whereby it was
further agreed that the lower hourly rate would also be applicable to any   **B**
full-time worker who persistently failed to work 40 hours per week.

The employers maintained the difference in pay rates as between full-
time and part-time workers to discourage absenteeism in their factory and
to try to ensure that all their expensive machinery was being used for as
many hours every day as was possible.

The applicant, who was regarded by the employers as expert at her   **C**
job, was engaged on like work with Mr. Bannan as a special machinist
(grade 2). She worked either a little more or a little less than 30 hours per
week. In the section where she worked there were 17 machines and five
machinists. None of the machines was regarded as being the applicant's
own particular machine. Some of the machines were used more often than
others, according to the work requirements, and when the work in hand did   **D**
not require the use of a particular machine that machine would stand idle.
Some of the machines were duplicated to cope with extra work. The applicant operated several machines, including the bluffing, basting and button-
holing machine. She might use four different machines in the course of two
hours depending on the type of work to be done.

Overtime was available to full-time workers who worked more than nine
hours a day, their normal working week of 40 hours being divided into   **E**
five days. Saturday morning overtime was available to both full-time and
part-time workers and the applicant sometimes worked on Saturday morn-
ings when she received her basic rate of pay plus a supplement of $37\frac{1}{2}$ per
cent. of her basic rate.

At the date of her application to the industrial tribunal the part-time
workers were all women. At the date of the hearing before the industrial   **F**
tribunal there was a male part-time worker who had recently retired and
had unusually been allowed to stay on beyond normal retiring age. His was
regarded as an exceptional case and he had worked 16 hours per week since
January 2, 1979, retaining his staff status and not clocking in but being
paid at 10 per cent. less than the hourly rate he had received before retirement. He was a skilled craftsman capable of doing almost all jobs in the
factory. It was a mutually convenient arrangement between him and the   **G**
employers but was subject to a six to eight week trial period.

By their decision of February 5, 1979, the industrial tribunal held that
(1) they were bound to follow the decision of the appeal tribunal in *Handley*
v. *H. Mono Ltd.* [1979] I.C.R. 147; (2) the applicant was working only 75
per cent. of a 40-hour week; and this was a substantial difference which
justified the difference in the hourly rate of pay between herself and Mr.   **H**
Bannan; (3) any difference in the basic rates as between full and part-time
workers " smacks of inequality among the sexes because by the very nature
of things the part-time workers are bound to be mostly women, even though
as in this case the [employers] had very good reason for paying the part-
time workers less."

The industrial tribunal accordingly upheld the employers' defence under
section 1 (3) of the Act of 1970 and rejected the applicant's claim. She

A   appealed to the appeal tribunal and initially contended that the proper interpretation of section 1 (3) of the Act was that, as a matter of law, a mere difference in the number of hours worked each week was not capable of affording the employers a defence.

In the course of argument, counsel for the applicant conceded that *Kearns* v. *Trust Houses Forte Catering Ltd.* (unreported), June 15, 1978; B   *Handley* v. *H. Mono Ltd.* [1979] I.C.R. 147 and *Durrant* v. *North Yorkshire Area Health Authority* [1979] I.R.L.R. 401, precluded him from succeeding under the Act of 1970 read in isolation from European Community law, but he reserved the applicant's right to contend on any appeal to the Court of Appeal that the previous cases had been wrongly decided.

Counsel for the applicant submitted that the equal pay provisions of article 119 of the E.E.C. Treaty and article 1 of Council Directive (75/117/ C   E.E.C.) affected the case and that there were questions of interpretation which ought to be immediately referred to the European Court of Justice. The employers did not oppose this course and the preliminary ruling of the European Court of Justice was accordingly requested on the following questions:

" 1. Does the principle of equal pay, contained in article 119 of the D   E.E.C. Treaty and article 1 of Council Directive (75/117/E.E.C.) require that pay for work at time rates shall be the same, irrespective: (a) of the number of hours worked each week, or (b) of whether it is of commercial benefit to the employer to encourage the doing of the maximum possible hours of work and consequently to pay a higher rate to workers doing 40 hours per week than to workers doing fewer E   than 40 hours per week?

" 2. If the answer to question 1(a) or (b) is in the negative, what criteria should be used in determining whether or not the principle of equal pay applies where there is a difference in the time rates of pay related to the total number of hours worked each week?

" 3. Would the answer to question 1(a) or (b) or 2 be different (and, F   if so, in what respects) if it were shown that a considerably smaller proportion of female workers than of male workers is able to perform the minimum number of hours each week required to qualify for the full hourly rate of pay?

" 4. Are the relevant provisions of article 119 of the E.E.C. Treaty or article 1 of the said Directive, as the case may be, directly applicable G   in member states in the circumstances of the present case? "

As appears from the decision of the European Court of Justice, in the United Kingdom 93 per cent. of all part-time workers are women. Therefore, not only in relation to these particular employers but in general, the impact of lower pay for part-time workers bears much more heavily on women than on men.

H   Two points should be noted at this stage. First, the agreed facts we have stated negate any intention by the employers to discriminate against women. Secondly, there is no finding by the industrial tribunal or agreement between the parties that the pay differential was in fact effective or required to reduce absenteeism or to increase the utilisation of the employers' machinery: the only finding or agreement is that it was for those purposes and with that intention that the employers maintained the pay differential. The importance of those points will emerge in due course.

The opinion of Advocate General J.-P. Warner was delivered on A
January 28, 1981, and the judgment of the full court of the European
Court of Justice was delivered on March 31, 1981: see [1981] 1 W.L.R.
972. We will have to refer to this judgment again in due course but at
this stage it is sufficient to state the formal ruling of the full court, at
p. 984:

"1. A difference in pay between full-time workers and part-time B
workers does not amount to discrimination prohibited by article 119
of the Treaty unless it is in reality merely an indirect way of reducing
the pay of part-time workers on the ground that that group of workers
is composed exclusively or predominantly of women.
"2. Where the national court is able, using the criteria of equal
work and equal pay, without the operation of Community or national
measures, to establish that the payment of lower hourly rates of re- C
muneration for part-time work than for full-time work represents discrimination based on difference of sex the provisions of article 119
of the Treaty apply directly to such a situation."

The case now comes back before us to apply those rulings in the present
case.

Section 1 (2) of the Equal Pay Act 1970, as amended, implies into every D
contract of employment an equality clause which has the effect that where
a woman is employed on "like work" with a man in the same employment
her pay for such work must be at the same rate as the man's pay. There is
no dispute that the applicant's work was like work to that done by one
of the full-time male employees. However, section 1 (3) provides:

"An equality clause shall not operate in relation to a variation between E
the woman's contract and the man's contract if the employer proves
that the variation is genuinely due to a material difference (other than
the difference of sex) between her case and his."

Article 119 of the E.E.C. Treaty provides:

"Each member state shall during the first stage ensure and subsequently maintain the application of the principle that men and women F
should receive equal pay for equal work.
"For the purpose of this article, 'pay' means the ordinary basic
or minimum wage or salary and any other consideration, whether in
cash or in kind, which the worker receives, directly or indirectly, in
respect of his employment from his employer.
"Equal pay without discrimination based on sex means: (a) that G
pay for the same work at piece rates shall be calculated on the basis
of the same unit of measurement; (b) that pay for work at time rates
shall be the same for the same job."

The questions which arise in this case as a result of the judgment of the
European Court of Justice are as follows. (1) Is the fact that the woman
is a part-time worker and the comparable man a full-time worker by H
itself, and without more, "a material difference" within section 1 (3) of the
Act of 1970 such as to prevent the equality clause from operating? (2) Is
the fact that the woman is a part-time worker and the comparable man
a full-time worker an irrelevant factor in considering whether there is a
material difference for the purposes of section 1 (3)? (3) Is the fact (if it be
a fact) that the differential in pay between part-time workers and full-time

A   workers encourages greater utilisation of the employers' plant and discourages absenteeism a relevant or sufficient material difference for the purposes of section 1 (3)? (4) Is it sufficient for the purposes of section 1 (3) of the Act of 1970 and article 119 for the employers to show only that they had no intention of discriminating or must they also show that the differential in pay is objectively justified for some other reason?

B   Before considering these questions we must say a word about the effect of article 119 on the internal United Kingdom law. It is now established that article 119 applies directly in the United Kingdom at least for the purposes of this case: see ruling 2 of the European Court of Justice. Therefore, under section 2 (1) of the European Communities Act 1972, article 119 is to be " recognised and available in law, and be enforced, allowed and followed accordingly." Under section 2 (4) of the Act " any enactment

C   passed or to be passed . . . shall be construed and have effect subject to the foregoing provisions of this section." Although difficult questions may arise in cases where the clear construction of the internal United Kingdom statute conflicts with article 119, where there is any ambiguity as to the ambit or meaning of an internal United Kingdom statute it ought to be construed so as to accord with article 119: see *Macarthys Ltd.* v. *Smith*

D   [1981] Q.B. 180, 201–202. In our view, there is an ambiguity as to the exact meaning of the words in section 1 (3) of the Act of 1970 " genuinely due to a material difference (other than the difference of sex) between her case and his." Therefore, to the extent that the judgment of the European Court of Justice indicates the effect of article 119, section 1 (3) of the Act of 1970 should be construed so far as possible as having the same effect. However, as we understand the matter, although the

E   United Kingdom statutes are to be construed as far as possible so as to confer rights at least as great as those conferred by article 119, there is in law no reason why the United Kingdom statutes should not confer greater rights than those conferred by article 119.

We turn then to the four questions mentioned above.

F   (1) *Is the difference between part-time and full-time work by itself a material difference?*

The decision of the appeal tribunal in *Kearns* v. *Trust Houses Forte Catering Ltd.* (unreported), June 15, 1978, is in our judgment a clear decision that the difference between part-time and full-time work is by itself " a material difference " for the purposes of section 1 (3). In *Handley*

G   v. *H. Mono Ltd.* [1979] I.C.R. 147 there are passages in the judgment which indicate the same view, although the *Kearns* case was not apparently cited: Slynn J. at p. 155F, referred to a part-time job being " basically a different kind of job in the quantitative sense." But in that case there were other material points which the appeal tribunal took into account in holding that, on the facts of that case, there was " a material difference," as Slynn J. pointed out on the first hearing of this case before the appeal tribunal.

H   Slynn J. also pointed out that there were material points (apart from the simple fact that the woman was a part-time worker) which arose for consideration in *Durrant* v. *North Yorkshire Area Health Authority* [1979] I.R.L.R. 401.

In our judgment the decision of the European Court of Justice clearly establishes that a differential in pay cannot be justified simply by showing that the women are part-time workers. The ruling we have already quoted

demonstrates that something more has to be shown. What that " something A
more " is, we will consider in dealing with question 4 below.

Therefore, in our judgment, where the circumstances are such that part-
time workers are wholly or mainly women, an employer cannot justify
paying less for like work to a part-time woman than to a full-time man by
simply relying on the fact that the woman is a part-time employee. *Kearns*
v. *Trust Houses Forte Catering Ltd.* can no longer be regarded as good law.
    B

(2) *Is the difference between full-time and part-time work an irrelevant
factor in considering whether there is a " material difference "?*

We are not sure whether Mr. Lester, for the applicant, ever put his case
as high as to submit that the difference between part-time and full-time
work was wholly irrelevant when considering the question whether there was C
a " material difference " for the purposes of section 1 (3). The judgment of
the European Court of Justice certainly establishes that this is a relevant
consideration which can in some circumstances justify a differential in pay.
What those circumstances are we will again consider when dealing with
question 4 below.

(3) *Is the fact that a differential in pay between part-time and full-time
workers achieves greater utilisation of plant or reduces absenteeism a
" material difference "?*   D

We must emphasise that this question arises only if employers prove
that the differential in pay in fact produces these results: it does not deal
with the case where an employer intends to produce these results without
showing that the results are in fact produced.   E

Mr. Lester submitted, in reliance on the decision of the Court of Appeal
in *Clay Cross (Quarry Services) Ltd.* v. *Fletcher* [1978] 1 W.L.R. 1429, that
the attainment by the employers of other objectives which relate solely
to the profitability of their business were extrinsic factors and could not be
regarded as relevant " material differences." In the *Clay Cross* case, the
employer relied on the fact that the man who was receiving higher pay had F
been the sole applicant for the job and had demanded higher pay. The
employer submitted that this constituted " a material difference." The
Court of Appeal rejected this submission, saying that to constitute a
material difference one had to look at the personal equations of the woman
and the man (i.e. matters personal to them and to their work) and that
reasons "personal to the employer " or " economic factors " were irrelevant. By analogy, Mr. Lester argued that considerations such as increasing G
the utilisation of plant were economic factors personal to the employers
which could not constitute a " material difference."

The first question put to the European Court of Justice was directed to
this submission. Before us, Mr. Lester accepted that the decision of the
European Court of Justice really concluded the point against him. Paragraph 12 of the judgment [1981] 1 W.L.R. 972, 983, gives as an example H
of a case where a pay differential may be justified where an " employer
is endeavouring, on economic grounds which may be objectively justified,
to encourage full-time work irrespective of the sex of the worker."

Therefore, in our judgment a differential in pay between part-time
workers, who are predominantly women, and full-time male workers can
be justified as being due to a material difference by showing that the pay
differential does in fact achieve economic advantages for the employer.

A (4) *Is it sufficient for the purposes of section 1 (3) of the Act of 1970 and article 119 for the employer to show only that he had no intention of discriminating or must he also show that the differential in pay is objectively justified for some other reason?*

This is the question which has caused us the greatest difficulty. It is highlighted in this case because of the findings of fact of the industrial tribunal and the facts agreed by the parties. No one has yet apparently con-
B sidered whether the payment of a lower rate of pay to part-time workers in this case is in fact an effective or necessary way to reduce absenteeism and increase utilisation of the employers' machinery. All that has been found is that the pay differential was introduced with that intention thereby ne-gating an intention to discriminate against women. Therefore, in order to decide this appeal, we have to answer this question: unfortunately it is not
C one on which the judgment of the European Court of Justice gives us clear guidance.

It is desirable first to state the sense in which we are using certain terminology. We use the phrase "direct discrimination" to mean cases where a distinction is drawn between the rights of men and the rights of women overtly on the ground of their sex. "Indirect discrimination" covers
D cases where, because a class of persons consist wholly or mainly of women, a difference drawn between that class and other persons operates in fact in a manner which is discriminatory against women, e.g. the present case. Indirect discrimination may itself be either intentional or unintentional. It is intentional if the employer (although not overtly discriminating) treats the class differently because he intends to differentiate on grounds of sex, i.e. he is dissimulating his real intentions. Indirect discrimination is uninten-
E tional where the employer has no intention of discriminating against women on the ground of sex but intends to achieve some different purpose, such as the greater utilization of his machinery.

The fact that indirect discrimination is unintentional does not necessarily mean that it is lawful. Thus, under the Sex Discrimination Act 1975, indirect discrimination is rendered unlawful by section 1 (1) (*b*) even if it is unin-
F tentional. To escape acting unlawfully, the alleged discriminator has to show that the requirement which operates in a discriminatory fashion is justi-fiable because, viewed objectively, the requirement is reasonably necessary to achieve some other purpose. The same is true in relation to racial dis-crimination under the Race Relations Act 1976, and under the law of the United States of America: see *Griggs* v. *Duke Power Co.* (1971) 401 U.S. 424. The question we have to decide is whether the same principle applies
G to section 1 (3) of the Act of 1970, or whether for the purposes of section 1 (3) it is enough to show that the employer had no actual covert intention of discriminating against women.

Were it not for the judgment of the European Court of Justice, we would have held that section 1 (3) requires an employer to do more than disprove an intention to discriminate. The equality clause implied by
H section 1 (2) of the Act of 1970 operates to counteract all discrimination whether direct or indirect and whether intentional or unintentional: it looks at the effect of the contractual terms, not at whether they are expressed in overtly discriminatory words or with any particular intention. Section 1 (3) then operates by taking out of subsection (2) those cases where the variation in the terms between men and women is "genuinely due to a material difference (other than the difference of sex) between her case and

his." The words "genuinely" and "other than the difference of sex" A
plainly prevent an employer who is intentionally discriminating (whether
directly or indirectly) from escaping the effect of the equality clause. In
our view, for the variation in pay to be "due to" a material difference it
would have to be shown that there was some other matter which in fact
justified the variation. It would not be enough simply to show that the employer had an intention to achieve some other legitimate objective (although
this might disprove any intention to discriminate): the employer would B
have to show that the pay differential actually achieved that different
objective.

This view is supported by authority. In *Shields* v. *E. Coomes (Holdings)
Ltd.* [1978] 1 W.L.R. 1408, the Court of Appeal held that so far as possible
the Sex Discrimination Act 1975 and the Equal Pay Act 1970 should be
construed together so as to produce a harmonious result. Bridge L.J. said, C
at pp. 1425–1426:

"In the sphere of employment the provisions of the Sex Discrimination Act 1975 and the Equal Pay Act 1970 aimed at eliminating discrimination on the ground of sex are closely interlocking and provide
in effect a single comprehensive code. The particular provisions
designed to prevent overlapping between the two statutes are complex, D
and it may often be difficult to determine whether a particular matter
of complaint falls to be redressed under one Act or the other. But what
is abundantly clear is that both Acts should be construed and applied
as a harmonious whole and in such a way that the broad principles
which underlie the whole scheme of legislation are not frustrated by a
narrow interpretation or restrictive application of particular provisions." E

To make section 1 (3) of the Act of 1970 accord harmoniously with section
1 (1) (b) of the Sex Discrimination Act 1975 requires that it should be
construed as imposing on the employer the onus of proving that the variation in pay is in fact reasonably required to achieve some other objective.

Moreover, in the *Clay Cross* case [1978] 1 W.L.R. 1429, Lord Denning F
M.R. treated the principles laid down in the *Griggs* case as applicable to
section 1 (3) of the Act of 1970. The principle of the *Griggs* case is that
requirements which operate in an indirectly discriminatory fashion have
to be objectively justified as being required for some purpose other than
a purpose linked to the sex of the person on whom the requirement is
imposed. This again indicates that section 1 (3) is not satisfied merely by
the employer showing that he had no intention to discriminate. G

However, when one turns to the judgment of the European Court of
Justice one is left in considerable doubt as to the effect of article 119 in
relation to unintentional indirect discrimination. There are passages in the
judgment which support the view that it is not enough for the employer
simply to show that he had no intention of discriminating. Thus in paragraph 11 [1981] 1 W.L.R. 972, 982–983, the judgment states that in cases H
where both male and female part-time workers are paid less than full-time
workers:

"the fact that work paid at time rates is remunerated at an hourly
rate which varies according to the number of hours worked per week
does not offend against the principle of equal pay laid down in article
119 of the Treaty in so far as the difference in pay between part-time

A   work and full-time work is attributable to factors which are objectively justified and are in no way related to any discrimination based on sex."

This approach is again reflected in paragraph 12 of the judgment and echoes the opinion of the advocate general. He adopted the approach of the United States Supreme Court in the *Griggs* case and plainly required that indirect

B   discrimination must be objectively justified irrespective of the employer's intention.

On the other hand the formal ruling of the full court seems to approach the matter on the basis that if, by showing some other intention, the employer negates any covert intention to discriminate there will be no infringement of article 119; this same approach is reflected in paragraphs 14 and 15 of the judgment.

C   We will assume, without deciding, that article 119 as construed by the European Court of Justice does not apply to cases of unintentional indirect discrimination. How then are we to construe the United Kingdom statute? Although we must construe the United Kingdom legislation so as not to conflict with article 119 and so far as possible to make it accord with article 119, it does not necessarily follow that the United Kingdom legisla-

D   tion must in all respects have the same effect as article 119. It would not contravene section 2 of the European Communities Act 1972 if the United Kingdom statutes conferred on employees greater rights than they enjoy under article 119. Since the Act of 1970 is an integral part of one code against sex discrimination and the rest of the code plainly renders unlawful indirect discrimination even if unintentional, it seems to us right that we should construe the Equal Pay Act 1970 as requiring any difference in pay to

E   be objectively justified even if this confers on employees greater rights than they would enjoy under article 119 of the E.E.C. Treaty. We therefore hold that in order to show a " material difference " within section 1 (3) of the Act of 1970 an employer must show that the lower pay for part-time workers is in fact reasonably necessary in order to achieve some objective other than an objective related to the sex of the part-time worker.

F   To sum up, an industrial tribunal in considering cases of part-time workers under the Act of 1970 will have to consider the following points. (1) Do the part-time workers consist mainly of women? (2) Do the part-time workers do " like work " to full-time male employees of the same employer? (3) If the answers to (1) and (2) are " yes ", the equality clause will apply unless the employer can justify the differential in pay by show-

G   ing a material difference for the purposes of section 1 (3). (4) If the industrial tribunal finds that the employer intended to discriminate against women by paying part-time workers less, the employer cannot succeed under section 1 (3). (5) Even if the employers had no such intention, for section 1 (3) to apply the employer must show that the difference in pay between full-time and part-time workers is reasonably necessary in order to obtain some result (other than cheap female labour) which the employer

H   desires for economic or other reasons.

Applying these principles to the present case, the industrial tribunal decided in favour of the employers on the short ground that the fact that the applicant was a part-time worker whereas the comparable man was a full-time worker was, by itself, a material difference for the purposes of section 1 (3). That is not a correct approach in law. We must therefore allow the appeal. We will remit the case to the industrial tribunal to find

whether the lower rate of pay for part-time workers paid by the employers A
in this case was in fact reasonably necessary in order to enable the employers to reduce absenteeism and to obtain the maximum utilisation of
their plant.

We are conscious that our decision may have far-reaching consequences. In particular it is likely to involve many industrial and other
employers in increased labour costs at a time when they and the country B
can ill afford it. This in turn may lead to a decrease in the total number
of women employed. But it is not our function to weigh these factors,
even if we were capable of assessing them, against the merits of the
social policy reflected in the Acts of 1970 and 1975. Our function is
simply to seek to apply the law as it now is. It is unfortunate that in a
case of such importance we have not had the advantage of legal argument C
on behalf of the employers and we would welcome an early consideration
of the matter by a higher court.

Finally we remit this case with considerable reluctance. The employers
are not a large company and, without having any evil discriminatory intentions, have been caught up in a long test case raising questions of fundamental importance to the Equal Opportunities Commission and to women
employees in general but of small importance to the employers. Not sur- D
prisingly, they have felt unable to go on incurring legal costs in these proceedings. We suggest that before the Equal Opportunities Commission and
the applicant put this small company to even more expense and trouble by
a further hearing before the industrial tribunal, consideration might be given
to whether it is not possible to reach agreement as to whether, in this particular case, the employers can or cannot satisfy the requirements we have
sought to summarise above.   E

                              Appeal allowed.
                              Case remitted to industrial tribunal.

Solicitors: *Mills, Curry & Gaskell.*

                                                        J. W.
                                                                         F

_____

[PRIVY COUNCIL]

* PERDANA PROPERTIES BHD.   .   .   .   .   APPELLANT

AND

UNITED ORIENT LEASING CO. SDN. BHD. . . RESPONDENT G

[APPEAL FROM THE FEDERAL COURT OF MALAYSIA]

1981   July 14;   Lord Diplock, Lord Russell of Killowen,
       Oct. 15   Lord Bridge of Harwich, Sir John Megaw
                                   and Sir Owen Woodhouse
                                                                         H

    *Bailment—Leasing agreement—Hire of equipment—Letter with-
       drawing lessor's consent to lessee's possession of equipment
       — Distress warrant issued against lessee's goods — Whether
       equipment in possession of lessee with owner's consent —
       Whether withdrawal of consent effective without termination
       of lease agreement*

        A tenant of premises leased equipment which it kept and
    used on the premises from a leasing company under a written

The Weekly Law Reports, December 11, 1981

1497

1 W.L.R.   Perdana Properties Bhd. v. United Orient Leasing Co. Sdn. Bhd. (P.C.)

A   lease agreement. Some of the tenant's creditors obtained judgments against it and the equipment was seized in execution.
On the same day the leasing company wrote a letter to the
tenant giving notice that as owner of the equipment the
company was assuming immediate possession of it. Some
days later, under an order of the court, the landlord of the
premises took out a warrant of distress for arrears of rent.
Subsequently the leasing company secured the release of its
B   equipment but it was immediately seized again in the landlord's suit for rent arrears. The leasing company applied to
the High Court under section 10 of the Distress Ordinance
1951 [1] for an order that the equipment should be released to
it as owner. The High Court refused the application on the
ground that the equipment was property held by the tenant
by consent of the owner in such circumstances that the tenant
was the reputed owner of it and that, therefore, it fell within
C   the exception to section 10 of the Ordinance created by
section 12.
        On the landlord's appeal to the Judicial Committee: —
        Held, dismissing the appeal, that a lessor's consent to a
lessee's continued possession of equipment hired to it under a
written agreement could be withdrawn without the necessity
for terminating the agreement itself and that since by its
terms the leasing company's letter to the tenant had been
D   sufficient to indicate that it withdrew its consent to the
tenant's continued possession of the equipment, the equipment
had not been in the tenant's possession by consent of its
owner, and that, therefore, section 12 of the Distress
Ordinance 1951 did not apply and the leasing company had
been entitled to have the equipment released to it on its
application under section 10 of the Ordinance (post, pp. 1499E–
G, 1500D–E).
E   Decision of the Federal Court of Malaysia affirmed.

The following cases are referred to in their Lordship's judgment:
Times Furnishing Co. Ltd. v. Hutchings [1938] 1 K.B. 775; [1938] 1 All
    E.R. 422.
Smart Brothers Ltd. v. Holt [1929] 2 K.B. 303, D.C.

F   No additional cases were cited in argument.

APPEAL (No. 35 of 1980) by Perdana Properties Bhd., the landlord,
from a judgment (April 2, 1980) of the Federal Court of Malaysia (Wan
Suleiman, Syed Othman and Ibrahim Manan F.JJ.) by which it allowed
an appeal by United Orient Leasing Co. Sdn. Bhd. from a judgment
(November 15, 1979) of Annuar J. in the High Court of Malaya by which
G   he dismissed the leasing company's application under section 10 of the
Distress Ordinance 1951 for the release of its equipment which had been
distrained in the landlord's suit against its tenant, Emporium President
and Supermarket, Johore Tower, Johore Bahru, for arrears of rent for
premises let by the landlord to the tenant.
    The facts are stated in the judgment of their Lordships.

H
    John Stuart Colyer Q.C. and Ong Ban Chai and G. J. Nijar (both
advocates and solicitors of the High Court of Malaya) for the landlord.
    Gerald Godfrey Q.C. and Wong Kim Fatt (advocate and solicitor of
the High Court of Malaya) for the leasing company.

                                                        Cur. adv. vult.

---

[1] Distress Ordinance 1951, s. 10: see post, pp. 1498H—1499A.
    S. 12: see post, p. 1499B–C.

October 15.   The judgment of their Lordships was delivered by A
LORD RUSSELL OF KILLOWEN.

This appeal involves a dispute between the appellant landlord, which
sought to distrain for rent arrears on equipment used by its tenant
Emporium President and Supermarket at Johore Tower, Johore Bahru,
and the respondent, the leasing company which owned the equipment
which it had leased to the tenant for use in its trade at those premises. B
Potentially the case raised a number of questions, but in the opinion of
their Lordships the answer to one question is fatal to the success of this
appeal, and it is not proposed to discuss other questions that otherwise
might have arisen.

The tenant ran into financial difficulties in 1979 and suffered judgments
at the suit of one or more creditors. On September 3, 1979, the equipment C
and no doubt other articles at the premises had been seized in execution
of those judgments under orders of the sessions court by the bailiff of that
court. On the same day the leasing company wrote to the tenant in the
following terms:

> "Re: lease agreements: 79–183; 79–199. It has come to our
> knowledge that your company's trading premises in the Johor Tower, D
> Johor Baru, is the subject of orders of attachment by your creditors
> today. Accordingly, in accordance with article 21 (b) of the lease
> agreements and also your failure to pay the overdue rents, we hereby,
> without prejudice to the terms and conditions of the above two lease
> agreements, give you notice that as owner of the equipment under
> lease to you, we are assuming immediate possession of our equipment
> under the above two lease agreements." E

On September 4, 1979, the landlord took out a warrant of distress for
rent arrears: this however was not pursuant to a relevant court authority
therefor, and on September 19, at the instance of the leasing company,
claiming ownership of the equipment, the High Court on that ground
discharged the warrant of distress. On the same date, September 19, 1979,
the landlord took out a warrant of distress, this time with the authority F
of a court order (suit No. 12 of 1979), and served it on the bailiff of the
sessions court. On October 22, 1979, the sessions court ordered the release
of the equipment to the leasing company, the execution creditors not
objecting. It would seem that the equipment was released to the leasing
company by the bailiff pursuant to that order on October 22, but
immediately afterwards was or was purported to be seized under the G
warrant of distress in suit No. 12 of 1979.

On October 23, 1979, the leasing company issued an originating motion
in the High Court in the proceedings the subject of this appeal, seeking
an order that the equipment be released to it. On November 15, 1979,
Anuar J. dismissed the motion with costs. On appeal by the leasing company the Federal Court allowed the appeal on April 2, 1980. Final leave H
to appeal to the Yang di-Pertuan Agong was granted by the Federal Court
on August 4, 1980.

The one question for discussion already mentioned arises under sections
10 and 12 of the Distress Ordinance 1951 (No. 28 of 1951). Section 10,
so far as now material, provides that:

> "Where any moveable property of—... (c) any ... person ... not
> being a tenant of the premises or of any part thereof, and not having

The Weekly Law Reports, December 11, 1981

1499

1 W.L.R.   Perdana Properties Bhd. v. United Orient Leasing Co. Sdn. Bhd. (P.C.)

A   any beneficial interest in any tenancy of the premises or any part
thereof, has been seized under a warrant of distress issued to recover
arrears of rent due to a superior landlord by his immediate tenant,
such ... person ... may apply to a judge ... to release a distrained
article . . ."

It is not disputed that the leasing company is the owner of the equip-
B ment and otherwise fulfils the criteria of section 10: thus there was
jurisdiction to order the release of the equipment in these proceedings to
the leasing company if section 10 applies. It was however contended for
the landlord that section 10 was excluded by section 12. Section 12, so far
as material, provides as follows:

     " The provisions of section 10 shall not apply—(1) ... to goods in the
C   possession, order, or disposition of such tenant by the consent and
permission of the true owner under such circumstances that such
tenant is the reputed owner thereof; ...."

The short point is whether in the light of the letter dated September 3,
1979, it could thereafter be said that the equipment was in the possession
of the tenant by the consent and permission of the leasing company.
D Counsel for the landlord accepted that he must surmount that hurdle at
the outset (and before any discussion of reputed ownership) if he was to
dispute the availability of section 10. It was accepted that consent to
possession could be effectively withdrawn by a communication simply
from the leasing company to the tenant, without the need to inform, e.g.
the landlord. But it was contended (1) that for effective withdrawal of
E consent it was necessary that the lease of the equipment should be wholly
determined, which the letter of September 3, did not purport to do; (2)
that that letter in the light of the language of the equipment leases was in
any event not an act which would convey to the tenant that consent was
withdrawn.

On point (1), their Lordships' attention was drawn to the cases of
Times Furnishing Co. Ltd. v. *Hutchings* [1938] 1 K.B. 775 and *Smart
F Bros. Ltd.* v. *Holt* [1929] 2 K.B. 303 in the first of which it was held that
though the hire purchase agreement was terminated the consent was not
withdrawn, and in the second of which the agreement was terminated.
These cases do not establish that the relevant consent cannot be withdrawn unless the relevant agreement of lease or hire is terminated, and
their Lordships do not accept the proposition. Suppose the letter of
G September 3 to have said expressly " accordingly our consent to your
continued possession of the equipment is hereby withdrawn," their Lordships do not see why that should not have effect according to its tenor:
and in their Lordships' view that express statement is inherent in the
letter which could not be understood in any other sense by the tenant.

On point (2) it is necessary to look at the clauses of the lease agree-
H ments (in identical form) referred to in the letter. Article 21, so far as
relevant, provides as follows:

     " Should any one of the following events take place, the [leasing
company] may without any prior notice or demand to the [tenant]
exercise any or all of the remedies as provided for in paragraph (1)
of article 17 hereof and the effects thereof shall be the same as
those provided for in paragraph (2) of article 17: . . . (b) on the

A

[tenant] being the subject of any writ of execution or distress, attachment or disposition (regardless of whether or not the same affects the equipment). . . ."

Article 17, so far as relevant, provides as follows:

" (1) If the [tenant] fails to pay the rent provided for in article 3 hereof after the same becomes due and payable or any other sums and moneys due and payable under this lease agreement or if the [tenant] fails to observe or perform all and any provision of this lease agreement or if the [leasing company] shall on any reasonable ground consider itself insecure the [leasing company] shall without prejudice to any pre-existing liability of the [tenant] to the [leasing company] have the right forthwith to exercise all or any of the following remedies without having to give any prior notice or demand to the [tenant]: . . . (b) to take possession of the equipment or demand its return; (c) to terminate the lease hereby created and to demand from the [tenant] the full amount of the agreed loss value and in addition thereto claim from the [tenant] for compensation for all loss and damages including but not limited to loss of profits. (2) Even if any of the remedies provided for in sub-paragraphs (a) and (b) of the paragraph (1) of this article have been taken by the [leasing company], the [tenant] shall not be relieved from any other liability under this lease agreement including but not limited to liability for damages."

B

C

D

The contention was that the letter of September 3 was a bad notice because it does not fit the language of articles 21 and 17 of the equipment leases. Their Lordships do not accept the relevance of that comment even if it were justified. The whole question is whether the letter sufficiently indicates a withdrawal of consent to continued possession of the equipment: and, as already stated, in their Lordships' opinion it clearly does.

E

Accordingly their Lordships are of the opinion that this appeal must be dismissed, with costs, and they advise His Majesty the Yang di-Pertuan Agong accordingly.

F

Solicitors: *Nabarro Nathanson; Coward Chance.*

T. J. M.

G

H

A

[QUEEN'S BENCH DIVISION]

* REGINA *v.* FOLKESTONE AND HYTHE JUVENILE COURT
JUSTICES, *Ex parte* R. (A JUVENILE)

B 1981 Oct. 6   Lord Lane C.J., Kilner Brown and McCullough JJ.

*Justices — Committal to Crown Court — Committal for sentence
— Transitional provisions — Proceedings commenced before
new Act in force—Court records showing committal under
new Act—Whether mistake vitiating proceedings—Whether
committal valid—Magistrates' Courts Act 1980 (c. 43), s. 37
(1), Sch. 8, para. 2 [1]—Magistrates' Courts Rules 1968 (S.I. 1968*
C   *No. 1920 (L. 20)), rr. 16 (1), 54 (as amended by the Magistrates' Courts (amendment) Rules 1973 (S.I. 1973 No. 790
(L. 11))) [2]*

       The applicant, who had previously pleaded guilty to three
charges of burglary, was committed on July 6, 1981, to the
Crown Court for consideration for borstal training. The entry
in the court register stated that he had been committed for
D   sentence under section 37 of the Magistrates' Courts Act 1980.
That section had come into force on the same day as the
applicant was committed for sentence but, under the transitional provisions of the Act, the previous, virtually identical,
provisions of section 28 of the Magistrates' Court Act 1952
applied as the proceedings against the applicant had commenced
before July 6.
       On an application for an order of certiorari to quash the
E   order made by the justices in respect of the committal to the
Crown Court: —
       Held, refusing the application, that although the justices
had no power to commit the applicant under section 37 of
the Magistrates' Courts Act 1980, there was no requirement
under rules 16 (1) and 54 of the Magistrates' Court Rules 1968
that the statutory provisions under which the applicant was
F   committed to the Crown Court should be recorded in the
register or the memorandum of the conviction entered in the
register sent to the Crown Court; that, since the justices had
complied with the statutory provisions applicable to a committal
under section 28 of the Act of 1952 until their adjudication
was recorded in the register, the unnecessary entry of section
37 of the Act of 1980 in the register should be disregarded and,
accordingly, the committal was valid (post, pp. 1506G—1507D,
1508H).
G   *Meek* v. *Powell* [1952] 1 K.B. 164, D.C. and *Reg.* v. *Kent
Justices, Ex parte Machin* [1952] 2 Q.B. 355, D.C. distinguished.

       The following cases are referred to in the judgment:

       Meek v. *Powell* [1952] 1 K.B. 164; [1952] 1 All E.R. 347, D.C.
       Reg. v. *Edgar* [1958] 2 All E.R. 494, C.C.A.
H

   [1] Magistrates' Courts Act 1980, s. 37 (1): see post, p. 1503B–C.
   Sch. 8, para. 2: see post, p. 1503E–G.
   [2] Magistrates' Courts Rules 1968, r. 16 (1): " Where a magistrates' court commits
an offender to the Crown Court under—. . . section 28 or 29 of the Act . . . after
convicting him of an offence, the clerk of the magistrates' court shall send to the
appropriate officer of the Crown Court—(*a*) a copy signed by the clerk of the
magistrates' court of the minute or memorandum of the conviction entered in the
register; . . ."
   R. 54: see post, p. 1506E.

Reg. v. *Huntingdon Justices, Ex parte Simpkin and Coombes* (1959) 123   A
    J.P. 166, D.C.
Reg. v. *Kent Justices, Ex parte Machin* [1952] 2 Q.B. 355; [1952] 1 All
    E.R. 1123, D.C.
Rex v. *Gee* [1936] 2 K.B. 442; [1936] 2 All E.R. 89, C.C.A.
Rex v. *Grant* (1944) 30 Cr.App.R. 99.
Rex v. *Wharmby* (1946) 31 Cr.App.R. 174.

                                                                          B

The following additional case was cited in argument:

Rex v. *Norfolk Justices, Ex parte Director of Public Prosecutions* [1950]
    2 K.B. 558; [1950] 2 All E.R. 346, D.C.

APPLICATION for judicial review.
   On July 1, 1981, the applicant, a juvenile, first appeared before the
juvenile court and on July 6, 1981, he pleaded guilty to three charges of   C
burglary. On July 27, 1981, he was committed by the justices to the
Maidstone Crown Court for consideration for borstal training and on
August 17 was sentenced to borstal training.
   The applicant applied for judicial review and an order of certiorari to
remove the order for committal into the High Court for the purpose of
its being quashed, on the ground that the justices' order was contrary to   D
the provisions of the Magistrates' Courts Act 1980 and the Schedules
thereunder, in that the proceedings having been commenced prior to
July 6, 1981, any committal for sentence should have been under section
28 of the Magistrates' Courts Act 1952 and not under section 37 of the
Magistrates' Courts Act 1980.
   The facts are stated in the judgment of Lord Lane C.J.   E

   John Hazan Q.C. and *Robert Cooney* for the applicant.
   Michael Hill Q.C. and *Allan Green* for the prosecutor.
   The justices did not appear and were not represented.

   LORD LANE C.J. This is an application by leave by way of judicial   F
review praying for an order of certiorari to remove into this court and to
quash an order made by a lower court in respect of the committal to the
Crown Court for sentence purportedly under section 37 of the Magistrates'
Courts Act 1980. It is said that the proceedings by which the applicant
was committed to the Crown Court with a view to a sentence of borstal
training were a nullity.
   It is a case which, if I may respectfully say so, has been argued with   G
great clarity and skill by counsel on each side, and we understand that it
is a matter which is likely to affect a very large number of cases up and
down the country where a similar error to the one committed in this case
has taken place.
   The facts which lie behind the case are these. The applicant was at
the material times a youth of 15. On May 31, 1981, he was arrested for a   H
breaking and entering offence at Sainsbury's in Folkestone. He was
released to the custody of his father. The offence was committed some-
time between May 29 and June 1. He was rearrested on June 30 and
charged with an offence at The Globe Public House, Folkestone, and
another offence at the premises of a concern called Spain & White. Those
were the first two charges eventually laid against him.
   On July 1 he made his first appearance in court in respect of these

The Weekly Law Reports, December 11, 1981

1503

1 W.L.R.   Reg. v. Folkestone JJ., Ex p. R. (D.C.)   Lord Lane C.J.

A   matters and he was remanded to a place called Oakhurst Home. On July 3 he was charged with the offence, which I have already mentioned, the Sainsbury's offence. He appeared at court on July 6 and pleaded guilty to all three offences. On July 27 he was committed for sentence, purportedly, as I say, under section 37 of the Act of 1980, and August 17 saw him before the Crown Court where he was sent to borstal training.

B   The terms of section 37 (1) of the Magistrates' Courts Act 1980 are as follows:

> " Where a person is convicted by a magistrates' court for an offence punishable on summary conviction with imprisonment, then, if on the day of the conviction he is not less than 15 but under 21 years old and is a person who under section 1 (2) and (4) of the Criminal Justice Act 1961 may be committed for a sentence of borstal training, the
C   court may commit him in custody or on bail to the Crown Court for sentence in accordance with the provisions of section 20 of the Criminal Justice Act 1948."

That particular section is in words which, to all intents and purposes, are precisely similar to those of the Act which preceded it, the relevant provision being section 28 (1) of the Magistrates' Courts Act 1952 (as
D   amended by section 41 (1) of and Schedule 4 to the Criminal Justice Act 1961). The only difference between the two Acts is simply a transposition of certain words which deal with the section of the Criminal Justice Act 1961; it is a distinction without any difference. The words are the same.

But the difficulty arises in this case in the following way. The appointed
E   day for the coming into operation of the Act of 1980 was July 6. That was the very day on which this young man pleaded guilty to the charges in the magistrates' court. There are tucked away in the Act transitional provisions which are to be found in Schedule 8, paragraph 2 and read:

> " (1) Where proceedings were commenced before the appointed day, the old enactments relating to the proceedings continue to apply and nothing in this Act affects those enactments. (2) Without prejudice to
F   the generality of sub-paragraph (1) above, the old enactments relating to proceedings which continue in force by virtue of it include any provision of those enactments which creates an offence, which relates to civil or criminal procedure, which relates to the punishment for an offence, or which relates to enforcing, appealing against, questioning,
G   varying or rescinding anything ordered or done in the proceedings."

Those provisions relate to penalties and also to procedures. They relate both to trial and to disposal of the offender after trial.

Happily, in this case we do not have to enter on to the vexed territory of what " proceedings were commenced " means. There is a wealth of authority on that subject, but it is conceded by both counsel—and indeed
H   is clear—that, whatever meaning may be given to the words " where proceedings were commenced," proceedings here had certainly commenced before July 6 because not only had this young man been charged with the various offences before that date, but he had also made his first appearance before the magistrates on July 1, which was five days before the Act came into force.

The way in which the minute of adjudication was sent forward to the Crown Court was as follows. The name of the informant or complainant

1504

in each of the three cases was Detective Constable Lloyd. The name of A
the defendant was N.J.R. in each case. There set out accurately in each
case is the nature of the offence; the Theft Act 1968 and the correct
section and subsection of the Theft Act which it was alleged had been
broken; the date of offence accurately set out in each of the three cases;
plea or consent to order in each case " Admits F.J.C. 6.7.81 "; and then
finally, in the final column " Minute of Adjudication "—and this is the
material part of course—" Committed in custody to Crown Court for B
sentence of borstal training (M.C.A. 1980, s. 37). Legal aid granted."
    It is plain, having read the transitional provisions and having set out
the chronology of events, that that was the incorrect way of stating
what the justices had done. In fact what they should have done to get
the matter correct was to have used exactly the same words in all the
columns, including the final column, save for the words in brackets. The C
words in brackets should have read " M.C.A. 1952, section 28 (1)."
    It is submitted by Mr. Hazan on behalf of the applicant that that error
vitiates the committal, which thereby becomes a nullity. He would submit,
and does submit, that in those circumstances the applicant is entitled to
succeed and entitled to have held in his favour that these proceedings were
void and should be quashed.
                                                                        D
    The way he puts the matter is this. He submits that magistrates' courts
in the exercise of their powers are creatures of statute. They must operate
strictly in accordance with the terms of their statute, and, if they deviate
from that straight and narrow way, what they do is without jurisdiction
and will be held to be null and void. Moreover, he says, statutes dealing
with the disposition of offenders must be strictly construed.
    He points correctly to the mistake procedure which exists under the E
new Act in section 142, which there is no need for me to read, imposing a
28-day limitation upon the correction of mistakes by the magistrates, and
to its precursor, which was section 41 of the Criminal Justice Act 1972,
which originally gave the same power but to a lesser extent because 14
days was originally the period during which the mistake had to be rectified, but that was enlarged a little later, in 1977, to a period of 28 days. F
He points out that those provisions show that, where there has been an
error of this sort, then the power to amend the error is one which itself
is limited very strictly by the statute which gives the power.
    The various authorities upon which Mr. Hazan relied can perhaps be
rather more briefly dealt with even than he himself dealt with them,
because there are certain of them which appear to me not to be relevant
at all. There are, however, two in his list of authorities to which it is G
necessary to refer.
    The first one of those is Reg. v. Kent Justices, Ex parte Machin [1952]
2 Q.B. 355. In that case the applicant had consented to be dealt with
summarily and was convicted by a court of summary jurisdiction of
obtaining credit by fraud and of larceny, and was committed to quarter
sessions for sentence under the Criminal Justice Act 1948. The error which H
the court made there was the failure to explain to the applicant that he
might be so committed, as was required by statute, and on the basis of
that error he applied for an order of certiorari.
    It was held by this court, under the presidency of Lord Goddard C.J.,
that the provisions of the statutes were peremptory, and, therefore, the
convictions were bad because the justices, although with the consent of
the applicant, had dealt with the cases summarily without complying with

The Weekly Law Reports, December 11, 1981

1505

1 W.L.R.   Reg. v. Folkestone JJ., Ex p. R. (D.C.)   Lord Lane C.J.

A   those provisions, and the order for certiorari was accordingly granted and
the conviction quashed. There is one passage of the report which is
rewarding to read, at p. 360:

"Following the reasoning of the court in *Reg.* v. *Cockshott* [1898] 1
Q.B. 582 we think we must give effect to [Schedule 9 to the Act of
1948], and therefore hold that certiorari must go and these convictions
B   must be quashed. The convictions must be quashed because the justices
took upon themselves, although with the consent of the prisoner, to
try offences summarily without a strict compliance with the provisions
of the Act, which alone allow an indictable offence to be dealt with
summarily. It was a very venial offence in the magistrates and one
can well understand their overlooking this provision tucked away in
the Schedule; but the prisoner is entitled to take advantage of it and
C   therefore the committal and the convictions were bad."

In that case the justices had omitted in the course of their trying of the
applicant, and in the course of their procedural behaviour had failed, to
take a step which the statute demanded that they must take before exercising their powers. Although in the circumstances of that particular case
it may have been something of a technicality because the man had con-
D   sented to be dealt with in that way, yet, nevertheless, an important procedural step had been omitted.

That is not the case here. It is conceded on all hands that everything
done by the justices was done strictly according to the book until it came
to the very last minute, namely, the recording of the Act under which
they were purporting to proceed. It seems to me that that case can easily
E   be distinguished on that basis.

The next case is another decision of this court, *Meek* v. *Powell* [1952]
1 K.B. 164. In that case the respondent was convicted by a court of summary jurisdiction on two informations charging him with offences under
section 24 of the Food and Drugs Act 1938. That section was repealed by,
but re-enacted in almost identical terms in section 9 of, the Food and
F   Drugs (Milk, Dairies and Artificial Cream) Act 1950, which came into
force on January 1, 1951. The respondent appealed against the convictions
of quarter sessions, who held the informations to be bad as charging an
offence under a repealed statute. They refused to amend them and quashed
the convictions.

It was held by the Divisional Court, consisting of Lord Goddard C.J.,
Byrne J. and Parker J., that the informations were not validated by the
G   provisions of section 36 of the Act of 1950, that the convictions were
bad for the reason given by quarter sessions and that quarter sessions had
power to amend an information only in cases where the court of summary
jurisdiction had that power, and the latter court had no power so to do
when once it had recorded a conviction on the information. Quarter
sessions, therefore, had no choice but to quash the convictions. Byrne J.,
H   who delivered the leading judgment, had this to say, at p. 167:

"But, it is nevertheless of importance that a conviction should be
obtained under the correct statute, although the wording of the
provision repealed may be reproduced in a later statute."

There again, although there are similarities between the present case
and *Meek* v. *Powell*, yet in that case it was a case of the information being
laid under the wrong Act and, therefore, the man, on the face of it, had

1506

been convicted under a non-existent Act. Conviction is one thing, but   A
disposal for sentence seems to me to be something entirely different.

We were referred by Mr. Hazan to four cases, the names of which I
will give simply for the purposes of completeness: *Rex* v. *Gee* [1936]
2 K.B. 442; *Rex* v. *Wharmby* (1946) 31 Cr.App.R. 174; *Reg.* v. *Edgar*
[1958] 2 All E.R. 494 and *Rex* v. *Grant* (1944) 30 Cr.App.R. 99. But it
seems to me that those cases do not really help us in coming to a con-   B
clusion as to whether his arguments are to be supported or not.

On the other side, Mr. Hill for the prosecutor, submits to us that, where
the justices have exercised a jurisdiction—which they undoubtedly have—
and do not go beyond the power which that jurisdiction gives them, an
error in the recording of the order does not vitiate either the proceedings
or the order itself.

The way in which he puts it is this. What is required from the justices   C
in circumstances such as this? When considering what it is that is required,
one bears in mind that not only is the old enactment in precisely the same
terms as the new to all intents and purposes but the old rules are also
identical with the new. He submits that the justices have to do this. They
have to hear the evidence. They have to consider the circumstances and
then they either deal with the young man, as they did in this case, there   D
and then, or they say, " We are committing you in custody to the Crown
Court with a view to borstal training."   That is all they have to do.

But certain procedural matters emerge from a consideration of the
rules. I turn first to rule 54 of the Magistrates' Courts Rules 1968 where
there is to be found the rules as to the register of convictions, which read:

> " (1) The clerk of every magistrates' court shall keep a register in   E
> which there shall be entered —(*a*) a minute or memorandum of every
> adjudication of the court; (*b*) a minute or memorandum of every other
> proceeding or thing required by these Rules or any other enactment
> to be so entered. (2) The register shall be in the prescribed form, and
> entries in the register shall include, where relevant, such particulars as
> are provided for in the said form. . . ."
>   F

One then turns to Form 146 of the Magistrates' Courts (Forms) Rules
1968 (S.I. 1968 No. 1919 (L. 19)), which has eight columns. Column 1 is
" Number "; column 2 is " Name of informant or complainant "; column
3 is " Name of defendant. Age, if known "; column 4 is " Nature of
offence or matter of complaint "; column 5 is " Date of offence or matter
of complaint "; column 6 is " Plea or consent to order "; column 7 is   G
" Minute of adjudication "; column 8 is " Time allowed for payment and
instalments."

It is to be noted that, in so far as those various columns are relevant,
they were all correctly filled in by the justices, with a possible exception of
column 7 as already mentioned. But there is no mention there of any
requirement that the statutory authority for doing what the justices did
has to be mentioned under the minute of adjudication heading, or indeed   H
under any other heading.

That takes me to the next provision, which is rule 16 (1) of the
Magistrates' Courts Rules 1968 (as amended) and it provides that, where a
magistrates' court commits an offender to the Crown Court under various
provisions, one of which is section 28 or 29 of the Act, the clerk of the
magistrates' court shall send to the appropriate officer of the Crown Court a

The Weekly Law Reports, December 11, 1981

1507

1 W.L.R.   Reg. v. Folkestone JJ., Ex p. R. (D.C.)   Lord Lane C.J.

A copy signed by the clerk of the magistrates' court of the minute or memorandum of the conviction entered in the register, which is precisely what he did; and once again there is no mention of the necessity to put in the name of the statute under which the justices say they are acting.

It seems to me that, without further authority on the point, the justices could properly in this case have simply said in their judgment to this young man: "You are committed in custody to the Crown Court for consideration of a sentence of borstal training," and that would have been a perfectly proper exercise of their powers to which no exception could properly have been taken anywhere.

Likewise it seems to me that, in Form 146 sent off to the Crown Court, if they had chosen under "Minute of adjudication" to do exactly the same, namely, to have said what they did on that form without the words in brackets, that is to say "Committed in custody to Crown Court for sentence of borstal training. Legal aid granted," that, likewise, would have been a perfectly proper exercise of their powers and jurisdiction, to which again no possible exception could have been taken. They had the power. They acted on it properly. They had the power to commit and it was unnecessary for them to state whether it was under Act "A" or Act "B" that they were acting.

The fact that they did so, subject to the case which I am about to cite, seems to me to make no difference. The use of the words "Magistrates' Courts Act 1980" was unnecessary; it was surplusage and can be disregarded.

But our attention was drawn, and very properly drawn by Mr. Hill as was his duty, to a decision of this court in 1959, which at first blush appears to be contrary to the point of view which I have been endeavouring to express. The name of the case is *Reg.* v. *Huntingdon Justices, Ex parte Simpkin and Coombes* (1959) 123 J.P. 166. What happened there is this. The two applicants were charged before the justices on two informations, the first of which alleged theft and the second receiving of certain motor car or lorry spares, a wheel and tyre. The justices dismissed the theft information but convicted on the receiving and committed the applicants to quarter sessions for sentence under section 29 of the Magistrates' Courts Act 1952. Their clerk then put an entry in the register, which under rule 54 of the Magistrates' Courts Rules 1952 (S.I. 1952 No. 2190 (L. 18)) it was the duty of their clerk to make. That entry was correct in respect of the adjudication on the information for larceny, but on the information with regard to the receiving in column 5, which provided for the date, what they put was the word "ditto," indicating that the date was the same as that for the larceny charges which had been dismissed. Under "Nature of offence" the words entered were "Received from some persons unknown a Bedford lorry spare wheel complete with tyre" of a certain size, "knowing the same to have been stolen." The minute of adjudication was: "Committed to quarter sessions for sentence in accordance with section 29 of the Criminal Justice Act 1948." The clerk of the justices sent to the clerk of peace a copy of both adjudications (that is the acquittal and the conviction) and the latter contained the aforementioned inaccuracies and omissions. On motion on behalf of the applicants to bring up and quash the record of the conviction on the ground that the record did not comply with rule 54, it was held that the contention of the applicants was right and that the entry must be quashed.

One turns then to the judgment of Lord Parker C.J., which was the

1508

leading judgment, to see on what basis the court came to that conclusion **A** so far as one can, and this is what Lord Parker C.J. said, at p. 168:

"In my judgment, it is imperative that convictions should be fully and accurately recorded, and this was not. In particular "—note those words—" there was no specific entry of the date of the offence. It was also suggested that the nature of the offence was not properly described in that it did not state where the receiving had taken place or **B** whose property the spare wheel was. I find it unnecessary to say whether those two matters should or should not have been entered, but there is no doubt that rule 54 (3) does provide that a description of the offence should be set out, and clearly that must be with sufficient detail so that it can be seen exactly in respect of what charge the prisoners were convicted. At any rate, in regard to the date of offence this record is not complete and not in accordance with the **C** rules. The effect of that not being in order was this. It is provided by rule 20 that in sending the case forward to quarter sessions, the clerk of the justices shall send to the clerk of the peace a copy signed by the clerk of the justices' court of the minute or memorandum of the conviction entered in the register. What went forward to quarter sessions in the present case was a copy of the two adjudications in **D** the register. If the clerk had sent forward the second adjudication, which was the one of conviction, it was clearly incomplete because it had no date, and in order that he should make it complete he had to send what I may call an omnibus copy, namely, a copy of both adjudications, the acquittal and the conviction. He also in that copy perpetuated the error which had already crept in of a committal under **E** section 29 of the Criminal Justice Act 1948."

In the short supporting judgment Donovan J. said, at p. 169:

"I agree. This case illustrates the difficulties which can arise through entries in the court's register being abbreviated in order to save an insignificant amount of time, and the clerk to the justices will, no doubt, be on guard to avoid any similar trouble in the future." **F**

In that case not only had there been an error in the statement of the provision under which the justices were purporting to act, but there had also been—and this is underlined by what Donovan J. said—material errors in the way in which the particulars had been set out in the document sent to quarter sessions.

One asks oneself what would have been the judgment of the court in **G** that case had there only been the error which had crept in relating to section 29 of the Criminal Justice Act 1948. I cannot help feeling that in those circumstances the result would have been different and the court would have come to the same conclusion as that which I have come to in the present case, namely, that this was an error which was an error of surplusage, one which can be disregarded, and that accordingly, in my judgment, **H** the committal here was perfectly valid and the appeal by way of judicial review fails.

KILNER BROWN J.   I agree entirely.

McCULLOUGH J.   I agree.   A statutory offence cannot be properly described without reference to the statute creating the offence, hence

The Weekly Law Reports, December 11, 1981

1509

1 W.L.R.   Reg. v. Folkestone JJ., Ex p. R. (D.C.)   McCullough J.

A the decision in *Meek* v. *Powell* [1952] 1 K.B. 164 where an offence was
described as being contrary to the statute which had been repealed. No
criminal offence can properly be described without reference to the date
upon which the offence was committed. This no doubt is why Form 146
in the Magistrates' Courts Forms Rules 1968 contained a column headed
" Date of offence or matter of complaint." This, to my mind, explains the
decision in *Reg.* v. *Huntingdon Justices, Ex parte Simpkin and Coombes,*
B 123 J.P. 166.

I do not in the circumstances here see any difficulty in distinguishing
either of those cases. There is no doubt about the offences of which R. was
convicted; nor is there any doubt that he was committed for borstal training exactly as the justices had power to commit him. All that has happened
is that an error was made in the magistrates' clerks' office when the com-
C pletion of the column headed " Minute of adjudication " was made and
reference was made to the wrong statute. I see no need for there to have
been any reference to any statute at all and I would regard the mistake
here as immaterial and having no more consequence than had a wrong
digit appeared by a typing error.

D   *Application refused.*
                                        Certificate under section 33 (2) *of
                                           Criminal Appeal Act* 1968 *that
                                           point of law of general public im-
                                           portance was involved in decision,
                                           namely:* " (1) *Whether in cases
                                           covered by the transitional provi-
E   sions of the Magistrates' Courts Act*
                                           1980 *proceedings in the magistrates'
                                           court are rendered null and void if
                                           the memorandum of the finding of
                                           guilt entered in the register shows
                                           that the committal for sentence pur-
F   ports to be under section* 37 *of that
                                           Act; and* (2) *if the proceedings are
                                           not null and void, does the Crown
                                           Court have jurisdiction to deal with
                                           the offender on receipt of such
                                           memorandum of finding of guilt?* "
                                        Leave to appeal refused.
G   *Legal aid granted to defendant to
                                           petition for leave to appeal.*

Solicitors: *Rootes & Alliott, Folkestone; Director of Public
Prosecutions.*

H   [Reported by COLIN BERESFORD, ESQ., Barrister-at-Law]

November 12. The Appeal Committee of the House of Lords (Lord
Wilberforce, Lord Russell of Killowen and Lord Bridge of Harwich) dismissed a petition by the applicant for leave to appeal.

A

* REGINA v. HALL (PETER MICHAEL)

1981 Oct. 20   Lord Lane C.J., Mustill and McCullough JJ.

B

*Justices—Committal to Crown Court—Committal for trial—Tran-
sitional provisions—Proceedings commenced before new Act
in force—Certificate sent to Crown Court wrongly stating
committal under relevant sections of new Act—Whether committal valid—Whether indictment valid—Magistrates' Courts
Rules 1968 (S.I. 1968 No. 1920), r. 10 (2) (b) (j)—Magistrates'
Courts Act 1980 (c. 43), Sch. 8, paras. 1, 2 (as amended by
Magistrates' Courts (Amendment) Rules 1973 (S.I. 1973 No.
790 (L. 11)), Sch., para. 5 (a))*

C

*Crown Court—Jurisdiction—Bill of indictment—Indictment drawn
from certificate erroneously reciting provisions of Magistrates'
Courts Act 1980—Recitation of previous legislation proper—
Whether indictment valid*

A committal for trial at the Crown Court is valid when
proceedings have been commenced before the Magistrates'
Courts Act 1980 came into operation, so that previous
legislation is applicable, notwithstanding that the certificate
and the statement required respectively by rule 10 (2) (b) and
(j) of the Magistrates' Courts Rules 1968 [1] erroneously recite
compliance with the relevant sections of the Act of 1980. A
bill of indictment can properly be founded on such a
committal (post, pp. 1514E–F, H—1515A, C–D).

D

Where, therefore, the appellant was committed for trial
in proceedings begun before the Act of 1980 came into
operation, he was convicted and he appealed on the grounds
that the committal was invalid because the certificate and the
statement recited compliance with inapplicable statutory
provisions and, alternatively, that the bill of indictment was
invalid in being founded on the committal: —

E

Held, that the appeal would be dismissed, for the committal was valid and the bill of indictment also was valid.

F

The following cases are referred to in the judgment:

Reg. v. *Folkestone and Hythe Juvenile Court Justices, Ex parte R. (A
Juvenile)* [1981] 1 W.L.R. 1501, D.C.

Rex v. *H. Sherman Ltd.* [1949] 2 K.B. 674; [1949] 2 All E.R. 207, C.C.A.

The following additional cases were cited in argument:

G

Moore v. *Hewitt* [1947] K.B. 831; [1947] 2 All E.R. 270, D.C.

Reg. v. *Urbanowski* [1976] 1 W.L.R. 455; [1976] 1 All E.R. 679, C.A.

APPEAL against conviction.

On August 28, 1981, at Dudley Crown Court before deputy circuit
judge R. F. Solman the appellant, Peter Michael Royston Hall, pleaded
guilty to two counts of unlawful wounding between December 30, 1980,
and January 2, 1981, contrary to section 20 of the Offences against the
Person Act 1861, in respect of which he had been committed for trial
by Wolverhampton Magistrates' Court on July 14, 1981. The certificate
sent to the Crown Court on his committal recited that he had been
committed under section 6 (2) of the Magistrates' Courts Act 1980 and

H

---

[1] Magistrates' Courts Rules 1968, r. 10 (1) (2): see post, p. 1514B–D.

A   that eight witness statements were tended in evidence under section 102 of the Act of 1980. He had been committed also for sentence on various offences including absconding after release on bail. He was sentenced to one day's detention for the bail offence concurrent with Borstal training in respect of the other offences. He applied for leave to appeal against conviction on the counts of unlawful wounding on the grounds that, since he had been committed for trial under section 6 (2) of the Act of
B   1980, the committal was void because, in view of the transitional provisions in Schedule 8 to the Act of 1980, the committal should have been under the previously existing legislation and that, in view of the references to the Act of 1980 in the certificate sent to the Crown Court on his committal, the bill of indictment was void. Leave to appeal was granted at the hearing.

C   The facts are stated in the judgment.

John Marriage Q.C. and *Martin Kingston* for the appellant.
Michael Hill Q.C. and *Allan Green* for the Crown.

LORD LANE C.J. gave the following judgment of the court. On August
D   28, 1981, at Dudley Crown Court before deputy circuit judge Solman, the appellant, as he now is (this court having granted him leave to appeal against his conviction), pleaded guilty to two counts of unlawful wounding laid under section 20 of the Offences against the Person Act 1861. He had been committed for sentence on two counts of burglary with one case taken into consideration, one count of going equipped for theft and also on a charge of absconding after release on bail. In the upshot the deputy
E   circuit judge sentenced him to Borstal training in respect of the first five offences and to one day's detention to run concurrently for the offence with regard to bail.

He now appeals to this court against his conviction of unlawful wounding. The appellant's ground of appeal in this respect is as follows. It is submitted that he was committed for trial under section 6 (2) of the
F   Magistrates' Courts Act 1980, but that that particular provision did not apply to the proceedings against him by virtue of the transitional provisions of that Act; consequently that the committal was bad, and that the bill of indictment based on the committal was, therefore, also bad.

A number of matters are not in dispute between the parties, and it is convenient that I should set those out. First of all there is no dispute that the proceedings here had commenced before the "relevant date,"
G   which was July 6, 1981. Secondly, it is agreed that the transitional provisions of the Act of 1980 applied. It is agreed that the examining justices could only receive the eight statements which existed in this case under the provisions of section 2 of the Criminal Justice Act 1967. There is no dispute but that the justices here could only commit under section 1 of the Act of 1967. Finally it is agreed that there is no difference of any
H   substance between the provisions of the Act of 1967 and the Act of 1980 as it affects this appeal.

The chronology of events was as follows. On New Year's Eve of 1980 the appellant was involved in a scuffle in a public house as a result of which the publican and his barman were cut by glass. That was the basis of the wounding counts. On January 2, 1981, the appellant was arrested and charged. That is probably—although we do not decide the point—the commencement of proceedings in this case. The case was listed twice. We

1512

need not bother about the first occasion. The second occasion was March A
23, 1981, when the appellant failed to surrender to his bail. Between
April 29 and May 2, 1981, he committed two burglaries in the company
of two other youths. On June 1 he was committed for trial with those two
youths for going equipped for burglary. On June 15 he was arrested and
remanded in custody. On July 14 at Wolverhampton Magistrates' Court
he was committed for trial on the unlawful wounding charges. On July 22, B
1981, he was committed for sentence in respect of other offences.

The Magistrates' Courts Act 1980 came into force on July 6, 1981,
by virtue of the Magistrates' Courts Act 1980 (Commencement Order) 1981
(S.I. 1981 No. 457 (c. 12)). Section 154 (2) of the Act gives effect to the
transitional provisions and in paragraphs 1 and 2 of Schedule 8, the
following provisions appear:

    " 1. In this Schedule references to the old enactments are to enact- C
    ments repealed or amended by this Act and references to the
    appointed day are to the day on which this Act comes into force "—
    namely, July 6, 1981. " 2. (1) Where proceedings were commenced
    before the appointed day, the old enactments relating to the proceed-
    ings continue to apply and nothing in this Act affects those enact-
    ments." D

The proceedings here commenced before July 6, and consequently the
provision under which the justices were acting was not the Act of 1980,
but section 1 of the Criminal Justice Act 1967 and section 2 (1) of the
Magistrates' Courts Act 1952. So much is agreed.

The Divisional Court in *Reg.* v. *Folkestone and Hythe Juvenile Court
Justices, Ex parte R. (A Juvenile)* [1981] 1 W.L.R. 1501 has already E
decided that a mistaken certificate does not invalidate a committal for
sentence when the mistake was similar to that in the present case. The
certificate here sent by the justices' clerk to the Crown Court was in the
following form. It is dated July 14, and the material part reads:

    " Having been committed for trial (in custody) under section . . ."—
    and crossed out is " 1 of the Criminal Justice Act 1967," and F
    inserted in its place is " 6 (2) Magistrates' Courts Act 1980 "— " I
    hereby certify that the eight statements purporting to be signed by the
    persons listed in Part II of Schedule 2 hereto were tendered in
    evidence under section . . ."—and crossed out is " 2 of the Criminal
    Justice Act 1967 " and inserted is " 102 Magistrates' Courts Act
    1980 "—" The court made no order under section 3 (2) of the G
    Criminal Justice Act 1967."

Then there are other matters which are not material. It is signed by the
justice of the peace.

There is no dispute that the alterations should not have been made.
If the certificate had been left in its original form, there would have been
no complaint. On the basis of that mistaken certificate Mr. Marriage H
contends that the committal was bad, and that the indictment resting
upon the committal is also bad. He seeks to distinguish the *Folkestone
Justices* case on the basis that there is a plain distinction between trying
an issue, deciding to convict and then deciding to send the defendant to
the Crown Court for sentence on the one hand and the present circumstance, where there has been a purported committal for trial, on the
other. In the *Folkestone Justices* case, he says, the wrong conduit pipe was

A   used, or a conduit pipe which was improperly labelled was used when
no label was necessary at all. Here, he says, the examining justice has
carried out a judicial function, that is to say, the committal, but he did
it under an Act which was not in operation, and, therefore, his actions
were invalid and void.

The case on which he very largely relied in support of his submission
was *Rex* v. *H. Sherman Ltd.* [1949] 2 K.B. 674. The headnote reads as
B   follows:

" When, as the result of proceedings before an examining magistrate
against a corporation in respect of an indictable offence, an order is
made by the magistrate pursuant to section 33 of the Criminal
Justice Act 1925, empowering the prosecutor to prefer a bill to
assizes against the corporation in respect of the offence named in
C   the order, it is essential that such order should be in writing, drawn
up under the hand of the presiding magistrate and bearing the seal of
the court, and, since the bill presented by the prosecutor becomes a
bill of indictment when signed by the clerk of assize, it is the duty of
the latter, in any case in which it is proposed to indict a company,
to satisfy himself, before signing the bill, that a proper order has been
D   made by the magistrate."

There is no doubt, if one reads the judgment of Lord Goddard C.J., in
that case, that had the wording of the Act in that case, section 33 (1) of
the Criminal Justice Act 1925 been similar to the wording of any Act
under which we were considering the present case, that judgment would
have been a powerful argument in favour of the appellant here. But in the
E   judgment of this court, *Rex* v. *H. Sherman Ltd.* is a very far distance
away from the facts of the present case. That dealt with the committal
for trial of a corporation, the distinction being an obvious one, that in
ordinary circumstances a person who is a human being is committed for
trial either in custody or on bail, but a corporation cannot be bailed and,
of course, cannot be committed in custody. Consequently the considerations
F   which affected the court in *Rex* v. *H. Sherman Ltd.* do not affect us here.
There is nothing in the present case equivalent to the " order " which was
required by section 33 (1) of the Act of 1925.

The matter is made even plainer perhaps by enactments subsequent
to the Criminal Justice Act 1925, which, no doubt as a result of the
judgment in *Rex* v. *H. Sherman Ltd.*, altered the wording of that particular
section. I do not need to read them. They are contained in section 36
G   of, and Schedule 2 to, the Magistrates' Courts Act 1952, and section 46 of,
and Schedule 3 to, the Magistrates' Courts Act 1980. But it will be plain, on
a consideration of *Rex* v. *H. Sherman Ltd.* and a consideration of the subsequent statutory enactments, that *Rex* v. *H. Sherman Ltd.* is no authority
for any of the propositions put forward by Mr. Marriage in the present case.

There are in this case two separate problems to be considered. The
H   first problem is, was there a valid committal? If there was not, then
that is the end of the matter and this appeal must succeed. If there was a
valid committal, then one has to ask the second question, was there a
valid bill of indictment? If there was, this appeal must fail. If there was
not, once again the appeal will succeed.

It is suggested that the statement of the wrong statute on the certificate
sent forward to the Crown Court invalidates the committal. It is suggested

1514

by Mr. Marriage that that certificate is, so to speak, the committal A
document.

In order to test the validity of that submission, it is necessary to turn
to the Magistrates' Court Rules 1968, in the course of which this certificate
is mentioned and which, in the judgment of this court, makes it plain
that the contention which I have just described is not a good one. Rule 10
(as amended) reads:

B

" (1) A magistrates' court that commits a person for trial shall,
unless there are reasons for not doing so, retain any documents and
articles produced by a witness who is subject to a conditional witness
order or in whose case the court has directed that a witness order
be treated as a conditional order. (2) As soon as practicable after the
committal of any person for trial, and in any case within four days
from the date of his committal . . . the clerk of the magistrates' court C
that committed him shall, subject to the provisions of section 5 of
the Prosecution of Offences Act 1879 . . . send to the appropriate
officer of the Crown Court— . . . (j) if the committal was under section
1 of the Criminal Justice Act 1967 (committal for trial without
consideration of the evidence), a statement to that effect; . . ."

D

Two things emerge from those words. First of all it is quite plain from
the opening words of rule 10 (2) that the certificate is not the committal.
The committal must have taken place before this document came into
existence. Although it is perhaps not necessary to decide the exact moment
when the committal takes place, it seems to this court highly likely to be
when the committing justice tells the defendant that he is to be committed;
that spoken order is probably the committal.

E

Secondly, it emerges from the words of the rule that this certificate
is something which the clerk sends forward to the committal court. If
there is a mistake on the face of the certificate, such as one which exists
here, it is a mistake of the clerk. But that is not the basis of our decision.

The justices undoubtedly had power to act as they did under section
7 (1) of the Magistrates' Courts Act 1952 so far as their power to commit F
for trial is concerned, and under section 1 of the Criminal Justice Act
1967, so far as their power to commit for trial without consideration of
the evidence is concerned. Consequently the fact that in the certificate
which comes into existence later the wrong Act was mentioned seems to
us in no way to invalidate the committal. That is enough so far as the first
part of the argument is concerned.

As there was a valid committal, it is then necessary to see whether G
there was a valid bill of indictment, and in order to decide that, one turns
to the provisions of the Administration of Justice (Miscellaneous Provisions) Act 1933. Section 2 of that Act reads:

" . . . (2) Subject as hereinafter provided no bill of indictment charging
any person with an indictable offence shall be preferred unless either—
(a) the person charged has been committed for trial for the offence; . . . H
(3) If a bill of indictment preferred otherwise than in accordance with
the provisions of the last foregoing subsection has been signed by the
proper officer of the court, the indictment shall be liable to be
quashed."

Those provisions, in the light of our decision that this was a valid
committal answer the second question. There was a committal for trial,

A and consequently the proper officer of the court, in basing his bill of indictment upon that committal for trial, was acting perfectly properly, and the bill of indictment is a good one.

For these reasons this appeal fails and must be dismissed.

Appeal dismissed.
Crown's costs out of central funds.

B October 23. Certificate under section 33 (2) of the Criminal Appeal Act 1968 that a point of law of general public importance was involved in the decision, namely:

" 1. In a case where proceedings have been commenced before the coming into force of the Magistrates' Courts Act 1980 (July 6, 1981), C and where the justices have purported to commit the accused person for trial at the Crown Court, is such a committal valid notwithstanding that the statement required by rule 10 (2) (*j*) of the Magistrates' Courts Rules 1968 recites that the committal was under section 6 (2) of the said Act (and notwithstanding that the certificate required by rule 10 (2) (*b*) of the said rules recites that written statements were tendered in evidence under section 102 of the said Act)? 2. In such D a case if the committal is valid can a bill of indictment properly be founded upon such committal notwithstanding the terms of the said statement (and of the said certificate)? "

Leave to appeal refused.
Legal aid for the appellant for two counsel
to petition the House of Lords for leave
E *to appeal.*

Solicitors: *A. Mervyn Williams, Bilston; Director of Public Prosecutions.*

L. N. W.

November 12. The Appeal Committee of the House of Lords (Lord F Wilberforce, Lord Russell of Killowen and Lord Bridge of Harwich) dismissed a petition by the appellant for leave to appeal.

[PRIVY COUNCIL]

G * NEVILLE NEMBHARD . . . . . . APPELLANT
AND
THE QUEEN . . . . RESPONDENT

[APPEAL FROM THE COURT OF APPEAL OF JAMAICA]

1981 July 6;   Lord Diplock, Lord Elwyn-Jones,
H   Oct. 6   Lord Edmund-Davies, Lord Roskill and
                                           Sir Owen Woodhouse

Crime—Evidence—Dying declaration—Evidence of identity—
Prosecution case solely dependent on dying declaration—
Whether corroboration necessary

The defendant was charged with the murder of a police officer who was shot outside his home and died about four hours later. There were no eye-witnesses and the assailant ran away. At

the trial the only evidence against the defendant was given by   A
the deceased's wife, who said that she had arrived at the scene
shortly after the shooting, that she had found that the deceased
was wounded and that he had made a statement to her. The
trial judge ruled that the statement was admissible as a dying
declaration. The wife's evidence was that the deceased had told
her he was dying and that it had been the defendant who had
shot him. The judge directed the jury that before they could
act on the dying declaration they had to be satisfied as to the   B
reliability of the wife and, if so satisfied, that they had to
assess the probative value of the declaration itself. The defendant was convicted. The Court of Appeal dismissed the
defendant's application for leave to appeal.

On the defendant's appeal to the Judicial Committee: —

Held, dismissing the appeal, that there was no rule of law
or of practice which required a trial judge admitting evidence
of a dying declaration under common law rules to warn a jury   C
specifically that it was dangerous to rely on it in the absence of
corroboration; that the trial judge, having correctly admitted
the deceased's statement in evidence, had given a direction to
the jury which had been fair, sensible and adequate in relation
to the declaration, and the defendant had been properly convicted (post, pp. 1518A–C, 1520D, 1521A–B).

Pius Jasunga s/o Akumu v. *The Queen* (1954) 21 E.A.C.A.
331 and *Terikabi* v. *Uganda* [1975] E.A. 60 distinguished.   D

Decision of the Court of Appeal of Jamaica affirmed.

The following cases are referred to in their Lordships' reasons:

Pius Jasunga s/o Akumu v. *The Queen* (1954) 21 E.A.C.A. 331.
Reg. v. *Turnbull* [1977] Q.B. 224; [1976] 3 W.L.R. 445; [1976] 3 All E.R.
    549, C.A.
Terikabi v. *Uganda* [1975] E.A. 60.   E

The following additional cases were cited in argument:

Ajodha v. *The State* [1981] 3 W.L.R. 1; [1981] 2 All E.R. 193, P.C.
Reg. v. *Angeli* [1979] 1 W.L.R. 26; [1979] 3 All E.R. 897, C.A.
Reg. v. *Jenkins* (1869) 11 Cox C.C. 250, C.C.A.
Reg. v. *Smith (Charlotte)* (1865) 10 Cox C.C. 82, C.C.A.
Rex v. *Booker* (1924) 88 J.P. 75, C.C.A.   F
Rex v. *Fitzpatrick* (1910) 46 I.L.T. 173; 129 L.T.J. 281, C.C.R.
Rex v. *Ngcobo,* S.A.L.R. [1925] A.D. 561.
Rex v. *Stephenson* [1947] N.I. 110, C.C.A.

APPEAL (No. 30 of 1979) with special leave by Neville Nembhard, the
defendant, from a decision of the Court of Appeal of Jamaica of November   G
9, 1977 refusing the defendant's application for leave to appeal against his
conviction for murder before Smith C.J. and a jury in the Home Circuit
Court for the parish of Kingston on April 15, 1977.

The facts are stated in their Lordships' judgment giving the reasons for
their decision.

At the close of the hearing before the Judicial Committee Lord Diplock
announced that their Lordships would advise that the appeal should be   H
dismissed for reasons to be delivered later.

Peter Martin for the defendant.
Ian X. Forte Q.C., Director of Public Prosecutions, Jamaica and
F. Algernon Smith, Deputy Director of Public Prosecutions, Jamaica for
the Crown.

Cur. adv. vult.

A   October 6. The reasons of their Lordships were delivered by SIR OWEN
WOODHOUSE.

      This appeal is concerned with evidence admitted by Smith C.J. as a
dying declaration at the trial of the defendant in the Supreme Court of
Jamaica on a charge of murder. He was found guilty by the jury and
applied unsuccessfully for leave to appeal against conviction to the Court
B of Appeal. On February 6, 1979, he was granted special leave to appeal
to the Judicial Committee of the Privy Council and the appeal was heard
by their Lordships on July 6, 1981. At the conclusion of argument they
announced that they would humbly advise Her Majesty that the appeal
should be dismissed. They now give their reasons.

      The deceased who was a police officer returned to his home in Kingston
C at about 8.30 one evening and there, at the gate, he was shot down by two
bullets fired at close range. His assailant immediately disappeared and there
were no eye-witnesses. But his wife had heard the shots fired and
immediately ran out to him from their house a few feet away. He was lying
inside the gate, bleeding profusely but still alive. In evidence she said that as
he lay there she took his head in her hands and he then said to her that he
was going to die and named his assailant. He was soon taken to the hospital
D where, she said, he further referred to the shooting both to her and to
another police officer. He had suffered a mortal wound in the upper
abdomen and he had also been struck in the neck. He died about four
hours after the shooting.

      At the point in her evidence when the wife was about to describe what
the deceased had said about the identity of the assailant objection was
E taken that the deceased's statement to her was not admissible and Smith
C.J. thereupon dealt with the issue. He did so in the presence of the jury
after being told by counsel for the defendant that it did not matter whether
they remained or not. The witness was then cross-examined upon alleged
inconsistencies in accounts she had given of what her husband had said;
and as an experienced nurse she was also asked for her own opinion as to
his condition after the shooting. His pulse was weak, she said, but he spoke
F in a strong voice. It was submitted to Smith C.J. that the deceased's statement should not qualify as a dying declaration because there was
insufficient evidence to satisfy the test that he was then in a hopeless
expectation of death; and in any event that the wife's version of what the
deceased had said could not safely be relied upon. In the result Smith C.J.
ruled that evidence could be given of what the deceased had said at the
G gate and, although he delayed a decision upon the subsequent conversation
at the hospital, he finally held that this other evidence should not go before
the jury. Before that later decision the wife gave an account of what the
deceased had said to her when she first ran to him. She repeated that he
had told her: " I am going to die," and then had said:

         " You are going to lose your husband. It is Neville Nembhard. Miss
H   Nembhard's grandson that shot me and take my gun. Your husband
         did not do him anything. Just as I came through the gate and turned to
         lock the gate I saw him over me, and your husband could not help
         himself."

She explained that the defendant had lived for 10 years with his grandmother in a house across the street from her own house and was well
known to her and her husband, as the defendant subsequently said when
he gave evidence himself.

Two independent grounds in support of the appeal were argued before A
their Lordships. The one is that in deciding to admit the critical evidence
of the dying declaration Smith C.J. had misdirected himself; that he had
failed to assess for himself the criticisms that had been made of the wife as
a witness and also that he had been in error when he held that there was
sufficient evidence to show that the deceased had a hopeless settled expectation of death when the statement was made. The other ground is that the
jury should have been warned, and they were not, that it is dangerous to B
rely upon the words of a dying declaration in the absence of corroboration.
It was this second matter which led to leave being granted to the defendant
to appeal to their Lordships' Board: in particular, a practice concerning
corroboration in such a context that was said to have developed in the
Court of Appeal for Eastern Africa. For that reason their Lordships will
consider this issue at once.   C

It is not difficult to understand why dying declarations are admitted in
evidence at a trial for murder or manslaughter and as a striking exception
to the general rule against hearsay. For example, any sanction of the oath
in the case of a living witness is thought to be balanced at least by the final
conscience of the dying man. Nobody, it has been said, would wish to die
with a lie on his lips. So it is considered quite unlikely that a deliberate untruth would be told, let alone a false accusation of homicide, by a man D
who believed that he was face to face with his own impending death. There
is the further consideration that it is important in the interests of justice
that a person implicated in a killing should be obliged to meet in court the
dying accusation of the victim, always provided that fair and proper precautions have been associated with the admission of the evidence and its subsequent assessment by the jury. In that regard it will always be necessary E
for the jury to scrutinise with care the necessarily hearsay evidence of what
the deceased was alleged to have said both because they have the problem
of deciding whether the deponent who has provided the evidence can be
relied upon and also because they will have been denied the opportunity of
forming a direct impression against the test of cross-examination of the
deceased's own reliability.

Against those considerations the question in this part of the case is F
simply whether the need for care in assessing the significance of a dying
declaration requires that a jury should be specifically directed that it would
be dangerous to convict on that evidence in the absence of corroboration.
Before providing the answer the practical implications and effect of the
directions actually given by Smith C.J. in the present case deserve to be
put beside the complaint that he should have said still more. In this part G
of the summing up Smith C.J. began by putting in contrast the evidence
given on oath by a witness who has appeared in person in the courtroom
and the hearsay evidence of a dying declaration. And he took pains to
describe the basis upon which a dying declaration was regarded as admissible and the tests which must be satisfied in that regard. He went on to
direct the jury that before they could act on the dying declaration they
themselves must be satisfied as to the reliability of the wife, both in terms H
of veracity and accuracy, and that if so satisfied then they must still assess
the probative value of the dying declaration itself. Inter alia, he said:

"Do you believe Mrs. Campbell? Do you believe her that she went out
there? Do you believe her that her husband told her the things which
she said she was told? That you have to decide first of all . . . If you
believe her that the deceased did tell her then, you have to examine

A the circumstances and say whether in the light of what he is supposed to have said, you are convinced by this, taking all the circumstances into account, so that you can feel sure that in fact it was this accused who shot the deceased." And later: " Now if you believe her that the deceased did tell her this, you will have to test the statement and say whether you can rely implicitly on it. If you believe the statement was made, Mr. Campbell is saying how he got his injuries and who caused

B them, if you believe he made the statement and he has described accurately what he said took place, were the circumstances such that he could identify positively the person who attacked him in order to convince you that a mistake has not been made in the identification of the person who shot him? In other words, you have to examine it in the same way as you would examine the evidence if he had come here

C and said the same thing."

At that point Smith C.J. expressly drew the attention of the jury to the fact that the dying declaration had not been tested by cross-examination. He said:

> " Another thing which you bear in mind when you consider evidence of this sort is that you have not had the advantage of the witness
D > coming here and having what he said tested by cross-examination. The statement is there, it is not tested, so it suffers or it is at a disadvantage in so far as you are concerned as against evidence given from the witness box where the witness states a fact and counsel can test him or her on it as to whether it is true or not."

E There follows a lengthy and entirely accurate warning concerning the various problems that can and do arise in the area of identification evidence and the circumstances that were relevant in assessing the deceased's identification of the defendant as his assailant. Then Smith C.J. summarised what he had been saying in the following way:

> " If you feel sure the statement was made to her you have to examine the circumstances which must have existed at the time when Mr.
F > Campbell was shot; you have to take into account his state of mind when he made the statement; was he in a state of mind where you would tell that you could safely rely on what he was saying, as being the truth? You have to take into account the caution that I have given about mistaken identity and whether the circumstances were such, having regard to distance, light and so forth, that you can feel that a
G > mistake was not made in the identity of the [defendant]. And if you are not sure whether a mistake was made or not, or if you do not think that you can safely rely at all on what the deceased is alleged to have said, then you must acquit the [defendant]."

Their Lordships have thought it appropriate to repeat the foregoing passages from the very fair and helpful summing up by Smith C.J. in this
H case because they demonstate so clearly, if demonstration were necessary, that adequate and proper directions to a jury do not require nor depend upon the strait-jacket of previous enunciation by the higher courts of some precisely worded formula. Certainly a jury must be given adequate assistance in respect of those questions of fact and law that seem to require it. But in general this is a responsibility that can be sufficiently discharged by the application of fairness and the good common sense of the judge.

 Some attempt was made by counsel to argue by analogy that the com-

paratively recent example of the decision in *Reg.* v. *Turnbull* [1977] Q.B.   A
224 justified the definition of a new rule of law as to the need for corroboration in the area of dying declarations. But their Lordships accept neither
the analogy nor its application in the present case. *Turnbull* does not purport to change the law. It provides a most valuable analysis of the various
circumstances which commonsense suggests or experience has shown may
affect the reliability of a witness's evidence of identification and make it
too dangerous in some of the circumstances postulated to base a conviction   B
on such evidence unless it is supported by other evidence that points to
the defendant's guilt. *Turnbull* sets out what the judgment itself described
as " guidelines for trial judges " who are obliged to direct juries in such
cases. But those guidelines are not intended as an elaborate specification to
be adopted religiously on every occasion. A summing up, if it is to be
helpful to the jury should be tailored to fit the facts of the particular case   C
and not merely taken ready-made " off the peg." In any event in the
present context their Lordships regard it as unnecessary and believe it
would be a mistake to lay down some new rule, whether of practice or of
law, that then might have to be followed almost verbatim before a judge
could feel sure that he had discharged his general duty to leave with the
jury a clear consciousness of their need for care in assessing the significance
of a dying declaration. Furthermore their Lordships are satisfied that the   D
eminently fair and sensible summing up in the present case was more than
adequate for the purpose of giving every necessary assistance and direction
to the jury.

A final observation should be made concerning the cases already
mentioned that have been decided in the Court of Appeal for Eastern
Africa. It appears that rule of practice has been developed that when a   E
dying declaration has been the only evidence implicating an accused person
a conviction usually cannot be allowed to stand where there had been a
failure to give a warning on the necessity for corroboration: see for
example *Pius Jasunga s/o Akumu* v. *The Queen* (1954) 21 E.A.C.A. 331
and *Terikabi* v. *Uganda* [1975] E.A. 60. But it is important to notice that
in the countries concerned, the admissibility of a dying declaration does not   F
depend upon the common law test: upon the deceased having at the time a
settled hopeless expectation of impending death. Instead there is the very
different statutory provision contained in section 32 (1) of the Indian
Evidence Act 1872. That section provides that statements of relevant facts
made by a person who is dead are themselves relevant facts:

> " When the statement is made by a person as to the cause of his   G
> death, or as to any of the circumstances of the transaction which re-
> sulted in his death, in cases in which the cause of that person's death
> comes into question. Such statements are relevant *whether the person
> who made them was or was not, at the time when they were made,
> under expectation of death,* and whatever may be the nature of the
> proceeding in which the cause of his death comes into question."
> (emphasis added).   H

In *Pius Jasunga s/o Akumu* v. *The Queen* it was pointed out (for the reason
associated with the italicised words in the subsection) that the weight to be
attached to a dying declaration admitted by reference to section 32 of the
Indian Evidence Act 1872 would necessarily be less than that attached to
a dying declaration admitted under the common law rules. The first kind of
statement would lack that special quality that is thought to surround a

A declaration made by a dying man who was conscious of his condition and who had given up all hope of survival. Accordingly it may not seem surprising that the courts dealing with such statements have felt the need to exercise even more caution in the use to be made of them than is the case where the common law test is applied. Be that as it may it is clear that the line of authority to which reference was made when the petition
B for special leave was under consideration has no relevance for present purposes.

The argument that Smith C.J. wrongly admitted the relevant evidence as a dying declaration can be dealt with shortly. As mentioned counsel contended both that there was insufficient evidence to justify a finding that at the crucial time the deceased was under a hopeless settled expectation of death and also that the Chief Justice had failed to assess the probative
C quality of the wife's evidence concerning the matter. They are issues that turn upon the record of what Smith C.J. said when ruling in favour of the evidence.

As to all this, their Lordships appreciate that there are references in the ruling to an assumption to be made concerning what the witness gave in evidence which, when examined in isolation from the surrounding record,
D may seem to carry a degree of ambiguity. It may appear at first sight that Smith C.J. was prepared to adopt the wife's evidence without assessing it. But their Lordships are of opinion that the approach was designed to test the wider significance of her evidence as it bore upon the true attitude of mind of the deceased himself. It is beyond argument that in the very context of the assumption there is further reference to an evaluation of the alleged inconsistencies already mentioned which counsel had relied upon to support
E his submission that the evidence was unreliable. The ruling was given orally and although the part of it under review is elliptical their Lordships are clearly of opinion that Smith C.J. did not misdirect himself: that he well understood the need to assess the quality of the deponent's evidence just as he then proceeded quite properly to test the statement said to have been made by the deceased himself against the latter's state of mind at the
F relevant time.

For these reasons this ground of appeal too must fail.

Solicitors: *Philip Conway, Thomas & Co.; Charles Russell & Co.*

T. J. M.

G

H

[QUEEN'S BENCH DIVISION]

* DUNKLEY v. EVANS AND ANOTHER

1981 March 24;   Ormrod L.J. and Webster J.
April 15

> *Statutory Instrument—Validity—Severability—Power under statute
> to make orders prohibiting fishing in designated areas—Order
> defining area to include parts of sea over which no ministerial
> power to make order—Whether invalid part of defined area
> severable — Validity of order — Sea Fish (Conservation) Act
> 1967 (c. 84), ss. 5 (2), 23 (1) (as amended by Fishery Limits
> Act 1976 (c. 86), s. 9 (1), Sch. 2, para. 16)—West Coast Her-
> ring (Prohibition of Fishing) Order 1978 (S.I. 1978 No. 930),
> art. 2, Sch.*

The defendants fished for herring in a prohibited area
within British fishing limits, contrary to the West Coast Herring
(Prohibition of Fishing) Order 1978. On the hearing of informations preferred against them, the defendants admitted that they
had fished in an area over which ministers had power to make
an order under section 5 (2) of the Sea Fish (Conservation)
Act 1967 [1] but contended that the Order of 1978 was invalid
because the prohibited area included Northern Irish waters
over which the ministerial power to make orders was excluded
by section 23 (1) of the Act. The justices accepted the submission and dismissed the informations.

On appeal by the prosecutor : —

Held, allowing the appeal, that, although the text of the
Order of 1978 did not lend itself to judicial deletion of words
that rendered part of the Order ultra vires, the omission of
the invalid parts would hardly affect the remainder and, since
the legislature would have enacted the valid provisions independently of the invalid parts, the Order was valid except in
so far as it affected the area of sea reserved by section 23 (1)
of the Act; and that, accordingly, the defendants had committed offences in fishing for herring in an area where such
fishing was validly prohibited by the Order (post, pp. 1525A–B,
F–G, H—1526A).

Dictum of Cussen J. in *Olsen* v. *City of Camberwell* [1926]
V.L.R. 58, 68 applied.

The following cases are referred to in the judgment:

Agricultural, Horticultural and Forestry Industry Training Board v.
Aylesbury Mushrooms Ltd. [1972] 1 W.L.R. 190; [1972] 1 All E.R.
280.

Carltona Ltd. v. *Works Commissioners* [1943] 2 All E.R. 560, C.A.

Hotel and Catering Industry Training Board v. *Automobile Proprietary
Ltd.* [1969] 1 W.L.R. 697; [1969] 2 All E.R. 582, H.L.(E.).

Olsen v. *City of Camberwell* [1926] V.L.R. 58.

Point of Ayr Collieries Ltd. v. *Lloyd-George* [1943] 2 All E.R. 546, C.A.

Potato Marketing Board v. *Merricks* [1958] 2 Q.B. 316; [1958] 3 W.L.R.
135; [1958] 2 All E.R. 538.

Strickland v. *Hayes* [1896] 1 Q.B. 290, D.C.

[1] Sea Fish (Conservation) Act 1967, s. 5, as amended: " (2) The power [to
prohibit fishing by order] shall, in relation to the imposition of any prohibition . . .
(b) on fishing for [herring] in any waters adjacent to Great Britain and within
[British fishery limits], be exercisable wherever it appears to the ministers to be
necessary or expedient . . ."

S. 23, as amended: " (1) Section 5 (2) of this Act shall not apply to the imposition of any prohibition or restriction on fishing within waters within British fishery
limits which are adjacent to Northern Ireland and [within certain defined limits]. . . ."

A   The following additional case was cited in argument:

> *Hoffmann-La Roche (F.) & Co. A.G.* v. *Secretary of State for Trade and Industry* [1975] A.C. 295; [1974] 3 W.L.R. 104; [1974] 2 All E.R. 1128, H.L.(E.).

CASE STATED by Humberside justices sitting at Great Grimsby.

B   On November, 12, 1979, informations were preferred by the prosecutor, David John Dunkley, against the defendants, Raymond Evans and Sandy Fishing Co. Ltd., that they did, on or about October 14, 1979, within British fishery limits, and within the area specified in the Schedule to the West Coast Herring (Prohibition of Fishing) Order 1978 as being an area in which such fishing is prohibited, being the master/owners of the British fishing vessel *Grimsby Lady,* fish for herring contrary to article 2 C of the Order, and section 5 (1) of the Sea Fish (Conservation) Act 1967.

The justices heard the informations on December 16, 1980, and found the following facts which had been formally admitted on behalf of the defendants. Raymond Evans was, from October 3, 1979, the master of the British fishing vessel *Grimsby Lady.* Sandy Fishing Co. Ltd. was, at all material times, the owner of the vessel. On or about October 14, 1979, Raymond Evans did fish for herring from the vessel within British fishery D limits at position 56°30′ north, 10°00′ west.

It was contended by the prosecutor that, although the Order was invalid as to part of the area included in the Schedule to the Order, i.e. an area adjacent to Northern Ireland, any offence committed in the remainder of the area should result in a conviction. The Northern Irish waters were clearly defined and severable. The *Grimsby Lady* was fishing E in that area for which the minister had power to make the Order. The part of the area which was invalid could be separated without altering the character of the rest of the Order.

It was contended by the defendants that where the good law was inextricably inseparable from the bad law in the Order whereby the Order needed rewriting, then the Order would be invalid. The wording of the Schedule to the Order and section 23 (1) of the Act of 1967 needed amend-F ment, it could not be made valid by striking out words in the Schedule.

The justices were of the opinion that the area described in the Schedule to the Order was unambiguous, but that it included Northern Ireland waters which the minister had no power to include in the Order and that the Order was ultra vires. The justices preferred the conten- tion of the defendants that severance of the invalid area from the area G described in the Schedule could not be supported by case law. The justices accordingly dismissed the informations.

The prosecutor appealed. The question for the opinion of the High Court was whether the justices were right in holding that the West Coast Herring (Prohibition of Fishing) Order 1978 was invalid.

H   *L. J. Davies Q.C.* and *P. G. Langdon-Davies* for the prosecutor.
N. A. Phillips Q.C. and *M. D. G. Cran* for the defendants.

Cur. adv. vult.

April 15. ORMROD L.J. read the following judgment of the court. This is an appeal by case stated, by the prosecutor from the dismissal on December 16, 1980, by Humberside justices sitting at Great Grimsby, of

informations alleging that the defendants on October 14, 1979, had fished A
for herring in a prohibited area, contrary to article 2 of the West Coast
Herring (Prohibition of Fishing) Order 1978.

It was admitted by the defendants that they had been fishing for herring
at a position 56°30′ north, 10°00′ west, which is within the area referred
to in the Order, contrary to article 2. The defence was that this Order
was ultra vires the minister who purported to make it under the terms of
the Sea Fish (Conservation) Act 1967. The justices accepted this submission and dismissed the informations. They now ask if they were right
to do so.

The point arises in this way. Under section 5 (2) of the Sea Fish
(Conservation) Act 1967, the ministers concerned may make orders prohibiting fishing within the area of the British fishery limits as defined in
the Act, as amended by section 9 (1) of and paragraph 16 of Schedule 2 C
to the Fishery Limits Act 1976.

The Order of 1978 prohibited fishing for herring within the area of
the sea defined in the Schedule, that is, the area lying within British
fishery limits and bounded by a line defined by a series of co-ordinates
set out in the Schedule. It was conceded that the defendants were fishing
for herring at a point which was within British fishery limits and within D
the area defined by the co-ordinates. However, section 23 (1) of the Act
of 1967, as amended by section 9 (1) of and paragraph 16 (7) of Schedule 2 to the Fishery Limits Act 1976, provides that the minister's powers
under the Act of 1967 shall not extend over a defined area of the sea
adjacent to the coast of Northern Ireland, 40 miles long by nine miles
wide. The prosecution conceded that the minister's power to make regulations did not extend over this relatively small area of the sea, notwith- E
standing that the Secretary of State for Northern Ireland was one of the
ministers who made the Order. Powers over this area were reserved to the
government of Northern Ireland. We understand that at present the power
to make prohibition orders in respect of this area of the sea is vested in
the Department of Agriculture (Northern Ireland), a statutory corporation
which can make the necessary orders itself. The Secretary of State for F
Northern Ireland has no power personally to make such orders.

The prosecutor submits that the fact that this Order is ultra vires in
so far as this area off the coast of Northern Ireland is concerned, does not
render the whole Order ultra vires. For the defence Mr. Phillips contended
that the whole Order is rendered invalid by including this area of the sea.
The offending area represents 0·8 per cent. of the area covered by the
Order. The only question, therefore, is whether it is possible to sever the G
invalid part from the valid part of the Order, or whether the whole Order
is invalidated by the inclusion of this small area.

The general principle is stated in *Halsbury's Laws of England,* 4th ed.,
vol. 1 (1973), para. 26:

"Unless the invalid part is inextricably interconnected with the valid,
a court is entitled to set aside or disregard the invalid part, leaving the H
rest intact."

The principle is more fully formulated in the judgment of Cussen J. sitting
in the Supreme Court of Victoria in *Olsen* v. *City of Camberwell* [1926]
V.L.R. 58, 68, where he said:

"If the enactment, with the invalid portion omitted, is so radically
or substantially different a law as to the subject-matter dealt with by

A   what remains from what it would be with the omitted portions forming part of it as to warrant a belief that the legislative body intended
it as a whole only, or, in other words, to warrant a belief that if all
could not be carried into effect the legislative body would not have
enacted the remainder independently, then the whole must fail."

We respectfully agree with and adopt this statement of the law. It would
B be difficult to imagine a clearer example than the present case of a law
which the legislative body would have enacted independently of the
offending portion and which is so little affected by eliminating the invalid
portion. This is clearly, therefore, an order which the court should not
strive officiously to kill to any greater extent than it is compelled to do.

Mr. Phillips, for the defendants, submitted that the court must confine
C the ministers " within the four corners of the powers given by the legisla-
ture," and referred us to two judgments by Lord Greene M.R. in *Point of
Ayr Collieries Ltd.* v. *Lloyd-George* [1943] 2 All E.R. 546 and *Carltona
Ltd.* v. *Works Commissioners* [1943] 2 All E.R. 560. That will be the
precise effect of eliminating the invalid portion of the Order in question.
He also submitted that the ministers did not apply their minds to the
right question. With respect, the question was the prohibition of herring
D fishing in an area off the west coast to which they clearly applied their
minds. Someone, however, overlooked the powers of the Department of
Agriculture (Northern Ireland) and probably failed to appreciate the
niceties of the present constitutional position of the Secretary of State for
Northern Ireland.

His main point, however, was that the court could not sever the invalid
E portion of this Order from the remainder because it was not possible to
excise from the text of the Order the words which rendered part of it
invalid. This is the so-called " blue pencil test." This test has been elaborated mainly in connection with covenants in restraint of trade. No
doubt the court will not and cannot rewrite contracts, and so confines
itself to deleting part of the text when it is able to do so. The same
F policy has been followed in relation to bye-laws where the text permitted
(*Strickland* v. *Hayes* [1896] 1 Q.B. 290), and to a demand for a return,
part of which could be struck out from a form (*Potato Marketing Board* v.
Merricks [1958] 2 Q.B. 316).

We can see no reason why the powers of the court to sever the invalid
portion of a piece of subordinate legislation from the valid should be
restricted to cases where the text of the legislation lends itself to judicial
G surgery, or textual emendation by excision. It would have been competent for the court in an action for a declaration that the provisions of
the Order in this case did not apply to the area of the sea off Northern
Ireland reserved by section 23 (1) of the Act of 1967, as amended, to
make the declaration sought, without in any way affecting the validity of
the Order in relation to the remaining 99·2 per cent. of the area referred
H to in the Schedule to the Order. Such an order was made, in effect, by the
House of Lords in *Hotel and Catering Industry Training Board* v. *Automobile Proprietary Ltd.* [1969] 1 W.L.R. 697, and by Donaldson J. in
Agricultural, Horticultural and Forestry Industry Training Board v. *Aylesbury Mushrooms Ltd.* [1972] 1 W.L.R. 190.

Accordingly we hold that the West Coast Herring (Prohibition of
Fishing) Order 1978 is not ultra vires the ministers who made the order,
save in so far as it affects the area of the sea reserved by section 23 (1) of

the Sea Fish (Conservation) Act 1967, as amended, and answer the question   A
put at the end of the case in the negative.

The appeal is, therefore, allowed. The case will be remitted to the
justices to convict the defendants and impose the appropriate penalty or
penalties.

                                          Appeal allowed with costs.

                                          Certificate that points of law of general   B
                                          public importance involved namely:
                                          " (1) Whether where a statutory
                                          instrument (upon the true construc-
                                          tion of which criminal liability de-
                                          pends) has been made partly ultra
                                          vires, the court can construe it and
                                          give effect to it in so far as it would   C
                                          probably have applied had it been
                                          made intra vires. (2) If so, in what
                                          circumstances and upon what prin-
                                          ciples should the court act in decid-
                                          ing whether so to construe and give
                                          effect to it? In particular, is the   D
                                          doctrine of severance applicable?
                                          If so, should the court apply the
                                          ' blue pencil test ' or some other,
                                          and if so what, test? "
                                          Leave to appeal refused.

                                                                                E

     Solicitors: *Solicitor, Ministry of Agriculture, Fisheries and Food;*
Sinclair, Roche & Temperley.

                                                                         H. J.

                                                                                F

                         [COURT OF APPEAL]

                      * PRACTICE DIRECTION
                        (TAPE RECORDERS)

1981 Nov. 19   Lord Lane C.J., Taylor and McCullough JJ.   G

          Contempt of Court — Tape recorder — Use in court — Discretion
               to grant or withhold leave — Contempt of Court Act 1981
               (c. 49), s. 9
          County Court—Tape recorder—Use in court—Discretion to grant
               or withhold leave—Contempt of Court Act 1981, s. 9

                                                                                H

     LORD LANE C.J. at the sitting of the court handed down the following
practice direction by the heads of divisions:

     1. Section 9 of the Contempt of Court Act 1981 contains provisions
governing the unofficial use of tape recorders in court. Among other things
it provides that it is a contempt of court to use in court, or bring into
court for use, any tape recorder or other instrument for recording sound,
except with the leave of the court; and it is also a contempt of court to

A   publish a recording of legal proceedings or to use any such recording in contravention of any conditions which the court may have attached to the grant of permission to use the machine in court. These provisions do not apply to the making or use of sound recordings for purposes of official transcripts of proceedings, upon which the Act imposes no restriction whatever.

B   2. The discretion given to the court to grant, withhold or withdraw leave to use tape recorders or to impose conditions as to the use of the recording is unlimited, but the following factors may be relevant to its exercise: (a) the existence of any reasonable need on the part of the applicant for leave, whether a litigant or a person connected with the press or broadcasting, for the recording to be made; (b) in a criminal case, or a civil case in which a direction has been given excluding one or more

C   witnesses from the court, the risk that the recording could be used for the purpose of briefing witnesses out of court; (c) any possibility that the use of a recorder would disturb the proceedings or distract or worry any witnesses or other participants.

3. Consideration should always be given whether conditions as to the use of a recording made pursuant to leave should be imposed. The identity and role of the applicant for leave and the nature of the subject matter of

D   the proceedings may be relevant to this.

4. The particular restriction imposed by section 9 (1) (b) applies in every case, but may not be present to the mind of every applicant to whom leave is given. It may, therefore, be desirable on occasion for this provision to be drawn to the attention of those to whom leave is given.

5. The transcript of a permitted recording is intended for the use of

E   the person given leave to make it and is not intended to be used as, or to compete with, the official transcript mentioned in section 9 (4).

LORD LANE C.J.
LORD DENNING M.R.
SIR JOHN ARNOLD P.
SIR ROBERT MEGARRY V.-C.

F

Unofficial use of tape recorders in county courts

The Lord Chancellor has directed, pursuant to his powers under Ord. 48, r. 1 (2) of the County Court Rules, that the *Practice Direction (Tape Recorders)* issued on November 19, 1981, by the heads of divisions giving guidance as to the unofficial use of tape recorders in the Supreme

G   Court shall apply also to the county courts.

H

1528

[1981]

A

[DIVISIONAL COURT]

* FAULKNER v. TALBOT

1981 April 2   Lord Lane C.J., Boreham and Drake JJ.

B

Crime—Sexual offences—Indecent assault—Boy under 16—Woman touching boy's penis—Whether act prior to sexual intercourse constituting indecent assault—Sexual Offences Act 1956 (4 & 5 Eliz. 2, c. 69), s. 15 (1) (2)

The Sexual Offences Act 1956 provides by section 15:
" (1) It is an offence for a person to make an indecent assault on a man. (2) A boy under the age of 16 cannot in law give any consent which would prevent an act being C an assault for the purposes of this section."

A boy, aged 14 years, who had left his parents and was living at the defendant's home, watched a horror film with the defendant and said that he was frightened. The defendant invited the boy to sleep with her if he wished to do so, which he did. When they were in bed the defendant invited the boy to have sexual intercourse with her. The boy resisted the defendant's attempts to put her hand on his penis, whereupon D she pulled the boy on top of her, took hold of his penis and placed it inside her vagina. The defendant was charged with indecent assault on a boy aged 14 years contrary to section 15 (1) of the Sexual Offences Act 1956. The justices convicted the defendant and she appealed to the Crown Court. That court, in dismissing her appeal, rejected her contention that, since there was no specific provision making the act of sexual intercourse between a woman and a boy under 16 an offence, E the touching of the boy as a prelude to sexual intercourse could not be an indecent assault under section 15 of the Act.

On appeal by the defendant: —

Held, dismissing the appeal, that since the defendant had intentionally touched the boy's penis that touching was an assault and by its nature indecent; that the boy, being under the age of 16, could not consent to her action by reason of F section 15 (2) of the Act of 1956 so that the touching was without lawful excuse and, accordingly, all the necessary ingredients of the offence of indecent assault pursuant to section 15 (1) were present (post, pp. 1534c–h, 1535g—1536a).

Reg. v. *McCormack* [1969] 2 Q.B. 442, C.A. applied.

Director of Public Prosecutions v. *Rogers* [1953] 1 W.L.R. 1017, D.C. explained.

Reg. v. *Mason* (1968) 53 Cr.App.R. 12 not followed.

G

The following cases are referred to in the judgment:

Director of Public Prosecutions v. *Rogers* [1953] 1 W.L.R. 1017; [1953] 2 All E.R. 644; 37 Cr.App.R. 137, D.C.

Fairclough v. *Whipp* [1951] 2 All E.R. 834, D.C.

Rex v. *Hare* [1934] 1 K.B. 354, C.C.A.

Reg. v. *Mason* (1968) 53 Cr.App.R. 12.

Reg. v. *McCormack* [1969] 2 Q.B. 442; [1969] 3 W.L.R. 175; [1969] 3 All H E.R. 371; 53 Cr.App.R. 514, C.A.

Reg. v. *Sutton (Terence)* [1977] 1 W.L.R. 1086; [1977] 3 All E.R. 476; 66 Cr.App.R. 21, C.A.

Reg. v. *Upward* (unreported), October 7, 1976, Wien J.

The following additional case was cited in argument:

Rex v. *Burrows (Note)* [1952] 1 All E.R. 58, 35 Cr.App.R. 180, C.C.A.

A   CASE STATED by Stafford Crown Court.

The prosecutor, Ian Keith Talbot, a police officer, charged the defendant, Patricia Ann Faulkner, on October 30, 1979, that at Stafford in the county of Stafford between September 1, 1979, and October 30, 1979, she did indecently assault a male person of 14 years of age contrary to section 15 (1) of the Sexual Offences Act 1956. The defendant was then bailed to appear at Stafford Magistrates' Court on November 26, 1979, to answer the charge. On November 26, 1979, before the justices sitting at Stafford Magistrates' Court the prosecutor laid an information against the defendant in terms of the charge. On February 5, 1980, the justices heard the information when both defendant and the prosecutor were represented. The justices convicted the defendant and committed her for sentence to Stafford Crown Court pursuant to the provision of section 29 of the Magistrates' Courts Act 1952.

By notice of appeal dated February 6, 1980, the defendant appealed to Stafford Crown Court against her conviction. Together with the justices who sat with him, the recorder heard the appeal on July 18, 1980, when the case was adjourned part heard. On July 21, 1980, the justices were not present or available and with the consent of counsel for the defendant and the prosecutor the recorder continued without them. The recorder found the following facts.

The defendant was convicted by the justices on February 5, 1980, of indecent assault on a boy then aged 14, contrary to section 15 (1) of the Sexual Offences Act 1956. The events giving rise to the charge happened at the defendant's home. The primary facts were not in dispute because the defendant, by her counsel, admitted the truth of the account of the boy set out in a statement in question and answer form which was before the court. The statement revealed that sexual intercourse, at any rate in the sense of penetration of the defendant by the boy, took place in her bedroom. At that time the boy had left his parents and was living at the defendant's home. Normally the defendant's boyfriend slept with her, but on the night in question he was away from home.

The defendant and the boy watched a horror film on television, and he apparently was scared of it. The defendant told him that he could sleep with her, and because he had been scared of the film he chose to do so. Once they were in bed together the defendant invited the boy to have intercourse with her. In the course of his account of what followed the boy stated that: "The defendant tried to put her hand on my thingy but I wouldn't let her because I have a rupture. She then pulled me on top of her. She was on her back with her legs open. She got hold of my thingy which was a bit hard and put it inside her."

The contentions of the defendant were that there was no provision of English law which made it an offence for a woman to have sexual intercourse with a boy under the age of 16, that is, an express offence. In those circumstances it was anomalous that a lesser act of sexual intimacy should be regarded as capable of founding an offence. Section 14 (3), which related to indecent assault on girls, relieved of guilt a man who believed the subject of the alleged offence to be his wife although she was in fact under 16, and the marriage was, therefore, invalid, while section 15 contained no parallel provision. For that reason section 15 might not have been intended to apply to an act of indecency committed by a woman against a man, but the Crown Court was bound by authorities to reject that proposition. Particular acts done in the course of the general act

of intercourse between a woman and a boy under 16, willingly under- A
taken by the boy, could not constitute an indecent assault on the boy by
the woman. For that proposition reliance was placed on the ruling of
Veale J. in *Reg.* v. *Mason* (1968) 53 Cr.App.R. 12 and the views expressed
by Wien J. in *Reg.* v. *Upward* (unreported), October 7, 1976. The position
where the subject of the alleged offence was under 16 was complicated by
the provision that a boy or girl under 16 could not consent to an indecent
assault.   B

It was contended by the prosecutor (i) that if the boy had not consented the acts of the defendant amounted to an assault on him; (ii) that
the assault was of an indecent nature so that the boy by virtue of his age
was incapable of giving his consent to it; (iii) that the fact that the assault
was committed immediately before an act of sexual intercourse by the boy
with the defendant was immaterial.   C

The recorder was of the opinion that from the most recent cases cited
to the court, *Reg.* v. *McCormack* [1969] 2 Q.B. 442 and *Reg.* v. *Sutton*
[1977] 1 W.L.R. 1086, it was possible to extract the following principles.
When faced with a charge of indecent assault on a person under 16,
whether the assailant or subject was male or female, it was necessary first
to ask: " Did the defendant do an act which the court was sure, if there   D
was no consent on the part of the subject, would be an assault? " If so, it
was necessary next to ask: " Did the subject in fact consent? " If he did
not consent then assault was proved and the question was whether it was
accompanied by indecency. Where the court was not satisfied that the
subject did not consent that is if the conclusion of fact was that he might
have consented, the question had to be asked: " Was the act alleged to
constitute the assault itself an indecent act? " If so, the consent would not E
avail. According to the evidence the defendant pulled the boy on top of
her, got hold of his penis and put it inside her. As a matter of law those
acts, if done without consent, would constitute an assault. But the boy
did or might have consented. The next question was whether those acts
were of themselves indecent. That was a question of fact. There could be
no doubt that those acts were in themselves indecent. Accordingly the   F
offence was proved. The recorder dismissed the appeal.

The question for the opinion of the High Court was whether the acts
of the defendant to which the boy consented in pulling him on top of her
and touching his penis immediately before sexual intercourse by him with
her were an indecent assault by the defendant on the boy contrary to
section 15 (1) of the Sexual Offences Act 1956.   G

Malcolm Lee for the defendant.
Anthony Barker for the prosecutor.

LORD LANE C.J. This is an appeal by way of case stated from the
Crown Court at Stafford in respect of an adjudication of that court sitting
then on appeal from the justices for the county of Stafford.   H

The way in which the case arises is this. The defendant, Patricia Ann
Faulkner, was convicted by the justices on February 5, 1980, of indecent assault on a boy, who was then aged 14 years, contrary to section
15 (1) of the Sexual Offences Act 1956. The events happened at the
defendant's home, and there is no dispute as to the material facts. The 14-
year-old boy was living in the defendant's home, having left his parents.
The defendant and the boy watched a horror film on the television; the

A boy was scared, or said he was scared, by the film. As a result of that the defendant told the boy that he could sleep with her if he wished. That he chose to do.

Once they were in bed together, the defendant invited the boy to have sexual intercourse with her. The boy's account, in so far as it was material, was this: the defendant tried to put her hand on his penis, but he would not let her. She then pulled the boy on top of her; she took hold of his

B penis and put it inside her vagina. On those facts the charge was laid.

It is a well-known fact that there is no statutory provision specifically forbidding a woman to have sexual intercourse with a boy of 14. But what section 15 of the Sexual Offences Act 1956, under which this case was brought, says is as follows:

C
"(1) It is an offence for a person to make an indecent assault on a man. (2) A boy under the age of sixteen cannot in law give any consent which would prevent an act being an assault for the purposes of this section."

The way in which Mr. Lee, in his attractive argument to this court, has put the matter is as follows. He submits that since the act of sexual intercourse in these circumstances is not an offence on the part of the

D woman, therefore that touching of the boy as a prelude to, or as part of, or as postlude to, the act of sexual intercourse cannot in logic itself be an offence.

He submits secondly, if, for example, in an act of sexual intercourse, in the way described by Wien J. in *Reg.* v. *Upward* (unreported), October 7, 1976, to which reference will be made later, a woman lies passively and

E does nothing at all except let the boy have sexual intercourse, that, suggests Mr. Lee, would be no offence; whereas if she took any part in the act, by touching the boy for instance on the buttock during the act of sexual intercourse, it would be an offence. That, Mr. Lee submits, is contrary to common sense and contrary to logic and, therefore, he goes on to argue, it cannot be right that the act of sexual intercourse under any

F circumstances can amount to indecent assault by the woman on the boy.

We have been referred to a number of authorities and it is right, both for the purpose of clarity and in deference to the arguments addressed to us, that I should refer to them.

The first case we were referred to was *Rex* v. *Hare* [1934] 1 K.B. 354. The appellant was a woman who had been convicted under section 62 of the Offences against the Person Act 1861 (which was a precursor of the

G Act of 1956), of indecent assault on a boy of 12. In so far as it was material, that section of the Act of 1861 read: "Whosoever . . . shall be guilty . . . of any indecent assault upon any male person shall be guilty of a misdemeanour."

The judgment of the court was delivered by Avory J. Having stated the facts, he continued, at pp. 355–356:

H
"We are asked in this case to hold that it was not competent to the recorder to leave the case to the jury or for the jury to convict the appellant. The argument put forward on behalf of the appellant is that the charge being laid under section 62 of the Offences against the Person Act 1861, no woman can be convicted of the offences charged. The boy, being under the age of sixteen, was by law incompetent to consent to any such conduct as took place between him and the appellant. There is no question that the nature of that which took

place between them was indecent. The whole question is, as has been A
concisely put by counsel for the appellant, whether the offence under
section 62 is to be limited to an indecent assault of a sodomitical
character. . . . there is no reason for saying that the phrase: ' Whosoever . . . shall be guilty . . . of any indecent assault,' does not
include a woman."

That case provides a formidable hurdle for Mr. Lee to clear.   B

The next case to which we were referred was the *Director of Public
Prosecutions* v. *Rogers* [1953] 1 W.L.R. 1017; 37 Cr.App.R. 137. That
was a case where the facts were somewhat special, as will be observed.
The headnote reads, at p. 137:

" On two occasions, the respondent, when alone in the house with his
daughter aged 11, put his arm round her and led her upstairs, and C
when they were upstairs exposed his person and invited her to
masturbate him, which she did. No compulsion or force was used by
the defendant, and the child neither objected nor resisted, but submitted to the defendant's request. Justices dismissed informations
charging the defendant with indecent assault on the child." The
Divisional Court held, on those facts: " that as the defendant had D
not used compulsion or force, or acted in a hostile manner towards
the child, there had been no assault, and consequently no indecent
assault on her, and that the decision of the justices was, therefore,
right."

The facts were that the father, being alone in the house with the little
daughter, put his arms round her and said " come upstairs." She made no E
objection or resistance and no force was used on either of the two occasions. That was the basis for the decision of the court, namely that the
justices were right and the appeal was dismissed.

It seems to me that the circumstances there were exceptional. There
was no reason why the father should not put his arm round the shoulder
of his daughter; there was a lawful excuse for doing that, because he was
the father. There was no touching of the child in an indecent way.   F

The next case was *Reg.* v. *Mason* (1968) 53 Cr.App.R. 12. The headnote reads as follows:

" The defendant, a married woman, was arraigned on a number of
counts, each alleging indecent assault against one of six different boys,
all between the ages of fourteen and sixteen years. Over a substantial
period of time she had been visited by the boys, sometimes singly, G
sometimes more than one at a time, and had had sexual intercourse
with them. There was no suggestion that she had used any force or
committed any hostile act against any of the boys. Intercourse had
taken place sometimes at her suggestion, sometimes at the suggestion
of the boys themselves.

" *Held,* that as there was no evidence of the use of any force or H
of any hostile act by the defendant, there had been no assault, and
consequently no indecent assault, so that the counts must be quashed."

I read one passage from the judgment of Veale J., which was really
the high spot of Mr. Lee's argument, at p. 18:

" I am further prepared to hold that acts of touching readily submitted to and enjoyed during or preliminary to intercourse in such

A   circumstances should be regarded as part of the intercourse and are equally not an assault by the woman on the boy."

Those words were echoed in a different form in a case to which we have been referred—an unreported case—*Reg.* v. *Upward* which was heard at Caernarvon before Wien J. and a jury on October 4 to 7, 1976. Wien J. was there, in the passage to which we have been referred, inform-

B   ing the jury of the reason why he was directing them to acquit the woman in similar circumstances to those which I have described in *Reg.* v. *Mason* 53 Cr.App.R. 12. Wien J., as I say, echoed and expanded the words used by Veale J. in *Reg.* v. *Mason.*

One turns now to consider whether those two passages correctly reflect the law as it stands at the moment, and in order to reach that deci-

C   sion, it is necessary to look at two more recent decisions. The first is *Reg.* v. *McCormack* [1969] 2 Q.B. 442; 53 Cr.App.R. 514. That was a decision of the Court of Appeal (Criminal Division), Fenton Atkinson L.J., Melford Stevenson and James JJ. The headnote reads as follows, at p. 514:

> " A charge of unlawful sexual intercourse with a girl under sixteen necessarily includes an allegation of indecent assault on the same girl and, where there is clear evidence of indecent assault, the judge should

D   leave this lesser offence also to the jury, even though the prosecution have not relied on it. When a man inserts his finger into the vagina of a girl under sixteen, this is an indecent assault, however willing and co-operative the girl may be."

I read a passage from the judgment of the court delivered by Fenton

E   Atkinson L.J., at pp. 517–518:

> " Then there followed an argument by Mr. Hunt, which he has repeated to this court and put very attractively before us, whether, in view of the girl's consent, there could be a conviction of indecent assault, there being here a willing girl and no evidence of any compulsion or hostility: and he referred to a line of authorities such as *Fairclough* v. *Whipp* (1951) 35 Cr.App.R. 138 and *Director of Public*

F   *Prosecutions* v. *Rogers* [1953] 1 W.L.R. 1017, cases which have shown that where the accused adult invites a child, for example, to touch his private parts, but exercises no sort of compulsion and there is no hostile act, the charge of indecent assault is not appropriate. But, in our view, that line of authorities has no application here, and, in the view of the members of this court, it is plain beyond argument that, if

G   a man inserts a finger into the vagina of a girl under sixteen, that is an indecent assault, in view of her age, and it is an indecent assault however willing and co-operative she may in fact be."

Finally, so far as authorities are concerned, I turn to *Reg.* v. *Sutton* (*Terence*) [1977] 1 W.L.R. 1086; 66 Cr.App.R. 21. In that case the facts were that the appellant took three boys, all under the age of 14, to his

H   home and photographed them partially clothed and in the nude. He remained fully clothed. He neither touched or fondled the boys, except touch them on the hands and legs and bodies in order to arrange their poses for the purpose of photography. The boys consented to these acts.

The appellant was charged with indecently assaulting the boys contrary to section 15 (1) of the Act of 1956. The jury were directed that any touching without consent was an assault and the law did not permit persons under 16 to consent to the touching, if it was accompanied by

1534

circumstances of indecency. The jury convicted. On appeal it was held by A
the Court of Appeal (Criminal Division) that they had been misdirected.

The holding was, 66 Cr.App.R. 21:

" that whereas section 15 (2) of the Sexual Offences Act 1956 bars
consent from preventing an act with a boy under 16 from being an
indecent assault—i.e. if the act alleged to constitute the assault is
itself an indecent act—and thus the defence of consent will not avail B
a defendant; in the present case the touching of the boys by the
appellant, which was merely to indicate a pose, was not of itself
indecent, was consented to and was not hostile or threatening, the
consent of the boys to the acts complained of prevented such acts
being an assault, and, therefore, an indecent assault; thus the question
of indecency did not arise; accordingly, the jury had been misdirected C
and the appeal would be allowed and the conviction quashed."

One turns, in the light of those authorities, to the present case. First of
all what is an assault? An assault is any intentional touching of another
person without the consent of that person and without lawful excuse. It
need not necessarily be hostile or rude or aggressive, as some of the cases
seem to indicate. If the touching is an indecent touching, as in this case it D
plainly was because the appellant took hold of the boy's penis, then the
provisions in section 15 (2) of the Sexual Offences Act 1956 come into
play, " A boy under the age of sixteen cannot in law give any consent
which would prevent an act being an assault for the purposes of this
section." Consequently, the touching undoubtedly being indecent, the boy
in this case, being aged 14, could not consent to it. It was intentional E
touching; it was touching without lawful excuse, and in view of section
15 (2) it was a touching to which the boy could not in law consent and
therefore did not consent. Accordingly, as I see it, one has all the necessary
ingredients of the offence of indecent assault, and the consequence is that
the recorder was correct in the conclusion to which he came.

The question which is asked by the case is as follows: " Whether the F
acts of the defendant to which the boy consented in pulling him on top of
her and touching his penis immediately before sexual intercourse by him
with her were an indecent assault by the defendant on the boy contrary to
section 15 (1) of the Sexual Offences Act 1956? " The answer I would give
to that is " Yes, it was an indecent assault." In my judgment the decision
of Veale J. in *Reg.* v. *Mason,* 53 Cr.App.R. 12 to which reference has
been made was wrong, and in so far as it is necessary to refer to the G
matter, where Wien J. was making explanation to the jury, he was likewise
in error.

For these reasons I would dismiss this appeal.

BOREHAM J. I agree for the reasons given by Lord Lane C.J. I add
only a few words of my own out of deference for the argument of Mr. Lee H
on behalf of the defendant.

Without going into detail, there is, in my judgment, now ample authority for this general proposition: where, in a charge of indecent assault on
a person under the age of 16, the act complained of is indecent and that
act would, if it were done without consent, be an assault, then the offence
is made out. The authority for that is to be found in a number of decisions
from *Fairclough* v. *Whipp* [1951] 2 All E.R. 834, to which Lord Lane C.J.

A has made reference, which was decided in 1951, to *Reg.* v. *Sutton* [1977] 1 W.L.R. 1086, more recently decided. That being so, section 15 (2) of the Sexual Offences Act 1956 provides that the consent of the complainant or the victim does not prevent it from constituting an offence.

In my judgment *Director of Public Prosecutions* v. *Rogers* [1953] 1 W.L.R. 1017 is entirely consistent with that proposition. Indeed the court there, through the words of Lord Goddard C.J., expressly confirmed the

B principle which had been laid down in *Fairclough* v. *Whipp* [1951] 2 All E.R. 834. In my judgment the problem which faced the prosecutor in *Director of Public Prosecutions* v. *Rogers* [1953] 1 W.L.R. 1017 was this, that the act which might have constituted an assault was not an indecent act. The defendant was the father who simply put his arm round the shoulder of his little daughter. The act which was indecent, namely her

C touching of his private parts at his behest, was not capable in the circumstances, for the reasons given in *Fairclough* v. *Whipp* [1951] 2 All E.R. 834, of constituting an assault. As Lord Goddard C.J. pointed out in *Director of Public Prosecutions* v. *Rogers* [1953] 1 W.L.R. 1017, the picture might have looked very different indeed if there had been evidence that that act by the little girl had been induced by threats or compulsion

D or by any hostile act. That was no more than a repetition of what was said in *Fairclough* v. *Whipp* [1951] 2 All E.R. 834.

In my judgment the reference to aggression, hostility, compulsion or the like has been misapplied in later decisions. It is unnecessary to go into detail. It is difficult to say that, in so far as Veale J. decided that it was necessary in cases of this kind that there should be evidence of aggres-

E sion or hostility, then I would respectfully disagree with him for the reasons given by Lord Lane C.J. The same applies to the observations made by Wien J. when explaining to a jury why he had decided to direct them to return verdicts of not guilty. I suspect, as Lord Lane C.J. has said in the course of argument, that Wien J. would be very surprised to know that his words to the jury by way of explanation were likely to be quoted in argument in later cases.

F I agree with the way the matter was put in *Reg.* v. *McCormack* [1969] 2 Q.B. 442; 53 Cr.App.R. 514. The headnote has already been read by Lord Lane C.J.; repetition of it would therefore be unhelpful. It is sufficient to quote one small passage of the judgment given by Fenton Atkinson L.J. He had referred to *Director of Public Prosecutions* v. *Rogers* and suggested that that line of authority had no application to the case with which the

G court was then dealing. He concludes [1969] 2 Q.B. 442, 445: ". . . it is plain beyond argument that if a man inserts a finger into the vagina of a girl under sixteen that is an indecent assault . . . however willing and co-operative she may in fact be."

If that is right, and if I may say so it clearly is right, why then, it seems to me that where roles of the sexes are reversed, where it is the woman

H who deliberately gets hold of the penis of a young boy, then she too is equally, and beyond dispute, guilty of indecent assault (and I quote the words again) " however willing and co-operative [the young boy] may be."

I have said enough I trust to do justice to the argument so attractively put before us. I respectfully agree with Lord Lane C.J.'s decision and with the reasons for that decision. In my judgment the answer to the question posed by the recorder here is an unqualified "Yes."

1536

A

DRAKE J. I also agree. I agree with everything that has been said by Lord Lane C.J. and Boreham J. and I would answer the question in the same way.

I would just add this, that the decision of Veale J. in *Reg.* v. *Mason,* 53 Cr.App.R. 12 and the view expressed by Wien J. in *Reg.* v. *Upward* are in fact both referred to in well-known textbooks, although they were not referred to in argument: that is to say *Smith and Hogan, Criminal Law,* 4th ed. (1978) and *Glanville Williams, Textbook of Criminal Law* (1978). Both of these learned writers came to the conclusion that the decision in *Reg.* v. *Mason,* 53 Cr.App.R. 12 of Veale J. and the views expressed by Wien J., are plainly wrong in law and unable to stand against the other authorities, particularly that of *Reg.* v. *McCormack* [1969] 2 Q.B. 442. The decision of this court confirms those views.

B

C

Appeal dismissed.
Costs out of central funds.

Solicitors: *Gregory, Rowcliffe & Co.* for *Pickering & Butters, Stafford; Kenneth Wainwright & Co., Stafford.*

[Reported by SUSAN DENNY, Barrister-at-Law]

D

[COURT OF APPEAL]

E

* REGINA v. DUNBAR

1981 Oct. 23   Lord Lane C.J., Mustill and McCullough JJ.

Crime—Drugs—Unauthorised possession of—Doctor possessing drugs on own authority for self-treatment—Whether " acting in his capacity " as practitioner—Whether possession unlawful —Misuse of Drugs Act 1971 (c. 38), ss. 5 (1), 7 (3) (a)— Misuse of Drugs Regulations 1973 (S.I. 1973 No. 797), regs. 8 (2), 10 (1)

F

The appellant, who was a registered medical practitioner, was tried on a count charging him with unlawful possession of controlled drugs, contrary to section 5 (1) of the Misuse of Drugs Act 1971.[1] His defence was that he had obtained the drugs himself for self-treatment in order to lift himself out of a severe depression from which he was suffering, so that he had the drugs in his possession for acting in his capacity as a practitioner within regulation 10 (1) of the Misuse of Drugs Regulations 1973.[2] The trial judge ruled that a doctor could not lawfully possess the drugs on his own authority to treat himself, so that on the appellant's own evidence he must be guilty as charged, and the jury, who were so directed, convicted him.

G

H

On appeal against conviction: —

Held, allowing the appeal, that a doctor bona fide treating himself was acting in his capacity as a practitioner although he was himself receiving the benefit of the drug; that it was for

[1] Misuse of Drugs Act 1971, s. 5 (1): see post, p. 1539c.
[2] Misuse of Drugs Regulations 1973, reg. 10 (1): see post, p. 1539G–H.

A   the jury to decide whether the appellant was or was not in fact acting in his capacity as a practitioner; that, therefore, the judge had erred in his direction and the conviction would be quashed.

No cases are referred to in the judgment.

B   The following case was cited in argument:
Keene v. *Muncaster* [1980] R.T.R. 377, D.C.

APPEAL against conviction.

On December 10, 1980, at Knightsbridge Crown Court (Judge Mendl) the appellant, Ian James Cameron Dunbar, a registered medical practitioner, on an amended indictment containing six counts, was convicted
C   by a majority of 10 to two on count 1 charging obtaining property by deception, contrary to section 15 (1) of the Theft Act 1968, in that he on September 12, 1978, dishonestly obtained from W. W. Brunton, Chemists, 10 × 10 mg. ampoules of diamorphine hydrochloride, 10 × 100 mg. ampoules of pethidine and 10 ampoules of sterile water with the intention of permanently depriving the chemists thereof by deception, namely, falsely
D   representing that he required them for professional use in the treatment of bona fide patients; by direction of the judge he was convicted on count 2 charging unlawful possession of a controlled drug in that he on September 12, 1978, did in contravention of section 5 (1) of the Misuse of Drugs Act 1971 unlawfully have in his possession controlled drugs of Class A, namely, 10 × 10 mg. ampoules of diamorphine hydrochloride and 10 × 100 mg. ampoules of pethidine; he pleaded guilty to counts 3 to 5 both
E   inclusive, being charges relating to a controlled drugs register and count 6, unlawful destruction of a controlled drug. He was in breach of a conditional discharge order made on June 17, 1977, in relation to offences concerning controlled drugs. He was sentenced on each count to three months' imprisonment suspended for two years with a similar sentence in respect of the offences for which he had been conditionally discharged. He
F   appealed against conviction on the grounds that, in relation to count 2, the trial judge erred in law in ruling that a registered medical practitioner could not lawfully treat himself with a controlled drug; and in relation to count 1 that in view of the jury having been directed by the judge that the appellant could not lawfully treat himself with controlled drugs, that knowledge could have influenced the decision on the question whether he had acted dishonestly in the circumstances.
G   The facts are stated in the judgment.

Diana Ellis (assigned by the Registrar of Criminal Appeals) for the appellant.
William Clegg for the Crown.

H   LORD LANE C.J. gave the following judgment of the court. On December 10, 1980, at the Crown Court at Knightsbridge the appellant faced an indictment containing six counts. He pleaded guilty to two counts of failing to make an entry in a controlled drugs register (counts 3 and 4) and to one count of failing to produce a controlled drugs register (count 5). He also pleaded guilty to a count of unlawful destruction of a controlled drug (count 6).

It is counts 1 and 2 which have occupied the attention of this court

this morning. On count 1 he was convicted by a majority verdict of the A
jury of obtaining property by deception contrary to section 15 (1) of the
Theft Act 1968, the allegation being that he dishonestly obtained a quantity
of diamorphine hydrochloride and pethidine from a chemist by deception, that is, by falsely representing that he required them for professional
use, for the treatment of bona fide patients. On count 2 he was convicted
by direction of the judge of unlawful possession of controlled drugs,
namely, diamorphine hydrochloride and pethidine.   B

He was sentenced to three months' imprisonment, suspended for two
years, on each count and an order was made in respect of a breach of a
conditional discharge to which he was previously subject.

We granted the necessary extension of time and we granted the application for leave to appeal against the conviction on count 1. The appeal
against the conviction on count 2 is on a point of law, and consequently C
no leave was required.

The facts of the case are these. The appellant is a registered medical
practitioner. On September 12, 1978, he obtained from a chemist's shop in
the Earls Court Road a quantity of diamorphine hydrochloride and
pethidine. For this purpose he handed over the counter an order on his
own headed notepaper, signed by him, saying " Please supply for professional purposes." The manager of the shop asked the appellant whether D
the drugs were required for surgery use, and he, according to the manager
of the shop, replied " Yes," although this matter was the subject of dispute
at the trial. In evidence the manager of the shop said that had he known
that the appellant was going to inject himself with the drugs, he would
not have supplied them to the appellant.

The appellant was interviewed by the police in April 1979. In short he E
admitted that he had obtained these drugs, and told the police, according
to them, that he had intended at the time of obtaining them to use them
to commit suicide. But after using some of them he felt better, and so he
flushed the remainder down the lavatory at his home. In evidence he said
that he had not in fact intended to commit suicide at all, but had obtained
the drugs in order to lift himself out of the severe depression from which F
he was suffering.

So far as the count of obtaining by deception was concerned, the
prosecution case was that he had obtained the drugs by the false representation that he required them for professional use for the treatment of
bona fide patients. The Crown's allegation was that when the drugs were
obtained, the appellant had no patients at all, that he wanted the drugs
for his own use to commit suicide, and accordingly was in unlawful G
possession of the drugs.

At the close of the defence case the judge was asked to consider the
situation in count 2, the unlawful possession count, and to rule whether
what had been said by the appellant in evidence on his own behalf could,
taken at its best from the point of view of the defence, amount to a
defence. The judge ruled against the appellant on that submission, and H
consequently held that, even on the evidence of the appellant himself, he
must be guilty of unlawful possession of controlled drugs, and so directed
the jury. Hence the conviction on count 2.

The basis of the judge's ruling was this. He first of all set out the
statutory provisions and the regulations, to which we will come in a
moment, and then he said:

" Can it be said that a person who is a doctor can have in his pos-

A   session a controlled drug of Class A when his authority for so doing is that of himself—ordering drugs for himself in order to treat himself? In my judgment he could not. I do not think that a doctor is entitled, under the Act and the Regulations to have a controlled drug in his possession except by virtue of some other regulation or provision, in other words it may be as a result of him having a drug prescribed by another doctor. . . . That being the case, whatever Dr.

B   Dunbar's understanding of the position may have been, it would seem to me that, subject to anything Miss Ellis may have to say, I will be obliged to direct the jury on the second count of the indictment that they must, on my direction, return a verdict of guilty."

That was in fact done.

C   We now turn to the statutory provisions and the regulations in order to see how the matter is set out. Section 5 (1) of the Misuse of Drugs Act 1971 provides:

" Subject to any regulations under section 7 of this Act for the time being in force, it shall not be lawful for a person to have a controlled drug in his possession."

D Section 7 provides:

" (1) The Secretary of State may by regulations . . . (b) make such other provision as he thinks fit for the purpose of making it lawful for persons to do things which under any of the following provisions of this Act, that is to say sections 4 (1), 5 (1) and 6 (1), it would otherwise be unlawful for them to do. . . . (3) Subject to subsection

E   (4) below, the Secretary of State shall so exercise his power to make regulations under subsection (1) above as to secure—(a) that it is not unlawful under section 4 (1) of this Act for a doctor, dentist, veterinary practitioner or veterinary surgeon, acting in his capacity as such, to prescribe, administer, manufacture, compound or supply a controlled drug, or for a pharmacist or a person lawfully conducting a retail pharmacy business, acting in either case in his capacity as

F   such, to manufacture, compound or supply a controlled drug; and (b) that it is not unlawful under section 5 (1) of this Act for a doctor, dentist, veterinary practitioner, veterinary surgeon, pharmacist or person lawfully conducting a retail pharmacy business to have a controlled drug in his possession for the purpose of acting in his capacity as such."

G   We turn then to the regulations made under the authority of that Act, which are to be found in the Misuse of Drugs Regulations 1973. Regulation 10 (1) reads as follows:

" Notwithstanding the provisions of section 5 (1) of the Act—(a) a person specified in regulation 8 (2) may have in his posession any drug specified in Schedule 2; (b) a person specified in regulation 9 (2)

H   may have in his possession any drug specified in Schedule 3, for the purpose of acting in his capacity as such."

Regulation 8 (2) reads as follows:

" Notwithstanding the provisions of section 4 (1) (b) of the Act any of the following persons, that is to say: — (a) a practitioner; (b) a pharmacist; (c) a person lawfully conducting a retail pharmacy business; . . . may, when acting in his capacity as such, supply or

offer to supply any drug specified in Schedule 1 or 2 to any person A
who may lawfully have that drug in his possession: . . . ."

The definition of practitioner is to be found in section 37 (1) of the Act,
and reads: ". . . 'practitioner' . . . means a doctor. . . . ." The only other
provision that it is necessary to read is regulation 10 (2):

" Notwithstanding the provisions of section 5 (1) of the Act a person
    may have in his possession any drug specified in Schedule 2 or 3 for B
    administration for medical, dental or veterinary purposes in accord-
    ance with the direction of a practitioner: Provided that this paragraph
    shall not have effect in the case of a person to whom the drug has
    been supplied by or on the prescription of a doctor. . . . ."

It is right that we should mention that the drugs with which we are C
concerned here are Schedule 2 drugs and so they come within the
provisions of the statute and regulations which we have read.

The way in which the matter is put before us by Miss Ellis on behalf
of the appellant is this. In her submission the words which have to be
considered, and really exclusively have to be considered, are those to be
found in regulation 10, that " a person specified," that is, a doctor, " may
have in his possession any drug specified in Schedule 2 . . . for the purpose D
of acting in his capacity " as a doctor. There is no doubt that the appellant
had in his possession Schedule 2 drugs. That is not in dispute. The only
question therefore that remains to be decided is: did he have them in his
possession in his capacity as a doctor?

It is very much a matter of first impression, as it so often is in this kind
of case. But the way in which it is put on behalf of the Crown is that, it is E
impossible for a person to act in his capacity as a doctor if he is not at the
time treating a patient, other than himself. Consequently a doctor who has
no patient, as was so in the case of the appellant, is not acting in his
capacity as a doctor.

That is a proposition which we find ourselves unable to accept. There
seem to us to be many occasions on which it can properly be said that a F
man is acting in his capacity as a doctor which have nothing to do with the
existence of any patients. If the Crown were correct, it would produce the
extraordinary result that no doctor, who had quite properly in his drug
cupboard a Schedule 2 drug, and who quite properly decided that he
required such a drug—for instance codeine—to alleviate either pain or
sickness in himself, could administer to himself such a drug without committing a criminal offence. Similarly the sort of situation propounded by G
Miss Ellis, where a doctor, again perfectly properly carrying morphine in
his bag in a car, suffers an accident as a result of which he is in acute
pain. If he were in those circumstances to remove an ampoule of morphine
from his bag and inject himself to relieve the pain with morphine, he once
again would be committing a criminal offence.

We find that as a proposition unattractive. Taking the words as they H
stand, it seems to us that the doctor bona fide treating himself in those
circumstances, is acting in his capacity as a practitioner, although it is he
himself who is receiving the benefit of the drug.

So much for that aspect. I emphasise the words " bona fide," because
there may well be cases, and the instant circumstances illustrate one of
them, where the actions of the doctor are not bona fide, and where they
might, on one view of the case, take him outside his acting in his capacity

A   as a doctor. For instance the suggestion made here, namely, it was said to the police that he intended to use these drugs to commit suicide, could scarcely be said, if that was his intention, that he would be acting either bona fide or in his capacity as a medical practitioner if with that view in mind he had possession of the drugs.

   What, in our judgment, it comes down to is this, that it is a matter for the jury to decide whether he was in fact acting in that capacity or not.

B   If in the present case the jury had come to the conclusion that they felt sure, whilst the drugs were in his possession, he intended to use them to commit suicide, then upon a proper direction one imagines the jury would have come to the conclusion that he was not acting in the proper capacity. But that was something which, by the judge's ruling, was withdrawn from their consideration.

C   We say straight away that this was not an easy problem for the judge to decide, and it has not been an easy problem for us to decide. No one must for a moment criticise the judge for taking the view which he did. We have come to the conclusion nevertheless that this was a matter which properly should have been left to the jury. To say, as the judge did, that because the doctor had no patient, because the only patient was the doctor

D   himself, ergo he was not acting in his capacity as a doctor, was wrong.

   We do not find it necessary to embark upon a discussion as to the meaning of regulation 10 (2), the contents of which we have already read. It may be that difficult problems would arise in determining the meaning of the words " administration for medical, dental or veterinary purposes in accordance with the direction of a practitioner."

E   Mr. Clegg on behalf of the Crown has painted a horrifying picture of what will happen as a result of this ruling which we are in the process of making. He submits that the whole Act was designed to restrict people administering prohibited drugs. With that we would agree. But he submits that if this court says that any doctor can administer to himself any quantity of drugs he wishes, the effect would be that very little control would exist over the destination of prohibited drugs. Doctors would have

F   drugs in their possession the destination of which it would be impossible to trace and he suggests that the regulations would be made of little effect by reason of this ruling.

   We do not accept the gloomy prognosis. It may be that things may be more difficult. We doubt it. If, unhappily, some doctors were to use these regulations in order to supply themselves with drugs which are going to be

G   illicitly used, no doubt they will in the end be brought to book. In any event the fact that the regulations as interpreted by this court may produce some difficulty is no reason for us to come to the conclusion other than that which appears to us to be right on the wording of the Act and the regulations as they stand. It follows that so far as count 2 is concerned, the conviction must be quashed, because it was not left for the determination

H   of the jury as it should have been.

   So far as count 1 is concerned, we can deal with that very briefly, because Mr. Clegg concedes that the way in which the judge summed the matter up to the jury imported so much consideration of matters which he had made in his direction on count 2 as to render the jury's verdict inevitable. In short the wrong decision on count 2 rubbed off on count 1 in such a way as to make that conviction unsafe and unsatisfactory.

1542

In the result the convictions on each of these two counts, and the   A
sentences which were imposed upon them must be quashed and this appeal
allowed.

Appeal allowed.
Convictions quashed.

Solicitor: *Director of Public Prosecutions.*

L. N. W.   B

[HOUSE OF LORDS]

* A.C.T. CONSTRUCTION LTD.   .   .   .   .   RESPONDENTS   C

AND

CUSTOMS AND EXCISE COMMISSIONERS   .   .   APPELLANTS

1981 Nov. 11   Lord Diplock, Lord Elwyn-Jones, Lord Keith of
      Dec. 3   Kinkel, Lord Scarman and Lord Roskill   D

Revenue—Value added tax—Zero-rating—Alteration of building—
Foundations underpinned to prevent subsidence—Whether work
of " repair or maintenance "—Whether zero-rated—" Altera-
tion "—Whether meaning structural alteration—Finance Act
1972 (c. 41), Sch. 4, Group 8, item 2, note (2) (as varied by
Value Added Tax (Consolidation) Order 1976 (S.I. 1976 No.
128), Sch. 1, Group 8, item 2, note (2) (a))   E

A construction company underpinned houses that had
foundations that were too shallow by constructing in each
case a further foundation, consisting of a new concrete beam
with pillars, beneath the existing foundation in order to
prevent subsidence. A value added tax tribunal upheld the
Customs and Excise Commissioners' assessment of the company to value added tax on the basis that, although the work   F
done was a service in the course of the alteration of a building
and so within item 2 of Group 8 of Schedule 4 to the Finance
Act 1972,[1] it was not zero-rated because it came within the
exception " maintenance " in note (2) (a) to Group 8. Drake J.
allowed the company's appeal, and the Court of Appeal dismissed an appeal by the commissioners from his decision.
On appeal by the commissioners by leave of the House of
Lords: —   G
Held, dismissing the appeal, (1) that " alteration " in item
2 of Group 8 of Schedule 4 to the Finance Act 1972 meant
an alteration involving some structural alteration.
Customs and Excise Commissioners v. *Morrison Dunbar*
Ltd. [1979] S.T.C. 406 approved.
(2) That the underpinning work done by the respondent
company, which had not been done to any existing part of a
building but had been entirely new work involving a radical   H
and fundamental alteration to the construction of the building
as it had been before by its extension in a downward direction
and resulting in the conversion of a building with a short life
into one with a long life, could not be classed as " repair or
maintenance " within the ordinary meaning of those words in
note (2) (a) to Group 8 of Schedule 4 to the Act of 1972.

---

[1] Finance Act 1972, Sch. 4, Group 8, item 2 and note (2) to item 2 (as varier):
see post, p. 1544F.

A   *Per curiam.* The words "repair" and "maintenance" are not used in antithesis to one another. The phrase "repair or maintenance" is a single composite phrase and in many cases there may well be an overlap between them, as also between "structural alteration" and "repair or maintenance." In some cases there may be room for dispute which side of the line particular work falls. If so, that would be a question of fact or degree for the tribunal of fact con-
B   cerned to determine (post, pp. 1546E, 1547B).

Decision of the Court of Appeal [1981] 1 W.L.R. 49; [1981] 1 All E.R. 324 affirmed.

The following case is referred to in the opinion of Lord Roskill:

Customs and Excise Commissioners v. *Morrison Dunbar Ltd.* [1979] S.T.C. 406.

C
The following additional case was cited in argument:

All Saints, Wellington, Parochial Church Council v. *Customs and Excise Commissioners* [1979] V.A.T.T.R. 207.

APPEAL from the Court of Appeal.

D   This was an appeal by the Customs and Excise Commissioners by leave of the House of Lords from the judgment of the Court of Appeal (Lord Denning M.R., Brandon and Ackner L.JJ.) on October 9, 1980, dismissing the commissioners' appeal from a decision of Drake J. [1979] 1 W.L.R. 870 on March 16, 1979. By that decision, Drake J. allowed an appeal by the respondents, A.C.T. Construction Ltd., from a decision of a value added tax tribunal sitting in London on August 8, 1978.
E   The Court of Appeal refused the commissioners leave to appeal from their decision, but on December 18, 1980, the Appeal Committee of the House of Lords (Lord Wilberforce, Lord Edmund-Davies and Lord Keith of Kinkel) allowed a petition by the commissioners for leave to appeal.

The facts are set out in the opinion of Lord Roskill.

F   *Simon D. Brown* and *Nicolas Bratza* for the commissioners.
Michael Beloff Q.C. and *David Pannick* for the respondents.

Their Lordships took time for consideration.

December 3. LORD DIPLOCK. My Lords, I have had the advantage of
G   reading in draft the speech prepared by my noble and learned friend, Lord Roskill. For the reasons he has given, I too would dismiss the appeal.

LORD ELWYN-JONES. My Lords, I have had the advantage of reading in draft the speech of my noble and learned friend, Lord Roskill. For the reasons he has given I would dismiss the appeal.

H
LORD KEITH OF KINKEL. My Lords, I agree with the speech of my noble and learned friend, Lord Roskill, which I have had the benefit of reading in draft. Accordingly I too would dismiss the appeal.

LORD SCARMAN. My Lords, I have had the advantage of reading in draft the speech to be delivered by my noble and learned friend, Lord Roskill. For the reasons he gives I also would dismiss the appeal.

1544

LORD ROSKILL. My Lords, this appeal by the Customs and Excise **A**
Commissioners against an order of the Court of Appeal (Lord Denning
M.R., Brandon and Ackner L.JJ.) dated October 9, 1980, whereby that
court affirmed an order of Drake J. dated March 16, 1979, raises directly
one short point of construction of Group 8 in Schedule 4 to the Finance
Act 1972 (" the Act of 1972 ") as amended by paragraph 3 of the Value
Added Tax (Consolidation) Order 1976 (" the Order of 1976 "). But, as
will later emerge, the appeal also raises, albeit indirectly, a second point **B**
of construction of that group upon which two members of the Court of
Appeal, Lord Denning M.R. and Ackner L.J., expressed their views, albeit
obiter.

My Lords, I should explain that section 12 (4), together with section
43 (2), of the Act of 1972 authorised the Treasury to amend Schedule 4
by statutory instrument by adding to, or deleting from, that Schedule any **C**
description or by varying any description for the time being specified in it,
subject to the parliamentary safeguard specified in section 43 (4); the
Order of 1976 was made pursuant to those powers on January 29, 1976. It
was duly laid before the House of Commons on February 10, 1976, and
came into operation on March 2, 1976.

My Lords, the provisions of Schedule 4, both before and after amendment by the Order of 1976, were concerned with zero-rating for the pur- **D**
poses of value added tax. Group 8 of that Schedule makes certain provisions for zero-rating in connection with " Construction of Buildings, etc."
Group 8 specifies three items, each numbered, which qualify for zero-
rating. Those three numbered items are followed by what are described
as " notes," four in number, each numbered. Section 46 (2) of the Act of
1972 enjoins, inter alia, that Schedule 4 " shall be interpreted in accord- **E**
ance with the   notes contained therein," power also being given by that
subsection to amend those notes along with the substantive provisions of
that Schedule.

My Lords, since everything in this appeal turns upon the construction
of item 2 of Schedule 4 and of note (2) (*a*) of the " notes " I set out the
relevant wording for ease of reference:
F
> " 2. The supply, in the course of the construction, alteration or demo-
> lition of any building or of any civil engineering work, of any ser-
> vices . . . *Notes*: . . . (2) Item 2 does not include—(*a*) any work of
> repair or maintenance; . . ."

My Lords, the facts which give rise to this dispute are set out in detail
in the carefully reasoned decision of the value added tax tribunal sitting **G**
in London, presided over by Mr. Neil Elles. Suffice it to say that the respondents are a construction company, and were employed to carry out
certain underpinning operations to a number of houses of which the original
foundations, which were laid in the 1930s and were acceptable under the
then current building regulations but no longer acceptable under those regulations in force when the work which led to the present dispute was done,
had been found seriously wanting as a result of the drought which took place **H**
in 1976. The respondents had developed a new method of underpinning
to avoid the subsidence which would otherwise have occurred. This new
method consisted of the construction of an additional foundation to the
affected building in danger of subsidence, that additional foundation being
not only additional to but also entirely separate from whatever original
foundations still existed. It follows that whatever remained of those original foundations, however defective they were or had become, was left

A unaltered. Your Lordships were shown a rough sketch of the under-pinning in question which illustrated this brief description.

My Lords, the appellants assessed certain underpinning work done by the respondents to value added tax in the sum of £1,072.44. This assessment followed certain correspondence. It related to four underpinning jobs carried out by the respondents—see the appellants' letter of January 9, 1978. The respondents appealed against that assessment but the value

B added tax tribunal in London, to which I have already referred, dis-missed this appeal on August 8, 1978. The respondents then appealed to the High Court. Drake J. allowed the appeal. An appeal by the appellants to the Court of Appeal was, as already mentioned, dismissed but your Lordships' House later gave leave to appeal against that decision.

My Lords, I said earlier that this appeal directly raised a single short

C point of construction, namely, whether the underpinning work which I have described was " repair or maintenance " within note (2). If it were, it is not zero-rated but positive-rated. But Mr. Simon Brown, for the appellants, urged your Lordships also to consider, when approaching this question of construction, the second question I have mentioned, namely, the meaning of the word " alteration " in item 2 in the context in which that word there appears, namely, ". . . in the course of the construction,

D alteration or demolition of any building. . . ." His contention was that in that context the word " alteration " meant " structural alteration " and he urged that if that contention, which had been rejected both by the learned Master of the Rolls and Ackner L.J., were right, it not only supported his submission as to the true construction of the phrase " any work of repair or maintenance " in note (2) (a) but vitiated much of the reasoning of the

E learned Master of the Rolls in the latter part of his judgment [1981] 1 W.L.R. 49, 55.

My Lords, in one sense it may be said that this second point does not arise, since Mr. Brown rightly conceded that the underpinning work which I have described was, in any event, a " structural alteration," and therefore even if the construction of the word for which he contended were correct,

F that prerequisite to zero-rating required by the relevant wording of item 2 was in any event satisfied. But since he urged that the determination of that true construction was essential to the proper interpretation of note (2), and that the views of the majority of the Court of Appeal, albeit obiter, could have far-reaching and perhaps unintended effects, I understand all your Lordships to agree that this House should now determine this matter as well as the other.

G My Lords, the meaning of " alteration " in this context had arisen in a previous value added tax case, *Customs and Excise Commissioners* v. *Morrison Dunbar Ltd.* [1979] S.T.C. 406, a decision by Neill J. about a fortnight before the hearing of the instant case before the value added tax tribunal, but not mentioned in their decision. That tribunal held that this underpinning work was an alteration.

H Neill J. said, at p. 413 :

"In dealing with a case to which item 2 of Group 8 is said to apply, I consider that one should first look to see whether the supply of the services in question is a supply in the course of the construction, alteration or demolition of a building. Each of these words is impor-tant and should be given its proper weight. The word ' alteration,' it is to be noted, is found between ' construction ' and ' demolition ' and it follows, in my view, that the alteration to which item 2 applies is an

alteration *of the building* and therefore one which involves some   A
structural alteration. . . ."

In the Court of Appeal in the present case, Lord Denning M.R. [1981]
1 W.L.R. 49, 53 after quoting this passage said that he could not agree with
it and that the adjective " structural " should not be inserted.   Ackner
L.J., at p. 57, agreed.   Brandon L.J. expressed no opinion.   Neither the
learned Master of the Rolls nor Ackner L.J. gave any reasons for their   B
disapproval of what Neill J. had said.   My Lords, with profound respect, I
agree with the view of Neill J., whose reasoning seems to me impeccable.
If the contrary view were right, the repainting of a house in a different
colour from that previously used would be an " alteration," a conclusion
which in this context, I venture to think, cannot be sustained.

My Lords, I therefore accept Mr. Brown's contention on this issue, and   C
turn to the question of construction of note (2) upon that basis.   It seems
to me clear that for the relevant work to qualify for zero-rating two requirements must be satisfied.   It must be a " structural alteration," and it must
not be " any work of repair or maintenance."   As already stated, the first
requirement is by concession satisfied; I therefore turn to the second.

My Lords, the argument in the courts below appears to have proceeded
upon the basis that the words " repair or maintenance " are used in anti-   D
thesis to one another.   Indeed, it was conceded in the Court of Appeal that
this underpinning could not be said to be a " repair " and therefore the
only question was whether it was maintenance : see the judgments of
Brandon L.J. [1981] 1 W.L.R. 49, 56 and Ackner L.J., at p. 58.   My
Lords, I think, as indeed Mr. Brown accepted in argument before your
Lordships' House, that this concession was wrongly made by him in the   E
Court of Appeal.   The two words are not used in antithesis to one another.
The phrase is a single composite phrase " repair or maintenance " and in
many cases there may well be an overlap between them, as indeed there
may also be between " structural alteration " on the one hand and " repair
or maintenance " on the other.

My Lords, Mr. Brown contended that this underpinning was " repair   F
or maintenance " because it was done to stop these buildings falling down.
He went so far as to submit that any work done to stop a building collap-
sing was " pure maintenance " since it was maintenance to promote the
essential safety of that structure.

My Lords, in the courts below there was much reference to well known
decisions in disputes between landlords and tenants arising from repairing
covenants in leases where contractual obligations to repair and maintain   G
had been assumed by tenants towards their landlords.   These decisions
are referred to in several of the judgments below and require no further
mention, but in my opinion they shed little or no light upon the construction
of the statutory instrument now in question.

My Lords, on the central question I find the reasoning in the judgment
of Brandon L.J. compelling.   The learned Lord Justice said, at p. 57:   H

" In the present case the work done was not done to any existing
part of a building; it was entirely new work.   It involved a radical
and fundamental alteration to the construction of the building as
it had been before.   It involved an extension of the existing building
in a downward direction.   Such work in my view is not capable
of coming within the expression ' maintenance ' in the ordinary and
natural meaning of that word.   It is conceded that, if that is right,

A   then the work was work of alteration within the meaning of that expression in item 2 of Group 8 and is accordingly zero-rated."

My Lords, I stress, like the learned Lord Justice, that this was new work which converted buildings which, apart from this work, would have had a short life into buildings which as a consequence of this work became endowed with a long life. This consequence was achieved only by the

B   installation of a new structure upon which the buildings thereafter rested. My Lords, I decline to attempt to define " repair or maintenance " when the Act of 1972 and the Order of 1976 do not do so, but leave those ordinary words which are in common use to be given their ordinary meaning. In some cases, there may be room for dispute which side of the line particular work falls. If so, that would be a question of fact or degree for the tribunal of fact concerned to determine. The problem should not

C   prove difficult of solution if their task is approached by applying the facts as that tribunal finds them to the relevant statutory provisions interpreted as I have endeavoured to state.

My Lords, in common with the courts below, I am unable to see how this underpinning work can possibly be classed as " repair or maintenance " within the ordinary meaning of those words. I would, therefore, dismiss

D   this appeal with costs.

Appeal dismissed with costs.

Solicitors : *Solicitor, Customs and Excise; Herbert Smith & Co.*

M. G.

E

———

[QUEEN'S BENCH DIVISION]

F   * IMPEX TRANSPORT AKTIESELSKABET *v.*
A.G. THAMES HOLDINGS LTD.
(TRADING AS JOHN GIBB & SONS)

1981   March 30;   Robert Goff J.
       May 22

G   *Practice—Pleadings—Counterclaim—C.M.R. contract to transport
      fruit—Writ issued by hauliers for sums due under contract—
      Defendants' intention to counterclaim in respect of damage to
      fruit stated in affidavit—Counterclaim served after expiry of
      time stipulated—Whether time-barred—Carriage of Goods by
      Road Act 1965 (c. 37), Sch., art. 32—R.S.C., Ord. 15, r. 2*

       The plaintiffs, a company of international road hauliers

H   incorporated in Denmark entered into a contract with the defendants, an English company, in October 1973, whereby the plaintiffs agreed to carry consignments of fruit for the defendants from Denmark to various United Kingdom destinations. The contract was subject to the Convention on the Contract for the International Carriage of Goods by Road, scheduled to the Carriage of Goods by Road Act 1965. On August 2, 1974, the plaintiffs issued a specially indorsed writ claiming the balance of freight charges and other expenses incurred in connection with consignments carried between October 29, 1973, and March 6,

1974. The plaintiffs issued a summons for judgment under A
R.S.C., Ord. 14 and swore an affidavit in support on September
18, 1974. The defendants in their affidavit dated October 18,
1974, stated the factual basis for a counterclaim they wished
to set off against the plaintiffs' claim. The counterclaim arose
from damage to goods carried between October 18, 1973, and
January 11, 1974, and would extinguish the plantiffs' claim.
The defendants were given leave to defend conditional upon
the payment into court of a sum of money. They served a B
defence and counterclaim on March 21, 1975. After delay by
both parties, on January 29, 1981, the plaintiffs were given
leave to amend their reply and defence to counterclaim to
rely upon, inter alia, article 32 which stipulated a time bar of
one year for an action arising out of carriage. The defendants
accepted that the contract was subject to the Convention, and
that time began to run from January 11, 1974, the date of the
last consignment the defendants sought to rely on. C

On the preliminary issue of whether the defendants' right
of action by way of counterclaim against the plaintiffs was
barred by lapse of time by virtue of article 32 of the
Convention : —

Held, that no counterclaim was made or set up or initiated
until the service of a pleading embodying a counterclaim, or
of some other document which by the order of the court was
to stand in the place of a pleading for the purpose of R.S.C., D
Ord. 15, r. 2; that until the service of a counterclaim no right
of action was exercised by way of counterclaim within article
32 of the Convention and since before January 11, 1975, the
defendants had merely adverted to a proposed counterclaim by
affidavit and no counterclaim was served until March 21, 1975,
that service was out of time, and accordingly any right of
action the defendants might have had against the plaintiffs
arising out of the carriage had been barred by lapse of time E
and might not be exercised by way of counterclaim or set-off
(post, pp. 1557H—1558A, H—1559C).

The Gniezno [1968] P. 418 considered.

Dicta of Sargant L.J. in *The Saxicava* [1924] P. 131, C.A.
applied.

The following cases are referred to in the judgment: F

Bildt v. *Foy* (1892) 9 T.L.R. 34, D.C.; 9 T.L.R. 83, C.A.
C.S.I. International Co. Ltd. v. *Archway Personnel (Middle East) Ltd.*
    [1980] 1 W.L.R. 1069; [1980] 3 All E.R. 215, C.A.
Fairplay XIV, The [1939] P. 57.
General Railway Syndicate, In re (Whiteley's Case) [1900] 1 Ch. 365, C.A.
Gniezno, The [1968] P. 418; [1967] 3 W.L.R. 705; [1967] 2 All E.R. 738.
Henriksens Rederi A/S v. *T.H.Z. Rolimpex* [1974] Q.B. 233; [1973] 3 G
    W.L.R. 556; [1973] 3 All E.R. 589, C.A.
Mondel v. *Steel* (1841) 8 M. & W. 858.
Salybia, The [1910] P. 25.
Saxicava, The [1924] P. 131, C.A.

No additional cases were cited in argument.

  H

PRELIMINARY ISSUE

The plaintiffs, Impex Transport Aktieselskabet, a company of international road hauliers incorporated in Denmark entered into an agreement
with the defendants, A.G. Thames Holdings Ltd., an English company
trading as John Gibb & Sons. The defendants agreed to carry for the
plaintiffs consignments of apples and pears from Funen in Denmark to a
number of destinations in the United Kingdom during 1973 and 1974. The

A plaintiffs issued a specially indorsed writ claiming £8,640·48 in respect of the balance of freight and certain other expenses arising from consignments transported between October 29, 1973, and March 6, 1974. They took out a summons for judgment under R.S.C., Ord. 14 and swore an affidavit in support on September 18, 1974. The defendants, on October 18, 1974, swore an affidavit deposing to damage to goods carried by the plaintiffs as a result of which they intended to counterclaim £28,136.

B The plaintiffs denied the defendants' allegations in an affidavit in reply. Further affidavits were sworn, and leave to defend was granted conditional upon a sum of money being paid into court. The defendants served a defence and counterclaim on March 21, 1975. The plaintiffs served a reply and defence to counterclaim on August 3, 1976. On January 29, 1981, the plaintiffs were granted leave to amend their reply and defence

C to counterclaim to rely on articles 17, 18, 30 and 32 of the Convention on Contracts for the International Carriage of Goods by Road, scheduled to the Carriage of Goods by Road Act 1965. An order was made for the trial of a preliminary issue on the question whether any right of action the defendants might have had against the plaintiffs arising out of the carriage had become barred by lapse of time and might not be exercised

D by way of counterclaim or set-off by virtue of article 32 of the Convention.

The facts are stated in the judgment.

Peter Birts for the plaintiffs.
Richard Nussey for the defendants.

Neither counsel was instructed before 1980.

E ROBERT GOFF J. There is before the court a preliminary issue in this action. The action itself has arisen out of a contract entered into in October 1973 under which the plaintiffs, Impex Transport Aktieselskabet, who are a company of international road hauliers incorporated in Denmark, agreed to carry consignments of apples and pears for the defendants, who are an English company, from the Danish island of

F Funen to various destinations in the United Kingdom during the season of 1973 to 1974. In the action, which was commenced by writ issued and served in 1974, the plaintiffs claimed a sum, Danish Kr. 121,398·80 or £8,640·48, in respect of the balance of freight and certain other expenses relating to a number of consignments carried between October 29, 1973, and March 6, 1974. Each consignment was carried in a road trailer.

G However, the defendants have alleged that certain consignments were, by reason of breaches of contract by the plaintiffs, subjected to delay in transit, in consequence of which the fruit was damaged; this damage they have assessed at £28,136, which of course far exceeds the amount of the plaintiffs' claim. The consignments in respect of which the defendants have complained were 25 in all, which were delivered on various dates between October 18, 1973 and January 11, 1974.

H As I have already indicated, the writ was issued and served on August 2, 1974, the statement of claim being specially indorsed on the writ. The plaintiffs then issued a summons for judgment under R.S.C., Ord. 14, their formal affidavit in support being sworn on September 18, 1974; and on October 18, 1974, an affidavit was sworn on behalf of the defendants, in which the facts giving rise to their counterclaim for damage to the goods were deposed to, on the basis of which they claimed to be entitled to set off part of their counterclaim in extinction of the plaintiffs'

claim. A detailed affidavit in reply, rejecting the defendants' allegations, A
was sworn on behalf of the plaintiffs on November 19, 1974; this was
followed by further affidavits on behalf of the defendants sworn on
February 3 and February 7, 1975, and on behalf of the plaintiffs also on
February 7, 1975. The summons for judgment was heard by the master
shortly thereafter, when he gave leave to defend conditional upon a sum
of money being paid into court. This was done, and the defendants'
defence and counterclaim were served on March 21, 1975. A reply and B
defence to counterclaim were served on August 3, 1976.

The matter next came before the court on January 29, 1981. In the
meantime neither party had pressed on with the action; I observe in
particular that the defendants had not pressed on with their counterclaim,
notwithstanding that it greatly exceeded the plaintiffs' claim. On January
29, 1981, leave was given by this court to the plaintiffs to amend their C
reply and defence to counterclaim, to rely upon certain provisions of the
Convention on the Contract for the International Carriage of Goods by
Road (" the Convention ") viz. articles 17 and 18 (concerned with the
carrier's responsibility for loss of or damage to goods), and articles 30 and
32 (which are concerned with time bars). Article 32, which is the relevant
article for the purposes of the preliminary issue now before the court,
provides as follows: D

" 1. The period of limitation for an action arising out of carriage
under this Convention shall be one year. Nevertheless, in the case of
wilful misconduct, or such default as in accordance with the law of
the court or tribunal seised of the case, is considered as equivalent to
wilful misconduct, the period of limitation shall be three years. The
period of limitation shall begin to run: (a) in the case of partial loss, E
damage or delay in delivery, from the date of delivery; (b) in the case
of total loss, from the thirtieth day after the expiry of the agreed time-
limit or where there is no agreed time-limit from the sixtieth day from
the date on which the goods were taken over by the carrier; (c) in all
other cases, on the expiry of a period of three months after the making
of the contract of carriage. The day on which the period of limitation F
begins to run shall not be included in the period.

" 2. A written claim shall suspend the period of limitation until
such date as the carrier rejects the claim by notification in writing
and returns the documents attached thereto. If a part of the claim is
admitted the period of limitation shall start to run again only in
respect of that part of the claim still in dispute. The burden of proof
of the receipt of the claim, or of the reply and of the return of the G
documents, shall rest with the party relying upon these facts. The
running of the period of limitation shall not be suspended by further
claims having the same object.

" 3. Subject to the provisions of paragraph 2 above, the extension
of the period of limitation shall be governed by the law of the court
or tribunal seised of the case. That law shall also govern the fresh H
accrual rights of action.

" 4. A right of action which has become barred by lapse of time
may not be exercised by way of counter-claim or set-off."

On the plaintiffs' application for leave to amend and to rely upon the
Convention, it was accepted that the contract or contracts in question were
indeed subject to the Convention. Furthermore, if the plaintiffs were

The Weekly Law Reports, December 18, 1981

1551

1 W.L.R.　　　Impex Transport Ltd. v. Thames Ltd. (Q.B.D.)　　Robert Goff J.

A entitled to invoke article 32 on the facts of the case, the effect would be that the whole of the defendants' counterclaim would be time-barred, and apart from certain very minor matters they would have no defence to the plaintiffs' claim. An order was therefore made for the trial of a pre-liminary issue on this point, which was identified as the issue arising under paragraph 15 of the plaintiffs' amended reply and defence to counterclaim, which reads:

B
　　" The plaintiffs further contend that any right of action the defendants
　　may have had against the plaintiffs arising out of the carriage has
　　become barred by lapse of time and may not be exercised by way of
　　counter-claim or set-off by virtue of the provisions of article 32 of the
　　Convention upon which the plaintiffs intend to rely.
　　　　　　　　　" Particulars
C
　　The date of delivery of the last consignment was January 11, 1974.
　　No written claim was made by the defendants prior to the delivery of
　　the counterclaim herein on March 21, 1975."

This is the preliminary issue now before the court.

The plaintiffs' case on this issue was very simple. By common consent,
D the relevant date from which the period of limitation ran was the date of delivery of the last consignment, viz. January 11, 1974. Accordingly, the period of limitation under article 32 expired on January 11, 1975. How-ever, the defendants did not serve their counterclaim until March 25, 1975. It was therefore submitted by the plaintiffs that, since the defendants' right of action, upon which they relied for their set-off and counterclaim, had become barred by January 12, 1975, they were no longer entitled to
E exercise their right of action by way of counterclaim served after that date. Accordingly, the plaintiffs asked that the preliminary issue should be decided in their favour, and that the defendants' set-off and counterclaim should be dismissed. In answer, the defendants submitted that by filing their affidavit dated October 18, 1974, they did an act which constituted the making of their counterclaim for the purposes of English law, and thereby
F exercised the right of action (which was the subject of their counterclaim) by way of a counterclaim made on that date, which was well within the one year limitation period specified in article 32 (1).

Now, in considering these submissions, it is necessary to inquire when, within the meaning of the words in article 32 (4) of the Convention, a right of action is exercised by way of set-off or counterclaim. It is clear
G from article 32 that the period of limitation will generally (unless it is suspended by reason of a written claim, by virtue of article 32 (2)) run until the period expires or action is brought in the sense that, if action is not brought within the relevant limitation period, the right of action will be time-barred unless extended under article 32 (3) by the court or tribunal seised of the case. Accordingly, subject to article 32 (2) and (3), it is essential that the claimant should actually bring an action within the
H period. This conclusion is to be derived from the opening words of article 32 (1), viz. " The period of limitation for an *action* arising out of carriage under this Convention shall be one year." So what is required within the one year period is the actual commencement of the action. That nothing less than the actual commencement of the action is enough, is underlined by the different provision relating to a written claim under article 32 (2). Of course, what constitutes the commencement of an action in any particular case must depend upon the procedural law of the

country where the action is commenced. In this country, no doubt it A would be the date of the issue of the writ.

So much is clear; but when we come to set-offs and counterclaims the matter becomes more complicated. In the English law of procedure, there is usually no problem in respect of limitation in relation to set-offs and counterclaims; because, by section 28 of the Limitation Act 1939 it is provided that: " For the purposes of this Act, any claim by way of set-off B or counterclaim shall be deemed to be a separate action and to have been commenced on the same date as the action in which the set-off or counter-claim is pleaded." So, provided that the main action has been commenced within the limitation period applicable to the cause of action which is the subject of the defendant's set-off or counterclaim pleaded in that action, the set-off or counterclaim will not become time-barred, even though it was not pleaded until after the expiry of the limitation period which C would have been applicable if the defendant's cause of action had been pursued by original action. However, it is plain that section 28 of the Limitation Act 1939 cannot apply to counterclaims to which the Conven-tion applies. This is because the effect of article 32 (4) is that, if a right of action is *not* exercised by way of counterclaim or set-off *before* it is barred by lapse of time, i.e. before the expiry of the one year (or three D year) period specified in article 32 (1) (subject to any extensions of time under article 32 (2) or (3)), then it can no longer be so exercised. It follows that this is not a case in which (as was accepted by the Court of Appeal in *Henriksens Rederi A/S* v. *T. H. Z. Rolimpex* [1974] Q.B. 233—see especially at p. 254, *per* Cairn L.J.—in relation to the period of limitation specified in the Hague Rules) a period of limitation specified in a conven-tion can, by analogy with section 28, be applied to a set-off or counterclaim E in the manner provided for in that section.

Equally, however, it is clear from article 32 (4) that if a right of action *is* exercised by way of counterclaim or set-off within the relevant period specified in the Convention, then the right of action will *not* be time-barred under the Convention—in other words, in such circumstances a separate action is not necessary for the purpose of stopping time running under the F Convention. The crucial question in a case such as the present is therefore this: was the defendant's right of action exercised by way of counterclaim or set-off before the expiry of the relevant limitation period? Furthermore, just as the question when an action has been commenced must be ascer-tained by reference to the procedural law of the country where the action is commenced, so the question when a right of action is exercised by way of counterclaim or set-off has to be ascertained by reference to the proce- G dural law of the country where the right of action is so exercised, in the present case English law.

I turn therefore to the English law of procedure for guidance. I can for present purposes ignore the fact that the defendants in the present case are seeking to set off part of the sum counterclaimed by them in extinction of the plaintiffs' claim. This is not a case in which they can simply plead H by way of defence that the debt is extinguished, on the principle in *Mondel* v. *Steel* (1841) 8 M. & W. 858; the existence of the defendants' right of set-off (if any) is entirely dependent upon their counterclaim, so that if the counterclaim is time-barred, their defence of set-off must fall to the ground. I have therefore to concentrate upon the defendants' counterclaim.

Here, however, I am faced at once with two difficulties. First, nowhere in the English Rules of the Supreme Court is there any definition of the

The Weekly Law Reports, December 18, 1981

1553

1 W.L.R.   Impex Transport Ltd. v. Thames Ltd. (Q.B.D.)   Robert Goff J.

A moment when a counterclaim is initiated. Secondly, by reason of section 28 of the Limitation Act 1939, it does not generally matter in English law when, for the purposes of a time-bar, a counterclaim is initiated or, to use the words of article 32 (4) of the Convention, a right of action is exercised by way of counterclaim.

However, the most relevant provision is R.S.C., Ord. 15, r. 2, which
B provides:

"(1) Subject to rule 5 (2), a defendant in any action who alleges that he has any claim or is entitled to any relief or remedy against a plaintiff in the action in respect of any matter (whenever and however arising) may, instead of bringing a separate action, make a counterclaim in respect of that matter; and where he does so he must
C add the counterclaim to his defence. (2) Rule 1 shall apply in relation to a counterclaim as if the counterclaim were a separate action and as if the person making the counterclaim were the plaintiff and the person against whom it is made a defendant. (3) A counterclaim may be proceeded with notwithstanding that judgment is given for the plaintiff in the action or that the action is stayed, discontinued or dismissed. (4) Where a defendant establishes a counterclaim against
D the claim of the plaintiff and there is a balance in favour of one of the parties, the court may give judgment for the balance, so, however, that this provision shall not be taken as affecting the court's discretion with respect to costs.

Of this rule, rule 2 (3), or rather its predecessor under the old Rules—Ord. 21, r. 16, has been the most productive of useful guidance in the authorities.
E This is of course because the question has arisen from time to time under this provision whether or not the defendant has initiated a counterclaim; for only if he has done so can he proceed with the counterclaim notwithstanding the circumstances specified in the present Ord. 25, r. 2 (3), or the old Ord. 21, r. 16. This could be important if the cause of action which was the subject of the counterclaim would otherwise be time-barred under
F the Limitation Act 1939. In point of fact, the language of the old Ord. 21, r. 16, was a little different from the present Ord. 15, r. 2 (3). It provided: "If, in any case in which the defendant sets up a counterclaim, the action of the plaintiff is stayed, discontinued, or dismissed, the counterclaim may nevertheless be proceeded with." So in cases under the old Ord. 21, r. 16, the question which arose was whether the defendant had "set up" a counterclaim, language which is not used in the present Ord. 15, r. 2 (3),
G though this does not, I think, affect the substance of the question.

The effect of these rules was examined by Brandon J. in *The Gniezno* [1968] P. 418, though the question he had to consider was somewhat different. In that case, following a collision at sea, the plaintiffs (the owners of one of the colliding ships) issued but did not serve a writ in rem against the defendants, the owners of the other ship involved in the
H collision. Nevertheless, despite the non-service of the writ, nearly two years later the defendants entered an appearance in the action and filed a notice of counterclaim. The plaintiffs applied to set aside both the appearance and the notice of counterclaim. Brandon J. held that the defendants were entitled to enter an appearance, despite the non-service of the writ; but he set aside the notice of counterclaim because it was not a proceeding recognised or directed by the Rules of the Supreme Court. It was on this latter point that he directed his attention to the effect of Ord. 15, r. 2, and he

1554

analysed a number of the authorities on the old Rules concerned with the
question of what constituted the setting up of a counterclaim. Among the
authorities he examined were *Bildt* v. *Foy* (1892) 9 T.L.R. 34, 83; *In re
General Railway Syndicate (Whiteley's Case)* [1900] 1 Ch. 365; *The Salybia*
[1910] P. 25; *The Saxicava* [1924] P. 131 and *Fairplay XIV* [1939] P. 57.
From these authorities he deduced that a counterclaim could only be set up
by a proceeding recognised or directed by the Rules of the Supreme Court;
and since a notice of counterclaim was not such a proceeding, and there was
no practice of the Admiralty Court that it should be regarded as such, he
decided that the notice of counterclaim must be set aside.

I must express my indebtedness to Brandon J.'s analysis of these
authorities. Even so, I have studied them myself, and from them I have
drawn the following conclusions, which do not entirely accord with his
analysis.

First, whether one uses the expression " set up " or " make " or
" raise " or " initiate " a counterclaim, the words have always to be read
in their context, and the same expression, e.g. " set up " a counterclaim
may have different meanings in different rules. This is made very clear in
the judgments of Bankes and Sargant L.JJ. in *The Saxicava* [1924] P. 131,
the leading case on the subject, when that case came before the Court of
Appeal. The question in that case was whether notice of a counterclaim
asserted in correspondence between the parties' solicitors was enough to
" set up " a counterclaim within the old Ord. 21, r. 16; it was held that it
was not. The point that the expression " set up " a counterclaim can have
different meanings in different rules was made very clear by Bankes L.J.,
when he said, at pp. 134–135:

"Now, the difficulty in which defendants, who have within the meaning of the rules set up a counterclaim, might be put in the event of
the plaintiff discontinuing, had to be met by a special rule—namely,
Ord. 21, r. 16: 'If, in any case in which the defendant sets up a
counterclaim, the action of the plaintiff is stayed, discontinued, or
dismissed, the counterclaim may nevertheless be proceeded with.' The
object of that rule and the necessity for it are obvious, because the
right of counterclaim takes its origin from section 24 of the Judicature
Act of 1873, which gives the court power to grant to a defendant all
such relief against a plaintiff as the defendant shall have properly
claimed by his pleadings. The effect of discontinuing is to remove
the plaintiff from the proceedings; and, therefore, unless the difficulty
was provided for by other rules dealing with the matter, the defendant's case would no longer come within the language of section 24 in
the event of the plaintiff disappearing from the action by means of discontinuance. Accordingly, this rule is framed, and it uses the
expression 'sets up,' of which there is no definition in the rules; but
from the rules themselves it appears that it is used in a different sense
with reference to different subject matters. For instance, Ord. 14, r. 4,
deals with a case of an application by a plaintiff under Ord. 14 for
judgment: 'If it appear that the defence set up by the defendant
applies only to a part of the plaintiff's claim,' and so forth. The
'setting up' there must necessarily refer to a setting up in an affidavit,
because at that stage of the proceedings there is no other process by
which the defendant can set up this defence. It is plain, therefore,
that the phrase 'set up' is not used in the rules always in the same
sense. But it seems to me that 'set up' can only refer to some step

The Weekly Law Reports, December 18, 1981

1555

1 W.L.R.   Impex Transport Ltd. v. Thames Ltd. (Q.B.D.)   Robert Goff J.

A   in the proceedings which is either directed by or recognised by the rules, because it is in reference to such matters only that the rules are dealing; and when it speaks of setting up a defence it must mean set up in some proceeding which is recognised or directed by the rules. Under Ord. 14 the proceeding is by way of affidavit, but when one comes a stage further and refers to pleadings it seems to me that Ord. 21, r. 16, in speaking of ' setting up,' must refer to a setting up

B   in a pleading, or, at any rate, in some proceeding which is recognised or directed by the rules, and which becomes part of the record, or something which is filed in the court."

The same view was expressed by Sargant L.J., at p. 139.

Secondly, the decided cases only go so far as to deciding that certain informal steps—such as the notice of counterclaim in *The Gniezno* [1968]

C   P. 418, or correspondence as in *The Salybia* [1910] P. 25 and *The Saxicava* [1924] P. 131, are insufficient to constitute a " setting up " of a counterclaim for the purpose of the old Ord. 21, r. 10, or the prerequisite for proceeding with a counterclaim for the purpose of the present Ord. 15, r. 2 (3). In no case has it been decided that an affidavit in opposition to a summons for judgment under Order 14 is sufficient for this purpose. If I

D   read the judgment of Brandon J. in *The Gniezno* [1968] P. 418 correctly, however, I understand that he considered the Divisional Court in *Bildt* v. *Foy* (1892) 9 T.L.R. 34 to have decided that such an affidavit could have this effect. Brandon J. said [1968] P. 418, 433:

". . . as I understand the decision of the Divisional Court it was that, where in Order 14 proceedings the defendant relies in his affidavit in

E   opposition to summary judgment on a counterclaim, he has set up a counterclaim within the meaning of the rules then in force."

With all respect, I am bound to say that I do not regard the decision of the Divisional Court in *Bildt* v. *Foy* (1892) 9 T.L.R. 34 as compelling me to reach any such conclusion. The case was not concerned with a summons for judgment under Order 14, but with an application for payment out of

F   a sum paid into court as a condition for obtaining an injunction; the case is very tersely reported in the Times Law Reports; and the two members of the Divisional Court proceeded on differing grounds—one of which, preferred by Wills J. and by the Court of Appeal which affirmed the decision of the Divisional Court, was that the money had been paid into court to abide the defendant's counterclaim, and that, therefore, it would be wrong to allow the plaintiff to withdraw his payment into court simply by dis-

G   continuing the action without any further order of the court. The Court of Appeal expressly reserved for later decision the question whether or not, in the circumstances of the case, the defendant had set up a counterclaim within Ord. 21, r. 16. Brandon J. also regarded *In re General Railway Syndicate (Whiteley's Case)* [1900] 1 Ch. 365 as indicating that a counterclaim can be raised by filing an affidavit in accordance with the rules

H   in Order 14 proceedings (see again p. 433 of the report). That case was concerned with the question whether a party had taken legal steps before the commencement of winding up to have his name removed from the register, and the Court of Appeal held that, by asserting, in an affidavit sworn under Order 14 in opposition to a summons for judgment in an action for calls, that he was entitled to repudiate the shares and have the contract rescinded, he had done all that could be reasonably expected of him to assert in a legal proceeding the right to repudiate the shares. Like

Sargant L.J. in *The Saxicava* [1924] P. 131, 139, I do not consider that that A
decision has any bearing upon the construction of the Rules of the
Supreme Court, and in particular the construction of the old Ord. 21, r. 16
or the present Ord. 15, r. 2.

Thirdly, although there is no decision to this effect, there are dicta in
the cases which support the view that to constitute the " setting up " of a
counterclaim under the old Ord. 21, r. 16, the service of a pleading containing a counterclaim, or some equivalent formal document, is necessary. B
Perhaps the strongest observation to this effect is that of Sargant L.J. in
The Saxicava [1924] P. 131, 138–139 when he said:

> " Order 21, r. 16, deals with the setting up of a counterclaim and
> refers to some definite step in the proceedings, but I do not think that
> the phrase ' sets up ' is satisfied by a general intimation outside the
> proceedings of the intention of the defendant to proceed by way of C
> counterclaim. The phrase ' sets up ' in that rule must have the same
> meaning as in the immediately preceding rule, and in the other two
> rules to which Scrutton L.J. has referred, rules 10 and 11. Each of these
> rules, as it seems to me, is a definite legal step in the delivery of the
> counterclaim, which is, for the purpose of the counterclaim, the
> commencement of the action. I agree with the view, which I think D
> was indicated by Bankes L.J., that in the case of an affidavit under
> Order 14, the setting up there is a setting up for the purpose of the
> particular proceeding contemplated by that Order, and I do not think
> myself that the filing of the affidavit under Order 14, could be a setting
> up of the counterclaim for any purpose except the purpose of reply-
> ing to the plaintiff's attempt to get judgment. It seems to me that in E
> the rules as to pleading under Order 21 the setting up of the counter-
> claim means the delivery of the counterclaim according to the rules."

It is significant that he regarded his view as being the same as that indicated by Bankes L.J. where he stated, in the passage I have just quoted,
that the expression " sets up " a counterclaim may be used in different
senses in different rules. In fact, I read the concluding sentence in the F
passage of Bankes L.J.'s judgment, at p. 135, which I have quoted, as
indicating that an affidavit under Order 14 is not generally sufficient to set
up a counterclaim for the purpose of the old Ord. 21, r. 16. It is also
significant that Scrutton L.J., at p. 138, appears to have regarded as open
the question whether setting up a counterclaim in an affidavit under Order
14 was a " setting up " of a counterclaim for the purpose of the old Ord.
21, r. 16—which indicates that he did not regard the point as having been G
settled by the decision of the Court of Appeal in *In re General Railway
Syndicate* [1900] 1 Ch. 365 which was cited to and considered by the court
and was (so far as relevant) binding upon the court. Furthermore, a
similar opinion to that expressed by Sargant L.J. was expressed by Sir
Boyd Merriman P. in *The Fairplay XIV* [1939] P. 57, 59.

It follows, in my judgment, that, on the balance of authority under the H
old rules, a counterclaim could be " set up " for the purposes of Ord. 21,
r. 16, when a pleading in the form of a counterclaim was served, or when
some equivalent document which was ordered to take the place of a pleading was served. If that is right, I can see no reason to apply any different
construction to the present Ord. 15, r. 2 (3).

I wish to add, however, that I find myself in respectful agreement with
the view expressed by Sargant L.J. in *The Saxicava* [1924] P. 131. The

The Weekly Law Reports, December 18, 1981

1557

1 W.L.R.   Impex Transport Ltd. v. Thames Ltd. (Q.B.D.)   Robert Goff J.

A whole tenor of Ord. 15, r. 2, presupposes, in my judgment, that a formal step should have been taken to initiate a counterclaim, so that the counterclaim shall be proceeded with as if it were an action. Thus rule 2 (1) provides that a counterclaim may be made, instead of bringing an action; and that where a counterclaim is made it must be added to the defence. Rule 2 (2) provides that Ord. 15, r. 1, shall apply in relation to a counterclaim as if the counterclaim were a separate action; and, as we have seen,

B rule 2 (3) provides for a counterclaim proceeding notwithstanding that the main action is no longer, for one of the reasons specified, in existence. An action is, of course, commenced by the formal step of the issue of a writ; one would expect to find a similar formal step for the initiation of a counterclaim, and the only comparable step appears to be the service of a counterclaim, either together with or subsequently added to the defence,

C or the service of some other document which, by virtue of some order of the court, is to stand as a counterclaim, as for example when the court makes an order dispensing with pleadings. It is difficult to see how (in the absence of some special order) an affidavit sworn in opposition to a summons for judgment under Order 14 can constitute such a document. In form, it is no more than evidence on affidavit of certain facts, which may

D form the basis of a counterclaim which the defendant wishes to advance and on the basis of which he asks the court either to give leave to defend, or to order a stay of execution. Thereafter he may or may not make a counterclaim. Furthermore, ordinarily no problem can arise in relation to limitation at the time of summons for judgment under Order 14; for so long as the plaintiff's action remains in existence, the defendant's counterclaim (if he has already pleaded it, or if he subsequently does so) will

E be deemed to have been commenced on the same date as the action, by virtue of section 28 of the Limitation Act 1939. If the defendant is at any time concerned about the time-bar position in relation to his cross-claim, his proper course is to serve a protective writ (a course which is frequently taken in relation to claims under commercial contracts, where a short time-bar may be imposed by the contract or by the terms of an international convention, such as the Hague Rules), or, after the plaintiff has served

F his statement of claim, to serve a defence and counterclaim within the limitation period. It is true that, after the plaintiff has commenced his action, and the defendant has sworn his affidavit and obtained either leave to defend or a stay of execution pending the determination of his counterclaim, the plaintiff may discontinue his action under Order 21 before the defendant had served his defence and counterclaim, in which

G event the defendant would be deprived of the opportunity of proceeding with his counterclaim by virtue of Ord. 15, r. 2 (2), and to that extent be deprived also of the benefit of section 28 of the Limitation Act 1939. But in these circumstances the defendant will no longer be exposed to the plaintiff's claim; moreover, he will not have taken any formal step to pursue his cross-claim until after the issue of the plaintiff's writ and if, in

H consequence, his cross-claim is time-barred, he has himself to blame because he did not preserve his position by issuing a protective writ.

For all these reasons I respectfully adopt the view expressed by Sargant L.J. (and, as I infer, also by Bankes L.J.) in *The Saxicava* [1924] P. 131 and by Sir Boyd Merriman P. in *The Fairplay XIV* [1939] P. 57, and I conclude that, for the purpose of Ord. 15, r. 2, of the present Rules of the Supreme Court, as for the purpose of the old Ord. 21, r. 16, no counterclaim is made or initiated or set up (whatever be the appropriate form of words) until the service of a pleading embodying the counterclaim, or of A some other document which, by the order of the court, is to stand in the place of such a pleading. Furthermore I am satisfied that, until such a step is taken, a right of action is not exercised by way of counterclaim within the meaning of those words as used in article 32 (4) of the Convention, in relation to a case of which an English court or tribunal is seised.

I wish to add that I was referred by counsel to the recent decision of B the Court of Appeal in *C.S.I. International Co. Ltd.* v. *Archway Personnel (Middle East) Ltd.* [1980] 1 W.L.R. 1069. In that case the question arose whether, assuming that a counterclaim had been " raised " by an affidavit sworn in opposition to a summons for judgment under Order 14, and the court had nevertheless refused leave to defend and a stay of execution and entered judgment for the plaintiff, the defendant could, after satisfaction C of the judgment, subsequently serve a counterclaim on the plaintiff pleading the matter formerly raised in his affidavit—this being done in order to establish English jurisdiction for the purposes of the counterclaim. The Court of Appeal held that such a counterclaim was irregular and must be set aside. Roskill L.J. said, at p. 1075:

> " I rest my decision on this simple point: where a counterclaim, even D if it has previously been raised, has not been the subject of a summons for directions or when required of a formal pleading before the time when the plaintiff had received full satisfaction of the judgment which he has obtained against the defendants, I do not think there is still extant any action by the plaintiffs in which the defendants could properly counterclaim against them. The action had, for all practical E purposes, come to an end when satisfaction of the judgment had been obtained."

The decision of the Court of Appeal does not, therefore, have any direct bearing on the problem in the present case. However, as I read it, the general tenor of the judgment of Roskill L.J. is consistent with the conclusion I have reached. In particular, Roskill L.J. was at pains to dis- F tinguish between the use of the words " any counterclaim made or raised " in Ord. 14, r. 3 (2), which provides that:

> " The court may by order and subject to such conditions, if any, as may be just, stay execution of any judgment given against a defendant under this rule until after the trial of any counterclaim made or raised by the defendant in the action," G

and the words " make a counterclaim " in Ord. 15, r. 2 (1). It may well be that, on the language of the Rules, a counterclaim may only be " made " within either Order 14 or Order 15 where it is embodied in a pleading, or in some other document which, by order of the court, is to stand as a pleading; but that the less formal expression " raised " was used in Ord. 14, r. 3 (2), to refer to the situation where a counterclaim has not H been pleaded but is only adumbrated in an affidavit. Be that as it may, the decision of the Court of Appeal in this case is, as I have said, at least consistent with the conclusion which I have reached.

For all these reasons. I am satisfied that the defendants did not exercise their right of action by way of counterclaim until after the expiry of the limitation period specified in article 32 (1) of the Convention. In particular, I am satisfied that the defendants' affidavit dated October 1, 1974, did not

The Weekly Law Reports, December 18, 1981

1559

1 W.L.R.   Impex Transport Ltd. v. Thames Ltd. (Q.B.D.)   Robert Goff J.

A amount to such an exercise of their right of action. At the best, it could only amount to a written claim within article 32 (2); though no documents appear to have been attached thereto as contemplated by that article. If it was such a written claim, it could only have been effective to suspend the running of the limitation period until the service, shortly after November 11, 1974, of the plaintiffs' affidavit rejecting the defendants' counterclaim

B In such event, it could only extend the limitation period by a little over six weeks; and as the defendants' defence and counterclaim was not served until two months and ten days after the expiry of the one year limitation period, the extension of time (if any) effected by the service of the defendants' affidavit of October 11, 1974, does not affect the decision in the case.

In the result I decide the preliminary issue in favour of the plaintiffs,
C and hold that any right of action the defendants may have had against the plaintiffs arising out of the carriage has been barred by lapse of time and may not be exercised by way of counterclaim or set-off.

Order accordingly.
Leave to appeal.

D
Solicitors: *Roche Hardcastles; Hicks, Arnold, Rose, Johnson.*

[Reported by SUSAN DENNY, Barrister-at-Law]

1560

A

[CHANCERY DIVISION]

* PRACTICE NOTE (CHANCERY: DEPOSITION)

1981 Oct. 28   Sir Robert Megarry V.-C.

B

*Evidence—Examination on oath—Order of court—Sufficient case
to be made out for examination before judge — Principles
governing conduct of examination—R.S.C., Ord. 39, r. 1 (1)
Practice—Chancery Division—Pleadings—Title—Listing of parties*

October 28. SIR ROBERT MEGARRY V.-C. read the following statement.
For the best part of the last two days I have been hearing the examination
of a witness in private under R.S.C., Ord. 39, in a substantial case which is
fixed for hearing in March 1982. The witness is in his eighties, and in the
circumstances of the case it was entirely proper for the parties to take the
precaution of obtaining an order for the examination of the witness in
advance of the hearing. What I am concerned with is the fact that the
order was treated as requiring an examination of the witness not before an
officer or examiner of the court, or some other person, but before a judge.
I think it desirable to say something about this in open court for guidance
in future cases.

    R.S.C., Ord. 39, r. 1 (1) allows the court, in any cause or matter where
it appears necessary for the purposes of justice, to make an order for " the
examination on oath " of a person " before a judge, an officer or examiner
of the court or some other person." I may leave out of account the special
provisions in rules 2 and 3 for examination out of the jurisdiction, and turn
to the provisions made by rules 4 to 14 for the general conduct of
examinations under the Order. It is plain that these rules govern all cases
where the examination is before " the examiner "; and by rule 4 (*a*) this
expression is defined in terms which include " an officer or examiner of
the court, or some other person." For instance, rule 10 provides that
questions of the admissibility of evidence are to be left for the court and
are not to be decided by the examiner, though he is to state his opinion
on the point. Yet he is not deprived of all power of decision, for according
to *The Supreme Court Practice* (1982), p. 689, he can allow a witness to
be treated as hostile by the party calling him, though it may be doubted
whether the authority cited, *Ohlsen* v. *Terrero* (1874) 10 Ch.App. 127, goes
quite as far as that. The rules deal with a variety of other matters on the
taking of evidence before an examiner, but I need not discuss them. What
I am concerned with is the position when evidence is taken before a judge
under the Order.

    The definition of " the examiner " in rule 4 (*a*) plainly seems to exclude
judges. The phrase " a judge, an officer or examiner of the court or some
other person " in rule 1 (1) contrasts with the definition of " the examiner "
in rule 4 (*a*) as " an officer or examiner of the court or some other person."
The omission of judges seems to be pointed, and so the detailed provisions
in rules 5 to 14 do not apply to them. If that is so, then there appears to be
no set of rules for examinations conducted before judges. I therefore
required counsel, before commencing the examination before me, to
consider what rules should apply; and in the end they agreed that I should
have a discretionary power either to rule on any objections to evidence or
to leave the ruling for the trial judge. Plainly there may be some objections

The Weekly Law Reports, December 18, 1981

1561

1 W.L.R.   Practice Note (Chancery: Deposition) (Ch.D.)   Sir Robert
                                                                        Megarry V.-C.

A to evidence which a judge who has neither been taken through the pleadings
nor heard the case opened may prefer to leave for the trial. It was also
agreed that the ordinary official transcript of the evidence would suffice,
and, indeed, be preferable to the mechanism of signed depositions envisaged
by rule 11.

B In the event, no objections to any of the evidence were taken, and so
for most of two days I simply sat and listened to the evidence, with
nothing to decide and no useful function to discharge. In those circumstances I think that I should provide some guidance for future cases. First,
I think that any litigant who wishes the examination of a witness under
Order 39 to take place before a judge and not an examiner must make out
a sufficient case for such an order to be made; and the burden is substantial.
The time of judges ought not to be spent on doing what can perfectly
C well be done by an examiner, and in the great majority of cases an examiner
will suffice. Only rarely will the greater authority of a judge be needed,
as where the witness is known to be recalcitrant or unruly. Most certainly
a judge is not to be had just for the asking.

Second, until the powers of a judge before whom an examination is
to be conducted are defined by rules of court, it behoves those who seek
D such an examination to agree beforehand, or to attempt to agree, what those
powers are to be. If the judge is to have no greater powers than an
examiner, it will usually be very difficult to establish a sufficient case for
having a judge rather than an examiner. Third, the extent of the powers
that the judge is to have should be defined in the order for the examination,
instead of being left for discussion when the examination is due to begin.
Fourth, the order for examination should make it explicit that it is to
E be before a judge, and not leave it optional for the parties to have it before
a judge or an examiner, as they choose. The master must exercise his
judgment, and decide whether or not it is a proper case for a judge.

In the present case the order does no credit to the Chancery Division.
It recites the application by the plaintiff, hearing her solicitors, and reading
a consent letter from solicitors for three of the nine defendants. Nothing
F is said about the solicitors for the various other parties (there are, I think,
six other firms involved), though I was told that in fact they all had assented
to the order, or at least not dissented from it. The body of the order then
proceeds to order that the witness " be orally examined by a judge or
commissioner by agreement or on failing such agreement by an examiner
of the court on a date and time to be mutually agreed." Nobody could
explain how the " commissioner " got into the order: I suppose he might
G be " some other person." The optional form of the order, giving a
three-fold choice, is deplorable; and certainly the word " by," on its first
and third appearances, should be " before."

At the conclusion of the examination I made various inquiries. In the
result, I came to the conclusion that the complex background to this family
dispute provided at least some grounds for asking for an examination
H before a judge, and that the fact that in the result I had had virtually no
function to perform, save to listen to the evidence, did not necessarily show
that the order should not have been made. Although in the result two
judicial days have been wasted, this has occurred through nothing worse
than a considerable degree of over-insurance. Having heard the explanations
of all concerned, I can well understand how that has come about; and
I utter no word of censure upon them, but merely give warning for the
future.

Practice Note (Chancery: Deposition) (Ch.D.)

There is one other procedural point which arose at the outset, and I   A
may mention now. This concerns the title of the case as it appears in the
pleadings. In the title the word " and " appears in an appropriate
superfluity. The proceedings are correctly stated to be " between " the
plaintiff " and " the first defendant; but then there appears the word
" and " between the names of each of the other eight defendants. Now the
proceedings are assuredly not between the first defendant " and " the
second defendant " and " the third defendant, who are all, in fact,   B
represented by the same counsel. In addition, each defendant is laboriously
described in the title as " seventh defendant," " eighth defendant " and
so on. Later on one comes to " second third party."

Nearly a year ago, in *Botton* v. *Remblance* (unreported), December 10,
1980, I inveighed against pleadings which showed multiple plaintiffs as
" sixth first plaintiff," " tenth first plaintiff," " second third plaintiff "   C
and so on; and I attempted to revive interest in *Practice Note* [1948]
W.N. 73. I shall try again. The simple and helpful Chancery practice where
there are multiple plaintiffs or defendants is to list the names in the title,
each on a separate line, with the appropriate numeral in brackets before
the name of each. When all the names of plaintiffs have been set out (and
not before) there should appear the single word " plaintiffs." Then, and
only then, there is an " and " separating all the plaintiffs from all the   D
defendants; and after that the defendants are similarly listed. If there are
third parties, there will be another " and," and they will be listed in the
same way; and so on. Brevity, clarity and simplicity are the hallmarks of
the skilled pleader; and those qualities should be extended to the titles
in his pleadings and not be confined to the text.

E

K. N. B.

F

G

H

END OF VOLUME 1

SUBJECT MATTER

(Vol. 1)

ADMIRALTY
Mortgage
Priorities
Sale of vessel—Order of priority of claims—Whether cost of discharging cargo before sale to become first charge of proceeds **The Jogoo,** Sheen J. **1376**

ADOPTION
Adoption order
Applications
Preliminary examination of jurisdiction—Procedure—Adoption (High Court) Rules 1976, r. 11 **Practice Direction (Adoption: Jurisdiction Application),** Fam.D. **1212**

AUSTRALIA
New South Wales
Contract
Unfair contract—Industrial Commission declaring void solus agreement granting licence to operate motor service station—Whether jurisdiction—Whether contract " whereby a person performs work in any industry "—Industrial Arbitration Act 1940 (1980 reprint), s. 88F (1) **Caltex Oil (Australia) Pty. Ltd. v. Feenan,** P.C. **1003**

BAILMENT
Leasing agreement
Hire of equipment
Letter withdrawing lessor's consent to lessee's possession of equipment—Distress warrant issued against lessee's goods—Whether equipment in possession of lessee with owner's consent—Whether withdrawal of consent effective without termination of lease agreement **Perdana Properties Bhd. v. United Orient Leasing Co. Sdn. Bhd.,**
P.C. **1496**

BANKING
Letter of credit
Proper law
Letter of credit issued by Kuwaiti bank through North Carolina bank—Buyers' provisional attachment order in Kuwait—Whether letter of credit enforceable by United States' sellers in England—Lex situs of debt
Power Curber International Ltd. v. National Bank of Kuwait S.A.K., C.A. **1233**

BANKRUPTCY
Bankruptcy notice
Application to set aside
Debtor's counterclaim, set-off or cross-demand—Affidavit—Time for filing—Whether jurisdiction in court to extend beyond 10 days from service of bankruptcy notice— Bankruptcy Act 1914, ss. 1 (1) (*g*), 109 (4) (as amended by Insolvency Act 1976, s. 4)—Bankruptcy Rules 1952, rr. 137 (*b*), 138, 139 (as amended by Bankruptcy (Amendment) Rules 1977, rr. 1 (3), 2)
In re **A Debtor (No. 6864 of 1980),** *Ex parte* **The Debtor v. Slater Walker Ltd.,**
C.A. **1205**

Bankruptcy notice file
Duty to search file before presenting petition—Requirement for affidavit of results of search **Practice Note (Bankruptcy: Affidavit of Search),** Ch.D. **474**

Trustee in bankruptcy
Release of trustee
Notice of intention to seek release sent to creditor care of solicitors—Affidavit in common form stating that notice sent to address on proof of debt—Whether release to be reversed or discharged—Bankruptcy Act 1914, s. 93 (1) (3)—Bankruptcy Rules 1952, r. 341 *In re* **Munro,** *Ex parte* **Singer v. Trustee in Bankruptcy,**
Walton J. **1358**

BARRISTER
Discipline
Disciplinary tribunal
Sentencing—Conviction for importuning in public place—Conduct unbecoming a barrister admitted before disciplinary tribunal—Sentence of suspension from practice—Whether not guilty plea to be taken into account in sentencing— Whether sentence in proportion to misconduct—Whether reprimand more appropriate *In re* **H. (A Barrister),** Gray's Inn Visitors **1257**

CARRIAGE BY LAND
International carriage of goods by road
Limitation of action see PRACTICE: **Pleadings:** *Counterclaim*

" Other means of transport "
  Damage to goods on trailer during loading on ship—Liability of carrier—Whether
  compensation to be calculated in accordance with law applicable to carriage by
  sea—Carriage of Goods by Road Act 1965, Sch., arts. 2, 17
                    Thermo Engineers Ltd. v. Ferrymasters Ltd., Neill J. **1470**

CHARITY
Cy-près doctrine
Impracticability of part of intention
  Bequests to found musical scholarships for absolute orphans from homes run by
  named charities—Refusal of bequests if restricted to absolute orphans from named
  charitable homes—Whether bequests to be applied cy-près
                    In re **Woodhams, decd.,** Vinelott J. **493**

CHILDREN AND YOUNG PERSONS
Care of
Intentional homelessness
  Families with young children—Local authority resolving that assistance with alter-
  native housing be not provided—Whether resolution ultra vires—Children and
  Young Persons Act 1963, s. 1 (1)
                    Attorney-General *ex rel.* **Tilley v. Wandsworth London Borough Council,**
                    C.A. **854**

CLUB
Construction of rules
Unincorporated international federation see CONTRACT

COMPANY
Charge
Registration
  Company's contingent right to grant of leases under building agreement—Interest
  charged to mortgagee as security for advances—Registration of mortgage against
  company under company legislation—No registration of equitable charge against
  freeholder—Leases granted and assigned—Whether leaseholders' interest in land
  subject to equitable charge created by mortgage—Companies Act 1948, s. 95—
  Land Charges Act 1925, s. 10 (1) (5)—Land Charges Act 1972, s. 3 (1) (7)
                    Property Discount Corpn. Ltd. v. Lyon Group Ltd.,
                    Goulding J. and C.A. **300**
Oppression
Compromise
  Application to enforce purchase of shares by company or directors—Action com-
  promised—Whether order in Tomlin form appropriate—Companies Act 1948, s. 210
                    In re **A Company (No. 003324 of 1979) (Practice Note),** Vinelott J. **1059**
Register
Restoration to register
  Winding up petition presented before dissolution of company—Winding up order
  made and perfected after dissolution—Court's discretion to declare dissolution
  void—Companies Act 1948, ss. 352 (1), 353 (5) (6)
                    In re **Thompson & Riches Ltd.,** Slade J. **682**
Shares
Compulsory acquisition see **Oppression**

Transfer
  Articles of private company restricting transfer of shares—Notice to be given of
  proposed transfer—Executor of deceased member holding shares for benefit of
  members of family—Whether " transfer " of shares
                    Safeguard Industrial Investments Ltd. v. National Westminster Bank Ltd.,
                    Vinelott J. **286**
Winding up
Petition
  Contributory's petition—Inspectors' report to Secretary of State—Whether evidence
  in support of contributor's petition—Companies Act 1948, s. 165 (*b*)—Companies
  Act 1967, s. 35 (1)   *In re* **St. Piran Ltd.,** Dillon J. **1300**

Preferential debt
  Group treatment for purposes of value added tax—Whether claim to tax preferential
  in winding up of non-representative member of group—Finance Act 1972,
  ss. 21 (1), 41   *In re* **Nadler Enterprises Ltd.,** Dillon J. **23**

CONFLICT OF LAWS
Contract
Proper law

Lloyd's average bond—Bond not specifying governing law—Bill of lading specifying that general average to be adjusted at such place as shipowners might select—Shipowners selecting London—Whether English law proper law—Whether shipowners' selection of London relevant—Whether proper law to be ascertained from circumstances at time of making of contract—R.S.C., Ord. 11, r. 1 (1) (*f*) (iii)

Armar Shipping Co. Ltd. v. Caisse Algérienne d'Assurance et de Réassurance, C.A. 207

CONTEMPT OF COURT
Tape recorder
Use in court

Discretion to grant or withhold leave—Contempt of Court Act 1981, s. 9

Practice Direction (Tape Recorders), C.A. 1526

CONTRACT
Condition or warranty
Mercantile contract

Sale of goods (f.o.b.)—Buyers to give 15 days' loading notice—Whether condition or intermediate term—GAFTA form 119, cl. 7

Bunge Corpn., New York v. Tradax Export S.A., Panama, H.L.(E.) 711

Construction
Rules of unincorporated international federation

Members of federation associations governing athletics in any " country "—Only one member permitted for each country—Taiwan association elected member in 1956 after China association elected—China association withdrawing in protest—China association re-elected as member representing mainland and Taiwan—Whether Taiwan " country " for purposes of rules—Validity of Taiwan's election

Reel v. Holder, C.A. 1226

F.o.b.
Loading

Buyers to give 15 days' loading notice—Whether notice given in time—Whether sellers entitled to hold buyers in default—Whether breach of condition or intermediate term—GAFTA form 119, cl. 7

Bunge Corpn., New York v. Tradax Export S.A., Panama, H.L.(E.) 711

Frustration
Remedy

Agreement to develop oil concession—Concession developed into oil field on stream—Agreement frustrated by Libyan Government expropriating one party's interest in field and excluding them from field—Resulting unjust enrichment of other party—Principles to be applied in awarding just sum—Currency of award—Whether interest payable on sum awarded—Law Reform (Miscellaneous Provisions) Act 1934, s. 3—Law Reform (Frustrated Contracts) Act 1943, ss. 1 (2) (3), 2 (3)

B.P. Exploration Co. (Libya) Ltd. v. Hunt (No. 2), C.A. 232

COPYRIGHT
Infringement
Literary work

Invented word—Whether " original literary work "—Copyright Act 1956, s. 2

Exxon Corpn. v. Exxon Insurance Consultants International Ltd., Graham J. 624

COSTS
Taxation
Value added tax

Solicitor's litigation on matter arising from practice—Tax not chargeable—Presentation of bill

Practice Direction (Taxation: VAT) (No. 3), Supreme Ct. Taxing Office 327

COUNTY COURT
Tape recorder
Use in court

Discretion to grant or withhold leave—Contempt of Court Act 1981, s. 9

Practice Direction (Tape Recorders), C.A. 1526

CRIME
Arson
Destroying or damaging property

Employee setting fire to employer's premises on employer's instructions—Intention to make fraudulent insurance claim—Whether employer " entitled to consent " to damage—Whether setting fire to own premises offence—Whether employee having " lawful excuse "—Criminal Damage Act 1971, ss. 1 (1) (3), 5 (2) (*a*)

Reg. v. Denton, C.A. 1446

CRIME—*continued*
Attempt
Causing noxious thing to be taken by another
   Drugs from sedative and sleeping tablets in milk—Little harm arising from toxicity
      of drugs—Danger to person carrying out potentially hazardous operation with
      faculties impaired—Whether " noxious thing "—Offences against the Person Act
      1861, s. 24   **Reg. v. Marcus, C.A. 774**

Coinage
Counterfeit coins
   Copies of current coinage—Whether intent to defraud necessary ingredient of offence
      —Coinage Offences Act 1936, s. 1 (1)   **Reg. v. Heron, C.A. 1480**

Common law offence
Attempt to pervert course of justice
   Witness's evidence conflicting with his statement—Witness either making false state-
      ments or committing perjury but neither proved—Whether permissible to charge
      witness with attempt to pervert course of justice
                                          Tsang Ping-nam v. The Queen, P.C. 1462

Costs
Central funds
   Crown Court—Acquitted defendant—Order for costs—Indictments Act 1915, ss. 5, 6
      —Costs in Criminal Cases Act 1973, s. 3
                      Practice Direction (Costs: Acquittal of Defendant), C.A. 1383

Court of Appeal
Sentence, appeal against
   Offence committed by young offender after release on licence on parole recommenda-
      tion—Whether " serving a sentence of imprisonment "—Criminal Justice Act 1961,
      s. 3 (1) (2) (3)—Criminal Justice Act 1967, s. 60   **Reg. v. Mellor, C.A. 1044**

   Young offender released on licence committing offence—Whether " serving a sentence
      of imprisonment "—Criminal Justice Act 1961, s. 3 (1) (2) (3)
                                               Reg. v. Orpwood, C.A. 1048

Drugs
Occupier of premises
   Cultivation of cannabis plants on premises—Whether occupier permitting production
      of controlled drug—Misuse of Drugs Act 1971, ss. 8, 37 (1) (as amended by
      Criminal Law Act 1977, s. 52)   **Taylor v. Chief Constable of Kent, D.C. 606**

Unauthorised possession of
   Doctor possessing drugs on own authority for self-treatment—Whether " acting in his
      capacity " as practitioner—Whether possession unlawful—Misuse of Drugs Act 1971,
      ss. 5 (1), 7 (3) (a)—Misuse of Drugs Regulations 1973, regs. 8 (2), 10 (1)
                                               Reg. v. Dunbar, C.A. 1536

Evidence
Corroboration
   Similar facts—Indecent assaults on girls—Circumstances similar to those leading to
      commission of offences—Evidence not disclosing offence—Whether admissible
                                            Reg. v. Barrington, C.A. 419

Dying declaration
   Evidence of identity—Prosecution case solely dependent on dying declaration—
      Whether corroboration necessary   **Nembhard v. The Queen, P.C. 1515**

Medical evidence
   Homicide—Tests for brain death—Suggestion of tests being insufficiently stringent
      and inadequately carried out—Whether admissible—Whether reception on appeal
      desirable, expedient or necessary—Criminal Appeal Act 1968, s. 23 (1) (2)
                                            Reg. v. Malcherek, C.A. 690

Firearms
Possession
   Pen gun used as toy gun—No certificate—No knowledge that gun lethal weapon—
      Whether absolute offence—Firearms Act 1968, s. 1 (1) (a)
                                         Reg. v. Hussain (Iftikhar), C.A. 416

Forgery
False document
   Falsification of witness statement—Statement tendered as evidence—Whether forgery
      of " document . . . made evidence by law "—Forgery Act 1913, s. 3 (3) (g)
                      Attorney-General's Reference (No. 2 of 1980), C.A. 148

Fraud
Conspiracy to defraud
   Bank director and employees using banking irregularities and malpractices followed
      by loss—Count to contain clear and concise particulars—Essential ingredient of
      offence—Whether dishonesty in mind or intention of person charged—Whether to be
      stressed in directing jury   **Reg. v. Landy, C.A. 355**

Evading liability by deception see **Theft**

CRIME—*continued*
    Fraud—*continued*
      Obtaining pecuniary advantage by deception
        Credit card used for purchases after credit limit exceeded—Whether representation of authority to use card—Whether shop assistant induced by false representation to sell goods on credit—Theft Act 1968, s. 16 (1)   **Reg. v. Lambie, C.A. 78**

    Homicide
      Causation
        Victim of assault connected by doctors to life-support machine—Machine disconnected on doctors' conclusion of victim's brain death—No evidence of original wound not being continuing and operating cause of victim's death—Whether causation issue for jury—Whether chain of causation broken
                    Reg. v. Malcherek, C.A. 690

      Manslaughter
        Death resulting from one or other act of assailant—Each act if causing death sufficient to establish manslaughter—Whether necessary to identify act causing death—Whether jury to be satisfied of each act being sufficient to establish offence whichever act resulting in death
            Attorney-General's Reference (No. 4 of 1980), C.A. 705

    Mens rea
      Harassment see LANDLORD AND TENANT

    Obscene libel
      Forfeiture
        Articles destined for publication abroad—Whether " kept for publication for gain " —Obscene Publications Act 1959, s. 3 (1) (3)
        Gold Star Publications Ltd. v. Comr. of Police of the Metropolis,
                         H.L.(E.) 732
      Obscene article
        Video cassette—Whether use publication of obscene article—Obscene Publications Act 1959, s. 1 (2) (3) (*b*)   **Attorney-General's Reference (No. 5 of 1980), C.A. 88**

    Practice
      Crown Court
        Distribution of business—Bail—Courts Act 1971, ss. 4 (5), 5 (4), Sch. 10
            Practice Direction (Crime: Crown Court Business) (No. 7), C.A. 1324
      Pre-trial review
        Papers in complicated case—Whether to be provided to judge well before review hearing   **Reg. v. Landy, C.A. 355**

      Submission of no case to answer
        Evidence of person charged committing crime alleged—Strength or weakness of evidence depending on view taken of witnesses—Whether for jury to determine
                  Reg. v. Galbraith, C.A. 1039

    Sentence
      Fine
        Imprisonment in default of payment—Offender failing to pay fine and emigrating—Extradition to United Kingdom on theft charges—Activation of imprisonment in default—Whether sentence for original offence—Whether detention unlawful—United States of America (Extradition) Order 1976, art. XII
            Reg. v. Uxbridge Justices, *Ex parte* Davies, D.C. 1080

    Sexual offences
      Indecent assault
        Boy under 16—Woman touching boy's penis—Whether act prior to sexual intercourse constituting indecent assault—Sexual Offences Act 1956, s. 15 (1) (2)
                  Faulkner v. Talbot, D.C. 1528

    Theft
      Dishonest appropriation
        Selection of goods in store with two different price labels—Intention to obtain goods at lower price—Cashier charging lower price—Whether contract of sale void—Whether appropriation of property belonging to another—Theft Act 1968, s. 1 (1)
            Kaur (Dip) v. Chief Constable for Hampshire, D.C. 578
      Evading liability by deception
        Diners in restaurant falsely claiming to have put money on table in payment of bill—Whether attempt to induce creditor to " forgo payment " with intent to make permanent default—Theft Act 1978, s. 2 (1)   **Reg. v. Holt, C.A. 1000**

      False accounting
        False material particulars—Personal loan proposal form with false statements—Whether document " required for any accounting purpose "—Theft Act 1968, s. 17 (1) (*a*)   **Attorney-General's Reference (No. 1 of 1980), C.A. 34**

CRIME—*continued*
  Theft—*continued*
    Handling stolen goods
      Evidence—Cheques obtained by deception—Cheques paid into bank account with
      other moneys—Cheque drawn on balance representing defendant's share of crime
      —Whether evidence of defendant handling stolen goods—Theft Act 1968,
      ss. 22 (1), 24 (2)   **Attorney-General's Reference (No. 4 of 1979), C.A. 667**

      " Realisation by or for the benefit of another person "—Innocent purchase of stolen
      goods—Subsequent suspicion of theft and realisation of goods by sale—Whether
      " for the benefit of " buyer—Theft Act 1968, s. 22 (1)   **Reg. v. Bloxham, C.A. 859**

CROWN
  Crown vehicles
    Road traffic offences
      Nominated person—Practical advantages in nominating John Doe—Road Traffic Act
      1972, s. 188 (8)   **Barnett v. French, D.C. 848**

CROWN COURT
  Jurisdiction
    Appeal against conviction
      Committal for sentence—Sentence imposed on applicant—Applicant seeking to
      appeal against conviction—Whether court functus officio
           Reg. v. Croydon Crown Court, Ex parte Bernard, D.C. 116

    Bill of indictment
      Indictment drawn from certificate erroneously reciting provisions of Magistrates'
      Courts Act 1980—Recitation of previous legislation proper—Whether indictment
      valid   **Reg. v. Hall (Peter Michael), C.A. 1510**

DAMAGES
  Contract
    Breach
      Non-payment of money due under contract—Loss suffered by reason of non-
      payment—Whether recoverable as special damages   **Wadsworth v. Lydall, C.A. 598**

  Earnings, loss of
    Future earnings
      Boy injured in accident—Future earning capacity impaired—Approach to assessment
      of damages   **Joyce v. Yeomans, C.A. 549**

    Supplementary benefit allowance
      Self-employed man injured in industrial accident—Cessation of unemployment benefit
      —Receipt of supplementary allowance—Whether benefit deductible from special
      damages   **Plummer v. P. W. Wilkins & Son Ltd., Latey J. 831**

  Personal injuries
    Loss of amenities
      Wife's inability to perform housekeeping duties—Husband's loss of earnings incurred
      as result of assisting wife—Estimated cost of employing domestic help—Whether
      proper measure of damages notwithstanding possibility of award not being used
      for that purpose—Whether husband's loss of earnings recoverable
           Daly v. General Steam Navigation Co. Ltd., C.A. 120

  Remoteness
    Foreseeability
      Ship's wrongful arrest—Expenses of obtaining release—High interest—Charges
      on overdraft to provide security—Whether damages or mitigation—Whether
      recoverable   **Compania Financiera " Soleada " S.A. v. Hamoor Tanker Corpn. Inc.,
                       C.A. 274**

  Sale of goods
    Construction of contract
      F.o.b. contract—Whether " default in shipment or delivery " confined to default by
      seller—Whether general principles of assessment of damages applicable where
      buyer defaults—GAFTA form 119, cl. 22
          Bunge Corpn., New York v. Tradax Export S.A., Panama, H.L.(E.) 711

DISCRIMINATION, SEX
  Equal pay
    Pension scheme
      Male bank clerks contributing to pension scheme—Women not contributing to scheme
      —Men receiving extra salary equivalent to contribution—Whether additional sum
      " pay "—Whether provision as to equal pay directly enforceable in member states—
      E.E.C. Treaty (Cmnd. 5170—II), art. 119—Council Directive (75/117/E.E.C.), art. 1
          Worringham v. Lloyd's Bank Ltd. (Case 69/80), E.C.J. 950

DISCRIMINATION, SEX—*continued*
    Equal pay—*continued*
        Variation due to material difference
            Hourly rates of pay—Full-time employees receiving higher rates than female part-time employees—Whether variation due to material difference other than sex—Effect of Community law on municipal law—Equal Pay Act 1970, s. 1 (3) (as amended by Sex Discrimination Act 1975, s. 8 (1))—E.E.C. Treaty (Cmnd. 5179-II), art. 119—Council Directive (75/117/E.E.C.), art. 1
                  Jenkins v. Kingsgate (Clothing Productions) Ltd., E.C.J. 972
                                        E.A.T. 1485

EASEMENT
    Right to draw water
        Statutory restriction
            Use of water from mill pond forming part of river—Occupier of dominant tenement having no statutory licence to abstract water—Increase of user during prescriptive period—Whether bar to prescription—Right to damages for interference with right—Effect of statute—Water Resources Act 1963, ss. 23 (1), 24 (1), 135 (8)
                                      Cargill v. Gotts, C.A. 441

ECCLESIASTICAL LAW
    Faculty
        Headstone see **Headstone**

        Memorial tablet
            Mural tablet in memory of benefactor of church and parish—Whether faculty to be granted—Relevant considerations
                  In re **St. Margaret's, Eartham,** Const.Ct. and Arches Ct. **1129**

        Organ
            Petition to install computer organ—Existing pipe organ unplayable but restorable—Relevance of comparative projected costs of introducing computer organ or restoring existing organ—Whether pipe organ to be restored—Whether faculty to be granted   *In re* **St. Martin's, Ashton-upon-Mersey,** Const.Ct. **1288**

Headstone
    Faculty
        Petition to erect headstone incorporating photographic reproductions—Whether appropriate memorial   *In re* **St. Mary's, Fawkham,** Arches Ct. **1171**

    Photographic reproduction
        Erection of headstone incorporating photographs—No indication of photographs on approved design—Whether photographs appropriate on headstone—Whether photographs should be removed   *In re* **St. Mark's, Haydock,** Const.Ct. **1164**

    Right to erect
        Permission to erect headstone sought by deceased's estranged widow and by woman with whom deceased associating—Appropriate inscription—Proper order
                  In re **St. Mark's, Haydock (No. 2),** Const.Ct. **1167**

EDUCATION
    School
        Education authority, statutory duties of
            Individual music tuition—Proposal by authority to charge fees—Whether instrumental tuition part of education—Whether authority entitled to charge—Education Act 1944, ss. 8, 61 (1)   **Reg. v. Hereford and Worcester Local Education Authority,** *Ex parte* **Jones,** Forbes J. **768**

            Travelling expenses—Pupil mistakenly thought to be living over three miles away from school—Season ticket granted—Whether authority entitled to revoke season ticket after discovering mistake in mileage—Whether authority estopped—Education Act 1944, ss. 39 (5), 55 (2) (as amended by Education (Miscellaneous Provisions) Act 1948, s. 11, Sch. 1, Pt. I)   **Rootkin v. Kent County Council,** C.A. **1186**

    Students' grants
        Overseas students
            Student entering United Kingdom to attend school—Student forming intention to remain in United Kingdom—Application to education authority for award for university course—Whether " ordinarily resident " in United Kingdom—Education Act 1962, s. 1 (1) (*a*)—Local Education Authority Awards Regulations 1979, reg. 13 (*a*)   **Cicutti v. Suffolk County Council,** Sir Robert Megarry V.-C. **558**

EMPLOYMENT
Contract of employment
Implied term
Statement of terms of employment containing no reference to sick pay—No wages paid during absence from work through ill-health—Whether term to be implied for payment of wages during period of sickness—Whether sickness benefit to be deducted—Employment Protection (Consolidation) Act 1978, s. 1 (3) (d)
                         Mears v. Safecar Security Ltd., E.A.T. 1214

Unfair dismissal
Excluded classes
Normal retiring age—Civil servant—Minimum retirement age of 50—Discretionary retention beyond minimum age—Civil servants usually allowed to complete 20 years' service—Civil servants in one department dismissed if 60 or over—Whether claim for unfair dismissal excluded—Trade Union and Labour Relations Act 1974, Sch. 1, para. 10 (b)
               Howard v. Department for National Savings, C.A. 542

Strike
Boilermakers on strike for more pay—Fitter refusing to cross picket line—Fitter returning to work before end of strike but subsequently dismissed for redundancy—Boilermaker on strike dismissed—Complaint of unfair dismissal—Whether fitter " relevant employee "—Employment Protection (Consolidation) Act 1978, s. 62 (2) (4)
                        McCormick v. Horsepower Ltd., C.A. 993

ESTOPPEL
Conduct, by
Development of law
Passing off action—Distinction between legal and equitable rights—Whether broader approach to estoppel now acceptable
                   Habib Bank Ltd. v. Habib Bank A.G. Zurich, C.A. 1265

Statutory discretion
Local education authority's discretion to pay travelling expenses—Season ticket granted in mistaken belief that pupil lived more than three miles from school—Whether local authority estopped from withdrawing ticket—Education Act 1944, s. 55 (2) (as amended)   **Rootkin v. Kent County Council, C.A. 1186**

EQUITY
Rectification
Lease
Rent revision clause failing to provide for default of agreement—Common intention that rent to be fixed by arbitrator in default of agreement—Execution of lease by tenant knowing omission due to landlord's mistake—Whether landlord entitled to rectification   **Thomas Bates and Son Ltd. v. Wyndham's (Lingerie) Ltd.,**
                                                     C.A. 505

EVIDENCE
Examination on oath
Order of court
Sufficient case to be made out for examination before judge—Principles governing conduct of examination—R.S.C., Ord. 39, r. 1 (1)
             Practice Note (Chancery: Deposition), Sir Robert Megarry V.-C. 1560

Expert evidence
Appellate court
Conflict of opinion between medical experts at trial—Judge preferring opinion of one expert—Extent of appellate court's powers of review   **Joyce v. Yeomans, C.A. 549**

Medical report
Action for negligence against medical practitioner—Joint report prepared by plaintiff's medical experts and settled by counsel—Whether undesirable practice
                          Whitehouse v. Jordan, H.L.(E.) 246

EXECUTION
Charging order on land
Trust for sale
Judgment debtor and his wife holding property under trust for sale—Whether judgment creditor entitled to have order imposed on judgment debtor's beneficial interest—Charging Orders Act 1979, s. 2
             National Westminster Bank Ltd. v. Stockman, Russell J. 67

EXTRADITION

Person surrendered by foreign state

Jurisdiction of English court

Extradition of offender on theft charges—Prohibition against proceeding against offender for any other matter—Non-payment of fine for offence previously committed—Imprisonment in default—Whether sentence for offence—Whether detention unlawful—United States of America (Extradition) Order 1976, art. XII

Reg. v. Uxbridge Justices, *Ex parte* **Davies,** D.C. **1080**

Treaty

Construction

Provision for admission of "sworn depositions or statements of witnesses" in extradition proceedings—Accomplices' unsworn statements—Acknowledgment of truth of statements on subsequent occasion in court after being told of penalties for perjury—Whether acknowledgment amounting to affirmation—Whether affirmation admissible under treaty—Extradition Treaty (Sweden and Norway), Order in Council, September 30, 1873, art. X—Extradition Act 1873, s. 4

Reg. v. Governor of Pentonville Prison, *Ex parte* **Singh (Harmohan),**
D.C. **1031**

FACT OR LAW

Value added tax

Qualifying activities see REVENUE: **Value added tax:** *Zero-rating*

FIJI

Crime

Evidence

Confession—Issue of admissibility—Whether issue for trial judge or assessors

Ragho Prasad v. The Queen, P.C. **469**

GAMING

Betting

Licensed betting office

Advertisement—Posters placed inside windows drawing attention to facilities available at betting offices—Posters placed inside windows only legible from outside—Whether posters published outside—Whether posters advertisements—Betting, Gaming and Lotteries Act 1963, s. 10 (5)

Windsors (Sporting Investments) Ltd. v. Oldfield, D.C. **1176**

GUARANTEE

Debt

Mortgage securing loan

Variation of mortgage without guarantor's consent—Mortgagee and mortgagor's agreement increasing mortgage interest rate and extending time for repayment of principal sum—Guarantee covering further advances—Whether variation " further advance "—Whether guarantor discharged from liability

Burns v. Trade Credits Ltd., P.C. **805**

HIRE-PURCHASE

Conditional sale agreement

Enforceability

Accelerated payment clause—Seller entitled to call for balance of purchase price and property in goods to pass to buyer—Default in payment of instalments—Seller claiming moneys due under accelerated payment clause—Whether clause void as restriction on buyer's right to terminate agreement—Whether unenforceable as penalty—Hire-Purchase Act 1965, ss. 27 (1), 29

Wadham Stringer Finance Ltd. v. Meaney, Woolf J. **39**

HONG KONG

Crime

Attempt to pervert course of justice see CRIME: **Common law offence**

Bribery

Control of assets disproportionate to official emoluments—Proof of cost of acquisition—Whether prosecution to prove value of assets at charge date—Prevention of Bribery Ordinance, s. 10 (1) (*b*)

Attorney-General of Hong Kong v. Ho Pui-yiu, P.C. **395**

Town planning

Director of Works

Tenants of Crown land seeking approval of Director for development—Approval conditional on payment of premium—Whether abuse of power

Hang Wah Chong Investment Co. Ltd. v. Attorney-General of Hong Kong,
P.C. **1141**

HOUSE OF LORDS
Costs
Security for
Increase in amount of security—Revision of forms of bill of costs for taxation
Practice Direction (House of Lords: Costs: Security), H.L. 1213

HUSBAND AND WIFE
Divorce
Ancillary relief
Court's jurisdiction
Wife seeking order for co-respondent to file affidavit of means—Whether jurisdiction to make order—Matrimonial Causes Rules 1977, r. 77 (5)
Wynne v. Wynne, C.A. 69

Children
Practice
Welfare officer's report—Court to specify matters on which report to be based —Welfare officer attending hearing
Practice Direction (Divorce: Welfare Report), Fam.D. 1162

Financial provision
Failure to maintain
Application to High Court
Hearing date in Principal Registry—Matrimonial Causes Act 1973, s. 27 (as amended by Domestic Proceedings and Magistrates' Courts Act 1978, s. 63)
Practice Direction (Divorce Registry: Failure to Maintain), Fam.D. 274

Pre-trial review
Procedures
Discontinuance of pre-trial review—Continuance of procedures incidental to review **Practice Direction (Pre-trial Review: Ancillary Relief), Fam.D. 1010**

Matrimonial home
Act of 1967
Registration of charge under Act
Sale of property owned by wife—Husband not intending to occupy property— Whether Class F charge registrable for purpose of freezing wife's assets —Matrimonial Homes Act 1967, s. 1 (1) (*b*) **Barnett v. Hassett, Wood J. 1385**

Practice
Affidavit
Principal Registry
Fixed date of hearing—Filing affidavits and documents
Practice Direction (Family Division: Filing Affidavits), Fam.D. 106

Property
Transfer of property
Avoidance of transaction
Land conveyed for valuable consideration to company—Company charging land to bank—Divorce—Wife seeking to set conveyance aside—Whether power to set aside bank's charge—Matrimonial Causes Act 1973, s. 37 (3)
Green v. Green, Eastham J. 391

IMMIGRATION
Limited leave to enter
Application to extend stay
Student expressing intention to remain in country after studies if permitted—Whether applicant disentitled to grant of extension—Statement of Immigration Rules for Control After Entry: E.E.C. and Other Non-Commonwealth Nationals (H.C. 82), para. 12 **Reg. v. Immigration Appeal Tribunal, *Ex parte* Shaikh (Munir Ahmed), Bingham J. 1107**

INDUSTRIAL RELATIONS
Employment Appeal Tribunal
Procedure
Appeals and interlocutory applications—Special procedure—Directions—Documents and exhibits—Complaints of bias—Employment Appeal Tribunal Rules 1980, r. 3
Practice Direction (E.A.T.: Procedure), E.A.T. 323

INJUNCTION
Domestic violence
Power of arrest
Injunction with power of arrest attached—Desirability of limiting order to period of not more than three months—Domestic Violence and Matrimonial Proceedings Act 1976, s. 2 **Practice Note (Domestic Violence: Power of Arrest), Fam.D. 27**

INJUNCTION—*continued*
Interlocutory
Jurisdiction to grant
Interlocutory order for payment of taxed costs—Order unenforceable pending taxation —Intention to defeat enforcement of order by disposal of assets—Injunction restraining disposal of assets before trial—Supreme Court of Judicature (Consolidation) Act 1925, s. 45 (1)   **Faith Panton Property Plan Ltd. v. Hodgetts,** C.A. **927**

Mareva injunction
Conditions—Application to restrain removal by defendant of any money in any bank account at specified branch—Whether plaintiff entitled to injunction—Whether plaintiff to pay bank's reasonable costs
Searose Ltd. v. Seatrain U.K. Ltd., Robert Goff J. **894**

——————Application to restrain removal by defendant of cargo laden on ship —Effect of injunction on port authority—Court's protection of interests of third parties   **Clipper Maritime Co. Ltd. of Monrovia v. Mineralimportexport,**
Robert Goff J. **1262**

INTEREST
Award of damages
Personal injury cases
Interest on amount for pain and suffering and loss of amenities
Daly v. General Steam Navigation Co. Ltd., C.A. **120**

JAMAICA
Crime
Evidence of dying declaration see CRIME: **Evidence**

JUSTICES
Clerk to justices
Functions
Responsibility of clerk to advise justices on law, practice and procedure—Manner in which functions to be performed
Practice Direction (Justices: Clerk to Court), Q.B.D. **1163**

Committal to Crown Court
Committal for sentence
Transitional provisions—Proceedings commenced before new Act in force—Court records showing committal under new Act—Whether mistake vitiating proceedings —Whether committal valid—Magistrates' Courts Act 1980, s. 37 (1), Sch. 8, para. 2— Magistrates' Courts Rules 1968, rr. 16 (1), 54 (as amended by Magistrates' Courts (Amendment) Rules 1973)
Reg. v. Folkestone and Hythe Juvenile Court Justices, *Ex parte* **R. (A Juvenile),**
D.C. **1501**

Committal for trial
Transitional provisions—Proceedings commenced before new Act in force—Certificate sent to Crown Court wrongly stating committal under relevant sections of new Act —Whether committal valid—Whether indictment valid—Magistrates' Courts Rules 1968, r. 10 (2) (*b*) (*j*) (as amended by Magistrates' Courts (Amendment) Rules 1973, Sch., para. 5 (*a*))—Magistrates' Courts Act 1980, Sch. 8, paras. 1, 2
Reg. v. Hall (Peter Michael), C.A. **1510**

Committal warrant
Non-payment of fines
Applicant in arrears—Justices' order fixing term of imprisonment for each fine— Warrant issued to total of periods fixed—Period in excess of period applicable to total amount of fines—Validity of warrant—Magistrates' Courts Act 1952, ss. 64 (1) (3), 65 (2), Sch. 3, para. 1 (as amended by Criminal Law Act 1977, s. 59)
Reg. v. Southampton Justices, *Ex parte* **Davies (Neil),** D.C. **374**

Costs
Property held by police
Claim for return of property—Whether "application" to be made by way of complaint—Jurisdiction to make order for costs—Police (Property) Act 1897, s. 1 (1)—Magistrates' Courts Act 1952, s. 55 (1)
Reg. v. Uxbridge Justices, *Ex parte* **Comr. of Police**
of the Metropolis, D.C. **112**

JUSTICES—*continued*
 Election for trial on indictment
  Criminal damage
    Criminal damage under £200 charged with three other offences all triable only sum-
    marily—Criminal damage triable either way if part of series of " offences of the
    same or a similar character "—Whether defendant entitled to elect trial on indict-
    ment—Criminal Law Act 1977, s. 23 (7)
                    Reg. v. Hatfield Justices, *Ex parte* **Castle,** D.C. **217**

 Peace
  Recognisance to keep
    Juveniles' refusal of consent to binding over—Jurisdiction to imprison for refusal—
    Whether power to bind over without juveniles' consent—Powers of Criminal Courts
    Act 1973, s. 19 (1)   **Veater v. G.,** D.C. **567**

 Summons
  Application for
    Clerk to justices refusing application—Whether justices required to reconsider
    application—Justices' Clerks Rules 1970, r. 3, Sch., para. 2
                    Reg. v. Worthing Justices, *Ex parte* **Norvell,** D.C. **413**

LAND CHARGE
 Register, vacation of
  Pending actions register
    Landlords' notices requiring repairs—Lessee's counter-notices preventing action for
    breach of covenant without leave of court—Cautions entered against houses—
    Landlords seeking leave to commence action in county court for breach of repair-
    ing covenants in leases—Whether pending action " relating to land "—Land
    Charges Act 1972, s. 17 (1)—Leasehold Property (Repairs) Act 1938, s. 1 (3)
                    Selim Ltd. v. Bickenhall Engineering Ltd.,
                    Sir Robert Megarry V.-C. **1318**

LAND REGISTRATION
 Register
  Rectification
    Squatter registered as proprietor of leasehold interest with possessory title—Lessee's
    title deleted—Whether freeholder entitled to possession—Whether squatter's title to
    be deleted and lessee's reinstated—Purported surrender of lease by lessee—Free-
    holder's right to possession—Land Registration Act 1925, ss. 11, 69 (1) (4), 75
                    Spectrum Investment Co. v. Holmes, Browne-Wilkinson J. **221**

LANDLORD AND TENANT
 Agreement for lease
  Usual covenants
    Business premises—Tenant allowed into immediate possession—Covenants to be
    included as usually to be found in 1971 commercial lease
                    Chester v. Buckingham Travel Ltd., Foster J. **96**

 Business premises (security of tenure)
  Application for new tenancy
    Notice to quit served on September 30—Tenant's application for new tenancy made
    on January 31—Whether application made within statutory four month period—
    Landlord and Tenant Act 1954, s. 29 (3)   **Dodds v. Walker,** H.L.(E.) **1027**

  Certificate of Secretary of State
    Local authority applying for certificate of change of use—Local authority wishing
    to store highways materials on site of premises—Whether change of use and
    occupation " requisite " for purposes of landlord—Landlord and Tenant Act
    1954, s. 57 (1)   **Reg. v. Secretary of State for the Environment,** *Ex parte* **Powis,**
                                                                    D.C. **584**

  Landlord's intention to occupy
    Premises consisting of vacant site—Landlord intending to erect building before
    occupying—Whether intention to occupy " the holding "—Landlord and Tenant
    Act 1954, s. 30 (1) (*g*)   **Cam Gears Ltd. v. Cunningham,** C.A. **1011**

 Harassment
  Residential occupier
    Mistaken belief that occupier not residential occupier—Mens rea—Whether necessary
    to show reasonable grounds for belief—Protection from Eviction Act 1977,
    s. 1 (3) (*a*)   **Reg. v. Phekoo,** C.A. **1117**

LANDLORD AND TENANT—*continued*
Lease
Rectification see EQUITY

Rent
Revision
No provision in event of failure to agree revised rent—Whether fair rent to be implied **Beer v. Bowden (Note), C.A. 522**

Revised rent to be fixed by arbitrator in default of agreement—Whether rent to be market rent or reasonable rent—No provision in event of failure to agree revised rent—Whether reasonable rent to be implied
Thomas Bates and Son Ltd. v. Wyndham's (Lingerie) Ltd., C.A. 505

Rent restriction
Personal occupation
Long tenancy at low rent—Penthouse comprising maisonette with self-contained flat attached—Original use as family home—Assignment of long lease—Subsequent sub-letting of maisonette for term of head lease less one day—Sub-tenant in unlawful occupation after term date—Tenant in occupation of flat—Tenant's intention to use whole premises as family home—Whether protected in respect of whole—Whether penthouse let as one separate dwelling—Landlord and Tenant Act 1954, ss. 1, 2 (1) (2), 22 (3)—Rent Act 1977, s. 2 (3)
Regalian Securities Ltd. v. Ramsden, H.L.(E.) 611

Personal representatives letting house held on trust for infant beneficiaries—Personal representatives seeking possession for occupation with beneficiaries—Whether " landlord " for purposes of application possession—Rent Act 1977, s. 98 (1) (*b*), Sch. 15, Case 9 **Patel (Mahendra Kumar) v. Patel (Bharat), C.A. 1342**

Rent assessment
Jurisdiction—Application by tenant to register fair rent—Issue whether protected tenant—Rent officer so satisfied—Adjournment of application to register fair rent pending court proceedings to determine nature of tenancy—Whether rent officer under duty to register fair rent prior to ruling of court
Reg. v. Camden London Borough Rent Officer, *Ex parte* Ebiri, D.C. 881

Repairs
Covenant implied by statute
Lease for seven years—Tenant covenanting to carry out internal repairs—Landlords' statutory obligation if lease for less than seven years—Entry into possession on date lease expressed to commence—Lease delivered 14 days later—Whether lease for seven years or less—Landlords accepting rent assessed by rent officer on basis of their liability for repairs—Tenant doing repairs and withholding part of rent—Landlords' claim for arrears of rent—Whether landlords estopped from denying liability for repairs—Housing Act 1961, ss. 32 (1), 33 (1) (3) (5)
Brikom Investments Ltd. v. Seaford, C.A. 863

Secure tenancy
Housing Act 1980
Notices to quit served on local authority tenants—Proceedings for possession brought before legislation coming into effect—Whether premises " let under a secure tenancy "—Whether tenants having licence to occupy—Housing Act 1980, ss. 28 (1), 33 (1), 34 (1), 48 (1)
Harrison v. Hammersmith and Fulham London Borough Council, C.A. 650

Surrender
Surrender by operation of law
Grant of new tenancy—Whether terminating tenant's right to remove tenant's fixtures
New Zealand Government Property Corpn. v. H.M. & S. Ltd., Woolf J. 870

LANDS TRIBUNAL
Case stated by
Interlocutory order
Application for discovery at hearing of appeal—Dismissal of application—Refusal of tribunal to state case on determination of application for discovery—Whether determination final " decision "—Lands Tribunal Act 1949, s. 3 (4)
Reg. v. Lands Tribunal, *Ex parte* City of London Corpn., Judge Newey Q.C. 985

LAW REFORM
  Whether necessary
    Recognisance to keep peace
      Juvenile defendant's refusal to be bound over—No jurisdiction in justices to impose
      sanction   **Veater v. G., D.C. 567**

LEGAL AID
  Certificate
    Ambit
      Certificate granted to plaintiff limited to representation at one hearing and thereafter
      obtaining counsel's opinion—Plaintiff ordered to pay costs of later interlocutory
      hearing—Certificate not discharged—Whether costs of later hearing covered by
      certificate—Legal Aid Act 1974, s. 8 (1) (e)   **Boorman v. Godfrey, C.A. 1100**

  Costs
    Charge on property
      Compromise of action—Action settled on terms that defendant discharge legally aided
      plaintiff's debts to amount of sum offered—Whether sum property " recovered or
      preserved " for plaintiff—Whether sum subject to statutory charge—Legal Aid Act
      1974, s. 9 (6) (7)   **Manley v. The Law Society, Bristow J. and C.A. 335**

LIBEL AND SLANDER
  Pleadings
    Innuendo
      Extrinsic facts in support of innuendo occurring after publication—Whether original
      words having defamatory meaning alleged in innuendo—Failure to plead names
      of individuals with knowledge of secondary meaning of statement—Whether cause
      of action complete on publication or on subsequent damage
                                        Grappelli v. Derek Block (Holdings) Ltd., C.A. 822

LIMITATION OF ACTION
  Personal injuries
    Time limit, power to override
      Writ not issued within three-year period due to negligence of solicitors—Plaintiff
      having unanswerable claim against solicitors—Whether jurisdiction in court to
      allow action to proceed—Whether plaintiff suffering no prejudice if action barred
      —Limitation Act 1939 (as amended by Limitation Act 1975, s. 1), s. 2D (1)
                                                          Thompson v. Brown, H.L.(E.) 744

LOCAL GOVERNMENT
  Contract
    Seal
      Council's resolution to accept fixed-price tender—Seal affixed to contract containing
      price fluctuation clause—Non-compliance with standing orders in affixing seal—
      Validity of contract—Local Government Act 1933, s. 266 (2)
                          **North West Leicestershire District Council v. East Midlands Housing
                                                                      Association Ltd., C.A. 1396**

  Housing
    Homeless persons
      Applicant claiming to be homeless with priority need—Previous application by inten-
      tionally homeless member of family—Applicant's conduct in acquiescing in decision
      resulting in family being homeless—Whether applicant " homeless intentionally "—
      Housing (Homeless Persons) Act 1977, ss. 4, 17
                          **Reg. v. North Devon District Council, *Ex parte* Lewis (J. P.),
                                                                                  Woolf J. 328**

MALAYSIA
  Bailment
    Leasing agreement see BAILMENT

  Land
    Stamp duty
      Date for assessing market value—Contract of sale followed by statutory memoran-
      dum of transfer—Collector's assessment at date of execution of memorandum—
      Whether proper—Stamp Ordinance 1949 (as amended by Stamp (Amendment) Act
      1967, Sch. 1), s. 12A
                          Chin Choy alias Chin Chong Kim v. Collector of Stamp Duties, P.C. 1201

MEDICAL PRACTITIONER
Negligence
Standard of care

Obstetrician—Use of forceps in delivery—Five or six pulls with forceps—Obstruction of ischial spines—Subsequent hospital report stating that infant's head disimpacted prior to Caesarean section—Whether evidence establishing negligence—Error of clinical judgment—Whether capable of amounting to negligence

Whitehouse v. Jordan, H.L.(E.) 246

Professional conduct
Medical reports

Practitioner suspended for criminal convictions—Fitness to resume practice—Professional Conduct Committee requiring evidence of practitioner's mental state—Whether entitled to confidential medical reports when considering habits and conduct since suspension—Whether failure to divulge contents breach of natural justice—Medical Act 1978, s. 6, Sch. 3, para. 5 (1)—General Medical Council Disciplinary Committee (Procedure) Rules Order of Council 1970, Appendix, r. 47, superseded by General Medical Council Preliminary Proceedings Committee and Professional Conduct Committee (Procedure) Rules Order of Council 1980, Appendix, r. 55 **Crompton v. General Medical Council, P.C. 1435**

MENTAL DISORDER
Court of Protection
Execution of statutory will

Application for order after patient's secret marriage—Husband not made party to application—Evidence of patient's incapability of making will—Order made on basis of urgency and doubt as to validity of marriage—Whether proper exercise of discretion to make order—Validity of will—Mental Health Act 1959, s. 103 (1) (*dd*) (3) (*b*) (as amended by Administration of Justice Act 1969, s. 17)

In re **Davey, Ct. of Protection 164**

MINOR
Custody
Interim order

Mother having custody of children sole tenant of council house—Breakdown of mother's health—Father moving into house at mother's request to look after children—Application by father for interim care and control and for injunction to exclude mother from house—Court's jurisdiction in emergency situation to interfere with tenant's right of occupation **Beard v. Beard, C.A. 369**

Ward of court
Jurisdiction

Child in care of local authority—Mother seeking custody of child—Local authority making child ward of court—No exceptional circumstances making it undesirable for mother to have care of ward—Whether correct test where local authority plaintiff to proceedings—Family Law Reform Act 1969, s. 7 (2)

In re **C. B. (A Minor) (Wardship: Local Authority), C.A. 379**

Children in care of local authority—Mother seeking custody of children—Local authority making children wards of court—Children with foster parents—Whether their care and control to be committed to local authority—Family Law Reform Act 1969, s. 7 (2) **Lewisham London Borough Council v. M., Hollings J. 1248**

Medical treatment

Newly born mongol child requiring operation to save life—Parents refusing consent—Whether operation in child's best interests

In re **B. (A Minor) (Wardship: Medical Treatment), C.A. 1421**

NATURAL JUSTICE
Disciplinary proceedings
Medical practitioner see MEDICAL PRACTITIONER: **Professional conduct:** *Medical reports*

Statutory board
Duty to be fair

Whether Parole Board and local review committee of prison obliged to give reasons for refusal of release on licence of prisoner

Payne v. Lord Harris of Greenwich, C.A. 754

PASSING OFF
Risk of confusion
Imitation of trading style
Use of name " Pub Squash " for lemon drink—Name, get-up and advertising cam-
paign imitative of slogans and visual images used in competitor's advertising—
Whether sufficient to establish passing off—Relevant date for establishing reputation
of product   **Cadbury-Schweppes Pty. Ltd. v. Pub Squash Co. Pty. Ltd.,** P.C. **193**

Use of family name
Banks incorporated by well known banking family—Banks in Pakistan and Switzer-
land closely associated with substantial business—Nationalisation of banks in
Pakistan—Whether Swiss bank passing off in carrying on independent trading—
Whether goodwill and reputation exclusive—Whether nationalised banks' claim
barred by acquiescence, laches and estoppel
                         Habib Bank Ltd. v. Habib Bank A.G. Zurich, C.A. **1265**

PRACTICE
Chancery Division
Pleadings
Title—Listing of parties
                    Practice Note (Chancery: Deposition), Sir Robert Megarry V.-C. **1560**

Trial
Setting action down for trial—Leave of court not required—R.S.C., Ord. 34, r. 2 (1)
                    Practice Direction (Chancery: Setting Down for Trial), Ch.D. **322**

Consent order
Application to discharge
Undertakings given until judgment or further order—Subsequent decision of Court
of Appeal—Whether sufficient grounds for setting aside order
                    Chanel Ltd. v. F. W. Woolworth & Co. Ltd., Foster J. and C.A. **485**

Discovery
Motion for
Undertaking not to use information disclosed save for purpose of passing off action
—Execution of order disclosing other counterfeit goods—Test purchase—Whether
fresh cause of action permissible on evidence of test purchase
                    Sony Corpn. v. Time Electronics, Goulding J. **1293**

Privilege
Professional privilege—Communication between plaintiffs and legal advisers—Part
of communication read by counsel in opening trial—No intention to waive any
privilege—Whether communication severable for purposes of privilege—Whether
privilege waived   **Great Atlantic Insurance Co. v. Home Insurance Co.,** C.A. **529**

Dismissal of action for want of prosecution
Second action
First action dismissed for failure to comply with peremptory order of court—Second
action in respect of same cause of action within limitation period—Whether second
action should be struck out—R.S.C., Ord. 18, r. 19 (1) (*d*) **Janov v. Morris,** C.A. **1389**

Family Division
Appeal
Appeal by case stated—Hearing by single judge—Application for hearing outside
London—R.S.C., Ord. 56, rr. 4A, 5
                    Practice Direction (Family Division: Case Stated), Fam.D. **138**

Immunity from suit
Potential witness see **Pleadings:** *Striking out*

Jury, civil action
Jurors
Inconvenience or hardship of lengthy trial—Necessity for accurate estimates
                    Practice Direction (Juries: Length of Trial), D.C. **1129**

Right to jury
Proceedings in Chancery Division—Allegation of fraud—Litigant requesting trial by
jury—Application to transfer action to Queen's Bench Division—Court's discretion
to transfer case to another division—Whether " fraud " in issue—Administration
of Justice (Miscellaneous Provisions) Act 1933, s. 6 (1)—R.S.C., Ord. 4, r. 3 (1)
                    Stafford Winfield Cook & Partners Ltd. v. Winfield,
                                                Sir Robert Megarry V.-C. **458**

Notice of intention to proceed
Validity
Notice served less than one year after last proceeding—Whether valid—R.S.C.,
Ord. 3, r. 6   **Suedeclub Co. Ltd. v. Occasions Textiles Ltd.,** Nourse J. **1245**

PRACTICE—*continued*
  Parties
    Representative action
      Infringement of copyright—Member suing in personal capacity and on behalf of class—Admissions by defendant—Whether member entitled to injunction and to inquiry as to damages in representative capacity
                                              E.M.I. Records Ltd. v. Riley, Dillon J. **923**

  Payment into court
    Several defendants
      Two defendants sued in one action in respect of breaches of separate contracts—Overlapping claims—Payment into court by one defendant accepted by plaintiff—Whether defendants " sued jointly "—Whether action against other defendant to be stayed in respect of overlapping items of claim—R.S.C., Ord. 22, r. 3 (4)
                                      Townsend v. Stone Toms & Partners, C.A. **1153**

  Pleadings
    Counterclaim
      CMR contract to transport fruit—Writ issued by hauliers for sums due under contract—Defendants' intention to counterclaim in respect of damage to fruit stated in affidavit—Counterclaim served after expiry of time stipulated—Whether time-barred —Carriage of Goods by Road Act 1965, Sch., art. 32—R.S.C., Ord. 15, r. 2
                              Impex Transport Aktieselskabet v. A.G. Thames Holdings Ltd.,
                                                                    Robert Goff J. **1547**

    Striking out
      Action for negligence—Post mortem investigation by defendants—Report to police indicating death due to poisoning—Arrest and prosecution of plaintiff for murder —Prosecution offering no evidence at trial—Plaintiff alleging contamination of organs due to defendants' negligence in post mortem investigation—Whether disclosing reasonable cause of action—Whether defendants immune from suit
                        Evans v. London Hospital Medical College (University of London),
                                                                        Drake J. **184**
  Possession of land
    Summary proceedings
      Short notice—Freehold owner planning redevelopment of building—Protesters opposed to redevelopment occupying to stop demolition—Leave to serve short notice—Owner's evidence not showing urgency—Whether summons to be dismissed or adjourned—Supreme Court of Judicature (Consolidation) Act 1925, s. 27 (1)— R.S.C., Ord. 113, r. 6 (1)   **Westminster City Council v. Monahan,** C.A. **698**

  Stay of proceedings
    Application
      Summons to set writ aside issued and served within 14 days—Failure to give grounds of application and serve affidavit within time limit—Whether procedural irregularity or nullity—Whether submission to jurisdiction—R.S.C., Ord. 2, r. 1 (1); Ord. 12, r. 8
                  Carmel Exporters (Sales) Ltd. v. Sea-Land Services Inc., Robert Goff J. **1068**

  Third party proceedings
    Service out of jurisdiction
      CMR contract for shipment of diesel engines from Scotland to Amsterdam—Goods shipped to Europoort by English carriers—Dutch carriers responsible for on-carriage of goods to Amsterdam—Accident causing loss while goods in possession of one carrier—Action for damages in England—Writ served only on English carrier— Whether English carrier entitled to serve third party notices on Dutch carriers —Carriage of Goods by Road Act 1965, Sch., art. 39—R.S.C., Ord. 11, r. 1 (1) (*l*)
                          Cummins Engine Co. Ltd. v. Davis Freight Forwarding (Hull) Ltd.,
                                                                        C.A. **1363**

  Trial
    Appropriate list
      London—Fixed date for hearing—Vacating list
                                      Practice Direction (Trials in London), Q.B.D. **1296**

PRISONS
  Prisoners' rights
    Release on licence
      Application for release—Recommendations to Secretary of State by Parole Board and local review committee of prison—Refusal to release on licence—Whether prisoner entitled to be given reasons for refusal—Criminal Justice Act 1967, ss. 59, 62
                                  Payne v. Lord Harris of Greenwich, C.A. **754**

PRIVY COUNCIL
Appeal as of right
Interpretation of Constitution
Whether genuine disputable question—Need for vigilance—Jamaica (Constitution)
Order in Council 1962, Sch. 2, ss. 20 (6) (*a*), 110 (1)
Frater v. The Queen (Note), P.C. 1468

Jurisdiction
Criminal matter
Appeal from Fiji—Basis for reviewing decision of local appellate court
Ragho Prasad v. The Queen, P.C. 469

PROBATE
Practice
Representation, grant of
Fee payable on grant—Form of oath—Inland Revenue account not required for
excepted estate—Capital Transfer Tax (Delivery of Accounts) Regulations 1981,
reg. 4—Non-Contentious Probate Fees Order 1981, art. 3, Sch.
Practice Direction (Probate: Representation Grant), Fam.D. 1185

PUBLIC HEALTH
Nuisance
Abatement notice
Noise made by lifts in block of flats—Validity of abatement notice unchallenged—
Failure to comply with notice—Whether common law defences to allegation of
nuisance "reasonable excuse" for non-compliance—Control of Pollution Act 1974,
s. 58 (1) (4)   **A. Lambert Flat Management Ltd. v. Lomas, D.C. 898**

Complaint by tenant
Statutory nuisance existing when informations laid—Repairs undertaken or tenants
removed to other properties before hearing—Properties left unoccupied—Whether
orders to be made—Costs—Public Health Act 1936, ss. 92 (1), 94 (2) (3), 99
Coventry City Council v. Doyle, D.C. 1325

Pollution, control of
Disposal licence
Conditions of licence relating to covering waste—Deposit of waste by company's
servants in contravention of conditions—Whether company "knowingly" permitting
deposit—Burden of proof—Whether for prosecution to prove knowledge of breach
of condition—Control of Pollution Act 1974, s. 3 (1) (*a*)
Ashcroft v. Cambro Waste Products Ltd., D.C. 1349

RATING
Unoccupied hereditament
Completion notice
Notice on photocopied form with blanks completed by rating authority assistant—
Assistant's opinion of expected date of completion—Validity of notice—Whether
provisions administrative in character—Treasurer validly appointed for proper
administration of rating authority's financial affairs—Whether including collection
of rates—Whether giving of notice making and levying rate—Whether action and
opinion of assistant part of proper administration—General Rate Act 1967, s. 17
(1), Sch. 1, paras. 1 (1), 8 (1) (4)—Local Government Act 1972, ss. 111 (1) (3), 151
Provident Mutual Life Assurance Association v. Derby City Council,
H.L.(E.) **173**

Surcharge
Commercial building unoccupied for more than six months—Legal charge in favour
of mortgagee prior in time to rating authority's charge—Whether rating authority's
charge on all interests in land—Whether binding on purchasers from mortgagee—
General Rate Act 1967, ss. 17A, 17B (3) (7) (as amended by Local Government
Act 1974, s. 16)   **Westminster City Council v. Haymarket Publishing Ltd., C.A. 677**

REVENUE
Capital gains tax
Tax avoidance
Taxpayer transferring shares to Guernsey company on trust for his benefit—Sale of
reversionary interest in trust fund for value—Subsequent sale of life interest to
company within exemption from charge to tax—Whether transfer of shares to
trustees "gift in settlement" so as to be deemed disposal at market value—
Whether tax chargeable on sale of reversionary interest as being part disposal—
Finance Act 1965, ss. 22 (2) (4), 25 (2), Sch. 7, paras. 17, 21 **Berry v. Warnett, C.A. 1**

REVENUE—*continued*
Corporation tax
Chargeable gains
  Allowable deductions—Investment company acquiring securities in exchange for issue of its own shares—Conditional agreement stipulating price of securities and number of shares to be issued in exchange—Market value of shares falling before completion of agreement—Value of consideration given for securities—Finance Act 1965, Sch. 6, para. 4 (1) (*a*)
  Stanton v. Drayton Commercial Investment Co. Ltd., C.A. 1425

Expenses of trade
  Parent company seconding employee to work for overseas subsidiary—Expenditure incurred by parent company in its own interest—Subsidiary benefiting from expenditure—Whether expenditure " wholly and exclusively " for purposes of parent company's trade—Whether capital payment—Income and Corporation Taxes Act 1970, s. 130 (*a*) (*f*)
  Robinson v. Scott Bader Co. Ltd., C.A. 1135

Group relief
  Tax avoidance scheme to provide relief by purchase of surplus capital allowances from shipping company—Whether " arrangements " in existence enabling purchasing company to be treated as a member of same group of companies as surrendering company—Whether group relief available—Income and Corporation Taxes Act 1970, s. 258 (1)—Finance Act 1973, s. 29 (1)
  Pilkington Brothers Ltd. v. Inland Revenue Comrs., Nourse J. 781

Development land tax
Compulsory acquisition
  Purchase notice for sale of land served and accepted by local authority—Introduction of tax—Subsequent agreement as to compensation—Date of " disposal and acquisition " of land—Whether deemed compulsory purchase—Whether transaction chargeable to tax—Town and Country Planning Act 1971, s. 181 (2)—Development Land Tax Act 1976, s. 45 (1) (2) (4)
  Inland Revenue Comrs. v. Metrolands (Property Finance) Ltd., Nourse J. 637

Income tax
Additional rate
  Settlement—Income of fund held on protective trusts for settlors' son—Trustees accumulating income in exercise of discretionary power conferred by trust deed—Whether additional rate tax chargeable on trust income to which beneficiary entitled subject only to trustees' power to accumulate—Finance Act 1973, s. 16 (1) (2)
  Inland Revenue Comrs. v. Berrill, Vinelott J. 1449

Assessment
  Notional income arising on sale of assets cum dividend—Basic rate of tax—Whether chargeable—Income and Corporation Taxes Act 1970, s. 30 (4) (as amended by Finance Act 1971, s. 37 (1), Sch. 6, Pt. I, para. 13)
  McCarney v. Freilich, Goulding J. 431

Earnings from work done abroad
  Relief for short or intermittent absences—Qualifying " day "—Whether employee working overseas during day but returning before midnight entitled to relief—Finance Act 1977, Sch. 7, para. 2
  Hoye v. Forsdyke, Vinelott J. 1442

Employment
  Benefits of directors and higher-paid employees—Employers settling funds on trustees—Trustees awarding scholarships to employees' children—Whether " benefits " accruing to employee—Income and Corporation Taxes Act 1970, s. 375—Finance Act 1976, s. 61 (1)
  Wicks v. Firth, Goulding J. 475

  Emolument—Local government officer receiving mileage allowance for essential travel in course of employment—Whether part of emoluments of employment—Whether cost of providing and maintaining care allowable deduction—Income and Corporation Taxes Act 1970, ss. 183 (1), 189 (1)
  Perrons v. Spackman, Vinelott J. 1411

Expenses of trade or profession (Schedule D)
  Barrister—Expenditure on replacing and cleaning professional clothes required to be worn in court—Whether incurred wholly and exclusively for purposes of profession—Whether deductible expense—Income and Corporation Taxes Act 1970, s. 130
  Mallalieu v. Drummond, Slade J. 908

Loan interest relief
  Licensee of public house acquiring mortgage to purchase house—Tenancy agreement requiring him to reside at licensed premises—Monthly visits to house—Whether house " only or main residence "—Whether entitled to relief for mortgage interest—Finance Act 1974, Sch. 1, para. 4 (1) (*a*)   **Frost v. Feltham, Nourse J. 452**

REVENUE—*continued*
  Income tax—*continued*
   Personal relief
    Polygamous marriage—Husband having domicile in Pakistan contracting second
    marriage under Muslim law—Husband maintaining second wife during subsistence
    of first marriage—Whether entitled to relief for maintenance of second wife—
    Income and Corporation Taxes Act 1970, s. 8 (1)
    Nabi (Ghulam) v. Heaton, Vinelott J. **1052**

   Tax avoidance
    Transaction in securities—Tax advantage—Relationship between transaction and
    receipt of dividend—Transaction " whereby " other person subsequently receives
    abnormal amount by way of dividend—Distribution of profits where company
    under " control " of not more than five persons—Date for determination—Income
    Tax and Corporation Taxes Act 1970, s. 461, paras. C (1), D (1)
    Inland Revenue Comrs. v. Garvin, H.L.(E.) **793**

   P.A.Y.E.
    Exploration work in designated areas of North Sea—Non-resident employer—
    Employees working in both United Kingdom and foreign sectors of North Sea—
    Whether employees' duties carried on in United Kingdom—Whether P.A.Y.E.
    provisions applicable to employer—Income and Corporation Taxes Act 1970,
    s. 204 (1)—Finance Act 1973, s. 38 (4) (6)
    Clark v. Oceanic Contractors Inc., Dillon J. **59**

  Value added tax
   Gift of goods under £10
    Company operating special retail schemes—Associated mail order company supplying
    goods without charge to agents under incentive scheme—Assessment by commis-
    sioners including tax on open market value of incentive supplies—Whether company
    accountable to tax on such supplies—Whether such supplies exempt as gifts—
    Finance Act 1972, s. 30 (3), Sch. 3, para. 6
    G.U.S. Merchandise Corpn. Ltd. v. Customs and Excise Comrs.,
    C.A. **1309**

   Group treatment
    Members of group jointly and severally liable—Whether claim to tax preferential
    debt in winding up of non-representative member of group—Finance Act 1972,
    ss. 21 (1), 41   *In re* **Nadler Enterprises Ltd.,** Dillon J. **23**

   Zero-rating
    Alteration of building—Foundations underpinned to prevent subsidence—Whether
    work of " repair or maintenance "—Whether zero-rated—" Alteration "—Whether
    meaning structural alteration—Finance Act 1972, Sch. 4, Group 8, item 2, note (2)
    (as varied by Value Added Tax (Consolidation) Order 1976, Sch. 1, Group 8,
    item 2, note 2 (*a*)) **A.C.T. Construction Ltd. v. Customs and Excise Comrs.,** C.A. **49**
    H.L.(E.) **1542**

ROAD TRAFFIC
  Arrest
   Validity
    Breath test—Police officers acting lawfully when requesting motorist to provide speci-
    men of breath—Motorist refusing to provide specimen—Officers entering without
    permission on motorist's property to arrest for such refusal—Whether arrest unlaw-
    ful—Whether invalidating subsequent request for specimen—Road Traffic Act 1972,
    s. 8 (5)   **Clowser v. Chaplin,** H.L.(E.) **837**

  Breath test
   Alcotest ® *80/A*
    Manufacturer's instructions to inflate bag fully in single breath—Bag inflated by series
    of short breaths—Breath test negative—Whether test valid—Whether subsequent
    evidence of blood analysis admissible—Road Traffic Act 1972, s. 12 (1) (3)
    Reg. v. Littell, C.A. **1146**

  Driving or attempting to drive
   " Driving "
    Motorist in driver's seat of towed vehicle with steering wheel and operative braking
    system—Whether driving—" Drives "—Road Traffic Act 1972, s. 99 (*b*)
    McQuaid v. Anderton, D.C. **154**

  Laboratory test
   Specimen
    Provision—Requirement for specimen made at one police station—Specimen taken
    at another police station—Whether specimen to be taken at same police station
    as requirement and breath test—Road Traffic Act 1972, ss. 9 (1), 11
    Pascoe v. Nicholson, H.L.(E.) **1061**

ROAD TRAFFIC—*continued*
Tyres
Defects
Vehicle owned by government department—Government employee nominated for purpose of proceedings relating to government vehicles—Whether criminally liable —Road Traffic Act 1972, s. 188 (8) (9)   **Barnett v. French,** D.C. **848**

SHIPPING
Bill of lading
Exemption clause
Goods discharged and placed in stevedore's warehouse—Goods obtained by thieves without presentation of bill of lading—Whether stevedore entitled to rely on exemption clause in bill of lading
                    **Port Jackson Stevedoring Pty. Ltd. v. Salmond and Spraggon
                                                 (Australia) Pty. Ltd.,** P.C. **138**
Charterparty
Time charter
Hire—Right to withdraw ship " failing . . . punctual . . . payment "—Payment of hire to be made " in cash "—Credit transfer on due date—Interest not to run until four days later—Whether payment " in cash "—Whether owners entitled to withdraw ship   **A/S Awilco of Oslo v. Fulvia S.p.A. di Navigazione of Cagliari,
                                                                          H.L.(E.) 314**
Ship's management
Dedicated pater familias
Agreement between owners and managers—Whether relationship of trustee and bene- ficiary created—Manager's liability for wrongful arrest—Extent
                    **Compania Financiera " Soleada " S.A. v. Hamoor Tanker Corpn. Inc.,
                                                                          C.A. 274**

SHIPS' NAMES
Borag   **Compania Financiera " Soleada " S.A. v. Hamoor Tanker Corpn. Inc.,
                                                                          C.A. 274**
Chikuma   **A/S Awilco of Oslo v. Fulvia S.p.A. di Navigazione of Cagliari,
                                                                          H.L.(E.) 314**
Dragon   **Daly v. General Steam Navigation Co. Ltd.,** C.A. **120**
Jogoo   **The Jogoo,** Sheen J. **1376**
New York Star   **Port Jackson Stevedoring Pty. Ltd. v. Salmond and Spraggon
                                                 (Australia) Pty. Ltd.,** P.C. **138**

SOCIAL SECURITY
Family income supplement
Entitlement
Claimant absent from work due to sickness at time of application—Whether engaged in full-time " work "—Family Income Supplements Act 1970, ss. 1 (1) (a), 6 (2) (a)   **Reg. v. Ebbw Vale and Merthyr Tydfil Supplementary Benefits
                                                 Appeal Tribunal,** *Ex parte* **Lewis,** D.C. **131**
Sickness benefit
False representation
Untrue statement made to deceive employer—No intention to obtain extra benefit— Whether offence—Social Security Act 1975, s. 146 (3)   **Barrass v. Reeve,** D.C. **408**

Supplementary benefit
Attendance allowance
Cooking for severely disabled person—Whether " attention . . . in connection with . . . bodily functions "—Social Security Act 1975, s. 35 (1) (a) (i)
                              Reg. v. National Insurance Comr., *Ex parte* **Secretary
                                                 of State for Social Services,** C.A. **1017**
False statement or representation
Dishonest statement by claimant that not working—Claimant dealing in scrap metal for no pecuniary reward—Whether " work "—Whether finding of dishonesty sufficient mens rea of offence—Supplementary Benefits Act 1976, s. 21
                                                            Clear v. Smith, D.C. **399**
Maintenance
Father's liability to maintain children—Consent order in divorce proceedings—Father to pay no maintenance for children but to transfer interest in matrimonial home— Effect of consent order on father's liability—Supplementary Benefits Act 1976, ss. 17 (1), 18 (3)   **Hulley v. Thompson,** D.C. **159**

Resources
Wages paid in advance—Claimant going on strike and obliged to repay in future— Whether payment " resources "—Supplementary Benefits Act 1976, Sch. 1, para. 27
                              Reg. v. Bolton Supplementary Benefits Appeal Tribunal,
                                                 Ex parte **Fordham,** C.A. **28**

SOLICITOR
  Costs
    Non-contentious business
      Recovery of costs—Omission to inform client company of its right to require
      solicitors to obtain certificate from Law Society that bill fair and reasonable—
      Petition to wind up company—Whether solicitors creditors—Whether petition
      abuse of process—Solicitors' Remuneration Order 1972, art. 3 (2)
                                  In re **Laceward Ltd.,** Slade J. **133**

STATUTE
  Construction
    International Convention
      Enforcement of carriers' right of recovery against other carriers—Competent court or
      tribunal—Court or tribunal where " one of the carriers concerned " ordinarily
      resident or carries on business—Meaning—Whether English carrier sued in England
      entitled to recover from Dutch carriers in English court—Carriage of Goods by
      Road Act 1965, Sch., arts. 37 (*a*), 39, para. 2
             Cummins Engine Co. Ltd. v. Davis Freight Forwarding (Hull) Ltd.,
                                           C.A. **1363**

    Meaning of word
      Word used in ordinary sense—Primary facts found by tribunal—Whether under-
      pinning work maintenance—Whether question of law
             A.C.T. Construction Ltd. v. Customs and Excise Comrs., C.A. **49**
                                        H.L.(E.) **1542**

STATUTORY INSTRUMENT
  Validity
    Severability
      Power under statute to make orders prohibiting fishing in designated areas—Order
      defining area to include parts of sea over which no ministerial power to make order
      —Whether invalid part of defined area severable—Validity of order—Sea Fish
      (Conservation) Act 1967, ss. 5 (2), 23 (1) (as amended by Fishery Limits Act 1976,
      s. 9 (1), Sch. 2, para. 16)—West Coast Herring (Prohibition of Fishing) Order 1978,
      art. 2, Sch.   **Dunkley v. Evans,** D.C. **1522**

TENANTS IN COMMON
  Ouster
    Occupation rent
      Assessment   **Dennis v. McDonald,** Purchas J. **810**

  Realty
    Family home
      House purchased as family home by man and woman living together—Woman leaving
      home with children because of man's violent behaviour—Man continuing to occupy
      house with some of children—Woman's application for order directing sale—Juris-
      diction to make orders other than order for sale—Whether woman excluded from
      premises—Whether entitled to occupation rent—Law of Property Act 1925, s. 30
                       Dennis v. McDonald, Purchas J. **810**

TOWN PLANNING
  Development
    Agreement
      Grant of planning permission in accordance with agreement necessarily involving
      demolition of buildings on site—Subsequent inclusion of site in conservation area—
      Whether planning authority able to exercise statutory power to prevent demolition
      of buildings—Town and Country Planning Act 1971, ss. 52 (3), 277A (as amended
      by Town and Country Amenities Act 1974, s. 1 (1))
                    Windsor and Maidenhead Royal Borough Council v.
                         Brandrose Investments Ltd., Fox J. **1083**

  Planning permission
    " *Material considerations* "
      Renewal of application for planning permission for residential development—
      Whether time-expired permission material consideration in determining whether
      to grant planning permission—Town and Country Planning Act 1971, s. 29 (1),
      Sch. 24, para. 19
          South Oxfordshire District Council v. Secretary of State for the Environment,
                                        Woolf J. **1092**

TRINIDAD AND TOBAGO
Constitution
Human rights and fundamental freedoms
High Court ordering journalist's imprisonment for contempt—Subsequent application for redress—Whether contravention of constitutional rights—Trinidad and Tobago (Constitution) Order in Council 1962, Sch. 2, ss. 1 (*a*), 6
Chokolingo v. Attorney-General of Trinidad and Tobago,
P.C. **106**

TRIBUNAL
Statutory
Disciplinary proceedings
Complaints of misconduct following criminal convictions—Effect of conditional discharge—Whether tribunal precluded from hearing evidence of facts which led to convictions—Powers of Criminal Courts Act 1973, s. 13
Reg. v. Statutory Committee of the Pharmaceutical Society of Great Britain,
Ex parte **Pharmaceutical Society of Great Britain,** D.C. **886**

TRUSTS
Distribution of fund
Appropriation to beneficiary
Life tenant's entitlement to one half—Half share paid to life tenant—Retained half share appreciating in value—Whether trustees having power to make further appropriation—Marquess of Abergavenny's Estate Act 1946, Sch. 7, Pt. I, para. 2 (ii)
In re **Marquess of Abergavenny's Estate Act Trusts,**
Goulding J. **843**

WILL
Mutual wills
Constructive trust
Husband and wife making wills in similar terms—Wife taking under husband's will—Wife making new will—Whether wife under legal obligation to bequeath her estate in terms of former will—Whether wife's executors holding estate on terms of former will
In re **Cleaver, decd.,** Nourse J. **939**

WORDS AND PHRASES
" *Acting in his capacity* "—Misuse of Drugs Regulations 1973, reg. 10 (1)
Reg. v. Dunbar, C.A. **1536**
" *Alteration* "—Finance Act 1972, Sch. 4, Group 8, item 2 (as varied)
A.C.T. Construction Ltd. v. Customs and Excise Comrs., H.L.(E.) **1542**
" *Application* "—Police (Property) Act 1897, s. 1 (1)
Reg. v. Uxbridge Justices, *Ex parte* **Comr. of Police of the Metropolis,** D.C. **112**
" *Arrangements* "—Finance Act 1973, s. 29 (1) (*b*)
Pilkington Brothers Ltd. v. Inland Revenue Comrs., Nourse J. **781**
" *Attention . . . in connection with . . . bodily functions* "—Social Security Act 1975, s. 35 (1) (*a*) (i)   **Reg. v. National Insurance Comr.,** *Ex parte* **Secretary of State for Social Services,** C.A. **1017**
" *Benefit* "—Finance Act 1976, s. 61 (1)   **Wicks v. Firth,** Goulding J. **475**
" *Days* "—Finance Act 1977, Sch. 7, para. 2   **Hoye v. Forsdyke,** Vinelott J. **1442**
" *Decision* "—Lands Tribunal Act 1949, s. 3 (4)
Reg. v. Lands Tribunal, *Ex parte* **City of London Corpn.,**
Judge Newey Q.C. **985**
" *Disposal and acquisition* "—Development Land Tax Act 1976, s. 45 (2) (4)
Inland Revenue Comrs. v. Metrolands (Property Finance) Ltd.,
Nourse J. **637**
" *Document . . . made evidence by law* "—Forgery Act 1913, s. 3 (3) (*g*)
Attorney-General's Reference (No. 2 of 1980), C.A. **148**
" *Drives* "—Road Traffic Act 1972, s. 99 (*b*)   **McQuaid v. Anderton,** D.C. **154**
" *Entitled to consent* "—Criminal Damage Act 1971, s. 5 (2) (*a*)   **Reg. v. Denton,** C.A. **1446**
" *Forgo payment* "—Theft Act 1978, s. 2 (1) (*b*)   **Reg. v. Holt,** C.A. **1000**
" *Fraud* "—Administration of Justice (Miscellaneous Provisions) Act 1933, s. 6 (1)
Stafford Winfield Cook & Partners Ltd. v. Winfield,
Sir Robert Megarry V.-C. **458**
" *Gift in settlement* "—Finance Act 1965, s. 25 (2)   **Berry v. Warnett,** C.A. **1**
" *Homeless intentionally* "—Housing (Homeless Persons) Act 1977, s. 17
Reg. v. North Devon District Council, *Ex parte* **Lewis (J. P.),**
Woolf J. **328**
" *Kept for publication for gain* "—Obscene Publications Act 1959, s. 3 (3)
Gold Star Publications Ltd. v. Comr. of Police of the Metropolis,
H.L.(E.) **732**
" *Knowingly* "—Control of Pollution Act 1974, s. 3 (1) (*a*)
Ashcroft v. Cambro Waste Products Ltd., D.C. **1349**

WORDS AND PHRASES—*continued*

" *Landlord* "—Rent Act 1977, Sch. 15, Case 9
       Patel (Mahendra Kumar) v. Patel (Bharat), C.A. 1342

" *Lawful excuse* "—Criminal Damage Act 1971, s. 1 (1)   **Reg. v. Denton, C.A. 1446**

" *Let under a secure tenancy* "—Housing Act 1980, ss. 33 (1), 34 (1)
    Harrison v. Hammersmith and Fulham London Borough Council,
                   C.A. 650

" *Maintenance* "—Finance Act 1972, Sch. 4, Group 8, item 2, note (2) (as varied)
    A.C.T. Construction Ltd. v. Customs and Excise Comrs., C.A. 49
                   H.L.(E.) 1542

" *Material considerations* "—Town and Country Planning Act 1971, s. 29 (1)
    South Oxfordshire District Council v. Secretary of State for the Environment,
                 Woolf J. 1092

" *Noxious thing* "—Offences against the Person Act 1861, s. 24 **Reg. v. Marcus, C.A. 774**

" *Offences of the same or a similar character* "—Criminal Law Act 1977, s. 23 (7) (*a*)
    Reg. v. Hatfield Justices, *Ex parte* Castle, D.C. 217

" *Only or main residence* "—Finance Act 1974, Sch. 1, para. 4 (1) (*a*)
            Frost v. Feltham, Nourse J. 452

" *Original literary work* "—Copyright Act 1956, s. 2
    Exxon Corpn. v. Exxon Insurance Consultants International Ltd.,
                 Graham J. 624

" *Other means of transport* "—Carriage of Goods by Road Act 1965, Sch., art. 2
    Thermo Engineers Ltd. v. Ferrymasters Ltd., Neill J. 1470

" *Pay* "—E.E.C. Treaty (Cmnd. 5179–II), art. 119
    Worringham v. Lloyds Bank Ltd. (Case 69/80), E.C.J. 950

" *Realisation by or for the benefit of another person* "—Theft Act 1968, s. 22 (1)
            Reg. v. Bloxham, C.A. 859

" *Reasonable excuse* "—Control of Pollution Act 1974, s. 58 (4)
    A. Lambert Flat Management Ltd. v. Lomas, D.C. 898

" *Recovered or preserved* "—Legal Aid Act 1974, s. 9 (6) (7)
    Manley v. The Law Society, Bristow J. and C.A. 335

" *Relating to land* "—Land Charges Act 1972, s. 17 (1)
    Selim Ltd. v. Bickenhall Engineering Ltd.,
          Sir Robert Megarry V.-C. 1318

" *Relevant employees* "—Employment Protection (Consolidation) Act 1978, s. 62 (4) (*b*)
        McCormick v. Horsepower Ltd., C.A. 993

" *Required for any accounting purpose* "—Theft Act 1968, s. 17 (1) (*a*)
    Attorney-General's Reference (No. 1 of 1980), C.A. 34

" *Requisite* "—Landlord and Tenant Act 1954, s. 57 (1)
    Reg. v. Secretary of State for the Environment, *Ex parte* Powis,
                   D.C. 584

" *Resources* "—Supplementary Benefits Act 1976, Sch. 1, para. 27
    Reg. v. Bolton Supplementary Benefits Appeal Tribunal,
            Ex parte **Fordham, C.A. 28**

" *Serving a sentence of imprisonment* "—Criminal Justice Act 1961, s. 3 (2)
            Reg. v. Mellor, C.A. 1044
            Reg. v. Orpwood, C.A. 1048

" *The holding* "—Landlord and Tenant Act 1954, s. 30 (1) (*g*)
        Cam Gears Ltd. v. Cunningham, C.A. 1011

" *Whereby* "—Income and Corporation Taxes Act 1970, s. 461, para. C (1)
        Inland Revenue Comrs. v. Garvin, H.L.(E.) 793

" *Whereby a person performs work in any industry* "—Industrial Arbitration Act 1940
(1980 reprint), s. 88F (1) (New South Wales)
    Caltex Oil (Australia) Pty. Ltd. v. Feenan, P.C. 1003

" *Work* "—Family Income Supplements Act 1970, s. 1 (1) (*a*)
    Reg. v. Ebbw Vale and Merthyr Tydfil Supplementary Benefits
        Appeal Tribunal, *Ex parte* Lewis, D.C. 131

ERRATA

[1981] 1 W.L.R.

Page 174A, lines 2–3: *for* " the treasurer's facsimile signature " *read* " the treasurer."

Page 218A, line 5: for " *John Howarth* " *read* " *Jonathan Haworth* "

Page 275C, line 18 *should read*: " On appeal by the managers: —"

Page 357D, line 22: *for* " £2,000 towards the costs of the prosecution " *read* " £2,000 towards the legal aid costs of his defence "

Page 470B: *delete* line 10.

Page 781E, line 22: *for* s. 528 (1) *read* s. 258 (1)

Page 794A, line 2: *for* informed *read* inferred

Page 806A, line 7: *for* [1977] Cr.A.R. 91 *read* [1977] W.A.R. 91

Page 937D, line 25: *for* " p. 26 " *read* " p. 261 "

Page 1000B, line 7: *for* " Theft Act 1968 " *read* " Theft Act 1978 "

Page 1562A, line 3: *for* " appropriate " *read* " inappropriate "